Japanese–English Learner's Dictionary

Published in collaboration with
Kenkyusha Limited

MERRIAM-WEBSTER, INCORPORATED
Springfield, Massachusetts

A GENUINE MERRIAM-WEBSTER

The name *Webster* alone is no guarantee of excellence.
It is used by a number of publishers and may serve
mainly to mislead an unwary buyer.

Merriam-Webster™ is the name you should look for
when you consider the purchase of dictionaries or
other fine reference books. It carries the reputation of
a company that has been publishing since 1831 and is
your assurance of quality and authority.

Merriam-Webster's Japanese–English Learner's Dictionary
Published in the United States by Merriam-Webster, Incorporated, by special
arrangement with Kenkyusha Ltd., Tokyo, Japan
Copyright © 1993 by Kenkyusha Ltd.
Originally published by Kenkyusha Ltd., Tokyo, Japan, under the title: The
Kenkyusha Japanese–English Learner's Dictionary

Library of Congress Cataloging-in-Publication Data
Main entry under title

Kenkyūsha Nichi-Ei jiten. English.
  Merriam-Webster's Japanese–English learner's dictionary.
      p.   cm.
  ISBN 0-87779-164-3
  1. Japanese language—Dictionaries—English.   I. Title.
PL679.K38213   1993
495.6′321—dc20   93-27294
                                                                                                       CIP

Made in the United States of America

12345RRD959493

Photo Credits

BOÑODORI Yasuo Kubo; BOÑSAI Yasuo Kubo; BOOSAÑ Yasuo Kubo; BUÑKA-KUÑSHOO Prime Minister's
Office; BUÑRAKU Yasuo Kubo; CHATSUMI Kyodo Photo Service; FUJI-SAÑ Kyodo Photo Service;
FUUZOKU-EEGYOO Kyodo Photo Service; HANAMI Kyodo Photo Service; HINADAÑ Yasuo Kubo;
IKEBANA Akihiro Kasuya, Ichiyo School; JUUDOO Kyodo Photo Service; KAÑNUSHI Yasuo Kubo; KARATE
Yasuo Kubo; KEÑDOO Yasuo Kubo; KOINOBORI Kyodo Photo Service; KOTATSU Yasuo Kubo; MATSURI
Kyodo Photo Service; NOO Yasuo Kubo; OSECHI Kyodo Photo Service; PACHIÑKO Kyodo Photo Service;
RAKUGO Yasuo Kubo; SADOO Shufunotomo Co., Ltd.; SHABUSHABU Kyodo Photo Service; SHIRO Kyodo
Photo Service; SUIBOKUGA Yasuo Kubo; SUMOO Kyodo Photo Service; SUSHIYA Yasuo Kubo; TAIKO Yasuo
Kubo; TAUE Kyodo Photo Service; TERA Yasuo Kubo; TSUZUMI Kyodo Photo Service; WASHITSU Yasuo
Kubo.

Contents

Contributors   iv

Preface   v

Guide to the Use of the Dictionary   vii

The Dictionary   1

Guide to Japanese Pronunciation   1098

Outline of Japanese Grammar   1106

Essential English–Japanese Vocabulary List   1115

Inside Front Cover:
A Table of Japanese Sounds

Inside Back Cover:
Map of Japan

Preface

MERRIAM-WEBSTER'S JAPANESE–ENGLISH LEARNER'S DICTIONARY is designed to meet the needs of students who wish to develop their skills in reading, writing, and speaking modern Japanese. It is intended to be a useful reference book for students at all levels of proficiency in the language; however, particular care has been taken to make the dictionary useful to beginners. It focuses, for instance, on the words that are most frequently encountered in everyday speech and writing. Example sentences and phrases are regularly given at most entries so that users can gain a better understanding of typical uses of commonly used words and phrases. English translations follow each example in order to make the meaning and grammatical structure of each phrase or sentence as clear as possible. For greater ease of reference, all vocabulary items, including phrases, prefixes, suffixes, and verb endings appear in a single alphabetical listing.

Illustrations are included at entries where they will add significantly to a user's understanding of a word or phrase. Typically, such entries are for words that refer to common aspects of Japanese life that may be unfamiliar to speakers of English.

Another noteworthy feature of this dictionary is the marking of accent on each headword. This is a guide to accepted pronunciation and serves to distinguish those Japanese words that differ only in ways that their syllables are accented.

The example phrases and sentences in this dictionary are shown in both romanized Japanese and in standard written Japanese. This makes it possible for students to familiarize themselves with the *hiragana, katakana,* and *kanji* characters used in writing Japanese.

The explanations of grammar and usage included in this dictionary are based on an analysis of modern Japanese as it is actually written and spoken. This analysis, which in places departs from traditional Japanese grammar, is intended to be easily understood and of immediate practical value to learners of Japanese.

MERRIAM-WEBSTER'S JAPANESE–ENGLISH LEARNER'S DICTIONARY was produced through a close collaboration between scholars of the Japanese and English languages and educators with long experience in teaching Japanese as a foreign language. The editors of Merriam-Webster and Kenkyusha Limited are grateful to all of those who helped create this new dictionary, and they join in the hope that this dictionary will prove helpful to both beginners and advanced students as they learn to speak, read, and write Japanese.

Guide to the Use of the Dictionary

1. Romanization

The romanization used in this dictionary is based on the standard Hepburn system with the following modifications:

1. 1 Long vowels are indicated by doubled vowel letters, '*aa, ii, uu, ee, oo,*' instead of the conventional transcription which, depending on the particular vowel, either uses macrons or doubles the vowel letter.

> **to⌐oki** とうき (earthenware)
> **shu⌐uchuu** しゅうちゅう (concentration)
> **pa⌐atii** パーティー (party)

1. 2 When the vowel sequence '*ei*' is pronounced as a long '*e*,' it is written as '*ee*.'

> **se⌐eto** せいと (pupil)
> **se⌐tsumee** せつめい (explanation)

But a word like けいと (knitting wool) is written as *keito* in order to show that it is composed of two separate word elements, *ke* (wool) and *ito* (thread).

1. 3 When there is a sequence of three or more identical vowel letters, a hyphen is used to clarify the word elements.

> **ke⌐e-ee** けいえい (management)
> **so⌐o-oñ** そうおん (noise)

1. 4 '*ñ*' is used to transcribe the syllabic '*n*' (ん/ン).

> **shi⌐ñbuñ** しんぶん (newspaper)
> **ke⌐ñkoo** けんこう (health)
> **ha⌐ñsamu** ハンサム (handsome)

1. 5 When the small 'っ/ッ' precedes a consonant, the sequence is transcribed as a double consonant, except in the case of '*ch*,' which is written '*tch*.'

> **a⌐ppaku** あっぱく (pressure)
> **hi⌐tto** ヒット (hit)
> **shu⌐tchoo** しゅっちょう (business trip)

1. 6 The small 'っ / ッ' in interjections such as 'あっ' and 'えっ' is transcribed with an apostrophe. This sign represents a glottal stop (an abrupt tightening of the vocal cords) after the preceding vowel.

> **a'** あっ (Oh!)
> **e'** えっ (Eh!)

2. Headwords

2. 1 Headwords are arranged in alphabetical order with accent marks. The accents of prefixes and suffixes are not given unless the accent of the derived compounds is invariant. Many compound nouns are listed under the headword which comprises the first element of the compound. For *kootsuu-dootoku* see '**kootsuu**,' and for *kooshuu-dootoku*, '**kooshuu**.'

2. 2 Headwords are written in roman letters followed by the standard writing in *hiragana* or *katakana* (the two Japanese syllabaries), and, where appropriate, *kanji* (Chinese characters). This is followed by an abbreviation indicating the part of speech.

> **aˈtama** あたま (頭) *n*. head
> **boˈoeki** ぼうえき (貿易) *n*. trade

2. 3 Numbered superscripts are used to distinguish different words with the same romanization.

> **haˈshi**[1] はし (bridge)
> **haˈshi**[2] はし (chopsticks)

2. 4 Prefixes are followed, and suffixes preceded, by a hyphen, thus indicating position at either the beginning or end of a word.

> **dai-** だい (big; large) > *dai*-**toshi** だいとし (a *large* city)
> **-**[1]**dan** だん (group) > **choosa-***dan* ちょうさだん (a survey *group*)

As a general principle, a word which can stand alone as a single unit is left as one word without a hyphen. However, in the case of examples which are listed under suffixes and prefixes which themselves constitute headwords, the hyphen is used to clarify the word elements.

da⌐iki⌐bo (大規模) (headword)
dai-**kibo** (大規模) (under headword, **dai**-)

ji⌐do⌐osha (自動車) (headword)
jidoo-*sha* (自動車) (under headword, **-sha**)

2. 5   The swung dash, ~, is used to avoid repetition of the Japanese headword.

u⌐ñdoo うんどう (exercise)
   uñdoo suru (~する) (take exercise)

2. 6   Set phrases are shown in boldfaced type.

abura o shiboru (~を絞る) haul over the coals
abura o uru (~を売る) sneak off from work

2. 7   The raised dot in a headword distinguishes the stem of verbs and adjectives from the part to be inflected.

ka⌐k·u かく (書く), **a⌐buna·i** あぶない (危ない)

2. 8   When a headword comprises more than one part of speech, each part is dealt with separately under a different subheading.

ma⌐ñzoku まんぞく (満足) *n.* satisfaction; contentment.
— *a.n.* (~ na, ni) satisfactory; contented.

The parts of speech of some words differ according to the context. In that case, they are given together.

o⌐oku おおく (多く) *n.*, *adv.* many; much.
n.   *Kare wa sono jikeñ ni tsutie* ooku *o kataranakatta.* (He did not say *much* about the affair.)
adv.   *Sono señkyo ni wa kane ga* ooku *ugoita.* (Money was involved *very much* in the election.)

3.   Meaning and usage

3. 1   Different senses of a headword which are subsumed under one meaning are separated by semicolons.

na⌐yami なやみ (悩み) *n.* worry; trouble; sufferings; anguish.

3. 2   When a headword has more than one meaning, each mean-

ing is listed in a numbered sequence, with the most common and important meaning shown first.

> **ho˺okoo** ほうこう (方向) *n.*
> 1 direction; way; course:
> 2 aim; object; course:

3. 3 Special notes on both the grammatical and social usage of words, and relevant cultural information are introduced by a ★. When a more detailed explanation is necessary, this is given in a box. Notes regarding use by sex or age (e.g. by men; used mainly by children, etc.) are to be regarded as guides and therefore interpreted flexibly.

4. Illustrative examples

4. 1 Example phrases and sentences are presented in the following order: romanized Japanese, normal Japanese orthography, the corresponding English translation.

> *Kono* basu *wa Shibuya e ikimasu ka*? (このバスは渋谷へ行きますか) Does this *bus* go to Shibuya?

4. 2 Romanized Japanese is printed in italics with the headword of that particular entry set in upright style. In the illustrative phrase or sentence, the English translation of the headword is given in italics. The user should note that the parts of speech of the Japanese headword and its English translation equivalent will often be different, and also that it is sometimes difficult to define precisely the exact English word or words that correspond to the Japanese headword.

4. 3 In example sentences featuring dialogue, Japanese style quotation marks, 「 」, are used in the Japanese text, and conventional English quotation marks in the romanization and translation.

> "*Kega wa arimaseñ ka?*" "*Ee,* daijoobu *desu.*" (「けがはありませんか」「ええ，だいじょうぶです」) "Did you hurt yourself?" "No, I'm *all right.*"

4. 4 Many of the Japanese sentences are subject to several interpretations depending on context, which of course cannot be given in any detail in a dictionary such as this. It should be

borne in mind that in Japanese the grammatical subject is often not expressed, and the distinction between singular and plural, or between definite (e.g. 'the pen') and indefinite (e.g. 'a pen'), is not as clearcut as in English.

4. 5 When giving examples of grammatical patterns, the verb '*suru*' is used to represent any appropriate verb.

> ... *suru toki* > *aruku toki*, *taberu toki*, etc.

5. Orthography

5. 1 The orthography of headwords and entries reflects current educated usage, while at the same time taking into account the recommendations of the Government Committee on 'Chinese Characters for Daily Use' (1981). The general principles that have been followed are:

5. 2 When there is a *kanji* listed after the *hiragana* immediately following the headword and all example phrases and sentences use that *kanji*, you may assume that the word is normally written in *kanji*, rather than *hiragana*.

> **na⌈game⌉ru** ながめる (眺める) *vt.* look at; watch; view:
> *Kanojo wa mado kara soto o* nagamete ita. (彼女は窓から外を眺めていた) She *was looking* out of the window.

5. 3 When there is a *kanji* listed after the *hiragana*, but no example phrases or sentences with that *kanji*, you may assume that whilst the *kanji* for that particular word does exist, it is common and perfectly acceptable not to use it in everyday written Japanese.

> **ma⌈ku** まく (蒔く) plant; sow:
> *Kadan ni hana no tane o* maita. (花壇に花の種をまいた) I *planted* flower seeds in the flower bed.

5. 4 You will also find illustrative examples in which example sentences using the headword is sometimes in *kana*, and sometimes in *kanji*. In such cases you may assume that both usages are perfectly acceptable, although some senses of the word may more commonly be written in *kana*, and other senses in *kanji*. (For example, see the entries under '**a⌈taru**.')

6. Conjugations of verbs

6. 1 Consonant-stem verbs

Consonant-stem verbs are marked Ⓒ in this dictionary and the two basic forms, to which '-*masu*' and '-*nai*' are attached, and the *te*-form are given in this order.

> **ka⌐k·u** かく (書く) *vt.* (kak·i-; kak·a-; ka·i-te Ⓒ)
> **no⌐mu** のむ (飲む) *vt.* (nom·i-; nom·a-; non̄-de Ⓒ)

6. 2 Vowel-stem verbs

Vowel-stem verbs are marked Ⓥ in this dictionary, and only the *te*-form is given, since the '-*masu*' and '-*nai*' are attached to the stem without any changes.

> **ta⌐be⌐·ru** たべる (食べる) *vt.* (tabe-te Ⓥ)

6. 3 Irregular verbs

Irregular verbs are marked Ⓘ in this dictionary, and the two basic forms, to which '-*masu*' and '-*nai*' are attached, and the *te*-form are given.

> **s·u⌐ru** する *vt.* (sh·i-; sh·i-; sh·i-te Ⓘ)
> **me⌐n̄s·u⌐ru** めんする (面する) *vi.* (men̄sh·i-; men̄sh·i-; men̄sh·i-te Ⓘ)
> **k·u⌐ru** くる (来る) *vi.* (ko-; ki-; ki-te Ⓘ)

6. 4 With longer verbs, the conjugational information is given in abbreviated form in the interests of both clarity and economy of space.

> **chi⌐rakas·u** ちらかす (散らかす) *vt.* (-kash·i-; -kas·a-; -sh·i-te Ⓒ)

7. Conjugation of adjectives

7. 1 Only the *ku*-form is given.

> **ta⌐ka⌐·i** たかい (高い) *a.* (-ku)

7. 2 Most adjectives are used attributively

> furui *yuujin̄* (an *old* friend)

and predicatively.

> *Chuugoku no rekishi wa* furui. (China's hisotry is *long*.)

But in those cases in which adjectives are restricted in their usage, those that are used only attributively are marked '*attrib.*' (attributive), and those used only predicatively are marked '*pred.*' (predicative).

8. Adjectival nouns

The entry that follows an adjectival noun is as follows:

> **shi˥zuka** しずか (静か) *a.n.* (~ na, ni) quiet

The word '*na*' is used to link the adjectival noun to a following noun or another adjectival noun which it modifies.

> shi˥zuka *na heya* (a *quiet* room)

The '*ni*' indicates that the adjectival noun can be adverbialized.

> shi˥zuka *ni nemutte iru* (be sleeping *peacefully*)

9. Adverbs

Inflected forms of some verbs or adjectives are used as adverbs, and when such a form is common, it is listed as a headword.

> **a˥a-shite** ああして *adv.* like that
> **a˥bunaku** あぶなく (危なく) *adv.* nearly

When adverbs are commonly followed by '*to*,' or '*suru*,' this information is given in brackets immediately following.

> **do˥shi˥n** どしん *adv.* (~ to) with a thud
> **fu˥rafura** ふらふら *adv.* (~ suru) feel dizzy

When '*to*' is optional, an attempt is made to show this in the illustrative examples.

10 Levels of usage

Levels of usage or register are indicated as follows:

formal	=	a word used in formal or official situations
informal	=	a word used in relaxed and friendly situations
colloquial	=	an informal word used in conversation
polite	=	a polite word
honorific	=	a word indicating respect for others
humble	=	a word indicating humility

brusque	=	a potentially rough or abrupt word
rude	=	a potentially impolite or offensive word
literary	=	a word used in the written language

The above is to be taken only as a guide. There will be great variations in usage amongst native speakers of Japanese.

11. Cross-references

Reference to another word with a related meaning is indicated by ((⇨)).

Reference to a word with a contrasting meaning is indicated by ((↔)).

12. Brackets in illustrative examples

11. 1   Round brackets (   ) indicate that omission is possible.

11. 2   Square brakets [   ] indicate alternative possibilities.

13. Abbreviations

a.	adjective	*int.*	interjection
a.n.	adjectival noun	*n.*	noun
adv.	adverb	*neg.*	negative
attrib.	attributive	*p.*	particle
colloq.	colloquial	*pred.*	predicative
conj.	conjunction	*pref.*	prefix
derog.	derogatory	*suf.*	suffix
fig.	figurative	*vi.*	intransitive verb
illus.	illustration	*vt.*	transitive verb
infl. end.	inflected ending		

A

a´¹ あっ *int.* oh; ah: ★ Used to express admiration, wonder, danger, etc.
A´, *wakatta*. (あっ、わかった) *Oh*, I see. / A´, *teeki o wasureta*. (あっ、定期を忘れた) *Oh*, I've forgotten my commuter ticket. / A´, *basu ga kita*. (あっ、バスが来た) *Look!* Here comes the bus. / A´, *señsee da*. (あっ、先生だ) *Oh!* It's the teacher. / A´, *abunai*. (あっ、危ない) *Look out*. That's dangerous.

a⌐a¹ ああ *adv.* such; that; to such a degree; to such an extent:
Niku ga aa takakute wa totemo kaemaseñ. (肉がああ高くてはとても買えません) If meat costs *that much*, I just cannot afford to buy it. / Aa *namakete ita ñ de wa shikeñ ni ochiru no mo toozeñ desu*. (ああ怠けていたんでは試験に落ちるのも当然です) Since he was *so* lazy, it is natural that he failed the exam. / *Watashi wa aa naru to omotte imashita*. (私はああなると思っていました) I thought it would turn out *that way*. / *Haha wa itsu-mo aa shiro koo shiro to iu*. (母はいつもああしろこうしろと言う) My mother is always telling me to do this and *that*. / Aa *ieba koo iu*. (ああ言えばこう言う) When I say *such and such*, he always says something else.
《⇨ doo¹; koo; soo¹》

a⌐a² ああ *int.* oh; ah; well; yes: ★ Used to express admiration, wonder, sorrow, etc.
Aa, *kiree da*. (ああ、きれいだ) *Oh*, that's beautiful. / Aa, *sugoi*. (ああ、すごい) *Wow!* that's great. / Aa, *kawaisoo ni*. (ああ、かわいそうに) *Oh*, how sad. / Aa, *samui*. (ああ、寒い) *Well*, it is cold. / Aa, *shukudai ga nakereba ii no ni*. (ああ、宿題がなければいいのに) *Ah!* If only we had no homework.

a⌐a-iu ああいう *attrib.* that; like that; that kind of; such:
"*Koñdo deta zasshi o doo omoimasu ka?*" "Aa-iu *zasshi ni wa kyoomi ga arimaseñ*." (「今度出た雑誌をどう思いますか」「ああいう雑誌には興味がありません」) "What do you think about the new magazine just published?" "I am not interested in *that kind* of magazine." / "*Kono-aida no fune no tabi wa ikaga deshita?*" "Aa-iu *tanoshii keekeñ wa hajimete desu*." (「この間の船の旅はいかがでした」「ああいう楽しい経験は初めてです」) "How was the recent cruise?" "That was the first time I've had *such* an enjoyable experience."
《⇨ doo-iu; koo-iu; soo-iu》

a⌐a-shite¹ ああして *adv.* like that; in that way:
Kanojo wa aa-shite itsu-mo hito ni damasareru. (彼女はああしていつも人にだまされる) She is always deceived *like that* by people. / *Kare wa itsu-mo aa-shite kure, koo-shite kure, to bakari itte iru*. (彼はいつもああしてくれ、こうしてくれ、とばかり言っている) He is always asking me to do this and *that* for him.
《⇨ doo-shite; koo-shite; soo-shite》

a⌐ba⌐k·u あばく (暴く) *vt.* (abak·i-; abak·a-; aba·i-te ⓒ) expose; disclose; reveal:
himitsu [iñboo] o abaku (秘密[陰謀]を暴く) *expose* a confidence [plot] / *shootai o abaku* (正体を暴く) *unmask* a person / *Kare wa sono fusee o abaita*. (彼はその不正を

暴いた) He *brought* the graft *to
light*.

aˈbare·ru あばれる (暴れる) *vi.*
(abare-te Ⓥ) **1** act violently;
rage; struggle:
*Kodomo wa chuusha o iyagatte
abareta.* (子どもは注射をいやがって暴れ
た) The child *struggled to get
away* from the injection. / *Kono
uma wa hidoku* abareru. (この馬はひ
どく暴れる) This horse *is* very
unruly.
2 do whatever one wants:
*Kyoo no shiai de wa omoikiri
abareru zo.* (きょうの試合では思い切り
暴れるぞ) I'm going to *give it my
all* in today's game.

aˈbekobe あべこべ *n.* (*informal*)
opposite; contrary; reverse:
abekobe *no kekka* (あべこべの結果)
the *opposite* result / *Kono e wa
jooge ga* abekobe *desu.* (この絵は上
下があべこべです) This painting is
upside down. / *Kono kami wa
omote to ura ga* abekobe *desu.* (こ
の紙は表と裏があべこべです) This
sheet of paper is *facing the wrong
way*.

aˈbi·ru あびる (浴びる) *vt.* (abi-te
Ⓥ) **1** bathe:
kawa de mizu o abiru (川で水を浴び
る) *bathe* in a river / *shawaa o*
abiru (シャワーを浴びる) *take* a shower / *hito-furo* abiru (ひと風呂浴びる)
take a bath.
2 get covered with:
hokori o abiru (ほこりを浴びる) *get
covered* with dust / *hooshanoo o*
abiru (放射能を浴びる) *get contami-
nated* by radioactivity.
3 bask:
nikkoo o abiru (日光を浴びる) *bask*
in the sun / *Yama ga asahi o
abite kagayaite iru.* (山が朝日を浴び
て輝いている) The mountains are
bright *under* the morning sun. /
Supotto-raito o abite *kashu ga toojoo shita.* (スポットライトを浴びて歌手

が登場した) The singer appeared
under the spotlight.
4 be an object of praise [attack;
criticism]:
zessañ o abiru (絶賛を浴びる)
receive great praise / *arashi no
yoo na hakushu o* abiru (嵐のような
拍手を浴びる) *win* a storm of ap-
plause / *Kare wa* hinañ *mo toozeñ da.* (彼は非難を浴びても当
然だ) It is quite natural that he *is
criticized.* (⇨ abiseru)

aˈbise·ru あびせる (浴びせる) *vt.*
(abise-te Ⓥ) **1** throw; pour
(water):
hito ni mizu o abiseru (人に水を浴
びせる) *throw* water on a person.
2 (*fig.*) shower (with questions);
heap (abuse on):
*Chooshuu wa kooshi ni shitsumoñ
o* abiseta. (聴衆は講師に質問を浴びせ
た) The audience *showered* questions on the lecturer. / *Kaku shiñbuñ wa seefu no yarikata ni hinañ
o* abiseta. (各新聞は政府のやり方に非
難を浴びせた) The newspapers
heaped condemnation on the
government for its actions.
(⇨ abiru)

aˈbuna·i あぶない (危ない) *a.* (-ku)
1 dangerous; risky:
Dooro de asobu no wa abunai. (道
路で遊ぶのは危ない) It is *dangerous*
to play in the road. / *Yamanobori de* abunai *me ni atta.* (山登
りで危ない目にあった) I had a *dan-
gerous* experience when mountain climbing.

ABUNAI SIGN

Abunai!! Koko de asoñde wa ikemaseñ.
(Danger!! Don't play here.)

2 critical:
Kaneko-sañ wa inochi ga abunai.
（金子さんは命が危ない）Mr. Kaneko
is in *critical* condition.
3 doubtful:
Kare ga tooseñ suru ka doo ka
abunai *mono da.*（彼が当選するかどう
か危ないものだ）It is *doubtful*
whether he will be elected.
abunai tokoro de（～ところで）nar-
rowly: *Abunai tokoro de tasu-*
katta.（危ないところで助かった）I *nar-*
rowly escaped.

a⌈**bunaku**　あぶなく（危なく）*adv.*
nearly; almost; narrowly.
abunaku ...suru tokoro datta
（～...するところだった）nearly: *Kabañ*
o abunaku deñwa-bokkusu ni
wasureru tokoro datta.（かばんを危な
く電話ボックスに忘れるところだった）I
nearly forgot my bag in the telephone booth. / *Sono ko wa abu-*
naku *kuruma ni hikareru tokoro*
deshita.（その子は危なく車にひかれると
ころでした）The child *came close to*
being hit by a car.

a⌈**bura**[1]　あぶら（油）*n.* oil:
kikai ni abura o sasu（機械に油をさ
す）*oil* a machine / *abura ga kireru*
（油が切れる）run short of *oil* / *sa-*
kana o abura de ageru（魚を油で揚
げる）deep-fry a fish in *oil*.
abura o shiboru（～を絞る）haul
over the coals: *Watashi-tachi wa*
señsee ni abura o shiborareta.（私
たちは先生に油を絞られた）We *were*
severely reprimanded by our
teacher.
abura o uru（～を売る）sneak off
from work; idle away one's time
(talking): *Doko de abura o utte*
ita ñ da?（どこで油を売っていたんだ）
Where *have* you *been goofing off?*

a⌈**bura**[2]　あぶら（脂）*n.* fat; grease.
《⇨ shiboo》
a⌈**bura**⌉**e**　あぶらえ（油絵）*n.* an oil
painting.
a⌈**burakko**⌉**・i**　あぶらっこい（脂っこい）

a. (-ku) greasy; oily.

a⌈**chi**⌉**-kochi**　あちこち *n.* here
and there; from place to place;
far and near: ★ Abbreviated
form of '*achira-kochira.*'
No no hana ga achi-kochi *ni saite*
ita.（野の花があちこちに咲いていた）
Wild flowers were blooming *here*
and there. / *Wakai koro wa* achi-
kochi *hikkoshi o shimashita.*（若い
ころはあちこち引っ越しをしました）I
moved *from place to place* when
I was young. / *Nihoñ-juu o* achikochi *ryokoo shite mitai.*（日本中をあ
ちこち旅行してみたい）I'd like to visit
various places in Japan. 《⇨ achi-
ra-kochira》

a⌈**chira**　あちら *n.* **1** that place;
that way; over there: ★ Refers
to a direction or a place at a distance from both the speaker and
the listener. More polite than
'*asoko*' and '*atchi.*'
Achira ni irassharu no wa donata
desu ka?（あちらにいらっしゃるのはどな
たですか）Who is that person *over*
there? (*polite*) / *O-kyaku-sama o*
achira *e go-añnai shite kudasai.*
（お客さまをあちらへご案内してください）
Please take the guests *over there.*
/ *Hokkaidoo kara korareta ñ desu*
ka? Achira wa samui deshoo.（北
海道から来られたんですか. あちらは寒いで
しょう）You have come from Hokkaido? It must be cold *up there.*
《⇨ dochira; kochira; sochira》
2 that thing; that person: ★ Refers to someone or something at
a distance from both the speaker
and the listener.
"Kono kabañ wa ki ni irimaseñ."
"Achira wa ikaga desu ka?"（「この
かばんは気に入りません」「あちらはいかが
ですか」）"I don't like this bag."
"How about *that one?*" / *Achira*
ga yuumee na Nakamura señsee
desu.（あちらが有名な中村先生です）
That person over there is the

famous Prof. Nakamura. / Achira *ni o-cha o sashiagete (kudasai).* (あちらにお茶を差し上げて(ください)) Will you please serve *that person* some tea?

aˈchira-koˈchira あちらこちら *n.* here and there; up and down: ★ Abbreviated to '*achi-kochi.*' *Kare wa kooeñ no* achira-kochira *o arukimawatta.* (彼は公園のあちらこちらを歩き回った) He walked *around* in the park. / Achira-kochira *de sakura ga saki-hajimemashita.* (あちらこちらで桜が咲き始めました) The cherry trees started to bloom *here and there.* 《⇨ achi-kochi》

aˈdaˈ あだ (仇) *n.* **1** vengeance; revenge: *chichi no* ada o utsu (父のあだを討つ) *avenge* one's father. **2** ill will; hostility: *oñ o* ada *de kaesu* (恩をあだで返す) return good with *evil.* 《⇨ kataki》

aˈeˈgˈu あえぐ (喘ぐ) *vi.* (aeg·i-; aeg·a-; ae·i-de Ⓒ) **1** pant; gasp: aegi aegi *yama o noboru* (あえぎあえぎ山を登る) climb a mountain, *gasping for* breath. **2** suffer: *fukyoo ni* aegu (不況にあえぐ) *suffer* an economic depression / *hiñkoñ ni* aegu (貧困にあえぐ) *suffer* from poverty / *atsusa ni* aegu (暑さにあえぐ) *find* the heat *unbearable.*

aˈete あえて (敢えて) *adv.* daringly; boldly. **aete...suru** (～...する) dare to do; venture to do: *Makeru towa-katte ite, kare wa* aete *tatakai o idoñda.* (負けるとわかっていて、彼はあえて戦いを挑んだ) He knew he would lose, but he *dared to challenge* them. / *Mooshiage nikui koto desu ga,* aete *shiñjitsu o* hanashi-masu. (申し上げにくいことですが、あえて真実を話します) This is not an easy

thing to say, but I have *decided to tell* you the truth. / *Anata no teeañ ni* aete *hañtai wa* shimaseñ. (あなたの提案にあえて反対はしません) I *have no particular* objection to your proposal.

aˈfureˈ·ru あふれる (溢れる) *vi.* (afure-te Ⓥ) **1** overflow; flood: *Oo-ame de kawa ga* afureta. (大雨で川があふれた) The river *overflowed* because of the heavy rain. / *Ka-nojo no me wa namida de* afurete *ita.* (彼女の目は涙であふれていた) Her eyes *were filled* with tears. / *Choo-shuu wa rooka made* afurete ita. (聴衆は廊下まであふれていた) The audience *spilled* into the corridors. **2** be crowded with: *Nichiyoobi no Shiñjuku wa hito de* afurete *iru.* (日曜日の新宿は人であふれている) Shinjuku on Sundays *is crowded* with people. **3** be full of: *Kare wa kiboo ni* afurete *iru.* (彼は希望にあふれている) He *is full* of hope. / *Wakamono-tachi wa geñki ni* afurete *iru.* (若者たちは元気にあふれている) The young people *are brimming* with energy.

Aˈfurika アフリカ *n.* Africa. 《⇨ tairiku》

aˈgarˈ·u あがる (上がる) *vi.* (agar·i-; agar·a-; agat-te Ⓒ) **1** go up; rise; come up: *Eñtotsu kara kemuri ga* agatte *iru.* (煙突から煙が上がっている) There is smoke *rising* from the chimney. / *Kare wa go-kai made aruite* agatta. (彼は5階まで歩いて上がった) He *walked up* to the fifth floor. / *Doozo* o-agari *kudasai.* (どうぞお上がりください) Please *come in* (to our house). **2** (of degree, quantity, prices, etc.) rise, be raised; be promoted: *Oñdo ga kyuu ni* agatta. (温度が急

に上がった) The temperature suddenly *rose*. / *Bukka wa* agari-*tsuzukete iru.* (物価は上がり続けている) Prices keep *rising*. / *Kare wa chii ga* agatta. (彼は地位が上がった) He *was promoted.* 《⇨ ageru¹》

3 improve; make progress:
seeseki ga agaru (成績が上がる) one's (school) grades *improve* / *Kare wa gorufu no ude ga* agatta. (彼はゴルフの腕が上がった) His skill at golf *improved.* 《⇨ ageru¹》

4 (of school) enter:
Kare no kodomo wa kotoshi shoogakkoo ni agarimashita. (彼の子どもは今年小学校に上がりました) His child *started* elementary school this year. 《⇨ ageru¹》

5 (of rain) stop; clear up:
Ame ga agarimashita. (雨が上がりました) The rain *has stopped.*

6 (of a person) get nervous; get stage fright:
Kanojo wa meñsetsu de agatte *shimatta.* (彼女は面接で上がってしまった) She *got nervous* at the interview.

7 (*polite*) eat; drink:
Doozo o-agari *kudasai.* (どうぞお上がりください) Please *help yourself.*

aˈgeku あげく (挙げ句) *n.* the end:
★ Follows the past-form of a verb and implies a result.
Iroiro kañgaeta ageku, *sono keekaku wa akiramemashita.* (いろいろ考えたあげく、その計画はあきらめました) *After* much thought, I gave up the plan.

ageku no hate (～の果て) finally; in the end: *Kare wa keeba de soñ o shi,* ageku no hate, *o-kane o zeñbu tsukatte shimatta.* (彼は競馬で損をし、あげくの果て、お金を全部使ってしまった) He lost on the horses, and *ended up* using up all his money.

aˈge·ru¹ あげる (上げる) *vt.* (age-te Ⅴ) **1** raise; lift:
Shitsumoñ ga areba te o age

nasai. (質問があれば手を上げなさい) If you have any questions, please *raise* your hands. 《⇨ agaru》

2 give:
Anata ni kono hoñ o agemasu. (あなたにこの本をあげます) I will *give* you this book. 《↔ kureru》

3 raise:
oñdo [nedañ] o ageru (温度[値段]を上げる) *raise* the temperature [price]. 《⇨ agaru》

4 improve; increase:
tenisu no ude o ageru (テニスの腕を上げる) *improve* one's skill at tennis / *shigoto no nooritsu o* ageru (仕事の能率を上げる) *improve* the efficiency of the work. 《⇨ agaru》

-te ageru (て～) (used when doing a favor for someone else):
Watashi wa kare ni kasa o kashite ageta. (私は彼に傘を貸してあげた) I *lent* him an umbrella. / *Kono nimotsu o* motte agemashoo *ka?* (この荷物を持ってあげましょうか) Shall I *carry* this baggage for you?

aˈge·ru² あげる (揚げる) *vt.* (age-te Ⅴ) deep-fry:
Yuushoku ni sakana o ageta. (夕食に魚を揚げた) I *deep-fried* fish for dinner. 《⇨ itameru (table)》

aˈgo¹ あご (顎) *n.* jaw; chin:
Kare wa ago *ni hige o hayashite ita.* (彼はあごにひげを生やしていた) He wore a beard on his *chin.*

ago de tsukau (～で使う) *vi.* order a person about.

ago o dasu (～を出す) *vi.* get tired out.

aˈgo¹hige あごひげ (顎髭) *n.* beard:
agohige *o hayasu* (あごひげを生やす) wear [grow] a *beard.* 《⇨ hige (table)》

aˈgura あぐら *n.* (way of sitting with one's legs crossed).

agura o kaku (～をかく) sit cross-legged.

aˈhaha¹ あはは *int.* used to

express loud laughter:
*Kare wa rakugo o kiki-nagara
'ahaha' to waratta.* (彼は落語を聞き
ながら「あはは」と笑った) He laughed
out *loud* as he was listening to
the comic monologue story
(*rakugo*).

a⌈hiru あひる (家鴨) *n*. domestic
duck. 《⇨ kamo》

a⌈i あい (愛) *n*. love:
ko ni taisuru haha no ai (子に対する
母の愛) a mother's *love* for her
child / *ai o chikau* (愛を誓う) swear
undying *love*. 《⇨ koi》

A⌈ichi⌉-ken あいちけん (愛知県) *n*.
Aichi Prefecture. Located in the
southwest section of the Chubu
district, facing the Pacific. It contains the third largest industrial
district of Japan. Capital city:
Nagoya (名古屋). 《⇨ map (E4)》

a⌈ida あいだ (間) *n*. **1** (of place)
between; among: ★ The space
between two things. Often used
in the pattern '*...no aida ni* [*de;
wa*].'
*Gyoo to gyoo no aida o sukoshi
ake nasai.* (行と行の間を少しあけなさ
い) Leave a little space *between*
the lines. / *Watashi-tachi wa ki
no* aida *ni teñto o hatta.* (私たちは木
の間にテントを張った) We pitched
our tents *among* trees.
2 (of time) for; while; during:
★ A certain interval of time.
Watashi wa nagai aida *matasareta.* (私は長い間待たされた) I was
kept waiting *for* a long time. /
Matte iru aida*, hoñ o yoñde ita.*
(待っている間, 本を読んでいた) I was
reading a book *while* I waited. /
Yasumi no aida*, zutto Tookyoo ni
imashita.* (休みの間, ずっと東京にいま
した) I stayed in Tokyo *right
through* the vacation. / *Miñna ga
nete iru* aida *ni kono shigoto o
sumaseta.* (みんなが寝ている間にこの仕
事をすませた) I finished up this

work *while* everyone was sleeping.
3 (of relations) between; among:
Sono jooyaku wa ryookoku no
aida *de musubareta.* (その条約は両
国の間で結ばれた) The treaty was
signed *between* the two countries.
/ *Kanojo wa daigakusee no* aida
de niñki ga aru. (彼女は大学生の間
で人気がある) She is popular *among*
college students. 《⇨ aidagara》

a⌈idagara あいだがら (間柄) *n*. relation; terms:
Ano-hito-tachi wa doo-iu aidagara
desu ka? (あの人たちはどういう間がらで
すか) What is the *relationship* between them? / *Takahashi to wa
shitashii* aidagara *desu.* (高橋とは
親しい間がらです) I'm on friendly
terms with Takahashi.

a⌈ide⌉a アイデア *n*. idea:
Sore wa ii aidea *desu.* (それはいいア
イデアです) That's a good *idea*. /
Subarashii aidea *o omoitsuita.* (す
ばらしいアイデアを思いついた) I hit on a
bright *idea*. 《⇨ kañgae》

a⌈ijiñ あいじん (愛人) *n*. lover;
love; mistress. 《⇨ koibito》

a⌈ijoo あいじょう (愛情) *n*. love;
affection; attachment:
Kare wa kanojo ni honoka na
aijoo *o idaite ita.* (彼は彼女にほのかな
愛情を抱いていた) He cherished a
faint feeling of *affection* for her. /
Watashi wa aijoo *no komotta
tegami o uketotta.* (私は愛情のこもっ
た手紙を受け取った) I received a letter full of *affection*.

a⌈ikagi あいかぎ (合鍵) *n*. duplicate key. 《⇨ kagi》

a⌈ikawarazu あいかわらず (相変わら
ず) *adv*. still; as ... as ever; as
usual:
"O-isogashii desu ka?" "Ee, aikawarazu.*"* (「お忙しいですか」「ええ, 相
変わらず」) "Are you busy?" "Yes,
as usual." / *Kanojo wa* aikawarazu *yoku hataraku.* (彼女は相変わらず

よく働く) She works *as* hard *as
ever.* / *Kare wa* aikawarazu *ichi-
nichi ni yoñjup-poñ mo tabako o
sutte iru.* (彼は相変わらず一日に40本
もたばこを吸っている) He *still* smokes
forty cigarettes in a day.

aˈikyoˈo あいきょう(愛敬) *n.*
charm; amiability:
Kanojo wa seeippai aikyoo *o furi-
maita.* (彼女は精いっぱい愛きょうを振り
まいた) She made every effort to
lay on the *charm.* / *Kare no hisho
wa* aikyoo *ga aru.* (彼の秘書は愛きょ
うがある) His secretary *is amiable
[charming].* ((⇨ aiso))

aˈima あいま(合間) *n.* interval;
recess:
Maku no aima *ni tabako o ippuku
sutta.* (幕の合間にたばこを一服吸った)
During the intermission of the
play, I had a smoke. / *Watashi
wa shigoto no* aima *ni sukoshi
uñdoo o shimasu.* (私は仕事の合間に
少し運動をします) I do some exer-
cise *during* my work breaks.

aˈimai あいまい(曖昧) *a.n.* (~ na,
ni) vague; ambiguous:
Kare wa aimai *na heñji o shita.*
(彼はあいまいな返事をした) He gave a
vague answer. / *Kono hyoogeñ wa*
aimai *da.* (この表現はあいまいだ)
This wording is *ambiguous.* /
Kanojo wa aimai *na taido o totta.*
(彼女はあいまいな態度をとった) She
took an *uncertain* attitude.

aˈiniku あいにく(生憎) *adv.* unfortunately; unluckily:
Ainiku *kare wa fuzai datta.* (あいに
く彼は不在だった) *Unfortunately,*
he was not at home.
—— *a.n.* (~ na/no) unfortunate;
unexpected:
Ainiku *no ame de eñsoku wa eñki
sareta.* (あいにくの雨で遠足は延期され
た) The excursion was postponed
on account of the *unexpected* rain.
/ *Kuruma ga koshoo suru to wa*
ainiku *deshita ne.* (車が故障するとは

あいにくでしたね) It was *too bad* that
your car happened to break
down.

aˈiroñ アイロン *n.* iron:
nuno ni airoñ *o kakeru* (布にアイロン
をかける) press cloth with an *iron.*

aˈisatsu あいさつ(挨拶) *n.*
1 greeting; salutation:
aisatsu *o kawasu* (あいさつを交わす)
exchange *greetings* / aisatsu *ni
atama o sageru* (あいさつに頭を下げ
る) bow one's head in *salutation.*
2 speech; address:
kaikai no aisatsu *o suru* (開会のあ
いさつをする) give an opening
address / *wakare no* aisatsu *o
noberu* (別れのあいさつを述べる) make
a farewell *speech* / *Kore o mochimashite go-*aisatsu *ni kaesasete
itadakimasu.* (これをもちましてごあいさ
つにかえさせていただきます) Please
accept what I have just said as
my *address.* ★ Set expression
used to close congratulatory
speeches, etc.
3 call; visit:
shiñneñ no aisatsu *ni mawaru* (新
年のあいさつに回る) make New
Year's *calls.*
aisatsu (o) suru (~(を)する) *vi.*
greet; salute: *Kanojo wa watashi
ni egao de* aisatsu *shita.* (彼女は私
に笑顔であいさつした) She *greeted* me
with a smile. / *Kare wa chooshuu
ni te o futte,* aisatsu *shita.* (彼は聴
衆に手をふって、あいさつした) With a
wave of his hand, he *saluted* the
audience.

aˈisoˈ あいそ(愛想) *n.* amiability;
sociability; civility:
Kanojo wa kare ni wa aiso *ga ii.*
(彼女は彼には愛想がいい) She *gets
along with him rather well.* / *Ano
mise no teñiñ wa* aiso *ga warui.*
(あの店の店員は愛想が悪い) The
clerks in that store *are rather
brusque.* / *Kare wa* aiso *no nai
heñji o shita.* (彼は愛想のない返事を

した）He gave me a *blunt* answer.

aiso ga tsukiru (～がつきる) be disgusted with: *Kare ni wa* aiso ga tsukita. (彼には愛想がつきた) I *am fed up* with him.

aiso o tsukasu (～をつかす) be out of patience with; be disgusted with: *Kanojo wa otto ni* aiso o tsukashite, *wakareta*. (彼女は夫に愛想をつかして、別れた) She *got completely fed up with* her husband and divorced him. 《⇨ aikyoo》

a⌐iso⌐o あいそう (愛想) *n.* = aiso.

a⌐isukuri⌐imu アイスクリーム *n.* ice cream.

a⌐is·u⌐ru あいする (愛する) *vt.* (ai-sh·i-; ais·a-; aish·i-te ⓒ) love: *watashi no* aisuru *kodomo-tachi* (私の愛する子どもたち) my *dear* children / *Dare yori mo anata o* aishite *imasu*. (だれよりもあなたを愛しています) I *love* you more than anyone else. / *Kare wa miñna ni* aisarete *iru*. (彼はみんなに愛されている) He *is loved* by all. / *Watashi wa nani yori mo heewa o* aisuru *mono da*. (私は何よりも平和を愛する者だ) I am a person who *loves* peace more than anything else. 《⇨ ai》

a⌐ite⌐ あいて (相手) *n.* mate; partner; opponent; companion: asobi-aite (遊び相手) a *playmate* / *tenisu no* aite (テニスの相手) a tennis opponent / *Wareware wa* aite *o roku tai ni de yabutta*. (われわれは相手を6対2で破った) We beat our *opponents* by a score of six to two. / *Kare ga* aite *de tanoshikatta*. (彼が相手で楽しかった) I enjoyed his *company*.

a⌐izu あいず (合図) *n.* signal; sign; alarm: *Beru ga hassha no* aizu *datta*. (ベルが発車の合図だった) The bell was the *signal* for the departure of the train. / *Watashi no* aizu *ga aru made koko ni i nasai*. (私の合図があるまでここにいなさい) Stay here until there is a *sign* from me.

...ni aizu (o) suru (…に～(を)する) *vi.* signal; make a sign: *Keekañ wa kuruma ni tomare to* aizu shita. (警官は車に止まれと合図した) The policeman *signaled* the car to stop. / *Kare wa watashi-tachi ni susume to* aizu shita. (彼は私たちに進めと合図した) He *made a sign* for us to go on.

a⌐ji[1] あじ (味) *n.* taste; savor; flavor: aji *o miru* (味をみる) test the *taste* / *nomimono ni* aji *o tsukeru* (飲み物に味をつける) add *flavor* to a drink / *Kore wa amai* aji *ga suru*. (これは甘い味がする) This has a sweet *taste*. / *Kono soosu wa niñniku no* aji *ga suru*. (このソースはにんにくの味がする) This sauce *tastes* of garlic.

amai	sweet; sugary
karai	hot; pungent
nigai	bitter
shibui	astringent
shiokarai	salty
suppai	sour; acid

a⌐ji[2] あじ (鯵) *n.* horse mackerel: aji *no hiraki* (あじの開き) a *horse mackerel* cut open and dried.

A SERVING OF AJI NO HIRAKI

A⌐jia アジア *n.* Asia. 《⇨ Toonañ-Ajia; tairiku》

a⌐jiwa⌐·u あじわう (味わう) *vt.* (aji-wa·i-; ajiwaw·a-; ajiwat-te ⓒ) **1** taste; relish: *suupu o* ajiwau (スープを味わう) *taste* the soup / *hoñba no Chuugoku-*

ryoori o ajiwau（本場の中国料理を味わう）*relish* real Chinese cooking.

2 enjoy; appreciate:
yoi oñgaku o ajiwau（良い音楽を味わう）*appreciate* good music / *Tanoshii tabi o* ajiwatta.（楽しい旅を味わった）I *enjoyed* a pleasant journey.

3 experience; go through:
kanashimi o ajiwau（悲しみを味わう）*experience* sorrow / *jiñsee no kuroo o* ajiwau（人生の苦労を味わう）*go through* the hardships of life / *... no suriru o* ajiwau（...のスリルを味わう）*get* a thrill *out of* ....

a「ka[1] あか（赤）*n.* red:
Shiñgoo ga aka *ni kawatta.*（信号が赤に変わった）The traffic light turned *red.*《⇨ akai》
aka no tanin（〜の他人）total stranger: *Ano hito wa watashi ni totte* aka no tanin *desu.*（あの人は私にとって赤の他人です）He is a *complete stranger* to me.

a「ka[12] あか（垢）*n.* dirt; grime.

a「ka-a「ka to あかあかと（赤々と）*adv.* brightly:
Hi ga aka-aka to *moete iru.*（火があかあかと燃えている）The fire is burning *brightly.* / *Yuuhi ga* aka-aka to *moete ita.*（夕日があかあかと燃えていた）The setting sun glowed *crimson.*

a「kachañ あかちゃん（赤ちゃん）*n.* baby: ★ Usually refers to someone else's baby.
Otaku no akachañ *wa nañ-sai desu ka?*（お宅の赤ちゃんは何歳ですか）How old is your *baby?*《⇨ akañboo》

a「ka·i あかい（赤い）*a.* (-ku) red; crimson; scarlet:
Yuuyake de sora ga akai.（夕焼けで空が赤い）The sky is *red* with the sunset. / *Ki no ha ga* akaku *natte kita.*（木の葉が赤くなってきた）The leaves are turning *red.* / *Hazuka-*

shikute, kao ga akaku *natta.*（恥ずかしくて、顔が赤くなった）I *blushed* for shame.

a「kaji あかじ（赤字）*n.* the red; red figures; deficit:
Koñgetsu wa goseñ-eñ no akaji *da.*（今月は 5,000 円の赤字だ）I'm 5,000 yen in *the red* this month. / *Shoobai ga* akaji *ni natta.*（商売が赤字になった）The business went into *the red.* / *Akaji o ume-nakereba naranai.*（赤字を埋めなければならない）We have to make up the *deficit.*《↔ kuroji》

a「kañboo あかんぼう（赤ん坊）*n.* baby.《⇨ akachañ》

a「kañtai あかんたい（亜寒帯）*n.* the subarctic [subantarctic] zone.

a「kari あかり（明り）*n.* light; lamp:
akari *o tsukeru* [*kesu*]（明りをつける [消す]）turn on [off] the *light* / *To-tsuzeñ,* akari *ga zeñbu kieta.*（突然、明りが全部消えた）Suddenly all the *lights* went out.

a「karu·i あかるい（明るい）*a.* (-ku)
1 bright; light:
akarui *hizashi*（明るい日差し）*bright* sunlight / akarui *iro*（明るい色）*bright* colors / *Soto ga dañdañ* akaruku *natte kita.*（外がだんだん明るくなってきた）It has become *light* outside.《↔ kurai》
2 cheerful; happy:
akarui *katee*（明るい家庭）a *happy* family / akarui *kibuñ*（明るい気分）a *happy* feeling / *Morita-sañ wa* akarui *seekaku desu.*（森田さんは明るい性格です）Miss Morita has a *cheerful* disposition.《↔ kurai》
3 (of prospects, etc.) bright:
akarui *mirai*（明るい未来）a *bright* future / *Keeki no mitooshi wa* akarui.（景気の見通しは明るい）The economic prospects are *bright.*《↔ kurai》[1]
4 be familiar with; be well informed:
Kare wa hooritsu ni akarui.（彼は

法律に明るい) He *is well versed in* the law. 《↔ kurai¹》《⇨ kuwashii》

aˈkashiˈñgoo あかしんごう (赤信号) *n.* red light; stoplight: *akashiñgoo de tomaru* (赤信号で止まる) stop at a *red light* / Sono kuruma wa akashiñgoo o mamoranakatta. (その車は赤信号を守らなかった) The car went through the *red light*. 《⇨ aoshiñgoo》

aˈkasˈu あかす (明かす) *vt.* (akash·i·; akas·a·; akash·i·te Ⓒ) **1** spend; pass (a night): *Watashi-tachi wa sono koya de ichi-ya o akashita.* (私たちはその小屋で一夜を明かした) We *spent* a night in that hut. **2** reveal; disclose (a secret, etc.): *Toki ga kureba, shiñjitsu o akashimasu.* (時が来れば真実を明かします) When the time comes, I will *tell* the truth.

aˈkegata あけがた (明け方) *n.* dawn; daybreak: *Ikkoo wa akegata ni shuppatsu shita.* (一行は明け方に出発した) The party set out at *dawn*. / Akegata chikaku kaji ga atta. (明け方近く火事があった) There was a fire toward *daybreak*.

aˈke·ru¹ あける (開ける) *vt.* (ake-te Ⓥ) open; unpack; unlock: *doa [hikidashi; kañzume] o akeru* (ドア[引き出し;缶詰]を開ける) *open* a door [drawer; can] / *kaateñ o akeru* (カーテンを開ける) *pull back* the curtains / *suutsukeesu o akeru* (スーツケースを開ける) *unpack* [*unlock*] one's suitcase / *Hoñ no juugo-peeji o ake nasai.* (本の15ページを開けなさい) *Open* your books to page fifteen. / *Kuchi o ookiku akete kudasai.* (口を大きく開けてください) Please *open* your mouth wide. / *Me o akete, yoku gorañ nasai.* (目を開けて,よくごらんなさい) *Open* your eyes and look carefully. / *Watashi wa itsu-mo mise*

o ku-ji ni akemasu. (私はいつも店を9時に開けます) I always *open* the shop at nine o'clock. 《↔ shimeru¹》 《⇨ aku》

aˈke·ru² あける (明ける) *vi.* (ake-te Ⓥ) **1** (of day) break; dawn: *Moo sugu yo ga akeru.* (もうすぐ夜が明ける) The day will *break* soon. **2** (of a new year) begin: *toshi ga akeru* (年が明ける) a new year *begins* / Akemashite omedetoo gozaimasu. (明けましておめでとうございます) *A Happy New Year!* **3** end; be over: *Yatto tsuyu ga aketa.* (やっと梅雨が明けた) At last the rainy season *is over*.

akete mo kurete mo (明けても暮れても) day in day out; always.

aˈke·ru³ あける (空ける) *vt.* (ake-te Ⓥ) **1** empty; vacate: *Kabiñ no mizu o nagashi ni aketa.* (花瓶の水を流しに空けた) I *emptied* the water in the vase into the sink. / *Koñgetsu-chuu ni heya o akete kudasai.* (今月中に部屋を空けてください) Please *vacate* the room within this month. / *Shigoto de ni, sañ-nichi ie o akemasu.* (仕事で2, 3日家を空けます) I will *be away* from home for two or three days on business. 《⇨ aku²》 **2** make room for: *Kyuukyuusha ga toorimasu. Michi o akete kudasai.* (救急車が通ります。道を空けてください) An ambulance is coming. Please *make way* for it. / *Isu to isu no aida o moo sukoshi akemashoo.* (いすといすの間をもう少しあけましょう) Let's *make* some more *room* between the chairs. / *Kotae wa ichi-gyoo zutsu aˈ.ete kaki nasai.* (答えは一行ずつあけて書きなさい) Write your answers on *every* other line. **3** make an opening: *kabe ni ana o akeru* (壁に穴を空ける) *make* a hole in the wall. 《⇨ aku²》

4 make time:
Chotto o-jikañ o akete kudasaimaseñ ka? (ちょっとお時間をあけてください ませんか) Can't you *spare* me a little time? / *Sono hi wa ichi-nichi karada o akete okimasu.* (その日は 一日体をあけておきます) On that day, I'll *make* myself *available* the whole day. 《⇨ aki; aku²》

aˈki¹ あき (秋) *n.* autumn; fall: *Aki wa ryokoo ni ichibañ yoi kisetsu desu.* (秋は旅行に一番良い季節で す) *Autumn* is the best season for traveling. / *Kono ki wa aki ni naru to kooyoo shimasu.* (この木は 秋になると紅葉します) The leaves of this tree turn red with the coming of *fall.* / aki-*bare* (秋晴れ) a fine *autumn* day / aki-*kaze* (秋風) an *autumn* breeze. 《⇨ kisetsu (table); shiki (table)》

aˈki² あき (空き) *n.* **1** vacancy: *Kono kaisha ni wa ima no tokoro aki ga arimaseñ.* (この会社には今のと ころ空きがありません) There are no *vacancies* at our company at the present time. 《⇨ aku²》
2 space; room: *Gyoo to gyoo no aida ni motto aki o tori nasai.* (行と行の間にもっと空き をとりなさい) Leave more *space* between lines. 《⇨ akeru³》
3 spare time: *Yotee ga tsumatte ite, kyoo no gogo wa aki ga arimaseñ.* (予定が 詰まっていて, きょうの午後は空きがありま せん) I have a tight schedule and have no *time to spare* this afternoon. 《⇨ akeru³》

aˈkichi あきち (空き地) *n.* vacant land; empty lot. 《⇨ tochi》

aˈkikañ あきかん (空き缶) *n.* empty can.

aˈkiˈraka あきらか (明らか) *a.n.* (~ na, ni) evident; obvious; clear: *Sono koto wa dare no me ni mo akiraka desu.* (そのことはだれの目にも 明らかです) That is *evident* to everybody. / *Sore wa akiraka na jijitsu da.* (それは明らかな事実だ) It is an *obvious* fact. / *Kare ga itte iru koto wa akiraka ni machigai da.* (彼が言っていることは明らかに間違いだ) What he says is *clearly* wrong. / *Seefu wa keñkai o akiraka ni shita.* (政府は見解を明らかにした) The government made its view *plain.*

aˈkirame あきらめ (諦め) *n.* resignation; abandonment: *Akirame ga kañjiñ desu.* (あきらめが 肝心です) We should know when to *give up.* / *Kare wa doo shite mo akirame ga tsukanakatta.* (彼は どうしてもあきらめがつかなかった) He couldn't for the life of him *resign himself* to fate. 《⇨ akirameru》

aˈkirameˈ・ru あきらめる (諦める) *vt.* (akirame-te Ⓥ) give up; abandon: *Teñki ga warukatta no de sono keekaku wa akirameta.* (天気が悪か ったのでその計画はあきらめた) We *gave up* the plan because of the bad weather. / *Watashi wa isha ni naru no o akirameta.* (私は医者にな るのをあきらめた) I *abandoned* the idea of becoming a doctor. / *Musuko wa shiñda mono to akiramete imasu.* (息子は死んだものとあきら めています) I *have given up* my son for dead. / *Uñmee to akirameta.* (運命とあきらめた) I *resigned* myself to my fate. 《⇨ akirame》

aˈkire・ru あきれる (呆れる) *vi.* (akire-te Ⓥ) be shocked; be astonished; be dumbfounded: *Kare no jooshiki no nasa ni wa akireta.* (彼の常識のなさにはあきれた) I *was shocked* by his lack of common sense. / *Añna hito ga shichoo ni natta to wa kiite,* akireru. (あんな人が市長になったとは聞いて, あき れる) I'm *astonished* to hear that a person like him became the

mayor. / *Akirete, mono mo ienai.*
(あきれて、ものも言えない) I'm *dumb-
founded.* / *Ware-nagara* akireru.
(われながらあきれる) I'm *disgusted*
with myself.

a⌈ki⌉·ru あきる(飽きる) *vi.* (aki-te
Ⅴ) get [be] tired of:
Tokai no seekatsu ni wa akita. (都
会の生活には飽きた) I *have become
weary* of city life. / *Kono ko wa
nani o yatte mo sugu* akiru. (この子
は何をやってもすぐ飽きる) This child
soon *loses interest* in whatever he
does. / *Sono hanashi wa kiki-
akita.* (その話しは聞き飽きた) I *am
tired* of hearing that story. /
Kono eega wa mi-akita. (この映画は
見飽きた) I *have seen enough* of
this movie.

A⌈kita⌉-keñ あきたけん(秋田県) *n.*
Akita Prefecture. Located near
the north end of Honshu, facing
the Sea of Japan on the west.
Sake brewing and the lumber
industry are the major industries.
Capital city: Akita. 《⇨ map
(G2)》

a⌈kiya あきや(空き家) *n.* vacant
[empty] house.

a⌈kka あっか(悪化) *n.* worsening;
deterioration; aggravation:
joosee no akka (情勢の悪化) a
worsening of the situation.
akka suru (～する) *vi.* become
worse; deteriorate: *Chichi no
byooki ga* akka shita. (父の病気が
悪化した) My father's illness *has
become worse.* / *Ryookoku no kañkee wa issoo* akka shita. (両国の関
係は一層悪化した) Relations be-
tween the two countries *have
further deteriorated.*

a⌈kkenai あっけない(呆気ない) *a.*
(-ku) disappointingly short
[brief; quick]:
Sono shiai wa akkenai *shiai datta.*
(その試合はあっけない試合だった) That
was a match which *ended too*

easily. / *Is-shuukañ ga* akkenaku
sugita. (一週間があっけなく過ぎた) A
week has passed *too quickly.*

a⌈kogare あこがれ(憧れ) *n.* yearning; longing; admiration:
Kare wa tokai no seekatsu ni akogare *o idaite ita.* (彼は都会の生活に
あこがれを抱いていた) He had a *yearning* for city life. / *Hawai wa* akogare *no tochi da.* (ハワイはあこがれの
土地だ) Hawaii is a place, I *long*
to visit. / *Kanojo wa wakai hito-
tachi no* akogare *no mato da.* (彼女
は若い人たちのあこがれの的だ) She is
the object of *admiration* of
young people. 《⇨ akogareru》

a⌈kogare·ru あこがれる(憧れる) *vt.*
(akogare-te Ⅴ) **1** long for;
yearn for:
Kanojo wa fasshoñ-moderu ni akogarete *iru.* (彼女はファッションモデルに
憧れている) She *longs* to become a
fashion model. / *Wakamono wa
tokai no seekatsu ni* akogareru.
(若者は都会の生活に憧れる) Young
people *have a yearning* for city
life. 《⇨ akogare》
2 admire:
*Joseeto-tachi wa hañsamu na señ-
see ni* akogarete *iru.* (女生徒たちは
ハンサムな先生に憧れている) The girl
pupils *admire* the handsome
teacher. 《⇨ akogare》

a⌈k·u あく(開く) *vi.* (ak·i-; ak·a-;
a·i-te Ｃ) open:

―――― **USAGE** ――――
「開く」can be read either as
'*hiraku*' or '*aku.*' The former
is usually written in *kanji*, and
the latter in *hiragana.*
――――――――――――――

Sono kagi de wa kono doa wa aki-
maseñ. (その鍵ではこのドアはあきません)
This door *will not open* with that
key. / *Kono doa wa sayuu [soto-
gawa; uchigawa] ni* akimasu. (この
ドアは左右[外側; 内側]にあきます)
This door *opens* sideways [out-

ward; inward]. / *Kaateñ ga hañbuñ* aite iru. (カーテンが半分あいてい
る) The curtains *are* half *open*. /
Mise wa juu-ji ni aite, *roku-ji ni
shimarimasu.* (店は10時にあいて, 6
時に閉まります) The store *opens* at
ten and closes at six. 《↔ shimaru¹》
《⇨ hiraku》

a⌐**k·u**² あく (空く) *vi.* (ak·i-; ak·a-;
a·i-te C) **1** get [be] empty
[vacant]:
Kono heya wa getsumatsu ni wa
akimasu. (この部屋は月末には空きま
す) This apartment will *become
vacant* by the end of the month.
/ *Sumimaseñ ga, sono seki wa*
aite imasu ka? (すみませんが, その席は
あいていますか) Excuse me, but *is*
that seat *occupied*? / *Buchoo no
isu ga* aite iru. (部長の椅子が空いて
いる) The post of department
chief *is open.* 《⇨ akeru³》
2 have a gap:
Hako ni sukima ga akanai *yoo ni
nani-ka tsumete kudasai.* (箱にすき
間が空かないように何か詰めてください)
Please fill up the box with something so that *no space remains.* /
*Kono eki wa deñsha to hoomu no
aida ga* aite imasu. (この駅は電車と
ホームの間が空いています) *There's* a
wide *gap* between the train and
the platform at this station.
《⇨ akeru³》
3 (of a hole) have an opening:
Kono poketto ni wa ana ga aite
imasu. (このポケットには穴があいていま
す) *There is a hole* in this pocket.
《⇨ akeru³》
4 be free:
Doyoobi no gogo nara aite imasu.
(土曜日の午後なら空いています) If you
make it Saturday afternoon, I'll
be free. 《⇨ akeru³》
5 finish with something:
Sono hasami ga aitara, *chotto
kashite kudasai.* (そのはさみがあいたら,
ちょっと貸してください) When you're

finished with the scissors, lend
them to me, please. / *Te ga aitara,
kono shigoto o tetsudatte kudasai.*
(手があいたら, この仕事を手伝ってくださ
い) When you're *finished*, please
help me with this job.

a⌐**ku**³ あく (悪) *n.* vice; evil:
aku *ni somaru* (悪に染まる) sink
into *vice* / aku *ni makeru* (悪に負け
る) surrender to *evil ways.*

a⌐**kubi** あくび (欠伸) *n.* yawn:
akubi *o suru* (あくびをする) give a
yawn / akubi *o osaeru* (あくびを抑え
る) stifle a *yawn.*

a⌐**kui** あくい (悪意) *n.* ill will;
malice; spite:
akui *o idaku* (悪意を抱く) bear *ill
will.*

a⌐**kuji** あくじ (悪事) *n.* evil [wick-
ed] deed; crime:
akuji *o hataraku* (悪事を働く) do
evil / akuji *o kasaneru* (悪事を重ね
る) commit one *crime* after another.

a⌐**kuma** あくま (悪魔) *n.* devil;
demon.

a⌐**ku**⌐**made (mo)** あくまで (も) (飽く
迄(も)) *adv.* to the last; persistently:
Kare-ra wa akumade (mo) *tatakau
kakugo da.* (彼らはあくまで(も)戦う覚
悟だ) They are prepared to fight
to the last. / *Kare wa* akumade
(mo) *shoogeñ o* kaenakatta. (彼はあ
くまで(も)証言を変えなかった) He vehe-
mently *adhered* to his testimony.
/ *Watashi wa* akumade (mo) *keekaku o jikkoo shimasu.* (私はあくま
で(も)計画を実行します) I am *firmly*
determined to carry out my plan.
/ *Kare wa* akumade (mo) *jibuñ no
ikeñ o toosoo to shita.* (彼はあくまで
(も)自分の意見を通そうとした) He *per-
sisted* in his opinion.

a⌐**kuniñ** あくにん (悪人) *n.* bad
[wicked] person; villain.

a⌐**kuru a**⌐**sa** あくるあさ (明くる朝) *n.*
= yokuasa.

a⌐**kuru hi**¹ あくるひ (明くる日) *n.*
= yokujitsu.

a⌐**kuru toshi**¹ あくるとし (明くる年)
n. = yokuneñ.

a⌐**kuseñto** アクセント *n.* **1** (pitch
or stress) accent: ★ Not used in
the sense of 'a (foreign) accent.'
Kono tañgo no akuseñto *wa doko
ni arimasu ka?* (この単語のアクセント
はどこにありますか) Where is the
accent on this word?
2 emphasis; stress; accent:
*Ooki-na riboñ ga kanojo no fuku
no* akuseñto *ni natte ita.* (大きなリボ
ンが彼女の服のアクセントになっていた) A
large ribbon *set off* her dress.

a⌐**kusesarii** アクセサリー *n.* accessory. ★ Usually refers to ornaments and decorations, such as
necklaces, brooches, etc., worn
by women.

a⌐**kushu** あくしゅ (握手) *n.* handshake; handclasp:
Wakareru mae ni futari wa katai
akushu *o kawashita.* (別れる前に二
人はかたい握手を交わした) They
shook hands firmly with each
other before parting.
akushu (o) suru (～ (を) する) *vi.*
shake hands.

a⌐**ma** アマ *n.* amateur. ★ Shortened form of '*amachua*.'
《↔ puro》

a⌐**machua** アマチュア *n.* amateur:
amachua *no gorufaa* (アマチュアのゴル
ファー) an *amateur* golfer / amachua *museñka* (アマチュア無線家) a
radio ham / *Kare wa* amachua *da
ga shashiñ no ude wa subarashii.*
(彼はアマチュアだが写真の腕はすばらしい)
Although he is an *amateur*, his
skill at photography is superb.

a⌐**ma**⌐**do** あまど (雨戸) *n.* sliding
storm door made of thin boards;
shutter:
amado *o shimeru* [*akeru*] (雨戸を
閉める[開ける]) close pull open the
shutters.

OLD-FASHIONED AMADO
IN CLOSED POSITION

a⌐**mae·ru** あまえる (甘える) *vi.*
(amae-te Ⅴ) **1** behave like a
spoiled child; have a coquettish
way:
Sono ko wa haha-oya ni amaeta.
(その子は母親に甘えた) The child
behaved like a baby with his
mother. / *Kanojo wa* amaeta *hanashikata o suru.* (彼女は甘えた話しかた
をする) She speaks in a *coquettish*
way.
2 depend on; take advantage of:
hito no kooi [*shiñsetsu*] *ni* amaeru
(人の好意[親切]に甘える) *depend* on
a person's good will [kindness] /
O-kotoba ni amaete *soo sasete itadakimasu.* (お言葉に甘えてそうさせてい
ただきます) Since you *are kind
enough* to say so, I will avail
myself of your suggestion.

a⌐**maga**⌐**sa** あまがさ (雨傘) *n.* umbrella. 《⇨ kasa》

a⌐**ma**⌐**gu** あまぐ (雨具) *n.* rain-
wear; umbrella; raincoat:
Furi-soo da kara amagu *o motte
itta hoo ga ii desu yo.* (降りそうだか
ら雨具を持って行ったほうがいいですよ)
It looks like rain, so you had better take *something to protect yourself from the rain*.

a⌐**ma·i** あまい (甘い) *a.* (-ku)
1 (of taste) sweet; sugary:
Kono suika wa amai. (このすいかは甘
い) This watermelon is *sweet*.
《⇨ aji (table)》
2 (of voice, melody, etc.) sweet;
attractive:

Kanojo wa amai *koe o shite iru.* (彼女は甘い声をしている) She has a *sweet* voice.

3 not salty:
Kyoo no misoshiru wa chotto amai. (きょうのみそ汁はちょっと甘い) Today's miso soup is *not salty* enough. 《↔ karai》

4 lenient; not severe in discipline:
Shujiñ wa kodomo ni amai. (主人は子どもに甘い) My husband is *too easy* on the children. 《↔ karai》

5 optimistic; easygoing; underestimating the results:
Kare no kañgaekata wa amai. (彼の考え方は甘い) He is too *optimistic*. / Amai *kitai wa idakanai hoo ga yoi.* (甘い期待は抱かないほうがよい) You had better not hold any *optimistic* expectations.

amai kotoba (〜言葉) honeyed words: Amai kotoba *ni ki o tsuke nasai.* (甘い言葉に気をつけなさい) Be careful of *sweet words.*

a⌈ma-no⌉-gawa あまのがわ（天の川） *n.* the Milky Way; the Galaxy. 《⇨ tanabata》

a⌈mari⌉[1] あまり（余り） *n.* the rest; the balance; remains:
Riñgo wa mittsu tabe, amari *wa ryoori ni tsukatta.* (りんごは三つ食べ、余りは料理に使った) We ate three apples and used *the rest* for cooking. / *Kuruma o katte,* amari *no o-kane wa chokiñ shimashita.* (車を買って、余りのお金は貯金しました) I bought a car and saved the money *left over.* 《⇨ amaru》

a⌈mari⌉[2] あまり（余り） *adv.* **1** too; very:
Amari *takusañ taberu to onaka o kowashimasu yo.* (あまりたくさん食べるとおなかをこわしますよ) If you eat *too* much, you will have an upset stomach. / *Kono ryoori wa* amari *karakute, watashi ni wa taberare-*

nai. (この料理はあまり辛くて、私には食べられない) This dish is *too* peppery for me to eat. / Amari *machigai ga ooi no de akirete shimatta.* (あまり間違いが多いのであきれてしまった) I was shocked to find *so* many mistakes.

2 (with a negative) not ... much; not very; seldom; rarely:
Yasai wa amari *suki de wa arimaseñ.* (野菜はあまり好きではありません) I don't like vegetables *very much.* / *Kare wa heya no sooji o* amari *shinai.* (彼は部屋の掃除をあまりしない) He *seldom* cleans his room. / *Sobo wa* amari *gaishutsu shimaseñ.* (祖母はあまり外出しません) My grandmother *rarely* goes out.

...no amari (...の〜) so...that:
Kanojo wa ureshisa no amari, *to-biagatta.* (彼女はうれしさのあまり、跳び上がった) She leapt *for joy.* / *Watashi wa odoroki no* amari, *kuchi mo kikenakatta.* (私は驚きのあまり、口もきけなかった) I was *so surprised that* I could not even speak.

-a⌉mari あまり（余り） *suf.* over...; more than...:
*Nihoñ ni kite moo sañ-neñ-*amari *ni narimasu.* (日本に来てもう3年あまりになります) I have been in Japan *over* three years now. / *Watashi wa ni-jikañ-*amari *matta.* (私は2時間あまり待った) I waited *more than* two hours.

a⌈ma⌉r·u あまる（余る） *vt.* (ama-r·i-; amar·a-; amat-te [C])
1 be left (over):
Juushichi o sañ de waru to go ga tatte, ni amaru. (17 を3で割ると5が立って、2余る) When you divide 17 by 3, you get 5, with 2 *left over.* / *Baageñ de yasuku kaeta no de, sañzeñ-eñ o-kane ga* amatta. (バーゲンで安く買えたので、3,000円お金が余った) As I could buy it at a bargain, I *saved* 3,000 yen.
《⇨ amari[1]》

2 be in excess; be more than enough:
Kono kaisha de wa hitode ga amatte *iru.* (この会社では人手が余っている) This company *is overstaffed.*

a⌈ma⌉s·u あます (余す) *vt.* (amash·i-; amas·a-; amash·i-te C)
1 leave:
Amasanai de, miñna tabe nasai. (余さないで、みんな食べなさい) *Don't leave* anything. Eat it all. 《⇨ no-kosu》
2 be left; remain:
Kotoshi mo amasu *tokoro wazuka futsuka desu.* (今年も余すところわずか二日です) There *remain* only two days of this year. / *Shikeñ made ato mikka o* amasu *bakari to natta.* (試験まであと三日を余すばかりとなった) We now have only three days *left* before the exams. 《⇨ no-kosu》

amasu tokoro naku (～ところなく) completely; fully: *Kono shoosetsu wa tooji no shakai o* amasu *tokoro naku egaite iru.* (この小説は当時の社会を余すところなく描いている) This novel gives a *complete* description of the society of the period. / *Kyoo no shiai de wa jibuñ no chikara o* amasu *tokoro naku hakki dekita.* (きょうの試合では自分の力を余すところなく発揮できた) I was able to display my ability *to the full* in today's match.

a⌈maya⌉dori あまやどり (雨宿り) *n.* taking shelter from the rain:
Watashi-tachi wa koya no naka de amayadori *o shita.* (私たちは小屋の中で雨宿りをした) We *sheltered* from the rain in a hut.

a⌈mayaka⌉s·u あまやかす (甘やかす) *vt.* (-kash·i-; -kas·a-; -kash·i-te C) spoil; pamper:
Kare wa chiisai koro kara amaya-kasarete *sodatta.* (彼は小さい頃から甘やかされて育った) He *has been spoilt* since he was small. / *Shiñ-*

nyuu-shaiñ o amayakasu *na.* (新入社員を甘やかすな) Don't *pamper* the new employees.

a⌈me¹ あめ (雨) *n.* rain:
Ame ga furi-soo da. (雨が降りそうだ) It looks like *rain.* / Ame ga furi-dashita. (雨が降りだした) It *began to rain.* / *Kinoo wa ichi-nichi-juu* ame ga futta. (きのうは一日中雨が降った) It *rained* all day yesterday. / Ame *wa moo sugu yamu [agaru] deshoo.* (雨はもうすぐやむ[あがる]でしょう) The *rain* is likely to let up soon. / Ame *no hi wa kuruma de eki made ikimasu.* (雨の日は車で駅まで行きます) On *rainy* days I go to the station by car. / *Koñgetsu wa* ame *ga ookatta.* (今月は雨が多かった) We have had a lot of *rain* this month. / *Kare wa* ame *no naka o dekaketa.* (彼は雨の中を出かけた) He went out in the *rain.* 《⇨ hare; kumori》

a⌈me² あめ (飴) *n.* candy; sweet; lollipop:
ame *o shaburu* (あめをしゃぶる) suck a piece of *candy.*

a⌈me⌉furi あめふり (雨降り) *n.* rain; rainy weather:
Amefuri *no toki wa eñsoku wa chuushi desu.* (雨降りのときは遠足は中止です) In the event of *rain,* the excursion will be canceled. 《⇨ ame》

A⌈merika アメリカ *n.* America.
★ North America is '*Kita-Ame-rika*' or '*Hoku-Bee,*' and the official name of the United States of America is '*Amerika-Gasshuu-koku.*'

A⌈merika⌉jiñ アメリカじん (アメリカ人) *n.* native or inhabitant of the U.S.A.

a⌈mi¹ あみ (網) *n.* net:
ami *o utsu* (網を打つ) cast a *net* / ami *o haru* (網を張る) lay a *net* / *Sakana ga* ami *ni kakatta.* (魚が網にかかった) A fish was caught in the

net. / *Kare wa* ami *de sakana o sukutta.* (彼は網で魚をすくった) He scooped up the fish with a *net.*

aˈmiˈmono あみもの (編み物) *n.* knitting; crochet:
Haha wa madobe de amimono *o shite imasu.* (母は窓辺で編み物をしています) My mother *is knitting* by the window.

aˈm·u あむ (編む) *vt.* (am·i-; am·a-; añ-de ⓒ) knit; crochet; braid; weave:
keito no seetaa o amu (毛糸のセーターを編む) *knit* a woolen sweater / *kami no ke o* amu (髪の毛を編む) *braid* one's hair / *take de kago o* amu (竹で篭を編む) *weave* a basket with bamboo.

aˈñ あん (案) *n.* plan; idea; proposal; draft:
añ *o tateru* (案を立てる) make a *plan* / añ *o dasu* (案を出す) make a *proposal* / añ *o jikkoo suru* (案を実行する) carry out a *plan* / *Sore wa ii* añ *da.* (それはいい案だ) That's a good *idea.* / *Kare wa sono* añ *ni sañsee* [*hañtai*] *shita.* (彼はその案に賛成[反対]した) He agreed [objected] to the *proposal.* (⇨ teeañ)

aˈnaˈ あな (穴) *n.* 1 hole; opening; perforation:
jimeñ ni ana *o horu* (地面に穴を掘る) dig a *hole* in the ground / *Kono kutsushita ni wa* ana *ga aru.* (この靴下には穴がある) There is a *hole* in this sock. / *Kabe ni* ana *ga aite iru.* (壁に穴があいている) There is an *opening* in the wall. / *Tama ga atatte, kabe ni* ana *ga aita.* (弾が当たって，壁に穴があいた) The bullet made a *hole* in the wall. / *Kiri de ita ni* ana *o aketa.* (きりで板に穴をあけた) I drilled a *hole* through the board. / *Semeñto de* ana *o umeta.* (セメントで穴をうめた) I filled up the *hole* with cement.
2 defect; deficit; loophole:
Kimi no keekaku ni wa ana *ga*

aru. (君の計画には穴がある) There is a *defect* in your plan. / *Kare wa choobo ni hyakumañ-eñ no* ana *o aketa.* (彼は帳簿に百万円の穴をあけた) He ran up a *deficit* of one million yen in the accounts. / *Kare wa jibuñ no kane de sono* ana *o umeta.* (彼は自分の金でその穴をうめた) He made up the *deficit* with his own money.
3 gap:
Sekiya-sañ no yasuñda ana *o umenakereba naranai.* (関谷さんの休んだ穴をうめなければならない) We have to fill the *gap* left by Mr. Sekiya's absence.

aˈnadorigataˈ·i あなどりがたい (侮り難い) *a.* (-ku) formidable; not easy:
anadorigatai *teki* (侮りがたい敵) a *formidable* enemy / *Kare wa keekeñ wa asai ga* anadorigatai. (彼は経験は浅いが侮りがたい) Though he has little experience, we *cannot make light of* his ability.

aˈnadoˈr·u あなどる (侮る) *vt.* (anador·i-; anador·a-; anadot-te ⓒ)
1 despise; look down on:
Wakai kara to itte kare o anadotte *wa ikenai.* (若いからといって彼を侮ってはいけない) You shouldn't *look down* on him just because he is young.
2 make light of:
Aite no chikara o anadoru *na.* (相手の力を侮るな) Don't *make light of* the ability of your opponent.

aˈnaˈta あなた *n.* you: ★ Plural forms are '*anata-tachi*,' '*anata-gata*' (*polite*) and '*anata-ra*' (*slightly derogatory*).
Anata-tachi [anata-gata] *no gakkoo wa doko ni arimasu ka?* (あなたたち[あなた方]の学校はどこにありますか) Where is *your* school?

──── **(USAGE)** ────
Not used when addressing one's superiors, and usually

omitted when speaking to one's subordinates. *e.g. Moo kono hoñ o yomimashita ka?* (もうこの本を読みましたか) Have you already read this book?
When speaking to subordinates, the family name is often used. *e.g. Takahashi-sañ wa doko ni suñde iru no?* (高橋さんはどこに住んでいるの) Where do *you* (= Mr. Takahashi) live?
To superiors a person's position is usually used instead of '*anata*.' *e.g.* Buchoo *wa nani o meshiagarimasu ka?* (部長は何を召し上がりますか) What would *you* (=the department chief) like to eat?
Often used by a wife when addressing her husband. Anata, *Yamamoto-sañ kara deñwa desu yo.* (あなた、山本さんから電話ですよ) *Darling*, there's a call from Mr. Yamamoto.

a￢nau￢ñsaa アナウンサー *n.* announcer.

a￢nau￢ñsu アナウンス *n.* announcement: ★ Comes from English 'announce.'
Hikooki no shuppatsu ga ichijikañ okureru to anauñsu *ga atta.* (飛行機の出発が1時間遅れるとアナウンスがあった) There was *announcement* that the departure of the flight would be an hour late.

a￢ñba￢rañsu アンバランス *a.n.* (~ na/ni) imbalance: ★ Comes from English 'unbalance,' and used in the sense of a lack of balance.
añbarañsu *na koosee* (アンバランスな構成) a structure that is *out of balance* / *juyoo to kyookyuu no* añbarañsu (需要と供給のアンバランス) the *imbalance* of supply and demand / *Yunyuu to yushutsu ga* añbarañsu ni natta. (輸入と輸出がア

ンバランスになった) The balance between imports and exports *became lopsided.*

a￢ñdo あんど (安堵) *n.* relief.
...ni añdo suru (...に~する) *vi.* be [feel] relieved: *Musuko no shuushoku ni* añdo shita. (息子の就職に安堵した) I *was relieved* by my son's getting a job.

a￢ne あね (姉) *n.* one's older [elder; big] sister:

──(USAGE)──
Used by an adult, referring to his or her own sister. When referring to someone else's, '*o-nee-sañ*' is used.

Kinoo, ane *to issho ni kaimono ni ikimashita.* (きのう、姉と一緒に買い物に行きました) I went shopping with my *older sister* yesterday. *cf. Kinoo kimi no* (o-)nee-sañ *to o-ai shimashita.* (きのう君の(お)姉さんとお会いしました) I met your *older sister* yesterday. 《↔ imooto》《⇨ ani; kazoku (table)》

ane (姉)	sister
imooto (妹)	

a￢ne￢ttai あねったい (亜熱帯) *n.* the subtropical zone. 《⇨ nettai》

a￢ñgai¹ あんがい (案外) *adv.* unexpectedly; against expectations: *Kono moñdai wa* añgai *muzukashii.* (この問題は案外難しい) This problem is *unexpectedly* difficult. / *Kono shigoto wa* añgai *jikañ ga kakatta.* (この仕事は案外時間がかかった) This work took *more* time *than I had expected.* / *Kare wa* añgai *yasashii tokoro ga aru.* (彼は案外優しいところがある) He is *more* tender at heart *than you might think.*

a￢ñgai² あんがい (案外) *a.n.* (~ na, ni) unexpected; surprising: *Takai to omotta ga* añgai *na nedaṅ datta.*(高いと思ったが案外な値段だった) I thought it would be expensive, but the price was *unexpectedly* low. / *Ano hito ga konna shippai o suru to wa* aṅgai *da.*(あの人がこんな失敗をするとは案外だ) It is *surprising* that that person should make such a blunder.

a⌐ṅgoo あんごう (暗号) *n.* code; cipher; cryptogram: aṅgoo *o kaidoku suru* (暗号を解読する) decipher a *code*.

a⌐ni あに (兄) *n.* one's older [elder; big] brother:

> **USAGE**
>
> Used by an adult, referring to his or her own brother. When referring to someone else's, '*o-nii-saṅ*' is used.

Ichibaṅ ue no ani *wa beṅgoshi desu.*(いちばん上の兄は弁護士です) *My oldest brother* is a lawyer. *cf. Kare no ichibaṅ ue no* (o-)nii-saṅ *wa seṅsee desu.*(彼のいちばん上の(お)兄さんは先生です) His *oldest brother* is a teacher. 《↔ otooto》《⇨ ane; kazoku (table)》

ani (兄)	brother
otooto (弟)	

a⌐ni あんい (安易) *a.n.* (～ na, ni) (*formal*) easy; easygoing; happy-go-lucky: aṅi *na seekatsu* (安易な生活) an *easy* life / *Tanaka-saṅ no shigoto ni taisuru kaṅgaekata wa* aṅi *da.*(田中さんの仕事に対する考え方は安易だ) Mr. Tanaka has a *happy-go-lucky* view of his work. / *Sono moṅdai ni* aṅi *ni torikumu to shippai shimasu yo.*(その問題に安易に取り組むと失敗しますよ) You'll fail if you take the problem *lightly*.

a⌐ṅji あんじ (暗示) *n.* hint; suggestion; intimation: aṅji *o ataeru* (暗示を与える) give a

hint / *Kanojo wa* aṅji *ni kakari-yasui.*(彼女は暗示にかかりやすい) She is easily influenced by *suggestion*.

aṅji suru (～する) *vt.* hint; suggest; imply: *Kono shoosetsu wa wareware no mirai o* aṅji shite iru.(この小説はわれわれの未来を暗示している) This novel *hints* at our future.

a⌐ṅjiˡ·ru あんじる (案じる) *vt.* (aṅjite V) worry; be anxious: *Kare wa chichi-oya no keṅkoo o* aṅjite *iru.*(彼は父親の健康を案じている) / He *is worried* about his father's health. / *Musuko no shoorai ga* aṅjirareru.(息子の将来が案じられる) My son's future *worries* me.

a⌐ṅki あんき (暗記) *n.* memorization; memorizing: aṅki-ryoku (暗記力) *memory.*

aṅki suru (～する) *vt.* memorize; learn by heart: *Kanojo wa jibuṅ no serifu o* aṅki shita.(彼女は自分のせりふを暗記した) She *memorized* her lines. / *Watashi wa sono shi o* aṅki shite imasu.(私はその詩を暗記しています) I *know* the poem *by heart.*

a⌐ṅma あんま (按摩) *n.* Japanese massage; masseur; masseuse: aṅma *o suru* [*shite morau*] (あんまをする[してもらう]) give [have] a *massage.* 《⇨ massaaji》

a⌐ṅmari あんまり *a.n.* (～ na/no, ni) beyond the ordinary degree; extreme: *Sore wa* aṅmari *da.*(それはあんまりだ) That's going *too far.*
— *adv.* (*colloq.*) = amari.

a⌐ṅmiṅ あんみん (安眠) *n.* sound [good] sleep: aṅmiṅ *o boogai suru* (安眠を妨害する) disturb a person's *sleep.*

a⌐ṅmoku あんもく (暗黙) *n.* implicitness; tacitness: *Watashi-tachi no aida ni wa* aṅmoku *no ryookai ga arimasu.*(私たちの間には暗黙の了解があります)

We have an *implicit* understanding between us.

a⌈ña あんな *attrib.* **1** such; like that: ★ Refers to something at a distance from the speaker and the listener.
Añna *tokoro de asoñde wa abunai na.* (あんな所で遊んでは危ないな) It is dangerous to play in *such* a place. / Añna *kuruma ni notte mitai desu ne.* (あんな車に乗ってみたいですね) I wish I could ride in a car *like that.*
2 such; that sort of: ★ Refers to a person or thing known to both the speaker and the listener.
Añna *tanoshii paatii wa hajimete deshita.* (あんな楽しいパーティーは初めてでした) I've never been to *such* an enjoyable party. / *Kare ga* añna *hito da to wa omowanakatta.* (彼があんな人だとは思わなかった) I never imagined that he was *such* a person. / *Hidoi jiko deshita ne.* Añna *jiko wa ni-do to okoshite wa ike-maseñ.* (ひどい事故でしたね。あんな事故は２度と起こしてはいけません) It was a terrible accident. We should never let *that sort of* accident happen again. 《⇨ doñna; koñna; soñna》

a⌈ña⌉i あんない (案内) *n.* **1** guidance; guide:
Kare no añnai *de Kyooto o keñbutsu shita.* (彼の案内で京都を見物した) I saw the sights of Kyoto under his *guidance*.
2 notice; invitation:
Watashi wa sono kai no añnai *o moratta.* (私はその会の案内をもらった) I received an *invitation* to the party. / añnai-*joo* (案内状) an *invitation* letter [card].
añnai suru (～する) *vt.* guide; show: *Kare wa eki made* añnai *shite kureta.* (彼は駅まで案内してくれた) He *guided* me to the station. / *Shanai o* go-añnai *shimashoo.* (社

内をご案内しましょう) I'll *show* you *around* the company.

a⌈ña ni あんなに *adv.* such; so:
Añna ni *kiree na keshiki wa mita koto ga nakatta.* (あんなにきれいな景色は見たことがなかった) I had never seen *such* a beautiful scene. / Añna ni *okoranakute mo yokatta no ni.* (あんなに怒らなくてもよかったのに) It was unnecessary for you to get *so* angry. / *Suzuki-sañ ga* añna ni *uta ga joozu da to wa shirimaseñ deshita.* (鈴木さんがあんなに歌がじょうずだとは知りませんでした) I didn't know Mrs. Suzuki was *so* good at singing. 《⇨ doñna ni; koñna ni; soñna ni》

a⌈no あの *attrib.* **1** that; the: ★ Refers to a person or thing that is located at some distance from both the speaker and the listener.
Mukoo ni takai biru ga mieru deshoo. Watashi no kaisha wa ano *naka ni arimasu.* (向こうに高いビルが見えるでしょう。私の会社はあの中にあります) You can see a tall building over there. My company is in *that* building. / *Asoko ni suwatte iru* ano *hito wa dare desu ka?* (あそこに座っているあの人はだれですか) Who is *that* person sitting over there? / *Ano hishaku no katachi o shite iru no ga hokuto-shichisee desu.* (あのひしゃくの形をしているのが北斗七星です) *The* group of stars in the shape of a dipper is the Big Dipper [the Plough].
2 that; the: ★ Refers to a person or thing that is, in time or space, distant from both the speaker and the listener.
"*Kinoo Akihabara e itte kimashita.*" "*Ano atari mo nigiyaka ni narimashita ne.*" (「きのう秋葉原へ行って来ました」「あの辺りもにぎやかになりましたね」) "I went to Akihabara yesterday." "*That* area has

become a lively place, hasn't it? "
3 that: ★ Refers to a person or thing known to both the speaker and the listener.
Sumisu-sañ wa Nihoñgo ga hoñtoo ni joozu desu. Ano hito no yoo ni hanasetara ii desu ne.(スミスさんは日本語が本当に上手です。あの人のように話せたらいいですね)Mr. Smith speaks Japanese really well. I wish I could speak like *him*. / *"Mada ano koto o ki ni shite iru ñ desu ka?" "Ano koto tte, nañ desu ka?"*(「まだあの事を気にしているんですか」「あの事って、何ですか」) "Are you still worried about *that* matter?" "What do you mean by *that* matter?"

ano koro [**toki**] (～ころ[とき]) that time: ★ Refers to a time known to both the speaker and the listener.
"Ryoo no chikaku no raameñya e yoku ikimashita ne." "Ano koro wa futari-tomo mazushikatta nee."(「寮の近くのラーメン屋へよく行きましたね」「あのころは二人とも貧しかったねえ」) "We often went to the noodle shop near the dormitory, didn't we?" "In *those days*, we were both poor, weren't we?" / *Kinoo jishiñ ga arimashita ga, ano toki doko ni imashita?*(きのう地震がありましたが、あのときどこにいました)We had an earthquake yesterday. Where were you *then*?
《⇨ dono; kono; sono》

a⌐no ne あのね *int.* well; listen; look here; I say:
Ano ne, tanomitai koto ga aru ñ desu ga.(あのね、頼みたいことがあるんですが)*I say*, there is something I want to ask of you.

a⌐noo あのう *int.* excuse me; say; well:
Anoo, Tookyoo-daigaku wa doo ittara ii deshoo ka?(あのう、東京大学はどう行ったらいいでしょうか)*Excuse me*, but how can I get to Tokyo University? / *Anoo, kippu o nakushite shimatta ñ desu kedo.*(あのう、切符をなくしてしまったんですけど)*Look*, I've lost my ticket.

a⌐ñpi あんぴ (安否) *n.* safety:
hito no añpi *o kizukau*(人の安否を気遣う)be concerned about a person's *safety* / *Kare no* añpi *ga shiñpai desu.*(彼の安否が心配です)I am worried about his *safety*.

A⌐ñpo-jo⌐oyaku あんぽじょうやく (安保条約) *n.* Japan-U.S. Security Treaty. ★ Abbreviated form of 'Nichi-Bee Añzeñ Hoshoo Jooyaku' (日米安全保障条約) Treaty of Mutual Cooperation and Security Between Japan and the United States of America. (signed in 1951).

a⌐ñsatsu あんさつ (暗殺) *n.* assassination.
añsatsu suru (～する) *vt.* assassinate.

a⌐ñsee あんせい (安静) *n.* rest; quiet; repose:
añsee ni suru (安静にする) lie quietly in bed; take bed rest.

a⌐ñshiñ あんしん (安心) *n.* peace of mind; relief:
O-kosañ wa buji desu kara, doozo go-añshiñ kudasai.(お子さんは無事ですから、どうぞご安心ください)Your child is safe, so *please don't worry*.
añshiñ suru (～する) *vi.* feel relieved [assured]: *Sono shirase o kiite* añshiñ shita.(その知らせを聞いて安心した)*It was a weight off my mind* to hear the news. / *Añshiñ shite kudasai. Shujutsu wa seekoo desu.*(安心して下さい。手術は成功です)*Don't worry*. The operation was a success.
— *a.n.* (～ na) safe; reassuring; secure: *Sore wa kare ni makasereba* añshiñ da.(それは彼に任せれば安心だ)If we leave it to him, *we'll have nothing to worry about*. /

Taifuu wa itte shimatta kara, moo añshiñ *desu.*（台風は行ってしまったから、もう安心です）Since the typhoon has gone on, we are *safe* now.

a⌐ñshoo あんしょう（暗礁）*n.*
1 reef:
Fune wa añshoo *ni noriagete ugokenaku natta.*（船は暗礁に乗り上げて動けなくなった）The ship ran up on a *reef* and got stuck.
2 (*fig.*) deadlock:
Kare-ra no hanashiai wa kañzeñ ni añshoo *ni noriageta.*（彼らの話し合いは完全に暗礁に乗り上げた）Their talks reached a complete *deadlock.*

a⌐ñshoo-ba⌐ñgoo （暗証番号）*n.* code number:
kyasshu-kaado no añshoo-bañgoo（キャッシュカードの暗証番号）a *code number* on a debit card / añshoo-bañgoo *o osu*（暗証番号を押す）enter one's *code number.*

a⌐ñta あんた *n.* (*informal*) = anata.

a⌐ñtee あんてい（安定）*n.* stability; balance; steadiness:
Kono isu wa añtee *ga ii [warui].*（このいすは安定がいい[悪い]）This chair *is stable [wobbly].* / *Booto wa* añtee *o ushinai, teñpuku shita.*（ボートは安定を失い、転覆した）The boat lost its *stability* and overturned.
añtee suru (～する) *vi.* become stable; be stabilized: *Seekyoku wa* añtee *shite iru.*（政局は安定している）The political situation *is stable.* / *Bukka ga* añtee *shita.*（物価が安定した）Prices *have been brought under control.* / *Kare-ra wa* añtee *shita seekatsu o nozoñde iru.*（彼らは安定した生活を望んでいる）They desire a *secure* life.

a⌐ñtena アンテナ *n.* antenna; aerial:
yane ni añtena *o tateru*（屋根にアンテナを立てる）put an *antenna* up on the roof.

a⌐ñzañ あんざん（暗算）*n.* mental arithmetic [calculation]:
Watashi wa añzañ *de keesañ shita.*（私は暗算で計算した）I calculated it *in my head.*
añzañ suru (～する) *vt.* do sums in one's head: *Kore o* añzañ *shi nasai.*（これを暗算しなさい）*Calculate* this *in your head.*

a⌐ñzeñ あんぜん（安全）*n.* safety; security:
Kare wa mi no añzeñ *o hakatte, nigeta.*（彼は身の安全を図って、逃げた）He fled for his own *safety.* / *Añzeñ no tame ni atarashii kagi o doa ni tsuketa.*（安全のために新しいかぎをドアにつけた）I put a new lock on the door just to *be safe.* / añzeñ-beruto（安全ベルト）a *safety* (seat) belt / *Añzeñ Dai-ichi.* (*sign*)（安全第一）*Safety* First.
— *a.n.* (～ na, ni) safe; secure:
Juumiñ wa añzeñ *na basho ni hinañ shita.*（住民は安全な場所に避難した）The inhabitants took refuge in a *safe* place. / *Kono kiñko nara* añzeñ *desu.*（この金庫なら安全です）If you use this safe, it will be *strong and reliable.*

a⌐ñzu あんず（杏）*n.* apricot.

a⌐o あお（青）*n.* **1** blue:
Ao to aka o mazeru to murasaki ni naru.（青と赤を混ぜると紫になる）When you mix *blue* and red, you get purple.
2 (of a traffic light, plants, vegetables, etc.) green:
Shiñgoo ga ao *ni kawatta.*（信号が青に変わった）The traffic light turned *green.* / ao-yasai（青野菜）*green* vegetables / ao-riñgo（青りんご）a *green* apple. 《⇨ aoi; aojiroi; midori》

USAGE

Traditionally, the Japanese color spectrum includes the colors known in English as 'blue' and 'green' within the category '*ao*.' Often, '*ao*' will correspond to English 'blue,' but in cases where specificity is called for, the speaker may use '*buruu*' for English 'blue' and '*guriiñ*' or '*midori*' for English 'green.'

a⌐oa⌐o to あおあおと（青々と）*adv.* (～ suru) (of trees, leaves, etc.) fresh and green; verdant.

a⌐oba あおば（青葉）*n.* green leaves [foliage].

a⌐o⌐g·u¹ あおぐ（仰ぐ）*vt.* (aog·i-; aog·a-; ao·i-de 〔C〕) **1** look up at:
sora no hoshi o aogu（空の星を仰ぐ）*look up* at the stars in the sky.
2 respect; look up to:
Miñna wa kare o shidoosha to shite aoide imasu.（みんなは彼を指導者として仰いでいます）They *look up* to him as their leader.

a⌐o⌐g·u² あおぐ（扇ぐ）*vt.* (aog·i-; aog·a-; ao·i-de 〔C〕) fan:
uchiwa de jibuñ o aogu（うちわで自分をあおぐ）*fan* oneself with a round fan / aoide *hi o okosu*（あおいで火を起こす）*fan* the fire.

a⌐o⌐i あおい（青い）*a.* (-ku) **1** blue:
★ See note under '*ao*.'
aoi *sora*（青い空）a *blue* sky / *Kabe o* aoi *peñki de nutta.*（壁を青いペンキで塗った）I painted the wall with *blue* paint. / *Kabe o peñki de* aoku *nutta.*（壁をペンキで青く塗った）I painted the wall *blue*.
2 green; unripe:
Kono riñgo wa mada aoi.（このりんごはまだ青い）This apple's still *green*.
3 (of a person's face, look) pale:
Kaoiro ga aoi *desu ne.*（顔色が青いですね）You look *pale*. / *Sono shirase o kiite, kanojo wa* aoku *natta.*（その知らせを聞いて、彼女は青くなった）She turned *pale* at the news.

a⌐ojiro⌐·i あおじろい（青白い）*a.* (-ku) **1** bluish white:
Hoshi ga aojiroi *hikari o hanatte iru.*（星が青白い光を放っている）The stars are giving off a *bluish-white* light.
2 pale; pallid:
Kare wa aojiroi *kao o shite iru.*（彼は青白い顔をしている）He looks *pale*. （⇨ aoi)

A⌐omori⌐-keñ あおもりけん（青森県）*n.* Aomori Prefecture. Located at Honshu's north end with two peninsulas. Apples are its most important product. Capital city: Aomori. 《⇨ map (G1)》

a⌐o⌐r·u あおる（煽る）*vt.* (aor·i-; ao-r·a-; aot-te 〔C〕) **1** fan; flap:
Kaze ni aorarete, *hi wa doñdoñ moe-hirogatta.*（風にあおられて、火はどんどん燃え広がった）*Fanned* by the wind, the fire spread rapidly. / *Kaateñ ga kaze ni* aorarete iru.（カーテンが風にあおられている）The curtains *are flapping* in the wind.
2 stir up; incite:
kyoosooshiñ o aoru（競争心をあおる）*arouse* a sense of rivalry / *Kare no kotoba wa gakusee no kookishiñ o* aotta.（彼の言葉は学生の好奇心をあおった）His words *gave rise to* curiosity among the students.

a⌐oshi⌐ñgoo あおしんごう（青信号）*n.* green light:
aoshiñgoo *de michi o wataru*（青信号で道を渡る）cross the road on the *green light* / *Aoshiñgoo ni naru made machimashoo.*（青信号になるまで待ちましょう）Let's wait until the *light turns green*. 《⇨ akashiñgoo》

a⌐ozame⌐·ru あおざめる（青ざめる）*vi.* (aozame-te 〔V〕) turn pale:
Sono shirase o kiita totañ, kare wa aozameta.（その知らせを聞いたとたん、彼は青ざめた）The moment he heard the news, he *turned pale*.

a⌐ozo⌐ra あおぞら（青空）*n.* the

blue (azure) sky.

a**ˈpaˈato** アパート n. an apartment; an apartment house: *Kare wa* apaato *ni suñde iru.* (彼はアパートに住んでいる) He lives in an *apartment house.* / *Watashi wa futa-ma no* apaato *o karita.* (私は二間のアパートを借りた) I rented a two-room *apartment.*

───── USAGE ─────

There are two Japanese words for 'apartment,' '*apaato*' and '*mañshoñ*.' '*Apaato*' customarily refers to one- or two-storied wooden structures with units divided by thin plaster walls on the inside that rent by the month. '*Mañshoñ*' are usually of three or more stories and of rather substantial construction, commonly reinforced concrete. '*Mañshoñ*' were originally mainly tenant-owned, and as such comparable to the North American 'condominium,' but now can denote rental units too.

─────────────────

a**ˈppaku** あっぱく (圧迫) n. pressure; oppression: appaku *o kuwaeru* (圧迫を加える) put *pressure* on / appaku *o ukeru* (圧迫を受ける) be under *pressure*.
appaku suru (〜する) vt. oppress; suppress: *Sono kuni no seefu wa geñroñ no jiyuu o* appaku *shita.* (その国の政府は言論の自由を圧迫した) The government of the country *suppressed* the freedom of speech. / *Iñfure wa kakee o* appaku suru. (インフレは家計を圧迫する) Inflation *strains* the family finances.

a**ˈra** あら int. my goodness; why: ★ Used by women to express wonder, surprise, etc. Men use '*are*.'
Ara, *niji da wa.* (あら, 虹だわ) *My goodness*, it's a rainbow. / *Ara, Su-*

zuki-sañ ja nai no. (あら, 鈴木さんじゃないの) *Why*, isn't it Miss Suzuki?

A**ˈrabia** アラビア n. Arabia.

a**ˈraˈi**[1] あらい (荒い) a. (-ku) rough; rude; violent: *Kyoo wa nami ga* arai. (きょうは波が荒い) The sea is *rough* today. / *Kare wa kishoo ga* arai. (彼は気性が荒い) He is a man of *violent* temper.

a**ˈraˈi**[2] あらい (粗い) a. (-ku) coarse; rough: arai *suna* (粗い砂) *coarse* sand / *Kono nuno wa tezawari ga* arai. (この布は手触りが粗い) This cloth feels *rough*. / *Kono ami wa me ga* arai. (この網は目が粗い) This net has *large* meshes. 《↔ komakai》

a**ˈrakajime** あらかじめ adv. beforehand; in advance: Arakajime *go-reñraku itadakereba, itsu de mo o-mukae ni mairimasu.* (あらかじめご連絡いただければ, いつでもお迎えにまいります) If you let me know *beforehand*, I will come to pick you up any time. / *Kare wa jikeñ no naiyoo o* arakajime *shitte ita.* (彼は事件の内容をあらかじめ知っていた) He knew the details of the affair *in advance*.

a**ˈrappoˈˈi** あらっぽい (荒っぽい) a. (-ku) rough; rude: arappoi *uñteñ* (荒っぽい運転) *unruly* driving / *Ano hito no shigoto wa* arappoi. (あの人の仕事は荒っぽい) He does his work in a very *rough and ready* manner. / *hito o* arappoku *atsukau* (人を荒っぽく扱う) treat someone *roughly*.

a**ˈrare** あられ n. hail; hailstone: *Sakuya* arare *ga futta.* (昨夜あられが降った) It *hailed* last night.

a**ˈrasaˈgashi** あらさがし n. fault-finding; picking flaws: *Kare wa itsu-mo hito no* arasagashi *o shite iru.* (彼はいつも人のあらさがしをしている) He *is* always *finding* *fault* with others.

a┌rashi あらし（嵐）*n.* storm; tempest:
Arashi ga hitoban-juu tsuzuita.（嵐が一晩中続いた）The *storm* raged all night. / *Fune wa hidoi arashi ni atta.*（船はひどい嵐にあった）The ship was caught in a heavy *storm.*

a┌raso┐i あらそい（争い）*n.* dispute; quarrel; trouble:
Dekiru koto nara arasoi wa saketai.（出来ることなら争いは避けたい）I wish to avoid a *dispute* if possible. / *Kare-ra wa tsumaranai koto de arasoi o shita.*（彼らはつまらないことで争いをした）They got into a *quarrel* over trifles. / *Sonna arasoi ni makikomaretaku nai.*（そんな争いに巻き込まれたくない）I don't want to be mixed up in such *trouble.* 《⇨ arasou》

a┌raso┐·u あらそう（争う）*vi.* (araso·i-; arasow·a-; arasot-te Ⓒ)
1 quarrel; dispute:
tochi no shoyuuken o arasou（土地の所有権を争う）*dispute* the ownership of land / *Kare-ra wa isan no koto de otagai ni arasotta.*（彼らは遺産のことでお互いに争った）They *quarreled* with each other over the legacy. 《⇨ arasoi》
2 compete:
Tanaka-san to Yamada-san wa itsu-mo toppu o arasotte iru.（田中さんと山田さんはいつもトップを争っている）Tanaka and Yamada *are* always *competing* for the top position. / *Jookyaku wa saki o arasotte, densha ni noroo to shita.*（乗客は先を争って、電車に乗ろうとした）The passengers *pushed* in front of one another to get on the train.

a┌ras·u あらす（荒らす）*vt.* (arash·i-; aras·a-; arash·i-te Ⓒ)
1 damage:
Hatake ga kuma ni hidoku arasareta.（畑が熊にひどく荒らされた）The fields *were* badly *ravaged* by

a bear. 《⇨ areru》
2 ransack; break in:
Doroboo ni heya o arasareta.（泥棒に部屋を荒らされた）My room was *ransacked* by a thief.

a┌rasuji あらすじ（粗筋）*n.* outline; synopsis; plot.

a┌rata あらた（新た）*a.n.* (~ na, ni) (*formal*) new; fresh:
Kare wa arata na shooko o teeshutsu shita.（彼は新たな証拠を提出した）He produced *new* evidence. / *Sono bamen o mite, kangeki mo arata datta.*（その場面を見て、感激も新だった）I was moved with *fresh* emotions at the sight. / *Seefu wa arata ni iinkai o setchi shita.*（政府は新たに委員会を設置した）The government *newly* set up a committee. / *Watashi wa ketsui o arata ni shita.*（私は決意を新たにした）I *renewed* my determination. 《⇨ atarashii》

a┌ratama┐r·u あらたまる（改まる）*vi.* (-mar·i-; -mar·a-; -mat-te Ⓒ)
1 be improved:
Kootsuu-kisoku ga oohaba ni aratamatta.（交通規則が大幅に改まった）The traffic regulations *were* greatly *improved.* 《⇨ aratameru》
2 (of a year, semester, etc.) begin; come around:
Toshi ga aratamatta.（年が改まった）The new year *has come around.* / *Gakki ga aratamaru to sugu shiken desu.*（学期が改まるとすぐ試験です）We are going to have an exam soon after the new term *begins.*
aratamatte（改まって）in a formal way: *Kare wa aratamatte, nani-ka ioo to shita.*（彼は改まって、何か言おうとした）He tried to say something *in a formal way.*
aratamatta 改まった *attrib.* formal; ceremonious:
Aratamatta seki de no supiichi wa nigate desu.（改まった席でのスピーチは苦手です）I'm not good at

making speeches on *formal* occasions.

a˥ratame˩·ru あらためる（改める）*vt.* (-me-te V) **1** change; renew: *fukusoo o* aratameru（服装を改める）*change* one's clothes / *keeyaku o* aratameru（契約を改める）*renew* a contract.《⇨ aratamaru》

2 correct; reform: *Watashi wa jibuñ no ketteñ o* aratametai.（私は自分の欠点を改めたい）I *want to correct* my shortcomings. / *Zeesee o* aratameru *hitsuyoo ga aru.*（税制を改める必要がある）It is necessary to *reform* the tax system.《⇨ aratamaru》

3 examine; check: *Keekañ wa kabañ no nakami o* aratameta.（警官はかばんの中身を改めた）The policeman *checked* the contents of the bag.

a˥rata˩mete あらためて（改めて）*adv.* **1** another time; again: *Kekka ga wakari shidai,* aratamete *kochira kara go-reñraku shimasu.*（結果がわかり次第、改めてこちらからご連絡します）As soon as the results are known, we will contact you *again*. / *Hoka ni yooji ga arimasu no de,* aratamete *o-jama itashimasu.*（ほかに用事がありますので、改めておじゃまいたします）Since I have other engagements, I would like to visit you at a *later date*.

2 anew; afresh: *Hanashi ni wa kiite imashita ga, Nara no Daibutsu o mite, sono ookisa ni* aratamete *odorokimashita.*（話には聞いていましたが、奈良の大仏を見て、その大きさに改めて驚きました）I had heard about the Great Buddha in Nara, but when I actually saw it, I was *still* surprised at its size.

a˥ra·u あらう（洗う）*vt.* (ara·i-; araw·a-; arat-te C) **1** wash; clean: *sara o* arau（皿を洗う）*wash* the dishes / *fuku o sekkeñ de* arau（服をせっけんで洗う）*wash* clothes with soap / *Yuushoku no mae ni te o* arai nasai.（夕食の前に手を洗いなさい）*Wash* your hands before dinner.

2 wash; flow against [over]: *Nami ga kishi o* aratte iru.（波が岸を洗っている）Waves *are washing* the beach.

a˥raware あらわれ（現れ）*n.* expression; sign; result: *doryoku no* araware（努力のあらわれ）the *result* of one's efforts / *Sore wa kare no iyoku no* araware *desu.*（それは彼の意欲のあらわれです）It is an *expression* of his eagerness.《⇨ arawareru》

a˥raware˩·ru あらわれる（現れる）*vi.* (-ware-te V) **1** appear; come out: *Kumo no aida kara tsuki ga* arawareta.（雲の間から月が現れた）The moon *appeared* from behind the clouds. / *Kusuri no kikime ga* arawarete *kimashita.*（薬の効き目があらわれてきました）The medicine is beginning to *take effect*. / *Tsukare ga kao ni* arawarete iru.（疲れが顔にあらわれている）Fatigue *is showing* on your face. / *Keeki-kaifuku no kizashi ga* arawareta.（景気回復のきざしが現れた）Signs of economic recovery *have appeared*.《⇨ arawasu²》

2 arrive; show up: *Sañjup-puñ matte, kare ga* arawarenakereba, *saki ni ikimashoo.*（30 分待って、彼が現れなければ、先に行きましょう）If he *doesn't show up* in thirty minutes, let's go on ahead.《⇨ arawasu²》

3 (of hidden nature, facts, etc.) be discovered; be revealed: *Kare wa you to hoñshoo ga* arawareru.（彼は酔うと本性が現れる）His true character *is revealed* when he gets drunk. / *Choosa no kekka,* atarashii jijitsu ga tsugi-tsugi ni arawareta.(調査の結果, 新しい事実が次々に現れた) New facts *were discovered*, one after another, as a result of the investigation.

a⌈rawa⌉s·u[1] あらわす (表す) *vt.* (-wash·i-; -was·a-; -wash·i-te C) **1** show; reveal: *Kanojo wa sugu kañjoo o omote ni arawasu.* (彼女はすぐ感情を表に表す) She *shows* her feelings easily.

2 express: *Kono yorokobi o kotoba de arawasu koto wa dekimaseñ.* (この喜びを言葉で表すことはできません) I can not *express* my joy in words. / *Kono e wa tooji no noomiñ no kurushii seekatsu o arawashite imasu.* (この絵は当時の農民の苦しい生活を表しています) This painting *indicates* the hard life of the farmers in those days.

3 signify; stand for; symbolize: *Kono kigoo wa nani o arawashite imasu ka?* (この記号は何を表しています か) What does this symbol *stand for?*

a⌈rawa⌉s·u[2] あらわす (現す) *vt.* (-wash·i-; -was·a-; -wash·i-te C) **1** show up; appear; reveal: *Hisashiburi ni kare wa paatii ni sugata o arawashita.* (久しぶりに彼はパーティーに姿を現した) He *showed up* at the party—the first time in quite a while. / *Mañgetsu ga higashi no sora ni yukkuri to sugata o arawashita.* (満月が東の空にゆっくりと姿を現した) The full moon *appeared* slowly in the eastern sky. / *Kare wa tootoo hoñshoo o arawashita.* (彼はとうとう本性を現した) At last he *has revealed* his true character. (⇨ arawareru)

2 take effect: *Kono kusuri wa sugu ni kooka o arawashimasu.* (この薬はすぐに効果を現します) This medicine will soon *take effect*. (⇨ arawareru)

a⌈rawa⌉s·u[3] あらわす (著す) *vt.* (-wash·i-; -was·a-; -wash·i-te C) (*formal*) write; publish: *Yamada señsee wa butsurigaku ni kañsuru hoñ o takusañ arawashite iru.* (山田先生は物理学に関する本をたくさん著している) Professor Yamada *has written* many books on physics.

a⌈rayu⌉ru あらゆる *attrib.* all; every: *kañgaerareru* arayuru *shudañ* (考えられるあらゆる手段) *every* method that can be thought of / arayuru *kikai o riyoo suru* (あらゆる機会を利用する) make use of *every* opportunity.

a⌈re⌉[1] あれ *n.* **1** that over there: ★ Refers to something located at some distance from both the speaker and the listener. *Are wa Tookyoo-tawaa desu.* (あれは東京タワーです) *That* is the Tokyo Tower. / *Chotto, are wa nañ desu ka? Ano, sora o toñde iru no wa?* (ちょっと, あれは何ですか. あの, 空を飛んでいるのは) Hey, what's *that*—the object flying in the sky? (⇨ dore; kore; sore)

2 that, it: ★ Refers to something, which is, in time or space, distant from both the speaker and the listener. *Kono mae, eizu no kiji o yomimashita yo. Are wa kowai byooki rashii desu ne.* (この前, エイズの記事を読みましたよ. あれはこわい病気らしいですね) I read an article about AIDS the other day. *It* seems to be a terrible disease. / *Kyoneñ wa yoku yuki ga futta deshoo. Are de yukiguni no hito-tachi no tsurasa ga wakarimashita yo.* (去年はよく雪が降ったでしょう. あれで雪国の人たちの辛さがわかりましたよ) It snowed frequently last year, didn't it? *It* made me understand the hardships of the lives of the people in

snowy districts. / Are *wa nañ-
neñ-mae deshita kke, Izu ni jishiñ
ga atta no wa?* (あれは何年前でしたっ
け，伊豆に地震があったのは) How
many years ago was *it* when
there was the earthquake in Izu?
3 that, it: ★ Refers to something known to both the speaker
and the listener.
*"Nee, are kaita?" "Are tte geñgo-
gaku no repooto no koto?"* (「ねえ，
あれ書いた」「あれって，言語学のレポート
のこと」) "Say, have you written
that?" "By 'that,' do you mean
the linguistics paper?"
4 she; he: ★ Refers to one's
wife or one's subordinate.
*Kanai desu ka? Are wa ima jikka
e ittemasu.* (家内ですか．あれは今実家
へ行ってます) My wife? *She* is visiting her parents' house. / *Kaisha
ni Tanaka to iu otoko ga iru daroo.
Are wa nakanaka kireru otoko da.*
(会社に田中という男がいるだろう．あれは
なかなか切れる男だ) You know the
fellow named Tanaka in our company. *He* is a pretty smart fellow.
are irai (～以来) since then: *Kono mae erebeetaa ni tojikomerareta deshoo. Are irai, kaidañ o tsukau koto ni shita no.* (この前エレベー
ターに閉じ込められたでしょう．あれ以来，
階段を使うことにしたの) Do you remember that I was stuck in the elevator the other day? *Since then*
I've decided to use the stairs.
《⇨ are-(k)kiri》
aˈre[2] あれ *int.* oh; look; really:
★ Used by men to express surprise, doubt, etc. Women use
'*ara*.'
Are, heñ da naa. (あれ，変だなあ)
Well, that really is strange! / *Are,
sore hoñtoo desu ka?* (あれ，それ本
当ですか) *Good heavens!* Is that
really true?
aˈre de あれで *adv.* **1** with that:
Are de kare wa jishiñ o torimodo-

shita. (あれで彼は自信を取り戻した)
With that, he regained his self-
confidence.
2 in one's own way:
*Kare wa are de nakanaka omoi-
yari ga aru.* (彼はあれでなかなか思いや
りがある) He is very considerate *in
his own way*.
aˈre kara あれから *adv.* since
then; after that:
Are kara kare to wa atte imaseñ.
(あれから彼とは会っていません) I have
not seen him *since then*. / *Are
kara doko e ikimashita ka?* (あれか
らどこへ行きましたか) Where did you
go *after that*? 《⇨ kore kara; sore
kara》
aˈre-(k)kiri あれ(っ)きり *adv.*
(with a negative) since then:
Are-(k)kiri kare ni atte imaseñ. (あ
れっきり彼に会っていません) I haven't
met him *since then*. 《⇨ kore-
(k)kiri; sore-(k)kiri》
aˈre]-kore あれこれ *adv.* this and
that; one thing and another; in
various ways:
Kyoo wa are-kore isogashii. (きょう
はあれこれ忙しい) Today I am busy
with *one thing and another*. /
*Are-kore yatte iru uchi ni, yoi hoo-
hoo ga mitsukatta.* (あれこれやっている
うちに，良い方法が見つかった) While
trying out *various ways*, I discovered a good method. / *Ima-
goro are-kore itte mo shoo ga nai.*
(今ごろあれこれ言ってもしょうがない) It
is no use talking *about this and
that* at this stage.
aˈre·ru あれる (荒れる) *vi.* (are-te
Ⅴ) **1** be stormy; be rough:
Umi wa arete imasu. (海は荒れてい
ます) The sea *is rough*.
2 lie waste; be dilapidated:
*Sono tochi wa arete ite, sakumo-
tsu no saibai ni wa futekitoo desu.*
(その土地は荒れていて，作物の栽培には
不適当です) The land *lies waste*
and it is unsuitable for growing

crops. / *Sono ie wa sumu hito mo
naku, arete ita.*(その家は住む人もなく、
荒れていた) The house had no one
living in it and *was dilapidated.*
3 (of lips and skin) become
rough:
Fuyu ni naru to te ga areru.(冬にな
ると手が荒れる) In winter, my
hands *become chapped.*
4 be in a bad mood:
*Kare wa shuushoku ni shippai
shite arete iru.*(彼は就職に失敗して
荒れている) He was unsuccessful in
getting the job and *is in a bad
mood.*

aˈreˈrugii アレルギー *n.* allergy:
*Watashi wa gyuunyuu o nomu to
arerugii o okosu.*(私は牛乳を飲むと
アレルギーを起す) I get an *allergic
reaction* when I drink milk.

aˈri あり (蟻) *n.* ant.

aˈrifureta ありふれた (有り触れた)
attrib. common; everyday; commonplace:
arifureta *hanashi* (ありふれた話) just
another story / *Soñna koto wa
goku* arifureta *koto desu.*(そんなこと
はごくありふれたことです) That sort of
thing is an *everyday* occurrence.

aˈrigataˈ·i ありがたい (有り難い) *a.*
(-ku) **1** thankful; grateful;
pleasant:
Tetsudatte itadaketara, arigatai
desu.(手伝っていただけたら、ありがたい
です) I would be *grateful* if you
helped me. / *Okurimono o arigataku choodai shita.*(贈り物をありがた
くちょうだいした) I accepted the
present *with thanks.* / *Arigatai
koto ni, keeshoo datta.*(ありがたいこ
とに、軽傷だった) *Fortunately*, the
injury was slight. / *Sore wa
amari* arigatai *hanashi de wa nai.*
(それはあまりありがたい話ではない) That
is not a very *pleasant* story.
2 edifying and merciful:
Kyoo wa boosañ kara arigatai
hanashi o kiita. (きょうは坊さんからあ

りがたい話を聞いた) I listened to the
edifying teachings of the Buddhist priest today.

aˈriˈgatoo ありがとう (有り難う)
thank you; thanks:
Arigatoo.(ありがとう) *Thanks.* / Arigatoo *gozaimasu.*(ありがとうございま
す) *Thank you* very much. /
Wazawaza kite kurete, arigatoo.
(わざわざ来てくれて、ありがとう) *Thank
you* for taking the trouble to
come.

aˈriˈsama ありさま (有様) *n.*
state; circumstances; scenes:
★ Often refers to a bad state.
Sono uchi wa hidoi arisama *datta.*
(その家はひどい有様だった) The house
was in a terrible *state.* / *Kono* arisama *de wa doo ni mo naranai.*(こ
の有様ではどうにもならない) Under the
circumstances, we can't help it. /
Sono arisama *ni miñna odoroita.*
(その有様にみんな驚いた) They were
surprised at the *scene.*

aˈru¹ ある (或る) *attrib.* a certain;
some:
Watashi wa aru *hito to au yakusoku ga arimasu.*(私はある人と会う
約束があります) I have an appointment to meet *a certain* person. /
*Aru hi kare ga totsuzeñ tazunete
kita.*(ある日彼が突然訪ねて来た) *One*
day he suddenly called on me. /
*Aru imi de kimi no hañdañ wa
tadashii.*(ある意味できみの判断は正し
い) In *one* sense, your decision is
right.

aˈrˈu² ある (有る・在る) *vi.* (ar·i-; atte Ⓒ) **1** be; exist; there is [are]:
Kagi wa tsukue no ue ni arimasu.
(鍵は机の上にあります) The key *is* on
the desk. / *Kono chikaku ni yuubiñkyoku wa* arimasu *ka?* (この近く
に郵便局はありますか) *Is there* a post
office in this neighborhood? /
Sono hoñ wa kono toshokañ ni wa
arimaseñ.(その本はこの図書館にはあり
ません) That book *is not* in this

library. 《↔ nai》《⇨ iru》
2 be located:
*Sono shiro wa yama no naka ni
arimasu.* (その城は山の中にあります)
The castle *is located* in the mountains. 《↔ nai》
3 have:
Kare ni wa takusañ o-kane ga aru.
(彼にはたくさんお金がある) He *has* a
lot of money. / *Kanojo ni wa e no
sainoo ga aru.* (彼女には絵の才能があ
る) She *has* a talent for painting.
《↔ nai》
4 (of quantity, height, width,
etc.) be:
Taijuu wa dono kurai arimasu ka?
(体重はどのくらいありますか) How
much *do* you *weigh*? / *Fuji-sañ no
takasa wa dono kurai arimasu ka?*
(富士山の高さはどのくらいありますか)
What *is* the height of Mt. Fuji?
5 be found:
*Kono ki wa Nihoñ-juu doko ni mo
arimasu.* (この木は日本中どこにもあり
ます) This tree *is found* throughout Japan. 《↔ nai》
6 have the experience of:
*Kare ni wa atta koto ga arimasu
ka?* (彼には会ったことがありますか) /
Have you *ever met* him? / *Sono
yoo na heñ na hatsugeñ wa kiita
koto ga arimaseñ.* (そのような変な発
言は聞いたことがありません) I *have
never heard* such a strange remark. 《⇨ koto¹》
7 happen:
Yuube kiñjo de kaji ga arimashita.
(ゆうべ近所で火事がありました) A fire
broke out in the neighborhood
last night.
8 take place; be held:
*Sakuneñ kono keñ de kokutai ga
arimashita.* (昨年この県で国体があり
ました) The National Athletic
Meet *was held* in this prefecture
last year.
a⌜ruba⌝ito アルバイト *n.* part-time
job; job on the side; part-timer:

★ From German 'Arbeit.' Often
connotes a student or young person.
Kare wa arubaito *o shite iru.* (彼は
アルバイトをしている) He is working
part-time. / *Kanojo wa* arubaito
de ueetoresu o shite iru. (彼女はアル
バイトでウエートレスをしている) She
moonlights as a waitress.
a⌜rubamu アルバム *n.* album:
shashiñ o arubamu *ni haru* (写真を
アルバムにはる) paste a photo in an
album / *Misora Hibari no hitto
kyoku no* arubamu (美空ひばりのヒッ
ト曲のアルバム) an *album* of the hit
songs of Hibari Misora.
a⌜rufabetto アルファベット *n.*
alphabet.
a⌜ru⌝iwa¹ あるいは (或は) *conj.*
(*formal*) or; either...or:
Anata ka aruiwa *watashi ga ikanakereba narimaseñ.* (あなたかあるいは
私が行かなければなりません) *Either*
you *or* I have to go. / *Sono jikkeñ ga seekoo suru ka,* aruiwa
*shippai suru ka, dare ni mo
wakarimaseñ.* (その実験が成功するか,
あるいは失敗するか, だれにもわかりません)
Nobody knows *whether* the
experiment will succeed *or* fail.
a⌜ru⌝iwa² あるいは (或は) *adv.*
perhaps; probably: ★ Usually
followed by '*ka mo shirenai.*'
Sono keekaku wa aruiwa *chuushi
ni naru ka mo shirenai.* (その計画は
あるいは中止になるかもしれない) The
project will *probably* be halted. /
*Aruiwa kanojo wa sono jijitsu o
shitte iru ka mo shirenai.* (あるいは
彼女はその事実を知っているかもしれない)
Perhaps she knows the truth.
a⌜rukari アルカリ *n.* alkali:
arukari-see (アルカリ性) *alkalinity.*
《↔ sañ²》
a⌜rukooru アルコール *n.* **1** alcohol.
2 alcoholic beverage:
arukooru-*isoñshoo* (アルコール依存
症) *alcohol* dependence.

aˈruˈk·u あるく (歩く) *vi.* (aruk·i-; aruk·a-; aru·i-te Ⓒ) walk: *Eki made* aruite *go-fuñ desu.* (駅まで歩いて5分です) It takes five minutes to *walk* to the station. / *Watashi wa itsu-mo* aruite *gakkoo e ikimasu.* (私はいつも歩いて学校へ行きます) I always go to school *on foot.* / *Kaigañ o burabura* aruita. (海岸をぶらぶら歩いた) I *strolled* along the shore.

aˈrumi アルミ *n.* aluminum: arumi *sasshi* (アルミサッシ) an *aluminum* window sash / arumihaku (アルミはく) *aluminum* foil. 《⇨ arumiñyuumu》

aˈrumiñyuˈumu アルミニューム *n.* aluminum.

aˈsa¹ あさ (朝) *n.* morning: *Fune wa* asa *hayaku shuppatsu shita.* (船は朝早く出発した) The ship sailed early in the *morning.* / *Asa no jugyoo wa ku-ji ni hajimarimasu.* (朝の受業は9時に始ります) *Morning* classes begin at nine. 《⇨ hiru (table)》

aˈsaˈ¹² あさ (麻) *n.* hemp; hemp plant [cloth].

aˈsabañ あさばん (朝晩) *n.* morning and evening: *Asabañ (wa) sukkari aki rashiku natte kimashita.* (朝晩(は)すっかり秋らしくなってきました) It has become quite autumnal in the *mornings and evenings.* 《⇨ asayuu》
— *adv.* always; from morning till night: *Kare wa* asabañ *yoku hataraku.* (彼は朝晩よく働く) He works hard *from morning till night.*

aˈsaˈgao あさがお (朝顔) *n.* morning glory plant.

aˈsagoˈhañ あさごはん (朝ご飯) *n.* breakfast. ★ More polite than '*asameshi.*' *Asagohañ wa karui mono o tabemasu.* (朝ご飯は軽いものを食べます) I eat something light for *breakfast.*

《⇨ gohañ; hirugohañ; bañgohañ》

aˈsahi あさひ (朝日) *n.* morning [rising] sun. 《↔ yuuhi》

aˈsa·i あさい (浅い) *a.* (-ku) **1** shallow: asai *nabe* (浅い鍋) a *shallow* pan / *Kono kawa wa* asai. (この川は浅い) This river is *shallow.* / *Isu ni* asaku *koshikaketa.* (椅子に浅く腰かけた) I sat *on the edge of* the chair. 《↔ fukai》
2 (of time, etc.) short: *Kono kaisha wa dekite kara, hi ga* asai. (この会社はできてから、日が浅い) This company was established *not so long ago.*
3 (of experience, knowledge) lacking; green; superficial: *Kare wa mada keekeñ ga* asai. (彼はまだ経験が浅い) He *doesn't have much* experience. / *Kare wa sono moñdai ni tsuite* asai *chishiki shika motte inai.* (彼はその問題について浅い知識しか持っていない) He has only a *superficial* knowledge of the problem.
4 light; slight: asai *kizu* (浅い傷) a *slight* cut / *Sakuya wa nemuri ga* asakatta. (昨夜は眠りが浅かった) I slept *lightly* last night. 《↔ fukai》

aˈsameshi あさめし (朝飯) *n.* (*slightly rude*) breakfast: **asameshi mae** (～前) **1** before breakfast. **2** very easy: *Soñna koto wa* asameshi *mae da.* (そんなことは朝飯前だ) That's quite an easy job (for me). 《⇨ asagohañ》

aˈsaˈne あさね (朝寝) *n.* late rising: *Watashi wa* asane *ga suki da.* (私は朝寝が好きだ) I like to *stay in bed late in the morning.* **asane (o) suru** (～ (を) する) *vi.* get up late. 《⇨ hirune》

aˈsa-neˈboo あさねぼう (朝寝坊) *n.* late riser: **asa-neboo (o) suru** (～ (を) する)

vi. get up late in the morning.

a⌈sa⌉tte あさって(明後日) *n.* the day after tomorrow: asatte *no asa* (あさっての朝) the morning *after next* / *Fune wa* asatte *shukkoo shimasu.* (船はあさって出港します) The ship sets sail *the day after tomorrow.* (⇨ kyoo (table))

a⌈sayake あさやけ(朝焼け) *n.* morning glow in the sky. (↔ yuu-yake)

a⌈sayuu あさゆう(朝夕) *n.* morning and evening: *Asayuu no deñsha wa mañiñ desu.* (朝夕の電車は満員です) The trains in the *mornings and evenings* are crowded. / *Asayuu taiheñ suzu-shiku narimashita.* (朝夕大変涼しくなりました) The *mornings and evenings* have become very much cooler. (⇨ asabañ)

a⌈se あせ(汗) *n.* sweat; perspiration: ase *ga deru* (汗が出る) *sweat* comes out / ase *o kaku* (汗をかく) *sweat*; *perspire* / ase *o fuku* [*nuguu*] (汗をふく[ぬぐう]) wipe the *sweat* / *Hitai kara* ase *ga nagare ochita.* (額から汗が流れ落ちた) The *sweat* ran down my brow. / *Kare wa* ase *bisshori datta.* (彼は汗びっしょりだった) He was all in a *sweat.*

a⌈se⌉r·u¹ あせる(焦る) *vi.* (aser·i-; aser·a-; aset-te Ⓒ) hurry; be impatient: *Aseranakute mo deñsha ni ma-ni-aimasu.* (焦らなくても電車に間にあいます) You *don't have to hurry.* You can catch the train. / *Aserazu jik-kuri yari nasai.* (焦らずじっくりやりなさい) You *don't need to be in a hurry.* Take your time. / *Doo-shite soñna ni kekkoñ o aseru ñ desu ka?* (どうしてそんなに結婚を焦るんですか) Why *are* you so *anxious* to get married?

a⌈se⌉r·u² あせる(褪せる) *vi.* (ase-

r·i-; aser·a-; aset-te Ⓒ) fade; be discolored: *Kaateñ no iro ga* asete kita. (カーテンの色があせてきた) The curtains *have faded.*

a⌈shi¹ あし(足・脚) *n.* 1 foot; leg; paw: ★ '脚' usually refers to some sort of support. ashi *ga ookii* (足が大きい) have large *feet* / ashi *ga nagai* (足が長い) have long *legs* / ashi *o fumi-hazusu* (足を踏みはずす) *miss one's step* / ashi *o kumu* [*nobasu*] (足を組む[伸ばす]) cross [stretch] one's *legs* / *Ashi ga itai.* (足が痛い) My *foot* hurts. / *Ashi ga shibireta.* (足がしびれた) My *feet* are asleep. / *Tsukue no* ashi *ga orete iru.* (机の脚が折れている) A *leg* of the desk is broken. (⇨ jiñtai (table))

2 step; pace: ashi *o hayameru* [*yurumeru*] (足を速める[ゆるめる]) quicken [slacken] one's *pace* / ashi *ga hayai* [*osoi*] (足が速い[遅い]) be quick [slow] of *foot*

3 means of transport: *Kootsuu suto ga shimiñ no* ashi *o ubatta.* (交通ストが市民の足を奪った) The transport strike deprived the citizens of *transportation.*

ashi ga deru (〜が出る) exceed the budget.

ashi no fumiba mo nai (〜の踏み場もない) there is no place to step: *Kare no heya wa chirakatte ite,* ashi no fumiba mo nakatta. (彼の部屋は散らかって, 足の踏み場もなかった) His room was in such a mess that *you could hardly find anywhere to stand.*

...kara ashi o arau (...から〜を洗う) wash one's hands of (crime).

...ni ashi o hakobu (...に〜を運ぶ) visit; make a call.

...no ashi o hipparu (...の〜を引っ張る) get in a person's way; hold back (from success, etc.)

aˈshiaˈto　あしあと（足跡）*n.* foot-print; track:

ashiato *o nokosu [tadoru; ou]* (足跡を残す[たどる；追う]) leave [follow] *footprints* / *Yuka no ue ni* ashiato *ga tsuite ita.* (床の上に足跡がついていた) There were *footprints* on the floor.

aˈshibuˈmi　あしぶみ（足踏み）*n.*
1 stepping; stamping:
2 standstill:
ashibumi-*jootai ni aru* (足踏み状態にある) be at a *standstill*.
　ashibumi (o) suru (〜を）する) *vi.* mark time.

aˈshidori　あしどり（足取り）*n.*
1 step; gate; pace:
Kare wa omoi [karui] ashidori *de ie e kaetta.* (彼は重い[軽い]足どりで家へ帰った) He returned home with heavy [light] *steps*.
2 trace; track:
Keesatsu wa hañniñ no ashidori *o otta.* (警察は犯人の足どりを追った) The police followed the *tracks* of the criminal.

aˈshigaˈkari　あしがかり（足掛かり）*n.* footing; foothold.

aˈshiˈkubi　あしくび（足首）*n.* ankle.

aˈshimotoˈ　あしもと（足元）*n.* at [near] one's foot:
ashimoto *ga furatsuku* (足元がふらつく) be unsteady *on one's feet* / Ashimoto *ni ki o tsuke nasai.* (足元に気をつけなさい) Watch your *step*!
　ashimoto ni hi ga tsuku (足元に火がつく) be in imminent danger. 《⇨ kikeñ'》

aˈshinami　あしなみ（足並み）*n.* (of two or more people) pace; step:
Kooshiñ-chuu ni miñna no ashi-nami *ga midareta.* (行進中にみんなの足並みが乱れた) They got out of *step* during the procession. / *sekai no nagare ni* ashinami *o*

soroeru (世界の流れに足並みをそろえる) *keep abreast* of the trends in society.

aˈshiotoˈ　あしおと（足音）*n.* sound of footsteps:
Dare-ka no ashioto *ga suru.* (だれかの足音がする) I hear somebody's *footsteps*.

aˈshitaˈ　あした（明日）*n.* tomorrow:
ashita *no asa* (あしたの朝) *tomorrow* morning / ashita *no shiñbuñ* (あしたの新聞) *tomorrow*'s newspaper. / Ashita *ukagaimasu.* (あした伺います) I'll call on you *tomorrow*. 《⇨ asu; kyoo (table)》

aˈsobi　あそび（遊び）*n.* play; game; fun ; amusement:
Kodomo-tachi wa asobi *ni mu-chuu da.* (子どもたちは遊びに夢中だ) The children are absorbed in their *play*. / *Watashi wa Kyuu-shuu e* asobi *ni itte kita.* (私は九州へ遊びに行ってきた) I've made a trip to Kyushu for *pleasure*. / *Ashita* asobi *ni irasshai.* (あした遊びにいらっしゃい) Please come around to *see* us tomorrow. 《⇨ asobu》

aˈsob·u　あそぶ（遊ぶ）*vi.* (asob·i-; asob·a-; asoñ-de Ⓒ) **1** play; amuse oneself:
inu to asobu (犬と遊ぶ) *play* with a dog / *kooeñ de* asobu (公園で遊ぶ) *play* in the park / *Kodomo-tachi wa geemu o shite* asoñde iru. (子どもたちはゲームをして遊んでいる) The children *are amusing themselves* by playing games. 《⇨ asobi》
2 be idle; idle away:
Kare wa shigoto ga nai no de asoñde ita. (彼は仕事がないので遊んでいた) He *was idle* because there was no work for him. / *Gogo wa* asoñde shimatta. (午後は遊んでしまった) I *idled away* the afternoon.
3 (of a place, a room, an instrument, etc.) be not in use:
asoñde iru *heya* (遊んでいる部屋) a

room *not in use* | *Kono kikai wa ima* asoñde imasu. (この機械は今遊んでいます) This machine *is not used* now.

asobi ni iku (遊びに行く) visit; call on: *Koñdo no nichiyoo, kare no tokoro e* asobi ni ikimaseñ *ka?* (こんどの日曜日, 彼のところへ遊びにいきませんか) How about *visiting* him next Sunday?

a⌈**soko** あそこ *n.* **1** that place; over there: ★ Refers to a place which is some distance away from both the speaker and the listener.
Asoko ni takai too ga mieru deshoo. (あそこに高い塔が見えるでしょう) You can see a tall tower *over there.* | Asoko *de shiñbuñ o yoñde iru no wa dare desu ka?* (あそこで新聞を読んでいるのはだれですか) Who is it reading a newspaper *over there*?

2 that place: ★ Refers to a place which is removed from both the speaker and the listener, but is known to them.
Izu mo ii kedo, watashi wa asoko *yori Shiñshuu no hoo ga suki desu.* (伊豆もいいけど, 私はあそこより信州の方が好きです) Izu is a nice place to visit, but I like Shinshu better. | "*Yuubiñkyoku no soba no akichi o oboete imasu ka?*" "*Ee, yoku* asoko *de asobimashita ne.*" (「郵便局のそばの空き地を覚えていますか」「ええ, よくあそこで遊びましたね」) "Do you remember the vacant lot next to the post office?" "Yes, we often played *there*, didn't we?" 《⇨ soko¹》

3 that place: ★ Refers to a place which the speaker expects the listener to know about.
"*Koñbañ* asoko *e nomi ni ikanai?*" "*Ii ne. Ikimashoo.*" (「今晩あそこへ飲みに行かない」「いいね. 行きましょう」) "How about going for a

drink at *that place* this evening?" "Yes. Let's go."

4 that: ★ Used to emphasize a degree.
Kare ga asoko *made gañbaru to wa omoimaseñ deshita.* (彼があそこまでがんばるとは思いませんでした) I never thought that he would try *that* hard. 《⇨ doko; koko; soko¹》

a⌈**ssa**⌉**ri** あっさり *adv.* (～ **to**) easily; readily:
Jitsuryoku nañbaa-wañ no chiimu to no shiai de watashi-tachi wa assari *(to) makete shimatta.* (実力ナンバーワンのチームとの試合で私たちはあっさり(と)負けてしまった) We *easily* lost in the game against the number one team. | *Shachoo to ikeñ ga tairitsu shite, ano hito wa* assari *(to) kaisha o yamete shimatta.* (社長と意見が対立して, あの人はあっさり(と)会社を辞めてしまった) The president and he had contradictory opinions and he resigned from the company *without hesitation.*

assari (**to**) **suru** (～(と)する) (of dish, appetite, desire, etc.) plain; simple; light: *Niku-ryoori no ato wa* assari *(to)* shita *mono ga tabetaku naru.* (肉料理の後はあっさり(と)したものが食べたくなる) After a meat dish, I feel like eating something *plain and simple.* | *Kare wa o-kane no koto ni wa* assari *(to)* shita *hito desu.* (彼はお金のことにはあっさり(と)した人です) He is a person who is *indifferent* to money.

a⌈**sseñ** あっせん (斡旋) *n.* good offices; mediation; help:
Boku wa Yamamoto-sañ no asseñ *de ima no shoku o eta.* (僕は山本さんの斡旋で今の職を得た) I got my present job through the *good offices* of Mr. Yamamoto.

asseñ suru (～する) *vt.* use one's good offices; mediate: *Watashi wa kare ni shoku o* asseñ shite *ageta.* (私は彼に職を斡旋してあげた) I *helped* him find employment.

a⌐su⌐ あす (明日) *n.* = ashita.

a⌐tae·ru あたえる (与える) *vt.* (atae-te Ⅴ) **1** give; award:
kodomo ni yoi omocha o ataeru (子どもに良いおもちゃを与える) *give* a child nice toys / *Kare ni moo ichi-do chañsu o* ataeyoo. (彼にもう一度チャンスを与えよう) *Let's give* him one more chance. / *Kono sakuhiñ ni kiñshoo ga* ataerareta. (この作品に金賞が与えられた) The gold prize *was awarded* for this work.
2 give; cause (shock, damage, pain, etc.):
Yuujiñ no shi wa kare ni ooki-na shokku o ataeta. (友人の死は彼に大きなショックを与えた) The death of his friend *gave* him a great shock.
3 afford (pleasure, etc.):
Koteñ wa dokusho no yorokobi o ataete *kureru.* (古典は読書の喜びを与えてくれる) Classical literature *affords* us reading pleasure.
4 assign; provide (a job, a question, etc.):
Hayashi-sañ wa ataerareta *shigoto o isshoo-keñmee yatte imasu.* (林さんは与えられた仕事を一生懸命やっています) Ms. Hayashi is putting her all into the work that *was assigned* to her. / *Moñdai ga muzukashikute,* ataerareta *jikañ de wa tokenakatta.* (問題が難しくて, 与えられた時間では解けなかった) The problem was so hard I couldn't solve it within the *given* time.

a⌐takushi あたくし *n.* (*informal*) = watakushi. ★ Used mainly by women.

a⌐tama⌐ あたま (頭) *n.* **1** head: ★ Usually indicates the portion from the eyebrows up or the top part covered with hair.
Booru ga atama *ni atatta.* (ボールが頭にあたった) The ball hit me on

the *head.* / Atama ga itai. (頭が痛い) *I have a headache* / *Shoobai fushiñ de* atama ga itai. (商売不振で頭が痛い) The slump in business *is a big headache.* 《⇨ jiñtai (illus.)》
2 brain:
atama ga ii (頭がいい) *be smart* / atama o tsukau (頭を使う) use one's *brains* / *Ii kañgae ga* atama ni ukañda. (いい考えが頭に浮かんだ) A good idea *occurred to me.*
3 hair:
atama o arau (頭を洗う) shampoo one's *hair* / Atama o katte moratta. (頭を刈ってもらった) I had my *hair* cut.

atama ga agaranai (頭が上がらない) cannot compete with; be indebted: *Ano hito ni wa* atama ga agaranai. (あの人には頭が上がらない) I *am greatly obliged* to him.

atama ga kireru (頭が切れる) have a sharp mind.

atama ga sagaru (頭が下がる) take off one's hat: *Kanojo no doryoku ni wa* atama ga sagaru. (彼女の努力には頭が下がる) I *take off my hat* to her efforts.

atama ni kuru (頭にくる) get angry: *Kare no taido wa* atama ni kuru. (彼の態度は頭にくる) His attitude *makes me mad.*

atama o hineru (〜をひねる) rack one's brains: *Kare wa sono moñdai ni* atama o hinetta. (彼はその問題に頭をひねった) He *gave a lot of thought* to the problem.

atama o itameru (頭を痛める) be worried: *Kare wa musuko no koto de* atama o itamete *iru.* (彼は息子のことで頭を痛めている) He *is quite concerned* about his son.

a⌐tamaka⌐zu あたまかず (頭数) *n.* the number of persons.
《⇨ niñzuu》

a⌐tamakiñ あたまきん (頭金) *n.* down payment.

a⌐tarashi⌐·i あたらしい (新しい) *a.*

(-ku) **1** new; latest:
Kono kuruma wa mada atarashii.
(この車はまだ新しい) This car is still
new. / *Kare wa* atarashii *sebiro o
kite, dekaketa.* (彼は新しい背広を着
て, 出かけた) He went out in his
new suit. / *Tanaka-sañ wa* atarashiku *kuwawatta meñbaa no hitori
desu.* (田中さんは新しく加わったメンバ
ーの一人です) Ms. Tanaka is one of
the *newly* joined members.
《↔ furui》
2 fresh:
Kono tamago wa atarashii. (この卵
は新しい) These eggs here are
fresh. / *Nani-ka* atarashii *nyuusu
wa arimaseñ ka?* (何か新しいニュース
はありませんか) Don't you have any
fresh news? 《↔ furui》《⇨ arata》

a'**tari** あたり (辺り) *n.* **1** neighborhood; vicinity:
Kono atari *ni yuubiñkyoku wa
arimasu ka?* (この辺りに郵便局はあり
ますか) Is there a post office in this
neighborhood?
2 about; around:
atari *o mimawasu* (辺りを見回す)
look *around* / *Tsugi no nichiyoo*
atari *o-hima desu ka?* (次の日曜あた
りおひまですか) Are you free sometime *around* next Sunday?

a'**tarimae** あたりまえ (当たり前)
a.n. (~ na/no, ni) **1** natural; reasonable:
Kare ga okoru no wa atarimae *da.*
(彼が怒るのはあたりまえだ) It is *natural* for him to get angry. / *Atarimae no koto o shita dake desu
kara, o-ree wa kekkoo desu.* (あたり
まえのことをしただけですから, お礼はけっ
こうです) I only did what *I should
have done*, so don't feel obligated.
/ *"Kono moñdai, dekiru?" "Atarimae deshoo."* (「この問題できる」「あた
りまえでしょう」) "Can you answer
this question?" "*Of course.*" /
*"Moo kore ijoo wa dame desu
ka?" "Atarimae deshoo."* (「もうこれ
以上はだめですか」「あたりまえでしょう」)
"Can't I ask for more?" "*Of
course not.*" 《⇨ toozeñ》
2 ordinary:
Atarimae *no hito nara, dare de mo
shitte iru koto desu.* (あたりまえの人
なら, だれでも知っていることです) It's
something that any *ordinary* person would know.

a'**tar·u** あたる (当たる) *vi.* (atar·i-;
atar·a-; atat-te [C]) **1** hit; strike:
*Booru ga toñde kite, kare no
atama ni* atatta. (ボールが飛んできて,
彼の頭に当たった) A ball came
flying and *hit* him on the head. /
Ya ga mato ni atatta. (矢が的に当た
った) The arrow *hit* the target. /
Kare wa tama ni atatte, *shiñda.*
(彼は弾に当たって, 死んだ) He *was
hit* by a bullet and killed.
《⇨ ateru》
2 (of a prediction, a forecast) be
right:
Kyoo no teñki-yohoo wa atatta. (き
ょうの天気予報は当たった) Today's
weather forecast *was right.* /
Kare no yosoo wa atatta. (彼の予想
は当たった) His prediction *proved
right.* 《⇨ ateru》
3 win:
Kono kuji ga it-too ni atarimashita. (このくじが一等に当たりました)
This lottery ticket *won* first prize.
《⇨ ateru》
4 make a hit; succeed:
Shiñ-seehiñ ga atatte, *kare wa
oomooke o shita.* (新製品が当たって,
彼は大もうけをした) The new prod-
uct *was a hit*, and he made a lot
of money out of it. / *Kore wa
kono natsu ichibañ* atatta *eega
desu.* (これはこの夏一番当たった映画で
す) This is the movie which *was*
the biggest *hit* this summer.
《⇨ ateru》
5 (of a date) fall on:
Koñdo no saijitsu wa doyoobi ni
atarimasu. (今度の祭日は土曜日に当

たります) The coming holiday *falls* on Saturday.

6 correspond; be equivalent to: *Ichi-doru wa ima hyaku-sañjuu-go-eñ ni* atarimasu. (1ドルは今135円に当たります) One dollar is now *equivalent* to about 135 yen. / *Kare wa watashi no gikee ni* atarimasu. (彼は私の義兄にあたります) He *is* my brother-in-law.

7 lie; be located: *Tookyoo wa Nihoñ no hobo chuuoo ni* ataru. (東京は日本のほぼ中央にあたる) Tokyo *lies* near the middle of Japan.

8 be assigned; be allotted; be called on: *Koñdo no geki de kanojo wa ii yaku ni* atatta. (今度の劇で彼女はいい役に当たった) In the recent play, she *was given* a good part. / *Watashi wa Eego no jikañ ni ni-kai* atatta. (私は英語の時間に2回当たった) I *was called on* twice during the English lesson. / *Kyoo, too-bañ ni* atatte iru *no wa dare desu ka?* (きょう、当番に当たっているのはだれですか) Who *is on* duty today? 《⇨ ateru》

9 (of light, rays, etc.) shine; get sunshine: *Tonari ni ooki-na biru ga tatta no de, sukkari hi ga* ataranaku natta. (隣に大きなビルが建ったので、すっかり日が当たらなくなった) Since a tall building was put up next to us, the sunlight *doesn't reach* us anymore. 《⇨ateru》

10 (of a person) be poisoned; get food poisoning: *fugu ni* ataru (ふぐにあたる) *be poisoned* by globefish.

11 consult; look up; check (a source of information): *Jisho ni* atatte, *kañji no imi o shirabeta.* (辞書にあたって、漢字の意味を調べた) I *looked* in the dictionary for the meaning of the

Chinese character. / *Chokusetsu hoñniñ ni* attate, *ikoo o kiite mimasu.* (直接本人にあたって、意向を聞いてみます) I will *ask* him in person for his views on the matter.

12 be hard on (a person): *Kimura-sañ wa itsu-mo watashi ni tsuraku* ataru. (木村さんはいつも私につらく当たる) Mr. Kimura *is* always *hard* on me.

13 undertake; be in charge of: *koohai no shidoo ni* ataru (後輩の指導に当たる) *guide* the younger students [employees] / *chiryoo ni* ataru (治療に当たる) *undertake* medical treatment / *Kare wa Nihoñ no daihyoo to shite koo-shoo ni* atatta. (彼は日本の代表として交渉に当たった) He *conducted* negotiations as the representative of Japan. 《⇨ ateru》

14 expose oneself to heat [wind, etc.]: *sutoobu ni* ataru (ストーブにあたる) *warm oneself* at the heater / *yo-kaze ni* ataru (夜風にあたる) *expose oneself* to the evening breeze. 《⇨ ateru》

...(suru) ni wa ataranai (…(する)にはあたらない) be not worth (doing): *Soñna koto wa* odoroku ni wa ataranai. (そんなことは驚くにはあたらない) That kind of thing *is nothing to be surprised about.*

...ni atari [attatte] (…にあたり[あたって]) (*formal*) on the occasion: *Kaikai* ni atari, *hitokoto go-aisatsu o mooshiagemasu.* (開会にあたり、一言ごあいさつを申し上げます) I would like to say a few words *at the start of* this meeting.

aˈtashi あたし *n.* (*informal*) = watakushi. ★ Used mainly by women.

aˈtataˈka あたたか (暖か) *a.n.* (~ na, ni) warm; mild: atataka *na hizashi* (暖かな日ざし) *warm* sunlight / *Kyoo wa* atataka *da.* (きょうは暖かだ) It is *warm* today. (⟹ atatakai))

a⌈**tataka**⌉**·i** あたたかい (暖かい・温かい) *a.* (-ku) (*informal* =attaka)
1 warm; mild:
atatakai *kooto* (暖かいコート) a *warm* coat / *Dañdañ atatakaku natte kita.* (だんだん暖かくなってきた) It has become *warmer and warmer.* (↔ samui (table)) (⟹ atataka))
2 warm-hearted; cordial:
Tanaka-sañ wa kokoro no atatakai *hito da.* (田中さんは心の温かい人だ) Mr. Tanaka is a *warm-hearted* man. / *Miñna wa kare o* atatakaku *mukaeta.* (みんなは彼を温かく迎えた) They gave him a *cordial* welcome. (↔ tsumetai))

a⌈**tatama**⌉**·u** あたたまる (暖まる・温まる) *vi.* (-mar·i-; -mar·a-; -matte C) get warm; warm up; be heated:
Kono heya wa yoku atatamatte *iru.* (この部屋はよく暖まっている) This room *is* well *heated.* / *Suupu ga hodoyoku* atatamatta. (スープがほどよく温まった) The soup *was* nice and *hot.* / *Furo ni haittara karada ga* atatamatta. (ふろに入ったら体が温まった) I *felt warm* after taking a bath. (⟹ atatameru))

a⌈**tatame**⌉**·ru** あたためる (暖める・温める) *vt.* (-me-te V) **1** warm (up); heat:
eñjiñ o atatameru (エンジンを暖める) *warm up* an engine / *reetoo-shokuhiñ o deñshi-reñji de* atatameru (冷凍食品を電子レンジで温める) *heat* frozen food in a microwave oven. / *Hi de te o* atatameta. (火で手を暖めた) I *warmed* my hands at the fire. / *Gyuunyuu o* atatamete *noñda.* (牛乳を温めて飲んだ) I *heated* the milk and drank it. (⟹ atatamaru))
2 nurse (a thought); have in mind:
Naganeñ atatamete *ita keekaku o*

jikkoo suru koto ni shita. (長年あたためていた計画を実行することにした) I've decided to carry out the plan I've *had in mind* for years.

a⌈**tchi**⌉ あっち *n.* (*colloq.*) =achira.
1 that; that way; over there:
Atchi *no kooto no hoo ga attakasoo da.* (あっちのコートのほうがあったかそうだ) *That* coat looks warmer. / Atchi *e itte miyoo.* (あっちへ行ってみよう) Let's go *that way.* / *Kodomo wa* atchi *de asobi nasai.* (子どもはあっちで遊びなさい) You children go and play *over there.*
2 (*informal*) that person:
Atchi *ga saki ni te o dashita ñ da.* (あっちが先に手を出したんだ) *He* was the one that started the fight. (⟹ dotchi; kotchi; sotchi))

a⌈**te** あて (当て) *n.* **1** object; aim; goal:
Kare wa ate *mo naku burabura aruita.* (彼は当てもなくぶらぶら歩いた) He wandered around *aimlessly.* / *Toku ni kore to itta* ate *wa arimaseñ.* (特にこれといった当てはありません) I have no definite *object* in mind.
2 expectation; hope:
ate *ga hazureru* (当てが外れる) *be disappointed* / *Kare ga kuru* ate *wa nai.* (彼が来る当てはない) There is no *hope* of his coming.
3 dependence; reliance:
Watashi-tachi wa anata o ate *ni shite imasu.* (私たちはあなたを当てにしています) We *depend* on you. / *Ano hito wa* ate *ni naranai.* (あの人は当てにならない) We can place no *reliance* on him.

-ate あて (宛) *suf.* addressed to:
Suzuki-sañ-ate *no kozutsumi* (鈴木さんあての小包) a parcel *addressed to* Miss Suzuki / *Anata*-ate *no tegami ga kite imasu.* (あなたあての手紙がきています) There is a letter *for* you.

a⌈**tehama**⌉**·ru** あてはまる (当てはまる) *vi.* (-hamar·i-; -hamar·a-;

-hamat-te ⒞） **1** hold true; fit: *Kono kotowaza wa geñdai ni mo* atehamaru.（このことわざは現代にも当てはまる）This proverb *holds true* even in our time. / *Sore wa kono baai ni* atehamaranai.（それはこの場合に当てはまらない）That *does not fit* this case. 《⇨ atehameru》 **2** fulfill: *Koo-iu jookeñ ni* atehamaru *hito wa nakanaka mitsukaranai.*（こういう条件に当てはまる人はなかなか見つからない）It is hard to find a person who *fulfills* these conditions. 《⇨ atehameru》 **3** apply: *Kono yakugo wa kono ba ni pittari* atehamaru.（この訳語はこの場にぴったり当てはまる）This translation exactly *applies* in this case. 《⇨ atehameru》

a⌈tehame⌉·ru あてはめる（当てはめる）*vt.* (-hame-te Ⓥ） **1** apply; adapt: *Gaikoku no shuukañ o subete Nihoñ ni* atehameru *wake ni wa ikanai.*（外国の習慣をすべて日本に当てはめるわけにはいかない）You cannot expect us to *adapt* all foreign customs to Japan. / *Sono hanashi o jibuñ no baai ni* atehamete mita.（その話を自分の場合に当てはめてみた）I *applied* that example to my case. 《⇨ atehamaru》 **2** fill in; fill out: *Kuusho ni tekitoo na go o* atehamete *buñ o kañsee shi nasai.*（空所に適当な語を当てはめて文を完成しなさい）*Fill* in the blank with a suitable word and complete the sentence. 《⇨ atehamaru》

a⌈tena あてな（宛名）*n.* address: *Kono* atena *wa chigatte iru.*（この宛名は違っている）This *address* is wrong.

a⌈te·ru あてる（当てる）*vt.* (ate-te Ⓥ） **1** hit; strike: *Kare wa ya o mato ni ateta.*（彼は

矢を的に当てた）He *shot* the arrow into the target. 《⇨ ataru》 **2** put: *Kanojo wa kodomo no hitai ni te o* ateta.（彼女は子どもの額に手を当てた）She *put* her hand to her child's forehead. **3** guess; give a right answer: *Kare ga dare da ka* atete *gorañ nasai.*（彼がだれだか当ててごらんなさい）Try *guessing* who he is. 《⇨ ataru》 **4** expose: *Nureta fuku o hi ni* atete *kawakashita.*（ぬれた服を日に当てて乾かした）I *put* the wet clothes out in the sun to dry them. 《⇨ ataru》 **5** (of a lottery) win: *Kare wa kuji de kaigai-ryokoo o* ateta.（彼はくじで海外旅行を当てた）He *won* an overseas trip in the lottery. 《⇨ ataru》 **6** use; spend (money, time, etc.): *Watashi wa hito-tsuki goseñ-eñ o hoñ-dai ni* atete imasu.（私はひと月5千円を本代に当てています）I *spend* 5,000 yen a month on books. / *Kanojo wa ichi-nichi ichi-jikañ o Nihoñgo no beñkyoo ni* atete iru.（彼女は1日1時間を日本語の勉強に当てている）She *devotes* an hour a day to studying Japanese. **7** call on (somebody): *Kyoo watashi wa señsee ni* aterareta.（きょう私は先生に当てられた）Today the teacher *called on* me in class. 《⇨ ataru》

a⌈tesaki あてさき（宛先）*n.* address; destination.

a⌈to¹ あと（後）*n.* **1** back; rear: ato o ou（後を追う）*pursue* / ato ni tsuzuku（後に続く）*follow* / ato ni mawasu（後に回す）*postpone* / *Ato e sagatte kudasai.*（後へ下がってください）Step *back*, please. 《↔ mae》 **2** after; later: ★ Usually in the pattern '(...*no*/-*ta*) ato *de*.' *Chuushoku no* ato *de tenisu o yaroo.*（昼食の後でテニスをやろう）

Let's play tennis *after* lunch. / *Kare ga itta* ato *de hanashimasu.* (彼が行った後で話します) I'll tell you *after* he has left. / Ato *de deñwa shimasu.* (後で電話します) I'll call you *later.* 《↔ mae》
3 rest; remainder:
Ato *wa raigetsu haraimasu.* (後は来月払います) I'll pay the *rest* next month.

a⌐to² あと (跡) *n.* mark; trace; track; ruins; remains:
kutsu no ato (靴の跡) the *marks* of shoes / *kuruma no* ato (車の跡) the *tracks* of a car / *kodai Rooma no* ato (古代ローマの跡) the *ruins* of ancient Rome / *Kare no hitai ni wa kizu no* ato *ga aru.* (彼の額には傷の跡がある) There is a *scar* on his forehead.

a⌐to⌐ashi あとあし (後足) *n.* (of an animal) hind leg. 《↔ maeashi》

a⌐toka⌐tazuke あとかたづけ (後片付け) *n.* clearing away:
shokuji no atokatazuke o suru (食事の後片付けをする) *clear* the table after a meal / *heya no* atokatazuke o suru (部屋の後片付けをする) *put* a room *back in order.*

a⌐tosaki あとさき (後先) *n.* **1** before and behind; both ends:
Atosaki *ni kuruma ga tsukaete ite, ugokenakatta.* (後先に車がつかえていて、動けなかった) There were cars *in front of and behind* me, and I was unable to make any progress.
2 consequences:
Kare wa atosaki *no kañgae mo naku, keeyakusho ni saiñ shita.* (彼は後先の考えもなく、契約書にサインした) He signed the contract without any consideration of the *consequences.* / Atosaki *no koto o yoku kañgae nasai.* (後先のことをよく考えなさい) You should reflect on the *consequences.*

a⌐toshi⌐matsu あとしまつ (後始末) *n.* **1** putting things in order:

hi no atoshimatsu o suru (火の後始末をする) *put out* a fire *completely.*
2 settlement:
Chichi ga watashi no shakkiñ no atoshimatsu o shite kureta. (父が私の借金の後始末をしてくれた) My father *settled* my debts for me.

ATS *n.* automatic train stop. (自動列車停止装置＝*jidoo ressha tee-shi soochi*)

a⌐tsugami あつがみ (厚紙) *n.* thick paper; cardboard; pasteboard.

a⌐tsugi あつぎ (厚着) *n.* heavy [thick] clothes [clothing]:
Kono ko wa atsugi *o shite iru.* (この子は厚着をしている) This child *is heavily clothed.* / *Kyoo wa* atsugi *o shita hoo ga yoi.* (きょうは厚着をしたほうがよい) You should *dress warmly* today. 《↔ usugi》

a⌐tsu⌐i¹ あつい (熱い) *a.* (-ku)
1 (of temperature) hot; heated:
atsui *o-cha* (熱いお茶) *hot* tea / *Chichi wa* atsui *furo ga suki desu.* (父は熱いふろが好きです) My father loves a *very hot* bath. 《↔ tsumetai; nurui》《⇨ atsusa²》
2 emotionally excited:
atsui *shiseñ* (熱い視線) a *passionate* look / *Sono kookee o mite, mune ga* atsuku *natta.* (その光景を見て、胸が熱くなった) I was *deeply moved* at the sight.

a⌐tsu⌐i² あつい (暑い) *a.* (-ku) hot; very warm:
Kyoo wa totemo atsui. (きょうはとても暑い) It is *very hot* today. / *Nihoñ de wa hachi-gatsu ga ichi-bañ* atsui *tsuki desu.* (日本では8月がいちばん暑い月です) August is the *hottest* month in Japan.
《↔ samui (table)》《⇨ atsusa¹》

a⌐tsu⌐i³ あつい (厚い) *a.* (-ku)
1 thick; heavy:
atsui *hoñ* (厚い本) a *thick* book / *Kono oreñji wa kawa ga* atsui. (このオレンジは皮が厚い) This orange

has a *thick* skin. / *Sora wa* atsui
kumo ni oowarete ita. (空は厚い雲に
おおわれていた) The sky was covered
with *heavy* cloud. 《↔ usui》
《⇨ atsusa³》
2 warm; hearty:
Watashi-tachi wa atsui *motenashi
o uketa.* (私たちは厚いもてなしを受けた)
We received a *warm and friendly* welcome. / *Inaka no hito wa
niñjoo ni* atsui. (いなかの人は人情に厚
い) Country people are *warm-
hearted.* / Atsuku *oñ-ree mooshiagemasu.* (*formal*) (厚く御礼申し上
げます) Please accept my *sincere*
thanks.

a⌈**tsukai** あつかい (扱い) *n.* handling; dealing; treatment:
Gasoriñ no atsukai *ni wa ki o tsukete kudasai.* (ガソリンの扱いには気を
つけてください) Please be careful
when *handling* gasoline. / *Watashi-tachi wa sono kaisha de hidoi*
atsukai *o uketa.* (私たちはその会社で
ひどい扱いをうけた) We *were* badly
treated at that company. 《⇨ atsu-
kau》

a⌈**tsukamashi**¹·**i** あつかましい (厚か
ましい) *a.* (-ku) impudent; shameless; presumptuous:
Atsukamashii *hito wa kirai da.* (厚
かましい人は嫌いだ) I don't like
impudent people. / *Kare wa* atsu-
kamashiku *mo, soo itta.* (彼は厚かま
しくも、そう言った) He *had the nerve*
to say that. / Atsukamashii *o-
negai de kyooshuku desu.* (*formal*) (厚かましいお願いで恐縮です) I
am ashamed to make this *presumptuous* request. 《⇨ zuuzuu-
shii》

a⌈**tsuka·u** あつかう (扱う) *vt.*
(-ka·i-; -kaw·a-; -kat-te ⓒ)
1 handle; operate:
Kono moñdai wa doo atsukatte
yoi ka wakarimaseñ. (この問題はどう
扱ってよいかわかりません) I don't
know how to *handle* this prob-

lem. / *Kono kabiñ wa ware-yasui
no de teenee ni* atsukatte *kudasai.*
(この花瓶は割れやすいのでていねいに扱っ
てください) This vase is fragile, so
handle it with care, please.
2 treat; take care of; deal with:
*Koko no teñiñ wa o-kyaku o taise-
tsu ni* atsukaimasu. (ここの店員はお
客を大切に扱います) The clerks in
this shop *treat* customers with
courtesy. / *Sono moñdai wa hoka
no ka de* atsukaimasu. (その問題はほ
かの課で扱います) That problem will
be treated in a different lesson.
3 accept; deal in:
*Kono madoguchi de wa kookuu-
biñ o* atsukatte *orimaseñ.* (この窓口
では航空便を扱っておりません) We
don't *accept* airmail at this window. / *Too-teñ de wa sono yoo na
shina wa* atsukatte *orimaseñ.* (当
店ではそのような品は扱っておりません)
We don't *deal in* such articles at
this store.
4 write up in a newspaper or a
magazine:
*Sono nyuusu wa chookañ no
toppu-kiji to shite* atsukawareta.
(そのニュースは朝刊のトップ記事として扱
われた) That news *was treated* as
the main story in the morning
papers.

a⌈**tsukurushi**¹·**i** あつくるしい (暑苦
しい) *a.* (-ku) sultry; humid and
uncomfortable:
Yuube wa atsukurushikute *nemurenakatta.* (ゆうべは暑苦しくて眠れなかっ
た) It was *uncomfortably hot* last
night and I could not sleep well.
/ *Deñsha wa koñde ite* atsukurushi-
katta. (電車は混んでいて暑苦しかった)
The train was crowded and
stuffy.

a⌈**tsumari**¹ あつまり (集まり) *n.*
1 meeting; gathering:
Kinoo no atsumari *wa doo deshita?* (きのうの集まりはどうでした)
How was yesterday's *meeting?* /

Kinoo sotsugyoosee no atsumari *ga atta.* (きのう卒業生の集まりがあった) There was a *get-together* of graduates yesterday. 《⇨ atsumaru》

2 attendance; collection: *Kyoo wa* atsumari *ga yoi [warui].* (きょうは集まりがよい[悪い]) There is a large [small] *attendance* today. / *Kifu no* atsumari *ga warui.* (寄付の集まりが悪い) *The amount of money collected* is unsatisfactory. 《⇨ atsumaru》

a⌈tsuma⌉r·u あつまる (集まる) *vi.* (-mar·i-; -mar·a-; -mat-te Ⓒ)
1 gather; assemble: *Gakusee wa zeñiñ kyooshitsu ni* atsumatte imasu. (学生は全員教室に集まっています) The students *have all assembled* in the classroom. / *Ashita no asa juu-ji ni eki no mae ni* atsumatte *kudasai.* (あしたの朝10時に駅の前に集まってください) Please *meet* in front of the station at ten o'clock tomorrow morning. 《⇨ atsumari; atsumeru》

2 be collected: *Koñkai no bazaa de wa zeñbu de juumañ-eñ hodo* atsumatta. (今回のバザーでは全部で10万円ほど集まった) A total of about 100,000 yen *was collected* at the bazaar. / *Hañtai-uñdoo no shomee ga zeñkoku kara* atsumatta. (反対運動の署名が全国から集まった) Signatures for the opposition movement *were collected* from throughout the country. 《⇨ atsumeru》

3 be concentrated; be centered: *Seefu no omo na kikañ wa Tookyoo ni* atsumatte iru. (政府の主な機関は東京に集まっている) The main administrative offices of the government *are concentrated* in Tokyo. / *Hitobito no doojoo ga kanojo ni* atsumatta. (人々の同情が彼女に集まった) Their sympathy *was centered* on her. 《⇨ atsumeru》

a⌈tsume⌉·ru あつめる (集める) *vt.* (-me-te Ⓥ) **1** gather; assemble: *gakusee o uñdoojoo ni* atsumeru (学生を運動場に集める) *assemble* the students on the sports field. 《⇨ atsumaru》

2 collect: *Yamada-sañ wa mezurashii kitte o takusañ* atsumete imasu. (山田さんは珍しい切手をたくさん集めています) Mr. Yamada *has collected* many rare stamps. / *Suzuki-sañ wa kaisha setsuritsu no tame shikiñ o* atsumeru *no ni isogashii.* (鈴木さんは会社設立のため資金を集めるのに忙しい) Mr. Suzuki is busy *raising* funds to establish his company. 《⇨ atsumaru》

3 attract: *Sono nyuusu wa hitobito no kañshiñ o* atsumeta. (そのニュースは人々の関心を集めた) The news *attracted* people's interest. / *Saikiñ no kare no sakuhiñ wa chuumoku o* atsumete iru. (最近の彼の作品は注目を集めている) His recent works *are attracting* attention. 《⇨ atsumaru》

a⌈tsurae⌉·ru あつらえる (誂える) *vt.* (-rae-te Ⓥ) order (goods): *Yuumee na mise de suutsu o* atsuraeta. (有名な店でスーツをあつらえた) I *ordered* a suit at a famous store. / *Sekkaku* atsuraeta *no ni kono kutsu wa umaku awanai.* (せっかくあつらえたのにこの靴はうまく合わない) Although I went to the trouble of having these shoes *made to order*, they don't fit well.

a⌈tsu⌉ryoku あつりょく (圧力) *n.* pressure; stress: *kuuki no* atsuryoku (空気の圧力) air *pressure* / *Kare-ra wa kaisha ni* atsuryoku *o kakeru tame ni sutoraiki-chuu desu.* (彼らは会社に圧力をかけるためにストライキ中です) They are on strike to put *pressure* on their company.

a￢tsusa¹ あつさ (暑さ) *n.* heat; hot weather; hotness:
Kono atsusa wa shibaraku tsuzuki-soo desu. (この暑さはしばらく続きそうです) This *hot weather* seems likely to continue for a while. / *Boku wa atsusa ni yowai.* (ぼくは暑さに弱い) I cannot stand *heat*. / *Kinoo wa hidoi atsusa datta.* (きのうはひどい暑さだった) Yesterday the *heat* was unbearable. ((↔ samusa)) ((⇨ atsui²; higañ))

a￢tsusa² あつさ (熱さ) *n.* hotness; heat; warmth:
furo no atsusa o miru (風呂の熱さをみる) check the *temperature* of a bath. ((⇨ atsui¹))

a￢tsusa³ あつさ (厚さ) *n.* thickness:
Kono ita wa atsusa ga go-señchi aru. (この板は厚さが5センチある) This board is five centimeters in *thickness*. ((⇨ atsui³))

a￢tta￢ka あったか (暖か) *a.n.* = atataka.

a￢ttoo あっとう (圧倒) *n.* being overwhelming.
attoo suru (〜する) *vt.* overwhelm; overpower: *Aite-chiimu no señshu no see ga takai no de attoo sareta.* (相手チームの選手の背が高いので圧倒された) We *were overpowered* by the opposing team because the players were very tall. / *Wareware wa kazu no ue de teki o attoo shita.* (われわれは数の上で敵を圧倒した) We *overwhelmed* the enemy numerically.

a￢ttoo-teki あっとうてき (圧倒的) *a.n.* (〜 na, ni) overwhelming: *attoo-teki tasuu* (圧倒的多数) an *overwhelming* majority / *attoo-teki na shoori* (圧倒的な勝利) an *overwhelming* victory / *Kekkoñ shite iru hito no hoo ga attoo-teki ni ooi.* (結婚している人のほうが圧倒的に多い) Married people were in the majority *by far*.

a￢u¹ あう (会う・逢う・遇う) *vi.* (a·i-; aw·a-; at-te C) meet; see; come across: ★ Used with 'ni [to].' A more polite expression is 'o-me-ni-kakaru.' (⇨ to³)
hito ni [to] au (人に[と]会う) *see* a person / *Watashi wa Giñza de kare ni battari atta.* (私は銀座で彼にばったり会った) I *came across* him in Ginza. / *Ashita Yamada-sañ to au yotee desu.* (あした山田さんと会う予定です) I am to *meet with* Mr. Yamada tomorrow. / *Kobayashi-sañ to wa ichi-do shika atta koto ga arimaseñ.* (小林さんとは一度しか会ったことがありません) I've *met with* Mr. Kobayashi only once.

a￢u² あう (合う) *vi.* (a·i-; aw·a-; at-te C) **1** fit; suit:
Kono fuku wa watashi ni pittari aimasu. (この服は私にぴったり合います) This dress *fits* me perfectly. / *Soo-iu iro wa watashi no shumi ni awanai.* (そういう色は私の趣味に合わない) Such colors *do not suit* my taste. / *Kono ryoori wa o-kuchi ni aimashita deshoo ka?* (この料理はお口に合いましたでしょうか) Did you *like* this food? / *Kare to watashi wa totemo ki ga atte imasu.* (彼と私はとても気が合っています) He and I *get along* very well.
2 agree with; correspond:
Watashi wa chichi to ikeñ ga mattaku awanai. (私は父と意見が全く合わない) My father and I *never agree* with each other. / *Kare no iu koto wa doomo jijitsu to atte inai.* (彼の言うことはどうも事実と合っていない) What he says does not seem to *correspond* with the facts.
3 (in the form of 'atte iru') be correct; be right:
Kono kotae wa atte imasu ka? (この答えは合っていますか) *Is* this answer *correct*? / *Kono tokee wa atte imasu.* (この時計は合っています) This clock *has the right time*.

4 (with a negative) pay:
Kore ijoo yasuku shite wa (*wari ni*) *awanai.* (これ以上安くしては(割に)合わない) It *does not pay* if I sell at a lower price. / *Isshoo-keñmee yatta no ni moñku o iwareta no de wa* (*wari ni*) *awanai.* (一生懸命やったのに文句を言われたのでは(割に)合わない) It *isn't worth* working so hard just to get complaints. 《⇨ wari》

a⌈·u⌉³ あう (遭う) *vi* (a·i-; aw·a-; at-te C) meet with; have an unfavorable experience:
jiko ni au (事故にあう) *meet with* an accident / *Sono teeañ wa miñna no hañtai ni atta.* (その提案はみんなの反対にあった) The proposal *met with* opposition from everyone. / *Watashi-tachi wa señsoo-chuu hidoi me ni aimashita.* (私たちは戦争中ひどい目にあいました) We *had* bitter experiences during the war.

a⌈wa⌉ あわ (泡) *n.* bubble; foam; lather:
sekkeñ no awa (せっけんの泡) soap *bubbles* / *biiru no awa* (ビールの泡) the *froth* on beer / *awa ga tatsu* (泡が立つ) *bubbles* form.
awa o kuu (泡を食う) be confused. (*literally* 'eat bubbles')

a⌈wa⌉·i あわい (淡い) *a.* (-ku) (*literary*) **1** pale; light:
awai aoiro (淡い青色) *pale* blue.
2 faint:
awai nozomi (淡い望み) a *faint* hope.
3 transitory; fleeting:
awai koi (淡い恋) a *fleeting* love.

a⌈ware⌉ あわれ (哀れ) *n.* pity:
Ryooshiñ o nakushita akañboo ga miñna no aware o sasotta. (両親を亡くした赤ん坊がみんなの哀れを誘った) The baby that was left behind by her parents' death aroused our *pity*.
— *a.n.* (~ na, ni) pitiful; miserable:
Hitori-gurashi no roojiñ o aware ni omou. (一人暮らしの老人を哀れに思う) I *pity* the old man living alone. / *Kare no ushiro-sugata wa aware datta.* (彼の後ろ姿は哀れだった) His appearance looked *miserable* from behind.

a⌈wase⌉·ru あわせる (合わせる) *vt.* (awase-te V) **1** put [join] together:
te (*to te*) *o awaseru* (手(と手)を合わせる) *put* one's hands *together* / *chikara o awaseru* (力を合わせる) *unite* efforts / *kokoro* [*kimochi*] *o awaseru* (心[気持ち]を合わせる) *cooperate* / *koe o awasete utau* (声を合わせて歌う) sing *in harmony*. 《⇨ au²》
2 add (up):
Watashi no kurasu wa dañjo awasete, nijuu-mee imasu. (私のクラスは男女合わせて, 20 名います) In my class, there are twenty boys and girls *in all*. / *Zeñbu awasete ikura desu ka?* (全部合わせていくらですか) How much does it come to *altogether*?
3 fit:
Karada ni awasete doresu o tsukutta. (体に合わせてドレスを作った) I had a dress made to *fit* me. 《⇨ au²》
4 adjust; set:
kamera no piñto o awaseru (カメラのピントを合わせる) *adjust* the focus of a camera / *Mezamashi-dokee o roku-ji ni awaseta.* (目覚まし時計を6時に合わせた) I *set* the alarm clock for six. / *Rajio no daiyaru o Enu-etchi-kee no dai-ichi ni awase nasai.* (ラジオのダイヤルをNHKの第1に合わせなさい) *Tune* the radio in to NHK Channel 1. 《⇨ au²》
5 accompany:
Watashi-tachi wa piano no bañsoo ni awasete utatta. (私たちはピアノの伴奏に合わせて歌った) We sang *to the accompaniment* of the piano.
6 adapt:

Watashi wa kare no yarikata ni awaseta.（私は彼のやり方に合わせた）I *adapted myself* to his way of working. / *Kare wa hito to umaku hanashi o awaseru koto ga deki-nai.*（彼は人とうまく話を合わせることができない）He cannot *fit in* with the conversation of other people easily. (⇨ au²)

7 mix:

Kechappu to mayoneezu o awa-sete, soosu o tsukutta.（ケチャップとマヨネーズを合わせて、ソースを作った）I made a sauce by *mixing* ketchup and mayonnaise.

aˈwatadashi¹·i あわただしい（慌ただしい）*a.* (-ku) hasty; hurried; quick; busy:

awatadashii tokai-seekatsu（あわただしい都会生活）the *bustle* of city life / *Kare wa* awatadashiku *heya kara dete itta.*（彼はあわただしく部屋から出て行った）He went out of the room in haste. / *Seeji-joosee ga* awatadashiku *natte kita.*（政治情勢があわただしくなってきた）The political situation has become *confused and hectic.*

aˈwatemono あわてもの（慌て者）*n.* rash person.

aˈwate·ru あわてる（慌てる）*vi.* (awate-te Ⅴ) **1** hurry; panic:

Awateru to korobimasu yo.（慌てると転びますよ）If you *hurry*, you'll fall over. / *Jishiñ no toki wa* awa-tenai *de, mazu hi o keshi nasai.*（地震のときは慌てないで、まず火を消しなさい）In the event of an earthquake, *keep calm*, and first turn off the gas. / *Awateta no de saifu o wasureta.*（慌てたので財布を忘れた）*In my haste*, I forgot to bring my purse. / *Awatete deñwa-bañgoo o machigaeta.*（あわてて電話番号を間違えた）*In my haste*, I called the wrong number.

2 get flustered; be confused:

Kodomo ga mienaku natta no de

kare wa hidoku awateta.（子どもが見えなくなったので彼はひどく慌てた）He lost sight of his child so he *was in* a terrible *fluster*. / *Igai na kekka ni sukkari* awatete *shi-matta.*（意外な結果にすっかり慌ててしまった）I *got completely flustered* at the unexpected outcome. / *Kare wa* awatete *jibuñ no hatsugeñ o torikeshita.*（彼はあわてて自分の発言を取り消した）*In confusion*, he withdrew his remarks.

aˈyafuya あやふや *a.n.* (~ na, ni) vague; uncertain:

ayafuya na heñji（あやふやな返事）a *vague* answer / *ayafuya na taido*（あやふやな態度）an *uncertain* attitude.

aˈyamachi¹ あやまち（過ち）*n.* mistake; error; fault; sin:

★ Most often connotes a mistake with an ethical or moral evaluation implied.

ayamachi o okasu（過ちを犯す）make a *mistake* / *Ayamachi wa dare ni de mo aru.*（過ちはだれにでもある）We are all liable to make *mistakes.* / *Kako no* ayamachi *o kuri-kaeshite wa ikenai.*（過去の過ちを繰り返してはいけない）Don't repeat the *errors* of the past. / *Doñna chiisa-na* ayamachi *de mo misugosu no wa yokunai.*（どんな小さな過ちでも見過ごすのはよくない）You should not overlook even a minor *fault.*

aˈyamari¹ あやまり（誤り）*n.* error; mistake; slip:

> **（USAGE）**
> Means something wrong or incorrect. Interchangeable with '*machigai*,' but more formal.

ayamari o tadasu（誤りを正す）rectify an *error* / *Señsee wa buñpoo-joo no* ayamari *o ikutsu-ka shi-teki shita.*（先生は文法上の誤りをいくつか指摘した）The teacher pointed

out some grammatical *mistakes.* /
Ayamari *ga attara, naoshi nasai.*
(誤りがあったら, 直しなさい) Correct
errors, if any. 《⇨ayamaru²》

a「yama」r·u¹ あやまる (謝る) *vt.*
(-mar·i-; -mar·a-; -mat-te Ⓒ)
apologize; beg a person's pardon:
Okureta koto o miñna ni ayamatta.
(遅れたことをみんなに謝った) I *apolo-
gized* to everyone for being late. /
*Kore wa ayamatte sumu moñdai
de wa nai.* (これは謝ってすむ問題ではな
い) This is not a matter that can
be settled with an *apology.* /
*O-niisañ ni hito-koto ayamatte ki
nasai.* (お兄さんに一言謝ってきなさい)
Go and *ask for* your brother's
pardon. / *Kazuko-sañ wa kare ni
"gomeñ nasai" to ayamatta.* (和子
さんは彼に「ごめんなさい」と謝った)
"I'm sorry," Kazuko *apologized*
to him.

a「yama」r·u² あやまる (誤る) *vi., vt.*
(-mar·i-; -mar·a-; -mat-te Ⓒ)
make a mistake:
hañdañ o ayamaru (判断を誤る)
make a mistake of judgment /
hoogaku o ayamaru (方角を誤る)
take the wrong direction / *señtaku o ayamaru* (選択を誤る) *make
the wrong* choice / *Kanojo wa ayamatte, koppu o watte shimatta.*
(彼女は誤って, コップを割ってしまった)
She broke a glass *by mistake.*

a「yame あやめ (菖蒲) *n.* sweet
flag; iris.

a「yashi·i あやしい (怪しい) *a.* (-ku)
1 suspicious; strange:
Kono nimotsu wa ayashii. (この荷
物は怪しい) This baggage is *suspicious.* / *Kono heñ de ayashii otoko
o mikakemseñ deshita ka?* (この
辺で怪しい男を見かけませんでしたか)
Didn't you see a *suspicious* man
around here? / *Niwa de ayashii
mono-oto ga shita.* (庭で怪しい物音
がした) I heard a *strange* noise in

the yard.
2 doubtful; dubious; uncertain:
Kare no seekoo wa ayashii. (彼の
成功は怪しい) I am *doubtful* of his
success. / *Teñki ga ayashii.* (天気
が怪しい) The weather looks *uncertain.*
3 clumsy; poor:
Kare wa ashimoto ga ayashikatta.
(彼は足元が怪しかった) He walked
unsteadily. / *Kanojo no Furañsu-
go wa ayashii.* (彼女のフランス語は怪
しい) Her French is rather *poor.*

a「ya」s·u あやす *vi.* (ayash·i-; aya-
s·a-; ayash·i-te Ⓒ) fondle; lull;
dandle; soothe:
akañboo o ayasu (赤ん坊をあやす)
cuddle a baby.

a「yau」·i あやうい (危うい) *a.* (-ku)
(*literary*) = abunai.

a「za」yaka あざやか (鮮やか) *a.n.*
(~ na, ni) **1** bright; vivid;
fresh:
azayaka na iro (鮮やかな色) a *bright*
color / *azayaka na iñshoo* (鮮やかな
印象) a *vivid* impression / *Ame no
ato de, ki no midori ga azayaka
datta.* (雨のあとで, 木の緑が鮮やかだっ
た) After the rain, the green of
the trees was *fresh.* / *Sono dekigoto wa ima de mo azayaka ni
oboete iru.* (その出来事はいまでも鮮や
かに覚えている) I still remember the
event *vividly.*
2 splendid, skillful:
azayaka na eñgi (鮮やかな演技) a
splendid performance / *Kare wa
sono moñdai o azayaka ni shori
shita.* (彼はその問題を鮮やかに処理し
た) He settled the matter in a
skillful way.

A「zuchi-Mo「moyama-ji」dai
あづちももやまじだい (安土桃山時代) *n.*
Azuchi-Momoyama Period (1573
to 1603). 《⇨ jidai (table)》

a「zuka」r·u あずかる (預かる) *vt.*
(-kar·i-; -kar·a-; -kat-te Ⓒ)
1 keep:

Yamada-sañ ga anata no nimotsu o azukatte imasu. (山田さんがあなたの荷物を預かっています) Mr. Yamada *has* your baggage. 《⇨ azukeru》

2 look after; take charge of: *Hoikueñ wa kodomo o go-ji made* azukatte *kureru.* (保育園は子どもを5時まで預かってくれる) At the nursery, they *look after* the children until five o'clock. / *Pairotto wa ooku no jiñmee o* azukatte iru. (パイロットは多くの人命を預かっている) The pilot of an airplane *has responsibility for* many people's lives. 《⇨ azukeru》

3 withhold: *Kimi no jihyoo wa toriaezu* azukatte *okoo.* (君の辞表はとりあえず預かっておこう) I will *sit on* your resignation for the time being. 《⇨ azukeru》

aˈzukeˈ·ru あずける(預ける) *vt.* (-ke-te Ⅴ) **1** leave: *Kurooku ni mochimono o* azuketa. (クロークに持ち物を預けた) I *left* my things in the cloakroom. / *Kono nimotsu o Saitoo-sañ ni* azukete *okoo.* (この荷物を斎藤さんに預けておこう) Let's *leave* this baggage in Miss Saito's care. 《⇨ azukaru》

2 deposit: *Giñkoo ni gomañ-eñ* azuketa. (銀行に5万円預けた) I *deposited* 50,000 yen in the bank. 《⇨ azukaru》

3 entrust: *Kodomo wa haha ni* azukete, *shigoto ni ikimasu.* (子どもは母に預けて, 仕事に行きます) I *entrust* my child to my mother's care and go to work. 《⇨ azukaru》

aˈzukiˈ あずき(小豆) *n.* adzuki bean.

B

ba ば〔場〕 *n.* **1** place; spot:
ba *o hazusu* (場を外す) leave the
room / ba *o fusagu* (場をふさぐ) take
up much *space* / *Sono* ba *de ni-
jikañ matta.* (その場で2時間待った)
I waited for two hours at the *spot.*
/ *Kare wa sono* ba *de taiho sareta.*
(彼はその場で逮捕された) He was ar-
rested *there.* 《⇨ basho》
2 occasion; case:
Kanojo wa sono ba *ni fusawashii
fuku o kite ita.* (彼女はその場にふさわ
しい服を着ていた) She wore clothes
suitable for the *occasion.*
3 (of a drama) scene:
Kare wa ni-maku sañ-ba *ni toojoo
shimasu.* (彼は2幕3場に登場します)
He appears in Act 2, *Scene* 3.

-ba¹ ば *infl. end.* [attached to the
conditional base of a verb, adjective or the copula]

USAGE

The *ba*-form of a verb is made
by dropping the final '-*u*' and
adding '-*eba*,' and the *ba*-form
of an adjective by dropping the
final '-*i*' and adding '-*kereba*.'
The *ba*-form of the copula '*da*'
is '*naraba*.'

---

1 if; provided; when:
a (the *ba*-form clause indicates a
condition and the following
clause the consequent result):
*Ame ga fureba eñsoku wa chuushi
desu.* (雨が降れば遠足は中止です) *If
it rains,* our outing will be canceled. / *Teñki ga yokereba koko
kara Fuji-sañ ga miemasu.* (天気が
良ければここから富士山が見えます)
When it is fine, we can see Mt.
Fuji from here. / *Namae o kikeba
dare da ka sugu wakaru deshoo.*
(名前を聞けばだれだかすぐわかるでしょう)
Once you hear the name, you will
soon realize who it is. / *Ima ikanakereba maniaimaseñ yo.* (今行か
なければ間に合いませんよ) You will
not be in time *unless you leave
now.* 《⇨ -tara》
b (the *ba*-form clause indicates
an assumed or possible situation
and the following clause the
speaker's intention, request,
advice, etc.):
*Tsukarete inakereba sañka shiyoo
to omoimasu.* (疲れていなければ参加し
ようと思います) I plan to participate
as long as I am not tired. / *Jikañ
ga areba Kyooto e mo ikitai to
omoimasu.* (時間があれば京都へも行き
たいと思います) *Provided there is
time,* I would like to go to Kyoto
as well. / *Deñsha no hoo ga haya-
kereba deñsha de itte kudasai.* (電
車のほうが速ければ電車で行ってください)
If the train is faster, take it. / *Shigoto ga owaranakereba yasuñde
wa ikemaseñ.* (仕事が終わらなければ
休んではいけません) You must not
stop *unless your work is finished.*
c (the *ba*-form clause indicates
an unfulfilled or unreal condition and the following clause the
speaker's judgment, wish, reaction, etc.):
*Kinoo ame ga furanakereba
yokatta ñ desu ga.* (きのう雨が降らな
ければ良かったんですが) *If only it
hadn't rained* yesterday. / *Moo
sukoshi gañbareba dekita to omoimasu.* (もう少しがんばればできたと思いま
す) I feel I could have succeeded
if I had tried a bit harder. / *Hayaku shikeñ ga owareba ii naa.*
(早く試験が終わればいいなあ) How I

wish *the exams were over soon!*
《⇨ -tara》

2 when; whenever: ★ The *ba-*
form clause indicates a habitual
action in the past and the following clause the consequence of
that action.
Chichi wa nomeba *kanarazu
utatta mono da.* (父は飲めば必ず歌っ
たものだ) My father always used to
sing *when he drank.* / *Izeñ wa*
mago ga asobi ni kureba *yuueñchi
ni tsurete itta mono desu.* (以前は
孫が遊びに来れば遊園地に連れて行った
ものです) In the old days, *whenever
our grandchild visited us*, I used
to take him to the amusement
park.

3 and; both...and; neither...nor:
★ Used to link similar items in a
parallel relationship.
Ano hito wa tabako mo sueba
sake mo nomu. (あの人はたばこも吸え
ば酒も飲む) He smokes *and* drinks.
/ *Watashi wa hima mo* nakereba
kane mo nai. (私は暇もなければ金もな
い) I have *neither* time *nor* money.

-¹ba² ば (羽) *suf.* counter for
birds and rabbits:
suzume sañ-ba (すずめ 3 羽) *three*
sparrows. 《⇨ -wa》

ba⌐a ばぁ *int.* boo; bo. ★ Used
when playing with babies.

ba⌐ai ばあい (場合) *n.* **1** case; occasion; circumstance:
Sono kisoku wa kono baai *ateha-
marimaseñ.* (その規則はこの場合あては
まりません) That rule does not ap-
ply in this *case.* / *Giroñ o shite iru*
baai *de wa nai.* (議論をしている場合
ではない) This is not the *place* for
an argument. / *Sore wa toki to*
baai *ni yorimasu.* (それは時と場合に
よります) That depends on the
time and the *situation.*
2 in case of; if; when:
Kaji no baai *wa beru ga narimasu.*
(火事の場合はベルがなります) *In the*

event of fire, the bell will ring. /
Ame no baai *wa uchi ni imasu.*
(雨の場合は家にいます) *If* it rains, I
will stay at home. / *Sañkasha ga
sukunai* baai, *ryokoo wa chuushi
desu.* (参加者が少ない場合, 旅行は中
止です) The trip will be canceled
if the number of participants is
small. 《⇨ toki》

ba⌐asañ ばあさん (婆さん) *n.* (*informal*) **1** one's grandmother:
Uchi no baasañ *wa mada ashi ga
tassha desu.* (うちの婆さんはまだ足が達
者です) Our *grandmother* still has
sturdy legs. 《⇨ kazoku (table)》
2 old woman.
《↔ jiisañ》《⇨ o-baasañ》

ba⌐chi¹ ばち (罰) *n.* punishment
inflicted by gods or Buddha:
bachi ga ataru (罰が当たる) *be punished; get it* / Bachi ga atatta ñ da.
(罰が当たったんだ) *It serves you right.*

ba⌐ggu バッグ *n.* bag. ★ Also
'*bakku.*' 《⇨ kabañ》

ba⌐i ばい (倍) *n.* double; twice:
Go-neñ de shuunyuu ga bai ni
natta. (5 年で収入が倍になった) My
income *doubled* in five years.
/ *Kyuuryoo o* bai ni shite *ageyoo.*
(給料を倍にしてあげよう) I will *double*
your pay. / *Kono heya wa watashi
no heya no* bai aru. (この部屋は私の
部屋の倍ある) This room is *twice*
as large as mine.

-bai¹ ばい (倍) *suf.* times; -fold:
Bukka ga sañ-bai *ni natta.* (物価が
3 倍になった) Prices *tripled.* / *Ano
biru no takasa wa kotchi no biru
no* ni-bai aru. (あのビルの高さはこっち
のビルの 2 倍ある) That building is
twice as tall as this one.

-bai² ばい (杯) *suf.* = -hai.

ba⌐ibai ばいばい (売買) *n.* buying
and selling; trade:
Kare wa sono baibai (no) *keeyaku
ni saiñ shita.* (彼はその売買(の)契約に
サインした) He signed the *trade*
agreement.

baibai suru (〜する) *vt.* deal in; trade: *Kare wa fudoosañ o* baibai shite iru.(彼は不動産を売買している) He *deals in* real estate.

ba⌐ieñ ばいえん(煤煙) *n.* soot; smoke: baieñ de yogoreta *teñjoo* (ばい煙で汚れた天井) a *smoke-stained* ceiling.

ba⌐ikai ばいかい(媒介) *n.* mediation; medium. **baikai suru** (〜する) *vt.* mediate; carry: *Mararia wa ka ni yotte* baikai sareru.(マラリアは蚊によって媒介される) Malaria *is carried* by mosquitoes.

ba⌐ikiñ ばいきん(ばい菌) *n.* germ; bacteria. ★ Informal equivalent for '*saikiñ*,' emphasizing filthiness. 《⇨ saikiñ²》

ba⌐imee ばいめい(売名) *n.* self-advertisement; publicity: baimee *o hakaru* (売名を図る) seek *publicity* / baimee-*kooi* (売名行為) a *publicity* stunt to make one's name famous.

ba⌐ioriñ バイオリン *n.* violin: baioriñ *o hiku* (バイオリンを弾く) play the *violin*.

ba⌐iritsu ばいりつ(倍率) *n.*
1 magnification; power: *Kono reñzu no* bairitsu *wa go-bai desu.*(このレンズの倍率は5倍です) The *magnification* of this lens is five times. / *Booeñkyoo wa* bairitsu *ga takakereba takai hodo yoku mieru.*(望遠鏡は倍率が高ければ高いほど良く見える) The higher the *power* of a telescope is, the better you can see.
2 competition: *Kono gakkoo wa* bairitsu *ga takai.*(この学校は倍率が高い) There is keen *competition* to enter this school.

ba⌐ishoo ばいしょう(賠償) *n.* reparation; compensation: baishoo *o suru* (賠償をする) pay *compensation* / baishoo *o yookyuu*

suru (賠償を要求する) demand *reparations* / baishoo *ni oojiru* (賠償に応じる) pay *reparations*.

ba⌐ishuñ ばいしゅん(売春) *n.* prostitution: baishuñ-fu (売春婦) a *prostitute*.

ba⌐ishuu ばいしゅう(買収) *n.*
1 buying up; purchase.
2 bribery; corruption.
baishuu (o) suru (〜(を)する) *vt.*
1 buy up; purchase: *tochi* [*tatemono*] *o* baishuu suru (土地[建物]を買収する) *purchase* land [a building].
2 bribe; corrupt: *shooniñ o* baishuu suru (証人を買収する) *corrupt* a witness.

ba⌐iteñ ばいてん(売店) *n.* stand; stall; kiosk; store: *shiñbuñ no* baiteñ (新聞の売店) a *newsstand* / *eki no* baiteñ (駅の売店) a station *kiosk*.

ba⌐iu ばいう(梅雨) *n.* the rainy season. 《⇨ tsuyu²》

ba⌐iyaku ばいやく(売約) *n.* sales contract: *Kono e wa* baiyaku-zumi desu.(この絵は売約ずみです) This painting *has been sold*.

ba⌐jji バッジ *n.* badge; pin. ★ Usually refers to the badge that businessmen wear on their lapels to identify their companies.

ba⌐ka ばか(馬鹿) *n.* fool; stupid [silly] person: *Baka! Yamero!* (ばか! やめろ!) You *fool*! Stop it! / *Soñna koto o suru to wa kanojo wa baka da.*(そんなことをするとは彼女はばかだ) She is a *fool* to do such a thing. / *Sore o shiñjiru to wa watashi mo baka datta.*(それを信じるとは私もばかだった) It was *stupid* of me to believe that.
baka ni naranai (〜にならない) be not negligible: *Yuubiñ-ryookiñ wa baka ni naranai.*(郵便料金はばかにならない) The postage *costs more than just a little.*

baka ni suru (〜にする) make a fool of: *Miñna ga kare o* baka ni *shita.*(みんなが彼をばかにした) Everyone *made a fool of* him.

baka o miru (〜を見る) feel like a fool: *Kare o matte ite,* baka o *mita.*(彼を待っていて、ばかを見た) *It was stupid of me* to waste my time waiting for him.

— *a.n.* (〜 na) foolish; stupid; ridiculous; unreasonable: *Damasareru nañte* baka *na hito da.* (だまされるなんてばかな人だ) You are a *fool* to be cheated. / *Doo-shite añ-na baka na machigai o shita ñ da-roo.*(どうしてあんなばかな間違いをしたんだろう) I don't know why I made such a *stupid* mistake. / *Nañte* baka *na kañgae da!* (何てばかな考えだ) What a *ridiculous* idea! / *Soñ-na baka na hanashi wa shiñjira-renai.*(そんなばかな話は信じられない) I cannot believe such an *unreasonable* story.

ba⌐ka- ばか (馬鹿) *pref.* too...; extremely; excessively: baka-*shoojiki* (ばか正直) *simple* honesty / baka-*teenee* (ばかていねい) *excessive* politeness / baka-*jikara* (ばか力) *enormous* strength.

ba⌐kabakashi⌐·i ばかばかしい (馬鹿馬鹿しい) *a.* (-ku) foolish; silly; absurd: *Soñna mono ni tagaku no kane o tsukau no wa* bakabakashii.(そんなものに多額の金を使うのはばかばかしい) It is *foolish* to spend a large sum of money on such a thing. / *Too-kyoo no tochi no nedañ wa* baka-bakashii *hodo takai.*(東京の土地の値段はばかばかしいほど高い) The price of land in Tokyo is *absurdly* high. (⇨ bakarashii)

ba⌐ka⌐geta ばかげた (馬鹿げた) *attrib.* ridiculous; foolish; silly: *Doo-shite soñna* bakageta *machi-gai o shita no ka wakaranai.*(どうしてそんなばかげた間違いをしたのかわからな

い) I have no idea why I made such a *foolish* mistake. (⇨ baka)

ba⌐ka⌐gete iru ばかげている (馬鹿げている) be ridiculous; be foolish; be silly: *Jitsu ni* bakagete iru.(実にばかげている) That's really *ridiculous.*

ba⌐ka ni ばかに (馬鹿に) *adv.* awfully; terribly; very: *Kyoo wa* baka ni *isogashii.*(きょうはばかに忙しい) I'm *terribly* busy today. / *Kare wa kyoo wa* baka ni *kigeñ ga yoi.*(彼はきょうはばかに機嫌がよい) He is in *very* good humor today.

ba⌐kañsu バカンス *n.* vacation; holidays. ★ From French, 'vacances.'

ba⌐karashi⌐·i ばからしい (馬鹿らしい) *a.* (-ku) foolish; silly; absurd; ridiculous: *Watashi wa* bakarashii *machigai o shita koto o kookai shite iru.*(私はばからしい間違いをしたことを後悔している) I regret having made a *silly* mistake. / *Yasui kyuuryoo de hataraku no ga* bakarashiku *natte kita.*(安い給料で働くのがばからしくなってきた) I have started to feel *fool-ish* working for a low salary.

ba⌐kari ばかり *p.*

> **USAGE**
>
> Follows a noun, adjective or the dictionary form of a verb, or the *te*-form of a verb in the pattern '*-te bakari iru.*'

1 only; no other than...; nothing but: *Sono mise no kyaku wa wakai hito* bakari *datta.*(その店の客は若い人ばかりだった) The customers at that shop were *all* young people. / *Señsee wa watashi* bakari *ni shi-tsumoñ suru.*(先生は私ばかりに質問する) The teacher asks questions to *no one but* me. / *Asoñde* bakari *iru to ii gakkoo e hairemaseñ yo.*

(遊んでばかりいるといい学校へ入れません
よ) If you do *nothing except* play
around, you will not be able to
get into a good school. / *Ano ko
wa naite* bakari *iru.* (あの子は泣いて
ばかりいる) That child *just* keeps
on crying. 《⇨ dake; nomi²》
2 just:
Nihoñ ni tsuita bakari *de mada
nani mo mite imaseñ.* (日本に着いた
ばかりでまだ何も見ていません) I've *just*
arrived in Japan, so I haven't yet
seen anything.
3 about; approximately; thereabouts:
Tomodachi ga juu-niñ bakari
asobi ni kite kureta. (友だちが 10 人
ばかり遊びに来てくれた) *About* ten of
my friends visited me. / *Kono shigoto wa is-shuukañ* bakari *areba,
dekimasu.* (この仕事は 1 週間ばかりあ
れば、できます) I can finish this job
if I have a week *or so.* / *Juugo-
fuñ* bakari *matte kudasai.* (15 分ば
かり待ってください) Please wait for
about fifteen minutes. / *Señ-eñ*
bakari *kashite kuremaseñ ka?* (千
円ばかり貸してくれませんか) Won't
you lend me a thousand yen, *or
thereabouts?* 《⇨ kurai²; hodo》
4 be about [ready] to do:
Kanojo wa ima ni mo naki-dasañ
bakari *datta.* (彼女はいまにも泣きださ
んばかりだった) She *was about to* cry.
/ *Itsu de mo shuppatsu dekiru* bakari *ni yooi wa dekite imasu.* (いつ
でも出発できるばかりに用意はできていま
す) We *are ready to* set off at any
time.
5 just [simply] because:
Sono kashu no kao o hitome mitai
bakari *ni, takai kippu o katte shimatta.* (その歌手の顔を一目見たいばか
りに、高い切符を買ってしまった) I
bought an expensive ticket *simply because* I wanted to get a
glimpse of the singer. / *Koñpyuutaa ga tsukaenai* bakari *ni, ii shi-*

goto ni tsukenakatta. (コンピューター
が使えないばかりに、いい仕事につけなかっ
た) *Just because* I can't use a computer, I couldn't get a decent job.
6 (used for emphasis): ★ Emphatic form is '*bakkari.*'
*Koñdo bakari wa gamañ ga deki-
nai.* (今度ばかりはがまんができない)
This time I am not going to put
up with it. / *Aitsu wa ookii bakari de nañ no yaku ni mo tatanai.*
(あいつは大きいばかりで何の役にもたたな
い) He *is big,* but utterly useless.

ba⌈ka⌉·s·u ばかす (化かす) *vt.* (ba-
kash·i-; bakas·a-; bakash·i-te
Ⓒ) bewitch; play a trick on:
Nihoñ de wa, kitsune ga hito o
bakasu *to iwareru.* (日本では、狐が
人を化かすと言われる) In Japan, it is
said that foxes *play tricks* on people. 《⇨ kitsune; tanuki》

ba⌈kemono⌉ ばけもの (化け物) *n.*
monster; ghost; specter.

ba⌈ke⌉·ru ばける (化ける) *vi.* (ba-
ke-te Ⓥ) **1** take the form of:
Mahootsukai ga raioñ ni baketa.
(魔法使いがライオンに化けた) The
witch *took the form of* a lion.
2 disguise oneself as:
Gootoo wa keekañ ni bakete ita.
(強盗は警官に化けていた) The rob-
ber *disguised himself* as a policeman.
3 (of money) be spent on:
Kyuuryoo no taihañ wa hoñ-dai ni
bakete shimatta. (給料の大半は本代
に化けてしまった) Most of his salary
was spent on books.

ba⌈ketsu バケツ *n.* bucket; pail:
baketsu *ni mizu o kumu* (バケツに水
をくむ) fill a *bucket* with water /
baketsu *de mizu o hakobu* (バケツで
水を運ぶ) carry water in a *bucket.*

ba⌈kka⌉ri ばっかり *p.* = bakari.

ba⌈kkiñ ばっきん (罰金) *n.* fine;
penalty:
bakkiñ *o harau* (罰金を払う) pay a
fine / *Supiido-ihañ de* bakkiñ o

sañmañ-eñ torareta. (スピード違反で罰金を3万円取られた) I *was fined* 30,000 yen for speeding.

ba⌐kku バック *n.* back; background:
taki o bakku *ni shashiñ o toru* (滝をバックに写真を撮る) take a picture with a waterfall for the *background* / *Kare no* bakku ni *wa seejika ga* iru. (彼のバックには政治家がいる) He *is supported* by a politician. 《⇒ haikee¹》

bakku suru (〜する) *vi.* reverse (a car).

ba⌐kuchi ばくち (博打) *n.* gambling; speculation:
bakuchi o utsu (ばくちを打つ) *gamble* / bakuchi de suru (ばくちでする) *gamble away* (*money*).

ba⌐kudai ばくだい (莫大) *a.n.*
(〜 na) huge; enormous; vast:
bakudai *na zaisañ* (莫大な財産) an *enormous* fortune / bakudai *na kiñgaku* (莫大な金額) a *huge* sum of money / *Damu no keñsetsu ni wa* bakudai *na hiyoo ga kakaru.* (ダムの建設には莫大な費用がかかる) It costs *a great deal* to construct a dam.

ba⌐kudañ ばくだん (爆弾) *n.* bomb:
bakudañ *o otosu* [*tooka suru*] (爆弾を落とす[投下する]) drop a *bomb* / *tatemono ni* bakudañ *o shikakeru* (建物に爆弾を仕掛ける) place a *bomb* in a building / *Eki de* bakudañ *ga haretsu shita.* (駅で爆弾が破裂した) A *bomb* burst in the station.

ba⌐kufu ばくふ (幕府) *n.* shogunate:
Kamakura bakufu (鎌倉幕府) the Kamakura *Shogunate* (1192–1333).

ba⌐kugeki ばくげき (爆撃) *n.* bombing:
bakugeki o ukeru (爆撃を受ける) *be bombed* / bakugeki-*ki* (爆撃機) a *bomber* (*airplane*).

bakugeki suru (〜する) *vt.* bomb:
machi o bakugeki suru (町を爆撃する) *bomb* a town.

ba⌐kuhatsu ばくはつ (爆発) *n.* explosion; eruption; burst:
Kinoo koko de gasu-bakuhatsu ga atta. (きのうここでガス爆発があった) A gas *explosion* occurred here yesterday. / *Machi zeñtai ga kazañ no* bakuhatsu *de higai o uketa.* (町全体が火山の爆発で被害を受けた) The whole town was damaged by the *eruption* of the volcano.

bakuhatsu suru (〜する) *vi.* explode; blow up; burst: *Bakudañ ga* bakuhatsu *shite, oozee no hito ga shiñda.* (爆弾が爆発して、大勢の人が死んだ) A bomb *exploded* and killed a large number of people. / *Sono koojoo de nani-ka ga* bakuhatsu *shita.* (その工場で何かが爆発した) Something *blew up* in the factory.

ba⌐kuro ばくろ (暴露) *n.* exposure; disclosure.

bakuro suru (〜する) *vt.* expose; disclose: *himitsu o* bakuro suru (秘密を暴露する) *disclose* a secret / *oshoku o* bakuro suru (汚職を暴露する) *expose* corruption / *Kare wa shootai o* bakuro shita. (彼は正体を暴露した) He *showed* his true self.

ba⌐kuzeñ ばくぜん (漠然) *adv.*
(〜 to) vaguely; aimlessly:
Kodomo no koro no koto wa bakuzeñ *to oboete imasu.* (子どものころのことは漠然と覚えています) I remember my childhood *vaguely*. / *Bakuzeñ to shigoto o shite ite mo nooritsu wa agaranai.* (漠然と仕事をしていても能率はあがらない) As long as you work *aimlessly*, efficiency will never improve.

bakuzeñ to suru (〜とする) be vague; be obscure: *Soñna* bakuzeñ to shita *keekaku wa ukeireraremaseñ.* (そんな漠然とした計画は受け入れられません) We cannot adopt such a *vague* plan. / *Kare no ha-*

tsugeñ no imi wa bakuzeñ to shite iru. (彼の発言の意味は漠然としている) The meaning of what he says *is obscure*.

ba¹meñ ばめん (場面) *n.* scene; sight; spectacle:
Bameñ *wa kawatte, Kyooto ni natta.* (場面は変わって，京都になった) The *scene* changed to one in Kyoto. / *Watashi wa sono* bameñ *ni kañdoo shita.* (私はその場面に感動した) I was moved by the *sight*.

ba⌐ñ¹ ばん (晩) *n.* evening; night:
Asu no bañ *wa uchi ni imasu.* (あすの晩は家にいます) I'll be at home tomorrow *evening*. / *Kare to wa nichiyoo no* bañ *ni aimashita.* (彼とは日曜の晩に会いました) I met him on Sunday *night* [*evening*]. 《⇨ hiru (table)》

koñbañ	tonight
sakubañ	last night
myoobañ	tomorrow night
maibañ	every night

ba⌐ñ² ばん (番) *n.* one's turn; order:
jibuñ no bañ *o matsu* (自分の番を待つ) wait for one's *turn* / *Koñdo wa kimi ga utau* bañ *da.* (今度は君が歌う番だ) Now it's your *turn* to sing.

ba⌐ñ³ ばん (番) *n.* watch; guard:
Watashi wa sono nimotsu no bañ *o kare ni tanoñda.* (私はその荷物の番を彼に頼んだ) I asked him to keep *watch* over the baggage. / *Sono keekañ wa hitobañ-juu* bañ *o shita.* (その警官は一晩中番をした) The policeman stood *guard* all night. / *Watashi ga mise no* bañ *o shimasu.* (私が店の番をします) I'll *tend* the shop.

ba⌐ñ⁴ ばん (盤) *n.* board; disk.

-¹bañ ばん (番) *suf.* **1** order in a series:

Kare wa ni-bañ *ni toochaku shita.* (彼は2番に到着した) He was the *second* to arrive.
2 number:
Nañ-bañ ni o-kake desu ka? (何番におかけですか) What *number* are you phoning? / *Sono ressha wa* sañ-bañ *hoomu ni tsukimasu.* (その列車は3番ホームに着きます) The train arrives at track *3*.

ba⌐ñana バナナ *n.* banana:
banana *hito-fusa* (バナナ一房) a bunch [hand] of *bananas*.

ba⌐ñcha ばんちゃ (番茶) *n.* coarse green tea. 《⇨ o-cha (table)》

ba⌐ñchi ばんち (番地) *n.* house [street] number; address: ★ A section of a '*choome*' comparable to a North American city block.
chizu de bañchi *o sagasu* (地図で番地を探す) look up the *house number* on a map / *Tanaka-sañ no uchi wa nañ-*bañchi *desu ka?* (田中さんの家は何番地ですか) What is Mr. Tanaka's *house number*? 《⇨ juusho》

ba⌐ñdo バンド *n.* **1** strap; band:
tokee no bañdo (時計のバンド) a *watchband*.
2 belt:
kawa no bañdo (皮のバンド) a leather *belt*.
3 musical band:
burasu-bañdo (ブラスバンド) a brass *band*.

ba¹ne バネ *n.* spring:
Kore wa bane *de ugokimasu.* (これはバネで動きます) This works by a *spring*.

ba⌐ñgo¹hañ ばんごはん (晩ご飯) *n.* dinner; supper: ★ More polite than '*bañmeshi*.'
Bañgohañ *wa nañ-ji desu ka?* (晩ご飯は何時ですか) What time is *dinner* served? 《⇨ gohañ; asagohañ; hirugohañ》

ba⌐ñgo¹o ばんごう (番号) *n.* number:

deñwa (*no*) bañgoo (電話(の)番号) a phone *number* / bañgoo-*juñ ni narabu* (番号順に並ぶ) line up in *numerical* order / bañgoo *o tsukeru* (番号をつける) attach a *number* / *Kono shorui ni wa* bañgoo ga tsuite iru. (この書類には番号がついている) These papers *are numbered.* / *Anata no zaseki no* bañgoo *wa nañ-bañ desu ka?* (あなたの座席の番号は何番ですか) What's your seat *number?* ★ When asking the number, say '*nañ-bañ*,' not '*nañ bañgoo*.' 《⇨ -bañ》

ba「ñgumi ばんぐみ (番組) *n.* program:
rajio [*terebi*] (*no*) bañgumi (ラジオ [テレビ](の)番組) a radio [television] *program* / *Sono* bañgumi *wa itsumo mite* [*kiite*] *imasu.* (その番組はいつも見て[聞いて]います) I always watch [listen to] that *program.*

ba「ñji ばんじ (万事) *n.* everything; all:
Bañji *umaku ikimashita.* (万事うまく行きました) *Everything* went well. / Bañji *kyuusu.* (万事休す) It is *all* over with us.

ba「ñkeñ ばんけん (番犬) *n.* watchdog. 《⇨ inu》

ba「ñku¹ruwase ばんくるわせ (番狂わせ) *n.* unexpected result; surprise; upset:
Kare no haiboku wa bañkuruwase *datta.* (彼の敗北は番狂わせだった) His defeat was a *surprise* to us.

-「bañme ばんめ (番目) *suf.* designates the place in a sequence:
Tookyoo-eki wa koko kara nañ-bañme *desu ka?* (東京駅はここから何番目ですか) *How many stops* are there from here to Tokyo Station? / *Watashi no seki wa mae kara* sañ-bañme *desu.* (私の席は前から3番目です) My seat is the *third* from the front. / Go-bañme *no eñsoosha ga ichibañ yokatta.* (5番目の演奏者がいちばん良かった) The

fifth musician's performance was the best.

ba「ñmeshi ばんめし (晩飯) *n.* (*informal*) supper. 《⇨ bañgohañ; yuushoku》

ba「ñneñ ばんねん (晩年) *n.* one's later years:
Kare no bañneñ *wa fukoo datta.* (彼の晩年は不幸だった) His *later years* were unhappy. / *Kare wa* bañneñ *ni kono shoosetsu o kaita.* (彼は晩年にこの小説を書いた) He wrote this novel *late in life.*

ba「ñni¹ñ ばんにん (番人) *n.* watchman; watch; guard.

ba「ñnoo ばんのう (万能) *n.* omnipotence:
bañnoo-*señshu* (万能選手) an *all-around* player / bañnoo-yaku (万能薬) a *cure-all* / *kagaku* bañnoo *no jidai* (科学万能の時代) the age in which science is *all powerful.*

ba「ñsañ ばんさん (晩餐) *n.* (*formal*) dinner; banquet:
Watashi wa kare o bañsañ *ni maneita.* (私は彼を晩餐に招いた) I invited him to *dinner.* / *Saigo no* bansañ (最後の晩餐) The Last Supper. 《⇨ yuushoku》

-bañseñ ばんせん (番線) *suf.* platform; track:
Señdai-yuki no ressha wa go-bañseñ *kara demasu.* (仙台行きの列車は5番線から出ます) The train for Sendai leaves from *track 5.*

ba「ñsoo ばんそう (伴奏) *n.* accompaniment:
piano no bañsoo *de utau* (ピアノの伴奏で歌う) sing to a piano *accompaniment.*

bañsoo (**o**) **suru** (〜(を)する) *vi.* accompany: *Kanojo wa piano de kare no* bañsoo *o shita.* (彼女はピアノで彼の伴奏をした) She *accompanied* him on the piano.

ba「ñsookoo ばんそうこう (絆創膏) *n.* sticking plaster; adhesive tape:

kizuguchi ni bañsookoo *o haru*
(傷口にばんそうこうを貼る) put a *plaster* on a cut.

ba⌐ñza⌐i ばんざい (万歳) *n.* cheers:
bañzai *o sañshoo suru* (万歳を三唱
する) give three *cheers.* ★ The
Japanese customarily shout
'*bañzai*' three times.

ba⌐ñzeñ ばんぜん (万全) *n.* absolute sureness:
Taifuu ni taisuru sonae wa bañzeñ *desu.* (台風に対する備えは万全で
す) We *are well prepared* against
typhoons. / *Ni-do to saigai ga
okoranai yoo ni, seefu wa* bañzeñ
no saku o koojita. (二度と災害が起こ
らないように, 政府は万全の策を講じた)
The government took *all possible*
measures to prevent another disaster.
bañzeñ o kisuru (〜を期する)
make doubly sure: Bañzeñ o
kishite, *hajime kara subete yarinaoshita.* (万全を期して, 初めからすべ
てやり直した) *To make doubly sure*,
I did the whole thing over again.

ba⌐ra ばら (薔薇) *n.* rose:
bara-iro (ばら色) *rose-color* / bara-
iro no *mirai* (ばら色の未来) a *rosy*
future.

ba⌐rabara[1] ばらばら *a.n.* (〜 na/
no, ni) apart; in [to] pieces:
Watashi wa jiteñsha o barabara
ni shita. (私は自転車をばらばらにした)
I took the bicycle *apart.* / *Kaze
de shorui ga* barabara *ni natte shimatta.* (風で書類がばらばらになってしま
った) The papers were *scattered*
by the wind. / *Señsoo de, sono
ikka wa* barabara *ni natta.* (戦争で,
その一家はばらばらになった) The fam-
ily were *broken up* owing to the
war.

ba⌐rabara[2] ばらばら *adv.* (〜 to)
(the sound of large drops of rain
or lots of small rocks pelting
down):
Barabara (*to*) *oto o tatete, yuu-*

dachi ga futte kita. (ばらばら(と)音をた
てて, 夕立が降ってきた) The evening
rain came *pelting down.* / *Hako o
hikkurikaeshitara, naka no mikañ
ga* barabara (*to*) *korogari deta.* (箱
をひっくり返したら, 中のみかんがばらばら
(と)転がり出た) I tipped the box
over, and the mandarin oranges
inside came *rolling out.*

ba⌐rama⌐k·u ばらまく (ばら蒔く) *vt.*
(-mak·i-; -mak·a-; -ma·i-te [C])
1 scatter; spread:
Koroñde, tsutsumi no nakami o
baramaite shimatta. (転んで, 包みの
中身をばらまいてしまった) I fell and
scattered the contents of the
package. / *Uwasa o* baramaita *no
wa kanojo desu.* (うわさをばらまいたの
は彼女です) It is she who *spread*
the rumor.
2 hand out indiscriminately;
throw around:
meeshi o baramaku (名刺をばらまく)
hand out name cards indiscriminately / *Kare wa señkyo ni katsu
tame ni kane o* baramaita. (彼は選
挙に勝つために金をばらまいた) He
passed a lot of money *around* to
win the election.

ba⌐rañsu バランス *n.* balance:
barañsu *o toru* [*tamotsu*] (バランスを
とる[保つ]) keep one's *balance* /
barañsu *o ushinau* (バランスを失う)
lose one's *balance* / barañsu no
toreta *shokuji* (バランスのとれた食事)
a *well-balanced* diet.

ba⌐ree バレエ *n.* ballet:
baree *o odoru* (バレエを踊る) dance
a *ballet.*

ba⌐ree-bo⌐oru バレーボール *n.*
volleyball: ★ Often abbreviated
to simply '*baree.*'
baree *o suru* (バレーをする) play *volleyball.*

ba⌐sho ばしょ (場所) *n.* **1** place;
spot; location:
Sono basho *o chizu de mitsuketa.*
(その場所を地図で見つけた) I found

the *place* on the map. / *Kono basho ni ie o tateru tsumori desu.* (この場所に家を建てるつもりです) I am planning to build my house on this *spot*. / *Watashi-tachi wa kyañpu ni tekitoo na basho o sagashita.* (私たちはキャンプに適当な場所を探した) We looked for a suitable *site* for the camp. 《⇨ ba》
2 space; room: *Piano wa basho o toru.* (ピアノは場所をとる) The piano takes up a lot of *space*. / *Basho o akete kudasai.* (場所をあけてください) Please make *room* for me.
3 (of sumo wrestling) tournament: *haru*-basho (春場所) the spring *sumo tournament*.

ba⌐ssui ばっすい (抜粋) *n.* extract; excerpt: *hoñ kara no* bassui (本からの抜粋) an *extract* from a book.
bassui suru (〜する) *vt.* extract; excerpt: *hoñ kara issettsu o* bassui suru (本から一節を抜粋する) *extract* a passage from a book.

ba⌐ss・uru ばっする (罰する) *vt.* (bassh・i-; bassh・i-; bassh・i-te ①) punish: *Warui koto o sureba* basserare-*masu.* (悪いことをすれば罰せられます) If you do something bad, you will *be punished*. 《⇨ batsu》

ba⌐su バス *n.* bus; coach: basu *ni noru* (バスに乗る) get on [take] a *bus* / basu *o* [*kara*] *oriru* (バスを[から]降りる) get off a *bus* / *Kono* basu *wa Shibuya e ikimasu ka?* (このバスは渋谷へ行きますか) Does this *bus* go to Shibuya? / *Ikebukuro-yuki no* basu *wa doko desu ka?* (池袋行きのバスはどこですか) Where can I take the *bus* for Ikebukuro?

ba⌐suketto-bo⌐oru バスケットボール *n.* basketball: ★ Often abbreviated to simply '*basuketto*.'

basuketto-booru *o suru* (バスケットボールをする) play *basketball*.

ba⌐sutee バスてい (バス停) *n.* bus stop. 《⇨ teeryuujo》

AN OLD-STYLE (left) AND NEW-STYLE (right) BASUTEE

ba⌐taa バター *n.* butter: *pañ ni* bataa *o nuru* [*tsukeru*] (パンにバターを塗る[つける]) spread *butter* on bread.

ba⌐tabata ばたばた *adv.* (〜 to)
1 (the sound of flapping, rattling or clattering): *Kaateñ ga kaze de* batabata (*to*) *oto o tatete iru.* (カーテンが風でばたばた(と)音をたてている) The curtains are *flapping* in the wind. / *Kodomo-tachi ga kaidañ o* batabata (*to*) *kakeorite kita.* (子どもたちが階段をばたばた(と)かけ降りて来た) The children came *clattering* down the stairs.
2 in a flurry: *Ano hito wa shikeñ no zeñjitsu ni naru to itsu-mo* batabata (*to*) *beñkyoo o hajimeru.* (あの人は試験の前日になるといつもばたばた(と)勉強を始める) He always begins to study *in a fluster* the day before the exams.
3 one after another: *Eñdaka no tame ni chiisa-na kaisha ga* batabata (*to*) *toosañ shita.* (円高のために小さな会社がばたばた(と)倒産した) Small firms went bank-

rupt *one after another* on account of the strong yen. / *Heeshi-tachi wa ue to samusa de* batabata *(to) taoreta.* (兵士たちは飢えと寒さでばたばた(と)倒れた) The soldiers fell over *one after another* from starvation and cold.

ba⌐tsu ばつ (罰) *n.* punishment; penalty:
Batsu *to shite heya no sooji o sase-rareta.* (罰として部屋の掃除をさせられた) I was made to clean the room as a *punishment.* (⇨ bassuru)

ba⌐tsuguñ ばつぐん (抜群) *a.n.* (~ no, ni) outstanding; unrivaled:
batsuguñ *no seeseki* (抜群の成績) an *outstanding* achievement / *Kare no Nihoñgo wa* batsuguñ *da.* (彼の日本語は抜群だ) His Japanese is *superb.* / *Kanojo wa uta ga* ba-tsuguñ *ni umai.* (彼女は歌が抜群にうまい) She *surpasses* others in singing.

ba⌐tta⌐ri ばったり *adv.* (~ to)
1 with a thud:
Kanojo wa battari *(to) taoreta.* (彼女はばったり(と)倒れた) She fell down *with a thud.*
2 unexpectedly; by chance:
Sakki ekimae de Tanaka-sañ to battari *aimashita.* (さっき駅前で田中さんとばったり会いました) I met Ms. Tanaka *by chance* near the station a little while ago.
3 suddenly:
Kare kara no tegami ga battari *konaku natta.* (彼からの手紙がばったり来なくなった) His letters *suddenly* stopped coming.

ba⌐tterii バッテリー *n.* car battery:
Batterii *ga agatte-shimatta.* (バッテリーが上がってしまった) The *battery* is dead. (⇨ deñchi)

ba⌐tto バット *n.* (baseball) bat.

-be べ (辺) *suf.* around; nearby; neighborhood:

kishi-be (岸辺) a *shore* / *mado*-be (窓辺) *by* the window / *umi*-be (海辺) *on* the sea.

be⌐ddo ベッド *n.* bed:
beddo *ni neru* (ベッドに寝る) lie down on the *bed.*

Be⌐ekoku べいこく (米国) *n.* America; the United States (of America).

be⌐esu ベース *n.* **1** base; basis:
chiñgiñ-beesu (賃金ベース) the wage *base.*
2 (of baseball) base.

be⌐esu-ap⌐pu ベースアップ *n.* pay raise [hike]:
Kore de wa beesu-appu *wa jisshi-tsu-teki ni zero da.* (これではベースアップは実質的にゼロだ) This means we have actually had no *raise.*

be⌐ki べき *n.* [follows the dictionary form of a verb, except that '*suru beki*' is usually '*su beki*.']
1 should; ought to:
Miñna ga kono teñ o kañgaeru beki *desu.* (みんながこの点を考えるべきです) Everyone *should* consider this point. / *Nani-ka nayami ga aru toki wa señsee ni soodañ su* beki *da.* (何か悩みがあるときは先生に相談すべきだ) When something is troubling you, you *ought to* consult the teacher. / *Soñna baka na koto wa su* beki *ja nakatta.* (そんなばかなことはすべきじゃなかった) I *should* not have done such a stupid thing. / *Aratameru* beki *teñ ga areba shiteki shite kudasai.* (改めるべき点があれば指摘してください) If there are any points I *should* improve, please point them out.
2 worthy of; deserve to be:
odoroku beki *dekigoto* (驚くべき出来事) a *remarkable* [*surprising*] incident / *kanashimu* beki *koto* (悲しむべきこと) a matter of *regret* / *Sore wa yorokobu* beki *koto desu.* (それは喜ぶべきことです) That is some-

thing to *rejoice about.* / *Kare wa soñkee su beki jiñbutsu desu.* (彼は尊敬すべき人物です) He is a person *worthy of respect.*

be⌐kkyo べっきょ (別居) *n.* living apart; separation:
bekkyo suru (〜する) *vi.* live apart; separate: *Kare-ra wa bekkyo shite iru.* (彼らは別居している) They *are separated.*

be⌐ñ べん (便) *n.* **1** convenience; facilities; service: *Kare no uchi wa kootsuu no beñ ga yoi.* (彼の家は交通の便が良い) His house *has easy access.* / *Hoteru made basu no beñ ga arimasu.* (ホテルまでバスの便があります) There is a bus *service* to the hotel.
2 feces; stool.

-beñ べん (遍) *suf.* (the number of) times. 《⇨ -heñ》

be⌐ñchi ベンチ *n.* bench: *beñchi ni suwaru* (ベンチに座る) sit on a *bench.*

be⌐ñgo べんご (弁護) *n.* (legal) defense; justification: *hito no beñgo o hikiukeru* (人の弁護を引き受ける) undertake a person's legal *defense.*
beñgo (o) suru (〜(を)する) *vt.* defend; justify: *Dare mo kare o beñgo shinakatta.* (だれも彼を弁護しなかった) *Nobody defended* him. / *Watashi wa kare no kooi o beñgo shita.* (私は彼の行為を弁護した) I *justified* his conduct.

be⌐ñgoniñ べんごにん (弁護人) *n.* defense lawyer; counsel.

be⌐ñgo⌐shi べんごし (弁護士) *n.* lawyer; attorney.

be⌐ñjo べんじょ (便所) *n.* toilet; lavatory.

(USAGE)
Avoid using this word in polite conversation. Use '*tearai*' (*literally* 'hand-washing place') or '*o-tearai*' (*polite*) instead. '*Toire*,' which is derived from English 'toilet,' is commonly used in daily conversation.

be⌐ñkai べんかい (弁解) *n.* excuse; explanation: *Kare no kooi wa beñkai no yochi ga nai.* (彼の行為は弁解の余地がない) There's no *excuse* for his conduct.
beñkai suru (〜する) *vt.* make excuses; explain: *Kare wa chikoku shita koto o iroiro beñkai shita.* (彼は遅刻したことをいろいろ弁解した) He *made* many *excuses* for being late.

be⌐ñkyoo べんきょう (勉強) *n.* **1** study: *Nihoñgo no beñkyoo* (日本語の勉強) the *study* of Japanese / *beñkyoo o namakeru* (勉強を怠ける) neglect one's *studies.*
2 experience; lesson: *Shippai ga ii beñkyoo ni natta.* (失敗がいい勉強になった) I *learned* much from my failure. / *Kaigairyokoo wa kichoo na beñkyoo ni narimashita.* (海外旅行は貴重な勉強になりました) The overseas trip taught me valuable *lessons.* 《⇨ taikeñ》
beñkyoo (o) suru (〜(を)する) *vi., vt.* **1** study; work: *Nihoñgo o beñkyoo suru* (日本語を勉強する) *study* Japanese / *Kare wa yoku beñkyoo suru.* (彼はよく勉強する) He *works* very hard.
2 make a discount; reduce the price: *Geñkiñ nara beñkyoo shimasu.* (現金なら勉強します) If you pay in cash, I'll *give you a discount.* / *Moo sukoshi beñkyoo shite kudasai.* (もう少し勉強してください) Will you please *take a little more off the price?* 《⇨ makeru》

be⌐ñpi べんぴ (便秘) *n.* constipation. *beñpi de nayamu* (便秘で悩む) suffer from *constipation*.

beñpi suru (〜する) *vi.* be constipated: *Kanojo wa* beñpi *shite iru.* (彼女は便秘している) She *is constipated*.

beñri べんり (便利) *a.n.* (〜 na, ni) convenient; useful; handy: *Kore wa* beñri *na doogu da.* (これは便利な道具だ) This is a *useful* tool. / *Kare no uchi wa eki ni chikakute* beñri *da.* (彼の家は駅に近くて便利だ) His house is *conveniently* near the station. / *Kono daidokoro wa* beñri *ni dekite iru.* (この台所は便利にできている) This kitchen is *efficiently* laid out. (↔ fubeñ)

beñshoo べんしょう (弁償) *n.* compensation; indemnification: *Sono soñgai ni taisuru* beñshoo *to shite ichimañ-eñ haratta.* (その損害に対する弁償として1万円払った) I paid 10,000 yen in *compensation* for the damage.
beñshoo (o) suru (〜(を)する) *vt.* compensate; indemnify; pay: *Kakatta hiyoo wa* beñshoo *shimasu.* (かかった費用は弁償します) I *will indemnify* you for expenses. / *Kowashita kabiñ no* beñshoo *o shita.* (壊した花瓶の弁償をした) I *paid* for the vase I broke.

beñtoo べんとう (弁当) *n.* packed [box] lunch; lunch box: beñtoo *o tsukuru [yooi suru]* (弁当を作る[用意する]) prepare a *lunch box* / beñtoo *o motte iku* (弁当を持って行く) take a *lunch box* with one.

berabera べらべら *adv.* (〜 to) glibly: *kudaranai koto o* berabera *(to) shaberu* (くだらないことをべらべら(と)しゃべる) *gab on* about worthless things / *himitsu o* berabera *(to) hanasu* (秘密をべらべら(と)話す) *babble out* a secret. (⇨ perapera)

berañda ベランダ *n.* veranda; porch.

beru ベル *n.* bell; doorbell: beru *o narasu [osu]* (ベルを鳴らす[押す]) ring [press] a *bell* / *Beru ga natte iru.* (ベルが鳴っている) I hear the *doorbell* ringing.

beruto ベルト *n.* belt: *Zuboñ no* beruto *o kitsuku shimeta.* (ズボンのベルトをきつく締めた) I tightened my trouser-*belt*. / *Shiito-*beruto *o shime nasai.* (シートベルトを締めなさい) Fasten your safety *belt*.

bessoo べっそう (別荘) *n.* country [summer] house; villa; cottage.

besuto ベスト *n.* best: besuto *o tsukusu* (ベストをつくす) do one's *best* / besuto*-teñ* (ベストテン) the *best* ten.

besuto-seraa ベストセラー *n.* best seller.

beterañ ベテラン *n.* expert; experienced person:

───(USAGE)───
Originally from English 'veteran,' but never used in the sense of a former member of the armed forces.
────────

beterañ *no kañgofu* (ベテランの看護婦) an *experienced* nurse / *Kare wa beñgoshi no* beterañ *desu.* (彼は弁護士のベテランです) He is an *expert* lawyer.

betsu[1] べつ (別) *n.* distinction; exception: *Dañjo no* betsu *naku oobo dekimasu.* (男女の別なく応募できます) Anyone can apply without *distinction* of sex.
betsu to shite (〜として) except: *Ame no hi wa* betsu to shite, *mainichi sañpo ni ikimasu.* (雨の日は別として, 毎日散歩に行きます) I go out for a walk every day *except* when it is rainy. / *Ookisa wa* betsu to shite, *iro ga ki ni iranakatta.* (大きさは別として, 色が気に入ら

なかった) *Regardless of* the size, I didn't like the color.

betsu ni shite (〜にして) without: *Zeekiñ o* betsu ni shite, *hasseñ-eñ ni narimasu.* (税金を別にして、8千円になります) It comes to 8,000 yen, *excluding* tax.

be⌈tsu² べつ (別) *a.n.* (〜 na/no, ni) another; different: *Shitte iru no to oshieru no to wa* betsu *desu.* (知っているのと教えるのは別です) Knowledge is one thing, and teaching is *another.* / Betsu *no kabañ o misete kudasai.* (別のかばんを見せてください) Please show me *another* bag. / *Kore wa* betsu *no kikai ni shimashoo.* (これは別の機会にしましょう) Let's take up this matter on *another* occasion. / *Watashi wa* betsu *no isha ni mite moratta.* (私は別の医者にみてもらった) I consulted a *different* doctor. / *Kono shorui wa* betsu *ni shite oite kudasai.* (この書類は別にしておいてください) Please keep these papers in a *different* place.

-betsu べつ (別) *suf.* classified by...; according to...: *shokugyoo*-betsu *deñwachoo* (職業別電話帳) a *classified* telephone directory / *see*-betsu *ni wakeru* (性別に分ける) classify *by* sex / *koomoku*-betsu *ni hyoo o tsukuru* (項目別に表を作る) make a table of items *under* different headings.

be⌈tsu ni べつに (別に) *adv.* (with a negative) particularly; in particular: *Ima no tokoro* betsu ni *suru koto wa arimaseñ.* (今のところ別にすることはありません) I have nothing *particular* to do at the moment. / *Kono yama wa* betsu ni *kiree na yama da to wa omoimaseñ.* (この山は別にきれいな山だとは思いません) I don't think that this mountain is a *particularly* beautiful one.

be⌈tsubetsu べつべつ (別々) *a.n.* (〜 na/no, ni) different(ly); separate(ly); respective(ly): *Kare-ra wa* betsubetsu *no yarikata de tameshite mita.* (彼らは別々のやり方で試してみた) They tried in *different* ways. / *Futari wa* betsubetsu *no michi o itta.* (二人は別々の道を行った) The two of them went their *respective* ways. / Betsubetsu *ni ikimashoo.* (別々に行きましょう) Let's go *separately.* / *Kono moñdai to sore wa* betsubetsu *ni kañgaeta hoo ga ii.* (この問題とそれは別々に考えたほうがいい) This matter and that should be considered *separately.*

be⌈tsujoo べつじょう (別状) *n.* (with a negative) something wrong; something unusual: *Eñjiñ ni* betsujoo wa nakatta. (エンジンに別状はなかった) *There was nothing wrong* with the engine. / *Kare wa atama ni kega o shita ga, inochi ni wa* betsujoo wa nakatta. (彼は頭にけがをしたが、命には別状なかった) He got hurt on the head, but his life *was not in danger.* / *Kazoku ni* betsujoo wa arimaseñ. (家族に別状はありません) My family *are all well.*

-bi び (日) *suf.* day: *kineñ*-bi (記念日) a memorial *day* / kayoo-bi (火曜日) *Tuesday.* (⇨ yoobi)

bi⌉deo ビデオ *n.* video (tape); videocassette recorder: *kekkoñ-shiki [bañgumi] o* bideo *ni toru [rokuga suru]* (結婚式[番組]をビデオに撮る[録画する]) record a wedding [program] on *videotape.*

bi⌈futeki ビフテキ *n.* beefsteak. (⇨ suteekī)

bii-esu *n.* = BS.

bi⌉iru ビール *n.* beer: biiru *ip-poñ* (ビール1本) a bottle of *beer* / biiru *ip-pai* (ビール1杯) a glass of *beer* / biiru-*biñ* (ビールびん) a *beer* bottle.

bi｢jiñ びじん（美人）*n.* good-looking [beautiful] woman; beauty.

bi｢jutsu びじゅつ（美術）*n.* art; fine arts:
Nihoñ no geñdai-bijutsu（日本の現代美術）Japanese modern art / *bijutsu-hiñ*（美術品）a work of *art*.

bi｢jutsu｢kañ びじゅつかん（美術館）*n.* art museum.

-biki びき（匹）*suf.* counter for small animals, fish and insects. 《⇨ -hiki》

bi｢kk｢uri gyo｢oteñ びっくりぎょうてん（びっくり仰天）*n.* astonishment.
bikkuri gyooteñ suru（～する）*vi.* be astounded:
Yosoo mo shinai kekka ni bikkuri gyooteñ shita.（予想もしない結果にびっくり仰天した）I *was astounded* by the unexpected result.

bi｢kku｢ri s･uru びっくりする *vi.* (sh･i-; sh･i-; shi-te ①) be surprised; be astonished; be amazed:
Sono shirase ni bikkuri shita.（その知らせにびっくりした）I *was surprised* at the news. / *Kare wa* bikkuri shite, *nigete itta.*（彼はびっくりして、逃げて行った）He ran away *in surprise.*

bi｢kubiku s･uru びくびくする *vi.* (sh･i-; sh･i-; shi-te ①) be timid [nervous; afraid]:
Nani o soñna ni bikubiku shite iru ñ desu ka?（何をそんなにびくびくしているんですか）What is it that you *are* so *nervous* about? / *Sono ko wa* bikubiku shi-nagara *uma ni chikazuita.*（その子はびくびくしながら馬に近づいた）The child *fearfully* approached the horse. / *Machigai o* bikubiku shite ite *wa Nihoñgo wa umaku narimaseñ.*（間違いをびくびくしていては日本語はうまくなりません）Your Japanese won't improve if you *are afraid* of mistakes. 《⇨ osoreru》

bi｢myoo びみょう（微妙）*a.n.* (～ na, ni) delicate; subtle; nice; fine:
bimyoo *na moñdai*（微妙な問題）a *delicate* matter / *iro no* bimyoo na *chigai*（色の微妙な違い）a *subtle* difference in color / *Ryoosha no ikeñ no aida ni wa* bimyoo na *chigai ga aru.*（両者の意見の間には微妙な違いがある）There are *subtle* differences in the opinions held by the two parties. / *Kare no tachiba ga* bimyoo *ni natte kita.*（彼の立場が微妙になってきた）His position has become very *delicate.*

bi｢ñ¹ びん（瓶）*n.* bottle; jar:
juusu o biñ *ni ireru*（ジュースをびんに入れる）put juice into a *bottle* / *jamu o* biñ *ni tsumeru*（ジャムをびんに詰める）put jam into a *jar* / *biñ-biiru*（びんビール）*bottled* beer / *aki-biñ*（空きびん）/ an empty *bottle.*

bi｢ñ² びん（便）*n.* flight; service:
Sono biñ *wa shoogo ni demasu.*（その便は正午に出ます）The *flight* leaves at noon. / *Kare wa nana-hyaku roku-biñ de tsukimasu.*（彼は706便で着きます）He arrives on *flight* 706.

bi｢ñboo びんぼう（貧乏）*n.* poverty; destitution:
Kanojo no uchi wa chichi-oya no shigo, biñboo *ni natta.*（彼女の家は父親の死後、貧乏になった）Her family fell into *poverty* after her father's death.
biñboo suru（～する）*vi.* be poor; be badly off: *Tooji wa zuibuñ* biñboo shita *mono da.*（当時はずいぶん貧乏したものだ）In those days, I *was* very *badly off.*
— *a.n.* (～ na, ni) poor; needy: *Kare wa* biñboo na *ie ni umareta.*（彼は貧乏な家に生まれた）He was born into a *poor* family. / *Sono koro kare wa hijoo ni* biñboo *datta.*（そのころ彼は非常に貧乏だった）He was very *poor* in those days.

bi｢ñbooniñ びんぼうにん（貧乏人）*n.*

poor person. 《↔ kanemochi》

bi⌐ni⌐iru ビニール *n.* plastic; vinyl.

biniiru (soft plastic)	plastic
purasuchikku (molded hard plastic)	

《⇨ purasuchikku》

bi⌐ñjoo びんじょう(便乗) *n.* free ride in a car.

biñjoo suru (〜する) *vi.* **1** get a lift: *Kare no kuruma ni* biñjoo *sasete moratta.* (彼の車に便乗させてもらった) I *got a lift* in his car. **2** take advantage of: *Kare-ra wa uñchiñ no neage ni* biñjoo *shite, nedañ o ageta.* (彼らは運賃の値上げに便乗して、値段を上げた) They *took advantage of* the rise in transport costs to increase their prices.

bi⌐ñkañ びんかん(敏感) *a.n.* (〜 na, ni) sensitive; susceptible: biñkañ *na mimi* (敏感な耳) a *sensitive* ear / *Wakamono wa ryuukoo ni* biñkañ *da.* (若者は流行に敏感だ) Young people are *susceptible* to changes in fashion. / *Doobutsu wa kikeñ o* biñkañ *ni kañji-toru.* (動物は危険を敏感に感じとる) Animals are *quick* in sensing danger. 《↔ doñkañ》

bi⌐ñseñ びんせん(便箋) *n.* letter paper; letterhead; writing pad.

bi⌐ñshoo びんしょう(敏捷) *a.n.* (〜 na, ni) agile; nimble; quick; prompt: biñshoo *na doobutsu* (敏しょうな動物) an *agile* animal / *Sono shoo-neñ wa hijoo ni* biñshoo *datta.* (その少年は非常に敏しょうだった) The boy was very *nimble.* / *Kanojo wa awatezu,* biñshoo *ni koodoo shita.* (彼女はあわてず、敏しょうに行動した) She acted *promptly*, without getting flustered.

bi⌐ñwañ びんわん(敏腕) *n.* (great) ability: biñwañ *o furuu* (敏腕をふるう) show one's *ability.* — *a.n.* (〜 na) able: ★ Highly competent in dealing with matters. biñwañ *na keeji* (敏腕な刑事) a *shrewd* detective.

bi⌐ñzume びんづめ(瓶詰) *n.* bottling; bottled food [beverage]: *hachimitsu no* biñzume (蜂蜜のびんづめ) honey *in a jar* / *jamu o* biñzume *ni suru* (ジャムをびんづめにする) *bottle* jam.

bi⌐ribiri びりびり *adv.* (〜 to) (the sound of trembling or ripping): *Jishiñ de garasu ga* biribiri (to) *furueta.* (地震でガラスがびりびり(と)震えた) The windowpanes *trembled* in the earthquake. / *Kare wa sono tegami o* biribiri (to) *yabuita.* (彼はその手紙をびりびり(と)やぶいた) He *tore* the letter into pieces. / *Burausu ga kugi ni hikkakatte* biribiri (to) *yabureta.* (ブラウスがくぎに引っかかってびりびり(と)破れた) My blouse got caught on a nail and *ripped*.

bi⌐roodo ビロード *n.* velvet.

bi⌐ru ビル *n.* building. ★ Shortened form of '*birudiñgu*' (building).

bi⌐rudiñgu ビルディング *n.* building. ★ Refers mainly to western-style structures three stories and over.

Bi⌐ruma ビルマ *n.* Burma. ★ Previous name of Myanmar.

Bi⌐rumago ビルマご(ビルマ語) *n.* the language of the Burmese.

Bi⌐ruma⌐jiñ ビルマじん(ビルマ人) *n.* native or inhabitant of Burma.

bi⌐shobisho びしょびしょ *a.n.* (〜 na/no, ni) wet through; soaked: *Mizu ga morete, daidokoro no yuka ga* bishobisho *ni natta.* (水が

漏れて, 台所の床がびしょびしょになった) There was a leakage of water and the kitchen floor got *thoroughly wet*. / *Niwaka-ame ni atte*, bisho-bisho *ni nurete shimatta*. (にわか雨にあって, びしょびしょに濡れてしまった) I was caught in a sudden shower and got *soaked through*.

bi⌐shoo びしょう (微笑) *n*. smile: *Oñna-no-ko wa* bishoo *o ukabete, te o futta*. (女の子は微笑を浮かべて, 手を振った) The girl waved to me with a *smile* on her face.
  bishoo suru (〜する) *vi*. make a smile: *Kanojo wa watashi o mite* bishoo shita. (彼女は私を見て微笑した) She *smiled* at me. (⇨ hoho-emu)

bi⌐suke⌐tto ビスケット *n*. cracker; cookie. ★ Comes from 'biscuit.'

bi⌐ta⌐miñ ビタミン *n*. vitamin: bitamiñ-*zai o nomu* (ビタミン剤を飲む) take a *vitamin* pill.

bi⌐yoo びよう (美容) *n*. beauty culture: *Earobikusu wa* biyoo *ni yoi*. (エアロビクスは美容に良い) Aerobics is good for *keeping your figure*.

bi⌐yo⌐oiñ びよういん (美容院) *n*. beauty shop [salon].

bi⌐za ビザ *n*. visa: *Biza wa hoomoñ-saki no kuni no taishikañ de moraimasu*. (ビザは訪問先の国の大使館でもらいます) You get a *visa* at the embassy of the country you are going to.

bo⌐chi ぼち (墓地) *n*. graveyard; cemetery.

bo⌐iñ ぼいん (母音) *n*. vowel: *tañ[choo]*-boiñ (短[長]母音) a short [long] *vowel*. (⇨ appendixes)

bo⌐ke·ru ぼける (惚ける) *vi*. (boke-te Ⓥ) grow senile: *Kare mo dañdañ* bokete kita. (彼もだんだんぼけてきた) He too *became* increasingly *affected by senility*.

bo⌐ki ぼき (簿記) *n*. bookkeeping: boki *o tsukeru* (簿記をつける) keep *books*.

bo⌐kiñ ぼきん (募金) *n*. fund-raising; collection of contributions: bokiñ *o aogu* (募金を仰ぐ) solicit *contributions* / bokiñ-*uñdoo* (募金運動) a *fund-raising* campaign.
  bokiñ suru (〜する) *vi*. raise funds; collect money: *kaikañ keñsetsu no tame ni* bokiñ *suru* (会館建設のために募金する) *collect money* for building a hall.

bo⌐koku ぼこく (母国) *n*. one's mother country; one's homeland.

bo⌐kokugo ぼこくご (母国語) *n*. one's mother tongue.

bo⌐koo ぼこう (母校) *n*. one's alma mater: *Koko ga watashi no* bokoo *desu*. (ここが私の母校です) This is *the school I attended*.

bo⌐ku ぼく (僕) *n*. I: ★ 'boku no' = my, 'boku ni/o' = me.

> ⸨ USAGE ⸩
> Plural forms are '*boku-tachi*' or '*boku-ra*' (*humble*). Used usually by boys and young men. Also used by adult men on informal occasions. It is better to use '*watashi*' or '*watakushi*' on formal occasions.

Boku wa tabako o suimaseñ. (ぼくはたばこを吸いません) *I* don't smoke. / *Kore wa* boku *no mono da*. (これはぼくのものだ) This is *mine*. (⇨ kimi[1]; kare; kanojo)

bo⌐kuchiku ぼくちく (牧畜) *n*. stock farming; cattle breeding.

bo⌐kujoo ぼくじょう (牧場) *n*. stock farm; pasture; ranch: bokujoo *o kee-ee suru* (牧場を経営する) run a *stock farm*.

bo⌐kushi ぼくし (牧師) *n*. clergyman; minister. (⇨ shiñpu)

bo⌐ñ[1] ぼん (盆) *n*. tray; server: ★ Usually with 'o-.'

Koppu o o-bon ni nosete, hakonda.
(コップをお盆にのせて、運んだ) I carried
the glasses on a *tray.*

bo⌐ñ² ぼん（盆）*n.* Bon Festival.
《⇨ boñ-odori》

USAGE

'*Bon*' is a Buddhist observance
celebrated on July 15 or August 15, depending on the
district. It is believed that an-
cestral spirits return to their
families on this day. Usually
called '*o-bon*' with an honorific
prefix, referring to the Bon
Festival which is held from
August 13–16.

-boñ ぼん（本）*suf.* counter for
long cylindrical objects. 《⇨ -hoñ》

bo⌐ñchi ぼんち（盆地）*n.* basin;
valley:
Kono atari wa boñchi *ni natte
imasu.* (この辺りは盆地になっています)
This area forms a *basin.* / *Koofu*
Boñchi (甲府盆地) the Kofu *Basin.*

bo⌐ñ-o⌐dori ぼんおどり（盆踊り）*n.*
Bon dances.

USAGE

Originally, dances performed
during the Bon Festival to
welcome the ancestors. Now
usually part of the secular cele-
brations held in conjunction
with the Bon Festival. 《⇨ boñ²》

BOÑ-ODORI

bo⌐ñsai ぼんさい（盆栽）*n.* potted
dwarf plant; bonsai:
boñsai *o ijiru* (盆栽をいじる) culture
[raise] *bonsai.*

BOÑSAI

bo⌐ñya⌐ri ぼんやり *adv.* (～ to;
～ suru) **1** absent-mindedly;
vacantly; carelessly:
Kare wa boñyari *(to) sora o mite
ita.* (彼はぼんやり（と）空を見ていた) He
was looking at the sky *absent-
mindedly.* / Boñyari *shite ite, oriru eki o machigaete shimaimashita.* (ぼんやりしていて、降りる駅を間違
えてしまいました) I *carelessly* went
and got off at the wrong station.
2 idly:
Boñyari *(to) tatte inai de tetsudai
nasai.* (ぼんやり（と）立っていないで手伝い
なさい) Don't stand there *idly.*
Give me a hand. / *Kare wa ichinichi-juu uchi de* boñyari *shite ita.*
(彼は一日中家でぼんやりしていた) He
stayed at home and *idled away*
the whole day.
3 (of memory, sight, etc.)
vaguely; unclearly; obscurely:
Kare no koto wa boñyari *(to)
shika oboete imaseñ.* (彼のことはぼん
やり（と）しか覚えていません) I only
vaguely remember him. / *Kiri de
sañchoo kara no keshiki wa* boñyari *(to) shite ita.* (霧で山頂からの景
色はぼんやり（と）していた) The view
from the top of the mountain
was *obscured* due to the mist. /
Terebi no gameñ ga boñyari *(to)*

shite iru. (テレビの画面がぼんやり(と)し
ている) The television picture is
fuzzy.
4 drowsy:
Ne-busoku de atama ga boñyari
(to) shite iru. (寝不足で頭がぼんやり
(と)している) I feel *drowsy* because
of lack of sleep.

bo⌐o ぼう(棒) *n.* stick; pole; rod:
boo *o furimawasu* (棒を振り回す)
brandish a *stick.*
 boo ni furu (〜に振る) *vt.* waste;
ruin: *Kare wa oshoku ni maki-
komare, isshoo o* boo ni futta. (彼
は汚職にまきこまれ、一生を棒に振った)
He was involved in a scandal and
it *ruined* his life.

bo⌐ochoo ぼうちょう(膨張) *n.* expansion; swelling:
Jiñkoo wa boochoo *o tsuzukeru
daroo.* (人口は膨張を続けるだろう)
The population will continue to
grow.
 boochoo suru (〜する) *vi.* expand; swell: *Kuuki wa netsu de*
boochoo suru. (空気は熱で膨張する)
Air *expands* with heat.

bo⌐odoo ぼうどう(暴動) *n.* riot:
boodoo *o okosu* (暴動を起こす)
start a *riot* / boodoo *o chiñatsu
suru* (暴動を鎮圧する) put down a
disturbance.

bo⌐oee ぼうえい(防衛) *n.* defense:
kuni no booee *no tame ni tatakau*
(国の防衛のために戦う) fight in
defense of one's country.
 booee suru (〜する) *vt.* defend:
kokkyoo o shiñryakusha kara
booee suru (国境を侵略者から防衛す
る) *defend* the frontier against
invaders.

Bo⌐oe⌐e-choo ぼうえいちょう(防衛
庁) *n.* Defense Agency:
Booee-choo *chookañ* (防衛庁長官)
the Director General of the
Defense Agency. 《⇨ choo⁴ (table)》

Bo⌐oeeshisetsu⌐-choo ぼうえ
いしせつちょう(防衛施設庁) *n.*

Defense Facilities Administration Agency:
Booeeshisetsu-choo *chookañ* (防衛
施設庁長官) the Director General
of the *Defense Facilities Administration Agency.* 《⇨ choo⁴ (table)》

bo⌐oeki ぼうえき(貿易) *n.* trade;
commerce:
booeki *no jiyuu-ka* (貿易の自由化)
liberalization of *trade* / Booeki
wa neñneñ fuete iru. (貿易は年々ふ
えている) *Trade* is increasing yearly.
 ...to booeki (o) suru (...と〜(を)す
る) *vi.* carry on trade: *Sono kaisha wa iroiro na kuni to* booeki *o
shite iru.* (その会社はいろいろな国と貿
易をしている) The company *trades*
with various countries.

bo⌐oeñkyoo ぼうえんきょう(望遠
鏡) *n.* telescope.

bo⌐ofuu ぼうふう(暴風) *n.* storm;
windstorm:
Boofuu *ga hitobañ-juu fukiareta.*
(暴風が一晩中吹き荒れた) The *storm*
raged all night.

bo⌐ogai ぼうがい(妨害) *n.* disturbance; obstruction; interference:
kootsuu no boogai *ni naru* (交通の
妨害になる) cause an *obstruction* to
traffic.
 boogai suru (〜する) *vt.* disturb;
obstruct; interfere:
añmiñ o boogai suru (安眠を妨害す
る) *disturb* a person's sleep / *hito
no eegyoo o* boogai suru (人の営業
を妨害する) *interfere* with a person's business / *Taoreta ki ga
tsuukoo o* boogai shite iru. (倒れた
木が通行を妨害している) A fallen
tree *obstructed* the traffic.

bo⌐ogyo ぼうぎょ(防御) *n.* defense; safeguard:
Koogeki wa sairyoo no boogyo *de
aru.* (攻撃は最良の防御である) Of-
fense is the best *defense.*
 boogyo suru (〜する) *vt.* defend:
shiro o teki kara boogyo suru (城を
敵から防御する) *defend* a castle

against the enemy.

boˈoi ボーイ *n.* waiter; bellboy; porter.

boˈoi-fureˈñdo ボーイフレンド *n.* boyfriend; male friend. ((⇨ aijiñ; koibito))

boˈoka ぼうか (防火) *n.* fire prevention:
Kono biru wa booka setsubi ga osomatsu da. (このビルは防火設備がお粗末だ) This building is poorly equipped *against fire.* / booka *kuñreñ* (防火訓練) a *fire* drill.

boˈokeñ ぼうけん (冒険) *n.* adventure; venture; risk:
Kare wa bookeñ ga suki da. (彼は冒険が好きだ) He is fond of *adventure.* / *Sono yama ni noboru no wa taiheñ na bookeñ da.* (その山に登るのは大変な冒険だ) It is quite an *adventure* to climb that mountain.
　bookeñ (o) suru (〜(を)する) *vi.* make a venture; run a risk: *Kare wa inochigake no bookeñ o shita.* (彼は命がけの冒険をした) He *risked* his life *in the adventure.*

boˈokoo ぼうこう (暴行) *n.* violence; assault; rape:
Miñna wa kare ni bookoo o kuwaeta. (みんなは彼に暴行を加えた) They did *violence* to him.
　bookoo suru (〜する) *vt.* use violence; make an assault; rape: *josee o bookoo suru* (女性を暴行する) *rape* a woman.

boˈomee ぼうめい (亡命) *n.* defection; asylum:
seeji-teki boomee (政治的亡命) political *asylum.*
　boomee suru (〜する) *vi.* defect; take [seek] asylum: *Kare wa Amerika ni boomee shita.* (彼はアメリカに亡命した) He *sought asylum* in the U.S.A.

boˈonasu ボーナス *n.* bonus.

((CULTURE))
Japanese 'full-time' workers usually receive extra wages, called '*boonasu*' twice a year in June and December. '*Arubaito*' and '*paato*' (part-time) are not eligible for this benefit. '*Boonasu*' may be cut rather easily, while salaries may not. '*Boonasu*' never refers to a gift of money given on a special occasion. ((⇨ shooyo))

boˈoneˈñkai ぼうねんかい (忘年会) *n.* year-end party. ★ Literally means 'a party for forgetting the year.' Usually held in December by people working together or close friends.

boˈoru[1] ボール *n.* ball:
booru o nageru [toru; utsu] (ボールを投げる[捕る; 打つ]) throw [catch; hit] a *ball.*

boˈoru[2] ボール *n.* (baseball) ball:
booru no tama o utsu (ボールの球を打つ) swing at a ball *which failed to pass through the strike zone.* ((↔ sutoraiku))

boˈorubako ボールばこ (ボール箱) *n.* cardboard box; carton.

boˈorugami ボールがみ (ボール紙) *n.* cardboard.

boˈoru-peñ ボールペン *n.* ballpoint pen:
booru-peñ de kaku (ボールペンで書く) write with a *ballpoint pen.*

boˈoryoku ぼうりょく (暴力) *n.* violence; force:
booryoku ni uttaeru (暴力に訴える) resort to *violence* / booryoku *o mochiiru* (暴力を用いる) use *force* / *Otto wa tsuma ni booryoku o furutta.* (夫は妻に暴力をふるった) The husband used *violence* against his wife.

boˈoryokuˈdañ ぼうりょくだん (暴力団) *n.* gang; a gang of racketeers:
booryokudañ-iñ (暴力団員) a *gangster.*

bo⌐osañ ぼうさん (坊さん) *n*. Buddhist priest; bonze.

BOOSAÑ

bo⌐oshi[1] ぼうし (帽子) *n*. hat; cap:
booshi *o kaburu* [*nugu; toru*] (帽子をかぶる[ぬぐ; とる]) put on [take off] a *cap* / *Kanojo wa suteki na* booshi *o kabutte ita*. (彼女はすてきな帽子をかぶっていた) She was wearing a lovely *hat*.

bo⌐oshi[2] ぼうし (防止) *n*. prevention; check:
hañzai no booshi (犯罪の防止) the *prevention* of crime.
booshi suru (～する) *vt*. prevent; check: *jiko o* booshi suru (事故を防止する) *prevent* accidents / *byooki no deñseñ o* booshi suru (病気の伝染を防止する) *check* the spread of a disease.

bo⌐osui ぼうすい (防水) *n*. waterproofing:
kooto ni boosui-*kakoo suru* (コートに防水加工する) make a coat *waterproof* / *Kono tokee wa* boosui *ni natte imasu*. (この時計は防水になっています) This watch is *waterproof*.

bo⌐oto ボート *n*. rowboat:
booto *o kogu* (ボートをこぐ) row a *boat*.

bo⌐ribori ぼりぼり *adv*. (～ to) (the sound of scratching, crunching, etc.):
ka ni sasareta tokoro o boribori (to) *kaku* (蚊に刺された所をぼりぼり(と)かく) *scratch away* at the place a

mosquito has bitten one / *señbee o* boribori (to) *taberu* (せんべいをぼりぼり(と)食べる) *munch* a rice-cracker.

bo⌐roboro[1] ぼろぼろ *a.n*. (～ na/ no, ni) (the state of being worn or torn):
jisho o boroboro *ni naru made tsukau* (辞書をぼろぼろになるまで使う) use a dictionary until it is *worn to tatters* / *Watashi no kutsu wa moo* boroboro *desu*. (私の靴はもうぼろぼろです) My shoes are completely *worn out*. / *Sono otoko wa* boroboro *no kimono o kite ita*. (その男はぼろぼろの着物を着ていた) The man was in *rags*.

bo⌐roboro[2] ぼろぼろ *adv*. (～ to) (the state of grains, drops, etc., falling down):
Furui kabe ga boroboro (to) *kuzure-ochita*. (古い壁がぼろぼろ(と)くずれ落ちた) The old wall *fell apart*.

bo⌐ruto[1] ボルト *n*. volt:
*Kono deñchi wa yaku juuni-*boruto *desu*. (この電池は約 12 ボルトです) This battery gives about twelve *volts*.

bo⌐ruto[2] ボルト *n*. bolt:
boruto *o shimeru* [*yurumeru*] (ボルトをしめる[ゆるめる]) fasten [loosen] a *bolt*.

bo⌐satsu ぼさつ (菩薩) *n*. bodhisattva. ★ A spiritual rank in Buddhism indicating one who has achieved great spirituality but vows not to become a Buddha until all other sentient beings have also attained this rank.

bo⌐shuu ぼしゅう (募集) *n*. recruitment; collection:
Taipisuto no boshuu *ni go-niñ ga oobo shita*. (タイピストの募集に 5 人が応募した) Five women applied for the *position of typist*. / *Sono kaisha de wa ima heñshuuiñ o* boshuu-chuu *desu*. (その会社では今編集員を募集中です) The company *is*

currently *seeking* editors.
boshuu suru (〜する) *vt.* recruit;
collect: *shiñ-kaiiñ o* boshuu suru
(新会員を募集する) *recruit* new
members.

BOSHUU SIGNBOARD

bo「sshuu ぼっしゅう (没収) *n.* confiscation; forfeit:
hoshoo-kiñ no bosshuu (保証金の没
収) security deposit *forfeiture*.
bosshuu suru (〜する) *vt.* confiscate; impound: *Zeekañ wa mitsuyunyuu-hiñ o* bosshuu shita.
(税関は密輸入品を没収した) Customs *confiscated* the smuggled
goods. (⇨ toriageru)

bo「tañ[1] ボタン *n.* button; push
button:
botañ *o kakeru* [*hazusu*] (ボタンをか
ける[はずす]) fasten [undo] a *button*
/ Botañ *ga hitotsu toreta* [*hazurete
iru*]. (ボタンが一つとれた[はずれている])
One *button* came off [is undone].

bo「tañ[2] ぼたん (牡丹) *n.* tree peony; *Paeonia suffruticosa*.

bo「tchañ ぼっちゃん (坊ちゃん) *n.*
1 (*polite*) your son:
Otaku no botchañ *wa o-ikutsu
desu ka?* (お宅の坊ちゃんはおいくつです
か) How old is *your son?*
(⇨ ojoosañ)
2 (*derog.*) naive person:
Kare wa sekeñ shirazu no botchañ *da.* (彼は世間知らずの坊ちゃんだ)
He is an *unsophisticated fellow*
who knows nothing of the world.

bo「ttoo ぼっとう (没頭) *n.* ab

sorption; devotion.
bottoo suru (〜する) *vi.* be absorbed; be devoted:
Kare wa dokusho ni bottoo shite
iru.* (彼は読書に没頭している) He *is
absorbed* in reading. / *Haha-oya
wa ikuji ni* bottoo shite iru. (母親
は育児に没頭している) The mother *is
devoted* to the care of her baby.

bo「ya ぼや *n.* small fire:
Kare no uchi de boya *ga atta.* (彼
の家でぼやがあった) A *small fire*
broke out in his house.

bo「yaboya s·uru ぼやぼやする *vi.*
(sh·i-; sh·i-; sh·i-te [1]) be careless; be absent-minded:
Boyaboya shite iru *to kuruma ni
hikaremasu yo.* (ぼやぼやしていると車
にひかれますよ) If *you are not on
your toes*, you will be hit by a car.
/ Boyaboya shite inai *de shigoto o
shi nasai.* (ぼやぼやしていないで仕事をし
なさい) Do your work *without going around in a daze.* / Boyaboya
suru na. (ぼやぼやするな) *Wake up!*
(⇨ boñyari)

BS *n.* broadcasting satellite. (放
送衛星＝hoosoo eesee)

bu[1] ぶ (分) *n.* advantage.
bu ga aru (〜がある) have an advantage: *Doo mite mo kare-ra no
hoo ni* bu ga aru. (どう見ても彼らのほ
うに分がある) In every way they
have the edge over us.
bu ga warui (〜が悪い) be at a disadvantage: *Ima wa* bu ga warui.
(今は分が悪い) We *are* now *in an
unfavorable situation.*

bu[2] ぶ (分) *n.* (a unit of rate) one
percent: ★ One tenth of '*wari*.'
Giñkoo wa hachi bu *no rishi de
kane o kashite kureta.* (銀行は8分
の利子で金を貸してくれた) The bank
lent me the money at eight *percent* interest.
...bu-doori (...〜どおり) ten percent: *Geñkoo wa* hachi-bu-doori
kañsee shimashita. (原稿は8分どお

り完成しました） I have finished eighty *percent* of the manuscript.

bu³ ぶ（部） *n.* **1** department: *hañbai*-bu（販売部）the sales *department*.

2 club: *tenisu*-bu（テニス部）a tennis *club*. 《⇨ gakubu》

-bu ぶ（部）*suf.* **1** part: *Kono shoosetsu wa sañ*-bu *kara naru.*（この小説は 3 部からなる）This novel consists of three *parts*.

2 copy: *Kono hoñ wa juumañ*-bu *ijoo uremashita.*（この本は 10 万部以上売れました）More than a hundred thousand *copies* of this book have been sold.

buʃaʔisoo ぶあいそう（無愛想）*a.n.* (~ na, ni) unsociable; blunt: buaisoo *na hito*（無愛想な人）an *unsociable* person / buaisoo *na taido*（無愛想な態度）a *cold* manner / *Ano mise no teñiñ wa* buaisoo *da.*（あの店の店員は無愛想だ）The clerks at that shop are *not courteous.* / *Kare wa* buaisoo *ni kotaeta.*（彼は無愛想に答えた）He answered *bluntly.* 《⇨ aiso》

buʃatsu·i ぶあつい（分厚い）*a.* (-ku) thick: buatsui *hoñ*（分厚い本）a *thick* book. 《⇨ atsui³》

buʔbuñ ぶぶん（部分）*n.* part; portion: *Kono kikai wa yottsu no* bubuñ *kara dekite imasu.*（この機械は 4 つの部分からできています）This machine is made up of four *parts.* / *Hoñ no kono* bubuñ *ga rikai dekinai.*（本のこの部分が理解できない）I cannot understand this *portion* of the book.

buʃbuñhiñ ぶぶんひん（部分品）*n.* parts. 《⇨ buhiñ》

buʃbuñ-teki ぶぶんてき（部分的）*a.n.* (~ na, ni) partial; partly: *Kono baai* bubuñ-teki *na tenaoshi*

de wa maniawanai.（この場合部分的な手直しでは間に合わない）A *partial* correction will not be good enough in this case. / *Kanojo no iu koto wa* bubuñ-teki *ni wa tadashii.*（彼女の言うことは部分的には正しい）What she says is *partly* right.

buʃchoo ぶちょう（部長）*n.* manager; the head [chief] of a department: Buchoo *wa dochira no shusshiñ desu ka?*（部長はどちらの出身ですか）Where do *you* come from? ★ Subordinates usually call their chief by the official title. / buchoo-*dairi*（部長代理）a deputy *general manager* / *hañbai*-buchoo（販売部長）the sales *manager* / *juñsa*-buchoo（巡査部長）a police *sergeant.* 《⇨ kaisha (table)》

buʃdoo ぶどう（葡萄）*n.* grape; grapevine: budoo *futa-fusa*（ぶどう二房）two *bunches* of grapes.

buʃdoʔoshu ぶどうしゅ（葡萄酒）*n.* wine.

buʃeʔñryo ぶえんりょ（無遠慮）*a.n.* (~ na, ni) rude; impolite: *Kare wa* bueñryo *na shitsumoñ o shita.*（彼は無遠慮な質問をした）He asked me *impolite* questions. 《↔ eñryo》

buʃhiñ ぶひん（部品）*n.* parts: *jidoosha no* buhiñ（自動車の部品）automobile *parts* / *yobi no* buhiñ（予備の部品）spare *parts*.

buʃji ぶじ（無事）*n.* safety; peace: *Ryokoo no* go-buji *o inorimasu.*（旅行のご無事を祈ります）I wish you a *safe* journey.

— *a.n.* (~ na, ni) safe; peaceful; all right: *Sono ko wa* buji *ni kyuushutsu sareta.*（その子は無事に救出された）The child was rescued *safely.* / *Taikai wa* buji *ni shuuryoo shimashita.*（大会は無事に終了しました）The meeting went off *without a hitch.* / *Kare wa* buji *desu.* (彼は無事です) He is *all right.*

bu｢joku ぶじょく (侮辱) *n.* insult; contempt; affront:
Kare no kotoba wa hidoi bujoku *da.* (彼の言葉はひどい侮辱だ) His remarks are a gross *insult.* / *Watashi wa sono* bujoku *o shinoñda.* (私はその侮辱を忍んだ) I swallowed the *insult.* / *Kanojo wa hidoi* bujoku *o uketa.* (彼女はひどい侮辱を受けた) She *was insulted.*
bujoku suru (〜する) *vt.* insult:
Kare wa miñna no mae de watashi o bujoku *shita.* (彼はみんなの前で私を侮辱した) He *treated* me *with contempt* in the presence of the others.

bu｢ka ぶか (部下) *n.* subordinate:
Kare wa watashi no buka *no hitori desu.* (彼は私の部下の一人です) He is one of *my men.* / *Kare wa* buka *ni shorui o juñbi suru yoo ni meejita.* (彼は部下に書類を準備するように命じた) He ordered his *subordinate* to get the documents ready.

bu｢ka¹kkoo ぶかっこう (不格好) *a.n.* (〜 na, ni) unshapely; awkward; clumsy:
bukakkoo *na booshi* (不格好な帽子) an *unshapely* hat / *Kare wa* bukakkoo *na tetsuki de kugi o utta.* (彼は不格好な手つきでくぎを打った) He drove in the nail in a *clumsy* manner. 《⇒ kakkoo》

bu｢ki ぶき (武器) *n.* arms; weapon; ordnance:
kuni no tame ni buki *o toru* (国のために武器をとる) take up *arms* for one's country / buki *o totte tatakau* (武器をとって戦う) fight with a *weapon* / *Buki o sutero.* (武器を捨てろ) Lay down your *arms!*

bu｢kimi ぶきみ (無気味) *a.n.* (〜 na, ni) weird; uncanny:
bukimi *na shizukesa* (無気味な静けさ) *uncanny* silence / *Yaneura de* bukimi *na oto ga shita.* (屋根裏で無気味な音がした) I heard a *weird* noise in the attic. / *Sono akiya wa* bukimi *datta.* (その空き家は無気味だった) The empty house had a *spooky* look.

bu｢ki¹yoo ぶきよう (不器用) *n.* clumsiness; awkwardness.
— *a.n.* **1** (〜 na, ni) clumsy; unskilled; awkward:
bukiyoo *na tetsuki de nuu* (不器用な手つきで縫う) sew with a *clumsy* hand / *Watashi wa totemo* bukiyoo *da.* (私はとても不器用だ) I'm *all thumbs.* 《↔ kiyoo》
2 unable to deal with a situation with finesse:
Watashi wa doomo bukiyoo *de oseji mo ienai.* (私はどうも不器用でお世辞も言えない) I am a *poor hand* at paying compliments.

bu｢kka ぶっか (物価) *n.* (commodity) prices: ★ Means general prices of commodities. The price of a specific article is 'nedañ.'
bukka *ga takai* [*yasui*] (物価が高い [安い]) *prices* are high [low] / *Bukka ga agatte* [*sagatte*] *kita.* (物価が上がって[下がって]きた) *Prices* have been rising [dropping].

Bu｢kkyoo ぶっきょう (仏教) *n.* Buddhism:
Bukkyoo *o shiñjiru* (仏教を信じる) believe in *Buddhism* / Bukkyoo-*to* (仏教徒) a *Buddhist.*

bu｢kubuku ぶくぶく *adv.* (〜 to, ni) **1** (the state of being fat or baggy):
Kare wa saikiñ bukubuku (*to* [*ni*]) *futotte kita.* (彼は最近ぶくぶく(と[に])太ってきた) He is getting *fatter* these days.
2 (〜 to) (the state of bubbling):
Kaitee kara awa ga bukubuku (*to*) *dete iru.* (海底から泡がぶくぶく(と)出ている) Bubbles are *rising* from the seabed. / *Fune wa* bukubuku (*to*) *shizuñde shimatta.* (船はぶくぶく(と)沈んでしまった) The ship sank, *leav-*

ing a trail of bubbles.

buˈñ[1] ぶん（文）*n.* sentence; composition:
Kono buñ wa nagasugiru. (この文は長すぎる) This *passage* is too long. / *Nihoñgo de buñ o kaku no wa muzukashii.* (日本語で文を書くのはむずかしい) It is difficult to write a *composition* in Japanese.

buˈñ[2] ぶん（分）*n.* **1** share; part; portion:
Kore wa kimi no buñ da. (これは君の分だ) This is your *share.* / *Nokotta buñ wa reezooko ni shimatte oki nasai.* (残った分は冷蔵庫にしまっておきなさい) Put away the *rest* in the refrigerator. / *Koñgetsu-buñ no kyuuryoo o mada moratte inai.* (今月分の給料をまだもらっていない) I haven't got my pay *for this month* yet.
2 place; station:
Kare wa jibuñ no buñ o wakimaete iru. (彼は自分の分をわきまえている) He knows his *place.*
3 condition:
Kono buñ nara, bañji umaku iku daroo. (この分なら，万事うまく行くだろう) Under the present *conditions,* everything will go well.
《⇨ -buñ; buñsuu》

-buñ ぶん（分）*suf.* (the amount or percentage contained in materials):
*too-*buñ （糖分）the *amount* [*percentage*] of sugar / *Sui-buñ ga sukoshi joohatsu shita.* (水分が少し蒸発した) A small amount of *water* has evaporated. / *Kono waiñ wa arukooru-buñ ga takai.* (このワインはアルコール分が高い) This wine has a high alcohol *content.* / *Kono suupu wa eñ-buñ ga ooi.* (このスープは塩分が多い) This soup contains a lot of *salt.*

buˈnañ ぶなん（無難）*n.* safety; security.
— *a.n.* (~ na, ni) safe; passable:

Hinañ sarenai yoo, bunañ na saku o totta. (批判されないよう，無難な策をとった) We took *precautions* to avoid criticism. / *Sono señshu wa eñgi o bunañ ni matometa.* (その選手は演技を無難にまとめた) The gymnast gave a *passable* performance. / *Sono koto ni tsuite wa damatte iru hoo ga bunañ da.* (そのことについてはだまっているほうが無難だ) Regarding that matter, it would be *safer* to keep silent.

buˈñbo ぶんぼ（分母）*n.* denominator. 《⇨ buñsuu》

buˈñboˈogu ぶんぼうぐ（文房具）*n.* stationery; writing materials.

buˈñboogu teñ ぶんぼうぐてん（文房具店）*n.* stationer's; stationery store.

buˈñbuñ ぶんぶん *adv.* (~ to) (the buzzing noise made when bees or flies are flying; the droning noise made by the rotation of motors):
katana [boo] o buñbuñ (to) furimawasu （刀[棒]をぶんぶん(と)振り回す) wave a sword [club] about *vigorously* / *Mitsubachi ga su no mawari o buñbuñ (to) toñde iru.* (蜜蜂が巣の回りをぶんぶん(と)飛んでいる) Honeybees are *buzzing* around their hive.

buˈñgaku ぶんがく（文学）*n.* literature:
Kare wa Nihoñ no buñgaku o keñkyuu shite iru. (彼は日本の文学を研究している) He is doing research in Japanese *literature.*

buˈñgaˈkusha ぶんがくしゃ（文学者）*n.* literary man; man of letters; writer.

buˈñgo ぶんご（文語）*n.* written [literary] language:
buñgo-tai （文語体）a *literary* style. 《↔ koogo》

buˈñka[1] ぶんか（文化）*n.* culture:
Kodai Girishajiñ wa takai buñka o motte ita. (古代ギリシャ人は高い文化

を持っていた) The ancient Greeks had a high level of *culture*. / buñka *no kooryuu* (文化の交流) *cultural* exchange. (⇨ buñkazai)

bu⌐ñka² ぶんか (文科) *n.* the department of liberal arts; the humanities: *Watashi wa* buñka-*kee desu.* (私は文化系です) I am studying *liberal arts*. (⇨ rika)

Bu⌐ñka⌐-choo ぶんかちょう (文化庁) *n.* Agency for Cultural Affairs: Buñka-choo *chookañ* (文化庁長官) the Director General of the *Agency for Cultural Affairs*. (⇨ choo⁴ (table))

bu⌐ñkai ぶんかい (分解) *n.* resolution; taking to pieces. **buñkai suru** (〜する) *vi., vt.* resolve; take to pieces: *Kono busshitsu wa shiboo o* buñkai *suru hataraki ga aru.* (この物質は脂肪を分解する働きがある) This substance has the function of *breaking down* fat. / *Kare wa eñjiñ o* buñkai *shita.* (彼はエンジンを分解した) He *took* the engine *to pieces*.

bu⌐ñka⌐jiñ ぶんかじん (文化人) *n.* person following an academic or artistic career; cultured person.

Bu⌐ñka-ku⌐ñshoo ぶんかくんしょう (文化勲章) *n.* Order of Culture. ★ On Culture Day (November 3), it is conferred upon those

BUÑKA-KUÑSHOO

who have rendered outstanding services for the promotion of culture.

Bu⌐ñka-no-hi ぶんかのひ (文化の日) *n.* Culture Day (November 3). (⇨ shukujitsu (table))

bu⌐ñka-teki ぶんかてき (文化的) *a.n.* (〜 na, ni) cultural; civilized: buñka-teki *na seekatsu o suru* [*okuru*] (文化的な生活をする[送る]) lead a *civilized* life.

bu⌐ñka⌐zai ぶんかざい (文化財) *n.* cultural property [assets]: *Sono shina wa juuyoo-*buñkazai *ni shitee sareta.* (その品は重要文化財に指定された) The article was designated as an Important *Cultural Property*.

bu⌐ñkeñ ぶんけん (文献) *n.* books or documents on a particular subject; literature: *Kodai ni kañsuru* buñkeñ *o sagashite iru tokoro desu.* (古代に関する文献を探しているところです) I'm looking for *books* on the ancient historical period.

bu⌐ñmee ぶんめい (文明) *n.* civilization: Buñmee *ga susumu.* (文明が進む) *Civilization* advances. / buñmee-*shakai* (文明社会) *civilized* society / *kikai*-buñmee (機械文明) industrial *civilization* / *busshitsu*-buñmee (物質文明) material *civilization*.

bu⌐ñmyaku ぶんみゃく (文脈) *n.* context: buñmyaku *kara imi o shiru* (文脈から意味を知る) know the meaning from the *context*.

bu⌐ñpai ぶんぱい (分配) *n.* distribution; division: *rieki no koohee na* buñpai (利益の公平な分配) a fair *distribution* of profit. **buñpai suru** (〜する) *vt.* distribute; divide: *Kare-ra wa sono* *kane o nakamauchi de* buñpai shita. (彼らはその金を仲間うちで分配した) They *divided* the money among themselves.

bu「ñpoo ぶんぽう (文法) *n.* grammar:
buñpoo-*joo no machigai* (文法上の間違い) an error in *grammar* / *Kono buñ wa* buñpoo-*teki ni okashii.* (この文は文法的におかしい) This sentence is *grammatically* strange.

bu「ñpu ぶんぷ (分布) *n.* distribution; spread:
Kono shokubutsu wa buñpu *ga kagirarete iru.* (この植物は分布が限られている) The *distribution* of this plant is limited. / buñpu-*zu* (分布図) a *distribution* map.
buñpu suru (〜する) *vi.* be distributed: *Kono hana wa Nihoñ-juu ni* buñpu *shite iru.* (この花は日本中に分布している) This flower *ranges* throughout Japan.

bu「ñraku ぶんらく (文楽) *n.* traditional Japanese puppet theater. (⇨ jooruri)

BUÑRAKU

bu「ñretsu ぶんれつ (分裂) *n.* split; division:
kaku-buñretsu (核分裂) nuclear *fission*.
buñretsu suru (〜する) *vi.* split; divide: *Too wa futatsu ni* buñretsu shita. (党は二つに分裂した) The party *split* into two factions. / *Saiboo ga* buñretsu suru *no o keñ-*

bikyoo de mita. (細胞が分裂するのを顕微鏡で見た) I saw the cells *divide* through the microscope.

bu「ñri ぶんり (分離) *n.* separation; disunion:
seeji to keezai no buñri (政治と経済の分離) the *separation* of politics and the economy.
buñri suru (〜する) *vi., vt.* separate: *gyuunyuu kara kuriimu o* buñri suru (牛乳からクリームを分離する) *separate* cream from milk.

bu「ñrui ぶんるい (分類) *n.* classification; grouping:
shokubutsu no buñrui (植物の分類) the *classification* of plants.
buñrui suru (〜する) *vt.* classify; group: *Deeta o koomoku-betsu ni* buñrui shita. (データを項目別に分類した) I *classified* the data by category. / *Kitte o ikutsu-ka no teema-betsu ni* buñrui shita. (切手をいくつかのテーマ別に分類した) I *grouped* the stamps into several categories.

bu「ñryo'o ぶんりょう (分量) *n.* quantity or amount that can be measured:
buñryoo *o hakaru* (分量をはかる) measure the *quantity* / *Satoo no* buñryoo *o herashita hoo ga yoi.* (砂糖の分量を減らしたほうがよい) You had better reduce the *amount* of sugar. / *Kusuri no* buñryoo *o machigaeta.* (薬の分量をまちがえた) I took the wrong *dose* of medicine. (⇨ ryoo¹)

bu「ñsañ ぶんさん (分散) *n.* dispersion; decentralization.
buñsañ suru (〜する) *vi., vt.* disperse; decentralize: *jiñkoo o* buñsañ suru (人口を分散する) *disperse* the population / *koojoo o* buñsañ suru (工場を分散する) *decentralize* a factory / *Seeto wa* buñsañ shite, *basu ni notta.* (生徒は分散して, バスに乗った) The pupils *broke up into groups* and got on the buses. (↔ shuuchuu)

bu「ñseki ぶんせき（分析）*n*. analysis:
shokuhiñ no buñseki（食品の分析）the *analysis* of food.
  buñseki suru（〜する）*vt*. make an analysis; analyze: *geñjoo o* buñseki suru（現状を分析する）*make an analysis* of the present situation / *Nihoñ-keezai o* buñseki suru（日本経済を分析する）*analyze* the Japanese economy.

bu「ñshi ぶんし（分子）*n*. 1 numerator. 《⇨ buñsuu》
  2 molecule.
  3 element: *guruupu-nai no fuhee* buñshi（グループ内の不平分子）the discontented *elements* in the group.

bu「ñsho ぶんしょ（文書）*n*. document; writing:
Watashi wa sono buñsho *ni shomee shita*.（私はその文書に署名した）I signed the *document*. / *Kare wa* buñsho *gizoo no tsumi de kiso sareta*.（彼は文書偽造の罪で起訴された）He was prosecuted for forgery of *documents*. / *Buñsho de kaitoo shite kudasai*.（文書で回答してください）Please reply in *writing*.

bu「ñshoo ぶんしょう（文章）*n*. sentences; writing:
buñshoo *o kakinaosu*（文章を書き直す）rewrite *sentences* / *kañgae o* buñshoo *ni matomeru*（考えを文章にまとめる）put one's ideas down in *writing* / *Kare wa* buñshoo *ga umai*.（彼は文章がうまい）He is a *good writer*.

bu「ñsu「u ぶんすう（分数）*n*. fraction. ★ The numerator is called '*buñshi*'（分子）, and the denominator '*buñbo*'（分母）. Y/X is read as '*X buñ no Y*.'

1/2	ni-buñ no ichi
2/3	sañ-buñ no ni
3/4	yoñ-buñ no sañ
4/5	go-buñ no yoñ
5/6	roku-buñ no go
6/7	nana-buñ no roku
7/8	hachi-buñ no nana
8/9	kyuu-buñ no hachi
9/10	juu-buñ no kyuu

bu「ñtai ぶんたい（文体）*n*. style of writing:
wakariyasui buñtai *de kaku*（わかりやすい文体で書く）write in an easily comprehensive *style*.

bu「ñtañ ぶんたん（分担）*n*. partial charge; allotment; share:
Wareware no shigoto no buñtañ *o kimete kudasai*.（われわれの仕事の分担を決めてください）Please decide *how you will allot* the work to each of us. / *Watashi no* buñtañ *wa owarimashita*.（私の分担は終わりました）I have done my *share* of the work.
  buñtañ suru（〜する）*vt*. share: *Sono hiyoo wa anata to futari de* buñtañ *shimashoo*.（その費用はあなたと二人で分担しましょう）*Let's share* the cost between the two of us. 《⇨ wakeru》

bu「ñtsuu ぶんつう（文通）*n*. correspondence:
Kare wa kanojo to buñtsuu *o hajimeta*.（彼は彼女と文通を始めた）He began a *correspondence* with her. 《⇨ tegami》
  buñtsuu suru（〜する）*vi*. correspond with; exchange letters: *Watashi wa ima de mo kare to* buñtsuu *shite iru*.（私は今でも彼と文通している）I still *exchange* letters with him.

bu「ñya ぶんや（分野）*n*. field; sphere; branch:
Kare wa kono buñya *de yuumee desu*.（彼はこの分野で有名です）He is famous in this *field*. / *Sono beñgoshi wa hiroi* buñya *de katsuyaku shite iru*.（その弁護士は広い分野で活躍している）The lawyer is active in many *spheres*.

bu˥rabura ぶらぶら *adv.* (~ to; ~ suru) **1** (the state of legs or arms hanging loosely, or of a pendulum swinging):
Isu ga takasugite kodomo no ashi ga burabura *shite iru.* (椅子が高すぎて子どもの足がぶらぶらしている) The chair is so high that the child's legs are *dangling down.* / *Jishiñ de teñjoo no shañderia ga* bura-bura *yureta.* (地震で天井のシャンデリアがぶらぶら揺れた) The chandelier on the ceiling swayed *back and forth* in the earthquake.
2 (the state of moving aimlessly about):
Teñki ga ii kara, kooeñ o bura-bura *sañpo shita.* (天気がいいから, 公園をぶらぶら散歩した) Since it was fine, I went out for a *stroll* around the park.
3 (the state of idling about):
Sotsugyoo shite kara, ano hito wa mainichi burabura *shite iru.* (卒業してから, あの人は毎日ぶらぶらしている) Since he graduated from school, he has been *lazing about* every day.

bu˥rañko ぶらんこ *n.* swing:
burañko *ni noru* (ぶらんこに乗る) get on a *swing* / burañko *de asobu* (ぶらんこで遊ぶ) play on a *swing.*

bu˥rasagar·u ぶらさがる (ぶら下がる) *vi.* (-sagar·i-; -sagar·a-; -sagat-te Ⓒ) **1** hang:
tetsuboo ni burasagaru (鉄棒にぶら下がる) *hang* from a horizontal bar / *tsurikawa ni* burasagaru (吊り革にぶら下がる) *hang* on to a strap (on the train) / *Teñjoo kara furui rañpu ga* burasagatte ita. (天井から古いランプがぶら下がっていた) An old lamp *hung* from the ceiling. 《⇨ burasageru》
2 dangle:
Kare no me no mae ni shachoo no chii ga burasagatte ita. (彼の目の前に社長の地位がぶら下がっていた) The

post of president of the company *was dangling* within his reach.

bu˥rasage·ru ぶらさげる (ぶら下げる) *vt.* (-sage-te Ⓥ) hang:
kata kara shorudaa-baggu o bura-sageru (肩からショルダーバッグをぶら下げる) *hang* a shoulder bag from one's shoulder / *kubi ni peñdañto o* burasageru (首にペンダントをぶら下げる) *wear* a pendant around one's neck / *Kare wa ryoote ni ooki-na nimotsu o* burasagete aruita. (彼は両手に大きな荷物をぶら下げて歩いた) He *carried* a large parcel in each hand. 《⇨ burasagaru》

bu˥rashi ブラシ *n.* brush:
uwagi ni burashi *o kakeru* (上着にブラシをかける) *brush* one's jacket [coat]. ★ The generic name for 'brush.' 《⇨ fude; hake》

bu˥ra˥usu ブラウス *n.* blouse:
Kanojo wa shiroi burausu *o kite ita.* (彼女は白いブラウスを着ていた) She was wearing a white *blouse.*

bu˥ree ぶれい (無礼) *n.* impolite behavior; rudeness:
buree *o hataraku* (無礼をはたらく) *be rude* / buree-*mono* (無礼者) an *impudent* fellow.
— *a.n.* (~ na) rude; impolite:
Heñji mo shinai nañte buree *na otoko da.* (返事もしないなんて無礼な男だ) What a *rude* fellow he is—not even giving a reply!

bu˥re˥eki ブレーキ *n.* brake:
bureeki *o kakeru* [*fumu*] (ブレーキをかける[ふむ]) put [step] on the *brakes* / Bureeki *ga kikanai.* (ブレーキが効かない) The *brakes* do not work. / *Kare wa kyuu-*bureeki *o kaketa.* (彼は急ブレーキをかけた) He slammed on the *brakes.*

-buri / -puri ぶり/ぷり (振り) *suf.*
1 [with a noun or the continuative base of a verb] manner; way:
*hanashi-*buri (話しぶり) someone's *way* of talking / *Kare no* seechoo-

buri *ni miñna ga odoroita.*(彼の成長ぶりにみんなが驚いた) Everyone was surprised at his rapid *growth.* / *Shaiñ no nesshiñ na shigoto*-buri *ni shachoo wa mañzoku shita yoo datta.*(社員の熱心な仕事ぶりに社長は満足したようだった) The president of the company seemed to be satisfied with the *way* the employees worked hard. / *Ano ko wa nomipp-puri ga ii nee.*(あの娘は飲みっぷりがいいねえ) I like the *way* she drinks.
2 after: ★ Used after words denoting duration and indicates that something occurred again after the interval of time stated. *Goneñ-buri ni furusato e kaetta.*(五年ぶりにふるさとへ帰った) I went back to my hometown *for the first time in five years.* / Is-shuu-kañ-buri *no aozora da.*(一週間ぶりの青空だ) *It's been a week since* we saw such a blue sky. / *Ara,* nañ-neñ-buri ka shira? *Zuibuñ ookiku natta wa ne.*(あら、何年ぶりかしら。ずいぶん大きくなったわね) *When was it* that I saw you last? My, you have grown! 《⇨ hisashiburi》

bu⌐riki ブリキ *n.* tinplate; tin: buriki no kañ (ブリキの缶) a *can* [*tin*].

-bu⌐r·u ぶる *suf.*(*vi.*)(-bur·i-; -bur·a-; -but-te ⒸC) pose as...; behave like...: ★ Used to form a verb from a noun, adjective, or adjectival noun. It conveys a derogatory meaning.
1 [after a noun] *Kare wa geeju-tsuka*-butte iru.(彼は芸術家ぶっている) He *poses as* an artist. / *Yamada señsee wa* gakusha-butta *toko-ro ga arimaseñ.*(山田先生は学者ぶったところがありません) There is nothing *pedantic* about the way Professor Yamada acts.
2 [after the stem of an adjective] *era*-buru (偉ぶる) *act big.*
3 [after an adjectival noun] *joo-*

hiñ-buru(上品ぶる) *put on* airs; *pretend* to be refined.

bu⌐ruburu ぶるぶる *adv.*(~ to)(the state of the body or limbs shaking or quivering from cold, fear, etc.): *Sono ko wa samusa no tame ni* buruburu *(to) furuete ita.*(その子は寒さのためにぶるぶる(と)震えていた) That child was *shivering* with cold. / *Watashi wa osoroshikute,* buru-buru (to) *furueta.*(私は恐ろしくて、ぶるぶる(と)震えた) I *trembled* with fear.

bu⌐sa⌐hoo ぶさほう(無作法) *n.* bad manners; breach of etiquette:
— *a.n.*(~ na, ni) ill-mannered; impolite: *Suwatta mama, meue no hito ni aisatsu suru no wa* busahoo *desu.*(座ったまま、目上の人に挨拶するのは無作法です) It is *bad manners* to greet your superiors while remaining seated. 《⇨ shitsuree》

bu⌐shi ぶし(武士) *n.* warrior; samurai. ★ A man of arms in the service of a feudal lord in Japan. 《⇨ shi-noo-koo-shoo (table)》

bu⌐sho⌐o ぶしょう(不精・無精) *n.* laziness; indolence: bushoo-*mono*(不精者) a *lazy* fellow / bushoo-hige(不精ひげ) a *stub-bly beard.*

bushoo suru(~する) *vi.* be lazy; be remiss: *Kesa wa* bushoo shite *kao o arawanakatta.*(今朝は不精して顔を洗わなかった) This morning I *was too lazy* to wash my face.
— *a.n.*(~ na, ni) lazy; indolent: *Musuko wa kono-goro* bushoo *ni natta.*(息子はこのごろ不精になった) Our son has grown *lazy* these days. / *Kare wa* bushoo *de, is-shuukañ heya no sooji o shina-katta.*(彼は不精で、一週間部屋の掃

除をしなかった) Because of his *indolence*, he did not clean his room for a week. / fude-bushoo *na hito* (筆不精な人) a *bad correspondent* / de-bushoo *na hito* (出不精な人) a *stay-at-home*.

buˈshu ぶしゅ (部首) *n.* the radical of a Chinese character:
★ Used as a classificatory element in *kañji*.
Kono kañji no bushu *wa nañ desu ka?* (この漢字の部首は何ですか) What is the *radical* of this character? 《⇨ heñ³; tsukuri》

bushu	kañji
木 kiheñ (tree)	松, 林
イ niñbeñ (person)	体, 住
⧾ kusa-kañmuri (grass)	草, 花
氵 sañzui (water)	池, 海
⻌ shiññyoo (advancing)	送, 返

-buˈsoku ぶそく (不足) *suf.* insufficient; short; lacking:
*shokuryoo-*busoku (食糧不足) a food *shortage* / *suimiñ-*busoku (睡眠不足) *insufficient* sleep / *uñdoo-*busoku (運動不足) *lack* of exercise. 《⇨ fusoku》

buˈsoo ぶそう (武装) *n.* armaments; military equipment:
busoo suru (〜する) *vt.* arm:
Sono otoko wa raifuru de busoo *shite ita.* (その男はライフルで武装していた) The man *was armed* with a rifle. 《↔ hibusoo》

buˈsshi ぶっし (物資) *n.* goods; necessities; supplies:
Watashi-tachi wa kare-ra ni sho-kuryoo ya ta no busshi *o ageta.* (私たちは彼らに食糧や他の物資をあげた) We gave them food and other *necessities.* / *Kare-ra wa kyuueñ-*busshi *o hitsuyoo to shite iru.* (彼らは救援物資を必要としている) They are in need of relief *supplies.*

buˈsshiki ぶっしき (仏式) *n.* Bud-dhist rites:
Nihoñ no sooshiki wa busshiki *de okonawareru koto ga ooi.* (日本の葬式は仏式で行なわれることが多い) In Japan it is customary to hold funerals according to *Buddhist rites.* 《⇨ shiñshiki》

buˈsshitsu ぶっしつ (物質) *n.* matter; substance.

buˈsshitsu-teki ぶっしつてき (物質的) *a.n.* (〜 na, ni) material; physical:
Kare-ra wa busshitsu-teki *na eñjo o hitsuyoo to shite iru.* (彼らは物質的な援助を必要としている) They need *material* aid. / *Kanojo wa* busshitsu-teki *ni megumarete iru.* (彼女は物質的に恵まれている) She is *well off.*

buˈssoˈo ぶっそう (物騒) *n.* lack of safety; danger.
— *a.n.* (〜 na, ni) unsafe; dangerous:
bussoo *na koto o iu* (物騒なことを言う) talk about *dangerous* things / *Kagi o kakenai de dekakeru no wa* bussoo *da.* (鍵をかけないで出かけるのは物騒だ) It is *unsafe* to go out leaving the door unlocked. / *Bussoo na yo-no-naka ni natte kita.* (物騒な世の中になってきた) We have come upon *troubled* times.

buˈta ぶた (豚) *n.* pig; hog:
buta *o kau* (豚を飼う) keep *pigs.* / *Buta ni shiñju.* (*proverb*) (豚に真珠) Cast pearls before swine. 《⇨ neko》

buˈtai ぶたい (舞台) *n.* 1 stage:
butai *ni tatsu* (舞台に立つ) appear on the *stage* / butai *de jooeñ suru* (舞台で上演する) act on the *stage.*
2 setting; scene:
Kyooto ga kono geki no butai *desu.* (京都がこの劇の舞台です) Kyoto is the *setting* for this play.
butai-ura (〜裏) backstage; behind the scenes: *Kare-ra wa* butai-ura *de torihiki o shita.* (彼ら

は舞台裏で取り引きをした) They made a deal *behind the scenes.*

bu⌐taniku ぶたにく (豚肉) *n.* pork.

bu⌐too ぶとう (舞踏) *n.* dance:
butoo-kai (舞踏会) a *ball.*
(⇨ odori)

-¹butsu ぶつ (物) *suf.* thing; object; matter:
iñsatsu-butsu (印刷物) printed *matter* / keñchiku-butsu (建築物) a *building* / *rakka*-butsu (落下物) a falling *object* / seesañ-butsu (生産物) a *product* / yuubiñ-butsu (郵便物) *mail.*

bu⌐tsubutsu¹ ぶつぶつ *adv.*
1 (the state of many small swellings appearing):
kao ni nikibi ga butsubutsu *dekiru* (顔ににきびがぶつぶつできる) have one's face come out in *pimples.*
2 (the state of talking to oneself in a low voice or mumbling complaints to someone):
Kare wa ki ni iranai to sugu butsubutsu *iu.* (彼は気に入らないとすぐぶつぶつ言う) When there is something he doesn't like, he soon *grumbles.*

bu⌐tsubutsu² ぶつぶつ *n.* rash; pimple:
Kao ni butsubutsu *ga dekita.* (顔にぶつぶつができた) A *rash* broke out on my face.

bu⌐tsudañ ぶつだん (仏壇) *n.* Buddhist family altar.

BUTSUDAÑ

bu⌐tsukar·u ぶつかる *vt.* (-kar·i-; -kar·a-; -kat-te Ⓒ) **1** bump into; crash against; collide:
Kuruma ga gaadoreeru ni butsukatta. (車がガードレールにぶつかった) A car *crashed into* the guardrail. / *Boñyari aruite itara mukoo kara kita hito ni* [*to*] butsukatta. (ぼんやり歩いていたら向こうから来た人に[と]ぶつかった) I was walking along absent-mindedly and *bumped* against the person coming from the opposite direction. (⇨ butsukeru)
2 encounter; run into; meet (difficulties, hardship, a problem, etc.):
Omoigakenai koññañ ni butsukatta. (思いがけない困難にぶつかった) We *encountered* unexpected difficulties. / *Zaisee-joo no kabe ni* butsukatte, *sono kikaku wa dame ni natta.* (財政上の壁にぶつかって, その企画はだめになった) They *ran into* financial difficulties and the project came to nothing.
3 (of dates) coincide; fall on:
Kotoshi no Seejiñ-no-hi wa nichi-yoobi to butsukaru. (今年の成人の日は日曜日とぶつかる) This year's Coming-of-Age Day *falls on* a Sunday. / *Kono jikañ wa rasshua-waa ni* butsukaru. (この時間はラッシュアワーにぶつかる) This time of day *coincides* with the rush-hour. / *Sotsugyoo-shiki to ane no kekkoñ-shiki ga* butsukatte shimatta. (卒業式と姉の結婚式がぶつかってしまった) The date of the graduation ceremony and my elder sister's wedding *clashed.*
4 wrangle; have a run-in with:
Shigoto no koto de jooshi to butsukatte shimatta. (仕事のことで上司とぶつかってしまった) I *had a disagreement* with my boss about the job.

bu⌐tsuke·ru ぶつける *vt.* (-ke-te Ⓥ) **1** bump; knock:
Ayamatte, kuruma o deñchuu ni butsukete shimatta. (誤って, 車を電

butsuri

柱にぶつけてしまった) I *drove* my car into a utility pole by mistake. / *Atama o hashira ni* butsuketa. (頭を柱にぶつけた) I *knocked* my head against a pole. 《⇨ butsukaru》

2 throw:
Neko ni ishi o butsukete *wa ike-maseñ*. (猫に石をぶつけてはいけません) Don't *throw* stones at the cat.

3 give vent to:
fumañ [*ikari; iraira*] *o hito ni* bu-tsukeru (不満[怒り;いらいら]を人にぶつける) *give vent* to one's discontent [anger; irritation] on somebody.

buˈtsuri ぶつり (物理) *n.* physics. ★ Shortened form of '*butsuri-gaku*.'

buˈtsuriˈgaku ぶつりがく (物理学) *n.* physics.

buˈttai ぶったい (物体) *n.* object; thing; substance:
marui buttai (丸い物体) a round *object*. / *Watashi wa nani-ka shiroi* buttai *o mita*. (私は何か白い物体を見た) I saw *something* white.

buˈumu ブーム *n.* boom; fad:
Wakai hito-tachi no aida de tenisu ga buumu *ni natte imasu*. (若い人たちの間でテニスがブームになっています) A tennis *boom* is on among young people. / *Sore wa tañ-naru* buumu *ni suginai*. (それは単なるブームにすぎない) It is only a passing *fad*.

buˈutsu ブーツ *n.* boots. 《⇨ naga-gutsu》

buˈyoˈojiñ ぶようじん (不用心) *a.n.* (~ na, ni) unsafe; careless:
Doa ni kagi o kakenai de oku no wa buyoojiñ *desu*. (ドアに鍵をかけないでおくのは不用心です) It is *unsafe* to leave the door unlocked. / *Sura-reru nañte kimi mo* buyoojiñ *datta ne*. (すられるなんてきみも不用心だったね) It was *careless* of you to get your pocket picked. 《↔ yoojiñ》

byoˈo¹ びょう (秒) *n.* second:
*Kono tokee wa go-*byoo *okurete iru*. (この時計は 5 秒遅れている) This watch is five *seconds* slow. / *Kare wa hyaku-meetoru o juuichi-*byoo *de hashiru*. (彼は 100 メートルを 11 秒で走る) He runs the one hundred meters in eleven *seconds*. 《⇨ hi¹ (table); fuñ¹》

byoˈo² びょう (鋲) *n.* tack; thumb-tack; drawing pin:
Posutaa o kabe ni byoo *de tometa*. (ポスターを壁に鋲で留めた) I fastened the poster to the wall with *thumb-tacks*.

-byoo びょう (病) *suf.* disease:
*deñseñ-*byoo (伝染病) an infectious *disease*; a contagious *disease* / *hifu-*byoo (皮膚病) a skin *disease* / *ichoo-*byoo (胃腸病) a stomach *disease* / *shiñzoo-*byoo (心臓病) heart *disease*.

byoˈobu びょうぶ (屏風) *n.* folding screen:
byoobu *o tateru* (びょうぶを立てる) set up a *folding screen* / byoobu *de heya o shikiru* (びょうぶで部屋を仕切る) divide a room with a *folding screen*.

BYOOBU

byoˈodoo びょうどう (平等) *n.* equality; impartiality:
*Kanojo-tachi wa dañjo-*byoodoo *o yookyuu shita*. (彼女たちは男女平等を要求した) The women called for sexual *equality*.
— *a.n.* (~ na, ni) equal; impartial; even:
Niñgeñ wa mina byoodoo *desu*.

（人間はみな平等です）All people are created *equal*. / *Mooke wa byoodoo ni wakeyoo.*（もうけは平等に分けよう）Let's divide the profit *evenly*.

byo「oiñ びょういん（病院）*n.* hospital:
Kare wa ichibañ chikai byooiñ e hakobareta.（彼はいちばん近い病院へ運ばれた）He was taken to the nearest *hospital*. / *Kanojo wa ichi-nichi-oki ni byooiñ ni kayotte iru.*（彼女は一日おきに病院に通っている）She goes to the *hospital* every other day. 《⇨ nyuuiñ; taiiñ》

gañka	ophthalmology
geka	surgery
hifuka	dermatology
hinyookika	urology
jibi-iñkooka	otolaryngology
keesee-geka	plastic surgery
naika	internal medicine
sañfujiñka	obstetrics and gynecology
seekee-geka	orthopedics
shika	dentistry
shiñkeeka	neurology
shoonika	pediatrics

byo「oki びょうき（病気）*n.* illness; sickness; disease:
byooki ga naoru（病気が治る）recover from one's *illness* / byooki ga yoku naru（病気が良くなる）*get well* / byooki ni naru（病気になる）become *ill* / *Kare wa byooki da.*（彼は病気だ）He is *ill*. / *Kanojo wa byooki de yasuñde imasu.*（彼女は病気で休んでいます）She is absent because of *sickness*. / *Kanojo wa omoi byooki ni kakatte iru.*（彼女は重い病気にかかっている）She is suffering from a serious *disease*. / *Wata-*

shi wa byooki *no kodomo o kañbyoo shita.*（私は病気の子どもを看病した）I looked after the *sick* child.

byo「oniñ びょうにん（病人）*n.* patient; sick person:
Byooniñ wa juutai desu.（病人は重体です）The *patient* is in critical condition. / *Byooniñ no sewa o suru no wa taiheñ da.*（病人の世話をするのは大変だ）It is hard work to look after a *sick person*. / *Atsusa no amari byooniñ ga deta.*（暑さのあまり病人がでた）It was so hot that *some people became ill*.

byo「osha びょうしゃ（描写）*n.* description; portrait:
tokai-seekatsu no migoto na byoosha（都会生活の見事な描写）a brilliant *portrait* of city life.
byoosha suru（〜する）*vt.* describe; portray: *Kono hoñ wa doobutsu no seetai o iki-iki to* byoosha shite iru.（この本は動物の生態を生き生きと描写している）This book *gives* a vivid *description* of the way of life of animals.

byo「oshi びょうし（病死）*n.* death from a disease.
byooshi suru（〜する）*vi.* die from an illness: *Sono sakka wa gaikoku de* byooshi shita.（その作家は外国で病死した）That author *died from an illness* while abroad.

byo「oshiñ びょうしん（秒針）*n.* second hand (of a timepiece). 《⇨ fuñshiñ》

byo「oshitsu びょうしつ（病室）*n.* sickroom; ward:
Tanaka-sañ no byooshitsu *ni mimai ni itta.*（田中さんの病室に見舞いに行った）I called on Miss Tanaka in her *sickroom*.

byo「otoo びょうとう（病棟）*n.* ward (in a hospital).

C

CD *n.* **1** compact disc.
2 cash dispenser; automated teller.

cha ちゃ (茶) *n.* **1** tea; green tea: ★ When referring to the beverage, it is usually called '*o-cha.*'
2 tea plant.
3 brown.
cha no kutsu (茶の靴) *brown* shoes. 《⇨ chairo》

cha「iro ちゃいろ (茶色) *n.* brown: chairo no kabañ (茶色のかばん) a *brown* bag.

cha「kk」ari ちゃっかり *adv.* (~ to; ~ suru)
shrewdly; smartly; cleverly: *Kare wa eñdaka ni tsukekoñde chakkari (to) mooketa.* (彼は円高につけ込んでちゃっかり(と)もうけた) He took advantage of the strong yen and *shrewdly* made a profit. / *Ano ko wa chakkari shite iru. O-tsuri o kaesanakatta.* (あの子はちゃっかりしている。お釣りを返さなかった) That boy *is shrewd.* He pocketed the change.

-chaku[1] ちゃく (着) *suf.* (after a numeral) the order of arrival; place: *Musuko wa sañ-chaku datta.* (息子は3着だった) My son finished in *third place.* / *Marasoñ de it-chaku ni natta.* (マラソンで1着になった) I came in *first* in the marathon.

-chaku[2] ちゃく (着) *suf.* [after a place name] arrival: *Gogo ni-ji Narita-chaku no biñ ni norimasu.* (午後2時成田着の便に乗ります) I'm going to travel on the plane *arriving* at Narita at two P.M.

-chaku[3] ちゃく (着) *suf.* counter for dresses, suits, etc.:

Wañpiisu o ni-chaku *kaimashita.* (ワンピースを2着買いました) I bought *two* ladies' suits.

cha「kuchaku ちゃくちゃく (着々) *adv.* (~ to) steadily; according to plan; step by step: *Kooji wa* chakuchaku *to susuñde imasu.* (工事は着々と進んでいます) The construction work is proceeding *according to plan.*

cha「kujitsu ちゃくじつ (着実) *a.n.* (~ na, ni) steady; sound; solid: chakujitsu *na yarikata* (着実なやり方) a *sound* method / *Keekaku wa* chakujitsu *ni susuñde imasu.* (計画は着実に進んでいます) The plan is making *steady* progress.

cha「kuriku ちゃくりく (着陸) *n.* landing: *Sono hikooki wa* chakuriku *ni shippai shita.* (その飛行機は着陸に失敗した) The plane failed to *land* safely.
chakuriku suru (~する) *vi.* make a landing; land: *Nanahyaku-nana-biñ wa teekoku ni* chakuriku *shita.* (707便は定刻に着陸した) Flight 707 *landed* on schedule. 《↔ ririku》

cha「kuseki ちゃくせき (着席) *n.* taking a seat; sitting: *"Kiritsu. Ree. Chakuseki."* (「起立! 礼! 着席!」) "Stand up! Bow! *Sit down!* "
chakuseki suru (~する) *vi.* sit down; have a seat: *Doozo* chakuseki *shite kudasai.* (どうぞ着席してください) Please *have a seat.* / *Chooshuu wa* chakuseki shita *mama de, dare mo tatanakatta.* (聴衆は着席したままで, だれも立たなかった) The audience remained *seated* and nobody stood up.

cha「kushoku ちゃくしょく (着色)

n. coloration; coloring: chakushoku-*garasu* (着色ガラス) *colored* glass / chakushoku-*ryoo* (着色料) a *coloring* agent / *shokuhiñ no* chakushoku-*zai* (食品の着色剤) food *coloring*.

chakushoku suru (〜する) *vt.* color; paint: *Shokuhiñ wa gaikeñ o yoku suru tame ni* chakushoku *sarete iru.* (食品は外見を良くするために着色されている) Foods *are* artificially *colored* to improve their appearance.

chaᵀkushu ちゃくしゅ (着手) *n.* start; commencement.

chakushu suru (〜する) *vi.* start; begin; set about: *Wareware wa sugu ni shigoto ni* chakushu *shita.* (われわれはすぐに仕事に着手した) We *got down* to work at once.

chaᵀkusoo ちゃくそう (着想) *n.* idea; conception.

-chañ ちゃん *suf.* (used after a given name to address children affectionately). ★ The first name is often shortened. *Sachiko>Sat*-chañ, *Hiroshi>Hiro*-chañ.

chaᵀññeru チャンネル *n.* (broadcast media) channel: chañneru *o kaeru* (チャンネルをかえる) change *channels*.

cha-ᵀno-ma ちゃのま (茶の間) *n.* living [sitting] room: cha-no-ma *de terebi o miru* (茶の間でテレビを見る) watch TV in the *living room* / *raikyaku o* cha-no-ma *ni toosu* (来客を茶の間に通す) show a visitor to the *living room*. (⇨ ima²)

cha-ᵀno-yu ちゃのゆ (茶の湯) *n.* tea ceremony. (⇨ sadoo (photo))

chaᵀñsu チャンス *n.* good chance; opportunity: ★ Used only with reference to a favorable occasion. *Ima ga nigeru* chañsu *da.* (今が逃げるチャンスだ) Now is the *chance* to escape. / *Chañsu o nogasu na.* (チャンスを逃すな) Don't miss the *chance*.

/ *Kimi no jitsuryoku o hakki suru yoi* chañsu *da.* (君の実力を発揮するよいチャンスだ) It is a *good opportunity* to show your real ability.

chaᵀñto ちゃんと *adv.* (〜 suru) (of an action) properly done; without fail; exactly: chañto *shita fukusoo* (ちゃんとした服装) *proper* dress / *Kono shorui wa* chañto *shimatte oite kudasai.* (この書類はちゃんとしまっておいてください) Please put these documents away *properly*. / *Kaze ga hairanai yoo ni doa o* chañto *shime nasai.* (風が入らないようにドアをちゃんと閉めなさい) Please shut the door *properly* to keep the wind out. / *Nimotsu wa* chañto *tsukimashita.* (荷物はちゃんと着きました) The parcel has arrived *safely*. (⇨ kichiñto)

chaᵀtsumi ちゃつみ (茶摘み) *n.* tea picking; a tea picker: chatsumi *o suru* (茶摘みをする) *pick tea*.

CHATSUMI

-chau ちゃう *suf.* ⇨ -shimau.

chaᵀwañ ちゃわん (茶碗) *n.* teacup; rice bowl.

CHAWAÑ

tea cup (left) and rice bowl (right)

che¹kku チェック *n.* check.
　chekku suru (〜する) *vt.* make sure; check: *meebo o* chekku *suru* (名簿をチェックする) *check* a name-list / *eñjiñ o* chekku *suru* (エンジンをチェックする) *check* the engine. (⇨ shiraberu)

chi¹ ち (血) *n.* **1** blood: chi *o tomeru* (血を止める) stop the *bleeding* / Chi *ga tomatta.* (血が止まった) The *bleeding* has stopped. **2** family relation: *Kare-ra wa* chi *no tsunagari ga aru.* (彼らは血のつながりがある) They are related by *blood.*
　chi mo namida mo nai (〜も涙もない) cold-blooded: *Kare wa* chi *mo namida mo nai.* (彼は血も涙もない) He is *heartless.*

chi¹² ち (地) *n.* the earth; the ground; district: *teñ to* chi (天と地) heaven and *earth* / *Kare wa* chi *ni ashi ga tsuite inai.* (彼は地に足がついていない) He does not have his feet on the *ground.*
　chi ni ochiru (〜に落ちる) be lost; be ruined: *Kare no meesee wa* chi *ni ochita.* (彼の名声は地に落ちた) He *has* now *lost* his reputation.

Chi「ba¹-keñ ちばけん (千葉県) *n.* Chiba Prefecture. Located in the southeast section of the Kanto district, facing the Pacific. Marine products and diary farming comprise the main industries. Capital city: Chiba. (⇨ map (G4))

chi「chi¹¹ ちち (父) *n.* **1** father:

──── USAGE ────
Used when an adult refers to his or her own father. The father of others is referred to as '*o-toosañ.*' Children usually address their own father as '*o-toosañ.*'

Chichi wa isha desu. (父は医者です) My *father* is a doctor. (↔ haha) ((⇨ chichi-oya; kazoku (table)))
2 originator: *Kare wa Nihoñ no kiñdai-kagaku no* chichi *desu.* (彼は日本の近代科学の父です) He is the *father* of modern science in Japan.

chi「chi¹² ちち (乳) *n.* milk: *akañboo ni* chichi *o nomaseru* (赤ん坊に乳を飲ませる) *breast-feed* a baby / *ushi no* chichi *o shiboru* (牛の乳をしぼる) *milk* a cow / *Kanojo wa* chichi *ga amari denai.* (彼女は乳があまり出ない) She doesn't produce much *milk.*

chi「chi¹³ ちち (遅々) *n.* slowing; lagging.
　chichi to suru (〜とする) (*formal*) be slow; be tardy: chichi *to shita shiñpo* (遅々とした進歩) *slow* progress / *Kooshoo wa* chichi *to shite susumanakatta.* (交渉は遅々として進まなかった) The negotiations made *little* progress. (⇨ osoi)

chi「chi¹-oya ちちおや (父親) *n.* male parent; father: *Ano ko no* chichi-oya *wa keesatsu-kañ desu.* (あの子の父親は警察官です) That boy's *father* is a policeman. ((↔ haha-oya) (⇨ chichi¹))

Chi「chu¹ukai ちちゅうかい (地中海) *n.* the Mediterranean (Sea).

chi「e ちえ (知恵) *n.* wisdom; sense; brains: chie *no aru hito* (知恵のある人) a man of *wisdom* / *Kare ni wa sore dake no* chie *ga nai.* (彼にはそれだけの知恵がない) He doesn't have enough *sense* to do it. / *Kare no* chie *wa karitakunai.* (彼の知恵は借りたくない) I don't need any *advice* from him.
　chie o shiboru (〜をしぼる) think hard: *Watashi-tachi wa miñna de* chie *o shibotta.* (私たちはみんなで知恵をしぼった) We all *racked our brains.* ((⇨ atama))

chi⌈gai ちがい (違い) *n*. difference; distinction; disparity:
Sono futatsu no chigai *ga wakaranai.* (その二つの違いがわからない) I cannot see the *difference* between the two. / *Hitsuji to yagi no* chigai *wa hakkiri shite imasu.* (羊とやぎの違いははっきりしています) The *distinction* between a sheep and a goat is clear.

-chigai ちがい (違い) *suf*. **1** mis-; error; mistake: ★ Attached to a noun or the continuative base of a verb.
keesañ-chigai (計算違い) a *mis*calculation / *kañ*-chigai (勘違い) a *mistaken* idea / *omoi*-chigai (思い違い) a *mis*apprehension / *kañgae*-chigai (考え違い) a *mis*understanding / *kiki*-chigai (聞き違い) a *mis*hearing / *yomi*-chigai (読み違い) *mis*reading
2 (with a numeral) difference: ★ Often the difference in age between siblings.
Watashi to ani wa mittsu-chigai *desu.* (私と兄は三つ違いです) My brother is three years *older* than me. / *Ip-puñ*-chigai *de deñsha ni noriokureta.* (1分違いで電車に乗り遅れた) I missed the train *by* one minute.

chi⌈gaina⌉i ちがいない must; be certain; be sure: ★ Polite equivalent is '*chigai arimaseñ*.'
Kare ga itte iru koto wa hoñtoo ni chigainai. (彼が言っていることは本当に違いない) What he says *must be* true. / *Juñko-sañ wa kyoo wa moo konai ni* chigainai. (純子さんはきょうはもう来ないにちがいない) *It is certain* that Junko will not come today. / *Kare wa seekoo suru ni* chigainai. (彼は成功するにちがいない) He *is sure* to succeed.
《⇨ tashika》

chi⌈ga·u ちがう (違う) *vi*. (chigai-; chigaw·a-; chigat-te [C])
1 be different; differ:
Kono kabañ wa watashi no to katachi ga onaji desu ga ookisa ga chigaimasu. (このかばんは私のと形が同じですが大きさが違います) This bag is the same shape as mine, but *differs* in size. / *Kuni ni yotte kotoba ya shuukañ ga* chigaimasu. (国によって言葉や習慣が違います) Language and customs *differ* from country to country. / *Chuugokugo to Nihoñgo no kañji wa yomikata ga zeñzeñ* chigau. (中国語と日本語の漢字は読み方が全然違う) The reading of Chinese characters in China and Japan *is* completely *different*. / *Mukashi wa ima to* chigatte *gasu mo deñki mo nakatta.* (昔は今と違ってガスも電気もなかった) In the old days, *unlike* the present, there used to be no gas or electricity.
2 wrong; incorrect:
Sañ-bañ no kotae ga chigatte *imasu.* (3番の答えが違っています) The answer to the third question *is wrong.* / *"Shitsuree desu ga, Tanaka-sañ desu ka?" "Iie,* chigaimasu." (「失礼ですが、田中さんですか」「いいえ、違います」) "Excuse me. Are you Mr. Tanaka?" "No, *I'm not*."

chi⌈gi⌉r·u[1] ちぎる (千切る) *vt*. (chigir·i-; chigir·a-; chigit·te [C])
tear off; tear to pieces:
Pañ o komakaku chigitte, *tori ni yatta.* (パンを細かくちぎって、鳥にやった) I *broke* the bread *into pieces* and gave it to the birds. / *Kare wa memo-yooshi o ichi-mai* chigitte, *deñwa-bañgoo o memo shita.* (彼はメモ用紙を1枚ちぎって、電話番号をメモした) He *tore* a leaf *off* the memo pad and made a note of the telephone number.

chi⌈gi⌉r·u[2] ちぎる (契る) *vt*. (chigir·i-; chigir·a-; chigit-te [C])
1 pledge; vow; promise:
Futari wa ee-eñ no ai o chigitta.

（二人は永遠の愛を契った）The two *pledged* their eternal love.
2 share a bed.

chiˈheeseñ ちへいせん（地平線）*n.* horizon: ★ The line where the sky and the land seem to meet. *Taiyoo ga chiheeseñ ni shizuñda.* （太陽が地平線にしずんだ）The sun went down below the *horizon*. 《⇨ suiheeseñ》

chiheeseñ	horizon
suiheeseñ	

chiˈhoˈo ちほう（地方）*n.* **1** district; region; area: ★ Refers to a particular region of a country. *Kesa Kañtoo-chihoo de jishiñ ga atta.* （今朝関東地方で地震があった）There was an earthquake in the Kanto *district* this morning. / *Taifuu ga Kyuushuu-chihoo nañbu o osotta.* （台風が九州地方南部を襲った）A typhoon hit the southern *part* of the Kyushu district. 《⇨ chiiki》
2 the country; the provinces: *Kare wa kinoo, chihoo kara jookyoo shita.* （彼はきのう，地方から上京した）He came up to Tokyo from *the country* yesterday. / chihoo *shusshiñ-sha* （地方出身者）a person from the *provinces*. 《⇨ inaka》

chiˈi ちい（地位）*n.* position; status; standing: chii *o eru [ushinau]* （地位を得る[失う]）obtain [lose] one's *position* / *Kare wa kaisha de juuyoo na chii ni tsuite iru.* （彼は会社で重要な地位についている）He occupies an important *position* in his company. / *Josee no shakai-teki chii wa koojoo shite iru.* （女性の社会的地位は向上している）The *status* of women in society is improving.

chiˈiki ちいき（地域）*n.* area;

region; zone: ★ '*Chiiki*' implies a more limited area than '*chihoo*.' *Hiroi* chiiki *ni watatte sakumotsu ga higai o uketa.* （広い地域にわたって作物が被害を受けた）The crops were badly damaged over a large *area*. / *Dañsui shita* chiiki *ni wa kyuusuisha ga shutsudoo shita.* （断水した地域には給水車が出動した）A water wagon was sent to the *area* where the water supply was cut off. / *Warui kaze ga kono* chiiki *ni hayatte iru.* （悪い風邪がこの地域にはやっている）Bad colds are prevalent *around* here. 《⇨ chihoo; chiku; chitai》

chiˈimu チーム *n.* team: *Uchi no yakyuu no* chiimu *wa tsuyoi.* （うちの野球のチームは強い）Our baseball *team* is strong. / *Watashi wa kare to* chiimu *o kuñda.* （私は彼とチームを組んだ）I *teamed up* with him.

chiˈisaˈ·i ちいさい（小さい）*a.* (-ku) **1** small; little: chiisai *kuruma* （小さい車）a *small* car / *Chiisai koro Hokkaidoo ni suñde imashita.* （小さいころ北海道に住んでいました）I lived in Hokkaido when I was *small*. / *Oto o* chiisa- *ku shite kudasai.* （音を小さくしてください）Please *turn down* the volume. 《↔ ookii》
2 trivial; petty: *Chiisai koto ni kuyokuyo suru no wa yame nasai.* （小さいことにくよくよするのはやめなさい）Don't worry about *trivial* matters. / *Kare wa niñgeñ ga* chiisai. （彼は人間が小さい）He is a *petty* person. 《↔ ookii》

chiisaku naru （小さくなる）**1** become small: *Kizuguchi wa dañ-dañ chiisaku natta.* （傷口はだんだん小さくなった）The wound has gradually *closed up*.
2 cower: *Erai hito bakari na no de sumi no hoo de chiisaku natte*

ita.（えらい人ばかりなので隅のほうで小さくなっていた）The others were all important people, so I was in a corner, trying to look *inconspicuous.*

chiᵣisa-na　ちいさな（小さな）*attrib.* small; little; trivial:

> **USAGE**
>
> The meaning is basically the same as '*chiisai*' but used only attributively before a noun.

chiisa-na *kaisha*（小さな会社）a *small* company / *Kare wa* chiisa-na *moñdai ni wa kodawaranai.*（彼は小さな問題にはこだわらない）He does not care about *trivial* matters. 《↔ ooki-na》《⇨ chiisai》

chiᵣizu　チーズ *n.* cheese.

chiᵣji　ちじ（知事）*n.* (prefectural) governor:
to-chiji（都知事）the *Governor* of Tokyo / *keñ[fu]*-chiji（県[府]知事）the *governor* of a prefecture.

chiᵣjimar·u　ちぢまる（縮まる）*vi.* (-mar·i-; -mar·a-; -mat·te C) get shorter or smaller:
Koñdo no taikai de kiroku ga ni-byoo chijimatta.（今度の大会で記録が 2 秒縮まった）In this meet, two seconds *were clipped off* the record. / *Ikura gañbatte mo toppu to no sa wa* chijimaranai.（いくらがんばってもトップとの差は縮まらない）No matter how hard I try, I *can't catch up with* the person at the top. / *Shiñkañseñ no okage de Tookyoo-Oosaka-kañ ga sañ-jikañ ni* chijimatta.（新幹線のおかげで東京大阪間が 3 時間に縮まった）Thanks to the Shinkansen, travel time by train between Tokyo and Osaka *has been shortened* to three hours. 《⇨ chijimeru》

chiᵣjime·ru　ちぢめる（縮める）*vt.* (-me·te V) **1** shorten; reduce:
sukaato no take o chijimeru（スカートの丈を縮める）*shorten* the length

of a skirt / *buñshoo o* chijimeru （文章を縮める）*condense* a written passage / *Kare wa hyaku-meetoru kyoosoo de sekai kiroku o ree-teñ-ni-byoo* chijimeta.（彼は 100 メートル競走で世界記録を 0.2 秒縮めた）He *bettered* the world record by 0.2 seconds in the hundred-meters. 《⇨ chijimaru》
2 lower or move (one's head or body suddenly):
Booru ga toñde kita no de omowazu kubi o chijimeta.（ボールが飛んできたので思わず首を縮めた）A ball came flying, so I instinctively *ducked* my head. 《⇨ chijimaru》

chiᵣjim·u　ちぢむ（縮む）*vi.* (chijim·i-; chijim·a-; chijiñ-de C) shrink; contract:
Kono shatsu wa aratte mo chijimanai.（このシャツは洗っても縮まない）This shirt *doesn't shrink* in the wash. / *Gomu wa nobitari* chijiñdari *suru.*（ゴムは伸びたり縮んだりする）Rubber stretches and *contracts.* / *Amari no osoroshisa ni jumyoo ga* chijiñda.（あまりの恐ろしさに寿命が縮んだ）The fearful experience *took a few years off* my life.

chiᵣjiñ　ちじん（知人）*n.* acquaintance; friend:
Kare wa watashi no chijiñ *desu.* （彼は私の知人です）He is one of my *acquaintances.* / *Kanojo wa* chijiñ *no kekkoñ-shiki ni shusseki shita.* （彼女は知人の結婚式に出席した）She attended the wedding of her *friend.*

chiᵣjire·ru　ちぢれる（縮れる）*vi.* (chijire-te V) (of hair) wave; curl; frizz:
Ano ko no kami wa shizeñ ni chijirete iru.（あの子の髪は自然に縮れている）Her hair *curls* naturally.

chiᵣjoo　ちじょう（地上）*n.* the ground; the land surface:
chijoo *juuni-kai no biru*（地上 12 階のビル）a building with twelve

stories above *the ground* / Chijoo *ni wa mada yuki ga ikura-ka nokotte iru.* (地上にはまだ雪がいくらか残っている) There is still some snow remaining on *the ground.* / *Kikyuu wa* chijoo *kara no aizu de orite kita.* (気球は地上からの合図で下りてきた) The balloon came down on a signal from *the ground.* / *Haru ni naru to iroiro na mushi ga* chijoo *ni dete kuru.* (春になるといろいろな虫が地上に出てくる) With the coming of spring, various insects come out from *the ground.* (↔ chika)

chi「ka」 ちか (地下) *n.* underground:
Sagyooiñ wa chika *ni mogutte, koshoo-kasho o shirabeta.* (作業員は地下に潜って、故障箇所を調べた) Workers went *underground* and checked the location where the trouble had developed. / *Atarashii biru wa chijoo nana-kai, chika ni-kai desu.* (新しいビルは地上7階、地下2階です) The new building has seven stories above and two stories *below the ground.* / *Chuushajoo wa* chika *ni arimasu.* (駐車場は地下にあります) The parking space is down in the *basement.* / chika-*gai* (地下街) an *underground* shopping area / chika-*sui* (地下水) *underground* water. (↔ chijoo)
chika ni moguru (〜に潜る) hide from public view: *Hañniñ wa* chika *ni mogutta.* (犯人は地下に潜った) The criminal *went underground.*

chi「ka」doo ちかどう (地下道) *n.* underground passage.

chi「ka」goro ちかごろ (近頃) *adv.* (〜 no) lately; recently; nowadays:
Chikagoro *koosoku-dooro de no jiko ga fuete kita.* (近ごろ高速道路での事故が増えてきた) Accidents on expressways have increased re-

cently. / *Añna ni juñshiñ na hito wa* chikagoro *mezurashii.* (あんなに純真な人は近ごろ珍しい) *Nowadays* one rarely comes across such a naive person. / Chikagoro *no wakai hito wa yoku kaigai e iku.* (近ごろの若い人はよく海外へ行く) *Today's* youngsters frequently go abroad.

chi「ka」・i[1] ちかい (近い) *a.* (-ku)
1 near; close:
chikai *shoorai* (近い将来) the *near* future / *Tookyoo-eki wa koko kara* chikai. (東京駅はここから近い) Tokyo Station is *near* here. / *Uchi wa shooteñ-gai ni* chikai. (家は商店街に近い) My house is *close* to the shopping area. (↔ tooi)
2 almost; nearly:
Natsu mo owari ni chikai. (夏も終わりに近い) Summer is *almost* over. / *Sore wa fukanoo ni* chikai. (それは不可能に近い) That's *next to* impossible. / *Señsoo de hyakumañ-niñ* chikai *hito ga ie o ushinatta.* (戦争で百万人近い人が家を失った) *Nearly* one million people lost their houses in the war.

chi「kai」[2] ちかい (誓い) *n.* oath; vow; pledge:
chikai *o tateru* (誓いをたてる) swear an *oath.* (⇒ chikau)

chi「ka」ku ちかく (近く) *n.* neighborhood:
Watashi no uchi wa eki no sugu chikaku *desu.* (私の家は駅のすぐ近くです) My house is right *near* the station. / *Kuwashii koto wa o-*chikaku *no yuubiñkyoku de o-kiki kudasai.* (詳しいことはお近くの郵便局でお聞きください) For further details, please ask at your *local* post office. / *Kono* chikaku *ni wa suupaa ga takusañ arimasu.* (この近くにはスーパーがたくさんあります) There are a lot of supermarkets *around here.* (↔ tooku) (⇒ chikai)
— *adv.* **1** almost; nearly:

★ Often with a numeral.
Kare wa moo ik-kagetsu chikaku
yasuñde iru. (彼はもう1か月近く休ん
でいる) He has been absent *nearly*
a month now. / *Ressha wa oo-
yuki no tame sañ-jikan* chikaku
mo okureta. (列車は大雪のため3時
間近くも遅れた) The train was delayed *nearly* three whole hours
due to the heavy snow. / *Yuugata* chikaku *ni natte kyuu ni ame
ga furidashita.* (夕方近くになって急に
雨が降りだした) It suddenly started
raining *toward* evening.
2 (of time) soon; before long:
Ano futari wa chikaku *kekkoñ
suru soo desu.* (あの二人は近く結婚す
るそうです) I hear that those two
are going to get married *soon*. /
Kare wa chikaku *Iñdo e iku koto
ni natte iru.* (彼は近くインドへ行くこと
になっている) He is scheduled to go
to India *in the near future*.

chi「ka¬michi ちかみち (近道) *n.*
shortcut; the shortest way:
chikamichi *o iku* (近道を行く) take
a *shortcut*. 《↔ toomawari》

chi「kara¬ ちから (力) *n.* **1** power;
ability:
Kono tori wa tobu chikara *ga nai.*
(この鳥は飛ぶ力がない) This bird has
no strength to fly. / *Watashi no*
chikara *de dekiru koto wa nañ de
mo yarimasu.* (私の力でできることは何
でもやります) I will do everything in
my *power*. / *Kare wa kaisha o
kee-ee suru* chikara *ga aru.* (彼は会
社を経営する力がある) He has the
ability to run a company.
2 strength; force; might:
Kare wa sugoku chikara *ga aru.*
(彼はすごく力がある) He has great
strength. / *Kaze no* chikara *de doa
ga shimatta.* (風の力でドアが閉まった)
The *force* of the wind closed the
door.
chikara-ippai (〜いっぱい) with all
one's might: *Kare wa* chikara-

ippai *sono tsuna o hiita.* (彼は力いっ
ぱいその綱を引いた) He pulled the
rope *as hard as he could*.
chikara o ireru (〜を入れる) make
efforts: *Motto señdeñ ni* chikara
o irenakereba naranai. (もっと宣伝
に力を入れなければならない) We *have
to put more effort* into publicity.
chikara o otosu (〜を落とす) be
discouraged: *Shippai shite mo*
chikara *o otosu na.* (失敗しても力を
落とすな) Even if you fail, *don't
lose heart*.

chi「karazuyo¬·i ちからづよい (力強
い) *a.* (-ku) powerful; strong; reassuring:
chikarazuyoi *koe* (力強い声) a *powerful* voice / *Kare kara* chikarazuyoi *hagemashi o uketa.* (彼から力強
い励ましを受けた) I received *reassuring* encouragement from him. /
*Chiimu ni ichiryuu señshu ga
kuwawatte, totemo* chikarazuyoku
natta. (チームに一流選手が加わって、と
ても力強くなった) Our team has become very *powerful* since a first-
rate player joined us.

chi「katetsu ちかてつ (地下鉄) *n.*
subway; underground railway:
Shiñjuku made nara, chikatetsu
no hoo ga hayai yo. (新宿までなら、
地下鉄のほうが速いよ) If it's to Shinjuku you want to go, the *subway*
is quicker.

SIGN AT CHIKATETSU ENTRANCE IN TOKYO

chi「ka¬·u ちかう (誓う) *vt.* (chika-
i-; chikaw·a-; chikat-te Ⓒ)
swear; pledge; vow:
Shooniñ wa shiñjitsu o noberu to
chikatta. (証人は真実を述べると誓っ
た) The witness *swore* to tell the
truth. / *Kare wa kanojo o itsu-*

made mo aisuru to chikatta. (彼は彼女をいつまでも愛すると誓った) He *pledged* himself to love her forever. (⇨ chikai)

chi「kayo」r・u ちかよる (近寄る) *vi.* (-yor・i-; -yor・a-; -yot-te) C approach; get near:
Abunai tokoro ni wa chikayoranai *hoo ga ii.* (危ないところには近寄らない方がいい) You'd better *keep away* from dangerous places.

chi「kazuke」・ru ちかづける (近付ける) *vt.* (-zuke-te) V bring close; move nearer:
Kore wa moeyasui kara hi ni chikazukenai *de kudasai.* (これは燃えやすいから火に近づけないでください) This is inflammable, so *don't bring* it *close* to the fire. / *Isu o motto tsukue ni* chikazuke *nasai.* (椅子をもっと机に近づけなさい) *Move* the chair *nearer* to the desk. (⇨ chikazuku)

chi「kazu」k・u ちかづく (近付く) *vi.* (-zuk・i-; -zuk・a-; -zu・i-te) C **1** approach; come [draw] near:
Kare wa osoruosoru ori ni chikazuita. (彼は恐る恐るおりに近づいた) He fearfully *drew near* the cage. / *Taifuu ga Nihoñ ni* chikazuite iru. (台風が日本に近づいている) A typhoon *is approaching* Japan. / *Shikeñ ga* chikazuku *to toshokañ ga komi-hajimeru.* (試験が近づくと図書館が込み始める) When the exams *draw near*, the library starts to get crowded. / *Natsu-yasumi ga* chikazuite kita. (夏休みが近づいてきた) The summer vacation *is coming soon*.
2 become acquainted; approach:
Kare wa zaisañ o meate ni kanojo ni chikazuita. (彼は財産を目当てに彼女に近づいた) He *approached* her with an eye to her fortune. / *Añna otoko ni wa* chikazukanai *hoo ga ii.* (あんな男には近づかないほうがいい) You had better *keep away from* such a fellow. (⇨ chikazukeru)

chi「kee」 ちけい (地形) *n.* the lay of the land; geographical features.

chi「koku」 ちこく (遅刻) *n.* late coming; being late.
chikoku suru (～する) *vi.* be [come] late: *gakkoo ni* chikoku suru (学校に遅刻する) *be late* for school / *Kare wa mata* chikoku shita. (彼はまた遅刻した) He *came late* again. / *Watashi wa kaigi ni jup-puñ* chikoku shita. (私は会議に10分遅刻した) I *was* ten minutes *late* for the meeting. (⇨ okureru)

chi「ku」 ちく (地区) *n.* district; zone; area: ★ Refers to a section or an area with some distinctive feature.
*toshi no shoogyoo-*chiku (都市の商業地区) the business *zone* of a city / *Kare wa kono* chiku *no daihyoo desu.* (彼はこの地区の代表です) He is the representative of this *district.* / *buñkyoo-*chiku (文教地区) a school *zone.* (⇨ chiiki)

chi「ku」bi ちくび (乳首) *n.* nipple; teat. (⇨ jiñtai (illus.))

chi「kuseki」 ちくせき (蓄積) *n.* accumulation:
shihoñ [*hiroo*] *no* chikuseki (資本 [疲労]の蓄積) the *accumulation* of capital [fatigue].
chikuseki suru (～する) *vt.* accumulate; store up: *tomi o* chikuseki suru (富を蓄積する) *accumulate* a fortune.

chi「kyuu」 ちきゅう (地球) *n.* the earth; the globe:
chikyuu-*joo ni sumu seebutsu* (地球上に住む生物) living creatures on *the earth* / *Chikyuu wa taiyoo no mawari o mawaru.* (地球は太陽のまわりを回る) *The earth* goes around the sun. / *Sono hikooki wa muchakuriku de* chikyuu *o isshuu shita.* (その飛行機は無着陸で地球を一周した) The plane made a non-stop flight around the *world.*

chi⌐**mamire** ちまみれ（血塗れ）*n.*
being bloody:
Geñba ni wa chimamire *no taoru
ga nokotte ita.*（現場には血まみれのタ
オルが残っていた）There was a *blood-
stained* towel left at the scene.

chi⌐**mee** ちめい（地名）*n.* place-
name:
Kono chimee *wa chizu ni notte
inai.*（この地名は地図にのっていない）
This *place-name* is not on the
map.

chi⌐**me¹eshoo** ちめいしょう（致命
傷）*n.* fatal wound [injury];
deathblow.

-**chiñ** ちん（賃）*suf.* pay; fare;
rate; charge:
deñsha-chiñ（電車賃）a train *fare* /
funa-chiñ（船賃）boat *fare* / kari-
chiñ（借り賃）a *rent*; *hire* / tema-
chiñ（手間賃）a *payment* for some
kind of service.《⇨ -ryoo; -dai²》

chi⌐**ñbotsu** ちんぼつ（沈没）*n.*
sinking (of a ship).
chiñbotsu suru（～する）*vi.* sink;
go down: *Fune wa a' to iu ma ni*
chiñbotsu shita.（船はあっという間に
沈没した）The ship *sank* in a very
short time.《⇨ shizumu》

chi¹**ñchiñ** ちんちん *adv.* (the
sound of whistling):
Yakañ ga chiñchiñ *natte iru.*（やかん
がちんちんなっている）The kettle is
singing.

chi¹**ñgiñ** ちんぎん（賃金）*n.* wages;
pay:
yasui [*takai*] chiñgiñ *de hataraku*
（安い[高い]賃金で働く）work at low
[high] *wages* / *Chiñgiñ wa getsumatsu ni moraimasu.*（賃金は月末に
もらいます）We get our *wages* at the
end of the month.《⇨ gekkyuu;
kyuuryoo》

chi⌐**ñmoku** ちんもく（沈黙）*n.* silence; reticence:
Totsuzeñ kare ga chiñmoku *o
yabutta.*（突然彼が沈黙を破った）All
of a sudden, he broke his *silence.*

/ *Kanojo wa sono keñ ni tsuite*
chiñmoku *o mamotta.*（彼女はその件
について沈黙を守った）She kept *silent*
about that matter.
chiñmoku suru（～する）*vi.* hold
one's tongue; be silent: *Kare wa
kaigi-chuu* chiñmoku shita *mama
datta.*（彼は会議中沈黙したままだった）
He remained *silent* for the whole
meeting.《⇨ damaru》

chi¹**noo** ちのう（知能）*n.* intelligence; mental ability:
Sono ko no chinoo *wa futsuu desu.*
（その子の知能は普通です）That boy
has average *intelligence.* / chinoo-
tesuto（知能テスト）an *IQ* test /
chinoo-*shisuu*（知能指数）an *intelligence* quotient.《⇨ chisee; chi-
teki》

chi⌐**ñretsu** ちんれつ（陳列）*n.* exhibition; display.
chiñretsu suru（～する）*vt.* exhibit; display: *Sono e wa ichibañ
yoi basho ni* chiñretsu sareta.（その
絵は一番良い場所に陳列された）The
painting *was exhibited* in the best
location. / *Shiñ-seehiñ wa tsugi
no heya ni* chiñretsu shite arimasu.
（新製品は次の部屋に陳列してあります）
The new products *are on display*
in the next room.

chi⌐**ñtai-ju¹utaku** ちんたいじゅうた
く（賃貸住宅）*n.* rental house
[apartment].

chi¹**ppu¹** チップ *n.* tip; gratuity:
chippu *o hazumu*（チップをはずむ）
give a generous *tip* / *Koko de wa
booi ni* chippu o yaru *hitsuyoo wa
arimaseñ.*（ここではボーイにチップをやる
必要はありません）You don't have to
tip the bellboys and waiters here.

chi¹**ppu²** チップ *n.* chip:
poteto chippu（ポテトチップ）potato
chips [*crisps*].

chi⌐**rabar·u** ちらばる（散らばる）*vi.*
(-bar·i-; -bar·a-; -bat·te [C]) scatter; be strewn:
Zeñkoku ni chirabatte ita *doo-*

kyuusee ga Tookyoo ni atsumatta. (全国に散らばっていた同級生が東京に集まった) The ex-classmates who *had scattered* all over Japan gathered in Tokyo. / *Akikañ ga hiroba ni takusañ* chirabatte iru. (空き缶が広場にたくさん散らばっている) Many empty cans *are strewn* over the square. (⇨ chiru)

chi⌐rachira ちらちら *adv.* (~ to; ~ suru) **1** (the state of something small and light falling slowly): *Yuki ga* chirachira (to) *furi-hajimeta.* (雪がちらちら(と)降り始めた) Snow has started to fall *lightly.* / *Hanabira ga* chirachira (to) *chitte iru.* (花びらがちらちら(と)散っている) The flower petals are *fluttering* to the ground.
2 (the state of small lights twinkling): *Tooku ni machi no akari ga* chirachira (to) *kagayaite iru.* (遠くに町の明かりがちらちら(と)輝いている) The lights of the town are *twinkling* in the distance. / *Terebi no gameñ ga* chirachira *shite minikui.* (テレビの画面がちらちらして見にくい) There is a *flutter* on the TV screen and it is uncomfortable to look at.
3 (the state of seeing or hearing on and off): *Kare wa* chirachira (to) *kochira o mita.* (彼はちらちら(と)こちらを見た) He kept *glancing* in my direction. / *Kumo no aida kara choojoo ga* chirachira (to) *mieta.* (雲の間から頂上がちらちら(と)見えた) The peak of the mountain was seen *on and off* from between the clouds.

chi⌐rakar·u ちらかる (散らかる) *vi.* (-kar·i-; -kar·a-; -kat-te C) be scattered; be littered; be untidy: *Kare no heya wa* chirakatte ita. (彼の部屋は散らかっていた) His room *was a mess.* (⇨ chirakasu)

chi⌐rakas·u ちらかす (散らかす) *vt.* (-kash·i-; -kas·a-; -kash·i-te C) scatter; litter: *Gomi o* chirakasanai de *kudasai.* (ごみを散らかさないでください) *Don't litter,* please. / *Omocha o* chirakashita *mama asobi ni itte wa ikemaseñ.* (おもちゃを散らかしたまま遊びに行ってはいけません) You mustn't go out to play with your toys left *scattered* all over. (⇨ chirakaru)

chi⌐ras·u ちらす (散らす) *vt.* (chirash·i-; chiras·a-; chirash·i-te C) (*literary*) scatter: *Kaze ga niwa ichimeñ ni ko no ha o* chirashita. (風が庭一面に木の葉を散らした) The wind *scattered* leaves all over the garden. (⇨ chiru)

chi⌐ri[1] ちり (塵) *n.* dust; dirt: *Tsukue ni* chiri *ga tsumotte iru.* (机にちりが積もっている) The desk is covered with *dust.* / *Kanojo wa teeburu no ue no* chiri *o haratta.* (彼女はテーブルの上のちりを払った) She brushed away the *dust* on the table. / *Chiri mo tsumoreba yama to naru.* (*saying*) (ちりも積もれば山となる) Many a little makes a mickle. (⇨ gomi; hokori[2])

chi⌐ri[2] ちり (地理) *n.* **1** geography. **2** geography of a neighborhood: *Kare wa kono heñ no* chiri *ni kuwashii.* (彼はこの辺の地理にくわしい) He is familiar with this *neighborhood.*

chi⌐rigami ちりがみ (ちり紙) *n.* tissue; toilet paper (in separate sheets).

chi⌐rigami-ko⌐okañ ちりがみこうかん (ちり紙交換) *n.* an exchange of old newspapers and magazines for tissue or toilet rolls: *Furu-shiñbuñ o* chirigami-kookañ *ni dashita.* (古新聞をちり紙交換に出した) I handed old newspapers to the *collector* in exchange for toilet paper. (⇨ photo (next page))

CHIRIGAMI-KOOKAN TRUCK

chiˈrijiri ちりぢり（散り散り） *n.* scattering; dispersion:
Miñna wa chirijiri *ni uchi e kaetta.* （みんなは散り散りに家へ帰った）Everyone returned home *separately.* / *Ikka wa sono jiko de* chirijiri ni *natta.* （一家はその事故で散り散りになった）The family *was broken up* by the accident. / *Kodomo-tachi wa itazura ga mitsukatte* chirijiri ni *nigeta.* （子どもたちはいたずらが見つかってちりぢりに逃げた）Having been caught in the act of mischief, the children ran away *in all directions.*

chiˈr·u ちる（散る）*vi.* (chir·i-; chir·a-; chit-te Ⓒ) **1** fall:
Ame de sakura no hana ga sukkari chitte *shimatta.* （雨で桜の花がすっかり散ってしまった）The cherry blossoms have all *fallen* in the rain. 《⇨ chirasu》
2 scatter; disperse:
Kooeñ ni kamikuzu ga chitte iru. （公園に紙くずが散っている）*There is* paper *all over* the park. / *Kumo ga* chitte, *taiyoo ga arawareta.* （雲が散って、太陽が現れた）The clouds *dispersed* and the sun appeared. / *Guñshuu wa patokaa ga kuru to satto* chitta. （群衆はパトカーが来るとさっと散った）The crowd soon *scattered* when the police car came. 《⇨ chirasu》
3 (of ink) spread; run:
Kono kami wa iñku ga chitte, *kaki-nikui.* （この紙はインクが散って、書きにくい）The ink *runs* on this paper

and it is difficult to write.

chiˈryoo ちりょう（治療）*n.* medical treatment:
Kare wa shiñzoobyoo no chiryoo *o ukete iru.* （彼は心臓病の治療を受けている）He *is being treated* for heart disease. / *Kare wa ikaiyoo no* chiryoo *no tame nyuuiñ shite imasu.* （彼は胃潰ようの治療のため入院しています）He is in the hospital for *treatment* of his stomach ulcer.
chiryoo suru （～する）*vt.* treat; cure: *Watashi wa me o* chiryoo *shite moratta.* （私は眼を治療してもらった）I *had* my eyes *treated.*

chiˈsee ちせい（知性）*n.* intellect; intelligence:
Kare wa chisee *ni kakete iru.* （彼は知性に欠けている）He lacks *intelligence.* / *Kanojo wa* chisee-teki *na josee da.* （彼女は知性的な女性だ）She is an *intelligent* woman. 《⇨ chiteki》

chiˈshiki ちしき（知識）*n.* knowledge; information; learning:
chishiki *o fuyasu* （知識をふやす）enrich one's *knowledge* / chishiki *o mi ni tsukeru* （知識を身につける）acquire *knowledge* / chishiki *ga kakete iru* （知識が欠けている）lack *knowledge [information]* / *Kare wa tashoo keezaigaku no* chishiki *ga aru.* （彼は多少経済学の知識がある）He has some *knowledge* of economics. / chishiki-jiñ （知識人）an *intellectual.*

chiˈsso ちっそ（窒素）*n.* nitrogen: chisso-sañkabutsu （窒素酸化物）*nitrogen* oxide.

chiˈssoku ちっそく（窒息）*n.* suffocation; choking.
chissoku suru （～する）*vi.* be suffocated; be choked: *Kare wa kemuri ni makarete,* chissoku suru *tokoro datta.* （彼は煙りにまかれて、窒息するところだった）He *was* almost *choked* when enveloped by the smoke.

chiˈtai ちたい (地帯) *n.* zone; area; region; belt:
anzen-chitai (安全地帯) a safety *zone* / *hibusoo*-chitai (非武装地帯) a demilitarized *zone* / *kazan*-chitai (火山地帯) a volcanic *belt* / *kokusoo*-chitai (穀倉地帯) a grain-producing *region* / *koogyoo*-chitai (工業地帯) an industrial *area*. 《⇨ chiiki; chiku》

chiˈteki ちてき (知的) *a.n.* (~ na, ni) intellectual; intelligent: chiteki *na hito* (知的な人) an *intellectual* person / *Sono megane o kakeru to* chiteki *ni miemasu.* (その眼鏡をかけると知的にみえます) You look *intelligent* when you put on those glasses. / chiteki-*suijun* (知的水準) *intellectual* level. 《⇨ chisee; chinoo》

chiˈtsuˈjo ちつじょ (秩序) *n.* order; system:
shakai no chitsujo *o midasu* (社会の秩序を乱す) disturb social [public] *order* / *Shuudan de seekatsu suru toki wa* chitsujo *o mamoru koto ga taisetsu desu.* (集団で生活するときは秩序を守ることが大切です) It is important to follow the *system* when you live in a group.

chiˈttoˈ-mo ちっとも *adv.* (with a negative) (not) a bit; (not) at all:
Kono bangumi wa chitto-mo *omoshirokunai.* (この番組はちっともおもしろくない) This program is *not at all* interesting. / *Nijup-pun mo matte iru no ni basu ga* chitto-mo *konai.* (20分も待っているのにバスがちっとも来ない) I have been waiting for twenty minutes, but the bus hasn't come *at all*. / "*Tsukaremashita ka?*" "*Iie,* chitto-mo." (「疲れましたか」「いいえ、ちっとも」) "Are you tired?" "No, *not a bit*." 《⇨ sukoshi mo》

chiˈzu ちず (地図) *n.* map; atlas; chart:
Eki made no chizu *o kaite kudasai.* (駅までの地図をかいてください) Will you please draw me a *map* to the station? / *Watashi wa sono shima o* chizu *de sagashita.* (私はその島を地図で探した) I searched for the island on the *map*. / *goman-bun no ichi no* chizu (五万分の一の地図) a *map* on a scale of 1 to 50,000.

-cho ちょ (著) *suf.* written by:
Kawabata Yasunari-cho "*Yukiguni*" (川端康成著『雪国』) "Snow Country" *written by* Yasunari Kawabata.

choˈchiku ちょちく (貯蓄) *n.* savings. ★ Used especially with reference to money set aside for unforeseen or future circumstances.
chochiku suru (~する) *vi.* save up: *Kare wa roogo ni sonaete* chochiku *shite iru.* (彼は老後に備えて貯蓄している) He *is saving up* for his old age. 《⇨ chokin; yokin》

choˈkin ちょきん (貯金) *n.* savings; deposit:
chokin *o orosu* (貯金をおろす) draw one's *savings* / *Watashi wa yuubinkyoku ni juuman-en* chokin *ga aru.* (私は郵便局に10万円貯金がある) I have 100,000 yen *deposited* in the post office. / chokin-tsuuchoo (貯金通帳) a *passbook*; a *bankbook*.
chokin suru (~する) *vi., vt.* save; deposit: *Watashi wa maitsuki sanman-en zutsu* chokin *shite imasu.* (私は毎月3万円ずつ貯金しています) I *save* 30,000 yen every month. / *Kare wa shuunyuu no ichibu o yuubinkyoku ni* chokin *shita.* (彼は収入の一部を郵便局に貯金した) He *deposited* part of his income in the post office. 《⇨ yokin; chochiku》

choˈkkaku ちょっかく (直角) *n.* right angle:
chokkaku *ni majiwaru* (直角に交わる) cross at *right angles*.

cho⌐kkee ちょっけい（直径）*n.* diameter:
Kono ana wa chokkee *ga ni-mee-toru aru.*（この穴は直径が 2 メートルある）This hole is two meters in *diameter.*

cho⌐kki チョッキ *n.* vest; waistcoat.

cho⌐kkoo ちょっこう（直行）*n.* going straight [direct].
chokkoo suru（〜する）*vi.* go straight [direct]: *Watashi wa kaijoo e* chokkoo *shimasu.*（私は会場へ直行します）I'll *go direct* to the meeting place.

cho⌐kore⌐eto チョコレート *n.* chocolate.

cho⌐kumeñ ちょくめん（直面）*n.* confrontation; facing.
chokumeñ suru（〜する）*vi.* be faced; be confronted: *Watashi-tachi wa muzukashii moñdai ni* chokumeñ *shite iru.*（私たちは難しい問題に直面している）We *are confronted* with a difficult problem. / *Kare wa kiki ni* chokumeñ *shite mo reesee datta.*（彼は危機に直面しても冷静だった）He remained calm even *in the face of* the crisis.

cho⌐kuseñ ちょくせん（直線）*n.* straight line:
chokuseñ *o hiku*（直線を引く）draw a *straight line* / *Eki made no* chokuseñ *kyori wa ni-kiro desu.*（駅までの直線距離は 2 キロです）It is two kilometers to the station *as the crow flies.*（↔ kyokuseñ）

cho⌐kusetsu ちょくせつ（直接）*adv.*（〜 no）directly; immediately:
Kare to chokusetsu *kooshoo shite mimasu.*（彼と直接交渉してみます）I will try to negotiate *directly* with him. / *Suhada no ue ni* chokusetsu *shatsu o kita.*（素肌の上に直接シャツを着た）I wore a shirt *next to* my skin. / *Norikaenai de* chokusetsu *soko e ikemasu.*（乗り換えない

で直接そこへ行けます）You can go *straight* there without transferring. / *Hooseki ni* chokusetsu *te o furenai de kudasai.*（宝石に直接手を触れないでください）Do not touch the jewelry *directly* with your hands. / *Jiko no* chokusetsu *no geñiñ wa uñteñshu no fuchuui datta.*（事故の直接の原因は運転手の不注意だった）The *direct* cause of the accident was the driver's carelessness.

cho⌐kusetsu-teki ちょくせつてき（直接的）*a.n.*（〜 na, ni）direct; immediate:
Kare ga kaisha o yameru chokusetsu-teki *na geñiñ wa jooshi to no fuwa desu.*（彼が会社をやめる直接的な原因は上司との不和です）The *immediate* cause of his quitting the company is the trouble with his superior.

cho⌐o[1] ちょう（腸）*n.* intestines; bowels:
Choo no guai ga warui.（腸の具合が悪い）I have an *intestinal* disorder.

cho⌐o[2] ちょう（兆）*n.* one trillion (U.S.); one billion (Brit.).
《⇒ suu[2] (table)》

cho⌐o[3] ちょう（蝶）*n.* butterfly.

choo[4] ちょう（庁）*n.* agency; government office. 《⇒ shoo[1] (table)》 《⇒ table (next page)》

cho⌐o- ちょう（超）*pref.* super-; ultra-:
choo-ichiryuu *no gakusha*（超一流の学者）a scholar of *the very first rank* / choo-koosoobiru（超高層ビル）a *skyscraper* / choo-mañiñ *no deñsha*（超満員の電車）an *overcrowded* train.

-cho⌐o[1] ちょう（町）*suf.* town; block; street: ★ An administrative division of a city or metropolitan area.
*Yuuraku-*choo（有楽町）Yurakucho (a district in Tokyo). 《⇒ -machi; juusho》

-cho⌐o[2] ちょう（長）*suf.* head;

boss; chief; leader:
bu-choo (部長) the *head* of a division / *ka*-choo (課長) the *chief* of a section / *kakari*-choo (係長) a *chief* clerk / eki-choo (駅長) a *stationmaster* / iiñ-choo (委員長) a *chairman* / *heñshuu*-choo (編集長) the *chief* editor / *toshokañ*-choo (図書館長) the *chief* librarian.

cho⌐obo ちょうぼ (帳簿) *n.* account book:
choobo *o tsukeru* [*shimeru*] (帳簿をつける[締める]) keep [close] the *accounts*.

cho⌐ochi⌐ñ ちょうちん (提灯) *n.* (paper) lantern.

CHOOCHIÑ
At Hie Jinja (left) and '*yakitoriya*' (right)

JAPANESE GOVERNMENT AGENCIES

Booee-choo (防衛庁) Defense Agency
Booeeshisetsu-choo (防衛施設庁) Defense Facilities Administration Agency
Buñka-choo (文化庁) Agency for Cultural Affairs
Chuushoo-kigyoo-choo (中小企業庁) Small and Medium Enterprise Agency
Hokkaidoo kaihatsu-choo (北海道開発庁) Hokkaido Development Agency
Kagaku-gijutsu-choo (科学技術庁) Science and Technology Agency
Kaijoohoañ-choo (海上保安庁) Maritime Safety Agency
Kainañshiñpañ-choo (海難審判庁) Marine Accidents Inquiry Agency
Kañkyoo-choo (環境庁) Environment Agency
Keesatsu-choo (警察庁) National Police Agency
Keñsatsu-choo (検察庁) Public Prosecutor's Office
Keezaikikaku-choo (経済企画庁) Economic Planning Agency
Kishoo-choo (気象庁) Meteorological Agency
Kokudo-choo (国土庁) National Land Agency
Kokuzee-choo (国税庁) National Tax Administration Agency
Kooañchoosa-choo (公安調査庁) Public Security Investigation Agency
Kunai-choo (宮内庁) Imperial Household Agency
Okinawa kaihatsu-choo (沖縄開発庁) Okinawa Development Agency
Riñya-choo (林野庁) Forestry Agency
Shakaihokeñ-choo (社会保険庁) Social Insurance Agency
Shigeñ-enerugii-choo (資源エネルギー庁) Agency of Natural Resources and Energy
Shokuryoo-choo (食糧庁) Food Agency
Shooboo-choo (消防庁) Fire Defense Agency
Soomu-choo (総務庁) Management and Coordination Agency
Suisañ-choo (水産庁) Fisheries Agency
Tokkyo-choo (特許庁) Patent Office

cho¹ocho(o) ちょうちょ(う)(蝶々)
n. = choo³.

cho「od¹ai ちょうだい(頂戴) please;
please do [give] ...:

> **USAGE**
>
> Used at the end of a sentence
> and follows a noun or the *te-*
> form of a verb. Informal equiv-
> alent of '*kudasai.*' Used mainly
> by children and women, and
> by men to their inferiors.

Kore o choodai. (これをちょうだい)
Please give this to me. / *Kono te-*
gami o kare ni watashite choodai.
(この手紙を彼に渡してちょうだい) *Please*
hand over this letter to him.

cho「odai s·uru ちょうだいする(頂
戴する) *vt.* (sh·i·; sh·i-; sh·i-te 1)
1 (*humble*) receive; get:
Koko ni iñkañ o choodai shitai *no*
desu ga. (ここに印鑑をちょうだいしたい
のですが) May I *have* your seal
impression here?
2 (*humble*) eat; drink:
"*Doozo go-eñryo naku meshi-*
agatte kudasai." "*Moo juubuñ*
choodai shimashita." (「どうぞ、ご遠
慮なく召し上がってください」「もう十分
ちょうだいしました」) "Help yourself,
please." "I *have had* enough,
thank you." (⇨ itadaku)

cho「odo ちょうど(丁度) *adv.*
just; exactly:
Ima choodo *shichi-ji desu.* (今ちょ
うど7時です) It is *exactly* seven
o'clock. / *Kore kara* choodo *deka-*
keru tokoro desu. (これからちょうど出
かけるところです) We are *just* going
out. / Choodo *shigoto ga owatta*
tokoro e tomodachi kara deñwa
ga kita. (ちょうど仕事が終わったところ
へ友だちから電話がきた) *Just* when I
had finished my work, I got a
call from a friend.

cho「ofuku ちょうふく(重複) *n.*
overlap; duplication: repetition:
choofuku *o sakeru* (重複を避ける)

avoid *duplication* / *Watashi wa*
koomoku no choofuku *o ikutsu-ka*
mitsuketa. (私は項目の重複をいくつか
見つけた) I found several *duplica-*
tions in the list of items.

choofuku suru (〜する) *vi.* repeat; overlap: *Meebo ni namae*
ga choofuku *shite iru.* (名簿に名前
が重複している) The same names
are repeated in the list. / *Kare-ra*
no hanashi wa bubuñ-teki ni choofuku *shite iru.* (彼らの話は部分的に重
複している) Their stories partly
agree.

cho¹ohoo ちょうほう(重宝) *a.n.*
(〜 na) useful; handy; helpful:
Kono naifu wa choohoo *da.* (このナ
イフは重宝だ) This knife is *useful.* /
Kare wa miñna ni choohoo-*gara-*
rete iru. (彼はみんなに重宝がられている)
He is considered by all to be a
helpful person. (⇨ beñri)
choohoo suru (〜する) *vt.* find
something handy [useful]: *Kono*
kañkiri wa choohoo *shite imasu.*
(このカン切りは重宝しています) I find
this can opener *handy.*

cho「ohookee ちょうほうけい(長方
形) *n.* rectangle.

cho「oiñ ちょういん(調印) *n.* signing; signature:
heewa-jooyaku no chooiñ (平和条
約の調印) the *signing* of a peace
treaty. (⇨ saiñ)
...ni chooiñ suru (...に〜する) *vi.*
sign (a treaty, contract, etc.):
Ryookoku no daihyoo wa sono joo-
yaku ni chooiñ *shita.* (両国の代表は
その条約に調印した) The representatives of the two nations *put their*
signatures to that treaty.

cho¹ojo ちょうじょ(長女) *n.* eldest
[oldest] daughter:

> **USAGE**
>
> The oldest daughter of the lis-
> tener is called '*ichibañ ue no o-*
> *joosañ*' or '*go-choojo.*'

Choojo *wa biyooshi desu.* (長女は美容師です) My *eldest daughter* is a beautician. / *Watashi wa* choojo *desu.* (私は長女です) I am the *oldest daughter*. 《↔ choonañ》《⇒ kyoodai (table)》

cho⌈ojo⌉o ちょうじょう（頂上）*n.* top; summit; peak: *Watashi-tachi wa yama no* choojoo *made nobotta.* (私たちは山の頂上まで登った) We climbed up to the *top* of the mountain.

cho⌈oka ちょうか（超過）*n.* excess; surplus: *yunyuu [shiharai] (no)* chooka (輸入[支払い](の)超過) an *excess* of imports [payment] / chooka-*kiñmu* (超過勤務) *overtime* work.
chooka suru (〜する) *vt.* exceed; be more than: *Kare wa seegeñsokudo o juk-kiro* chooka *shita.* (彼は制限速度を 10 キロ超過した) He *exceeded* the speed limit by ten kilometers per hour. / *Yosañ o* chooka *shite shimatta.* (予算を超過してしまった) We *have gone over* our budget. 《⇒ koeru²》

cho⌈okañ¹ ちょうかん（朝刊）*n.* morning paper; the morning edition of a paper. 《↔ yuukañ》《⇒ shiñbuñ》

cho⌈okañ² ちょうかん（長官）*n.* the director [head] of a (government) office.

cho⌈oki ちょうき（長期）*n.* a long (period of) time: Chooki *no taizai de shuppi ga kasañda.* (長期の滞在で出費がかさんだ) The *long* stay pushed the expenses up. / *Sono kooshoo wa* chooki *ni watatta.* (その交渉は長期にわたった) The negotiations extended over a *long period of time.* / *Teñki no* chooki *yohoo wa ate ni naranai.* (天気の長期予報はあてにならない) The *long-range* weather forecast is unreliable. 《↔ tañki¹》

cho⌈okoku ちょうこく（彫刻）*n.*
sculpture; carving: *Watashi wa Iñdo no* chookoku *o hitotsu katta.* (私はインドの彫刻を一つ買った) I bought an Indian *carving.*
chookoku suru (〜する) *vt.* sculpt; carve: *Watashi wa ita ni hana no moyoo o* chookoku *shita.* (私は板に花の模様を彫刻した) I *carved* flower patterns on a board.

cho⌈oku チョーク *n.* chalk: chooku *ip-poñ* (チョーク１本) a piece of *chalk.*

cho⌈ome ちょうめ（丁目）*n.* chome: ★ A section of a city, larger than '*bañchi.*' *Giñza yoñ*-choome (銀座４丁目) Ginza 4-chome. 《⇒ bañchi; juusho》

cho⌈ome⌉ñ ちょうめん（帳面）*n.* notebook; account book: choomeñ *o tsukeru* (帳面をつける) keep an *account book.* 《⇒ choobo; nooto》

cho⌈omi⌉ryoo ちょうみりょう（調味料）*n.* seasoning; flavoring: *Moo sukoshi* choomiryoo *o kuwaereba aji ga yoku naru.* (もう少し調味料を加えれば味が良くなる) If you add a little more *seasoning*, the taste will improve.

cho⌈ona⌉ñ ちょうなん（長男）*n.* eldest [oldest] son:

> **USAGE**
> When referring to the oldest son of the listener, unlike '*choojo,*' only '*go-choonañ*' is used.

Choonañ *wa daigaku ichi-neñ desu.* (長男は大学一年です) My *eldest son* is a college freshman. / *Boku wa* choonañ *desu.* (僕は長男です) I am the *oldest son*. 《↔ choojo》《⇒ kyoodai (table)》

cho⌈ori⌉shi ちょうりし（調理師）*n.* qualified cook.

cho⌐osa ちょうさ (調査) *n*. investigation; survey; research:
Choosa *no kekka wa matomattara, happyoo shimasu.* (調査の結果はまとまったら, 発表します) We will publish the results of the *research* when it is completed. / *Kaji no geñiñ wa* choosa-chuu *desu.* (火事の原因は調査中です) The cause of the fire is *under investigation.*
choosa suru (～する) *vt*. investigate; make a survey: *Sono moñdai ni tsuite wa yoroñ o* choosa suru *hitsuyoo ga arimasu.* (その問題については世論を調査する必要があります) It is necessary to *make a survey* of public opinion on that matter.

cho⌐osa⌐dañ ちょうさだん (調査団) *n*. survey group; investigating commission:
choosadañ *o soshiki suru* (調査団を組織する) organize a *survey group* / choosadañ *o mookeru* (調査団を設ける) establish an *investigatory commission.*

cho⌐osee ちょうせい (調整) *n*. adjustment; regulation:
Ikeñ no choosee *ga hitsuyoo da.* (意見の調整が必要だ) An *adjustment* of opinions must be made. / *eñjiñ no* choosee (エンジンの調整) an engine *tune-up.*
choosee suru (～する) *vt*. adjust; regulate: *Bureeki o* choosee *shite moratta.* (ブレーキを調整してもらった) I *had* the breaks *adjusted.* / *Kono kikai wa kono botañ de* choosee suru *yoo ni natte imasu.* (この機械はこのボタンで調整するようになっています) This machine *is controlled* by this button.

cho⌐oseñ ちょうせん (挑戦) *n*. challenge; attempt:
Watashi wa tenisu no shiai de kare no chooseñ *ni oojita.* (私はテニスの試合で彼の挑戦に応じた) I accepted his *challenge* to a game of ten-

nis. / chooseñ-sha (挑戦者) a *challenger.*
chooseñ suru (～する) *vi*. challenge; attempt; try: *Ano yama ni moo ichido* chooseñ *shite mitai.* (あの山にもう一度挑戦してみたい) I'd like to *have one more go* at climbing that mountain. / *Kare wa hyaku-meetoru kyoosoo de sekai kiroku ni* chooseñ shita. (彼は100メートル競争で世界記録に挑戦した) He *made an attempt* on the world record for the 100-meters.

Cho⌐oseñ ちょうせん (朝鮮) *n*. the historical Korea:
Chooseñ-*hañtoo wa kita to minami ni nibuñ sarete iru.* (朝鮮半島は北と南に二分されている) The *Korean* Peninsula is divided into two parts, north and south.
《⇒ Kañkoku; Kita-chooseñ》

cho⌐osetsu ちょうせつ (調節) *n*. control; adjustment; regulation.
choosetsu suru (～する) *vt*. control; adjust; regulate:
shitsunai no oñdo o choosetsu suru (室内の温度を調節する) *regulate* the room temperature.

cho⌐oshi ちょうし (調子) *n*.
1 condition:
Kono kuruma wa chooshi *ga yoi.* (この車は調子が良い) This car is in good *condition.* / *Kyoo wa karada no* chooshi ga okashii. (きょうは体の調子がおかしい) I *don't feel well* today. / *Kono bideo wa* chooshi ga warui. (このビデオは調子が悪い) This video *does not work well.*
2 way; manner:
Sono chooshi *de yari nasai.* (その調子でやりなさい) Keep trying in that *way.* / *Kono* chooshi *de wa ichineñ kakaru.* (この調子では一年かかる) At this *rate*, it will take a year.
3 tune; tone:
Kono gitaa wa chooshi *ga atte [hazurete] iru.* (このギターは調子が合って[はずれて]いる) This guitar is in

[out of] *tune*. / *Kare wa shizuka na* choosh *de hanashita.* (彼は静かな調子で話した) He spoke in a quiet *tone*.

chooshi ga deru (～が出る) get into one's stride: *Dandan* chooshi ga dete kita. (だんだん調子が出てきた) I gradually *got into the swing of things*.

chooshi ni noru (～に乗る) be carried away; be elated: *Kare wa sugu* chooshi ni noru. (彼はすぐ調子に乗る) He is apt to *let himself loose*.

chooshi o awaseru (～を合わせる) adapt oneself; humor: *Watashi wa kare ni umaku* chooshi o awaseta. (私は彼にうまく調子を合わせた) I skillfully got on the right side of him by *humoring* him.

cho¹osho ちょうしょ (長所) *n.* strong [good] point; merit; advantage: choosho *o ikaseru shigoto* (長所を生かせる仕事) a job in which one can *make full use* of one's strong points. (↔ tañsho)

cho⌐oshoku ちょうしょく (朝食) *n.* breakfast: chooshoku *o taberu* [*toru*] (朝食を食べる[とる]) have *breakfast* / Chooshoku *ni toosuto o tabeta.* (朝食にトーストを食べた) I had toast for *breakfast*. (⇒ asameshi; asagohañ)

cho⌐oshuu ちょうしゅう (聴衆) *n.* audience; attendance.

cho¹oteñ ちょうてん (頂点) *n.* peak; top; climax: chooteñ *ni tassuru* (頂点に達する) reach the *peak*.

cho⌐owa ちょうわ (調和) *n.* harmony: choowa *o tamotsu* [*midasu*] (調和を保つ[乱す]) maintain [spoil] the *harmony* / Heya no iro wa choowa *ga torete iru.* (部屋の色は調和がとれている) The colors of the room are in *harmony*.

choowa suru (～する) *vi.* harmonize; match: *Kono iro wa sono iro to yoku* choowa suru *deshoo.* (この色はその色とよく調和するでしょう) This color should *harmonize* well with that color.

cho¹sha ちょしゃ (著者) *n.* writer of a book; author.

cho¹sho ちょしょ (著書) *n.* book written by the author; work: *Kore ga kare no saisho no* chosho *desu.* (これが彼の最初の著書です) This is his first *book*.

cho⌐su¹ichi ちょすいち (貯水池) *n.* reservoir.

cho¹tto ちょっと *adv.* **1** (of degree, quality, quantity, etc.) just a little; slightly: *Kyoo wa* chotto *atsui.* (きょうはちょっと暑い) It is *slightly* hot today. / *Moo* chotto *gañbareba, seeseki wa agarimasu.* (もうちょっとがんばれば, 成績は上がります) Try *just a little* harder, and your grades will go up. / *Satoo o moo* chotto *irete kudasai.* (砂糖をもうちょっと入れてください) Please add *a little more* sugar.

2 (of time) just a minute; for a moment: Chotto *o-machi kudasai.* (ちょっとお待ちください) Please wait *a moment*. / Chotto *yotte ikimaseñ ka?* (ちょっと寄って行きませんか) Won't you drop in *for a moment*?

3 rather; pretty: *Sore wa* chotto *omoshiro-soo desu ne.* (それはちょっとおもしろそうですね) That sounds *rather* interesting.

4 (with a negative) just; easily: *Kare ni doko de atta ka* chotto *omoidasenai.* (彼にどこで会ったかちょっと思い出せない) I *just* cannot remember where I met him. / *Sore wa dare de mo* chotto *dekimaseñ.* (それはだれでもちょっとできません) Nobody can do that *easily*. / "*Koñ-bañ ip-pai doo desu ka?*" "*Kyoo*

wa chotto..." (「今晩一杯どうですか」「きょうはちょっと…」) "How about having a drink this evening?" "Sorry, but I *just* cannot."
★ An expression of refusal.

chotto shita (〜した) quite; slight; pretty; fairly: *Gookee suru to* chotto shita *kiñgaku ni narimasu*. (合計するとちょっとした金額になります) When added up, the total comes to *quite* a bit of money. / *Ano hito wa sono buñya de wa* chotto shita *yuumeejiñ desu*. (あの人はその分野ではちょっとした有名人です) He is *quite* a famous person in that field / *Ano hito wa* chotto shita *koto de sugu okoru*. (あの人はちょっとしたことですぐ怒る) He easily gets angry at the *slightest* thing.

cho⌐zoo ちょぞう (貯蔵) *n.* storage; preservation; stock.

chozoo suru (〜する) *vt.* store; preserve: *Jagaimo wa chika ni* chozoo *sarete imasu*. (じゃがいもは地下に貯蔵されています) The potatoes *are stored* in the cellar.

chu⌐u¹ ちゅう (中) *n.* middle; medium; average: *Kare no seeseki wa* chuu *no joo desu*. (彼の成績は中の上です) His school record is slightly above *average*. / *Kono iremono no* chuu *no saizu wa arimasu ka?* (この入れ物の中のサイズはありますか) Do you have a *medium-size* container of this type?

size	degree
dai (large)	joo (good)
chuu (medium)	chuu (fair)
shoo (small)	ge (poor)

chu⌐u² ちゅう (注) *n.* note; annotation: chuu o ⌐tsukeru (注をつける) *annotate*.

-chuu ちゅう (中) *suf.* **1** (used to express time) in; during; within; through; throughout: *Gozeñ-*chuu *wa isogashikatta*. (午前中は忙しかった) I was busy *all morning*. / *Koñshuu-*chuu *ni reñraku itashimasu*. (今週中に連絡いたします) I will get in touch with you *during* the week.

USAGE

'-*chuu*' refers to a length of time, and '-*chuu ni*' to an occurrence within a length of time.

2 (used to express a continuing state, condition or situation) under; in; during: *Sono dooro wa ima kooji-*chuu *desu*. (その道路は今工事中です) The road is now *under* construction. / *Watashi no rusu-*chuu *ni dare-ka kimashita ka?* (私の留守中にだれか来ましたか) Did anyone come *while* I was out? / *Yamada wa* gaishutsu-chuu *desu*. (山田は外出中です) Yamada *is out* now. / *Deñwa wa* hanashi-chuu *desu*. (電話は話し中です) The line *is busy*.

3 out of (the stated number): *Juuniñ-*chuu *hachi-niñ ga sono añ ni sañsee shita*. (10人中8人がその案に賛成した) Eight *out of* ten were in favor of the proposal.

Chu⌐u-Bee ちゅうべい (中米) *n.* Central America. (⇨ Hoku-Bee; Nañ-Bee)

Chu⌐ubu ちゅうぶ (中部) *n.* Chubu, the central district in Honshu, comprising Shizuoka, Aichi, Gifu, Nagano, Yamanashi, Niigata, Toyama, Ishikawa and Fukui prefectures. (⇨ map (inside back cover))

chu⌐uburu ちゅうぶる (中古) *n.* used [secondhand] article: chuuburu *no taipuraitaa [jiteñsha]* (中古のタイプライター[自転車]) a *used* typewriter [bicycle]. (⇨ chuuko)

chu¹ucho ちゅうちょ (躊躇) *n.*
hesitation; indecision.
　chuucho suru (〜する) *vi.* hesitate; waver: *Michi o wataru mae ni isshuñ* chuucho shita. (道を渡る前に一瞬ちゅうちょした) I *hesitated for a moment before crossing the street.* / *Watashi wa* chuucho sezu *ni sono yaku o hikiuketa.* (私はちゅうちょせずにその役を引き受けた) I accepted the role *without having to think twice.*

chu⌈udañ ちゅうだん (中断) *n.* discontinuance; interruption.
　chuudañ suru (〜する) *vi., vt.* stop; discontinue; interrupt: *Shiai wa ame de* chuudañ sareta. (試合は雨で中断された) The game *was interrupted* by rain.

chu¹udoku ちゅうどく (中毒) *n.* poisoning:
*shoku[gasu]-*chuudoku (食[ガス]中毒) food [gas] *poisoning.*
　chuudoku suru (〜する) *vi.* be poisoned: *Sono beñtoo o tabete, go-niñ ga* chuudoku shita. (その弁当を食べて、5人が中毒した) Five people *got food poisoning* after eating the box lunch.

chu⌈udoo-se⌉etoo ちゅうどうせいとう (中道政党) *n.* centrist [middle-of-the-road] political party.

chu⌈uga⌉eri ちゅうがえり (宙返り) *n.* somersault; looping.
　chuugaeri (o) suru (〜(を)する) *vi.* turn a somersault; loop the loop: *Kare wa* chuugaeri o *ni-kai* shita. (彼は宙返りを2回した) He *turned* two *somersaults.* / *Hikooki ga* chuugaeri suru *no o mimashita ka?* (飛行機が宙返りするのを見ましたか) Did you see the plane *loop the loop?*

chu⌈uga⌉kkoo ちゅうがっこう (中学校) *n.* junior high school; lower secondary school. 《⇒ gakkoo》

chu¹ugaku ちゅうがく (中学) *n.* Shortened form of '*chuugakkoo*'

(junior high school).

chu⌈uga⌉kusee ちゅうがくせい (中学生) *n.* junior high school pupil.

chu⌈ugata ちゅうがた (中型) *n.* medium size:
chuugata *no kuruma* (中型の車) a *medium-sized* car. 《⇒ oogata; kogata》

chu⌈ugeñ ちゅうげん (中元) *n.* midyear gift. ★ Usually used with an honorific '*o-*.' In appreciation of special favors received, it is sent between July and August. 《⇒ (o)seebo》

Chu¹ugoku¹ ちゅうごく (中国) *n.* Chugoku, the western district in Honshu, comprising Okayama, Hiroshima, Yamaguchi, Tottori and Shimane prefectures.
《⇒ map (C3)》

Chu¹ugoku² ちゅうごく (中国) *n.* China.

Chu⌈ugokugo ちゅうごくご (中国語) *n.* the Chinese language; Chinese.

Chu⌈ugoku⌉jiñ ちゅうごくじん (中国人) *n.* a [the] Chinese.

chu¹ui ちゅうい (注意) *n.* **1** attention:
Dare mo kare no itta koto ni chuui *o harawanakatta.* (だれも彼の言ったことに注意を払わなかった) Nobody paid *attention* to what he said. / *Kanojo no fuku wa miñna no* chuui *o hiita.* (彼女の服はみんなの注意を引いた) Her dress drew everyone's *attention.*

2 care; caution:
Kono shigoto wa tokubetsu no chuui *ga iru.* (この仕事は特別の注意がいる) This work needs special *care.*

3 warning:
Kanojo wa watashi no chuui *o mushi shita.* (彼女は私の注意を無視した) She disregarded my *warning.*
　chuui suru (〜する) *vi.* take care; caution; advise; warn: *Koro-*

banai yoo ni chuui shi nasai.(ころば
ないように注意しなさい) *Take care*
that you don't fall. / *Kare ni,
okurenai yoo ni* chuui shita.(彼に,
遅れないように注意した) I *cautioned*
him not to be late.

chuˈuibukaˈ·i ちゅういぶかい (注意
深い) *a.* (-ku) careful; cautious;
watchful:
chuuibukai *hito* (注意深い人) *a cautious* person / chuuibukaku *kañsatsu suru* (注意深く観察する) observe
carefully. 《⇒ shiñchoo; yoojiñbu-
kai》

chuˈujitsu ちゅうじつ (忠実) *a.n.*
(～ na, ni) **1** loyal; faithful:
Kare ni wa chuujitsu *na buka ga
oozee iru.*(彼には忠実な部下がおおぜ
いいる) He has many *loyal* people
working under him. / *Guñtai de
wa meeree o* chuujitsu *ni mamoranakereba naranai.*(軍隊では命令を
忠実に守らなければならない) In the
army, one must obey orders
faithfully.
2 true to fact:
Kore wa geñbuñ ni chuujitsu *na
yaku da.*(これは原文に忠実な訳だ)
This is a translation *true* to the
original. / *Jijitsu o* chuujitsu *ni
hanashite kudasai.*(事実を忠実に話
してください) Please try to give a
true account of the matter.

chuˈujuñ ちゅうじゅん (中旬) *n.*
the middle ten days of a month:
Kare wa shi-gatsu (no) chuujuñ *ni
Nihoñ e kimasu.*(彼は4月(の)中旬
に日本へ来ます) He is coming to
Japan in the *middle* of April.
《⇒ joojuñ; gejuñ》

chuˈukai ちゅうかい (仲介) *n.* in-
termediation; mediation; agency.
chuukai (o) suru (～(を)する) *vt.*
mediate: *ryoosha no* chuukai o
suru(両者の仲介をする) *mediate* between two parties.

chuˈukañ ちゅうかん (中間) *n.* interim; middle:

chuukañ *hookoku* (中間報告) an
interim report / chuukañ *shikeñ*
(中間試験) a *mid-term* examination / *Eki wa sono futatsu no
machi no* chuukañ *ni dekimasu.*
(駅はその二つの町の中間にできます)
The train station will be built *in
between* the two towns.

chuˈuka-ryoˈori ちゅうかりょうり
(中華料理) *n.* Chinese dishes
[food]; Chinese cooking [cuisine].

chuˈuka-soˈba ちゅうかそば (中華
そば) *n.* Chinese noodles. 《⇒ raa-
meñ》

chuˈukee ちゅうけい (中継) *n.*
relay; hookup; transmission:
chuukee *hoosoo* (中継放送) *relay*
broadcasting / *zeñkoku* chuukee
hoosoo (全国中継放送) a nationwide *hookup*.
chuukee suru (～する) *vt.* relay:
Sono bañgumi wa eesee de chuukee sareta.(その番組は衛星で中継さ
れた) The program *was relayed* by
satellite.

chuˈuko ちゅうこ (中古) *n.* used
[secondhand] article:
chuuko-*sha* (中古車) a *secondhand*
car / chuuko-*hiñ* (中古品) a *used*
article. 《⇒ chuuburu》

chuˈukoku ちゅうこく (忠告) *n.*
advice; counsel:
Kare no chuukoku *o kiki nasai.*(彼
の忠告を聞きなさい) Listen to his
advice. / *Watashi-tachi wa kare
no* chuukoku *ni shitagatta.*(私たちは
彼の忠告に従った) We followed his
advice.
chuukoku suru (～する) *vt.* advise; counsel: *Isha wa kare ni
tabako o yameru yoo ni* chuukoku
shita.(医者は彼にたばこをやめるように
忠告した) The doctor *advised* him
to stop smoking.

chuˈukoˈoneñ ちゅうこうねん (中高
年) *n.* (people of) middle and
advanced age; senior citizen.

chuˈukyuu ちゅうきゅう (中級) *n.*

medium level: *Nihoñgo no* chuukyuu *kurasu* [*koosu*] (日本語の中級クラス[コース]) the *intermediate* Japanese class [course] / chuukyuu *Eego* (中級英語) *intermediate* English. 《⇨ shokyuu; jookyuu》

chu⌐umoku ちゅうもく (注目) *n.* attention; notice: *Sono hoñ wa sekeñ no* chuumoku *o atsumeta.* (その本は世間の注目を集めた) The book attracted public *attention.* / *Kore wa* chuumoku *ni atai suru hatsumee da.* (これは注目に値する発明だ) This is an invention worthy of *notice.*
chuumoku suru (〜する) *vi., vt.* pay attention; watch: *Miñna wa sono nariyuki ni chuumoku shite iru.* (みんなはその成り行きに注目している) Everybody *is watching* the course of events.

chu⌐umoñ ちゅうもん (注文) *n.*
1 order (of goods): *Kyoo wa ooguchi no chuumoñ o uketa.* (きょうは大口の注文を受けた) We received a big *order* today. / *Chuumoñ o sabaku no ni isogashii.* (注文をさばくのに忙しい) We are busy filling *orders.*
2 request; demand: *Soñna chuumoñ ni wa oojirarenai.* (そんな注文には応じられない) I cannot comply with such a *demand.*
chuumoñ suru (〜する) *vt.* give an order; order: *Sono hoñ o shuppañsha ni chuumoñ shita.* (その本を出版社に注文した) I *ordered* the book from the publisher. / *Kore wa watashi ga chuumoñ shita mono to chigau.* (これは私が注文したものと違う) This differs from what I *ordered.*

chu⌐uneñ ちゅうねん (中年) *n.* middle age: chuuneñ *no fuufu* (中年の夫婦) a *middle-aged* couple.

chu⌐uo⌐o ちゅうおう (中央) *n.* cen-

ter; middle: *Gakkoo wa shi no* chuuoo *ni arimasu.* (学校は市の中央にあります) The school is in the *center* of the city. / *Teeburu o heya no* chuuoo *ni oita.* (テーブルを部屋の中央に置いた) I put the table in the *middle* of the room. / *Kono koto ni tsuite wa, mazu* chuuoo *no seefu ga ugokidasu beki da.* (この事については、まず中央の政府が動き出すべきだ) As regards this matter, the *central* government should first take the initiative.

chu⌐urippu チューリップ *n.* tulip.

chu⌐uritsu ちゅうりつ (中立) *n.* neutrality: chuuritsu *o mamoru* (中立を守る) observe *neutrality* / chuuritsu-*koku* (中立国) a *neutral* nation.

chu⌐uryuu ちゅうりゅう (中流) *n.*
1 middle class: *Kare wa* chuuryuu *no katee ni sodatta.* (彼は中流の家庭に育った) He grew up in a *middle-class* family. 《⇨ jooryuu; kasoo》
2 the middle of a river.

chu⌐usai ちゅうさい (仲裁) *n.* arbitration; mediation.
chuusai (o) suru (〜(を)する) *vt.* arbitrate; mediate: *Futari no keñka o chuusai shita no wa Yamada-sañ desu.* (二人のけんかを仲裁したのは山田さんです) It was Mr. Yamada who *arbitrated* the dispute between the two of them.

chu⌐usee ちゅうせい (中世) *n.* the Middle Ages; medieval times.
★ The Japanese Middle Ages comprise the Kamakura period (12th century) to the Azuchi-Momoyama period (late 16th–early 17th centuries). 《⇨ jidai (table)》

chu⌐useñ ちゅうせん (抽選) *n.* drawing; lot: *Tooseñ-sha wa* chuuseñ *de kimerareta.* (当選者は抽選で決められた)

The winners were decided by *lot.* / *Watashi wa* chuuseñ *ni atatta* [*hazureta*]. (私は抽選に当たった[はずれた]) I *drew a winning* [*losing*] *number.*

chu⌈usha¹ ちゅうしゃ (駐車) *n.* parking:
Koko ni chuusha *dekimasu ka?* (ここに駐車できますか) *Can I park here?* / *Koko wa* chuusha-*kiñshi desu.* (ここは駐車禁止です) *Parking is prohibited here.* / Chuusha-*ihañ de bakkiñ o torareta.* (駐車違反で罰金をとられた) I was fined for a *parking* violation. / chuusha-*ryookiñ* (駐車料金) a *parking* fee.
chuusha suru (〜する) *vi.* park:
Chuusha suru *basho o sagashite iru tokoro desu.* (駐車する場所を探しているところです) I am looking for a *parking* space. 《⇨ chuushajoo》

CHUUSHA-KIÑSHI SIGN

chu⌈usha² ちゅうしゃ (注射) *n.* injection; shot:
Sono chuusha *de netsu ga sagatta.* (その注射で熱が下がった) The *injection* lowered the fever. / *Penishiriñ no* chuusha *o shite moratta.* (ペニシリンの注射をしてもらった) I had a *shot* of penicillin.
chuusha suru (〜する) *vt.* inject:
Isha wa kare ni atarashii kusuri o chuusha *shita.* (医者は彼に新しい薬を注射した) The doctor *injected* him with a new drug.

chu⌈ushajoo ちゅうしゃじょう (駐車場) *n.* parking lot; car park:
Kono chikaku ni chuushajoo *wa arimaseñ ka?* (この近くに駐車場はありませんか) Isn't there a *parking lot* near here? 《⇨ chuusha》

chu⌈ushi ちゅうし (中止) *n.* stoppage; discontinuance; suspension:
Shiai wa ame de chuushi *ni natta.* (試合は雨で中止になった) The game *was called off* because of rain.
chuushi suru (〜する) *vt.* stop; call off; discontinue; suspend:
Watashi wa sono zasshi no koodoku o chuushi *shita.* (私はその雑誌の購読を中止した) I *discontinued* my subscription to the magazine.

chu⌈ushiñ ちゅうしん (中心) *n.*
1 center:
Sono biru wa shi no chuushiñ *ni aru.* (そのビルは市の中心にある) That building is in the *center* of the city. / *Okada-sañ ga iiñkai no* chuushiñ *to natte imasu.* (岡田さんが委員会の中心となっています) Mr. Okada is the *key figure* on the committee.
2 focus; core:
Kuruma no yushutsu ga wadai no chuushiñ *datta.* (車の輸出は話題の中心だった) Car exports were the *focus* of our discussions.

chu⌈ushoku ちゅうしょく (昼食) *n.* (*formal*) lunch:
chuushoku *o taberu* [*toru*] (昼食を食べる[とる]) have *lunch* / Chuushoku *ni sañdoitchi o tabeta.* (昼食にサンドイッチを食べた) I had sandwiches for *lunch.* 《⇨ hirumeshi; hirugohañ》

chu⌈ushoo ちゅうしょう (中傷) *n.* slander.
chuushoo suru (〜する) *vt.* slander; speak ill of: *Kare ga kage de watashi no koto o* chuushoo *shite iru no wa shitte imasu.* (彼が陰で私のことを中傷しているのは知っています) I know that he *is saying some-*

thing nasty about me behind my back.

chuʳushoo-kiˀgyoo　ちゅうしょうきぎょう（中小企業）*n.* small and medium-sized enterprises: *Kare no kaisha wa* chuushoo-kigyoo *da ga keeki ga ii.*（彼の会社は中小企業だが景気がいい）His firm is *small*, but business is good.

Chuʳushoo-kigyoˀo-choo　ちゅうしょうきぎょうちょう（中小企業庁）*n.* Small and Medium Enterprise Agency: Chuushoo-kigyoo-choo *chookañ*（中小企業庁長官）the Director General of the *Small and Medium Enterprise Agency.* 《⇨ choo⁴ (table)》

chuʳushoo-teki　ちゅうしょうてき（抽象的）*a.n.* (~ na, ni) abstract: *Kare no hanashi wa* chuushoo-teki *de yoku wakaranai.*（彼の話は抽象的でよくわからない）What he says is too *abstract* for me to understand properly. / Chuushoo-teki *na giroñ bakari de keekaku ga chitto-mo susumanai.*（抽象的な議論ばかりで計画がちっとも進まない）With nothing but *abstract* discussion, the plan is not making any progress. 《↔ gutai-teki》

chuʳutai　ちゅうたい（中退）*n.* leaving school in mid-course.
chuutai suru (~する) *vi.* drop out; quit school: *Kare wa katee no jijoo de daigaku o* chuutai *shita.*（彼は家庭の事情で大学を中退した）He *quit* the university for reasons having to do with his family.

chuʳuto　ちゅうと（中途）*n.* middle; the midway point: *Teñki ga warui no de* chuuto *de hikikaeshita.*（天気が悪いので中途で引き返した）We turned back *halfway* because the weather was bad.

Chuʳutoo　ちゅうとう（中東）*n.* the Middle East.

D

da だ *copula.* (*informal*)

> **USAGE**
>
> Used in both the written and spoken languages. The corresponding formal equivalent in the written language is '*de aru*,' and the polite colloquial equivalent is '*desu*.' '*Da*' is usually avoided at the end of sentences in women's speech, because it can sound rude or abrupt. The negative of '*da*' is '*de wa nai*,' which becomes '*ja nai*' in colloquial speech. The past and provisional forms are '*datta*' and '*nara(ba)*.'

1 be [am/is/are]: ★ Indicates that the subject equals the complement.
Kare wa haisha da. (彼は歯医者だ) He *is* a dentist. / *Kono madogarasu o watta no wa dare* da? (この窓ガラスを割ったのはだれだ) Who *is* it that broke this windowpane? / *Kono kasa wa watashi no* de wa nai. (この傘は私のではない) This umbrella *is not* mine.
2 be located in a certain place:
"Boku no kuruma wa doko da?" *"Chuushajoo ni aru yo."* (「僕の車はどこだ」「駐車場にあるよ」) "Where *is* my car?" "It is in the parking lot."
3 (indicates a situation or condition):
Koko wa shizuka da. (ここは静かだ) This place *is* very quiet. / *Kare wa shitsugyoo-chuu* da. (彼は失業中だ) He *is* out of work. / *Kyoo wa ichi-nichi* ame datta. (きょうは一日雨だった) It *rained* all day today.
4 (used as a verb substitute):

"Nomimono wa nani ni shimasu ka?" "Boku wa koohii da." (「飲物は何にしますか」「僕はコーヒーだ」) "What would you like to drink?" "I'll *drink* coffee."

da¹asu ダース *n.* dozen:
Eñpitsu o ni-daasu *kudasai.* (鉛筆を2ダース下さい) Please give me two *dozen* pencils. / *Sañ-niñ de* ichi-daasu *no biiru o noñde shimatta.* (三人で1ダースのビールを飲んでしまった) The three of us emptied a *dozen* bottles of beer.

da「budabu だぶだぶ *a.n.* (~ na, ni) too large; baggy:
dabudabu *na zuboñ* (だぶだぶなズボン) *baggy* trousers / *Kono fuku wa* dabudabu da. (この服はだぶだぶだ) These clothes are *too loose*.

da¹ ga だが *conj.* but; however: ★ Used at the beginning of a sentence.
Kiki wa satta. Da ga *yudañ wa dekinai.* (危機は去った. だが油断はできない) The danger has passed. *However*, we must be careful. / *Kare wa byooiñ e katsugi-komareta.* Da ga *osokatta.* (彼は病院へかつぎ込まれた. だが遅かった) He was carried into the hospital. *But* it was too late. 《⇨ desu ga》

...no da ga (...のだが) though; but: ★ In conversation, '*no*' often becomes '*ñ*.' *Sore o kaitai* no [ñ] da ga *ima o-kane ga arimaseñ.* (それを買いたいの[ん]だが今お金がありません) I wish to buy it, *but* I have no money now.

da「geki だげき (打撃) *n.* **1** hard hit; blow:
Kare wa atama ni dageki *o ukete taoreta.* (彼は頭に打撃を受けて倒れた) He got a *blow* on the head and

fell to the ground.

2 damage:

Noomiñ wa kañbatsu de hidoi dageki o uketa. (農民はかんばつでひどい打撃を受けた) The farmers suffered serious *damage* because of the drought.

3 emotional disturbance; shock:

Haha no shi wa kanojo ni totte ooki-na dageki datta. (母の死は彼女にとって大きな打撃だった) Her mother's death was a great *shock* to her.

4 (of baseball) batting:

Shiai no mae ni dageki no reñshuu o shita. (試合の前に打撃の練習をした) We practiced *batting* before the game.

da「ha だ (打破) *n.* breaking; overthrow:

daha suru (〜する) *vt.* break down; overthrow: *warui shuukañ o daha suru* (悪い習慣を打破する) *break down* evil customs.

da「i¹ だい (大) *n.* bigness; large size:

Dai wa shoo o kaneru. (*saying*) (大は小をかねる) 'Big' always includes '*small*.' / *Keeki no ookisa ni wa dai, chuu, shoo ga arimasu.* (ケーキの大きさには大中小があります) The cake comes in three sizes: *large*, medium and small. / *Kare wa koe o dai ni shite sakeñda.* (彼は声を大にして叫んだ) He *raised his voice* and shouted. 《⇨ chuu¹ (table)》

da「i² だい (代) *n.* generation; time:

Sono mise wa kare no dai ni sakaeta. (その店は彼の代に栄えた) The shop flourished in his *time*. / *Chichi-oya ga nakunari, musuko no dai ni natta.* (父親が亡くなり, 息子の代になった) The father died and he *was succeeded* by his son.

da「i³ だい (題) *n.* subject; theme: *'Watashi no shumi' to iu dai de sakubuñ o kaita.* (「私の趣味」という

題で作文を書いた) I wrote an essay on the *theme* of 'My Hobby.'

da「i-¹ だい (大) *pref.* **1** big; large:

dai-*toshi* (大都市) a *large* city / dai-*hooru* (大ホール) a *large* hall / dai-*kibo* (大規模) *large*-scale / dai-*gaisha* (大会社) a *big* company. 《↔ shoo-》

2 great:

dai-*sakka* (大作家) a *great* writer / dai-*gakusha* (大学者) a *great* scholar / dai-*seekoo* (大成功) a *great* success.

3 serious; grave:

dai-*moñdai* (大問題) a *serious* issue.

da「i-² だい (第) *pref.* (indicates an ordinal number):

dai-ichi (第一) *the first* / dai-ni (第二) *the second* / dai-nijuuyoñ-kai *Oriñpikku* (第 24 回オリンピック) *the 24th* Olympiad / dai-niji *sekai-taiseñ* (第二次世界大戦) *the Second* World War.

-dai¹ だい (台) *suf.* **1** (counter for relatively large vehicles or machines):

Jidoosha o ichi-dai katta. (自動車を 1 台買った) I bought *a* car. / *Uchi ni wa terebi ga ni-dai aru.* (うちにはテレビが 2 台ある) We have *two* TVs at home.

2 mark:

Kabuka ga niseñ-eñ-dai ni tasshita. (株価が 2,000 円台に達した) The price of the stock reached the 2,000-yen *mark*. / *Ano marasoñ señshu wa ni-jikañ-jup-puñ-dai o kiru daroo.* (あのマラソン選手は 2 時間 10 分台を切るだろう) The marathon runner will beat the 2-hour 10-minute *mark*.

3 between...and...:

Sañmañ-eñ-dai no teepu rekoodaa ga yoku urete iru. (三万円台のテープレコーダーがよく売れている) Tape recorders *in the 30,000–40,000 yen-price range* are selling well. / *Asa* shichi-ji-dai *no deñsha wa totemo koñde imasu.* (朝 7 時台の電車はとても混んでいます) The trains *between seven and eight* in the morning are very crowded.

-dai² -だい (代) *suf.* fare; rate; charge:
takushii-dai (タクシー代) a taxi *fare* / *heya*-dai (部屋代) room *rent* / *hoteru*-dai (ホテル代) hotel *rates* / *kuriiniñgu*-dai (クリーニング代) *charges* for cleaning. 《⇨ -chiñ; -ryoo》

-¹dai³ だい (代) *suf.* age; period:
Kare wa mada sañjuu-dai *desu.* (彼はまだ 30 代です) He is still in his *thirties.* / Señ-kyuuhyaku-rokujuu-neñ-dai *wa fukeeki datta.* (1960 年代は不景気だった) Business was slack in the *1960s.*

da「ibe¹ñ だいべん (大便) *n.* feces; stool; excrement:
daibeñ o suru (大便をする) *defecate*; *have a movement of the bowels.* 《⇨ kuso》

da「ibu だいぶ (大分) *adv.* considerably; quite; very:
Ku-gatsu ni natte, daibu *suzushiku natte kita.* (九月になって, だいぶ涼しくなってきた) It has become *considerably* cool since September. / *Isha ni yoru to chichi no byooki wa* daibu *omoi soo desu.* (医者によると父の病気はだいぶ重いそうです) According to the doctor, my father's sickness is *very* serious. / *Eki made aruku to* daibu *arimasu.* (駅まで歩くとだいぶあります) It is a *good* walk to the station. 《⇨ kanari》

da「ibu¹buñ だいぶぶん (大部分) *n.* the greater part; most:
Sono kuni no daibubuñ *wa señsoo de higai o uketa.* (その国の大部分は戦争で被害を受けた) *The greater part* of the country was damaged in the war. / Daibubuñ *no hito wa sono hooañ ni hañtai desu.* (大部分

の人はその法案に反対です) *Most* of the people are against the bill.
— *adv.* mostly:
Shigoto wa daibubuñ *owatta.* (仕事は大部分終わった) The work is *mostly* finished. 《⇨ hotoñdo》

da「ibutsu だいぶつ (大仏) *n.* huge statue of Buddha. ★ Refers to the huge, seated figures of the Buddha; in Kamakura, outdoors, and Nara, inside.

DAIBUTSU IN KAMAKURA

da「idai だいだい (代々) *n.* from generation to generation; generation after generation:
Kore wa daidai *uchi ni tsutawaru takara desu.* (これは代々うちに伝わる宝です) This is a treasure handed down *from generation to generation* in our family.

da「idoko(ro) だいどこ(ろ) (台所) *n.* kitchen:
Haha wa daidokoro *de shokuji no shitaku o shite imasu.* (母は台所で食事の支度をしています) My mother is preparing the meal in the *kitchen.* 《⇨ katte¹》

da「igaku だいがく (大学) *n.* university; college:
daigaku ni hairu (大学に入る) matriculate at a *college* / daigaku o sotsugyoo suru (大学を卒業する) graduate from a *university* / *Musuko wa Tokyo no* daigaku *ni kayotte imasu.* (息子は東京の大学に

通っています) My son attends a *university* in Tokyo.

da⌐igaku⌐iñ だいがくいん (大学院) *n.* graduate school.

da⌐iga⌐kusee だいがくせい (大学生) *n.* university [college] student; undergraduate.

da⌐igi⌐shi だいぎし (代議士) *n.* Diet member. ★ Usually refers to a member of the House of Representatives (*Shuugiiñ*).

da⌐ihyoo だいひょう (代表) *n.* representative; delegate: *Watashi wa kaisha no* daihyoo *to shite sono kai ni shusseki shita.* (私は会社の代表としてその会に出席した) I attended the convention as a *representative* of our company. / *Kare wa Amerika e iku* daihyoo *no hitori desu.* (彼はアメリカへ行く代表の一人です) He is one of the *delegates* going to America.

daihyoo suru (〜する) *vt.* represent: *Kare wa sañbyaku-niñ no roodoosha o* daihyoo suru *kumiai no shidoosha desu.* (彼は300人の労働者を代表する組合の指導者です) He is a leader of a union *representing* 300 workers. / *Watashi wa guruupu o* daihyoo shite *hatsugeñ shita.* (私はグループを代表して発言した) I spoke *on behalf of* the group.

da⌐ihyoo-teki だいひょうてき (代表的) *a.n.* (〜 na) typical; representative: *Sukiyaki wa* daihyoo-teki *na Nihoñ-ryoori desu.* (すきやきは代表的な日本料理です) Sukiyaki is a *typical* Japanese dish. / *Kare no* daihyoo-teki *na sakuhiñ o atsumeta teñrañkai ga atta.* (彼の代表的な絵を集めた展覧会があった) There was an exhibition of his *main* works.

da⌐i-ichi だいいち (第一) *n.* the first; the most important thing: dai-ichi-ji *sekai-taiseñ* (第一次世界大戦) *The First* World War /

Añzeñ Dai-ichi. (安全第一) Safety First. / *Keñkoo ga* dai-ichi *da.* (健康が第一だ) Health is *everything*. / *Maitsuki* dai-ichi *mokuyoobi ni kaigi ga arimasu.* (毎月第一木曜日に会議があります) We have a meeting on *the first* Thursday of every month.

— *adv.* first; to begin with: *Mazu* dai-ichi *ni kono moñdai o kaiketsu shinakereba narimaseñ.* (まず第一にこの問題を解決しなければなりません) *First* of all, we must solve this problem. / Dai-ichi *sore wa takasugimasu.* (第一それは高すぎます) *To begin with*, it is too expensive.

da⌐iji[1] だいじ (大事) *a.n.* (〜 na, ni) important; valuable; precious: Daiji *na kabiñ o kowashite shimatta.* (大事な花瓶をこわしてしまった) I broke a *valuable* vase. / Daiji *na moñdai o mazu hanashiaimashoo.* (大事な問題をまず話し合いましょう) Let's discuss *important* problems first. / *Toshiyori wa* daiji *ni shinai to ikemaseñ.* (年寄りは大事にしないといけません) We must take *good care* of old people. 《⇨ taisetsu; juuyoo》

O-daiji ni (お大事に) (to a sick person) Take care of yourself.

da⌐iji[2] だいじ (大事) *n.* serious matter; crisis; emergency: *kokka no* daiji (国家の大事) a national *crisis* / *Uñ-yoku kaji wa* daiji *ni itaranakatta.* (運良く火事は大事に至らなかった) Luckily the fire did not get *serious*. 《⇨ ichidaiji》

daiji o toru (大事を取る) be on the safe side: Daiji o totte, *futari hakeñ shita.* (大事を取って、二人派遣した) They dispatched two persons, *just to be on the safe side*.

da⌐ijiñ だいじん (大臣) *n.* minister; secretary; cabinet member. 《⇨ shoo[1]》

da⌐ijo⌐obu だいじょうぶ (大丈夫)

a.n. (~ na) **1** all right; sure: *"Kega wa arimaseñ ka?" "Ee,* daijoobu *desu."* (「けがはありませんか」「ええ, だいじょうぶです」) "Did you hurt yourself?" "No, I'm *all right."* / *Watashi wa hitori de* daijoobu *desu.* (私は一人でだいじょうぶです) I can *manage* it by myself. **2** (of buildings, equipment, instruments, etc.) resistant; proof: *Kono biru wa jishiñ ga kite mo* daijoobu *desu.* (このビルは地震が来てもだいじょうぶです) This building is earthquake-*proof.*

da┌iki┌bo だいきぼ (大規模) *a.n.* (~ na, ni) large-scale: daikibo *na toshi-kaihatsu* (大規模な都市開発) a *large-scale* urban development / *Choosa ga* daikibo *ni okonawareta.* (調査が大規模に行なわれた) The investigation was carried out on a *large scale.* 《⇨ oogakari》

da┌ikiñ だいきん (代金) *n.* price; charge; bill: *Kuriiniñgu no* daikiñ *wa haraimashita.* (クリーニングの代金は払いました) I paid the cleaning *charges.* / Daikiñ *wa tsuide no toki de kekkoo desu.* (代金はついでのときで結構です) You may *pay* at your convenience. / *Kono* daikiñ *wa watashi ga haraimasu.* (この代金は私が払います) I'll pay this *bill.* / *Shinamono wa* daikiñ *hikikae ni o-watashi shimasu.* (品物は代金引き換えにお渡しします) We will hand over the goods on receiving *payment.* 《⇨ ryookiñ》

da┌ikirai だいきらい (大嫌い) *a.n.* (~ na) have a strong dislike; hate: *Kare wa watashi no* daikirai *na taipu da.* (彼は私の大嫌いなタイプだ) He is the type of man *I hate.* / *Watashi wa atsui no ga* daikirai *desu.* (私は暑いのが大嫌いです) I *hate* hot weather. 《⇨ kirai》

da┌ikoñ だいこん (大根) *n.* Japanese white radish. ★ Japanese radishes are long and thick. The small, roundish red radish is referred to as 'hatsuka-daikoñ.' 《⇨ yasai (illus.)》

da┌iku だいく (大工) *n.* carpenter. 《⇨ nichiyoo daiku》

-daime だいめ (代目) *suf.* the order of generations: *Kare wa kono mise no* sañ-daime *no shujiñ desu.* (彼はこの店の3代目の主人です) He is the *third*-generation owner of this shop. / *Tanaka-shi wa* go-daime *no shachoo ni natta.* (田中氏は5代目の社長になった) Mr. Tanaka became the *fifth* president of the company.

da┌imee だいめい (題名) *n.* title: *hoñ ni* daimee *o tsukeru* (本に題名をつける) give a *title* to a book.

da┌ime┐eshi だいめいし (代名詞) *n.* **1** pronoun. **2** synonym: *Ekonomikku animaru to iu kotoba ga Nihoñjiñ no* daimeeshi *ni tsukawareta jiki ga arimashita.* (エコノミックアニマルという言葉が日本人の代名詞に使われた時期がありました) At one time, 'economic animal' was used as a *synonym* for the Japanese people.

da┌imyo┐o だいみょう (大名) *n.* daimyo. ★ Japanese feudal lord.

da┌inashi だいなし (台無し) *n.* ruining; spoiling: *Ame de ryokoo ga* dainashi *ni natta.* (雨で旅行が台なしになった) Our trip *was spoiled* by the rain. / *Inu ni kadañ o* dainashi *ni sareta.* (犬に花壇を台なしにされた) My flower bed *was ruined* by the dog. / *Kodomo no koe de koñsaato wa* dainashi *datta.* (子どもの声でコンサートは台なしだった) The concert *was spoiled* by children talking.

da┌iri だいり (代理) *n.* representative; proxy:

Watashi ga kare no dairi *to shite kai ni shusseki shimashita.*（私が彼の代理として会に出席しました）I attended the party *on his behalf.* / *Kachoo ga shutchoo no aida, watashi ga* dairi o tsutomemashita.（課長が出張の間, 私が代理をつとめました）I *acted* for the section chief during his business trip.

da⌐ishoo だいしょう（大小）*n.* size; measure:
Daishoo *ni kañkee naku, nedañ wa onaji desu.*（大小に関係なく, 値段は同じです）The price is the same, regardless of *size.* / *Hako no naka ni* daishoo samazama *na jagaimo ga atta.*（箱の中に大小さまざまなじゃがいもがあった）There were potatoes, both *large and small*, in the box.《⇒ ookisa》

da⌐isuki だいすき（大好き）*a.n.* (〜 na) favorite:
daisuki *na tabemono*（大好きな食べ物）one's *favorite* food / *Tanakasañ wa gorufu ga* daisuki *desu.*（田中さんはゴルフが大好きです）Mr. Tanaka *loves* golf.《⇒ suki》

da⌐itai だいたい（大体）*n.* outline; summary; sketch:
Keekaku no daitai *no tokoro o ohanashi shimashoo.*（計画の大体のところをお話ししましょう）I will give you an *outline* of our plan. / *Nihoñ keezai no* daitai *wa kono hoñ o yomeba wakarimasu.*（日本経済の大体はこの本を読めばわかります）If you read this book, you can get a *general idea* about Japan's economy.
— *adv.* **1** about; almost; generally:
Kono gakkoo ni wa gakusee ga daitai *sañbyaku-niñ imasu.*（この学校には学生が大体 300 人います）There are *about* 300 students at this school. / *Kare no toshi wa* daitai *watashi to onaji-gurai desu.*（彼の年は大体私と同じぐらいです）He

is *almost* as old as I am. / Daitai *ima-goro wa ame ga ooi.*（大体今ごろは雨が多い）*Generally speaking*, we have a lot of rain about this time of the year.
2 originally:
Daitai *koko wa watashi no tochi datta ñ desu.*（大体ここは私の土地だったんです）This land *originally* belonged to me.

da⌐itaⁿñ だいたん（大胆）*a.n.* (〜 na, ni) daring; bold:
daitañ *na hatsugeñ*（大胆な発言）a *daring* comment / daitañ *na omoitsuki*（大胆な思いつき）a *bold* idea / *Kare wa* daitañ *ni mo, chañpioñ ni chooseñ shita.*（彼は大胆にも, チャンピオンに挑戦した）He *daringly* challenged the champion.

da⌐ito⌐oryoo だいとうりょう（大統領）*n.* president (of a country).

da⌐iya[1] ダイヤ *n.* train [bus] schedule; timetable:

> **USAGE**
> From '*daiyaguramu*' (train diagram), it specifically refers to the detailed charts the railroad uses to coordinate the running of trains, but it is often used as a synonym for '*jikoku-hyoo*' in conversation.

Yuki no tame daiya *ga midarete iru.*（雪のためダイヤが乱れている）*Train schedules* have been disrupted owing to the snow. / *Shi-gatsu kara* daiya *ga kaisee saremasu.*（四月からダイヤが改正されます）The *timetables* will be revised from April.

da⌐iya[2] ダイヤ *n.* diamond:
daiya *no yubiwa*（ダイヤの指輪）a *diamond* ring.

da⌐iyaru ダイヤル *n.* dial:
daiyaru *o mawasu*（ダイヤルを回す）turn a *dial* / daiyaru *o sañ ni awaseru*（ダイヤルを 3 に合わせる）turn the *dial* to 3.
daiyaru suru (〜する) *vi.* call on

the phone; dial: *Zero-sañ no sañ-ni-ichi-sañ no yoñ-ni-sañ-ni e* daiyaru shite *kudasai.* (03–3213–4232 へダイヤルしてください) Please *dial* 03-3213-4232.

da「iyoo だいよう (代用) *n.* substitution:
Kono iremono wa kabiñ no daiyoo *ni naru.* (この入れ物は花瓶の代用になる) This container will *serve as* a flower vase. / daiyoo-hiñ (代用品) a *substitute* (*article*).

da「izu だいず (大豆) *n.* soybean.

da¹kara だから *conj.* so; therefore: ★ In this usage, used only at the beginning of a sentence.
Kinoo wa netsu ga atta. Da kara *gakkoo o yasuñda.* (きのうは熱があった. だから学校を休んだ) I had a temperature yesterday. *That's why* I took the day off from school. / Da kara *itta ja nai ka.* (だから言ったじゃないか) Didn't I tell you *so?*
...no da kara (...のだから) because; since; as: ★ In conversation, '*no*' often becomes '*ñ*.' *Kimi ga yatta* no [ñ] da kara *kimi ga sekiniñ o tori nasai.* (君やったの[ん]だから君が責任を取りなさい) *Since* you have done it, you should take the responsibility.

da「ke だけ (丈) *p.* [follows a noun, the dictionary form and *ta*-form of a verb or adjective, an adjectival noun with '*na*' or particles]
1 only; just; no more: ★ Used to indicate a limit.
Sore o shitte iru no wa watashi dake *desu.* (それを知っているのは私だけです) I am the *only* person who knows that. / *Hoñtoo no koto wa kare ni* dake *hanashimashita.* (本当のことは彼にだけ話しました) I told the truth to him, and *no one else.* / *Watashi-tachi wa ichi-jikañ* dake *kyuukee shimashita.* (私たちは1時間だけ休憩しました) We took a

break for *just* one hour. / *Kao o mita* dake *de kare ga doñna hito ka wakatta.* (顔を見ただけで彼がどんな人かわかった) By *merely* looking at his face, I understood what kind of person he was.
2 as ... as; enough to do: ★ Used for emphasis or to indicate a limit.
Doozo suki na dake *meshiagatte kudasai.* (どうぞ好きなだけ召し上がってください) Please go ahead and eat *as much as* you wish. / *Futsuu no seekatsu o shite ikeru* dake *no shuunyuu wa arimasu.* (普通の生活をしていけるだけの収入はあります) I get an income *sufficient* to lead an ordinary life. / *Tonikaku dekiru* dake *no koto wa yatte mimasu.* (とにかくできるだけのことはやってみます) Anyway, I will do *the best I can.* 《⇨ nomi²; shika³》

da¹kedo だけど *conj.* (*informal*) = da keredo (mo).

da¹keredo (mo) だけれど(も) *conj.* but; however; yet: ★ In this usage, used only at the beginning of a sentence.
Ano hito wa uñdoo wa nañ de mo tokui desu. Da keredo (mo) *oyogemaseñ.* (あの人は運動は何でも得意です. だけれど(も)泳げません) He excels at all sorts of sports. *However,* he cannot swim.
...no da keredo mo (...のだけれども) though; but: ★ In conversation, '*no*' often becomes '*ñ*.' *Motto tabetai* no [ñ] da keredo mo, *moo onaka ga ippai desu.* (もっと食べたいの[ん]だけれども, もうおなかがいっぱいです) I'd like to eat much more, *but* I am already full.

da「ketsu だけつ (妥結) *n.* agreement; compromise settlement:
daketsu-*gaku* (妥結額) the average pay raise *agreed upon* between management and labor.
daketsu suru (〜する) *vi.* come to

an agreement [a settlement]: *Kai-sha to no chiñgiñ kooshoo wa sakuya osoku* daketsu shita. (会社との賃金交渉は昨夜遅く妥結した) We *came to an agreement* with the management about the pay raise late last night.

da「kia」·u だきあう(抱き合う) *vi.* (-a·i-; -a·wa-; -at-te C) embrace [hug] each other: *Futari wa shikkari to* dakiatta. (二人はしっかりと抱き合った) The two *embraced each other* tightly.

da「kko だっこ *n.* carrying [holding] (a baby) in one's arms.

dakko suru (〜する) *vt.* carry [hold] (a baby) in one's arms: *Sono ko wa "dakko shite " to itte naita.* (その子は「だっこして」と言って泣いた) The child cried and said, "*Carry me!*" 《⇨ daku》

da「k·u だく(抱く) *vt.* (dak·i-; dak·a-; dai-te C) **1** hold (a thing; a person) in one's arms; hug; embrace: *Oñna-no-ko wa niñgyoo o mune ni* daite ita. (女の子は人形を胸に抱いていた) The girl *was holding* a doll *to her chest.* / *Akañboo wa* haha-oya ni dakarete *suyasuya nemutte iru.* (赤ん坊は母親に抱かれてすやすや眠っている) The baby is sleeping peacefully *in its mother's arms.* / *Kanojo wa obiete iru kodomo o yasashiku* daita. (彼女はおびえている子どもを優しく抱いた) She gently *hugged* the frightened child. 《⇨ dakko》

2 (of a bird) sit on an egg: *Tori ga tamago o daite iru.* (鳥が卵を抱いている) A bird *is sitting on its eggs.*

da「kuoñ だくおん(濁音) *n.* syllables in Japanese that have a voiced consonant. ★ Indicated in writing with '゛' on the upper right-hand side of the *kana* letters. ガ (*ga*), ザ (*za*), ダ (*da*), バ (*ba*).

《⇨ hañ-dakuoñ; seeoñ》

da「kyoo だきょう(妥協) *n.* compromise; agreement: dakyoo *ni oojiru* (妥協に応じる) agree to a *compromise* / *Ryoosha no aida ni* dakyoo *ga seeritsu shita.* (両者の間に妥協が成立した) An *understanding* was reached between the two parties. / Dakyoo *no yochi wa nai.* (妥協の余地はない) There is no room for *compromise.* / Dakyoo ni itaru *made ni wa jikañ ga kakaru.* (妥協に至るまでには時間がかかる) It will take some time to *come to terms.*

dakyoo suru (〜する) *vi.* compromise: *Soñna jookeñ de wa kare-ra to* dakyoo suru *koto wa dekinai.* (そんな条件では彼らと妥協することはできない) We cannot *compromise* with them on such conditions.

da「ma」r·u だまる(黙る) *vi.* (da-mar·i-; damar·a-; damat-te C) **1** stop talking [crying]: Damare! (黙れ) (*rude*) *Shut up!* / Damari nasai! (黙りなさい) *Stop talking.*

2 keep silent: *Kono koto wa doo ka* damatte ite *kudasai.* (このことはどうか黙っていてください) Please *keep silent* about this matter. / Damatte ita *ñ de wa wakaranai yo.* (黙っていたんではわからないよ) If you *keep things to yourself* like this, I cannot make out what you are thinking. / *Kaisha no katte na iibuñ ni, moo* damatte *irarenai.* (会社の勝手な言い分に、もう黙っていられない) We can no longer *put up with* the company's unreasonable demands.

da「mashi-da」mashi だましだまし *adv.* coaxingly: *Kono kuruma o* damashi-damashi *hashirasete, moo juu-neñ ni narimasu.* (この車をだましだまし走らせて、もう10年になります) I have been *coax-*

ing this old car to run for ten years now.

da「ma」s·u だます（騙す）*vt.* (damash·i-; damas·a-; damash·i-te C) **1** cheat; trick; deceive:
Kare wa hito o damasu *teñsai da.* (彼は人をだます天才だ) He is a genius at *tricking* people. / *Seerusumañ (no kotoba) ni umaku* damasareta. (セールスマン（の言葉）にうまくだまされた) I *was* neatly *taken in* by (the words of) the salesman.
2 coax (a child); use every trick to coax:
naku ko o o-kashi de damasu (泣く子をお菓子でだます) *coax* a child with candy to stop crying.

da「ma」tte だまって（黙って）*adv.*
1 without telling a person:
Shujiñ wa watashi ni damatte, *uchi o dete ikimashita.* (主人は私に黙って、家を出て行きました) My husband left home *without letting me know.* / Damatte *ireba, dare ni mo wakarimaseñ yo.* (黙っていれば、だれにもわかりませんよ) If we keep *mum*, nobody will be aware of it.
2 without permission [notice]:
Damatte, *hito no mono o tsukatte wa ikemaseñ.* (黙って、人の物を使ってはいけません) You mustn't use other people's things *without permission.* / *Satoo-sañ wa kinoo* damatte, *gakkoo o yasuñda.* (佐藤さんはきのう黙って、学校を休んだ) Sato was absent from school yesterday *without notice.*
3 without complaints:
Kare wa tsurai shigoto o damatte *yatta.* (彼はつらい仕事を黙ってやった) He carried out the hard work *without complaints.*

da「me」 だめ（駄目）*a.n.* (～ na, ni)
1 no good; useless:
Kore wa dame *da.* (これはだめだ) This is *no good.* / *Kare wa mattaku* dame *na otoko da.* (彼は全くだめな男だ) He is an absolute *good-*

for-nothing fellow. / *Kono kamisori wa zeñzeñ* dame *da.* (このかみそりは全然だめだ) This razor is completely *useless.*
2 vain; of no use:
Doryoku shita ga dame *datta.* (努力したがだめだった) I made every effort, but *in vain.* / *Koogi shite mo* dame *desu.* (抗議してもだめです) There is *no use* protesting.
《⇨ muda》
3 fail:
Shikeñ wa dame *datta.* (試験はだめだった) I *failed* in the examination. / *Keekaku wa* dame *deshita.* (計画はだめでした) The plan *failed.*
4 cannot do; be poor at:
Moo dame *desu.* (もうだめです) I *can not do* any more. / *Ryoori wa* dame *na ñ desu.* (料理はだめなんです) I am *not good* at cooking. / *Yooji ga atte, ashita wa* dame *desu.* (用事があって、あしたはだめです) I have things to do, so tomorrow is *out of the question.*
5 must not do; should not do:
Sake o noñde wa dame *desu.* (酒を飲んではだめです) You *shouldn't* drink. / *"Soto de asoñde mo ii?" "*Dame *yo."* (「外で遊んでもいい」「だめよ」) "Can we play outside?" "No, you *can't!*" / *Motto reñshuu shinai to* dame *da.* (もっと練習しないとだめだ) You *must* practice harder.
《⇨ ikenai》

dame ni naru (～になる) *vi.* be spoiled; be ruined; go bad:
Taifuu de ine ga dame *ni natta.* (台風で稲がだめになった) The rice plants *were ruined* by the typhoon. / *Atatakai tokoro ni oita no de gyuunyuu ga* dame *ni natta.* (暖かい所に置いたので牛乳がだめになった) Since the milk was left in a warm place, it *went bad.*

dame ni suru (～にする) *vt.* spoil; ruin:
Soñna ni amayakasu to kodomo o

dame ni shimasu *yo*. (そんなに甘やか
すと子どもをだめにしますよ) If you are
so lenient with the children, you
will *spoil* them. / *Sake ga kare no
isshoo o dame ni shita*. (酒が彼の一
生をだめにした) Drink *ruined* his life.
　dame o osu (～を押す) double-
check.

da¹mu ダム *n*. dam.

da¹ñ¹ だん (段) *n*. **1** step; stair;
rung:
*Hashigo no ichibañ shita no dañ
ga orete iru*. (はしごのいちばん下の段が
折れている) The bottom *rung* of
the ladder is broken.
2 column:
shiñbuñ no go-dañ *kookoku* (新聞
の 5 段広告) a five-*column* newspaper advertisement.
3 (in judo, kendo, karate, go,
shogi, etc.) a degree of proficiency:
juudoo sañ-dañ (柔道 3 段) a third
degree black belt in judo.
4 the holder of *dan*:
Kare wa go no sañ-dañ *da*. (彼は碁
の 3 段だ) His rank in go is the
third *grade*. 《⇨ kyuu²》

da¹ñ² だん (壇) *n*. platform;
podium:
dañ *ni tatsu* (壇に立つ) stand on a
platform / dañ *ni agaru* (壇に上が
る) step up onto a *platform*.

-¹dañ だん (団) *suf*. group;
troupe; party:
choosa-dañ (調査団) a survey
group / *ooeñ*-dañ (応援団) a *group*
of cheerleaders.

da¹ñatsu だんあつ (弾圧) *n*. oppression; suppression; pressure:
roodoosha ni dañatsu *o kuwaeru*
(労働者に弾圧を加える) put *pressure*
on the laborers.
　dañatsu suru (～する) *vt*. oppress; suppress: *Seefu wa geñroñ no jiyuu o* dañatsu *shiyoo to
shite iru*. (政府は言論の自由を弾圧し
ようとしている) The government is

attempting to *suppress* freedom
of speech.

da¹ñboo だんぼう (暖房) *n*. heating of a room, building, etc.:
dañboo *o ireru* [*kiru*] (暖房を入れる
[切る]) turn the *heater* on [off] /
Kono heya wa dañboo *ga nai*. (この
部屋は暖房がない) This room has
no *heating*. / *Kyooshitsu wa* dañboo *ga kiki-sugite iru*. (教室は暖房
がききすぎている) The classroom *is
overheated*.
　dañboo suru (～する) *vt*. heat:
Dañboo suru *no wa mada hayai*.
(暖房するのはまだ早い) It is a little
too early to *turn on the heating*.
《↔ reeboo》

da¹ñbooru だんボール (段ボール) *n*.
corrugated cardboard:
dañbooru *no hako* (段ボールの箱) a
corrugated cardboard box.

da¹ñchi だんち (団地) *n*. public
apartment [housing] complex:
Kare wa Mogusa dañchi *ni suñde
iru*. (彼は百草団地に住んでいる) He
lives in the Mogusa *housing complex*.

da¹ñdañ だんだん (段々) *adv*.
(～ to, ni) gradually; little by
little; one after another:
Ki no ha ga dañdañ *kiiroku natta*.
(木の葉がだんだん黄色くなった) The
leaves have *gradually* turned yellow. / *Kare no seekaku ga* dañdañ (*to*) *wakatte kita*. (彼の性格がだ
んだん(と)わかってきた) I have come to
understand his personality *little
by little*. / *Tanaka-sañ no byooki
wa* dañdañ (*to*) *waruku natta*. (田
中さんの病気はだんだん(と)悪くなった)
Ms. Tanaka's sickness *slowly*
worsened.

da¹ñjo だんじょ (男女) *n*. man and
woman; both sexes:
Kono kurasu wa dañjo *awasete
sañjuu-niñ imasu*. (このクラスは男女
合わせて 30 人います) There are thirty *boys and girls* in this class. /

Dañjo o towazu, *oobo dekimasu.* (男女を問わず、応募できます) *Anybody can apply regardless of sex.*

da⌐ñjo byo⌐odoo だんじょびょうどう (男女平等) *n.* equality between men and women.

da⌐ñjo do⌐oken だんじょどうけん (男女同権) *n.* equal rights for men and women.

da⌐ñjo kyo⌐ogaku だんじょきょうがく (男女共学) *n.* coeducation.
★ Sometimes abbreviated to '*kyoogaku.*'

da⌐ñkai だんかい (段階) *n.* **1** step; stage; phase:
Kore wa jikkeñ no dai-ichi dañkai *desu.* (これは実験の第一段階です) This is the first *step* in the experiment. / *Ima no* dañkai *de wa happyoo dekimaseñ.* (今の段階では発表できません) We cannot make an announcement at this *stage.* / *Kooshoo wa atarashii* dañkai *ni haitta.* (交渉は新しい段階に入った) The negotiations have entered a new *phase.*
2 grade; rank; level:
Gakkoo no seeseki wa itsutsu no dañkai *ni wakete, hyooka saremasu.* (学校の成績は五つの段階に分けて、評価されます) Schoolchildren's performance is rated according to five *levels.*

da⌐ñketsu だんけつ (団結) *n.* union; solidarity:
dañketsu-*ryoku* (団結力) the power of *unity* / dañketsu *o katameru* (団結を固める) strengthen *solidarity.*

dañketsu suru (〜する) *vi.* unite:
Machi no juumiñ wa dañketsu *shite, hañtai-uñdoo ni tachiagatta.* (町の住民は団結して、反対運動に立ち上がった) The inhabitants of the town *joined together* and rose up in a movement of protest.

dano だの *p.* and; or; and the like; and so forth; and what not:

USAGE
Used to link nouns, verbs or adjectives which are viewed as representative examples of their class.

Watashi wa jisho dano *sañkoosho* dano *o tsukatte shirabemashita.* (私は辞書だの参考書だのを使って調べました) I checked it using dictionaries, reference books *and so forth.* / *Uchi no ko wa atsui* dano *tsukareta* dano *to itte zeñzeñ beñkyoo shinai.* (うちの子は暑いだの疲れただのと言って全然勉強しない) Our child doesn't study at all, saying it is too hot, *or* he is too tired, *or something or the other.* 《⇨ ya¹; to ka》

da⌐ no ni だのに *conj.* (*informal*) but; nevertheless: ★ Used at the beginning of a sentence.
Kanojo ni wa nañ do mo tegami o dashimashita. Da no ni heñji o kuremaseñ. (彼女には何度も手紙を出しました。だのに返事をくれません) I have written to her many times. *But* she has never answered me.

da⌐ñsee だんせい (男性) *n.* adult man; male:
Ano kashu wa chuuneñ no dañsee *ni niñki ga aru.* (あの歌手は中年の男性に人気がある) The singer is popular among middle-aged *men.* / *Sono kaisha de wa* dañsee *no shaiñ o boshuu shite iru.* (その会社では男性の社員を募集している) The company is advertising for *male* employees. 《↔ josee》《⇨ dañshi; otoko》

da⌐ñsee-teki だんせいてき (男性的) *a.n.* (〜 na, ni) (of men, women and things) manly; masculine; mannish:
dañsee-teki *na hito* (男性的な人) a *manly* man / dansee-teki *na ara-arashii yama* (男性的な荒々しい山) jagged *manly* mountains /

Tanaka-sañ ni wa dañsee-teki *na tokoro ga aru.* (田中さんには男性的なところがある) Ms. Tanaka has some *mannish* characteristics. 《⇨ otokorashii》

da⌐ñshi だんし (男子) *n.* **1** boy: *Kono kurasu no* dañshi *to joshi no wariai wa sañ tai ni desu.* (このクラスの男子と女子の割合は3対2です) The ratio of *boys* to girls in this class is three to two. / dañshi-*koo* (男子校) a *boys'* school.
2 man; male: dañshi-*yoo toire* (男子用トイレ) the *men's* toilet / *Ano mise wa* dañshi-*gakusee ni niñki ga aru.* (あの店は男子学生に人気がある) That store is popular among *male* students. 《↔ joshi》《⇨ dañsee》

da⌐ñsu ダンス *n.* dance: ★ '*dañsu-paatii*' (from 'dance party') means a social gathering for dancing.
Sakuya wa dañsu-*paatii e itta.* (昨夜はダンスパーティーへ行った) I went to a *dance* last night.

da⌐ñtai だんたい (団体) *n.* party; group; body: *Juugo-mee no* dañtai *o soshiki shita.* (十五名の団体を組織した) We formed a *party* of fifteen. / *Sañjuu-mee ijoo no* dañtai *ni wa waribiki ga arimasu.* (三十名以上の団体には割り引きがあります) There is a discount for *groups* of thirty people or more. / dañtai-*ryokoo* (団体旅行) a *group* tour.

da⌐ñtee だんてい (断定) *n.* conclusion; decision: dañtee *o kudasu* (断定を下す) make one's *conclusion* / *Ima no tokoro* dañtee *wa dekinai.* (今のところ断定はできない) We cannot make a *decision* at the moment.
dañtee suru (～する) *vt.* conclude; decide: *Keesatsu wa sono otoko o jisatsu to* dañtee *shita.* (警察はその男を自殺と断定した) The

police *concluded* that the man committed suicide.

da⌐ñtoo だんとう (暖冬) *n.* mild winter: Dañtoo-*iheñ de sutoobu ga urenakatta.* (暖冬異変でストーブが売れなかった) Heaters did not sell well because of the abnormally *warm winter.*

-da⌐rake だらけ *suf.* (*n.*) [after a noun] be full of; be covered with: ★ Used in an unfavorable situation.
*Kare no te wa chi[doro]-*darake *datta.* (彼の手は血[泥]だらけだった) His hands *were covered* with blood [mud]. / *Kono hoñyaku wa machigai-*darake *da.* (この翻訳は間違いだらけだ) This translation *is full of* mistakes. / *Heya ga gomi-*darake *da.* (部屋がごみだらけだ) The room *is littered* with trash. / *Fuku ga abura-*darake *da.* (服が油だらけだ) The clothes *are smeared* with oil.

da⌐rashina⌐·i だらしない *a.* (-ku)
1 slovenly; sloppy; untidy: *Fukusoo ga* darashinai *to darashinai niñgeñ da to omowareru.* (服装がだらしないとだらしない人間だと思われる) If you are *sloppily* dressed, you will be considered a *sloppy* person. / *Kare no heya wa* darashinaku *chirakatte ita.* (彼の部屋はだらしなく散らかっていた) His room was *messy* and everything was scattered around.
2 weak-willed; spineless: *Sono-gurai de akirameru nañte* darashinai *na.* (そのぐらいであきらめるなんてだらしないな) How *spineless* of you to give up at this point!

USAGE
Also '*darashi (ga) nai.*' There are two polite forms: '*darashi (ga) nai desu*', and '*darashi (ga) arimaseñ.*'

da⌐re だれ（誰）*n.* who; whose; whom:

Dare *ga soo iimashita ka?* (だれがそう言いましたか) *Who* said so? / *Kore wa* dare *no kutsu desu ka?* (これはだれの靴ですか) *Whose* shoes are these? / *Dare ni aitai no desu ka?* (だれに会いたいのですか) *Who* is it you wish to see? / *Dare mo sono shitsumoñ ni kotaerarenakatta.* (だれもその質問に答えられなかった) *Nobody* could answer the question. 《⇨ donata》

da⌐re-ka だれか（誰か）*n.* someone; anyone:

Dare-ka *kono nimotsu o mite ite kuremaseñ ka?* (だれかこの荷物を見ていてくれませんか) Won't *someone* watch this baggage for me? / Dare-ka *kanojo no juusho o shirimaseñ ka?* (だれか彼女の住所を知りませんか) Doesn't *anyone* know her address?

da⌐re⌐・ru だれる *vi.* (dare-te Ⅴ) **1** become dull; become tedious: *Kono shoosetsu wa nagasugite, tochuu de darete shimau.* (この小説は長すぎて、途中でだれてしまう) This novel is so long that it *becomes tedious* by the middle.
2 become listless: *Reñkyuu de* darete *shimatta.* (連休でだれてしまった) I *became listless* because of the consecutive holidays.

daroo だろう [follows a verb, noun, adjectival noun, or adjective] (*polite*=deshoo) I think; I suppose; I wonder: *Kare mo iku* daroo. (彼も行くだろう) *I think* he will also go. / *Ame wa furanai* daroo. (雨は降らないだろう) *I* don't *think* it will rain. / *Ano hito wa dare* daroo. (あの人はだれだろう) *I wonder* who that man is. / *Asoko wa shizuka* daroo naa. (あそこは静かだろうなあ) *I think* that place is quiet. / *Kono kuruma wa takai*

daroo *ne.* (この車は高いだろうね) *I suppose* this car is very expensive. 《⇨ da; deshoo》

da⌐ru⌐・i だるい *a.* (-ku) listless; feel languid [tired]: *Netsu wa sagatta ga, mada karada ga* darui. (熱は下がったが、まだ体がだるい) The fever has gone, but I still feel *listless*. / *Ashi ga* darui. (足がだるい) My legs feel *heavy*.

da⌐sseñ だっせん（脱線）*n.* derailment; digression.
dasseñ suru (〜する) *vi.* be derailed; digress: *Ressha ga* dasseñ *shita.* (列車が脱線した) The train *ran off the track*.

da⌐s・u だす（出す）*vt.* (dash·i-; das·a-; dash·i-te Ⓒ) **1** hold out; stick out: *Deñsha no mado kara te o* dasanai *de kudasai.* (電車の窓から手を出さないでください) *Don't stick* your hands out of the train window. / *Sono ko wa watashi ni mukatte, shita o* dashita. (その子は私に向かって、舌を出した) The boy *stuck out* his tongue at me.
2 take out: *kabañ kara kyookasho o* dasu (かばんから教科書を出す) *take* a textbook out of a bag / *kodomo o soto e* dashite *asobaseru* (子どもを外へ出して遊ばせる) *send* a child *out* to play / *kimerareta basho ni gomi o* dasu (決められた場所にごみを出す) *take* the garbage *out* to the designated place.
3 issue; publish: *Sono kaisha wa zasshi o go-shurui* dashite *iru.* (その会社は雑誌を5種類出している) The company *issues* five kinds of magazines. / *Koñdo Eego no hoñ o* dashimasu. (今度英語の本を出します) I will *publish* an English book shortly. / *Sono kashu wa hajimete rekoodo o* dashita. (その歌手は初めてレコードを

出した) The singer *made* a record for the first time. 《⇨ hakkoo; shuppañ》

4 give; hand in:
nyuukoku no kyoka o dasu (入国の許可をだす) *give* permission to enter a country / *Señsee wa gakusee ni takusañ shukudai o* dashita. (先生は学生にたくさん宿題を出した) The teacher *gave* the students lots of homework. / *Kare wa jihyoo o* dashita. (彼は辞表をだした) He *handed in* his resignation.

5 send:
Tegami o sokutatsu de dashita. (手紙を速達で出した) I *sent* a letter by special delivery. / *Gañsho wa* dashimashita *ka?* (願書は出しましたか) Have you *sent in* your application form? / *Yamada-sañ o daihyoo ni* dashimashoo. (山田さんを代表に出しましょう) Let's *send* Ms. Yamada as our representative. 《⇨ okuru¹》

6 serve (a dish); pay (expenses):
o-kyaku ni koohii o dasu (お客にコーヒーを出す) *serve* coffee to a visitor / *Chichi ga gakuhi o* dashite kureta. (父が学費を出してくれた) My father *financed* my way through college.

7 give out; break out:
hanaji o dasu (鼻血を出す) *have* a nose bleed. / *Kaze o hiite, netsu o* dashita. (かぜを引いて、熱を出した) I caught a cold and *ran* a fever. / *Odoroite, koe o* dashite shimatta. (驚いて、声を出してしまった) I *gave out* a cry in surprise.

8 show; display:
paatii ni kao o dasu (パーティーに顔を出す) *make an appearance* at a party / *Soñna koto o iu nara, shooko o* dase. (そんなことを言うなら証拠を出せ) If you so insist, *show* me the evidence. / *Kare wa mado kara hata o* dashita. (彼は窓から旗を出した) He *displayed* the flag from the window.

9 put forth; stir (power, energy, etc.):
chikara o dasu (力を出す) *put forth* one's strength / *supiido o* dasu (スピードを出す) *gather* speed. / *Geñki o* dashi nasai. (元気を出しなさい) *Cheer up!* / *Yuuki o* dashi nasai. (勇気を出しなさい) *Summon up* your courage!

10 start; result in; cause (a fire, casualties, etc.):
Yuube kiñjo no apaato ga kaji o dashita. (ゆうべ近所のアパートが火事を出した) Last night a fire *started* at an apartment in the neighborhood. / *Koñkai no jiko wa ooku no shishoosha o* dashita. (今回の事故は多くの死傷者を出した) The accident *resulted in* many dead and injured.

11 draw; work out (a conclusion, an answer, etc.):
Ketsuroñ o dasu *no wa mada hayai.* (結論を出すのはまだ早い) It is still too early to *draw* a conclusion. / *Kare wa tadashii kotae o* dashita. (彼は正しい答えを出した) He *worked out* the correct answer.

12 open (a shop):
Shiñjuku ni mise o dasu *ni wa taiheñ na kane ga iru.* (新宿に店を出すにはたいへんな金がいる) It costs a lot to *open* a shop in Shinjuku. / *Sono kaisha wa Amerika ni shiteñ o* dashita. (その会社はアメリカに支店を出した) That company *opened* a branch office in America.

-da¹s·u だす (出す) (-dash·i-; -das·a-; -dash·i-te Ⓒ) ★ Occurs as the second element of compound verbs. Added to the continuative base of a verb.

1 [with a transitive verb] take out; put out; bring out:
oshi-dasu (押し出す) push *out* / *tori*-dasu (取り出す) take *out* / *hiki*-dasu (引き出す) pull *out* / *mochi-*

dasu (持ち出す) carry *out* / *oi*-dasu (追い出す) drive *away* / *hoori*-dasu (放り出す) throw *out* / *shime*-dasu (締め出す) shut *out*.

2 [with an intransitive verb] go out; come out:

nige-dasu (逃げ出す) run *away* / *nuke*-dasu (抜け出す) sneak *out* / *hai*-dasu (はい出す) crawl *out* / *tobi*-dasu (飛び出す) jump *out*.

3 [with a transitive or intransitive verb] start; begin:

yomi-dasu (読み出す) *start* to read / *utai*-dasu (歌い出す) *start* singing / *aruki*-dasu (歩き出す) *start* walking / *furi*-dasu (降り出す) *begin* to rain [snow] / *naki*-dasu (泣き出す) *burst out* crying. 《⇨ -hajimeru》

da⌐too だとう (妥当) *a.n.* (～ na) appropriate; proper; reasonable: *Sono handan wa* datoo *na tokoro deshoo.* (その判断は妥当なところでしょう) I think the judgment is *appropriate*.

da⌐ttai だったい (脱退) *n.* withdrawal; secession.

dattai suru (～する) *vt.* withdraw; secede: *Sono kuni wa doomee kara* dattai shita. (その国は同盟から脱退した) The nation *withdrew* from the alliance. 《↔ kanyuu》

da⌐ttara だったら *conj.* (*informal*) if so: ★ In this usage, used only at the beginning of a sentence. Dattara, *doo sureba ii n desu ka?* (だったら、どうすればいいんですか) *If that is the case*, what should I do? / Dattara, *ayamareba ii ja nai desu ka?* (だったら、謝ればいいじゃないですか) *If so*, why don't you apologize?

datte[1] だって *p.* [an informal variant of '*de mo*' and follows a noun] **1** even:

a (used to give an extreme example).

Sonna mono, inu datte *tabenai yo.*

(そんなもの、犬だって食べないよ) *Even* a dog wouldn't eat something like that. / *Konna kantan na koto, kodomo* datte *shitte iru yo.* (こんな簡単なこと、子どもだって知っているよ) *Even* a child knows something as simple as this. / *Asu* datte, *asatte* datte *kamaimasen.* (明日だってあさってだってかまいません) It doesn't matter *even if* it is tomorrow or the day after tomorrow. 《⇨ de mo[1]》

b (with a number or quantity expression, indicates an emphatic negative):

Ano ko wa ichi-do datte *chikoku o shita koto ga arimasen.* (あの子は一度だって遅刻をしたことがありません) That child has not been late *even* once. / *Ano hito ni wa ichi-en* datte *kashitaku arimasen.* (あの人には一円だって貸したくありません) I wouldn't lend him *even* one *single* yen.

2 always; everyone; everywhere: ★ Used with interrogatives such as '*itsu*,' '*dare*,' and '*doko*.'

Ano hito wa itsu datte *hima soo da.* (あの人はいつだって暇そうだ) She *always* seems to have time on her hands. / *Kono-goro wa doko no resutoran* datte *kineńseki o mookete iru.* (この頃はどこのレストランだって禁煙席を設けている) These days *all* restaurants have no-smoking sections. / *Sonna koto wa* dare datte *wakaru.* (そんなことはだれだってわかる) *Anyone* can understand something like that. 《⇨ de mo[1]》

da⌐tte[2] だって *conj.* (*informal*) because; but: ★ Used at the beginning of a sentence.

"Doo-shite okureta no?" "Datte basu ga okureta n da mono" (「どうして遅れたの」「だってバスが遅れたんだもの」) "Why are you late?" "Well, *because* the bus was late." / *"Hayaku oki nasai." "Datte nemui ń*

da mono." (「早く起きなさい」「だって
眠いんだもの」) "Hurry up and get
out of bed." "*But* I'm sleepy."
《⇨ de mo²》

de¹ で *p.* [follows a noun]
1 (indicates the location of an
action) at; in; on:
Gakkoo de *kookai-kooza ga arimasu.* (学校で公開講座があります)
There is an open lecture *at* the
school. / *Kono dooro* de *asoñde
wa ikemaseñ.* (この道路で遊んではいけ
ません) Don't play *on* this street. /
Doko de *shokuji o shimashoo ka?*
(どこで食事をしましょうか) *Where* shall
we eat? / *Giñza* de *eega o mimashita.* (銀座で映画を見ました) I saw a
movie *in* Ginza.
2 (indicates a means or method)
by; with; in:
Takushii de *ikimashoo.* (タクシーで
行きましょう) Let's go *by* taxi. / *Peñ*
de *kaite kudasai.* (ペンで書いてくださ
い) Please write *with* a pen. /
Kagu wa torakku de *hakobima-
shita.* (家具はトラックで運びました) We
moved the furniture *by* truck. /
Sono nyuusu wa kesa no shiñbuñ
de *shirimashita.* (そのニュースは今朝
の新聞で知りました) I heard about
the news *in* this morning's paper.
3 (indicates a substance or material) of; with:
Kono niñgyoo wa kami de *dekite
imasu.* (この人形は紙でできています)
This doll is made *of* paper. /
Kono yubiwa wa kiñ de *mekki
shite arimasu.* (この指輪は金でめっき
したあります) This ring is *gold*
plated.
4 (sets the limits of a time or
space) in:
Nihoñ de *ichi-bañ takai yama wa
Fuji-sañ desu.* (日本で一番高い山は
富士山です) The highest mountain
in Japan is Mt. Fuji. / *Ichi-neñ*
de *ichibañ ii kisetsu wa itsu desu
ka?* (一年で一番いい季節はいつですか)

What is the best season *in* the
year?
5 (indicates cause or reason)
because of; by; owing to:
Byooki de *kaisha o yasumimashita.* (病気で会社を休みました) I was
absent from the company *due to*
illness. / *Jiko* de *dooro ga koñde
imasu.* (事故で道路が込んでいます)
The road is crowded *because of*
the accident. / *Kimi wa* nañ de
gakkoo e konakatta ñ desu ka?
(君は何で学校へ来なかったんですか)
Why is it that you didn't come to
school? / *Watashi wa* sukii de
ashi o orimashita. (私はスキーで足を
折りました) I broke my leg *skiing.* /
Jishiñ de *ooku no kaoku ga
kowaremashita.* (地震で多くの家屋が
壊れました) Many buildings were
destroyed *by* the earthquake. /
Kare wa shigoto de *gaikoku e ikimashita.* (彼は仕事で外国へ行きまし
た) He went overseas *on* business.
6 (delimits the time in which an
action or event occurs) in:
Is-shuukañ de *sañ-satsu hoñ o
yomimashita.* (一週間で3冊本を読
みました) I read three books *in* a
week. / *Sañjup-puñ* de *sono shigoto wa dekimaseñ.* (三十分でその
仕事はできません) I cannot do that
work *in* thirty minutes. / *Ichi-
jikañ* de *shokuji o sumasete kudasai.* (一時間で食事をすませてください)
Please finish up your meal *in* one
hour. / *Shikeñ wa ato jup-puñ* de
owari desu. (試験はあと10分で終わり
です) The exam will be over *in*
ten minutes.
7 (sets the limits of a price or
quantity) for; by:
Riñgo wa sañ-ko de *hyaku-eñ
desu.* (りんごは3個で100円です) Ap-
ples are 100 yen *for* three. / *Sono
terebi wa ikura* de *kaimashita ka?*
(そのテレビはいくらで買いましたか) *How
much* did you pay for that televi-

sion? / *Soñna koto* boku hitori de *kimeraremaseñ.*(そんなことぼく一人で決められません) I cannot decide that kind of thing *on my own.*

de[2] で *copula* [the *te*-form of '*da*'] be:
Gogo wa kumori de, ashita wa ame deshoo.(午後は曇りで、あしたは雨でしょう) It *will be* cloudy this afternoon and it will rain tomorrow. / *Imooto wa daigakusee de, eebuñgaku o señkoo shite imasu.*(妹は大学生で、英文学を専攻しています) My younger sister *is* a university student studying English literature. / *Chichi wa isha de, ani wa kyooshi desu.*(父は医者で、兄は教師です) My father *is* a doctor and my older brother is a teacher.

de「a·u であう (出会う) *vi.* (dea·i-; deaw·a-; deat-te Ⓒ) **1** come across; run into; meet:
Kitaku no tochuu de battari kyuuyuu ni deatta.(帰宅の途中でばったり旧友に出会った) I *ran into* an old friend on the way home. / *Watashi wa paatii de kare ni* [to] *hajimete deaimashita.*(私はパーティーで彼に[と]初めて出会いました) I *met* him for the first time at the party.
2 encounter (difficulties, hardship, etc.):
Ikite iku aida ni wa samazama na koñnañ ni deau mono desu.(生きていく間にはさまざまな困難に出会うものです) It is natural to *encounter* various difficulties in our lifetimes.

de「do」koro でどころ (出所) *n.* source; origin:
Sono uwasa no dedokoro o shitte imasu ka?(そのうわさの出どころを知っていますか) Do you know the *source* of that rumor? / *Kare ni sono kane no dedokoro o tazuneta.*(彼にその金の出どころをたずねた) I asked him *where that money came from.*

de「eto デート *n.* date:

Sañ-ji ni kanojo to deeto *no yakusoku ga arimasu.*(3時に彼女とデートの約束があります) I have a *date* with her at three o'clock. / *Kanojo ni* deeto *o mooshikoñda ga kotowarareta.*(彼女にデートを申し込んだが断られた) I asked her for a *date* but was turned down.
deeto suru (〜する) *vi.* have a date: *Watashi wa kinoo Yamadasañ to* deeto *shita.*(私はきのう山田さんとデートした) I *had a date* with Miss Yamada yesterday.

de「fure デフレ *n.* deflation:
defure *ni naru* (デフレになる) sink into *deflation.* 《↔ iñfure》

de「guchi でぐち (出口) *n.* exit; way out:
Deguchi *wa doko desu ka?* (出口はどこですか) Where is the *exit*? / Deguchi *wa kochira desu.*(出口はこちらです) This is the *way out.* 《↔ iriguchi》

de「iri でいり (出入り) *n.* going in and out:
Kare no tokoro wa hito no deiri *ga ooi.*(彼の所は人の出入りが多い) He *has a lot of visitors.*
deiri suru (〜する) *vi.* go in and out: *Kuukoo ni* deiri suru *hito wa miñna bodii-chekku o ukemasu.*(空港に出入りする人はみんなボディチェックを受けます) Everyone who *goes in and out* of the airport undergoes a body-check.

de「iriguchi でいりぐち (出入り口) *n.* entrance; doorway; gateway:
Deiriguchi *ni tatanai de kudasai.*(出入り口に立たないでください) Don't stand in the *doorway.*

de「kake·ru でかける (出掛ける) *vi.* (dekake-te Ⓥ) go out; leave the house:
Yamada-sañ wa sañpo ni dekakemashita.(山田さんは散歩に出かけました) Mr.Yamada *has gone out* for a walk. / *Kachoo wa tadaima shutchoo de Oosaka ni* dekakete ori-

masu.(課長はただいま出張で大阪に出かけております) The section chief *is* presently in Osaka on business. / *Choodo* dekakeyoo *to shita tokoro e o-kyaku ga kita.*(ちょうど出かけようとしたところへお客が来た) Just as I was about to *go out*, a visitor arrived. / *Dochira e* o-dekake *desu ka?*(どちらへお出かけですか) Where *are* you *off to*?

> (USAGE)
> Japanese people often use this expression by way of greeting. They do not mean to be inquisitive. The usual answer is '*Chotto, soko made.*' (Just over there).

o-dekake kudasai (お出かけください) come and visit: *Sono uchi zehi ichi-do* o-dekake kudasai.(そのうちひ一度お出かけください) *Please come and visit* us sometime.

de⌈ki でき (出来) *n.* **1** workmanship; make: *Kono urushi no hako wa subarashii* deki *da.*(この漆の箱はすばらしい出来だ) This lacquered box is a fine piece of *workmanship*.
2 crop; harvest: *Kotoshi wa jagaimo no* deki *ga yokatta* [*warukatta*].(今年はじゃがいもの出来が良かった[悪かった]) The potato *crop* was good [poor] this year.
3 result: *Shiken no* deki *wa maamaa datta.*(試験の出来はまあまあだった) The *result* of the examination was not so bad.

deki no yoi [**warui**] (〜の良い[悪い]) good [bad]: deki no yoi [warui] *gakusee* (出来の良い[悪い]学生) a *bright* [*dull*] student.

de⌈kiagari できあがり (出来上がり) *n.* completion; workmanship: Dekiagari *wa itsu desu ka?* (出来上がりはいつですか) When will it be

completed? / Dekiagari *wa joojoo da.*(出来上がりは上々だ) The *workmanship* is excellent. (⇨ deki)

de⌈kiagar·u できあがる (出来上がる) *vi.* (-agar·i-; -agar·a-; -agat-te Ⓒ) be completed; be finished: *Kono apaato wa* dekiagaru *made ni dono-kurai kakarimasu ka?* (このアパートはでき上がるまでにどのくらいかかりますか) How long will it take for this apartment building to *be completed*? / *Genkoo wa getsumatsu made ni wa* dekiagarimasu.(原稿は月末までにはでき上がります) The manuscript will *be completed* by the end of this month. / *Seetaa ga yatto* dekiagatta.(セーターがやっとでき上がった) The sweater *is finished* at last. / *Ryoori ga* dekiagarimashita.(料理ができ上がりました) The meal *is ready*. / *Sentakuya kara sentakumono ga* dekiagatte kita.(洗濯屋から洗濯物ができ上がって来た) The clothes *came back* from the laundry.

de⌈ki⌉goto できごと (出来事) *n.* occurrence; happening; event; accident: *Watashi-tachi wa sono fushigi na* dekigoto *ni tsuite hanashiatta.*(私たちはその不思議な出来事について話し合った) We talked about the strange *happenings*. / *Kotoshi no omo-na* dekigoto *wa nan desu ka?* (今年の主な出来事は何ですか) What were the chief *events* of this year?

de⌈kimo⌉no できもの (出来物) *n.* boil; tumor; eruption: *O-shiri ni* dekimono *ga dekita rashii.*(おしりにできものができたらしい) It seems that a *boil* has broken out on my bottom.

de⌈ki⌉·ru できる (出来る) *vi.* (deki-te Ⓥ) **1** be able to do; can do: *Kare wa suiee ga yoku* dekiru.(彼は水泳がよくできる) He *can* swim very well. / *Watashi wa kuruma no unten ga* dekimasu.(私は車の運

転ができます) I *can* drive a car. / *Añna hidoi koto wa watashi ni wa totemo* dekinai. (あんなひどいことは私にはとてもできない) I *could never do* such a terrible thing. / *Sore wa* dekinai *soodañ desu.* (それはできない相談です) That is an *impossible* proposition.

> **(USAGE)**
>
> A less common variant of the potential is made with verb＋'*koto ga dekiru.*' e.g. *hanasu koto ga dekiru* (話すことができる) = *hanaseru* (話せる) I can speak.

2 be competent; be capable:
Kare wa nakanaka dekiru *otoko da.* (彼はなかなかできる男だ) He is a very *competent* man. / *Kanojo wa suugaku ga* dekiru. (彼女は数学ができる) She *is good* at mathematics.
3 be completed; be organized:
Sono biru wa ku-gatsu ni deki-masu. (そのビルは9月にできます) The building will *be completed* in September. / *Uchi no kaisha ni mo roodoo-kumiai ga* dekita. (うちの会社にも労働組合ができた) A labor union *was set up* in our company as well.
4 be ready:
Yuushoku no yooi ga dekimashita. (夕食の用意ができました) Dinner *is ready.* / *Shuppatsu no juñbi wa* dekimashita *ka?* (出発の準備はできましたか) *Are* you *all set* to depart?
5 be made:
Kono supuuñ wa suteñresu de dekite iru. (このスプーンはステンレスでできている) This spoon *is made* of stainless steel. / *Kono kutsu wa gañjoo ni* dekite iru. (この靴はがんじょうにできている) These shoes *are made* strong.
6 form:
Kao ni nikibi ga dekita. (顔ににきびができた) Pimples have *come out* on my face. / *I ni kaiyoo ga* dekita.

(胃に潰ようができた) An ulcer has *formed* in my stomach. / *Tsuma ni kodomo ga* dekita. (妻に子どもができた) My wife has *become pregnant.*
7 grow; yield:
Kono chihoo de wa riñgo ga deki-masu. (この地方ではりんごができます) Apples *are grown* in this district.

de⌐kiru dake できるだけ (出来る丈) *adv.* as ... as possible; to the best of one's ability:
Dekiru dake *hayaku kite kudasai.* (できるだけ早く来てください) Please come *as* early *as possible.* / *Yasai wa* dekiru dake *shiñseñ na mono o katta hoo ga yoi.* (野菜はできるだけ新鮮なものを買ったほうがよい) You'd better buy the freshest vegetables *available.* / Dekiru dake *heya o kiree ni shite mimasu.* (できるだけ部屋をきれいにしてみます) I will *do my best* to clean the room. / Dekiru dake *no koto wa yatte mimasu.* (できるだけのことはやってみます) I will do everything *in my power.*

de⌐koboko でこぼこ (凸凹) *a.n.* (〜 na, ni) uneven; rough:
dekoboko *na dooro* (でこぼこ道路) a *rough* road / *Kono michi wa* dekoboko *shite iru.* (この道はでこぼこしている) This road is very *bumpy.*

de mo[1] でも *p.* [the *te*-form of '*da*' plus the particle '*mo*']
1 even:
a (used to give an extreme example):
Soñna kañtañ na koto wa kodomo de mo *dekimasu.* (そんな簡単なことは子どもでもできます) *Even* a child can do something as simple as that. / *Wakai koro wa yuki no hi* de mo *jogiñgu shita mono desu.* (若い頃は雪の日でもジョギングしたものです) In my youth, I used to go jogging *even* on snowy days. / *Ame* de mo *uñdookai wa okonaimasu.* (雨でも運動会は行います) *Even* if it rains,

we will hold sports day.
《⇨ datte¹》
b (used to emphasize the preceding noun):
Hitori de mo *ooku no seeto ga shiken ni gookaku sureba ureshii.* (一人でも多くの生徒が試験に合格すればうれしい) I would be pleased if *even* one additional student were to pass the exam. / *Kau toki wa ichi-en* de mo *yasuku kaitai mono desu.* (買うときは 1 円でも安く買いたいものです) It is natural that we want to buy things *even* one yen more cheaply. 《⇨ datte¹》
2 any: ★ Used with interrogatives such as '*itsu*,' '*dare*,' and '*doko*.'
Hoomon-sha wa itsu de mo *kangee itashimasu.* (訪問者はいつでも歓迎いたします) Visitors are welcome at *any time*. / *Dare* de mo *hitotsu gurai tokui na mono ga aru mono desu.* (だれでも一つくらい得意なものがあるものです) *Anyone* is good at one thing at least. / *Sono shina wa* do-ko de mo *te ni hairimasu.* (その品はどこでも手に入ります) The goods are available *anywhere*. 《⇨ datte¹》
3 or something: ★ Used to casually introduce an example when making suggestions, giving invitations, etc.
O-hima nara eega de mo *mimasen ka?* (おひまなら映画でも見ませんか) If you have time, why don't we, *say*, watch a movie? / *Sono hen de koohii* de mo *ikaga desu ka?* (その辺でコーヒーでもいかがですか) What about having a coffee *or something* over there?

de mo² でも *conj.* (*informal*) but; and yet: ★ In this usage, used only at the beginning of a sentence.
Kinoo wa netsu ga atta. De mo *shigoto ni ikimashita.* (きのうは熱があった. でも仕事に行きました) I had a tem-perature yesterday, *but* went to work. / De mo *watashi wa hantai desu.* (でも私は反対です) *But* I am against it. 《⇨ datte²》

de⸢mukae でむかえ (出迎え) *n.* meeting; reception:
Eki made demukae *ni kite kudasai.* (駅まで出迎えに来てください) Please come to the station to *meet* me. / *Kare wa oozee no hito no* demukae *o uketa.* (彼は大勢の人の出迎えを受けた) He *was greeted* by many people. / *Eki-mae wa kare no* demukae *no hito de ippai datta.* (駅前は彼の出迎えの人でいっぱいだった) The station square was full of people *welcoming* him. 《↔ mio-kuri》

de⸢mukae·ru でむかえる (出迎える) *vt.* (-kae-te Ⅴ) meet; greet; receive:
Kuukoo de [ni] tomodachi o demu-kaeru *koto ni natte imasu.* (空港で[に]友だちを出迎えることになっています) I am to *meet* my friends at the airport. / *Eki made kanojo o* demu-kae *ni itta.* (駅まで彼女を出迎えに行った) I went to the station to *meet* her. / *O-*demukae *arigatoo gozai-masu.* (お出迎えありがとうございます) Thank you for coming out to *meet* me.

de⸢natsu でんあつ (電圧) *n.* volt-age:
Denatsu *ga takai [hikui].* (電圧が高い[低い]) The *voltage* is high [low]. / denatsu *o ageru [sageru]* (電圧を上げる[下げる]) increase [decrease] the *voltage*.

de⸢nchi でんち (電池) *n.* battery; (electric) cell:
Kono kamera no denchi *o tori-kaete kudasai.* (このカメラの電池を取り換えてください) Please replace the *cell* of this camera with a new one. / *Rajio no* denchi *wa utte imasu ka?* (ラジオの電池は売っていますか) Do you sell radio *batteries*? /

Kono deñchi *wa kirete iru.*（この電池は切れている）This *battery* is dead. / *kañ*-deñchi（乾電池）a dry *cell* [*battery*] / *chiku*-deñchi（蓄電池）a storage *cell* [*battery*] / *tañ-ichi* deñchi（単一電池）a size D *battery* / *tañ-ni* deñchi（単二電池）a size C *battery* / *tañ-sañ* deñchi（単三電池）a size AA *battery*. ★ A car battery is usually called '*batterii*'（バッテリー）.

de「ñchuu でんちゅう（電柱）*n.* utility pole; electric light [telephone] pole.

de「ñeñ でんえん（田園）*n.* the country; rural districts: deñeñ-*seekatsu*（田園生活）a *country* life / deñeñ-*fuukee*（田園風景）*rustic* scenery.

de「ñgeñ でんげん（電源）*n.* power supply; switch; outlet: deñgeñ o ireru [kiru]（電源を入れる[切る]）*turn the switch on* [*off*].

de「ñki でんき（電気）*n.* **1** electricity: *Kono omocha wa* deñki *de ugoku.*（このおもちゃは電気で動く）This toy works by *electricity*. / *Keekootoo wa amari* deñki *o kuwanai.*（蛍光灯はあまり電気を食わない）Fluorescent lamps do not use much *electricity*. / deñki-*ryookiñ*（電気料金）*electric* charges / deñki-*kigu*（電気器具）*electric* appliances. **2** electric light: deñki o tsukeru [kesu]（電気をつける[消す]）turn on [off] the *light*.

de「ñki-go」tatsu でんきごたつ（電気炬燵）*n.* electric foot warmer. 《⇨ kotatsu (photo)》

de「ñki-sooji」ki でんきそうじき（電気掃除機）*n.* vacuum cleaner.

de「ñki-suta」ñdo でんきスタンド（電気スタンド）*n.* desk lamp; floor lamp.

de「ñkyuu でんきゅう（電球）*n.* electric light bulb: deñkyuu o torikaeru（電球を取り換

える）change the *bulb* / *Ima no* deñkyuu *ga kireta.*（居間の電球が切れた）The *bulb* in the living room has burned out. 《⇨ tama¹》

de「ñpa でんぱ（電波）*n.* electric wave; radio wave: deñpa o dasu [ukeru]（電波を出す[受ける]）transmit [receive] *radio waves*.

de「ñpoo でんぽう（電報）*n.* telegram; wire; telegraph: *Kare ni o-iwai no* deñpoo *o utta.*（彼にお祝いの電報を打った）I sent a congratulatory *telegram* to him. / deñpoo-*ryoo*（電報料）a *telegram* charge / deñpoo *deñwa kyoku*（電報電話局）a *telegraph* and telephone office.

de「ñryoku でんりょく（電力）*n.* electric power; electricity: deñryoku o setsuyaku [muda ni] suru（電力を節約[無駄に]する）save [waste] *electricity*.

de「ñryuu でんりゅう（電流）*n.* electric current.

de「ñseñ¹ でんせん（電線）*n.* electric wire; telephone line.

de「ñseñ² でんせん（伝染）*n.* contagion; infection. **deñseñ suru**（～する）*vi.* be contagious; be infectious: *Kaze wa* deñseñ suru.（かぜは伝染する）Colds *are contagious*. / *Hashika wa* deñseñ suru byooki desu.（はしかは伝染する病気です）Measles is an *infectious* disease.

de「ñsetsu でんせつ（伝説）*n.* legend; tradition.

de「ñsha でんしゃ（電車）*n.* (electric) train; streetcar; tram (car): ★ For specificity, a streetcar or tram may be referred to as '*romeñ deñsha*.' *Kaisha e wa* deñsha *de ikimasu.*（会社へは電車で行きます）I go to my office by *train*. / *Ueno e iku ni wa dono* deñsha *ni noru ñ desu ka?*（上野へ行くにはどの電車に乗るんですか）

Which *train* do I take for Ueno? / *Tsugi no eki de* deñsha *o ori nasai.* (次の駅で電車を降りなさい) Get off the *train* at the next station. 《⇨ ressha; kisha》

Densha ga kimasu. (Train is coming.) Sign hanging above platforms in urban areas that flashes to signal the approach of a train.

de⌈ñshi-re⌉ñji でんしレンジ (電子レンジ) *n.* microwave oven.

de⌈ñtaku でんたく (電卓) *n.* desk [pocket] calculator.

de⌈ñtoo¹ でんとう (電灯) *n.* electric light: deñtoo *o tsukeru* [*kesu*] (電灯をつける[消す]) switch on [off] the *light.*

de⌈ñtoo² でんとう (伝統) *n.* tradition; heritage: deñtoo *o mamoru* [*omoñjiru*] (伝統を守る[重んじる]) maintain [value] a *tradition* / *Kono kaisha wa nanajuu-neñ no* deñtoo *ga arimasu.* (この会社は70年の伝統があります) This company has a *tradition* of seventy years.

de⌈ñtoo-teki でんとうてき (伝統的) *a.n.* (~ na, ni) traditional: deñtoo-teki *na Nihoñ keñchiku* (伝統的な日本建築) *traditional* Japanese architecture / *Kono gakkoo wa* deñtoo-teki *ni yakyuu ga tsuyoi.* (この学校は伝統的に野球が強い) This school is *traditionally* good at baseball.

de⌈ñwa でんわ (電話) *n.* **1** telephone: deñwa *o hiku* [*toritsukeru*] (電話を引く[取り付ける]) install a *telephone* / deñwa *de hanasu* (電話で話す) talk on the *telephone* / *Kono* deñwa *o o-kari dekimasu ka?* (この電話をお借りできますか) May I use this

telephone?

2 (tele)phone call: deñwa *o kakeru* [*kiru*] (電話をかける[切る]) dial [hang up] / *Tanaka-sañ kara* o-deñwa *desu.* (田中さんからお電話です) There is a *phone call* for you from Mr. Tanaka. / *Nyuu Yooku e kokusai* deñwa *o kaketai ñ desu ga.* (ニューヨークへ国際電話をかけたいんですが) I want to make an overseas *phone call* to New York. / *Deñwa o sono mama kirazu ni ite kudasai.* (電話をそのまま切らずにいてください) Please *do not hang up.*

deñwa (o) suru (~(を)する) *vt.* call up; telephone: *Ato de* deñwa *shimasu.* (後で電話します) I'll *call* you back later. / *Deñwa o shite, takushii o yoñde kudasai.* (電話をして、タクシーを呼んでください) Please *telephone* for a taxi.

de⌈ñwa-ba⌉ñgoo でんわばんごう (電話番号) *n.* telephone number: Deñwa-bañgoo *ga chigaimasu.* (電話番号が違います) You have the wrong *number.* / Deñwa-bañgoo *wa nañ-bañ desu ka?* (電話番号は何番ですか) What is your *phone number?* / *Uchi no* deñwa-bañgoo *wa sañ-nii-kyuu-yoñ no sañ-nana-goo-roku desu.* (うちの電話番号は3294-3756です) My *phone number* is 3294-3756.

de⌈ñwachoo でんわちょう (電話帳) *n.* telephone book [directory].

de⌈pa⌉ato デパート *n.* department store: *Sono* depaato *e wa yoku kaimono ni ikimasu.* (そのデパートへはよく買い物に行きます) I often go shopping at that *department store.*

de⌈∙ru でる (出る) *vi.* (de-te Ⅴ) **1** go out; leave; depart: *Heya kara deyoo to shitara,* deñwa *ga natta.* (部屋から出ようとしたら、電話が鳴った) Just as I was about to *go out* of the room, the phone rang. / *Watashi wa maiasa hachi-*

ji ni ie o demasu. (私は毎朝 8 時に家を出ます) I *leave* the house at eight every morning. / *Oosaka-yuki no deñsha wa ichi-bañ señ kara* demasu. (大阪行きの電車は 1 番線から出ます) The train for Osaka *departs* from track 1. 《⇨ shuppatsu》

2 go to; get to:
chikatetsu de Shiñjuku ni deru (地下鉄で新宿に出る) *go* to Shinjuku by subway / *Kono michi o massugu ni iku to eki ni* demasu. (この道をまっすぐに行くと駅に出ます) Go straight along this road, and you'll *get to* the station.

3 attend; take part in:
jugyoo [kaigi] ni deru (授業[会議]に出る) *attend* class [a meeting] / *shiai ni* deru (試合に出る) *take part* in a match / *señkyo ni* deru (選挙に出る) *run* for election. 《⇨ sañka¹》

4 appear; come out:
Nishi no sora ni tsuki ga deta. (西の空に月が出た) The moon *appeared* in the western sky. / *Yamada-sañ ga terebi ni* deta. (山田さんがテレビに出た) Mr. Yamada *appeared* on television. / *Suiseñ no me ga* deta. (水仙の芽が出た) The narcissus buds have *come out.*

5 graduate:
Daigaku o deta *no wa go-neñ mae desu.* (大学を出たのは 5 年前です) It is five years since I *graduated* from university. / *Kono daigaku kara wa yuushuu na sotsugyoosee ga oozee* dete iru. (この大学からは優秀な卒業生が大勢出ている) Many outstanding graduates *have come* from this university. 《⇨ sotsugyoo》

6 produce; yield:
Kono chihoo de wa oñseñ ga deru. (この地方では温泉が出る) There *are* hot springs in this area. / *Kore de*

wa rieki ga denai. (これでは利益が出ない) This *yields little* profit. / *Kono kuruma wa kanari supiido ga* demasu. (この車はかなりスピードが出ます) This car can *run* pretty *fast.*

7 (of physiological phenomena) have:
kushami ga deru (くしゃみが出る) *have* a sneeze / *Yoñjuu-do chikai netsu ga* deta. (40度近い熱が出た) I *had* a fever of almost forty degrees.

8 (of liquid) run; flow; come out:
Jaguchi kara mizu ga dete iru. (蛇口から水が出ている) Water *is flowing* from the tap. / *Kemuri ga shimite, namida ga* deta. (煙がしみて、涙が出た) The smoke made my eyes *water.* / *Hana ga* dete iru yo. (はなが出ているよ) Your nose *is running.*

9 (of emotions and spirits) show; raise:
Kare wa kañjoo ga sugu kao ni deru. (彼は感情がすぐ顔に出る) His emotions easily *show* on his face. / *Kore o nomeba geñki ga* demasu. (これを飲めば元気が出ます) Drinking this will *raise* your spirits. / *Sono kotoba de yuuki ga* deta. (その言葉で勇気が出た) With those words I *found* my courage.

10 stick out:
Kare wa chuuneñ ni natte, o-naka ga dete kita. (彼は中年になって、おなかが出てきた) When he reached middle age, his stomach *began to bulge.* / *Koñna tokoro ni kugi ga* dete iru. (こんなところにくぎが出ている) There's a nail *sticking out* here.

11 be published; be printed:
Kono hoñ wa deta *bakari desu.* (この本は出たばかりです) This book *has* just *been published.* / *Kare no kiji ga zasshi ni* deta. (彼の記事が雑誌に出た) His article *came out* in a magazine. 《⇨ shuppañ¹》

12 be given:
Meeree [Kyoka] ga shachoo kara deta.(命令[許可]が社長から出た) The order [permission] *issued* from the president. / *Boonasu wa neñ ni ni-do demasu.*(ボーナスは年に2度出ます) A bonus *is given* twice a year. / *Señsee kara shukudai ga deta.*(先生から宿題が出た) Our teacher *gave* us homework.
13 be reached; come up with:
Yatto ketsuroñ ga deta.(やっと結論が出た) At last a conclusion *was reached*. / *Hayashi-sañ kara ii aidea ga deta.*(林さんからいいアイデアが出た) Ms. Hayashi *came up with* a good idea.
14 be found; turn up:
Otoshita saifu wa nakanaka denai mono desu.(落とした財布はなかなか出ないものです) A lost purse seldom *turns up* again. / *Ikura sagashite mo ano tegami ga dete konai.*(いくら探してもあの手紙が出てこない) Although I've looked everywhere, the letter *has not been found*.
15 exceed; be over:
Kono kabiñ wa gomañ-eñ o sukoshi deta.(この花瓶は5万円を少し出た) This vase *cost* me a little *over* 50,000 yen. / *Kanojo wa sañjuu o sukoshi dete iru.*(彼女は30を少し出ている) She *is* a little *over* thirty.
16 sell:
Kono hoñ wa saikiñ yoku demasu.(この本は最近良く出ます) This book *has been selling* very well recently. / *Kono fuyu wa kono te no kooto ga yoku demashita.*(この冬はこの手のコートがよく出ました) This kind of coat *sold* well this winter. 《⇨ ureru¹》
17 take an attitude:
Aa-iu hito ni wa tsuyoku [shitate ni] denakute wa dame da.(ああいう人には強く[下手に]出なくてはだめだ) You should *take* a firm [deferential] attitude toward a person like

him. / *Aite ga doo deru ka ga moñdai desu.*(相手がどう出るかが問題です) It is a question of what move the other party *makes*.

-de·ru でる (出る) (-de-te Ⓥ)
★ Occurs as the second element of compound verbs.
1 [with an intransitive verb] appear; come out:
waki-deru (沸き出る) gush *forth* / *tobi*-deru (飛び出る) *protrude; project* / *tsuki*-deru (突き出る) stick *out* / *shimi*-deru (しみ出る) ooze *out*.
2 [with a transitive verb] apply; announce:
mooshi-deru (申し出る) *offer* / *todoke*-deru (届け出る) *report* / *negai*-deru (願い出る) *apply* / *nanori*-deru (名乗り出る) *announce; declare*.

de⌐shi¹ でし (弟子) *n.* pupil; apprentice; disciple.

de⌐shitara でしたら *conj.* = dattara.

deshoo でしょう I suppose [wonder]: ★ Polite equivalent of 'daroo.'
Chichi wa osoraku uchi ni iru deshoo.(父はおそらく家にいるでしょう) *I think* my father will probably be at home. / *Kare wa tabako o yamenai deshoo.*(彼はたばこをやめないでしょう) *I suppose* he will not give up smoking. / *Ano hito wa shiñyoo dekimasu deshoo ka?*(あの人は信用できますでしょうか) *I wonder* if we can trust him. / *Kore wa nañ deshoo?*(これは何でしょう) *I wonder* what this is. / *Sore wa nani-ka no machigai deshoo.*(それは何かの間違いでしょう) *I think* that is a mistake of some sort. 《⇨ da; daroo》

desu です *copula.* (*polite*) (*informal* = da) **1** be [am/is/are]: ★ Indicates that the subject equals the complement.
Ano hito ga watashi no señsee desu.(あの人が私の先生です) That

person *is* my teacher. / *Kono tate-mono ga watashi-tachi no gakkoo desu.* (この建物が私たちの学校です) This building *is* our school. / *"Anata wa gakusee* desu *ka?"* *"Hai, soo* desu. *[Iie, soo* de wa arimaseñ.*]"* (「あなたは学生ですか」「はい、そうです[いいえ、そうではありません]」) *" Are* you a student? " "Yes, I *am.* [No, I *am not.*]" ★ The negative form of '*desu*' is '*de wa arima-señ,*' which becomes '*ja arimaseñ*' in colloquial speech. / *Koko wa moto kooeñ* deshita. (ここはもと公園でした) This place *used to be* a park. ★ '*Deshita*' is the past affirmative form of '*desu*' and '*de wa [ja] arimasen deshita*' is the past negative form.

2 be located in a certain place: *Omocha-uriba wa sañ-gai desu.* (おもちゃ売り場は3階です) The toy section *is* on the third floor. / *Giñ-koo wa eki no mae desu.* (銀行は駅の前です) The bank *is* in front of the station. 《⇨ aru²》

3 (indicates a situation or condition): *Kanojo wa byooki* desu. (彼女は病気です) She *is* sick. / *Sono dooro wa kooji-chuu desu.* (その道路は工事中です) The road *is* under construction.

4 (used as a verb substitute): *"Anata wa nani o chuumoñ shima-shita ka?" "Watashi wa o-sushi desu."* (「あなたは何を注文しましたか」「私はおすしです」) "What did you order?" " I *ordered* sushi. "

5 (after an adjective, makes the expression polite): *Kono riñgo wa totemo oishii* desu. (このりんごはとてもおいしいです) This apple *is* very delicious.

de¹su ga ですが *conj.* (*polite*) but; however; though: ★ In this usage, used only at the beginning of a sentence.

Amari mikomi wa arimaseñ. Desu ga, watashi wa akiramemaseñ. (あまり見込みはありません。ですが、私はあきらめません) There is hardly any hope. *However,* I am not going to give up. 《⇨ da ga》

...no desu ga (...のですが) though; but: ★ In conversation, '*no*' often becomes '*ñ.*' *Kono hoñ o yomitai no* [ñ] *desu ga, jikañ ga arimaseñ.* (この本を読みたいの[ん]ですが、時間がありません) I would like to read this book, *but* I have no time.

de¹su kara ですから *conj.* (*polite*) ＝da kara.

...no desu kara (...のですから) because; since; as: ★ In conversation, '*no*' often becomes '*ñ.*' *Koko made kita no* [ñ] *desu kara ano mise ni yotte ikimashoo.* (ここまで来たの[ん]ですからあの店に寄って行きましょう) We have come all the way, *so* why don't we look into that shop?

de¹tarame でたらめ (出鱈目) *n.* nonsense; irresponsible remark; lie: *detarame o oshieru* (でたらめを教える) give *inaccurate information* / *Detarame o iu na!* (でたらめを言うな) Don't talk *nonsense!*

— *a.n.* (～ na, ni) random; haphazard; irresponsible: *Detarame ni erañdara, seekai datta.* (でたらめに選んだら、正解だった) I made a *haphazard* guess, but it was the correct answer. / *Ano uwasa wa detarame da.* (あのうわさはでたらめだ) That rumor is *untrue.* / *Añna detarame na hito to issho ni shigoto wa dekinai.* (あんなでたらめな人と一緒に仕事はできない) I can't work with such an *irresponsible* person. / *Kono fuku no tsukuri-kata wa detarame da.* (この服の作り方はでたらめだ) This dress is a *slipshod* piece of work.

de wa¹ では [used in conditional

sentences] with: ★ The 'de wa' clause indicates the condition and the second clause the natural or obvious result.
Koñna ni shizuka de wa *kaette sabishii kurai da.* (こんなに静かではかえってさびしいくらいだ) *With* it quiet like this, it actually feels lonely. / *Kono chooshi* de wa *kotoshi no keeki wa kitai dekimaseñ.* (この調子ではことしの景気は期待できません) *If* things are like this, we cannot expect good business this year.

...de wa ikenai [dame da] (...〜いけない[だめだ]) can [must; should] not do: *Kono shigoto wa* josee de wa *dame da.* (この仕事は女性ではだめだ) *Women* can't do this job. / *Tabako o suu no wa koko* de wa *dame desu.* (たばこを吸うのはここではだめです) Smoking is not allowed *here*.

(USAGE)

'*de wa*' becomes '*jaa*' in informal speech. *e.g. Koñna heta na ji* jaa *yomemaseñ.* (こんなへたな字じゃあ読めません) I can't read such poor *handwriting*.

de¹ wa² では *conj.* then; well; if so: ★ In this usage, used only at the beginning of a sentence.
"Ima wa isogashikute dame desu." *"De wa itsu nara yoroshii desu ka?"* (「今は忙しくてだめです」「ではいつならよろしいですか」) "I am too busy to do it now." "*In that case*, when would be convenient?" / *"Watashi wa biiru ni shimasu."* *"De wa watashi mo soo shimasu."* (「私はビールにします」「では私もそうします」) "I will have beer." "*Then* I will have the same." / De wa *kore kara kaigi o hajimemasu.* (ではこれから会議を始めます) *Well then*, we will now start the meeting.

de¹ wa ma⌈ta ではまた (では又) so long; see you later:

De wa mata *ashita.* (ではまたあした) *So long*, see you again tomorrow.

de⌈za⌉iñ デザイン *n.* design; pattern; figure; plan; cutting for an article of clothing:
Kotoshi no suutsu wa eri no de-zaiñ *ga poiñto desu.* (今年のスーツは襟のデザインがポイントです) With this year's suits, the *shape* of the lapels is the fashion point. / *shoo-gyoo*-dezaiñ (商業デザイン) commercial *design* / *koogyoo*-dezaiñ (工業デザイン) industrial *design* / *gurafik-ku*-dezaiñ (グラフィックデザイン) graphic *design* / *iñteria*-dezaiñ (インテリアデザイン) interior *design [decoration]*.

dezaiñ (o) suru (〜(を)する) *vt.* design; plan: *Jibuñ de fuku no* dezaiñ *o suru hito wa kekkoo ooi.* (自分で服のデザインをする人はけっこう多い) There are quite a few people who *design* their own clothes.

do ど (度) *n.* 1 (of myopia, glasses) degree:
do *no tsuyoi [yowai] megane* (度の強い[弱い]眼鏡) *strong [weak]* glasses / do *ga susumu* (度が進む) *grow more near[far]sighted.*
2 extent; amount; limit.

do ga sugiru (〜が過ぎる) carry things too far: *Kimi no joodañ wa* do ga sugiru. (君の冗談は度が過ぎる) You *have gone too far* in your jokes.

do o sugosu (〜を過ごす) go to excess: *Arukooru wa* do o sugo-sanai *yoo ni shi nasai.* (アルコールは度を過ごさないようにしなさい) You should *take* alcohol *in moderation.*

-do ど (度) *suf.* 1 (a unit of measure) degree:
sesshi nijuu-do (摂氏 20 度) twenty *degrees* centigrade / *hokui sañjuu-hachi*-do (北緯 38 度) latitude 38 *degrees* north / *sañjuu*-do *no kaku* (30 度の角) an angle of

thirty *degrees*.
2 time:
ichi-do (一度) *once* / ni-do (二度) *twice* / *sañ*-do (三度) three *times* / *Anata wa nañ*-do *soko e ikimashita ka?* (あなたは何度そこへいきましたか) How many *times* have you been there? 《⇨ -kai¹》

do】a ドア *n.* door:
doa *o akeru* [*shimeru*] (ドアを開ける [閉める]) open [close] a *door*.

do「buꟀ」ñ どぶん *adv.* (~ to) with a plop; with a splash: ★The sound of an object falling into water.
Kare wa dobuñ *to kawa e tobiko-ñda.* (彼はどぶんと川へ飛び込んだ) He dived into the river *with a splash*.

do】chira どちら *n.* ★ More polite than '*doko*' and '*dotchi*.'
1 where:
Deguchi wa dochira *desu ka?* (出口はどちらですか) *Where* is the exit? / *O-kuni wa* dochira *desu ka?* (お国はどちらですか) *Where* do you come from? / *Kaze wa* dochira *kara fuite imasu ka?* (風はどちらから吹いていますか) *From which way* is the wind blowing?
2 which:
Koohii to koocha to dochira *ga suki desu ka?* (コーヒーと紅茶とどちらが好きですか) *Which* do you like better, coffee or tea?
3 who:
Dochira-sama deshoo ka? (どちら様でしょうか) *May I have your name?* (*literally Who* would you be?)
《⇨ achira; kochira; sochira》

do】chira mo どちらも both; either:
Ryooshiñ wa dochira mo *señsee desu.* (両親はどちらも先生です) *Both* of my parents are teachers. / *Ano futari wa* dochira mo *shirimaseñ.* (あの二人はどちらも知りません) I don't know *either* of them.

Do】itsu ドイツ (独逸) *n.* Ger-many: Doitsu *no kuruma* (ドイツの車) a *German* car.

Do「itsugo ドイツご (独逸語) *n.* the German language; German.

Do「itsu」jiñ ドイツじん (独逸人) *n.* a German; the Germans.

do「ke・ru どける (退ける) *vt.* (doke-te Ⓥ) remove; take away:
Sono nimotsu o hoka e dokete *kuremaseñ ka?* (その荷物をほかへどけてくれませんか) Would you please *move* that luggage to another place? / *Sono te o* dokete *choodai.* (その手をどけてちょうだい) *Get* your hand *out of my way*. 《⇨ doku¹》

do】kidoki どきどき *adv.* (~ to; ~ suru) (the state of one's heart beating faster):
Shikeñ no beru o kiku to shiñzoo ga dokidoki (*to*) *natta.* (試験のベルを聞くと心臓がどきどき(と)鳴った) My heart started *thumping* when I heard the bell for the exam. / *Mune ga* dokidoki *shita.* (胸がどきどきした) *There was a pounding* in my chest.

do】ko どこ (何処) *n.* where; wherever:
Koobañ wa doko *desu ka?* (交番はどこですか) *Where* is the police box? / *Natsu-yasumi wa* doko *e ikimasu ka?* (夏休みはどこへ行きますか) *Where* are you going for your summer vacation? / *Watashi no booshi wa* doko *ni arimasu ka?* (私の帽子はどこにありますか) *Where* is my hat? / *Watashi wa kare ni* doko *e ittara ii no ka tazuneta.* (私は彼にどこへ行ったらいいのか尋ねた) I asked him *where* I should go. / *Doko de mo suki na tokoro e iki nasai.* (どこでも好きな所へ行きなさい) You may go *wherever* you like. 《⇨ dochira; dotchi》

do】ko-ka どこか (何処か) some-where; someplace:
Doko-ka shizuka na tokoro e ryokoo shite mitai. (どこか静かな所へ旅

行してみたい) I want to take a trip to *someplace* quiet. / *Sore ni nita hanashi o* doko-ka *de yoñda koto ga arimasu.* (それに似た話をどこかで読んだことがあります) I have read a similar story *somewhere else.*
— *adv.* somewhat; something: *Nisemono wa hoñmono no yoo ni mieru ga* doko-ka *chigau.* (にせものは本物のように見えるがどこか違う) An imitation looks genuine, but *somewhat* different. / *Yamada-sañ wa* doko-ka *kurai kañji ga suru.* (山田さんはどこか暗い感じがする) There is *something* gloomy about Mr. Yamada. / *Kikai ga* doko-ka *okashii.* (機械がどこかおかしい) There is *something* wrong with the machine.

do¹ko made mo どこまでも (何処迄も) *adv.* to the last; endlessly: doko made mo *massugu ni nobiru michi* (どこまでもまっすぐに延びる道) an *endlessly* straight road / *Umi wa* doko made mo *aoku utsukushikatta.* (海はどこまでも青く美しかった) The sea was blue and beautiful *as far as the eye could see.* / *Kare wa* doko made mo *jibuñ no ikeñ o shuchoo shita.* (彼はどこまでも自分の意見を主張した) He *persistently* held to his opinion.

do¹ko mo どこも (何処も) *adv.* everywhere; (*neg.*) nowhere: *Natsu-yasumi ni naru to kaisui-yokujoo wa* doko mo *hito de ippai ni naru.* (夏休みになると海水浴場はどこも人でいっぱいになる) With summer break starting, beaches *everywhere* become crowded. / *Kono machi o deru to* doko mo *shizuka na tokoro bakari desu.* (この町を出るとどこも静かな所ばかりです) Once you go out of this city, it is quiet *wherever you go.* / *Nihoñ no kañkoochi wa mada* doko mo *itta koto ga arimaseñ.* (日本の観光地はまだどこも行ったことがありません) I

haven't been to *any* sightseeing spots in Japan. / *Kuruma no eñjiñ wa* doko mo *okashi-na tokoro wa arimaseñ.* (車のエンジンはどこもおかしなところはありません) There's *nothing* wrong with the engine of the car.

> **(USAGE)**
> The forms '*doko e mo*' and '*doko ni mo*' are often used with a negative. *e.g. Kyoo wa* doko e mo *ikimaseñ.* (きょうはどこへも行きません) Today, I'm not going *anywhere.* / *Boku no kabañ ga heya no* doko ni mo *nai.* (ぼくのかばんが部屋のどこにもない) My bag is *nowhere* in the room.

dokoro ka どころか *p.* [precedes a contradictory or qualifying statement]
1 far from; on the contrary: *Kare wa byooki* dokoro ka, *totemo geñki desu.* (彼は病気どころか, とても元気です) *Far from* being ill, he is in excellent health. / *Kotoshi no tsuyu wa ame ga furu* dokoro ka, *o-teñki-tsuzuki deshita.* (ことしの梅雨は雨が降るどころか, お天気続きでした) During the rainy season, we had no rain; *on the contrary*, we had a long spell of fine weather.
2 not to mention; to say nothing of: *Uchi de wa jidoosha* dokoro ka, *jiteñsha mo arimaseñ.* (うちでは自動車どころか, 自転車もありません) We do not have a bicycle, *not to mention* a car. / *Ano hito wa Nihoñgo* dokoro ka *Chuugokugo mo hanasemasu.* (あの人は日本語どころか中国語も話せます) He can *not only* speak Japanese, but also Chinese.

do¹k·u¹ どく (退く) *vi.* (dok·i-; dok·a-; do·i-te 〔C〕) move; make room; step aside: *Jama da kara soko o* doki nasai. (じゃまだからそこをどきなさい) You're in the way. *Move!* / *Abunai kara doite i nasai.* (危ないからどいていなさい) As it's dangerous, *keep out of the way.* (⇨ dokeru)

do｢ku｣[12] どく（毒）*n.* **1** poison: doku o nomu（毒を飲む）swallow [take] *poison.*
2 harm: *Tabako wa karada ni doku da.* (たばこは体に毒だ) Smoking is *bad* for your health.

do｢kuji｣ どくじ（独自）*a.n.* (～ na/ no, ni) one's own; unique; original; personal: *Kore wa watashi dokuji no kañgae desu.* (これは私独自の考えです) This is my *original* idea. / *Kare wa dokuji ni koto o hakoñda.* (彼は独自に事を運んだ) He carried out things in *his own way.*

do｢kuritsu｣ どくりつ（独立）*n.* independence: dokuritsu o señgeñ suru（独立を宣言する）declare *independence.*
dokuritsu suru (～する) *vi.* become independent: *Sono kuni wa señ kyuu-hyaku yoñjuu go-neñ ni dokuritsu shita.* (その国は1945年に独立した) The country *became independent* in 1945. / *Kanojo wa Tookyoo de dokuritsu shita seekatsu o shite iru.* (彼女は東京で独立した生活をしている) She is leading an *independent* life in Tokyo. / *Kare wa sorosoro dokuritsu shite mo ii koro da.* (彼はそろそろ独立してもいいころだ) It is about time he *earned his own living.*

Do｢kuritsu Ko｣kka Kyo｢odo-otai （独立国家共同体）*n.* the Commonwealth of Independent States. ★ The successor to the Soviet Union.

do｢kusai｣ どくさい（独裁）*n.* dictatorship; despotism.

do｢kuseñ｣ どくせん（独占）*n.* monopoly; exclusive possession.
dokuseñ suru (～する) *vt.* monopolize: *Kare wa kanojo no ai o dokuseñ shitagatte iru.* (彼は彼女の愛を独占したがっている) He *wants to monopolize* her love. / *Sono kaisha no seehiñ ga shijoo o dokuseñ shite iru.* (その会社の製品が市場を独占している) The products of the company *are monopolizing* the market. / *Kanojo wa subete no taitoru o dokuseñ shita.* (彼女はすべてのタイトルを独占した) She *made a clean sweep* of all the titles.

do｢kusha｣ どくしゃ（読者）*n.* subscriber; reader.

do｢kushiñ｣ どくしん（独身）*n.* bachelorhood; spinsterhood: dokushiñ no hito（独身の人）an *unmarried* person; a *single* man [woman] / *Kanojo wa dokushiñ desu ka?* (彼女は独身ですか) *Is* she *unmarried?* / *Kare wa mada dokushiñ desu.* (彼はまだ独身です) He still remains *single.*

do｢kushi｣ñsha どくしんしゃ（独身者）*n.* bachelor; unmarried woman.

do｢kusho｣ どくしょ（読書）*n.* reading (a book): *Dokusho no shuukañ o tsuke nasai.* (読書の習慣をつけなさい) Try to acquire the habit of *reading books.* / dokusho-ryoku（読書力）*reading* ability.
dokusho (o) suru (～(を)する) *vi.* read (a book): *Ame no hi wa dokusho suru no mo ii desu ne.* (雨の日は読書するのもいいですね) It's also a good idea to *read books* on rainy days.

do｢kutoku｣ どくとく（独特）*a.n.* (～ na/no, ni) characteristic; peculiar; unique: dokutoku na katachi o shita geñdai-keñchiku（独特な形をした現代建築）modern architecture with a *unique* style / *Kono kudamono ni wa dokutoku no kaori ga aru.* (この果物には独特の香りがある) This fruit has a *characteristic* pleasant smell. / *Ano hanashi-kata wa kare dokutoku no mono da.* (あの話し方は彼独特のものだ) That is *his own way* of speaking. 《⇨ tokuyuu》

do⌐kuyaku どくやく (毒薬) *n.* poison:
dokuyaku *o nomu* (毒薬を飲む) take *poison.* 《⇨ gekiyaku》

-do⌐mo ども (共) *suf.* (used to form the plural of a noun):
1 (expresses humility): ★ Attached to a noun indicating the speaker.
Watashi-domo ni o-makase kudasai. (私どもにおまかせください) Please leave it to *us.*
2 (implies a contemptuous or belittling attitude): ★ Attached to a noun indicating others.
Wakamono-domo wa mattaku reegi o shiranai. (若者どもはまったく礼儀を知らない) *Young people* have no manners at all.

do⌐na⌐r・u どなる (怒鳴る) *vi.* (donar・i-; donar・a-; donat-te ⓒ)
1 shout; cry:
Soñna ni ooki-na koe de donaranakute mo chañto kikoemasu. (そんなに大きな声でどならなくてもちゃんと聞こえます) You don't have to *shout* so loudly. I can hear you perfectly well. / *Tooku ni iru hito ni (mukatte) tasukete kure to donatta.* (遠くにいる人に(向かって)助けてくれとどなった) I *cried* for help to a person in the distance.
2 yell:
Shukudai o wasurete, señsee ni donarareta. (宿題を忘れて、先生にどなられた) I *was yelled at* by the teacher, because I forgot my homework. / *Kare wa ki ni iranai to sugu (ni) donaru.* (彼は気に入らないとすぐ(に)どなる) He always starts *yelling* when he is not pleased.

do⌐nata どなた (何方) *n.* (*polite*) = dare.

who; whose; whom:
"*Donata desu ka?*" "*Yamada desu.*" (「どなたですか」「山田です」) "*May I have your name? (lit. Who* are you?)" "I'm Yamada." / *Kore wa* donata *no kasa desu ka?* (これはどなたの傘ですか) *Whose* umbrella is this? / Donata *o matte iru ñ desu ka?* (どなたを待っているんですか) *For whom* are you waiting?

do⌐nata-ka どなたか (何方か) *n.* anyone: ★ Polite equivalent of '*dare-ka.*'
Donata-ka *tetsudatte kureru hito wa imaseñ ka?* (どなたか手伝ってくれる人はいませんか) Isn't there *anyone* who can help me?

do⌐ñbu⌐ri どんぶり (丼) *n.* porcelain bowl; large rice bowl:
doñburi-*mono* (どんぶり物) a meal served in a *bowl* / unagi-doñburi (うなぎどんぶり) a *bowl* of rice and broiled eel / oyako-doñburi (親子どんぶり) a *bowl* of rice topped with chicken and eggs / tamago-doñburi (卵どんぶり) a *bowl* of rice with eggs.

DOÑBURI (left) CHAWAÑ (right)

do⌐ñdoñ[1] どんどん *adv.* (~ to) rapidly; steadily:
Yama-kaji ga doñdoñ *(to) moe-hirogatta.* (山火事がどんどん(と)燃え広がった) The forest fire spread *rapidly.* / *Ame ga furanai no de mizuumi no mizu ga* doñdoñ *(to) hette kite iru.* (雨が降らないので湖の水がどんどん(と)減っている) Since we have had little rain, the water in the lake is *rapidly* going down. / *Tsukihi ga* doñdoñ *(to) tatte iku.* (月日がどんどん(と)たっていく) Time *really* flies.

do˹ñdoñ[2] どんどん *adv.* (~ **to**) (the sound made when knocking strongly on a door or beating a drum):
Dare-ka ga yonaka ni to o doñdoñ *(to) tataita.* (だれかが夜中に戸をどんどん(と)たたいた) Someone *banged* at the door in the middle of the night. / *Tooku de taiko ga* doñdoñ *(to) natte iru no ga kikoeru.* (遠くで太鼓がどんどん(と)鳴っているのが聞こえる) I can hear the *roll* of a drum in the distance.

do˹ñkañ どんかん (鈍感) *a.n.* (~ **na, ni**) insensible; insensitive; dull:
Tanaka-sañ wa doñkañ *da kara hiniku o itte mo tsuujinai.* (田中さんは鈍感だから皮肉を言っても通じない) Mr. Tanaka is *insensitive*, so even if you say something sarcastic, it won't get through to him. / *Yakamashii kooji-geñba ni ita no de mimi ga* doñkañ *ni natte shimatta.* (やかましい工事現場にいたので耳が鈍感になってしまった) Since I was on a noisy construction site, my hearing *has been dulled*.

do˹ñkoo どんこう (鈍行) *n.* (*informal*) local [slow] train. 《⇨ futsuu¹; kyuukoo¹ (table)》

do˹ñna どんな *attrib.* **1** what; what kind of:
Saikiñ doñna *mono o yomimashita ka?* (最近どんなものを読みましたか) *What* have you read recently? / *Doñna supootsu ga suki desu ka?* (どんなスポーツが好きですか) *What kind of* sports do you like?
2 however; no matter how:
Doñna chiisa-na koto de mo kiroku shite kudasai. (どんな小さなことでも記録してください) *However* minor it is, please make a record of it. / *Doñna koto ga atte mo kore dake wa kañsee shimasu.* (どんなことがあってもこれだけは完成します) *Whatever* happens, this I will at least complete. / Doñna *iiwake o shite mo dame desu.* (どんな言い訳をしてもだめです) No matter *what* excuse you make, it won't do you any good.
3 any; every:
Soñna koto wa doñna hito *de mo shitte iru.* (そんなことはどんな人でも知っている) *Everyone* is aware of such a thing. 《⇨ añna; koñna; soñna》

do˹ñna ni どんなに *adv.* **1** how; how much; to what extent:
Ano hito to kekkoñ dekitara, doñna ni *subarashii deshoo.* (あの人と結婚できたら、どんなに素晴らしいでしょう) *How* wonderful it would be if I could marry her! / *Geñki na toki wa keñkoo ga* doñna ni *taisetsu ka wakaranai mono desu.* (元気なときは健康がどんなに大切かわからないものです) When we are enjoying good health, we don't realize *how* important it is to be healthy. 《⇨ ika ni》
2 (with a negative) no matter how; whatever; however:
Doñna ni *gañbatte mo sore o isshuukañ de kañsee suru koto wa dekimaseñ.* (どんなにがんばってもそれを1週間で完成することはできません) No matter *how* hard I try, I cannot complete it in a week. / Doñna ni *ooki-na jishiñ de mo kono biru wa taoremaseñ.* (どんなに大きな地震でもこのビルは倒れません) *However* great the earthquake may be, this building will not collapse. 《⇨ añna ni; koñna ni; soñna ni》

do˹no どの *attrib.* **1** which; what; who:
Dono *waapuro o erabimashita ka?* (どのワープロを選びましたか) *Which* word processor have you chosen? / Dono *kisetsu ga ichibañ suki desu ka?* (どの季節が一番好きですか) *Which* season do you like best? / *Suzuki-sañ wa* dono hito *desu ka?* (鈴木さんはどの人ですか)

Which one is Mr. Suzuki?
2 any; every:
Dono jisho de mo kekkoo desu. (どの辞書でもけっこうです) *Any* dictionary will do. / *Koñshuu wa* dono *hi mo isogashii.* (今週はどの日も忙しい) I am busy *every* day this week. / *Ima wa taitee* dono *uchi ni mo terebi ga arimasu.* (今はたいていどの家にもテレビがあります) Almost *every* house has a television now. 《⇨ ano; kono; sono》

-do￺no どの (殿) *suf.* (one of the titles used after the addressee's name in a formal letter):
★ Used by public offices while '*-sama*' is used by private individuals.
Yamada Taroo-dono (山田太郎殿) *Mr.* Taro Yamada.

do￺no-kurai どのくらい (どの位) *adv.* (〜 no) how much [many; long; far, etc.]: ★ Also '*donogurai*'.
Anata no uchi kara eki made dono-kurai *kakarimasu ka?* (あなたの家から駅までどのくらいかかりますか) *How long* does it take to go to the station from your house? / *Ichi-nichi ni tabako o* dono-kurai *suimasu ka?* (一日にたばこをどのくらい吸いますか) *How many* cigarettes do you smoke in a day? / *Kono suutsukeesu no omosa wa* dono-kurai *desu ka?* (このスーツケースの重さはどのくらいですか) *How much* does this suitcase weigh?

do￺ñteñ どんてん (曇天) *n.* cloudy weather. 《↔ seeteñ; uteñ》

do￺o[1] どう *adv.* **1** how:
Kono tañgo wa doo *yomu no desu ka?* (この単語はどう読むのですか) *How* do you read [pronounce] this word? / *Kibuñ wa* doo *desu ka?* (気分はどうですか) *How* are you feeling? / *Ashita tenisu wa* doo *desu ka?* (あしたテニスはどうですか) *How* about some tennis tomorrow?

2 what:
Moshi shippai shitara, doo *shimasu ka?* (もし失敗したら、どうしますか) *What* if you should fail? / *Doo shite ii no ka wakarimaseñ.* (どうしていいのかわかりません) I don't know *what* to do. 《⇨ aa[1]; koo; soo》

do￺o[2] どう (胴) *n.* the trunk of the body: ★ The body not including the head and limbs.
Kare wa doo *ga nagai.* (彼は胴が長い) He has a long *trunk.* / *Kono kooto wa* doo *no tokoro ga kitsui.* (このコートは胴のところがきつい) This coat is tight in the *body.* 《⇨ jiñtai (illus.)》

do￺o[3] どう (銅) *n.* copper; bronze:
Kare wa doo-*medaru o totta.* (彼は銅メダルをとった) He won a *bronze* medal.

doo[4] どう (道) *n.* an administrative division of Japan, but only used with reference to Hokkaido (北海道). 《⇨ fu; keñ[1]; to[4]》

doo- どう (同) *pref.* **1** the same:
Oosaji sañ-bai no shooyu to doo-*ryoo no sake o iremasu.* (大さじ3杯のしょうゆと同量の酒を入れます) Add three tablespoons of soy sauce and *the same* amount of sake. / *Kare wa* doo-*sedai no wakamono no aida de niñki ga aru.* (彼は同世代の若者の間で人気がある) He is popular among the youth of *his generation.* / *Kare wa Hideyoshi to* doo-*jidai no hito datta.* (彼は秀吉と同時代の人だった) He was a *contemporary* of Hideyoshi.

2 (used in documents, newspaper articles, etc. to avoid repetition of the same word):
Higaisha wa chikaku no byooiñ ni hakobare, doo-*byooiñ de teate o uketa.* (被害者は近くの病院に運ばれ、同病院で手当を受けた) The injured were taken to a nearby hospital and treated in *that* hospital.

do￺o i￺tashima￺shite どういたし

まして（どう致しまして）you're welcome; don't mention it; not at all; it's my pleasure.

do⸢obutsu どうぶつ（動物）*n.*
1 animal: ★ Any living thing that is not a plant.
Niñgeñ mo inu mo doobutsu *desu.* （人間も犬も動物です）Human beings and dogs are *animals.*
2 any animal other than man: doobutsu *o hogo* [*gyakutai*] *suru* （動物を保護[虐待]する）protect [be cruel to] *animals* / Doobutsu *ni esa o yaranai de kudasai.* （動物に餌をやらないでください）Please don't feed the *animals.*

do⸢obutsu⸥eñ どうぶつえん（動物園）*n.* zoo. 《⇨ shokubutsueñ》

do⸢odoo どうどう（堂々）*adv.*
（～ to）**1** in a dignified manner; magnificently:
Doodoo to *mune o hatte kooshiñ shi nasai.* （堂々と胸を張って行進しなさい）March *proudly* with your head held high.
2 (of competition, play, etc.) fairly:
Makete mo ii kara, doodoo to *tatakai nasai.* （負けてもいいから、堂々と戦いなさい）It doesn't matter if you lose. Play *fair.*

doodoo to shita （～とした）dignified; imposing; magnificent:
Kare wa doodoo to shita *taido de eñzetsu o shita.* （彼は堂々とした態度で演説をした）He made a speech in a *dignified* manner.

do⸢ofuu どうふう（同封）*n.* enclosing:
doofuu-butsu（同封物）an *enclosure.*
doofuu suru （～する）*vt.* enclose:
Shashiñ o ichi-mai doofuu shimasu. （写真を一枚同封します）I *enclose* one photograph. / *Tegami ni wa kitte ga* doofuu shite atta. （手紙には切手が同封してあった）A postage stamp *was enclosed* with the letter.

do⸢ogu⸥ どうぐ（道具）*n.* tool;

utensil; instrument:
*daiku-*doogu（大工道具）carpenter's *tools* / *daidokoro-*doogu（台所道具）kitchen *utensils.*

do⸢ohañ どうはん（同伴）*n.* company; accompanying:
Kare wa fujiñ doohañ *de Kyooto e ikimashita.* （彼は夫人同伴で京都へ行きました）He went to Kyoto *with* his wife. / doohañ-sha（同伴者）a *companion.*
doohañ suru （～する）*vt.* go with; accompany; escort: *Sono gakusee wa ryooshiñ o* doohañ *shite ita.* （その学生は両親を同伴していた）The student *was accompanied* by his parents.

do⸢oi どうい（同意）*n.* agreement; consent; assent:
Sore ni wa kare no dooi *ga hitsuyoo desu.* （それには彼の同意が必要です）For that, his *agreement* is necessary. / *Yatto chichi no* dooi *ga erareta.* （やっと父の同意が得られた）I finally obtained my father's *consent.*
dooi suru （～する）*vt.* agree; consent: *Sono teeañ ni* dooi shimasu. （その提案に同意します）I *agree* to the proposal. / *Watashi wa musume ga Yooroppa e iku no ni* dooi shita. （私は娘がヨーロッパへ行くのに同意した）I *consented* to my daughter's going to Europe.

do⸢oigo どういご（同意語）*n.* synonym:
'Ashita' to 'asu' wa dooigo *desu.* （「あした」と「あす」は同意語です）*'Ashita'* and *'asu'* are *synonyms.* 《↔ hañigo》

do⸢oitsu どういつ（同一）*a.n.*
（～ na/no, ni）identical; the same:
dooitsu *jiñbutsu*（同一人物）*the same* person / Dooitsu *no jookeñ de jikkeñ o kurikaeshita.* （同一の条件で実験を繰り返した）We repeated the experiment under *the*

same conditions. / *Sore to kore o* dooitsu *ni roñjiru koto wa dekinai.* (それとこれを同一に論じることはできない) We cannot discuss this and that on *the same level.*

do｢o-iu どういう (どう言う) *attrib.* how; why; what: *Kore wa* doo-iu *fuu ni shitara ii desu ka?* (これはどういうふうにしたらいいですか) *How* should I do this? / Doo-iu *wake de soñna koto o shita ñ desu ka?* (どういう訳でそんなことをしたんですか) *Why* did you do something like that? / *Suzuki-sañ wa* doo-iu *hito desu ka?* (鈴木さんはどういう人ですか) *What* sort of person is Mr. Suzuki? / *Sore wa* doo-iu *koto desu ka?* (それはどういうことですか) *What* do you mean by that? (⇨ aa-iu; koo-iu; soo-iu)

do｢oji どうじ (同時) *n.* simultaneity; occurrence at the same time: *Futari ga arawareta no wa hotoñ-do* dooji *datta.* (二人が現れたのはほとんど同時だった) The two appeared *at* almost *the same time.*

do｢oji ni どうじに (同時に) *adv.* **1** at the same time; simultaneously: *Futari wa* dooji ni *sono hoshi o hakkeñ shita.* (二人は同時にその星を発見した) The two people discovered the star *at the same time.* **2** soon; immediately: *Kare wa gakkoo no sotsugyoo to* dooji ni *Amerika e itta.* (彼は学校の卒業と同時にアメリカへ行った) *On* leaving school, he went to America. / *Yo ga akeru to* dooji ni *ame ga furi-dashita.* (夜が明けると同時に雨が降りだした) *At* the break of day, it started to rain. ★ The dictionary form of a verb or a noun precedes 'to dooji ni.' **3** as well as; while: *Watashi-tachi wa kare-ra ni taberu mono to* dooji ni *kiru mono mo*

ataeta. (私たちは彼らに食べる物と同時に着る物も与えた) We gave them clothes *as well as* food. / *Kanemo-chi mo iru ga* dooji ni *biñbooniñ mo iru.* (金持ちもいるが同時に貧乏人もいる) *While* there are rich people, there are also poor people.

do｢oji-tsu｣uyaku どうじつうやく (同時通訳) *n.* simultaneous interpretation; simultaneous interpreter: *Kanojo wa Furañsugo o Nihoñgo ni* dooji-tsuuyaku *dekimasu.* (彼女はフランス語を日本語に同時通訳できます) She can *interpret simultaneously* from French to Japanese. **dooji-tsuuyaku (o) suru** (～(を) する) *vt.* provide simultaneous interpretation: *Kono kaigi de wa sañkasha no kotoba goto ni* dooji-tsuuyaku shimasu. (この会議では参加者の言葉ごとに同時通訳します) We will *provide simultaneous interpretation* at this conference for each participant's language. (⇨ tsuuyaku)

do｢ojoo どうじょう (同情) *n.* sympathy; compassion: doojoo *o hiku* [*shimesu*] (同情をひく[示す]) *arouse* [offer] *sympathy.* **(ni) doojoo suru** ((に)～する) *vt.* sympathize: Dare mo *kare ni* doojoo shinakatta. (だれも彼に同情しなかった) *No one sympathized* with him.

do｢o ka どうか *adv.* **1** please: Doo ka *o-kane o kashite kudasai.* (どうかお金を貸してください) *Please* lend me some money. / Doo ka *ano hito no byooki ga yoku nari-masu yoo ni.* (どうかあの人の病気が良くなりますように) *I hope* that he gets over his illness. **2** if; whether: *Sore ga hoñtoo ka* doo ka *shirima-señ.* (それが本当かどうか知りません) I don't know *whether* that is true or not.

doo ka shite iru (〜している) be strange; be wrong: *Futtari tettari kyoo no teñki wa doo ka shite iru.* (降ったり照ったりきょうの天気はどうかしている) Raining one minute, and sunny the next; the weather *is strange* today.

doo ka to omou (〜と思う) think something is a bit off: *Señsee ni añna hanashi-kata o suru wa doo ka to omou.* (先生にあんな話し方をするのはどうかと思う) I *think it's not proper* for you to speak to your teacher like that.

do「okañ どうかん (同感) n. agreement; feeling the same way: *Watashi mo kare no ikeñ ni dookañ da.* (私も彼の意見に同感だ) I am also in *agreement* with his opinion. / *Kare wa sono keekaku o yameru beki da to iu ga, watashi mo* dookañ desu. (彼はその計画をやめるべきだと言うが私も同感です) He says that we should give up the plan, and I *feel the same way.*

dookañ suru (〜する) vi. agree; sympathize; feel the same way: *Kare no ikeñ ni wa ooi-ni dookañ shita.* (彼の意見には大いに同感した) I *was quite agreeable* to his views.

do「oki どうき (動機) n. motive; motivation; reason: *Anata ga Nihoñgo o beñkyoo shiyoo to omotta dooki wa nañ desu ka?* (あなたが日本語を勉強しようと思った動機は何ですか) What was your *motive* for starting to study Japanese?

do「omee[1] どうめい (同盟) n. alliance; league; union: doomee o musubu [*haki suru*] (同盟を結ぶ[破棄する]) conclude [renounce] an *alliance.*

(**to**) **doomee suru** ((と)〜する) vi. make an alliance with; ally: *Señ kyuu-hyaku ni-neñ ni Nihoñ wa Igirisu to* doomee shita. (1902年に日本はイギリスと同盟した) In 1902,

Japan *formed an alliance* with Britain.

do「omee[2] どうめい (同名) n. the same name: *Kono kurasu ni wa* doomee *no hito ga sañ-niñ iru.* (このクラスには同名の人が3人いる) In this class, there are three persons who have *the same name.*

do「omo どうも adv. **1** very: Doomo *arigatoo gozaimasu.* (どうもありがとうございます) Thank you *very* much. / Doomo *sumimaseñ deshita.* (どうもすみませんでした) I am *very* sorry to have troubled you.

(**USAGE**)

'*Doomo*' is often used as an abbreviation of either '*doomo arigatoo*' or '*doomo sumimaseñ.*' In that sense, '*doomo*' is more like 'thank you' or 'I'm sorry.' It is also used merely as an intensifier. *e.g.* Doomo *shitsuree shimashita.* (どうも失礼しました) I'm *very* sorry for taking your time.

---

2 it seems...: ★ Used when making unfavorable judgments or predictions. In this usage '*yoo da*' or '*rashii*' often come at the end of the sentence. Doomo *ano hanashi wa uso no yoo da.* (どうもあの話はうそのようだ) The story *seems* like a lie. / Doomo *kare wa shiñsetsu na hito de wa nai rashii.* (どうも彼は親切な人ではないらしい) It *seems* that he is just not a kind person.

3 (with a negative) just cannot; there is no way: Doomo *kono Nihoñgo wa Eego ni umaku yakusemaseñ.* (どうもこの日本語は英語にうまく訳せません) There is *just no way* to translate this Japanese smoothly into English. / *Urusai oñgaku wa* doomo *suki ni naremaseñ.* (うるさい音楽はどうも

好きになれません) I *just don't seem able to enjoy loud music.*
4 somehow:
Doomo *watashi-tachi wa itsu-mo keñka ni natte shimau.* (どうも私たちはいつもけんかになってしまう) *Somehow we always end up arguing.*

do⌐oni ka どうにか *adv.*
= nañto ka.

-do⌐ori どおり *suf.* = -toori.

do⌐oro どうろ (道路) *n.* road; way; street:
dooro *o oodañ suru* (道路を横断する) cross a *road* / Dooro *de asoñde wa ikemaseñ.* (道路で遊んではいけません) Don't play on the *road.*
《⇒ koosoku-dooro》

do⌐osa どうさ (動作) *n.* movement; manners; action:
Kare wa doosa *ga nibui.* (彼は動作がにぶい) He is slow in his *movements.*

do⌐ose どうせ *adv.* **1** after all:
★ Used when past experience suggests an unfavorable result.
Kare kara no tanomi nara, doose *meñdoo na koto daroo.* (彼からの頼みなら、どうせ面倒なことだろう) *Since* it is a request from him, I expect it will be something troublesome. / *Soñna hanashi wa* doose *uso ni kimatte iru.* (そんな話はどうせうそに決まっている) *After all*, such a story must be a lie.
2 as a matter of course; anyhow: ★ Used when a certain limit is known and the speaker is pessimistic.
Doose *watashi no inochi wa nagaku nai no da.* (どうせ私の命は長くないのだ) *Anyhow*, I know that I cannot live long. / *Anata wa* doose *moo watashi ni ai ni kite kurenai no deshoo?* (あなたはどうせもう私に会いに来てくれないのでしょう) You won't come and see me *anymore*, will you?
doose...nara (〜…なら) if...at all:

Doose *kau* nara, *kookyuuhiñ o kai nasai.* (どうせ買うなら、高級品を買いなさい) *If* you're going to buy one *at all*, buy a high-quality one. / Doose *shinakereba naranai shigoto* nara, *hayaku shita hoo ga ii.* (どうせしなければならない仕事なら、早くしたほうがいい) *If* it is a job you must do *anyway*, you might as well do it as soon as possible.

do⌐osee¹ どうせい (同性) *n.* **1** the same sex:
doosee *no hito* (同性の人) a member of *the same sex* / doosee-*ai* (同性愛) *homosexual* love.
2 person of the same sex.

do⌐osee² どうせい (同姓) *n.* the same family name:
doosee *doomee* (同姓同名) *the same family* and given *names.*

do⌐osee³ どうせい (同棲) *n.* cohabitation; living together.
doosee suru (同せいする) cohabit; live together: *Kare wa kanojo to hañtoshi* doosee *shita.* (彼は彼女と半年同せいした) He *cohabited* with her for half a year.

do⌐oshi どうし (動詞) *n.* verb.
《⇒ appendixes》

-do⌐oshi¹ どうし (同士) *suf.*
1 persons who belong to the same group or class:
Tomodachi-dooshi *de mo o-kane no kashi-kari wa shinai hoo ga yoi.* (友だちどうしでもお金の貸し借りはしない方がよい) You shouldn't lend or borrow money, even *among friends.* / *Kodomo*-dooshi *de keñka o hajimeta.* (子どもどうしでけんかを始めた) The children began to quarrel *among themselves.*
2 persons who stand in the same relationship to each other:
Futari wa koibito-dooshi *da.* (二人は恋人どうしだ) They are *lovers.* / *Isañ o megutte,* kyoodai-dooshi *ga arasotte iru.* (遺産をめぐって、兄弟どうしが争っている) The *brothers* are

quarreling over a legacy.

-dooshi[2] どおし（通し）*suf.* keep doing: ★ Added to the stem of a verb.

Asa kara tachi-dooshi *de tsukareta.*（朝から立ち通しで疲れた）As I *have been standing* since morning, I am tired. / *Sañ-jikañ* aruki-dooshi *de, yatto mokutekichi ni tsuita.*（三時間歩き通して、やっと目的地に着いた）I *kept on walking* for three hours, and at last arrived at my destination. / *Wakai koro wa* shippai no shi-dooshi *datta.*（若いころは失敗のし通しだった）In my youth, I *was always making* mistakes.

doˈo-shite どうして *adv.* **1** why: Doo-shite *Sumisu-sañ wa añna ni joozu ni Nihoñgo ga hanaseru no desu ka?*（どうしてスミスさんはあんなに上手に日本語が話せるのですか）*Why* is it that Mr. Smith is so good at speaking Japanese? / Doo-shite *koñna koto ni natta no ka, setsumee shite kudasai.*（どうしてこんなことになったのか、説明してください）Please explain *why* this happened.
2 how: *Kono moñdai wa* doo-shite *toku ñ desu ka?*（この問題はどうして解くんですか）*In what way* can we solve this problem? / *Kono futa wa* doo-shite *akeru no?*（このふたはどうして開けるの）*How* shall we take this lid off?

doˈo-shite mo どうしても *adv.* **1** by all means; at any cost: *Watashi wa sono hoñ ga* doo-shite mo *hoshikatta.*（私はその本がどうしても欲しかった）I wanted the book *at any cost.* / *Kono keekaku wa* doo-shite mo *jitsugeñ suru hitsuyoo ga aru.*（この計画はどうしても実現する必要がある）We must *absolutely* carry out this plan.
2（with a negative）just cannot: *Kare no iu koto wa* doo-shite mo *shiñjirarenai.*（彼の言うことはどうして

も信じられない）I *just cannot* believe what he says. / *Watashi wa* doo-shite mo *kare no namae ga omoidasenai.*（私はどうしても彼の名前が思い出せない）I *cannot for the life of me* remember his name.

doo-shite mo...suru（〜...する）cannot help doing: *Musuko no kao o miru to* doo-shite mo *"Beñkyoo shiro" to itte shimau.*（息子の顔を見るとどうしても「勉強しろ」と言ってしまう）Every time I see my son's face, I *can't stop* myself *saying,* "Go study."

doˈosoˈokai どうそうかい（同窓会）*n.* alumni association [reunion].

doˈotai どうたい（胴体）*n.* trunk; body; torso: *hikooki no* dootai（飛行機の胴体）the *fuselage* of an airplane.《⇨ doo[2]》

doˈotoku どうとく（道徳）*n.* morality; morals: dootoku *kyooiku*（道徳教育）*moral* education.

doˈotoku-teki どうとくてき（道徳的）*a.n.*（〜 na, ni）moral; morally: Dootoku-teki *na bañgumi wa gaishite tsumaranai.*（道徳的な番組は概してつまらない）*Morally* uplifting programs are generally boring. / *Hooritsu-teki ni wa tadashii ga* dootoku-teki *ni wa moñdai ga aru.*（法律的には正しいが道徳的には問題がある）It is legally right, but from the *moral* point of view there are problems.

doˈowa どうわ（童話）*n.* fairy [nursery] tale; children's story.

doˈo-yara どうやら *adv.* **1** probably; apparently: ★ Usually occurs with 'rashii,' 'yoo da,' etc. Doo-yara *taifuu ga Kyuushuu ni jooriku suru rashii.*（どうやら台風が九州に上陸するらしい）The typhoon will *probably* hit Kyushu. / Doo-yara *Satoo-sañ wa sootoo no kane-*

mochi rashii. (どうやら佐藤さんは相当な金持ちらしい) Mrs. Sato is *apparently* quite rich. / Doo-yara *hare-soo da.* (どうやら晴れそうだ) It is *likely* to clear up. / *Ashita wa* doo-yara *ame no yoo desu.* (あしたはどうやら雨のようです) It *certainly* looks like rain tomorrow.

2 somehow:
Doo-yara *shujutsu wa seekoo shita.* (どうやら手術が成功した) The operation was *somehow* a success.

do「oyoo¹ どうよう（同様）*a.n.*
(～ na, ni) the same; similar:
Dooyoo *na ikeñ wa hoka kara mo deta.* (同様な意見はほかからも出た) *Similar* opinions were given by other people. / *Tanaka-sañ wa inu o kazoku* dooyoo *ni kawai-gatte iru.* (田中さんは犬を家族同様にかわいがっている) Ms. Tanaka loves her dog *as if* it were a member of the family. 《⇨ onaji》

— *adv.* in the same way; like-wise:
Kinoo to dooyoo, *kyoo mo atsui ichi-nichi ni naru deshoo.* (きのうと同様, きょうも暑い一日になるでしょう) *Like* yesterday, it is expected to be another hot day today. / *"Tsuki wa chikyuu no mawari o mawatte iru. Dooyoo ni chikyuu mo taiyoo no mawari o mawatte iru.* (月は地球の周りを回っている. 同様に地球も太陽の周りを回っている) The moon goes round the earth. *In the same way* the earth moves round the sun.

do「oyoo² どうよう（動揺）*n.* shaki-ness; disturbance; agitation:
Kanojo wa kokoro no dooyoo o kakusoo to shita. (彼女は心の動揺を隠そうとした) She tried to hide her *lack of emotional balance.* 《⇨ fuañ》

dooyoo suru (～する) *vi.* shake; be disturbed: *Kare wa sono shirase ni* dooyoo *shita.* (彼はその

知らせに動揺した) He *was shaken* by the news. / *Kanojo ga nyuuiñ shita to kiite, watashi wa* dooyoo *shita.* (彼女が入院したと聞いて, 私は動揺した) I *was disturbed* when I heard she was in the hospital.

do「oyoo³ どうよう（童謡）*n.* chil-dren's song; nursery rhyme.

do「ozo どうぞ（何卒）*adv.*
1 please:
Doozo *o-kake kudasai.* (どうぞお掛けください) *Please* have a seat. / *Moo ip-pai* doozo. (もう一杯どうぞ) *Please* drink another glass.

2 certainly; sure; of course:
"Deñwa o o-kari dekimasu ka?" "Ee, doozo.*"* (「電話をお借りできますか」「ええ, どうぞ」) "May I use your telephone?" "*Certainly.*" / *"Tabako o sutte mo ii desu ka?" "Doozo.*"* (「たばこを吸ってもいいですか」「どうぞ」) "May I smoke?" "*Sure.*"

do「ra「ibu ドライブ *n.* trip in a car; drive:
Watashi-tachi wa kaiteki na dora-ibu *o tanoshiñda.* (私たちは快適なドライブを楽しんだ) We enjoyed a pleas-ant *drive.*

doraibu suru (～する) *vi.* take a drive for pleasure: *Kinoo wa Hakone made* doraibu *shita.* (きのうは箱根までドライブした) We *enjoyed a drive* to Hakone yesterday.

do「rama ドラマ *n.* drama; play (especially for TV or radio).

do「re¹ どれ（何れ）*n.* **1** which:
★ Used when choosing one out of three or more things.
Dore *ga anata no nimotsu desu ka?* (どれがあなたの荷物ですか) *Which* one is your baggage? / *Ichibañ yasui no wa* dore *desu ka?* (一番安いのはどれですか) *Which* is the cheap-est one?

2 whichever:
Dore *de mo ichibañ suki na mono o tori nasai.* (どれでも一番好きなものをとりなさい) Take *whichever* one

you like best.

3 all:

Karita hoñ wa dore mo omoshiroku nakatta. (借りた本はどれも面白くなかった) *All* the books I borrowed were boring. 《⇨ are[1]; kore; sore[1]》

do「re[2] どれ *int.* now; well; let me see: ★ Used when starting something.

Dore, shigoto o hajimeru ka. (どれ、仕事を始めるか) *Now*, shall I get to work? / *Dore, misete gorañ.* (どれ、見せてごらん) *Well*, let me have a look at it.

do「ro[1] どろ (泥) *n.* mud:

Doro ga kutsu ni tsuita. (泥が靴についた) *Mud* stuck to my shoes. / *Sono kuruma wa doro-darake da.* (その車は泥だらけだ) The car is covered with *mud*.

do「roboo どろぼう (泥棒) *n.* thief; robber; burglar:

Sakuya kare no uchi ni doroboo ga haitta. (昨夜彼の家にどろぼうが入った) A *thief* broke into his house last night.

doroboo (o) suru (〜(を)する) *vi.* steal a thing from a person:

Kare wa kane ni komatte, doroboo (o) shita. (彼は金に困って、どろぼう(を)した) He was hard up so he *committed theft*.

do「ru ドル (弗) *n.* dollar:

Doru no kawase reeto wa ikura desu ka? (ドルの為替レートはいくらですか) What's the exchange rate for the *dollar*? / *Doru o eñ ni kaete kudasai.* (ドルを円に替えてください) Will you please exchange *dollars* into Japanese yen? / *Doru wa koko ichi-neñkañ ni nihyaku nijuu-eñ kara hyaku yoñjuu-eñ ni sagatta.* (ドルはここ一年間に220円から140円に下がった) During the past year, the *dollar* fell from 220 to 140 yen. 《⇨ dorudaka; doruyasu》

do「rubako ドルばこ (弗箱) *n.* money-maker; gold mine:

Kono seehiñ wa waga-sha no doru bako da. (この製品は我が社のドル箱だ) This product is a *real gold mine* for our company.

do「rudaka ドルだか (弗高) *n.* strong dollar; appreciation of the dollar. 《↔ doruyasu》

do「ruyasu ドルやす (弗安) *n.* weak dollar; depreciation of the dollar:

Kore ijoo no eñdaka doruyasu ga atte wa naranai. (これ以上の円高ドル安があってはならない) There should be no further *depreciation of the dollar* against the yen. 《↔ dorudaka》

do「ryoku どりょく (努力) *n.* effort; endeavor:

Doryoku no kai mo naku, kare wa shippai shita. (努力のかいもなく彼は失敗した) Despite his *efforts*, he failed. / *Kare no doryoku ga yatto mi o musuñda.* (彼の努力がやっと実を結んだ) His *efforts* bore fruit at last. / doryoku-ka (努力家) a *hard worker*.

doryoku suru (〜する) *vi.* make efforts; endeavor: *Go-kiboo ni sou yoo doryoku itashimasu.* (ご希望にそうよう努力いたします) We will *make every effort* to meet your expectations. / *Dekiru dake doryoku shita ga dame datta.* (できるだけ努力したがだめだった) I *tried* as *hard* as I could, but in vain.

do「shiñ どしん *adv.* (〜 to) with a thud [thump]; plump: ★The sound of something hitting something else, or falling down. *Kodomo ga beddo kara doshiñ to ochita.* (子どもがベッドからどしんと落ちた) The child fell out of bed *with a thud*. / *Kuruma ga hee ni doshiñ to butsukatta.* (車が塀にどしんとぶつかった) The car *thudded* into the wall.

do「soku どそく (土足) *n.* with one's shoes on:

Kare wa dosoku *no mama uchi ni agatta.*（彼は土足のまま家にあがった）He entered the house *without removing his shoes.* / Dosoku Geñkiñ. (*sign*)（土足厳禁）*Remove Shoes Before Entry.*

DOSOKU GEÑKIÑ SIGN

do⌐tchi どっち *n.* ★ Informal equivalent of '*dochira.*'
1 which:
Waiñ wa aka to shiro, dotchi *ni shimasu ka?*（ワインは赤と白、どっちにしますか）*Which* will you have, red or white wine? / *Miñna wa* dotchi *e ikimashita ka?*（みんなはどっちへ行きましたか）*Which* way did they go?
2 both; either:
Watashi-tachi wa dotchi *mo sarariimañ desu.*（私たちはどっちもサラリーマンです）We are *both* office workers. / *"Dochira ni shimasu ka?" "Dotchi de mo kekkoo desu."*（「どちらにしますか」「どっちでも結構です」）"Which would you prefer?" "*Either* will do."
《⇒ atchi; kotchi; sotchi》

do⌐tchimichi どっちみち *adv.* anyway; in either case; sooner or later:
Dotchimichi *kare-ra wa tasuka-ranai deshoo.*（どっちみち彼らは助からないでしょう）*In either case,* they will not be able to survive. / Dotchimichi *suupaa e ikimasu kara, anata no mono mo katte kite agemasu yo.*（どっちみちスーパーへ行きますから、あなたの物も買ってきてあげますよ）I'm going to the supermarket *anyway,* so I'll buy your things, too.

do⌐te どて（土手）*n.* bank; embankment.

do⌐tto どっと *adv.* **1** (the state of giving a roar of laughter):
Kañkyaku wa dotto *waratta.*（観客はどっと笑った）The audience *burst* into laughter.
2 in a rush; all of a sudden:
Deñsha kara hito ga dotto *orita.*（電車から人がどっと降りた）People *rushed* off the train. / *Shikeñ ga owaru to tsukare ga* dotto *deta.*（試験が終わると疲れがどっと出た）I *suddenly* felt tired when the exam finished.

do⌐yadoya どやどや *adv.* (～ to) (the state of many people moving together in a crowd):
Siñbuñ-kisha ga shizuka na kaijoo ni doyadoya (*to*) *haitte kita.*（新聞記者が静かな会場にどやどや（と）入って来た）The reporters rushed *noisily* into the quiet meeting room.

do⌐yo⌐o(bi) どよう（び）（土曜（日））*n.* Saturday:
Giñkoo wa doyoobi *wa yasumi desu.*（銀行は土曜日は休みです）The banks are closed on *Saturdays.*
《⇒ yoobi (table)》

E

e¹¹ え (絵) *n.* picture; drawing; painting:
e o kaku (絵をかく) draw a *picture* / Kare wa e ga umai. (彼は絵がうまい) He is good at *painting.* / Sono keshiki wa e no yoo ni utsukushikatta. (その景色は絵のように美しかった) The view was as beautiful as a *picture.* (⇨ kaiga)

e² え (柄) *n.* handle (of a tool, etc.):
kasa no e (かさの柄) the *handle* of an umbrella.

e³ へ *p.* [follows a noun and indicates a direction or goal]
1 to; for:
Ginza e itte, eega o mimashoo. (銀座へ行って、映画を見ましょう) Let's go *to* Ginza and see a film. / Ashita Hoñkoñ e tachimasu. (あした香港へ発ちます) I leave *for* Hong Kong tomorrow.
2 on; onto:
Kono hako o tana no ue e oite kudasai. (この箱を棚の上へ置いてください) Please put this box *on* the shelf. / Kare wa yuka no ue e hoñ o otoshita. (彼は床の上へ本を落とした) He dropped the book *onto* the floor.
3 in; into:
Shorui wa hikidashi e iremashita. (書類は引き出しへ入れました) I put the papers *in* the drawer. / Uchi no naka e hairi nasai. (家の中へ入りなさい) Come *into* the house.

⎯⎯⎯ USAGE ⎯⎯⎯
In the above examples 'ni' can be used instead of 'e.' However, before the particle 'no,' only 'e' can be used. *e.g.* yuujiñ e no tegami (a letter *to* a friend). (⇨ ni²)

e' えっ *int.* oh; hah; eh: ★ Used when one fails to hear what is said, or to indicate surprise.
E', nañ desu ka? (えっ、何ですか) *What?* What did you say? / E', sore hoñtoo kai? (えっ、それ本当かい) *What!* Is that really true?

-e え (重) *suf.* fold; ply; layer:
hito-e (一重) single; one *layer*; one *fold* / futa-e (二重) two *layers*; double; two-*ply* / ya-e (八重) eight *fold*; (of flowers) multi-petalled / iku-e (幾重) so many *folds* / to-e hata-e no hitogaki (十重二十重の人垣) a *thick* wall of spectators.

e⎡akoñ エアコン *n.* air conditioner; air conditioning. (⇨ kuuraa)

e⎡bi えび (海老) *n.* lobster; prawn; shrimp.

⎯⎯⎯ USAGE ⎯⎯⎯
Lobsters are called 'ise-ebi,' prawns, 'kuruma-ebi,' and shrimps 'ko-ebi.'

e⎡chiketto エチケット *n.* etiquette; good manners:
echiketto o mamoru (エチケットを守る) observe the rules of *etiquette.*

e⎡da えだ (枝) *n.* branch; bough; twig; sprig:
eda o oru [harau] (枝を折る[払う]) break [trim] a *branch* / eda o kiru (枝を切る) cut a *branch* off.

E⎡do えど (江戸) *n.* Edo; Yedo:
★ The former name of Tokyo, changed to Tokyo in 1868.
Edo-jidai (江戸時代) Edo Period (1603-1867) ★ Tokugawa Ieyasu made himself shogun and established his government in Edo in 1603. Also known as '*Tokugawa-jidai*' (Tokugawa Period).

《⇨ jidai (table)》

e¹e ええ *int.* **1** yes; no:

> ---
> **USAGE**
>
> '*Ee*' literally means 'That's right' and is used to confirm a statement, whether affirmative or negative. Note that this use is different from that of 'yes' and 'no' in English. '*Hai*' is the more polite form.
> ---

"*Anata wa Nihoñjiñ desu ka?*" "*Ee, soo desu.*" (「あなたは日本人ですか」「ええ、そうです」) "Are you Japanese?" "*Yes,* I am." / "*Kore wa anata no kasa de wa arimaseñ ne?*" "*Ee, chigaimasu.*" (「これはあなたの傘ではありませんね」「ええ、違います」) "Isn't this your umbrella?" "*No,* it isn't." 《⇨ hai¹; iie》 **2** well; let's see: *Ee, nañ to ittara yoi ka.* (ええ、何と言ったらよいか) *Well,* I don't quite know what to say.

e「ebuñ えいぶん (英文) *n.* English; English sentence: *eebuñ o nihoñbuñ ni yakusu* (英文を日本文に訳す) translate *English* into Japanese / *eebuñ de tegami o kaku* (英文で手紙を書く) write a letter in *English*.

e「ebu¹ñgaku えいぶんがく (英文学) *n.* English literature: *eebuñgaku-ka* (英文学科) the Department of *English Literature*. 《⇨ buñgaku》

e「e-eñ えいえん (永遠) *n.* eternity; permanence: *Futari wa ee-eñ no ai o chikatta.* (二人は永遠の愛を誓った) The two pledged their *eternal* love.
— *a.n.* (～ na, ni) eternal; permanent: *Oriñpikku no hi wa ee-eñ ni tsuzuku daroo.* (オリンピックの火は永遠に続くだろう) The Olympic Flame will last *forever*.

e「ega えいが (映画) *n.* movie; the movies; film: *Koñya eega ni ikimaseñ ka?* (今夜映画に行きませんか) How about going to the *movies* tonight? / *Puraza-gekijoo de, ima yoi eega o yatte imasu.* (プラザ劇場で、今良い映画をやっています) There's a good *movie* on at the Plaza.

e「ega¹kañ えいがかん (映画館) *n.* movie theater; cinema.

E「ego えいご (英語) *n.* English; the English language: *Anata wa Eego o hanasemasu ka?* (あなたは英語を話せますか) Can you speak *English?* / *Kore wa Eego de nañ to iimasu ka?* (これは英語で何と言いますか) What is this called in *English?* / *Watashi wa Eego o tsukau shigoto o sagashite imasu.* (私は英語を使う仕事を探しています) I am looking for a job where I can use my *English*.

e「egyoo えいぎょう (営業) *n.* sales; business; trade: *Eegyoo-hookoku wa kakimashita ka?* (営業報告は書きましたか) Have you written the *sales* report? / *eegyoo-añnai* (営業案内) a catalog of *business* activities / *eegyoo-chuu* (sign) (営業中) *Open* (for business) / *eegyoo-jikañ* (営業時間) *business* [*office*] hours / *eegyoo-teeshi* (営業停止) suspension of *business*.

EEGYOO-CHUU SIGN

eegyoo suru (～する) *vi.* do business: *Kono mise wa nichiyoo mo eegyoo shite iru.* (この店は日曜も営業している) This shop *is open* even on Sundays.

E⌐ekoku えいこく（英国）*n.* Great Britain; England; the United Kingdom.《⇨ Igirisu》

e⌐ekyoo えいきょう（影響）*n.* influence; effect; impact: eekyoo o oyobosu（影響を及ぼす）exert *influence* / eekyoo ga aru（影響がある）have an *effect* / *Sono hoñ wa wakai hito-tachi ni tsuyoi eekyoo o ataeta.*（その本は若い人たちに強い影響を与えた）The book had a strong *influence* on young people. / *Kodomo wa sugu ni terebi no eekyoo o ukeru.*（子どもはすぐにテレビの影響を受ける）Children *are* easily *influenced* by TV. / *Sono jikeñ no shakai-teki eekyoo wa ooki-katta.*（その事件の社会的影響は大きかった）The social *impact* of the event was very great. / *Jishiñ no eekyoo de ressha ga okureta.*（地震の影響で列車が遅れた）The train was delayed *because of* the earthquake.

(ni) eekyoo suru《(に)～する》*vi.* influence; affect: *Kioñ ga sakumotsu no shuukaku ni eekyoo suru koto ga yoku aru.*（気温が作物の収穫に影響することがよくある）The temperature often *influences* the harvest.

e⌐ekyuu えいきゅう（永久）*a.n.* (～ no, ni) permanent; eternal: eekyuu no heewa o negau（永久の平和を願う）wish for *eternal* peace / *Nihoñ kokumiñ wa eekyuu ni señsoo o hooki shita.*（日本国民は永久に戦争を放棄した）The Japanese people renounced war *forever.*《⇨ ee-eñ》

e⌐enichi-ji⌐teñ えいにちじてん（英日辞典）*n.* English-Japanese dictionary for English speaking people.《⇨ eewa-jiteñ; nichiee-jiteñ; waee-jiteñ》

e⌐esee[1] えいせい（衛生）*n.* hygiene; sanitation; health:

Natsu wa eesee ni ki o tsuketa hoo ga yoi.（夏は衛生に気をつけたほうが良い）You had better be careful about *sanitation* in summer. / *Namamizu o nomu no wa eesee-joo yoku nai.*（生水を飲むのは衛生上良くない）It is not good for *health* to drink unboiled water.

e⌐esee[2] えいせい（衛星）*n.* satellite: eesee-hoosoo（衛星放送）*satellite* broadcasting / eesee-chuukee（衛星中継）transmission via *satellite*.

e⌐esee-teki えいせいてき（衛生的）*a.n.* (～ na, ni) sanitary: *Shokudoo no eesee-teki na kañri ga hitsuyoo desu.*（食堂の衛生的な管理が必要です）Conditions in restaurants must be kept *sanitary*.

ee-tii-esu *n.* = ATS.

e⌐eto ええと *int.* let me see; well: *"Ima nañ-ji desu ka?" "Eeto, sañ-ji go-fuñ desu."*（「今何時ですか」「えеと、3 時 5 分です」）"What is the time?" "*Let me see*, it is five past three."

e⌐ewa-ji⌐teñ えいわじてん（英和辞典）*n.* English-Japanese dictionary for Japanese people.《⇨ ee-nichi-jiteñ; nichiee-jiteñ; waee-jiteñ》

e⌐eyoo えいよう（栄養）*n.* nutrition; nourishment: *Motto eeyoo no aru mono o tabe nasai.*（もっと栄養のある物を食べなさい）You should eat more *nutritious* food.

e⌐eyuu えいゆう（英雄）*n.* hero.

e⌐ga⌐k·u えがく（描く）*vt.* (egak·i-; egak·a-; ega·i-te Ⓒ) **1** paint; draw: *Fusuma ni wa shiki no hana ga egakarete ita.*（ふすまには四季の花が描かれていた）Flowers of the four seasons *were painted* on the sliding paper door. **2** take form; describe: *Booru wa aozora ni ko o egaite*

toñde itta.（ボールは青空に弧を描いて
飛んで行った）The ball went flying,
describing an arc against the sky.
3 form a picture in the mind;
imagine:
*Watashi wa hajimete otozureru
machi no yoosu o kokoro ni* egaita.
（私は初めて訪れる町の様子を心に描い
た）I *imagined* in my mind's eye
what the town I was visiting for
the first time would look like.

eˈgao えがお（笑顔）*n.* smile; smiling [beaming] face:
Miñna wa kare o egao *de mukaeta.*（みんなは彼を笑顔で迎えた）They
welcomed him with a *smile*.

e-ˈhaˈgaki えはがき（絵葉書）*n.*
picture postcard. （⇨ hagaki）

Eˈhimeˈ-keñ えひめけん（愛媛県）*n.*
Ehime Prefecture. Located in
the west of Shikoku. The annual
output of oranges is the largest
in Japan. Capital city: Matsu-
yama（松山）. （⇨ map (C5)）

eˈhoˈñ えほん（絵本）*n.* picture
[illustrated] book.

eˈizu エイズ *n.* AIDS:
eizu *ni kañseñ suru*（エイズに感染す
る）get [contract] *AIDS*.

eˈki えき（駅）*n.* (railroad) station:
eki *no minami[kita]-guchi*（駅の南
[北]口）the south [north] entrance
of a *station* / *Tsugi no* eki *de orimasu.*（次の駅で降ります）I'm get-
ting off at the next *station*. / *Tookyoo*-eki *wa ikutsu-me desu ka?*
（東京駅はいくつ目ですか）How many
stops are there from here to
Tokyo *Station*? / *Chikatetsu no*
eki *made, aruite go-fuñ desu.*（地
下鉄の駅まで，歩いて5分です）It is a
five-minute walk to the subway
station.

ekˈibeñ えきべん（駅弁）*n.* box
lunch sold at a railroad station.
★ It contains a variety of local
specialties.

EKIBEÑ

eˈkichoo えきちょう（駅長）*n.*
stationmaster:
ekichoo-*shitsu*（駅長室）a *stationmaster's* office.

eˈkiˈiñ えきいん（駅員）*n.* station
employee; station staff.

eˈkimae えきまえ（駅前）*n.* the
place [street] in front of [near] a
(railroad) station:
ekimae-*hiroba*（駅前広場）an open
space *in front of a station* / Eki-
mae *ni koobañ ga arimasu.*（駅前に
交番があります）There is a police
box *near the station*.

eˈkitai えきたい（液体）*n.* liquid;
fluid. （⇨ kitai²; kotai）

eˈma えま（絵馬）*n.* votive picture
tablet.

───(CULTURE)───

A piece of wood offered to a
Shinto shrine or a Buddhist
temple with prayers written on
it. Students often offer such
tablets to pray for their success
in entrance examinations.

EMA

e˼**mono** えもの（獲物）*n.* game;
catch; take:
Emono *o ni-too shitometa.*（獲物を
2頭しとめた）I shot two head of
game. / *Kyoo wa* emono *ga suku-nai.*（きょうは獲物が少ない）We had a
small *catch* today. / *Ichi-nichi aru-ki-mawatta ga taishita* emono *wa
nakatta.*（一日歩きまわったがたいした獲
物はなかった）I hunted all day, but
there was not much *game.* / Emo-no *ga wana ni kakatta.*（獲物がわな
にかかった）There was an *animal*
caught in the trap.

e˼**ñ**[1] えん（円）*n.* yen: ★ The
monetary unit of Japan.
*señ-*eñ（千円）one thousand *yen* /
*Kono baggu wa goseñ-*eñ *de kai-mashita.*（このバッグは5千円で買いま
した）I bought this bag for 5,000
yen. / Eñ *ga mata tsuyoku natta.*
（円がまた強くなった）The *yen* has got-ten stronger again.（⇨ eñdaka;
eñyasu）

e˼**ñ**[2] えん（円）*n.* circle:
eñ *o egaku*（円を描く）draw a *circle.*

e˼**ñ**[3] えん（縁）*n.* relation; connec-tion; affinity:
Kare to wa nañ no eñ *mo arima-señ.*（彼とは何の縁もありません）I have
nothing *to do* with him. / *Ano hi-to to wa* eñ *o kirimashita.*（あの人と
は縁を切りました）I broke off *rela-tions* with him. / *Fushigi na* eñ
de kare to tomodachi ni natta.（不
思議な縁で彼と友達になった）I be-came friends with him by a sin-gular *chance.* / *Watashi wa kane
mooke ni wa* eñ *ga nai.*（私は金もう
けには縁がない）I *am no good* at mak-ing money.

e˼**ñchoo** えんちょう（延長）*n.* ex-tension; prolongation:
Fukuseñ-kukañ no eñchoo *o kee-kaku-chuu desu.*（複線区間の延長を
計画中です）They are planning an
extension of the double track rail-way. / *Kaiki no* eñchoo *ni wa hañ-tai desu.*（会期の延長には反対です）I
am against the *extension* of this
session.（↔ tañshuku）

eñchoo suru（〜する）*vt.* extend;
lengthen; prolong: *Kare wa Pari
e yoru tame ni kyuuka o* eñchoo
shita.（彼はパリへ寄るために休暇を延長
した）He *prolonged* his vacation in
order to visit Paris. / *Sono dooro
wa Niigata made* eñchoo *sareta.*
（その道路は新潟まで延長された）The
road *was extended* to Niigata.

e˼**ñdaka** えんだか（円高）*n.* strong
yen; appreciation of the yen:
Eñdaka *doruyasu de yushutsu ga
kurushii.*（円高ドル安で輸出が苦しい）
It is hard to export because of
the *strong yen* against the dollar.
（↔ eñyasu）

e˼**ñdañ** えんだん（縁談）*n.* an offer
of marriage; marriage arrange-ments:
eñdañ *ni oojiru*（縁談に応じる）ac-cept an *offer of marriage* / eñdañ
o kotowaru（縁談を断る）refuse an
offer of marriage / *Kare ga sono*
eñdañ *o matometa.*（彼がその縁談を
まとめた）He arranged the *marriage.*
/ *Sono* eñdañ *wa kowareta.*（その縁
談はこわれた）The *marriage arrange-ment* has broken down.

e˼**ñdoo** えんどう（沿道）*n.* route;
roadside: Eñdoo *wa keñbutsuniñ
de ippai datta.*（沿道は見物人でいっ
ぱいだった）*Both sides of the street*
were crowded with spectators.

e˼**ñgañ** えんがん（沿岸）*n.* coast;
shore:
Sono toshi wa Nihoñkai eñgañ *ni
aru.*（その都市は日本海沿岸にある）
The city is on the *coast* of the
Sea of Japan.

e˼**ñgawa** えんがわ（縁側）*n.* corri-dor-like veranda. ★ A long, nar-row wooden floor laid outside
the rooms of a Japanese house. It
usually faces onto a garden.
（⇨ illus. (next page)）

EṄGAWA

e⌐ṅgee えんげい（園芸）*n.* gardening; horticulture.

e⌐ṅgeki えんげき（演劇）*n.* play; theatrical performance. ★ Usually refers to dramatic performances as a branch of art.

e⌐ṅgi[1] えんぎ（演技）*n.* performance; acting: *Kanojo no* eṅgi *wa subarashikatta.* （彼女の演技は素晴らしかった）Her *performance* was superb. / *Kare wa* eṅgi *ga umai [heta da].* （彼は演技がうまい[下手だ]）He is good [poor] at *acting.*

e⌐ṅgi[2] えんぎ（縁起）*n.* omen; luck; portent: eṅgi *no yoi [warui] kotogara* （縁起のよい[悪い]事柄）an event of good [bad] *omen* / *Kore wa* eṅgi *ga yoi [warui].* （これは縁起がよい[悪い]）This is a sign of good [bad] *luck.* **eṅgi o katsugu** （〜をかつぐ）be superstitious: *Watashi wa* eṅgi *o katsugimaseṅ.* （私は縁起をかつぎません）I'm *not superstitious.*

e⌐ṅjiṅ エンジン *n.* engine: eṅjiṅ *o kakeru [tomeru]* （エンジンをかける[止める]）start [stop] an *engine* / *Eṅjiṅ no chooshi ga okashii.* （エンジンの調子がおかしい）Something is wrong with the *engine.*

e⌐ṅji⌐nia エンジニア *n.* engineer. 《⇨ gishi》

e⌐ṅji·ru えんじる（演じる）*vt.* (eṅjite [V]) perform; play; act: *Kare wa Yoshitsune no yaku o* *ikiiki to* eṅjita. （彼は義経の役を生き生きと演じた）He *acted* the part of Yoshitsune with élan. / *Kooshoo ni atari, kare wa juuyoo na yakuwari o* eṅjita. （交渉にあたり、彼は重要な役割を演じた）He *played* an important role in the negotiation. / *Kanojo wa hitomae de wa yoki tsuma o* eṅjite ita. （彼女は人前では良き妻を演じていた）In the presence of others, she *acted* like a good wife.

e⌐ṅjo えんじょ（援助）*n.* help; aid; assistance; support: eṅjo *o ukeru* （援助を受ける）receive *support* / eṅjo *o ataeru* （援助を与える）give *assistance* / eṅjo *o uchikiru* （援助を打ち切る）discontinue *aid* / *Watashi wa kare ni* eṅjo *o motometa.* （私は彼に援助を求めた）I asked him for his *help.* / *Watashi wa kare no* eṅjo *o kotowatta.* （私は彼の援助を断った）I refused his *help.* / *Zaisee-teki* eṅjo *ga hitsuyoo da.* （財政的援助が必要だ）We need financial *aid.* / *Anata no* go-eṅjo *o kaṅsha shimasu.* （あなたのご援助を感謝します）I thank you for your *assistance.*

eṅjo suru （〜する）*vt.* help; aid; assist; support: *sono kuni no keezai-fukkoo o* eṅjo suru （その国の経済復興を援助する）*aid* the economic revival of the country / *Kanojo wa paato de hataraite, kakee o* eṅjo shite iru. （彼女はパートで働いて、家計を援助している）She is working part-time to *help out* with the family finances.

e⌐ṅka えんか（演歌）*n.* traditional Japanese popular songs. ★ Typically with sad lyrics and melancholy melodies.

e⌐ṅkai えんかい（宴会）*n.* party; dinner (party); banquet: *Kare no tame ni* eṅkai *o hiraita.* （彼のために宴会を開いた）We held a *dinner* in his honor. / *Kono* eṅkai *no kakari wa dare desu ka?* (この宴会の係りはだれですか) Who is looking after this *banquet*?

e⌐ñkatsu えんかつ（円滑）*a.n.* (～ na, ni) smooth; without a hitch: *Hanashiai wa* eñkatsu *ni susuñda.* (話し合いは円滑に進んだ) The talks went off *smoothly.*

e⌐ñki えんき（延期）*n.* postponement; adjournment.
　eñki suru (～する) *vt.* postpone; put off; adjourn: *Shiai wa teñki ni naru made* eñki shimasu. (試合は天気になるまで延期します) The game will *be put off* until the weather clears up. / *Kai wa raishuu made* eñki sareta. (会は来週まで延期された) The meeting *was postponed* until next week.

e⌐nogu えのぐ（絵の具）*n.* paints; colors: *abura*-enogu (油絵の具) oil *colors* / *suisai*-enogu (水彩絵の具) water *colors.*

e⌐ñpitsu えんぴつ（鉛筆）*n.* pencil: eñpitsu *de kaku* (鉛筆で書く) write in *pencil* / eñpitsu *o kezuru* (鉛筆を削る) sharpen a *pencil* / *Kono* eñpitsu *no shiñ wa sugu oreru.* (この鉛筆のしんはすぐ折れる) The lead of this *pencil* is easily broken.

e⌐ñryo えんりょ（遠慮）*n.* reserve; restraint; modesty: *Ano hito wa* eñryo *ga nai.* (あの人は遠慮がない) He has no *modesty.* / *Eñryo no nai ikeñ o kikasete kudasai.* (遠慮のない意見を聞かせてください) I'd appreciate your *frank* opinion. / *Kanojo ni wa* eñryo *ga atta yoo da.* (彼女には遠慮があったようだ) She seemed to *be reserved.*
《⇨ bueñryo》
　eñryo suru (～する) *vi., vt.* **1** reserve: *Watashi no hihañ wa* eñryo shite okimasu. (私の批判は遠慮しておきます) I will *reserve* my crit-

icism.
2 refrain: *Tabako wa* eñryo shite *kudasai.* (たばこは遠慮してください) Please *refrain* from smoking. / *Sore o taberu no wa* eñryo shita. (それを食べるのは遠慮した) I *refrained* from eating it.
　eñryo naku (～なく) without reserve: *Kare wa* eñryo naku *jibuñ no ikeñ o nobeta.* (彼は遠慮なく自分の意見を述べた) He expressed his own opinion *without reserve.* / *"Kono kuruma o doozo go-*eñryo naku *o-tsukai kudasai." "Hai sore de wa* (eñryo naku)." (「この車をどうぞご遠慮なくお使いください」「はいそれでは（遠慮なく）」) "Please *feel free* to use this car." "Thank you. Then I'll go ahead and accept your kind offer (*without reserve*)."

e⌐ñshi えんし（遠視）*n.* farsightedness; longsightedness: *Watashi wa* eñshi *desu.* (私は遠視です) I *am farsighted.* 《↔ kiñshi²》

e⌐ñshutsu えんしゅつ（演出）*n.* production; direction: *Sono gakkoo-geki wa señsee no* eñshutsu *de jooeñ sareta.* (その学校劇は先生の演出で上演された) The school play was presented under the *direction* of the teacher. / eñshutsu-ka (演出家) a *director* (for the stage); a *producer* (for the mass media).
　eñshutsu suru (～する) *vt.* produce; direct: *Sono geki wa dare ga* eñshutsu shimashita ka? (その劇はだれが演出しましたか) Who *produced* the play? / *Yamada-sañ ga* eñshutsu shita *geki o mimashita.* (山田さんが演出した劇を見ました) I saw a play *directed* by Mr. Yamada.

e⌐ñshuu えんしゅう（演習）*n.* **1** maneuvers: *Jieetai ga tokubetsu*-eñshuu *o oko-*

natta.(自衛隊が特別演習を行なった) The Self-Defense Forces held special *maneuvers.*
2 seminar:
Nihoñ-buñgaku no eñshuu (日本文学の演習) a *seminar* in Japanese literature / eñshuu-*shitsu* (演習室) a *seminar* room.

e⌈**ñsoku** えんそく (遠足) *n.* outing; excursion; hike:
Watashi-tachi wa kaigañ e eñshuu *ni itta.*(私たちは海岸へ遠足に行った) We went on an *outing* to the seaside. / *Asu wa* eñsoku *desu.*(あすは遠足です) We have an *excursion* tomorrow.

e⌈**ñsoo** えんそう (演奏) *n.* (musical) performance; recital:
Kare no eñsoo *wa subarashikatta.*(彼の演奏はすばらしかった) His *performance* was fantastic. / eñsoo-*kai* (演奏会) a *concert.*
eñsoo suru (〜する) *vt.* play; perform: *Kanojo wa piano de Shopañ o* eñsoo *shita.*(彼女はピアノでショパンを演奏した) She *played* Chopin on the piano.

e⌈**ñtotsu** えんとつ (煙突) *n.* chimney; stovepipe; funnel.

E⌈**nu-etchi-ke**⌉**e** *n.* = NHK.

E⌈**nu-tii-ti**⌉**i** *n.* = NTT.

e⌈**ñyasu** えんやす (円安) *n.* weak yen; depreciation of the yen. 《↔ eñdaka》

e⌈**ñzetsu** えんぜつ (演説) *n.* address; speech; oration:
Ano hito no eñzetsu *wa kiita koto ga aru.*(あの人の演説は聞いたことがある) I've heard him make an *address.* / señkyo-eñzetsu (選挙演説) a campaign *speech* / gaitoo-eñzetsu (街頭演説) / street *oratory.*
eñzetsu (o) suru (〜(を)する) *vt.* make a speech; speak; give an address: *Kare wa mijikai* enzetsu *o shita.*(彼は短い演説をした) He *made* a short *speech.* / *Hito no mae de* eñzetsu suru *no wa nigate*

desu.(人の前で演説するのは苦手です) I'm no good at *speaking* in public. 《⇨ kooeñ²》

e⌈**ra** えら (鰓) *n.* gills.

e⌈**ra**⌉**b·u** えらぶ (選ぶ) *vt.* (erab·i-; erab·a-; erañ-de Ⓒ) **1** choose; select:
Chokoreeto ka kyañdii ka suki na hoo o erabi nasai.(チョコレートかキャンディーか好きなほうを選びなさい) *Select* whatever you like, chocolates or candies. / *Kare wa takusañ no oobosha no naka kara chuuseñ de erabareta.*(彼はたくさんの応募者の中から抽選で選ばれた) He *was chosen* by lot from many applicants. / *Kare wa shusse no tame nara shudañ o erabanai.*(彼は出世のためなら手段を選ばない) As long as it furthers his career, he *is not choosy* about what he does.
2 elect:
Señkyo no kekka Yoshida-shi ga shichoo ni erabareta.(選挙の結果吉田氏が市長に選ばれた) As a result of the election, Mr. Yoshida *was elected* mayor.

e⌈**ra**⌉**·i**¹ えらい (偉い) *a.* (-ku) **1** distinguished; high:
Erai hito to au toki wa nekutai o shimeta hoo ga ii.(偉い人と会うときはネクタイを締めたほうがいい) When meeting a *distinguished* person, you should wear a tie.
2 great; admirable:
Jibuñ de hataraite, daigaku o deta nañte erai desu ne.(自分で働いて，大学を出たなんて偉いですね) It is *admirable* that you worked your way through college. 《⇨ rippa》

e⌈**ra**⌉**·i**² えらい *a.* (-ku) serious; awful: ★ This is a dialectal usage from Kansai that can be heard nationwide. It is still considered colloquial.
Erai koto ni natta zo.(えらいことになったぞ) Now we are *in a fix.* / *Erai samusa da naa.*(えらい寒さだなあ)

It's *awfully* cold.

e⌈rebe⌉etaa　エレベーター　*n.* elevator; lift: Erebeetaa *ni notte, gokai made itta.* (エレベーターに乗って, 5階まで行った) I took an *elevator* to the fifth floor.

e⌈ri⌉　えり (襟)　*n.* collar; neck; neckband; lapel:
Kare wa watashi no eri *o tsukañda.* (彼は私のえりをつかんだ) He seized me by the *collar.* / *Samui no de kooto no* eri *o tateta.* (寒いのでコートのえりを立てた) It was so cold that I turned up the *collar* of my overcoat.
eri o tadasu (〜を正す) shape up; behave oneself.

e⌈·ru　える (得る)　*vt.* (e-te Ⓥ) gain; obtain; get:
Kare wa arubaito o shite seekatsuhi o ete iru. (彼はアルバイトをして生活費を得ている) He *earns* his living from a part-time job. / *Kanojo wa señsee no shikaku o eru tame ni beñkyoo shite imasu.* (彼女は先生の資格を得るために勉強しています) She is studying to *obtain* a teaching certificate. / *Wareware wa hoñ kara chishiki o* eru. (われわれは本から知識を得る) We *acquire* knowledge from books. / *Kare wa daigaku ni shoku o eta.* (彼は大学に職を得た) He *gained* a position in the university. / *Kanojo wa oya no yurushi o ete, Amerika e itta.* (彼女は親の許しを得て, アメリカへ行った) After *obtaining* the consent of her parents, she went to America.

/ *Kono bañgumi kara* eru *tokoro ga ookikatta.* (この番組から得るところが大きかった) I *learned* a lot from this program.
-zaru o enai (ざるを得ない) can do nothing but...:

> ┌──── (USAGE) ────
> Attached to the negative base of a verb; '*suru*' is irregular: '*sezaru o enai.*'

Sono keekaku wa akiramezaru o enai. (その計画はあきらめざるを得ない) We *can do nothing but give up* the plan. / *Watashi wa kaisha o* yamezaru o enaku narimashita. (私は会社を辞めざるを得なくなりました) *It came to my having no choice but to quit the company.*

e⌈sa⌉　えさ (餌)　*n.* bait; food; feed:
Sakana ni esa *o torareta.* (魚にえさをとられた) The *bait* was carried away by a fish. / *Neko ga* esa *o hoshigatte naite iru.* (猫がえさを欲しがってないている) The cat is meowing for *food.* / *Doobutsu ni* esa *o yaranai de kudasai.* (動物にえさをやらないでください) Please *don't feed* the animals.

e⌈sukare⌉etaa　エスカレーター　*n.* escalator:
eskareetaa *ni noru* (エスカレーターに乗る) take an *escalator* / eskareetaa *de agaru* [*kudaru*] (エスカレーターで上がる[下る]) go up [down] on an *escalator.*

F

fa┌ito ファイト *n.* fight; fighting spirit:
faito o moyasu (ファイトを燃やす) be full of *fight*.
— *int.* a shout given when encouraging other people:
Faito! (ファイト) *Stick to it [Come on]!*

fa┌kkusu ファックス *n.* fax; facsimile: *Tegami wa* fakkusu *de okurimasu.* (手紙はファックスで送ります) I'll send the letter by *fax*.

fa┌ñ ファン *n.* fan; passionate admirer:
Watashi wa Jaiañtsu (no) fañ *desu.* (私はジャイアンツ(の)ファンです) I am a Giants *fan.* / fañ-*retaa* (ファンレター) a *fan* letter; *fan* mail.

fa┌sunaa ファスナー *n.* zipper; zip fastener:
baggu no fasunaa o akeru [shimeru] (バッグのファスナーを開ける[締める]) *zip* a bag *open* [*closed*].

fi┌rumu フィルム *n.* film:
sañjuugo-miri no firumu (35 ミリのフィルム) 35 mm *film* / *Nijuuyoñ-mai-dori no* firumu *o ip-poñ kudasai.* (二十四枚撮りのフィルムを1本下さい) I'd like a roll of *film* with twenty-four exposures / *Kono kamera ni wa karaa* firumu *ga haitte imasu.* (このカメラにはカラーフィルムが入っています) This camera is loaded with color *film*.

fo┌oku フォーク *n.* table fork:
Kare wa naifu to fooku *no tsukai-kata ga heta da.* (彼はナイフとフォークの使い方が下手だ) He is not good at using a knife and *fork*.

fu ふ (府) *n.* prefecture: ★ An administrative division of Japan, but only used with reference to Osaka (大阪) and Kyoto (京都).

Oosaka-fu (大阪府) Osaka *Prefecture.* (⇨ keñ┐)

fu- ふ (不) *pref.* not; un-; in-:
★ Gives a negative or contrary meaning to a word.
fu-*goori na* (不合理な) *ir*rational / fu-*hitsuyoo na* (不必要な) *un*necessary / fu-*jiyuu* (不自由) *in*convenience / fu-*juubuñ* (不十分) *in*sufficiency / fu-*kakujitsu* (不確実) *un*certainty / fu-*kañzeñ* (不完全) *im*perfection.

fu┌añ ふあん (不安) *n.* worry; uneasiness; anxiety:
fuañ *o kañjiru* (不安を感じる) feel *anxiety* / *Kono kusuri wa añzeñ-see ni* fuañ *ga aru.* (この薬は安全性に不安がある) There is *anxiety* over the safety of this medicine.
— *a.n.* (~ na, ni) afraid; uneasy; anxious; worried:
Hidoi oo-ame de fuañ *na ichiya o sugoshita.* (ひどい大雨で不安な一夜を過ごした) With the heavy rain, I passed an *uneasy* night. / *Haha-oya ga nakanaka kaette konai no de, kodomo wa* fuañ *ni natte kita.* (母親がなかなか帰って来ないので、子どもは不安になってきた) Since his mother did not come home for a long time, the child began to *get worried.* / *Shiñnyuu-shaiñ ni ooki-na shigoto o makaseru no wa chotto* fuañ *desu.* (新入社員に大きな仕事をまかせるのはちょっと不安です) I feel a bit *uneasy* about entrusting an important job to a new employee. (⇨ shiñpai)

fu┌beñ ふべん (不便) *n.* inconvenience; unhandiness:
Go-fubeñ o okake-shite mooshi-wake arimaseñ. (ご不便をおかけして申し訳ありません) I'm sorry to have

caused you *inconvenience*.

fubeñ (o) suru (~(を)する) *vi*. suffer inconvenience; feel inconvenienced: *Teedeñ de zuibuñ* fubeñ (o) shita. (停電でずいぶん不便(を)した) We *were put to great inconvenience* because of the power failure.

— *a.n.* (~ na, ni) inconvenient; not handy:
Watashi no uchi wa kootsuu ga fubeñ *da*. (私の家は交通が不便だ) My house is *difficult to get to* by public transport. / *Deñwa ga soba ni nai to shigoto ni* fubeñ *desu*. (電話がそばにないと仕事に不便です) It is *inconvenient* working unless a phone is near at hand. (↔ beñri)

fuｌbeｌñkyoo ふべんきょう (不勉強) *n*. laziness (in one's studies):
Fubeñkyoo o hañsee shite imasu. (不勉強を反省しています) I'm sorry I *didn't study hard enough*.

— *a.n.* (~ na) idle; lazy:
★ Not trying hard enough to acquire knowledge.
fubeñkyoo na *hito* (不勉強な人) an *idle* person / *Fubeñkyoo de yoku shirimaseñ*. (不勉強でよく知りません) I'm afraid I *have been inattentive to that matter*, and I don't know about it very well.

fuｌbo ふぼ (父母) *n*. parents; one's father and mother:
fubo-kai (父母会) a *Parent-Teacher* Association. (⇒ fukee)

fuｌbuki ふぶき (吹雪) *n*. snowstorm; blizzard:
Yama de fubuki *ni atta*. (山で吹雪にあった) We were overtaken by a *blizzard* in the mountains.

fuｌchi ふち (縁) *n*. brim; rim; edge; brink:
fuchi *no hiroi kabiñ* (縁の広い花瓶) a vase with a broad *brim* / *Kono chawañ wa* fuchi *ga kakete iru*. (この茶碗は縁が欠けている) The *rim* of

this cup is broken. / *Koppu o teeburu no* fuchi *ni oite wa ikemaseñ*. (コップをテーブルの縁に置いてはいけません) Don't put the glass on the *edge* of the table. / fuchi-nashi *megane* (縁なし眼鏡) *rimless* spectacles.

fuｌchuｌui ふちゅうい (不注意) *n*. carelessness; negligence:
Sono jiko wa watashi no fuchuui *kara desu*. (その事故は私の不注意からです) The accident was from *carelessness* on my part.

— *a.n.* (~ na) careless; thoughtless; negligent:
Fuchuui *na ayamari o shinai yoo ni*. (不注意な誤りをしないように) Avoid making *careless* mistakes. / *Keeyaku suru toki ni* fuchuui *de soñ o shita*. (契約をするときに不注意で損をした) I was *thoughtless* at the time of signing the contract, and suffered a loss.

fuｌda ふだ (札) *n*. check; tag; card:
torañpu no fuda (トランプの札) a playing *card*.

fuｌdañ ふだん (普段) *n., adv.* usual(ly); ordinary; ordinarily; always:
Fudañ (wa) *watashi wa ichi-nichi ni tabako o nijup-poñ kurai suimasu*. (普段(は)私は一日にたばこを20本くらい吸います) I *usually* smoke around twenty cigarettes a day. / *Yamada-sañ wa* fudañ *nara añna tsumaranai koto de okorimaseñ*. (山田さんは普段ならあんなつまらないことで怒りません) *Ordinarily*, Mr. Yamada would not have gotten angry at such trifles. / *Tanaka-sañ wa* fudañ *to kawaranai fukusoo o shite imashita*. (田中さんは普段と変わらない服装をしていました) Miss Tanaka wore the same clothes as *always*. / *Reegi-sahoo wa* fudañ *kara chuui shite oku hitsuyoo ga arimasu*. (礼儀作法は普段から注意し

ておく必要があります) One must *always* pay attention to manners.

fuˈdañgi¹ ふだんぎ (普段着) *n.* everyday clothes; casual wear:
Watashi wa soko e fudañgi no mama de itta. (私はそこへふだん着のままで行った) I went there in my *everyday clothes.*

fuˈde ふで (筆) *n.* writing brush (for Japanese calligraphy); brush for painting a picture:
fude *de kaku* (筆で書く) write with a *writing brush* / fude-bushoo na hito (筆不精な人) a *bad correspondent.*

fude ga tatsu (〜が立つ) be a very good writer.

fude o toru (〜をとる) put pen to paper.

fuˈdoosañ ふどうさん (不動産) *n.* real estate [property]; immovables:
fudoosañ-*gyoo* (不動産業) the *real estate* business / fudoosañ-ya (不動産屋) a *real estate* agent.

FUDOOSAÑ-YA OFFICE

fuˈe ふえ (笛) *n.* flute; whistle:
fue *o fuku* (笛を吹く) play the *flute*; blow a *whistle.*

fuˈeˈ·ru ふえる (増える・殖える) *vi.* (fue-te [V]) **1** increase:
Neñshoosha no jisatsu ga neñneñ fuete iru. (年少者の自殺が年々増えている) Suicide by young people *is increasing* every year. / *Señgetsu ni kurabe, taijuu ga ichi-kiro* fueta. (先月に比べ, 体重が 1 キロ増えた)

Compared to last month, I *have gained* a kilo in weight. / *Shiñgata kikai no doonyuu de seesañryoo ga* ni-bai ni fueta. (新型機械の導入で生産量が 2 倍に増えた) With the introduction of new machines, production *has doubled.* / *Taifuu no tame ni kawa no mizu ga kanari* fuete iru. (台風のために川の水がかなり増えている) The water of the river *has risen* considerably due to the typhoon. 《↔ heru¹》
2 breed; propagate:
Uchi de wa neko ga fuete, *komatte iru.* (うちでは猫が殖えて, 困っている) We don't know what to do about the cats *breeding* at our house.

fuˈgoo ふごう (符号) *n.* sign; mark; symbol: 《⇨ kigoo》
purasu no fugoo (プラスの符号) the plus *sign* / *Kore wa nañ no* fugoo *desu ka?* (これは何の符号ですか) What does this *mark* stand for?

fuˈhee ふへい (不平) *n.* dissatisfaction; discontent; complaint:
Ano hito wa itsu-mo fuhee bakari *itte iru.* (あの人はいつも不平ばかり言っている) He *is* always *complaining.*

fuˈhitsuˈyoo ふひつよう (不必要) *a.n.* (〜 na, ni) unnecessary; needless:
Fuhitsuyoo *na mono wa nani mo motte konai de kudasai.* (不必要なものは何も持って来ないでください) Don't bring any *unnecessary* articles with you. / *Suzuki-sañ no setsumee wa* fuhitsuyoo *ni nagai.* (鈴木さんの説明は不必要に長い) Mr. Suzuki's explanation is *unnecessarily* long. 《↔ hitsuyoo》

fuˈi ふい (不意) *n.* unexpectedness; suddenness; surprise.
fui o tsuku (〜をつく) catch a person off guard: *Hañniñ wa keesatsukañ no* fui o tsuite, *nigeta.* (犯人は警察官の不意をついて, 逃げた) The criminal *took* the policeman

unawares and ran away. / *Wata-shi wa fui o tsukarete sugu ni heñji ga dekinakatta.* (私は不意をつかれてすぐに返事ができなかった) I *was caught off guard* and was unable to answer immediately.
— *a.n.* (~ na/no, ni) unexpected; sudden; all of a sudden: *Fui no tanomi de, doo-shite ii ka wakaranakatta.* (不意の頼みで、どうしていいかわからなかった) It was an *unexpected* request, and I didn't know what to do. / *Mukashi no tomoda-chi ga fui ni yatte kita.* (昔の友だちが不意にやって来た) An old friend *unexpectedly* dropped by. / *Kare wa fui ni tachidomatta.* (彼は不意に立ち止まった) He *suddenly* stopped.

fui⌐rumu フィルム *n.* film. 《⇨ firumu》

fu⌐jiñ[1] ふじん（夫人）*n.* **1** wife: *shushoo* fujiñ（首相夫人）the *wife* of the prime minister / *Saitoo-sañ wa* fujiñ *doohañ de ryokoo shita.* (斎藤さんは夫人同伴で旅行した) Mr. Saito went on a trip with his *wife*.
2 Mrs.: *Hiroma de Satoo* fujiñ *ni shookai sareta.* (広間で佐藤夫人に紹介された) I was introduced to *Mrs.* Sato in the hall.

fu⌐jiñ[2] ふじん（婦人）*n.* lady; female; adult woman. 《⇨ josee; joshi; oñna》

fu⌐jiñka ふじんか（婦人科）*n.* gynecology. 《⇨ sañfujiñka》

fu⌐jiñka⌐-i ふじんかい（婦人科医）*n.* gynecologist.

fu⌐jiñke⌐ekañ ふじんけいかん（婦人警官）*n.* policewoman.

Fu⌐ji-sañ ふじさん（富士山）*n.* Mt. Fuji. ★ The highest mountain in Japan (3,776 meters).

fu⌐jiyuu ふじゆう（不自由）*a.n.* (~ na) **1** (of one's lifestyle) inconvenient; needy: *Deñwa ga nai to nani-ka to* fujiyuu

FUJI-SAÑ

desu. (電話がないと何かと不自由です) It is somewhat *inconvenient* to be without a telephone. / *Fujiyuu na kurashi ni wa narete imasu.* (不自由な暮らしには慣れています) I am used to living in *straitened circumstances.*
2 physically handicapped; disabled: *me no* fujiyuu *na hito*（目の不自由な人）a person with *weak* eyes; a *blind* person. ★ '...*no* fujiyuu *na*...' is a euphemism for the loss of function of body parts. *Sobo wa ashi ga* fujiyuu *desu.*（祖母は足が不自由です）My grandmother has *lost the use* of her legs.

fujiyuu suru (~する) *vi.* be inconvenient; be needy; be short of: *Kare wa o-kane ni* fujiyuu *shita ko-to ga nai.*（彼はお金に不自由したことがない）He *has* always *had plenty of* money. / *Suzuki-sañ nara gai-koku de mo kotoba ni* fujiyuu *shi-nai.*（鈴木さんなら外国でも言葉に不自由しない）Ms. Suzuki *won't have problems* abroad with language. / *Techoo o nakushite, zuibuñ* fuji-yuu *shita.*（手帳をなくして、ずいぶん不自由した）I *was put to great inconvenience* when I lost my pocket diary.

fu⌐ju⌐ubuñ ふじゅうぶん（不十分）*a.n.* (~ na) not enough; unsatisfactory; imperfect: *Kono kiñgaku de wa waapuro o* *kau no ni* fujuubuñ *desu.*(この金額ではワープロを買うのに不十分です) This money is *not enough* to buy a word processor. / *Setsumee ga* fujuubuñ *de, tsukaikata ga mada yoku wakaranai.*(説明が不十分で、使い方がまだよくわからない) The explanation is *insufficient* so I still don't know how to use this. / *Kare no roñbuñ wa* fujuubuñ *na deki datta.*(彼の論文は不十分な出来だった) His thesis was an *unsatisfactory* piece of work. 《↔ juubuñ》

fu「ka」 ふか (不可) *n.* (of a grade rating) failure; F in schoolwork: *Kare wa suugaku de* fuka *o totta.* (彼は数学で不可をとった) He got an *F* in mathematics. 《⇨ seeseki (table)》

fu「ka」·i ふかい (深い) *a.* (-ku)
1 deep:
fukai *kawa* (深い川) a *deep* river / fukai *kizu* (深い傷) a *deep* wound / *Mizuumi wa koko ga ichibañ* fukai.(湖はここが一番深い) The lake is *deepest* at this point. / *Mada yuki wa* fukai.(まだ雪は深い) The snow is still *deep.* 《↔ asai》
2 profound; deep:
gakushiki no fukai *hito* (学識の深い人) a man of *deep* learning / fukai *kanashimi* (深い悲しみ) *deep* sorrow / *Seefu wa sono moñdai ni* fukai *kañshiñ o yosete iru.*(政府はその問題に深い関心を寄せている) The government takes a *profound* interest in the issue.
3 dense; thick:
fukai *kiri* (深い霧) a *dense* fog / fukai *yami* (深い闇) *thick* darkness.

fu「kama」r·u ふかまる (深まる) *vi.* (-mar·i-; -mar·a-; -mat-te C) deepen; become deeper: *Nihoñgo e no kyoomi ga* fukamatta.(日本語への興味が深まった) My interest in the Japanese language *has deepened.* / *Kare-ra no yuujoo wa* fukamatta.(彼らの友情は

深まった) Their friendship *deepened.* / *Yoru mo* fukamatte kita. (夜も深まってきた) The night *is far advanced.* 《⇨ fukameru》

fu·kame」·ru ふかめる (深める) *vt.* (-me-te V) deepen; enrich: *chishiki o* fukameru (知識を深める) *deepen* one's knowledge / *keekeñ o* fukameru (経験を深める) *enrich* one's experience / *yuujoo o* fukameru (友情を深める) *cement* a friendship / *Sono jooyaku wa ryookoku no kañkee o* fukameta.(その条約は両国の関係を深めた) The treaty *further improved* relations between the two countries. 《⇨ fukamaru》

fu「ka」noo ふかのう (不可能) *n.* impossibility; impracticability: *Sono keekaku wa* fukanoo *ni chikai.*(その計画は不可能に近い) The plan is almost *impossible* to carry out.
— *a.n.* (~ na, ni) impossible; impracticable:
Sono yama ni noboru no wa fukanoo *desu.*(その山に登るのは不可能です) It is *impossible* to climb that mountain. / *Kare ni totte* fukanoo *na koto wa nani mo arimaseñ.*(彼にとって不可能なことは何もありません) Nothing is *impossible* for him. 《↔ kanoo》

fu「ka」ñzeñ ふかんぜん (不完全) *a.n.* (~ na) incomplete; imperfect: *Kare no hooritsu no chishiki wa* fukañzeñ *desu.*(彼の法律の知識は不完全です) His knowledge of the law is *imperfect.* / *Futa no shimekata ga* fukañzeñ *de, gasoriñ ga morete shimatta.*(ふたの締め方が不完全で、ガソリンが漏れてしまった) As the cap was *not put on properly,* some gasoline leaked out. / fukañzeñ-*neñshoo* (不完全燃焼) *incomplete* combustion. 《↔ kañzeñ》

fu「ka」sa ふかさ (深さ) *n.* depth: *Kono kawa wa* fukasa *ga go-meetoru aru.* (この川は深さが5メート

ルある) This river is five meters *deep*. / *Kono mizuumi no fukasa wa dono kurai desu ka?* (この湖の深さはどの位ですか) What is the *depth* of this lake?

fuˈkaˈs·u[1] ふかす (吹かす) *vt.* (fukash·i-; fukas·a-; fukash·i-te [C])
1 puff:
tabako o fukasu (たばこを吹かす) *puff on* a cigarette.
2 race (an engine):
eñjiñ o fukasu (エンジンを吹かす) *race* an engine.

fuˈkaˈs·u[2] ふかす (蒸かす) *vt.* (fukash·i-; fukas·a-; fukash·i-te [C])
steam:
jagaimo [gohañ] o fukasu (じゃがいも[ご飯]をふかす) *steam* potatoes [rice].

fuˈkeˈe ふけい (父兄) *n.* parents of schoolchildren. ★ Literally 'father and older brother.' 《⇨ fubo》

fuˈkeˈeki ふけいき (不景気) *n.* economic depression; hard times; recession; slump:
Yushutsu-sañgyoo wa fukeeki ni kurushiñde iru. (輸出産業は不景気に苦しんでいる) The export industry is suffering from a *slump*. 《⇨ fukyoo》
── *a.n.* (~ na) **1** dull; slack; depressed:
Doko mo fukeeki de, tabete iku no ga yatto da. (どこも不景気で、食べていくのがやっとだ) Business is *slack* everywhere and it is hard to just make a living.
2 (*informal*) cheerless; gloomy:
Fukeeki na koto o iu na yo. (不景気なことを言うなよ) Don't say such a *depressing* thing. / *Kare wa fukeeki na kao o shite ita.* (彼は不景気な顔をしていた) He looked *gloomy*. 《⇨ keeki²》

fuˈkeˈ·ru[1] ふける (老ける) *vi.* (fuke-te [V]) grow old; look old for ones's age:
Haha wa kono suu-neñ de mekkiri fuketa. (母はこの数年でめっきり老けた) Mother *has* really *shown her age* in the last few years. / *Kare wa toshi no wari ni fukete mieru.* (彼は年のわりに老けて見える) He looks *old* for his age.

fuˈkeˈ·ru[2] ふける (更ける) *vi.* (fuke-te [V]) grow late:
Yoru mo daibu fukete kimashita kara sorosoro o-itoma itashimasu. (夜もだいぶ更けてきましたからそろそろおいとま致します) As *it is getting* quite late, I must be leaving now. / *Aki mo fuke, hadasamui hi ga tuzuite imasu.* (秋も更け、肌寒い日が続いています) It's *late* autumn, and the chilly days are continuing.

fuˈketsu ふけつ (不潔) *a.n.*
(~ na) unclean; dirty; filthy; unsanitary:
Sono fuketsu na shatsu o hayaku nugi nasai. (その不潔なシャツを早く脱ぎなさい) Take off that *dirty* shirt at once. / *Ryoo no señmeñjo wa fuketsu datta.* (寮の洗面所は不潔だった) The lavatory in the dormitory was *unsanitary*. 《↔ seeketsu》

fuˈkiˈñ ふきん (付近) *n.* neighborhood; vicinity:
Kono fukiñ ni yuubiñkyoku wa arimasu ka? (この付近に郵便局はありますか) Is there a post office in this *neighborhood*? / *Kono fukiñ ittai wa moto wa hatake deshita.* (この付近一帯はもとは畑でした) The *area* all around here used to be fields.

fuˈkiˈsoku ふきそく (不規則) *a.n.*
(~ na, ni) irregular:
fukisoku na seekatsu o suru (不規則な生活をする) lead an *irregular* life / *Ikeda-sañ no shigoto wa jikañ ga fukisoku da.* (池田さんの仕事は時間が不規則だ) Ms. Ikeda's work requires *irregular* hours.

fuˈkitobaˈs·u ふきとばす (吹き飛ばす) *vt.* (-tobash·i-; -tobas·a-; -tobash·i-te [C]) blow off:
Kaze de booshi o fukitobasareta.

(風で帽子を吹き飛ばされた) My hat *was blown off* by the wind. (⇨ fukitobu))

fuˈkitobˑu ふきとぶ (吹き飛ぶ) *vi.* (-tobˑi-; -tobˑa-; -toñ-de C)
1 blow off:
Shorui ga kaze de fukitoñda. (書類が風で吹き飛んだ) The papers *flew away* in the wind.
2 (*fig.*) be dispelled:
Señsee no kotoba o kiite, kanojo no shiñpai wa fukitoñda. (先生の言葉を聞いて、彼女の心配は吹き飛んだ) Her fears *were dispelled* on hearing her teacher's words. (⇨ fukitobasu))

fuˈkitsu ふきつ (不吉) *a.n.* (~ na)
ominous; unlucky:
Fukitsu na yokañ ga suru. (不吉な予感がする) I have an *ominous* presentiment. / 'Yoñ' wa Nihoñ de wa fukitsu na kazu to sarete imasu. (「四」は日本では不吉な数とされています) In Japan, the number 'four' is considered *unlucky*.

fuˈkitsukeˈˑru ふきつける (吹き付ける) (-tsuke-te V) **1** *vi.* blow against:
Kaze ga shoomeñ kara hageshiku fukitsuketa. (風が正面から激しく吹き付けた) The wind *blew* violently from in front.
2 *vt.* spray:
kabe ni peñki o fukitsukeru (壁にペンキを吹き付ける) *spray* paint on the wall.

fuˈkkatsu ふっかつ (復活) *n.* revival; restoration; resurgence.
fukkatsu suru [saseru] (~する[させる]) *vi., vt.* come [bring] back; revive; restore: Kare-ra wa sono furui matsuri o fukkatsu saseyoo to doryoku shite iru. (彼らはその古い祭を復活させようと努力している) They are making efforts to *revive* that old festival. / Yosañ kara kezurareta koomoku o fukkatsu suru no wa muzukashii. (予算から削られた項目を復活するのはむずかしい) It is difficult to *restore* the item deleted from the budget.

Fuˈkkatsuˈsai ふっかつさい (復活祭) *n.* Easter; Easter Day [Sunday].

fuˈkoˈo ふこう (不幸) *n.* **1** unhappiness; misfortune:
Kare wa jibuñ no fukoo o nageita. (彼は自分の不幸を嘆いた) He bewailed his *misfortune*. (⇨ fushiawase))
2 death:
Kanojo no uchi de fukoo ga atta rashii. (彼女の家で不幸があったらしい) She seems to have had a *death* in the family.
— *a.n.* (~ na, ni) unhappy; unlucky; unfortunate:
Ano hito no bañneñ wa fukoo datta. (あの人の晩年は不幸だった) He led an *unhappy* life in his later years. / Sakuneñ wa fukoo na jikeñ ga takusañ atta. (昨年は不幸な事件がたくさんあった) There were many *unfortunate* occurrences last year. / Fukoo ni mo kare wa ashi ni kega o shita. (不幸にも彼は足にけがをした) *Unfortunately*, he got hurt in the leg.
fukoo chuu no saiwai (~中の幸い) a stroke of good luck in the midst of ill fortune.

fuˈkoˈohee ふこうへい (不公平) *n.* unfairness; partiality; injustice:
fukoohee o tadasu (不公平を正す) redress an *injustice*.
— *a.n.* (~ na, ni) unfair; partial; unjust:
Ryoohoo no ikeñ o kikanai no wa fukoohee da. (両方の意見を聞かないのは不公平だ) It is *unfair* not to listen to both sides. / Ano kaisha de wa josee-shaiñ ga fukoohee na atsukai o ukete iru. (あの会社では女性社員が不公平な扱いを受けている) Female workers receive *unfair* treatment at that firm.

fuˈk·u[1] ふく (吹く) (fuk·i-; fuk·a-; fu·i-te Ⓒ) *vi.* blow:
Kaze ga fuite iru. (風が吹いている) The wind *is blowing.* / *Kaateṅ ga kaze ni* fukarete, *maiagatta.* (カーテンが風に吹かれて, 舞い上がった) The curtains *were blown* up by the wind.
— *vt.* **1** play a musical instrument:
fue [*toraṅpetto*] *o* fuku (笛[トランペット]を吹く) *play* the flute [trumpet].
2 send forth air; blow:
Atsui koohii o fuite, *samashita.* (熱いコーヒーを吹いて, 冷ました) I *blew* on the hot coffee to cool it. / *Kare wa roosoku no hi o* fuite, *keshita.* (彼はろうそくの火を吹いて, 消した) He *blew* out the candle.
3 put forth a bud:
Sakura no ki ga me o fuita. (桜の木が芽をふいた) The cherry trees *have put forth* buds.

fuˈku[2] ふく (服) *n.* clothes; dress; suit:
fuku *o kiru* [*nugu*] (服を着る[脱ぐ]) put on [take off] one's *clothes* / *Kanojo wa* fuku *o kigaeru tame ni heya kara dete itta.* (彼女は服を着替えるために部屋から出て行った) She went out of the room to change her *dress.* / *Ano hito wa itsu-mo jimi na* fuku *o kite iru.* (あの人はいつも地味な服を着ている) She always wears *plain* clothes.

fuˈk·u[3] ふく (拭く) *vt.* (fuk·i-; fuk·a-; fu·i-te Ⓒ) **1** wipe (off); clean:
Mado o fuite, *kiree ni shita.* (窓をふいて, きれいにした) I *wiped* the windows clean. / *Shokuji no mae ni teeburu no ue o* fuki nasai. (食事の前にテーブルの上をふきなさい) *Wipe* the table before the meal.
2 dry:
Haṅkachi de namida [*ase*] *o* fuita. (ハンカチで涙[汗]をふいた) I *dried* my tears [perspiration] with my handkerchief. / *O-furo kara agattara, taoru de yoku karada o* fuki nasai. (お風呂から上がったら, タオルでよく体をふきなさい) *Dry* youself well with a towel after getting out of the bath.

fuˈku[4] ふく (福) *n.* good luck [fortune]; happiness:
fuku *no kami* (福の神) the god of *good fortune* / *Kono okimono wa* fuku *o motarasu to iwarete imasu.* (この置物は福をもたらすと言われています) This ornament is said to bring *good luck.* / "Fuku *wa uchi, oni wa soto.*" (「福は内, 鬼は外」) " In with *good fortune!* Out with the devils! " ★ Shout given while throwing roasted beans on the day of 'setsubuṅ' (節分) (Feb. 2 or 3).

fuˈku- ふく (副) *pref.* vice; deputy; assistant:
fuku-*chiji* (副知事) a *deputy* governor / fuku-*gichoo* (副議長) a *vice*-chairman / fuku-*shihainiṅ* (副支配人) an *assistant* manager.

Fuˈkui[1]**-keṅ** ふくいけん (福井県) *n.* Fukui Prefecture. Located at the west end of Honshu, facing Sea of Japan. The textile industry is widespread and fabric production is the highest of any prefecture in Japan. Capital city: Fukui. 《⇨ map (E3)》

fukˈumaku ふくまく (腹膜) *n.* peritoneum.

fuˈkumeˈ·ru ふくめる (含める) *vt.* (fukume-te Ⓥ) include:
Meṅbaa wa watashi mo fukumete, *zeṅbu de juu-niṅ desu.* (メンバーは私も含めて, 全部で10人です) There are ten members all together, *including* me. / *Riṅgo wa sooryoo o* fukumete, *rokuseṅ-eṅ desu.* (りんごは送料を含めて, 6千円です) The apples will be 6,000 yen, *including* delivery charges. 《⇨ fukumu》

fuˈkuˈm·u ふくむ (含む) *vt.*

(fukum·i-; fukum·a-; fukuñ-de
C) **1** contain; include:
*Hooreñsoo wa bitamiñ o takusañ
fukuñde iru.* (ほうれん草はビタミンをたく
さん含んでいる) Spinach *contains*
plenty of vitamins. / *Kono nedañ
wa zeekiñ o fukuñde imasu.* (この値
段は税金を含んでいます) This price
includes tax. ((⇨ fukumeru))
2 hold a thing in one's mouth:
*Mizu o kuchi ni fukuñde, ugai o
shita.* (水を口に含んで, うがいをした)
I *held* water in my mouth and
gargled. ((⇨ fukumeru))
3 imply:
*Kare no kotoba wa hiniku o fuku-
ñde ita.* (彼の言葉は皮肉を含んでいた)
There was sarcasm in his words.
/ *Kanojo wa uree o fukuñda kao o
shite iru.* (彼女は憂いを含んだ顔をして
いる) She *has* a sorrowful look.
4 bear in mind:
*Doo ka kono teñ o o-fukumi oki
kudasai.* (どうかこの点をお含みおきくだ
さい) Please *bear* this point *in
mind.*
...o fukumu (...を〜) including:
*Josee ni-mee o fukumu go-niñ no
paatii ga Eberesuto ni nobotta.* (女
性2名を含む5人のパーティーがエベレス
トに登った) A party of five, *including* two women, climbed Mt.
Everest.

Fu⌈kuoka⌉-keñ   ふくおかけん (福岡
県) *n.* Fukuoka Prefecture. Located in the northern part of
Kyushu, facing the Sea of Japan
on the north and the northwest
and the Inland Sea on the east.
The northeastern part is an industrial area with many modern
factories. Capital city: Fukuoka.
((⇨ map (B5)))

fu⌈kurahagi   ふくらはぎ (張ら脛) *n.*
calf of the leg. ((⇨ jiñtai (illus.)))

fu⌈kuramas·u   ふくらます (膨らます)
vt. (-mash·i-; -mas·a-; -mash·i-
te C) **1** inflate; swell; blow up:

kuchi de fuusen o fukuramasu (口
で風船をふくらます) *blow up* a balloon / *Kuuki o irete, taiya o fuku-
ramashita.* (空気を入れて, タイヤをふく
らました) I pumped air in the tire
and *inflated* it. ((⇨ fukuramu))
2 puff out; expand:
*Kare wa fumañ soo ni hoo o fuku-
ramashita.* (彼は不満そうにほおをふく
らました) He *puffed out* his cheeks
with apparent dissatisfaction.
((⇨ fukureru))

fu⌈kuram·u   ふくらむ (膨らむ) *vi.*
(-ram·i-; -ram·a-; -rañ-de C)
1 swell; expand:
*Hana no tsubomi ga fukurami-
hajimeta.* (花のつぼみがふくらみ始めた)
The flower buds *have begun to
swell.* / *Kuuki o iretara, taiya ga
fukurañda.* (空気を入れたら, タイヤがふ
くらんだ) The tire *expanded* when I
pumped air into it. ((⇨ fukureru))
2 bulge:
*Kabañ wa nimotsu de fukurañde
ita.* (かばんは荷物でふくらんでいた) The
bag *was bulgy* with its contents.

fu⌈kure·ru   ふくれる (膨れる) *vi.*
(fukure-te V) **1** swell:
Mochi wa yaku to fukureru. (もちは
焼くとふくれる) Rice cakes *swell*
when grilled. / *Shigañsha wa sañ-
bai ni fukureta.* (志願者は3倍にふく
れた) The number of applicants
has grown three-fold.
2 sulk; become sulky:
*Kare wa shikarareru to sugu ni
fukureru.* (彼はしかられるとすぐにふくれ
る) He soon *sulks* when he is
scolded.

fu⌈kuro⌉   ふくろ (袋) *n.* bag; sack;
pouch:
hoñ o kami no fukuro ni ireru (本を
紙の袋に入れる) put a book in a
paper *bag* / *jagaimo o fukuro ni
tsumeru* (じゃがいもを袋に詰める) fill a
sack with potatoes / *Kare wa
fukuro kara nani-ka toridashita.*
(彼は袋から何か取り出した) He took

something out of the *bag*.

fu⌐kusa⌐yoo ふくさよう（副作用）*n.*
side effect:
*Sono kusuri wa fukusayoo no aru
koto ga wakatta.*（その薬は副作用の
あることがわかった）It was discovered
that the drug had *side effects.*

fu⌐kuseñ ふくせん（複線）*n.* two-
track line; double track:
fukuseñ no tetsudoo（複線の鉄道）a
double-track railroad. 《↔ tañseñ》

fu⌐ku-sha⌐choo ふくしゃちょう（副
社長）*n.* executive vice president.
《⇨ kaisha (table)》

fu⌐ku⌐shi¹ ふくし（福祉）*n.* welfare; well-being:
fukushi o zooshiñ suru（福祉を増進
する）promote *welfare* / *fukushi-
jigyoo*（福祉事業）*welfare* work /
shakai-fukushi（社会福祉）social
welfare.

fu⌐kushi² ふくし（副詞）*n.* adverb.

Fu⌐kushima⌐-keñ ふくしまけん
（福島県）*n.* Fukushima Prefecture. Located in the south of the
Tohoku district, facing the Pacific. Lake Inawashiro and Mt. Ban-
dai are well-known scenic spots.
Capital city: Fukushima.
《⇨ map (G3)》

fu⌐kushuu ふくしゅう（復習）*n.*
review; revision:
*Kyoo no jugyoo no fukushuu wa
moo sumimashita.*（きょうの授業の復
習はもうすみました）I have finished
the *review* of today's lessons.
fukushuu suru（～する）*vt.* review
[go over] one's lessons: *Shikeñ
ni sonaete kyookasho o fukushuu
shita.*（試験に備えて教科書を復習した）
I *reviewed* my textbooks before
the test.

fu⌐kusoo ふくそう（服装）*n.* dress;
costume; clothes:
seeshiki [futsuu] no fukusoo（正式
[普通]の服装）a formal [an infor-
mal] *dress* / *fukusoo o totonoeru*
（服装を整える）straighten up one's

clothes / *Uchi no musuko wa* fukusoo *o amari kamawanai.*（うちの息
子は服装をあまり構わない）My son
doesn't care much about his
clothes.

fu⌐kuzatsu ふくざつ（複雑）*a.n.*
（～ na, ni) complicated; complex; intricate:
fukuzatsu na koozoo（複雑な構造）a
complex structure / *fukuzatsu na
kimochi*（複雑な気持ち）*mixed* feelings / *fukuzatsu na niñgeñ-kañkee*
（複雑な人間関係）*complicated* human relationships / *Kono kikai
wa tsukaikata ga* fukuzatsu *de,
yoku wakaranai.*（この機械は使い方
が複雑で、よくわからない）This ma-
chine is so *intricate* I don't know
how to use it. / *Kono moñdai no
ura ni wa* fukuzatsu *na jijoo ga
aru.*（この問題の裏には複雑な事情があ
る）There are *complicated* circumstances behind this problem.
《↔ kañtañ》

fu⌐kyoo ふきょう（不況）*n.* recession; depression; slump:
fukyoo o norikiru（不況を乗り切る）
get over a *recession.* 《↔ kookyoo²》
《⇨ fukeeki》

fu⌐kyuu ふきゅう（普及）*n.* popu-
larization; spread; diffusion:
kyooiku no fukyuu（教育の普及）the
spread of education / *chishiki no*
fukyuu（知識の普及）the *diffusion*
of knowledge / *suiseñ-beñjo no*
fukyuu *ni tsutomeru*（水洗便所の普
及に努める）work toward the *popu-
larization* of the flush toilet.
fukyuu suru（～する）*vi.* spread;
diffuse; popularize: *Nihoñ de wa
karaa terebi ga hiroku* fukyuu
shite iru.（日本ではカラーテレビが広く
普及している）Color TV sets *are
very common* in Japan.
《⇨ hiromaru》

fu⌐ma⌐jime ふまじめ（不真面目）
a.n.（～ na, ni) not serious; frivolous; insincere:

Kare wa señsee ni fumajime *na heñji o shita.* (彼は先生にふまじめな返事をした) He gave a *frivolous* reply to his teacher. / *Kare wa kiñmu-taido ga* fumajime *da.* (彼は勤務態度がふまじめだ) He is *not* working *seriously.* ((↔ majime))

fu⌈mañ ふまん (不満) *n.* dissatisfaction; discontent:
fumañ *o idaku* (不満を抱く) feel *dissatisfaction* / *Fumañ ga aru nara, watashi ni ii nasai.* (不満があるなら, 私に言いなさい) If there is *something that displeases you,* tell me. / *Tabemono ni tsuite wa* fumañ *wa arimaseñ.* (食べ物については不満はありません) I have no *complaints* about the food.
— *a.n.* (~ na, ni) unsatisfactory; unsatisfied; dissatisfied:
Ima no kyuuryoo ni wa fumañ *desu.* (今の給料には不満です) I am *dissatisfied* with my present salary. / *Shikeñ no yarikata o* fumañ *ni omotte iru hito wa ooi.* (試験のやり方を不満に思っている人は多い) There are many people who *are not satisfied* with the examination system. ((↔ mañzoku))

fu⌈mee ふめい (不明) *a.n.* (~ na/no) unclear; obscure; unknown:
kokuseki fumee *no hikooki* (国籍不明の飛行機) an aircraft of *unidentified* nationality / *Fumee na teñ ga arimashitara, o-toiawase kudasai.* (不明な点がありましたら, お問い合わせください) If there are any *unclear* points, please inquire. / *Hañkoo no dooki wa* fumee *da.* (犯行の動機は不明だ) The motive for the crime is *unknown.*

fu⌈me⌉eyo ふめいよ (不名誉) *a.n.* (~ na) disgraceful; shameful; discreditable:
Booryoku o furuu no wa fumeeyo *na koto da.* (暴力をふるうのは不名誉なことだ) It is a *disgraceful* act to use violence. ((↔ meeyo))

fu⌈mikiri ふみきり (踏切) *n.* railroad crossing; level crossing:
*mujiñ-*fumikiri (無人踏切) an unattended *crossing* / *Kodomo-tachi wa chuui shi-nagara* fumikiri *o watatta.* (子どもたちは注意しながら踏切を渡った) The children went over the *crossing* carefully.

MUJIÑ-FUMIKIRI

fu⌈mitsuke⌉ru ふみつける (踏み付ける) *vt.* (-tsuke-te Ⅴ) trample; stamp:
Watashi wa akikañ o fumitsukete *tsubushita.* (私は空き缶を踏みつけてつぶした) I *stamped* on the empty can and made it flat. / *Dare-ka ga kadañ o* fumitsuketa. (だれかが花壇を踏みつけた) Someone *trampled down* the flower bed.

fu⌈moto⌉ ふもと (麓) *n.* lowest part of a mountain; foot of a hill.

fu⌈m·u ふむ (踏む) *vt.* (fum·i-; fum·a-; fuñ-de Ⓒ) **1** trample; step:
bureeki o fumu (ブレーキを踏む) *step* on the brakes / *jiteñsha no pedaru o* fumu (自転車のペダルを踏む) *pedal* a bicycle / *Mañiñ deñsha de hito ni ashi o* fumareta. (満員電車で人に足を踏まれた) In the crowded train my foot *was stepped on* by someone. / *Yuki o* fuñde *kata-meta.* (雪を踏んで固めた) I *stamped down* the snow.
2 set foot on:
Kare wa hajimete Amerika no chi o fuñda. (彼は初めてアメリカの地を踏ん

だ) He *set foot* on American soil for the first time.

3 go through; follow (a procedure):
seeki no tetsuzuki o fumu (正規の手続きを踏む) *go through* the due formalities / *ittee no tejuñ o* fumu (一定の順序を踏む) *follow* the regular procedures.

4 estimate (value):
Sore wa takakute mo, ichimañ-eñ to fuñda. (それは高くても、1万円と踏んだ) I *estimated that* it would cost 10,000 yen at most. / *Mikka mo areba dekiru to* fuñde imasu. (三日もあればできると踏んでいます) I *think* I can do it in three days.

fu⌐ñ¹ ふん (分) *n.* minute:
*Sañ-ji go-*fuñ *mae* [*sugi*] *desu.* (3時5分前[過ぎ]です) It is five *minutes* to [past] three. / *Eki made aruite juugo-*fuñ *desu.* (駅まで歩いて15分です) It is a fifteen-*minute* walk to the station. / *Shikeñ ga owaru made nañ-*puñ *nokotte imasu ka?* (試験が終わるまで何分残っていますか) How many *minutes* remain until the end of the test? ★ Notice the sound changes. (⇨ hi¹ (table))

1	i⌐p-puñ	7	na⌐na⌐-fuñ
2	ni⌐-fuñ	8	ha⌐p-puñ
3	sa⌐ñ-puñ	9	kyu⌐u-fuñ
4	yo⌐ñ-puñ	10	ji⌐p-puñ
5	go⌐-fuñ		(ju⌐p-puñ)
6	ro⌐p-puñ	?	na⌐ñ-puñ

fu⌐ñ² ふん (糞) *n.* excrement; feces; dung. (⇨ kuso)

fu⌐nabiñ ふなびん (船便) *n.* sea [surface] mail:
Hoñ wa funabiñ *de okurimashita.* (本は船便で送りました) I sent the book by *sea mail*.

fu⌐ñba⌐r·u ふんばる (踏ん張る) *vi.* (-bar·i-; -bar·a-; -bat-te C)
1 stand firm; brace one's legs:

Deñsha no naka de taorenai yoo ni (*ashi o*) fuñbatta. (電車の中で倒れないように(足を)踏ん張った) I *took a balanced stance* on the train so as not to fall over.
2 hold out:
Akirameru na. Ima koso fuñbaru *toki da.* (あきらめるな。今こそ踏ん張るときだ) Don't give up. Now is the time to *hang on*.

fu⌐ne ふね (舟・船) *n.* boat; ship; vessel:

USAGE
'舟' usually refers to a small vessel like a rowboat, and '船' to a large vessel like a steamship.

fune *ni noru* (船に乗る) board a *ship* / fune *o oriru* (船を降りる) leave a *ship* / Fune *de ryokoo o shitai.* (船で旅行をしたい) I wish to go on a *sea voyage*. / Fune *de kawa o watatta.* (舟で川を渡った) I crossed the river by *boat*.

fu⌐neñ ふねん (不燃) *n.* nonflammability; incombustibility:
funeñ*-butsu* (不燃物) *incombustibles*.

fu⌐ñeñ ふんえん (噴煙) *n.* smoke of a volcano:
Kazañ kara fuñeñ *no agaru no ga mieru.* (火山から噴煙の上がるのが見える) We can see the *smoke* rising from the volcano.

fu⌐ñgai ふんがい (憤慨) *n.* indignation; resentment.
fuñgai suru (〜する) *vi.* resent; be indignant: *Kanojo ga* fuñgai *suru no wa mottomo da.* (彼女が憤慨するのはもっともだ) It is natural that she should *be indignant*. / *Kare wa futoo ni atsukawarete,* fuñgai *shita.* (彼は不当に扱われて、憤慨した) He *resented* being treated unfairly.

fu⌐ñi⌐ki ふんいき (雰囲気) *n.* mood; atmosphere; ambience:

katee-teki na fuñiki *no aru resu-torañ* (家庭的な雰囲気のあるレストラン) a restaurant with a homelike *atmosphere* / *Watashi wa sono guruupu no* fuñiki *ni najimenai.* (私はそのグループの雰囲気になじめない) I cannot get used to the *mood* of that group.

fuˈñka ふんか(噴火) *n.* eruption; volcanic activity.
fuñka suru (〜する) *vi.* erupt: *Mihara-yama ga totsuzeñ* fuñka shita. (三原山が突然噴火した) Mt. Mihara suddenly *erupted*.

fuˈñkaˈkoo ふんかこう(噴火口) *n.* volcanic crater.

fuˈñshiñ ふんしん(分針) *n.* (of a clock) minute hand. (⇨ byoo-shiñ)

fuˈñshitsu ふんしつ(紛失) *n.* loss.
fuñshitsu suru (〜する) *vt.* (*formal*) lose; miss: *Gakuseeshoo o* fuñshitsu shita *baai wa sumiyaka ni todokederu koto.* (学生証を紛失した場合はすみやかに届け出ること) In the event of a *loss* of your student ID, it must be promptly reported. / fuñshitsu-*butsu* (紛失物) a *lost* article / fuñshitsu-*todoke* (紛失届) a report of the *loss* of an article. (⇨ nakusuˈ)

fuˈñwaˈri ふんわり *adv.* (〜 to) softly; lightly; gently: *Akañboo ni moofu o* fuñwari (*to*) *kaketa.* (赤ん坊に毛布をふんわり(と)掛けた) I put a blanket *gently* over the baby. (⇨ fuwari)

fuˈñzukeˈru ふんづける(踏ん付ける) *vt.* (-zuke-te Ⅴ) (*informal*) = fumitsukeru.

fuˈrafura[1] ふらふら *a.n.* (〜 na, ni) unsteady; staggering; groggy: *Marasoñ no saigo no soosha wa* furafura *ni natte, gooru-iñ shita.* (マラソンの最後の走者はふらふらになって、ゴールインした) The last marathon runner crossed the finish line *staggering.* / *Kare wa* furafura *to*

tachiagatta. (彼はふらふらと立ち上がった) He *unsteadily* got to his feet.

fuˈrafura[2] ふらふら *adv.* (〜 to; 〜 suru) **1** impulsively; unconsciously: *Kanojo wa* furafura *to kare no sasoi ni notte shimatta.* (彼女はふらふらと彼の誘いに乗ってしまった) She yielded to his temptation *in spite of herself.*
2 feel dizzy; be faint; waver: *Onaka ga suite* furafura *suru.* (おなかがすいてふらふらする) I am *faint* with hunger. / *Jibuñ no shoorai o kimeru no ni* furafura *shite wa ikenai.* (自分の将来を決めるのにふらふらしてはいけない) When deciding your own future, you must not *waver.*

fuˈrai フライ *n.* fried food: *ebi-*furai (えびフライ) *fried* prawns.

fuˈraipañ フライパン *n.* frying pan; skillet.

Fuˈrañsu フランス(仏蘭西) *n.* France.

Fuˈrañsugo フランスご(仏蘭西語) *n.* the French language; French.

Fuˈrañsuˈjiñ フランスじん(仏蘭西人) *n.* Frenchman; Frenchwoman; the French.

fuˈreˑru ふれる(触れる) *vi.* (fure-te Ⅴ) **1** touch; feel: *E ya chookoku ni te o furenai de kudasai.* (絵や彫刻に手を触れないでください) *Don't touch* the paintings and sculptures. / *Akañboo no te ni* furete mitara, *totemo yawaraka datta.* (赤ん坊の手に触れてみたら、とても柔らかだった) I *felt* the baby's hand and found it very soft.
2 mention; refer to: *Sono moñdai wa kono hoñ de wa* furerarete imaseñ. (その問題はこの本では触れられていません) The problem *is not referred to* in this book. / *Kare wa jibuñ no misu ni tsuite hitokoto mo* furenakatta. (彼は自分のミスについて一言も触れなかった) He *did not mention* even one word

about his blunder. / *Kare no hatsugeñ wa jikeñ no kakushiñ ni* fureru *mono datta.*（彼の発言は事件の核心に触れるものだった）His remark was what *touched* the heart of the matter.
3 affect the emotions or feelings of (a person):
Shachoo no ikari ni furete, *kare wa kubi ni natta.*（社長の怒りに触れて, 彼は首になった）Having *incurred* the president's anger, he was fired.
4 perceive; experience:
Me ni fureru *mono subete ga watashi ni wa mezurashii.*（目に触れるものすべてが私には珍しい）Everything that I *see* is new to me. / *Hoomusutee o shite, Nihoñjiñ no seekatsu ni* furete mitai.（ホームステイをして, 日本人の生活に触れてみたい）I *want to experience* the Japanese way of life through a homestay.
5 infringe (a law, a regulation, a rule, etc.):
Soñna koto o sureba, hoo ni furemasu *yo.*（そんなことをすれば, 法に触れますよ）If you do such a thing, it will *violate* the law.

fu⌐ri[1]   ふり (不利) *n.* disadvantage; handicap:
furi *o maneku* (不利を招く) incur a *disadvantage.*
── *a.n.* (〜 na, ni) disadvantageous; unfavorable:
Kyoo no teñkoo wa marasoñ señshu ni totte furi *da.*（きょうの天候はマラソン選手にとって不利だ）Today's weather will be a *disadvantage* to the marathon runners. / *Jookyoo wa waga-sha ni* furi *ni natte kita.*（状況はわが社にとって不利になってきた）The situation has become *unfavorable* to our firm. / *Kare ni totte* furi *na shooko ga mitsukatta.*（彼にとって不利な証拠が見つかった）A piece of evidence *against* him has been found. 《↔ **yuuri**》

fu⌐ri[2]   ふり (振り) *n.* swing:
Kare wa batto no furi *ga surudoi.*（彼はバットの振りが鋭い）His *swing* is quick and accurate. 《⇨ **furu**[2]》
...furi o suru (〜をする) pretend; affect; feign: *neta* furi o suru (寝たりをする) *pretend* to be asleep / *shiranai* furi o suru (知らないふりをする) *affect* ignorance / *byooki no* furi o suru (病気のふりをする) *feign* illness.

fu⌐rigana   ふりがな (振り仮名) *n.* 'kana' written next to or above Chinese characters to show the pronunciation:
furigana *o tsukeru* [furu] (ふりがなをつける[ふる]) give the *reading in kana.*

とうきょう　辞じ
東京　　　書しょ

EXAMPLES OF FURIGANA

fu⌐rika⌐er·u   ふりかえる (振り返る) *vi.* (-kaer·i-; -kaer·a-; -kaet-te C) **1** turn around; look back:
Watashi wa namae o yobarete furikaetta.（私は名前を呼ばれて振り返った）Hearing my name called, I *turned around.* / *Kanojo ga soto o aruite iru to, dare mo ga miñna* furikaeru.（彼女が外を歩いていると, だれもがみんな振り返る）When she is out walking, everyone *turns* to look at her.
2 recollect; look back:
kako [gakusee jidai] *o* furikaeru (過去[学生時代]を振り返る) *look back* on the past [one's college days] / *Moo ichi-do* furikaette, *jiko no geñiñ o shirabete mimasu.*（もう一度振り返って, 事故の原因を調べてみます）I will *look over* the facts once more to find out the cause of the accident.

fu⌐rimu⌐k·u   ふりむく (振り向く) *vi.* (-muk·i-; -muk·a-; -mu·i-te C) **1** turn one's face; turn around:
Kare wa watashi no hoo o furimuite, *te o futta.*（彼は私の方を振り向い

て, 手を振った) He *turned* toward me and waved his hand. / *Totsuzeñ kata o tatakarete, omowazu* furimuita. (突然肩をたたかれて, 思わず振り向いた) I was suddenly tapped on the shoulder, so I *turned around* instinctively.

2 (with a negative) pay attention to; care for: *Kanojo wa kanemochi igai no otoko ni wa* furimuki mo shinai. (彼女は金持ち以外の男には振り向きもしない) She *doesn't care for* men unless they are rich.

fu⌐ro⌐ ふろ (風呂) *n.* **1** bath; bathtub: ★ Often with '*o-*.' furo *o wakasu* [*taku*] (風呂をわかす[たく]) prepare a *bath* / furo *ni hairu* (風呂に入る) take a *bath* / furo *kara deru* [*agaru*] (風呂から出る[上がる]) get out of a *bath* / Furo *ga wakimashita.* (風呂がわきました) The *bath* is ready.

2 public bath: furo *ni iku* (風呂に行く) go to the *public bath.* ★ The public bath is called '*furoya*' or '*señtoo.*' ((⇨ nyuuyoku (illus.); señtoo³ (illus.)))

fu⌐roba⌐ ふろば (風呂場) *n.* a room with a bathtub; bathroom.

> **USAGE**
> Traditionally, Japanese bathrooms are not equipped with toilets, and the word '*furoba*' is never used to mean 'toilet.'

FUROBA

fu⌐roku ふろく (付録) *n.* supplement; appendix:

zasshi no furoku (雑誌の付録) a *supplement* to a magazine.

fu⌐roñto フロント *n.* (of a hotel) front desk; reception desk.

fu⌐roñto-ga⌐rasu フロントガラス *n.* windshield; windscreen.

fu⌐roshiki ふろしき (風呂敷) *n.* wrapping cloth: ★ A square scarf-like cloth used for wrapping and carrying things. *shorui o* furoshiki *ni tsutsumu* (書類をふろ敷に包む) wrap documents up in a *cloth* / furoshiki-*zutsumi* (ふろ敷包み) a parcel wrapped with a *furoshiki*.

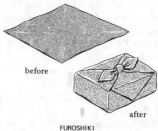

before
after
FUROSHIKI

fu⌐ro⌐ya ふろや (風呂屋) *n.* public bath. ((⇨ señtoo³))

fu⌐r·u¹ ふる (降る) *vi.* (fur·i-; fur·a-; fut-te Ⓒ) **1** (of rain, snow, hail) fall: *Tsuyu ni haitte, mainichi ame ga* futte iru. (梅雨に入って, 毎日雨が降っている) The rainy season has set in, and it *is raining* every day. / *Ima ni mo yuki ga* furi-soo da. (今にも雪が降りそうだ) It is threatening to *snow* at any moment. / *Ame wa kyoo ichi-nichi* futtari yañdari de-shoo. (雨はきょう一日降ったりやんだりでしょう) I expect it will *rain* off and on all day today. / *Kitaku suru tochuu de ame ni* furareta. (帰宅する途中で雨に降られた) I *was caught in the rain* on my way home.

2 (of ash, dust, etc.) fall; come down: *Sora kara kazañbai ga* futte kita.

(空から火山灰が降ってきた) Volcanic ash *fell* on us from the sky.

fu⌐r·u² ふる (振る) *vt.* (fur·i-; fur·a-; fut-te Ⓒ) **1** shake; move: *Kare wa batto o ookiku* futta.(彼はバットを大きく振った) He *gave* the bat *a good swing*. ((⇨ furi²)) / *Keekañ wa te o futte, tomare to aizu shita.*(警官は手を振って、止まれと合図した) The policeman *waved* his hand to signal me to halt. / *Nama-juusu wa biñ o yoku* futte *kara nomi nasai.*(生ジュースはびんをよく振ってから飲みなさい) *Shake* the bottle of fresh fruit juice well before drinking.
2 sprinkle: *Niku ni shio to koshoo o karuku* futta.(肉に塩とこしょうを軽く振った) I lightly *sprinkled* the meat with salt and pepper.
3 assign; add (a letter, a number, etc.): *Kañji ni furigana o* futta.(漢字にふりがなを振った) I *put* the corresponding 'furigana' next to the Chinese characters. / *Kaado ni ichi kara hyaku made bañgoo o furimashita.*(カードに1から100まで番号を振りました) I *numbered* the cards from 1 to 100. ((⇨ tsukeru¹))
4 (often in the passive) refuse; abandon: *Kare wa koibito ni furareta.*(彼は恋人に振られた) He *was jilted* by his girlfriend.

fu⌐rue·ru ふるえる (震える) *vi.* (furue-te Ⓥ) tremble; shake; shiver; shudder: *Samusa de te-ashi ga* furueta.(寒さで手足が震えた) My hands and legs *trembled* with cold. / *Kare wa kyoofu [kiñchoo] no amari karada ga* furueta.(彼は恐怖[緊張]のあまり体が震えた) He *shuddered* with fear [tension]. / *Te ga* furuete, *umaku ji ga kakenai.*(手が震えて、

うまく字が書けない) My hand *is shaking* and I cannot write very well. ((⇨ furuwaseru))

fu⌐ru¹·i ふるい (古い) *a.* (-ku) **1** old; stale: furui *yuujiñ* (古い友人) an *old* friend / furui *niku* (古い肉) *stale* meat /*Chuugoku no rekishi wa* furui.(中国の歴史は古い) China's history is *long*. / *Sono tatemono wa* furuku *natta no de torikowasareta.*(その建物は古くなったので取り壊された) Since the building became *old*, it was pulled down. ((↔ atarashii))
2 old-fashioned; out-of-date: *Sono hyoogeñ wa moo* furui.(その表現はもう古い) That expression is rather *old-fashioned*. / *Soñna* furui *kañgae wa sute nasai.*(そんな古い考えは捨てなさい) Dismiss such *old-fashioned* ideas. ((↔ atarashii))

fu⌐ruma¹·u ふるまう (振る舞う) *vi.* (-ma·i-; -maw·a-; -mat-te Ⓒ) **1** behave; act: *Kare wa shachoo-rashiku* furumatta.(彼は社長らしく振る舞った) He *behaved* just as the president of a company should. / *Ano hito wa marude raihiñ no yoo ni* furumatte iru.(あの人はまるで来賓のように振る舞っている) He *is carrying on* just as if he were the guest of honor.
2 treat; entertain: *Satoo-sañ wa watashi ni go-chisoo o* furumatte kureta.(佐藤さんは私にごちそうを振る舞ってくれた) Mr. Sato *treated* me to dinner.

fu⌐ru¹sato ふるさと (故郷) *n.* one's home; one's hometown.

fu⌐rushi¹ñbuñ ふるしんぶん (古新聞) *n.* old newspaper: furushiñbuñ *no kaishuu* (古新聞の回収) the collection of *old newspapers* (for recycling). ((⇨ chirigami-kookañ))

fu⌐ruwase·ru ふるわせる (震わせる) *vt.* (furuwase-te Ⓥ) cause to tremble:

Shoojo wa samu-soo ni karada o furuwasete ita. (少女は寒そうに体を震わせていた) The girl *was shaking* all over as if she were cold. / *Kanojo wa ikari ni koe o furuwasenagara otto o semeta.* (彼女は怒りに声を震わせながら夫を責めた) She reproached her husband with her voice *trembling* in anger.
《⇨ furueru》

fuˈryoo ふりょう (不良) *a.n.*
(~ na/no) bad; poor; defective:
Kotoshi wa ine no sakugara ga furyoo da. (今年は稲の作柄が不良だ) We had a *poor* rice crop this year. / *Teñkoo furyoo no tame shiai wa eñki sareta.* (天候不良のため試合は延期された) The game was postponed due to *bad* weather.
《⇨ yoi》

fuˈsa ふさ (房) *n.* tuft; fringe; tassel; bunch:
umoo no fusa (羽毛の房) a *tuft* of feathers / *budoo no fusa* (ぶどうの房) a *bunch* of grapes.

fuˈsagar·u ふさがる (塞がる) *vi.*
(fusagar·i-; fusagar·a-; fusagatte C) 1 close; be closed:
Kizuguchi ga yatto fusagatta. (傷口がやっとふさがった) The wound has *closed up* at last. 《⇨ fusagu》
2 be blocked; be packed:
Jiko de dooro ga fusagatte, ugokenakatta. (事故で道路がふさがって、動けなかった) The road *was blocked* by the accident and we were stuck. 《⇨ fusagu》
3 be occupied; be used:
Zaseki wa miñna fusagatte imasu. (座席はみんなふさがっています) The seats *are* all *occupied.* / *Dono hoteru mo heya ga fusagatte iru.* (どのホテルも部屋がふさがっている) The rooms at all the hotels *are taken.* / *Ima te ga fusagatte iru no de ato ni shite kuremaseñ ka?* (今手がふさがっているので後にしてくれませんか) As

I'*m busy* now, could you come back later?

fuˈsag·u ふさぐ (塞ぐ) *vt.* (fusag·i-; fusag·a-; fusa·i-de C)
1 stop; cover:
Ana o ishi de fusaida. (穴を石でふさいだ) I *stopped up* the hole with a stone. / *Kami o hatte, kabe no sukima o fusaida.* (紙を貼って、壁のすき間をふさいだ) I *covered* the opening in the wall by pasting paper over it. 《⇨ fusagaru》
2 block; occupy:
Ooki-na torakku ga michi o fusaide ita. (大きなトラックが道をふさいでいた) A large truck *was blocking* the road. / *Kono nimotsu wa basho o fusagu.* (この荷物は場所をふさぐ) This package *takes up* a lot of space. 《⇨ fusagaru》
3 close; shut:
Booru ga toñde kita no de omowazu me o fusaida. (ボールが飛んで来たので思わず目をふさいだ) A ball came flying toward me, and I *shut* my eyes instinctively. / *Kanojo wa watashi no iu koto ni mimi o fusaide kikoo to shinai.* (彼女は私の言うことに耳をふさいで聞こうとしない) She *closes* her ears to all I say and doesn't even try to listen.

fuˈsaˈi ふさい (夫妻) *n.* husband and wife:
Tanaka-fusai (田中夫妻) *Mr. and Mrs.* Tanaka; *Mr.* Tanaka and his *wife.*

fuˈsawashiˈ·i ふさわしい *a.* (-ku) suitable; proper; appropriate:
Kanojo wa sono ba ni fusawashii fuku o kite ita. (彼女はその場にふさわしい服を着ていた) She wore clothes *suitable* for the occasion. / *Suzuki-sañ wa kono shigoto ni fusawashiku nai.* (鈴木さんはこの仕事にふさわしくない) Mrs. Suzuki is not *suited* to this job. / *Motto fusawashii iikata wa arimaseñ ka?* (もっとふさわしい言い方はありませんか) Isn't

there a *better* way of saying it? / *Kare koso hyooshoo sareru no ni* fusawashii *senshu da.*(彼こそ表彰されるのにふさわしい選手だ) He is the very player who *deserves* to win official commendation. 《⇨ tekitoo》

fu˻se˺ekaku ふせいかく (不正確) *n.*, *a.n.* (~ na, ni) incorrect; inaccurate; inexact; uncertain: fuseekaku *na keesan* (不正確な計算) an *inaccurate* calculation / *Kono hoodoo wa* fuseekaku *da.* (この報道は不正確だ) This report is *inaccurate.* 《↔ seekaku²》

fu˻se˺g·u ふせぐ (防ぐ) *vt.* (fuseg·i-; fuseg·a-; fuse·i·de C)
1 protect; defend:
Samusa o fusegu *tame ni, janpaa o kita.* (寒さを防ぐために, ジャンパーを着た) I wore a windbreaker to *protect* myself from the cold.
2 guard; prevent:
doroboo no shinnyuu o fusegu (泥棒の侵入を防ぐ) *guard* against burglary / *jiko o* fusegu (事故を防ぐ) *prevent* an accident / *Gokai o* fusegu *tame ni, arakajime o-kotowari shite okimasu.*(誤解を防ぐために, あらかじめお断りしておきます) To *prevent* misunderstandings, I want to start by making myself clear. 《⇨ booshi²》

fu˻se˺·ru ふせる (伏せる) *vt.* (fuse-te V)
1 put a thing upside down; put a thing face down:
Koppu o aratte fuseta. (コップを洗って伏せた) I washed the glasses and *placed* them *upside down.* / *Kare wa hon o* fusete, *heya kara dete itta.* (彼は本を伏せて, 部屋から出て行った) He *laid* the book *face down* and went out of the room.
2 look downward; lower one's eyes:
Kanojo wa hazukashi-soo ni me [*kao*] *o* fuseta. (彼女は恥ずかしそうに目[顔]を伏せた) She *lowered* her

eyes [*looked down*] bashfully. / *Kare wa namida o misemai to kao o* fuseta.(彼は涙を見せまいと顔を伏せた) He *hung* his head to hide his tears.
3 keep a thing secret:
Kono koto wa Yamada-san ni fusete *okimashoo.* (このことは山田さんに伏せておきましょう) Let's *keep* this matter *secret* from Mr. Yamada. / *Konna himitsu o watashi hitori no mune ni* fusete oku *koto wa dekimasen.* (こんな秘密を私一人の胸に伏せておくことはできません) I cannot *keep* such a *secret* locked up in my heart.

fu˻shi˺¹ ふし (節) *n.* **1** knot: *Kono ita wa fushi ga ooi.* (この板は節が多い) This plank is full of knots.
2 joint:
take no fushi (竹の節) a *joint* in a piece of bamboo.

fu˻shi˺² ふし (節) *n.* melody; tune; strain:
Sono fushi wa yoku oboete imasu. (その節はよく覚えています) I remember the *melody* well.

fu˻shia˺wase ふしあわせ (不幸せ) *n.* unhappiness; misfortune.
— *a.n.* (~ na, ni) unhappy; unfortunate:
fushiawase *na kodomo-tachi* (不幸せな子どもたち) *unhappy* children / *Kanojo wa* fushiawase *datta.* (彼女は不幸せだった) She was *unfortunate.* 《↔ shiawase》《⇨ fukoo》

fu˻shi˺bushi ふしぶし (節々) *n.* joints; points:
Fushibushi *ga itamu.* (節々が痛む) My *joints* ache.

fu˻shigi ふしぎ (不思議) *n.* wonder; mystery; miracle:
Kare ga kanemochi ni natta no mo fushigi *wa nai.* (彼が金持になったのも不思議はない) It is no *wonder* that he became rich.
— *a.n.* (~ na, ni) difficult to ex-

plain the reason or cause; mysterious; strange:
Sono shorui ga nakunatta no wa fushigi *da.*(その書類がなくなったのは不思議だ) It is *strange* that the papers have disappeared. / *Kare ga gichoo ni erabareta no mo* fushigi *de wa nai.*(彼が議長に選ばれたのも不思議ではない) It is not *surprising* that he was elected chairman. / *Kare wa shiai ni naru to* fushigi ni *yoku hitto o utsu.*(彼は試合になると不思議によくヒットを打つ) *Strangely enough*, he hits well in an actual game.

fushigi to (〜と) *adv.* strangely; miraculously: *Watashi ga dekakeru hi ni wa* fushigi to *itsu-mo ame ga furu.*(私が出かける日には不思議といつも雨が降る) *Strange to say*, it always rains on the days that I go out.

fuˈshiˈmatsu ふしまつ (不始末) *n.* carelessness; misconduct:
Kaji no geñiñ wa tabako no hi no fushimatsu *datta.*(火事の原因はたばこの火の不始末だった) The cause of the fire was *careless handling* of cigarette butts. / *Kare wa* fushimatsu *o shite kubi ni natta.*(彼は不始末をして首になった) He was fired for his *misconduct*.

fuˈshiˈñsetsu ふしんせつ (不親切) *a.n.* (〜 na, ni) unkind; insufficient:
Kare wa roojiñ ni fushiñsetsu *datta.*(彼は老人に不親切だった) He was *unkind* to the old man. / *Kono ryokoo-añnai wa* fushiñsetsu *da.*(この旅行案内は不親切だ) This guidebook is *inadequate*. / *Ano mise no teñiñ wa* fushiñsetsu *da.*(あの店の店員は不親切だ) The clerks at that store are *inconsiderate*. 《↔ shiñsetsu》

fuˈshiˈzeñ ふしぜん (不自然) *a.n.* (〜 na, ni) unnatural; artificial; forced:

fushizeñ *na kakkoo o suru* (不自然な格好をする) assume an *unnatural* posture / *Kare ga soñna koto o suru no wa* fushizeñ *da.*(彼がそんなことをするのは不自然だ) It is *not natural* for him to do such a thing. / *Yoogisha no zuboñ no poketto wa* fushizeñ *ni fukurañde ita.*(容疑者のズボンのポケットは不自然にふくらんでいた) The trouser pockets of the suspect were bulging in an *unnatural way*. 《↔ shizeñ》

fuˈshoo ふしょう (負傷) *n.* injury; wound; cut; bruise:
fushoo-sha (負傷者) a *wounded* [an *injured*] *person*.

fushoo suru (〜する) *vi.* be injured; be wounded: *Kare wa sono jiko de* fushoo shita.(彼はその事故で負傷した) He *was injured* in the accident. / *Sono otoko wa naifu de sasarete,* fushoo shita.(その男はナイフで刺されて、負傷した) The man was stabbed with a knife and *wounded*.

fuˈsoku ふそく (不足) *n.* shortage; lack; want; insufficiency:
Oozee no hito ga shokuryoo no fusoku *de gashi shite iru.*(大勢の人が食糧の不足で餓死している) Many people are starving from *lack* of food. / fusoku-buñ (不足分) *shortage*. 《⇒ -busoku》

fusoku suru (〜する) *vi.* be short; be lacking: *O-tsuri ga sañjuu-eñ* fusoku shite imasu.(おつりが30円不足しています) The change is thirty yen *short*.

fuˈsuma ふすま (襖) *n.* Japanese sliding door. ★ Both sides are covered with thick paper; used as a partition between rooms. 《⇒ photo (next page)》

fuˈta ふた (蓋) *n.* lid; cap; cover:
biñ no futa *o akeru* (びんのふたをあける) take off the *cap* of a bottle / *nabe ni* futa *o suru* (なべにふたをする) put the *lid* on a pot.

FUSUMA

fu⌈ta- ふた (二) *pref.* double; two:
futa-*keta* (二桁) *double* digits / futa-*kumi* (二組) *two* pairs / futa-*tsuki* (二月) *two* months / futa-*toori* (二通り) *two* ways.

fu⌈tañ ふたん (負担) *n.* burden; load; charge; obligation:
Oya ni futañ *wa kaketaku nai.* (親に負担はかけたくない) I don't want to be a *burden* to my parents.
futañ suru (〜する) *vt.* bear; share; cover: *Dare-ka ga sono hiyoo o* futañ *shinakereba naranai.* (だれかがその費用を負担しなければならない) Someone *must bear* the expenses. / *Sooryoo wa kochira de* futañ *shimasu.* (送料はこちらで負担します) We *will cover* the postage.

fu⌈tari⌉ ふたり (二人) *n.* two persons; couple:
Kanojo to futari *de resutorañ de shokuji o shita.* (彼女と二人でレストランで食事をした) I had dinner *together with* her at a restaurant.

fu⌈ta⌉shika ふたしか (不確か) *a.n.* (〜 na, ni) uncertain; unreliable:
futashika *na joohoo* (不確かな情報) *unreliable* information / *Shoorai no koto wa* futashika *desu.* (将来のことは不確かです) The future is *uncertain*. (↔ tashika)

fu⌈tatabi ふたたび (再び) *adv.* again; once more; for the second time: ★ Similar in meaning to '*mata*' but slightly formal.
Futatabi o-ai dekiru koto o negatte imasu. (再びお会いできることを願っています) I hope we have a chance to meet *again*. / *Nichi-Bee no kooshoo ga* futatabi *hajimatta.* (日米の交渉が再び始まった) Japan-U.S. negotiations have started *once more*. / *Ni-do to* futatabi *kuni ni kaeru tsumori wa arimaseñ.* (二度と再び国に帰るつもりはありません) I have no intention of *ever* returning to my country.

fu⌈tatsu ふたつ (二つ) *n.* couple; two: ★ Used when counting.
keeki o futatsu *ni wakeru* (ケーキを二つに分ける) cut a cake in *two* / futatsu-*me* (二つ目) *the second*. 《⇒ ni¹; kazu (table)》

fu⌈te⌉kitoo ふてきとう (不適当) *a.n.* (〜 na, ni) unsuitable; unfit:
Kono eega wa kodomo ni wa futekitoo *desu.* (この映画は子どもには不適当です) This movie is *unsuitable* for children. (↔ tekitoo)

fu⌈to ふと *adv.* suddenly; by chance; unexpectedly:
Sañpo no tochuu de futo *ii aidea ga ukañda.* (散歩の途中でふといいアイデアが浮かんだ) *Suddenly* a good idea came to me in the middle of my stroll. / *Futo miru to kare no kuruma ga soko ni atta.* (ふと見ると彼の車がそこにあった) I noticed his car there quite *unexpectedly*.
futo shita (〜した) by chance; accidentally: *Futo shita koto kara kare to tomodachi ni natta.* (ふとしたことから彼と友だちになった) *By mere chance*, I made friends with him.

fu⌈to⌉・i ふとい (太い) *a.* (-ku)
1 (of round objects such as sticks or string) thick; bold:
futoi *keito* (太い毛糸) *thick* wool / futoi *señ* (太い線) a *bold* line / *Sukeeto no señshu wa momo ga* futoi. (スケートの選手はももが太い) Pro-

fessional skaters have *big* thighs.
/ *Uesuto ga* futoku *natta.* (ウエストが
太くなった) I've grown *fat* around
the waist. ((↔ hosoi))
2 (of a voice) deep:
Kare wa koe ga futoi. (彼は声が太
い) He has a *deep* voice. ((↔ hosoi))

fu⌈tokoro ふところ (懐) *n.* breast;
bosom; one's pocket:
Akañboo wa haha-oya no futokoro
ni dakarete ita. (赤ん坊は母親のふと
ころに抱かれていた) The baby was
held in his mother's *bosom.* /
Kare wa sono kane o futokoro *ni
shimatta.* (彼はその金をふところにしまっ
た) He stowed the money away in
his *breast pocket.* ((⇨ mune; wafuku (illus.)))
futokoro ga atatakai (〜が暖かい)
have a lot of money; have a fat
purse.
futokoro ga sabishii (〜が寂しい)
be pressed for money; be hard
up for money.

fu⌈tomomo ふともも (太股) *n.*
thigh. ((⇨ jiñtai (illus.)))

fu⌈toñ ふとん (布団) *n.* padded
floor mattress used as a bed; bedding; quilt:
futoñ *o shiku* (ふとんを敷く) spread
a *mattress* on the floor; make a
bed / futoñ *o kakeru* (ふとんを掛ける)
put a *quilt* (over a baby) / futoñ *o
tatamu* (ふとんを畳む) fold up the
bedding / futoñ *o oshiire ni shimau* (ふとんを押し入れにしまう) stow
away the *bedding* in a closet.
((⇨ oshiire (illus.)))

──────(CULTURE)──────
The '*futoñ*' is folded and put
away in a large closet during
the day, and spread on the
tatami floor at night. Strictly
speaking, that which serves as
the mattress is called '*shikibutoñ*' and the covering is
called '*kakebutoñ.*'
────────────────────

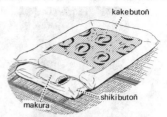

kakebutoñ

shikibutoñ

makura

FUTOÑ SPREAD OUT FOR SLEEPING

fu⌈too ふとう (不当) *a.n.* (〜 na,
ni) unfair; unjust; unreasonable:
futoo *na shudañ* (不当な手段) *unjust* means / *Kare-ra no yookyuu
wa* futoo *da.* (彼らの要求は不当だ)
Their demands are *unreasonable.*
/ *Kore wa* futoo *ni takasugiru.* (こ
れは不当に高すぎる) This is *unreasonably* expensive. ((↔ seetoo'))

fu⌈to⌉r·u ふとる (太る) *vi.* (futor·i-;
futor·a-; futot-te C) **1** grow fat;
gain weight:
Watashi wa kore ijoo futoritaku
arimaseñ. (私はこれ以上太りたくありま
せん) I don't want to *gain any
more weight.* / *Señgetsu yori mo
ni-kiro* futotta. (先月よりも2キロ太っ
た) I've *gained* as much as two
kilos since last month.
2 be fat; be plump: ★ '*Futotte
iru*' is the pattern used in this
sense.
Ano hito wa zuibuñ futotte iru. (あ
の人はずいぶん太っている) He *is* very
fat. / Futotte iru *hito wa tsukare-
yasui.* (太っている人は疲れやすい) *Fat*
people get tired easily.

fu⌈tsuka ふつか (二日) *n.* two
days; the second day:
Roñdoñ ni futsuka *taizai shita.* (ロ
ンドンに二日滞在した) I stayed in
London for *two days.* / *Sañ-gatsu*
futsuka *ni Oosaka e ikimasu.* (三月
2日に大阪へ行きます) I am going to
Osaka on the *second* of March.
((⇨ tsuitachi (table)))

fu⌈tsukayoi ふつかよい (二日酔い)

n. hangover (from alcohol).

fuˈtsuu¹ ふつう (普通) *a.n.* (~ na/ no, ni) common; ordinary; normal; usual; average:
futsuu *no hito* (普通の人) an *ordinary* person / futsuu *no seekatsu* (普通の生活) an *average* life / *"Yamada-sañ wa paatii de doo deshita?" "Itsu-mo to kawarazu,* futsuu *deshita yo."*(「山田さんはパーティーでどうでした」「いつもと変わらず、普通でしたよ」) "How was Mr. Yamada at the party?" "There was *nothing out of the ordinary* about him." / *Nihoñ de wa busshiki no sooshiki ga* futsuu *desu.*(日本では仏式の葬式が普通です) In Japan Buddhist funerals are the *norm.*
— *adv.* usually; commonly; ordinarily; normally:
Watashi wa futsuu *(wa) shichi-ji made ni wa uchi ni kaerimasu.*(私は普通(は)7時までには家に帰ります) I'm *usually* home by seven./ Futsuu *(wa) hitomae de wa sonna koto wa shimaseñ.*(普通(は)人前ではそんなことはしません) We *usually* don't do such things in public.

fuˈtsuu² ふつう (普通) *n.* local train; one that stops at every station along the line:
Mitaka de kyuukoo kara futsuu *ni norikae nasai.*(三鷹で急行から普通に乗り換えなさい) Transfer from the express to a *local* at Mitaka.
《⇨ doñkoo; kyuukoo¹ (table)》

fuˈtsuu³ ふつう (不通) *n.* interruption; suspension:
Yamanote-señ wa ima futsuu *desu.*(山の手線はいま不通です) The Yamanote Line *is not in service* now. / *Deñwa ga* futsuu *ni natta.*(電話が不通になった) Telephone communication *broke down.*

fuˈttoboˈoru フットボール *n.* American football:

── **USAGE** ──
'*Futtobooru*' refers to American football, although to be more specific, '*Amerikañ futtobooru*' or in normal conversation, '*Amefutto*' can be used. Association football is called '*sakkaa*' and Rugby fooball, '*ragubii.*'

futtobooru *o suru* (フットボールをする) play *football.*

fuˈttoo ふっとう (沸騰) *n.* boiling; seething.
futtoo suru (~する) *vi.* 1 boil; come to the boil: *Suupu wa ichido* futtoo shitara *hi o tomemasu.*(スープは一度沸騰したら火を止めます) Once the soup *comes to the boil*, turn off the gas.
2 be heated:
Giroñ ga futtoo shita.(議論がふっとうした) The discussion *became heated.*

fuˈu¹ ふう (風) *n.* 1 look; appearance; air:
Kare wa nanigenai fuu *o shite ita.*(彼は何気ない風をしていた) He *pretended* nonchalance.
2 way; manner:
Sore wa koñna fuu *ni yatte gorañ nasai.*(それはこんな風にやってごらんなさい) Try to do it *in this manner.*

fuˈu² ふう (封) *n.* seal:
tegami no fuu *o suru [kiru]* (手紙の封をする[切る]) *seal [open]* a letter.

-fuu ふう (風) *suf.* style; type:
Watashi wa Nihoñ-fuu *no furo ga suki desu.*(私は日本風のふろが好きです) I like Japanese *style* baths.

fuˈufu ふうふ (夫婦) *n.* man [husband] and wife; married couple:
Ano futari wa fuufu *desu.*(あの二人は夫婦です) Those two are a *married couple.* / *Kare-ra wa* fuufu-*naka ga yoi.*(彼らは夫婦仲がよい) They are a happy *couple.* / fuufu-*geñka* (夫婦げんか) a quarrel between *husband and wife.*

fuˈufuu ふうふう *adv.* (~ to)

1 (used when blowing on something hot to cool it):
misoshiru o fuufuu *samasu* (みそ汁をふうふう冷ます) cool *miso* soup by *blowing* on it / *Miñna* fuufuu *ii-nagara sukiyaki o tabeta.* (みんなふうふう言いながらすき焼きを食べた) Everyone was *blowing* on the sukiyaki as they ate it.

2 (used when a person is short of breath or does something with difficulty):
Watashi wa fuufuu *ii-nagara kare ni tsuite hashitta.* (私はふうふう言いながら彼について走った) I *panted* along behind him. / *Koñna kañtañ na shigoto de* fuufuu *itte ite wa, kore-kara ga taiheñ da.* (こんな簡単な仕事でふうふう言っていては、これからが大変だ) If you're having a *hard time* with a simple job like this, from now on things are going to be really tough.

fuˈukee ふうけい (風景) *n.* landscape; scene; scenery:
Kono fuukee *o miru to kokyoo o omoidasu.* (この風景を見ると故郷を思い出す) This *scenery* reminds me of my hometown. / fuukee-*ga* (風景画) a *landscape* painting.

fuˈuki ふうき (風紀) *n.* social morality; discipline:
fuuki *o midasu* (風紀を乱す) corrupt *public morals* / *Kono atari wa* fuuki *ga yoku nai.* (この辺りは風紀がよくない) *Public conduct* in this area is very poor.

fuˈuñ¹ ふうん *int.* hum; oh:

┌─ **USAGE** ─────────┐
Used to express a half-hearted reply. It is rude to use this expression in reply to one's superiors.
└──────────────────┘

"Yuki ga futte kita yo." "Fuuñ, (soo kai)." (「雪が降ってきたよ」「ふうん、(そうかい)」) "Look, it has started snowing." "*Oh,* (really)?"

fuˈuñ² ふうん (不運) *n.* bad luck; misfortune:
Kono tokoro fuuñ *ga tsuzuita.* (このところ不運が続いた) I have had a succession of *bad luck* recently.
— *a.n.* (~ na, ni) unlucky; unfortunate:
Tanaka-sañ wa fuuñ *na hito da.* (田中さんは不運な人だ) Ms. Tanaka is an *unlucky* person. / *Sore wa* fuuñ *na jiko datta.* (それは不運な事故だった) It was an *unfortunate* accident. (↔ koouñ)

fuˈuseñ ふうせん (風船) *n.* balloon:
fuuseñ *o fukuramasu* [*tobasu*] (風船をふくらます[飛ばす]) inflate [send up] a *balloon* / fuuseñ-*dama* (風船玉) a toy *balloon* / fuuseñ-*gamu* (風船ガム) *bubble* gum / kami-fuuseñ (紙風船) a paper *balloon*.

KAMI-FUSEÑ

fuˈushuu ふうしゅう (風習) *n.* custom; manners; practices:
fuushuu *ni shitagau* (風習に従う) follow a *custom* / *Kare wa Nihoñ no* fuushuu *o yoku shitte iru.* (彼は日本の風習をよく知っている) He is familiar with the *customs* of Japan. / *Jidai ga kawareba,* fuushuu *mo kawarimasu.* (時代が変われば、風習も変わります) Other times, other *manners*.

fuˈutoo ふうとう (封筒) *n.* envelope:
Futtoo ni kitte o haru no o wasureta. (封筒に切手を貼るのを忘れた) I forgot to put a stamp on the *envelope*.

fu⌐u-u ふうう（風雨）*n.* wind and rain; storm:
Koñya wa fuu-u ga tsuyoku narisoo da.（今夜は風雨が強くなりそうだ）It seems that we'll have a *strong wind with heavy rain* tonight.

fu⌐uzoku ふうぞく（風俗）*n.* manners; public morals:
Nihoñgo no beñkyoo ni wa Nihoñ no fuuzoku shuukañ no chishiki ga taisetsu desu.（日本語の勉強には日本の風俗習慣の知識が大切です）Acquaintance with Japanese *manners* and customs is important for the study of Japanese.

fu⌐uzoku-e⌐egyoo ふうぞくえいぎょう（風俗営業）*n.* entertainment and amusement trades. ★ Usually used as a euphemism for prostitution.

ENTERTAINMENT DISTRICT

fu⌐wafuwa[1] ふわふわ *a.n.*（～ no, ni) gentle; soft: ★ Used for objects which are light and fluffy.
fuwafuwa no kusshoñ（ふわふわのクッション）a *soft* cushion / *Kono señzai de arau to, seetaa ga fuwafuwa ni narimasu.*（この洗剤で洗うと、セーターがふわふわになります）If you use this detergent, your sweaters will become *fluffy*.

fu⌐wafuwa[2] ふわふわ *adv.*（～ to, ～ suru) **1** lightly; buoyantly:
Sono fuuseñ wa doko-ka e fuwafuwa (to) toñde itta.（その風船はどこかへふわふわ（と）飛んで行った）The balloon *gently* floated away somewhere.
2 restless; unsettled: ★ Used about people who cannot settle down or pay attention to what they should be doing.
Fuwafuwa shite inai de, sukoshi wa shigoto de mo shitara doo desu ka?（ふわふわしていないで、少しは仕事でもしたらどうですか）What about getting down to at least some work, instead of *fooling* around?

fu⌐wa⌐ri ふわり *adv.*（～ to) gently; softly; lightly: ★ Used for objects moving slowly in the air. '*Fuñwari*' is also used when referring to something softer or lighter.
Kikyuu ga fuwari to tobitatta.（気球がふわりと飛び立った）The (observation) balloon *lightly* rose up into the air. / *Parashuuto wa fuwari to chijoo ni chakuriku shita.*（パラシュートはふわりと地上に着陸した）The parachute *softly* settled down on the ground. / *Haha-oya wa nete iru akachañ ni fuwari to moofu o kakete yatta.*（母親は寝ている赤ちゃんにふわりと毛布をかけてやった）The mother *gently* laid the blanket over her sleeping baby.（⇨ fuñwari)

fu⌐ya⌐s·u ふやす（増やす）*vt.*（fuyash·i-; fuyas·a-; fuyash·i-te [C]）increase; add to:
hito o fuyasu（人を増やす）*increase* the staff / *zaisañ o fuyasu*（財産を増やす）*add to* one's fortune / *chishiki o fuyasu*（知識を増やす）*enrich* one's knowledge.

fu⌐yu[1] ふゆ（冬）*n.* winter:
Kotoshi no fuyu wa samukatta.（ことしの冬は寒かった）We had a cold *winter* this year. / *Fuyu wa sukii o shimasu.*（冬はスキーをします）I go

skiing in *winter*. 《⇨ shiki¹ (table);
kisetsu (table)》

fu⌐yu⌐kai ふゆかい (不愉快) *a.n.*
(~ na, ni) unpleasant; disagreeable:
Kinoo wa totemo fuyukai *na omoi
o shita*. (きのうはとても不愉快な思いを
した) I had a very *unpleasant* experience yesterday. / Fuyukai *na
uwasa ga nagarete iru*. (不愉快なう
わさが流れている) An *unpleasant*
rumor is going around. / *Kare no
taido wa* fuyukai *da*. (彼の態度は不
愉快だ) I am *displeased* with his
attitude. 《↔ yukai》

fu⌐yu-ya⌐sumi ふゆやすみ (冬休み)
n. winter vacation: ★ Schools
are on vacation between the last
ten days of December and the
first ten days of January, depending on schools and districts.
*Fuyu-yasumi ni wa uchi e kaeri-
masu*. (冬休みには家に帰ります) I
return home during the *winter
vacation*.

fu⌐zai ふざい (不在) *n.* absence:
Anata no fuzai-*chuu ni raikyaku
ga arimashita*. (あなたの不在中に来客
がありました) A visitor came to see
you during your *absence*. / *Kare
wa* fuzai *desu*. (彼は不在です) He *is
not at home*.

fu⌐zake⌐·ru ふざける (巫山戯る) *vi.*
(fuzake-te Ⅴ) **1** joke; jest; talk
nonsense:
Kare ga fuzakete *itta koto nado,
ki ni suru na*. (彼がふざけて言ったこと

など, 気にするな) Don't worry about
what he said *in jest*. / Fuzaketa
*koto o ittenai de, majime ni kotae
nasai*. (ふざけたことを言ってないで, まじ
めに答えなさい) Stop *talking nonsense*, and answer properly. / Fuza-
keru *na!* (*rude*) (ふざけるな) *Stop
your nonsense!*
2 frisk; frolic:
Kodomo-tachi ga koe o agete fuza-
ke-mawatte *iru*. (子どもたちが声を上
げてふざけまわっている) Children are
shouting and *running about play-
fully*. / *Shoogakusee ga deñsha
no naka de* fuzakete *ita*. (小学生が
電車の中でふざけていた) Elementary
school children *were frolicking*
on the train.
3 (of lovers) flirt:
Futari wa hitomae de mo heeki de
fuzakete *ita*. (二人は人前でも平気で
ふざけていた) The couple *were carrying on* without any shame right
in front of other people.

fu⌐zoku ふぞく (付属) *n.* attachment; accessory:
*Kono gakkoo wa Meeji-daigaku
no* fuzoku *desu*. (この学校は明治大学
の付属です) This school *is attached*
to Meiji University. / fuzoku-hiñ
(付属品) *accessories*.

fuzoku suru (~する) *vi.* be attached [affiliated]: *Kono byooiñ
wa Keeoo-daigaku ni* fuzoku shite
iru. (この病院は慶応大学に付属してい
る) This hospital *is affiliated* with
Keio University.

G

ga[1] が *p.* **1** (used to mark the topic of a sentence): *Kyooto ni wa furui* tatemono ga *takusañ arimasu.* (京都には古い建物がたくさんあります) There are a lot of old *buildings* in Kyoto. / Deñsha ga *hoomu ni haitte kita.* (電車がホームに入って来た) The *train* drew into the platform.

> **USAGE**
>
> Generally speaking, '*ga*' is used to stress the subject and '*wa*' is used to emphasize the predicate. When a noun is first mentioned, it is usually followed by '*ga*,' but on later mentions, by '*wa.*' *e.g. Eki no soba ni* kooeñ ga *arimasu. Sono* kooeñ wa *hirokute, totemo kiree desu.* (駅のそばに公園があります。その公園は広くて、とてもきれいです) There is *a park* next to the station. *The park* is spacious and very pretty. (⇨ wa³)

2 [follows a nominalized verb which is the subject of its clause]: *Yasumi ni wa* oñgaku o kiku no ga *nani yori no tanoshimi desu.* (休みには音楽を聞くのがなによりの楽しみです) Nothing is more enjoyable than *listening to music* on my days off.

3 (used with certain expressions indicating likes, dislikes, desires and wishes): *Watashi wa* yasai ga *kirai desu.* (私は野菜がきらいです) I dislike *vegetables.* / *Anata wa doñna* eega ga *suki desu ka?* (あなたはどんな映画が好きですか) What kind of *movies* do you like? / *Atarashii* kuruma ga *hoshii.* (新しい車が欲しい) I want a new *car.* / *Nani-ka* oishii mono ga *tabetai.* (何かおいしいものが食べたい) I feel like eating *something tasty.*

> **USAGE**
>
> Both '*o*' and '*ga*' are used in '*-tai*' patterns. *e.g. Omoshiroi* eega ga [o] *mitai naa.* (おもしろい映画が[を]見たいなあ) I want to see an interesting *movie.* (⇨ o²)

4 (used with certain expressions indicating ability or skill): *Yamada-sañ wa* sukii ga *joozu desu.* (山田さんはスキーが上手です) Mrs. Yamada is good at *skiing.* / *Watashi wa* kuruma no uñteñ ga *dekimaseñ.* (私は車の運転が出来ません) I don't know how to *drive* a car. / *Kare wa* Doitsugo ga [o] *hanasemasu.* (彼はドイツ語が[を]話せます) He can speak *German.*

> **USAGE**
>
> *Both* '*ga*' and '*o*' are used, but '*ga*' is traditionally correct and is therefore generally safer to use than '*o.*' (⇨ o²)

ga[2] が *p.* **1** but; although:
a (used to link two clauses, the second of which is an unexpected outcome or result of the first): *Zuibuñ hanashiaimashita* ga, *kekkyoku ketsuroñ wa demaseñ deshita.* (ずいぶん話し合いましたが、結局結論は出ませんでした) We talked a great deal *but* in the end came to no conclusion. / *Yuujiñ ni ai ni ikimashita* ga, *ainiku rusu deshita.* (友人に会いに行きましたが、あいにく留守でした) I went to see my friend, *but* unfortunately she was not at

home. / *Iroiro shirabete mima-shita* ga, *wakarimaseñ deshita.* (い
ろいろ調べてみましたが, わかりませんでし
た) *Although* I checked in every
way, I could not find out about
it. ((⇨ kakawarazu; keredo mo; no
ni))
b (used to link two clauses that
are in direct contrast):
Tanaka-sañ wa kimashita ga, *Ya-mada-sañ wa mada desu.* (田中さん
は来ましたが, 山田さんはまだです) Mr.
Tanaka has arrived, *but* Mr. Ya-
mada hasn't yet. / *Peñ wa arima-su* ga, *kami ga arimaseñ.* (ペンはあり
ますが, 紙がありません) I have a pen,
but no paper. / *Gozeñ-chuu wa
ame ga furimashita* ga, *gogo kara
haremashita.* (午前中は雨が降りまし
たが, 午後から晴れました) *Although* it
rained in the morning, it cleared
up in the afternoon.
((⇨ kakawarazu; keredo mo; no ni))
2 (used in a non-contrastive way
to link two clauses, the first of
which is a preliminary to the
second):
Sumimaseñ ga, *eki e wa doo ike-ba ii ñ deshoo ka?* (すみませんが, 駅へ
はどう行けばいいんでしょうか) *Excuse
me*, but what would be the best
way of going to the station? /
Watashi wa Yamada to mooshi-masu ga, *Kobayashi señsee wa
go-zaitaku deshoo ka?* (私は山田と
申しますが, 小林先生はご在宅でしょう
か) My name is Yamada; I wonder if Professor Kobayashi is at
home now.
3 and also: ★ Used to link two
clauses, the second of which sup-
plements the first.

((**USAGE**))
Similar to the particle '*shi*'
and the conjunction '*sore ni*'
in meaning. Also used with the
particle '*mo*.' ((⇨ shi¹; mo²))

Kanojo wa kiryoo mo ii ga, *atama
mo ii.* (彼女は器量もいいが, 頭もいい)
She is good-looking, *and* what is
more, clever. / *Kyooto mo kiree
da* ga, *Nikkoo mo nakanaka ii.* (京
都もきれいだが, 日光もなかなかいい)
Kyoto is pretty *and* Nikko is *also*
very nice.
4 (used at the end of an unfinished sentence to politely express
modesty or reserve, or to avoid
making an overly direct statement):
Anoo, sore watashi no na ñ desu
ga... (あのう, それ私のなんですが...)
Excuse me, but I *think* that is
mine. / *Kyoo wa chotto tsugoo ga
warui ñ desu* ga... (きょうはちょっと都
合が悪いんですが...) Today is a bit
inconvenient, *so*...

ga⌐aru-fure⌐ñdo ガールフレンド *n.*
girlfriend.

ga⌐bugabu がぶがぶ *adv.* (~ to)
(the sound of noisily drinking a
liquid): ★ Not used to describe
eating.
Kare wa uma-soo ni mizu o nañ-bai mo gabugabu (*to*) *noñda.* (彼は
うまそうに水を何杯もがぶがぶ(と)飲んだ)
He *noisily* drank several cups of
water with evident pleasure.
((⇨ gatsugatsu))

ga⌐byoo がびょう (画鋲) *n.* thumb-
tack; drawing pin:
e o kabe ni gabyoo de tomeru (絵
を壁に画鋲でとめる) *tack* a picture
on the wall. ((⇨ byoo²))

-gachi がち (勝ち) *suf.* tend to
do; be apt [liable] to do:
★ Added to a noun or the stem
of a verb. Often used when the
tendency is unfavorable.
*Gaishoku bakari shite iru to eeyoo
ga* katayori-gachi *ni naru.* (外食ば
かりしていると栄養がかたよりがちになる)
If you eat out all the time, your
diet will *tend to be unbalanced.* /
Kare wa karada ga yowai no de

gakkoo o yasumi-gachi *desu.*(彼は体が弱いので学校を休みがちです) Since he is physically delicate, he *is often absent* from school. / *Kanojo wa* byooki-gachi *no kodomo o kakaete iru.*(彼女は病気がちの子どもをかかえている) She has a child who *gets sick easily.*

ga┌i がい(害) *n.* harm; damage: *Kono kusuri wa mainichi noñde mo* gai *wa arimaseñ.*(この薬は毎日飲んでも害はありません) Even if you take this medicine every day, it will not do you any *harm.* / *Tabako wa keñkoo ni* gai ga aru.(たばこは健康に害がある) Smoking *is harmful* to your health.

-gai がい(外) *suf.* outside: *moñdai[roñ]*-gai (問題[論]外) *out of* the question / *yosoo*-gai (予想外) *unexpected* / jikañ-gai *roodoo* (時間外労働) *overtime* work.

ga┌iatsu がいあつ(外圧) *n.* external pressure: gaiatsu *ni makeru* (外圧に負ける) yield to *external pressure* / gaiatsu *ni taeru* (外圧に耐える) withstand *pressure from outside.*

ga┌ibu がいぶ(外部) *n.* **1** outside; exterior: *Tatemono no* gaibu *wa tsuta de oowarete ita.*(建物の外部はつたで覆われていた) The *exterior* of the building was covered with ivy. 《↔ ┌naibu》 **2** outside (one's circle); external (to one's interests): *Himitsu ga* gaibu *ni moreta.* (秘密が外部に漏れた) The secret leaked to *outsiders.* 《↔ ┌naibu》

ga┌ido ガイド *n.* guide: *Watashi ga minasañ no* gaido *o tsutomemasu.*(私がみなさんのガイドをつとめます) I will be acting as your *guide.* / *Eego no hanaseru* gaido *o gozoñji desu ka?* (英語の話せるガイドをご存じですか) Do you know a *guide,* who can speak English? /

Gaido-sañ, kono basu wa itsu demasu ka? (ガイドさん、このバスはいつ出ますか) Excuse me (*guide*). When does this bus leave?

ga┌ido-bu┐kku ガイドブック *n.* **1** guidebook for travelers or tourists. **2** manual; handbook.

ga┌ijiñ がいじん(外人) *n.* foreigner. ★ Abbreviation of '*gaikokujiñ.*'

ga┌ika がいか(外貨) *n.* foreign currency [money]: Gaika *o kakutoku suru no ni kañkoo wa juuyoo desu.*(外貨を獲得するのに観光は重要です) The tourist industry is important for earning *foreign currency.*

ga┌ikañ がいかん(外観) *n.* appearance; exterior view: *Sono tatemono no* gaikañ *wa shiro no yoo da.*(その建物の外観は城のようだ) The *exterior* of the building looks like a castle.

ga┌ikoku がいこく(外国) *n.* foreign country [land]: *Kare wa* gaikoku *ni suñde imasu.* (彼は外国に住んでいます) He lives in a *foreign country.* / gaikoku-*booeki* (外国貿易) *foreign* trade / gaikoku-*kawase* (外国為替) *foreign* exchange / gaikoku-*yuubiñ* (外国郵便) *mail from abroad.*

ga┌ikokugo がいこくご(外国語) *n.* foreign language: *Kare wa ikutsu mo* gaikokugo *ga hanasemasu.*(彼はいくつも外国語が話せます) He can speak a number of *foreign languages.*

ga┌ikoku┐jiñ がいこくじん(外国人) *n.* foreigner; alien.

ga┌ikoo がいこう(外交) *n.* **1** diplomacy; foreign affairs: *Kare-ra wa sono kuni to* gaikoo *kañkee o musuñda [tatta].*(彼らはその国と外交関係を結んだ[断った]) They established [broke off] *diplomatic* relations with that country. / *Seefu no* gaikoo-*hooshiñ wa*

hakkiri shinai. (政府の外交方針ははっきりしない) The *foreign* policy of the government is not clear. / *Sore wa* gaikoo-*joo no himitsu desu.* (それは外交上の秘密です) It is a *diplomatic* secret.
2 door-to-door sales:
Kanojo wa hokeñ no gaikoo o *shite iru.* (彼女は保険の外交をしている) She *goes from house to house* selling insurance.

ga⌈iko⌉oiñ がいこういん (外交員) *n.* salesman; saleswoman:
Kanojo wa hokeñ no gaikooiñ *desu.* (彼女は保険の外交員です) She is an insurance *saleswoman.*

ga⌈iko⌉okañ がいこうかん (外交官) *n.* diplomat.

Ga⌈imu-da⌉ijiñ がいむだいじん (外務大臣) *n.* Minister of Foreign Affairs.

Ga⌈imu⌉-shoo がいむしょう (外務省) *n.* Ministry of Foreign Affairs. 《⇒ shoo¹ (table)》

ga⌈ineñ がいねん (概念) *n.* notion; general idea; concept.

ga⌈iraigo がいらいご (外来語) *n.* loan word; Japanized foreign word. ★ Usually written in 'katakana.'

ga⌈ishite がいして (概して) *adv.* (*formal*) generally; in general; on the whole:
Nihoñ no dooro wa Amerika no yori gaishite *semai.* (日本の道路はアメリカのより概して狭い) Roads in Japan are *generally* narrower than those in the U.S. / *Kono heñ wa* gaishite *yuki ga ooi.* (この辺は概して雪が多い) *Generally* speaking, it snows a lot in this area.

ga⌈ishoku がいしょく (外食) *n.* eating out:
Koñya wa gaishoku *ni shimashoo.* (今夜は外食にしましょう) Let's *eat out* tonight.

Ga⌈ishoo がいしょう (外相) *n.* Foreign Minister. ★ Abbrevi-

ated form of '*Gaimu-daijiñ.*'

ga⌈ishutsu がいしゅつ (外出) *n.* going out:
Yakañ no gaishutsu *wa kiñjirarete imasu.* (夜間の外出は禁じられています) *Going out* at night is prohibited. / Gaishutsu-*saki o oshiete kudasai.* (外出先を教えてください) Tell me *where you are going.*
gaishutsu suru (〜する) *vi.* go out: *Gogo wa* gaishutsu *shimasu.* (午後は外出します) I will *go out* this afternoon. / *Kare wa ima* gaishutsu *shite imasu.* (彼は今外出しています) He *is out* now.

ga⌈isoo がいそう (外装) *n.* the exterior (of a building, car, etc.); external ornament:
Ima ie no gaisoo *no shiage o shite iru tokoro desu.* (今家の外装の仕上げをしているところです) We are now at the stage of finishing off the *exterior* of the house. 《↔ naisoo》

ga⌈is·u がいす (害す) *vt.* (gaish·i·te Ⓥ) injure; hurt:
Kare no kotoba wa watashi no kañjoo o gaishita. (彼の言葉は私の感情を害した) His words *hurt* my feelings. / *Kare wa kañjoo o* gaishita *rashii.* (彼は感情を害したらしい) He seems to *be offended.* / *Tabako wa keñkoo o* gaisu. (たばこは健康を害す) Smoking *injures* your health.

ga⌈itoo¹ がいとう (該当) *n.* application; correspondence.
gaitoo suru (〜する) *vi.* come [fall] under; apply; correspond:
Sore wa kono keeyaku no dai-sañ-joo ni gaitoo suru. (それはこの契約の第3条に該当する) That *comes under* Article 3 of this contract. / *Sore wa kono baai ni* gaitoo shinai. (それはこの場合に該当しない) It *doesn't apply* in this case. / Gaitoo suru *koomoku o maru de kakomi nasai.* (該当する項目を○で囲みなさい) Circle each *applicable*

item. 《⇨ atehamaru》

ga⌈itoo² がいとう（街頭）*n.* street:
Watashi-tachi wa gaitoo *de shomee o atsumeta.* (私たちは街頭で署名を集めた) We collected signatures on the *street*. / gaitoo-*bokiñ* (街頭募金) collecting contributions on the *street* / gaitoo-*eñzetsu* (街頭演説) a speech on the *street*.

ga⌈itoo³ がいとう（街灯）*n.* street lamp:
Kuraku naru to kono gaitoo *wa shizeñ ni tomorimasu.* (暗くなるとこの街灯は自然にともります) When it gets dark, these *street lamps* automatically come on.

ga⌈ito⌉osha がいとうしゃ（該当者）*n.* applicable person:
Sono shoo no gaitoosha *wa inakatta.* (その賞の該当者はいなかった) There was nobody *deserving* of the prize.

ga⌈iyoo がいよう（概要）*n.* outline; summary:
Shi tookyoku wa keekaku no gaiyoo *o hapyoo shita.* (市当局は計画の概要を発表した) The city authorities announced the *outline* of the plan. / *Kono shoo no* gaiyoo *o nobe nasai.* (この章の概要を述べなさい) Please give a *summary* of this chapter. 《↔ shoosai》

ga⌈ka がか（画家）*n.* painter; artist.

-gakari¹ がかり（係）*suf.* **1** clerk:
añnai-gakari (案内係) a *receptionist*; an *usher* / kaikee-gakari (会計係) an *accountant* / settai-gakari (接待係) a *receptionist*.
2 section (of a company, organization, etc.) 《⇨ kakari》

-gakari² がかり（掛かり）*suf.* take; require:
Sañ-niñ-gakari *de piano o ugokashita.* (三人がかりでピアノを動かした) It *took* three people to move the piano. / *Byooiñ e iku no wa ichi-nichi*-gakari *da.* (病院へ行くのは1日がかりだ) It *takes* the whole day when you go to the hospital. / *Kare wa ni-neñ*-gakari *de sono hoñ o kaita.* (彼は2年がかりでその本を書いた) It *took* him two years to write the book.

ga⌈ke がけ（崖）*n.* cliff; precipice; bluff:
Sono kuruma wa gake *kara ochita.* (その車はがけから落ちた) The car fell over a *precipice*. / *Watashi wa* gake *no fuchi ni tatte, shita o mioroshita.* (私はがけのふちに立って、下を見下ろした) I stood at the edge of the *bluff* and looked down.

ga⌈keku⌉zure がけくずれ（崖崩れ）*n.* landslide:
Goou de gakekuzure *ga okita.* (豪雨で崖崩れが起きた) The *heavy rain* set off a landslide.

ga⌈kka がっか（学科）*n.* **1** department (of a university):
seeji-gakka (政治学科) the *department* of political science.
2 subject; a course of study:
Gakka *ni wa jishiñ ga aru ga jitsugi wa nigate da.* (学科には自信があるが実技は苦手だ) In *academic subjects* I have confidence, but I am poor in practical skills.

ga⌈kkai がっかい（学会）*n.* learned society; academic conference:
gakkai *ni shusseki suru* (学会に出席する) attend an *academic meeting* / *Butsuri*-gakkai *ga Kyooto de hirakareta.* (物理学会が京都で開かれた) The *physics convention* was held in Kyoto.

ga⌈kka⌉ri がっかり *adv.* (～ suru) be disappointed; lose heart:
Ichi-do kurai no shippai de soñna ni gakkari *suru koto wa arimaseñ.* (一度くらいの失敗でそんなにがっかりすることはありません) You shouldn't *lose heart* over just one failure. / *Shiai ga ame de chuushi ni nari,* gakkari *shita.* (試合が雨で中止になり、が

っかりした) I *was* very *disappointed*, because the game was rained out. 《⇨ shitsuboo》

ga「kki[1] がっき (学期) *n.* term; semester:
ichi[ni; sañ]-gakki (一 [二; 三] 学期) the first [second; third] *term.*
★ Japanese elementary schools and junior and senior high schools have three terms. Universites and colleges have two terms.

ga「kki[2] がっき (楽器) *n.* (musical) instrument:
gakki o hiku (楽器をひく) play an *instrument.*

ga「kkoo がっこう (学校) *n.* school:

CULTURE

Usually refers to the compulsory six years of elementary school and the three years of junior high school, plus the optional three years of senior high school. Informally refers to a university.

---

gakkoo e iku (学校へ行く) go to *school* / gakkoo kara kaeru (学校から帰る) return home from *school* / gakkoo o yasumu (学校を休む) be absent from *school* / gakkoo ni hairu (学校に入る) enroll in *school* / gakkoo o sotsugyoo suru (学校を卒業する) graduate from *school* / gakkoo de beñkyoo suru (学校で勉強する) study at *school* / Gakkoo wa hachi-ji-hañ ni hajimarimasu. (学校は 8 時半に始まります) *School* begins at 8:30.

ga「ku[1] がく (額) *n.* sum; amount:
Bokiñ wa yotee shita gaku ni tasshita. (募金は予定した額に達した) The money collected reached the expected *amount.* / Tsukatta gaku wa yosoo o uwamawatta. (使った額は予想を上回った) The *amount* of the money spent was more than we had expected.

ga「ku[2] がく (額) *n.* framed pic-

ture; frame:
e o gaku ni ireru (絵を額に入れる) set a picture in a *frame* / Gaku o kabe ni kaketa. (額を壁に掛けた) I hung a *framed picture* on the wall.

ga「ku[3] がく (学) *n.* learning; knowledge; education:
Ano hito wa gaku ga aru. (あの人は学がある) He *is well-educated.*

-gaku がく (学) *suf.* science; study:
butsuri-gaku (物理学) *physics* / shakai-gaku (社会学) social *science* / geñgo-gaku (言語学) *linguistics* / ka-gaku (化学) *chemistry.*

ga「kubu がくぶ (学部) *n.* college; faculty; department; school:
koo-gakubu (工学部) the *college* of engineering / hoo-gakubu (法学部) the *faculty* of law / i-gakubu (医学部) the medical *school* / buñ-gakubu (文学部) the *department* of literature / ri-gakubu (理学部) the *college* of science / keezai-gakubu (経済学部) the *department* of economics. (⇨ bu[1])

ga「kuchoo がくちょう (学長) *n.* the president of a university; chancellor.

ga「kufu がくふ (楽譜) *n.* (sheet) music; score:
gakufu o yomu (楽譜を読む) read *music.*

ga「kuhi がくひ (学費) *n.* school expenses; tuition:
gakuhi o kasegu (学費を稼ぐ) earn one's *school expenses.*

ga「ku」moñ がくもん (学問) *n.* learning; study; education:
gakumoñ no aru hito (学問のある人) a person of *learning* / Kare wa isshoo o gakumoñ ni sasageta. (彼は一生を学問に捧げた) He devoted his whole life to *study.*

ga「kuneñ がくねん (学年) *n.* school [academic] year; grade:
Nihoñ no chuugaku wa sañ gaku-

neñ *aru.*（日本の中学は3学年ある）
Junior high schools in Japan
have three *grades.* / *Nihoñ no shiñ*
gakuneñ *wa shi-gatsu ni hajimarimasu.*（日本の新学年は四月に始まりま
す）The Japanese *school year* begins in April.

ga⌐kureki　がくれき（学歴）*n.* educational background; schooling:
Nihoñ de wa gakureki *ga mono o
iu.*（日本では学歴がものを言う）In
Japan, *educational background*
counts a great deal. / *Kare wa
hotoñdo* gakureki *ga nakatta.*（彼は
ほとんど学歴がなかった）He had little
schooling.

ga⌐kuryoku　がくりょく（学力）*n.*
academic ability; scholarship:
Gakusee no gakuryoku *wa zeñtai
to shite agatte iru.*（学生の学力は全
体として上がっている）The overall
academic ability of the students
is improving.

ga⌐kusee　がくせい（学生）*n.*
student:

(USAGE)

Refers to older students, especially college students. Junior
and senior high school students are usually called '*seeto.*'

Watashi wa kono daigaku no
gakusee *desu.*（私はこの大学の学生で
す）I am a *student* at this univer-

detachable collar

GAKUSEE-FUKU

sity. / gakusee-*seekatsu o tanoshimu*（学生生活を楽しむ）enjoy
one's *student* life / gakusee-*fuku*
（学生服）a *school* uniform, especially for a male student / gaku-
see-*shoo*（学生証）a *student* identification card.

ga⌐kusetsu　がくせつ（学説）*n.*
theory.

ga⌐kusha　がくしゃ（学者）*n.*
scholar; learned man.

ga⌐kushuu　がくしゅう（学習）*n.*
learning; study. ★ Usually refers to the process of studying.
　gakushuu suru（～する）*vt.* learn;
study: *Eego wa chuugaku de* gakushuu shimasu.（英語は中学で学習
します）We *study* English at junior
high school.

ga⌐kushu⌐usha　がくしゅうしゃ（学
習者）*n.* learner.

ga⌐mañ　がまん（我慢）*n.* endurance; patience; preserverance:
Moo gamañ *no geñkai desu.*（もう
我慢の限界です）I've come to the
end of my *patience.* / *Kare no
busahoo wa* gamañ *dekinakatta.*
（彼の不作法は我慢できなかった）I
could not stand his rudeness.
　gamañ suru（～する）*vt.* **1** endure; stand; put up with: *Itai no
o* gamañ shita.（痛いのを我慢した）I
endured the pain. / *Soo-oñ ga*
gamañ dekinai.（騒音が我慢できない）
I *cannot put up with* the noise.
2 manage; make do with: *Koñgetsu no o-kozukai wa kore de*
gamañ shi nasai.（今月のお小遣いは
これで我慢しなさい）Please try to
manage with this much allowance this month. / *Kono fuyu wa
furui oobaa de* gamañ shita.（この
冬は古いオーバーで我慢した）I *made
do with* my old overcoat this winter.
3 let off: *Koñdo dake wa* gamañ
shite *yaru.*（今度だけは我慢してやる）
I'll *let* you *off* just this once.

gamañ ga naranai (～がならない) cannot stand: *Kono atsusa wa* gamañ ga naranai. (この暑さは我慢がならない) I *cannot stand* this heat. / *Kare ni wa moo* gamañ ga naranai. (彼にはもう我慢がならない) I *have lost patience with* him.

gamañ-zuyoi (～強い) be very patient.

-gamashiˈi がましい *suf.* (*a.*) (-ku) sound like; smack of: *Kare no setsumee wa iiwake-*gamashikatta. (彼の説明は言い訳がましかった) His explanation *sounded like* an excuse. / *Taniñ-*gamashii *koto wa yoshimashoo.* (他人がましいことはよしましょう) Please don't behave *like* a stranger.

gaˈmigami がみがみ *adv.* (～ to) (the manner of insisting or needlessly saying something): *Soñna chiisa-na koto de* gamigami iu *no wa yoshi nasai.* (そんな小さなことでがみがみ言うのはよしなさい) Don't *go on so* about such a trivial matter. / *Uchi no kachoo wa itsu-mo* gamigami (to) urusai. (うちの課長はいつもがみがみ(と)うるさい) Our section chief *is* always *nagging* us. / *Kare wa kodomo-tachi o* gamigami (*to*) *shikatta.* (彼は子どもたちをがみがみ(と)しかった) He *snappishly* scolded the children.

gaˈñ がん (癌) *n.* cancer: *Kare wa hai[i]-*gañ *de shiñda.* (彼は肺[胃]がんで死んだ) He died of lung [stomach] *cancer.*

gaˈñbaˈr·u がんばる (頑張る) *vi.* (-bar·i-; -bar·a-; -bat·te C) **1** work hard; persevere: Gañbatte, *repooto o kakiageta.* (頑張って、レポートを書き上げた) I *worked hard* and finished writing the paper. / *Atarashii shokuba de* gañbarimasu. (新しい職場で頑張ります) I will *do my utmost* in my new place of work. / *Saigo made* gañbare. (最後まで頑張れ) *Stick it out* to the last!

2 insist: *Kare wa jibuñ ga tadashii to* gañbatta. (彼は自分が正しいと頑張った) He *insisted* that he was right.

3 refuse to move; block: *Gaadomañ ga iriguchi ni* gañbatte ita. (ガードマンが入り口に頑張っていた) A security guard *was blocking* the entrance. / *Kodomo ga terebi no mae ni* gañbatte ite, ugokanai. (子どもがテレビの前に頑張っていて、動かない) The child is in front of the television, *refusing to move.*

gañbatte (ne) (頑張って(ね)) good luck: *Shikeñ* gañbatte ne! (試験頑張ってね) *Good luck* in your exams! ★ Used in giving encouragement.

gaˈñjitsu がんじつ (元日) *n.* New Year's Day. 《⇨ shoogatsu; shukujitsu (table)》

gaˈñjoo がんじょう (頑丈) *a.n.* (～ na, ni) strong; firm; sturdy: gañjoo *na kuruma* (がんじょうな車) a *solidly-built* car / *Kono hoñbako wa* gañjoo *ni dekite iru.* (この本箱はがんじょうにできている) This bookcase is *well put together.*

gaˈñka がんか (眼科) *n.* ophthalmology: gañka-i (眼科医) an *eye doctor.* 《⇨ byooiñ (table)》

gaˈñkiñ がんきん (元金) *n.* monetary principal: *Juumañ-eñ no* gañkiñ *ni rokuseñ-eñ no rishi ga tsuita.* (十万円の元金に6千円の利子がついた) The *principal* of 100,000 yen yielded an interest of 6,000 yen. 《↔ rishi》

gaˈñko がんこ (頑固) *a.n.* (～ na, ni) **1** (of a person) stubborn; obstinate: *Chichi wa* gañko *da.* (父はがんこだ) My father is *stubborn.* / *Suzuki-sañ wa mukashi kara no yarikata o* gañko *ni mamotte iru.* (鈴木さんは昔からのやり方をがんこに守っている) Mr.

Suzuki has *stubbornly* kept to the old ways.
2 (of a disease, stains, etc.) incurable; stubborn:
gañko *na byooki* (がんこな病気) a disease which is very *difficult to treat* / Gañko *na yogore ni kono señzai ga yoi.* (がんこな汚れにこの洗剤がよい) This detergent is good for *stubborn* stains.

ga⌐ñpeki　がんぺき (岸壁) *n.* quay; wharf:
fune o gañpeki *ni tsukeru* (船を岸壁につける) bring a ship alongside the *wharf.*

ga⌐ñrai　がんらい (元来) *adv.* originally; by nature. 《⇨ hoñrai (wa)》

ga⌐ñsho　がんしょ (願書) *n.* (written) application; written request:
Gañsho *no shimekiri wa koñgetsu matsu desu.* (願書の締め切りは今月末です) The deadline for *applications* is the end of this month.

ga⌐ppee　がっぺい (合併) *n.* merger; combination; amalgamation:
Sono futatsu no kaisha no gappee *ga uwasa sarete iru.* (その二つの会社の合併がうわさされている) Rumor has it there will be a *merger* of the two companies.
gappee suru (〜する) *vi., vt.* merge; combine: *Sono futatsu no giñkoo wa* gappee *shita.* (その二つの銀行は合併した) The two banks *merged.* / *Futatsu no mura wa* gappee *shite, shi ni natta.* (二つの村は合併して、市になった) The two villages *combined* to become a city.

ga⌐ra　がら (柄) *n.* **1** pattern; design:
hade na [*shibui*] gara (派手な[渋い]柄) showy [sober] *patterns* / *Hoka no* gara *wa arimaseñ ka?* (ほかの柄はありませんか) Don't you have any other *patterns?* / *Kono kire no* gara *wa sukoshi hade sugiru.* (この布の柄は少し派手すぎる) The *design* of this material is a little too loud.

2 build:
Kare wa gara *ga ookii.* (彼は柄が大きい) He *has a large build.*
gara ga warui (〜が悪い) be vulgar; have coarse manners.
gara ni mo naku (〜にもなく) be quite unlike oneself: *Kare wa* gara ni mo naku, *kookyuusha o norimawashite iru.* (彼は柄にもなく, 高級車を乗り回している) It *is quite unlike him*—driving around in a luxury car.

-gara　がら (柄) *suf.* **1** pattern:
hana-gara *no sukaato* (花柄のスカート) a skirt with a flower *pattern.*
2 pertinent to the situation:
Koko wa gakkoo desu kara, ba-sho-gara *o wakimaete koodoo shi nasai.* (ここは学校ですから, 場所柄をわきまえて行動しなさい) Since this is a school, please behave in a manner *appropriate to the place.* / Shigoto-gara *sake o nomu kikai ga ooi.* (仕事柄酒を飲む機会が多い) *My job being what it is,* I often have occasion to drink.

ga⌐ragara¹　がらがら *a.n.* (〜 na/no, ni) empty:
Heejitsu no eegakañ wa hotoñdo itsu-mo garagara *desu.* (平日の映画館はほとんどいつもがらがらです) Movie theaters on weekdays are almost always *empty.* / *Tookyoo-eki o sugiru to deñsha wa* garagara *ni natta.* (東京駅を過ぎると電車はがらがらになった) After stopping at Tokyo Station, the train became *empty.*

ga⌐ragara²　ガラガラ *adv* (the sound of things crashing or collapsing):
Jishiñ de tatemono ga garagara (to) *kuzureta.* (地震で建物がガラガラ(と)崩れた) The earthquake caused the building to *come crashing down.* / *Kodomo no omocha ga* garagara (to) *oto o tatete, urusa-katta.* (子どものおもちゃがガラガラ(と)音をたてて, うるさかった) The child's

toy made an annoying *rattling noise.*

ga⌐ra⌐ri to がらりと *adv.* **1** with a clatter [noise]:
to o garari to akeru (戸をがらりと開ける) slide open a door *with a noise.* ★ Used only for sliding doors.
2 (of attitude, situation, etc.) completely; suddenly:
Shiñkañseñ no kaitsuu de sono machi no yoosu wa garari to kawatta. (新幹線の開通でその町のようすはがらりと変わった) With the opening of the Shinkansen, the look of that town has changed *completely.* / *Kare wa garari to taido o kaeta.* (彼はがらりと態度を変えた) He *suddenly* changed his attitude.

ga⌐rasu ガラス *n.* glass; pane:
Mado no garasu o watta no wa dare desu ka? (窓のガラスを割ったのはだれですか) Who is it that broke the *windowpane?*

ga⌐reeji ガレージ *n.* garage:

> **USAGE**
>
> Refers to a private garage usually built next to a house. Japanese '*gareeji*' does not refer to a place where cars are repaired and gasoline sold.

Kuruma o gareeji ni ireta. (車をガレージに入れた) I put the car into the *garage.* 《⇨ shako》

-gari がり *suf.* (*n.*) (refers to a person sensitive to the quality suggested by the adjective): ★ Attached to the stem of an adjective to form a noun. It is often followed by '*-ya* (*-sañ*),' which implies familiarity.
kowa-gari (怖がり) a *timid person* / *samu-gari no hito* (寒がりの人) a person *sensitive to the cold* / *sabishi-gari-ya* (寂しがり屋) a person *who always feels lonely and longs for*

company / *tsuyo-gari o iu* (強がりを言う) bluff; talk big.

ga⌐roo がろう (画廊) *n.* gallery.
★ Refers to a store that sells art work, usually Western art. A gallery in an art museum is a '*teñji-shitsu.*'

-ga⌐r·u がる *suf.* (*vi.*) (*-gar·i-; -gar·a-; -gat-te* Ⓒ) [attached to the stem of an adjective or adjectival noun] ★ Not used when asking others about their feelings, emotions, etc.
1 (expresses the feelings or emotions of someone other than the speaker):
atsu-garu (暑がる) *feel hot* / *hoshi-garu* (欲しがる) *want* / *fushigi-garu* (不思議がる) *wonder* at / *kayu-garu* (かゆがる) *itch* / *Kodomo-tachi wa miñna samu-gatte iru.* (子どもたちはみんな寒がっている) The children are all *complaining that they are cold.* / *Kowa-garanakute mo daijoobu desu.* (恐がらなくても大丈夫です) You don't need to *fear.* / *Kanojo wa meñdookusa-gatte heya no sooji o shinai.* (彼女は面倒くさがって部屋の掃除をしない) She *is* too *lazy* to clean her room.
2 pretend:
Kare wa tsuyo-gatte iru dake da. (彼は強がっているだけだ) He is only *pretending to be strong.*

ga⌐soriñ ガソリン *n.* gasoline; petrol:
Gasoriñ o nijuu-rittaa irete kudasai. (ガソリンを20リッター入れてください) Please put in twenty liters of *gasoline.* / *Gasoriñ ga kirete shimatta.* (ガソリンが切れてしまった) We have run out of *gasoline.*

ga⌐soriñ-suta⌐ñdo ガソリンスタンド *n.* [filling] station:
Kono chikaku ni gasoriñ-sutañdo wa arimasu ka? (この近くにガソリンスタンドはありますか) Is there a *gas station* around here?

ga⌐sshoo がっしょう（合唱）*n.* chorus; concerted singing.
gasshoo suru （～する）*vi.* sing in chorus: *Watashi-tachi wa miñna de* gasshoo shita.（私たちはみんなで合唱した）We all *sang together*.

ga⌐sshuku がっしゅく（合宿）*n.* lodging together for training.
gasshuku suru （～する）*vi.* lodge together; have a training camp: *Tenisubu wa Karuizawa de isshuukañ* gasshuku shita.（テニス部は軽井沢で1週間合宿した）The tennis club *had a training camp* at Karuizawa for a week.

ga⌐su ガス *n.* **1** gas: gasu *o tsukeru* [*kesu*]（ガスをつける［消す］）turn on [off] the *gas* / Gasu *ga morete imasu.*（ガスが漏れています）The *gas* is leaking.
2 dense fog: Gasu *ga dete kita.*（ガスが出てきた）A *dense fog* has set in.

-gata がた（方）*suf.* toward: *ake*-gata（明け方）daybreak / *yuu*-gata（夕方）evening.

ga⌐tagata[1] がたがた *adv.* （～ to; suru）**1** rattle; clatter: *Tsuyoi kaze de mado ga* gatagata (to) natta.（強い風で窓ががたがた(と)鳴った）The windows *rattled* in the strong wind. / *Kuruma wa yama no naka no michi o* gatagata (to) hashitta.（車は山の中の道をがたがた(と)走った）The car went *clattering* along the mountain road.
2 shiver; tremble: *Samukute, karada ga* gatagata (to) furueta.（寒くて、体ががたがた(と)震えた）My body *trembled* with cold. / *Kiñchoo no amari ashi ga* gatagata shite, *tomaranakatta.*（緊張のあまり足ががたがたして、止まらなかった）I was so nervous that I could not keep my legs from *shaking*.

ga⌐tagata[2] がたがた *a.n.* （～ na/ no, ni）shaky; rickety: *Koñna* gatagata *no teeburu wa moo tsukaenai.*（こんながたがたのテーブルはもう使えない）I can no longer use such a *rickety* table. / *Kono hashigo wa* gatagata *da.*（このはしごはがたがただ）This ladder is *unsteady*.

-ga⌐tai -がたい（難い）*suf.* (*a.*) (-ku) (*formal*) difficult; impossible: ★ Added to the stem of a verb.
Kare no koodoo wa rikai shi-gatai.（彼の行動は理解しがたい）His behavior *is difficult* to understand. / *Ano hito wa nañ to naku chikayori*-gatai.（あの人は何となく近寄りがたい）I don't know why, but he *is difficult* to approach. 《↔ -yasui》《⇨ -nikui; -zurai》

-ga⌐tera (ni) がてら（に）*suf.* while; at the same time; by way of: ★ Attached to the stem of volitional verbs or nouns that denote action. Note that the last verb phrase indicates the main action.
Yooji o shi-gatera, *asobi ni itta.*（用事をしがてら、遊びに行った）I went out and enjoyed myself *while doing* some errands *at the same time.* / *Sañpo*-gatera (ni), *chotto yotte mita dake desu.*（散歩がてら(に)、ちょっと寄ってみただけです）I just dropped by *while taking a walk.* / *Uñdo*-gatera (ni), *shiba de mo karoo.*（運動がてら(に)、芝でも刈ろう）I think I will cut the grass, and get some exercise *while I am at it.*

─(**USAGE**)─
Note that '-*katagata*' is similar in meaning and can be substituted for '-*gatera*' in the above sentences.

ga⌐tsugatsu がつがつ *adv.* （～ to; ～ suru）hungrily; greedily: ★ Used only to refer to eating.
Soñna ni gatsugatsu (to) *taberu no*

wa yoshi nasai. (そんなにがつがつ(と)食べるのはよしなさい) Don't eat *greedily* like that. (⇨ gabugabu))

ga「wa がわ(側) *n.* side:
Kare-ra ni wa sabetsu sareru gawa no kimochi ga wakaranai. (彼らには差別される側の気持ちがわからない) They are unable to understand the feelings of *those* suffering from discrimination. / *Kootsuu-hi wa kaisha-gawa de dashimasu.* (交通費は会社側で出します) The *company* will pay for transportation expenses. / *Aite-gawa no misu no okage de, karoojite katsu koto ga dekita.* (相手側のミスのおかげで, かろうじて勝つことができた) We just managed to win owing to the *opponent's* error. / *migi* [*hidari*]-gawa (右[左]側) the right [left] *side* / *ryoo*-gawa (両側) both *sides* / *kochira*-gawa (こちら側) this *side*; our *side*.

-gawa がわ(川) *suf.* river.
★ The initial /k/ of '*kawa*' is often changed to /g/ when preceded by the name of the river. *Fuji*-gawa (富士川) the Fuji *River*. (⇨ kawa)

ga「yagaya がやがや *adv.* (~ to) (the noise made by many people talking and laughing):
Kyooshitsu de kodomo-tachi ga gayagaya (to) sawaide iru. (教室で子どもたちががやがや(と)騒いでいる) The children are making *a lot of noise* in the classroom. (⇨ zawazawa))

ge「 げ(下) *n.* lowest grade [class]; inferiority:
Kare no seeseki wa chuu no ge desu. (彼の成績は中の下です) His class standing is in the lower part of the middle grades. (⇨ chuu[1] (table); joo[1]))

-ge げ(気) *suf.* (*a.n.*) (~ na, ni) (indicates the feeling or appearance of others): ★ Attached to the stem of an adjective.

Kazuko wa itsu-mo sabishi-ge na yoosu o shite ita. (和子はいつもさびしげな様子をしていた) Kazuko always looked *sad*. / *Tonari no heya kara tanoshi-ge na waraigoe ga kikoete kita.* (隣の部屋から楽しげな笑い声が聞こえてきた) *Happy* laughter could be heard from the next room. / *Haha-oya wa musuko o hokorashi-ge ni miageta.* (母親は息子を誇らしげに見上げた) The mother *proudly* looked up to her son. / *Shachoo to shitashi-ge ni hanashite iru ano hito wa dare desu ka?* (社長と親しげに話しているあの人はだれですか) Who is that person talking with the president in a *friendly way*?

ge「e げい(芸) *n.* **1** art; skill:
gee o mi ni tsukeru (芸を身につける) acquire a special *art* / *gee o migaku* (芸をみがく) improve one's *skill*.
2 trick:
Inu ni gee o shikoñda. (犬に芸を仕込んだ) I taught my dog *tricks*.

ge「ejitsu = geejutsu.

ge「ejutsu げいじゅつ(芸術) *n.* art; fine arts:
Geejutsu wa nagaku, jiñsee wa mijikai. (芸術は長く, 人生は短い) *Art is long, life is short* (*Ars longa, vita brevis.*)

ge「ejutsuka げいじゅつか(芸術家) *n.* artist.

ge「emu ゲーム *n.* game:
Paatii de wa doñna geemu o shimashita ka? (パーティーではどんなゲームをしましたか) What *games* did you play at the party? / *Geemu setto.* (ゲームセット) The *game* is over.
★ Used when a game of baseball or tennis is finished.

ge「enoo げいのう(芸能) *n.* public entertainment; performing arts:
geenoo-jiñ (芸能人) *public entertainer; show business personality* / *geenoo-kai* (芸能界) the world of

show business.

geˈeto-boˈoru ゲートボール *n.*
'gate ball.' ★ A variant of croquet created in Japan and given a name that corresponds to the words 'gate ball' in English. A popular recreation among the elderly.

GEETO-BOORU

geˈhiˈñ げひん (下品) *a.n.* (~ na, ni) vulgar; coarse; unrefined: *gehiñ na share* (下品なしゃれ) a *vulgar* joke / *Kare wa tokidoki* gehiñ *na kotoba o tsukau.* (彼はときどき下品な言葉を使う) He sometimes uses *coarse* language. 《↔ joohiñ》

geˈjuñ げじゅん (下旬) *n.* the last ten days of a month: *Sañ-gatsu* (*no*) gejuñ *wa neñdo-matsu de isogashii.* (三月(の)下旬は年度末で忙しい) We are busy toward *the end of* March because it is the end of the fiscal year. 《⇨ chuujuñ; joojuñ》

geˈka げか (外科) *n.* surgery: geka-i (外科医) a *surgeon.* 《⇨ byooiñ (table)》

geˈki げき (劇) *n.* drama; play: geki *o jooeñ suru* (劇を上演する) stage a *drama* / *Kono* geki *no shuyaku wa dare desu ka?* (この劇の主役はだれですか) Who plays the lead in this *play?*

geˈkijoo げきじょう (劇場) *n.* theater; playhouse.

geˈkiree げきれい (激励) *n.* encouragement; urging: *Shichoo wa daihyoo señshu ni* gekiree *no kotoba o okutta.* (市長は代表選手に激励の言葉を贈った) The mayor spoke some words of *encouragement* to the representatives of the athletes.

gekiree suru (~する) *vt.* encourage; cheer up: *Kare o* gekiree suru *tame ni kai o hiraita.* (彼を激励するために会を開いた) We gave a party to *cheer* him *up.*

geˈkiyaku げきやく (劇薬) *n.* powerful drug; poison. 《⇨ dokuyaku》

geˈkkañ げっかん (月間) *n.* by the month; monthly: gekkañ *no uriage* (月間の売り上げ) *monthly* sales / *Kono koñpyuutaa no seesañ-daka wa* gekkañ *goseñ-dai desu.* (このコンピューターの生産高は月間5千台です) Five thousand units of this computer are produced *monthly.* 《⇨ neñkañ》

geˈkkyuu げっきゅう (月給) *n.* monthly pay [salary]: *Kare wa kekkoo ii* gekkyuu *o moratte iru.* (彼は結構いい月給をもらっている) He gets a very decent *monthly salary.* / gekkyuu-*tori* (月給取り) a *salaried* employee. 《⇨ chiñgiñ》

geˈkoo げこう (下校) *n.* leaving school: Gekoo *no tochuu de ame ni furareta.* (下校の途中で雨に降られた) I was caught in the rain on my way home *from school.*

gekoo suru (~する) *vi.* leave school: *Moo* gekoo suru *jikañ da.* (もう下校する時間だ) Now it is time to *go home.* 《↔ tookoo》

geˈñba げんば (現場) *n.* the scene; the spot: *Kare wa* geñba *ni kaketsuketa.* (彼は現場にかけつけた) He rushed to the *scene.* / *Koko ga jiko-*geñba *desu.* (ここが事故現場です) This is the *spot* where the accident occurred. / *Sagyoo-*geñba *de wa herumetto o kaburu koto.* (作業現場ではヘルメットをかぶること) Helmets must be worn on the work *site.* /

Suri wa geñba *o osaerareta.* (すりは現場を押さえられた) The pickpocket was caught *in the act of* stealing.

ge⌐ñbaku げんばく (原爆) *n.* = geñshi-bakudañ.

ge⌐ñchi げんち (現地) *n.* the spot; the place: Geñchi *kara no hookoku wa mada kite imaseñ.* (現地からの報告はまだ来ていません) Reports from *the scene* have not yet come in. / *Kare wa sugu ni* geñchi *e toñda.* (彼はすぐに現地へ飛んだ) He flew to *the place* immediately. / geñchi-*jikañ* (現地時間) *local* time.

ge⌐ñdai げんだい (現代) *n.* the present age [day]; today: Geñdai *wa koñpyuutaa no jidai desu.* (現代はコンピューターの時代です) *Now* is the age of the computer. / geñdai-*buñgaku* (現代文学) *contemporary* literature / geñdai-*oñgaku* (現代音楽) *modern* music.

ge⌐ñdai-teki げんだいてき (現代的) *a.n.* (~ na, ni) modern: geñdai-teki *na keñchiku* (現代的な建築) *modern* architecture / *Ano hito wa rokku ga daisuki na* geñdai-teki *na obaasañ da.* (あの人はロックが大好きな現代的なおばあさんだ) She is a *modern* old lady who just loves rock 'n' roll.

ge⌐ñdo げんど (限度) *n.* limit; limitations; bounds: geñdo *o koeru* (限度を越える) exceed the *limit* / *Nanigoto ni mo* geñdo *ga aru.* (何事にも限度がある) There is a *limit* to everything. / *O-kane wa* geñdo-*nai nara, ikura de mo kariraremasu.* (お金は限度内なら、いくらでも借りられます) You can borrow as much money as you want within the *limit.*

ge⌐ñgo げんご (言語) *n.* language; speech; words: geñgo-*shoogai* (言語障害) a *speech* defect.

ge⌐ñgo⌐gaku げんごがく (言語学)

n. linguistics.

ge⌐ñgo⌐o げんごう (元号) *n.* name of an era.

Meeji	September 8, 1868– July 30, 1912
Taishoo	July 30, 1912– December 25, 1926
Shoowa	December 25, 1926– January 7, 1989
Heesee	January 8, 1989–

ge⌐ñiñ げんいん (原因) *n.* cause; factor; origin. *Sono jiko wa yopparai-uñteñ ga* geñiñ *datta.* (その事故は酔っ払い運転が原因だった) Drunken driving was the *cause* of the accident. / *Keesatsu wa kaji no* geñiñ *o shirabete iru.* (警察は火事の原因を調べている) The police are trying to find the *cause* of the fire. 《↔ kekka》

ge⌐ñjitsu げんじつ (現実) *n.* actuality; reality: Geñjitsu *wa kimi ga kañgaete iru yori mo kibishii.* (現実は君が考えているよりも厳しい) *Reality* is tougher than you think. / *Sore wa* geñjitsu *ni okotta koto desu.* (それは現実に起こったことです) It is something which *actually* happened. / *Yume ga* geñjitsu *to natta.* (夢が現実となった) The dream came *true.*

ge⌐ñjitsu-teki げんじつてき (現実的) *a.n.* (~ na, ni) realistic; down-to-earth: *Motto* geñjitsu-teki *na seesaku o toru hitsuyoo ga aru.* (もっと現実的な政策をとる必要がある) It is necessary to adopt a more *realistic* policy. / *Sono keekaku wa* geñjitsu-teki *de wa nai.* (その計画は現実的ではない) The plan is not *realistic.*

ge⌐ñjoo げんじょう (現状) *n.* the present condition: *Watashi-tachi wa* geñjoo *ni mañzoku shite imasu.* (私たちは現状に満

足しています) We are content with *the present situation.* / Geñjoo o iji suru no wa muzukashii.(現状を維持するのは難しい) It is difficult to maintain *the existing state of affairs.*

ge「ñjuu　げんじゅう (厳重) *a.n.* (～ na, ni) strict; severe; strong: geñjuu na keñsa (厳重な検査) a *close* inspection / geñjuu ni tsutsumu (厳重に包む) wrap *carefully and thoroughly* / Kyootee-ihañ ni taishite, geñjuu ni koogi shita.(協定違反に対して、厳重に抗議した) We made a *strong* protest against their breach of the agreement. / Keesatsu wa yopparai-uñteñ o geñjuu ni torishimaru beki da.(警察は酔っ払い運転を厳重に取り締まるべきだ) The police should exercise *strict* control over drunken driving.

ge「ñju」usho　げんじゅうしょ (現住所) *n.* one's present address. 《⇒ juusho》

ge「ñkai　げんかい (限界) *n.* boundary; limit; limitations: niñgeñ no chishiki no geñkai (人間の知識の限界) the *boundaries* of human knowledge / Shuuyoo nooryoku ni wa geñkai ga arimasu.(収容能力には限界があります) There is a *limit* to how many people we can accommodate. / Watashi wa tairyoku no geñkai ni chikakatta.(私は体力の限界に近かった) I was near the *limits* of my physical strength. / Sore wa watashi no nooryoku no geñkai o koete imasu.(それは私の能力の限界を越えています) That is beyond the *limit* of my ability.

ge「ñkañ　げんかん (玄関) *n.* front door; entrance; porch: Geñkañ kara haitte kudasai.(玄関から入ってください) Please come in by *the front door.*

ge「ñki　げんき (元気) *n.* spirits; vigor; energy:

Kodomo-tachi wa geñki ga ii [nai].(子どもたちは元気がいい[ない]) The children are in high [low] *spirits.* / Totemo tsukarete, hanasu geñki mo nai.(とても疲れて、話す元気もない) I'm so tired I *don't even feel like* talking. / Motto geñki o dashi nasai.(もっと元気を出しなさい) *Cheer up!*

geñki-zukeru　(～づける) *vt.* encourage: Señsee no kotoba ni geñki-zukerareta.(先生の言葉に元気づけられた) I *was encouraged* by the teacher's words.

— *a.n.* (～ na, ni) **1** well; fine; healthy: ★ The honorific 'o' ('o-geñki') is often used when enquiring about someone's health, but never used when referring to oneself, one's family members, etc.

"O-geñki desu ka?" "Hai, geñki desu."(「お元気ですか」「はい、元気です」) "How are you?" "*Fine,* thank you." / Kazoku wa miñna geñki desu.(家族はみんな元気です) My family are all *well.* / Kaze ga naotte, geñki ni narimashita.(かぜが治って、元気になりました) My cold got better and I *perked up.*
2 lively; high-spirited; energetic; vigorous; active: Shachoo wa hachijus-sai da ga totemo geñki desu.(社長は80歳だがとても元気です) The president is eighty years old, but he is very *energetic.* / O-matsuri ni geñki na wakamono-tachi ga atsumatta.(お祭りに元気な若者たちが集まった) *Active and vigorous* young people got together at the festival. / Motto geñki ni utai nasai.(もっと元気に歌いなさい) Sing with more *spirit.*

ge「ñki」ñ　げんきん (現金) *n.* cash: geñkiñ de harau (現金で払う) pay in *cash* / Geñkiñ o mochi-aruku no wa abunai.(現金を持ち歩くのは危な

い) It is not safe to carry *cash* around with you.

ge⌐ñki⌐ñ² げんきん (現金) *a.n.* (~ na, ni) calculating; mercenary:
Kare wa geñkiñ *na otoko da.* (彼は現金な男だ) He is a *calculating* fellow.

ge⌐ñki⌐ñ³ げんきん (厳禁) *n.* strict prohibition:
chuusha geñkiñ (*sign*) (駐車厳禁) *No* Parking / *kaki* geñkiñ (*sign*) (火気厳禁) *Caution*: Inflammable Materials / *Kikeñ-buppiñ mochikomi* geñkiñ. (*sign*) (危険物品持ち込み厳禁) Dagerous Articles *Prohibited*.

VARIOUS GEÑKIÑ SIGNS

geñkiñ suru (~する) *vt.* strictly prohibit [forbid]: *Kono heya ni hairu koto wa* geñkiñ *sarete iru.* (この部屋に入ることは厳禁されている) Entry into this room *is strictly forbidden*.

ge⌐ñkoo げんこう (原稿) *n.* manuscript; copy:
geñkoo-*ryoo* (原稿料) a payment for a *written contribution*.

ge⌐ñkoo-yo⌐oshi げんこうようし (原稿用紙) *n.* manuscript [writing] paper:
yoñhyaku-ji-zume geñkoo-yooshi (四百字詰め原稿用紙) *manuscript paper* with four hundred squares for characters. ★ The customary way of submitting compositions and manuscripts for publication.

ge⌐ñ ni げんに (現に) *adv.* actually; really:
Watashi wa geñ ni *sore o kono me de mimashita.* (私は現にそれをこの目で見ました) I *actually* saw it with my own eyes.

ge⌐ñpatsu げんぱつ (原発) *n.* nuclear power plant. ★ Abbreviation of '*geñshiryoku hatsudeñsho*.' (⇨ geñshiryoku)

ge⌐ñri げんり (原理) *n.* principle; theory.

ge⌐ñroñ げんろん (言論) *n.* speech; writing:
geñroñ *no jiyuu* (言論の自由) freedom of *speech*.

ge⌐ñryo⌐o げんりょう (原料) *n.* raw materials; ingredient:
Nihoñ wa gomu no geñryoo *o yunyuu shite iru.* (日本はゴムの原料を輸入している) Japan imports *natural* rubber. / *Pañ no* geñryoo *wa komugiko desu.* (パンの原料は小麦粉です) The *basic ingredient* of bread is flour. / *Uisukii no* geñryoo *wa nañ desu ka?* (ウイスキーの原料は何ですか) What are the *basic ingredients* of whisky?

ge⌐ñsaku げんさく (原作) *n.* the original (work).

ge⌐ñshi げんし (原子) *n.* atom.

ge⌐ñshi-ba⌐kudañ げんしばくだん (原子爆弾) *n.* atomic bomb. (⇨ geñbaku)

ge⌐ñshi⌐kaku げんしかく (原子核) *n.* atomic nucleus.

ge⌐ñshi⌐ro げんしろ (原子炉) *n.* nuclear reactor.

ge⌐ñshi⌐ryoku げんしりょく (原子力) *n.* atomic energy; nuclear power:
geñshiryoku *hatsudeñ* (原子力発電) *nuclear power* generation / geñshiryoku *señsuikañ* (原子力潜水艦) a *nuclear* submarine / geñshiryoku *kuubo* (原子力空母) a *nuclear-powered* aircraft carrier.

ge⌐ñsho げんしょ (原書) *n.* the

original (book) written in a foreign language:
Eego no geñsho (英語の原書) an English book in the *original* / *Watashi wa 'Geñji Monogatari' o* geñsho *de yoñda.* (私は「源氏物語」を原書で読んだ) I read *The Tale of Genji* in the *original.*

ge⌐ñshoo[1] (減少) *n.* decrease; diminution.

geñshoo suru (〜する) *vi.* decrease; diminish; lessen: *Jiñkoo wa sukoshi-zutsu* geñshoo shite *imasu.* (人口は少しずつ減少しています) The population *is decreasing* little by little. / *Oobosha no kazu wa sañ-buñ no ichi ni* geñshoo shite shimatta. (応募者の数は1/3に減少してしまった) The number of the applicants *was reduced* to one-third. (↔ zoodai; zooka)

ge⌐ñshoo[2] げんしょう (現象) *n.* phenomenon:
shizeñ geñshoo (自然現象) a natural *phenomenon* / *Fushigi na* geñshoo *ga okita.* (不思議な現象が起きた) A strange *phenomenon* occurred.

ge⌐ñshu げんしゅ (厳守) *n.* strict observance; rigid adherence:
Kaigi (ni) wa jikañ geñshu *no koto.* (会議(に)は時間厳守のこと) *Strict punctuality* for meetings is required.

geñshu suru (〜する) *vt.* observe strictly: *Kisoku wa* geñshu shinakereba narimaseñ. (規則は厳守しなければなりません) We *must strictly observe* the rules.

ge⌐ñshuu げんしゅう (減収) *n.* decrease in income [revenue]:
Kanojo wa paato o yametara, go-mañ-eñ no geñshuu *ni natta.* (彼女はパートをやめたら、5万円の減収になった) When she quit her part-time job, her income *decreased* by 50,000 yen. (↔ zooshuu)

ge⌐ñso げんそ (元素) *n.* chemical element.

ge⌐ñsoku げんそく (原則) *n.* principle; general rule:
geñsoku *o tateru* [*mamoru*] (原則をたてる[守る]) formulate [observe] a *principle* / *keezai no* geñsoku (経済の原則) economic *principles.*

geñsoku to shite (〜として) in principle: Geñsoku to shite *sono kañgae ni wa hañtai desu.* (原則としてその考えには反対です) *In principle*, I object to the idea.

ge⌐ñzai げんざい (現在) *n.* the present time; now:
Watashi wa geñzai *koko ni suñde imasu.* (私は現在ここに住んでいます) I live here *now*. / *Kore ga watashi no* geñzai *no kaisha desu.* (これが私の現在の会社です) This is my *present* company. / *Geñzai no tokoro, subete wa umaku itte imasu.* (現在のところ、すべてはうまく行っています) Everything is going well *at present*. (⇒ ima[1])

...geñzai (...〜) as of...: *Hachi-gatsu tooka* geñzai, *oobosha wa gojuu-niñ desu.* (8月10日現在、応募者は50人です) The number of applicants is fifty *as of* August 10.

kako	geñzai	mirai
the past	the present	the future

ge⌐ñzoo げんぞう (現像) *n.* development.

geñzoo suru (〜する) *vt.* develop: *Kono fuirumu o* geñzoo shite *kudasai.* (このフイルムを現像してください) Please *develop* this film.

ge⌐ppu げっぷ (月賦) *n.* monthly installment [payment]:
kuuraa o geppu *de kau* (クーラーを月賦で買う) buy an air conditioner in *monthly installments* / geppu *de shiharau* (月賦で支払う) make payment by *monthly installments.*

ge¹ragera げらげら *adv.* (~ to)
(the act of laughing loudly):
*Sono okashi-na hanashi o kiite
miñna wa* geragera *(to) waratta.*
(そのおかしな話を聞いてみんなはゲラゲラ
(と)笑った) Everyone *guffawed*
when they heard the funny story.

ge⌐ri げり (下痢) *n.* diarrhea:
geri *o suru [tomeru]* (下痢をする[止
める]) suffer from [cure] *diarrhea.*
《⇨ kudaru》

ge⌐sha げしゃ (下車) *n.* getting off
(a train).
gesha suru (~する) *vi.* get off (a
train): *Tsugi no eki de* gesha shimasu. (次の駅で下車します) I *get off*
at the next station. 《⇨ tochuu-
gesha; oriru》

ge⌐shi げし (夏至) *n.* summer solstice (about June 21). 《⇨ tooji》

ge⌐shuku げしゅく (下宿) *n.*
1 boardinghouse; rooming
house:
Watashi wa ima geshuku *o sagashite imasu.* (私は今下宿を探していま
す) I am now looking for a *boardinghouse.*
2 boarding; lodging.
geshuku suru (~する) *vi.* board;
live in a rooming house: *Kare
wa oji-sañ no ie ni* geshuku shite
iru. (彼はおじさんの家に下宿している)
He *is boarding* at his uncle's.
★ There are few actual boarding
houses left, but persons fifty or
older may refer to a student
living alone in a wooden apartment house as '*geshuku shite iru.*'

ge⌐ssha げっしゃ (月謝) *n.*
monthly tuition; tuition fee:
gessha *o osameru [harau]* (月謝を
納める[払う]) pay one's *tuition fee.*

ge⌐sshoku げっしょく (月食) *n.*
lunar eclipse. 《⇨ nisshoku》

ge⌐ta げた (下駄) *n.* Japanese
wooden sandals:
geta *o haku [nugu]* (げたをはく[ぬぐ])
put on [take off] geta.

PAIR OF GETA

ge⌐tsumatsu げつまつ (月末) *n.*
the end of the month:
Daikiñ wa getsumatsu *made ni
shiharaimasu.* (代金は月末までに支
払います) I will make payment by
the end of the month. 《⇨ shuumatsu; neñmatsu》

ge⌐tsuyo¹o(bi) げつよう(び) (月曜
(日)) *n.* Monday: Getsuyoobi *wa
itsu-mo ki ga omoi.* (月曜日はいつも
気が重い) I always feel blue on
Mondays. 《⇨ yoobi (table)》

gi¹choo ぎちょう (議長) *n.* chairperson; the speaker:
Miñna wa kare o gichoo *ni erañda.*
(みんなは彼を議長に選んだ) They all
chose him *chairman.*

gi⌐dai ぎだい (議題) *n.* topic [sub-
ject] for discussion; agenda:
Sono moñdai wa kyoo no gidai *ni
arimasu.* (その問題はきょうの議題にあ
ります) The question is on today's
agenda. | *Sono keñ wa* gidai *ni
toriagerarenakatta.* (その件は議題に
取り上げられなかった) The matter
was not brought up for *discussion.*

Gi⌐fu-ke¹ñ ぎふけん (岐阜県) *n.*
Gifu Prefecture. An inland prefecture nearly in the center of
Honshu. Home industry is the
mainstay; some of the products
are Japanese paper, lanterns, fans,
umbrellas and lacquerware. Capital city: Gifu.
《⇨ map (E4)》

gi¹iñ ぎいん (議員) *n.* Diet member; member of an assembly:
keñ[shi]-gikai giiñ (県[市]議会議
員) a *member* of the prefectural

[municipal] *assembly*.
《⇨ Shuugiiñ; Sañgiiñ》

giˈjitsu = gijutsu.

giˈjutsu ぎじゅつ（技術）*n.* technique; technology; art; skill:
Nihoñ no gijutsu *wa takaku hyooka sarete iru.*（日本の技術は高く評価されている）Japanese *technology* is highly regarded. / *Nani-ka* gijutsu *o mi ni tsuke nasai.*（何か技術を身につけなさい）Try to acquire some kind of *skill.* / *keñchiku*-gijutsu（建築技術）the *art* of building.

giˈkai ぎかい（議会）*n.* assembly; the Diet; Congress; Parliament.
keñ [*shi*] gikai（県[市]議会）the prefectural [municipal] *assembly.*

giˈkyoku ぎきょく（戯曲）*n.* play; drama:
gikyoku *o kaku*（戯曲を書く）write a *drama.*

-gimi ぎみ（気味）*suf.* touch; shade:
Watashi wa kaze-gimi *desu.*（私はかぜぎみです）I have a *bit* of a cold. / *Kyoo wa* tsukare-gimi *da.*（きょうは疲れぎみだ）I'm *a little tired* today.

giˈmoñ ぎもん（疑問）*n.* question; doubt; problem:
Nani-ka gimoñ *wa arimaseñ ka?*（何か疑問はありませんか）Do you have any *questions*? / *Sono keñ ni tsuite wa* gimoñ *no yochi ga nai.*（その件については疑問の余地がない）There is no room for *doubt* concerning that matter. / *Kare ga kuru ka doo ka* gimoñ *desu.*（彼が来るかどうか疑問です）It is *doubtful* whether he will come or not.
《⇨ utagai》

giˈmu ぎむ（義務）*n.* duty; obligation:
gimu *o hatasu* [*okotaru*]（義務を果たす[怠る]）perform [neglect] one's *duty* / *Wareware wa zeekiñ o osameru* gimu *ga aru.*（われわれは税金を納める義務がある）We have an *obligation* to pay our taxes. / gimu-

kyooiku（義務教育）*compulsory* education.

giˈñ ぎん（銀）*n.* silver.

giˈñkoo ぎんこう（銀行）*n.* bank:
Watashi wa sono giñkoo *ni yokiñ ga arimasu.*（私はその銀行に預金があります）I have a savings account at that *bank.* / *Sono o-kane wa* giñkoo *ni yokiñ shimashita.*（そのお金は銀行に預金しました）I deposited the money in the *bank.*

giˈñkoˈoiñ ぎんこういん（銀行員）*n.* bank clerk.

Giˈñza ぎんざ（銀座）*n.* Ginza.
★ One of the shopping quarters in Tokyo, well-known for its specialty stores.

giˈragira ぎらぎら *adv.* (~ to)
(the state of shining with unpleasant brightness):
giragira (to) suru（ぎらぎら(と)する）*glare* / *Taiyoo ga* giragira (to) *teritsukete ita.*（太陽がぎらぎら(と)照りつけていた）The sun *was glaring down.* / *Kare wa me o* giragira (to) *sasete ita.*（彼は目をぎらぎら(と)させていた）His eyes *were glaring.*
《⇨ kirakira》

giˈriˈ ぎり（義理）*n.* duty; obligation; debt of gratitude:
giri *o tateru* [*kaku*]（義理を立てる[欠く]）do [fail to do] one's *duty* / giri *to niñjoo no itabasami ni naru*（義理と人情の板ばさみになる）be torn between *duty* and love / *Watashi wa kare ni* giri *ga aru.*（私は彼に義理がある）I am under an *obligation* to him. / *Kare wa* giri-*gatai.*（彼は義理がたい）He has a strong sense of *obligation.*

giri no...（~の...）...-in-law: giri no *chichi* [*imooto*]（義理の父[妹]）a father[sister]-*in-law.*

giˈroñ ぎろん（議論）*n.* argument; discussion; dispute:
Giroñ o kasaneta ga ketsuroñ wa denakatta.（議論を重ねたが結論は出なかった）In spite of much *discussion,*

we didn't come to a conclusion. / *Sore wa* giroñ *no yochi wa nai.* (それは議論の余地はない) It is beyond *dispute.*

giroñ (o) suru (〜(を)する) *vt.* argue; discuss; dispute: *Kare-ra wa sono moñdai ni tsuite oogoe de* giroñ *shita.* (彼らはその問題について大声で議論した) They *argued* loudly about the problem. / *Kare to* giroñ *shite mo muda da.* (彼と議論してもむだだ) It's no use *arguing* with him.

gi⌐see ぎせい (犠牲) *n.* **1** sacrifice:
Oya wa kodomo no kyooiku ni ooki-na gisee *o haratte iru.* (親は子どもの教育に大きな犠牲を払っている) Parents make great *sacrifices* to educate their children. / *Doñna ni* gisee *o haratte mo, sore o yaritogemasu.* (どんなに犠牲を払っても, それをやりとげます) *No matter what the cost is,* I will accomplish that.
2 victim:
Chichi wa señsoo no gisee *to natte shiñda.* (父は戦争の犠牲となって死んだ) My father died, a *victim* of war. / *Sono jiko de ooku no* gisee-sha *ga deta.* (その事故で多くの犠牲者がでた) There were a lot of *casualties* in the accident.

gi⌐shi ぎし (技師) *n.* engineer. 《⇒ eñjinia》

gi⌐sshi⌐ri ぎっしり *adv.* (〜 to) closely; tightly; to the full: *Hoñbako ni hoñ ga* gisshiri (*to*) *tsumatte iru.* (本箱に本がぎっしり(と)詰まっている) The bookcase is *tightly* packed with books. / *Deñsha wa* gisshiri *mañiñ datta.* (電車はぎっしり満員だった) The train was *jam-packed.* / *Koñgetsu wa yoyaku de* gisshiri *desu.* (今月は予約でぎっしりです) This month we are *completely* booked up. / *Kanojo wa tañsu ni irui o* gisshiri (*to*) *tsumeta.* (彼女はたんすに衣類をぎ

っしり(と)詰めた) She *stuffed* the clothes into the wardrobe.

gi⌐taa ギター *n.* guitar: gitaa *o hiku* (ギターをひく) play the *guitar.*

go[1] ご (語) *n.* **1** language: *Kare wa sañ-ka-koku-*go *o shaberemasu.* (彼は 3 か国語をしゃべれます) He can speak three *languages.* / *Nihoñ-*go (日本語) the Japanese *language* / *Ee-*go (英語) the English *language* / *gaikoku-*go (外国語) a foreign *language.*
2 word:
Kono go *no imi wa nañ desu ka?* (この語の意味は何ですか) What does this *word* mean? / *gairai-*go (外来語) a *loanword* / *ruigi-*go (類義語) a *synonym.*
3 term:
*señmoñ-*go (専門語) a technical *term.*

go[12] ご (碁) *n.* (the game of) go: go *o utsu* (碁を打つ) play *go.*

GO BOARD LAID OUT WITH STONES

go[13] ご (五) *n.* five. 《⇒ itsutsu; suu[2] (table)》

go- ご (御) *pref.* [added to a noun, usually of Chinese origin]
1 (indicates respect toward the listener):
Go-kazoku *wa o-geñki desu ka?* (ご家族はお元気ですか) Are *your family* all well? / Go-kekkoñ *wa itsu desu ka?* (ご結婚はいつですか) When is *your marriage?*
2 (indicates humility on the part of the speaker):

Watashi ga go-aññai *itashimasu.*
(私がご案内いたします) I'll *show* you
around. / *Kañgee no* go-aisatsu *o
hito-koto mooshiagemasu.* (歓迎の
ご挨拶を一言申し上げます) Please
allow me to say *a few words* of
welcome.
★ Note that the '*go-*' in the following examples is part of the
word: *gohañ, gochisoo,* etc.

-go ご (後) *suf.* after; in:
Mikka-go ni mata kite kudasai.
(三日後にまた来てください) Please
come again *in three days.* / *Kare
no shujutsu-go no keeka wa ryookoo desu.* (彼の手術後の経過は良好で
す) He is doing well *after* the
operation. 《⇨ -mae¹》

go「bogobo ごぼごぼ *adv.* (〜 to)
(gurgling sound):
Oñseñ ga gobogobo *(to) waite iru
no o mimashita.* (温泉がゴボゴボ(と)わ
いているのを見ました) I saw hot
spring water welling up with a
gurgling sound.

go-「busata ごぶさた (御無沙汰) *n.*
long silence (not having been in
touch): ★ Humble form of
'*busata.*' This word is only used
with reference to oneself.
Nagai go-busata *o o-yurushi kudasai.* (長いご無沙汰をお許しください)
Please forgive me for *not getting
in touch with you* for such a long
time.
go-busata suru (〜する) *vi.* do
not see [write] for a long time:
Go-busata shite imasu [shima-
shita] (ご無沙汰しています[しました]) I
haven't seen [*written to*] you *for a
long time.* / Go-busata shite, *mooshiwake arimaseñ.* (ご無沙汰して、
申し訳ありません) I apologize for *my
long silence.*

go「chisoo ごちそう (御馳走) *n.*
treat; feast; entertainment:
*Kanojo wa watashi-tachi no tame
ni* gochisoo *o tsukutte kureta.* (彼

女は私たちのためにごちそうを作ってくれ
た) She prepared a *feast* for us. /
Moo juubuñ ni gochisoo *ni narimashita.* (もう十分にごちそうになりまし
た) I've eaten enough.
gochisoo (o) suru (〜を)する) *vt.*
treat; feast; entertain: *Kare wa
watashi ni teñpura o* gochisoo
shite kureta. (彼は私にてんぷらをごちそ
うしてくれた) He *treated* me to tempura.

go「chisoosama ごちそうさま (御
馳走さま) **1** (used to express
thanks after a meal): ★ The
literal translation is 'It was a nice
feast.'
Gochisoosama (*deshita*) (ごちそうさ
ま(でした)) *Thank you. I really enjoyed the meal.* 《⇨ itadakimasu》 /
Señjitsu wa gochisoosama
deshita. (先日はごちそうさまでした)
Thank you for treating me the
other day.
2 (used to express thanks for hospitality):
Kyoo wa hoñtoo ni gochisoosama
deshita. (きょうは本当にごちそうさまでし
た) *Thank you very much for
your hospitality* today.

go「gaku ごがく (語学) *n.* language study; linguistics:
Kanojo wa gogaku *no sainoo ga
aru.* (彼女は語学の才能がある) She
has a talent for *languages.* / *Kare
wa* gogaku *ga tassha da.* (彼は語学
が達者だ) He is proficient in *languages.*

go「-gatsu ごがつ (五月) *n.* May:
Kodomo no hi wa go-gatsu *itsuka
desu.* (子どもの日は五月五日です)
Children's Day falls on *May* 5.
《⇨ tsuki¹ (table)》

go「geñ ごげん (語源) *n.* origin of
a word; etymology.

go「go ごご (午後) *n.* afternoon;
P.M.:
Ashita no gogo *wa aite imasu.* (あ
したの午後はあいています) I am free

tomorrow *afternoon.* 《↔ gozeñ》
《⇨ hiru (table)》

go⌐hañ ごはん (ご飯) *n.*
1 (cooked [boiled]) rice:
gohañ *o taku* (ご飯を炊く) cook
[boil] *rice* / Gohañ *o ni-hai tabeta.*
(ご飯を2杯食べた) I ate two bowls
of *rice.* / *Pañ yori* gohañ *no hoo
ga suki desu.* (パンよりご飯のほうが好
きです) I prefer *rice* to bread.
《⇨ kome (table)》
2 meal; food:
Haha wa gohañ *no shitaku de isogashii.* (母はご飯の支度で忙しい)
Mother is busy preparing the
meal. / Gohañ *desu yo.* (ご飯ですよ)
Breakfast [*Lunch, Dinner*] *is
ready!* / *Ohiru da kara* gohañ *ni
shiyoo.* (お昼だからご飯にしよう) Since
it is noon, let's have *lunch.*
《⇨ asagohañ; bañgohañ; hirugo-
hañ》

go⌐i ごい (語彙) *n.* vocabulary:
goi *o fuyasu* (語いをふやす) increase
one's *vocabulary* / *Kono jisho wa*
goi *ga hoofu da.* (この辞書は語いが豊
富だ) This dictionary has a large
number of *words.*

go⌐ju⌐u ごじゅう (五十) *n.* fifty.

go⌐juu-no⌐-too ごじゅうのとう (五
重の塔) *n.* five-storied pagoda.

GOJUU-NO-TOO

go⌐ju⌐uoñ ごじゅうおん (五十音) *n.*
the Japanese syllabary. 《⇨ inside
front cover》

go⌐kai ごかい (誤解) *n.* misunderstanding; misapprehension:
gokai *o maneku* [*toku*] (誤解を招く
[解く]) cause [clear up] a *misunderstanding.*

gokai (o) suru (~(を)する) *vt.* mis-
understand; mistake: *Miñna wa
kimi o* gokai shite iru. (みんなは君を
誤解している) Everyone *misunder-
stands* you. / *Kimi wa boku no
kotoba o* gokai shite iru. (君は僕の
言葉を誤解している) You *have mis-
taken* my meaning.

go⌐kaku-kee ごかくけい (五角形)
n. pentagon.

go⌐kiburi ごきぶり *n.* cockroach.

-go⌐kko ごっこ *suf.* play...:
o-isha-sañ-gokko *o suru* (お医者さ
んごっこをする) play *doctor* / o-mise-
ya-sañ-gokko *o suru* (お店屋さんごっ
こをする) play *store.*

-gokochi ごこち (心地) *suf.* feeling:
nori-gokochi *ga ii* [*warui*] (乗り心
地がいい[悪い]) be comfortable
[uncomfortable] to *ride in* / ne-
gokochi *ga ii* (寝心地がいい) be
comfortable to *sleep in* / sumi-
gokochi *ga ii* (住み心地がいい) be
comfortable to *live in.*

go⌐ku ごく (極) *adv.* (*formal*)
very; extremely:
Goku *mare ni shika kare ni aimaseñ.* (ごくまれにしか彼に会いません) I
only meet him *very* infrequently.
/ *Sore wa* goku *saikiñ no dekigoto
desu.* (それはごく最近のでき事です)
That is a *very* recent occurrence.
/ *Sono shiñsoo o shitte iru no wa*
goku *shoosuu no hito desu.* (その真
相を知っているのはごく少数の人です) It
is an *exceedingly* small number of
people who know the truth.

go⌐ku⌐roo ごくろう (ご苦労) *n.*
trouble:
Gokuroo *o kakete, mooshiwake
arimaseñ.* (ご苦労をかけて、申し訳あり
ません) I am very sorry for causing

so much *trouble*.

— *a.n.* (～ na/no) painful; hard: ★ Sometimes used sarcastically. *Kono samui no ni suiee to wa gokuroo na koto da.* (この寒いのに水泳とはご苦労なことだ) It is an *ordeal* to go swimming when it is cold like this. (⇨ gokuroosama)

go「ku「roosama ごくろうさま (御苦労様) thank you for your trouble; thank you very much.

─ USAGE ─
Used to express thanks for a task well done or trouble expended. Not used to superiors. '*Gokuroosama deshita* [*desu*]' sounds more polite. '*Gokuroo-sañ*' is more informal.

go「maka「s·u ごまかす (誤魔化す) *vt.* (-kash·i-; -kas·a-; -kash·i-te Ⓒ) **1** cheat; deceive: *Kare wa kanojo o gomakashite, kane o totta.* (彼は彼女をごまかして、金を取った) He *cheated* her out of her money. / *Soñna koto o itte mo watashi wa gomakasarenai.* (そんなことを言っても私はごまかされない) No matter what you may say, I *will not be taken in*.
2 tell a lie: *Kanojo wa neñree o gomakashite, hatachi da to itta.* (彼女は年齢をごまかして、20歳だと言った) *Lying* about her age, she said that she was twenty years old.
3 gloss over: *Kare wa shippai o waratte gomakashita.* (彼は失敗を笑ってごまかした) He *laughed off* his blunder.
4 embezzle; (of accounts) cook: *Dare-ka ga kaisha no kane o gomakashita.* (だれかが会社の金をごまかした) Someone *embezzled* company money. / *Kare wa choobo o gomakashita.* (彼は帳簿をごまかした) He *cooked* the books.

go「meñ[1] ごめん (御免) excuse me; pardon me; I'm sorry. ★ '*Go-meñ nasai*' is more polite. (⇨ go-meñ kudasai)

go「meñ[2] ごめん (御免) *n.* (used to express refusal): *Soñna shigoto wa gomeñ da.* (そんな仕事はごめんだ) That kind of job *is not for me*.

go「meñ kudasa「i ごめんください (御免下さい) **1** excuse me: ★ Used when arriving or taking one's leave. *Kare wa doa no mae de '*gomeñ kudasai*' to nañ-do ka itta.* (彼はドアの前で「ごめんください」と何度か言った) He called out "*Excuse me*" several times in front of the door. / *Kore de shitsuree shimasu. Gomeñ kudasai.* (これで失礼します。ごめんください) I will now say good-bye here. *Please excuse me*.
2 I am sorry; pardon [forgive] me. (⇨ gomeñ[1])

go「meñ nasa「i ごめんなさい (御免なさい) I am sorry; excuse me; forgive me: *Okurete, gomeñ nasai.* (遅れて、ごめんなさい) *I'm sorry* to be late. / *Mae o gomeñ nasai.* (前をごめんなさい) *Excuse me* for passing in front of you. / *O-saki ni gomeñ nasai.* (お先にごめんなさい) *Excuse me* for leaving before you.

go「mi[1] ごみ (塵・芥) *n.* trash; rubbish; litter; garbage: *moeru gomi to moenai gomi o kubetsu suru* (燃えるごみと燃えないごみを区別する) separate *trash* into burnables and unburnables / *Gomi o sutenai de kudasai.* (*sign*) (ごみを捨てないでください) Don't *litter* please. / *Sono gomi o kono hako ni ire nasai.* (そのごみをこの箱に入れなさい) Put the *trash* in this box. / gomi-*shuushuu* (ごみ収集) *trash* collection / gomi-*suteba* (ごみ捨て場) a *dumping* ground. (⇨ photo (next page))

GOMI SHUUSHUU SCHEDULE SIGN
Schedule for trash pick-up posted
at a local collection point.

go⌐mi¹bako　ごみばこ（ごみ箱）*n.*
trash [garbage] can; dustbin.

go¹mu　ゴム *n.* rubber.

-goo　ごう（号）*suf.* **1** number:
*taifuu juusañ-*goo（台風 13 号）
Typhoon *No.* 13.
2 issue (of a magazine):
*fujiñ-zasshi no sañ-gatsu-*goo（婦
人雑誌の 3 月号）the March *issue*
of a women's magazine.
3 building number.（⇨ *juusho*）

go⌐oiñ　ごういん（強引）*a.n.*（～ na,
ni）forcible; high-handed:
gooiñ *na seerusumañ*（強引なセール
スマン）a *high-handed* salesman
/ *Buchoo wa* gooiñ *ni jibuñ no añ o
tooshita.*（部長は強引に自分の案を通
した）The manager pushed his
plan through *high-handedly.*

go⌐oka　ごうか（豪華）*a.n.*（～ na,
ni）luxurious; magnificent:
oosetsuma o gooka *ni kazaru*（応
接間を豪華に飾る）decorate a draw-
ing room *gorgeously* / *Kare-ra wa*
gooka *na kekkoñ-shiki o ageta.*
（彼らは豪華な結婚式を挙げた）They
held a *splendid* wedding ceremony. / *Kare wa* gooka *na uchi ni
suñde iru.*（彼は豪華な家に住んでいる）
He lives in a *magnificent* house.

go⌐okaku　ごうかく（合格）*n.* passing (an examination); success:
gookaku-*hiñ*（合格品）an article
which has passed (*quality control*)
inspection / gookaku-*sha*（合格者）

a *successful* candidate.
gookaku suru（～する）*vi.* pass;
succeed: *keñsa ni* gookaku suru
（検査に合格する）*pass* an inspection
/ *Kare wa nyuugaku shikeñ ni*
gookaku shita.（彼は入学試験に合格
した）He *passed* the school entrance examination.

go⌐okee　ごうけい（合計）*n.* total;
sum; the sum total:
Gookee *wa nimañ-eñ ni narimasu.*
（合計は 2 万円になります）The *total*
comes to 20,000 yen. / *Shishoosha no* gookee *wa gohyaku-niñ ni
tasshita.*（死傷者の合計は 500 人に達
した）The *total number* of dead
and injured rose to 500.
gookee suru（～する）*vt.* sum up;
total: *Kiñgaku o* gookee shite
kudasai.（金額を合計してください）
Please *total up* the amount of
money.

go⌐orika　ごうりか（合理化）*n.* rationalization:
goorika *hañtai uñdoo*（合理化反対
運動）a movement against *rationalization* (of working conditions, etc.)
goorika suru（～する）*vt.* rationalize: *sañgyoo o* goorika suru（産業
を合理化する）*rationalize* an industry.

go⌐ori-teki　ごうりてき（合理的）
a.n.（～ na, ni）rational; reasonable; practical:
goori-teki *na setsumee*（合理的な説
明）a *rational* explanation / *kaji o*
goori-teki ni suru（家事を合理的にす
る）*streamline* housework / *Kee-
eesha wa* goori-teki *na kañgaekata o shinakereba ikenai.*（経営者
は合理的な考え方をしなければいけない）
A manager should have a *practical* way of thinking.

go¹oru　ゴール *n.* goal; finish
(line):
gooru *ni hairu*（ゴールに入る）reach
the *finish* line.

go「orudeñ-ui「iku ゴールデンウイーク n. 'Golden Week.' ★ Refers to the period from April 29 to May 5, which is full of national holidays. (⇨ shukujitsu)

go「oru「-iñ ゴールイン n. finish; breasting the tape:
gooru-iñ suru (〜する) 1 reach the finish line: *Kare wa ni-chaku de* gooru-iñ *shita.* (彼は2着でゴールインした) He was the second to *cross the finish line.*
2 get married: *Futari wa yatto* gooru-iñ *shita.* (二人はやっとゴールインした) The two of them finally *got married.*

go「osee ごうせい (合成) n. synthesis; composition:
goosee-*jushi* (合成樹脂) *synthetic* resin / goosee-*señi* (合成繊維) *synthetic* fiber.
goosee suru (〜する) vt. compose; synthesize: *tañpakushitsu o* goosee suru (たんぱく質を合成する) *synthesize* proteins.

go「otoo ごうとう (強盗) n. 1 burglar; robber:
Sakuya kono mise ni gootoo *ga haitta.* (昨夜この店に強盗が入った) A *burglar* broke into this store last night.
2 robbery:
gootoo *o hataraku* (強盗をはたらく) commit a *robbery.*

go「raku ごらく (娯楽) n. amusement; recreation; entertainment:
goraku-*bañgumi* (娯楽番組) an *entertainment* program (on TV).

go「rañ ごらん (ご覧) (honorific)
1 see; look at:
Kore o gorañ *kudasai.* (これをご覧ください) Please *look at* this. / *Kare no e wa* gorañ *ni narimashita ka?* (彼の絵はご覧になりましたか) *Have* you *seen* his painting? / *Gorañ no toori, watashi wa geñki desu.* (ご覧のとおり，私は元気です) I'm in good health, *as you see.*

2 try:
Moo ichi-do yatte gorañ *nasai* (もう一度やってご覧なさい) *Try* it again.

-go「ro ごろ (頃) suf. about; around:
*Juuji-*go*ro uchi ni kite kudasai.* (10時ごろうちに来てください) I would like you to come to my house at *about* ten o'clock. / *Kono biru wa haru-*go*ro ni kañsee suru yotee desu.* (このビルは春ごろに完成する予定です) This building is scheduled to be completed *sometime* within the spring. / *"Itsu-*go*ro kara jogiñgu o hajimemashita ka?" "Go-neñ mae kara desu."* (「いつごろからジョギングを始めましたか」「5年前からです」) "*About* when did you take up jogging?" "It's five years ago." (⇨ koro)

go「rogoro ごろごろ adv. (〜 to)
1 (the sound of rolling, rumbling or purring):
Kaminari ga tooku de gorogoro (to) *natte iru.* (雷が遠くでゴロゴロ(と)鳴っている) The thunder *is rolling* in the distance. / *Onaka ga suku to,* gorogoro (to) *naru.* (おなかがすくと，ゴロゴロ(と)鳴る) When one is hungry, one's stomach *rumbles.* / *Neko wa nodo o* gorogoro (to) *narashita.* (猫はのどをゴロゴロ(と)鳴らした) The cat *purred.*
2 (the state of something rolling):
Ooki-na iwa ga yama no shameñ o gorogoro (to) *ochite itta.* (大きな岩が山の斜面をゴロゴロ(と)落ちて行った) A large rock *rolled down* the mountainside.
3 (the state of being plentiful):
Suisu de wa ni-ka-koku-go o hanaseru hito ga gorogoro *iru.* (スイスでは2か国語を話せる人がごろごろいる) In Switzerland *there are many who can speak two languages.*
4 (the state of being lazy):
Kare wa yasumi-juu ie de goro-

goro (to) shite ita. (彼は休み中家でごろごろ(と)していた) He *lolled around* the house all through the holidays.

go⌐ro⌐ri ごろり *adv.* (~ to) (used to express the action of lying down):

Kare wa gorori *to tatami no ue ni yoko ni natta.* (彼はごろりと畳の上に横になった) He *plopped himself down* full length on the tatami.

go⌐rufu ゴルフ *n.* golf:

gorufu *o suru* (ゴルフをする) play *golf.*

-goshi ごし (越し) *suf.* 1 through; over:

Tonari no hito to hee-goshi *ni oshaberi o shita.* (隣の人と塀越しにおしゃべりをした) I had a chat with my neighbor *over* the fence. / *Kuruma no mado*-goshi *ni Yamada-sañ o mikakemashita.* (車の窓越しに山田さんを見かけました) I saw Mrs. Yamada *through* the window of the car. / *Kare wa megane*-goshi *ni watashi o niramitsuketa.* (彼は眼鏡越しに私をにらみつけた) He glared at me *over* his glasses.

2 [after a noun denoting a long period of time] for; over:

Go-neñ-goshi *no koi ga minotte, futari wa kekkoñ shita.* (五年越しの恋が実って、二人は結婚した) Their love of *five years* gradually matured and they got married. / *Ni-neñ*-goshi *no moñdai ga yatto kaiketsu shita.* (二年越しの問題がやっと解決した) The problem which had been *pending for* two years was solved at last.

-goto ごと *suf.* and all; together with:

riñgo o kawa-goto *taberu* (りんごを皮ごと食べる) eat an apple, peel *and all* / *sakana o maru*-goto *ryoori suru* (魚をまるごと料理する) cook a fish *whole.*

-go⌐to ni ごとに *suf.* 1 every; each:

Sooji toobañ wa ik-kagetsu-goto *ni kawarimasu.* (掃除当番は1か月ごとに替わります) Cleaning duty changes *every* month. / *Kurasu*-goto ni *ikeñ o dasu yoo ni tanoñda.* (クラスごとに意見を出すように頼んだ) I asked *each* class to present its ideas.

2 every time; whenever; whoever:

Kare wa au hito-goto ni *sono hanashi o shite iru.* (彼は会う人ごとにその話をしている) He tells that story to *whoever* he meets. / *Kikai ga aru*-goto ni *watashi wa kare ni tabako o yameru yoo ni itte imasu.* (機会があるごとに私は彼にたばこをやめるように言っています) *Whenever* I get an opportunity, I tell him to give up smoking.

go⌐zaima⌐su ございます (御座居ます) be; have; there is [are]:

★ Polite equivalent of '*arimasu.*' The polite equivalent of '*desu*' is '*de gozaimasu.*'

Nani-ka go-yoo ga gozaimashitara, o-shirase kudasai. (何かご用がございましたら、お知らせください) If *there is* anything I can do for you, please let me know. / *Heñji ga okurete mooshiwake* gozaimaseñ. (返事が遅れて申しわけございません) *I am* very sorry for the delay in my reply. / *Shitagi uriba wa sañgai de* gozaimasu. (下着売り場は3階でございます) The underwear section *is* on the third floor. / *O-kawari* gozaimaseñ ka? (お変わりございませんか) *Are* you keeping in good health?

Arigatoo gozaimasu. (ありがとうございます) Thank you very much.

Ohayoo gozaimasu. (お早うございます) Good morning.

go⌐zeñ ごぜん (午前) *n.* forenoon; morning; A.M.:

Kare wa gozeñ *ku-ji ni tsukimasu.* (彼は午前9時に着きます) He will

arrive at nine *in the morning*. /
Kiñyoo no gozeñ *wa aite imasu.*
（金曜の午前はあいています）I am free
on Friday *before twelve*. 《↔ gogo》
《⇨ asa; hiru (table)》

go「**zeñ-chuu**　ごぜんちゅう（午前中）
n., adv. in the morning; any
time from sunrise to noon:
Watashi wa gozeñ-chuu *hima
desu.*（私は午前中ひまです）I am free
all morning. / *Asu* gozeñ-chuu *ni
ukagaimasu.*（あす午前中に伺います）
I will pay you a visit *by noon* tomorrow. / *Kinoo wa netsu o dashite,* gozeñ-chuu *nete imashita.*
（きのうは熱を出して、午前中寝ていまし
た）Yesterday I had a fever and
stayed in bed *all morning*.

go「**zo**]**ñji**　ごぞんじ（ご存じ）(*honorific*) know; be aware:
Kare no atarashii juusho o gozoñji *desu ka?*（彼の新しい住所をご
存じですか）*Do* you *know* his new
address? / *Gozoñji no yoo ni Yamada-sañ wa nyuuiñ-chuu desu.*
（ご存じのように山田さんは入院中です）
As you *are aware*, Mr.Yamada is
in the hospital. 《⇨ zoñjiru》

gu「**ai**　ぐあい（具合）*n.* **1** condition:
Kono kuruma no guai *wa hijoo ni
yoi.*（この車のぐあいは非常に良い）This
car is in excellent *condition*. /
Onaka no guai *ga okashii.*（おなかの
ぐあいがおかしい）I *am sick* to my
stomach. / *Terebi no* guai *ga heñ
da.*（テレビのぐあいが変だ）*There is
something wrong* with the TV.
2 convenience:
Kare wa guai *no warui toki ni
yatte kita.*（彼はぐあいの悪いときにやっ
て来た）He showed up at an *inconvenient* time.
3 manner; way:
Koñna guai *ni yareba, umaku ikimasu.*（こんなぐあいにやれば、うまく行き
ます）If you do it *this way*, you
will succeed.

gu」**ñ**[1]　くん（群）*n.* group; crowd:
Tori wa guñ *o nashite, tobi-satta.*
（鳥は群をなして、飛び去った）The
birds flew away in *flocks*.
《⇨ mure》

guñ o nuku （〜を抜く）excel [sur-
pass] all: *Nihoñgo o hanasu koto
de wa kare wa* guñ *o nuite iru.*（日
本語を話すことでは彼は群を抜いている）
He *is well above the average* in
speaking Japanese.

gu」**ñ**[2]　くん（軍）*n.* force; army;
troops:
riku-guñ（陸軍）the *army* / kai-guñ
（海軍）the *navy* / kuu-guñ（空軍）
the *air force*. 《⇨ jieetai》

gu」**ñ**[3]　くん（郡）*n.* county; district:
*Chiba-keñ, Iñba-*guñ（千葉県印旛
郡）Inba County, Chiba Prefecture. ★ A '*guñ*' may contain one
or more '*machi*' and/or '*mura*.'
There are no '*guñ*' in urban
areas. The term is used only for
postal addresses and has no administrative function.

gu」**ñbi**　くんび（軍備）*n.* armaments; military preparations:
guñbi *o kakuchoo* [*shukushoo*]
suru（軍備を拡張［縮小］する）expand
[reduce] *armaments*.

gu」**ñguñ**　くんくん　*adv.* (〜 to)
quickly; rapidly; steadily:
Kare no Nihoñgo wa guñguñ *jootatsu shite imasu.*（彼の日本語はぐんく
ん上達しています）His Japanese is
rapidly improving. / *Kare wa
kuruma o* guñguñ *(to) tobashita.*
（彼は車をぐんぐん（と）飛ばした）He
drove *very fast*. / *Taroo wa chuugaku ni haitte kara shiñchoo ga*
guñguñ *(to) nobita.*（太郎は中学に入
ってから身長がぐんぐん（と）伸びた）Taro
has shot up in height since he
entered junior high school. /
Hikooki wa ririku-go guñguñ *(to)
koodo o ageta.*（飛行機は離陸後ぐん
ぐん（と）高度をあげた）The plane *rap-*

idly gained altitude after taking off.

gu⌐nji-eñjo ぐんじえんじょ（軍事援助）*n.* military aid.

gu⌐ñjiñ ぐんじん（軍人）*n.* military man; soldier; sailor; airman.

gu⌐ñkañ ぐんかん（軍艦）*n.* warship; man-of-war.

Gu⌐ñma⌐-keñ ぐんまけん（群馬県）*n.* Gunma Prefecture. An inland prefecture almost in the center of Honshu. Sericulture is a major industry and there are many spinning and weaving factories. Capital city: Maebashi (前橋). 《⇨ map (F3)》

gu⌐ñshuu ぐんしゅう（群衆）*n.* crowd; throng; mob:
Guñshuu *wa kare no eñzetsu ni nesshiñ ni mimi o katamuketa.*（群衆は彼の演説に熱心に耳を傾けた）The *crowd* listened attentively to his speech. / *Kare wa* guñshuu *ni kakomareta.*（彼は群衆に囲まれた）He was surrounded by a *crowd.* / guñshuu-*shiñri*（群衆心理）*mass* psychology.

gu⌐ñtai ぐんたい（軍隊）*n.* armed forces; troops.

gu⌐ñtoo ぐんとう（群島）*n.* a group of islands; archipelago. 《⇨ rettoo¹》

gu⌐rabu グラブ *n.* (of baseball and boxing) glove.

gu⌐rafu グラフ *n.* graph:
gurafu *o kaku*（グラフをかく）draw a *graph* / *Kotoshi no uriage o* gurafu *ni shita.*（今年の売上をグラフにした）I made a *graph* of this year's sales figures.

gu⌐ragura ぐらぐら *adv.* (～ to)
1 (unstable shaking or moving):
Jishiñ de ie ga guragura (*to*) *yureta.*（地震で家がぐらぐら（と）揺れた）The house shook *unsteadily* in the earthquake.
2 (the state of water boiling):
Yakañ no yu ga guragura (*to*)

nitatte iru.（やかんの湯がぐらぐら（と）煮立っている）The water in the kettle is boiling *vigorously.*

gu⌐rai ぐらい *p.* = kurai².

gu⌐ramu グラム *n.* gram:
Buta-niku wa hyaku guramu *hyakusañjuu-eñ desu.*（豚肉は100 グラム130 円です）The pork costs 130 yen per 100 *grams.*

gu⌐rañdo グランド *n.* playground; sports ground; stadium:
Kodomo-tachi wa yasumi jikañ ni gurañdo *de asoñda.*（子どもたちは休み時間にグランドで遊んだ）The children played in the *playground* during the break.

gu⌐riiñsha グリーンしゃ（グリーン車）*n.* 'green car'; first-class railway carriage.

gu⌐ro⌐obu グローブ *n.* = gurabu.

gu⌐ruguru ぐるぐる *adv.* (～ to)
(the state of something moving around or rotating continuously):
Tori no mure ga umi no ue o guruguru (*to*) *toñde iru.*（鳥の群れが海の上をぐるぐる（と）飛んでいる）A flock of birds is flying *in circles* above the sea. / *Kare wa te o* guruguru (*to*) *mawashite aizu shita.*（彼は手をぐるぐる（と）回して合図した）He signaled by *waving* his hand *around.*

gu⌐ru⌐tto ぐるっと *adv.* (the action of looking around or the feeling of being completely surrounded):
Kare wa atari o gurutto *miwatashita.*（彼はあたりをぐるっと見渡した）He looked *all around* him. / *koosoo-biru ni* gurutto *torikakomareta kooeñ*（高層ビルにぐるっと取り囲まれた公園）a park *completely* surrounded by high-rise buildings.

gu⌐ru⌐upu グループ *n.* group:
guruupu *o tsukuru*（グループを作る）form a *group* / *Kare no* guruupu *wa juu-niñ iru.*（彼のグループは10 人いる）There are ten people in his

group. / *Zeñtai o mittsu no guruupu ni waketa*. (全体を三つのグループに分けた) We divided it all into three *groups*.

guˈssuˈri ぐっすり *adv*. (〜 to) (the state of sleeping soundly): *Akañboo wa gussuri (to) nete iru*. (赤ん坊はぐっすり(と)寝ている) The baby is sleeping *like a log*. / *Yuube wa gussuri (to) nemureta*. (ゆうべはぐっすり(と)眠れた) I was able to sleep *soundly* last night.

guˈtai-teki ぐたいてき (具体的) *a.n*. (〜 na, ni) concrete; definite: *Keekaku wa gutai-teki na dañkai ni haitta*. (計画は具体的な段階に入った) The plan entered its *concrete* stage. / *Gutai-teki na ree o agete, setsumee shimashoo*. (具体的な例をあげて、説明しましょう) Let me explain by giving *concrete* examples. / *Moo sukoshi gutai-teki ni hanashite kudasai*. (もう少し具体的に話してください) Please speak more *specifically*. ((↔ chuushoo-teki))

guˈtto ぐっと *adv*. **1** suddenly; firmly; fast; hard: *supiido o gutto ageru* (スピードをぐっとあげる) *suddenly* increase speed / gutto *tsukamu* (ぐっとつかむ) grasp *firmly* / gutto *hipparu* (ぐっと引っ張る) pull *with a jerk* / gutto *nomu* (ぐっと飲む) drink *in one gulp* / gutto *niramu* (ぐっとにらむ) stare *hard*.
2 much; by far: *Kotchi no hoo ga gutto hikitatsu*. (こっちのほうがぐっと引き立つ) This one looks *much* better.

guˈuguu ぐうぐう *adv*. (〜 to) (the sound of snoring or that of an empty stomach): *Kare wa guuguu (to) ooki-na ibiki o kaite ita*. (彼はグウグウ(と)大きないびきをかいていた) He was snoring *loudly*. / *Kuufuku de onaka ga guuguu (to) natte iru*. (空腹でおなかが

グウグウ(と)鳴っている) My stomach *is rumbling* with hunger.

guˈusuˈu ぐうすう (偶数) *n*. even number(s). ((↔ kisuu))

guˈuzeñ ぐうぜん (偶然) *a.n*. (〜 na/no, ni) chance; accident: *guuzeñ no dekigoto* (偶然の出来事) a *chance* occurrence / *guuzeñ no itchi* (偶然の一致) a *strange* coincidence / *Wareware no shoori wa kesshite guuzeñ de wa arimaseñ*. (われわれの勝利は決して偶然ではありません) Our victory was by no means a *fluke*.
— *adv*. by chance: *Watashi wa guuzeñ, sono jiko geñba ni ita*. (私は偶然、その事故現場にいた) I just *happened to be* at the scene of the accident.

guˈzuguzu ぐずぐず *adv*. (〜 to; 〜 suru) slowly; lazily: *Kare wa guzuguzu (to) shigoto o nobashita*. (彼はぐずぐず(と)仕事を延ばした) He *put off* getting down to work. / *Guzuguzu suru na!* (ぐずぐずするな) Don't be so *slow*! / *Guzuguzu shite iru to, okuremasu yo*. (ぐずぐずしていると、遅れますよ) If you *dawdle along*, you will be late. / *Koñna tokoro de guzuguzu (to) shite wa irarenai*. (こんなところでぐずぐず(と)してはいられない) We cannot *linger* in a place like this.
guzuguzu iu (〜言う) grumble; complain: *Kare wa itsu-mo nani-ka guzuguzu itte iru*. (彼はいつも何かぐずぐず言っている) He *is* always *grumbling* about something. ((⇒ fuhee))

gyaˈku ぎゃく (逆) *n*. reverse; contrary; opposite: *Gyaku mo mata shiñjitsu desu*. (逆もまた真実です) The *opposite* is also true. / gyaku-*muki* (逆向き) facing *backward*.
— *a.n*. (〜 na/no, ni) reverse; contrary; opposite: gyaku *no hookoo* (逆の方向) the *op-*

posite direction / *Kekka wa yosoo to wa* gyaku *datta.* (結果は予想とは逆だった) The result was *contrary* to our expectations. / *Suuji ga* gyaku *ni natte iru.* (数字が逆になっている) The numbers are in *reverse* order.

gyoˈgyoo ぎょぎょう (漁業) *n.* fishery; fishing industry.
《⇨ noogyoo》

gyoˈkuro ぎょくろ (玉露) *n.* green tea of the highest quality.
《⇨ o-cha (table)》

gyoˈo ぎょう (行) *n.* **1** row of words; line:
Ichi gyoo *oki ni kaki nasai.* (一行おきに書きなさい) Write on every other *line.* / *Ue* [*Shita*] *kara go-*gyoo-*me ni goshoku ga aru.* (上 [下] から5行目に誤植がある) There is a misprint on the fifth *line* from the top [bottom].
2 (of the Japanese syllabary) series:
gojuuoñ-zu no ka gyoo (五十音図のカ行) the 'k' *series* in the list of the Japanese syllabary. 《⇨ inside front cover》

gyoˈogi ぎょうぎ (行儀) *n.* manners; behavior:
Kare no musuko wa gyoogi *ga yoi* [*warui*]. (彼の息子は行儀が良い[悪い]) His son has good [bad] *manners.* / *O-kyaku-sañ ga kitara,* gyoogi *yoku shi nasai.* (お客さんが来たら, 行儀よくしなさい) When guests come, *behave nicely.*

gyoˈoji ぎょうじ (行事) *n.* event; function:
Hina-matsuri wa haru no omo-na gyooji *no hitotsu desu.* (ひな祭は春の主な行事の一つです) The Doll Festival is one of the chief *events* of spring. / *Sono* gyooji *wa yotee doori okonawareta.* (その行事は予定どおり行われた) The *function* took place as scheduled.

gyoˈoretsu ぎょうれつ (行列) *n.*

1 line; queue:
gyooretsu *o tsukuru* (行列を作る) form a *queue* / *Iriguchi no mae ni* gyooretsu *ga dekita.* (入り口の前に行列が出来た) A *line* formed in front of the entrance.
2 procession; parade:
Soogi no gyooretsu *ga shizuka ni susuñda.* (葬儀の行列が静かに進んだ) The funeral *procession* moved forward slowly.

gyooretsu suru (〜する) *vi.* stand in line; queue up: *Watashi-tachi wa* gyooretsu *shite, takushii o matta.* (私たちは行列して, タクシーを待った) We *stood in line* waiting for a taxi.

gyoˈosee ぎょうせい (行政) *n.* administration:
gyoosee-*kaikaku* (行政改革) *administrative* reform / gyoosee-*shidoo* (行政指導) *administrative* guidance. 《⇨ sañkeñ-buñritsu》

gyoˈoseki ぎょうせき (業績) *n.* achievements; results; work:
Kare wa subarashii gakumoñ-teki gyooseki *o ageta* (彼は素晴らしい学問的業績を上げた) He produced outstanding academic *achievements.* / *Kaisha no* gyooseki *wa amari yoku arimaseñ.* (会社の業績はあまり良くありません) Company *business* is not so good.

gyoˈosha ぎょうしゃ (業者) *n.* dealer; trader; manufacturer:
*Kyoo wa kañkee-*gyoosha *no atsumari ga aru.* (きょうは関係業者の集まりがある) We have a meeting of the *traders* concerned today. / *Sono keñ wa* gyoosha *ni makemashita.* (その件は業者にまかせました) We left the matter to the *manufacturer.*

gyoˈoza ぎょうざ *n.* Chinese dumplings. ★ Stuffed with vegetables and ground meat, and fried in oil or steamed.
《⇨ photo (next page)》

GYOOZA

gyo⌐señ　ぎょせん（漁船）　*n.* fishing boat [vessel].

gyo⌐soñ　ぎょそん（漁村）　*n.* fishing village.

gyo⌐tto s·uru　ぎょっとする　*vi.* (-sh·i-; -sh·i-; -sh·i-te ①) be startled; be frightened:
Dare mo inai hazu no heya kara koe ga suru no de gyotto shita. （誰もいないはずの部屋から声がするのでぎょっとした）I *was startled* to hear voices coming from a room that was supposed to be empty. / *Omowazu,* gyotto shite *tachisukuñda.* （思わず，ぎょっとして立ちすくんだ）I *was startled* and couldn't move.

gyu⌐ugyuu　ぎゅうぎゅう　*adv.* (~ to, ni) (the state of squeezing something or of it being tightly packed):
Watashi wa kabañ ni irui o gyuugyuu (*to* [*ni*]) tsumeta. （私はかばんに衣類をぎゅうぎゅう（と[に]）詰めた）I *squeezed* my clothes into the bag. / *Tsuukiñ deñsha wa maiasa* gyuugyuu-zume *da.* （通勤電車は毎朝ぎゅうぎゅう詰めだ）Every morning the commuter trains are *jam-packed.* / *Señsee wa shukudai de gakusee o* gyuugyuu shibotta. （先生は宿題で学生をぎゅうぎゅうしぼった）The teacher really *made* the students *work hard* with the homework she assigned them.

gyu⌐u-niku　ぎゅうにく（牛肉）　*n.* beef. 《⇨ niku》

gyu⌐unyuu　ぎゅうにゅう（牛乳）　*n.* cow's milk:
koppu ip-pai no gyuunyuu （コップ一杯の牛乳）a glass of *milk* / gyuunyuu-*pakku* （牛乳パック）a *milk* carton.

H

ha⌐¹ は（歯）*n.* tooth:
ha o migaku（歯を磨く）brush one's *teeth* / Ha ga itamu.（歯が痛む）My *tooth* hurts. / Ha o nuite moratta.（歯を抜いてもらった）I had a *tooth* out. / Akañboo ni ha ga hae-hajimeta.（赤ん坊に歯が生え始めた）The baby began to cut its *teeth*.
ha ga tatanai（〜がたたない）be beyond one's power.

ha⌐² は（刃）*n.* edge; blade:
kamisori no ha（かみそりの刃）a razor *blade* / Hoochoo no ha o toide moratta.（包丁の刃を研いでもらった）I had the *edge* of the kitchen knife sharpened. / Naifu no ha ga kakete shimatta.（ナイフの刃が欠けてしまった）The *blade* of the knife got chipped.

ha³ は（葉）*n.* leaf; foliage:
Ki [Ko] no ha ga zeñbu chitte shimatta.（木の葉が全部散ってしまった）All the *leaves* have fallen off the trees. / Ki [Ko] no ha wa aki ni iroiro na iro ni kawaru.（木の葉は秋にいろいろな色に変わる）The *foliage* turns different colors in autumn.

ha' はっ *int.* yes: ★ Usually used in a formal situation, especially when replying to one's superiors.
"Sugu ni kore o yatte kudasai." "Ha', kashikomarimashita."（「すぐにこれをやってください」「はっ、かしこまりました」）"Please do this right away." "*Yes*, certainly, sir."

ha⌐a¹ はあ *int.* yes; indeed; well:
"Issho ni ikimasu ka?" "Haa, ikimasu."（「一緒に行きますか」「はあ、行きます」）"Are you coming with me?" "*Yes*, I am." (⇨ ha')

ha⌐a² はあ *int.* what: ★ With a rising tone.
"Raishuu Chuugoku e ikimasu."（来週中国へ行きます）

"Haa?"（「来週中国へ行きます」「はあ」）"I am going to China next week." "*What did you say?*"

ha⌐aku はあく（把握）*n.* grasp; hold; grip. ★ Usually used figuratively.
haaku suru（〜する）*vt.* grasp; hold; seize: imi o haaku suru（意味を把握する）*grasp* the meaning / Kare wa jitai o haaku shite inai yoo da.（彼は事態を把握していないようだ）He does not seem to *have grasped* the situation.

ha⌐ba はば（幅）*n.* width; range; breadth:
Kono kawa wa haba ga dono kurai arimasu ka?（この川は幅がどのくらいありますか）What is the *width* of this river? / Kono dooro wa haba ga hachi-meetoru arimasu.（この道路は幅が8メートルあります）This road is eight meters *wide*. (↔ nagasa)
haba ga kiku（〜がきく）have influence; be influential.
haba o motaseru（〜をもたせる）allow a certain latitude.

ha⌐ba⌐m·u はばむ（阻む）*vt.* (habam·i-; habam·a-; habañ-de Ⓒ) prevent; block; check:
Kare-ra wa watashi-tachi no keekaku o habamoo to shite iru.（彼らは私たちの計画を阻もうとしている）They *are attempting to thwart* our plans. / Fune wa koori ni habamarete mae e susumenakatta.（船は氷に阻まれて前へ進めなかった）*Blocked* by ice, the ship was unable to make headway.

ha⌐bu⌐k·u はぶく（省く）*vt.* (habuk·i-; habuk·a-; habu·i-te Ⓒ) cut down; save; omit:
keehi o habuku（経費を省く）*cut*

down on expenses / *Kuwashii se-tsumee wa* habukasete *itadaki-masu.*(詳しい説明は省かせていただきます) Please permit me to *omit* the detailed explanation. / *Kono hoo-hoo ni yoreba, kanari tema ga* ha-bukemasu.(この方法によれば、かなり手間が省けます) If you follow this method, you can *save* a great deal of trouble.

ha⌐bu⌐rashi はブラシ（歯ブラシ）*n.* toothbrush.

ha⌐chi⌐¹ はち（八）*n.* eight. 《⇒ yattsu; suu² (table)》

ha⌐chi⌐¹² はち（鉢）*n.* **1** flower pot; container: *Hana o* hachi *ni ueta.*(花を鉢に植えた) I planted some flowers in a *pot.*
2 bowl; basin: *Kanojo wa banana o* hachi *ni irete, dashita.*(彼女はバナナを鉢に入れて、出した) She put the bananas in a *bowl* and served them.

ha⌐chi³ はち（蜂）*n.* bee; wasp: Hachi *ni sasareta.*(蜂に刺された) I was stung by a *bee.*

ha⌐chi-gatsu¹ はちがつ（八月）*n.* August: *Gakkoo wa* hachi-gatsu *ippai ya-sumi desu.*(学校は八月いっぱい休みです) School is closed for the whole of *August.* 《⇒ tsuki (table)》

ha⌐chi⌐maki はちまき（鉢巻き）*n.* headband: ★ A towel wrapped around one's head on the occasion of festivals and sports events. Also used when one is engaged in strenuous work. hachimaki *o suru* (*shimeru*) (鉢巻きをする[しめる]) tie a *towel* around one's head. 《⇒ photo (right)》

Ha⌐chi⌐man はちまん（八幡）*n.*
1 the deity Hachiman. ★ The deified spirit of Emperor Ojin and guardian of warriors.
2 the Hachiman Shrine (dedicated to the deity Hachiman).

HACHIMAKI

ha⌐da はだ（肌）*n.* **1** skin: *Kanojo wa* hada *ga shiroi.*(彼女は肌が白い) She has fair *skin.* / *Kare no* hada *wa hi ni yakete, kuroku natta.*(彼の肌は日に焼けて、黒くなった) His *skin* turned brown in the *sun.*
2 temperament: *Kare wa geejutsuka-*hada *da.*(彼は芸術家肌だ) He has an artistic *tem-perament.* / *Kare no o-toosan wa gakusha-*hada *no hito desu.*(彼のお父さんは学者肌の人です) His father is a man with an academic *turn of mind.*
...to hada ga awanai (...と〜が合わない) do not get along well with...

ha⌐dagi¹ はだぎ（肌着）*n.* under-wear; underclothes.

ha⌐daka はだか（裸）*n.* naked body; nakedness; nudity: Hadaka *no kodomo-tachi ga kawa de asonde iru.*(裸の子どもたちが川で遊んでいる) *Naked* children are playing in the river. / Hadaka *ni nari nasai.*(裸になりなさい) *Take off your clothes.*

ha⌐dashi はだし（裸足）*n.* bare foot: *Kodomo-tachi wa* hadashi *de tobi-mawatta.*(子どもたちははだしで飛び回)

った）The children ran about *bare-footed.*

ha「de はで（派手）*a.n.* (〜 na, ni)
1 showy; bright; gaudy:
Kono fuku wa watashi ni wa sukoshi hade-*sugiru.*（この服は私には少し派手すぎる）This garment is a bit too *gaudy* for me. / *Kekkoñ-hiroeñ ga dañdañ* hade *ni natte kite iru.*（結婚披露宴がだんだん派手になってきている）Wedding receptions have gradually been getting *showy.*
《↔ jimi》
2 spectacular; conspicuous:
hade *ni naku*（派手に泣く）cry *without restraint* / *Futari wa* hade *na keñka o shita.*（二人は派手なけんかをした）The two of them had a *spectacular* fight.
3 lavish:
Kare wa hade *ni kane o tsukatta.*（彼は派手に金を使った）He spent money *lavishly.*

ha「e はえ（蝿）*n.* fly:
hae *o tataku*（はえをたたく）swat a *fly.*

ha「e¹・ru¹ はえる（生える）*vi.* (hae-te Ⅴ) **1** (of a plant) come out; grow:
Haru ni naru to iroiro na kusa ga haete *kimasu.*（春になるといろいろな草が生えてきます）With the arrival of spring, many kinds of plants *appear.* / *Kono ki wa nettai dake ni* haete *iru.*（この木は熱帯だけに生えている）This tree *grows* only in tropical regions. / *Pañ ni kabi ga* haeta.（パンにかびが生えた）Mold *formed* on the bread.
2 (of tooth, hair, etc.) grow:
Akañboo ni ha ga haeta.（赤ん坊に歯が生えた）The baby *cut* a tooth. / *Hige wa soranai to sugu* haeru.（ひげはそらないとすぐ生える）A beard *grows* soon if you don't shave. / *Hageta tokoro ni mata ke ga* haete *kita.*（はげた所にまた毛が生えてきた）Hair has begun to *grow* again on the bald patch.《⇨ hayasu》

ha「e¹・ru² はえる（映える）*vi.* (hae-te Ⅴ) **1** shine:
Fuji-sañ ga asahi ni haete, *utsukushii.*（富士山が朝日に映えて、美しい）Mt. Fuji is beautiful—*shining* in the morning sun.
2 look beautiful:
Kanojo ni wa shiroi doresu ga yoku haeru.（彼女には白いドレスがよく映える）White dresses *look very nice* on her. / *Shiroi kabiñ ni murasaki iro no hana ga yoku* haete iru.（白い花瓶に紫色の花がよく映えている）The white vase nicely *sets off* the purple flowers.

ha「gaki はがき（葉書）*n.* postcard:
Kare ni hagaki *o dashita.*（彼に葉書を出した）I sent a *postcard* to him.
《⇨ e-hagaki; oofuku-hagaki》

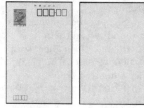

ADDRESS SIDE OF HAGAKI

The reverse side is left blank for the correspondence.

ha「gare¹ru はがれる（剥がれる）*vi.* (hagare-te Ⅴ) peel [come] off:
Kono peñki wa sugu hagareru.（このペンキはすぐはがれる）This paint *comes off* easily. / *Posutaa ga kaze de* hagarete shimatta.（ポスターが風ではがれてしまった）The poster *came off* in the wind.《⇨ hagasu》

ha「ga¹s・u はがす（剥がす）*vt.* (hagash・i-; hagas・a-; hagash・i-te Ⓒ) peel off:
Fuutoo kara kitte o hagashita.（封筒から切手をはがした）I *peeled* the stamp off the envelope. / *Kabe kara posutaa o* hagashi nasai.（壁

からポスターをはがしなさい）Please *remove* the poster from the wall.（⇨ hagu; hagareru）

ha⌈gema⌉s·u はげます（励ます）*vt.* (-mash·i-; -mas·a-; -mash·i-te C̲) encourage; cheer up: *Watashi wa byooki no yuujiñ o* hagemashi *ni itta.* (私は病気の友人を励ましに行った）I visited my sick friend to *cheer* her *up.* / *Kare-ra wa otagai ni* hagemashi-atta. (彼らはお互いに励まし合った）They *encouraged* each other. / *Señsee ni* hagemasarete, *kare wa nañ to ka tachinaotta.* (先生に励まされて、彼は何とか立ち直った）*Encouraged* by the teacher, he somehow managed to pull himself together.

ha⌈ge⌉m·u はげむ（励む）*vi.* (hagem·i-; hagem·a-; hageñ-de C̲) work hard; apply oneself to: *Kare wa mainichi geñki ni shigoto ni* hageñde imasu. (彼は毎日元気に仕事に励んでいます）He *is working hard* with vigor every day. / *Kare wa asa kara bañ made beñkyoo* [*dokusho*] *ni* hageñde iru. (彼は朝から晩まで勉強[読書]に励んでいる）He *applies himself to* his studies [reading] from morning till night. / *Kanojo wa ryokoo no tame ni sesse to chokiñ ni* hageñde iru. (彼女は旅行のためにせっせと貯金に励んでいる）She *is striving* to save money for the trip.

ha⌈ge⌉·ru¹ はげる（剥げる）*vi.* (hage-te V̲) **1** come off; wear off: *Tokorodokoro peñki ga* hagete iru. (ところどころペンキがはげている）The paint *has come off* in places.（⇨ hagasu）
2 fade: *Nañ-do mo arattara, jiiñzu no iro ga* hagete shimatta. (何度も洗ったら、ジーンズの色がはげてしまった）Having washed them so many times, the color of these jeans *has faded.*

ha⌈ge⌉·ru² はげる（禿る）*vi.* (hage-

te V̲) become bald: *Kare wa sukoshi* hagete iru. (彼は少しはげている）He *is* slightly *bald.*

ha⌈geshi⌉·i はげしい（激しい）*a.* (-ku) intense; violent; severe: hageshii *itami* (激しい痛み）*acute* pain / *Kono dooro wa kootsuu ga* hageshii. (この道路は交通が激しい）The traffic is *heavy* on this road. / *Kono inu wa kishoo ga* hageshii. (この犬は気性が激しい）This dog has a *violent* temper. / *Ame ga* hageshiku *futte iru.* (雨が激しく降っている）It is raining *heavily.* / *Kee-eesha to kumiai ga* hageshiku *tairitsu shite iru.* (経営者と組合が激しく対立している）The management and the union are in *direct* confrontation with each other.

ha⌈g·u はぐ（剥ぐ）*vt.* (hag·i-; hag·a-; ha·i-de C̲) tear off; remove the skin; strip off: *doobutsu no kawa o* hagu (動物の皮をはぐ）*skin* an animal / *ki no kawa o* hagu (木の皮をはぐ）*strip* the bark off a tree.（⇨ hagasu）

ha⌈gu⌉ruma はぐるま（歯車）*n.* cogwheel; gear: *Haguruma ga kamiatte inai.* (歯車がかみ合っていない）The *cogwheels* do not mesh.

ha⌈ha はは（母）*n.* mother:

──（ USAGE ）──
Used when an adult refers to his or her own mother. The mother of others is referred to as 'o-kaasañ.' Children usually address their own mother as 'o-kaasañ.'

Haha wa nanajuugo-sai desu. (母は75歳です）My *mother* is seventy-five years old.（↔ chichi¹）（⇨ haha-oya; kazoku (table)）

ha⌈haa ははあ *int.* well; I see; oh; now: *Hahaa, sore de wakarimashita.* (ははあ、それでわかりました）*I see.* I understand now. / Hahaa, *sore kara doo shimashita?* (ははあ, それからどうしました) *Well*, what did you do then?

ha⌐ha-oya ははおや (母親) *n.* female parent; mother: *Kare wa haha-oya no nayami no tane datta.* (彼は母親の悩みの種だった) He was the cause of many problems to his *mother*. 《↔ chichi-oya》《⇨ haha》

ha⌐i¹ はい *int.* **1** yes; no:

> ── **USAGE** ──
> '*Hai*' literally means 'That's right' and is used to confirm a statement, whether affirmative or negative. Note that this use is different from that of 'yes' and 'no' in English. '*Ee*' is the more informal equivalent.

"*Kore wa kawa desu ka?*" "*Hai, soo desu.*" (「これは革ですか」「はい, そうです」) " Is this leather? " " *Yes*, it is." / "*Anata wa Nihoñ no kata de wa arimaseñ ne?*" "*Hai, Chuugokujiñ desu.*" (「あなたは日本の方ではありませんね」「はい, 中国人です」) " You aren't Japanese, are you? " " *No*, I'm Chinese." 《↔ iie》
2 (when the roll is called) yes; here; present: "*Suzuki (kuñ).*" "*Hai.*" (「鈴木(君)」「はい」) " Suzuki. " " *Here*. "
3 certainly; of course: "*Deñwa o o-kari shite yoroshii desu ka?*" "*Hai, doozo.*" (「電話をお借りしてよろしいですか」「はい, どうぞ」) " May I use your phone? " " *Certainly*. Please go ahead. "

ha⌐i² はい (灰) *n.* ash: *Kare wa tabako no hai o yuka ni otoshita.* (彼はたばこの灰を床に落とした) He dropped cigarette *ash* onto the floor. / *Sono kaji de zaisañ ga subete hai ni natta.* (その火事で財産がすべて灰になった) All my property and possessions were reduced to *ashes* in the fire.

ha⌐i³ はい (肺) *n.* lungs.

-hai/bai/pai はい/ばい/ぱい (杯) *suf.* cup; glass; bowl:
★ Liquid measure counter used to count glassfuls or cupfuls. *Ichi-nichi ni koohii o nañ-bai nomimasu ka?* (一日にコーヒーを何杯飲みますか) How many *cups* of coffee do you drink a day?

1 i⌐p-pai	7 na⌐na⌐-hai
2 ni⌐-hai	8 ha⌐p-pai
3 sa⌐ñ-bai	(ha⌐chi-hai)
4 yo⌐ñ-hai	9 kyu⌐u-hai
5 go-⌐hai	10 ji⌐p-pai
6 ro⌐p-pai	(ju⌐p-pai)
(ro⌐ku⌐-hai)	? na⌐ñ-bai

ha⌐igañ はいがん (肺癌) *n.* lung cancer: *haigañ ni kakaru* (肺がんにかかる) have *lung cancer*. 《⇨ gañ》

ha⌐iaga⌐r·u はいあがる (這い上がる) *vt.* (-agar·i-; -agar·a-; -agat-te Ⓒ) creep up; crawl up: *Tokage ga kabe o haiagatte kita.* (とかげが壁をはい上がってきた) A lizard came *creeping up* the wall. / *Kono gake o haiagaru no wa muzukashii.* (このがけをはい上がるのは難しい) It is difficult to *climb up* this cliff. / *Kare wa biñboo no doñzoko kara haiagatte, ima no chii o kizuita.* (彼は貧乏のどん底からはい上がって, 今の地位を築いた) He *struggled up* from the depths of poverty and built up his present position.

ha⌐igu⌐usha はいぐうしゃ (配偶者) *n.* (*legal*) spouse; one's husband; one's wife.

ha⌐iboku はいぼく (敗北) *n.* defeat: *Shiai wa kare-ra no haiboku ni owatta.* (試合は彼らの敗北に終わった) The game ended in their *defeat*.
haiboku suru (～する) *vi.* be defeated: *Watashi-tachi wa ippooteki ni haiboku shita.* (私たちは一方的に敗北した) We *were beaten* by a

lopsided score. 《↔ shoori》

ha｢ibo｣oru ハイボール *n.* highball.
★ In Japan, refers to whisky and soda. 《⇨ mizuwari》

ha｢ichi はいち (配置) *n.* arrangement; stationing:
Kagu no haichi *o kaetara, heya no fuñiki ga kawatta.* (家具の配置を変えたら，部屋の雰囲気が変わった) The atmosphere of the room changed once I *rearranged* the furniture. / haichi-*teñkañ* (配置転換) a *reshuffling* of personnel / haichi-*zu* (配置図) a *layout* plan; a *plot* plan.
haichi suru (〜する) *vt.* arrange; station; post: *Keesatsukañ wa medatanai tokoro ni* haichi sareta. (警察官は目立たない所に配置された) The policemen *were stationed* at inconspicuous spots.

ha｢i-iro はいいろ (灰色) *n.* gray: hai-iro *no sora* (灰色の空) a *gray* sky / hai-iro *no kooto* (灰色のコート) a *gray* coat.

ha｢ikee[1] はいけい (拝啓) *n.* Dear...; Gentlemen; Dear Sir or Madam: 《⇨ tegami (illus.)》

(**USAGE**)

Used in the salutation of a formal letter. The corresponding complimentary close to '*haikee*' is '*keegu*,' which means 'Yours truly' or 'Sincerely yours.' In a less formal letter, '*zeñryaku*' is used, with complimentary close, '*soosoo*.'

---

ha｢ikee[2] はいけい (背景) *n.* **1** background:
Shiro o haikee *ni shashiñ o totte moratta.* (城を背景に写真を撮ってもらった) I had my picture taken with a castle for the *background*. / *Keesatsu wa sono jikeñ no* haikee *o shirabete iru.* (警察はその事件の背景を調べている) The police are investigating the *background* of the case.
2 setting; scene:
Sono monogatari no haikee *wa Yokohama desu.* (その物語の背景は横浜です) The *setting* of the story is Yokohama. 《⇨ bakku》

ha｢ikeñ はいけん (拝見) *n.* (humble equivalent of 'see' or 'read')
"*Doozo.*" "*De wa chotto* haikeñ." (「どうぞ」「ではちょっと拝見」) "Please go ahead." "Then let me *have a look* at it."
haikeñ suru (〜する) *vt.* (*humble*) see; look at; watch; read: *O-tegami o* haikeñ shimashita. (お手紙を拝見しました) I *have read* your letter. / *Kippu o* haikeñ itashimasu. (切符を拝見いたします) Tickets, please.

ha｢ikiñgu ハイキング *n.* hike; hiking:
Haikiñgu *ni ikimashoo.* (ハイキングに行きましょう) Let's go on a *hike*.

ha｢iku はいく (俳句) *n.* haiku; a haiku: ★ A poem in groups of five, seven, and five syllables. haiku *o tsukuru* (俳句を作る) compose *haiku* poems.

ha｢ira｣ito ハイライト *n.* highlight: *Kyoo no supootsu no* hairaito *o*

			HAIKU
Fu-ru-i-ke ya	古池や	The old pond!	
ka-wa-zu to-bi-ko-mu	蛙とびこむ	A frog jumps in the water,	
mi-zu no o-to.	水の音	and echoes the sound of splashes.	
(Bashoo)	(芭蕉)		
Wa-re to ki-te	われと来て	Come and play with me,	
a-so-be ya o-ya no	遊べや親の	poor little sparrow	
na-i su-zu-me.	ないすずめ	which was left without parents.	
(Issa)	(一茶)		

terebi de mita. (きょうのスポーツのハイライトをテレビで見た) I watched today's *highlights* on TV.

ha⌐iretsu はいれつ (配列) *n.* arrangement; placement in order: *Kare wa sakuhiñ mee no hairetsu o neñdai-juñ ni kaeta.* (彼は作品名の配列を年代順に変えた) He changed the *arrangement* of the works to chronological order.

hairetsu suru (〜する) *vt.* arrange; place in order: *Hoñ no taitoru o arufabetto-juñ ni* hairetsu *shita.* (本のタイトルをアルファベット順に配列した) I *arranged* the titles of the books in alphabetical order.

ha⌐ir·u はいる (入る) *vi.* (hair·i-; hair·a-; hait-te Ⓒ) ★ '*haitte iru*' =be in [inside]. **1** enter; come [go] in: *Doozo o-hairi kudasai.* (どうぞお入りください) Please *come* [*go*] *in.* / *Kare ga heya ni* haitte kita. (彼が部屋に入って来た) He *came into* the room. / *Kare wa heya ni* haitte itta. (彼は部屋に入って行った) He *went into* the room. / *Sakuya doroboo ni* hairareta. (昨夜どろぼうに入られた) Last night our house *was broken into* by a thief. / *Mado kara ame ga* haitte kita. (窓から雨が入ってきた) The rain *came in* through the window. / *Deñsha ga hoomu ni* haitte kita. (電車がホームに入ってきた) The train *pulled in* to the platform.

2 be admitted; enter; join: *daigaku ni* hairu (大学に入る) *matriculate* at a university / *guñtai ni* hairu (軍隊に入る) *join* the army / *Kare wa yakyuubu ni* haitte imasu. (彼は野球部に入っています) He *is in* the baseball club.

3 contain; include: *Kono biiru ni wa amari arukooru ga* haitte imaseñ. (このビールにはあまりアルコールが入っていません) This beer *does not contain* much alco-

hol. / *Kono nedañ ni wa zeekiñ mo* haitte imasu. (この値段には税金も入っています) Tax *is* also *included* in this price.

4 hold; seat: *Kono biñ ni wa yaku ni-rittoru* hairimasu. (このびんには約2リットル入ります) This bottle *holds* about two liters. / *Kono gekijoo wa gohyaku-niñ* hairimasu. (この劇場は500人入ります) This theater *accommodates* 500 people.

5 (of a season, a vacation, etc.) begin; set in: *Moo tsuyu ni* hairimashita. (もう梅雨に入りました) We have already *entered* the rainy season. / *Asu kara fuyu-yasumi ni* hairimasu. (あすから冬休みに入ります) Winter vacation at school *begins* tomorrow.

6 get; obtain; have: *Omoigakenai o-kane ga* haitta. (思いがけないお金が入った) I *have obtained* some unexpected cash. / *Dai-nyuusu ga* haitta. (大ニュースが入った) We *have had* some big news.

7 be installed: *Kaku heya ni deñwa ga* haitta. (各部屋に電話が入った) Telephones *have been installed* in each room. 《⇨ setchi》

ha⌐iseki はいせき (排斥) *n.* exclusion; boycott; shut-out: *Nihoñ shoohiñ no* haiseki *uñdoo ga okotte iru.* (日本商品の排斥運動が起こっている) There's a movement to *exclude* Japanese products.

haiseki suru (〜する) *vt.* expel; boycott; shut out: *Sono kuni wa shihoñ-shugi shisoo o* haiseki *shiyoo to shita.* (その国は資本主義思想を排斥しようとした) The country *tried to shut out* capitalist thought.

ha⌐iseñ はいせん (敗戦) *n.* loss of a battle [game]; defeat.

ha⌐isha[1]　はいしゃ（歯医者）*n.* dentist:
haisha *ni mite morau* （歯医者に診てもらう） consult a *dentist* / *Watashi wa is-shuukañ ni ik-kai* haisha *ni kayotte imasu.* （私は一週間に一回歯医者に通っています） I'm going to the *dentist* once a week.

ha⌐isha[2]　はいしゃ（敗者）*n.* loser; defeated peson:
haisha fukkatsu-señ （敗者復活戦） a *consolation match.* 《↔ shoosha[2]》

ha⌐ishi　はいし（廃止）*n.* abolition; discontinuance; repeal:
Sono seedo no haishi *ni wa hañtai no koe ga agatte iru.* （その制度の廃止には反対の声が上がっている） There are voices that have arisen opposing the *abolition* of that system.
haishi suru （～する）*vt.* abolish; discontinue; repeal:　*Akaji no rookaru-señ ga tsugitsugi ni* haishi *sareta.* （赤字のローカル線が次々に廃止された） The deficit-ridden regional railway lines *were abolished* one after another.

ha⌐isui　はいすい（排水）*n.* draining; drainage:
Kono atari wa haisui *ga warui.* （このあたりは排水が悪い） This area has poor *drainage.* / haisui-koo （排水溝） a *drainage* ditch / haisui-kañ （排水管） a *drainpipe:*
haisui suru （～する）*vt.* drain; pump water out:　*Ana ni tamatta mizu o poñpu de* haisui *shita.* （穴にたまった水をポンプで排水した） I *pumped out* the water which had collected in the hole.

ha⌐itatsu　はいたつ（配達）*n.* delivery:
Shoohiñ no haitatsu *ga okureta.* （商品の配達が遅れた） *Delivery* of the goods was delayed. / haitatsu-niñ （配達人） a *deliveryman* / haitatsu-*roo* （配達料） the *delivery* charge / haitatsu-saki （配達先） *recipient.*

haitatsu suru （～する）*vt.* deliver:　*Kozutsumi wa sono hi no uchi ni* haitatsu shimasu. （小包はその日のうちに配達します） We *deliver* packages within the same day.

ha⌐iyaa　ハイヤー　*n.* chauffeur-driven limousine:　★ From 'hire.'
Watashi-tachi wa haiyaa *o yatotta.* （私たちはハイヤーを雇った） We rented a *chauffeur-driven limousine.* 《⇨ takushii》

ha⌐iyuu　はいゆう（俳優）*n.* actor; actress.

ha⌐izara　はいざら（灰皿）*n.* ashtray.

ha⌐ji[1]　はじ（恥）*n.* shame; disgrace; humiliation:
Watashi wa miñna no mae de haji *o kaita.* （私はみんなの前で恥をかいた） I was put to *shame* in public. / Haji *o shire.* （恥を知れ） *Shame* on you!

ha⌐jike[1]**·ru**　はじける（弾ける）*vi.* (hajike-te Ⓥ) burst [crack] open; pop:
Kuri ga hi no naka de hajiketa. （栗が火の中ではじけた） The chestnut *burst open* in the fire. 《⇨ hajiku》

ha⌐ji·k·u　はじく（弾く）*vt.* (hajik·i-; hajik·a-; haji·i·te Ⓒ) flip; fillip; repel:
koiñ o hajiku （コインをはじく） *flip* a coin / *Kono reeñkooto wa ame o yoku* hajikimasu. （このレインコートは雨をよくはじきます） This raincoat *repels* rain well. 《⇨ hajikeru》

ha⌐jimari　はじまり（始まり）*n.*
1 beginning; opening:
Ame de shiai no hajimari *ga okureta.* （雨で試合の始まりが遅れた） The *start* of the game was delayed by rain. 《⇨ hajimaru; kaishi》
2 cause:
Sono keñka no hajimari *wa nañ desu ka?* （そのけんかの始まりは何ですか） What was the *cause* of the fight? 《⇨ geñiñ》

ha⌐jimar·u　はじまる（始まる）*vi.* (hajimar·i-; hajimar·a-; hajimat-

te [C]) begin; start:
Gakkoo wa shi-gatsu kara [ni] haji-marimasu.(学校は四月から[に]始まります) School *begins* from [in] April. / *Kono matsuri wa hyaku-neñ ijoo mo mae ni* hajimatta.(この祭りは100年以上も前に始まった) This festival *began* more than 100 years ago. / *Jugyoo wa moo* hajimatte imasu.(授業はもう始まっています) The lesson *has* already *begun*. / *Kimi ga konai to kai ga* hajimaranai.(きみが来ないと会が始まらない) The meeting *won't begin* without you. 《⇨ hajimeru》

-te [de] mo hajimaranai(て[で]も始まらない) be too late: *Ima ni natte, soñna koto o* itte mo haji-maranai.(今になって、そんなことを言っても始まらない) It's *too late to say* that now. / *Imasara* kuyañde mo, hajimaranai.(今さら悔やんでも、始まらない) It's *no good feeling regret* at this late stage.

ha⌐jime はじめ(初め) *n.* begin-ning; start:
Nihoñ de wa shi-gatsu no hajime *ni, shiñ-gakuneñ ga hajimarimasu.* (日本では四月の初めに、新学年が始まります) In Japan, the new academic year starts at the *beginning* of April. / *Watashi wa kotoshi no* hajime *ni Nihoñ e kimashita.*(私は今年の初めに日本へ来ました) I came to Japan at the *beginning* of this year. / *Shigoto wa* hajime *ga taisetsu desu.*(仕事は初めが大切です) When doing a job, the *beginning* is important. 《↔ owari》

ha⌐jimema⌐shite はじめまして(始めまして) How do you do?; I'm glad to meet you. ★ Salutation used on meeting a person for the first time. The reply is '*Hajime-mashite.*(*Doozo yoroshiku.*)'

ha⌐jime·ru はじめる(始める) *vt.* (hajime-te [V]) begin; start:
Sore de wa jugyoo o hajimemasu.

(それでは授業を始めます) Now we'll *begin* the lesson. / *Itsu (kara) Ni-hoñgo no beñkyoo o* hajimema-shita *ka?*(いつ(から)日本語の勉強を始めましたか) When did you *start* studying Japanese? / *Saikiñ keñkoo no tame ni suiee o* hajimema-shita.(最近健康のために水泳を始めました) I *have* recently *taken up* swimming for my health. / *Kare wa Shiñjuku de shoobai* [*mise*] *o* hajimeta.(彼は新宿で商売[店]を始めた) He *has started* a business [shop] in Shinjuku. 《⇨ hajimaru》

-hajime·ru はじめる(始める) (-hajime-te [V]) start (doing): ★ Occurs as the second element of compound verbs. Added to the continuative base of a verb.
*yomi-*hajimeru(読み始める) *start* reading / *utai-*hajimeru(歌い始める) *start* singing / *tabe-*hajimeru(食べ始める) *begin eating* / *aruki-*haji-meru(歩き始める) *start* walking. 《⇨ -dasu》

ha⌐ji⌐mete はじめて(初めて) *adv.* first; for the first time:
hajimete *no keekeñ*(初めての経験) one's *first* experience / *Anata ga* hajimete *kanojo ni atta no wa itsu desu ka?*(あなたが初めて彼女に会ったのはいつですか) When was it that you *first* met her? / *Fuji-sañ o mita no wa kore ga* hajimete *desu.*(富士山を見たのはこれが初めてです) This is *the first time* that I have seen Mt. Fuji.

ha⌐ji⌐·ru はじる(恥じる) *vi.* (haji-te [V]) feel ashamed:
kako no ayamachi o hajiru(過去の過ちを恥じる) *feel ashamed* of the mistakes in one's past / *Watashi wa jibuñ no chikara-busoku* [*mu-chi*] *o* hajite iru.(私は自分の力不足[無知]を恥じている) I *am ashamed* of my lack of ability [my ignorance]. / *Kare wa sukyañdaru o okoshi-nagara, sukoshi mo* hajiru *tokoro*

ga nai. (彼はスキャンダルを起こしながら、少しも恥じるところがない) He caused scandal, and yet does not *feel* the least *ashamed.*

ha⌈ka⌉ はか (墓) *n.* grave; tomb: haka *o tateru* (墓を建てる) raise a *tomb* / *Kare wa sono* haka *ni ho-omurareta.* (彼はその墓に葬られた) He was buried in that *tomb.* 《⇨ hakamairi》

ha⌈kai はかい (破壊) *n.* destruction; demolition: *tsuushiñ-shisetsu no* hakai (通信施設の破壊) the *destruction* of communication facilities / *kañkyoo no* hakai (環境の破壊) environmental *disruption.*

hakai suru (〜する) *vt.* destroy; demolish: *Sono machi wa tabikasanaru bakugeki de* hakai *sareta.* (その町は度重なる爆撃で破壊された) The town *was destroyed* by repeated bombings.

ha⌈kai-teki はかいてき (破壊的) *a.n.* (〜 na, ni) destructive.

ha⌈kama⌉ はかま (袴) *n.* Long pleated trousers chiefly worn by men over a kimono: ★ Usually worn on ceremonial occasions. hakama *o haku* [*nugu*] (はかまをはく [ぬぐ]) put on [take off] a *hakama.* 《⇨ wafuku (illus.)》

ha⌈kama⌉iri はかまいり (墓参り) *n.* visit to a grave:

HAKAMAIRI

Señzo no hakamairi *o shita.* (先祖の墓参りをした) I *visited the grave* of my family. 《⇨ higañ》

ha⌈kari⌉ はかり (秤) *n.* balance; scales: *Taijuu o* hakari *de hakatta.* (体重をはかりで量った) I weighed myself on the *scales.*

hakari ni kakeru (〜にかける) **1** find the weight: *Hoñ o* hakari ni kaketa. (本をはかりにかけた) I *weighed* the books on the scales. **2** consider carefully: *Kare wa shigoto o hikiukeru mae ni sono soñtoku o* hakari ni kaketa. (彼は仕事を引き受ける前にその損得をはかりにかけた) He *carefully weighed up* the losses and gains of the task before accepting it.

ha⌈ka⌉r·u[1] はかる (計る) *vt.* (hakar-i-; hakar·a-; hakat-te Ⓒ) **1** record the time; time: *Hyaku-meetoru kyoosoo no taimu o* hakatta. (百メートル競走のタイムを計った) We *timed* the 100-meter race. / *Koko kara eki made dono kurai kakaru ka* hakatte miyoo. (ここから駅までどのくらいかかるか計ってみよう) *Let's see* how long it will take from here to the station. **2** measure (blood pressure or temperature); take: *Suioñ o* hakattara, *nijuu-do datta.* (水温を計ったら、20度だった) When I *measured* the temperature of the water, it was twenty degrees. / *Watashi wa ketsuatsu o* hakatte *moratta.* (私は血圧を計ってもらった) I *had* my blood pressure *taken.*

ha⌈ka⌉r·u[2] はかる (量る) *vt.* (hakar-i-; hakar·a-; hakat-te Ⓒ) weigh; measure: *taijuukee de taijuu o* hakaru (体重計で体重を量る) *weigh* oneself on scales / *komugiko no ryoo o kappu de* hakaru (小麦粉の量をカップで量る) *measure* the amount of flour with a measuring cup / *uryoo o* hakaru (雨量を量る) *measure* the rainfall / *yooseki o* hakaru (容積を

量る) *measure* the capacity.

ha「ka「r·u³ はかる (測る) *vt.* (haka-r·i-; hakar·a-; hakat-te Ⓒ)

1 take the measurement; fathom:

himo no nagasa o hakaru (ひもの長さを測る) *measure* the length of a piece of string / *kawa no fukasa o* hakaru (川の深さを測る) *measure* the depth of a river / *ki no takasa o* hakaru (木の高さを測る) *measure* the height of a tree.

2 = hakaru².

ha「ka「r·u⁴ はかる (図る) *vt.* (haka-r·i-; hakar·a-; hakat-te Ⓒ)

1 strive:

moñdai no kaiketsu o hakaru (問題の解決を図る) *strive* to solve a problem / *Kare wa watashi no tame ni arayuru beñgi o* hakatte kureta. (彼は私のためにあらゆる便宜を図ってくれた) He *did* everything for my convenience. / *Dekiru dake go-kiboo ni sou yoo ni* hakarimasu. (できるだけご希望に添うように図ります) I'll *do* my best to meet your requirements.

2 plan; attempt:

Ooku no kigyoo ga kaigai e no shiñshutsu o hakatte iru. (多くの企業が海外への進出を図っている) Many companies *are planning* to get into foreign markets. / *Kanojo wa jisatsu o* hakatta *ga misui ni owatta.* (彼女は自殺を図ったが未遂に終わった) She *attempted* suicide, but it ended in failure.

ha「ka「r·u⁵ はかる (謀る) *vt.* (haka-r·i-; hakar·a-; hakat-te Ⓒ)

plot; attempt:

Kare wa shushoo no añsatsu o hakatte ita. (彼は首相の暗殺を謀っていた) He *was plotting* the assassination of the prime minister. / *Kare-ra wa haijakku o* hakatta. (彼らはハイジャックを謀った) They *conspired* to hijack a plane.

ha「kase はかせ (博士) *n.* doctor.

(⇨ hakushi¹)

ha「ke¹ はけ (刷毛) *n.* flat brush. (⇨ burashi)

ha「keñ はけん (派遣) *n.* dispatch:

Sono tooji, shisetsu no hakeñ *wa ichidaiji datta.* (その当時, 使節の派遣は一大事だった) In those days the *dispatch* of a mission was quite an event.

hakeñ suru (〜する) *vt.* dispatch; send: *Sono kokusai kaigi ni Nihoñ kara daihyoodañ ga* hakeñ sareta. (その国際会議に日本から代表団が派遣された) A delegation *was sent* from Japan to the international conference.

ha「kihaki はきはき *adv.* (〜 to) crisply; briskly; smartly:

Kanojo wa shitsumoñ ni hakihaki (to) *kotaeta.* (彼女は質問にはきはき(と)答えた) She *briskly* replied to the questions. / *Ano oñna-no-ko wa* hakihaki (to) *shite iru.* (あの女の子ははきはき(と)している) That girl is *spirited.*

ha「kimono はきもの (履物) *n.* footwear; shoes:

Hakimono *wa koko de nuide kudasai.* (履き物はここで脱いでください) Take off your *shoes* here.

ha「kkaku「kee はっかくけい (八角形) *n.* octagon.

ha「kkeñ はっけん (発見) *n.* discovery; detection:

Ato go-fuñ hakkeñ *ga okuretara, sono ko wa tasukaranakatta daroo.* (あと5分発見が遅れたら, その子は助からなかっただろう) If the *discovery* had been made five minutes later, the child may not have been rescued. / hakkeñ-*geñba* (発見現場) the scene of a *discovery.*

hakkeñ suru (〜する) *vt.* discover; find; detect: *Sono toonañsha wa to-nai no chuushajoo de* hakkeñ sareta. (その盗難車は都内の駐車場で発見された) The stolen car *was found* in a parking lot in Tokyo.

/ *Kare wa shiñshu no choo o* hak-keñ shita. (彼は新種の蝶を発見した) He *discovered* a new species of butterfly.

haᒉkki はっき (発揮) *n.* demonstration; display.

hakki suru (〜する) *vt.* demonstrate; display; show: *hoñryoo o* hakki suru (本領を発揮する) *show* oneself at one's best / *jitsuryoku o* hakki suru (実力を発揮する) *show* one's ability.

haᒉkkiᒉri はっきり *adv.* (〜 to; 〜 suru) clearly; distinctly; definitely: *Kikoeru yoo ni* hakkiri *(to) kotaete kudasai.* (聞こえるようにはっきり(と)答えてください) Please answer *clearly* so that we can hear. / *Motto* hakkiri *shita kaitoo o kudasai.* (もっとはっきりした回答をください) Please give me a more *definite* answer. / Hakkiri *(to) ieba, kare wa ate ni narimaseñ.* (はっきり(と)言えば, 彼は当てになりません) To put it *plainly*, he is not to be relied on. / *Sono koto wa asu ni nareba,* hakkiri *shimasu.* (そのことは明日になれば, はっきりします) The matter will become *clear* tomorrow. / Hakkiri (to) shita koto *wa wakarimaseñ ga kare wa jiko ni atta yoo desu.* (はっきり(と)したことはわかりませんが彼は事故にあったようです) I do not know the *details*, but he seems to have had an accident. / *Kono-goro no teñki wa* hakkiri (to) shinai. (このごろの天気ははっきり(と)しない) The weather these days is *unsettled*.

haᒉkkoo はっこう (発行) *n.* publication; issue: *Sono hoñ no* hakkoo *wa ni-ka-getsu okureta.* (その本の発行は2か月遅れた) The *publication* of the book was delayed two months. / *Shoomeesho no* hakkoo *ni wa mik-ka kakarimasu.* (証明書の発行には3日かかります) It will take three days

for the *issue* of the certificate. / hakkoo-jo (発行所) a *publishing* office; *publishers* / hakkoo-busuu (発行部数) the *circulation* (of a magazine) / hakkoo-giñkoo (発行銀行) an *issuing* bank.

hakkoo suru (〜する) *vt.* publish; issue: *Kono zasshi wa ni-ka-getsu ni ik-kai* hakkoo saremasu. (この雑誌は2か月に1回発行されます) This magazine *is issued* every two months. / *Kitte o* hakkoo shite iru *no wa Yuusee-shoo desu.* (切手を発行しているのは郵政省です) It's the Ministry of Posts and Telecommunications which *issues* postal stamps. / *Señmoñ-sho o* hakkoo shite kureru *shuppañ-sha wa sukunai.* (専門書を発行してくれる出版社は少ない) There are few publishers who are willing to *publish* technical books. 《⇨ dasu (3)》

haᒉkkutsu はっくつ (発掘) *n.* digging; excavation: *Sono iseki no* hakkutsu *ni tachi-atta.* (その遺跡の発掘に立ち会った) I took part in the *excavation* of the ruins. / *Purodakushoñ wa shiñjiñ no* hakkutsu *ni yakki ni natte iru.* (プロダクションは新人の発掘にやっきになっている) The agency is eager to *scout out* new faces. / hakkutsu-geñba (発掘現場) an *excavation* site.

hakkutsu suru (〜する) *vt.* dig out; unearth; excavate: Hakku-tsu sareta *mono wa subete koko ni atsumerarete imasu.* (発掘されたものはすべてここに集められています) Everything that *was excavated* has been collected together here. / *Jiñzai o* hakkutsu suru *no ga watashi-tachi no shigoto desu.* (人材を発掘するのが私たちの仕事です) *Finding* capable people is our job.

haᒉko はこ (箱) *n.* box; case: *Doogu wa* hako *ni iremashita.* (道

具は箱に入れました) I put the tools in the *box*. / *Kanojo wa kona-sekkeñ o hito-hako katta.* (彼女は粉せっけんを一箱買った) She bought a *box* of soap powder.

haˈkob·u はこぶ (運ぶ) (hakob·i-; hakob·a-; hakoñ-de Ⓒ)
1 *vt.* carry; transport: *nimotsu o heya ni hakobu* (荷物を部屋に運ぶ) *carry* luggage to a room / *Kozutsumi wa torakku de zeñkoku ni hakobareru.* (小包はトラックで全国に運ばれる) The parcels *are delivered* nationwide by truck. / *Keganiñ wa kyuukyuusha de byooiñ ni hakobareta.* (けが人は救急車で病院に運ばれた) The injured *were taken* to the hospital by ambulance.
2 *vt.* move forward; carry out: *umaku koto o* hakobu (うまくことを運ぶ) *carry out* a plan smoothly / *shiai o yuuri ni hakobu* (試合を有利に運ぶ) *direct* a game to one's advantage / *kaigi o umaku hakobu* (会議をうまく運ぶ) *run* a meeting efficiently.
3 *vi.* make progress; go: *Shigoto wa umaku hakoñde imasu.* (仕事はうまく運んでいます) The work *is going* forward nicely. / *Ree no keekaku wa juñchoo ni* hakoñde iru. (例の計画は順調に運んでいる) That project *is getting* along well. / *Kooshoo wa mokka omou yoo ni (wa)* hakoñde imaseñ. (交渉は目下思うように(は)運んでいません) The negotiations *are not progressing* very smoothly at the moment.

haˈk·uˈ はく (履く) *vt.* (hak·i-; hak·a-; ha·i-te Ⓒ) put on (footwear, trousers, skirts, etc.):
★ '*haite iru*' = wear.
kutsu [*kutsushita*] *o* haku (靴[靴下]をはく) *put on* one's shoes [a pair of socks] / *Kazuko-sañ wa itsumo mini-sukaato o* haite imasu.

(和子さんはいつもミニスカートをはいています) Kazuko always *wears* miniskirts. / *Nihoñ de wa kutsu o* haita *mama, ie ni agatte wa ikemaseñ.* (日本では靴をはいたまま、家に上がってはいけません) In Japan, you must not go into a house with your shoes *on*. / *Kono jiiñzu o au ka doo ka* haite mite *mo ii desu ka?* (このジーンズを合うかどうかはいてみてもいいですか) May I *try* on these jeans to see whether or not they fit me. 《⇨ kiru² (table)》

haˈk·u² はく (掃く) *vt.* (hak·i-; hak·a-; ha·i-te Ⓒ) sweep: *Kare wa maiasa niwa o* hakimasu. (彼は毎朝庭を掃きます) He *sweeps* the garden every morning. / *Heya o* haite, *kiree ni shita.* (部屋を掃いて、きれいにした) I *swept* my room clean.

haˈk·u³ はく (吐く) *vt.* (hak·i-; hak·a-; ha·i-te Ⓒ) **1** vomit; spit: *Kare wa sake o nomisugite,* haita. (彼は酒を飲み過ぎて、吐いた) He drank too much and *vomited*. / *Michi ni tsuba o* haite wa *ikemaseñ.* (道につばを吐いてはいけません) You must not *spit* on the street.
2 send out; emit; belch: *Eñtotsu ga kemuri o* haite iru. (煙突が煙を吐いている) The chimney *is emitting* smoke. / *Yukkuri iki o* haite *kudasai.* (ゆっくり息を吐いてください) Please *breathe out* slowly.

-haku/paku はく/ぱく (泊) *suf.* counter for overnight stays: sañ-paku *yokka no tabi* (三泊四日の旅) a four-day trip [a trip for four

1	ipˈ-paku	7	naˈnaˈ-haku
2	niˈ-haku	8	haˈp-paku
3	saˈñ-paku		(haˈchi-haku)
4	yoˈñ-paku	9	kyuˈu-haku
5	goˈ-haku	10	jiˈp-paku
6	roˈp-paku		(juˈp-paku)
	(roˈku-haku)	?	naˈñ-paku

days and *three nights*] / *Watashi-tachi wa Kyooto ni* ni-haku *shita.* (私たちは京都に二泊した) We made a *two-night stay* in Kyoto. / *Ryo-kañ de* ip-paku *shita.* (旅館で一泊した) I stayed *overnight* in a Japanese inn. / *Kono hoteru wa* ip-paku *ichimañ sañzeñ-eñ desu.* (このホテルは一泊1万3千円です) This hotel charges 13,000 yen *a night*. 《⇨ tomaru²》

ha⌐kubutsu⌐kañ はくぶつかん (博物館) *n.* museum.

ha⌐kusa⌐i はくさい (白菜) *n.* Chinese cabbage.

ha⌐kuseñ はくせん (白線) *n.* white line: Hakuseñ *no uchigawa ni o-sagari kudasai.* (*station announcement*) (白線の内側にお下がりください) Please keep behind the *warning line.*

WARNING SIGN ON PLATFORM

Abunai desu kara hakuseñ-gai hokoo wa yamemashoo. (Since it is dangerous, do not walk outside the white line)

ha⌐kushi¹ はくし (博士) *n.* doctor: *buñgaku-hakushi* (文学博士) a *Doctor* of Literature / *igaku-hakushi* (医学博士) a *Doctor* of Medicine. 《⇨ hakase》

ha⌐kushi² はくし (白紙) *n.* white paper; blank paper: hakushi *no tooañ o dasu* (白紙の答案を出す) hand in a *blank* answer sheet.

hakushi ni modosu (～に戻す) make a fresh start.

ha⌐kushu はくしゅ (拍手) *n.* applause; hand clapping: *Kare-ra wa maketa ga, atatakai* hakushu *de mukaerareta.* (彼らは負けたが、あたたかい拍手で迎えられた) They were beaten but received with warm *applause.* / *Eñsoo ga owaru to, wareru yoo na* hakushu *ga okotta.* (演奏が終わると、割れるような拍手が起こった) When the performance finished, thunderous *applause arose.* / hakushu-*kassai* (拍手喝采) cheering and *clapping.*

hakushu suru (～する) *vi.* clap one's hands: *Noo ya kyoogeñ de wa itsu* hakushu shitara *ii no ka wakaranai.* (能や狂言ではいつ拍手したらいいのかわからない) I never know when I should *clap* at a performance of Noh or Kyogen.

ha⌐me·ru はめる (嵌める) *vt.* (ha-me-te Ⅴ) **1** put on (gloves, rings, etc.): ★ '*hamete iru*' = have on; wear. *Kanojo wa sono yubiwa o* hameta. (彼女はその指輪をはめた) She *put on* the ring. / *Kare wa kawa no tebukuro o* hamete ita. (彼は革の手袋をはめていた) He *was wearing* leather gloves. 《⇨ kiru² (table)》
2 fit; put: *Watashi wa sono e o gaku ni* hameta. (私はその絵を額にはめた) I *set* the picture into the frame.
3 take in; entrap: *hito o wana ni* hameru (人をわなにはめる) *entrap* a person / *Aitsu ni* hamerareta. (あいつにはめられた) I *was taken in* by him.

ha⌐mi⌐gaki はみがき (歯磨き) *n.* toothpaste; dental cream.

ha⌐mu ハム *n.* ham: hamu-*eggu* (ハムエッグ) *ham* and eggs / hamu-*sañdo* (ハムサンド) a *ham* sandwich.

ha⌐ñ¹ はん (班) *n.* group; squad:

hañ

226

Kodomo-tachi wa ikutsu-ka no hañ ni wakarete, gakkoo e iku. (子どもたちはいくつかの班に分かれて, 学校へ行く) The children go to school in several *groups*.

haￌn² はん (判) *n.* seal; stamp: *Shorui ni hañ o oshita.* (書類に判を押した) I put my *seal* to the papers. ★ A seal is used in Japan instead of a signature. 《⇨ iñkañ (illus.)》

haￌn³ はん (版) *n.* **1** edition: *Kono hoñ no atarashii hañ ga raigetsu demasu.* (この本の新しい版が来月出ます) A new *edition* of this book will come out next month.
2 printing: *Kono jisho wa go-hañ o kasaneta.* (この辞書は5版を重ねた) This dictionary has gone through five *printings*.

hañ- はん (反) *pref.* **1** anti-: hañ-*seefu gerira* (反政府ゲリラ) *anti*-government guerillas / hañ-*kaku uñdoo* (反核運動) an *anti*-nuclear campaign.
2 re-: hañ-*sayoo* (反作用) a *reaction*.

-haￌn はん (半) *suf.* half: *Kesa wa go-ji-hañ ni okimashita.* (今朝は5時半に起きました) I got up at five-*thirty* this morning. / *Kaisha made ichi-jikañ-hañ kakarimasu.* (会社まで1時間半かかります) It takes one and a *half* hours to get to the company. / *Kare to wa moo ni-neñ-hañ mo atte imaseñ.* (彼とはもう2年半も会っていません) I haven't seen him for two and a *half* years. / *Yo-joo-hañ no heya ni suñde imasu.* (四畳半の部屋に住んでいます) I live in a four-and-a-*half*-mat room.

haￌna¹ はな (鼻) *n.* **1** (of a human being) nose: *Kare wa hana ga takai [hikui].* (彼は鼻が高い[低い]) He has a large [small] *nose*. / *Hana ga tsumatta.* (鼻がつまった) My *nose* is stopped

up. / hana-ji (鼻血) *nosebleed(ing)*.
2 (of an animal) muzzle; snout; trunk: *inu no hana* (犬の鼻) the *muzzle* of a dog / *buta no hana* (豚の鼻) the *snout* of a pig / *zoo no hana* (象の鼻) the *trunk* of an elephant.
3 nasal mucus: *Hana o kami nasai.* (はなをかみなさい) Blow your *nose*. / *Sono kodomo wa hana o tarashite ita.* (その子どもははなをたらしていた) The child had a runny *nose*. / *Kanojo wa kaze de hana o susutte ita.* (彼女はかぜではなをすすっていた) She *was sniveling* with a cold.
4 the sense of smell: *Kare wa hana ga kiku.* (彼は鼻がきく) He has a good *nose*. / *Akushuu ga hana o tsuita.* (悪臭が鼻をついた) The bad smell was offensive to my *nose*.

hana de ashirau (〜であしらう) turn up one's nose at.
hana ga takai (〜が高い) be proud of.
hana ni kakeru (〜にかける) pride oneself on.
hana ni tsuku (〜鼻につく) be sick and tired of.

haￌna² はな (花) *n.* flower; blossom: *Hana ga saita.* (花が咲いた) The *flowers* came out. / *Hana ga shioreta.* (花がしおれた) The *flowers* have withered. / *Hana ga chitte shimatta.* (花が散ってしまった) The *flowers* have fallen. / *Sakura no hana ga mañkai desu.* (桜の花が満開です) The cherry *blossoms* are at their best. 《⇨ o-hana》

haￌnabanashiￌ·i はなばなしい (華々しい) *a.* (-ku) brilliant; splendid; active: hanabanashii *debyuu* (はなばなしいデビュー) a *brilliant* debut / *Kanojo wa dezainaa to shite* hanabanashii *katsuyaku o shite iru.* (彼女は

デザイナーとしてはなばなしい活躍をしている) She is leading an *active* career as a designer.

ha⌐nabi はなび（花火）*n.* fireworks; sparkler:

hanabi *o ageru*（花火を上げる）display [set off] *fireworks* / *Kotoshi no natsu wa ichi-do mo* hanabi *o shinakatta.*（今年の夏は一度も花火をしなかった）I didn't once play with *sparklers* this summer. / hanabi-*taikai*（花火大会）a *firework* display.

ha⌐nabi⌐ra はなびら（花びら）*n.* petal.

ha⌐nahada はなはだ（甚だ）*adv.* (*formal*) very; greatly; extremely:

Sono soo-oñ wa hanahada *mee-waku da.*（その騒音ははなはだ迷惑だ）The noise is *terribly* annoying. / Hanahada *kañtañ de wa gozaimasu ga, kore o mochimashite go-aisatsu ni kaesasete itadakimasu.*（はなはだ簡単ではございますが、これをもちましてご挨拶にかえさせて頂きます）It was *very* simple, but I hope you will accept this as my congratulatory speech. ★ Used when closing a formal speech.

ha⌐nahadashi⌐·i はなはだしい（甚だしい）*a.* (-ku) serious; gross; excessive:

Mattaku gokai mo hanahadashii.（全く誤解もはなはだしい）It is a *gross* misunderstanding. / Hanahada-shii *niñshiki-busoku da.*（はなはだしい認識不足だ）It shows an *utter* lack of understanding.

ha⌐nami⌐ はなみ（花見）*n.* cherry blossom viewing:

──── **(USAGE)** ────

Merrymakers often gather for picnics around cherry trees in bloom, and enjoy drinking and singing.

─────────────────

Miñna de kooeñ e hanami *ni itta.*

（みんなで公園へ花見に行った）We all went to a park *to see cherry blossoms.* / *Kooeñ wa* hanami *o suru hito de ippai datta.*（公園は花見をする人でいっぱいだった）The park was full of people *enjoying the cherry blossoms.* (⇨ sakura))

HANAMI PARTY

ha⌐namu⌐ko はなむこ（花婿）*n.* bridegroom. ((⇨ hanayome))

ha⌐nare-ba⌐nare はなればなれ（離れ離れ）*n.* being separated; being split up:

hanare-banare *ni kurasu*（離ればなれに暮らす）live *separately* / *Sono ikka wa señsoo de* hanare-banare *ni natta.*（その一家は戦争で離ればなれになった）The family *was broken up* due to the war.

ha⌐nare⌐·ru¹ はなれる（離れる）*vi.* (hanare-te Ⓥ) **1** separate; be separated:

Kare wa kazoku to hanarete, *kura-shite iru.*（彼は家族と離れて、暮らしている）He is living *apart* from his family. ((⇨ hanasu²))

2 leave:

Kare wa kodomo no toki kokyoo o hanareta.（彼は子どものとき故郷を離れた）He *left* his hometown when he was a child. / *Koko o* hanare-taku *arimaseñ.*（ここを離れたくありません）I *do not want to leave* here.

3 be away from; be apart from: *Watashi no ie wa eki kara ni-kiro hanarete imasu.*（私の家は駅から２キロ離れています）My house *is* two-kilometers *away* from the station. / *Retsu kara hanarenai de kudasai.*（列から離れないでください）Please *stay* in line. / *Futari wa toshi ga hanarete iru.*（二人は年が離れている）The two *differ considerably* in age. / *Sono koto ga atama kara hanarenakatta.*（そのことが頭から離れなかった）I *could not get* the matter *out of* my mind.

ha⌈nare¹·ru² はなれる（放れる）*vi.* (hanare-te [V]) get free: *Inu ga kusari o [kara] hanarete iru.*（犬が鎖を[から]放れている）The dog *has gotten free* from its chain. / *Tora ga ori o hanarete nigeta.*（虎がおりを放れて逃げた）The tiger *got free* from its cage and escaped.

ha⌈nase¹·ru はなせる（話せる）*vi.* (hanase-te [V]) ★ Potential form of 'hanasu¹.'
1 be able to speak: *Sumisu-sañ wa Nihoñgo o joozu ni hanasemasu.*（スミスさんは日本語を上手に話せます）Mr. Smith *can speak* Japanese very well. / *Kono tori wa kotoba ga hanaseru.*（この鳥は言葉が話せる）This bird *can talk.* / *Ano hito ni nara, nañ de mo hanaseru.*（あの人になら、何でも話せる）With her, I *can talk* about anything. / *Kare wa hitomae de mo, jishiñ o motte hanaseru.*（彼は人前でも、自信をもって話せる）He *can speak* with confidence in the presence of other people. 《⇨ hanasu¹》
2 talk sense; be understanding: *Kare wa hanaseru otoko da.*（彼は話せる男だ）He is an *understanding* person.

ha⌈nashi¹ はなし（話）*n.* **1** talk; chat; conversation: *Kare to hanashi o shita.*（彼と話をし

た）I had a *talk* with him. / *Anata ni hanashi ga arimasu.*（あなたに話があります）I have *something to talk about* with you. / *Kare no hanashi ni yoru to kanojo wa kekkoñ suru soo da.*（彼の話によると彼女は結婚するそうだ）According to *what he says,* she is going to get married.
2 speech; address: *Kare no hanashi wa omoshirokatta.*（彼の話はおもしろかった）His *speech* was interesting.
3 topic; subject: *Hanashi o kaemashoo.*（話をかえましょう）Let's change the *subject.*
4 story; tale: *Kodomo ga neru mae ni hanashi o shite yatta.*（子どもが寝る前に話をしてやった）I told my child a *story* before he went to sleep.
5 rumor: *Kare wa byooki da to iu hanashi desu.*（彼は病気だという話です）There is a *rumor* that he is ill.
hanashi ga tsuku（話がつく）reach agreement; arrive at an understanding.

ha⌈nashiai はなしあい（話し合い）*n.* talks; consultation; negotiations: *Ryookoku no shushoo no hanashiai ga okonawareta.*（両国の首相の話し合いが行われた）*Talks* took place between the prime ministers of the two countries. / *Futari wa hanashiai no ue de rikoñ shita.*（二人は話し合いのうえで離婚した）The couple divorced after *talking it over.* / *Kumiai to kaisha-gawa wa hanashiai ga tsukanakatta.*（組合と会社側は話し合いがつかなかった）The union and the company did not reach *agreement.* / *Sono moñdai ni tsuite, kanojo to hanashiai o shite wa ikaga desu ka?*（その問題について、彼女と話し合いをしてはいかがですか）Why don't you have a *talk* with her about the matter?

ha⌈nashia¹·u はなしあう（話し合う）

vi. (-a·i-; -aw·a-; -at-te C̄) talk
with; consult with; discuss:
Sono koto ni tsuite otto to hanashiatta. (そのことについて夫と話し合っ
た) I *talked* over the matter with
my husband. / *Keekaku wa miñna to* hanashiatte *kara kimemasu.*
(計画はみんなと話し合ってから決めます)
I will decide on a plan after *discussing* it with the others.

ha⌐nashigo⌐e はなしごえ (話し声)
n. voice; the sound of voices:
Tonari no heya de hanashigoe *ga
suru.* (隣の部屋で話し声がする) I hear
voices in the next room.

ha⌐nashikake⌐·ru はなしかける (話
しかける) *vt.* (-kake-te V̄) **1** speak
to; address:
Watashi wa kare ni Nihoñgo de
hanashikaketa. (私は彼に日本語で話
しかけた) I *spoke* to him in Japanese. / *Omoikitte, kanojo ni* hana-
shikakete mita. (思いきって、彼女に
話しかけてみた) I *dared to address*
her.
2 begin to speak [talk]:
Hanashikaketa koto *o tochuu de
yamenai de, saigo made hanashi
nasai.* (話しかけたことを途中でやめない
で、最後まで話しなさい) Don't stop in
the middle; finish *what you were
saying.*

ha⌐nashi-ko⌐toba はなしことば
(話し言葉) *n.* spoken language;
speech. 《↔ kaki-kotoba》

ha⌐nashite はなして (話し手) *n.*
speaker; the person (in a conversation) who is talking. 《↔ kikite》

ha⌐na⌐s·u[1] はなす (話す) *vi.* (ha-
nash·i-; hanas·a-; hanash·i-te
C̄) talk; speak; tell:
*Watashi-tachi wa Nichi-Bee
booeki-masatsu ni tsuite* hanashita. (私たちは日米貿易摩擦について
話した) We *talked* about the trade
friction between Japan and the
U.S. / *Motto yukkuri* hanashite
kudasai. (もっとゆっくり話してください)

Will you please *speak* a little
more slowly? / *Kanojo wa Kyooto
no o-tera ni tsuite* hanashite kureta. (彼女は京都のお寺について話して
くれた) She *talked* to us about the
temples of Kyoto. / *Sono koto o
kare ni* hanashimashita ka? (そのこ
とを彼に話しましたか) *Have* you *told*
him that? / *Kore ga señjitsu* hanashita hoñ desu. (これが先日話した本
です) This is the book I *talked
about* the other day. 《⇒ hanaseru; kataru》

ha⌐na⌐s·u[2] はなす (離す) *vt.* (ha-
nash·i-; hanas·a-; hanash·i-te
C̄) **1** separate; part; keep apart;
isolate:
*Keñka o shinai yoo ni, ni-hiki no
inu o* hanashita. (けんかをしないように
2匹の犬を離した) In order to prevent fights I *separated* the two
dogs. / *Tsukue no aida o tooreru
yoo ni* hanashite *kudasai.* (机の間を
通れるように離してください) Please
make a space between the desks
so I can pass between them.
2 (with a negative) do without:
Kono jiteñ wa hanasu *koto ga
dekinai.* (この辞典は離すことができない)
I *cannot do without* this dictionary.

ha⌐na⌐s·u[3] はなす (放す) *vt.* (ha-
nash·i-; hanas·a-; hanash·i-te
C̄) **1** let go; take one's hand
off:
Kare wa roopu kara te o hanashita. (彼はロープから手を放した) He
let go of the rope.
2 let loose; set free (an animal):
Sakana o kawa e hanashite yatta.
(魚を川へ放してやった) I *put* the fish
back into the river. / *Inu o* hanashite *wa dame desu.* (犬を放してはだ
めです) You mustn't *let* your dog
loose.

ha⌐na⌐ts·u はなつ (放つ) *vt.* (ha-
nach·i-; hanat·a-; hanat-te C̄)
1 give off; emit (light):

hikari o hanatsu (光を放つ) *give off* light.

2 set (fire):

Doroboo ga ie ni hi o hanatte, nigeta. (泥棒が家に火を放って、逃げた) The robber *set* fire to the house and fled.

3 shoot; fire; hit:

ya o hanatsu (矢を放つ) *shoot* an arrow / *dañgañ o* hanatsu (弾丸をはなつ) *fire* a shot / *Kare wa kyuukai ni hoomurañ o hanatta.* (彼は9回にホームランを放った) He *hit* a home run in the ninth inning.

ha⌐na⌐wa はなわ (花輪) *n.* floral wreath: ★ Natural or artificial flowers arranged in a circle on a board. Black-and-white wreaths are presented at funerals and red-and-white ones are given on festive occasions, such as at the opening of a store.

hanawa *o* sonaeru (花輪を供える) offer a *floral wreath.*

HANAWA

ha⌐na⌐yaka はなやか (華やか) *a.n.* (~ na, ni) bright; flowery; gorgeous; luxurious:

hanayaka *na doresu* (華やかなドレス) a *gorgeous* dress / *Ooganemochi ni natte,* hanayaka *ni kurashite mitai.* (大金持ちになって、華やかに暮らしてみたい) I'd like to become a millionaire and live *luxuriously.*

ha⌐na⌐yome はなよめ (花嫁) *n.* bride. 《↔ hanamuko》

ha⌐ñbai はんばい (販売) *n.* sale; selling; marketing:

Sono seehiñ no hañbai *wa kare ni makaseta.* (その製品の販売は彼にまかせた) We placed the *sale* of the product in his hands. / hañbai-iñ (販売員) a *salesperson* / hañbai-*kakaku* (販売価格) the *selling* (retail) price / hañbai-teñ (販売店) a *store* [*shop*].

ha⌐ñbai suru (~する) *vt.* sell; deal: *Kono kaisha wa sono seehiñ o itte ni* hañbai *shite iru.* (この会社はその製品を一手に販売している) This company *sells* that product exclusively. / *Kono shoohiñ wa depaato de shika* hañbai *sarete imaseñ.* (この商品はデパートでしか販売されていません) These goods *are sold* only in department stores.

ha⌐ñ-Bee はんべい (反米) *n.* anti-American: hañ-Bee-*kañjoo* (反米感情) *anti-American* sentiment. 《↔ shiñ-Bee》

ha⌐ñbu⌐ñ はんぶん (半分) *n.* half: *Hako no naka no riñgo o* hañbuñ *agemashoo.* (箱の中のりんごを半分あげましょう) I will give you *half* of the apples in the box. / *Watashi wa anata no o-kane no* hañbuñ *shika motte imaseñ.* (私はあなたのお金の半分しか持っていません) I only have *half* as much money as you. —*adv.* half: *Shigoto wa* hañbuñ *owarimashita.* (仕事は半分終わりました) The work is now *half* finished. / *Kono inu wa moo* hañbuñ *shiñde iru.* (この犬はもう半分死んでいる) This dog is already *half* dead.

ha⌐ñ-da⌐kuoñ はんだくおん (半濁音) *n. kana* letters with '゜' attached. These change the original consonant pronunciation to '*p*': パ (*pa*), ピ (*pi*), プ (*pu*), ペ (*pe*) and ポ (*po*). 《⇒ dakuoñ; seeoñ; see inside front cover》

ha⌐ñdañ はんだん (判断) *n.*

judgment; decision:
hañdañ *o ayamaru* (判断を誤る)
make an error in *judgment* / hañdañ *o aogu* (判断を仰ぐ) ask for a
person's *decision* / hañdañ *o kudasu* (判断を下す) pass *judgment* /
Kare no hañdañ *wa tadashikatta
[ayamatte ita]*. (彼の判断は正しかった
[誤っていた]) His *judgment* was
right [wrong]. / *Watashi wa tossa
no* hañdañ *de hañdoru o hidari ni
kitta.* (私はとっさの判断でハンドルを左に
切った) *Deciding* instantaneously,
I swung the steering wheel to
the left. / *Iiñkai naibu de* hañdañ
ga wakareta. (委員会内部で判断が
分かれた) The committee mem-
bers were divided among themselves regarding their *decision.* /
Dochira ga hoñmono ka hañdañ
ga tsukanai. (どちらが本物か判断がつ
かない) I *cannot tell* which is genuine.
hañdañ suru (～する) *vt.* judge;
decide: *Hito wa mikake de hañdañ shite wa ikenai.* (人は見かけで判
断してはいけない) We should not
judge others by their appearance.
/ *Kare no kotoba kara* hañdañ suru
*to shigoto ga umaku ittenai ra-
shii.* (彼の言葉から判断すると仕事がう
まくいってないらしい) *Judging* from
what he says, his work doesn't
seem to be doing well.
haˈñdo-baˈggu ハンドバッグ *n.*
handbag; purse.
haˈñdoru ハンドル *n.* **1** steering
wheel:
kuruma no hañdoru *o nigiru* (車の
ハンドルを握る) take the *wheel* of a
car / *Kare wa kaabu de* hañdoru *o
kiri-sokonatta.* (彼はカーブでハンドルを
切りそこなった) He *could not make
the corner.*
2 (of a bicycle) handlebars.
haˈne はね (羽) *n.* feather; wing;
plume:
Kujaku ga hane *o hirogeta.* (くじゃ

くが羽を広げた) The peacock spread
its *feathers.*
haˈñee[1] はんえい (繁栄) *n.* prosperity:
Anata no kaisha no hañee *o inorimasu.* (あなたの会社の繁栄を祈ります)
I wish your company *prosperity.*
hañee suru (～する) *vi.* prosper;
thrive; flourish: *Kare no uchi wa
chichi-oya no dai ni* hañee shite
ita. (彼の家は父親の代に繁栄していた)
His family *prospered* in his father's time.
haˈñee[2] はんえい (反映) *n.* reflection.
hañee suru (～する) *vt.* reflect:
*Gakkoo-gawa no kettee wa seeto
no ikeñ o mattaku* hañee shite *inakatta.* (学校側の決定は生徒の意見を
全く反映していなかった) The school's
decision did not *reflect* the pupils' opinion at all. / *Sakusha no
seekaku wa sono sakuhiñ ni*
hañee sareru *koto ga aru.* (作者の
性格はその作品に反映されることがある)
The author's personality *is* sometimes *reflected* in his works.
haˈnekaesˈu はねかえす (跳ね返す)
vt. (-kaesh·i-; -kaes·a-; -kae-
sh·i-te C) repel; reject:
Teki no koogeki o hanekaeshita.
(敵の攻撃を跳ね返した) We *repelled*
the attack of the enemy. / *Aite no
yookyuu o* hanekaeshita. (相手の要
求を跳ね返した) I *rejected* the other
party's demand.
haˈneˈru はねる (跳ねる) *vi.* (hanete V) **1** jump; leap; spring;
bound:
Koi ga ike de haneta. (こいが池で跳
ねた) A carp *jumped* in the pond.
2 (of mud, water, etc.) splash:
Doro ga kanojo no sukaato ni haneta. (泥が彼女のスカートに跳ねた)
The mud *splashed* her skirt.
3 (of a performance) close; be
over:
Shibai wa hanemashita *ka?* (芝居

はねましたか) *Is* the play *over?*

ha⌐ñga はんが (版画) *n.* woodblock print; woodcut.

HAÑGA BY HOKUSAI

ha⌐ñgaa ハンガー *n.* hanger: hañgaa *ni yoofuku o kakeru* [*tsurusu*] (ハンガーに洋服を掛ける[つるす]) hang clothes on a *hanger*.

ha⌐ñgaku はんがく (半額) *n.* half the price: *Kono terebi wa* hañgaku *de katta.* (このテレビは半額で買った) I bought this TV at *half price.* / *Kodomo wa* hañgaku *desu.* (子どもは半額です) Children are *half price.*

ha⌐ñgeki はんげき (反撃) *n.* counterattack: *Aite wa mamori kara* hañgeki *ni teñjita.* (相手は守りから反撃に転じた) Our opponents switched from defending to *counterattacking.*

hañgeki suru (～する) *vi.* counterattack; fight back: *Kare-ra wa sugu ni* hañgeki shite *konai to omou.* (彼らはすぐに反撃してこないと思う) I don't think they will *counterattack* soon. / Hañgeki suru *yooi wa dekite imasu.* (反撃する用意はできています) We are ready to *fight back.*

ha⌐ñhañ はんはん (半々) *n.* half-and-half; fifty-fifty: *rieki o* hañhañ *ni wakeru* (利益を半々にわける) divide the profit *equally* / *Kono kurasu wa dañshi to joshi ga* hañhañ *desu.* (このクラスは男子と女子が半々です) In this class, there are an *equal number*

of boys and girls. / *Kare ga seekoo suru chañsu wa* hañhañ *da.* (彼の成功するチャンスは 半々だ) He has a *fifty-fifty* chance of success.

ha⌐ñi はんい (範囲) *n.* scope; sphere; range: *Katsudoo* hañi *o motto hirogetai.* (活動範囲をもっと広げたい) I want to enlarge the *scope* of my activities. / *Kare no kyoomi wa hiroi* hañi *ni wataru.* (彼の興味は広い範囲にわたる) His interests are wide *ranging.* / *Niñgeñ no chishiki no* hañi *wa kagirarete iru.* (人間の知識の範囲は 限られている) The *breadth* of humanity's knowledge is limited. / *Yosañ wa* hañi-*nai ni osameru koto ga dekita.* (予算は範囲内に収めることができた) We were able to keep the budget within *limits.*

ha⌐ñi⌐go はんご (反意語) *n.* antonym. ((↔ dooigo))

ha⌐ñji はんじ (判事) *n.* judge.

ha⌐ñjoo はんじょう (繁盛) *n.* (of business) prosperity: *Shoobai* hañjoo *o kami ni inotta.* (商売繁盛を神に祈った) I prayed to God for a *prosperous* business.

hañjoo suru (～する) *vi.* (of business) prosper; thrive, flourish: *Kare no shoobai wa* hañjoo shite *iru.* (彼の商売は繁盛している) His business *is flourishing.* / Hañjoo shite iru *isha ga kanarazu shimo umai to wa kagiranai.* (繁盛している 医者が必ずしもうまいとは限らない) A *prosperous* doctor is not necessarily a good one.

ha⌐ñjuku はんじゅく (半熟) *n.* half-boiled egg. ((⇒ tamago))

ha⌐ñkachi ハンカチ *n.* handkerchief.

ha⌐ñkañ はんかん (反感) *n.* antipathy; ill feeling: *Kare wa watashi ni* hañkañ *o motte iru yoo da.* (彼は私に反感を持っているようだ) He seems to have *ill feelings* toward me. / *Kare no eñ-*

zetsu wa chooshuu no haṅkaṅ *o katta.* (彼の演説は聴衆の反感を買った) His speech provoked the *antipathy* of the audience.

ha⌐ṅkee はんけい（半径）*n.* radius: haṅkee *jus-seṅchi no eṅ o egaku* (半径10センチの円を描く) draw a circle with a *radius* of ten centimeters.

ha⌐ṅko⌐ はんこ（判子）*n.* seal; stamp: haṅko *o osu [tsuku]* (はんこを押す[つく]) affix a *seal*. 《⇨ iṅkaṅ (illus.)》

ha⌐ṅkyoo はんきょう（反響）*n.*
1 echo.
2 sensation; repercussion: *Sono eega wa ooki-na* haṅkyoo *o yoṅda.* (その映画は大きな反響を呼んだ) The movie created a great *sensation*.
haṅkyoo suru (～する) *vi.* echo; reverberate: *Koe ga toṅneru no naka de* haṅkyoo *shita.* (声がトンネルの中で反響した) Our voices *echoed* in the tunnel.

ha⌐ṅnichi はんにち（半日）*n.* half a day; a half day: *Sono shigoto wa* haṅnichi *kakatta.* (その仕事は半日かかった) That job took *half a day*. / *Kinoo wa* haṅnichi *nete sugoshimashita.* (きのうは半日寝て過ごしました) Yesterday I spent *half the day* sleeping. / *Soko made* haṅnichi *de wa ikemaseṅ.* (そこまで半日では行けません) You can't go there in *half a day*.

ha⌐ṅniṅ はんにん（犯人）*n.* criminal; culprit; offender: *Sono* haṅniṅ *wa mada tsukamaranai.* (その犯人はまだつかまらない) The *criminal* is still at large. / *Keṅjuu o hassha shita* haṅniṅ *wa dare desu ka?* (拳銃を発射した犯人はだれですか) Who is the *culprit* that fired the gun?

ha⌐ṅnoo はんのう（反応）*n.* reaction; response; effect: *Kare-ra wa watashi no teeaṅ ni* tsumetai haṅnoo *o shimeshita.* (彼らは私の提案に冷たい反応を示した) They showed a cool *response* to my proposal. / *Kare wa chooshuu no* haṅnoo *o mi-nagara hanashi o susumeta.* (彼は聴衆の反応を見ながら話を進めた) He proceeded with his talk, watching the audience's *reaction*.
haṅnoo suru (～する) *vi.* react: respond: *Seeto-tachi wa seṅsee no kotoba ni biṅkaṅ ni* haṅnoo *shita.* (生徒たちは先生の言葉に敏感に反応した) The pupils *responded* sensitively to what the teacher said. 《⇨ eekyoo》

ha⌐ṅraṅ はんらん（反乱）*n.* rebellion; revolt; insurrection: *Shokumiṅchi no juumiṅ wa seefu ni taishite* haṅraṅ *o okoshita.* (植民地の住民は政府に対して反乱を起こした) The colonized people *rebelled* against the government. / *Haṅraṅ wa sugu ni shizumerareta.* (反乱はすぐに鎮められた) The *revolt* was put down immediately.

haṅsamu ハンサム *a.n.* (～ na) handsome; good-looking.

ha⌐ṅsee はんせい（反省）*n.* reflection; reconsideration; introspection: *Watashi wa kare-ra ni* haṅsee *o unagashita.* (私は彼らに反省を促した) I urged them to *reflect* on what they had done. / *Haṅniṅ wa* haṅsee *no iro ga mattaku mirarenakatta.* (犯人は反省の色が全く見られなかった) The criminal showed absolutely no sign of *repentance*.
haṅsee suru (～する) *vt.* reflect; feel sorry: Haṅsee *shite miru to watashi ga machigatte ita yoo ni omou.* (反省してみると私が間違っていたように思う) *On reflection*, I seem to have been wrong. / *Jibuṅ no shita koto o* haṅsee *shite imasu.* (自分のしたことを反省しています) I *am sorry* for what I did.

ha「ñsha はんしゃ（反射）*n.* reflection; reflex:
Tsuyoi hikari no hañsha *de mabushikatta.* （強い光の反射でまぶしかった） The *reflection* of the strong light dazzled me.
hañsha suru （〜する）*vt.* reflect:
Shiroi kabe wa hikari o hañsha suru. （白い壁は光を反射する） A white wall *reflects* light.

ha「ñsha-teki はんしゃてき（反射的）*a.n.* （〜 ni） reflexively; instinctively; instantly:
Watashi wa namae o yobarete, hañsha-teki *ni tachiagatta.* （私は名前を呼ばれて、反射的に立ち上がった） On hearing my name called, I stood up *instinctively.*

ha「ñshite はんして（反して）be contrary to: ★ Used in the pattern '*...ni hañshite.*'
Yosoo ni hañshite, *Suzuki-sañ ga yuushoo shita.* （予想に反して、鈴木さんが優勝した） *Contrary to* expectations, Ms. Suzuki took first prize. / *Kare wa oya no kiboo ni* hañshite, *isha ni naranakatta.* （彼は親の希望に反して、医者にならなかった） *Contrary to* his parents' wishes, he did not become a doctor. / *Kanojo ga ureshi-soo na no ni* hañshite, *kare wa geñki ga nai.* （彼女が嬉しそうなのに反して、彼は元気がない） *Whereas* she looks very happy, he looks depressed. （⇨ hañsuru）

ha「ñshoku はんしょく（繁殖）*n.* breeding; propagation:
gaichuu no hañshoku （害虫の繁殖） the *propagation* of vermin.
hañshoku suru （〜する）*vi.* breed; propagate: *Nezumi wa* hañshoku suru *no ga hayai.* （ねずみは繁殖するのが早い） Mice *breed* quickly. / *Bakuteria wa kono jookeñ de wa* hañshoku shimaseñ. （バクテリアはこの条件では繁殖しません） Bacteria *won't propagate* under these conditions.

ha「ñsu「・ru はんする（反する）*vi.* （hañsh·i-; hañsh·i-; hañsh·i-te □） be against; breach (a regulation, rule, contract, etc.):
Sore wa keeyaku ni hañsuru. （それは契約に反する） That *breaches* the contract. / *Kare no yarikata wa moraru ni* hañsuru. （彼のやり方はモラルに反する） His methods *go against* public morality. / *Kiñeñsha de tabako o suu no wa kisoku ni* hañsuru. （禁煙車でたばこを吸うのは規則に反する） It *is against* the rules to smoke in a nonsmoking (railway) car. （⇨ hañshite; ihañ）

ha「ñtai はんたい（反対）*n.* **1** opposite; contrary:
hañtai *no hoogaku* （反対の方角） the *opposite* direction / *Kono e wa jooge* hañtai *da.* （この絵は上下反対だ） This picture is *upside-down.*
2 opposition; objection:
Watashi wa sono ikeñ ni hañtai *desu.* （私はその意見に反対です） I am *against* that opinion. / *Sono añ wa sañsee rokujuugo-hyoo,* hañtai *juuhachi-hyoo de kaketsu saremashita.* （その案は賛成65票, 反対18票で可決されました） The proposal was approved by 65 ayes to 18 *nays.* （↔ sañsee'）
hañtai suru *vi.* oppose: *Ooku no josee ga see-sabetsu ni* hañtai shite iru. （多くの女性が性差別に反対している） Many women *are opposed* to sexual inequality.

ha「ñ-ta「isee はんたいせい（反体制）*n.* anti-establishment:
hañ-taisee *no sakka* （反体制の作家） an *anti-establishment* novelist.

ha「ñtee はんてい（判定）*n.* judgment; decision:
Ishi ga nooshi no hañtee *o kudashite mo, kazoku wa nattoku shinakatta.* （医師が脳死の判定を下しても、家族は納得しなかった） Although the doctor gave a *judgment* of brain death, the family remained

unconvinced. / hañtee-*gachi* (判定勝ち) victory by a *decision*.

hañtee suru (～する) *vt.* judge; decide: *Kikaku no zehi o* hañtee suru *no wa rijikai desu.* (企画の是非を判定するのは理事会です) It is the board of directors that will *make a decision* on the advisability of the plan.

ha「ñtoo はんとう (半島) *n.* peninsula:
Izu hañtoo (伊豆半島) the Izu *Peninsula*.

ha「ñtoshi はんとし (半年) *n.* six months; half a year:
Watashi wa hañtoshi *ni ik-kai shigoto de Oosutoraria e ikimasu.* (私は半年に一回仕事でオーストラリアへ行きます) Once in *six months* I go to Australia on business. / *Kare wa* hañtoshi *Oosaka ni ita koto ga arimasu.* (彼は半年大阪にいたことがあります) He has lived in Osaka for *half a year*. / *Kotoshi mo ato* hañtoshi *desu.* (今年もあと半年です) We are *halfway through the year*.

ha「ñtsuki¹ はんつき (半月) *n.* fortnight; two weeks; half a month:
Koko e kite, hañtsuki *sugimashita.* (ここへ来て，半月過ぎました) *Half a month* has passed since we came here. / *Kaigi wa* hañtsuki *goto ni hirakaremasu.* (会議は半月ごとに開かれます) Meetings are held *semimonthly*.

ha「ñzai はんざい (犯罪) *n.* crime; offense; delinquency:
hañzai *o okasu* (犯罪を犯す) commit a *crime* / *Shooneñ no* hañzai *ga fuete iru.* (少年の犯罪が増えている) Juvenile *delinquency* is increasing.

ha「ori はおり (羽織り) *n.* short overgarment. ★ Usually worn over a kimono. 《⇨ wafuku (illus.)》

ha「ppi はっぴ (法被) *n.* happi coat. ★ Often bears a crest or the name of the employer on the back. Worn mainly by craftsmen, and during festivals by men and women.

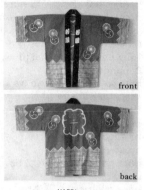

front

back

HAPPI

ha「ppyoo はっぴょう (発表) *n.* announcement; publication; release:
Gookakusha no happyoo *wa gozeñ juu-ji desu.* (合格者の発表は午前10時です) The *announcement* of the successful candidates' names will be made at 10:00 A.M. / *Toosseñsha no* happyoo *wa shoohiñ no hassoo o motte kaesasete itadakimasu.* (当選者の発表は賞品の発送をもってかえさせていただきます) The prizewinners will receive their prizes by mail. / *shiñbuñ*-happyoo (新聞発表) a press *release*.

happyoo suru (～する) *vt.* announce; publish; release: *Seefu wa zeesee moñdai ni tsuite keñkai o* happyoo shita. (政府は税制問題について見解を発表した) The government *released* its view on the tax issue. / *Tsugi no gakkai de keñkyuu no seeka o* happyoo shitai *to omoimasu.* (次の学会で研究の成果を発表したいと思います) I *would like to present* the results of my research at the next conference. 《⇨ dasu (**3**)》

ha┌ra┐¹ はら (腹) *n.* **1** belly; bowels; stomach: ★ Informal expression used by men. '*Onaka*' is more polite.
Hara ga itai. (腹が痛い) I *have a stomachache.* / Hara *o kowashite iru.* (腹をこわしている) I have loose *bowels.* / Hara ga hetta. (腹がへった) I *am hungry.* 《⇨ jiñtai (illus.)》
2 mind; heart:
Hara *no naka de kanojo wa kare o keebetsu shite ita.* (腹の中で彼女は彼を軽蔑していた) She despised him in her *heart.*
hara ga futoi (〜が太い) be broad-minded.
hara ga tatsu (〜が立つ) be [get] angry.
hara o kimeru (〜を決める) make up one's mind.
hara o saguru (〜を探る) sound out another person's intentions.
hara o tateru (〜を立てる) lose one's temper.
hara o yomu (〜を読む) read another person's mind.
ha┌ra┐² はら (原) *n.* field; plain. 《⇨ nohara》
ha┌ra┐gee はらげい (腹芸) *n.* implicit mutual understanding.
ha┌rahara はらはら *adv.* (〜 suru) (the state of being nervous or uneasy):
Kare ga nani o ii-dasu ka wakaranai no de harahara *shita.* (彼が何を言い出すかわからないのではらはらした) I didn't know what he was going to say, so I felt *uneasy.* / *Dochira ga katsu ka* harahara *shi-nagara sono shiai o mita.* (どちらが勝つかはらはらしながらその試合を見た) I watched the game *in suspense,* wondering which side would win. / *Amari hito o* harahara *saseru na yo.* (あまり人をはらはらさせるなよ) Don't make me so *nervous.*
ha┌ra┐i はらい (払い) *n.* payment; bill:

Koñgetsu wa harai *ga ookatta.* (今月は払いが多かった) This month the *bill* was steep. / *Sono* harai *wa sumasemashita ka?* (その払いは済ませましたか) Have you completed the *payment?* / *Kare wa* harai *ga yoi [warui].* (彼は払いがよい[悪い]) He is always punctual [late] in *paying his bills.* 《⇨ harau》
ha┌rappa はらっぱ (原っぱ) *n.* field; plain.
ha┌ra┐·u はらう (払う) *vt.* (hara·i-; haraw·a-; harat-te ⓒ) **1** pay; pay back:
Kare ni sugu haratte *kudasai.* (彼にすぐ払ってください) Please *pay* him right away. / *Kare ni gomañ-eñ* haraimasu. (彼に5万円払います) I'll *pay* him 50,000 yen. / *Kuruma ni nihyakumañ-eñ* haratta. (車に200万円払った) I *paid* two million yen for the car. / *Kanojo ni shakkiñ o* harawanakereba naranai. (彼女に借金を払わなければならない) I *have to pay* her *back* the loan. 《⇨ harai》
2 dust; brush; clear:
hoñ no hokori o harau (本のほこりを払う) *dust* the books / *kooto no chiri o burashi de* harau (コートのちりをブラシで払う) *brush* the dust off one's coat.
3 pay; show (attention):
Hokoosha no añzeñ ni chuui o harai nasai. (歩行者の安全に注意を払いなさい) You should *pay* attention to the safety of pedestrians. 《⇨ shimesu》
ha┌re┐ はれ (晴れ) *n.* fine [clear] weather:
Asu wa hare *deshoo.* (あすは晴れでしょう) It is likely to be *fine* tomorrow. 《⇨ hareru¹; ame¹; kumori》
hare no (〜の) **1** fine; fair:
hare no *hi* (晴れの日) a *clear* day.
2 auspicious; grand: hare no *hi* (晴れの日) an *auspicious* day / hare no *butai* (晴れの舞台) a *grand* occasion / hare no *basho* (晴れの場所) a

formal occasion.

ha⌈re⌉·ru[1] はれる（晴れる）*vi.* (hare-te V̄) **1** (of weather, sky) clear up; become clear:
Asu wa tabuñ hareru deshoo.（あすはたぶん晴れるでしょう）I think it may *be fine* tomorrow. / *Sora ga harete kita.*（空が晴れてきた）The sky *has cleared up.* 《⇨ hare》

2 be cheered up; be refreshed:
Sañpo de mo sureba ki ga hare-masu yo.（散歩でもすれば気が晴れますよ）If you were to, say, go for a stroll, you'd *feel much better.*

3 be cleared; be dispelled:
Kare ni taisuru utagai ga hareta.（彼に対する疑いが晴れた）The suspicion against him *has been dispelled.*

ha⌈re·ru[2] はれる（腫れる）*vi.* (hare-te V̄) swell up; become swollen:
Mushi ni sasarete, te ga hareta.（虫に刺されて、手がはれた）I was stung by an insect and my hand *became swollen.*

ha⌈ri[1] はり（針）*n.* **1** needle:
hari *ni ito o toosu*（針に糸を通す）thread a *needle.*

2 the hands of a clock:
Tokee no hari *ga shichi-ji o sashi-te iru.*（時計の針が7時を指している）The *hands* of the clock show seven o'clock.

3 fishhook. 《⇨ tsuri[1]》

ha⌈ri[2] はり（鍼）*n.* acupuncture:
hari *o utte morau*（はりを打ってもらう）receive *acupuncture* treatment.

ha⌈rigane はりがね（針金）*n.* wire:
harigane *de shibaru*（針金でしばる）bind with *wire.*

ha⌈riki⌉r·u はりきる（張り切る）*vi.* (-kir·i-; -kir·a-; -kit-te C̄) be in high spirits; be full of vitality; be fired up:
Kanojo wa atarashii shigoto ni harikitte imasu.（彼女は新しい仕事に張り切っています）She *is very enthu-*

siastic about her new job.

ha⌈ru[1] はる（春）*n.* spring:
Moo sugu haru *ga kuru.*（もうすぐ春が来る）*Spring* will come soon. / *Shiñ-gakki wa* haru *ni hajimaru.*（新学期は春に始まる）The new term begins in *spring.* / haru-*kaze*（春風）a *spring* breeze. 《⇨ shiki[1] (table); kisetsu (table)》

ha⌈r·u[2] はる（貼る）*vt.* (har·i-; ha-r·a-; hat-te C̄) put; stick:
kabe ni posutaa o haru（壁にポスターをはる）*stick* a poster on the wall / *Ryookiñ-busoku desu kara sañ-juu-eñ kitte o moo ichi-mai* hatte *kudasai.*（料金不足ですから30円切手をもう1枚はってください）The postage is insufficient, so please *put on* another 30-yen stamp. / *Kuu-poñ-keñ o hagaki ni* hatte, *dashita.*（クーポン券をはがきにはって、出した）I *stuck* a coupon on the postcard and sent it off.

ha⌈r·u[3] はる（張る）*vi., vt.* (har·i-; har·a-; hat-te C̄) **1** set up; put up; spread:
teñto o haru（テントを張る）*pitch* a tent / *ho o* haru（帆を張る）*set* a sail / *Kono ki wa ne ga yoku* hatte iru.（この木は根がよく張っている）This tree *is deep-rooted.*

2 stretch; strain:
Geñba ni wa tsuna ga hatte atte, dare mo hairemaseñ.（現場には綱が張ってあって、だれも入れません）A rope *is stretched* around the spot and no one can get in.

3 cover; freeze; tile:
Ike ni koori ga hatta.（池に氷が張った）Ice *covered* the pond. / *Furoba ni wa tairu ga* hatte arimasu.（風呂場にはタイルが張ってあります）The bathroom *is tiled.*

ha⌈ruba⌉ru はるばる（遥々）*adv.*
(〜 to) all the way; from afar:
Kinoo haha ga kyoori kara haru-baru (*to*) *dete kimashita.*（きのう母が郷里からはるばる（と）出てきました）Yes-

terday my mother came up *all the way* from our hometown.

ha⌐ruka はるか (遥か) *adv.* **1** (of distance) far away:
Haruka *mukoo ni Fuji-sañ ga mieta.* (はるか向こうに富士山が見えた) I could see Mt. Fuji *far away.*
2 (of time) far back:
Haruka *mukashi no koto na no de yoku oboete imaseñ.* (はるか昔のことなのでよく覚えていません) It is something that happened *a very long time ago*, so I don't remember clearly.

ha⌐ruka ni はるかに (遥かに) *adv.* much; by far:
Kono kuruma no hoo ga haruka ni *seenoo ga ii.* (この車のほうがはるかに性能がいい) This car's performance is *far* better. 《⇨ zutto》

ha⌐ru-ya⌐sumi はるやすみ (春休み) *n.* spring vacation. ★ Schools are on vacation from the middle of March until the beginning of April. 《⇨ yasumi》

ha⌐sami はさみ (鋏) *n.* scissors; shears:
kami o hasami *de kiru* (紙をはさみで切る) cut paper with *scissors.*

ha⌐sa⌐m·u はさむ (挟む) *vt.* (hasam·i-; hasam·a-; hasañ-de Ⓒ) put in; insert; catch in:
shiori o hoñ ni hasamu (しおりを本に挟む) *insert* a bookmark in a book / *tabemono o hashi de* hasamu (食べ物を箸で挟む) *pick* food *up* between one's chopsticks / *Kare wa deñsha no doa ni yubi o hasamareta.* (彼は電車のドアに指を挟まれた) He *got* his fingers *caught* in the train door.

ha⌐sañ はさん (破産) *n.* bankruptcy; insolvency:
Kare wa hasañ *no señkoku o uketa.* (彼は破産の宣告を受けた) He was declared *bankrupt.* / *Kee-ee ga akka shite,* hasañ *no mooshitate o shinakereba naranaku natta.*

(経営が悪化して, 破産の申し立てをしなければならなくなった) Business went bad and we were forced to petition for *bankruptcy.* / *Sono kaisha no* hasañ *de, ooku no hito ga eekyoo o uketa.* (その会社の破産で, 多くの人が影響を受けた) Many people were affected by the company's *bankruptcy.*

hasañ suru (〜する) *vi.* go bankrupt: *Kare wa jigyoo ni shippai shite,* hasañ shita. (彼は事業に失敗して, 破産した) He failed in his business and *went bankrupt.*

ha⌐shi¹ はし (橋) *n.* bridge:
kawa ni hashi *o kakeru* (川に橋をかける) build a *bridge* across a river / hashi *o wataru* (橋を渡る) cross a *bridge.*

ha⌐shi² はし (箸) *n.* chopsticks:
hashi *ichi-zeñ* (箸一膳) a pair of *chopsticks* / hashi *de taberu* (箸で食べる) eat with *chopsticks.*

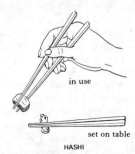

in use

set on table

HASHI

ha⌐shi³ はし (端) *n.* end; edge:
Kare wa beñchi no hashi *ni suwatta.* (彼はベンチの端に座った) He sat at the *end* of the bench.

ha⌐shigo はしご (梯子) *n.* ladder; stairs:
hashigo *o noboru* [*oriru*] (はしごをのぼる[おりる]) go up [climb down] a *ladder* / *Yane ni* hashigo *o kaketa.* (屋根にはしごを掛けた) I set up a *ladder* against the roof.

ha⌐shira はしら (柱) *n.* pillar; post; column:

Kakine no hashira *o ni-meetoru-oki ni tateta.* (垣根の柱を 2 メートルおきに立てた) I set the fence *posts* two meters apart. / *Futoi* hashira *ga yane o sasaete ita.* (太い柱が屋根を支えていた) The thick *pillars* supported the roof.

ha⌐shi⌐r·u はしる (走る) *vi.* (hashir·i-; hashir·a-; hashit-te Ⓒ)
1 (of people and animals) run; dash; rush; jog:
Uma wa zeñsokuryoku de hashitte ita. (馬が全速力で走っていた) The horse *was galloping* at full tilt. / *Deñsha ni maniau yoo ni eki e* hashitta. (電車に間に合うように駅へ走った) I *ran* to the station to be in time for the train.
2 (of vehicles) run; travel:
Kono dooro wa basu ga hashitte imasu. (この道路はバスが走っています) Buses *run* along this street. / *Kuruma de ichi-jikañ* hashittara, *soko ni tsukimashita.* (車で 1 時間走ったら、そこに着きました) I *traveled* an hour by car and arrived there.
3 (of a railroad, a road, etc.) run:
Kono michi wa toozai ni hashitte imasu. (この道は東西に走っています) This road *runs* east-west.

ha⌐shiwa⌐tashi はしわたし (橋渡し) *n.* mediation; go-between:
Kare wa Nichi-Bee-kañ no hashiwatashi *o shita.* (彼は日米間の橋渡しをした) He *mediated* between the U.S.A. and Japan.

ha⌐soñ はそん (破損) *n.* damage; breakage:
Paipu no hasoñ-*kasho o shuuri shita.* (パイプの破損箇所を修理した) I repaired the *damaged* parts of the pipe. / *Taifuu ni yoru kaoku no* hasoñ *wa hyaku-keñ ni nobotta.* (台風による家屋の破損は 100 軒にのぼった) The number of houses *damaged* by the typhoon reached 100.
hasoñ suru (～する) *vi.* be dam-

aged; be broken: Hasoñ shita *fune wa chikaku no minato ni haitta.* (破損した船は近くの港に入った) The *damaged* ship entered a nearby port. / *Kono zaishitsu no utsuwa wa* hasoñ shi-yasui. (この材質の器は破損しやすい) Utensils made of this material are *fragile.*

ha⌐ssee はっせい (発生) *n.* occurrence; outbreak:
Jishiñ no hassee *wa yochi dekinai.* (地震の発生は予知できない) We cannot predict the *occurrence* of earthquakes. / *Jikeñ no* hassee *kara juu-jikañ ga tatta.* (事件の発生から 10 時間がたった) Ten hours have passed since the *occurrence* of the event.
hassee suru (～する) *vi.* occur; break out: *Jiko ga* hassee shita *tame, koosoku-dooro wa geñzai juutai shite imasu.* (事故が発生したため、高速道路は現在渋滞しています) Since an accident has *occurred*, the freeway is at present jammed with traffic.

ha⌐ssha はっしゃ (発車) *n.* (of a train, bus, etc.) departure:
Hassha *no beru ga natte iru.* (発車のベルが鳴っている) The bell signaling *departure* is ringing. / Hassha oorai. (発車オーライ) Ready for *departure!* ★ Shout given by platform attendant to conductor to indicate it is safe to depart.
(⇨ shuppatsu)
hassha suru (～する) *vi.* start; leave; depart: *Takasaki-yuki no ressha wa ni-bañseñ kara* hassha shimasu. (高崎行きの列車は 2 番線から発車します) The train for Takasaki *leaves* from track 2. / *Basu wa ato go-fuñ de* hassha shimasu. (バスはあと 5 分で発車します) The bus will *depart* in five minutes.

ha⌐sumu⌐kai はすむかい (斜向かい) *n.* the diagonally opposite side:
hasumukai *no ie* (はす向かいの家) a

house standing *diagonally opposite*.

ha「ta」 はた (旗) *n.* flag; banner:
hata *o kakageru [orosu]* (旗を掲げる[おろす]) put up [take down] a *flag* / hata *o furu* (旗を振る) wave a *flag* / Hata *ga kaze ni hatameite iru.* (旗が風にはためいている) The *flag* is fluttering in the wind.

ha「tachi はたち (二十歳) *n.* twenty years of age:
Musume wa hatachi *desu.* (娘ははたちです) My daughter is *twenty.* / *Kanojo wa* hatachi *de kekkon shita.* (彼女ははたちで結婚した) She got married at *the age of twenty.*

ha「take はたけ (畑) *n.* field; farm:
hatake *o tagayasu* (畑を耕す) plow a *field* / Hatake *ni mugi no tane o maita.* (畑に麦の種をまいた) I sowed wheat in the *field.*
hatake chigai (〜違い) outside one's field: *Kagaku wa* hatake chigai *desu.* (化学は畑違いです) Chemistry is *outside my field.*

ha「taki」 はたき (叩き) *n.* duster:
★ Made of strips of cloth tied at the end of a long stick.
hataki *o kakeru* (はたきをかける) remove dust by using a *duster.*

HATAKI

ha「tame」k・u はためく *vi.* (-mek・i-; -mek・a-; -me・i-te C) flutter; wave:
Hata ga kaze ni hatameite iru. (旗が風にはためいている) The flag *is fluttering* in the wind.

ha「tan」 はたん (破綻) *n.* failure; breakdown; rupture:
too-zai kankee no hatan (東西関係

の破たん) a *rupture* in East-West relations.
hatan suru (〜する) *vi.* fail; break down; rupture: *Kare-ra no keekaku wa* hatan shita. (彼らの計画は破たんした) Their plan *failed.*

ha「taraki はたらき (働き) *n.*
1 work; service:
hataraki *ni deru* (働きに出る) go to *work.*
2 function; operation:
i no hataraki (胃の働き) the *function* of the stomach.
hataraki o suru (〜をする) *vi.* do work; make a contribution:
★ Preceded by a modifier.
Kare wa mezamashii hataraki o shita. (彼は目覚ましい働きをした) He *has done* remarkable *work.* / *Kare wa sono kurabu no tame ni ookina* hataraki o shimashita. (彼はそのクラブのために大きな働きをしました) He *made* great *contributions* for the sake of the club.

ha「tarak・u はたらく (働く) *vi., vt.* (hatarak・i-; hatarak・a-; hatara・ite C) **1** work; labor; serve:
Kare wa yoku hatarakimasu. (彼はよく働きます) He *works* well. / *Kanojo wa ginkoo de* hataraite imasu. (彼女は銀行で働いています) She *works* at a bank. / *Nihonjin wa* hataraki-*sugiru to iwareru.* (日本人は働き過ぎるといわれる) It is said that the Japanese *work* too much.
2 function; work:
Kyoo wa atama ga hatarakanai. (きょうは頭が働かない) My brain *is not working* today. / *Bureeki ga* hatarakanai *de, jiko ni natta.* (ブレーキが働かないで、事故になった) The breaks *did not function*, and there was an accident.
3 commit (violence, a crime, etc.):
nusumi o hataraku (盗みを働く) *commit* theft / *ranboo o* hataraku (乱暴を働く) *commit* violence.

ha「ta」shite はたして (果たして) *adv.*

(often in questions) really; as was expected; sure enough:
Kare wa jishiñ o motte soo itta ga hatashite *hoñtoo daroo ka.*(彼は自信を持ってそう言ったがはたしてほんとうだろうか) He said so with confidence, but I *really* wonder if it is true. / *Shiñpai shite ita ga,* hatashite *kare wa jiko o okoshita.*(心配していたが, はたして彼は事故を起した) I was concerned about him, and *as I expected,* he caused an accident.

ha⌐to はと (鳩) *n.* pigeon; dove.

ha⌐tsu- はつ (初) *pref.* first:
hatsu-*koi* (初恋) one's *first* love / hatsu-*shukkiñ* (初出勤) one's *first* day at work / hatsu-*yuki* (初雪) the *first* snow of the winter / *Nihoñ* hatsu-*kookai no e* (日本初公開の絵) a picture exhibited in Japan for the *first time.*

-hatsu[1] はつ (発) *suf.* **1** (of a train, bus, etc.) leaving:
Ueno-hatsu *no shiñdaisha* (上野発の寝台車) the sleeper *leaving* Ueno / *roku-ji*-hatsu *no 'Hikari'* (6時発の「ひかり」) the 'Hikari' *leaving* at six o'clock.
2 (of a news source) from; datelined:
Pekiñ-hatsu *no nyuusu* (北京発のニュース) news *datelined* Beijing.

-hatsu[2]/**patsu** はつ/ぱつ (発) *suf.* counter for bullets, shells and large fireworks:

1 i⌐p-patsu⌐	7 na⌐na⌐-hatsu
2 ni⌐-hatsu	8 ha⌐p-patsu⌐
3 sa⌐ñ-patsu	(ha⌐chi-hatsu)
4 yo⌐ñ-patsu	9 kyu⌐u-hatsu
5 go⌐-hatsu	10 ji⌐p-patsu
6 ro⌐p-patsu⌐	(ju⌐p-patsu)
(ro⌐ku-hatsu)	? na⌐ñ-patsu

Tama wa nañ-patsu *nokotte imasu ka?* (弾は何発残っていますか) *How many bullets* are left? / *Hanabi ga* go-hatsu *uchiagerareta.*

(花火が5発打ち上げられた) *Five fireworks* were shot off.

ha⌐tsubai はつばい (発売) *n.* sale:
Shiñ-seehiñ no hatsubai *wa raigetsu desu.*(新製品の発売は来月です) The new product will *be put on sale* next month. / hatsubai-*kiñshi* (発売禁止) prohibition of *sales.* ★ Often shortened '*hakkiñ* (発禁)' / hatsubai-*moto* (発売元) a *sales* agency.
hatsubai suru (〜する) *vt.* sell; put on sale: *Shiteeseki-keñ wa joosha suru hi no ik-kagetsu mae kara* hatsubai saremasu. (指定席券は乗車する日の1か月前から発売されます) Tickets for reserved seats *are sold* one month before the day of travel. / *Sono jisho wa raineñ* hatsubai saremasu.(その辞書は来年発売されます) The dictionary is due to *come out* next year.

ha⌐tsubyoo はつびょう (発病) *n.* onset of a disease; attack:
Kare wa jibuñ no hatsubyoo *ni ki ga tsukanakatta.* (彼は自分の発病に気がつかなかった) He did not realize that he *had contracted an illness.*
hatsubyoo suru (〜する) *vi.* become sick; be taken ill: *Eizu no uirusu ni kañseñ shite mo* hatsubyoo *shinai hito mo imasu.* (エイズのウイルスに感染しても発病しない人もいます) There are some people who *do not fall ill* even if they are infected with the AIDS virus.

ha⌐tsugeñ はつげん (発言) *n.* speech; remark:
Kare wa jibuñ no hatsugeñ *o torikeshita.*(彼は自分の発言を取り消した) He retracted his *remark.* / hatsugeñ-*ryoku* (発言力) an influential *voice* / hatsugeñ-sha (発言者) a *speaker.*
hatsugeñ suru (〜する) *vi.* speak; utter; say a word: *Shussekisha wa tsugitsugi to* hatsugeñ shita.(出席者は次々と発言した) Those

present *made remarks* one after another. / *Watashi ni mo* hatsugeñ sasete *kudasai.* (私にも発言させてください) Please *let* me also *say a word.*

ha⌐tsu-hi⌐node はつひので (初日の出) *n.* the sunrise on New Year's Day. ★ It is a Japanese custom to greet and pay respects to the first sunrise of the year.

ha⌐tsuiku はついく (発育) *n.* development; growth: *Kono ki wa* hatsuiku ga yoi [warui] (この木は発育が良い[悪い]) This tree *is growing quickly* [*slowly*]. / *Kono ko wa* hatsuiku *ga osoi yoo ni miemasu ga shiñpai wa irimaseñ.* (この子は発育が遅いように見えますが心配はいりません) This boy seems slow in *development,* but you don't have to worry.

hatsuiku suru (～する) *vi.* grow; develop: *Kyoneñ ueta nae wa juñchoo ni* hatsuiku shite imasu. (去年植えた苗は順調に発育しています) The seedlings we planted last year *are growing* well.

hatsuiku-zakari (～ざかり) growing; developing: Hatsuiku-zakari *no kodomo wa shokuyoku ga oosee da.* (発育ざかりの子どもは食欲が旺盛だ) A *growing* child has a hearty appetite.

ha⌐tsuka はつか (二十日) *n.*
1 twenty days: *Shuppatsu made ato* hatsuka *aru.* (出発まであと二十日ある) There are *twenty days* before departure.
2 the twentieth: *Watashi no tañjoobi wa shichigatsu* hatsuka *desu.* (私の誕生日は七月二十日です) My birthday is July *20.* 《⇨ tsuitachi (table)》

ha⌐tsuka-da⌐ikoñ はつかだいこん (二十日大根) *n.* radish. 《⇨ daikoñ》

ha⌐tsumee はつめい (発明) *n.* invention:

deñwa [*terebi*] *no* hatsumee (電話 [テレビ]の発明) the *invention* of the telephone [television] / hatsumee-hiñ (発明品) an *invention* / hatsumee-ka (発明家) an *inventor.*

hatsumee suru (～する) *vt.* invent: *Deñwa o* hatsumee shita *no wa dare desu ka?* (電話を発明したのはだれですか) Who is it that *invented* the telephone? / *Kare wa omoshiroi kikai o* hatsumee shita. (彼はおもしろい機械を発明した) He *invented* a very interesting machine.

ha⌐tsumo⌐ode はつもうで (初詣) *n.* the first New Year's visit to a shrine or a temple. ★ It is a Japanese custom to pay a visit on New Year's Day to a shrine or temple in the neighborhood to pray for a long life, and happiness during the year.

TYPICAL HATSUMOODE SCENE

ha⌐tsuoñ[1] はつおん (発音) *n.* pronunciation: '山' *ni wa* '*yama*' *to* '*sañ*' *no futatsu no kotonatta* hatsuoñ *ga arimasu.* (「山」には「やま」と「さん」の二つの異なった発音があります) There are two different *pronunciations* for '山': '*yama*' and '*sañ*.'
hatsuoñ suru (～する) *vt.* pronounce: *Kono go o* hatsuoñ shite *mite kudasai.* (この語を発音してみてください) Please try *pronouncing* this word. 《⇨ appendixes》

ha⌐tsuoñ[2] はつおん (撥音) *n.* the Japanese syllabic nasal, written '*ñ*' in this dictionary:

hatsuoñ-*biñ* (はつ音便) the *nasal sound* change. 《⇨ sokuoñ; yoo-oñ; appendixes》

ha⌐ttatsu はったつ (発達) *n.* development; growth:
Saikiñ no waapuro no hattatsu *wa mezamashii.* (最近のワープロの発達はめざましい) Recent *developments* in word processors are remarkable. / *Supootsu wa shiñshiñ no* hattatsu *ni juuyoo na yakuwari o hatashimasu.* (スポーツは心身の発達に重要な役割を果たします) Sports play an important role in the *growth* of mind and body.
hattatsu suru (〜する) *vi.* grow; develop: *Taifuu ga minami no kaijoo de* hattatsu shite iru. (台風が南の海上で発達している) A typhoon *is developing* over the ocean in the south. / *Nihoñ wa shakai hoshoo seedo ga juubuñ ni* hattatsu shite iru *kuni to wa ienai.* (日本は社会保障制度が十分に発達している国とはいえない) Japan cannot be considered a country in which the social welfare system *is* fully *developed.* 《⇨ hatteñ》

ha⌐tteñ はってん (発展) *n.* expansion; development; progress:
Sono kaisha wa koko juu-neñkañ ni mezamashii hatteñ *o togeta.* (その会社はここ10年間にめざましい発展を遂げた) The company has made a remarkable *expansion* in the past ten years. / *Miñna wa sono jikeñ no* hatteñ *o mimamotta.* (みんなはその事件の発展を見守った) Everybody watched the *development* of that affair. / *Saigo ni Ikeda-kuñ no masumasu no go*-hatteñ *o o-inori itashimasu.* (最後に池田君のますますのご発展をお祈りいたします) In conclusion, I would like to wish Mr. Ikeda *further success.*
hatteñ suru (〜する) *vi.* develop; grow; expand: *Kono machi wa koojoo ga dekite kara* hatteñ shita.

(この町は工場ができてから発展した) This town *has become prosperous* since the factory was built. / *Kono shoosha wa kaigai e* hatteñ suru *koto o keekaku shite iru.* (この商社は海外へ発展することを計画している) This trading company plans to *expand* overseas. / *Arata na shoogeñ de, jikeñ wa igai na hookoo e* hatteñ shita. (新たな証言で, 事件は意外な方向へ発展した) With the appearance of new testimony, the case *developed* in an unexpected direction. 《⇨ hattatsu》

ha⌐tteñ-tojo⌐o-koku はってんとじょうこく (発展途上国) *n.* developing country.

ha⌐tto はっと *adv.* (〜 suru) (the state of being startled or surprised):
Watashi wa ushiro kara yobikakerarete, hatto shita. (私は後ろから呼びかけられて, はっとした) I was *startled* when called to from behind. / *Kare wa señsee no koe ni* hatto *shite tachi-agatta* (彼は先生の声にはっとして立ち上がった) He *started* from his seat at the teacher's voice. / *Kanojo wa* hatto *me o samashita.* (彼女ははっと目を覚ました) She awoke with a *start.*

ha⌐·u はう (這う) *vi.* (ha·i-; ha-w·a-; hat-te 〔C〕) creep; crawl:
Akañboo ga hai-*hajimeta.* (赤ん坊がはいはじめた) The baby has started to *crawl.* / *Hebi ga tamago no hoo e* hatte itta. (蛇は卵のほうへはって行った) The snake *slithered* toward the egg.

ha⌐usu ハウス *n.* hothouse; (plastic) greenhouse:
hausu-*saibai no tomato* (ハウス栽培のトマト) tomatoes grown in a *hothouse.*

ha⌐ya⌐·i[1] はやい (早い) *a.* (-ku) (of time) early; soon:
Akirameru no wa mada hayai. (あきらめるのはまだ早い) It is still too

early to give up. / *Watashi wa asa* hayaku *okimasu.* (私は朝早く起きます) I get up *early* in the morning. / Hayaku *haru ni naru to ii naa.* (早く春になるといいなあ) I hope spring will come *soon.* / Haya-kereba hayai *hodo ii desu.* (早ければ早いほどいいです) The *sooner,* the better. ((↔ osoi))

ha「ya」·i[2] はやい (速い) *a.* (-ku) (of motion) fast; quick; rapid; speedy:
Hikari wa oto yori mo hayai. (光りは音よりも速い) Light is *faster* than sound. / *Kono kawa wa nagare ga* hayai. (この川は流れが速い) The current in this river is very *fast.* / *Suzuki-sañ wa shigoto ga* hayai. (鈴木さんは仕事が速い) Mr. Suzuki does his work *quickly.* / *Motto* hayaku *hashiri nasai.* (もっと速く走りなさい) Run *faster.* ((↔ osoi))

ha「ya」kuchi はやくち (早口) *n.* fast talking:
Kanojo wa hayakuchi *da.* (彼女は早口だ) She *talks fast.* / *Kare wa* ha-yakuchi *da kara itte iru koto ga yoku wakaranai.* (彼は早口だから言っていることがよくわからない) He *talks so fast* that I cannot follow what he is saying.

ha「yama」r·u はやまる (早まる) *vi.* (-mar·i-; -mar·a-; -mat-te [C]) (of time) be made earlier; be brought forward:
Dañtoo de sakura no kaika ga ha-yamatta. (暖冬で桜の開花が早まった) Because of the warm winter, the opening of the cherry blossoms *occurred early.* ((⇨ hayameru[1]))

ha「yame」·ru[1] はやめる (早める) *vt.* (-me-te [V]) 1 hasten; speed up:
Karoo ga kare no shi o hayameta. (過労が彼の死を早めた) Overwork *hastened* his death. / *Kono hiryoo wa sakumotsu no seechoo o* haya-memasu. (この肥料は作物の生長を早めます) This fertilizer *speeds up* the

growth of the crops. ((⇨ haya-maru))
2 advance; bring forward:
Kare-ra wa kekkoñ-shiki o ni-shuukañ hayameta. (彼らは結婚式を2週間早めた) They *advanced* their wedding by two weeks. / *Tsugoo de kaikai no jikañ o* hayameta. (都合で開会の時間を早めた) Owing to circumstances, we *brought forward* the time for the start of the meeting. ((⇨ hayamaru))

ha「yame」·ru[2] はやめる (速める) *vt.* (-me-te [V]) quicken; hasten:
Basu ni maniau yoo ni ashi o haya-meta. (バスに間に合うように足を速めた) I *quickened* my pace so as to be in time for the bus. / *Kuruma wa supiido o* hayameta. (車はスピードを速めた) The car *speeded up.*

ha「ya」ne はやね (早寝) *n.* going to bed early:
Hayane hayaoki *no shuukañ o tsuke nasai.* (早寝早起きの習慣をつけなさい) Get into the habit of *going to bed early* and getting up early. ((↔ hayaoki))
hayane (o) suru (～(を)する) *vi.* go to bed early: Hayane suru *hito wa asa mo hayai.* (早寝する人は朝も早い) Those who *go to bed early* also rise early in the morning.

ha「ya」oki はやおき (早起き) *n.* early rising:
hayaoki no hito (早起きの人) an *early riser* / Hayaoki wa sañ-moñ no toku. (*saying*) (早起きは三文の得) *The early bird catches the worm.* ((↔ hayane))
hayaoki (o) suru (～(を)する) *vi.* get up early; rise early: Hayaoki shite, *hito-mawari sañpo o shite kimashita.* (早起きして、一回り散歩をしてきました) I *got up early* and took a walk around. / *Ashita wa toobañ na no de* hayaoki shina-kereba *narimaseñ.* (あしたは当番なので早起きしなければなりません) I'm on

duty tomorrow, so I have to *get up early.*

ha⌐ya⌐r·u はやる（流行る）*vi.* (hayar·i-; hayar·a-; hayat-te C)
1 be popular; be in fashion:
Ima sono uta ga hayatte imasu. （今その歌がはやっています）That song *is* now *popular.* / *Kore ga ima* hayatte iru *fukusoo desu.* （これが今はやっている服装です）These are the clothes that *are* now *in fashion.*
2 (of a shop, an enterprise, etc.) prosper; do good business:
Ano mise wa hayatte iru. （あの店ははやっている）That shop *is doing well.*
3 (of disease) be raging; be prevalent:
Ryuukañ ga Nihoñ-juu de hayatte imasu. （流感が日本中ではやっています）Influenza *is prevalent* throughout Japan.

ha⌐yasa はやさ（速さ）*n.* speed; quickness; rapidity:
hikari [oto] no hayasa （光[音]の速さ）the *speed* of light [sound] / *kaifuku no* hayasa （回復の速さ）the *speed* of recovery (from an illness) / *Taioo no* hayasa *ni odoroita.* （対応の速さに驚いた）I was surprised at the *quickness* of the response. 《⇨ sokudo; supiido》

ha⌐yashi はやし（林）*n.* grove; woods: ★ A large area of land more thickly covered with trees than '*hayashi*' is called '*mori*' （森）.
Hayashi *no naka ni komichi ga ippoñ tootte iru.* （林の中に小道が一本通っている）There is one path running through the *woods.*

ha⌐ya⌐s·u はやす（生やす）*vt.* (hayash·i-; hayas·a-; hayash·i-te C) grow (a beard, etc.): ★ '*hayashite iru*'＝wear.
Hatake ni kusa o hayashite *wa ikemaseñ.* （畑に草を生やしてはいけません）You must not let weeds *grow*

in the fields. / *Kare wa hige o* hayashite iru. （彼はひげを生やしている）He *wears* a beard. 《⇨ haeru'》

ha⌐zu はず（筈）*n.* supposed; expected:
Tanaka-sañ wa jimusho ni iru hazu *desu.* （田中さんは事務所にいるはずです）Miss Tanaka is *supposed* to be in the office. / *Kimi wa sono koto o shitte iru* hazu *da.* （君はそのことを知っているはずだ）You *ought to* know it. / *Kare ga uso o tsuku* hazu *wa arimaseñ.* （彼がうそをつくはずはありません）*One would not expect* him to tell a lie. 《⇨ hazu wa nai》

ha⌐zukashi⌐·i はずかしい（恥ずかしい）*a.* (-ku) ashamed; shameful:
Koñna kañtañ na koto ga dekinakute, hazukashii. （こんな簡単なことができなくて、恥ずかしい）I feel *ashamed* that I cannot do such a simple thing. / *Sono oñna-no-ko wa* hazukashi-soo *ni heñji o shita.* （その女の子は恥ずかしそうに返事をした）The girl answered *bashfully.*

ha⌐zumi はずみ（弾み）*n.* momentum; impulse:
Jiteñsha wa saka o kudaru ni tsurete hazumi *ga tsuita.* （自転車は坂を下るにつれてはずみがついた）As the bicycle went down the slope, it gained *momentum.* 《⇨ hazumu》

hazumi de (〜で) by chance [accident]: *Ano chiimu wa nani-ka no* hazumi de *yuushoo suru ka mo shirenai.* （あのチームは何かのはずみで優勝するかも知れない）That team may come in first *by some lucky chance.*

ha⌐zum·u はずむ（弾む）*vi.* (hazum·i-; hazum·a-; hazuñ-de C)
1 bounce; bound:
Kono booru wa yoku hazumu. （このボールはよく弾む）This ball *bounces* well. 《⇨ hazumi》
2 become lively; bound:
Watashi-tachi no hanashi wa hazuñda. （私たちの話は弾んだ）Our

conversation *became lively.* | *Kanojo no mune wa yorokobi ni* hazuñda. (彼女の胸は喜びに弾んだ) Her heart *jumped* for joy.

ha「zure·ru はずれる (外れる) *vi.* (hazure-te Ⅴ) **1** come off; be undone; be out of joint: *Botañ ga* hazurete imasu yo. (ボタンがはずれていますよ) Your button *is undone.* | *Juwaki ga* hazurete imasu. (受話器がはずれています) The receiver *is off the hook.* | *To ga* hazureta. (戸が外れた) The door *was unhinged.* 《⇨ hazusu》
2 miss (a target); fail; (of a prediction, a forecast, a guess, etc.) prove wrong: *Tama wa mato o* hazureta. (弾は的を外れた) The bullet *missed* the target. | *Teñki yohoo ga* hazureta. (天気予報がはずれた) The weather forecast *was wrong.* | *Watashi no ate wa* hazureta. (私の当てははずれた) My expectations *were off the mark.*
3 be out of the way; be contrary: *chuushiñ kara* hazureru (中心からはずれる) *be off* center | *kisoku ni* hazureta *kooi* (規則にはずれた行為) an act *contrary* to the rules.

ha「zus·u はずす (外す) *vt.* (hazush·i-; hazus·a-; hazush·i-te Ⅽ) **1** take off; remove: *megane [tokee] o* hazusu (眼鏡[時計]を外す) *take off* one's glasses [watch] | *botañ o* hazusu (ボタンをはずす) *undo* a button | *Kare no namae wa señshu no meebo kara* hazusareta. (彼の名前は選手の名簿からはずされた) His name *was removed* from the list of competitors. 《⇨ hazureru》
2 leave (one's seat); slip away from: *Kare wa kaigi-chuu, seki o* hazushita. (彼は会議中, 席をはずした) He *left* his seat in the middle of the

meeting.

ha「zu wa na「i はずはない (筈は無い) (*formal* = 'hazu wa arimaseñ') be hardly possible; cannot expect: *Ano hito ga Taguchi-sañ no hazu wa nai. Kare wa ima Pari ni iru ñ da kara.* (あの人が田口さんのはずはない. 彼は今パリにいるんだから) *It is hardly possible* that that man is Taguchi, since he is now in Paris. | *Kare wa shikeñ ni ochita bakari de, geñki na* hazu wa nai. (彼は試験に落ちたばかりで, 元気なはずはない) He has just failed the exam, so *it's only natural* that he doesn't feel cheerful. | *Aa-iu hito ga majime ni shigoto o suru* hazu wa arimaseñ. (ああいう人がまじめに仕事をするはずはありません) You *cannot expect* a person like that to work properly. | *Ano futari ga koñbañ no paatii ni shusseki suru* hazu wa arimaseñ. (あの二人が今晩のパーティーに出席するはずはありません) That couple *are not expected* to attend tonight's party. | *Hitori-gurashi no seekatsu ga tanoshii* hazu wa nai. (一人暮らしの生活が楽しいはずはない) *It is hardly possible* that living alone is enjoyable. | *Soñna* hazu wa nai. (そんなはずはない) That's *impossible.*

― (**USAGE**) ―

Note the use of a double negative, '*nai hazu wa nai*': *Kimi ga sore o* shiranai hazu wa nai. (君がそれを知らないはずはない) *There is no reason* for you *not to know* that.

---

he「bi へび (蛇) *n.* snake; serpent.
he「e へい (塀) *n.* wall; fence: *Ie no mawari o burokku no* hee *de kakoñda.* (家の回りをブロックの塀で囲んだ) I built a *wall* of concrete blocks around the house. | *Niwa wa ki no* hee *de kakomarete iru.* (庭は木の塀で囲まれている) The gar-

den is surrounded by a wooden *fence.*

He⌈eañ-ji⌉dai へいあんじだい (平安時代) *n.* Heian Period (794 to 1192). 《⇨ jidai (table)》

he⌈eboñ へいぼん (平凡) *a.n.* (〜 na, ni) ordinary; common; uneventful:
heeboñ *na aidea* (平凡なアイデア) an *ordinary* idea / Heeboñ *da keredo, shiawase na mainichi o okutte imasu.* (平凡だけど、幸せな毎日を送っています) I lead an *uneventful,* but happy life.

he⌈ehoo へいほう (平方) *n.* square:
ni-meetoru heehoo (2 メートル平方) 2 meters *square* / *ni*-heehoo *meetoru* (2 平方メートル) two *square* meters / *Yoñ-meetoru* heehoo *no yuka meñseki wa juuroku* heehoo *meetoru desu.* (4 メートル平方の床面積は 16 平方メートルです) Floor space of four meters *square* is sixteen *square* meters. / *Kono tochi wa hyaku* heehoo-*meetoru arimasu.* (この土地は 100 平方メートルあります) This plot of land measures one hundred *square* meters. / heehoo-koñ (平方根) a *square* root.
heehoo suru (〜する) *vt.* square: *Juu o* heehoo suru *to hyaku ni naru.* (10 を平方すると 100 になる) If you *square* ten, you get a hundred. 《↔ rippoo¹》

he⌈ejitsu へいじつ (平日) *n.* weekday; workday:
Nihoñ no shooteñ wa futsuu doyoobi mo heejitsu *to onajiku hiraite imasu.* (日本の商店はふつう土曜日も平日と同じく開いています) Japanese stores are usually open on Saturdays just as on *working days.* / Heejitsu *no gogo nara daitai jimusho ni imasu.* (平日の午後なら大体事務所にいます) If it's a weekday afternoon, I am usually in the office. 《⇨ kyuujitsu; shukujitsu》

he⌈ejoo へいじょう (平常) *n.* normal; usual:
Shiñkañseñ no daiya wa heejoo *ni modotta.* (新幹線のダイヤは平常にもどった) The schedule of the Shinkansen has returned to *normal.* / *Basu wa* heejoo-doori *ugoite imasu.* (バスは平常どおり動いています) The buses are running *as usual.* 《⇨ futsuu¹》

he⌈ekai へいかい (閉会) *n.* closing of a meeting [session]:
heekai *no ji o noberu.* (閉会の辞を述べる) give a *closing* address. / *Kokkai wa* heekai-chuu desu. (国会は閉会中です) The Diet *is not in session.* / heekai-shiki (閉会式) a *closing* ceremony.
heekai suru (〜する) *vi.* close [adjourn] a meeting: *Kokkai wa kyoo kaiki o oe,* heekai shimashita. (国会はきょう会期を終え、閉会しました) The Diet finished its session and *was adjourned* today. 《↔ kaikai》

he⌈eki¹ へいき (平気) *n.* indifference; calmness:
Kanojo wa heeki *o yosootta.* (彼女は平気を装った) She assumed an air of *indifference.*
— *a.n.* (〜 na, ni) calm; cool; indifferent; unconcerned:
Nani o iwarete mo watashi wa heeki *desu.* (何を言われても私は平気です) I *do not care* what is said to me. / *"Hitori de daijoobu?" "Heeki desu."* (「一人でだいじょうぶ?」「平気です」) "Are you all right by yourself?" " "I'm *O.K.*" / *Kare wa* heeki *de uso o tsuku.* (彼は平気でうそをつく) He *makes no bones* about telling lies.

he⌈eki² へいき (兵器) *n.* weapon; arms:
kaku-heeki (核兵器) nuclear *weapons* / *tsuujoo*-heeki (通常兵器) conventional *weapons.*

he⌈ekiñ¹ へいきん (平均) *n.* average; mean:

heekiñ *o dasu* (平均を出す) find the *average* / *Seeseki ga* heekiñ *ijoo nara, kono gakkoo ni hairemasu.* (成績が平均以上なら、この学校に入れます) If your academic grades are above *average*, you will be able to enter this school. / *Kare no tooji no gekkyuu wa* heekiñ *no sañ-bai datta.* (彼の当時の月給は平均の3倍だった) His monthly salary in those days was three times the *average*. / *Haitatsuniñ wa is-shuukañ ni* heekiñ *sañ-kai kimasu.* (配達人は一週間に平均3回来ます) The deliveryman comes three times a week on the *average*. / heekiñ-*chi* (平均値) the *mean* (value) / heekiñ-*jumyoo* (平均寿命) the *average* life span / heekiñ-*teñ* (平均点) the *average* score.
heekiñ suru (～する) *vi.* calculate the average: Heekiñ shite, *futari ni hitori ga megane o kakete imasu.* (平均して、二人に一人がめがねをかけています) On the average, every second person wears glasses. / *Kono meekaa no shinamono wa hiñshitsu ga* heekiñ shite iru. (このメーカーの品物は品質が平均している) The products of this manufacturer *are of uniform* quality. / *Nihoñjiñ zeñtai de* heekiñ *sureba, chochiku wa sore hodo ooku arimaseñ.* (日本人全体で平均すれば、貯蓄はそれほど多くありません) If you *work out the average* savings of all Japanese, you will find it is not so high.

he「ekiñ² へいきん (平均) *n.* balance:
heekiñ *o tamotsu* [ushinau] (平均を保つ[失う]) keep [lose] one's *balance* / heekiñ-*dai* (平均台) a *balance* beam.

he「ekoo¹ へいこう (平行) *n.* parallel:
Kono nihoñ no señ wa heekoo *desu.* (この2本の線は平行です) These

two lines are *parallel*.

he「ekoo² へいこう (並行) *n.* going side by side.

he「ekoo³ へいこう (閉口) *n.* being annoyed; being bothered.
heekoo suru (～する) *vi.* be annoyed; be bothered: *Kodomo-tachi no gyoogi no warui no ni wa* heekoo shita. (子どもたちの行儀の悪いのには閉口した) I *was embarrassed* by the bad behavior of the children. / *Shichoo no nagai eñzetsu ni wa* heekoo shita. (市長の長い演説には閉口した) We *got fed up* with the mayor's long speech.

he「ekoo-shite へいこうして (並行して) *adv.* 1 parallel; side by side:
Koosoku-dooro to tetsudoo ga hee-koo-shite *hashitte iru.* (高速道路と鉄道が並行して走っている) The highway and the railroad run *parallel* to each other.
2 (of two events) concurrently; at the same time:
Choosa to heikoo-shite *kikaku-kaigi ga okonawareta.* (調査と並行して企画会議が行われた) The planning meetings were held *concurrently* with the survey.

he「emeñ へいめん (平面) *n.* level; plane.

he「eme¹ñzu へいめんず (平面図) *n.* floor [ground] plan:
Kore ga uchi no heemeñzu *desu.* (これが家の平面図です) This is the *floor plan* of our house.

He「esee へいせい (平成) *n.* Heisei. ★ The name of the Japanese era beginning in 1989. 《⇨ geñgoo (table); jidai (table)》

he「etai へいたい (兵隊) *n.*
1 a group of soldiers; troops.
2 soldier; sailor. ★ Especially those lower in rank. Often figuratively refers to a common company employee. 《⇨ guñjiñ》

he「ewa へいわ (平和) *n.* peace:

heewa *o negau* (平和を願う) pray for *peace* / heewa *o mamoru* (平和を守る) preserve *peace* / *katee no* heewa (家庭の平和) domestic *tranquility* / *Sono seejika wa sekai no* heewa *no tame ni tsukushita.* (その政治家は世界の平和のために尽くした) The politician worked hard for world *peace*.
— *a.n.* (~ na, ni) peaceful: heewa *na shakai* (平和な社会) a *peaceful* society / *Señgo, hitobito wa* heewa *ni kurashite iru.* (戦後、人々は平和に暮らしている) People have been living in *peace* since after the war. ((↔ señsoo))

he⌈eya へいや (平野) *n.* plain; open field:
*Kañtoo-*heeya (関東平野) the Kanto *plain*.

he⌈ñ⌉¹ へん (変) *a.n.* (~ na, ni) strange; odd; queer; peculiar:
heñ *na gaijiñ* (変な外人) a *strange* foreigner / *Kono kuruma wa tokidoki* heñ *na oto ga suru.* (この車はときどき変な音がする) This car sometimes makes a *strange* noise. / *Kare ga konai no wa* heñ *da.* (彼が来ないのは変だ) His not coming is *strange*. / *Sono iikata wa Nihoñgo to shite chotto* heñ *desu.* (その言い方は日本語としてちょっと変です) That expression is a bit *odd* in Japanese. / *Ano hito, atsusa de atama ga* heñ *ni natta no ka shira.* (あの人、暑さで頭が変になったのかしら) I wonder if the heat has made him go a bit *queer* in the head.

heñ² へん (辺) *n.* **1** part; region; neighborhood:
Kare no ie wa kono heñ *ni aru hazu desu.* (彼の家はこの辺にあるはずです) His house should be *around* here. / *Kono* heñ *de wa riñgo wa toremaseñ.* (この辺ではりんごは採れません) Apples are not grown in these *parts*. ((⇨ atari))
2 degree; range; limit:

Kyoo wa kono heñ *de owari ni shiyoo.* (きょうはこの辺で終わりにしよう) Let's finish up *here* today. / *Sono koto ni tsuite dono* heñ *made shitte imasu ka?* (そのことについてどの辺まで知っていますか) *How much* do you know about that matter? / *Kono mae wa kyookasho no dono* heñ *made susumimashita ka?* (この前は教科書のどの辺まで進みましたか) *How far* did we get to in the textbook last time?

he⌈ñ⌉³ へん (偏) *n.* the left-hand radical of a Chinese character. ((⇨ bushu (table); tsukuri))

-he⌈ñ⌉/be⌈ñ⌉/pe⌈ñ へん/べん/ぺん (遍) *suf.* counter for the number of times:

1	i⌈p-pe⌉ñ	7	na⌈na⌉-heñ
2	ni-⌈he⌉ñ	8	ha⌈p-pe⌉ñ
3	sa⌈ñ-be⌉ñ	9	kyu⌉u-heñ
4	yo⌈ñ-heñ	10	ji⌈p-pe⌉ñ
5	go-⌈he⌉ñ		(ju⌈p-pe⌉ñ)
6	ro⌈p-pe⌉ñ	?	na⌈ñ-beñ

*Nañ-*beñ *ittara wakaru ñ da?* (何べん言ったらわかるんだ) How many *times* do I have to tell you? / "*Koko ni wa nañ-*beñ *(ka) kita koto ga arimasu ka?*" "*Ip-*peñ *mo arimaseñ.*" (「ここには何べん(か)来たことがありますか」「一ぺんもありません」) "Have you been here several *times*?" "Not even *once*." / *Kono hoñ wa sañ-*beñ *mo yomimashita.* (この本は3べんも読みました) I have read this book three *times*. ((⇨ -kai¹))

he⌈ñi へんい (変異) *n.* variation:
totsuzeñ-heñi (突然変異) *mutation*.

he⌈ñji⌉ へんじ (返事) *n.* answer; reply:
heñji *o dasu* (返事を出す) send a *reply* to a letter / heñji o kaku (返事を書く) *write back* / *Tegami no* heñji *ga mada konai.* (手紙の返事がまだ来ない) I still haven't received

a *reply* to my letter. / *Deñwa de sugu* heñji *o kudasai.* (電話ですぐ返事を下さい) Please let me have your *reply* by telephone. / *Geñkañ no beru o narashite mo* heñji *ga nakatta.* (玄関のベルを鳴らしても返事がなかった) I rang the doorbell, but there was no *answer.*

heñji (**o**) **suru** (〜(を)する) *vi.* answer; reply: *Yobaretara, sugu* heñji *o shi nasai.* (呼ばれたら、すぐ返事をしなさい) *Answer* immediately when your name is called.

he⌐ñka へんか (変化) *n.*

1 change; variation; alteration: *Shoku seekatsu wa jidai no* heñka *to tomo ni kawatte kita.* (食生活は時代の変化とともに変わってきた) Our eating habits have altered with the *changes* in the times. / *Meeji-ishiñ ni Nihoñ wa ooki-na* heñka *o togeta.* (明治維新に日本は大きな変化を遂げた) Japan went through a great *change* during the Meiji Restoration. / *Heñka no nai seekatsu ni wa moo akita.* (変化のない生活にはもう飽きた) I'm sick and tired of this *monotonous* life. / *Kono atari no keshiki wa* heñka *ni toñde iru.* (この辺りの景色は変化に富んでいる) The landscapes around here are full of *variety.*

2 inflection; conjugation: *dooshi no* heñka (動詞の変化) *conjugation* of verbs / *kaku-*heñka (格変化) case *declension.*

heñka suru (〜する) *vi.* **1** change; vary; alter: *Teñki ga kyuu ni* heñka *shita.* (天気が急に変化した) The weather *changed* suddenly. / *Oñdo ni yotte, taiseki wa* heñka *shimasu.* (温度によって、体積は変化します) Volume *varies* according to temperature.

2 inflect; conjugate: *Kono dooshi wa fukisoku ni* heñka *shimasu.* (この動詞は不規則に変化します) This verb *conjugates* irregularly.

he⌐ñkeñ へんけん (偏見) *n.* prejudice; bias: *Kare wa josee ni taishite,* heñkeñ *o motte iru.* (彼は女性に対して、偏見を持っている) He has a *prejudice* against women. / *Jiñshu-teki* heñkeñ *wa sute nasai.* (人種的偏見は捨てなさい) You must get rid of racial *prejudice.* / *Kare-ra wa* heñkeñ *no nai hito o shidoosha ni erañda.* (彼らは偏見のない人を指導者に選んだ) They chose an *impartial* person as their leader.

he⌐ñkoo へんこう (変更) *n.* change; alteration; modification: heñkoo *o kuwaeru* (変更を加える) make a *change* / *Puroguramu wa ichibu* heñkoo *ni natta.* (プログラムは一部変更になった) Some *changes* have been made in the program.

heñkoo suru (〜する) *vt.* change; alter; modify: *Naiyoo wa yoko-ku nashi ni* heñkoo *suru koto ga arimasu.* (内容は予告なしに変更することがあります) The contents are subject to *change* without notice. / *Yotee o* heñkoo *shite, tochuu Tookyoo ni yotta.* (予定を変更して、途中東京に寄った) I *changed* my schedule and broke my journey at Tokyo.

he⌐ñsai へんさい (返済) *n.* repayment; refund: *Shakkiñ no* heñsai *o semararete iru.* (借金の返済を迫られている) I am being pressed for *repayment* of the debt. / *heñsai-kigeñ* (返済期限) the time limit for *repayment.*

heñsai suru (〜する) *vt.* pay back; repay; refund: *Sono o-kane o* heñsai *suru tame ni ie o utta.* (そのお金を返済するために家を売った) I sold my house to *pay back* the money.

he⌐ñshuu へんしゅう (編集) *n.* editing; compilation: *Jisho no* heñshuu *wa taiheñ na sagyoo desu.* (辞書の編集はたいへんな

作業です) The *compilation* of a dictionary is a hard task. / heñshuu-bu (編集部) an *editorial* department / heñshuu-sha (編集者) an *editor*.

heñshuu suru (〜する) *vi.* edit; compile: *zasshi o* heñshuu suru (雑誌を編集する) *edit* a magazine / *Bideo o* heñshuu shite, *bañgumi o tsukutta*. (ビデオを編集して、番組を作った) We made a TV program by *editing* video tapes.

heｒñshuｒuchoo へんしゅうちょう (編集長) *n.* editor-in-chief; chief editor.

heｒras·u へらす (減らす) *vt.* (herash·i-; heras·a-; herash·i-te Ⓒ) reduce; decrease; cut down; diminish: *Anata wa taijuu o* herashita *hoo ga yoi*. (あなたは体重を減らしたほうがよい) You should *lose* weight. / *Kootsuu jiko o* herasanakereba naranai. (交通事故を減らさなければならない) We have to *cut down* on the number of traffic accidents. / *Kare wa keñkoo no tame ni sake o* herashita. (彼は健康のために酒を減らした) He has *cut back* on his drinking for the sake of his health. 《⇨ heru¹》

heｒrikoｒputaa ヘリコプター *n.* helicopter: herikoputaa *o soojuu suru* (ヘリコプターを操縦する) pilot a *helicopter*. 《⇨ hikooki》

heｒr·u¹ へる (減る) *vi.* (her·i-; her·a-; het-te Ⓒ) **1** become less [fewer]; decrease: *Kootsuu-jiko [Jiñkoo] ga* hetta. (交通事故[人口]が減った) The number of traffic accidents [The population] *has decreased*. / *Watashi no shuunyuu wa* herimashita. (私の収入は減りました) My income *has gone down*. / *Kuruma no gasoriñ ga* hette kita. (車のガソリンが減ってきた) The car *has run low* on gas. 《↔ fueru》《⇨ herasu》

2 (of shoes, tires) wear out: *Kono kutsu wa* heru *no ga hayai*. (この靴は減るのが早い) These shoes *wear out* quickly.

3 get hungry: *Onaka ga* hette kita. (おなかが減ってきた) I've gotten hungry. ★ 'Onaka ga suite kimashita' is more polite.

heｒr·u² へる (経る) *vi.* (he-te Ⓥ) experience: *Wareware wa ooku no koñnañ o* hete kimashita. (われわれは多くの困難を経てきました) We *have experienced* a lot of difficulties. 《⇨ hete》

heso へそ (臍) *n.* navel. ★ Often 'o-heso.' 《⇨ jiñtai (illus.)》

heｒta へた (下手) *a.n.* (〜 na, ni) poor; bad: *ji no* heta na hito (字のへたな人) a person whose penmanship is *poor* / *Watashi wa uñteñ ga* heta desu. (私は運転がへたです) I am *not* very *good* at driving. / *Uchi no ko wa hashi o tsukau no ga mada* heta desu. (うちの子ははしを使うのがまだへたです) Our child *can't use* chopsticks *properly* yet. 《↔ joozu》

heta o suru to (〜をすると) if one is not careful; if not properly handled: Heta o suru to *jikañ made ni soko ni tsukanai ka mo shirenai*. (へたをすると時間までにそこに着かないかも知れない) *If things do not go well*, we may not get there in time.

heｒte へて (経て) via; by way of: ★ *te*-form of the verb, 'heru².' *Kare wa Hawai o* hete *Tookyoo ni tsukimashita*. (彼はハワイを経て東京に着きました) He arrived in Tokyo *via* Hawaii. 《⇨ heru²; keeyu¹》

heｒya へや (部屋) *n.* room; chamber; apartment: heya *ni hairu* (部屋に入る) enter a *room* / heya *kara deru* (部屋から出る) go out of a *room* / *Koko wa roku-joo no* heya desu. (ここは6畳

の部屋です) This is a six-mat *room*.

hi¹ ひ (日) *n*. **1** day (24 hours);
time:
Sono hi *wa ame datta.* (その日は雨だった) It rained on that *day*. / Hi *ni*
hi *ni atatakaku natte kuru.* (日に日に暖かくなってくる) It's getting warmer *day* by *day*. / *Kare wa Nihoñ e kite kara, mada* hi *ga asai.* (彼は日本へ来てから、まだ日が浅い) It's been only a *short time* since he came to Japan. / *Doñdoñ* hi *ga tatte yuku.* (どんどん日がたってゆく) The *days* go by so quickly.

seeki	世紀	century
neñ	年	year
tsuki	月	month
shuu	週	week
hi	日	day
ji	時	hour
fuñ	分	minute
byoo	秒	second

《⇨ hiru (table)》
2 date:
Haha ga umareta hi *wa go-gatsu nijuuhachi-nichi desu.* (母が生まれた日は5月28日です) The *date* of my mother's birth is May 28. / *Shuppatsu no* hi *wa mitee desu.* (出発の日は未定です) The *date* of departure is not fixed yet.

hi² ひ (日) *n*. **1** the sun:
hi *ga noboru* [*shizumu*] (日が昇る[沈む]) *the sun* rises [sets] / Hi *wa mada takai.* (日はまだ高い) *The sun* is still high.
2 sun (=sunbeam):
Kono heya ni wa hi *ga sasanai.* (この部屋には日がささない) The *sun* does not shine into this room. / *Taoru o* hi *ni atete, kawakashita.* (タオルを日に当てて、乾かした) I dried the towel by putting it in the *sun*.
3 period of light; day (as opposed to night):
Hi *ga nagaku* [*mijikaku*] *natta.* (日

が長く[短く]なった) The *days* are getting longer [shorter].

hi¹³ ひ (火) *n*. fire:
matchi de hi *o tsukeru* (マッチで火をつける) kindle a *fire* with a match / *tabako ni* hi *o tsukeru* (たばこに火をつける) *light* a cigarette / hi *o taku* (火をたく) start a *fire* / hi *o kesu* (火を消す) put out a *fire* / *Kami wa* hi *ga tsuki-yasui.* (紙は火がつきやすい) Paper catches *fire* easily. / *Kyañpaa-tachi wa yagai de* hi *o okoshita.* (キャンパーたちは野外で火をおこした) The campers built a *fire* in the open air. / Hi *no nai tokoro ni kemuri wa tatanai.* (*saying*) (火のない所に煙は立たない) There is no smoke without *fire*.

hi¹⁴ ひ (灯) *n*. light:
hi *o tomosu* [*kesu*] (灯をともす[消す]) turn on [off] a *light* / *Tooku ni machi no* hi *ga mieta.* (遠くに町の灯が見えた) We saw the *lights* of the town in the distance.

hi¹⁵ ひ (比) *n*. ratio. 《⇨ hiritsu》

hi⁶ ひ (碑) *n*. monument:
Kare o kineñ shite, hi *o tateta.* (彼を記念して、碑を建てた) We built a *monument* in memory of him.

hi¹- ひ (非) *pref*. un-; non-:
hi-*booryoku-shugi* (非暴力主義) *nonviolence* / hi-*geñjitsu-teki na kañgaekata* (非現実的な考え方) an *un*realistic way of thinking / hi-*kyooryoku-teki na taido* (非協力的な態度) an *un*cooperative attitude.

-hi ひ (費) *suf*. expenses:
koosai-hi (交際費) an *expense* account; *expenses* for entertainment / *kootsuu*-hi (交通費) traveling *expenses* / *seekatsu*-hi (生活費) living *expenses* / *shoku*-hi (食費) *money* for food / *shukuhaku*-hi (宿泊費) hotel *charges* / *iji*-hi (維持費) maintenance *costs*.

hi「atari ひあたり (日当たり) *n*. exposure to the sun; sunshine:
hiatari *no yoi heya* (日当たりのよい

部屋) a *sunny* room. 《⇨ hikage; hinata》

hi「bachi ひばち (火鉢) *n.* hibachi: ★ The hibachi has no grill. It is used basically for heating, not cooking.
hibachi *ni ataru* (火鉢に当たる) warm oneself at a *brazier*.

tetsubiñ ‥‥ hibashi

HIBACHI

hi「bana ひばな (火花) *n.* sparks:
Kireta deñseñ kara hibana *ga toñda.* (切れた電線から火花が飛んだ) *Sparks* flew up from the broken electric cable.
hibana o chirasu (～を散らす) have a heated argument: *Futari wa* hibana o chirashite, *roñsoo shita.* (二人は火花を散らして，論争した) The two of them had a quarrel, *with sparks flying*.

hi「bari ひばり (雲雀) *n.* skylark; lark.

hi「bashi ひばし (火箸) *n.* chopsticks made of metal. ★ Used like tongs and fire irons to tend heated charcoal, etc. 《⇨ hibachi (illus.)》

hi「bi[1] ひび *n.* **1** crack:
Kono koppu ni wa hibi *ga haitte iru.* (このコップにはひびが入っている) There is a *crack* in this glass. / *Booru ga atatte, mado-garasu ni* hibi ga haitta. (ボールが当たって，窓ガラスにひびが入った) The windowpane *cracked* when a ball hit it.
2 split:
Sono koto de futari no kañkee ni hibi *ga haitta.* (そのことで二人の関係

にひびが入った) The incident caused a *split* in their relationship.

hi「biki[1] ひびき (響き) *n.* sound; peal; echo:
Tooku kara kane no hibiki *ga ki-koeru.* (遠くから鐘の響きが聞こえる) I can hear the *peal* of a bell a long way off. / *Sono namae wa* hibiki *ga yokunai.* (その名前は響きが良くない) That name has an unpleasant *sound* to it. 《⇨ hibiku》

hi「bi·k·u ひびく (響く) *vi.* (hibik·i-; hibik·a-; hibi·i-te Ⓒ) **1** sound; ring; resound; echo:
Tera no kane ga mura-juu ni hibi-ita. (寺の鐘が村中に響いた) The bell of a temple *sounded* throughout the village. / *Toñneru no naka de wa koe ga* hibiku. (トンネルの中では声が響く) Our voice *echoes* in the tunnel. 《⇨ hibiki》
2 affect; have an unfavorable influence on:
Naga-ame ga sakumotsu no shuu-kaku ni hibiita. (長雨が作物の収穫に響いた) The long rains *had an adverse effect* on the harvest. / *Yuki-busoku ga sukiijoo no kee-ee ni* hibikanakereba *ii ga.* (雪不足がスキー場の経営に響かなければいいが) I hope the lack of snow will *not affect* the ski resort's business.

hi「bu「soo ひぶそう (非武装) *n.* demilitarization:
kuni o hibusoo-ka *suru* (国を非武装化する) *demilitarize* a nation / hibusoo-*chitai* ひぶそうちたい (非武装地帯) a *demilitarized* zone.
《↔ busoo》

hi「dari ひだり (左) *n.* left:
neji o hidari *e mawasu* (ねじを左へ回す) turn a screw to the *left* / *Tsugi no koosateñ de* hidari *e magari nasai.* (次の交差点で左へ曲りなさい) Turn to the *left* at the next intersection. / *Hidari ni mi-eru no ga Tookyoo-eki desu.* (左に見えるのが東京駅です) That you can

see on your *left* is Tokyo Station. (↔ migi)

hi「darigawa ひだりがわ (左側) *n.*
left side:
Kanojo wa watashi no hidarigawa *ni suwatta.* (彼女は私の左側に座った) She sat on my *left side.* / *Kuruma wa* hidarigawa *tsuukoo desu.* (車は左側通行です) Cars must keep to the *left.* (↔ migigawa)

hi「darikiki ひだりきき (左利き) *n.*
left-handed person:
Kare wa hidarikiki *da.* (彼は左利きだ) He is *left-handed.* (↔ migi-kiki)

hi「darite ひだりて (左手) *n.*
1 left hand:
Kanojo wa hidarite *de kaku.* (彼女は左手で書く) She writes with her *left hand.* / *Kare wa* hidarite *ni kega o shita.* (彼は左手にけがをした) He got hurt in the *left hand.* (↔ migite)
2 left direction:
Hidarite *ni kawa ga mieru.* (左手に川が見える) I can see a river on the *left.* (↔ migite)

hi「do」・i ひどい (酷い) *a.* (-ku) **1** serious; hard; violent:
hidoi *kega* (ひどいけが) a *serious* injury / hidoi *machigai* (ひどい間違い) a *gross* mistake / hidoi *seeseki* (ひどい成績) *awful* (academic) grades / *Ame ga* hidoku *natte kita.* (雨がひどくなってきた) It has started to rain *hard.*
2 cruel; terrible:
Ano otoko wa hidoi *yatsu da.* (あの男はひどいやつだ) He is a *cruel* man. / *Kanojo ni* hidoi *koto o iwanai de kudasai.* (彼女にひどいことを言わないでください) Don't say such *terrible* things to her.

hi「e」・ru ひえる (冷える) *vi.* (hie-te Ⅴ) get cold [chilly; cool]:
Yoru ni natte, dañdañ hiete *kita.* (夜になって、だんだん冷えてきた) It *is* gradually *getting cold* as night

comes on. / *Kesa wa* hiemasu *ne.* (今朝は冷えますね) It *is chilly* this morning, isn't it? / *Tsumetai kaze ni atatte, karada ga* hieta. (冷たい風に当たって、体が冷えた) I was in a cold wind and *got chilled.* / *Reezooko no biiru wa* hiemashita *ka?* (冷蔵庫のビールは冷えましたか) *Has* the beer in the fridge *chilled?* (⇒ hiyasu)

hi「fu ひふ (皮膚) *n.* skin:
Watashi wa hifu *ga yowai.* (私は皮膚が弱い) I have delicate *skin.* / hifu-*byoo* (皮膚病) a *skin* disease.

hi「fuka ひふか (皮膚科) *n.* dermatology. (⇒ byooiñ (table))

hi「gaeri」 ひがえり (日帰り) *n.*
day-trip; one day trip:
higaeri *no shutchoo* (日帰りの出張) a *day* business *trip* / *Hakone made* higaeri *de itta.* (箱根まで日帰りで行った) I made a *day-trip* to Hakone. / *Hokkaidoo e* higaeri *de oofuku suru no wa muri desu.* (北海道へ日帰りで往復するのは無理です) It is difficult to *get* to Hokkaido and *back in a day.*

hi「gai ひがい (被害) *n.* **1** damage:
Taifuu wa sakumotsu ni ooki-na higai *o ataeta.* (台風は作物に大きな被害を与えた) The typhoon caused a lot of *damage* to the crops. / *Sono mura wa koozui de ooki-na* higai *o koomutta.* (その村は洪水で大きな被害を被った) The village suffered serious *damage* from the flood. / *Watashi-tachi wa uñ-yoku* higai *o manugareta.* (私たちは運よく被害を免れた) Fortunately we have escaped *damage.*
2 loss:
Sono kaisha no uketa higai *wa wazuka datta.* (その会社の受けた被害はわずかだった) The *loss* the company sustained was slight.

hi「ga」isha ひがいしゃ (被害者) *n.*
victim; sufferer.

hi「ga」ñ ひがん (彼岸) *n.* the equinoctial week: ★ Politely '*o-hi-gañ.*' *Atsusa samusa mo* higañ *made.*(暑さ寒さも彼岸まで) Mild weather comes with the *equinox.*

CULTURE

It is a Japanese custom to visit one's family grave during the spring and autumn equinoctial weeks. 《⇨ hakamairi (photo)》

hi「gashi」 ひがし (東) *n.* east; (~ ni/e) eastward:
Kaze wa higashi *kara fuite imasu.* (風は東から吹いています) The wind is blowing from the *east.* / *Taifuu wa Señdai no* higashi *sañbyaku-kiro no kaijoo desu.*(台風は仙台の東300キロの海上です) The typhoon is at sea, 300 kilometers to the *east* of Sendai. / *Kawa wa machi no* higashi-*gawa o nagarete imasu.* (川は町の東側を流れています) The river flows through the *eastern* part of the town. / *Kono heya wa* higashi *muki desu.* (この部屋は東向きです) This room faces *east.* 《↔ nishi》

hi「ge」 ひげ (髭) *n.* general term for facial hair:
hige *o hayasu* (ひげを生やす) grow a *beard* / *Kare wa koi* hige *o hayashite iru.* (彼は濃いひげを生やしている) He has a heavy *mustache* and *beard.* / Hige *o sori nasai.* (ひげをそりなさい) *Shave your face.*

ago-hige	beard
kuchi-hige	mustache
hoo-hige	whiskers

hi「geki」 ひげき (悲劇) *n.* tragedy:
higeki *no shujiñkoo* (悲劇の主人公) the hero(ine) of the *tragedy.* 《↔ kigeki》

hi「goro」 ひごろ (日頃) *n.* everyday; always; usually:
Higoro *no doryoku ga taisetsu desu.* (日ごろの努力が大切です) One's *daily* efforts are important. / *Yatto* higoro *no kiboo ga jitsugeñ shimashita.*(やっと日ごろの希望が実現しました) At last my *long-cherished* wish was realized. / Higoro, *musume ga o-sewa ni natte imasu.* (日ごろ、娘がお世話になっています) I thank you for the kindness my daughter *always* receives from you.

hi「hañ」 ひはん (批判) *n.* criticism:
hihañ *o abiru* (批判を浴びる) be exposed to *criticism* / hihañ *o ukeru* (批判を受ける) face *criticism* / *Tochi seesaku ga* hihañ *no mato ni natte iru.*(土地政策が批判の的になっている) The land policy is the target of *criticism.*

hihañ suru (~する) *vt.* criticize:
Taniñ o hihañ suru *no wa yasashii.* (他人を批判するのはやさしい) It is easy to *criticize* others.

hi「hyoo」 ひひょう (批評) *n.* comment; criticism; review:
Kare wa zasshi ni eega no hihyoo *o kaita.* (彼は雑誌に映画の批評を書いた) He wrote a film *review* in a magazine. / hihyoo-*ka* (批評家) a *critic*; a *reviewer.*

hihyoo suru (~する) *vt.* criticize; review; comment: *Kono sakuhiñ o doozo jiyuu ni* hihyoo shite *kudasai.*(この作品をどうぞ自由に批評してください) Please feel free to *criticize* this work.

hi「itaa」 ヒーター *n.* heater:
hiitaa *o tsukeru* [*kesu*] (ヒーターをつける[消す]) turn on [off] the *heater.*

hi「ji」 ひじ (肘) *n.* elbow:
teeburu no ue ni hiji *o tsuku* (テーブルの上にひじをつく) rest one's *elbows* on a table / hiji *o haru* (ひじを張る) spread one's *elbows.* 《⇨ jiñtai (illus.)》

hi「joo」 ひじょう (非常) *n.* emergency; contingency:
Hijoo *no baai wa koko kara derare-masu.* (非常の場合はここから出られま

す) You can go out this way in an *emergency*. / Hijoo-jitai *ga hassee shita*. (非常事態が発生した) An *emergency* has occurred. / *Kare-ra wa* hijoo *shudañ o totta*. (彼らは非常手段をとった) They took *emergency* measures.
— *a.n.* (~ na, ni) great; extreme; very:
hijoo *na hayasa* (非常な速さ) *great* speed / hijoo *na yorokobi* (非常な喜び) *extreme* joy / *Imiñ-tachi wa* hijoo *na doryoku o shita*. (移民たちは非常な努力をした) The immigrants made *great* efforts. / *Kanoosee wa* hijoo *ni hikui*. (可能性は非常に低い) The possibility is *extremely* low. / *Sono shikeñ wa* hijoo ni *muzukashikatta*. (その試験は非常に難しかった) The examination was *very* difficult. / *Kare wa* hijoo ni *yorokoñde imashita*. (彼は非常に喜んでいました) He was *absolutely* delighted. ★ '*Hijoo da*' is not used.

hi「jo「oguchi ひじょうぐち (非常口) *n.* emergency exit.

HIJOOGUCHI SIGNS

hi「joo ni ひじょうに (非常に) *adv.* ⇨ hijoo.

hi「jooseñ ひじょうせん (非常線) *n.* police cordon:
hijooseñ *o haru* [*toppa suru*] (非常線を張る[突破する]) set up [break through] a *cordon*.

hi「jo「oshiki ひじょうしき (非常識) *a.n.* (~ na, ni) lacking in com-

mon sense; unreasonable:
Kooto o kita mama, teeburu ni tsuku nañte hijooshiki *da*. (コートを着たまま、テーブルにつくなんて非常識だ) It shows a *lack of knowledge of how people usually behave* to sit at the table with your coat on. / Hijooshiki *na koto o iu no wa yoshi nasai*. (非常識なことを言うのはよしなさい) Stop talking *nonsense*.

hi「kae「shitsu ひかえしつ (控室) *n.* anteroom; waiting room.

hi「kage ひかげ (日陰) *n.* shade:
Watashi-tachi wa hikage *de yasuñda*. (私たちは日陰で休んだ) We had a rest in the *shade*. 《↔ hinata》

hi「kaku ひかく (比較) *n.* comparison; parallel:
Eego to Nihoñgo no hikaku *keñkyuu wa yoku okonawaremasu*. (英語と日本語の比較研究はよく行われます) *Comparative* studies of English and Japanese are frequently carried out. / *Sore to kore de wa* hikaku *ni naranai*. (それとこれでは比較にならない) There is no *comparison* between this and that.
hikaku suru (~する) *vt.* compare:
Ni-mai no shashiñ o hikaku shite *mita*. (2枚の写真を比較してみた) I *compared* the two photographs. / *Ani to* hikaku sareru *no wa iya desu*. (兄と比較されるのは嫌です) I don't like to *be compared* with my older brother.

hi「kaku-teki ひかくてき (比較的) *adv.* comparatively; relatively:
★ Note that this word is an adverb, not an adjectival noun. *Moñdai wa* hikaku-teki *yasashikatta*. (問題は比較的やさしかった) I found the problems *comparatively* easy. / *Kotoshi no natsu wa* hikaku-teki *suzushii*. (今年の夏は比較的涼しい) Summer this year is *relatively* cool.

hi「kari」 ひかり (光) *n.* light; ray:
taiyoo no hikari (太陽の光) *rays* of

the sun / tsuki no hikari (月の光)
moonbeams / *roosoku no* hikari (ろ
うそくの光) candle *light* / Hikari *wa
oto yori mo hayai.* (光は音よりも速
い) *Light* is faster than sound.

hi⌈ka⌉r·u ひかる (光る) *vi.* (hikar·i-; hikar·a-; hikat-te [C])
1 shine; twinkle; gleam; glitter:
Yozora ni hoshi ga hikatte iru. (夜
空に星が光っている) The stars *are
twinkling* in the night sky. /
Tooku de nani-ka ga hikatta. (遠く
で何かが光った) Something *glinted*
in the distance. / *Yuki ga hi o
abite,* hikatte iru. (雪が日を浴びて,
光っている) The snow, bathed in
the sunshine, *is shining.*
2 stand out; be prominent:
Kono zasshi de wa kare no shoosetsu ga hikatte iru. (この雑誌では彼の
小説が光っている) His novel *figures
prominently* in this magazine.

hi⌈kiage⌉·ru ひきあげる (引き上げる・
引き揚げる) *vt.* (-age-te [V])
1 pull up; salvage:
Chiñbotsu shita fune o hikiageta.
(沈没した船を引き揚げた) We *salvaged* the sunken ship.
2 raise:
maku o hikiageru (幕を引き上げる)
raise a stage curtain / *chiñgiñ o*
hikiageru (賃金を引き上げる) *raise*
wages. 《↔ hikisageru》[C]
3 withdraw (an army):
guñtai o hikiageru (軍隊を引き揚げ
る) *withdraw* troops.

-hiki/biki/piki ひき/びき/ぴき (匹)
suf. counter for small animals,
fish and insects:

1 i⌈p-piki⌉	7 na⌈na⌉-hiki
2 ni⌉-hiki	8 ha⌈p-piki
3 sa⌈ñ-biki	(ha⌈chi⌉-hiki)
4 yo⌈ñ-hiki	9 kyu⌈u-hiki
5 go⌉-hiki	10 ji⌈p-piki⌉
6 ro⌈p-piki⌉	(ju⌈p-piki⌉)
(ro⌈ku-hiki)	? na⌉ñ-biki

Kono ike ni wa koi ga nañ-biki
gurai imasu ka? (この池にはこいが何
匹ぐらいいますか) *How many* carp
are there in this pond?

hi⌈kidashi ひきだし (引き出し) *n.*
drawer:
hikidashi *o akeru* [*shimeru*] (引き
出しを開ける[閉める]) open [shut] a
drawer.

hi⌈kida⌉s·u ひきだす (引き出す) *vt.*
(-dash·i-; -das·a-; -dash·i-te [C])
1 draw (a conclusion, etc.):
ketsuroñ o hikidasu (結論を引き出
す) *draw* a conclusion.
2 draw (money from a deposit):
*Kare wa giñkoo kara hyakumañ-
eñ* hikidashita. (彼は銀行から 100 万
円引き出した) He *withdrew* one
million yen from the bank.

hi⌈kihana⌉s·u ひきはなす (引き離す)
vt. (-hanash·i-; -hanas·a-; -hanash·i-te [C]) **1** outdistance;
outrun:
Watashi wa hyaku-meetoru kyoosoo de, kare o sañ-meetoru hikihanashita. (私は 100 メートル競走で,
彼を 3 メートル引き離した) I *outran*
him by three meters in the hundred meter race.
2 separate:
Osanai kodomo o haha-oya kara
hikihanasu *no wa zañkoku desu.*
(幼い子どもを母親から引き離すのは残酷
です) It is cruel to *separate* a very
young child from its mother.
《⇨ hanasu²》

hi⌈kika⌉es·u ひきかえす (引き返す)
vi. (-kaesh·i-; -kaes·a-; -kaesh·i-te [C]) come [go] back; return:
*Hikooki wa eñjiñ no koshoo de
tochuu kara* hikikaeshita. (飛行機
はエンジンの故障で途中から引き返した)
The plane *turned back* halfway
because of engine trouble. / *Watashi-tachi wa michi ni mayoi,
moto no tokoro e* hikikaeshita. (私
たちは道に迷い, 元の所へ引き返した)

We got lost and *returned* to our starting point.

hi⌈kiniku ひきにく（挽き肉）*n.*
ground meat; mincemeat:
gyuu [buta] no hikiniku（牛[豚]のひ
き肉）*ground* beef [pork].

hi⌈kinobashi[1] ひきのばし（引き延ば
し）*n.* delaying; postponement:
Kare-ra wa kooshoo no hikinobashi *o hakatte iru.*（彼らは交渉の引き
延ばしをはかっている）They are trying
to *drag out* the negotiations.
（⇨ hikinobasu[1]）

hi⌉kinobashi[2] ひきのばし（引き伸ば
し）*n.* enlargement:
shashiñ no hikinobashi（写真の引き
伸ばし）an *enlargement* of a photo.
（⇨ hikinobasu[2]）

hi⌈kinoba⌉s・u[1] ひきのばす（引き延ば
す）*vt.* (-nobash・i-; -nobas・a-;
-nobash・i-te Ⓒ) extend; prolong; put off:
Shiharai kigeñ o hikinobashite
moratta.（支払い期限を引き延ばしても
らった）The payment deadline *was
extended* for me. （⇨ hikinobashi[1]）

hi⌈kinoba⌉s・u[2] ひきのばす（引き伸ば
す）*vt.* (-nobash・i-; -nobas・a-;
-nobash・i-te Ⓒ) enlarge:
Watashi wa sono shashiñ o hikinobashite *moratta.*（私はその写真を引
き伸ばしてもらった）I *had* the photograph *enlarged.* （⇨ hikinobashi[2]）

hi⌈kinu⌉k・u ひきぬく（引き抜く）*vt.*
(-nuk・i-; -nuk・a-; -nu・i-te Ⓒ)
1 pull out; draw; extract:
kugi o hikinuku（くぎを引き抜く）
pull out a nail.
2 hire away; transfer:
*Uchi no kaisha de wa shaiñ o sañ-
niñ* hikinukareta.（うちの会社では社
員を3人引き抜かれた）Three people
were hired away from our company.

hi⌈kisaga⌉r・u ひきさがる（引き下が
る）*vi.* (-sagar・i-; -sagar・a-; -sa-
gat-te Ⓒ) withdraw; leave:
Kumiaiiñ-tachi wa sunao ni hikisa-

garanakatta.（組合員たちは素直に引
き下がらなかった）The union mem-
bers *did not withdraw* obediently.
（⇨ hiku[1]）

hi⌈kisage⌉・ru ひきさげる（引き下げ
る）*vt.* (-sage-te Ⓥ) lower;
reduce; cut [bring] down:
nedañ o hikisageru（値段を引き下げ
る）*lower* the price / *maku o* hikisa-
geru（幕を引き下げる）*lower* a stage
curtain. （⇨ hikiageru）

hi⌈kitate⌉・ru ひきたてる（引き立てる）
vt. (-tate-te Ⓥ) **1** favor; patron-
ize; support:
Kachoo wa itsu-mo kare o hikitatete *iru.*（課長はいつも彼を引き立ててい
る）Our boss *is* always *favoring*
him.
2 set off:
*Bakku no aozora ga kanojo no
fukusoo o* hikitatete *iru.*（バックの青
空が彼女の服装を引き立てている）The
blue sky in the background *sets
off* her clothes. （⇨ hikitatsu）

hi⌈kita⌉ts・u ひきたつ（引き立つ）*vi.*
(-tach・i-; -tat・a-; -tat-te Ⓒ) look
nice; be set off:
Soko ni hana o ikeru to issoo hiki-
tachimasu.（そこに花を生けるといっそう
引き立ちます）If you put a flower
arrangement there, the place will
look much better. （⇨ hikitateru）

hi⌈kitome⌉・ru ひきとめる（引き止め
る・引き留める）*vt.* (-tome-te Ⓥ)
keep; prevent:
*O-hikitome shite mooshiwake ari-
maseñ.*（お引き止めして申し訳ありませ
ん）I am very sorry to *have kept
you from going.* / *Kare o* hikito-
meru *koto wa dekinakatta.*（彼を引
き止めることはできなかった）We could
not *prevent* him *from leaving.*

hi⌈kito⌉r・u ひきとる（引き取る）*vt.*
(-tor・i-; -tor・a-; -tot-te Ⓒ)
1 take [buy] back:
Urenokotta shinamono wa hikitori-
masu.（売れ残った品物は引き取ります）
We will *take back* unsold goods.

2 take care of; take in (a child, an old person, etc.):
Kanojo wa sono koji o hikitotta. (彼女はその孤児を引き取った) She *took in* the orphan.

hi「kitsuke⌉·ru ひきつける (引き付ける) *vt.* (-tsuke-te Ⓥ) **1** attract; charm; magnetize:
Kare no eñzetsu wa chooshuu o hikitsuketa. (彼の演説は聴衆を引きつけた) His speech *charmed* the audience. / *Kanojo no yasashisa ni kodomo-tachi wa* hikitsukerareta. (彼女の優しさに子どもたちは引き付けられた) The children *were attracted* by her kindness.
2 (of a magnet) attract:
Jishaku wa tetsu o hikitsukeru. (磁石は鉄を引き付ける) A magnet *attracts* iron.

hi「kiuke⌉·ru ひきうける (引き受ける) *vt.* (-uke-te Ⓥ) take; undertake:
Sono yakume wa watashi ga hikiukemasu. (その役目は私が引き受けます) I will *undertake* that duty.

hi「kiwake⌉ ひきわけ (引き分け) *n.* drawn game; draw; tie:
Shiai wa hikiwake *ni owatta.* (試合は引き分けに終わった) The game ended in a *draw*. (⇨ hikiwakeru)

hi「kiwake⌉·ru ひきわける (引き分ける) *vi., vt.* (-wake-te Ⓥ) draw; tie:
Jaiañtsu wa Taigaasu to no shiai o hikiwaketa. (ジャイアンツはタイガースとの試合を引き分けた) The Giants *drew* in the game with the Tigers. (⇨ hikiwake)

hi「kiwata⌉s·u ひきわたす (引き渡す) *vt.* (-watash·i-; -watas·a-; -watash·i-te Ⓒ) hand over; deliver:
Kare-ra wa doroboo o keesatsu ni hikiwatashita. (彼らは泥棒を警察に引き渡した) They *handed* the thief *over* to the police. / *Shinamono wa ashita* hikiwatashimasu. (品物はあした引き渡します) We will *deliver* the goods tomorrow. (⇨ watasu)

hi「ki⌉zañ ひきざん (引き算) *n.* subtraction:
hikizañ o suru (引き算をする) *subtract*. (↔ tashizañ) (⇨ keesañ (table); hiku')

hi「kizur·u ひきずる (引きずる) *vt.* (-zur·i-; -zur·a-; -zut-te Ⓒ) drag; trail:
ashi o hikizuru (足を引きずる) *drag* one's feet / *kimono no suso o* hikizuru (着物のすそを引きずる) *trail* the hem of one's kimono.

hi「kkaka⌉r·u ひっかかる (引っ掛かる) *vi.* (-kakar·i-; -kakar·a-; -kakat-te Ⓒ) **1** get caught:
Zuboñ ga kugi ni hikkakatta. (ズボンがくぎに引っ掛かった) My trousers *got caught* on a nail. (⇨ hikkakeru)
2 fall for; be deceived:
Kanojo wa sagi ni hikkakatta. (彼女は詐欺に引っ掛かった) She *fell for* a confidence trick. (⇨ hikkakeru)

hi「kkake⌉·ru ひっかける (引っ掛ける) *vt.* (-kake-te Ⓥ) **1** catch:
Kare wa shatsu o kugi ni hikkaketa. (彼はシャツをくぎに引っ掛けた) He *caught* his shirt on a nail. (⇨ hikkakaru)
2 (of clothes) throw on:
Kare wa uwagi o hikkakete, *soto ni deta.* (彼は上着を引っ掛けて、外に出た) He *threw on* his jacket and went out.
3 splash:
Kodomo-tachi wa otagai ni mizu o hikkakete, *asoñda.* (子どもたちはお互いに水を引っ掛けて、遊んだ) The children played, *splashing* water at each other. (⇨ hikkakaru)
4 deceive; trap; seduce:
Kare o hikkakeyoo *to shite mo, muda desu.* (彼を引っ掛けようとしても、無駄です) It is no use trying to *deceive* him. / *Kare wa toori de oñna-no-ko o* hikkaketa. (彼は通りで女の子を引っ掛けた) He *picked up* a girl on the street. (⇨ hikkakaru)

hi￹kki￺ ひっき（筆記）*n.* note-taking; writing:
hikki-*shiken*（筆記試験）a *written* examination / hikki-*gu[yoogu]*（筆記具[用具]）*writing* implements / hikki-*yooshi*（筆記用紙）writing paper.

hikki suru（〜する）*vt.* take notes; write down: *koogi o* hikki suru（講義を筆記する）*take notes* of a lecture / *kooen o* hikki suru（講演を筆記する）*write down* someone's speech.

hi￹kko￺m·u ひっこむ（引っ込む）*vi.* (-kom·i-; -kom·a-; -koñ-de Ⓒ) **1** retire; withdraw:
Kare wa kokyoo ni hikkoñda.（彼は故郷に引っ込んだ）He *retired* to his hometown. / *Omae wa* hikkoñde iro.（お前は引っ込んでいろ）*Mind your own business.*
2 stand back:
Kare no ie wa dooro kara yaku gojuu-meetoru hikkoñde iru.（彼の家は道路から約50メートル引っ込んでいる）His house *stands back* about fifty meters from the road.

hi￹kkoshi￺ ひっこし（引っ越し）*n.* move; removal:
Hikkoshi *wa kinoo owarimashita.*（引っ越しはきのう終わりました）The *move* to our new house was completed yesterday. 《⇨ hikkosu》

hi￹kko￺s·u ひっこす（引っ越す）*vi.* (-kosh·i-; -kos·a-; -kosh·i-te Ⓒ) move:
Ikka wa Nagoya kara Oosaka e hikkoshita.（一家は名古屋から大阪へ引っ越した）The family *moved* from Nagoya to Osaka. 《⇨ hikkoshi》

hi￹kkurika￺er·u ひっくりかえる（ひっくり返る）*vi.* (-kaer·a-; -kaer·i-; -kaet-te Ⓒ) overturn; upset:
Tsuri-bune ga hikkurikaetta.（釣り舟がひっくり返った）The fishing boat *overturned.* 《⇨ hikkurikaesu》

hi￹kkurika￺es·u ひっくりかえす（ひっくり返す）*vt.* (-kaesh·i-; -kaes·a-; -kaesh·i-te Ⓒ) turn over; upset:
Kodomo wa omocha-bako o hikkurikaeshita.（子どもはおもちゃ箱をひっくり返した）The child *turned over* the toy box. / *Kare wa koppu o* hikkurikaeshita.（彼はコップをひっくり返した）He *upset* the glass. 《⇨ hikkuraeru》

hi￹koo￺ ひこう（飛行）*n.* flight; flying:
Tenki ga warui no de hikoo wa *chuushi sareta.*（天気が悪いので飛行は中止された）The *flight* was canceled because of bad weather.

hikoo suru（〜する）*vi.* fly; make a flight: *Janboki wa daitai koodo ichiman-meetoru no tokoro o* hikoo shimasu.（ジャンボ機はだいたい高度1万メートルのところを飛行します）Jumbo jets *fly* at an altitude of about ten thousand meters.

hi￹koojoo￺ ひこうじょう（飛行場）*n.* airfield; airport. 《⇨ kuukoo》

hi￹ko￺oki ひこうき（飛行機）*n.* airplane; plane:
Rondon-yuki no hikooki *ni noru*（ロンドン行きの飛行機に乗る）get on the *plane* for London / hikooki *kara oriru*（飛行機から降りる）get off a *plane* / Hikooki *wa ma-mo-naku ririku shimasu.*（飛行機は間もなく離陸します）The *plane* will soon be taking off. / Hikooki *wa buji cha-kuriku shita.*（飛行機は無事着陸した）The *plane* landed safely. / *Hokkaidoo made* hikooki *de itta.*（北海道まで飛行機で行った）I went to Hokkaido by *plane.*

hi￹koosen￺ ひこうせん（飛行船）*n.* airship; dirigible; blimp.

hi￹k·u￺[1] ひく（引く）*vt.* (hik·i-; hik·a-; hi·i-te Ⓒ) **1** pull; draw; tow; tug:
kaaten o hiku（カーテンを引く）*draw* the curtains / *Himo o* hiite, *denki o tsuketa.*（ひもを引いて、電気をつけた）

I switched on the light by *pulling* the cord.

2 lead by the hand:

Kanojo wa kodomo no te o hiite, *aruita.* (彼女は子どもの手を引いて、歩いた) She walked along, *leading* her child *by the hand.*

3 catch; attract:

chuui o hiku (注意を引く) *attract* someone's attention / *hitome o* hiku (人目を引く) *catch* someone's attention / *Kare wa kanojo ni kokoro o* hikareta. (彼は彼女に心を引かれた) He was *attracted* to her.

4 consult (a dictionary); look up:

Jisho o hiite, *sono imi o shirabeta.* (辞書を引いて、その意味を調べた) I *consulted* a dictionary and checked the meaning.

5 lay; install:

suidoo o hiku (水道を引く) *lay* a water pipe / *gasu o* hiku (ガスを引く) *lay* on gas / *deñwa o* hiku (電話を引く) *install* a telephone / *Sono mura ni wa mada deñki ga* hiite *nai.* (その村にはまだ電気が引いてない) Electricity has not been *supplied* to that village yet.

6 draw (a line):

señ o hiku (線を引く) *draw* a line.

7 subtract; take:

Juu kara sañ o hiku *to nana nokorimasu.* (10 から 3 を引くと 7 残ります) *Take* 3 from 10 and it leaves 7. 《↔ tasu》

8 catch (a cold):

Kaze o hiite shimatta. (かぜをひいてしまった) I *have caught* a cold.

9 *vi.* go down; subside; ebb:

Netsu wa hikimashita *ka?* (熱は引きましたか) *Has* the fever *subsided?* / *Shio ga* hiki-*hajimeta.* (潮が引き始めた) The tide began to *ebb.*

10 *vi.* yield; pull out:

Kare wa ip-po mo ato e hikanakatta. (彼は一歩も後へ引かなかった) He *did not yield* a single step. / *Kare wa sono shoobai kara mi o*

hiita. (彼はその商売から身を引いた) He *pulled out* of that business. 《⇨ yameru》

hi「k·u² ひく (弾く) *vt.* (hik·i-; hik·a-; hi·i-te ⒞) play (a musical instrument):

Kanojo wa joozu ni piano o hiku. (彼女は上手にピアノを弾く) She *plays* the piano well. / *Kono kyoku o baioriñ de* hiku *no wa muzukashii.* (この曲をバイオリンで弾くのは難しい) It's difficult to *play* this tune on the violin.

hi「k·u³ ひく (轢く) *vt.* (hik·i-; hik·a-; hi·i-te ⒞) hit; run over [down]:

Kare no kuruma wa neko o hiita. (彼の車は猫をひいた) His car *ran over* a cat.

hi「ku」·i ひくい (低い) *a.* (-ku)

1 (of height) low; short:

hikui *yama* (低い山) *a low* mountain / *Chichi wa watashi yori se ga* hikui. (父は私より背が低い) My father is *shorter* than me. / *Kono ko wa hana ga* hikui. (この子は鼻が低い) This child has a *flat* nose. / *Herikoputaa ga* hikuku *toñde ita.* (ヘリコプターが低く飛んでいた) A helicopter was flying *low.* 《↔ takai》

2 (of a position, degree, level) low:

shakai-teki chii no hikui *hito-tachi* (社会的地位の低い人たち) people in a *low* social position / hikui *seekatsu-suijuñ* (低い生活水準) a *low* standard of living / *Kyoo wa kinoo yori oñdo ga* hikui. (きょうはきのうより温度が低い) Today the temperature is *lower* than yesterday. / *Saikiñ ketsuatsu ga* hikuku *natta.* (最近血圧が低くなった) My blood pressure has recently become *lower.* 《↔ takai》

3 (of sound, voice) not loud; low:

hikui *koe de hanasu* (低い声で話す)

speak in a *low* voice. (↔ takai)

hiˈkyoˈo ひきょう (卑怯) *a.n.*
(~ na, ni) foul; unfair; cowardly; mean:
Hikyoo *na shudañ o tsukau na.* (ひ
きょうな手段を使うな) Don't use
unfair means. / *Imasara te o hiku
nañte* hikyoo *da.* (いまさら手を引くな
んてひきょうだ) It is *cowardly* of you
to back out now.

hiˈma ひま (暇) *n.* time; free
time; leisure:
Hima *o mitsukete, gorufu no reñshuu o shite imasu.* (暇を見つけて, ゴ
ルフの練習をしています) I manage to
find *time* to practice golf. / *Isogashikute, shiñbuñ o yomu* hima *ga
arimaseñ.* (忙しくて, 新聞を読む暇があ
りません) I am so busy that I have
no *time* to read the newspaper. /
Terebi o miru hima *ga attara, beñkyoo shi nasai.* (テレビを見る暇があっ
たら, 勉強しなさい) If you have *time*
to watch TV, you should study
instead. / *Kare wa* hima *o mote-
amashite iru.* (彼は暇を持て余してい
る) He has too much *time* on his
hands:
hima o dasu (~を出す) dismiss;
fire.
— *a.n.* (~ na) free:
Hima *na toki wa nani o shimasu
ka?* (暇なときは何をしますか) What do
you do when you are *free*? /
Kyoo wa kyaku ga sukunakute,
hima *desu.* (きょうは客が少なくて, 暇で
す) There are only a few customers today, so we are *not busy*.

hiˈmee ひめい (悲鳴) *n.* shriek;
scream:
Tonari no heya kara himee *ga
kikoeta.* (隣の部屋から悲鳴が聞こえた)
A *shriek* came from the next
room. / *Kanojo wa osoroshikute,*
himee *o ageta.* (彼女は恐ろしくて, 悲
鳴を上げた) She gave a *scream* of
terror.

hiˈmitsu ひみつ (秘密) *n.* secret:

himitsu *o mamoru* [*morasu*] (秘密
を守る[漏らす]) keep [disclose] a *secret* / *Kono koto wa kare-ra ni*
himitsu *ni shite okoo.* (このことは彼
らに秘密にしておこう) Let's keep this
matter *secret* from them.

hiˈmo ひも (紐) *n.* string; cord;
band:
himo *o musubu* [*toku*] (ひもを結ぶ
[解く]) tie [untie] a *string* / *Shiñbuñshi wa gomu no* himo *de shi-
batte atta.* (新聞紙はゴムのひもで縛って
あった) The newspapers were held
together with a rubber *band*.

hiˈñ ひん (品) *n.* elegance; grace;
refinement:
hiñ *no yoi fujiñ* (品の良い婦人) an
elegant lady / *Kono kabiñ wa* hiñ
no aru katachi o shite iru. (この花瓶
は品のある形をしている) This vase has
a *graceful* shape. / *Kare wa tokidoki* hiñ *no nai kotoba o tsukau.*
(彼はときどき品のない言葉を使う) He
sometimes uses *vulgar* language.

hiˈna ひな (雛) *n.* chick; young
bird:
Hina *ga go-wa kaetta.* (ひなが5羽か
えった) Five *chickens* hatched.

hiˈnamaˈtsuri ひなまつり (雛祭り)
n. the Doll Festival celebrated
on March 3.

HINADAÑ

CULTURE

Also known as the Girls' Festival. 'Hina' dolls in ancient costumes are displayed on a tier of shelves (*hinadañ*) to celebrate the growth and health of the young girl(s) in a family.

hi¹nañ¹ ひなん (非難) *n.* blame; criticism; attack:

hinañ *o abiru* (非難を浴びる) be subjected to *criticism* / hinañ *o ukeru* (非難を受ける) encounter *criticism* / hinañ *o maneku* (非難を招く) invite *criticism* / *Kare no taimañ wa* hinañ *no mato to natta.* (彼の怠慢は非難の的となった) His negligence became the target of *attack*.

hinañ suru (〜する) *vt.* criticize; blame; attack: *Kare wa watashi ga okureta koto o* hinañ shita. (彼は私が遅れたことを非難した) He *blamed* me for being late. / *Kanojo wa fuchuui o* hinañ sareta. (彼女は不注意を非難された) She *was criticized* for carelessness.

hi¹nañ² ひなん (避難) *n.* shelter; refuge; evacuation:

Tsunami no osore ga aru no de keesatsu wa juumiñ ni hinañ *o meejita.* (津波の恐れがあるので警察は住民に避難を命じた) Because of the fear of a tidal wave, the police ordered the inhabitants *to evacuate.*

hinañ suru (〜する) *vi.* take shelter [refuge]; evacuate: *Watashitachi wa nadare o sakete, koya ni* hinañ shita. (私たちはなだれを避けて、小屋に避難した) We *took shelter* from the avalanche in a cabin.

hi¹nani¹ñgyoo ひなにんぎょう (雛人形) *n.* a doll made of paper or clay, usually colorfully clad. (⇨ hinamatsuri)

hi¹nata ひなた (日向) *n.* sunny place:

Señtakumono o hinata *ni hoshita.*

(洗濯物を日なたに干した) I dried the wash in the *sun*. (↔ hikage) (⇨ hiatari)

hinata-bokko (〜ぼっこ) sunbath: hinata-bokko o suru (日なたぼっこをする) *bask in the sun.*

hi¹ne¹r·u ひねる (捻る) *vt.* (hiner-i-; hiner·a-; hinet-te C)

1 turn (a faucet, tap, knob): *suidoo no señ o* hineru (水道の栓をひねる) *turn* on a tap.

2 twist: *Kare wa sukeeto de ashi o* hinetta. (彼はスケートで足をひねった) He *twisted* his foot ice-skating.

hi¹ñi ひいん (品位) *n.* dignity; grace; elegance:

hiñi *o tamotsu* [*otosu*] (品位を保つ [落とす]) keep [lose] one's *dignity* / *Ano hito wa* hiñi *ni kakeru.* (あの人は品位に欠ける) He is wanting in *dignity*. (⇨ hiñ)

hi¹niku ひにく (皮肉) *n.* irony; sarcasm; cynicism:

Sore wa hiniku *desu ka?* (それは皮肉ですか) Is that meant to be *sarcastic*? / *Hara ga tatta no de* hiniku *o itte yatta.* (腹が立ったので皮肉を言ってやった) I got angry so I made *cynical remarks* to him.

— *a.n.* (〜 na, ni) ironic: hiniku *na ketsumatsu* (皮肉な結末) an *ironic* outcome / hiniku *na uñmee* (皮肉な運命) an *ironic* fate / *Gyaku no kekka ni naru to wa* hiniku *da.* (逆の結果になるとは皮肉だ) It's *ironic* that things turned out exactly opposite.

hi¹ñjaku ひんじゃく (貧弱) *a.n.* (〜 na, ni) poor; feeble: hiñjaku *na karadatsuki* (貧弱な体つき) a *feeble* body / *Kono roñbuñ wa nakami ga* hiñjaku *da.* (この論文は中身が貧弱だ) This essay is *thin* in content.

hi¹node ひので (日の出) *n.* sunrise:

Hinode *o ogamu tame ni hayaoki*

o shita. (日の出を拝むために早起きをした) I got up early to pay my respects to the *rising sun.* 《↔ hino-iri》《⇨ hiru (table)》

hi⌐noiri ひのいり (日の入り) *n.* sunset. 《↔ hinode》《⇨ hiru (table)》

hi⌐ñshi ひんし (品詞) *n.* part of speech.

hi⌐ñshitsu ひんしつ (品質) *n.* quality:
Kono kiji wa hiñshitsu ga yoi [warui]. (この生地は品質が良い[悪い]) This cloth is good [bad] in *quality.* / Hiñshitsu o kairyoo suru yochi ga aru. (品質を改良する余地がある) There is some room for improvement in *quality.*

hi⌐nyookika ひにょうきか (泌尿器科) *n.* urology department. 《⇨ byooiñ (table)》

hi⌐ppa⌐r·u ひっぱる (引っ張る) *vt.* (-par·i-; -par·a-; -pat-te 〔C〕)
1 pull; tug; jerk:
Himo o hippatte, akari o tsuketa. (ひもを引っ張って、明かりをつけた) I *pulled* the cord and switched on the light. / Dare-ka ga watashi no sode o hippatta. (誰かが私の袖を引っ張った) Someone *tugged* at my sleeve.
2 bring; take (a person):
Yatsu o hippate koi. (やつを引っ張って来い) *Bring* that fellow *along.* / Kare wa keesatsu e hipparareta. (彼は警察へ引っ張られた) He *was taken along* to the police.
3 lead:
Kare wa chiimu no hoka no mono o yoku hippatte iru. (彼はチームの他の者をよく引っ張っている) He *leads* the others in the team well.

hi⌐raga⌐na ひらがな (平仮名) *n.* the Japanese cursive syllabary:
Hiragana de tsugi no kañji no yomikata o kaki nasai. (ひらがなで次の漢字の読み方を書きなさい) Write the readings of the following Chinese characters in *hiragana.*

《⇨ inside front cover》

hi⌐rahira ひらひら *adv.* (~ to) (the motion of light, thin or soft things, fluttering, swaying, or falling):
Sakura no hana ga hirahira (to) chiri-hajimeta. (桜の花がひらひら(と)散り始めた) The cherry blossoms have started to fall, *fluttering* down. / Choochoo ga hirahira (to) toñde iru. (蝶々がひらひら(と)飛んでいる) The butterflies are *fluttering* around.

hi⌐rake⌐·ru ひらける (開ける) *vi.* (hirake-te 〔V〕) **1** (of a place) become modernized [civilized]; develop:
Kono machi wa saikiñ hirakemashita. (この町は最近開けました) This town *has* recently *developed.*
2 (of scenery) open; spread out:
Me no mae ni utsukushii keshiki ga hiraketa. (目の前に美しい景色が開けた) A beautiful view *opened* in front of our eyes.
3 fortune smiles (on a person):
Kare ni uñ ga hirakete kita. (彼に運が開けてきた) Fortune *has come to smile* on him.

hi⌐raki ひらき (開き) *n.*
1 opening:
Kono tobira wa hiraki ga warui. (このとびらは開きが悪い) This door *won't open easily.* 《⇨ hiraku》
2 difference:
Futari no ikeñ ni wa ooki-na hiraki ga aru. (二人の意見には大きな開きがある) There is a great *difference* of opinion between them.
3 fish cut open, flattened and dried:
aji no hiraki (あじの開き) a horse mackerel *cut open and dried.* 《⇨ aji² (photo)》

hi⌐ra⌐k·u ひらく (開く) (hirak·i-; hirak·a-; hira·i-te 〔C〕)
1 *vt.* open; undo; unpack; unseal:

tsutsumi [*tegami*] *o* hiraku (包み[手紙]を開く) *open* a parcel [letter] / *Moñ o* hiraite *hoodoojiñ o ireta.* (門を開いて報道陣を入れた) We opened the gate and *let in* the reporters. / *Kare wa doa o* hiraite, *heya ni haitta.* (彼はドアを開いて、部屋に入った) He *opened* the door and went into the room. 《⇨ aku¹》
2 *vi.* (of an office, shop, etc.) start; begin; establish; found: *Yuubiñkyoku wa ku-ji ni* hiraki-masu. (郵便局は9時に開きます) The post office *opens* at nine. / *Kono hakubutsukañ wa gojuu-neñ mae ni* hirakaremashita. (この博物館は50年前に開かれました) This museum *was established* fifty years ago. 《⇨ aku¹》
3 *vt.* hold; give: *kaigi o* hiraku (会議を開く) *hold* a meeting / *paatii o* hiraku (パーティーを開く) *give* a party.
4 *vi.* (of flowers) come out: *Sakura ga* hiraki-*hajimemashita.* (桜が開き始めました) The cherry blossoms have started to *open.*

hi「rata·i ひらたい (平たい) *a.* (-ku) flat; even: hiratai *sara* (平たい皿) *a flat* plate / *hyoomeñ o* hirataku *suru* (表面を平たくする) make a surface *even.* 《⇨ taira》
hirataku iu (平たく言う) speak plainly: Hirataku ieba, *kudaranai to iu koto desu.* (平たく言えば、くだらないということです) *Plainly speaking*, it is nonsense.

hi「ritsu ひりつ (比率) *n.* ratio; percentage: *Sañsee to hañtai no* hiritsu *wa sañ tai ni datta.* (賛成と反対の比率は3対2だった) The *ratio* between the pros and cons was three to two. / *Rieki wa shi bu roku no* hiritsu *de waketa.* (利益は四分六の比率で分けた) We divided the profits in the *proportion* of four to six.

hi「roba ひろば (広場) *n.* open space; square; plaza: *Ekimae no* hiroba *wa señkyo eñzetsu ni yoi basho da.* (駅前の広場は選挙演説に良い場所だ) The *square* in front of the station is a good place for a campaign speech.

hi「rogar·u ひろがる (広がる) *vi.* (hirogar·i-; hirogar·a-; hirogat-te Ⓒ) **1** extend; expand; widen: *Me no mae ni bokujoo ga* hiro-gatte ita. (目の前に牧場が広がっていた) The pastures *extended* in front of us. / *Eki no mae no michi ga* hirogatta. (駅の前の道が広がった) The road in front of the station *widened.* 《⇨ hirogeru》
2 (of a rumor) spread: *Uwasa wa sugu ni* hirogaru. (うわさはすぐに広がる) Rumors *spread* quickly. / *Kaji wa shihoo ni* hiro-gatta. (火事は四方に広がった) The fire *spread* in all directions. 《⇨ hirogeru》

hi「roge·ru ひろげる (広げる) *vt.* (hiroge-te Ⓥ) **1** spread; unfold; unroll: *shiñbuñ o* hirogeru (新聞を広げる) *open* a newspaper / *Sono tori wa tsubasa o* hirogeta. (その鳥は翼を広げた) The bird *spread* its wings. 《⇨ hirogaru》
2 widen (a field of activity); enlarge; extend: *shoobai o* hirogeru (商売を広げる) *expand* one's business / *Sono michi wa* hirogeru *keekaku desu.* (その道は広げる計画です) We are planning to *widen* the road. 《⇨ hiro-garu》

hi「ro⌐·i ひろい (広い) *a.* (-ku) large; big; wide; broad: hiroi *ie* (広い家) *a roomy* house / hiroi *chishiki* (広い知識) *broad* knowledge / *Eki kara* hiroi *toori o aruite kite kudasai.* (駅から広い通りを歩いて来てください) Please come from the station by walking along the *wide* road. / *Tanaka-san wa shiya ga hiroi.*（田中さんは視野が広い）Mr. Tanaka has a *broad* outlook. / *Kare wa juudoo no shidoo-sha to shite* hiroku *katsuyaku shite imasu.*（彼は柔道の指導者として広く活躍しています）He is very *active* as a judo instructor. / *Motto* hiroi *kokoro o mochi nasai.*（もっと広い心を持ちなさい）Be more *broad-minded.* (↔ semai)

hiʳromar·u ひろまる（広まる）*vi.* (hiromar·i-; hiromar·a-; hiro-mat-te Ⓒ) spread; come into fashion; be circulated: *Sono uwasa wa machi-juu ni* hiromatta.（そのうわさは町中に広まった）The rumor *spread* throughout the town. / *Kono kabañ wa wakai hito-tachi no aida ni* hiromatte *imasu.*（このかばんは若い人たちの間に広まっています）These bags *are* now *in fashion* with young people. (⇨hiromeru)

hiʳrome·ru ひろめる（広める）*vt.* (hirome-te Ⓥ) spread; popularize: *uwasa o* hiromeru（うわさを広める）*spread* a rumor / *Kokumiñ no aida ni kañkyoo-hakai ni kañsuru chishiki o* hiromeru *hitsuyoo ga arimasu.*（国民の間に環境破壊に関する知識を広める必要があります）It is necessary to *spread* knowledge about environmental destruction among citizens. (⇨ hiromaru)

hiʳroo[1] ひろう（疲労）*n.* fatigue; tiredness; exhaustion: Hiroo *ga kaifuku shita.*（疲労が回復した）I have recovered from my *exhaustion.* / Hiroo *ga toreru yoo ni yoku yasumi nasai.*（疲労がとれるようによく休みなさい）Take a good rest to get over your *tiredness.* / *Kare wa* hiroo *no iro o misena-katta.*（彼は疲労の色を見せなかった）He showed no signs of *fatigue.*

hiroo suru (〜する) *vi.* be tired; be fatigued; be exhausted: *Señ-shu-tachi wa* hiroo *shite iru yoo ni mieta.*（選手たちは疲労しているように見えた）The players looked *exhausted.*

hiʳroo[2] ひろう（披露）*n.* introduction; announcement: *kaiteñ*-hiroo（開店披露）an *announcement* of the opening of a store / *kekkoñ*-hiroo-*eñ*（結婚披露宴）a wedding *reception.*

hiroo suru (〜する) *vt.* introduce; announce; show: *Kare wa wata-shi-tachi ni atarashii sakuhiñ o* hiroo *shita.*（彼は私たちに新しい作品を披露した）He *showed* us his new work.

hiʳrosa ひろさ（広さ）*n.* area; extent; size; width: *Sono heya no* hirosa *wa dono kurai desu ka?*（その部屋の広さはどのくらいですか）What is the *size* of that room? / *Kare no chishiki no* hirosa *ni wa odorokimashita.*（彼の知識の広さには驚きました）We were amazed by his *breadth* of knowledge.

Hiʳroshima[1]**-keñ** ひろしまけん（広島県）*n.* Hiroshima Prefecture. Located near the west end of Honshu, facing the Inland Sea on the south. The capital city, Hiroshima, was the first city to be subject to an attack by an atomic bomb. (⇨ map (C4))

hiʳro·u ひろう（拾う）*vt.* (hiro·i-; hirow·a-; hirot-te Ⓒ) **1** pick up; find: *gomi o* hirou（ごみを拾う）*pick up* trash / *Saifu o* hirotte, *keesatsu ni todoketa.*（財布を拾って、警察に届けた）I *picked up* a wallet and turned it in to the police.
2 get; pick up (a taxi): *Tsukareta no de takushii o* hirotte *kaetta.*（疲れたのでタクシーを拾って帰った）As I was tired, I *got* a taxi and

came back.

hiˈru ひる (昼) *n.* noon; day; daytime:

Hiru-*goro gaishutsu shimasu.* (昼ごろ外出します) I go out about *noon.* / *Kare wa* hiru *mo yoru mo hataraita.* (彼は昼も夜も働いた) He worked both *day* and night.

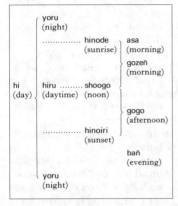

《⇨ asa; bañ[1] (table)》

hiˈrugoˈhañ ひるごはん (昼ご飯) *n.* lunch: ★ More polite than '*hirumeshi.*'

Hirugohañ *ni soba o tabeta.* (昼ご飯にそばを食べた) I had buckwheat noodles for *lunch.* / Hirugohañ *ni shiyoo.* (昼ご飯にしよう) Let's eat *lunch.* 《⇨ gohañ; asagohañ; bañgohañ》

hiˈruma ひるま (昼間) *n.* daytime:

Hiruma *no biñ wa mañseki desu.* (昼間の便は満席です) All seats on the *daytime* flights are filled. / *Hito wa* hiruma *hataraite, yoru yasumu no ga shizeñ desu.* (人は昼間働いて、夜休むのが自然です) It is natural for people to work in the *daytime* and sleep at night. / Hiruma *wa hima desu.* (昼間は暇です) I'm free during the *daytime.*

hiˈrumeshi ひるめし (昼飯) *n.* (*informal*) lunch. 《⇨ hirugohañ;

chuushoku》

hiˈruˈmˈu ひるむ (怯む) *vi.* (hirum·i-; hirum·a-; hiruñ-de Ⓒ) flinch (from); shrink (from): *Watashi wa kare no te no naifu o mite, isshuñ* hiruñda. (私は彼の手のナイフを見て一瞬ひるんだ) I *flinched* for a moment at the sight of the knife in his hand. / *Kare wa kikeñ ni mo* hirumanakatta. (彼は危険にもひるまなかった) He *did not shrink* from danger.

hiˈrune ひるね (昼寝) *n.* nap: hirune *o suru* (昼寝をする) take a *nap.*

hiˈruyaˈsumi ひるやすみ (昼休み) *n.* lunch break; noon recess: Hiruyasumi *ni hoñya e itta.* (昼休みに本屋へ行った) I went to a bookshop during the *lunch break.* / Hiruyasumi *wa ichi-jikañ desu.* (昼休みは1時間です) The *lunch break* is one hour.

hiˈryoo ひりょう (肥料) *n.* manure; fertilizer: *Hatake ni* hiryoo *o hodokoshita.* (畑に肥料を施した) I spread *manure* over the fields.

hiˈsaˈisha ひさいしゃ (被災者) *n.* victim (of a disaster); sufferer.

hiˈsañ ひさん (悲惨) *a.n.* (~ na, ni) wretched; miserable; terrible; tragic: hisañ *na jiko* (悲惨な事故) a *tragic* accident / hisañ *na jookyoo* (悲惨な状況) a *miserable* situation / *Kaji de kazoku mo zaisañ mo nakushi, kare wa* hisañ *na kurashi o shite iru.* (火事で家族も財産もなくし、彼は悲惨な暮らしをしている) Having lost both family and fortune in the fire, he is now leading a *wretched* life.

hiˈsashi ひさし (庇) *n.* **1** eaves. **2** visor (to a cap).

hiˈsashiburi ひさしぶり (久し振り) *a.n.* (~ na/no, ni) after a long time [silence; separation]:

Hisashiburi *desu ne.* (久しぶりですね)
It's *a long time* since I saw you
last. ★In greetings, '*O-hisashi-
buri desu ne*' is more polite. /
Hisashiburi *de [ni] Asakusa no
Kañnoñ-sama ni o-mairi o shita.*
(久しぶりで[に]浅草の観音さまにお参りを
した) *For the first time in quite a
while,* I visited the Kannon Temple at Asakusa. / Hisashiburi *no
ame de damu no mizu ga fueta.*
(久しぶりの雨でダムの水が増えた) With
the *first rain for ages,* the water
behind the dam rose.

hi⌐sa⌐shiku ひさしく (久しく) *adv.*
(*formal*) for a long time:
Suzuki-sañ to wa hisashiku *atte
imaseñ.* (鈴木さんとは久しく会っていま
せん) I haven't met Mrs. Suzuki
for a long time.

hi⌐sho¹ ひしょ (秘書) *n.* secretary:
Kanojo wa uchi no shachoo no
hisho *desu.* (彼女はうちの社長の秘書
です) She is the *secretary* to the
president of our company.

hi⌐sho² ひしょ (避暑) *n.* sum-
mering; going somewhere cool
during the hot months:
Watashi wa maitoshi Nagano e
hisho *ni ikimasu.* (私は毎年長野へ
避暑に行きます) Every year I go to
Nagano to *escape the hot weather.*

hi⌐so⌐ka ひそか (密か) *a.n.* (~ na,
ni) in secret; in private:
Kagekiha wa hisoka *ni bakudañ o
tsukutte ita.* (過激派はひそかに爆弾を
作っていた) The radicals were *secretly* making bombs. / *Tanaka-
sañ wa kare ni* hisoka *na omoi o
yosete iru.* (田中さんは彼にひそかな思
いを寄せている) Miss Tanaka *secretly* loves him. ★'*Hisoka da*' is
not common.

hi⌐ssha ひっしゃ (筆者) *n.* writer;
author.

hi⌐sshi ひっし (必死) *a.n.* (~ na/
no, ni) desperate; frantic:

hisshi *no soosaku* (必死の捜索) a
frantic search / *Kare wa* hisshi *ni
nigeta.* (彼は必死に逃げた) He ran
away *desperately.*

hi⌐sso⌐ri ひっそり *adv.* (~ to;
~ suru) (the state of being quiet,
still or deserted):
Mori no naka wa hissori (*to*) *shite
ita.* (森の中はひっそり(と)していた) All
was *hushed* in the forest. / *Aki ni
naru to sono hamabe wa* hissori
(*to*) *shite shimau.* (秋になるとその浜
辺はひっそり(と)してしまう) With
autumn, the beach becomes *deserted.* / *Kare wa inaka de* hissori
(*to*) *kurashite iru.* (彼はいなかでひっそ
り(と)暮らしている) He lives *quietly*
in the country.

hi⌐tai ひたい (額) *n.* forehead;
brow:
hiroi [*semai*] hitai (広い[狭い]額) a
broad [narrow] *forehead* / *Kare
wa* hitai *ni shiwa o yoseta.* (彼は
額にしわを寄せた) He *knitted his
brows.*

hi⌐tar·u ひたる (浸る) *vi.* (hitar·i-;
hitar·a-; hitat-te Ⓒ) **1** be
flooded; be under water:
Koozui de hatake ga mizu ni
hitatta. (洪水で畑が水に浸った) The
fields *were inundated* because of
flooding. 《⇨ hitasu》
2 be immersed in; be given to:
sake ni hitaru (酒に浸る) *give oneself over* to drinking / *Kare wa
sono ba no tanoshii fuñiki ni*
hitatta. (彼はその場の楽しい雰囲気に
浸った) He *steeped himself* in the
merry atmosphere of the place.

hi⌐tas·u ひたす (浸す) *vt.* (hita-
sh·i-; hitas·a-; hitash·i-te Ⓒ)
dip; soak:
mame o mizu ni hitasu (豆を水に浸
す) *soak* beans in water / *pañ o
miruku ni* hitasu (パンをミルクに浸す)
dip bread in milk. 《⇨ hitaru》

hi⌐tee ひてい (否定) *n.* denial;
negation:

Sono jijitsu wa hitee dekimaseñ. (その事実は否定できません) The fact *is undeniable.* / hitee-*buñ* (否定文) a *negative* sentence.

hitee suru (〜する) *vt.* deny; make a denial: *Kanojo wa sono uwasa o kippari* hitee shita. (彼女はそのうわさをきっぱり否定した) She flatly *denied* the rumor. 《↔ kootee¹》

hiˈto ひと (人) *n.* **1** person; man; woman: ★ In polite speech, '*kata*' is used.
Ano hito *wa dare desu ka?* (あの人はだれですか) Who is that *man* [*woman*]? / *Kare wa ii* hito *da.* (彼はいい人だ) He is a nice *person.* / *Kanojo wa ki no kawariyasui* hito *da.* (彼女は気の変わりやすい人だ) She is a *woman* of moods.
2 (other) people:
Wakai hito *ga urayamashii.* (若い人がうらやましい) I envy young *people.* / Hito *no warukuchi o iu no wa yoshi nasai.* (人の悪口を言うのはよしなさい) Don't speak ill of *other people.*
3 human being; man:
Hito *wa dare de mo shinu.* (人はだれでも死ぬ) *Man* is mortal.
4 worker; hand:
Hito *ga tarinai.* (人が足りない) We are short of *workers.* 《⇨ hitode》
hito ga warui (〜が悪い) mean; spiteful: *Ano majime na hito o karakau nañte, anata mo* hito ga warui. (あのまじめな人をからかうなんて, あなたも人が悪い) It's *mean* of you to make fun of such a serious person.

hiˈto-¹ ひと (一) *pref.* one: hito-*kañ* (一缶) *one* can / hito-*kumi* (一組) *one* group; *one* pair / *Kono gakkoo wa* hito-*kurasu nijuu-niñ desu.* (この学校は一クラス20人です) There are twenty students in *one* class at this school. / *Watashi wa ichi-nichi ni tabako o*

hito-*hako suimasu.* (私は一日にたばこを一箱吸います) I smoke *a* pack of cigarettes a day.

hiˈto-² ひと (一) *pref.* a [an]:
★ Precedes a noun and indicates one (short) action.
hito-*shigoto suru* (一仕事する) do *a* job of work / hito-*oyogi suru* (一泳ぎする) have *a* swim / hito-*nemuri suru* (一眠りする) have *a* nap.

hiˈtoˈbito ひとびと (人々) *n.* (many) people:
Sono eega wa hitobito *o fukaku kañdoo saseta.* (その映画は人々を深く感動させた) The movie moved *people* deeply.

hiˈtochiˈgai ひとちがい (人違い) *n.* mistaking a person for somebody else:
Yamada-sañ da to omottara, hito-chigai *datta.* (山田さんだと思ったら, 人違いだった) I thought he was Yamada, but I *made a mistake.* / *Gomeñ nasai.* Hitochigai deshita. (ごめんなさい. 人違いでした) I'm sorry. I *took you for someone I know.* 《⇨ -chigai》

hiˈtode ひとで (人手) *n.*
1 worker; hand:
Hitode *ga tarinai.* (人手が足りない) We are short of *hands.* 《⇨ hito》
2 another's help:
Kono shigoto wa hitode *o karizu ni, yarimashita.* (この仕事は人手を借りずに, やりました) I have done this work without *anyone else's help.*
3 another's possession:
Sono uchi wa tsui-ni hitode *ni watatta.* (その家はついに人手に渡った) The house finally passed into *another's possession.*

hiˈtodoori ひとどおり (人通り) *n.* pedestrian traffic:
Kono toori wa hitodoori *ga ooi* [*sukunai*]. (この通りは人通りが多い[少ない]) This street is *full* [*not full*] *of people.*

hiˈtoˈe ni ひとえに *adv.* (*formal*)

wholly; sincerely:
Wareware ga koñnichi koko ni ari-masu no mo hitoe ni *minasama no okage desu.* (われわれが今日ここにありますもひとえに皆さまのおかげです) The fact that we are here today is *entirely* thanks to you all. / *Shitsuree no dañ,* hitoe ni *o-yurushi kudasai.* (失礼の段, ひとえにお許しください) I *sincerely* ask you to forgive me for being impolite.

hiˈ**togara** ひとがら (人柄) *n.* personality; personal character:
Watashi wa kanojo no hitogara *ni hikareta.* (私は彼女の人柄にひかれた) I was attracted by her *personality.* / *Tanaka-sañ wa* hitogara *ga yoi.* (田中さんは人柄が良い) Mr. Tanaka is *good-natured.*

hiˈ**togomi** ひとごみ (人込み) *n.* crowd:
Hitogomi o kakiwakete susumu no wa taiheñ datta. (人込みをかき分けて進むのは大変だった) It was hard to push my way through the *crowd.* / *Kare wa* hitogomi *ni magirete shimatta.* (彼は人込みにまぎれてしまった) He was lost in the *crowd.* / *Depaato wa taiheñ na* hitogomi *datta.* (デパートは大変な人込みだった) The department store was very *crowded.*

hiˈ**togoto** ひとごと (人事) *n.* other people's affairs: ★ Often used with a negative.
Sono jiko wa hitogoto *de wa nai.* (その事故はひと事ではない) *Everyone has the possibility* of encountering such an accident. / *Sore wa* hitogoto *to wa omoenai.* (それはひと事とは思えない) I *can well appreciate* such a situation. / *Kare wa sono moñdai o* hitogoto *no yoo ni kañgaete iru.* (彼はその問題をひと事のように考えている) He thinks that the problem is *nothing to do with him.*

hiˈ**tokage** ひとかげ (人影) *n.*

shadow of a person; human figure:
Toori ni wa hitokage *ga nakatta.* (通りには人影がなかった) There were no *people* in sight on the street.

hiˈ**to**ˈ**koto** ひとこと (一言) *n.* single word:
Kare wa Nihoñgo ga hitokoto *mo shaberemaseñ.* (彼は日本語がひと言もしゃべれません) He can't speak *a single word* of Japanese. / *Hitokoto iwasete kudasai.* (ひと言言わせてください) Let me say just *one word.* / *Kare wa kaigi-chuu,* hitokoto *mo shaberanakatta.* (彼は会議中, ひと言もしゃべらなかった) He *remained silent* during the meeting.

hiˈ**toma**ˈ**kase** ひとまかせ (人任せ) *n.* leaving a matter to others:
Kare wa nañ de mo hitomakase *da.* (彼は何でも人まかせだ) He *leaves everything to others.* / *Kono shigoto wa* hitomakase *ni dekinai.* (この仕事は人まかせにできない) I cannot *leave this work to others.*

hiˈ**tomane** ひとまね (人真似) *n.* (of people) mimicry; imitation:
Oomu wa hitomane *ga umai.* (おうむは人まねがうまい) Parrots are good at *copying what people say.* / *Hitomane o shite iru dake de wa shiñpo dekinai.* (人まねをしているだけでは進歩できない) You can make no progress by just *imitating* others.

hiˈ**to**ˈ**mazu** ひとまず *adv.* first (of all); for a while; for the time being:
Hitomazu, kono shigoto o katazukeyoo. (ひとまず, この仕事を片づけよう) *First of all,* let's finish this work. / *Hitomazu, yasumi o torimashoo.* (ひとまず, 休みをとりましょう) Let's take a break *for a while.* / *Kore de* hitomazu *añshiñ desu.* (これでひとまず安心です) With this, I feel relieved *for the time being.*

hiˈ**to**ˈ**me**[1] ひとめ (一目) *n.* look; sight; glance:

Kore o mae kara hitome *mitai to omotte imashita.* (これを前からひと目見たいと思っていました) I had wanted to have *a look* at this for a long time. / *Kare wa* hitome *de kanojo ga suki ni natta.* (彼はひと目で彼女が好きになった) With *one glance*, he took a fancy to her.

hi「tome[2] ひとめ (人目) *n.* public attention; notice:
Soñna tokoro e oitara, hitome ni tsuku. (そんな所へ置いたら、人目につく) If you put it there, *everyone will notice* it. / *Sono atarashii biru wa* hitome *o hiita.* (その新しいビルは人目を引いた) The new building attracted *public attention.* / *Kare-ra wa* hitome o shinoñde, *atta.* (彼らは人目を忍んで、会った) They met *in secret.*

hi「to」mi ひとみ (瞳) *n.* pupil of the eye:
hitomi o korasu (瞳を凝らす) *stare intently.*

hi「to」ri ひとり (一人) *n.* one (person); each; by [for] oneself:
Kare wa koko no kaiiñ no hitori *desu.* (彼はここの会員の一人です) He is *one* of the members of this society. / *Hitori, ik-ko totte kudasai.* (一人、1個取ってください) Please take one *each.* / *Kare wa mada* hitori *desu.* (彼はまだ一人です) He is still *single.* / hitorik-ko (ひとりっ子) an *only* child / hitori-*musuko* (ひとり息子) an *only* son / hitori-*musume* (ひとり娘) an *only* daughter.
hitori de (〜で) by oneself: *Kanojo wa* hitori de *kurashite imasu.* (彼女は一人で暮らしています) She lives *by herself.* / *Shukudai wa* hitori de *yari nasai.* (宿題は一人でやりなさい) Do your homework *by yourself.*

hi「toridachi ひとりだち (独り立ち) *n.* independence.
hitoridachi suru (〜する) *vi.* become independent; stand on

one's own feet: *Kare mo sorosoro* hitoridachi *shite ii koro da.* (彼もそろそろ独り立ちしていいころだ) It is about time for him to *stand on his own feet.* 《⇨ dokuritsu》

hi「toride ni ひとりでに (独りでに) *adv.* by itself; automatically:
Doa ga hitoride ni *hiraita.* (ドアがひとりでに開いた) The door opened *by itself.* / *Kono deñtoo wa kuraku naru to* hitoride ni *tsukimasu.* (この電灯は暗くなるとひとりでにつきます) When it gets dark, this light comes on *automatically.* 《⇨ shizeñ ni》

hi「torigoto ひとりごと (独り言) *n.* soliloquy; talking to oneself:
Kare wa hitorigoto *o iu kuse ga aru.* (彼は独り言を言う癖がある) He has a habit of *talking to himself.*

hi「tori-hito」ri ひとりひとり (一人一人) *n.* every one; one by one; one after another:
Paatii de kaichoo wa hitori-hitori *ni hanashikaketa.* (パーティーで会長は一人一人に話しかけた) At the party the chairman spoke to *everyone.* / *Miñna* hitori-hitori *ikeñ o happyoo shita.* (みんな一人一人意見を発表した) *One by one*, we expressed our opinions.

hi「tosashi」yubi ひとさしゆび (人差し指) *n.* forefinger; index finger. 《⇨ yubi (illus.)》

hi「toshi」・i ひとしい (等しい) *a.* (-ku)
1 equal; the same:
Kono futatsu no kozutsumi wa mekata ga hitoshii. (この二つの小包みは目方が等しい) These two parcels are *equal* in weight. / *Rieki wa* hitoshiku *wakemashita.* (利益は等しく分けました) We divided the profit into *equal* parts.
2 (*pred.*) almost; practically:
Rieki ga tatta señ-eñ de wa nai ni hitoshii. (利益がたった千円ではないに等しい) The profit was only one thousand yen, which is *almost*

nothing.

hi⌐to⌐tobi ひととび（一飛び）*n.*
jump; hop:
Hikooki nara, Tookyoo to Fukuoka wa hitotobi desu.（飛行機なら、東京と福岡はひととびです）It is just a *hop* between Tokyo and Fukuoka if you go by airplane. / *Kare wa sono ogawa o hitotobi de toñda.*（彼はその小川をひととびでとんだ）He got across the stream with a *leap*.

hi⌐totoori ひととおり（一通り）*n.*
all; generality; ordinariness:
hitotoori *no chishiki*（一通りの知識）a *general* knowledge (of something) / hitotoori *no setsumee*（一通りの説明）a *general* explanation / *Kare no kuroo wa* hitotoori *de wa nakatta.*（彼の苦労は一通りではなかった）He went to *extraordinary* trouble. 《⇨ futsuu¹》
— *adv.* (~ no) briefly; hurriedly; roughly:
Maiasa dekakeru mae ni hitotoori *shiñbuñ ni me o tooshimasu.*（毎朝出かける前に一通り新聞に目を通します）I glance *through* the newspaper every morning before leaving home. / *Sono kiji wa* hitotoori *yomimashita.*（その記事は一通り読みました）I read through the article *in a cursory manner.* 《⇨ zatto》

hi⌐to⌐tsu¹ ひとつ（一つ）*n.* **1** one; single: ★ Used when counting.
Kore o hitotsu *kudasai.* (*at a store*)（これを一つ下さい）Give me *one* of these, please. / *Kono riñgo wa* hitotsu *ikura desu ka?*（このりんごは一ついくらですか）How much is *one* of these apples? / *Kono iñsatsu ni wa* hitotsu *mo machigai ga nai.*（この印刷には一つも間違いがない）There is not a *single* mistake in this printed material. / *Hitotsu machigaeba, taiheñ na koto ni narimasu.*（ひとつ間違えば、大変なことになります）Even a *single* mistake will cause serious trouble. / hitotsu-

me（一つ目）the *first*. 《⇨ ichi¹; kazu (table)》
2 one-year old:
Kono ko wa hitotsu *hañ desu.*（この子は一つ半です）This child is *one* and a half years old.

hi⌐to⌐tsu² ひとつ *adv.* just; anyway; at any rate:
Mono wa tameshi da. Hitotsu yatte miyoo.（ものは試しだ。ひとつやってみよう）You will never know if you don't try. Let's have *a go.* / *Hitotsu yoroshiku onegai itashimasu.*（ひとつよろしくお願いいたします）I *would appreciate your kind consideration.* 《⇨ doo ka》

hi⌐to⌐tsuki ひとつき（一月）*n.* one month:
Sono shigoto wa hitotsuki *kakarimasu.*（その仕事は一月かかります）The job will take *one month.* / *Watashi wa* hitotsuki *ni, ni-kai Oosaka e shutchoo shimasu.*（私は一月に、2回大阪へ出張します）I go to Osaka on business twice *a month.* 《⇨ tsuki¹ (table)》

hi⌐to⌐yasumi ひとやすみ（一休み）*n.* a short rest; break.
hitoyasumi suru (~する) *vi.* take a short rest: *Hitoyasumi shite, ippuku tsukemashoo.*（一休みして、一服つけましょう）Let's *take a break* for a cigarette. 《⇨ kyuukee》

hi⌐tsuji ひつじ（羊）*n.* sheep:
hitsuji *no mure*（羊の群れ）a flock of *sheep* / hitsuji *no niku*（羊の肉）*mutton.*

hi⌐tsuyoo ひつよう（必要）*n.* necessity; need:
hitsuyoo *saishoogeñ*（必要最少限）a minimum *necessity* / *Ayamaru* hitsuyoo *wa arimaseñ.*（謝る必要はありません）You *don't have to* apologize. / *Hitsuyoo ni semararete Nihoñgo no beñkyoo o hajimemashita.*（必要に迫られて日本語の勉強を始めました）I started my study of Japanese out of *necessity.* / hitsu-

yoo-*keehi* (必要経費) *necessary* expenses.
— *a.n.* (～ na, ni) necessary; essential; indispensable: Hitsuyoo *na mono ga attara, osshatte kudasai.* (必要なものがあったら、おっしゃってください) If there is anything you *need*, please let me know. / *Kodomo ni wa aijoo o shimesu koto ga* hitsuyoo *desu.* (子どもには愛情を示すことが必要です) It's *necessary* to show affection to children. / *Kono jitensha wa shuuri ga* hitsuyoo *da.* (この自転車は修理が必要だ) This bicycle *needs* repairing. 《↔ fuhitsuyoo》

hi「tsuzen-teki ひつぜんてき (必然的) *a.n.* (～ na, ni) necessary; natural; inevitable: hitsuzen-teki *na kekka* (必然的な結果) an *inevitable* result / *Shiñriñ no geñshoo ni tomonai, yachoo no kazu mo* hitsuzen-teki *ni hette kite imasu.* (森林の減少に伴い、野鳥の数も必然的に減ってきています) With the disappearance of wooded areas, the number of wild birds has *inevitably* decreased.

hi「tto ヒット *n.* **1** (of baseball) hit; single: hitto *o utsu* (ヒットを打つ) hit a *single*.
2 great success; hit.
hitto suru (～する) *vi.* make a hit: *Sono uta wa* dai-hitto *shita.* (その歌は大ヒットした) The song *was quite a hit.*

hi「ya-a」se ひやあせ (冷や汗) *n.* cold sweat: hiya-ase *o kaku* (冷や汗をかく) break into a *cold sweat*.

hi「yaka」s·u ひやかす (冷やかす) *vt.* (hiyakash·i-; hiyakas·a-; hiyakash·i-te Ⓒ) **1** make fun of; tease: *Futari ga aruite iru no o mite,* hiyakashite *yatta.* (二人が歩いているのを見て、冷やかしてやった) We saw

the couple strolling and *made fun of* them.
2 window-shop: *Mise o* hiyakashite *jikañ o tsubushita.* (店を冷やかして時間をつぶした) I idled away the time *window-shopping.*

hi「yake ひやけ (日焼け) *n.* sunburn; suntan: hiyake-*dome* (日焼けどめ) *sunburn* cream [oil].
hiyake suru (～する) *vi.* get sunburned; get a suntan: *Kanojo wa sugu* hiyake suru. (彼女はすぐ日焼けする) She *gets a suntan* easily. / *Kare wa makkuro ni* hiyake shita. (彼は真っ黒に日焼けした) He *was* well *suntanned.*

hi「ya」s·u ひやす (冷やす) *vt.* (hiyash·i-; hiyas·a-; hiyash·i-te Ⓒ) cool; ice; refrigerate: *reezooko de biiru o* hiyasu (冷蔵庫でビールを冷やす) *cool* beer in the fridge / *Kanojo wa tsumetai kaze ni atatte, karada o* hiyashita. (彼女は冷たい風に当たって、体を冷やした) She *cooled herself off* in the cold breeze. / *Atama o* hiyashite, *kañgae nasai.* (頭を冷やして、考えなさい) *Calm down* and think. 《⇒ hieru》

hi「ya」yaka ひややか (冷ややか) *a.n.* (～ na, ni) cold; coldhearted; cool; icy: hiyayaka *na taido* (冷ややかな態度) a *cool* attitude / hiyayaka *ni kotaeru* (冷ややかに答える) give a *chilly* reply / *Kare wa* hiyayaka *na me de watashi o mita.* (彼は冷ややかな目で私を見た) He gave me a *cold* look.

hi「yoko ひよこ *n.* chick; chicken.
hi「yoo ひよう (費用) *n.* expense; expenditure; cost: Hiyoo *wa kochira de futañ shimasu.* (費用はこちらで負担します) We will cover the *cost.* / Hiyoo *wa ikura kakarimasu ka?* (費用はいくらかかりますか) How much does it

cost? / Hiyoo *wa zeñbu de sañ-man-eñ kakatta.* (費用は全部で3万円かかった) The *expenses* amounted to 30,000 yen in total. / *Kaisha no* hiyoo *de paatii o hiraita.* (会社の費用でパーティーを開いた) We held a party at company *expense*.

hi⌈za　ひざ (膝) *n.* knee; lap: *Akañboo o* hiza *ni daita.* (赤ん坊をひざに抱いた) I held the baby on my *lap*. 《⇨ jiñtai (illus.)》

　　hiza o kuzusu (〜をくずす) sit comfortably: ★ This expression is used with reference to sitting on the floor, Japanese style.
Doozo hiza o kuzushite *kudasai.* (どうぞひざをくずしてください) Please *sit at ease*.

hi⌈zashi　ひざし (日差し) *n.* sunlight; sun:
Hizashi *ga mabushii.* (日ざしがまぶしい) The *sunlight* is bright. / Hizashi *ga tsuyoi* [*yowai*]. (日ざしが強い[弱い]) The *sunlight* is strong [weak].

hi⌈zuke　ひづけ (日付) *n.* date:
Kono tegami ni wa hizuke *ga nai.* (この手紙には日付がない) This letter has no *date*. / *Kogitte ni* hizuke *o ireru no o wasureta.* (小切手に日付を入れるのを忘れた) I forgot to put the *date* on the check.

hi⌈zumi　ひずみ (歪み) *n.* warp; distortion:
ita no hizumi (板のひずみ) a *warp* in a board / *oto no* hizumi (音のひずみ) a *distortion* in sound / *keezai no* hizumi (経済のひずみ) *distortions* in the economy.

ho¹¹　ほ (穂) *n.* (of a plant) ear:
Ine no ho *ga desorotta.* (稲の穂が出そろった) The rice plants came into *ears*.

ho¹²　ほ (帆) *n.* sail:
ho *o ageru* [*orosu*] (帆を揚げる[下ろす]) hoist [lower] a *sail*.

-¹ho/po　ほ/ぽ (歩) *suf.* counter for steps:

1	i⌈p-po	7	na⌈na¹-ho
2	ni¹-ho	8	ha¹p-po
3	sa⌈ñ-po		(ha⌈chi¹-ho)
4	yo⌈ñ-ho	9	kyu⌈u-ho
5	go¹-ho	10	ji¹p-po
6	ro¹p-po		(ju¹p-po)
	(ro⌈ku-ho)	?	na⌈ñ-po

Ip-po mae e de nasai. (一歩前へ出なさい) Please move one *step* forward. / *Sañ-po ushiro e sagari nasai.* (三歩後へ下がりなさい) Take three *steps* backward.

ho¹bo　ほぼ *adv.* almost; nearly; about:
Biru wa hobo *dekiagarimashita.* (ビルはほぼでき上がりました) The building is *almost* completed. / *A wa B no* hobo *sañ-bai no hiyoo ga kakarimasu.* (AはBのほぼ3倍の費用がかかります) A costs *about* three times as much as B.

hodo　ほど (程) *p.* **1** about; some:
Jagaimo o sañ-kiro hodo *kudasai.* (じゃがいもを3キロほど下さい) Please give me *some* three kilos of potatoes. / *Ato juugo-fuñ* hodo *de Narita ni tsukimasu.* (あと15分ほどで成田に着きます) We will be arriving at Narita in *about* fifteen minutes. 《⇨ kurai²》

2 not as [so]...as: ★ Follows a noun and used with a negative.
Kotoshi no natsu wa kyoneñ hodo *atsuku nai.* (今年の夏は去年ほど暑くない) This summer is *not as* hot *as* last year's. / *Watashi wa anata* hodo *tsukarete imaseñ.* (私はあなたほど疲れていません) I am *not as* tired *as* you. / *Kare* hodo *yuunoo na hito wa metta ni imaseñ.* (彼ほど有能な人はめったにいません) There is scarcely anyone *as* talented *as* him.

3 the more...the more:
Reñshuu sureba suru hodo *umaku narimasu.* (練習すればするほどうまくな

ります) *The more* you practice, *the better* you become. / *Kañgaereba kañgaeru* hodo *wakaranaku naru.* (考えれば考えるほどわからなくなる) *The more* I think about it, *the less* I understand. / *Beñri de areba aru* hodo *nedañ mo takai.* (便利であればあるほど値段も高い) *The more* convenient something is, *the more* expensive it is.

4 so...that:
Tsukarete, moo ip-po mo arukenai hodo *datta.* (疲れて、もう一歩も歩けないほどだった) I was *so* exhausted *that* I was unable to take even one step more.

5 almost:
Sono shirase o kiite tobiagaru hodo *bikkuri shita.* (その知らせを聞いて飛び上がるほどびっくりした) On hearing the news, I *almost* jumped up in surprise.

ho⌈do⌉k·u ほどく (解く) *vt.* (hodok·i-; hodok·a-; hodo·i-te C) undo; untie; unpack; unfasten: *kozutsumi o* hodoku (小包みをほどく) *untie* a parcel / *kutsu no himo o* hodoku (靴のひもをほどく) *untie* one's shoe laces / *musubi o* hodoku (結びをほどく) *untie* a knot / *seetaa o* hodoku (セーターをほどく) *unravel* a sweater.

ho⌈doo ほどう (歩道) *n.* sidewalk; pavement:
hodoo o aruku (歩道を歩く) walk on the *sidewalk.*

ho⌈dookyoo ほどうきょう (歩道橋) *n.* pedestrian overpass:

HODOOKYOO

hodookyoo o wataru (歩道橋を渡る) go across a *pedestrian overpass.*

ho⌈e⌉l·ru ほえる (吠える) *vi.* (hoe-te V) bark; howl; roar:
Sono inu wa watashi ni mukatte hoeta. (その犬は私に向かってほえた) The dog *barked* at me.

ho⌈ga⌉raka ほがらか (朗らか) *a.n.* (~ na, ni) cheerful; bright:
hogaraka na seekaku (朗らかな性格) a *cheerful* disposition / *hogaraka de yoku shaberu hito* (朗らかでよくしゃべる人) a *cheerful* and talkative person / *hogaraka ni warau* (朗らかに笑う) laugh *merrily.*

ho⌉go ほご (保護) *n.* protection; guardianship; preservation:
hogo o ataeru [*ukeru*] (保護を与える [受ける]) give [receive] *protection* / *shiñriñ no* hogo (森林の保護) *preservation* of a forest / *hogo-choo* (保護鳥) a *protected* bird / *hogo-sha* (保護者) a *guardian* / *hogo-booeki* (保護貿易) *protective* trade.
hogo suru (~ する) *vt.* **1** protect; take care of; preserve: *Atama o* hogo suru *no ni herumetto ga hitsuyoo desu.* (頭を保護するのにヘルメットが必要です) You need a helmet to *protect* your head.
2 take into protective custody; shelter: *Keesatsu wa sono iede shooneñ o* hogo shita. (警察はその家出少年を保護した) The police *took* the runaway boy *into custody.*

ho⌉ho ほほ (頬) *n.* cheek. ((⇨ hoo³))

ho⌈hoe⌉m·u ほほえむ (微笑む) *vi.* (-em·i-; -em·a-; -eñ-de C) smile:
Kanojo wa kodomo-tachi ni hohoeñda. (彼女は子どもたちにほほえんだ) She *smiled* at the children.

ho⌈ka ほか (外・他) *n.* other; another; else:
Kono kutsu wa sukoshi ooki-sugimasu. Hoka no o misete kudasai. (この靴は少し大き過ぎます。ほかのを見せてください) These shoes are a bit

too big. Can you show me some *others*? / Hoka *no hito no ikeñ mo kiite mimashoo.* (ほかの人の意見も聞いてみましょう) Let's try asking some *other* people their opinions.

...hoka shikata ga nai (...〜しかたがない) there is nothing for it but to...: *Zettai añsee o señkoku sareta no de, nete iru yori* hoka shikata ga nai. (絶対安静を宣告されたので, 寝ているよりほかしかたがない) Since I was warned that I should have absolute rest, *I have no choice but to* stay in bed.

hoˈka ni ほかに (他に) *adv.* **1** besides; else; as well as: Hoka ni *nani-ka suru koto wa arimasu ka?* (ほかに何かすることはありますか) Is there anything *else* left to do? / *Kare wa Nihoñgo no* hoka ni *Chuugokugo mo hanasemasu.* (彼は日本語のほかに中国語も話せます) He can speak Chinese *as well as* Japanese.
2 except (for): *Kare no* hoka ni *sore ga dekiru mono wa imaseñ.* (彼のほかにそれができる者はいません) *Except for* him, there is no one who can do that.

hoˈkahoka ほかほか *a.n.* (〜 no) nice and warm; steaming hot: hokahoka *no futoñ* (ほかほかのふとん) a *nice, warm* futon / hokahoka *no satsumaimo* (ほかほかのさつまいも) *steaming* hot sweet potatoes.
—— *adv.* (〜 suru) warm: *Furo ni hairu to karada ga* hokahoka *suru.* (ふろに入ると体がほかほかする) You will feel *warm* after taking a bath.

hoˈkañ ほかん (保管) *n.* safekeeping; custody; storage: hokañ-*ryoo* (保管料) charges for *custody*; a *storage* fee.
hokañ suru (〜する) *vt.* keep; have a thing in one's custody: *Ryooshuusho o nakusanai yoo ni,* hokañ shite *oite kudasai.* (領収書をなくさないように, 保管しておいてください)

Please *keep* the receipts *in a safe place* so that you don't lose them. / *Shorui wa giñkoo ni* hokañ shite *arimasu.* (書類は銀行に保管してあります) The documents *are in the custody* of a bank.

hoˈkeñ[1] ほけん (保険) *n.* insurance; assurance: hokeñ *ni hairu* (保険に入る) buy *insurance* / hokeñ *o kaiyaku suru* (保険を解約する) cancel an *insurance policy* / *Kuruma ni* hokeñ *o kaketa.* (車に保険をかけた) I've taken out *insurance* on my car. / *Kare wa isseñmañ-eñ no seemee* hokeñ *ni haitte iru.* (彼は1,000万円の生命保険に入っている) He carries ten million-yen *insurance* on his life. / hokeñ-*ryoo* (保険料) an *insurance* premium / hokeñ-*kiñ* (保険金) *insurance* money.

hoˈkeñ[2] ほけん (保健) *n.* preservation of health; health: *Kono kaisha wa shaiñ no* hokeñ *o juushi shite iru.* (この会社は社員の保健を重視している) This company attaches importance to the *health* of its employees.

hoˈkeñjo ほけんじょ (保健所) *n.* health center.

hoˈkeˈñshoo ほけんしょう (保険証) *n.* = keñkoo-hokeñshoo.

hoˈkeñ-taˈi·iku ほけんたいいく (保健体育) *n.* health and physical education.

Hoˈkkaˈidoo ほっかいどう (北海道) *n.* Hokkaido. An island situated at the north end of Japan, administered as one unit. The output of dairy products is the highest in Japan. Capital city: Sapporo (札幌). 《⇨ inside back cover》.

Hoˈkkaˈidoo kaˈihaˈtsu-choo ほっかいどうかいはつちょう (北海道開発庁) *n.* Hokkaido Development Agency: Hokkaidoo kaihatsu-choo *chookañ* (北海道開発庁長官) the Director

General of the *Hokkaido Development Agency*. 《⇨ choo⁴ (table)》

Ho「kkyoku ほっきょく (北極) *n*. North Pole. 《↔ Nañkyoku》

ho「kori¹ ほこり (誇り) *n*. pride: *Kare wa kono machi no* hokori *da*. (彼はこの町の誇りだ) He is the *pride* of this town. / *Kimi wa kanojo no* hokori *o kizutsuketa*. (君は彼女の誇りを傷つけた) You've hurt her *pride*. / *Kare wa musuko o* hokori *ni omotte iru*. (彼は息子を誇りに思っている) He takes *pride* in his son.

ho「kori² ほこり (埃) *n*. dust: *Tsukue no ue no* hokori *o haratta*. (机の上のほこりを払った) I brushed the *dust* off the desk. / *Tana no ue wa* hokori-*darake datta*. (棚の上はほこりだらけだった) The top of the shelves was covered with *dust*. / *Hokori o tatenai de*. (ほこりを立てないで) Don't raise *dust*. 《⇨ chiri¹》

ho「korobi¹・ru ほころびる (綻びる) *vi*. (hokorobi-te Ⓥ) **1** be torn; come apart: *nuime ga* hokorobiru (縫い目がほころびる) *come apart* at the seams / *Kimono no suso ga* hokorobita. (着物のすそがほころびた) The hem of the kimono *has come undone*. **2** (*of a flower bud*) begin to bloom: *Sakura ga* hokorobi-*hajimeta*. (桜がほころび始めた) The cherry trees have begun to *bloom*.

ho「kor・u ほこる (誇る) *vt*. (hokor・i-; hokor・a-; hokot-te Ⓒ) be proud; boast; brag: *Kare wa umare no yoi no o* hokotte iru. (彼は生まれの良いのを誇っている) He *is proud* of being well-born.

Ho「ku-Bee ほくべい (北米) *n*. North America. 《⇨ Nañ-Bee; Chuu-Bee》

Ho「kuriku ほくりく (北陸) *n*. the district which comprises the four prefectures of Fukui, Ishikawa, Toyama, and Niigata. 《⇨ inside back cover》

ho「me¹・ru ほめる (褒める) *vt*. (home-te Ⓥ) praise; speak well of; compliment: *Señsee wa kare no Nihoñgo no hatsuoñ o* hometa. (先生は彼の日本語の発音をほめた) The teacher *praised* his Japanese pronunciation. / *Kare wa metta ni hito o* homenai. (彼はめったに人をほめない) He *rarely praises* other people. / *Kare no koto wa dare mo* homenai. (彼のことはだれもほめない) *No one speaks well of* him. / *Kare wa watashi no ryoori o* homete kureta. (彼は私の料理をほめてくれた) He *complimented* me on my cooking.

ho「ñ ほん (本) *n*. book; volume: hoñ *o yomu* [*kaku*] (本を読む[書く]) read [write] a *book* / hoñ *o dasu* (本を出す) publish a *book* / *Sono mise de* hoñ *o ni-satsu katta*. (その店で本を2冊買った) I bought two *books* at the bookshop. / *Sono* hoñ *wa shinagire desu*. (その本は品切れです) The *book* is out of stock.

hoñ- ほん (本) *pref*. **1** real; genuine; regular: hoñ-*shiñju* (本真珠) a *genuine* pearl / hoñ-*shikeñ* (本試験) the *final* examination / hoñ-*kaigi* (本会議) a *plenary* meeting. **2** (*formal*) this; current: hoñ-*añ* (本案) *this* plan / hoñ-*keñ* (本件) *this* affair.

-hoñ/boñ/poñ ほん/ぼん/ぽん (本) *suf*. counter for long, cylindrical objects:

1	i「p-poñ	7	na「na¹-hoñ
2	ni¹-hoñ	8	ha「p-poñ
3	sa「ñ-boñ		(ha「chi¹-hoñ)
4	yo「ñ-hoñ	9	kyu「u-hoñ
5	go-「hoñ	10	ji「p-poñ
6	ro「p-poñ		(ju「p-poñ)
	(ro「ku¹-hoñ)	?	na「ñ-boñ

eñpitsu ip-poñ (鉛筆 1 本) *a* pencil / *biiru* ni-hoñ (ビール 2 本) *two bottles* of beer / *Roosoku wa* nañ-boñ *hitsuyoo desu ka?* (ろうそくは何本必要ですか) *How many* candles do you need?

hoˈñba ほんば (本場) *n.* center of production; home:
Riñgo no hoñba *wa Aomori desu.* (りんごの本場は青森です) The *home* of Japanese apple *production* is Aomori. / *Kono atari wa o-cha no* hoñba *to shite shirarete imasu.* (このあたりはお茶の本場として知られています) This district is famous as a tea-growing *center.* / hoñba *no sukotchi uisukii* (本場のスコッチウィスキィー) *genuine* Scotch whisky.

hoˈñbako ほんばこ (本箱) *n.* bookcase.

hoˈñbuñ ほんぶん (本文) *n.* text; body:
keeyakusho no hoñbuñ (契約書の本文) the *text* of a contract.

hoˈñdana ほんだな (本棚) *n.* bookshelf.

hoˈne ほね (骨) *n.* **1** bone:
Kare wa migi ude no hone *o otta.* (彼は右腕の骨を折った) He broke a *bone* in his right arm. / *Kono sakana wa* hone *ga ooi.* (この魚は骨が多い) This fish has a lot of *bones.*
2 rib; frame:
Kasa no hone *ga ip-poñ orete shimatta.* (傘の骨が一本折れてしまった) A *rib* of my umbrella broke.
3 hardness; difficulty:
Sono yama ni noboru no wa hone *da.* (その山に登るのは骨だ) It *is hard* to climb that mountain.
4 backbone; pluck:
Kare wa hone *no aru otoko da.* (彼は骨のある男だ) He is a man with *backbone.*

hone no oreru (～の折れる) hard; laborious: *Kare wa* hone *no oreru shigoto wa yaritagaranai.* (彼は骨の折れる仕事はやりたがらない)

He avoids *laborious* tasks.

hone o oru (～を折る) take great pains: *Kare wa watashi no shuushoku no tame ni* hone *o otte kureta.* (彼は私の就職のために骨を折ってくれた) He *took great pains* to find a job for me.

hoˈneoˈr·u ほねおる (骨折る) *vi.* (-or·i-; -or·a-; -ot-te Ⓒ) take pains; make efforts:
Honeotte *yatta no ni kekka wa fuseekoo datta.* (骨折ってやったのに結果は不成功だった) Despite my *great efforts,* the outcome was not successful. / *Watashi-tachi wa yukimichi o* honeotte *susuñda.* (私たちは雪道を骨折って進んだ) We proceeded *laboriously* along the snow-covered road.

hoˈñgoku ほんごく (本国) *n.* one's own country; one's home country:
Kare wa kyoosee-teki ni hoñgoku *e kaesareta.* (彼は強制的に本国へ帰された) He was forcibly returned to *his own country.*

hoˈñjitsu ほんじつ (本日) *n.* today; this day. ★ Formal equivalent of '*kyoo.*'

hoˈñkaku-teki ほんかくてき (本格的) *a.n.* (～ na, ni) full; full-scale; real:
hoñkaku-teki *na choosa* (本格的な調査) a *full-scale* investigation / hoñkaku-teki *na Furañsu ryoori* (本格的なフランス料理) *real* French cooking / *Kooji ga* hoñkaku-teki *ni hajimatta.* (工事が本格的に始まった) The construction work has started in *earnest.*

hoˈñkañ ほんかん (本館) *n.* the main building; this building.

hoˈñki ほんき (本気) *n.* earnestness; seriousness:
Tanaka-sañ wa joodañ o hoñki *ni shita.* (田中さんは冗談を本気にした) Ms. Tanaka *took* the joke *seriously.* 《⇒ majime》

— *a.n.* (∼ na, ni) earnest; serious:

Hoñki *desu ka?* (本気ですか) Are you *serious?* / *Shikeñ ga chikai no de ani wa* hoñki *de beñkyoo shite iru.* (試験が近いので兄は本気で勉強している) His exam is soon, so my elder brother is studying *seriously.* / *Kare-ra wa* hoñki *ni natte, choosa o hajimeta.* (彼らは本気になって, 調査を始めた) They have become *serious* and started the investigation.

Hoｰñkoｰñ ほんこん (香港) *n.* Hong Kong.

hoｰñmono ほんもの (本物) *n.* genuine article; the real thing:

Kore wa hoñmono *no daiyamoñdo desu.* (これは本物のダイヤモンドです) This is a *genuine* diamond. / *Dochira ga* hoñmono *ka miwake ga tsukanai.* (どちらが本物か見分けがつかない) It is difficult to tell which is the *original.*

hoｰñmyoo ほんみょう (本名) *n.* one's real name. 《⇨ namae》

hoｰñne ほんね (本音) *n.* real intention [feeling]:

hoñne *o haku* (本音を吐く) confess one's *real intention [feeling]* / *Ano hito wa nakanaka* hoñne *o iwanai.* (あの人はなかなか本音を言わない) He doesn't readily disclose his *real intentions [feelings].* 《⇨ tatemae》

hoｰñneñ ほんねん (本年) *n.* the current year; this year: ★ More formal than '*kotoshi.*'

hoñneñ *no gyooji yotee* (本年の行事予定) *this year*'s schedule of events / hoñneñ-*do no yosañ* (本年度の予算) the budget for *the current year* / *Shiñ-gaisha wa* hoñneñ *setsuritsu to kettee shimashita.* (新会社は本年設立と決定しました) We have decided to establish the new company *this year.* / Hoñneñ *mo yoroshiku onegai itashi-*

masu. (本年もよろしくお願いいたします) I would appreciate your continuing favor *this year.* ★ A greeting given at the beginning of the New Year.

hoｰñniñ ほんにん (本人) *n.* the person in question:

Hoñniñ *wa sono jijitsu o hitee shite imasu.* (本人はその事実を否定しています) *The man himself* denies the fact. / *Moñdai no* hoñniñ *ga arawareta.* (問題の本人が現れた) *The person in question* has appeared. 《⇨ tooniñ》

hoｰñno ほんの (本の) *attrib.* only; mere; just:

Shio o hoñno *sukoshi irete kudasai.* (塩をほんの少し入れてください) Please add *just* a little salt. / Hoñno *kimochi dake desu ga, doozo o-uketori kudasai.* (ほんの気持ちだけですが, どうぞお受け取りください) It is *just* a token of my gratitude, but I would like you to accept this.

hoｰñnoo ほんのう (本能) *n.* instinct:

doobutsu no hoñnoo (動物の本能) the *instinct* of animals.

hoｰñnoo-teki ほんのうてき (本能的) *a.n.* (∼ na, ni) instinctive:

Doobutsu wa hoñnoo-teki *ni kikeñ o kañjiru.* (動物は本能的に危険を感じる) Animals sense danger *instinctively.*

hoｰnoo ほのお (炎) *n.* flame; blaze:

roosoku no honoo (ろうそくの炎) the *flame* of a candle / *Uchi wa isshuñ no uchi ni* honoo *ni tsutsumareta.* (家は一瞬のうちに炎に包まれた) The house was enveloped in *flames* in an instant. / *Kuruma ga patto* honoo *o agete, moeta.* (車がぱっと炎を上げて, 燃えた) The car burst into *flames* and burned.

hoｰñrai (wa) ほんらい(は) (本来(は)) *adv.* 1 originally; by nature:

Sushi wa hoñrai (wa) hozoñshoku de atta. (すしは本来(は)保存食であった) Sushi was *originally* a preserved food. / *Kodomo wa* hoñrai *(wa) soto de asobu no ga suki na mono da.* (子どもは本来(は)外で遊ぶのが好きなものだ) Children, *by nature*, like to play outdoors.

2 essentially:

Kore to sore wa hoñrai *(wa) betsu no mono da.* (これとそれは本来(は)別のものだ) This and that are *essentially* different matters.

hoñrai nara (〜なら) ought to [should] have been (done):

★ Used with reference to an action that should have been performed, but was not.

Hoñrai nara, *anata ga ayamaru beki desu.* (本来なら、あなたが謝るべきです) You *ought to* have apologized. / Hoñrai nara, *watashi ga shachoo ni naru tokoro datta.* (本来なら、私が社長になるところだった) I *should* have become president of the company.

hoñrai no (〜の) original; primary; real: *Kare wa* hoñrai *no niñmu o wasurete shimatta rashii.* (彼は本来の任務を忘れてしまったらしい) It seems that he has fogotten his *primary* duty. / *Kare no* hoñrai *no jitsuryoku wa sonna mono de wa nai.* (彼の本来の実力はそんなものではない) Such is not his *real* ability.

《⇨ gañrai; motomoto》

hoˈñryoo ほんりょう (本領) *n.* one's real ability; one's specialty: *Kare wa hañbaibu de* hoñryoo *o hakki shita.* (彼は販売部で本領を発揮した) He showed *what he could do* in the sales department.

hoˈñshitsu ほんしつ (本質) *n.* essence; substance; real nature: *Kare-ra no ikeñ wa* hoñshitsu *ni oite onaji desu.* (彼らの意見は本質において同じです) Their opinions are the same in *essence.*

hoˈñshitsu-teki ほんしつてき (本質的) *a.n.* (〜 na, ni) essential; intrinsic: *Ryoosha no aida ni* hoñshitsu-teki *na chigai wa nai.* (両者の間に本質的な違いはない) There is not an *essential* difference between the two of them. / *Kono jikeñ wa* hoñshitsu-teki *ni wa miñzoku-kañ no arasoi desu.* (この事件は本質的には民族間の争いです) This affair is *in essence* an ethnic dispute.

Hoˈñshuu ほんしゅう (本州) *n.* Honshu, the largest of the four principal islands of Japan. 《⇨ inside back cover》

hoˈñteñ ほんてん (本店) *n.* head office; main store: *Kare wa* hoñteñ *e teñkiñ ni natta.* (彼は本店へ転勤になった) He was transferred to *the head office.*

hoˈñto ほんと *n.* = hoñtoo.

hoˈñtoo ほんとう (本当) *n.* truth; fact; reality:

Hoñtoo? (本当) *Really?* / Hoñtoo *no koto o itte kudasai.* (本当のことを言ってください) Please tell me the *truth.* / Hoñtoo *wa byooki ja nakatta ñ desu.* (本当は病気じゃなかったんです) *In fact*, I was not ill.

—*a.n.* (〜 na, ni) true; actual; real:

Sono hanashi wa hoñtoo *desu.* (その話は本当です) The story is *true.* / Hoñtoo *ni mita ñ desu ka?* (本当に見たんですか) Did you *really* see it? / *Kare no eñsoo wa* hoñtoo *ni subarashii.* (彼の演奏は本当にすばらしい) His musical performances are *really* wonderful.

hoˈñya ほんや (本屋) *n.* bookstore; bookshop: *Kono hoñ wa ekimae no* hoñya *de kaimashita.* (この本は駅前の本屋で買いました) I bought this book at the *bookstore* in front of the station.

hoˈñyaku ほんやく (翻訳) *n.* translation:

Sono hoñ wa hoñyaku *de yomima-shita.*(その本は翻訳で読みました) I read the book in *translation.* / *Kare wa* hoñyaku *ga umai.*(彼は翻訳がうまい) He is good at *translation.* / hoñyaku-*keñ*(翻訳権) the *translation* rights / hoñyaku-sha (翻訳者) a *translator* / hoñyaku-sho (翻訳書) a *translation.*

hoñyaku suru (〜する) *vt.* translate: *Kono tegami o Nihoñgo ni* hoñyaku shite *kudasai.*(この手紙を日本語に翻訳してください) Please *translate* this letter into Japanese. / *Haiku o Eego ni* hoñyaku suru *no wa muzukashii.*(俳句を英語に翻訳するのは難しい) It is difficult to *translate* haiku into English. ((⇒ yaku⁴))

ho⌐o¹ ほう(法) *n.* **1** law: hoo *o mamoru* [*okasu*] (法を守る[犯す]) observe [break] the *law* / hoo *ni shitagau* (法に従う) obey the *law* / *Kimi no kooi wa* hoo *ni hañ-suru.*(君の行為は法に反する) Your conduct is against the *law.*
2 method; way: *Nihoñgo ni jootatsu suru* hoo *wa nañ desu ka?* (日本語に上達する法は何ですか) What's the best *way* to make progress in Japanese? / *Watashi wa ii keñkoo-*hoo *o shitte imasu.*(私はいい健康法を知っています) I know a very effective *way* of keeping one's health. ((⇒ hoohoo))

ho⌐o² ほう(方) *n.* **1** direction: *Kare wa dotchi no* hoo *e ikima-shita ka?* (彼はどっちの方へ行きましたか) In which *direction* did he go? / *Hikooki wa nishi no* hoo *e toñde ikimashita.*(飛行機は西の方へ飛んで行きました) The airplane flew away *toward* the west.
2 (as far as) something [someone] (is concerned): ★ Used in comparison or contrast. *Boku no* hoo *ga kare yori mo se ga takai.*(ぼくのほうが彼よりも背が高

い) I am taller than him. / *Sono ko wa ookii* hoo *o erañda.*(その子は大きいほうを選んだ) The child took the larger *one.* / *Warui no wa kare no* hoo *desu.*(悪いのは彼のほうです) It is *he* who is wrong.

ho⌐o³ ほお(頬) *n.* cheek: *Sono ko wa* hoo *o fukuramaseta.* (その子はほおを膨らませた) The boy puffed out his *cheeks.* / *Kanojo wa señsee ni homerarete* hoo *o akarameta.*(彼女は先生にほめられてほおを赤らめた) Her *cheeks* turned red when she was praised by the teacher.

hoo o someru (〜を染める) blush.

ho⌐o ga i⌐i ほうがいい (方が良い)

USAGE

Used in the patterns, '*n.*+*no hoo ga ii; a.n.*+*na hoo ga ii; v.* [*a.; attrib.*]+*hoo ga ii.*' Before '*hoo ga ii*' a negative verb is in the present tense, but an affirmative verb is usually in the past.

1 be better: "*Kore to sore to dochira ga ii desu ka?*" "*Kono* hoo *ga ii desu.*" (「これとそれとどちらがいいですか」「このほうがいいです」) "Which is better, this or that?" "This one *is better.*" / *Chiisai no yori ookii* hoo *ga ii.* (小さいのより大きいほうがいい) The big one *is better* than the small one. / *Terebi nara, Amerika no yori mo Nihoñ-see no* hoo *ga ii.* (テレビなら, アメリカのよりも日本製のほうがいい) As far as televisions are concerned, a Japanese-made one *is better* than an American one.
2 I suggest...; be better; had better (do); should (do): ★ Used in making recommendations. *Hokkaidoo nara, hikooki de itta* hoo *ga ii ka mo shiremaseñ.* (北海道なら, 飛行機で行ったほうがいいかもしれません) If you are going to Hok-

kaido, *it might be better* to go by plane. / *Moo jikañ da kara hajimeta* hoo ga ii *to omoimasu.* (もう時間だから始めたほうがいいと思います) It's time, so I think we *had better* start. / *Kimi no baai nani mo iwanai* hoo ga ii. (君の場合何も言わないほうがいい) In your case, you *had better* say nothing at all. / *Sono kaigi ni wa shusseki shita* hoo ga ii *deshoo ne.* (その会議には出席したほうがいいでしょうね) I suppose I *ought to* attend that meeting.

ho⌐oañ ほうあん (法案) *n.* bill: hooañ *o shiñgi suru* (法案を審議する) debate a *bill* / *Sono* hooañ *wa gikai o tsuuka shita.* (その法案は議会を通過した) The *bill* passed the Diet.

ho⌐obi ほうび (褒美) *n.* reward; prize: *Watashi wa* hoobi *ni mañneñhitsu o moratta.* (私はほうびに万年筆をもらった) I got a fountain pen as a *prize.*

ho⌐oboo ほうぼう (方々) *n.* every direction; everywhere; here and there: *Kagi o* hooboo *sagashita ga, mitsukaranakatta.* (鍵をほうぼう探したが、見つからなかった) I searched for the key *high and low*, but it did not turn up. / *Kyooto wa* hooboo *ikimashita ga kono o-tera ga ichibañ desu.* (京都はほうぼう行きましたがこのお寺が一番です) I have been *everywhere* in Kyoto, but this temple is the best. / *Kooeñ no* hooboo *de sakura ga saite imasu.* (公園のほうぼうで桜が咲いています) The cherry trees are in blossom *all over* the park.

ho⌐ochi ほうち (放置) *n.* leaving (a thing): *Kono moñdai wa* hoochi *dekinai.* (この問題は放置できない) This problem cannot *be left as it is.*
hoochi suru (〜する) *vt.* leave; let

alone: *Jiteñsha o koko ni* hoochi *shinai de kudasai.* (自転車をここに放置しないでください) Please *don't leave* your bicycle here.

HOOCHI SIGN

Musekiniñ na jiteñsha no hoochi wa yamemashoo. (Don't leave unattended bicycles here.)

ho⌐ochoo ほうちょう (包丁) *n.* kitchen knife.

HOOCHOO

ho⌐odoo ほうどう (報道) *n.* news; report; information: *Hoodoo wa seekaku de nakereba naranai.* (報道は正確でなければならない) *News* must be accurate. / hoodoo-kiñkañ (報道機関) *news* media.
hoodoo suru (〜する) *vt.* report; inform: *Sono jiko wa shiñbuñ de ookiku hoodoo sareta.* (その事故は新聞で大きく報道された) The accident *made headlines* in newspapers.

ho⌐odo⌐ojiñ ほうどうじん (報道陣) *n.* a group of reporters; the press.

ho⌐ofu ほうふ (豊富) *a.n.* (〜 na, ni) plentiful; ample; rich: hoofu *na chishiki* (豊富な知識) *ample* knowledge / *Kono kuni wa teñneñ shigeñ ga* hoofu *desu.* (この国は天然資源が豊富です) This country is *rich* in natural resources. / *Ano kañgofu-sañ wa keekeñ ga* hoofu *desu*. (あの看護婦さんは経験が豊富です) That nurse has *a lot of* experience. / *Shinamono wa* hoofu *ni arimasu*. (品物は豊富にあります) We keep *plenty of* goods in stock.

ho⌐ogaku ほうがく (方角) *n*. direction; bearings: *Kare wa hañtai no* hoogaku *e iki-mashita*. (彼は反対の方角へ行きました) He went in the opposite *direction*. / Hoogaku *o machigaeta*. (方角を間違えた) I took the wrong *direction*. / *Fune wa* hoogaku *o miushinatta*. (船は方角を見失った) The ship lost her *bearings*.

ho⌐oge⌐ñ ほうげん (方言) *n*. dialect: *Kyuushuu* hoogeñ *de hanasu* (九州方言で話す) speak in a Kyushu *dialect*.

ho⌐ohige ほおひげ (頬髭) *n*. whiskers. 《⇨ hige (table)》

ho⌐ohoo ほうほう (方法) *n*. method; way; measure: *Shiharai* hoohoo *o oshiete kuda-sai*. (支払い方法を教えてください) Please let me know the *method* of payment. / *Nihoñgo o manabu ichibañ yoi* hoohoo *wa mainichi reñshuu suru koto desu*. (日本語を学ぶ一番良い方法は毎日練習することです) The best *way* to learn Japanese is to practice it every day. / *Kare wa kootsuu añzeñ no tame no atarashii* hoohoo *o teeañ shita*. (彼は交通安全のための新しい方法を提案した) He proposed new *measures* for traffic safety. / *Kono moñdai o toku* hoohoo *ga waka-ranai*. (この問題を解く方法がわからない) I don't know *how to* solve this problem. 《⇨ hoo¹》

ho⌐oji·ru ほうじる (報じる) *vt*. (hooji-te Ⅴ) report; inform; broadcast; televise: *Dono shiñbuñ mo sono kuni no jishiñ no koto o* hoojita. (どの新聞も

その国の地震のことを報じた) All the newspapers *reported* the earthquake. / *Kesa fune no shoototsu jiko ga atta to terebi de* hoojirareta. (けさ船の衝突事故があったとテレビで報じられた) It *was reported* on television that there was a collision between two ships this morning.

ho⌐okai ほうかい (崩壊) *n*. collapse; breakdown; disintegration: hookai *o maneku* (崩壊を招く) cause a *collapse* / *Kai wa uchiwa-mome de* hookai *suñzeñ datta*. (会は内輪もめで崩壊寸前だった) The association was on the verge of a *breakup* owing to internal trouble.

hookai suru (〜する) *vi*. collapse; disintegrate; decay: *Hashi ga jishiñ de* hookai *shita*. (橋が地震で崩壊した) The bridge *collapsed* in the earthquake. / *Naikaku wa ma-mo-naku* hookai *suru daroo*. (内閣は間もなく崩壊するだろう) The cabinet will *fall* before long.

ho⌐okeñ-shu⌐gi ほうけんしゅぎ (封建主義) *n*. feudalism.

ho⌐okeñshugi-teki ほうけんしゅぎてき (封建主義的) *a.n*. (〜 na, ni) feudalistic; feudal. 《⇨ hookeñ-teki》

ho⌐okeñ-teki ほうけんてき (封建的) *a.n*. (〜 na, ni) feudal; feu-dalistic: hookeñ-teki *na kañgaekata* (封建的な考え方) a *feudalistic* way of thinking. 《⇨ hookeñshugi-teki》

ho⌐oki¹ ほうき (放棄) *n*. abandon-ment; renunciation: *señsoo no* hooki (戦争の放棄) the *renunciation* of war.

hooki suru (〜する) *vt*. give up; abandon; renounce: *keekaku o* hooki suru (計画を放棄する) *give up* a plan / *Oya to shite no sekiniñ o* hooki shite *shimau hito ga iru*. (親

としての責任を放棄してしまう人がいる）There are some people who *abandon* their duty as parents. / *Kumiai-iñ wa demo ni sañka suru tame ni, shokuba o hooki shita.* (組合員はデモに参加するために、職場を放棄した) The union members *deserted* their jobs to join the demonstration.

hoˈoki² ほうき (箒) *n.* broom: *Heya o hooki de haita.* (部屋をほうきで掃いた) I swept my room with a *broom*.

for a garden

for a room

HOOKI

hoˈokoku ほうこく (報告) *n.* report: *Sono* hookoku *wa mada ukete imaseñ.* (その報告はまだ受けていません) I have not received the *report* yet. / *Iiñkai wa saikiñ chuukañ* hookoku *o matometa.* (委員会は最近中間報告をまとめた) The committee recently made an interim *report*. / hookoku-sho (報告書) a *report*.

hookoku suru (～する) *vt.* report; inform; give an account: *Nanika attara, sugu ni* hookoku shite kudasai. (何かあったら、すぐに報告してください) If anything happens, *report* it to me immediately. / *Kare wa gakkai de* hookoku suru *koto ni natte imasu.* (彼は学会で報告することになっています) He is scheduled to *read a paper* at the academic conference.

hoˈokoo ほうこう (方向) *n.*
1 direction; way; course: *Watashi mo onaji* hookoo *e ikimasu.* (私も同じ方向へ行きます) I'm going in the same *direction* as well. / *Eki wa dochira no* hookoo *desu ka?* (駅はどちらの方向ですか) Which *way* is the station. / *Fune wa* hookoo *o kaeta.* (船は方向を変えた) The ship changed its *course*.
2 aim; object; course: *jibuñ no shoorai no* hookoo *o kimeru* (自分の将来の方向を決める) make a decision about the future *course* of one's life / *Shi-gatsu ni kaikoo no* hookoo *de keñtoo shite kudasai.* (四月に開校の方向で検討してください) Please examine it with the *aim* of opening the school in April.

hoˈoku ホーク *n.* fork. 《⇒ fooku》

hoˈomeˈñ ほうめん (方面) *n.*
1 district: *Taifuu wa Shikoku* hoomeñ *o osotta.* (台風は四国方面を襲った) The typhoon hit the Shikoku *district*.
2 direction: *Kare wa Ueno* hoomeñ *e ikimashita.* (彼は上野方面へ行きました) He went in the *direction* of Ueno.
3 field: *Yamada hakase wa kono* hoomeñ *no keñi desu.* (山田博士はこの方面の権威です) Dr. Yamada is an authority in this *field*.

hoˈomoñ ほうもん (訪問) *n.* visit; call: hoomoñ *o ukeru* (訪問を受ける) receive a *visit* / hoomoñ-gi (訪問着) a *semi-formal* kimono / hoomoñ-kyaku (訪問客) a *visitor*; a *guest* / katee-hoomoñ (家庭訪問) a home *visit* by a teacher.
hoomoñ suru (～する) *vt.* call at [on]; visit: *Gogo Yamada-sañ o* hoomoñ suru *yotee desu.* (午後山田さんを訪問する予定です) I'm going to *visit* Miss Yamada this afternoon.

ho⸢omu[1] ホーム *n.* platform:
Kare wa hoomu *de matte ite kureta.* (彼はホームで待っていてくれた) He was waiting for me on the *platform.*

ho⸢omu[2] ホーム *n.* home; asylum:
roojiñ-hoomu (老人ホーム) an old people's *home.*

ho⸢omu[3] ホーム *n.* (of baseball) home plate.

Ho⸢omu-da⸤ijiñ ほうむだいじん (法務大臣) *n.* Minister of Justice.

ho⸢omu⸤rañ ホームラン *n.* (of baseball) home run; homer:
hoomurañ *o utsu* (ホームランを打つ) hit a *home run.*

ho⸢omu⸤r·u ほうむる (葬る) *vt.* (hoomur·i-; hoomur·a-; hoomut-te ⓒ) **1** bury (a dead body):
Kare wa kono bochi ni hoomurarete imasu. (彼はこの墓地に葬られています) He *is buried* in this graveyard.
2 shelve (a plan); hush up (an incident):
Sono oshoku-jikeñ wa yami ni hoomurareta. (その汚職事件は闇に葬られた) The corruption case *was swept under the carpet.*

Ho⸢omu-shoo ほうむしょう (法務省) *n.* Ministry of Justice.
《⇨ shoo[1] (table)》

ho⸢omustee ホームステイ *n.* homestay:
Nihoñ no katee ni hoomustee *o shitai.* (日本の家庭にホームステイをしたい) I want to *stay with* a Japanese *family.*

ho⸢oreñsoo ほうれんそう (菠薐草) *n.* spinach:
hooreñsoo *ichi-wa* (ほうれん草一把) a bunch of *spinach.*

ho⸢oritsu ほうりつ (法律) *n.* law:
hooritsu *o seetee suru* (法律を制定する) enact a *law* / *Kono* hooritsu *wa raineñ shi-gatsu kara shikoo saremasu.* (この法律は来年四月から施行されます) This *law* will go into effect next April. / *Kore wa* hooritsu *ihañ da.* (これは法律違反だ) This is against the *law.*

ho⸢or·u[1] ほうる (放る) *vt.* (hoor·i-; hoor·a-; hoot-te ⓒ) throw; toss; pitch:
Sono booru o hootte *kudasai.* (そのボールを放ってください) Please *throw* the ball to me. 《⇨ nageru》

ho⸢oru[2] ホール *n.* hall: ★ Used for public events.
koñsaato-hooru (コンサートホール) a concert *hall.*

ho⸢osaku[1] ほうさく (豊作) *n.* good crop; rich harvest:
Kotoshi wa kome ga hoosaku *da.* (今年は米が豊作だ) We have a *good crop* of rice this year.

ho⸢osaku[2] ほうさく (方策) *n.* measures; plan; means:
Kare-ra no hoosaku *wa nakanaka kimaranakatta.* (彼らの方策はなかなか決まらなかった) Their *plan* was not decided on for a long time. / *Kore ga dame nara, hoka no* hoosaku *o tatenakereba naranai.* (これがだめなら、ほかの方策を立てなければならない) If this fails, we will have to work out some other *measures.*

ho⸢oseki ほうせき (宝石) *n.* jewel; gem; jewelry:
hooseki *o mi ni tsukeru* (宝石を身につける) put on *jewelry.*

ho⸢oshi ほうし (奉仕) *n.* service:
hooshi-*katsudoo* (奉仕活動) voluntary *service* / hooshi-*hiñ* (奉仕品) a *bargain* / hooshi-*kakaku* (奉仕価格) a *bargain* price.
hooshi suru (～する) *vt.* serve:
Watashi wa nani-ka shite, shakai ni hooshi *shitai.* (私は何かして、社会に奉仕したい) I wish to do something to *serve* the community.

ho⸢oshiñ ほうしん (方針) *n.* policy; course; principle:
Atarashii hooshiñ *o tatenakereba naranai.* (新しい方針を立てなければなら

ない) We have to make a new *policy*. / Hooshiñ *o ayamatta yoo da.*(方針を誤ったようだ) We seem to have chosen the wrong *course*. / *Waga-sha no* hooshiñ *wa kaigai hañro no kakudai ni aru.* (わが社の方針は海外販路の拡大にある) The *policy* of our company lies in developing a foreign market.

ho⌜oshuu ほうしゅう (報酬) *n.* remuneration; reward; fee: *Sono shigoto no* hooshuu *to shite gomañ-eñ moratta.*(その仕事の報酬として5万円もらった) I received 50,000 yen as a *reward* for the job. / *Sono koto ni taishite watashi wa nañ no* hooshuu *mo kitaishite imaseñ.*(そのことに対して私は何の報酬も期待していません) I expect no *remuneration* for that. / *Beñgo-shi no* hooshuu *wa takai.*(弁護士の報酬は高い) Lawyers' *fees* are very high.

ho⌜osoku ほうそく (法則) *n.* law; rule: *iñryoku no* hoosoku (引力の法則) the *law* of gravity / *juyoo to kyoo-kyuu no* hoosoku (需要と供給の法則) the *law* of supply and demand.

ho⌜osoo¹ ほうそう (放送) *n.* broadcasting; broadcast: hoosoo *o kiku* (放送を聞く) listen to a *broadcast* / *Sono bañgumi no* hoosoo *wa chuushi sareta.*(その番組の放送は中止された) The *broadcasting* of the program was canceled. / hoosoo-*bañgumi* (放送番組) a *radio* [*TV*] program / hoo-soo-*eesee*(放送衛星) a *broadcasting* satellite.

hoosoo suru (〜する) *vt.* broadcast; televise; put on the air: *Sono geki wa koñya* hoosoo sa-remasu.*(その劇は今夜放送されます) The drama will *be broadcast* this evening. / *Dono kyoku mo sono nyuusu o* hoosoo shita. (どの局もそ

のニュースを放送した) All the stations *put* that news *on the air.*

ho⌜osoo² ほうそう (包装) *n.* packing; wrapping: *kozutsumi no* hoosoo *o toku* (小包の包装を解く) open [*unwrap*] a parcel / hoosoo-*shi* (包装紙) *wrapping* paper.

hoosoo suru (〜する) *vt.* pack; wrap: *Kabiñ ga kowarenai yoo ni teenee ni* hoosoo shita.(花瓶がこわれないようにていねいに包装した) I *packed* the vase carefully so that it would not break. / *Okurimono o kiree na kami de* hoosoo shite moratta.(贈り物をきれいな紙で包装してもらった) I *had* my gift *wrapped* in pretty paper.

ho⌜oso⌜ogeki ほうそうげき (放送劇) *n.* radio [TV] drama.

ho⌜oso⌜okyoku ほうそうきょく (放送局) *n.* broadcasting station; radio [TV] station.

ho⌜otai ほうたい (包帯) *n.* bandage; dressing: hootai *o maku* (包帯を巻く) apply a *bandage* / hootai *o toru* [*torikaeru*] (包帯を取る[取り替える]) remove [*change*] a *bandage* / *Kare wa kizuguchi ni* hootai *o shita.* (彼は傷口に包帯をした) He put a *bandage* on the wound.

ho⌝ra ほら *int.* look; look here; listen: Hora, *mukoo ni shima ga mieru yo.*(ほら、向こうに島が見えるよ) *Look!* You can see an island over there. / Hora, *watashi ga itta toori ja nai no.*(ほら、私が言った通りじゃないの) *There you are!* Isn't it just as I said?

ho⌜ra-ana ほらあな (洞穴) *n.* cave; cavern.

ho⌝ri¹ ほり (堀) *n.* moat; canal: hori *o horu* [*umeru*] (堀を掘る[埋める]) dig [fill in] a *moat* / hori *o me-gurashita shiro* (掘りをめぐらした城) a castle surrounded by a *moat.*

ho「robi¹・ru ほろびる (滅びる) *vi.*
(horobi-te V) fall; die out; be
ruined; perish:
Sono kuni wa sañzeñ-neñ mae ni
horobimashita. (その国は3千年前に
滅びました) That country *perished*
3,000 years ago. / *Kono shu no
tori wa* horobite *shimaimashita.*
(この種の鳥は滅びてしまいました) This
species of bird *has died out.*
《⇨ horobosu》

ho「robo¹s・u ほろぼす (滅ぼす) *vt.*
(horobosh・i-; horobos・a-; horo-
bosh・i-te C) destroy; ruin:
Kaku-señsoo wa jiñrui o horobo-
shimasu. (核戦争は人類を滅ぼします)
Nuclear war will *destroy* humanity. / *Sono tatakai de Hoojoo-shi
wa Hideyoshi ni* horobosareta. (そ
の戦いで北条氏が秀吉に滅ぼされた)
The Hojo family *was destroyed*
by Hideyoshi in that battle. /
Kare wa kakegoto de mi o horobo-
shita. (彼は賭けごとで身を滅ぼした)
He *ruined* his life by gambling.
《⇨ horobiru》

ho「r・u¹ ほる (掘る) *vt.* (hor・i-; ho-
r・a-; hot-te C) dig; excavate:
ana o horu (穴を掘る) *dig* a hole /
jagaimo o horu (じゃがいもを掘る) *dig
up* potatoes / *toñneru o* horu (トン
ネルを掘る) *make* a tunnel / *sekitañ
o* horu (石炭を掘る) *mine* coal.

ho「r・u² ほる (彫る) *vt.* (hor・i-; ho-
r・a-; hot-te C) carve; engrave;
chisel; inscribe:
Kare wa ki o hotte *niñgyoo o tsukutta.* (彼は木を彫って人形を作った)
He made a doll by *carving* the
wood.

ho「ryo ほりょ (捕虜) *n.* prisoner
(of war); captive:
Kare wa horyo *ni natta.* (彼は捕虜
になった) He was taken *prisoner.*

ho「shi ほし (星) *n.* star:
Sora ni wa hoshi *ga matataite ita.*
(空には星がまたたいていた) *Stars* were
twinkling in the sky.

ho「shi¹・i ほしい (欲しい) *a.* (-ku)
want; would like; wish; hope:
Motto jikañ ga hoshii. (もっと時間が
欲しい) I *want* more time. / *Kimi
no* hoshii *mono wa nañ de mo
katte ageru yo.* (君の欲しいものは何で
も買ってあげるよ) I'll buy you anything you *want.* / *Kyuuryoo o
agete* hoshii *desu.* (給料を上げて欲し
いです) I *would like* to have my
pay raised. / *Sono koto wa iwanai
de* hoshikatta. (そのことは言わないで欲
しかった) I *wish* you had not mentioned that. / *Kuruma nañka* hoshiku nai. (車なんか欲しくない) I
don't want to have a car, or anything like that.

hoshimono ほしもの (干し物) *n.*
washing; clothes for drying:
hoshimono *o suru* (干し物をする)
hang out the *washing* / hoshimono *o ireru* (干し物を入れる) bring
in the *washing.* 《⇨ señtaku¹》

ho「shoo¹ ほしょう (保証) *n.* guarantee; warranty; assurance:
Kono rajio ni wa nineñ-kañ no
hoshoo *ga tsuite imasu.* (このラジオ
には2年間の保証が付いています) This
radio has a two-year *guarantee.*
/ *Seekoo suru to iu* hoshoo *wa nani
mo arimaseñ.* (成功するという保証は
何もありません) There is no *assurance* at all that we will succeed. /
hoshoo-*sho* (保証書) a written
guarantee.

hoshoo suru (〜する) *vt.* guarantee; warrant; assure: *Kare no
shoorai wa* hoshoo *sarete iru.* (彼
の将来は保証されている) His future *is
guaranteed.* / *Kare ga soñna hito
de nai koto wa* hoshoo *shimasu.*
(彼がそんな人でないことは保障します) I
assure you that he is not such a
person.

ho「shoo² ほしょう (保障) *n.* security:
*shakai-*hoshoo (社会保障) social
security / *añzeñ-*hoshoo *jooyaku*

(安全保障条約) a *security pact*.
hoshoo suru (〜する) *vt.* secure; guarantee: *Anata no añzeñ wa hoshoo shimasu.* (あなたの安全は保障します) We *guarantee* your safety. / *Geñroñ no jiyuu wa keñpoo de hoshoo sarete iru.* (言論の自由は憲法で保障されている) Freedom of speech *is guaranteed* by the Constitution.

ho⌐shoo³ ほしょう (補償) *n.* compensation; indemnity: hoshoo *o yookyuu suru* (補償を要求する) demand *compensation* / hoshoo-*kiñ* (補償金) monetary *compensation*.
hoshoo suru (〜する) *vt.* compensate; indemnify: *Kaisha-gawa wa higaisha ni sono soñshitsu o hoshoo shita.* (会社側は被害者にその損失を補償した) The company *compensated* the victims for their loss.

ho⌐shooniñ ほしょうにん (保証人) *n.* guarantor: *Oji ga kare no hoshooniñ desu.* (おじが彼の保証人です) His uncle is his *guarantor*. / *Watashi wa kare ni hoshooniñ ni natte kureru yoo ni tanoñda.* (私は彼に保証人になってくれるように頼んだ) I asked him to be my *guarantor*.

ho⌐shu ほしゅ (保守) *n.* conservatism: hoshu-*too* (保守党) a conservative party. 《↔ kakushiñ²》

ho⌐shu-teki ほしゅてき (保守的) *a.n.* (〜 na, ni) conservative: hoshu-teki *na seekatsu-yooshiki* (保守的な生活様式) a *conservative* way of life / *Mura no hito-tachi no kañgaekata wa hijoo ni hoshu-teki de atta.* (村の人たちの考え方は非常に保守的であった) The thinking of the villagers was very *conservative*. 《↔ shiñpo-teki》

ho⌐so⌐i ほそい (細い) *a.* (-ku)
1 (of round objects such as sticks or string) thin; small; fine: hosoi *hari* (細い針) a *thin* needle / hosoi *señ* (細い線) a *fine* line / hosoi *michi* (細い道) a *narrow* street / *Suzuki-sañ wa hosoi yubi o shite iru.* (鈴木さんは細い指をしている) Ms. Suzuki has *slender* fingers. 《↔ futoi》
2 (of a voice) thin: *Kanojo wa koe ga hosoi.* (彼女は声が細い) She has a *thin* voice. 《↔ futoi》

ho⌐sonaga⌐i ほそながい (細長い) *a.* (-ku) long and narrow; slender: hosonagai *boo* (細長い棒) a *long, thin* stick / *Kono heya wa hosonagakute tsukainikui.* (この部屋は細長くて使いにくい) This room is *long and narrow*, and awkward to use.

ho⌐ssoku ほっそく (発足) *n.* start; inauguration: *jigyoo no* hossoku (事業の発足) the *start-up* of a business.
hossoku suru (〜する) *vi.* make a start; be inaugurated: *Arata ni futatsu no kyookai ga hossoku shita.* (新たに二つの協会が発足した) Another two associations *have been inaugurated*. / *Seefu wa jiko choosa iiñkai o hossoku saseta.* (政府は事故調査委員会を発足させた) The government *set up* an accident investigatory committee.

ho⌐s·u ほす (干す) *vt.* (hosh·i-; hos·a-; hosh·i-te Ⓒ) **1** dry: *señtakumono o hosu* (洗濯物を干す) *hang* the washing *out to dry* / *Kanojo wa nureta taoru o hinata ni hoshita.* (彼女はぬれたタオルを日なたに干した) She *dried* the wet towel in the sun.
2 drink up; empty: *Kare wa koppu no biiru o hoshita.* (彼はコップのビールを干した) He *drained* the glass of beer.

ho⌐taru ほたる (蛍) *n.* firefly.

ho⌐tchikisu ホッチキス *n.* stapler: *shorui o hotchikisu de tomeru* (書類をホッチキスでとめる) *staple* papers together.

ho⌐teru ホテル *n*. hotel:
Watashi wa kono hoteru *ni tomatte imasu.* (私はこのホテルに泊まっています) I am staying at this *hotel.* / Hoteru *no yoyaku wa sumasemashita ka?* (ホテルの予約はすませましたか) Have you reserved a room in the *hotel?*

ho⌐toke ほとけ (仏) *n*. **1** the Buddha:
hotoke *o ogamu* (仏を拝む) worship *the Buddha.*
2 the deceased:
hotoke *ni hana o sonaeru* (仏に花を供える) offer flowers before *the deceased.*

ho⌐to⌐ñdo ほとんど (殆ど) *n., adv.* **1** almost; nearly:
Kita hito no hotoñdo *wa josee datta.* (来た人のほとんどは女性だった) *Almost* all the people who came were women. / Hotoñdo *no hito ga sono añ ni sañsee shita.* (ほとんどの人がその案に賛成した) *Almost* everyone agreed to the plan. / *Sono ie wa* hotoñdo *dekiagarimashita.* (その家はほとんどでき上がりました) The house is *nearly* completed.
2 (with a negative) hardly; few; little:
Watashi wa sore ni tsuite wa hotoñdo *shirimaseñ.* (私はそれについてはほとんど知りません) I *hardly* know anything about that. / *Saikiñ wa* hotoñdo *ame ga furimaseñ.* (最近はほとんど雨が降りません) It has *hardly* rained recently. / *Soñna baka na koto o suru hito wa* hotoñdo *inai.* (そんなばかなことをする人はほとんどいない) There are *few* people who would do that kind of stupid thing. / *Tañku ni wa sekiyu ga* hotoñdo *nakatta.* (タンクには石油がほとんどなかった) There was *little* kerosene in the tank.

ho⌐tto ほっと *adv*. (〜 suru) (the state of being relieved):

Shikeñ ga owatte, hotto shita. (試験が終わって、ほっとした) I *was relieved* when the exam was over. / *Kanojo wa* hotto *tameiki o tsuita.* (彼女はほっとため息をついた) She breathed a sigh of *relief.* / Hotto suru *no wa mada hayai. Kore kara ga taiheñ da.* (ほっとするのはまだ早い。これからがたいへんだ) It is too early to *feel relieved.* From now on things will be tough.

ho⌐yahoya ほやほや *n*. (the state of being new or fresh):
hoyahoya *no satsumaimo* (ほやほやのさつまいも) a sweet potato *fresh from the oven* / *nyuusha* hoyahoya *no shaiñ* (入社ほやほやの社員) an employee *who has just joined a company* / *Kare-ra wa shinkoñ* hoyahoya *desu.* (彼らは新婚ほやほやです) They have *just* married.

ho⌐zoñ ほぞん (保存) *n*. preservation; conservation:
hozoñ *jootai ga ii* [*warui*] (保存状態がいい[悪い]) be in a good [poor] state of *preservation* / *Kono hamu wa* hozoñ *ga kikimasu.* (このハムは保存がききます) This ham *can be kept* long.
hozoñ suru (〜する) *vt*. preserve; keep: *Niku wa reezooko ni* hozoñ shimashita. (肉は冷蔵庫に保存しました) I *kept* the meat in the refrigerator. / *Kichoo na shorui wa sooko ni* hozoñ sarete imasu. (貴重な書類は倉庫に保存されています) The valuable papers *are preserved* in the warehouse.

ho⌐zo⌐ñshoku ほぞんしょく (保存食) *n*. preserved food; emergency provisions.

hya⌐kkaji⌐teñ ひゃっかじてん (百科事典) *n*. encyclopedia:
hyakkajiteñ *o hiku* (百科事典を引く) consult an *encyclopedia* / *Sono sakana o* hyakkajiteñ *de shirabeta.* (その魚を百科事典で調べた) I looked up the fish in the *encyclopedia.*

hya⌈ku⌉ ひゃく (百) *n.* one hundred:
hyaku-*gojuu-hachi* (158); sañ-byaku (300); rop-pyaku (600).
《⇨ suu² (table)》

hya⌈kuniñ i⌉sshu ひゃくにんいっしゅ (百人一首) *n.* Japanese traditional playing cards based on one hundred well-known 'tanka' poems by celebrated ancient poets. 《⇨ karuta》

HYAKUNIÑ ISSHU

hyo⌈ito ひょいと *adv.* unexpectedly; suddenly; casually; lightly:
Kare no tokoro ni hyoito *tachi-yotta ga rusu datta.* (彼の所にひょいと立ち寄ったが留守だった) I *casually* dropped in at his house, but he was not at home. / *Michi no kado kara* hyoito *jiteñsha ga dete kite, bikkuri shita.* (道の角からひょいと自転車が出て来て, びっくりした) I was surprised when a bicycle *suddenly* came around the corner. / *Kare wa* hyoito *ogawa o tobikoeta.* (彼はひょいと小川を飛び越えた) He *nimbly* jumped across the stream. / *Kare wa sono omoi nimotsu o* hyoito *mochiageta.* (彼はその重い荷物をひょいと持ち上げた) He *lightly* lifted up the heavy baggage.

hyo⌈o ひょう (表) *n.* table; list:
Deeta o hyoo *ni shita.* (データを表にした) I organized the data into a *table*. / *Kare no namae ga* hyoo *ni notte inai.* (彼の名前が表にのっていない) His name is not on the *list*.

hyo⌈obañ ひょうばん (評判) *n.* reputation; popularity; rumor:
Kanojo wa hyoobañ *ga yoi [warui].* (彼女は評判が良い[悪い]) She has a good [bad] *reputation*. / *Sono terebi dorama wa zeñkoku-teki ni* hyoobañ *ni natta.* (そのテレビドラマは全国的に評判になった) The TV drama became *popular* all over the country. / *Kanojo wa kare to kekkoñ suru to iu* hyoobañ *da.* (彼女は彼と結婚するという評判だ) It *is rumored* that she will marry him.

hyo⌈ogeñ ひょうげん (表現) *n.* verbal expression; representation:
Kare wa furui hyoogeñ *o tsukatta.* (彼は古い表現を使った) He used old-fashioned *expressions*. / hyoogeñ *no jiyuu* (表現の自由) freedom of *expression* / hyoogeñ-*ryoku* (表現力) the ability to *express oneself*.

hyoogeñ suru (〜する) *vt.* express; represent: *Kare wa jibuñ no kañgae o hakkiri* hyoogeñ *dekinakatta.* (彼は自分の考えをはっきり表現できなかった) He *couldn't express* his ideas clearly. / *Kono e wa fuyu no Nihoñkai o* hyoogeñ *shita mono desu.* (この絵は冬の日本海を表現したものです) This picture is one *representing* the Sea of Japan in winter.

Hyo⌈ogo⌉-keñ ひょうごけん (兵庫県) *n.* Hyogo Prefecture. Located in the west of the Kinki district, facing the Sea of Japan on the north and the Inland Sea on the south. The capital city, Kobe (神戸), has the second largest port in Japan. 《⇨ map (D4)》

hyo⌈ojo⌉o ひょうじょう (表情) *n.* facial expression; look:
hyoojoo *ni tomu [toboshii]* (表情に富む[乏しい]) *be expressive [expressionless]* / *Sono joyuu wa shujiñ-koo o* hyoojoo *yutaka ni eñjita.* (その女優は主人公を表情豊かに演じた)

The actress played the part of the heroine with much *expression*. / *Kare wa sono shirase ni* hyoojoo *o kaeta.* (彼はその知らせに表情を変えた) He changed his *expression* at the news. / *Kare wa kurai* hyoojoo *o shite, kaette kita.* (彼は暗い表情をして、帰って来た) He came home with a gloomy *look* on his face.

hyoˈojuñ ひょうじゅん (標準) *n.* standard; normal; average: hyoojuñ *o sadameru* (標準を定める) fix a *standard* / *Kono hiñshitsu wa* hyoojuñ *ni tasshite inai.* (この品質は標準に達していない) The quality of this product is not up to *standard*. / *Ketsuatsu ga* hyoojuñ *yori yaya takai.* (血圧が標準よりやや高い) My blood pressure is a little higher than *normal*. / *Kare no shuunyuu wa* hyoojuñ *nami desu.* (彼の収入は標準なみです) His income is just about *average*.

hyoˈojuñgo ひょうじゅんご (標準語) *n.* the standard language: ★ Often called '*kyootsuugo*' (共通語) (=common language). *Nihoñ no* hyoojuñgo (日本の標準語) the *standard language* of Japan.

hyoˈojuñ-teki ひょうじゅんてき (標準的) *a.n.* (~ na, ni) standard; average; typical: hyoojuñ-teki *na gakusee* (標準的な学生) an *average* student / hyoojuñ-teki *na hatsuoñ* (標準的な発音) *standard* pronunciation / *Hyoojuñ-teki na sarariimañ katee no neñshuu wa yaku roppyakumañ-eñ desu.* (標準的なサラリーマン家庭の年収は約600万円です) The annual income of the *average* office-worker's family is about six million yen.

hyoˈoka ひょうか (評価) *n.* valuation; appraisal; rating; assessment: *takai* hyooka *o eru* (高い評価を得る) gain a high *assessment* / *seeseki*

no go-dañkai hyooka (成績の5段階評価) a *rating* of (academic) performance on five levels.
hyooka suru (～する) *vt.* value; appraise; estimate: *Señmoñka ni sono uchi o* hyooka *shite moratta.* (専門家にその家を評価してもらった) I *had* the house *appraised* by an expert. / *Kare wa nakama kara takaku* hyooka *sarete iru.* (彼は仲間から高く評価されている) He *is* highly *thought of* by his colleagues.

hyoˈomeˈñ ひょうめん (表面) *n.*
1 surface:
Teeburu no hyoomeñ *wa pika-pika shite ita.* (テーブルの表面はぴかぴかしていた) The *surface* of the table was shiny.
2 outside:
Tatemono no hyoomeñ *wa rippa datta.* (建物の表面はりっぱだった) The *outside* of the building was gorgeous.
3 appearance:
Kare wa hyoomeñ *wa otonashi-soo ni mieru.* (彼は表面はおとなしそうに見える) In *appearance*, he seems easy to deal with.

hyoˈoroñ ひょうろん (評論) *n.* criticism; review; critical essay: *Ano hito wa yoku zasshi ni buñ-gee*-hyooroñ *o kaite iru.* (あの人はよく雑誌に文芸評論を書いている) He often writes literary *criticism* for magazines. / hyooroñ-ka (評論家) a *critic*; a *reviewer*.
hyooroñ (o) suru (～(を)する) *vt.* criticize; review; comment: *Kare wa terebi de eega no* hyooroñ *o shita.* (彼はテレビで映画の評論をした) He *commented* on movies on television.

hyoˈoryuu ひょうりゅう (漂流) *n.* drifting: hyooryuu-butsu (漂流物) *driftwood; flotsam*.
hyooryuu suru (～する) *vt.* drift:

Sono booto wa hyooryuu shite iru *tokoro o tasukerareta.*（そのボートは漂流しているところを助けられた）The boat was rescued when it *had been adrift.*

hyo⌐oshi¹ ひょうし（表紙）*n.* the cover of a book or a magazine. ★ Often refers to the jacket of a book.《⇨ kabaa》

hyo⌐rohyoro¹ ひょろひょろ *adv.* (~ to; ~ suru) **1** tall and thin: hyorohyoro *(to) nobita kusa*（ひょろひょろ（と）伸びた草）grass which has grown *tall and thin.*
2 staggeringly; totteringly: *Kare wa sake ni yotte* hyorohyoro (to) aruita.（彼は酒に酔ってひょろひょろ（と）歩いた）He *staggered* along drunk. / *Sono roojiñ no aru-kikata wa* hyorohyoro (to) shite ita.（その老人の歩き方はひょろひょろ（と）していた）The old man's way of walking was *unsteady.*《⇨ yoro-yoro》

hyo⌐rohyoro² ひょろひょろ *a.n.* (~ na, ni) lanky; slender; frail; feeble: Hyorohyoro *na nae de wa ii mi ga narimaseñ.*（ひょろひょろな苗ではいい実がなりません）Good fruit do not come from *feeble* seedlings. / *Kare wa karada ga* hyorohyoro *de tayorinai.*（彼は体がひょろひょろで頼りない）He is *tall and slim* and looks unreliable.

I

i い（胃）*n.* stomach:
Kare wa i ga yowai [joobu da].（彼は胃が弱い[丈夫だ]）He has a weak [strong] *stomach.* / *I ga itamu.*（胃が痛む）My *stomach* aches. / *I no chooshi ga okashii.*（胃の調子がおかしい）I have an upset *stomach.* / *i-gañ*（胃がん）cancer of the *stomach.*

-i[1] い（位）*suf.* place; rank:
Hyaku-meetoru kyoosoo de ni-i ni natta.（百メートル競走で2位になった）I came in *second* in the 100-meter race. / *Shoosuu dai sañ-i ika o kirisute nasai.*（小数第3位以下を切り捨てなさい）Omit the figures after the *second decimal place.*

-i[2] い（医）*suf.* medical doctor; general practitioner:
gañka-i（眼科医）an eye *doctor* / *geka-i*（外科医）a *surgeon* / *naika-i*（内科医）a *physician.* ⟪⇨ isha⟫

I¯baraki¯-keñ いばらきけん（茨城県）*n.* Ibaraki Prefecture. Located northeast of Tokyo, facing the Pacific on the east. One of the most famed Japanese gardens, Kairakuen, is located in the capital city, Mito（水戸）. ⟪⇨ map (G3)⟫

i¯ba¯r·u いばる（威張る）*vi.* (ibar·i-; ibar·a-; ibat-te Ⓒ) put on airs; boast; be haughty:
Kare wa itsu-mo buka no mae de ibatte iru.（彼はいつも部下の前で威張っている）He always *acts in an overbearing manner* in front of his subordinates. / *Kare no ibatta taido wa suki de nai.*（彼の威張った態度は好きでない）I don't like his *arrogant* attitude. / *Shooneñ wa chichi-oya ga kanemochi da to ibatte iru.*（少年は父親が金持ちだと威張っている）The boy *boasts* that his father is a rich man.

i¯basho いばしょ（居場所）*n.* whereabouts:
Kare wa dare ni mo ibasho o shirasenakatta.（彼はだれにも居場所を知らせなかった）He didn't give out his *whereabouts* to anyone. / *Ibasho wa wakaru yoo ni shite oite kudasai.*（居場所はわかるようにしておいてください）Please keep us informed of *where you are.*

i¯biki[1] いびき（鼾）*n.* snore:
Kare wa hoñtoo ni ooki-na ibiki o kaku.（彼はほんとうに大きないびきをかく）He really *snores* loudly.

i¯chi[1] いち（一・壱）*n.* one; the first; No. 1:
ni-buñ no ichi（2分の1）one half / *Nihoñ-ichi*（日本一）No. 1 in Japan / *sekai-ichi no koosoo biru*（世界一の高層ビル）the *tallest* building in the world. ⟪⇨ hitotsu[1]; suu[2] (table)⟫

ichi ka bachi ka（～か八か）all or nothing; take a chance: Ichi ka bachi ka *yatte miyoo.*（一か八かやってみよう）It's *all or nothing;* I'll have a go.

ichi mo ni mo naku（～も二もなく）readily; at once: *Kare wa* ichi mo ni mo naku *sañsee shita.*（彼は一も二もなく賛成した）He *readily* agreed.

i¯chi[2] いち（位置）*n.* position; location; situation:
Taiyoo no ichi de jikañ o shiru koto ga dekimasu.（太陽の位置で時間を知ることができます）You can tell the time by the *position* of the sun. / *Sono machi no ichi o chizu de mitsuketa.*（その町の位置を地図でみつけた）I found the *position* of the town on the map. / *Deguchi no ichi ga wakaranakatta.*（出口の

位置がわからなかった）We could not find the *location* of the exit. / Ichi *ni tsuite.*（位置について）On your *mark*!

ichi suru（～する）*vi.* lie; be located: *Minato wa shi no minami, yoñ-kiro ni* ichi shite imasu.（港は市の南、4 キロに位置しています）The harbor *is located* four kilometers south of the city.

i⌈chiba⌉ いちば（市場）*n.* market:
★ Never used to mean 'supermarket' or 'store.'
Watashi wa ichiba *de yasai o katta.*（私は市場で野菜を買った）I bought some vegetables at the *market.*

ICHIBA (fish market)

i⌈chi⌉bañ[1] いちばん（一番）*n.* first:
Kare wa kurasu de ichibañ *da.*（彼はクラスで 1 番だ）He is *first* in his class. / *Yamada-sañ ga* ichibañ *ni yatte kimashita.*（山田さんが 1 番にやって来ました）Mr. Yamada was the *first* to come.

i⌈chibañ[2] いちばん（一番）*adv.* most; best:
Dono kisetsu ga ichibañ *suki desu ka?*（どの季節がいちばん好きですか）Which season do you like *best*? / *Hana wa sakura ga* ichibañ *desu.*（花は桜がいちばんです）The cherry is the *most beautiful* of flowers.

i⌈chi⌉bañ[3] いちばん（一番）*n.* bout; round; game:
Kono ichibañ *de kyoo no torikumi wa owari desu.*（この一番できょうの取組は終わりです）Today's sumo matches end with this *bout.*

i⌈chi⌉bu いちぶ（一部）*n.* (a) part; portion; section:
Kono hoñ wa mada ichibu *shika yoñde imaseñ.*（この本はまだ一部しか読んでいません）I have as yet read only *part* of this book. / *Ichibu no hito ga sono teeañ ni hañtai shite imasu.*（一部の人がその提案に反対しています）*Some* of the people are against the proposal.
— *adv.* partially; in part:
Kono sekkee wa ichibu *shuusee suru hitsuyoo ga arimasu.*（この設計は一部修正する必要があります）It is necessary to correct this design *in part.*

ichibu shijuu（～始終）everything; all the details; the whole story: *Kanojo wa sono jikeñ ni tsuite* ichibu shijuu *(o) hanashita.*（彼女はその事件について一部始終（を）話した）She told us *everything* there was to know about that affair.

i⌈chibu⌉buñ いちぶぶん（一部分）*n.* (a) part; section. 《⇨ ichibu》

i⌈chida⌉iji いちだいじ（一大事）*n.* serious [grave] matter:
Kono shigoto ga okuretara ichidaiji *da.*（この仕事が遅れたら一大事だ）If this work is delayed, it will cause *serious trouble.*

i⌈chidan いちだん（一団）*n.* group; party; body:
kañkookyaku no ichidañ（観光客の一団）a *party* of tourists / *Kare-ra wa* ichidañ *to natte heya kara dete itta.*（彼らは一団となって部屋から出て行った）They walked out of the room *in a body.* 《⇨ -dañ; guruupu》

i⌈chido いちど（一度）*n.* once; one time.

i⌈chido⌉ ni いちどに（一度に）*adv.* all at once; at a time; at the same time:
Ichido ni *takusañ tabete wa ikemaseñ.*（一度にたくさん食べてはいけません）You must not eat a lot *at one*

time. | *Niwa no hana ga* ichido ni *saki-dashita.* (庭の花が一度に咲き出した) The flowers in the garden came into blossom *all at once.* | *Isu wa* ichido ni *futatsu zutsu hakoñde kudasai.* (いすは一度に２つずつ運んでください) Please carry two chairs *at a time.*

i¯**chido**¯o　いちどう (一同)　*n.* everyone; all present:
Watashi-tachi ichidoo *wa geñki ni kurashite orimasu.* (私たち一同は元気に暮らしております) We are *all* getting along fine. | *Kare wa* ichidoo *o daihyoo shite, aisatsu shita.* (彼は一同を代表して、挨拶した) He made the address as the representative of *all those present.*

ichidoo sorotte (〜揃って) all together: *Kare-ra wa* ichidoo sorotte *ryokoo ni dekaketa.* (彼らは一同そろって旅行に出かけた) They set out *all together* on a trip.

i¯**chi**¯**gai ni**　いちがいに (一概に)　*adv.* (〜 *wa*) (with a negative) generally; necessarily; indiscriminately:
Kare ga machigatte iru to wa ichigai ni (*wa*) *kimeraremaseñ.* (彼が間違っているとは一概に(は)決められません) We cannot *necessarily* conclude that he is wrong. | *Roojiñ no kañgae wa hoshu-teki de aru to* ichigai ni (*wa*) *iemaseñ.* (老人の考えは保守的であると一概に(は)言えません) One cannot *necessarily* say that old people's ways of thinking are conservative.

i¯**chi-gatsu**¯　いちがつ (一月)　*n.* January:
Watashi wa ichi-gatsu *ni Hawai e ikimasu.* (私は一月にハワイへ行きます) I'm going to Hawaii in *January.* | *Kare no tañjoobi wa* ichi-gatsu *mikka desu.* (彼の誕生日は一月三日です) His birthday is on *January* 3. | *Sono kai wa* ichi-gatsu *no joo-juñ* [*chuujuñ; gejuñ*] *ni hirakare-*

masu. (その会は一月の上旬[中旬, 下旬]に開かれます) The party will be held in the first [second; last] ten days of *January.* 《⇨ tsuki¹ (table)》

i¯**chigo**　いちご (苺)　*n.* strawberry.

i¯**chiguñ**　いちぐん (一軍)　*n.* (of baseball) the first team; major league. 《⇨ niguñ》

i¯**chiha**¯**yaku**　いちはやく (逸早く)　*adv.* quickly; without delay:
Sono hoñ no kookoku o mite, kare wa ichihayaku *chuumoñ shita.* (その本の広告を見て、彼はいち早く注文した) Seeing the advertisement of that book, he was *quick* to place an order. | *Sono keekaku wa* ichi-hayaku *jikkoo ni utsusareta.* (その計画はいち早く実行に移された) The plan was carried out *without a moment's delay.*

i¯**chi**¯**ichi**　いちいち (一々)　*adv.* in detail; one by one:
Riyuu wa ichiichi *nobenakute mo yoi.* (理由はいちいち述べなくてもよい) You do not have to give *each individual* reason. | *Chichi wa watashi no suru koto ni* ichiichi *kuchi o dasu.* (父は私のすることにいちいち口を出す) My father meddles in *everything* I do. | *Kanojo wa* ichiichi *iwareru mae ni chañto shigoto o shimasu.* (彼女はいちいち言われる前にちゃんと仕事をします) She does her work properly without being told everything *in detail.*

i¯**chi**¯**ji**　いちじ (一時)　*adv.* **1** once; at one time:
Sono uta wa ichiji *hayatta koto ga arimasu.* (その歌は一時はやったことがあります) That song was *at one time* popular.
2 for a while; for the time being:
Watashi wa sañ-neñ hodo mae ni ichiji *koko ni suñde ita koto ga arimasu.* (私は三年ほど前に一時ここに住んでいたことがあります) Three years ago I used to live here *for a while.* | *Kono kane wa* ichiji *giñ-*

koo ni azukete okimashoo.(この金は一時銀行に預けておきましょう) Let's deposit this money in the bank *for the time being.*

3 (～ no) passing; temporary:
Kono sutairu wa ichiji no ryuukoo ni suginai.(このスタイルは一時の流行に過ぎない) This style is nothing more than just a *passing* fad.

i⌈**chijirushi**⌉**・i** いちじるしい (著しい) *a.* (-ku) remarkable; marked; noticeable:
Kono chihoo wa asa-bañ no oñdo-sa ga ichijirushii.(この地方は朝晩の温度差が著しい) The temperature range between daytime and night-time is *very great* in this area. / *Ryoosha no aida ni ichijirushii chigai wa miraremaseñ.*(両者の間に著しい違いは見られません) We cannot find any *marked* difference between the two. / *Koñgetsu no uriage wa ichijirushiku zooka shimashita.*(今月の売り上げは著しく増加しました) This month's sales have increased *remarkably.*

i⌈**chimeñ** いちめん (一面) *n.* **1** one side; one aspect:
Anata wa yo-no-naka no ichimeñ shika mite inai.(あなたは世の中の一面しか見ていない) You have only seen *one side* of life.

2 the front page of a newspaper:
Sono kiji wa ichimeñ ni notte imashita.(その記事は一面に載っていました) The article was on *the front page.*
— *adv.* **1** on the other hand:
Kanojo wa yasashii ga ichimeñ kibishii tokoro mo aru.(彼女は優しいが一面厳しい所もある) She is tender-hearted, but *on the other hand* she has a strict side.

2 all over; the whole place:
Atari (wa) ichimeñ yuki datta.(辺り(は)一面雪だった) There was snow *all over.* / *Mizuumi wa ichimeñ koori de oowarete ita.*(湖は一面氷でおおわれていた) *The whole surface* of the lake was covered with ice.

i⌈**chinichi-juu** いちにちじゅう (一日中) *adv.* all day (long):
Kinoo wa ichinichi-juu ie ni imashita.(きのうは一日中家にいました) I was at home *all day long* yesterday.

i⌈**chioo** いちおう (一応) *adv.* anyway; just in case; for the time being:
Kare ga iru ka doo ka wakaranai ga, ichioo reñraku shite mimashoo.(彼がいるかどうかわからないが、一応連絡してみましょう) I don't know if he is there or not, but *anyway* let's try to get in touch with him. / *Hañko wa iranai to omou keredo, ichioo motte iki nasai.*(はんこは要らないと思うけれど、一応持って行きなさい) I don't think you need your seal, but *just in case*, take it with you. / *Kono wadai wa kore de ichioo owari ni shimashoo.*(この話題はこれで一応終わりにしましょう) Let's now finish with this topic *for the present.*

i⌈**chiritsu** いちりつ (市立) *n.* = shiritsu².

i⌈**chiryuu** いちりゅう (一流) *n.* first-class; first-rate:
ichiryuu no hoteru (一流のホテル) a *first-rate* hotel / *ichiryuu señshu* (一流選手) a *ranking* player / *Tanaka kyooju wa keezai gakusha to shite ichiryuu desu.*(田中教授は経済学者として一流です) As an economist, Professor Tanaka is of the *first rank.* 《⇨ niryuu; sañryuu》

i⌈**chi**⌉**ya** いちや (一夜) *n.* a [one] night:
Watashi wa sono koya de ichiya o sugoshita.(私はその小屋で一夜を過ごした) I spent *a night* in the hut. / *Yuki ga ichiya de nijus-señchi tsumotta.*(雪が一夜で20センチ積もった) Snow piled up twenty centimeters deep *overnight.*

i⌈**chiyoo ni** いちように（一様に）*adv.* equally; unanimously:
Shussekisha wa ichiyoo ni *sono teeañ ni sañsee shita.* (出席者は一様にその提案に賛成した) Those present were *unanimously* in favor of the proposal.

i⌈**dai** いだい（偉大）*a.n.* (〜 na, ni) great; grand:
Kawabata Yasunari wa idai *na sakka desu.* (川端康成は偉大な作家です) Yasunari Kawabata is a *great* novelist. / *Mae no shachoo no kooseki wa* idai *desu.* (前の社長の功績は偉大です) The former president left behind *great* accomplishments.

i⌈**da⌉k·u** いだく（抱く）*vt.* (idak·i-; idak·a-; ida·i-te Ⓒ) **1** hold; embrace:
akañboo o mune ni idaku (赤ん坊を胸に抱く) *hold* a baby to one's breast. 《⇨ daku》
2 harbor; bear; cherish:
Kare wa watashi ni urami o idaite *iru yoo da.* (彼は私に恨みを抱いているようだ) He *seems to bear* me a grudge. / *Kanojo wa kañgofu ni naru kiboo o* idaite iru. (彼女は看護婦になる希望を抱いている) She *cherishes* the hope of becoming a nurse.

i⌈**do** いど（井戸）*n.* well:
ido *o horu* (井戸を掘る) sink a *well* / ido *kara mizu o kumu* (井戸から水を汲む) draw water from a *well.*

i⌈**do⌉m·u** いどむ（挑む）*vt.* (idom·i-; idom·a-; idoñ-de Ⓒ) try; challenge; defy:
shiñ-kiroku ni idomu (新記録に挑む) *try to set* a new record / *Watashi-tachi wa kare no chiimu ni* idoñde *makashita.* (私たちは彼のチームに挑んで負かした) We *challenged* and beat his team. / *Kare wa sono moñdai de watashi ni* idoñde kita. (彼はその問題で私に挑んできた) He *defied* me on that matter. 《⇨ chooseñ》

i⌈**doo**[1] いどう（移動）*n.* **1** movement; transfer:
Kono machi wa juumiñ no idoo *ga hageshii.* (この町は住民の移動が激しい) The *movement* of residents in this town is very frequent. / *Kamotsu no* idoo *ni jikañ ga kakatta.* (貨物の移動に時間がかかった) It took time to *move* the freight.
2 removal; migration:
miñzoku no idoo (民族の移動) a racial *migration.*
idoo suru (〜する) *vi., vt.* move; travel; migrate: *Shikyuu kuruma o* idoo shite *kudasai.* (至急車を移動してください) *Move* your car at once. / *Kare-ra wa ressha de achikochi* idoo shita. (彼らは列車であちこち移動した) They *traveled* from one place to another by train.

i⌈**doo**[2] いどう（異動）*n.* personnel change:
Raigetsu idoo *ga aru soo desu.* (来月異動があるそうです) I hear that there will be some *personnel changes* next month. / *Koñdo no* idoo *de, kare wa Nagoya e teñkiñ ni narimashita.* (今度の異動で, 彼は名古屋へ転勤になりました) In the recent *re-organization of personnel*, he was transferred to Nagoya. / *jinji-*idoo (人事異動) personnel *change*(s) / *naikaku no* idoo (内閣の異動) a Cabinet *reshuffle.*

i⌈**e**[1] いえ（家）*n.* home; house:
★ A little more formal than '*uchi.*'
Watashi wa maiasa hachi-ji ni ie *o demasu.* (私は毎朝8時に家を出ます) I leave *home* at eight every morning. / *Nichiyoo wa* ie *ni imasu.* (日曜は家にいます) I'll be at *home* on Sunday. / *Kotoshi-juu ni* ie *o tateru yotee desu.* (今年中に家を建てる予定です) I am planning to build a *house* within this year.
ie o tsugu (〜を継ぐ) succeed to one's family business.

i⌐**e**¹² いえ *int.* no. ★ Less formal than '*iie.*'

i⌐**ede** いえで（家出）*n.* running away from home:
iede-niñ（家出人）a *runaway.*
iede (o) suru（～（を）する）*vi.* go [run] away from home; elope:
Riyuu mo naku, iede (o) suru *kodomo ga ooi.*（理由もなく、家出（を）する子どもが多い）There are many children who *run away from home* for no reason.

i⌐**emoto**¹ いえもと（家元）*n.* master [leader] of a school (of flower arrangement, tea ceremony, etc.)

i⌐**fuku** いふく（衣服）*n.* clothes; clothing:
ifuku o aratameru（衣服を改める）*dress oneself properly.*

i⌐**gai** いがい（意外）*a.n.*（～ na, ni）unexpected; surprising:
igai na dekigoto（意外な出来事）an *unexpected* occurrence / *Yamadasañ ga Chuugokugo o hanaseru nañte,* igai *da.*（山田さんが中国語を話せるなんて、意外だ）It is *surprising* that Mr. Yamada can speak Chinese. / *Shikeñ wa* igai *ni yasashikatta.*（試験は意外にやさしかった）The examination was easier *than I had expected.*
igai to（～と）unexpectedly: Igai to *jikañ ga kakatta.*（意外と時間がかかった）*Unexpectedly,* it took a long time.

-i⌐**gai** いがい（以外）*suf.* **1** except; but; other than:
*Mokuyoo-*igai *nara, itsu de mo kekkoo desu.*（木曜以外なら、いつでもけっこうです）As long as it is a day *other than* Thursday, anytime is fine. / *Kono koto wa anata-*igai *ni wa hanashite imaseñ.*（このことはあなた以外には話していません）I have spoken about this matter to nobody *but* you. / *Nigeru-*igai *ni hoohoo wa nakatta.*（逃げる以外に方法はなかった）There was nothing for it *but* to escape.
2 in addition to; besides:
*Kare wa hyooroñ-*igai *ni shoosetsu mo kakimasu.*（彼は評論以外に小説も書きます）*In addition to* reviews, he also writes novels.

i⌐**gaku** いがく（医学）*n.* medical science; medicine:
igaku-bu（医学部）the department of *medicine* / igaku-hakase（医学博士）a doctor of *medicine.*

i⌐**gañ** いがん（胃癌）*n.* stomach [gastric] cancer:
igañ *ni kakaru*（胃がんにかかる）have stomach cancer.（⇨ gañ）

i⌐**geñ** いげん（威厳）*n.* dignity; majesty:
igeñ *o tamotsu* [sokonau]（威厳を保つ[損なう]）maintain [impair] one's *dignity* / *Kare wa doko-ka* igeñ *ga aru.*（彼はどこか威厳がある）There is something *dignified* about him.

i⌐**gi**¹ いぎ（意義）*n.* meaning; significance:
Jiñsee no igi *ni tsuite shiñkeñ ni kañgaeta.*（人生の意義について真剣に考えた）I thought seriously about the *meaning* of life. / *Watashitachi wa hijoo ni* igi *no aru tooroñ o shita.*（私たちは非常に意義のある討論をした）We had a very *meaningful* discussion. / *Oriñpikku wa sañka suru koto ni* igi *ga aru.*（オリンピックは参加することに意義がある）In the Olympics, the *importance* lies in participating.

i⌐**gi**² いぎ（異議）*n.* objection; dissent; protest:
igi *o tonaeru*（異議を唱える）raise an *objection* / *Igi no aru kata wa te o agete kudasai.*（異議のある方は手をあげてください）Will those who have *objections,* please raise their hands. / *Igi nashi.*（異議なし）No *objection.*

I⌐**girisu** イギリス *n.* England; (loosely) Great Britain; the United Kingdom. 《⇨ **Eekoku**》

I「**girisujiñ** イギリスじん（イギリス人）
n. the British; the English.

i「**go**¹ いご（以後）*n.* after this;
from that time on; ever since:
Koñbañ shichi-ji igo, *o-deñwa o
kudasai.*（今晩 7 時以後, お電話をく
ださい）Please phone me *after*
seven this evening. / Igo, *ki o
tsuke nasai.*（以後, 気をつけなさい）
Be more careful *from now on.* /
Sore igo, *kanojo ni wa atte imaseñ.*（それ以後, 彼女には会っていません）
Since then I have not met her. /
Sono kaisha wa sekiyu shokku
igo, *sugu ni tachinaorimashita.*（そ
の会社は石油ショック以後, すぐに立ち
直りました）The company recov-
ered soon *after* the oil crisis.
《↔ **izeñ**¹》

i「**go**² いご（囲碁）*n.* the game of go.
《⇨ **go**² (photo)》

i「**hañ** いはん（違反）*n.* violation;
breach:
Keesatsu wa chuusha ihañ *o kibishiku torishimatta.*（警察は駐車違
反を厳しく取り締まった）The police
took strict measures against *illegal* parking. / *Sore wa keeyaku*
ihañ *da.*（それは契約違反だ）That is
a *breach* of contract.

　ihañ suru（〜する）*vt.* violate;
break: *Kare no kooi wa kootsuu
hooki ni* ihañ suru.（彼の行為は交通
法規に違反する）His act *violates* the
traffic rules.

i「**i** いい（良い）*a.* good; nice; fine:

―――（**USAGE**）―――
Used only in this form. More
informal than '*yoi*' and often
used ironically. Note the following examples where '*yoi*'
cannot be used.
―――――――――――

Ii *kimi da.*（いい気味だ）Serves you
right! / *Kanojo wa kyooiku-mama
no* ii *mihoñ da.*（彼女は教育ママのいい
見本だ）She is a *good* example of a

mother who pushes her children
to study. / *Kanojo wa fukusoo no
señsu ga* ii.（彼女は服装のセンスがい
い）She has *good* taste in clothes. /
Ii *toshi o shite, soñna koto o suru
no wa mittomonai.*（いい年をして, そ
んなことをするのはみっともない）It is disgraceful for someone of *your age*
to behave like that.

i「**iarawa**「**s·u** いいあらわす（言い表す）
vt. (-arawash·i-; -arawas·a-;
-arawash·i-te C) say; express;
describe:
*Jibuñ ga omotte iru koto o hak-
kiri* iiarawashi nasai.（自分が思って
いることをはっきり言い表しなさい）
Clearly *say* what you think. /
Kono kimochi wa nañ to iiarawa-
shite *yoi ka wakarimaseñ.*（この気
持ちは何と言い表してよいかわかりません）
I don't know how I can *express*
these feelings.

i「**ia**「**·u** いいあう（言い合う）*vt.* (-a·i-;
-aw·a-; -at-te C) quarrel; dispute:
*Kare-ra wa sono moñdai de hage-
shiku* iiatta.（彼らはその問題で激しく
言い合った）They *quarreled* violently about the problem.

i「**ida**「**s·u** いいだす（言い出す）*vt.*
(-dash·i-; -das·a-; -dash·i-te C)
start speaking; propose; suggest:
Kore wa dare ga iidashita *no desu
ka?*（これはだれが言い出したのですか）
Who *proposed* this? / *Kare wa haikiñgu ni ikoo to* iidashita.（彼はハイ
キングに行こうと言い出した）He *sug-
gested* going hiking.

i「**ie**「 いいえ *int.* no; yes:

―――（**USAGE**）―――
'*Iie*' literally means 'That's
wrong,' and is used to confirm a
statement, whether affirmative
or negative. Note that this use
is different from that of 'yes'
and 'no' in English. '*Iya*' is
the more informal equivalent.
―――――――――――

"Ima isogashii desu ka?" *"Iie, iso-gashiku arimaseñ."* (「今忙しいです か」「いいえ、忙しくありません」) "Are you busy now?" "*No*, I am not." / *"Moo sukoshi o-nomi ni narima-señ ka?"* *"Iie, moo kekkoo desu."* (「もう少しお飲みになりませんか」「いいえ、もう結構です」) "Won't you have a bit more to drink?" "*No*, thank you." / *"O-sake wa nomanai ñ desu ka?"* *"Iie, nomimasu yo."* (「お酒は飲まないんですか」「いいえ、飲みますよ」) "You don't drink?" "*Yes*, I do." (↔ hai)

i⌐ika⌐es·u いいかえす (言い返す) *vi.* (-kaesh·i-; -kaes·a-; -kaesh·i·te C) talk back; retort: *Sono seeto wa señsee ni* iikae-shita. (その生徒は先生に言い返した) The pupil *talked back* to the teacher. / *"Watashi wa hañtai desu,"* to kanojo wa iikaeshita. (「私は反対です」と彼女は言い返した) "I am against it," she *retorted*.

i⌐ikageñ いいかげん (いい加減) *a.n.* (~ na, ni) irresponsible; non-committal; vague: iikageñ *ni kotaeru* (いいかげんに答える) give a *vague* reply / likageñ *na koto o iu na.* (いいかげんなことを言うな) Do not make *irresponsible* state-ments. / *Kare wa suru koto ga* iikageñ *da.* (彼はすることがいいかげんだ) He *never takes responsibility* for what he does.
— *adv.* rather; pretty: *Tañjuñ na shigoto na no de* iika-geñ *iya ni natta.* (単純な仕事なのでいいかげんいやになった) Since it is a monotonous job, I am *rather* bored with it.

iikageñ ni suru (~にする) **1** do one's work sloppily: *Kare wa toki-doki shigoto o* iikageñ ni suru. (彼はときどき仕事をいいかげんにする) He sometimes *does his work sloppily*. **2** (with the imperative) stop doing:

Itazura wa iikageñ *ni shi nasai.* (いたずらはいいかげんにしなさい) *Stop fooling around!*

Iikageñ ni shinai ka. (~にしないか) That's enough! Come off it!

i⌐ikata いいかた (言い方) *n.* expres-sion; way of speaking: *Kanojo wa mono no* iikata *ga tee-nee da.* (彼女は物の言い方が丁寧だ) Her *manner of speaking* is polite. / *Kore wa yoku tsukawareru* iikata *desu.* (これはよく使われる言い方です) This is a frequently used *expression*. / *Kare wa motte ma-watta* iikata o suru. (彼は持って回った言い方をする) He *talks* in a round-about *way*. / *Soo iu* iikata *wa nai deshoo.* (そういう言い方はないでしょう) You *should not speak* like that.

i⌐ikikase⌐·ru いいきかせる (言い聞かせる) *vi.* (-kikase-te V) tell a per-son to do; persuade; admonish: *Señsee wa sono ko ni chikoku shinai yoo ni* iikikaseta. (先生はその子に遅刻しないように言い聞かせた) The teacher *admonished* the child not to be late for school.

i⌐iñ いいん (委員) *n.* member of a committee: *Kare wa sono* iiñ *ni niñmee sareta.* (彼はその委員に任命された) He was appointed a *member of the com-mittee*.

i⌐i⌐ñchoo いいんちょう (委員長) *n.* chairman; chairperson: liñchoo, *shitsumoñ ga arimasu.* (委員長、質問があります) *Mr. Chair-man*, I have a question.

i⌐i⌐ñkai いいんかい (委員会) *n.* com-mittee; committee meeting: iiñkai *o hiraku* (委員会を開く) hold a *committee meeting* / *Sono teeañ wa* iiñkai *ni kakerareta.* (その提案は委員会にかけられた) The proposal was presented to the *committee*.

i⌐itsuke⌐·ru いいつける (言い付ける) *vi., vt.* (-tsuke-te V) **1** tell a per-son to (do):

Kare wa musuko ni shigoto o te-tsudau yoo iitsuketa. (彼は息子に仕事を手伝うよう言いつけた) He *told* his son to help him with his work.
2 tell on:
Soñna koto o shitara, señsee ni ii-tsukemasu *yo.* (そんなことをしたら、先生に言いつけますよ) If you do such a thing, I will *tell* the teacher *on* you.

i˞itsutae いいつたえ (言い伝え) *n.*
tradition; legend:
Kono numa ni wa mukashi kappa ga suñde ita to iu iitsutae *ga arimasu.* (この沼には昔かっぱが住んでいたという言い伝えがあります) There is a *legend* that in the old days a 'kappa' (water imp) lived in this marsh.

i˞iwake いいわけ (言い訳) *n.* excuse; explanation; justification:
Kore de rippa ni iiwake *ga tatsu yo.* (これで立派に言い訳が立つよ) This affords us a good *excuse.*
iiwake (o) suru (〜(を)する) *vi.*
make an excuse; justify oneself:
Sekiniñsha wa kurushii iiwake o shita. (責任者は苦しい言い訳をした) The person in charge *made* a poor *excuse.*
iiwake-gamashii (〜がましい) try to justify oneself: *Kare wa* ii-wake-gamashii *koto wa iwana-katta.* (彼は言い訳がましいことは言わなかった) He didn't *try to justify himself.*

i˞iji[1] いじ (意地) *n.* **1** pride:
Watashi ni mo iji *ga aru.* (私にも意地がある) I, too, have my *pride.*
2 nature; disposition:
Ano hito wa iji *ga warui.* (あの人は意地が悪い) She is *ill-natured.*
iji de mo (〜でも) for one's pride:
Iji de mo *kono shigoto o yatte misemasu.* (意地でもこの仕事をやってみせます) *My pride forces me* to carry through with this work.
iji ga kitanai (〜が汚い) be

greedy: *Iji ga kitanai koto wa yame nasai.* (意地が汚いことはやめなさい) Don't *be so greedy.*
iji ni natte (〜になって) stubbornly: *Kare wa* iji ni natte, *sono kee-kaku ni hañtai shita.* (彼は意地になって、その計画に反対した) He *persistently* opposed the plan.
iji o haru (〜をはる) do not give in: *Kare wa tsumaranai koto ni* iji o hatta. (彼はつまらないことに意地をはった) He *was stubborn* over trifles.
iji o toosu (〜を通す) have one's own way: *Kare wa itsu-mo* iji o toosoo *to suru.* (彼はいつも意地を通そうとする) He always *sticks to his guns.*

i˞iji[2] いじ (維持) *n.* maintenance; upkeep:
Kono tatemono wa iji *ni kane ga kakaru.* (この建物は維持に金がかかる) This building costs a lot in *upkeep.* / *Geñjoo* iji *wa muzukashii.* (現状維持はむずかしい) It is difficult to *maintain* the present situation. / iji-hi (維持費) *maintenance* costs.
iji suru (〜する) *vt.* maintain; keep up: *keñkoo o* iji suru (健康を維持する) *keep* oneself in good health / *Sekai no heewa ga* iji sareru *koto o nozomimasu.* (世界の平和が維持されることを望みます) I hope that world peace will *be maintained.*

i˞ime·ru いじめる (苛める) *vt.* (iji-me-te Ⅴ) tease; annoy; bully:
Kodomo-tachi wa ishi o nagete, inu o ijimeta. (子どもたちは石を投げて、犬をいじめた) The children *maltreated* the dog by throwing stones at it. / *Sono oñna-no-ko wa otoko-no-ko-tachi ni* ijimerareta. (その女の子は男の子たちにいじめられた) The girl *was teased* by the boys. / *Yowai mono o* ijimeru *no wa yoshi nasai.* (弱い者をいじめるのはよしなさい) Don't *bully* weaker people.

i┌jiwa┐ru いじわる (意地悪) *n.* nastiness; maliciousness:
Tomodachi ni ijiwaru o shite wa dame desu yo. (友達に意地悪をしてはだめですよ) You must not be *nasty* to your friends.
— *a.n.* (~ na, ni) nasty; ill-natured; malicious:
Ano hito wa hoñto ni ijiwaru da. (あの人はほんとに意地悪だ) He is really *nasty.* / *Kare wa yoku ijiwaru na shitsumoñ o suru.* (彼はよく意地悪な質問をする) He often asks *teasing* questions.

i┌joo┐¹ いじょう (以上) *n.* **1** the above; the foregoing:
Ijoo no toori sooi arimaseñ. (以上の通り相違ありません) I affirm that *the above* is correct. ★ Used when attesting to the veracity of a document. / *Ijoo ga watashi no kiita koto no subete desu.* (以上が私の聞いたことのすべてです) *The foregoing* is everything I heard. ((↔ ika))
2 that's all; concluded:
Ijoo, watashi no kañgae o nobesasete itadakimashita (以上，私の考えを述べさせていただきました) *That is* what I wanted to say. ★ Used to close an announcement or speech. / *Ijoo desu.* (以上です) *That's all.*

i┌joo┐² いじょう (以上) *conj.* since; once; as long as:
Yakusoku shita ijoo, watashi wa kanarazu jikkoo shimasu. (約束した以上，私は必ず実行します) *Once* I have made a promise, I will certainly carry it out. / *Nihoñ ni suñde iru ijoo Nihoñ no shuukañ ni shitagawanakereba narimaseñ.* (日本に住んでいる以上日本の習慣に従わなければなりません) *As long as* you live in Japan, you have to follow Japanese customs.

i┌joo┐³ いじょう (異常) *a.n.* (~ na, ni) abnormal; unusual; extraordinary:
ijoo na niñki (異常な人気) *extraordinary* popularity / *Kono atsusa wa ijoo desu.* (この暑さは異常です) This heat is very *unusual.* / *Ijoo na jitai ga hassee shita.* (異常な事態が発生した) An *abnormal* state of affairs has developed. / *Jikkeñshitsu no oñdo ga ijoo ni agatta.* (実験室の温度が異常に上がった) The temperature in the laboratory went up *extraordinarily.* / *ijoo-kishoo* (異常気象) *abnormal* weather.

-i┌joo┐ いじょう (以上) *suf.* **1** above; over; not less than:
Juuhas-sai-ijoo nara dare de mo meñkyo ga toremasu. (18歳以上ならだれでも免許が取れます) Anybody who is eighteen *and over* can get a driver's license. / *Kare wa sono e ni sukunaku-tomo hyakumañ-eñ-ijoo wa haratta.* (彼はその絵に少なくとも100万円以上は払った) He paid a million yen *or more*, at least, for that picture. ((↔ -ika))

> **(USAGE)**
> '*-ijoo*' includes the preceding number, so, strictly speaking, '18-*ijoo*' means 'more than 17.'

2 more than:
Kono mae kanojo ni atte kara ichi-neñ-ijoo ni narimasu. (この前彼女に会ってから一年以上になります) It is now *more than* a year since I last met her. / *Omotte ita-ijoo no kifu ga atsumarimashita.* (思っていた以上の寄付が集まりました) A *larger* contribution *than* we had expected was collected.

i┌juu いじゅう (移住) *n.* migration; emigration; immigration:
ijuu-sha (移住者) an *emigrant*; an *immigrant.*
ijuu suru (~ する) *vi.* migrate; emigrate; immigrate: *Kare no ikka wa Burajiru e ijuu shita.* (彼の一家はブラジルへ移住した) His family

emigrated to Brazil. / *Amerika e ijuu shite kita hito wa ooi.* (アメリカへ移住してきた人は多い) There are many people who *immigrated* to the United States.

i⌐ka¹ いか (以下) *n.* the following; as follows:
Kare kara kiita hanashi wa ika no toori desu. (彼から聞いた話は以下の通りです) What I heard from him is *as follows:* / *Ika raigetsu-goo ni tsuzuku.* (以下来月号に続く) *Continued* in next month's issue (of this magazine). 《↔ ijoo¹》

i⌐ka² いか (烏賊) *n.* cuttlefish; squid. ★ Sashimi from '*ika*' is called '*ikasashi.*' 《⇨ surume》

IKA

-i⌐ka いか (以下) *suf.* **1** less than:
Kono kuruma wa juumañ-eñ ika no kachi shika nai. (この車は10万円以下の価値しかない) This car only has a value of *less than* 100,000 yen. / *Nihoñ de wa juukyuu-sai ika no hito wa señkyo de toohyoo dekimaseñ.* (日本では19歳以下の人は選挙で投票できません) In Japan, people nineteen *and under* cannot vote in elections. 《↔ -ijoo》

USAGE

'*-ika*' includes the preceding number, so, strictly speaking, '19 *ika*' means 'less than 20.' 《⇨ -mimañ》

---

2 below; under:
Koñdo no watashi no seeseki wa heekiñ-ika datta. (今度の私の成績は平均以下だった) My grades this time were *below* average.

i⌐kada いかだ (筏) *n.* raft:
ikada de kawa o kudaru (いかだで川を下る) go down a river on a *raft.*

i⌐ka⌐ga いかが (如何) *adv.* [usually used with the copula '*da.*']
1 how:
Go-kigeñ ikaga desu ka? (ご機嫌いかがですか) *How* are you getting along? / *O-karada wa ikaga desu ka?* (お体はいかがですか) *How* is your health? / *O-aji wa ikaga deshoo ka?* (お味はいかがでしょうか) *How do you like* the taste? / *Señdai de no seekatsu wa ikaga deshita ka?* (仙台での生活はいかがでしたか) *What was it like* living in Sendai?
2 Would you like...?: ★ Used when offering food, etc.
Biiru wa ikaga desu ka? (ビールはいかがですか) *Would you like* some beer? / *O-cha o ip-pai ikaga desu ka?* (お茶を一杯いかがですか) *How about* a cup of tea?
3 how [what] about...?:
Kare o sasottara ikaga desu ka? (彼を誘ったらいかがですか) *What about* inviting him?
4 what:
Anata no go-ikeñ wa ikaga desu ka? (あなたのご意見はいかがですか) *What* is your opinion?

i⌐ka⌐iyoo いかいよう (胃潰瘍) *n.* an ulcer of the stomach:
ikaiyoo ni naru (胃かいようになる) get a *stomach ulcer.*

i⌐ka⌐ ni いかに (如何に) *adv.* **1** (of degree) how:
Itte minai to sono taki ga ika ni ookii ka wakarimaseñ. (行って見ないとその滝がいかに大きいかわかりません) You will not appreciate *how* large the waterfall is unless you go and see for yourself. / *Nihoñgo kaiwa no reñshuu ga ika ni taisetsu ka wakatte imasu.* (日本語会話の練習がいかに大切かわかっています) I know *how* important practice in

spoken Japanese is.

2 (of manner) how:
Taisetsu na no wa shiai o ika ni tatakau ka desu. (大切なのは試合をいかに戦うかです) What is important is the *way* you play the game. / Ika ni *shite uriage o nobasu ka ga mondai desu.* (いかにして売上を伸ばすかが問題です) The question is *how* to increase sales.

3 (*formal*) however:
Ika ni *kurushikute mo kono shigoto o tsuzukeru tsumori desu.* (いかに苦しくてもこの仕事を続けるつもりです) *However* painful it is, I intend to continue this work.

i「ka」 ni mo いかにも (如何にも) *adv.* really; truly; typically:
Kanojo wa ika ni mo *komatta yoosu datta.* (彼女はいかにも困った様子だった) She looked as if she were *truly* troubled. / *Sono hanashi wa* ika ni mo *hontoo ni kikoeru.* (その話はいかにもほんとうに聞こえる) That story sounds as if it were *really* true. / *Sonna koto o suru nante,* ika ni mo *kare-rashii.* (そんなことをするなんて、いかにも彼らしい) Doing something like that—it's *just* like him.

i「kari いかり (怒り) *n.* anger; rage; wrath:
Watashi no kotoba ga kare no ikari *o maneita.* (私の言葉が彼の怒りを招いた) My words provoked his *anger.* (⇨ okoru²)

i「ka」s·u いかす (生かす) *vt.* (ika-sh·i-; ikas·a-; ikash·i-te [C]) make the most of:
jibun no chishiki [*sainoo; keeken*] *o* ikasu (自分の知識[才能; 経験]を生かす) *make good use of* one's knowledge [talent; experience].

i「ke」 いけ (池) *n.* pond.
★ A small body of water usually made artificially, while '*numa*' is a pool of shallow muddy water formed naturally.

i「ke」bana いけばな (生け花) *n.* flower arrangement:
Kanojo wa Yamada sensee ni tsuite ikebana *o naratte iru.* (彼女は山田先生について生け花を習っている) She is studying *flower arrangement* under Mrs. Yamada.

IKEBANA

i「kemase」n いけません ★ Polite equivalent of '*ikenai.*'

1 must not (do); will not (do); be no good:
"*Tabe-hajimete mo ii desu ka?*" "*Iie,* ikemasen." (「食べ始めてもいいですか」「いいえ、いけません」) "Can I start eating?" "No, *you can't.*" / *Uchi no inu o ijimete wa* ikemasen. (うちの犬をいじめてはいけません) You *must not* tease our dog. / *Koko made kita no da kara, akiramete wa* ikemasen. (ここまで来たのだから、あきらめてはいけません) Now we have come this far, *it just won't do* to give up. (⇨ dame)

2 (with a negative verb) must (do); have to (do):
Anata wa kanojo ni ayamaranakute wa ikemasen. (あなたは彼女に謝らなくてはいけません) You *must* apologize to her. / *Shokuji wa chanto toranakute wa* ikemasen. (食事はちゃんととらなくてはいけません) You *have to* eat properly. (⇨ beki; dame)

i｢ke̅ñ いけん（意見）n. **1** opinion; view:
Kare wa jibuñ no ikeñ o nobeta. （彼は自分の意見を述べた）He expressed his *opinion.* / *Watashi mo anata to onaji* ikeñ *desu.* （私もあなたと同じ意見です）I share your *view.* / *Kare to wa* ikeñ *ga atta* [*awanakatta*].（彼とは意見が合った［合わなかった］）I *agreed* [*disagreed*] with him.
2 idea:
Kono keñ ni tsuite anata no ikeñ *o kikasete kudasai.* （この件についてあなたの意見を聞かせてください）Please let us hear your *ideas* on this matter.
3 advice:
Isha no ikeñ *ni shitagatta.* （医者の意見に従った）I followed my doctor's *advice.*

i｢kena･i いけない *a.* (-ku) bad; wrong:
Doko-ka ikenai tokoro ga arimasu ka? （どこかいけないところがありますか）Is there anything *wrong* with it? / *"Señsee, netsu ga aru ñ desu." "Sore wa* ikemaseñ *ne."* （「先生, 熱があるんです」「それはいけませんね」）"Doctor, I have a temperature." "*I'm sorry.*" / *Ano kaisha wa moo* ikenai *rashii.* （あの会社はもういけないらしい）I hear the company is on the verge of *bankruptcy.* / *A', ikenai. Wasuremono o shita.* （あ, いけない. 忘れ物をした）Oh, *that won't do.* I've forgotten something.
-te wa ikenai （ては〜）must not do; should not do: *Keñka o shite wa ikemaseñ.* （けんかをしてはいけません）You *must not* quarrel. / *Soñna koto o shite wa ikenai.* （そんなことをしてはいけない）You *should not do* such a thing. 《⇨ **dame**》
...to ikenai kara [**no de**] （...と〜から［ので］）in case: *Ame ga furu to ikenai kara, kasa o motte iki nasai.* （雨が降るといけないから, 傘を持って行きなさい）Take an umbrella with you *in case* it rains. ★ Po-

lite forms are '*ikenai desu, ikemaseñ.*'

i｢ke̅･ru いける（生ける）*vt.* (ike-te Ⅴ) arrange (flowers):
Kanojo wa hana o ikeru no ga joozu da. （彼女は花を生けるのが上手だ）She is good at *arranging* flowers. 《⇨ **ikebana**》

i｢ki̅ いき（息）*n.* breath; breathing:
iki *o suu* [*haku*]（息を吸う［吐く］）*breathe in* [*out*] / iki *ga arai* （息が荒い）one's *breathing* is rough / iki *ga kireru* （息が切れる）run out of *breath* / *Watashi-tachi wa ookiku* iki *o shita.* （私たちは大きく息をした）We *breathed* deeply.
iki ga au （〜が合う）get along well; be in perfect harmony:
Futari no haiyuu wa iki ga atte *ita.* （二人の俳優は息が合っていた）The two actors *worked in perfect harmony.*
iki ga kireru （〜が切れる）be out of breath: *Kaidañ o noboru to iki ga kireru.* （階段を上ると息が切れる）Whenever I go up stairs, I *get short of* breath.
iki ga nagai （〜が長い）exist for a long time: *Kono bañgumi wa* iki ga nagai. （この番組は息が長い）This is a *long-running* program.
iki o fukikaesu （〜を吹き返す）come to life; be revived: *Kare wa kiseki-teki ni* iki o fukikaeshita. （彼は奇跡的に息を吹き返した）He *came to life* by a miracle.
iki o hikitoru （〜を引き取る）breathe one's last: *Haha wa kesa* iki o hikitorimashita. （母は今朝息を引き取りました）My mother *expired* this morning.
iki o korosu （〜を殺す）hold one's breath: *Miñna wa* iki o koroshite *sore o mitsumeta.* （みんなは息を殺してそれを見つめた）Everyone watched it *with bated breath.*
iki o nomu （〜をのむ）catch one's

breath: *Sono kookee ni omowazu iki o noñda.* (その光景に思わず, 息をのんだ) I involuntarily *held my breath* at the sight.

iki o tsuku (〜をつく) take a rest: *Isogashikute iki o tsuku hima mo nai.* (忙しくて息をつくひまもない) I am too busy to *even pause for breath*.

i꜀ki² いき (行き) *n.* (=yuki²) going (to the destination): *Iki mo kaeri mo Shiñkañseñ deshita.* (行きも帰りも新幹線でした) The trips *there* and back were both by Shinkansen. / *Iki wa takushii, kaeri wa basu deshita.* (行きはタクシー, 帰りはバスでした) I *went there* by taxi and came back by bus. 《↔ kaeri》

i꜀ki³ いき (粋) *a.n.* (〜 na, ni) chic; stylish; smart: *iki na sugata* (いきな姿) a *stylish* appearance / *Iki na wakamono ga mikoshi o katsuide iru.* (いきな若者がみこしを担いでいる) Some *stylish* young people are carrying the portable shrine on their shoulders.

i꜀kichigai いきちがい (行き違い) *n.* crossing each other. 《⇨ yukichigai》

i꜀kidomari いきどまり (行き止まり) *n.* dead end. 《⇨ yukidomari》

i꜀kigire いきぎれ (息切れ) *n.* being short of breath: *Kaidañ o ni-dañ zutsu nobottara, ikigire ga shita.* (階段を2段ずつのぼったら, 息切れがした) I *ran out of breath* after going up the stairs two at a time.

i꜀ki-i꜀ki いきいき (生き生き) *adv.* (〜 to) vividly: *Sono hoñ ni wa shomiñ no seekatsu ga iki-iki to egakarete imasu.* (その本には庶民の生活が生き生きと描かれています) In that book, the life of common people is *vividly* depicted. / *Mizu o yattara, nae ga iki-iki to shite kita.* (水をやったら, 苗が生き生きとしてきた) When I watered the young plants, they *freshened up*. / *Kodomo-tachi wa iki-iki to shite iru.* (子どもたちは生き生きとしている) The children are *full of life*.

i꜀kikaer·u いきかえる (生き返る) *vi.* (-kaer·i-; -kaer·a-; -kaet-te Ⓒ)
1 revive; come to life: *Sono ko wa jiñkoo-kokyuu de iki-kaetta.* (その子は人口呼吸で生き返った) The child *was resuscitated* by artificial respiration.
2 feel refreshed: *Tsumetai shawaa o abitara, iki-kaetta yoo na kokochi ga shita.* (冷たいシャワーを浴びたら, 生き返ったような心地がした) I *felt refreshed* after taking a cold shower.

i꜀kimono いきもの (生き物) *n.* living thing; creature; animal: *Kare wa iroiro na ikimono o katte iru.* (彼はいろいろな生き物を飼っている) He keeps various *animals*. 《⇨ seebutsu》

i꜀kinari いきなり *adv.* all of a sudden; abruptly; without notice: *Kare wa ikinari donari-dashita.* (彼はいきなり怒鳴りだした) *All of a sudden*, he started shouting. / *Kodomo ga ikinari dooro ni tobidashita.* (子どもがいきなり道路に飛び出した) A child *abruptly* ran out into the road. / *Ikinari namae o yobarete, magotsuita.* (いきなり名前を呼ばれて, まごついた) I lost my composure when my name was *suddenly* called.

i꜀kinoko꜀r·u いきのこる (生き残る) *vi.* (-nokor·i-; -nokor·a-; -nokot-te Ⓒ) survive: *Sono jiko de sañ-niñ dake ikinokotta.* (その事故で3人だけ生き残った) Only three people *survived* that accident.

i꜀kio꜀i いきおい (勢い) *n.* force; might; vigor; energy; influence: *kaze [mizu] no ikioi* (風[水]の勢い)

the *force* of the wind [of water] / *Miñna de booto o* ikioi yoku *koida.* (みんなでボートを勢いよくこいだ) We all rowed the boat *powerfully.* / *Kare wa sake no* ikioi *de keñka o shita.* (彼は酒の勢いでけんかをした) He had a fight under the *influence* of alcohol.

i「kio¬i² いきおい (勢い) *adv.* in the course of; consequently; naturally; necessarily: Ikioi, *sono yaku o hikiukeru koto ni natte shimatta.* (勢い, その役を引き受けることになってしまった) *By force of circumstances*, I ended up accepting the role.

i「ki¬·ru いきる (生きる) *vi.* (iki-te Ⅴ) **1** live: ★ '*ikite iru*' = be alive. *Doobutsu wa kuuki ga nai to* ikite *yukemaseñ.* (動物は空気がないと生きてゆけません) Animals cannot *live* without air. / *Sofu wa kyuujuu made* ikimashita. (祖父は 90 まで生きました) My grandfather *lived* to the age of ninety. / *Sono inu wa mada* ikite *imasu.* (その犬はまだ生きています) The dog *is* still *alive.* / *Kono tori wa nani o tabete,* ikite *iru ñ desu ka?* (この鳥は何を食べて, 生きているんですか) What do these birds *live* on?

2 (of a rule, convention, etc.) be valid; be good; live: ★ Usually used in '*ikite iru.*' *Kono kisoku wa mada* ikite imasu. (この規則はまだ生きています) This rule still *applies.* / *Kare no seeshiñ wa wareware no kokoro no naka de* ikite imasu. (彼の精神はわれわれの心の中で生きています) His spirit *lives on* in our hearts.

i「kisatsu いきさつ (経緯) *n.* circumstances; story; reason: *Kanojo to shiriatta* ikisatsu *o kare ni hanashita.* (彼女と知り合ったいきさつを彼に話した) I told him the *story* of how I had come to know her.

/ *Doo iu* ikisatsu *de koko ni sumu yoo ni natta no desu ka?* (どういういきさつでここに住むようになったのですか) *How* was it that you came to live here? / *Kare ga kaisha o yameta* ikisatsu *wa shirimaseñ.* (彼が会社をやめたいきさつは知りません) I don't know the *circumstances* surrounding his quitting the company.

i「kka いっか (一家) *n.* family: *Kare wa* ikka *no choo desu.* (彼は一家の長です) He is the head of his *family.* / *Kanojo no* ikka *wa kyuuka de Hawai e itta.* (彼女の一家は休暇でハワイへ行った) Her *whole family* went to Hawaii on vacation. / *Yamada-sañ* ikka *wa Yokohama e hikkoshimashita.* (山田さん一家は横浜へ引っ越しました) *The Yamadas* moved to Yokohama. 《⇨ kazoku (table)》

ik「koo¹ いっこう (一行) *n.* party; group; company: *Watashi-tachi* ikkoo *wa hachi-niñ datta.* (私たち一行は 8 人だった) Our *party* was made up of eight in all. / *Ikkoo wa yama no fumoto ni go-go toochaku shita.* (一行は山のふもとに午後到着した) The *party* arrived at the foot of the mountain in the afternoon. / *Watashi wa kare no* ikkoo *ni kuwawaranakatta.* (私は彼の一行に加わらなかった) I didn't join his *group.*

i「kkoo² いっこう (一向) *adv.* (~ ni) (with a negative) at all; in the least: *Kare no gorufu wa* ikkoo *ni jootatsu shinai.* (彼のゴルフは一向に上達しない) His golf does not improve *at all.* / *Soñna koto wa* ikkoo *(ni) kamaimaseñ.* (そんなことは一向(に)かまいません) I am not *in the least* worried about that kind of thing.

i「kkyuu いっきゅう (一級) *n.* first class [rate]; top grade: ikkyuu-hiñ (一級品) *first-class* goods. 《⇨ ichiryuu; saikoo》

-i⌐koo いこう（以降）*suf.* after; on or after:
Yoru hachi-ji-ikoo ni o-deñwa o kudasai.（夜8時以降にお電話を下さい）Please phone me *after* eight in the evening. / *Kaigi wa go-gatsu too-ka-ikoo ni eñki saremashita.*（会議は5月10日以降に延期されました）The meeting was postponed *until* May 10, *or later*.

(USAGE)
'*-ikoo*' includes the preceding number, so, strictly speaking, '*sañ-ji-ikoo*' means 'at and after three o'clock.'

---

i⌐k·u いく（行く）*vi.* (ik·i-; ik·a-; it-te Ⓒ)

(USAGE)
'行く' is also pronounced '*yu-ku*,' an alternate form of '*iku*,' which is somewhat formal and old-fashioned but is used in forming compounds.

---

1 go away; leave:
Kare wa moo ikimashita.（彼はもう行きました）He *has* already *left.* / *Mukoo e iki nasai.*（向こうへ行きなさい）*Go* over there.
2 go; come:
Kare wa maiasa hachi-ji ni gak-koo e ikimasu.（彼は毎朝8時に学校へ行きます）He *goes* to school at eight every morning. / *Kanojo wa kotoshi Oosutoraria ni ikimasu.*（彼女は今年オーストラリアに行きます）She *is going* to Australia this year. / *Sochira ni ni-ji ni itte yoroshii desu ka?*（そちらに2時に行ってよろしいですか）May I *visit* you at two? 《↔ kaeru¹》
3 go doing: ★ Used with a noun in '*... ni iku.*'
Kanojo wa suupaa e kaimono ni ikimashita.（彼女はスーパーへ買い物に行きました）She *has gone* shopping

at the supermarket. / *Watashi wa señshuu, Zaoo e sukii ni itta.*（私は先週、蔵王へスキーに行った）Last week I *went* to Zao to ski.
4 go in order to do: ★ Used with a verb in '*... ni iku.*'
Kinoo wa eega o mi ni ikimashita.（きのうは映画を見に行きました）I *went* to see a movie yesterday. / *Kare-ra wa kooeñ e tenisu o shi ni iki-mashita.*（彼らは公園へテニスをしに行きました）They *went* to the park to play tennis.
5 proceed; go:
Subete ga umaku ikimashita.（すべてがうまくいきました）Everything *went* smoothly. / *Sore wa watashi no omotta toori ni itta.*（それは私の思った通りにいった）It *went off* just as I had expected. / *Keekaku wa yotee-doori itte imasu.*（計画は予定通りいっています）The plan *is pro-ceeding* as scheduled. / *Futari no naka wa umaku itte imaseñ.*（二人の仲はうまくいっていません）The two of them *are not getting on* well. 《⇨ wake ni wa ikanai》

(USAGE)
Note that '*iku*' is equivalent to 'come' in the following kind of situation: "*Hayaku, kochira ni kite kudasai.*" "*Hai, ima iki-masu.*"（「早く、こちらに来てください」「はい、いま行きます」）"Please come here quickly." "All right, I'*m coming* (lit. 'going') now."

---

i⌐ku- いく（幾）*pref.* (*formal*)
1 how many:
Fune de iku-nichi kakarimashita ka?（船で幾日かかりましたか）*How many* days did it take by ship? / *Iku-niñ kega o shimashita ka?*（幾人けがをしましたか）*How many* people were injured? 《⇨ nañ》
2 some; several:
Iku-nichi ka tatte, netsu ga sagatta.（幾日かたって、熱が下がった）After

some days, my fever went away. /
Sono jiko de iku-*niñ mo keganiñ
ga deta.* (その事故で幾人もけが人がで
た) *Several* people were injured in
that accident. 《⇨ nañ》

i⌐**kubuñ** いくぶん（幾分）*adv.*
(～ *ka*) a little; somewhat; more
or less:
Kare wa ikubuñ (*ka*) *geñki ni
natta.* (彼はいくぶん（か）元気になった)
He has *somewhat* recovered. /
Asa-bañ ikubuñ *hiete kimashita.*
(朝晩いくぶん冷えてきました) It has
become *a bit* chilly in the mornings and evenings. 《⇨ ikura-ka》

i⌐**kudo** いくど（幾度）*adv.* **1** how
often:
Ikudo *ittara wakaru ñ da.* (いくど言
ったらわかるんだ) *How many times* do
I have to tell you before you
understand?
2 (～ *mo*) very often; again and
again:
Watashi wa kare ni ikudo mo
chuui shita. (私は彼にいくども注意し
た) I warned him *again and again*.

i⌐**kuji ga nai** いくじがない（意気地が
ない) chickenhearted; cowardly:
Kare wa ikuji ga nai. (彼は意気地が
ない) He has *no guts*.

i⌐**kunichi mo** いくにちも（幾日も）
adv. for days:
Kaze wa ikunichi mo *naorana-
katta.* (かぜは幾日も治らなかった) My
cold did not get better *for days*. /
Watashi wa kare no heñji o iku-
nichi mo *matta.* (私は彼の返事を幾
日も待った) I waited for his answer
for days.

i⌐**kura** いくら（幾ら）*adv.* (of a
price) how much:
Kono hoñ wa ikura *desu ka?* (この
本はいくらですか) *How much* is this
book? / *Sono tokee wa* ikura *shimashita ka?* (その時計はいくらしました
か) *How much* did that watch
cost? / Ikura *de kono uchi o o-uri
ni naru tsumori desu ka?* (いくらでこ

の家をお売りになるつもりですか) *How
much* do you intend to sell this
house for?

ikura mo (～も) (with a negative)
not many [much]: *Kono biñ ni
wa uisukii ga* ikura mo *nokotte
inai.* (このびんにはウイスキーがいくらも残
っていない) There is *not much*
whisky left in this bottle.

ikura -te [de] mo (～て[で]も)
(with a negative) no matter how;
however:
Ikura *hayaku aruite mo, kare ni oi-
tsukenakatta.* (いくら速く歩いても、彼
に追いつけなかった) *No matter how
fast I walked*, I could not catch
up with him. / Ikura *tabete mo,
tabekirenai.* (いくら食べても、食べ切れ
ない) *However much you eat*, you
can not finish it up. / Ikura *kare
de mo, sore wa dekinai deshoo.* (い
くら彼でも、それはできないでしょう) *Even
if it is him*, that he surely will be
unable to do.

i⌐**kura ka** いくらか（幾らか）*adv.*
a little; somewhat; more or less:
Kyoo wa kinoo yori ikura ka
samui. (きょうはきのうよりいくらか寒い)
Today it is *a bit* colder than yesterday. / Ikura ka *o-kane o motte
imasu ka?* (いくらかお金を持っています
か) Do you have *some* money with
you? / *Kanojo wa* ikura ka *Nihoñgo ga hanasemasu.* (彼女はいくらか
日本語が話せます) She can speak
Japanese *after a fashion*. / *Anata
mo* ikura ka *warui.* (あなたもいくらか
悪い) You too are *somewhat* to
blame. 《⇨ ikubuñ》

i⌐**kusaki** いくさき（行く先）*n.* destination. 《⇨ yukusaki》

i⌐**kutsu** いくつ（幾つ）*adv.* **1** (of a
number, age) how many; how
old:
Kago ni riñgo wa ikutsu *arimasu
ka?* (かごにりんごはいくつありますか)
How many apples are there in the
basket? / *Kono ko wa* ikutsu *desu*

ka? (この子はいくつですか) *How old* is
this child?
2 (〜 ka) some; (〜 mo) a lot of:
*Kono hoñyaku ni wa ikutsu ka
[ikutsu mo] machigai ga aru.* (この
翻訳にはいくつか[いくつも]間違いがある)
There are *some* [*a lot of*] mistakes
in this translation.
ikutsu de mo (〜でも) as many as
(you like); any number:
*Ikutsu de mo, suki na dake totte
kudasai.* (いくつでも、好きなだけ取って
ください) Please take just *as many*
as you wish.
i¹ma¹ いま（今）*n.* now; at present; at the moment:
Ima nañ-ji desu ka? (今何時ですか)
What is the time *now*? / *Ima kara
de mo osoku arimaseñ ka?* (今から
でも遅くありませんか) Is it not too
late *now*? / *Ima no shushoo wa
dare desu ka?* (今の首相はだれですか)
Who is the *current* prime minister? / *Kare wa ima mo soko ni
suñde imasu.* (彼は今もそこに住んでい
ます) He is *still* living there.
— *adv.* **1** at once; right [just]
now:
Ima (sugu) ikimasu. (今(すぐ)行きま
す) I am coming (right) *now.* /
*Ima kono shorui ni kinyuu shite
kudasai.* (今この書類に記入してくださ
い) Please fill out these forms
right now. / *Kare wa ima kaette
kimashita.* (彼は今帰って来ました)
He has *just* come back.
2 more:
Ima shibaraku matte kudasai. (今
しばらく待ってください) Please wait a
little *longer.* / *Ima ik-kai yatte
mimashoo.* (今一回やってみましょう)
Let us try doing it once *more.*
i¹ma¹² いま（居間）*n.* living room;
sitting room:
O-kyaku o ima ni tooshita. (お客を
居間に通した) I showed the visitor
into the *living room.*
i¹magoro いまごろ（今頃）*n.*

now; (about) this time:
*Kyoneñ no imagoro wa motto sa-
mukatta.* (去年の今ごろはもっと寒かっ
た) It was colder *this time* last
year. / *Kare ga notta hikooki wa
imagoro doko o toñde iru ka shira?* (彼が乗った飛行機は今ごろどこを飛
んでいるかしら) I wonder where the
plane he boarded is *now* flying. /
*Kanojo wa imagoro ni natte, ika-
nai to iidashita.* (彼女は今ごろになっ
て、行かないと言い出した) *At this
stage* she has announced that she
is not going.
i¹ma ma¹de いままで（今迄）*adv.*
(〜 no) until now; so far:
*Ima made, doko e itte ita ñ desu
ka?* (今まで、どこへ行っていたんですか)
Where have you been *until now*?
/ *Ima made hoñ o yoñde imashita.*
(今まで本を読んでいました) I have
been reading *up to now.* / *Ima made no tokoro ijoo arimaseñ.* (今まで
のところ異常ありません) *So far* everything is normal. / *Ima made (ni)
Hokkaidoo e itta koto wa arimaseñ.* (今まで(に)北海道へ行ったことはあ
りません) *Up to now* I have never
been to Hokkaido. / *Koñna ni
ooki-na inu wa ima made mita
koto ga arimaseñ.* (こんなに大きな犬
は今まで見たことがありません) *Until
now* I have never seen such a
large dog.
i¹ma ni いまに（今に）*adv.* soon;
before long:
*Ima ni anata mo Nihoñgo ga hana-
seru yoo ni narimasu yo.* (今にあなた
も日本語が話せるようになりますよ) *Be-
fore long* you too will be able to
speak Japanese. / *Koñna koto o
shite iru to ima ni komatta koto ni
narimasu yo.* (こんなことをしていると今
に困ったことになりますよ) If you do
this kind of thing, you will *soon*
get into trouble. / *Ima ni mite ite
kudasai.* (今に見ていてください) *One
of these days* I'll show you.

i⌐ma ni mo いまにも（今にも）*adv.*
at any moment; be ready to:
Ima ni mo *ame ga furi-soo da.* (今
にも雨が降りそうだ) It looks as if it
will rain *at any moment.*

i⌐masara いまさら（今更）*adv.*
1 (with a negative) now; after so
long; at this late stage:
Imasara, *iya to wa ienai.* (いまさら,
いやとは言えない) I can't say no *at
this stage.* / Imasara, *kookai shite
mo hajimaranai.* (いまさら, 後悔しても
始まらない) It is too late *now* to feel
regret.
2 (with a negative) again:
Imasara *iu made mo nai ga, ashita
wa chikoku shinai yoo ni.* (いまさら
言うまでもないが, あしたは遅刻しないよう
に) It is hardly necessary to tell
you *again,* but make sure that
tomorrow you are not late.

i⌐meeji イメージ *n.* image; picture; impression:
'Nihoñ' *to kiite doñna* imeeji *ga
ukabimasu ka?* (「日本」と聞いてどん
なイメージが浮かびますか) What *image*
comes to mind when you hear
the word 'Japan'? / *Sono jikeñ
wa kaisha no* imeeji *o kizutsuketa.*
(その事件は会社のイメージを傷つけた)
The incident hurt the *image* of
the company.

i⌐meeji-a⌐ppu イメージアップ *n.*
improving one's image:
*Chiimu no yuushoo wa sono gak-
koo no* imeeji-appu *ni natta.* (チーム
の優勝はその学校のイメージアップになっ
た) The victory of the team was a
boost to the image of the school. /
Sono kaisha wa imeeji-appu *o
hakatte iru.* (その会社はイメージアップ
をはかっている) The company is
striving to create a *better image.*
imeeji-appu (**o**) **suru** (〜(を)する)
vi. improve one's image: *Sono
daigaku wa* imeeji-appu suru
tame ni namae o kaeta. (その大学は
イメージアップするために名前を変えた)

That university changed its
name to *project a better image.*
《↔ imeeji-dauñ》

i⌐meeji-che⌐ñji イメージチェンジ *n.*
changing one's image:
Sono mise wa imeeji-cheñji *o
hakatte iru.* (その店はイメージチェンジを
はかっている) The store is striving
to *change its image.*
imeeji-cheñji (**o**) **suru** (〜(を)する)
vi. change one's image: *Kanojo
wa* imeeji-cheñji o suru *tame ni
kamigata o kaeta.* (彼女はイメージチ
ェンジをするために髪形を変えた) She
changed her hairstyle to *give herself a new look.*

i⌐meeji-da⌐uñ イメージダウン *n.*
damaging one's image:
Kono kookoku wa kaisha no
imeeji-dauñ *ni naru.* (この広告は会
社のイメージダウンになる) This adver-
tisement will *harm the image* of
the company.
imeeji-dauñ (**o**) **suru** (〜(を)する)
vi. damage one's image: *Fusee
jikeñ de sono giñkoo wa* imeeji-
dauñ shita. (不正事件でその銀行はイ
メージダウンした) Because of the scandal, the *reputation* of the bank
was damaged. 《⇨ imeeji-appu》

i⌐mi いみ（意味）*n.* **1** meaning;
sense:
Kono tañgo no imi *o oshiete kudasai.* (この単語の意味を教えてください)
Will you please tell me the
meaning of this word? / *Kono go
ni wa iroiro na* imi *ga arimasu.* (こ
の語にはいろいろな意味があります) This
word has a variety of *senses.*
2 implication:
Kono go ni warui imi *wa arimaseñ.* (この語に悪い意味はありません)
This word has no bad *implica-
tions.*
3 significance:
Kare no shite iru koto wa imi *ga
arimasu.* (彼のしていることは意味があり
ます) What he is doing has *signifi-

cance. / *Soñna koto o shite mo* imi
ga arimaseñ.（そんなことをしても意味
がありません）Even if you do something like that, it will have no *effect.*

imi suru（～する）*vt.* mean; imply: *Kono hyooshiki wa nani o*
imi shite iru *ñ desu ka?*（この標識は
何を意味しているんですか）What does
this sign *stand for*? / *Kare-ra no
chiñmoku wa nani o* imi suru *no
daroo ka?*（彼らの沈黙は何を意味する
のだろうか）I wonder what their
silence *implies.*

i⌐**miñ**　いみん（移民）*n.* **1** emigration; immigration.
2 emigrant; immigrant:
imiñ suru（～する）*vi.* emigrate;
immigrate: *Kare no ikka wa Ka-
nada e* imiñ suru *kyoka o moratta.*
（彼の一家はカナダへ移民する許可をもら
った）His family received permission to *emigrate* to Canada.

i⌐**mo**⌐　いも（芋）*n.* potato; sweet
potato; taro.

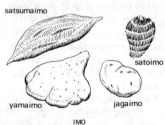

satsumaimo

satoimo

yamaimo　　jagaimo

IMO

i⌐**mooto**　いもうと（妹）*n.* one's
younger sister: ★ When referring to someone else's sister,
'*imooto-sañ*' is usually used.
Imooto-sañ *wa nani o shite imasu
ka?*（妹さんは何をしていますか）What
does your *younger sister* do? /
Imooto *wa giñkoo ni tsutomete
imasu.*（妹は銀行に勤めています）My
younger sister works for a bank.
《↔ ane》《⇨ kazoku (table)》

-⌐**iñ**　いん（員）*suf.* person in
charge; member:

eki-iñ（駅員）a station *employee* /
kaisha-iñ（会社員）a company
worker / *kakari*-iñ（係員）an *official* in charge.

i⌐**na**　いな（否）*n.* (*formal*) no; nay:
Watashi no teeañ ni kare wa ina
to kotaeta.（私の提案に彼は否と答え
た）He said *no* to my proposal. /
Iku no ka ina *ka hakkiri kotae
nasai.*（行くのか否かはっきり答なさい）
Answer me definitely whether
you are going or *not.*

...ya ina ya（...や否や）as soon as;
hardly...when: *Kodomo-tachi wa
watashi o miru* ya ina ya *nigedashita.*（子どもたちは私を見るや否や逃げ
出した）*The moment* the children
saw me, they ran away.《⇨ ka²》

-i⌐**nai**　-いない（以内）*suf.* within;
in:
Paatii no yosañ wa goseñ-eñ-inai
desu.（パーティーの予算は5千円以内
です）The budget for the party is
within 5,000 yen. / *Hoñ wa ni-
shuukañ*-inai *ni kaeshite kudasai.*
（本は2週間以内に返してください）
Please return the book *in* two
weeks. / *Kare no seeseki wa itsu-
mo juu-bañ*-inai *desu.*（彼の成績は
いつも10番以内です）His grades
always put him *in* the top ten in
the class.

―――――（USAGE）―――――
'*-inai*' includes the preceding
number, so, strictly speaking,
'*hyaku-eñ-inai*' means '100 yen
or less than 100 yen.'
――――――――――――――――

i⌐**naka**　いなか（田舎）*n.* **1** the
country; the countryside:
Iñtai shitara, ato wa inaka *de kurashitai.*（引退したら、後は田舎で暮らし
たい）When I retire, I want to live
in *the country.* / *Watashi wa*
inaka *no seekatsu ga suki da.*（私
は田舎の生活が好きだ）I like the
rural life.
2 one's home; one's hometown:

Ryooshiñ wa inaka *ni suñde ima-su.*（両親は田舎に住んでいます）My parents live in our *hometown.* / *Watashi no* inaka *wa Aomori desu.*（私の田舎は青森です）My *home* is in Aomori. （⇨ chihoo）

i**ˈnariˈzushi** いなりずし（稲荷鮨）*n.* vinegared rice ball stuffed into a bag of fried bean curd. ★ The fried bean curd was named '*inari*' in the belief that it was the favorite food of foxes, considered to be messengers of the deity '*O-inarisañ.*'

INARIZUSHI

i**ˈnazuma** いなずま（稲妻）*n.* lightning.

i**ˈñboo** いんぼう（陰謀）*n.* plot; intrigue; conspiracy:
Kare-ra wa kodomo o yuukai suru iñboo *o kuwadateta.*（彼らは子どもを誘拐する陰謀を企てた）They hatched a *plot* to kidnap a child.

i**ˈñchiki** いんちき *n.* (*colloq.*) fake; fraud; forgery:
Iñchiki *o suru na yo.*（いんちきをするなよ）Don't *cheat.*
— *a.n.* (~ na, ni) fake; fraudulent; bogus:
Kono shorui wa iñchiki *da.*（この書類はいんちきだ）These documents are *forgeries.* / *Kare-ra wa* iñchiki *na shoobai de kane o mooketa.*（彼らはいんちきな商売で金をもうけた）They made money in a *fraudulent* business.

I**ˈñdo** インド *n.* India.

I**ˈñdoˈjiñ** インド人 *n.* an Indian.

I**ˈñdoneˈsia** インドネシア *n.* Indonesia.

I**ˈñdonesiaˈjiñ** インドネシア人 *n.* an Indonesian.

i**ˈne** いね（稲）*n.* rice plant:
ine *o karu*（稲を刈る）reap *rice* / Ine *wa atatakai chihoo de dekiru.*（稲は暖かい地方でできる）*Rice* grows in warm regions. （⇨ kome (table)）

i**ˈñfure** インフレ *n.* inflation. （↔ defure）

i**ˈñkañ** いんかん（印鑑）*n.* personal seal; stamp:
shorui ni iñkañ *o osu*（書類に印鑑を押す）put one's *seal* to a document / iñkañ-*shoomee*（印鑑証明）proof of *seal* design and ownership.

> **USAGE**
> In Japan, an '*iñkañ*' has legal force and is used instead of a signature on formal or legal documents, including bankbooks.

SHORUI NI IÑKAÑ O OSU

i**ˈñki** インキ *n.* = iñku.

i**ˈñku** インク *n.* ink:
iñku *de kaku*（インクで書く）write in *ink* / *Kono mañneñhitsu wa* iñku *ga kirete iru.*（この万年筆はインクが切れている）This fountain pen has no *ink* left in it.

i**ˈñmetsu** いんめつ（隠滅）*n.* destruction; disappearance.
iñmetsu suru (~ する) *vt.* destroy: *shooko o* iñmetsu suru（証拠を隠滅する）*destroy* evidence.

i**ˈnochi** いのち（命）*n.* life:
Inochi *o taisetsu ni shiyoo.*（命を大

切にしよう) We should value *life*. /
Sono jiko de shichi-niñ ga inochi
o ushinatta. (その事故で7人が命を失
った) Seven people lost their *lives*
in that accident.

inochi-gake de (〜がけで) at the
risk of one's life: *Kare wa* inochi-gake de *sono ko o sukutta.* (彼
は命がけでその子を救った) He saved
the child *at the risk of his life*.

inochi-karagara (〜からがら) for
one's life: *Watashi wa* inochi-
karagara *nigeta.* (私は命からがら逃げ
た) I ran *for dear life*.

i⌈noko⌉r·u いのこる (居残る) *vi.*
(inokor·i-; inokor·a-; inokot-te
Ⓒ) stay; remain; work overtime:
Kare wa sono ba ni inokotte, *nimotsu no bañ o shita.* (彼はその場に
居残って、荷物の番をした) He *re-
mained* there to look after the
baggage. / *Koñshuu wa isogashikute, yoku* inokotta. (今週は忙しくて、
よく居残った) This week I was so
busy that I often *stayed late* at
the office.

i⌈nori⌉ いのり (祈り) *n.* prayer;
grace:
kami ni inori *o sasageru* (神に祈り
を捧げる) offer *prayers* to God.
((⇨ inoru))

i⌈no⌉r·u いのる (祈る) *vi., vt.* (ino-
r·i-; inor·a-; inot-te Ⓒ) pray;
wish:
*Watashi wa Kitano Teñmañguu
ni omairi o shite, gookaku o*
inotta. (私は北野天満宮にお参りをして、
合格を祈った) I visited the Kitano
Shrine and *prayed* that I would
pass the entrance examinations. /
Koouñ [Seekoo] o inorimasu. (幸運
[成功]を祈ります) I *wish* you good
luck [success]. / *Ichi-nichi mo
hayai zeñkai o* inorimasu. (一日も
早い全快を祈ります) I *hope* you will
recover soon. ((⇨ inori))

i⌈ñryoku いんりょく (引力) *n.* gravi-

tation.

i⌈ñryo⌉osui いんりょうすい (飲料水)
n. drinking water.

i⌈ñsatsu いんさつ (印刷) *n.* printing; print; press:
Kono geñkoo o iñsatsu *ni mawashite kudasai.* (この原稿を印刷に回し
てください) Please send in this
manuscript for *printing*.

iñsatsu suru (〜する) *vt.* print;
put into print: *Kono hoñ wa
Nihoñ de* iñsatsu shita *mono desu.*
(この本は日本で印刷したものです) This
book is one which *was printed* in
Japan.

i⌈ñsatsu⌉butsu いんさつぶつ (印刷
物) *n.* printed matter:
Iñsatsubutsu *zaichuu.* (*on an envelope*) (印刷物在中) *Printed Matter*.

i⌈ñshi いんし (印紙) *n.* = shuunyuu-
iñshi.

i⌈ñshoo いんしょう (印象) *n.* impression:
Kanojo no dai-ichi iñshoo *wa doo
deshita?* (彼女の第一印象はどうでし
た) What was your first *impression of* her? / *Kare wa miñna ni
yoi* iñshoo *o ataeta.* (彼はみんなに良
い印象を与えた) He made a good
impression on everybody.

i⌈ñshoo-teki いんしょうてき (印象
的) *a.n.* (〜 na, ni) impressive:
Kare wa totemo iñshoo-teki *na
hito deshita.* (彼はとても印象的な人で
した) He was a very *impressive* person. / *Sono bameñ wa hijoo ni*
iñshoo-teki *datta.* (その場面は非常に
印象的だった) The scene was very
impressive.

iñ⌈sutañto ra⌉ameñ インスタント
ラーメン *n.* instant Chinese noodles. ((⇨ raameñ))
((⇨ photo (next page)))

i⌈ñteri インテリ *n.* intellectual;
the intelligentsia.

i⌈ñtone⌉eshoñ イントネーション *n.*
intonation.

i⌈nu⌉ いぬ (犬) *n.* dog:

INSUTAÑTO RAAMEÑ

inu *o kau* (犬を飼う) keep a *dog* /
Sono inu *wa watashi o mite, hoeta.*
(その犬は私を見て、ほえた) The *dog*
saw me and barked. 《⇨ **bañkeñ**》

i｢**nugoya** いぬごや(犬小屋) *n.*
doghouse; kennel.

i｢**ñyoo** いんよう(引用) *n.* quotation; citation:
*Kono ichi-gyoo wa Sheekusupia
kara no* iñyoo *desu.* (この一行はシェ
ークスピアからの引用です) This line is
a *quotation* from Shakespeare.

iñyoo suru (〜する) *vt.* quote;
cite: *Kare wa ree o shiñbuñ kara*
iñyoo *shita.* (彼は例を新聞から引用し
た) He *quoted* the example from a
newspaper. / *Kanojo wa yoku Seesho o* iñyoo *suru.* (彼女はよく聖書を
引用する) She often *cites* the Bible.

i｢**ppai**[1] いっぱい(一杯) *n.* **1** a cup
[glass; bowl]:
Koohii o ippai *ikaga desu ka?* (コ
ーヒーを一杯いかがですか) What about
a cup of coffee? / *Atsui hi no*
ippai *no biiru wa oishii.* (暑い日の
一杯のビールはおいしい) *A glass* of
beer on a hot day tastes wonderful. 《⇨ **-hai**》
2 (having) a drink:
Kaeri ni ippai *yarimaseñ ka?* (帰り
に一杯やりませんか) Won't you have
a drink on the way back? / *Biiru
o* ippai *yari-nagara hanashi o shimashoo.* (ビールを一杯やりながら話をし
ましょう) Let's have a talk over *a
beer.*

ippai kuwasu (〜食わす) deceive;
cheat: *Kare ni* ippai kuwasareta.
(彼にいっぱい食わされた) I *was taken
in* by him.

i｢**ppai**[2] いっぱい *a.n.* (〜 na/no, ni)
be full; be filled; be crowded:
Depaato wa hito de ippai *datta.* (デ
パートは人でいっぱいだった) The de-
partment store was *crowded* with
people. / *Moo onaka ga* ippai *de,
taberaremaseñ.* (もうおなかがいっぱいで、
食べられません) I am already *full* so
I cannot eat any more. / *Kanojo
wa ureshisa de, mune ga* ippai
datta. (彼女はうれしさで、胸がいっぱいだ
った) Her heart was *filled* with
joy. / *Kare wa o-kane o* ippai
motte iru. (彼はお金をいっぱい持ってい
る) He has *heaps of* money. / *Iitai
koto wa* ippai *arimasu.* (言いたいこ
とはいっぱいあります) There is *a lot*
that I want to say.

i｢**ppai**[3] いっぱい *adv.* until (the
end of):
Kono shigoto wa koñgetsu ippai
kakarimasu. (この仕事は今月いっぱい
かかります) This job will take *until
the end of* this month. / *Sono
moñdai o toku no ni jikañ* ippai
kakatta. (その問題を解くのに時間いっ
ぱいかかった) I used *all the time* to
solve the problem.

i｢**ppañ ni** いっぱんに(一般に) *adv.*
generally; in general:
*Ippañ ni Nihoñjiñ wa hataraki-
sugimasu.* (一般に日本人は働き過ぎ
ます) *Generally speaking*, Japanese
people work too much. / *Nana
wa eñgi ga ii suu to* ippañ ni *shiñ-
jirarete imasu.* (七は縁起がいい数と
一般に信じられています) It is *generally* believed that seven is a
lucky number.

i｢**ppoo**[1] いっぽう(一方) *n.* **1** one
end [side]; the other end [side]:
Kono eñpitsu wa ippoo *ga aka de
moo* ippoo *ga ao desu.* (この鉛筆は
一方が赤でもう一方が青です) *One end*

of this pencil is red and *the other end* is blue./ *Booto ga* ippoo *ni ookiku katamuita.* (ボートが一方に大きく傾いた) The boat heeled heavily to *one side.*

2 one-way:
ippoo-*tsuukoo* (一方通行) *one-way* traffic.

3 continuation:
Tochi no nedañ wa agaru ippoo *desu.* (土地の値段は上がる一方です) Land prices *continue* to rise.

i⌐ppo⌐o² いっぽう (一方) *conj.* on the other hand; while:
Shuunyuu wa fueta ga, ippoo, *isogashiku natta.* (収入は増えたが、一方、忙しくなった) My income has gone up, but, *on the other hand,* I have become busier. / *Kanojo wa isshoo-keñmee hataraite iru no ni,* ippoo *kare wa namakete ita.* (彼女は一生懸命働いているのに、一方彼は怠けていた) She was working really hard, *while* he was lazing around.

i⌐rai いらい (依頼) *n.* **1** request:
hito no irai *ni oojiru* (人の依頼に応じる) respond to a person's *request* / *hito no* irai *o kotowaru* (人の依頼を断る) decline a person's *request.*

2 dependence; reliance:
Kanojo wa irai-*shiñ ga tsuyoi.* (彼女は依頼心が強い) She *relies too much* on other people.

irai suru (～する) *vt.* ask; request:
Sono kaisha ni shijoo-choosa o irai *shita.* (その会社に市場調査を依頼した) We *asked* the company to make a market survey.

-i⌐rai いらい (以来) *suf.* since; after:
*Sotsugyoo-*irai *kare to wa atte imaseñ.* (卒業以来彼とは会っていません) I have not seen him *since* graduation. / *Kishoochoo kaisetsu-*irai *no ooyuki ga futta.* (気象庁開設以来の大雪が降った) We had the heaviest snowfall *since* the establishment of the Meteorologi-

cal Agency.

i⌐raini̅ñ いらいにん (依頼人) *n.* client. (⇨ kyaku)

i⌐raira いらいら *adv.* (～ suru) (the state of being impatient [nervous]):
Kare o matte mo konai no de iraira *shite kita.* (彼を待っても来ないのでいらいらしてきた) I waited for him but he did not come, so I got *impatient.* / *Ano hito no buree na taido ni wa* iraira *suru.* (あの人の無礼な態度にはいらいらする) His rude manner *irritates* me.

I⌐raku イラク *n.* Iraq.

Ir⌐aku⌐jiñ イラク人 *n.* an Iraqi.

i⌐rassha⌐i (いらっしゃい) = irasshaimase.

i⌐rasshaima⌐se いらっしゃいませ
1 (to a visitor) welcome:
Irasshaimase. *Doozo o-hairi kudasai.* (いらっしゃいませ。どうぞお入りください) *Welcome.* Please come in.

2 (to a customer at a store) welcome:
Irasshaimase. *Nani o o-sagashi desu ka?* (いらっしゃいませ。何をお探しですか) *Welcome.* Is there something you are looking for?

┌─────── USAGE ───────┐
Store clerks and restaurant employees often shout out '*Irasshaimase*' (less formal '*Irasshai*') to greet their customers, but it is usually not necessary to reply to them.
└─────────────────────┘

i⌐rassha⌐r·u いらっしゃる *vi.* (irassha·i-; irasshar·a-; irasshat-te Ⓒ) ★ Honorific form of '*kuru, iku, iru.*' The *te*-form is often pronounced '*irashite.*'
1 come:
Yoku irasshaimashita. (よくいらっしゃいました) I am glad you *have come.* / *Mata kochira ni* irasshai. (またこちらにいらっしゃい) Please *come* again.

2 go:
Kyooto e wa itsu itsu irasshaimasu ka? (京都へはいついらっしゃいますか) When *are* you *going* to Kyoto?
3 be; be present:
Señsee wa ima irasshaimasu ka? (先生は今いらっしゃいますか) Is the teacher *in* now? / *Itsu-mo waka-kute irasshaimasu ne.* (いつも若くていらっしゃいますね) You *are* as young as ever.

iˈrechigai ni いれちがいに (入れ違いに) *adv.* passing [crossing] each other:
Anata to irechigai ni Tanaka-sañ ga miemashita. (あなたと入れ違いに田中さんが見えました) *Just as you went out*, Miss Tanaka came to see you.

iˈreˈesai いれいさい (慰霊祭) *n.* memorial service.

iˈrekaeˈ·ru いれかえる (入れ替える) *vt.* (-kae-te Ⅴ) **1** replace; substitute; change:
señshu o irekaeru (選手を入れ替える) *change* players / *Terebi o atarashii no ni irekaeta.* (テレビを新しいのに入れ替えた) I *replaced* the television with a new one. (⇨ irekawaru)
2 refresh:
kuuki o irekaeru (空気を入れ替える) *change* the air (of a room) / *o-cha o irekaeru* (お茶を入れ替える) *make fresh* tea.

iˈrekawaˈr·u いれかわる (入れ代わる) *vi.* (-kawar·i-; -kawar·a-; -kawat-te Ⓒ) be replaced; change:
Kaichoo ga irekawatta. (会長が入れ代わった) The company chairman *was replaced.* / *Watashi wa kare to seki o irekawatta.* (私は彼と席を入れ代わった) I *changed* seats with him. (⇨ irekaeru)

iˈremono いれもの (入れ物) *n.* container; vessel:
Kono chiizu no iremono wa doko

desu ka? (このチーズの入れ物はどこですか) Where is the *container* for this cheese? / *Wain o tooki no iremono ni ireta.* (ワインを陶器の入れ物に入れた) I put the wine in an earthenware *vessel*.

iˈre·ru いれる (入れる) *vt.* (ire-te Ⅴ) **1** put in [into]; pour; fill:
koohii ni satoo o ireru (コーヒーに砂糖を入れる) *put* sugar into coffee / *kuruma ni gasoriñ o ireru* (車にガソリンを入れる) *put* gas in a car / *O-kane wa kiñko ni iremashita.* (お金は金庫に入れました) I *put* the money in a safe. / *Poketto ni te o ireta mama, hanasu no wa shitsuree desu.* (ポケットに手を入れたまま, 話すのは失礼です) It is rude to talk *with* your hands *in* your pockets.
2 insert; enclose:
Sono go no ato ni tooteñ o ire nasai. (その語のあとに読点を入れなさい) *Put* a period after that word. / *Tegami ni shashiñ o ireta.* (手紙に写真を入れた) I *enclosed* some photos with the letter.
3 let in:
Sono ko o naka ni irete yari nasai. (その子を中に入れてやりなさい) *Let* that child *in.* / *Mado o akete shiñseñ na kuuki o ireta.* (窓を開けて新鮮な空気を入れた) I opened the windows and *let in* some fresh air.
4 send (a person to school, an organization, etc.):
Kare wa musuko o gaikoku no daigaku ni ireta. (彼は息子を外国の大学に入れた) He *sent* his son to a university overseas.
5 include:
Tesuuryoo o irete, goseñ-eñ ni narimasu. (手数料を入れて, 5 千円になります) It comes to 5,000 yen, *including* commission. / *Nakama ni irete kudasai.* (仲間に入れてください) Please *include* me in your group.
6 admit:
Keganiñ wa chikaku no byooiñ ni

irerareta. (けが人は近くの病院に入れられた) The injured *were admitted* to a nearby hospital. / *Sono kai no meñbaa ni* irete moratta. (その会のメンバーに入れてもらった) I *was admitted* as a member of the society.

7 accept (a demand, request, etc.): *Kaisha-gawa wa kumiai no yookyuu o* ireta. (会社側は組合の要求を入れた) The management *accepted* the union's demands.

8 switch on: *terebi no suitchi o* ireru (テレビのスイッチを入れる) *switch on* the television.

i⌐riguchi いりぐち (入り口) *n.* entrance; way in; doorway: Iriguchi *kara haitte kudasai*. (入り口から入ってください) Please come in by the *entrance*. / Iriguchi *ga wakarimaseñ*. (入り口がわかりません) I can't find my *way in*. / Iriguchi *o fusaganai de kudasai*. (入り口をふさがないでください) Don't block the *doorway*. ((↔ deguchi))

i⌐rita⌐mago いりたまご (炒り卵) *n.* scrambled eggs.

i⌐ro⌐ いろ (色) *n.* **1** color; tint: *hade [jimi] na* iro (派手[じみ]な色) a loud [quiet] *color* / *Kare no me no* iro *wa kuro desu*. (彼の目の色は黒です) The *color* of his eyes is black. / *Kimi no kuruma wa nani* iro *desu ka?* (君の車は何色ですか) What *color* is your car? / *Moo sukoshi* iro *no usui [koi] mono o kudasai*. (もう少し色の薄い[濃い]ものを下さい) Please give me one of a lighter [deeper] *color*.

2 complexion: *Kanojo wa* iro *ga shiroi*. (彼女は色が白い) She has a fair *complexion*. / *Sono shirase ni kare wa* iro *o ushinatta*. (その知らせに彼は色を失った) The *color* drained from his face at the news.

3 sensual pleasures; love affair; lover: *Eeyuu,* iro *o konomu*. (*saying*) (英雄、色を好む) Heroes *are amorous*.

iro o tsukeru (〜をつける) add a little something extra: *Yoku yatte kureta no de, señ-eñ bakari* iro *o tsukete haraimashoo*. (よくやってくれたので、千円ばかり色をつけて払いましょう) Since you have done a good job, I will pay you 1,000 yen *extra*.

i⌐roiro[1] いろいろ (色々) *n.* variety: *choo no* iroiro (蝶のいろいろ) a *variety* of butterflies.

— *a.n.* (〜 na, ni) various; all kinds of: ★ '*Iroiro na*' is often pronounced '*iroñna*' in informal speech.
iroiro *na shurui* (いろいろな種類) *various* kinds / *Depaato de wa* iroiro *na mono o utte imasu*. (デパートではいろいろな物を売っています) They sell *all kinds of* things at department stores. / Iroiro *na kuni kara señshu ga atsumarimashita*. (いろいろな国から選手が集まりました) The players came from *many different* countries. / *Hito ni yotte kañgae-kata mo* iroiro *desu*. (人によって考え方もいろいろです) Ways of thinking *vary* from person to person. / *Kono shoosetsu wa* iroiro *ni kaishaku dekimasu*. (この小説はいろいろに解釈できます) One can interpret this novel in *various ways*.

i⌐roiro[2] いろいろ (色々) *adv.* (〜 to) variously; differently; all kinds of:
Iroiro *kufuu shite mite kudasai*. (いろいろ工夫してみてください) Please try *various ways* of doing it. / Iroiro *(to) kañgaete mimashita ga, ii añ ga ukabimaseñ*. (いろいろ(と)考えてみましたが、いい案が浮かびません) I have tried thinking about it *in different ways*, but no good ideas occur to me. / *Muzukashii moñdai ga* iroiro *(to) arimasu*. (むずかしい問

題がいろいろ(と)あります) There are *all kinds of* difficult problems. / Iroiro (*to*) *arigatoo gozaimashita.* (いろいろ(と)ありがとうございました) Thank you for *everything*.

i⌐**rojiro** いろじろ(色白) *a.n.* (~ na/no) fair-complexioned: *irojiro no bijiñ* (色白の美人) a *fair-skinned* beauty.

i⌐**roñna** いろんな *attrib.* (*informal*) = iroiro¹.

i・⌐**ru**¹ いる(居る) *vi.* (i-te Ⓥ)
1 (of a person, animal) be; there is [are]; exist:

──── **USAGE** ────
When the subject is animate (a person or animal), '*iru*' is used, while '*aru*' is used to indicate the existence of something inanimate (a thing or plant).
─────────────────

Kare wa niwa ni imasu. (彼は庭にいます) He *is* in the garden. / *Tsukue no shita ni neko ga iru.* (机の下に猫がいる) There *is* a cat under the desk. / *Kono kawa ni wa sakana wa imaseñ.* (この川には魚はいません) There *are no* fish in this river. / *Watashi wa ima hoteru ni imasu.* (私は今ホテルにいます) I *am* now *staying* at a hotel.
2 have:
Watashi ni wa ani ga hitori imasu. (私には兄が一人います) I *have* one older brother. / *Oosaka ni oba ga imasu.* (大阪におばがいます) I *have* an aunt in Osaka.
3 live:
Ryooshiñ wa Hokkaidoo ni imasu. (両親は北海道にいます) My parents *live* in Hokkaido. / *Ano hito wa moo Nihoñ ni sañ-neñ imasu.* (あの人はもう日本に3年います) He *has* already *been* in Japan for three years.
4 be present:
Anata ga ite kuretara, tasukarimasu. (あなたがいてくれたら、助かります)

Your *presence* will be of great help to us.
-te [de] iru (て[で]~)

──── **USAGE** ────
Follows to the *te*-form of a verb, it indicates a continuing action, the state of being engaged in something, or a resulting state.
─────────────────

Chichi wa shiñbuñ o yoñde imasu. (父は新聞を読んでいます) My father *is reading* the newspaper. / *Kanojo wa gakkoo de Nihoñgo o oshiete imasu.* (彼女は学校で日本語を教えています) She *teaches* Japanese at a school. / *Mado ga hiraite ita.* (窓が開けていた) The window *was open*. / *Yuki ga tsumotte ita.* (雪が積もっていた) The snow *lay deep*.

i⌐**r・u**² いる(要る) *vi.* (ir・i-; ir・a-; it-te Ⓒ) need; want; be necessary:
Nani-ka iru mono ga arimasu ka? (何か要るものがありますか) Is there anything you *need*? / *Kono shorui ni wa iñkañ ga irimasu.* (この書類には印鑑が要ります) Your seal *is necessary* on this document. / *Kono hoñ wa moo irimaseñ.* (この本はもう要りません) I *no longer need* this book.

i⌐**r・u**³ いる(煎る) *vt.* (ir・i-; ir・a-; it-te Ⓒ) roast; parch:
Kono mame o kogasanai yoo ni itte kudasai. (この豆をこがさないようにいってください) Please *roast* these beans without scorching them.

i⌐**r・u**⁴ いる(射る) *vt.* (i-te Ⓥ) shoot; hit:
ya o iru (矢を射る) *shoot* an arrow.

i⌐**r・u**⁵ いる(入る) *vi.* (ir・i-; ir・a-; it-te Ⓒ) **1** go in; set:
hibi ga iru (ひびが入る) *be cracked* / *Hi wa nishi ni iru.* (日は西に入る) The sun *sets* in the west.
((⇒ hairu))
2 (used for emphasis): ★ Follows the continuative base of a

verb.
naki iru (泣き入る) weep *bitterly* /
Osore irimashita. (恐れ入りました) I
am *very much* obliged to you.

i⌐**rui** いるい (衣類) *n.* clothing;
clothes; garments:
Watashi-tachi wa higaisha ni irui
o okutta. (私たちは被害者に衣類を送
った) We sent *clothes* to the victims.

i⌐**ryoo**[1] いりょう (医療) *n.* medical
treatment:
iryoo-*hi* (医療費) *medical* expenses.

i⌐**ryoo**[2] いりょう (衣料) *n.* clothing; clothes:
iryoo-*hi* (衣料費) *clothing* expenses.

iryoohiñ いりょうひん (衣料品) *n.*
articles of clothing:
iryoohiñ-*teñ* (衣料品店) a *clothing*
store.

i⌐**samashi**⌐**i** いさましい (勇ましい) *a.*
(-ku) brave; courageous:
isamashiku *tatakau* (勇ましく戦う)
fight *bravely* / *Shiyakusho ni
hitori de koogi ni iku to wa* isama-
shii. (市役所にひとりで抗議に行くとは
勇ましい) It is *brave* of him to go
alone to the city hall to make a
protest.

i⌐**see**[1] いせい (異性) *n.* the opposite [other] sex.

i⌐**see**[2] いせい (威勢) *n.* spirits:
Ryooshi-tachi wa isee *ga ii.* (漁師
たちは威勢がいい) The fishermen are
high-spirited. / *Kare-ra wa* isee
yoku, shuppatsu shita. (彼らは威勢
よく、出発した) They set out *in
high spirits.*

i⌐**sha** いしゃ (医者) *n.* doctor;
physician:
isha *ni mite morau* (医者に診てもら
う) consult a *doctor* / isha *o yobu*
(医者を呼ぶ) send for a *doctor* /
isha *no teate o ukeru* (医者の手当を
受ける) be treated by a *doctor*.

i⌐**shi**[1] いし (石) *n.* stone; rock;

pebble:
Kare-ra wa keekañ ni ishi *o nageta.* (彼らは警官に石を投げた) They
threw *rocks* at the policemen.

ishi ni kajiritsuite mo (〜にかじり
ついても) at any cost; by all means:
Ishi ni kajiritsuite mo *kono keekaku wa yaritogemasu.* (石にかじり
ついてもこの計画はやりとげます) I'll
carry this plan through, *no matter what.*

i⌐**shi**[2] いし (意志) *n.* will:
Kare wa ishi *ga tsuyoi* [yowai].
(彼は意志が強い[弱い]) He is a man
of strong [weak] *will.* / *Watashi
wa jibuñ no* ishi *de sono moo-
shide o kotowatta.* (私は自分の意志
でその申し出を断った) I turned down
the offer of my own free *will.*

i⌐**shi**[3] いし (意思) *n.* intention:
jibuñ no ishi *o noberu* (自分の意思
を述べる) state one's *intention* /
Soko e iku ishi *wa arimaseñ.* (そこ
へ行く意思はありません) I have no
intention of going there. / *Otagai
no* ishi *ga tsuujita.* (お互いの意思が
通じた) We *understood* each other.

ishi[4] いし (医師) *n.* doctor:
ishi-*kai* (医師会) a *medical* association.

i⌐**shido**⌐**oroo** いしどうろう (石灯籠)
n. stone lantern. ★ Originally
placed to provide illumination,
but now used as an artistic
object in a Japanese garden.

ISHIDOORO

I「shikawa」-keñ いしかわけん（石川県）*n.* Ishikawa Prefecture. Located in the northwest of the Chubu district, with Japan's largest peninsula stretching into the Sea of Japan. The capital city, Kanazawa（金沢）, is the cultural center of this region and the hub of its commerce and industry. ((⇨ map (E3)))

i「shiki いしき（意識）*n.* consciousness; one's senses:
ishiki *o ushinau*（意識を失う）lose *consciousness* / ishiki *o kaifuku suru* [*torimodosu*]（意識を回復する[取り戻す]）recover *consciousness* / *Sono ko ni wa tsumi no* ishiki *ga nakatta.*（その子には罪の意識がなかった）The child had no *sense* of guilt.
ishiki suru（〜する）*vt.* be conscious [aware] of: *isee o* ishiki suru（異性を意識する）*be conscious* of the presence of the opposite sex.

i「shoku いしょく（移植）*n.* transplantation; grafting:
shiñzoo-ishoku-*shujutsu*（心臓移植手術）a heart *transplant* operation.
ishoku suru（〜する）*vt.* transplant; graft: *Watashi wa niwa ni matsu no ki o* ishoku shita.（私は庭に松の木を移植した）I *transplanted* a pine tree to my garden.

i-「shoku」-juu いしょくじゅう（衣食住）*n.* food, clothing and shelter:
Señsoo chokugo wa miñna i-shoku-juu *ni fujiyuu shimashita.*（戦争直後はみんな衣食住に不自由しました）Immediately after the war, everyone had a hard time getting *food, clothing and housing.*

i「shoo いしょう（衣装）*n.* clothes; dress; costume:
ishoo *o tsukeru*（衣装を着ける）put on *clothes* / *Hanayome no* ishoo *wa subarashikatta.*（花嫁の衣装は素晴らしかった）The bride's wedding *dress* was very beautiful.

i「sogashi」-i いそがしい（忙しい）*a.* (-ku) busy:
isogashii *hito*（忙しい人）a *busy* man / *Neñmatsu wa me ga mawaru hodo* isogashii.（年末は目が回るほど忙しい）At the end of the year I am so *busy* that I am run off my feet. / *Musuko wa jukeñ-beñkyoo de* isogashii.（息子は受験勉強で忙しい）My son is *busy* studying for the entrance exams. / *Kare wa mainichi kaisha de* isogashiku *hataraite iru.*（彼は毎日会社で忙しく働いている）He is working *busily* in his office every day.

i「soga」s·u いそがす（急がす）*vt.* (isogash·i-; isogas·a-; isogash·i-te C) hurry; hasten:
Soñna ni isogasanai *de kudasai.*（そんなに急がさないでください）*Don't hurry* me like that. / Isogashite *sumimaseñ ga, kore o ashita no asa made ni shiagete kudasai.*（急がしてすみませんが、これをあしたの朝までに仕上げてください）I don't like to *hurry* you, but would you please finish this by tomorrow morning? ((⇨ isogu))

i「so」g·u いそぐ（急ぐ）*vi.* (isog·i-; isog·a-; iso·i-de C) hurry; make haste; hasten:
Kodomo-tachi wa gakkoo e isoida.（子どもたちは学校へ急いだ）The children *hurried* to school. / Isoganai *to deñsha ni okuremasu yo.*（急がないと電車に遅れますよ）If you *don't hurry*, you'll miss the train. / *Soñna ni* isoganakute yoi.（そんなに急がなくてよい）You *don't have to rush* like that. ((⇨ isogasu))

i「ssai いっさい（一切）*n.* all; everything:
Sore ni kañsuru issai *no joohoo o kare ni oshiete yatta.*（それに関する一切の情報を彼に教えてやった）I gave him *all* the information about it.

— *adv*. (with a negative) not at all:

Watashi wa sono moñdai to issai *kañkee arimaseñ.* (私はその問題と一切関係ありません) I am *not in any way* connected with that matter. / *Sono koto ni kañshite wa* issai *zoñjimaseñ.* (そのことに関しては一切存じません) I know *nothing at all* concerning that.

i⌈**ssaku**⌉**jitsu** いっさくじつ（一昨日）*n*. the day before yesterday. ★ Formal equivalent of '*ototoi*.' 《⇨ ototoi; kyoo (table)》

i⌈**ssakuneñ** いっさくねん（一昨年）*n*. =ototoshi.

i⌈**ssee**[1] いっせい（一斉）*adv*. (~ ni) at the same time; all together; simultaneously:

Marasoñ no señshu wa issee *ni sutaato shita.* (マラソンの選手は一斉にスタートした) The competitors in the marathon started *at the same time.* / *Kañshuu wa* issee *ni hakushu shita.* (観衆は一斉に拍手した) The spectators *all together* broke into applause. / issee-*keñsa* (一斉検査) a *spot* check.

i⌈**ssee**[2] いっせい（一世）*n*. Issei; Japanese immigrant, usually to North and South American countries. 《⇨ nisee; sañsee》

i⌈**sshi**⌉**ñ** いっしん（一心）*n*. desire: *Kanojo wa haha-oya ni aitai* isshiñ *de Chuugoku kara yatte kita.* (彼女は母親に会いたい一心で中国からやって来た) She came over from China with a *strong desire* to see her mother.

i⌈**sshi**⌉**ñ ni** いっしんに（一心に）*adv*. earnestly; fervently: *Shooneñ wa* isshiñ ni *gameñ o mitsumete ita.* (少年は一心に画面を見つめていた) The boy was watching the screen *intently.* / *Kanojo wa* isshiñ ni *chichi-oya no kañbyoo o shita.* (彼女は一心に父親の看病をした) She nursed her father *with single-minded devotion.*

i⌈**ssho** いっしょ（一緒）*n*. the same: *Watashi wa shoogakkoo jidai Yamada to kurasu ga zutto* issho *datta.* (私は小学校時代山田とクラスがずっと一緒だった) I was in *the same* class as Yamada all the time I was in elementary school. / *Suzuki to Tanaka wa daigaku ni nyuugaku shita no ga* issho *da.* (鈴木と田中は大学に入学したのが一緒だ) Suzuki and Yamada entered university in *the same* year.

i⌈**ssho ni** いっしょに（一緒に）*adv*. (all) together; at the same time: Issho ni *ikimashoo.* (いっしょに行きましょう) Let's go *together.* / Issho ni *tenisu o shimaseñ ka?* (いっしょにテニスをしませんか) Won't you play tennis *with* us? / *Soñna ni takusañ no koto wa* issho ni *wa dekimaseñ.* (そんなにたくさんのことはいっしょにはできません) I cannot do that many things *at the same time.*

issho ni naru (~なる) **1** meet: *Eki de* issho ni naroo. (駅でいっしょになろう) *Let's meet* at the station. / *Kinoo, depaato de señsee to* issho ni natta. (きのう、デパートで先生といっしょになった) I *bumped* into my teacher at a department store yesterday.

2 get married: *Futari wa señgetsu* issho ni natta. (二人は先月いっしょになった) They *got married* last month.

issho ni suru (~する) put together; mix up: *Watashi no kañjoo wa kare no to* issho ni shite *kudasai.* (私の勘定は彼のといっしょにしてください) Please *put* my bill *together* with his. / *Yatsu to boku o* issho ni shinai de *kure.* (やつとぼくをいっしょにしないでくれ) Don't *lump* that fellow *together* with me.

i⌈**sshoo** いっしょう（一生）*n*. lifetime; life:

Sore wa kare no isshoo no shigoto *datta.*(それは彼の一生の仕事だっ
た) That was his *lifework.* / *Kanojo wa koofuku na* isshoo *o okutta.*
(彼女は幸福な一生を送った) She
lived a happy *life.* / *Kare wa*
isshoo *dokushiñ de sugoshita.*(彼
は一生独身で過ごした) He was a
bachelor *all his life.* / *Go-oñ wa*
isshoo *wasuremaseñ.*(ご恩は一生忘
れません) I will not forget your
kindness *as long as I live.*

i｢**sshoo-ke**｣**ñmee** いっしょうけんめ
い (一生懸命) *a.n.* (～ na, ni) very
hard; with all one's might:
*Watanabe-sañ wa ima roñbuñ o
kaku no ni* isshoo-keñmee *desu.*
(渡辺さんはいま論文を書くのに一生懸
命です) Mr. Watanabe is now
working *all out* to write his thesis. / *Kare wa* isshoo-keñmee *ni
hataraite, kane o tameta.*(彼は一生
懸命に働いて，金をためた) He worked
as hard as he could and saved
money. / Isshoo-keñmee *(ni) kañgaemashita ga mada wakarimaseñ.*(一生懸命(に)考えましたがまだわか
りません) I have thought about it
very hard, but I still do not
understand. (⇨ keñmee[2])

i｢**sshu** いっしゅ (一種) *n.* kind;
sort; variety:
Kono ki wa sakura no isshu *desu.*
(この木は桜の一種です) This tree is *a
variety* of cherry. / *Sono kañgae
wa* isshu *no heñkeñ desu.*(その考え
は一種の偏見です) That way of
thinking is *a kind* of prejudice.

isshu dokutoku (～独特) peculiar; strange: *Kanojo wa* isshu
dokutoku *no hanashikata o suru.*
(彼女は一種独特の話し方をする) She
has *a peculiar way* of talking. /
Kare no utaikata wa isshu dokutoku *desu.*(彼の歌い方は一種独特で
す) His way of singing is *unique.*

i｢**sshuñ** いっしゅん (一瞬) *n.* an instant; a moment:

Isshuñ *no fuchuui ga ooki-na jiko
o okosu koto ga arimasu.*(一瞬の不
注意が大きな事故を起こすことがありま
す) *A moment*'s carelessness can
sometimes cause a serious accident. / *Sore wa* isshuñ *no dekigoto deshita.*(それは一瞬の出来事で
した) It was something that happened in *an instant.*
— *adv.* for a moment:
Kare wa isshuñ *ishiki o ushinatta.*
(彼は一瞬意識をうしなった) He lost
consciousness *for just a moment.*

i｢**sshuu** いっしゅう (一周) *n.* one
round:
Natsu-yasumi ni Hokkaidoo
isshuu *no doraibu o shimashita.*
(夏休みに北海道一周のドライブをしまし
た) During the summer vacation
I drove all *round* Hokkaido.

isshuu suru (～する) *vi.* go
around: *Itsu-ka sekai o* isshuu
shitai. (いつか世界を一周したい) I
would like to travel around the
world someday. / *Kono mizuumi
o* isshuu suru *no ni dono kurai
kakarimasu ka?* (この湖を一周する
のにどのくらいかかりますか) How long
will it take to *go around* this
lake?

i｢**sso** いっそ *adv.* rather; preferably; once and for all:
*Byooki de koñna ni kurushimu
nara,* isso *shiñde shimaitai.*(病気
でこんなに苦しむなら，いっそ死んでしまい
たい) I would *rather* die than suffer this much from illness.

isso no koto (～の事) rather;
preferably: Isso no koto *saisho
kara yarinaoshita hoo ga ii to
omoimasu.*(いっその事最初からやり直
したほうがいいと思います) I think we
had better do it all over again
from the beginning.

i｢**ssoo** いっそう (一層) *adv.* (～ no)
all the more; further; still:
Sore irai, kare wa kanojo ga issoo
suki ni natta.(それ以来，彼は彼女がい

っそう好きになった) After that, he grew to like her *even more.* / *Kyoo wa kinoo yori issoo samuku natta.* (きょうはきのうよりいっそう寒くなった) Today has become *considerably* colder than yesterday. / *Anata wa kore kara issoo no doryoku ga hitsuyoo desu.* (あなたはこれからいっそうの努力が必要です) From now on an *even* greater effort is required of you.

i「su いす (椅子) *n.* **1** chair; stool: isu *ni suwaru* [*koshikakeru*] (いすに座る[腰掛ける]) sit on a *chair* / isu *kara tachiagaru* (いすから立ち上がる) rise from a *chair* / *Kono* isu *ni o-kake kudasai.* (このいすにお掛けください) Please sit in this *chair.*
2 post; position: *Kare wa shachoo no* isu *o neratte iru.* (彼は社長のいすをねらっている) He is aiming for the *post* of president.

i「ta いた (板) *n.* board; plank: *nokogiri de* ita *o kiru* (のこぎりで板を切る) cut a *board* with a saw / *kabe ni* ita *o haru* (壁に板を張る) cover the wall with *boards* / ita *no ma* (板の間) a room with a *wooden* floor / ita-bari (板張り) *boarding; planking.*

i「taba」sami いたばさみ (板挟み) *n.* dilemma; fix: *giri to ninjoo no* itabasami ni naru (義理と人情の板挟みになる) *be torn between* duty and sentiment / *Futari no aide de* itabasami ni natte komatte imasu. (二人の間で板挟みになって困っています) *Placed between* two of them, I am at a loss what to do.

i「tadakima」su いただきます (頂きます・戴きます) ★ This is what the Japanese say before they start eating. Literally it means, "We are going to eat [partake]." 《⇨ itadaku; gochisoo-sama》

i「tadak・u いただく (頂く・戴く) *vt.*

(itadak・i-; itadak・a-; itada・i-te [C])
1 (*humble*) have; get; take; receive: *Kono hoñ o* itadakimasu. (この本をいただきます) I *will take* this book. / *Kinoo, o-tayori o* itadakimashita. (きのう, お便りをいただきました) I *received* your letter yesterday. 《⇨ morau》
2 (*humble*) eat; drink: *Moo juubuñ* itadakimashita. (もう十分いただきました) I *have had* plenty, thanks. / *O-cha o ippai* itadakemaseñ ka? (お茶を一杯いただけませんか) May I *have* a cup of tea? 《⇨ itadakimasu; taberu; nomu》
3 be capped: *yuki o* itadaita *yama* (雪をいただいた山) a mountain *capped* with snow. 《⇨ -te itadaku》

i「ta」・i いたい (痛い) *a.* (-ku) painful; sore: *Ha ga* itai. (歯が痛い) I *have a toothache.* / *Atama ga itakute tamaranai.* (頭が痛くてたまらない) I cannot stand this *headache.* / Itai. (痛い) *Ouch!*
itai tokoro (~所) (*fig.*) a raw spot: Itai tokoro *o kare ni tsukareta.* (痛い所を彼につかれた) He took advantage of my *weak point.*
itaku mo kayuku mo nai (痛くもかゆくもない) couldn't care less: *Soñna koto* itaku mo kayuku mo arimaseñ. (そんなこと痛くもかゆくもありません) I *don't give a fig* about that kind of thing.

i「tame」・ru いためる (炒める) *vt.* (itame-te [V]) fry; panfry; sauté: *yasai o* itameru (野菜をいためる) *fry* vegetables / *niku o abura de* itameru (肉を油でいためる) *fry* meat in oil. 《⇨ ageru²》

itameru	fry
ageru	

i「tami」 いたみ（痛み）*n.* pain; ache:
hageshii [nibui] itami（激しい[鈍い]痛み）a severe [dull] *pain* / *i no* itami（胃の痛み）a *pain* in the stomach / *kokoro no* itami（心の痛み）a *wound* to one's heart / *Senaka ni* itami *o kañjiru.*（背中に痛みを感じる）I can feel a *pain* in my back. 《⇨ itamu》

i「ta」m·u いたむ（痛む）*vi.* (itam·i-; itam·a-; itañ-de Ⓒ) **1** hurt; ache; have a pain:
Ha ga mada itamu.（歯がまだ痛む）My tooth still *hurts.* / *Senaka ga sukoshi* itamimasu.（背中が少し痛みます）I *have* a slight *pain* in the back. 《⇨ itami》
2 (of one's heart) ache:
Ryooshiñ ga itamu.（良心が痛む）My conscience *pricks* me. / *Sono ko no koto o omou to kanojo wa kokoro ga* itañda.（その子のことを思うと彼女は心が痛んだ）When she thought of the child, her heart *ached.* 《⇨ itami》

I「taria」 イタリア *n.* Italy.

I「tariajiñ」 イタリア人 *n.* an Italian.

i「tashima」su いたします（致します）*vt.* = itasu.

i「tas·u」 いたす（致す）*vt.* (itash·i-; itas·a-; itash·i-te Ⓒ) do:
★ The humble form of '*suru.*' Usually used in the *masu*-form. *Asu o-ukagai* itashimasu.（あすお伺いいたします）I *will* call on you tomorrow. / *Yamakawa-sañ o go-shookai* itashimashoo ka?（山川さんをご紹介いたしましょうか）*May* I introduce Miss Yamakawa to you? / *Nañ no o-kamai mo* itashimaseñ *de, shitsuree shimashita.*（何のお構いもいたしませんで、失礼しました）I'm sorry I *could do nothing* to entertain you. ★ A set expression used after entertaining a guest. / *Go-busata* itashite *orimasu.*（ご無沙汰いたしております）I'm

sorry I *haven't been* in touch with you for a long time.

i「tawa」r·u いたわる（労る）*vt.* (itawar·i-; itawar·a-; itawat-te Ⓒ) treat kindly; be kind; take care of:
roojiñ o itawaru（老人をいたわる）*be kind* to old people / *karada o* itawaru（体をいたわる）*take care of* oneself.

i「tazura」 いたずら（悪戯）*n.* mischief; prank:
Itazura *o shite wa ikemaseñ yo.*（いたずらをしてはいけませんよ）You must not play any *naughty tricks.* / itazura-*deñwa*（いたずら電話）a *prank* phone call.
— *a.n.* (～ na) naughty; mischievous:
Itazura *na ko ne.*（いたずらな子ね）What a *naughty* boy you are!

i「tchi」 いっち（一致）*n.* agreement; accord; coincidence:
Ikeñ no itchi *o miru made jikañ ga kakatta.*（意見の一致を見るまで時間がかかった）It took time before they came to *unanimous agreement.* 《⇨ mañjoo-itchi》
itchi suru (～する) *vi.* match; agree; accord; coincide: *Sono shimoñ wa hañniñ no mono to* itchi shita.（その指紋は犯人のものと一致した）The fingerprint *matched* that of the criminal. / *Kimi no setsumee wa jijitsu to* itchi shinai.（君の説明は事実と一致しない）Your explanation *does not agree* with the facts. / *Watashi-tachi wa* itchi shite *sono moñdai o kaiketsu shita.*（私たちは一致してその問題を解決した）We *worked together* and solved the problem.

i「to」[1] いと（糸）*n.* thread; yarn; string:
hari ni ito *o toosu*（針に糸を通す）put a *thread* through the eye of a needle.

i「to」[2] いと（意図）*n.* intention; purpose:

*Kare wa satsugai no ito o motte
sono uchi ni shiññyuu shita.* (彼は
殺害の意図をもってその家に侵入した)
He broke into the house with
murder *in mind.* / *Kare no ito ga
doko ni aru no ka wakaranai.* (彼の
意図がどこにあるのかわからない) I don't
know what his *purpose* is.
ito suru (～する) *vt.* intend; aim
at: *Seefu wa hooañ no seeritsu o
ito shite ita.* (政府は法案の成立を意
図していた) The government *intended* to have the bill passed.

i˺**to˺guchi** いとぐち (糸口) *n.*
1 the end of a thread.
2 beginning; clue; lead:
shusse no itoguchi (出世の糸口)
the *beginning* of one's success in
life / hanashi no itoguchi *o mitsukeru* (話の糸口を見つける) try to
break the ice in a conversation /
*Nokosareta shimoñ ga jikeñ kai-
ketsu no* itoguchi to natta. (残され
た指紋が事件解決の糸口となった) The
fingerprints left *led* to the solution of the case.

i˺**to˺ko** いとこ (従兄弟・従姉妹) *n.*
cousin. ★'従兄弟' is used to
refer to male cousins or a mixed
group of male and female cousins. '従姉妹' refers to female
cousins.

i˺**toma** いとま (暇) *n.* **1** spare
time:
O-kyaku ga oozee kite, yasumu
itoma *mo nakatta.* (お客がおおぜい来
て休むいとまもなかった) We had a lot
of customers and didn't even
have *time* to take a rest. (⇨ hima)
2 taking one's leave: ★ Often
with 'o-.'
Moo o-itoma *shinakereba narimaseñ.* (もうおいとましなければなりません) I
must *be leaving* now.
3 dismissal; discharge:
tsuma ni itoma *o dasu* (妻にいとまを
出す) *divorce* one's wife.

i˺**tona˺m·u** いとなむ (営む) *vt.*
(itonam·i-; itonam·a-; itonañ·de
Ⓒ) run; be engaged in; lead:
Kare wa ryokañ o itonañde iru.
(彼は旅館を営んでいる) He *runs* a
Japanese inn. / *Kare no ikka wa
noogyoo o* itonañde imasu. (彼の一
家は農業を営んでいます) His family *is
engaged in* agriculture. / *Kare-ra
wa shisso na seekatsu o* itonañde
imashita. (彼らは質素な生活を営んで
いました) They *led* a simple life.
《⇨ kee-ee》

i˺**tsu** いつ (何時) *adv.* when; what
time:
Kono koinu wa itsu *umarema-
shita?* (この小犬はいつ生まれました)
When was this puppy born? /
Anata wa itsu *Nihoñ e korarema-
shita ka?* (あなたはいつ日本へ来られま
したか) *When* did you come to
Japan? / *Itsu kara Nihoñgo o naratte iru ñ desu ka?* (いつから日本語
を習っているんですか) *When* did you
start learning Japanese? / *Fuyu-
yasumi wa* itsu *kara hajimarimasu ka?* (冬休みはいつから始まります
か) *When* does the winter vacation start? /*Anata wa* itsu *made
Hokkaidoo ni iru yotee desu ka?*
(あなたはいつまで北海道にいる予定です
か) *How long* do you plan to stay
in Hokkaido?

i˺**tsu de mo** いつでも (何時でも)
adv. **1** always; all the time:
Kare wa hima ga areba, itsu de
mo *hoñ o yoñde iru.* (彼はひまがあれ
ば, いつでも本を読んでいる) When he
has time, he is *always* reading.
2 at any time; whenever:
*Itsu de mo suki na toki ni kite
kudasai.* (いつでも好きなときに来てくだ
さい) Please come around *any
time* you like. / *Kaesu no wa* itsu
de mo *kekkoo desu.* (返すのはいつ
でもけっこうです) You can return it
anytime.

i˺**tsu made mo** いつまでも (何時

迄も) *adv.* forever; endlessly; as long as (one likes):
Anata no koto wa itsu made mo *wasuremaseñ.* (あなたのことはいつまでも忘れません) I will *never* forget you. / Itsu made mo *suki na dake koko ni ite kudasai.* (いつまでも好きなだけここにいてください) Please stay here just *as long as* you like. / *Ima no seefu ga* itsu made mo *tsuzuku to wa omoimaseñ.* (今の政府がいつまでも続くとは思いません) I don't think that the current government will last *forever.*

i「**tsuka** いつか (五日) *n.* five days; the fifth day of the month:
Itsuka *inai ni kono shigoto wa shiagemasu.* (五日以内にこの仕事は仕上げます) I will finish this task within *five days.* / *Gogatsu* itsuka *wa kodomo no hi desu.* (五月五日は子どもの日です) May *5* is Children's Day. 《⇨ tsuitachi (table)》

i「**tsu-ka** いつか (何時か) *adv.*
1 (of future) someday; sometime:
Sono shiñsoo wa itsu-ka *wakaru deshoo.* (その真相はいつかわかるでしょう) The truth will come out *someday.* / *Sono uchi* itsu-ka *o-tazune shimasu.* (そのうちいつかお訪ねします) I will call on you *sometime* in the future.
2 (of the past) once; before:
Kanojo ni wa itsu-ka *doko-ka de atta oboe ga arimasu.* (彼女にはいつかどこかで会った覚えがあります) I have a recollection of meeting her somewhere *sometime before.*
itsu-ka no (〜の) the other day:
Itsu-ka no *hanashi wa doo narimashita ka?* (いつかの話はどうなりましたか) How did that matter we were *recently* talking about turn out?

i「**tsu-mo** いつも (何時も) *adv.*
(〜 no) **1** always:
Katoo-sañ wa itsu-mo *hito no warukuchi bakari itte iru.* (加藤さ

んはいつも人の悪口ばかり言っている)
Mr. Kato is *always* saying bad things about other people. / *Okinawa no hoo ga Hoñshuu yori* itsu-mo *atsui to iu wake de wa arimaseñ.* (沖縄のほうが本州よりいつも暑いというわけではありません) It does not follow that Okinawa is *always* hotter than Honshu.
2 usually:
Itsu-mo *neru mae ni shawaa o abimasu.* (いつも寝る前にシャワーを浴びます) I *usually* take a shower before going to bed. / Itsu-mo *no yoo ni hatsuoñ-reñshuu kara hajimemashoo.* (いつものように発音練習から始めましょう) Let's start *as usual* with pronunciation practice. / Itsu-mo *no tokoro de go-ji ni matte imasu.* (いつもの所で5時に待っています) I'll be waiting at the *usual* place at five.

i「**tsu-no-ma-ni**「-ka いつのまにか (何時の間にか) *adv.* before one knows it; too soon:
Itsu-no-ma-ni-ka *kanojo wa inaku natte ita.* (いつの間にか彼女はいなくなっていた) She disappeared *before we even realized it.* / Itsu-no-ma-ni-ka *ichi-neñ ga sugita.* (いつの間にか一年が過ぎた) A year has gone by *in no time at all.*

i「**tsu**「**tsu** いつつ (五つ) *n.* five:
★ Used when counting.
Watashi no musuko wa itsutsu *desu.* (私の息子は五つです) My son is *five.* / itsutsu-me (五つ目) *the fifth.* 《⇨ go³; kazu (table)》

i「**ttai**¹ いったい (一体) *n.* one; one body: ★ Usually used in the expression, '*ittai to naru.*'
Kare-ra wa ittai *to natte koñnañ ni uchikatta.* (彼らは一体となって困難に打ち勝った) *Shoulder to shoulder*, they overcame the difficulty. / *Seefu yotoo ga* ittai *to natte, kokkai o uñee shite iru.* (政府与党が一体となって, 国会を運営している) The

government party as *one body* manages the Diet. / *Futatsu no kaisha ga gappee shite,* ittai to natta. (二つの会社が合併して、一体となった) The two companies merged and became *one*.

i˹**ttai**² いったい (一体) *adv.* (with an interrogative) on earth; in the world; even:
Ittai *nani ga okotta no desu ka?* (いったい何が起こったのですか) What *on earth* has happened? / Ittai *kanojo wa doko e itta no daroo.* (いったい彼女はどこへ行ったのだろう) I wonder where *on earth* she has gone. / Ittai *doo shita ñ desu ka? Koñna machigai o shite.* (いったいどうしたんですか。こんな間違いをして) *Whatever* is the matter—making a mistake like this?

i˹**ttai ni** いったいに (一体に) *adv.* on the whole; generally (speaking):
Kotoshi wa ittai ni *hoosaku deshita.* (ことしは一体に豊作でした) This year the harvest was *on the whole* good.

i˹**ttañ** いったん (一旦) *adv.* 1 once:
Ittañ *hajimeta koto wa saigo made yari nasai.* (いったん始めたことは最後までやりなさい) *Once* you have started something, continue until you have finished it.
2 temporarily; for a while:
Ittañ *(wa) soo omoimashita ga kañgae o kaemashita.* (いったん(は)そう思いましたが考えを変えました) I thought so *for a while*, but I have changed my opinion. / *Watashi wa raishuu* ittañ *kuni ni kaerimasu.* (私は来週いったん国に帰ります) I am going home *for just a short while* next week.

i˹**tte** いって (一手) *n.* 1 monopoly; exclusiveness:
Kono shina wa kare no kaisha ga itte *ni hañbai shite iru.* (この品は彼の会社が一手に販売している) This

article is sold *exclusively* by his company.
2 (of chess, etc.) move:
Saigo no itte *de makete shimatta.* (最後の一手で負けてしまった) I lost the game on my last *move*.

i˹**ttee** いってい (一定) *n.* fixed (condition); definite (condition); uniform (circumstances):
ittee no (〜の) 1 fixed; regular:
Nae o ittee *no kañkaku de ueta.* (苗を一定の間隔で植えた) We planted seedlings at regular intervals. / *Watashi wa* ittee *no sokudo de uñteñ shita.* (私は一定の速度で運転した) I drove at a *steady* speed.
2 to some [a certain] degree:
Sakuya no roo-shi-kañ no kooshoo de wa ittee *no zeñshiñ ga mirareta.* (昨夜の労使間の交渉では一定の前進が見られた) Last night's collective bargaining between management and labor yielded *some* progress.
ittee suru (〜する) *vi.,vt.* fix; set; standardize: *Kono buhiñ no ookisa wa* ittee *shite imasu.* (この部品の大きさは一定しています) The size of this (machinery) part *is standardized*. / *Okiru jikañ wa* ittee *shite imaseñ.* (起きる時間は一定していません) The time I get up *is irregular*.

i˹**tte-kimasu** いってきます (行って来ます) I'll go and come back. ★ A set expression used when leaving home, especially when responding to the greeting, '*Itte-(i)rasshai.*' A more polite form is '*Itte-mairimasu.*' 《⇨ itte-(i)rasshai》

i˹**tte-(i)rasshai** いって(い)らっしゃい (行って(い)らっしゃい) Please go and come back. ★ A set expression used when someone is going out. The usual answer is '*itte-kimasu [mairimasu]*.' 《⇨ itte-kimasu》

i˹**ttoo** いっとう (一等) *n.* first class;

first prize; first place:
Kare wa kyoosoo de ittoo *ni natta.*
(彼は競争で一等になった) He won
first place in the race. / ittoo *señ-*
shitsu (一等船室) a *first-class*
ship's cabin. 《⇨ nitoo》

i·「u　いう (言う) *vt.* (i·i-; iw·a-; it-te
C)

> ──(**USAGE**)──
> '言う' (*iu*) is always pronounced
> '*yuu*.' In the *te*-form and the
> past '*yutte*' and '*yutta*' are
> common, but slightly more
> informal than the equivalent
> standard forms, '*itte*' and '*itta*.'

1 say; tell; talk; speak:
Kare wa watashi ni "Isoge" to
itta. (彼は私に「急げ」と言った) He
said "Hurry up" to me. / *Ano*
hito no iu *koto wa shiñjiru na.* (あの
人の言うことは信じるな) Do not
believe what he *says.* / *Ooki-na*
koe de itte *kudasai.* (大きな声で言っ
てください) Please *speak* in a loud
voice. / *Hoñtoo no koto o* ii *nasai.*
(本当のことを言いなさい) *Tell* the
truth. / *Kare wa miñna kara yoku*
iwarete iru. (彼はみんなからよく言われ
ている) He *is* well *spoken of* by
everyone.
2 mention; refer to:
Kare wa anata no koto o nani mo
itte *imaseñ deshita.* (彼はあなたのこと
を何も言っていませんでした) He has
mentioned nothing about you. /
Shachoo wa atarashii keekaku ni
tsuite nani mo iwanakatta. (社長は
新しい計画について何も言わなかった)
The president *did not refer* to
the new project.
3 express; call:
Anata no kañgae o itte *kudasai.*
(あなたの考えを言ってください) Please
express your thoughts. / *Kono*
hana wa Nihoñgo de nañ to
iimasu ka? (この花は日本語で何と言
いますか) What do you *call* this

flower in Japanese? / *Tanaka-sañ*
to iu *kata ga miemashita.* (田中さん
という方が見えました) A person
called Tanaka came to see you.
4 tell; order:
Kare-ra ni sugu dete iku yoo ni
itta. (彼らにすぐ出て行くように言った) I
told them to get out at once. /
Watashi wa tabako o suwanai yoo
ni to iwareta. (私はたばこを吸わないよ
うにと言われた) I *was ordered* not to
smoke.
...to iu (...と~) **1** people say:
Kare wa kaisha o yameru to iu
uwasa ga aru. (彼は会社をやめるとい
ううわさがある) Rumor has it *that*
he will quit his company. /
Kanojo wa kodomo ga sañ-niñ iru
to iu. (彼女は子どもが 3 人いるという)
They say that she has three children.
2 (used for emphasis or explanation): *Ichioku-eñ* to iu *kiñgaku*
wa ookii. (一億円という金額は大きい)
The sum *of* 100 million yen is
large. / *Watashi wa mada tako* to
iu *mono o tabeta koto ga nai.* (私は
まだたこというもの食べたことがない) I
have not yet eaten *octopus.*
《⇨ to iu koto da》

i「wa」　いわ (岩) *n.* rock; crag.
《⇨ ishi¹》

i「waba　いわば (言わば) *adv.* so to
speak; as it were, in a sense; practically:
Kaichoo wa iwaba, *namae dake*
no sekiniñsha desu. (会長はいわば,
名前だけの責任者です) The chair-
man is, *as it were,* a figurehead. /
Kare wa iwaba, *kage no jitsuryo-*
kusha desu. (彼はいわば, 陰の実力者
です) He is, *so to speak,* the power
behind the throne.

i「wa」i　いわい (祝い) *n.* **1** celebration; congratulation:
shiñneñ no o-iwai (新年のお祝い) a
New Year *celebration* / *Kokoro*
kara o-iwai *mooshiagemasu.* (心か

らお祝い申し上げます) I would like to offer you my heartiest *congratulations*. 《⇨ iwau》

2 present: *kekkoñ no* o-iwai (結婚のお祝い) a wedding *present*.

i「**washi** いわし (鰯) *n*. sardine.

I「**wate**1**-keñ** いわてけん (岩手県) *n*. Iwate Prefecture. Located near the north end of Honshu, facing the Pacific on the east. In the south stands Chusonji Temple, where important works of art are preserved. Capital city: Morioka (盛岡). 《⇨ map (G2)》

i「**wa**1**·u** いわう (祝う) *vt*. (iwa·i-; iwaw·a-; iwat-te C) celebrate; congratulate: *tañjoobi o* iwau (誕生日を祝う) *celebrate* a birthday / *Machi o agete, koomiñkañ no kañsee o iwatta.* (町をあげて, 公民館の完成を祝った) All the townspeople *celebrated* the completion of the public hall. 《⇨ iwai》

i「**wa**1**yuru** いわゆる (所謂) *attrib*. what is called; so-called: *Kare wa iwayuru eriito shaiñ da.* (彼はいわゆるエリート社員だ) He is *what you call* an elite employee. / *Kare wa iwayuru shusse koosu ni notte iru.* (彼はいわゆる出世コースに乗っている) He is on the *so-called* promotional track to the top.

i「**ya**1 いや (嫌) *a.n.* (~ na, ni) disagreeable; disgusting; horrible: iya *na kao o suru* (いやな顔をする) make a *sour* face / *Iya na nioi ga suru.* (いやなにおいがする) There is a *nasty* smell. / *Nani-ka* iya *na koto de mo atta ñ desu ka?* (何かいやなことでもあったんですか) Has something or other *bad* happened to you? / *Koñna shigoto wa* iya *da.* (こんな仕事はいやだ) I *don't like* this kind of work. / *Beñkyoo ga* iya *ni natta.* (勉強がいやになった) I *am fed up*

with my studies.

i「**ya**12 いや *int*. no; yes:

────(USAGE)────

'*Iya*' literally means 'That's wrong,' and is used to confirm a statement, whether affirmative or negative. Note that the use is different from that of 'yes' and 'no' in English. '*Iie*' is more polite.

"*Kare wa kimasu ka?*" "*Iya, konai to omoimasu.*" (「彼は来ますか」「いや, 来ないと思います」) "Is he coming?" "*No, I do not think so.*" / "*Mada ame wa yamimaseñ ka?*" "*Iya, yamimashita.*" (「まだ雨はやみませんか」「いや, やみました」) "Hasn't the rain stopped yet?" "*Yes, it has.*" 《⇨ iie》

iya to iu (~ と言う) say no: *Kare wa kesshite* iya *to iwanai.* (彼は決していやと言わない) He never *says no*.

i「**yagarase** いやがらせ (嫌がらせ) *n*. harassment: Iyagarase *no deñwa ga kakatte kita.* (嫌がらせの電話がかかってきた) I got a *harassing* phone call. / *Kare wa tokidoki* iyagarase *o iu.* (彼はときどき嫌がらせを言う) Sometimes he says *unpleasant things* to me. / *Kanojo ni* iyagarase *o suru no wa yoshi nasai.* (彼女に嫌がらせをするのはよしなさい) Stop *annoying* her. / *see-teki* iyagarase (性的嫌がらせ) sexual *harassment*. 《⇨ sekuhara》

i「**yaga**1**r·u** いやがる (嫌がる) *vt*. (iyagar·i-; iyagar·a-; iyagat-te C) dislike; hate; be unwilling; be reluctant: *Sono ko wa haisha e iku no o* iyagatta. (その子は歯医者へ行くのを嫌がった) The child *was reluctant* to go to the dentist. / *Kanojo wa hito no* iyagaru *shigoto o susuñde hikiuketa.* (彼女は人の嫌がる仕事を進んで引き受けた) She willingly undertook the work that others *hated* to do.

i｢**yaiya** いやいや *adv.* unwillingly; reluctantly; against one's will: *Kare wa* iyaiya *kane o kashite kureta.* (彼はいやいや金を貸してくれた) He *reluctantly* lent me the money. / *Watashi wa* iyaiya *kare no teeañ ni sañsee shita.* (私はいやいや彼の提案に賛成した) I *unwillingly* agreed to his proposal.

i｢**yarashi¹·i** いやらしい *a.* (-ku) disgusting; offensive; nasty: *Uwayaku no go-kigeñ bakari totte ite,* iyarashii *yatsu da.* (上役のご機嫌ばかりとっていて, いやらしいやつだ) He is a *nasty* fellow, always currying favor with his superiors. / *Suzuki-sañ wa sugu* iyarashii *koto o iu.* (鈴木さんはすぐいやらしいことを言う) Mr. Suzuki is all too ready to make *dirty* remarks. / *Uchi no kachoo wa eñkai no seki de, watashi ni* iyarashii *koto o shita.* (うちの課長は宴会の席で, 私にいやらしいことをした) The chief of our section behaved *indecently* toward me at the party.

i｢**yashi·i** いやしい (卑しい) *a.* (-ku) **1** vulgar; coarse; mean: iyashii *waraikata* (卑しい笑い方) a *coarse* way of laughing / *Kokoro no* iyashii *niñgeñ ni naru na.* (心の卑しい人間になるな) Do not become a *base*-minded person.
2 greedy; gluttonous: iyashii *tabekata* (卑しい食べ方) a *gluttonous* way of eating / *Kare wa kane ni* iyashii. (彼は金に卑しい) He is *mean* with money.

iyo｢iyo いよいよ *adv.* **1** more and more; all the more: *Juuni-gatsu ni natte,* iyoiyo *samuku natte kita.* (十二月になって, いよいよ寒くなってきた) With the arrival of December, it has become *even colder.*
2 at last; finally: Iyoiyo *ashita wa nyuugaku-shikeñ*

da. (いよいよあしたは入学試験だ) Tomorrow is the entrance exam *at long last.*

iyoiyo no [to iu] toki ni (～の[という]ときに) at the last moment; at the eleventh hour: Iyoiyo to iu *toki ni naranai to kare wa majime ni shigoto o shinai.* (いよいよというときにならないと彼はまじめに仕事をしない) He never works seriously unless it is *at the eleventh hour.* / Iyoiyo no *toki ni wa kare mo yaru deshoo.* (いよいよのときには彼もやるでしょう) When it comes to *the critical moment,* he will act.

i｢**yoku** いよく (意欲) *n.* will; eagerness: *Sono roojiñ wa ikiru* iyoku *ga nakatta.* (その老人は生きる意欲がなかった) The old man had no *will* to live. / *Kanojo ni wa beñkyoo shitai to iu* iyoku *ga aru.* (彼女には勉強したいという意欲がある) She *is eager* to study.

i｢**yoku-teki** いよくてき (意欲的) *a.n.* (～ na, ni) eager; active; positive: iyoku-teki *na taido* (意欲的な態度) a *positive* attitude / *Sono gaka wa* iyoku-teki *ni shigoto o shite imasu.* (その画家は意欲的に仕事をしています) That painter does his work *enthusiastically.*

i｢**zeñ**¹ いぜん (以前) *n.* **1** before a certain time: *Watashi wa Meeji* izeñ *no chizu ni kyoomi o motte imasu.* (私は明治以前の地図に興味を持っています) I am interested in *pre*-Meiji era maps. 《↔ igo¹》
2 ago; once; formerly: *Kare ni atta no wa zutto* izeñ *desu.* (彼に会ったのはずっと以前です) It was a long time *ago* that I met him. / *Kanojo wa* izeñ *yori mo yoku natta mitai da.* (彼女は以前よりも良くなったみたいだ) She seems to be much better than *before.* / *Wata-*

shi wa izeñ *isha ni naritakatta.* (私は以前医者になりたかった) I *once* wanted to be a doctor.

i「**zeñ**² いぜん (依然) *adv.* (~ **to shite**) still; as ever; as before: *Eñ wa* izeñ (*to shite*) *agari tsuzukete iru.* (円は依然(として)上がり続けている) The Japanese yen *still* shows a tendency to go up. / *Sono chiimu ga yuushoo-kooho de aru koto ni wa* izeñ (*to shite*) *kawari wa nai.* (そのチームが優勝候補であることには依然(として)変わりはない) The fact that the team is the favorite in the championship *still* remains unchanged.

i「**zumi** いずみ (泉) *n.* spring; fountain.

i「**zure** いずれ (何れ) *adv.* (~ **no**) some day; one day; before long: *Izure, kare mo kookai suru toki ga kuru deshoo.* (いずれ, 彼も後悔するときが来るでしょう) The time for him to feel remorse will come *before long.* / *Izure mata, o-ai shimashoo.* (いずれまた, お会いしましょう) Let's meet again *sometime.* / *Izure mata, o-shirase itashimasu.* (いずれまた, お知らせいたします) We will inform you *in due course.*

izure ni shite mo [seyo] (~にしても[せよ]) in any event; at any rate: *Izure ni shite mo [Izure ni seyo] sono hi wa shusseki dekimaseñ.* (いずれにしても[いずれにせよ]その日は出席できません) *At any rate*, I can not attend on that day.

i「**zure mo** いずれも (何れも) *adv.* both; either; any; all: *Sono ni-satsu no shoosetsu wa* izure mo *yomimashita.* (その2冊の小説はいずれも読みました) I have read *both* those novels. / *Kare-ra wa* izure mo *rippa na hito-tachi desu.* (彼らはいずれも立派な人たちです) They are *all* fine people.

J

ja じゃ *conj.* = jaa.

JA ジェイエイ *n.* abbreviation of 'Japan Agriculture' (農協＝*Nookyoo*).

ja⌐a じゃあ *conj.* (*formal*＝de wa) well; then:
Jaa, sono uwasa wa hoñtoo datta ñ desu ne. (じゃあ、そのうわさは本当だったんですね) *Well then*, the rumor was true, wasn't it? / *Jaa, mata ashita.* (じゃあ、またあした) *Well*, I'll see you tomorrow. / *Jaa ne.* (じゃあね) *Goodbye.* ★ Informal expression used when leaving.

ja⌐anari⌐suto ジャーナリスト *n.* journalist.

ja⌐bujabu じゃぶじゃぶ *adv.* (～ *to*) (the sound or action of water splashing around):
kawa o jabujabu (*to*) *wataru* (川をじゃぶじゃぶ(と)渡る) *splash* one's way across a river / *tabemono ni soosu o* jabujabu (*to*) *kakeru* (食べ物にソースをじゃぶじゃぶ(と)かける) *smother* food with sauce.

JAF ジャフ *n.* abbreviation of 'Japan Automobile Federation' (日本自動車連盟＝*Nihoñ Jidoosha Reñmee*).

Ja⌐fu ジャフ *n.* = JAF.

ja⌐gaimo じゃがいも (じゃが芋) *n.* potato. 《⇨ imo (illus.)》

ja⌐guchi じゃぐち (蛇口) *n.* tap; faucet:
jaguchi *o akeru* [*shimeru*] (蛇口を開ける[閉める]) turn on [off] a *faucet.*

ja⌐ma じゃま (邪魔) *n.* disturbance; hindrance; interference:
jama ga hairu (じゃまが入る) *be troubled* / jama-mono (じゃま者) a person who is a *nuisance.*
jama (o) suru (～(を)する) *vt.*

1 disturb; hinder; interfere:
Shigoto no jama o shinai de kudasai. (仕事のじゃまをしないでください) Please *do not disturb* me when I am working.
2 visit:
Asu o-jama shite yoroshii desu ka? (あすおじゃましてよろしいですか) Is it all right if I *visit* you tomorrow?
— *a.n.* (～ *na*, *ni*) obstructive; hampering; burdensome:
Soko ni iru to jama *desu.* (そこにいるとじゃまです) You are *in the way.* / *Sono moñdai ga kare no shusse no* jama *ni natta.* (その問題が彼の出世のじゃまになった) That matter became an *obstacle* to his advancement.

ja⌐mu ジャム *n.* jam:
ichigo no jamu (いちごのジャム) strawberry *jam* / *pañ ni* jamu *o nuru* [*tsukeru*] (パンにジャムを塗る[つける]) spread *jam* on bread.

ja⌐ñkeñ じゃんけん *n.* the game of 'paper, scissors, stone.'

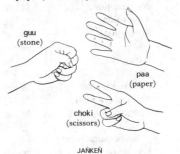

JAÑKEÑ

ja⌐re⌐·ru じゃれる *vi.* (jare-te Ⅴ) play with:
Neko ga mari to jarete iru. (猫がまりとじゃれている) The cat *is playing* with a ball.

JAS ジャス *n*. **1** abbreviation of
'Japanese Agricultural Standard'
(日本農林規格＝*Nihoñ Nooriñ
Kikaku*). ★ Usually appears as
'JAS' even within Japanese script.
2 Japan Air System (日本エアシステ
ム＝*Nihoñ Ea Shisutemu*).
Ja┐su ジャス *n*. ＝ JAS.
-jau じゃう *suf*. ＝ -shimau.
Je┌e-a┐aru ジェイアール *n*. ＝ JR.
Je┌e-e┐e ジェイエイ *n*. ＝ JA.
JES ジェス *n*. abbreviation of
'Japan Engineering Standard'
(日本技術標準規格＝*Nihoñ Gijutsu
Hyoojuñ Kikaku*). ★ Usually
appears as 'JES' even within
Japanese script.
Je┐su ジェス *n*. ＝ JES.
je┌tto┐ki ジェットき（ジェット機）*n*.
jet (plane).
ji¹ じ（字）*n*. **1** letter; character:
Kono ji *wa nañ to yomu no desu
ka?* (この字は何と読むのですか) How
do you read this *character*? /
Motto ooki-na ji *de kaite kudasai*.
(もっと大きな字で書いてください) Please
write in bigger *characters*.
2 handwriting:

Kare wa ji *ga umai [heta da]*. (彼は
字がうまい[下手だ]) He *writes a good
[poor] hand*. / *Kare no* ji *wa yominikui*. (彼の字は読みにくい) His *handwriting* is hard to read.
-ji¹ じ（時）*suf*. o'clock:
gozeñ roku-ji (午前 6 時) *six* in the
morning / *Jugyoo wa* sañ-ji *hañ
ni owarimasu*. (授業は 3 時半に終わ
ります) The lesson finishes at
three-thirty. 《⇨ hi¹ (table)》
-ji² じ（寺）*suf*. temple:
Hooryuu-ji (法隆寺) Horyuji *Temple*.
-ji³ じ（次）*suf*. the number in a
series; order:
ichi-ji (一次) the *first* / ni-ji (二次)
the *second* / (*dai*) ichi-ji *shikeñ*
((第)一次試験) a *preliminary* examination / juñ-ji (順次) *in order* /
seki-ji (席次) seating *order* / neñ-ji
yosañ (年次予算) an *annual* budget.
ji┌bi-iñkooka じびいんこうか（耳鼻
咽喉科）*n*. otolaryngology; ear,
nose and throat department.
《⇨ byooiñ (table)》
ji┌bika じびか（耳鼻科）*n*. ＝ jibi-

JAPANESE HISTORICAL PERIODS AND ERAS   After 1868, '*jidai*' refers to eras.

Joomoñ-jidai	縄 文 時 代	8,000 – 300 B.C.
Yayoi-jidai	弥 生 時 代	300 B.C. – A.D. 300
Kofuñ-jidai	古 墳 時 代	A.D. 300 – 710
Nara-jidai	奈 良 時 代	710 – 794
Heeañ-jidai	平 安 時 代	794 – 1192
Kamakura-jidai	鎌 倉 時 代	1192 – 1333
Muromachi-jidai	室 町 時 代	1336 – 1573
Señgoku-jidai	戦 国 時 代	ca. 1480 – ca. 1570
Azuchi-Momoyama-jidai	安土・桃山時代	1573 – 1603
Edo-jidai	江 戸 時 代	1603 – 1867
Meeji-jidai	明 治 時 代	1868 – 1912
Taishoo-jidai	大 正 時 代	1912 – 1926
Shoowa-jidai	昭 和 時 代	1926 – 1989
Heesee-jidai	平 成 時 代	1989 –

iñkooka.

ji⌐biki じびき (字引) *n.* dictionary.
★ Not as common as '*jisho*' anymore. 《⇨ jisho²》

ji⌐buñ じぶん (自分) *n.* oneself:
Kanojo wa kagami no naka no jibuñ o mita. (彼女は鏡の中の自分を見た) She looked at *herself* in the mirror. / *Jibuñ no koto wa jibuñ de shi nasai.* (自分のことは自分でしなさい) *You yourself* do *your own* business. / *Jibuñ no ie ga hoshii.* (自分の家が欲しい) I want to have a house of *my own*.

ji⌐chi じち (自治) *n.* self-government; autonomy:
jichi-keñ (自治権) the right of local *self-government* / jichi-tai (自治体) a *self-governing* body.

Ji⌐chi-da⌐ijiñ じちだいじん (自治大臣) *n.* Minister of Home Affairs.

Ji⌐chi⌐-shoo じちしょう (自治省) *n.* Ministry of Home Affairs. 《⇨ shoo¹ (table)》

ji⌐choo じちょう (次長) *n.* deputy chief; vice-director. 《⇨ kaisha (table)》

ji⌐dai じだい (時代) *n.* **1** era; period; age:
Meeji-jidai (明治時代) the Meiji *era* (1868–1912) / *Ima wa geñshi-ryoku no jidai desu.* (今は原子力の時代です) This is the *age* of nuclear power. 《⇨ table (previous page)》
2 days:
Kanojo wa gakusee jidai ni Pari e itta. (彼女は学生時代にパリへ行った) She went to Paris in her student *days*.
3 times:
Jidai wa kawatta. (時代は変わった) *Times* have changed / *Kimi no kañgae wa jidai-okure da.* (君の考えは時代遅れだ) You ideas are behind the *times*.

ji⌐dai-sa⌐kugo じだいさくご (時代錯誤) *n.* anachronism:

jidai-sakugo *no shisoo* (時代錯誤の思想) an *anachronistic* way of thinking.

ji⌐doo¹ じどう (自動) *n.* automatic:
jidoo-*shooteñ no kamera* (自動焦点のカメラ) an *automatic* focusing camera / *Kono doa wa* jidoo-teki *ni hirakimasu.* (このドアは自動的に開きます) This door opens *automatically.* / jidoo-*hañbaiki* (自動販売機) a *vending* machine / jidoo-*kaisatsuguchi* (自動改札口) an *automatic* wicket (ticket barrier).

JIDOOHAÑBAIKI FOR SUBWAY TICKETS

ji⌐doo² じどう (児童) *n.* child; juvenile:
jidoo *muke no hoñ* (児童向けの本) a book for *children*.

ji⌐do⌐osha じどうしゃ (自動車) *n.* car; automobile; motor vehicle:
jidoosha *o uñteñ suru* (自動車を運転する) drive a *car* / *Jidoosha ga tochuu de koshoo shita.* (自動車が途中で故障した) The *car* broke down on the way. / *Koko kara Shiñjuku made* jidoosha *de nijup-puñ desu.* (ここから新宿まで自動車で20分です) It takes twenty minutes by *car* from here to Shinjuku. / *Jidoosha Tsuukoodome* (*sign*) (自動車通行止) No Entry for *Motor Vehicles*.

ji⌐do⌐oshi じどうし (自動詞) *n.* intransitive verb. 《↔ tadooshi》 《⇨ appendixes》

ji「ee じえい（自衛）*n.* self-defense:
jiee *saku* [*shudañ*] *o toru*（自衛策
[手段]を取る）take *self-defensive*
measures / jiee-*keñ*（自衛権）the
right of *self-defense* / jiee-*kañ*（自
衛艦）a warship of *the Maritime
Self-Defense Force.*
jiee suru（～する）*vi.* defend oneself.

Ji「eetai じえいたい（自衛隊）*n.* the
Self-Defense Forces:
Rikujoo [*Kaijoo; Kookuu*] jieetai
（陸上[海上；航空]自衛隊）the
Ground [Maritime; Air] *Self-
Defense Force.*

──(**USAGE**)──
For constitutional and political
reasons, the Japanese armed
forces are not called 'Army,'
'Navy,' and 'Air Force.'
《⇨ guñ²》

ji「goku¹ じごく（地獄）*n.* hell.

ji「gyoo じぎょう（事業）*n.* business; enterprise:
jigyoo *ni seekoo* [*shippai*] *suru*（事
業に成功[失敗]する）succeed [fail]
in *business* / jigyoo *o kakudai* [*shukushoo*] *suru*（事業を拡大[縮小]する）
expand [reduce] *business / shakai*
jigyoo（社会事業）social *work* / ji-
gyoo-*ka*（事業家）an *entrepreneur;
a businessman.*

ji「hi「biki じひびき（地響き）*n.* rumbling of the ground:
Sono ki wa jihibiki *o tatete, taoreta.*（その木は地響きを立てて、倒れた）
The tree fell *with a thud.* / *Torakku ga* jihibiki *o tatete, tootta.*
（トラックが地響きを立てて、通った）A
truck *rumbled* past.

ji「isañ じいさん（爺さん）*n.* (*informal*) **1** one's grandfather:
Uchi no jiisañ *wa mimi ga tooi.*（う
ちのじいさんは耳が遠い）Our *grand-
father* is hard of hearing.
2 old man.
《↔ baasañ》《⇨ o-jiisañ》

ji「jitsu¹ じじつ（事実）*n.* fact;
truth; reality:
Kare no itte iru koto wa jijitsu
desu.（彼の言っていることは事実です）
What he says is an *actual fact.* /
Kono shoosetsu wa jijitsu *ni motozuite imasu.*（この小説は事実に基づい
ています）This novel is based on
fact. / Jijitsu *o yugameru koto wa
watashi ni wa dekimaseñ.*（事実を
ゆがめることは私にはできません）To dis-
tort the *truth* is not something I
can do.
jijitsu joo (no)（事実上（の））ac-
tual: *Kare wa* jijitsu joo (no) *shachoo no yoo ni furumatte iru.*（彼は
事実上（の）社長のように振る舞っている）
He carries on as if he were the
actual president.

ji「jitsu² じじつ（事実）*adv.* as a
matter of fact; actually:
Jijitsu *kare wa soo iimashita.*（事
実彼はそう言いました）*As a matter of
fact,* he said so.

ji「jo じじょ（次女・二女）*n.* one's
second daughter. 《⇨ kyoodai
(table)》

ji「joo じじょう（事情）*n.* **1** circumstances; conditions:
Jijoo *ga yuruseba sono kai ni
shusseki shimasu.*（事情が許せばその
会に出席します）I'll attend the
party if *circumstances* permit. /
Koo iu jijoo *de wa doo suru koto
mo dekimaseñ.*（こういう事情ではどう
することもできません）Under these *circumstances,* we can do nothing.
2 reasons:
Kanojo wa katee no jijoo *de kaisha o yamemashita.*（彼女は家庭の
事情で会社をやめました）She left the
company for family *reasons.*
3 affairs:
Kare wa Nihoñ no jijoo *o yoku
shitte iru.*（彼は日本の事情をよく知っ
ている）He is familiar with Japanese *affairs.*

ji「kai じかい（次回）*n.* next; next

time:
Jikai *no kaigi wa shi-gatsu mikka desu*. (次回の会議は4月3日です) The *next* meeting will be held on April 3.

ji「kaku じかく (自覚) *n.* consciousness; awareness:
Kare wa jikaku *ni kakeru*. (彼は自覚に欠ける) He has no *sense of responsibility*. / jikaku *shoojoo* (自覚症状) *subjective* symptoms.

jikaku suru (〜する) *vt.* realize; awaken; be aware of: *Watashi wa chiimu no kyaputeñ to shite* jikaku *shite imasu*. (私はチームのキャプテンとして自覚しています) *I am well aware* that I am captain of this team.

ji「kañ じかん (時間) *n.* **1** time; period:
jikañ *o kasegu* [*tsubusu*] (時間をかせぐ[つぶす]) play for [kill] *time* / *Jikañ wa juubuñ ni arimasu*. (時間は十分にあります) We have plenty of *time*. / *Jikañ wa amari arimaseñ*. (時間はあまりありません) There is not much *time* left.

2 time; hour:
Kaikai no jikañ *ni maniatta* [*okurete shimatta*]. (開会の時間に間に合った[遅れてしまった]) I was in *time* [late] for the opening. / *Chooshoku no* jikañ *wa shichi-ji desu*. (朝食の時間は7時です) *Breakfast* is at seven o'clock. / *Shuppatsu no* jikañ *ga heñkoo ni natta*. (出発の時間が変更になった) The *hour* of departure has been changed.

3 lesson; class:
Tsugi no jikañ *wa suugaku desu*. (次の時間は数学です) The next *lesson* is mathematics. / *Nihoñgo no* jikañ *wa gogo desu*. (日本語の時間は午後です) Japanese *class* is in the afternoon.

-ji「kañ じかん (時間) *suf.* hour:
*Hakone made kuruma de sañ-*jikañ *kakatta*. (箱根まで車で3時間か

かった) It took three *hours* to Hakone by car. / *Watashi-tachi wa ni-*jikañ *mo matasareta*. (私たちは2時間も待たされた) We were kept waiting for two *hours*.

ji「ka ni じかに (直に) *adv.* directly; at first hand; in person:
Sono hanashi wa kare kara jika ni *kikimashita*. (その話は彼からじかに聞きました) I heard the news *directly* from him. / *Atsui nabe o* jika ni *motsu to yakedo o shimasu yo*. (熱いなべをじかに持つとやけどをしますよ) If you hold the hot pot with your *bare* hands, you'll get a burn. / *Kono shorui o kare ni* jika ni *watashite kudasai*. (この書類を彼にじかに渡してください) Please present these documents to him *in person*.
(⇨ chokusetsu)

ji「kañwari じかんわり (時間割) *n.* class schedule.

ji「keñ じけん (事件) *n.* **1** event; affair:
Sono kaisha no toosañ wa ooki-na jikeñ *datta*. (その会社の倒産は大きな事件だった) The bankruptcy of the company was quite an *event*. / *Kare wa sono* jikeñ *ni makikomareta*. (彼はその事件に巻き込まれた) He was involved in that *affair*.

2 incident; case:
Sono jikeñ *no nyuusu wa shiñbuñ de yomimashita*. (その事件のニュースは新聞で読みました) I read the news about the *incident* in the newspaper. / *satsujiñ-*jikeñ (殺人事件) a murder *case*.

ji「ki[1] じき (時期) *n.* **1** time:
Ima ga ichineñ-juu de ichibañ isogashii jiki *desu*. (今が一年中で一番忙しい時期です) This is the busiest *time* of the whole year. / *Imagoro no* jiki *wa taifuu ga ooi*. (今頃の時期は台風が多い) We have lots of typhoons at around this *time*.

2 season:
Aki wa ryokoo o suru no ni ichi-

bañ ii jiki *desu.*（秋は旅行をするのに一番いい時期です）Autumn is the best *season* for traveling.

ji⎡ki² じき（時機）*n.* opportunity; chance:
jiki *o matsu*（時機を待つ）wait for an *opportunity* / jiki *o nogasu*（時機を逃す）miss one's *chance*.

ji⎡ki³ じき（磁器）*n.* porcelain; china.

ji⎡ki ni じきに（直に）*adv.* **1** soon; in a moment:
Shujiñ wa jiki ni *modotte kimasu.*（主人はじきに戻ってきます）My husband will *soon* be back. / *Ichi-nichi nete ireba,* jiki ni *netsu wa sagarimasu.*（一日寝ていれば、じきに熱は下がります）Stay in bed for a day, and your fever will *soon* go down.
2 easily; readily:
Yasui shinamono wa jiki ni *kowareru.*（安い品物はじきに壊れる）Cheap goods *easily* break.

ji⎡kkañ じっかん（実感）*n.* actual feeling; realization:
Yuushoo shita to iu jikkañ *ga mada wakanai.*（優勝したという実感がまだわからない）I still don't *really feel* that I've won.
jikkañ suru（～する）*vt.* fully realize: *Sekiniñ no omomi o* jikkañ *shita.*（責任の重みを実感した）I *was fully aware of* the importance of my responsibility.

ji⎡kkeñ じっけん（実験）*n.* experiment; test:
Kare wa jikkeñ *ni yotte sore o shoomee shita.*（彼は実験によってそれを証明した）He proved it by *experiment.* / *kaku*-jikkeñ（核実験）nuclear *tests.*
jikkeñ (o) suru（～（を）する）*vt.* make an experiment: *Sono kasetsu ga tadashii ka doo ka,* jikkeñ *shite mita.*（その仮説が正しいかどうか、実験してみた）I *carried out an experiment* to see if the hypothesis

was right. / *Kore kara kagaku no* jikkeñ *o suru tokoro desu.*（これから化学の実験をするところです）We are now going to *carry out an experiment* in chemistry.

ji⎡kkeñdai じっけんだい（実験台）*n.*
1 laboratory table.
2 the subject of an experiment: jikkeñdai *ni sareru*（実験台にされる）be used as a *guinea pig.*

ji⎡kke⎤ñshitsu じっけんしつ（実験室）*n.* laboratory.

ji⎡kkoo じっこう（実行）*n.* practice; action; execution:
keekaku o jikkoo *ni utsusu*（計画を実行に移す）put a plan into *practice* / *Kare wa* jikkoo-ryoku *no aru otoko da.*（彼は実行力のある男だ）He is a man of *action.*
jikkoo suru（～する）*vt.* carry out; execute: *yakusoku o* jikkoo suru（約束を実行する）*fulfill* a promise / *Kimi no añ wa ii ga,* jikkoo suru *no wa muzukashii.*（君の案はいいが、実行するのは難しい）Your idea sounds good, but *carry it out* is hard.

ji⎡kku⎤ri じっくり *adv.*（～ to）closely; carefully; thoroughly:
Watashi wa kanojo to sono koto ni tsuite jikkuri（to）*hanashiatta.*（私は彼女とそのことについてじっくり（と）話し合った）I discussed the matter *thoroughly* with her. / *Kono shigoto wa jikañ o kakete* jikkuri（to）*yari nasai.*（この仕事は時間をかけてじっくり（と）やりなさい）Please take your time and do this job *carefully.*

ji⎡ko¹ じこ（事故）*n.* accident:
jiko *o okosu*（事故を起こす）cause an *accident* / jiko *ni au*（事故にあう）meet with an *accident* / *Kare wa kootsuu-*jiko *de kega o shita.*（彼は交通事故でけがをした）He was injured in a traffic *accident.*

ji⎡ko² じこ（自己）*n.* self; oneself:
jiko-*mañzoku*（自己満足）*self*-satisfaction / jiko-*shuchoo*（自己主張）

self-assertion.

ji˺koku じこく（時刻）*n.* time: *Jikoku wa ku-ji juuni-fuñ desu.* (時刻は9時12分です) The *time* is 9:12. / *Tokee o tadashii* jikoku *ni awaseta.* (時計を正しい時刻に合わせた) I set my watch to the right *time*.

ji˻kokuhyoo じこくひょう（時刻表）*n.* (train) schedule; timetable. 《⇨ daiya¹》

ji˻ko-sho˺okai じしょうかい（自己紹介）*n.* self-introduction. **jiko-shookai (o) suru** (～（を）する) *vi.* introduce oneself: *Kare ga saisho ni* jiko-shookai shita. (彼が最初に自己紹介した) First of all, he *introduced himself*.

ji˻ku˺ じく（軸）*n.* axis; axle; shaft.

ji˻mañ じまん（自慢）*n.* pride; boast: *Kare wa haha-oya no* jimañ no tane da. (彼は母親の自慢の種だ) He is his mother's *pride*. / *Kanojo no* jimañ-banashi *wa kiki-akita.* (彼女の自慢話は聞き飽きた) I am sick of her *bragging*. **jimañ (o) suru** (～（を）する) *vt.* be proud of; boast; brag: *Kanojo wa jibuñ no ko o* jimañ shite iru. (彼女は自分の子を自慢している) She *is proud* of her children.

ji˺meñ じめん（地面）*n.* surface of the earth; ground.

ji˻mi˺ じみ（地味）*a.n.* (～ na, ni) plain; quiet; modest: *Watashi wa* jimi *na fuku de meñsetsu ni dekaketa.* (私は地味な服で面接に出かけた) I went for the interview in *conservative* clothes. / *Kono shigoto wa* jimi *da ga, watashi ni wa omoshiroi.* (この仕事は地味だが、私にはおもしろい) This job is *nothing special*, but to me it is interesting. / *Suzuki-sañ wa* jimi *na hito desu.* (鈴木さんは地味な人です) Mr. Suzuki is a *modest* person. 《↔ hade》

Ji˻miñtoo じみんとう（自民党）*n.* = Jiyuu Miñshutoo.

ji˺mu じむ（事務）*n.* office [clerical] work; business: *Kanojo wa booekigaisha de* jimu *o totte iru.* (彼女は貿易会社で事務を執っている) She does *clerical work* at a trading company. / *Watashi wa kare kara* jimu *o hikitsuida.* (私は彼から事務を引き継いだ) I took over the *business* from him.

ji˻mu˺iñ じむいん（事務員）*n.* office worker; clerk; secretary.

ji˻mu˺shitsu じむしつ（事務室）*n.* office room.

ji˻mu˺sho じむしょ（事務所）*n.* office: *Sono beñgoshi wa Kañda ni* jimusho *o motte iru.* (その弁護士は神田に事務所を持っている) That lawyer has an *office* in Kanda.

-˺jiñ じん（人）*suf.* person: *geenoo*-jiñ (芸能人) a show business [TV] *personality* / chishiki-jiñ (知識人) an *intellectual* / shiñ-jiñ (新人) a *newcomer* / shakai-jiñ (社会人) a fully-fledged *member* of society / *Kañsai*-jiñ (関西人) a *person* from the Kansai.

ji˺nañ じなん（次男・二男）*n.* one's second son. 《⇨ kyoodai (table)》

ji˻ñbuñka˺gaku じんぶんかがく（人文科学）*n.* the humanities.

ji˻ñbutsu じんぶつ（人物）*n.* 1 character: *Kare no* jiñbutsu *wa hoshoo shimasu.* (彼の人物は保証します) I vouch for his *character*. 2 person; figure: *Ano hito wa kaisha no juuyoo* jiñbutsu *no hitori desu.* (あの人は会社の重要人物の一人です) He is one of the top *men* in our company. / *Kare wa sono guruupu no chuushiñ* jiñbutsu *desu.* (彼はそのグループの中心人物です) He is a key *figure* in the group.

ji˺ñja じんじゃ（神社）*n.* Shinto

shrine. ★ A place where the Shinto gods are enshrined.

JIÑJA

ji「ñji¹ じんじ（人事）*n.* personnel affairs:
Atarashii jiñji *ga happyoo ni natta.* （新しい人事が発表になった）The new *personnel appointments* were announced. / jiñji-*idoo*（人事異動）*personnel* changes.

ji「ñji² じんじ（人事）*n.* human business:
Jiñji o tsukushite, *teñmee o matsu.* （人事をつくして、天命を待つ）We have to *do our best* and leave the rest to providence.

ji「ñkaku じんかく（人格）*n.* **1** character:
jiñkaku *o migaku*（人格を磨く）cultivate one's *character* / *Kare wa sugureta* jiñkaku *no mochinushi desu.*（彼はすぐれた人格の持ち主です）He is a man of outstanding *character.*
2 personality:
Kodomo no jiñkaku *mo soñchoo shinakereba ikemaseñ.*（子どもの人格も尊重しなければいけません）One must respect children's *personalities* as well.

ji「ñkoo じんこう（人口）*n.* population:
Kono machi wa jiñkoo *ga ooi* [*sukunai*].（この町は人口が多い[少ない]）This town has a large [small] *population.* / jiñkoo-*mitsudo*（人口密度）*population* density.

ji「ñkoo-e」esee じんこうえいせい

（人工衛星）*n.* artificial satellite. 《⇨ eesee²》

ji「ñkoo-ko」kyuu じんこうこきゅう（人工呼吸）*n.* artificial respiration:
Isha wa kare ni jiñkoo kokyuu *o hodokoshita.*（医者は彼に人工呼吸を施した）The doctor gave him *artificial respiration.*

ji「ñkoo-teki じんこうてき（人工的）*a.n.* (~ na, ni) artificial:
Jiñkoo-teki *ni ame o furaseru no wa muzukashii.*（人工的に雨を降らせるのは難しい）It is difficult to make rain fall *artificially.*

ji「ñmee じんめい（人命）*n.* human life:
Sono jishiñ de ooku no jiñmee *ga ushinawareta.*（その地震で多くの人命が失われた）A great number of *lives* were lost in that earthquake. / jiñmee-*kyuujo*（人命救助）the saving of a *life.*

ji「ñmi」ñ じんみん（人民）*n.* the people; the members of a nation-state.

ji「ñrui じんるい（人類）*n.* humankind; the human race:
jiñrui *no rekishi*（人類の歴史）the history of the *human race* / jiñrui-*gaku*（人類学）*anthropology.* 《⇨ niñgeñ》

ji「ñsee じんせい（人生）*n.* human life; life:
Kare wa jiñsee *o tanoshiñde iru.* （彼は人生を楽しんでいる）He is enjoying *life.* / *Kanojo wa shiawase na* jiñsee *o okutta.*（彼女は幸せな人生を送った）She lived a happy *life.*

ji「ñshu じんしゅ（人種）*n.* race; ethnic group:
hakushoku [*ooshoku*] jiñshu（白[黄]色人種）the white [yellow] *race* / jiñshu-*moñdai*（人種問題）the *race* problem / jiñshu-*sabetsu* （人種差別）*racial* discrimination.

ji「ñtai じんたい（人体）*n.* human body:

Kono satchuuzai wa jiñtai *ni gai wa arimaseñ.*（この殺虫剤は人体に害はありません）This insecticide is harmless to *humans.* / jiñtai-kaiboozu（人体解剖図）an *anatomical chart.* 《⇨ illus. (below)》

ji⌐nushi じぬし（地主）*n.* landowner; landlord. 《⇨ ooya》

ji⌐rojiro じろじろ *adv.* (～ to) **jirojiro (to) miru**（～（と）見る）stare at: *Kare wa heñ na booshi o kabutte ita no de miñna ni* jirojiro (to) mirareta.（彼は変な帽子をかぶっていたのでみんなにじろじろ（と）見られた）He *was stared at* by everyone, because he was wearing a strange hat. / *Takusañ no yajiuma ga hañzai-geñba o* jirojiro (to) mite ita.（たくさんのやじ馬が犯罪現場をじろじろ（と）見ていた）Lots of curious onlookers *were gaping* at the scene of the crime.

JIS ジス *n.* abbreviation of 'Japan Industrial Standard'（日本工業規格＝*Nihoñ Koogyoo Kikaku*）. ★ Usually appears as 'JIS' even within Japanese script.

ji⌐satsu じさつ（自殺）*n.* suicide: jisatsu *o hakaru*（自殺を図る）attempt *suicide* / jisatsu-*kooi*（自殺行為）a *suicidal* act / jisatsu-*misui*（自殺未遂）an attempted *suicide.*
jisatsu suru（～する）*vi.* commit suicide; kill oneself: *Sono otoko wa* kubi o tsutte jisatsu shita.（その男は首をつって自殺した）The man *hanged himself.*

ji⌐shiñ¹ じしん（自信）*n.* confidence; assurance: jishiñ *o eru* [*ushinau*]（自信を得る［失う］）gain [lose] *confidence* / *Watashi wa shikeñ ni ukaru* jishiñ ga aru.（私は試験に受かる自信がある）I *am confident* of passing the examination. / *Nihoñgo ni wa* jishiñ *ga arimaseñ.*（日本語には自信がありません）I have no *confidence* in my Japanese. / *Kare wa* jishiñ *mañmañ datta.*（彼は自信満々だった）He was brimming with *confidence.*

ji⌐shiñ² じしん（地震）*n.* earthquake; earth tremor: *Sañ-ji-goro ni* jishiñ *ga atta.*（3時ごろに地震があった）There was an *earthquake* at about three o'clock. / *Ima no* jishiñ *wa shiñdo sañ*

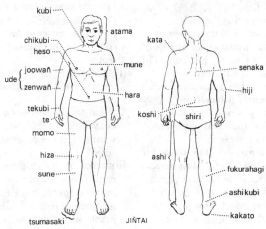

JIÑTAI

gurai desu. (今の地震は震度 3 ぐらい
です) The *earthquake* we felt just
now would be about 3 on the
Japanese seismic scale.

ji˩shiñ³ じしん(自身) *n.* oneself;
itself:
Kare jishiñ *ga soo iimashita.* (彼自
身がそう言いました) He told me so
himself. / *Watashi* jishiñ *no kañ-
chigai deshita.* (私自身の勘違いでし
た) It was my *own* misunderstanding.

ji˩sho¹ じしょ(地所) *n.* land;
ground; lot:
Kono jisho *no shoyuusha wa dare
desu ka?* (この地所の所有者はだれです
か) Who owns this *land?* / *Semai*
jisho *ni ie ga ni-keñ tatta.* (狭い地
所に家が 2 軒建った) Two houses
were built on a small *lot.*

ji˩sho² じしょ(辞書) *n.* dictionary:
★ More formal than '*jibiki.*'
jisho *o hiku* (辞書を引く) consult a
dictionary / Jisho *de sono tañgo
no imi o shirabete gorañ.* (辞書でそ
の単語の意味を調べてごらん) Look up
the meaning of the word in your
dictionary. 《⇨ jibiki; jiteñ》

ji˥shuu じしゅう(自習・自修) *n.*
studying for [by] oneself:
*Kokugo no jikañ wa señsee ga
yasumi de* jishuu *ni natta.* (国語の
時間は先生が休みで自習になった) The
Japanese class became a *free
study period*, because the teacher
was absent. / jishuu-*jikañ* (自習時
間) a *study* period / jishuu-*shitsu*
(自習室) a *study* hall / jishuu-sho
(自習書) a *workbook*.
jishuu suru (〜する) *vi.* study for
[by] oneself: *Kono jikañ wa sorezore* jishuu shite *kudasai.* (この時間
はそれぞれ自習してください) *Study by
yourselves* during this period.

ji˥ssai じっさい(実際) *n.* fact;
truth; practice:
Sono hanashi wa jissai *to chigaimasu.* (その話は実際と違います) Your

story differs from the *facts.* / *Riroñ to* jissai *wa chigau koto ga arimasu.* (理論と実際は違うことがありま
す) Theory and *practice* are sometimes different. / *Kanojo wa* jissai
yori mo wakaku mieru. (彼女は実際
よりも若く見える) She looks younger than she *actually* is.

jissai wa (〜は) as a matter of
fact: *Kare wa reetañ ni mieru ga*
jissai wa *shiñsetsu na hito desu.*
(彼は冷淡に見えるが実際は親切な人で
す) He appears coldhearted, but
he is *really* a kind man.
— *adv.* (〜 no, ni) actually;
really:
Sore wa jissai *(ni) atta hanashi
desu.* (それは実際(に)あった話です) It is
a tale that *actually* took place. /
Watashi mo jissai *(ni) kono me de
sore o mimashita.* (私も実際(に)この
目でそれを見ました) I, too, *actually*
saw it with my own eyes. / *Kono
hoohoo de* jissai *ni moñdai ga kaiketsu dekiru deshoo ka?* (この方法
で実際に問題が解決できるでしょうか)
Can we *actually* solve the problem in this way? / *Jissai, kare mo
komatta koto o shite kureta mono
da.* (実際、彼も困ったことをしてくれたも
のだ) *As a matter of fact*, he did
something that caused us a lot of
trouble.

ji˥ssai-teki じっさいてき(実際的)
a.n. (〜 na, ni) practical; matter-
of-fact:
Jissai-teki *na chishiki o mi ni tsuketai.* (実際的な知識を身につけたい) I
want to acquire *practical* knowledge.

ji˥sseki じっせき(実績) *n.* actual
results; one's achievements:
jisseki *o ageru* (実績を上げる) give
satisfactory results / *Sakuneñ no*
jisseki *wa akaji datta.* (昨年の実績
は赤字だった) Last year's *business
results* were in the red. / *Kare wa
gakumoñ-joo no* jisseki *wa nani*

mo nai.(彼は学問上の実績は何もない) He has no academic *achievements.*

ji⌐sseñ じっせん (実践) *n.* practice: *jisseñ o tsuujite manabu* (実践を通じて学ぶ) learn through *practice.*

jisseñ suru (〜する) *vt.* practice: *Jibuñ ga shiñjiru yoo ni* jisseñ shi nasai.(自分が信じるように実践しなさい) *Act* in accordance with your beliefs.

ji⌐sshi じっし (実施) *n.* enforcement; operation: jisshi *ni fumikiru* (実施に踏み切る) decide to put into *operation* / ... *no* jisshi *o miokuru* (...の実施を見送る) put off the *implementation* of....

jisshi suru (〜する) *vt.* enforce; carry out; put into force: *Sono hooritsu wa raigetsu kara* jisshi saremasu.(その法律は来月から実施されます) The law *comes into force* next month.

ji⌐sshitsu-teki じっしつてき (実質的) *a.n.* (〜 na, ni) substantial; essential; material: *Iiñkai wa mada* jisshitsu-teki *na shiñgi ni wa haitte inai.*(委員会はまだ実質的な審議には入っていない) The committee has not yet started *substantive* deliberations. / *Sono kaisha wa* jisshitsu-teki *ni wa sude ni toosañ shite iru.*(その会社は実質的にはすでに倒産している) *To all intents and purposes*, the firm has already gone bankrupt.

ji⌐sshuu じっしゅう (実習) *n.* practice; practical training: jisshuu-see (実習生) a *trainee* / *kyooiku*-jisshuu (教育実習) *practice* teaching.

jisshuu (o) suru (〜(を)する) *vt.* practice; have practical training: *ryoori no* jisshuu o suru (料理の実習をする) *practice* cooking.

Ji⌐su ジス *n.* = JIS.

ji⌐tai じたい (事態) *n.* situation: *Jitai wa akka shite iru.*(事態は悪

化している) The *situation* is worsening. / *Jitai o kaizeñ shinake-reba naranai.*(事態を改善しなければならない) We must improve the *situation.* / *Saiaku no jitai wa sakerareta.*(最悪の事態は避けられた) We were able to avert *the worst.* / *Kare-ra wa* jitai *no shuushuu o hakatta.*(彼らは事態の収拾をはかった) They strived to settle the *matter.*

ji⌐taku じたく (自宅) *n.* one's own house; one's home: *Señsee no* jitaku *o hoomoñ shita.* (先生の自宅を訪問した) I visited my teacher at his *house.* / *Asu wa* jitaku *ni imasu.*(あすは自宅にいます) I will be at *home* tomorrow.

ji⌐teñ じてん (辞典) *n.* dictionary: ★ More formal than '*jisho.*' Usually used in the title of a dictionary. *ee-wa* jiteñ (英和辞典) an English-Japanese dictionary. 《⇨ jisho; jibiki》

ji⌐teñsha じてんしゃ (自転車) *n.* bicycle: jiteñsha *ni noru* (自転車に乗る) ride a *bicycle* / jiteñsha *o kogu* (自転車をこぐ) pedal a *bicycle* / *Kare wa* jiteñsha *de gakkoo e itte imasu.* (彼は自転車で学校へ行っています) He goes to school by *bicycle.*

ji⌐tsubutsu じつぶつ (実物) *n.* real thing; original: *Kono e wa* jitsubutsu *sokkuri da.* (この絵は実物そっくりだ) This picture looks just like the *real thing.* / *Kore wa* jitsubutsu *de naku, kopii desu.*(これは実物でなく、コピーです) This is not the *original*, but a copy. / *Kono shashiñ wa* jitsubutsu-*dai desu.*(この写真は実物大です) This photograph shows the *actual* size.

ji⌐tsugeñ じつげん (実現) *n.* realization; materialization: *...no* jitsugeñ *o mezasu* (...の実現を目指す) aim at *making a reality* of... / *Sono keekaku wa yatto* jitsu-geñ *no hakobi to natta.* (その計画は やっと実現の運びとなった) The plan was at long last all set to *be put into action.* / *Sore wa* jitsugeñ-see *ga nai.* (それは実現性がない) That is not *realistic.*

jitsugeñ suru (～する) *vi., vt.* come true; realize: *Kanojo no naganeñ no yume ga* jitsugeñ *shita.* (彼女の長年の夢が実現した) Her long-cherished dream *has come true.* / *Kare no kiboo o* jitsu-geñ suru *no wa muzukashii.* (彼の 希望を実現するのはむずかしい) It is difficult to *realize* his hope.

ji⌐tsujoo じつじょう (実情) *n.* ac-tual circumstances; the real state of affairs: jitsujoo *o shiraberu* (実情を調べる) look into the *actual circum-stances* / *Sono kuni no* jitsujoo *wa hisañ desu.* (その国の実情は悲惨です) The *real state of affairs* in that country is miserable.

ji⌐tsu⌐ ni じつに (実に) *adv.* very; terribly; really; extremely: *Kono shoosetsu wa* jitsu ni *omo-shirokatta.* (この小説は実におもしろか った) This novel was *extremely* interesting. / *Kyoo wa* jitsu ni *ii teñki da.* (きょうは実にいい天気だ) Today the weather is *really* good. / *Koko kara miru Fuji-sañ wa* ji-tsu ni *utsukushii.* (ここから見る富士 山は実に美しい) Mt. Fuji seen from here is *very* beautiful.

ji⌐tsuree じつれい (実例) *n.* ex-ample; instance: *Kare wa* jitsuree *o agete, setsu-mee shita.* (彼は実例をあげて, 説明し た) He explained by giving *exam-ples.* / *Soñna* jitsuree *wa kako ni nai.* (そんな実例は過去にない) Such an *example* is without precedent.

ji⌐tsuryoku じつりょく (実力) *n.*
1 real ability; merit: jitsuryoku *o hakki suru* (実力を発

揮する) demonstrate one's *ability* / *Kare wa Nihoñgo no* jitsuryoku *ga aru.* (彼は日本語の実力がある) He has a *good command* of Japanese. / *Kare wa* jitsuryoku *de shachoo ni natta.* (彼は実力で社長になった) He became president of the com-pany on his own *merits.* / jitsu-ryoku-*sha* (実力者) an *influential* person.
2 force: jitsuryoku *ni uttaeru* (実力に訴える) resort to *force* / jitsuryoku *o koo-shi suru* (実力を行使する) use *force.*

ji⌐tsu⌐-wa じつは (実は) *adv.* to tell the truth; actually; as a mat-ter of fact: Jitsu-wa *watashi ga kare ni yara-seta ñ desu.* (実は私が彼にやらせたんで す) *To tell you the truth,* I made him do it. / Jitsu-wa *watashi wa ano hito ga suki ja arimaseñ.* (実は 私はあの人が好きじゃありません) *The fact* is I do not like him.

⌐**USAGE**⌐

This phrase often has no sub-stantial meaning, just being used as a rhetorical signal for starting a conversation or dis-cussion: *e.g.* Jitsu-wa *ni, sañ-nichi ie o rusu ni suru koto ni narimashite...* (実は2, 3日家を留 守にすることになりまして...) *As a matter of fact,* I will be away for a few days...

ji⌐tsuyoo じつよう (実用) *n.* prac-tical use; utility: *Kono doogu wa* jitsuyoo *ni wa yakudatanai.* (この道具は実用には役 立たない) This tool is of little *prac-tical use.* / jitsuyoo-*hiñ* (実用品) a *useful article; daily necessaries.*

ji⌐tsuyooka じつようか (実用化) *n.* practical use.

jitsuyooka suru (～する) *vt., vi.* put [turn] a thing to practical use: *Sono hatsumee ga* jitsuyooka sareru *ni wa jikañ ga kakaru deshoo.*(その発明が実用化されるには時間がかかるでしょう) It will take some time before that invention *is put to practical use.*

ji⌐tsuyoo-teki じつようてき (実用的) *a.n.* (~ na, ni) practical: *Kono kabiñ wa kiree da kedo* jitsuyoo-teki *de wa nai.*(この花瓶はきれいだけど実用的ではない) This vase is pretty, but *not practical.* / *Sono keñkyuu wa mada* jitsuyoo-teki *na dañkai ni wa tasshite inai.*(その研究はまだ実用的な段階には達していない) The research has not yet reached the stage of *practical* application.

ji⌐ttai じったい (実態) *n.* actual condition: *Roodoosha no* jittai *o shirabeta.*(労働者の実態を調べた) We researched the *actual conditions* of the workers.

ji⌐tto じっと *adv.* **1** still; quietly; motionlessly: *Kare-ra wa* jitto *tatte, sono shiai o mite ita.*(彼らはじっと立って、その試合を見ていた) They stood *still* as they watched the game. / *Keeba no aru hi wa kare wa* jitto shite irarenaku *naru.*(競馬のある日は彼はじっとしていられなくなる) On horse-racing days he gets very *restless.* / *Shashiñ o torimasu kara* jitto *shite ite kudasai.*(写真を撮りますからじっとしていてください) I am going to take a photo, so please keep *still.*
2 fixedly; steadily; intently; attentively: *Kanojo wa kagami no naka no jibuñ no kao o* jitto *mitsumeta.*(彼女は鏡の中の自分の顔をじっと見つめた) She stared *intently* at her own face in the mirror.
3 patiently: *Watashi wa sono itami o* jitto *gamañ shita.*(私はその痛みをじっと我慢した) I *patiently* endured the

pain. / *Kanojo wa otto ga jibuñ no tokoro e modotte kuru no o* jitto *matte ita.*(彼女は夫が自分のところへ戻ってくるのをじっと待っていた) She *patiently* waited for her husband to return to her.

ji⌐yoo じよう (滋養) *n.* nourishment; nutrition. 《⇨ eeyoo》

ji⌐yu⌐u じゆう (自由) *n.* freedom; liberty: *Hyoogeñ no jiyuu wa keñpoo de hoshoo sarete imasu.*(表現の自由は憲法で保障されています) *Freedom* of expression is guranteed by the Constitution. / *Iku ikanai wa kimi no jiyuu da.*(行く行かないは君の自由だ) It is *up to* you whether you go or not.
— *a.n.* (~ na, ni) free; easy: jiyuu *na jikañ*(自由な時間) *free* time / *Kega de migiude ga* jiyuu *ni naranai.*(けがで右腕が自由にならない) Owing to an injury, I can not use my right arm *freely.* / *Dokushiñ no hito wa* jiyuu *de urayamashii.*(独身の人は自由でうらやましい) I envy unmarried people because they are *free.* / *Kono taipuraitaa wa doozo go-*jiyuu *ni o-tsukai kudasai.*(このタイプライターはどうぞご自由にお使いください) Please feel *free* to use this typewriter.

Ji⌐yu⌐u Mi⌐ñshutoo じゆうみんしゅとう (自由民主党) *n.* Liberal Democratic Party. 《⇨ seetoo² (table)》

ji⌐yuushu⌐gi じゆうしゅぎ (自由主義) *n.* liberalism.

ji⌐zeñ じぜん (慈善) *n.* charity: jizeñ *o okonau*(慈善を行う) give to *charity* / jizeñ *no tame ni kane o atsumeru*(慈善のために金をあつめる) collect money for *charity* / jizeñ-*jigyoo*(慈善事業) a *philanthropic* work / jizeñ-*dañtai*(慈善団体) a *charitable* organization.

ji⌐zoo じぞう (地蔵) *n.* guardian deity of children and travelers.

JIZOO

★ Stone statues of '*jizoo*' usually stand along country roads.

-jo じょ (所) *suf.* office; institute; works:
iñsatsu-jo (印刷所) printing *plant* / *keñkyuu*-jo (研究所) a research *institute* / seesaku-jo (製作所) a *factory*. 《⇨ -sho¹》

joˈdoˈoshi じょどうし (助動詞) *n.* auxiliary verb.

joˈgai じょがい (除外) *n.* exclusion; exception.
jogai suru (〜する) *vt.* exclude; except: *Kono baai, shiññyuusee wa jogai shita hoo ga yoi.* (この場合、新入生は除外したほうがよい) In this case, we had better *exclude* the new students.

joˈkoo じょこう (徐行) *n.* going slow:

Kooji-chuu ni tsuki jokoo o-negai shimasu.
(Under construction; please drive slowly.)
JOKOO SIGN

jokoo *kukañ* (徐行区間) a section of road where one must *drive slowly* / Jokoo. (*sign*) (徐行) *Go Slow*.

jokoo suru (〜する) *vi.* go slow; slow down: *Kuruma wa kiri de jokoo shita.* (車は霧で徐行した) The cars *slowed down* on account of the fog.

joˈkyoˈoju じょきょうじゅ (助教授) *n.* assistant professor. 《⇨ kyooju (table)》

joˈoˈ¹ じょう (情) *n.* **1** affection; love:
oyako no joo (親子の情) the *affection* between parent and child.
2 feeling; sentiment:
joo ni atsui [usui] *hito* (情に厚い[薄い]人) a *warmhearted* [*coldhearted*] person / *Kare wa joo ni moroi.* (彼は情にもろい) He *is easily moved emotionally*.
joo ga utsuru (〜が移る) become attached: *Kare wa kanojo ni joo ga utsutta yoo da.* (彼は彼女に情が移ったようだ) He seems to *have become attached* to her.

joˈoˈ² じょう (上) *n.* the best; the top:
Kono shina wa joo no bu desu. (この品は上の部です) This article is one of the *best*.
《⇨ chuu¹ (table)》

-joo¹ じょう (場) *suf.* ground; links; track:
uñdoo-joo (運動場) a *playground* / yakyuu-joo (野球場) a baseball *ground* / gorufu-joo (ゴルフ場) golf *links* / keeba-joo (競馬場) a race *track*.

-joo² じょう (状) *suf.* letter:
shootai-joo (招待状) an *invitation* / suiseñ-joo (推薦状) a *letter* of recommendation.

-joo³ じょう (状) *suf.* -like; -shaped; form:
kyuu-joo no (球状の) *globular* / eñsui-joo no (円錐状の) *cone-*

shaped / kuriimu-joo no (クリーム状
の) *creamy*.

-joo[4] じょう（上）*suf.* concerning;
from the viewpoint of:
kigyoo-joo no *himitsu* (企業上の秘
密) a *company* secret / koozoo-joo
no *kekkañ* (構造上の欠陥) a *structural* defect / kyooiku-joo *konomashiku nai* (教育上好ましくない) be
unsuitable *from the educational
point of view*.

-joo[5] じょう（畳）*suf.* counter for
tatami mats:

USAGE

A standard size (with some
variation between eastern versus western Japan, and apart-
ment-house size versus house
size) for measuring the area of
a room. Typical tatami floor
sizes are '*sañ-joo*' (three-mat
room), '*yo-joo-hañ*' (four-and-a
half-mat room), '*roku-joo*' (six-
mat room), '*hachi-joo*' (eight-
mat room), and '*juu-joo*' (ten-
mat room).

---

roku-joo *ma* (6 畳間) a six-*mat*
room / hachi-joo *no heya* (8 畳の部
屋) a room with eight *mats*.
《⇒ tatami》

ROKU-JOO MA

jo⌐obu じょうぶ（丈夫）*a.n.* (～ *na,
ni*) **1** (of a person) healthy:
Kare wa joobu *de zeñzeñ kaze o*
hikanai. (彼はじょうぶでぜんぜんかぜを
引かない) He is *healthy*, so he does
not catch colds at all.
2 (of substance) strong; durable; firm; tough:
joobu *na nuno* (じょうぶな布) *strong
and durable* cloth / *Nairoñ wa*
joobu *desu.* (ナイロンはじょうぶです)
Nylon is *tough*. / *Kono suutsukeesu wa* joobu *ni dekite iru.* (この
スーツケースはじょうぶにできている) This
suitcase is *solidly* made.

jo⌐ocho じょうちょ（情緒）*n.* **1** atmosphere:
Yokohama no ikoku-joocho *o tanoshiñda.* (横浜の異国情緒を楽しんだ) I
enjoyed the exotic *atmosphere* of
Yokohama.
2 emotion:
Kare wa joocho *ga fuañtee da.* (彼
は情緒が不安定だ) He is *emotion-
ally* unstable.

jo⌐odañ じょうだん（冗談）*n.*
1 joke; humor:
joodañ *o iu* (冗談を言う) tell a *joke*
/ *Kanojo wa* joodañ *o ma ni uketa.*
(彼女は冗談を真に受けた) She took
the *joke* seriously. / *Kare ni wa*
joodañ *ga tsuujinai.* (彼には冗談が
通じない) He has no sense of *humor*.
2 fun:
Joodañ *hañbuñ ni itta dake desu.*
(冗談半分に言っただけです) I just
said it in *fun*.
joodañ deshoo (～でしょう) you're
kidding.
joodañ ja nai (～じゃない) you
can't be serious.
joodañ wa sate oki (～はさておき)
joking apart: Joodañ wa sate oki,
kare wa nañ to itta no desu ka?
(冗談はさておき, 彼は何と言ったのですか)
Serious now, what is it he said?

jo⌐oee じょうえい（上映）*n.* showing of a movie.
jooee suru (～する) *vt.* show;
present: *Sono eegakañ de wa*

ima nani o jooee shite imasu *ka?* (その映画館ではいま何を上映しています か) What film *is* now *showing* at that movie theater?

jo⌐oeñ じょうえん（上演）*n.* presentation; performance: Jooeñ-*chuu wa ushiro kara o-hairi kudasai.*（上演中は後ろからお入りくだ さい）Enter from the rear door during the *performance.*

jooeñ suru（〜する）*vt.* present; perform; put on the stage: *Ano gekijoo de wa raigetsu "Chuushiñgura" o* jooeñ *shimasu.*（あの劇場で は来月「忠臣蔵」を上演します）They are going to *present* "Chushingura" at that theater next month.

jo⌐oge じょうげ（上下）*n.* **1** upper and lower parts: *sebiro no* jooge（背広の上下）the *jacket and trousers* of a suit.

2 social standing: jooge *kañkee*（上下関係）the *pecking order.*

3 up and down: *hata o* jooge *ni furu*（旗を上下に振 る）wave a flag *up and down* / Jooge-*señ tomo futsuu desu.*（上下 線とも不通です）Both *up and down* train service is suspended.

jooge suru（〜する）*vi.* rise and fall; fluctuate: *Oñdo wa ree-do to go-do no aida o* jooge *shite ita.* （温度は零度と 5 度の間を上下していた） The temperature *was fluctuating* between 0°C and 5°C.《↔ sayuu》 《⇨ ueshita》

jo⌐ohatsu じょうはつ（蒸発）*n.* **1** evaporation; vaporization. **2** (of people) disappearance.

joohatsu suru（〜する）*vi.* **1** evaporate; vaporize: *Mizu wa* joohatsu shite *kumo ni naru.*（水は蒸発し て雲になる）Water *evaporates* to form clouds.

2 (of people) disappear; run away: *Kanojo no otto wa sañ-neñ mae ni* joohatsu shita.（彼女の夫は 3 年前に 蒸発した）Her husband *vanished* three years ago.

jo⌐ohi⌐ñ じょうひん（上品）*a.n.* （〜 na, ni）graceful; elegant; refined: joohiñ *na iro no fuku*（上品な色の 服）clothes of *refined* color / *Suzuki fujiñ wa* joohiñ *na hito desu.* （鈴木夫人は上品な人です）Mrs. Suzuki is a *graceful* lady. / *Motto* joohiñ *na kotoba o tsukai nasai.* （もっと上品な言葉を使いなさい）Please use more *refined* language. 《↔ gehiñ》

jo⌐ohoo じょうほう（情報）*n.* information; intelligence: joohoo *o eru*（情報を得る）obtain *information* / *Nani-ka atarashii* joohoo *wa arimasu ka?*（何か新しい 情報はありますか）Is there any new *information?* / *Sono* joohoo *o teekyoo shita no wa dare desu ka?* （その情報を提供したのはだれですか） Who is it that gave you that *information?*

jo⌐ojuñ じょうじゅん（上旬）*n.* the first ten days of a month: *Nyuugaku shikeñ wa sañ-gatsu* (no) joojuñ *ni arimasu.*（入学試験は 3 月(の)上旬にあります）We have entrance examinations at *the beginning* of March.《⇨ chuujuñ; gejuñ》

jo⌐okeñ じょうけん（条件）*n.* condition; terms: jookeñ *o mitasu*（条件を満たす）satisfy the *conditions* / jookeñ *o ukeireru* [*nomu*]（条件を受け入れる[飲 む]）accept a *condition* / *Getsumatsu made ni kaesu to iu* jookeñ *de kane o karita.*（月末までに返すとい う条件で金を借りた）I borrowed money on the *condition* that I pay it back by the end of this month. / *Kanojo wa motto yoi* jookeñ *no shigoto o sagashite iru.*（彼 女はもっと良い条件の仕事を探している）

She is looking for a job with better *conditions*.

jookeñ tsuki (～つき) conditional: jookeñ tsuki (no) keeyaku (条件つき(の)契約) a *conditional* contract / Jookeñ tsuki de sono añ ni sañsee shita. (条件つきでその案に賛成した) I agreed to the plan *conditionally*.

jo⌐oki じょうき (蒸気) *n.* steam; vapor:
Yakañ kara jooki ga agatte iru. (やかんから蒸気があがっている) *Steam* is coming from the kettle. / Mizu wa nessuru to jooki ni naru. (水は熱すると蒸気になる) If you heat water it becomes *vapor*.

jo⌐oki⌐geñ じょうきげん (上機嫌) *n.* good humor; high spirits:
Kare wa jookigeñ datta. (彼は上きげんだった) He was in *good humor*.

jo⌐oko⌐okyaku じょうこうきゃく (乗降客) *n.* passengers getting on and off.

jo⌐okuu じょうくう (上空) *n.* the sky:
Kikyuu wa haruka jookuu ni kieta. (気球ははるか上空に消えた) The (weather) balloon disappeared far up in *the sky*. / Hikooki wa Tookyoo-wañ jookuu o señkai shita. (飛行機は東京湾上空を旋回した) The airplane circled *over* Tokyo Bay.

jo⌐okyaku じょうきゃく (乗客) *n.* passenger.

jo⌐okyoo[1] じょうきょう (状況) *n.* situation; circumstances; conditions:
Wareware wa hijoo ni komatta jookyoo ni aru. (われわれは非常に困った状況にある) We are in a very awkward *situation*. / Ima no jookyoo de wa rieki o ageru no wa muzukashii. (今の状況では利益を上げるのは難しい) Under the present *circumstances*, it is difficult to make a profit. / Jookyoo kara hañdañ shite, sore wa mazu fukanoo de-

shoo. (状況から判断して，それはまず不可能でしょう) Judging from the present *conditions*, it will almost certain be impossible.

jo⌐okyoo[2] じょうきょう (上京) *n.* going [coming] up to Tokyo.
jookyoo suru (～する) *vi.* go [come] up to Tokyo: Oji ga raigetsu jookyoo shite kimasu. (おじが来月上京して来ます) My uncle will *come up* to Tokyo next month.

jo⌐okyuu じょうきゅう (上級) *n.* advanced course:
Nihoñgo no jookyuu kurasu [koosu] (日本語の上級クラス[コース]) the *advanced* Japanese class [course] / jookyuu Eego (上級英語) *advanced* English. 《⇨ chuukyuu; shokyuu》

jo⌐omae じょうまえ (錠前) *n.* lock:
to ni joomae o kakeru (戸に錠前を掛ける) *lock* a door. 《⇨ kagi》

Jo⌐omoñ-ji⌐dai じょうもんじだい (縄文時代) *n.* Jomon Period (ca. 8,000 to ca. 300 B.C.): Joomoñ-shiki doki (縄文式土器) *straw-rope pattern* pottery; *Jomon* ware. 《⇨ jidai (table)》

jo⌐omu (to⌐rishimari⌐yaku) じょうむ(とりしまりやく) (常務(取締役)) *n.* managing director. 《⇨ kaisha (table)》

jo⌐onetsu じょうねつ (情熱) *n.* passion; enthusiasm:
Kare wa joonetsu o komete katatta. (彼は情熱を込めて語った) He spoke with *passion*. / Kare wa mada sono keñkyuu ni joonetsu o moyashite iru. (彼はまだその研究に情熱を燃やしている) He *is* still *enthusiastic* about his research.

jo⌐onetsu-teki じょうねつてき (情熱的) *a.n.* (～ na, ni) passionate; enthusiastic; ardent:
joonetsu-teki na odori (情熱的な踊り) a *passionate* dance.

jo-⌐o⌐o じょおう (女王) *n.* queen:
Eekoku no jo-oo (英国の女王) the

Queen of the United Kingdom / *tenisu* [*sukeeto*] *no* jo-oo (テニス[スケート]の女王) the *queen* of tennis [skating]. 《⇨ oo'》

jo'o-oñ じょうおん（常温）*n.* normal [room] temperature; fixed temperature:
niku o joo-oñ *de kaitoo suru* (肉を常温で解凍する) defrost meat at *room temperature*.

jo'oriku じょうりく（上陸）*n.* landing; disembarkation.
jooriku suru (～する) *vi.* land; disembark: *Taifuu ga Kyuushuu ni* jooriku *shita.* (台風が九州に上陸した) The typhoon *came ashore* in Kyushu.

jo'oruri じょうるり（浄瑠璃）*n.* narrative ballad sung for traditional puppet theater.
《⇨ buñraku (photo)》

jo'oryuu じょうりゅう（上流）*n.*
1 the upper course [reaches] of a river:
Kono kawa no jooryuu *ni damu ga arimasu.* (この川の上流にダムがあります) There is a dam on *the upper reaches* of this river. / *Watashi-tachi wa* jooryuu *ni mukatte booto o koida.* (私たちは上流に向かってボートをこいだ) We rowed our boat *upstream.* 《↔ karyuu》
2 the upper class:
Kono yoochieñ wa jooryuu *katee no kodomo ga ooi.* (この幼稚園は上流家庭の子どもが多い) This kindergarten has a lot of children from *upper-class* families. 《⇨ chuuryuu; kasoo》

jo'osee じょうせい（情勢）*n.* the state of affairs; situation; conditions:
Joosee wa taezu heñka shite iru. (情勢は絶えず変化している) *The state of affairs* is changing every moment. / *Kare wa sekai no* joosee *ni tsuujite iru.* (彼は世界の情勢に通じている) He is well versed in the

world *situation.* / *Mokka no* joo-see *de wa kachime ga nai.* (目下の情勢では勝ち目がない) Under the present *conditions*, we have no chance of winning. / *Joosee o tekikaku ni hañdañ shi nasai.* (情勢を的確に判断しなさい) Please judge the *situation* accurately.

jo'osha じょうしゃ（乗車）*n.* boarding a train [bus]; taking a taxi:
joosha-*guchi* (乗車口) the door to a bus, train / joosha-*kyohi* (乗車拒否) a taxi driver's refusal to *pick up a passenger* / joosha-*hoomu* (乗車ホーム) a *boarding* platform.
joosha suru (～する) *vt.* get on a train [bus, etc.]: *Jookyaku wa ichiretsu ni narañde* joosha shita. (乗客は一列に並んで乗車した) The passengers lined up and *got on* the bus. / *Doozo* go-joosha *kudasai.* (どうぞご乗車ください) All *aboard!*

jo'osha'keñ じょうしゃけん（乗車券）*n.* train [bus] ticket:
Joosha-keñ *o haikeñ shimasu.* (by a conductor in the train) (乗車券を拝見します) (Let me see) your *tickets*, please.

jo'oshi じょうし（上司）*n.* one's superior; boss.

jo'oshiki じょうしき（常識）*n.* common knowledge; common sense:
Sore wa watashi-tachi no aida de wa jooshiki *desu.* (それは私たちの間では常識です) It is *a matter of common knowledge* among us. / *Kare wa* jooshiki *ni kakete iru.* (彼は常識に欠けている) He lacks in *common sense.* / *Soñna koto o suru nañte* jooshiki *de wa kañgaerarenai.* (そんなことをするなんて常識では考えられない) A person of *ordinary intelligence* would never do such a thing.
jooshiki hazure (～はずれ) eccen-

tric; absurd: jooshiki hazure *no furumai* (常識はずれの振る舞い) *senseless* behavior.

jo⌐oshiki-teki じょうしきてき (常識的) *a.n.* (~ na, ni) commonsense; practical; ordinary; commonplace:
jooshiki-teki *na mikata* (常識的な見方) a *commonsense* view / *Sono nedañ wa* jooshiki-teki *da to omoimasu.* (その値段は常識的だと思います) I think that price is *reasonable.*

jo⌐oshoo じょうしょう (上昇) *n.* rise; ascent:
jooshoo *o tadoru* (上昇をたどる) continue to *rise* / jooshoo-*kiryuu* (上昇気流) an *ascending* air current.
jooshoo suru (~する) *vi.* rise; go up: *Iñfure de bukka ga* jooshoo shita. (インフレで物価が上昇した) As a result of inflation, prices *have gone up.* 《↔ kakoo²》

jo⌐otai じょうたい (状態) *n.* state; condition:
Kono ie wa hidoi jootai *da.* (この家はひどい状態だ) This house is in a bad *state.* / *Kañja wa kikeñ na* jootai *ni arimasu.* (患者は危険な状態にあります) The patient is in critical *condition.*

jo⌐otoo じょうとう (上等) *a.n.* (~ na, ni) of good quality; excellent:
jootoo *na niku* (上等な肉) meat of *superior quality* / *Kono mise wa takai kedo,* jootoo *na shinamono o oite iru.* (この店は高いけど，上等な品物を置いている) This shop is expensive, but it carries *high quality* goods.

jo⌐owañ じょうわん (上腕) *n.* upper arm. 《⇨ ude; jiñtai (illus.)》

jo⌐oyaku じょうやく (条約) *n.* treaty:
jooyaku *o musubu* [*haki suru*] (条約を結ぶ[破棄する]) conclude [abrogate] a *treaty* / jooyaku *ni chooiñ suru* (条約に調印する) sign a *treaty.*

jo⌐oyoo-ka⌐ñji じょうようかんじ (常用漢字) *n.* Chinese characters in common use. ★ The 1945 characters designated by the Cabinet in 1981 for everyday use. 《⇨ kañji²》

jo⌐ozu じょうず (上手) *a.n.* (~ na, ni) good; well:
oshieru no ga joozu *na señsee* (教えるのがじょうずな先生) a teacher who is *good* at teaching / *Suzuki-sañ wa e ga* joozu *desu.* (鈴木さんは絵がじょうずです) Mr. Suzuki paints *well.* / *Zuibuñ* joozu *ni narimashita ne.* (ずいぶんじょうずになりましたね) You have become really *good.* / *Nakanaka* joozu *ni utaenai.* (なかなかじょうずに歌えない) I can't sing at all *well.* 《↔ heta》《⇨ umai》

jo⌐see じょせい (女性) *n.* adult woman; lady; female: ★ A more refined word than 'oñna,' which often sounds rude.
Kare wa wakai josee *ni niñki ga aru.* (彼は若い女性に人気がある) He is popular among *young women.* / *Kanojo wa* josee-rashii *mono no kañgaekata o shite iru.* (彼女は女性らしいものの考え方をしている) She has *womanly* views. 《↔ dañsee》《⇨ fujiñ²; joshi¹; oñna》

jo⌐see-teki じょせいてき (女性的) *a.n.* (~ na, ni) (of women, men and things) womanly, feminine; womanish:
josee-teki *na ji* (女性的な字) *womanly* handwriting / josee-teki *na fuñiki no otoko* (女性的な雰囲気の男) a man with a *feminine* air / *Kono shoosetsu wa kiwamete* josee-teki *na sakuhiñ da.* (この小説はきわめて女性的な作品だ) This novel is a very *feminine* work. 《↔ dañsee-teki》《⇨ oñna-rashii》

jo⌐shi¹ じょし (女子) *n.* **1** girl:
joshi-*koo* (女子校) a *girls'* school / *Kono kurasu ni wa* joshi *ga nijuu-niñ imasu.* (このクラスには女子が 20 人います) There are twenty *girls* in

this class.

2 woman; lady; female: joshi-*yoo toire* (女子用トイレ) the *ladies'* toilet / *Kotoshi wa* joshi *no kyuujiñ mooshikomi ga sukoshi arimasu.* (今年は女子の求人申し込みが少しあります) There are a few job offers for *women* this year. 《↔ dañshi》《⇨ fujiñ²; josee》

jo⌐shi² じょし (助詞) *n.* (postpositional) particle.

jo⌐shidai じょしだい (女子大) *n.* women's university. ★ Shortened form of '*joshi-daigaku.*'

jo⌐shi-da⌐igaku じょしだいがく (女子大学) *n.* women's university. 《⇨ daigaku; joshidai》

jo⌐shu じょしゅ (助手) *n.* assistant; helper; tutor: joshu *o tsutomeru* (助手を務める) serve as an *assistant* / *Kare wa igakubu no* joshu *o shite imasu.* (彼は医学部の助手をしています) He is an *instructor* in a medical college.

jo⌐yuu じょゆう (女優) *n.* actress.

JR ジェーアール *n.* the Japan Railway Company. ★ Collective name for the group of companies that comprise the former Japan National Railways, '*Kokutetsu*' (国鉄).

ju⌐gyoo じゅぎょう (授業) *n.* lesson; class; school: *Kyoo no gogo wa* jugyoo *ga arimaseñ.* (きょうの午後は授業がありません) We have no *class* this afternoon. / *Imai señsee no* jugyoo *o uketa koto ga arimasu.* (今井先生の授業を受けたことがあります) I have taken *lessons* from Mr. Imai. / jugyoo-*ji-kañ* (授業時間) *school* hours / ju-gyoo-*nissuu* (授業日数) the number of *school* days / jugyoo-*ryoo* (授業料) *school* fees; *tuition.*

jugyoo (o) suru (～(を)する) *vi.* teach; give lessons: *Señsee wa Nihoñgo de* jugyoo (o) shita. (先生は日本語で授業(を)した) The teacher *conducted her class* in Japanese.

ju⌐keñ じゅけん (受験) *n.* taking an (entrance) examination: jukeñ *no juñbi o suru* (受験の準備をする) prepare for an *entrance examination* / jukeñ-*see* (受験生) a student *preparing for an examination* / jukeñ-*ryoo* (受験料) an *examination* fee / jukeñ-*kamoku* (受験科目) *examination* subjects.

jukeñ suru (～する) *vt.* take an (entrance) examination: *Kotoshi wa kokuritsu daigaku o* jukeñ shimasu. (今年は国立大学を受験します) I am going to *take the entrance examination* for a national university this year.

ju⌐kugo じゅくご (熟語) *n.* **1** compound word consisting of two or more Chinese characters. *e.g.* 手荷物 (*tenimotsu*), 登山 (*tozañ*).
2 idiom; set phrase.

ju⌐ku⌐s·u じゅくす (熟す) *vi.* (jukush·i-; jukus·a-; jukush·i-te ⓒ)
1 ripen: *Kono kaki wa* jukushite iru. (この柿は熟している) This persimmon *is ripe.* / *Kudamono no ooku wa aki ni* jukushimasu. (果物の多くは秋に熟します) Most fruits *ripen* in autumn.
2 (of opportunity, etc.) be ripe: *Ki no* jukusu *no o matoo.* (機の熟すのを待とう) Let's wait until the time *is ripe.*

ju⌐myoo じゅみょう (寿命) *n.* life span; life: jumyoo *ga nagai* [*mijikai*] (寿命が長い[短い]) be *long-lived* [*short-lived*] / *Ippañ-teki ni heekiñ* jumyoo *wa nobite imasu.* (一般的に平均寿命は延びています) Generally speaking, the average *life span* has become longer. / *Kono deñchi wa* jumyoo da. (この電池は寿命だ) This battery *has run down.*

jumyoo ga chijimaru (～が縮まる) one's life is shortened: *Sono jiko* *de* jumyoo ga chijimatta. (その事故で寿命が縮まった) The accident *took years off my life.*

ju「ñ¹ じゅん (順) *n.* order; turn:
Juñ *ga kurutte shimatta.* (順が狂ってしまった) The *order* was mixed up. / *Se no takai* juñ *ni narabi nasai.* (背の高い順に並びなさい) Line up in *order* of height. / *Tañgo o a-i-u-e-o* juñ *ni hairetsu shita.* (単語をあいうえお順に配列した) I arranged the words in the *order* of the Japanese syllabary. 《⇨ juñbañ; juñjo》
　juñ o otte (〜を追って) in the proper order: *Sono keeka o* juñ o otte, *setsumee shita.* (その経過を順を追って, 説明した) I explained the development *in the proper sequence.*

ju「ñ² じゅん (純) *a.n.* (〜 na) pure; innocent; simplehearted:
Juñ *na hito hodo damasare-yasui.* (純な人ほどだまされやすい) Those who are *unsophisticated* are apt to be taken in easily.

juñ-¹ じゅん (準) *pref.* quasi-; semi-; associate:
juñ-*kyuu* (ressha) (準急(列車)) a *semi*-express train / juñ-*kesshoo* (準決勝) a *semi*-final match [game] / juñ-*kaiiñ* (準会員) an *associate* member.

ju「ñ-² じゅん (純) *pref.* pure; all:
juñ-*kiñ* (純金) *pure* gold / juñ-*moo* (純毛) *all* wool.

ju「ñbañ じゅんばん (順番) *n.* one's turn:
Narañde, juñbañ *o matta.* (並んで, 順番を待った) I lined up and waited for my *turn.* / *Kodomo-tachi wa* juñbañ *ni burañko ni notta.* (子どもたちは順番にぶらんこに乗った) The children got on the swing *in turns.*

ju「ñbi じゅんび (準備) *n.* preparation; arrangements:
juñbi *o totonoeru* (準備を整える) make *preparations* / *Taikai no* juñbi *wa chakuchaku to susuñde imasu.* (大会の準備は着々と進んでいます) The *arrangements* for the conference are well under way. / Juñbi *ga dekitara, hayaku ne nasai.* (準備ができたら, 早く寝なさい) Go to bed as soon as you're *ready.* / Juñbi-*busoku de setsumeekai wa hirakenakatta.* (準備不足で説明会は開けなかった) We were unable to hold the orientation meeting because of insufficient *preparation.* / juñbi-chuu (準備中) *Closed* / juñbi-*taisoo* [*uñdoo*] (準備体操[運動]) *warm-up* gymnastics [exercise]. 《⇨ yooi¹》

ju「ñbi (**o**) **suru** (〜(を)する) *vt.* prepare; make ready: *ryokoo no* juñbi o suru (旅行の準備をする) *make ready* for a trip / *Gekai-tachi wa shujutsu no* juñbi o shita. (外科医たちは手術の準備をした) The surgeons *made preparations* for the operation.

JUÑBI-CHUU SIGN

ju「ñchoo じゅんちょう (順調) *a.n.* (〜 na, ni) smooth; favorable; all right:
Shujutsu-go no keeka wa juñchoo *desu.* (手術後の経過は順調です) Post-operative progress has been *satisfactory.* / *Kooji wa* juñchoo *ni susuñde imasu.* (工事は順調に進んでいます) The construction work is proceeding *smoothly.*

ju「ñeñ じゅんえん (順延) *n.* postponement of something scheduled:

Kaigi wa raishuu made juñeñ *ni natta.* (会議は来週まで順延になった) The meeting *was put off* until next week. / *Uteñ* juñeñ *desu.* (雨天順延です) In the event of rain, it will *be postponed* until the first clear day.

juñeñ suru (〜する) *vt.* postpone; put off: *Oñgakukai wa yamu o enai jijoo de* juñeñ *sareta.* (音楽会はやむをえない事情で順延された) The concert *was postponed* due to unavoidable circumstances.

ju「ñjo じゅんじょ (順序) *n.* order: *Kono kaado wa* juñjo *ga kurutte iru.* (このカードは順序が狂っている) These cards are out of *order*. / *Juñjo ga gyaku desu.* (順序が逆です) The *order* is reversed.

ju「ñjoo じゅんじょう (純情) *a.n.* (〜 na) unsophisticated; naive; pure: *Sono otoko wa* juñjoo *na kookoosee o damashita.* (その男は純情な高校生をだました) That man deceived some *naive* high school students. / *Kare wa* juñjoo *de, josee no mae ni deru to sugu akaku naru.* (彼は純情で、女性の前に出るとすぐ赤くなる) Being *unsophisticated*, he easily blushes in front of girls.

ju「ñju「ñ ni じゅんじゅんに (順々に) *adv.* one by one: *Kare wa tanomareta shigoto o* juñjuñ ni *katazuketa.* (彼は頼まれた仕事を順々に片づけた) *One by one* he carried out the tasks he had been asked to do.

ju「ñkañ じゅんかん (循環) *n.* circulation; rotation: juñkañ-*ki* (循環器) a *circulatory* organ / *aku-*juñkañ (悪循環) a vicious *circle*.

juñkañ suru (〜する) *vi.* circulate; cycle: *Ketsueki wa karada no naka o* juñkañ *shite iru.* (血液はから

だの中を循環しいる) Blood *circulates* through the body.

ju「ñkyuu じゅんきゅう (準急) *n.* semi-express train. 《⇨ kyuukoo[1] (table)》

ju「ñsa じゅんさ (巡査) *n.* policeman (the lowest rank in the police).

ju「ñsui じゅんすい (純粋) *a.n.* (〜 na, ni) pure; genuine: juñsui *na Akita-keñ* (純粋な秋田犬) a *pure-blooded* Akita dog / *Kodomo no* juñsui *na kimochi wa taisetsu ni shitai.* (子どもの純粋な気持ちは大切にしたい) We should treasure the *unsophisticated* feelings of children. / *Sore wa* juñsui *na shiñsetsu-shiñ kara shita koto desu.* (それは純粋な親切心からしたことです) That is something I did out of *simple* kindness.

ju「tsugo じゅつご (術語) *n.* technical term: *señmoñ-teki na* jutsugo (専門的な術語) special *technical terms*.

ju「u[1] じゅう (十) *n.* ten. **jut-chuu hakku** (〜中八九) highly likely to occur. 《⇨ too[1]; suu[2] (table)》

ju「u[2] じゅう (銃) *n.* gun; rifle: *mato ni mukete,* juu *o kamaeru* (的に向けて、銃を構える) level one's *gun* at a target.

-juu[1] じゅう (中) *suf.* **1** through; throughout: *Natsuyasumi-*juu *isogashikatta.* (夏休み中忙しかった) I was busy *throughout* the summer vacation. / *Ichinichi-*juu *ame ga futta.* (一日中雨が降った) It rained *all* day *long*. / *ichineñ-*juu (一年中) *right through* the year. 《⇨ -chuu》
2 all over: *Ie-*juu *sagashita ga, sono tegami wa nakatta.* (家中探したが、その手紙はなかった) I looked *all over* the house, but the letter was nowhere. / *Kare wa sekai-*juu *o ryo-*

koo shita.（彼は世界中を旅行した）He has traveled *all over* the world.

-「juu[2] じゅう（重）*suf.* -fold: ni-juu no（二重の）*twofold* / sañ-juu no（三重の）*threefold* / go-juu-no-too（五重の塔）a *five-storied* pagoda.《⇨ gojuu-no-too》

ju「ubu」ñ[1] じゅうぶん（十分）*a.n.* (～ na, ni) enough; sufficient; ample: juubuñ *na shokuryoo*（十分な食料）*sufficient* food supplies / juubuñ *ni shiraberu*（十分に調べる）examine *thoroughly* / *Sañmañ-eñ areba* juubuñ *desu.*（3万円あれば十分です）Thirty thousand yen would be *ample.* / *Jikañ wa* juubuñ *ni arimasu.*（時間は十分にあります）We have *plenty of* time.《↔ fujuubuñ》 —*adv.* enough; to the full; thoroughly: Juubuñ *kañgaete kara kime nasai.*（十分考えてから決めなさい）Make your decision after considering *carefully.* / *Añzeñ ni* juubuñ *go-chuui kudasai.*（安全に十分ご注意ください）Please pay *close* attention to safety.

ju「udai じゅうだい（重大）*a.n.* (～ na) serious; important; grave: juudai *na ayamari*（重大な誤り）a *serious* mistake / *Kare no sekiniñ wa* juudai *desu.*（彼の責任は重大です）His responsibility is *great.* / *Anata to* juudai *na hanashi ga arimasu.*（あなたと重大な話があります）I have something *important* to talk about with you.

ju「udeñ じゅうでん（充電）*n.* charge of electricity: juudeñ-shiki *no higesori*（充電式のひげそり）a *rechargeable* shaver.

juudeñ suru (～する) *vt.* charge: *chiku-deñchi o* juudeñ suru（蓄電池を充電する）*charge* a (storage) battery.

ju「udoo じゅうどう（柔道）*n.* judo: juudoo *o suru*（柔道をする）practice *judo*.

JUUDOO MATCH

ju「ufuku じゅうふく（重複）*n.* = choofuku.

ju「u-gatsu じゅうがつ（十月）*n.* October: *Taiiku-no-hi wa* juu-gatsu *tooka desu.*（体育の日は10月10日です）Health-Sports Day is on *October* 10.《⇨ tsuki[1]（table）》

ju「ugoya じゅうごや（十五夜）*n.* a full moon night.

ju「ugyo」oiñ じゅうぎょういん（従業員）*n.* employee; worker.《⇨ shaiñ》

ju「uichi-gatsu」 じゅういちがつ（十一月）*n.* November: *Buñka-no-hi wa* juuichi-gatsu *mikka desu.*（文化の日は11月3日です）Culture Day is on *November* 3.《⇨ tsuki[1]（table）》

ju「uji」ro じゅうじろ（十字路）*n.* crossroads.《⇨ koosateñ》

ju「ujitsu じゅうじつ（充実）*n.* fullness; substantiality: *naiyoo no* juujitsu *o hakaru*（内容の充実を図る）seek to *enrich* the content / juujitsu-*kañ o ajiwau*（充実感を味わう）enjoy a sense of *fulfillment*.

juujitsu suru (～する) *vi.* be rich in content: juujitsu shita *seeka-tsu o okuru*（充実した生活を送る）live a *full* life / *Kono gakkoo wa uñdoo shisetsu ga* juujitsu shite iru.（この学校は運動施設が充実している）

This school has a *full range* of sports facilities.

ju⌐ujuu じゅうじゅう（重々）*adv.* (*formal*) very much; fully:
Soñna koto wa juujuu shoochi shite imasu.（そんなことはじゅうじゅう承知しています）I am *fully* aware of that sort of thing. / *Shitsuree no dañ, juujuu o-wabi mooshiagemasu.*（失礼の段，じゅうじゅうお詫び申し上げます）I *deeply* apologize for having been rude.

ju⌐ukyo じゅうきょ（住居）*n.* dwelling; residence:
Kare wa Oosaka ni juukyo o sadameta.（彼は大阪に住居を定めた）He took up *residence* in Osaka.

ju⌐umiñ じゅうみん（住民）*n.* inhabitant; dweller; resident:
Juumiñ wa sono biru no keñsetsu ni hañtai shite iru.（住民はそのビルの建設に反対している）The *residents of the area* are against the construction of that building. / juumiñ-*hyoo*（住民票）a certificate of *residence* / juumiñ-*tooroku*（住民登録）*resident* registration / juumiñ-*uñdoo*（住民運動）concerted action by the *residents* / juumiñ-*zee*（住民税）a *resident* tax.

ju⌐uni-gatsu⌐ じゅうにがつ（十二月）*n.* December:
Juuni-gatsu ni wa suru koto ga takusañ aru.（十二月にはすることがたくさんある）In *December* there are a lot of things I have to do. 《⇨ tsuki¹ (table)》

ju⌐uni⌐shi じゅうにし（十二支）*n.* the twelve Chinese year signs.
ne (子)＝rat, ushi (丑)＝cow, tora (寅)＝tiger, u (卯)＝rabbit, tatsu (辰)＝dragon, mi (巳)＝snake, uma (午)＝horse, hitsuji (未)＝sheep, saru (申)＝monkey, tori (酉)＝rooster, inu (戌)＝dog, i (亥)＝boar.
★ Used for reckoning the names of the years. *e.g.* 1990＝*uma doshi* (horse year).

ju⌐urai じゅうらい（従来）*n.* being traditional [conventional; old]:
juurai *no yarikata*（従来のやり方）the *traditional* way of doing things / *Kee-eesha wa kawarimashita ga, mise wa* juurai *doori ee-gyoo o tsuzukemasu.*（経営者は代わりましたが，店は従来通り営業を続けます）The management has changed, but this shop will continue business *as in the past.*

ju⌐usho じゅうしょ（住所）*n.* one's address; one's dwelling place:
Koko ni juusho *o kaite kudasai.*（ここに住所を書いてください）Please write *your address* here. / *Kono tegami no* juusho *wa machigatte imasu.*（この手紙の住所は間違っています）The *address* on this letter is wrong. / *Kanojo no* juusho *wa fumee desu.*（彼女の住所は不明です）Her *address* is unknown.

hagaki

fuutoo

JUUSHO

── (CULTURE) ──
An address written in Japanese starts with the largest unit and finishes with the smallest one. In the case of a large city this may start with prefecture, city, and '*ku*' (ward). This is followed by a smaller division that often bears an area name. Next comes a still smaller area called '*choome*' (丁目). The

next division is '*bañchi*' (番地) and finally '*goo*' (号＝building number).

東京都千代田区富士見 2 丁目
11 番地 3 号
11-3, Fujimi 2-chome
Chiyoda-ku, Tokyo

The '*choome*,' '*bañchi*,' and '*goo*' are also written: 2-11-3. 《⇨ atena》

ju⌐usu ジュース *n.* soft drink; juice. ★ Usually refers to sweetened and flavored carbonated drinks. Fruit and vegetable juice is called '*nama (no) juusu*' (fresh juice).

juutaku じゅうたく（住宅）*n.* house; housing: *Kono atari wa* juutaku *ga misshuu shite iru.*（この辺りは住宅が密集している）The *houses* stand close together in this area. / juutaku-*moñdai* (住宅問題) the *housing* problem / juutaku-*nañ* (住宅難) a *housing* shortage / *koomuiñ*-juutaku (公務員住宅) *housing* for government employees / *kooee*-juutaku (公営住宅) public *housing* / *koodañ*-juutaku (公団住宅) a Japan Housing Corporation *apartment*.

ju⌐utañ じゅうたん（絨毯）*n.* carpet; rug: juutañ *o shiku* (じゅうたんを敷く) spread a *carpet*.

ju⌐uteñ じゅうてん（重点）*n.* stress; importance; priority: *Kono gakkoo de wa supootsu ni* juuteñ *o oite iru.*（この学校ではスポーツに重点を置いている）This school lays *stress* on sports. / *Atarashii hooritsu wa roojiñ no fukushi ni* juuteñ *ga aru.*（新しい法律は老人の福祉に重点がある）The new law attaches *importance* to the welfare

of old people.

ju⌐uteñ-teki じゅうてんてき（重点的）*a.n.* (～ na, ni) intensive; preponderant: juuteñ-teki *na eñjo* (重点的な援助) aid on a *priority basis* / *Keesatsu wa kono atari o* juuteñ-teki *ni soosaku shita.*（警察はこのあたりを重点的に捜索した）The police made an *intensive* search around here.

ju⌐uyaku じゅうやく（重役）*n.* corporate executive; company director. 《⇨ kaisha (table)》

ju⌐uyoo じゅうよう（重要）*a.n.* (～ na) important; major; essential: *Juuyoo na shorui wa kiñko ni shimaimashita.*（重要な書類は金庫にしまいました）I put the *important* documents away in the safe. / *Sore wa kaisha ni totte,* juuyoo *na moñdai desu.*（それは会社にとって、重要な問題です）That is a *vital* question for our company. / juuyoo-*jiñbutsu* (重要人物) an *important* person; a VIP.

ju⌐uyu じゅうゆ（重油）*n.* heavy oil. 《↔ keeyu⌐》

ju⌐wa⌐ki じゅわき（受話器）*n.* (telephone) receiver: juwaki *o toru* (受話器をとる) lift the *receiver*.

ju⌐yoo じゅよう（需要）*n.* demand; request: *Kome no* juyoo *ga hette iru.*（米の需要が減っている）The *demand* for rice is declining. / *Kyookyuu ga* juyoo *ni oitsukanai.*（供給が需要に追いつかない）The supply does not meet the *demand*. / juyoo *to kyookyuu* (需要と供給) supply and *demand*. ★ Note that the word order is reversed in Japanese. 《↔ kyookyuu》

ju⌐yo⌐osha じゅようしゃ（需要者）*n.* consumer; user; customer.

K

ka[1] か (蚊) *n.* mosquito:
Ka ni kuwareta. (蚊に食われた) I
was bitten by a *mosquito*.

ka[12] か (可) *n.* **1** (of a grade rating) being passable; C or D in
schoolwork:
Suugaku wa ka *datta.* (数学は可だっ
た) I got a C in mathematics.
《⇨ seeseki (table)》
2 (*formal*) approval:
Sono teeañ o ka *to suru mono ga
ookatta.* (その提案を可とする者が多か
った) There were a lot of people
who were in *favor* of the proposal. 《↔ ina》
ka mo nashi fuka mo nashi
(〜もなし不可もなし) neither good
nor bad.

ka[3] か *p.* **1** (used to make questions): ★ Changes an ordinary
declarative sentence to an interrogative sentence.
Kore wa nañ desu ka? (これは何です
か) *What* is this? / *Anata wa
Tanaka-sañ desu* ka? (あなたは田中
さんですか) *Are you* Mrs. Tanaka? /
Eñpitsu wa arimasu ka? (鉛筆はあ
りますか) *Do you have* a pencil? /
Kono heñ ni deñwa wa arimaseñ
ka? (この辺に電話はありませんか) *Isn't
there* a phone around here?
2 won't you...; what about...;
shall I [we]...: ★ Used in invitations, requests or proposals.
Koohii de mo nomimaseñ ka? (コー
ヒーでも飲みませんか) *What about
having* a coffee? / *Issho ni eega ni*
ikimaseñ ka? (いっしょに映画に行きま
せんか) *Won't you come* to the
movies with me? / *Chotto te o
kashite* kuremaseñ ka? (ちょっと手を
貸してくれませんか) *Won't you just
lend* me a hand? / *Sorosoro deka-*

kemashoo ka? (そろそろ出かけましょう
か) *Shall we be getting along* now?
/ *Watashi ga soko e* mairimashoo
ka? (わたしがそこへ参りましょうか)
Shall I come there?
3 I wonder: ★ Used with the
tentative of the copula.
Ashita wa teñki ni naru daroo ka?
(あしたは天気になるだろうか) *I wonder*
if it will be fine tomorrow. / *Koñna koto o shite, shikararenai
daroo* ka? (こんなことをして, しかられな
いだろうか) If I do this kind of
thing, *I wonder* if I will be scolded. / *Ano hito ga soñna warui
koto o suru deshoo* ka? (あの人がそ
んな悪いことをするでしょうか) *Do you
suppose* he would do something
bad like that?
4 (used rhetorically when confirming a fact to oneself):
Are, moo koñna jikañ ka. (あれ, もう
こんな時間か) What! *Is it already so
late?* / *Yappari* soo datta no ka.
(やっぱりそうだったのか) *It was just as*
I had thought.
5 (used rhetorically when encouraging oneself to do something):
Sorosoro kaeru ka. (そろそろ帰るか) I
must be off on my way now. /
Teñki ga ii kara sañpo de mo suru
ka. (天気がいいから散歩でもするか)
The weather is fine, so *I think* I
will go for a walk.
6 (used when questioning or re-
futing someone's opinion):
Soñna kodomo ni nani ga dekiru
ka. (そんな子どもに何ができるか) *What
can* a child like that *do?* / *Kimi
nañka ni boku no kimochi ga* wakaru ka. (君なんかにぼくの気持ちがわか
るか) Someone like you *could*

never understand my feelings.

ka[4] か *p.* **1** (used after interrogatives to form indefinites):
Dare-ka *kimashita ka?* (だれか来ましたか) Did *someone* come? / **Doko-ka** *atatakai tokoro e ikitai.* (どこか暖かい所へ行きたい) I want to go *somewhere* warm. / **Nani-ka** *tsumetai mono o kudasai.* (何か冷たいものを下さい) Please give me *something* cold to drink. / **Mata** itsu-ka *o-ai shimashoo.* (またいつかお会いしましょう) Let's get together again *sometime.* / **Dare-ka** *Eego no hanaseru hito wa imaseñ ka?* (だれか英語の話せる人はいませんか) Isn't there *anyone* who speaks English?

2 perhaps [probably] because:
★ Used to indicate a possible reason or cause.
Tsukarete iru see ka *shokuyoku ga arimaseñ.* (疲れているせいか食欲がありません) *Perhaps* it is *because* I am tired, but I have no appetite. / **Kinoo nomi-sugita kara** ka *atama ga itai.* (きのう飲み過ぎたからか頭が痛い) It is *probably because* I drank too much yesterday that my head hurts.

3 or: ★ Used when listing examples from among two or more alternatives.
Ashita ka *asatte issho ni shokuji o shimashoo.* (あしたかあさって一緒に食事をしましょう) Let's have a meal together either tomorrow *or* the day after. / **Tanaka-sañ** ka *dare-ka ni kiite kudasai.* (田中さんかだれかに聞いてください) Please ask Mr. Tanaka *or* someone. / **Kyooto** ka *Nara e ikitai.* (京都か奈良へ行きたい) I want to go to *either* Kyoto *or* Nara. / **Daigaku e iku** ka *shuushoku suru* ka *mada kimete imaseñ.* (大学へ行くか就職するかまだ決めていません) I haven't yet decided *whether* I'll go to university *or* get a job.

4 (used with embedded questions):
Kore wa nani ka *gozoñji desu ka?* (これは何かご存じですか) Do you know *what this is?* / **Tsugi no deñsha wa** nañ-ji ni deru ka *shitte imasu ka?* (次の電車は何時に出るか知っていますか) Do you know *what time the next train leaves?* / **Yamada-sañ ni ashita** nani o suru ka *kiite miyoo.* (山田さんにあした何をするか聞いてみよう) Let's ask Miss Yamada *what she is doing* tomorrow. / **Doo shitara ii** ka *kañgaete kudasai.* (どうしたらいいか考えてください) Please think about *what we should do.* / **Sore o doko de katta** ka *oshiete kudasai.* (それをどこで買ったか教えてください) Please tell me *where you bought it.*

5 whether or...; whether or not:
★ Used with embedded alternate questions.
Doyoo ni iku ka, *nichiyoo ni iku* ka, *mada wakarimaseñ.* (土曜に行くか、日曜に行くか、まだわかりません) I don't know yet *whether* I will go on Saturday *or* go on Sunday. / **Kare ni heñji o dashita** ka *doo* ka *oboete imaseñ.* (彼に返事を出したかどうか覚えていません) I can't remember *whether* I sent him the answer *or not.*

USAGE

Note that '*ka*' can be followed by other particles, particularly '*wa*,' '*ga*' and '*o*.' *e.g.* Doko e iku ka wa, *mada kimete imaseñ.* (どこへ行くかは、まだ決めていません) I have not yet decided *where to go.* / Doo kaiketsu suru ka ga, *moñdai desu.* (どう解決するかが、問題です) The problem is *how we should solve it.* / Ashita no kaigi ni shusseki suru ka, *shinai* ka o *hayaku reñraku shite kudasai.* (あしたの会議に出席するか、しないかを早く連絡してください) Please let us know promptly *whether or not* you are attending tomorrow's meeting.

-ka[1] か（日）*suf.* day:
futsu-ka（二日）the 2nd (*day*); two *days* / *mik-ka*（三日）the 3rd (*day*); three *days* / *too-ka*（十日）the 10th (*day*); ten *days* / *hatsu-ka*（二十日）the 20th (*day*); twenty *days*. 《⇨ tsuitachi (table)》

-¹ka[2] か（下）*suf.* under; below:
...no shihai-ka（...の支配下）*under* the rule of... / *...no kañtoku-ka ni*（...の監督下に）*under the* supervision of... / *ree-ka*（零下）below zero (degrees).

-ka[3] か（化）*suf.* -ization: ★ A change into the stated condition. *eega-ka*（映画化）*making* into a movie / *goori-ka*（合理化）*rationalization* / *jiyuu-ka*（自由化）*liberalization*.
　　-ka suru（〜する）-ize: ★ Forms verbs. kikai-ka suru（機械化する）*mechanize* / goohoo-ka suru（合法化する）*legalize* / soshiki-ka suru（組織化する）*systematize*.

-ka[4] か（科）*suf.* course; department; studies:
Nihoñgo gak-ka（日本語学科）a Japanese language *course* / *nai-ka*（内科）the *department* of internal medicine / *shakai-ka*（社会科）social *studies*.

-ka[5] か（課）*suf.* 1 lesson; work:
dai ik-ka（第一課）*Lesson* 1 / *nik-ka*（日課）daily *work*.
　　2 section (of a company):
jiñji-ka（人事課）the personnel *section*.

-ka[6] か（家）*suf.* 1 (signifies a possessor):
shihoñ-ka（資本家）a *capitalist* / zaisañ-ka（財産家）a *man* of wealth.
　　2 a person of the stated quality or tendency:

kuusoo-ka（空想家）a *dreamer* / joonetsu-ka（情熱家）an *enthusiast*.
　　3 specialist.
oñgaku-ka（音楽家）a *musician* / shuukyoo-ka（宗教家）a *man* of religion.

-ka[7] か（箇）*suf.* counter used with numerals: ★ Sometimes 'ケ' is used instead of 'か.'
ni-ka-*getsu*（二か月）*two* months / sañ-ka-*neñ*（三か年）*three* years / go-ka-*koku*（五か国）*five* countries / nana-ka-*sho*（七か所）*seven* places.

ka¹ado カード *n.* card; a slip of paper:
Toshokañ de mokuroku no kaado o mekutte, hoñ o sagashita.（図書館で目録のカードをめくって、本を探した）In the library I went through the index *cards* looking for the book.

kaasañ かあさん（母さん）*n.* (*informal*) momma; mother.
　　★ Usually with 'o-.' 《↔ toosañ》《⇨ o-kaasañ》

ka¹ateñ カーテン *n.* curtain:
kaateñ o hiku（カーテンを引く）draw a *curtain* / kaateñ o tsurusu（カーテンをつるす）hang *curtains*.

ka¹baa カバー *n.* 1 cover; covering:
sofaa ni kabaa o kakeru（ソファーにカバーをかける）put a *cover* on the sofa.
　　2 dust jacket; wrapper.
《⇨ hyooshi》
　　kabaa suru（〜する）*vt.* 1 cover; make up: *akaji o* kabaa suru（赤字をカバーする）*make up* the deficit.
　　2 (of baseball) cover; back up: *Shooto ga sekañdo o* kabaa shita.（ショートがセカンドをカバーした）The shortstop *covered* the second baseman.

ka「bañ かばん（鞄）*n.* bag; satchel; briefcase:
kabañ o akeru [shimeru]（かばんを開ける[しめる]）open [close] a *bag* / *Kare wa kuroi* kabañ *o motte ita.*

（彼は黒いかばんを持っていた）He was carrying a black *briefcase*.

ka⌐ba⌐·u かばう（庇う）*vt.* (kaba·i-; kabaw·a-; kabat-te Ⓒ) protect; defend:
Dare mo kanojo o kabawanakatta. （だれも彼女をかばわなかった）*Nobody pleaded* for her. / *Tooshu wa ashi no kega o* kabai-nagara *nageta.* （投手は足のけがをかばいながら投げた）The pitcher pitched hard, *keeping the strain off* his injured leg.

ka⌐bayaki かばやき（蒲焼き）*n.* broiled eels. ★ Eels are split and barbecued over a charcoal fire. 《⇨ unagi》

ka⌐be かべ（壁）*n.* **1** wall: Kabe *ni e o kaketa.* （壁に絵を掛けた）I hung a picture on the *wall*. **2** obstacle; deadlock: *Jiñshu-moñdai ga* kabe *ni natte iru.* （人種問題が壁になっている）The racial problem constitutes an *obstacle*. / *Kare no keekaku wa* kabe *ni butsukatta.* （彼の計画は壁にぶつかった）His plan ran up against a *problem*.

ka⌐bi かび（黴）*n.* mold: *Kono pañ ni wa* kabi *ga haete iru.* （このパンにはかびが生えている）There is *mold* on this bread.

ka⌐biñ かびん（花瓶）*n.* flower vase: Kabiñ *ni hana o iketa.* （花瓶に花を生けた）I arranged some flowers in the *vase*.

ka⌐bocha かぼちゃ *n.* pumpkin; squash. 《⇨ yasai (illus.)》

ka⌐bu⌐ かぶ（株）*n.* **1** stock; share: *Watashi wa kono kaisha no* kabu *o motte imasu.* （私はこの会社の株を持っています）I have *stock* in this company. **2** roots; stump: *Pañjii no nae o sañ-*kabu *katta.* （パンジーの苗を3株買った）I bought three pansy *seedlings*.

ka⌐bu² かぶ（蕪）*n.* turnip. 《⇨ yasai (illus.)》

ka⌐bukeñ かぶけん（株券）*n.* stock [share] certificate.

ka⌐buki かぶき（歌舞伎）*n.* Japanese traditional drama. ★ All the roles are played by male actors wearing traditional costumes.

KABUKI (stamp)

ka⌐bu⌐nushi かぶぬし（株主）*n.* stockholder; shareholder: kabunushi-*sookai* （株主総会）a general meeting of *stockholders*.

ka⌐bu⌐r·u かぶる（被る）*vt.* (kabur·i-; kabur·a-; kabut-te Ⓒ) **1** put on (headwear): ★ '*kabutte iru*' ＝wear. 《⇨ kiru² (table)》 *booshi o* kaburu （帽子をかぶる）*put on* one's hat / *Giñkoo-gootoo wa fukumeñ o* kabutte ita. （銀行強盗は覆面をかぶっていた）The bank robber *wore* a mask. 《⇨ kabuseru》 **2** be covered: *Tsukawanai kagu ga monooki de hokori o* kabutte iru. （使わない家具が物置でほこりをかぶっている）The unused furniture *is covered* with dust in the storeroom. 《⇨ kabuseru》 **3** take on (responsibility): *Kare wa hitori de sono jikeñ no sekiniñ o* kabutta. （彼は一人でその事件の責任をかぶった）He alone *took* responsibility for the affair.

ka⌐buse⌐·ru かぶせる（被せる）*vt.* (kabuse-te Ⓥ) put...on; cover... with:

Haha-oya wa kodomo ni booshi o kabusete yatta.（母親は子どもに帽子をかぶせてやった）The mother *put* a cap on her child's head. / *Hana ni biniiru o* kabusete, *samusa o fuseide yatta.*（花にビニールをかぶせて、寒さを防いでやった）I *covered* the flowers with plastic sheets to protect them from the cold. 《⇨ kaburu》

ka⌐bushikiga¬isha　かぶしきがいしゃ（株式会社）*n.* incorporated company; joint-stock company. 《⇨ kaisha》

ka˥chi¹　かち（価値）*n.* worth; value; merit:
Kono e wa hyakumañ-eñ no kachi *ga aru.*（この絵は100万円の価値がある）This picture is *worth* one million yen. / *Kono hoñ wa yomu* kachi *ga aru.*（この本は読む価値がある）This book is *worth* reading. / *Kono hooseki no* kachi *wa dono kurai desu ka?*（この宝石の価値はどのくらいですか）What is the *value* of this gem?

ka⌐chi¬²　かち（勝ち）*n.* victory:
Anata no kachi *desu.*（あなたの勝ちです）You *win*. / *Go tai sañ de wareware ga* kachi *o osameta.*（5対3でわれわれが勝ちを収めた）We gained *victory* by 5 to 3. / *Kachi make wa toki no uñ desu.*（勝ち負けは時の運です）*Victory* or defeat depends on chance. 《↔ make》

ka⌐chikachi¬¹　かちかち *a.n.*
(～ no, ni) **1** be frozen hard:
Ike (no mizu) ga kachikachi *ni kootte iru.*（池（の水）がかちかちに凍っている）The (water in the) pond is frozen *hard*.
2 tense:
Sono oñna-no-ko wa kiñchoo shite, kachikachi *ni natte ita.*（その女の子は緊張して、かちかちになっていた）The girl was *rigid* with tension.

ka˥chikachi²　カチカチ *adv.*
(～ to) (tick of a clock):

Kono tokee wa amari kachikachi (to) *iwanai.*（この時計はあまりカチカチ（と）いわない）This clock hardly makes any *ticking sound*.

ka⌐chiku　かちく（家畜）*n.* livestock; domestic animal:
kachiku *o kau*（家畜を飼う）raise *livestock*.

ka⌐choo　かちょう（課長）*n.* section chief; manager.
kachoo-*dairi*（課長代理）an acting *manager*. 《⇨ kaisha (table)》

ka⌐dai　かだい（課題）*n.* **1** problem; question:
Sore wa koñgo no kadai *desu.*（それは今後の課題です）That is the *problem* we have to deal with from now on.
2 assignment:
Señsee wa seeto ni natsu-yasumi no kadai *o takusañ ataeta.*（先生は生徒に夏休みの課題をたくさん与えた）The teacher gave his pupils a lot of *assignments* for the summer vacation.

ka⌐do¬¹　かど（角）*n.* corner:
Kodomo ga tsukue no kado *ni atama o butsuketa.*（子どもが机の角に頭をぶつけた）The little boy struck his head on the *corner* of the desk. / *Eki wa tsugi no* kado *o magaru to sugu desu.*（駅は次の角を曲がるとすぐです）The station is just around the next *corner*. / *Watashi no uchi wa* kado *kara sañ-geñme desu.*（私の家は角から3軒めです）My house is the third one from the *corner*.

kado ga tatsu（角が立つ）create hard feelings: *Soñna koto o ittara,* kado ga tachimasu.（そんなことを言ったら、角が立ちます）If you say such a thing, it will *give rise to ill feelings*.

ka˥do²　かど（過度）*a.n.* (～ no, ni) excessive; too much:
Kado *no kitai wa kiñmotsu desu.*（過度の期待は禁物です）You should

not expect *too much.* / Kado no uñdoo wa karada ni yoku nai. (過度の運動は体に良くない) *Excessive* exercise is not good for you. / Kare wa hihyoo ni taishite, kado ni biñkañ da. (彼は批評に対して、過度に敏感だ) He is *over*-sensitive to criticism.

ka「do¹matsu かどまつ (門松) *n.* New Year's pine decorations. ★ Set up outside homes and offices with the hope that the new year will bring longevity and prosperity.

KADOMATSU

ka「eri¹ かえり (帰り) *n.* return: O-kaeri wa itsu-mo nañ-ji desu ka? (お帰りはいつも何時ですか) What time *do* you always *go back?* / Koñya wa kaeri ga osoku narimasu. (今夜は帰りが遅くなります) I will *be coming home* late this evening. / Kaeri ni kaimono o shite kuremaseñ ka? (帰りに買い物をしてくれませんか) Would you do some shopping for me *on the way back?* / kaeri-michi (帰り道) one's *way home.* 《↔ iki²; yuki²》

ka「erimi¹·ru かえりみる (顧みる) *vt.* (kaerimi-te Ⓥ) **1** look back on: Jibuñ no kako o kaerimiru to, hazukashiku naru. (自分の過去を顧みると、恥ずかしくなる) When I *look back on* my past I feel ashamed. **2** think of; pay attention: Isogashikute, kazoku o kaerimiru hima mo nakatta. (忙しくて、家族を

顧みるひまもなかった) I was so busy that I did not even have time to *consider* my family. / Kare wa kikeñ mo kaerimizu, kawa ni tobi-koñde, kodomo o tasuketa. (彼は危険も顧みず、川に飛び込んで、子どもを助けた) *Ignoring* the danger, he jumped into the river and rescued the child.

ka「er·u¹ かえる (帰る) *vi.* (kaer·i-; kaer·a-; kaet-te Ⓒ) (of a person) come back; return:

―― **USAGE** ――
'*Kaeru*' and '*modoru*' are often used interchangeably. However, the former implies returning to a place where one spends most of one's time (home, workplace); the latter implies leaving the place at which one is temporarily, and subsequently returning there.

Yamada-sañ wa Sooru kara kaetta tokoro desu. (山田さんはソウルから帰ったところです) Mr. Yamada *has* just *returned* from Seoul. / Watashi wa moo kuni e kaeru tsumori wa arimaseñ. (私はもう国へ帰るつもりはありません) I no longer have any intention of *returning* to my country. / Moo kaeranakereba narimaseñ. (もう帰らなければなりません) I *must be going* now. / Uchi ni kaeru tochuu de tomodachi ni atta. (家に帰る途中で友だちに会った) *On my way* home I met a friend. 《↔ iku》

kaeranu hito (帰らぬ人) a dead person: Kanojo wa kaeranu hito to natta. (彼女は帰らぬ人となった) She *has been taken from us.*

ka「er·u² かえる (返る) *vi.* (kaer·i-; kaer·a-; kaet-te Ⓒ) (of an object) return; get back: Nusumareta e wa buji ni mochinushi no tokoro e kaetta. (盗まれた絵は無事に持ち主の所へ返った) The stolen picture *was* safely *returned* to its owner. / *Kare ni kashita o-kane wa tabuñ* kaette *konai de-shoo.*(彼に貸したお金はたぶん返ってこないでしょう) The money I lent him will probably not *be returned.* / *Señsoo ga owatte, heewa na jidai ni* kaetta.(戦争が終わって、平和な時代に返った) The war finished and we *returned* to a period of peace. 《⇨ modoru》

ka「e・ru³ かえる (変える) *vt.* (kae-te Ⅴ) change; alter:
Taifuu wa shiñro o kaeta. (台風は進路を変えた) The typhoon *altered* its course. / *Kaisha wa kee-ee hoo-shiñ o* kaeta. (会社は経営方針を変えた) The company *changed* its management policy. / *Koñpyuu-taa no fukyuu wa hito no seeka-tsu-yooshiki o* kaeru *deshoo.*(コンピューターの普及は人の生活様式を変えるでしょう) The spread of computers will probably *change* people's lifestyles. / *Sono shirase ni kare wa* kaoiro o kaeta. (その知らせに彼は顔色を変えた) He *turned pale* at the news. 《⇨ kawaru¹》

ka「e・ru⁴ かえる (代える・替える・換える) *vt.* (kae-te Ⅴ) change:
Ichimañ-eñ satsu o señ-eñ satsu ni kaete *moraemasu ka?* (一万円札を千円札にかえてもらえますか) Could you please *change* a 10,000-yen bill into 1,000-yen bills? / *Kibuñ-teñkañ ni heya no* kaateñ *o* kaete *mita.*(気分転換に部屋のカーテンをかえてみた) For a change of mood, I tried *replacing* the curtains in the room. / *Hito no inochi wa* nani-mono ni mo kaerarenai. (人の命は何物にもかえられない) *Nothing is more precious* than a human life.

ka「e・ru⁵ かえる (孵る) *vi.* (kaer・i-; kaer・a-; kaet-te Ⅽ) hatch; be hatched:
Hina ga go-wa kaetta.(ひなが5羽かえった) Five chicks *hatched.*

ka「e・ru⁶ かえる (蛙) *n.* frog; toad:
Kaeru ga naite iru.(蛙が鳴いている) *Frogs* are croaking.

ka「es・u かえす (返す) *vt.* (kaesh・i-; kaes・a-; kaesh・i-te Ⅽ) return; give back:
O-kane wa kijitsu made ni kana-razu kaeshimasu.(お金は期日までに必ず返します) I will without fail *return* the money by the due date. / *O-kashi shita hoñ o* kae-shite *kudasai.*(お貸しした本を返してください) Please *return* the book I lent you. 《⇨ modosu》

ka「ette かえって (却って) *adv.* on the contrary; after all; rather:
Shiñsetsu no tsumori de shita koto ga, kaette *kanojo no mee-waku ni natte shimatta.*(親切のつもりでしたことが、かえって彼女の迷惑になってしまった) What I did with the intention of being kind has, *on the contrary*, ended up causing her trouble. / *Kuruma yori aruita hoo ga,* kaette *hayai koto ga ari-masu.*(車より歩いたほうが、かえって早いことがあります) Walking, *rather* than going by car, is sometimes quicker. / *Uñdoo no shi-sugi wa,* kaette *karada ni warui toki ga arimasu.*(運動のし過ぎは、かえって体に悪いときがあります) Too much exercise sometimes does *more* harm *than* good. / *Aa-iu ketteñ ga aru kara,* kaette *kare ga suki desu.*(ああいう欠点があるから、かえって彼が好きです) I like him *all the more* be-cause he has those sorts of failings.

ka「fuñshoo かふんしょう (花粉症) *n.* hay fever; pollen allergy.

ka「gaku¹ かがく (科学) *n.* science:
Geñdai-kagaku no shiñpo wa me-zamashii.(現代科学の進歩は目覚ましい) The progress of modern *science* is remarkable. / *shakai [shizeñ]-kagaku* (社会[自然]科学) social [natural] *science.*

ka⌐gaku² かがく (化学) *n.* chemistry: ★ Sometimes called '*bakegaku*' to distinguish it from '*kagaku*¹.'
kagaku-*hañnoo* (化学反応) a *chemical* reaction / kagaku-*hiryoo* (化学肥料) *chemical* fertilizer / *yuuki* [*muki*]-kagaku (有機[無機]化学) organic [inorganic] *chemistry*.

Ka⌐gaku-gijutsu⌐-choo かがくぎじゅつちょう (科学技術庁) *n.* Science and Technology Agency: Kagaku-gijutsu-choo *chookañ* (科学技術庁長官) the Director General of the *Science and Technology Agency*. 《⇨ choo⁴ (table)》

ka⌐ga⌐kusha¹ かがくしゃ (科学者) *n.* scientist.

ka⌐ga⌐kusha² かがくしゃ (化学者) *n.* chemist.

ka⌐gaku-teki かがくてき (科学的) *a.n.* (~ na, ni) scientific: kagaku-teki *na hoohoo* (科学的な方法) a *scientific* method / kagaku-teki *ni setsumee suru* (科学的に説明する) explain something *scientifically*.

ka⌐game·ru かがめる (屈める) *vt.* (kagame-te Ⅴ) bend; stoop: *senaka o* kagameta *roojiñ* (背中をかがめた老人) an old man *stooped* with age / *Watashi wa mi o* kagamete *yuka no ue no eñpitsu o hirotta.* (私は身をかがめて床の上の鉛筆を拾った) I *bent down* and picked up the pencil on the floor. 《⇨ kagamu》

ka⌐gami¹ かがみ (鏡) *n.* mirror; looking glass: kagami *o miru* [*nozoku*] (鏡を見る[のぞく]) look in a *mirror* / kagami *ni utsuru* (鏡に映る) be reflected in a *mirror* / *Kanojo wa* kagami *ni jibuñ no sugata o utsushite mita.* (彼女は鏡に自分の姿を映して見た) She looked at herself in the *mirror*. / *Mizuumi wa* kagami *no yoo ni shizuka datta.* (湖は鏡のように静か

だった) The lake was calm like a *mirror*.

ka⌐gami⌐-mochi かがみもち (鏡餅) *n.* round rice cake offered to gods at New Year's time.

KAGAMI-MOCHI

ka⌐gam·u かがむ (屈む) *vi.* (kagam·i-; kagam·a-; kagañ-de C) bend; stoop; crouch: *Kare wa* kagañde *kusa o totta.* (彼はかがんで草を取った) He *bent down* and pulled up the weeds. 《⇨ kagameru》

Ka⌐gawa⌐-keñ かがわけん (香川県) *n.* Kagawa Prefecture. Located in the northwest of Shikoku. The climate is mild and the chief industries include growing olives and manufacturing salt. Capital city: Takamatsu (高松). 《⇨ map (C4)》

ka⌐gayaki¹ かがやき (輝き) *n.* brightness; brilliance; radiance: *taiyoo no* kagayaki (太陽の輝き) the *brilliance* of the sun / *Kare no me no* kagayaki *ga iñshoo-teki datta.* (彼の目の輝きが印象的だった) The *brightness* of his eyes was impressive. 《⇨ kagayaku》

ka⌐gaya⌐k·u かがやく (輝く) *vi.* (-yak·i-; -yak·a-; -ya·i-te C) **1** shine; flash; glitter; twinkle: *Taiyoo ga akaruku* kagayaite iru. (太陽が明るく輝いている) The sun *is shining* brightly. / *Yozora ni hoshi ga* kagayaite iru. (夜空に星が輝いている) The stars *are twinkling* in the night sky.
2 be radiant; sparkle: *Shoojo no kao wa yorokobi de* kagayaite ita. (少女の顔は喜びで輝い

ていた) The girl's face *was radiant* with joy.

ka`ge`[1] かげ (影) *n.* **1** shadow: *Eñtotsu ga jimeñ ni nagai kage o otoshite ita.* (煙突が地面に長い影を落としていた) The smokestack cast a long *shadow* on the ground.
2 silhouette: *Shooji ni hito no kage ga utsutta.* (障子に人の影が映った) *The outline of a figure* was cast onto the paper sliding door.
3 reflection: *Mizuumi ni yama no kage ga utsutte iru.* (湖に山の影が映っている) The *image* of the mountain is reflected in the lake.
kage mo katachi mo nai (〜も形もない) (with a negative) disappear without a trace: *Modotte mitara, watashi no suutsukeesu wa kage mo katachi mo nakatta.* (戻ってみたら, 私のスーツケースは影も形もなかった) When I returned, *there was no trace of* my suitcase.

ka`ge`[2] かげ (陰) *n.* **1** shade: *Ano ki no kage de yasumoo.* (あの木の陰で休もう) Let's take a rest in the *shade* of that tree. / *Sabaku de kage ni natte iru tokoro o sagasu no wa muzukashii.* (砂漠で陰になっている所を捜すのは難しい) In the desert, it is hard to find anyplace *shady*.
2 back; rear: *Otoko wa kaateñ no kage ni kakureta.* (男はカーテンの陰に隠れた) The man hid *behind* the curtain.
3 behind one's back; behind the scenes: *Kage de hito no warukuchi o iu no wa yoshi nasai.* (陰で人の悪口を言うのはよしなさい) Don't speak ill of others *behind their backs*. / *Kare wa kage no jitsuryokusha desu.* (彼は陰の実力者です) He is the strong man *behind the scenes*.

ka`geki` かげき (過激) *a.n.* (〜 na,

ni) extreme; radical: **kageki** *na shisoo* (過激な思想) *radical* ideology / kageki-ha (過激派) the *extremists*.

ka`geñ` かげん (加減) *n.* **1** addition and subtraction.
2 state; condition: ★ Often used as a suffix attached to a noun. *Kyoo no kañja no* kageñ *wa yosa* [waru]-soo da. (きょうの患者のかげんは良さ[悪]そうだ) The *condition* of the patient today seems to be good [bad]. / *Kyoo wa* o-kageñ *wa ikaga desu ka?* (きょうはおかげんはいかがですか) *How are you feeling* today? / *Aji (no)* kageñ *wa doo desu ka?* (味(の)かげんはどうですか) How do you like the *taste?* / Yu-kageñ *wa choodo yoi.* (湯かげんはちょうどよい) The *bath water* is just right.
kageñ suru (〜する) *vt.* regulate; adjust (something physical): *heya no oñdo o* kageñ suru (部屋の温度を加減する) *regulate* the temperature of the room / *reeboo o* kageñ suru (冷房を加減する) *adjust* the air-conditioning.

ka`gi`[1] かぎ (鍵) *n.* key: ★ Can also refer to a lock. For instances where specificity is necessary, use '*joomae*' (錠前) (padlock).

kagi (鍵)	key
	lock

kagi o kakeru [akeru] (鍵をかける[開ける]) *lock* [*unlock*] / kagi *o mawasu* (鍵を回す) turn a *key* / *Kore ga geñkañ no* kagi *desu.* (これが玄関の鍵です) This is the *key* to the front door. / *Doroboo wa* kagi *o kowashite, haitta.* (どろぼうは鍵を壊して, 入った) The burglar got in by breaking the *lock*. / *Seekoo e no* kagi *wa doryoku desu.* (成功への鍵

は努力です) The *key* to success is hard work. / kagi-ana (鍵穴) a *key-hole* / ai-kagi (合鍵) a skelton *key*.

ka「giri¹ かぎり (限り) *n*. **1** limit: *Wareware wa chikara no* kagiri *o tsukushita*. (われわれは力の限りを尽くした) We exerted ourselves to the *limits* of our strength. / *Joodañ ni mo*, kagiri *ga aru*. (冗談にも, 限りがある) Even joking has its *limits*. / *Niñgeñ no yokuboo ni wa* kagiri *ga nai*. (人間の欲望には限りがない) There are no *bounds* to human greed. (⇨ kagiru)
2 end: *Kono teñrañkai wa koñgetsu-ka-giri de owari desu*. (この展覧会は今月限りで終わりです) This exhibition finishes at the *end* of this month.
...kagiri (...限り) as long as; as far as: *Watashi ga ikite iru* kagiri, *fujiyuu wa sasemaseñ*. (私が生きている限り, 不自由はさせません) *As long as* I am alive, I will not let you want for anything. / *Miwatasu* kagiri, *umi ga hirogatte ita*. (見渡す限り, 海が広がっていた) The sea extended *as far as* the eye could see.
...(shi)nai kagiri (...(し)ない限り) unless; if not: *Yohodo beñkyoo shinai kagiri, anata wa shikeñ ni gookaku shimaseñ*. (よほど勉強しない限り, あなたは試験に合格しません) *Unless* you study exceptionally hard, you will not pass the exam.

ka「gi¹r・u かぎる (限る) *vt*. (kagi-r・i-; kagir・a-; kagit-te Ⓒ)
1 limit; restrict: *Hatsugeñ wa sañ-puñ inai ni ka-girimasu*. (発言は3分以内に限ります) Your talk *is limited* to three minutes. / *Nissuu o* kagitte, *kare ni sono shigoto o tanoñda*. (日数を限って, 彼にその仕事を頼んだ) I asked him to finish the work within a *set* number of days. / *Kono shoo-hiñ wa kazu ga* kagirarete imasu.

(この商品は数が限られています) These goods *are limited* in quantity. (⇨ kagiri)
2 be (the) best; be (the) most suitable: *Natsu wa biiru ni* kagirimasu. (夏はビールに限ります) In summer *there is nothing like* beer. / *Sake wa Nada ni* kagiru. (酒は灘に限る) As for Japanese sake, that from the Nada district *is best*.
...ni kagiri (...に限り) just: *Koñdo ni kagiri, muryoo to shimasu*. (今度に限り, 無料とします) *Just this once*, we will make it free. / *Señ-chaku hyaku-mee ni kagiri, so-shina zootee*. (先着100名に限り, 粗品贈呈) *The first one hundred persons to arrive* will be presented with a gift.
...ni kagitte (...に限って) be the last person: *Kare ni kagitte, soñna koto wa shimaseñ*. (彼に限って, そんなことはしません) *He is the last person* to do a thing like that. / *Uchi no ko ni kagitte, soñna wa-rusa o suru hazu ga arimaseñ*. (うちの子に限って, そんな悪さをするはずがありません) I cannot believe that *our child, of all people*, would do something naughty like that.

ka「go かご (籠) *n*. basket; cage: kago *o amu* (かごを編む) fashion a *basket*.

ka「goo かごう (化合) *n*. chemical combination: kagoo-*butsu* (化合物) a *chemical* compound.
kagoo suru (〜する) *vi*. combine with: *Suiso to sañso ga* kagoo *shite, mizu ni naru*. (水素と酸素が化合して, 水になる) Hydrogen *combines* with oxygen to form water.

Ka「goshima¹-keñ かごしまけん (鹿児島県) *n*. Kagoshima Prefecture. Located at the south end of Kyushu. An active volcano, Sakurajima, is located within the capital city, Kagoshima. 《⇨ map (B6)》

ka¹gu¹ かぐ（家具）*n.* furniture: Kagu-tsuki *no ie o karita.*（家具付きの家を借りた）I rented a *furnished* house.

ka⌐g·u² かぐ（嗅ぐ）*vt.* (kag·i-; kag·a-; ka·i-de [C]) smell; scent; sniff: *Kanojo wa bara no hana no nioi o* kaida.（彼女はばらの花のにおいをかいだ）She *smelled* the roses. / *Inu wa taberu mae ni sono niku o* kaida.（犬は食べる前にその肉をかいだ）The dog *sniffed* at the meat before eating it.

ka⌐ha¹ñsuu かはんすう（過半数）*n.* majority; the greater number: *Iiñ no* kahañsuu *ga sono añ ni sañsee shita.*（委員の過半数がその案に賛成した）The *majority* of the committee members were in favor of the proposal. / *Sono too wa Shuugiiñ de* kahañsuu *o shimeru koto ga dekinakatta.*（その党は衆議院で過半数を占めることができなかった）The party was unable to get a *majority* in the House of Representatives.

ka¹hee かへい（貨幣）*n.* money; currency.

ka¹i¹ かい（会）*n.* **1** meeting; party; assembly; gathering: kai *o hiraku* [*tojiru*]（会を開く[閉じる]）open [close] a *meeting* / *Kanojo wa sono* kai *ni shusseki shita.*（彼女はその会に出席した）She attended the *party*.
2 society; club: *Yamada-shi o ooeñ suru* kai *o tsukutta.*（山田氏を応援する会をつくった）We organized a *society* in support of Mr. Yamada. / *Kare wa sono* kai *no kaiiñ no hitori desu.*（彼はその会の会員の一人です）He is one of the members of the *club*.

ka¹i² かい（貝）*n.* shellfish; shell: *Kodomo-tachi wa kaigañ de* kai *o*

takusañ hirotta.（子どもたちは海岸で貝をたくさん拾った）The children collected many *shells* on the beach.

kai³ *p.* (an informal sentence final question particle): *Kore taberu* kai?（これ食べるかい）*Would you like* to eat this? / *Chotto tetsudatte kurenai* kai?（ちょっと手伝ってくれないかい）*Could* you give me a hand for a while? / *Boku ga soñna koto o suru* niñgeñ kai?（ぼくがそんなことをする人間かい）I am *the last person* to do such a thing.

-kai¹ かい（回）*n.* **1** time: ik-kai（1 回）*once* / ni-kai（2 回）*twice* / sañ-kai（3 回）three *times* / *Watashi wa ik-kagetsu ni* ni-kai *Oosaka e ikimasu.*（私は1か月に2回大阪へ行きます）I go to Osaka *twice* a month. / *Sono eega wa* nañ-kai *mo mita.*（その映画は何回も見た）I've seen the movie many *times.* 《⇨ -do》

1	i⌐k-ka¹i	7	na⌐na¹-kai
2	ni-⌐ka¹i	8	ha⌐chi-kai
3	sa⌐ñ-ka¹i		(ha⌐k-ka¹i)
4	yo¹ñ-kai	9	kyu¹u-kai
5	go-⌐ka¹i	10	ji⌐k-ka¹i
6	ro⌐k-ka¹i		(ju⌐k-ka¹i)
		?	na¹ñ-kai

2 (of baseball) inning: *Kare wa sañ-kai no omote ni hoomurañ o utta.*（彼は3回の表にホームランを打った）He hit a home run in the first half of the third *inning.*

-kai² かい（界）*suf.* community; world; circle; kingdom: *buñgaku*-kai（文学界）the literary *world* / *keezai*-kai（経済界）financial *circles* / *doobutsu*-kai（動物界）the animal *kingdom.*

-kai³ かい（階）*n.* **1** (used for counting floors): *ik*-kai（1 階）the first *floor* / ni-kai

(2 階) the second *floor* / *Kono biru wa nañ-kai arimasu ka?* (このビルは何階ありますか) How many *floors* does this building have?

- **USAGE** -
The floors of a house or a building are counted in the same way as in the U.S.A., the ground floor being the first floor.

2 (used for naming floors): *Omocha wa go-*kai *de utte imasu.* (おもちゃは5階で売っています) Toys are sold on the fifth *floor.* / *ni-*kai-*date no ie* (二階建ての家) a two-*story* house.

1	iʳk-kai	8	haʳchi-kai
2	ni-ʳkai		(haʳk-kai)
3	saʳñ-gai	9	kyuʳu-kai
4	yoʳñ-kai	10	jiʳk-kai
5	go-ʳkai		(juʳk-kai)
6	roʳk-kai	?	naʳñ-gai
7	naʳna-kai		(naʳñ-kai)

-kai⁴ かい (会) *suf.* party; gathering: *kañgee-*kai (歓迎会) a welcome *party* / *soobetsu-*kai (送別会) a farewell *party* / *doosoo-*kai (同窓会) a class *reunion* / *oñgaku-*kai (音楽会) a *concert.*

-kai⁵ かい (海) *suf.* sea: *Nihoñ-*kai (日本海) the *Sea* of Japan / *Kasupi-*kai (カスピ海) the Caspian *Sea.*

kaʳiage かいあげ (買い上げ) *n.* buying; purchase: *O-kaiage no shina wa is-shuukañ inai nara kookañ itashimasu.* (お買い上げの品は一週間以内なら交換いたします) We will exchange articles you *have purchased* if you return them within a week. 《⇨ kaiageru》

kaʳiageˈru かいあげる (買い上げる) *vt.* (-age-te Ⅴ) (of a govern-

ment) buy; purchase: *Seefu wa kome o nooka kara* kaiagete iru. (政府は米を農家から買い上げている) The government *purchases* rice from farmers. 《⇨ kaiage》

kaʳichoo かいちょう (会長) *n.* the president (of a company); the chairman (of a corporation). 《⇨ kaisha (table)》

kaʳichuudeˈñtoo かいちゅうでんとう (懐中電灯) *n.* flashlight; electric torch: kaichuudeñtoo *o tsukeru* [*kesu*] (懐中電灯をつける[消す]) turn on [off] a *flashlight.*

kaʳichuudoˈkee かいちゅうどけい (懐中時計) *n.* pocket watch. 《⇨ tokee (table)》

kaʳidañ¹ かいだん (階段) *n.* stairs; steps; staircase: kaidañ *o agaru* [*noboru*] (階段を上がる[上る]) go up the *stairs* / kaidañ *o oriru* (階段を降りる) go down the *stairs* / *Kare wa* kaidañ *o kakeashi de nobotta.* (彼は階段を駆け足で上った) He ran up the *stairs.*

kaʳidañ² かいだん (会談) *n.* talks; conference: *shunoo* kaidañ *o hiraku* (首脳会談を開く) hold a summit *conference.* **kaidañ suru** (〜する) *vi.* talk together; confer: *Kare wa shushoo to* kaidañ *shita.* (彼は首相と会談した) He *conferred* with the prime minister.

kaʳifuku かいふく (回復) *n.* **1** recovery: *Kare no* kaifuku *wa hayakatta.* (彼の回復は早かった) He made a quick *recovery.*

2 restoration: *shiñyoo no* kaifuku *o hakaru* (信用の回復を図る) seek to *restore* one's reputation. **kaifuku suru** (〜する) *vt., vi.* restore; improve; recover: *meeyo o* kaifuku suru (名誉を回復する) *regain* one's honor / *Kanojo wa* *sugu ni ishiki o* kaifuku shita. (彼女はすぐに意識を回復した) She soon *regained* consciousness. / *Teñki ga* kaifuku shita. (天気が回復した) The weather *has improved*.

ka⌐iga かいが (絵画) *n.* picture; painting:
kaiga *o kañshoo suru* (絵画を鑑賞する) appreciate *pictures*. 《⇨ e¹》

ka⌐igai かいがい (海外) *n.* lands beyond the sea; overseas countries:
Kanojo wa kaigai-*ryokoo-chuu desu.* (彼女は海外旅行中です) She is on an *overseas* trip. / *Ashita wa* kaigai *kara o-kyaku ga kimasu.* (あしたは海外からお客がきます) We will have guests from *abroad* tomorrow. / *Kare wa* kaigai (*no*) *jijoo ni kuwashii.* (彼は海外(の)事情に詳しい) He is conversant with *foreign* affairs. / *Yamada-sañ wa* kaigai-*seekatsu ga nagai.* (山田さんは海外生活が長い) Mr. Yamada lived *abroad* for many years. 《↔ kokunai》 《⇨ kokugai》

ka⌐igañ かいがん (海岸) *n.* seashore; coast; beach:
Kare no uchi wa kaigañ *ni tatte iru.* (彼の家は海岸に建っている) His house stands on the *seashore*. / *Yatto* kaigañ *ga miete kita.* (やっと海岸が見えてきた) The *coastline* came into view at last. / *Kodomotachi wa* kaigañ *de asoñda.* (子どもたちは海岸で遊んだ) The children played on the *beach*.

ka⌐igara かいがら (貝殻) *n.* seashell.

ka⌐igi かいぎ (会議) *n.* conference; meeting; council:
kaigi *ni shusseki* [*kesseki*] *suru* (会議に出席[欠席]する) attend [be absent from] a *meeting* / *Kare wa* kaigi-*chuu desu.* (彼は会議中です) He is in *conference*. / *Kaigi wa asu ni eñki sareta.* (会議はあすに延期された) The *meeting* was ad-

journed until tomorrow. / *Kaigi-chuu* (*sign*) (「会議中」) In *Session*.

ka⌐igo かいご (介護) *n.* nursing; care:
roojiñ no kaigo (老人の介護) the *care* of elderly people.
kaigo suru (〜する) *vt.* nurse; look after; care for: *Kanojo wa netakiri no haha-oya o* kaigo shite iru. (彼女は寝たきりの母親を介護している) She *looks after* her bedridden mother.

ka⌐igoo かいごう (会合) *n.* meeting; gathering; assembly:
kaigoo o hiraku (会合を開く) hold a *meeting* / *Sono moñdai ni tsuite, nañ-kai mo* kaigoo *o kasaneta.* (その問題について、何回も会合を重ねた) We repeatedly had *meetings* about that problem.
kaigoo suru (〜する) *vi.* meet; gather; assemble: *Watashi-tachi wa tsuki ni, ik-kai* kaigoo shimasu. (私たちは月に、1回会合します) We *get together* once a month.

ka⌐iguñ かいぐん (海軍) *n.* navy; naval forces. 《⇨ rikuguñ; kuuguñ; jieetai》

ka⌐ihatsu かいはつ (開発) *n.* development; exploitation:
kaihatsu *o susumeru* (開発を進める) press forward with *development* / *shiñ-seehiñ no* kaihatsu *ni doryoku suru* (新製品の開発に努力する) make efforts to *develop* new products.
kaihatsu suru (〜する) *vt.* develop; exploit: *atarashii gijutsu o* kaihatsu suru (新しい技術を開発する) *develop* new technology / *umi no shigeñ o* kaihatsu suru (海の資源を開発する) *exploit* the resources of the sea.

ka⌐ihoo¹ かいほう (解放) *n.* release; liberation:
kaihoo-*kañ o ajiwau* (解放感を味わう) enjoy the feeling of *freedom* /

kaihoo-*uñdoo* (解放運動) a *liberation* movement.

kaihoo suru (～する) *vt.* release; free; liberate: *hitojichi o* kaihoo suru (人質を解放する) *free* the hostages / *Sono shokumiñchi wa taikoku no shihai kara* kaihoo sareta. (その植民地は大国の支配から解放された) The colony *was freed* from the rule of the great power.

ka⌐ihoo² かいほう (開放) *n.* opening.

kaihoo suru (～する) *vt.* open; leave open: *Kono gakkoo no kootee wa nichiyoobi wa ippañ ni* kaihoo sarete imasu. (この学校の校庭は日曜日は一般に開放されています) The playground of this school *is open* to the public on Sundays.

ka⌐ihyoo かいひょう (開票) *n.* ballot [vote] counting: *Kaihyoo no kekka wa ashita no shoogo made ni wa wakarimasu.* (開票の結果はあしたの正午までにはわかります) The results of *vote counting* will be known by noon tomorrow.

kaihyoo suru (～する) *vi.* count the ballots [votes]: *señkyo no sono hi ni* kaihyoo suru (選挙のその日に開票する) *open the ballots* on the same day as the election.

ka⌐iiñ かいいん (会員) *n.* member; membership: *Kare wa sono kurabu no* kaiiñ *ni natta.* (彼はそのクラブの会員になった) He became a *member* of the club.

ka⌐ijoo¹ かいじょう (会場) *n.* meeting place; site: *Kaijoo wa doko desu ka?* (会場はどこですか) Where is the *meeting place*? / *Teñjikai no* kaijoo *wa go-kai desu.* (展示会の会場は5階です) The *site* of the exhibition is on the fifth floor.

ka⌐ijoo² かいじょう (海上) *n.* the sea: *Sono booto wa* kaijoo *o hyooryuu shita.* (そのボートは海上を漂流した) The boat was adrift on *the sea.* 《↔ rikujoo》

Ka⌐ijoohoa⌐ñ-choo かいじょうほあんちょう (海上保安庁) *n.* Maritime Safety Agency: *Kaijoohoañ-choo chookañ* (海上保安庁長官) the Director-General of the *Maritime Safety Agency.* 《⇒ choo⁴ (table)》

ka⌐ikai かいかい (開会) *n.* the opening of a meeting [session]: kaikai *no ji o noberu* (開会の辞を述べる) give an *opening* address / kaikai-*shiki* (開会式) an *opening* ceremony / *Kokkai wa* kaikai-*chuu desu.* (国会は開会中です) The Diet is *in session.*

kaikai suru (～する) *vi., vt.* open a meeting: *Kaigi wa sañ-ji ni* kaikai shimasu. (会議は3時に開会します) The meeting will *be opened* at three. / *Kokkai wa raishuu* kaikai saremasu. (国会は来週開会されます) The Diet will *be opened* next week. 《↔ heekai》

ka⌐ikaku かいかく (改革) *n.* reform; revision: kaikaku *o susumeru* (改革を進める) carry out a *reform* / *Kyooiku-seedo no* kaikaku *ga semararete iru.* (教育制度の改革が迫られている) A *revision* in the system of education is required.

kaikaku suru (～する) *vt.* reform; revise: *zeesee o* kaikaku suru (税制を改革する) *make reforms* in the taxation system.

ka⌐ikee かいけい (会計) *n.* **1** accounts; accounting: kaikee *o keñsa suru* (会計を検査する) examine the *accounts* / kaikee-*neñdo* (会計年度) a *fiscal* year / kaikee-*kañsa* (会計監査) an *audit* / kaikee-*hookoku* (会計報告) a *financial* report / kaikee-shi (会計士) an *accountant.*

2 payment; check; bill:

Kaikee *wa sumasemashita*. (会計は済ませました) I paid the *bill*. / Ano *madoguchi de* kaikee *o shite kudasai*. (あの窓口で会計をしてください) Please make your *payment* at that window. / Kaikee *o o-negai shimasu*. (会計をお願いします) *Bill*, please.

ka⌐ikeñ かいけん (会見) *n.* interview:
shachoo ni kaikeñ *o motomeru* (社長に会見を求める) ask for an *interview* with the president.
kaikeñ suru (～する) *vi.* have an interview: *Watashi wa gaishoo to* kaikeñ *shita*. (私は外相と会見した) I *had an interview* with the foreign minister.

ka⌐iketsu かいけつ (解決) *n.* solution; settlement:
fuñsoo no kaiketsu *ni ataru* (紛争の解決に当たる) make efforts to *settle* a dispute / *moñdai* kaiketsu *no itoguchi o tsukamu* (問題解決の糸口をつかむ) find a clue to the *solution* of a problem. (↔ mikaiketsu)
kaiketsu suru (～する) *vi.*, *vt.* solve; settle; clear up: *Jikeñ wa ichi-neñ-buri ni* kaiketsu *shita*. (事件は一年ぶりに解決した) The case *was solved* after a year. / *Ryoosha no arasoi wa heewa-teki ni* kaiketsu *saremashita*. (両者の争いは平和的に解決されました) The dispute between the two *was settled* peacefully.

ka⌐iko かいこ (解雇) *n.* dismissal; discharge; layoff:
Kare wa kaiko *no tsuuchi o uketotta*. (彼は解雇の通知を受け取った) He received a *dismissal* notice.
kaiko suru (～する) *vt.* dismiss; lay off: *Fukyoo no tame, hyakuniñ ga* kaiko *sareta*. (不況のため、百人が解雇された) A hundred people *were laid off* because of the depression. (⇨ kubi)

ka⌐ikyoo かいきょう (海峡) *n.*

strait; channel:
Tsugaru-kaikyoo (津軽海峡) the Tsugaru *Straits*.

Ka⌐ikyoo かいきょう (回教) *n.* Islam:
kaikyoo-to (回教徒) a *Muslim*.

ka⌐ikyuu かいきゅう (階級) *n.*
1 class:
jooryuu [chuuryuu; kasoo] kaikyuu (上流 [中流; 下層] 階級) the upper [middle; lower] *class* / kaikyuu-*seedo* (階級制度) the *class* system.
2 rank:
Ano keesatsukañ no kaikyuu *wa nañ desu ka?* (あの警察官の階級は何ですか) What is that policeman's *rank*?

ka⌐imono かいもの (買い物) *n.* shopping; purchase:
kaimono *ni iku* (買い物に行く) go *shopping* / *Kanojo wa depaato de takusañ* kaimono *o shita*. (彼女はデパートでたくさん買い物をした) She made many *purchases* at the department store. / *Koko de chotto* kaimono *o shite ikimasu*. (ここでちょっと買い物をしていきます) I'm going to do some *shopping* here. / kaimono-*kyaku* (買い物客) a *shopper* / kaimono-*bukuro* (買い物袋) a *shopping* bag.

ka⌐inañ かいなん (海難) *n.* shipwreck; sea disaster; marine accident:
kainañ-*kyuujo* (海難救助) *sea* rescue / kainañ-*shiñpañ* (海難審判) a *marine accident* inquiry.

Ka⌐inañshiñpa⌐ñ-choo かいなんしんぱんちょう (海難審判庁) *n.* Marine Accidents Inquiry Agency. (⇨ choo⁴ (table))

ka⌐iryoo かいりょう (改良) *n.* improvement; reform:
kairyoo *o hodokosu* (改良を施す) bring about *improvement* / *Kairyoo no yochi ga nai*. (改良の余地がない) There is no room for further

improvement.

kairyoo suru (〜する) *vt.* improve; reform: *seedo o* kairyoo suru (制度を改良する) *reform* the system / *Kono kikai wa* kairyoo sarete *tsukai-yasuku natta.* (この機械は改良されて使いやすくなった) This machine *has been improved* and is now easier to use. (⇨ kaizeñ)

ka⌐iryuu かいりゅう (海流) *n.* ocean current: *Nihoñ*-kairyuu (日本海流) the Japan *Current.*

ka⌐isai かいさい (開催) *n.* holding (of a conference, exhibition, etc.): *hakurañkai no* kaisai-chi (博覧会の開催地) the *site* of an exposition / *Oriñpikku no* kaisai-koku (オリンピックの開催国) the *host country* for the Olympic Games.

kaisai suru (〜する) *vt.* hold; open: *Shikiteñ wa juu-ji kara* kaisai saremasu. (式典は10時から開催されます) The ceremony *will be held* from ten o'clock. / *Teñrañkai wa is-shuukañ ni watatte,* kaisai sareta. (展覧会は1週間にわたって、開催された) The exhibition *was held* for a period of a week. (⇨ hiraku)

ka⌐isañ かいさん (解散) *n.* breakup; dissolution: *Sono guruupu wa* kaisañ *suñzeñ desu.* (そのグループは解散寸前です) That group is on the brink of a *breakup.* / *Kokkai no* kaisañ *wa jikañ no moñdai desu.* (国会の解散は時間の問題です) The *dissolution* of the Diet is a matter of time. / kaisañ-*jikañ* [*basho*] (解散時間[場所]) the *breakup* time [the place where a party *breaks up*].

kaisañ suru (〜する) *vi., vt.* break up; dissolve: *Ikkoo wa Tookyoo-eki de* kaisañ shita. (一行は東京駅で解散した) The group *separated* at Tokyo Station. / *Shuugiiñ ga* kai-

sañ shita. (衆議院が解散した) The House of Representatives *was dissolved.*

ka⌐isatsu かいさつ (改札) *n.* examination of tickets: ★ A ticket inspector punches your ticket as you go into the station and collects it at your destination. With an automatic ticket gate, put your ticket in the slot. ka⌐isatsu-guchi (改札口) ticket barrier; platform wicket.

kaisatsu suru (〜する) *vt.* punch [inspect] tickets.

KAISATSU-GUCHI

ka⌐isee¹ かいせい (改正) *n.* revision; amendment: kaisee-*añ* (改正案) a proposed *amendment.*

kaisee suru (〜する) *vt.* revise; amend: *Raigetsu kara daiya ga* kaisee saremasu. (来月からダイヤが改正されます) The train timetable *will be revised* as of next month.

ka⌐isee² かいせい (快晴) *n.* fine weather: *Sono hi wa* kaisee *ni megumareta.* (その日は快晴に恵まれた) We were favored with *fine weather* on that day. (⇨ teñki)

ka⌐isetsu¹ かいせつ (解説) *n.* explanation; commentary: ★ Given by an expert. *nyuusu no* kaisetsu (ニュースの解説) a news *commentary* / kaisetsu-*kiji* (解説記事) an *interpretive* article /

kaisetsu-sha (解説者) a *commentator*; an *analyst*.

kaisetsu suru (〜する) *vt.* explain, comment: *Kono rañ wa jiji-moñdai o wakari-yasuku* kaisetsu shite iru. (この欄は時事問題をわかりやすく解説している) This column *comments* on current events in a manner easy to understand.

ka⌐isetsu² かいせつ (開設) *n.* establishment; foundation; inauguration:
Kono mura no juumiñ wa byooiñ no kaisetsu *o nozoñde iru.* (この村の住民は病院の開設を望んでいる) The people of this village are hoping for the *establishment* of a hospital.

kaisetsu suru (〜する) *vt.* establish; set up: *Kare wa toshiñ ni jibuñ no jimusho o* kaisetsu shita. (彼は都心に自分の事務所を開設した) He *set up* his own office in the center of Tokyo.

ka⌐isha かいしゃ (会社) *n.* **1** company; corporation; firm:
Kare wa kono kaisha *ni tsutomete imasu.* (彼はこの会社に勤めています) He works at this *company.* /

Kono kaisha *ni haitta no wa go-neñ mae desu.* (この会社に入ったのは5年前です) It is five years since I joined this *company.* / *Kanojo wa señgetsu* kaisha *o yamemashita.* (彼女は先月会社を辞めました) She left her *company* last month.
2 office:
Kaisha o deru no wa roku-ji-goro desu. (会社を出るのは6時ごろです) It is at about six o'clock that I leave the *office.*

ka⌐isha⌐iñ かいしゃいん (会社員) *n.* company employee; office worker: ★ Considered an occupational category.
Musuko wa kaishaiñ *desu.* (息子は会社員です) My son is a *company employee.*

ka⌐ishaku かいしゃく (解釈) *n.* interpretation; explanation:
Kore ijoo kaishaku *o kuwaeru hitsuyoo wa nai to omoimasu.* (これ以上解釈を加える必要はないと思います) I think there is no need to add further *explanation.* / *Sono moñdai wa iroiro ni* kaishaku ga dekiru. (その問題はいろいろに解釈ができる) The problem *can be interpreted*

A TYPICAL RANKING SYSTEM IN A JAPANESE COMPANY

Kaichoo	Chairman
Shachoo	President
Fuku-shachoo	Executive Vice President
Señmu Torishimariyaku	Executive Managing Director
Joomu Torishimariyaku	Managing Director
Torishimariyaku	Director
Buchoo	General Manager
Buchoo-dairi	Acting General Manager
Jichoo	Deputy General Manager
Kachoo	Manager
Kachoo-dairi	Acting Manager
Kakarichoo	Group Chief

in many ways.

kaishaku suru (〜する) *vt.* interpret; construe: *Kore igai ni kaishaku (no) shiyoo ga nai.* (これ以外に解釈(の)しようがない) It *cannot be interpreted* in any other way. / *Kare wa monogoto o jibuń no tsugoo no ii yoo ni kaishaku suru.* (彼はものごとを自分の都合のいいように解釈する) He *interprets* matters in a way that suits him.

ka「ishi かいし (開始) *n.* beginning; start; opening: *Shiai no kaishi wa ame de ichijikań okureta.* (試合の開始は雨で1時間遅れた) The *beginning* of the game was delayed an hour due to rain.

kaishi suru (〜する) *vt.* begin; start; open: *Keesatsu wa sugu ni choosa o kaishi shita.* (警察はすぐに調査を開始した) The police *started* the investigation immediately. (↔ shuuryoo)

ka「ishoo かいしょう (解消) *n.* cancellation; annulment: *keeyaku no kaishoo* (契約の解消) the *cancellation* of a contract.

kaishoo suru (〜する) *vt.* cancel; annul; break off: *Kanojo wa totsuzeń końyaku o kaishoo shita.* (彼女は突然婚約を解消した) She suddenly *broke off* her engagement.

ka「isu「iyoku かいすいよく (海水浴) *n.* sea bathing: *kaisuiyoku o suru* (海水浴をする) *bathe in the sea* / kaisuiyoku *ni iku* (海水浴に行く) go *swimming in the sea* / *kaisuiyoku-joo* (海水浴場) a *bathing* resort.

ka「isu「u かいすう (回数) *n.* the number of times; frequency: *Basu no deru kaisuu wa ichi-jikań ni ni-hoń desu.* (バスの出る回数は1時間に2本です) The bus runs twice each hour. / *Fuńka no kaisuu wa hi ni dono kurai desu ka?* (噴火の回数は日にどのくらいですか)

How many *times* does the volcano become active in a day?

ka「isu「ukeń かいすうけん (回数券) *n.* coupon; ticket: *juu-mai tsuzuri no kaisuukeń* (十枚つづりの回数券) a book of 10 *bus* [*train*] *tickets.*

ka「itaku かいたく (開拓) *n.* **1** reclamation; cultivation: kaitaku-*chi* (開拓地) *newly developed* land.

2 opening up.

kaitaku suru (〜する) *vt.* **1** reclaim; cultivate: *arechi o kaitaku suru* (荒れ地を開拓する) *cultivate* waste land.

2 open up a new field [market, etc.]: *Kono shoohiń no atarashii shijoo o kaitaku shiyoo to shite iru tokoro desu.* (この商品の新しい市場を開拓しようとしているところです) We are now trying to *develop* a new market for this product. / *Kare wa seebutsu-gaku no atarashii buńya o kaitaku shita.* (彼は生物学の新しい分野を開拓した) He *has opened up* a new field in biology.

ka「iteń[1] かいてん (回転) *n.* **1** revolution; rotation; spin: kaiteń-*isu* (回転いす) a *swivel* chair / kaiteń-*doa* (回転ドア) a *revolving* door / kaiteń-*zushi* (回転ずし) a sushi restaurant where customers can take their choice of prepared sushi from a conveyor belt that circles the counter.

2 turnover; circulation: kaiteń-*shikiń* (回転資金) a *revolving* fund / *Ano mise wa kyaku no kaiteń ga ii.* (あの店は客の回転がいい) That store has a *constant flow* of customers.

kaiteń suru (〜する) *vi.* **1** revolve; rotate; spin: *Eńjiń wa yukkuri kaiteń shi-hajimeta.* (エンジンはゆっくり回転し始めた) The engine *started to turn over* slowly.

2 circulate; turn over: *Shikiń*

wa hayaku kaiteñ *sasenakereba naranai.*(資金は速く回転させなければ ならない) You *have to turn over* your money quickly.

ka⌐iteñ² かいてん(開店) *n.* opening of a store:
Depaato no kaiteñ *wa juu-ji kara desu.*(デパートの開店は10時からです) The department store *opens* at ten o'clock. / kaiteñ *oo-uridashi* (開店大売り出し) a grand *opening* sale.

kaiteñ suru (〜する) *vt., vi.* open [set up] a store: *Kiñjo ni ooki-na suupaa ga* kaiteñ *shita.*(近所に大き なスーパーが開店した) A large supermarket *was opened* in my neighborhood.

ka⌐itoo¹ かいとう(回答) *n.* reply; answer:
kaitoo *o yookyuu suru* (回答を要求 する) ask for a *reply* / kaitoo *o hiki-dasu* (回答を引き出す) draw a *reply* / *Watashi-tachi wa* kaitoo *o sema-rarete iru.*(私たちは回答を迫られてい る) We are being pressed for an *answer.*

kaitoo suru (〜する) *vt.* reply; answer: *Sono yookyuu ni taishite, buñsho de* kaitoo *shita.*(その要求に 対して、文書で回答した) We *replied* in writing to the demand.

ka⌐itoo² かいとう(解答) *n.* solution; answer:
shikeñ-moñdai no kaitoo *o kaku* (試験問題の解答を書く) write *an-swers* to the examination questions / *kaitoo-yooshi*[*rañ*] (解答用 紙[欄]) an *answer* sheet [column].

kaitoo (*o*) **suru** (〜(を)する) *vt.* an-swer; solve: *Kare wa tadashiku* kaitoo *shita.*(彼は正しく解答した) He *answered* correctly. / *Sono moñdai wa* kaitoo *suru koto ga dekinakatta.*(その問題は解答すること ができなかった) I couldn't *solve* the problem. 《⇒ toku¹》.

ka⌐itoo³ かいとう(解凍) *n.* thaw-

ing; defrosting.

kaitoo suru (〜する) *vt.* thaw; defrost: *reetoo-shokuhiñ o* kaitoo suru (冷凍食品を解凍する) *thaw out* frozen food.

ka⌐iwa かいわ(会話) *n.* conver-sation; talk; dialogue:
Kare wa Nihoñgo no kaiwa *ga umai.*(彼は日本語の会話がうまい) He is good at Japanese *conversation.* / *Kanojo wa watashi-tachi no* kaiwa *ni kuwawaranakatta.*(彼女 は私たちの会話に加わらなかった) She didn't join in our *conversation.*

kaiwa suru (〜する) *vi.* converse; talk: *Kare wa kanojo to Furañsu-go de* kaiwa shita.(彼は彼女とフラン ス語で会話した) He *talked* with her in French.

ka⌐iyoo かいよう(潰瘍) *n.* ulcer:
I wa kaiyoo *ga dekiyasui.*(胃はかい ようができやすい) *Ulcers* easily form in the stomach. 《⇒ ikaiyoo》

ka⌐izeñ かいぜん(改善) *n.* im-provement; betterment:

> ⓘ **USAGE**
> Usually used for something abstract. For concrete things, '*kairyoo*' is used.

taiguu no kaizeñ *o yookyuu suru* (待遇の改善を要求する) seek *im-provement* in working conditions / *taishitsu no* kaizeñ *o hakaru* (体 質の改善を図る) aim to *build up* one's physical constitution.

kaizeñ suru (〜する) *vt.* improve; better: *Nañ to ka ima no seeka-tsu-jootai o* kaizeñ *shitai to omot-te imasu.*(なんとか今の生活状態を改 善したいと思っています) Somehow or other I *want to improve* my present living conditions.

ka⌐ji¹ かじ(家事) *n.* housework; household chores; housekeep-ing:
Kanojo wa yoku haha-oya no kaji *o tetsudau.*(彼女はよく母親の家事を

手伝う) She often helps her mother with the *housework*. / Kaji *ni owarete, isogashii.*(家事に追われて、忙しい) I am busy with my *household chores*. / *Kodomo-tachi ga kootai de* kaji *o shimasu.*(子どもたちが交替で家事をします) The children take turns at doing *housework*.

kaji no tsugoo (〜の都合) family reasons: *Kyoo wa* kaji no tugoo *de yasumimasu.*(きょうは家事の都合で休みます) I will be absent today for *family reasons*.

ka⌐ji² かじ (火事) *n.* fire: *Sakuya kiñjo de* kaji *ga atta.*(昨夜近所で火事があった) There was a *fire* in the neighborhood last night. / Kaji *wa sono hoteru de okita.*(火事はそのホテルで起きた) The *fire* broke out in that hotel. / Kaji *wa sugu ni kieta.*(火事はすぐに消えた) The *fire* was put out soon. / Kaji *no geñiñ wa tabako datta.*(火事の原因はたばこだった) The cause of the *fire* was a cigarette.

ka⌐ji³ かじ (舵) *n.* tiller; rudder; helm: kaji *o hidari* [*migi*] *ni toru* (かじを左[右]にとる) turn a *tiller* to the left [right].

ka⌐jiritsu⌐k·u かじりつく (齧り付く) *vt.* (-tsuk·i-; -tsuk·a-; -tsu·i-te Ⓒ) **1** bite at [into]: *Kare wa ooki-na riñgo ni* kajiritsuita.(彼は大きなりんごにかじりついた) He *bit* into a large apple.
2 hold on to; cling to: *Kanojo wa sutoobu ni* kajiritsuite ita.(彼女はストーブにかじりついていた) She *stayed close up to* the heater.

ka⌐ji⌐r·u かじる (齧る) *vt.* (kajir·i-; kajir·a-; kajit-te Ⓒ) **1** gnaw; bite: *Inu ga hone o* kajitte iru.(犬が骨をかじっている) The dog *is gnawing* on the bone. / *Sono kaki o* kajit- *tara, shibukatta.*(その柿をかじったら、

渋かった) When I *took a bite* of the persimmon, it was bitter.
2 know a little of (learning): *Watashi wa Rateñgo o sukoshi* kajirimashita.(私はラテン語を少しかじりました) I *have learned* a bit of Latin.

ka⌐kae·ru かかえる (抱える) *vt.* (kakae-te Ⓥ) **1** have [hold] (a parcel, bag, baggage, etc.) in [under] one's arms: *Kare wa ryoote ni, nimotsu o* ka- kaete ita.(彼は両手に、荷物を抱えていた) He *had* baggage *under* both *arms*. / *Kanojo wa migi-ude ni hoñ o* kakaete ita.(彼女は右腕に本を抱えていた) She *was holding* a book in her right arm.
2 have (a problem, difficulty, etc.): *Kare wa dai-kazoku o* kakaete iru.(彼は大家族を抱えている) He *has* a large family to support. / *Kare wa muzukashii moñdai o* kakaete iru.(彼は難しい問題を抱えている) He *has* a difficult problem to solve.

ka⌐kage·ru かかげる (掲げる) *vt.* (kakage-te Ⓥ) fly; put up; hang up (a flag, sign, etc.): *hata o* kakageru (旗を掲げる) *fly* a flag / *kañbañ o* kakageru (看板を掲げる) *put up* a signboard.

ka⌐kaku かかく (価格) *n.* **1** price; cost: kakaku *o ageru* [*sageru*] (価格を上げる[下げる]) raise [lower] the *price* / *Shijoo-*kakaku *wa añtee shite iru.*(市場価格は安定している) The market *price* remains stable.
2 value: *Tochi no* kakaku *wa jooshoo o tsu- zukete iru.*(土地の価格は上昇を続けている) The *value* of land continues to go up.

ka⌐kari かかり (係り) *n.* charge; duty: *Kare wa eñkai no* kakari *desu.*(彼は宴会の係りです) He is in *charge* of the banquet. / *Tadaima,* kakari *no mono wa seki o hazushite ima-su.*(ただいま, 係りの者は席をは外しています) The person in *charge* is not at his desk right now.

ka⌈kari⌉choo かかりちょう (係長) *n.* group chief; chief clerk. 《⇨ kaisha (table)》

ka⌈ka⌉r·u[1] かかる (掛かる) *vi.* (ka-kar·i-; kakar·a-; kakat-te ⌒C)

1 (of time) take:
Koko kara eki made aruite, dono kurai kakarimasu ka? (ここから駅まで歩いて, どのくらいかかりますか) How long does it *take* to walk from here to the station? / *Kono shi-goto o owaraseru no ni ni-jikañ kakarimashita.*(この仕事を終わらせるのに 2 時間かかりました) It *took* me two hours to finish this work. 《⇨ kakeru²》

2 (of money) cost:
Hokkaidoo made iku no ni, ikura kakarimasu ka? (北海道まで行くのに, いくらかかりますか) How much does it *cost* to go to Hokkaido? / *Terebi no shuuri ni goseñ-eñ kakatta.* (テレビの修理に 5 千円かかった) The television repair *cost* me five thousand yen. 《⇨ kakeru²》

3 hang:
Kabe ni hana no e ga kakatte ima-su. (壁に花の絵が掛かっています) There is a picture of flowers *hanging* on the wall. 《⇨ kakeru¹》

4 be locked; button:
Kono kuruma wa kagi ga kakatte inai.(この車は鍵がかかっていない) This car *is not locked.* / *Kono fuku wa botañ ga nakanaka kakaranai.* (この服はボタンがなかなかかからない) This garment *won't button* easily. 《⇨ kakeru¹》

5 be caught:
Kare wa wana ni kakatta. (彼はわなにかかった) He *was caught* in a trap. / *Sakana ga hari ni kakatta.* (魚が針にかかった) The fish *was caught* on a hook.

6 splash:
Mizu ga zuboñ ni kakatta. (水がズボンにかかった) Water *splashed* on my trousers. 《⇨ kakeru¹》

7 (of suspicion) rest:
Kare ni utagai ga kakatta. (彼に疑いがかかった) Suspicion *has rested* on him.

8 (of tax) be imposed:
Gasoriñ ni wa zeekiñ ga kakatte imasu. (ガソリンには税金がかかっています) *There is* a tax on gasoline.

9 consult (a doctor):
Hayaku isha ni kakari nasai. (早く医者にかかりなさい) You should *consult* a doctor immediately.

10 be telephoned:
Kanojo kara deñwa ga kakatta. (彼女から電話がかかった) *There was* a phone call from her. 《⇨ kakeru¹》

11 work:
Kuruma no eñjiñ wa sugu ni ka-katta. (車のエンジンはすぐにかかった) The car engine soon *started.* / *Kono jiteñsha wa bureeki ga kakaranai.* (この自転車はブレーキがかからない) The brakes *do not work* on this bicycle. 《⇨ kakeru¹》

12 be covered:
Sora ni kumo ga kakatte kita. (空に雲がかかってきた) The sky *became cloudy.*

13 begin:
shigoto ni kakaru (仕事にかかる) *start* a job.

...ni kakatte wa (...にかかっては) play [fight] against: *Aitsu ni ka-katte wa kanawanai.* (あいつにかかってはかなわない) I am no match *for him.*

ka⌈ka⌉r·u² かかる (架かる) *vi.* (ka-kar·i-; kakar·a-; kakat-te ⌒C) span:
Kono kawa ni chikai uchi ni hashi ga kakarimasu. (この川に近いうちに橋がかかります) A bridge will *span* this

river in the near future. 《⇨ kake-ru⁵》

ka⌈ka⌉r·u³ かかる (罹る) *vi.* (kakar·i-; kakar·a-; kakat-te 〇) become [fall] sick [ill]; catch (a disease):
Watashi wa kodomo no toki ha-shika ni kakarimashita. (私は子どものときはしかにかかりました) I *caught* the measles when I was a child. / *Kono ko wa kaze ni kakari-yasui.* (この子はかぜにかかりやすい) This child *catches* colds *easily*.

ka⌈ka⌉r·u⁴ かかる (懸かる) *vi.* (kakar·i-; kakar·a-; kakat-te 〇) appear; form:
Sora ni niji ga kakatta. (空に虹がかかった) A rainbow *formed* in the sky.

ka⌈kato かかと *n.* heel:
kakato *no takai* [*hikui*] *kutsu* (かかとの高い[低い]靴) high [low]-*heeled* shoes / *Kono kutsu no kakato wa surihette iru.* (この靴のかかとはすり減っている) The *heels* of these shoes are worn down. / *Kono kutsu o haku to kakato ga itai.* (この靴をはくとかかとが痛い) When I wear these shoes, they hurt my *heels*. 《⇨ jiñtai (illus.)》

ka⌈kawa⌉razu かかわらず (拘らず) irrespective of; regardless of:
★ Used in the pattern, '...*ni ka-kawarazu*.'
Neñree ni kakawarazu, dare de mo sañka dekimasu. (年齢にかかわらず、だれでも参加できます) Anyone can take part, *irrespective of* age. / *Teñkoo ni kakawarazu, watashi-tachi wa ashita shuppatsu shi-masu.* (天候にかかわらず、私たちはあした出発します) We will set off tomor-row, rain *or* shine.

...ni mo kakawarazu (...にも〜) although; in spite of: *Nañ-do mo chuui shita* ni mo kakawarazu, *kare wa aikawarazu kuru no ga osoi.* (何度も注意したにもかかわらず、彼

は相変わらず来るのが遅い) *Although* I have repeatedly warned him, he still continues to arrive late. / *Doryoku shita* ni mo kakawarazu, *seeseki wa warukatta.* (努力したにもかかわらず、成績は悪かった) *In spite of* all my efforts, my grades were poor. ★ Similar to '*no ni*' but more common in writing.
《⇨ ga²; no ni》

ka⌈kawa⌉r·u かかわる (関わる) *vi.* (kakawar·i-; kakawar·a-; kaka-wat-te 〇) **1** have to do with; concern; affect:
Sore wa hito no inochi ni kaka-waru moñdai desu. (それは人の命にかかわる問題です) That is a problem *affecting* people's lives. / *Sore wa kanojo no meeyo ni kakawaru.* (それは彼女の名誉にかかわる) That *con-cerns* her honor.
2 get involved; involve oneself with:
Yopparai ni wa kakawaranai hoo ga yoi. (酔っ払いにはかかわらないほうがよい) You had better *not get in-volved* with drunks.

ka⌈ke¹ かけ (賭け) *n.* bet; stake; gamble:
kake *ni katsu* [*makeru*] (賭けに勝つ[負ける]) win [lose] a *bet* / *Dotchi ga katsu ka* kake *o shiyoo.* (どっちが勝つか賭けをしよう) Let's make a *bet* as to which side will win. / *Sore wa chotto shita* kake *da.* (それはちょっとした賭けだ) It's a bit of a *gamble*.
《⇨ kakeru⁴》

ka⌈ke⌉ashi かけあし (駆け足) *n.* run; gallop:
Kodomo-tachi wa kakeashi *de yatte kita.* (子どもたちは駆け足でやって来た) The children came at a *run*.
kakeashi de (〜で) hurriedly: *Watashi wa Amerika o* kakeashi *de ryokoo shita.* (私はアメリカを駆け足で旅行した) I made a *quick* tour of the United States. / *Kono kuni no rekishi o* kakeashi de *mite mi-*

yoo. (この国の歴史を駆け足で見てみよう) Let's take a *brief* look at the history of this country.

ka⌈kebu¹toñ かけぶとん (掛け布団) *n.* covers; quilt; eiderdown. 《⇨ futoñ (illus.)》

ka⌈kedas·u かけだす (駆け出す) *vi.* (-dash·i-; -das·a-; -dash·i-te [C]) run out; start running: *Kodomo-tachi wa issee ni* kakedashita. (子どもたちはいっせいに駆け出した) The children *started running* at the same time. / *Jishiñ ga kita no de miñna awatete, heya kara* kakedashita. (地震が来たのでみんなあわてて, 部屋から駆け出した) An earthquake struck, so everyone *ran out* of the room in confusion.

ka⌈kedo¹kee かけどけい (掛け時計) *n.* wall clock. 《⇨ tokee (table)》

ka⌈kee かけい (家計) *n.* family budget; housekeeping expenses: *Kanojo wa nañ to ka* kakee no *yarikuri o shita.* (彼女はなんとか家計のやりくりをした) She somehow managed to *make both ends meet at home.* / kakee-*bo* (家計簿) a *household* account book.

ka⌈kego¹e かけごえ (掛け声) *n.* shout; cheer: *Watashi wa kare-ra no* kakegoe ni *hagemasareta.* (私は彼らの掛け声に励まされた) I was encouraged by their *shouts.* / *Watashi-tachi wa furee furee to* kakegoe o kaketa. (私たちはフレーフレーと掛け声をかけた) We gave three *cheers.* / *Kare wa 'gañbare' to* kakegoe o kaketa. (彼は「がんばれ」と掛け声をかけた) He *shouted,* "Come on."

kakegoe dake ni owaru (～だけに終わる) fizzle out: *Sono keekaku wa* kakegoe dake ni owatta. (その計画は掛け声だけに終わった) The plan *came to nothing.*

ka⌈ke¹goto かけごと (賭事) *n.* gambling: kakegoto *o suru* (かけ事をする) *gam-*

ble; make a *bet* / *Kare wa* kakegoto *de isshoo o dainashi ni shita.* (彼はかけ事で一生を台なしにした) He ruined his career by *gambling.* 《⇨ bakuchi; kake》

ka⌈ke¹jiku かけじく (掛け軸) *n.* hanging scroll. ★ Traditionally hung in the '*tokonoma.*' 《⇨ washitsu (illus.)》

ka⌈kekomi かけこみ (駆け込み) *n.* running into: Kakekomi-*joosha wa kikeñ desu.* (駆け込み乗車は危険です) It is dangerous to try to *dash onto a train* just before it leaves. 《⇨ kakekomu》

Abunai desu kara kakekomi-joosha wa yamemashoo. (Don't try to rush onto the train; it's dangerous.)

ka⌈kekomu かけこむ (駆け込む) *vi.* (-kom·i-; -kom·a-; -koñ-de [C]) run into; seek refuge: *Ame ga futte kita no de, kodomo-tachi wa ie no naka ni* kakekoñda. (雨が降ってきたので, 子どもたちは家の中に駆け込んだ) It began to rain, so the children *rushed into* the house. / *Kanojo wa tasuke o motomete koobañ ni* kakekoñda. (彼女は助けを求めて交番に駆け込んだ) Seeking help, she *took refuge* in a police box. 《⇨ kakekomi》

ka⌈kemawar·u かけまわる (駆け回る) *vi.* (-mawar·i-; -mawar·a-; -mawat-te [C]) **1** run about: *Kodomo-tachi wa nohara o* kakemawatta. (子どもたちは野原を駆け回った) The children *ran about* the field. 《⇨ kakeru》

2 busy oneself (doing):
Kare-ra wa kifu-atsume ni kake-mawatte iru.(彼らは寄付集めに駆け回っている) They *are busying themselves* collecting contributions.

ka「kera かけら(欠片) *n.* fragment; broken piece:
doki no kakera (土器のかけら) *fragments* of earthenware / *garasu no kakera* (ガラスのかけら) *broken pieces* of glass.

kakera mo nai (〜もない) without a trace of: *Kare no taido ni wa hañsee no kakera mo nakatta.*(彼の態度には反省のかけらもなかった) *There was not an ounce* of self-examination in his attitude.

ka「ke」・ru¹ かける(掛ける・懸ける) *vt.* (kake-te V) **1** hang:
Kare wa heya no kabe ni e o kaketa.(彼は部屋の壁に絵をかけた) He *hung* a picture on the wall of his room. / *Booshi wa koko ni kakete kudasai.*(帽子はここにかけてください) Please *hang* your hat here. 《⇨ kakaru¹》

2 set up:
yane ni hashigo o kakeru (屋根にはしごをかける) *set up* a ladder against the roof. 《⇨ kakaru²》

3 place; put:
Hi ni nabe o kakete kudasai.(火になべをかけてください) Please *put* the pot on the fire.

4 put on: ★'*kakete iru*'＝ wear. *Kanojo wa hoñ o yomu toki, itsumo megane o kakete iru.*(彼女は本を読むとき、いつも眼鏡をかけている) She always *wears* glasses for reading. / *Kare wa kaze yoboo no masuku o kaketa.*(彼はかぜ予防のマスクをかけた) He *put on* a flu mask. 《⇨ kiru² (table)》

5 cover; lay; put:
Samui no de hiza ni moofu o kaketa.(寒いのでひざに毛布をかけた) It was cold, so I *covered* my knees with a blanket. / *Watashi wa sofaa ni kabaa o kaketa.*(私はソファーにカバーをかけた) I *put* a cover on the sofa.

6 lock:
Mado ni kagi o kakeru no o wasurenai yoo ni.(窓に鍵をかけるのを忘れないように) Don't forget to *lock* the window. 《⇨ kakaru¹》

7 telephone; make a phone call:
Ato de deñwa o kakete kudasai.(あとで電話をかけてください) Please *phone* me later. / *Yuube kare ga deñwa o kakete kita.*(ゆうべ彼が電話をかけてきた) He *gave* me *a call* last night. 《⇨ kakaru¹》

8 play; start; switch on:
rekoodo o kakeru (レコードをかける) *put* a record on / *rajio o kakeru* (ラジオをかける) *turn on* the radio / *eñjiñ o kakeru* (エンジンをかける) *start* an engine. 《⇨ kakaru¹》

9 sit down; take a seat:
Doozo o-kake kudasai.(どうぞおかけください) Please *take a seat.* / *Kare wa kooeñ no beñchi ni koshi o kaketa.*(彼は公園のベンチに腰をかけた) He *sat down* on a bench in the park.

10 fasten; tie; bind:
Watashi wa furu-shiñbuñ no taba ni himo o kaketa.(私は古新聞の束にひもをかけた) I *bound up* a sheaf of old newspapers with a cord.

11 pour; sprinkle; splash; water:
Toñkatsu ni soosu o kake nasai.(トンカツにソースをかけなさい) *Pour* some sauce over your pork cutlet. / *Hana ni mizu o kakemashita ka?*(花に水をかけましたか) *Have* you *watered* the flowers? / *Sono kuruma wa watashi no fuku ni doromizu o kaketa.*(その車は私の服に泥水をかけた) The car *splashed* muddy water on my clothes. 《⇨ kakaru¹》

ka「ke」・ru² かける(掛ける) *vt.* (kake-te V) spend; take:

Kare wa kuruma ni takusañ no kane o kaketa. (彼は車にたくさんの金をかけた) He *spent* a lot of money on the car. / *Kare wa sono sakuhiñ no kañsee ni go-neñ* kaketa. (彼はその作品の完成に5年かけた) He *took* five years to complete the work. ((⇨ kakaru[1]))

ka⌐ke⌐·ru[3] かける (掛ける) *vt.* (kake-te Ⓥ) multiply:
Sañ kakeru ni wa roku desu. (3掛ける2は6です) Three *times* two is six. ((↔ waru)) ((⇨ keesañ (table)))

ka⌐ke⌐·ru[4] かける (賭ける) *vt.* (kake-te Ⓥ) **1** bet; stake; gamble:
Kare wa sono reesu ni gomañ-eñ kaketa. (彼はそのレースに5万円賭けた) He *bet* 50,000 yen on the race. / *Torañpu de kane o* kakeru *no wa yoku nai.* (トランプで金を賭けるのはよくない) It is not good to *gamble* at cards. ((⇨ kake))
2 risk:
Dare mo soñna koto ni inochi o kakeru *mono wa imaseñ.* (だれもそんなことに命を賭ける者はいません) There is no one who will *risk* his life for such a thing.

ka⌐ke⌐·ru[5] かける (架ける) *vt.* (kake-te Ⓥ) build; span:
Kare-ra wa sono kawa ni tsuribashi o kaketa. (彼らはその川につり橋をかけた) They *built* a suspension bridge across the river.
((⇨ kakaru[2]))

ka⌐ke·ru[6] かける (欠ける) *vi.* (kake-te Ⓥ) **1** chip; break:
Kono chawañ wa fuchi ga kakete *iru.* (この茶碗は縁が欠けている) The rim of this rice bowl *is chipped.* / *Naifu no ha ga* kakete *shimatta.* (ナイフの刃が欠けてしまった) The blade of the knife *got chipped.*
2 lack; want; missing:
Kono hoñ wa ni-peeji kakete *imasu.* (この本は2ページ欠けています) This book *is missing* two pages. / *Kare ni wa yuuki ga* kakete *iru.*

(彼には勇気が欠けている) He *is lacking* in courage.

ka⌐ke⌐·ru[7] かける (駆ける) *vi.* (kake-te Ⓥ) run:
Deñsha ni maniau yoo ni eki made kaketa. (電車に間に合うように駅まで駆けた) I *ran* to the station to be in time for the train.

ka⌐ketsuke·ru かけつける (駆け付ける) *vi.* (-tsuke-te Ⓥ) run [rush] to; come running:
Keekañ ga sugu sono geñba ni kaketsuketa. (警官がすぐその現場に駆けつけた) A policeman *rushed* to the scene immediately. / *Watashi ga taoreta toki, kare wa sugu* kaketsukete *okoshite kureta.* (私が倒れたとき、彼はすぐ駆けつけて起こしてくれた) When I fell down, he soon *came running* to help me up.
((⇨ isogu))

ka⌐keyor·u かけよる (駆け寄る) *vi.* (-yor·i-; -yor·a-; -yot-te Ⓒ) run up:
"Abunai" to itte kanojo wa kodomo ni kakeyotta. (「危ない」と言って彼女は子どもに駆け寄った) Saying "Look out," she *ran toward* her child.

ka⌐ke⌐zañ かけざん (掛け算) *n.* multiplication:
kakezañ o suru (掛け算をする) *multiply.* ((⇨ kakeru[3]; keesañ (table)))
((↔ warizañ))

ka⌐ki[1] かき (柿) *n.* persimmon.

ka⌐ki[2] かき (牡蠣) *n.* oyster:
kaki-*furai* (かきフライ) deep-fried *oysters.*

ka⌐ki[3] かき (夏期) *n.* summer; summertime:
kaki-*kooshuukai* (夏期講習会) *summer* school / kaki-*kooza* (夏期講座) a *summer* course / kaki-*kyuuka* (夏期休暇) *summer* vacation [holidays]. ((⇨ tooki[4]; shuñki; shuuki[2]))

ka⌐kiarawa⌐s·u かきあらわす (書き表す) *vt.* (-arawash·i-; -arawas-

a-; -arawash·i-te C) describe in writing:
Sono kimochi wa kotoba de wa kakiarawasemaseñ. (その気持ちは言葉では書き表せません) I *cannot express* that feeling in writing.

ka⌈kidas·u かきだす (書き出す) *vt.* (-dash·i-; -das·a-; -dash·i-te C) make a list of:
Kanojo wa kau mono o kakidashita. (彼女は買う物を書き出した) She *made a* shopping *list*.

ka⌈kiire·ru かきいれる (書き入れる) *vt.* (-ire-te V) write [put] in; enter:
Koko ni o-namae to juusho o kakiirete *kudasai*. (ここにお名前と住所を書き入れてください) Please *enter* your name and address here.

ka⌈kikae·ru かきかえる (書き換える) *vt.* (-kae-te V) **1** rewrite; retell; paraphrase:
Kono buñshoo o motto yasashii Nihoñgo ni kakikaete *kudasai*. (この文章をもっと易しい日本語に書き換えてください) Please *rewrite* this sentence in easier Japanese. / *Kono monogatari wa kodomo ga wakaru yoo ni* kakikaete arimasu. (この物語は子どもがわかるように書き換えてあります) This tale *is rewritten* so that children can understand it.
2 renew (a license, certificate, etc.):
Uñteñ-meñkyo o kakikaenakereba naranai. (運転免許を書き換えなければならない) I *have to renew* my driver's license.

ka⌈kika⌉ta かきかた (書き方) *n.* manner of writing; how to write; how to fill in [out]:
Kono shorui no kakikata *o oshiete kudasai*. (この書類の書き方を教えてください) Please tell me *how to fill in* these papers.

ka⌈kikom·u かきこむ (書き込む) *vt.* (-kom·i-; -kom·a-; -koñ-de C) write; jot down; fill in [out]:

Techoo ni kanojo no deñwa-bañgoo o kakikoñda. (手帳に彼女の電話番号を書き込んだ) I *jotted down* her telephone number in my notebook. / *Kono yooshi ni shimee to juusho o* kakikoñde *kudasai*. (この用紙に氏名と住所を書き込んでください) Please *write in* your name and address on this form.

ka⌈ki-ko⌉toba かきことば (書き言葉) *n.* written language; literary expression. 《↔ hanashi-kotoba》

ka⌈kimawas·u かきまわす (掻き回す) *vt.* (-mawash·i-; -mawas·a-; -mawash·i-te C) **1** stir; rummage:
miruku o saji de kakimawasu (ミルクをさじでかき回す) *stir* milk with a spoon / *Hikidashi o* kakimawashite *hañko o sagashita*. (引き出しをかき回してはんこを捜した) I *rummaged around* in the drawer looking for my seal.
2 ruin; throw into confusion:
Iiñkai wa kare hitori ni kakimawasarete iru. (委員会は彼一人にかき回されている) The committee *has been thrown into confusion* just by him.

ka⌈kinaos·u かきなおす (書き直す) *vt.* (-naosh·i-; -naos·a-; -naosh·i-te C) rewrite; write again:
Watashi wa sono tegami o kakinaoshita. (私はその手紙を書き直した) I *rewrote* the letter. 《⇨ kakikaeru》

ka⌈kine かきね (垣根) *n.* fence; hedge:
ie no mawari ni kakine *o megurasu* (家の周りに垣根をめぐらす) make a *fence* around the house.

ka⌈kitate·ru かきたてる (書き立てる) *vt.* (-tate-te V) write up:
Shiñbuñ wa issee ni sono jikeñ o kakitateta. (新聞は一斉にその事件を書き立てた) All the newspapers *played up* that affair.

ka⌈kitome かきとめ (書留) *n.*

registered mail:
Kogitte wa kakitome *de okurima-shita.* (小切手は書留で送りました) I sent the check by *registered mail.* / *O-kane wa geñkiñ-kakitome ni shite kudasai.* (お金は現金書留にしてください) Please have the cash sent by *currency registration.*

ka「**kitome·ru** かきとめる（書き留める）*vt.* (-tome-te V) write [jot] down:
Wasurenai yoo ni, kanojo no juusho o techoo ni kakitometa. (忘れないように、彼女の住所を手帳に書き留めた) I *jotted down* her address in my memobook so as not to forget it. / *Kare wa jikeñ no keeka o hitotsu hitotsu* kakitomete ita. (彼は事件の経過をひとつひとつ書き留めていた) He *wrote down*, step by step, the development of the affair.

ka「**kitori** かきとり（書き取り）*n.* dictation:
kakitori *o suru* (書き取りをする) take *dictation* / kakitori *no shikeñ* (書き取りの試験) a *dictation* test / *kañji no* kakitori (漢字の書き取り) a *kanji dictation.*

ka「**kitor·u** かきとる（書き取る）*vt.* (-tor·i-; -tor·a-; -tot-te C) write down; dictate; copy:
Watashi wa kare no kotoba o kakitotta. (私は彼の言葉を書き取った) I *wrote down* his words. / *Señsee wa watashi-tachi ni Nihoñgo no buñ o* kakitoraseta. (先生は私たちに日本語の文を書き取らせた) The teacher *made us take dictation* of Japanese sentences.

ka「**kitsuke·ru** かきつける（書き付ける）*vt.* (-tsuke-te V) note [jot] down:
Omoi-ukañda koto o nooto ni kakitsuketa. (思い浮かんだことをノートに書き付けた) In my notebook I *jotted down* what had occurred to me.

ka「**kizome** かきぞめ（書き初め）*n.* the New Year's writing. ★ A Japanese custom of practicing calligraphy with a brush for the first time in the New Year, usually on January 2.

KAKIZOME

ka「**kko** かっこ（括弧）*n.* parentheses; brackets; braces:
tañgo o kakko *ni ireru* (単語を括弧に入れる) put a word in *parentheses* / *tañgo o* kakko *de kukuru* (単語を括弧でくくる) enclose a word with *parentheses.*

( )	maru-kakko	parentheses
[ ]	kaku-kakko	brackets
{ }	dai-kakko	braces

kakko suru (〜する) *vt.* parenthesize.

ka「**kkoi¹·i** かっこいい *a.* (kakkoyoku) (*informal*) good-looking; handsome; stylish: ★ Abbreviation of '*kakkoo ga ii.*'
Kare wa kakkoii *kuruma o motte iru.* (彼はかっこいい車を持っている) He has a *stylish* car.

ka「**kkoku** かっこく（各国）*n.* every country; each nation; various countries:
Kakkoku *no daihyoo ga sono kaigi ni shusseki shita.* (各国の代表がその会議に出席した) Representatives of *various countries* attended the conference.

ka「**kkoo¹** かっこう（格好）*n.* appearance; shape; style:
kakkoo *no ii ootobai* (格好のいいオートバイ) a *stylish* motorcycle / *Heñ*

na kakkoo *de neta kara, kubi ga itai.*(変な格好で寝たから、首が痛い) My neck hurts since I slept in an odd *position.* / *Aratamatta kakkoo de paatii ni deta.*(改まった格好でパーティーに出た) I attended the party in formal *attire.*

kakkoo ga warui (～が悪い) feel awkward: *Shitsumoñ ni kotaerarenakute,* kakkoo ga warukatta. (質問に答えられなくて、格好が悪かった) I couldn't answer the question so I *didn't look so good.*

— *a.n.* (～ na/no) suitable; fit; ideal: *Haikiñgu ni wa* kakkoo *no teñki da.*(ハイキングには格好の天気だ) It is *ideal* weather for hiking. / *Koko wa kodomo-tachi ni totte* kakkoo *no asobiba da.*(ここは子どもたちにとって格好の遊び場だ) This is an *ideal* playground for children.

kaꜜkkoo[2] かっこう(郭公) *n.* Japanese cuckoo.

kaꜜko かこ(過去) *n.* the past: *Kako no koto wa wasuremashoo.*(過去のことは忘れましょう) Let's forget *the past.* / *Kare wa* kako *juuneñ-kañ mujiko desu.*(彼は過去10年間無事故です) He has not had a driving accident for *the past* ten years. 《⇨ geñzai (table)》

kaꜜkoi かこい(囲い) *n.* enclosure; fence; railing: *Niwa ni* kakoi *o shite moratta.*(庭に囲いをしてもらった) I had the garden *enclosed* with a fence. 《⇨ kakou》

kaꜜkom·u かこむ(囲む) *vt.* (kakom·i-; kakom·a-; kakoñ-de [C]) **1** enclose; surround: *Sono mura wa yama ni* kakomarete iru.(その村は山に囲まれている) The village *is surrounded* by mountains. / *Shiñsetsu na tomodachi ni* kakomarete, *tanoshii gakkoo-seekatsu o sugoshimashita.* (親切な友だちに囲まれて、楽しい学校生

活を過ごしました) *With* kind friends *all around me,* I had an enjoyable school life. / *Watashi-tachi wa teeburu o* kakoñde *suwatta.* (私たちはテーブルを囲んで座った) We sat *around* the table.

2 circle: *Tadashii kotae o maru de* kakomi nasai.(正しい答えを丸で囲みなさい) *Circle* the correct answers.

kaꜜkoo[1] かこう(加工) *n.* processing; manufacturing: kakoo-*hiñ* (加工品) *processed* goods.

kakoo suru (～する) *vt.* process; manufacture; work: *geñryoo o* kakoo suru(原料を加工する) *process* raw materials.

kaꜜkoo[2] かこう(下降) *n.* descent; fall; downturn: *Tochi no nedañ wa* kakoo *no keekoo ni aru.*(土地の値段は下降の傾向にある) Land prices are tending to *fall.*

kakoo suru (～する) *vi.* go down; descend; decline: *Hikooki wa jojo ni* kakoo shita.(飛行機は徐々に下降した) The airplane gradually *lost altitude.* / *Kare no niñki wa ikki ni* kakoo shita.(彼の人気は一気に下降した) His popularity *has* suddenly *declined.* (↔ jooshoo)

kaꜜko·u かこう(囲う) *vt.* (kako·i-; kakow·a-; kakot-te [C]) enclose; fence: *Shikichi o saku de* kakotta.(敷地を柵で囲った) I *enclosed* the site with a fence. / *Nawa de* kakotta *basho ni hairanai de kudasai.*(なわで囲った場所に入らないでください) Please do not enter the areas which *are cordoned off.* 《⇨ kakoi》

kaꜜk·u[1] かく(書く) *vt.* (kak·i-; kak·a-; ka·i-te [C]) write: *peñ de kañji o* kaku(ペンで漢字を書く) *write* a Chinese character with a pen / *tegami [shi] o* kaku(手紙

kaku

386

[詩]を書く) *write* a letter [poem] / *shoosetsu o* kaku (小説を書く) *write* a novel / × (=*batsu*) *o* kaku (×を書く) *mark* ×.

kaite aru (書いてある) be written; say: *Shiñbuñ* [*Tegami*] *ni wa nañ to* kaite arimasu *ka?* (新聞[手紙]には何と書いてありますか) What does it *say* in the paper [letter]?

ka⌐k·u² かく (描く) *vt.* (kak·i-; ka-k·a-; ka·i-te Ⓒ) draw; paint: *Seeto-tachi wa chuurippu no e o kaite ita.* (生徒たちはチューリップの絵をかいていた) The pupils *were drawing* pictures of tulips. / *Eki made no chizu o* kaite *moraemasu ka?* (駅までの地図をかいてもらえますか) Can you *draw* me a map of the way to the station?

ka⌐k·u³ かく (掻く) *vt.* (kak·i-; ka-k·a-; ka·i-te Ⓒ) **1** scratch: *kayui tokoro o* kaku (かゆい所をかく) *scratch* where it itches / *atama o* kaku (頭をかく) *scratch* one's head. **2** shovel: *yuki o* kaku (雪をかく) *shovel* snow away.

ka⌐ku⁴ かく (格) *n.* status; rank; class; grade: kaku *ga agaru* [*sagaru*] (格が上がる[下がる]) rise [fall] in *rank* / *Kono hoteru wa kono chiiki de wa ichi-bañ* kaku *ga takai.* (このホテルはこの地域ではいちばん格が高い) This hotel is the highest *class* in this area.

kaku ga chigau (〜が違う) be not comparable: *Kare to watashi de wa* kaku ga chigau. (彼と私では格が違う) I *am just not in his class.*

ka⌐ku⁵ かく (核) *n.* **1** nucleus: kaku-*jikkeñ* (核実験) a *nuclear* test / kaku-*kazoku* (核家族) a *nuclear* family. **2** core; kernel.

ka⌐ku⁶ かく (角) *n.* angle. 《⇨ kakudo; shikaku》

ka⌐ku- かく (各) *pref.* each: kaku-*gakkoo* (各学校) *each* school

/ *Señsee wa sono koto o seeto no* kaku-*katee ni reñraku shita.* (先生はそのことを生徒の各家庭に連絡した) The teacher informed *each* pupil's family of the matter.

-⌐kaku かく (画) *suf.* **1** (of rooms) partition: ik-kaku (一画) a *partition.* **2** (of Chinese characters) stroke: rok-kaku *no kañji* (6 画の漢字) a Chinese character of six *strokes.*

ka⌐kuchi かくち (各地) *n.* various parts: *Taifuu ga* kakuchi *ni higai o motarashita.* (台風が各地に被害をもたらした) The typhoon caused damage to *various parts* of the country.

ka⌐kudai かくだい (拡大) *n.* expansion; magnification: *ryoodo no* kakudai (領土の拡大) *expansion* of territory / kakudai-*kyoo* (拡大鏡) a *magnifying* glass.

kakudai suru (〜する) *vi., vt.* expand; magnify; enlarge: *Seefu wa kaigai-eñjo no waku o* kakudai shita. (政府は海外援助の枠を拡大した) The government *increased* the range of overseas aid. / *Boodoo wa shi zeñiki ni* kakudai shita. (暴動は市全域に拡大した) The riot *spread* all over the city. 《↔ shukushoo》

ka⌐kudo かくど (角度) *n.* **1** angle: kakudo *o hakaru* (角度を測る) measure an *angle* / *Kono shameñ no* kakudo *wa sañ-juu-do ijoo arimasu.* (この斜面の角度は 30 度以上あります) The *angle* of this slope is more than thirty degrees. **2** viewpoint: *Sono moñdai o chigau* kakudo *kara keñtoo shite mimashoo.* (その問題を違う角度から検討してみましょう) Let's examine the problem from a different *viewpoint.*

ka⌐kugo かくご (覚悟) *n.* **1** preparedness; readiness: *Hinañ wa* kakugo *no ue desu.* (非

難は覚悟のうえです) I *am prepared*
for criticism. / Kakugo wa ii *desu*
ka? (覚悟はいいですか) *Are you*
ready?
2 resolution; determination:
Watashi wa jihyoo o dasu kakugo
desu. (私は辞表を出す覚悟です) I *am*
determined to hand in my resignation.
kakugo suru (〜する) *vt.* **1** be
prepared; be ready: *Saiaku no*
jitai wa kakugo shite imasu. (最悪
の事態は覚悟しています) I *am pre-*
pared for the worst.
2 be determined; be resigned:
Kare wa shi o kakugo shite ita
yoo da. (彼は死を覚悟していたようだ)
He seems to *be resigned* to death.
ka˥kuho かくほ (確保) *n.* securing; ensuring; guarantee:
Tomaru tokoro no kakuho *ga mu-*
zukashikatta. (泊まる所の確保が難し
かった) *Securing* a place to stay
was difficult.
kakuho suru (〜する) *vt.* secure;
ensure: *zaseki o* kakuho suru (座
席を確保する) *secure* a seat / *Saikiñ*
wa kañgofu no kazu o kakuho suru
no ga koñnañ desu. (最近は看護婦
の数を確保するのが困難です) These
days it is difficult to *ensure* an
adequate number of nurses.
ka˥kuji かくじ (各自) *n.* (*formal*)
each person:
Kakuji beñtoo o motte kuru koto.
(各自弁当を持って来ること) *Each per-*
son is requested to bring his or
her own lunch.
ka˥kujitsu かくじつ (確実) *a.n.*
(〜 na, ni) certain; sure:
Tanaka-shi no tooseñ wa hobo
kakujitsu *desu.* (田中氏の当選はほぼ
確実です) Mr. Tanaka's victory in
the election is almost *certain.* /
Kakujitsu ni mookaru kabu wa ari-
maseñ. (確実にもうかる株はありません)
There are no stocks which will
definitely yield a profit.

ka˥kumee かくめい (革命) *n.* revolution:
Furañsu-kakumee (フランス革命)
the French *Revolution* / *Deñki-*
seehiñ no kaihatsu wa shufu no
seekatsu ni kakumee *o motara-*
shita. (電気製品の開発は主婦の生活
に革命をもたらした) The develop-
ment of electrical appliances has
brought about a *revolution* in
housewives' lives.
ka˥kumee-teki かくめいてき (革命
的) *a.n.* (〜 na, ni) revolutionary:
kakumee-teki *na hatsumee* (革命的
な発明) a *revolutionary* invention
/ *Kare no yarikata wa* kakumee-
teki *datta.* (彼のやり方は革命的だった)
His method was *revolutionary.*
ka˥kuneñ かくねん (隔年) *n.* every
other [second] year.
ka˥kuniñ かくにん (確認) *n.* confirmation; verification:
kakuniñ *o eru* (確認を得る) receive
confirmation / *Niñzuu no* kakuniñ
o shite kudasai. (人数の確認をしてく
ださい) Please *count heads* to see if
everybody is here.
kakuniñ suru (〜する) *vt.* confirm; make sure: *Hoteru no yo-*
yaku o kakuniñ shita. (ホテルの予約
を確認した) I *confirmed* the hotel
reservation. / *Wasuremono ga nai*
koto o kakuniñ shita. (忘れ物がない
ことを確認した) I *made sure* that I
hadn't left anything.
ka˥kure˥ñbo(o) かくれんぼ(う) (隠
れん坊) *n.* hide-and-seek:
kakureñbo *o suru* (かくれんぼをする)
play hide-and-seek.
ka˥kure·ru かくれる (隠れる) *vi.*
(kakure-te [V̄]) hide; hide oneself:
Kodomo-tachi wa doko ni kakurete iru *ñ dai?* (子どもたちはどこに隠れ
ているんだい) Where *are* the children *hiding?* / *Kanojo wa doa no*
ushiro ni kakureta. (彼女はドアの後

ろに隠れた) She *hid herself* behind
the door. / *Tsuki ga kumo ni* kakureta. (月が雲に隠れた) The moon
disappeared behind a cloud.
《⇨ kakusu》
kakurete (隠れて) in secret: *Sono
ko wa* kakurete, *tabako o sutte iru.*
(その子は隠れて, たばこを吸っている)
The child is smoking *in secret.*

ka⌐kuritsu[1] かくりつ (確立) *n.*
establishment.
kakuritsu suru (〜する) *vi., vt.*
establish; build up: *meesee o*
kakuritsu suru (名声を確立する) *establish* one's reputation / *Ryookoku wa yuukoo-kaṅkee o* kakuritsu shita. (両国は友好関係を確立し
た) The two countries *built up*
friendly relations.

ka⌐kuritsu[2] かくりつ (確率) *n.*
probability; likelihood:
Wareware ga yuushoo suru kakuritsu *wa gojup-paaseṅto desu.* (われわ
れが優勝する確率は 50% です) The
probability of our winning the
championship is fifty percent. /
Kare ga seekoo suru kakuritsu *wa
takai* [*hikui*]. (彼が成功する確率は高
い[低い]) There is a good [small]
chance of his success.

ka⌐kushiṅ[1] かくしん (確信) *n.*
conviction; confidence:
*Kare wa jibuṅ ga tadashii to tsu-
yoi* kakushiṅ *o idaite iru.* (彼は自分
が正しいと強い確信を抱いている) He
has the strong *conviction* that he
is right. / *Watashi wa* kakushiṅ *o
motte kotaeta.* (私は確信をもって答え
た) I answered with *confidence.*
kakushiṅ suru (〜する) *vt.* be convinced; strongly believe: *Kare
no mujitsu o* kakushiṅ shite imasu.
(彼の無実を確信しています) I *strongly
believe* that he is innocent.

ka⌐kushiṅ[2] かくしん (革新) *n.*
1 reform; innovation:
gijutsu no kakushiṅ (技術の革新)
technological *innovation.*

2 reformist; progressive; reformist [progressive] party:
Chiji-seṅkyo de kakushiṅ *ga ho-
shu ni katta.* (知事選挙で革新が保守
に勝った) The *progressive camp*
won against the conservatives in
the gubernatorial election.
《↔ hoshu》
kakushiṅ suru (〜する) *vt.* reform; innovate: *kyooiku-seedo o*
kakushiṅ suru (教育制度を革新する)
reform the education system.

ka⌐kushu かくしゅ (各種) *n.* various kinds; all kinds:
Kare wa kakushu *no raṅ o soda-
tete iru.* (彼は各種のらんを育てている)
He grows *various kinds* of or-
chids. / *Watashi-domo de wa
mihoṅ o* kakushu *torisoroete orimasu.* (私どもでは見本を各種とりそろえ
ております) We have *all kinds* of
samples.

ka⌐kushuu かくしゅう (隔週) *n.*
every other [second] week.

ka⌐ku⌐s·u かくす (隠す) *vt.* (kaku-
sh·i-; kakus·a-; kakush·i-te [C])
1 hide; put out of sight:
*Kare wa sono memo o hoṅ no
naka ni* kakushita. (彼はそのメモを本
の中に隠した) He *hid* the note inside the book. / *Kanojo wa kaateṅ
no kage ni mi o* kakushita. (彼女は
カーテンの陰に身を隠した) She *hid herself* behind the curtain.
《⇨ kakureru》
2 keep secret from; conceal;
cover up:
Kare wa sono koto o oya ni kakushita. (彼はそのことを親に隠した) He
kept the matter from his parents.
/ *Nanimo-kamo* kakusazu ni hanashi nasai. (何もかも隠さずに話しなさい)
Speak out *without concealing* anything.

ka⌐kutee かくてい (確定) *n.* decision; settlement:
Tooseṅ ga kakutee *shidai shirasete kudasai.* (当選が確定次第知らせ

てください) Please let us know as soon as the success in the election *is assured.*

kakutee suru (〜する) *vi.*, *vt.* decide; settle; fix: *Nittee ga kakutee shimashita.*(日程が確定しました) The schedule *has been worked out.* / *Hikoku no yuuzai ga* kakutee shita.(被告の有罪が確定した) The defendant's guilt *was decided.* / *Kaisha wa kongo no hooshiñ o* kakutee shita.(会社は今後の方針を確定した) The company *decided* on its future policy.

ka⌐kutoku かくとく(獲得) *n.* acquisition; acquirement: *Kaku chiimu tomo yuumee señshu no* kakutoku *ni yakki to natte iru.*(各チームとも有名選手の獲得に躍起となっている) Each team is very eager to *acquire* star players.

kakutoku suru (〜する) *vt.* acquire; win; obtain: *Kanojo wa koñtesuto de it-too-shoo o* kakutoku shita.(彼女はコンテストで一等賞を獲得した) She *won* first prize in the contest.

ka⌐ma¹ かま(釜) *n.* iron pot; kettle.

ka⌐ma² かま(鎌) *n.* sickle; scythe.

ka⌐mae⌐·ru かまえる(構える) *vt.* (kamae-te Ⅴ) **1** take a posture; prepare oneself: *Kare wa pisutoru o* kamaeta.(彼はピストルを構えた) He *had* a pistol *ready.*
2 set up; build: *mise o* kamaeru (店を構える) *set up* a shop / *ikka o* kamaeru (一家を構える) *set up* housekeeping on one's own.

Ka⌐makura かまくら(鎌倉) *n.* a city located in Kanagawa Prefecture; a popular tourist spot, about an hour by train from Tokyo. The great bronze image of Buddha is famous.

Ka⌐makura-ji⌐dai かまくらじだい (鎌倉時代) *n.* Kamakura Period (1192 to 1333).《⇨ jidai (table)》

ka⌐ma⌐·u かまう(構う) *vi.*, *vt.* (kama·i-; kamaw·a-; kamat-te Ⓒ) **1** (with a negative) (not) mind: *Doo natte mo* kamaimaseñ.(どうなってもかまいません) I *do not care* what happens. / *Sore ga jijitsu de atte mo nakute mo,* kamaimaseñ.(それが事実であってもなくても、かまいません) Whether it is true or not, it *makes no difference.* / *"Tabako o sutte mo* kamaimaseñ *ka?" "Ee,* kamaimaseñ.*"*(「たばこを吸ってもかまいんせんか」「ええ、かまいません」) "Do you *mind* if I smoke?" "No, I *don't.*" / *Suiri-shoosetsu nara, nañ de mo* kamaimaseñ *kara kashite kudasai.*(推理小説なら、何でもかまいませんから貸してください) It *doesn't matter* what it is, as long as it is a mystery novel, so will you please lend it to me? / *Doozo* kamawanai *de kudasai.*(どうぞかまわないでください) Please *don't trouble yourself.*
2 (with a negative) meddle; interfere: *Hito* [*Watashi*] *ni* kamau *na.*(ひと[私]にかまうな) *Leave* me alone. / *O-mae nañka ni* kamatte *irarenai.*(お前なんかにかまっていられない) I *have no time to waste* on people like you.
3 (in the negative) (not) look after; (not) care for; (not) pay attention to: *Gorufu bakari shite, otto wa watashi o* kamatte *kurenai.*(ゴルフばかりして、夫は私をかまってくれない) My husband always goes golfing, and does not *pay any attention* to me.

...mo kamawanai (...もかまわない) do not mind [matter]; do not cause any problem: *Koko ni oite mo* kamaimaseñ *ka?*(ここに置いてもかまいませんか) Is it *all right* if I place it here? / *Itsu oide ni natte mo* kamawanai *desu.*(いつおいでになって

ってもかまわないです) It *does not matter* when you come. ★ '*kamaimaseñ*' and '*kamawanai desu*' are polite forms.

ka⌐me かめ (亀) *n.* tortoise; turtle. 《⇨ tsuru³》

ka⌐mera カメラ *n.* camera: kamera *ni fuirumu o ireru* (カメラに フィルムを入れる) load a *camera* / kamera *no shattaa o kiru* (カメラのシ ャッターを切る) click the shutter of a *camera* / *sañjuugo-miri* kamera (35 ミリカメラ) a 35 millimeter *camera* / *ichi-gañ refu* kamera (一 眼レフカメラ) a single-lens reflex *camera*.

ka⌐mera⌐mañ カメラマン *n.* photographer; cameraman. ★ Professional photographers are usually called '*kameramañ*' regardless of sex.

ka⌐mi¹ かみ (紙) *n.* paper: Kami *o ichi-mai kudasai.* (紙を 1 枚 下さい) Please give me a sheet of *paper.* / *Okurimono o* kami *ni tsutsuñda.* (贈り物を紙に包んだ) I wrapped the present in *paper.* / kami-*bukuro* (紙袋) a *paper* bag / kami-*kire* (紙切れ) a slip of *paper* / kami-*koppu* (紙コップ) a *paper* cup.

ka⌐mi² かみ (髪) *n.* hair: kami *o tokasu* (髪をとかす) comb one's *hair* / kami *o wakeru* (髪を 分ける) part one's *hair* / kami *o arau* (髪を洗う) wash one's *hair* / Kami *o mijikaku katte moratta.* (髪を短く刈ってもらった) I had my *hair* cut close.

ka⌐mi³ かみ (神) *n.* deity; god; God: ★ Often called '*kamisama.*' kami *o shiñjiru* (神を信じる) believe in *God* [a *god*].

ka⌐mi- かみ (上) *pref.* **1** upper: kami-*te* (上手) the *upper* part; the right of the stage / kami-*za* (上座) the seat of *honor.* 《↔ shimo-》 **2** the first:

kami-*hañki* (上半期) the *first* half of the year. 《↔ shimo-》

ka⌐mia⌐·u かみあう (噛み合う) *vi.* (-a·i-; -aw·a-; -at-te Ⓒ) **1** (of gears) mesh; engage: Kono haguruma wa kamiawanai. (この歯車はかみ合わない) These gears *won't mesh.* **2** (of an opinion, view, etc.) agree: ★ Used usually in the negative. Futari no ikeñ wa kamiawanakatta. (二人の意見はかみ合わなかった) They *argued on different planes.*

ka⌐mifu⌐buki かみふぶき (紙吹雪) *n.* confetti: Pareedo no hito no ue de kamifubuki ga matta. (パレードの人の上で 紙吹雪が舞った) *Confetti* floated over the people in the parade.

ka⌐mikuda⌐k·u かみくだく (噛み砕 く) *vt.* (-kudak·i-; -kudak·a-; -kuda·i-te Ⓒ) **1** crush with one's teeth: ame o kamikudaku (あめをかみくだく) *crunch up* candy. **2** explain in easy words: Watashi wa sono koto o kodomo ni kamikudaite hanashita. (私はその ことを子どもにかみくだいて話した) I told it to the child *in simple words.*

ka⌐miku⌐zu かみくず (紙屑) *n.* wastepaper: kamikuzu-kago (紙屑かご) a *wastebasket.*

ka⌐mina⌐ri かみなり (雷) *n.* thunder; lightning: Tooku de kaminari ga natte iru. (遠くで雷が鳴っている) I hear the rumble of *thunder* in the distance. / Kaminari ga uraniwa no ki ni ochita. (雷が裏庭の木に落ちた) *Lightning* struck the tree in the backyard. 《⇨ illus. (next page)》

ka⌐mi-no⌐-ke かみのけ (髪の毛) *n.* hair of the head: Kanojo wa kami-no-ke ga nagai. (彼女は髪の毛が長い) She has long

PERSONIFIED KAMINARI

hair. | *Suupu ni* kami-no-ke *ga ip-poṅ haitte ita.* (スープに髪の毛が1本入っていた) I found a *hair* in the soup. 《⇨ kami²; ke¹》

ka⌐misama かみさま（神様）*n.* deity; god; God. 《⇨ kami³》

ka⌐misori¹ かみそり（剃刀）*n.* razor: Kamisori *de hige o sotta.* (剃刀でひげをそった) I shaved my face with a *razor.* | kamisori *no ha* (剃刀の刃) a *razor* blade | *deṅki-*kamisori (電気剃刀) an electric *razor.*

ka⌐mo かも（鴨）*n.* wild duck. 《⇨ ahiru》

ka⌐moku かもく（科目）*n.* subject; course of study: Watashi no suki na kamoku *wa rekishi desu.* (私の好きな科目は歴史です) My favorite *subject* is history. | *hisshuu-*kamoku (必修科目) a required *subject* | *seṅtaku-*kamoku (選択科目) an elective *subject.*

ka⌐ mo shirenai かもしれない（かも知れない）(*polite* = '*ka mo shirema-seṅ*' or '*ka mo shirenai desu*')
1 it may be; perhaps: Soo ka mo shirenai *shi, soo de nai* ka mo shirenai. (そうかもしれないし、そうでないかもしれない) It *may be* so, or *may not be.* | *Sore wa tsukuribana-shi* ka mo shirenai. (それは作り話かもしれない) It *might be* a made-up story. | *Isoide ikeba maniau* ka mo shirenai. (急いで行けば間に合うか

もしれない) If you hurry along, you *may* make it.
2 there is no way to tell...: *Itsu ame ga furi-hajimeru* ka mo shirenai *kara kasa o motte iki na-sai.* (いつ雨が降り始めるかもしれないから傘を持って行きなさい) *There is no telling* when it might start raining, so take an umbrella with you.

ka⌐motsu かもつ（貨物）*n.* freight; goods; cargo: Torakku wa omoi kamotsu *o tsu-ṅde ita.* (トラックは重い貨物を積んでいた) The truck was loaded with heavy *freight.* | *Shinamono wa kookuu-*kamotsu *de okurimasu.* (品物は航空貨物で送ります) We will send the goods by air *cargo.* | kamotsu-*ressha* (貨物列車) a *freight* [*goods*] train.

ka⌐m·u かむ（噛む）*vt.* (kam·i-; kam·a-; kaṅ-de Ｃ) bite; chew; gnaw: tabemono o kamu (食べ物をかむ) *chew* one's food | *tsume o* kamu (つめをかむ) *bite* one's nails | *Inu ni te o* kamareta. (犬に手をかまれた) My hand *was bitten* by a dog.

ka⌐ṅ¹ かん（缶）*n.* can; tin: sake no kaṅ *o akeru* (鮭の缶を開ける) open a *can* of salmon | kaṅ-*biiru* (缶ビール) a *can* of beer | kaṅ-*kiri* (缶切り) a *can* opener.

ka⌐ṅ² かん（管）*n.* pipe; tube. 《⇨ shikeṅkaṅ; shiṅkuukaṅ; sui-dookaṅ》

ka⌐ṅ³ かん（勘）*n.* intuition; perception: kaṅ *o hatarakasu* (勘を働かす) use one's *intuition* | *Watashi wa* kaṅ *de wakatta.* (私は勘でわかった) I felt it *intuitively.* | *Kare wa* kaṅ *ga ii* [*warui*]. (彼は勘がいい[悪い]) He has quick [slow] *perception.*

-kaṅ¹ かん（間）*suf.* **1** (of places, persons, etc.) between; among: Tookyoo Oosaka-kaṅ (東京・大阪

間) *between* Tokyo and Osaka /
sañsha-kaṅ *de hanashiau* (三者間で
話し合う) discuss something
among three parties.
2 (of time, period) in; for;
during:
Sono shigoto wa futsuka-kaṅ *de
owatta.* (その仕事は 2 日間で終わった)
The job was finished *in* two days.
/ *Is-shuu*-kaṅ *Seṅdai ni taizai shita.* (一週間仙台に滞在した) I stayed
in Sendai *for* a week. / *Moo ik-
kagetsu*-kaṅ *ame ga futte inai.* (も
う 1 か月間雨が降っていない) We have
had no rain *for* a month.

-kaṅ[2] かん(巻) *suf.* volume; reel:
★ Counter for books, dictionaries, and reels of film.
ni-kaṅ *kara naru jisho* (2 巻からなる
辞書) a dictionary consisting of
two *volumes* / *sañ*-kaṅ-*mono no
eega* (3 巻ものの映画) a movie of
three *reels*.

ka「na かな(仮名) *n.* Japanese syllabary: ★ There are two sys-
tems, '*hiragana*' and '*katakana*.'
kañji ni kana o furu (漢字にかなをふ
る) show the reading of a Chinese
character by adding *kana* / *waapuro o kana de nyuuryoku suru*
(ワープロをかなで入力する) input
words into a word-processor by
means of *kana*. 《⇨ furigana; see
inside front cover》

ka「 na かな *p.* **1** I wonder (if):

(USAGE)

Usually used in addressing oneself. Most often used by men;
women use '*ka shira.*' '*Ka naa*'
is a variant.

Ashita wa teṅki ka na? (あしたは天
気かな) Will the weather be fine
tomorrow, *I wonder*? / *Koñna shigoto boku hitori de dekiru* ka na?
(こんな仕事ぼく一人でできるかな) *I won-
der* if I can manage this kind of
job by myself.

2 I don't know (whether or
not):
Kimi ni kore wakaru ka na? (君に
これわかるかな) *I don't know whether
or not* you can understand this.
/ "*Yamamoto kuru* ka na?" "*Saa,
doo* ka naa." (「山本来るかな」「さあ，
どうかなあ」) "*Do you reckon* Yamamoto is coming?" "Well, *I just
don't know.*"

...nai ka na(a) (ない〜(あ)) I wish:
Hayaku yasumi ni naranai ka na.
(早く休みにならないかな) *Would that
the holidays were here!* / *Shikeñ
ga hayaku owaranai ka naa.* (試験
が早く終わらないかなあ) *How I wish
the tests would soon be over.*

ka「naa かなあ *p.* = ka na.

Ka「nagawa」-keñ かながわけん (神
奈川県) *n.* Kanagawa Prefecture.
Located in the southwest of the
Kanto district. Heavy-chemical
factories are clustered on the
eastern coast near Tokyo. The
capital city, Yokohama (横浜), is
the largest port in Japan.
《⇨ map (F4)》

ka「nai かない(家内) *n.* one's own
wife:
Kanai wa jikka ni kaerimashita.
(家内は実家に帰りました) *My wife*
has returned to her parents'
home. 《↔ otto; shujiñ》《⇨ tsuma》

ka「namonoya かなものや (金物屋)
n. hardware dealer; hardware
store; ironmonger.

ka「narazu」 かならず (必ず) *adv.*
certainly; surely; without fail;
by all means:
Kare wa kanarazu *kuru to itte imashita.* (彼は必ず来ると言っていました)
He said that he would come
without fail. / *Kono shigoto wa*
kanarazu *kañsee sasemasu.* (この仕
事は必ず完成させます) We will com-
plete this job *by all means.* /
Ashita kanarazu *juu-ji ni kite
kudasai.* (あした必ず 10 時に来てくださ

い) Please *be sure* to come at ten tomorrow. / *Watashi wa moratta tegami ni wa* kanarazu *heñji o dashimasu.* (私はもらった手紙には必ず返事を出します) I *always* answer the letters I get.

ka「narazu¹-shimo かならずしも (必ずしも) *adv.* (with a negative) always; necessarily:
Jisho ni aru kara to itte, kanarazu-shimo *tadashii wake de wa arimaseñ.* (辞書にあるからと言って、必ずしも正しいわけではありません) Just because it is in the dictionary does not *necessarily* mean it is correct. / *Gakkoo no seeseki to shakai ni dete kara no katsuyaku wa* kanarazu-shimo *itchi shimaseñ.* (学校の成績と社会に出てからの活躍とは必ずしも一致しません) School grades do not *necessarily* match the activities of a person who has gone out into the world.

ka¹nari かなり (可成) *adv.* pretty; fairly; considerably:
Kyoo wa kanari *samui desu ne.* (きょうはかなり寒いですね) It is *quite* cold today, isn't it? / *Yasuñdara,* kanari *geñki ni narimashita.* (休んだら、かなり元気になりました) I took a day off, so I feel *pretty* good now. / *Kanari no kiñgaku ga koogai-taisaku ni tsukawarete imasu.* (かなりの金額が公害対策に使われています) A *considerable* amount of money is used for antipollution measures. (⇨ daibu)

ka「nashi·i かなしい (悲しい) *a.* (-ku) sad; sorrowful:
kanashii *monogatari* (悲しい物語) a *sad* tale / *Oyako de kimochi ga tsuujinai no wa* kanashii *koto desu.* (親子で気持ちが通じないのは悲しいことです) It is a *sad* thing when parents and children cannot communicate with each other. / *Sono shirase o kiite, watashi wa* kana-shikute *tamaranakatta.* (その知らせを

聞いて、私は悲しくてたまらなかった) I felt unbearably *sad* when I heard the news. (↔ ureshii)
(⇨ kanashimi; kanashimu)

ka「nashimi かなしみ (悲しみ) *n.* sadness; sorrow; grief:
fukai kanashimi (深い悲しみ) deep *grief* / kanashimi *ni shizumu* (悲しみに沈む) be deep in *grief* / kanashimi *ni taeru* (悲しみに耐える) endure *sorrow* / kanashimi *o nori-koeru* (悲しみを乗り越える) overcome *sorrow*. (↔ yorokobi)
(⇨ kanashimu; kanashii)

ka「nashi¹m·u かなしむ (悲しむ) *vt.* (kanashim·i-; kanashim·a-; kanashiñ-de C) feel sad; grieve; mourn; lament:
Kanojo wa neko no shi o kanashi-ñda. (彼女は猫の死を悲しんだ) She *felt sad* about her cat's death. / *Ryooshiñ wa jiko de shiñda musuko no koto o* kanashiñde imasu. (両親は事故で死んだ息子のことを悲しんでいます) The parents *are grieving* for their son who was killed in an accident. / *Kootsuu-jiko ga zooka shite iru no wa* kanashimu *beki koto da.* (交通事故が増加しているのは悲しむべきことだ) The fact that the number of traffic accidents is increasing is something *to be deplored*. (↔ yorokobu) (⇨ kanashimi; kanashii)

ka「na¹·u かなう (適う) *vi.* (kana·i-; kanaw·a-; kanat-te C) suit; meet; serve:
mokuteki ni kanau (目的にかなう) *serve* a purpose / *yookyuu ni* ka-nau (要求にかなう) *answer* a demand / *Sore wa rikutsu ni* kanat-te iru. (それは理屈にかなっている) That *is in conformity* with logic.

ka「nawa¹nai かなわない (適わない) cannot bear [compete]: ★ The *nai*-form of the verb '*kanau*.'
Mushiatsukute kanawanai. (蒸し暑くてかなわない) I *cannot stand* this

sultry weather. / *Kare no shitsu-kosa ni wa* kanawanai.(彼のしつこさにはかなわない) I *cannot tolerate* his stubborn persistence.

★ '*Kanaimaseñ*' and '*kanawanai desu*' are polite forms.

ka⌐nazu⌐chi かなづち(金槌) *n.*
1 hammer:
kanazuchi *de kugi o utsu* (金づちで釘を打つ) drive a nail in with a *hammer*.
2 (*colloq.*) a person who can not swim at all.

ka⌐nazu⌐kai かなづかい(仮名遣) *n.* rules for the use of *kana*.

ka⌐ñbañ かんばん(看板) *n.* signboard; sign:
kañbañ *o dasu* (看板を出す) put up a *signboard* / *Kono* kañbañ *wa nañ to kaite aru ñ desu ka?* (この看板は何と書いてあるんですか) What does this *sign* say?

ka⌐ñbatsu かんばつ(干魃) *n.* drought; dry weather.

ka⌐ñbeñ かんべん(勘弁) *n.* pardon; excuse; tolerance:
Ittañ o-kaiage no shina no kookañ wa go-kañbeñ kudasai.(いったんお買い上げの品の交換はご勘弁ください) *We regret that we are unable* to exchange goods that have already been purchased.

kañbeñ suru (〜する) *vt.* **1** pardon; forgive; excuse: *Watashi ni meñjite kono ko o* kañbeñ shite *yatte kudasai.*(私に免じてこの子を勘弁してやってください) Please *forgive* this child for my sake. / *Chikoku shimashita ga* kañbeñ shite *kudasai.*(遅刻しましたが勘弁してください) Please *excuse* me for being late.
2 put up with; bear; stand: *Kare no taido wa* kañbeñ *dekinai.*(彼の態度は勘弁できない) I *cannot put up with* his manner.

Ka⌐ñboo-cho⌐okañ かんぼうちょうかん(官房長官) *n.* Chief Cabinet Secretary. 《⇨ choo⁴ (table)》

ka⌐ñbu かんぶ(幹部) *n.* management; executives; leaders:
Kare wa kono kaisha no kañbu *no hitori desu.*(彼はこの会社の幹部の一人です) He is one of *the executives* of this company. / *kumiai no* kañbu (組合の幹部) the union *leaders*.

ka⌐ñbyoo かんびょう(看病) *n.* nursing; attendance:
Byooniñ no kañbyoo *de tsukaremashita.*(病人の看病で疲れました) I was tired from *nursing* the patient.

kañbyoo (o) suru (〜を(を)する) *vt.* nurse; attend: *Haha wa nenai de,* kañbyoo shite *kureta.*(母は寝ないで、看病してくれた) Mother *nursed* me without taking any sleep. / *Watashi-tachi wa kootai de byooniñ o* kañbyoo shita.(私たちは交替で病人を看病した) We *attended* the patient in turns.

ka⌐ñchoo かんちょう(官庁) *n.* government office.
《⇨ choo⁴ (table)》

ka⌐ñdañkee かんだんけい(寒暖計) *n.* thermometer. 《⇨ oñdokee》

ka⌐ñdoo かんどう(感動) *n.* deep emotion; strong impression:
Sono shoosetsu wa ooku no hito no kañdoo o *yoñda.*(その小説は多くの人の感動を呼んだ) The novel *moved* many readers.

kañdoo suru (〜する) *vi.* be impressed; be moved; be touched:
Sono hanashi ni kañdoo shite, *nakidasu hito mo ita.*(その話に感動して、泣き出す人もいた) Some people *were moved* to tears at the story.

ka⌐ñdo⌐oshi かんどうし(感動詞) *n.* (of grammar) interjection.
《⇨ appendixes》

ka⌐ne¹ かね(金) *n.* money:
★ Often used with '*o-.*'
kane *o harau* (金を払う) pay *money* / kane *o kasegu* (金を稼ぐ) earn *money* / kane *o tameru* (金をためる) save *money* / *Giñkoo de* kane *o*

karita. (銀行で金を借りた) I borrowed *money* from the bank. / *Kare wa* kane *ni komatte iru yoo da.* (彼は金に困っているようだ) He seems to be pressed for *money.* / O-kane *o nakushimashita.* (お金をなくしました) I've lost my *money.* / Kane *wa zeñbu tsukatte shimaimashita.* (金は全部使ってしまいました) I've spent all my *money.* / O-kane *wa ikura kakarimasu ka?* (お金はいくらかかりますか) How much *money* does it cost? / Kane *ga mono o iu.* (金がものを言う) *Money* talks. 《⇨ kooka³; shihee》

ka⌈ne² かね (鐘) *n.* bell; gong; chime: kane o narasu [tsuku] (鐘を鳴らす [突く]) ring [strike] a *bell* / *Mainichi go-ji ni tera no* kane *ga naru.* (毎日 5 時に寺の鐘が鳴る) Every day, the temple *bell* tolls at five.

ka⌈nemo⌉chi かねもち (金持ち) *n.* rich person; wealthy person; the rich. 《↔ biñbooniñ》

ka⌈ne⌉・ru かねる (兼ねる) *vt.* (kane-te [V]) serve both as; double as: *Kono heya wa shosai to oosetsuma o* kanete *imasu.* (この部屋は書斎と応接間を兼ねています) This room *serves both as* a study and a reception room. / *Kare wa señshu to koochi o* kanete *iru.* (彼は選手とコーチを兼ねている) He *acts as both* a player and the coach. / *Kore wa shumi to jitsueki o* kaneta *shigoto desu.* (これは趣味と実益を兼ねた仕事です) This is a job which gives me pleasure and profit *at the same time.*

-kane⌉・ru かねる (-kane-te [V]) cannot; be unable to; be not allowed to: ★ Occurs as the second element of compound verbs. Added to the continuative base of a verb. *Nañ to mo mooshiage-*kanemasu. (何とも申し上げかねます) I *am not in a position* to make any comment. / *Ano hito nara sore o yari-*kanenai. (あの人ならそれをやりかねない) He *is likely* to do that. / *Musuko wa iede mo shi-*kanenai. (息子は家出もしかねない) My son *is quite capable* of running away from home.

ka⌉nete かねて (予て) *adv.* before; beforehand; previously: Kanete *yotee sarete ita yoo ni, ashita kaigi ga arimasu.* (かねて予定されていたように, あした会議があります) As *previously* scheduled, the meeting will be held tomorrow. / *Sono koto wa watashi mo* kanete *kara yosoo shite imashita.* (そのことは私もかねてから予想していました) I also had foreseen that *for some time.* / *Watashi no* kanete *kara no yume ga jitsugeñ shimashita.* (私のかねてからの夢が実現しました) My *long-cherished* dream has come true.

ka⌈netsu¹ かねつ (加熱) *n.* heating.

kanetsu suru (〜する) *vt.* heat; cook: *Namamono wa sake, ichi-do* kanetsu shita *mono o tabe nasai.* (生ものは避け, 一度加熱したものを食べなさい) Avoid raw food, and eat things that *have been cooked.* 《↔ reekyaku》

ka⌈netsu² かねつ (過熱) *n.* overheating: ★ Figuratively refers to the state of being excessively absorbed in something. *Sono moñdai o meguru roñgi wa saikiñ* kanetsu-*gimi da.* (その問題をめぐる論議は最近過熱気味だ) The argument over that problem has recently tended to *go too far.*

kanetsu suru (〜する) *vi.* **1** overheat: *Eñjiñ ga* kanetsu shita *rashii.* (エンジンが過熱したらしい) The engine seems to *have overheated.* **2** (*fig.*) go to excess:

Señkyo-uñdoo ga kanetsu shite kita. (選挙運動が過熱してきた) The election campaign *has gone too far.*

ka⌐ñga⌐e かんがえ (考え) *n.*
1 thought:
kañgae *ni fukeru* (考えにふける) be deep in *thought* / kañgae *o matomeru* (考えをまとめる) collect one's *thoughts.* 《⇨ kañgaeru》
2 idea:
Sore wa yoi kañgae *da.* (それはよい考えだ) That is a good *idea.* / *Ii* kañgae *ga atama ni ukañda.* (いい考えが頭に浮かんだ) A good *idea* has occurred to me.
3 opinion; view:
Watashi no kañgae *de wa, anata no* kañgae *wa machigatte imasu.* (私の考えでは、あなたの考えは間違っています) In my *opinion*, your *view* is wrong.
4 intention:
Anata o damasu kañgae *wa arimaseñ.* (あなたをだます考えはありません) I have no *intention* of deceiving you. / *Ima no shigoto wa yameru* kañgae *desu.* (今の仕事はやめる考えです) I *intend* to quit my present job.

ka⌐ñgaeko⌐m·u かんがえこむ (考え込む) *vi.* (-kom·i-; -kom·a-; -koñde C) think hard; brood over:
Musuko no hañtai ni atte, kare wa sukkari kañgaekoñde shimatta. (息子の反対にあって、彼はすっかり考え込んでしまった) He *got* completely *lost in thought* when he came up against his son's opposition. / *Sore wa soñna ni* kañgaekomu *koto de wa arimaseñ.* (それはそんなに考え込むことではありません) That is not something to *think about so deeply.*

ka⌐ñgaenao⌐s·u かんがえなおす (考え直す) *vt.* (-naosh·i-; -naos·a-; -naosh·i-te C) reconsider; rethink; give up:

Sono koto wa kañgaenaoshita *hoo ga ii desu yo.* (そのことは考え直したほうがいいですよ) You had better *think about* that *again.*

ka⌐ñgae⌐·ru かんがえる (考える) *vt.* (kañgae-te V) **1** think; consider:
Watashi mo soo kañgaemasu. (私もそう考えます) I *think* so, too. / *Sono añ ni tsuite doo* kañgaemasu *ka?* (その案についてどう考えますか) What do you *think* of that idea? / *Yoku* kañgaete *kara kimetai to omoimasu.* (よく考えてから決めたいと思います) I would like to decide after I *have considered* carefully. 《⇨ kañgae》
2 expect; imagine:
Sono shigoto wa kañgaete *ita yori mo kañtañ datta.* (その仕事は考えていたよりも簡単だった) The job was easier than I *had expected.* / *Nihoñ ga koñna ni atsui to wa* kañgaete *mo imaseñ deshita.* (日本がこんなに暑いとは考えてもいませんでした) I *never even imagined* that Japan would be hot like this. 《⇨ omou》
3 regard; take; believe:
Watashi wa ima made ano hito o shiñshi da to kañgaete imashita. (私は今まであの人を紳士だと考えていました) Up to now I *had believed* that he was a gentleman.
4 devise:
Kore wa watashi ga kañgaeta *omocha desu.* (これは私が考えたおもちゃです) This is a toy which I *thought up.*

ka⌐ñgaetsu⌐k·u かんがえつく (考え付く) *vt.* (-tsuk·i-; -tsuk·a-; -tsui-te C) think of; hit upon; call to mind; recollect:
Yoi aidea o kañgaetsuita. (良いアイデアを考えついた) I *hit upon* a good idea.

ka⌐ñgai¹ かんがい (感慨) *n.* deep emotion:
Waga ko no seechoo o miru to

kañgai-bukai *mono ga aru.* (わが子の成長を見ると感慨深いものがある) My heart *is filled with deep emotion* when I see my children grown up. / *Kako no kuroo o omou to* kañgai muryoo da. (過去の苦労を思うと感慨無量だ) When I look back on the past hardships, I *am stirred with emotion.*

ka⌐ñgai² かんがい (灌漑) *n.* irrigation.

kañgai suru (～する) *vt.* irrigate; water: *tochi o* kañgai suru (土地をかんがいする) *irrigate* land.

ka⌐ñga⌐ruu カンガルー *n.* kangaroo.

ka⌐ñgee かんげい (歓迎) *n.* welcome; reception:

kañgee *no ji o noberu* (歓迎の辞を述べる) give a *welcoming* address / *Kare wa atatakai* kañgee *o uketa.* (彼は温かい歓迎を受けた) He received a warm *welcome.* / kañgee-*kai* (歓迎会) a *welcome* party.

kañgee suru (～する) *vt.* welcome: *Watashi-tachi wa kare o kokoro kara* kañgee shita. (わたしたちは彼を心から歓迎した) We *gave* him a hearty *welcome.* / *Yaru ki no aru hito nara, dare de mo* kañgee shimasu. (やる気のある人なら、だれでも歓迎します) We *welcome* anyone who is keen and willing. / *Sono fasshoñ wa wakai hito-tachi ni* kañgee sareta. (そのファッションは若い人たちに歓迎された) That fashion *was received favorably* by young people.

ka⌐ñgeki かんげき (感激) *n.* deep emotion; strong impression: kañgeki *o arata ni suru* (感激を新たにする) recall something with renewed *emotion* / *Nyuushi ni gookaku shita toki no* kañgeki *wa isshoo wasurenai.* (入試に合格したときの感激は一生忘れない) As long as I live, I'll never forget the *excitement* I felt when I passed the

entrance examination.

kañgeki suru (～する) *vi.* be deeply moved; be impressed: *Sono shoosetsu ni* kañgeki shite, *chosha ni tegami o kaita.* (その小説に感激して、著者に手紙を書いた) *Deeply moved* by the novel, I wrote a letter to the author.

ka⌐ñgo かんご (看護) *n.* nursing: *Kare wa byooiñ de teatsui* kañgo *o uketa.* (彼は病院で手厚い看護を受けた) He received tender *care* in the hospital. / kañgo-shi (看護士) a *male nurse.*

kañgo suru (～する) *vt.* nurse; look after: *Kanojo wa tetsuya de otto o* kañgo shita. (彼女は徹夜で夫を看護した) She *looked after* her husband right through the night.

ka⌐ñgo⌐fu かんごふ (看護婦) *n.* female nurse. 《⇨ kañgo》

ka⌐ni かに (蟹) *n.* crab.

ka⌐ñja かんじゃ (患者) *n.* patient; sufferer; case: *Eizu no* kañja *ga mata hitori deta.* (エイズの患者がまた一人でた) Another *case* of AIDS has appeared.

ka⌐ñji¹ かんじ (感じ) *n.* **1** impression: *Kare wa* kañji *ga yoi* [*warui*]. (彼は感じが良い[悪い]) He makes a good [bad] *impression.*
2 feeling; feel: *Watashi no* kañji *de wa kare wa konai to omou.* (私の感じでは彼は来ないと思う) I have a *feeling* that he will not come. / *Samukute, ashi no* kañji *ga nakunatta.* (寒くて、足の感じがなくなった) Since it was so cold, I lost all *feeling* in my feet. / *Kono nuno wa kinu no* kañji *ga suru.* (この布は絹の感じがする) This cloth *feels* like silk.

ka⌐ñji² かんじ (漢字) *n.* Chinese character; 'kanji': kañji *no kakitori-reñshuu o suru* (漢字の書き取り練習をする) practice *kanji* dictation / *Nihoñgo no shiñ-*

buñ o yomu ni wa kanji *o niseñ-ji kurai oboeru hitsuyoo ga arimasu.* (日本語の新聞を読むには漢字を 2 千字くらい覚える必要があります) It is necessary to learn about 2,000 *Chinese characters* to read a Japanese newspaper. (⇨ jooyoo kanji)

ka⌐ñji³ かんじ (幹事) *n.* secretary; manager; steward:
Kare wa kono kyookai no kanji *o shite iru.* (彼はこの協会の幹事をしている) He is a *secretary* of this association. / *Watashi wa booneñ-kai no* kanji *o tsutometa.* (私は忘年会の幹事を務めた) I acted as *organizer* of our year-end party. / kanji-choo (幹事長) the chief *secretary*.

ka⌐ñjiñ かんじん (肝心) *a.n.* (~ na, no) essential; important; critical:
Kanjiñ no shuyaku ga byooki ni natte shimatta. (肝心の主役が病気になってしまった) The *all-important* leading actor has fallen ill. / *Nañ de mo hajime ga* kanjiñ *desu.* (何でも初めが肝心です) In all things the first step is the most *important*. (⇨ juuyoo)

ka⌐ñji·ru かんじる (感じる) *vt.* (ka-ñji-te Ⅴ) feel; sense; be impressed:
kuufuku o kanjiru (空腹を感じる) *feel* hungry / *hiroo o* kanjiru (疲労を感じる) *feel* tired / *Sono eega o mite, doo* kanjimashita *ka?* (その映画を見て、どう感じましたか) How did you *feel* when you saw the film? / *Watashi wa nani-ka kikeñ o* kanjita. (私は何か危険を感じた) I *sensed* some danger. / *Nihoñ ni kite,* kanjita *koto o kaki nasai.* (日本に来て、感じたことを書きなさい) Write about your *feelings* since coming to Japan.

ka⌐ñjo⌐o¹ かんじょう (勘定) *n.*
1 calculation; count:
Sono ko wa kanjoo *o machigaeta.* (その子は勘定を間違えた) The boy

made a mistake in *calculation*. / *Gookee no* kanjoo *ga awanai.* (合計の勘定が合わない) The *figures* for the total do not come out right.
2 account; payment; bill:
Kanjoo *wa watashi ga haraimasu.* (勘定は私が払います) I'll pay the *bill*. / *Kanjoo o o-negai shimasu.* (勘定をお願いします) *Check*, please. / *Kanjoo wa ikura desu ka?* (勘定はいくらですか) How much is the *bill*?
3 consideration; account:
Kare no koto wa kanjoo *ni irete nakatta.* (彼のことは勘定に入れてなかった) I did not take him into *consideration*.

kanjoo-dakai (~高い) calculating; closefisted: *Ano hito wa* kanjoo-dakai. (あの人は勘定高い) He *is calculating*.

kanjoo suru (~する) *vt.* count; calculate: *Shussekisha no kazu o* kanjoo shite *kudasai.* (出席者の数を勘定してください) Please *count* the number of those present.

ka⌐ñjo⌐o² かんじょう (感情) *n.* feeling(s); emotion; sentiment:
kanjoo *ni hashiru* (感情に走る) give way to one's *feelings* / kanjoo *o osaeru* (感情を押さえる) control one's *feelings* / *Kare wa* kanjoo *o sugu ni soto ni dasu.* (彼は感情をすぐに外に出す) He easily betrays his *emotions*. / *Kare no kotoba wa kanojo no* kanjoo *o gaishita.* (彼の言葉は彼女の感情を害した) His words hurt her *feelings*.

ka⌐ñjoo-teki かんじょうてき (感情的) *a.n.* (~ na, ni) emotional; sentimental:
kanjoo-teki *na giroñ* (感情的な議論) an *emotional* argument / *Kanojo wa* kanjoo-teki *ni natte, nakidashita.* (彼女は感情的になって、泣きだした) She got *emotional* and started to cry. / *Kare wa sugu* kanjoo-teki *ni naru.* (彼はすぐ感情的になる) He soon *gives way to his*

feelings.

ka⌐ñkaku¹ かんかく（間隔）*n.*

1 interval:
Basu wa juugo-fuñ-kañkaku de hashitte imasu. (バスは15分間隔で走っています) Buses leave at fifteen-minute *intervals.* / *Ki wa ittee no* kañkaku o oite uerareta. (木は一定の間隔を置いて植えられた) The trees were planted at regular *intervals.*
2 space:
Ie to ie to no kañkaku *ga hotoñdo nai.* (家と家との間隔がほとんどない) There is little *space* between houses.

ka⌐ñkaku² かんかく（感覚）*n.*
sense; sensation:
*Kanojo wa shikisai-*kañkaku *ga sugurete iru.* (彼女は色彩感覚がすぐれている) She has an excellent *sense* of color. / *Hookoo-*kañkaku o ushinatte shimatta. (方向感覚を失ってしまった) I've lost my *sense* of direction. / *Samukute, yubi no* kañkaku *ga nakunatta.* (寒くて、指の感覚がなくなった) My fingers *got numb* with the cold.

ka⌐ñkaku-teki かんかくてき（感覚的）*a.n.* (~ na, ni) sensuous; related to the senses.

ka⌐ñkañ¹ かんかん *adv.* (~ to)
1 (used to describe the heat and brightness of the sun):
Soto wa hi ga kañkañ (to) tette imasu. (外は日がかんかん(と)照っています) Outside the sun *is blazing hot.*
2 clang; loud ringing sound:
Sono koojoo kara kañkañ to iu oto ga kikoete kita. (その工場からかんかんという音が聞こえてきた) The *clanging* sounds from the factory reached our ears.

ka⌐ñkañ² かんかん *a.n.* (~ ni)
furious:
Chichi wa kañkañ ni natte okotta. (父はかんかんになって怒った) My father *flew into a rage.*

ka⌐ñkee かんけい（関係）*n.*

1 connection:
kañkee *o musubu* [*tatsu*] (関係を結ぶ[断つ]) form [break] a *connection* / *Sore to kore wa nani-ka* kañkee *ga arimasu ka?* (それとこれは何か関係がありますか) Is there any *connection* between this and that? / *Kare wa shigoto no* kañkee *de Oosaka e ikimashita.* (彼は仕事の関係で大阪へ行きました) He went to Osaka *in connection with* his business.
2 relation; relationship:
Kanojo wa watashi no uchi to nañ no kañkee *mo arimaseñ.* (彼女は私の家と何の関係もありません) She is of no *relation* to my family. / *Taijuu wa keñkoo to missetsu na* kañkee *ga arimasu.* (体重は健康と密接な関係があります) Body weight has a close *relation* to health.
3 concern; involvement:
Anata ni wa kañkee *no nai koto desu.* (あなたには関係のないことです) It is *none of your business.*
4 influence:
Teñkoo wa shuukaku ni juuyoo na kañkee *ga arimasu.* (天候は収穫に重要な関係があります) The weather has an important *influence* on the harvest.
5 relations with the opposite sex:
Kare wa sono josee to izeñ kara kañkee *ga atta rashii.* (彼はその女性と以前から関係があったらしい) He seems to have been on *intimate terms* with her for some time.

kañkee suru (~する) *vi.* **1** be concerned; be involved: *Kare wa sono jigyoo ni* kañkee shite iru. (彼はその事業に関係している) He *is involved* in that business.
2 be related; be affected:
Kakaku wa seesañryoo ni mo kañkee shite iru. (価格は生産量にも関係している) The price *is* also *affected* by the volume of output.

ka⌐ñke⌐esha かんけいしゃ(関係者)
n. person concerned:
Kañkeesha igai *tachiiri kiñshi.*
(*sign*)(関係者以外立ち入り禁止) No
Entry to *Unauthorized Persons.*

KAÑKEESHA IGAI TACHIIRI KIÑSHI SIGN

ka⌐ñkeezuke⌐·ru かんけいづける
(関係付ける) *vt.* (-zuke-te Ⅴ) connect; relate:
Sono jikeñ o kore to kañkeezukeru
koto wa dekimaseñ.(その事件をこれ
と関係づけることはできません) We can
not *connect* that case with this.

ka⌐ñki[1] かんき(喚起) *n.* arousing;
stirring up.
kañki suru (〜する) *vt.* arouse; stir
up: *hitobito no chuui o* kañki
suru(人々の注意を喚起する) *arouse*
the attention of people / *seeji-
kaikaku no yoroñ o* kañki suru (政
治改革の世論を喚起する) *stir up* public opinion for government reform.

ka⌐ñki[2] かんき(乾期) *n.* dry season.
《↔ uki[1]》

Ka⌐ñkoku かんこく(韓国) *n.*
South Korea. ★ The official
name is '*Daikañmiñkoku*' (大韓民
国) The Republic of Korea.
《⇨ Chooseñ; Kita-chooseñ》

ka⌐ñkoo かんこう(観光) *n.* sightseeing; tourism:
Kare no ikka wa Kyooto e kañkoo
ni itta.(彼の一家は京都へ観光に行っ
た) His family went *sightseeing* in
Kyoto. / kañkoo-kyaku(観光客) a

tourist; a *sightseer* / kañkoo-
gyoosha (観光業者) a *travel* agent
/ kañkoo-ryokoo (観光旅行) a *sightseeing* tour.
kañkoo suru (〜する) *vt.* see the
sights: *shinai o* kañkoo suru(市
内を観光する) *go sightseeing* in a
city.

ka⌐ñkyaku かんきゃく(観客) *n.*
audience; spectator:
Kyoo wa kañkyaku *ga ookatta*
[*sukunakatta*]. (きょうは観客が多かっ
た[少なかった]) There was a large
[small] *audience* today.

ka⌐ñkyoo かんきょう(環境) *n.*
1 environment; surroundings:
Kodomo wa katee no kañkyoo *ni
eekyoo o ukeru.*(子どもは家庭の環境
に影響を受ける) Children are influenced by their home *environment.* / Kare wa atarashii kañkyoo *ni sugu nareta.*(彼は新しい環
境にすぐ慣れた) He soon adapted
himself to the new *surroundings.*
2 natural environment:
Gorufujoo keñsetsu no tame, shizeñ no kañkyoo *ga hakai sarete
iru.*(ゴルフ場建設のため, 自然の環境が
破壊されている) The *natural environment* is being destroyed due
to the construction of golf courses. / kañkyoo-hogo (環境保護)
environmental protection / kañkyoo-hogo uñdooka (環境保護運動
家) an *enviromentalist.*

Ka⌐ñkyo⌐o-choo かんきょうちょう
(環境庁) *n.* Environment
Agency:
Kañkyoo-choo chookañ (環境庁長
官) the Director General of *the
Environment Agency.* 《⇨ choo[4]
(table)》

ka⌐ñkyoo-e⌐esee (環境衛生) *n.*
environmental hygiene [sanita-
tion].

ka⌐ñkyoo-ha⌐kai かんきょうはかい
(環境破壊) *n.* environmental destruction:

Kore ijoo no kankyoo-hakai *wa yurusenai.*(これ以上の環境破壊は許せない) We can not allow any further *environmental destruction.*

ka⌐nmuri かんむり (冠) *n.* crown: kanmuri *o kaburu* (冠をかぶる) put on a *crown.*

ka⌐nnen かんねん (観念) *n.*
1 sense:
Kare wa jikan no kannen *ga nai.* (彼は時間の観念がない) He has no *sense* of time.
2 idea:
Kimi wa sonna kotee-kannen *o suteru beki da.*(君はそんな固定観念を捨てるべきだ) You should get rid of such fixed *ideas.*

kannen suru (〜する) *vi.* give up; resign oneself to: *Moo ii kagen* kannen shi nasai.(もういいかげん観念しなさい) It's time you *gave up.*

Ka⌐nnon かんのん (観音) *n.* Avalokitesvara. ★ A bodhisattva ('*bosatsu*') of great compassion. Its name literally means 'regarder of the cries of the world.' Often mistakenly called 'goddess of mercy.'

KANNON

ka⌐nnushi かんぬし (神主) *n.* Shinto priest. 《⇨ photo (right)》

ka⌐nojo かのじょ (彼女) *n.* **1** she: ★ 'kanojo no'＝her; 'kanojo o'＝ her. 《⇨ kare-ra》
Kanojo no engi wa kanpeki datta. (彼女の演技は完璧だった) *Her* acting was flawless. / *Watashi wa ima*

KANNUSHI

de mo kanojo o *aishite imasu.*(私は今でも彼女を愛しています) I still love *her.* / *Watashi wa* kanojo ni *okurimono o shita.*(私は彼女に贈り物をした) I gave *her* a present.
2 girlfriend:
Kare ni wa kanojo *ga iru.* (彼には彼女がいる) He has a *girlfriend.*
《↔ kare》

ka⌐noo かのう (可能) *a.n.* (〜 na, ni) possible; practicable:
Kono keekaku wa kanoo *daroo ka?* (この計画は可能だろうか) I wonder if this plan is *practicable.* / *Ima nara, henkoo wa* kanoo *desu.* (今なら, 変更は可能です) Provided it is now, it is *possible* to make a change. 《↔ fukanoo》

ka⌐noosee かのうせい (可能性) *n.* possibility; potentiality:
Kono kazan wa bakuhatsu suru kanoosee *ga takai* [*hikui*].(この火山は爆発する可能性が高い[低い]) There is a good [small] *possibility* of this volcano erupting.

ka⌐npa カンパ *n.* fund-raising campaign; contribution.
kanpa suru (〜する) *vt.* make a contribution: *Kono kai no tame ni* kanpa shite *kudasai.*(この会のためにカンパしてください) Please *make a contribute* for this association.

ka⌐npai かんぱい (乾杯) *n.* toast: kanpai *no ondo o toru* (乾杯の音頭を取る) propose a *toast* / *Kanpai.*

(乾杯) *Cheers!*; *Here's to you.*

kañpai suru (〜する) *vi.* toast; drink: *Satoo-kuñ no zeñto o shukushite,* kañpai shiyoo. (佐藤君の前途を祝して、乾杯しよう) *Let's drink a toast* to Mr. Sato, wishing him success in the future.

ka⌈ñreñ かんれん (関連) *n.* relation; connection; association: *Keesatsu wa sono futatsu no jikeñ no* kañreñ *o shirabete iru.* (警察はその二つの事件の関連を調べている) The police are investigating the *relation* between the two cases. / *Kare no itta koto wa kono keñ to nañ no* kañreñ *mo arimaseñ.* (彼の言ったことはこの件と何の関連もありません) What he said *has nothing* at all *to do with* this matter. / kañreñ-*gaisha* (関連会社) an *associated* company.

kañreñ suru (〜する) *vi.* be related; be connected: *Kono koto ni* kañreñ shite, *kare wa jibuñ no ikeñ o nobeta.* (この事に関連して、彼は自分の意見を述べた) He expressed his own opinion *in this connection.*

ka⌈ñri かんり (管理) *n.* administration; management; control: *Niwa no* kañri *o kare ni tanoñda.* (庭の管理を彼に頼んだ) I asked him to take *care* of my garden. / kañri-*sha* (管理者) an *administrator*; a *manager* / kañri-*shoku* (管理職) a *managerial* position; a *managerial* staff member / kañri-niñ (管理人) a *janitor*; a *concierge.*

kañri suru (〜する) *vt.* administer; manage; take care of: *Dare ga kanojo no zaisañ o* kañri shite *iru no desu ka?* (だれが彼女の財産を管理しているのですか) Who *administers* her property?

ka⌈ñroku かんろく (貫録) *n.* presence; dignity: *Kare wa* kañroku *ga aru.* (彼は貫録がある) He is a man of *presence.*

ka⌈ñryoo¹ かんりょう (完了) *n.* completion: *Kooji no* kañryoo *made ato ik-ka-getsu kakarimasu.* (工事の完了まであと一か月かかります) It will take another one month before the *completion* of the construction work. / *Juñbi* kañryoo. (準備完了) Everything *is ready.*

kañryoo suru (〜する) *vt.* complete; finish: *Teñkeñ wa subete* kañryoo shimashita. (点検はすべて完了しました) I *have finished* checking everything.

ka⌈ñryoo² かんりょう (官僚) *n.* bureaucrat; bureaucracy.

ka⌈ñryoo-teki かんりょうてき (官僚的) *a.n.* (〜 na, ni) bureaucratic.

Ka⌈ñsai かんさい (関西) *n.* the district which comprises the three prefectures of Hyogo, Kyoto and Osaka. 《↔ Kañtoo》 《⇨ inside back cover》

ka⌈ñsañ かんさん (換算) *n.* (of numerical units) conversion; change: kañsañ-*hyoo* (換算表) a *conversion* table.

kañsañ suru (〜する) *vt.* convert; change: *eñ o doru ni* kañsañ suru (円をドルに換算する) *convert* yen into dollars / *mairu o kiro-meetoru ni* kañsañ suru (マイルをキロメートルに換算する) *convert* miles into kilometers.

ka⌈ñsatsu かんさつ (観察) *n.* observation. *Kare wa* kañsatsu *ga surudoi.* (彼は観察が鋭い) He *has an observant eye.*

kañsatsu suru (〜する) *vt.* observe; watch: *hoshi no ugoki o* kañsatsu suru (星の動きを観察する) *observe* the movement of the stars / *teki no koodoo o* kañsatsu suru (敵の行動を観察する) *watch* the movements of the enemy.

ka⌈ñsee かんせい (完成) *n.* com-

pletion; perfection:
Toñneru ga kañsee *ni chikazuita.*
(トンネルが完成に近づいた) The tunnel is near *completion.* / *Kare wa sono biru no* kañsee *o mizu ni nakunatta.* (彼はそのビルの完成を見ずに亡くなった) He died before seeing the *completion* of the building.
kañsee suru (～する) *vt., vi.* complete; finish: *Sono hashi wa kyoneñ* kañsee *shimashita.* (その橋は去年完成しました) The bridge *was completed* last year. / *Kono dooro o hayaku* kañsee *shite hoshii.* (この道路を早く完成してほしい) I wish for this road to *be completed* as soon as possible.

kaｰñseñ かんせん (感染) *n.* infection; contagion; transmission.
kañseñ suru (～する) *vi.* catch; contract: *Eizu ni* kañseñ *shinai yoo ni ki o tsuke nasai.* (エイズに感染しないように気をつけなさい) Take care *not to contract* AIDS.

kaｰñsetsu[1] かんせつ (間接) *n.* indirectness; being secondhand: *Sono koto wa* kañsetsu *ni kikimashita.* (そのことは間接に聞きました) I heard it *indirectly.* / *Satoo kyooju kara wa chokusetsu,* kañsetsu *ni ooki-na eekyoo o ukemashita.* (佐藤教授からは直接, 間接に大きな影響を受けました) I was strongly influenced, directly and *indirectly,* by Professor Sato. / kañsetsu-*zee* (間接税) an *indirect* tax. 《↔ chokusetsu》

kaｰñsetsu[2] かんせつ (関節) *n.* (of a body) joint: *hiji no* kañsetsu (ひじの関節) an elbow *joint* / kañsetsu-*eñ* (関節炎) *arthritis.*

kaｰñsetsu-teki かんせつてき (間接的) *a.n.* (～ na, ni) indirect; secondhand:
jiko no kañsetsu-teki *na geñiñ* (事故の間接的な原因) the *indirect* cause of an accident / *Sono hana-*

shi wa kañsetsu-teki *ni kikimashita.* (その話は間接的に聞きました) I heard the story *indirectly.*
《↔ chokusetsu-teki》

kaｰñsha かんしゃ (感謝) *n.* thanks; gratitude: kañsha *no i o arawasu* (感謝の意を表す) express one's *thanks* / *Kore wa watashi no* kañsha *no shirushi desu.* (これは私の感謝の印です) This is a token of my *gratitude.*
kañsha suru (～する) *vt., vi.* thank; be grateful; be thankful: *Go-shiñsetsu ni* kañsha *shimasu.* (ご親切に感謝します) I *thank* you for your kindness. / *Watashi wa koouñ o* kañsha *shita.* (私は幸運を感謝した) I *was thankful* for my good fortune.

kaｰñshi かんし (監視) *n.* watch; surveillance:
kañshi *no me o hikaraseru* (監視の目を光らせる) keep a *close* eye on / *Koko wa* kañshi *no me ga kibishii.* (ここは監視の目が厳しい) We are placed under strict *surveillance* here. / kañshi-*niñ* (監視人) a *watchman.*
kañshi suru (～する) *vt.* watch; observe: *Kimi no koodoo wa* kañshi *sarete imasu.* (きみの行動は監視されています) Your behavior *is being watched.*

kaｰñshiñ[1] かんしん (感心) *n.* admiration.
kañshiñ suru (～する) *vi.* be impressed; admire: *Ano hito ga yoku hataraku no ni wa* kañshiñ *suru.* (あの人がよく働くのには感心する) I *am impressed* with how hard she works. / *Kimi no yarikata wa amari* kañshiñ *shimaseñ.* (きみのやり方はあまり感心しません) I *do not much like* the way you do things.
— *a.n.* (～ na) admirable; good; praiseworthy:
Oya no tetsudai o suru to wa kañshiñ *na ko da.* (親の手伝いをするとは

感心な子だ) You are a *good* child to give your parents a helping hand.

ka⌐nshiñ² かんしん (関心) *n.* interest; concern:

Kokumiñ wa kono moñdai ni kañshiñ *ga takai [hikui].* (国民はこの問題に関心が高い[低い]) The nation feels great [little] *interest* in this issue. / *Señkyo no kekka ni wa miñna ga* kañshiñ *o motte iru.* (選挙の結果にはみんなが関心を持っている) The election results are a matter of public *concern*.

ka⌐nshoo¹ かんしょう (鑑賞) *n.* (usually of works of art, etc.) appreciation:

Watashi no shumi wa eega no kañshoo *desu.* (私の趣味は映画の鑑賞です) My interest is *watching* movies.

kañshoo suru (〜する) *vt.* appreciate; enjoy: *oñgaku o* kañshoo suru (音楽を鑑賞する) *listen to and enjoy* music.

ka⌐nshoo² かんしょう (干渉) *n.* interference; intervention:

Hoka no hito no kañshoo *wa uketaku arimaseñ.* (ほかの人の干渉は受けたくありません) I don't like to have other people *meddle* in my affairs. / *naisee*-kañshoo (内政干渉) *interference* in the internal affairs of another country.

kañshoo suru (〜する) *vi.* interfere; meddle: *Kare no koto ni wa* kañshoo *shinai hoo ga yoi.* (彼のことには干渉しないほうが良い) We had better *not interfere* in his affairs.

ka⌐nshuu¹ かんしゅう (慣習) *n.* custom; convention:

kañshuu *ni shitagau* (慣習に従う) follow a *custom* / kañshuu *o yaburu* (慣習を破る) break a *custom* / *Sono furui* kañshuu *wa ima mo nokotte imasu.* (その古い習慣は今も残っています) That old *custom* is

still kept even now.

ka⌐nshuu² かんしゅう (観衆) *n.* audience; spectators:

Kañshuu *no taihañ wa wakai hitotachi datta.* (観衆の大半は若い人たちだった) Most of the *audience* were young people. / *Sutajiamu wa* kañshuu *de mañiñ datta.* (スタジアムは観衆で満員だった) The stadium was filled with *spectators*.

ka⌐nsoku かんそく (観測) *n.* **1** observation:

kishoo no kañsoku (気象の観測) meteorological *observation*.

2 prediction; conjecture: *kiboo-teki* kañsoku (希望的観測) wishful *thinking*.

kañsoku suru (〜する) *vt.* **1** observe: *Shima de wa kesa chiisana jishiñ ga* kañsoku *sareta.* (島では今朝小さな地震が観測された) A slight earthquake *was recorded* on the island this morning.

2 predict:

Koñrañ wa izure osamaru daroo to señmoñka wa kañsoku *shite imasu.* (混乱はいずれ収まるだろうと専門家は観測しています) The experts *predict* that the confusion will eventually subside.

ka⌐nsoo¹ かんそう (乾燥) *n.* dryness:

Ijoo-kañsoo-*chuuihoo ga dete imasu.* (異常乾燥注意報が出ています) A *dry* weather warning has been issued. / kañsoo-*zai* (乾燥剤) a *desiccant*.

kañsoo suru (〜する) *vt., vi.* dry; desiccate: *Kuuki ga* kañsoo *shite iru.* (空気が乾燥している) The air *is dry*. / *Kore wa sakana o* kañsoo *saseta mono desu.* (これは魚を乾燥させたものです) This one is a fish which *is dried*.

ka⌐nsoo² かんそう (感想) *n.* impression; thoughts; comment:

Kare wa sono hoñ ni tsuite no kañsoo *o nobeta.* (彼はその本についての感

想を述べた) He gave his *impressions* of the book. / *Sono moñdai ni tsuite anata no* kañsoo *o kikasete kudasai.* (その問題についてあなたの感想を聞かせてください) I'd like to hear your *thoughts* on that matter.

ka「ñs·u「ru かんする (関する) *vi.* (kañsh·i-; kañsh·i-; kañsh·i-te [1]) concern.

...ni kañshite (...に関して) concerning; about: *Sono koto* ni kañshite, *shitte iru koto o o-hanashi shimasu.* (そのことに関して、知っていることをお話しします) I will tell you what I know *concerning* that matter.

...ni kañsuru (...に関する) concerning; about: *Nihoñ* ni kañsuru *hoñ* (日本に関する本) a book *about* Japan / *kuruma* ni kañsuru *joohoo* (車に関する情報) a report *concerning* vehicles / *Kore wa seeshi* ni kañsuru *moñdai desu.* (これは生死に関する問題です) This is a matter *of* life and death. / *Watashi* ni kañsuru *kagiri, igi wa arimaseñ.* (私に関する限り、異議はありません) As far as I *am concerned*, there are no objections.

ka「ñtai かんたい (寒帯) *n.* frigid zone: kañtai-*doobutsu* (寒帯動物) a *polar* animal. 《↔ nettai》 《⇨ kikoo (table)》

ka「ñtañ かんたん (簡単) *a.n.* (~ na, ni) **1** easy; simple: kañtañ *na koozoo* (簡単な構造) *a simple* structure / *Beñgoshi ni naru no wa* kañtañ *de wa nai.* (弁護士になるのは簡単ではない) It is not *easy* to become a lawyer. / *Soñna moñdai wa* kañtañ *ni tokemasu.* (そんな問題は簡単に解けます) I can *easily* solve a problem like that. **2** brief: kañtañ *ni ieba* (簡単に言えば) *briefly* speaking.

ka「ñtoku かんとく (監督) *n.* **1** supervision: *Watashi-tachi wa kare no* kañtoku *no moto ni hataraita.* (私たちは彼の監督のもとに働いた) We worked under his *supervision*. **2** supervisor; superintendent: *Ano hito ga kono eega no* kañtoku *desu.* (あの人がこの映画の監督です) He is the *director* of this movie. / geñba-kañtoku (現場監督) a *foreman*. **3** manager: *yakyuu-chiimu no* kañtoku (野球チームの監督) the *manager* of a baseball team.

kañtoku suru (~ する) *vt.* supervise: *Kimi wa kodomo no koodoo o* kañtoku su beki da. (君は子どもの行動を監督すべきだ) You *should supervise* the children's activities.

Ka「ñtoo かんとう (関東) *n.* Kanto, the central eastern district on Honshu. It comprises Tokyo, Saitama, Kanagawa, Chiba, Ibaraki, Tochigi and Gunma prefectures: Kañto-*heeya* (関東平野) the *Kanto* plain. 《↔ Kañsai》 《⇨ inside back cover》

ka「ñtsuu かんつう (貫通) *n.* penetration.

kañtsuu suru (~ する) *vi.* penetrate; go through: *Tama wa kabe o* kañtsuu *shite ita.* (弾は壁を貫通していた) The bullet *went through* the wall.

ka「ñwa かんわ (緩和) *n.* relaxation; mitigation: *kiñchoo no* kañwa (緊張の緩和) *relaxation* of tensions.

kañwa suru (~ する) *vt., vi.* relax; ease: *seegeñ o* kañwa *suru* (制限を緩和する) *relax* restrictions / *Tsuukiñ-rasshu o* kañwa saseru *yoo ni doryoku shite iru tokoro desu.* (通勤ラッシュを緩和させるように努力しているところです) We are now making every effort to *ease* the commuter rush.

ka⌐ñwa-ji⌐teñ かんわじてん (漢和辞典) *n.* dictionary of Chinese explained in Japanese.

ka⌐nyuu かにゅう (加入) *n.* joining; entry; admission: *kurabu e no* kanyuu *o mooshi-komu* (クラブへの加入を申し込む) apply for *admission* to a club.
kanyuu suru (〜する) *vi.* join; enter: *kumiai ni* kanyuu suru (組合に加入する) *become* a member of a union / *seemee-hokeñ ni* kanyuu suru (生命保険に加入する) *take out* life insurance. 《↔ dattai》

ka⌐nyu⌐usha かにゅうしゃ (加入者) *n.* member; subscriber: *hokeñ* kanyuusha (保険加入者) a *holder* of an insurance policy / *deñwa* kanyuusha (電話加入者) a telephone *subscriber*.

ka⌐ñzee かんぜい (関税) *n.* customs; tariff: kañzee *o kakeru* (関税をかける) impose *customs duty* / *Hoñ ni wa* kañzee *ga kakarimaseñ.* (本には関税がかかりません) Books *are duty-free.* / kañzee-*shooheki* (関税障壁) a *customs* [*tariff*] barrier.

ka⌐ñzeñ かんぜん (完全) *n.* perfection; completeness: kañzeñ *o nozomu* (完全を望む) expect *perfection* / kañzeñ-*hañzai* (完全犯罪) a *perfect* crime.
—*a.n.* (〜 na, ni) perfect; complete; fully: *Iseki ga* kañzeñ *na katachi de hakkeñ sareta.* (遺跡が完全な形で発見された) The remains were discovered in *perfect* condition. / *Jikkeñ wa* kañzeñ *ni shippai datta.* (実験は完全に失敗だった) The experiment was a *total* failure. / *Kono señtakumono wa* kañzeñ *ni kawaite inai.* (この洗濯物は完全に乾いていない) This washing is not *completely* dry. 《↔ fukañzeñ》

ka⌐ñzoo かんぞう (肝臓) *n.* liver.

ka⌐ñzume かんづめ (缶詰) *n.* canned [tinned] food: *Sake no* kañzume *o aketa.* (鮭の缶詰を開けた) I opened a *can* of salmon.

ka⌐o かお (顔) *n.* **1** face; features: kao *o arau* (顔を洗う) wash one's *face* / *Kare wa hori no fukai* kao *o shite iru.* (彼は彫りの深い顔をしている) He has clear-cut *features.* / *Kare wa itami de* kao *o shikameta.* (彼は痛みで顔をしかめた) He *grimaced* with pain.
2 look; expression: *Kanojo wa kanashi-soo na* kao *o shite ita.* (彼女は悲しそうな顔をしていた) She *looked* sad. / *Kare wa ukanu* kao *o shite, modotte kita.* (彼は浮かぬ顔をして、もどって来た) He returned *looking* depressed. / *Chichi wa* kao *o kumoraseta.* (父は顔を曇らせた) The expression on my father's *face* turned gloomy.
3 head: ★ The part of the head where hair grows is called '*atama.*' kao *o somukeru* (顔をそむける) turn one's *head* / *Mado kara* kao *o dashite wa ikemaseñ.* (窓から顔を出してはいけません) Don't put your *head* out of the window.
4 honor; influence: kao *ni kakawaru moñdai* (顔にかかわる問題) an affair which affects one's *honor* / *Kare wa oji no* kao *de kono kaisha ni haitta.* (彼は叔父の顔でこの会社に入った) He got into this company through the *influence* of his uncle.

kao ga hiroi (〜が広い) know a lot of people: *Ano hito wa seekai ni* kao ga hiroi. (あの人は政界に顔が広い) He *is well connected* in the political world.

kao ga kiku (〜がきく) have influence: *Ano hito wa kono machi de* kao ga kiku. (あの人はこの町で顔がきく) He *has a lot of influence* in this town.

kao ga sorou(〜がそろう)be present: *Kañkeesha wa zeñbu kao ga soroimashita.*(関係者はぜんぶ顔がそろいました)All the persons concerned *are present.*

kao ga ureru(〜が売れる)be well known: *Kare wa kiñyuu-suji de kao ga urete iru.*(彼は金融筋で顔が売れている)He *is well known* in financial circles.

kao kara hi ga deru(〜から火が出る)be flushed with shame: *Kare ni machigai o shiteki sarete,* kao kara hi ga deru omoi datta.(彼に間違いを指摘されて、顔から火が出る思いだった)When my mistake was pointed out by him, I *burned with embarrassment.*

kao ni doro o nuru(〜に泥を塗る)stain a person's reputation: *Kare wa oya no* kao ni doro o nutta.(彼は親の顔に泥を塗った)He *disgraced his parents.*

kao o dasu(〜を出す)make an appearance: *Sono kai ni wa tokidoki* kao o dashimasu.(その会にはときどき顔を出します)I *show up* at that society's meeting once in a while.

kao o tateru(〜を立てる)save a person's face: *Kare wa watashi no* kao o tatete kureta.(彼は私の顔を立ててくれた)He *saved me from looking bad.*

kao o tsubusu(〜をつぶす)disgrace: *Kare wa jooshi no* kao o tsubushita.(彼は上司の顔をつぶした)He made his boss *lose face.*

ka⌐odachi かおだち(顔立ち)*n.* features; looks: *Kare no musuko wa* kaodachi *ga ii.*(彼の息子は顔立ちがいい)His son is good-*looking.* / *Kanojo no* kaodachi *wa haha-oya ni nite iru*(彼女の顔立ちは母親に似ている)Her *features* resemble her mother's. / *Ano hito wa totonotta* kaodachi *o shite iru.*(あの人は整った顔立ちをして

いる)He has regular *features.*

ka⌐oiro かおいろ(顔色)*n.* complexion; look; expression: *Kare wa* kaoiro *ga ii [warui].*(彼は顔色がいい[悪い])He *looks healthy [unhealthy].* / *Kanojo wa kaette kita toki, hidoi* kaoiro o shite ita.(彼女は帰って来たとき、ひどい顔色をしていた)She *looked* awfully pale when she came back.

kaoiro o kaeru(〜を変える)change color: *Kare wa* kaoiro o *kaete okotta.*(彼は顔色を変えて怒った)He *turned red* with anger.

kaoiro o ukagau(〜をうかがう)be sensitive to a person's moods: *Kare wa itsu-mo jooshi no* kaoiro o ukagatte iru.(彼はいつも上司の顔色をうかがっている)He *is* always *sensitive* to his boss's *moods.*

ka⌐oku かおく(家屋)*n. (literary)* house; building: *Furui* kaoku *o kowashite, atarashii biru o tateta.*(古い家屋をこわして、新しいビルを建てた)We pulled down the old *houses* and put up a new building.

ka⌐ori かおり(香り)*n.* smell; fragrance; aroma: *Kono bara wa yoi* kaori *ga suru.*(このバラはよい香りがする)This rose *smells* sweet.《⇨ nioi》

ka⌐otsuki かおつき(顔付き)*n.* looks; countenance: *Kare wa kiñchoo shita* kaotsuki *de arawareta.*(彼は緊張した顔つきで現れた)He appeared with a strained *look.* / *Kanojo wa tsukareta yoo na* kaotsuki o shite ita.(彼女は疲れたような顔つきをしていた)She *looked* tired.

ka⌐ppa かっぱ(河童)*n.* imaginary Japanese river-sprite.《⇨ illus. (next page)》

ka⌐ppatsu かっぱつ(活発)*a.n.* (〜 na, ni) lively; active: kappatsu *na oñna-no-ko*(活発な女の子)a *lively* girl / *Shoohisha-*

KAPPA

dañtai ga kappatsu *ni katsudoo shite iru.* (消費者団体が活発に活動している) The consumer groups are now very *active*. / *Giroñ ga* kappatsu *ni natte kita.* (議論が活発になってきた) The discussion has become *heated*.

ka¹ppu カップ *n.* (coffee) cup; trophy cup; measuring cup:
kome o kappu de hakaru (米をカップで計る) measure rice with a *cup*. (⇒ koppu)

KOOHII KAPPU   KOPPU

ka⌐ra⌐¹ から (空) *n.* emptiness:
kara *no biñ* (空のびん) an *empty* bottle / *Sono hako wa* kara *desu.* (その箱は空です) The box is *empty*. / *Kanojo wa sono iremono o* kara *ni shita.* (彼女はその入れ物を空にした) She *emptied* the container.

ka⌐ra⌐¹² から (殻) *n.* shell; husk; hull:
yude-tamago no kara *o muku* (ゆで卵の殻をむく) *shell* a boiled egg.
kara ni tojikomoru (〜に閉じこもる) withdraw into one's shell:

Kare wa jibuñ no kara *ni toji-komotte iru no de, nani o kañ-gaete iru no ka wakaranai.* (彼は自分の殻に閉じこもっているので，何を考えているのかわからない) He *has built a wall around himself* so I don't know what he is thinking.

kara³ から *p.* [follows a noun]
1 (indicates a point of origin in time or space) from:
Soko wa eki kara *aruite, dono kurai kakarimasu ka?* (そこは駅から歩いて，どのくらいかかりますか) How long does it take to go there on foot *from* the station? / *Ashita wa ku-ji* kara *kaigi ga arimasu.* (あしたは9時から会議があります) We will have a meeting *from* nine o'clock tomorrow. (↔ made)

2 (indicates a source) from:
Sono hanashi wa dare kara *kiki-mashita ka?* (その話はだれから聞きましたか) Who did you hear that story *from*? / *Toshokañ* kara *hoñ o ka-rita.* (図書館から本を借りた) I borrowed a book *from* the library. / *Tomodachi* kara *purezeñto o mo-raimashita.* (友達からプレゼントをもらいました) I received a present *from* a friend.

3 (indicates origin or provenance) from:
Waiñ wa budoo kara *tsukurare-masu.* (ワインはぶどうから作られます) Wine is made *from* grapes. / *Hira-gana wa kañji* kara *dekimashita.* (ひらがなは漢字からできました) Hiragana developed *from* Chinese characters.

4 (indicates movement or action from or through a place) from; through:
Watashi no ie kara *Fuji-sañ ga miemasu.* (私の家から富士山が見えます) Mt. Fuji is visible *from* my house. / *Soko* kara *o-hairi kuda-sai.* (そこからお入りください) Please go in *through* there.

5 (indicates the first item in a series) from:

Sono hoñ wa kodomo kara *otona made, miñna ni yomarete imasu.* (その本は子どもから大人まで、みんなに読まれています) The book is read by everyone *from* children to adults. / *Chiisai hito* kara *juñ ni narañde kudasai.* (小さい人から順に並んでください) Please line up in order, starting *with* the smaller children.

6 (indicates cause or reason) from:

Chotto shita kooroñ kara *oogeñka ni natta.* (ちょっとした口論から大げんかになった) A big fight developed *from* a minor argument.

kara[4] から *p.* so; therefore; because: ★ Follows a verb, adjective or the copula and indicates cause or reason.

Sugu iku kara, *chotto matte ite kudasai.* (すぐ行くから、ちょっと待っていてください) I'm coming in a minute, *so* just wait a bit please. / *Sukoshi samui* kara *sutoobu o tsukemashoo ka?* (少し寒いからストーブをつけましょうか) *As* it's a bit chilly, shall I put on the heater? / *Kodomo ga byooki da* kara, *byooiñ e tsurete ikimashita.* (子どもが病気だから、病院へ連れて行きました) I took my child to the hospital *because* he was ill. 《⇨ da kara; no de》

...kara da (...~だ) because: *Nihoñgo o narai-hajimeta no wa Nihoñ de beñkyoo shitakatta* kara desu. (日本語を習い始めたのは日本で勉強したかったからです) It is *because* I wanted to study in Japan that I started studying Japanese. / *Kyoo wa doko mo hito ga ooi no wa yasumi de teñki ga ii* kara desu. (きょうはどこも人が多いのは休みで天気がいいからです) The reason why there are lots of people everywhere today is *that* it is a holiday and the weather is fine.

ka˥**raa**[1] カラー *n.* color: karaa-*fuirumu* (カラーフイルム) a *color* film / karaa-*shashiñ* (カラー写真) a *color* photo / karaa-*shatsu* (カラーシャツ) a *colored* shirt / karaa-*terebi* (カラーテレビ) a *color* television.

ka˥**raa**[2] カラー *n.* collar.

ka˥**rada** からだ (体) *n.* **1** body; physique; build; constitution: karada *o kitaeru* (体を鍛える) build up one's *physique* / *Kare wa ii* karada *o shite iru.* (彼はいい体をしている) He has a well-built *body*. / *Rizumu o* karada *de oboeta.* (リズムを体で覚えた) By moving my *body* to the rhythm, I learned it.

2 health:

Karada *no guai ga yoi* [*warui*]. (体の具合が良い[悪い]) I am in good [poor] *health*. / *Kare wa karoo de* karada *o kowashita.* (彼は過労で体をこわした) He injured his *health* by overwork.

karada o haru (~を張る) risk one's neck: *Kare-ra wa* karada *o hatte teeboo o mamotta.* (彼らは体を張って堤防を守った) They protected the embankment *at the risk of their lives*.

ka˥**radatsuki** からだつき (体つき) *n.* one's figure; build: *Kanojo wa hossori shita* karadatsuki *o shite iru.* (彼女はほっそりした体つきをしている) She has a slender *build*.

ka˥**ra**˥**·i** からい (辛い) *a.* (-ku) **1** salty; hot; peppery; spicy: karai *misoshiru* (辛いみそ汁) *salty* miso-soup / *Kono karee wa* karakute *taberarenai.* (このカレーは辛くて食べられない) This curry is so *spicy* that I cannot eat it. 《⇨ aji[1] (table)》

2 severe; strict: *Ano señsee wa saiteñ ga* karai. (あの先生は採点が辛い) That teacher is *strict* in grading. 《↔ amai》

ka⌐rai⌐bari からいばり（空ら威張り）
n. bravado; bluff:
Kare no wa karaibari *da.*（彼のはか
ら威張りだ）His behavior is an *act
of bravado.*
karaibari suru（〜する）*vi.* blus-
ter; bluff: *Kimi ga* karaibari
shite *mo, kowai no wa wakatte
iru yo.*（きみがから威張りしても、恐いの
はわかっているよ）Even if you *try to
bluff,* I know you are afraid.
《⇨ ibaru》

ka⌐rakara からから *a.n.*（〜 na/no,
ni）dry; thirsty:
*Karakara no teñki ga nañ-nichi
mo tsuzuita.*（からからの天気が何日も
続いた）The *dry* weather continued for many days. / *Watashi wa
nodo ga* karakara *da.*（私はのどがから
からだ）My throat is *parched.* /
Ame ga furanai no de ike ga karakara *ni natte shimatta.*（雨が降らな
いので池がからからになってしまった）It
has not rained, so the pond has
dried up.

ka⌐raka⌐·u からかう *vt.*（karaka-
i-; karakaw·a-; karakat-te C）
tease; play a trick; make fun of:
Kare wa watashi o karakatta.*（彼
は私をからかった）He *teased* me.

ka⌐raoke カラオケ *n.* karaoke;
recorded musical backing for
vocal accompaniment:
karaoke *de utau*（カラオケで歌う）
sing into a microphone to a *taped
music accompaniment.*

KARAOKE

ka⌐rappo からっぽ *a.n.*（〜 na/
no, ni）empty:

Kono uisukii no biñ wa karappo
da.（このウイスキーのびんはからっぱだ）
This whisky bottle is *empty.* /
Sono hako no naka wa karappo
datta.（その箱の中はからっぱだった）
The interior of the box was
empty. 《⇨ kara¹》

ka⌐rashi からし（芥子）*n.* mustard.

ka⌐rasu¹ からす（烏）*n.* crow;
raven.

ka⌐ras·u² からす（枯らす）*vt.*（kara-
sh·i-; karas·a-; karash·i-te C）
wither; kill (a plant):
Matsu no boñsai o karashite *shimatta.*（松の盆栽を枯らしてしまった）I
let my pine bonsai *wither.* 《⇨ ka-
reru》

ka⌐rasumu⌐gi からすむぎ（烏麦）*n.*
oats. 《⇨ mugi (table)》

ka⌐rate¹ からて（空手）*n.* state of
being empty-handed:
*Kanojo wa kaimono ni itta hazu
na no ni* karate *de kaette kita.*（彼
女は買い物に行ったはずなのに空手で帰っ
て来た）I thought she went shopping, but she came back *empty-
handed.*

ka⌐rate² からて（空手）*n.* karate:
karate-*choppu*（空手チョップ）a *karate* chop / *Supootsu wa* karate *o
shite imasu.*（スポーツは空手をしていま
す）For sports, I do *karate.*

KARATE

ka⌐re かれ（彼）*n.* **1** he: ★ 'kare
no'＝his, 'kare o'＝him.
Kare *wa shutchoo-chuu desu.*（彼は
出張中です）*He* is on a business
trip. / *Tsugi wa* kare no *bañ da.*

(次は彼の番だ) Next it's *his* turn. / *Kanojo wa ima de mo kare o nikuñde iru.* (彼女は今でも彼を憎んでいる) She still hates *him.* / *Kare ni wa ashita deñwa shimasu.* (彼にはあした電話します) I'll call *him* tomorrow.

2 boyfriend:
Kanojo no kare wa supootsukaa o motte iru. (彼女の彼はスポーツカーを持っている) Her *boyfriend* has a sports car. ((↔ kanojo))

ka⌐ree カレー *n.* curry:
karee-*ko* (カレー粉) *curry* powder / karee-*raisu* (カレーライス) *curry* and rice.

ka⌐re⌐ñdaa カレンダー *n.* calendar:
kareñdaa *o mekuru* (カレンダーをめくる) turn over a *calendar.*

ka⌐re-ra かれら (彼ら) *n.* they:
★ 'kare-ra no'＝their, 'kare-ra o' ＝them.
Kare-ra *wa sekiniñkañ ga nai.* (彼らは責任感がない) *They* have no sense of responsibility. / Kare-ra *no keekaku wa shippai shita.* (彼らの計画は失敗した) *Their* plan failed. / *Kare-ra o settoku shiyoo to shite mo muda da.* (彼らを説得しようとしてもむだだ) It is no use trying to persuade *them.* / *Subete wa* kare-ra *ni makaseta.* (すべては彼らにまかせた) I left everything up to *them.*

ka⌐re·ru かれる (枯れる) *vi.* (karete Ⓥ) (of a plant) die; wither:
Kono ki wa karete *shimatta.* (この木は枯れてしまった) This tree *has* withered. ((⇨ karasu²))

ka⌐ri かり (借り) *n.* debt:
Kare ni wa ooki-na kari *ga aru.* (彼には大きな借りがある) I am greatly in *debt* to him. ((↔ kashi²)) ((⇨ kariru))

ka⌐ri ni かりに (仮に) *adv.* **1** if; even if; supposing:
Kari ni *anata ga watashi datta to shitara, nañ to iiwake o shimasu*

ka? (かりにあなたが私だったとしたら, 何と言い訳をしますか) *Supposing* you were me, what excuse would you make? / Kari ni *anata ga chuukoku shita to shite mo kare wa iu koto o kikanai deshoo.* (かりにあなたが忠告したとしても彼は言うことを聞かないでしょう) *Even if* you were to warn him, he would not pay attention to what you say.

2 for the time being; temporarily:
Kono heya wa kari ni *kyooshitsu ni shiyoo shite imasu.* (この部屋はかりに教室に使用しています) We are using this room as a classroom *for the time being.* / *Kono añ o* kari ni *A-añ to shite okimashoo.* (この案をかりにA案としておきましょう) Let us *provisionally* call this plan Plan A.

ka⌐ri·ru かりる (借りる) *vt.* (kari-te Ⓥ) **1** borrow; rent; lease:
Kare kara señ-eñ karita. (彼から千円借りた) I *borrowed* 1,000 yen from him. ((⇨ kari)) / *Kyooto de wa reñtakaa o* karimashita. (京都ではレンタカーを借りました) I *rented* a car in Kyoto. / *Kare wa* karite iru *tochi ni ie o tateta.* (彼は借りている土地に家を建てた) He built his house on *leased* land. ((↔ kasu))

kariru			
borrow	rent	use	lease

2 use (equipment, facilities, etc.):
Deñwa o o-kari *dekimasu ka?* (電話をお借りできますか) Can I *use* your phone? / *Toire o* o-kari *shite ii desu ka?* (トイレをお借りしていいですか) May I *use* the toilet? ((↔ kasu))
3 receive; need:
hito no chikara o kariru (人の力を借りる) *receive* someone's help / *chie o* kariru (知恵を借りる) *ask for* advice / *Anata no o-te o* o-kari *shitai ñ desu ga.* (あなたのお手をお借りしたい

んですが) I *need* your assistance.

ka「roñji·ru かろんじる（軽んじる）*vt.*
(karoñji-te [V]) neglect; make little [light] of:
*Mainichi no reñshuu o karoñjite
wa ikemaseñ.* (毎日の練習を軽んじて
はいけません) You should not *take*
your daily practice *lightly.*
(↔ omoñjiru)

ka「roo かろう（過労）*n.* overwork;
strain:
*Kare wa karoo kara byooki ni
natta.* (彼は過労から病気になった) He
fell ill from *overwork.*

ka「ro」ojite かろうじて（辛うじて）
adv. barely; narrowly:
*Kare wa karoojite shikeñ ni
ukatta.* (彼はかろうじて試験に受かった)
He *barely* passed the examination. / *Sono torakku wa semai
michi o karoojite tootta.* (そのトラッ
クは狭い道をかろうじて通った) That
truck passed along the narrow
road *with difficulty.*

ka「rooshi[1] かろうし（過労死）*n.*
death from overwork:
*Otto wa karooshi datta to fujiñ wa
uttaeta.* (夫は過労死だったと夫人は訴
えた) The wife claimed that her
husband *had died from overwork.*
(⇨ karoo)

ka「r·u かる（刈る）*vt.* (kar·i-; ka-
r·a-; kat-te [C]) cut; reap; crop;
mow:
shibafu o karu (芝生を刈る) *mow* a
lawn / *Kami o mijikame ni katte
kudasai.* (髪を短めに刈ってください)
Please *cut* my hair a bit short.

ka「ru·i かるい（軽い）*a.* (-ku) 1 (of
weight) light:
karui nimotsu (軽い荷物) *light* baggage / *Yasete, karada ga karuku
natta.* (やせて、体が軽くなった) I have
lost weight, and I am now *lighter*
than I used to be. (↔ omoi[1])
2 easy:
Koñna shigoto wa karui. (こんな仕
事は軽い) This sort of job is *easy.* /

*Watashi wa karui kimochi de
demo ni sañka shita.* (私は軽い気持
ちでデモに参加した) I *casually* partici-
pated in the demonstration. /
Jitai o karuku mite wa ikenai. (事
態を軽く見てはいけない) We must not
regard the situation *lightly.*
3 (of crime, disease, etc.) slight;
minor:
Karui kaze o hiita. (軽いかぜをひいた)
I have caught a *slight* cold. /
Soñna no wa karui tsumi da. (そんな
のは軽い罪だ) That's a *minor* crime.
(↔ omoi[1])
4 relieved; relaxed:
Ima wa kibuñ mo karui. (今は気分
も軽い) I feel *relieved* now. / *Kore
de watashi no sekiniñ mo karuku
naru.* (これで私の責任も軽くなる)
Because of this my responsibility
will become *less.* (↔ omoi[1])

ka「ruta カルタ *n.* cards; card
game:
iroha-garuta (いろはガルタ) 'iroha'
cards; the 'iroha' *card game.*

CULTURE

Each card of one set contains
one letter from the Japanese
syllabary with a picture of
something that begins with
that letter. Each card of the
other set contains a proverb
headed by the word contained
on the other corresponding set.

Shoogatsu ni wa karuta o shimasu.
(正月にはカルタをします) We play
cards during New Year. (⇨ hyakuniñ isshu)

KARUTA

ka⸢ryoku かりょく（火力）*n.* heat;
heating power:
Kono reñji wa karyoku *ga tsuyoi
[yowai].*（このレンジは火力が強い[弱
い]）This range has a strong
[weak] *flame.* / karyoku-*hatsu-
deñsho*（火力発電所）a *thermal*
power plant. 《↔ suiryoku》

ka⸢ryuu かりゅう（下流）*n.* lower
course [reaches] of a river:
*Sono koojoo wa kono kawa no ka-
ryuu ni arimasu.*（その工場はこの川の
下流にあります）That factory is on
the lower reaches of this river. /
Kare no booto wa ni-kiro karyuu
de hakkeñ sareta.（彼のボートは2キロ
下流で発見された）His boat was
found two kilometers *down-
stream.* 《↔ jooryuu》

ka⸢sa かさ（傘）*n.* umbrella; para-
sol:
kasa *o sasu [hirogeru]*（傘をさす[広
げる]）put up [open] an *umbrella* /
kasa *o tatamu [subomeru]*（傘をたた
む[すぼめる]）fold [close] an *umbrella.* 《⇨ amagasa》

ka⸢sai かさい（火災）*n.* fire:
★ More formal than '*kaji.*'
Shiñriñ ni kasai ga hassee shita.
（森林に火災が発生した）A *fire* broke
out in the forest. / kasai-*hokeñ*
（火災保険）*fire* insurance / kasai-
hoochiki（火災報知機）a *fire* alarm.

KASAI-HOOCHIKI

ka⸢sakasa[1] カサカサ *adv.* (~ to)
(rustling sound): ★ The sound

of a thin, light object moving.
Ochiba ga kaze ni fukarete kasakasa *(to) oto o tatete ita.*（落ち葉が
風に吹かれてカサカサ(と)音をたてていた）
The fallen leaves, blown by the
wind, were making a *rustling*
sound.

ka⸢sakasa[2] かさかさ *a.n.* (~ no,
ni) (the state of being dry):
Fuyu ni naru to te ga kasakasa *ni
naru [kasakasa shite kuru].*（冬にな
ると手がかさかさになる[かさかさしてくる]）
Whenever winter comes, my
hands get *dry.*

ka⸢sanar·u かさなる（重なる）*vi.*
(kasanar·i-; kasanar·a-; kasa-
nat-te Ⓒ) **1** happen at the same
time; occur one after another:
Kinoo wa kootsuu-jiko ga kasa-
natta.*（きのうは交通事故が重なった）
Yesterday traffic accidents *occurred one after another.* / *Kyuujitsu ga nichiyoo to* kasanaru *no
de koñdo no getsuyoo wa yasumi
desu.*（休日が日曜と重なるので今度の
月曜は休みです）Since the public
holiday *falls* on Sunday, this
Monday will be a holiday.
2 pile up:
Tsukue no ue ni shorui ga kasa-
natte iru.*（机の上に書類が重なってい
る）There *are* papers *piled up* on
the desk. 《⇨ kasaneru》

ka⸢sane·ru かさねる（重ねる）*vt.*
(kasane-te Ⓥ) **1** pile up; put on
top:
Kare wa tsukue no ue ni hoñ o
kasaneta.*（彼は机の上に本を重ねた）
He *piled* the books *up* on the
desk. / *Kanojo wa shitagi o ni-mai
kasanete kita.*（彼女は下着を2枚重
ねて着た）She wore two sets of
underwear, *one over the other.*
《⇨ kasanaru》
2 repeat:
jikkeñ o kasaneru（実験を重ねる）
carry out an experiment *repeatedly* / *Kare no* kasaneta *kuroo ga*

mi o musuñda.(彼の重ねた苦労が実を結んだ) His *repeated* toil produced favorable results.

ka⌐se⌐gi かせぎ(稼ぎ) *n.* income; earnings:
Kare wa kasegi *ga ii.*(彼は稼ぎがいい) He *earns* a good income. / *Kasegi ga warui kara mada kekkoñ dekimaseñ.*(稼ぎが悪いからまだ結婚できません) My *earnings* are not enough for me to get married yet. ((⇨ kasegu; shuunyuu))

ka⌐se⌐gu かせぐ(稼ぐ) *vt.* (kaseg·i-; kaseg·a-; kase·i-de C)
earn; make money; work:
Kare wa ikka no seekatsu-hi o kaseganeba naranai.(彼は一家の生活費を稼がねばならない) He has to *earn* the living expenses for his family. / *Arubaito o shite, sañ-mañ-eñ kaseida.*(アルバイトをして、3万円稼いだ) I worked part-time and *earned* 30,000 yen. ((⇨ kasegi))

ka⌐seki かせき(化石) *n.* fossil.

ka⌐se⌐tto カセット *n.* cassette:
kasetto *o kakeru*(カセットをかける) play a *cassette* / kasetto-*teepu*(カセットテープ) a *cassette* tape / kasetto-*rekoodaa*(カセットレコーダー) a *cassette* recorder.

ka⌐shi[1] かし(菓子) *n.* confectionery; cake; candy; sweets. ★ Often 'o-kashi.' Cookies, crackers and pastries are also called '(o-)kashi.' ((⇨ keeki[1]))

ka⌐shi[2] かし(貸し) *n.* loan: ★ Used both literally and figuratively.
Kare ni wa takusañ kashi *ga aru.*(彼にはたくさん貸しがある) He *owes me* a lot. ((↔ kari)) ((⇨ kasu (table)))

ka⌐shidashi かしだし(貸し出し) *n.* loan; lending service:
Sono hoñ wa kashidashi-*chuu desu.*(その本は貸し出し中です) That book is out on *loan*. ((⇨ kashidasu))

ka⌐shida⌐s·u かしだす(貸し出す) *vt.* (-dash·i-; -das·a-; -dash·i-te C) lend [loan] out; rent:
kane o kashidasu(金を貸し出す) *lend* money / *Kono toshokañ wa kasetto teepu o* kashidashimasu.(この図書館はカセットテープを貸し出します) This library *lends out* cassette tapes. ((⇨ kashidashi))

ka⌐shiko かしこ *n.* Yours sincerely. ★ Used at the end of a woman's letter. ((⇨ keegu; tegami))

ka⌐shiko⌐·i かしこい(賢い) *a.* (-ku) wise; clever; smart:
kashikoi *ko*(賢い子) a *bright* child / *Kare no ketsudañ wa* kashiko-katta.(彼の決断は賢かった) His decision was *wise*. / *Shoohisha wa motto* kashikoku *naru hitsuyoo ga aru.*(消費者はもっと賢くなる必要がある) Consumers need to become *better informed*. ((⇨ rikoo))

ka⌐shikomarima⌐shita かしこまりました(畏まりました) certainly: ★ Indicates that the speaker will carry out an order or request given by a superior. Often used by service personnel to customers.
"Kono hañkachi o kudasai." "Ka-shikomarimashita."(「このハンカチをください」「かしこまりました」) "Please let me have this handkerchief." "*Certainly.*"

ka⌐shima かしま(貸間) *n.* = kashishitsu.

ka shira かしら *p.* (*informal*)
1 I wonder: ★ Used, often rhetorically, to indicate a question or express doubt. Used mainly by women. Men use '*ka na.*' ((⇨ na[3]))
Ano hito wa ima-goro nani o shite iru ka shira.(あの人は今ごろ何をしているかしら) *I wonder* what he is doing at the moment. / *Kono shigoto wa watashi hitori de dekiru*

ka shira. (この仕事は私一人でできるか
しら) *Would* I be able to do this
job by myself? ★ Sometimes
used with other particles. *e.g.*
Ashita wa ame ga furu ka shira *ne*.
(あしたは雨がふるかしらね) *I wonder* if
it will rain tomorrow. ((⇨ ne³))
2 (used to pose a question):
Anata wa kore o-suki ka shira. (あ
なたはこれお好きかしら) *I wonder* if
you like this. / *Anata wa ashita o-
taku ni* irassharu ka shira. (あなたは
あしたお宅にいらっしゃるかしら) *Are*
you *going to be* home tomorrow?
-nai ka shira (ない〜) I hope; I
would like: *Hayaku yasumi ni
naranai ka shira*. (早く休みにならない
かしら) *I hope* the vacation begins
soon. / *Shiken ga hayaku
owaranai ka shira*. (試験が早く終わ
らないかしら) *I'd like* the test to be
over soon.

ka⌐shishitsu かししつ (貸し室) *n.*
room for rent; room to let:
Kashishitsu (*sign*) (貸室) *Rooms
for Rent*.

KASHISHITSU SIGN

ka⌐shiya¹ かしや (貸家) *n.* house
for rent; house to let:
kashiya o sagasu (貸家を探す) look
for a *house for rent* / *Kashiya arimasu*. (*sign*) (貸家あります) *House
for Rent*.

ka⌐shi⌐ya² かしや (菓子屋) *n.*
confectioner; confectionery.

ka⌐sho かしょ (箇所) *n.* place;
spot; point:
Kono shirushi wa kiken na kasho

o shimeshimasu. (この印は危険なか
所を示します) These marks show
the dangerous *places*. / *Koko ga
jiko no atta* kasho *desu*. (ここが事故
のあったか所です) This is the *spot*
where the accident occurred.
((⇨ basho))

-ka⌐sho かしょ (箇所) *suf.* part;
place; passage:
Shiken de ni-kasho machigaeta.
(試験で 2 か所間違えた) I made *two*
mistakes in the examination. /
Kare wa sono hon kara suu-kasho
inyoo shita. (彼はその本から数か所引
用した) He quoted *several passages*
from the book.

ka⌐shu かしゅ (歌手) *n.* singer;
vocalist.

ka⌐soo かそう (下層) *n.* **1** lower
layer [stratum]:
*Kasoo kara kaseki ga hakken
sareta*. (下層から化石が発見された) A
fossil was discovered in the *lower
stratum*.
2 the lower class:
kasoo-kaikyuu no hito-tachi (下層
階級の人たち) people of the *lower
class*. ((⇨ chuuryuu; jooryuu))

ka⌐s·u かす (貸す) *vt.* (kash·i-; ka-
s·a-; kash·i-te [C]) **1** lend; loan;
rent; lease:
*Kare wa watashi ni ichiman-en
kashite kureta*. (彼は私に 1 万円貸し
てくれた) He *lent* me 10,000 yen. /
*Sono rentakaa no kaisha wa fu-
tsuusha dake o* kashimasu. (そのレ
ンタカーの会社は普通車だけを貸します)
That car-rental company only
rents standard size cars. / *Watashi wa sono tochi o kare ni* kashite imasu. (私はその土地を彼に貸し
ています) I *have leased* the land to
him. ((↔ kariru))((⇨ kashi²))

kasu		
lend, loan	rent (out)	lease

2 let use (equipment, facilities,

etc.):
Deñwa o kashite *itadakemasu ka?*
(電話を貸していただけますか) Would
you please *let me use* your telephone? 《↔ kariru》
3 give:
hito ni chikara o kasu (人に力を貸
す) *give* a person assistance / *hito
ni chie o* kasu (人に知恵を貸す) *give*
a person advice / *hito ni mimi o*
kasu (人に耳を貸す) *give* ear to a
person / *Chotto te o* kashite *moraemasu ka?* (ちょっと手を貸してもらえ
ますか) Can you *give* me a helping
hand? 《↔ kariru》

ka¹suka かすか (微か) *a.n.* (~ na,
ni) faint; vague; dim:
kasuka *na nozomi* (かすかな望み) a
faint hope / kasuka *na kioku* (かす
かな記憶) a *vague* recollection /
Tooku ni akari ga kasuka *ni mieta.*
(遠くに明りがかすかに見えた) I could
see a light shining *dimly* in the
distance. / *Niwa de* kasuka *na
mono-oto ga shita.* (庭でかすかな物音
がした) I heard a *faint* sound in
the garden.

ka⌈sumi かすみ (霞) *n.* haze;
mist:
Yama ni wa kasumi *ga kakatte ita.*
(山にはかすみがかかっていた) There was
a *haze* hanging over the mountains.

ka⌈sum·u かすむ (霞む) *vi.* (kasu-
m·i-; kasum·a-; kasuñ-de Ⓒ)
1 (of a view, sky, etc.) be hazy:
Yama ga tooku ni kasuñde iru. (山
が遠くにかすんでいる) The mountains
are hazy in the distance.
2 (of vision) be blurred:
Me ga namida de kasuñde shimatta. (目が涙でかすんでしまった) My
vision *was blurred* with tears.

ka⌈ta¹ かた (肩) *n.* shoulder:
kata *o sukumeru* (肩をすくめる)
shrug one's *shoulders* / Kata *ga
kotte iru.* (肩がこっている) My *shoulders* are stiff. / *Dare-ka ga wata-*

shi no kata *o tataita.* (だれかが私の肩
をたたいた) Someone patted me on
the *shoulder.* / *Kare wa kamera o*
kata *ni sagete ita.* (彼はカメラを肩に
下げていた) He was carrying a
camera slung over his *shoulder.* /
Futari wa kata *o narabete aruita.*
(二人は肩を並べて歩いた) The two of
them walked *side by side.*
《⇨ jiñtai (illus.)》

kata no koranai (~のこらない)
light; easy; informal: Kata no
koranai *hoñ wa arimaseñ ka?* (肩
のこらない本はありませんか) Aren't
there any books for *light reading?*

kata no ni ga oriru (~の荷がおり
る) a load off one's mind: *Yatto*
kata no ni ga orita. (やっと肩の荷が
おりた) At last I felt *a load slip off
my shoulders.*

kata o motsu (~をもつ) take
sides: *Kanojo wa itsu-mo kare no*
kata o motsu. (彼女はいつも彼の肩を
もつ) She always *takes sides* with
him.

kata o otosu (~を落とす) **1** drop
one's shoulders.
2 be disappointed.

ka⌈ta¹² かた (型) *n.* **1** pattern:
Kanojo wa kami de doresu no
kata *o totta.* (彼女は紙でドレスの型を
とった) She made a *pattern* of a
dress out of paper.
2 type; style; model:
Kare wa furui kata *no niñgeñ da.*
(彼は古い型の人間だ) He is a man of
the old *style.* / *Kore ga kotoshi no
ichibañ atarashii* kata *no kuruma
desu.* (これが今年の一番新しい型の車
です) This car is this year's latest
model.
3 mold:
zerii o kata *ni nagashikomu* (ゼリー
を型に流し込む) pour jelly into a
mold.

kata ni hamatta (~にはまった)
stereotyped; conventional: *Wa-*

tashi wa kata *ni hamatta koto wa kirai desu.*(私は型にはまったことは嫌いです) I don't like *stereotyped* things.

ka「ta[13] かた (方) *n.* (*polite*) person; lady; gentleman: *Ano* kata *wa donata desu ka?* (あの方はどなたですか) Who is that *gentleman* [*lady*]? / *Kono* kata *ga Suzuki-sañ desu.* (この方が鈴木さんです) This *lady* is Miss Suzuki. (⇨ hito)

-kata[1] かた (方) *suf.* care of: *Itoo-sama*-kata *Suzuki sama* (伊藤様方鈴木様) Mr. Suzuki *c/o* Mr. Ito.

-kata[2] かた (方) *suf.* way; manner: ★ Added to the continuative base of a verb. *kuruma no uñteñ no shi*-kata (車の運転の仕方) *how to* drive a car / *Kanojo no kuchi no kiki*-kata *ga ki ni iranai.*(彼女の口の利き方が気に入らない) I do not like her *way of* talking. / *Kono kudamono no tabe*-kata *ga wakarimaseñ.* (この果物の食べ方がわかりません) I don't know *how to* eat this fruit. / *Umai yari*-kata *o omoitsuita.* (うまいやり方を思いついた) I hit upon an excellent *method.*

ka「tachi かたち (形) *n.* **1** shape: *Kore to onaji* katachi *no hako wa arimasu ka?* (これと同じ形の箱はありますか) Do you have a box which has the same *shape* as this? / *Kono kabiñ wa kawatta* katachi *o shite iru.* (この花瓶は変わった形をしている) This vase has a strange *shape.*
2 form: Katachi *yori naiyoo ga taisetsu desu.* (形より内容が大切です) Content is more important than *form.* / *Doñna* katachi *no mono de mo, uñdoo wa kirai desu.* (どんな形のものでも, 運動はきらいです) I don't like exercise in any *shape* or *form.* /

Shiki to itte mo, katachi *dake no mono datta.* (式と言っても, 形だけのものだった) Although it was a ceremony, it was only a matter of *form.*

ka「tachizuku「r・u かたちづくる (形作る) *vt.* (-zukur・i-; -zukur・a-; -zukut-te [C]) make; form; shape: *Jiñkaku wa yooji no toki* katachi-zukurareru *to iwareru.* (人格は幼児のとき形作られると言われる) It is said that one's personality *is formed* in infancy.

ka「tagaki かたがき (肩書) *n.* title; degree: *Nihoñ de wa* katagaki *ga mono o iu.* (日本では肩書がものをいう) In Japan *titles* have weight. / *Kare wa hakase no* katagaki *o motte iru.* (彼は博士の肩書を持っている) He has a doctor's *degree.*

ka「ta「gata かたがた (方々) *n.* (*polite*) the people (concerned): *go-shusseki no* katagata (ご出席の方々) *those* present / *Kore made iroiro na* katagata *no o-sewa ni narimashita.* (これまでいろいろな方々のお世話になりました) So far I have received assitance and kindness from many *people.*

-ka「ta「gata かたがた *suf.* = -gatera.

ka「tagawa かたがわ (片側) *n.* one side: *Kooji no tame kuruma wa michi no* katagawa *shika toorenakatta.* (工事のため車は道の片側しか通れなかった) Vehicles could pass on only *one side* of the road because of construction work. (⇨ ryoogawa)

ka「tagu「ruma かたぐるま (肩車) *n.* riding on someone's shoulders. **kataguruma suru** (〜する) *vt.* give someone a piggyback: *Watashi wa sono ko o* kataguruma *shite yatta.* (私はその子を肩車してやった)

I *carried* the child *on my shoulders.*

KATAGURUMA

ka⌈tahashi かたはし (片端) *n.* one end; one side:
Kono tsuna no katahashi *o hippatte kudasai.* (この綱の片端を引っ張ってください) Please pull *one end* of this rope. 《↔ ryoohashi》

ka⌈ta⌉hoo かたほう (片方) *n.* one side; one of a pair; the other:
Tebukuro no katahoo *o nakushite shimatta.* (手袋の片方をなくしてしまった) I have lost *one of* my gloves. / *Ni-mai no shatsu no uchi,* katahoo *wa ii ga, moo* katahoo *wa ki ni iranai.* (二枚のシャツのうち, 片方はいいが, もう片方は気に入らない) Of these two shirts, *one of* them is fine, but I do not like *the other.* / *Me wa* katahoo-zutsu *keñsa shimasu.* (目は片方ずつ検査します) I am going to check your right and left eyes *separately.* 《↔ ryoohoo》

ka⌈ta·i かたい (堅い・固い・硬い) *a.* (-ku) **1** hard; solid; stiff; firm; tough:
katai *jimeñ* (固い地面) *hard* ground / katai *koori* (堅い氷) *solid* ice / katai *burashi* (堅いブラシ) a *stiff* brush / katai *mattoresu* (堅いマットレス) a *firm* mattress / *Kono niku wa* katai. (この肉は堅い) This meat is *tough.* / *Daiyamoñdo wa* katai. (ダイヤモンドは硬い) Diamonds

are *hard.* 《↔ yawaraka; yawarakai》
2 stiff:
katai *hyoojoo* (硬い表情) *a stiff* expression / *Kare wa* katai *buñshoo o kaku.* (彼は硬い文章を書く) He writes in a *stiff* style.
3 firm; tight:
katai *ketsui* (固い決意) a *firm* determination / *Kono musubime wa* katakute, *hodokenai.* (この結び目は固くて, ほどけない) This knot is so *tight* I cannot undo it.
4 sure:
Ano señshu no nyuushoo wa katai. (あの選手の入賞は堅い) That player's winning the prize is a *sure* thing.
5 steady; sound; serious:
Motto katai *shigoto ni tsuki nasai.* (もっと堅い仕事につきなさい) You should get a *steadier* job. / *Katai hanashi wa kore-gurai ni shimashoo.* (堅い話はこれぐらいにしましょう) Let's talk no more of *serious* matters.
6 obstinate; stubborn:
Uchi no kachoo wa atama ga katai. (うちの課長は頭が固い) Our section chief is *obstinate* in his way of thinking.

ka⌈taka⌉na かたかな (片仮名) *n.* one of the Japanese syllabaries:
Gairaigo wa katakana *de kakimasu.* (外来語はカタカナで書きます) Words borrowed from foreign languages are written in *katakana.* 《⇨ inside front cover》

ka⌈taki⌉ かたき (敵) *n.* **1** enemy; foe:
Ano futari wa naka ga yokatta ga, ima wa kataki-*dooshi da.* (あの二人は仲がよかったが, 今は敵同士だ) The two of them used to be very good friends but now are *enemies.*
2 rival:
shoobai-gataki (商売がたき) a *rival* in business / *koi*-gataki (恋いがたき)

a *rival* in love. ★ The initial /k/ changes to /g/ in compounds.
kataki o utsu (〜を討つ) revenge oneself: *Kono* kataki wa utsu *zo.* (この敵は打つぞ) I'll *get my own back on* him for this.

ka⌈tamari かたまり(塊) *n.* lump; mass; clod; chunk:
koori no katamari (氷の塊) a *lump* of ice / *koñkuriito no* katamari (コンクリートの塊) a *mass* of concrete / *tsuchi no* katamari (土の塊) a *clod* of soil / *niku no* katamari (肉の塊) a *chunk* of meat.

ka⌈tamar·u かたまる(固まる) *vi.* (-mar·i-; -mar·a-; -mat·te Ⓒ) become hard; harden; set:
Kono semeñto wa mada katamatte *imaseñ.* (このセメントはまだ固まっていません) This cement *has* not *set* yet. 《⇨ katameru》

ka⌈tame·ru かためる(固める) *vt.* (-me·te Ⓥ) **1** harden:
Koñkuriito o hayaku katameru *tame ni wa yakuzai o tsukaimasu.* (コンクリートをはやく固めるためには薬剤を使います) We use chemicals to *harden* concrete quickly. 《⇨ katamaru》
2 strengthen; tighten; fortify: *chii* [*mamori*] *o* katameru (地位[守り]を固める) *strengthen* one's position [the defense] / *ketsui o* katameru (決意を固める) *make a firm* resolution. 《⇨ katamaru》

ka⌈tamichi かたみち(片道) *n.* one-way (ticket):
Atami made katamichi *ichi-mai kudasai.* (熱海まで片道1枚下さい) One *one-way ticket* to Atami, please. / *Katamichi yori oofuku-kippu o katta hoo ga toku desu.* (片道より往復切符を買ったほうが得です) It is to your advantage to buy a round-trip ticket instead of two *one-way tickets.* 《↔ oofuku》

ka⌈tamuke⌉·ru かたむける(傾ける) *vt.* (-muke·te Ⓥ) **1** incline;

lean; slant; tilt:
Kare wa karada o katamukete, *booru o yoketa.* (彼は体を傾けて、ボールをよけた) *Leaning to one side*, he dodged the ball. 《⇨ katamuku》
2 devote (one's energy):
Watashi wa sono shigoto ni zeñ-ryoku o katamuketa. (私はその仕事に全力を傾けた) I *devoted* all my energies to the job.

ka⌈tamuki⌉ かたむき(傾き) *n.*
1 slant; slope; tilt:
Kono yuka wa sukoshi katamuki *ga aru.* (この床は少し傾きがある) This floor has a slight *tilt*. 《⇨ katamuku》
2 tendency; trend:
Kare wa monogoto o karuku miru katamuki *ga aru.* (彼は物事を軽く見る傾きがある) He has a *tendency* to take things lightly.

ka⌈tamu⌉k·u かたむく(傾く) *vi.* (-muk·i-; -muk·a-; -mu·i·te Ⓒ)
1 lean; slope; slant; tilt:
Kono uchi wa sukoshi katamuite *iru.* (この家は少し傾いている) This house *leans* slightly to one side. / *Migi e kyuu-kaabu o kitta toki, basu wa ookiku* katamuita. (右へ急カーブを切ったとき、バスは大きく傾いた) The bus *leaned over* as it made a sharp turn to the right. 《⇨ katamukeru; katamuki; keesha》
2 be inclined; lean:
Kare wa tasuu-ha ni katamuite iru. (彼は多数派に傾いている) He *is inclining* toward the majority faction.
3 (of the sun or the moon) go down; sink; set:
Hi wa nishi ni katamuite ita. (日は西に傾いていた) The sun *was setting* in the west.

ka⌈tana⌉ かたな(刀) *n.* sword: katana *o nuku* (刀を抜く) draw a *sword* / katana *o saya ni osameru* (刀をさやにおさめる) sheathe a *sword* / katana *o sasu* (刀を差す) carry a *sword.*

ka⌐tar·u かたる（語る）*vt.* (katar·i-; katar·a-; katat-te Ⓒ) (*slightly formal*) talk; tell; relate:
Kare wa Nihoñ no gakusee-see-katsu ni tsuite katatta.（彼は日本の学生生活について語った）He *talked* about student life in Japan. / *Kanojo wa shiñjitsu o* katatta.（彼女は真実を語った）She *spoke* the truth.
《⇨ hanasu; shaberu》

ka⌐tasa かたさ（堅さ・固さ・硬さ）*n.*
1 hardness; solidity; firmness; stiffness:
Kiñ to giñ de wa katasa *ga dono kurai chigaimasu ka?*（金と銀では硬さがどの位違いますか）What is the difference in *hardness* between gold and silver? 《⇨ katai》
2 stubbornness: *Kare no atama no* katasa *ni wa aiso ga tsukita.*（彼の頭の固さには愛想がつきた）I am totally disappointed with his *stubbornness.* 《⇨ katai》

ka⌐tate かたて（片手）*n.* one hand:
Kare wa katate *de sono suutsu-keesu o mochiageta.*（彼は片手でそのスーツケースを持ち上げた）He lifted the suitcase with *one hand.* / *Kanojo wa* katate *ni nani-ka motte ita.*（彼女は片手に何か持っていた）She had something in *one hand.*
《⇨ ryoote》

ka⌐tayo⌐r·u かたよる（偏る）*vi.* (-yor·i-; -yor·a-; -yot-te Ⓒ) be partial; be prejudiced; be slanted:
Kono shiñbuñ-kiji wa katayotte iru.（この新聞記事はかたよっている）This newspaper article *is slanted.*

ka⌐tazuke⌐·ru かたづける（片付ける）*vt.* (-zuke-te Ⓥ) 1 put in order; tidy up; put away:
Heya (no naka) o katazuke nasai.（部屋（の中）を片づけなさい）*Tidy up* the room. / *Kanojo wa kodomo-tachi ni shokki o* katazuke saseta.（彼女は子どもたちに食器を片づけさせた）She made the children *put away* the dishes.
2 settle (a dispute); solve (a problem); finish (a job):
Kare wa sono moñdai o umaku katazukeru *koto ga dekita.*（彼はその問題をうまく片づけることができた）He was able to skillfully *deal with* the problem. / *Shukudai o koñ-shuu-chuu ni* katazukenakereba naranai.（宿題を今週中に片づけなければならない）I *have to finish up* my homework within this week.

ka⌐tee¹ かてい（家庭）*n.* home; family:
Kare wa mazushii katee *ni so-datta.*（彼は貧しい家庭に育った）He grew up in a poor *home.* / *Terebi wa doko no* katee *ni mo aru.*（テレビはどこの家庭にもある）There is a TV in every *household.* / katee-ryoori（家庭料理）*home* cooking.
katee o motsu（～を持つ）start married life.

ka⌐tee² かてい（仮定）*n.* assumption; supposition; hypothesis:
Katee no moñdai ni wa o-kotae dekimaseñ.（仮定の問題にはお答えできません）I am not in a position to answer concerning *hypothetical* problems. / katee-kee（仮定形）*provisional* form (of a verb).
katee suru（～する）*vi., vt.* assume; suppose; postulate: *Kari ni kono hañdañ ga tadashii to* katee shimasu.（仮にこの判断が正しいと仮定します）*Let us assume* that this decision is correct. / *Hyaku-neñ mae no Tookyoo ni kono yoo na jookyoo o* katee shite mima-shoo.（百年前の東京にこのような状況を仮定してみましょう）*Let us imagine* this kind of situation in the Tokyo of one hundred years ago.

ka⌐tee³ かてい（過程）*n.* process; course:
*Seezoo-*katee *de nani-ka machigai*

ga atta rashii. (製造過程で何か間違いがあったらしい) Something seems to have gone wrong in the *course* of production. / *Kooshoo no* katee *o koohyoo suru koto wa dekimaseñ*. (交渉の過程を公表することはできません) We cannot disclose the *course* of the negotiations.

ka⌐tee-teki かていてき (家庭的) *a.n.* (~ na, ni) homely; homelike; domestic:
Kanojo wa totemo katee-teki *na josee da*. (彼女はとても家庭的な女性だ) She is a very *domestic* woman. / *Kono resutorañ wa* katee-teki *na fuñiki ga aru*. (このレストランは家庭的な雰囲気がある) This restaurant has a *homely* atmosphere.

ka⌐ts·u[1] かつ (勝つ) *vi.* (kach·i-; kat·a-; kat-te ⌐C⌐) **1** win; beat; defeat:
tatakai ni katsu (戦いに勝つ) *win* a battle / *Uchi no chiimu wa ni tai ichi de shiai ni* katta. (うちのチームは2対1で試合に勝った) Our team *won* the game by 2 to 1. 《↔ makeru》
2 overcome (temptation, difficulties, etc.):
Kare wa yuuwaku ni katsu *koto ga dekinakatta*. (彼は誘惑に勝つことができなかった) He *could not overcome* temptation. 《↔ makeru》

ka⌐tsu[2] かつ (且つ) *conj.* (*formal*) and; moreover; also:
hitsuyoo katsu *juubuñ na jookeñ* (必要かつ十分な条件) a necessary *and* sufficient condition / *Watashi-tachi wa ooi-ni nomi* katsu *utatta*. (私たちは大いに飲みかつ歌った) We drank freely *and* sang a lot.

ka⌐tsudoo かつどう (活動) *n.* activity; action; operation:
kurabu [*kagai*]-katsudoo (クラブ[課外]活動) club [extracurricular] *activities* / katsudoo-ka (活動家) a man of *action*; an *active* person.
katsudoo suru (~する) *vi.* be

active; work: *Kono yama wa mata itsu* katsudoo shi-dasu *ka wakarimaseñ*. (この山はまたいつ活動しだすかわかりません) Nobody knows when this volcano will *become active* again. / *Kare-ra wa chika ni mogutte,* katsudoo shita. (彼らは地下に潜って、活動した) They went underground and *carried out* their *activities*.

ka⌐tsudoo-teki かつどうてき (活動的) *a.n.* (~ na, ni) active; energetic.

ka⌐tsu⌐g·u かつぐ (担ぐ) *vt.* (katsug·i-; katsug·a-; katsu·i-de ⌐C⌐)
1 carry (a burden) on one's shoulder:
Kare wa ooki-na nimotsu o katsuide *ita*. (彼は大きな荷物をかついでいた) He was *carrying* a large load on his shoulders.
2 play a trick on; make a fool of; take in:
Kare ni wa sukkari katsugareta. (彼にはすっかりかつがれた) I *was taken in* completely by him.

ka⌐tsuji かつじ (活字) *n.* printing type:
katsuji *o kumu* (活字を組む) set *type* / *Kono hoñ no* katsuji *wa chiisa-sugiru*. (この本の活字は小さすぎる) The *type* in this book is too small.

ka⌐tsute かつて (曽て) *adv.* (~ no) **1** once; at one time; formerly.
Katsute *kanojo wa niñki-kashu datta*. (かつて彼女は人気歌手だった) She was a popular singer *at one time*. / *Kare ni* katsute *no omokage wa nakatta*. (彼にかつての面影はなかった) He was not *what he used to be*.
2 ever; never:
Koñna keekeñ wa imada katsute *shita koto ga arimaseñ*. (こんな経験はいまだかつてしたことがありません) So far I have *never* had this kind of

experience.

ka「tsuyaku かつやく (活躍) *n.*
remarkable activity:
Kono buñya de mo Nihoñjiñ no katsuyaku *ga medatte kita.* (この分野でも日本人の活躍が目立ってきた) The *activities* of Japanese people have become conspicuous in this field, too. / *Señshu-tachi no* katsuyaku *o kitai shitai.* (選手たちの活躍を期待したい) We look forward to remarkable *achievements* on the part of the players.

katsuyaku suru (〜する) *vi.* take an active part; participate actively: *Kotoshi terebi de mottomo* katsuyaku shita *hito ga hyooshi ni notta.* (テレビで最も活躍した人が表紙に載った) The people most *active* in TV this year appeared on the cover.

ka「tsuyoo かつよう (活用) *n.*
1 practical use; utilization:
Yoka no katsuyoo *o kañgaeru beki desu.* (余暇の活用を考えるべきです) You must think of *ways to utilize* your leisure time.
2 (of grammar) inflection; conjugation:
katsuyoo-*kee* (活用形) a *conjugated* form.

katsuyoo suru (〜する) **1** *vt.* make use of; utilize; make the most of: *Ima aru mono o saidaigeñ ni* katsuyoo shi nasai. (今あるものを最大限に活用しなさい) You must *make the most of* what you now have.
2 *vi.* inflect; conjugate:
Kono dooshi wa dono yoo ni katsuyoo shimasu ka? (この動詞はどのように活用しますか) How does this verb *conjugate*?

ka「tte¹ かって (勝手) *n.* **1** kitchen: ★ Usually with '*o-.*'
Haha wa o-katte *de yuuhañ no juñbi o shite imasu.* (母はお勝手で夕飯の準備をしています) Mother is pre-

paring dinner in the *kitchen.* / katte-*guchi* (勝手口) *kitchen* entrance; backdoor. (⇨ daidokoro)
2 way; convenience:
Kono apaato wa katte ga warui. (このアパートは勝手が悪い) This apartment *is inconvenient.* / *Kono atari wa* katte ga wakarimaseñ. (この辺りは勝手がわかりません) I *am a stranger* here.

ka「tte² かって (勝手) *n.* selfishness; willfulness:
Soñna katte *wa yurusenai.* (そんな勝手は許せない) I won't stand for that sort of *selfish behavior.*
(⇨ wagamama)
— *a.n.* (〜 na, ni) selfish:
Ano hito wa zuibuñ katte *na hito da.* (あの人はずいぶん勝手な人だ) He is a very *selfish* man. / *Kare wa nañ de mo* katte *ni yaritagaru.* (彼は何でも勝手にやりたがる) He likes to do everything *in his own way.* / Katte *ni shi nasai.* (勝手にしなさい) Do *what the hell you want to.* / Katte *ni jiteñsha o tsukatte, sumimaseñ deshita.* (勝手に自転車を使って、すみませんでした) I am sorry for using your bicycle *without your permission.* / *Kono heya ni* katte *ni haitte wa komarimasu.* (この部屋に勝手に入っては困ります) I do not like it when you come into this room *without asking.*

ka「tto カット *n.* haircut; cut:
Katto *to paama o o-negai shimasu.* (カットとパーマをお願いします) I'd like a *cut* and a perm. (⇨ paama)

ka・「u¹ かう (買う) *vt.* (ka・i-; kaw・a-; kat-te Ⓒ) **1** buy; purchase; get:
Depaato de seetaa o katta. (デパートでセーターを買った) I *bought* a sweater at the department store. / *Kono kamera wa baageñ de yasuku* katta *mono desu.* (このカメラはバーゲンで安く買ったものです) This camera is something I *got* cheaply at a

sale. / *Kanojo wa tokee o ichimañ-eñ de* katta. (彼女は時計を1万円で買った) She *bought* a watch for 10,000 yen. / *Kodomo ni omocha o* katte yatta. (子どもにおもちゃを買ってやった) I *bought* the child a toy. / *Shiñkañseñ no kippu wa doko de* kau *ñ desu ka?* (新幹線の切符はどこで買うんですか) Where does one *buy* tickets for the Shinkansen? 《↔ uru¹》

2 incur; take up (an ill feeling, quarrel, etc.):
hito no urami o kau (人の恨みを買う) *incur* a person's ill will / *keñka o* kau (けんかを買う) *accept* a challenge to fight.

3 recognize; think much of (a person's ability):
Shachoo wa kare no nooryoku o takaku katte iru. (社長は彼の能力を高く買っている) The president *thinks highly of* his ability. / *Watashi wa kare o amari takaku* katte imaseñ. (私は彼をあまり高く買っていません) I don't *think much of* him.

ka⌐i·u² かう (飼う) *vt.* (ka·i-; ka·w·a-; kat·te C) keep; have; raise; rear:
Watashi wa neko o sañ-biki katte imasu. (私は猫を3匹飼っています) I *keep* three cats. / *Kono atari no nooka wa kachiku o* katte imasu. (このあたりの農家は家畜を飼っています) The farmers here *raise* livestock.

ka⌐wa¹¹ かわ (川) *n.* river; stream; brook:
kawa *o noboru* [*kudaru*] (川を上る[下る]) go up [down] a *river* / *Watashi-tachi wa kobune de* kawa *o watatta.* (私たちは小舟で川を渡った) We crossed the *river* in a boat. / *Tone*-gawa (利根川) the Tone *River.* ★ The initial /k/ of 'kawa' often changes to /g/ in proper names. 《⇨ -gawa》

ka⌐wa¹² かわ (皮) *n.* skin; hide; peel; rind; bark:
banana no kawa (バナナの皮) the *skin* of a banana / *meroñ no* kawa (メロンの皮) the *rind* of a melon / *remoñ no* kawa (レモンの皮) the *peel* of a lemon / *ki no* kawa (木の皮) the *bark* of a tree / *jagaimo no* kawa o *muku* (ジャガイモの皮をむく) *peel* potatoes / *shika no* kawa o *hagu* (鹿の皮をはぐ) *skin* a deer / kawa o *namesu* (皮をなめす) tan a *hide*.

ka⌐wa¹³ かわ (革) *n.* leather:
kawa *no tebukuro* (革の手袋) *leather* gloves / kawa *no kabañ* (革のかばん) a *leather* bag.

ka⌐wa⁴ かわ (側) *n.* = gawa.

ka⌐waiga⌐r·u かわいがる (可愛がる) *vt.* (-gar·i-; -gar·a-; -gat·te C) love; pet; caress:
Kanojo wa mago o totemo kawaigatte iru. (彼女は孫をとてもかわいがっている) She *is very attached* to her grandchild.

ka⌐wai¹·i かわいい (可愛い) *a.* (-ku)
1 cute; pretty; lovely:
kawaii *kodomo* (かわいい子ども) a *cute* child / kawaii *niñgyoo* (かわいい人形) a *lovely* doll / *Sono oñna-no-ko wa* kawaii *kao o shite ita.* (その女の子はかわいい顔をしていた) The girl looked very *pretty.* / *Kono riboñ o tsukeru to, motto* kawaiku *mieru yo.* (このリボンをつけると, もっとかわいく見えるよ) If you put this ribbon on, you will look *prettier.*
2 dear:
Seeto wa miñna kawaii. (生徒はみんなかわいい) My pupils are all *dear* to me. / *Suzuki-sañ wa mago ga* kawaikute *tamaranai yoo da.* (鈴木さんは孫がかわいくてたまらないようだ) It seems that Mr. Suzuki cannot help *loving* his grandchild so much.
3 (of a vehicle, instrument, etc.) little; tiny:
Yuueñchi ni wa kawaii *ressha ga*

hashitte iru. (遊園地にはかわいい列車が走っている) A *small* train runs in the amusement park.

ka⌐wairashi¬·i かわいらしい (可愛らしい) *a.* (-ku) = kawaii.

ka⌐waiso¬o かわいそう (可哀相) *a.n.* (~ na, ni) poor; pitiful; miserable; sad:
Sono kawaisoo *na tori wa hane ga orete ita.* (そのかわいそうな鳥は羽が折れていた) The *poor* bird had a broken wing. / *Kawaisoo ni, sono oñna-no-ko wa haha-oya o nakushita.* (かわいそうに、その女の子は母親を亡くした) *Sad* to say, she lost her mother. / *Sono hanashi o kiite, roojiñ ga* kawaisoo *ni natta.* (その話を聞いて、老人がかわいそうになった) I felt *sorry* for the old man when I heard the story. / *Inu o tsunaide oite, sañpo o sasenai no wa* kawaisoo *da.* (犬をつないでおいて、散歩をさせないのはかわいそうだ) Keeping a dog tied up, and not walking it, is *cruel.*

ka⌐waka¬s·u かわかす (乾かす) *vt.* (-kash·i-; -kas·a-; -kash·i-te C̲) dry:
Kanojo wa señtakumono o hi ni hoshite kawakashita. (彼女は洗濯物を日に干して乾かした) She put out the washing and *dried* it in the sun. (⟹ kawaku)

ka⌐wa¬k·u かわく (乾く) *vi.* (kawak·i-; kawak·a-; kawa·i-te C̲) dry:
Teñki ga yoi no de señtakumono ga hayaku kawaita. (天気が良いので洗濯物が早く乾いた) The weather was good so the washing *dried* quickly. / *Kuuki ga* kawaite iru *no de, hi no moto ni chuui shite kudasai.* (空気が乾いているので、火の元に注意してください) As the air *is dry,* take precautions against fire. (⟹ kawakasu)

ka⌐wara かわら (瓦) *n.* tile:
kawara *de yane o fuku* (瓦で屋根を

ふく) roof a house with *tiles.*

KAWARA

ka⌐wari かわり (代わり) *n.* substitute; replacement:
Dare ga kare no kawari *o tsutomemashita ka?* (だれが彼の代わりをつとめましたか) Who acted as his *substitute?* / *Kare no* kawari *o mitsukeru no wa muzukashii.* (彼の代わりを見つけるのは難しい) It will be difficult to find a *replacement* for him.

ka⌐wari ni かわりに (代わりに) *adv.*
1 instead (of):
Kare ga ikenakereba, watashi ga kawari ni *ikimasu.* (彼が行けなければ、私が代わりに行きます) If he cannot go, I will go *instead.* / *Kesa wa koohii no* kawari ni *koocha o noñda.* (今朝はコーヒーの代わりに紅茶を飲んだ) This morning I had tea *instead of* coffee.
2 in return; in exchange:
Kono hoñ o kashimasu kara kawari ni *sono rekoodo o kashite kudasai.* (この本を貸しますから代わりにそのレコードを貸してください) I'll lend you this book, so please lend me that record *in return.* / *Furushiñbuñ o dasu to* kawari ni *toiretto-peepaa o kuremasu.* (古新聞を出すと代わりにトイレットペーパーをくれます) When you put out old newspapers, you get toilet paper *in exchange.* (⟹ chirigami-kookañ)

ka⌐war·u¬ かわる (変わる) *vi.* (kawar·i-; kawar·a-; kawat-te C̲)
1 change; turn:
Shiñgoo ga aka kara ao ni kawatta. (信号が赤から青に変わった) The traffic light *changed* from red to green. / *Ki no ha ga kiiro*

ni kawatta. (木の葉が黄色に変わった) The leaves *have turned* yellow. / *Yama no teñki wa* kawari-yasui. (山の天気は変わりやすい) The weather in the mountains *is changeable.* / *Kare wa gakusee-jidai to* kawatta. (彼は学生時代と変わった) He *has changed* from the days when he was a student. ((⇨ kaeru³))

2 differ; vary: *Kuni ni yotte fuuzoku shuukañ wa* kawarimasu. (国によって風俗習慣は変わります) Manners and customs *differ* from country to country. ((⇨ kaeru³))

3 move (to a new house): *Kare wa juusho ga* kawarimashita. (彼は住所が変わりました) He *has moved.*

ka⌐war·u² かわる(代わる・替わる) *vi.* (kawar·i-; kawar·a-; kawat-te Ⓒ) replace; displace; substitute: *Saikiñ wa taipuraitaa ni* kawatte *waapuro ga* tsukawarete iru. (最近はタイプライターに代わってワープロが使われている) Recently word processors *have been replacing* typewriters. / *Kaeri wa watashi ga kuruma no uñteñ o kare to* kawatta. (帰りは私が車の運転を彼と代わった) On the way back I did the driving *instead of* him. / *Ima* kawarimasu. *(on the telephone)* (今代わります) I'll *put* him *on.* ((⇨ kaeru⁴))

ka⌐waru-ga⌐waru かわるがわる (代わる代わる) *adv.* (~ ni) by turns; in turn: *Watashi-tachi wa* kawaru-gawaru *(ni) kuruma o uñteñ shita.* (私たちは代わる代わる(に)車を運転した) We *took turns* driving the car. / *Kare-ra wa suki na uta o* kawaru-gawaru *(ni)* utatta. (彼らは好きな歌を代わる代わる(に)歌った) They sang their favorite songs *in turn.* ((⇨ kootai))

Ka⌐wasaki かわさき (川崎) *n.* a large city in Kanagawa Prefec-

ture, a major industrial center.

ka⌐wase かわせ (為替) *n.*

1 money order: *Sookiñ wa* kawase *de o-negai shimasu.* (送金は為替でお願いします) Please send your remittance by *money order.*

2 monetary exchange: kawase-*sooba* (為替相場) the *exchange* rate / kawase-*tegata* (為替手形) a bill of *exchange.*

Gaikoku kawase kooñiñ giñkoo
SIGN ON BANK WHERE EXCHANGE IS POSSIBLE

ka⌐yo⌐o(bi) かよう(び)(火曜(日)) *n.* Tuesday: *Raishuu no* kayoobi *ni kare to aimasu.* (来週の火曜日に彼と会います) I'll see him next *Tuesday.* ((⇨ yoobi (table)))

ka⌐yo⌐okyoku かようきょく (歌謡曲) *n.* popular song: kayookyoku *o utau* (歌謡曲を歌う) sing a *popular song.*

ka⌐yo·u かよう (通う) *vi.* (kayo·i-; kayow·a-; kayot-te Ⓒ) **1** go; commute: *Kodomo-tachi wa aruite gakkoo e* kayotte imasu. (子どもたちは歩いて学校へ通っています) The children *go* to school on foot. / *Kare wa kuruma de kaisha e* kayotte imasu. (彼は車で会社へ通っています) He *commutes* to his office by car. / *Kanojo wa maishuu getsuyoobi ni byooiñ e* kayotte imasu. (彼女は毎週月曜日に病院へ通っています) Every week she *goes* to the hospital on Monday.

2 (of a vehicle) run: *Sono machi made basu ga* kayotte

imasu.(その町までバスが通っています) There are buses *running* as far as that town.

ka⌐yowa⌐·i かよわい (か弱い) *a.* (-ku) weak; frail; helpless: kayowai *josee o itawaru* (か弱い女性をいたわる) be kind to a *frail* woman.

ka⌐yu⌐·i かゆい (痒い) *a.* (-ku) itchy; itching: *Senaka ga kayui.*(背中がかゆい) My back is *itching.* / *Me ga* kayuku *natte kita.*(目がかゆくなってきた) My eyes have started to feel *itchy.*

ka⌐zañ かざん (火山) *n.* volcano: *Kazañ ga bakuhatsu shita.*(火山が爆発した) The *volcano* erupted. / kazañ-*bai* (火山灰) *volcanic* ash / *kak*-kazañ (活火山) an active *volcano* / *kyuu*-kazañ (休火山) a dormant *volcano* / *shi*-kazañ (死火山) an extinct *volcano.*

ka⌐zari かざり (飾り) *n.* decoration; ornament. ((⇨ kazaru))

ka⌐zar·u かざる (飾る) *vt.* (kazar·i-; kazar·a-; kazat-te C) 1 decorate; ornament: *Heya o hana de* kazatta.(部屋を花で飾った) I *decorated* the room with flowers. ((⇨ kazari)) 2 display: *Heya ni Nihoñ-niñgyoo o* kazatta. (部屋に日本人形を飾った) I *displayed* a Japanese doll in my room. / *Shoo-uiñdoo ni hooseki ga* kazatte atta.(ショーウインドーに宝石が飾ってあった) The jewelry *was displayed* in the show window.

ka⌐ze¹ かぜ (風) *n.* wind; draft; breeze: *Kaze ga dete kita.*(風が出てきた) The *wind* is picking up. / *Kaze ga fuite iru.*(風が吹いている) The *wind* is blowing. / *Kaze ga yañda.* (風がやんだ) The *wind* has died down. / *Kyoo wa kaze ga tsuyoi.* (きょうは風が強い) It is *windy* today. / *Mado kara suzushii* kaze ga

haitte kuru.(窓から涼しい風が入ってくる) There's a cool *breeze* coming in from the window.

ka⌐ze² かぜ (風邪) *n.* cold; influenza: *Kaze o hiita rashii.*(かぜをひいたらしい) I seem to have caught a *cold.* / *Kare wa kaze o hiite, nete imasu.* (彼はかぜをひいて、寝ています) He is in bed with a *cold.* / *Kaze ga naotta.* (かぜが治った) I have gotten over a *cold.* / *Kanojo wa kaze-gimi desu.* (彼女はかぜ気味です) She has a bit of a *cold.* / *Kaze ga hayatte iru.* (かぜがはやっている) There is a *cold* going about.

ka⌐zoe⌐doshi かぞえどし (数え年) *n.* a person's age counted on the basis of the calendar year:

CULTURE

According to this old Japanese way of counting, at birth a baby was considered one year old, and everyone became one year older on January 1. This meant that, for example, a baby born on December 31 became two years old on January 1. The modern way of counting, with age counted from zero, is called '*mañ-neñree.*'

Kazuko wa kazoedoshi *de juunana-sai desu.*(和子は数え年で17歳です) Kazuko is in her seventeenth *calendar year.*

ka⌐zoe⌐·ru かぞえる (数える) *vt.* (kazoe-te V) count: *ichi kara juu made* kazoeru (1から10まで数える) *count* from one to ten / *Hako no naka no riñgo o* kazoete *kudasai.*(箱の中のりんごを数えてください) Will you please *count* the apples in the box?

ka⌐zoku かぞく (家族) *n.* family: kazoku *ga ooi* [*sukunai*](家族が多い[少ない]) have a large [small] *family* / Kazoku *wa miñna geñki desu.*(家族はみんな元気です) My *family* are all well. / Go-kazoku *wa nañ-niñ desu ka?*(ご家族は何人ですか) How large is your *family?* / *Uchi wa roku-niñ* kazoku *desu.* (うちは6人家族です) We have six *family members.* 《⇨ below》

ka¹zu かず(数) *n.* number: ★ There are two ways of counting in Japanese: one is the native Japanese system (*hitotsu, futatsu... too*), and the other is borrowed from the Chinese (*ichi, ni, sañ...*) 《⇨ suu² (table)》 kazu *ga ooi* [*sukunai*](数が多い[少ない]) be large [small] in *number* / *Gakusee no* kazu *ga hette imasu.* (学生の数が減っています) The *number* of students is decreasing. / *Shussekisha no* kazu *o kazoe nasai.*(出席者の数をかぞえなさい) Count the *number* of those present.

Native Japanese
counting system

1	hi⌐to⌐tsu	6	mu⌐ttsu⌐
2	fu⌐tatsu⌐	7	na⌐na⌐tsu
3	mi⌐ttsu⌐	8	ya⌐ttsu⌐
4	yo⌐ttsu⌐	9	ko⌐ko⌐notsu
5	i⌐tsu⌐tsu	10	to⌐o
		?	i⌐kutsu

KDD ケイディーディー *n.* abbrevia-

tion of 'Kokusai Denshin Denwa Co., Ltd.'(国際電信電話株式会社).

ke¹ け(毛) *n.* **1** (body) hair: *Kare wa* ke *ga koi* [*usui*].(彼は毛が濃い[薄い]) He has thick [thin] *hair.* / *Ke wa sugu ni haemasu.* (毛はすぐに生えます) *Hair* grows soon. 《⇨ kami-no-ke》
2 fur; feather; wool: *Uchi no neko wa chairoi* ke *o shite iru.*(うちの猫は茶色い毛をしている) Our cat has brown *fur.* / *Kono kutsushita wa* ke *de dekite imasu.*(この靴下は毛でできています) These socks are made of *wool.*

ke² け(気) *n.* sign; touch; taste: *Doko ni mo hi no* ke *wa nakatta.* (どこにも火の気はなかった) There was no *sign* of fire. / *Kono ko wa zeñsoku no* ke *ga aru.*(この子はぜんそくの気がある) This child has a *touch* of asthma. / *Kono suupu wa shioke ga tarinai.*(このスープは塩気が足りない) This soup needs a *touch* of salt.

-ke け(家) *suf.* family: *Yamada-*ke(山田家) the Yamada *family* / Maeda-ke(前田家) *the Maedas.*

ke¹chi けち *n.* stinginess; stingy person; miser: *Aitsu wa* kechi *da.*(あいつはけちだ) He is a *stingy fellow.* ——*a.n.* (~ na, ni) **1** stingy; mean; miserly:

FAMILY RELATIONS

| o-jiisañ (grandfather) | o-baasañ (grandmother) | o-jiisañ (grandfather) | o-baasañ (grandmother) |

oji (uncle) — chichi (father) — haha (mother) — oba (aunt)

imooto (younger sister) — otooto (younger brother) — ane (older sister) — ani (older brother)

watashi (I) — tsuma (wife) / otto (husband)

musuko (son) — musume (daughter)

Kare wa saikiñ kechi *ni natta.*(彼は最近けちになった) He has grown *stingy* these days.
2 narrow-minded:
kechi *na kañgae* (けちな考え) a *narrow-minded* idea.

ke⌐damono けだもの (獣) *n.* beast; brute: ★ More emphatic than '*kemono*' and often has a derogatory connotation.
Aitsu wa kedamono *no yoo na yatsu da.* (あいつは獣のようなやつだ) He is a *beast* of a man.

ke⌐do (mo) けど(も) *conj.* a shortened informal variant of '*keredo (mo).*'

ke⌐e[1] けい (刑) *n.* punishment; penalty; sentence:
Kare no kee *wa karukatta.* (彼の刑は軽かった) He was given a light *punishment.* / *Kare wa* kee *ni fukushite iru.* (彼は刑に服している) He is serving his *sentence.*

ke⌐e[2] けい (計) *n.* **1** total; sum:
kee *o dasu* (計を出す) figure out a *sum* / *Kyoo no uriage wa* kee *juu-gomañ-eñ desu.* (きょうの売上は計15万円です) Today's sales come to 150,000 yen in *total.*
2 plan; plot:
Ichi-neñ no kee *wa gañtañ ni ari.* (一年の計は元旦にあり) New Year's Day is the day to make your *plans* for the year. (⇨ keekaku)

-kee けい (形) *suf.* shape; form; type:
*kyuu-*kee (球形) a round *shape* / *chi-*kee (地形) the *lay* of the land.

ke⌐eba けいば (競馬) *n.* horse racing:
Keeba de mooketa [*soñ o shita*]. (競馬でもうけた[損をした]) I made [lost] money at the *races.* / *keeba-joo* (競馬場) a *race* track.

ke⌐ebetsu けいべつ (軽蔑) *n.* contempt; scorn; disdain:
Watashi wa kanojo no keebetsu *ni taerarenakatta.* (私は彼女の軽蔑に耐

えられなかった) I could not put up with her *scorn.* (↔ soñkee)
keebetsu suru (～する) *vt.* look down on; despise; disdain: *Sugu oseji o iu hito o* keebetsu *hito mo imasu.* (すぐお世辞を言う人を軽蔑する人もいます) Some people *look down on* those who are too quick to flatter others. / *Uso o tsuku to* keebetsu *saremasu yo.* (うそをつくと軽蔑されますよ) You will *be despised* if you tell a lie.

ke⌐e-ee けいえい (経営) *n.* management; administration.
Kono byooiñ wa kee-ee *ga kurushii rashii.* (この病院は経営が苦しいらしい) This hospital seems to be undergoing *financial difficulties.* / kee-ee-gaku (経営学) the academic study of *business administration.*
kee-ee suru (～する) *vt.* manage; operate; run: *Kare wa mise o go-keñ* kee-ee *shite iru.* (彼は店を5軒経営している) He *operates* five shops. (⇨ itonamu)

ke⌐e-e⌐esha けいえいしゃ (経営者) *n.* manager; the management; proprietor:
Kare ga kono koojoo no kee-ee-sha *desu.* (彼がこの工場の経営者です) He is the *person who runs* this factory.

ke⌐ego けいご (敬語) *n.* honorific; polite expression: ★ Comprising the three categories of honorific, polite and humble expressions.
keego *o tsukau* (敬語を使う) use *polite expressions* / '*Meshiagaru*' *wa* '*taberu*' *no* keego *desu.* (「召し上がる」は「食べる」の敬語です) '*Meshiagaru*' is an *honorific expression* for '*taberu.*'

ke⌐egu けいぐ (敬具) *n.* Yours truly; Sincerely yours. ★ Used in the complimentary close of a letter. (⇨ haikee[1]; tegami)

ke⌐ehi けいひ (経費) *n.* expense;

cost; upkeep:
keehi o kiritsumeru (経費を切り詰める) cut down on *expenses* / *Sono keehi wa kaisha ga haraimasu.* (その経費は会社が払います) The company will pay the *expenses.* / *Kuruma no keehi wa kanari kakaru.* (車の経費はかなりかかる) The *upkeep* of a car comes to quite a bit. / *hitsuyoo-keehi* (必要経費) necessary *expenses.*

ke⌐eji けいじ (刑事) *n.* **1** (police) detective.
2 criminal affairs:
keeji-*jiken* (刑事事件) a *criminal* case / keeji-*soshoo* (刑事訴訟) a *criminal* action. (⇒ minji)

ke⌐eka けいか (経過) *n.* **1** progress; development; course:
Shujutsu-go no keeka wa ryookoo desu. (手術後の経過は良好です) His *progress* after the operation is good. / *Kore made no keeka o hanashite kudasai.* (これまでの経過を話してください) Please tell me the *sequence* of events up to now.
2 lapse; passage:
Ip-pun keeka. (1 分経過) One minute *has passed.*
keeka suru (～する) *vi.* pass:
★ More formal than '*tatsu.*'
Sutaato shite kara sanjup-pun keeka shimashita. (スタートしてから 30 分経過しました) Thirty minutes *have passed* since they started.

ke⌐ekai¹ けいかい (警戒) *n.* caution; precaution; watch; guard:
Gojuu-nin no keekan ga keekai ni atatta. (50 人の警官が警戒に当たった) Fifty policemen were put on *guard.* / keekai-*shin* (警戒心) sense of *precaution* / keekai-*keehoo* (警戒警報) a *warning* siren / *hijoo*-keekai (非常警戒) extraordinary *security.*
keekai suru (～する) *vt.* be cautious of; look [watch] out for; guard against: *Minna keekai*

shite, *kuchi o hirakanakatta.* (みんな警戒して、口を開かなかった) Everyone *was cautious* and wouldn't say anything. / *Shoohisha wa futoo na neage o* keekai su beki da. (消費者は不当な値上げを警戒すべきだ) Consumers *should be on guard* against unjustified price raises.

ke⌐ekai² けいかい (軽快) *a.n.* (～ na, ni) light; nimble:
Kodomo-tachi wa keekai *na ashidori de aruita.* (子どもたちは軽快な足どりで歩いた) The children walked with *light steps.* / *Risu no ugoki wa* keekai *desu.* (りすの動きは軽快です) Squirrels are *nimble.*

ke⌐ekaku けいかく (計画) *n.* plan; design; project; scheme:
natsu-yasumi no keekaku *o tateru* (夏休みの計画を立てる) make *plans* for the summer vacation / *Keekaku wa matomari shidai, jikkoo ni utsushimasu.* (計画はまとまり次第、実行に移します) We will carry out the *plan* as soon as it is fixed. / *go-ka-nen*-keekaku (五か年計画) a five-year *plan.*
keekaku suru (～する) *vt.* plan; project; scheme: *Kare wa Nihon isshuu o* keekaku *shite iru.* (彼は日本一周を計画している) He *is planning* to make a tour around Japan. / *Kare-ra wa sono kane o nusumoo to* keekaku *shite ita.* (彼らはその金を盗もうと計画していた) They *were scheming* to steal the money.

ke⌐ekan けいかん (警官) *n.* policeman; police officer. ★ More formal than '*omawari-san.*'
(⇒ omawari-san; keesatsu)

ke⌐eken けいけん (経験) *n.* experience:
keeken *ga asai [yutaka da]* (経験が浅い[豊かだ]) have little [a lot of] *experience* / keeken *o tsumu* (経験を積む) gain *experience* / keeken *o ikasu* (経験を生かす) make use of

one's *experience* / *Kono shigoto de wa* keekeñ *ga mono o iimasu.* (この仕事では経験がものを言います) *Experience is of the utmost importance in this job.* / *Torihiki de wa nigai* keekeñ *o shita koto ga arimasu.* (取引では苦い経験をしたことがあります) *I have had bitter experiences in business dealings.* / keekeñ-*sha* (経験者) *a person with experience.*

keekeñ suru (〜する) *vt.* experience; go through; undergo: *Kare wa toosañ o* keekeñ *shite iru.* (彼は倒産を経験している) *He has experienced bankruptcy.*

ke⌐eki[1] ケーキ *n.* cake: ★ Japanese confectionery is called 'kashi.'
keeki *ik-ko* (ケーキ1個) a piece [slice] of *cake* / *Tañjoo-iwai no* keeki *o yaita.* (誕生祝いのケーキを焼いた) I baked a birthday *cake.* (⇨ kashi[1])

ke⌐eki[2] けいき (景気) *n.* business; economy; economic conditions: Keeki *ga yoi* [*warui*]. (景気が良い[悪い]) *Business is brisk* [*slow*]. / Keeki *wa doo desu ka?* (景気はどうですか) *How is your business?* / Keeki *wa ma-mo-naku kaifuku suru deshoo.* (景気は間もなく回復するでしょう) *The economy will soon recover.* / Keeki *wa jojo ni yoku natte imasu.* (景気は徐々に良くなっています) *Economic conditions are gradually improving.* / *Kare no mise wa* keeki *ga ii.* (彼の店は景気がいい) *His store is doing well.*

ke⌐eko けいこ (稽古) *n.* practice; exercise; lesson; rehearsal: *Koochi ga mainichi* keeko *o tsukete kureta.* (コーチが毎日けいこをつけてくれた) *The coach helped us with our practice every day.* / (o-) keeko-*goto* ((お)けいこ事) *lesssons* (in dancing, piano, etc.)

keeko (o) suru (〜(を)する) *vt.* practice; exercise; take lessons: *Watashi wa señsee ni tsuite koto no* o-keeko *o shite imasu.* (私は先生に就いて琴のおけいこをしています) *I am taking lessons* in 'koto' from a teacher.

ke⌐ekoku けいこく (警告) *n.* warning; caution: keekoku *o hassuru* [*ukeru*] (警告を発する[受ける]) give [receive] a *warning* / keekoku *o mushi suru* (警告を無視する) ignore a *warning.*

keekoku suru (〜する) *vt.* warn; caution: *Koko de oyoganai yoo ni kodomo-tachi ni* keekoku *shita.* (ここで泳がないように子どもたちに警告した) *I warned the children not to swim here.*

ke⌐ekoo けいこう (傾向) *n.* tendency; trend; inclination: *Wakai hito-tachi wa hoñ o yomanai* keekoo *ga aru.* (若い人たちは本を読まない傾向がある) *Young people have a tendency* not to read books. / *Kabu wa sagaru* keekoo *ni aru.* (株は下がる傾向にある) *There is a downward trend in stock prices.* / *Kare wa chikagoro mono-wasure o suru* keekoo *ga aru.* (彼は近ごろ物忘れをする傾向がある) *He is inclined* to be forgetful these days.

ke⌐ekootoo けいこうとう (蛍光灯) *n.* fluorescent lamp.

ke⌐ekoo-to⌐ryoo けいこうとりょう (蛍光塗料) *n.* fluorescent [luminous] paint.

ke⌐ereki けいれき (経歴) *n.* career; background; one's personal history: *Kare wa kagakusha to shite subarashii* keereki *o motte iru.* (彼は科学者としてすばらしい経歴を持っている) *He has a brilliant background* as a scientist. / *Kare wa doo iu* keereeki *no hito desu ka?* (彼はどういう経歴の人ですか) *He is a person with what sort of background?*

Ke⌈eroo-no-hi⌉ (敬老の日) *n.*
Respect-for-the-Aged Day. (Sept.
15) 《⇨ shukujitsu (table)》

ke⌈esai けいさい (掲載) *n.* publication; insertion:
sono kiji no keesai-*shi* (その記事の
掲載誌) a magazine which *carries*
the article in question.
　keesai suru (〜する) *vt.* publish;
insert; print: *Sono kookoku wa
Asahi-shiñbuñ ni* keesai sareta.
(その広告は朝日新聞に掲載された)
That advertisement *appeared* in
the Asahi.

ke⌈esañ けいさん (計算) *n.* calculation; sums; figures:
keesañ *ga hayai* [*osoi*] (計算が速い
[遅い]) be quick [slow] at *figures* /
Kono keesañ *wa machigatte iru
yoo desu.* (この計算は間違っているよう
です) This *calculation* seems to be
wrong.

tashizañ	$5 + 3 = 8$
	(go tasu sañ wa hachi)
hikizañ	$7 - 2 = 5$
	(nana hiku ni wa go)
kakezañ	$4 \times 3 = 12$
	(yoñ kakeru sañ wa juuni)
warizañ	$6 \div 2 = 3$
	(roku waru ni wa sañ)

　keesañ-hazure (〜はずれ) contrary to expectation: *Kekka wa*
keesañ-hazure *datta.* (結果は計算は
ずれだった) The results were *contrary to expectation.*
　keesañ ni ireru (〜に入れる) take
account of: *Soñna koto ga okoru
to wa* keesañ ni irete *nakatta.* (そん
なことが起こるとは計算に入れてなかった)
We didn't *allow* for something
like that occurring.
　keesañ suru (〜する) *vt.* **1** calculate; count: *Sore wa dono kurai
kakaru ka* keesañ *shite kudasai.*
(それはどの位かかるか計算してください)
Please *calculate* how much it will
cost.

2 reckon; figure:
Subete keesañ shita *toori umaku
itta.* (すべて計算した通りうまくいった)
Everything went off well, as we
reckoned it would.
　keesañ-zuku (〜ずく) calculated:
Kare wa nañ de mo keesañ-zuku
de yaru. (彼は何でも計算ずくでやる)
He does everything in a *calculated manner.*

ke⌈esa⌉ñki けいさんき (計算機) *n.*
calculator:
takujoo keesañki (卓上計算機) a
desk *calculator.*

ke⌈esatsu けいさつ (警察) *n.* the
police; police station:
keesatsu *ni todokeru* (警察に届ける)
report (something) to the *police* /
keesatsu *o yobu* (警察を呼ぶ) call
the *police* / keesatsu *ni shiraseru*
(警察に知らせる) inform the *police* /
Keesatsu *wa sono jikeñ o shirabete iru tokoro desu.* (警察はその事
件を調べているところです) The *police*
are investigating the case. / *Kono
koto wa* keesatsu-*zata ni shitaku
nai.* (このことは警察ざたにしたくない) I
don't want to make this an affair
for the *police.* / keesatsu-*kañ* (警
察官) a *police* officer. 《⇨ keekañ》

THE KEESATSU EMBLEM

Ke⌈esatsu⌉-choo けいさつちょう
(警察庁) *n.* National Police
Agency:
Keesatsu-choo *chookañ* (警察庁長
官) the Commissioner General
for the *National Police Agency.*
《⇨ choo⁴ (table)》

ke⌈esatsusho けいさつしょ (警察
署) *n.* police station.

ke⌐esee けいせい (形成) *n.* formation; building:
jiñkaku no keesee (人格の形成) character *building*.
keesee suru (～する) *vt.* form; shape: *jiñkaku o* keesee suru (人格を形成する) *shape* one's character. (⇨ tsukuru¹)

ke⌐esee-ge⌐ka けいせいげか (形成外科) *n.* plastic surgery. (⇨ byooiñ (table))

ke⌐esha けいしゃ (傾斜) *n.* slant; slope; inclination:
Keesha *ga kyuu da.* (傾斜が急だ) The *slope* is steep.
keesha suru (～する) *vi.* incline; slant; slope; descend: *Michi wa kawa e mukatte, yuruku* keesha shite ita. (道は川へ向かって、ゆるく傾斜していた) The road gently *sloped* down to the river. (⇨ katamuku)

Ke⌐eshi⌐-choo けいしちょう (警視庁) *n.* Metropolitan Police Department.

ke⌐eshiki けいしき (形式) *n.* form; formality:
Keeshiki *yori mo naiyoo ga juuyoo da.* (形式よりも内容が重要だ) The substance is more important than the *form.* / *Kare wa* keeshiki *ni kodawarisugiru.* (彼は形式にこだわりすぎる) He sticks too much to *formalities.* (↔ naiyoo)

ke⌐eshiki-teki けいしきてき (形式的) *a.n.* (～ na, ni) formal; perfunctory:
Keeshiki-teki *na aisatsu* (形式的なあいさつ) a *perfunctory* greeting / *Kare-ra wa tada* keeshiki-teki *ni kaigi o hiraita dake da.* (彼らはただ形式的に会議を開いただけだ) They held the meeting just as a mere *formality.*

ke⌐esotsu けいそつ (軽率) *a.n.* (～ na, ni) careless; rash; hasty:
Kasa o deñsha no naka ni wasureru to wa kimi mo keesotsu *datta ne.* (かさを電車の中に忘れるとは君も軽率だったね) It was *careless* of you to leave your umbrella on the train. / Keesotsu *ni ketsuroñ o dasanai yoo ni.* (軽率に結論を出さないように) Don't jump to a *hasty* conclusion. (↔ shiñchoo)

ke⌐etai けいたい (携帯) *n.* carrying:
keetai-hiñ (携帯品) *personal belongings* / keetai-yoo *taipuraitaa* (携帯用タイプライター) a *portable* typewriter.
keetai suru (～する) *vt.* carry:
Gaishutsu suru toki wa mibuñshoomeesho o keetai suru *koto.* (外出するときは身分証明書を携帯すること) Personal identification must *be carried* when going out.

ke⌐eto けいと (毛糸) *n.* = keito.

ke⌐etoo けいとう (系統) *n.*
1 system:
Meeree-keetoo *ga barabara da.* (命令系統がばらばらだ) The *system* of command is in disorder. / *shiñkee*-keetoo (神経系統) nervous *system.*
2 lineage; descent:
Ano hito wa Geñji no keetoo *o hiite iru.* (あの人は源氏の系統を引いている) He *is descended* from the Genji family.
keetoo-datete (～だてて) systematically: *Kare wa* keetoo-datete, *setsumee shita.* (彼は系統だてて、説明した) He explained it *systematically.*

ke⌐etoo-teki けいとうてき (系統的) *a.n.* (～ na, ni) systematic.

ke⌐eyaku けいやく (契約) *n.* contract; agreement:
keeyaku *o musubu* (契約を結ぶ) conclude a *contract* / keeyaku *o rikoo suru* (契約を履行する) carry out a *contract* / keeyaku *o kaijo* [*haki*] *suru* (契約を解除[破棄]する) cancel [repudiate] a *contract* / keeyaku *ni ihañ suru* (契約に違反する) breach a *contract* / keeyaku *no*

furikoo (契約の不履行) non-fulfillment of a *contract*.

keeyaku suru (〜する) *vi*. contract: *Meekaa to chokusetsu keeyaku shita hoo ga ii.* (メーカーと直接契約したほうがいい) You had better *make a contract* directly with the manufacturer.

ke⌐eyakusho けいやくしょ (契約書) *n*. (written) contract: keeyakusho *o torikawasu* (契約書を取り交わす) exchange *written contracts* / keeyakusho *ni sain suru* (契約書にサインする) sign a *contract*.

ke⌐eyoo けいよう (掲揚) *n*. (of a flag) hoist; fly.

keeyoo suru (〜する) *vt*. hoist; raise: *Shukujitsu ni wa kokki o* keeyoo suru *uchi ga ooi.* (祝日には国旗を掲揚する家が多い) There are many families who *hoist* the national flag on national holidays.

ke⌐eyu[1] けいゆ (経由) *n*. by way of; via: *Arasuka* keeyu *de Pari e itta.* (アラスカ経由でパリへ行った) I went to Paris *via* Alaska.

keeyu suru (〜する) *vt*. go by way of: *Kono shoohin wa Honkon o* keeyu shite, *yunyuu sarete imasu.* (この商品は香港を経由して, 輸入されています) These goods are imported *through* Hong Kong. 《⇨ hete》

ke⌐eyu[2] けいゆ (軽油) *n*. light oil. 《↔ juuyu》

ke⌐ezai けいざい (経済) *n*. economy; finance: *Endaka wa Nihon no* keezai *ni ooki-na eekyoo o ataeta.* (円高は日本の経済に大きな影響を与えた) The strong yen had a great effect on the Japanese *economy*. / *Bukkadaka wa katee no* keezai *no obiyakashite iru.* (物価高は家庭の経済をおびやかしている) The high prices are a threat to family *finances*.

Ke⌐ezaikika⌐ku-choo けいざいき

かくちょう (経済企画庁) *n*. Economic Planning Agency: Keezaikikaku-choo *chookan* (経済企画庁長官) the Director General of the *Economic Planning Agency*. 《⇨ choo[4] (table)》

ke⌐ezai-teki けいざいてき (経済的) *a.n.* (〜 na, ni) **1** economic; financial: Keezai-teki *na kiki* (経済的な危機) an *economic* crisis / *Sono kuni wa* keezai-teki *ni tsumazuite iru.* (その国は経済的につまづいている) The country is *financially* on its last legs. / *Kare wa* keezai-teki *ni mondai ga aru yoo da.* (彼は経済的に問題があるようだ) He seems to have *financial* problems.
2 economical: keezai-teki *na danbookigu* (経済的な暖房器具) an *economical* heater / *Chiisai kuruma no hoo ga* keezai-teki *da.* (小さい車のほうが経済的だ) Small cars are more *economical*.

keezai-teki	economic
	economical

ke⌐ezoku けいぞく (継続) *n*. continuation; renewal: keezoku-*kikan* (継続期間) a period of *duration* / keezoku-*shingi* (継続審議) deliberations *continued in the next session* (of the Diet).

keezoku suru (〜する) *vi*., *vt*. continue; go on: ★ More formal than 'tsuzuku.' *Kono ken no shingi wa raiki mo* keezoku suru *koto ga kimatta.* (この件の審議は来期も継続することが決まった) It has been decided to *continue* deliberations on this matter in the coming session. / *Ano kenkyuukai wa mada* keezoku shite imasu. (あの研究会はまだ継続しています) That study group *is still in existence*.

ke⌐ga[1] けが (怪我) *n*. injury; hurt; wound:

Kare wa jiko de ashi ni kega *o shita.* (彼は事故で足にけがをした) He got *hurt* in the leg in an accident. / *Hito ni* kega *o sasenai yoo ni ki o tsuke nasai.* (人にけがをさせないように気をつけなさい) Be careful *not to injure* other people. / *Saiwai ni mo, karui* kega *de sunda.* (幸いにも, 軽いけがですんだ) Fortunately, I got off with only a slight *injury.* / kega-*niñ* (けが人) an *injured* [*wounded*] person / *oo*-kega (大けが) a serious *injury.*

kega (o) **suru** (〜を する) *vt.* injure; wound; hurt: *Sono kañja wa ude ni* kega (o) *shite iru yoo datta.* (その患者は腕にけが(を)しているようだった) It seemed that the patient *had injured* her arm.

ke⌐hai けはい (気配) *n.* sign; indication:
Heya ni wa hito no kehai *wa nakatta.* (部屋には人の気配はなかった) There were no *signs* of life in the room. / *Bukka jooshoo no* kehai *ga aru.* (物価上昇の気配がある) There are some *indications* of a rise in the prices.

ke⌐ito けいと (毛糸) *n.* woolen yarn; knitting wool:
keito *no kutsushita* (毛糸の靴下) *woolen* socks / keito *o maku* (毛糸を巻く) wind up *wool* / keito de *tebukuro o amu* (毛糸で手袋を編む) *knit* gloves.

ke⌐kka けっか (結果) *n.* result; effect; consequence; outcome: *geñiñ to* kekka (原因と結果) cause and *effect* / *Shikeñ no* kekka *wa asu happyoo saremasu.* (試験の結果はあす発表されます) The *results* of the examination will be announced tomorrow. / *Shujutsu no* kekka *wa yokatta.* (手術の結果は良かった) The *outcome* of the surgical operation was satisfactory. / *Kare wa karoo no* kekka, *byooki ni natta.* (彼は過労の結果, 病気になっ

た) He became ill as a *result* of overwork. 《↔ **geñiñ**》

ke⌐kkaku けっかく (結核) *n.* tuberculosis:
kekkaku *ni kakaru* (結核にかかる) contract *tuberculosis.*

ke⌐kkañ[1] けっかん (欠陥) *n.* flaw; defect; shortcomings:
Kono kikai ni wa wazuka da ga kekkañ *ga aru.* (この機械にはわずかだが欠陥がある) This machine has a *defect,* albeit a small one. / *Kekkañ no aru shoohiñ o uru koto wa dekinai.* (欠陥のある商品を売ることはできない) We cannot sell *defective* merchandise. / kekkañ-*sha* (欠陥車) a *defective* car. 《⇒ **ketteñ**》

ke⌐kkañ[2] けっかん (血管) *n.* blood vessel; vein; artery.

ke⌐kkoñ けっこん (結婚) *n.* marriage; matrimony:
Tanaka-sañ kara kekkoñ *o mooshikomareta.* (田中さんから結婚を申し込まれた) I have received a proposal of *marriage* from Mr. Tanaka. / *Go-*kekkoñ *omedetoo gozaimasu.* (ご結婚おめでとうございます) Congratulations on your *marriage.* / kekkoñ-*kineñbi* (結婚記念日) a *wedding* anniversary / kekkoñ-*hirooeñ* (結婚披露宴) a *wedding* reception / kekkoñ-*yubiwa* (結婚指輪) a *wedding* ring.

kekkoñ suru (〜する) *vi.* marry; get married: *Taroo wa Hanako to* kekkoñ *shita.* (太郎は花子と結婚した) Taro *married* Hanako. / *Kanojo wa* kekkoñ *shite imasu.* (彼女は結婚しています) She *is married.* / *Kekkoñ shite, moo juu-neñ ni narimasu.* (結婚して, もう 10 年になります) I *have been married* for ten years.

ke⌐kko⌐ñshiki けっこんしき (結婚式) *n.* wedding ceremony:
kekkoñshiki *o ageru* (結婚式を挙げる) hold a *wedding ceremony* / kekkoñshiki *ni shusseki suru* (結婚式

に出席する) attend a *wedding ceremony* / kekkoñshiki *ni shootai sareru* [*yobareru*] (結婚式に招待される[呼ばれる]) be invited to a *wedding ceremony*.

(**CULTURE**)

Traditionally only close family members attend the wedding ceremony, most of the invited guests attending only the reception afterward. '*Kekkoñshiki*' sometimes refers to this wedding reception.

---

ke˥kkoo[1] けっこう (結構) *a.n.*
(～ na, ni) good; nice; excellent; splendid:
Kono ryoori wa kekkoo *na aji desu.* (この料理は結構な味です) This food tastes *very nice*. / Kekkoo *na mono o itadaki, arigatoo gozaimashita.* (結構なものをいただき, ありがとうございました) Thank you very much for the *splendid* gift you gave me.
kekkoo desu (～です) **1** fine:
★ Acceptance of an invitation, offer, etc. *"Kaeri ni ip-pai yarimasu ka?" "Kekkoo desu ne. Yarimashoo."* (「帰りに一杯やりますか」「結構ですね. やりましょう」) "Won't you have a drink on the way home?" "*Fine*. Let's do that." / *Nani-ka kakumono o kashite kudasai. Nañ de mo* kekkoo desu. (何か書くものを貸してください. 何でも結構です) Please lend me something to write with. Anything is *fine*.
2 (*refusal*) no, thank you: *"Moo ip-pai biiru o ikaga desu ka?" "Moo* kekkoo desu. *Juubuñ itadakimashita."* (「もう一杯ビールをいかがですか」「もう結構です. 十分いただきました」) "What about another glass of beer?" "*No, thank you*. I have had plenty."
ke˥kkoo[2] けっこう (結構) *adv.*
fairly; quite; rather:
Kanojo no Nihoñgo wa kekkoo umai. (彼女の日本語はけっこううまい) Her Japanese is *rather* good. / *Sono gekijoo wa heejitsu de mo* kekkoo *koñde imasu.* (その劇場は平日でもけっこう込んでいます) The theater is *quite* crowded even on weekdays.

ke˩kkoo[3] けっこう (決行) *n.* carrying out as scheduled:
Sutoraiki kekkoo-*chuu.* (*sign*) (ストライキ決行中) *On Strike*.
kekkoo suru (～する) *vt.* carry out as scheduled: *Shiai wa kosame nara* kekkoo shimasu. (試合は小雨なら決行します) In the event of light rain, the game *will be played as scheduled*.

ke˩kkoo[4] けっこう (欠航) *n.* cancellation (of a flight, voyage):
Watashi-tachi no biñ ga yuki no tame kekkoo *ni natta.* (私たちの便が雪のため欠航になった) Our flight *was canceled* because of snow.
kek˩koo suru (～する) *vi.* do not fly [sail]: *Kono fune wa ashita wa* kekkoo shimasu. (この船はあしたは欠航します) This ship *will not sail* tomorrow.

ke˩kkyoku けっきょく (結局) *adv.* after all; in the end; in the long run:
Tameratte ita ga kekkyoku *kare wa nani mo shinakatta.* (ためらっていたが結局彼は何もしなかった) He was hesitating, but he did nothing *after all*. / *Iroiro kañgaeta ga* kekkyoku *onaji ketsuroñ ni tasshita.* (いろいろ考えたが結局同じ結論に達した) I tried thinking in different ways, but *in the end* I came to the same conclusion. / Kekkyoku *wa seegi ga katsu to shiñjite imasu.* (結局は正義が勝つと信じています) I believe that right is bound to prevail *in the long run*.

ke˩mono けもの (獣) *n.* beast; wild animal. 《⇒ kedamono》

ke˩mu·i けむい (煙い) *a.* (-ku)

smoky:

Takibi ga kemui.(たき火が煙い)
The bonfire is *smoky*. / *Heya ga*
kemuku *natte kita*.(部屋が煙くなって
きた) The room has gotten *full of
smoke*. / Kemukattara, *itte kudasai*.(煙かったら、言ってください) *If it is
smoky*, please tell me so.

ke⌐muri けむり (煙り) *n.* smoke;
fumes:

Kuroi kemuri *ga sono sooko kara
dete ita*.(黒い煙がその倉庫から出てい
た) Black *smoke* was rising from
the warehouse. / *Tabako no* kemuri *wa meewaku da*.(たばこの煙は
迷惑だ) Cigarette *smoke* is annoying. ((⇨ kemuru))

ke⌐mur·u けむる (煙る) *vi.* (kemu-
r·i-; kemur·a-; kemut-te Ⓒ)
1 smoke; smolder:

Kono danro wa hidoku kemuru.(こ
の暖炉はひどく煙る) This fireplace
smokes badly. ((⇨ kemuri))
2 look dim; be obscured:

Shima wa kiri ni kemutte ita.(島
は霧に煙っていた) The island *was
shrouded* in fog.

ke⌐muta·i けむたい (煙たい) *a.* (-ku)
1 smoky:

Heya ga kemutai. *Mado o akete
kure*.(部屋が煙たい。窓を開けてくれ)
The room is *smoky*. Please open
the window. ((⇨ kemui))
2 unapproachable; uncomfortable:

Kono-goro chichi ga kemutaku
natte kita.(このごろ父が煙たくなってき
た) These days I have begun to
feel *awkward* in my father's
presence.

ke⌐ñ¹ けん (県) *n.* prefecture:
★ A basic administrative unit in
Japan.

Shikoku ni wa keñ *ga yottsu arimasu*.(四国には県が四つあります)
There are four *prefectures* in Shikoku. / *Saitama*-keñ (埼玉県) Saitama *Prefecture* / keñ-*chiji* (県知

事) a *prefectural* governor.
((⇨ inside back cover))

ke⌐ñ² けん (券) *n.* ticket; coupon:
Keñ *ga nakereba nyuujoo dekimaseñ*.(券がなければ入場できません) You
cannot gain admittance without
a *ticket*. / *Kono* keñ *ga areba, jup-
paaseñto waribiki shite moraemasu*.(この券があれば、10パーセント割
り引きしてもらえます) If you have this
coupon, you can get a ten percent
discount.

-keñ¹/geñ -けん/げん (軒) *suf.*
house; door:

1	i⌐k-keñ	7	na⌐na⌐-keñ
2	ni⌐-keñ	8	ha⌐k-keñ
3	sa⌐ñ-geñ	9	kyu⌐u-keñ
4	yo⌐ñ-keñ	10	ji⌐k-keñ
5	go⌐-keñ		(ju⌐k-keñ)
6	ro⌐k-keñ	?	na⌐ñ-geñ

Kono mura ni wa ie ga sañjuk-keñ
aru.(この村には家が30軒ある) There
are thirty *houses* in this village. /
Kare wa koko kara ni-keñ *saki ni
sunde imasu*.(彼はここから2軒先に
住んでいます) He lives two *doors*
from here.

-keñ² -けん (権) *suf.* right:
señkyo-keñ (選挙権) the *right* to
vote / *jiñ*-keñ (人権) human *rights*.

ke⌐nas·u けなす (貶す) *vt.* (kena-
sh·i-; kenas·a-; kenash·i-te Ⓒ)
speak ill of; run down; criticize:
Kare wa koochi o kenashite ita.
(彼はコーチをけなしていた) He *was running down* the coach. / *Sono e wa
miñna ni* kenasareta.(その絵はみんな
にけなされた) The painting *was
severely criticized* by everybody.

ke⌐ñbeñ けんべん (検便) *n.* stool
test:

Keñshiñ de wa keñbeñ *mo arimasu*.(検診では検便もあります) The
medical checkup includes a *stool
test*.

keñbeñ (o) suru (〜(を)する) *vi.*

examine a person's stool: *Byooiñ de* keñbeñ shite moratta. (病院で検便してもらった) I *had my stool examined* in the hospital.

ke⌐ñbutsu けんぶつ (見物) *n.*

1 sightseeing; visit: *Koñdo no yasumi ni Kamakura* keñbutsu *ni ikimaseñ ka?* (今度の休みに鎌倉見物に行きませんか) Why don't we go *sightseeing* in Kamakura during the coming holiday? / keñbutsu-kyaku (見物客) a *spectator.*

2 sightseer; spectator: *Sono misemono ni wa* keñbutsu *ga oozee ita.* (その見世物には見物が大勢いた) There were a lot of *spectators* at the show.

keñbutsu suru (～する) *vt.* see; see the sights of; watch: *O-matsuri ga atta no de* keñbutsu shi *ni itta.* (お祭りがあったので見物しに行った) There was a festival so I went to *see* it.

ke⌐ñbutsuniñ けんぶつにん (見物人) *n.* spectator; onlooker: *Ooku no* keñbutsuniñ *ga sono shiai o mita.* (多くの見物人がその試合を見た) Many *spectators* watched the game. / *Jiko no mawari ni* keñbutsuniñ *ga atsumatta.* (事故のまわりに見物人が集まった) A crowd of *onlookers* gathered at the scene of the accident.

ke⌐ñchi けんち (見地) *n.* viewpoint; standpoint: *Kare wa kotonatta* keñchi *kara ikeñ o nobeta.* (彼は異なった見地から意見を述べた) He expressed his opinion from a different *viewpoint.*

ke⌐ñ-chi⌐ji けんちじ (県知事) *n.* (prefectural) governor. 《⇨ chiji》

ke⌐ñchiku けんちく (建築) *n.* building; construction; architecture: *Sono biru wa ima* keñchiku-*chuu desu.* (そのビルは今建築中です) The

building is now under *construction.* / keñchiku-butsu (建築物) a *building*; a *structure* / *koosoo* [*mokuzoo*]-keñchiku (高層[木造]建築) a tall [wooden] *building* / keñchiku-ka (建築家) an *architect.* 《⇨ tatemono》

keñchiku suru (～する) *vt.* build; put up: ★ More formal than '*tateru.*' *Koosha o* keñchiku suru *hiyoo o atsumete iru tokoro desu.* (校舎を建築する費用を集めているところです) We are collecting funds to *put up* a school building.

ke⌐ñchoo けんちょう (県庁) *n.* prefectural office.

ke⌐ñdoo けんどう (剣道) *n.* Japanese swordsmanship [fencing]; kendo: *Ano hito wa* keñdoo *sañ-dañ desu.* (あの人は剣道3段です) He holds a third grade in *kendo.*

KEÑDOO MATCH

ke⌐ñgaku けんがく (見学) *n.* study by observation; study visit: *Kurasu de koojoo* keñgaku *ni itta.* (クラスで工場見学に行った) Our class took a *field trip* to the factory. / keñgaku-sha (見学者) a *visitor*; an *observer.*

keñgaku suru (～する) *vt.* **1** visit for study; tour: *Shiñbuñsha no naibu o* keñgaku sasete moratta. (新聞社の内部を見学させてもらった) We *were given a tour* of the newspaper office.

2 observe: *Ashi o kega shita no*

de, taiiku wa keñgaku shita. (足を
けがしたので, 体育は見学した) As I
had injured my leg, I only *ob-
served* the physical education
class.

ke⌐ñi けんい（権威）*n.* authority;
expert:
saibañsho no keñi *o mamoru* (裁判
所の権威を守る) maintain the *dignity* of a court of justice / *Yamada hakase wa ideñshi-koogaku no*
keñi *desu.* (山田博士は遺伝子工学の
権威です) Dr. Yamada is an *authority* on genetic engineering.

ke⌐ñji けんじ（検事）*n.* public prosecutor.

ke⌐ñka けんか（喧嘩）*n.* quarrel;
fight; brawl:
Ano futari wa itsu-mo keñka *ga
taenai.* (あの二人はいつもけんかが絶えな
い) Those two *are always quarreling* with each other. / keñka-
bayai (けんか早い) quick to *quarrel*
/ *fuufu*-geñka (夫婦げんか) a marital
spat.

keñka-goshi (〜腰) be ready for
a fight: *Kare wa haitte kita toki
kara* keñka-goshi *datta.* (彼は入って
きたときからけんか腰だった) His atti-
tude was *defiant* from the time
he came in.

keñka (o) suru (〜（を）する) *vi.*
quarrel; have a fight: *Kodomo
no koro wa otagai ni yoku naguriai no* keñka *o shita mono da.* (子
どものころはお互いによく殴り合いのけんか
をしたものだ) When we were children, we often used to *come to
blows* with each other.

keñka o uru (〜を売る) pick a
fight: *Yotta otoko ga kare ni*
keñka *o utta.* (酔った男が彼にけんかを
売った) A drunkard *started a quarrel* with him.

ke⌐ñkai けんかい（見解）*n.* opinion; view; outlook:
Sore wa keñkai *no moñdai desu.*
（それは見解の問題です）That is a mat-

ter of *opinion.* / *Kare to watashi
wa* keñkai *ga itchi shita.* (彼と私は
見解が一致した) He and I held the
same *opinion.*

ke⌐ñketsu けんけつ（献血）*n.*
blood donation:
Watashi wa kare ni keñketsu *o
onegai shita.* (私は彼に献血をお願いし
た) I asked him to *give blood.*

keñketsu (〜する) *vi.* donate
[give] blood: *Watashi wa ima
made ni sañ-do* keñketsu shimashita. (私は今までに３度献血しました)
So far I *have donated blood* three
times.

Ke⌐ñkoku-ki⌐ñeñ-no-hi （建国
記念の日）*n.* National Foundation Day (Feb. 11). 《⇨ shukujitsu
(table)》

ke⌐ñkoo けんこう（健康）*n.*
health:
keñkoo *o tamotsu* (健康を保つ)
keep one's *health* / *Keñkoo ni wa
ki o tsuke nasai.* (健康には気をつけな
さい) Take care of your *health.* /
Haha wa keñkoo *o kaifuku shimashita.* (母は健康を回復しました) My
mother has regained her good
health. / keñkoo-*shiñdañ* (健康診
断) a *medical* checkup / keñkoo-
hokeñ (健康保険) *health* insurance.
— *a.n.* (〜 na, ni) healthy;
healthful:
keñkoo *na hito* (健康な人) a
healthy person / *Kazoku zeñiñ*
keñkoo *ni kurashite imasu.* (家族
全員健康に暮らしています) Our
whole family is *in good health.*

ke⌐ñkoo-hoke⌐ñshoo けんこうほ
けんしょう（健康保険証）*n.* health
insurance card.

ke⌐ñkyuu けんきゅう（研究）*n.*
study; research; investigation:
keñkyuu *ni torikumu* (研究に取り組
む) begin *research* / keñkyuu *ni
juuji suru* (研究に従事する) be engaged in *research* / *Kare wa* keñkyuu nesshiñ *na hito desu.* (彼は研

究熱心な人です) He is a very *studious* person. / keñkyuu-*jo* (研究所) a *research* institute / keñkyuu-*kai* (研究会) a *research* group / keñkyuu-*sha* (研究者) a *researcher* / keñkyuu-shitsu (研究室) a *laboratory*; a *teacher's office*.

keñkyuu (o) suru (〜(を)する) *vt.* study; do research: *Watashi wa yuki ni kañsuru* keñkyuu o suru *tsumori desu.* (私は雪に関する研究をするつもりです) I plan to *do research* concerning snow.

ke⌐ñmee¹ けんめい (賢明) *a.n.* (〜 na, ni) wise; sensible; judicious.
keñmee *na hoohoo* (賢明な方法) a *sensible* method / *Sore ni wa chikazukanai hoo ga* keñmee *desu.* (それには近づかない方が賢明です) It would be *wise* not to get near that.

ke⌐ñmee² けんめい (懸命) *a.n.* (〜 na/no, ni) eager; hard; strenuous:
Keñmee *na soosa ga tsuzukerareta.* (懸命な捜査が続けられた) A *diligent* investigation was carried out. / *Kare wa nyuushi o mae ni* keñmee *ni beñkyoo shite iru.* (彼は入試を前に懸命に勉強している) With the entrance examination close at hand, he is studying *hard*. (⇨ isshoo-keñmee)

ke⌐ñpoo けんぽう (憲法) *n.* constitution:
keñpoo *o mamoru* (憲法を守る) abide by a *constitution* / keñpoo *o seetee* [*kaisee*] *suru* (憲法を制定 [改正]する) establish [revise] a *constitution* / keñpoo-*ihañ* (憲法違反) a breach of the *constitution*.

Ke⌐ñpoo-kine⌐ñbi けんぽうきねんび (憲法記念日) *n.* Constitution Day (May 3). (⇨ shukujitsu (table))

ke⌐ñri けんり (権利) *n.* right; claim; privilege:
kyooiku o ukeru keñri (教育を受ける権利) the *right* to receive an education / *Taniñ no* keñri *o shiñgai shite wa ikenai.* (他人の権利を侵害してはいけない) You should not infringe on other people's *rights*. / *Kimi ni wa kare o semeru* keñri *wa nai.* (君には彼を責める権利はない) You have no *right* to blame him. / *Sono o-kane wa seekyuu suru* keñri *ga aru.* (そのお金は請求する権利がある) You have the *right* to make a claim for that money.

ke⌐ñrikiñ けんりきん (権利金) *n.* key money; premium. ★ Money additional to the rent requested when renting an apartment or house. (⇨ shikikiñ)

ke⌐ñryoku けんりょく (権力) *n.* power; authority; influence:
Kare wa shushoo to shite keñryoku *o furutta.* (彼は首相として権力を振るった) He wielded his *authority* as the prime minister. / *Watashi wa* keñryoku-*arasoi ni makikomaretaku nai.* (私は権力争いに巻き込まれたくない) I don't want to be involved in a struggle for *power*. / *Kare wa kono kaisha de* keñryoku *ga aru.* (彼はこの会社で権力がある) He is an *influential man* in this company. / keñryoku-*sha* (権力者) a man of *power* [*influence*].

ke⌐ñsa けんさ (検査) *n.* inspection; examination; test:
keñsa *o ukeru* (検査を受ける) receive an *inspection* / *Hokeñjo wa kyoo, sono mise no tachiiri-* keñsa *o okonatta.* (保健所はきょう、その店の立ち入り検査を行った) Today the Health Department made a spot *inspection* of that shop. / *Kono seehiñ wa* keñsa *ni gookaku shinakatta.* (この製品は検査に合格しなかった) This product did not pass the *inspection*. / *Kono nimotsu wa moo zeekañ no* keñsa *o tootte imasu.* (この荷物はもう税関の

検査を通っています) This luggage has already gone through customs *inspection*.

keñsa (o) suru (~(を)する) *vt.* inspect; examine; test: *Kono bumoñ de wa omo ni hiñshitsu no* keñsa *o shite imasu.* (この部門では主に品質の検査をしています) In this section, they mainly *carry out* quality *inspections*.

ke⌐ñsaku けんさく (検索) *n.* reference; access: *joohoo no* keñsaku (情報の検索) *access* to information.

keñsaku suru (~する) *vt.* refer to; get: *Hitsuyoo na koomoku o* keñsaku *shite, ichirañ-hyoo ni shita.* (必要な項目を検索して、一覧表にした) I *accessed* the necessary items and organized them into a table.

ke⌐ñsatsu[1] けんさつ (検札) *n.* inspection of tickets: *Shashoo ga* keñsatsu *ni mawatte kita.* (車掌が検札に回って来た) A conductor came around to *inspect tickets*.

ke⌐ñsatsu[2] けんさつ (検察) *n.* prosecution: *Kare wa* keñsatsu-gawa *no shooniñ ni tatta.* (彼は検察側の証人に立った) He took the stand as a witness for the *prosecution*. / keñsatsu-kañ (検察官) a *public prosecutor*.

Ke⌐ñsatsu⌐-choo けんさつちょう (検察庁) *n.* Public Prosecutor's Office. 《⇨ choo[4] (table)》

ke⌐ñsetsu けんせつ (建設) *n.* construction; establishment: *buñka-kokka no* keñsetsu *o mezasu* (文化国家の建設を目指す) aim at the *establishment* of a civilized nation / *Sono biru wa ima* keñsetsu-chuu desu. (そのビルは今建設中です) The building is under *construction* now. / keñsetsu-*gaisha* (建設会社) a *construction* company / keñsetsu-*yoochi* (建設用地)

a *building* lot.

keñsetsu suru (~する) *vt.* build; construct; establish: *Sono hashi wa* keñsetsu suru *no ni go-neñ kakatta.* (その橋は建設するのに 5 年かかった) It took five years to *build* that bridge.

Ke⌐ñsetsu-da⌐ijiñ (建設大臣) *n.* Minister of Construction.

Ke⌐ñsetsu⌐-shoo けんせつしょう (建設省) *n.* Ministry of Construction. 《⇨ shoo[1] (table)》

ke⌐ñshoo けんしょう (懸賞) *n.* prize; prize contest; reward: keñshoo *ni oobo suru* (懸賞に応募する) enter a *prize contest* / *Eegagaisha ga* keñshoo-*tsuki de kyakuhoñ o boshuu shita.* (映画会社が懸賞つきで脚本を募集した) A movie company solicited scripts, and offered a *prize*. / *Keñshoo ni tooseñ suru no wa muzukashii.* (懸賞に当選するのは難しい) It is difficult to win the *prize*. / *Sono sumoo no torikumi ni wa* keñshoo *ga nijuu mo tsuita.* (そのすもうの取組には懸賞が 20 もついた) Sponsors put up as many as twenty *prizes* for the sumo bout.

keñshu⌐usee けんしゅうせい (研修生) *n.* trainee.

ke⌐ñsoñ けんそん (謙遜) *n.* modesty; humility: *Soñna koto o osshatte* go-keñsoñ *deshoo.* (そんなことをおっしゃってご謙そんでしょう) It's out of *modesty* that you say so.

keñsoñ suru (~する) *vi.* be modest; be humble: *Ano hito wa* keñsoñ *shite, soo itta no desu.* (あの人は謙そんして、そう言ったのです) He said that *out of modesty*. / *Soñna* go-keñsoñ *nasarazu ni.* (そんなご謙そんなさらずに) *Don't be so modest*.

ke⌐ñto⌐o[1] けんとう (見当) *n.*

1 guess; estimate; idea: *Keñtoo ga hazureta yoo da.* (見当がはずれたようだ) I seem to have made a wrong *guess*. / *Hiyoo no daitai no* keñtoo *o keesañ shita.* (費用の大体の見当を計算した) I made out a rough *estimate* of the expenses. / *Dare ga yuushoo suru no ka sappari* keñtoo *ga tsukanai.* (だれが優勝するのかさっぱり見当がつかない) I don't have the foggiest *idea* who will win the victory.

2 direction:

Byooiñ wa daitai kono keñtoo *ni arimasu.* (病院は大体この見当にあります) The hospital is roughly in this *direction*.

keñtoo-chigai[hazure] (～違い[はずれ]) be wrong: *Kare no hatsu-geñ wa* keñtoo-chigai[hazure] *da.* (彼の発言は見当違い[はずれ]だ) His remark is *off the point*.

ke⌐ñtoo² けんとう (検討) *n.* examination; study; investigation: keñtoo *o kuwaeru* (検討を加える) *look into*; *study* / *sai-*keñtoo *o semarareru* (再検討を迫られる) be obliged to carry out a second *investigation* / Keñtoo *no yochi ga aru.* (検討の余地がある) There is room for *examination*.

keñtoo suru (～する) *vt.* examine; study; investigate: *Kono kekka o* keñtoo *shite kara de nai to ketsuroñ wa dasemaseñ.* (この結果を検討してからでないと結論は出せません) We cannot draw a conclusion until after we *have examined* these results.

ke⌐ñtoo³ けんとう (健闘) *n.* good fight; strenuous efforts: *Shiai ni wa maketa ga miñna wa sono chiimu no* keñtoo *o tataeta.* (試合には負けたがみんなはそのチームの健闘をたたえた) Although it lost the game, everyone praised the team's *good fight*.

keñtoo suru (～する) *vi.* put up a good fight; make strenuous efforts: *Nihoñ-chiimu wa Doitsu-chiimu o aite ni* keñtoo *shita.* (日

本チームはドイツチームを相手に健闘した) The Japanese team *fought hard* against the German team.

ke⌐ñyaku けんやく (倹約) *n.* thrift; economy: keñyaku *o yobikakeru* (倹約を呼びかける) advise *thrift* / keñyaku-*ka* (倹約家) a *thrifty* person.

keñyaku suru (～する) *vt.* save; economize: *Shokuhi o* keñyaku *shite mo, taishite o-kane wa tamaranakatta.* (食費を倹約しても、たいしてお金はたまらなかった) Though I *economized* on food expenses, I did not save much money.

《↔ roohi》《⇒ setsuyaku》

ke⌐ñzeñ けんぜん (健全) *a.n.* (～ na, ni) healthy; wholesome; sound: keñzeñ *na seeshiñ* (健全な精神) a *sound* mind / keñzeñ *na yomi-mono* (健全な読み物) *wholesome* reading / *kodomo o* keñzeñ *ni sodateru* (子どもを健全に育てる) bring up one's child in a *wholesome* manner.

ke⌐ppaku けっぱく (潔白) *n.* innocence; guiltlessness: *Kare wa mi no* keppaku *o shoo-mee shita.* (彼は身の潔白を証明した) He proved his *innocence*. / *Kano-jo wa* keppaku *de aru to watashi wa shiñjimasu.* (彼女は潔白であると私は信じます) I believe that she is *innocent*.

ke⌐redo (**mo**) けれど(も) *conj.* but; however: *Tashika ni kore wa nedañ ga takai.* Keredo (mo) *shitsu wa taiheñ yoi.* (確かにこれは値段が高い。けれど(も)質はたいへん良い) This certainly is expensive. *However*, the quality is excellent. / *Yakyuu mo kekkoo desu.* Keredo mo *beñkyoo mo gañ-bari nasai.* (野球も結構です。けれども勉強もがんばりなさい) Baseball is fine. *But* be sure to try hard in your studies. / *Kanojo wa kai ni shoo-*

tai sareta keredo mo *shusseki shi-nakatta.*(彼女は会に招待されたけれども出席しなかった)*Though* she was invited, she did not attend the party. / *Kare no musuko wa wakai* keredo (mo) *shikkari shite iru.*(彼の息子は若いけれど(も)しっかりしている)His son is young, *but* reliable. 《⇒ ga²; kakawarazu》

ke⌐r·u ける(蹴る)*vt.* (ker·i-; ke-r·a-; ket-te Ⓒ) **1** kick: *booru o* keru (ボールをける) *kick* a ball / *Kare wa okotte, isu o* ketta.(彼は怒って、いすをけった)He *kicked* the chair in anger.
2 reject; refuse (a request, demand, etc.): *Kare wa watashi-tachi no yookyuu o* ketta.(彼は私たちの要求をけった)He *rejected* our demands.

ke⌐sa けさ(今朝)*n.* this morning: *Kesa wa samukatta.*(けさは寒かった)It was cold *this morning.* / *Kanojo wa kesa Oosaka ni mukatte tachimashita.*(彼女はけさ大阪に向かって発ちました)She left for Osaka *this morning.* 《↔ myoochoo; yokuasa》

ke⌐shigomu けしごむ(消しゴム)*n.* eraser; rubber: *señ o* keshigomu *de kesu* (線を消しゴムで消す) rub out a line with an *eraser.*

ke⌐shiki けしき(景色)*n.* scenery; scene; landscape; view: *Kanojo wa fuyu no* keshiki *o e ni kaita.*(彼女は冬の景色を絵にかいた)She portrayed winter *scenes* in her paintings. / *Yama no ue kara no* keshiki *wa subarashikatta.*(山の上からの景色は素晴らしかった)The *view* from the top of the mountain was spectacular.

ke⌐sho⌐o けしょう(化粧)*n.* makeup: keshoo *o naosu [otosu]* (化粧を直す[落とす])adjust [remove] one's

makeup / keshoo *ga atsui [usui]* (化粧が厚い[薄い]) wear heavy [light] *makeup* / keshoo-hiñ (化粧品) *cosmetics* / keshoo-doogu (化粧道具) a *toilet* set / keshoo-sui (化粧水) *face lotion* / keshoo-shitsu (化粧室) a *toilet*; a *restroom.*

SIGN INDICATING KESHOO-SHITSU FOR MEN

keshoo (o) suru (～(を)する)*vi.* make oneself up; paint: *Tanaka-sañ wa fudañ* (wa) metta ni keshoo o shinai.(田中さんはふだん(は)めったに化粧をしない)Ordinarily, Ms. Tanaka *seldom wears makeup.*

ke⌐ssaku けっさく(傑作)*n.* masterpiece.

ke⌐ssañ けっさん(決算)*n.* closing accounts; settlement of accounts: *Kessañ wa neñ ni-kai desu.*(決算は年2回です)We *settle accounts* twice a year. / kessañ-*hookoku* (決算報告) a statement of *accounts.*
kessañ (o) suru (～(を)する)*vt.* settle [balance] accounts: *Hañto-shi-goto ni* kessañ suru *kaisha wa ooi.*(半年ごとに決算する会社は多い) There are many companies which *settle accounts* every six months.

ke⌐ssee けっせい(結成)*n.* organization; formation.
kessee suru (～する)*vt.* organize; form: *Kare-ra wa atarashii too o* kessee shita.(彼らは新しい党を結成した)They *formed* a new political party. / *Choosa no tame tokubetsu no iiñkai ga* kessee sareta.(調査のため特別の委員会が結成された)A special committee *was organized* for the investigation.

ke⌐sseki けっせき (欠席) *n.* absence:

Kono kurasu wa saikiñ kesseki *ga ooi.* (このクラスは最近欠席が多い) Recently many people *have been absent* from this class. / kessekisha (欠席者) an *absentee* / kessekitodoke (欠席届) a notice of *absence* / mudañ-kesseki (無断欠席) an *absence* without notice.

kesseki suru (～する) *vt.* stay away; absent oneself: *Kossetsu shite ik-kagetsu gakkoo o* kesseki shita. (骨折して1か月学校を欠席した) I *was absent* from school for a month with a broken bone. 《↔ shusseki》

ke⌐sshiñ けっしん (決心) *n.* decision; determination; resolution: *Señsee no sono kotoba de yatto* kesshiñ *ga tsuita.* (先生のその言葉でやっと決心がついた) When I heard the teacher's words, I was finally able to reach a *decision*. / *Moo nani o itte mo, ano hito no* kesshiñ *wa kawarimaseñ.* (もう何を言っても、あの人の決心は変わりません) No matter what you say, he won't change his *mind*.

kesshiñ suru (～する) *vi., vt.* make up one's mind; decide; determine; resolve: *Itsu-ka Nihoñ ni ryuugaku shiyoo to* kesshiñ shita. (いつか日本に留学しようと決心した) I *resolved* to go to study in Japan some day. / *Kanojo wa kañgofu ni naru koto o* kesshiñ shita. (彼女は看護婦になることを決心した) She *made up her mind* to be a nurse.

ke⌐sshite けっして (決して) *adv.* (with a negative) never; by no means; not at all: *Kanojo wa* kesshite *yakusoku o yaburimaseñ.* (彼女は決して約束を破りません) She *never* breaks a promise. / *Nihoñgo wa* kesshite *muzukashiku arimaseñ.* (日本語は決して難しくありません) Japanese is *not at all* difficult. / *Anata ni wa* kesshite *meewaku o kakemaseñ.* (あなたには決して迷惑をかけません) I will *never* cause you any trouble.

ke⌐sshoo[1] けっしょう (決勝) *n.* final game [match]; finals: *Sono chiimu wa juñ-kesshoo ni katte,* kesshoo *ni susuñda.* (そのチームは準決勝に勝って、決勝に進んだ) The team won in the semifinals and advanced to the *finals*.

ke⌐sshoo[2] けっしょう (結晶) *n.*
1 crystal; crystallization.
2 (*fig.*) result; fruit: *ase no* kesshoo (汗の結晶) the *result* of much effort / *ai no* kesshoo (愛の結晶) the *fruit of love* (i. e. a *child*).

ke⌐ssoñ けっそん (欠損) *n.* deficit; loss: kessoñ *o umeru* (欠損を埋める) make up a *loss* / *Koñgetsu wa hyakumañ-eñ no* kessoñ *o dashite shimatta.* (今月は100万円の欠損を出してしまった) We had a *deficit* of a million yen this month. 《↔ rieki》

ke⌐s·u けす (消す) *vt.* (kesh·i-; kes·a-; kesh·i-te Ⓒ) **1** extinguish; put out; blow out: *kaji o* kesu (火事を消す) *extinguish* a fire / *akari o* kesu (明かりを消す) *put out* a light / *roosoku (no hi) o* kesu (ろうそく(の火)を消す) *blow out* (the flame of) a candle. 《⇨ kieru》
2 switch off; turn off: *Rajio o* keshite *kudasai.* (ラジオを消してください) Please *turn off* the radio.
3 erase; rub [wipe] off; cross out: *kokubañ (no ji) o* kesu (黒板(の字)を消す) *erase* (the writing on) the blackboard / *Kare wa kanojo no namae o meebo kara* keshita. (彼は彼女の名前を名簿から消した) He *crossed* her name *off* the list.
4 remove; deaden; absorb:

iya na nioi o kesu (いやなにおいを消
す) *get rid of* a bad smell / *oto o*
kesu (音を消す) *deaden* a sound.
《⇨ kieru》

ke⌐tobas·u けとばす (蹴飛ばす) *vt.*
(-tobash·i-; -tobas·a-; -tobash·i-
te [C]) kick (away). 《⇨ keru》

ke⌐tsuatsu けつあつ (血圧) *n.*
blood pressure:
Ketsuatsu *ga agatta* [*sagatta*]. (血
圧が上がった[下がった]) The *blood
pressure* rose [went down]. / Ketsuatsu *o hakatte moratta*. (血圧を
測ってもらった) I had my *blood pressure* taken. / *Kare wa* ketsuatsu
ga takai [*hikui*]. (彼は血圧が高い[低
い]) He has a high [low] *blood
pressure*.

ke⌐tsudañ けつだん (決断) *n.* decision; determination; resolution:
Kare wa ketsudañ *ga hayai* [*osoi*].
(彼は決断が早い[遅い]) He is quick
[slow] to make *decisions*. / *Wareware wa sono keekaku no* ketsudañ *o semararete iru*. われわれはその
計画の決断を迫られている) We are
being urged to make a *definite
decision* on the project.
ketsudañ suru (～する) *vi.* decide; determine; resolve: *Kooshoo o uchikiru ka doo ka*, ketsudañ suru *no wa mada hayai*. (交渉
を打ち切るかどうか, 決断するのはまだ早
い) It is still too early to *make a
final decision* whether we should
break off the negotiations or not.

ke⌐tsu⌐eki けつえき (血液) *n.*
blood:
ketsueki *no juñkañ* (血液の循環)
the circulation of the *blood* / ke-
tsueki-*gata* (血液型) a *blood* type.

ke⌐tsui けつい (決意) *n.* determination; resolution:
ketsui *o katameru* (決意を固める)
make a firm *resolution* / ketsui *o
arata ni suru* (決意を新たにする)
renew one's *determination*.
ketsui suru (～する) *vt.* deter-

mine; resolve: *Ika no riyuu ni
yori, jiniñ o* ketsui shimashita. (以
下の理由により, 辞任を決意しました)
For the following reasons, I *have
decided* to resign my post.

ke⌐tsuroñ けつろん (結論) *n.* conclusion:
ketsuroñ *o dasu* (結論を出す) form
a *conclusion* / ketsuroñ *ga deru*
(結論が出る) come to a *conclusion* /
ketsuroñ *o kudasu* (結論を下す)
draw a *conclusion* / ketsuroñ *ni
tassuru* (結論に達する) arrive at a
conclusion.

ke⌐ttee けってい (決定) *n.* decision; determination; conclusion;
settlement:
kettee *o okonau* (決定を行う) make
a *decision* / *Iiñkai wa niñka no* kettee *o kudashita*. (委員会は認可の決
定を下した) The committee made a
decision of approval. / *Watashi-
tachi wa sono keekaku ni taisuru
taido no* kettee *o semararete
imasu*. (私たちはその計画に対する態度
の決定を迫られています) We are
being pressed to *decide* our position regarding that project.
kettee suru (～する) *vi., vt.* decide; determine; conclude; settle: *Jiki Oriñpikku no kaisaichi
ga* kettee shita. (次期オリンピックの
開催地が決定した) The venue of
the next Olympics *was decided*. /
Dai-ichi-i wa Satoo-sañ ni kettee
shimashita. (第1位は佐藤さんに決定
しました) It *was decided* to award
first place to Ms. Sato. / *Tsugi ni
nani o suru ka o* kettee shinakereba naranai. (次に何をするかを決
定しなければならない) We *have to
decide* what to do next. 《⇨ kimeru; kimaru》

ke⌐tte⌐ñ けってん (欠点) *n.* fault;
drawback; weak point:
jibuñ no ketteñ *o naosu* (自分の欠
点を直す) correct one's *weak
points*. 《↔ choosho》《⇨ tañsho》

ke⌈washi⌉¹·i けわしい（険しい）*a.*
(-ku) **1** steep:
kewashii *yama-michi* (険しい山道)
a *steep* mountain path.
2 grim; severe; critical:
kewashii *kaotsuki* (険しい顔つき) a
stern countenance / *Joosee ga*
kewashiku *natte kita.* (情勢が険しく
なってきた) The situation has
become *grave.*

ke⌈zur·u けずる（削る）*vt.* (kezur·i-; kezur·a-; kezut-te Ⓒ)
1 shave; plane; sharpen:
ita o taira ni kezuru (板を平らに削る)
plane a board smooth / *eñpitsu o*
kezuru (鉛筆を削る) *sharpen* a pencil.
2 delete; cross out:
Kare wa yobuñ na go o kezutta.
(彼は余分な語を削った) He *deleted*
the unnecessary words.
3 reduce; curtail; cut:
koosaihi o kezuru (交際費を削る)
cut down on entertainment expenses.

ki⌉¹ き（木）*n.* **1** tree; shrub:
ki *o ueru* (木を植える) plant a *tree* /
ki *ni noboru* (木に登る) climb up a
tree.
2 wood; lumber; timber:
Kono omocha wa ki *de dekite imasu.* (このおもちゃは木でできています)
This toy is made of *wood.*

ki² き（気）*n.* **1** mind; mood; feeling:
Shikeñ no kekka ga ki *ni kakaru.*
(試験の結果が気にかかる) The results
of the exam are weighing on my
mind. / *Tsukarete ite, hoñ o yomu*
ki *ga shinai.* (疲れていて, 本を読む気
がしない) I am tired and not in the
mood to read books. / *Kare wa
shippai suru yoo na* ki *ga suru.* (彼
は失敗するような気がする) I have a
feeling that he will fail.
2 nature; disposition; temper:
Kare wa ki *ga ii.* (彼は気がいい) He
is kind by *nature.* / *Uchi no bosu*

wa ki *ga mijikai.* (うちのボスは気が短
い) Our boss has a quick *temper.* /
Kare no musume wa ki *ga tsuyoi
ga, musuko wa* ki *ga yowai.* (彼の
娘は気が強いが, 息子は気が弱い) His
daughter is *unyielding*, but his
son is *timid.*
3 intention; will:
Ano hito to kekkoñ suru ki *wa arimaseñ.* (あの人と結婚する気はありませ
ん) I have no *intention* of marry-
ing him. / *Kare ni wa yaroo to
suru* ki *ga nai.* (彼にはやろうとする気が
ない) He has no *intention* of doing
it.

ki ga au (〜が合う) get along well:
Ano futari wa ki *ga au.* (あの二人は
気が合う) That two of them *get
along well.*

ki ga chiisai (〜が小さい) be timid:
Kare wa ki *ga chiisai kara hitori
de ikenakatta.* (彼は気が小さいから一
人で行けなかった) He was so *inhib-
ited* that he could not go alone.

ki ga chiru (〜が散る) be distracted: *Terebi no oto de* ki *ga chitte
hoñ ga yomenakatta.* (テレビの音で気
が散って本が読めなかった) *Distracted*
by the sound of the TV, I was
unable to read.

ki ga ki de nai (〜が〜でない) feel
uneasy: *Kare ga mata hema o
suru no de wa nai ka to* ki *ga ki
de nakatta.* (彼がまたへまをするのではな
いかと気が気でなかった) I *was worried
sick* that he would make a blunder again.

ki ga kiku (〜が利く) be considerate; be attentive: *Ano teñiñ wa
yoku* ki *ga kiku.* (あの店員はよく気が
利く) That sales clerk *is* very
thoughtful.

ki ga omoi (〜が重い) be heavy-
hearted: *Shakkiñ no koto o kañgaeru to* ki *ga omoi.* (借金のことを考
えると気が重い) When I think of
my debt, I *feel depressed.*

ki ga shirenai (〜が知れない) cannot understand: *Kare ga añna koto o suru nañte ki ga shirenai.* (彼があんなことをするなんて気が知れない) *It is beyond my comprehension* why he did such a thing.

ki ga sumu (〜が済む) be satisfied: *Ki ga sumu made yari nasai.* (気が済むまでやりなさい) Do it until you *are satisfied*.

ki ga tsuku (〜がつく) notice; come to one's senses: *Sono machigai ni sugu ki ga tsuita.* (そのまちがいにすぐ気がついた) I immediately *noticed* the mistake.

ki ni iru (〜に入る) like; be pleased: *Kanojo wa sono okurimono ga ki ni itta yoo datta.* (彼女はその贈り物が気に入ったようだった) She seemed to *be pleased* with the present.

ki ni kuwanai (〜に食わない) be disagreeable: *Hito no mono o damatte tsukau nañte ki ni kuwanai ne.* (人の物をだまって使うなんて気に食わないね) I *don't like* you to use my things without permission.

ki ni naru (〜になる) bother; get on one's nerves: *Kare no itta koto ga ki ni naru.* (彼の言ったことが気になる) What he said *bothers* me.

ki ni suru (〜にする) worry; mind; care: *Kanojo ga dare to kekkoñ shiyoo to ki ni shimaseñ.* (彼女がだれと結婚しようと気にしません) I *don't care* who she marries.

ki ni yamu (〜に病む) feel nervous [bad] about: *Soñna sasai na koto o ki ni yamu no wa yoshi nasai.* (そんなささいなことを気に病むのはよしなさい) Don't let such a trifling matter *weigh on your mind.*

ki o hiku (〜を引く) draw a person's attention: *Sono ko wa haha-oya no ki o hikoo to shite ita.* (その子は母親の気を引こうとしていた) The child was trying to *get* his mother's *attention.*

ki o kubaru (〜を配る) be attentive to: *kodomo-tachi no añzeñ ni ki o kubaru* (子どもたちの安全に気を配る) *pay attention* to the safety of children / *roojiñ ni ki o kubaru* (老人に気を配る) *take care of* old people.

ki o momu (〜をもむ) be worried; be anxious: *Kanojo wa otto no añpi ni ki o moñda.* (彼女は夫の安否に気をもんだ) She *was in suspense* regarding her husband's safety.

ki o tsukeru (〜をつける) be careful; take care: *Michi o wataru toki wa ki o tsuke nasai.* (道を渡るときは気をつけなさい) *Take care* when you cross the road.

ki o waruku suru (〜を悪くする) be offended; feel hurt: *Moshi watashi ga korarenakute mo, ki o waruku shinai de kudasai.* (もし私が来られなくても，気を悪くしないでください) I hope you *won't be upset* if I can not come.

ki o yoku suru (〜をよくする) be in a good mood: *Kanojo wa shikeñ ni ukatte, ki o yoku shite iru.* (彼女は試験に受かって，気をよくしている) She has passed the exam, so she *is in a good mood.*

-ki[1] き (器) *suf.* **1** -ware; utensil; apparatus: *shok-ki* (食器) *tableware* / *too-ki* (陶器) ceramic *ware* / *gak-ki* (楽器) a musical *instrument* / *juwa-ki* (受話器) a telephone *receiver* / *deñnetsu-ki* (電熱器) an electric *heater.*

2 organ: *shooka-ki* (消化器) the digestive *organs.*

-ki[2] き (機) *suf.* **1** plane: *hikoo-ki* (飛行機) an *airplane* / *jetto-ki* (ジェット機) a jet *plane.*

2 machine: *señtaku-ki* [*sentak-ki*] (洗濯機) a washing *machine* / *señpuu-ki* (扇風機) an electric *fan.*

ki⌐atsu きあつ (気圧) *n.* atmospheric pressure.

ki「bishi¹·i きびしい (厳しい) *a*. (-ku)
severe; stern; strict:
kibishii *hito* (厳しい人) *a strict* person / kibishii *hyoojoo* (厳しい表情)
a *stern* look / kibishii *atsusa*
[*samusa*] (厳しい暑さ[寒さ]) *great*
heat [*intense* cold] / *Kanojo wa
kodomo ni* kibishii. (彼女は子どもに
厳しい) She is *strict* with her children. / *Geñjitsu wa* kibishii. (現実
は厳しい) Reality is *harsh*. / *Señsee
wa kodomo-tachi o* kibishiku *shikatta*. (先生は子どもたちを厳しくしかっ
た) The teacher *sternly* scolded
the children.

ki「bo きぼ (規模) *n*. scale; size:
Kibo *ga ookii* [*chiisai*]. (規模が大き
い[小さい]) The *scale* is large
[small]. / *Sono taikai wa kokusai-
teki na kibo de hirakareta*. (その大
会は国際的な規模で開かれた) The
convention was held on an international *scale*.

ki「boo きぼう (希望) *n*. hope;
wish; request; expectation:
kiboo *o idaku* (希望を抱く) cherish
a *hope* / kiboo *o ushinau* (希望を失
う) lose *hope* / Kiboo *ga kanatta*.
(希望がかなった) My *wish* was realized. / *Go-kiboo ni oojite, juñbi
itashimasu*. (ご希望に応じて、準備い
たします) We will prepare everything in accordance with your
wishes. / kiboo-sha (希望者) an
applicant.

kiboo suru (〜する) *vt*. hope;
wish: *Ryookoku no kooyuu-
kañkee ga suenagaku kawaranai
koto o* kiboo shimasu. (両国の交友
関係が末長く変わらないことを希望しま
す) I *hope* that the friendly relations between both countries continue unchanged forever.
《⇨ nozomu¹》

ki「buñ きぶん (気分) *n*. feeling;
mood; sentiment:
Kare no kotoba de kanojo wa kibuñ *o gaishita*. (彼の言葉で彼女は気
分を害した) With his words, her
feelings were hurt. / Kibuñ *wa
doo desu ka?* (気分はどうですか)
How are you *feeling*? / *Kyoo wa*
kibuñ *ga yoi* [*warui*]. (きょうは気分が
良い[悪い]) I [*don't*] *feel well* today.
/ *Totemo eega ni iku* kibuñ *ni
narenai*. (とても映画に行く気分になれ
ない) I'm not at all in the *mood* to
go to the movies. / Kibuñ-teñkañ
ni soto de shokuji o shita. (気分転
換に外で食事をした) We dined out
for a *change*.

ki「chi きち (基地) *n*. base:
guñji-kichi (軍事基地) a military
base.

ki「chi¹ñto きちんと *adv*. neatly;
exactly; properly; in good order:
Kare wa kichiñto *shita fukusoo o
shite ita*. (彼はきちんとした服装をしてい
た) He was *neatly* dressed. / *Imooto no heya wa itsu-mo* kichiñto
shite imasu. (妹の部屋はいつもきちんと
しています) My sister's room is
always kept *neat and tidy*. / *Sono
ko wa* kichiñto *ojigi o shita*. (その
子はきちんとおじぎをした) The child
bowed *properly*. / *Hikidashi o* kichiñto *seeri shite oki nasai*. (引き
出しをきちんと整理しておきなさい)
Please keep the drawers *tidy*.
《⇨ chañto》

ki「choo きちょう (貴重) *a.n*.
(〜 na) precious; valuable:
kichoo *na taikeñ* (貴重な体験) a
precious experience / *Ima no wareware ni wa sukoshi no jikañ mo*
kichoo *desu*. (今のわれわれには少しの
時間も貴重です) For us in our
present situation, even a little
time is *valuable*.

ki「choohiñ きちょうひん (貴重品) *n*.
(one's) valuables.

ki「dootai きどうたい (機動隊) *n*.
riot police [squad].

ki「dor·u きどる (気取る) *vi*., *vt*.
(kidor·i-; kidor·a-; kidot-te Ⓒ)

1 put on airs; give oneself airs: *Kanojo wa* kidotte iru. (彼女は気取っている) She *gives herself airs*.
2 pose as: *Kare wa gakusha o* kidotte iru. (彼は学者を気取っている) He *affects* to be a scholar.

kiˈe·ru きえる (消える) *vi.* (kie-te Ⓥ) **1** (of a fire, light, etc.) go out; die out: *Totsuzeñ akari ga* kieta. (突然明かりが消えた) Suddenly the lights *went out*. / *Hi wa* kiemashita *ka?* (火は消えましたか) Did the fire *go out?* 《⇨ kesu》
2 disappear; vanish; go out of sight: *Niji ga* kieta. (虹が消えた) The rainbow *has disappeared.* / *Fune ga suiheeseñ no kanata ni* kieta. (船が水平線のかなたに消えた) The ship *went out of sight* beyond the horizon.
3 (of snow) melt away: *Haru ga kuru to kono yama no yuki wa* kiemasu. (春が来るとこの山の雪は消えます) The snow on this mountain *melts away* as spring comes.
4 go away; die out: *Itami ga* kieta. (痛みが消えた) The pain *has gone away.* / *Deñtoo ga* kieta. (伝統が消えた) The tradition *has died out.*

kiˈfu きふ (寄付) *n.* contribution; donation: kifu *o atsumeru* (寄付を集める) collect *contributions* / kifu-kiñ (寄付金) a *contribution*; a *donation*.
kifu suru (〜する) *vt.* contribute; donate: *Watashi wa isañ no ichibu o jizeñ-jigyoo ni* kifu shimashita. (私は遺産の一部を慈善事業に寄付しました) I *donated* part of my inheritance to charitable organizations.

kiˈgae きがえ (着替え) *n.* change of clothes:
Kigae *o motte iki nasai.* (着替えを持って行きなさい) Take along a *change of clothes.*
kigae (o) suru (〜(を)する) *vi.* change one's clothes: Kigae *o shitara, sugu ikimasu.* (着替えをしたら, すぐ行きます) I am coming as soon as I *have changed my clothes.* 《⇨ kigaeru》

kiˈgaeˈ·ru きがえる (着替える) *vt.* (kigae-te Ⓥ) change one's clothes:
Kare wa sooji no tame ni kigaeta. (彼は掃除のために着替えた) He *changed his clothes* to do the cleaning. 《⇨ kigae》

kiˈgai きがい (機外) *n.* outside an airplane. 《↔ kinai》

kiˈgaˈkari きがかり (気掛り) *a.n.* (〜 na, ni) worry; anxiety; concern:
Musuko no shoorai ga kigakari *desu.* (息子の将来が気がかりです) We *are worried* about our son's future. / *Nani-ka* kigakari *na koto de mo aru ñ desu ka?* (何か気がかりなことでもあるんですか) Is there something or other *which is troubling you?* 《⇨ shiñpai》

kiˈgane きがね (気兼ね) *n.* constraint:
Ano hito to wa nañ de mo kigane *nashi ni hanashiaemasu.* (あの人とは何でも気兼ねなしに話し合えます) I can *freely* talk with him about anything at all.
kigane suru (〜する) *vi.* feel constrained; worry about giving trouble: *Shuuto ni wa* kigane *shite imasu.* (しゅうとには気兼ねしています) I *feel ill at ease* with my mother-in-law.

kiˈgaru きがる (気軽) *a.n.* (〜 na, ni) lighthearted; cheerful; buoyant:
kigaru *na tabi* (気軽な旅) a *casually* undertaken trip / *Kyoo wa shigoto mo nakute* kigaru *da.* (きょ

うは仕事もなくて気軽だ) I feel *free and lighthearted* today; I do not even have any work to do. / *Kigaru ni asobi ni kite kudasai.* (気軽に遊びに来てください) Please feel *free* to come and visit us.

ki⌐geki きげき (喜劇) *n.* comedy. 《↔ higeki》

ki⌐geñ¹ きげん (期限) *n.* time limit; deadline: *Repooto no teeshutsu-kigeñ wa ashita desu.* (レポートの提出期限はあしたです) The *deadline* for the term paper is tomorrow. / *Koñgetsu de keeyaku no kigeñ ga kiremasu.* (今月で契約の期限が切れます). The agreement *expires* this month. / *Kono pasupooto no yuukoo-kigeñ wa go-neñ desu.* (このパスポートの有効期限は5年です) This passport is *good* for five years.

ki⌐geñ² きげん (機嫌) *n.* humor; temper; mood: *Kare wa kyoo wa kigeñ ga ii [warui].* (彼はきょうはきげんがいい[悪い]) He is in good [bad] *humor* today. / *Kanojo no kigeñ o sokonawanai yoo ni ki o tsuke nasai.* (彼女のきげんを損なわないように気をつけなさい) Be careful *not to offend* her *feelings.* / *Go-kigeñ ikaga desu ka?* (ごきげんいかがですか) How are you?
kigeñ o toru (～を取る) play up to: *Kare wa uwayaku no go-kigeñ o totta.* (彼は上役のごきげんを取った) He *got on the right side of* his boss.

ki⌐geñ³ きげん (起源) *n.* origin; beginning: *buñmee no kigeñ o tazuneru* (文明の起源をたずねる) trace civilization to its *origin.*

ki⌐goo きごう (記号) *n.* mark; sign; symbol: *kigoo de kaku* (記号で書く) write in *symbols* / *Kono kigoo wa nani o arawashite iru no desu ka?* (この記号は何を表しているのですか) What does this *mark* stand for?

ki⌐gu きぐ (器具) *n.* appliance; utensil; instrument: *Kare wa beñri na deñki-kigu o takusañ motte iru.* (彼は便利な電気器具をたくさん持っている) He has many useful electrical *appliances.* / *Kono kigu no atsukai ni chuui shi nasai.* (この器具の扱いに注意しなさい) Be careful when handling this *instrument.*

ki⌐gyoo きぎょう (企業) *n.* company; business; enterprise: *Kare wa dai-kigyoo ni shuushoku o kiboo shite iru.* (彼は大企業に就職を希望している) He wants to get a job in a big *company.*

ki⌐hoñ きほん (基本) *n.* fundamentals; basics; basis; standard: *Kihoñ o wasureru na.* (基本を忘れるな) Never forget *basics.* / *Nihoñ-go o kihoñ kara yarinaosu koto ni shita.* (日本語を基本からやり直すことにした) I decided to study Japanese again, starting from the *basics.*

ki⌐hoñ-teki きほんてき (基本的) *a.n.* (～ na, ni) fundamental; basic: *Kihoñ-teki na jijitsu ni ikutsu-ka machigai ga aru.* (基本的な事実にいくつか間違いがある) There are a number of mistakes in the *basic* facts. / *Kihoñ-teki ni wa kimi ga tadashii.* (基本的にはきみが正しい) You are *fundamentally* correct. / *kihoñ-teki-jiñkeñ* (基本的人権) *fundamental* human rights.

ki⌐i キー *n.* key. 《⇨ kagi》

ki⌐iro きいろ (黄色) *n.* yellow: *kiiro no enogu* (黄色の絵の具) *yellow* paint / *Shiñgoo ga ao kara kiiro ni kawatta.* (信号が青から黄色に変わった) The traffic light changed from green to *yellow.* 《⇨ kiiroi》

ki⌐iro·i きいろい (黄色い) *a.* (-ku) yellow:

kiiroi *bara* (黄色いバラ) *a yellow rose* / *Ki no ha ga* kiiroku *natte kita.* (木の葉が黄色くなってきた) The leaves of the trees have turned *yellow.* (⇨ kiiro)

ki⌐ji[1] きじ (記事) *n.* news; article: *shuukañshi no* kiji (週刊誌の記事) an *article* in a weekly magazine / *Sono* kiji *wa kesa no shiñbuñ de yomimashita.* (その記事は今朝の新聞で読みました) I read the *news* in this morning's paper.

ki⌐ji[2] きじ (生地) *n.* cloth; material; texture.

ki⌐ji[3] きじ (雉) *n.* pheasant.

ki⌐jitsu きじつ (期日) *n.* fixed date; deadline; appointed day: *Tsugi no kaigi no* kijitsu *o kime-mashoo.* (次の会議の期日を決めましょう) Let's set the *date* for our next meeting. / *Kare wa itsu-mo* kijitsu *o mamoranai.* (彼はいつも期日を守らない) He always fails to meet the *deadline.* / *Kono shigoto wa* kiji-tsu *made ni wa shiagemasu.* (この仕事は期日までには仕上げます) I will finish this work by the *appointed day.*

ki⌐juñ[1] きじゅん (基準) *n.* standard; criterion; basis: *Kare no chiñgiñ wa* kijuñ *o shita-mawatte iru.* (彼の賃金は基準を下回っている) His wages are below *standard.* / *Sono hañdañ no* kijuñ *wa nañ desu ka?* (その判断の基準は何ですか) What was the *basis* of that decision? / *Yosañ wa sakuneñ-do no jisseki o* kijuñ *ni shite iru.* (予算は昨年度の実績を基準にしている) The budget was made on the *basis* of last year's actual results.

ki⌐juñ[2] きじゅん (規準) *n.* norm; standard.

ki⌐ka[1][1] きかい (機械) *n.* machine; machinery: *Kono* kikai *wa koshoo shite imasu.* (この機械は故障しています) This *machine* is out of order. / *Kono* kikai

no atsukai-kata o shitte imasu ka? (この機械の扱い方を知っていますか) Do you know how to work this *machine?*

ki⌐ka[1][2] きかい (機会) *n.* opportunity; chance; occasion: *Ii* kikai *da kara, kare ni shookai shimasu.* (いい機会だから、彼に紹介します) This is a good *opportunity,* so I will introduce you to him. / *Kikai ga attara, o-ukagai shimasu.* (機会があったら、お伺いします) I will visit you if I have the *chance.* / *Kono* kikai *o nogasazu ni nyuukai shi nasai.* (この機会を逃さずに入会しなさい) Don't miss this *chance;* join the club. / *Kore made Nihoñgo o hanasu* kikai *wa hotoñdo arima-señ deshita.* (これまで日本語を話す機会はほとんどありませんでした) I have so far had almost no *occasions* to speak Japanese.

ki⌐kaika きかいか (機械化) *n.* mechanization. **kikaika suru** (〜する) *vt.* mechanize: *noogyoo o* kikaika suru (農業を機械化する) *mechanize* farming.

ki⌐kaku[1] きかく (企画) *n.* plan; project; planning: kikaku *o tateru* (企画を立てる) make a *plan.* **kikaku suru** (〜する) *vt.* plan; arrange: *Sono hi ni awasete, toku-betsu-bañgumi o* kikaku shima-shita. (その日に合わせて、特別番組を企画しました) We *have planned* special programs for that day.

ki⌐kaku[2] きかく (規格) *n.* standard; requirements: *Kono seehiñ wa jisu-*kikaku *ni atte imasu.* (この製品は JIS 規格に合っています) This product meets the JIS (=Japanese Industrial Standard) *requirements.* / kikaku-*hazure no seehiñ* (規格はずれの製品) a *below-standard* article.

ki⌐kañ きかん (期間) *n.* term; period:

Keeyaku no kikañ *wa go-neñ desu.* (契約の期間は 5 年です) The *term* of the contract is five years. / *Watashi wa hoñno shibaraku no* kikañ *soko ni taizai shita koto ga arimasu.* (私はほんのしばらくの期間そこに滞在したことがあります) I once stayed there for a very short *period*.

-ki「kañ きかん (機関) *suf.* **1** engine:
*jooki-*kikañ (蒸気機関) a steam *engine*.
2 institution; system; means:
*kyooiku-*kikañ (教育機関) an educational *institution* / *gyoosee-*kikañ (行政機関) an administrative *organ* / *kootsuu-*kikañ (交通機関) a *means* of transport / *hoodoo-*kikañ (報道機関) news *media*.

ki「ka¬ñsha きかんしゃ (機関車) *n.* locomotive.

ki「kas·u きかす (聞かす) *vt.* (kikash·i-; kikas·a-; kikash·i-te Ⓒ) tell; let hear.
Sono hanashi wa nañ-do mo kikasareta. (その話は何度も聞かされた) I *was told* the story many times. 《⇨ kiku¹》

ki「keñ¹ きけん (危険) *n.* danger; peril; risk; hazard:
kikeñ *kara mi o mamoru* (危険から身を守る) protect oneself against a *danger* / kikeñ *o kañjiru* (危険を感じる) sense *danger* / kikeñ *o okasu* (危険をおかす) brave *danger* / *Koko wa koozui ni naru* kikeñ *wa arimaseñ.* (ここは洪水になる危険はありません) There is no *danger* of this area being flooded.
— *a.n.* (~ na) dangerous; perilous; risky; hazardous; unsafe:
kikeñ *na shigoto* (危険な仕事) *hazardous* work / kikeñ *na jiñbutsu* (危険な人物) a *dangerous* character / *Dooro de asobu no wa* kikeñ *desu.* (道路で遊ぶのは危険です) It is *dangerous* to play on the road.

ki「keñ² きけん (棄権) *n.* abstention; withdrawal:
Toohyoo no kekka wa sañsee nana, hañtai sañ, kikeñ *ni deshita.* (投票の結果は賛成 7, 反対 3, 棄権 2 でした) The voting was seven for, three against, with two *abstentions*. / *Aite-chiimu no* kikeñ *de uchi ga kachimashita.* (相手チームの棄権でうちが勝ちました) We won the game because of our opponent's *withdrawal*. / kikeñ-*sha* (棄権者) an *abstainer*; a *nonvoter*.
kikeñ suru (~する) *vt.* abstain; withdraw; default: *Watashi wa toohyoo o* kikeñ *shita.* (私は投票を棄権した) I *abstained* from voting. / *Kare wa reesu no tochuu de* kikeñ shita. (彼はレースの途中で棄権した) He *dropped out* halfway through the race.

ki¬ki きき (危機) *n.* crisis; emergency.
Seefu wa zaisee-joo no kiki *ni chokumeñ shite iru.* (政府は財政上の危機に直面している) The government is facing a financial *crisis*. / kiki-*kañ* (危機感) a sense of impending *crisis*.
kiki-ippatsu (~一髪) a hair's breadth: *Kare wa* kiki-ippatsu *de shi o manugareta.* (彼は危機一髪で死を免れた) He escaped death *by the skin of his teeth*.

ki「kiaki¬·ru ききあきる (聞き飽きる) *vi.* (-aki-te Ⓥ) be tired of hearing:
Kanojo no fuhee wa kikiakita. (彼女の不平は聞き飽きた) I *am tired of hearing* her complaints. 《⇨ akiru》

ki「kichigae¬·ru ききちがえる (聞き違える) *vt.* (-chigae-te Ⓥ) mishear:
Doomo kare ga itta koto o kikichigaeta rashii. (どうも彼が言ったことを聞き違えたらしい) I *seem to have incorrectly heard* what he said.

《⇨ kikichigai》

ki⌈kichigai ききちがい（聞き違い）*n.*
hearing wrongly:
Sore wa anata no kikichigai *desu.*
（それはあなたの聞き違いです）You
didn't hear me *correctly.*《⇨ kiki-
chigaeru》

ki⌈kida⌉s·u ききだす（聞き出す）*vt.*
(-dash·i-; -das·a-; -dash·i·te Ⓒ)
get (information); find out:
Kare kara nani mo kikidasu *koto
ga dekinakatta.*（彼から何も聞き出す
ことができなかった）We could not
find out anything from him.

ki⌈kigurushi⌉·i ききぐるしい（聞き
苦しい）*a.* (-ku) disagreeable to
hear; harsh to the ear:
*O-*kikigurushii *tokoro ga arimashita koto o o-wabi itashimasu.*（お
聞き苦しいところがありましたことをおわび
いたします）We apologize for *these
problems with the sound.* (*said by
a TV* [*radio*] *announcer*) / *Kare
no iiwake wa* kikigurushikatta.（彼
の言い訳は聞き苦しかった）I *could not
bear* to listen to his excuses.

ki⌈kika⌉es·u ききかえす（聞き返す）
vt. (-kaesh·i-; -kaes·a-; -kae-
sh·i·te Ⓒ) repeat a question:
Wakaranai toki wa kikikaeshite
kudasai.（わからないときは聞き返してく
ださい）When you do not understand, please *ask again.*《⇨ kiki-
naosu》

ki⌈kimachigae⌉·ru ききまちがえる
（聞き間違える）*vt.* (-machigae·te
Ⓥ) mishear:
Kare no kotoba o kikimachigaeta
rashii.（彼の言葉を聞き間違えたらしい）
I seem to *have misheard* what he
said.《⇨ machigaeru》

ki⌈kime ききめ（効き目）*n.* effect;
efficacy; virtue:
zutsuu ni kikime *no aru kusuri*（頭
痛に効き目のある薬）medicine *good
for* a headache / *Kono kusuri wa
sugu ni* kikime *ga arawaremasu.*
（この薬はすぐに効き目が現れます）This

medicine takes *effect* immediately. / *Kare ni chuukoku shite mo,*
kikime *wa nakatta.*（彼に忠告しても，
効き目はなかった）Although I
warned him, it had no *effect.*

ki⌈kinao⌉s·u ききなおす（聞き直す）
vt. (-naosh·i-; -naos·a-; -nao-
sh·i·te Ⓒ) ask again:
*Kare no itta koto ga wakaranai no
de* kikinaoshita.（彼の言ったことがわ
からないので聞き直した）I did not
understand what he had said, so
I *asked again.*《⇨ kikikaesu》

ki⌈kinoga⌉s·u ききのがす（聞き逃す）
vt. (-nogash·i-; -nogas·a-; -no-
gash·i·te Ⓒ) fail to hear:
Sono nyuusu wa kikinogashima-
shita.（そのニュースは聞き逃しました）I
failed to hear the news.

ki⌈kisokona⌉·u ききそこなう（聞き損
なう）*vt.* (-sokona·i-; -sokona-
w·a-; -sokonat·te Ⓒ) hear
amiss; fail to catch:
Kare ga itta koto o kikisokonai-
mashita.（彼が言ったことを聞き損ない
ました）I *could not catch* what he
said.

ki⌈kite ききて（聞き手）*n.* hearer;
listener; interviewer; audience:
Kare wa kikite *ni mawatta.*（彼は聞
き手に回った）He took the part of
the *listener.* / Kikite *no hañnoo wa
nekkyoo-teki datta.*（聞き手の反応は
熱狂的だった）The response of the
audience was enthusiastic.
《↔ hanashite》

ki⌈kito⌉r·u ききとる（聞き取る）*vt.*
(-tor·i-; -tor·a-; -tot·te Ⓒ) hear;
catch:
Watashi no iu koto ga kikitore-
masu *ka?*（私の言うことが聞き取れます
か）*Can* you *hear* what I am
saying?

ki⌈koe·ru きこえる（聞こえる）*vi.*
(kikoe·te Ⓥ) **1** hear; be audible:
Tooku de kane no naru no ga
kikoeta.（遠くで鐘の鳴るのが聞こえた）

I *heard* a bell ring in the distance. / *Deñwa ga tookute, yoku* kikoe-masen. (電話が遠くて、よく聞こえませ ん) I *cannot hear* you properly because of the bad phone connection. / *Kanojo wa yatto* kikoeru *yoo na koe de sasayaita.* (彼女はや っと聞こえるような声でささやいた) She whispered in a barely *audible* voice.
2 sound (like …):
Anata no kotoba wa iiwake ni kikoeru. (あなたの言葉は言い訳に聞こ える) What you say *sounds* like an excuse.

ki「koku きこく (帰国) *n.* return to one's country [homeland]: kikoku *no to ni tsuku* (帰国の途につ く) set out on *one's journey home.*
kikoku suru (〜する) *vi.* return to one's country [homeland]: *Kono keñkyuu ga owattara,* kikoku shi-masu. (この研究が終わったら、帰国しま す) Once this research is com-pleted, I will *go home.* / *Kare wa ichiji,* kikoku shite imasu. (彼は一 時、帰国しています) He *has returned home* for a short while. 《↔ shuk-koku》

ki「koku-shi」jo きこくしじょ (帰国 子女) *n.* Japanese children [stu-dents] who have recently re-turned home from living abroad.

ki「koo きこう (気候) *n.* climate; weather:
Nihoñ wa kikoo *ga oñwa desu.* (日 本は気候が温和です) Japan has a mild *climate.* / Kikoo *wa maitoshi ima-goro fujuñ desu.* (気候は毎年今 ごろ不順です) Every year the *weather* is unsettled around now.

kañtai	the frigid zone
oñtai	the temperate zone
nettai	the torrid zone

ki「k・u」[1] きく (聞く・聴く・訊く) *vt.* (ki-k・i-; kik・a-; ki・i-te ⓒ)

1 listen to:
oñgaku o kiku (音楽をきく) *listen to* music / *Maiasa shichi-ji no nyuu-su o* kikimasu. (毎朝 7 時のニュースを ききます) Every morning I *listen to* the seven o'clock news.
2 hear of [about]:
Soñna koto wa kiita *koto ga arima-señ.* (そんなことは聞いたことがありません) I *have* never *heard of* such a thing. / *Kare ga nyuuiñ shite iru koto* kikimashita *ka?* (彼が入院して いること聞きましたか) *Have* you *heard* that he is in the hospital?
3 ask; inquire:
Keesatsukañ ni eki e iku michi o kiita. (警察官に駅へ行く道を聞いた) I *asked* a policeman the way to the station. / *Kanojo ni o-kaasañ no yoosu o* kiite mita. (彼女にお母さんの 様子を聞いてみた) I *inquired* after her mother's health.
4 obey; follow:
Sono ko wa oya no iu koto o yoku kiku. (その子は親の言うことをよく聞く) That boy faithfully *obeys* what his parents tell him. / *Kare wa señsee no chuui o* kikanakatta. (彼 は先生の注意を聞かなかった) He *did not obey* his teacher's warning. 《⇒ shitagau》

ki「k・u」[2] きく (効く・利く) *vi.* (kik・i-; kik・a-; ki・i-te ⓒ) **1** (of medi-cine, remedy, etc.) have an effect; work:
Kono kusuri wa yoku kikimasu. (この薬はよく効きます) This medicine *works* well.
2 (of apparatus) act; work:
Kono jiteñsha wa bureeki ga kikanai. (この自転車はブレーキが利かな い) The brakes on this bicycle *do not work.*
...ga kiku (...が〜) can be done: señtaku ga kiku (洗濯がきく) *be washable* / shuuri ga kiku (修理がき く) *be repairable* / *Kanojo wa muri ga kikanai.* (彼女は無理がきかない)

She *is unable to push herself too hard.* ((⇨ dekiru))

ki「ku[3] きく (菊) *n.* chrysanthe-mum.

KIKU EXHIBITION

ki「ku｣bari きくばり (気配り) *n.* attention; care; consideration:
kikubari *ni kakeru* (気配りに欠ける) lack *consideration* / *Watashi wa* kanojo no kikubari *ni kañsha shite imasu.* (私は彼女の気配りに感謝しています) I am grateful to her for her *attention.*

ki「kyoo ききょう (帰郷) *n.* home-coming.
kikyoo suru (〜する) *vi.* return to one's hometown: *Tookyoo ni dete kite kara, mada ichi-do mo* kikyoo shite imaseñ. (東京に出て来てから, まだ一度も帰郷していません) Since coming to Tokyo, I *have not* yet *returned* to my home-town even once.

ki「mae きまえ (気前) *n.* ⇨ kimae ga ii.

ki「mae ga i｣i きまえがいい (気前がいい) generous; liberal; open-handed:
Ano hito wa itsu-mo kimae ga ii. (あの人はいつも気前がいい) He *is* always *generous* with his money. / *Chichi wa sake o nomu ni tsurete,* kimae ga yoku natta. (父は酒を飲むにつれて, 気前がよくなった) As our father drank more sake, he *became more liberal and open-handed.*

ki「magure きまぐれ (気紛れ) *n.* caprice; whim; fancy:
Ichiji no kimagure *de shita koto desu.* (一時の気まぐれでしたことです) It is something I did on a *whim.*
— *a.n.* (〜 na, ni) capricious; whimsical:
kimagure *na hito* (気まぐれな人) a *capricious* person / *Kimagure ni itta koto ga hoñtoo ni natta.* (気まぐれに言ったことが本当になった) What I had said *frivolously* came true.

ki「mama きまま (気まま) *a.n.* (〜 na, ni) easy; carefree:
kimama *ni seekatsu o suru* (気ままに生活をする) live just *as one pleases* / *Chichi wa inaka de* kimama *na kurashi o shite imasu.* (父はいなかで気ままな暮らしをしています) My father has a *carefree* existence in the country.

ki「mari きまり (決まり) *n.* **1** rule; regulation:
kimari *o tsukuru* (決まりを作る) lay down a *rule* / kimari *o mamoru* [*yaburu*] (決まりを守る[破る]) obey [break] a *rule.*
2 settlement; conclusion:
Sono moñdai wa yatto kimari ga tsuita. (その問題はやっと決まりがついた) The problem *has been settled* at last. / *Hayaku kono shigoto ni* kimari o tsuketai. (早くこの仕事に決まりをつけたい) I *want to finish up* this job as soon as possible.
3 habit; custom:
Yuuhañ mae ni biiru o nomu no ga kare no kimari desu. (夕飯前にビールを飲むのが彼の決まりです) It is his *custom* to have a beer before dinner.

ki「mari ga waru｣i きまりがわるい (きまりが悪い) feel embarrassed:
Heñ na tokoro de señsee ni atte, kimari ga warukatta. (変な所で先生に会って, きまりが悪かった) I *felt awkward and ashamed* when I met my teacher in rather a strange

place. (⇨ hazukashii)

ki⌐mar·u きまる (決まる) *vi.* (ki-mar·i-; kimar·a-; kimat-te C)
be decided; be settled; be fixed: *Kore kara no nittee ga* kimarimashita. (これからの日程が決まりました) The schedule from now on *has been fixed.* / *Sono hanashi wa sugu ni* kimatta. (その話はすぐに決まった) The negotiations *were* soon *concluded.* (⇨ kimeru)

kimatta (決まった) regular: *Kare ni wa* kimatta *shoku ga nai.* (彼には決まった職がない) He has no *regular* job.

kimatte (決まって) always: *Kaigi ni kare wa* kimatte *okureru.* (会議に彼は決まって遅れる) He is *always* late for meetings.

...ni [to] kimatte iru (...に[と]決まっている) be certain: *Kare wa katsu* ni [to] kimatte iru. (彼は勝つに[と]決まっている) It *is certain* that he will win.

ki⌐me·ru きめる (決める) *vt.* (kime-te V) **1** decide; determine: *Kare wa tabako o yameru koto ni* kimeta. (彼はたばこをやめることに決めた) He *has decided* to give up smoking. / *Natsu-yasumi ni doko e iku ka mada* kimete *imaseñ.* (夏休みにどこへ行くかまだ決めていません) I have not yet *made up my mind* where to go during the summer vacation. (⇨ kimaru)
2 arrange (a time, a place, etc.); fix; settle:
Watashi-tachi wa tsugi no kaigi no hi o kimeta. (私たちは次の会議の日を決めた) We *fixed* the day of the next meeting. (⇨ kimaru)

...to [ni] kimete iru (...と[に]決めている) **1** make it a rule: *Kare wa maiasa sañpo suru koto* ni kimete iru. (彼は毎朝散歩することに決めている) He *makes it a rule* to go for a walk every morning.
2 assume that: *Wareware wa katsu mono* to kimete ita. (われわれは勝つものと決めていた) We *were sure that* we would win.

ki⌐mi¹ きみ (君) *n.* you: ★ The plural forms are 'kimi-tachi' and 'kimi-ra (slightly derogatory).'

> **USAGE**
>
> Used by a man when talking to a close friend or to his subordinates or juniors (*e.g.* a teacher talking to a student).

Tsugi wa kimi *no bañ da.* (次は君の番だ) Next it's *your* turn. / *Kimi-tachi ga suki na yoo ni shi nasai.* (君たちが好きなようにしなさい) Do as *you all* please. (⇨ anata)

ki⌐mi¹² きみ (気味) *n.* **1** feeling; sensation:
Ii kimi *da.* (いい気味だ) *It serves you right.*
2 tendency.

kimi ga aru (〜がある) tend: *Kare wa hataraki-sugi no* kimi ga aru. (彼は働き過ぎの気味がある) He *tends* to overwork.

kimi ga ii (〜がいい) feel satisfied: *Kare ga yarikomerarete,* kimi ga yokatta. (彼がやり込められて、気味がよかった) I *felt satisfied* that he was talked down.

kimi ga warui (〜が悪い) weird; creepy; uncanny: *Kono e wa* kimi ga warui. (この絵は気味が悪い) This picture *is eerie.* / *Hebi o mitara* kimi ga waruku *natta.* (蛇を見たら気味が悪くなった) I *felt a horrid sensation* when I saw the snake.

kimi no warui (〜の悪い) uncanny; weird; spooky: kimi no warui *koe* (気味の悪い声) an *uncanny* voice / kimi no warui *hanashi* (気味の悪い話) a *weird* story.

ki⌐mitsu きみつ (機密) *n.* secret [classified] information: kimitsu-*buñsho* (機密文書) *secret* [*confidential*] document.

kiˈmochi きもち（気持ち）n. feeling; mood:
Watashi wa kañsha no kimochi *o nobeta.* (私は感謝の気持ちを述べた) I expressed my *feelings* of gratitude. / *Kare no* kimochi *wa wakaru.* (彼の気持ちはわかる) I know *how he feels.* / *Nakitai* kimochi *da.* (泣きたい気持ちだ) I *feel like* crying. / *Hoñniñ no* kimochi *ni wa hakarishirenai mono ga aru.* (本人の気持ちには計り知れないものがある) There is something one cannot fathom in his *feelings.*
kimochi ga warui (〜が悪い) feel sick: Kimochi ga warui *no de, ie ni imashita.* (気持ちが悪いので家にいました) As I *didn't feel well,* I stayed home.
kimochi ga yoi (〜がよい) feel good: *Ii teñki de* kimochi ga yoi. (いい天気で気持ちがよい) It's nice weather, and I *feel great.*
kimochi no warui (〜の悪い) unpleasant; disagreeable: kimochi no warui *oto* (気持ちの悪い音) an *unpleasant* sound.
kimochi no yoi (〜のよい) pleasant; comfortable: *Kare wa* kimochi no yoi *otoko da.* (彼は気持ちのよい男だ) He is an *agreeable* person.

kiˈmono きもの（着物）n. 1 kimono; traditional Japanese costume:
Kanojo wa kiree na kimono *o kite ita.* (彼女はきれいな着物を着ていた) She was wearing a beautiful *kimono.* 《⇨ wafuku (illus.)》
2 clothes; clothing:
kimono *o kiru* [nugu] (着物を着る[脱ぐ]) put on [take off] one's *clothes.*

kiˈmuzukashiˈi きむずかしい（気難しい）n. (-ku) hard to please; grouchy:
Kaneko-sañ wa kimuzukashii *kara tsukiai-nikui.* (金子さんは気難しいからつきあいにくい) Since Mr. Kaneko is *hard to please,* it is difficult to get along with him. / *O-kyaku ga* kimuzukashii *kao o shite haitte kita.* (お客が気難しい顔をして入って来た) A customer came in with a *sour* look on his face.

kiˈmyoo きみょう（奇妙）a.n. (〜 na, ni) strange; odd; queer:
Kimi ga sono koto o shiranai nañte kimyoo *da.* (きみがそのことを知らないなんて奇妙だ) It is rather *odd* that you know nothing about that. / *Kono-goro wa* kimyoo *na jikeñ ga ooi.* (このごろは奇妙な事件が多い) Recently, there have been many *strange* incidents.

kiˈñ[1] きん（金）n. gold:
kiñ *no yubiwa* (金の指輪) a *gold* ring / kiñ *no kusari* (金の鎖) a chain made of *gold.*

kiˈñ[2] きん（菌）n. germ; bacterium; fungus.

kiˈnai きない（機内）n. inside an airplane:
Kinai *ni wa ooki-na nimotsu wa mochikomemaseñ.* (機内には大きな荷物は持ち込めません) You are not allowed to take large items of luggage *onto the plane.* / kinai-*shoku* (機内食) a meal *on the plane.* 《↔ kigai》

kiˈñbeñ きんべん（勤勉）n. diligence; industry:
Señsee wa kare no kiñbeñ *o hometa.* (先生は彼の勤勉をほめた) The teacher praised him for his *hard work.*
— a.n. (〜 na, ni) hardworking; diligent:
kiñbeñ *na hito* (勤勉な人) a *hardworking* person / kiñbeñ *ni hataraku* (勤勉に働く) work *diligently* / *Ano hito wa* kiñbeñ *da.* (あの人は勤勉だ) He is *industrious.*

kiˈñchoo きんちょう（緊張）n.
1 strain; tension:
kiñchoo *o hogusu* (緊張をほぐす) ease *tension.*

2 tensions:
kiñchoo *kañwa* (緊張緩和) a decrease in *tensions* / *Ryookoku wa* kiñchoo-*jootai ga tsuzuite iru.* (両国は緊張状態が続いている) The *tense* situation between the two countries still continues.

kiñchoo suru (〜する) *vi.* feel nervous: *Maiku no mae de* kiñchoo *shite shimatta.* (マイクの前で緊張してしまった) I *tensed up* in front of the microphone.

kiˈñdai きんだい (近代) *n.* modern ages [times]:
Jiñkoo ga kyuu ni fue-hajimeta no wa kiñdai *ni natte kara desu.* (人口が急に増え始めたのは近代になってからです) It is from the beginning of the *modern era* that the population started to increase rapidly. / kiñdai-*kokka* (近代国家) a *modern* nation / kiñdai-*sañgyoo* (近代産業) *modern* industry. 《⇨ geñdai》

kiˈñdaika きんだいか (近代化) *n.* modernization:
koojoo no kiñdaika (工場の近代化) the *modernization* of a factory.

kiñdaika suru (〜する) *vt.* modernize: *mura o* kiñdaika *suru* (村を近代化する) *modernize* a village.

kiˈñeñ きねん (記念) *n.* souvenir; commemoration:
Sono koishi o kiñeñ *ni totte oku koto ni shita.* (その小石を記念にとっておくことにした) I have decided to keep that stone as a *souvenir*. / kiñeñ-*bi* (記念日) a day of *remembrance*; an *anniversary* / kiñeñ-hi (記念碑) a *monument* / kiñeñ-hiñ (記念品) a *memento* / kiñeñ-*kitte* (記念切手) a *commemorative* stamp / kiñeñ-*shashiñ* (記念写真) a *souvenir* photo.

kiñeñ suru (〜する) *vt.* commemorate: *Sooritsu hyaku-shuuneñ o* kiñeñ *shite, shikiteñ ga okonawareta.* (創立 100 周年を記念して、式典が行われた) *Commemorating* the

100th anniversary of the founding, ceremonies were held.

kiˈñeñ きんえん (禁煙) *n.* prohibition of smoking:
Shanai wa kiñeñ *desu.* (車内は禁煙です) Smoking *is prohibited* in the train. / kiñeñ-*kukañ* (禁煙区間) a *no-smoking* section of a (train) route / kiñeñ-*sha* (禁煙車) a *no-smoking* (railroad) car.

kiñeñ suru (〜する) *vi.* give up smoking: *Kotoshi koso* kiñeñ *shiyoo to omoimasu.* (今年こそ禁煙しようと思います) I've told myself that this is the year I *will stop smoking.*

Shuujitsu kiñeñ. (No smoking all day)
KIÑEÑ SIGN

kiˈneˈñbi きねんび (記念日) *n.* memorial [commemoration] day; anniversary:
Kyoo wa watashi-tachi no kekkoñ kiñeñbi *desu.* (きょうは私たちの結婚記念日です) Today is our wedding *anniversary.*

kiˈñgaku きんがく (金額) *n.* amount [sum] of money:
Higai no kiñgaku *wa hyakumañ-eñ ni tasshita.* (被害の金額は 100 万円に達した) The *sum* of the damages came to a million yen.

kiˈñgañ きんがん (近眼) *n.* nearsightedness; shortsightedness:
Watashi wa kiñgañ *desu.* (私は近眼です) I am *nearsighted.*

kiˈñgyo きんぎょ (金魚) *n.* goldfish:
kiñgyo *o kau* (金魚を飼う) keep *goldfish* / *O-matsuri de* kiñgyo-

sukui o shite, asoñda. (お祭りで金魚すくいをして、遊んだ) I played at trying to scoop up *goldfish* at the festival.

ki「ñiro きんいろ (金色) *n.* color of gold; gold.

ki「ñji·ru きんじる (禁じる) *vt.* (kiñjite ▽) forbid; prohibit; ban: *Daigaku no ryoo de wa gakusee no gaihaku o* kiñjite *iru.* (大学の寮では学生の外泊を禁じている) At the college dormitory, they *forbid* the students from staying out at night. / *Koko de wa kitsueñ ga* kiñjirarete imasu. (ここでは喫煙が禁じられています) Smoking *is prohibited* here.

kiñji enai (禁じ得ない) (*formal*) cannot help: *Aware na kodomo-tachi e no doojoo o* kiñji enakatta. (哀れな子どもたちへの同情を禁じ得なかった) I *could not help* feeling sympathy toward the poor children. / *Sono hanashi o kiite, watashi wa namida o* kiñji enakatta. (その話を聞いて、私は涙を禁じ得なかった) On hearing that story, I *couldn't stop myself* crying.

ki「ñjo きんじょ (近所) *n.* neighborhood; vicinity: *Uchi no* kiñjo *ni kooeñ ga arimasu.* (うちの近所に公園があります) There is a park in my *neighborhood.* / *Yamada-sañ no o-taku wa watashi no* kiñjo *desu.* (山田さんのお宅は私の近所です) Mr. Yamada's house is *near* mine. / *Kiñjo no hito wa miñna sono jikeñ no koto o hanashite imasu.* (近所の人はみんなその事件のことを話しています) The people in the *neighborhood* have been talking about that affair.

ki「ñjo-me」ewaku (近所迷惑) *n.* a nuisance to the neighbors.

Ki「ñki きんき (近畿) *n.* the central western district in Honshu. It comprises Kyoto, Osaka, and Nara, Hyogo, Wakayama, Mie and Shiga prefectures. (⇨ inside back cover)

ki「ñko きんこ (金庫) *n.* safe: *Kare wa kichoohiñ o giñkoo no* kiñko *ni azuketa.* (彼は貴重品を銀行の金庫に預けた) He kept his valuables in a *safe* at the bank.

ki「ñkoo きんこう (均衡) *n.* balance; equilibrium: *chikara no* kiñkoo *o tamotsu [yaburu]* (力の均衡を保つ[破る]) maintain [upset] the *balance* of power / kiñkoo *no toreta yosañ* (均衡のとれた予算) a *balanced* budget.

ki「ñkyuu きんきゅう (緊急) *n.* emergency; urgency: *Kore wa* kiñkyuu *o yoosuru moñdai desu.* (これは緊急を要する問題です) This is a matter which requires great *urgency.* / *Kiñkyuu no baai wa kono doa o akete kudasai.* (緊急の場合はこのドアを開けてください) Please open this door in an *emergency.*
— *a.n.* (~ na, ni) urgent; pressing; immediate: *Kiñkyuu na yooji ga dekimashita.* (緊急な用事ができました) Some *pressing* business has come up. / *Kiñkyuu ni kaigi o hirakaneba narimaseñ.* (緊急に会議を開かねばなりません) We have to hold a meeting *urgently.*

ki「ñmotsu きんもつ (禁物) *n.* prohibited thing; taboo: *Sono hanashi wa ima wa* kiñmotsu *desu.* (その話は今は禁物です) That topic of conversation is now *taboo.* / *Yudañ wa* kiñmotsu *desu.* (油断は禁物です) Carelessness is *not tolerated*

ki「ñmu きんむ (勤務) *n.* service; duty; work: *Kare wa ima* kiñmu-chuu *desu.* (彼は今勤務中です) He is now *at work.* / kiñmu-*hyootee* (勤務評定) an *efficiency rating* / kiñmu-*jikañ* (勤務時

間) *office* hours / kiñmu-*saki* (勤務先) one's place of *employment*.
kiñmu suru (〜する) *vi.* be on duty; be at work: *Watashi wa Tochoo ni sañjuu-neñ* kiñmu shimashita. (私は都庁に 30 年勤務しました) I *worked* for the Tokyo Metropolitan Government for thirty years.

ki˥ñniku きんにく (筋肉) *n.* muscle; brawn:
Uñdoo suru to kiñniku *ga tsuku.* (運動すると筋肉がつく) If you do exercises, you will develop your *muscles.* / *Kare wa* kiñniku *takumashii ude o shite iru.* (彼は筋肉たくましい腕をしている) He has *brawny* arms.

ki˥nodoku きのどく (気の毒) *a.n.* (〜 na, ni) pitiable; pitiful; unfortunate; regrettable; sorry: kinodoku *na hito* (気の毒な人) a person *to be pitied* / Kinodoku ni natte, *sono roojiñ ni o-kane o ageta.* (気の毒になって、その老人にお金をあげた) I gave the old man some money *out of pity.* / Kinodoku ni, *kanojo no go-shujiñ ga kinoo nakunarimashita.* (気の毒に、彼女のご主人がきのう亡くなりました) *Tragically*, her husband died last night. / *Sore wa o-*kinodoku *desu.* (それはお気の毒です) I'm *sorry* to hear that.

ki˥noko きのこ *n.* mushroom: kinoko-*gari ni iku* (きのこ狩りに行く) go *mushrooming.*

ki˥no˥o[1] きのう (昨日) *n.* yesterday:
kinoo *no asa* (きのうの朝) *yesterday morning* / kinoo *no bañ* (きのうの晩) *last* night / kinoo *no shiñbuñ* (きのうの新聞) *yesterday's* newspaper / Kinoo *wa kyuujitsu datta.* (きのうは休日だった) *Yesterday* was a holiday. / Kinoo *Yamada-sañ ni atta.* (きのう山田さんに会った) I saw Mr. Yamada *yesterday.* 《↔ ashita》

《⇨ kyoo (table)》

ki˥noo[2] きのう (機能) *n.* function: kinoo-*shoogai* (機能障害) a *functional* disorder (of the body).
kinoo suru (〜する) *vi.* function; work: *Keeki-rui wa subete seejoo ni* kinoo shite imasu. (計器類はすべて正常に機能しています) The instruments *are* all *working* normally.

ki˥ñpatsu きんぱつ (金髪) *n.* blond [golden] hair.

Ki˥ñroo-ka˥ñsha-no-hi (勤労感謝の日) *n.* Labor Thanksgiving Day (Nov. 23). 《⇨ shukujitsu (table)》

ki˥ñseñ きんせん (金銭) *n.* money; cash:
Kare wa sono moñdai o kiñseñ *de kaiketsu shita.* (彼はその問題を金銭で解決した) He settled the matter with *money.* / *Kare-ra wa* kiñseñ-*joo no koto de mometa.* (彼らは金銭上のことでもめた) There was some trouble between them concerning *monetary* matters.

ki˥ñshi[1] きんし (禁止) *n.* prohibition; ban:
Koko wa chuusha kiñshi *desu.* (ここは駐車禁止です) Parking *is prohibited* here. / *Shuryoo* kiñshi *wa kinoo tokemashita.* (狩猟禁止はきのう解けました) The hunting *prohibition* was lifted yesterday. / tachi-iri kiñshi (*sign*) (立ち入り禁止) *Keep Out.* / tsuukoo kiñshi (*sign*) (通行禁止) *No* Through Traffic.
kiñshi suru (〜する) *vt.* prohibit; forbid; ban: *Gakkoo wa seeto no yakañ hitori-aruki o* kiñshi shita. (学校は生徒の夜間一人歩きを禁止した) The school *prohibited* pupils from going out alone at night. / *Kikeñbutsu no mochikomi wa* kiñshi sarete imasu. (危険物の持ち込みは禁止されています) Entry with dangerous articles *is forbidden.*
《↔ kyoka》

ki「ñshi[2] きんし (近視) *n.* near-sightedness; shortsightedness. 《↔ eñshi》《⇨ kiñgañ》

Ki「ñtoo きんとう (近東) *n.* Near East.

ki「nu きぬ (絹) *n.* silk.

ki「ñyo「o(bi) きんよう(び) (金曜(日)) *n.* Friday: *Kyoo wa juusañ-nichi no* kiñ-yoobi *da.* (きょうは 13 日の金曜日だ) Today is *Friday* the thirteenth. 《⇨ yoobi (table)》

ki「nyuu きにゅう (記入) *n.* entry: kinyuu-more (記入漏れ) an *omission* (in a list).
kinyuu (o) suru (～(を)する) *vt.* make an entry; write; fill out: *Kono waku no naka dake* kinyuu shite *kudasai.* (この枠の中だけ記入してください) Please *write* only inside this box. / *Kaado ni namae to neñ-ree o* kinyuu shita. (カードに名前と年令を記入した) I *wrote* my name and age on the card.

ki「ñzoku きんぞく (金属) *n.* metal: kiñzoku-*hiroo* (金属疲労) *metal* fatigue / kiñzoku-*seehiñ* (金属製品) *metal* goods.

ki「oku きおく (記憶) *n.* memory; recollection; remembrance: kioku *ni todomeru* [*nokoru*] (記憶にとどめる[残る]) register [remain] in one's *memory* / kioku *kara kieru* (記憶から消える) fade from one's *memory* / *Doo-shite keñka ni natta no ka* kioku *ga nai.* (どうしてけんかになったのか記憶がない) I have no *recollection* of why we started fighting. / *Sono jikeñ wa mada miñna no* kioku *ni atarashii.* (その事件はまだみんなの記憶に新しい) That incident is still fresh in everyone's *mind.* / kioku-*ryoku* (記憶力) one's powers of *memory* / kioku-*sooshitsu* (記憶喪失) loss of *memory* / kioku-*soo-chi* (記憶装置) a computer *memory.*

kioku suru (～する) *vt.* remember; memorize: *Ano futari wa sono go, kekkoñ shita to* kioku shite imasu. (あの二人はその後, 結婚したと記憶しています) I *remember* that the two of them got married later. / *Kono deeta wa koñpyuu-taa ni* kioku sasete okoo. (このデータはコンピューターに記憶させておこう) *Let's enter* these data into the computer.

ki「oñ きおん (気温) *n.* (atmo-spheric) temperature: Kioñ *ga agatta* [*sagatta*]. (気温が上がった[下がった]) The *temperature* rose [fell]. / *Kyoo no saikoo*-kioñ *wa sesshi sañjuuni-do datta.* (きょうの最高気温は摂氏 32 度だった) To-day's highest *temperature* was thirty-two degrees centigrade. 《⇨ oñdo (table)》

ki「ppa「ri きっぱり *adv.* (～ to) flatly; definitely; for good: *Kare ni shakkiñ o tanoñda ga* kip-pari (to) *kotowarareta.* (彼に借金を頼んだがきっぱり(と)断られた) I asked him for a loan of money, but I was *flatly* turned down. / *Kare wa* kippari (to) *sake o yameta.* (彼はきっぱり(と)酒をやめた) He has given up drinking *for good.*

ki「ppu きっぷ (切符) *n.* ticket: kippu *o kiru* (切符を切る) punch a *ticket* / *Koñsaato no* kippu *wa doko de kau no desu ka?* (コンサートの切符はどこで買うのですか) Where does one buy *tickets* for the con-cert? / *Señdai made no oofuku*-kippu *o kudasai.* (仙台までの往復切符を下さい) Please give me a round-trip *ticket* to Sendai. / kippu-*uriba* (切符売り場) a *ticket* office; a *box* office. 《⇨ keñ[2]》

ki「rai きらい (嫌い) *a.n.* (～ na) dislike; hate: *Toku ni* kirai *na tabemono wa ari-maseñ.* (特に嫌いな食べ物はありません) There isn't any food I *dislike* in particular. / *Gehiñ na hito wa kirai desu.* (下品な人は嫌いです) I *hate* vulgar people. (↔ suki[1]) (⇨ kirau)

ki˺rakira きらきら *adv.* (~ to) (the state of things that shine brightly):
kirakira (to) hikaru (きらきら(と)光る) *glitter; glisten / Daiyamoñdo ga hikari o ukete kirakira (to) hikatta.* (ダイヤモンドが光を受けてきらきら(と)光った) The diamond *glittered* in the light. / *Sora ni hoshi ga kirakira (to) kagayaite ita.* (空に星がきらきら(と)輝いていた) The stars *were twinkling* in the sky. (⇨ giragira)

ki˺raku きらく (気楽) *a.n.* (~ na, ni) carefree; easy; comfortable:
kiraku na shigoto [kurashi] (気楽な仕事[暮らし]) an *easy* job [life] / *O-kane ga ari, shiñpai ga nakereba jiñsee wa kiraku desu.* (お金があり, 心配がなければ人生は気楽です) Provided you have money, and you have no worries, life is *comfortable and easy.* / *Doozo,* kiraku ni shite kudasai. (どうぞ, 気楽にしてください) Please make yourself *comfortable.* / *Kiraku ni yari nasai.* (気楽にやりなさい) Take it *easy.*
(⇨ noñbiri; noñki)

ki˺ra˺ri きらり *adv.* (~ to) shine or glitter briefly:
Kanojo no me ni namida ga kirari to hikatta. (彼女の目に涙がきらりと光った) The tears *glistened* in her eyes. / *Yami no naka de nani-ka ga kirari to hikatta.* (闇の中で何かがきらりと光った) Something *shone briefly* in the darkness. / *Kare no hatsugeñ ni wa kirari to hikaru mono ga atta.* (彼の発言にはきらりと光るものがあった) There were some *fine* points in his speech.

ki˺ra·u きらう (嫌う) *vt.* (kira·i-; kiraw·a-; kirat-te Ⓒ) dislike; hate:
Miñna ga watashi no koto o

kiratte iru yoo desu. (みんなが私のことを嫌っているようです) Everyone seems to *dislike* me. / *Soñna koto o suru to hito ni kirawareru yo.* (そんなことをすると人に嫌われるよ) If you do that kind of thing, you will *be disliked* by everyone. (⇨ kirai)

ki˺re[1] きれ (切れ) *n.* cloth; rag. (⇨ nuno)

-kire -きれ (切れ) *suf.* piece; slice; strip:
niku go-kire (肉 5 切れ) five *pieces* of meat / *pañ hito-kire* (パン 1 切れ) a *slice* of bread.

ki˺ree きれい (綺麗) *a.n.* (~ na, ni) **1** beautiful; pretty; lovely:
kiree na josee [keshiki] (きれいな女性[景色]) a *beautiful* woman [view] / *Shoojo wa toshi goto ni kiree ni natta.* (少女は年ごとにきれいになった) Each year the girl became *lovelier.* / *Koko kara miru Fuji-sañ ga ichibañ kiree desu.* (ここから見る富士山がいちばんきれいです) Mt. Fuji, as seen from here, is most *beautiful.* (⇨ utsukushii)
2 clean; clear; tidy; neat:
kiree na daidokoro (きれいな台所) a *clean and tidy* kitchen / *Heya o kiree ni sooji shita.* (部屋をきれいに掃除した) I *cleaned* the room thoroughly. / *Kono kawa no mizu wa kiree da.* (この川の水はきれいだ) The water in this river is *clear.*
(↔ kitanai)
3 (~ ni) completely; wholly; entirely:
Sono koto wa kiree ni wasurete ita. (そのことはきれいに忘れていた) I had *completely* forgotten that. / *Shakkiñ wa kiree ni haraimashita.* (借金はきれいに払いました) I *completely* paid off my debts. (⇨ sukkari)
4 (~ na) (of politics) fair; clean:
kiree na señkyo (きれいな選挙) a *clean and fair* election / *kiree na seeji* (きれいな政治) *clean* politics.

ki「re¹・ru きれる（切れる）*vi.* (kire-te
Ⅴ) 1 (of a blade, knife, sword,
etc.) cut; be sharp:
Kono naifu wa (yoku) kireru. (この
ナイフは(よく)切れる) This knife *cuts*
well.
2 (of a thread, rope, etc.) break;
be broken; snap:
Ito [Tsuna] ga kireta. (糸[綱]が切れ
た) The thread [rope] *broke*.
《⇒ kiru¹》
3 (of a telephone, communication, relations, etc.) cut off:
Deñwa ga tochuu de kireta. (電話
が途中で切れた) I *was cut off* in the
middle of my phone call. / *Geñzai sono kaisha to no kañkee wa*
kirete imasu. (現在その会社との関係
は切れています) At present, relations
between that company and us
are ruptured. 《⇒ kiru¹》
4 (of a bank, dam) collapse;
burst:
Dote ga kireta. (土手が切れた) The
embankment *collapsed*. / *Totsuzeñ damu ga kireta.* (突然ダムが切れ
た) The dam suddenly *burst*.
5 (of food, goods) run out; be
out of stock:
Bataa ga kirete shimatta. (バターが
切れてしまった) The butter *has run
out*. / *Sono shina wa kirete imasu.*
(その品は切れています) Those goods
are out of stock.
6 (of a contract, deadline, etc.)
expire:
*Kono keeyaku wa kotoshi de kire-
masu.* (この契約は今年で切れます)
This contract *expires* this year. /
*Kono fuirumu wa kigeñ ga kirete
imasu.* (このフィルムは期限が切れていま
す) The expiry date of this roll of
film *has passed.*
7 (of a person) able; competent:
Kanojo wa kireru. (彼女は切れる)
She is *very able.*

ki「ri¹ きり（霧）*n.* fog; mist:
Kiri wa ma-mo-naku hareru de-

shoo. (霧は間もなく晴れるでしょう)
The *fog* will soon clear up. /
Kesa wa kiri ga fukai. (今朝は霧が
深い) It *is foggy* this morning. /
Yama wa kiri ni tsutsumarete ita.
(山は霧に包まれていた) The moun-
tains were covered with *mist.*

ki「ri² きり（錐）*n.* drill; gimlet;
awl:
kiri *de ana o akeru* (錐で穴を開ける)
bore a hole with a *gimlet.*

-kiri きり（切り）*suf.* 1 only:
★ The emphatic form is '-*kkiri*.'
Josee wa watashi hitori-kiri *datta.*
(女性は私一人きりだった) I was the
only woman there. / *Watashi wa
asa kara mizu*-kiri *noñde inai.* (私
は朝から水きり飲んでいない) I have
had *nothing but* water since this
morning. / *O-kane wa kore*-kkiri
desu. (お金はこれっきりです) This is
the last of my money.
2 since:
Kare wa itta-kiri *kaette konakatta.*
(彼は行ったきり帰って来なかった) He
has never returned *since* he left.

ki「riage・ru きりあげる（切り上げる）
vt. (-age-te Ⅴ) 1 knock off;
leave off; finish:
*Watashi-tachi wa go-ji ni shigoto
o* kiriageta. (私たちは5時に仕事を切
り上げた) We *knocked off* work at
five.
2 raise; round up:
Shoosuu-teñ ika wa kiriageru *koto
ni shita.* (小数点以下は切り上げること
にした) We decided to *raise* the
decimals to the nearest whole
number. 《⇒ kirisuteru; shisha-
gonyuu》
3 revalue:
tsuuka o juugo-paaseñto kiriageru
(通貨を15%切り上げる) *revalue* the
currency by fifteen percent.

ki「ridas・u きりだす（切り出す）*vi.*,
vt. (-dash・i-; -das・a-; -dash・i-te
Ⅽ) 1 begin to talk:
Kare wa yooyaku sono moñdai o

kiridashita.（彼はようやくその問題を切り出した）He finally *broached* the matter.
2 cut down; log; quarry: *ki o* kiridasu（木を切り出す）*cut down* a tree / *ishi o* kiridasu（石を切り出す）*quarry* stone.

ki⌐rihana⌐s·u きりはなす（切り離す） *vt.* (-hanash·i·; -hanas·a·; -hanash·i·te C) cut off; separate: *Kono futatsu no moñdai wa* kirihanasemaseñ.（この二つの問題は切り離せません）We *cannot separate* these two problems. / *Mae no niryoo wa kono eki de* kirihanashimasu.（前の2両はこの駅で切り離します）They *uncouple* the first two cars at this station.

ki⌐rikae·ru きりかえる（切り替える） *vt.* (-kae-te V) change; renew; switch: *chañneru o* kirikaeru（チャンネルを切り替える）*change* the (TV) channel / *wadai o* kirikaeru（話題を切り替える）*change* a topic of conversation / *atama o* kirikaeru（頭を切り替える）*alter* one's way of thinking / *Watashi wa uñteñ-meñkyo o* kirikaeta.（私は運転免許を切り替えた）I *renewed* my driver's license. 《⇨ kirikawaru》

ki⌐rikawa⌐r·u きりかわる（切り替わる） *vi.* (-kawar·i·; -kawar·a·; -kawat-te C) change over; switch; be replaced: *Natsu-jikañ ni* kirikawaru *no wa itsu kara desu ka?*（夏時間に切り替わるのはいつからですか）When do they *change over* to daylight saving time? / *Oñdo ga agaru to suitchi wa jidoo-teki ni ofu ni* kirikawarimasu.（温度が上がるとスイッチは自動的にオフに切り替わります）When the temperature goes up, the switch automatically *turns* to 'off.' 《⇨ kirikaeru》

ki⌐rinuk·u きりぬく（切り抜く） *vt.* (-nuk·i·; -nuk·a·; -nu·i·te C)

clip; cut out: *Watashi wa sono kiji o shiñbuñ kara* kirinuita.（私はその記事を新聞から切り抜いた）I *clipped* the article out of the newspaper.

ki⌐risage·ru きりさげる（切り下げる） *vt.* (-sage-te V) **1** cut; reduce: *Nedañ wa subete go-paaseñto* kirisagemashita.（値段はすべて5%切り下げました）We *reduced* all prices by five percent.
2 devalue: *tsuuka o juugo-paaseñto* kirisageru（通貨を15%切り下げる）*devalue* the currency by fifteen percent.

ki⌐risute·ru きりすてる（切り捨てる） *vt.* (-sute-te V) round down; cut off; omit: *hasuu o* kirisuteru（端数を切り捨てる）*cut off* fractions. 《⇨ kiriageru; shisha-gonyuu》

Ki⌐risuto キリスト *n.* Christ.

Ki⌐risuto-kyoo キリストきょう（基督教） *n.* Christianity: Kirisuto-kyooto（キリスト教徒）a *Christian.* 《⇨ kurisuchañ》

ki⌐ritor·u きりとる（切り取る） *vt.* (-tor·i·; -tor·a·; -tot-te C) cut away [off]; clip: *ki no eda o* kiritoru（木の枝を切り取る）*cut away* the branches of a tree / *niku o hito-kire* kiritoru（肉を一切れ切り取る）*cut off* a slice of meat.

ki⌐ritsu きりつ（規律） *n.* **1** rules; regulations: kiritsu *o mamoru* [*yaburu*]（規律を守る[破る]）observe [break] the rules.
2 order; discipline: *Kare-ra wa itsu-mo* kiritsu *tadashii.*（彼らはいつも規律正しい）They always maintain good *order.* / *Kono gakkoo wa* kiritsu *ga kibishii.*（この学校は規律が厳しい）The *discipline* in this school is rigid.

ki⌐ritsume⌐·ru きりつめる（切り詰め

る) *vt.* (-tsume-te Ⅴ) cut down; reduce; shorten:
beruto o kiritsumeru (ベルトを切り詰める) *shorten* a belt *by cutting* it / *keehi o* kiritsumeru (経費を切り詰める) *cut down* on expenses.

kiˉro キロ *n.* ★Shortened form of '*kiromeetoru*' and '*kiro-guramu.*'
1 kilometer:
*Koko kara eki made yaku ni-*kiro *arimasu.* (ここから駅まで約 2 キロあります) It is about two *kilometers* from here to the station. / *Kare wa jisoku gojuk-*kiro *de uñteñ shita.* (彼は時速 50 キロで運転した) He drove at a speed of fifty *kilometers* per hour.
2 kilogram:
*Jagaimo o sañ-*kiro *katta.* (ジャガイモを 3 キロ買った) I bought three *kilograms* of potatoes.

kiˉroguˉramu キログラム *n.* kilogram. 《⇨ kiro》

kiˉroku きろく (記録) *n.* record; minutes:
kaigi no kiroku *o toru* (会議の記録をとる) keep the *minutes* of a meeting / *Kyoo no toogi no naiyoo wa* kiroku *ni nokosu hitsuyoo ga arimasu.* (きょうの討議の内容は記録に残す必要があります) It is necessary to place the substance of today's debate on *record.* / *Sono señshu wa kyoogikai no tabi ni* kiroku *o kooshiñ shite iru.* (その選手は競技会のたびに記録を更新している) That athlete establishes a new *record* at every tournament. / kiroku-*eega* (記録映画) a *documentary* film / kiroku-*hojisha* (記録保持者) a *record* holder.
kiroku suru (〜する) *vt.* record; write down: *kaigi no naiyoo o* kiroku suru (会議の内容を記録する) *record* the content of a meeting / *Kyoo wa kotoshi ni haitte saikoo no kioñ o* kiroku *shimashita.* (きょう

はことしに入って最高の気温を記録しました) Today *registered* the highest temperature since the year started.

kiˉromeˉetoru キロメートル *n.* kilometer. 《⇨ kiro》

kiˉrˉu[1] きる (切る) *vt.* (kir·i-; kir·a-; kit-te Ⓒ) **1** cut; chop; slice; saw; shear:
eda o kiru (枝を切る) *cut down* branches / *chiizu o* kiru (チーズを切る) *cut off* a piece of cheese / *daikoñ o* kiru (大根を切る) *slice* a Japanese radish / *tamanegi o komakaku* kiru (たまねぎを細かく切る) *slice* an onion finely / *riñgo o futatsu ni* kiru (りんごを 2 つに切る) *cut* an apple in two / *nokogiri de ita o* kiru (のこぎりで板を切る) *cut* a plank of wood with a saw / *Kanojo wa hoochoo de yubi o* kitta. (彼女は包丁で指を切った) She *cut* her finger with a kitchen knife.
2 sever (relations):
Kare wa sono kai to eñ o kitta. (彼はその会と縁を切った) He *severed* his connection with the society. 《⇨ kireru》
3 hang up (a telephone):
Deñwa o kiranai de kudasai. (電話を切らないでください) Please *do not hang up.* 《⇨ kireru[1]》
4 switch off:
deñki (*no suitchi*) *o* kiru (電気(のスイッチ)を切る) *switch off* the electricity.
5 punch (a ticket):
kippu o kitte morau (切符を切ってもらう) *get* one's ticket *punched.*
6 drain:
hooreñsoo no mizu o kiru (ほうれん草の水を切る) *drain* water from spinach.
7 be less than...:
Kare wa hyaku-meetoru de juuichi-byoo o kitta. (彼は 100 メートルで 11 秒を切った) He *did* 100 meters *in less than* eleven seconds.

8 shuffle:

toranpu o kiru（トランプを切る）*shuffle* playing cards.

ki·「ru[2] きる（着る）*vt.* (ki-te ⩒)

1 put on:

uwagi [pajama] o kiru（上着[パジャマ]を着る）*put on* one's jacket [pajamas] / *Kare wa oobaa o* kinai de soto e deta.（彼はオーバーを着ないで外へ出た）He went out *without putting on* his overcoat. / *Kanojo wa kau mae ni sono fuku o* kite mita.（彼女は買う前にその服を着てみた）She *tried on* the dress before buying it.《⇨ kiseru》

2 wear; have on: ★ Used in '*kite iru*.'

Yamada-san wa wafuku o kite ita.（山田さんは和服を着ていた）Miss Yamada *was wearing* Japanese clothes. / *Ano kuroi fuku o* kite iru *josee wa donata desu ka?*（あの黒い服を着ている女性はどなたですか）Who is that woman *in* black?

	put on	wear
clothes	kiru	kite iru
shoes	haku	haite iru
trousers	haku	haite iru
hat	kaburu	kabutte iru
glasses	kakeru	kakete iru
necktie	shimeru	shimete iru
gloves	hameru	hamete iru
scarf	suru	shite iru
ribbon	tsukeru	tsukete iru

ki「sen きせん（汽船）*n.* steamer; steamship; steamboat.

ki「se·ru きせる（着せる）*vt.* (kise-te ⩒) dress; clothe:

Kanojo wa kodomo ni wafuku o kiseta.（彼女は子どもに和服を着せた）She *dressed* her child in Japanese style clothes.《⇨ kiru²》

ki「se」tsu きせつ（季節）*n.* season; time of the year:

Sakura no kisetsu *wa moo sugu*

desu.（桜の季節はもうすぐです）The cherry blossom *season* is coming soon. / *Kisetsu no kawarime ni wa yoku kaze o hikimasu.*（季節の変わり目にはよくかぜを引きます）One is apt to catch a cold at the change of *seasons.* / *Ima-goro no* kisetsu *ni wa yoku tsuyoi kaze ga fukimasu.*（今ごろの季節にはよく強いかぜが吹きます）It often blows hard at this *time of the year.*

haru （春）	March April May	aki （秋）	September October November
natsu （夏）	June July August	fuyu （冬）	December January February

ki「sha[1] きしゃ（記者）*n.* reporter; journalist:

Kare wa moto shuukanshi no kisha *datta.*（彼はもと週刊誌の記者だった）He used to be a *reporter* for a weekly magazine.

ki「sha[2] きしゃ（汽車）*n.* train: ★ Originally referred to a long-distance train pulled by a steam locomotive.

kisha *de ryokoo suru*（汽車で旅行する）travel by *train.*《⇨ ressha; densha》

ki「sha-ka」iken きしゃかいけん（記者会見）*n.* press conference: kisha-kaiken *o okonau*（記者会見を行う）hold a *press conference.*

ki「shi[1] きし（岸）*n.* bank; shore; coast:

Watashi-tachi wa mizuumi no kishi *ni sotte aruita.*（私たちは湖の岸に沿って歩いた）We walked along the *shore* of the lake.

ki「shitsu きしつ（気質）*n.* disposition; temper; nature:

Kare wa kimuzukashii [yasashii] kishitsu *no otoko da.*（彼は気難しい[やさしい]気質の男だ）He is a man of grumpy [affectionate] *disposition*.

ki「shoo[1] きしょう（気性）*n.* temper; disposition; nature:
Kare wa kishoo *ga hageshii.* (彼は気性が激しい) He has a fiery *temper*. / *Kanojo no* kishoo *wa yoku wakatte imasu.* (彼女の気性はよくわかっています) I know her *nature* well. / *Ishiyama-sañ wa sappari shita* kishoo *da.* (石山さんはさっぱりした気性だ) Mr. Ishiyama has an open *disposition*. 《⇨ kishitsu》

ki「shoo[2] きしょう（気象）*n.* weather conditions:
kishoo *no kañsoku* (気象の観測) the observation of *weather conditions* / kishoo-*eesee* (気象衛星) a *weather* satellite / kishoo-*dai* (気象台) a *weather* station.

ki「shoo[3] きしょう（起床）*n.* getting up; rising:
kishoo-*jikañ* (起床時間) the hour of *rising*.
kishoo suru (〜する) *vi.* rise from one's bed: *Watashi-tachi wa roku-ji ni* kishoo *shite, heya o sooji shita.* (私たちは6時に起床して、部屋を掃除した) We *got up* at six and cleaned our room. 《⇨ okiru》

Ki「sho」o-choo きしょうちょう（気象庁）*n.* Meteorological Agency:
Kishoo-choo *chookañ* (気象庁長官) the Director General of the *Meteorological Agency*.
《⇨ choo[4] (table)》

ki「so[1] きそ（基礎）*n.* foundation; basis; base; basics:
Nanigoto mo kiso *ga taisetsu desu.* (何事も基礎が大切です) In everything, the *basics* are important. / *Kare no riroñ wa* kiso *ga shikkari shite iru.* (彼の理論は基礎がしっかりしている) His theory has a solid *basis*. / *Nihoñgo o* kiso *kara beñkyoo shitai.* (日本語を基礎から勉強したい) I want to study Japanese from the *basics*. / kiso-*kooji* (基礎工事) the *foundation* work of a building. 《⇨ kihoñ》

ki「so」ku きそく（規則）*n.* rule; regulations:
kisoku *o mamoru* [*yaburu*] (規則を守る[破る]) observe [break] a *rule* / kisoku *ni shitagau* [*ihañ suru*] (規則に従う[違反する]) follow [violate] the *rules* / *kootsuu-*kisoku (交通規則) traffic *rules* / *añzeñ-*kisoku (安全規則) safety *regulations*.
《⇨ ruuru》

ki「soku-teki きそくてき（規則的）*a.n.* (〜 na, ni) regular; systematic:
kisoku-teki *na seekatsu o suru* (規則的な生活をする) lead a *well-regulated* life / *Kai wa sañ-shuukañ oki ni* kisoku-teki *ni hirakaremasu.* (会は3週間おきに規則的に開かれます) The meetings are held *regularly* every three weeks.

ki「so-teki きそてき（基礎的）*a.n.* (〜 na, ni) fundamental; basic; elementary:
kiso-teki *na buñpoo* (基礎的な文法) *elementary* grammar.

ki「ssa」teñ きっさてん（喫茶店）*n.* coffeehouse; coffee shop; tearoom. ★ Serves coffee, black tea (not green tea), and other refreshments.

ki「su」u きすう（奇数）*n.* odd number. 《↔ guusuu》

ki「ta きた（北）*n.* north; (〜 ni/e) northward:
Kono heya wa kita-*muki da kara fuyu wa samui.* (この部屋は北向きだから冬は寒い) This room is *north* facing, so in winter it is cold. / *Koobe no machi wa* kita *ni yama, minami ni umi ga aru.* (神戸の町は北に山、南に海がある) The town of Kobe has mountains to the *north* and the sea to the south. / *Saikaihatsu wa shi no* kita *kara hajimatta.* (再開発は市の北から始まった) Redevelopment has started from the *north* of the city. 《↔ minami》

Ki⌐ta-choose⌐n きたちょうせん (北朝鮮) *n.* North Korea. ★ Officially, '*Chooseñ Miñshushugi Jiñmiñ Kyoowakoku*' (朝鮮民主主義人民共和国) the Democratic People's Republic of Korea. 《⇨ Chooseñ; Kañkoku》

ki⌐tae⌐·ru きたえる (鍛える) *vt.* (ki-tae-te [V]) train; build up; strengthen:
Wakai uchi ni karada o kitae nasai. (若いうちに体を鍛えなさい) *Harden* your body while young. / *Oriñpikku ni wa* kitaerareta señshu-tachi ga atsumaru. (オリンピックには鍛えられた選手たちが集まる) In the Olympics, *well-trained* athletes get together.

ki⌐tai¹ きたい (期待) *n.* expectation; anticipation; hope:
kitai o idaku (期待を抱く) cherish a *hope* / kitai o uragiru (期待を裏切る) run contrary to one's *expectations*; *let down a person* / kitai ni hañsuru (期待に反する) be contrary to one's *expectations* / *Kare wa musuko ni* kitai o kakete iru. (彼は息子に期待をかけている) He places his *hopes* on his son. / *Zañneñnagara, go-*kitai *ni wa soemaseñ.* (残念ながら、ご期待には添えません) Unfortunately, we cannot meet your *expectations*. / kitai-hazure (期待外れ) a *disappointment*.
kitai suru (〜する) *vt.* count on; expect; anticipate; hope for:
Koñdo no kachoo ni wa kitai shite imasu. (今度の課長には期待しています) I *am expecting* much from the new section chief. / *Hito no zeñi o* kitai suru *hoo ga machigatte iru.* (人の善意を期待するほうが間違っている) It is a mistake to *count on* other people's good intentions.

ki⌐tai² きたい (気体) *n.* gas. 《⇨ ekitai; kotai》

ki⌐taku きたく (帰宅) *n.* returning home:

Kare wa kitaku no tochuu de jiko ni atta. (彼は帰宅の途中で事故にあった) He had an accident *on his way home.*
kitaku suru (〜する) *vi.* return home: *Shujiñ wa mada* kitaku shite orimaseñ. (主人はまだ帰宅しておりません) My husband *has not yet come back home.* 《⇨ kaeru¹》

ki⌐tana⌐·i きたない (汚い) *a.* (-ku)
1 dirty; filthy; foul:
kitanai zuboñ (汚いズボン) *dirty* trousers / Kitanai *te o koko de arai nasai.* (汚い手をここで洗いなさい) Wash your *dirty* hands here. / *Heya no kuuki ga* kitanaku *natte kita.* (部屋の空気が汚くなってきた) The air in the room has become *foul.* 《↔ kiree》
2 mean; low; dirty:
kitanai shudañ o tsukau (汚い手段を使う) use *dirty* tricks / *Ano hito wa o-kane ni* kitanai. (あの人はお金に汚い) He is *mean* with his money.
3 indecent; filthy; nasty:
kitanai kotoba (汚い言葉) *indecent* words

ki⌐tee きてい (規定) *n.* rule; regulation; stipulation:
kitee o tsukuru (規定を作る) make a *regulation* / kitee ni shitagau (規定に従う) follow the *regulations* / kitee ni hañsuru (規定に反する) be against the *rules* / *Kono daigaku wa ryuugakusee no tame ni tokubetsu na* kitee o mookete imasu. (この大学は留学生のために特別な規定を設けています) This university has laid down special *provisions* for overseas students. / kitee-*shumoku* (規定種目) *compulsory* exercises (in gymnastics).
kitee suru (〜する) *vt.* prescribe; provide for: *Sono keñ ni tsuite wa keñchiku-hoo de* kitee sarete imasu. (その件については建築法で規定されています) As far as that matter

is concerned, it *is provided for* in the building code.

ki「teñ きてん (起点) *n.* starting point:
Mukashi wa Tookaidoo no kiteñ *wa Nihoñbashi datta.* (昔は東海道の起点は日本橋だった) Years ago, the *starting point* of the Tokaido highway was at Nihonbashi.

ki「tsu·i きつい *a.* (-ku) **1** tight:
Kono sukaato wa sukoshi kitsui. (このスカートは少しきつい) This skirt is a bit *tight.* / *Kare wa sono tsu-tsumi o* kitsuku *shibatta.* (彼はその包みをきつく縛った) He tied up the parcel *tightly.* (↔ yurui)
2 hard; severe:
kitsui *shigoto* (きつい仕事) a *hard* job / kitsui *nittee* (きつい日程) a *demanding* schedule / *Kono-goro no samusa wa* kitsui. (この頃の寒さはきつい) The recent cold weather has been *severe.*
3 stern; strong-minded:
kitsui *seekaku* (きつい性格) a *stern* and *strong-minded* personality.

ki「tsune きつね (狐) *n.* fox.
★ In Japan, tradition says that foxes and racoon dogs bewitch people. (⇨ bakasu; tanuki)

ki「tte きって (切手) *n.* postage stamp:
Fuutoo ni kitte *o haru no o wasureta.* (封筒に切手を貼るのを忘れた) I forgot to put a *stamp* on the envelope. / *Rokujuuni-eñ* kitte *o go-mai kudasai.* (62円切手を5枚下さ

KITTE

い) Please give me five 62-yen *stamps.* / *Kono tegami ni wa iku-ra no* kitte *o hareba ii no desu ka?* (この手紙にはいくらの切手を貼ればいいのですか) How much *postage* should I put on for this letter?

ki「tto きっと *adv.* surely; without fail; undoubtedly:
Kare wa kitto *kimasu.* (彼はきっと来ます) He will *certainly* come. / *Kanojo wa* kitto *katsu deshoo.* (彼女はきっと勝つでしょう) She will *undoubtedly* win. / *Kare wa* kitto *ima-goro wa Roñdoñ ni tsuita koro desu.* (彼はきっと今ごろはロンドンに着いたころです) He *must be* in London by now.

ki「wa」mete きわめて (極めて) *adv.* (*formal*) extremely; exceedingly:
Sono daigaku ni hairu no wa ki-wamete *muzukashii.* (その大学に入るのはきわめて難しい) It is *extremely* difficult to get into that university. / *Kore wa* kiwamete *juudai na moñdai desu.* (これはきわめて重大な問題です) This is an *exceedingly* serious problem.

ki「yo」·i きよい (清い) *a.* (-ku) (*literary*) clean; pure:
kiyoi *kokoro* (清い心) a *pure* heart / kiyoku *suñda nagare* (清く澄んだ流れ) a *crystal clear* stream. (⇨ kiyoraka)

ki「yoo きよう (器用) *a.n.* (～ na, ni) **1** skillful; handy; deft:
Kanojo wa tesaki ga kiyoo *da.* (彼女は手先が器用だ) She is *good* with her hands. / *Kare wa* kiyoo *ni sekeñ o watatta.* (彼は器用に世間を渡った) He *skillfully* made his way in the world. (↔ bukiyoo)
2 clever:
kiyoo *na hito* (器用な人) a *clever* person.

ki「yo」raka きよらか (清らか) *a.n.* (～ na, ni) (*literary*) pure; clear; noble:
kiyoraka *na hitomi* (清らかなひとみ)

bright, clear eyes. (⇨ kiyoi)

ki⌐zam·u きざむ (刻む) *vt.* (kizam·i-; kizam·a-; kizañ-de C)
1 mince; chop up:
tamanegi o kizamu (たまねぎを刻む) *chop up* an onion.
2 carve; engrave:
ishi ni shi o kizamu (石に詩を刻む) *engrave* a poem on a stone / *Kare wa ki o kizañde, niñgyoo o tsukutta.* (彼は木を刻んで、人形を作った) He made a doll by *carving* wood.

ki⌐zetsu きぜつ (気絶) *n.* fainting; faint; swoon.
kizetsu suru (～する) *vi.* faint:
Kanojo wa kizetsu shite taoreta. (彼女は気絶して倒れた) She fell *in a faint*.

ki⌐zoku きぞく (貴族) *n.* aristocracy; noble; nobleman; peer; peeress.

ki⌐zu¹ きず (傷) *n.* injury; wound; hurt; cut:
kizu o ou (傷を負う) *get injured [wounded]* / Kizu *ga mada itai.* (傷がまだ痛い) The *wound* still hurts me. / Kizu *no teate o shite moratta.* (傷の手当てをしてもらった) I had my *injury* treated.

ki⌐zu² きず (疵) *n.* crack; flaw; bruise; defect:
hooseki no kizu (宝石のきず) *flaws* in a jewel / *Kono koppu ni wa chiisa-na kizu ga aru.* (このコップには小さなきずがある) There is a small *crack* in this glass. / *Kono riñgo ni wa kizu ga aru.* (このりんごにはきずがある) This apple has *bruises*.
kizu o tsukeru (～をつける) damage; ruin; spoil: *Kare no okonai wa kaisha no hyoobañ ni kizu o tsuketa.* (彼の行いは会社の評判にきずをつけた) His behavior *damaged* the reputation of his company.

ki⌐zu⌐kai きづかい (気遣い) *n.* worry; fear:
O-kizukai wa muyoo desu. (お気遣いは無用です) You needn't *worry*

about me. / *Kare ga shippai suru kizukai wa arimaseñ.* (彼が失敗する気遣いはありません) There is no *fear* of his failing. (⇨ kizukau)

ki⌐zuka⌐u きづかう (気遣う) *vt.* (kizuka·i-; kizukaw·a-; kizukatte C) be anxious about; worry about:
Kazoku-tachi wa soonañsha no añpi o kizukatte iru. (家族たちは遭難者の安否を気づかっている) The families *are anxious* about the safety of those involved in the disaster. / *Kanojo wa taniñ no koto o amari kizukawanai.* (彼女は他人のことをあまり気づかわない) She *does not pay* much *attention* to others. (⇨ kizukai)

ki⌐zu⌐k·u¹ きづく (気付く) *vi.* (kizuk·i-; kizuk·a-; kizu·i-te C) become aware; notice; find out:
kikeñ ni kizuku (危険に気づく) *become aware* of danger / *Kare wa buñshoo no ayamari ni kizuita.* (彼は文章の誤りに気づいた) He *noticed* a mistake in the sentence. / *Watashi wa tori ga kago kara nigeta no ni kizukanakatta.* (私は鳥がかごから逃げたのに気づかなかった) I *did not notice* that the bird had escaped from the cage. / *Keesatsu wa kare-ra no keekaku ni kizuita.* (警察は彼らの計画に気づいた) The police *found out* about their plan.

ki⌐zu⌐k·u² きづく (築く) *vt.* (kizuk·i-; kizuk·a-; kizu·i-te C) build; construct; erect:
shiro o kizuku (城を築く) *build* a castle / *Kare wa ooki-na zaisañ o kizuita.* (彼は大きな財産を築いた) He *built up* a large fortune.

ki⌐zuna きずな (絆) *n.* bond; ties:
Futari wa tsuyoi yuujoo no kizuna de musubarete ita. (二人は強い友情のきずなで結ばれていた) The two of them were bonded together by firm *ties* of friendship.

ki⌐zutsuke⌐·ru きずつける (傷付け

る) *vt.* (-tsuke-te V) wound;
injure; hurt (physically or mentally):
Kare wa koroñde, ashi o kizutsuketa. (彼は転んで, 足を傷つけた) He
fell over and *injured* his foot. /
*Kare no kotoba wa kanojo no ko-
koro o* kizutsuketa. (彼の言葉は彼女
の心を傷つけた) His words *cut* her
to the quick. / *Neko ga doa o* kizu-
tsukete iru. (猫がドアを傷つけている)
The cat *is scratching* at the door.
《⇨ kizutsuku》

ki「zutsu」k·u きずつく (傷付く) *vi.*
(-tsuk·i-; -tsuk·a-; -tsu·i-te C)
be [get] injured; be [get] hurt
(usually mentally):
*Sono uwasa de kanojo no kokoro
wa* kizutsuita. (その噂で彼女の心は傷
ついた) She *was deeply hurt* by the
rumor. 《⇨ kizutsukeru》

kke っけ *p.* (*informal*) [follows
the past of a verb, adjective or
the copula]
1 used to: ★ Used to recall or
reflect on the past.
*Kodomo no koro wa koko de yoku
asoñda* kke. (子どものころはここでよく
遊んだっけ) I *used to* play a lot here
when I was a child. / *Mukashi
wa kono heñ mo midori ga ookatta* kke. (昔はこの辺も緑が多かったっ
け) In the old days, there *used to*
be a lot of trees in this area.
★Sometimes used with other
particles. *e.g. Yoku issho ni beñkyoo shita* kke *ne.* (よく一緒に勉強し
たっけね) We often *used to* study
together, didn't we? 《⇨ ne³》
2 (used when trying to recall
something or when encouraging
someone to give an answer):
Ee to, ano hito wa dare datta kke?
(ええと, あの人はだれだったっけ) Let me
see. Who *was* that man? / *Tanaka-sañ no tañjoobi wa itsu datta*
kke? (田中さんの誕生日はいつだったっ
け) Now, when *was* Miss Tana-

ka's birthday? / *Kono hoñ wa
doko de katta* kke? (この本はどこで買
ったっけ) Where *was* it that I bought this book?

ko こ (子) *n.* **1** child; son;
daughter: ★ Usually used with
a modifier.
otoko-no-ko (男の子) a *boy* / oñna-
no-ko (女の子) a *girl* / *Ano* ko *o
shitte imasu ka?* (あの子を知っていま
すか) Do you know that *child*? /
Uchi no ko *wa roku-sai desu.* (うち
の子は6歳です) Our *son* [*daughter*]
is six years old. / *O-*ko *sañ wa
nañ-niñ desu ka?* (お子さんは何人です
か) How many *children* do you
have? 《↔ oya》《⇨ kodomo》
2 (of animals) the young:
inu no ko (犬の子) a *puppy* / neko
no ko (猫の子) a *kitten.* 《↔ oya》

ko-¹ こ (小) *pref.* small; little:
ko-*tori* (小鳥) a *little* bird / ko-
zeni (小銭) *small* change / ko-
same (小雨) *light* rain / ko-*goe* (小
声) a *low* voice / ko-michi (小道) a
path

ko¹⁻² こ (故) *pref.* the late; the
deceased:
ko-*Yamada-shi* (故山田氏) *the late*
Mr. Yamada.

-ko¹ こ (個) *suf.* piece; item:
★ Counter for small objects.
tamago sañ-ko (卵3個) *three eggs*
/ *sekkeñ* go-ko (石けん5個) *five
cakes* of soap / *Keeki o* rok-ko
katta. (ケーキを6個買った) I bought
six *pieces* of cake.

-ko² こ (戸) *suf.* house:
nijuk-ko *no ie* (20戸の家) twenty
houses.

-ko³ こ (粉) *suf.* powder; flour:
*fukurashi-*ko (ふくらし粉) baking
powder / *karee-*ko (カレー粉) curry
powder / *komugi-*ko (小麦粉)
wheat *flour.*

-ko⁴ こ (湖) *suf.* lake:
*Kawaguchi-*ko (河口湖) *Lake*
Kawaguchi / *Yamanaka-*ko (山中

湖) *Lake* Yamanaka.

ko˺ara コアラ *n.* koala.

ko˹ba˺m·u こばむ (拒む) *vt.* (kobam·i-; kobam·a-; kobañ-de C) refuse (a demand, request); decline:
Kare wa wareware no yookyuu o kobañda. (彼はわれわれの要求を拒んだ) He *refused* our demands. / *Watashi-tachi wa nyuujoo o* kobamareta. (私たちは入場を拒まれた) We *were refused* admission.

ko˹bore˺·ru こぼれる (零れる) *vi.* (kobore-te V) (of fluid, grains, etc.) fall; slop; spill:
Kanojo no me kara namida ga koboreta. (彼女の目から涙がこぼれた) Tears *fell* from her eyes. / *Baketsu kara mizu ga* koboreta. (バケツから水がこぼれた) Water *slopped* out of the bucket. (⇨ kobosu)

ko˹bo˺s·u こぼす (零す) *vt.* (kobosh·i-; kobos·a-; kobosh·i-te C)
1 spill (fluid, grains, etc.); shed; drop:
yuka ni mizu o kobosu (床に水をこぼす) *spill* water on the floor / *namida o* kobosu (涙をこぼす) *shed* tears / *kometsubu o* kobosu (米粒をこぼす) *drop* grains of rice. (⇨ koboreru)
2 complain; grumble:
Kanojo wa itsu-mo kodomo no koto o koboshite iru. (彼女はいつも子どものことをこぼしている) She *is* always *grumbling* about her children.

ko˹chira こちら *n.* **1** this place; this way; here: ★ Refers to a direction or a place close to the speaker. More polite than '*koko*' and '*kotchi*.'
Doozo kochira *e irasshite kudasai*. (どうぞこちらへいらっしてください) Please come *over here*. / *Kochira ga o-tearai desu*. (こちらがお手洗いです) *This* is the bathroom. / *Shashiñ o* torimasu. Kochira *o muite, hai* waratte. (写真を撮ります. こちらを向いて, はい笑って) I am going to take your picture. Please turn *this way*. Okay smile. (⇨ mukoo˺)
2 this thing; this person:
★ More polite than '*kore*.'
Kochira *wa hoñjitsu no tokubetsu ryoori desu*. (こちらは本日の特別料理です) *This* is today's special dish. / *"Dochira ni shimasu ka?" "Ko*chira *ni shimasu."* (「どちらにしますか」「こちらにします」) "Which would you like?" "I'll take *this*." / Kochira *ga Tamura-sañ desu*. (こちらが田村さんです) *This* is Mr. Tamura.
3 I; we:
Ato de kochira *kara moo ichido o-deñwa itashimasu*. (あとでこちらからもう一度お電話いたします) *I* will call you back again later. / Kochira *to shite wa sono yookyuu ni oojiru wake ni wa ikimaseñ*. (こちらとしてはその要求に応じるわけにはいきません) For *our part*, we are not really in a position to meet those demands. (⇨ achira; dochira; sochira)

ko˹choo こちょう (誇張) *n.* exaggeration; overstatement:
Ano hito no hanashi ni wa kochoo *ga aru*. (あの人の話には誇張がある) There is *exaggeration* in what he says. / *Sore wa* kochoo *desu*. (それは誇張です) That is an *overstatement*.
kochoo suru (～する) *vt.* exaggerate; overstate: *Kare wa jibuñ no taikeñ o* kochoo shite *hanashita*. (彼は自分の体験を誇張して話した) He related his experiences *with exaggeration*.

ko˺dai こだい (古代) *n.* ancient times; remote ages:
kodai *kara geñdai made o kabaa shita rekishi hyakka-jiteñ* (古代から現代までをカバーした歴史百科事典) an encyclopedia of history covering the period from *ancient times* to

the present day / kodai-*buñmee*
(古代文明) *ancient* civilization.
《⇨ jidai (table)》

ko「doku こどく (孤独) *n.* loneliness; solitude:
kodoku *ni taeru* (孤独に耐える)
endure *loneliness*.
— *a.n.* (～ na, ni) lonely; solitary:
kodoku *na seekatsu o suru* (孤独な生活をする) lead a *solitary* life /
Watashi wa kodoku *da.* (私は孤独だ) I am *lonely*.

ko「domo こども (子供) *n.* child;
boy; girl:
Kono hoñ wa kodomo *ni mo otona
ni mo omoshiroi.* (この本は子どもにも大人にもおもしろい) This book is
interesting for both *children* and
adults. / Kodomo *no koro yoku
koko de asobimashita.* (子どものころよくここで遊びました) I used to play
here when I was a *child*. / Kodomo-*tachi wa miñna geñki desu.*
(子どもたちはみんな元気です) The *children* are all well. 《↔ otona》《⇨ ko》

Ko「domo-no-hi「」 (子供の日) *n.*
Children's Day (May 5). 《⇨ shukujitsu (table)》

ko「e こえ (声) *n.* **1** human voice;
cry:
koe *o ageru* [*otosu*] (声を上げる[落とす]) raise [lower] one's *voice* / koe
o dashite, hoñ o yomu (声を出して、本を読む) read a book *aloud* / *ooki-
na* koe *de hanasu* (大きな声で話す)
speak in a loud *voice* / *Sono ka-
shu wa ii* koe *o shite iru.* (その歌手はいい声をしている) The singer has a
sweet *voice*. / *Akañboo no naku*
koe *ga kikoeru.* (赤ん坊の泣く声が聞こえる) I hear a baby *crying*.
2 sound; note; song:
sora de saezuru tori no koe (空でさえずる鳥の声) the *sound* of birds
chirping in the sky / *mushi no*
koe *o kiku* (虫の声を聞く) listen to
the *singing* of insects.

3 opinion; view:
Seefu wa kokumiñ no koe *ni mimi
o katamukeru beki da.* (政府は国民の声に耳を傾けるべきだ) The government should pay attention to the
opinions of the people.

ko「e·ru「1」 こえる (越える) *vi.* (koe-te
Ⅴ) go beyond; go over:
yama o koeru (山を越える) *go over* a
mountain / *kawa o* koeru (川を越える) *cross* a river.

ko「e·ru「2」 こえる (超える) *vi.* (koe-te
Ⅴ) **1** exceed; be more than:
Kanojo wa sañjuu o koete iru. (彼女は30を超えている) She *is more
than* thirty. / *Higai wa watashi-
tachi no soozoo o* koete ita. (被害は私たちの想像を超えていた) The damage was *beyond* our imagination.
《⇨ chooka》
2 excel; be above:
Suugaku de wa kare o koeru
mono wa imaseñ. (数学では彼を超える者はいません) There is nobody
who *excels* him in mathematics.

ko「e「」·ru「3」 こえる (肥える) *vi.* (koe-te
Ⅴ) **1** be fertile:
Kono tochi wa koete iru. (この土地は肥えている) This soil *is fertile*.
2 grow fat; put on flesh:
Buta ga koete kita. (豚が肥えてきた)
The pigs *have fattened up*.
...ga koete iru (...が肥えている)
have a delicate ...: me ga koete
iru (目が肥えている) *have an eye for*
(beauty) / mimi [shita] ga koete
iru (耳[舌]が肥えている) *have a sensitive ear* [*delicate palate*].

ko「fuñ こふん (古墳) *n.* old
mound; ancient tomb. 《⇨ kofuñ-
jidai》

Ko「fuñ-ji「」dai こふんじだい (古墳時代) *n.* Kofun Period (ca. A.D. 300
to 710). 《⇨ jidai (table)》

ko「ga「s·u こがす (焦がす) *vt.* (ko-
gash·i-; kogas·a-; kogash·i-te
Ⓒ) burn; singe; scorch:
Kanojo wa pañ o kuroku koga-

shite shimatta. (彼女はパンを黒く焦がしてしまった) She *burned* the toast black. / *Airoñ de shatsu o* kogashite shimatta. (アイロンでシャツを焦がしてしまった) I *scorched* my shirt with the iron. 《⇨ kogeru》

ko⌐gata こがた (小型) *n.* small size; pocket size:
kogata *no kuruma* (小型の車) a *small* car / kogata *no rajio* (小型のラジオ) a *portable* radio / kogata *no kamera* (小型のカメラ) a *pocket* camera. 《⇨ oogata; chuugata》

ko⌐ge⌐·ru こげる (焦げる) *vi.* (ko-ge-te Ⅴ) burn; scorch:
Mochi ga makkuro ni kogete shimatta. (餅が真っ黒に焦げてしまった) The rice cake *has been burned* black. 《⇨ kogasu》

ko⌐gi⌐tte こぎって (小切手) *n.* check; cheque:
Ichimañ-eñ no kogitte *o furidashita.* (一万円の小切手を振り出した) I drew a *check* for 10,000 yen. / *Kogitte de haratte mo ii desu ka?* (小切手で払ってもいいですか) Can I pay by *check?* / *Kono* kogitte *ni uragaki o shite kudasai.* (この小切手に裏書をしてください) Please endorse this *check.* / *Kono* kogitte *o geñkiñ ni shitai ñ desu ga.* (この小切手を現金にしたいんですが) I'd like to cash this *check.*

ko⌐goe こごえ (小声) *n.* low voice; whisper:
Futari wa nani-ka kogoe *de hanashite ita.* (二人は何か小声で話していた) The two of them were talking about something in a *low voice.* 《↔ oogoe》

ko⌐goe·ru こごえる (凍える) *vi.* (ko-goe-te Ⅴ) freeze; be frozen:
Samukute, te ga kogoeta. (寒くて, 手が凍えた) My hands *were numb* with the cold.

ko⌐g·u こぐ (漕ぐ) *vt.* (kog·i-; ko-g·a-; ko-i-de Ⓒ) **1** row; paddle:
Watashi-tachi wa mizuumi de

booto *o* koida. (私たちは湖でボートをこいだ) We *rowed* a boat on the lake. **2** pedal; swing:
jiteñsha o kogu (自転車をこぐ) *pedal* a bicycle / *burañko o* kogu (ぶらんこをこぐ) *swing* on a swing.

ko⌐·i¹ こい (濃い) *a.* (-ku) **1** (of color) dark; deep:
koi *iro* (濃い色) a *dark* color / koi *aka* (濃い赤) *deep* red. 《↔ usui》
2 (of taste, density, etc.) thick; strong; dense:
koi *suupu* (濃いスープ) *thick* soup / *Ani wa hige ga* koi. (兄はひげが濃い) My brother has a *thick* beard. / *Kiri ga* koku *natte kita.* (霧が濃くなってきた) The fog has *closed in.* / *O-cha o* koku *irete kudasai.* (お茶を濃く入れてください) Please make the tea *strong.* 《↔ usui》
3 (of degree) strong:
Kare ga sore o shita utagai ga koi. (彼がそれをした疑いが濃い) The suspicion he did that is *strong.*

ko⌐i² こい (恋) *n.* love:
koi *ni ochiru* (恋に落ちる) *fall in love* / koi *ni nayamu* (恋に悩む) *be lovesick* / koi *o uchiakeru* (恋を打ち明ける) confess one's *love* / *Kare wa kanojo ni* koi *o shite ita.* (彼は彼女に恋をしていた) He was in *love* with her. 《⇨ ai》

ko⌐i³ こい (故意) *n.* intention; deliberation; purpose:
Watashi wa koi *ni okureta wake de wa arimaseñ.* (私は故意に遅れたわけではありません) I did not come late *intentionally.* 《⇨ waza-to》

ko⌐i⁴ こい (鯉) *n.* carp. ★ In Japan, the carp is prized for its strength because it fights its way up swift streams. 《⇨ koinobori》

ko⌐ibito こいびと (恋人) *n.* boyfriend; girlfriend; love: ★ Refers to a steady male or female companion.
Ano futari wa koibito *dooshi da.* (あの二人は恋人同士だ) They *are in*

love with each other. ((⇨ aijiñ))

ko⌐ino⌐bori こいのぼり（鯉のぼり）*n.* carp streamer. ★ Carp-shaped streamers traditionally flown on Children's Day (May 5).

KOINOBORI

ko⌐ishi こいし（小石）*n.* small stone [rock]. ((⇨ ishi¹))

ko⌐ishi⌐·i こいしい（恋しい）*a.* (-ku) miss; long for; beloved: koishii *hito* (恋しい人) a *beloved* person / *Haha ga* koishii. (母が恋しい) My heart *aches* for my mother. / *Kokyoo ga* koishiku *natte kita.* (故郷が恋しくなってきた) I have come to *long for* my hometown.

ko⌐is·u·ru こいする（恋する）*vt.* (ko-ish·i-; koish·i-; koish·i-te ①) be in love: *Kare wa kanojo ni* koishite iru. (彼は彼女に恋している) He *is in love* with her.

ko⌐ji こじ（孤児）*n.* orphan.

ko⌐jiñ¹ こじん（個人）*n.* **1** individual: kojiñ *no jiyuu* [*keñri*] (個人の自由 [権利]) the freedom [rights] of the *individual*. **2** each person: *Mochimono wa* kojiñ kojiñ *de chuui shite kudasai.* (持ち物は個人個人で注意してください) *Each person* please take care of his or her possessions. / kojiñ-*kyooju* (個人教授) a *private* lesson / kojiñ-*takushii* (個人タクシー) a *privately-owned* taxi.

ko⌐jiñ² こじん（故人）*n.* the deceased: *Takahashi-sañ wa señgetsu* kojiñ *to nararemashita.* (高橋さんは先月故人となられました) Mr. Takahashi *passed away* last month.

ko⌐jiñ-teki こじんてき（個人的）*a.n.* (~ na, ni) personal; private: *Kore wa* kojiñ-teki *na moñdai desu.* (これは個人的な問題です) This is a *personal* matter. / *Kare wa* kojiñ-teki *na riyuu de tsutome o yamemashita.* (彼は個人的な理由で勤めをやめました) He quit his job for *private* reasons. / *Ano hito wa* kojiñ-teki *ni wa shirimaseñ.* (あの人は個人的には知りません) I do not know him *personally.* / *Watashi wa* kojiñ-teki *ni kaisha no hooshiñ ni hañtai desu.* (私は個人的に会社の方針に反対です) *For my part,* I am against the company's policy.

ko⌐ke こけ（苔）*n.* moss.

ko⌐kka¹ こっか（国家）*n.* nation; state; country: *Afurika ni atarashii* kokka *ga tañjoo shita.* (アフリカに新しい国家が誕生した) A new *nation* was established in Africa. / kokka-*koomuiñ* (国家公務員) a *national* government worker [official] / kokka-*shikeñ* (国家試験) a *state* [*national*] examination.

ko⌐kka² こっか（国歌）*n.* national anthem: *Kaikaishiki de* kokka *ga eñsoo sareta.* (開会式で国歌が演奏された) The *national anthem* was played at the opening ceremony.

ko⌐kka³ こっか（国花）*n.* national flower: *Sakura wa Nihoñ no* kokka *desu.* (桜は日本の国花です) The cherry is the *national flower* of Japan.

ko⸢kkai こっかい（国会）*n.* national assembly; legislature of a nation; the Diet:

> ━━━ (CULTURE) ━━━
> The Japanese Diet is made up of the House of Representatives (*Shuugiiñ*) and the House of Councilors (*Sañgiiñ*).

kokkai *o shooshuu* [*kaisañ*] *suru* （国会を招集[解散]する）convene [dissolve] *the Diet* / Kokkai *wa ima kaikai*[*heekai*]-*chuu desu.*（国会は今開会[閉会]中です）*The Diet* is now in session [recess]. / kokkai-*giiñ*（国会議員）a member of *the Diet* / kokkai-*gijidoo*（国会議事堂）the *Diet* Building.
《⇨ Shuugiiñ; Sañgiiñ》

KOKKAI-GIJIDOO

ko⸢kkee こっけい（滑稽）*a.n.* (~ na, ni) funny; humorous; comical; ridiculous:
Kare wa kokkee *na koto o itte miñna o warawaseta.*（彼は滑稽なことを言ってみんなを笑わせた）He made everyone laugh by saying something *foolishly comical.* / *Kare no shita koto ga* kokkee *ni mieta.*（彼のしたことが滑稽に見えた）His actions looked *ridiculously funny.* / *Aitsu ga ĝiiñ ni naritai nañte* kokkee *da.*（あいつが議員になりたいなんて滑稽だ）His desire to become a member of the Diet is *laughable.*

ko⸢kki こっき（国旗）*n.* national flag:
kokki *o keeyoo suru*（国旗を掲揚する）hoist a *national flag.*

ko⸢kkoo こっこう（国交）*n.* diplomatic relations; national friendship:
kokkoo *o musubu* [*juritsu suru*]（国交を結ぶ[樹立する]）establish *diplomatic relations* / kokkoo *o tatsu* [*dañzetsu suru*]（国交を断つ[断絶する]）break off *diplomatic relations* / kokkoo *o seejooka suru*（国交を正常化する）normalize *diplomatic relations* / *Nihoñ wa sono kuni to* kokkoo *ga nai.*（日本はその国と国交がない）Japan has no *diplomatic relations* with that country.

ko⸢kku⸥ri こっくり *adv.* (~ to) nod:
kokkuri o suru（こっくりをする）*nod one's head* (in agreement); *fall asleep* (unintentionally) / *Kanojo wa* kokkuri to unazuita.（彼女はこっくりとうなずいた）She *nodded in assent.*

ko⸢kkyoo こっきょう（国境）*n.* national border; frontier of a country:
kokkyoo *o mamoru*（国境を守る）guard the *border* / kokkyoo *o koeru*（国境を越える）cross the *frontier.*

ko⸢ko[1] ここ（此処）*n.* **1** here; this place: ★ Refers to a place close to the speaker.
Koko *kara eki made dono kurai arimasu ka?*（ここから駅までどのくらいありますか）How far is it from *here* to the station? / *"Boku no megane wa doko ni aru ka shitte imasu ka?" "*Koko *ni arimasu yo."*（「ぼくの眼鏡はどこにあるか知っていますか」「ここにありますよ」）"Do you know where my glasses are?" "They're *here.*" / *Sono kabañ wa* koko *ni oki nasai.*（そのかばんはここに置きなさい）Please put that bag *here.*
2 here; this place: ★ Used when the speaker indicates a location by way of explanation, etc.
Kono chizu no koko *ga watashi-*

tachi no machi desu.(この地図のここ
が私たちの町です) *This part* of the
map is our town. / *Zumeñ o gorañ kudasai.* Koko ga daidokoro
desu.(図面をご覧ください. ここが台所
です) Please look at the plan. *Here*
is the kitchen.

3 this: ★ Refers to something
the speaker has just mentioned
or intends to mention.
Kyoo no koogi wa koko *made
desu.*(きょうの講義はここまでです)
This concludes my lecture for
today. / *Koko ga juuyoo desu
kara yoku kiite kudasai.*(ここが重
要ですからよく聞いてください) *What I
am going to say* is very important,
so please listen carefully.

4 next; past: ★ Refers to a
period of time.
Kare wa koko *shibaraku byooki
deshita.*(彼はここしばらく病気でした)
He has been sick for some time
past. / *Kooshoo wa* koko *ni, sañ-
nichi de matomaru deshoo.*(交渉は
ここ 2, 3 日でまとまるでしょう) The
negotiations should be concluded in the *next* few days.

5 so far: ★ Refers to a time in
the present.
Koko *made wa subete umaku ikimashita.*(ここまではすべてうまくいきまし
た) *So far* everything has gone
well. 《⇨ asoko; doko; soko[1]》

ko￢ko[2] ここ(個々) *n.* (*formal*) individual; each:
Sore wa koko *no hito no sekiniñ
desu.*(それは個々の人の責任です)
Each individual person is responsible for it. / *Sono moñdai wa ato
de* koko *ni atsukaimasu.*(その問題
は後で個々に扱います) We will deal
with each of the problems *separately* later.

ko￢kochi ここち(心地) *n.* feeling;
sensation:
Kono isu wa kokochi *ga yoi.*(この
いすは心地がよい) This chair *is com-*

fortable. / *Ureshikute yume no
yoo na* kokochi *datta.*(うれしくて夢
のような心地だった) I was so happy—
I *felt* as if I was in a dream. /
Hikooki ga yurete iru aida, ikita
kokochi *ga shinakatta.*(飛行機が揺
れている間, 生きた心地がしなかった) I
felt more dead than alive as the
plane was pitching and rolling. /
Kono kuruma wa nori-gokochi *ga
ii.*(この車は乗り心地がいい) This car
gives a smooth ride. ★ The initial /k/ changes to /g/ in compounds.

ko￢koku ここく(故国) *n.* homeland [country]:
Kare wa kokoku *o hanarete kara
go-neñ ni naru.*(彼は故国を離れてか
ら 5 年になる) He has been away
from *home* for five years.

ko￢konoka ここのか(九日) *n.*
nine days; the ninth day of the
month:
Shikeñ made ato kokonoka *desu.*
(試験まであと 9 日です) We have *nine
days* left before the exam. / *shi-
gatu* kokonoka (四月九日) April 9.
《⇨ tsuitachi (table)》

ko￢ko￢notsu ここのつ(九つ) *n.*
nine: ★ Used when counting.
Uchi no musuko wa kotoshi kokonotsu *desu.*(うちの息子は今年九つで
す) My son is *nine* years old this
year. / *Riñgo wa zeñbu de* kokonotsu *arimasu.*(りんごは全部で九つあり
ます) There are *nine* apples in all.
/ kokonotsu-me (九つ目) *the ninth.*
《⇨ ku[1]; kyuu[5]; kazu (table)》

ko￢ko￢ro こころ(心) *n.* heart;
mind; spirit:
Kanojo wa yasashii kokoro *no
mochinushi desu.*(彼女は優しい心の
持ち主です) She is a person with a
kind *heart.* / *Kanojo wa* kokoro *o
komete, sono tegami o kaita.*(彼女
は心を込めて, その手紙を書いた) She
put her *heart* into writing the letter. / *Mada* kokoro *o kimete ima-*

señ.(まだ心を決めていません) I have not made up my *mind* yet. / *Sono koto o* kokoro *ni tomete okimasu.* (そのことを心に留めておきます) I will keep it in *mind*.

kokoro kara (〜から) from the bottom of one's heart: Kokoro kara *o-ree mooshiagemasu.* (心から お礼申し上げます) I thank you *from the bottom of my heart.*

kokoro ni mo nai (〜にもない) something one does not mean: *Kare wa* kokoro ni mo nai *o-seji o itta.* (彼は心にもないお世辞を言った) He paid me *empty* compliments.

kokoro o irekaeru (〜を入れ替える) turn over a new leaf: *Kare wa* kokoro o irekaeta *yoo da.* (彼は心を入れ替えたようだ) He seems to *have reformed himself.*

kokoro o utsu (〜を打つ) strike home: *Sono eega wa kañkyaku no* kokoro o utta. (その映画は観客の心を打った) The film *struck home* to the audience.

ko⌐koroa⌐tari こころあたり(心当たり) *n.* idea; clue: *Kare ga doko ni iru ka* kokoro-atari *wa arimasu ka?* (彼がどこにいるか心当たりはありますか) Do you have any *idea* where he is? / *Dare ga soñna koto o shita no ka* kokoro-atari *wa arimaseñ.* (だれがそんなことをしたのか心当たりはありません) I don't have a *clue* who it was that did something like that.

ko⌐koroboso⌐·i こころぼそい(心細い) *a.* (-ku) lonely; helpless; uncertain: *Dare mo tasukete kurezu,* kokorobosoi *omoi o shita.* (だれも助けてくれず, 心細い思いをした) Nobody would give me a hand and I felt *helpless*. / Kokorobosoi *koto o iwanai de yo.* (心細いことを言わないでよ) Don't talk in such a *discouraging* way.

ko⌐koro⌐e こころえ(心得) *n.* knowledge; skill:

Kanojo wa ikebana no kokoroe *ga arimasu.*(彼女は生け花の心得があります) She has a good *knowledge* of flower arrangement. / *Kare wa e no* kokoroe *ga arimasu.* (彼は絵の心得があります) He has some *skill* at painting.

ko⌐koroe⌐·ru こころえる(心得る) *vt.* (kokoroe-te ⓥ) know; be aware: *Sono heñ no jijoo wa yoku* kokoroete imasu.*(その辺の事情はよく心得ています) I *am well aware* of that situation.

ko⌐korogake こころがけ(心掛け) *n.* care; prudence; intention: *Kare wa itsu-mo* kokorogake ga yoi.*(彼はいつも心がけがよい) He *is always prudent.* 《⇨ kokorogakeru》

ko⌐korogake⌐·ru こころがける(心掛ける) *vt.* (-gake-te ⓥ) try; keep in mind; do one's best: *Kare wa chikoku shinai yoo ni* kokorogakete iru.*(彼は遅刻しないように心がけている) He *is doing his best* not to be late. 《⇨ kokorogake》

ko⌐korogurushi⌐·i こころぐるしい (心苦しい) *a.* (-ku) feel sorry; painful: *Go-meewaku o kakeru no o* kokorogurushiku *omotte imasu.*(ご迷惑をかけるのを心苦しく思っています) I feel *sorry* to cause you trouble. 《⇨ sumanai》

ko⌐koromi こころみ(試み) *n.* trial; attempt; test: Kokoromi *ni sore o yatte mi nasai.* (試みにそれをやってみなさい) Give it a *try*. / *Kare-ra no* kokoromi *wa see-koo shita.* (彼らの試みは成功した) Their *attempt* succeeded. 《⇨ kokoromiru》

ko⌐koromi⌐·ru こころみる(試みる) *vt.* (-mi-te ⓥ) try; attempt; experiment: *Jookyaku wa hikooki no soto e deyoo to* kokoromita. (乗客は飛行

機の外へ出ようと試みた) The passengers *tried* to get out of the plane. 《⇨ kokoromi》

ko⌈koromochi こころもち（心持ち）*adv.* a little; a bit; slightly: *Kyoo wa* kokoromochi *atatakai.* （きょうは心持ち暖かい）It is *a bit* warm today. / *Kare wa itsu-mo yori,* kokoromochi *hayaku okita.* （彼はいつもより、心持ち早く起きた）He got up *a little* earlier than usual.

ko⌈koroyo¹·i こころよい（快い）*a.* (-ku) pleasant; agreeable; delightful: Kokoroyoi *kaze ga fuite kita.* （快い風が吹いてきた）A *pleasant* breeze came up. / *Suzuki-sañ wa sono shigoto o* kokoroyoku *hikiukete kureta.* （鈴木さんはその仕事を快く引き受けてくれた）Mr. Suzuki *cheerfully* accepted the task.

ko⌈korozashi こころざし（志）*n.* one's will; resolution; ambition: kokorozashi *o tateru* （志を立てる）make up *one's mind* / *Kare wa chichi-oya no* kokorozashi *ni shitagatte, isha ni natta.* （彼は父親の志に従って、医者になった）Following his father's *wishes,* he became a doctor. 《⇨ kokorozasu》

ko⌈koroza¹s·u こころざす（志す）*vt.* (-zash·i-; -zas·a-; -zash·i-te [C]) intend; aim; plan: *Kare wa sakka o* kokorozashite *iru.* （彼は作家を志している）He *has set his heart* on becoming a writer. 《⇨ kokorozashi》

ko⌈korozu⌈kai こころづかい（心遣い）*n.* thoughtfulness; consideration: *Seki o yuzutte kureta kare no* kokorozukai *ga ureshikatta.* （席を譲ってくれた彼の心づかいがうれしかった）I was grateful to him for *being kind enough* to give up his seat.

ko⌈korozuyo¹·i こころづよい（心強い）*a.* (-ku) reassuring: ★ Feeling secure because there is some-

one [something] to depend upon. *Anata ga ite kureru to* kokorozuyoi. （あなたがいてくれると心強い）Your presence *reassures* me.

ko⌈kubañ こくばん（黒板）*n.* blackboard: kokubañ *ni ji o kaku* （黒板に字を書く）write letters on the *blackboard* / kokubañ *o fuku* （黒板をふく）erase the *blackboard* / kokubañ-*fuki* （黒板ふき）a *blackboard* eraser.

ko⌈kuboo こくぼう（国防）*n.* national defense: kokuboo-*hi* （国防費）*national defense* expenditure.

ko⌈kudo こくど（国土）*n.* country; territory; land: *Nihoñ no* kokudo *no yoñ-buñ no sañ wa sañchi desu.* （日本の国土の4分の3は山地です）Three-fourths of Japan's *land area* is mountains.

Ko⌈kudo¹-choo こくどちょう（国土庁）*n.* National Land Agency: Kokudo-choo *chookañ* （国土庁長官）the Director General of the *National Land Agency.* 《⇨ choo⁴ (table)》

ko⌈ku¹gai こくがい（国外）*n.* outside the country; abroad; overseas: *Kare wa go-neñkañ* kokugai *de kurashita.* （彼は5年間国外で暮らした）He lived *abroad* for five years. / *Kare wa* kokugai *ni tsuihoo sareta.* （彼は国外に追放された）He *was deported.* （↔ kokunai） 《⇨ kaigai》

ko⌈kugo こくご（国語）*n.* 1 Japanese language (as an academic subject in Japan): *Kare wa* kokugo *no señsee desu.* （彼は国語の先生です）He is a teacher of *Japanese.* / kokugo-*jiteñ* （国語辞典）a *Japanese* dictionary. 《⇨ Nihoñgo》
2 language; one's mother tongue: *Kanojo wa sañ-ka-*kokugo *ga hanaseru.* （彼女は3か国語が話せる）She

can speak three *languages*.
《⇨ geñgo》

ko⌐kuhaku こくはく（告白）*n.* confession; declaration:
shiñkoo no kokuhaku（信仰の告白）a *confession* of faith / *ai no* kokuhaku（愛の告白）a *declaration* of love.

kokuhaku suru（〜する）*vt.* confess; declare: *Kare wa jibuñ no tsumi o* kokuhaku shita.（彼は自分の罪を告白した）He *confessed* his crimes.

ko⌐kuhoo こくほう（国宝）*n.* National Treasure:
Sono e wa kokuhoo *ni shitee sareta.*（その絵は国宝に指定された）The picture was designated as a *National Treasure*.

ko⌐kumee こくめい（国名）*n.* name of a country.

ko⌐kumiñ こくみん（国民）*n.*
1 nation; people:
Nihoñjiñ wa kiñbeñ na kokumiñ *da to omowarete imasu.*（日本人は勤勉な国民だと思われています）The Japanese are considered an industrious *people*. / kokumiñ *no gimu*（国民の義務）a *national* obligation / kokumiñ *no shukujitsu*（国民の祝日）a *national* holiday. 《⇨ shukujitsu (table)》
2 citizen:
Nihoñ no kokumiñ *to shite hazukashii omoi o shita.*（日本の国民として恥ずかしい思いをした）I felt embarrassed as a Japanese *citizen*.

ko⌐kumu-da⌐ijiñ（国務大臣）*n.* minister of state.

ko⌐ku⌐nai こくない（国内）*n.* inside the country; domestic; home:
kokunai *no sañgyoo o hogo suru*（国内の産業を保護する）protect *home* industries / *Kare wa* Nihoñ kokunai *o jiteñsha de ryokoo shita.*（彼は日本国内を自転車で旅行した）He has traveled *around*

Japan by bicycle. / kokunai-*moñdai*（国内問題）a *domestic* problem.
《↔ kokugai; kaigai》

Ko⌐kureñ こくれん（国連）*n.* U.N.
★ Abbreviation of '*Kokusai Reñgoo*'（国際連合）the United Nations.

ko⌐kuritsu こくりつ（国立）*n.* national; state:
kokuritsu-*daigaku*（国立大学）a *national* university / kokuritsu-*kooeñ*（国立公園）a *national* park / kokuritsu-*byooiñ*（国立病院）a *national* hospital.

ko⌐kusai- こくさい（国際）*pref.* international:
kokusai-*joosee*（国際情勢）the *international* situation / kokusai-*deñwa*（国際電話）an *international* telephone call; a telephone from which one can make an *international* call / kokusai-*kekkoñ*（国際結婚）an *international* marriage.

SIGN INDICATING PUBLIC PHONE
THAT HANDLES KOKUSAI DEÑWA

ko⌐kusaika こくさいか（国際化）*n.* internationalization:
kokusaika *o susumeru*（国際化を進める）promote *internationalization*.

kokusaika suru（〜する）*vi.* internationalize: *Kono moñdai wa* kokusaika *shi-soo da.*（この問題は国際化しそうだ）I am afraid this problem will *become a matter of international concern*.

ko⌐kusai-teki こくさいてき（国際的）*a.n.*（〜 na, ni）international:
kokusai-teki *na moñdai*（国際的な問題）an *international* issue / ko-

kusai-teki *ni katsuyaku shite iru
pianisuto* (国際的に活躍しているピアニ
スト) a pianist who is active *on the
world stage.*

ko｢kusañ こくさん (国産) *n.* domestic production; home-produced:
Kokusañ-*hiñ o motto tsukau beki
da.* (国産品をもっと使うべきだ) We
should use more *domestic* products. / kokusañ-*sha* (国産車) a *domestically produced* car.

ko｢kuseki こくせき (国籍) *n.*
(country of) nationality; citizenship:
Kokuseki *o koko ni kinyuu shite
kudasai.* (国籍をここに記入してくださ
い) Please fill in your *nationality*
here. / *Kare no* kokuseki *wa Nihoñ desu.* (彼の国籍は日本です) His
country of nationality is Japan. /
Nihoñ no kokuseki *o shutoku suru
koto wa kanoo desu.* (日本の国籍を
取得することは可能です) It is possible
to acquire Japanese *citizenship.*

Ko｢kutai こくたい (国体) *n.* National Athletic Meet.
★ Shortened form of '*Kokumiñ
Taiiku Taikai*' (国民体育大会).

ko｢kuyuu こくゆう (国有) *n.* national; state:
kokuyuu-*chi* (国有地) *national*
land / kokuyuu-*riñ* (国有林) a *state*
forest / kokuyuu-*zaisañ* (国有財産)
national property.

Ko｢kuze｣e-choo こくぜいちょう
(国税庁) *n.* National Tax Administration Agency:
Kokuzee-choo *chookañ* (国税庁長
官) the Director General of the
*National Tax Administration
Agency.* 《⇨ choo⁴ (table)》

ko｣kyoo こきょう (故郷) *n.* one's
home; one's birthplace; hometown:
Watashi no kokyoo *wa Hokkaidoo desu.* (私の故郷は北海道です) I
come from Hokkaido.

ko｢kyuu こきゅう (呼吸) *n.*
1 breathing; respiration:
Byooniñ wa kokyuu *ga arakatta.*
(病人は呼吸が荒かった) The patient
was *breathing* hard. / *Kare no* kokyuu *ga tomatta.* (彼の呼吸が止まっ
た) He *breathed* his last. / kokyuu-*ki* (呼吸器) the *respiratory* organs.
《⇨ iki¹》
2 knack; trick; craft:
Watashi wa yatto sono shigoto no
kokyuu *ga nomikometa.* (私はやっと
その仕事の呼吸が飲み込めた) Finally
I got the *hang* of how to do the
work.
3 harmony:
Shikisha to eñsoosha no kokyuu
wa pittari atte ita. (指揮者と演奏者
の呼吸はぴったり合っていた) The conductor and musicians were in perfect *harmony.*
kokyuu suru (〜する) *vi., vt.*
breathe; respire: *Watashi-tachi
wa yama no shiñseñ na kuuki o*
kokyuu shita. (私たちは山の新鮮な空
気を呼吸した) We *breathed* in the
fresh mountain air.

ko｢ma｣ka こまか (細か) *a.n.* (〜na,
ni) fine; attentive; detailed:
komaka *na ame* (細かな雨) *fine*
rain / komaka *na chuui* (細かな注
意) *meticulous* care / komaka *ni
shiraberu* (細かに調べる) examine
minutely. 《⇨ komakai》

ko｢maka｣·i こまかい (細かい) *a.*
(-ku) **1** (of grains, particles, etc.)
very small; fine:
komakai *yuki* (細かい雪) *fine* snow
/ *Tamanegi o* komakaku *kizañda.*
(玉ねぎを細かく刻んだ) I chopped the
onion *finely.* 《↔ arai²》
《⇨ komaka》
2 (of money) small:
Kono señ-eñ satsu o komakaku
dekimasu ka? (この千円札を細かくで
きますか) Could you *change* this
one-thousand-yen bill? / *Ainiku,
komakai o-kane o mochiawasete*

imaseñ. (あいにく, 細かいお金を持ち合わせていません) Unfortunately, I have no *small* change with me.
3 detailed; careful:
Komakai koto wa ato de setsumee shimasu. (細かいことはあとで説明します) I will explain the *details* later. / *Ano kañgofu wa* komakai *koto ni yoku ki ga tsuku.* (あの看護婦は細かいことによく気がつく) That nurse has the sensitivity to notice *little* things.
4 minor; trifling:
Komakai koto de kuyokuyo suru no wa yoshi nasai. (細かいことでくよくよするのはよしなさい) Don't worry about *trifling* matters.
5 thrifty; stingy:
Kare wa kane ni komakai. (彼は金に細かい) He is *tight* with money.

ko⌐mane⌐zumi こまねずみ (独楽鼠) *n.* Asian species of mouse (*Mus musculus wagneri*):
komanezumi *no yoo ni hataraku* (こまねずみのように働く) work like a *beaver.*

ko⌐ma⌐r·u こまる (困る) *vi.* (komar·i-; komar·a-; komat-te ⌊C⌋)
1 be in an awkward position; be in a fix; have a hard time:
Kagi o nakushite komatte imasu. (鍵をなくして困っています) I have lost the key, so I *am in an awkward position.* / *Jikañ ga nakute* komarimashita. (時間がなくて困りました) I *was in a fix* because there was no time left. / *Nihoñgo ga tsuujinakute* komarimashita. (日本語が通じなくて困りました) I *had a hard time* because my Japanese was not intelligible. / *Komatta. Doo shiyoo.* (困った。どうしよう) I *am in a jam.* What shall I do?
2 be in financial difficulties; be hard up:
Kare wa o-kane ni komatte iru *yoo da.* (彼はお金に困っているようだ) He seems to *be in* financial dif-

ficulties. / *Sono kuni no hito-tachi wa shokuryoo ni* komatte iru. (その国の人たちは食糧に困っている) The people in that country *are short of* food.

ko⌐me こめ (米) *n.* rice:
★ With '*o-*' in polite speech.
kome *o tsukuru* (米を作る) raise *rice* / kome *o taku* (米を炊く) cook *rice* / *Watashi-tachi wa* kome *o jooshoku to shite imasu.* (私たちは米を常食としています) We eat *rice* as our staple food. / kome-*tsubu* (米粒) a grain of *rice.*

ine	rice plant
kome	uncooked rice
gohañ (served in a bowl)	boiled rice
raisu (served on a plate)	

ko⌐me⌐·ru こめる (込める) *vt.* (kome-te ⌊V⌋) load:
juu ni tama o komeru (銃に弾を込める) *load* a gun.

ko⌐mori⌐uta こもりうた (子守歌) *n.* lullaby:
komoriuta *o utau* (子守歌を歌う) sing a *lullaby.*

ko⌐m·u こむ (込む・混む) *vi., vt.* (kom·i-; kom·a-; koñ-de ⌊C⌋) be crowded; be packed; be full; be jammed:
Deñsha wa koñde ita. (電車は込んでいた) The train *was crowded.* / *Eegakañ wa soñna ni* koñde inakatta. (映画館はそんなに込んでいなかった) The movie theater *was not* that *crowded.*

ko⌐mu⌐gi こむぎ (小麦) *n.* wheat. 《⇨ mugi (table)》

ko⌐mugiko こむぎこ (小麦粉) *n.* wheat flour.

ko⌐ñ こん (紺) *n.* dark blue; navy blue:
koñ *no sebiro* (紺の背広) a *dark-*

blue suit.

ko⌐ñ- こん（今）*pref.* this; the present; the coming:
koñ-*neñdo*（今年度）*this* year / koñ-*seeki*（今世紀）*the present* century / koñ-*shiizuñ*（今シーズン）*the current* (baseball) season.

ko⌐na こな（粉）*n.* powder; flour; meal:
komugi o hiite, kona *ni suru*（小麦を引いて, 粉にする）grind wheat into *flour* / kona-*gusuri*（粉薬）*powdered* medicine / kona-*miruku*（粉ミルク）*powdered* milk.

ko⌐naida こないだ *n.* (*informal*) recently; the other day.
Sore wa tsui konaida *no dekigoto da.*（それはついこないだの出来事だ）That is a very *recent* event. / Konaida *mukashi no tomodachi ni atta.*（こないだ昔の友だちに会った）*The other day* I met a former friend. 《⇨ kono-aida》

ko⌐ñbañ こんばん（今晩）*n.* this evening; tonight:
Kare wa koñbañ *kaette kimasu.*（彼は今晩帰って来ます）He returns home *this evening.* / Koñbañ *wa hiekomi-soo da.*（今晩は冷え込みそうだ）It seems as if it is going to get cold *tonight.* 《⇨ bañ¹ (table)》

ko⌐ñbañ wa⌐ こんばんは（今晩は）Good evening.

ko⌐ñbu こんぶ（昆布）*n.* sea tangle; kelp. ★ Also called '*kobu.*'

ko⌐ñchuu こんちゅう（昆虫）*n.* insect; bug. 《⇨ mushi¹》

ko⌐ñdate こんだて（献立）*n.* menu:
Kyoo no koñdate *wa nañ desu ka?*（きょうの献立は何ですか）What is on the *menu* today?

ko⌐ñdo こんど（今度）*n.* **1** this time; now:
Isshoo-keñmee yareba, koñdo *wa seekoo shimasu.*（一生懸命やれば, 今度は成功します）If you try hard, *this time* you will succeed. /

Koñdo *wa kimi no bañ desu.*（今度は君の番です）Now, it's your turn.
2 next time:
Koñdo *wa itsu kimasu ka?*（今度はいつ来ますか）When are you coming *next time?* / Koñdo *no nichi-yoo ni Nyuu Yooku e ikimasu.*（今度の日曜にニューヨークへ行きます）I am going to New York *next* Sunday.

SIGN ABOVE PLATFORM INDICATING DESTINATION
koñdo (next train); *tsugi* (train after next)

3 recently:
Kare wa koñdo *hoñ o dashita.*（彼は今度本を出した）He has *recently* published a book.

ko⌐ñgetsu こんげつ（今月）*n.* this month:
Koñgetsu *wa kyuujitsu ga ooi.*（今月は休日が多い）There are a lot of holidays *this month.* / *Kanojo wa* koñgetsu *kekkoñ shimasu.*（彼女は今月結婚します）She is getting married *this month.* / Koñgetsu *no owari wa isogashiku narimasu.*（今月の終わりは忙しくなります）I will be busy at the end of *this month.* 《↔ señgetsu; raigetsu》

ko⌐ñgo こんご（今後）*n., adv.* after this; from now on; in the future:
Koñgo *zutto koko ni sumimasu.*（今後ずっとここに住みます）I am going to live here *from now on.* / Koñgo *nani ga okoru ka dare ni mo wakarimaseñ.*（今後何が起こるかだれにもわかりません）Nobody knows what will happen *in the future.* / Koñgo *no yotee wa mada tatete imaseñ.*（今後の予定はまだ立てていません）I have not worked out the *future*

schedule yet.

koñgo tomo (～とも) continually: Koñgo tomo *yoroshiku o-negai ita-shimasu.* (今後ともよろしくお願いいたします) I'm looking forward to enjoying good relations with you. ★ Set phrase used upon meeting someone for the first time.

ko「ñgoo こんごう(混合) *n.* mixing; mixture: koñgoo-butsu (混合物) a *mixture*; a *compound*.

koñgoo suru (～する) *vi., vt.* mix; mingle; blend: *Abura to mizu wa* koñgoo shimaseñ. (油と水は混合しません) Oil and water *do not mix.* / *Watashi wa suna to semeñto o mizu de* koñgoo shita. (私は砂とセメントを水で混合した) I *mixed* sand and cement with water. 《⇨ majiru; mazeru》

ko「ñjoo こんじょう(根性) *n.* spirit; guts: koñjoo *no aru otoko* (根性のある男) a man of *spirit* / *Ano hito ni wa sore o suru dake no* koñjoo *ga nai.* (あの人にはそれをするだけの根性がない) He does not have the *guts* for it.

ko「ñkai こんかい(今回) *n.* this time: Koñkai *wa nyuushoo shita hito ga inakatta.* (今回は入賞した人がいなかった) There was nobody who won the prize *this time.* / Koñkai *dake oome ni mite kudasai.* (今回だけ大目に見てください) Please overlook it just *this once.*

ko「ñkuri¬ito コンクリート *n.* concrete: koñkuriito *no tatemono* (コンクリートの建物) a *concrete* building.

ko「ñku¬uru コンクール *n.* contest; competition: oñgaku-koñkuuru (音楽コンクール) a musical *contest* / shashiñ-koñkuuru (写真コンクール) a photo *contest* / koñkuuru *ni sañka suru* (コンクールに参加する) take part in a com-

petition.

ko「ñkyo こんきょ(根拠) *n.*
1 basis; foundation; ground: *Anata no shuchoo no* koñkyo *wa nañ desu ka?* (あなたの主張の根拠は何ですか) What is the *basis* for your claim? / *Sono uwasa wa mattaku* koñkyo *ga arimaseñ.* (そのうわさは全く根拠がありません) The rumor is completely without *foundation.*
2 reason: *Kare ga soo iu no ni wa* koñkyo *ga aru.* (彼がそう言うのには根拠がある) He has his *reasons* for saying so.

ko「ñmo¬ri こんもり *adv.* (～ to; ～ suru) thick; dense: koñmori to shita *mori* (こんもりとした森) *thick* woods.

ko「ñna こんな *attrib.* this; like this: ★ Refers to something close to the speaker. Koñna *sakana wa mita koto ga arimaseñ.* (こんな魚は見たことがありません) I have never seen a fish *like this.* / Koñna *hi wa gaishutsu shitaku arimaseñ.* (こんな日は外出したくありません) I don't want to go out on a day *like this.* / *Hana wa* koñna *fuu ni ikereba yoi desu ka?* (花はこんなふうに生ければよいですか) Is it all right to arrange the flowers *like this?* / Koñna *koto ni naru to wa omotte mo inakatta.* (こんなことになるとは思ってもいなかった) I never thought for a moment that things would turn out *like this.* 《⇨ añna; doñna; soñna》

ko「ñna ni こんなに *adv.* this; like this; so: Koñna ni *osoku made doko ni itañ desu?* (こんなに遅くまでどこにいたんです) Where have you been until *so* late? / *Ima made* koñna ni *kiree na yuuhi wa mita koto ga arimaseñ.* (今までこんなにきれいな夕日は見たことがありません) I have never seen as beautiful a sunset *as this.* / *Sañ-gatsu ni* koñna ni *ame ga*

furu no wa mezurashii. (三月にこん なに雨が降るのは珍しい) It is rare to have *so* much rain in March.
《⇨ añna ni; doñna ni; soñna ni》

ko¬ññañ こんなん (困難) *n.* difficulty; hardship; trouble: koññañ *ni taeru* (困難に耐える) endure *hardships* / koññañ *o nori-koeru* (困難を乗り越える) overcome *difficulties* / koññañ *to tatakau* (困難と戦う) struggle with a *difficulty*. — *a.n.* (~ na, ni) difficult; hard; troublesome: koññañ *na shigoto* (困難な仕事) a *tough* job / *Seekatsu ga* koññañ *ni natte kita.* (生活が困難になってきた) Life has become *harder*. / *Kono moñdai wa kaiketsu ga* koññañ *desu.* (この問題は解決が困難です) It is *difficult* to solve this problem.

ko¬ññichi こんにち (今日) *n.* today; the present day: koññichi *no sekai* (今日の世界) the world of *today* / koññichi *no Nihoñ* (今日の日本) *today*'s Japan.
《⇨ hoñjitsu; kyoo》

ko¬ññichi wa こんにちは (今日は) Good day; Good morning; Good afternoon; Hello.

ko¬ññyaku こんにゃく *n.* devil's tongue. ★ Jelly-like food made from the starch of devil's tongue root.

ko¬no この (此の) *attrib.* **1** this: ★ Refers to a person or thing that is close to the speaker. *Kono fairu o tana ni modoshite kudasai.* (このファイルを棚に戻してください) Please put *this* file back on the shelf. / *Kono niñgyoo wa kawaii desu ne.* (この人形はかわいいですね) *This* doll is cute, isn't it? / *Kono hito ga Satoo-sañ desu.* (この人が佐藤さんです) *This* is Mr. Sato.
2 this: ★ Refers to a time in the immediate future. *Kono natsu-yasumi wa doko-ka e*

ikimasu ka? (この夏休みはどこかへ行きますか) Are you going anywhere *this* summer vacation? / *Kono juugo-nichi ni kare wa Amerika e ikimasu.* (この15日に彼はアメリカへ行きます) He leaves for America on the fifteenth of *this* month.
3 this: ★ Introduces something as a subject of conversation. *Kono go-oñ wa isshoo wasuremaseñ.* (このご恩は一生忘れません) I will never forget *this* kindness all my life. / *Kono koto wa dare ni mo iwanai de kudasai.* (このことはだれにも言わないでください) Please don't tell anybody about *this*.
《⇨ ano; dono; sono》

ko¬no-aida このあいだ (此の間) *n.* the other day; some time ago; recently: ★ *informal* = konaida. *Kono-aida wa o-sewa ni narimashita.* (この間はお世話になりました) Thank you for the kindness I received *the other day*. / *Kono-aida kara kaze o hiite nakanaka naorimaseñ.* (この間から風邪をひいてなかなか治りません) I caught a cold *some time ago*, and it just will not go away. / *Kono-aida, Tanaka-sañ kara tegami o moraimashita.* (この間, 田中さんから手紙をもらいました) I *recently* received a letter from Mr. Tanaka. 《⇨ kono-mae》

ko¬no-goro このごろ (此の頃) *adv.* (~ no) now; these days; recently: *Nañ da ka* kono-goro *karada no chooshi ga yoku nai.* (何だかこのごろ体の調子がよくない) Somehow I don't feel very well *these days*. / *Kono-goro wa soo de mo arimaseñ ga, izeñ wa taiki-oseñ ga hidoi mono deshita.* (このごろはそうでもありませんが, 以前は大気汚染がひどいものでした) It isn't so *now*, but air pollution used to be really terrible. / *Kono-goro ni natte kare mo yatto sore ni ki ga tsuita.* (このごろに

なって彼もやっとそれに気がついた) He noticed it only *recently*. / Kono-goro *no gakusee wa kanemochi da*. (このごろの学生は金持ちだ) *Today's* students are rich. (⇨ chika-goro; saikiñ²)

ko⌈no-ma⌉e このまえ (此の前) *n.* the other day; last; the last time: Kono-mae *no kaigi ni wa demaseñ deshita*. (この前の会議には出ませんでした) I did not attend the *last* meeting. / *Kore ga* kono-mae *o-hanashi shita hoñ desu*. (これがこの前お話しした本です) This is the book I mentioned *the other day*. / Kono-mae *atta toki, kare wa soñna koto wa itte imaseñ deshita*. (この前会ったとき, 彼はそんなことは言っていませんでした) He did not say anything like that when I met him *the last time*. (⇨ kono-aida)

ko⌈no-mama このまま (此の儘) *n.* the present state; as it is; as they are: Kono-mama *no jootai de wa mañzoku dekimaseñ*. (このままの状態では満足できません) I am dissatisfied with the *present* situation. / Kono-mama *de wa chikyuu no oseñ wa susumu bakari desu*. (このままでは地球の汚染は進むばかりです) If things continue *like this*, global pollution will just get worse. / *Kono shorui wa* kono-mama *koko ni oite oite kudasai*. (この書類はこのままここに置いておいてください) Please leave these papers here *just as they are*. (⇨ mama¹)

ko⌈nomashi⌉¹-i このましい (好ましい) *a.* (-ku) good; desirable; favorable: konomashii *seeneñ* (好ましい青年) a *nice* young man / konomashiku nai *jiñbutsu* (好ましくない人物) an *undesirable* person / konomashii [konomashiku nai] *iñshoo o ataeru* (好ましい[好ましくない]印象を与える) give a *favorable* [an *unfavorable*]

impression / *Kitsueñ wa keñkoo-joo* konomashiku *arimaseñ*. (喫煙は健康上好ましくありません) Smoking is not *good* for the health.

ko⌈nomi⌉ このみ (好み) *n.* liking; taste; fancy: *Sore wa kaku-jiñ no* konomi *no moñdai desu*. (それは各人の好みの問題です) That is a question of each person's *taste*. / *Kono nekutai wa watashi no* konomi *ni atte iru*. (このネクタイは私の好みに合っている) This tie is to my *taste*. / Konomi *wa hito ni yotte chigaimasu*. (好みは人によって違います) *Tastes* differ according to the individual. (⇨ konomu)

ko⌈no⌉m-u このむ (好む) *vt.* (ko-nom-i-; konom-a-; konoñ-de Ⓒ) like; prefer: ★ 'suki da [desu]' is more common. *Watashi wa* konoñde, *kono yaku o hikiuketa wake de wa arimaseñ*. (私は好んで, この役を引き受けたわけではありません) It does not mean that I have taken on this role *by choice*. **konomu to konomazaru to ni kakawarazu** (〜と好まざるとにかかわらず) whether one likes it or not: Konomu to konomazaru to ni kakawarazu, *anata wa soko ni ikaneba narimasen*. (好むと好まざるとにかかわらず, あなたはそこに行かねばなりません) *Regardless of whether you wish to or not*, you have to go there. (⇨ konomi)

ko⌈no⌉¹-tabi このたび (此の度) *n.* (*formal*) this (present; previous) time [occasion]: Kono-tabi *no go-shooshiñ omede-too gozaimasu*. (この度のご昇進おめでとうございます) Congratulations on your *recent* promotion. / Kono-tabi *wa iroiro go-meewaku o o-kake shimashita*. (この度はいろいろご迷惑をおかけしました) *This time* I have caused you a lot of trouble. / *Watashi wa* kono-tabi *Shiñga-*

pooru ni teñkiñ to narimashita. (私はこの度シンガポールに転勤となりました) I have been transferred to Singapore *this time.* ((⇨ koñdo))

ko「no-tsugi¹ このつぎ (此の次) *n.* next:
Kono-tsugi no deñsha ni noroo. (この次の電車に乗ろう) Let's take the *next* train. / *Kono-tsugi no nichi-yoo wa o-hima desu ka?* (この次の日曜はお暇ですか) Are you free *this coming* Sunday? / *Kono-tsugi wa itsu aemasu ka?* (この次はいつ会えますか) When can we meet *next?*

ko「no-ue このうえ (此の上) *n.* more; further; in addition to this:
Kono-ue nani mo nozomimaseñ. (この上何も望みません) I do not want anything *more.* / *Kono-ue anata ni go-meewaku o o-kake suru wake ni wa ikimaseñ.* (この上あなたにご迷惑をおかけするわけにはいきません) It just will not do for me to cause you any *further* inconvenience.

kono-ue (mo) nai (〜（も）ない) most; greatest: *O-me ni kakarereba,* kono-ue mo nai *kooee desu.* (お目にかかれれば、この上もない光栄です) It would be the *greatest* honor if I could meet with you.

kono-ue (mo) naku (〜（も）なく) most; greatest: *Kare wa hitori-musume o* kono-ue naku *taisetsu ni omotte iru.* (彼は一人娘をこの上なく大切に思っている) He feels that there is *nothing more* precious than his only daughter.

ko「ñpakuto-ka¹mera コンパクトカメラ *n.* small [compact] camera. ★ Usually fully automatic.

ko「ñpoñ こんぽん (根本) *n.* foundation; basis; root:
Koñdo no señsoo no koñpoñ-*geñiñ wa nañ desu ka?* (今度の戦争の根本原因は何ですか) What is the *basic* cause of the present war? / *Sore wa* koñpoñ *kara yarinaoshi da.* (そ

れは根本からやり直しだ) We have to do it over from the *very beginning.*

ko「ñpoñ-teki こんぽんてき (根本的) *a.n.* (〜 na, ni) fundamental; basic:
Kono seedo wa koñpoñ-teki *na kaikaku ga hitsuyoo desu.* (この制度は根本的な改革が必要です) A *fundamental* revision of this system is necessary. / *Kimi wa* koñpoñ-teki *ni machigatte iru.* (きみは根本的に間違っている) You are *fundamentally* wrong.

ko「ñrañ こんらん (混乱) *n.* confusion; disorder; chaos:
Taikai wa koñrañ *no uchi ni owatta.* (大会は混乱のうちに終わった) The convention ended in *chaos.* / koñrañ *jootai* (混乱状態) a state of *disorder.*

koñrañ suru (〜する) *vi.* be confused; be mixed up: *Kare no hatsugeñ de kaigi ga* koñrañ *shita.* (彼の発言で会議が混乱した) The meeting *was thrown into confusion* by his remark. / *Jishiñ no tame ressha no daiya ga* koñrañ *shita.* (地震のため列車のダイヤが混乱した) The train schedule *was disrupted* because of the earthquake.

ko「ñsaato コンサート *n.* concert.

ko「ñseñto コンセント *n.* electrical outlet; wall socket:
koñseñto *ni sashikomu* (コンセントに差し込む) *plug in* / koñseñto *o nuku* (コンセントを抜く) *unplug.*

ko「ñshuu こんしゅう (今週) *n.* this week:
Koñshuu wa zutto isogashikatta. (今週はずっと忙しかった) I have been busy all *this week.* / *Koñshuu no yotee o o-kikase kudasai.* (今週の予定をお聞かせください) Please let me know *this week*'s schedule. / *Koñshuu-juu ni kono shigoto o oenakereba naranai.* (今週中にこの仕事を終えなければならない) I have to finish

up this work within *the week*. /
Koñshuu *no doyoo ni Kyooto e ikimasu*. (今週の土曜に京都へ行きます) I
am going to Kyoto *this* Saturday.
《⇨ shuu¹ (table)》

ko¹ñya こんや (今夜) *n.* this evening; tonight:
Koñya *o-hima desu ka?* (今夜おひま
ですか) Are you free *this evening*? /
Koñya *wa koko ni tomete kudasai*.
(今夜はここに泊めてください) Please let
me stay here *tonight*. / Koñya *wa
Kurisumasu-ibu desu*. (今夜はクリス
マスイブです) *Tonight* is Christmas
Eve. / *Ashita wa yasumi da kara*
koñya *wa osoku made okite ite
mo ii desu yo*. (あしたは休みだから今
夜は遅くまで起きていてもいいですよ) To-
morrow is a holiday, so you may
stay up late *tonight*. 《⇨ sakuya》

ko¹ñyaku こんやく (婚約) *n.* marriage engagement:
Go-koñyaku *omedetoo gozaimasu*.
(ご婚約おめでとうございます) Congratu-
lations on your *engagement*. / koñ-
yaku-sha (婚約者) a *fiancé(e)* / koñyaku yubiwa (婚約指輪) an *engagement* ring.
 koñyaku suru (〜する) *vi.* get engaged: *Futari wa medetaku* koñyaku shimashita. (二人はめでたく婚
約しました) They happily *got engaged*.

ko¹ñzatsu こんざつ (混雑) *n.* congestion; jam:
Watashi wa koñzatsu *o sakete,
heejitsu ni ryokoo shita*. (私は混雑
を避けて, 平日に旅行した) I traveled
on a weekday, avoiding the *congestion*. / *Kaijoo wa taiheñ na* koñzatsu deshita. (会場は大変な混雑でし
た) The hall *was* very *crowded*.
 koñzatsu suru (〜する) *vi.* be
crowded; be jammed: *Ressha
wa sukii ni dekakeru hito de* koñzatsu shite ita. (列車はスキーに出かけ
る人で混雑していた) The train *was
jam-packed* with people going off

to ski.

ko¹o こう (斯う) *adv.* **1** this; like
this: ★ Refers to something
close to the speaker.
Koo *atsukute wa gaishutsu shitaku nai*. (こう暑くては外出したくない)
I don't want to go out in *such*
heat. / *Jidoosha no uñteñ ga* koo
*muzukashii to wa omoi mo shima-
señ deshita*. (自動車の運転がこうむず
かしいとは思いもしませんでした) I didn't
for a moment think it would be
this hard to drive a car. / *Hashi
wa* koo *mochi nasai*. (はしはこう持ち
なさい) Hold your chopsticks *like
this*.
2 this: ★ Refers to something
just mentioned or about to be
mentioned.
Kono hoñ ni wa koo *kaite arimasu*.
(この本にはこう書いてあります) This
book says *as follows*: / *Koo shitara doo deshoo. Anata to watashi
ga saki ni iku ñ desu*. (こうしたらどう
でしょう. あなたと私が先に行くんです)
How about doing it *like this*:
You and I go first? 《⇨ aa¹;
doo¹; soo》

-koo こう (港) *suf.* port; harbor:
Yokohama-koo (横浜港) Yokohama *Harbor* / *Niigata-koo* (新潟
港) the *port* of Niigata.

Ko¹oañchoosa¹-choo こうあん
ちょうさちょう (公安調査庁) *n.* Pub-
lic Security Investigation
Agency:
Kooañchoosa-choo *chookañ* (公安
調査庁長官) the Director General
of the *Public Security Investigation Agency*. 《⇨ choo⁴ (table)》

ko¹oba¹ こうば (工場) *n.* factory;
workshop: ★ Refers to a small
factory, often under private
management.
kooba *de hataraku* (工場で働く)
work in a *factory*. 《⇨ koojoo¹》

ko¹obai¹ こうばい (勾配) *n.* slope;
grade; slant:

Watashi-tachi wa kyuu na koobai *no yama-michi o nobotta.*(私たちは急な勾配の山道を登った) We climbed a mountain path with a steep *slope.* / *Michi wa yurui kudari* koobai *datta.*(道はゆるい下り勾配だった) The road was a gentle downward *slope.*

ko⌐bañ こうばん(交番) *n.* police box:

> **(USAGE)**
>
> A small box-like construction located at important street corners. The policemen stationed there look after the safety and protection of people.

Jiko o koobañ *ni shiraseta.*(事故を交番に知らせた) I reported the accident to the *police box.*

KOOBAÑ

Ko⌐obe こうべ(神戸) *n.* the capital of Hyogo Prefecture, a seaport and a commercial city. 《⇨ map (D4)》

ko⌐obutsu[1] こうぶつ(好物) *n.* one's favorite food:
Sushi wa watashi no koobutsu *desu.*(すしは私の好物です) Sushi is one of my *favorite dishes.* / *Kanojo wa amai mono ga* koobutsu *da.*(彼女は甘いものが好物だ) She *is fond of* sweet things.

ko⌐obutsu[2] こうぶつ(鉱物) *n.* mineral.

ko⌐ocha こうちゃ(紅茶) *n.* black tea:
koocha *o ireru [dasu]*(紅茶を入れる

[出す]) make [serve] *tea* / koocha *o nomu*(紅茶を飲む) drink *tea.* 《⇨ o-cha》

ko⌐ochi[1] コーチ *n.* coach:
Kare wa koochi *to señshu o kanete ita.*(彼はコーチと選手を兼ねていた) He acted as the *coach* and as a player.

koochi suru (～する) *vt.* coach:
Yamada-sañ wa watashi-tachi ni tenisu o koochi *shite kureta.*(山田さんは私たちにテニスをコーチしてくれた) Mr. Yamada *coached* us in tennis.

ko⌐ochi[2] こうち(耕地) *n.* cultivated land; arable land.

ko⌐ochi[3] こうち(高地) *n.* highlands; upland. 《↔ teechi》

Ko⌐ochi-keñ こうちけん(高知県) *n.* Kochi Prefecture. Located in the south of Shikoku. The climate is mild and rice is harvested twice a year. Capital city: Kochi. 《⇨ map (C5)》

ko⌐ochoo[1] こうちょう(好調) *a.n.* (～ na, ni) in good shape [condition]; favorable; satisfactory:
Señshu wa zeñiñ koochoo *desu.*(選手は全員好調です) The competitors are all in *fine form.* / *Kare-ra wa* koochoo *na sutaato o kitta.*(彼らは好調なスタートを切った) They made a *promising* start. / *Subete* koochoo *ni hakoñde imasu.*(すべて好調に運んでいます) Everything is progressing *favorably.*

ko⌐ochoo[2] こうちょう(校長) *n.* principal; headmaster; headmistress.

ko⌐odai こうだい(広大) *a.n.* (～ na) extensive; vast:
koodai *na sabaku*(広大な砂漠) an *extensive* desert.

ko⌐odeñ こうでん(香典) *n.* monetary offering to a departed soul:
★ Usually given at a funeral service. koodeñ-*gaeshi*(香典返し) a present given in return for a *funeral offering.*

ko┐odo[1] コード *n.* electrical cord; flex:
koodo o tsunagu (コードをつなぐ) connect *cords* / eñchoo koodo (延長コード) an extension *cord*.

ko┐odo[2] こうど (高度) *n.* height; altitude:
koodo goseñ-meetoru (高度 5 千メートル) a *height* of 5,000 meters / Hikooki wa koodo o ageta [sageta]. (飛行機は高度を上げた[下げた]) The plane increased [lowered] its *altitude*.

ko┐odo[3] こうど (高度) *a.n.* (~ na/ no, ni) advanced; highly developed:
koodo na [no] buñmee (高度な[の]文明) an *advanced* civilization / koodo ni hattatsu shita kagaku-gijutsu (高度に発達した科学技術) scientific technology which has developed to a *high level*.

ko┐odo[4] こうど (硬度) *n.* hardness.

ko┌odoo[1] こうどう (行動) *n.* act; action; behavior; conduct:
koodoo o toru [okosu] (行動をとる[起こす]) take *action* / Watashi ni wa kare no koodoo ga rikai deki-maseñ. (私には彼の行動が理解できません) I cannot understand his *actions*. / Gogo wa jiyuu-koodoo desu. (午後は自由行動です) We *are free* in the afternoon.
koodoo suru (~する) *vi.* act; behave; conduct oneself: Watashi-tachi wa shiñchoo ni koodoo shimashita. (私たちは慎重に行動しました) We *conducted ourselves* with discretion.

ko┌odoo[2] こうどう (講堂) *n.* lecture hall; auditorium; assembly hall.

ko┌oeñ[1] こうえん (公園) *n.* park; public playground:
Kooeñ o sañpo shita. (公園を散歩した) I took a walk in the *park*. / Kodomo-tachi wa kooeñ de aso-ñde imasu. (子どもたちは公園で遊んで

います) The children are having fun in the *playground*.

ko┌oeñ[2] こうえん (講演) *n.* lecture; speech; talk:
Watashi wa sono sakka no kooeñ o kikimashita. (私はその作家の講演を聞きました) I listened to the *lecture* by the author. / kooeñ-kai (講演会) a *lecture* meeting / kooeñ-sha (講演者) a *lecturer*.
kooeñ (o) suru (~(を)する) *vi.* give a lecture; make a speech: Sono hyooroñka wa Chuutoo no joosee ni tsuite kooeñ shita. (その評論家は中東の情勢について講演した) The critic *gave a talk* on the situation in the Middle East. 《⇒ eñzetsu》

ko┌oeñ[3] こうえん (公演) *n.* public performance:
Sono gekidañ no kooeñ wa raigetsu Kabukiza de okonawaremasu. (その劇団の公演は来月歌舞伎座で行われます) The *performance* of the theatrical company will be put on at the Kabukiza next month. / Yoru no kooeñ wa chuushi ni narimashita. (夜の公演は中止になりました) The evening *performance* was canceled.
kooeñ suru (~する) *vt.* perform; present: Sono shibai wa ima Kokuritsu Gekijoo de kooeñ sarete imasu. (その芝居は今国立劇場で公演されています) That play *is presently being performed* at the National Theater. 《⇒ jooeñ》

ko┌oeñ[4] こうえん (後援) *n.* support; sponsorship:
Sono teñrañkai wa Moñbu-shoo no kooeñ de hirakareta. (その展覧会は文部省の後援で開かれた) The exhibition was held under the *sponsorship* of the Ministry of Education. / kooeñ-kai (後援会) a *supporters*' association; a *fan* club.
kooeñ suru (~する) *vt.* support; sponsor: Watashi-tachi wa Ya-

mada-sañ o kooen shite, *kai o tsu-kutta.* (私たちは山田さんを後援して, 会を作った) We formed a society to *support* Mr. Yamada.

ko⌐ofu こうふ (交付) *n.* issue; grant:
meñkyoshoo no koofu (免許証の交付) the *issue* of a driver's license.
koofu suru (~する) *vt.* issue; grant: *Pasupooto wa doko de* koofu shite imasu *ka?* (パスポートはどこで交付していますか) Where do they *issue* passports? / *Kare wa neñkiñ o* koofu sarete imasu. (彼は年金を交付されています) He *has been granted* a pension.

ko⌐ofuku こうふく (幸福) *n.* happiness; fortune:
koofuku *o tsukamu* (幸福をつかむ) achieve *happiness* / Go-koofuku *o o-inori mooshiagemasu.* (ご幸福をお祈り申し上げます) I wish you every *happiness.*
—— *a.n.* (~ na, ni) happy; fortunate:
koofuku *na katee* (幸福な家庭) a *happy* family / koofuku *ni kurasu* (幸福に暮らす) live a *happy* life / *Watashi-tachi wa ima,* koofuku *desu.* (私たちは今, 幸福です) We are now very *happy.* 《⇨ shiawase》

ko⌐ofuñ こうふん (興奮) *n.* excitement; stimulation:
Kañshuu no koofuñ *wa ma-mo-naku shizumatta.* (観衆の興奮は間もなく静まった) The audience's *excitement* soon died down. / koofuñ-zai (興奮剤) a *stimulant.*
koofuñ suru (~する) *vi.* be [get] excited: *Soñna ni* koofuñ suru *no wa yoshi nasai.* (そんなに興奮するのはよしなさい) Don't *get* so *excited.* / *Watashi wa* koofuñ shite, *nemure-nakatta.* (私は興奮して, 眠れなかった) I *was* so *excited* that I could not sleep. / *Kare wa* koofuñ shite, *su-gu okoru.* (彼は興奮して, すぐ怒る) He *gets excited* and soon becomes angry.

ko⌐ogai[1] こうがい (郊外) *n.* suburbs; outskirts:
Watashi wa Tookyoo no koogai *ni suñde imasu.* (私は東京の郊外に住んでいます) I live in the *suburbs* of Tokyo. / *Kare wa* koogai *no ie ni hikkoshita.* (彼は郊外の家に引っ越した) He moved to a house on the *outskirts of town.* 《⇨ shigai[2]》

ko⌐ogai[2] こうがい (公害) *n.* pollution; public nuisance:
*Juumiñ wa soo-oñ-*koogai *ni na-yañde iru.* (住民は騒音公害に悩んでいる) The residents are suffering from noise *pollution.* / koogai-moñdai (公害問題) the issue of *pollution.*

ko⌐ogaku こうがく (高額) *n.* large sum of money:
Kare wa koogaku *no kifu o shita.* (彼は高額の寄付をした) He made a *large* contribution. / koogaku-shotokusha (高額所得者) a person with a *high income.* 《↔ teegaku》

ko⌐ogeehiñ こうげいひん (工芸品) *n.* craftwork.

ko⌐ogeki こうげき (攻撃) *n.* attack; criticism; offensive:
Teki wa koogeki *o kaishi shita.* (敵は攻撃を開始した) The enemy opened an *attack.* / *Naikaku wa yoroñ no* koogeki *ni tae-kanete, soojishoku shita.* (内閣は世論の攻撃に耐えかねて, 総辞職した) The cabinet could not stand the severe *criticism* of the public and resigned en masse. / *Kare no koodo wa* koogeki *no mato to natta.* (彼の行動は攻撃の的となった) His behavior became the target of *criticism.*
koogeki suru (~する) *vt.* attack; criticize: *Yatoo wa seefu no see-saku o* koogeki shita. (野党は政府の政策を攻撃した) The opposition *criticized* the government's policy. / *Sono machi wa sora kara* koogeki sareta. (その町は空から攻撃された)

The town *was attacked* from the air. 《↔ boogyo》

ko⌐ogeñ こうげん（高原）*n.* plateau; tableland; highlands.

ko⌐ogi[1] こうぎ（抗議）*n.* protest; objection:
koogi *o mooshikomu*（抗議を申し込む）lodge a *protest* / koogi-*buñ*（抗議文）a written *objection* / koogi *shuukai*（抗議集会）a *protest* rally.
koogi suru（～する）*vi.* protest; object: *Oozee no hito ga sono kaku-jikkeñ ni* koogi shita.（大勢の人がその核実験に抗議した）A large number of people *protested* against the nuclear experiment.

ko⌐ogi[2] こうぎ（講義）*n.* lecture: *Gogo no* koogi *ni wa demashita ka?*（午後の講義には出ましたか）Did you attend the *lecture* in the afternoon? / *Watashi wa Tanaka kyooju no shakaigaku no* koogi *o ukete imasu.*（私は田中教授の社会学の講義を受けています）I'm attending Professor Tanaka's *lectures* on sociology.
koogi (o) suru（～（を）する）*vt.* give a lecture; lecture: *Kyooju wa Nihoñ-buñgaku ni tsuite* koogi shita.（教授は日本文学について講義した）The professor *lectured* on Japanese literature.

ko⌐ogo こうご（口語）*n.* spoken [colloquial] language:
koogo-*tai*（口語体）*colloquial* style. 《↔ buñgo》

ko⌐ogo ni こうごに（交互に）*adv.* by [in] turns; alternately: *Futari wa* koogo ni *keebi ni tsuite ita.*（二人は交互に警備についていた）The two persons were on guard *in turns.* / *Nichi-Bee-shunoo-kai-dañ wa Tookyoo to Washiñtoñ de maitoshi* koogo ni *hirakareru.*（日米首脳会談は東京とワシントンで毎年交互に開かれる）The Japanese-American summit meetings are held each year in Tokyo and Washing-ton *alternately.*

ko⌐ogo⌐o こうごう（皇后）*n.* empress:
Koogoo *Heeka*（皇后陛下）Her Majesty the *Empress.* 《⇨ teñnoo》

ko⌐ogu こうぐ（工具）*n.* tool; implement:
koogu *isshiki*（工具一式）a set of *tools* / koogu-*bako*（工具箱）a *tool box.*

ko⌐ogyoo[1] こうぎょう（工業）*n.* industry: *Kono chihoo de wa seemitsu*-ki-kaikoogyoo *ga sakañ desu.*（この地方では精密機械工業が盛んです）The precision machinery *industry* thrives in this area. / *juu[kee]*-koogyoo（重[軽]工業）heavy [light] *industries* / koogyoo-*toshi*（工業都市）an *industrial* city / koogyoo-chitai（工業地帯）an *industrial* district.

ko⌐ogyoo[2] こうぎょう（鉱業）*n.* mining (industry).

ko⌐ohai こうはい（後輩）*n.* one's junior; underclassman: *Watashi wa kare no ichi-neñ* koo-hai *desu.*（私は彼の一年後輩です）I am his *junior* by a year. 《↔ señpai》

ko⌐ohaku こうはく（紅白）*n.* red and white:
koohaku *no maku*（紅白の幕）a *red-and-white* curtain / koohaku-*jiai*（紅白試合）a match [game] between the *red* and *white* teams.

ko⌐ohañ こうはん（後半）*n.* second [latter] half: 《↔ zenhañ》 *nijus-seeki* koohañ（20世紀後半）*the second half* of the twentieth century / *Shiai no* koohañ *wa omoshiroku nakatta.*（試合の後半はおもしろくなかった）*The second half* of the game was not interesting. / *Komaasharu no ato,* koohañ *o gorañ itadakimasu.*（コマーシャルのあと、後半をご覧いただきます）Join us for *the second half* after the commercials. (*TV announcement*)

ko⌐ohee こうへい (公平) *n.* fairness; impartiality:
koohee o kaku (公平を欠く) *be unfair.*
— *a.n.* (~ na, ni) fair, just; impartial:
koohee na saiban (公平な裁判) a *fair* trial / koohee na iken (公平な意見) an *impartial* opinion / Tanaka sensee wa dono gakusee ni mo koohee da. (田中先生はどの学生にも公平だ) Mr. Tanaka is *impartial* to every student.
《↔ fukoohee》

ko⌐ohii コーヒー (咖啡) *n.* coffee:
koohii o ireru [nomu] (コーヒーを入れる[飲む]) make [drink] *coffee* / Koohii o ip-pai ikaga desu ka? (コーヒーを一杯いかがですか) Would you like a cup of *coffee*? / Koohii ni satoo [kuriimu] o iremasu ka? (コーヒーに砂糖[クリーム]を入れますか) Do you want sugar [cream] in your *coffee*?

ko⌐oho こうほ (候補) *n.* **1** candidacy; candidature; candidate:
kooho ni tatsu (候補に立つ) *run [stand] for election* / Kare wa shichoo-sen no kooho no hitori desu. (彼は市長選の候補の一人です) He is one of the *candidates* for mayor.
2 favorite:
Kare no chiimu wa yuushoo kooho da. (彼のチームは優勝候補だ) His team is the top *favorite*.

ko⌐ohoo¹ こうほう (広報) *n.* public information; public relations:
koohoo-katsudoo o kappatsu ni okonau (広報活動を活発に行う) actively do *public realtions* work.

ko⌐ohoo² こうほう (公報) *n.* official bulletin:
shi no koohoo (市の公報) the *official bulletin* of a city.

ko⌐oi¹ こうい (行為) *n.* act; action; deed; behavior; conduct:
shinsetsu na kooi (親切な行為) an

act of kindness / Sono kooi wa ihoo desu. (その行為は違法です) That *act* is illegal. / Kare wa kuchisaki dake de, kooi ga tomonawanai. (彼は口先だけで、行為が伴わない) He is a man of words, not of *deeds.*

ko⌐oi² こうい (好意) *n.* goodwill; kindness; favor:
kooi o shimesu (好意を示す) show *goodwill* / Go-kooi o kansha shimasu. (ご好意を感謝します) I appreciate your *kindness.* / Kanojo wa kimi ni kooi o motte iru yoo da. (彼女は君に好意を持っているようだ) She seems to *be fond of* you.
《↔ tekii》

ko⌐oin こういん (工員) *n.* factory worker.

ko⌐oi-teki こういてき (好意的) *a.n.* (~ na, ni) friendly; kind; favorable:
Minna watashi-tachi ni kooi-teki datta. (みんな私たちに好意的だった) They were all very *friendly* to us. / Kare wa kooi-teki na henji o kureta. (彼は好意的な返事をくれた) He gave me a *favorable* reply.

ko⌐o-iu こういう (斯ういう) *attrib.* like this; thus: ★ Refers to something close to the speaker.
Sonna koto wa koo-iu basho de iu beki de wa nai. (そんなことはこういう場所で言うべきではない) That is not the kind of thing you should say in a place *like this.* / Koo-iu nagai sukaato ga kotoshi no ryuukoo desu. (こういう長いスカートが今年の流行です) *This sort of* long skirt is in fashion this year. / Hana wa koo-iu fuu ni ikeru to umaku ikimasu. (花はこういうふうに生けるとうまくいきます) If you arrange the flowers *like this*, they will look nice. 《⇒ aa-iu; doo-iu; soo-iu》

ko⌐oji こうじ (工事) *n.* construction work:
Raishuu kara hashi no kooji ga

hajimarimasu.（来週から橋の工事が始まります）The *construction* of the bridge will start next week. / Kooji-*chuu.* (*sign*)（工事中）Under *Construction.* / kooji-*genba*（工事現場）a *construction* site.

kooji suru（～する）*vi.* construct; work on: *Kono saki wa* kooji shite iru *kara tooremasen.*（この先は工事しているから通れません）The road ahead *is under construction*, so you cannot go through.

ko⌐oji·ru こうじる（講じる）*vt.* (kooji-te Ⓥ) **1** (*formal*) give a lecture: *Watanabe kyooju wa Nihon-dai-gaku de Chuugokushi o* koojite *iru.*（渡辺教授は日本大学で中国史を講じている）Professor Watanabe *lectures* on the history of China at Nihon University.

2 take measures: *Kootsuu-jiko o booshi suru tame ni nanra-ka no saku o* koojinake-reba *naranai.*（交通事故を防止するために何らかの策を講じなければならない）We *must take* some *measures* to prevent traffic accidents.

ko⌐ojoo[1] こうじょう（工場）*n.* factory; mill; plant; workshop: ★ Refers to a larger, well-equipped factory. More formal than '*kooba.*' koojoo *o tateru*（工場を建てる）build a *factory* / *Chichi wa kono machi no* koojoo *de hataraite imasu.*（父はこの町の工場で働いています）My father works at the *factory* in this town. / *jidoosha-*koo-joo（自動車工場）an automobile *plant* / *seeshi-*koojoo（製紙工場）a paper *mill* / koojoo-*haikibutsu*（工場廃棄物）*factory* waste.

ko⌐ojoo[2] こうじょう（向上）*n.* rise; improvement; progress: *seekatsu-suijun no* koojoo（生活水準の向上）a *rise* in the standard of living / *gijutsu no* koojoo（技術の向上）an *improvement* in techniques / koojoo-*shin*（向上心）a desire to *improve oneself.*

koojoo suru（～する）*vi.* rise; improve; progress: *Saikin josee no chii ga* masumasu koojoo shite kimashita.（最近女性の地位がますます向上してきました）Recently the position of women *has been getting better and better.*

ko⌐oka[1] こうか（効果）*n.* effect; efficacy; efficiency: kooka ga aru [nai]（効果がある[ない]）*be effective* [*ineffective*] / *Kono kusuri wa zutsuu ni* kooka ga ari-masu.（この薬は頭痛に効果があります）This medicine *is effective* for headaches. / *Isshoo-kenmee yatta ga* kooka wa nakatta.（一生懸命やったが効果はなかった）I tried my hardest, but I *was not successful.*

ko⌐oka[2] こうか（高価）*a.n.* (～ na, ni) expensive; high-priced; costly: kooka *na shinamono*（高価な品物）*high-priced* goods. 《↔ yasui》《⇒ takai》

ko⌐oka[3] こうか（硬貨）*n.* coin. 《⇒ shihee》

500 yen　　100 yen　　50 yen

10 yen　　5 yen　　1 yen

KOOKA IN CURRENT USE

ko⌐okai[1] こうかい（公開）*n.* open to the public: Kookai *no seki de hanasu no wa nigate desu.*（公開の席で話すのは苦手です）I am poor at speaking in *pub-lic.* / kookai-*kooza*（公開講座）an *extension* course; a lecture *open to the public* / kookai-*soosa* (公開捜査) an *open* criminal investigation / kookai-*tooroñkai* (公開討論会) an *open* forum.

kookai suru (～する) *vt.* make public; exhibit; release: *Kono gakkoo no kootee wa kyuujitsu wa ippañ ni kookai sarete imasu.* (この学校の校庭は休日は一般に公開されています) This school's playground *is open* to the general public on holidays. / *Sono kokuhoo wa neñ ni ichi-do kookai saremasu.* (その国宝は年に一度公開されます) That National Treasure *is exhibited* once a year.

ko⌐okai² こうかい (航海) *n.* voyage; navigation; cruise; sailing: *Sono fune wa sekai isshuu no kookai ni shuppatsu shita.* (その船は世界一周の航海に出発した) The ship set out on a round-the-world *voyage.* / *Tanoshii kookai o o-inori itashimasu.* (楽しい航海をお祈りいたします) I pray that you have a pleasant *voyage.*

kookai suru (～する) *vi.* go by sea; sail; cruise: *Shoowa-maru wa ima Taiseeyoo o kookai shite imasu.* (昭和丸は今大西洋を航海しています) The Showa-maru *is* now *sailing* across the Atlantic.

ko⌐okai³ こうかい (後悔) *n.* regret; repentance: *Kookai saki ni tatazu.* (*saying*) (後悔先に立たず) It is no use crying over spilt milk.

kookai suru (～する) *vi., vt.* regret; repent: *Ato de kookai shimasu yo.* (後で後悔しますよ) You will *regret* it later. / *Watashi wa jibuñ no shita koto o ima kookai shite imasu.* (私は自分のしたことを今後悔しています) I now *feel remorse* for what I did.

ko⌐okai⁴ こうかい (公海) *n.* the high seas.

ko⌐okañ こうかん (交換) *n.* exchange; replacement; barter: *Kono kamera to kookañ ni, nani o kuremasu ka?* (このカメラと交換に, 何をくれますか) What will you give me in *exchange* for this camera? / kookañ *gakusee* [*kyooju*] (交換学生[教授]) an *exchange* student [professor] / kookañ *jookeñ* (交換条件) a *bargaining* point.

kookañ suru (～する) *vt.* change; exchange; replace; barter: *akañ-boo no omutsu o* kookañ suru (赤ん坊のおむつを交換する) *change* a baby's diaper / *buhiñ o* kookañ suru (部品を交換する) *replace* a part / *Furyoo-hiñ wa itsu de mo* kookañ itashimasu. (不良品はいつでも交換いたします) We are always ready to *replace* defective articles. / *Kurisumasu ni wa purezeñto o* kookañ shimasu. (クリスマスにはプレゼントを交換します) People *exchange* presents on Christmas Day. / *Watashi wa taiya o* kookañ shite moratta. (私はタイヤを交換してもらった) I *had* the tires *changed.* (⇨ torikaeru)

ko⌐oka-teki こうかてき (効果的) *a.n.* (～ na, ni) effective; successful: *Jiko o booshi suru no ni, nani-ka kooka-teki na hoohoo wa arimasu ka?* (事故を防止するのに, 何か効果的な方法はありますか) Is there any *effective* way to prevent accidents? / *Doo sureba, iñfurueñza o* kooka-teki *ni yoboo dekimasu ka?* (どうすれば, インフルエンザを効果的に予防できますか) How can we *effectively* prevent the flu?

ko⌐okee こうけい (光景) *n.* scene; sight; view: *Sono tani no kookee wa ima de mo oboete imasu.* (その谷の光景は今でも覚えています) I still remember the *view* of that valley. / *Hi no shizumu kookee wa subarashi-katta.* (日の沈む光景は素晴らしかった)

The *sight* of the sunset was spectacular.

ko⌐oki こうき（後期）*n.* latter half of the year; second term [semester]:
Edo no kooki (江戸の後期) the *later* Edo *period* / Kooki *no shiken wa getsuyoo kara hajimarimasu.* (後期の試験は月曜から始まります) The *final* exams start on Monday. 《↔ zeñki》

ko⌐oki⌐shiñ こうきしん（好奇心）*n.* curiosity; inquisitiveness:
Kare wa kookishiñ *ga tsuyoi.* (彼は好奇心が強い) He *is very inquisitive.* / *Watashi wa* kookishiñ *kara sono kai ni shusseki shite mita.* (私は好奇心からその会に出席してみた) I attended the party out of *curiosity.* 《⇒ kyoomi》

ko⌐okoku こうこく（広告）*n.* advertisement:
shiñbuñ ni kookoku *o dasu* [*noseru*] (新聞に広告を出す[載せる]) put an *advertisement* in a newspaper / *Watashi wa* kookoku *o mite, sono hoñ o kaimashita.* (私は広告を見て、その本を買いました) I bought the book after seeing the *advertisement.* / kookoku-*ryoo* (広告料) *advertising* rates.
kookoku suru (〜する) *vt.* advertise: *Sono depaato wa terebi de oo-uridashi o* kookoku shita. (そのデパートはテレビで大売り出しを広告した) That department store *advertised* a big sale on television.

ko⌐okoo[1] こうこう（高校）*n.* (senior) high school: ★ Shortened form of '*kootoo-gakkoo.*'
kookoo *o jukeñ suru* (高校を受験する) take the entrance examination for a *high school* / kookoo *ni nyuugaku suru* (高校に入学する) enter a *high school.*

ko⌐okoo[2] こうこう（孝行）*n.* being obedient (to one's parents):
Oya (*ni*) kookoo (*o*) *shi nasai.* (親(に)孝行(を)しなさい) Make sure you are *affectionate and dutiful* toward your parents. / *oya*-kookoo (親孝行) filial *piety.*
— *a.n.* (〜 na) good; obedient; dutiful:
kookoo *na musuko* (孝行な息子) a *dutiful* son.

ko⌐oko⌐osee こうこうせい（高校生）*n.* (senior) high school student.

ko⌐okuubiñ こうくうびん（航空便）*n.* airmail:
Kore o Furañsu e kookuubiñ *de okuru to ikura ni narimasu ka?* (これをフランスへ航空便で送るといくらになりますか) How much will it cost if I send this to France by *airmail?*

kooku⌐ukeñ こうくうけん（航空券）*n.* airline ticket.

kooku⌐uki こうくうき（航空機）*n.* airplane; aircraft.

Ko⌐okyo こうきょ（皇居）*n.* the Imperial Palace. ★ The bridge over the moat is called '*Nijuubashi* (二重橋),' (the Double-Arched Bridge) and is often used to signify the Imperial Palace.

NIJUU-BASHI

ko⌐okyoo[1] こうきょう（公共）*n.* the community; public:
kookyoo *no fukushi* (公共の福祉) *public* welfare / kookyoo-*no tatemono* (公共の建物) a *public* building / kookyoo-*shisetsu* (公共施設) facilities belonging to the *community* / kookyoo-*jigyoo* (公共事業) a *public* enterprise / kookyoo-*ryookiñ* (公共料金) *public* utility

charges.

ko`okyoo`² こうきょう（好況）*n.*
brisk market; prosperous conditions:
Nihoñ no sañgyoo-kai wa koo-kyoo desu.（日本の産業界は好況です）The Japanese industrial world *is thriving.* / *Kono kookyoo wa mada tsuzuku deshoo.*（この好況はまだ続くでしょう）These *prosperous conditions* are likely to further continue.《↔ fukyoo》

ko`okyuu` こうきゅう（高級）*a.n.*
（～ na, ni) high-class; high-grade; exclusive:
kookyuu (na) hoteru（高級（な）ホテル）an *exclusive* hotel / *kookyuu-sha*（高級車）a *high-class* car.

Ko`omeetoo` こうめいとう（公明党）*n.* Komeito Party.《⇨ seetoo²(table)》

ko`omi`ñkañ こうみんかん（公民館）*n.* public hall; community center.

ko`omiñ`keñ こうみんけん（公民権）*n.* civil rights.

ko`omoku` こうもく（項目）*n.*
item; heading; clause:
Risuto ni wa koomoku ga ikutsu arimasu ka?（リストには項目がいくつありますか）How many *headings* are there on the list? / *Kaku koomoku wa ooki-na katsuji de iñsatsu sarete ita.*（各項目は大きな活字で印刷されていた）Each *heading* was printed in large type.

ko`omu`iñ こうむいん（公務員）*n.*
public worker; government employee; civil servant:
kokka[chihoo]-koomuiñ（国家[地方]公務員）a national [local] *government worker.*

ko`omu`r·u こうむる（被る）*vt.*
(-mur·i-; -mur·a-; -mut-te [C])
receive; sustain; suffer:
Sono mura wa taifuu de ooki-na higai o koomutta.（その村は台風で大きな被害を被った）The village *suffered* heavy damage from the typhoon.

ko`omyoo` こうみょう（巧妙）*a.n.*
（～ na, ni) clever; cunning; smart; crafty:
koomyoo na yarikata（巧妙なやり方）a *clever* trick / *koomyoo ni hito o damasu*（巧妙に人をだます）*cunningly* deceive people / *Kare no hanashikata wa koomyoo datta.*（彼の話し方は巧妙だった）His way of speaking was *clever.*

ko`onyuu` こうにゅう（購入）*n.* purchase; buying:
Watashi wa sono pasokoñ no koonyuu o miawaseta.（私はそのパソコンの購入を見合わせた）I decided to put off the *purchase* of that personal computer. / *koonyuu-sha*（購入者）a *buyer* / *koonyuu-kakaku*（購入価格）the *purchase* price.
　koonyuu suru（～する）*vt.* buy; purchase: *Kare wa atarashii uchi o koonyuu shita.*（彼は新しい家を購入した）He *purchased* a new house.《⇨ kau¹》

ko`o-oñ` こうおん（高温）*n.* high temperature:
Koo-oñ ni tsuki chuui. (*sign*)（高温につき注意）Caution: *High Temperatures.*《↔ teeoñ》

ko`ora` コーラ *n.* cola. ★ Any carbonated soft drink.《⇨ saidaa》

ko`ori` こおり（氷）*n.* ice:
Mizuumi ni koori ga hatta.（湖に氷が張った）*Ice* has formed in the lake. / *Koori ga toketa.*（氷が解けた）The *ice* has melted. / *Waiñ o koori de hiyashita.*（ワインを氷で冷やした）I cooled the wine in *ice.* / *koori-mizu*（氷水）*ice* water; shaved *ice.*

ko`oritsu`¹ こうりつ（公立）*n.*
public; prefectural; municipal:
kooritsu no gakkoo（公立の学校）a *public* school / *kooritsu no toshokañ*（公立の図書館）a *public* library.

《↔ shiritsu¹》

ko˞oritsu² こうりつ（効率）*n.* efficiency:
kooritsu *o takameru*（効率を高める）increase the *efficiency* | *Kono eñjiñ wa* kooritsu ga yoi [warui].（このエンジンは効率が良い[悪い]）This engine *is efficient* [*inefficient*].

ko˞oritsu-teki こうりつてき（効率的）*a.n.* (~ na, ni) efficient:
kooritsu-teki *na kikai*（効率的な機械）an *efficient* machine | *Hoka ni motto* kooritsu-teki *na hoohoo wa arimaseñ ka?*（ほかにもっと効率的な方法はありませんか）Isn't there any other method that is more *efficient?*

ko˞or·u こおる（凍る）*vi.* (koor·i-; koor·a-; koot-te Ⓒ) freeze:
Kesa niwa no ike ga kootta.（けさ庭の池が凍った）This morning the pond in the garden *was frozen.*

ko˞oryo こうりょ（考慮）*n.* (*formal*) consideration:
Kimi wa kanojo no kimochi o kooryo *ni ireru hitsuyoo ga arimasu.*（君は彼女の気持ちを考慮に入れる必要があります）You should take her feelings into *account.* | *Sono moñdai wa mada* kooryo *no yochi ga arimasu.*（その問題はまだ考慮の余地があります）As far as that matter goes, there is still room for *consideration.* | *Sono kikaku wa* kooryo-*chuu desu.*（その企画は考慮中です）The project is now under *consideration.*

kooryo suru (~する) *vt.* consider; take into account: *Hiyoo no moñdai o* kooryo suru *hitsuyoo ga arimasu.*（費用の問題を考慮する必要があります）It is necessary to *take* the question of expenses *into account.* | *Iroiro na jijoo o* kooryo shite, keekaku wa chuushi suru koto ni itashimashita.（いろいろな事情を考慮して, 計画は中止することにいたしました）*Taking* all the circumstances into *consideration*, we have decided to cancel the plan.

ko˞oryoku こうりょく（効力）*n.* effect; force; validity:
kooryoku *o hassuru*（効力を発する）come into *effect* | *Sono hooritsu wa mada* kooryoku *ga arimasu.*（その法律はまだ効力があります）That law is still in *force.* | *Kore-ra no kisoku wa* kooryoku *o ushinatte imasu.*（これらの規則は効力を失っています）These regulations are no longer in *effect.*

ko˞osa こうさ（交差）*n.* crossing; intersection:
rittai koosa *no shita o kuruma de tooru*（立体交差の下を車で通る）drive under an *overpass.*

koosa suru (~する) *vi.* cross; intersect: *Kono michi wa kono saki de ooki-na michi to* koosa shimasu.（この道はこの先で大きな道と交差します）This road *joins* a wider one straight ahead.

ko˞osai こうさい（交際）*n.* company; association; friendship; acquaintance:
Kare wa koosai *ga hiroi.*（彼は交際が広い）He has a large circle of *acquaintances.* | *Watashi wa ano hito to wa* koosai *ga arimaseñ.*（私はあの人とは交際がありません）I *do not associate* with him. | *Kare wa kanojo ni* koosai *o mooshikoñda.*（彼は彼女に交際を申し込んだ）He asked her if they could start *going out together.* | koosai-*hi*（交際費）an *expense* account; *entertainment* [*social*] expenses.

koosai suru (~する) *vi.* keep company; associate: *Anata wa tonari kiñjo to umaku* koosai shite imasu ka?（あなたは隣近所とうまく交際していますか）Do you *get on well* with your neighbors?

ko˞osaku¹ こうさく（工作）*n.*
1 handicraft; woodwork:
Kyoo wa koosaku *de take no fue o*

tsukutta. (きょうは工作で竹の笛を作った) I made a bamboo flute in *handicraft class.*
2 maneuvering; move:
Kare wa kooshoo no ura de koosaku o shita. (彼は交渉の裏で工作をした) He *maneuvered* behind the scenes at the negotiations.

ko⌈osaku² こうさく(耕作) *n.* cultivation:
koosaku-*chi* (耕作地) *cultivated* land / koosaku-*butsu* (耕作物) *agricultural* products.
koosaku suru (～する) *vt.* cultivate: *Kare no uchi de wa hiroi noochi o* koosaku *shite imasu.* (彼の家では広い農地を耕作しています) His family *cultivates* a very large area of land.

ko⌈osa⌉ten こうさてん(交差点) *n.* crossing; intersection:
Kesa kono koosateñ *de kuruma no shoototsu jiko ga atta.* (けさこの交差点で車の衝突事故があった) A crash between cars occurred at this *intersection* this morning. / *Tsugi no* koosateñ *o migi ni magatte kudasai.* (次の交差点を右に曲がってください) Please turn to right at the next *crossing.*

ko⌈osee¹ こうせい(構成) *n.* make-up; organization; composition; structure:
buñ no koosee (文の構成) the *structure* of a sentence / *Kono kurasu no* koosee *wa dañjo hañhañ desu.* (このクラスの構成は男女半々です) This class *is composed of* the same number of boys and girls. / koosee-*iñ* (構成員) a *member* (of an organization).
koosee suru (～する) *vt.* make up; organize; compose: *Iiñkai wa shichi-niñ de* koosee *sarete imasu.* (委員会は7人で構成されています) The committee *is made up of* seven members.

ko⌈osee² こうせい(校正) *n.* proof-

reading:
koosee-*zuri* (校正刷り) a *printer's proof.*
koosee (o) suru (～(を)する) *vt.* proofread: *zasshi o* koosee suru (雑誌を校正する) *read proofs* of a magazine.

Ko⌈osee-da⌉ijiñ (厚生大臣) *n.* Minister of Health and Welfare.

Ko⌈ose⌉e-shoo こうせいしょう(厚生省) *n.* Ministry of Health and Welfare. 《⇨ shoo⁴ (table)》

ko⌈oseñ こうせん(光線) *n.* light; beam; ray:
taiyoo no kooseñ (太陽の光線) the *rays* of the sun.

ko⌉osha¹ こうしゃ(校舎) *n.* school building; schoolhouse. 《⇨ gakkoo》

ko⌉osha² こうしゃ(後者) *n.* (*formal*) the latter:
Washitsu to yooshitsu de wa, koosha *no hoo ga suki desu.* (和室と洋室では, 後者のほうが好きです) Between a Japanese-style room and a western-style room, I prefer *the latter.* 《↔ zeñsha》

ko⌉oshi¹ こうし(講師) *n.* lecturer; instructor:
señniñ[hijookiñ]-kooshi (専任[非常勤]講師) a full-time [part-time] *lecturer* [*instructor*] / *Kare wa sono atsumari de* kooshi *o tsutometa.* (彼はその集まりで講師を勤めた) He *gave a lecture* at the meeting. 《⇨ kyooju (table)》

ko⌉oshi² こうし(公使) *n.* minister (in the diplomatic service):
chuu-Nichi Furañsu kooshi (駐日フランス公使) the French *minister* to Japan. 《⇨ taishi (table)》

ko⌉oshi⌉kañ こうしかん(公使館) *n.* legation. 《⇨ taishikañ (table)》

ko⌉oshiki¹ こうしき(公式) *n.* official; formal:
Daihyoosha no namae ga kooshiki *ni happyoo ni natta.* (代表者の名前が公式に発表になった) The names of

the representatives were *officially* announced. / kooshiki-*seemee* (公式声明) an *official* statement / kooshiki-*hoomoñ* (公式訪問) a *formal* visit.

ko⌈oshiki[2] こうしき (公式) *n.* formula:
suugaku no kooshiki (数学の公式) a mathematical *formula.*

ko⌈oshiñ こうしん (行進) *n.* march; parade:
guñtai no kooshiñ (軍隊の行進) a military *parade* / kooshiñ-*kyoku* (行進曲) a musical *march.*

  kooshiñ suru (〜する) *vi.* march; parade: *Yuushoo chiimu wa oo-doori o* kooshiñ *shita.* (優勝チームは大通りを行進した) The victorious team *paraded* down the main street.

ko⌈oshi⌉see こうせい (高姿勢) *n.* aggressive [high-handed] attitude:
Aite-gawa wa wareware ni tai-shite kooshisee *ni deta.* (相手側はわれわれに対して高姿勢に出た) The other party adopted a *high-handed attitude* toward us. 《↔ teeshisee》

ko⌈o-shite こうして *adv.* in this way:
Nekutai wa koo-shite *musubi-masu.* (ネクタイはこうして結びます) You tie a necktie *like this.* / Koo-shite *watashi wa sainañ kara umaku nogaremashita.* (こうして私は災難からうまく逃れました) *This* is how I successfully avoided the disaster. / Koo-shite *ojiisañ wa kane-mochi ni narimashita.* (こうしておじいさんは金持ちになりました) And *thus* the old man became rich. / *Isoga-shikute,* koo-shite *jitto suwatte wa irarenai.* (忙しくて、こうしてじっと座ってはいられない) I am too busy to sit around *in this way* doing nothing. 《⇨ aa-shite; soo-shite》

ko⌈oshoo こうしょう (交渉) *n.*

1 negotiations; talks:
Kooshoo *wa ma-mo-naku saikai sareru deshoo.* (交渉は間もなく再開されるでしょう) The *negotiations* will soon be resumed. / *Sono* kooshoo *wa matomarimashita.* (その交渉はまとまりました) The *negotiations* were concluded.

2 connection; relations:
Watashi wa seejika to wa nañ no kooshoo *mo arimaseñ.* (私は政治家とは何の交渉もありません) I have no *connections* with politicians.

  kooshoo suru (〜する) *vt.* negotiate: *Keeyaku ni tsuite wa ima aite to* kooshoo *shite iru tokoro desu.* (契約については今相手と交渉しているところです) Regarding the contract, we *are* now *negotiating* with the other party.

ko⌈oshuu こうしゅう (公衆) *n.* the general public:
Kooshuu *no meñzeñ de haji o kakasareta.* (公衆の面前で恥をかかされた) I was put to shame in *public.* / kooshuu-*dootoku* (公衆道徳) *public* morality / kooshuu-*eesee* (公衆衛生) *public* health [hygiene]

ko⌈oshuu-be⌉ñjo こうしゅうべんじょ (公衆便所) *n.* public lavatory [toilet].

KOOSHUU-BEÑJO

ko⌈oshuu-de⌉ñwa こうしゅうでんわ (公衆電話) *n.* public telephone; pay phone. 《⇨ deñwa》

───(**CULTURE**)───
There are several kinds of public telephones in Japan, depending on the kind of payment

they take, their range of operation, and who operates them. '*Aka-deñwa*' (red phones) and '*piñku-deñwa*' (pink phones) accept only 10-yen coins, can be used for calling anywhere in Japan, and are operated by the proprietors of the place they are located. '*Kiiro-deñwa*' (yellow phones) are operated directly by the phone company, take both 10- and 100-yen coins, and can be used for domestic calls, although there are a few from which one can make international calls. The last category of phone does not have a specific name per se. They are green, also operated directly by the phone company, and take both coins and pre-paid telephone cards ('*terehoñ-kaado*,' or '*tereka*'). Many are designated also for international use. None of the coin-operated phones give change for the coin unit being used.

ko⌐oshuu-do⌐otoku （公衆道徳） *n.* public morals. （⇨ *dootoku*）

ko⌐osoku-do⌐oro こうそくどうろ （高速道路） *n.* expressway; freeway; motorway. （⇨ *dooro*）

ko⌐osoo こうそう（構想） *n.* plan; idea; design; plot:
koosoo *o tateru* [*neru*] （構想を立てる[練る]）map out [refine] a *plan* / *Shiñ-kuukoo keñsetsu no* koosoo *wa juñchoo ni shiñkoo shite imasu.* （新空港建設の構想は順調に進行しています）The *plan* to build a new airport is proceeding smoothly. / *Shoosetsu no* koosoo *wa dekimashita ka?* （小説の構想はできましたか）Have you worked out the *plot* of your novel?
　koosoo suru （〜する） *vt.* plan; design; plot: *Shi tookyoku wa*

kono chiiki ni shoppiñgu señtaa o koosoo *shite imasu.* （市当局はこの地域にショッピングセンターを構想しています）The municipal authorities *are planning* a shopping center in this area.

ko⌐osu コース *n.* **1** (of lessons) course:
Nihoñgo no shokyuu [*chuukyuu; jookyuu*] koosu （日本語の初級[中級;上級]コース）the beginners' [intermediate; advanced] Japanese *course*.
2 (of a race) course; lane: *dai-sañ* koosu *o hashiru* （第3コースを走る）run in *Lane* No. 3.
3 (of a meal) course: *furu*-koosu *no shokuji* （フルコースの食事）a meal with all the *courses*.

ko⌐osui こうすい（香水） *n.* perfume; scent:
koosui *o tsukeru* （香水をつける）put on *perfume*.

ko⌐otai こうたい（交替） *n.* shift; change:
Watashi-tachi wa kootai *de uñteñ o shimashita.* （私たちは交替で運転をしました）We took *turns* doing the driving. / *Kañgofu wa ichi-nichi sañ*-kootai *de hataraite imasu.* （看護婦は一日三交替で働いています）Nurses work one of three *shifts* a day. / kootai-*jikañ* （交替時間）the time of the *shift change*.
　kootai suru （〜する） *vi.* take turns; change: *Sooji toobañ wa maishuu* kootai *shimasu.* （掃除当番は毎週交替します）The person in charge of cleaning *changes* every week. / *Kare ga watashi to* kootai *shite kuremashita.* （彼が私と交替してくれました）He was kind enough to *take my place*.

ko⌐otee¹ こうてい（肯定） *n.* affirmation; affirmative:
kootee-*buñ* （肯定文）an *affirmative* sentence.
　kootee suru （〜する） *vt.* affirm;

acknowledge; confirm: *Kare wa sono uwasa o* kootee *mo hitee mo shinakatta.*(彼はそのうわさを肯定も否定もしなかった) He neither *confirmed* nor denied the rumor. 《↔ hitee》

ko⌐otee[2] こうてい（皇帝）*n.* emperor. ★ The Japanese emperor is known as 'teñnoo.'

ko⌐oteñ-teki こうてんてき（後天的）*a.n.* (~ na, ni) acquired; a posteriori:
kooteñ-teki *na seekaku* (後天的な性格) a personality *acquired because of one's upbringing and environment.* 《↔ señteñ-teki》

ko⌐oto[1] コート *n.* coat; overcoat; raincoat; trenchcoat.

ko⌐oto[2] コート *n.* court:
tenisu kooto (テニスコート) a tennis *court.*

ko⌐otoo こうとう（高等）*a.n.* (~ na) high; higher; advanced:
kootoo *na gijutsu* (高等な技術) *advanced* technology / kootoo-*kyooiku* (高等教育) *higher* education / kootoo-*doobutsu* (高等動物) the *higher* animals.

ko⌐otoo-ga⌐kkoo こうとうがっこう（高等学校）*n.* senior high school; upper secondary school. 《⇨ koo-koo》

ko⌐otsuu こうつう（交通）*n.* traffic; transportation; communication.
Kono toori wa kootsuu *ga hageshii* [*sukunai*].(この通りは交通が激しい[少ない]) The *traffic* is heavy [light] on this street. / *Kare no uchi wa* kootsuu *no beñ ga yoi.* (彼の家は交通の便が良い) His house is convenient for *public transport.* / kootsuu-*hyooshiki* (交通標識) a *traffic* sign / kootsuu-*joohoo* (交通情報) a *traffic* report / kootsuu-*juutai* (交通渋滞) a *traffic* jam / kootsuu-*kikañ* (交通機関) a means of *transport.*

ko⌐otsuu-do⌐otoku （交通道徳）*n.* good driving manners; consideration for others when driving. 《⇨ dootoku》

ko⌐otsuu⌐uhi こうつうひ（交通費）*n.* traveling expenses; carfare.

ko⌐otsuu-ji⌐ko こうつうじこ（交通事故）*n.* traffic accident:
kootsuu-jiko *ni au* (交通事故にあう) meet with a *traffic accident* / *Koko de sakuya* kootsuu-jiko *ga atta.*(ここで昨夜交通事故があった) A *traffic accident* occurred here last night. / *Kare wa* kootsuu-jiko *de kega o shita.*(彼は交通事故でけがをした) He was injured in a *traffic accident.*

ko⌐ouñ こううん（幸運）*n.* good luck [fortune]:
Koouñ o inorimasu. (幸運を祈ります) I wish you *good luck.* 《⇨ uñ¹》
— *a.n.* (~ na, ni) lucky; fortunate:
koouñ *na hito* (幸運な人) a *fortunate* person / *Kimi wa sono hikooki ni noranakute,* koouñ *datta.* (君はその飛行機に乗らなくて、幸運だった) It was *lucky* that you did not travel on that plane. 《↔ fuuñ²》
koouñ ni mo (~にも) luckily; fortunately: *Chichi wa* koouñ ni mo *inochi ga tasukatta.* (父は幸運にも命が助かった) *As luck would have it,* my father's life was saved.

ko⌐oyoo こうよう（紅葉）*n.* red leaves; autumn colors [tints]:
Sono yama wa kooyoo *de moete ita.*(その山は紅葉で燃えていた) The mountainside was ablaze with *autumn colors.*
kooyoo suru (~する) *vi.* turn red [yellow]: *Kono heñ no yama wa itsu-goro* kooyoo *shimasu ka?* (この辺の山はいつごろ紅葉しますか) When do the mountains around here *take on their autumn colors?*

ko⌐ozañ[1] こうざん（鉱山）*n.* mine.

ko⌐ozañ[2] こうざん（高山）*n.* high

mountain:
koozañ-*shokubutsu* (高山植物) an
alpine plant / koozañ-*byoo* (高山
病) *mountain* sickness.

ko⌐ozeñ こうぜん (公然) *a.n.*
(~ to; ~ taru) open; public:
Sono seejika wa koozeñ *to shushoo o hinañ shita.* (その政治家は公
然と首相を非難した) The politician
publicly criticized the prime minister.
koozeñ no himitsu (~の秘密) an
open secret: *Sore wa* koozeñ no
himitsu *desu.* (それは公然の秘密です)
It is an *open secret.*

ko⌐ozoo こうぞう (構造) *n.* structure; construction:
buñ no koozoo (文の構造) the *structure* of a sentence / *shakai no* koozoo (社会の構造) the *structure* of
society / *Kono tatemono no* koozoo *wa gañjoo da.* (この建物の構造は
がんじょうだ) The *construction* of
this building is solid. / *Sono kuruma wa* koozoo-joo no *kekkañ
ga atta.* (その車は構造上の欠陥があっ
た) The car had *structural* defects.

ko⌐ozui こうずい (洪水) *n.* flood;
inundation:
Oo-ame de koozui *ni natta.* (大雨で
洪水になった) The heavy rain
caused a *flood.*

ko⌐pii コピー *n.* copy; photocopy:

――――(**USAGE**)――――
Comes from English, 'copy,'
but not used in the sense of a
single example of a magazine,
book, etc.

Watashi wa sono tegami no kopii
o totta. (私はその手紙のコピーをとった)
I made a *copy* of the letter. /
kakudai [*shukushoo*] kopii (広大
[縮小]コピー) an enlarged [a re-
duced] *copy.*
kopii suru (~する) *vt.* copy; photocopy: *Kono shorui o* kopii shite *kudasai.* (この書類をコピーしてくださ

い) Please *copy* these documents.

ko⌐ppu コップ *n.* glass; tumbler:
koppu *ip-pai no mizu* (コップ一杯の
水) a *glass* of water. 《⇨ kappu
(photo)》

ko⌐ra こら *int.* (*rude*) hey (you)!;
hi!; there! ★ Used by men
when reprimanding someone.
Kora, itazura wa yoshi nasai. (こら,
いたずらはよしなさい) *Come on!*
Stop fooling around.

ko⌐rae⌐·ru こらえる (堪える) *vt.*
(korae-te Ⅴ) **1** bear; stand;
endure:
itami o koraeru (痛みをこらえる)
endure pain / *kuufuku o* koraeru
(空腹をこらえる) *bear* hunger.
2 control; subdue; suppress:
namida o koraeru (涙をこらえる)
keep back one's tears / *warai o*
koraeru (笑いをこらえる) *suppress* a
laugh / *akubi o* koraeru (あくびをこ
らえる) *stifle* a yawn.

ko⌐re これ (此れ) *n.* **1** this:
★ Refers to something or someone that is close to the speaker.
Kore wa dare no hoñ desu ka? (こ
れはだれの本ですか) Whose book is
this? / *Sumimaseñ,* kore *o katazu-
kete kudasai.* (すみません, これを片づけ
てください) Excuse me, but could
you put *this* away?
2 this: ★ Introduces or refers
to one's own wife or child.
Kore ga uchi no kanai [*musuko*]
desu. (これがうちの家内[息子]です)
This is my wife [son].
3 this; it: ★ Refers to something or someone that was previously mentioned or that is
about to be mentioned.
Kodomo no seeseki ga waruku,
kore *ga nayami no tane desu.* (子ど
もの成績が悪く, これが悩みの種です)
My son is doing poorly at school,
and *this* is the source of my distress. / *Zairyoo o yoku maze,* kore
ni tamago o kuwaemasu. (材料をよ

く混ぜ, これに卵を加えます) Mix the ingredients well, and then add the egg to *it*.

4 this; that: ★ Refers to a continuing state or action.

Kore *de yoshi*. (これでよし) *This* will do. / *Kyoo wa* kore *de owari ni shiyoo*. (きょうはこれで終わりにしよう) Let's finish off *here* for today.

5 this; that: ★ Used for emphasis.

Kore *wa hidoi netsu da*. (これはひどい熱だ) What a fever *this* is! / Kore *wa sugoi*. (これはすごい) *That's* great! 《⇨ are¹; dore¹; sore¹》

ko⌈re de⌉ これで (此れで) *adv.*
now; under the circumstances; with this:

Ko⌈re de *añshiñ shita*. (これで安心した) I *now* feel relieved. / Kore de *ano jikeñ kara sañ-neñ ni naru*. (これであの事件から3年になる) It is *now* three years since that incident. / Kore de *watashi no yume mo tsubureta*. (これで私の夢もつぶれた) *With this* my dream has been destroyed. / Kore de *jiko no gisee-sha wa sañ-juu mee ni narimashita*. (これで事故の犠牲者は30名になりました) *With this* the number of victims of the accident has reached thirty. / Kore de *watashi no hanashi wa owari desu*. (これで私の話は終わりです) *This* winds up my story.

ko⌈re kara⌉ これから (此れから)
1 now:

Kore kara *shusseki o torimasu*. (これから出席をとります) I am *now* going to take attendance. / Kore kara *iku tokoro desu*. (これから行くところです) I am *now* leaving.

2 from now on; after this; in the future:

Kore kara *wa motto chuui shimasu*. (これからはもっと注意します) I will be more careful *from now on*. / Kore kara *doo shite ii ka wakari-*

maseñ. (これからどうしていいかわかりません) I am at a loss what to do *in the future*. 《⇨ are kara; sore kara》

ko⌈re-(k)kiri これっきり (此れっきり)
adv. (with a negative) **1** (of future) never:

Kore-kkiri *kanojo to wa aenai ka mo shirenai*. (これっきり彼女とは会えないかもしれない) I'm afraid I will *never* be able to see her again.

2 (of a thing) only:

O-kane wa kore-kkiri *shika motte imaseñ*. (お金はこれっきりしか持っていません) This is the *only* money I have. 《⇨ are-(k)kiri》

ko⌈re ma⌉de これまで (此れ迄)
1 so far; until now:

Kare wa kore made *gakkoo o yasuñda koto ga arimaseñ*. (彼はこれまで学校を休んだことがありません) *So far* he has not missed a day from school. / Kore made *no keeka o go-hookoku itashimasu*. (これまでの経過をご報告いたします) I will now report on the progress *up to now*. / Kore made *no koto wa wasurete kudasai*. (これまでのことは忘れてください) Please forget about everything *so far*.

2 here:

Kyoo wa kore made. (きょうはこれまで) Let us finish *here* today.

3 what I am; what it is:

Watashi ga kore made *(ni) nareta no mo mina-sañ no okage desu*. (私がこれまで(に)なれたのも皆さんのお陰です) It is thanks to all of you that I am now *what I am*.

ko⌈ri¹·ru こりる (懲りる) *vi.* (kori-te Ⅴ) **1** learn a lesson:

Kare wa mada sono shippai ni korinai yoo da. (彼はまだその失敗に懲りないようだ) It seems he *has not learned a lesson* from his failure. / *Kore ni korite, kore kara wa ki o tsukemasu*. (これに懲りて, これからは気をつけます) *Having learned* from

this, I will take care from now on.
2 have enough (on); be soured: *Kekkoñ ni wa* korite imasu. (結婚には懲りています) I've *had a bitter experience* with marriage.

ko⌐ro ころ (頃) *n.* the time: *Sakura wa ima ga ichibañ ii* koro *desu.* (桜は今がいちばんいいころです) Now is the best *time* for cherry blossoms. / *Moo sorosoro kare ga kuru* koro *desu.* (もうそろそろ彼が来るころです) It will soon be *time* for him to arrive. / *Kodomo no* koro *kono kawa de yoku oyoida mono desu.* (子どものころこの川でよく泳いだものです) In my *childhood* I often used to swim in this river. / *Omae wa sorosoro dokuritsu shite mo ii* koro *da.* (お前はそろそろ独立してもいいころだ) It is about *time* for you to go out in the world on your own. / *Sono* koro (*wa*) *watashi wa mada shoogakusee deshita.* (そのころ(は)私はまだ小学生でした) I was still an elementary school pupil at that *time.* 《⇨ -goro》

ko⌐rob·u ころぶ (転ぶ) *vi.* (korob·i-; korob·a-; koroñ-de Ⓒ) fall; tumble: *Kare wa ne ni tsumazuite* koroñda. (彼は根につまずいて転んだ) He tripped on a root and *fell.* 《⇨ taoreru》

ko⌐rogar·u ころがる (転がる) *vi.* (-gar·i-; -gar·a-; -gat-te Ⓒ) **1** roll; fall; tumble: *Booru ga saka o* korogatte *itta.* (ボールが坂を転がっていった) The ball *rolled down* away the slope. 《⇨ korogasu》
2 lie down: *Tsukareta no de shibafu ni* korogatte *yasuñda.* (疲れたので芝生に転がって休んだ) I was tired, so I *lay down* on the lawn to take a rest.

ko⌐rogas·u ころがす (転がす) *vt.* (-gash·i-; -gas·a-; -gash·i-te Ⓒ)

roll; tumble over: *Sono ooki-na ishi o* korogashite *ugokashita.* (その大きな石を転がして動かした) We moved that large stone by *rolling* it along. 《⇨ korogaru》

ko⌐rokoro ころころ *adv.* (~ to) (the sound or manner of a small, round object rolling): *Booru ga* korokoro (to) *korogatte kita.* (ボールがころころ(と)転がって来た) A ball came *rolling up* to me.
korokoro (to) kawaru (~(と)変わる) change easily: *Kare wa ikeñ ga* korokoro (to) *kawaru.* (彼は意見がころころ(と)変わる) His opinion is *always changing.*

ko⌐ro⌐ri ころり *adv.* (~ to) **1** easily; suddenly: *Shiai ni* korori *to makete shimatta.* (試合にころりと負けてしまった) We lost the game *easily.* / *Kanojo wa kare ni* korori *to damasareta.* (彼女は彼にころりとだまされた) She was *easily* taken in by him.
2 quite; entirely: *Sono yakusoku o* korori *to wasurete ita.* (その約束をころりと忘れていた) I *quite* forgot the appointment.

ko⌐ros·u ころす (殺す) *vt.* (korosh·i-; koros·a-; korosh·i-te Ⓒ)
1 kill; murder: *Kare wa* korosu *to itte, watashi o odoshita.* (彼は殺すと言って、私を脅した) He threatened to *kill* me. / *Sono señsoo de ooku no hito ga* korosareta. (その戦争で多くの人が殺された) A large number of people *were killed* in that war.
2 suppress (breathing, a yawn, etc.); restrain: *iki o* korosu (息を殺す) *hold* one's breath / *Kanojo wa koe o* koroshite *naita.* (彼女は声を殺して泣いた) She cried in a *suppressed* tone of voice.

ko⌐r·u¹ こる (凝る) *vi.* (kor·i-; kor·a-; kot-te Ⓒ) be crazy; be devoted:

Kare wa gorufu ni kotte iru. (彼は
ゴルフに凝っている) He *is crazy*
about golf.

ko¹r·u² こる (凝る) *vi.* (kor·i-; ko-
r·a·-; kot-te Ⓒ) (of shoulders) be
stiff:
Konogoro yoku kata ga koru. (この
ごろよく肩が凝る) My shoulders *are*
frequently *stiff* these days.

ko¹same こさめ (小雨) *n.* light
rain; drizzle:
Kosame ga furi-dashita. (小雨が降
り出した) A *light rain* began to fall.
《↔ oo-ame》

ko¹see こせい (個性) *n.* individ-
ulality; personality:
kosee ga aru [nai] (個性がある[ない])
have [lack] *individuality* / *kosee
o nobasu* (個性を伸ばす) develop
one's *individuality* / *kosee o
hakki suru* (個性を発揮する) exhibit
one's *originality* / *Kanojo wa tsuyoi* kosee *no mochinushi da.* (彼女
は強い個性の持ち主だ) She is the
possessor of a strong *personality.*

ko¹see-teki こせいてき (個性的)
a.n. (~ na, ni) distinctive:
*kosee-teki ni sekkee sareta tate-
mono* (個性的に設計された建物) a
building of *unusual design* / *Ano
haiyuu wa* kosee-teki *na kao o
shite iru.* (あの俳優は個性的な顔をして
いる) The actor has a *distinctive*
face.

ko¹seki こせき (戸籍) *n.* family
register.

━━━ (CULTURE) ━━━
Under the Japanese legal system, the record of birth, marriage, divorce and death of
each person is registered in a
family register with municipal,
town or village offices, and the
copy of the official entry is
issued on demand for identification. An exact copy of one's
family registration is called
'koseki *toohoñ*' (戸籍謄本) and

an extract, 'koseki *shoohoñ*' (戸
籍抄本). The latter is used as a
birth certificate as in Europe
and North America.

ko¹shi こし (腰) *n.* waist; hip:
koshi *o mageru* (腰を曲げる) bend
one's *back* / koshi o nobasu (腰を
伸ばす) *stretch oneself* / isu ni koshi o orosu (椅子に腰を下ろす) *sit*
on a chair / ryoote o koshi *ni
attete tatsu* (両手を腰にあてて立つ)
stand with one's hands on one's
hips / koshi *ni beruto o tsukeru*
(腰にベルトをつける) wear a belt
around one's *waist* / *Koshi ga itai.*
(腰が痛い) I have a pain in my
lower back. / koshi-*mawari* (腰まわ
り) one's *waist* measurement.
《⇨ shiri》

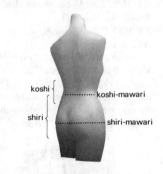

koshi {
koshi-mawari
shiri {
shiri-mawari

koshi ga hikui (~ が低い) be polite [modest]: *Kare wa* koshi ga
hikui. (彼は腰が低い) He *is unas-
suming.*
koshi ga omoi (~ が重い) be slow
to act: *Kanojo wa* koshi ga omoi.
(彼女は腰が重い) She *is slow to take
action.*
ko¹shikake¹ こしかけ (腰掛け) *n.*
1 chair; stool:
koshikake *ni suwaru* (腰掛けに座る)
sit on a *chair.* 《⇨ isu; koshika-
keru》
2 temporary work; makeshift

job:

Kanojo no shigoto wa kekkoñ made no koshikake da. (彼女の仕事は結婚までの腰掛けだ) Her job is a *temporary one* until marriage. 《⇨ riñji》

ko⌈shikake⌉·ru こしかける (腰掛ける) *vi.* (-kake-te Ⓥ) sit down; take a seat:

Kare wa kooeñ no beñchi ni koshi-kaketa. (彼は公園のベンチに腰掛けた) He *sat down* on the park bench. 《⇨ koshikake》

ko⌈shirae-ru こしらえる (拵える) *vt.* (-rae-te Ⓥ) make; build:

Kare wa jibuñ de inugoya o ko-shiraeta. (彼は自分で犬小屋をこしらえた) He *made* a doghouse by himself. / *Kono ryoori wa dare ga ko-shiraemashita ka?* (この料理はだれがこしらえましたか) Who *cooked* this meal? 《⇨ tsukuru¹》

ko⌈shoo¹ こしょう (故障) *n.* breakdown; trouble:

Kuruma ga eñjiñ no koshoo o oko-shita ga sugu ni naotta. (車がエンジンの故障を起こしたがすぐに直った) The car developed engine *trouble* but it soon went away. / Koshoo-chuu. *(sign)* (故障中) *Out of Order.*

KOSHOO-CHUU SIGN

koshoo suru (～する) *vi.* go out of order; break down; be in trouble: *Kono heya no ruumu-kuuraa wa ima koshoo shite imasu.* (この部屋のルームクーラーは今故障しています) The air conditioner in this room *is not working* now.

ko⌈sho⌉o² こしょう (胡椒) *n.* pepper:

koshoo o kakeru (こしょうをかける) put *pepper* on.

koso こそ *p.* indeed; just:

★ Used to emphasize the preceding word.

"Hajimemashite. Doozo yoroshiku." "Kochira koso." (「はじめまして。どうぞよろしく」「こちらこそ」) "How do you do? It is a pleasure to meet you." "*The same* here." / *Yoo koso irasshaimashita.* (ようこそいらっしゃいました) You are *indeed* welcome. / *Ano hito wa gaikeñ koso warui ga totemo ii hito desu.* (あの人は外見こそ悪いがとてもいい人です) That man, *in appearance*, does not look so attractive, but he is a very nice person. / *Koñdo koso seekoo shite miseru.* (今度こそ成功して見せる) *This one time* I will show you I can succeed. / *Tomo-dachi da kara koso ii-nikui koto mo ieru no desu.* (友だちだからこそ言いにくいことも言えるのです) I can tell you that which is hard to say, *precisely because* you are my friend.

...koso sure (...～すれ) surely; far from (being): ★ Stresses the occurrence of a certain action or fact in contrast to the non-occurrence of another.

Gogo ni natte kaze wa tsuyoku nari koso sure, yowaku wa narana-katta. (午後になって風は強くなりこそすれ、弱くはならなかった) In the afternoon, the wind, *rather than* abating, became stronger. / *Chi-chi ga sono shirase o kiitara, yoro-kobi koso sure, okoru hazu wa ari-maseñ.* (父がその知らせを聞いたら、喜びこそすれ、怒るはずはありません) When my father hears that news he *will surely be pleased* with it and have no reason to be angry.

ko⌈sso⌉ri こっそり *adv.* (～ to)

secretly; stealthily; in private:
Kare wa kanojo ni kossori *(to)*
atte ita. (彼は彼女にこっそり(と)会って
いた) He was meeting with her *secretly.* / *Watashi wa* kossori *(to)*
kaijoo kara nukedashita. (私はこっそ
り(と)会場から抜け出した) I *stealthily*
slipped out of the hall.

ko⌐s·u¹ こす (越す) *vt.* (kosh·i-;
kos·a-; kosh·i-te Ⓒ) **1** go over;
cross:
Kare no utta booru wa feñsu o
koshita. (彼の打ったボールはフェンスを
越した) The ball he hit *went over*
the fence.
2 move (to a new house):
Raigetsu atarashii ie e koshimasu.
(来月新しい家へ越します) We *are
moving* to a new house next
month.
3 spend (time):
*Kare wa Hokkaidoo de sukii o
shite, fuyu o* koshita. (彼は北海道で
スキーをして、冬を越した) He *spent*
winter skiing in Hokkaido.

ko⌐s·u² こす (超す) *vt.* (kosh·i-;
kos·a-; kosh·i-te Ⓒ) be over;
be more than:
Shachoo wa nanajuu o koshite iru.
(社長は70を超している) Our presi-
dent *is more than* seventy. / *Kare
wa seegeñ sokudo o nijuk-kiro* koshite, *tsukamatta.* (彼は制限速度を
20キロ超して、捕まった) He was ar-
rested for driving twenty k.p.h.
over the speed limit.

ko⌐su⌐r·u こする (擦る) *vt.* (kosur-
r·i-; kosur·a-; kosut-te Ⓒ) rub;
scrub:
Kare wa nemui me o kosutta. (彼
は眠い目をこすった) He *rubbed* his
sleepy eyes. / *Kanojo wa yuka o
burashi de* kosutta. (彼女は床をブラ
シでこすった) She *scrubbed* the floor
with a brush.

ko⌐ta⌐e こたえ (答え) *n.* answer;
reply; response:
kotae *o dasu* (答えを出す) get an

answer (to a problem) / *Kono* kotae *wa atte [machigatte] imasu.* (こ
の答えはあって[間違って]います) This
answer is right [wrong]. / *Doa o
nokku shita ga* kotae *ga nakatta.*
(ドアをノックしたが答えがなかった) I
knocked at the door, but there
was no *response.* (⟷ toi)
(⇨ kotaeru)

ko⌐tae⌐·ru こたえる (答える) *vi.*
(kotae-te Ⓥ) answer; reply:
Namae o yoñdara, kotae nasai.
(名前を呼んだら、答えなさい) When I
call out your names, please *answer.* / *Sono ko wa nani o kiite mo*
kotaenakatta. (その子は何を聞いても
答えなかった) Whatever I asked the
child, he *did not reply.* / *Sono shitsumoñ ni dare mo* kotaerarenakatta. (その質問にだれも答えられなかっ
た) *Nobody could answer* the question. (⇨ kotae)

ko⌐tai こたい (固体) *n.* solid.
(⇨ ekitai; kitai²)

ko⌐tatsu こたつ (炬燵) *n.* Japanese foot warmer. ★ A traditional heating device with frame
and coverlet over it. As a heat
source, an electric heater is used

KOTATSU

INSIDE A DEÑKI-GOTATSU

today instead of a charcoal bur-
ner. (⇨ deñki-gotatsu)

ko⌈tchi⌉ こっち *n.* ★ Informal
equivalent of '*kochira.*'
1 this; here:
*"Dochira ni shimasu ka?" "Kotchi
ni shimasu."* (「どちらにしますか」「こっ
ちにします」) "Which do you like?"
"I'll take *this.*" / *Kotchi no heya
no hoo ga sotchi yori hiroi.* (こっち
の部屋のほうがそっちより広い) *This*
room is larger than that. / *Kare
wa ma-mo-naku* kotchi *e kimasu.*
(彼は間もなくこっちへ来ます) He will
be *here* very soon.
2 we; I:
Kotchi ni wa sekiniñ wa arimaseñ.
(こっちには責任はありません) *We* are
not to blame. / *Deñwa wa* kotchi
kara kakemasu. (電話はこっちからかけ
ます) *I'*ll give you a call. (⇨ atchi;
dotchi; sotchi)

ko⌈tee⌉ こてい (固定) *n.* fixation:
kotee-*kyaku* (固定客) a *regular*
customer / kotee-*shisañ zee* (固定
資産税) a *fixed* property tax /
kotee-*shuunyuu* (固定収入) a *fixed*
income.
kotee suru (〜する) *vt.* fix; settle:
Kono tsukue wa yuka ni kotee
shite arimasu. (この机は床に固定して
あります) This desk *is bolted* to the
floor.

ko⌈teñ⌉ こてん (古典) *n.* classics:
Nihoñ no koteñ (日本の古典) the
Japanese *classics* / koteñ-*oñgaku*
(古典音楽) *classical* music.

ko⌈to⌉¹ こと (事) *n.* **1** thing; matter; affair; fact: ★ The meaning
is defined by the preceding noun
or modifier.
Kyoo wa suru koto *ga takusañ aru.*
(きょうはすることがたくさんある) I have
a lot of *things to do* today. / *Kare
no* koto *ga wasurerarenai.* (彼のこ
とが忘れられない) I cannot forget
about him. / *Koñna* koto *wa hajimete desu.* (こんなことは始めてです)

This is the first time I've experienced *anything like this.* / *Kuwashii* koto *wa shirimaseñ.* (詳しいこと
は知りません) I don't know about
the *details.* / *Yakkai na* koto *ni
natta.* (やっかいなことになった) We are
in *trouble* now. / *Kanojo no* koto
kikimashita ka? (彼女のこと聞きまし
たか) Have you heard the *rumor
about her.* / *Geñroñ no jiyuu wa*
toozeñ *no* koto *desu.* (言論の自由は
当然のことです) Freedom of speech
is a *matter of course.* / *Kootsuu-
jiko wa mainichi no* koto *desu.*
(交通事故は毎日のことです) Traffic
accidents are *everyday occurrences.*
2 incident; problem; plan:
*Koto wa juñchoo ni susuñde ima-
su.* (ことは順調に進んでいます) The
plan is well under way. / *Nani-ka*
koto *ga attara, sugu shirasete kudasai.* (何かことがあったら、すぐ知らせて
ください) If *anything* happens, let
me know immediately. / *Sore wa*
koto *desu yo.* (それはことですよ)
That's a serious *problem.*
3 (used in giving impersonal orders or instructions):
Shimee oyobi juusho o kinyuu no
koto. (氏名および住所を記入のこと)
Enter both full name and address.
...koto ga aru (...〜がある) have
experienced: ★ Preceded by the
past form of a verb and refers to
experiences in the past. *Watashi
wa mada Iñdo e itta* koto ga arimaseñ. (私はまだインドへ行ったことが
りません) I *have not been* to India
yet. / *Kare wa chuugaku de oshieta* koto ga arimasu. (彼は中学で教え
たことがあります) He *has experience*
of teaching at a junior high
school.
...koto ga dekiru (...〜ができる) be
able to do: ★ Preceded by the
dictionary form of a verb. *Sono*

ooki-na iwa wa ugokasu koto ga dekinakatta.（その大きな岩は動かすことができなかった）We *were unable to move that large rock.*

...koto ni natte iru（...～になっている）be supposed [scheduled] to do: ★ Preceded by the dictionary form of a verb. *Kare to wa go-ji ni au* koto ni natte imasu.（彼とは5時に会うことになっています）I *am set to* meet him at five.

...koto ni shite iru（...～にしている）make it a rule to do: ★ Preceded by the dictionary form of a verb. *Asa wa hayaku okiru* koto ni shite imasu.（朝は早く起きることにしています）I *make it a rule to* get up early in the morning.

...koto ni suru（...～にする）decide to do: ★ Preceded by the dictionary form of a verb. *Kuuraa o kau* koto ni shimashita.（クーラーを買うことにしました）I *decided to* buy an air conditioner. / *Moo kare wa shiñyoo shinai* koto ni shita.（もう彼は信用しないことにした）I *am determined* never *to* trust him again.

ko⌉to² こと（琴）*n.* koto; traditional Japanese harp:
koto *o hiku*（琴をひく）play the *koto.*

KOTO

ko⌉to³ こと（古都）*n.* ancient city [capital]. ★ Often refers to Kyoto or sometimes to Nara.

ko⌈toba⌉ ことば（言葉）*n.* language; word; speech:
Anata wa doñna kotoba *o hanashimasu ka?*（あなたはどんな言葉を話しますか）What *language* do you speak? / *Kanojo wa hijoo ni teenee na* kotoba *o tsukau.*（彼女は非

常に丁寧な言葉を使う）She uses very polite *language.* / *Umai* kotoba *ga mitsukaranai.*（うまい言葉が見つからない）I can't find the right *words.* / *Nihoñ no hyoojuñgo wa Tookyoo no* kotoba *desu.*（日本の標準語は東京の言葉です）The standard language of Japan is the *speech* of Tokyo. / *hanashi[kaki]-*kotoba（話し[書き]言葉）spoken [written] *language.*

ko⌈tobazu⌉kai ことばづかい（言葉遣い）*n.* wording; language; one's way of speaking:
Ano ko wa kotobazukai *ga teenee [rañboo] da.*（あの子は言葉づかいが丁寧[乱暴]だ）That child *speaks politely [rudely].* / Kotobazukai *ni ki o tsuke nasai.*（言葉づかいに気をつけなさい）Watch your *language.* / *Kanojo wa joohiñ na* kotobazukai *o suru.*（彼女は上品な言葉づかいをする）She has a refined *manner of speaking.*

ko⌈togara⌉ ことがら（事柄）*n.* thing; matter; subject:
Kore wa hijoo ni juuyoo na kotogara *desu.*（これは非常に重要な事柄です）This is a very important *matter.*《⇨ koto¹》

ko⌈togo⌉to ni ことごとに（事毎に）*adv.* (*formal*) in everything; in every way:
Kare wa watashi no iu koto ni, kotogoto ni *hañtai suru.*（彼は私の言うことに，ことごとに反対する）He opposes *in every way* what I say.

ko⌈togo⌉toku ことごとく（悉く）*adv.* (*formal*) entirely; utterly:
Yatoo wa yotoo no teeañ ni, kotogotoku *hañtai shite iru.*（野党は与党の提案に，ことごとく反対している）The opposition is *utterly* against the ruling party's proposal.

ko⌉tokoto ことこと *adv.* (～ to) (the sound of food simmering):
Mame o kotokoto (to) *nita.*（豆をことこと（と）煮た）I *simmered* the

beans.

ko「tona」r·u ことなる (異なる) *vi.*
(-nar·i-; -nar·a-; -nat-te C) differ; vary; be different: ★ More
formal than '*chigau.*'
Watashi-tachi no kañgae-kata wa
kotonatte iru. (私たちの考え方は異な
っている) Our ways of thinking *are*
different. / *Eñ sooba wa hi ni yot-*
te kotonarimasu. (円相場は日によっ
て異なります) The exchange rate for
the yen *varies* daily.

ko「to ni ことに (殊に) *adv.* (*for-*
mal) especially; particularly:
Supootsu wa nañ de mo suki desu
ga, koto ni *tenisu ga suki desu.* (ス
ポーツは何でも好きですが, ことにテニスが
好きです) When it comes to sports,
I like everything, *especially* tennis. / *Koko wa yuki no ooi koto*
de yuumee desu ga, kotoshi wa
koto ni *yoku furimashita.* (ここは雪
の多いことで有名ですが, ことしはことによ
く降りました) This place is famous
for having a lot of snow, but this
year *in particular* it has snowed
heavily. 《⇨ toku ni》

ko「to ni yoru to ことによると (事
に依ると) *adv.* probably; possibly:
Koto ni yoru to *gogo wa ame ga*
furu ka mo shirenai. (ことによると午
後は雨が降るかもしれない) There will
probably be rain in the afternoon.
/ Koto ni yoru to *ashita no asa wa*
okureru ka mo shiremaseñ. (ことに
よるとあしたの朝は遅れるかもしれません) I
may *possibly* be late tomorrow
morning.

ko「tori ことり (小鳥) *n.* little bird:
kotori *o kau* (小鳥を飼う) keep a *lit-*
tle bird.

ko「toshi ことし (今年) *n.* this
year:
Kotoshi *wa Oriñpikku no toshi*
desu. (今年はオリンピックの年です)
This year is the year of the Olympics. / Kotoshi *wa reeneñ ni naku*
atatakai. (今年は例年になく暖かい)

This year it is warmer than usual.
/ Kotoshi *no natsu wa Hokkaidoo*
e ikimasu. (今年の夏は北海道へ行き
ます) I'll go to Hokkaido *this* summer. / Kotoshi *mo moo sugu*
owari desu. (今年ももうすぐ終わりで
す) *The year* is almost over.

ototoshi	the year before last
kyoneñ	last year
kotoshi	this year
raineñ	next year
saraineñ	the year after next

ko「towa」r·u ことわる (断る) *vt.*
(-war·i-; -war·a-; -wat-te C)
1 refuse (a demand, request,
admission, etc.); decline; reject;
turn down:
Watashi wa kare no yookyuu o
kotowatta. (私は彼の要求を断った) I
turned down his demand. / *Kare*
wa sono shootai o kotowatta. (彼は
その招待を断った) He *declined* the
invitation. / *Kanojo wa nyuujoo o*
kotowarareta. (彼女は入場を断られ
た) She *was refused* admission.
2 get permission:
Kuruma o tsukau toki wa watashi
ni kotowatte *kudasai.* (車を使うとき
は私に断ってください) When you are
going to use the car, please *get*
permission from me.
3 give notice:
Kare wa arakajime kotowaranai
de kaisha o yamete shimatta. (彼は
あらかじめ断らないで会社を辞めてしまっ
た) *Without giving notice* beforehand, he just went and quit the
company.

ko「towaza ことわざ (諺) *n.* proverb; saying:
"*Toki wa kane nari*" *to iu furui*
kotowaza *ga arimasu.* (「時は金な
り」という古いことわざがあります) There
is an old *saying* that "Time is
money."

ko「tozuke」·ru ことづける (言付ける)

vt. (-zuke-te V̄) leave a message; ask a person to do:
Ato de deñwa suru yoo, kare ni kotozukete *kudasai.* (あとで電話するよう, 彼に言づけてください) Please *ask him* to phone me later. 《⇨ tanomu》

koˈtsu こつ (骨) *n.* knack; secret:
Kare wa tsuri no kotsu *o shitte iru.* (彼は釣りのこつを知っている) He has the *knack* of fishing. / *Sono* kotsu *o nomikomu no ni jikañ ga kakatta.* (そのこつを飲み込むのに時間がかかった) It took me some time to get the *hang* of that.

koˈtsukotsu こつこつ *adv.*
(〜 to) 1 (the sound of a step; tap):
Kotsukotsu *to dare-ka no kutsu no oto ga kikoeru.* (こつこつとだれかの靴の音が聞こえる) I hear the *clicking* sound of someone's heels.
2 steadily; patiently; little by little:
kotsukotsu (*to*) *kane o tameru* (こつこつ(と)金をためる) save money *little by little* / kotsukotsu (*to*) *hataraku* (こつこつ(と)働く) *plod away* at a task / *Kanojo wa mainichi* kotsukotsu (*to*) *beñkyoo shite imasu.* (彼女は毎日こつこつ(と)勉強しています) She studies every day *with steady determination.*

koˈuri こうり (小売り) *n.* retail:
Kore wa kouri *de gohyaku-eñ desu.* (これは小売りで 500 円です) This is 500 yen *retail.* / *Haha wa keshoohiñ no* kouri *o shite imasu.* (母は化粧品の小売りをしています) My mother *retails* cosmetic products. / kouri-*kakaku* (小売価格) the *retail* price / kouri-shooniñ (小売商人) a *retailer* / kouri-teñ (小売店) a *retail* shop. 《⇨ oroshi²》

koˈwagaˈru こわがる (怖がる) *vi.*
(-gar·i-; -gar·a-; -gat-te C̄) be afraid; be frightened; be scared:
Kanojo wa takai tokoro o kowa-

garu. (彼女は高い所を怖がる) She *is afraid* of heights. / *Kodomo wa kaminari no oto o* kowagatta. (子どもは雷の音を怖がった) The child *was frightened* by the sound of thunder. 《⇨ kowai》

koˈwaˈ·i こわい (怖い) *a.* (-ku)
1 dreadful; horrible; frightening:
Kinoo wa kowai *omoi o shita.* (きのうは怖い思いをした) I had a *frightening* experience yesterday. / *Watashi wa takai tokoro ga* kowai. (私は高い所が怖い) I am *afraid* of heights. / *Sono eega o mite,* kowaku natta. (その映画を見て, 怖くなった) I *got scared* when I saw the movie. 《⇨ kowagaru》
2 strict:
Yamada señsee wa kowai. (山田先生は怖い) Our teacher, Mr. Yamada, is very *strict.*

koˈwareˈ·ru こわれる (壊れる) *vi.*
(koware-te V̄) 1 break; be broken; be damaged:
Kabiñ ga yuka ni ochite kowareta. (花びんが床に落ちてこわれた) The vase fell on the floor and *broke.* / *Kono isu wa* kowarete iru. (このいすはこわれている) This chair *is broken.* / *Kuruma ga butsukatte, moñ ga* kowareta. (車がぶつかって, 門がこわれた) The gate *was damaged* when the car ran into it. 《⇨ kowasu》
2 get out of order:
Kono terebi wa kowarete imasu. (このテレビはこわれています) This television *is out of order.* 《⇨ koshoo¹》
3 (of a hope, dream, etc.) be destroyed; be broken off:
Watashi no yume wa kowareta. (私の夢はこわれた) My dream *was destroyed.* / *Kanojo no eñdañ wa* kowareta. (彼女の縁談はこわれた) The arrangements for her marriage *were stopped.* 《⇨ kowasu》

koˈwaˈs·u こわす (壊す) *vt.* (ko-wash·i-; kowas·a-; kowash·i-te

C) **1** break; pull down:
Dare-ka ga doa o kowashita. (だれかがドアをこわした) Someone *broke* the door. / *Kono biru wa ma-monaku* kowasaremasu. (このビルは間もなくこわされます) This building will *be pulled down* in the near future. 《⇨ kowareru》
2 wreck; destroy; ruin; spoil (a hope, dream, etc.):
shizeñ o kowasu (自然をこわす) *destroy* nature / *yume o* kowasu (夢をこわす) *ruin* one's dreams / *fuñiki o* kowasu (雰囲気をこわす) *spoil* the atmosphere. 《⇨ kowareru》
3 injure (health); upset:
Kare wa muri o shite karada o kowashita. (彼は無理をして体をこわした) He *injured* his health by overworking. / *Tabe-sugite onaka o* kowashita. (食べ過ぎておなかをこわした) I *upset* my stomach by eating too much.

ko⌐ya こや (小屋) *n.* hut; shack; shed:
koya *o tateru* (小屋を建てる) put up a *hut* / *Nihoñ no uchi wa yoku* usagi-goya *to iwareru koto ga aru.* (日本の家はよくうさぎ小屋といわれることがある) Japanese houses are often referred to as *rabbit hutches*. ★ The initial /k/ of '*koya*' changes to /g/ in compounds.

ko⌐yomi⌐ こよみ (暦) *n.* calendar; almanac.

ko⌐yubi こゆび (小指) *n.* little finger; little toe. 《⇨ yubi (illus.)》

ko⌐yuki こゆき (小雪) *n.* light snow:
Kesa wa koyuki *ga futta.* (けさは小雪が降った) We had some *light snow* this morning. 《⇨ ooyuki》

ko⌐yuu こゆう (固有) *a.n.* (~ na/ no, ni) peculiar; characteristic; inherent:
Shiñtoo wa Nihoñ koyuu *no shuu-kyoo desu.* (神道は日本固有の宗教です) Shinto is a religion *peculiar* to Japan.

ko⌐zukai こづかい (小遣い) *n.* allowance; pocket money:
Kozukai *wa is-shuukañ goseñ-eñ desu.* (小遣いは一週間5千円です) My weekly *allowance* is 5,000 yen.

ko⌐zu⌐tsumi こづつみ (小包) *n.* parcel; package; parcel post:
Hoñ wa kozutsumi *de okurimashi-ta.* (本は小包で送りました) I sent the book by *parcel post*. / *Kore o* ko-zutsumi *ni shite kudasai.* (これを小包にしてください) Will you please do this up in a *package*?

ku⌐1 く (九) *n.* nine: ★ 「九」 is also sometimes pronounced '*kyuu.*'
ku-*ji* (九時) *nine* o'clock / ku [kyu-u]-*niñ* (九人) *nine* people. ★ For counting days, the ninth day is pronounced '*kokonoka.*' 《⇨ suu² (table); kokonotsu》

ku² く (区) *n.* **1** ward: ★ The basic administrative unit in metropolitan areas. In Tokyo, '*ku*' have the same administrative rank as '*shi*' (市), cities.
*Chiyoda-*ku (千代田区) Chiyoda *Ward*. 《⇨ kuyakusho》
2 district; zone:
Basu wa ik-ku *hyakurokujuu-eñ desu.* (バスは1区160円です) The bus fare is 160 yen per *zone*. / *señkyo-*ku (選挙区) an electoral *district*.

ku¹³ く (句) *n.* phrase:
*meeshi-*ku (名詞句) a noun *phrase* / *see-*ku (成句) a set *phrase*.

ku⌐ba⌐r·u くばる (配る) *vt.* (kubar-i-; kubar·a-; kubat-te C) distribute; deliver; pass out:
bira o kubaru (ビラを配る) *distribute* handbills / *shiñbuñ o* kubaru (新聞を配る) *deliver* newspapers / *Yuu-biñ wa ichi-nichi ni ichi-do* kuba-raremasu. (郵便は一日に一度配られます) The mail *is delivered* once a

day. / *Hisaisha ni shokuryoo ga* kubarareta. (被災者に食料が配られた) Provisions *were delivered* to the victims of the disaster.

ku｢betsu くべつ (区別) *n*. distinction; difference:
Kodomo ni zeñ aku no kubetsu *o oshieru koto wa taisetsu desu.* (子どもに善悪の区別を教えることは大切です) It is important to teach children the *difference* between right and wrong. / *Kono e wa hoñmono ka nisemono ka* kubetsu *ga tsukanai.* (この絵は本物か偽物か区別がつかない) I *cannot tell* whether this picture is the real thing or a forgery.

　kubetsu suru (〜する) *vt*. tell... from; distinguish; discriminate:
Moeru gomi to moenai gomi o kubetsu *shite kudasai.* (燃えるごみと燃えないごみを区別してください) Please *sort out* your trash into burnable and non-burnable.

ku｢bi くび (首) *n*. **1** neck:
★ Refers to the part of the body between the head and the shoulders, and sometimes to the head itself. (⇨ jiñtai (illus.))
Kare wa kubi *ga futoi.* (彼は首が太い) He has a thick *neck*. / *Kanojo wa* kubi *ni sukaafu o maite ita.* (彼女は首にスカーフを巻いていた) She wore a scarf around her *neck*.
2 head:
Mado kara kubi *o dasu to kikeñ desu.* (窓から首を出すと危険です) It is dangerous to stick your *head* out of the window. (⇨ atama)

　kubi ga mawaranai (〜が回らない) be up to one's neck: *Kare wa shakkiñ de* kubi ga mawaranai. (彼は借金で首が回らない) He is in debt *up to his neck*.

　kubi ga tobu (〜が飛ぶ) be fired: *Soñna koto o shitara* kubi ga tobimasu. (そんなことをしたら首が飛びます) If I did something like that, I

would *get the chop*.

　kubi ni naru (〜になる) be dismissed [fired].

　kubi ni suru (〜にする) dismiss [fire].

　kubi o furu (〜を振る) nod; shake one's head: *Kanojo wa dooi shite,* kubi o tate ni futta. (彼女は同意して, 首を縦に振った) She *nodded her head* in agreement. / *Kare wa* kubi *o yoko ni futte 'dame da' to itta.* (彼は首を横に振って「だめだ」と言った) He *shook his head* and said, 'No.'

　kubi o nagaku shite matsu (〜を長くして待つ) wait eagerly: *Kare wa kimi no heñji o* kubi o nagaku shite matte iru. (彼は君の返事を首を長くして待っている) He *is anxiously awaiting* your reply.

　kubi o tsukkomu (〜を突っ込む) consciously involve oneself: *Jibuñ ni kañkee no nai koto ni wa* kubi o tsukkomitaku arimaseñ. (自分に関係のないことには首を突っ込みたくありません) I *don't want to stick my nose* into matters that are no concern of mine.

ku｢cha｣kucha くちゃくちゃ *adv*. (〜 to) (the sound of chewing things):
Mono o taberu toki, kuchakucha (to) *oto o saseru no wa gehiñ desu.* (物を食べるとき, くちゃくちゃ(と)音をさせるのは下品です) It is rude to make a *smacking* noise while eating food.

ku｢chi¹ くち (口) *n*. **1** mouth:
kuchi *o akeru [tojiru]* (口を開ける[閉じる]) open [shut] one's *mouth* / *paipu o* kuchi *ni kuwaeru* (パイプを口にくわえる) have a pipe in one's *mouth*.
2 (of a container) mouth:
biñ no kuchi (びんの口) the *mouth* of a bottle.

　aita kuchi ga fusagaranai (開いた〜がふさがらない) be dumbfounded: *Sore o mite,* aita kuchi ga fusagaranakatta. (それを見て, 開いた口がふさがらなかった) I *was open-mouthed* with amazement on seeing it.

kuchi de iu (〜で言う) tell: *Donna ni ureshikatta ka* kuchi de wa ienai. (どんなにうれしかったか口では言えない) I *can't tell* how happy I was.

kuchi ga karui (〜が軽い) indiscreet; talkative: *Kanojo wa* kuchi ga karui. (彼女は口が軽い) She *cannot keep a secret.*

kuchi ga omoi (〜が重い) be close-mouthed: *Ano hito wa* kuchi ga omoi. (あの人は口が重い) He is *a man of few words.* 《⇨ mukuchi》

kuchi ga suberu (〜が滑る) let slip: *Tsui* kuchi ga subette, *sono himitsu o morashite shimatta.* (つい口が滑って, その秘密を漏らしてしまった) I inadvertently *let* the secret *slip out.*

kuchi ga umai (〜がうまい) be a smooth talker.

kuchi ga warui (〜が悪い) have a sharp tongue: *Kare wa* kuchi wa warui *ga hito wa ii.* (彼は口は悪いが人はいい) He *has a sharp tongue* but he is kind at heart.

kuchi ni au (〜に合う) suit one's taste: *Kono niku wa watashi no* kuchi ni awanai. (この肉は私の口に合わない) This meat *is not to my taste.*

kuchi o kiku (〜をきく) talk; speak: *Kare wa* ooki-na kuchi o kiku. (彼は大きな口をきく) He *has a big mouth.* | *Ano hito to wa* kuchi o kiita koto ga arimaseñ. (あの人とは口をきいたことがありません) I've *never talked* with her.

ku⌈chi² くち (口) n. job; position; opening: *Kanojo wa taipisuto no* kuchi o mitsuketa. (彼女はタイピストの口を見つけた) She found a *job* as a typist.

ku⌈chibeni くちべに (口紅) n.

rouge; lipstick: *kuchi ni* kuchibeni o nuru (口に口紅を塗る) put *lipstick* on one's lips.

ku⌈chibiru くちびる (唇) n. lip: kuchibiru o kamu (唇を噛む) bite one's *lip* | uwa-kuchibiru (上唇) the upper *lip* | shita-kuchibiru (下唇) the lower *lip.*

ku⌈chi¹guchi ni くちぐちに (口々に) adv. unanimously; in unison; at once: *Sono shuukai no sañkasha wa* kuchiguchi ni *seefu ni taisuru fumañ o nobeta.* (その集会の参加者は口々に政府に対する不満を述べた) The participants at the meeting *unanimously* expressed their dissatisfaction with the government. | *Miñna wa* kuchiguchi ni *kanojo no e o hometa.* (みんなは口々に彼女の絵を褒めた) They were *all* in agreement in praising her painting.

ku⌈chihige くちひげ (口髭) n. mustache. 《↔ hige (table)》

ku⌈da くだ (管) n. pipe; tube: kuda *ni mizu o toosu* (管に水を通す) run water through a *pipe.*

ku⌈dake¹·ru くだける (砕ける) vi. (kudake-te Ⅴ) break; go to pieces: *Ishi ga atatte, kagami ga* kudaketa. (石が当たって, 鏡が砕けた) A stone hit the mirror and it *smashed.* | *Nami ga iwa ni atatte* kudaketa. (波が岩に当たって砕けた) The waves *broke* against the rocks. 《⇨ kudaku》

ku⌈da¹keta くだけた 1 (of language) colloquial; informal: kudaketa *iikata* (くだけた言いかた) a *colloquial* expression. 2 (of a person) affable: kudaketa *hito* (くだけた人) an *affable* person.

ku⌈da¹k·u くだく (砕く) vt. (kudak·i-; kudak·a-; kuda·k·i·te Ⓒ) 1 break; smash; shatter; crush: *Koori o* kudaite *koppu ni ireta.* (氷

を砕いてコップに入れた) I *crushed* the ice and put it in the glass.
2 destroy; ruin (a hope, dream, etc.):
Kanojo no yume wa kudakareta. (彼女の夢は砕かれた) Her dream *was shattered*. 《⇨ kudakeru》

ku「da」mono くだもの (果物) *n.* fruit:
Dezaato ni kudamono *ga deta*. (デザートに果物が出た) *Fruit* was served for dessert. / kudamono-ya (果物屋) a *fruit* store.

ku「darana·i くだらない *a.* (-ku)
1 worthless; trivial:
Kudaranai *koto ni kane o tsukau na*. (くだらないことに金を使うな) Don't spend money on *worthless* things. / *Kare-ra wa* kudaranai *moñdai de keñka o shita*. (彼らはくだらない問題でけんかをした) They quarreled over a *trivial* matter. 《⇨ tsumaranai》
2 absurd; nonsense:
Kudaranai *koto o iu na*. (くだらないことを言うな) Don't talk *nonsense*.

ku「dari くだり (下り) *n.* **1** descent; downhill slope:
Michi wa koko kara kudari *desu*. (道はここから下りです) The road is *downhill* from here. / kudari-zaka (下り坂) a *downward slope*; a *downhill*. 《↔ nobori》《⇨ kudaru》
2 down train: ★ The train going away from Tokyo or a major city.
Tsugi no kudari *wa juuni-ji juu-go-fuñ desu*. (次の下りは 12 時 15 分です) The next *down train* leaves at 12:15. / kudari *no saishuu* (下りの最終) the last *down train*. 《↔ nobori》

ku「dar·u くだる (下る) *vi.* (kudar·i-; kudar·a-; kudat-te Ⓒ)
1 descend; go down; come down:
Watashi-tachi wa kuraku naranai uchi ni yama o kudatta. (私たちは暗くならないうちに山を下った) We *came*

down from the mountain before it got dark. / *Byooiñ wa kono saka o* kudatta *tokoro ni arimasu*. (病院はこの坂を下った所にあります) The hospital is *at the bottom of* this hill. 《↔ noboru¹》
2 (of an order) be passed; be issued:
Kare-ra ni shuppatsu no meeree ga kudatta. (彼らに出発の命令が下った) The order for departure *was issued* to them.
3 have loose bowels:
Watashi wa o-naka ga kudatte *iru*. (私はおなかが下っている) My bowels *are loose*. 《⇨ geri》

kudaranai (下らない) be not less than...: *Kono eki no ichi-nichi no jookoo-kyaku wa juumañ-niñ o* kudarimaseñ. (この駅の一日の乗降客は 10 万人を下りません) The number of passengers getting on and off trains at this station *is not less than* a hundred thousand per day.

ku「dasa」i ください (下さい) [the imperative of '*kudasaru*']
1 (*polite*) please give me; let me have: ★ Preceded by a noun＋ '*o*.' *Kono hoñ o* kudasai. (*at a store*) (この本を下さい) *I would like* this book. / *O-cha o ip-pai* kudasai. (お茶を一杯下さい) *Please give me* a cup of tea.
2 (*polite*) please do (for me): ★ Preceded by the *te*-form of a verb. *Koko ni go-juusho o kaite* kudasai. (ここにご住所を書いてください) *Please write* your address here. / *Moo sukoshi yukkuri hanashite* kudasai. (もう少しゆっくり話してください) *Speak* more slowly, *please*.
3 (*honorific*) please do: ★ Preceded by '*o-*' ＋ the continuative base of a verb. *Doozo o-kake* kudasai. (どうぞお掛けください) *Please have a seat*. / *Kochira no deñwa o* o-tsukai kudasai. (こちらの電話をお

使いください) *Please use* this telephone.

-nai de kudasai (ないで〜) (*polite*) please do not: *Doo-ka ikanai de kudasai.* (どうか行かないでください) *Please don't go away.* / *Sakuhiñ ni wa te o* furenai de kudasai. (*sign*) (作品には手を触れないでください) *Please Do Not Touch* the Works of Art.

ku⌐dasa⌐r·u くださる(下さる) *vt.* (-sa·i-; -sar·a-; -sat-te ⒞) give me [us] (something): ★ Honorific alternative of '*kureru*.' *Señsee wa watashi ni nooto o* kudasatta. (先生は私にノートを下さった) The teacher *gave me* a notebook.

-te kudasaru (て〜) (used when a person's superior does something for that person): *Sono hoñ o* okutte kudasareba *arigataku omoimasu.* (その本を送ってくださればありがたく思います) I should be very much obliged *if you would send me* that book. / *Kore wa ano yuumee na gaka ga* kaite kudasatta *e desu.* (これはあの有名な画家がかいてくださった絵です) This is the picture which that famous painter *drew* for me.

ku⌐fuu くふう(工夫) *n.* idea; device; contrivance: *Nani-ka yoi* kufuu *wa arimasu ka?* (何かよい工夫はありますか) Do you have any good *ideas?* / *Dekiru dake* kufuu o kasanete *mi nasai.* (できるだけ工夫を重ねてみなさい) Try to *devise* all possible means.

kufuu suru (〜する) *vt.* devise; contrive; think out: *Watashi-tachi wa nañ to ka* kufuu shite, *shi-kiñ o atsumeta.* (私たちはなんとか工夫して, 資金を集めた) We somehow *contrived* to raise funds.

ku⌐-gatsu くがつ(九月) *n.* September: *Ku-gatsu wa mada zañsho ga kibishii.* (九月はまだ残暑が厳しい) The lingering heat of summer is still severe in *September.* (⇨ tsuki (table))

ku⌐gi くぎ(釘) *n.* nail: kugi *o utsu [nuku]* (釘を打つ[抜く]) drive [pull out] a *nail.*

ku⌐gi⌐r·u くぎる(区切る) *vt.* (kugir·i-; kugir·a-; kugit-te ⒞) divide; partition; space; punctuate: *heya o futatsu ni* kugiru (部屋を2つに区切る) *divide* a room into two / *ichi-go ichi-go* kugitte *hanasu* (一語一語区切って話す) speak, *separating* each word / *hyaku-tsubo no tochi o yottsu ni* kugitte *uru* (100坪の土地を4つに区切って売る) *divide* a 100-*tsubo* plot of land into four sections and sell them.

ku⌐izu クイズ *n.* quiz: ★ Not used in the sense of a short exam. kuizu *bañgumi* (クイズ番組) a *quiz* show.

ku⌐ji くじ(籤) *n.* lot; lottery: kuji *o hiku* (くじを引く) draw *lots* / *Kuji ga atatta.* (くじが当たった) I won in the *lottery.*

ku⌐ji⌐k·u くじく(挫く) *vt.* (kujik·i-; kujik·a-; kuji·i-te ⒞) 1 sprain; wrench: *ashikubi o* kujiku (足首をくじく) *sprain* one's ankle.
2 frustrate; baffle; crush: *yowaki o tasuke, tsuyoki o* kujiku (弱きを助け, 強きをくじく) help the weak and *crush* the strong / *Kanojo no kiboo wa* kujikareta. (彼女の希望はくじかれた) Her hopes *were frustrated.*

ku⌐ki¹ くき(茎) *n.* stalk; stem.

ku⌐kyoo くきょう(苦境) *n.* difficult situation; adversity: *Kare wa ima* kukyoo *ni tatte iru.* (彼は今苦境に立っている) He is now in *difficulty.* / *Dare mo watashi o* kukyoo *kara sukutte kurenakatta.* (だれも私を苦境から救ってくれなかった) Nobody would help me out of the *difficulties.*

ku⸢ma⸣ くま (熊) *n.* bear.

Ku⸢mamoto⸣-keñ くまもとけん (熊本県) *n.* Kumamoto Prefecture. Located on the west coast of central Kyushu. Mt. Aso, an active volcano with the world's largest caldera formation, is located in the prefecture. Capital city: Kumamoto. 《⇨ map (B5)》

ku⸢mi⸣ くみ (組) *n.* **1** class: *Watashi-tachi wa onaji* kumi *desu.* (私たちは同じ組です) We are in the same *class.* 《⇨ kurasu²》
2 group; party; team: *Go-niñ-zutsu, sañ-*kumi *ni wakareta.* (五人ずつ, 3 組に分かれた) We were divided into three *groups* of five.
3 set; pair: *Kono sara wa go-ko de, hito-*kumi *desu.* (この皿は 5 個で, ひと組です) These plates come five to a *set.* / *sukii futa* kumi (スキーふた組) two *pairs* of skis.

ku⸢miai くみあい (組合) *n.* union; association:
kumiai *o tsukuru* (組合を作る) organize a *union* / kumiai *ni kanyuu suru* (組合に加入する) become a member of a *union* / roodoo-kumiai (労働組合) a labor [trade] *union* / kyoodoo-kumiai (協同組合) a cooperative *association.*

ku⸢miawase くみあわせ (組み合わせ) *n.* combination; pairing:
sañ-shoku *no* kumiawase (三色の組み合わせ) a three color *combination* / shiai *no* kumiawase (試合の組み合わせ) the *pairings* for a tournament. 《⇨ kumiawaseru》

ku⸢miawase·ru くみあわせる (組み合わせる) *vt.* (-awase-te Ⅴ) put together; combine; match:
suuji to moji o kumiawasete, *fugoo o tsukuru* (数字と文字を組み合わせて, 符号を作る) make a code by *combining* numbers and letters /

Dai-ichi shiai wa A chiimu to B chiimu ga kumiawaserareta. (第一試合は A チームと B チームが組み合わせられた) In the first game, team A and team B *were matched* against each other. 《⇨ kumiawase》

ku⸢mitate くみたて (組み立て) *n.* assembly; structure; construction; composition:
buhiñ no kumitate (部品の組み立て) the *assembly* of parts / *mokee-hikooki no* kumitate *o suru* (模型飛行機の組み立てをする) *put together* a model airplane / kumitate-shiki *no hoñbako* (組み立て式の本箱) a *knockdown* bookcase / *jidoosha no* kumitate-*koojoo* (自動車の組み立て工場) an auto *assembly* plant. 《⇨ kumitateru》

ku⸢mitate⸣·ru くみたてる (組み立てる) *vt.* (-tate-te Ⅴ) put together; assemble; construct; compose:
mokee hikooki o kumitateru (模型飛行機を組み立てる) *build* a model airplane / *jidoosha o* kumitateru (自動車を組み立てる) *assemble* a car / *jiteñsha no buhiñ o* kumitateru (自転車の部品を組み立てる) *put together* the parts of a bicycle. 《⇨ kumitate》

ku⸣mo¹ くも (雲) *n.* cloud:
Sora ni wa kumo *hitotsu nakatta.* (空には雲ひとつなかった) There was not a *cloud* in the sky. / *Kumo ga dete kita.* (雲が出てきた) The *clouds* are gathering.

ku⸣mo² くも (蜘蛛) *n.* spider:
kumo *no ito* (くもの糸) a *spider's* thread / kumo *no su* (くもの巣) a *spider's* web.
kumo no ko o chirasu yoo ni (〜の子を散らすように) in all directions: *Kodomo-tachi wa* kumo no ko o chirasu yoo ni *nigete itta.* (子どもたちはくもの子を散らすように逃げて行った) The children ran away, *fleeing every which way.*

ku⸢mori⸣ くもり (曇り) *n.* cloudi-

ness; cloudy weather:
Hare nochi kumori.(晴れのち曇り)
Fine, *cloudy* later. / *Asu wa*
kumori *deshoo*.(あすは曇りでしょう)
Tomorrow will probably be
cloudy. 《⇨ ame¹; hare; kumoru》

ku⌈mori-ga⌉rasu くもりガラス(曇
りガラス) *n.* frosted glass; ground
glass. 《⇨ garasu》

ku⌈mo⌉r·u くもる(曇る) *vi.* (ku-
mor·i-; kumor·a-; kumot-te [C])
1 become cloudy; cloud over;
become overcast:
Kyuu ni kumotte *kita*.(急に曇ってき
た) It has suddenly *become cloudy*.
《↔ hareru¹》《⇨ kumori》
2 fog up; cloud up; collect moisture:
Yuge de megane ga kumotta.(湯
気で眼鏡が曇った) My glasses
misted up with the steam.
3 (of a facial expression) grow
cloudy:
Sore o kiku to kanojo no kao wa
kumotta.(それを聞くと彼女の顔は曇っ
た) When she heard that, her
expression *grew cloudy*.

ku⌉m·u¹ くむ(組む) *vt.* (kum·i-;
kum·a-; kuñ-de [C]) **1** cross;
fold:
ude o kumu(腕を組む) *fold* one's
arms / *Futari wa* ude o kuñde
aruite ita.(二人は腕を組んで歩いてい
た) The couple were walking *arm
in arm*. / *Kanojo wa ashi o* kuñde
isu ni suwatta.(彼女は足を組んでいす
に座った) She sat on the chair with
her legs *crossed*.
2 cooperate; pair with:
Sono futari wa kuñde, *shigoto o
hajimeta*.(その二人は組んで, 仕事を
始めた) The two of them started
the job *together*. / *Watashi wa
tenisu de Yamada-sañ to* kuñda.
(私はテニスで山田さんと組んだ) I
paired up with Mr. Yamada for
tennis.
3 put together; assemble:

retsu o kumu(列を組む) *form* a line.

ku⌈m·u⌉² くむ(汲む) *vt.* (kum·i-;
kum·a-; kuñ-de [C]) **1** draw;
ladle; scoop up; pump:
baketsu ni mizu o kumu(バケツに水
をくむ) *ladle* water into a bucket /
ido kara poñpu de mizu o kumu
(井戸からポンプで水をくむ) *pump up*
water from a well.
2 understand (a person's feeling); take into consideration:
Kare wa watashi no kimochi o
kuñde *kureta*.(彼は私の気持ちをくん
でくれた) He *took* my feelings *into
consideration*.

ku⌈ñ くん(訓) *n.* the Japanese
reading of a Chinese character:
★ A single Chinese character
with different meanings may
have more than one '*kuñ*' reading.
kañji o kuñ *de yomu*(漢字を訓で読
む) read Chinese characters in *the
Japanese way* / '川' *to iu ji no*
kuñ *wa* '*kawa*' *de oñ wa* '*señ*'
desu.(「川」という字の訓は「かわ」で音
は「せん」です) The *kuñ-reading* of
the Chinese character, '川,' is
'*kawa*' and the *oñ*-reading is '*señ*.'
《⇨ oñ² (table)》

-kuñ くん(君) *suf.* Mr.:
★ Added to either the given or
family name of male friends or
someone of lower status.
《⇨ -sañ¹》
Suzuki-kuñ(鈴木君) (Mr.) Suzuki.

Ku⌈nai-choo くないちょう(宮内
庁) *n.* Imperial Household
Agency:
Kunai-choo *chookañ*(宮内庁長官)
the Director Grneral of the *Imperial Household Agency*.
《⇨ choo⁴ (table)》

ku⌈ni くに(国) *n.* **1** country;
nation:
Iroiro na kuni *e itte mitai*.(いろいろ
な国へ行ってみたい) I want to go to
various *countries*. / *Ano kata wa*

doko no kuni *no hito desu ka?* (あの方はどこの国の人ですか) Which *country* is that person from?
2 home; hometown:
kuni *e kaeru* (国へ帰る) go back to one's *hometown* / *O*-kuni *wa dochira desu ka?* (お国はどちらですか) *Where* do you come from?

ku¬ñreñ くんれん (訓練) *n.* training; drill; practice:
Jisshuu o shite, kyooshi to shite no kuñreñ *o uketa.* (実習をして、教師としての訓練を受けた) I did my teaching practice, receiving *training* as a teacher.
kuñreñ (o) suru (〜(を)する) *vt.* train; drill: *heeshi o* kuñreñ suru (兵士を訓練する) *drill* soldiers / *Kanojo o tsuuyaku to shite* kuñreñ shita. (彼女を通訳として訓練した) We *trained* her as an interpreter.

ku¬rabe·ru くらべる (比べる) *vt.* (kurabe-te Ⅴ) compare:
Waga-sha no seehiñ to K-sha no seehiñ o kurabete *mite kudasai.* (わが社の製品とK社の製品を比べてみてください) Please *compare* our products with those of K company. / *Kotoshi no fuyu wa kyoneñ ni* kurabete [kuraberu to] *atatakai.* (今年の冬は去年に比べて[比べると]暖かい) This winter is warm *compared* with last year's. [If you *compare* this winter with last year's, it is warm.]

ku¬rabu クラブ *n.* club; school club:
tenisu kurabu *ni hairu* (テニスクラブに入る) join a tennis *club* / kurabu *katsudoo* (クラブ活動) *extracurricular* activities / kurabu-*iñ* (クラブ員) a member of a *club*.

ku¬ra·i¹ くらい (暗い) *a.* (-ku)
1 dim; dark:
Kono deñtoo wa kurai. (この電灯は暗い) This light is *dim*. / *Soto ga* kuraku *natte kita.* (外が暗くなってきた) It is getting *dark* outside.

《↔ akarui》
2 (of character, mood, etc.) gloomy; shadowy:
kurai *seekaku* (暗い性格) a *gloomy* disposition / kurai *kako* (暗い過去) a *shadowy* past / *Suzuki-sañ wa itsu-mo* kurai kao o shite iru. (鈴木さんはいつも暗い顔をしている) Miss Suzuki always *has a long face*. 《↔ akarui》
3 (of prospects, etc.) gloomy; dark:
Keezai no mitooshi wa kurai. (経済の見通しは暗い) The economic outlook is *gloomy*. / *Kare no zeñto wa* kurai. (彼の前途は暗い) He has a *bleak* future. 《↔ akarui》
4 (of knowledge) be unfamiliar with:
Watashi wa hooritsu ni kurai. (私は法律に暗い) I am *unfamiliar* with the law. 《↔ akarui》

ku¬rai²/gu¬rai くらい/ぐらい (位) *p.*
★ In the following examples, '*kurai*' can be replaced by '*gurai*.' 《⇒ bakari; hodo》
1 (of time and quantity) about; approximately:
Uchi kara kaisha made kuruma de sañjup-puñ kurai *kakarimasu.* (家から会社まで車で30分くらいかかります) It takes *about* thirty minutes by car from home to work. / *Go-fuñ* kurai *de modorimasu.* (5分くらいで戻ります) I will be back in *approximately* five minutes.

─ **USAGE** ─
'*Goro*' refers to an approximate point in time, and '*gurai*' traditionally indicates approximate time or quantity, but is sometimes used in place of '*goro*' in modern usage. *e.g. Kaeri wa san-ji* goro [gurai] *ni narimasu.* (帰りは3時くらい[ごろ]になります) I will be back at *about* three o'clock.

2 like; such that:
Yamada-san kurai *shigoto ga dekireba ii naa.* (山田さんくらい仕事ができればいいなあ) I wish I could do my work *like* Mr. Yamada. / *Konna koto* kurai *kodomo datte dekiru.* (こんなことくらい子どもだってできる) Even a child can do something *like* this. / *Kare wa hotondo kikoenai* kurai *no koe de hanashita.* (彼はほとんど聞こえないくらいの声で話した) He spoke in a voice *such that* you could hardly hear.

3 too...to:
Watashi wa ip-po mo arukenai kurai *tsukareta.* (私は一歩も歩けないくらい疲れた) I was *too* tired *to* take another step forward.

4 not as [so]...as: ★ Follows nouns and occurs with a negative.
Katoo-san kurai, *wagamama na hito wa inai.* (加藤さんくらい, わがままな人はいない) There is *no one as* selfish *as* Mr. Kato. / *Anata* kurai *isogashii hito wa hoka ni imasen.* (あなたくらい忙しい人はほかにいません) There is *no one* who is *as* busy *as* you.

5 only; at least:
Sonna baka na koto o kangaeru no wa kimi kurai *no mono da.* (そんなばかなことを考えるのは君くらいのものだ) You are the *only* person that would think of something idiotic like that. / *Watashi ga shite agerareru no wa hanashi o kiite ageru koto* kurai *desu.* (私がしてあげられるのは話を聞いてあげることくらいです) The *least* I can do for you is to listen to what you have to say.

kurai nara (〜なら) if: *Tochuu de nagedasu* kurai nara, *hajime kara yaranai hoo ga ii.* (途中で投げ出すくらいなら, 初めからやらないほうがいい) *If* you are going to give up halfway through, you had better not start at all. / *Anna yatsu to shigoto o suru* kurai nara, *hitori de yatta*

hoo ga mashi da. (あんな奴と仕事をするくらいなら, 一人でやったほうがましだ) *If* it is a question of doing the job with someone like him, I'd rather do it alone.

ku˺rashi くらし (暮らし) *n.* life; living; livelihood:
kurashi *o tateru* (暮らしを立てる) make a *living* / *Kono kyuuryoo de wa* kurashi *ga tatanai.* (この給料では暮らしが立たない) I can't earn a *livelihood* on this salary. / *Tokai no* kurashi *wa tanoshii [kurushii].* (都会の暮らしは楽しい[苦しい]) *Life* in the city is enjoyable [hard].

ku˺rashi˺kku (o˺ngaku) クラシック(音楽) *n.* classical music.

ku˺ras·u˺¹ くらす (暮らす) *vi., vt.* (kurash·i-; kuras·a-; kurash·i-te Ⓒ) live; make a living; get along; stay:
Shiawase ni kurashitai. (幸せに暮らしたい) I *wish to live* happily. / *Kare wa ryooshi o shite* kurashite imasu. (彼は漁師をして暮らしています) He *makes a living* as a fisherman. / *Ikaga* o-kurashi desu ka? (いかがお暮らしですか) How *are* you *getting along*? / *Sono sakka wa ik-ka-getsu hoteru de* kurashita. (その作家は一か月ホテルで暮らした) The author *stayed* at a hotel for a month.

ku˺rasu˺² クラス *n.* class:
Nihongo no shokyuu [chuukyuu; jookyuu] kurasu (日本語の初級[中級;上級]クラス) the beginners' [intermediate; advanced] Japanese *class* / *Kare to watashi wa onaji* kurasu *desu.* (彼と私は同じクラスです) He and I are in the same *class*. / kurasu-kai (クラス会) a *class* meeting [reunion] / kurasu-iin (クラス委員) a *class* representative.

ku˺re くれ (暮れ) *n.* end of the year:
Moo sugu (toshi no) kure *desu.* (もうすぐ(年の)暮れです) *The end of the year* is near. / *Kure no uchi ni*

sono shakkiñ o haraitai.(暮れのうち
にその借金を払いたい) I want to
repay the loan before *the end of
the year.*《⇨ kureru²》

ku｢regu｣re mo くれぐれも（呉々も）
adv. please: ★ Used as an intensifier in expressions indicating
one's sincere desire.
Kuregure mo keñkoo ni go-chuui
kudasai.(くれぐれも健康にご注意くださ
い) *Please* take good care of yourself. / Kuregure mo *go-ryooshiñ ni
yoroshiku o-tsutae* kudasai.(くれぐ
れもご両親によろしくお伝えください)
Please give my best regards to
your parents.

ku｢re｣jitto クレジット *n.* credit:
kurejitto-*kaado*(クレジットカード)
credit card.

ku｢re·ru｣¹ くれる（呉れる）*vt.* (kurete Ⓥ) give: ★ '*Kudasaru*' is the
honorific alternative.
Kare wa watashi ni jisho o kureta.
(彼は私に辞書をくれた) He *gave* me a
dictionary. / *Musuko wa motto
kozukai o* kure *to itta.*(息子はもっと
小遣いをくれと言った) My son asked
me to *give* him more pocket money. / *Kare wa watashi ni deñwa o*
kureta.(彼は私に電話をくれた) He
gave me a phone call.
-te kureru (て〜) (used when a
person's equal or subordinate
does something for that person):
Kare wa sono hoñ o watashi ni
kashite kureta.(彼はその本を私に貸し
てくれた) He *lent* me the book. /
*Yamada-sañ wa shiñsetsu ni mo
watashi o eki made* okutte kureta.
(山田さんは親切にも私を駅まで送ってく
れた) Mr. Yamada was kind
enough to *take* me to the station.
/ *O-kane wa itsu* kaeshite kuremasu *ka?*(お金はいつ返してくれますか)
When can you *return* the money
to me? 《↔ ageru¹》

ku｢re·ru｣² くれる（暮れる）*vi.* (kurete Ⓥ) **1** (of a day) get dark:

Hi ga kurete kita.(日が暮れてきた) It
is getting dark. / *Hi ga* kurenai
uchi ni kaerimashoo.(日が暮れない
うちに帰りましょう) Let's return
before it *gets dark.*
2 (of a year) draw to an end:
Kotoshi mo kurete kita.(今年も暮れ
てきた) The year *is drawing to an
end.* 《⇨ kure》
...ni kureru (...に暮れる) be lost (in
thought): *Doo shite yoi ka* tohoo
ni kureta.(どうしてよいか途方に暮れた)
I *was at a loss* what to do. /
*Kodomo ga shiñda toki, kanojo
wa* kanashimi ni kureta.(子どもが死
んだとき, 彼女は悲しみに暮れた) She
was overcome with sorrow when
her child died.

ku｢ri·imu クリーム *n.* **1** (of milk)
cream:
*aisu-*kuriimu(アイスクリーム) ice
cream
2 (of cosmetics) cream:
higesori kuriimu(ひげそりクリーム)
shaving *cream* / *koorudo* kuriimu
(コールドクリーム) cold *cream.*

ku｢ri｣iniñgu クリーニング *n.* cleaning; laundry:
Zuboñ o kuriiniñgu *ni dashita.*(ズボ
ンをクリーニングに出した) I sent my
trousers to the *cleaner's.* / *Kare
wa sebiro no* kuriiniñgu o shite
moratta.(彼は背広のクリーニングをして
もらった) He *had his suit cleaned* at
the laundry. / kuriiniñgu-*ya*(クリー
ニング屋) a *laundry*; a *laundryman.*

ku｢rika｣es·u くりかえす（繰り返す）
vt. (-kaesh·i-; -kaes·a-; -kae-
sh·i-te Ⓒ) repeat; do over
again:
*Kanojo wa kare no tegami o nañ-
do mo* kurikaeshite *yoñda.*(彼女は
彼の手紙を何度も繰り返して読んだ)
She read over his letter *again and
again.* / *Onaji machigai o* kurikae-
sanai *yoo ni ki o tsuke nasai.*(同じ
間違いを繰り返さないように気をつけなさ
い) Take care that you *do not*

repeat the same mistake.

ku⌈ri⌉suchan クリスチャン *n.* a Christian.

Ku⌈risu⌉masu クリスマス *n.* Christmas:
Kurisumasu *o iwau* (クリスマスを祝う) celebrate *Christmas* / Kurisumasu *ibu* (クリスマスイブ) *Christmas* Eve.

ku⌈ro くろ (黒) *n.* **1** black; brown:
kuro *no kutsu* (黒の靴) *black* shoes / kuro *iñku* (黒インク) *black* ink. 《↔ shiro[1]》
2 guilty:
Kare wa kuro *da to omou.* (彼は黒だと思う) I think he is *guilty*. 《↔ shiro[1]》

ku⌈ro⌉·i くろい (黒い) *a.* (-ku)
1 black; dark; tanned:
kuroi *kami* (黒い髪) *black* hair / *Taitee no Nihoñjiñ wa me ga* kuroi. (たいていの日本人は目が黒い) Most Japanese have *dark* eyes. / *Hi ni yakete,* kuroku *natta.* (日に焼けて, 黒くなった) I got *suntanned.* 《⇨ kuro》
2 (of rumors, etc.) dark:
Ano kaisha wa saikiñ kuroi *uwasa ga aru.* (あの会社は最近黒いうわさがある) Recently there have been *dark* rumors concerning that company.

ku⌈roji くろじ (黒字) *n.* black-ink balance; surplus:
Kaisha wa kuroji *desu.* (会社は黒字です) Our company is in the *black*. 《↔ akaji》

ku⌈roo くろう (苦労) *n.* trouble; difficulty; hardship; pains:
Ryooshiñ ni wa kuroo *o kakema-shita.* (両親には苦労をかけました) I caused my parents much *anxiety and trouble.* / *Anata wa mada* kuroo *ga tarinai.* (あなたはまだ苦労が足りない) You are still lacking in *experience.* / Kuroo *no tane wa tsu-kinai mono da.* (苦労の種は尽きないものだ) *Worries* are unending.

kuroo suru (〜する) *vi.* have trou-ble [difficulty]; have a hard time:
Natsu-yasumi no shukudai ni wa kuroo *shimashita.* (夏休みの宿題には苦労しました) I *had a tough time* with my summer vacation assign-ments. / *Kare wa wakai toki* ku-roo *shita.* (彼は若いとき苦労した) He *suffered many hardships* in his youth. 《⇨ gokuroosama》

ku⌈rooto くろうと (玄人) *n.* ex-pert; professional; specialist:
Kare wa kono michi no kurooto *desu.* (彼はこの道の玄人です) He is an *expert* in this line.

kurooto hadashi (〜はだし) put the professionals to shame: *Ano hito no e wa* kurooto hadashi *da.* (あの人の絵は玄人はだしだ) Her paint-ing *is more than just the work of a simple amateur.* 《↔ shirooto》

k·u⌈ru くる (来る) *vi.* (ki-; ko-; ki-te ①) **1** come; arrive:

Deñsha ga... (The train...)
kuru = is going to arrive.
kita = has appeared.
kite iru = has arrived and is here now.

Koko ni kite *kudasai.* (ここに来てください) Please *come* here. / *Haru ga* kita. (春が来た) Spring *has come.* / *Koko wa mae ni* kita *koto ga ari-masu.* (ここは前に来たことがあります) I *have been* here before. / *Koñdo itsu* koraremasu *ka?* (今度いつ来られますか) When *can* you *come* next time? / *Watashi no kawari ni, kanai o kosasete mo ii desu ka?* (私の代わりに, 家内を来させてもいいですか) Is it all right if I *send* my wife in my place? 《↔ iku》
2 come from; be caused:
'Arubaito' to iu go wa Doitsugo kara kite *imasu.* (「アルバイト」という語はドイツ語からきています) The word *'arubaito' comes* from German. /

Kare no byooki wa karoo kara kita.(彼の病気は過労からきた) His illness *was caused* by overwork.

-te kuru (て〜) become [come to]...: *Kare wa* fukete kita.(彼は老けてきた) He *has grown old.* | *Dañdañ samuku* natte kita.(だんだん寒くなってきた) It *has become* colder and colder. | *Kare no kimochi ga* wakatte kita.(彼の気持ちがわかってきた) I *have come to understand* how he feels.

ku¹rukuru くるくる *adv.* (〜 to)
1 (used to express an object rotating):
Fuusha ga kurukuru *to mawatte ita.*(風車がくるくると回っていた) The sails of the windmill were turning *round and round.*
2 (used to express the state of being unstable):
Kare wa kañgae ga kurukuru (to) *kawaru.*(彼は考えがくるくる(と)変わる) His ideas are *always* changing.

ku¹ruma くるま(車) *n.* **1** vehicle; car; automobile:
kuruma *ni noru* (車に乗る) get into a *car* | kuruma *kara oriru* (車から降りる) get out of a *car* | Kuruma *de ikimasu.*(車で行きます) I'll go by *car.*
2 taxi:
Kuruma *o yoñde kudasai.*(車を呼んでください) Please call me a *taxi.*
3 wheel; caster:
kuruma *o mawasu* (車を回す) turn a *wheel* | *Kono beddo ni wa* kuruma *ga tsuite iru.*(このベッドには車がついている) This bed has *casters* attached.

ku¹ru¹m·u くるむ *vt.* (kurum·i-; kurum·a-; kuruñ-de ⨍) wrap:
Kanojo wa akañboo o moofu de kuruñda.(彼女は赤ん坊を毛布でくるんだ) She *wrapped* her baby in a blanket.

ku¹ru¹ri to くるりと *adv.* **1** (used to express the action of turning

around):
Kare wa kururi *to ushiro o furi-muita.*(彼はくるりと後ろを振り向いた) He *spun around* and looked back.
2 suddenly; abruptly:
Kare wa kururi *to keekaku o kaeta.*(彼はくるりと計画を変えた) He *suddenly* changed his plan.

ku¹rushi¹·i くるしい(苦しい) *a.*
(-ku) **1** painful; hard:
kurushii *shigoto* (苦しい仕事) an *arduous* task | *Sono tozañ wa* kurushikatta.(その登山は苦しかった) The mountain climb was *very hard.*
《⇨ kurushimi》
2 needy:
Koñgetsu wa kakee ga kurushii.(今月は家計が苦しい) This month we are in financially *straitened circumstances* at home.
3 awkward:
kurushii *iiwake* (苦しい言い訳) a *lame* excuse | *Watashi no tachiba ga* kurushiku *natte kita.*(私の立場が苦しくなってきた) My position has become *awkward.*

ku¹rushime¹·ru くるしめる(苦しめる) *vt.* (-shime-te Ⓥ) distress; annoy; torment:
Sono ryooshu wa noomiñ o kurushimeta.(その領主は農民を苦しめた) The feudal lord *persecuted* the farmers. | *Kare wa wakai toki, byooki ni* kurushimerareta.(彼は若いとき, 病気に苦しめられた) When he was young, he *was afflicted* with disease. | *Shakkiñ ga kare o* kurushimete iru.(借金が彼を苦しめている) The loan *is causing* him *distress.*
《⇨ kurushimu》

ku¹rushimi¹ くるしみ(苦しみ) *n.* pain; hardship; agony:
kurushimi *ni taeru* (苦しみに耐える) bear *hardship* | *Jiñsee wa* kurushimi *mo areba, raku mo aru.*(人生は苦しみもあれば, 楽もある) In life, if there is *pain*, there is also pleasure. 《⇨ kurushimu》

ku⌈rushi⌉m·u くるしむ (苦しむ) *vi.*
(-shim·i-; -shim·a-; -shiñ-de Ⓒ)
1 suffer from; feel pain; be afflicted:
Yuube wa ha ga itakute, kurushi-ñda. (ゆうべは歯が痛くて, 苦しんだ)
Last night I *suffered* from a toothache. / *Ue ni* kurushiñde iru *hito wa oozee imasu.* (飢えに苦しんでいる人は大勢います) There are many people who *are suffering* from hunger. 《⇨ kurushimeru; kurushimi》
2 be troubled; be worried; be at a loss:
Kare wa iiwake ni kurushiñda. (彼は言い訳に苦しんだ) He *was at a loss* for an excuse.
3 have difficulty:
Kare no koodoo wa rikai ni kurushimu. (彼の行動は理解に苦しむ) I *have difficulty* in understanding his behavior.

ku⌈sa くさ (草) *n.* grass; weed:
★ Useless or unwanted plants are called '*zassoo*' and the lawn '*shibafu.*'
kusa *o karu* (草を刈る) cut the *grass* / *niwa no* kusa *o toru* (庭の草をとる) *weed* the garden. 《⇨ zassoo; shiba; shibafu》

ku⌈sa⌉bana くさばな (草花) *n.* flowering plant.

ku⌈sa⌉·i くさい (臭い) *a.* (-ku)
1 smelly; stinking:
Kono kutsushita wa kusai. (この靴下は臭い) These socks are *smelly.* / *Kono* kusai *nioi wa gamañ dekinai.* (この臭いにおいはがまんできない) I cannot stand this *stinking* smell.
2 suspicious; dubious; fishy:
Ano hito wa kusai. (あの人は臭い) There is something *fishy* about him. / *Sono hanashi wa* kusai. (その話は臭い) That story is *dubious.*

-ku⌈sa⌉i くさい (臭い) *suf.*
1 smelly; stinking:
ase-kusai (汗臭い) *stink* of sweat /

gasu-kusai (ガス臭い) *smell* of gas / *koge*-kusai (焦げ臭い) have a burnt *smell* / *sake*-kusai (酒臭い) *reek* of alcohol.
2 seem; look; sound:
iñchiki-kusai (インチキくさい) be phony *sounding* / *shiroto*-kusai (素人くさい) *be like* a rank amateur / *uso*-kusai (嘘くさい) *seem like* a lie.
3 (used as an intensifier):
baka-kusai (ばかくさい) *completely* foolish / *kechi*-kusai (けちくさい) *really* stingy / *meñdoo*-kusai (面倒くさい) *very* troublesome.

ku⌈sa⌉ki くさき (草木) *n.* grass and trees; plants.

ku⌈sari くさり (鎖) *n.* chain:
Inu o ki ni kusari *de tsunaida.* (犬を木に鎖でつないだ) I *chained* my dog to a tree.

ku⌈sa⌉r·u くさる (腐る) *vi.* (kusar·i-; kusar·a-; kusat-te Ⓒ) **1** go bad; decay; rot:
Natsu wa tabemono ga sugu kusaru. (夏は食べ物がすぐ腐る) In summer, food soon *goes bad.* / *Kono tamago wa* kusatte iru. (この卵は腐っている) This egg *is addled.*
2 be discouraged:
Koto ga umaku ikanakute, kare wa kusatte iru. (ことがうまくいかなくて, 彼はくさっている) Things have gone wrong for him, so he *is discouraged.* / Kusarazu *ni gañbaroo.* (くさらずにがんばろう) Let's stick it out *without getting discouraged.*

ku⌈se⌉ くせ (癖) *n.* **1** habit:
Kare ni wa yofukashi no kuse *ga aru.* (彼には夜更かしの癖がある) He is in the *habit* of staying up late at night. / Kuse *wa tsuki-yasuku, naoshi-nikui.* (癖はつきやすく, 直しにくい) *Habits* are easy to fall into, but difficult to break.
2 peculiarity:
Kare wa kuse *no aru ji o kaku.* (彼は癖のある字を書く) He writes in a *characteristic* way. / *Kare wa*

Chuugokujiñ da ga kuse no nai *Nihoñgo o hanasu.* (彼は中国人だが癖のない日本語を話す) Although he is Chinese, he speaks *completely natural* Japanese. / *Watashi no kami wa* kuse ga tsuki-yasui. (私の髪は癖がつきやすい) My hair *tends to curl easily.*

kuˈseˈ ni くせに (癖に) although; when; in spite of: ★ Usually belittling or disparaging. *Kareˈ wa nani mo shiranai* kuse ni, *nañ de mo shitte iru yoo ni hanasu.* (彼は何も知らないくせに、何でも知っているように話す) *Although* he knows nothing, he talks as if he knew everything. / *Kimi wa Kyooto shusshiñ no* kuse ni, *Kyooto no koto wa nani mo shiranai ñ da ne.* (君は京都出身のくせに、京都のことは何も知らないんだね) *Although* you come from Kyoto, you don't know anything about the town, do you?

kuˈshakusha くしゃくしゃ *adv.* (~ no, ni) (used to express something that is wrinkled, creased or crumpled): *kami o* kushakusha *ni marumeru* (紙をくしゃくしゃに丸める) *crumple up* paper into a ball / *Zuboñ ga suutsukeesu no naka de* kushakusha *ni natta.* (ズボンがスーツケースの中でくしゃくしゃになった) My trousers got *rumpled* in the suitcase. / *Kami no ke ga* kushakusha *da.* (髪の毛がくしゃくしゃだ) My hair is all *messed up.*

kuˈshaˈmi くしゃみ *n.* sneeze: *Watashi wa* kushami *o gamañ shita.* (私はくしゃみを我慢した) I held back a *sneeze.*

kushami (o) suru (~(を)する) *vi.* have a sneeze: *Kare wa nañ-do mo* kushami (o) shita. (彼は何度もくしゃみ(を)した) He *sneezed* many times.

kuˈshiˈ くし (櫛) *n.* comb:

kushi *de kami o* tokasu (くしで髪をとかす) *comb* one's hair / *Kanojo wa kami ni itsu-mo* kushi *o sashite iru.* (彼女は髪にいつもくしをさしている) She always wears a *comb* in her hair.

kuˈshiˈñ くしん (苦心) *n.* pains; hard work; effort: *Kare no* kushiñ *ga mi o musuñda.* (彼の苦心が実を結んだ) His *hard work* has produced results. / *Watashi no* kushiñ *wa muda ni natte shimatta.* (私の苦心は無駄になってしまった) My *efforts* have come to nothing. / *Kore wa sono sakka no* kushiñ *no saku desu.* (これはその作家の苦心の作です) This is the work which the author *toiled over.*

kushiñ suru (~する) *vi.* take pains; work hard: *Nihoñ ni saisho ni kita toki Nihoñgo o manabu no ni* kushiñ shita. (日本に最初に来たとき日本語を学ぶのに苦心した) When I first arrived in Japan I *made great efforts* to learn Japanese.

kuˈsoˈ くそ (糞) *n.* shit: ★ Often used as an exclamation of disgust, anger, etc. kuso o suru (くそをする) *have a shit.* (⇨ daibeñ; fuñ[2])

kuˈsudama くすだま (薬玉) *n.*
1 decorative paper ball.

KUSUDAMA BEING OPENED

★ It is usually hung on festive occasions.

2 ornamental scent bag.

ku⌐sugur·u くすぐる (擽る) *vt.* (-gur·i-; -gur·a-; -gut-te Ⓒ) tickle:
Kodomo wa watashi no ashi no ura o kusugutta. (子どもは私の足の裏をくすぐった) The child *tickled* the soles of my feet.

ku⌐sugutta⌐·i くすぐったい *a.* (-ku) tickling; ticklish:
Senaka ga kusuguttai. (背中がくすぐったい) My back is *ticklish.*

ku⌐su⌐kusu くすくす *adv.* (~ to) (used to express the manner of giggling [tittering; chuckling]):
Oñna-no-ko-tachi wa nani ga oka-shii no ka kusukusu (to) waratte ita. (女の子たちは何がおかしいのかくすくす(と)笑っていた) I do not know why, but the girls *were giggling* about something. / *Kare wa sono koto o omoidashite, hitori de* kusukusu (to) waratta. (彼はそのことを思い出して, ひとりでくすくす(と)笑った) When he recalled that, he *chuckled* to himself.

ku⌐suri くすり (薬) *n.* medicine; drug: ★ '*Kusuri*' has a broad meaning and it also refers to other chemicals.
Kono kusuri *o maishoku-go ni nomi nasai.* (この薬を毎食後に飲みなさい) Take this *medicine* after every meal. / *Kono* kusuri *wa yoku kikimasu.* (この薬はよく効きます) This *medicine* is very effective. / *Kono* kusuri *wa zassoo o toru no ni tsukawaremasu.* (この薬は雑草をとるのに使われます) This *chemical* is used to kill weeds.

ku⌐suriya くすりや (薬屋) *n.* pharmacy; drugstore. 《⇨ yak-kyoku》

ku⌐suri⌐yubi くすりゆび (薬指) *n.* ring finger. 《⇨ yubi (illus.)》

ku⌐tabire⌐·ru くたびれる *vi.* (-bi-

re-te Ⓥ) **1** be tired; get tired; get exhausted:
Kyoo wa yamanobori de kuta-bireta. (きょうは山登りでくたびれた) Today I *am exhausted* from the mountain climbing. / *Kanojo wa sugu ni* kutabireru. (彼女はすぐにくたびれる) She soon *gets tired out.*
2 (of clothes) be worn out:
Kare wa kutabireta *kutsu o haite ita.* (彼はくたびれた靴をはいていた) He was wearing *worn-out* shoes.

ku⌐takuta くたくた *adv.* (~ ni) dead tired; exhausted:
Kare wa tsukarete kutakuta *datta.* (彼は疲れてくたくただった) He was *utterly exhausted.* / *Watashi wa tetsuya no shigoto de* kutakuta *ni tsukareta.* (私は徹夜の仕事でくたくたに疲れた) I was *dead tired* after working right through the night.

ku⌐teñ くてん (句点) *n.* period. ★ The Japanese period is '。' 《⇨ tooteñ》

ku⌐to⌐oteñ くとうてん (句読点) *n.* punctuation marks:
kutooteñ o tsukeru (句読点をつける) *punctuate.* 《⇨ kuteñ; tooteñ》

ku⌐tsu⌐ くつ (靴) *n.* shoes; boots:
kutsu is-soku (靴一足) a pair of *shoes* / kutsu o haku [nugu] (靴をはく[脱ぐ]) put on [take off] one's *shoes* / *Kono* kutsu *wa sukoshi ki-tsui.* (この靴は少しきつい) These *shoes* are a little too tight for me. / Kutsu *o migaite kudasai.* (靴を磨いてください) Please polish my *shoes.*

ku⌐tsu⌐shita くつした (靴下) *n.* socks; stockings: ★ Women's socks are usually called '*sokkusu.*'
kutsushita is-soku (靴下一足) a pair of *socks* / kutsushita o haku [nugu] (靴下をはく[脱ぐ]) put on [take off] one's *socks* / *Fujiñ-yoo no* kutsushita *wa arimasu ka?* (婦人用の靴下はありますか) Do you have ladies' *socks?*

ku⌐tsuu くつう (苦痛) *n.* pain;

pang; agony:

kutsuu *o kaṅjiru* (苦痛を感じる) feel *pain* / kutsuu *o yawarageru* (苦痛を和らげる) relieve *pain* / *Roojiṅ ni totte deṅsha no naka de tatte iru no wa* kutsuu *desu.* (老人にとって電車の中で立っているのは苦痛です) It is *painful* for elderly people to remain standing on trains.

ku˥·u くう (食う) *vt.* (ku·i-; ku·w·a-; kut-te Ⓒ) **1** (*rude*) eat: ★ '*Taberu*' is more polite and usual.

Hiru wa kutta *kai?* (昼は食ったかい) You *ate* lunch? / *Kyoo wa mada nani mo* kutte inai. (きょうはまだ何も食っていない) I *have not eaten* anything yet.

2 (*slightly rude*) live; earn a living: ★ '*Taberu*' is more polite. *Kare wa arubaito o shite,* kutte iru. (彼はアルバイトをして、食っている) He *gets by* doing a part-time job.

3 (of an insect) eat; bite: *Kono moofu wa mushi ga* kutte iru. (この毛布は虫が食っている) The moths *have eaten* this blanket. / *Ni wa ni ite ka ni* kuwareta. (庭にいて蚊に食われた) I *got bitten* by a mosquito when in the garden.

4 (of time, fuel, etc.) consume; waste: *Ookii kuruma wa gasoriṅ o* kuu. (大きい車はガソリンを食う) Large cars *consume* lots of gasoline. / *Kare o matte ite, jikaṅ o* kutte shimatta. (彼を待っていて、時間を食ってしまった) I *have wasted* my time waiting for him.

5 be taken in: *Kare ni kaṅzeṅ ni ippai* kuwasareta. (彼に完全にいっぱい食わされた) I *was* completely *taken in* by him. / *Sono te wa* kuwanai *zo.* (その手は食わないぞ) I *will not fall* for that trick.

ku˥uchuu くうちゅう (空中) *n.* the air; the sky:

Fuuseṅ ga kuuchuu *ni tadayotte iru.* (風船が空中に漂っている) A balloon is floating in the *air.* / kuuchuu *buṅkai* (空中分解) a breakup in *midair* / kuuchuu-seṅ (空中戦) an *air battle*; a *dogfight.* 《⇨ kaijoo²; rikujoo》

ku˥ude˥taa クーデター *n.* coup d'état: kuudetaa *o okosu* (クーデターを起こす) start a *coup d'état.*

ku˥ufuku くうふく (空腹) *n.* hunger; empty stomach: kuufuku *o kaṅjiru* (空腹を感じる) feel *hungry* / kuufuku *o mitasu* (空腹を満たす) satisfy one's *hunger.*

ku˥uguṅ くうぐん (空軍) *n.* air force. 《⇨ rikuguṅ; kaiguṅ》

ku˥ukaṅ くうかん (空間) *n.* space; room: *jikaṅ to* kuukaṅ (時間と空間) time and *space* / kuukaṅ *o akeru* (空間をあける) make *room.*

ku˥uki くうき (空気) *n.* air: *Mado o akete, shiṅseṅ na* kuuki *o ireta.* (窓を開けて、新鮮な空気を入れた) I opened the window and let in the fresh *air.* / *Jiteṅsha no taiya ni moo sukoshi* kuuki *o ire nasai.* (自転車のタイヤにもう少し空気を入れなさい) Put a little more *air* in the bicycle tires.

ku˥ukoo くうこう (空港) *n.* airport: *Narita* Kuukoo (成田空港) Narita *Airport.* ★ The official name is '*Shiṅ Tookyoo Kokusai Kuukoo*' (新東京国際空港) New Tokyo International Airport. 《⇨ hikoojoo》

ku˥upoṅ˥keṅ クーポンけん (クーポン券) *n.* coupon ticket.

ku˥uraa クーラー *n.* air conditioner: *Kono heya wa* kuuraa *ga kiite iru.* (この部屋はクーラーが利いている) This room *is well air-conditioned.*

ku˥uraṅ くうらん (空欄) *n.* blank

column [space]:
kotae o kuurañ *ni kakikomu* (答え を空欄に書き込む) fill in the *blanks* with the proper words.

ku「usoo くうそう (空想) *n.* fancy; imagination; daydream:
Kanojo wa mado kara soto o minagara, kuusoo *ni fuketta.* (彼女は 窓から外を見ながら, 空想にふけった) She indulged in *fancies,* staring out of the window. / kuusoo *no sañbutsu* (空想の産物) a figment of one's *imagination* / kuusoo-ka (空想家) a *dreamer.*

kuusoo suru (〜する) *vt.* fancy; imagine; daydream: *Kanojo wa puro no kashu ni natta jibuñ o* kuusoo *shita.* (彼女はプロの歌手になった 自分を空想した) She *imagined* herself as a professional singer.

ku「wadate¹•ru くわだてる (企てる) *vt.* (-date-te Ⅴ) **1** attempt; try:
Kanojo wa jisatsu o kuwadateta. (彼女は自殺を企てた) She *attempted* suicide.
2 plan:
Sono kaisha wa atarashii koojoo no keñsetsu o kuwadatete iru. (その 会社は新しい工場の建設を企てている) The company *is planning* the construction of a new factory.

ku「wae•ru くわえる (加える) *vt.* (-e-te Ⅴ) **1** add; sum up; include; join:
Satoo o moo sukoshi kuwaete *kudasai.* (砂糖をもう少し加えてくださ い) Please *add* a little more sugar. / *Shoohizee o* kuwaeru *to señ-ni-hyaku-sañjuuroku-eñ ni narimasu.* (消費税を加えると 1,236 円になります) It comes to 1,236 yen, *including* the consumption tax. / *Watashi mo nakama ni* kuwaete *kudasai.* (私も仲間に加えてください) Please *include* me in your group.
2 increase; gather; pick up:
Kuruma wa shidai ni sokudo o kuwaeta. (車は次第に速度を加えた)

The car gradually *picked up* speed. / *Jitai wa shiñkokusa o* kuwaete imasu. (事態は深刻さを加え ています) The situation *is increasing* in gravity. 《⇨ kuwawaru》
3 give; put; deal:
hito ni atsuryoku o kuwaeru (人に 圧力を加える) *put* pressure on a person / *koogeki o* kuwaeru (攻撃 を加える) *press on* an attack / *soñgai o* kuwaeru (損害を加える) *inflict* damage.

ku「washi¹•i くわしい (詳しい) *a.* (-ku) **1** full; detailed; minute:
Kono hoñ wa Nihoñgo no buñpoo ga kuwashii. (この本は日本語の文法 が詳しい) This book treats Japanese grammar in *detail.* / Kuwashii *koto wa shirimaseñ.* (詳しいこと は知りません) I do not know the *full details.* / Kuwashiku *setsumee shite kudasai.* (詳しく説明して ください) Please explain it *fully.*
2 (of knowledge) well versed; familiar:
Kuwashii *joohoo wa mada haitte kite orimaseñ.* (詳しい情報はまだ入っ てきておりません) We have not received *detailed* information yet. / *Suzuki-sañ wa hooritsu ni* kuwashii. (鈴木さんは法律に詳しい) Miss Suzuki is *well versed* in the law.

ku「wawa¹r•u くわわる (加わる) *vi.* (-war-i-; -war-a-; -wat-te Ⓒ)
1 join; take part in:
Kanojo mo sono asobi ni kuwawatta. (彼女もその遊びに加わった) She too *joined* in the game. / *Sono kuni wa Oriñpikku ni* kuwawaranakatta. (その国はオリンピックに 加わらなかった) That country *did not take part* in the Olympics. 《⇨ kuwaeru》
2 increase; gain:
Higoto ni samusa ga kuwawatte imasu. (日ごとに寒さが加わっています) It *is getting* colder day by day.

ku「ya¹kusho くやくしょ (区役所) *n.*

ward office: ★ The equivalent of city hall in metropolitan areas. *Shiñjuku* kuyakusho (新宿区役所) the Shinjuku *Ward Office*. (⇨ ku²; shiyakusho)

ku「yashi」・i くやしい (悔しい) *a.* (-ku) mortifying; regrettable: *Makete* kuyashii. (負けて悔しい) How *mortifying* it is to be defeated. / *Kodomo no koro wa biñboo de* kuyashii omoi o shimashita. (子どものころは貧乏で悔しい思いをしました) When I was a child I *was vexed and chagrined* about our poverty. / kuyashi-*namida* (悔し涙) tears of *regret*.

ku「zu くず (屑) *n.* 1 waste; rubbish; trash: Kuzu *wa kono hako ni irete kudasai.* (くずはこの箱に入れてください) Please put the *waste* in this box. / Kuzu *o chirakasanai de kudasai.* (くずを散らかさないでください) Don't scatter *wastepaper* around. / kuzu-kago (くずかご) a *wastebasket* / kuzu-ire (くず入れ) a *trash* can.
2 (*informal*) worthless [useless] person: *Aitsu wa niñgeñ no* kuzu *da.* (あいつは人間のくずだ) He is a *good-for-nothing*.

ku「zure」・ru くずれる (崩れる) *vi.* (-re-te V) 1 collapse; break; be destroyed; give way: *Dote ga* kuzureta. (土手がくずれた) The embankment *collapsed*. / *Toñneru ga* kuzureta. (トンネルがくずれた) The tunnel *caved in*. / *Shiro ga* kuzureta. (城がくずれた) The castle *crumbled down*. (⇨ kuzusu)
2 lose shape: *Sono fuku wa katachi ga* kuzurete iru. (その服は形がくずれている) Those clothes *have lost* their shape.
3 (of weather) change; deteriorate: *Teñki ga* kuzure-soo da. (天気がくずれそうだ) The weather is likely to

deteriorate.
4 (of money) be changed: *Ichimañ-eñ satsu* kuzuremasu ka? (一万円札くずれますか) Can you *change* a ¥10,000 note? (⇨ kuzusu)

ku「zu」s・u くずす (崩す) *vt.* (-sh・i-; -s・a-; -sh・i-te C) 1 break down; pull down: *Furui biru o* kuzushite, *atarashii biru o tateru keekaku desu.* (古いビルをくずして、新しいビルを建てる計画です) We are planning to *knock down* the old building and put up a new one. (⇨ kuzureru)
2 change (money); break: *Ichimañ-eñ o* kuzushite, *señ-eñ satsu ni shita.* (一万円をくずして、千円札にした) I *have changed* ¥10,000 into thousand yen notes. (⇨ kuzureru)
3 write (letters, characters) in a cursive style: Kuzushita *moji wa yominikui.* (くずした文字は読みにくい) Letters *written in cursive style* are difficult to read.

kya「betsu キャベツ *n.* cabbage: kyabetsu *ikko* (キャベツ1個) a head of *cabbage*.

kya「kkañ-teki きゃっかんてき (客観的) *a.n.* (~ na, ni) objective: kyakkañ-teki *na mikata* (客観的な見方) an *objective* point of view / *Jitai o* kyakkañ-teki *ni haaku suru hitsuyoo ga aru.* (事態を客観的に把握する必要がある) It is necessary to grasp the situation *objectively*. (↔ shukañ-teki)

kya「ku きゃく (客) *n.* 1 caller; visitor; guest: ★ Polite form is 'o-kyaku(-sañ).'
Kyoo wa o-kyaku *ga kuru koto ni natte imasu.* (きょうはお客が来ることになっています) I am expecting a *visitor* today. / *Kanojo wa paatii ni* o-kyaku *o nijyuu-niñ maneita.* (彼女はパーティーにお客を20人招いた) She

invited twenty *guests* to her party.
2 customer; client:
Kono mise wa wakai kyaku *ga ooi.*
(この店は若い客が多い) This store
has many young *customers.*
3 audience; spectator:
Kyaku *wa sukunakatta.* (客は少なか
った) There was a small *audience.*
4 passenger.

kya⌐kuhoñ きゃくほん (脚本) *n.*
play; drama; scenario; screen-
play:
kyakuhoñ-ka (脚本家) a *play-
wright*; a *dramatist.*

kya⌐kuma きゃくま (客間) *n.*
drawing room; guest room:
kyaku o kyakuma *ni toosu* (客を客
間に通す) show a visitor into the
drawing room.

kya⌐kuseñ きゃくせん (客船) *n.*
passenger boat [ship].

kya⌐kushoku きゃくしょく (脚色)
n. dramatization; adaptation:
kyakushoku-sha (脚色者) a *drama-
tizer.*
　kyakushoku suru (～する) *vt.*
dramatize; adapt: *shoosetsu o
eega muki ni* kyakushoku suru (小
説を映画向きに脚色する) *adapt* a
novel for the screen.

kya⌐sshu-ka⌐ado キャッシュカード
n. debit card; bank card.

─ **CULTURE** ─
A plastic card issued by a bank.
It is used when depositing,
withdrawing or transferring
money, and not used for purchasing goods.

kyo⌐dai きょだい (巨大) *a.n.* (～ na,
ni) huge; gigantic:
kyodai *na iwa* (巨大な岩) a *huge*
rock / kyodai *na tatemono* (巨大な
建物) a *huge* building / kyodai-
toshi (巨大都市) a *megalopolis.*
《⇨ ookii》

kyo⌐hi きょひ (拒否) *n.* refusal;
rejection; denial; veto:

takushii no joosha kyohi (タクシーの
乗車拒否) *refusal* by a taxi driver
to let someone get into the taxi /
kyohi-*keñ* (拒否権) a *veto* right.
　kyohi suru (～する) *vt.* refuse;
reject; deny; turn down; veto:
liñkai wa watashi no teeañ o
kyohi shita. (委員会は私の提案を拒
否した) The committee *refused* to
accept my proposal.

kyo⌐ka きょか (許可) *n.* permission; license; approval; leave:
gaishutsu no kyoka *o morau* (外出
の許可をもらう) get *permission* to go
out / *shokuhiñ no eegyoo* kyoka *o
shiñsee suru* (食品の営業許可を申請
する) apply for a *license* to deal in
foodstuffs / kyoka-shoo (許可証) a
permit; a *license.*
　kyoka suru (～する) *vt.* permit;
allow; license; approve: *Kanojo
no chichi-oya wa kanojo ga gaikoku e iku no o* kyoka shita. (彼女
の父親は彼女が外国へ行くのを許可し
た) Her father *permitted* her to go
abroad. / *Kare wa sono daigaku
ni nyuugaku o* kyoka sareta. (彼は
その大学に入学を許可された) He *was
admitted* to the university.
《↔ kiñshi[1]》《⇨ yurusu》

kyo⌐ku きょく (曲) *n.* music;
tune:
kookyoo-kyoku (交響曲) a *symphony.*

-kyoku きょく (局) *suf.* **1** bureau; department:
Seesoo-kyoku (清掃局) Public
Sanitation *Department.* 《⇨ -ka[5]》
2 office; station:
yuubiñ-kyoku (郵便局) a post *office*; *heñshuu*-kyoku (編集局) an
editorial *office*; *hoosoo*-kyoku (放
送局) a broadcasting *station.*

kyo⌐kuseñ きょくせん (曲線) *n.*
curve; curved line. 《⇨ chokuseñ》

kyo⌐kuta⌐ñ きょくたん (極端) *n.*
extreme:
kyokutañ *ni hashiru* (極端に走る)

go to *extremes.*

— *a.n.* (~ na, ni) extreme; radical.

kyokutañ *na ikeñ*（極端な意見）an *extreme* opinion / *Anata no kañgae wa* kyokutañ *desu.*（あなたの考えは極端です）Your view is too *radical.* / *Kanojo wa* kyokutañ *ni shiñkeeshitsu da.*（彼女は極端に神経質だ）She is *extremely* nervous.

kyo¹neñ きょねん（去年）*n.* last year:

Watashi wa kyoneñ *no juu-gatsu ni Nihoñ ni kimashita.*（私は去年の10月に日本に来ました）I came to Japan in October of *last year.* 《⇨ kotoshi (table)》

kyo¹o きょう（今日）*n.* today; this day:

kyoo *no gogo*（きょうの午後）*this* afternoon / kyoo *no shiñbuñ*（きょうの新聞）*today*'s newspaper / *raishuu* [*señshuu*] *no* kyoo（来週[先週]のきょう）*this day* next [last] week / *Kyoo wa kayoobi desu.*（きょうは火曜日です）*Today* is Tuesday. / *Tegami wa* kyoo *uketorimashita.*（手紙はきょう受け取りました）I received your letter *today.*

ototoi	the day before yesterday
kinoo	yesterday
kyoo	today
ashita	tomorrow
asatte	the day after tomorrow

-kyoo きょう（鏡）*suf.* -scope: booeñ-kyoo（望遠鏡）a *telescope* / keñbi-kyoo（顕微鏡）a *microscope.*

kyo⌐ochoo きょうちょう（強調）*n.* emphasis; stress.

kyoochoo suru (~する) *vt.* emphasize; stress: *Shachoo wa añzeñ uñteñ o* kyoochoo shita.（社長は安全運転を強調した）The president *stressed* the importance of safe driving.

kyo¹odai きょうだい（兄弟）*n.* sibling; brother; sister:

(USAGE)

Refers to one's own brother or sister. When referring to someone else's, '*go-kyoodai*' is used.

Go-kyoodai *wa nañ-niñ desu ka?*（ご兄弟は何人ですか）How many *brothers and sisters* do you have? / Kyoodai *wa ane ga hitori to otooto ga futari desu.*（兄弟は姉が一人と弟が二人です）I have one older *sister* and two younger *brothers.* / *Watashi wa sañ-niñ* kyoodai *no suekko desu.*（私は三人兄弟の末っ子です）I am the youngest of the three *children* in my family. / kyoodai-*geñka*（兄弟げんか）a quarrel between *brothers* [*sisters*]. 《⇨ kazoku (table)》

	sons	daughters
oldest	choonañ	choojo
second	jinañ	jijo
third	sañnañ	sañjo
fourth	yoñnañ	yoñjo

kyo⌐odoo きょうどう（共同）*n.* collaboration; partnership:

Watashi wa Yamada-shi to kyoodoo *de sono hoñ o kaita.*（私は山田氏と共同でその本を書いた）I wrote the book in *collaboration* with Mr. Yamada. / *Sono mise wa kare to* kyoodoo *de kee-ee shite imasu.*（その店は彼と共同で経営しています）I run that shop in *partnership* with him. / kyoodoo *bokiñ*（共同募金）a *community* chest / kyoodoo *jigyoo*（共同事業）a *joint* venture / kyoodoo *seemee*（共同声明）a *joint* statement.

kyoodoo suru (~する) *vt.* share; combine one's efforts: *Watashi-*

tachi wa kono heya o kyoodoo shite *tsukatte imasu.* (私たちはこの部屋を共同して使っています) We *share* this room.

kyoᒐofu きょうふ (恐怖) *n.* fear; terror; horror:
Kyoofu *de koe mo denakatta.* (恐怖で声も出なかった) In my *terror*, even words failed me.

kyoᒐogeᒐñ きょうげん (狂言) *n.*
1 traditional comic drama.
★ Performed as supplementary entertainment to fill the intervals between Noh plays.
2 sham; make-believe:
Kare no shita koto wa kyoogeñ *datta.* (彼のしたことは狂言だった) What he did was a *sham*. 《⇨ shibai》

kyoᒐogi¹ きょうぎ (競技) *n.* contest; competition; match; game; event:
kyoogi *de katsu* [*makeru*] (競技で勝つ[負ける]) win [lose] a *match* / *Kare wa sono* kyoogi *de yuushoo shita.* (彼はその競技で優勝した) He won first prize in the *contest*. / *rikujoo*-kyoogi (陸上競技) track and field *events* / *suiee*-kyoogi (水泳競技) a swimming *competition* / kyoogi-*joo* (競技場) a *sports ground*; a *stadium*.

kyoogi suru (～する) *vt.* play a game; have a contest; compete:
Kono taiikukañ de wa iroiro na shumoku o kyoogi shimasu. (この体育館ではいろいろな種目を競技します) We *have* various *events* in this gymnasium.

kyoᒐogi² きょうぎ (協議) *n.* conference; discussion; deliberation:
Kyoogi *no kekka, sono kai wa eñki suru koto ni natta.* (協議の結果、その会は延期することになった) As a result of the *deliberations*, it was decided to postpone the meeting. / kyoogi-*rikoñ* (協議離婚) a di-

vorce by *consent*.

kyoogi suru (～する) *vt.* discuss; talk; consult: *Sono keñ ni tsukimashite wa ashita* kyoogi shimasu. (その件につきましてはあした協議します) We will *hold discussions* concerning that matter tomorrow.

kyoᒐoguu きょうぐう (境遇) *n.* surroundings; circumstances:
Kanojo wa megumareta kyooguu *ni sodatta.* (彼女は恵まれた境遇に育った) She grew up in favorable *surroundings*. / *Kare wa doñna* kyooguu *ni atte mo isshoo-keñmee hataraita.* (彼はどんな境遇にあっても一生懸命働いた) He worked hard, whatever the *circumstances*.

kyoᒐohaku きょうはく (脅迫) *n.* threat; intimidation; menace:
Kare wa booryokudañ no kyoohaku *ni hirumanakatta.* (彼は暴力団の脅迫にひるまなかった) He didn't shrink from the gangsters' *intimidation*. / kyoohaku-*deñwa* (脅迫電話) a *threatening* phone call / kyoohaku-*joo* (脅迫状) a *threatening* [*blackmail*] letter.

kyoohaku suru (～する) *vt.* threaten; intimidate; menace: *Gootoo wa sawagu to utsu zo to* kyoohaku shita. (強盗は騒ぐと撃つぞと脅迫した) The robber *threatened* us, " Make a noise and I'll shoot. "

kyoᒐoiku きょういく (教育) *n.* education; teaching; training:
Kono kuni no kyooiku *teedo wa takai.* (この国の教育程度は高い) The standard of *education* in this country is high. / *Watashi-tachi no señsee wa Doitsu de* kyooiku *o uketa.* (私たちの先生はドイツで教育を受けた) Our teacher *was educated* in Germany. / kyooiku-*iiñkai* (教育委員会) the Board of *Education* / kyooiku-*mama* (教育ママ) an *education-minded* mother / kyooiku-*sha* (教育者) an *educator*.

kyooiku suru (～する) *vt.* edu-

cate; train: *Kodomo o* kyooiku
suru *no wa oya no tsutome desu.*
(子どもを教育するのは親の務めです) It
is the duty of parents to *educate*
their children.

kyoˈoiñ きょういん（教員）*n.*
teacher:
kookoo no kyooiñ（高校の教員）a
high school *teacher* / kyooiñ-
shitsu（教員室）a *teachers'* room.
《⇨ señsee》

kyoˈoju きょうじゅ（教授）*n.* (full)
professor: 《⇨ table (bottom)》
daigaku kyooju（大学教授）a university [college] *professor.*

kyoˈoka きょうか（強化）*n.*
strengthening; reinforcement;
buildup:
kyooka-*garasu*（強化ガラス）*reinforced* glass / kyooka-gasshuku
（強化合宿）*camp training.*
kyooka suru（〜する）*vt.* strength-
en; reinforce; build up: *keebi o*
kyooka suru（警備を強化する）
strengthen the guard / *kiñniku o*
kyooka suru（筋肉を強化する）*build
up* one's muscles.

kyoˈokai[1] きょうかい（境界）*n.*
boundary; border:
*Kono kawa ga Tookyoo to Chiba-
keñ no* kyookai *to natte iru.*（この川
が東京と千葉県の境界となっている）
This river forms a *boundary* between Tokyo and Chiba Prefecture. / kyookai-señ（境界線）a *bor-
derline*; a *demarcation line.*

kyoˈokai[2] きょうかい（教会）*n.*
church.

kyoˈokaˈsho きょうかしょ（教科書）
n. textbook; schoolbook:

Nihoñgo no kyookasho（日本語の
教科書）a Japanese-language *textbook.*

kyoˈokuñ きょうくん（教訓）*n.*
lesson; moral:
Sono shippai wa yoi kyookuñ *ni
natta.*（その失敗は良い教訓になった）
The failure was a good *lesson* to
me. / *Kono hanashi ni wa juuyoo
na* kyookuñ *ga fukumarete iru.*（こ
の話には重要な教訓が含まれている）
This story has an important
moral to it.

kyoˈokyuu きょうきゅう（供給）*n.*
supply:
Sono kuni de wa shokuryoo no
kyookyuu *ga fusoku shite iru.*（その
国では食糧の供給が不足している）
Food *supplies* are inadequate in
that country. / *Kyookyuu ga juyoo ni oitsukanai.*（供給が需要に追
いつかない）The *supply* cannot meet
the demand. 《↔ juyoo》
kyookyuu suru（〜する）*vt.* supply; provide: *Watashi-tachi wa
hisaisha ni tabemono to nomimono o* kyookyuu shita.（私たちは被災
者に食べ物と飲物を供給した）We *pro-
vided* the victims of the disaster
with food and drink.

kyoˈomi きょうみ（興味）*n.* interest:
Kare wa sono hanashi ni kyoomi *o
shimeshita.*（彼はその話に興味を示し
た）He showed an *interest* in the
story. / *Watashi wa seeji ni wa*
kyoomi *ga nai.*（私は政治には興味が
ない）I have no *interest* in politics.
/ *Kanojo wa eñgee ni* kyoomi *o
motte iru.*（彼女は園芸に興味を持って

U.S.A.	Japan	U.K.
(full) professor	kyooju（教授）	professor
associate professor	jokyooju（助教授）	reader
assistant professor		
instructor	kooshi（講師）	lecturer

いる) She *is interested* in gardening. 《⇨ kookishiñ》

kyo「oretsu きょうれつ (強烈) *a.n.*
(~ na, ni) strong; intense:
kyooretsu *na iñshoo* (強烈な印象) a
powerful impression / kyooretsu
ni hañnoo suru (強烈に反応する)
react very *strongly* / *Sono jishiñ
wa* kyooretsu *datta.* (その地震は強烈
だった) The earthquake was very
strong.

kyo「ori きょうり (郷里) *n.* one's
hometown; one's home:
Watashi no kyoori *wa Kanazawa
desu.* (私の郷里は金沢です) My
hometown is Kanazawa. / Kyoori
wa dochira desu ka? (郷里はどちらで
すか) Where do you come from?

kyo「oryoku きょうりょく (協力) *n.*
cooperation; collaboration; working together:
*Go-*kyooryoku *o zehi onegai itashimasu.* (ご協力をぜひお願いいたします)
We earnestly request your *cooperation.* / *Wareware wa* kyooryoku
o oshimimaseñ. (われわれは協力を惜
しみません) We will not stint in our
collaboration. / kyooryoku-sha (協
力者) a *co-worker.*
kyooryoku suru (~する) *vi.* cooperate; collaborate; work together: *Watashi-tachi wa keesatsu no
choosa ni* kyooryoku shita. (私たち
は警察の調査に協力した) We *cooperated* with the police investigation.
/ *Futari de* kyooryoku shite, *sono
shigoto o kañsee shimashoo.* (二人
で協力して、その仕事を完成しましょう)
Let the two of us *cooperate* and
complete the work.

kyo「oryoku きょうりょく (強力)
a.n. (~ na, ni) strong; powerful:
kyooryoku *na shiji* (強力な支持)
strong support / *Kono eñjiñ wa*
kyooryoku *desu.* (このエンジンは強力
です) This engine is *powerful.* /
Watashi-tachi wa sono keekaku o

kyooryoku *ni susumeta.* (私たちはそ
の計画を強力に進めた) We *strongly*
pushed forward with the plan.
《⇨ chikarazuyoi》

kyo「osañshu「gi きょうさんしゅぎ
(共産主義) *n.* communism.

Kyo「osañtoo きょうさんとう (共産
党) *n.* = Nihoñ Kyoosañtoo.

kyo「osee きょうせい (強制) *n.*
compulsion; coercion:
Sore o gakusee-tachi ni kyoosee
wa dekimaseñ. (それを学生たちに強
制はできません) We are unable to
compel the students to do that. /
kyoosee-*shikkoo* (強制執行) *compulsory* implementation / kyoosee-*sookañ* (強制送還) *enforced*
repatriation.
kyoosee suru (~する) *vt.* force;
compel; coerce: *Kare-ra wa watashi ni sono kai ni hairu koto o* kyoosee shita. (彼らは私にその会に入るこ
とを強制した) They *forced* me to
become a member of the association.

kyo「osee-teki きょうせいてき (強制
的) *a.n.* (~ na, ni) compulsory;
obligatory:
Watashi-tachi wa kyoosee-teki *ni
sore o yarasareta.* (私たちは強制的に
それをやらされた) We were made to
do it *by force.*

kyo「oshi きょうし (教師) *n.* teacher; instructor:
suugaku no kyooshi (数学の教師) a
teacher of mathematics / *Nihoñ-go no* kyooshi (日本語の教師) an
instructor in Japanese. 《⇨ señ-see》

kyo「oshi「ñshoo きょうしんしょう
(狭心症) *n.* angina (pectoris).

kyo「oshitsu きょうしつ (教室) *n.*
classroom; schoolroom:
Kyooshitsu *de wa shizuka ni shi
nasai.* (教室では静かにしなさい) Keep
quiet in the *classroom.*

kyo「oshuku きょうしゅく (恐縮) *n.*
being obliged; feeling sorry:

Wazawaza oide itadaite, kyoo-shuku *desu.*（わざわざお出でいただいて，恐縮です）I *am much obliged* to you for taking the trouble to come. / Kyooshuku *desu ga, issho ni kite itadakemasu ka?*（恐縮ですが，一緒に来ていただけますか）I *am sorry to trouble you,* but would you mind coming with me?

kyooshuku suru（〜する）*vi.* be obliged; feel sorry: *Taiheñ na machigai o shite,* kyooshuku shite orimasu.（大変な間違いをして，恐縮しております）I *feel ashamed* for having made a terrible mistake.

kyoˈosoñ きょうそん（共存）*n.* co-existence:
Jiñrui ga ikinokoru michi wa heewa kyoosoñ *igai ni nai.*（人類が生き残る道は平和共存以外にない）There is no way apart from peaceful *coexistence* that humanity can survive.

kyoosoñ suru（〜する）*vi.* coexist; live together: *Sono kuni ni wa hañee to hiñkoñ ga* kyoosoñ *shite iru.*（その国には繁栄と貧困が共存している）Prosperity and poverty *exist side by side* in that country.

kyoˈosoo きょうそう（競争）*n.* competition; contest:
kyoosoo *ni katsu [makeru]*（競争に勝つ［負ける］）win [lose] in a *competition* / *Suugaku de wa kare to wa* kyoosoo *ni naranai.*（数学では彼とは競争にならない）I *am no match* for him in mathematics. / kyoosoo *aite*（競争相手）a *rival* / kyoosoo-*shiñ*（競争心）the spirit of *competitiveness.*

kyoosoo suru（〜する）*vt.* compete; contest: *Sono futari no see-to wa beñkyoo de* kyoosoo shite iru.（その二人の生徒は勉強で競争している）Those two pupils *are competing* against each other in their studies.

Kyoˈotoˈ-fu きょうとふ（京都府）*n.* Kyoto Prefecture. Located northeast of Osaka, facing the Sea of Japan on the north. The capital city, Kyoto, was the capital of Japan from 794 to 1868. There are many spots of scenic beauty and historic interest.
《⇨ map (D4)》

kyoˈotsuu きょうつう（共通）*a.n.* (〜 na/no, ni) common; mutual:
kyootsuu *no yuujiñ*（共通の友人）a *mutual* friend / *Sore wa oya ga* kyootsuu *ni motsu nayami desu.*（それは親が共通に持つ悩みです）That is a worry parents have *in common.*

kyootsuu suru（〜する）*vi.* have in common: *Sore wa ryookoku ni* kyootsuu suru *moñdai desu.*（それは両国に共通する問題です）That is a problem the two nations *have in common.*

kyoˈotsuugo きょうつうご（共通語）*n.* common language. ★ In Japan's case, the language used by the broadcast media, based primarily on the Tokyo dialect.
《⇨ kokugo》

kyoˈowaˈkoku きょうわこく（共和国）*n.* republic:
Chuuka Jiñmiñ Kyoowakoku（中華人民共和国）the People's *Republic* of China.

kyoˈoyoo きょうよう（教養）*n.* culture; education:
kyooyoo *o mi ni tsukeru*（教養を身につける）acquire *education and culture* / *bijutsu no* kyooyoo *o takameru*（美術の教養を高める）cultivate one's *interest* in art / *Yamada-sañ wa* kyooyoo *no aru hito desu.*（山田さんは教養のある人です）Mr. Yamada is a man of *culture.* / kyooyoo-*gakubu*（教養学部）a faculty of *general education.*

kyoˈri きょり（距離）*n.* distance; interval:
kyori *o hakaru*（距離を測る）mea-

sure the *distance* / *Koko kara Oosaka made no* kyori *wa dono kurai desu ka?* (ここから大阪までの距離はどのくらいですか) What is the *distance* from here to Osaka? / *Sono* kyori *nara ichi-jikañ de ikemasu.* (その距離なら1時間で行けます) We can cover that *distance* in one hour.

kyoˈrokyoro きょろきょろ *adv.* (～ to; ～ suru) (used to express the action of looking around nervously or restlessly): *Shooneñ wa kaijoo ni hairu to atari o* kyorokyoro *(to) mimawashita.* (少年は会場に入ると辺りをきょろきょろ(と)見回した) The boy *looked all about him curiously* when he entered the hall. / *Kyorokyoro shinai de, kokubañ o mi nasai.* (きょろきょろしないで黒板を見なさい) Stop *looking around restlessly* and take a look at the blackboard.

kyuˈu¹ きゅう(急) *n.* emergency; urgency: kyuu *(no baai) ni sonaeru* (急の(場合)に備える) prepare against an *emergency* / *Kono keñ wa* kyuu *o yoo shimasu.* (この件は急を要します) This matter demands *immediate attention*.
— *a.n.* (～ na, ni) 1 urgent; pressing: *Kare wa* kyuu *na yooji de Oosaka e ikimashita.* (彼は急な用事で大阪へ行きました) He went to Osaka on *urgent* business.
2 sudden; unexpected: *teñkoo no* kyuu *na heñka* (天候の急な変化) a *sudden* change in the weather / *Kare no shi wa amari ni mo* kyuu *datta.* (彼の死はあまりにも急だった) His death was very *sudden*. / *Kare wa* kyuu *ni Nagoya e teñkiñ to natta.* (彼は急に名古屋へ転勤となった) He was transferred to Nagoya *unexpectedly*.
3 steep; sharp:

Kono saka wa kyuu *da.* (この坂は急だ) This slope is *steep*. / *Kono saki ni* kyuu *na magarikado ga arimasu.* (この先に急な曲がり角があります) There is a *sharp* corner ahead.
4 swift; rapid: *Koko wa nagare ga* kyuu *da.* (ここは流れが急だ) The flow of the river is *swift* hereabouts.

kyuˈu² きゅう(級) *n.* 1 class; grade; rank: *goseñ-toñ* kyuu *no fune* (5,000トン級の船) a ship in the 5,000-ton *class* / *daijiñ* kyuu *no jiñbutsu* (大臣級の人物) a person of ministerial *rank* / *Kare wa watashi no* ik-kyuu *ue [shita] desu.* (彼は私の一級上[下]です) He is one *grade* above [below] me.
2 (in judo, kendo, karate, go, shogi, etc.) the name for the degree given to the less proficient: *karate no ni*-kyuu (空手の2級) a second *grade* in karate.
3 the holder of *kyuu*: *Watashi wa keñdoo no sañ*-kyuu *desu.* (私は剣道の3級です) I am a third *grade in* 'kendo'. ⟪⇨ **dañ¹**⟫

kyuˈu³ きゅう(旧) *n.* old; former: kyuu *no shoogatsu* (旧の正月) New Year's Day according to the *old [lunar] calendar* / kyuu *ni modosu* (旧に戻す) restore to the *former state*.
— *pref.* ex-: kyuu-*shichoo* (旧市長) an *ex-*mayor. ⟪⇨ **moto²**⟫

kyuˈu⁴ きゅう(球) *n.* globe; sphere; ball; bulb.

kyuˈu⁵ きゅう(九) *n.* nine: ★ Also pronounced '*ku.*' kyuu-*niñ* (9人) *nine* people / kyuu-*kai* (9階) the *ninth* floor. ⟪⇨ kokonotsu; suu² (table)⟫

kyuˈubyoo きゅうびょう(急病) *n.* sudden illness; acute disease: *Kare wa* kyuubyoo *de nyuuiñ* *shita.*（彼は急病で入院した）He was hospitalized because of *sudden illness.* / kyuubyoo-*niñ*（急病人）an *emergency* case.

kyu⌐ugaku きゅうがく（休学）*n.* temporary absence from school: kyuugaku *negai o dasu*（休学願いを出す）submit a request for *temporary withdrawal* from school.
kyuugaku suru（～する）*vi.* withdraw from school temporarily: *Tanaka-sañ wa byooki de ichineñ-kañ* kyuugaku shita.（田中さんは病気で一年間休学した）Miss Tanaka *was absent from school* for a year due to illness.

kyu⌐ugeki きゅうげき（急激）*a.n.* (～ *na, ni*) sudden; abrupt; rapid: *jiñkoo no* kyuugeki *na zooka*（人口の急激な増加）a *rapid* increase in population / *Oñdo ga* kyuugeki *ni sagatta.*（温度が急激に下がった）The temperature *suddenly* dropped. / *Saikiñ no yo-no-naka wa heñka ga* kyuugeki *desu.*（最近の世の中は変化が急激です）The changes in recent society are very *rapid.*

kyu⌐ugyoo きゅうぎょう（休業）*n.* suspension of business; shutdown: *Sono koojoo wa* kyuugyoo-*chuu desu.*（その工場は休業中です）The factory is now *idle.*

HOÑJITSU KYUUGYOO
(Closed Today)

kyuugyoo suru（～する）*vi.* suspend business; be closed; take a holiday: *Kooji no tame ichiji* kyuugyoo shimasu.（工事のため一時休業します）On account of the construction work, we *are* temporarily *closed for business.* / *Asu wa riñji ni* kyuugyoo shimasu.（あすは臨時に休業します）We will *take* an unscheduled *holiday* tomorrow.

kyu⌐ujiñ きゅうじん（求人）*n.* offer of a situation [job]: kyuujiñ-*kookoku ni oobo suru*（求人広告に応募する）apply for a job in the *wanted* ads. / Kyuujiñ. (*sign*) *Help Wanted.* / kyuujiñ-*rañ*（求人欄）a *help-wanted* column.

kyu⌐ujitsu きゅうじつ（休日）*n.* holiday: *Kono mise wa* kyuujitsu *mo hiraite imasu.*（この店は休日も開いています）This store is also open on *holidays.* 《⇨ heejitsu; shukujitsu (table)》

kyu⌐uka きゅうか（休暇）*n.* vacation; holiday: *is-shuukañ no* kyuuka *o toru*（一週間の休暇をとる）take a week's *vacation* / *Kare wa* kyuuka-*chuu Hoñkoñ e itta.*（彼は休暇中ホンコンへ行った）He went to Hong Kong during his *vacation.* / *Isogashikute,* kyuuka *ga torenai.*（忙しくて、休暇がとれない）I am too busy to *take time off.* 《⇨ yasumi》

kyu⌐ukee きゅうけい（休憩）*n.* break; rest; intermission: kyuukee *nashi ni hataraku*（休憩なしに働く）work without a *break* / kyuukee-*jikañ*（休憩時間）a *recess*; an *intermission* / kyuukee-*jo*（休憩所）a *resting* place. 《⇨ kyuusoku; yasumi》
kyuukee suru（～する）*vt.* take [have] a break [rest]: *Kore kara jup-puñ* kyuukee shimasu.（これから10分休憩します）We will now *take* a ten-minute *break.* 《⇨ hitoyasumi》

kyu⌐ukoo[1] きゅうこう（急行）*n.* express train.

tokkyuu	limited express train
kyuukoo	express train
juñkyuu	semi-express train
futsuu	local [slow] train

★ These are the basic categories although there are variants between different companies.

kyu⌐ukoo[2] きゅうこう（休講）*n.* no lecture.

kyuukoo suru (〜する) *vt.* cancel a class [lecture]: *Ano kyooju wa yoku* kyuukoo suru. （あの教授はよく休講する）That professor often *cancels* his lectures.

kyu⌐ukutsu きゅうくつ（窮屈）*a.n.* (〜 na, ni) **1** small; close; tight: kyuukutsu *na nittee* （窮屈な日程）a *tight* schedule / *Kono kuruma wa roku-niñ noru to,* kyuukutsu *desu.* （この車は6人乗ると，窮屈です）If six people get in this car, it will *be cramped.* / *Zuboñ ga* kyuukutsu *ni natte kita.* （ズボンが窮屈になってきた）These trousers have become *too close fitting.*
2 (of regulations, etc.) strict; rigid: *Kono gakkoo no kisoku wa* kyuukutsu *da.* （この学校の規則は窮屈だ）The rules at this school are *strict.*
3 stiff; formal; serious; uncomfortable: kyuukutsu *na kaigoo* （窮屈な会合）a *stiff and formal* gathering / *Soñna ni* kyuukutsu *ni kañgaenai de kudasai.* （そんなに窮屈に考えないでください）Don't take it so *seriously.*

kyu⌐ukyuu きゅうきゅう（救急）*n.* emergency. kyuukyuu-*bako* （救急箱）a *first-aid* kit / kyuukyuu-*byooiñ* （救急病院）an *emergency* hospital / kyuukyuu-kyuumeeshi （救急救命士）a *parame-*dic / kyuukyuu-sha （救急車）an *ambulance.*

kyu⌐uri きゅうり（胡瓜）*n.* cucumber.

kyu⌐uryoo きゅうりょう（給料）*n.* pay; wages; salary: Kyuuryoo *wa getsumatsu ni moraimasu.* （給料は月末にもらいます）We get our *pay* at the end of the month. / *Ima no* kyuuryoo *de nañ to ka yatte imasu.* （今の給料でなんとかやっています）I somehow manage to make do on my present *salary.* / Kyuuryoo *ga agatta.* （給料が上がった）I *got a raise.* 《⇨ chiñgiñ》

kyu⌐ushoku[1] きゅうしょく（求職）*n.* job hunting: kyuushoku *no mooshikomi o suru* （求職の申し込みをする）ask for *employment* [*a position*] / *Watashi wa ima* kyuushoku-chuu *desu.* （私は今求職中です）I *am looking for* a job. / kyuushoku-rañ （求職欄）the *classified ads section.*

kyu⌐ushoku[2] きゅうしょく（給食）*n.* provision of meals; school meal [lunch].

kyuushoku suru (〜する) *vt.* provide lunches [meals] (for schoolchildren, employees, etc.)

KYUUSHOKU

kyuˈushuu きゅうしゅう (吸収) *n.*
absorption; suction:
shooka to kyuushuu (消化と吸収)
digestion and *absorption* / *kaisha
no* kyuushuu *gappee* (会社の吸収合
併) a business *takeover*.
  kyuushuu suru (〜する) *vt.* absorb; suck in: *gaikoku no buñka
o* kyuusuu suru (外国の文化を吸収す
る) *absorb* the cultures of other
countries / *Kono supoñji wa mizu
o yoku* kyuushuu suru. (このスポンジは
水をよく吸収する) This sponge *sucks
up* water well.

Kyuˈushuu きゅうしゅう (九州) *n.*
Kyushu, the southernmost of
the four principal islands of
Japan. It contains Fukuoka, Oita,
Kumamoto, Miyazaki, Kago-
shima, Saga and Nagasaki prefectures. 《⇨ map (B5)》

kyuˈusoku きゅうそく (休息) *n.*
rest; repose:
Anata wa kyuusoku *ga hitsuyoo
desu.* (あなたは休息が必要です) You
need some *rest.* / *Sukoshi* kyuusoku *o tori nasai.* (少し休息を取りな
さい) Take a short *rest.*
  kyuusoku suru (〜する) *vi.* take
[have] a rest: *Watashi-tachi wa
aruku no o yamete, chotto* kyuusoku shita. (私たちは歩くのをやめて、ち
ょっと休息した) We stopped walk-
ing and *rested* for a while.
《⇨ kyuukee》

kyuˈuyoo きゅうよう (急用) *n.* urgent business:
Kare wa kyuuyoo *de Oosaka e itta.*
(彼は急用で大阪へ行った) He went
to Osaka on *urgent business.*

M

ma ま(間) *n*. **1** time; interval: *Isogashikute, yasumu ma mo arimaseñ.* (忙しくて、休む間もありません) I am so busy I do not even have *time* to rest. / *Shikeñ made ni wa mada ma ga arimasu.* (試験までにはまだ間があります) There is still some *time* left before the test. / *Sore wa a' to iu ma no dekigoto deshita.* (それはあっと言う間の出来事でした) It was something which happened *in the twinkling of an eye.* / *Nihoñ ni kite, mada ma ga arimaseñ.* (日本に来て、まだ間がありません) *It is only a while ago* that I came to Japan.
2 interval; space: *Ie to dooro no aida ni wa ittee no ma o toranakereba narimaseñ.* (家と道路の間には一定の間を取らなければなりません) You have to leave a certain *space* between your house and the road.
3 room: *Tsugi no ma de, o-machi kudasai.* (次の間で、お待ちください) Please wait in the next *room.* 《⇨ heya; -ma》

ma ga [no] warui (〜が[の]悪い)
1 unlucky; unfortunate: *Ma ga warui koto ni, kare wa shutchoochuu datta.* (間が悪いことに、彼は出張中だった) *Unfortunately* he was away on business.
2 be embarrassed; feel awkward: *Soñna tokoro de señsee ni atte, ma no warui omoi o shita.* (そんな所で先生に会って、間の悪い思いをした) I *felt embarrassed* meeting our teacher in a place like that. 《⇨ maniau》

-ma ま(間) *suf*. room: ★ Also used as counter for rooms. *Nihoñ-ma* (日本間) a Japanese-style *room* / *yoo-ma* (洋間) a Western-style *room* / *roku-joo-ma* (六畳間) a six-tatami-mat *room.* / *Kono ie wa iku-ma arimasu ka?* (この家はいく間ありますか) How many *rooms* are there in this house? 《⇨ heya; ma》

maa¹ まあ *adv*. **1** (*informal*) just: *Maa chotto yatte mimashoo.* (まあちょっとやってみましょう) I will *just* have a quick try. / *Maa tabete mite kudasai.* (まあ食べてみてください) *Just* try a bite. / *Jiñsee nañte, maa soñna mono desu.* (人生なんて、まあそんなものです) Life is *just* like that.
2 well; say; probably; now: ★ Used to soften a statement or opinion. *Maa kañgaete okimasu.* (まあ考えておきます) *Well,* I will give it some thought. / *Maa kyoo wa kono heñ de yame ni shimashoo.* (まあきょうはこの辺でやめにしましょう) *Well,* let us pack it in here for today.
3 about; by and large: *Kanojo wa maa sañ-juu gurai desu.* (彼女はまあ30ぐらいです) She would be, *about,* thirty. / *Maa daitai umaku iku to omoimasu.* (まあだいたいうまくいくと思います) I think it will, *by and large,* work out. / *Eki e wa maa jup-puñ hodo de ikeru deshoo.* (駅へはまあ10分ほどで行けるでしょう) I suppose I can get to the station in *about* ten minutes.

maa² まあ *int*. oh; well; good heavens; goodness: ★ Used by women to express surprise, embarrassment or admiration. *Maa, odoroita.* (まあ、驚いた) *Well!* I am surprised! / Maa, *komatta. Doo shimashoo.* (まあ, 困った. どうしましょう) *Goodness me!* I am in a fix. What shall I do? / Maa *suteki na fuku da koto.* (まあ素敵な服だこと) *Oh!* What a lovely dress!

ma⌐aku マーク *n.* mark; sign; insignia; design: *Watashi wa suutsukeesu ni kiiroi maaku o tsukete oita.* (私はスーツケースに黄色いマークをつけておいた) I put a yellow *mark* on my suitcase.

maaku suru (〜する) *vt.* 1 mark: *Juuyoo na tango o aka de maaku shita.* (重要な単語を赤でマークした) I *marked* the important words in red.
2 keep an eye on: *Keesatsu de wa kare o maaku shite iru.* (警察では彼をマークしている) The police *are keeping a close eye* on him.

ma⌐amaa まあまあ *adv.* so-so; not so bad; all right: *Kotoshi no kome no shuukaku wa maamaa datta.* (今年の米の収穫はまあまあだった) The rice harvest this year was *not so bad.*
— *int.* come now; well: *Maamaa, sonna ni koofun shinai de.* (まあまあ, そんなに興奮しないで) *Come now*, do not get so excited. / *Maamaa kore de ii to shimashoo.* (まあまあ, これでいいとしましょう) *Well,* let's assume this is all right.

ma⌐bushi⌐·i まぶしい (眩しい) *a.* (-ku) glaring; dazzling: *mabushii hizashi* (まぶしい日ざし) *dazzling* sunlight / *Mabushii no de kaaten o shimete kuremasen ka.* (まぶしいのでカーテンを閉めてくれませんか) As it is *rather bright*, will you please draw the curtains? / *Mae kara kuru kuruma no raito ga mabushikatta.* (前から来る車のライトがまぶしかった) The lights of the car coming from the other direction were *glaring.*

ma⌐buta まぶた (瞼) *n.* eyelid.
ma⌐chi⌐ まち (町・街) *n.* 1 town; city: *machi e iku* (町へ行く) go to *town* / *Kare wa kono machi ni sunde imasu.* (彼はこの町に住んでいます) He lives in this *town*. (⇨ mura)
2 street: *Watashi wa kanojo ga machi o aruite iru no o mimashita.* (私は彼女が街を歩いているのを見ました) I saw her walking along the *street.*

shi (市)	city
machi (町)	town
	village
mura (村)	hamlet

-machi まち (町) *suf.* town; block; street: ★ An administrative division of a town. *Kooji-machi* (麹町) (an area in Tokyo). (⇨ -choo⌐)

ma⌐chia⌐ishitsu まちあいしつ (待合室) *n.* waiting room.
ma⌐chiawase まちあわせ (待ち合わせ) *n.* meeting by appointment: *Kanojo to no machiawase basho wa kissaten desu.* (彼女との待ち合わせ場所は喫茶店です) The place *I am meeting* with her is a coffee shop. / *Donata to o-machiawase desu ka?* (どなたとお待ち合わせですか) With whom do you have an *appointment*? (⇨ machiawaseru)
ma⌐chiawase·ru まちあわせる (待ち合わせる) *vt.* (-awase-te Ⓥ) meet; wait for: *Watashi wa kanojo to roku-ji ni machiawaseru koto ni shita.* (私は彼女と6時に待ち合わせることにした) I have made an arrangement to *meet* her at six. (⇨ machiawase)
ma⌐chidooshi⌐·i まちどおしい (待ち遠しい) *a.* (-ku) look forward to; wait anxiously for; long for:

Kanojo to au no ga machidooshii. (彼女と会うのが待ち遠しい) I am *looking forward to* seeing her. / *Natsu-yasumi ga* machidooshii. (夏休みが待ち遠しい) It seems like the summer vacation will *never come*.

ma⌈chigae⌉·ru まちがえる (間違える) *vt.* (-gae-te Ⓥ) **1** make a mistake; make an error:

Watashi wa yoku kañji o machigaemasu. (私はよく漢字を間違えます) I often *make mistakes* with Chinese characters. / *Michi o* machigaeta *yoo da.* (道を間違えたようだ) I seem *to have taken the wrong* way.

2 mistake; confuse:

Dare-ka ga machigaete, *watashi no kutsu o haite itta.* (だれかが間違えて、私の靴をはいて行った) Someone *mistakenly* put on my shoes and went off. 《⇨ machigai》

ma⌈chiga⌉i まちがい (間違い) *n.*

1 mistake; error; blunder; fault:

Machigai wa dare ni de mo arimasu. (間違いはだれにでもあります) Everyone makes *mistakes*. / *Señsee ni Nihoñgo no buñ no* machigai *o naoshite moratta.* (先生に日本語の文の間違いを直してもらった) I had the *mistakes* in my Japanese sentences corrected by the teacher. 《⇨ machigau》

2 accident; trouble:

Kodomo no kaeri ga osoi no de haha-oya wa nani-ka machigai *ga atta no ka to shiñpai shita.* (子どもの帰りが遅いので母親は何か間違いがあったのかと心配した) Since her child was late coming home, the mother worried whether there had been some *accident*.

machigai naku (～なく) without fail: *Asu wa* machigai naku *ikimasu.* (あすは間違いなく行きます) I will go tomorrow *without fail*.

ma⌈chiga⌉·u まちがう (間違う) *vi.*, *vt.* (-ga·i-; -gaw·a-; -gat-te Ⓒ)

be wrong: ★ Usually in the phrase '*machigatte iru*.'

Watashi ga machigatte imashita. (私が間違っていました) I *was wrong*. / *Kono deñwa bañgoo wa* machigatte imasu. (この電話番号は間違っています) This telephone number *is wrong*. 《⇨ machigaeru; machigai》

ma⌈chikane·ru まちかねる (待ち兼ねる) *vt.* (-kane-te Ⓥ) wait impatiently:

Kodomo-tachi wa natsu-yasumi o machikanete iru. (子どもたちは夏休みを待ち兼ねている) The children *can't wait* for their summer vacation to come.

ma⌈chi⌉machi まちまち *a.n.*

(～ na/no, ni) different; various; divided:

machimachi *no hyooka* (まちまちの評価) *various* assessments / *Ikeñ ga* machimachi *ni wakareta.* (意見がまちまちに分かれた) Opinion was divided *in many ways*. / *Watashi-tachi no neñree wa* machimachi *desu.* (私たちの年齢はまちまちです) Our ages are *different*.

ma⌈chinozom·u まちのぞむ (待ち望む) *vt.* (-nozom·i-; -nozom·a-; -nozoñ-de Ⓒ) wait for; look forward to:

Miñna atarashii kooeñ no kañsee o machinozoñde imasu. (みんな新しい公園の完成を待ち望んでいます) Everyone *is looking forward* to the completion of the new park. 《⇨ machidooshii》

ma⌈da まだ (未だ) *adv.* **1** (with a negative) yet:

Kanojo wa mada *kite imseñ.* (彼女はまだ来ていません) She has not come *yet*. / "*Shukudai wa moo yarimashita ka?*" "*Mada desu.*" (「宿題はもうやりましたか」「まだです」) "Have you finished your homework *yet*?" "Not *yet*." / *Ima no tokoro kawatta koto wa* mada *okotte imaseñ.* (今のところ変わったことはまだ起こっていません) So far nothing out of the ordinary has happened *yet.*

2 still:

Anata wa mada *wakai.* (あなたはまだ若い) You are *still* young. / *Kare wa* mada *miseeneñ desu.* (彼はまだ未成年です) He is *still* under age. / *Ame wa* mada *futte imasu ka?* (雨はまだ降っていますか) Is it *still* raining? / *Kaigi ga hajimaru made,* mada *ichi-jikañ arimasu.* (会議が始まるまで、まだ1時間あります) There is *still* an hour before the meeting starts.

3 more:

Taifuu wa mada *yatte kuru deshoo.* (台風はまだやって来るでしょう) Some *more* typhoons will be coming our way.

4 only:

Nihoñ ni kite, mada *hañtoshi desu.* (日本に来て、まだ半年です) It is *only* six months since I came to Japan.

ma¹damada まだまだ (未だ未だ) *adv.* still; (not) yet:

Kare wa señshu to shite wa madamada *(dame) desu.* (彼は選手としてはまだまだ(だめ)です) He is *still* no good as a player. / *Kono shoobai wa* madamada *kore kara nobimasu yo.* (この商売はまだまだこれから伸びますよ) This business will expand *still* more from now. / *Madamada samuku narimasu.* (まだまだ寒くなります) It will get *even* colder.

ma¹de まで (迄) *p.* **1** to; till; as far as: ★ Indicates the forward limits of an action or state in time or space. Often used with '*kara³*.'

Mainichi asa ku-ji kara gogo go-ji made *hatarakimasu.* (毎日朝9時から午後5時まで働きます) I work from nine in the morning *till* five in the afternoon every day. / *Tookyoo kara Oosaka* made *Shiñ-kañseñ de ikimashita.* (東京から大阪まで新幹線で行きました) I traveled by Shinkansen from Tokyo *to* Osaka. / *Kore o Satoo-sañ no uchi* made *todokete kudasai.* (これを佐藤さんの家まで届けてください) Please deliver this *to* Mr. Sato's. / *Señdai* made *otona ichi-mai ikura desu ka?* (仙台まで大人1枚いくらですか) How much is a ticket for one adult *to* Sendai? / *Watashi-tachi wa Fuji-sañ no go-goo-me* made *nobotta.* (私たちは富士山の5合目まで登った) We climbed up *as far as* the fifth station on Mt. Fuji. (⟨↔ kara³⟩)

2 till: ★ Follows the dictionary form of a verb and indicates the time limit of an action or state.

Kare ga kuru made *koko de matte imasu.* (彼が来るまでここで待っています) I'll wait here *until* he comes. / *Shiñbuñ o yomu* made *sono jikeñ no koto wa shiranakatta.* (新聞を読むまでその事件のことは知らなかった) I didn't know about the incident *till* I read the paper. (⟨⇒ made ni⟩)

3 also; even: ★ Emphasizes an extreme limit.

Kodomo ni made *baka ni sareta.* (子どもにまでばかにされた) I was made a fool of *even* by the children. / *Ame dake de naku, yuki* made *futte kita.* (雨だけでなく雪まで降ってきた) Not only did it rain, but it *also* started to snow. / *Kare wa soñna koto* made *itta ñ desu ka?* (彼はそんなことまで言ったんですか) You mean to say that he went *so far as* to say something like that?

...made mo nai (...～もない) needless; do not need to (do): *Iu made mo naku, gaikokugo no beñkyoo ni wa mainichi no reñshuu ga taisetsu desu.* (言うまでもなく、外国語の勉強には毎日の練習が大切です) *Needless to say,* in the study of foreign languages, daily practice is important. / *Ano hito ga warui koto wa* shiraberu made mo nai. (あの人が悪いことは調べるまでもない) You *do not need to take the trouble* to verify that he is in the wrong.

ma¹de ni までに (迄に) **1** by; before; not later than: ★ Follows time expressions. 《⇨ made》 *Kono shigoto wa getsumatsu* made ni *shiagete kudasai*. (この仕事は月末までに仕上げてください) Please finish up this work *by* the end of this month. / *Ashita no asa wa ku-ji* made ni *kite kudasai*. (あしたの朝は9時までに来てください) Tomorrow morning please come *no later than* nine o'clock.
2 by the time: ★ Follows the dictionary form of a verb. *Kodomo-tachi ga kaette kuru* made ni *yuuhañ no shitaku o shita*. (子どもたちが帰って来るまでに夕飯の支度をした) I had prepared dinner *by the time* the children got back.
made ni naru (〜なる) reach the stage: *Sono ko wa yatto hitori de arukeru* made ni *natta*. (その子はやっと一人で歩けるまでになった) The child has finally *reached the stage* where she can walk by herself.
made ni wa (〜は) by the desired time: *Kotoshi no sakura wa nyuugaku-shiki* made ni wa *saku deshoo*. (ことしの桜は入学式までには咲くでしょう) The cherries this year should blossom *in time for* the school entrance ceremony. / *Keekaku shita jikañ* made ni wa *oeru koto ga dekinakatta*. (計画した時間までには終えることができなかった) I couldn't finish it *by the time* I had planned.

ma¹do まど (窓) *n.* window: mado *o akeru* [*shimeru*] (窓を開ける [閉める]) open [shut] the *window* / *Kare wa shibaraku* mado *kara soto o mite ita*. (彼はしばらく窓から外

を見ていた) He was looking out the *window* for a while. / mado-garasu (窓ガラス) a *windowpane*.

ma¹do¹guchi まどぐち (窓口) *n.* window; wicket: *Kono* madoguchi *no kakari wa dare desu ka?* (この窓口の係りはだれですか) Who is the clerk at this *window*? / *Sañ-bañ no* madoguchi *de shiharatte kudasai*. (三番の窓口で支払ってください) Please pay at *window* No. 3.

ma¹e まえ (前) *n.* **1** front: ★ '*mae*' covers the meanings 'front' and 'in front (of).' *e.g.* biru no mae=the front of the building; in front of the building.
mae *kara sañ-bañ-me no retsu* (前から3番目の列) the third row from the *front* / *Kare no uchi no* mae *ni wa ooki-na sakura no ki ga arimasu*. (彼の家の前には大きな桜の木があります) There is a large cherry tree in *front* of his house. 《↔ ura; ushiro》
2 the first part: *Sono monogatari no* mae *no bubuñ wa taikutsu desu*. (その物語の前の部分は退屈です) The *first part* of the story is tedious. 《↔ ato¹》
3 the previous [former] time; ago; before: *Kare wa* mae *yori mo akaruku natta*. (彼は前よりも明るくなった) He has become more cheerful than *before*. / Mae *wa koko ni eki ga arimashita*. (前はここに駅がありました) In *former times* there was a station here.

-mae¹ まえ (前) *suf.* **1** in front of: *Kono basu wa shiyakusho*-mae *ni tomarimasu*. (このバスは市役所前に止まります) This bus stops *in front of* the city hall.
2 ago; before: *Kanojo wa hito-tsuki*-mae *ni*

Nihoñ e kimashita.（彼女は一月前に日本へ来ました）She came to Japan one month *ago.* 《⇨ -go》

-mae[2] まえ（前）*suf.* for (the stated number of people):
Shokuji o go-niñ-mae tanoñde kudasai.（食事を5人前頼んでください）Please order food *for five.*

ma⌐eashi まえあし（前足）*n.* (of an animal) forefoot: foreleg.
《↔ atoashi》

ma⌐egaki まえがき（前書き）*n.* preface; foreword:
Señsee ga sono hoñ no maegaki *o kaite kureta.*（先生がその本の前書きを書いてくれた）My teacher wrote the *preface* to my book.

ma⌐emuki まえむき（前向き）*n.*
1 facing front.
2 positive attitude:
Kono moñdai ni motto maemuki *ni torikuñde kudasai.*（この問題にもっと前向きに取り組んでください）I would like you to take a more *positive attitude* to this problem.
《⇨ sekkyoku-teki》

ma⌐furaa マフラー *n.* scarf; muffler:
Shoojo wa akai mafuraa *o shite ita.*（少女は赤いマフラーをしていた）The girl wore a red *muffler.*

ma⌐garikado まがりかど（曲がり角）*n.* **1** street corner; bend; turn:
Magarikado de wa ki o tsuke nasai.（曲がり角では気をつけなさい）Be careful at the *corner.* / *Kono saki ni kyuu na* magarikado *ga arimasu.*（この先に急な曲がり角があります）There is a sharp *bend* ahead.
2 turning point:
Gakkoo kyooiku wa magarikado *ni kite iru.*（学校教育は曲がり角に来ている）School education is now at a *turning point.*

ma⌐gar·u まがる（曲がる）*vi.* (magar·i-; magar·a-; magat-te [C])
1 bend; curve:
Sono toshiyori wa koshi ga ma-

gatte ita.（その年寄りは腰が曲がっていた）The old man *was bent over* at the waist. 《⇨ mageru》
2 turn; wind:
Tsugi no shiñgoo o hidari ni magari nasai.（次の信号を左に曲がりなさい）*Turn* left at the next traffic light. / *Yuubiñkyoku wa kado o* magatta *tokoro ni arimasu.*（郵便局は角を曲がった所にあります）The post office is just *around the corner.*

ma⌐ge·ru まげる（曲げる）*vt.* (mage-te [V]) **1** bend:
harigane o mageru（針金を曲げる）*bend* a wire / *hiza o* mageru（ひざを曲げる）*bend* one's knees.
《⇨ magaru》
2 depart from (one's principles); deviate from:
shiñneñ o mageru（信念を曲げる）*deviate from* one's convictions / *kisoku o* mageru（規則を曲げる）*bend* a rule / *Watashi no kotoba o* magete *toranai de kudasai.*（私の言葉を曲げて取らないでください）Please do not *wrongly interpret* my words.

ma⌐gira⌐s·u まぎらす（紛らす）*vt.* (-rash·i-; -ras·a-; -sh·i-te [C]) divert; beguile:
Watashi wa oñgaku o kiite ki o magirashita.（私は音楽を聞いて気を紛らした）I *diverted myself* by listening to music. / *Kare wa sake o noñde kanashimi o* magirasoo to shita.（彼は酒を飲んで悲しみを紛らそうとした）He *tried to drown* his sorrows in drink. 《⇨ magireru》

ma⌐gire⌐·ru まぎれる（紛れる）*vi.* (-re-te [V]) **1** get mixed up:
Shashiñ ga shorui ni magirete *doko e itta ka wakaranai.*（写真が書類に紛れてどこへ行ったかわからない）The photo *was mixed up* with papers and I had no idea where it had gotten to. / *Sono otoko wa yami ni* magirete *nigeta.*（その男は

闇に紛れて逃げた) That man ran away *under cover of* darkness.
2 be diverted:
Tabi ni dereba ki ga magireru *de-shoo.* (旅に出れば気が紛れるでしょう) If you go on a trip, you will *be diverted from worry.* / *Isogashisa ni* magirete, *kare ni deñwa o suru no o wasureta.* (忙しさに紛れて、彼に電話をするのを忘れた) I *was so busy* that I forgot to call him.
《⇨ magirasu》

maˈgoˈ まご (孫) *n.* grandchild; grandson; granddaughter.

maˈgomago まごまご *adv.*
(~ suru) **1** get confused; lose one's presence of mind:
Shiñkañseñ no noriba ga wakaranakute magomago shite shimatta. (新幹線の乗り場がわからなくてまごまごしてしまった) I could not easily find the Shinkansen platforms, and I *ended up in a fluster.*
2 loiter; hang around:
Magomago shite iru *to deñsha ni maniaimaseñ yo.* (まごまごしていると電車に間に合いませんよ) If you *waste time,* we will not be in time for the train.

maˈgotsukˈu まごつく *vi.* (-tsuk-i-; -tsuk-a-; -tsu-i-te [C]) get confused; be embarrassed; be at a loss:
Totsuzeñ supiichi o tanomarete, magotsuita. (突然スピーチを頼まれて、まごついた) I *was at a loss* when suddenly asked to make a speech.

maˈguro まぐろ (鮪) *n.* tuna:
maguro *no sashimi* (まぐろの刺身) slices of raw *tuna.*

maˈhi まひ (麻痺) *n.* paralysis; numbness:
migi hañshiñ no mahi (右半身のまひ) *paralysis* on the right side / *suto ni yoru kootsuu* mahi (ストによる交通まひ) a transport *stoppage* due to a strike / *shiñzoo-*mahi (心臓まひ) heart *failure.*

mahi suru (~する) *vi.* be paralyzed; be numbed: *Samusa de yubi no saki ga* mahi shite shimatta. (寒さで指の先がまひしてしまった) I *lost the feeling* in my fingers because of the cold. / *Kare wa ryooshiñ ga* mahi shite iru. (彼は良心がまひしている) He is *without* any conscience.

maˈhoo まほう (魔法) *n.* magic; witchcraft:
mahoo *o tsukau* (魔法を使う) use *magic* / *hito ni* mahoo o kakeru (人に魔法をかける) *cast a spell* over a person.

mai- まい (毎) *pref.* every; each:
mai-*nichi* (毎日) *every* day / mai-*shuu* (毎週) *every* week / mai-*tsuki* (毎月) *every* month / mai-*toshi* (毎年) *every* year.

-maiˈ まい *infl. end.* [attached to the dictionary form of a consonant-stem verb or the continuative base of a vowel-stem verb]

(USAGE)

Note that 'surumai' usually becomes 'sumai.' This form is mainly literary, and in the modern spoken language '*nai daroo*' and '*shitaku nai*' are more common.

---

1 think not; probably not:
Tabuñ soo de wa arumai. (たぶんそうではあるまい) I *suppose not.* / *Osoraku kare wa* ikumai. (おそらく彼は行くまい) Probably he *will not go.* / *Konna mono wa inu de mo* tabemai. (こんなものは、犬でも食べまい) Even a dog *wouldn't eat* stuff like this. 《⇨ daroo》
2 do not want to: ★ Often in the pattern 'ni-do to ...-mai to omou.'
Kare ni wa ni-do to aumai *to omotte imasu.* (彼には二度と会うまいと思っています) I am determined *never to meet* him again.

-mai² まい〈枚〉 *suf.* sheet; piece; leaf; slice: ★ Counter for flat objects such as sheets of paper, tickets, slices of bread, pictures, records, etc.
kami yoñ-mai〈紙4枚〉four *sheets* of paper / *garasu ni-mai*〈ガラス2枚〉two *panes* of glass / *pañ ichi-mai*〈パン1枚〉a *slice* of bread / *rokujuuni-eñ kitte juu-mai*〈62円切手10枚〉*ten* 62-yen stamps / *nyuu-joo-keñ ni-mai*〈入場券2枚〉*two* tickets for admission / *hañkachi ichi-mai*〈ハンカチ1枚〉*one* handkerchief / *ichimañ-eñ satsu nana-mai*〈一万円札7枚〉*seven* 10,000-yen bank notes.

maiasa まいあさ〈毎朝〉*n.* every morning:
Watashi wa maiasa kooeñ de jogiñgu o shimasu.〈私は毎朝公園でジョギングをします〉I jog *every morning* in the park.

maibañ まいばん〈毎晩〉*n.* every evening; every night:
Kare wa maibañ kaeri ga osoi.〈彼は毎晩帰りが遅い〉He returns home late *every night*. 《⇨ bañ¹ (table)》

maido まいど〈毎度〉*n.* every [each] time; always:
Kare ga moñku o iu no wa maido no koto da.〈彼が文句を言うのは毎度のことだ〉His complaining is an *everyday affair*.
— *adv.* often; frequently:
Kare wa maido machigai bakari shite iru.〈彼は毎度間違いばかりしている〉He *frequently* makes mistakes. 《⇨ itsu-mo》
maido arigatoo〈～ありがとう〉thank you: *Maido arigatoo gozaimasu.*〈毎度ありがとうございます〉*Thank you* very much. ★ A set phrase used by service personnel.

maigetsu まいげつ〈毎月〉*n.* every [each] month. 《⇨ maitsuki》

maigo まいご〈迷子〉*n.* lost [stray; missing] child:
Maigo no kodomo o miñna de sagashita.〈迷子の子どもをみんなで探した〉We all searched for the *missing* child. / *Sono ko wa doobutsu-eñ de maigo ni natta.*〈その子は動物園で迷子になった〉The child *got lost* in the zoo.

mai-hoomu マイホーム *n.* one's own home: ★ From English 'my home.'
Mai-hoomu o tateru no ga kare no yume desu.〈マイホームを建てるのが彼の夢です〉It is his dream to build *his own house*. / mai-hoomu-*shugi*〈マイホーム主義〉a *family-oriented* way of thinking / mai-hoomu-shugisha〈マイホーム主義者〉a *family man*.

mai-kaa マイカー *n.* one's own car; private [family] car: ★ From English 'my car.'
Mai-kaa no retsu ga sañ-kiro mo tsuzuita.〈マイカーの列が3キロも続いた〉*Private cars* stood in a line for all of three kilometers. / mai-kaa-zoku〈マイカー族〉*owner drivers*.

maikai まいかい〈毎回〉*adv.*
1 every [each] time:
Watashi ga teeañ suru to kare wa maikai hañtai shita.〈私が提案すると彼は毎回反対した〉I made a proposal, and he opposed it every time.
2 every inning [round]:
Kare wa maikai sañshiñ o ubatta.〈彼は毎回三振を奪った〉He struck out batters *every inning*. / *Kare wa maikai dauñ o kisshita.*〈彼は毎回ダウンを喫した〉He was downed *every round*.

maiku マイク *n.* microphone:
maiku *de hanasu*〈マイクで話す〉speak through a *microphone*.

mainasu マイナス *n.* 1 minus:
Kesa wa mainasu go-do datta.〈今朝はマイナス5度だった〉It was five degrees *below zero* this morning.

/ *Ni hiku sañ wa* mainasu *ichi.* (2 引く 3 はマイナス 1) Three from two is *minus* one. / mainasu-*kigoo* (マイナス記号) a *minus* sign.
2 disadvantage; handicap: *Sono koto wa wareware ni totte* mainasu *da.* (そのことはわれわれにとってマイナスだ) That is a *disadvantage* to us. 《↔ purasu》
mainasu suru (〜する) *vt.* subtract: *Gookee kara, hyaku o* mainasu shite *kudasai.* (合計から, 100 をマイナスしてください) Please *subtract* 100 from the total.

maⁱineñ まいねん (毎年) *n.* every [each] year. 《⇨ maitoshi》

maⁱinichi まいにち (毎日) *n.* every day: *Kare wa* mainichi *sañjup-puñ sañpo shimasu.* (彼は毎日 30 分散歩します) He takes a thirty-minute walk *every day.* / *Suimiñ-busoku wa* mainichi *no shigoto ni sashitsukaemasu.* (睡眠不足は毎日の仕事に差し支えます) Lack of sleep will adversely affect one's *daily* work.

maⁱir·u¹ まいる (参る) *vi.* (mair·i-; mair·a-; mait-te C) **1** (*humble*) go; come: ★ Not used for one's superiors. *Sugu* mairimasu. (すぐ参ります) I *am coming* right away. / *Kinoo kochira ni* mairimashita. (きのうこちらに参りました) I *came* here yesterday. / *Itte* mairimasu. (行って参ります) I *am going out* (*and will be back soon*). ★ Used when going out. '*Tadaima*' is used when one returns.
2 visit a shrine [temple]; go to worship. 《⇨ sañpai (photo)》
-te mairu (てまいる) (*polite*) become; come to: *Aki ga* fukamatte mairimashita. (秋が深まってまいりました) We *are well into* autumn now.

maⁱir·u² まいる (参る) *vi.* (mair·i-; mair·a-; mait-te C) **1** cannot stand; give up: *Kono atsusa ni wa* maitta. (この暑さには参った) I *cannot stand* this heat.
2 be defeated: *Kare wa* maitta *to itta.* (彼は参ったと言った) He admitted his *defeat.*
3 be at a loss; be embarrassed: *Doo shite yoi ka wakarazu,* maitta. (どうしてよいかわからず, 参った) I *was at a loss* what to do.

maⁱishuu まいしゅう (毎週) *n.* every week: *Kono zasshi wa* maishuu *mokuyoobi ni demasu.* (この雑誌は毎週木曜日に出ます) This magazine comes out *weekly* on Thursday. / *Watashi wa* maishuu *ichi-do haha ni deñwa shimasu.* (私は毎週一度母に電話します) I phone my mother once a *week.*

maⁱitoshi まいとし (毎年) *n.* every [each] year: *Kare wa* maitoshi *Kurisumasu kaado o kuremasu.* (彼は毎年クリスマスカードをくれます) He sends me a Christmas card *every year.* / *Sono matsuri wa* maitoshi *ku-gatsu ni okonawaremasu.* (その祭りは毎年 9 月に行われます) That festival is held *every* September. / *Kore wa* maitoshi *no gyooji no hitotsu desu.* (これは毎年の行事の一つです) This is one of the *yearly* events.

maⁱitsuki まいつき (毎月) *n.* every [each] month: *Kono zasshi wa* maitsuki *juushichi-nichi ni hatsubai saremasu.* (この雑誌は毎月 17 日に発売されます) This magazine comes out *every month* on the seventeenth. / *Kare wa* maitsuki *ichi-do Oosaka e iku.* (彼は毎月 1 度大阪へ行く) He goes to Osaka once a *month.* / *Maitsuki no harai ga tamatte shimatta.* (毎月の払いがたまってしまった) I have fallen into arrears with my *monthly* payments.

maⁱjime まじめ (真面目) *a.n.*

(~ na, ni) serious; honest; sober; earnest:
"Joodañ deshoo." "Iya, boku wa majime *desu."* (「冗談でしょう」「いや、ぼくはまじめです」) "You're kidding!" "No, I'm *serious.*" / *Tanaka-sañ wa* majime *na hito desu.* (田中さんは真面目な人です) Ms. Tanaka is a *serious* woman. / *Fuzakete inai de* majime *ni kiki nasai.* (ふざけていないで真面目に聞きなさい) Stop fooling around, and listen *seriously.* / *Chichi wa kyooshi to shite sañjuu-neñkañ* majime *ni hataraite kita.* (父は教師として 30 年間真面目に働いてきた) My father has worked *earnestly* as a teacher for thirty years. 《↔ fumajime》

ma「ji¹r・u まじる（混じる）*vi.* (majir・i-; majir・a-; majit-te C) be mixed; be mingled:
Mizu to abura wa majiranai. (水と油は混じらない) Oil and water *do not mix.* / *Kare no atama ni wa shiraga ga* majitte iru. (彼の頭には白髪が混じっている) He *has* gray hairs on his head. 《⇨ mazeru》

ma「jiwa¹r・u まじわる（交わる）*vi.* (-war・i-; -war・a-; -wat-te C)
1 cross; intersect:
Sono futatsu no dooro wa yaku ichi-kiro saki de majiwatte *imasu.* (その二つの道路は約 1 キロ先で交わっています) The two roads *cross each other* about one kilometer ahead.
2 associate (with a person); get along with:
Iroiro na kuni no hito to majiwaru *koto ga taisetsu desu.* (いろいろな国の人と交わることが大切です) It is important to *get along well* with the people of various countries.

ma「kase¹・ru まかせる（任せる）*vt.* (makase-te V) leave; trust:
Sono shigoto wa watashi ni makase *nasai.* (その仕事は私に任せなさい) Please *leave* that job to me. / *Sore wa anata no go-soozoo ni*

makasemasu. (それはあなたのご想像に任せます) I will *leave* it to your imagination.

ma「kas・u まかす（負かす）*vt.* (makash・i-; makas・a-; makash・i-te C) beat; defeat:
Kare wa tooroñ de aite o makashita. (彼は討論で相手を負かした) He *defeated* his opponent in the debate. 《⇨ makeru》

ma「ke まけ（負け）*n.* defeat; loss; lost game:
Watashi no make *da.* (私の負けだ) It is my *defeat.* / *Sono saibañ wa kare-ra no* make *ni owatta.* (その裁判は彼らの負けに終わった) The court case ended with their *defeat.* 《↔ kachi²》《⇨ makeru》

ma「keoshimi まけおしみ（負け惜しみ）*n.* sour grapes:
makeoshimi *o iu* (負け惜しみを言う) cry *sour grapes* / *Kare wa* makeoshimi *ga tsuyoi.* (彼は負け惜しみが強い) He is a *bad loser.*

ma「ke・ru まける（負ける）*vi.* (make-te V) **1** be beaten [defeated]; lose:
Kare wa kesshoo de maketa. (彼は決勝で負けた) He *was beaten* in the finals. / *Kare wa señkyo de* maketa *koto ga nai.* (彼は選挙で負けたことがない) He *has* never *lost* an election. / *Kono saibañ wa* makeru *deshoo.* (この裁判は負けるでしょう) We will *lose* this lawsuit. 《⇨ makasu; make》
2 discount; reduce; cut:
Sukoshi makete *kuremseñ ka?* (少しまけてくれませんか) Can't you *reduce* the price slightly? / *Geñkiñ nara ichi-wari* makemashoo. (現金なら 1 割まけましょう) If you pay in cash, I will *give* you a ten percent *discount.*
3 give in (to temptation); yield:
Kanojo wa yuuwaku ni maketa. (彼女は誘惑に負けた) She *gave in* to temptation. / *Niwa no matsu no*

ki ga atsusa ni makete, *kareta.*(庭
の松の木が暑さに負けて, 枯れた) The
pine tree in the garden withered,
overcome by the heat. 《↔ katsu》

ma⌈kiage⌉・ru まきあげる(巻き上げ
る) *vt.* (-age-te [V]) rob of; take
away; swindle:
Kare wa roojiñ kara hyakumañ-eñ
makiageta. (彼は老人から 100 万円
巻き上げた) He *swindled* the old
man out of a million yen.

ma⌈kichiras・u まきちらす(撒き散ら
す) *vt.* (-chirash・i-; -chiras・a-;
-chirash・i-te [C]) scatter; sprinkle:
Kaze ga shorui o yuka ni maki-
chirashita. (風が書類を床にまき散らし
た) The wind *scattered* the papers
all over the floor.

ma⌈kiko⌉m・u まきこむ(巻き込む)
vt. (-kom・i-; -kom・a-; -koñ-de
[C]) involve:
Watashi wa sono keñka ni maki-
komarete shimatta. (私はそのけんかに
巻き込まれてしまった) I *got involved*
in the fight.

ma⌈kka⌉ まっか(真っ赤) *a.n.*
(～ na, ni) (deep) red; crimson;
scarlet:
makka *na hana* (まっかな花) a *bright
red* flower / *Sensee wa* makka *ni
natte, okotta.* (先生はまっかになって,
怒った) Our teacher became *red*
with anger. 《↔ massao》
makka na uso (～なうそ) a down-
right lie.

ma⌈kko⌉o kara まっこうから(真っ
向から) *adv.* head-on; squarely:
Kare wa sono keekaku ni makkoo
kara *hañtai shita.* (彼はその計画にま
っこうから反対した) He opposed that
plan *head-on.*

ma⌈kku⌉ra まっくら(真っ暗) *a.n.*
(～ na, ni) pitch-dark:
makkura *na heya* (真っ暗な部屋) a
pitch-black room / *Hi ga kurete,*
makkura *ni natta.* (日が暮れて, 真っ
暗になった) Night fell and it be-

came *pitch-dark.*
osaki makkura (お先～) hold no
prospects: *Watashi wa* osaki makkura *da.* (私はお先真っ暗だ) My future *is bleak.*

ma⌈kku⌉ro まっくろ(真っ黒) *a.n.*
(～ na, ni) coal-black; tanned all
over:
makkuro *na kami* (真っ黒な髪)
raven-black hair / *Sumi de te ga*
makkuro *ni natte shimatta.* (墨で手
が真っ黒になってしまった) My hands
got *completely black* with the
Indian ink. / *Kare no kao wa hi
ni yakete* makkuro *da.* (彼の顔は日
に焼けて真っ黒だ) His face is *deeply
sun-tanned.* 《↔ masshiro》

ma⌈koto ni まことに(誠に) *adv.*
(*formal*) very; very much; truly:
Makoto ni *arigatoo gozaimasu.* (ま
ことにありがとうございます) Thank you
very much. / Makoto ni *mooshiwake arimaseñ deshita.* (まことに申
しわけありませんでした) I am *sincerely*
sorry.

ma⌈k・u⌉¹ まく(巻く) *vt.* (mak・i-;
mak・a-; ma・i-te [C]) 1 wind;
wrap:
ude ni hootai o maku (腕に包帯を巻
く) *wind* a bandage around one's
arm / *kubi ni taoru o* maku (首にタ
オルを巻く) *wrap* a towel around
one's neck.
2 roll up; coil up:
roopu o guruguru maku (ロープをぐ
るぐる巻く) *coil* a rope *up.*

ma⌈ku⌉¹² まく(幕) *n.* 1 curtain:
Maku *wa shichi-ji ni agari[ori]-
masu.* (幕は 7 時に上がり[下り]ます)
The *curtain* rises [falls] at seven.
2 act:
sañ-maku *no kigeki* (3 幕の喜劇) a
comedy in three *acts.*

ma⌉k・u³ まく(蒔く) *vt.* (mak・i-;
mak・a-; ma・i-te [C]) plant; sow:
Kadañ ni hana no tane o maita.
(花壇に花の種をまいた) I *planted*
flower seeds in the flower bed.

ma⌐ku¹⁴ まく（膜）*n.* membrane; film.

ma⌐ku-no⌐-uchi(-be⌐ntoo) まくのうち（べんとう）（幕の内（弁当）) *n.* Japanese-style variety box lunch.

—（ CULTURE ）—
Foods arranged in a wooden box consist of small rice balls and an assortment of fish, meat, egg and vegetables.

MAKU-NO-UCHI

ma⌐kura まくら（枕）*n.* pillow: makura o suru（枕をする）rest one's head on a *pillow*. 《⇨ futoñ (illus.)》

ma⌐ma¹¹ まま（儘）*n.* **1** remaining in the same state [condition]: Deñsha wa mañiñ de, zutto tatta mama datta.（電車は満員で、ずっと立ったままだった）The train was full, and I *remained standing* all the way. / Futari wa nagai aida damatta mama aruita.（二人は長い間黙ったまま歩いた）They both walked along for quite a while *without saying anything*. / Kare wa mukashi no mama da.（彼は昔のままだ）He is just *as* he used to be. 《⇨ kono-mama; sono-mama》
2 with; having: Kanojo wa booshi o kabutta mama, heya ni haitta.（彼女は帽子をかぶったまま、部屋に入った）She entered the room *with* her hat on.
3 as it is. Watashi wa mita mama (no koto) o keesatsu ni hanashita.（私は見たま

ま(のこと)を警察に話した）I reported it to the police just *as I saw it happen*. / Anata no kañjita mama (no koto) o hanashite kudasai.（あなたの感じたまま(のこと)を話してください）Please tell us *how you really felt*.
4 in accordance with; as: Watashi wa iwareru (ga) mama ni soko e itta.（私は言われる(が)ままにそこへ行った）I went there *as I was told to*. / Kodomo wa ryooshiñ no iu (ga) mama ni naru to wa kagiranai.（子どもは両親の言う(が)ままになるとは限らない）Children do not necessarily do *just as their parents tell them*.

ma⌐ma² ママ *n.* mom; mum; mommy; mammy; mother. 《⇨ papa》

ma⌐mahaha ままはは（継母）*n.* stepmother.

ma⌐me¹¹ まめ（豆）*n.* bean; pea: mame o niru（豆を煮る）cook *beans*.

ma⌐me¹² まめ *n.* blister; corn: Kakato ni mame ga dekita.（かかとにまめができた）I got a *blister* on my heel.

ma⌐me³ まめ *a.n.* (～ na, ni) hardworking: mame na hito（まめな人）a *hardworking* person / Daidokoro wa mame ni sooji shinai to sugu ni yogoreru.（台所はまめに掃除しないとすぐに汚れる）If you do not clean the kitchen *carefully and regularly* it will soon get dirty.

ma⌐metsu まめつ（摩滅）*n.* wear and tear: bureeki no mametsu（ブレーキの摩滅）*wear* on vehicle brakes.
mametsu suru (～する) *vi.* be worn down [out]: Taiya ga sukkari mametsu shite shimatta.（タイヤがすっかり摩滅してしまった）The tires *have* completely *worn down*. 《⇨ heru¹》

-mamire まみれ（塗れ）*suf.* (n.) [after a noun] be covered:

★ Used in an unfavorable situation.
ase-mamire (汗まみれ) *covered* in sweat / *chi*-mamire (血まみれ) *all bloody* / *doro*-mamire (泥まみれ) *smeared* with mud / *hokori*-mamire (ほこりまみれ) dust-*covered*.

ma⌈mire⌉·ru まみれる (塗れる) *vi.* (mamire-te Ⅴ) be covered; be smeared:
Kare no zuboñ wa doro ni mamirete ita. (彼のズボンは泥にまみれていた) His trousers *were covered* in mud.

ma-⌈mo⌉-naku まもなく (間も無く) *adv.* soon; shortly; before long:
Ressha wa ma-mo-naku hassha shimasu. (*station announcement*) (列車はまもなく発車します) The train will leave *shortly*. / Ma-mo-naku *natsu-yasumi desu.* (まもなく夏休みです) The summer vacation will *soon* start. / *Watashi wa* ma-mo-naku *sañjuu ni narimasu.* (私はまもなく30になります) I will turn thirty *soon*. / *Anata ga dekakete kara* ma-mo-naku *deñwa ga arimashita.* (あなたが出かけてからまもなく電話がありました) *Just* after you left, there was a phone call for you.

ma⌈mono まもの (魔物) *n.* devil; demon.

ma⌈mo⌉r·u まもる (守る) *vt.* (mamor·i-; mamor·a-; mamot-te Ⓒ)
1 defend:
kuni o mamoru (国を守る) *defend* one's country / *gooru o* mamoru (ゴールを守る) *defend* a (soccer) goal / *Kare wa shooto o* mamotta. (彼はショートを守った) He *played* as shortstop. (↔ semeru¹))
2 protect; guard:
Kodomo-tachi o kootsuu-jiko kara mamoranakereba *narimaseñ.* (子どもたちを交通事故から守らなければなりません) We must *protect* children from traffic accidents.
3 keep (a promise); observe (a rule, etc.):

yakusoku o mamoru (約束を守る) *keep* a promise / *kisoku o* mamoru (規則を守る) *observe* a rule / *Sekai no heewa o* mamoranakereba *naranai.* (世界の平和を守らなければならない) We have to *preserve* world peace.

ma⌉ñ まん (万) *n.* ten thousand. ((⇨ suu² (table)))

ma⌉naa マナー *n.* manners:
Ima no wakamono wa manaa *ga yoku nai.* (今の若者はマナーがよくない) The youth of today have no *manners*.

ma⌈nab·u まなぶ (学ぶ) *vt.* (manab·i-; manab·a-; manañ-de Ⓒ) learn; study:
Watashi-tachi wa keekeñ kara ooku o manabu. (私たちは経験から多くを学ぶ) We *learn* much from experience. / *Kanojo wa daigaku de Nihoñgo o* manañda. (彼女は大学で日本語を学んだ) She *studied* Japanese at university. ((⇨ narau))

ma⌈ne まね (真似) *n.* **1** imitation; mimicry:
Sono ko wa señsee no mane *o shita.* (その子は先生のまねをした) The child did an *imitation* of his teacher.
2 behavior; action:
Baka na mane *wa yoshi nasai.* (ばかなまねはよしなさい) Stop *playing the fool*.

ma⌈neki¹ まねき (招き) *n.* invitation:
maneki *ni oojiru* (招きに応じる) accept an *invitation* / maneki *o kotowaru* (招きを断わる) decline an *invitation* / O-maneki *arigatoo gozaimasu.* (お招きありがとうございます) Thank you very much for your kind *invitation*. / *Oosutoraria no shushoo ga seefu no* maneki *de rainichi shita.* (オーストラリアの首相が政府の招きで来日した) The prime minister of Australia came to Japan at the *invitation*

of the government. 《⇨ maneku; shootai[1]》

ma˥ne˩k·u まねく (招く) *vt.* (manek·i-; manek·a-; mane·i-te C)
1 invite; call:
Kanojo wa watashi o paatii ni maneite kureta. (彼女は私をパーティーに招いてくれた) She *invited* me to the party. / *Sono sakka o* maneite, *kooeñ o shite moratta.* (その作家を招いて, 講演をしてもらった) We *invited* the novelist and had him give a lecture. 《⇨ maneki》
2 beckon; gesture:
Watashi wa sono ko o te de maneita. (私はその子を手で招いた) I *beckoned* the child over. 《⇨ temaneki (illus.)》
3 cause (an accident, trouble, etc.); result in; bring about:
Fuchuui ga ooki-na jiko o maneku *koto ga arimasu.* (不注意が大きな事故を招くことがあります) Carelessness can sometimes *cause* serious accidents.

ma˥ne·ru まねる (真似る) *vt.* (mane-te V) imitate; copy; mimic:
Kodomo wa otona o maneru. (子どもは大人をまねる) Children *imitate* adults. / *Kare wa sono e o* manete kaita. (彼はその絵をまねてかいた) He *copied* the picture.

ma˥ñga まんが (漫画) *n.* cartoon; comics; caricature:
mañga-*boñ* [*zasshi*] (漫画本[雑誌]) a *comic* book [magazine] / mañga-ka (漫画家) a *cartoonist*.

ma˥ñgetsu まんげつ (満月) *n.* full moon. 《⇨ tsuki[2]》

ma˥nia˩·u まにあう (間に合う) *vi.* (-a·i-; -aw·a-; -at-te C)
1 be in time:
Isogeba, shuudeñ ni maniaimasu. (急げば, 終電に間に合います) If you hurry, you will *be in time* for the last train.
2 be useful; be enough; do:
Kono jisho de maniaimasu. (この辞書で間に合います) I can make *do* with this dictionary. / *Anata ga korarenakute mo,* maniaimasu. (あなたが来られなくても, 間に合います) We can *get by* even if you cannot come. 《⇨ ma》

ma˥nichi まんいち (万一) *n.* emergency; the worst: ★ Literally 'one out of ten thousand.'
Mañichi *ni sonaete, chokiñ o shite imasu.* (万一に備えて, 貯金をしています) I am saving up money in order to provide for an *emergency*. / Mañichi *no baai wa koko ni reñraku shite kudasai.* (万一の場合はここに連絡してください) In the event of an *unforseen occurrence*, please contact this place. / *Kare ni* mañichi *no koto ga attara, dare ga kazoku o miru no desu ka?* (彼に万一のことがあったら, だれが家族をみるのですか) If he *should happen to die*, who would take care of his family?
—— *adv.* in case; by some chance:
Mañichi *kanojo ga konakattara, doo shimasu ka?* (万一彼女が来なかったら, どうしますか) What will we do if *by some chance* she happens not to come?

ma˥ñiñ まんいん (満員) *n.* being full; no vacancy; full house:
Basu wa mañiñ *datta.* (バスは満員だった) The bus was *full* of passengers. / *Kaijoo wa* mañiñ *datta.* (会場は満員だった) The assembly hall *was filled to capacity.* / mañiñ-deñsha (満員電車) a *crowded* train.

ma˥ñjoo-itchi まんじょういっち (満場一致) *n.* unanimity:
Sono keekaku wa mañjoo-itchi *de kimatta.* (その計画は満場一致で決まった) The plan was *unanimously* adopted. 《⇨ itchi》

ma˥ññaka まんなか (真ん中) *n.* the middle; center:
Michi no maññaka *ni ooki-na ana*

ga atta. (道の真ん中に大きな穴があった) There was a big hole in the *middle* of the road. / *Shi-yakusho wa shi no* mañnaka *ni arimasu.* (市役所は市の真ん中にあります) The city hall is in the *center* of the city.

ma⌐ñne⌐ñhitsu まんねんひつ (万年筆) *n.* fountain pen.

ma⌐ñseki まんせき (満席) *n.* full house; the seats being filled: *Sono oñgaku-kai wa* mañseki *datta.* (その音楽会は満席だった) All the seats in the concert hall *were filled.*

ma⌐ñshoñ マンション *n.* **1** condominium; apartment complex. **2** individual unit of same. ★ From English 'mansion.'

─────── **USAGE** ───────
'*Mañshoñ*' refers to an apartment house in which individual apartments are mostly owner-occupied. '*Apaato*' is less prestigious and rented. 《⇨ apaato》

ma⌐ñte⌐ñ まんてん (満点) *n.* full marks; perfect score: *Shikeñ de* mañteñ *o toru no wa muzukashii.* (試験で満点を取るのは難しい) It is difficult to get *full marks* in the examination.

ma⌐ñza⌐i まんざい (漫才) *n.* comic dialogue on stage. ★ A vaudeville act performed by a pair of comedians. There is also a traditional form of '*mañzai*' performed during the New Year season; one person sings cheerful songs while the other dances to a hand drum.

ma⌐ñzoku まんぞく (満足) *n.* satisfaction; contentment: *Kare wa watashi-tachi ga* mañzoku *no iku yoo ni setsumee shite kureta.* (彼は私たちが満足のいくように説明してくれた) He explained it to

us to our *satisfaction.* / *O-kyaku-sama ga* mañzoku o erareru yoo doryoku itashimasu. (お客様が満足を得られるよう努力いたします) We will make efforts so that the customers *are satisfied.*

mañzoku suru (〜する) *vi.* be satisfied: *Watashi wa ima no seekatsu ni* mañzoku shite imasu. (私は今の生活に満足しています) I *am satisfied* with my present way of life.
── *a.n.* (〜 na, ni) **1** satisfactory; contented: *Watashi wa ima no kyuuryoo de juubuñ* mañzoku *desu.* (私は今の給料で十分満足です) I am quite *contented* with my present salary. / *Kare kara* mañzoku *na kaitoo wa erarenakatta.* (彼から満足な回答は得られなかった) I was unable to get a *satisfactory* reply from him.
2 enough; complete; proper: *Isogashikute, kono mikka-kañ* mañzoku *na shokuji o shite imaseñ.* (忙しくて、この3日間満足な食事をしていません) I have not had a *proper* meal these three days as I have been so busy. / *Ima no wakai hito-tachi no naka ni wa* mañzoku *ni aisatsu mo dekinai hito ga iru.* (今の若い人たちのなかには満足にあいさつもできない人がいる) Among modern-day youngsters, there are those who cannot even give a *proper* greeting.

ma⌐ppu⌐tatsu まっぷたつ (真っ二つ) *n.* right in half [two]: *Suika o* mapputatsu *ni kitta.* (すいかを真っ二つに切った) I cut the watermelon *right in half.* / *Ikeñ wa* mapputatsu *ni wareta.* (意見は真っ二つに割れた) Opinion was *completely* divided *in two.*

ma⌐re まれ (希) *a.n.* (〜 na, ni) rare; uncommon; unusual: mare *na ree* (まれな例) an *unusual* example / mare *ni miru teñsai* (まれに見る天才) a person of *rare* genius / *Kono jiki ni koko de yuki ga furu no wa* mare *na koto desu.* (この時期にここで雪が降るのはまれなことです) It is *unusual* for it to snow here at this time of the year.

ma⌐ri⌐ まり (鞠) *n.* ball. 《⇨ booru¹》

ma⌐ru まる (丸) *n.* circle: *Tadashii kotae o* maru *de kakomi nasai.* (正しい答えを丸で囲みなさい) Mark the right answers with a *circle.* 《⇨ marui》

ma⌐ru- まる (丸) *pref.* full; whole: maru-*ichi-nichi* (丸一日) a *full* day / *Kañsee made ni wa* maru-*ik-ka-getsu kakarimasu.* (完成までには丸1か月かかります) It will take a *whole* month before completion.

-maru まる (丸) *suf.* (attached to the name of a Japanese civilian vessel): *Aruzeñchiñ*-maru *wa takusañ no Nihoñ no imiñ o Nañ-Bee ni hako-bimashita.* (あるぜんちん丸はたくさんの日本の移民を南米に運びました) The Aruzenchin-*maru* transported many Japanese immigrants to South America. ★ '*Goo*' (号) is used as the suffix for foreign civilian vessels.

ma⌐rude まるで (丸で) *adv.*
1 (with a negative) absolutely; entirely; quite; altogether: *Sono eega wa* marude *omoshiroku nakatta.* (その映画はまるでおもしろくなかった) The film was *utterly* uninteresting. / *Watashi no Nihoñgo wa* marude *dame desu.* (私の日本語はまるでだめです) My Japanese is *absolutely* useless. / *Kimi no hanashi wa kare no hanashi to* marude *chigau.* (きみの話は彼の話とまるで違う) What you say is *quite* different from what he says.
2 just (like; as if): ★ Used with '*yoo da.*' *Sono oñna-no-ko wa* marude *otona*

no yoo *na kuchi o kiku.* (その女の子はまるで大人のような口をきく) The girl talks *just as if* she were an adult. / *Sono koto wa* marude *kinoo no koto no* yoo *ni oboete imasu.* (そのことはまるできのうのことのように覚えています) I remember the event *just as if* it happened yesterday. / *Kanojo wa* marude *Nihoñjiñ no* yoo *ni Nihoñgo o hanashimasu.* (彼女はまるで日本人のように日本語を話します) She speaks Japanese *just like* a Japanese.

ma⌐ru·i まるい (丸い) *a.* (-ku)
1 round; spherical; circular: marui *ishi* (丸い石) a *round* stone / marui *o-boñ* (丸いお盆) a *circular* tray / *Maruku, wa ni natte, suwari nasai.* (丸く、輪になって、座りなさい) Please sit in a *circle.* 《⇨ maru》 《↔ shikakui》
2 plump; chubby: *akañboo no* marui *hoo* (赤ん坊の丸いほお) the *chubby* cheeks of a baby.
3 bent; stooped: *Kare wa toshi o totte, senaka ga* maruku *natte kita.* (彼は年をとって、背中が丸くなってきた) As he grew older, he became *stooped.*
...o maruku **osameru** (...を丸く治める) settle...amicably: *arasoi o* maruku osameru (争いを丸く治める) *settle* a dispute *amicably.*

ma⌐rume·ru まるめる (丸める) *vt.* (marume-te Ⓥ) form into a ball; roll (up): *Kare wa sono kami o* marumete, *kuzukago ni hoorikoñda.* (彼はその紙を丸めて、くずかごに放り込んだ) He *made a ball* of the paper and threw it into the wastebasket.

ma⌐saka まさか *adv.* surely (not); cannot be: ★ Used to express unlikelihood or unwillingness to believe. *Sore wa* masaka *hoñtoo no hanashi ja nai deshoo ne?* (それはまさか本

当の話じゃないでしょうね) That is not *really* a true story, is it? / "*Kare ga taiho sareta yo.*" "*Masaka.*" (「彼が逮捕されたよ」「まさか」) "He has been arrested." "*Impossible.*"

masaka no toki (〜のとき) in case of emergency [need]: Masaka no toki *wa yoroshiku onegai itashimasu.* (まさかのときはよろしくお願いいたします) Please help me *if something unforeseen occurs.*

ma⌐sa¬ni まさに (正に) *adv.*
1 just; exactly; really; surely: *Kono hoñ wa* masa ni *watashi ga sagashite ita hoñ desu.* (この本はまさに私が探していた本です) This book is *exactly* the one I have been looking for. / Masa ni *anata no ossharu toori desu.* (まさにあなたのおっしゃるとおりです) It is *just* as you say. / *Kare wa* masa ni *meejiñ desu.* (彼はまさに名人です) He is *truly* an expert.
2 be about to (do); be just going to (do): *Eki ni tsuitara, deñsha ga* masa ni *deyoo to shite ita.* (駅に着いたら, 電車がまさに出ようとしていた) When I arrived at the station, the train was *just about to* pull out.

ma⌐sa¬r・u まさる (勝る) *vi.* (masar・i-; masar・a-; masat-te Ⓒ) surpass; excel; exceed: *Aite chiimu no hoo ga chikara ga* masatte ita. (相手チームのほうが力が勝っていた) The other team *was stronger.* / *Kore ni* masaru *hoohoo wa nai daroo.* (これに勝る方法はないだろう) There is no other way that would be *better* than this.

ma⌐satsu まさつ (摩擦) *n.* **1** rubbing; friction: Masatsu *de netsu ga shoojiru.* (摩擦で熱が生じる) *Friction* causes heat.
2 conflict; friction: *booeki-*masatsu *o okosu* (貿易摩擦を起こす) give rise to trade *friction.*

masatsu suru (〜する) *vt., vi.* rub: *Sono bubuñ wa* masatsu shite, *hidoku surihette ita.* (その部分は摩擦して, ひどくすり減っていた) The parts *rubbed together* and were badly worn down.

ma¬shite まして *adv.* **1** (with a negative) much [still] less; let alone: *Chuugokugo wa hanasemaseñ shi,* mashite *kaku koto wa dekimaseñ.* (中国語は話せませんし, まして 書くことはできません) I cannot speak Chinese, *much less* write it.
2 (with an affirmative) much [still] more; even more: *Hisaichi ni wa iyaku-hiñ o okuru hitsuyoo ga arimasu.* Mashite *shokuryoo wa toozeñ okuranakereba narimaseñ.* (被災地には医薬品を送る必要があります. まして食料は当然送らなければなりません) We have to send medical supplies to the stricken areas. *And even more* so, we must naturally send food.

ma⌐ssa¬aji マッサージ *n.* massage: massaaji *o suru* [*ukeru*] (マッサージをする[受ける]) give [have] a *massage.* (⇒ añma)

ma⌐ssa¬ichuu まっさいちゅう (真っ最中) *n.* right in the middle (of); (at) the height (of): *Ima wa sotsugyoo shikeñ no* massaichuu *desu.* (今は卒業試験の真っ最中です) We are now *in the middle* of graduation exams. / *Kare wa shiai no* massaichuu *ni taoreta.* (彼は試合の真っ最中に倒れた) He collapsed right *in the middle* of the match. (⇒ -chuu¹)

ma⌐ssa¬ki まっさき (真っ先) *n.* the very first; (at) the head (of): *Kanojo wa Nihoñ ni tsuitara,* massaki *ni Kyooto e itta.* (彼女は日本に着いたら, 真っ先に京都へ行った) She went *straight* to Kyoto after arriving in Japan. / *Shichoo wa* *gyooretsu no* massaki *ni tatte aruita.*（市長は行列の真っ先に立って歩いた）The mayor walked *at the head* of the procession.

ma⌈ssa⌉o まっさお（真っ青）*a.n.*
(~ na, ni) **1** (deep) blue; azure: massao *na umi*（真っ青な海）*azure* sea / *Kyoo no sora wa* massao *da.*（きょうの空は真っ青だ）The sky today is *clear and blue.*
2 pale; white:
Kare wa kyoofu de massao *ni natta.*（彼は恐怖で真っ青になった）He grew *pale* with terror. 《↔ makka》

ma⌈sshi⌉ro まっしろ（真っ白）*a.n.*
(~ na, ni) pure-white; white as snow:
masshiro *na hada*（真っ白な肌）*lily-white* skin / *Yuki ga* masshiro *ni kagayaite iru.*（雪が真っ白に輝いている）The snow is shining *white.* / *Hatake wa shimo de* masshiro *da.*（畑は霜で真っ白だ）The fields are *pristine white* with frost. 《↔ makkuro》

ma⌈sshiro⌉·i まっしろい（真っ白い）*a.* (-ku) pure-white; white as snow:
Fuji-san no choojoo ga yuki de masshiroku *natta.*（富士山の頂上が雪で真っ白くなった）The summit of Mt. Fuji became *immaculately white* with snow.

ma⌈ssu⌉gu まっすぐ（真っ直ぐ）*a.n.*
(~ na, ni) **1** straight; direct: massugu *na michi*（真っすぐな道）a *straight* road / *Yuubinkyoku wa kono michi o* massugu *ni iki nasai.*（郵便局はこの道を真っすぐに行きなさい）Walk *straight* down this road for the post office. / *Kare wa* massugu *(ni) ie ni kaetta.*（彼は真っすぐ（に）家へ帰った）He went *straight* back home. / *Karada o* massugu *ni shi nasai.*（体を真っすぐにしなさい）Hold yourself up *straight.*
2 upright; honest:
Kare wa massugu *na seekaku o*

shite iru.（彼は真っすぐな性格をしている）He has an *honest and upright* personality. / *Jinsee wa* massugu *ni iki nasai.*（人生は真っすぐに生きなさい）Make sure you live your life *honestly.*

ma⌈s·u⌉¹ ます（増す）*vi.* (mash·i-; mas·a-; mash·i-te C̲) increase; gain; add: ★ Slightly more formal than '*fueru.*'
Ame de kawa no mizu ga mashita.（雨で川の水が増した）The amount of water in the river *increased* with the rain. / *Kare wa taijuu ga go-kiro* mashita.（彼は体重が5キロ増した）He *gained* five kilograms in weight.

ma⌈su⌉¹² ます（鱒）*n.* trout.

ma⌈su⌉¹³ ます（升）*n.* small square measuring box.

-masu ます *infl. end.* [attached to the continuative base of a verb]

> ⟨USAGE⟩
> Used to make the style of speech polite without adding any concrete meaning. The negative form is '-*masen*,' past form is '-*mashita*,' and tentative form is '-*mashoo.*'

Watashi wa maiasa shinbun o yomimasu.（私は毎朝新聞を読みます）I *read* the newspaper every morning. / *Yamada-san wa doko ni* imasu ka?（山田さんはどこにいますか）Where *is* Mr. Yamada? / *Watashi wa tabako o* suimasen.（私はたばこを吸いません）I *don't smoke.* / *Ashita mata* hanashimashoo.（あしたまた話しましょう）*Let's talk* again tomorrow. / *O-hiru wa nani o* tabemashoo ka?（お昼は何を食べましょうか）What *shall* we *eat* for lunch? / '*Nara e wa* ikimashita ka?' '*Iie,* ikimasen deshita.'（「奈良へは行きましたか」「いいえ、行きませんでした」）'*Did* you *go* to Nara?' 'No, I *didn't.*'

ma⌐sukomi マスコミ *n.* mass
media; journalism. ★ Abbreviation of '*masu-komyunikeeshoñ*'
(mass communication), but usually refers to newspapers, the
radio and television.

ma⌐suku マスク *n.* mask:
kafuñ-shoo yoke ni masuku *o kakeru [suru]* (花粉症よけにマスクをかけ
る[する]) put on a *mask* to prevent
hay fever / *Nihoñjiñ wa kaze o
hiku to yoku* masuku *o shimasu.*
(日本人はかぜをひくとよくマスクをします)
Japanese people often wear a *face
mask* when they catch a cold.

MASUKU

ma⌐su⌐masu ますます (益々) *adv.*
more and more; less and less;
increasingly:
Tochi no nedañ ga masumasu
agatte iru. (土地の値段がますます上が
っている) The price of land is going up *more and more.* / *Jitai wa
wareware ni totte* masumasu *furi
ni natte kite iru.* (事態はわれわれにと
ってますます不利になってきている) The
situation is getting *less and less*
favorable for us. / *Kare ni mo
ketteñ ga aru to wakari,* masumasu *suki ni natta.* (彼にも欠点があると
わかり、ますます好きになった) When I
realized that even he had his
faults, I came to like him *all the
more.*

ma⌐sutaa¹ マスター *n.* mastery.
masutaa suru (~する) *vt.* master: *Nihoñgo o* masutaa suru (日
本語をマスターする) *master* the Japanese language.

ma⌐sutaa² マスター *n.* owner (of
a bar, club, etc.); proprietor.

ma⌐ta¹¹ また (股) *n.* crotch; thigh.
mata ni kakeru (~にかける) travel
all over (a country): *Kare wa
sekai o* mata ni kakete aruita.* (彼
は世界をまたにかけて歩いた) He *trav-
eled all over* the world.

ma⌐ta² また (又) *adv.* **1** again:
Mata, kare wa chikoku da. (また,
彼は遅刻だ) He is late *again.* / Mata, *itsu-ka o-ai shimashoo.* (また, い
つかお会いしましょう) Let's get to-
gether *again* someday. / Mata,
ato de kimasu. (また, 後で来ます) I
will be back *again* in a while.
2 also; too:
*Soogi ni wa koochoo ga sañretsu
shita.* Mata señsee *mo suu-niñ
shusseki shita.* (葬儀には校長が参列
した. また先生も数人出席した) The
principal attended the funeral,
and several teachers were *also*
present. / *Kare wa isha de ari,
mata sakka de mo aru.* (彼は医者で
あり, また作家でもある) He is a doctor and *also* a writer. / *Koo-iu
kuruma mo* mata *ii mono desu ne.*
(こういう車もまたいいものですね) This
kind of car is *also* a nice one.
mata no (~の) some other
(time): *Sekkaku desu ga* mata
no *kikai ni shite kudasai.* (せっかく
ですがまたの機会にしてください) I know
you have gone to some trouble,
but could you make it *some other*
time?

ma⌐ta³ また (又) *conj.* moreover;
besides; what is more:
hitotsu mata *hitotsu* (一つまた一つ)
one *after* another.
《⇨ sara ni》

ma⌐taga⌐r·u またがる (跨る) *vi.*
(matagar·i-; matagar·a-; mata-
gat-te C) **1** straddle; sit
astride:
Sono ko wa ki no eda ni matagatte ita.* (その子は木の枝にまたがって
いた) The child *was sitting astride*
the branch.

2 extend; span:
Fuji-sañ wa futatsu no keñ ni ma-tagatte imasu. (富士山は2つの県にまたがっています) Mt. Fuji *sits on* two prefectures. / *Taoreta ki ga michi ni matagatte ita.* (倒れた木が道にまたがっていた) A fallen tree *lay across* the road.

ma⌐ta⌐g·u またぐ (跨ぐ) *vt.* (matag·i-; matag·a-; mata·i-de C) step over; cross:
Kare wa mizutamari o mataida. (彼は水たまりをまたいだ) He *stepped over* the puddle.

ma⌐ta⌐-wa または (又は) *conj.* or:
Kuro mata-wa ao no boorupeñ de kaite kudasai. (黒または青のボールペンで書いてください) Please write with a black *or* a blue ballpoint pen. / *Mooshikomi wa deñwa mata-wa hagaki de onegai shimasu.* (申し込みは電話または葉書でお願いします) Please make the application by telephone *or* by postcard.

ma⌐tchi マッチ *n.* match:
matchi *o suru* (マッチをする) strike a *match* / matchi *de tabako ni hi o tsukeru* (マッチでたばこに火をつける) light a cigarette with a *match*.

ma⌐to まと (的) *n.* **1** mark; target:
Ya ga mato *ni atatta* [mato *o hazu-shita*]. (矢が的に当たった[的を外した]) The arrow hit [missed] the *mark*.
2 object; focus:
akogare no mato (あこがれの的) an *object* of admiration / *chuumoku no* mato (注目の的) the *focus* of public attention.
mato-hazure (〜外れ) off the point: *Kare no ikeñ wa* mato-hazure *da.* (彼の意見は的外れだ) His opinion *completely misses the point.*

ma⌐tomari まとまり (纏り) *n.*
1 unity; organization; solidarity:
Kono chiimu wa matomari *ga ii* [*warui*]. (このチームはまとまりがいい[悪い]) This team works [does not work] *together well*. 《⇨ matomaru》
2 coherence; order:
Kare no hanashi wa matomari *ga nai.* (彼の話はまとまりがない) His talk lacks *coherence*.

ma⌐tomar·u まとまる (纏まる) *vi.* (matomar·i-; matomar·a-; matomat-te C) **1** be collected; be brought together:
Kare no tañpeñ wa matomatte, *is-satsu no hoñ ni natta.* (彼の短編はまとまって、1冊の本になった) His short stories *were brought together* into one volume. 《⇨ matomeru》
2 be united; be organized:
Sono soshiki wa yoku matomatte iru. (その組織はよくまとまっている) The organization *is* closely *knit*. / *Kañgae wa mada* matomatte imaseñ. (考えはまだまとまっていません) My thoughts *are not organized* yet. 《⇨ matomeru; matomari》
3 (of a negotiation, contract, etc.) be settled; be concluded; come to an agreement:
Sono kooshoo wa sugu ni mato-matta. (その交渉はすぐにまとまった) The negotiations *were* soon *concluded*. 《⇨ matomeru》

ma⌐tome まとめ (纏め) *n.* summary; conclusion. 《⇨ matomeru》

ma⌐tome·ru まとめる (纏める) *vt.* (matome-te V) **1** collect; gather together:
Kare wa kamikuzu o matomete *moyashita.* (彼は紙屑をまとめて燃やした) He *collected* the wastepaper and burned it.
2 arrange; put into shape; sum up:
Kare wa sono eñdañ o matometa. (彼はその縁談をまとめた) He *arranged* the marriage. / *Kanojo wa jibuñ no kañgae o* matometa. (彼女は自分の考えをまとめた) She *put* her

ideas *into shape*. / *Kono buñ no
naiyoo o gojuu-ji inai ni* matome
nasai. (この文の内容を 50 字以内にま
とめなさい) *Sum up* the contents of
this passage in fifty characters or
less. ⟪⇨ matomaru; matome⟫
3 settle (a negotiation, contract,
etc.); mediate:
Kare wa M-sha to no keeyaku o
matometa. (彼は M 社との契約をまと
めた) He *wrapped up* the contract
with M company. ⟪⇨ matomaru⟫

ma⌐ts·u¹ まつ (待つ) *vt.* (mach·i-;
mat·a-; mat-te C) wait; look forward to:
Chotto matte *kudasai.* (ちょっと待っ
てください) *Wait* a minute, please. /
Dare o matte *iru ñ desu ka?* (誰を
待っているんですか) Who *are* you
waiting for? / *Kanojo wa kimi no
heñji o* matte *iru yo.* (彼女は君の返
事を待っているよ) She *is waiting* for
your reply. / *Kodomo-tachi wa
shoogatsu o tanoshimi ni* matte
imasu. (子どもたちは正月を楽しみに待
っています) The children *are looking forward* to the New Year.

ma⌐tsu² まつ (松) *n.* pine (tree):
matsu-*kazari* (松飾り) the New
Year's pine decorations. ⟪⇨ kado-
matsu⟫

-matsu まつ (末) *suf.* the end:
shuu-matsu (週末) the week-*end* /
getsu-matsu (月末) the *end* of the
month / *neñ*-matsu (年末) the *end*
of the year / *seeki*-matsu (世紀末)
the *end* of the century.

ma⌐tsuri まつり (祭り) *n.* festival;
fete. ⟪⇨ photo (right)⟫

ma⌐tsur·u まつる (祭る) *vt.* (ma-
tsur·i-; matsur·a-; matsut-te C)
deify; enshrine:
Kono jiñja ni wa dare ga matsutte
arimasu ka? (この神社にはだれが祭っ
てありますか) Who *is deified* at this
shrine?

ma⌐tsutake まつたけ (松茸) *n.*
matsutake. ★ A large brown edi-

ble mushroom. ⟪⇨ kinoko⟫

MATSURI

ma⌐tsuwa⌐r·u まつわる (纏わる) *vi.*
(-war·i-; -war·a-; -wat-te C) be
associated; be concerned:
Watashi wa kono tera ni matsu-
waru *omoshiroi hanashi o shitte
imasu.* (私はこの寺にまつわるおもしろい
話を知っています) I know an interesting story *associated with* this
temple. / *Kare no shi ni* matsu-
waru *heñ na uwasa ga aru.* (彼の死
にまつわる変なうわさがある) There is a
strange rumor *concerning* his
death.

ma⌐ttaku まったく (全く) *adv.*
1 completely; utterly:
Sore wa mattaku *bakageta hanashi da.* (それはまったくばかげた話だ)
That is an *utterly* ridiculous
story. / *Kore kara noberu koto wa*
mattaku *no shiñjitsu desu.* (これから
述べることはまったくの真実です) What
I am going to tell you now is the
absolute truth.
2 (with a negative) (not) at all:
Watashi wa mattaku *oyogemaseñ.*
(私はまったく泳げません) I cannot
swim *at all*. / *Watashi wa sono
koto ni tsuite wa* mattaku *shirimaseñ.* (私はそのことについてはまったく知り
ません) I do not know anything *at
all* about that.
3 really; indeed:
*"Kyoo wa ii teñki desu ne." "Mat-
taku desu."* (「きょうはいい天気ですね」
「まったくです」) "It is nice weather

today." "It *certainly* is." / Mattaku *heñna koto ni natta mono da.* (まったく変なことになったものだ) Things have *really* turned out strange.

ma·「u まう（舞う）*vi.* (ma·i-; ma-w·a-; mat-te Ⓒ) dance; flutter; whirl:
mai o mau（舞いを舞う）*perform* a dance / *Choo ga* matte *iru.* (蝶が舞っている) A butterfly *is fluttering about.* / *Kono ha ga kaze ni* matte *iru.* (木の葉が風に舞っている) The leaves *are whirling* in the wind.

ma「wari まわり（回り・周り）*n.*
1 circumference; edge:
Futari wa ike no mawari *o aruita.* (二人は池の周りを歩いた) The two of them walked around the *edge* of the pond.
2 neighborhood; environment:
Watashi no ie no mawari *ni takusañ ie ga tachimashita.* (私の家の周りにたくさん家が建ちました) Many houses were built in my *neighborhood.* / *Tabako o suu hito wa* mawari *no hito ni meewaku desu.* (たばこを吸う人は周りの人に迷惑です) People who smoke are an annoyance to the people *around* them.
3 spread:
Hi no mawari *ga hayaku, sono ie wa sugu ni moete shimatta.* (火の回りが早く，その家はすぐに燃えてしまった) The *spread* of the fire was fast and the house burnt down in no time. 《⇨ mawaru》
4 effect:
Kare wa sake no mawari *ga hayai.* (彼は酒の回りが早い) Alcohol soon has an *effect* on him.

ma「wari」michi まわりみち（回り道）*n.* detour; roundabout course:
Hashi ga kooji-chuu na no de mawarimichi *o shita.* (橋が工事中なので回り道をした) The bridge was being repaired, so I made a *detour.*

MAWARIMICHI SIGN

ma「war·u まわる（回る）*vi.* (ma-war·i-; mawar·a-; mawat-te Ⓒ)
1 turn; rotate; revolve; spin:
Sono jiñkoo-eesee wa mada chikyuu no mawari o mawatte imasu. (その人口衛星はまだ地球の周りを回っています) The artificial satellite *is* still *circling* around the earth. / *Kono koma wa yoku* mawaru. (このこまはよく回る) This top *spins* well. 《⇨ mawasu》
2 make the rounds; look around:
Keekañ ga kono heñ o mawatte *iru no o mimashita.* (警官がこの辺を回っているのを見ました) I saw a policeman *making the rounds* in this area.
3 come around; go around:
Uraguchi e mawatte *kudasai.* (裏口へ回ってください) Please *come around* to the back door. / *Watashi wa sono hoñ o sagashite, nañ-geñ mo hoñya o* mawatta. (私はその本を探して，何軒も本屋を回った) I *went around* many bookshops looking for the book.

-mawar·u まわる（回る）(-mawar·i-; -mawar·a-; -mawat-te Ⓒ)
★ Occurs as the second element of compound verbs. Added to the continuative base of a verb. go about; move around:
*aruki-*mawaru（歩き回る）walk *about* / *kake-*mawaru（駆け回る）run *around* / *nige-*mawaru（逃げ回る）run *about* trying to escape /

tobi-mawaru (飛び回る) rush *around*; fly *about*.

ma「was·u まわす (回す) *vt.* (ma-wash·i-; mawas·a-; mawash·i-te C) **1** turn; rotate; spin: *daiyaru o* mawasu (ダイヤルを回す) *dial* a number / *totte o* mawasu (取っ手を回す) *rotate* a handle / *koma o* mawasu (こまを回す) *spin* a top. ((⇨ mawaru))

2 send around; pass; forward: *Sono shio o* mawashite *kudasai.* (その塩を回してください) *Pass* me the salt, please. / *Kono tegami wa sochira ni* mawashimasu. (この手紙はそちらに回します) I will *forward* this letter to you.

3 (of a phone call) transfer: *Naisen roku-goo ni* mawashimasu. (内線65に回します) I will *transfer* you to Extension 65.

ma「yo」naka まよなか (真夜中) *n.* midnight; the middle of the night: Mayonaka *ni denwa ga natta.* (真夜中に電話が鳴った) The phone rang in the *middle of the night.*

ma「yone」ezu マヨネーズ *n.* mayonnaise: *sarada ni* mayoneezu *o kakeru* (サラダにマヨネーズをかける) pour *mayonnaise* over a salad.

ma「yo」·u まよう (迷う) *vi.* (mayoi-; mayow·a-; mayot-te C) **1** get lost; lose one's way: *Tochuu de michi ni* mayottara *denwa o kudasai.* (途中で道に迷ったら電話をください) If you *get lost* on the way, give me a call.

2 be puzzled; be at a loss: *Watashi wa nan to itte yoi ka* mayotta. (私は何と言ってよいか迷った) I *was at a loss* what to say.

3 hesitate; be undecided; waver: *Kare wa dare ni toohyoo suru ka mada* mayotte *iru.* (彼はだれに投票するかまだ迷っている) He *is* still *unde-*

cided who to vote for.

ma「yu」 まゆ (眉) *n.* eyebrow: mayu *o hisomeru* (眉をひそめる) knit one's *eyebrows.*

ma「yuge」 (眉毛) *n.* eyebrow.

ma「za」r·u まざる (混ざる) *vi.* (ma-zar·i-; mazar·a-; mazat-te C) = majiru. ((⇨ mazeru))

ma「ze」·ru まぜる (混ぜる) *vt.* (ma-ze-te V) mix; combine; mingle; blend: *semento to suna o* mazeru (セメントと砂を混ぜる) *mix* cement and sand / *Kuro to shiro o* mazeru *to haiiro ni narimasu.* (黒と白を混ぜると灰色になります) If you *mix* black and white, it makes gray. / *Komugi-ko to soba-ko o 7-3 no wari de* mazeta. (小麦粉とそば粉を7-3の割で混ぜた) I *mixed* wheat flour and buckwheat flour in proportions of seven to three. ((⇨ majiru))

ma「zu」 まず (先ず) *adv.* **1** first of all; to begin with: Mazu *chuushoku o sumaseyoo.* (まず昼食を済ませよう) *First of all*, let's finish lunch. / Mazu *dai-ichi ni sore wa nedan ga takasugiru.* (まず第一にそれは値段が高すぎる) *To begin with*, the main thing is that the price is too high.

2 probably; almost certainly: *Gogo wa* mazu *ame deshoo.* (午後はまず雨でしょう) It will *probably* rain this afternoon. / *Kare no yuu-shoo wa* mazu *machigai ga nai.* (彼の優勝はまずまちがいがない) It is *almost* certain that he will win the championship.

ma「zu」·i[1] まずい (不味い) *a.* (-ku) **1** (of taste) not good; bad: *Kono pan wa* mazui. (このパンはまずい) This bread tastes *bad.* / *Ano mise no karee wa* mazukatta. (あの店のカレーはまずかった) The curry at that restaurant was *awful.* / *Kudamono wa hayaku tabenai to* mazuku *naru.* (果物は早く食べないとま

ずくなる）If you do not eat fruit quickly, it *no longer tastes good.* 《↔ oishii》

2 awkward; unfavorable; unwise:

Kanojo wa mazui *toki ni kita.* (彼女はまずいときに来た) She showed up at an *awkward* moment. / *Jijitsu o kakushite oita no wa* mazukatta. (事実を隠しておいたのはまずかった) It was *unwise* of me to have kept the truth hidden. / *Mazui koto ni natta.* (まずいことになった) Things have turned out *badly.*

ma⌈zu⌉·i²（拙い）*a.* (-ku) (of skill) clumsy; poor:

mazui *hoñyaku* (まずい翻訳) a *poor* translation / *Kare wa ji ga* mazui. (彼は字がまずい) He writes a *poor* hand.

ma⌈zushi⌉·i　まずしい（貧しい）*a.* (-ku) poor; needy:

Watashi wa ie ga mazushikute, *daigaku e ikenakatta.* (私は家が貧しくて、大学へ行けなかった) My family was *poor* and I could not go on to university. 《⇨ biñboo》

me¹¹　め（目）*n.* **1** eye:

me *o akeru* [*hiraku*] (目をあける[開く]) open one's *eyes* / me *o tsuburu* [*tojiru*] (目をつぶる[閉じる]) close one's *eyes* / me *o hosomeru* (目を細める) screw one's *eyes* up / me *o hanasu* (目を離す) take one's *eyes* off / me *o korasu* (目をこらす) strain one's *eyes* / me *o sorasu* (目をそらす) turn one's *eyes* away from / *Haha wa hidari no* me *ga mienai.* (母は左の目が見えない) My mother is blind in the left *eye.* / *Kare wa* tsumetai me *de watashi o mita.* (彼は冷たい目で私を見た) He looked at me *coldly.*

2 eyesight; sight:

me *ga yoi* [*warui*] (目が良い[悪い]) have good [bad] *eyesight* / *Me ga waruku natte kita.* (目が悪くなってきた) My *sight* began to fail.

3 viewpoint:

gaikokujiñ no me *kara mita Nihoñ no buñka* (外国人の目から見た日本の文化) Japanese culture seen from a foreigner's *viewpoint* / *Oya no* me *kara mireba, dono ko mo kawaii.* (親の目から見れば、どの子もかわいい) In the *eyes* of the parents, all children are sweet and dear.

4 bad experience:

Watashi wa osoroshii me *ni atta.* (私は恐ろしい目にあった) I had a frightening *experience.* / *Ikka wa hidoi* me *ni atta.* (一家はひどい目にあった) The whole family had a very bad *experience.*

5 eye-like object:

hari no me (針の目) the *eye* of a needle / *taifuu no* me (台風の目) the *eye* of a typhoon / *amimono no* me (編み物の目) a *stitch.*

me ga aru [kiku] (～がある[利く]) have an eye for (beauty): *Kare wa yakimono ni* me ga aru [kiku]. (彼は焼き物に目がある[利く]) He *is a connoisseur* of pottery.

me ga mawaru (～が回る) feel giddy: *Watashi wa takai tokoro ni agaru to* me ga mawaru. (私は高いところに上がると目が回る) I *feel giddy* when I go up to high places. / *Kyoo wa* me ga mawaru hodo *isogashikatta.* (きょうは目が回るほど忙しかった) I was so busy today that I *was rushed off my feet.*

me ga nai (～がない) be very fond of: *Kare wa uisukii ni* me ga nai. (彼はウイスキーに目がない) He *is very fond of* whisky.

me ga takai (～が高い) have an expert eye: *Kore o erabu to wa kimi mo* me ga takai. (これを選ぶとはきみも目が高い) Picking this one shows that you *have an expert eye.*

me ga todoku (～が届く) keep an eye on; look after: *Koñna ni seeto ga ookute wa* me ga todo-

kanai.(こんなに生徒が多くては目が届か
ない) There are such a large number of pupils that I *cannot look
after* all of them.

me ni amaru (〜に余る) be unpardonable: *Kare no shitsuree na
taido wa* me ni amaru.(彼の失礼な
態度は目に余る) His rude behavior
is inexcusable.

me ni tomaru (〜に留まる) catch a
person's eye: *Kanojo no eñgi ga
kañtoku no* me ni tomatta.(彼女の
演技が監督の目に留まった) Her act-
ing *caught the director's eye.*

me ni tsuku (〜につく) attract a
person's attention: *Kare no akai
shiñsha wa miñna no* me ni tsuita.
(彼の赤い新車はみんなの目についた) His
red new car *was highly conspicuous.*

me no kataki ni suru (〜の敵にす
る) hate all the time: *Kare wa
watashi no koto o* me no kataki ni
shite iru.(彼は私のことを目の敵にして
いる) He always *treats me like an
enemy.*

me o hikaraseru (〜を光らせる)
keep a sharp eye out: *Zeekañ wa
mayaku no mitsuyu ni* me o hika-
rasete iru.(税関は麻薬の密輸に目を
光らせている) The customs *keep a
sharp eye out* for drug smuggling.*

me o hiku (〜を引く) attract a person's attention: *Kanojo no e ga
tokubetsu watashi-tachi no* me o
hiita.(彼女の絵が特別私たちの目を引
いた) Her painting especially *attracted our attention.*

me o kakeru (〜を掛ける) favor;
be kind: *Señsee wa watashi ni*
me o kakete kureta.(先生は私に目
をかけてくれた) The teacher *treated
me with kindness and consideration.*

me o mawasu (〜を回す) faint;
be astonished: *Kare wa seekyuusho no kiñgaku o mite,* me o ma-
washita.(彼は請求書の金額を見て,

目を回した) He *was astonished*
when he saw the amount on the
bill.

me o nusumu (〜を盗む) do something behind a person's back:
Kare wa oya no me o nusuñde, *tabako o sutta.* (彼は親の目を盗んで、た
ばこを吸った) He smoked, *unknown*
to his parents.

me o toosu (〜を通す) run one's
eye over: *Kono shorui ni* me o
tooshite *oite kudasai.* (この書類に目
を通しておいてください) Please *glance
through* these papers.

me o tsuburu (〜をつぶる) close
one's eyes; ignore: *Kare wa watashi no machigai ni* me o tsu-
butte kureta.(彼は私の間違いに目をつ
ぶってくれた) He *turned a blind eye*
to my mistake.

me o tsukeru (〜をつける) have
one's eye (on something): *Kare
wa eki-mae no tochi ni* me o tsukete ita.(彼は駅前の土地に目をつけて
いた) He *had his eye* on the land
in front of the station.

o-me ni kakaru (お〜にかかる)
(*polite*) see; meet: *Koko de* o-me
ni kakareta *koto o ureshiku omoimasu.* (ここでお目にかかれたことをうれし
く思います) I am very happy I
could *see* you here.

o-me ni kakeru (お〜にかける)
(*polite*) show: *Watashi no e wa
totemo* o-me ni kakeru *yoo na mono de wa arimaseñ.* (私の絵はとても
お目にかけるようなものではありません)
My painting is not the kind of
thing I could *show* you.

me[12] め (芽) *n.* shoot; sprout;
bud:
Ki ga me o dashi-hajimeta.(木が芽
を出し始めた) The trees *have started sprouting* their leaves. / *Chuurippu no* me ga deta.(チューリップの
芽が出た) The tulips are in *bud.*

-me[1] め (目) *suf.* (the position of
something in an ordered group

or arrangement):

mae kara go-bañ-me *no seki* (前か
ら5番目の席) the *fifth* seat from
the front / *hidari kara* ni-keñ-me
no uchi (左から2軒目の家) the
second house from the left / *Koko
kara* mittsu-me *no eki de ori nasai.* (ここから3つ目の駅で降りなさい)
Get off at the *third* stop from
here.

-me² め *suf.* (degree or tendency): ★ Added to the stem of an
adjective.
haya-me ni shuppatsu suru (早めに
出発する) start *earlier than scheduled* / *ooki-me no kutsu* (大きめの
靴) a pair of shoes *on the large
side* / *mijika-me ni kiru* (短めに切る)
cut *a bit short.*

me「atarashi」·i めあたらしい (目新
しい) *a.* (-ku) new; fresh; novel;
original:
meatarashii shoohiñ (目新しい商品)
a *novel* product / *Sono aidea wa
meatarashii mono de wa arimaseñ.*
(そのアイデアは目新しいものではありませ
ん) There is nothing *original*
about the idea. 《⇨ atarashii》

me「ate めあて (目当て) *n.* **1** aim;
object:
*Kare no meate wa kanojo no zai-
sañ da.* (彼の目当ては彼女の財産だ)
His *aim* is her money. / *Watashi
wa nañ no meate mo naku, bura-
bura aruita.* (私は何の目当てもなく、ぶ
らぶら歩いた) I strolled around
without any particular *aim.*
2 guide; landmark:
*Ano takai biru o meate ni aruite
iki nasai.* (あの高いビルを目当てに歩い
て行きなさい) Continue walking,
keeping an eye on that tall building.

me「chakucha めちゃくちゃ *a.n.*
(~ na, ni) messy; unreasonable;
reckless:
*Kare no yookyuu wa mechakucha
da.* (彼の要求はめちゃくちゃだ) His

demands are *unreasonable.* / *Kare
no mechakucha na uñteñ ni akireta.* (彼のめちゃくちゃな運転にあきれた)
I was appalled at his *reckless* driving.

me「chamecha めちゃめちゃ *a.n.*
(~ na, ni) (*informal*) smashed
up; ruined; messed up: ★ Used
in '~ *ni naru* [*suru*].'
*Kuruma wa hee ni shoototsu shite,
mechamecha ni natta.* (車は塀に衝
突して、めちゃめちゃになった) The car
ran into a wall and was *smashed
up.* / *Sono jikeñ wa kare no sono-
go no jiñsee o mechamecha ni shite shimatta.* (その事件は彼のその後の
人生をめちゃめちゃにしてしまった) The
incident ended up making a *mess*
of his subsequent life.

me「da「ts·u めだつ (目立つ) *vi.*
(medach·i-; medat·a-; medat-te
Ⓒ) stand out; be conspicuous;
be prominent:
*Kare wa see ga takai no de doko
e itte mo medatsu.* (彼は背が高いので
どこへ行っても目だつ) He is tall, so
he *stands out* wherever he goes. /
Kare wa kurasu de amari meda-
tanakatta. (彼はクラスであまり目だたな
かった) He *was not very noticeable*
in our class. / *Kanojo wa saikiñ*
medatte, *Nihoñgo ga joozu ni
natta.* (彼女は最近目だって、日本語が
上手になった) Recently her Japanese has improved *remarkably.*

me「deta」·i めでたい (目出度い) *a.*
(-ku) happy; joyful:
medetai shirase (めでたい知らせ) *joyful* news / *Musuko wa* medetaku
daigaku ni gookaku shimashita.
(息子はめでたく大学に合格しました)
Happily my son was able to pass
the exam to university.

me「e めい (姪) *n.* niece.
★ When another family's niece is
referred to, '*meego-sañ*' is used.
《↔ oi¹》

me「e- めい (名) *pref.* famous;

great; excellent:

mee-*bameñ* (名場面) a *famous* scene / mee-*pianisuto* (名ピアニスト) an *excellent* pianist / mee-*señshu* (名選手) a *star* player.

-mee めい (名) *suf.* number of people:

nijuu-mee (20 名) twenty *people*.

me⌐eañ[1] めいあん (名案) *n.* good idea; splendid plan:

meeañ *ga ukabu* (名案が浮かぶ) hit on a *good idea* / *Sore wa* meeañ *da.* (それは名案だ) That's a *wonderful idea.*

me⌐eañ[2] めいあん (明暗) *n.* light and shade; bright and dark sides:

meeañ *no hakkiri shita e* (明暗のはっきりした絵) a painting which shows a clear contrast between *light and shade.*

meeañ o wakeru (〜を分ける) decide: *Sono dekigoto ga kare no jiñsee no* meeañ *o waketa.* (その出来事が彼の人生の明暗を分けた) The incident *decided* his fate.

me⌐ebo めいぼ (名簿) *n.* name list; directory; roll:

kaiiñ no meebo *o tsukuru* (会員の名簿を作る) make a *list* of the members of a society / *jookyaku no* meebo (乗客の名簿) a passenger *list.*

me⌐ebutsu めいぶつ (名物) *n.* special [noted] product; specialty.

me⌐echuu めいちゅう (命中) *n.* hit.

meechuu suru (〜する) *vt.* hit the target: *Tama wa mato no mañnaka ni* meechuu *shita.* (弾は的の真ん中に命中した) The bullet *hit the target* right in the center.

me⌐ehaku めいはく (明白) *a.n.* (〜 na, ni) clear; obvious; plain; evident:

meehaku *na jijitsu* (明白な事実) an *obvious* fact / *Kare ga koñdo no jikeñ ni kañkee ga aru no wa* meehaku *desu.* (彼が今度の事件に関係が

あるのは明白です) It is *evident* that he is involved in this affair. / *Sono koto wa keeyakusho ni* meehaku *ni kakarete imasu.* (そのことは契約書に明白に書かれています) That matter is *clearly* stated in the contract.

Me⌐eji めいじ (明治) *n.* Meiji:

★ The name of a Japanese emperor and of his reign.

Meeji *jidai* (明治時代) the *Meiji* era (1868–1912) / Meeji *Ishiñ* (明治維新) the *Meiji* Restoration.

《⇒ geñgoo (table); jidai (table)》

me⌐eji⌐ñ めいじん (名人) *n.* expert; master:

go no meejiñ (碁の名人) a *master* 'go' player / *Kare wa tsuri no* meejiñ *da.* (彼はつりの名人だ) He is an *expert* at fishing.

me⌐eji·ru めいじる (命じる) *vt.* (meeji-te Ⅴ) **1** tell; order; command.

Keesatsu wa demo-tai ni soko kara tachisaru yoo ni meejita. (警察はデモ隊にそこから立ち去るように命じた) The police *ordered* the demonstrators to leave the area. / *Saibañsho wa kare ni bakkiñ o* meejita. (裁判所は彼に罰金を命じた) The court *ordered* him to pay a fine.

2 appoint; place:

Kare wa koochoo ni meejirareta. (彼は校長に命じられた) He *was appointed* school principal.

me⌐ekaku めいかく (明確) *a.n.* (〜 na, ni) clear and accurate; distinct; definite:

meekaku *na kaitoo* (明確な回答) a *clear and accurate* answer / meekaku *ni setsumee suru* (明確に説明する) explain *explicitly* / *Dare ni sekiniñ ga aru no ka* meekaku *de nai.* (だれに責任があるのか明確でない) It is not *clear* who bears responsibility.

me⌐eme⌐e めいめい (銘々) *n.* (〜 ni) each; individually:

Miñna ga meemee *no ikeñ o no-beta.* (みんながめいめいの意見を述べた) Everyone expressed their *individual* opinions. / *Asu wa* mee-mee *beñtoo o motte kite kudasai.* (あすはめいめい弁当を持ってきてください) Please bring *your own* lunches tomorrow.

me⌐eree めいれい (命令) *n.* order; command; instructions:
meeree *ni shitagau* [*somuku*] (命令に従う[背く]) follow [disobey] an *order* / Meeree-doori *ni shi nasai.* (命令どおりにしなさい) Do *as you are instructed to.*
meeree suru (〜する) *vt.* order; command; instruct: *Shachoo wa watashi ni sugu kaisha ni modoru yoo* meeree *shita.* (社長は私にすぐ会社に戻るよう命令した) The president *ordered* me to immediately return to the company.

me⌐eroo めいろう (明朗) *a.n.*
(〜 na, ni) **1** cheerful; open-hearted:
Suzuki-sañ wa meeroo *de ii hito desu.* (鈴木さんは明朗でいい人です) Mr. Suzuki is a nice *openhearted* person. (⇨ hogaraka)
2 (of accounts, bills, etc.) clean; aboveboard:
meeroo *na señkyo* (明朗な選挙) a *clean and honest* election / *kaikee o* meeroo ni suru (会計を明朗にする) *put* the accounting *on an aboveboard* basis.

me⌐eryoo めいりょう (明瞭) *a.n.*
(〜 na, ni) clear; evident; articulate:
meeryoo *na hatsuoñ* (明瞭な発音) *clear* pronunciation / meeryoo *ni setsumee suru* (明瞭に説明する) explain *articulately* / *Sono jijitsu wa dare ni mo* meeryoo *desu.* (その事実はだれにも明瞭です) That fact is *evident* to everyone.

me⌐esaku めいさく (名作) *n.* fine work; masterpiece.

me⌐eshi[1] めいし (名刺) *n.* calling [visiting] card; business card:

meeshi *o kookañ suru* (名刺を交換する) exchange *cards* / *O*-meeshi *o itadakemasu ka?* (お名刺をいただけますか) May I have your *card*? / *Watashi wa kare ni* meeshi *o watashita.* (私は彼に名刺を渡した) I gave him my *card*.

MEESHI

me⌐eshi[2] めいし (名詞) *n.* noun; substantive. 《⇨ appendixes》

me⌐eshiñ めいしん (迷信) *n.* superstition:
meeshiñ *o shiñjiru* (迷信を信じる) believe in a *superstition* / meeshiñ *o daha suru* (迷信を打破する) break down a *superstition*.

me⌐esho めいしょ (名所) *n.* noted place; place of interest; sights to see:
Kare ni Tookyoo no meesho *o añnai shite yatta.* (彼に東京の名所を案内してやった) I showed him the *sights* of Tokyo. / meesho-*kyuuseki* (名所旧跡) *places of scenic beauty* and historical interest.

me⌐eshoo めいしょう (名称) *n.* name; title:
shiñ-seehiñ ni meeshoo *o tsukeru* (新製品に名称をつける) give a *name* to a new product.

me⌐etaa メーター *n.* meter:

gasu [suidoo; deñki] no meetaa (ガス[水道; 電気]のメーター) a gas [water; electricity] *meter* / meetaa *o shiraberu* (メーターを調べる) read the *meter*.

meˈetoru メートル（米） *n.* meter: *Kono michi wa haba ga hachi-meetoru arimasu.* (この道は幅が8メートルあります) This road is eight *meters* wide.

meˈewaku めいわく（迷惑） *n.* trouble; annoyance; nuisance: *Meewaku o o-kake shite, mooshi-wake arimaseñ.* (迷惑をおかけして、申し訳ありません) I am sorry for causing you so much *trouble*.

Meewaku chuusha wa yameyoo. (Don't park and inconvenience others.)

NO PARKING SIGN

meewaku suru (～する) *vi.* be annoyed; be bothered: *Tonari no piano no oto ni wa* meewaku shite imasu. (隣のピアノの音には迷惑しています) We *are bothered* by the noise of our neighbor's piano.

— *a.n.* (～ na) annoying; bothering; troublesome; inconvenient: *Kuruma o michi no mañnaka ni tomeru no wa* meewaku *da.* (車を道の真ん中に止めるのは迷惑だ) It is *annoying* for a car to be parked in the middle of the road. / *Mee-waku de nakereba, issho ni tsu-rete itte kudasai.* (迷惑でなければ、一緒に連れて行ってください) If it is not a *nuisance* to you, please take me along with you.

meˈeyo めいよ（名誉） *n.* honor; glory: *hito no* meeyo *o kizutsukeru* (人の名誉を傷つける) *bring discredit* on a person's *name* / meeyo *o bañkai suru* (名誉をばんかいする) retrieve one's *honor* / *Subarashii shoo o itadaite* meeyo *ni omoimasu.* (素晴らしい賞をいただいて名誉に思います) I *am honored* to have received such a wonderful prize. / meeyo-*shi-miñ* (名誉市民) an *honorary* citizen / meeyo-*kyooju* (名誉教授) a professor *emeritus*.

— *a.n.* (～ na) honorable: *Yuushoo wa waga koo ni totte* meeyo *na koto desu.* (優勝はわが校にとって名誉なことです) It is an *honor* for our school to have won the prize. ((↔ fumeeyo))

meˈeyokisoñ めいよきそん（名誉棄損） *n.* defamation; libel; slander.

meˈgakeˈ·ru めがける（目掛ける） *vt.* (megake-te Ⅴ) aim: *Shooneñ wa hebi o* megakete, *ishi o nageta.* (少年は蛇を目がけて、石を投げた) The boy *aimed* at the snake and threw a stone.

meˈgane めがね（眼鏡） *n.* glasses; spectacles: megane *o kakeru [hazusu]* (眼鏡をかける[はずす]) put on [take off] one's *glasses* / *Kare wa kiñbuchi no* megane *o kakete ita.* (彼は金縁の眼鏡をかけていた) He wore gold-rimmed *glasses*.

meˈgumareˈ·ru めぐまれる（恵まれる） *vi.* (megumare-te Ⅴ) **1** be blessed; be gifted: *Kare wa keñkoo ni* megumarete *iru.* (彼は健康に恵まれている) He *is blessed* with good health.
2 be rich: *Sono kuni wa teñneñ shigeñ ni* megumarete *iru.* (その国は天然資源に恵まれている) That country *is rich* in natural resources.

meˈgum·u めぐむ（恵む） *vt.* (me-gum·i-; megum·a-; meguñ·de C)

give in charity; do a person a kindness:
Kare wa sono hito ni tabemono o meguñda. (彼はその人に食べ物を恵んだ) He *gave* that man some food *out of kindness.*

me⌈gur·u めぐる (巡る) *vt.* (me-gur·i-; megur·a-; megut-te Ⓒ)
1 come around; make a tour:
Mata yuki no kisetsu ga megutte kita. (また雪の季節が巡ってきた) The season of snow *has come around* again. / *Watashi-tachi wa shima o meguru kañkooseñ ni notta.* (私たちは島を巡る観光船に乗った) We went aboard the sightseeing ship *making a tour* through the islands.
2 concern; relate:
geñdai no kyooiku o meguru moñdai (現代の教育を巡る問題) a problem *concerning* contemporary education / *Isañ o megutte, kyoodai ga arasotte iru.* (遺産を巡って兄弟が争っている) The brothers are fighting *over* the legacy.

me⌈gu⌉suri めぐすり (目薬) *n.* eyewash; eye lotion:
megusuri o sasu (目薬をさす) apply *eye lotion.*

me⌉isha めいしゃ (目医者) *n.* eye doctor; oculist. (⇨ gañka)

me⌈kata めかた (目方) *n.* weight:
tsutsumi no mekata o hakaru (包みの目方を計る) *weigh* a parcel / *Kore wa mekata ga go-kiro aru.* (これは目方が5キロある) This *weighs* five kilograms. / *Kono suutsukeesu wa mekata ga sukoshi chooka shite imasu.* (このスーツケースは目方が少し超過しています) This suitcase *is* a little *too heavy.* (⇨ omosa)

me⌈kki めっき (鍍金) *n.* plating; gilding:
giñ-mekki no supuuñ (銀めっきのスプーン) a silver-*plated* spoon / *Kono saji wa mekki ga hagete iru.* (このさじはめっきがはげている) The *plating* of this spoon is coming off.

mekki ga hageru (～がはげる) be unmasked: *Mekki wa sugu ni hageru.* (めっきはすぐにはげる) False pretenses will soon *be detected.*

mekki suru (～する) *vt.* plate; gild: *Kore wa kiñ-mekki shita mono desu.* (これは金めっきしたものです) This is one which *is plated* with gold.

me⌈kur·u めくる (捲る) *vt.* (me-kur·i-; mekur·a-; mekut-te Ⓒ)
turn over [up]:
peeji o mekuru (ページをめくる) *turn over* a page / *torañpu no kaado o mekuru* (トランプのカードをめくる) *turn up* a playing card.

me⌈ma⌉i めまい (眩暈) *n.* giddiness; dizziness:
Nañ da ka memai ga suru. (なんだかめまいがする) I don't know why, but I *feel dizzy.*

me⌉mo メモ *n.* memo; note:
memo o toru (メモを取る) make a *memo* / *memo o mi-nagara hanasu* (メモを見ながら話す) speak from *notes* / *memo-yooshi* (メモ用紙) *memo* paper / *memo-choo* (メモ帳) *memo* pad; *scratch* pad.

memo suru (～する) *vt.* put down; make a note of: *Kare no eñzetsu no yooteñ o memo shita.* (彼の演説の要点をメモした) I *noted down* the key points of his speech.

me⌈mori⌉ めもり (目盛り) *n.* scale; graduation:
oñdokee no memori o yomu (温度計の目盛りを読む) read the *graduations* on a thermometer / *biñ ni memori o tsukeru* (ビンに目盛りをつける) mark a *scale* on a bottle.

me⌈ñ⌉ めん (面) *n.* 1 mask; face guard:
meñ o tsukeru [kaburu] (面をつける[かぶる]) put on a *mask.*
2 plane; surface:
suihee-meñ (水平面) a horizontal *plane.*
3 aspect; side:

monogoto no akarui meñ *o miru* (物事の明るい面を見る) look on the bright *side* of things.
4 (of a newspaper) page: *shiñbuñ no dai ichi-*meñ (新聞の第一面) the front *page* of a newspaper.
meñ to mukkatte (〜と向かって) to a person's face: *Kare ni wa* meñ *to mukatte, nani mo ienakatta.* (彼には面と向かって, 何も言えなかった) I could say nothing *to him face to face.*

me¬ñ² めん(綿) *n.* cotton: meñ*-seehiñ* (綿製品) *cotton* goods / meñ *no kutsushita* (綿の靴下) *cotton* socks. 《⇨ wata》

me¬ñbaa メンバー *n.* member (of a club, society, etc.).

me¬ñboku めんぼく(面目) *n.* honor; face; prestige: meñboku *o tamotsu* [*ushinau*] (面目を保つ[失う]) save [lose] *face*.
meñboku nai (〜ない) be ashamed: *Añna machigai o shite,* meñboku nai. (あんな間違いをして, 面目ない) I *am ashamed* of having made such a mistake.

me¬ñdo¬o めんどう(面倒) *n.*
1 trouble; inconvenience: *Hito ni* meñdoo *wa kaketaku arimaseñ.* (人に面倒はかけたくありません) I don't want to cause any *trouble* to others.
2 care: *Ane ga byooki no haha no* meñdoo *o mite imasu.* (姉が病気の母の面倒を見ています) My sister takes *care* of our sick mother.
meñdoo-mi ga ii (〜見がいい) take good care of: *Ano señsee wa gakusee no* meñdoo-mi ga ii. (あの先生は学生のめんどう見がいい) That teacher *takes good care of* her students.
— *a.n.* (〜 na, ni) troublesome; difficult; complicated.
Meñdoo *na koto ni natte kita.* (面

倒なことになってきた) The situation has become *complicated.* / *Kare wa sono* meñdoo *na shigoto o hikiuketa.* (彼はその面倒な仕事を引き受けた) He took on that *troublesome* job.

me¬ñdookusa¬·i めんどうくさい(面倒臭い) *a.* (-ku) troublesome; wearisome; reluctant: meñdookusai *shigoto* (面倒くさい仕事) a *troublesome* job / *Ame ga futte iru no de gaishutsu suru no wa* meñdookusai. (雨が降っているので外出するのは面倒くさい) It is raining, so I am *reluctant* to go out. / *Kono moñdai wa* meñdookusaku *nari-soo da.* (この問題は面倒くさくなりそうだ) This matter looks as if it is going to cause us a lot of *trouble.*

me¬ñji·ru めんじる(免じる) *vt.* (meñji-te Ⅴ) (*formal*) exempt; excuse: *shikeñ o* meñjiru (試験を免じる) *exempt* a person from an examination / *shiharai o* meñjiru (支払を免じる) *excuse* a person from payment. 《⇨ meñjo》
...ni meñjite (...に免じて) in consideration of: *Watashi* ni meñjite *kare o yurushite yatte kudasai.* (私に免じて彼を許してやってください) Please forgive him *for my sake.*

me¬ñjo めんじょ(免除) *n.* exemption; remission: *gakuhi no* meñjo (学費の免除) a *remission* of school fees.
meñjo suru (〜する) *vt.* exempt; remit: *Zeekiñ ga* meñjo *sareru no wa doo-iu baai desu ka?* (税金が免除されるのはどういう場合ですか) In what cases *are* taxes exempted?

me¬ñkai めんかい(面会) *n.* interview; meeting: meñkai *o mooshikomu* (面会を申し込む) request an *interview* / *Watashi wa kare to no* meñkai *o kotowatta.* (私は彼との面会を断わった) I refused to *see* him. / *Sono kañja wa* meñkai *shazetsu desu.* (その患者は面会謝絶です) No visitors are allowed to *see* the patient. / meñkai-*jikañ* (面会時間) *visiting* [*consulting*] hours.

meñkai suru (～する) *vt.* see; meet; visit: *Señsee wa sono ko no haha-oya to* meñkai shita. (先生はその子の母親と面会した) The teacher *interviewed* the child's mother.

me⌐ñkyo めんきょ (免許) *n.* license: uñteñ-meñkyo *o toru* (運転免許を取る) obtain a driver's *license* / meñkyo *teeshi* (免許停止) suspension of a *license.*

me⌐ñkyo⌐joo めんきょじょう (免許状) *n.* license; certificate: *kyooiñ* meñkyojoo (教員免許状) a teaching *certificate.*

me⌐ñkyo⌐shoo めんきょしょう (免許証) *n.* license; driver's license.

me⌐ñmoku めんもく (面目) *n.* honor. 《⇨ meñboku》

me⌐ñseki めんせき (面積) *n.* area; size: *Kono heya no* meñseki *wa yaku gojuu heehoo-meetoru arimasu.* (この部屋の面積は約 50 平方メートルあります) The *area* of this room is about fifty square meters. 《⇨ taiseki》

me⌐ñs·u⌐ru めんする (面する) *vi.* (meñsh·i-; meñsh·i-; meñsh·i-te Ⅰ) face; look out: *Sono heya wa minami* [*umi*] *ni* meñshite iru. (その部屋は南[海]に面している) The room *faces* south [the sea].

me⌐ñyuu メニュー *n.* menu; bill of fare.

me⌐ñzee めんぜい (免税) *n.* tax exemption: *Kono uisukii wa* meñzee *de kaimashita.* (このウイスキーは免税で買いました) I bought this whisky *duty-free.* / meñzee-*hiñ* (免税品) a *duty-free* article.

meñzee suru (～する) *vt.* exempt from taxation: *Mise ni yotte wa shoohi-zee ga* meñzee *sareru tokoro mo aru.* (店によっては消費税が免税されるところもある) Depending on the store, some *are exempted from* the consumption *tax.*

me⌐rodii メロディー *n.* melody; tune.

-me⌐ru める *suf.* (*v.*) (-me-te Ⅴ) make; -en: ★ Added to the stem of an adjective describing quality. haya-meru (早める) *hasten*; *quicken* / usu-meru (薄める) *make* thinner / *gasu o* yowa-meru (ガスを弱める) *turn down* the gas / *kañshiñ o* taka-meru (関心を高める) *heighten* interest.

me⌐shi めし (飯) *n.* ★ Used by men. **1** (*informal*) (cooked [boiled]) rice: meshi *o taku* (飯を炊く) cook [boil] *rice.* 《⇨ kome (table)》 **2** (*informal*) meal; food: *Saa* meshi *ni shiyoo.* (さあ飯にしよう) Let's have *breakfast* [*lunch, dinner*]. / *Saa* meshi *no jikañ da.* (さあ飯の時間だ) Well, now it's time *to eat.* 《⇨ asameshi; hirumeshi; bañmeshi》 **3** (*informal*) living; livelihood: meshi *no tane* (飯の種) a means of *living* / *Kono kyuuryoo de wa* meshi *wa kuenai.* (この給料では飯は食えない) I *cannot make a living* on this salary.

me⌐shiagar·u めしあがる (召し上がる) *vt.* (-agar·i-; -agar·a-; -agatte Ⓒ) ★ Honorific equivalent of '*taberu*' and '*nomu.*' eat; drink; have: *Nani o* meshiagarimasu *ka?* (何を召し上がりますか) What would you like to *have?* / *Doozo* meshiagatte *kudasai.* (どうぞ召し上がってください)

Please go ahead and *help yourself.*

me⌐shita⌐ めした（目下）*n.* one's inferior; subordinate. 《↔ meue》

me⌐su⌐ めす（雌）*n.* female; she: mesu no niwatori (めすの鶏) a *hen* / mesu inu (めす犬) a *female* dog. 《↔ osu²》

me⌐tsuboo⌐ めつぼう（滅亡）*n.* fall; downfall: kuni no metsuboo (国の滅亡) the *collapse* of a country.

metsuboo suru (～する) *vi.* fall; perish: Kamakura bakufu wa juuyoñ-seeki ni metsuboo shita. (鎌倉幕府は14世紀に滅亡した) The Kamakura Shogunate *collapsed* in the fourteenth century.

me⌐tsuki⌐ めつき（目付き）*n.* look; eyes: Ano otoko wa metsuki ga warui. (あの男は目つきが悪い) That man has an evil *look* in his eyes. / Kare wa metsuki ga surudoi. (彼は目つきが鋭い) He has a piercing *look.*

me⌐tta⌐ めった（滅多）*a.n.* (～ na) rash; thoughtless; reckless: Metta na koto wa iwanai hoo ga ii desu yo. (めったなことは言わないほうがいいですよ) You had better *be careful* about what you say.

me⌐tta ni⌐ めったに（滅多に）*adv.* (with a negative) rarely; seldom; hardly ever: Saikiñ wa kare to metta ni aimaseñ. (最近は彼とめったに会いません) I *hardly ever* see him these days. / Gaishoku wa metta ni shimaseñ. (外食はめったにしません) I *rarely* eat out. / Koñna ii chañsu wa metta ni arimaseñ. (こんないいチャンスはめったにありません) One *seldom* has a chance as good as this.

me⌐ue⌐ めうえ（目上）*n.* one's superior. 《↔ meshita》

me⌐zamashi⌐·i めざましい（目覚ましい）*a.* (-ku) remarkable; startling; wonderful:

mezamashii hatteñ (めざましい発展) *remarkable* development / Shiai de no Yamada no katsuyaku wa mezamashikatta. (試合での山田の活躍はめざましかった) Yamada's performance in the match was *spectacular.*

me⌐za⌐s·u めざす（目指す）*vt.* (mezash·i-; mezas·a-; mezash·i-te Ⓒ) aim: Fune wa Ooshima o mezashite shukkoo shita. (船は大島を目指して出港した) The ship left port, *heading for* Oshima. / Kare-ra wa yuushoo o mezashite, isshoo-keñmee reñshuu shita. (彼らは優勝を目指して、一生懸命練習した) *With an eye on* victory, they trained very hard. / Kanojo wa mezasu daigaku ni nyuugaku dekita. (彼女は目指す大学に入学できた) She could enter the college of *her choice.*

me⌐zurashi⌐·i めずらしい（珍しい）*a.* (-ku) rare; unusual; uncommon: mezurashii doobutsu (珍しい動物) a *rare* animal / mezurashii dekigoto (珍しい出来事) an *uncommon* occurrence / Nihoñ ni kita bakari no toki wa, subete ga mezurashikatta. (日本に来たばかりのときは、すべてが珍しかった) Everything was *strange* to me when I first arrived in Japan. / Koosoku-dooro no juutai wa mezurashiku arimaseñ. (高速道路の渋滞は珍しくありません) Traffic jams on the expressway are not *uncommon.* / Kyoo no señsee wa mezurashiku okotte ita. (きょうの先生は珍しく怒っていた) Today our teacher, *unlike his usual self,* was angry.

mi¹ み（身）*n.* **1** one's body; person; oneself: Sono ko wa doa no ushiro ni mi o kakushita. (その子はドアの後ろに身を隠した) The child hid *himself* behind the door. / Watashi wa mi no keppaku o shoomee shita. (私は身の潔白を証明した) I proved *my* innocence. / *Kare wa hirari to* mi o kawashita. (彼はひらりと身をかわした) He *dodged aside* quickly.

2 position; place: *Watashi no* mi *ni mo natte kudasai.* (私の身にもなってください) Please put yourself in my *place*. / *Kare wa itsu de mo* mi *o hiku kakugo de imasu.* (彼はいつでも身を引く覚悟でいます) He is resolved to resign his *position* at any time.

mi ni amaru (～に余る) be too great for one: *Kono yoo na shoo wa* mi ni amaru *kooee desu.* (このような賞は身に余る光栄です) An award like this is an honor that *I do not deserve.*

mi ni shimiru (～にしみる) touch one's heart: *Kare no shiñsetsu ga* mi ni shimita. (彼の親切が身にしみた) His kindness *deeply impressed me.*

mi ni tsukeru (～につける) put on; acquire: *Kare wa isoide fuku o* mi ni tsuketa. (彼は急いで服を身につけた) He hurriedly *put on* his clothes. / *Nani-ka gijutsu o* mi ni tsuketai. (何か技術を身につけたい) I *want to acquire* some technical skill.

mi o katameru (～を固める) settle down: *Kare wa kekkoñ shite,* mi o katameta. (彼は結婚して、身を固めた) He got married and *settled down*. ★ Usually said of a man.

mi o tateru (～をたてる) establish oneself: *Gaka to shite* mi o tateru *no wa muzukashii.* (画家として身をたてるのはむずかしい) It is difficult to *establish oneself* as a painter.

mi o yoseru (～を寄せる) live with: *Kare wa ojisañ no tokoro ni* mi o yosete imasu. (彼はおじさんのところに身を寄せています) He *stays with* his uncle.

mi[2] み (実) *n.* fruit; nut; berry: *Kono ki wa* mi *ga naranai.* (この木は実がならない) This tree does not bear *fruit*.

mi o musubu (～を結ぶ) **1** yield fruit: *Subete no ki ga* mi o musubu *wake de wa nai.* (すべての木が実を結ぶわけではない) Not all trees *produce fruit.*

2 (*fig.*) bear fruit: *Kare no doryoku wa* mi o musuñda. (彼の努力は実を結んだ) His efforts *bore fruit.*

mi- み (未) *pref.* un-: mi-*tee* (未定) *undecided* / mi-*kañsee* (未完成) *unfinished* / mi-*harai* (未払い) *unpaid*.

-mi み (味) *suf.* taste: ama-mi (甘味) *sweetness* / kara-mi (辛味) a hot *taste* / niga-mi (苦味) a bitter *taste* / (*fig.*) niñjoo-mi (人情味) *human kindness*.

mi⌈age·ru みあげる (見上げる) *vt.* (-age-te Ⅴ) look up at; raise one's eyes toward: *sora [sañchoo] o* miageru (空[山頂]を見上げる) *look up* at the sky [summit]. 《↔ miorosu》

miageta (見上げた) praiseworthy: *Kare no kooi wa* miageta *mono da.* (彼の行為は見上げたものだ) His action *is admirable.*

mi⌈ai みあい (見合い) *n.* an arranged meeting with a view to marriage:

(**CULTURE**)

The meeting is arranged by a '*nakoodo*' (go-between), who helps exchange information concerning the families of the prospective couple.

---

miai-*kekkoñ* (見合い結婚) an *arranged* marriage.

miai (o) suru (～(を)する) *vi.* see each other with a view to marriage: *Futari wa kinoo* miai shita. (二人はきのう見合いした) The two of them *met* yesterday *with the idea of a possible marriage in mind.* / *Kinoo sañjuu-go sai no o-isha no hito to* miai o shimashita. (きのう35歳のお医者の人と見合いをしました) Yesterday I *met* a thirty-five-year-old doctor *as a possible future husband.*

miˈawase·ru みあわせる（見合わせる） *vt.* (**-awase-te** Ⅴ) **1** look at each other:
Futari wa otagai ni kao o miawaseta.（二人はお互いに顔を見合わせた）They both *looked at each other.*
2 put off; postpone:
Sono keekaku wa miawaseru koto ni shita.（その計画は見合わせることにした）We have decided to *put off* that project.

miˈbuñ みぶん（身分） *n.* social status [standing]; position:
mibuñ no takai [hikui] hito（身分の高い[低い]人）a person of high [humble] *standing* / *Anata no mibuñ ga urayamashii.*（あなたの身分がうらやましい）I envy you your *position.* / *Kare to watashi de wa mibuñ ga tsuriawanai.*（彼と私では身分がつり合わない）*There is a wide social gap* between him and me.

miˈbuñ-shoomeesho みぶんしょうめいしょ（身分証明書） *n.* identification card; ID (card):
Anata no mibuñ-shoomeesho o misete kudasai.（あなたの身分証明書を見せてください）Please show me your *ID card.*

miˈburi みぶり（身振り） *n.* gesture; motion; way of acting:
oogesa na miburi（大げさな身ぶり）an exaggerated *gesture* / *Kotoba ga tsuujinai no de miburi teburi de hanashita.*（言葉が通じないので身ぶり手ぶりで話した）I could not make myself understood, so we communicated *with signs and gestures.* / *Chichi wa miburi de boku ni damare to itta.*（父は身ぶりでぼくに黙れと言った）My father *motioned* me to be quiet.

miˈchi[1] みち（道） *n.* **1** road; way; street; path:
michi o aruku（道を歩く）walk along a *road* / *michi o oodañ suru*（道を横断する）cross a *road* / *Eki e iku michi o oshiete kudasai.*（駅へ行く道を教えてください）Please tell me the *way* to the station. / *Michi ni mayotte shimatta.*（道に迷ってしまった）I lost my *way.* / *Michi de asobu no wa kikeñ desu.*（道で遊ぶのは危険です）It is dangerous to play on the *street.*
2 course; means:
Kore ga nokosareta tada hitotsu no michi desu.（これが残されたただ一つの道です）This is the only *course* left open to us. / *seekee no michi*（生計の道）a *means* of living.
3 field:
Yamada-shi wa kono michi no keñi desu.（山田氏はこの道の権威です）Mr. Yamada is an authority in this *field.*
4 public morals; the path of righteousness:
Kare wa hito no michi o ayamatta.（彼は人の道を誤った）He strayed from the *right path.*

miˈchi[2] みち（未知） *n.* unknown:
michi no sekai（未知の世界）the *unknown* world / *michi no basho*（未知の場所）an *unknown* place.

miˈchibiˈk·u みちびく（導く） *vt.* (**-bik·i-; -bik·a-; -bi·i·te** Ｃ) guide; lead:
Kakegoto ga kare o hametsu e michibiita.（賭け事が彼を破滅へ導いた）Gambling *led* him to his ruin.

miˈchigae·ru みちがえる（見違える） *vt.* (**-gae-te** Ⅴ) mistake for:
Kare to kare no niisañ o michigaete shimatta.（彼と彼の兄さんを見違えてしまった）I *mistook* his older brother for him. / *Kanojo wa michigaeru hodo utsukushiku natta.*（彼女は見違えるほど美しくなった）She became so beautiful that I *could hardly recognize her.*

miˈchijuñ みちじゅん（道順） *n.* route; way; course:

Kare ni yuubiñkyoku made no michijuñ *o oshiete yatta.* (彼に郵便局までの道順を教えてやった) I told him the *way* to the post office.

mi「chimichi みちみち (道々) *adv.* on the way; while walking; all the way:
Kare wa kaeri no michimichi *sono koto o kañgae-tsuzuketa.* (彼は帰りの道々そのことを考え続けた) He continued to think about it *on his way* home.

mi「chi¹・ru みちる (満ちる) *vi.* (michi-te V) **1** be filled; be full:
Sono machi wa kakki ni michite *ita.* (その町は活気に満ちていた) The town *was full* of activity.
2 (of the tide) rise; come in:
Shio ga michite *kita.* (潮が満ちて来た) The tide *is coming in.*
(↔ hiku¹)

mi「dare¹・ru みだれる (乱れる) *vi.* (midare-te V) be in disorder; be in a mess; be confused; be disrupted:
Yuki de ressha no daiya ga mida-reta. (雪で列車のダイヤが乱れた) The train timetable *was disrupted* because of the snow. / *Machi no fuuki wa kanari* midarete *ita.* (町の風紀はかなり乱れていた) Public morals in the town *were* rather *corrupt.* (⇨ midasu)

mi「da¹s・u みだす (乱す) *vt.* (midash・i-; midas・a-; midash・i-te C) put into disorder; disturb; confuse; disrupt:
chitsujo o midasu (秩序を乱す) *disturb* peace and order / *Retsu o* midasanai *de kudasai.* (列を乱さないでください) Please *do not fall out of* line. (⇨ midareru)

mi「dori みどり (緑) *n.* **1** green:
Midori to kiiro wa yoku au. (緑と黄色はよく合う) *Green* and yellow go well together.
2 greenery; verdure:
Tookyoo wa midori *ga sukunai.*

(東京は緑が少ない) There's little *greenery* in Tokyo. / *Haru wa* midori *ga kiree da.* (春は緑がきれいだ) The *green of the trees* is beautiful in the spring time. (⇨ ao; midori-iro)

mi「doriiro みどりいろ (緑色) *n.* green color:
midoriiro *no boorupeñ* (緑色のボールペン) a *green* ball-point pen.
(⇨ ao; midori)

Mi「dori-no-hi みどりのひ (緑の日) *n.* Greenery Day (Apr. 29)
(⇨ shukujitsu (table))

Mi「e¹-keñ みえけん (三重県) *n.* Mie Prefecture. Located at the east end of the Kinki district with a large peninsula stretching into the Pacific. In the eastern part, Ise Jingu Shrine is a representative of ancient Japanese architecture. Capital city: Tsu (津). (⇨ map (E4))

mi「e¹・ru みえる (見える) *vi.* (mie-te V) **1** be seen; be visible; be in sight:
Tooku ni akari ga mieta. (遠くに明かりが見えた) A light *was visible* in the distance. / *Umi ga* miete *kita.* (海が見えて来た) The sea *came into view.* / *Kiri de nani mo* miena-katta. (霧で何も見えなかった) We *could see nothing* because of the fog. / *Shitagi ga* miemasu *yo.* (下着が見えますよ) Your underwear *is showing.* (⇨ miru)
2 look; seem:
Kanojo wa toshi yori mo wakaku mieru. (彼女は年よりも若く見える) She *looks* young for her age. / *Kore ga ichibañ ii yoo ni* mieru. (これが一番いいように見える) This *seems* best to me.
3 (*honorific*) come; appear:
Shachoo wa mada miemaseñ. (社長はまだ見えません) The president *has not appeared* yet.

mi「gak・u みがく (磨く) *vt.* (miga-

k·i-; migak·a-; miga·i·te Ⓥ)
1 polish; shine; brush:
garasu o migaku (ガラスを磨く)
polish a windowpane / *kutsu o*
migaku (靴を磨く) *shine* one's
shoes / *ha o* migaku (歯を磨く)
brush one's teeth.
2 improve (one's skill):
Yoku reñshuu shite, ude o migaki
nasai. (よく練習して, 腕を磨きなさい)
Practice hard and *improve* your
skill.

mi˺gi みぎ (右) *n.* right:
tsumami o migi *e mawasu* (つまみを
右へ回す) turn a handle to the
right / *Tsugi no kado de* migi *e
magari nasai.* (次の角で右へ曲がりな
さい) Turn to the *right* at the next
corner. / *Migi ni mieru no ga gijidoo desu.* (右に見えるのが議事堂です)
What you see on your *right* is
the Diet building. 《↔ hidari》

mi˺gigawa みぎがわ (右側) *n.*
right side:
Kare wa watashi no migigawa *ni
suwatta.* (彼は私の右側に座った) He
sat on my *right-hand side.* / *Hokoosha wa* migigawa *tsuukoo desu.* (歩行者は右側通行です) Pedes-
trians must keep to the *right.*
《↔ hidarigawa》

mi˺gikiki みぎきき (右利き) *n.*
right-handed person:
Watashi wa migikiki *desu.* (私は右
利きです) I am *right-handed.*
《↔ hidarikiki》

mi˺gite みぎて (右手) *n.* **1** right
hand:
Kodomo-tachi wa migite *o agete,
dooro o oodañ shita.* (子どもたちは右
手を上げて, 道路を横断した) The chil-
dren raised their *right hands* and
crossed the street. 《↔ hidarite》
2 right direction:
Migite ni Fuji-sañ ga mieta. (右手
に富士山が見えた) We saw Mt. Fuji
on our *right.* 《↔ hidarite》

mi˺goto みごと (見事) *a.n.* (~ na,

ni) splendid; wonderful; excellent; beautiful:
migoto *na sakuhiñ* (みごとな作品) a
splendid work of art / *Kare wa
sono shiai ni* migoto *ni katta.* (彼は
その試合にみごとに勝った) He won
the match *in fine form.* / *Shiñkañseñ kara mita Fuji-sañ wa jitsu ni*
migoto *datta.* (新幹線から見た富士
山は実にみごとだった) The Mt. Fuji
we saw from the Shinkansen was
absolutely *wonderful.* / *O-*migoto!
(おみごと) *Wonderful!*

mi˺gurushi˺·i みくるしい (見苦しい)
a. (-ku) unsightly; indecent; disgraceful:
migurushii *furumai* (見苦しい振る舞
い) *indecent* behavior / *Heta na
iiwake wa* migurushii. (下手な言い
訳は見苦しい) It is *disgraceful* to
make lame excuses.

mi˺harashi みはらし (見晴らし) *n.*
view:
miharashi *no yoi heya* (見晴らしのよ
い部屋) a room with a good *view* /
Ano oka no ue kara no miharashi
wa subarashii. (あの丘の上からの見晴
らしはすばらしい) The *view* from that
hilltop is splendid.

mi˺hari みはり (見張り) *n.* watch;
guard:
iriguchi ni mihari *o oku* (入り口に
見張りを置く) post a *guard* at the
entrance / *Koko de watashi ga*
mihari *o shimasu.* (ここで私が見張り
をします) I will *keep watch* here.

mi˺har·u みはる (見張る) *vt.* (-har-
r·i-; -har·a-; -hat-te Ⓒ) keep
watch; keep a lookout:
Gaadomañ ga nañ-niñ ka soto de
mihatte *ita.* (ガードマンが何人か外で見
張っていた) Several guards *were
keeping watch* outside. / *Kono
nimotsu o chotto* mihatte *ite kudasai.* (この荷物をちょっと見張っていてくだ
さい) Will you please *watch* this
baggage for a few moments?

mi˺hoñ みほん (見本) *n.* sample;

specimen:
Kore wa mihoñ *to onaji de wa nai.*
(これは見本と同じではない) This does
not correspond to the *sample.* /
Mihoñ *ga attara, misete kudasai.*
(見本があったら、見せてください) If you
have a *sample*, please show it to
me.

mi⌐idas·u みいだす (見い出す) *vt.*
(-dash·i-; -das·a-; -dash·i-te ⓒ)
find; discover:
Watashi-tachi wa nañ to ka kaike-
tsu-saku o miidashita. (私達はなんと
か解決策を見いだした) We managed
somehow to *find* the solution. /
Kare wa sono shigoto ni yorokobi
o miidashita. (彼はその仕事に喜びを
見いだした) He *discovered* joy in
the job.

mi⌐jika みぢか (身近) *a.n.* (~ na,
ni) familiar; close; near oneself:
mijika *na wadai* (身近な話題) a *fa-*
miliar topic / mijika *na hito-tachi*
(身近な人たち) people in one's
immediate circle / *Watashi wa*
sono chosha o mijika *ni kañjita.*
(私はその著者を身近に感じた) I felt
myself *close* to the author.

mi⌐jika⌐·i みじかい (短い) *a.* (-ku)
1 (of length, distance) short:
Byooniñ wa mijikai *kyori nara aru-*
kemasu. (病人は短い距離なら歩けます)
Provided it is a *short* distance,
the patient can walk it. / *Kanojo*
wa kami o mijikaku *shite iru.* (彼
女は髪を短くしている) She wears her
hair *short.* / *Kono zuboñ no suso o*
mijikaku shite *kudasai.* (このズボンの
すそを短くしてください) Please *shorten*
these trousers. 《↔ nagai》
2 (of time) short; brief:
Kare no supiichi wa mijikakatta.
(彼のスピーチは短かった) His speech
was *short.* / *Hoñno* mijikai *aida*
Iñdo ni itta koto ga arimasu. (ほん
の短い間インドへ行ったことがあります) I
have been to India for just a
short while. / *Hi ga dañdañ* miji-

kaku *natte kita.* (日がだんだん短くなっ
てきた) The days have gradually
grown *shorter.* 《↔ nagai》

mi⌐jime みじめ (惨め) *a.n.* (~ na,
ni) miserable; wretched; pitiful:
mijime *na seekatsu o okuru* (惨めな
生活を送る) lead a *miserable* life /
Kotoba ga tsuujinakute mijime *na*
omoi o shita. (言葉が通じなくて惨めな
思いをした) I felt *miserable* when I
could not make myself understood. / *Sono maigo no oñna-no-*
ko ga mijime *ni mieta.* (その迷子の
女の子が惨めに見えた) The girl who
got separated from her parents
looked *pitiful.*

mi⌐ka⌐iketsu みかいけつ (未解決)
n., a.n. (~ na/no, ni) unsolved;
unsettled:
Sono moñdai wa mada mikaiketsu
desu. (その問題はまだ未解決です) The
problem is *not yet settled.* / *Keesa-*
tsu wa mikaiketsu *no jikeñ o taku-*
sañ kakaete iru. (警察は未解決の事
件をたくさんかかえている) The police
have a lot of *unsolved* cases on
their hands. 《↔ kaiketsu》

mi⌐kake みかけ (見掛け) *n.* appearance; look; show:
Hito wa mikake *ni yoranai.* (人は見
かけによらない) *Appearances* are de-
ceptive.

mikake-daoshi (見かけ倒し) decep-
tive: *Kare no jitsuryoku wa* mikake-daoshi *da.* (彼の実力は見かけ倒
しだ) He looks an able man, but it
is a *false impression.*

mi⌐kake·ru みかける (見掛ける) *vt.*
(-kake-te Ⓥ) happen to see;
come across; catch sight of:
Kinoo eegakañ de kare o mikakemashita. (きのう映画館で彼を見かけま
した) I *happened to see* him yesterday at the movie theater.

mi⌐kañ みかん (蜜柑) *n.* mandarin
orange. 《⇒ photo (next page)》
mi⌐ka⌐ñsee みかんせい (未完成)
a.n. (~ na/no, ni) unfinished; in-

MIKAÑ

complete:
Sono sakuhiñ wa mikañsee *no mama ni natte iru.* (その作品は未完成のままになっている) The work remains *unfinished.* / *Kono hashi wa sañ-neñ mae wa* mikañsee *datta.* (この橋は 3 年前は未完成だった) This bridge was *unfinished* three years ago. 《↔ kañsee》

mi「kata」[1] みかた (見方) *n.* point of view; standpoint; attitude:
Hito wa sorezore mono no mikata *ga chigaimasu.* (人はそれぞれものの見かたが違います) Different people have different *points of view.* / *Kare no kotoba wa* mikata *ni yotte wa kooi to mo toremasu.* (彼の言葉は見かたによっては好意ともとれます) *In a way,* we can also interpret his words favorably.

mi「kata」[2] みかた (味方) *n.* friend; side; ally; supporter:
Ano hito wa watashi-tachi no mikata *desu.* (あの人は私たちのみかたです) He is *on our side.* / *Kimi wa dochira no* mikata *o shimasu ka?* (君はどちらのみかたをしますか) Which side will you *support?* / *seegi no* mikata (正義のみかた) a *champion* of justice. 《↔ teki》

mi「kazuki」 みかづき (三日月) *n.* crescent; new moon. 《⇨ tsuki[2]》

mi「ki」 みき (幹) *n.* main stem of a tree; trunk.

mi「kka」 みっか (三日) *n.* three days; the third day of the month:
Watashi wa mikka *gakkoo o yasumimashita.* (私は 3 日学校を休みました) I was absent from school for *three days.* / *Sañ-gatsu* mikka *wa hina-matsuri de, oñna-no-ko no hi desu.* (三月三日はひな祭りで, 女の子の日です) March *3* is a day for girls, celebrated as the Doll Festival. / mikka-boozu (三日坊主) a *quitter.* 《⇨ tsuitachi (table)》

mi「komi」 みこみ (見込み) *n.*
1 hope; chance; possibility:
Kare ga kaifuku suru mikomi *wa hotoñdo arimaseñ.* (彼が回復する見込みはほとんどありません) There is little *hope* of his recovery. / *Seekoo no* mikomi *wa gobu-gobu desu.* (成功の見込みは五分五分です) There is a fifty-fifty *chance* of success. 《⇨ chañsu》
2 expectation; prospect:
Watashi-tachi no mikomi *wa atatta [hazureta].* (私たちの見込みは当たった[はずれた]) Our *expectations* proved right [wrong].
mikomi no aru (～のある) promising: *Kare wa* mikomi no aru *otoko da.* (彼は見込みのある男だ) He is a *promising* man.

mi「koñ」 みこん (未婚) *n.* unmarried; single:
Kanojo wa mikoñ *desu.* (彼女は未婚です) She is *unmarried.* / mikoñ *no haha* (未婚の母) an *unmarried* mother.

mi「kudas·u」 みくだす (見下す) *vt.* (-kudash·i-; -kudas·a-; -kudash·i-te [C]) look down on; despise:
Kare wa watashi o mikudashite *iru.* (彼は私を見下している) He *looks down on* me. 《↔ miageru》

mi「kurabe·ru」 みくらべる (見比べる) *vt.* (-kurabe-te [V]) compare:
Mihoñ to jitsubutsu o yoku mikurabe nasai. (見本と実物をよく見比べなさい) Carefully *compare* the sample and the actual article. 《⇨ kuraberu》

mi「mai」 みまい (見舞い) *n.* **1** visit

(to a hospital or a sick person); call; inquiry: ★ Usually with '*o-*.'
Watashi wa byooiñ e kare no mimai *ni itta.* (私は病院へ彼の見舞いに行った) I paid him a *visit* in the hospital. / *Shochuu* o-mimai *mooshiagemasu.* (*letter*) (暑中お見舞い申し上げます) I *hope you will take good care of youself* in the hot season. 《⇨ mimau》

2 expression of one's sympathy [concern]:
Shichoo wa higaisha ni mimai *no kotoba o nobeta.* (市長は被害者に見舞いの言葉を述べた) The mayor expressed his *sympathy* for the victims.

-mi⌐ma¬ñ みまん (未満) *suf.* under; below; less than:
Juuhas-sai-mimañ *wa nyuujo dekimaseñ.* (18歳未満は入場できません) Those *under* eighteen years of age are not permitted to enter. / *Hyaku-eñ*-mimañ *wa kirisute desu.* (百円未満は切り捨てです) Amounts *smaller than* 100 yen will be ignored. 《⇨ -ika》

⌐ USAGE ¬
'*-mimañ*' does not include the preceding number, so, strictly speaking, '*jus-sai-mimañ*' is 'under nine years of age.'

mi⌐ma¬u みまう (見舞う) *vt.* (mima·i-; mimaw·a-; mimat-te C)
1 visit; inquire after:
Kinoo nyuuiñ-chuu no itoko o mimatta. (きのう入院中のいとこを見舞った) Yesterday I *visited* my cousin who is in the hospital. 《⇨ mimai》
2 (of disaster) hit; strike:
Maitoshi natsu ni naru to, Nihoñ wa taifuu ni mimawaremasu. (毎年夏になると, 日本は台風に見舞われます) Every year when summer comes, Japan *is struck* by typhoons.

mi⌐mawari みまわり (見回り) *n.* patrol; inspection:
mimawari *ni dekakeru* (見回りに出かける) go out on *patrol* / *koojoo no* mimawari *o suru* (工場の見回りをする) make an *inspection* visit to a factory. 《⇨ mimawaru》

mi⌐mawar·u みまわる (見回る) *vt.* (-mawar·i-; -mawar·a-; -mawat-te C) patrol; make one's rounds; inspect:
Keesatsukañ ga teeki-teki ni kono atari o mimawatte imasu. (警察官が定期的にこの辺りを見回っています) Policemen *patrol* this area regularly. 《⇨ mimawari》

mi⌐mawas·u みまわす (見回す) *vt.* (-mawash·i-; -mawas·a-; -mawash·i-te C) look around [about]:
Atari o mimawashita *ga dare mo inakatta.* (辺りを見回したがだれもいなかった) I *looked around* but nobody was there.

mi⌐mi¬ みみ (耳) *n.* **1** ear:
mimi *ni te o ateru* (耳に手をあてる) cup a hand behind one's *ear* / *Kare wa watashi no* mimi-*moto de nani-ka sasayaita.* (彼は私の耳もとで何かささやいた) He whispered something in my *ear*. 《⇨ jiñtai (illus.)》
2 hearing:
Kare wa mimi *ga tooi.* (彼は耳が遠い) He is hard of *hearing*.

mimi ga hayai (～が早い) get hold of information quickly.

mimi ni suru (～にする) hear:
Kare ni tsuite, heñ na uwasa o mimi *ni shita.* (彼について, 変なうわさを耳にした) I *heard* a strange rumor about him.

mimi ni tsuku (～につく) be disturbed by a sound: *Tonari no heya no oto ga* mimi *ni tsuite, yoku nemurenakatta.* (隣の部屋の音が耳について, よく眠れなかった) *Disturbed by the sound* in the next room, I could not sleep well.

mimi o kasanai (〜を貸さない)
turn a deaf ear: *Kanojo wa watashi no chuukoku ni* mimi o kasanakatta. (彼女は私の忠告に耳を貸さなかった) She *disregarded* my advice.

mimi o sumasu (〜を澄ます)
strain one's ears; listen carefully: *Watashi wa* mimi o sumashite *sono rajio no nyuusu o kiita.* (私は耳を澄ましてそのラジオのニュースを聞いた) I *listened carefully* to the news on the radio.

mimi o utagau (〜を疑う) cannot believe one's ears: *Sono jiko no koto o kiite, watashi wa* mimi o utagatta. (その事故のことを聞いて、私は耳を疑った) When I heard about the accident, I *could not believe my ears*.

mi⌐na⌐ みな (皆) *n., adv.* all; everyone; everything:
Kokyoo no kazoku wa mina *geñki desu.* (故郷の家族は皆元気です) *All* the family back home are fine. / *Kare-ra wa* mina *sorotte, dekaketa.* (彼らは皆そろって、出かけた) They went out *all* together. / *Kare wa sono kane o hito-bañ de* mina *tsukatte shimatta.* (彼はその金を一晩で皆使ってしまった) He spent *all* the money in one night.
《⇨ miñna》

mi⌐nami みなみ (南) *n.* south; (〜ni/e) southward:
Watashi no heya wa minami *ni meñshite imasu.* (私の部屋は南に面しています) My room faces *south*. / *Ikkoo wa* minami ni mukatte *tabi o shita.* (一行は南に向かって旅をした) The party traveled *southward*. / *Kanojo no ie wa mizuumi no* minami-*gawa ni arimasu.* (彼女の家は湖の南側にあります) Her house is on the *south* side of the lake.
《↔ kita》

mi⌐nara⌐u みならう (見習う) *vt.* (-nara·i-; -naraw·a-; -narat-te [C]) follow a person's example;

copy; imitate:
Niisañ o minaratte *motto beñkyoo shi nasai.* (兄さんを見習ってもっと勉強しなさい) *Follow the example* of your older brother and study harder.

mi⌐nari みなり (身なり) *n.* appearance; dress; clothes:
Kare wa minari *o kamawanai.* (彼は身なりを構わない) He is indifferent about his *appearance*. / *Kanojo wa misuborashii* minari o shite ita. (彼女はみすぼらしい身なりをしていた) She *was* shabbily *dressed*. / Minari o kichiñ to *shi nasai* (身なりをきちんとしなさい) Try to *look neat*.
《⇨ fukusoo》

mi⌐na⌐-sama みなさま (皆様) *n.* (*honorific*) = mina-sañ.
everybody; everyone; all:
Watashi ga koñnichi aru no wa mina-sama *no okage desu.* (私が今日あるのは皆さまのおかげです) I owe what I am now to *all of you*.

mi⌐na⌐-sañ みなさん (皆さん) *n.*
1 everybody; everyone; all:
Mina-sañ, *ohayoo gozaimasu.* (皆さん、お早うございます) Good morning, *everybody*. / *Go-kazoku wa* mina-sañ *o-geñki desu ka?* (ご家族は皆さんお元気ですか) Are your family *all* well?
2 ladies and gentlemen:
Mina-sañ, *kore o gorañ kudasai.* (皆さん、これをご覧ください) *Ladies and gentlemen*, please look at this.
《⇨ mina-sama》

mi⌐nas·u みなす (見なす) *vt.* (minash·i-; minas·a-; minash·i-te [C]) regard; consider:
Sañjup-puñ ijoo tatte mo konai hito wa kesseki to minashimasu. (30 分以上たっても来ない人は欠席とみなします) Those who are over thirty minutes late will *be considered* absent. / *Kare wa sono buñya no keñisha no hitori to* minasarete *imasu.* (彼はその分野の

権威者の一人とみなされています) He *is considered* to be one of the authorities in the field.

mi⌈nato みなと (港) *n.* port; harbor:

minato *ni hairu* (港に入る) enter a *port* / minato *o deru* (港を出る) sail from a *port* / minato *ni hinañ suru* (港に避難する) take refuge in a *harbor*.

mi⌈ne みね (峰) *n.* mountain peak; ridge.

mi⌈niku⌉·i[1] みにくい (見難い) *a.* (-ku) hard [difficult] to see:

Koko kara de wa sono too wa minikui. (ここからではその塔は見にくい) From here, we *cannot see* the tower *well*.

mi⌈niku⌉·i[2] みにくい (醜い) *a.* (-ku)

1 ugly:

minikui *kao* (醜い顔) an *ugly* face / minikuku *mieru* (醜く見える) look *ugly*.

2 (of conduct, trouble, etc.) scandalous; ignoble:

minikui *arasoi* (醜い争い) a *scandalous* dispute / minikui *okonai* (醜い行い) an *ignoble* action.

mi⌉ñji みんじ (民事) *n.* (of law) civil affairs:

miñji-*jikeñ* (民事事件) a *civil* case / miñji-*soshoo* (民事訴訟) a *civil* action. 《⇨ keeji》

mi⌈ñkañ みんかん (民間) *n.* private; civilian:

miñkañ-*kigyoo* (民間企業) a *private* enterprise / miñkañ-*jiñ* (民間人) a *civilian* / miñkañ-*hoosoo* (民間放送) *commercial* broadcasting.

mi⌈ñna[1] みんな (皆) *n., adv.* all; everyone; everything:

Miñna *de issho ni ikimashoo.* (みんなで一緒に行きましょう) Let's *all* go together. / Miñna *no ikeñ o kiite kara kimemasu.* (みんなの意見を聞いてから決めます) I will decide after listening to *everyone*'s opinion. / *Kurasu no* miñna *ga eñsoku ni sañka*

shita. (クラスのみんなが遠足に参加した) *Everyone* in the class took part in the excursion. / *Kyoo no yotee no shigoto wa* miñna *owarimashita.* (きょうの予定の仕事はみんな終わりました) I have finished *all* the work scheduled for today. 《⇨ mina》

mi⌈no⌉r·u みのる (実る) *vi.* (minor·i-; minor·a-; minot-te [C])

1 bear fruit:

Kono ki ni wa riñgo ga takusañ minorimasu. (この木にはりんごがたくさん実ります) This tree *bears* many apples.

2 (of an effort, etc.) have results:

Kare no doryoku wa amari minoranakatta. (彼の努力はあまり実らなかった) His efforts *hardly produced anything*.

mi⌈noshirokiñ みのしろきん (身代金) *n.* ransom:

Yuukai-hañ wa deñwa de minoshirokiñ *o yookyuu shite kita.* (誘拐犯は電話で身代金を要求してきた) The kidnapper demanded a *ransom* over the telephone.

mi⌈noue みのうえ (身の上) *n.*

1 one's personal affairs:

Watashi wa señsee ni minoue *o soodañ shita.* (私は先生に身の上を相談した) I asked for my teacher's advice about my *personal affairs*.

2 one's personal history:

Kanojo wa watashi-tachi ni minoue-*banashi o kikaseta.* (彼女は私たちに身の上話を聞かせた) She told us the story of her *life*.

Mi⌉ñshatoo みんしゃとう (民社党) *n.* Japan Democratic Socialist Party. 《⇨ seetoo²(table)》

mi⌈ñshuku みんしゅく (民宿) *n.* private home which takes in paying guests. ★ Like a 'Bed & Breakfast' establishment, it provides meals and lodging for tourists.

mi⌈ñshu-shu⌉gi みんしゅしゅぎ (民主主義) *n.* democracy:

miñshu-shugi *o yoogo suru*（民主主義を擁護する）protect *democracy*.

mi˺nu˺k·u みぬく（見抜く）*vt.* (-nuk·i-; -nuk·a-; -nu·i-te [C]) see through; figure out; perceive: *Kare wa musuko no uso o sugu ni* minuita.（彼は息子のうそをすぐに見抜いた）He immediately *saw through* his son's lie. / *Watashi wa kare no kañgae ga* minukenakatta.（私は彼の考えが見抜けなかった）I *was not able to figure out* what he was thinking.

mi˹ñyoo みんよう（民謡）*n.* folk song; popular ballad: miñyoo *o utau*（民謡を歌う）sing a *folk song*.

mi˹ñzoku みんぞく（民族）*n.* race; people; nation: miñzoku *no dai-idoo*（民族の大移動）the migration of *nations* / *yuuboku*-miñzoku（遊牧民族）a nomadic *people* / *shoosuu*-miñzoku（少数民族）a minority *race* / miñzoku-*ishoo*（民族衣装）*native* costume / miñzoku-shugi（民族主義）*nationalism* / miñzoku-shugisha（民族主義者）a *nationalist*.

mi˹oboe みおぼえ（見覚え）*n.* recognition; remembrance: *Ano otoko ni wa* mioboe ga aru.（あの男には見覚えがある）I *remember* having seen that man.

mi˹okuri みおくり（見送り）*n.* send-off: *Watashi-tachi wa eki de kare no* miokuri o shita.（私達は駅で彼の見送りをした）We *saw* him *off* at the station. 《↔ demukae》《⇨ miokuru》

mi˹okur·u みおくる（見送る）*vt.* (-okur·i-; -okur·a-; -okut-te [C]) **1** see off: *Tookyoo-eki de Oosaka e teñkiñ suru kare o* miokutta.（東京駅で大阪へ転勤する彼を見送った）We *saw* him *off* at Tokyo Station when he was being transferred to Osaka. 《⇨ miokuri》

2 pass up (one's turn, opportunity, etc.): *Kare wa sono kikai o yamu o ezu* miokutta.（彼はその機会をやむを得ず見送った）He unavoidably had to *pass up* the chance.

mi˹oros·u みおろす（見下ろす）*vt.* (-orosh·i-; -oros·a-; -orosh·i-te [C]) look down; overlook; command: *Watashi-tachi wa sono shiro kara machi o* mioroshita.（私たちはその城から町を見下ろした）We *looked down* on the town from the castle. 《↔ miageru》

mi˹otoshi みおとし（見落とし）*n.* oversight; careless mistake: *Dare mo sono* miotoshi *ni ki ga tsukanakatta*.（だれもその見落としに気がつかなかった）Nobody was aware of the *oversight*. 《⇨ miotosu》

mi˹otos·u みおとす（見落とす）*vt.* (-otosh·i-; -otos·a-; -otosh·i-te [C]) overlook; miss: *Watashi wa sono machigai o* miotoshite ita.（私はその間違いを見落としていた）I *missed* the mistake. 《⇨ miotoshi》

mi˹rai みらい（未来）*n.* future: *Mirai no koto wa dare ni mo wakaranai*.（未来のことはだれにもわからない）No one knows what will happen in the *future*. / *Ano hito ga watashi no* mirai *no otto desu*.（あの人が私の未来の夫です）He is my *future* husband. 《⇨ geñzai (table)》

mi˹ri ミリ（粍）*n.* millimeter; milligram: ★ Shortened form of '*miri-meetoru*' and '*miri-guramu*.' *Is-señchi wa juu*-miri *desu*.（1センチは10ミリです）Ten *millimeters* make one centimeter.

mi˹ri-gu˹ramu ミリグラム（瓱）*n.* milligram. ★ Shortened form, '*miri*' is more common. 《⇨ miri》

mi˹ri-me˹etoru ミリメートル（粍）*n.* millimeter. ★ Shortened

form, '*miri*' is more common. 《⇨ miri》

mi「ri-ri「ttoru ミリリットル (竓) *n.* milliliter.

mi」・ru みる (見る・診る) *vt.* (mi-te Ⅴ) **1** see; look at; watch: *Sono eega wa kinoo* mimashita. (その映画はきのう見ました) I *saw* the movie yesterday. / *Kare wa terebi de sumoo o* mite imasu. (彼はテレビですもうを見ています) He *is watching* sumo on TV. / *Kagami de jibuñ no kao o* mite mi nasai. (鏡で自分の顔を見てみなさい) *Take a look at* yourself in the mirror.
2 read; look through: *Kyoo no shiñbuñ o* mimashita ka? (きょうの新聞を見ましたか) *Have you read* today's paper? / *Kare wa sono shorui o ima* mite iru *tokoro desu.* (彼はその書類を今見ているところです) He *is* just *looking through* the documents.
3 inspect; check; consult: *Haisha de ha o* mite moratta. (歯医者で歯を診てもらった) I *had* my teeth *looked at* by the dentist. / *Bureeki o* mite *kudasai.* (ブレーキを見てください) Please *check* the brakes. / *Jisho o* mite, *sono imi o shirabeta.* (辞書を見て, その意味を調べた) I *consulted* the dictionary to find the meaning.
4 look after; help: *Toire ni itte kuru aida, kono kabañ o* mite ite *kudasai.* (トイレに行って来る間, このかばんを見ていてください) Will you please *keep an eye on* this bag while I go to the toilet? / *Dare ga byooki no o-toosañ o* mite iru *ñ desu ka?* (だれが病気のお父さんを見ているんですか) Who *is looking after* your sick father? / *Otooto no shukudai o* mite yatta. (弟の宿題を見てやった) I *helped* my brother with his homework.
mite minu furi o suru (見て見ぬふりをする) look the other way: *Watashi wa kare no shite iru koto o* mite minu furi o shita. (私は彼のしていることを見て見ぬふりをした) I *pretended not to notice* what he was doing.
-te miru (て〜) try doing: *Atarashii waapuro wa tsukatte* mimashita ka? (新しいワープロは使ってみましたか) *Have you tried using* your new word processor?

mi「ruku ミルク *n.* milk: ★ Often refers to processed milk and creamers. Cows' milk is called '*gyuunyuu.*' *kona*-miruku (粉ミルク) dried [powdered] *milk.* 《⇨ gyuunyuu》

mi「ryoku みりょく (魅力) *n.* charm; attraction; appeal; fascination: *Kanojo no koe wa dokutoku no* miryoku *ga aru.* (彼女の声は独特の魅力がある) Her voice has a special *charm.* / *Kyooto no* miryoku *no hitotsu wa Nihoñ tee-eñ desu.* (京都の魅力の一つは日本庭園です) One of the *attractions* of Kyoto is the Japanese gardens. / *Kono terebi bañgumi wa* miryoku *ga nai.* (このテレビ番組は魅力がない) This TV program is not *appealing* to me.
miryoku no aru (〜のある) charming; attractive; appealing; fascinating.

mi「sage・ru みさげる (見下げる) *vt.* (misage-te Ⅴ) = mikudasu.

mi「saki みさき (岬) *n.* cape; promontory: *Ashizuri*-misaki (足摺岬) *Cape Ashizuri.*

mi「se」 みせ (店) *n.* store; shop: mise o kee-ee suru (店を経営する) run a *store* / mise o dasu (店を出す) open one's own *shop* / mise o tatamu (店をたたむ) close down a *store* / *Kono mise wa juu-ji ni hiraku* [shimaru]. (この店は10時に開く[閉まる]) This *store* opens [closes] at ten o'clock.

mi⌈sebiraka⌉s·u みせびらかす (見せびらかす) *vt.* (-kash·i-; -kas·a-; -kash·i-te Ⓒ) show off: *Kanojo wa atarashii kegawa no kooto o misebirakashita.* (彼女は新しい毛皮のコートを見せびらかした) She *showed off* her new fur coat.

mi⌈semono⌉ みせもの (見せ物) *n.* show; exhibition.

mi⌈se⌉·ru みせる (見せる) *vt.* (mise-te Ⓥ) **1** show; display; let a person see: *Anata no arubamu o misete kudasai.* (あなたのアルバムを見せてください) Please *show* me your photograph album. / *Ano uiñdoo no naka no nekkuresu o misete itadakemasu ka?* (あのウインドーの中のネックレスを見せていただけますか) Can you *show* me the necklace in that window, please? / *Kanojo wa fukuzatsu na hyoojoo o miseta.* (彼女は複雑な表情を見せた) She *displayed* mixed feelings.
2 show on purpose; pretend: *waratte miseru* (笑って見せる) laugh *on purpose* / *shiñshi-butte miseru* (紳士ぶって見せる) *pretend* to be a gentleman / *Heya o hiroku miseru tame ni teeburu o ugokashita.* (部屋を広く見せるためにテーブルを動かした) I moved the table so that the room *would look* larger.
-te miseru (て～) **1** show how to do: *oyoide miseru* (泳いで見せる) *show* someone *how to swim* / *tañgo o hatsuoñ shite miseru* (単語を発音して見せる) *show* someone *how to pronounce* a word.
2 show a firm decision: *Koñdo koso kare o makashite miseru.* (今度こそ彼を負かして見せる) You just *watch* me *beat* him this time.

mi⌈shiñ ミシン *n.* sewing machine: *sukaato ni mishiñ o kakeru* (スカートにミシンをかける) sew a skirt on a *sewing machine*.

mi⌈so みそ (味噌) *n.* soybean paste; miso.

mi⌈soshi⌉ru みそしる (味噌汁) *n.* miso soup. ★ Served with a Japanese-style meal.

MISOSHIRU

mi⌈ssetsu みっせつ (密接) *a.n.* (～ na, ni) close; closely related: *Bukka wa watashi-tachi no seekatsu to missetsu na kañkee ga arimasu.* (物価は私たちの生活と密接な関係があります) Prices have a *close* relation to our daily lives. / *Ryoosha wa missetsu ni kañkee shite iru.* (両者は密接に関係している) Both the parties are *closely* related.

mi⌈su⌉[1] ミス *n.* mistake; error: ★ Shortened form of 'misu-teeku' (English 'mistake'). *Kono taipu-geñkoo wa misu ga ooi.* (このタイプ原稿はミスが多い) There are many *mistakes* in this typed material.
misu (o) suru (～(を)する) *vi.* make a mistake: *Mata misu shite shimatta.* (またミスしてしまった) I've *made a mistake* again. 《⇨ machigai》

mi⌈su⌉[2] ミス *n.* Miss; being single: *Misu Yamada* (ミス山田) *Miss Yamada* / *Misu Nihoñ* (ミス日本) *Miss Japan* / *Kanojo wa mada misu desu.* (彼女はまだミスです) She is still *single*.

mi⌈suborashi⌉·i みすぼらしい *a.* (-ku) humble; scruffy; shabby; wretched: *misuborashii ie* (みすぼらしい家) a *humble* house / *Sono toki no kare wa* misuborashiku *mieta.*（そのときの彼はみすぼらしく見えた）He looked very *scruffy* in those days.

mi⌈sui みすい（未遂）*n.* attempt: *Kare no keekaku wa* misui ni owatta.（彼の計画は未遂に終わった）His plot *ended in failure.* / *satsujiñ*-misui（殺人未遂）an *attempted* murder.

mi⌈sumisu みすみす *adv.* before one's eyes; helplessly: *Ie o* misumisu *yaite shimatta.*（家をみすみす焼いてしまった）I had my house burn down *before my eyes.* / *Kare wa* misumisu *sono kikai o nogashite shimatta.*（彼はみすみすその機会を逃してしまった）He *helplessly* let the chance slip by.

mi⌈su-puri⌉ñto ミスプリント *n.* misprint: misu-puriñto *o teesee suru*（ミスプリントを訂正する）correct *printing errors.*

mi⌈sute·ru みすてる（見捨てる）*vt.* (-sute-te V) forsake; desert; leave: *Kanojo wa kodomo o* misutete, *ie-de shita.*（彼女は子どもを見捨てて、家出した）She left home, *deserting* her children.

mitai みたい *a.n.* (~ na, ni) [immediately follows a preceding noun or adjectival noun]
1 similar to; like: *Ano fuufu wa marude koibito dooshi* mitai *da.*（あの夫婦はまるで恋人同士みたいだ）That married couple look just *like* lovers. / *Sore wa yume* mitai *na hanashi datta.*（それは夢みたいな話だった）It was a story *like* a dream.
2 such as; like: ★ Refers to something by way of example. *Kare* mitai *ni atama no yoi hito ni wa atta koto ga nai.*（彼みたいに頭のよい人には会ったことがない）I have never met a smart person *like*

him.
3 seem; appear: *Kare wa shippai shita* mitai *da.*（彼は失敗したみたいだ）/ He *seems* to have failed. / *Kanojo wa kanemochi* mitai *da.*（彼女は金持ちみたいだ）She *appears* to be rich. / *Shiai wa ni-ji kara* mitai *da.*（試合は2時からみたいだ）*It seems* that the game will start from two o'clock. / *Kaigi wa sañ-ji made* mitai *desu.*（会議は3時までみたいです）The meeting *seems likely* to continue until three o'clock. 《⇒ yoo²; soo¹; rashii》

mi⌈ta⌉s·u みたす（満たす）*vt.* (mitash·i-; mitas·a-; mitash·i-te C)
1 fill up: *Kare wa koppu ni biiru o* mitashita.（彼はコップにビールを満たした）He *filled* the glass with beer.
2 satisfy (desire); meet (a condition, etc.): *jookeñ o* mitasu（条件を満たす）*fulfill* the conditions / *yokuboo o* mitasu（欲望を満たす）*satisfy* one's desires / *yookyuu o* mitasu（要求を満たす）*meet* the demands

mi⌈tee みてい（未定）*n.* undecided; uncertain: *Tsugi no kaigoo no nichiji wa* mitee *desu.*（次の会合の日時は未定です）The time and date of the next meeting are *undecided.*

mi⌈tome·ru みとめる（認める）*vt.* (mitome-te V) **1** recognize; admit; concede: *Kare wa jibuñ no machigai o* mitometa.（彼は自分の間違いを認めた）He *admitted* his mistake. / *Tooshu wa señkyo de no haiboku o* mitometa.（党首は選挙での敗北を認めた）The party leader *conceded* defeat in the election.
2 allow; approve: *Chichi wa watashi no gaihaku o* mitomete kuremaseñ.（父は私の外泊を認めてくれません）My father *does*

not allow me to sleep out.

3 see; find; notice (an unusual thing, change, etc.):

Eṅjiṅ ni wa nani mo ijoo wa mito-merarenakatta. (エンジンには何も異状は認められなかった) We *could find nothing* unusual with the engine.

mi⌐tooshi みとおし（見通し）*n.*

1 visibility:

Kono atari wa mitooshi *ga ii* [*warui*]. (このあたりは見通しがいい[悪い]) *Visibility* is good [poor] around here.

2 prospects; outlook:

Shoobai no mitooshi *wa akarui.* (商売の見通しは明るい) Business *prospects* are bright.

mi⌐tsu みつ（蜜）*n.* honey; molasses; treacle.

mi⌐tsu⌐bachi みつばち（蜜蜂）*n.* honeybee.

mi⌐tsudo みつど（密度）*n.* density:

Nihoṅ wa jiṅkoo no mitsudo *ga takai.* (日本は人口の密度が高い) Japan has a high population *density*.

mi⌐tsukar·u みつかる（見付かる）*vi.* (-kar·i-; -kar·a-; -kat-te C) be found; be discovered; be caught:

Nakushita kagi ga mitsukatta. (なくした鍵が見つかった) The lost key *was found.* / *Sono gakusee wa kaṅniṅgu shite iru tokoro o* mitsukatta. (その学生はカンニングしているところを見つかった) The student *got caught* cheating on an examination. 《⇨ mitsukeru》

mi⌐tsuke·ru みつける（見付ける）*vt.* (-tsuke-te V) find; discover; catch:

Nakushita saifu o mitsuketa. (なくした財布を見つけた) I *found* the wallet that I had lost. / *Kinoo yasui mise o* mitsukemashita. (きのう安い店を見つけました) Yesterday I *found* a shop with good prices. 《⇨ mi-

tsukaru; sagasu》

mi⌐tsume·ru みつめる（見詰める）*vt.* (-tsume-te V) gaze; stare; study:

Kare wa jitto sono shashiṅ o mitsumeta. (彼はじっとその写真を見つめた) He *stared* intently at the photo.

mi⌐tsumori みつもり（見積もり）*n.* estimate:

Heya no shuuri no mitsumori *o shite moratta.* (部屋の修理の見積もりをしてもらった) I had an *estimate* made for repairs to my apartment. 《⇨ mitsumoru》

mi⌐tsumor·u みつもる（見積もる）*vt.* (-tsumor·i-; -tsumor·a-; -tsumot-te C) make an estimate:

Sono hiyoo no daitai o mitsumotte *kudasai.* (その費用の大体を見積もってください) Will you please *make a rough estimate* of the expenses? 《⇨ mitsumori》

mi⌐tto ミット *n.* (of baseball) mitt.

mi⌐ttomona⌐·i みっともない *a.* (-ku) shabby; clumsy-looking; shameful; disgraceful:

Kare wa mittomonai *fuku o kite ita.* (彼はみっともない服を着ていた) He was wearing a *shabby* jacket. / *Yuube wa yotte,* mittomonai koto *o shita.* (ゆうべ酔って、みっともないことをした) Last night I got drunk and *behaved disgracefully*.

mi⌐ttsu⌐ みっつ（三つ）*n.* three:

★ Used when counting.

mittsu-me (三つめ) *the third*. 《⇨ saṅ³; kazu (table)》

mi⌐ushina·u みうしなう（見失う）*vt.* (-ushina·i-; -ushinaw·a-; -ushi-nat-te C) lose sight [track] of:

Eki no hitogomi de yuujiṅ o miu-shinatte shimatta. (駅の人込みで友人を見失ってしまった) I *lost sight of* my friend in the crowd at the station.

mi⌐wake·ru みわける（見分ける）*vt.*

(-wake-te V) distinguish; tell from:
Sake to masu o miwakeru *koto ga dekimasu ka?* (さけとますを見分けることができますか) Can you *tell* salmon *from* trout?

mi⌈watas·u みわたす (見渡す) *vt.* (-watash·i-; -watas·a-; -watash·i-te C) look around; survey: *Kare wa dañ no ue kara chooshuu o miwatashita.* (彼は壇の上から聴衆を見渡した) He *surveyed* the audience from the platform.
　miwatasu kagiri (～限り) as far as the eye can see: *Sabaku ga miwatasu kagiri hirogatte iru.* (砂漠が見渡す限り広がっている) The desert stretches on all sides *as far as the eye can see.*

mi⌈yage みやげ (土産) *n.* present; souvenir: ★ Something you buy as a present when returning from a trip or visiting someone. *Kono hoñ wa ii o-*miyage *ni naru.* (この本はいいおみやげになる) This book will make a good *present.* / *Hawai no* miyage *ni painappuru o katta.* (ハワイのみやげにパイナップルを買った) I bought some pineapples as *something to take home* from Hawaii. 《⇨ o-miyage》

Mi⌈yagi⌉-keñ みやぎけん (宮城県) *n.* Miyagi Prefecture. Located in almost the center of the Tohoku district, facing the Pacific on the east. The capital city, Sendai (仙台), is the cultural center of northeastern Japan. 《⇨ map (G2)》

mi⌈yako みやこ (都) *n.* capital; metropolis; city.

Mi⌈yazaki⌉-keñ みやざきけん (宮崎県) *n.* Miyazaki Prefecture. Located in the southeast of Kyushu, facing the Pacific on the east. Forestry is one of the important industries. Capital city: Miyazaki. 《⇨ map (B6)》

mi⌈zo みぞ (溝) *n.* 1 ditch; gutter. mizo *o horu* (溝を掘る) dig a *ditch* / *Mizo ga tsumatte shimatta.* (溝が詰まってしまった) The *gutter* has gotten blocked up.
　2 groove:
ki ni mizo *o tsukeru* (木に溝をつける) cut a *groove* in a tree.
　3 gap; gulf:
Futari no aida ni mizo *ga dekita.* (二人の間に溝ができた) A *gulf* has developed between the couple.

mi⌈zu みず (水) *n.* water; cold water:
Mizu o ip-pai kudasai. (水を一杯下さい) May I have a glass of *water?* / *Mizu ga morete imasu.* (水が漏れています) There is *water* leaking.
　mizu ni nagasu (～に流す) forgive and forget: *Kako no koto wa* mizu ni *nagashimashoo.* (過去のことは水に流しましょう) *Let bygones be bygones.*

mi⌈zugi みずぎ (水着) *n.* swimsuit; bathing suit.

mi⌈zuiro みずいろ (水色) *n.* pale [light] blue.

mi⌈zukara みずから (自ら) *adv.* personally; in person:
Shachoo mizukara *sono kooshoo ni atatta.* (社長自らその交渉にあたった) The president *personally* carried on the negotiations.

mi⌈zumushi みずむし (水虫) *n.* athlete's foot.

mi⌈zusashi⌉ みずさし (水差し) *n.* pitcher; water jug.

mi⌈zuu⌉mi みずうみ (湖) *n.* lake:

――――(USAGE)――――
'*Mizuumi*' is an area of fresh water surrounded by land and larger than '*ike*' (pond).
――――――――――――

Mizuumi no mawari o sañpo shita. (湖のまわりを散歩した) I strolled along the bank of the *lake.* 《⇨ ike》

mi⌈zuwari みずわり (水割り) *n.*

whisky and water:
Mizuwari o ip-pai kudasai. (水割り
を 1 杯下さい) Please give me a
whisky and water. (⇨ haibooru))

mo[1] も (藻) *n.* waterweed; seaweed.

mo[2] も *p.* **1** also; too; besides:
*Kare wa Chuugokugo ga hanase-
masu shi, Kañkokugo* mo *dekimasu.* (彼は中国語が話せますし, 韓国
語もできます) He can speak Chinese
and *also* Korean. / *Watashi* mo
ikitai. (私も行きたい) I want to go,
too. / *Kaigi ni wa Ajia kara* mo
daihyoo ga kimashita. (会議にはアジ
アからも代表が来ました) Representa-
tives from Asia *also* came to the
conference.
2 both...and; either...or; neither...nor: ★ Usually occurs as a
pair.
Oosaka mo *Nagoya* mo *ooki-na
toshi desu.* (大阪も名古屋も大きな都
市です) *Both* Osaka *and* Nagoya
are big cities. / *Kare wa sukii* mo
sukeeto mo *dekimasu.* (彼はスキーも
スケートもできます) He can *both* ski
and skate. / *Ano hito to wa aitaku*
mo *hanashitaku* mo *nai.* (あの人とは
会いたくも話したくもない) I do not
want to *either* see him *or* talk to
him. / *Watashi wa hima* mo
okane mo *arimaseñ.* (私は暇もお金も
ありません) I have *neither* time *nor*
money.
3 even: ★ Used to emphasize a
situation by giving one extreme
negative example.
Isogashikute, deñwa mo *kakera-
renai.* (忙しくて, 電話もかけられない)
I'm so busy that I can't *even*
make a phone call. / *Kare wa tsukarete ite, tachiagaru koto* mo *dekinakatta.* (彼は疲れていて, 立ち上がる
こともできなかった) He was very tired
and couldn't *even* stand up.
((⇨ sae; sura))
4 (used with interrogatives to

emphasize a negative):
Kinoo wa doko e mo *ikanakatta.*
(きのうはどこへも行かなかった) I did
not go *anywhere* yesterday. / *Kare wa koñdo no jikeñ ni tsuite*
nani mo *shiranakatta.* (彼は今度の
事件について何も知らなかった) He
knew *nothing* about the recent
incident.
5 as many as; as much as:
★ Used with a number or quantity expression to emphasize that
the number or quantity is unexpectedly either large or small.
*Kootsuu-juutai no tame, uchi kara
eki made sañjup-puñ* mo *kakatta.*
(交通渋滞のため, 家から駅まで 30 分も
かかった) It took *all of* half an hour
from my house to the station
because of a traffic jam. / *Kekkoñ-shiki ni hyaku-niñ* mo *kite
kureta.* (結婚式に 100 人も来てくれた)
A *full* hundred people came to
our wedding. / *Kono kamera wa
nimañ-eñ* mo *shinakatta.* (このカメラ
は 2 万円もしなかった) This camera
did not cost *as much as* 20,000
yen.
6 within, as little as: ★ Used
with number or quantity expressions to indicate a limit.
Ichi-neñ mo *sureba, shigoto ni nareru deshoo.* (一年もすれば, 仕事に慣
れるでしょう) I am sure you will get
used to the job *in* a year. / *Ato
sañjup-puñ* mo *sureba, kare wa
kimasu.* (あと 30 分もすれば, 彼は来ま
す) He will be here *in* about half
an hour. / *Kono nekutai wa sañzeñ-eñ* mo *daseba, kaemasu.* (この
ネクタイは 3 千円も出せば, 買えます)
You can buy this tie with *as little as* 3,000 yen.
7 not one; not any; not a single:
★ Follows counters and used
with a negative for emphasis.
Kanojo wa tomodachi ga hitori
mo *inakatta.* (彼女は友だちが一人もい

なかった) She *did not have a single
friend.* / *Gaikoku e wa* ichi-do mo
itta koto ga arimaseñ. (外国へは一
度も行ったことがありません) I have not
been abroad *even once.* / *Soñna
koto wa* ik-kai mo shita koto ga
arimaseñ. (そんなことは一回もしたこと
がありません) I *have absolutely never
done* anything like that.
8 (used in sentences expressing
emotion, especially nostalgia):
★ '*Wa*' does not convey this
nuance. 《⇨ wa³》
Natsu-yasumi mo *moo owari da.*
(夏休みももう終わりだ) *Ah! The summer vacation* is now over. / *Kyoodai geñka mo ima wa ii omoide
da.* (兄弟げんかも今はいい思い出だ)
The fights between us brothers are
now a pleasant memory to me.
mo「chi もち (餅) *n.* rice cake:
★ Traditionally eaten on New
Year's Day or on other festive
occasions.
mochi o tsuku (餅をつく) *pound
steamed rice into cake.* 《⇨ mochitsuki (photo)》

Abekawa (coated with soy bean powder)

Isobe (wrapped with nori sheet)
MOCHI

mo「chiage・ru もちあげる (持ち上げ
る) *vt.* (-age-te ⊻) **1** lift; heave:
Kare wa sono tsukue o hitori de

mochiageta. (彼はその机を一人で持ち
上げた) He *lifted* the desk by himself.
2 flatter; cajole:
Kare wa mochiagerarete *jookigeñ
datta.* (彼は持ち上げられて上機嫌だっ
た) He *was flattered* into good
spirits.
mo「chidas・u もちだす (持ち出す)
vt. (-dash・i-; -das・a-; -dash・i-te
ⓒ) **1** take out:
Kono hoñ wa damatte, mochidasanai de *kudasai.* (この本は黙って，
持ち出さないでください) Please *do not
take out* this book without asking.
2 bring up; propose (a plan, suggestion, etc.):
Kare wa kaigi de atarashii añ o
mochidashita. (彼は会議で新しい案を
持ち出した) He *brought up* a new
proposal at the meeting.
mo「chii¹・ru もちいる (用いる) *vt.*
(mochi・i-te ⊻) use; make use of:
Nani-ka hoka no hoohoo o mochiiru *koto wa dekinai ñ desu ka?* (何
かほかの方法を用いることはできないんです
か) Can't you *use* some other
methods? / *Kono go wa futsuu
ukemi de* mochiiraremasu. (この語
は普通受け身で用いられます) This
word *is* generally *used* in the passive.
mo「chikomi もちこみ (持ち込み) *n.*
bringing in:
Shikeñ ni jisho no mochikomi *wa
yurusarete imaseñ.* (試験に辞書の持
ち込みは許されていません) You are not
allowed to *take* dictionaries *into*
the examination. / *Kikeñbutsu no*
mochikomi *kiñshi.* (sign) (危険物の
持ち込み禁止) Dangerous Articles
Prohibited. 《⇨ mochikomu》
mo「chikom・u もちこむ (持ち込む)
vt. (-kom・i-; -kom・a-; -koñ-de
ⓒ) bring into; carry into:
Kono tsutsumi wa kinai ni mochikomu *koto wa dekimaseñ.* (この包み
は機内に持ち込むことはできません) You

are not allowed to *carry* this package *onto* the airplane. / *Nihoñjiñ wa yoku tsutomesaki no shigoto o ie ni made* mochikomu. (日本人はよく勤め先の仕事を家にまで持ち込む) Japanese people often *bring* office work home. / *Kare wa watashi ni yakkai na moñdai o* mochikoñde kita. (彼は私にやっかいな問題を持ち込んで来た) He *came* to me *with* a troublesome problem. 《⇨ mochikomi》

mo「chi¬mono もちもの (持ち物) *n.* one's belongings; one's property; one's personal effects: *Kono kuruma wa watashi no* mochimono *desu.* (この車は私の持ち物です) This car is my *property.* / *Kuukoo de* mochimono *o shirabe-rareta.* (空港で持ち物を調べられた) I had my *baggage* checked at the airport.

mo「chi¬nushi もちぬし (持ち主) *n.* owner; possessor; proprietor: *Kono kasa no* mochinushi *wa dare desu ka?* (この傘の持ち主はだれですか) Who is the *owner* of this umbrella? / *Kono resutorañ no* mochinushi *wa nañ-do mo kawatta.* (このレストランの持ち主は何度も替わった) The *owners* of this restaurant have changed many times.

mo「chi¬roñ もちろん (勿論) *adv.* **1** of course; certainly; sure: *"Shiai o mi ni kite kuremasu ka?" "Mochiroñ desu."* (「試合を見に来てくれますか」「もちろんです」) "Could you come to see our game?" "Yes, *of course.*" **2** (~ *no koto*) not to mention; to say nothing of: *Kanojo wa Nihoñ no geñdai-buñ wa* mochiroñ (*no koto*), *koteñ mo yomemasu.* (彼女は日本の現代文はもちろん(のこと)、古典も読めます) She can read the Japanese classics, *to say nothing of* contemporary writing.

mo「chitsuki¬ もちつき (餅つき) *n.* making of rice cake. ★ Steamed glutinous rice is pounded in a large wooden mortar at the end of the year as part of New Year's preparations. 《⇨ mochi》

MOCHITSUKI

mo「dañ モダン *a.n.* (~ *na*) modern; nice: modañ *na tatemono* (モダンな建物) a *modern* building.

mo「do¬r·u もどる (戻る) *vi.* (modor·i-; modor·a-; modot-te Ⓒ) **1** go [come] back; return: *Sugu* modorimasu. (すぐ戻ります) I will *be back* in a minute. / *Kare wa itsu Nihoñ ni* modorimasu *ka?* (彼はいつ日本に戻りますか) When will he *be coming back* to Japan? / *Nakushita saifu ga* modorima-shita. (なくした財布が戻りました) The wallet I had lost *was returned.* 《⇨ kaeru¹; kaeru²》 **2** be restored; regain: *Shiñkañseñ no daiya wa heejoo ni* modorimashita. (新幹線のダイヤは平常に戻りました) The Shinkansen schedule *has been restored* to normal. / *Kanojo no ishiki wa sugu ni* modorimashita. (彼女の意識はすぐに戻りました) She *regained* consciousness soon. 《⇨ modosu》

mo「do¬s·u もどす (戻す) *vt.* (modosh·i-; modos·a-; modosh·i-te Ⓒ) **1** put back; return; restore:

Jisho wa tsukattara tana ni modo-shite oki nasai.(辞書は使ったら棚に戻しておきなさい) *Put* the dictionary *back* on the shelf when you've finished with it. / *Watashi wa tokee o go-fuñ modoshita.*(私は時計を5分戻した) I *put* my watch *back* five minutes. / *Hanashi o moto ni modoshimashoo.*(話を元に戻しましょう) *Let's return* to the previous subject. 《⇨ modoru》

2 throw up; vomit:
Kare wa sake o nomisugite, modo-shita.(彼は酒を飲み過ぎて, もどした) He *vomited* from drinking too much.

mo⌐e·ru もえる (燃える) *vi.* (moe-te Ⓥ) **1** burn; blaze:
Kono maki wa yoku moeru.(このまきはよく燃える) This firewood *burns* well. / *Yuuhi ga akaku moete iru.*(夕日が赤く燃えている) The setting sun *is burning* red.
2 glow (with hope, ambition, etc.); burn:
Kanojo wa kiboo ni moete ita.(彼女は希望に燃えていた) She *was burning* with hope. 《⇨ moyasu》

mo⌐ga¬k·u もがく *vi.* (mogak·i-; mogak·a-; moga·i-te Ⓒ) struggle; writhe:
Inu wa ana kara deyoo to mogaite ita.(犬は穴から出ようともがいていた) The dog *was struggling* to get out of the hole.

mo¬g·u もぐ *vt.* (mog·i-; mog·a-; mo·i-de Ⓒ) pick; pluck:
Kare wa kaki o eda kara moida.(彼は柿を枝からもいだ) He *picked* a persimmon from the branch.

mo¬gumogu もぐもぐ *adv.*
(~ to) mumblingly:
Shooneñ wa utsumuite, nani-ka mogumogu (to) itta.(少年はうつむいて, 何かもぐもぐ(と)言った) The boy hung down his head and *mumbled* something.

mo⌐gu¬r·u もぐる (潜る) *vi.* (mo-gur·i-; mogur·a-; mogut-te Ⓒ)
1 dive; go [stay] underwater:
Watashi-tachi wa sakana o toru tame ni mogutta.(私たちは魚をとるために潜った) We *dived down* to catch fish. / *Kare wa suichuu ni ni-fuñ mogutte ita.*(彼は水中に2分潜っていた) He *stayed* underwater for two minutes.
2 get into (a hole, the ground, etc.); creep into; hide:
ana ni moguru (穴に潜る) *creep into* a hole / *chika ni moguru* (地下に潜る) *go* underground.

mo⌐hañ もはん (模範) *n.* model; example; pattern:
Kare wa chichi-oya o mohañ to shita.(彼は父親を模範とした) He took his father for his *model.* / *Kodomo-tachi ni yoi mohañ o shi-meshi nasai.*(子どもたちに良い模範を示しなさい) Set a good *example* to the children. / *Yukari wa kurasu no mohañ-see da.*(ゆかりはクラスの模範生だ) Yukari is a *model* student in her class.

mo¬haya もはや (最早) *adv.* now; by now; already:
Mohaya ososugimasu.(もはや遅すぎます) It is too late *now.* / *Are kara mohaya go-neñ sugimashita.*(あれからもはや5年過ぎました) Five years have *already* passed since then. / *Mohaya iku hitsuyoo wa arimaseñ.*(もはや行く必要はありません) It is *no longer* necessary to go. / *Mohaya kore made desu.*(もはやこれまでです) It's all over with us *now.*

mo¬ji もじ (文字) *n.* letter; character:
Nihoñgo wa kañji, hiragana, kata-kana no sañ-shurui no moji o omo ni tsukaimasu.(日本語は漢字, ひらがな, カタカナの3種類の文字を主に使います) In Japanese, Chinese characters, 'hiragana' and 'katakana' are the three main types of *writing* that are used.

mo｢ji˺moji もじもじ *adv.* (~ to;
~ suru) hesitatingly; timidly;
reservedly:
Kanojo wa meñsetsu no toki moji-
moji *(to) shite ita.*(彼女は面接のとき
もじもじ(と)していた) She acted *nervously* at the interview.

mo｢kee もけい(模型) *n.* model;
miniature:
Fuji-sañ no mokee (富士山の模型)
a *model* of Mt. Fuji / mokee *hikooki* (模型飛行機) a *model* plane /
jitsubutsu-dai no mokee (実物大の
模型) a *mock-up.*

mo｢kka もっか(目下) *n., adv.*
(*formal*) now; currently; at present:
mokka *no jootai* (目下の状態) the
present circumstances / *Sono moñdai wa* mokka *keñtoo-chuu desu.*
(その問題は目下検討中です) That
matter is *presently* under consideration.

mo｢kuhi˺keñ もくひけん(黙秘権)
n. the right of silence:
Kare wa mokuhikeñ *o tsukatta.*(彼
は黙秘権を使った) He exercised his
right to refuse to answer questions.

mo｢kuhyoo もくひょう(目標) *n.*
goal; target; object; mark:
mokuhyoo *o tateru* (目標を立てる)
set a *goal* / *Kotoshi no* mokuhyoo
wa tassee shita.(今年の目標は達成
した) We attained the *goal* for this
year. / *Anata no uchi no chikaku
ni wa nani-ka* mokuhyoo *ni naru
mono ga arimasu ka?* (あなたの家の
近くには何か目標になるものがありますか)
Is there anything for a *landmark*
near your house?

mo｢kuji もくじ(目次) *n.* table of
contents.

mo｢kumoku もくもく(黙々) *adv.*
(~ to) in silence; without saying
anything:
Kare wa mokumoku *to hataraita.*
(彼は黙々と働いた) He worked
without saying anything.

mo｢kuroku もくろく(目録) *n.*
catalog; list.

mo｢kuromi˺ もくろみ(目論見) *n.*
plan; scheme; intention:
Watashi no mokuromi *wa hazureta.*(私のもくろみははずれた) My *plan*
fell through. 《⇨ mokuromu》

mo｢kuro˺m·u もくろむ(目論む) *vt.*
(-rom·i-; -rom·a-; -roñ-de Ⓒ)
plan; scheme; intend:
kanemooke o mokuromu (金もうけを
もくろむ) *plan* to make money /
Kare wa nani-ka mokuroñde iru.
(彼は何かもくろんでいる) He *is up to*
something. 《⇨ mokuromi》

mo｢kuteki もくてき(目的) *n.*
purpose; aim; objective:
Ryokoo no mokuteki *wa nañ desu
ka?* (旅行の目的は何ですか) What is
the *purpose* of your trip? / *Mokuteki o tassee suru no ni sañ-neñ
kakatta.* (目的を達成するのに3年かか
った) It took three years to
achieve our *objective.*

mo｢kuteki˺chi もくてきち(目的地)
n. destination:
Kuraku naranai uchi ni mokutekichi *ni tsuita.*(暗くならないうちに目的
地に着いた) We arrived at our *destination* before it got dark.

mo｢kuyo˺o(bi) もくよう(び)(木曜
(日)) *n.* Thursday:
Mokuyoobi *wa uchi ni imasu.*(木
曜日は家にいます) I am at home on
Thursdays. 《⇨ yoobi (table)》

mo｢ku˺zai もくざい(木材) *n.*
wood; lumber; timber.

mo｢kuzoo もくぞう(木造) *n.*
made of wood; wooden:
mokuzoo *no fune* (木造の船) a
wooden ship / *Kono jiñja wa* mokuzoo *desu.* (この神社は木造です) This
shrine is *built of wood.*

mo｢meñ もめん(木綿) *n.* cotton;
cotton thread:
momeñ-*ito* (木綿糸) *cotton* thread
/ momeñ *no kutsushita* (木綿の靴
下) *cotton* socks. 《⇨ meñ²; wata》

mo⌐me·ru もめる（揉める）*vi.* (mo-me-te Ⅴ) have trouble; have an argument:
Sono oyako wa itsu-mo momete iru. (その親子はいつももめている) That parent and child *are* always *quarreling*. | *Anata-gata wa nani o momete iru ñ desu ka?* (あなたがたは何をもめているんですか) What *are* you all *arguing* about?

mo⌐miji もみじ（紅葉）*n.* maple; autumn [red] leaves.
momiji suru (〜する) *vi.* turn red [crimson]: *Aki no yama ga kiree ni momiji shite ita.* (秋の山がきれいにもみじしていた) The mountains in autumn *were* beautifully *red*. (⇨ **kooyoo**)

mo⌐mo¹ もも（股）*n.* thigh. (⇨ **jiñtai** (illus.))

mo⌐mo² もも（桃）*n.* peach; peach tree: ★ Japanese peaches are larger than those of Europe and North America.
momo no sekku (桃の節句) *Peach Festival.* ★ Known as '*Hina Matsuri*' (Doll Festival), which is celebrated on March 3.

mo⌐moiro ももいろ（桃色）*n.* pink. ★ Has a pornographic implication like English 'blue.' (⇨ **piñku**)

mo⌐m·u もむ（揉む）*vt.* (mom·i-; mom·a-; moñ-de Ⓒ) massage; rub:
Watashi wa haha no kata o moñde ageta. (私は母の肩をもんであげた) I *massaged* my mother's shoulders. (⇨ **massaaji**)

mo⌐ñ もん（門）*n.* gate:
moñ o akeru [shimeru] (門を開ける [閉める]) open [close] a *gate*. | *Sono moñ wa itsu-mo shimatte iru.* (その門はいつも閉まっている) That *gate* is always closed.

mo⌐naka もなか（最中）*n.* Japanese wafer cake. ★ Sweet bean jam is sandwiched between wafers. (⇨ **wagashi**)

MONAKA

Mo⌐ñbu-da⌐ijiñ （文部大臣）*n.* Minister of Education.

Mo⌐ñbu⌐-shoo もんぶしょう（文部省）*n.* Ministry of Education. (⇨ **shoo⁴** (table))

mo⌐ñdai もんだい（問題）*n.*
1 question; issue; problem:
moñdai o kaiketsu suru (問題を解決する) settle a *question* | *Sore wa kokusai* moñdai *ni natta.* (それは国際問題になった) It became an international *issue*. | *Kore ga* moñdai *no shashiñ desu.* (これが問題の写真です) This is the photograph in *question*. | *juutaku-moñdai* (住宅問題) the housing *problem*.
2 problem (to be answered):
moñdai o toku (問題を解く) solve a *problem* | *Suugaku no* moñdai *wa yasashikatta.* (数学の問題はやさしかった) The math *problem* was easy. | moñdai-*yooshi* (問題用紙) a sheet of *problems*; a *question* sheet. (↔ **tooañ**)
3 matter:
Sore wa betsu moñdai *desu.* (それは別問題です) That is another *matter*.
4 trouble:
Kare wa mata moñdai *o okoshita.* (彼はまた問題を起こした) He has once more caused *trouble*. | *Taroo wa* moñdai-*ji da.* (太郎は問題児だ) Taro is a *problem* child.

mo⌐ñdo⌐o もんどう（問答）*n.* argument; questions and answers:
Kono keñ ni tsuite wa moñdoo

muyoo desu. (この件については問答無用です) I *have no intention of wasting time arguing* about this matter.

moñdoo suru (〜する) *vi.* have an argument: *Añna hito to* moñdoo shite *mo muda desu.* (あんな人と問答してもむだです) It's useless *arguing* with a person like that.

mo⌐ñku もんく (文句) *n.* **1** words; phrase:

uta no moñku (歌の文句) the *words* of a song / *kimari*-moñku (決まり文句) a set *phrase.*

2 complaint; objection:

moñku *o iu* (文句を言う) make a *complaint* / *Watashi no teeañ ni nani-ka* moñku *ga arimasu ka?* (私の提案に何か文句がありますか) Do you have any *objections* to my proposal?

mo⌐no¹ もの (物) *n.* **1** thing; material; article:

Kare wa itsu-mo ii mono *o mi ni tsukete iru.* (彼はいつもいい物を身につけている) He always wears fine *things.* / *Nani-ka taberu* mono *wa arimasu ka?* (何か食べる物はありますか) Is there any*thing* to eat? / *Kore wa choodo watashi ga sagashite ita* mono *desu.* (これはちょうど私が探していた物です) This is just *what* I have been looking for.

2 one's possessions:

Kono mañneñhitsu wa dare no mono *desu ka?* (この万年筆はだれの物ですか) This fountain pen *belongs to whom?* / *Kono suutsukeesu wa watashi no* mono *desu.* (このスーツケースは私の物です) This suitcase is *mine.*

3 quality:

Kono shina wa mono *ga ii.* (この品は物がいい) This article is of good *quality.*

4 word:

Tsukarete, mono *mo ienai.* (疲れて、物も言えない) I am too tired to

even say a *word.*

mono ni naru (〜になる) make good: *Sono keekaku wa* mono ni *naranakatta.* (その計画はものにならなかった) The plan *did not materialize.*

mono ni suru (〜にする) master: *Kare wa sañ-neñ de Nihoñgo o* mono ni shita. (彼は3年で日本語をものにした) He *mastered* Japanese in three years.

mono o iu (〜を言う) talk: *Kane ga* mono o iu. (*saying*) (金がものをいう) Money *talks.* / *Koo iu baai ni wa keekeñ ga* mono o iu. (こういう場合には経験がものをいう) In this case, experience is *most important.*

mo⌐no¹² もの (者) *n.* person; fellow; one:

Watashi wa Yamada *to iu* mono *desu.* (私は山田という者です) My name is *Yamada.* / *Kare wa kono kaisha no* mono *de wa arimaseñ.* (彼はこの会社の者ではありません) He is not an *employee* of this company. / *Watashi wa kiñjo no* mono *desu.* (私は近所の者です) I am *one* of your neighbors. 《⇨ hito; kata³》

mono³ [**moñ**] もの [もん] *p.*
★ Used mainly by women and children.

1 (*colloq.*) because: ★ Used to justify or assert oneself by giving a reason.

"Doo shite Nihoñgo ga kirai na no?" "Datte, señsee no koto kirai na ñ da mono.*"* (「どうして日本語がきらいなの」「だって先生のこときらいなんだもの」) "Why don't you like Japanese?" "*Because* I don't like the teacher."

2 (*colloq.*) (expresses the speaker's assertion or determination): *Soñna koto zettai ni shite nai moñ.* (そんなこと絶対にしてないもん) I *have never done* such a thing. / *Soñna koto (o) iu nara, watashi hitori de dekakeru mono.* (そんなこと言うなら私

一人で出かけるもの) If that's what you think, I'll *go out on my own!*

-mono もの (物) *suf.* thing; article; clothes:
uri-mono (売り物) an *article* for sale / *fuyu*-mono (冬物) winter *clothes* / seńtaku-mono (洗濯物) *washing.*

mo⌐no˥ da ものだ **1** be natural: ★ Polite form is '*mono desu.*'

(USAGE)

Denotes that a certain result or consequence is natural under given circumstances. The subject is often omitted.

Ryokoo ni deru to hoń ga yomi-taku naru mono da. (旅行に出ると本が読みたくなるものだ) When one goes on a trip, one *usually* feels like reading a book.
2 used to (do): ★ Refers to past habits and states.
Mukashi wa kono atari ni norainu ga takusań ita mono desu. (昔はこのあたりに野良犬がたくさんいたものです) There *used to* be many stray dogs around this place a while back. / *Izeń wa dańsee ga kono yoo na shigoto o shita* mono da. (以前は男性がこのような仕事をしたものだ) In former days, men *used to do* this kind of work.
3 should (do): ★ Denotes obligation or duty.
Hito ni mono o morattara, oree o iu mono da. (人に物をもらったら、お礼をいうものだ) When you receive something from someone, you *should* say 'thank you.' / *Kodomo wa hayaku neru* mono desu. (子どもは早く寝るものです) Children *should* go to bed early.
4 how...! ★ Denotes the speaker's sentiment.
Hito no isshoo wa mijikai mono da. (人の一生は短いものだ) *How* short life is!

5 how could...? ★ Denotes the speaker's criticism or judgment.
Baka na koto o shita mono da. (ばかなことをしたものだ) *It was* very foolish of me. / *Yoku ańna otoko to kekkoń shita* mono da. (よくあんな男と結婚したものだ) *How could* she marry such a man?

mo⌐noga˥tari ものがたり (物語) *n.* story; tale; narrative.

mo⌐nogata˥r·u ものがたる (物語る) *vt.* (-gatar·i-; -gatar·a-; -gatat-te Ⓒ) show; describe; prove:
Sono jijitsu wa mińshushugi no juuyoo na koto o monogatatte imasu. (その事実は民主主義の重要なことを物語っています) That fact *shows* the importance of democracy.

mo⌐no˥goto ものごと (物事) *n.* things; everything:
Anata wa monogoto *o majime ni kańgae-sugiru.* (あなたは物事をまじめに考え過ぎる) You take *things* too seriously. / *Monogoto ni wa ura-omote ga aru.* (物事には裏表がある) There are good and bad sides to *everything.* / *Nakanaka* monogoto *wa warikirenai.* (なかなか物事は割り切れない) It is difficult to do *everything* in a businesslike manner.

mo⌐no˥ ka ものか never: ★ Placed at the end of a sentence to express strong negation.
Ańna yatsu to moo kuchi o kiku mono ka. (あんなやつともう口をきくものか) *Do you expect* me to talk to a fellow like him again? / *Moo ańna tokoro e iku* mono ka. (もうあんなところへ行くものか) *You can be sure* that I'll *never* go to such a place again.

mo⌐no-o˥boe ものおぼえ (物覚え) *n.* memory:
Kare wa mono-oboe *ga ii.* (彼は物覚えがいい) He has a good *memory.* / *Saikiń* mono-oboe *ga waruku natta.* (最近物覚えが悪くなった) My *memory* has begun to fail these

days. ⟪⇨ kioku⟫

mo⌈nooki⌉ ものおき (物置) n.
storeroom; shed; closet.

mo⌈nooto⌉ ものおと (物音) n.
(strange) sound; noise:
Monooto *de me ga sameta.* (物音で
目が覚めた) I was awakened by a
noise.

mo⌈nosa⌉shi ものさし (物差し) n.
ruler; measure.

mo⌈nosugo⌉·i ものすごい (物凄い)
a. (-ku) (*informal*) terrible; terrific:
monosugoi *supiido* (ものすごいスピー
ド) a *terrific* speed / Monosugoi
yuudachi deshita ne. (ものすごい夕立
でしたね) It was a *terrible* evening
shower, wasn't it? / *Soko no
keshiki wa* monosugoku *yokatta.*
(そこの景色はものすごく良かった) The
scenery there was *absolutely* fantastic. / *Kare wa kimi no koto o*
monosugoku *okotte iru zo.* (*by
men*) (彼は君のことをものすごく怒ってい
るぞ) He is *hopping* mad at you.

mo⌈no⌉zuki ものずき (物好き) n.
strange [eccentric] person:
Yo-no-naka ni wa iroiro to monozuki *ga iru mono da.* (世の中にはいろ
いろと物好きがいるものだ) There are
many kinds of *strange people* in
this world.
— *a.n.* (~ na, ni) curious;
weird; eccentric:
*Anna otoko o oikakeru nante, ka-
nojo mo* monozuki *da.* (あんな男を追
いかけるなんて, 彼女も物好きだ) She is
a bit *weird* to chase after a man
like that. / *Monozuki ni mo kare
wa tooku made sono kaji o mi ni
itta.* (物好きにも彼は遠くまでその火事を
見に行った) *Just out of curiosity,*
he went quite some way to see
the fire.

mo⌈o⌉ もう adv. 1 already; yet;
now:
Shukudai wa moo *sumasemashita.*
(宿題はもう済ませました) I have al-

ready finished my homework. /
Depaato wa moo *hiraite imasu
ka?* (デパートはもう開いていますか) Are
the department stores open *yet?*
/ *Kare wa* moo *Sendai ni tsuita
deshoo.* (彼はもう仙台に着いたでしょう)
I think he has *already* arrived in
Sendai. / *Kekka wa* moo *akiraka
desu.* (結果はもう明らかです) The
results are *now* quite obvious.
2 more; further; again:
Moo *ichi-do sono eega o mitai.* (も
う一度その映画を見たい) I would like
to see that film once *more.* / *Shi-
tsumon no aru kata wa* moo *imasen ka?* (質問のある方はもういませんか)
Aren't there any *more* people
with questions? / Moo *shibaraku
o-machi kudasai.* (もうしばらくお待ち
ください) Please wait *a little* longer.
/ Moo *kore ijoo matemasen.* (もうこ
れ以上待てません) We cannot wait
any longer. / *Joodan wa* moo *ii
kagen ni shite kudasai yo.* (冗談は
もういい加減にしてくださいよ) No *more*
of your jokes!
3 soon; before long:
Moo *sorosoro kanojo wa kuru to
omoimasu.* (もうそろそろ彼女は来ると
思います) I think she will be coming *soon.* ⟪⇨ moo sugu⟫

mo⌈o-⌉ もう (猛) *pref.* hard;
heavy; intensive:
moo-*benkyoo* (猛勉強) *hard* study
/ moo-*renshuu* (猛練習) *intensive*
training / moo-*hangeki* (猛反撃) a
fierce counterattack.

mo⌈ochoo もうちょう (盲腸) n.
appendix:
moochoo-*en* (盲腸炎) *appendicitis.*
★ '*Chuusuien*' (虫垂炎) is the
technical term.

mo⌈ofu もうふ (毛布) n. blanket:
kodomo ni moofu *o kakeru* (子ども
に毛布をかける) put a *blanket* over a
child / *Akanboo wa* moofu *ni ku-
rumatte nete imasu.* (赤ん坊は毛布
にくるまって寝ています) The baby is

sleeping wrapped in a *blanket.*

mo「o jiki もうじき *adv.* soon; shortly. 《⇨ moo sugu》

mo「oka¹r・u もうかる(儲かる) *vi.* (-kar・i-; -kar・a-; -kat-te C) make money; make a profit; be profitable: *Koñdo no torihiki de hyakumañ-eñ* mookatta.(今度の取引で 100 万円もうかった) I *made a profit* of one million yen on this deal. / *Kono shigoto wa* mookaranai.(この仕事はもうからない) This job *does not pay.* 《⇨ mookeru¹; mooke》

mo「oke もうけ(儲け) *n.* profit; gains: *Koñgetsu wa* mooke *ga sukunakatta.*(今月はもうけが少なかった) This month, the *profits* were small. / Mooke *wa futari de yamawake shimashoo.*(もうけは二人で山分けしましょう) Let's divide the *profits* between the two of us. 《↔ soñ》 《⇨ mookeru¹; mookaru; rieki》

mo「oke¹・ru¹ もうける(儲ける) *vt.* (-ke-te V) make money; make a profit: *Ikura* mookemashita *ka?*(いくらもうけましたか) How much *did you make?* / *Kare wa kabu de ni-hyakumañ-eñ* mooketa.(彼は株で 200 万円もうけた) He *made* two million yen on stocks. / *Kare wa raku o shite o-kane o* mookeyoo *to shite iru.*(彼は楽をしてお金をもうけようとしている) He is trying to *make money* the easy way. 《⇨ mookaru; mooke》

mo「oke¹・ru² もうける(設ける) *vt.* (-ke-te V) set up (an organization, rule, etc.); lay down: *iiñkai o* mookeru(委員会を設ける) *form* a committee / *kisoku o* mookeru(規則を設ける) *lay down* rules / *Sono kaisha wa Nagoya ni shiteñ o* mooketa.(その会社は名古屋に支店を設けた) The company *set up* a branch in Nagoya.

mo「omoo もうもう *adv.* (~ to) (used to express swirling steam, clouds of dust, etc.): *Fuñkakoo kara kemuri ga* moomoo (to) dete iru.(噴火口から煙がもうもう(と)出ている) The smoke *is swirling up* from the crater. / *Kuruma wa hokori o* moomoo (to) tatete, hashirisatta.(車はほこりをもうもう(と)立てて, 走り去った) The car drove away, *raising clouds* of dust. / *Heya wa tabako no kemuri de* moomoo *o shite ita.*(部屋はたばこの煙でもうもうとしていた) The room *was thick* with cigarette smoke.

mo「oretsu もうれつ(猛烈) *a.n.* (~ na, ni) violent; fierce; terrible: *Kotoshi no natsu no atsusa wa* mooretsu *da.*(今年の夏の暑さは猛烈だ) This summer's heat is *fierce.* / Mooretsu *na taifuu ga Shikoku ni chikazuite iru.*(猛烈な台風が四国に近づいている) A *violent* typhoon is approaching Shikoku. / *Kare wa ima Nihoñgo o* mooretsu *ni beñkyoo shite imasu.*(彼はいま日本語を猛烈に勉強しています) He is now studying Japanese *very hard.* / mooretsu-*shaiñ*(猛烈社員) an employee who *puts everything into his work.*

mo「oshiage・ru もうしあげる(申し上げる) *vt.* (-age-te V) express; say: ★ Humble equivalent of '*iu.*' More humble than '*moosu.*' Mooshiagemasu.(申し上げます) *May I have your attention,* please? / *Go-kyooryoku ni taishi, kokoro kara o-ree* mooshiagemasu.(ご協力に対し, 心からお礼申し上げます) I *express* thanks from the bottom of my heart for your cooperation. / *Hoñ-neñ mo yoroshiku onegai* mooshiagemasu.(*on a New Year's card*)(本年もよろしくお願い申し上げます) I *would appreciate* your further kindness this year.

o[go]-... mooshiagemasu (お[ご]...
申し上げます) (*humble*) will do:
O-seki e go-añnai mooshiagemasu.
(お席へご案内申し上げます) I *will
show* you to your seat.

mo⌐oshide·ru もうしでる (申し出
る) *vt.* (-de-te Ⅴ) propose; offer;
request; apply for:
*Watashi-tachi wa kare-ra ni eñjo
o* mooshideta. (私たちは彼らに援助を
申し出た) We *offered* them assistance. / *Kanojo wa sono kaigi e
sañka o* mooshideta. (彼女はその会
議へ参加を申し出た) She *requested*
to take part in the conference.

mo⌐oshikomi もうしこみ (申し込み)
n. application; offer; proposal;
request:
*Mooshikomi wa deñwa de mo kek-
koo desu.* (申し込みは電話でも結構で
す) *Applications* by telephone are
also acceped. / *Katarogu wa* mooshikomi *o itadaki shidai, o-okuri
shimasu.* (カタログは申し込みをいただき
次第, お送りします) We will send
you the catalog on receipt of
your *request.* / *Hoteru no yoyaku
no* mooshikomi *o shita.* (ホテルの予
約の申し込みをした) I *have requested*
hotel reservations. / mooshikomi-
yooshi (申し込み用紙) an *application* form.
《⇨ mooshikomu》

mo⌐oshikom·u もうしこむ (申し込
む) *vt.* (-kom·i-; -kom·a-; -koñ-
de Ⅽ) apply for; propose:
shoogakukiñ o mooshikomu (奨学
金を申し込む) *apply* for a scholarship / *Kare wa kanojo ni kekkoñ o*
mooshikoñda. (彼は彼女に結婚を申
し込んだ) He *proposed* marriage to
her. / *Watashi wa sono koñtesuto
ni sañka o* mooshikoñda. (私はその
コンテストに参加を申し込んだ) I *ap-
plied* to take part in the contest. /
Kare wa sono zasshi no yoyaku o
mooshikoñda. (彼はその雑誌の予約を
申し込んだ) He *applied* for a sub-

scription to that magazine.
《⇨ mooshikomi》

mo⌐oshiwake もうしわけ (申し訳)
n. apology; excuse:
Kore de wa mooshiwake *ga tachimaseñ.* (これでは申し訳が立ちません) I
don't know how to make an
excuse for this.

mooshiwake arimaseñ (〜ありま
せん) I am sorry; excuse me:
Okurete mooshiwake arimaseñ.
(遅れて申し訳ありません) *I am sorry* I
am late. / *Mooshiwake arimaseñ
ga, eki e iku michi o oshiete kudasai.* (申し訳ありませんが, 駅へ行く道を
教えてください) *Excuse me*, but
could you tell me the way to the
station? 《⇨ mooshiwake nai》

mo⌐oshiwake na]·i もうしわけな
い (申し訳ない) (-ku) be sorry:

⦅USAGE⦆

Polite forms are '*mooshiwake
gozaimaseñ, mooshiwake arimaseñ, mooshiwake nai desu.*'

Okurete mooshiwake nai. (遅れて
申し訳ない) *I am sorry* for being
late. / *Go-meewaku o o-kakeshite,
mattaku* mooshiwake *naku omotte orimasu.* (ご迷惑をおかけして, まった
く申し訳なく思っております) *I feel very
sorry* for causing you so much
trouble.

mo⌐os·u もうす (申す) *vt.* (moo-
sh·i-; moos·a-; moosh·i-te Ⅽ)
(*humble*) say; tell; call:
Chichi wa sugu ni mairu to mooshite *orimasu.* (父はすぐに参ると申し
ております) My father *says* that he
will soon come. / *Watashi wa
Suzuki to* mooshimasu. (私は鈴木と
申します) My name *is* Suzuki.

o-...mooshimasu (お...申します)
(*humble*) will do: *Nochi-hodo o-
ukagai* mooshimasu. (後ほどお伺い
申します) I *will call on* you later. /
O-machi mooshimasu. (お待ち申しま
す) I *will wait* for you. 《⇨ moo-

shiageru》

mo⌐o su⌐gu もうすぐ *adv.* soon; shortly; before long:
Moo sugu *yo-ji ni narimasu.* (もうすぐ４時になります) It's *almost* four o'clock. / Moo sugu *Kurisumasu desu.* (もうすぐクリスマスです) Christmas is *just around the corner.* / Isha wa moo sugu *kuru to omoimasu.* (医者はもうすぐ来ると思います) The doctor will *soon* be here.

mo⌐otaa モーター *n.* motor:
mootaa o ugokasu [*tomeru*] (モーターを動かす[止める]) start [cut off] a *motor.* 《⇨ eñjiñ》

mo⌐ppara もっぱら (専ら) *adv.* exclusively; wholly; mostly:
Sono gaka wa moppara *umi no fuukee o egaita.* (その画家はもっぱら海の風景を描いた) The painter drew pictures of *nothing but* seascapes. / Kare wa saikiñ moppara *gorufu ni uchikoñde iru.* (彼は最近もっぱらゴルフに打ち込んでいる) Recently he has been devoting himself *wholeheartedly* to golf.

mo⌐ra⌐s·u もらす (漏らす) *vt.* (morash·i·; moras·a·; morash·i·te Ⓒ) 1 let leak:
Kono biniiru no fukuro wa mizu o morashimaseñ. (このビニールの袋は水を漏らしません) This plastic bag *does not leak* water. 《⇨ moreru》
2 let out (a secret, complaint, etc.):
Kono keekaku o morasanai de kudasai. (この計画を漏らさないでください) *Do not let* these plans *get out.* / Kare wa fumañ o morashita. (彼は不満を漏らした) He *revealed* his feelings of dissatisfaction.
3 fail to do: ★ Attached to the continuative base of a verb.
kiki-morasu (聞き漏らす) *fail to* hear / kaki-morasu (書き漏らす) *fail to* write down.

mo⌐ra·u もらう (貰う) *vt.* (mora·i·; moraw·a·; morat-te Ⓒ) get; receive:

Watashi wa kanojo kara purezeñto o moratta. (私は彼女からプレゼントをもらった) I *received* a present from her. / Kare kara tegami o moraimashita *ka?* (彼から手紙をもらいましたか) *Did* you *get* a letter from him? / Kare wa takai kyuuryoo o moratte iru. (彼は高い給料をもらっている) He *gets* a good salary.
-te morau (て～) ★ Used when asking someone to do something, or when receiving benefit from someone.
Anata ni soko e itte moraitai. (あなたにそこへ行ってもらいたい) I *would like you to go* there. / Kare ni Nihoñgo o oshiete moraimashita. (彼に日本語を教えてもらいました) I *learned* Japanese *from him.* / Kanojo ni tegami o taipu shite moratta. (彼女に手紙をタイプしてもらった) I *had* her *type* the letter *for me.* 《⇨ itadaku》

mo⌐re⌐·ru もれる (漏れる) *vi.* (more-te Ⓥ) 1 leak; escape:
Paipu kara mizu ga morete iru. (パイプから水が漏れている) Water *is leaking* from the pipe. / Kabe no sukima kara akari ga morete ita. (壁のすき間から明かりが漏れていた) *There was* light *coming* through a chink in the wall. 《⇨ moru'》
2 (of a secret) leak out:
Shiranai ma ni himitsu ga morete ita. (知らない間に秘密が漏れていた) Before we knew it, the secret *had leaked out.* 《⇨ morasu》
3 be left out (of a list, selection, etc.); be omitted:
Watashi no namae ga meebo kara morete imasu. (私の名前が名簿から漏れています) My name *is omitted* from the list. / Kare no e wa señ ni moreta. (彼の絵は選に漏れた) His painting *was left out* of the selection.

mo⌐ri もり (森) *n.* woods; forest. 《⇨ hayashi》

mo「ribachi もりばち (盛り鉢) *n.*
bowl. ★ Placed in the center of a
table to serve fruit or vegetables.
《⇨ waň¹》

mo「ro」・i もろい (脆い) *a.* (-ku)
1 fragile; weak:
*Toshi o toru to hone ga moroku
narimasu.* (年を取ると骨がもろくなりま
す) As you grow older, your
bones become *fragile.* / *Sono too
wa jishiň de moroku mo kuzure
ochita.* (その塔は地震でもろくも崩れ落
ちた) The tower *easily* fell down
in the earthquake.
2 (of feeling, motion, etc.) be
moved easily:
Haha wa joo ni moroi. (母は情にも
ろい) My mother *is easily moved*
emotionally.

mo「r・u」¹ もる (漏る) *vi.* (mor・i-;
mor・a-; mot-te C) leak:
Kono heya wa ame ga moru. (この
部屋は雨が漏る) Rain *leaks* into
this room. / *Suidoo no mizu ga
motte iru.* (水道の水が漏っている)
The water from the pipe *is leaking.* 《⇨ moreru》

mo「r・u」² もる (盛る) *vt.* (mor・i-;
mor・a-; mot-te C) pile up; heap
up:
*Kodomo-tachi wa suna o motte,
chiisa-na yama o tsukutta.* (子ども
たちは砂を盛って, 小さな山を作った)
The children *heaped up* sand and
made a small mound. / *Kare wa
chawaň ni gohaň o yama no yoo
ni motta.* (彼は茶碗にご飯を山のように
盛った) He *piled up* the rice like a
mountain in his bowl.

mo」shi (mo) もし(も) (若し(も))
adv. if; in case: ★ '*Moshi mo*' is
used to form an emphatic conditional.
*Moshi mo ashita yoi teňki nara,
pikunikku ni ikimasu.* (もしもあした
良い天気なら, ピクニックに行きます) We
are going on a picnic *if* it is fine
tomorrow. / *Moshi sono kuruma o

mitsuketara, sugu shirasete kudasai.* (もしその車を見つけたら, すぐ知らせ
てください) *If* you happen to find
the car, please let me know at
once.

mo」shi-ka shitara もしかしたら
(若しかしたら) *adv.* perhaps; maybe; possibly:
*Moshi-ka shitara, gogo wa ame
ka mo shirenai.* (もしかしたら, 午後は
雨かもしれない) *Perhaps* it will rain
in the afternoon.

mo」shi-ka suru to もしかすると
(若しかすると) *adv.* = moshi-ka shitara.

mo」shikuwa もしくは (若しくは)
conj. (*formal*) or:
honniň moshikuwa *dairiniň* (本人
もしくは代理人) *either* the person in
question *or* his or her representative. 《⇨ mata-wa》

mo」shimoshi もしもし *int.*
1 hello: ★ Used when answering a telephone call.
*Moshimoshi, Yamada-saň desu
ka?* (もしもし, 山田さんですか) Hello.
Is that Mrs. Yamada?
2 excuse me: ★ Used when
addressing a stranger.
*Moshimoshi, kippu o otoshima-
shita yo.* (もしもし, 切符を落としました
よ) *Excuse me.* You have dropped
your ticket.

mo「tara」s・u もたらす *vt.* (-ra-
sh・i-; -ras・a-; -rash・i-te C)
bring (about); lead to:
*Terebi no fukyuu wa hitobito no
seekatsu ni ooki-na heňka o motarashita.* (テレビの普及は人々の生活に
大きな変化をもたらした) The spread
of television *has brought about*
great changes in people's lives.
《⇨ shoojiru》

mo「tare」・ru もたれる (凭れる) *vi.*
(-re-te V) 1 lean:
Kare wa kabe ni motarete ita. (彼
は壁にもたれていた) He *was leaning*
against the wall.

2 (of food) sit heavy on one's stomach; be hard to digest: *Abura no ooi tabemono wa i ni motaremasu.* (脂の多い食べ物は胃にもたれます) Greasy food *sits heavy* on the stomach.

mo⌐tenas‧u もてなす (持て成す) *vt.* (-nash‧i-; -nas‧a-; -nash‧i‧te C) entertain; treat: *Kare wa watashi o taiheñ motenashite kureta.* (彼は私をたいへんもてなしてくれた) He *entertained* me exceedingly well.

mo⌐te¬‧ru もてる (持てる) *vi.* (mo-te-te V) be popular; be a favorite: *Kare wa oñna-no-ko ni yoku moteru.* (彼は女の子によくもてる) He *is very popular* with the girls.

mo⌐to¹ もと (元・基・本・素) *n.*
1 cause; beginning; origin: *Kare-ra no keñka no moto wa nañ desu ka?* (彼らのけんかの元は何ですか) What was the *cause* of their quarrel?
2 basis; foundation: *Kono deeta wa nani o moto ni shite imasu ka?* (このデータは何を基にしていますか) What is the *basis* for these data?
3 material; basic ingredient: *Miso no moto wa daizu desu.* (みその素は大豆です) The *basic material* for miso is soybeans.
4 capital; funds. 《⇨ motode》

mo¬to² もと (元・旧) *n.* original [former] state: moto-*shushoo* (元首相) the *former* prime minister 《⇨ -zeñ²》 / *Tsukatta doogu wa moto no basho ni modoshi nasai.* (使った道具はもとの場所に戻しなさい) Return the tools you used to their *original* place. / *Teeburu o moto no toori narabete kudasai.* (テーブルをもとの通り並べてください) Please put the tables *as they were.* / *Watashi wa moto koko ni suñde imashita.* (私はもとここ

に住んでいました) I used to live here *before.*

mo⌐tode もとで (元手) *n.* capital; funds: *Doñna shoobai de mo hajimeru ni wa motode ga iru.* (どんな商売でも始めるには元手が要る) You need *capital* in order to start any kind of business.

mo⌐tome¬‧ru もとめる (求める) *vt.* (-me-te V) **1** request; demand: *kyooryoku o motomeru* (協力を求める) *request* a person's cooperation / *setsumee o motomeru* (説明を求める) *demand* an explanation / *Kare-ra wa shichoo ni meñkai o motometa.* (彼らは市長に面会を求めた) They *made a request* to the mayor for an interview.
2 seek; look for: *koofuku [heewa] o motomeru* (幸福[平和]を求める) *seek* happiness [peace] / *Kanojo wa shoku o motomete iru.* (彼女は職を求めている) She *is looking for* employment.
3 buy; purchase: *Sono shina wa yuumee depaato de o-motome ni naremasu.* (その品は有名デパートでお求めになれます) You can *buy* that article at well-known department stores.

mo⌐tomoto もともと (元々) *adv.* from the first [beginning]; by nature: *Sono keekaku wa motomoto zusañ datta.* (その計画はもともとずさんだった) The plan was faulty *from the beginning.* / *Kare wa motomoto kimae ga ii.* (彼はもともと気前がいい) He is generous *by nature.*

motomoto da (～だ) remain unchanged: *Soñ shite [Kotowararete], motomoto da.* (損して[断わられて], もともとだ) Even if I lose money [am refused], I will be *none the worse* for it.

motomoto wa (～は) originally; primarily. 《⇨ hoñrai (wa)》

moˈtozuˈk·u もとづく (基づく) *vi.*
(-zuk·i-; -zuk·a-; -zu·i-te C) be
based on; be founded on:
Kono shoosetsu wa jijitsu ni moto-
zuite imasu. (この小説は事実に基づい
ています) This novel *is based* on
fact. / *Riidaa no shiji ni motozuite*
koodoo shi nasai. (リーダーの指示に
基づいて行動しなさい) Act *in accor-*
dance with the leader's instructions.

moˈts·u もつ (持つ) *vt.* (moch·i-;
mot·a-; mot-te C) **1** take; hold;
carry:
Sono nimotsu wa watashi ga mo-
chimashoo. (その荷物は私が持ちましょ
う) I'll *take* that luggage. / *Te ni*
nani o motte iru ñ desu ka? (手に
何を持っているんですか) What *are* you
holding in your hand? / *Kare wa*
suutsukeesu o motte ita. (彼はスー
ツケースを持っていた) He *was carry-*
ing a suitcase.
2 possess; own: ★ Usually used
in the form '*motte iru.*'
"Kurejitto kaado o motte imasu
ka?" "Hai, motte imasu.*" (「クレジッ
トカードを持っていますか」「はい, 持ってい
ます」) "Do you *have* a credit
card?" "Yes, I *do.*" / *Kare wa*
supootsukaa o motte iru. (彼はスポ
ーツカーを持っている) He *has* a sports
car. / *Tanaka-sañ wa ooki-na uchi*
o motte iru. (田中さんは大きな家を持
っている) Mr. Tanaka *possesses* a
large house. / *Kanojo wa sugureta*
kiokuryoku o motte imasu. (彼女は
優れた記憶力を持っています) She *has*
an excellent memory.
3 cherish (a feeling); harbor (a
desire):
Watashi wa Nihoñ no rekishi ni
kyoomi o motte imasu. (私は日本の
歴史に興味を持っています) I *have* an
interest in Japanese history. /
Kanojo wa kare ni urami o motte
ita. (彼女は彼に恨みを持っていた) She
harbored a grudge against him.

4 last; hold; keep; wear:
Kono teñki wa asu made motsu
daroo *ka.* (この天気はあすまでもつだろう
か) I wonder if this weather *will*
hold until tomorrow. / *Kono sa-*
kana wa reezooko ni irete okanai
to mochimaseñ *yo.* (この魚は冷蔵庫
に入れておかないともちませんよ) If you
do not put this fish in the fridge,
it *will not keep.* / *Kono fuku wa*
ato go-neñ mochimasu. (この服はあと
5年もちます) These clothes *will*
last five more years. / *Byooniñ wa*
ichi-neñ motanai *ka mo shirenai.*
(病人は1年もたないかもしれない) The
patient *will* probably *not hold*
out a year.
5 bear; cover; pay:
Kañjoo wa kare ga motta. (勘定は
彼が持った) He *paid* the bill.
《⇨ harau》
6 take charge of; be in charge
of:
Sono kurasu o motte iru no wa
Tanaka señsee desu. (そのクラスを持
っているのは田中先生です) It is Mrs.
Tanaka who *is in charge of* that
class.

moˈttainaˈ·i もったいない (勿体無
い) *a.* (-ku) **1** wasteful:
Koñna koto o shite ite wa jikañ
ga mottainai. (こんなことをしていては
時間がもったいない) It is a *waste* of
time to be doing something like
this. / *Koñna ii kabañ o tsuka-*
wanai nañte, mottainai. (こんないい
かばんを使わないなんて, もったいない) It
is a real *waste* not to use a good
bag like this.
2 too good:
Watashi ni wa mottainai *heya de-*
su. (私にはもったいない部屋です) This
is a room that is *too good* for me.
/ *Koñna ni kiree na ehagaki o*
suteru no wa mottainai. (こんなにき
れいな絵葉書を捨てるのはもったいない)
It is a shame to throw away such
pretty postcards. 《⇨ oshii》

mo｢tte ik･u もっていく（持って行く）
vi. (ik･i-; ik･a-; it-te C) take;
carry:
*Watashi-tachi wa pikunikku ni
iroiro na tabemono o motte itta.*
（私たちはピクニックにいろいろな食べ物を
持って行った）We *took* various
foods to the picnic. 《↔ motte
kuru》

mo｢tte k･u｣ru もってくる（持って来
る）*vi.* (k･i-; k･o-; k･i-te I)
bring; get:
*Kasa o motte kuru no o wasurete
shimatta.* （かさを持って来るのを忘れて
しまった）I forgot to *bring* my
umbrella. 《↔ motte iku》

mo｢tto もっと *adv.* more:
Motto *motte kite kudasai.* （もっと持
って来てください）Please bring some
more. / Motto *beñkyoo shi nasai.*
（もっと勉強しなさい）Study *harder.* /
Kono moñdai wa motto *choosa
suru hitsuyoo ga aru.* （この問題はも
っと調査する必要がある）This prob-
lem requires *more* investigation. /
Motto *nedañ no yasui mono wa
arimaseñ ka?* （もっと値段の安いものは
ありませんか）Isn't there anything *a
bit* cheaper?

mo｢tto｣mo¹ もっとも（最も）*adv.*
most:
Nihoñ de mottomo *takai yama wa
Fuji-sañ desu.* （日本で最も高い山は
富士山です）The *highest* mountain
in Japan is Mt. Fuji. / *Kare wa
Nihoñ de* mottomo *yuumee na
sakka no hitori desu.* （彼は日本で最
も有名な作家の一人です）He is one
of the *most* famous authors in
Japan. / *Kono e no naka de* mottomo *suki na no wa dore desu ka?*
（この絵のなかで最も好きなのはどれですか）
Which do you like *best* of these
pictures?

mo｢ttomo² もっとも（尤も）*a.n.*
(～ na, ni) reasonable; natural;
right:
Mottomo na go-ikeñ desu. （もっとも

なご意見です）Your point of view is
reasonable. / *Kare ga okoru no mo
mottomo da.* （彼が怒るのももっともだ）
It is quite *natural* that he got
angry.

mo｢ttomo³ もっとも（尤も）*conj.*
however; but; though:
Kanojo wa keesañ ga hayai. Mottomo *tokidoki machigaeru kedo
ne.* （彼女は計算が速い. もっともときどき
間違えるけどね）She is quick at figures. *But* she sometimes makes
mistakes.

mo｢yas･u もやす（燃やす）*vt.* (mo-
yash･i-; moyas･a-; moyash･i-te
C) burn:
Uraniwa de kamikuzu o moyashita. （裏庭で紙くずを燃やした）I
burned the wastepaper in the
back yard. 《⇨ moeru》

mo｢yoo もよう（模様）*n.* **1** pattern; design:
hana no moyoo *no kabegami* （花の
模様の壁紙）wallpaper with a floral *pattern* / *Kono hako no* moyoo
wa nañ desu ka? （この箱の模様は何
ですか）What does this *design* on
the box stand for?
2 look; appearance:
sora moyoo （空もよう）the *appearance* of the sky / *Kaigi wa eñki ni
naru* moyoo *da.* （会議は延期になるも
ようだ）It *looks like* the meeting is
going to be postponed.
3 development; circumstances:
Kare wa sono kuni no saikiñ no
moyoo *o hanashite kureta.* （彼はそ
の国の最近のもようを話してくれた）He
told us about the latest *developments* in the country.
《⇨ yoosu》

mo｢yooshi もよおし（催し）*n.*
meeting; party; function:
moyooshi o okonau （催しを行う）
hold a *meeting* [*party*] / *seefu shusai no* moyooshi （政府主催の催し）a
party held under the auspices of
the government. 《⇨ moyoosu》

mo「yoos·u もよおす (催す) *vt.* (mo-yoosh·i-; moyoos·a-; moyoo-sh·i-te ⓒ) **1** hold; have; give: *Kiñyoobi no bañ watashi no ie de paatii o* moyooshimasu. (金曜日の晩私の家でパーティーを催します) On Friday evening we *are having* a party at my house. 《⇨ moyooshi》
2 feel: *nemuke o* moyoosu (眠気を催す) *feel* sleepy / *samuke o* moyoosu (寒気を催す) *feel* a chill / *hakike o* moyoosu (吐き気を催す) *feel like* vomiting.

mu¹ む (無) *n.* nothing; naught; nil: *Watashi-tachi no doryoku wa subete* mu *ni natta.* (私たちの努力はすべて無になった) All our efforts have come to *nothing.* / *Kare wa wareware no kooi o* mu *ni shita.* (彼はわれわれの好意を無にした) He *did not avail himself* of our kindness.

mu- む (無) *pref.* un-; -less; free: mu-*yoku* (無欲) / *unselfish* / mu-*zai* (無罪) *innocent* / mu-*zee* (無税) *free* of duty.

mucha むちゃ (無茶) *n.* being unreasonable; being absurd: *Mucha o suru no wa yoshi nasai.* (むちゃをするのはよしなさい) Do not act *unreasonably.* / *Soñna* mucha *o iwarete mo komarimasu.* (そんなむちゃを言われても困ります) You are *asking too much* of me.
— *a.n.* (~ na, ni) unreasonable; absurd; reckless: *Kare no yookyuu wa sukoshi* mu-cha *da.* (彼の要求は少しむちゃだ) His demand is rather *unreasonable.* / *Mucha na uñteñ wa jiko ni tsunagarimasu.* (むちゃな運転は事故につながります) *Reckless* driving leads to accidents.

mu「chakucha むちゃくちゃ (無茶苦茶) *a.n.* (~ na, ni) (*informal*) absurd; reckless; awful: *Mattaku* muchakucha *na giroñ da.*

(まったくむちゃくちゃな議論だ) It's an utterly *unreasonable* argument. / *Kare no iu koto wa* muchakucha *da.* (彼の言うことはむちゃくちゃだ) What he says is *absurd.* / *Kesa no deñsha wa* muchakucha *ni koñde ita.* (今朝の電車はむちゃくちゃに混んでいた) This morning's train was *awfully* crowded. 《⇨ mucha》

mu「chi¹ むち (無知) *n.* ignorance; innocence: *Jibuñ no* muchi *ga hazukashii.* (自分の無知が恥ずかしい) I am ashamed of my *ignorance.*
— *a.n.* (~ na) ignorant: muchi *na taishuu* (無知な大衆) the *ignorant* masses / *Watashi wa kabu no koto wa mattaku* muchi *desu.* (私は株のことは全く無知です) I am completely *ignorant* about matters concerning stocks.

mu「chi² むち (鞭) *n.* whip; lash: muchi *de utsu* (むちで打つ) strike with a *whip.*

mu「chuu むちゅう (夢中) *a.n.* (~ na, ni) absorbed; crazy: *Kodomo-tachi wa terebi-geemu ni* muchuu *ni natte iru.* (子どもたちはテレビゲームに夢中になっている) The children *are absorbed* in the video game. / *Kanojo wa jazu-dañsu ni* muchuu *da.* (彼女はジャズダンスに夢中だ) She is *crazy* about jazz dancing.

muchuu de (~ で) for one's life: *Watashi wa* muchuu de *nigeta.* (私は夢中で逃げた) I ran *for my life.*

mu「da むだ (無駄) *n.* waste; uselessness: muda *o habuku* (無駄を省く) cut down on *waste.*
— *a.n.* (~ na, ni) wasteful; useless: *Soñna koto o shiyoo to shite mo* muda *desu.* (そんなことをしようとしても無駄です) There is *no use* trying to do something like that. / *Watashi wa* muda *na doryoku o shite kita.*

(私は無駄な努力をしてきた) I have been making *useless* efforts. / *Mizu o muda ni shite wa ikenai.* (水を無駄にしてはいけない) You must not *waste* water. 《⇨ dame》

mu「dañ むだん (無断) *n.* without permission [leave; notice]: *Kakari ni mudañ de hoñ o mochidasanai de kudasai.* (係に無断で本を持ち出さないでください) Please do not take out books *without asking* the person in charge. / *Kanojo wa mudañ de gakkoo o yasuñda.* (彼女は無断で学校を休んだ) She was absent from school *without notice.* / mudañ-*gaihaku* (無断外泊) staying out at night *without permission* / mudañ-*kesseki* (無断欠席) an *unauthorized* absence.

mu「dazu¹kai むだづかい (無駄遣い) *n.* waste; wasting: *Sore wa zeekiñ no mudazukai da.* (それは税金のむだづかいだ) That is a *waste* of tax money. / *O-kane no mudazukai wa yame nasai.* (お金のむだづかいはやめなさい) Stop *wasting* money.
mudazukai suru (〜する) *vt.* waste: *Kañgaete miru to, wareware wa shigeñ o daibu mudazukai shite iru.* (考えてみると、われわれは資源をだいぶむだづかいしている) When you stop to think about it, you realize that we *are* greatly *wasting* resources.

mu¹eki むえき (無益) *a.n.* (〜 na, ni) useless; futile: *Soñna* mueki *na arasoi wa yameta hoo ga ii.* (そんな無益な争いはやめたほうがいい) You had better put an end to such a *useless* controversy. 《↔ yuueki》

mu¹gai むがい (無害) *a.n.* (〜 na, ni) harmless; innocuous: mugai *na teñkabutsu* (無害な添加物) a *harmless* additive / *Kono satchuuzai wa jiñtai ni* mugai *desu.* (この殺虫剤は人体に無害です) This

insecticide is *harmless* to people. 《↔ yuugai》

mu「geñ むげん (無限) *n.* boundless; limitless: mugeñ *no yorokobi* (無限の喜び) *boundless* joy / mugeñ *no kanoosee* (無限の可能性) *limitless* potential.
— *a.n.* (〜 na, ni) infinite; boundless; limitless: *Uchuu wa* mugeñ *da to iu no wa hoñtoo desu ka?* (宇宙は無限だというのは本当ですか) Is it true that the universe is *infinite?* / *Teñneñshigeñ wa* mugeñ *ni aru mono de wa nai.* (天然資源は無限にあるものではない) Natural resources do not exist *without limit.*

mu¹gi むぎ (麦) *n.* wheat; barley; oats: mugi-*wara* (麦わら) *straw* / mugi-*wara booshi* (麦わら帽子) a *straw* hat.

	karasumugi	oats
mugi	komugi	wheat
	oomugi	barley
	raimugi	rye

mu「goñ むごん (無言) *n.* silence; muteness: *Kare wa* mugoñ *de [no mama] heya kara dete itta.* (彼は無言で[のまま]部屋から出て行った) He went out of the room *without a word.* / mugoñ *no teekoo* (無言の抵抗) a *silent* protest.

mu¹hoñ むほん (謀反) *n.* rebellion: muhoñ *o okosu* (謀反を起こす) *rebel.*

mu「ika むいか (六日) *n.* six days; the sixth day of the month: *Kyuuka de* muika-*kañ Karuizawa ni imashita.* (休暇で六日間軽井沢にいました) I spent *six days* on holiday in Karuizawa. / *sañgatsu* muika (三月六日) March *6.* 《⇨ tsuitachi (table)》

mu⌈i⌉mi むいみ (無意味) *a.n.*
(～ na, ni) meaningless; sense-less:
Ima ni natte, soñna koto o shite mo muimi *desu.* (今になって, そんなことをしても無意味です) At this stage, it would be *meaningless* to do that. / *Koñna* muimi *na giroñ wa yame ni shiyoo.* (こんな無意味な議論はやめにしよう) Let us stop this kind of *senseless* discussion. / *Kare wa* muimi *ni nagai setsumee o shita.* (彼は無意味に長い説明をした) He made a *meaninglessly* long explanation.

mu⌉jaki むじゃき (無邪気) *a.n.*
(～ na, ni) innocent; childlike:
Kodomo wa mujaki *da.* (子どもは無邪気だ) Children are *without guile.* / *Kare wa* mujaki *na kao o shite iru.* (彼は無邪気な顔をしている) He has an *innocent, childlike* expression. / *Kanojo wa* mujaki *ni waratta.* (彼女は無邪気に笑った) She laughed *artlessly.*

mu⌉ji むじ (無地) *n.* plain; having no pattern or design:
muji *no kire* (無地のきれ) *plain* cloth.

mu⌈jiñ むじん (無人) *n.* vacant; uninhabited:
mujiñ-*fumikiri* (無人踏切) an *un-attended* railroad crossing / mu-jiñ-*roketto* (無人ロケット) an *un-manned* rocket / mujiñ-*too* (無人島) an *uninhabited* island.

mu⌈juñ むじゅん (矛盾) *n.* contra-diction; inconsistency; incom-patibility:
Anata no itte iru koto ni wa mujuñ *ga aru.* (あなたの言っていることには矛盾がある) There is an *inconsistency* in what you say.
mujuñ suru (～する) *vi.* contra-dict; be inconsistent; be incom-patible: *Kare wa iu koto to yaru koto ga* mujuñ *shite iru.* (彼は言うこととやることが矛盾している) His ac-tions *contradict* his words.

mu⌈kae むかえ (迎え) *n.* person sent to meet one; meeting:
Eki ni mukae *ga kite ita.* (駅に迎えが来ていた) *Someone* was at the sta-tion *to meet* us. / *O-mukae no kuruma ga kimashita.* (お迎えの車が来ました) *The car they sent* has ar-rived. (⇨ mukaeru)

mu⌈kae·ru むかえる (迎える) *vt.*
(mukae-te Ⓥ) **1** meet; come to meet; welcome; receive:
Watashi-tachi wa kare o eki de mukaemashita. (私たちは彼を駅で迎えました) We *met* him at the sta-tion. / *Kare wa o-kyaku hitori hitori o akushu shite,* mukaeta. (彼はお客一人一人を握手して, 迎えた) One by one, he shook hands with the guests and *welcomed* them. (⇨ mukae)

2 invite:
Koñbañ no paatii ni wa Chuugoku no kata o futari mukaemasu. (今晩のパーティーには中国の方を二人迎えます) We *have invited* two Chinese people to the party this evening.

3 greet (a new year); see (one's birthday); attain:
Ato hito-tsuki de mata shiñneñ o mukaemasu. (あと一月でまた新年を迎えます) In one month, we *greet* the New Year once more. / *Chichi wa raigetsu nanajus-sai no tañ-joobi o* mukaemasu. (父は来月70歳の誕生日を迎えます) My father *will see* his seventieth birthday come round next month.

mu⌈kai むかい (向かい) *n.* opposite side [place]:
Mukai *no uchi ni wa yuumee na sakka ga suñde imasu.* (向かいの家には有名な作家が住んでいます) In the house *opposite*, a famous novelist lives. / *Gakkoo no* mukai *ni hoñya ga arimasu.* (学校の向かいに本屋があります) There is a bookstore *across* from the school. (⇨ mukau)

mu「ka¹ñkee むかんけい（無関係）
a.n. (～ na, ni) unrelated; irrelevant:
Watashi wa koñdo no jikeñ to wa
mukañkee *desu.*（私は今度の事件とは
無関係です）I *have nothing to do*
with this affair. / *Kono* moñdai to
mukañkee *na go-shitsumoñ ni wa
o-kotae shikanemasu.*（この問題と無
関係なご質問にはお答えしかねます）I
am not in a position to answer
questions *unrelated* to this subject. / *Hanashi wa gidai to wa*
mukañkee *ni susuñda.*（話は議題と
は無関係に進んだ）The talk continued in a manner *unrelated* to
the topic of discussion.

mu「kashi むかし（昔）*n.* the past;
old days; ancient times:
mukashi *no yuujiñ*（昔の友人）a
friend from the *old days* / mukashi *kara no chijiñ*（昔からの知人）an
acquaintance one has known for
a long time / *Watashi-tachi wa*
mukashi *no koto o hanashiatta.*（私
たちは昔のことを話し合った）We
talked about the *old days*. / *Kono
mura wa* mukashi no mama *da.*
（この村は昔のままだ）This village remains *just as it used to be*. / *Mukashi koko ni kita koto ga arimasu.*
（昔ここに来たことがあります）I came
here *a long time ago*. （↔ ima¹）

mu「kashi-ba¹nashi むかしばなし
（昔話）*n.* old tale [story].

mu「kashi-mukashi むかしむかし
（昔々）*n.* once upon a time:
★ Used as the beginning of a
tale.
Mukashi-mukashi *aru tokoro ni o-
jiisañ to o-baasañ ga suñde imashita.*（昔々ある所におじいさんとおばあさ
んが住んでいました）*Once upon a time*
in a certain place, there lived an
old man and his wife.

mu「ka·u むかう（向かう）*vi.* (muka-
i-; mukaw·a-; mukat-te C)
1 face; front:
kagami ni mukau（鏡に向かう）*look*
in a mirror / *tsukue ni* mukau（机
に向かう）*sit* at one's desk / Mukatte *migi ni mieru no ga shiyakusho desu.*（向かって右に見えるのが市役
所です）The building *you can see*
on the right is the town hall.
（⇨ mukai）
2 head; leave for...:
*Hikooki wa Tookyoo kara Oosaka
e* mukatta.（飛行機は東京から大阪へ
向かった）The airplane *set course*
from Tokyo for Osaka. / *Taifuu
wa Kyuushuu ni* mukatte imasu.
（台風は九州に向かっています）The
typhoon *is heading* for Kyushu.
3 against; to:
Señsee ni mukatte, *soñna koto o
itte wa ikemaseñ.*（先生に向かって、
そんなことを言ってはいけません）You
must not say that kind of thing
directly *to* your teacher.

-muke むけ（向け）*suf.* for:
*Amerika-*muke *no kuruma*（アメリカ
向けの車）cars *for* America / *ko-
domo-*muke *no bañgumi*（子ども向
けの番組）a program *for* children.
（⇨ muki）

mu「ke·ru むける（向ける）*vt.* (mu-
ke-te Ⅴ) **1** turn; direct:
Kare wa kanojo no hoo ni me o
muketa.（彼は彼女のほうに目を向けた）
He *turned* his eyes toward her. /
*Watashi-tachi wa umi no hoo ni
ashi o* muketa.（私たちは海のほうに足
を向けた）We *turned out* steps in
the direction of the sea.
（⇨ muku¹）
2 aim; point:
Gootoo wa keekañ ni juu o
muketa.（強盗は警官に銃を向けた）
The robber *aimed* his pistol at
the policeman.

mu¹ki むき（向き）*n.* **1** way; direction:
Kaze no muki *ga kawatta.*（風の向
きが変わった）The *direction* of the
wind has changed. / *Watashi no*

heya wa minami-muki *desu.* (私の部屋は南向きです) My room *faces* south. 《⇨ muku¹》

2 suitable; suited:
Kono fuku wa wakai hito muki *desu.* (この服は若い人向きです) These clothes are *suitable* for young people. / *Kare wa shoobai-niñ* muki *da.* (彼は商売人向きだ) He is *suited* to being a tradesman. 《⇨ muku¹》

muˈko むこ (婿) *n.* **1** bridegroom:
muko ni iku (婿に行く) *marry into a woman's family* and take her family name. 《↔ yome》

2 son-in-law.

muˈkoo¹ むこう (向こう) *n.* **1** the other [opposite] side; over there:
Mukoo *ni aru no ga Suzuki-sañ no ie desu.* (向こうにあるのが鈴木さんの家です) The house *over there* is Mr. Suzuki's. / *Yuubiñ-posuto wa to-ori no* mukoo(gawa) *desu.* (郵便ポストは通りの向こう(側)です) The post box is on *the other side* of the street. 《↔ kochira》

2 (used to refer to the third person) the other party; he; she; they:
Warui no wa mukoo *da.* (悪いのは向こうだ) It is *they* who are in the wrong. / Mukoo *no iu koto mo kiite miyoo.* (向こうの言うことも聞いてみよう) Let's listen to what *they* say. 《↔ kochira》

3 destination:
Mukoo *ni tsuitara, o-shirase shimasu.* (向こうに着いたら、お知らせします) I will let you know when I reach my *destination.*

4 the near future; the coming period of time:
Mukoo *ichi-neñkañ no keekaku wa mada tatte imaseñ.* (向こう一年間の計画はまだ立っていません) The plans for the *coming* year have not been made yet. / Mukoo *is-*

shuukañ kyuugyoo shimasu. (向こう一週間休業します) We will be closed for business for the *next* week.

muˈkoo² むこう (無効) *a.n.* (~ na) invalid; no good; void:
Kono keñ wa mukoo *desu.* (この券は無効です) This ticket is *invalid.* / *Sono keeyaku wa kigeñ ga kireta no de,* mukoo *desu.* (その契約は期限が切れたので、無効です) That contract is *null and void* since it has expired. 《↔ yuukoo》

muˈkoozune むこうずね (向こう脛) *n.* shin. 《⇨ jiñtai (illus.)》

muˈkˑu¹ むく (向く) *vi.* (mukˑi-; mukˑa-; muˑiˑte C) **1** turn; look:
ushiro o muku (後ろを向く) *look back* / *migi o* muku (右を向く) *look to the right.* 《⇨ mukeru》

2 face:
Watashi no heya wa nishi ni mui-te imasu. (私の部屋は西に向いています) My room *faces* west. 《⇨ mukeru; muki》

3 be fit; be suitable; suit:
Kono shigoto wa kanojo ni muite iru. (この仕事は彼女に向いている) This work *suits* her. / *Kanojo wa kono shigoto ni* muite iru. (彼女はこの仕事に向いている She *is suited* to this work. 《⇨ muki》

muˈkˑu² むく (剥く) *vt.* (mukˑi-; mukˑa-; muˑiˑte C) peel; pare:
banana no kawa o muku (バナナの皮をむく) *peel* a banana / *riñgo no kawa o* muku (りんごの皮をむく) *pare* an apple.

muˈkuchi むくち (無口) *a.n.* (~ na) taciturn; reticent:
Kare wa mukuchi *desu.* (彼は無口です) He *does not talk much.* / *Watashi wa* mukuchi *na hito ga suki da.* (私は無口な人が好きだ) I like *reticent* people. 《⇨ kuchi¹》

muˈmee むめい (無名) *n.* nameless; unknown:

mumee no *sakka* (無名の作家) an *obscure* writer / *Kanojo wa* mumee *da ga e no sainoo ga aru.* (彼女は無名だが絵の才能がある) She is *unknown to the world*, but she has a talent for painting. 《↔ yuumee》

mu⌈nashi⌉·i むなしい (空しい) *a.* (-ku) fruitless; futile; empty: munashii *doryoku* (むなしい努力) *futile* efforts / *Jiñsee wa* munashii *to omou hito mo imasu.* (人生はむなしいと思う人もいます) There are those who think life is *without meaning*. / *Natsu-yasumi o* munashiku *sugoshite shimatta.* (夏休みをむなしく過ごしてしまった) I ended up *idling away* the summer holidays. 《⇨ muda》

mu⌈ne⌉ むね (胸) *n.* **1** chest; breast; bust: mune *o haru* (胸を張る) *throw* one's chest *out* / mune *no poketto* (胸のポケット) a *breast* pocket.
2 heart: *Mada* mune *ga dokidoki shite iru.* (まだ胸がどきどきしている) My *heart* is still pounding.

mune ga fukuramu (～がふくらむ) be full of: *Watashi wa kiboo ni* mune ga fukurañda. (私は希望に胸がふくらんだ) I *was full of* expectations.

mune ga ippai ni naru (～がいっぱいになる) one's heart is full of (emotion): *Kañgeki de* mune ga ippai ni natta. (感激で胸がいっぱいになった) *My heart was overflowing* with emotion.

mune ga itamu (～が痛む) pain one's heart: *Kare no jiko no koto o omou to* mune ga itamu. (彼の事故のことを思うと胸が痛む) *My heart aches* to think of his accident.

mune o utareru (～を打たれる) be impressed: *Kanojo no sakuhiñ ni* mune o utareta. (彼女の作品に胸を打たれた) I *was impressed* by her artistic work.

mu⌈noo⌉ むのう (無能) *a.n.* (～ na) incompetent; incapable: munoo *na niñgeñ* (無能な人間) a *useless* person / *Kare wa seejika to shite* munoo *da.* (彼は政治家として無能だ) He is *incompetent* as a politician. 《↔ yuunoo》

mura むら (村) *n.* village: mura-*yakuba* (村役場) a *village* office. 《⇨ machi (table)》

-mu⌈ra⌉ むら (村) *suf.* village: ★ An administrative division within a '*guñ.*' *Ogawa*-mura (小川村) Ogawa *Village.* 《⇨ -machi (table)》

mu⌈ra⌉saki むらさき (紫) *n.* purple; violet.

mu⌈re⌉ むれ (群れ) *n.* group; crowd: mure o nasu (群れをなす) *flock [group] together* / *hitsuji no* mure (羊の群れ) a *flock* of sheep / *ushi no* mure (牛の群れ) a *herd* of cattle / *mitsubachi no* mure (蜜蜂の群れ) a *swarm* of bees / *iwashi no* mure (いわしの群れ) a *shoal* of sardines.

mu⌈ri むり (無理) *n.* unreasonable; unjust: muri o toosu (無理を通す) *get one's own way* / *Amari* muri *o iwanai de kudasai.* (あまり無理を言わないでください) Do not be so *unreasonable.* / *Kare ga soo iu no mo* muri wa arimaseñ. (彼がそう言うのも無理はありません) *It is natural* that he says so.

muri (o) suru (～(を)する) *vi.* overwork; strain oneself: *Amari* muri *o shinai yoo ni shite imasu.* (あまり無理をしないようにしています) I take care *not to overwork.* / *Kaze o hiite imasu ga,* muri shite *dete kimashita.* (かぜをひいていますが、無理して出て来ました) Although I have a cold, I *forced myself* to come here.
— *a.n.* (～ na, ni) impossible; unreasonable; unjust:

Sonna koto wa totemo muri *desu.*
(そんなことはとても無理です) It is absolutely *impossible* for me to do such
a thing. / *Sore wa* muri *na chuu-
mon desu.* (それは無理な注文です)
That is an *unreasonable* request.
/ *Watashi wa* muri *ni soko e ika-
sareta.* (私は無理にそこへ行かされた) I
was sent there *against my wishes.*

mu⌐ri⌐kai むりかい (無理解) *n., a.n.*
(~ na) lack of understanding
[sympathy]:
tsuma no shumi ni murikai *na otto*
(妻の趣味に無理解な夫) a husband
who *does not understand* his
wife's interests / *Kanojo wa chichi-oya no* murikai *ni nayande iru.*
(彼女は父親の無理解に悩んでいる)
She is distressed by her father's
lack of understanding. 《↔ rikai》

mu⌐ri-shi⌐njuu むりしんじゅう (無
理心中) *n.* forced double suicide.
《⇨ shinjuu》

Mu⌐romachi-ji⌐dai むろまちじだい
(室町時代) *n.* Muromachi Period
(1336 to 1573). 《⇨ jidai (table)》

mu⌐ron むろん (無論) *adv.* = mo-
chiron.

mu⌐ryoku むりょく (無力) *a.n.*
(~ na/no) powerless; helpless;
incompetent:
Ningen wa shizen ni taishite muryoku *da.* (人間は自然に対して無力だ)
Human beings are *powerless*
before nature. / *Kare ni tasuke o
motometa ga, kare wa kekkyoku*
muryoku *da to wakatta.* (彼に助けを
求めたが、彼は結局無力だとわかった)
We asked for his help, but he
turned out to be *incompetent.*
《↔ yuuryoku》

mu⌐ryoo むりょう (無料) *n.* no
charge; free:
Sooryoo wa muryoo *desu.* (送料は
無料です) The postage is *free.* /
Eki no chikaku ni muryoo *no chuushajoo ga arimasu.* (駅の近くに無料
の駐車場があります) There is *free*

parking space near the station. /
Nyuujoo muryoo (*sign*) (入場無料)
Admission *Free.* 《↔ yuuryoo》

mu⌐sen むせん (無線) *n.* radio;
wireless:
tsuushin o musen *de okuru* (通信を
無線で送る) send a message by
radio / musen-*renraku* (無線連絡)
radio communications / musen-
soojuu (無線操縦) *radio* control.

mu⌐shi[1] むし (虫) *n.* insect; bug;
worm; vermin:
mushi *ni sasareru* (虫に刺される) be
stung by an *insect* / *Kono ringo
wa* mushi *ga kutte iru.* (このりんごは
虫が食っている) There is a *worm* in
this apple. / *Niwa de* mushi *ga
naite iru.* (庭で虫が鳴いている) *Insects*
are chirping in the yard.

mushi ga [no] sukanai (~ が[の]
好かない) don't like: *Ano hito wa*
mushi *ga sukanai.* (あの人は虫が好か
ない) I *don't like* him.

mushi ga [no] yoi (~ が[の]よい)
be selfish: *Sore wa* mushi *ga yo-
sugiru.* (それは虫がよすぎる) That is
too selfish of you.

mushi mo korosanai (~ も殺さな
い) be incapable of hurting a fly:
Kare wa mushi *mo korosanai yoo
na kao o shite iru ga zankoku da.*
(彼は虫も殺さないような顔をしているが残
酷だ) He looks as if he *would not
hurt a fly*, but he is cruel.

mu⌐shi[2] むし (無視) *n.* disregard;
neglect:
shingoo mushi (信号無視) *ignoring*
traffic lights.

mushi suru (~ する) *vt.* ignore;
disregard: *Kare wa isha no chuukoku o* mushi *shita.* (彼は医者の忠
告を無視した) He *took no notice* of
his doctor's warning. / *Watashi
no hatsugen wa* mushi *sareta.* (私
の発言は無視された) My comment
was ignored.

mu⌐shiatsu⌐i むしあつい (蒸し暑い)
a. (-ku) sultry; hot and humid:

Kyoo wa mushiatsui. (きょうは蒸し暑い) It is very *sultry* today. / *Oosaka no natsu wa* mushiatsui. (大阪の夏は蒸し暑い) Summer in Osaka is *hot and humid*. 《⇨ musu》

mu⌈shiba むしば (虫歯) *n.* decayed [bad] tooth; cavity; caries.

mu⌈shiro むしろ (寧ろ) *adv.* rather (than):
Kono uñdoo [geemu] wa wakamono-muki to iu yori, mushiro *chuukooneñ-muki da.* (この運動[ゲーム]は若者向きというより, むしろ中高年向きだ) This exercise [game] is suitable for the middle-aged and the elderly, *rather* than for young people. / *Kare wa shoosetsuka to iu yori,* mushiro *shijiñ desu.* (彼は小説家というより, むしろ詩人です) He is *more* of a poet than a novelist.

mu⌈shir·u むしる *vt.* (mushir·i-; mushir·a-; mushit-te [C]) pull up; pluck:
niwatori no ke o mushiru (鶏の毛をむしる) *pluck* a chicken's feathers / *kusa o* mushiru (草をむしる) *pull up* weeds.

mu⌉s·u むす (蒸す) (mush·i-; mus·a-; mush·i-te [C]) **1** *vt.* steam:
Kanojo wa jagaimo o mushita. (彼女はじゃがいもを蒸した) She *steamed* the potatoes.
2 *vi.* (of weather, place, etc.) be sultry; be stuffy:
Yuube wa mushita. (ゆうべは蒸した) It *was sultry* yesterday evening. / *Kono heya wa* mushite iru. (この部屋は蒸している) This room *is stuffy*.

mu⌈subi むすび (結び) *n.* **1** end; finish; conclusion:
musubi *no ichibañ* (結びの一番) the *last [final]* bout / *Kare ni* musubi *no kotoba o tanoñda.* (彼に結びの言葉を頼んだ) We asked him to make some *closing* remarks. 《⇨ musubu》

2 rice ball: ★ Usually with '*o-.*'
musubi *o nigiru* (むすびを握る) make a *rice ball*. 《⇨ onigiri (illus.)》

mu⌈subitsuke⌉·ru むすびつける (結び付ける) *vt.* (-tsuke-te [V])
1 tie; fasten:
Kare wa inu no kusari o ki ni musubitsuketa. (彼は犬の鎖を木に結び付けた) He *fastened* the dog's chain to a tree.
2 link; relate:
Sono futatsu no hañzai o musubitsukeru *shooko wa nani mo nai.* (その二つの犯罪を結び付ける証拠は何もない) There is no evidence at all that *links* the two crimes.

mu⌈sub·u むすぶ (結ぶ) *vt.* (musub·i-; musub·a-; musuñ-de [C])
1 tie; knot:
himo o musubu (ひもを結ぶ) *knot* a piece of string / *riboñ o* musubu (リボンを結ぶ) *tie* a ribbon / *nekutai o* musubu (ネクタイを結ぶ) *put on* a tie. 《⇨ musubi》
2 link; connect:
Hoñshuu to Shikoku o musubu *hashi ga kañsee shita.* (本州と四国を結ぶ橋が完成した) The bridges which *link* Honshu and Shikoku have been completed. 《⇨ musubitsukeru》
3 (*fig.*) bind:
Kare-ra wa yuujoo de musubarete *ita.* (彼らは友情で結ばれていた) They *were bound* together by their friendship.
4 conclude (a treaty, contract); form (an alliance):
jooyaku o musubu (条約を結ぶ) *conclude* a treaty / *doomee o* musubu (同盟を結ぶ) *form* an alliance / *keeyaku o* musubu (契約を結ぶ) *make* a contract / *Kare-ra wa wareware to te o* musuboo *to kiboo shite iru.* (彼らはわれわれと手を結ぼうと希望している) They want to *join hands* with us.

mu⌈suko むすこ (息子) *n.* son:

Kare wa hitori-musuko desu. (彼は
ひとり息子です) He is the only *son*. /
Musuko-*sañ wa o-geñki desu ka?*
(息子さんはお元気ですか) How is
your *son?* ★ Another person's
son is called '*musuko-sañ.*'
《↔ musume》《⇨ kazoku (table)》

mu⌐sume¹ むすめ (娘) *n.*
1 daughter:
Musume *wa futari desu.* (娘は二人
です) I have two *daughters.* / Mu-
sume-*sañ wa o-ikutsu desu ka?*
(娘さんはおいくつですか) How old is
your *daughter?* ★ Another person's daughter is called '*musume-sañ.*' 《↔ musuko》《⇨ kazoku
(table)》
2 unmarried young woman;
girl:
Ano musume-*sañ wa dare desu
ka?* (あの娘さんはだれですか) Who is
that *girl?*

musu⌐u むすう (無数) *a.n.* (~ ni)
countless; numberless:
Hoshi no kazu wa musuu *desu.* (星
の数は無数です) The stars are *numberless.* / *Taiheeyoo ni wa shima
ga* musuu *ni arimasu.* (太平洋には島
が無数にあります) There are *innu-
merable* islands in the Pacific
Ocean.

mu⌐ttsu むっつ (六つ) *n.* six:
★ Used when counting.
Machigai o muttsu *mitsukemashita.* (間違いを6つ見つけました) I
have found *six* mistakes. / mut-
tsu-me (六つ目) *the sixth.*
《⇨ roku; kazu (table)》

mu⌐udo ムード *n.* atmosphere:
★ From English 'mood,' but not
used in the sense of 'bad temper.'
muudo *no aru resutorañ* (ムードのあ
るレストラン) a restaurant with a
pleasant ambience / *Kai no* muudo
wa nagoyaka datta. (会のムードは和
やかだった) The *atmosphere* of the
meeting was friendly.

mu⌐yami むやみ (無闇) *a.n.* (~ na,

ni) **1** reckless; excessive:
muyami *na home-kotoba* (むやみな褒
め言葉) *excessive* praise / Muyami
*ni uñdoo suru no wa karada ni
yoku nai.* (むやみに運動するのは体によ
くない) Exercising *excessively* is
not good for you.
2 indiscriminate:
Muyami *ni kodomo o shikaranai
hoo ga yoi.* (むやみに子どもをしからない
ほうがよい) You should not *indiscriminately* scold children.

mu⌐yoku むよく (無欲) *a.n.* (~ na,
ni) disinterested; unselfish:
muyoku *no shoori* (無欲の勝利) an
unsolicited victory / *Kare wa kanemooke ni taishite wa* muyoku
desu. (彼は金もうけにたいしては無欲で
す) He is *indifferent* to making
money. 《↔ yokubari》

mu⌐yoo むよう (無用) *a.n.* (~ na,
ni) unnecessary; useless:
Shiñpai wa muyoo *desu.* (心配は無
用です) There is *no need* to worry.
/ Muyoo *na mono wa motte konai
koto.* (無用なものは持って来ないこと)
Do not bring *unnecessary* articles
with you.

mu⌐zukashi·i むずかしい (難しい) *a.*
(-ku) **1** hard; difficult:
muzukashii *hoñ* (難しい本) a *difficult* book / muzukashii *shitsumoñ*
(難しい質問) a *hard* question /
Kyoo no tesuto wa muzukashikatta. (きょうのテストは難しかった)
Today's test *was difficult.*
《↔ yasashii¹》
2 (of a procedure, a situation,
etc.) troublesome; complicated:
★ Often used as a euphemism
for the impossible.
muzukashii *kyokumeñ ni tatasa-
reru* (難しい局面に立たされる) be put
in a *troublesome* situation / *Yushutsu no tetsuzuki wa* muzukashiku *arimaseñ.* (輸出の手続きは難し
くありません) The export proce-
dures are not *complicated.* / *Sono*

koto wa amari muzukashiku *kañgaenai hoo ga ii desu yo.* (そのことはあまり難しく考えないほうがいいですよ) You had better not think about the matter too *seriously.*
3 (of character, personality, etc.) difficult to please; particular: *Kanojo no chichi-oya wa* muzukashii *hito desu.* (彼女の父親は難しい人です) Her father is *hard* to please. / *Kesa no kachoo wa* muzukashii *kao o shite iru.* (今朝の課長は難しい顔をしている) The boss this morning has a *glum* expression.

mya「ku」 みゃく(脈) *n.* pulse: myaku *o toru* (脈をとる) take one's *pulse* / *Kimi no* myaku *wa sukoshi haya[oso]sugiru.* (君の脈は少し速[遅]すぎる) Your *pulse* is a little too fast [slow].
myaku ga aru (〜がある) be hopeful: *Kare no hanashi de wa mada* myaku ga ari-soo da. (彼の話ではまだ脈がありそうだ) According to him, there still *seems to be some hope.*

Mya「ñmaa」 ミャンマー *n.* Myanmar. ★ New name of the Union of Burma.

myo「o」 みょう(妙) *a.n.* (〜 na, ni) strange; queer; funny; odd: *Ima* myoo *na oto ga shita.* (今妙な音がした) I just heard a *strange* noise. / *Kodomo-tachi wa kyoo wa* myoo *ni otonashii.* (子どもたちはきょうは妙におとなしい) The children are *strangely* well-behaved today. / *Kare ga mada konai no wa* myoo *da.* (彼がまだ来ないのは妙だ) It is *odd* that he has not come yet.

myo「oban」 みょうばん(明晩) *n.* (*formal*) tomorrow evening; tomorrow night: *Shuppatsu wa* myoobañ *desu.* (出発は明晩です) I am departing *tomorrow evening.* 《⇨ bañ¹ (table)》

myo「ochoo」 みょうちょう(明朝) *n., adv.* (*formal*) tomorrow morning: Myoochoo *ku-ji ni o-ukagai shimasu.* (明朝9時にお伺いします) I will call on you at nine *tomorrow morning.* 《↔ kesa》

myo「ogo」nichi みょうごにち(明後日) *n.* the day after tomorrow. ★ Formal equivalent of '*asatte.*' 《⇨ kyoo (table)》

myo「oji」 みょうじ(名字) *n.* family name; surname. 《⇨ namae》

┌─ **CULTURE** ─┐
In Japan the family name is placed before the given name. In '*Yoshida Shigeru*,' '*Yoshida*' is the family name and '*Shigeru*' the given name. The Imperial Family have no family names. 《⇨ see³》
└────────────┘

THE TEN MOST COMMON JAPANESE
FAMILY NAMES

1	Satoo (佐藤)	6	Itoo (伊藤)
2	Suzuki (鈴木)	7	Yamamoto (山本)
3	Takahashi (高橋)	8	Kobayashi (小林)
4	Tanaka (田中)	9	Saitoo (斎藤)
5	Watanabe (渡辺)	10	Nakamura (中村)

myo「onichi みょうにち(明日) *n.* tomorrow. ★ Formal equivalent of '*ashita.*' 《⇨ kyoo (table)》

N

na¹ な(名) *n.* **1** name; title:
Kono hana no na *o shitte imasu ka?* (この花の名を知っていますか) Do you know the *name* of this flower? 《⇨ namae》
2 fame; reputation:
Kare wa Nihoñ de wa na *ga shirarete iru.* (彼は日本では名が知られている) He is *well-known* in Japan.
na bakari no (〜ばかりの) in name only: *Watashi wa* na bakari no *kaiiñ desu.* (私は名ばかりの会員です) I am a member of the club *in name only.*
na mo nai (〜もない) nameless; obscure: Na mo nai *sakka ga sono shoo o totta.* (名もない作家がその賞を取った) An *obscure* novelist won the prize.
na o uru (〜を売る) make oneself well known: *Dono seejika mo jibuñ no na o uritagatte iru.* (どの政治家も自分の名を売りたがっている) Every politician *wants to make himself well known.*
...no na ni hajinai (...の〜に恥じない) be worthy of: *Kare no tsuyosa wa chañpioñ no* na ni hajinai. (彼の強さはチャンピオンの名に恥じない) His superior power *is worthy of* a champion. 《⇨ hajiru》

na² な *p.* (*rude*) do not (do):
★ Used to indicate prohibition or to give a negative order. Used usually by men.
Soñna abunai koto wa suru na. (そんな危ないことはするな) *Do not do* such a dangerous thing. / *Yakusoku wa* wasureru na. (約束は忘れるな) *Do not forget* the appointment. / *Shibafu ni* hairu na. (芝生に入るな) *Do not walk* on the grass.

na³ な *p.* (*rude*) (used to give an order): ★ An abbreviation of '(*shi*) *nasai.*'
Motto hayaku aruki na. (もっと速く歩きな) *Walk* faster. / *Hitori de* yari na. (一人でやりな) *Do it* by yourself.

na(a) な(あ) *p.* **1** (used to indicate emotion):
Ii teñki da na. (いい天気だな) *What* nice weather it is! / *Yukkuri yasumitai* na. (ゆっくり休みたいな) *I wish* I could just relax. / *O-kane ga takusañ attara* naa. (お金がたくさんあったらなあ) *If only* I had lots of money. / *Komatta* na. (困った) *Oh dear,* I am in a fix.
2 (used when seeking agreement): ★ Used mainly by men.
Ashita wa atsui deshoo na. (あしたは暑いでしょうな) It will be hot tomorrow, *won't it?* / *Kore wa nañ desu ka* na? (これは何ですかな) *I wonder* what this could be.

na⌐be なべ (鍋) *n.* pan; pot:
nabe *o hi ni kakeru* (なべを火にかける) put a *pan* over the fire / nabe-mono (*ryoori*) (なべ物(料理)) a dish cooked in a *large pot,* often at the table.

na⌐bi⌐k·u なびく (靡く) *vi.* (nabik·i-; nabik·a-; nabi·i-te Ⓒ) flutter; wave; stream:
Hata ga kaze ni nabiite iru. (旗が風になびいている) The flag *is fluttering* in the breeze. / *Ine no ho ga kaze ni* nabiite iru. (稲の穂が風になびいている) The rice ears *are swaying* in the wind.

Na⌐da なだ (灘) *n.* the area located east of Kobe, Hyogo Prefecture. Famous for the Japanese rice wine brewed in this area.

na⌐daka⌐·i なだかい (名高い) *a.*

(**-ku**) famous; well-known; noted:

sekai-teki ni nadakai *gakusha* (世界的に名高い学者) a world-*famous* scholar / *Kono chiiki wa orimono no sañchi to shite* nadakai. (この地域は織物の産地として名高い) This area is *well-known* as a textile-producing region. 《⇨ yuumee》

na「dare」 なだれ (雪崩) *n.* snowslide; avalanche.

na「de」・ru なでる (撫でる) *vt.* (na-de-te V) stroke; pat; pet:
kodomo no atama o naderu (子どもの頭をなでる) *stroke* a child's head / *neko o* naderu (猫をなでる) *pet* a cat.

na「do など (等) *p.* 1 such as; and the like: ★ Used to give examples.

(**USAGE**)

Follows nouns, usually in the pattern 'ya...(ya)...nado.' '*Nañka*' is the informal variant, and a little brusque.

Nihoñ no tabemono de wa teñpura ya sushi nado *ga suki desu.* (日本の食べ物ではてんぷらや寿司などが好きです) When it comes to Japanese food, I am fond of tempura, sushi, *and the like.* / *Kono machi ni wa jiñja ya tera* nado *furui tatemono ga takusañ arimasu.* (この町には神社や寺など古い建物がたくさんあります) In this town there are lots of old buildings, *such as* temples and shrines.

2 or whatever: ★ Used when giving one representative example.
Sono heñ de biiru nado *ip-pai ikaga desu ka?* (その辺でビールなど一杯いかがですか) What about a beer, *or whatever*, over there?

3 (used to express humility when referring to oneself, one's relatives, or one's possessions):
Watashi nado *ni wa soñna muzu-*

kashii koto wa totemo dekimaseñ. (私などにはそんな難しいことはとてもできません) Someone *the likes of* me cannot possibly do such a difficult thing. / *Watashi no koto* nado *doozo o-kamai naku.* (私のことなどどうぞおかまいなく) Please don't worry yourself *about me.*

4 (used in expressions of negation, disavowal, or scorn): ★ Follows a noun, or a verb in the *te*-form. 《⇨ nañte²》
Rokku nado *yakamashikute kirai desu.* (ロックなどやかましくて嫌いです) I dislike music *such as* rock, because it is so noisy. / *Ore wa aitsu* nado *ni hanashitaku nai.* (おれはあいつなどに話したくない) I do not want to talk to *the likes of* him. / *Kimi ni tetsudatte* nado *hoshiku nai.* (君に手伝ってなどほしくない) I do not need help, *or anything else*, from you. / *Koñna tsumaranai koto de keñka* nado *yoshi nasai.* (こんなつまらないことでけんかなどよしなさい) Don't argue about *something* that is as unimportant as this.

5 (used to add emphasis):
Kare wa uso nado *tsuku yoo na hito de wa arimaseñ.* (彼はうそなどつくような人ではありません) He is not the kind of person that would do *something like* tell a lie.

na「e」 なえ (苗) *n.* seedling; young plant:
nae *o ueru* (苗を植える) plant a *seedling.*

na「fuda なふだ (名札) *n.* name tag; nameplate:
Miñna uwagi ni nafuda *o tsukete ita.* (みんな上着に名札をつけていた) Everyone had a *name tag* on his or her coat.

na「ga- なが (長) *pref.* long; many:
naga-*ame* (長雨) a *long* rain / naga-*banashi* (長話) a *long* talk / naga-*neñ* (長年) *many* years.

na⌐gabi⌐k·u ながびく（長引く）*vi.*
(-bik·i-; -bik·a-; -bi·i-te Ⓒ) be
prolonged; drag on:
Sono kaigi wa nagabiita.（その会議
は長引いた）The meeting *dragged
on.* / *Kare no kaze wa* nagabiite
imasu.（彼のかぜは長引いています）It *is
taking* him *a long time* to get
over his cold.

na⌐gagutsu ながぐつ（長靴）*n.*
boots; rubber boots; Wellington
boots:
nagagutsu *is-soku*（長靴一足）a
pair of *boots* / nagagutsu *o haku
[nugu]*（長靴をはく[ぬぐ]）put on
[take off] *boots.*《⇨ buutsu》

na⌐ga⌐·i ながい（長い）*a.* (-ku)
1 (of length, distance) long:
Kono kutsu wa nagai *kyori o aruku no ni wa mukanai.*（この靴は長い
距離を歩くのには向かない）These
shoes are not suitable for walking *long* distances. / *Nihoñ de ichibañ* nagai *kawa wa Shinano-gawa
desu.*（日本で一番長い川は信濃川で
す）The *longest* river in Japan is
the Shinano River.《↔ mijikai》
2 (of time) long:
*Koochoo señsee no hanashi wa
totemo* nagakatta.（校長先生の話は
とても長かった）The headmaster's
speech was very *long.* / *Sono shigoto wa* nagai *jikañ ga kakarimashita.*（その仕事は長い時間がかかりまし
た）The job took a *long* time. / *Hi
ga dañdañ* nagaku *natte kita.*（日が
だんだん長くなってきた）The days
have gradually grown *longer.*
《↔ mijikai》《⇨ nagasa》

na⌐gaiki⌐ ながいき（長生き）*n.* long
life; longevity:
*Nagaiki no hiketsu o oshiete kuda-
sai.*（長生きの秘訣を教えてください）
Please tell me the secret of *longevity.*
　　nagaiki (o) suru（〜(を)する）*vi.*
live long; outlive: *Uchi no neko
wa* nagaiki *o shita.*（うちのねこは長生

きをした）Our cat *lived long.* / *Ippañ ni josee wa dañsee yori mo*
nagaiki *suru to iwarete iru.*（一般に
女性は男性よりも長生きすると言われてい
る）Generally speaking, women
are said to *outlive* men.

na⌐game⌐ ながめ（眺め）*n.* view;
scene:
Kono hashi kara no nagame *wa
subarashii.*（この橋からの眺めはすばらし
い）The *view* from this bridge is
wonderful.《⇨ nagameru》

na⌐game⌐·ru ながめる（眺める）*vt.*
(nagame-te Ⓥ) look at; watch;
view:
Kanojo wa mado kara soto o naga-
mete ita.（彼女は窓から外を眺めてい
た）She *was looking* out of the window. / *Watashi-tachi wa oka no
ue kara yuuhi ga shizumu no o*
nagameta.（私たちは丘の上から夕日が
沈むのを眺めた）From the top of the
hill we *watched* the evening sun
sink down.《⇨ nagame》

na⌐ganeñ ながねん（長年）*n.* many
years; a long time:
Yatto naganeñ *no keñkyuu ga kañsee shimashita.*（やっと長年の研究が
完成しました）At last my *many
years* of research have been completed. / *Watashi wa* naganeñ *koko ni suñde imasu.*（私は長年ここに
住んでいます）I have lived here for
a long time. / *Kare wa watashi no*
naganeñ *no tomo desu.*（彼は私の長
年の友です）He is an *old* friend of
mine.

Na⌐gano⌐-keñ ながのけん（長野県）
n. Nagano Prefecture. Located
in almost the center of Japan.
One of the important industries
is the precision-machinery manufacture of such items as watches,
cameras and music boxes. Capital city: Nagano.《⇨ map (E3)》

-nagara ながら（乍ら）*suf.* [at-
tached to the continuative base
of a verb, an adjectival noun or

the dictionary form of an adjective]
1 while; as: ★ Used to show that two actions are simultaneous. The subject of both verbs must be the same, and the final verb indicates the main action.
Watashi wa sutereo o kiki-nagara, *beñkyoo shimasu.* (私はステレオを聞きながら, 勉強します) I study *while* listening to the stereo. / Tabe-nagara, *aruite wa ikemaseñ.* (食べながら, 歩いてはいけません) You must not walk *and* eat *at the same time.* / Kañgaegoto o shi-nagara *aruite ita no de kuruma ni ki ga tsukanakatta.* (考えごとをしながら歩いていたので車に気がつかなかった) Since I was walking along, *absorbed in thought*, I did not notice the car.
2 though; yet: ★ Used to indicate a contrast or an unexpected result or situation.
Karada ni warui to shiri-nagara, *tabako wa yameraremaseñ.* (体に悪いと知りながら, たばこはやめられません) *Though* I know cigarettes are bad for me, I cannot give them up. / *Ano ko wa* kodomo-nagara, *yoku keñtoo shimashita.* (あの子は子どもながら, よく健闘しました) *Child though he is*, he put up a good fight. / *Kono kamera wa* chiisai-nagara, *seenoo ga ii.* (このカメラは小さいながら, 性能がいい) This camera *is small, but* it works well.
3 (used in fixed, introductory expressions):
Zañneñ-nagara, *koñkai no jiko de ooku no kata ga nakunarimashita.* (残念ながら, 今回の事故で多くの方が亡くなりました) *To my deep regret*, a great many people died in this accident. / Shitsuree-nagara, *sono go-ikeñ ni wa sañsee dekimaseñ.* (失礼ながら, そのご意見には賛成できません) *Forgive my rudeness*, but I am unable to agree with that opinion.

na⌈gare⌉ ながれ (流れ) *n.* **1** flow; stream:
Kono kawa wa nagare ga hayai. (この川は流れが速い) This river *flows fast.* / *Kare wa* nagare *ni sotte* [*sakaratte*] *oyoida.* (彼は流れに沿って[逆らって]泳いだ) He swam with [against] the *stream.* / *Kono dooro wa kuruma no* nagare *ga togirenai.* (この道路は車の流れが途切れない) There is an unending *flow* of traffic along this road. ⟪⇨ nagareru⟫
2 current; momentum:
Kare wa toki no nagare *ni umaku notta.* (彼は時の流れにうまくのった) He skillfully took advantage of the *current* of the times. / *Koohañ ni natte, shiai no* nagare *ga kawatta.* (後半になって, 試合の流れが変わった) In the latter half, the *momentum* of the game changed.

na⌈gare⌉·ru ながれる (流れる) *vi.* (nagare-te [V]) **1** flow; run; stream:
Sumida-gawa wa Tookyoo o nagarete iru. (隅田川は東京を流れている) The Sumida *flows* through Tokyo. / *Shoojo no me kara namida ga* nagareta. (少女の目から涙が流れた) Tears *streamed down* from the girl's eyes. ⟪⇨ nagare; nagasu⟫
2 (of a bridge, building, etc.) be washed away:
Oo-ame de hashi ga nagareta. (大雨で橋が流れた) The bridge *was washed away* by the heavy rains. ⟪⇨ nagasu⟫
3 pass:
Are kara juu-neñ no saigetsu ga nagareta. (あれから10年の歳月が流れた) Ten years *have passed* since then. ⟪⇨ nagare⟫
4 (of a game, meeting, etc.) be rained out:
Ame de tenisu no shiai ga nagareta. (雨でテニスの試合が流れた) The

tennis tournament *was rained out.* ((⇨ chuushi))

na⌐gasa ながさ（長さ） *n.* length: *Kono hashi no* nagasa *wa dono kurai arimasu ka?*（この橋の長さはどのくらいありますか）What is the *length* of this bridge? / *Nagasa sañ-meetoru no koodo ga hitsuyoo desu.*（長さ3メートルのコードが必要です）We need a cord three meters in *length.* / *Kanojo wa sono kaapetto no* nagasa *o hakatta.*（彼女はそのカーペットの長さを測った）She measured the *length* of the carpet. ((↔ haba)) ((⇨ nagai))

Na⌐gasaki⌐-keñ ながさきけん（長崎県） *n.* Nagasaki Prefecture. Located in northwest Kyushu. It includes more than 600 islands, spread along the coast. Its capital, Nagasaki, was the second city to be atom-bombed. ((⇨ map (A5)))

na⌐gashi⌐¹ ながし（流し） *n.* sink: nagashi *de sara o arau*（流しで皿を洗う）wash dishes in a *sink.*

na⌐gashi² ながし（流し） *n.* cruising (taxi): *Umaku* nagashi *no takushii o hirou koto ga dekita.*（うまく流しのタクシーを拾うことができた）Luckily, I could get a *cruising* taxi.

na⌐ga⌐s·u ながす（流す） *vt.* (nagash·i-; nagas·a-; nagash·i-te C̄) **1** pour; let flow; shed: *furo no mizu o* nagasu（風呂の水を流す）*let* the bath water *out* / *jaguchi kara suidoo no mizu o* nagasu（蛇口から水道の水を流す）*run* water from a tap / *toire no mizu o* nagasu（トイレの水を流す）*flush* a toilet / *namida o* nagasu（涙を流す）*shed* tears. ((⇨ nagareru)) **2** wash away (a bridge, building, etc.): *Taifuu de hashi ga* nagasareta.（台風で橋が流された）A bridge *was washed away* in the typhoon. / *Koozui de ie ga sañ-geñ* naga-

sareta.（洪水で家が3軒流された）Three houses *were washed away* in the flood. ((⇨ nagareru)) **3** wash down: *Señtoo de kare no senaka o* nagashite yatta.（銭湯で彼の背中を流してやった）I *washed down* his back in the public bath.

na⌐ge⌐k·u なげく（嘆く） *vi.* (nagek·i-; nagek·a-; nage·i-te C̄) grieve; deplore: *Kanojo wa kodomo no shi o* nageita.（彼女は子どもの死を嘆いた）She *grieved* over her child's death. / *Wakamono no hikoo o* nageku *hito wa ooi.*（若者の非行を嘆く人は多い）There are many people who *deplore* the delinquency of youth.

na⌐ge⌐·ru なげる（投げる） *vt.* (nage-te V̄) **1** throw; hurl; fling; pitch; toss: *booru o* nageru（ボールを投げる）*throw* [*pitch*] a ball / *Inu ni ishi o* nageru *no wa yame nasai.*（犬に石をなげるのはやめなさい）Stop *throwing* stones at the dog. ((⇨ hooru¹)) **2** abandon (a plan, attempt, etc.); give up: *Kare wa sono keekaku o tochuu de* nagete shimatta.（彼はその計画を途中で投げてしまった）He *gave up* the plan halfway.

na⌐gori¹ なごり（名残） *n.* **1** parting; farewell: *Futari wa* nagori *o oshiñda.*（二人は名残を惜しんだ）The couple were *reluctant to part.* **2** trace; remains: *Sono mura ni wa mada señsoo no* nagori *ga atta.*（その村にはまだ戦争の名残があった）There were still *traces* of the war in the village.

Na⌐goya なごや（名古屋） *n.* an industrial center and the capital of Aichi Prefecture. ((⇨ map (E4)))

na⌐go⌐yaka なごやか（和やか） *a.n.* (~ na, ni) peaceful; friendly: *Kooshoo wa* nagoyaka *na fuñiki*

de okonawareta. (交渉はなごやかな雰
囲気で行われた) The negotiations
were conducted in a *friendly* atmosphere.

na⌐gu⌐r·u なぐる (殴る) *vt.* (nagur-
r·i-; nagur·a-; nagut-te C)
strike; hit; knock; beat:
Kare wa watashi no kao o nagutta.
(彼は私の顔を殴った) He *hit* me in
the face.

na⌐gusame⌐·ru なぐさめる (慰める)
vt. (nagusame-te V) comfort;
console; cheer up:
Higaisha o nagusameru *tame ni
nani-ka o shitai.* (被害者を慰めるた
めに何かをしたい) I wish to do something to *comfort* the victims. /
Sono ko no egao ni nagusamera-
reta. (その子の笑顔に慰められた) I *was
consoled* by that child's smile.

na⌐·i ない (無い) *a.* (-ku) ★ Not
used attributively. Polite forms
are 'arimaseñ' and 'nai desu.'
1 no; do not exist:
Kono chikaku ni yuubiñkyoku wa
nai. (この近くに郵便局はない) There
is *no* post office near here. / *Kono
buñ ni machigai wa* nai. (この文に
間違いはない) There are *no* mistakes in this sentence. 《↔ aru²》
2 no; do not have:
Moo o-kane ga nai. (もうお金がない)
I *have no* money left. / *Hoñ o yomu hima ga* nai. (本を読む暇がない)
I *have no* time to read. / *Kasa ga*
nakute *komatta.* (傘がなくて困った) I
was at a loss as I *didn't have* an
umbrella. 《↔ aru²》
3 be free (from):
*Kare no seekatsu wa mattaku ku-
roo ga* nai. (彼の生活はまったく苦労が
ない) His life *is* quite *free* from
care. 《↔ aru²》
4 (of a thing, an article, etc.) be
missing:
Watashi no megane ga nai. (私の
眼鏡がない) My glasses *are missing.*
《↔ aru²》

Follows the *ku*-form of other
adjectives to make the negative
form. *Kyoo wa isogashiku* nai.
(きょうは忙しくない) I am *not* busy
today. / *Kono hoñ wa omoshiroku* nakatta. (この本はおもしろくな
かった) This book was *not* interesting. / *Soko e wa ikitaku* nai.
(そこへは行きたくない) I *don't* want
to go there.

-na·i¹ ない *infl. end.* (-ku) [at-
tached to the negative base of a
verb, and inflected like an adjec-
tive] do not; will not; cannot:
Kono mado wa dooshite mo akanai. (この窓はどうしても開かない) This
window *won't* open. / Umaku
ikanai *koto mo arimasu.* (うまくいか
ないこともあります) Things some-
times *do not go well.* / *Koñsaato
ni ikenakute, zañneñ deshita.* (コン
サートに行けなくて、残念でした) I regret
that I *was not able to go* to the
concert. / *Iya nara* tabenakute *mo
ii desu yo.* (いやなら食べなくてもいいで
すよ) If you don't like it, you
needn't eat it. / *Moo* kaeranakute
wa ikemaseñ. (もう帰らなくてはいけま
せん) I *must be going* now.
-nai de (~で) not... (but); without...: *Watashi wa Kyooto ni*
ikanai de, *Nara e ikimashita.* (私は
京都に行かないで、奈良へ行きました) I
went to Nara, *not* Kyoto. / *Kare
wa nani mo iwanai de, heya kara
dete itta.* (彼は何も言わないで、部屋か
ら出て行った) *Not saying* anything,
he left the room. / *Kekkoñ shita
koto o dare ni mo* shirasenai de
oita. (結婚したことをだれにも知らせない
でおいた) I *didn't let* anyone *know*
that I had gotten married.
-na·i² ない (無い) *suf.* (*a.*) (-ku)
[added to a limited number of
nouns to make a negative adjec-
tive]

nasake-nai (情けない) *shameful* / shikata-nai (仕方ない) *unavoidable* / tayori-nai (頼りない) *unreliable.*

-nai³ -ない (内) *suf.* in; inside; within:

shitsu-nai (室内) *inside* a room / *yosañ no waku*-nai (予算の枠内) *within* the budget / *Sha*-nai *no o-tabako wa go-eñryo kudasai.* (車内のおたばこはご遠慮ください) Please refrain from smoking *in* the vehicle.

na⌐ibu ないぶ (内部) *n.* **1** inside; interior:

Kuruma no naibu *o kiree ni sooji shita.* (車の内部をきれいに掃除した) I cleaned the *inside* of the car well. / *Kyookai no* naibu *wa sukkari arete ita.* (教会の内部はすっかり荒れていた) The *interior* of the church was quite dilapidated. 《↔ gaibu》 **2** internal affairs:

Kare wa sono kaisha no naibu *ni kuwashii.* (彼はその会社の内部に詳しい) He is well acquainted with the *internal affairs* of the company. / *Kore wa* naibu no mono no shiwaza *ni chigainai.* (これは内部の者のしわざに違いない) This must have been an *inside job.* 《↔ gaibu》

na⌐ifu ナイフ *n.* knife: naifu *de sasu* (ナイフで刺す) stab with a *knife.* ★ 'Kitchen knife' is called '*hoochoo.*'

na⌐ifuku⌐yaku ないふくやく (内服薬) *n.* medicine to be taken internally.

na⌐ika ないか (内科) *n.* internal medicine:

naika-i (内科医) a *physician.* 《⇨ geka; byooiñ (table)》

na⌐ikaku ないかく (内閣) *n.* cabinet:

naikaku *o soshiki [kaizoo] suru* (内閣を組織[改造]する) form [reshuffle] a *cabinet.*

Na⌐ikaku so⌐orida⌐ijiñ (内閣

総理大臣) *n.* the Prime Minister. ★ Often abbreviated to '*Soori.*'

na⌐iroñ ナイロン *n.* nylon: nairoñ *no kutsushita* (ナイロンの靴下) *nylon* stockings.

na⌐ishi ないし (乃至) *conj.* (*formal*) **1** from...to...; between...and..:

Kono shigoto wa kañsee made ni, tooka naishi *ni-shuukañ kakarimasu.* (この仕事は完成までに、10日ないし2週間かかります) It will take *between* ten days *and* two weeks before this job is finished. 《⇨ mata-wa》

2 or:

Dairiniñ wa haiguusha naishi *oyako ni kagirimasu.* (代理人は配偶者ないし親子に限ります) The proxy must be a spouse, *or* parent or child.

na⌐ishiñ ないしん (内心) *n., adv.* one's inmost heart; at heart; inwardly:

Kare wa naishiñ *bikubiku shite ita.* (彼は内心びくびくしていた) He was *inwardly* nervous. / *Sore o kiite* naishiñ *(de wa) hotto shita.* (それを聞いて内心（では）ほっとした) I was *inwardly* relieved to hear that. 《⇨ kokoro》

na⌐isho¹ ないしょ (内緒・内証) *n.* secrecy; secret:

Kono keekaku wa kare ni wa naisho *ni shite kudasai.* (この計画は彼にはないしょにしてください) Please keep this plan a *secret* from him. / *Kare-ra wa* naisho *de atte ita rashii.* (彼らはないしょで会っていたらしい) They seem to have been meeting in *secret.*

na⌐isoo ないそう (内装) *n.* interior decoration [furnishings]; upholstery:

Kono heya no naisoo *wa sharete iru.* (この部屋の内装はしゃれている) The *interior decoration* of this room is very stylish. 《↔ gaisoo》

na⌐iyoo ないよう (内容) *n.* contents; substance:

Sono tegami no naiyoo *o hana-shite kudasai.*（その手紙の内容を話してください）Please tell me the *contents* of the letter. / *Kare no eñzetsu wa* naiyoo *ga nakatta.*（彼の演説は内容がなかった）His speech had no *substance*. 《↔ keeshiki》

na⌐iyoo-mi⌐hoñ ないようみほん（内容見本）*n.* sample papes; prospectus.

na⌐izoo ないぞう（内臓）*n.* internal organs.

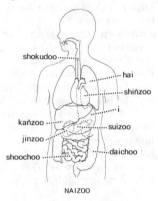

shokudoo

hai

shiñzoo

i

kañzoo

suizoo

jinzoo

shoochoo

daichoo

NAIZOO

na⌐ka[1] なか（中）*n.* **1** inside; interior:

Kono koppu wa naka *ga yogorete iru.*（このコップは中が汚れている）This glass is dirty on the *inside*. / *Kare wa teñto no* naka *ni imasu.*（彼はテントの中にいます）He is *inside* the tent. 《↔ soto》《⇨ uchi[2]》

2 in; into:

Kono hako no naka *wa nañ desu ka?*（この箱の中は何ですか）What is *in* this box? / *Uchi no* naka *e hairi nasai.*（家の中へ入りなさい）Please come *into* the house. 《↔ soto》

3 middle:

Kare-ra wa fubuki no naka *o deka-keta.*（彼らは吹雪の中を出かけた）They went out in the *middle* of the blizzard.

4 of; among:

Kare ga watashi-tachi no naka *de ichibañ se ga takai.*（彼が私たちの中で一番背が高い）He is the tallest *of* us all. / *Sono shinamono no* naka *ni wa furyoohiñ ga atta.*（その品物の中には不良品があった）There were some defective items *among* the goods.

naka kara （～から）of; out of:

Kono naka kara *hitotsu erabi na-sai.*（この中から一つ選びなさい）Pick one *out of* these.

na⌐ka[2] なか（仲）*n.* relation; terms:

Ryookoku no naka *wa yuukoo-te-ki desu.*（両国の仲は友好的です）The *relations* between the two countries are friendly. / *Yamada-sañ to Suzuki-sañ wa* naka *ga ii* [*warui*].（山田さんと鈴木さんは仲がいい[悪い]）Mr. Yamada and Mr. Suzuki are on good [bad] *terms*. / *Dare mo futari no* naka *o saku koto wa dekimaseñ.*（だれも二人の仲を裂くことはできません）No one can *separate* that couple.

na⌐kaba[1] なかば（半ば）*n.* **1** middle; halfway:

Sono biru wa sañ-gatsu nakaba *ni kañsee shimasu.*（そのビルは三月半ばに完成します）The building will be completed in *mid*-March. / *Raishuu no* nakaba-*goro ni o-ukagai shimasu.*（来週の半ばごろにお伺いします）I will visit you about the *middle* of next week. / *Kare wa hana-shi* nakaba *de seki o tatta.*（彼は話し半ばで席をたった）He left his seat in the *middle* of the talk. / *Ichi-neñ mo* nakaba *o sugimashita.*（一年も半ばを過ぎました）We are now *halfway* through the year.

— *adv.* half; partly:

Shigoto wa nakaba *owarimashita.*（仕事は半ば終わりました）The job is *half* finished. / *Ima no wa* nakaba *joodañ desu.*（今のは半ば冗談です）I was *half* joking. / *Sono uwasa wa nakaba hoñtoo desu.* (そのうわさは半ば本当です) That rumor is *partly* true. (⇨ **hañbuñ**)

na⌈kama⌉¹ なかま (仲間) *n.* friend; fellow; comrade:
Kare wa shigoto no nakama desu. (彼は仕事の仲間です) He is one of my *workmates.* / *Watashi wa sono nakama ni haitta.* (私はその仲間に入った) I joined in the *group.* / *asobi*-nakama (遊び仲間) *friends* who have a good time together.

na⌈ka⌉mi なかみ (中身) *n.* contents; substance:
Kono hako no nakami wa nañ desu ka? (この箱の中身は何ですか) What are the *contents* of this box? / *Toogi no nakami wa usukatta.* (討議の中身は薄かった) There was little *substance* in the discussion.

na⌈kanaka なかなか (中々) *adv.*
1 very; quite:
Kanojo no Nihoñgo wa nakanaka umai. (彼女の日本語はなかなかうまい) Her Japanese is *pretty* good. / *Kare no gorufu no ude wa nakanaka datta.* (彼のゴルフの腕はなかなかだった) His skill at golf was *very impressive.*
2 (with a negative) easily; readily:
Kare wa watashi no ikeñ ni nakanaka sañsee shinakatta. (彼は私の意見になかなか賛成しなかった) He would not *readily* agree with my opinion. / *Kono futa wa naka-naka torenai.* (このふたはなかなか取れない) This lid will not come off *easily.*

na⌈kana⌉ori なかなおり (仲直り) *n.* reconciliation:
Ano futari no nakanaori wa muzukashii. (あの二人の仲直りは難しい) A *reconciliation* between the two of them will be difficult.
nakanaori suru (〜する) *vi.* be reconciled; make up: *Sono fuufu*

wa keñka o shita ga sugu naka-naori shita. (その夫婦はけんかをしたがすぐ仲直りした) The husband and wife quarreled, but soon *made up.*

Na⌈kase⌉ñdoo なかせんどう (中山道) *n.* one of the main highways in the Edo period. The road started at Nihonbashi in Edo (now Tokyo) and ended at Kusatsu, where it joined the Tokaido. (⇨ **Tookaidoo**)

na⌈kas·u なかす (泣かす) *vt.* (nakash·i-; nakas·a-; nakash·i-te Ⓒ) = nakaseru.

na⌈kase·ru なかせる (泣かせる) *vt.* (nakase-te Ⓥ) **1** make a person cry; move a person to tears:
Kono ko o nakaseta no wa dare desu ka? (この子を泣かせたのはだれですか) Who is it that *made* this child *cry*? / *Kono eega wa nakasemasu yo.* (この映画は泣かせますよ) This movie will *move you to tears.* / nakaseru hanashi (泣かせる話) a *touching* story. (⇨ **naku⌉**)
2 (*fig.*) cause trouble [a problem]:
Kore ijoo oya o nakasenai yoo ni shi nasai. (これ以上親を泣かせないようにしなさい) You should *not cause* any further *trouble* to your parents.

na⌈kayoku s·uru なかよくする (仲良くする) *vi.* (sh·i-; sh·i-; sh·i-te Ⅰ) make friends with; get on well:
Kanojo wa kurasu no hito, miñna to nakayoku shita. (彼女はクラスの人, みんなと仲良くした) She *got on well* with everyone in her class. / *Kare to wa nakayoku shitai to omotte imasu.* (彼とは仲良くしたいと思っています) I want to *make friends* with him.

na⌈ka⌉yubi なかゆび (中指) *n.* middle finger. (⇨ **yubi** (illus.))

-na⌈kereba i⌈kenai なければいけな

い (*polite*='-*nakereba ikemaseñ*') must do (something): ★ Literally 'Unless someone does..., it cannot go.'
Isha ni kono kusuri o nomanakereba ikenai *to iwareta*.(医者にこの薬を飲まなければいけないと言われた) I was told by the doctor that I *had to take* this medicine. / *Tsukue no ue wa kichiñto* katazukenakereba ikenai.(机の上はきちんと片づけなければいけない) You *must tidy up* your desk neatly. / *Roojiñ ni wa itsu-mo shiñsetsu ni* shite agenakereba ikenai.(老人にはいつも親切にしてあげなければいけない) You *must always be kind* to old people.

-na「kereba nara」nai なければならない (*polite*='-*nakereba narimaseñ*') must do (something): ★ Literally, 'Unless someone does..., it will not do.'
Kyoo wa hayaku ikanakereba naranai.(きょうは早く行かなければならない) I *must leave* early today. / *Koñshuu-chuu ni kore o* shinakereba naranai.(今週中にこれをしなければならない) I *must finish* this within this week.

na「kigo」e[1] なきごえ(泣き声) *n.* cry; sob; whine:
Doko-ka de akañboo no nakigoe *ga suru*.(どこかで赤ん坊の泣き声がする) I hear a baby *crying* somewhere. / *Sono ko wa haha-oya ni* nakigoe *de nedatta*.(その子は母親に泣き声でねだった) Using a *tearful voice*, the child tried to get his own way with his mother. 《↔ waraigoe》

na「kigo」e[2] なきごえ(鳴き声) *n.* song; note; bark:
kotori no nakigoe (小鳥の鳴き声) a little bird's *song* / *inu no* nakigoe (犬の鳴き声) the *bark* of a dog / *mushi no* nakigoe (虫の鳴き声) the *chirp* of an insect / *kaeru no* nakigoe (かえるの鳴き声) the *croak* of a

frog. 《⇨ naku²》

na「ko」odo なこうど(仲人) *n.* matchmaker; go-between:
Ano futari ga kekkoñ suru toki watashi ga nakoodo *o tsutomemashita*.(あの二人が結婚するとき私が仲人を務めました) I acted as *matchmaker* when they were getting married. / *Kare wa hajimete* nakoodo *o shita*.(彼は初めて仲人をした) He acted as *go-between* for the first time. 《⇨ miai》

na「k·u」[1] なく(泣く) *vi.* (nak·i-; nak·a-; na·i-te [C]) cry; weep; sob; shed tears:
Akachañ ga naite imasu yo.(赤ちゃんが泣いていますよ) The baby *is crying*. / *Kanojo wa sono shirase o kiite*, naita.(彼女はその知らせを聞いて、泣いた) She *wept* on hearing the news. 《⇨ nakaseru》

na「k·u」[2] なく(鳴く) *vi.* (nak·i-; nak·a-; na·i-te [C]) **1** (of insects, birds) sing; cry:
Mushi ga kusa no naka de naite *iru*.(虫が草の中で鳴いている) There are insects *singing* in the grass.
2 (of animals) bark; roar; bleat.

na「kunar·u」[1] なくなる(無くなる) *vi.* (-nar·i-; -nar·a-; -nat·te [C])
1 run out:
O-cha ga nakunatta.(お茶がなくなった) We *are out of* tea. / *Kozukai ga* nakunatte shimatta.(小遣いがなくなってしまった) I *have used up* all my pocket money. 《⇨ nakusu¹》
2 be missing:
Kono hoñ wa ni-peeji nakunatte iru.(この本は2ページなくなっている) This book *is missing* two pages.
3 be gone; disappear:
Ha no itami ga nakunatta.(歯の痛みがなくなった) The pain in my tooth *has gone*.

na「kunar·u」[2] なくなる(亡くなる) *vi.* (-nar·i-; -nar·a-; -nat·te [C]) pass away; die: ★ Euphemistic equivalent of '*shinu*.'

Tanaka-sañ no o-kaasañ ga kinoo shiñfuzeñ de nakunatta *soo desu.* (田中さんのお母さんがきのう心不全で亡くなったそうです) I hear that Miss Tanaka's mother *died* of heart failure yesterday. 《⇨ nakusu²》

na⌈kus·u⌉¹ なくす (無くす) *vt.* (na-kush·i-; nakus·a-; nakush·i-te C) **1** lose:
Watashi wa kurejitto kaado o nakushite shimatta. (私はクレジットカードをなくしてしまった) I *have lost* my credit card. 《⇨ nakunaru¹》
2 get rid of; abolish:
Koñna warui shuukañ wa nakusu *beki da.* (こんな悪い習慣はなくすべきだ) This kind of evil custom should *be abolished.* 《⇨ nakunaru¹》

na⌈kus·u⌉² なくす (亡くす) *vt.* (na-kush·i-; nakus·a-; nakush·i-te C) lose (a close relative); be bereft of:
Kare wa tsuma o gañ de naku-shita. (彼は妻をがんで亡くした) He *lost* his wife to cancer. 《⇨ naku-naru²》

na⌉ma なま (生) *n.* **1** raw; uncooked:
Kono sakana wa nama *de tabe-raremasu.* (この魚は生で食べられます) You can eat this fish *raw.* / *Kono niku wa mada* nama *da.* (この肉はまだ生だ) This meat is still *underdone.*
2 live; direct:
Nama *no oñgaku wa subarashii.* (生の音楽は素晴らしい) *Live* music is wonderful. / *Seejika wa koku-miñ no* nama *no koe o kiku beki da.* (政治家は国民の生の声を聞くべきだ) Politicians should listen to the *real* voice of the people.

na⌈ma- なま (生) *pref.* **1** raw; fresh:
nama-*tamago* (生卵) a *raw* egg / nama-*yasai* (生野菜) *raw* vegetables / nama-*mizu* (生水) *unboiled* water.

2 live:
nama-*hoosoo* (生放送) a *live* broadcast.

na⌈ma-bi⌉iru (生ビール) draft beer. ★ Beer not sterilized by heating.

na⌈mae なまえ (名前) *n.* **1** name:
O-namae *wa?* (お名前は) May I have your *name*? / *Kono eki no* namae *wa nañ desu ka?* (この駅の名前は何ですか) What is the *name* of this station?
2 given name. 《⇨ myooji; na¹》

na⌈magusa⌉·i なまぐさい (生臭い) *a.* (-ku) (of smell) fishy:
namagusai *nioi* (生臭いにおい) a *fishy* smell.

na⌈maiki なまいき (生意気) *a.n.* (~ na, ni) cheeky; saucy; impudent; impertinent:
namaiki *na taido* (生意気な態度) an *impudent* attitude / *Ano ko wa* namaiki *na koto o iu.* (あの子は生意気なことを言う) That child makes *cheeky* comments. / *Uchi no musuko wa konogoro* namaiki *ni natte kita.* (うちの息子はこのごろ生意気になってきた) Our son has recently become rather *impertinent.*

na⌈make⌉·ru なまける (怠ける) *vi.* (namake-te V) be lazy; idle away; neglect:
Kare wa mata namakete iru. (彼はまた怠けている) He *is idling away* his time again. / *Kanojo wa kes-shite shigoto o* namakenai. (彼女は決して仕事を怠けない) She *does not* in the least *neglect* her work. 《↔ kiñbeñ》

na⌈manuru⌉i なまぬるい (生温い) *adj.* **1** (of liquid) lukewarm; tepid:
namanuri *biiru* (なまぬるいビール) *lukewarm* beer / *Kono o-cha wa* namanurui. (このお茶はなまぬるい) This tea is *tepid.*
2 (of a method) mild; soft; wishy-washy:

Kimi no yarikata wa namanurui. *Motto kibishiku yari nasai.* (きみのやり方はなまぬるい。もっと厳しくやりなさい) Your methods are *too soft*. Be tougher.

naˈmari[1] なまり (訛) *n.* dialect; accent:
Kare ni wa Toohoku namari *ga aru.* (彼には東北なまりがある) He has a Tohoku *accent*.

naˈmari[12] なまり (鉛) *n.* lead.

naˈma-taˈmago なまたまご (生卵) *n.* raw egg:
Nihoñjiñ wa chooshoku ni yoku nama-tamago *o tabemasu.* (日本人は朝食によく生卵を食べます) Japanese people often eat *raw eggs* for breakfast.

naˈmeˈraka なめらか (滑らか) *a.n.* (~ na, ni) smooth:
nameraka *na hada* (滑らかな肌) *smooth* skin / *Ita no hyoomeñ o* nameraka ni shita. (板の表面を滑らかにした) I *leveled* the surface of the board.

naˈmeˈ·ru なめる (嘗める) *vt.* (na-me-te Ⓥ) **1** lick; lap:
Inu ga sono ko no kao o nameta. (犬がその子の顔をなめた) The dog *licked* the child's face. / *Neko ga sara no miruku o* namete iru. (猫が皿のミルクをなめている) The cat *is lapping up* the milk in the saucer. / *Suupu o* namete, *aji o mita.* (スープをなめて、味をみた) I *took a sip* of the soup to see what it tasted like.
2 suck (candy); eat:
ame o nameru (あめをなめる) *suck* a candy.
3 make light of:
Aite o namete *wa ikemaseñ.* (相手をなめてはいけません) Do not *underestimate* your rival. / *Shikeñ o* namete ite, shippai shita. (試験をなめていて、失敗した) I failed the exam because I *did not take it seriously*.

naˈmi[1] なみ (並) *n.* average; medium:

Kare no gakuryoku wa nami *yori ue desu.* (彼の学力は並より上です) He is above *average* in his academic ability. / *Nami no sariimañ de wa totemo kaenai uchi da.* (並のサラリーマンではとても買えない家だ) This is a house that *ordinary* office workers absolutely cannot afford to buy.

naˈmi[12] なみ (波) *n.* wave; surf:
nami *ni noru* (波に乗る) ride on the *surf*. / *Kyoo wa* nami *ga takai.* (きょうは波が高い) The *waves* are high today.

-nami なみ (並み) *suf.* ordinary; the same level:
*Kare wa kazoku-*nami *ni atsukawareta.* (彼は家族並に扱われた) He was treated *like* a member of the family. / *Sekeñ-*nami *no seekatsu wa shite imasu.* (世間並みの生活はしています) I live an *ordinary* life.

naˈmida なみだ (涙) *n.* tear:
namida *o nagasu* (涙を流す) shed *tears* / namida *o fuku* (涙をふく) wipe one's *tears* away / *Namida ga kanojo no hoo o tsutawatta.* (涙が彼女の頬を伝わった) *Tears* rolled down her cheeks.

naˈmiki なみき (並木) *n.* row of trees:
namiki-michi (並木道) a *tree-lined street*; an *avenue*.

naˈṅ なん (何) *n.* ★ Variant of '*nani*.' 《⇨ nani》
1 what:
Are wa nañ *desu ka?* (あれは何です か) *What* is that? / *Kanojo no namae wa* nañ *desu ka?* (彼女の名前は何ですか) *What* is her name? / *Ima* nañ-*ji desu ka?* (今何時ですか) *What* time is it now? / *Nañ de kono señ o nukimashita?* (何でこの栓を抜きました) *What* did you pull out this cork with?
2 how:
Anata wa kono kaisha ni nañ-*neñ tsutomemashita ka?* (あなたはこの会

社に何年勤めましたか) *How* many years have you worked for this company? / *Kono ike ni koi wa nañ-biki imasu ka?* (この池にこいは何匹いますか) *How* many carp are there in this pond?

3 many:

Kono shigoto o oeru no ni nañ-neñ mo kakarimashita. (この仕事を終えるのに何年もかかりました) It took *many* years to finish this work.

na⌐na なな (七) *n.* seven: ★ Usually used in a compound.

nana iro (七色) *seven* colors / nana fushigi (七不思議) *seven* wonders (of the world). 《⇒ nanatsu; shichi; suu² (table)》

na⌐na⌐me ななめ (斜め) *a.n.* (~ no, ni) **1** oblique; slant:

naname no señ o hiku (斜めの線を引く) draw an *oblique* line / *Michi o naname ni oodañ suru no wa kikeñ desu.* (道を斜めに横断するのは危険です) It is dangerous to cross the road *diagonally.* / *Tana ga sukoshi naname da.* (棚が少し斜めだ) The shelf has a slight *slant.*

2 in a bad humor:

Kanojo wa ima go-kigeñ *naname da.* (彼女は今ご機嫌斜めだ) She is now *in a bad mood.*

na⌐na⌐tsu ななつ (七つ) *n.* seven; the seventh: ★ Used when counting.

Kare wa watashi yori nanatsu *ue desu.* (彼は私より七つ上です) He is *seven years* older than me. / *Tamago wa zeñbu de* nanatsu *arimasu.* (卵は全部で七つあります) There are *seven* eggs in all. / nanatsu-me (七つ目) *the seventh.* 《⇒ nana; shichi; kazu (table)》

Na⌐ñ-Bee なんべい (南米) *n.* South America:

Nañ-Bee-tairiku (南米大陸) the *South American* Continent. 《⇒ Hoku-Bee; Chuu-Bee》

na⌐ñboku なんぼく (南北) *n.*

north and south: 《⇒ toozai》

Sono kawa wa nañboku *ni nagarete imasu.* (その川は南北に流れています) The river flows *north-south.* / nañboku moñdai (南北問題) the *North-South* problem.

na⌐ñ da なんだ (何だ) *int.* what!; why!:

Nañ da, *kimi ka.* (なんだ、きみか) *Why!* It's you.

na⌐ñ da ka なんだか (何だか) *adv.* somehow; somewhat:

Kyoo wa nañ da ka *kibuñ ga warui.* (きょうは何だか気分が悪い) Today I feel *somewhat* out of sorts. / Nañ da ka *gaikoku ni iru yoo na ki ga suru.* (何だか外国にいるような気がする) *Somehow* I feel as if I am in a foreign country.

na⌐ñ de なんで (何で) *adv.* why:

Kare wa nañ de *okotta ñ desu ka?* (彼は何で怒ったんですか) *Why* is it that he got angry? / *Watashi wa señsee ni* nañ de *okureta ka setsumee shita.* (私は先生に何で遅れたか説明した) I explained to my teacher *why* I was late. 《⇒ naze》

na⌐ñ de mo なんでも (何でも) *adv.*

1 anything; everything; whatever:

Nañ de mo *hoshii mono ga attara, ii nasai.* (何でも欲しいものがあったら、言いなさい) If there is *anything* you want, please mention it. / *Anata no tame nara* nañ de mo *itashimasu.* (あなたのためなら何でもいたします) If it is for you, I will do *anything* at all. / *Kare wa supootsu nara* nañ de mo *dekimasu* (彼はスポーツなら何でもできます) When it comes to sports, he can do *everything.*

2 I hear; they say: ★ Used to avoid direct agreement, judgment, or opinion.

Nañ de mo *kare no byooki wa omoi rashii.* (何でも彼の病気は重いらしい) *They say* that his illness seems grave. / Nañ de mo *ano*

futari wa rikoñ suru soo da. (何でも
あの二人は離婚するそうだ) *I hear* that
they are going to get divorced.
3 (with a negative) nothing:
Koñna shigoto wa nañ de mo *nai.*
(こんな仕事は何でもない) There is
nothing to this kind of job. /
"Doo ka shimashita ka?" "Iya,
nañ de mo *arimaseñ."* (「どうかしまし
たか」「いや, 何でもありません」) "Did
something happen?" "No, it is
nothing at all."

na⌐ñ-do なんど (何度) *adv.*
1 how many times; how often:
Nañ-do ittara wakaru ñ da. (何度
言ったらわかるんだ) *How many times*
do I have to tell you that! /
Kyooto ni wa nañ-do *ikimashita
ka?* (京都には何度行きましたか) *How
often* have you been to Kyoto?
2 how many degrees:
Netsu wa nañ-do *arimasu ka?* (熱
は何度ありますか) *How much* is your
temperature? / *Kyoo no saikoo
kioñ wa* nañ-do *deshita ka?* (きょう
の最高気温は何度でしたか) *What* was
today's maximum temperature? /
Kono saka no koobai wa nañ-do
arimasu ka? (この坂のこうばいは何度
ありますか) *What* is the gradient of
this slope?
nañ-do mo (～も) many times:
Hokkaidoo ni wa nañ-do mo *ikimashita.* (北海道には何度も行きまし
た) I have been to Hokkaido
many times. / Nañ-do mo *onaji
koto o iwasenai de kudasai.* (何度
も同じことを言わせないでください) Do
not make me tell you the same
thing *over and over again.*

na⌐ni なに (何) *n.* what:
Nani ga atta ñ desu ka? (何があった
んですか) *What* happened? / *Nani o
o-sagashi desu ka?* (何をお探しです
か) *What* are you looking for? /
Kare ga nani *o itte mo, ki ni suru
na.* (彼が何を言っても, 気にするな)
Whatever he may say, don't wor-

ry about it. 《⇨ nani-ka》
— *int.* what; why:
Nani, kare ga jiko o okoshita tte.
(なに, 彼が事故を起こしたって) *What!*
You mean he has caused an accident! / Nani, *sonna koto kañtañ
desu yo.* (何, そんなこと簡単ですよ)
Why, that kind of thing is simple.

na⌐ni-buñ なにぶん (何分) *adv.*
1 anyway:
Nani-buñ *kodomo ga shita koto
desu no de o-yurushi kudasai.* (な
にぶん子どもがしたことですのでお許しくだ
さい) *Anyway*, it is something that
children have done, so please
excuse them.
2 please:
Kono koto wa nani-buñ *naisho ni
o-negai shimasu.* (このことはなにぶん
ないしょにお願いします) I ask you to
please keep this matter secret.

na⌐ni-ka なにか (何か) *n., adv.*
something; anything:
Nani-ka *hikaru mono ga mukoo ni
miemasu.* (何か光るものが向こうに見え
ます) I can see *something* shining
over there. / Nani-ka *nomimono o
kudasai.* (何か飲み物を下さい) Please
give me *something* to drink. /
Kare kara nani-ka *itte kimashita
ka?* (彼から何か言ってきましたか) Have
you heard *anything* from him?

na⌐ni-mo なにも (何も) *adv.*
(with a negative) be no reason
[need]:
*Nani-mo sonna ni okoranakute mo
ii ja nai desu ka.* (何もそんなに怒らな
くてもいいじゃないですか) There is *no
reason* to be so angry, is there? /
Nani-mo isogu koto wa arimaseñ.
(何も急ぐことはありません) There is *no
need* to hurry.

na⌐ni mo なにも (何も) *adv.*
(with a negative) nothing:
Watashi wa kare to nani mo *kañkee arimaseñ.* (私は彼と何も関係あり
ません) I have *nothing* to do with
him. / *Ima wa* nani mo *tabetaku*

arimaseñ. (今は何も食べたくありません)
I do not want to eat *anything*
now.

na⌐ni-shiro なにしろ (何しろ) *adv.*
at any rate; anyway:
Nani-shiro *yatte miru koto desu.*
(何しろやってみることです) *At any rate,*
the important thing is to try. /
Nani-shiro *shiñjiñ na no de nani-
mo wakarimaseñ.* (何しろ新人なので
何もわかりません) *Anyway,* I am a
newcomer and know nothing.

na⌐ni-yara なにやら (何やら) *adv.*
some; something:
Nani-yara *heñ na oto ga suru.* (何
やら変な音がする) There is *some*
strange noise. / *Inaka kara* nani-
yara *okutte kita.* (田舎から何やら送っ
てきた) I have received *something*
sent from the country.

na⌐ni-yori なにより (何より) *adv.*
(～ no) better [more] than anything else:
Keñkoo ga nani-yori *desu.* (健康が
何よりです) Health is the *most important* thing. / *Atsui hi wa biiru
ga* nani-yori *desu.* (暑い日はビールが
何よりです) There is *nothing like*
beer on a hot day. / Nani-yori *mo
kiso o beñkyoo shi nasai.* (何よりも
基礎を勉強しなさい) *Most of all,*
study the basics.

na⌐ni yue なにゆえ (何故) *adv.*
why: ★ Formal equivalent of
'*naze.*'
Nani yue *koñna koto o shinakereba naranai ñ da?* (なにゆえこんな
ことをしなければならないんだ) *Why*
must I do something like this? /
Nani yue *sono kekka o hookoku
shinakatta ñ da?* (なにゆえその結果を
報告しなかったんだ) *Why* did you fail
to report the result to me?

nañka なんか *p.* = nado.

na⌐ñ-ka なんか (何か) *n.* (*informal*)
= nani-ka.

na⌐ñkañ なんかん (難関) *n.* difficulty; obstacle; barrier:

nañkañ *ni butsukaru* (難関にぶつか
る) encounter *difficulties* / nañkañ
o norikoeru (難関を乗り越える) overcome an *obstacle* / *Sono shikeñ
wa juu-niñ ni hitori to iu* nañkañ
datta. (その試験は 10 人に 1 人という難
関だった) The examination was
very competitive, and one person
out of ten passed it.

na⌐ñkyoku なんきょく (難局) *n.*
difficult situation; difficulty:
nañkyoku *ni chokumeñ suru* (難局
に直面する) face a *difficult situation* / *Watashi-tachi wa nañ to ka*
nañkyoku *o norikoeta.* (私たちはなん
とか難局を乗り越えた) We somehow
managed to get through the
crisis.

Na⌐ñkyoku なんきょく (南極) *n.*
South Pole:
Nañkyoku-*tairiku* (南極大陸) the
Antarctic Continent. 《↔ Hok-
kyoku》

na⌐noka なのか (七日) *n.* seven
days; the seventh day of the
month: ★ Also pronounced
'*nanuka.*'
Kanojo wa nanoka-*kañ nyuuiñ
shita.* (彼女は 7 日間入院した) She
was in the hospital for *seven days.*
/ *Tanabata wa shichi-gatsu* nanoka *desu.* (七夕は七月七日です) The
Star Festival is celebrated on
July 7. 《⇒ tsuitachi (table)》

na⌐ñra-ka なんらか (何らか) *n.*
some; any:
Fukeeki ni taishite nañra-ka *no
taisaku o tateru hitsuyoo ga aru.*
(不景気に対してなんらかの対策を立てる
必要がある) We have to take *some*
measures against the business
depression. / *Kare kara* nañra-ka
no heñji ga attara oshiete kudasai.
(彼からなんらかの返事があったら教えてく
ださい) If there is *any* answer from
him, please let me know.

na⌐ñte なんて (何て) *adv.* how;
what:

Kesa wa nañte *samui ñ daroo.* (今朝は何て寒いんだろう) *How* cold it is this morning! / Nañte *ooki-na ki da.* (何て大きな木だ) *What* a large tree! / Nañte *koto da.* (何てことだ) *What* a situation!

nañte[2] なんて *p.* such; like:
★ Colloquial variant of '*nado to wa.*' Follows a noun or the dictionary form of a verb and implies a degree of criticism.
Ano hito ga nusumi o suru nañte *shiñjirarenai.* (あの人が盗みをするなんて信じられない) I cannot believe that he would do *such* a thing *as* steal. / *Tabako* nañte *warui shuukañ wa yame nasai.* (たばこなんて悪い習慣はやめなさい) You must give up bad habits *like* smoking. / *Jiñsee* nañte *soñna mono sa.* (人生なんてそんなものさ) *Such* is life.

na⌐ñ to なんと (何と) *adv.*
1 what: ★ Used in a question.
Kare wa ima nañ to *iimashita ka?* (彼はいま何と言いましたか) *What* did he say just now? / *Michi o kiku toki Nihoñgo de wa* nañ to *iimasu ka?* (道を聞くとき日本語では何と言いますか) *What* does one say in Japanese when asking the way?
2 how; in what way:
Nañ to *o-wabi shite yoi ka wakarimaseñ.* (何とおわびしてよいかわかりません) I do not kow *how* I can apologize.
3 what; how: ★ Used in an exclamation of surprise.
Kesa wa nañ to *samui ñ daroo.* (今朝は何と寒いんだろう) *What* a cold morning it is! / Nañ to *kare wa mata makete shimatta.* (何と彼はまた負けてしまった) *What a shame* that he has gone and lost again! / Nañ to *kare wa kyuujus-sai datta.* (何と彼は90歳だった) *To my surprise*, he was ninety.

na⌐ñ to ka なんとか (何とか) *adv.*
one way or another; anyhow; somehow:
Nañ to ka *shikeñ ni gookaku shimashita.* (何とか試験に合格しました) I *barely* passed the exam. / Nañ to ka *futari de seekatsu dekiru dake no shuunyuu wa arimasu.* (何とか二人で生活できるだけの収入はあります) Our income is just enough for the two of us to get by in *one way or another.*

nañ to ka (shite) (～(して)) somehow: Nañ to ka (shite) *Oriñpikku de yuushoo shitai.* (何とか(して)オリンピックで優勝したい) I wish to *somehow* win in the Olympics. / Nañ to ka (shite) *koñshuu-chuu ni o-kane o kaesanakereba naranai.* (何とか(して)今週中にお金を返さなければならない) *Somehow or other*, I must return the money within the week.

⌐USAGE⌐
Either '*nañ to ka*' or '*nañ to ka shite*' can be used when the predicate is imperative, or a wish or request is expressed.

nañ to ka naru (～なる) manage to do: *Kippu wa* nañ to ka naru *deshoo.* (切符は何とかなるでしょう) We *will be able* to get the tickets *somehow.* / *Shikeñ no juñbi wa is-shuukañ areba,* nañ to ka narimasu. (試験の準備は一週間あれば、何とかなります) I can *somehow manage* to prepare for the exams if I have one week.

nañ to ka suru (～する) manage to do: *Kono keñ wa getsumatsu made ni* nañ to ka shimasu. (この件は月末までに何とかします) I will *manage to do* it by the end of this month. / *Kore wa anata no sekiniñ desu.* Nañ to ka shite *kudasai.* (これはあなたの責任です。何とかしてください) You are responsible for this. *Do something* about it.

na⌐ñ-to-na⌐ku なんとなく (何と無

く) *adv.* somehow; vaguely; for some reason or other:
Kyoo wa nañ-to-naku, *sore o yaru ki ga shinai.*(きょうは何となく、それをやる気がしない) *Somehow* I have no mind to do it today. / *Kanojo wa* nañ-to-naku *eñryo shita tokoro ga aru.*(彼女は何となく遠慮したところがある) There is *something* reserved about her manner. / *Sono hanashi wa* nañ-to-naku *uso no yoo na ki ga suru.*(その話は何となくうそのような気がする) I have a feeling that the story is *in some way* a lie. / *Kare no kimochi ga* nañ-to-naku *wakatta.*(彼の気持ちが何となくわかった) I *more or less* understood his feelings.

na「nuka なぬか (七日) *n.* = nanoka. 《⇨ tsuitachi (table)》

na「o¹ なお (尚) *adv.* still; even:
Kore dake de mo juubuñ da ga ookereba nao yoi.(これだけでも十分だが多ければなおよい) This is enough, but it would be *still* better if there were more. / *Daibu yoku natte kimashita ga* nao *chuui ga hitsuyoo desu.*(だいぶよくなってきましたがなお注意が必要です) You have gotten much better, but care is *still* necessary. / *Sofu wa ima* nao *geñki ni hataraite imasu.*(祖父は今なお元気に働いています) My grandfather *even* now does his work with vigor.

na「o² なお (尚) *conj.* furthermore:
Nao, *shoosai wa nochi-hodo o-shirase itashimasu.*(なお、詳細は後ほどお知らせいたします) *Furthermore,* we will inform you of the details later.

na「o「r・u¹ なおる (直る) *vi.* (naor・i-; naor・a-; naot-te Ⓒ) **1** be fixed; be mended; be repaired:
Jiteñsha no pañku wa naorimashita ka?(自転車のパンクは直りましたか) *Is* the puncture in the bicycle tire *fixed?* / *Kono señtakuki wa*

moo naorimseñ.(この洗濯機はもう直りません) This washing machine *is beyond repair.* 《⇨ naosu¹》
2 (of a mistake) be corrected:
Iñsatsu no machigai wa naorimashita.(印刷の間違いは直りました) The misprints *have been corrected.* / *Kare no chikoku no kuse wa* naoranai *deshoo.*(彼の遅刻の癖は直らないでしょう) His habit of being late is not likely to *get better.* 《⇨ naosu¹》
3 (of a mood, temper) be restored:
Kanojo no kigeñ ga naotta.(彼女の機嫌が直った) Her good mood *has been restored.* 《⇨ naosu¹》

na「o「r・u² なおる (治る) *vi.* (naor・i-; naor・a-; naot-te Ⓒ) (of a person, injury, illness, etc.) recover; get well; be cured; be healed:
Kare wa sugu ni naoru *deshoo.*(彼はすぐに治るでしょう) He will soon *recover.* / *Kega no kizu ga* naotte kita.(けがの傷が治ってきた) The cut from my injury *is healing.* / *Kotoshi wa kaze ga nakanaka* naorimseñ.(ことしはかぜがなかなか治りません) This year my cold just *will not go away.* 《⇨ naosu²》

na「o-sara なおさら (尚更) *adv.* all the more; still more:
Kare no seejitsusa ga wakari, nao-sara *suki ni natta.*(彼の誠実さがわかり、なおさら好きになった) On discovering his honesty, I came to like him *all the more.* / *Shite wa ikenai to iwareru to* nao-sara *shitaku narimasu.*(してはいけないと言われるとなおさらしたくなります) If we are told that we must not do something, we want to do it *all the more.*

na「o「s・u¹ なおす (直す) *vt.* (naosh・i-; naos・a-; naosh・i-te Ⓒ)
1 mend; repair; fix:
Kare wa isu o jibuñ de naoshita.(彼はいすを自分で直した) He *repaired* the chair by himself. / *Watashi*

wa tokee o naoshite moratta. (私は時計を直してもらった) I *had* my watch *fixed.* (⇨ naoru¹)

2 correct (a mistake); remedy: *Tsugi no buñshoo no machigai o* naoshi nasai. (次の文章の間違いを直しなさい) *Correct* the errors in the following sentences. (⇨ naoru¹)

3 adjust: *tokee no hari o* naosu (時計の針を直す) *adjust* a watch / *kami o na-*osu (髪を直す) *adjust* one's hair.

4 translate; convert; turn: *Nihoñgo o Eego ni* naosu (日本語を英語に直す) *translate* Japanese into English / *yaado o meetoru ni* naosu (ヤードをメートルに直す) *convert* yards into meters.

na⌐o⌐s·u² なおす (治す) *vt.* (naosh·i-; naos·a-; naosh·ite Ⓒ) cure; heal: *Gañ o* naosu *hoohoo ga iroiro keñ-kyuu sarete imasu.* (がんを治す方法がいろいろ研究されています) Many ways to *cure* cancer are being investigated. / *Yakedo o* naosu *ni wa kono kusuri ga yoi.* (やけどを治すにはこの薬がよい) This medicine is good for *healing* burns. (⇨ naoru²)

nara なら [provisional form of '*da*'] ★ The more literary variant '*naraba*' can be used to emphasize the idea of condition.

1 when it comes to...; as far as... is concerned; if: *Deñsha* nara, *nijip-puñ mo kakari-maseñ.* (電車なら, 20分もかかりません) *If* you go by train, it won't even take twenty minutes. / *Kañji* nara *sukoshi wa yomemasu.* (漢字なら少しは読めます) *When it comes to* Chinese characters, I can read them a bit. / *Watashi* nara, *kes-shite ayamarimasen.* (私なら, 決して謝りません) *If* I were in your place, I certainly would not apologize.

2 provided that; if:

Sore ga uso nara, *kimi wa kubi da ze.* (それがうそなら, 君はくびだぜ) *If* that is a lie, you will be fired. / *Yasui no* nara, *dore de mo ii desu.* (安いのなら, どれでもいいです) Any one of them will be fine *as long as* it is cheap. / *Tanaka-sañ ga ikanai no* nara, *boku mo ikimaseñ.* (田中さんが行かないのなら, 僕も行きません) *If* Miss Tanaka does not go, I will not go, either.

3 the more...the more: *Fukuzatsu* nara *fukuzatsu na ho-do tsukai nikui.* (複雑なら複雑なほど使いにくい) *The more* complicated it is, *the harder* it is to use.

★ Only adjectival nouns are used in this pattern. (⇨ -ba¹; to¹; -tara)

na⌐rabe·ru ならべる (並べる) *vt.* (narabe-te Ⓥ) **1** arrange; line up: *Tsukue o ichi-retsu ni* narabe *nasai.* (机を一列に並べなさい) *Arrange* the desks in one row. / *Saa, ohinasama o* narabemashoo. (さあ, おひなさまを並べましょう) Now, let's *line up* the 'hina' dolls. / *Kaado o arufabetto-juñ ni* narabeta. (カードをアルファベット順に並べた) I *arranged* the cards in alphabetical order. (⇨ narabu)

2 display; spread (dishes): *Hooseki wa kochira no heya ni* narabete *arimasu.* (宝石はこちらの部屋に並べてあります) The jewelry *is displayed* in this room. / *Teeburu ni ryoori o* narabete *kudasai.* (テーブルに料理を並べてください) Please *put* the food *out* on the table. (⇨ narabu)

na⌐rabi ni ならびに (並びに) *conj.* (formal) and; as well as: *Nihoñ* narabi ni *Kañkoku* (日本ならびに韓国) Japan *and* Korea. (⇨ soshite; to²)

na⌐rab·u ならぶ (並ぶ) *vi.* (narab·i-; narab·a-; narañ-de Ⓒ)

1 stand in a row; form a line [queue]:
Señchaku-juñ ni narañde *kudasai.* (先着順に並んでください) Please *line up* in the order of arrival. / *Koko no toori ni wa hoñya ga takusañ* narañde *imasu.* (ここの通りには本屋がたくさん並んでいます) There *are* many bookstores *along* this street. / *Futari wa* narañde suwatta. (二人は並んで座った) The two of them *sat side by side.* / *Gaadomañ wa nyuujoosha o sañ-retsu ni* narabaseta. (ガードマンは入場者を3列に並ばせた) The guard *made* the people waiting to enter *stand* in three rows. 《⇨ naraberu》
2 rank; be equal:
Watashi-tachi no aida de wa gorufu de kare ni narabu *mono wa imaseñ.* (私たちの間ではゴルフで彼に並ぶものはいません) In our group, there is no one *equal* to him in golf.

Na⌐ra-ji⌐dai ならじだい (奈良時代) *n.* Nara Period (710 to 794). 《⇨ jidai (table)》

Na⌐ra⌐-keñ ならけん (奈良県) *n.* Nara Prefecture. Located in the center of the Kinki district. The capital city, Nara, surrounded by ranges of mountains on all sides, was the capital of Japan in the eighth century and there are many places of historic interest. 《⇨ map (D4)》

na⌐ra⌐nai ならない (*polite* = *narimaseñ*) **1** must not (do); should not (do): ★ Used in the pattern '*-te wa naranai*' to indicate prohibition.
Koko de tabako o sutte wa naranai. (ここでたばこを吸ってはならない) You *must not* smoke here. / *Kono koto o kare ni itte wa* naranai. (このことを彼に言ってはならない) You *should not* tell him about this matter.
2 must (do); have to (do); need

to (do): ★ Used in the pattern '*-nakereba* [*-nakute wa*] *naranai*' to indicate necessity.
Moo ikanakereba naranai. (もう行かなければならない) I *must* be going now. / *Kare ni heñji o dasanakute wa* naranai. (彼に返事を出さなくてはならない) I *have to* write an answer to him.
3 cannot help (doing): ★ Used with a *te*-form of a verb, adjective or the copula to indicate that one cannot prevent oneself from doing something.
Kare wa uso o tsuite iru yoo ni omowarete naranai. (彼はうそをついているように思われてならない) I *cannot help* thinking that he is telling a lie. / *Shikeñ ni ukatta no de ureshikute* naranai. (試験に受かったのでうれしくてならない) Since I have passed the examination, I *am beside myself* with joy. / *Kanojo ni aenakatta no ga* zañneñ de naranai. (彼女に会えなかったのが残念でならない) *It is very regrettable* that I was unable to meet her.
4 cannot (do):
Moo gamañ ga naranai. (もうがまんがならない) I *cannot* stand any more.

na⌐ras·u¹ ならす (鳴らす) *vt.* (narash·i-; naras·a-; narash·i-te Ⓒ) **1** ring; sound; blow:
beru o narasu (ベルを鳴らす) *ring* a bell / *keeteki o* narasu (警笛を鳴らす) *sound* a horn / *Kyuukyuusha ga saireñ o* narashi-nagara *yatte kita.* (救急車がサイレンを鳴らしながらやってきた) An ambulance approached, *sounding* its siren. 《⇨ naru²》
2 (of a person) be popular:
Kanojo wa kashu to shite narashita *toki mo atta.* (彼女は歌手として鳴らした時もあった) There was a time when she *was popular* as a singer.

na⌐ras·u² ならす (慣らす) *vt.* (na-

rash·i-; naras·a-; narash·i-te Ⓒ) accustom; train:
Nihoñgo no hatsuoñ ni mimi o narasu koto ga taisetsu desu. (日本語の発音に耳を慣らすことが大切です) It is important to *accustom* your ears to the pronunciation of Japanese. / *Hokkaidoo e iku mae ni karada o samusa ni narasana-kute wa.* (北海道へ行く前に体を寒さに慣らさなくては) I have to *get accus-tomed* to the cold before I go to Hokkaido. ((⇨ nareru))

na⌐ra⌐·u ならう (習う) *vt.* (nara·i-; naraw·a-; narat-te Ⓒ) learn; study; practice; take lessons:
Nihoñgo wa sañ-neñkañ naraima-shita. (日本語は3年間習いました) I studied Japanese for three years. / *Suiei wa dare ni naraimashita ka?* (水泳はだれに習いましたか) Who *did* you *learn* swimming from? / *Kanojo wa ikebana o naratte ima-su.* (彼女は生け花を習っています) She *is taking lessons* in flower arrange-ment. ((⇨ manabu))

na⌐renareshi⌐·i なれなれしい (馴れ馴れしい) *a.* (-ku) overfamiliar; too friendly:
narenareshii *taido* (なれなれしい態度) an *overfamiliar* attitude / *Shira-nai hito ga* narenareshiku *hanashi-kakete kita.* (知らない人がなれなれしく話しかけてきた) A stranger talked to me in an *overly familiar* manner.

na⌐re⌐·ru なれる (慣れる) *vi.* (nare-te Ⓥ) become accustomed:
Kanojo wa Nihoñ no seekatsu ni narete kita. (彼女は日本の生活に慣れてきた) She *has become accustomed* to life in Japan. / *Kono shigoto ni* nareta *hito o shirimaseñ ka?* (この仕事に慣れた人を知りませんか) Don't you know anyone who *is accus-tomed* to doing this job? ((⇨ na-rasu²))

nari¹ なり *p.* or: ★ Follows a noun or the dictionary form of a verb and implies a choice among two or more alternatives, but does not exclude other possibili-ties.
Koñdo no getsuyoobi nari *kayoobi* nari *ni oide kudasai.* (今度の月曜日なり火曜日なりにおいでください) Please visit us, *say,* this Monday *or* Tuesday. / *Wakaranai toki wa señsee ni kiku* nari *jisho de shira-beru* nari *shi nasai.* (わからないときは先生に聞くなり辞書で調べるなりしなさい) When you do not understand, ask the teacher, look it up in your dictionary, *or* do something.

nari² なり *p.* as soon as: ★ Fol-lows the dictionary form of a verb.
Kare wa kaette kuru nari, *nete shi-matta.* (彼は帰ってくるなり、寝てしまった) He went straight to sleep *as soon as* he returned.

-nari なり *suf.* appropriate to; ex-pected of:
Jibuñ wa jibuñ-nari ni ikite ikitai. (自分は自分なりに生きていきたい) I want to start living *in my own way.*

na⌐ritats·u なりたつ (成り立つ) *vi.* (-tach·i-; -tat·a-; -tat-te Ⓒ)
1 be made up; consist:
Kono kaisha wa nanatsu no bu kara naritatte imasu. (この会社は7つの部から成り立っています) This com-pany *is made up* of seven depart-ments.
2 materialize; be realized:
Shikiñ ga areba kono kikaku wa naritachimasu. (資金があればこの企画は成り立ちます) Provided we have the funds, this project will *be realized.* / *Kimi no riroñ wa kono baai* naritachimaseñ. (君の理論はこの場合成り立ちません) Your theory *does not hold* good in this case. ((⇨ seeritsu))

na⌐r·u⌐¹ なる (成る) *vi.* (nar·i-; na-r·a-; nat-te Ⓒ) **1** (of a person) become; grow:

kanemochi ni naru (金持ちになる)
become rich / *byooki ni* naru (病気
になる) *fall* ill / *Kare wa isha* ni
natta. (彼は医者になった) He *became*
a doctor. / *Sotsugyoo shitara, nañ
ni* narimasu *ka?* (卒業したら, 何にな
りますか) After you graduate, what
are you going to *be?* / *Kare no
musuko wa kono mae atta toki
kara zuibuñ ookiku* natta. (彼の息
子はこの前会ったときからずいぶん大きくな
った) His son *has* really *grown*
since I saw him last.

2 (of time, season, etc.) come;
grow; set in:
Yatto haru ni natta. (やっと春になっ
た) At last spring *has come.* / *Gogo
wa yuki ni* nari-soo da. (午後は雪に
なりそうだ) *It seems as if it will
snow* in the afternoon. / *Dañdañ
hi ga mijikaku* natte kita. (だんだん
日が短くなってきた) Gradually the
days *have become* shorter. / *Shiga-
tsu ni* naru *to isogashiku narimasu.* (四月になると忙しくなります) I
will become busy *in* April.

3 come to do; begin to do:
Watashi wa kare ga suki ni natta.
(私は彼が好きになった) I *have come* to
like him. / *Nihoñgo ga dañdañ
wakaru yoo ni* narimashita. (日本
語がだんだんわかるようになりました) I *am*
gradually *beginning* to understand Japanese.

4 change; turn:
Shiñgoo ga ao ni natta. (信号が青に
なった) The traffic light *turned*
green. / *Kanojo wa hito ga kawatta yoo ni* natta. (彼女は人が変わ
ったようになった) Her personality
has changed.

5 become of:
Sono go kare ga doo natta *ka shirimaseñ.* (その後彼がどうなったか知りま
せん) I do not know what *became
of* him after that. / *Kaji de yaketa
ie wa doo* natta *daroo.* (火事で焼け

た家はどうなっただろう) What *has
become of* the house which was
burned in the fire?

6 (of a number, quantity, etc.)
amount; total:
*Shishoosha no kazu wa gookee
juuhachi-mee to* natta. (死傷者の数
は合計 18 名となった) The dead and
injured *totaled* eighteen. / *Zeñbu
de ikura ni* narimasu *ka?* (全部でい
くらになりますか) How much does it
come to altogether?

7 (of age) reach:
Kanojo wa raineñ hatachi ni narimasu. (彼女は来年二十歳になります)
She will *be* twenty next year. /
Kare wa gojus-sai ni natta. (彼は
50 歳になった) He *has reached* fifty
years of age.

8 (*formal*) (of time) pass:
Nihoñ ni kite, ni-neñ ni narimasu.
(日本に来て, 2 年になります) Two
years *have passed* since I came to
Japan.

9 act; serve:
Kare wa geki de Hamuretto ni
natta. (彼は劇でハムレットになった) He
acted Hamlet in the play. / *Kare
wa sono kaigi de gichoo to* natta.
(彼はその会議で議長となった) He *was
elected* chairman at the meeting.

10 be made up; consist:
*Kono kurasu wa yoñjuugo-niñ
kara* natte imasu. (このクラスは 45 人
からなっています) This class *is made
up* of forty-five people.

─── **(USAGE)** ───

Honorific expressions are
formed with '*o-*' plus the continuative base of a verb plus
'*ni naru.*' e.g. *Kono hoñ o* o-
yomi ni narimasu *ka?* (この本をお
読みになりますか) Would you like
to *read* this book? / *Nani o* o-
nomi ni narimasu *ka?* (何をお飲み
になりますか) What would you
like to *drink?*

na⌈r･u² なる (鳴る) *vi.* (nar･i-; na-r･a-; nat-te ⌊C⌋) ring; sound; chime; toll:
Geñkañ no beru ga natta. (玄関のベルが鳴った) The front-door bell *rang.* / *Deñwa ga* natte imasu *yo.* (電話が鳴っていますよ) The phone *is ringing.* / *Kyuukyuusha no saireñ ga* natte iru. (救急車のサイレンが鳴っている) There is an ambulance siren *sounding.* 《⇨ narasu¹》

na⌈r･u³ なる (生る) *vi.* (nar･i-; na-r･a-; nat-te ⌊C⌋) (of a plant) bear fruit; (of fruit) grow:
Kono budoo no ki wa yoku mi ga narimasu. (このぶどうの木はよく実がなります) This grapevine *bears* well. / *Kaki ga ippai* natte iru. (柿がいっぱいなっている) There *are* a lot of persimmons on the tree.

na⌈rubeku なるべく (成る可く) *adv.*
1 as ... as possible; to the best of one's ability:
Narubeku *ooki-na koe de hana-shite kudasai.* (なるべく大きな声で話してください) Please speak *as loudly as possible.* / Narubeku *kiree na hana o erañde kudasai.* (なるべくきれいな花を選んでください) Please choose the *prettiest* flowers. / Narubeku *okurenai yoo ni shimasu.* (なるべく遅れないようにします) I will *do my best* not to be late.
2 if possible:
Tabako wa narubeku (nara) *ya-meta hoo ga yoi.* (たばこはなるべく(なら)やめたほうがよい) *If it's possible,* you had better quit smoking. / Narubeku (nara) *ashita made ni kono shigoto o shiagete kudasai.* (なるべく(なら)あしたまでにこの仕事を仕上げてください) I want you to finish this work by tomorrow, *if possible.*

na⌈ruhodo なるほど (成る程) *adv.*
1 I see; I admit:
"*Kootsuu-jiko de okuremashita.*" "Naruhodo, *sore de wa shooganai*

na.*" (「交通事故で遅れました」「なるほど、それではしょうがないな」) "I was late because of a traffic accident." "*I see.* That is quite natural." / Naruhodo, *watashi no machigai deshi-ta.* (なるほど、私の間違いでした) I *admit* it was my mistake.
2 indeed; to be sure:
Naruhodo *kanojo wa atama wa kireru ga sukoshi unuborete iru.* (なるほど彼女は頭は切れるが少しうぬぼれている) She is sharp, *to be sure,* but a bit vain.

na⌈sa⌉i なさい (used to express an imperative): ★ The imperative form of '*nasaru.*' Follows the continuative base of a verb.
Tsugi no moñdai o toki nasai. (次の問題を解きなさい) *Solve* the following problems.

na⌈sake なさけ (情け) *n.* sympathy; mercy; charity; kindness:
Komatte iru hito ni wa nasake *o kakete yari nasai.* (困っている人には情けをかけてやりなさい) You should show *compassion* to those who are in difficult circumstances. / *Hito no* nasake *ga tsukuzuku ari-gatakatta.* (人の情けがつくづくありがたかった) I deeply appreciated the *kindness* of others. / Nasake *wa hito no tame narazu.* (情けは人のためならず) (*saying*) He who gives to another bestows on himself.

na⌈sakebuka⌉･i なさけぶかい (情け深い) *a.* (-ku) kindhearted; warm-hearted; merciful:
nasakebukai *hito* (情け深い人) a *kindhearted* person.

na⌈sakena⌉･i なさけない (情けない) *a.* (-ku) shameful; deplorable; miserable:
nasakenai *seeseki* (情けない成績) *disgraceful* school grades / *Ima no seejika wa* nasakenai. (今の政治家は情けない) Politicians these days are *despicable.* / *Jibuñ no shita koto o* nasakenaku *omoimasu.* (自

分のしたことを情けなく思います) I feel *ashamed* of what I have done.

na⌈sa⌉r·u なさる（為さる）*vt.* (nasa-i-; nasar·a-; nasat-te Ⓒ) do: ★ Honorific equivalent of '*suru*.' *Ashita wa doo* nasaimasu *ka?* (あしたはどうなさいますか) What are you going to *do* tomorrow? / *O-furo wa doo* nasaimasu *ka?* (お風呂はどうなさいますか) What do you want to *do* about your bath? / *Doozo go-eñryo* nasaranai de *kudasai.* (どうぞご遠慮なさらないでください) Please *do not* stand on ceremony. 《⇨ nasai》

na⌉shi[1] なし（無し）*n.* nothing: *Ijoo* nashi. (異常なし) There is *nothing* abnormal. / *Kore de* ka-shi-kari wa nashi *ni shimashoo.* (これで貸し借りはなしにしましょう) With this, let us *call it quits* between us. 《⇨ nai》

na⌈shi⌉[2] なし（梨）*n.* pear; pear tree.

nashi no tsubute (〜のつぶて) hear nothing from: *Kare ni te-gami o dashita ga* nashi no tsu-bute *datta.* (彼に手紙を出したが梨のつぶてだった) I sent a letter to him, but I *have not heard a word* in reply.

na⌉su[1] なす（茄子）*n.* eggplant. ★ Japanese eggplants are smaller and not as round as those of Europe and America. 《⇨ yasai (illus.)》

na⌉s·u[2] なす（為す）*vt.* (nash·i-; na-s·a-; nash·i-te Ⓒ) (*formal*) do: *Kare ni wa kare no* nasu *beki koto ga aru.* (彼には彼のなすべきことがある) He has to do what he has to *do.*

na⌈tsu なつ（夏）*n.* summer: *Nihoñ no* natsu *wa atsui.* (日本の夏は暑い) *Summer* in Japan is hot. / *Kotoshi no* natsu *wa yama e iki-masu.* (ことしの夏は山へ行きます) I'm going to the mountains this *sum-mer.* 《↔ fuyu》《⇨ shiki[1] (table);

kisetsu (table)》

na⌈tsukashi⌉·i なつかしい（懐かしい）*a.* (-ku) dear; good old; longed-for: *Furusato ga* natsukashii. (ふるさとが懐かしい) I *long for* my hometown. / *Yuube rajio de* natsukashii *uta o takusañ kiita.* (ゆうベラジオで懐かしい歌をたくさん聞いた) Last night on the radio I listened to a lot of the *good old* songs. / *Kono shashiñ o miru to mukashi ga* natsukashiku *naru.* (この写真を見ると昔が懐かしくなる) Whenever I look at this picture I *feel nostalgic.*

na⌈tsumi⌉kañ なつみかん（夏蜜柑）*n.* Chinese citron.

na⌈tsu-ya⌉sumi なつやすみ（夏休み）*n.* summer vacation: *Gakkoo wa itsu kara* natsu-yasu-mi *desu ka?* (学校はいつから夏休みですか) When do you break up for the *summer holidays?* 《⇨ yasumi》

na⌈ttoku なっとく（納得）*n.* un-derstanding; satisfaction: *Kare ga naze heñji o kurenai no ka* nattoku *ga ikanai.* (彼がなぜ返事をくれないのか納得がいかない) I *cannot understand* why he does not re-ply to us. / *Watashi-tachi wa sono moñdai o* nattoku *ga iku made hanashiatta.* (私たちはその問題を納得がいくまで話し合った) We dis-cussed the problem until *every-one was convinced.*

nattoku saseru (〜させる) *vt.* con-vince; persuade: *Watashi wa kanojo ni kikeñ no nai koto o* nat-toku saseta. (私は彼女に危険のないことを納得させた) I *convinced* her that there was no danger.

nattoku suru (〜する) *vi.* under-stand; be satisfied: *Watashi no kuwashii setsumee de aite wa* nat-toku shita. (私の詳しい説明で相手は納得した) They *were satisfied* by my detailed explanation.

na⌈tto⌉o なっとう（納豆）*n.* fermented soybeans.

NATTOO

na⌈wa⌉ なわ (縄) *n.* rope; cord: nawa *de shibaru* (なわでしばる) bind with a *rope* / *tsutsumi ni* nawa *o kakeru* (包みになわをかける) put a *rope* around a parcel / nawa-*tobi* (なわ飛び) *rope* skipping / nawa-*bashigo* (なわばしご) a *rope* ladder.

na⌈yamashi⌉·i なやましい (悩ましい) *a.* (-ku) sexy; amorous; voluptuous: nayamashii *koe* (悩ましい声) a *sexy* voice / *Koñya no kanojo wa* naya-mashii. (今夜の彼女は悩ましい) She looks *sexy* tonight.

na⌈yami⌉ なやみ (悩み) *n.* worry; trouble; sufferings; anguish: *Kanojo wa nani-ka* nayami *ga aru yoo da.* (彼女は何か悩みがあるようだ) It seems that she has some *troubles.* / *Watashi no* nayami *wa haha no byooki desu.* (私の悩みは母の病気です) My *worry* is my mother's sickness. / *Watashi wa* naya-mi *o subete kare ni uchiaketa.* (私は悩みをすべて彼に打ち明けた) I told him all my *troubles.* (⇨ nayamu)

nayami no tane (〜の種) the source of one's distress: *Musuko no shoorai ga kare no* nayami *no tane datta.* (息子の将来が彼の悩みの種だった) His son's future was a *headache* to him.

na⌈ya⌉m·u なやむ (悩む) *vi.* (na-yam·i-; nayam·a-; nayañ-de [C])

worry; suffer: *Kare wa doo shitara yoi ka* naya-ñde imasu. (彼はどうしたらよいか悩んでいます) He *is worrying* about what to do. / *Kanojo wa musuko no see-seki no koto de* nayañde ita. (彼女は息子の成績のことで悩んでいた) She *was worrying* about her son's school grades. / *Sono kuni wa bo-oeki fushiñ de* nayañde iru. (その国は貿易不振で悩んでいる) The country *is suffering* from a slump in trade. (⇨ nayami)

na⌈ze なぜ (何故) *adv.* why; what for: Naze *paatii ni konakatta ñ desu ka?* (なぜパーティーに来なかったんですか) *Why* didn't you come to our party? / *Kanojo wa* naze *añna koto o shita no daroo.* (彼女はなぜあんなことをしたのだろう) I wonder *why* it is that she did such a thing. / *"Sore wa tabenai hoo ga ii desu yo." "Naze desu ka?"* (「それは食べないほうがいいですよ」「なぜですか」) "You had better not eat that." " *Why* not?"

na⌈ze nara(ba) なぜなら(ば) (何故なら(ば)) *conj.* the reason is; that is so because: ★ Used at the beginning of a sentence. *Soko e wa ikitaku arimaseñ.* Naze naraba *ima isogashii kara desu.* (そこへは行きたくありません. なぜならば今忙しいからです) I don't wish to go there. *The reason is* I am busy now.

na⌈zo なぞ (謎) *n.* mystery; enigma; riddle; puzzle: nazo *o toku* (謎を解く) solve a *mystery* [*riddle*] / *Sono o-kane ga na-kunatta no wa mattaku no* nazo *desu.* (そのお金がなくなったのは全くの謎です) The disappearance of the money is a complete *riddle.* / *Subete ga watashi ni totte* nazo *datta.* (すべてが私にとって謎だった) Everything was a *mystery* to me.

/ *Sono go no kare no yukue wa nazo ni tsutsumarete iru.* (その後の彼の行方は謎に包まれている) His whereabouts after that are cloaked in *mystery*.

na「zonazo なぞなぞ (謎々) *n.* riddle:
Nazonazo o shiyoo. (なぞなぞをしよう) Let's play *riddles*. / Nazonazo o hitotsu dashimasu yo. (なぞなぞを一つ出しますよ) I'll ask you a *riddle*.
《⇨ nazo》

na「zuke¹·ru なづける (名付ける) *vt.* (nazuke-te [V]) name; call:
Ryooshiñ wa kodomo o Akemi to nazuketa. (両親は子どもを明美と名づけた) The parents *named* their child Akemi. / Sono seehiñ wa hatsumeesha ni chinañde nazukerareta. (その製品は発明者にちなんで名づけられた) The product *was named* after its inventor.
《⇨ namae》

ne¹¹ ね (根) *n.* **1** root:
Sono ki wa sugu ni ne ga tsuita. (その木はすぐに根がついた) The tree soon took *root*.
2 (*fig.*) root:
aku no ne o tatsu (悪の根を断つ) eradicate the *root* of evil.
ne ni motsu (～に持つ) have a grudge: Kare wa watashi no koto o mada ne ni motte iru yoo da. (彼は私のことをまだ根に持っているようだ) He still seems to *have a grudge* against me.

ne² ね (値) *n.* price; cost:
Yasai no ne ga agatta [sagatta]. (野菜の値が上がった[下がった]) The *price* of vegetables has gone up [down]. / Kono nekutai wa chotto ne ga hatta. (このネクタイはちょっと値が張った) This tie *was* a little too *expensive*.

ne³ ね *p.* **1** (used when seeking agreement from someone):
Ashita kimasu ne. (あした来ますね) You are coming tomorrow,

aren't you? / Tetsudatte ne. (手伝ってね) Help me, *won't you?* / Kore wa oishii ne. (これはおいしいね) This is delicious, *isn't it?* / "Jaa ne." "Uñ, mata ne." (「じゃあね」「うん、またね」) "Well then..." "All right, see you soon, *okay?*"
2 (used after a phrase to obtain confirmation from the listener):
★ Overuse sounds too familiar.
Ano ne, kinoo ne, Giñza de ne, shokuji shite ne... (あのね、きのうね、銀座でね、食事してね...) *Look*...yesterday, *okay?* In Ginza, *understand?* We had a meal, *right?*
3 (used as an exclamation, or to indicate surprise):
Zuibuñ muzukashii desu ne. (ずいぶん難しいですね) Well, it is very difficult, *isn't it?* / Ano kata wa yuushuu desu ne. (あの方は優秀ですね) He's great, *isn't he?*
4 (used to slightly emphasize one's opinion):
Hayaku kaetta hoo ga ii to omoimasu ne. (早く帰ったほうがいいと思いますね) *I think* you had better go back soon. / Sono shigoto wa kyoo yarimasu. Ashita wa isogashii desu kara ne. (その仕事はきょうやります。あしたは忙しいですからね) I'll finish up the work today, because, *as you know*, we will be busy tomorrow.

ne¹⁴ ね *int.* look; listen; say:
★ Used to call attention.
Ne, kore kiree deshoo. (ね、これきれいでしょう) *Look*, isn't this lovely? / Ne, soo deshoo. (ね、そうでしょう) *Say*, that is right, isn't it?
《⇨ nee¹》

ne「a¹gari ねあがり (値上がり) *n.* increase in price; appreciation:
kookyoo-ryookiñ no neagari (公共料金の値上がり) an *increase in* utility *charges* / eñ [doru] no neagari (円[ドル]の値上がり) an *appreciation in the value* of the yen [dollar].

neagari suru (～する) *vi.* rise; go up: *Tochi wa sara ni* neagari suru *deshoo.* (土地はさらに値上がりするでしょう) Land prices are likely to further *go up.* ((↔ nesagari))

ne⌐age ねあげ (値上げ) *n.* price rise; increase; raise: *Koñgetsu kara yachiñ ga* neage *ni narimashita.* (今月から家賃が値上げになりました) Beginning this month, my rent *has been raised.*

　neage suru (～する) *vt.* raise the price: *Biiru-gaisha ga biiru no kouri kakaku o raigetsu kara* neage suru *to happyoo shita.* (ビール会社がビールの小売価格を来月から値上げすると発表した) Beer companies announced that they would *raise* the retail *prices* of beer from next month. ((↔ nesage))

ne⌐bari⌐ ねばり (粘り) *n.* **1** stickiness; adhesiveness: *Kono mochi wa* nebari *ga nai.* (この餅は粘りがない) This rice cake is not *nice and sticky.* ((⇨ nebaru)) **2** tenacity; perseverance: *Kimi wa* nebari *ga tarinai.* (きみは粘りが足りない) You lack *tenacity.* ((⇨ nebaru))

ne⌐ba⌐r·u ねばる (粘る) *vi.* (nebar·i-; nebar·a-; nebat-te Ⓒ) **1** be sticky; be glutinous: *Kono mochi wa yoku* nebaru. (このもちはよく粘る) This rice cake *is* nice and *glutinous.* ((⇨ nebari)) **2** (of a person) stick; persist: *Kare wa yookyuu ga tooru made* nebatta. (彼は要求が通るまで粘った) He *persisted* until his demands were met. ((⇨ nebari))

ne⌐biki ねびき (値引き) *n.* discount; reduction in price: *sañ-wari no* nebiki *de uru* (3割の値引きで売る) sell at a thirty percent *discount.*

　nebiki suru (～する) *vt.* discount; reduce a price: *Kono booshi wa hiyake shite imasu kara* nebiki shimasu. (この帽子は日焼けしていますから値引きします) This hat has been damaged by sunlight, so I will *give* you *a reduction.* / *Kono mise de wa zeñ shoohiñ o ni-wari* nebiki shite imasu. (この店では全商品を2割値引きしています) At this store, *they have reduced* all articles by twenty percent.

ne⌐boke⌐·ru ねぼける (寝惚ける) *vi.* (-boke-te Ⓥ) be half asleep; be not fully awake: Nebokete ita *no de nañ to itta ka oboete imaseñ.* (寝ぼけていたので何と言ったか覚えていません) I *was half asleep,* so I do not remember what I said. / Nebokeru *na!* (寝ぼけるな) *Wake up!*

ne⌐boo ねぼう (寝坊) *n.* late riser; sleepyhead; oversleeping: *Watashi wa* neboo *desu.* (私は寝坊です) I am a *late riser.*

　neboo suru (～する) *vt.* oversleep; get up late: *Kesa wa* neboo shite, *gakkoo ni okurete shimatta.* (今朝は寝坊して、学校に遅れてしまった) I *overslept* this morning and was late for school.

　— *a.n.* (～ na) oversleeping; sleepyheaded: *Uchi no musuko wa* neboo *na ko de komatte imasu.* (うちの息子は寝坊な子で困っています) We really have a hard time with our *sleepyheaded* son.

ne⌐dañ ねだん (値段) *n.* price; cost: *Kono tokee no* nedañ *wa ikura desu ka?* (この時計の値段はいくらですか) What is the *price* of this watch? / *Sono* nedañ *wa datoo [tegoro] da to omoimasu.* (その値段は妥当[手ごろ]だと思います) I think the *price* is reasonable. / *Kono hoñ wa* nedañ *ga takai [yasui].* (この本は値段が高い[安い]) The *price* of this book is high [low].

ne⌐da⌐r·u ねだる *vt.* (nedar·i-;

nedar·a-; nedat·te C) ask; beg;
press:
*Sono ko wa haha-oya ni omocha o
katte kure to* nedatta. (その子は母親
におもちゃを買ってくれとねだった) The
child *pleaded* with his mother to
buy him a toy.

neˈdoko ねどこ(寝床) *n.* bed:
nedoko *ni hairu* (寝床に入る) go to
bed / nedoko *kara okiru* (寝床から
起きる) get out of *bed*.

neˈe[1] ねえ *int.* (used as a form of
address between husband and
wife):
Nee, *chotto matte.* (ねえ、ちょっと待っ
て) Wait a moment, *darling.* / Nee,
soko de nani shite iru no. (ねえ、そこ
で何しているの) What are you doing
there, *my dear*? 《⇨ neˈe[4]》

nee[2] ねえ *p.* = ne[3].

neˈesañ ねえさん(姉さん) *n.* one's
own older sister. ★ When addressing one's own older sister,
'(o)nee-sañ' is used instead of
her first name. 《⇨ ane, niisañ》

neˈfuda ねふだ(値札) *n.* price tag
[label]:
kabañ ni nefuda *o tsukeru* (かばんに
値札を付ける) put a *price tag* on a
bag.

neˈgaˈi ねがい(願い) *n.* wish;
desire; request:
heewa e no negai (平和への願い)
desire for peace / *Wareware no*
negai *ga kanaimashita.* (われわれの
願いがかないました) Our *wish* has
been fulfilled. 《⇨ o-negai; negau》

neˈgaˈ·u ねがう(願う) *vt.* (nega·i-;
negaw·a-; negat·te C) wish;
desire; hope:
Dare mo ga heewa o negatte imasu. (だれもが平和を願っています) Every-
one *desires* peace. / *Mata o-me ni
kakareru koto o* negatte imasu. (ま
たお目にかかれることを願っています) I
hope to see you again. 《⇨ negai》

neˈgi ねぎ(葱) *n.* Welsh onion;
scallion. ★ Onions are called

'*tamanegi.*' 《⇨ yasai (illus.)》

neˈji ねじ *n.* **1** screw:
neji *o shimeru* [*yurumeru*] (ねじを締
める[ゆるめる]) turn [loosen] a *screw*
/ neji *de tomeru* (ねじで留める) fasten with a *screw*.
2 the spring of a watch:
Tokee no neji o maku *no o wasureta.* (時計のねじを巻くのを忘れた) I
forgot to *wind* the clock.
neji o maku (～を巻く) get a person moving: *Kare wa namakete
iru kara* neji o maite yatta. (彼は怠
けているからねじを巻いてやった) Since
he was taking things too easy, I
got him moving.

neˈjireˈ·ru ねじれる(捩れる) *vi.* (ne-
jire·te V) be twisted:
Kono himo wa nejirete iru. (このひも
はねじれている) This string *is twisted.*
《⇨ nejiru》

neˈjiˈr·u ねじる(捩る) *vt.* (nejir·i-;
nejir·a-; nejit·te C) twist;
screw; wring:
futa o nejitte *shimeru* [*akeru*] (ふた
をねじって閉める[開ける]) *screw* a cap
on [off] / *Kare wa watashi no ude
o* nejitta. (彼は私の腕をねじった) He
twisted my arm. 《⇨ nejireru》

neˈkase·ru ねかせる(寝かせる) *vt.*
(nekase·te V) put to bed; let
sleep. 《⇨ nekasu》

neˈkas·u ねかす(寝かす) *vt.* (ne-
kash·i-; nekas·a-; nekash·i-te
C) put to bed; let sleep:
Yurikago o yusutte, akañboo o ne-
kashita. (揺りかごをゆすって、赤ん坊を
寝かした) I rocked the baby to
sleep in its cradle / *Moo kodomo-
tachi o* nekasu *jikañ desu.* (もう子ど
もたちを寝かす時間です) It's already
time to *put* the children *to bed.* /
Asu wa osoku made nekashite
kudasai. (あすは遅くまで寝かしてくださ
い) Please *let* me *sleep* in late
tomorrow. 《⇨ neru[1]》

neˈkkuresu ネックレス *n.* necklace:

Kanojo wa kubi ni shiñju no nek-kuresu *o shite ita.* (彼女は首に真珠の ネックレスをしていた) She was wearing a pearl *necklace.*

ne¦ko ねこ (猫) *n.* cat:
neko *o kau* (猫を飼う) keep a *cat* / *Neko ni kobañ.* (*proverb*) (猫に小判) Pearls cast before swine. (literally 'Coins to *cats*') ((⇨ buta))

ne¦koro¦b·u ねころぶ (寝転ぶ) *vi.* (-korob·i-; -korob·a-; -koroñ-de Ⓒ) lie down; throw oneself down:
Kare wa kooeñ no shibafu ni neko-roñda. (彼は公園の芝生に寝転んだ) He *threw himself down* on the grass in the park.

ne¦kutai ネクタイ *n.* necktie; bow tie:
nekutai *o shimeru* [*hazusu*] (ネクタイを締める[はずす]) put on [take off] a *necktie* / nekutai *o naosu* (ネクタイを直す) straighten a *necktie* / nekutai *o yurumeru* (ネクタイをゆるめる) loosen a *necktie* / *Ii* nekutai *o shite imasu ne.* (いいネクタイをしていますね) That is a nice *necktie* you have on. / nekutai-piñ (ネクタイピン) a *tiepin.*

ne¦maki ねまき (寝巻) *n.* nightclothes; nightgown; pajamas.

ne¦mu·i ねむい (眠い) *a.* (-ku) sleepy; drowsy:
Kaigi no toki, totemo nemukatta. (会議のとき、とても眠かった) I *felt* very *drowsy* during the meeting. / *Moo* nemuku *natte kita.* (もう眠くなってきた) I have already become *sleepy.*

ne¦mure·ru ねむれる (眠れる) *vi.* (nemure-te Ⓥ) be able to sleep:
Sakuya wa yoku nemurenakatta. (昨夜はよく眠れなかった) Last night I *was not able to sleep* well. ((⇨ ne-muru))

ne¦mur·u ねむる (眠る) *vi.* (ne-mur·i-; nemur·a-; nemut-te Ⓒ) sleep; fall asleep:

Yuube wa yoku nemurimashita *ka?* (ゆうべはよく眠りましたか) *Did* you *sleep* well last night? / *Akañ-boo wa gussuri* nemutte imasu. (赤ん坊はぐっすり眠っています) The baby *is sleeping* soundly. ((⇨ ne-mureru; neru¦))

ne¦muta·i ねむたい (眠たい) *a.* (-ku) = nemui.

ne¦ñ¹ ねん (年) *n.* **1** year:
Kare wa neñ *ni ichi-do gaikoku e iku.* (彼は年に一度外国へ行く) He goes abroad once a *year.* / *Chichi wa sañ-*neñ *mae ni nakunarima-shita.* (父は3年前に亡くなりました) My father died three *years* ago. / *Shoowa gojuu-*neñ *wa señ kyuu-hyaku nanajuu go-*neñ *desu.* (昭和50年は1975年です) The fiftieth *year* of Showa is 1975. ((⇨ hi¹ (table)))
2 grade:
*Musuko wa kookoo ichi-*neñ *desu.* (息子は高校1年です) My son is in the first *year* of high school. ((⇨ gakuneñ))

ne¦ñ² ねん (念) *n.* sense; feeling:
Kimi wa kañsha no neñ *ga tarinai.* (きみは感謝の念が足りない) You lack a *sense* of gratitude. / *Miñna ga kare ni soñkee no* neñ *o idaite iru.* (みんなが彼に尊敬の念を抱いている) Everyone has a *feeling* of respect for him.

neñ no tame (〜のため) just in case: Neñ no tame *kasa o motte yuki nasai.* (念のため傘を持って行きなさい) Take an umbrella *just in case.*

neñ o ireru (〜を入れる) do with great care: *Motto* neñ *o irete sooji o shi nasai.* (もっと念を入れて掃除しなさい) Clean the room *more carefully.* / *Neñ ni wa* neñ *o ireta hoo ga yoi.* (念には念を入れたほうがよい) You had better *make doubly sure.*

neñ o osu (〜を押す) remind:

Sore o wasurenai yoo ni kare ni
neñ o oshita. (それを忘れないように彼に念を押した) I *reminded* him not to forget about it.

neｒñbutsu ねんぶつ (念仏) *n*. Buddhist invocation.
neñbutsu *o tonaeru* (念仏を唱える) chant a *Buddhist invocation*.

neｒñchoo ねんちょう (年長) *n*. seniority:
Kare wa watashi yori mittsu neñ-choo desu. (彼は私より3つ年長です) He is *older* than me by three years. / neñchoo-sha (年長者) a *senior*; an *elder person*.

neｒñdai ねんだい (年代) *n*. generation; date; age; period:
Kare to watashi de wa nendai *ga chigau.* (彼と私では年代が違う) We are of different *generations*. / *Kanojo wa rekishi no* nendai *o yoku oboete iru.* (彼女は歴史の年代をよく覚えている) She has a good memory for historical *dates*.

neｒñdo[1] ねんど (年度) *n*. year; fiscal [financial] year:
Gakkoo no nendo *wa shi-gatsu ni hajimarimasu.* (学校の年度は四月に始まります) The school *year* begins in April. / *Rai-*nendo *no yosañ ga kimatta.* (来年度の予算が決まった) The budget for the next *year* has been decided on.

neｒñdo[2] ねんど (粘土) *n*. clay:
neñdo-zaiku (粘土細工) *claywork*.

neｒñga ねんが (年賀) *n*. New Year's greetings:
neñga *ni iku* (年賀に行く) pay a *New Year's call* / neñga *no aisatsu o kawasu* (年賀のあいさつを交わす) exchange *New Year's greetings*.

neｒñga-haｒgaki ねんがはがき (年賀葉書) *n*. New Year's greeting postcard. ★ The postal card for New Year's greetings issued by the post office has a lottery number printed on it. 《⇨ neñgajoo》

NEÑGA-HAGAKI

neｒñgajoo ねんがじょう (年賀状) *n*. New Year's card:
neñgajoo *o dasu* (年賀状を出す) send a *New Year's card*. 《⇨ neñga-hagaki》

(CULTURE)

In Japan, New Year's cards are more popular than Christmas cards. Mail with '年賀' printed in red is usually posted in middle or late December and delivered on the morning of New Year's Day.

NEÑGAJOO

neｒñgaｒppi ねんがっぴ (年月日) *n*. date:
Koko ni neñgappi *o kaite kudasai.* (ここに年月日を書いてください) Please write the *date* here.

neｒñgetsu ねんげつ (年月) *n*. time; years:
Kare ga nakunatte kara hachi-neñ no neñgetsu *ga tatta.* (彼が亡くなってから8年の年月がたった) Eight *years* have passed since he died. / *Sono toñneru o kañsee suru no ni nagai* neñgetsu *ga kakatta.* (そのトンネルを

完成するのに長い年月がかかった）It took many *years* to build the tunnel. 《⇨ tsukihi》

ne￢ngo￢o ねんごう（年号）*n.* the name of an era; the posthumous name of a Japanese emperor and of his reign:
Ima no neñgoo *wa Heesee desu.* （今の年号は平成です）The current *era* is Heisei. 《⇨ geñgoo (table)》

ne￢ñjuu ねんじゅう（年中）*n., adv.* all the year round; throughout the year; always:
Sono mise wa neñjuu *eegyoo shite imasu.* （その店は年中営業しています）That shop is open *throughout the year.* / *Ano futari wa* neñjuu *keñka o shite iru.* （あの二人は年中けんかをしている）The two of them are *always* qaurreling.

ne￢ñkañ ねんかん（年間）*n.* year:
Neñkañ *keekaku o tatenakereba naranai.* （年間計画を立てなければならない）We must set up a plan *for the year.* / *Watashi wa* juugo-neñkañ *mujiko desu.* （私は15年間無事故です）I've had a clean driving record *for fifteen years.* / neñkañ-*shuunyuu* （年間収入）an *annual* income. 《⇨ gekkañ》

ne￢ñmatsu ねんまつ（年末）*n.* the end of the year:
neñmatsu *oo-uridashi* （年末大売り出し）a *year-end* bargain sale. 《↔ neñtoo》《⇨ getsumatsu; shuumatsu》

ne￢ñree ねんれい（年齢）*n.* age:
Musuko-sañ no neñree *wa o-iku-tsu desu ka?* （息子さんの年齢はおいくつですか）What is the *age* of your son? / *Kare to watashi wa* neñree *ga onaji desu.* （彼と私は年齢が同じです）He and I are of the same *age.* 《⇨ toshi¹》

ne￢ñryo￢o ねんりょう（燃料）*n.* fuel:
Neñryoo *ga tarinai.* （燃料が足りない）We are short of *fuel.* / neñryoo-

hi （燃料費）*fuel* expenses.

-ne￢ñsee ねんせい（年生）*suf.* a student of the stated academic year:
*shoogaku roku-*neñsee （小学6年生）a sixth *year* elementary school pupil / *chuugaku sañ-*neñsee （中学3年生）a junior high school pupil in the third *year* / *kookoo sañ-*neñsee （高校3年生）a third *year* high school student / *daigaku yo-*neñsee （大学4年生）a university student in the fourth *year*; a *senior.*

ne￢ñtoo ねんとう（年頭）*n.* the beginning of a year:
Shachoo ga neñtoo *no aisatsu o nobeta.* （社長が年頭の挨拶を述べた）The president made a *New Year's* speech. 《↔ neñmatsu》

ne￢rai ねらい（狙い）*n.* **1** aim; mark; target:
Kare wa mato ni nerai *o sadameta.* （彼は的にねらいを定めた）He took *aim* at the target. / Nerai *ga hazurete shimatta.* （ねらいが外れてしまった）I missed the *mark.* 《⇨ nerau》
2 purpose; aim:
Kare no nerai *wa motto yoi kyuu-ryoo o morau koto ni aru.* （彼のねらいはもっとよい給料をもらうことにある）His *aim* is to get a higher salary. 《⇨ nerau》

ne￢ra·u ねらう（狙う）*vt.* (nera·i-; neraw·a-; nerat-te Ⓒ) **1** take aim; set one's sights:
Mato no mañnaka o yoku neratte, *uchi nasai.* （的の真ん中をよくねらって，撃ちなさい）*Take* careful *aim* at the center of the target and shoot. 《⇨ nerai》
2 aim (a goal, victory, success, etc.):
Watashi-tachi wa yuushoo o neratte imasu. （私たちは優勝をねらっています）We *are aiming* for victory. / *Kare wa buchoo no isu o* neratte iru. （彼は部長のいすをねらって

いる) He *has an eye* on the post of general manager. 《⇨ nerai》

ne·「ru¹   ねる (寝る) *vi.* (ne-te V)

1 go to bed; sleep:

> ――― USAGE ―――
>
> The basic meaning of '*neru*' is to lie down, while '*nemuru*' more specifically means 'sleep.' However, '*neru*' is often used with the meaning of '*nemuru*.'

Watashi wa juuni-ji mae ni ne-masu. (私は 12 時前に寝ます) I *go to bed* before twelve. / *Kanojo wa otto ga kaette kuru made,* nenai *de matte ita.* (彼女は夫が帰って来るまで、寝ないで待っていた) She *stayed up* waiting until her husband came back. / *Kare wa mada* nete imasu. (彼はまだ寝ています) He *is* still *asleep.* 《⇨ nekasu》

2 be sick in bed:

Kinoo wa kaze de nete imashita. (きのうはかぜで寝ていました) I *was sick in bed* with a cold yesterday. / *Kare wa* neta-kiri *ni natte shi-matta.* (彼は寝たきりになってしまった) He became *bedridden.*

3 lie down:

aomuke ni neru (仰向けに寝る) *lie down* on one's back / *Watashi wa sofaa no ue ni* nete, *terebi o mita.* (私はソファーの上に寝て、テレビを見た) I *lay down* on the sofa watching TV. 《⇨ nekasu》

ne「r·u²   ねる (練る) *vi.* (ner·i-; ne-r·a-; net-te C) **1** knead:

komugi-ko no kiji o neru (小麦粉の生地を練る) *knead* dough.

2 work out (a plan, etc.) carefully; elaborate:

keekaku o neru (計画を練る) *work out* one's plans *carefully* / *buñ-shoo o* neru (文章を練る) *polish* one's prose.

ne「sagari   ねさがり (値下がり) *n.* fall in price; depreciation:

eñ [doru] no nesagari (円[ドル]の値下がり) a *depreciation* in the value of the yen [dollar]. 《↔ neagari》

nesagari suru (～する) *vi.* fall; go down: *Saikiñ kookyuuhiñ ga zee no hikisage de* nesagari shima-shita. (最近高級品が税の引き下げで値下がりしました) Luxury goods *have* recently *become cheaper* because of the reductions in taxes.

ne「sage   ねさげ (値下げ) *n.* reduction in price; price cut: *Sono waapuro no furui kata wa* nesage ni natta. (そのワープロの古い型は値下げになった) The old model of that word processsor *has been reduced in price.* / nesage *kyoo-soo* (値下げ競争) a *price* war. 《↔ neage》

nesage suru (～する) *vt.* reduce; cut the price: *Jidoosha wa ko-toshi no shi-gatsu kara* nesage shita. (自動車は今年の 4 月から値下げした) They *marked down* the prices of cars from this April.

ne「sobe「r·u   ねそべる (寝そべる) *vi.* (nesober·i-; nesober·a-; neso-bet-te C) lie down; sprawl; stretch: *Kare wa kooeñ no beñchi ni* neso-bette ita. (彼は公園のベンチに寝そべっていた) He *lay sprawled out* on the park bench.

ne「sshiñ   ねっしん (熱心) *a.n.* (～ na, ni) eager; hardworking; devoted: nesshiñ *na señsee* (熱心な先生) a *devoted* teacher / *Kare wa shigoto ni* nesshiñ *da.* (彼は仕事に熱心だ) He is *devoted* to his work. / *Su-zuki-sañ wa totemo* nesshiñ *ni beñkyoo shite iru.* (鈴木さんはとても熱心に勉強している) Mr. Suzuki is studying *very hard.* / *Amari* nes-shiñ *ni sasou no de kotowarena-katta.* (あまり熱心に誘うので断れなかった) As he *eagerly* invited me, I couldn't refuse.

ne「ss·u「ru   ねっする (熱する) *vi., vt.*

(nessh·i-; nessh·i-; nessh·i-te
①) heat; become hot:
Kono mizu ga futtoo suru made
nesshi nasai. (この水が沸騰するまで熱
しなさい) *Heat* this water until it
boils. / *Mizu wa* nessuru *to sui-
jooki ni naru.* (水は熱すると水蒸気に
なる) Water turns into steam
when it *is heated*.
nesshi-yasuku same-yasui (熱
し易く冷め易い) easily get excited
and easily cool off: *Kare wa* nesshi-yasuku same-yasui. (彼は熱し易
く冷め易い) He *is easily excited and
cools down quickly*.

ne⌐**takiri** ねたきり(寝たきり) *n.*
bedridden:
Chichi wa netakiri *desu.* (父は寝た
きりです) My father is *bedridden*. /
netakiri-*roojiñ* (寝たきり老人) a
bedridden old man [woman].

ne⌐**tsu**⌐ ねつ(熱) *n.* **1** heat:
taiyoo no netsu (太陽の熱) the *heat*
of the sun.
2 fever; temperature:
netsu *o hakaru* (熱をはかる) take
one's *temperature* / *Kono ko wa*
netsu *ga aru.* (この子は熱がある) This
child has a *fever*. / *Netsu wa sa-
garimashita ka?* (熱は下がりましたか)
Has your *temperature* gone
down?
3 enthusiasm; craze:
Kare wa netsu *no komotta eñzetsu o shita.* (彼は熱のこもった演説をし
た) He made a speech with *enthusiasm*. / *Saikiñ wa kabu no* netsu
mo sukkari sagatte shimatta. (最
近は株の熱もすっかり下がってしまった)
Recently the stock market *craze*
has completely abated.

ne⌐**ttai** ねったい(熱帯) *n.* torrid
zone; tropics:
nettai-*gyo* (熱帯魚) a *tropical* fish.
《↔ kañtai》《⇨ kikoo (table)》

ne⌐**ttoo** ねっとう(熱湯) *n.* boiling
water.

ne⌐**uchi** ねうち(値打ち) *n.* value;
worth; price:
Kore wa taiheñ neuchi *no aru kabiñ desu.* (これはたいへん値打ちのある
花瓶です) This is a vase of great
value. / *Sore wa yatte miru* neuchi *ga arimasu.* (それはやってみる値打
ちがあります) That is *worth* trying.
《⇨ kachi¹》

ne⌐**zumi** ねずみ(鼠) *n.* mouse;
rat: ★ Those that live in houses
in Japan are rats. Mice are specifically called '*hatsuka nezumi*.'
Kono daidokoro ni wa nezumi *ga
iru.* (この台所にはねずみがいる) There
is a *house rat* in this kitchen.

NHK *n.* Japan Broadcasting Corporation. (日本放送協会 = *Nippoñ
Hoosoo Kyookai*)

ni¹¹ に(二) *n.* two:
ni-*mai no kami* (2枚の紙) *two*
sheets of paper / ni-*kai* (2回)
twice / ni-*bañme no hito* (二番目の
人) the *second* person. 《⇨ futatsu;
suu² (table)》

ni² に *p.* **1** (indicates a place):
a at; in: ★ Indicates existence
at a location.
Eki no mae ni depaato ga arimasu.
(駅の前にデパートがあります) There is
a department store *in front of*
the station. / *Ashita wa watashi
wa uchi* ni *imasu.* (あしたは私は家に
います) I will be *at* home tomorrow. / *Tookyoo de wa apaato* ni
suñde imashita. (東京ではアパートに
住んでいました) I lived *in* an apartment in Tokyo. / *Kyooto* ni *wa
yuumee na tera ga takusañ arimasu.* (京都には有名な寺がたくさんあり
ます) There are many famous temples *in* Kyoto. / *Kanojo wa giñkoo* ni *tsutomete imasu.* (彼女は銀
行に勤めています) She works *at* a
bank. ★ Use '*de*' to indicate the
location of an action. 《⇨ de¹》
b on; onto: ★ Indicates the
final location of an object that is
moved.

Hoñ wa tsukue no ue ni *oite kudasai.*(本は机の上に置いてください) Put the book *on* the desk, please. / *Soko* ni *mono o sutete wa ikemaseñ.*(そこに物を捨ててはいけません) You must not throw things away *there.*

c to; toward: ★ Indicates direction or final destination. Used with verbs of movement.
Watashi wa mainichi gakkoo ni *ikimasu.*(私は毎日学校に行きます) I go *to* school every day. / *Kare wa kesa Tookyoo-eki* ni *tsukimashita.*(彼は今朝東京駅に着きました) He arrived *at* Tokyo Station this morning. / *Tsugi no kado o hidari* ni *magatte kudasai.*(次の角を左に曲がってください) Turn *to* the left at the next corner. ★ Direction can also be indicated by 'e.' 《⇨ e³》

2 to; from; by: ★ Indicates the direction of giving or receiving.
Nokorimono o inu ni *yatta.*(残り物を犬にやった) I gave the leftovers *to* the dog. / *Señsee* ni *purezeñto o itadaita.*(先生にプレゼントをいただいた) I got a present *from* my teacher. / *Tanaka-sañ* ni *omoshiroi hanashi o shite moratta.*(田中さんにおもしろい話をしてもらった) I was told an interesting story *by* Ms. Tanaka. 《⇨ kara³》

3 at; in: ★ Indicates the time of an action or event.
Watashi wa maiasa roku-ji ni *okimasu.*(私は毎朝6時に起きます) I get up *at* six every morning. / *Sono hoñ wa ku-gatsu* ni *shuppañ saremasu.*(その本は9月に出版されます) The book will be published *in* September. / *Hima na toki ni kono hoñ o yomi nasai.*(暇なときにこの本を読みなさい) Read this book *when* you have time.

4 in; to: ★ Used in expressions of frequency or proportion.

Kare wa ichi-nichi ni *tabako o futa-hako suimasu.*(彼は1日にたばこを2箱吸います) He smokes two packs of cigarettes *in* a day. / *Riñgo o hitori* ni *sañ-ko zutsu agemashita.*(りんごを一人に3個ずつあげました) I gave three apples *to* each person.

5 to; into: ★ Indicates a change or resulting condition.
Shiñgoo ga aka kara ao ni *kawatta.*(信号が赤から青にかわった) The traffic lights changed from red *to* green. / *Haru ni naru to sakura ga sakimasu.*(春になると桜が咲きます) *When spring comes,* the cherry trees blossom. / *Gogo kara* ame ni natta.(午後から雨になった) *It started raining* in the afternoon.

6 (used with verbs of decision): *Kaisha o* yameru koto ni *kimeta.*(会社をやめることに決めた) I have decided *to quit* the company. / "Nani ni *shimasu ka.*" "Koohii ni *shimasu.*"(「何にしますか」「コーヒーにします」) "*What* would you like?" "I'll have *a cup of coffee.*"

7 to: ★ Indicates a recipient.
Gaikoku no tomodachi ni *tegami o kaita.*(外国の友だちに手紙を書いた) I wrote a letter *to* a friend abroad. / *Kore o anata* ni *agemashoo.*(これをあなたにあげましょう) I will give this *to* you.

8 by: ★ Indicates the agent of a passive sentence.
Kyoo wa señsee ni *homerareta.*(きょうは先生にほめられた) I was praised *by* my teacher today. / *Sono hoñ wa ooku no hito* ni *yomarete imasu.*(その本は多くの人に読まれています) That book has been read *by* many people. / *Kare no keñkyuu wa sekai-juu no kagakusha* ni *chuumoku sarete imasu.*(彼の研究は世界中の科学者に注目されています) His research is attracting the attention of scientists all over the

world. ★ '*Kara*' can also be used. 《⇨ kara³》

9 (indicates the person who is made or allowed to do an action): ★ Used with a causative verb.

Kodomo ni *motto hoñ o yomase nasai.* (子どもにもっと本を読ませなさい) Encourage *children* to read more books. / *Sono shigoto o* watashi ni *sasete kudasai.* (その仕事を私にさせてください) I beg you to let *me* do the job.

10 for: ★ Used when comparing, differentiating, estimating, etc.

Kono doresu wa watashi ni *choo-do ii.* (このドレスは私にちょうどいい) This dress is just right *for* me. / *Kono hoñ wa kodomo* ni *wa muzu-kashi-sugimasu.* (この本は子どもには難しすぎます) This book is too difficult *for* children. / *Kono akachañ wa chichi-oya* ni *nite iru.* (この赤ちゃんは父親に似ている) This baby looks *like* his father. / *Koko wa tsuri* ni *ii basho da.* (ここは釣りにいい場所だ) This ia a good place *for* fishing.

11 in order to; for the purpose of: ★ Indicates purpose or reason. Used with verbs of movement, especially '*iku*' and '*kuru*.'

Watashi wa Nihoñ e Nihoñgo o narai ni *kimashita.* (私は日本へ日本語を習いに来ました) I came to Japan *to* learn Japanese. / *Sañpo* ni *iki-mashoo.* (散歩に行きましょう) Let's go *for* a walk. / *O-cha o nomi* ni *kimaseñ ka?* (お茶を飲みに来ませんか) Won't you come and have a cup of tea?

12 for; as: ★ Indicates purpose or means.

Kono sakana wa shokuyoo ni *na-ranai.* (この魚は食用にならない) This fish is not fit *for* food. / *Kono heya wa kodomo-beya* ni *tsukatte*

imasu. (この部屋は子ども部屋に使っています) We use this room *as* the children's room.

13 from; by: ★ Indicates the cause or reason for a state or situation.

Shigoto ni *tsukaremashita.* (仕事に疲れました) I am tired *from* work. / *O-kane* ni *komatte imasu.* (お金に困っています) I am *in* financial difficulties. / *Mono-oto* ni *odoroite me ga sameta.* (物音に驚いて目が覚めた) I woke up, alarmed *by* a noise. / *Ano hito no hanashi* ni *wa itsu-mo kañdoo shimasu.* (あの人の話にはいつも感動します) I am always moved *by* his stories.

14 at; in: ★ Used in expressions indicating ability, skill or knowledge.

Kare wa suugaku ni *tsuyoi.* (彼は数学に強い) He is good *at* math. / *Ano hito wa seeyoo no rekishi* ni *kuwashii.* (あの人は西洋の歴史に詳しい) He is well versed *in* European history.

15 in (a stated way): ★ Used in expressions indicating manner.

Sore wa koñna fuu ni *yatte wa doo desu ka?* (それはこんなふうにやってはどうですか) How about doing it *in* this manner? / *Kare wa sono buñ-shoo o* machigawazu ni *yoñda.* (彼はその文章を間違わずに読んだ) He read the sentence *faultlessly*.

ni³ に *p.* and: ★ Used in listing, recalling or restating items.

"Kinoo dare ga paatii ni *kima-shita?" "Eeto, Tanaka-sañ* ni, *Yamada-sañ* ni, *sore kara Katoo-sañ mo kimashita."* (「きのうだれがパーティーに来ました」「ええと、田中さんに、山本さんに、それから加藤さんも来ました」) "Who came to the party yesterday?" "Let me see... Miss Tanaka *and* Mr. Yamamoto, *and* also Miss Kato, were there." / *Kyoo kau mono wa tamago* ni *mi-*

ruku ni, *sore kara retasu* ni *tomato desu.*(きょう買うものは、卵にミルクに、それから、レタスにトマトです) Today I have to buy eggs *and* milk, and also lettuce *and* tomatoes. / *Sono hito wa jiiñzu* ni *T-shatsu to iu kakkoo de meñsetsu ni kita.*(その人はジーンズにTシャツというかっこうで面接に来た) He came to the interview dressed in jeans *and* a T-shirt. 《⇨ to²; ya¹; yara》

ni¹⁴ に (荷) *n.* load; freight; cargo:
kuruma ni ni *o tsumu* (車に荷を積む) *load up* a car / *kuruma kara* ni *o orosu* (車から荷を降ろす) remove a *load* from a car.

ni⌐aꜜ·u にあう (似合う) *vi.* (nia·i-; niaw·a-; niat-te ⓒ) suit; become:
Sono megane wa anata ni yoku niatte imasu.(その眼鏡はあなたによく似合っています) Those glasses really *suit* you. / *Kare wa shiñshi ni* niawanai *koto o shita.* (彼は紳士に似合わないことをした) He did something *unbecoming* of a gentleman.

ni⌐buꜜ·i にぶい (鈍い) *a.* (-ku)
1 (of sound) dull:
nibui *oto* (鈍い音) a *dull* sound.
2 (of a knife) blunt:
ha no nibui *naifu* (刃の鈍いナイフ) a *blunt* knife. 《↔ surudoi》
3 (of a pain, motion, etc.) dull; slow:
nibui *itami* (鈍い痛み) a *dull* pain / *Toshi o toru to ugoki ga* nibuku *naru.*(年をとると動きが鈍くなる) One's actions *slow down* as one becomes older. 《↔ surudoi》
4 (of a person) slow; thickheaded:
Mada ki ga tsukanai nañte kare mo nibui *desu ne.*(まだ気がつかないなんて彼も鈍いですね) He still does not understand. He is a bit *slow*, isn't he? 《↔ surudoi》

-nichi にち (日) *suf.* day:

*Kyoo wa nañ-*nichi *desu ka?* (きょうは何日ですか) What *day* of the month is it today? / *Kono shigoto wa ichi-*nichi *de wa dekimaseñ.* (この仕事は1日ではできません) This job cannot be done in a *day*. / *Ni, sañ-*nichi *koko ni taizai shimasu.* (2, 3日ここに滞在します) I will stay here for a few *days*.

ni⌐chiee-jiꜜteñ (日英辞典) *n.* a Japanese-English dictionary for English-speaking people. ★ A Japanese-English dictionary for Japanese is called '*waee-jiteñ*' (和英辞典). 《⇨ jiteñ》

ni⌐chiji にちじ (日時) *n.* time and date:
nichiji *o kimeru* (日時を決める) fix the *time and date* / *Shuppatsu no* nichiji *wa mitee desu.*(出発の日時は未定です) The *time and date* of departure are undecided yet.

ni⌐chijoo-kaꜜiwa (日常会話) *n.* everyday conversation.

ni⌐chijoo-seꜜekatsu (日常生活) *n.* daily life.

ni⌐chiyoo daꜜiku (日曜大工) *n.* Sunday [weekend] carpenter. 《⇨ daiku》

ni⌐chiyoꜜo(bi) にちよう(び) (日曜(日)) *n.* Sunday:
Kyoo wa nichiyoobi *desu.*(きょうは日曜日です) Today is *Sunday*. / *Kono mise wa* nichiyoo *ga yasumi desu.*(この店は日曜が休みです) This store is closed on *Sundays*. / *Tsugi no* nichiyoo *ni wa yakyuu no shiai ga arimasu.*(次の日曜には野球の試合があります) There is a baseball game next *Sunday*. 《⇨ yoobi (table)》

ni⌐chiyoohiñ にちようひん (日用品) *n.* daily necessities.

ni⌐eꜜ·ru にえる (煮える) *vi.* (nie-te Ⓥ) cook; be cooked:
Jagaimo wa sugu ni niemaseñ.(じゃがいもはすぐに煮えません) Potatoes *do not cook* quickly. 《⇨ niru¹》

ni「ga」·i にがい（苦い）*a.* (-ku)
1 (of taste) bitter:
Kono kusuri wa nigai. (この薬は苦い) This medicine is *bitter*.
《↔ amai》《⇨ aji¹ (table)》
2 (of experience) hard; bitter:
Koñna nigai keekeñ wa hajimete desu. (こんな苦い経験は初めてです) This is the first time I have had a *bitter* experience like this.
3 (of a countenance) sour; unpleasant:
Chichi wa watashi no itta koto ni taishite nigai kao o shita. (父は私の言ったことに対して苦い顔をした) My father made a *wry* face in response to what I said.

ni「ga」s·u にがす（逃がす）*vt.* (nigash·i-; nigas·a-; nigash·i-te C)
set free; let go; let escape:
Sakana o nigashite yatta. (魚を逃がしてやった) I *have released* the fish.
| *Keesatsu wa yoogisha o nigashite shimatta.* (警察は容疑者を逃がしてしまった) The police *have gone and let* the suspect *escape*. | *Kono yoi kikai o nigasanai yoo ni shiyoo.* (この良い機会を逃がさないようにしよう) Let's *not miss* this great opportunity. 《⇨ nigeru》

ni「gate」 にがて（苦手）*a.n.* (～ na)
1 weak point:
Rika wa nigate desu. (理科は苦手です) Science is my *weak point*. | *Anata no nigate na kamoku wa nañ desu ka?* (あなたの苦手な科目は何ですか) What is your *weak* subject at school? 《↔ tokui》
2 person who is hard to deal with; tough customer:
Ano hito wa nigate da. (あの人は苦手だ) I just *cannot deal with* him. | *Tsugi no taiseñ aite wa nigate na chiimu da.* (次の対戦相手は苦手なチームだ) The opposing team in the next game will be a *tough customer*.

ni-「gatsu」 にがつ（二月）*n.* February:
Ni-gatsu mikka no yoru ni wa mamemaki o shimasu. (二月三日の夜には豆まきをします) We throw roasted beans on the evening of *February* 3. 《⇨ tsuki¹ (table)》

ni「gedas·u にげだす（逃げ出す）*vi.* (-dash·i-; -das·a-; -dash·i-te C)
run away; take to one's heels:
Keekañ ga kuru to kare-ra wa nigedashita. (警官が来ると彼らは逃げ出した) They *ran away* as the policeman approached.

ni「ge」·ru にげる（逃げる）*vi.* (nige-te V) run away; escape; flee:
Doroboo wa subayaku nigeta. (泥棒はすばやく逃げた) The thief nimbly *escaped*. | *Raioñ ga ori kara nigete, oosawagi ni natta.* (ライオンがおりから逃げて、大騒ぎになった) The lion *escaped* from its cage and caused a great disturbance. 《⇨ nigasu》

ni「giri にぎり（握り）*n.* **1** grip; handle:
nigiri *no futoi* [*hosoi*] *raketto* (握りの太い[細い]ラケット) a racket with a thick [thin] *grip*. 《⇨ nigiru》
2 = nigirizushi.

ni「giri」zushi にぎりずし（握り鮨）*n.* hard-rolled sushi. ★ Small vinegared rice balls topped with a variety of ingredients. Often shortened to 'nigiri.' 《⇨ sushi》

ni「gir·u にぎる（握る）*vt.* (nigir·i-; nigir·a-; nigit-te C) **1** grasp; grip; hold:
Kodomo wa haha-oya no te o nigitte ita. (子どもは母親の手を握っていた) The child *was holding* his mother's hand. 《⇨ nigiri》
2 dominate (an organization); rule; control:
Kare ga kaisha no subete o nigitte iru. (彼が会社のすべてを握っている) He *controls* everything in the company.

ni「giwa」·u にぎわう（賑わう）*vi.*

(-wa·i-; -waw·a-; -wat·te C̄)
be crowded; be alive; be prosperous:
Yuueñchi wa hito de nigiwatte ita.
(遊園地は人でにぎわっていた) The amusement park *was bustling* with people. 《⇨ nigiyaka》

ni⌈gi⌉yaka にぎやか (賑やか) *a.n.*
(～ na, ni) **1** (of place) busy; crowded:
Eki-mae no toori wa itsu-mo nigiyaka *desu.* (駅前の通りはいつもにぎやかです) The street in front of the station is always *busy.* / *Kono shooteñgai wa yuugata ni naru to* nigiyaka *ni narimasu.* (この商店街は夕方になるとにぎやかになります) This shopping center becomes *crowded* in the evening. 《⇨ nigiwau》
2 (of people, crowds, etc.) merry; lively; cheerful; noisy:
nigiyaka *na waraigoe* (にぎやかな笑い声) *merry* laughter / nigiyaka *na paatii* (にぎやかなパーティー) an *animated* party / *Eñkai de wa miñna ga* nigiyaka *ni noñdari utattari shita.* (宴会ではみんながにぎやかに飲んだり歌ったりした) Everyone was *cheerfully* drinking and singing at the party. / *Soto wa matsuri no taiko no oto de* nigiyaka *datta.* (外は祭りの太鼓の音でにぎやかだった) With the sound of the festival drum, it was *noisy* outside.

ni⌈gori⌉[1] にごり (濁り) *n.* **1** muddiness; unclearness:
nigori *no aru iro* (濁りのある色) a *muddy* color / *Kono mizu wa* nigori *ga aru.* (この水は濁りがある) This water is *not clear.* 《⇨ nigoru》
2 voiced consonant. 《⇨ dakuoñ; nigoru》

ni⌈go⌉r·u にごる (濁る) *vi.* (nigor·i-; nigor·a-; nigot·te C̄)
1 become muddy; become cloudy:
Oo-ame de kawa no mizu ga ni-

gotta. (大雨で川の水が濁った) The river *became muddy* with the heavy rain. 《⇨ nigori》
2 (of some *kana* letters) be voiced:
'*Ta*' *ga* nigoru *to* '*da*' *ni narimasu.* (「た」が濁ると「だ」になります) '*Da*' is the *voiced* equivalent of '*ta*.' 《⇨ nigori》

ni⌈guñ にぐん (二軍) *n.* (of baseball) farm team [club]; the minors. 《⇨ ichiguñ》

Ni⌈ho⌉ñ にほん (日本) *n.* Japan:
★ Also '*Nippoñ*.' 《⇨ Nippoñ》

Compounds with '*Nihoñ*'

-cha (日本茶) *Japanese* tea
-eega (日本映画) *Japanese* movie
-ga (日本画) *Japanese* painting
-gami (日本髪) traditional *Japanese* women's hairstyle
-ma (日本間) *Japanese*-style room
-ryoori (日本料理) *Japanese* cooking
-shu (日本酒) *Japanese* rice wine

Ni⌈hoñgo にほんご (日本語) *n.* Japanese language; Japanese:
Nihoñgo *de hanasu* (日本語で話す) speak in *Japanese* / Nihoñgo *o manabu* (日本語を学ぶ) learn *Japanese* / Nihoñgo *kaiwa* (日本語会話) *Japanese* conversation. 《⇨ kokugo》

Ni⌈hoñji⌉ñ にほんじん (日本人) *n.* Japanese people; Japanese:
Nihoñjiñ *no gakusee* (日本人の学生) a *Japanese* student.

Ni⌈ho⌉ñkai にほんかい (日本海) *n.* Sea of Japan.

Ni⌈ho⌉ñ Kyo⌈osañtoo にほんきょうさんとう (日本共産党) *n.* Japanese Communist Party. 《⇨ seetoo[2] (table)》

Ni「ho¹ñ Sha「kaitoo にほんしゃかいとう（日本社会党）*n.* Social Democratic Party of Japan. 《⇨ seetoo² (table)》

Ni「igata¹-keñ にいがたけん（新潟県）*n.* Niigata Prefecture. Located in the northeast of the Chubu district, facing the Sea of Japan. The lowlands extending along two rivers form the best rice-producing district in Japan. Capital city: Niigata. 《⇨ map (F3)》

ni「isañ にいさん（兄さん）*n.* one's own older brother. ★ When addressing one's own older brother, '(*o*)*niisañ*' is used instead of his first name. 《⇨ ani; neesañ》

ni「ji にじ（虹）*n.* rainbow:
Sora ni niji ga deta.（空に虹が出た）A *rainbow* appeared in the sky.

ni「ji¹m·u にじむ（滲む）*vi.* (nijim·i-; nijim·a-; nijiñ-de Ⓒ) run; blot; get blurred:
Kono kami wa iñku ga nijimu.（この紙はインクがにじむ）Ink *runs* on this paper. / *Kare no te wa ase de nijiñde ita.*（彼の手は汗でにじんでいた）His hands *were stained* with sweat.

ni「kai にかい（二階）*n.* the second (American) floor; the first (British) floor:
nikai e agaru（二階へ上がる）*go up-stairs* / nikai kara oriru（二階から降りる）*go downstairs* / nikai-ya（二階家）a *two-storied* house.

ni「kka にっか（日課）*n.* one's daily work [task]:
Kyoo no nikka *wa oemashita.*（きょうの日課は終えました）I have done today's *work*. / *Maiasa jogiñgu o suru no ga* nikka *desu.*（毎朝ジョギングをするのが日課です）I make a *practice* of jogging every morning.

ni「kki にっき（日記）*n.* diary:
nikki o tsukeru（日記をつける）keep a *diary*.

ni「kkoo にっこう（日光）*n.* sun-light; sunshine; sun:
Kono heya wa nikkoo *ga ataranai.*（この部屋は日光があたらない）The *sun-light* does not come into this room. / nikkoo-yoku（日光浴）a *sunbath*.

Ni¹kkoo にっこう（日光）*n.* city in Tochigi Prefecture. Well-known for Toshogu Shrine, the Kegon Falls and Lake Chuzenji.

ni「kko¹ri にっこり *adv.* (~ to; ~ suru) with a smile:
Sono oñna-no-ko wa watashi ni mukatte nikkori *(to) waratta.*（その女の子は私に向かってにっこり（と）笑った）The girl gave me a *smile*.

ni¹koniko にこにこ *adv.* (~ to; ~ suru) with a smile:
Kanojo wa itsu-mo nikoniko *shite iru.*（彼女はいつもにこにこしている）She is always *smiling cheerfully*.

ni「ku¹ にく（肉）*n.* meat; flesh:
Kono niku *wa yawarakai [katai].*（この肉はやわらかい[堅い]）This *meat* is tender [tough]. / buta-niku（豚肉）*pork* / tori-niku（鳥肉）*chicken*.

ni「ku¹·i にくい（憎い）*a.* (-ku)
1 hateful:
Watashi wa ano hito ga nikui.（私はあの人が憎い）He is *hateful* to me. / *Ani o koroshita señsoo ga* nikui.（兄を殺した戦争が憎い）I *detest* the war which killed my brother.
2 (*ironic*) smart; clever:
Kare mo nikui *ne.*（彼も憎いね）He is a *clever* fellow, isn't he? / *Kimi mo nakanaka* nikui *koto o iu ne.*（君もなかなか憎いことを言うね）*Well* said.

-niku¹i にくい（難い）*suf.* (*a.*) (-ku) hard; difficult: ★ Added to the stem of a volitional verb.
*Kare no ji wa yomi-*nikui.（彼の字は読みにくい）His handwriting is *hard* to read. / *Kono doogu wa tsukai-*nikui.（この道具は使いにくい）This tool is *difficult* to handle.
《↔ -yasui》《⇨ -gatai》

ni￼ku￼m·u にくむ（憎む）*vt.* (ni-kum·i-; nikum·a-; nikuñ-de 🄲) hate; abhor; despise:
fusee o nikumu（不正を憎む）*despise* injustice / *Kanojo wa kare o* niku-ñde iru.（彼女は彼を憎んでいる）She *hates* him. (⇨ nikushimi)

ni￼kurashi￼·i くらしい（憎らしい）*a.* (-ku) hateful; spiteful:
Nañte nikurashii *ko daroo.*（何て憎らしい子だろう）What a *spiteful* child he is. / *Dañdañ kare ga* niku-rashiku *natte kita.*（だんだん彼が憎らしくなってきた）He has gradually become *detestable* to me.

ni￼kushimi にくしみ（憎しみ）*n.* hatred; hate; enmity:
Kanojo wa kare ni nikushimi *o idaite iru.*（彼女は彼に憎しみを抱いている）She bears *enmity* toward him. (⇨ nikumu; nikui)

ni￼kutai にくたい（肉体）*n.* body; the flesh:
nikutai-*roodoo*（肉体労働）*physical* labor.

ni￼ku￼ya にくや（肉屋）*n.* butcher; meat shop.

ni￼kyuu にきゅう（二級）*n.* second class; second rate:
nikyuu-*hiñ*（二級品）*second-class* goods. (⇨ ikkyuu)

ni￼ mo ka￼kawa￼razu にもかかわらず（にも拘らず）⇨ kakawarazu.

ni￼motsu にもつ（荷物）*n.* load; baggage; luggage:
Kono nimotsu *wa omosugite, hitori de wa hakobemaseñ.*（この荷物は重すぎて、一人では運べません）This *baggage* is too heavy for you to carry alone.

-niñ にん（人）*suf.* counter for people:
O-ko-sañ wa nañ-niñ *desu ka?*（お子さんは何人ですか）*How many* children do you have? / *Kodomo wa* sañ-niñ *desu.*（子どもは 3 人です）I have *three* children. ★ Exceptions are '*hitori*' (one person)

and '*futari*' (two persons).

ni￼na￼·u になう（担う）*vt.* (nina·i-; ninaw·a-; ninat-te 🄲) (*formal*) bear; take:
Kare wa kaisha saikeñ no sekiniñ o ninatte imasu.（彼は会社再建の責任をになっています）He *bears* the responsibility for the reconstruction of the company.

ni￼ñgeñ にんげん（人間）*n.* human being; man:
Watashi wa Tookyoo no niñgeñ *desu.*（私は東京の人間です）I am a *Tokyoite.*

ni￼ñgyoo にんぎょう（人形）*n.* doll; puppet:
niñgyoo-*geki*（人形劇）a *puppet* show.

NIHOÑ-NIÑGYOO

ni￼ñjiñ にんじん（人参）*n.* carrot. (⇨ yasai (illus.))

ni￼ñjoo にんじょう（人情）*n.* human nature; humanity; kindness:
Kare wa niñjoo *no atsui [usui] otoko da.*（彼は人情の厚い[薄い]男だ）He is a *warmhearted [coldhearted]* man.

ni￼ñki にんき（人気）*n.* popularity; public interest:
Sono sakka wa wakai hito ni niñ-ki *ga aru.*（その作家は若い人に人気がある）That author is *popular* with young people. / *Sono kashu wa saikiñ* niñki *ga ochita.*（その歌手は最近人気が落ちた）The singer has

653   **Nippoñ**

recently become less *popular*.

niˌñmu にんむ (任務) *n.* duty;
task; office:
niñmu o hatasu [*okotaru*] (任務を果
たす[怠る]) fulfill [neglect] one's
duty / *Kare wa jibuñ no* niñmu *ni
chuujitsu datta.* (彼は自分の任務に
忠実だった) He was faithful to his
duties.

niˌñshiki にんしき (認識) *n.* understanding; knowledge; recognition:
niñshiki *ga asai* (認識が浅い) have
only a superficial *understanding* /
niñshiki *ga tarinai* (認識が足りない)
have little *understanding* / niñshiki *o fukameru* (認識を深める)
deepen one's *knowledge* / *Kare no
eñzetsu o kiite kare ni taisuru* niñshiki o aratameta. (彼の演説を聞い
て彼に対する認識を改めた) Listening
to his speech, I *came to look at
him in a new light*. / niñshiki-
busoku (認識不足) lack of *understanding*.
niñshiki suru (～する) *vt.* understand; recognize; be aware of:
Sono koto no juuyoo-see wa yoku
niñshiki shite imasu. (その事の重要
性はよく認識しています) I thoroughly
understand the importance of
that matter.

niˌñshiñ にんしん (妊娠) *n.* preg-
nancy:
Kanojo wa niñshiñ *rok-kagetsu
desu.* (彼女は妊娠6か月です) She is
six months *pregnant*.
niñshiñ suru (～する) *vi.* become
pregnant: *Kanojo wa kekkoñ shite, sugu* niñshiñ shita. (彼女は結婚
して, すぐ妊娠した) She *became pregnant* soon after getting married.

niˌñzuu にんずう (人数) *n.* the
number of people:
niñzuu *o kazoeru* (人数を数える)
count the *number of people* / *O-
kyaku no* niñzuu *wa juugo-niñ
datta.* (お客の人数は15人だった) The

guests were fifteen in *number*.

niˌoˌi におい (匂い・臭い) *n.* smell;
odor; fragrance:

> **(USAGE)**
> Usually preceded by a modifi-
> er. Refers to both good and
> bad smells, while '*kaori*' (香り)
> is used exclusively for a good
> smell.

Heñ na nioi *ga suru.* (変な匂いがす
る) There is a strange *smell*. /
Kanojo wa sono koosui no nioi o
kaide mita. (彼女はその香水の匂いを
嗅いでみた) She took a *smell* of the
perfume. 《⇨ kaori; niou》
ni「oˌite において (に於いて) ⇨ oite.
niˌokeˌru における (に於ける)
⇨ okeru.
niˌoˌ·u におう (匂う・臭う) *vi.* (nio-
i-; niow·a-; niot-te C) smell; be
fragrant; stink:
Gasu ga niou. (ガスがにおう) There is
a smell of gas. / *Kanojo wa koosui
ga* niou *hañkachi o motte ita.* (彼
女は香水がにおうハンカチを持っていた)
She carried a handkerchief
which *smelled* of perfume. / *Kono
nagashi wa* niou. (この流しはにおう)
This sink *smells bad*. 《⇨ nioi》
Niˌppoˌñ にっぽん (日本) *n.* Japan.
★ Used often with proper names
and official names such as on
postage stamps and bank notes,
and sometimes for emphasis.
Both '*Nippoñ*' and '*Nihoñ*' are often used in isolation interchangeably. Generally, however,
'*Nihoñ*' is preferred when forming compounds. 《⇨ Nihoñ》

Compounds with '*Nippoñ*'

-Arupusu (日本アルプス) the
 Japan Alps
-Giñkoo (日本銀行) the Bank
 of *Japan*
-ichi (日本一) No. 1 in *Japan*
-jiñ (日本人) *Japanese* people

-juu（日本中）all over *Japan*
-koku（日本国）the Nation of *Japan* (the official name of Japan in Japanese)
-rettoo（日本列島）the *Japanese* Islands
-too（日本刀）*Japanese* sword

ni⸢ra⸣m·u にらむ（睨む）*vt.* (niram·i-; niram·a-; niran-de [C])
1 glare; stare:
Kare wa watashi o niranda.（彼は私をにらんだ）He *stared* at me.
2 (in the passive) be in disfavor:
Kare wa buchoo ni niramarete iru.（彼は部長ににらまれている）He *is in disfavor* with the general manager.
3 suspect; spot:
Keesatsu wa sore o kagekiha no hankoo to nirande iru.（警察はそれを過激派の犯行とにらんでいる）The police *suspect* that it is a crime by extremists.

ni·⸢ru¹ にる（煮る）*vt.* (ni-te [V])
boil; simmer; cook:
Ima jagaimo o nite iru *tokoro desu.*（今じゃがいもを煮ているところです）I *am* now *cooking* the potatoes. / *Mame o torobi de ichi-jikan* nita.（豆をとろ火で1時間煮た）I *simmered* the beans over a low heat for one hour. 《⇨ nieru》

ni·⸢ru² にる（似る）*vi.* (ni-te [V])
resemble; be like; be similar:
Kare wa niisan to yoku nite iru.（彼は兄さんとよく似ている）He *looks just like* his elder brother. / *Kanojo wa haha-oya ni* nite, *bijin da.*（彼女は母親に似て、美人だ）She is a beauty *just like* her mother. / *Kare wa oya ni* nizu *se ga takai.*（彼は親に似ず背が高い）*Unlike* his parents, he is tall. / *Kare to watashi wa* nita *shumi o motte iru.*（彼と私は似た趣味を持っている）He and I have *similar* tastes.

ni⸢ryuu にりゅう（二流）*n.* second-class; second-rate:
niryuu *no hoteru*（二流のホテル）a *second-class* hotel. 《⇨ ichiryuu; sanryuu》

ni⸢se にせ（偽）*n.* sham; counterfeit; imitation:
nise *no daiya*（偽のダイヤ）a *fake* diamond / nise *no joohoo*（偽の情報）*false* information.

ni⸢see にせい（二世）*n.* Nisei; the second-generation of Japanese immigrants; a member of this generation. 《⇨ issee²; sansee》

ni⸢semono にせもの（偽物）*n.* forgery; counterfeit; imitation.

ni ⸢se⸣yo にせよ ＝ ni shiro.

ni⸢shi にし（西）*n.* west; (～ni/e) westward:
Kono heya wa nishi-muki de, nishi-bi *ga sasu.*（この部屋は西向きで、西日がさす）The room faces *west* and the *afternoon sun* shines in. / *Kono dooro no* nishi *wa betsu no machi desu.*（この道路の西は別の町です）It is a different town to the *west* of this road. / *Kare-ra wa* nishi ni mukatte *kookai shita.*（彼らは西に向かって航海した）They sailed *westward.* 《↔ higashi》

ni ⸢shiro にしろ

┌─── **USAGE** ───┐

The particle '*ni*' plus the imperative of '*suru.*' '*Ni*' plus the literary imperative '*seyo*' may also be used but mainly as a written form.

1 even if: ★ Used to form a weak conditional.
Oseji ni shiro, *homerarereba dare de mo warui ki wa shinai.*（お世辞にしろ、ほめられればだれでも悪い気はしない）*Even if* it is flattery, no one feels displeased when he is praised. / *Izure dare ka ni tanomu* ni shiro, *dekiru dake jibun de yari nasai.*（いずれだれかに頼むにしろ、

出来るだけ自分でやりなさい) *Even if* you ask someone later on, try to do as much as possible by yourself.

2 and; or: ★ Used to give illustrative examples or possibilities. *Beñkyoo* ni shiro *uñdoo* ni shiro, *mainichi no doryoku ga taisetsu desu.* (勉強にしろ運動にしろ, 毎日の努力が大切です) In *both* studies *and* physical training, continued daily effort is important. / *Iku* ni shiro *ikanai* ni shiro, *tonikaku deñwa o kudasai.* (行くにしろ行かないにしろ, とにかく電話を下さい) *Whether* you are going *or* not, please give me a call. / *Nihoñ no natsu wa Tookyoo* ni shiro *Kyooto* ni shiro, *atsukute tamaranai.* (日本の夏は東京にしろ京都にしろ, 暑くてたまらない) Summer in Japan, be it in Tokyo *or* Kyoto, is unbearably hot. ★ Note: in **1** and **2**, similar expressions such as '*ni shite mo, ni shitatte*' can also be used.

ni shiˈtagaˈtte にしたがって (に従って) ⇨ shitagatte.

ni shiˈteˈ mo にしても even if:

> **USAGE**
> Used when the speaker partially accepts the situation or explanation in the first clause but is still not completely satisfied or convinced.

Joodañ ni shite mo, *do ga sugiru.* (冗談にしても, 度が過ぎる) *Even if* you did it in jest, you've carried things too far. / *Isogashii* ni shite mo, *deñwa gurai kakerare soo na mono da.* (忙しいにしても, 電話ぐらいかけられそうなものだ) *No matter how* busy you may be, you should at least be able to make a phone call. / *Zañgyoo* ni shite mo, *kyoo wa kare no kaeri ga osoi.* (残業にしても, きょうは彼の帰りが遅い) *Even if* he is doing overtime, he is still late in coming home today.

niˈ shiˈteˈ wa にしては **1** even if; for:

> **USAGE**
> Used when the speaker accepts the situation or explanation in the first clause, but finds that the consequent result, as specified in the second clause, is contrary to normal expectation.

Nayamigoto ga aru ni shite wa, *kare wa geñki-soo da.* (悩みごとがあるにしては, 彼は元気そうだ) *Even if* there is something troubling him, he looks fine. / *Kare wa daigaku o deta* ni shite wa, *jooshiki ni kakete iru.* (彼は大学を出たにしては, 常識に欠けている) *For* someone who graduated from college, he lacks common sense.

2 considering; for:

> **USAGE**
> Follows a noun and indicates that, considering the characteristics normally associated with that noun, the judgment the speaker makes is contrary to expectation.

Ano mise wa Giñza ni shite wa, *yasui.* (あの店は銀座にしては, 安い) That is an inexpensive store *considering* it is in Ginza. / *Ano hito wa gaikoku-jiñ* ni shite wa, *Nihoñgo ga umai.* (あの人は外国人にしては, 日本語がうまい) *For* a foreigner, his Japanese is good.

niˈsshoku にっしょく (日食) *n.* solar eclipse. (⇨ gesshoku)

niˈssuˈu にっすう (日数) *n.* the number of days; time: nissuu o kazoeru (日数を数える) count the *number of days* / *Kañsee made* nissuu *wa dono kurai kakarimasu ka?* (完成まで日数はどのくらいかかりますか) How many *days* will it take until completion? /

Kono shigoto wa nissuu *ga kakatta*. (この仕事は日数がかかった) This job took me *quite a few days*.

ni「ta」ishite にたいして (に対して) ⇨ taishite.

ni「ta」ts・u にたつ (煮立つ) *vi.* (-tach・i-; -tat・a-; -tat-te Ⓒ) (of water, vessel) boil; come to a boil:
Nabe ga nitatte *imasu yo*. (なべが煮立っていますよ) The pot *is boiling*.

ni「tchuu にっちゅう (日中) *n.* the daytime:
Nitchuu *wa harete ita ga, yuugata ni natte, ame ga furi-dashita.* (日中は晴れていたが、夕方になって、雨が降りだした) The weather was fine *during the day*, but it started to rain toward evening. 《↔ yakañ¹》

ni「too にとう (二等) *n.* second class; second prize; second place:
Watashi wa koñtesuto de nitoo *ni natta.* (私はコンテストで二等になった) I won the *second prize* in the contest. / nitoo-*señshitsu* (二等船室) a *second-class* cabin. 《⇨ ittoo》

ni 「to」tte にとって ⇨ totte.
ni 「tsu」ite について ⇨ tsuite.
ni 「tsu」ki につき ⇨ tsuite.
ni「ttee にってい (日程) *n.* one's day's schedule; itinerary:
Kyoo wa nittee *ga tsumatte imasu.* (きょうは日程が詰まっています) I have a tight *schedule* for today. / *Ryokoo no* nittee *wa ima tsukutte iru tokoro desu.* (旅行の日程はいま作っているところです) I am now preparing the *itinerary*.

ni「wa にわ (庭) *n.* garden; yard; court:
niwa *no teire o suru* (庭の手入れをする) care for a *garden* / *Kare no uchi no* niwa *wa hiroi [semai].* (彼の家の庭は広い[狭い]) The *yard* at his house is large [small].

ni「wa には *p.* for; to; in:

Kore wa watashi ni wa *taisetsu na shashiñ desu.* (これは私には大切な写真です) This is a photo which is important *for* me. 《⇨ ni²; wa¹》

ni「waka にわか (俄か) *a.n.* (~ na, ni) sudden; immediate; unexpected:
Niwaka *ni heñji wa dekimaseñ.* (にわかに返事はできません) I can't reply on *the spur of the moment*. / Niwaka *ni ame ga furidashita.* (にわかに雨が降りだした) It *suddenly* started raining.

ni「waka-a」me にわかあめ (俄か雨) *n.* rain shower:
niwaka-ame *ni au* (にわか雨にあう) be caught in a *shower*.

ni「watori にわとり (鶏) *n.* chicken; rooster; hen. 《⇨ hiyoko》

ni「yaniya にやにや *adv.* (~ to; ~ suru) (the manner of grinning [smirking]):
Kare wa sono mañga o mite, niyaniya *(to) waratte ita.* (彼はその漫画を見て、にやにや(と)笑っていた) He was *grinning broadly* as he read the comic. / *Kare wa* niyaniya *(to) shi-nagara kanojo o mite ita.* (彼はにやにや(と)しながら彼女を見ていた) He was looking at her *with a smirk*.

ni yo「re」ba によれば ⇨ yoreba.
ni yo「tte によって ⇨ yotte.
ni「zu」kuri にづくり (荷造り) *n.* packing:
nizukuri *o toku* (荷造りを解く) *unpack* / *Kono* nizukuri *wa shikkari shite iru.* (この荷造りはしっかりしている) This *packing* is well done.
nizukuri (o) suru (~を)する *vt.* pack (up): *Kinoo hikkoshi no* nizukuri *o shimashita.* (きのう引っ越しの荷造りをしました) I *did the packing* for moving yesterday.

no¹ の *p.* **1** of; at; in; on:
★ Used to link two nouns. The first noun describes the latter in some way.
kinu no *hañkachi* (絹のハンカチ) a

silk handkerchief / *watashi* no *hoñ* (私の本) a book *of* mine / chi-chi no *ie* (父の家) my *father's* house / *eki* no *baiteñ* (駅の売店) a kiosk *at* the station / *machi* no *yuubiñkyoku* (町の郵便局) a post office *in* town / *kabe* no *e* (壁の絵) a picture *on* the wall.

> **USAGE**
>
> Also note the pattern: noun＋particle＋'*no*'＋noun. *e.g.* *tomodachi* kara no *deñwa* (友だちからの電話) a phone call *from* a friend / *haha* e no *tegami* (母への手紙) a letter *to* my mother.

2 (used as the subject marker in a clause modifying a noun): ★ '*ga*' can also be used. *Watashi* no *yomitai hoñ wa kore desu*. (私の読みたい本はこれです) The book *I* want to read is this one. / *Tomodachi* no *kaita hoñ ga besuto-seraa ni natta*. (友だちの書いた本がベストセラーになった) The book my *friend* wrote became a best-seller. / *Atama* no *itai hito wa kono kusuri o doozo*. (頭の痛い人はこの薬をどうぞ) People *with headaches*, try this medicine.

3 (used to link two nouns, which are in apposition): *beñgoshi* no *Tanaka-sañ* (弁護士の田中さん) Mr. Tanaka, *who is* a lawyer / *imooto* no *Kazuko* (妹の和子) my younger sister Kazuko.

> **USAGE**
>
> Note the ambiguity: '*isha* no *tomodachi*' (医者の友だち) has two meanings, 'the doctor's friend' (as in **1**) and 'my friend, who is a doctor' (as in **3**).

4 (used to link quantity expressions to a following noun): *sañ-biki* no *kobuta* (三匹のこぶた) *three* little pigs / *hyaku gojuu-eñ* no *kippu* (150円の切符) a *150-yen*

ticket / *tatta hitori* no *yuujiñ* (たった一人の友人) *my one and only* friend / *oozee* no *hito* (大勢の人) *a great number of* people / *takusañ* no *purezeñto* (たくさんのプレゼント) *many* presents.

no² の *n*. **1** one: ★ Used to substitute for another noun and often modified by a verb or adjective. *Motto yasui* no *wa arimaseñ ka?* (もっと安いのはありませんか) Isn't there a cheaper *one*? / *Kono koppu o kowashita* no *wa watashi desu*. (このコップをこわしたのは私です) I am *the person who* broke this glass. / *Kimi ga kiita* no *wa doñna hanashi desu ka?* (きみが聞いたのはどんな話ですか) What kind of *story* is it *that* you heard? / *"Toire o tsukatte ii desu ka?" "Ni-kai* no *o tsukatte kudasai."* (「トイレを使っていいですか」「2階のを使ってください」) "May I use the toilet?" "Please use the upstairs *one*."

2 the fact; that: ★ Used to nominalize the previous clause. *Watashi wa kanojo ga utatte iru* no *o kikimashita*. (私は彼女が歌っているのを聞きました) I heard her *singing* a song. / *Kanojo ga nyuuiñ shita* no *o shitte imasu ka?* (彼女が入院したのを知っていますか) Do you know *that* she was hospitalized? / *Kono moñdai o toku* no *wa muzukashii*. (この問題を解くのはむずかしい) *Solving* this problem is difficult. / *Kare ga mukoo ni hashitte iku* no *o mimashita*. (彼が向こうへ走って行くのを見ました) I saw him *running* in that direction. / *Doko-ka de kodomo ga naite iru* no *ga kikoeru*. (どこかで子どもが泣いているのが聞こえる) I hear a child *crying* somewhere.

3 (used in giving explanations, or in eliciting or confirming information): ★ Added to the end of

a clause as '*no da*' or '*no desu.*' In speech, usually '*ñ da*' or '*ñ desu.*'
Sono hoñ o sagashita *no desu ga* mitsukarimaseñ deshita. (その本を探したのですが見つかりませんでした) I *looked for* the book, but could not find it. / *Nani-ka* atta ñ *desu ka?* (何かあったんですか) *Has* something *happened*?

no[3] の *p.* (*colloq.*) [added to the end of a sentence]
1 (signifies a question): ★ With rising intonation. Equivalent to '*no desu ka.*'
Doko e iku no? (どこへ行くの) Where *are* you *off* to? / *Sore itsu* katta *no?* (それいつ買ったの) When *did* you *buy* that?
2 (suggests an explanation): ★ With falling intonation. Used mainly by women and children. Equivalent to '*no desu.*'
"*Doo shita?*" "*Atama ga itai* no." (「どうした」「頭が痛いの」) "What's the matter?" " I have a headache. " / "*Eega e ikanai?*" "*Kyoo wa chotto tsugoo ga warui* no." (「映画へ行かない」「きょうはちょっとつごうが悪いの」) "What about going to the movies?" "Today is a bit inconvenient."

no[4] の (野) *n.* field:
no no hana (野の花) a *wildflower.* (⇨ nohara)

no「ba」s·u[1] のばす (伸ばす) *vt.* (nobash·i-; nobas·a-; nobash·i-te C) **1** lengthen:
Kare wa zuboñ no take o sukoshi nobashita. (彼はズボンの丈を少し伸ばした) He *lengthened* his trousers a bit.
2 straighten; stretch; reach:
Watashi wa karada o nobashite *akubi o shita.* (私は体を伸ばしてあくびをした) I *stretched* and yawned. / *Kanojo wa te o* nobashite *posutaa o hagashita.* (彼女は手を伸ばしてポス

ターをはがした) She *reached out* and pulled down the poster.
3 smooth out (a wrinkle, surface, etc.); iron out:
Kanojo wa hañkachi no shiwa o airoñ de nobashita. (彼女はハンカチのしわをアイロンで伸ばした) She *ironed out* the creases in the handkerchief. (⇨ nobiru[1])
4 let grow (a beard, hair):
kami [*hige*] *o* nobasu (髪[ひげ]を伸ばす) *let* one's hair [beard] *grow* / *Kare wa hige o nagaku* nobashite iru. (彼はひげを長く伸ばしている) He *wears* his beard long. (⇨ nobiru[1])
5 develop; improve; better:
Nihoñgo no chikara o nobashitai *to omotte imasu.* (日本語の力を伸ばしたいと思っています) I *want to improve* my Japanese ability. / *Kare wa mata kiroku o* nobashimashita. (彼はまた記録を伸ばしました) He *bettered* his record once more. / *Sono kaisha wa biiru no hañbai o ookiku* nobashita. (その会社はビールの販売を大きく伸ばした) The company greatly *increased* its sales of beer. (⇨ nobiru[1])

no「ba」s·u[2] のばす (延ばす) *vt.* (nobash·i-; nobas·a-; nobash·i-te C) **1** extend; prolong:
Kare wa Nihoñ de no taizai kikañ o nobashita. (彼は日本での滞在期間を延ばした) He *extended* his length of stay in Japan. (⇨ nobiru[2])
2 postpone; put off:
Shuppatsu o kore ijoo nobasu *koto wa dekimaseñ.* (出発をこれ以上延ばすことはできません) I cannot *postpone* my departure any longer. (⇨ nobiru[2])

no」be- のべ (延べ) *pref.* aggregate; total number:
nobe-*nissuu* (延べ日数) *the total number of days* / *Nyuujoosha wa* nobe-*hasseñ-niñ ni tasshita.* (入場者は延べ 8,000 人に達した) *The total number* of visitors reached 8,000.

no⌐be⌐·ru のべる（述べる）*vt.* (no-be-te $\boxed{V}$) state; express; mention:
Miñna ga hitori hitori ikeñ o nobeta.（みんなが一人一人意見を述べた）One by one, they all *stated* their opinions.

no⌐bi⌐·ru[1] のびる（伸びる）*vi.* (nobite $\boxed{V}$) **1** (of a plant, hair, etc.) grow:
Watashi no hige wa sugu nobiru.（私のひげはすぐ伸びる）My beard *grows* rapidly. / *Ame no ato, zassoo ga kyuu ni nobita.*（雨のあと、雑草が急に伸びた）After the rain, the weeds *grew* rapidly. / *Asagao no tsuru ga nobite, hisashi ni karamatta.*（朝顔のつるが伸びて、ひさしにからまった）The morning glory vine *grew* and wound itself around the eaves. 《⇨ nobasu[1]》
2 lengthen; extend:
Kare wa saikiñ shiñchoo ga kyuu ni nobita.（彼は最近身長が急に伸びた）He *has* recently *shot up* in height.
3 improve; develop; increase:
Kono hoñ o tsukaeba anata no Nihoñgo no chikara wa kitto nobimasu.（この本を使えばあなたの日本語の力はきっと伸びます）Your skill in Japanese will surely *improve* if you use this book. / *Yushutsu wa nobiru keekoo ni arimasu.*（輸出は伸びる傾向にあります）Exports show a tendency to *increase*. 《⇨ nobasu[1]》
4 (*colloq.*) be tired out; pass out:
Kinoo wa nomisugite, nobite shimatta.（きのうは飲み過ぎて、伸びてしまった）Yesterday I drank so much that I *passed out*.

no⌐bi⌐·ru[2] のびる（延びる）*vi.* (nobite $\boxed{V}$) **1** lengthen; be extended:
Hi ga nobimashita ne.（日が延びましたね）The days *have gotten longer*, haven't they? / *Tetsudoo ga kono mura made nobite kimashita.*（鉄道がこの村まで延びてきました）The railroad *has been extended* to this village.
2 be postponed; be delayed:
Ame de shiai wa asu ni nobimashita.（雨で試合はあすに延びました）The match *was postponed* until tomorrow because of the rain. / *Shiñkañseñ no shuppatsu ga ichijikañ nobite shimatta.*（新幹線の出発が1時間延びてしまった）The departure of the Shinkansen *has been delayed* one hour. 《⇨ nobasu[2]》

no⌐bori のぼり（上り）*n.* **1** ascent:
Michi wa koko kara nobori desu.（道はここから上りです）The road starts its *ascent* from here. 《↔ kudari》
2 up train:

USAGE

'*Nobori*' is a train going in the direction of a major city, especially Tokyo, and '*kudari*' is a train going out of a major city.

Koñdo no nobori wa go-fuñ okurete imasu.（今度の上りは5分遅れています）The next *up train* is five minutes behind schedule. 《↔ kudari》

no⌐bor·u[1] のぼる（上る）*vi.* (nobor·i-; nobor·a-; nobot-te $\boxed{C}$) **1** go up; ascend:
kaidañ [saka] o noboru（階段[坂]を上る）*go up* stairs [a slope] / *booto de kawa o noboru*（ボートで川を上る）*go up* a river by boat. 《↔ kudaru》
2 amount to; reach:
Sono jiko ni yoru shishoosha wa gojuu-niñ ijoo ni nobotta.（その事故による死傷者は50人以上に上った）The dead and injured in the accident *reached* more than fifty.
3 rise:
Kare wa gojuu de shachoo no chii ni nobotta.（彼は50で社長の地位に上った）He *rose* to the position of president at fifty.

4 = noboru².

no「bor・u² のぼる（昇る）*vi.* (nobor・i-; nobor・a-; nobot-te [C]) go up; rise:
Fuuseñ wa yukkuri sora e no-botte itta.（風船はゆっくり空へ昇って行った）The balloon slowly *rose* skywards.

no「bor・u³ のぼる（登る）*vi.* (nobor・i-; nobor・a-; nobot-te [C]) climb:
ki ni noboru（木に登る）*climb* a tree / *Fuji-sañ ni nobotta koto wa ari-masu ka?*（富士山に登ったことはありますか）*Have* you ever *climbed* Mt. Fuji?

no「chi¹ のち（後）*n.* later; after:
Ikkoo wa hoteru ni toochaku shita nochi, *tadachi ni kañkoo ni deka-keta.*（一行はホテルに到着したのち、ただちに観光に出掛けた）Immediately *after* the group arrived at the hotel, they went out for sight-seeing. / *Nochi no koto o kañga-ete, koodoo shi nasai.*（のちのことを考えて、行動しなさい）Think of *what will happen* and then act accord-ingly. / *Asu wa yuki* nochi *ame deshoo.*（あすは雪のち雨でしょう）To-morrow there will be snow, *followed by* rain.

no「chi-hodo のちほど（後程）*adv.* later (on):
Nochi-hodo go-reñraku itashima-su.（後ほどご連絡いたします）I will get in touch with you *later on.* / *De wa,* nochi-hodo.（では、後ほど）See you *later.*

no de ので because; so; owing to: ★ Used to refer to an actual fact as it is objectively, while 'kara' is used to emphasize the reason subjectively. 'No de' is more commonly used in formal situations.
Ame ga futta no de, *shiai wa chuu-shi ni narimashita.*（雨が降ったので、試合は中止になりました）The match

was canceled *because* it rained. / *Sakuya wa osoku made shigoto o shita* no de, *nemui.*（昨夜は遅くまで仕事をしたので、眠い）I worked late last night and I am *therefore* sleepy. / *Isogimasu* no de, *kyoo wa shitsuree shimasu.*（急ぎますので、きょうは失礼します）I am in a hurry, *so* will you please excuse me for today. / *Kodomo ga byooki na* no de *isha ni kite moratta.*（子どもが病気なので医者に来てもらった）Our child was sick, *so* I called in the doctor. / *Ima isogashii* no de *ato ni shite kudasai.*（今忙しいのであとにしてください）*As* I am busy now, please make it later. (⇨ kara⁴)

no「do のど（喉）*n.* throat:
Nodo ga itai.（のどが痛い）I have a sore *throat.* / *Nodo ga kawaita.*（のどが渇いた）I *am thirsty.* / *Shiñ-pai de shokuji ga nodo o toorana-katta.*（心配で食事がのどを通らなかった）I was so worried I *couldn't eat a bite.*

no「doka のどか（長閑）*a.n.* (~ na, ni) calm; peaceful:
nodoka *na haru no hi*（のどかな春の日）a *calm* spring day / nodoka *ni kurasu*（のどかに暮らす）live *peace-fully.*

no「gare¹・ru のがれる（逃れる）*vi.* (nogare-te [V]) escape; run away; avoid:
Hañniñ wa gaikoku e nogareta.（犯人は外国へ逃れた）The criminal *escaped* abroad. / *Kare wa kikeñ kara umaku* nogareta.（彼は危険からうまく逃れた）He skillfully *avoided* the danger. / *Kare wa shakkiñ kara* nogareru *koto ga dekina-katta.*（彼は借金から逃れることができなかった）He was unable to *rid him-self of* his debts. (⇨ nigeru; no-gasu)

no「ga¹s・u のがす（逃す）*vt.* (nogash・i-; nogas・a-; nogash・i-te [C]) miss (a chance, an opportunity,

etc.); lose; let slip:
Kare wa zekkoo no kikai o nogashita. (彼は絶好の機会を逃した) He
missed a golden opportunity. /
Keesatsu wa misumisu hañniñ o
nogashite shimatta. (警察はみすみす
犯人を逃がしてしまった) The police
let the criminal *escape* before
their very eyes. 《⇨ nigasu; no-
gareru》

no「hara のはら (野原) *n.* field;
plain. 《⇨ hara²》

no「iro」oze ノイローゼ *n.* neuro-
sis; nervous breakdown:
Kanojo wa noirooze *da.* (彼女はノイ
ローゼだ) She is suffering from a
nervous breakdown.

no「ki のき (軒) *n.* eaves:
Tsubame ga noki *no shita ni su o
tsukutta.* (ツバメが軒の下に巣を作った)
Swallows made a nest under the
eaves.

noki-nami (〜並み) every; all:
Taifuu de sono mura wa noki-
nami *higai o uketa.* (台風でその村は
軒並み被害を受けた) *All the houses*
in the village were damaged by
the typhoon.

no「kku ノック *n.* **1** knock.
2 (of baseball) hitting grounders
and flies for practice.
nokku suru (〜する) *vt.* rap on a
door; knock: *doa o* nokku suru
(ドアをノックする) *knock* on a door.

no「kogiri のこぎり (鋸) *n.* saw:
ita o nokogiri *de kiru* (板をのこぎり
で切る) cut a board with a *saw.*

no「ko」razu のこらず (残らず) *adv.*
all; entirely; without exception:
Sono ko wa kozukai o nokorazu
tsukatte shimatta. (その子はこづかいを
残らず使ってしまった) The child used
up his pocket money, *not leaving
any.* / *Jishiñ de sono mura no kaoku ga* nokorazu *taoreta.* (地震でそ
の村の家屋が残らず倒れた) *Every sin-
gle* house in the village collapsed
in the earthquake. / *Shitte iru*
koto wa nokorazu *hanasu tsumori
desu.* (知っていることは残らず話すつもり
です) I am going to tell you *everything* I know.

no「kori のこり (残り) *n.* the remainder; the rest; leftovers:
Booru wa sañ-ko tsukai, nokori
wa totte okoo. (ボールは 3 個使い, 残
りは取って置こう) Let's use three of
the balls and put the *rest* aside. /
Gakusee-seekatsu mo nokori sukunaku natte kita. (学生生活も残り
少なくなってきた) My student life *is
nearly over* now. / *Shokuji no*
nokori *wa kachiku no esa ni shimasu.* (食事の残りは家畜のえさにしま
す) The *leftovers* from our meals
are used as food for the animals.

no「ko」r・u のこる (残る) *vi.* (nokor-
r・i-; nokor・a-; nokot-te ⓒ)
remain; be left:
Watashi wa shibaraku sono ba ni
nokotta. (私はしばらくその場に残った)
I *remained* there for a short
while. / *Saifu ni wa isseñ mo* nokotte *inakatta.* (財布には 1 銭も残っ
ていなかった) There was not a single
penny *left* in my purse. / *Jishiñ
de sono biru dake ga* nokotta. (地
震でそのビルだけが残った) That build-
ing was the only one that *survived* the earthquake.
《⇨ nokosu》

no「ko」s・u のこす (残す) *vt.* (nokosh-
sh・i-; nokos・a-; nokosh・i-te ⓒ)
leave (behind); set aside; reserve:
Chichi wa kanari zaisañ o nokoshimashita. (父はかなり財産を残しました)
Our father *left behind* a considerable estate. / *Kare wa kazoku o*
nokoshite, *hitori de tabi ni deta.*
(彼は家族を残して, 一人で旅に出た)
Leaving his family behind, he set
out on a journey by himself. /
Yuushoku o sukoshi nokoshite shimatta. (夕食を少し残してしまった) I
have left some of the evening

meal unfinished. / *Kanojo wa ko-domo no gakuhi no tame ni hyaku-mañ-eñ* nokoshite oita. (彼女は子どもの学費のために100万円残しておいた) She *set aside* a million yen for her children's school fees.
((⇨ nokoru))

no¹mi¹ のみ (鑿) *n.* chisel.

no¹mi² のみ *p.* (*formal*) only; alone: ★ Used after a noun or verb to express a limit.
Hito wa pañ nomi de wa ikirare-nai. (人はパンのみでは生きられない) Man cannot live on bread *alone.* / *Watashi wa jibuñ ga shitte iru koto* nomi *hanashita.* (私は自分が知っていることのみ話した) I told *only* what I knew. / *Oya to shite wa kodomo no shiawase o negau* nomi *desu.* (親としては子どもの幸せを願うのみです) As a parent, I wish for *nothing but* my child's happiness. ((⇨ bakari; dake; shika³))
...nomi narazu...mo (...～ならず...も) not only...but also: *Kono hoñ wa kodomo* nomi narazu *otona ni mo omoshiroi.* (この本は子どものみならず大人にも面白い) This book is interesting, *not only* for children, *but also* for adults. / *Kare wa ji-gyoo ni seekoo shita* nomi narazu *kuni kara hyooshoo mo sareta.* (彼は事業に成功したのみならず国から表彰された) He succeeded in his business, and *moreover* got a commendation from the nation.

no¹mikom·u のみこむ (飲み込む) *vt.* (-kom·i-; -kom·a-; -koñ-de C̄) 1 swallow; gulp; choke down: *Kare wa juusu o ikki ni* nomiko-ñda. (彼はジュースを一気に飲み込んだ) He *downed* his juice in one gulp. / *Mochi o* nomikoñde *iki ga kuru-shikatta.* (もちを飲み込んで息が苦しかった) When I *swallowed* the rice-cake I almost choked.
2 understand; learn; grasp: *Kanojo wa watashi no setsumee o*

sugu nomikoñda. (彼女は私の説明をすぐ飲み込んだ) She *grasped* my explanation right away. / *Sono ko-tsu o* nomikomu *made jikañ ga ka-katta.* (そのこつを飲み込むまで時間がかかった) It took some time before I *got* the knack of it.

no¹mi¹mizu のみみず (飲み水) *n.* drinking water:
Kono mizu wa nomimizu *ni teki-sanai.* (この水は飲み水に適さない) This water is not fit for *drinking.*

no¹mi¹mono のみもの (飲み物) *n.* drink; beverage:
Nani-ka nomimono *o kudasai.* (何か飲み物を下さい) Give me *some-thing to drink*, please.

no¹m·u のむ (飲む) *vt.* (nom·i-; nom·a-; noñ-de C̄) 1 drink: *Watashi wa maiasa gyuunyuu o* nomimasu. (私は毎朝牛乳を飲みます) I *drink* milk every morning.
2 take alcohol; drink: *Yuube wa zuibuñ* noñda. (ゆうべはずいぶん飲んだ) I *drank* a lot last night. / *Noñdara noru na.* (*slogan for preventing traffic accidents*) (飲んだら乗るな) If you *drink*, don't drive.
3 take (medicine): ★ Used also for medicine, such as pills and tablets, which are non-liquid.
Kono i no kusuri o nomi nasai. (この胃の薬を飲みなさい) Please *take* this stomach medicine.
4 accept (a demand, request, etc.); agree:
Shiyoosha-gawa wa kumiai no yookyuu o noñda. (使用者側は組合の要求を飲んだ) The employers *accepted* the union's demands.

no¹ñbi¹ri のんびり *adv.* (～ to; ～ suru) leisurely; quietly; peacefully:
Kore kara wa inaka de noñbiri *(to) kurashitai.* (これからはいなかでのんびり(と)暮らしたい) From now on I want to live *quietly* in the coun-

try. / *Kinoo wa ichi-nichi* noñbiri (to) shite imashita. (きのうは一日のんびり(と)していました) Yesterday I *took things easy* the whole day. / *Kare wa* noñbiri *shita seekaku no hito desu.* (彼はのんびりした性格の人です) He is a person with an *easygoing disposition.*

no ni のに although; but; in spite of: ★ Used to link two clauses, which are in contrast or opposition. Often implies dissatisfaction.

Nañ-do mo tanoñda no ni *kare wa tetsudatte kurenakatta.* (何度も頼んだのに彼は手伝ってくれなかった) *Although* I asked him time and time again, he would not help me out. / *Isshoo-keñmee hataraite iru* no ni *seekatsu wa raku ni naranai.* (一生懸命働いているのに生活は楽にならない) *In spite of* my working hard, life has not become any easier. / *Samui* no ni *kare wa kooto o kite inakatta.* (寒いのに彼はコートを着ていなかった) He was not wearing a overcoat, *though* it was cold. / *Kare wa sono hoñ o yomanakatta* no ni *yoñda furi o shita.* (彼はその本を読まなかったのに読んだふりをした) He did not read the book *but* pretended that he had.

《⇨ ga²; kakawarazu; keredo (mo)》

noⁿki のんき (呑気) *a.n.* (~ na, ni) easygoing; happy-go-lucky; carefree; optimistic: *Kare wa* noñki *da.* (彼はのんきだ) He is *easygoing.* / Noñki *ni kurashitai.* (のんきに暮らしたい) I want to live in a *happy-go-lucky* fashion.

noo¹ のう (脳) *n.* brain; brains: noo-*geka* (脳外科) *brain* surgery.

noo² のう (能) *n.* Noh play. ★ A classical highly-stylized Japanese dance-drama. The actors wear wooden masks. 《⇨ photo (right)》

noochi のうち (農地) *n.* farm-

NOO STAGE

NOO MASK

land; agricultural land.

nooeñ のうえん (農園) *n.* farm; plantation. 《⇨ noojoo》

noogyoo のうぎょう (農業) *n.* agriculture; farming: noogyoo *ni tazusawaru* (農業にたずさわる) be engaged in *farming.*

noogyoo-kyoodoo-kumiai のうぎょうきょうどうくみあい (農業共同組合) *n.* agricultural cooperative association. ★ Often shortened to '*nookyoo*' (農協). 《⇨ JA》

nooikketsu のういっけつ (脳溢血) *n.* cerebral hemorrhage.

noojoo のうじょう (農場) *n.* farm; ranch: noojoo *o kee-ee suru* (農場を経営する) run a *farm.*

nooka のうか (農家) *n.* farmhouse; farmer: *Kare no uchi wa* nooka *desu.* (彼の家は農家です) His is a *farming family.* / Nooka *wa ima ga ichi-bañ isogashii toki da.* (農家は今がいちばん忙しいときだ) It is the busiest season for *farming households* now.

nooke**sseñ** のうけっせん (脳血栓) *n.* cerebral thrombosis.

no「oko「osoku のうこうそく (脳梗塞) *n.* cerebral infarction.

no「okyoo のうきょう (農協) *n.* a contraction of '*noogyoo-kyoodoo-kumiai*' (農業共同組合) ((⇨ JA))

no「omiñ のうみん (農民) *n.* landed farmer; peasant. ((⇨ shi-noo-koo-shoo (table)))

No「oriñ-suisañ-da「ijiñ のうりんすいさんだいじん (農林水産大臣) *n.* Minister of Agriculture, Forestry and Fisheries.

No「oriñ-suisa「ñ-shoo のうりんすいさんしょう (農林水産省) *n.* Ministry of Agriculture, Forestry and Fisheries. ((⇨ shoo¹ (table)))

no「oritsu のうりつ (能率) *n.* efficiency:
shigoto no nooritsu *o ageru* (仕事の能率を上げる) improve the *efficiency* of the work. / *Kono yarikata wa* nooritsu *ga warui.* (このやり方は能率が悪い) This method is *inefficient*.

no「oritsu-teki のうりつてき (能率的) *a.n.* (~ na, ni) efficient:
Kore wa nooritsu-teki *na yarikata da.* (これは能率的なやり方だ) This is an *efficient* method. / *Moo sukoshi* nooritsu-teki *ni yari nasai.* (もう少し能率的にやりなさい) Try to do it a little more *efficiently*.

no「oryoku のうりょく (能力) *n.* ability; capacity; faculty:
Kanojo ni wa kono shigoto o suru nooryoku *ga juubuñ ni arimasu.* (彼女にはこの仕事をする能力が十分にあります) She has quite enough *ability* to do this job. / *Kare ni wa shiharai* nooryoku *ga arimaseñ.* (彼には支払い能力がありません) He does not have the *ability* to pay.

no「oshi のうし (脳死) *n.* brain death.

no「osoñ のうそん (農村) *n.* farm village; farming district.

no「oto ノート *n.* **1** notebook:
Señsee ga kokubañ ni kaku koto o nooto *ni utsushita.* (先生が黒板に書くことをノートに写した) I copied into my *notebook* what the teacher wrote on the board. ((⇨ choomeñ)) **2** note:
nooto *o toru* (ノートを取る) take *notes*.

nooto suru (~ する) *vt.* write down; take notes: *Kore kara watashi ga iu koto o* nooto shi nasai. (これから私が言うことをノートしなさい) *Make notes* of what I am now going to say.

no「oyaku のうやく (農薬) *n.* artificially synthesized fertilizers and pesticides.

no「rainu のらいぬ (野良犬) *n.* homeless dog; stray dog.

no「reñ のれん (暖簾) *n.* short split curtain: ★ Hung outside the entrance of a Japanese-style shop, restaurant, bar, etc.
nawa-noreñ (なわのれん) a rope *curtain*.

NOREÑ (soba shop)

NAWA-NOREÑ (bar)

no「ri¹¹ のり (糊) *n.* glue; paste; starch:
E no ura ni nori *o tsuketa.* (絵の裏にのりをつけた) I put some *glue* on the back of the picture. / *Kabe ni kami o* nori *de hatta.* (壁に紙をのりで貼った) I *pasted* the paper onto the wall. ((⇨ norizuke))

no「ri¹² のり (海苔) *n.* laver; seaweed:

Dried laver, '*asakusa-nori*,' usually comes in square sheets. It is used in wrapping up sushi rice and also eaten with warm rice.

yaki-nori (焼きのり) a sheet of toasted *laver*. 《⇨ norimaki (illus.)》

NORI

no⌐riage⌐·ru のりあげる (乗り上げる) *vi.* (-age-te V) run onto; run aground:
Kare no kuruma wa hodoo ni noriageta. (彼の車は歩道に乗り上げた) His car *ran onto* the sidewalk. / *Fune wa iwa ni* noriageta. (船は岩に乗り上げた) The vessel *ran aground* on the rocks.

no⌐riba のりば (乗り場) *n.* stop; stand; platform:
Chikatetsu no noriba *wa doko desu ka?* (地下鉄の乗り場はどこですか) *Where* can I take the subway? / *Yokohama hoomeñ no basu*-noriba *wa doko desu ka?* (横浜方面のバス乗り場はどこですか) *Where* can I get a bus for Yokohama? / *takushii*-noriba (タクシー乗り場) a taxi *stand* [*rank*].

no⌐rida⌐s·u のりだす (乗り出す) *vi.* (-dash·i-; -das·a-; -dash·i-te C)
1 sail out:
Kare-ra wa araumi ni noridashita. (彼らは荒海に乗り出した) They *sailed out* on the rough sea.
2 set about; embark; start (an enterprise):
Kare wa atarashii jigyoo ni nori-dashita. (彼は新しい事業に乗り出した) He *has embarked* on a new business.
3 lean forward:
Kodomo-tachi wa mado kara nori-dashite, *sono gyooretsu o mita.* (子どもたちは窓から乗り出して, その行列を見た) The children *leaned* out of the window and watched the parade.

no⌐riire のりいれ (乗り入れ) *n.*
1 driving (a car) into:
Kuruma no noriire *kiñshi* (*sign*) (車の乗り入れ禁止) No *Entry* for Motor Vehicles. 《⇨ noriireru》
2 the extension of (a railroad line) into (another line):
chikatetsu no Seebu-señ e no noriire (地下鉄の西武線への乗り入れ) the *use* by the subway of the Seibu Line tracks. 《⇨ noriireru》

no⌐riire⌐·ru のりいれる (乗り入れる) *vi.* (-ire-te V) **1** drive into; ride into:
Uñdoojoo ni kuruma o noriirete *wa ikemaseñ.* (運動場に車を乗り入れてはいけません) You must not *drive* your car *into* the playground.
2 extend into:
Raineñ wa chikatetsu ga kono eki made noriiremasu. (来年は地下鉄がこの駅まで乗り入れます) The subway will *be extended* to this station next year. 《⇨ noriire》

no⌐rikae のりかえ (乗り換え) *n.* change; transfer:
Giñza-señ wa koko de norikae *desu.* (銀座線はここで乗り換えです) *Change* here for the Ginza Line. / *Tookyoo-eki made* norikae *nashi de ikemasu ka?* (東京駅まで乗り換え無しで行けますか) Can I go to Tokyo Station without *changing*? 《⇨ norikaeru》

no⌐rikae⌐·ru のりかえる (乗り換える) *vi.* (-kae-te V) change; transfer:
Asakusa ni iku ni wa doko de nori-kaeru *ñ desu ka?* (浅草に行くにはど

こで乗り換えるんですか) Where do we *change* to get to Asakusa? / *Tsugi no eki de* norikaemasu. (次の駅で乗り換えます) I *change* at the next station. / *Giñza-señ e wa Ueno de* norikaete *kudasai*. (銀座線へは上野で乗り換えてください) Please *change* at Ueno for the Ginza Line. 《⇨ norikae》

no「rikoe」·ru のりこえる (乗り越える) *vi.* (-koe-te V) get over; climb over; overcome:
Kodomo-tachi wa kakine o norikoeta. (子どもたちは垣根を乗り越えた) The children *climbed over* the hedge. / *Kanojo wa samazama na koñnañ o* norikoeta. (彼女はさまざまな困難を乗り越えた) She *overcame* all sorts of hardships.

no「riko」m·u のりこむ (乗り込む) *vi.* (-kom·i-; -kom·a-; -koñ-de C)
1 get on [in] (a vehicle); board:
takushii ni norikomu (タクシーに乗り込む) *get in* a taxi / *basu* [*fune*] *ni* norikomu (バス[船]に乗り込む) *board* a bus [boat].
2 show up; arrive:
Shuzai no tame, oozee no kisha ga Nihoñ ni norikoñde kita. (取材のため、大勢の記者が日本に乗り込んで来た) A large number of reporters *arrived* in Japan to cover the news.

no「rikoshi のりこし (乗り越し) *n.* riding beyond one's station (unintentionally):
norikoshi *no seesañ o suru* (乗り越しの清算をする) pay the *excess* fare / *Norikoshi no kata wa oide ni narimasu ka?* (*by a conductor*) (乗り越しの方はおいでになりますか) Are there any passengers who *have traveled beyond their station*? 《⇨ norikosu》

no「riko」s·u のりこす (乗り越す) *vt.* (-kosh·i-; -kos·a-; -kosh·i-te C) ride past one's station (unintentionally):

Watashi wa Tookyoo-eki o norikoshite, *Ueno made itte shimatta.* (私は東京駅を乗り越して、上野まで行ってしまった) I *went past* Tokyo Station and was taken on to Ueno. 《⇨ norikoshi》

no「ri」maki のりまき (海苔巻き) *n.* vinegared rice rolled in dried laver. 《⇨ nori²》

NORIMAKI MAKING

no「rimono のりもの (乗り物) *n.* vehicle; conveyance:
Norimono *wa chikatetsu o riyoo suru no ga beñri desu.* (乗り物は地下鉄を利用するのが便利です) As a *means of transport*, it is convenient to use the subway.

no「riokure」·ru のりおくれる (乗り遅れる) *vi.* (-okure-te V) fail to catch; miss:
Shuusha ni noriokurete shimatta. (終車に乗り遅れてしまった) I *missed* the last train.

no「ri」ori のりおり (乗り降り) *n.* getting on and off:
Chiisai kodomo no basu no noriori *wa taiheñ desu.* (小さい子どものバスの乗り降りは大変です) It is difficult for little children to *get on and off* the bus. / *Noriori wa o-hayaku negaimasu.* (乗り降りはお速く願います) Please *get on and off* the train quickly. (*station announcement*)

noriori suru (〜する) *vi.* get on and off: *Kono eki de wa oozee no tsuukiñ-kyaku ga* noriori shimasu. (この駅では大勢の通勤客が乗り降りします) Lots of commuters *get on and off* at this station.

no⌐risokona¬·u のりそこなう (乗り損なう) *vt.* (-sokona·i-; -soko-naw·a-; -sokonat-te Ⓒ) fail to catch (a train [bus], etc.): *Saishuu deñsha ni* norisokonatta. (最終電車に乗り損なった) I *failed to catch* the last train.

no⌐rizuke のりづけ (糊付け) *n.* pasting; gluing.

norizuke (ni) suru (〜(に)する) *vt.* paste; glue: *Kabe ni posutaa o* norizuke ni shita. (壁にポスターをのりづけにした) I *pasted* a poster onto the wall. 《⇨ nori¹》

no⌐ro¬·i のろい (鈍い) *a.* (-ku) (*colloq.*) (of motion, work, etc.) slow; dull: *Kare wa shigoto ga* noroi. (彼は仕事がのろい) He is *slow* at his work.

no⌐ronoro のろのろ *adv.* (〜 to; 〜 suru) slowly; sluggishly: *Kare-ra wa* noronoro (*to*) *shigoto o shita.* (彼らはのろのろ(と)仕事をした) They did their work very *slowly*. / *Kuruma ga koñde ite,* noronoro (*to*) *shika susumenakatta.* (車が込んでいて、のろのろ(と)しか進めなかった) The traffic was congested, and we could only proceed *at a snail's pace*.

no⌐r·u¹ のる (乗る) *vi.* (nor·i-; nor·a-; not-te Ⓒ) **1** take; ride; get on: *basu [ressha; takushii] ni* noru (バス[列車;タクシー]に乗る) *take* a bus [train; taxi] / *jiteñsha [uma] ni* noru (自転車[馬]に乗る) *ride* a bicycle [horse] / *Kono basu wa* noru *toki ni ryookiñ o haraimasu.* (このバスは乗るときに料金を払います) You have to pay the fare as you *get on* this bus. / *Fune ni* notte ite, yotte shimatta. (船に乗っていて、酔ってしまった) I got seasick *traveling* on the ship. 《↔ oriru》《⇨ noseru¹》

2 step on; get on: *Kanojo wa isu ni* notte, *sono hoñ o totta.* (彼女はいすに乗って、その本を取った) She *got on* a chair and took the book.

3 give advice; take an interest: *Kare wa watashi no soodañ ni* notte kureta. (彼は私の相談に乗ってくれた) He was kind enough to *give* me *advice*. / *Kare-ra wa sono keekaku ni* notte kita. (彼らはその計画に乗ってきた) They *took an interest* in the scheme.

no⌐r·u² のる (載る) *vi.* (nor·i-; nor·a-; not-te Ⓒ) **1** lie on; rest: *Shiryoo wa anata no tsukue no ue ni* notte imasu. (資料はあなたの机の上にのっています) The data *are on* your desk.

2 (of an article, advertisement, etc.) appear (in a magazine, newspaper, etc.); (of a name, etc.) be listed: *Sono kookoku wa kinoo no shiñbuñ ni* norimashita. (その広告はきのうの新聞に載りました) The advertisement *appeared* in yesterday's paper. / *Kare no namae wa meebo ni* notte inakatta. (彼の名前は名簿に載っていなかった) His name *was not* on the list. 《⇨ noseru²》

no⌐se·ru¹ のせる (乗せる) *vt.* (nose-te Ⓥ) give a ride; load; pick up: *Kare o eki made kuruma ni* nose-te yatta. (彼を駅まで車に乗せてやった) I *gave* him *a ride* to the station. / *Sono takushii wa josee no o-kya-ku o futari* noseta. (そのタクシーは女性のお客を二人乗せた) The taxi *picked up* two female passengers. 《↔ orosu¹》《⇨ noru¹》

no⌐se·ru² のせる (載せる) *vt.* (nose-te Ⓥ) **1** put on; load: *Watashi wa sono tsutsumi o tana no ue ni* noseta. (私はその包みを棚の

上に載せた) I *put* the parcel on the shelf. / *Torakku wa nimotsu o ippai* nosete ita. (トラックは荷物をいっぱい載せていた) The truck *was* fully *loaded* with goods.

2 publish:
Kono kiji wa sañ-gatsu-goo ni nosemasu. (この記事は 3 月号に載せます) We are going to *publish* this article in the March issue. 《⇨ noru²》

no「shi¹ のし (熨斗) *n.* decoration for gifts. ★ Thin strip of dried abalone wrapped in red and white paper. The stretched abalone is a symbol of longevity. These days the abalone is usually omitted.

noshi-*gami*[-*bukuro*] (のし紙[袋]) wrapping paper [envelope] with a *noshi* decoration printed on it.

NOSHI-BUKURO

no「zok·u¹ のぞく (除く) *vt.* (nozok·i-; nozok·a-; nozo·i-te Ⓒ) remove; exclude; get rid of: *Watashi-tachi wa taoreta ki o dooro kara* nozoita. (私たちは倒れた木を道路から除いた) We *removed* the fallen tree from the road.

...o nozoite (...を除いて) except; excluding: *Kare o* nozoite, *hachi-niñ ga shusseki shimashita.* (彼を除いて、8 人が出席しました) Eight people attended, *excluding* him. 《↔ fukumeru》

no「zok·u² のぞく (覗く) *vt.* (nozok·i-; nozok·a-; nozo·i-te Ⓒ) peep; look in:

Kare wa kagiana kara naka o nozoita. (彼は鍵穴から中をのぞいた) He *peeped* in through the keyhole. / *Kaeri ni sono atarashii mise o* nozoite mita. (帰りにその新しい店をのぞいてみた) On my way home, I *looked in* at the new store.

no「zomashi¹·i のぞましい (望ましい) *a.* (-ku) desirable; preferable: *kodomo no kyooiku ni* nozomashii *kañkyoo* (子どもの教育に望ましい環境) a *desirable* environment for children's education / *Kaigi ni wa dekiru dake ooku no hito ga shusseki suru koto ga* nozomashii. (会議にはできるだけ多くの人が出席することが望ましい) It is *desirable* that as many people as possible attend the conference. / *Jitai wa* nozomashiku nai *hookoo ni mukatte iru.* (事態は望ましくない方向に向かっている) The situation is developing in an *unwelcome* direction. 《⇨ konomashii》

no「zomi のぞみ (望み) *n.* **1** wish; desire; hope; dream: *Watashi no* nozomi *wa Chuugoku e iku koto desu.* (私の望みは中国へ行くことです) My *wish* is to go to China. / *Yatto kanojo no* nozomi *ga kanatta.* (やっと彼女の望みがかなった) At last her *dream* has come true. 《⇨ nozomu¹》

2 chance; prospect; likelihood: *Shoori no* nozomi *wa mada juubuñ ni arimasu.* (勝利の望みはまだ十分にあります) We still have a good *chance* of victory. / *Kare ga kaifuku suru* nozomi *wa hotoñdo arimaseñ.* (彼が回復する望みはほとんどありません) There is little *prospect* of his recovery. 《⇨ nozomu¹》

no「zom·u¹ のぞむ (望む) *vt.* (nozom·i-; nozom·a-; nozoñ-de Ⓒ)

1 want; wish; hope for: *Watashi-tachi wa miñna heewa o* nozoñde imasu. (私たちはみんな平和

を望んでいます) We all *want* peace. /
Kare wa kimi no eñjo o nozoñde
iru.(彼は君の援助を望んでいる) He *is
hoping* for your help. 《⇨ nozomi》
2 like; prefer:
*Inaka no seekatsu o nozomu hito
ga ooi.*(田舎の生活を望む人が多い)
There are many people who *prefer* life in the country. 《⇨ no-
zomi》

no「zom·u² のぞむ(臨む) *vi.* (nozo-
m·i-; nozom·a-; nozoñ-de Ⓒ)
1 face (a place); overlook:
Sono heya wa mizuumi ni nozoñde imasu.(その部屋は湖に臨んでいま
す) The room *overlooks* the lake.
2 attend (a ceremony):
Chiji wa kaikai-shiki ni nozoñda.
(知事は開会式に臨んだ) The gover-
nor *attended* the opening ceremony.
3 face (danger, crisis, etc.):
Kare wa kikeñ ni nozoñde *mo, reesee datta.*(彼は危険に臨んでも、冷静
だった) Although *facing* danger,
he was calm.

NTT *n.* Nippon Telegraph and
Telephone Corporation. (日本電
信電話公社 = *Nihoñ Deñshiñ Deñwa Koosha*).

nu「g·u ぬぐ(脱ぐ) *vt.* (nug·i-; nu-
g·a-; nu·i-de Ⓒ) take off; get un-
dressed:
uwagi [kutsushita; booshi] o nugu
(上着[靴下; 帽子]をぬぐ) *take off*
one's jacket [socks; hat] / *Nihoñ
de wa zashiki ni agaru toki kutsu
o* nugimasu.(日本では座敷に上がると
き靴を脱ぎます) In Japan you *take
off* your shoes when entering a
room with 'tatami' mats.

nu「karumi ぬかるみ(泥濘) *n.*
mud; muddy place:
nukarumi *ni hamaru* (ぬかるみにはま
る) get stuck in the *mud*.

nu「keda」s·u ぬけだす(抜け出す) *vi.*
(-dash·i-; -das·a-; -dash·i-te Ⓒ)
1 get away; slip away:

*Kanojo wa dare mo shiranai ma ni
heya kara* nukedashita.(彼女はだれ
も知らない間に部屋から抜け出した) She
slipped out of the room without
anyone noticing.
2 get out of:
Sono chiimu wa yatto reñpai kara
nukedashita.(そのチームはやっと連敗か
ら抜け出した) The team at last
broke their string of losses.

nu「ke·ru ぬける(抜ける) *vi.* (nukete Ⓥ) **1** come out; fall (out):
Maeba ga nukete shimatta.(前歯が
抜けてしまった) A front tooth *came
out.* / *Kugi ga nakanaka* nukenai.
(くぎがなかなか抜けない) The nail
won't come out easily. 《⇨ nuku》
2 come off; go off; wear off:
Baketsu no soko ga nukete shimatta.(バケツの底が抜けてしまった)
The bottom of the bucket *came
out.* / *Koosui no kaori ga* nukete
shimatta.(香水の香りが抜けてしまっ
た) The perfume *has worn off.*
《⇨ nuku》
3 be missing; be left out:
Kono geñkoo wa sañ-mai nukete
imasu.(この原稿は3枚抜けています)
This manuscript *is missing* three
pages. / *Kanojo no namae ga meebo kara* nukete ita.(彼女の名前が
名簿から抜けていた) Her name *was
missing* from the list. 《⇨ nuku》
4 go through:
Deñsha wa toñneru o nuketa.(電車
はトンネルを抜けた) The train *went*
through the tunnel.
5 leave (a group, organization,
etc.); quit:
Kare wa roodoo kumiai o nuketa.
(彼は労働組合を抜けた) He *left* the
labor union. 《⇨ nuku》

nu「kito」r·u ぬきとる(抜き取る) *vt.*
(-tor·i-; -tor·a-; -tot-te Ⓒ) pull
out; extract; take out:
Kare wa yubi ni sasatta toge o
nukitotta.(彼は指に刺さったとげを抜き
取った) He *pulled out* the thorn

which was stuck in his finger. / *Kare-ra wa sañpuru o* nuki totte, *hiñshitsu o keñsa shita.* (彼らはサンプルを抜き取って、品質を検査した) They *took* samples and examined for quality.

nu「k·u ぬく (抜く) *vi., vt.* (nuk·i-; nuk·a-; nu·i-te C) **1** pull out; extract: *kugi* [*kusa*] *o* nuku (くぎ[草]を抜く) *pull out* a nail [weeds] / *ha o* nuku (歯を抜く) *extract* a tooth / *Kono biiru no señ o* nuite *kudasai.* (このビールの栓を抜いてください) Please *open* this bottle of beer. 《⇨ nukeru》 **2** take out; remove (a stain): *Kono shimi wa* nuku *koto ga dekimasu ka?* (この染みは抜くことができますか) Is it possible to *take out* this stain? 《⇨ nukeru》 **3** beat; outrun; outstrip: *Hyaku-meetoru kyoosoo de watashi wa kare o* nuita. (百メートル競走で私は彼を抜いた) I *outran* him in the 100 meter race. / *Kare wa mae o hashitte iru kuruma o* nuita. (彼は前を走っている車を抜いた) He *overtook* the car traveling in front.

nu「ma」 ぬま (沼) *n.* swamp; marsh: ★ An area of shallow, muddy water with wild plants growing in it. *Deñsetsu ni yoru to kono* numa *no nushi wa ryuu da to iu koto desu.* (伝説によるとこの沼の主は竜だということです) According to legend, the spirit of this *swamp* is a dragon. 《⇨ ike》

nu「no」 ぬの (布) *n.* cloth: nuno-*kire* (布切れ) a piece of *cloth.*

nu「ras·u ぬらす (濡らす) *vt.* (nurash·i-; nuras·a-; nurash·i-te C) wet; moisten; dampen: *Mizu o koboshite, yuka o* nurashite *shimatta.* (水をこぼして、床をぬらしてしまった) I have spilled the water and *wet* the floor. 《⇨ nureru》

nu「re·ru ぬれる (濡れる) *vi.* (nurete V) get wet; be moistened: *Ame de* nurete *shimatta.* (雨でぬれてしまった) I *got wet* in the rain. / *Nureta te de sawaranai de kudasai.* (ぬれた手で触らないでください) Do not touch with *wet* hands. 《⇨ nurasu》

nu「r·u ぬる (塗る) *vt.* (nur·i-; nur·a-; nut-te C) paint; spread; plaster; apply: *pañ ni bataa o* nuru (パンにバターを塗る) *spread* butter on bread / *te ni kuriimu o* nuru (手にクリームを塗る) *apply* cream to one's hands / *Kare wa kabe o shiroku* nutta. (彼は壁を白く塗った) He *painted* the wall white. / *Peñki* nuritate. (*sign*) (ペンキ塗りたて) *Wet* Paint. 《⇨ tsukeru¹》

nu「ru」·i ぬるい (温い) *a.* (-ku) lukewarm; tepid: nurui *o-cha* (ぬるいお茶) *lukewarm* tea / *Furo ga* nuruku *natte shimatta.* (ふろがぬるくなってしまった) The bathwater has become *lukewarm.* 《⇨ atsui¹》

nu「shi」 ぬし (主) *n.* the person: *Ano hito ga uwasa no* nushi *desu.* (あの人がうわさの主です) He is *the person* we have been talking about.

nu「sumi」 ぬすみ (盗み) *n.* theft; pilferage; stealing: nusumi *o hataraku* (盗みを働く) commit *theft* / nusumi *ni hairu* (盗みに入る) *break into a house* / *Sono otoko wa* nusumi *de taiho sareta.* (その男は盗みで逮捕された) That man was arrested for *theft.* 《⇨ nusumu》

nu「su」m·u ぬすむ (盗む) *vt.* (nusum·i-; nusum·a-; nusuñ-de C) steal; rob; pilfer: *Dare-ka ga kiñko kara kane o* nusuñda. (だれかが金庫から金を盗んだ) Someone *stole* money from the safe. / *Kare wa kuukoo de kamera o* nusumareta. (彼は空港でカメラを盗

まれた) He *had* his camera *stolen* at the airport. 《⇨ nusumi》

nu¹·u ぬう(縫う) *vt.* (nu·i-; nu-w·a-; nut-te C) sew; stitch: *Kanojo wa jibuñ no fuku o* nutte *iru tokoro desu.* (彼女は自分の服を縫っているところです) She *is* now *sewing* her own dress. / *Isha wa kizuguchi o go-hari* nutta. (医者は傷口を5針縫った) The doctor *sewed up* the wound with five stitches.

nutte aruku [iku] (縫って歩く[行く]) weave one's way: *Kanojo wa kodomo o mitsukeru tame ni, hitogomi no naka o* nutte aruita. (彼女は子どもを見つけるために、人込みの中を縫って歩いた) She *wove her way* through the crowds to find her child.

nyu¹añsu ニュアンス *n.* nuance; shade of meaning: *'Yooboo' to 'yoosee' de wa sukoshi* nyuañsu *ga chigaimasu.* (「要望」と「要請」では少しニュアンスが違います) There is a slight difference in *nuance* between '*yooboo*' and '*yoosee.*'

nyo¹o にょう(尿) *n.* urine: nyoo *(no) keñsa* (尿(の)検査) *urine* analysis.

nyu⌈u- にゅう(入) *pref.* entry; entrance: nyuu-*koku* (入国) *entry* into a country / nyuu-*koo* (入港) *arrival* of a ship in port.

nyu⌈ugaku にゅうがく(入学) *n.* entrance into a school; admission to a school: *Watashi wa sono gakkoo ni* nyuugaku *o yurusareta.* (私はその学校に入学を許された) I *was admitted* to the school. / nyuugaku-*gañsho* (入学願書) an application for a school / nyuugaku-*kiñ* (入学金) an *entrance* fee / nyuugaku-*shikeñ* (入学試験) an *entrance* examination ★ Often abbreviated to '*nyuushi.*'

/ nyuugaku-*shiki* (入学式) a school *entrance* ceremony / nyuugaku-*tetsuzuki* (入学手続き) school *entrance* procedures.

nyuugaku suru (〜する) *vi.* enter school; be admitted to a school: *Musume wa kotoshi no shi-gatsu shoogakkoo ni* nyuugaku shimasu. (娘は今年の4月小学校に入学します) My daughter *starts* elementary school in April of this year. 《↔ sotsugyoo》

nyu¹ugañ にゅうがん(乳癌) *n.* breast cancer: nyuugañ *ni kakaru* (乳がんにかかる) have *breast cancer.* 《⇨ gañ》

nyu⌈uiñ にゅういん(入院) *n.* admission to a hospital; hospitalization: nyuuiñ-*kañja* (入院患者) an *inpatient* / nyuuiñ-*ryoo* (入院料) *hospital* charges / nyuuiñ-*tetsuzuki* (入院手続き) procedures connected with *hospitalization.*

nyuuiñ suru (〜する) *vi.* be hospitalized; enter the hospital: *Chichi wa kinoo* nyuuiñ shimashita. (父はきのう入院しました) My father *was hospitalized* yesterday. / *Kare wa ima* nyuuiñ *shite imasu.* (彼は今入院しています) He *is* now *in the hospital.* 《↔ taiiñ》

nyu⌈ujoo にゅうじょう(入場) *n.* entrance; admission: nyuujoo *o kyoka* [*kyohi*] *suru* (入場を許可[拒否]する) give permission for [refuse] *entrance* / *Kono keñ de* nyuujoo *dekimasu ka?* (この券で入場できますか) Can I gain *admittance* with this ticket? / nyuujoo-*ryoo* (入場料) an *admission* charge / nyuujoo-*sha* (入場者) a *visitor*; a *spectator.*

nyuujoo suru (〜する) *vi.* enter; be admitted: *Sono shiai ni oozee no kañkyaku ga* nyuujoo shita. (その試合に大勢の観客が入場した) A large number of spectators *were* *admitted* to the match. 《↔ tai-joo》《⇒ hairu》

nyu⌈ujo⌉okeñ にゅうじょうけん（入場券）*n.* admission ticket.

nyu⌈ukoku にゅうこく（入国）*n.* entry into a country:
Sono otoko wa Nihoñ e no nyuu-koku *o mitomerarenakatta.*（その男は日本への入国を認められなかった）He was refused *entry* to Japan. / *fu-hoo*-nyuukoku（不法入国）illegal *entry* / nyuukoku-*biza*（入国ビザ）an *entry* visa / nyuukoku-*tetsuzu-ki*（入国手続き）*immigration* forma-lities.
nyuukoku suru（～する）*vi.* enter a country: *Iroiro tetsuzuki o shi-te, yatto watashi wa sono kuni ni* nyuukoku shita.（いろいろ手続きをして、やっと私はその国に入国した）After go-ing through many procedures, I finally *entered* that country. 《↔ shukkoku》

nyu⌈usha にゅうしゃ（入社）*n.* join-ing a company:
Nyuusha *wa itsu desu ka?*（入社はいつですか）When did you *join* this company? / nyuusha-*shikeñ*（入社試験）a *company entrance* exam.
nyuusha suru（～する）*vi.* join a company: *Watashi wa go-neñ mae ni kono kaisha ni* nyuusha shi-mashita.（私は5年前にこの会社に入社しました）I *joined* this company five years ago. 《↔ taisha》

nyu⌈ushoo にゅうしょう（入賞）*n.* winning a prize:
nyuushoo-*sakuhiñ*（入賞作品）a *prize-winning* work / nyuushoo-sha（入賞者）a *prize-winner*.
nyuushoo suru（～する）*vi.* win a prize: *Watashi no kaita e ga* nyuushoo shimashita.（私のかいた絵が入賞しました）The picture I drew *received a prize.*

nyu⌈usu ニュース *n.* **1** news:
rajio no nyuusu（ラジオのニュース）the

news on the radio / *Terebi no* nyuusu *ni yoru to kesa Uñzeñdake ga bakuhatsu shita rashii.*（テレビのニュースによるとけさ雲仙岳が爆発したらしい）According to the TV *news*, it seems that Unzendake erupted this morning.
2 personal news:
Nani-ka ii nyuusu *wa arimasu ka?*（何かいいニュースはありますか）Do you have any good *news*? / *Kanojo no kekkoñ no* nyuusu *o kikimashita ka?*（彼女の結婚のニュースを聞きましたか）Have you heard the *news* of her marriage?

nyu⌈uyoku にゅうよく（入浴）*n.* bath; bathing:

┌─── **CULTURE** ───┐
In Japan, people wash them-selves outside the bathtub, not inside. The bath water must be kept clean, because several people use the same bath in turn.
└──────────────┘

Haha wa nyuuyoku-chuu *desu.*（母は入浴中です）My mother is *in the bath.* / *Kanojo wa akañboo ni* nyuuyoku *o saseta.*（彼女は赤ん坊に入浴をさせた）She gave her baby a *bath.* 《⇒ furo》
nyuuyoku suru（～する）*vi.* take a bath: *Watashi wa mainichi* nyuu-yoku shimasu.（私は毎日入浴します）I *take a bath* daily.

NYUUYOKU

O

o¹ お (尾) *n*. **1** tail. 《⇨ shippo》
2 (of a comet) trail.

o² を *p*. [follows a noun]
1 (indicates the direct object):
Maiasa shiñbuñ o *yomimasu*. (毎朝新聞を読みます) I read the *newspaper* every morning. / *Watashi wa Nihoñgo de* tegami o *kaita*. (私は日本語で手紙を書いた) I wrote a *letter* in Japanese. / *Nani-ka* nomimono o *kudasai*. (何か飲み物を下さい) Please give me *something to drink*. / *Anata no* heñji o *matte imasu*. (あなたの返事を待っています) I am waiting for your *answer*.
2 (indicates location or movement):
Kono michi o *massugu iki nasai*. (この道をまっすぐ行きなさい) Go straight along this *road*. / *Tsugi no* kado o *hidari e magari nasai*. (次の角を左へ曲がりなさい) Turn left *at the next corner*. / *Michi no* migigawa o *arukanakereba ikemaseñ*. (道の右側を歩かなければいけません) You should walk *on the right side* of the road. / *Rooka o [de] hashiranai yoo ni*. (廊下を[で]走らないように) Do not run *in the corridors*.
3 (indicates movement away from a place, institution, etc):
Kyoneñ koko no daigaku o *demashita*. (去年ここの大学を出ました) I graduated *from a university* here last year. / *Kanojo wa* kokyoo o *[kara] hanarete, Tookyoo de shuushoku shita*. (彼女は故郷を[から]離れて、東京で就職した) She left her *hometown* and got employment in Tokyo. / *Maiasa nañ-ji ni* o-taku o *demasu ka?* (毎朝何時にお宅を出ますか) What time do you leave *home* every morning?

o- お *pref*. [added to a noun, verb or adjective to indicate respect, humility or politeness]
1 (respect toward the listener):
O-tegami *arigatoo gozaimashita*. (お手紙ありがとうございました) Thank you for *your letter*. / *Kono shiñbuñ wa* o-yomi *ni narimashita ka?* (この新聞はお読みになりましたか) *Have* you *read* this newspaper? / *Yamada-sañ wa* o-isogashi-soo da. (山田さんはお忙しそうだ) Mr. Yamada seems to be *busy*.

──── (USAGE) ────
Verbs are used in the following pattern: '*o-* + *v*. (continuative base) + *ni naru*.' 《⇨ naru¹》

2 (humility on the part of the speaker):
Ato de o-deñwa *itashimasu*. (あとでお電話いたします) I'll give you a *call* later. / *Watashi no* sakuhiñ o *o-*mise *shimashoo*. (私の作品をお見せしましょう) I'll *show* you my work.

──── (USAGE) ────
Verbs are used in the following pattern: '*o-* + *v*. (continuative base) + *suru* [*shimasu; itashimasu*].' 《⇨ suru¹》

3 (politeness):
o-kashi (お菓子) *sweets* / o-kane (お金) *money* / o-kome (お米) *rice* / *Ano hito wa* o-sake ni *tsuyoi*. (あの人はお酒に強い) He *can drink a lot*.

──── (USAGE) ────
It is not usual to place '*o-*' before foreign loan words, but some people say '*o-biiru*' (beer), '*o-soosu*' (sauce), etc.

o⌈ba おば（伯母・叔母）n. one's aunt:

> **(USAGE)**
> Older sisters of one's father or
> mother are '伯母,' and younger
> sisters are '叔母.'

Oba *wa keeki o tsukuru no ga
joozu desu.*（おばはケーキを作るのが上
手です）My *aunt* is good at baking
cakes. 《⇨ obasañ; kazoku (table)》

o-⌈ba⌉asañ おばあさん（お祖母さん・お
婆さん）n. ★ '祖母' is used for **1**,
while '婆' is used for **2**.
1 one's grandmother:
Kare wa o-baasañ *ni sodaterareta.*
（彼はおばあさんに育てられた）He was
brought up by his *grandmother.* /
O-baasañ wa o-geñki desu ka?（お
ばあさんはお元気ですか）Is your *grandmother* in good health? 《⇨ sobo;
kazoku (table)》
2 old woman:
O-baasañ ni seki o yuzutte ageta.
（おばあさんに席を譲ってあげた）I gave
up my seat to an *old lady.*

o⌈basañ おばさん（伯母さん・叔母さ
ん・小母さん）n. ★ '伯母, 叔母' are
used for **1**, while '小母' is used
for **2**. 《⇨ oba》
1 one's aunt:
*Obasañ no uchi made deñsha de
dono kurai kakarimasu ka?*（おばさ
んの家まで電車でどのくらいかかりますか）
How long does it take to go to
your *aunt's* house by train?
2 middle-aged woman:
Shiranai o-basañ *ni eki made no
michi o oshiete ageta.*（知らないおば
さんに駅までの道を教えてあげた）I told
a *woman* I didn't know the way
to the station.

o⌈bi おび（帯）n. obi; belt for a kimono; broad sash:
obi *o shimeru*（帯をしめる）tie an *obi.*
《⇨ illus. (right)》

o⌈biyaka⌉s·u おびやかす（脅かす）vt.
(-kash·i-; -kas·a-; -kash·i·te C)
threaten; menace; frighten:

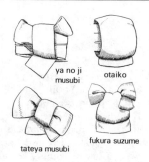

ya no ji
musubi

otaiko

tateya musubi

fukura suzume

A FEW TYPICAL OBI

*Kakuheeki wa sekai heewa o obi-
yakashimasu.*（核兵器は世界平和を
おびやかします）Nuclear weapons
threaten world peace. / *Sono chiimu wa shui no za o obiyaka-
sarete iru.*（そのチームは首位の座をおび
やかされている）The team's leading
ranking *is being threatened.*

o⌈bo⌉e おぼえ（覚え）n. memory;
remembrance; recollection:
*Kanojo ni wa mae ni doko-ka de
atta* oboe *ga aru.*（彼女には前にどこか
で会った覚えがある）I *remember* seeing her somewhere before. / *Kare
ga sono o-kane o kaeshite kureta*
oboe *wa arimaseñ.*（彼がそのお金を
返してくれた覚えはありません）I have
no *recollection* that he returned
the money to me. 《⇨ kioku》

o⌈boe⌉·ru おぼえる（覚える）vt.
(oboe-te V) **1** remember;
memorize:
Kare no namae wa oboete *imaseñ.*
（彼の名前は覚えていません）I *don't remember* his name. / *Sono shi wa
oboemashita ka?*（その詩は覚えました
か）*Have* you *memorized* the
poem? 《⇨ omoidasu》
2 learn:
*Yaku ni tatsu Nihoñgo no hyoo-
geñ o takusañ oboemashita.*（役に
立つ日本語の表現をたくさん覚えました）
I *have learned* a lot of useful Japanese expressions. / *Suiee wa
doko de oboemashita ka?*（水泳は

どこで覚えましたか) Where *did* you *learn* swimming?

3 (*formal*) feel:
kuufuku o oboeru (空腹を覚える) *feel* hungry.

o-「boosañ おぼうさん (お坊さん) *n.* Buddhist priest; bonze.
《⇨ boosañ (photo)》

o「bore·ru おぼれる (溺れる) *vi.* (o-bore-te Ⓥ) **1** (almost) drown; be (almost) drowned: ★ '*Obore-ru*' is used in two senses, 'almost drown' and 'drown.'
Kare wa oborete iru kodomo o tasuketa. (彼はおぼれている子どもを助けた) He rescued the *drowning* boy. / *Kono kawa de sañ-niñ ga oborete shinimashita.* (この川で3人がおぼれて死にました) Three people *drowned* in this river.
2 indulge in:
Sore irai kanojo wa sake ni oboreta. (それ以来彼女は酒におぼれた) Since then she *has abandoned herself* to drink.

o「busa「r·u おぶさる (負ぶさる) *vi.* (obusar·i-; obusar·a-; obusat-te Ⓒ) ride on a person's back:
Kodomo no koro yoku chichi ni obusarimashita. (子どものころよく父におぶさりました) When I was a child I *was* often *carried on* my father's *back.*

o-「cha おちゃ (お茶) *n.* **1** tea; green tea:
o-cha o ireru [nomu] (お茶を入れる [飲む]) make [drink] *tea.* / *O-cha o nomimaseñ ka?* (お茶を飲みませんか) How about a cup of *tea*? ★ This expression often implies "Let's have a chat." 《⇨ cha》

KINDS OF JAPANESE TEA

gyokuro (玉露)	the highest quality
señcha (煎茶)	middle grade
bañcha (番茶)	coarse

2 tea break:
O-cha ni shimashoo. (お茶にしましょう) Let's have a *tea break.*
3 tea ceremony:
o-cha o narau (お茶を習う) learn the *tea ceremony.*

o-cha o nigosu (～をにごす) get by in an awkward situation by being evasive: *Kare wa kañjiñ na koto ni naru to o-cha o nigosu.* (彼は肝心なことになるとお茶を濁す) He *evades the issue* when it comes to the crux of the problem.
《⇨ gomakasu》

o「chiba おちば (落ち葉) *n.* fallen leaves:
ochiba o haku [taku] (落ち葉を掃く [たく]) rake up [burn] *fallen leaves.*

o「chi「·ru おちる (落ちる) *vi.* (ochite Ⓥ) **1** come [go] down; fall; drop:
Hi ga ochite, kuraku natta. (日が落ちて、暗くなった) The sun *went down* and it became dark. / *Kanojo wa kaidañ kara ochite, kega o shita.* (彼女は階段から落ちて、けがをした) She *fell down* the stairs and injured herself. / *Hikooki wa umi ni ochita rashii.* (飛行機は海に落ちたらしい) The airplane seems to *have come down* in the sea. 《⇨ otosu》
2 fall [drop] off:
Koñgetsu wa uriage ga ochita. (今月は売上が落ちた) This month's sales *have fallen off.* / *Kanojo wa niñki ga ochite iru.* (彼女は人気が落ちている) Her popularity *is waning.* / *Gakkoo no seeseki ga ochite shimatta.* (学校の成績が落ちてしまった) My grades at school *have gotten worse.*
《↔ agaru》
3 fail an examination:
Shikeñ ni ochitara, doo suru ñ desu ka? (試験に落ちたら、どうするんですか) What are you going to do if you *fail* the examination? / *Kare wa kotoshi no nyuushi ni ochita.*

（彼は今年の入試に落ちた）He *failed* this year's entrance examination. 《⇨ otosu》

4 (of stains) come out [off]: *Kono shimi wa sekkeñ de araeba, ochimasu.* (このしみはせっけんで洗えば、落ちます) This stain will *come off* if you wash it with soap. 《⇨ otosu》

5 (of a name, item, etc.) be missing: *Watashi no namae ga meebo kara ochite imasu.* (私の名前が名簿から落ちています) My name *is not* on the list. 《⇨ otosu》

o「chitsuk·u おちつく (落ち着く) *vi.* (-tsuk·i-; -tsuk·a-; -tsu·i-te Ⓒ)
1 calm down; cool down: *Shikeñ no kekka ga shiñpai de, ochitsukanakatta.* (試験の結果が心配で、落ち着かなかった) I was anxious about the result of the examination and *could not keep calm.* / Ochitsuki nasai. (落ち着きなさい) *Calm yourself.*
2 (of trouble, a quarrel, etc.) subside; die down: *Sawagi wa ma-mo-naku ochitsuita.* (騒ぎは間もなく落ち着いた) It was not long before the uproar *subsided.*
3 settle down: *Shiñkoñ no futari wa apaato ni ochitsuita.* (新婚の二人はアパートに落ち着いた) The newly married couple *have settled down* in their apartment.

o-「chuugeñ おちゅうげん (お中元) *n.* = chuugeñ.

o-「dai おだい (お代) *n.* price; rate; charge; fare: *O-dai wa zeñbu de ikura desu ka?* (お代は全部でいくらですか) What is the total *price?* / O-dai wa moo itadakimashita. (お代はもういただきました) We have already received *payment.* 《⇨ -dai²》

o-「daiji ni おだいじに (お大事に) take care of yourself: ★ An idiomatic expression of sympathy to a sick person. *O-karada o o-daiji ni.* (お体をお大事に) Please *take care of yourself.*

o「date·ru おだてる (煽てる) *vt.* (odate-te Ⓥ) flatter; incite: *Kare o odatete, sono shigoto o hikiukesaseta.* (彼をおだてて、その仕事を引き受けさせた) I *wheedled* him into undertaking the task. / Odatete mo dame desu yo. (おだててもだめですよ) It's no use trying to *soft-soap* me. / Soñna ni odatenai de kudasai yo. (そんなにおだてないでくださいよ) *Don't flatter* me like that.

o「da」yaka おだやか (穏やか) *a.n.* (~ na, ni) **1** calm; quiet; peaceful: *Kyoo no umi wa odayaka da.* (きょうの海は穏やかだ) The sea today is *calm.* / Kare wa odayaka na seekatsu o okutte iru. (彼は穏やかな生活を送っている) He leads a *quiet* life.
2 (of personality, atmosphere, etc.) mild; gentle; amicable: *Kanojo wa odayaka na hito desu.* (彼女は穏やかな人です) She is a person of *mild* disposition. / Watashi-tachi wa odayaka ni hanashi-aimashita. (私たちは穏やかに話し合いました) We talked together *amicably.*

o「de」ki おでき *n.* = dekimono.

o「de」ñ おでん *n.* Japanese hotchpotch. ★ Consists of a variety of ingredients: tofu, eggs, cuttlefish, Japanese radish, fish-paste cake, devil's-tongue, kelp, etc.

ODEÑ

o⌈**dokas·u** おどかす (脅かす) *vt.*
(odokash·i-; odokas·a-; odo-
kash·i·te C) **1** threaten:
*Sono otoko wa korosu zo to wata-
shi o odokashita.* (その男は殺すぞと
私を脅かした) The man *threatened*
me, saying, "I will kill you."
《⇨ odosu》
2 frighten; startle:
*Kare wa sono inu o odokashite
oiharatta.* (彼はその犬を脅かして追い
払った) He *frightened* away the
dog.

o⌈**do-odo** おどおど *adv.* timidly;
shyly.
odo-odo suru (～する) *vi.* be timid.

o⌈**dori** おどり (踊り) *n.* dance;
dancing:
Kanojo wa odori ga umai. (彼女は
踊りがうまい) She is good at *dancing.* 《⇨ odoru》

o⌈**doriba** おどりば (踊り場) *n.* landing (of stairs).

o⌈**doroka⌉s·u** おどろかす (驚かす) *vt.*
(-kash·i-; -kas·a-; -kash·i·te C)
surprise; astonish; startle:
*Kare wa kurayami kara kyuu ni
arawarete kodomo-tachi o odoro-
kashita.* (彼は暗闇から急に現れて子ど
もたちを驚かした) He came out of
the darkness suddenly, *frightening* the children. / *Ike no tori o
odorokashite wa ikemaseñ.* (池の
鳥を驚かしてはいけません) Don't *star-
tle* the birds in the pond. / *Soñna
ni odorokasanai de kudasai yo.* (そ
んなに驚かさないでくださいよ) *Don't surprise* me like that. 《⇨ odoroku》

o⌈**doroki⌉** おどろき (驚き) *n.* surprise; astonishment; shock:
odoroki no koe o ageru (驚きの声を
あげる) express one's *surprise* / *Kare o mita toki no odoroki to ittara.*
(彼を見たときの驚きといったら) Imag-
ine my *astonishment* when I saw
him! 《⇨ odoroku》

o⌈**doro⌉k·u** おどろく (驚く) *vi.* (o-
dorok·i-; odorok·a-; odoro·i·te

C) **1** be surprised; be astonished; be shocked:
Totsuzeñ no juusee ni odoroita.
(突然の銃声に驚いた) I *was sur-
prised* at the sudden report of a
gun. / *Kanojo wa* odoroite, *watashi o mita.* (彼女は驚いて、私を見た)
She looked at me *in astonishment.*
/ *Odoroita koto ni wa, kare wa watashi o uragitta.* (驚いたことには、彼は
私を裏切った) To my *astonishment,*
he betrayed me. 《⇨ odorokasu》
2 wonder; marvel:
*Sono sakuhiñ no amari no deki-
bae ni* odorokimashita. (その作品の
あまりのできばえに驚きました) I *mar-
veled* at that wonderful work.
《⇨ odoroki》
odoroku ni (wa) ataranai (～に
(は)当たらない) it is no wonder:
*Kare ga Nihoñgo o yoku hanasu
no wa odoroku ni (wa) atarimaseñ.*
(彼が日本語をよく話すのは驚くに(は)当
たりません) *It is quite natural* that
he speaks Japanese well.

o⌈**dor·u** おどる (踊る) *vi.* (odor·i-;
odor·a-; odot·te C) dance:
Kanojo wa koto ni awasete odotta.
(彼女は琴に合わせて踊った) She
danced to the Japanese harp. /
Issho ni odotte moraemasu ka? (い
っしょに踊ってもらえますか) Can I ask
you for a *dance?* 《⇨ odori》

o⌈**doshi** おどし (脅し) *n.* threat;
menace; bluff:
odoshi o kakeru (脅しをかける)
threaten / *Kimi no odoshi nado
kowaku nai.* (きみの脅しなど怖くない)
I'm not afraid of your *threats.* /
*Kono ko wa odoshi no kiku yoo
na ko de wa nai.* (この子は脅しのきく
ような子ではない) This is not the
sort of child against which *threats*
have any effect. 《⇨ odosu》

o⌈**dos·u** おどす (脅す) *vt.* (odo-
sh·i-; odos·a-; odosh·i·te C)
threaten; menace:
Sono otoko wa naifu de watashi o

odoshita. (その男はナイフで私を脅した) The man *threatened* me with a knife. ((⇨ odoshi))

o⌈**e·ru** おえる (終える) *vt.* (oe-te [V]) finish; end; complete: *Kyoo no shigoto wa* oemashita. (きょうの仕事は終えました) I *have finished* today's work. / *Shokuji o* oetara, *atokatazuke o tanomimasu yo.* (食事を終えたら、後片付けを頼みますよ) Please clean up once you *have finished* your meal. / *Roñbuñ no shippitsu wa* oemashita *ka?* (論文の執筆は終えましたか) *Have* you *finished* writing your thesis? / *Kare wa mijikai shoogai o* oeta. (彼は短い生涯を終えた) He *ended* his brief life. ((⇨ owaru))

o⌈**ga**⌉**m·u** おがむ (拝む) *vt.* (ogam·i-; ogam·a-; ogañ-de [C]) pray; worship: *hotoke-sama o* ogamu (仏様を拝む) *worship* the Buddha / *jiñja no mae de te o awasete* ogamu (神社の前で手を合わせて拝む) put one's hands together and *pray* in front of a shrine.

o⌈**gawa** おがわ (小川) *n.* brook; small stream.

o⌈**gina**⌉·**u** おぎなう (補う) *vt.* (ogina·i-; oginaw·a-; oginat-te [C]) make up for; compensate; fill: *Kanojo wa akaji o* oginau *no ni kuroo shite iru.* (彼女は赤字を補うのに苦労している) She is having a hard time *making up* the deficit. / *Kuusho ni tekitoo na go o* oginai *nasai.* (空所に適当な語を補いなさい) *Fill in* the blanks with suitable words.

o⌈**gor·u**¹ おごる (奢る) *vt.* (ogor·i-; ogor·a-; ogot-te [C]) treat: *Kyoo no o-hiru wa watashi ga* ogorimasu. (きょうのお昼は私がおごります) I'll *treat* you to lunch today. / *Kare wa watashi ni aisukuriimu o* ogotte kureta. (彼は私にアイスクリームをおごってくれた) He *treated* me to

an ice cream.

o⌈**gor·u**² おごる (驕る) *vi.* (ogor·i-; ogor·a-; ogot-te [C]) be proud; be haughty: *Saikiñ yuumee ni natte, kare wa sukoshi* ogotte iru. (最近有名になって、彼は少しおごっている) Recently he has become famous and *is* a little *proud and arrogant.* / Ogoru *Heeke wa hisashikarazu.* (*saying*) (おごる平家は久しからず) *Pride* comes before the fall. (literally 'The haughty Heike family will not be that way long.')

─(**CULTURE**)─
The Heike family enjoyed prosperity and lived in luxury, but this lasted only a short period before they were destroyed by the Minamoto family in 1185.

o⌈**go**⌉**soka** おごそか (厳か) *a.n.* (~ na, ni) solemn; grave; dignified: *Ireesai wa* ogosoka *ni okonawaremashita.* (慰霊祭は厳かに行われました) The memorial service was *solemnly* performed.

o⌈**ha**⌉**gi** おはぎ (お萩) *n.* glutinous rice ball coated with sweet red-bean paste or soybean powder. ★ Traditionally eaten at the spring or autumn equinox.

OHAGI

o-⌈**hana** おはな (お花) *n.* flower arrangement; ikebana: o-hana *o narau* (お花を習う) learn *flower arrangement* / o-hana *no señsee* (お花の先生) a teacher of *flower arrangement* / o-hana *ni* *tsukau hana* (お花に使う花) flowers for *ikebana.* 《⇨ ikebana》

o-「**hanami** おはなみ (お花見) *n.* = hanami.

o「**hayoo** おはよう (お早よう) Good morning.

─(**USAGE**)─
Expression used when people first see each other in the early morning. '*Ohayoo*' is used between close friends or when addressing a person lower in status. The more polite expression is '*Ohayoo gozaimasu.*'

o-「**hi**」**ru** おひる (お昼) *n.* **1** noon: O-hiru *sugi ni o-tazune shimasu.* (お昼すぎにお訪ねします) I'll visit you after *noon.* 《⇨ hiru (table)》 **2** lunch: O-hiru *wa doko de tabemashita ka?* (お昼はどこで食べましたか) Where did you have *lunch*?

o「**i**」**¹** おい (甥) *n.* nephew. ★ When another family's nephew is referred to, '*oigo-sañ*' is used. 《↔ mee》

o「**i**」**²** おい *int.* hey; hi; say; hello; look: ★ Used by men. Oi. *Doko e iku ñ da.* (おい。どこへ行くんだ) *Hey*! Where are you going?

o「**ida**」**s·u** おいだす (追い出す) *vi.* (-dash·i-; -das·a-; -dash·i-te Ⓒ) drive out; expel; oust: Niwa ni haitte kita inu o oida-shita. (庭に入ってきた犬を追い出した) I *drove out* the dog which had come into our garden. / Kare wa sono kurabu kara oidasareta. (彼はそのクラブから追い出された) He *was expelled* from the club.

o「**ide** おいで (お出で) *n.* ★ Both '*oide desu*' and '*oide ni naru*' are honorific equivalents of '*iru,*' '*kuru*' and '*iku.*'

1 presence: O-kaasañ *wa* oide *desu ka?* (お母さんはおいでですか) *Is* your mother *in*?

/ O-toosañ *wa* oide *ni narimasu ka?* (お父さんはおいでになりますか) *Is* your father *at home*? 《⇨ iru'》

2 coming: Doozo oide *kudasai.* (どうぞおいでください) Please *come and visit* us. / Watashi to issho ni oide *ni narimasu ka?* (私といっしょにおいでになりますか) Will you *be coming* with me? 《⇨ kuru》

3 going: Dochira e oide *desu ka?* (どちらへおいでですか) Where *are* you *going*? / Ashita wa dochira e oide *ni narimasu ka?* (あしたはどちらへおいでになりますか) Where *are* you *going* tomorrow? 《⇨ iku》

4 be present; go; come: ★ Shortened form of '*oide nasai,*' which implies an order or request. Koko ni shibaraku oide. (ここにしばらくおいで) *Stay* here for a while. / Hayaku gakkoo e oide. (早く学校へおいで) *Go* to school quickly. / Kotchi e oide. (こっちへおいで) *Come* here.

o「**ihara**」**·u** おいはらう (追い払う) *vt.* (-hara·i-; -haraw·a-; -harat-te Ⓒ) (*informal* = opparau) drive [turn] away; disperse: Kare wa norainu o oiharatta. (彼はのら犬を追い払った) He *drove* a stray dog away. / Keekañ wa yajiuma o oiharatta. (警官はやじ馬を追い払った) The policemen *dispersed* the onlookers.

o「**ikake**」**·ru** おいかける (追い掛ける) *vt.* (-kake-te Ⓥ) run after; chase; pursue: Keekañ wa hañniñ o oikaketa ga miushinatta. (警官は犯人を追いかけたが見失った) The policeman *chased* the criminal but lost track of him.

o「**iko**」**s·u** おいこす (追い越す) *vt.* (-kosh·i-; -kos·a-; -kosh·i-te Ⓒ) pass; overtake; outstrip: Sakamichi de hoka no kuruma o oikosu no wa kikeñ desu. (坂道でほ

かの車を追い越すのは危険です) It is dangerous to *overtake* other cars on a slope. / *Jii-enu-pii de Nihoñ wa sono kuni o* oikoshita. (GNP で日本はその国を追い越した) Japan *outstripped* that country in GNP. (⇨ oitsuku)

O-「i」narisañ おいなりさん (お稲荷さん) *n.* **1** Inari shrine. ★ Inari, whose messenger is considered to be the fox, was originally the guardian deity of farmers, but since the sixteenth century has also been known as a guardian of commerce.
2 = inarizushi.

o「inu」k·u おいぬく (追い抜く) *vt.* (-nuk·i-; -nuk·a-; -nu·i-te Ⓒ) overtake. (⇨ oikosu)

o-「isha-sañ おいしゃさん (お医者さ ん) *n.* (medical) doctor; family doctor. (⇨ isha)

o「ishi·i おいしい (美味しい) *a.* (-ku) delicious; tasty; good: *Kono mise no suteeki wa* oishii. (この店のステーキはおいしい) The steaks served at this restaurant are very *good.* / *Daidokoro kara* oishi-soo *na nioi ga shite kita.* (台 所からおいしそうなにおいがしてきた) A *delicious* smell came from the kitchen. (↔ mazui') (⇨ umai)

o「ite おいて (於いて)

──(USAGE)──
Used in the pattern '…*ni oite.*' Compared to '*de,*' it is a written form. Before a noun '…*ni okeru*' or '…*ni oite no.*'
──────────

1 in: ★ Indicates location in place or time.
Shikeñ wa kaigishitsu ni oite *okonawareta.* (試験は会議室において行わ れた) The examination was given *in* the conference room. / *Nihoñ no shakai* ni okeru [oite no] *josee no chii wa mada hikui.* (日本の社会 における[おいての]女性の地位はまだ低い)

The status of women *in* Japanese society is still low.
2 as for; in the matter of: *Kono teñ* ni oite *watashi wa kare to ikeñ ga kuichigatte imasu.* (この 点において私は彼と意見が食い違ってい ます) *As for* this point, my opinion differs from his. / *Kono soochi wa añzeñsee* ni oite *hoka no mono yori otoru.* (この装置は安全性 においてほかのものより劣る) *Regarding* safety, this device is inferior to others.

o「itsu」k·u おいつく (追い付く) *vt.* (-tsuk·i-; -tsuk·a-; -tsu·i-te Ⓒ) catch up with; overtake: *Isoide aruite, kare ni* oitsukoo. (急 いで歩いて、彼に追いつこう) Let's walk quickly to *catch up with* him. / *Watashi wa hoka no seeto ni* oitsuku *tame ni isshoo-keñmee beñkyoo shita.* (私はほかの生徒に追いつく ために一生懸命勉強した) I studied hard to *catch up with* the other pupils. (⇨ oikosu)

o「ji おじ (伯父・叔父) *n.* one's uncle:

──(USAGE)──
Older brothers of one's father or mother are '伯父,' and younger brothers are '叔父.'
──────────

Daigaku-jidai wa oji no ie ni geshuku shite imashita. (大学時代は おじの家に下宿していました) When I was in college, I boarded at my *uncle's.* (⇨ ojisañ; kazoku (table))

o「jigi おじぎ (お辞儀) *n.* bow: *Kare wa* ojigi *no shikata o shiranai.* (彼はおじぎのしかたを知らない) He does not know how to *bow* properly.
ojigi (o) suru (〜(を)する) *vi.* bow: *Sono ko wa watashi ni teenee ni* ojigi *o shita.* (その子は私にていねいにお じぎをした) The child *bowed* politely to me.

o-「ji」isañ おじいさん (お祖父さん・お爺

さん) *n.* ★ '祖父' is used for **1**, while '爺' is used for **2**.

1 one's grandfather:

O-jiisañ *wa o-ikutsu desu ka?* (おじいさんはおいくつですか) How old is your *grandfather?* / *Ano hito no* o-jiisañ *wa shichoo deshita.* (あの人のおじいさんは市長でした) His *grandfather* was mayor. 《⇨ sofu; kazoku (table)》

2 old man:

O-jiisañ *ga kooeñ de kodomo to asoñde iru.* (おじいさんが公園で子どもと遊んでいる) An *old man* is playing with the children in the park.

o「jisañ おじさん (伯父さん・叔父さん・小父さん) *n.* ★ '伯父, 叔父' is used for **1**, while '小父' is used for **2**.

1 one's uncle:

Kono tokee wa ojisañ *kara no purezeñto desu.* (この時計はおじさんからのプレゼントです) This watch is a present from my *uncle.* 《⇨ oji》

2 middle-aged man:

Shiranai ojisañ *ni tsuite itte wa ikemaseñ.* (知らないおじさんについて行ってはいけません) You mustn't go along with middle-aged men you don't know.

o-「jo」osañ おじょうさん (お嬢さん) *n.*

1 your [his; her] daughter:

O-joosañ *wa o-geñki desu ka?* (お嬢さんはお元気ですか) How is your *daughter?* / *Yamada-sañ no* o-joosañ *wa biyooshi desu.* (山田さんのお嬢さんは美容師です) Mr. Yamada's *daughter* is a beautician.

2 young lady; girl. 《↔ botchañ》

o「ka おか (丘) *n.* hill; heights:

Asoko no oka *ni noboru to umi ga miemasu.* (あそこの丘に登ると海が見えます) If you go up the *hill* over there, you can see the sea. 《⇨ yama》

o-「ka」achañ おかあちゃん (お母ちゃん) *n.* mother; mom. ★ Used chiefly by small children, but also by adults in the Kansai area.

《↔ o-toochañ》

o-「ka」asañ おかあさん (お母さん) *n.* mother; mom:

O-kaasañ *ni kore o watashite kudasai.* (お母さんにこれを渡してください) Please give this to your *mother.* / *Akañboo ga* o-kaasañ *no senaka de suyasuya nemutte iru.* (赤ん坊がお母さんの背中ですやすや眠っている) The baby is sleeping quietly on its *mother*'s back. 《↔ o-toosañ》《⇨ haha》

o「kaeri nasa」i おかえりなさい (お帰りなさい) Welcome home; I'm glad you're home again. ★ Literally 'You've come home.' A set phrase used in response to '*Tadaima.*' (I'm home.) 《⇨ tadaima²》

o「kage おかげ (お陰) *n.* thanks to; owing to: ★ Usually used for actions that are favorable to the speaker. Unfavorable actions are usually described using '*see,*' although '*okage*' can be used ironically.

Anata ga tetsudatte kureta okage *de, mikka de shigoto ga owarimashita.* (あなたが手伝ってくれたおかげで、3日で仕事が終わりました) *Thanks to* your help, I was able to finish the work in three days. / *Subete wa anata no* okage *desu.* (すべてはあなたのおかげです) We *owe* everything to you. / *Aitsu no* okage *de haji o kaita.* (あいつのおかげで恥をかいた) *Thanks to* him, I was put to shame. 《⇨ see⁵》

okagesama de おかげさまで (お陰さまで) ★ An idiomatic expression used in response to a greeting.

"*O-geñki desu ka?*" "*Okagesama de.*" (「お元気ですか」「おかげさまで」) "How are you?" "*I'm fine, thank you.*"

o-「kane おかね (お金) *n.* = kane¹.

o-「ka」shi おかし (お菓子) *n.* confectionery; cake; sweets; candy. 《⇨ kashi¹》

o⌈**kashi**⌉·**i** おかしい（可笑しい）*a.*
(-ku) **1** amusing; funny; ridiculous:
Kare no okashii *hanashi o kiite, miñna ga waratta.*（彼のおかしい話を聞いて, みんなが笑った）Everyone laughed on hearing his *funny* story. / *Sono mañzai wa sukoshi mo* okashiku *nakatta.*（その漫才は少しもおかしくなかった）The 'manzai' comic dialogue was not at all *amusing.* 《⇨ okashi-na》
2 strange; odd:
Kare ga mada konai no wa okashii.（彼がまだ来ないのはおかしい）It is *strange* that he has not come yet. / *Kare no riroñ wa* okashii.（彼の理論はおかしい）His theory *does not make sense.*
3 queer; unusual:
I no guai ga chotto okashii.（胃の具合がちょっとおかしい）My stomach feels a bit *queer.*

o⌈**ka**⌉**shi-na** おかしな（可笑しな）*attrib.* **1** amusing; funny; ridiculous:
Kare wa okashi-na *koto o itte, hito o warawaseta.*（彼はおかしなことを言って, 人を笑わせた）He made people laugh by saying something *funny.*
2 strange; queer; odd:
Kanojo no hanashi ni wa okashi-na *teñ ga aru.*（彼女の話にはおかしな点がある）There are some *odd* points in her story. 《⇨ okashii》

o⌈**ka**⌉**s·u**¹ おかす（犯す）*vt.* (oka-sh·i-; okas·a-; okash·i-te Ⓒ)
commit; violate; break.
tsumi o okasu（罪を犯す）*commit* a crime / *hooritsu o* okasu（法律を犯す）*break* a law / *josee o* okasu（女性を犯す）*rape* a woman.

o⌈**ka**⌉**s·u**² おかす（侵す）*vt.* (oka-sh·i-; okas·a-; okash·i-te Ⓒ)
invade; infringe; violate:
hoka no hito no puraibashii o okasu（他の人のプライバシーを侵す）*invade* another person's privacy /

takoku no ryookai o okasu（他国の領海を侵す）*violate* another country's territorial waters.

O⌈**kayama**⌉**-keñ** おかやまけん（岡山県）*n.* Okayama Prefecture. Located in the southeast of the Chubu district, facing the Inland Sea on the south. The capital city, Okayama, is home to Korakuen, one of the three most famous public gardens in Japan. 《⇨ map (C4)》

o⌈**kazu** おかず（お数）*n.* side dish:

CULTURE

Rice is considered the main part ('*shushoku*') of any Japanese meal. Any other foods served in addition to it are considered '*okazu.*'

Kyoo no okazu *wa nañ desu ka?*（きょうのおかずは何ですか）What are today's *dishes?*

o⌈**ke** おけ（桶）*n.* tub; pail; wooden bucket.

o⌈**ke**⌉**ru** おける（於ける）at; in:
★ Used in the pattern '*...ni okeru.*'
Igaku ni okeru *shiñpo wa subarashii.*（医学における進歩はすばらしい）The progress *in* medical science is remarkable. / *Hokkaidoo ni* okeru *shitsugyoo-sha no jittai o choosa shita.*（北海道における失業者の実態を調査した）We investigated the actual conditions of the unemployed *in* Hokkaido. / *Kodomo no seechooki ni* okeru *hahaoya no yakuwari wa juuyoo desu.*（子どもの成長期における母親の役割は重要です）The mother's role *during* the growth of a child is very important. 《⇨ oite》

o⌈**ki** おき（沖）*n.* offing; open sea:
oki no hañseñ（沖の帆船）a sailing vessel in the *offing.*

-o⌈**ki** おき（置き）*suf.* every; at intervals of:
*Kono zasshi wa isshuu-*oki *ni hak-*

koo saremasu. (この雑誌は一週おきに発行されます) This magazine is published *every other* week. | *Ichimeetoru-*oki *ni kui o utta.* (1 メートルおきに杭を打った) I drove in the stakes *at intervals of* one meter.

o「**kiba**」 おきば (置き場) *n.* place; space; room:
Koko wa jitensha no okiba *de wa arimasen.* (ここは自転車の置き場ではありません) This is not a *place* where you can leave bicycles. | *Sonna ooki-na honbako no* okiba *wa arimasen.* (そんな大きな本箱の置き場はありません) There is no *room* for such a big bookcase.

o「**kido**「**kee** おきどけい (置き時計) *n.* table [desk; mantel] clock. 《⇨ tokee (table)》

o「**kimono** おきもの (置物) *n.* ornament: ★ China, carving, figurines, etc. that are displayed in one's home.
tokonoma no okimono (床の間の置物) an *ornament* in the alcove. 《⇨ washitsu (illus.)》

O「**kinawa**」**-ken** おきなわけん (沖縄県) *n.* Okinawa Prefecture. Comprising most of the islands of the Ryukyu chain, between Kyushu and Taiwan. Principle industries are agriculture, tourism and catering to the U.S. military. Capital city: Naha (那覇). 《⇨ map (inside back cover)》

O「**kinawa ka**「**ihatsu**」**-choo** おきなわかいはつちょう (沖縄開発庁) *n.* Okinawa Development Agency: Okinawa kaihatsu-choo *chookan* (沖縄開発庁長官) the Director General of the *Okinawa Development Agency.* 《⇨ choo⁴ (table)》

o「**ki**」**·ru** おきる (起きる) *vi.* (oki-te V) **1** get up; rise:
Watashi wa maiasa roku-ji-han ni okimasu. (私は毎朝6時半に起きます) I *get up* at 6:30 every morning. 《⇨ kishoo³; okosu》

2 wake up; stay awake:
Shizuka ni shinai to akanboo ga okimasu *yo.* (静かにしないと赤ん坊が起きますよ) Please be quiet, or the baby will *wake up.* | *Sakuya wa yonaka made* okite imashita. (昨夜は夜中まで起きていました) Last night I *stayed up* until the middle of the night. 《⇨ okosu》
3 happen; occur. 《⇨ okoru¹》

o「**kiwasure**」**·ru** おきわすれる (置き忘れる) *vt.* (-wasure-te V) leave; forget; put down and forget:
Densha no naka ni kasa o okiwasurete shimatta. (電車の中に傘を置き忘れてしまった) I *left* my umbrella in the train.

o「**kona·u** おこなう (行う) *vt.* (okona·i-; okonaw·a-; okonat-te C) hold; give; practice:
senkyo o okonau (選挙を行う) *hold* an election | *shiken o* okonau (試験を行う) *give* an examination | *Sono shuukan wa ima de mo kono chihoo de* okonawarete imasu. (その習慣は今でもこの地方で行われています) That custom *is* even now *practiced* in this area.

o「**kori**」 おこり (起こり) *n.* **1** cause:
Koto no okori *wa nan desu ka?* (事の起こりは何ですか) What is the *cause* of this?
2 origin; source:
bunmee no okori (文明の起こり) the *origin* of civilization.

o「**ko**」**r·u**¹ おこる (起こる) *vi.* (oko-r·i-; okor·a-; okot-te C)
1 happen; occur; take place:
Kanojo no mi ni nani-ka okotta *ni chigainai.* (彼女の身に何か起こったに違いない) Something must *have happened* to her. | *Sono jiko wa doko de* okorimashita *ka?* (その事故はどこで起こりましたか) Where did the accident *occur?*
2 be caused; stem from:
Sono jiko wa fuchuui kara okotta. (その事故は不注意から起こった) The

accident *stemmed* from carelessness. 《⇨ okiru; okosu》

o｢ko｣r・u² おこる (怒る) (okor・i-; okor・a-; okot-te Ⓒ) **1** *vi.* get angry; lose one's temper: *Kare ga okoru no mo muri wa nai.* (彼が怒るのも無理はない) It is natural that he should *get angry.* / *Anata wa nani o okotte iru ñ desu ka?* (あなたは何を怒っているんですか) What *are* you *angry* about?
2 *vt.* scold: *Kanojo wa kodomo ga namakete iru no de* okotta. (彼女は子どもが怠けているので怒った) She *scolded* her child for being idle.

o｢ko｣r・u³ おこる (興る) *vi.* (okor・i-; okor・a-; okot-te Ⓒ) spring up; come into existence: *Sono kuni de wa ima iroiro na sañgyoo ga* okotte imasu. (その国では今いろいろな産業が興っています) Various industries *are coming into existence* in that country.

o-｢kosañ おこさん (お子さん) *n.* (*polite*) someone else's child: *O-kosañ wa o-ikutsu desu ka?* (お子さんはおいくつですか) How old is your *child?*

o｢ko｣s・u おこす (起こす) *vt.* (okosh・i-; okos・a-; okosh・i-te Ⓒ) **1** wake up; awake: *Asu no asa roku-ji ni* okoshite *kudasai.* (あすの朝6時に起こしてください) Please *wake* me *up* at six tomorrow morning. / *Amari sawagu to akachañ o* okoshite shimaimasu yo. (あまり騒ぐと赤ちゃんを起こしてしまいますよ) If you make such a noise, you will *wake up* the baby. 《⇨ okiru》
2 raise; set up: *Kare wa taoreta saku o* okoshita. (彼は倒れたさくを起こした) He *raised* the fallen fence.
3 cause (an accident, trouble); bring about: *jiko [moñdai] o* okosu (事故[問題]を起こす) *cause* an accident [trouble] / *soodoo o* okosu (騒動を起こす) *raise* a commotion. 《⇨ okiru》
4 start (a movement): *shoohisha-uñdoo o* okosu (消費者運動を起こす) *start* a consumer movement. 《⇨ okiru》
5 produce: *deñki o* okosu (電気を起こす) *produce* electricity. 《⇨ okiru》

o-｢kotowari おことわり (お断り) *n.* refusal; rejection; prohibition: ★ Used as a warning. *Meñkai wa* o-kotowari *desu.* (面会はお断りです) We *cannot accept* visitors. / *Nyuujoo* o-kotowari (*sign*) (入場お断り) *No* Admittance. / *Chuusha* o-kotowari (*sign*) (駐車お断り) *No* Parking.

CHUUSHA O-KOTOWARI SIGN

o｢k・u¹ おく (置く) *vt.* (ok・i-; ok・a-; o・i-te Ⓒ) **1** put; keep; place: *Kasa wa doko ni* oitara *yoi deshoo ka?* (傘はどこに置いたらよいでしょうか) Where should I *put* my umbrella? / *Kono niku wa reezooko ni* oite *kudasai.* (この肉は冷蔵庫に置いてください) Please *keep* this meat in the fridge. / *Kare wa kurushii tachiba ni* okarete iru. (彼は苦しい立場に置かれている) He *has been placed* in a very difficult position.
2 leave: *Kagi o doko e* oita *ka wasurete shimatta.* (鍵をどこへ置いたか忘れてしまった) I have forgotten where I

left the keys.

3 have for sale; deal in: *Kono mise wa iroiro na buñboogu o oite imasu.* (この店はいろいろな文房具を置いています) At this shop they *handle* a variety of stationery goods.

4 take in; have: *Kare wa shiyooniñ o oite imasu.* (彼は使用人を置いています) He *has* a servant.

-te oku (ておく) leave a thing as it is; do something in advance: *Tomodachi ga sugu kuru kara doa o akete oite kudasai.* (友だちがすぐ来るからドアを開けておいてください) A friend is coming soon, so please *leave* the door *open.* / *Ashita tsukau no de kyoo* katte okimashita. (あした使うのできょう買っておきました) I *went ahead and bought* it today.

o｢ku² おく (奥) *n.* inner part; interior; back: *O-kyaku o* oku *no heya ni tooshita.* (お客を奥の部屋に通した) I showed the visitor into an *inner* room. / *Kono mori no* oku *ni taki ga arimasu.* (この森の奥に滝があります) There is a waterfall in the *depths* of this forest. / *Sono himitsu wa kokoro no* oku *ni shimatte okimasu.* (その秘密は心の奥にしまっておきます) I will keep the secret locked away *deep* in my heart.

o｢ku³ おく (億) *n.* one hundred million. (⇨ suu² (table))

o｢kubyo｣o おくびょう (臆病) *a.n.* (~ na, ni) cowardly; timid: okubyoo *na hito* (臆病な人) a *cowardly* person.

o｢kujoo おくじょう (屋上) *n.* roof; rooftop: *Kono biru no* okujoo *ni wa tenisu kooto ga arimasu.* (このビルの屋上にはテニスコートがあります) There is a *roof* of this building. (↔ chika)

o｢kurase·ru おくらせる (遅らせる) *vt.* (okurase-te ▽) delay; put off; turn back: *Kare-ra wa shiai kaishi o okuraseta.* (彼らは試合開始を遅らせた) They *delayed* the start of the game. / *Kaigi wa mik-ka* okuraseru *koto ni kettee shita.* (会議は3日遅らせることに決定した) We decided to *put off* the meeting for three days. / *Tokee o ni-fuñ* okuraseta. (時計を2分遅らせた) I *put* the clock *back* two minutes. (⇨ okureru)

o｢kure おくれ (遅れ) *n.* delay: *Kootsuu juutai ga* okure *no geñiñ datta.* (交通渋滞が遅れの原因だった) The traffic jam was the cause of the *delay.* / *Shigoto no* okure *o torimodosanakereba narimaseñ.* (仕事の遅れを取り戻さなければなりません) We have to make up for the *time lost* in the work. / *Kare ni wa* okure *o toritaku arimaseñ.* (彼には遅れを取りたくありません) I do not wish to *fall behind* him. (⇨ okureru)

o｢kure·ru おくれる (遅れる) *vi.* (okure-te ▽) **1** be late; be behind time: *Yakusoku no jikañ ni* okurete shimatta. (約束の時間に遅れてしまった) I *was later* than the time agreed on. / *Ressha wa ichi-jikañ* okurete, *toochaku shita.* (列車は1時間遅れて, 到着した) The train arrived one hour *behind schedule.* (⇨ chikoku; okure)

2 (of a clock, watch) be slow; lose: *Kono tokee wa is-shuukañ ni sañpuñ* okuremasu. (この時計は一週間に3分遅れます) This watch *loses* three minutes a week. / *Tokee ga go-fuñ* okurete imasu. (時計が5分遅れています) The clock *is* five minutes *slow.* (↔ susumu)

3 fall behind; be behind:
Sañ-niñ no soosha ga shidai ni okurete kita. (三人の走者がしだいに遅れてきた) The three runners *fell behind* one by one. / *Nagaku gakkoo o yasuñde, beñkyoo ga okurete shimatta.* (長く学校を休んで、勉強が遅れてしまった) I was away from school for a long time, so I *have fallen behind* in my studies. / *Yo-no-naka ni okurenai yoo ni beñkyoo shi nasai.* (世の中に遅れないように勉強しなさい) Study hard so that you *do not fall behind* the times. 《⇨ okuraseru》

o「kurigana おくりがな (送り仮名) *n.* (inflectional) 'kana' ending:
★ The 'kana' added to a Chinese character to help show its Japanese grammatical ending.
'通' *to iu kañji wa* 'る' *to iu okurigana no toki wa* 'tooru' *to yomi,* 'う' *to iu okurigana no toki wa* 'kayou' *to yomimasu.* (「通」という漢字は「る」という送り仮名のときは「とおる」と読み、「う」という送り仮名のときは「かよう」と読みます) When the *ending* 'ru' is added to the Chinese character '通,' the reading is 'tooru'; when the *okurigana* is 'u,' you read it 'kayou.'

o「kurimono おくりもの (贈り物) *n.* present; gift:
Kanojo ni tañjoobi no okurimono o shita. (彼女に誕生日の贈り物をした) I gave her a birthday *present.* 《⇨ miyage; purezeñto》

o「kur·u¹ おくる (送る) *vt.* (okur·i-; okur·a-; okut-te [C]) **1** send:
Kare ni kookuubiñ de hoñ o okutta. (彼に航空便で本を送った) I *sent* him a book by airmail.
2 see off; see home; take:
Watashi wa eki o oba o okuri ni itta. (私は駅へおばを送りに行った) I went to the station to *see off* my aunt. / *Kanojo o uchi made okutte yari nasai.* (彼女を家まで送ってやりな

さい) Please *see* her home. / *Nomura-sañ wa maiasa kodomo o yoochieñ ni okutte ikimasu.* (野村さんは毎朝子どもを幼稚園に送って行きます) Mrs. Nomura *takes* her child to kindergarten every morning.
3 pass; spend; lead:
Kare wa megumareta seekatsu o okutte imasu. (彼は恵まれた生活を送っています) He *leads* a privileged life.

o「kur·u² おくる (贈る) *vt.* (okur·i-; okur·a-; okut-te [C]) give; present:
Kanojo no kekkoñ iwai ni kabiñ o okutta. (彼女の結婚祝いに花瓶を贈った) I *gave* her a vase for a wedding present.

o「kusama おくさま (奥様) *n.* (*polite*) someone else's wife; married woman. 《⇨ okusañ》

o「kusañ おくさん (奥さん) *n.* someone else's wife; married woman:

┌─ **USAGE** ─┐
Used when addressing someone else's wife or referring to her. A more polite word is 'okusama.' The speaker's wife is referred to as 'kanai.'
└────────┘

Kare no okusañ wa biyooshi desu. (彼の奥さんは美容師です) His *wife* is a beautician.

o-「kyaku-sañ おきゃくさん (お客さん) *n.* **1** (*polite*) caller; visitor; guest:
Kyoo no o-kyaku-sañ wa dare desu ka? (きょうのお客さんはだれですか) Who was today's *visitor?*
2 customer; client:
Kyoo wa o-kyaku-sañ ga sukunakatta. (きょうはお客さんが少なかった) There were only a few *customers* today.
3 audience; spectator.
4 passenger.
《⇨ kyaku》

o╹**machidoosama** おまちどうさま
（お待ちどうさま）(*informal*) = omatase shimashita.

o╹**mae** おまえ（お前）*n.* (*rude*) you:
★ Used by men in addressing
inferiors, particularly children.
The plural forms are 'omae-
tachi' and (*derog.*) 'omae-ra.'
Omae mo kuru ka? (おまえも来るか)
You coming with me? / *Omae,
mada kore o yatte inai no ka?* (おま
えまだこれをやっていないのか) *You*
haven't finished it yet, have you?
/ *Ore to omae ga kumeba kitto
umaku iku ze.* (おれとおまえが組めばき
っとうまくいくぜ) If *you* and me
work together, we're bound to
succeed. (⇨ ore)

o╹**mairi** おまいり（お参り）*n.* visit to
a temple [shrine]; going to worship at a temple [shrine]. (⇨ sañpai (photo))

omairi suru (～する) *vi.* visit [go
to] a temple [shrine]: *Señshuu
no nichiyoo wa ryooshiñ no haka
ni omairi o shimashita.* (先週の日
曜は両親の墓にお参りをしました) I *vis-
ited* the grave of my parents last
Sunday. (⇨ hakamairi (photo))

o╹**mamori** おまもり（お守り）*n.*
good luck talisman [charm].
kootsuu-añzeñ no omamori (交通
安全のお守り) a *lucky charm* for
traffic safety.

OMAMORI

o╹**matase shima╹shita** おまた
せしました（お待たせしました）(*humble*
= 'omatase itashimashita')

I am sorry to have kept you waiting:
Omatase shimashita. *Tadaima
kara kaikai itashimasu.* (お待たせし
ました. ただ今から開会いたします) *We
are sorry to have kept you waiting.*
The meeting will now come to
order. / *Biiru ni-hoñ.* Omatase shimashita. (ビール 2 本. お待たせしまし
た) *Here you are.* Two beers.

o╹**ma╹wari-sañ** おまわりさん（お巡
りさん）*n.* policeman; cop:
Omawari-sañ *ni michi o tazuneta.*
(お巡りさんに道を尋ねた) I asked the
policeman for directions.
((⇨ keekañ))

o╹**medeta** おめでた（御目出度）*n.*
happy event: ★ Often used with
reference to a forthcoming birth.
Omedeta *wa itsu desu ka?* (おめでた
はいつですか) When is the *happy
event?* / *Yamada-sañ wa raigetsu
omedeta da soo desu.* (山田さんは来
月おめでただそうです) I hear that Mrs.
Yamada *is expecting a baby* next
month.

o╹**medeta·i** おめでたい（お目出度い）
a. (-ku) **1** = medetai.
2 (*derog.*) simple-minded:
★ Used always in this form, 'omedetai.'
Kimi wa hoñtoo ni omedetai *ne.*
(君は本当におめでたいね) You are
really *simple-minded*, aren't you?

o╹**medetoo** おめでとう（御目出度う）
congratulations: ★ '*Omedetoo
gozaimasu*' is more polite.
Shiñneñ omedetoo (*gozaimasu*).
(新年おめでとう（ございます）) *Happy
New Year.* / *Tañjoobi* omedetoo.
(誕生日おめでとう) *Many happy
returns of the day.* / *Sotsugyoo*
omedetoo. (卒業おめでとう) *Congratulations* on your graduation. /
Gookaku omedetoo. (合格おめでとう)
Congratulations on passing the
examination.

o╹**medetoo gozaima╹su** おめで

とうございます (御目出度う御座います)
= omedetoo.

o⌐me-ni-kaka⌐r·u おめにかかる (お
目に掛かる) *vt.* (-kakar·i-; -kaka-
r·a-; -kakat-te Ⓒ) meet; see:
★ Humble equivalent of '*au.*'
*Mata ome-ni-kakarete ureshii de-
su.* (またお目にかかれてうれしいです) I'm
glad to *see* you again. / *Sono hito
ni ome-ni-kakaritai to omoimasu.*
(その人にお目にかかりたいと思います) I
would like to meet him.

om⌐ikuji おみくじ (御神籤) *n.* sacred lot from a shrine; written
oracle:
omikuji o hiku (おみくじを引く) draw
a *sacred lot.*

> (**CULTURE**)
>
> The fortune is written on a
> slip of paper. Suppliants draw
> it from a box in front of the
> shrine and after reading it, tie
> it onto the branch of a tree
> within the shrine's precincts.

OMIKUJI TIED TO A TREE

o-⌐miyage おみやげ *n.* present;
gift; souvenir:
*Kodomo-tachi no o-miyage ni na-
ni o kaimashita ka?* (子どもたちのおみ
やげに何を買いましたか) What did
you buy as *souvenirs* for your
children? / o-miyageya (おみやげ屋)
a *souvenir shop.* (⇨ miyage; okurimono)) ((⇨ photo (right))

o⌐mo⌐cha おもちゃ *n.* toy; play-
thing:
omocha-ya (おもちゃ屋) a *toyshop.*
omocha ni suru (〜にする) toy

OMIYAGE-YA

[play] with: *Sono ko wa kamera
o omocha ni shite ita.* (その子はカメ
ラをおもちゃにしていた) The child *was
playing with* a camera.

o⌐mo·i[1] おもい (重い) *a.* (-ku)
1 heavy:
Kono kaban wa baka ni omoi. (この
かばんはばかに重い) This bag is very
heavy. / *Kono ishi wa* omokute
mochiagaranai. (この石は重くて持ち
上がらない) This stone is too *heavy*
to lift. ((↔ karui)) ((⇨ omosa))
2 important; grave:
omoi *chii* (重い地位) an *important*
position / *Watashi wa sono* omoi
sekinin o hikiukeru koto ni shita.
(私はその重い責任を引き受けることにし
た) I've decided to assume that
grave responsibility. ((↔ karui))
3 (of crime, disease, etc.)
serious:
Satsujin wa tsumi ga omoi. (殺人
は罪が重い) Murder is a very
serious crime. / *Kare no byooki
wa* omoku *natta.* (彼の病気は重くなっ
た) His sickness has become *serious.* ((↔ karui))
ki ga omoi (気が〜) ⇨ ki[2].
kuchi ga omoi (口が〜) ⇨ kuchi[1].

o⌐mo⌐i[2] おもい (思い) *n.*
1 thought; idea:
omoi *ni fukeru* (思いにふける) be
lost in *thought.*
2 wish; expectation:
Yatto naganen no omoi *ga kanatta.*
(やっと長年の思いがかなった) At last

my long-cherished *wish* was fulfilled. / *Subete wa* omoi-doori
umaku ikimashita.(すべては思い通り
うまくいきました)Everything went
off well, *as we had wished.*
3 attachment; affection:
Kare wa kanojo ni omoi *o yosete
ita.*(彼は彼女に思いを寄せていた)He
had an *attachment* for her. / *Kanojo wa chichi-oya* omoi *da.*(彼女
は父親思いだ)She *is* always *thinking* of her father.
4 feeling:
hazukashii omoi *o suru*(恥ずかしい
思いをする)*feel ashamed* / *Kodomo
ni wa* kanashii omoi *o sasetaku
nai.*(子どもには悲しい思いをさせたくな
い)I do not want to make my children *feel sad.*

o⌐**moichigai** おもいちがい(思い違い)
n. misunderstanding; mistake:
Sore wa kare no omoichigai *to wakarimashita.*(それは彼の思い違いとわ
かりました)It turned out to be his
misunderstanding. / *Ukkari* omoichigai *o shite imashita.*(うっかり思
い違いをしていました)I carelessly
made a *mistake.*

o⌐**moida⌐s·u** おもいだす(思い出す)
vt. (-dash·i-; -das·a-; -dash·i-te
Ⓒ) remember; recall; remind:
Doo-shite mo kare no namae ga
omidasenai.(どうしても彼の名前が思
い出せない)I just *cannot remember*
his name. / *Kono uta o kiku to
kodomo no koro o* omoidashimasu.
(この歌を聞くと子どものころを思い出しま
す)Whenever I hear this song, it
reminds me of my childhood.

o⌐**moide** おもいで(思い出)*n.* recollections; memory; reminis-
cence:
*watashi no wakaki hi no Roñdoñ
no* omoide(私の若き日のロンドンの思
い出)my *memory* of the days I
spent in London when young /
Tabi no omoide *wa iroiro arimasu.*
(旅の思い出はいろいろあります)I have

many *memories* of my trip. / *Kare
wa shooneñ jidai no* omoide *ni
tsuite katatta.*(彼は少年時代の思い
出について語った)He spoke about
his *recollections* of boyhood.

o⌐**moigakena⌐·i** おもいがけない(思
いがけない)*a.* (-ku) unexpected:
Omoigakenaku, *tomodachi ga tazunete kita.*(思いがけなく、友だちが訪
ねて来た)A friend *unexpectedly*
visited me. / *Jiñsee ni wa* omoigakenai *koto ga okoru mono desu.*
(人生には思いがけないことが起こるもので
す)The *unexpected* is likely to
occur in life. / Omoigakenaku *mo,
riñji shuunyuu ga atta.*(思いがけなく
も、臨時収入があった)*Unexpectedly*
I have earned some extra income.

o⌐**moikiri**¹ おもいきり(思い切り)*n.*
decisiveness; decision:
Kare wa omoikiri *ga yoi [warui].*
(彼は思い切りがよい[悪い])He *is* deci-
sive [indecisive]. / *Ooki-na shigoto
o suru toki wa* omoikiri *ga taisetsu desu.*(大きな仕事をするときは思い
切りが大切です)When doing a
major piece of work, *decisiveness*
is very important. (⇨ omoikiru)

o⌐**moikiri**² おもいきり(思い切り)
adv. thoroughly; to one's heart's
content:
Hisashiburi no kyuujitsu de omoikiri *gorufu o tanoshiñda.*(久しぶりの
休日で思い切りゴルフを楽しんだ)I en-
joyed my golf *thoroughly* on my
first day off in a long time. / *Jibuñ no heya ni modotte kara, kanojo wa* omoikiri *naita.*(自分の部
屋に戻ってから、彼女は思い切り泣いた)
She *cried her eyes out* after returning to her room. / *Watashi
wa sono booru o* omoikiri *tsuyoku
ketobashita.*(私はそのボールを思い切り
強くけ飛ばした)I kicked the ball
away *with all my might.*

o⌐**moiki⌐r·u** おもいきる(思い切る)
vt. (-kir·i-; -kir·a-; -kit-te Ⓒ)
give up:

Kare ni sono keekaku o omoikira-
seta. (彼にその計画を思い切らせた) I
made him *give up* the project.
《⇨ omoikiri¹; omoikitte》

o「**mo¹ikitte** おもいきって (思い切っ
て) *adv.* decisively; resolutely:
Kanojo wa omoikitte *señsee ni hoñtoo no koto o hanashita.* (彼女は思
い切って先生にほんとうのことを話した)
She *dared* to tell the truth to her
teacher. / *Kare-ra wa* omoikitte
sono horaana no naka ni haitta. (彼
らは思い切ってそのほら穴の中に入った)
They *resolutely* entered the cave.
omoikitte...suru (～...する) make
up one's mind to do: *Watashi
wa* omoikitte *shiñsha o kau koto
ni shimashita.* (私は思い切って新車を
買うことにしました) I *have made up
my mind* to buy a new car.

o「**moiko¹m·u** おもいこむ (思い込む)
vi. (-kom·i-; -kom·a-; -koñ-de
Ⓒ) **1** believe; be under the impression:
*Kanojo wa sono uwasa wa hoñtoo
da to* omoikoñde imasu. (彼女はその
うわさは本当だと思い込んでいます) She
believes that the rumor is true.
2 take...for granted:
*Miñna kare ga yuushoo suru mo-
no to* omoikoñde ita. (みんな彼が優
勝するものと思い込んでいた) Everyone
took it for granted that he would
win the championship.

o「**moi-no-hoka** おもいのほか (思い
の外) *adv.* unexpectedly; surprisingly:
Mooke wa omoi-no-hoka *sukunakatta.* (もうけは思いのほか少なかった)
The profits were *unexpectedly*
small. / *Sono shigoto wa* omoi-
no-hoka *hayaku owatta.* (その仕事は
思いのほか早く終わった) We finished
the job *surprisingly* quickly.
《⇨ añgai¹》

o「**moitodoma¹r·u** おもいとどまる
(思い止まる) *vt.* (-todomar·i-; -to-
domar·a-; -todomat-te Ⓒ)

change one's mind; hold oneself
back:
Kare wa teñshoku o omoitodo-
matta. (彼は転職を思いとどまった) He
changed his mind about changing
his job. / *Chichi-oya wa kanojo no
kekkoñ o* omotodomaraseyoo *to
shita.* (父親は彼女の結婚を思いとどま
らせようとした) Her father tried to
make her give up the idea of marriage.

o「**moitsuki** おもいつき (思い付き) *n.*
idea; thought:
Sore wa yoi omoitsuki *desu.* (それは
良い思いつきです) That is a good
idea. 《⇨ omoitsuku》
omoitsuki de (～で) off the top
of one's head: *Kare wa yoku*
omoitsuki de *koodoo suru.* (彼はよ
く思いつきで行動する) He often acts
on impulse.

o「**moitsu¹k·u** おもいつく (思い付く)
vt. (-tsuk·i-; -tsuk·a-; -tsu·i-te
Ⓒ) hit on; think of:
*Sono moñdai o kaiketsu suru
umai kañgae o* omoitsuita. (その問
題を解決するうまい考えを思いついた) I
hit on a good idea which would
solve the problem. 《⇨ omoitsuki》

o「**moiyari** おもいやり (思いやり) *n.*
consideration; thoughtfulness;
sympathy:
Kare wa hoka no hito ni taishite
omoiyari ga aru. (彼はほかの人に対し
て思いやりがある) He *is considerate*
to others. / *Watashi wa kanojo no*
omoiyari no nai *kotoba ni hara o
tateta.* (私は彼女の思いやりのない言葉
に腹を立てた) I got angry at her
unkind words.

o「**mokurushi¹·i** おもくるしい (重苦
しい) *a.* (-ku) heavy; gloomy; op-
pressive; stifling:
Kaijoo wa omokurushii *fuñiki ni
tsutsumarete ita.* (会場は重苦しい雰
囲気に包まれていた) The hall was
enveloped in a mood of *gloom.* /
Tabesugite, i ga omokurushii. (食

べ過ぎて, 胃が重苦しい) Having eaten too much, my stomach feels *uncomfortably full*.

o⌐**momuki** おもむき (趣) *n*. **1** attractive atmosphere; charm: *Kono niwa wa* omomuki *ga aru*. (この庭には趣がある) This garden has its *charm*.
2 look; appearance: *Kaateñ de heya no* omomuki *ga kawatta*. (カーテンで部屋の趣が変わった) Because of the curtains the *appearance* of the room changed.
3 purpose; aim: *Go-yoo no* omomuki *o ukagaimashoo*. (ご用のおもむきをうかがいましょう) May I ask you the *purpose* of your visit?

o⌐**mo-na** おもな (主な) *attrib*. chief; principal; main; leading: *Hañtai no* omo-na *riyuu wa nañ desu ka*? (反対の主な理由は何ですか) What is the *principal* reason for your opposition? / *Nihoñ no* omo-na *toshi wa hotoñdo miñna mawarimashita*. (日本の主な都市はほとんどみんな回りました) I have visited almost all the *major* cities in Japan.

o⌐**moni** おもに (重荷) *n*. **1** heavy load [burden].
2 burden; load: *Ryooshiñ no kitai ga kare no* omoni *datta*. (両親の期待が彼の重荷だった) The expectations of his parents were a *burden* to him. / *Kare no kotoba de kokoro no* omoni *ga toreta*. (彼の言葉で心の重荷が取れた) With his words, a *weight* was removed from my mind.

o⌐**mo ni** おもに (主に) *adv*. chiefly; mainly; mostly: *Jiko no sekiniñ wa* omo ni *doraibaa ni atta*. (事故の責任は主にドライバーにあった) The blame for the accident was *chiefly* with the driver. / *Rokku-koñsaato no kañkyaku wa* omo ni *wakai hito-tachi datta*.

(ロックコンサートの観客は主に若い人たちだった) The audience at the rock concert was *mainly* young people.

o⌐**moñji⌐·ru** おもんじる (重んじる) *vt*. (omoñji-te Ⅴ) respect; make much of; value: *hooritsu o* omoñjiru (法律を重んじる) *respect* the law / *Shachoo wa kare no teeañ o* omoñjite iru. (社長は彼の提案を重んじている) The president *thinks much of* his suggestions. (↔ karoñjiru)

o⌐**mo-omoshi⌐·i** おもおもしい (重重しい) *a*. (-ku) (of speech, attitude, etc.) grave; dignified; serious: omo-omoshii *taido o toru* (重々しい態度をとる) assume a *dignified* air / *Jitai wa shiñkoku da to, kare wa* omo-omoshiku *katatta*. (事態は深刻だと, 彼は重々しく語った) He *gravely* announced that the state of affairs was serious.

o⌐**mosa** おもさ (重さ) *n*. weight: *Kono suutsukeesu wa dono kurai (no)* omosa *ga arimasu ka*? (このスーツケースはどのくらい(の)重さがありますか) What is the *weight* of this suitcase? / *Kono kozutsumi no* omosa *o hakatte kudasai*. (この小包の重さを量ってください) Please *weigh* this parcel. (⇒ omoi¹; mekata)

o⌐**moshiro⌐·i** おもしろい (面白い) *a*. (-ku) interesting; amusing; funny; exciting: *Sono eega wa totemo* omoshirokatta. (その映画はとてもおもしろかった) That film was very *interesting*. / *Nihoñgo no beñkyoo ga* omoshiroku *natte kimashita*. (日本語の勉強がおもしろくなってきました) The study of Japanese has become more *interesting* for me. / *Otto to kuchigeñka o shita no de ichinichi-juu* omoshiroku nakatta. (夫と口げんかをしたので一日中おもしろくなかった) I had an argument with my husband, so the whole day was miserable. 《↔ tsumaranai》

o⌈**mota·i** おもたい（重たい）*a.* (-ku)
heavy:
Kono hako wa omotakute, *hitori
de wa hakobemaseñ.* (この箱は重たく
て，一人では運べません) This box is
too *heavy* for one person to carry.
《⇨ omoi¹》

o⌈**mote**⌉ おもて（表）*n.* **1** front;
the right side; surface:
fuutoo no omote (封筒の表) the
front of an envelope / *Kono kami
wa dochira ga* omote *desu ka?* (こ
の紙はどちらが表ですか) Which is the
right side of this sheet of paper?
《↔ ura》
2 front door:
Omote *kara haitte kudasai.* (表から
入ってください) Please come in
through the *front door.* 《↔ ura》
3 outside; the outdoors:
Omote *ni dare-ka tatte imasu.* (表
にだれか立っています) There is someone standing *outside.* / *Kodomo-
tachi wa* omote *de asoñde imasu.*
(子どもたちは表で遊んでいます) The
children are playing *outside.*
《↔ ura》
4 (baseball) the first half:
Ima sañ-kai no omote *ga owarimashita.* (今 3 回の表が終わりました)
The *first half* of the third inning
has just finished. 《↔ ura》

o⌈**motemoñ**⌉ おもてもん（表門）*n.*
front gate. 《↔ uramoñ》

o⌈**mo**⌉**·u** おもう（思う）*vt.* (omo·i-;
omow·a-; omot-te Ⓒ)

omou	(I) think
	(I) hope
	(I) fear, (I'm) afraid

★ '*Omou*' refers to having
thoughts and '*kañgaeru*' implies
thinking about, pondering, considering, but there is some overlap in meaning.
1 think; believe:

Sore wa uso da to omoimasu. (それ
はうそだと思います) I *think* that is a
lie. / *Kare wa konai to* omoimasu.
(彼は来ないと思います) I don't *think*
he will come. ★ Note the positions of '*nai*' and 'not.' / *Ashita
wa harereba yoi to* omoimasu. (あ
したは晴れればよいと思います) I *hope* it
will be fine tomorrow. / *Kare wa
okureru to* omoimasu. (彼は遅れると
思います) I'm *afraid* he will be late.
/ *Kanojo wa jibuñ ga bijiñ da to*
omotte iru. (彼女は自分が美人だと思
っている) She *believes* herself to be
a beauty.
2 consider; regard:
Kare wa yuushuu na señshu da to
omoimasu. (彼は優秀な選手だと思い
ます) I *consider* him to be an excellent player.
3 expect:
Omotta *toori kare wa shippai
shita.* (思った通り彼は失敗した) Just
as I *had expected*, he failed. / *Soko de kare ni au to wa* omowanakatta. (そこで彼に会うとは思わなかった)
I *never expected* I would meet
him there.
4 want; wish; hope:
Monogoto wa omou *yoo ni ikanai
mono desu.* (物事は思うように行かない
ものです) Things do not go as one
would *wish.* / *Yoroshikereba, sochira ni ukagaitai to* omoimasu.
(よろしければ，そちらにうかがいたいと思い
ます) Provided it is convenient, I
would like to pay you a visit. /
*Anata ni kono shigoto o yatte mo-
raitai to* omotte imasu. (あなたにこの
仕事をやってもらいたいと思っています) I
would like you to do this task.

──── (**USAGE**) ────
In the pattern '*...tai to omou*,'
'*omou*' is used to soften the
force of '*tai*' and as such does
not have a very specific meaning.

Anata to issho ni ikereba yoi to omoimasu.（あなたと一緒に行ければよいと思います）I *wish* I could go with you.

5 intend; be going to:
Kare wa isha ni naroo to omotte iru.（彼は医者になろうと思っている）He *intends* to become a doctor. / *Natsu-yasumi ni wa Hokkaidoo e iko-o ka to omotte imasu.*（夏休みには北海道へ行こうかと思っています）I *am considering* going to Hokkaido during the summer holidays.
★ In the pattern '*-yoo/-oo ka to omotte iru,*' the '*ka*' makes the intention less firm.

6 think of:
Kare wa itsu-mo byooki no haha no koto o omotte iru.（彼はいつも病気の母のことを思っている）He always *thinks of* his sick mother.
《⇨ kañgaeru》

o「mo」u-zoñbuñ おもうぞんぶん（思う存分）*adv.* (~ ni) to the full; to one's heart's content:
Natsu-yasumi no aida omou-zoñbuñ (ni) asoñda.（夏休みの間思う存分(に)遊んだ）I enjoyed myself *to the full* during the summer vacation. / *Kanashii toki wa omou-zoñbuñ naki nasai.*（悲しいときは思う存分泣きなさい）Have a *good* cry when you are sad.

o「mowaku」 おもわく（思惑）*n.* expectation; calculation:
Kooshoo wa omowaku doori ni itta.（交渉は思惑どおりにいった）The negotiations proceeded *as we had expected.* / *Watashi no omowaku wa hazureta.*（私の思惑ははずれた）My *calculations* turned out to be wrong.

o「mowashi」・i おもわしい（思わしい）*a.* (-ku) satisfactory; desirable:
★ Usually used with a negative.
Kanojo kara omowashii heñji ga moraenakatta.（彼女から思わしい返事がもらえなかった）I was not able to get a *satisfactory* reply from her.

o「mo」wazu おもわず（思わず）*adv.* involuntarily; unconsciously; instinctively:
Tossa no shitsumoñ ni omowazu hoñtoo no koto o itte shimatta.（とっさの質問に思わず本当のことを言ってしまった）I *unwittingly* went and revealed the truth in reply to a sudden question. / *Sono shashiñ o mite, omowazu waratte shimatta.*（その写真を見て、思わず笑ってしまった）I *could not help* laughing when I saw the picture.

o「muretsu」 オムレツ *n.* omelette.

o「mu」subi おむすび（お結び）*n.* rice ball. 《⇨ onigiri (illus.)》

o「mu」tsu おむつ *n.* diaper; nappy:
akañboo ni omutsu o suru（赤ん坊におむつをする）put a *diaper* on a baby's bottom / *akañboo no omutsu o torikaeru*（赤ん坊のおむつを取り替える）change a baby's *diaper.*

o「ñ」¹ おん（恩）*n.* obligation; favor; kindness:
oñ ni kiru（恩に着る）*be grateful [obliged]* / *oñ o ada de kaesu*（恩をあだで返す）return evil for *good.* / *Yamada-sañ ni wa oñ o kañjite imasu.*（山田さんには恩を感じています）I feel under an *obligation* to Mr. Yamada. / *Kare no oñ wa kaeshimashita.*（彼の恩は返しました）I repaid his *favor.* / *Go-oñ wa wasuremaseñ.*（ご恩は忘れません）I will never forget your *kindness.*

o「ñ」² おん（音）*n.* **1** (phonetics) speech sound.
2 the reading of a Chinese character taken from the original Chinese pronunciation: 《⇨ kuñ》
'山' *to iu ji no* 'oñ' *wa* 'sañ' *de* 'kuñ' *wa* 'yama' *desu.*（「山」という字の音は「さん」で訓は「やま」です）The *Chinese-style pronunciation* of the character '山' is '*sañ*' and the Japanese-style pronunciation

is 'yama.' / *kañji o* oñ *de yomu*
(漢字を音で読む) read Chinese
characters with the *Chinese style
pronunciation.*

o「ñ- おん (御) *pref.* (used to indicate respect or politeness):
★ More formal than '*o-,*' but
limited in use.
On-ree *mooshi agemasu.* (御礼申し
上げます) Please accept my *sincere
thanks.*

o「naji おなじ (同じ)

> **(USAGE)**
>
> '*Onaji*' is the form that pre-
> cedes a noun. It is not fol-
> lowed by '*na*' or '*no.*' Instead
> of '*onaji (yoo) ni,*' the form
> '*onajiku*' is sometimes used.

1 same; similar; alike:
Watashi mo kore to onaji *jisho o
motte imasu.* (私もこれと同じ辞書を
持っています) I have the *same* dictionary as this. / *Kare to watashi
wa* onaji *toshi desu.* (彼と私は同じ
年です) He and I are the *same* age.
/ *Kare-ra wa watashi o kaiiñ to*
onaji *ni atsukatte kureta.* (彼らは私
を会員と同じに扱ってくれた) They
were nice enough to treat me *like*
a member of their club. / *Tanaka-sañ to* onaji *yoo ni shite kudasai.* (田中さんと同じようにしてください)
Please do it in the *same way* as
Miss Tanaka. (⇨ onajiku)
2 equivalent; equal:
Kono Nihoñgo to mattaku onaji
Eego wa arimaseñ. (この日本語とま
ったく同じ英語はありません) There is
no English expression that is
exactly *equivalent* to this Japanese. (⇨ dooyoo¹)

o「na「jiku おなじく (同じく) *adv.*
similarly; in like manner:
Kare mo kimi to onajiku *gorufu
ga suki da.* (彼も君と同じくゴルフが好
きだ) He is fond of playing golf
like you. / *Nihoñ wa anata no*

kuni to onajiku *kome ga shushoku
desu.* (日本はあなたの国と同じく米が主
食です) In Japan rice is our staple
food *as* it is in your country.
(⇨ onaji)

o「naka おなか (お腹) *n.* bowels;
stomach: ★ More polite than
'*hara.*'
Onaka ga suita. (おなかがすいた) I *am
hungry.* / Onaka *ga ippai desu.* (お
なかがいっぱいです) My *stomach* is
full. / Onaka ga itai. (おなかが痛い) I
have a stomachache. / *Tabesugite,*
onaka *ga hatte iru.* (食べ過ぎて、おな
かが張っている) I have overloaded
my *stomach* by eating too much.
/ *Soñna ni taberu to* onaka *o kowashimasu yo.* (そんなに食べるとおなかを
こわしますよ) If you eat so much,
you will get *stomach* trouble.
onaka ga ookii (〜が大きい) *(euphemistic)* be pregnant: *Kanojo
wa* onaka ga ookii. (彼女はおなかが
大きい) She *is in the family way.*
(⇨ hara¹)

o「ñbiñ おんびん (音便) *n.* euphonic
change in the pronunciation of a
word:
*i-*oñbiñ (イ音便) the '*i*' sound
change. *e.g. kaku—kaite* / *soku-*
oñbiñ (促音便) the geminate consonant sound change. *e.g. toru—
totte* / *hatsu-*oñbiñ (撥音便) the
nasal sound change. *e.g. tobu—
toñde* (⇨ appendixes)

o「ñbu おんぶ *n.* piggyback; picka-
back. (⇨ illus. (next page))
oñbu suru (〜する) *vt.* **1** carry a
child piggyback: *Haha-oya wa
akañboo o* oñbu shite ita. (母親は
赤ん坊をおんぶしていた) The mother
had her baby strapped to her back.
2 rely on; depend upon: *Nañ de
mo anata ni* oñbu suru *wake ni wa
ikimaseñ.* (何でもあなたにおんぶする訳
にはいきません) It just will not do
for me to *rely on* you for everything.

OÑBU

o「ñchuu おんちゅう (御中) *n.* (*formal*) Messrs: ★ Used after the name of a firm or office on an envelope when writing to the organization, rather than to a specific person within it.
Yamada Shookai oñchuu (山田商会御中) *Messrs.* Yamada & Co. 《⇨ tegami》

o「ñdañ おんだん (温暖) *a.n.* (~ na, ni) temperate; mild:
oñdañ *na kikoo* (温暖な気候) a *temperate* climate / *Kono heñ wa kikoo ga* oñdañ *desu.* (この辺は気候が温暖です) The climate is *mild* around here.

o「ñdo おんど (温度) *n.* temperature; heat:

	kioñ	atmospheric temperature
oñdo	shitsuoñ	room temperature
	suioñ	water temperature
	taioñ	body temperature

oñdo *o hakaru* (温度を測る) take the *temperature* / Oñdo *ga go-do agatta* [*sagatta*]. (温度が5度上がった[下がった]) The *temperature* rose [fell] five degrees. / *Ima no* oñdo *wa nañ-do desu ka?* (今の温度は何度ですか) What's the *temperature* now?

o「ñdokee おんどけい (温度計) *n.* thermometer: ★ In Japan, the temperature is measured in Celsius. 《⇨ sesshi》
Oñdokee *wa sañjuu-do o shimeshite ita.* (温度計は30度を示していた) The *thermometer* read 30 degrees. 《⇨ oñdo》

o-「ne「esañ おねえさん (お姉さん) *n.*
1 someone else's older sister:
O-neesañ *wa kekkoñ sarete imasu ka?* (お姉さんは結婚されていますか) Is your *older sister* married? 《↔ o-niisañ》
2 (as a term of address) my older sister. ★ When referring to one's own older sister, '*ane*' is used.

o-「negai おねがい (お願い) *n.* favor; request:
O-negai *ga aru ñ desu ga.* (お願いがあるんですが) I have a *favor* to ask of you. / O-negai *da kara shizuka ni shite kudasai.* (お願いだから静かにしてください) *For goodness sake*, will you be quiet!
o-negai suru (~する) *vt.* request; ask: *Kore kara mo yoroshiku* o-negai shimasu. (これからもよろしくお願いします) I'd *appreciate* your support in the future. 《⇨ negai》

o「ñgaku おんがく (音楽) *n.* music; the musical art:
shii-dii de oñgaku *o kiku* (CDで音楽を聞く) listen to *music* on a CD. 《⇨ CD》

o「ñgakuka おんがくか (音楽家) *n.* musician.

o「ñgaku「kai おんがくかい (音楽会) *n.* concert:
oñgakukai *o hiraku* (音楽会を開く) give a *concert*. 《⇨ koñsaato》

o「ni「 おに (鬼) *n.* **1** demon; fiend; ogre:
Kare wa shigoto no oni *da.* (彼は仕事の鬼だ) He is a *demon* for work.
2 (of the game of tag) "it."
《⇨ illus. (next page)》

ONI

o⌐**ni**⌐**giri** おにぎり（お握り）*n.* rice ball. 《⇨ omusubi》

MAKING ONIGIRI

o⌐**ni-go**⌐**kko** おにごっこ（鬼ごっこ）*n.* tag:
oni-gokko *o suru* （鬼ごっこをする） play *tag*.

o-⌐**ni**⌐**isan** おにいさん（お兄さん）*n.*
1 someone else's older brother: O-niisan *wa o-geñki desu ka?* （お兄さんはお元気ですか）How is your older *brother*?
2 (as a term of address) my older brother. ★ When referring to one's own older brother, '*ani*' is used.

o⌐**nna**⌐ おんな（女）*n.* woman; female: ★ Often has a derogatory connotation; '*josee*' is preferable in many uses.
Ano oñna no hito *wa shirimaseñ.* （あの女の人は知りません）I don't know that *woman.* / *Kanojo wa ichiniñmae no* oñna *ni natta.* （彼女は一人前の女になった）She became a grown-up *woman.* 《↔ otoko》

《⇨ fujiñ²; josee》

o⌐**ñnade** おんなで（女手）*n.* female breadwinner:
Kanojo wa oñnade *hitotsu de sañ-niñ no kodomo o sodateta.* （彼女は女手ひとつで３人の子どもを育てた）She brought up three children all by *herself.*

o⌐**ñna**⌐**-no-ko** （女の子）*n.*
1 girl:
Sono oñna-no-ko *wa naite ita.* （その女の子は泣いていた）The *girl* was crying. 《↔ otoko-no-ko》
2 daughter:
Kanojo ni wa oñna-no-ko *ga hitori iru.* （彼女には女の子が一人いる）She has a *daughter.* 《↔ otoko-no-ko》

o⌐**ñnarashi**⌐**·i** おんならしい（女らしい）*a.* (-ku) womanly; feminine; ladylike:
Kanojo wa ichidañ to oñnarashiku *natta.* （彼女は一段と女らしくなった）She has become more *womanly.* / *Kanojo no furumai wa* oñnarashiku *nai.* （彼女のふるまいは女らしくない）Her behavior is not *ladylike.* 《↔ otokorashii》《⇨ josee-teki》

o⌐**no**⌐**-ono** おのおの（各々）*n.* (*slightly formal*) each:
ono-ono *no ikeñ o kiku* （おのおのの意見を聞く）listen to *each* opinion / *Hito ni wa* ono-ono *choosho to tañsho ga arimasu.* （人にはおのおの長所と短所があります）*Each* person has merits and shortcomings. 《⇨ kakuji; meemee》

o⌐**ñsee** おんせい（音声）*n.* voice; vocal sound:
oñsee-gaku （音声学）*phonetics* / oñsee-tajuu-*hoosoo* （音声多重放送）*multiplex* broadcasting.

o⌐**ñseñ** おんせん（温泉）*n.* hot spring; spa:
┌─── CULTURE ───┐
Japanese hot springs are recreational rather than medicinal.

oñseñ *ni hairu* (温泉に入る) take a *hot spring bath* / oñseñ-*chi* (温泉地) a hot spring resort.

o⌐**ñsetsu** おんせつ（音節） *n.* syllable:
tañgo o oñsetsu *de wakeru* (単語を音節で分ける) divide a word into *syllables.*

o⌐**ñshiñ-futsuu** おんしんふつう（音信不通） *n.* no news; no correspondence:
Kare to wa ni-neñ ijoo mo oñshiñ-futsuu *desu.* (彼とは2年以上も音信不通です) I *haven't heard from him* for more than two years.

o⌐**ñshitsu** おんしつ（温室） *n.* hothouse; greenhouse.

o⌐**ñtai** おんたい（温帯） *n.* temperate zone:
oñtai-*shokubutsu* (温帯植物) the flora of the *temperate zone.*
《⇨ kikoo (table)》

o⌐**o**[1] おう（王） *n.* **1** king. 《↔ jo-oo》
2 king; magnate:
hyaku-juu no oo (百獣の王) the *king* of beasts / *sekiyu*-oo (石油王) an oil *magnate.*

o⌐**o**[2] おお *int.* oh; aah; well:
★ Used to express admiration, wonder, sorrow, etc.
Oo, *suteki da.* (おお, すてきだ) *Oh,* how fantastic. / Oo, *atsui.* (おお, 暑い) *Well,* it is hot! 《⇨ aa[2]》

oo- おお（大） *pref.* big; many; heavy; special:
oo-*ame* (大雨) *heavy* rain / oo-*doori* (大通り) a *main* street / oo-*goe* (大声) a *loud* voice / oo-*machigai* (大間違い) a *huge* mistake / oo-*sawagi* (大騒ぎ) a *big* fuss / oo-*uridashi* (大売出し) a *bargain sale.*

-oo *infl. end.* [attached to the stem of a consonant-stem verb]
《⇨ -yoo》
1 intend; want:
Boku wa beñgoshi ni naroo *to omotte imasu.* (ぼくは弁護士になろう

と思っています) I *intend to become* a lawyer. / *Shukudai wa kore kara* yaroo *to omotte imasu.* (宿題はこれからやろうと思っています) I *intend to do* my homework now. / *Mise wa tokka-hiñ o* kaoo *to suru hito-tachi de ippai datta.* (店は特価品を買おうとする人たちでいっぱいだった) The store was full of people *wanting to get* good bargains.
2 be about to do:
Hi wa shizumoo *to shite ita.* (日は沈もうとしていた) The sun *was about to set.* / *Nani-ka ijoo na koto ga* okoroo *to shite ita.* (何か異常なことが起ころうとしていた) Something unusual *was about to happen.* / *Kare no uchi e* ikoo *to shitara, kare ga tazunete kita.* (彼の家へ行こうとしたら, 彼が訪ねてきた) I *was on the point of going* to his house, when he came to see me.
3 let's:
Teñrañ-kai o mi ni ikoo. (展覧会を見に行こう) *Let's go* to see the exhibition.

o⌐**oame** おおあめ（大雨） *n.* heavy rain:
Kinoo wa ooame *ga futta.* (きのうは大雨が降った) We had a *heavy rain* yesterday. 《↔ kosame》

o⌐**obaa** オーバー *a.n.* (～ na, ni) exaggerated: ★ Comes from English 'over.'
oobaa *na iikata* (オーバーな言いかた) an *exaggerated* way of speaking / *Kare no hanashi wa itsu-mo* oobaa *da.* (彼の話はいつもオーバーだ) His stories are always *exaggerated.*
《⇨ oogesa》

oobaa suru (～する) *vi.* exceed; go beyond: *seegeñ-sokudo o* oobaa suru (制限速度をオーバーする) *exceed* the speed limit / *Yosañ ga ichimañ-eñ* oobaa shita. (予算が1万円オーバーした) Actual expenditure *exceeded* the budget by 10,000 yen.

Oˈobee おうべい（欧米）*n.* Europe and North America. 《⇨ Yooroppa; Amerika》

oˈobo おうぼ（応募）*n.* application; entry: oobo-sha（応募者）an *applicant*. **oobo suru**（〜する）*vi.* apply for; enter for: *Kare wa sono shuppañ-sha no heñshuusha boshuu ni oo-bo shita.*（彼はその出版社の編集者募集に応募した）He *applied for* a position as an editor in the publishing company. / *Watashi wa sono keñshoo ni oobo shimashita.*（私はその懸賞に応募しました）I *entered* the prize contest.

oˈobuñ オーブン *n.* oven: *oobuñ de keeki o yaku*（オーブンでケーキを焼く）bake a cake in the *oven*.

oˈodañ[1] おうだん（横断）*n.* crossing; traversing: *oodañ-hodoo*（横断歩道）a pedestrian *crossing* / *Oodañ kiñshi.*（*sign*）（横断禁止）No *Crossing* Here.

OODAÑ KIÑSHI SIGN

oodañ suru（〜する）*vt.* go across; cross; traverse: *Dooro o oodañ suru toki wa sayuu o yoku mi na-sai.*（道路を横断するときは左右をよく見なさい）Carefully look right and left before you *cross* the street. / *Kare wa oyoide, sono kawa o oodañ shita.*（彼は泳いで、その川を横断した）He *swam across* the river.

oˈodañ[2] おうだん（黄疸）*n.* jaundice.

oˈodoˈori おおどおり（大通り）*n.* main street; thoroughfare.

oˈoeñ おうえん（応援）*n.* help; support; backing: *Isogashii no de kare ni ooeñ o ta-noñda.*（忙しいので彼に応援を頼んだ）Since I am busy, I have asked him to *help me out*. / ooeñ *eñze-tsu*（応援演説）a speech *in support of someone*.

ooeñ suru（〜する）*vt.* **1** help; support; back up: *Watashi-tachi wa sono koohosha o ooeñ shita.*（私たちはその候補者を応援した）We *supported* the candidate.

2 cheer: *Kañshuu wa yowai hoo no chiimu o ooeñ shita.*（観衆は弱いほうのチームを応援した）The spectators *cheered* the weaker team.

oˈoeˈñdañ おうえんだん（応援団）*n.* cheering party; rooters: ooeñdañ *o tsukuru*（応援団をつくる）form a *cheering party*.

oˈo-eˈru オーエル *n.* female office worker. ★ Often written as 'OL,' an abbreviation of 'office lady.'

oˈofuku おうふく（往復）*n.* coming and going; going and returning: *Jikañ wa* oofuku *dono kurai ka-karimasu ka?*（時間は往復どのくらいかかりますか）How long does it take *there and back*? / oofuku-*kippu*（往復切符）a *two-way* ticket / oo-fuku-*uñchiñ*（往復運賃）a *round-trip* fare. 《↔ katamichi》

oofuku suru（〜する）*vi.* go and come back; make a round trip: *Kyoo wa Shiñkañseñ de Tookyoo to Kyooto o oofuku shimashita.*（きょうは新幹線で東京と京都を往復しました）Today I *made* the Tokyo-Kyoto *round trip* by Shinkansen.

oˈofuku-haˈgaki おうふくはがき（往復葉書）*n.* reply-paid postcard. 《photo (next page)》 ★ A reply-prepaid postcard is attached.（⇨ hagaki）

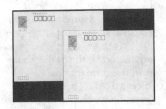

OOFUKU-HAGAKI

oˈogaˈkari　おおがかり（大掛かり）
a.n. (~ na, ni) great; large-
scale:
oogakari *na kooji* (大がかりな工事)
large-scale construction works /
Damu no keñsetsu ga oogakari *ni
susumerarete imasu.* (ダムの建設が
大がかりに進められています) The con-
struction works on the dam are
under way on *a large scale.*
《⇨ daikibo》

oˈogata　おおがた（大型）*n.* large
size:
oogata *no taifuu* (大型の台風) a
large typhoon / oogata *no reezooko* (大型の冷蔵庫) a *large* refrigerator / oogata *no shiñjiñ* (大
型の新人) a new face of *high caliber.* 《⇨ chuugata; kogata》

oˈogesa　おおげさ（大袈裟）*a.n.*
(~ na, ni) exaggerated:
Kare no hanashi wa itsu-mo oogesa *da.* (彼の話はいつも大げさだ) His
stories are always *exaggerated.* /
Shiñbuñ wa sono jikeñ o oogesa
ni hoodoo shita. (新聞はその事件を
大げさに報道した) The newspapers
played up the incident.

oˈogoˈe　おおごえ（大声）*n.* loud
voice:
oogoe *o dasu* (大声を出す) *raise
one's voice* / oogoe *de hanasu* (大
声で話す) speak in a *loud voice.*
《↔ kogoe》

oˈoguchi　おおぐち（大口）*n.* **1** big
[large] mouth:
ooguchi *o akete warau* (大口を開け
て笑う) laugh *with one's mouth*

wide open.
2 big:
ooguchi *no chuumoñ o morau* (大
口の注文をもらう) receive a *big* order.

oˈohaba　おおはば（大幅）*a.n.*
(~ na, ni) large; big; drastic;
substantial:
oohaba *na kaikaku* (大幅な改革) a
sweeping reform / oohaba *ni heñkoo suru* (大幅に変更する) change
drastically / *Jugyoo-ryoo ga* oohaba *ni agatta.* (授業料が大幅に上が
った) Tuition fees have gone up
substantially.

oˈoˈi　おおい（多い）*a.* (-ku) many;
much; numerous:
*Kono sakubuñ wa kañji no machi-
gai ga* ooi. (この作文は漢字の間違い
が多い) There are *lots of* errors in
Chinese characters in this essay.
/ *Nihoñ wa jishiñ ga* ooi. (日本は
地震が多い) Earthquakes are *common* in Japan. / *Kotoshi wa yuki
ga* ookatta. (今年は雪が多かった) We
have had *much* snow this year.
《↔ sukunai》

oˈoi ni　おおいに（大いに）*adv.*
greatly; very (much):
Sore o kiite kare wa ooi ni *mañzoku shita.* (それを聞いて彼はおおいに
満足した) He was *very* satisfied
when he heard that. / *Sakumotsu
no deki wa teñkoo to* ooi ni *kañkee ga arimasu.* (作物の出来は天候
とおおいに関係があります) Crop yields
are *closely* related to the weather.

oˈoiˈsogi　おおいそぎ（大急ぎ）*n.* being urgent; being pressed:
ooisogi *no shigoto* (大急ぎの仕事)
an *urgent* task / *Itsu-mo no deñsha ni noru tame ni* ooisogi *de eki
e itta.* (いつもの電車に乗るために大急ぎ
で駅へ行った) I *rushed* to the station to catch my usual train.

Oˈoitaˈ-keñ　おおいたけん（大分県）
n. Oita Prefecture. Located in
northeast Kyushu, it contains

Japan's largest hot spring resort, Beppu (別府). Capital city: Oita. 《⇨ map (B5)》

o「**oji·ru** おうじる (応じる) *vi.* (ooji-te ☑) **1** answer; respond; accept:
shitsumoñ ni oojiru (質問に応じる) *answer* a question / *chooseñ ni* oojiru (挑戦に応じる) *accept* a challenge / *Zañneñ nagara anata no teeañ ni wa* oojiraremaseñ. (残念ながらあなたの提案には応じられません) I regret it, but I *cannot accept* your proposal.
2 meet (a demand, order, etc.); accept; satisfy:
chuumoñ ni oojiru (注文に応じる) *accept* an order / *Juyoo ni* oojiru *tame ni seesañ o fuyashita.* (需要に応じるために生産を増やした) We have increased production to *meet* demand.
3 apply:
Kanojo wa shaiñ boshuu ni oojite, *rirekisho o okutta.* (彼女は社員募集に応じて、履歴書を送った) *In response to* an advertisement for employees, she sent in her personal history.
4 be appropriate; be suitable (to one's ability):
Nooryoku ni oojita *shoku o sagashi nasai.* (能力に応じた職を探しなさい) Please look for employment that *is appropriate* to your abilities.

o「**okata**[1] おおかた (大方) *adv.*
1 probably; perhaps:
Ookata *soñna koto daroo to omotte imashita.* (おおかたそんなことだろうと思っていました) I thought that was *perhaps* the case.
2 almost; nearly:
Sono atarashii ie wa ookata *dekiagarimashita.* (その新しい家はおおかたでき上がりました) The new house is *almost* finished.

o「**okata**[2] おおかた (大方) *n.* peo-

ple in general:
Ookata no yosoo-doori, *Seebu ga yuushoo shimashita.* (おおかたの予想通り, 西武が優勝しました) *As generally expected*, the Seibu Lions won the pennant.

o「**oke**]**sutora** オーケストラ *n.* (symphony) orchestra; orchestral music.

o「**oki**]**·i** おおきい (大きい) *a.* (-ku)
1 big; large:
ookii *tsukue* (大きい机) a *large* desk / *hyaku yori* ookii *kazu* (100 より大きい数) a number *larger* than one hundred / *Pañda wa atama ga* ookii. (パンダは頭が大きい) The panda has a *big* head. / *Kare wa kañgaeru koto ga* ookii. (彼は考えることが大きい) He always thinks *big.* 《↔ chiisai》《⇨ ooki-na》
2 (of degree) great:
Fugookaku no shokku wa ookikatta. (不合格のショックは大きかった) Failure in the exam came as a *great* shock. / *Kagaku-gijutsu wa kono juu-neñ de* ookiku *shiñpo shita.* (科学技術はこの 10 年で大きく進歩した) Scientific techniques have improved *greatly* in the past decade.
ookiku naru (大きくなる) grow up:
Ookiku *nattara kashu ni naritai.* (大きくなったら歌手になりたい) I want to be a singer when I *grow up.*

o「**oki-na** おおきな (大きな) *attrib.*

─ (USAGE) ─
The meaning is basically the same as '*ookii,*' but used only attributively before a noun.

big; large; great:
ooki-na *inu* (大きな犬) a *big* dog / *Yotee ni* ooki-na *heñkoo wa nakatta.* (予定に大きな変更はなかった) There was no *great* change in the schedule.
ooki-na kao o suru (～顔をする) be haughty: *Kare wa* ooki-na kao

o shite *ita*. (彼は大きな顔をしていた)
He *was arrogant* to us.

Ooki-na o-sewa da. (〜お世話だ)
It's *none of your business.*
《(↔ chiisa-na)》《⇨ ookii》

oˈokisa おおきさ (大きさ) *n.* size;
dimensions; volume:
hoñ no ookisa (本の大きさ) the *size*
of a book / oto no ookisa (音の大き
さ) *loudness* / Ookisa *wa dono kurai desu ka?* (大きさはどのくらいですか)
How *big* is it? / Ookisa *o hakatte
mimashoo.* (大きさを測ってみましょう)
Let's measure the *size.* / *Kore wa*
ookisa ga *sore no* ni-bai aru. (これ
は大きさがそれの2倍ある) This is
twice as large as that.
《⇨ daishoo》

oˈoku おおく (多く) *n.*, *adv.*
many; much:
Kañkyaku no ooku wa *kodomo-
tachi datta.* (観客の多くは子どもたちだ
った) *Most* of the audience were
children. / *Kare wa sono jikeñ ni
tsuite* ooku *o kataranakatta.* (彼はそ
の事件について多くを語らなかった) He
did not say *much* about the affair.
/ *Sono señkyo ni wa kane ga* ooku
ugoita. (その選挙には金が多く動いた)
Money was *very much* involved
in the election.

Oˈokura-daˈijiñ おおくらだいじん
(大蔵大臣) *n.* Minister of Finance.

Oˈokuraˈ-shoo おおくらしょう (大
蔵省) *n.* Ministry of Finance.
《⇨ shoo¹ (table)》

oˈokyuu おうきゅう (応急) *n.* emergency; temporary; makeshift:
★ Usually used in compounds.
Kega o shita hito ni ookyuu-teate
o shita. (けがをした人に応急手当をし
た) We gave the injured people
first aid. / ookyuu-*shochi* (応急処
置) an *emergency* measure / oo-
kyuu-*shuuri* (応急修理) *temporary*
repairs.

oˈomiˈzu おおみず (大水) *n.* flood:

oomizu ga deru (大水が出る) *be
flooded.*

oˈomuˈgi おおむぎ (大麦) *n.* barley.
《⇨ mugi (table)》

oˈomuˈkashi おおむかし (大昔) *n.*
ancient times; antiquity:
oomukashi *no juukyo* (大昔の住居)
a dwelling of *great antiquity* /
Kore wa oomukashi *kara tsutawatte iru hanashi desu.* (これは大昔
から伝わっている話です) This is a
story handed down from *ancient
times.* / Oomukashi *(wa) kono
atari wa umi deshita.* (大昔(は)この
辺りは海でした) This area was sea a
long time ago.

oˈopuñ¹ オープン *n.* opening:
Shiñ-kyuujoo no oopuñ *wa raineñ
no shi-gatsu desu.* (新球場のオープン
は来年の四月です) The *opening* of
the new stadium will be in April
next year. / oopuñ-*señ* (オープン戦)
a *pre-seasonal exhibition* game.

oopuñ suru (〜する) *vi.* open:
Atarashii depaato wa ku-gatsu ni
oopuñ shimasu. (新しいデパートは九
月にオープンします) The new department store will *open* in September.

oˈopuñ² オープン *a.n.* (〜 na, ni)
frank; open to the public:
Oopuñ *ni hanashiaimashoo.* (オープ
ンに話し合いましょう) Let's talk
frankly. / *Kaigi no ketsuroñ wa*
oopuñ *ni su beki da.* (会議の結論は
オープンにすべきだ) We should make
public the conclusions of the
meeting.

oˈorai オーライ *n.* all right; O.K.:
Hassha oorai. (発車オーライ) It is
all right to depart. (*said by train
conductors, etc.*)

Oˈosakaˈ-fu おおさかふ (大阪府) *n.*
Osaka Prefecture. Located in the
center of the Kinki district between Kobe and Kyoto. The
capital city, Osaka, is the second
largest city in Japan and the cen-

ter of administration, economy, and culture in western Japan. 《⇨ map (D4)》

o⌐osee おうせい (旺盛) *a.n.* (~ na, ni) full of energy; eager: *Chichi wa geñki oosee desu.* (父は元気おうせいです) My father is in *high* spirits. / *Kodomo-tachi wa shokuyoku oosee da.* (子どもたちは食欲おうせいだ) Children have a *good* appetite.

o⌐osetsu おうせつ (応接) *n.* reception (of a visitor).
oosetsu suru (~する) *vt.* receive (a guest).

o⌐osetsuma おうせつま (応接間) *n.* drawing room: *o-kyaku o oosetsuma ni toosu* (お客を応接間に通す) show a visitor into the *drawing room*.

o⌐osetsu⌐shitsu おうせつしつ (応接室) *n.* reception room.

O⌐osutora⌐ria オーストラリア *n.* Australia.

O⌐osutoraria⌐jiñ オーストラリアじん (オーストラリア人) *n.* Australian.

o⌐otai おうたい (応対) *n.* reception; meeting: *Kare no hisho wa kyaku no ootai ga joozu [heta] da.* (彼の秘書は客の応対がじょうず[へた]だ) His secretary is good [poor] at *dealing with* guests. / *Kyoo wa kyaku no ootai de isogashikatta.* (きょうは客の応対で忙しかった) Today I was very busy *meeting with* customers.
ootai suru (~する) *vi.* receive; deal with; meet: *Sono teñiñ wa o-kyaku ni teenee ni ootai shite ita.* (その店員はお客に丁寧に応対していた) The shop clerk *was* politely *attending* to the customers.

o⌐oteñ (横転) *n.* turning sideways; overturning; rolling over: *ressha no ooteñ jiko* (列車の横転事故) an accident involving the *overturning* of a train.
ooteñ suru (~する) *vi.* turn side-

ways; overturn: *Sono kuruma wa kabe ni gekitotsu shite, ooteñ shita.* (その車は壁に激突して, 横転した) The car crashed into the wall and *rolled sideways*.

o⌐oto⌐bai オートバイ *n.* motorcycle; motorbike: *ootobai ni noru* (オートバイに乗る) ride on a *motorcycle*.

o⌐o⌐·u おおう (覆う) *vt.* (oo·i-; oo-w·a-; oot-te Ⓒ) cover; veil; envelop: *Kanojo wa nete iru akañboo o moofu de ootta.* (彼女は寝ている赤ん坊を毛布で覆った) She *covered* the sleeping baby with a blanket. / *Yama wa yuki de oowarete ita.* (山は雪で覆われていた) The mountains *were covered* with snow.

o⌐oya おおや (大家) *n.* owner of a house for rent; landlord; landlady. 《⇨ jinushi》

o⌐oyoo おうよう (応用) *n.* application; adaptation; practice: *Kono riroñ wa ooyoo ga kikimasu.* (この理論は応用がききます) This theory has a wide range of *applications*. / *ooyoo-kagaku* (応用科学) *applied* science / *ooyoo-moñdai* (応用問題) a *practice* exercise.
ooyoo suru (~する) *vt.* apply; adapt; put to use: *keñkyuu no seeka o jissai ni ooyoo suru* (研究の成果を実際に応用する) *put* the results of research *to practical use.*

o⌐oyo⌐rokobi おおよろこび (大喜び) *n.* delight; glee; joy: *Sono ko wa o-kane o morai, ooyorokobi de kaimono ni dekaketa.* (その子はお金をもらい, 大喜びで買い物に出かけた) The child *gleefully* went out shopping after getting the money. / *Kare-ra wa shiai ni katte, ooyorokobi datta.* (彼らは試合に勝って, 大喜びだった) They *were overjoyed* at winning the match.

o⌐oyoso おおよそ (大凡) *n.* outline:

Keekaku no ooyoso *o hanashite kudasai.* (計画のおおよそを話してください) Please tell us the *general outline* of your plan.
— *adv.* roughly; approximately; about:

Ik-ka-getsu no shuunyuu wa ooyoso *dono kurai desu ka?* (一か月の収入はおおよそどのくらいですか) *About* how much is your monthly income? (⇨ oyoso)

o⌈**oyuki**⌉ おおゆき (大雪) *n.* heavy fall of snow; heavy snowfall:
Yama wa ooyuki *desu.* (山は大雪です) It *is snowing hard* in the mountains. (↔ koyuki) (⇨ yuki¹)

o⌈**oza**⌉**ppa** おおざっぱ (大雑把) *a.n.* (～ na, ni) rough; general:
oozappa *na keekaku* (おおざっぱな計画) a *rough* plan / *Oozappa ni mitsumotte, hyakumañ-eñ kakarimasu.* (おおざっぱに見積もって, 100万円かかります) Estimating *roughly*, it will cost a million yen.

o⌈**oze**⌉**e** おおぜい (大勢) *n., adv.* crowd (of people):
Sono kashu wa oozee *no fuañ ni torikakomareta.* (その歌手は大勢のファンに取り囲まれた) The singer was surrounded by a *crowd* of fans. / *Kare no eñzetsu o kiku tame ni,* oozee *atsumatta.* (彼の演説を聞くために, 大勢集まった) A *crowd* gathered to hear his speech.

o⌈**pera**⌉ オペラ *n.* opera.
o⌈**pere**⌉**tta** オペレッタ *n.* operetta.
o⌈**ppai**⌉ おっぱい *n.* = chichi².
★ Infant word for mother's milk or breast.

op⌈**para**⌉**·u** おっぱらう (追っ払らう) *vt.* (-para·i-; -paraw·a-; -parat-te ⟨C⟩) = oiharau.

O⌈**rañda**⌉ オランダ *n.* the Netherlands; Holland.
O⌈**rañda**⌉**jiñ** オランダじん (オランダ人) *n.* the Dutch.
o⌈**re**⌉ おれ (俺) *n.* (*rude*) I:

★ Used by men. The plural form is '*ore-tachi*.'
Ore ni tsuite koi. (おれについて来い) Follow *me*! / *Saa,* ore *no iu koto o yoku kike.* (さあ, おれの言うことをよく聞け) Now, listen to *me*. (⇨ omae)

o-⌈**ree**⌉ おれい (お礼) *n.* ★ Polite form of '*ree*.'
1 thanks; gratitude:
Sono uchi o-ree *ni ukagaimasu.* (そのうちお礼に伺います) I will shortly pay you a visit *to thank you*. / *Nañ to* o-ree *o mooshite yoi ka wakarimaseñ.* (何とお礼を申してよいかわかりません) I do not know how to express my *gratitude*. (⇨ ree²)
2 reward; fee; remuneration:
Beñgoshi no o-ree *wa haraimashita ka?* (弁護士のお礼は払いましたか) Have you paid the lawyer's *fee*?

o-ree (o) suru (～(を)する) *vt.* give a reward; pay a fee: *Sono hito ni dono kurai* o-ree *o shitara yoi deshoo ka?* (その人にどのくらいお礼をしたら良いでしょうか) What would be a suitable sum to *give* him *as a 'thank you'*?

o⌈**re**⌉**ñji** オレンジ *n.* orange:
oreñji-*juusu* (オレンジジュース) *orange* juice / oreñji-*iro* (オレンジ色) *orange* color.

or⌈**eñji-ka**⌉**ado** オレンジカード *n.* a magnetic card with which one can buy Japan Railway tickets from vending machines.

OREÑJI KAADO

o⌐re⌐·ru おれる（折れる）*vi.* (ore-te
Ⓥ) **1** break; give way:
*Yuki no omomi de ki no eda ga
oreta.*（雪の重みで木の枝が折れた）
The branches *broke* under the
weight of the snow. 《⇨ oru¹》
2 give in; yield to:
*Kare no hoo ga orete, kanojo no
yookyuu o noñda.*（彼のほうが折れて、
彼女の要求を飲んだ）He, on his part,
gave in and accepted her demand.
3 turn:
Sono kuruma wa hidari ni oreta.
（その車は左に折れた）The car *turned*
left.

o⌐ri⌐ おり（折）*n.* occasion; time;
chance:
*Kono tsugi kare ni atta ori, yoro-
shiku o-tsutae kudasai.*（この次彼に
会った折、よろしくお伝えください）
Please give him my best regards
the next *time* you see him.
ori o mite （〜をみて）at the first
opportunity： *Ori o mite, kare no
byooki-mimai ni ikimashoo.*（折を
みて、彼の病気見舞いに行きましょう）
Let's visit him in the hospital *at
a convenient time.*
ori yoku （〜よく）fortunately；
luckily： *Totsuzeñ tazuneta ga,
ori yoku kare ga ita.*（突然訪ねたが、
折よく彼がいた）I visited him without warning, but *luckily* he was
in.

o⌐ri⌐gami おりがみ（折り紙）*n.* origami; colored paper for paper folding:
origami o otte tsuru o tsukuru （折

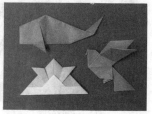

ORIGAMI

り紙を折ってつるを作る）fold *colored
paper* into a crane.

o⌐rimono おりもの（織物）*n.* textile; fabric:
orimono o oru （織物を織る）weave
a *fabric* / *kinu*-orimono（絹織物）
silk *fabrics* / *ke*-orimono（毛織物）
woolen *textiles.*

O⌐riñpi⌐kku オリンピック *n.* Olympic Games; Olympiad:
Oriñpikku-shumoku （オリンピック種
目）*Olympic* events / *Kokusai
Oriñpikku liñkai* （国際オリンピック委
員会）the International *Olympic*
Committee / *tooki* Oriñpikku（冬
季オリンピック）the Winter *Olympic*
Games.

o⌐ri⌐·ru おりる（降りる・下りる）*vi.*
(ori-te Ⓥ) **1** get off (a vehicle);
step off:
*Watashi wa Tookyoo-eki de ori-
masu.*（私は東京駅で降ります）I *am
getting out* at Tokyo Station. /
*Basu kara oriru toki wa ki o tsuke
nasai.*（バスから降りるときは気をつけな
い）Be careful when you *step off*
the bus. 《↔ noru¹》《⇨ orosu¹》
2 come [go] down; step down:
yama o oriru（山を下りる）*go down* a
mountain / *kaidañ o oriru*（階段を
下りる）*go down* stairs.
3 (of frost and dew) fall:
Kesa wa hidoi shimo ga orita.（今
朝はひどい霜が降りた）This morning
the frost *was thick.*
4 quit (a position, etc.); resign:
*Kare wa ima no chii kara oritai to
omotte iru.*（彼は今の地位から降りたい
と思っている）He *wants to resign*
from his present position.

o⌐ritatam·u おりたたむ（折り畳む）
vt. (-tatam·i-; -tatam·a-; -tatañ-
de Ⓒ) fold; collapse (an umbrella):
Isu o oritatañde katazuketa.（いすを
折り畳んで片づけた）I *folded* the
chair and put it away. / *Kono
kasa wa futatsu ni oritatamu koto*

ga dekimasu. (このかさは二つに折り畳むことができます) You can *collapse* this umbrella in half.

o⌐roka おろか (愚か) *a.n.* (~ na, ni) foolish; silly; stupid:
oroka *na okonai* (愚かな行い) a *foolish* act / *Soñna hanashi o shiñjiru nañte boku mo* oroka *datta.* (そんな話を信じるなんてぼくも愚かだった) I was a *fool* to believe that sort of tale. / *Watashi wa* oroka *ni mo kanojo ni damasareta.* (私は愚かにも彼女にだまされた) I was *foolish* enough to be deceived by her.

o⌐roshi おろし (卸し) *n.* wholesale:
oroshi *de kau* (卸して買う) buy at a *wholesale* price / oroshi-uri-gyoosha (卸し売り業者) a *wholesaler*.
(⇨ kouri; orosu[2])

o⌐ro⌐soka おろそか (疎か) *a.n.* (~ na, ni) neglectful; negligent:
Beñkyoo o orosoka *ni shite wa ikemaseñ.* (勉強をおろそかにしてはいけません) Don't *neglect* your studies.

o⌐ro⌐s·u[1] おろす (降ろす・下ろす) *vt.* (orosh·i-; oros·a-; orosh·i-te ⓒ)
1 drop; let off:
Tsugi no shiñgoo de oroshite *kudasai.* (次の信号で降ろしてください) Please *drop* me *off* at the next traffic light. (↔ noseru[1]) (⇨ oriru)
2 unload; discharge; take down:
Miñna de torakku kara piano o oroshita. (みんなでトラックからピアノをおろした) Everyone together *unloaded* the piano from the truck. / *Tana kara ano hako o* oroshite *kudasai.* (棚からあの箱をおろしてください) Please *take* that box *down* from the shelf.
3 pull down; roll down; lower:
buraiñdo o orosu (ブラインドを下ろす) *lower* the blinds.
4 withdraw (a deposit):
Kanojo wa giñkoo kara gomañ-eñ oroshita. (彼女は銀行から5万円おろした) She *withdrew* 50,000 yen

from the bank.

o⌐ro⌐s·u[2] おろす (卸す) *vt.* (orosh·i-; oros·a-; orosh·i-te ⓒ)
sell; wholesale:
Kono shoohiñ wa hitotsu señ-eñ de oroshite imasu. (この商品は一つ千円で卸しています) We *wholesale* these goods at 1,000 yen apiece.

o⌐r·u[1] おる (折る) *vt.* (or·i-; or·a-; ot-te ⓒ) **1** break; snap:
Kare wa hidari-ashi no hone o otta. (彼は左足の骨を折った) He *broke* a bone in his left leg. / *Sakura no eda o* otte *wa ikemaseñ.* (桜の枝を折ってはいけません) You mustn't *break off* the cherry branches.
2 fold:
Kanojo wa origami o otte, *tsuru o tsukutta.* (彼女は折り紙を折って、つるを作った) She *folded* a piece of paper into a crane.

o⌐r·u[2] おる (織る) *vt.* (or·i-; or·a-; ot-te ⓒ) weave:
Kore wa kinu de otta *mono desu.* (これは絹で織ったものです) This is something *woven* from silk.

o⌐r·u[3] おる (居る) *vi.* (or·i-; or·a-; ot-te ⓒ) be; exist:
1 [with an animate subject] (humble equivalent of '*iru*'):
Shujiñ wa ima ie ni orimasu. (主人は今家におります) My husband *is* at home now. / *Takeda wa ima gaishutsu shite* orimasu. (竹田は今外出しております) Takeda *is* now out on business.
2 [with an inanimate subject] (polite equivalent of '*(-te) iru*'):
Kochira wa ima yuki ga futte orimasu. (こちらは今雪が降っております) It *is* now snowing here.
3 (indicates an arrogant attitude on the part of the speaker):
Washi wa sakki kara koko ni oru. (わしはさっきからここにおる) I *have been* here for a while now. (*by men*)

o⌐rugañ オルガン *n.* organ:

orugañ *o hiku* (オルガンをひく) play the *organ*. ★ Usually refers to a reed organ or a harmonium. The pipe organ is always called '*paipu orugañ*.'

o⌐sae⌐·ru¹ おさえる (押さえる) *vt.* (osae-te Ⓥ) **1** hold (down): *Kono roopu o shikkari* osaete *kudasai.* (このロープをしっかり押さえてください) Please *hold* this rope tightly. **2** catch; arrest: *Doroboo wa geñkoohañ de* osae-rareta. (泥棒は現行犯で押さえられた) The thief *was caught* red-handed.

o⌐sama⌐r·u¹ おさまる (収まる) *vi.* (osamar·i-; osamar·a-; osamat-te Ⓒ) **1** fit; be kept: *Sono tana ni kono hoñ ga zeñbu* osamarimasu ka? (その棚にこの本が全部収まりますか) Will these books all *fit* onto that shelf? (⇨ osa-meru¹) **2** take office: *Kare wa kaichoo ni* osamatta. (彼は会長に収まった) He *took* the post of chairman.

o⌐sama⌐r·u² おさまる (治まる) *vi.* (osamar·i-; osamar·a-; osamat-te Ⓒ) **1** settle (down); be settled: *Sawagi wa sugu ni* osamatta. (騒ぎはすぐに治まった) The turmoil *was* soon *settled*. (⇨ osameru²) **2** calm down; die down: *Kaze ga* osamatta. (風が治まった) The wind *has died down*. / *Kare no ikari wa* osamaranakatta. (彼の怒りは治まらなかった) His anger *did not die down*.

o⌐sama⌐r·u³ おさまる (納まる) *vi.* (osamar·i-; osamar·a-; osamat-te Ⓒ) be paid: *Anata no zeekiñ ga mada* osa-matte *imaseñ*. (あなたの税金がまだ納まっていません) Your taxes *have* not *been paid* yet. (⇨ osameru³)

o⌐same⌐·ru¹ おさめる (収める) *vt.* (osame-te Ⓥ) **1** put away (in);

store; keep: *Tsukatta doogu wa moto no tokoro ni* osamemashita. (使った道具は元の所に収めました) I *put* the tools *away* in their proper place. (⇨ osamaru¹) **2** get (a grade, mark); obtain; gain; attain: *Kare wa yuushuu na seeseki o* osameta. (彼は優秀な成績を収めた) He *obtained* distinguished grades.

o⌐same⌐·ru² おさめる (治める) *vt.* (osame-te Ⓥ) **1** rule; govern; reign: *kuni o* osameru (国を治める) *govern* a country. **2** settle; put down: *sawagi o* osameru (騒ぎを治める) *settle* a disturbance. (⇨ osamaru²)

o⌐same⌐·ru³ おさめる (納める) *vt.* (osame-te Ⓥ) **1** pay (a fee, charge, tax, etc.): *jugyoo-ryoo [zeekiñ] o* osameru (授業料[税金]を納める) *pay* one's tuition [tax]. (⇨ osamaru³) **2** supply; deliver: *Chuumoñ no shina wa getsumatsu made ni* osamemasu. (注文の品は月末までに納めます) We will *deliver* the goods ordered by the end of the month. (⇨ osamaru³) **3** accept: *Doo-ka kore o* o-osame *kudasai.* (どうかこれをお納めください) Please *accept* this.

o⌐sana⌐·i おさない (幼い) *a.* (-ku) **1** very young: *Kare no futari no kodomo wa ma-da* osanai. (彼の二人の子どもはまだ幼い) His two children are still *very young*. / *Watashi wa* osanai *koro koko ni suñde imashita*. (私は幼いころここに住んでいました) I used to live here when I was a *small child*. **2** childish; immature: *Ano hito wa toshi no wari ni* osa-nai. (あの人は年の割に幼い) He is very *immature* for his age.

o-「satsu おさつ（お札）*n.* paper money; bill; note:
Kono o-satsu *o kuzushite kudasai.* （このお札をくずしてください）Please change this *bill.* 《⇨ shihee (photo)》

o「sechi-ryo¬ori おせちりょうり（お節料理）*n.* special dishes served on the first three days of the New Year. ★ Consists of a variety of ingredients associated with wishes for health, happiness, and a good harvest: fish-paste cake, black beans, herring roe, chestnuts in mashed sweet potato, vinegared Japanese radish, lotus root, etc.

OSECHI-RYOORI

o-「seebo おせいぼ（お歳暮）*n.*
= seebo.

o「seji おせじ（お世辞）*n.* compliment; flattery: ★ Note the two meanings of 'a sincere compliment' and 'insincere flattery.'
Kare wa kanojo ni ryoori ga umai to oseji *o itta.* （彼は彼女に料理がうまいとお世辞を言った）He *flattered* her by telling her her cooking was good. / *Kare wa* oseji *ga umai.* （彼はお世辞がうまい）He is good at *compliments.*

o「sha¬beri おしゃべり（お喋り）*n.* chat; chatter:
Wakai onna-no-ko wa oshaberi *ga suki da.* （若い女の子はおしゃべりが好きだ）Young girls like to *chatter.*
oshaberi (o) suru （～（を）する）*vi.* chat; chatter: *Hito ga hanashi o shite iru toki ni* oshaberi o shite *wa ikemaseñ.* （人が話をしているときにおしゃべりをしてはいけません）You must not *chatter away* while someone is talking.
— *a.n.* （～ na) talkative; gossipy:
Kanojo wa oshaberi *da.* （彼女はおしゃべりだ）She is very *talkative.* / Oshaberi *na hito wa hito no uwasa ga suki da.* （おしゃべりな人は人のうわさが好きだ）A *chatterbox* likes gossiping about others.

o「sha¬re おしゃれ（お洒落）*n.* dressing up; smart dresser:
Kanojo wa oshare *o tanoshiñde iru.* （彼女はおしゃれを楽しんでいる）She takes pleasure in *being well-dressed.* / *Watashi-tachi no señsee wa* oshare *da.* （私たちの先生はおしゃれだ）Our teacher is a *smart dresser.*
oshare (o) suru （～（を）する）*vi.* get dressed up: *Kanojo wa* oshare o shite, *deeto ni dekaketa.* （彼女はおしゃれをして、デートに出かけた）She *got dressed up* and went out on her date. / *Chikagoro wa* oshare o suru *wakai dañsee ga ooi.* （近いごろはおしゃれをする若い男性が多い）Nowadays there are many young men who *get themselves all done up.*

o「shie おしえ（教え）*n.* teaching; instruction:
Kirisuto no oshie （キリストの教え）the *teachings* of Christ. 《⇨ oshieru》

o「shie·ru おしえる（教える）*vt.* (oshie-te ▽) **1** teach (a lesson); instruct:
Kookoo de nani o oshiete iru ñ *desu ka?* （高校で何を教えているんですか）What do you *teach* at a high school? / *Watashi wa kanojo ni ikebana o* oshieta. （私は彼女に生け花を教えた）I *taught* her ikebana. /

*Kono hoñ wa iroiro na koto o oshi-
ete kuremasu.* (この本はいろいろなこと
を教えてくれます) This book *teaches*
us a lot. (⇨ oshie; osowaru)
2 tell (information); show (the
way):
*Shiyakusho e iku michi o oshiete
kudasai.* (市役所へ行く道を教えてくだ
さい) Could you *tell* me the way
to the city hall? / *Kare ga kitara,*
oshiete *kudasai.* (彼が来たら、教えて
ください) Please *let me know* when
he has arrived. (⇨ osowaru)

oˈshiˈ·i おしい (惜しい) *a.* (-ku)
1 regrettable; unlucky:
Oshii machigai o shite shimatta.
(惜しい間違いをしてしまった) I have
made a *regrettable* mistake. / *Ii
chañsu o nogashite, oshii koto o
shita.* (いいチャンスを逃して、惜しいこと
をした) It was too *bad* that I let a
great opportunity slip by. / *Oshii
tokoro de makete shimatta.* (惜しい
ところで負けてしまった) We *almost*
won the game. / *Oshikatta ne.* (惜
しかったね) What *a shame*!
2 precious; dear:
Dare de mo inochi ga oshii. (誰でも
命が惜しい) Life is *dear* to everyone. / *Jikañ ga oshii kara, shigoto o tsuzukeyoo.* (時間が惜しいから、
仕事を続けよう) Time is *precious*,
so let's continue the work. / *Watashi-tachi wa oshii hito o nakushita.* (私たちは惜しい人を亡くした)
We have lost a person very *important* to us. (⇨ oshimu)
3 too good:
*Kono mañneñhitsu wa suteru no
ga oshii.* (この万年筆は捨てるのが惜し
い) This fountain pen is *too good*
to throw away. (⇨ mottainai)

oˈshiire おしいれ (押し入れ) *n.*
closet; storage cupboard:
futoñ o oshiire ni shimau (ふとんを
押し入れにしまう) put bedding away
in a *closet*. (⇨ photo (right))

oˈshiˈkko おしっこ *n.* pee; urine;

closed   open
OSHIIRE

piddle: ★ Often used by
young children.
oshikko *o suru* (おしっこをする) have
a *pee*; *piddle*. (⇨ shoobeñ)

oˈshikoˈm·u おしこむ (押し込む) *vi.*
(-kom·i-; -kom·a-; -koñ-de C)
push; thrust; stuff:
*Kare wa kabañ ni hoñ o oshiko-
ñda.* (彼はかばんに本を押し込んだ) He
stuffed the books into his bag.

oˈshimai おしまい (お仕舞い) *n.*
end; finish:
Sake wa kore de oshimai desu.
(酒はこれでおしまいです) With this we
have come to the end of the sake.
/ *Kyoo wa kore de oshimai ni shiyoo.* (きょうはこれでおしまいにしよう)
Let's finish off here for today. /
Sono jikeñ de kare mo oshimai da.
(その事件で彼もおしまいだ) Things
were finished for him because of
that affair. (⇨ shimai²)

oˈshiˈm·u おしむ (惜しむ) *vt.* (o-
shim·i-; oshim·a-; oshiñ-de C)
1 grudge; spare:
roo o oshimu (労を惜しむ) *grudge*
pains / *Kare wa musume no tame
ni hiyoo o oshimanakatta.* (彼は娘
のために費用を惜しまなかった) He
spared no expense for his
daughter.
2 regret:
*Muda ni sugoshita jikañ ga oshi-
mareru.* (むだに過ごした時間が惜しまれ
る) The time I wasted away *is
regretted*. / *Miñna ga kare no shi*

o oshiñda. (みんなが彼の死を惜しんだ) Everybody *regretted* his death. 《⇨ oshii》

3 value; hold dear:
Wakamono wa motto inochi o oshimu beki da. (若者はもっと命を惜しむべきだ) Young people should *hold* life more *dearly*.

o⌐**shiroi** おしろい (白粉) *n.* face powder:
kao ni oshiroi o nuru (顔に白粉を塗る) put *powder* on one's face.

o⌐**shitsuke**⌐**ru** おしつける (押し付ける) *vt.* (-tsuke-te ▽) **1** push against; press against; thrust:
Kanojo wa jibuñ no hoo o kodomo no hoo ni oshitsuketa. (彼女は自分のほおを子どものほおに押しつけた) She *pressed* her cheek against her child's cheek.

2 force (an unwelcome job) onto:
Kare wa muzukashii shigoto wa hito ni oshitsukeru. (彼は難しい仕事は人に押つける) He *forces* difficult jobs onto others. / *Kanojo wa pii-tee-ee no yakuiñ o oshitsukerareta.* (彼女は PTA の役員を押しつけられた) She *was forced* into being a PTA official.

o⌐**shiyose**⌐**ru** おしよせる (押し寄せる) *vi.* (-yose-te ▽) crowd; throng; surge:
Oozee no hito ga shiñ-kyuujoo ni oshiyoseta. (大勢の人が新球場に押し寄せた) Many people *crowded* into the new ballpark. / *Ooki-na nami ga oshiyosete kita.* (大きな波が押し寄せて来た) Great waves *surged* toward us.

o⌐**shoku** おしょく (汚職) *n.* corruption; graft; bribery:
Oshoku-jikeñ wa ato o tatanai. (汚職事件は後を絶たない) There is no end to the *corruption* cases.

o-⌐**shoosui** おしょうすい (お小水) *n.* urine. ★ A common euphemism used in hospitals. 《⇨ shoobeñ》

o⌐**so·i** おそい (遅い) *a.* (-ku) **1** (of time) late:
Kinoo no yoru wa osoku nema-shita. (きのうの夜は遅く寝ました) I went to bed *late* last night. / *"Suzuki-sañ osoi desu ne."* (「鈴木さん遅いですね」) "Mr. Suzuki is *late*, isn't he?" / *Kotoshi wa haru ga osoi.* (今年は春が遅い) Spring is *late* in coming this year. / *Aya-matte mo, moo osoi.* (謝っても, もう遅い) It is too *late* to apologize. 《↔ hayai¹》

2 (of motion) slow:
Watashi wa taberu no ga osoi. (私は食べるのが遅い) I am a *slow* eater. / *Ano yakusho wa taioo ga osoi.* (あの役所は対応が遅い) They are *slow* at that government office. 《↔ hayai¹》

o⌐**sonae** おそなえ (お供え) *n.* **1** offering:
osonae-mono o suru (お供え物をする) make a *votive offering*.
2 rice-cake offering. 《⇨ kagami-mochi (photo)》

osonae suru (～する) *vt.* offer:
butsudañ ni hana o osonae suru (仏壇に花をお供えする) *offer* flowers at a Buddhist family altar.

o⌐**so**⌐**raku** おそらく (恐らく) *adv.* perhaps; probably; possibly; likely:
Ashita wa osoraku ame deshoo. (あしたはおそらく雨でしょう) It will *probably* rain tomorrow. / *Kare wa osoraku konai deshoo.* (彼はおそらく来ないでしょう) He is not *likely* to come. / *Kanojo wa osoraku sono jijitsu o shitte iru deshoo.* (彼女はおそらくその事実を知っているでしょう) She *probably* knows the fact. 《⇨ tabuñ; tashika》

o⌐**sore**⌐¹ おそれ (虞れ) *n.* **1** fear:
Kyoo wa ame no osore wa arima-señ. (きょうは雨のおそれはありません) There is no *fear* of rain today.
2 possibility; likelihood:

Sono jikkeñ wa shippai suru oso-re ga arimasu. (その実験は失敗するおそれがあります) The experiment *is likely* to fail.

o⌐sore[12] おそれ (恐れ) *n.* terror; horror; dread:
Kodomo-tachi wa sono inu o mite, osore o kañjita. (子どもたちはその犬を見て, 恐れを感じた) The children felt *frightened* when they saw the dog. (⇨ osoreru)

o⌐so⌐reirimasu おそれいります (恐れ入ります) (*humble*) thank you very much:
O-kokorozukai osoreirimasu. (お心づかい恐れ入ります) Your kind consideration *is much appreciated.*

osoreirimasu ga (〜が) excuse me, but: *Osoreirimasu ga eki e iku michi o oshiete itadakemasu ka?* (恐れ入りますが駅へ行く道を教えていただけますか) *Excuse me, but* would you be kind enough to tell me the way to the station? / *Oso-reirimasu ga mado o shimete ita-dakemaseñ ka?* (恐れ入りますが窓を閉めていただけませんか) *Excuse me, but* would you mind closing the window?

o⌐sore⌐ru おそれる (恐れる) *vi.* (osore-te Ⅴ) fear; dread; be afraid; be frightened:
Wareware wa nanigoto mo osore-maseñ. (われわれは何事も恐れません) We *fear nothing* at all. / *Kikeñ o osorete ite wa, sono shigoto wa dekimaseñ.* (危険を恐れていては, その仕事はできません) If you *fear* the danger, you will be unable to do the job. / *Kare wa chichi-oya o osorete ita.* (彼は父親を恐れていた) He *was in fear* of his father. (⇨ osore²; osoroshii)

o⌐soroshi⌐i おそろしい (恐ろしい) *a.* (-ku) fearful; terrible; horrible:
Kiñjo de osoroshii satsujiñ-jikeñ ga atta. (近所で恐ろしい殺人事件があった) There was a *terrible* murder

in my neighborhood. / *Saikiñ hikooki ni noru no ga* osoroshiku *narimashita.* (最近飛行機に乗るのが恐ろしくなりました) I have recently become *frightened* of flying. (⇨ osoreru; kowai)

o⌐soro⌐shiku おそろしく (恐ろしく) *adv.* very; awfully; terribly:
Kyoo wa osoroshiku *samui hi desu ne.* (きょうはおそろしく寒い日ですね) Today is a *terribly* cold day, isn't it?

o⌐so⌐u おそう (襲う) *vt.* (oso·i-; osow·a-; osot-te Ⓒ) 1 attack; assault; raid:
teki o haigo kara osou (敵を背後から襲う) *attack* an enemy from behind / *Sakuya josee ga sono kooeñ de* osowaremashita. (昨夜女性がその公園で襲われました) A woman *was assaulted* in that park last night.
2 (of disaster, tragedy, etc.) hit; strike:
Taifuu ga Kañtoo chihoo o osotta. (台風が関東地方を襲った) A typhoon *struck* the Kanto district. / *Fukyoo ni osowarete, ooku no kaisha ga toosañ shita.* (不況に襲われて, 多くの会社が倒産した) *Hit by* the recession, many companies went bankrupt.

o⌐sowar·u おそわる (教わる) *vi.* (osowar·i-; osowar·a-; osowat-te Ⓒ) be taught; learn:
Watashi wa Tanaka señsee kara Nihoñgo o osowatte *imasu.* (私は田中先生から日本語を教わっています) I *am learning* Japanese from Miss Tanaka. (↔ oshieru)

o⌐ssha⌐r·u おっしゃる (仰る) *vt.* (ossha·i-; osshar·a-; osshat-te Ⓒ) say: ★ Honorific equivalent of '*iu.*'
Nañ to osshaimashita ka? (何とおっしゃいましたか) What was it you *said?* / *Anata no ossharu toori desu.* (あなたのおっしゃる通りです) It is

just as you *say*.

o⌈s·u⌉¹ おす (押す) *vt.* (osh·i-; o-s·a-; osh·i·te Ⓒ) **1** push; press; shove; thrust:
Kono botañ o osu to beru ga narimasu. (このボタンを押すとベルが鳴ります) If you *press* this button, the bell rings. / *Ushiro kara osanai de kudasai.* (後ろから押さないでください) *Do not push* from behind.
2 stamp; seal:
Fuutoo ni jibuñ no namae o hañ de oshita. (封筒に自分の名前を判で押した) I *stamped* my name onto the envelope. / *Koko ni hañ o oshite kudasai.* (ここに判を押してください) Please *affix* your seal here.
3 overwhelm:
Watashi-tachi wa kazu no ue de kare-ra ni osarete ita. (私たちは数の上で彼らに押されていた) We *were* numerically *overwhelmed* by them.

o⌈su⌉¹² おす (雄) *n.* male; he:
osu *no saru* (雄の猿) a *male* monkey / osu-neko (雄猫) a *tomcat.* 《↔ mesu》

o⌈tagaisama⌉ おたがいさま (お互い様) being in the same circumstances:
Kyuuryoo ga yasui no wa otagaisama da. (給料が安いのはお互いさまだ) You are not the only person who is poorly paid. *I am in the same boat.*

o⌈taku⌉ おたく (お宅) *n.* **1** someone else's house: ★ Usually refers to the house of the listener.
Asu o-taku ni ukagaimasu. (あすお宅に伺います) I'll visit *your house* tomorrow. / *Moshi moshi, Yamada-sañ no o-taku desu ka?* (*over the telephone*) (もしもし、山田さんのお宅ですか) Hello, is this Mr. Yamada's *home?*
2 you: ★ Polite equivalent of '*anata.*'
Kono kabañ wa o-taku no mono desu ka? (このかばんはお宅のものですか)

Is this bag *yours*? / *O-taku no go-shoobai wa?* (お宅のご商売は) What business are *you* in?

o-⌈tazune⌉¹ おたずね (お尋ね) *n.* (*polite*) question; inquiry.
o-tazune suru (〜する) *vt.* ask; inquire; question: O-tazune shitai *koto ga aru ñ desu ga, yoroshii desu ka?* (お尋ねしたいことがあるんですが、よろしいですか) There is something I would like to *ask* you. Would that be all right?

o-⌈tazune⌉² おたずね (お訪ね) *n.* (*polite*) visit.
o-tazune suru (〜する) *vt.* pay a visit: *Ichido otaku o* o-tazune shite *mo yoroshii desu ka?* (一度お宅をお訪ねしてもよろしいですか) May I *call on* you at home sometime? / *Kinoo* o-tazune shimashita *ga o-rusu deshita.* (きのうお訪ねしましたがお留守でした) I *visited* your house yesterday, but you were not in.

o-⌈tea⌉rai おてあらい (お手洗い) *n.* (*polite*) toilet; lavatory: O-tearai *o kashite kudasai.* (お手洗いをかしてください) May I use the *toilet?* 《⇒ tearai; beñjo; toire》

O-TEARAI SIGN

o-⌈te⌉tsudai-sañ おてつだいさん (お手伝いさん) *n.* home help; housemaid.

o⌈to⌉¹ おと (音) *n.* sound; noise: oto *o tateru* (音をたてる) make a *noise* / *Soto de heñ na* oto *ga shita.* (外で変な音がした) I heard a strange *noise* outside. / *Sono* oto *wa tonari no heya kara kikoete kita.* (その音は隣の部屋から聞こえてきた) The *sounds* came from the next room. / *Terebi no* oto *o ookiku [chiisaku] shite kudasai.* (テレビの音を大

きく[小さく]してください) Please *turn up* [*down*] the TV.
oto o shiboru (〜を絞る) turn down (the radio, TV, etc.)

o「**togiba**」**nashi** おとぎばなし (お伽話) *n.* fairy tale; nursery tale. 《⇨ doowa》

o「**toko**」 おとこ (男) *n.* man; male: ★ Has no derogatory connotation like 'oñna.'
Ano otoko *no hito wa dare desu ka?* (あの男の人はだれですか) Who is that *man?* / *Kare wa koñjoo no aru* otoko *da.* (彼は根性のある男だ) He is a *man* with guts. 《↔ oñna》 《⇨ dañsee》

o「**toko**」**-no-ko** (男の子) *n.*
1 boy:
Watashi wa sono otoko-no-ko *ni eki e iku michi o kiita.* (私はその男の子に駅へ行く道を聞いた) I asked the *boy* the way to the station. 《↔ oñna-no-ko》
2 son:
Kare ni wa otoko-no-ko *ga hitori iru.* (彼には男の子が一人いる) He has one *son.* 《↔ oñna-no-ko》

o「**tokorashi**」**·i** おとこらしい (男らしい) *a.* (-ku) (*appreciative*) manly; masculine:
Otokorashikute *tanomoshii hito wa josee ni niñki ga aru.* (男らしくて頼もしい人は女性に人気がある) A *manly* and reliable man is popular with women. / Otokorashiku *sekiniñ o tottara doo da.* (男らしく責任をとったらどうだ) Why don't you take the responsibility *like a man?* 《↔ oñnarashii》《⇨ dañsee-teki》

o-「**tokui(-sañ)** おとくい(さん) (お得意(さん)) *n.* good customer:
Kanojo wa uchi no o-tokui-sañ *no hitori desu.* (彼女はうちのお得意さんの一人です) She is one of our *good customers.*

o「**tona** おとな (大人) *n.* grown-up; adult:

Otona *ni nattara, isha ni narimasu.* (おとなになったら, 医者になります) I am going to become a doctor when I *grow up.* / Otona *ichi-mai, kodomo ni-mai kudasai.* (*at a ticket office*) (おとな1枚, 子ども2枚下さい) One *adult* and two children, please. 《↔ kodomo》

o「**tonashi**」**·i** おとなしい (大人しい) *a.* (-ku) **1** (of a disposition) quiet; gentle; mild; meek; obedient; tame:
Kyoo wa kodomo-tachi ga otona-shii. (きょうは子どもたちがおとなしい) Today the children are very *quiet.* / *Kare wa* otonashiku *ryooshiñ no iu koto ni shitagatta.* (彼はおとなしく両親の言うことに従った) He *meekly* obeyed what his parents said. / Otonashiku *shi nasai.* (おとなしくしなさい) *Behave* yourself!
2 (of a color, a pattern) quiet; soft; sober:
otonashii *iro* (おとなしい色) a *quiet* color.

o-「**to**」**ochañ** おとうちゃん (お父ちゃん) *n.* father; dad. ★ Used chiefly by small children and often by adults in the Kansai area. 《↔ o-kaachañ》

o-「**to**」**osañ** おとうさん (お父さん) *n.* father; dad:
Kimi no o-toosañ *to boku wa dookyuusee da.* (君のお父さんとぼくは同級生だ) Your *father* and I were classmates. / *O-toosañ, kyoo no shiñbuñ wa doko?* (お父さん, きょうの新聞はどこ) *Dad,* where is today's paper? 《↔ o-kaasañ》《⇨ chichi》

o「**tooto**」 おとうと (弟) *n.* one's younger brother: ★ When referring to someone else's, 'otootosañ' is usually used.
Otooto-*sañ wa nañ-neñsee desu ka?* (弟さんは何年生ですか) What school grade is your *younger brother* in? / Otooto *wa kookoo ni-neñ desu.* (弟は高校二年です) My

younger brother is a second year high school student. 《↔ ani》 《⇨ kazoku (table)》

o「**toroe**」 おとろえ (衰え) *n.* decline; weakening; failing: *ashikoshi no* otoroe (足腰の衰え) the *decline* of one's bodily strength / *kiokuryoku no* otoroe (記憶力の衰え) the *failing* of one's memory. 《⇨ otoroeru》

o「**toroe**」**·ru** おとろえる (衰える) *vi.* (otoroe-te ⓥ) become weak; fail; decline: *Kare wa toshi de tairyoku ga* otoroete iru. (彼は年で体力が衰えている) He *is weak* because of age. / *Taifuu wa* otoroete kita. (台風は衰えてきた) The typhoon *has lost its force.* / *Kanojo no niñki wa shidai ni* otoroete imasu. (彼女の人気は次第に衰えています) Her popularity *is* gradually *declining.* 《⇨ otoroe》

o「**tor·u**」 おとる (劣る) *vi.* (otor·i-; otor·a-; otot-te ⓒ) be inferior; fall below: *Kono kamera wa kimi no kamera yori seenoo ga* ototte iru. (このカメラは君のカメラより性能が劣っている) This camera *is inferior* in efficiency to yours. / *Kare wa suugaku de wa dare ni mo* otorimaseñ. (彼は数学ではだれにも劣りません) In mathematics, he *is second to none.*

o「**toshimono**」 おとしもの (落とし物) *n.* lost article [property]; something dropped by mistake: *Ima* otoshimono *o sagashite iru tokoro desu.* (今落とし物を探しているところです) I am now looking for *what I lost.* / Otoshimono o shinai *yoo ni, ki o tsuke nasai.* (落とし物をしないように、気をつけなさい) Be careful *not to lose anything.* / otoshimono-*toriatsukaijo* (落とし物取扱所) a *lost-and-found* office.

o「**to**」**s·u** おとす (落とす) *vt.* (otosh·i-; otos·a-; otosh·i-te ⓒ) **1** drop:

Kare wa fooku o yuka ni otoshita. (彼はフォークを床に落とした) He *dropped* his fork on the floor. 《⇨ ochiru》

2 lose: *Saifu o doko de* otoshita *no ka wakarimaseñ.* (財布をどこで落としたのかわかりません) I do not know where I *lost* my purse.

3 reduce; lower: *supiido o* otosu (スピードを落とす) *reduce* speed / *koe o* otosu (声を落とす) *lower* one's voice. 《⇨ ochiru》

4 remove makeup; take out (stains, etc.): *Kanojo wa keshoo o* otoshita. (彼女は化粧を落とした) She *removed* her makeup. 《⇨ ochiru》

5 fail (an examinee): *Sono daigaku wa jukeñ-sha no hañsuu o* otoshita. (その大学は受験者の半数を落とした) The university *failed* half of the examinees. 《⇨ ochiru》

o「**toto**」**i** おととい (一昨日) *n.* the day before yesterday: ototoi *no yoru* (おとといの夜) the night *before last* / Ototoi *wa kanojo no tañjoobi datta.* (おとといは彼女の誕生日だった) *The day before yesterday* was her birthday. / *Watashi wa* ototoi *Nihoñ ni tsukimashita.* (私はおととい日本に着きました) I arrived in Japan *the day before yesterday.* 《⇨ kyoo (table)》

o「**to**」**toshi** おととし (一昨年) *n.* the year before last: Ototoshi *wa Oriñpikku no toshi deshita.* (おととしはオリンピックの年でした) *The year before last* was the year of the Olympics. / *Watashi no chichi wa* ototoshi *nakunarimashita.* (私の父はおととし亡くなりました) My father died *the year before last.* 《⇨ kotoshi (table)》

o「**tozure**」**·ru** おとずれる (訪れる) *vi.* (otozure-te ⓥ) visit; call: *Kinoo tomodachi no kaisha o* oto-

zureta. (きのう友だちの会社を訪れた)
Yesterday I *visited* my friend's
company.

o-「tsuri おつり (お釣り) *n.* change:
Gojuu-eñ no o-tsuri *desu.* (50 円のお
釣りです) Here is fifty yen *change.*
/ O-tsuri *wa totte oite kudasai.* (お
釣りはとっておいてください) Please
keep the *change.* (⇨ tsuri²)

o「tsu」uji おつうじ (お通じ) *n.*
= tsuuji.

o「tto おっと (夫) *n.* husband:
★ '*Otto*' refers either to one's
own husband, or is used as a generic term for husband. '*Shujiñ*'
is used only in the first sense.
Otto *wa kyooshi o shite imasu.* (夫
は教師をしています) My *husband* is a
teacher. / *Hokeñ-kiñ o meate ni
tsuma ga* otto *o korosu jikeñ ga
yoku aru.* (保険金を目当てに妻が夫を
殺す事件がよくある) There are quite
a number of cases in which
wives kill *husbands* for the
insurance money. (↔ tsuma)
(⇨ kazoku (table))

o・「u¹ おう (追う) *vt.* (o・i-; ow・a-;
ot-te C) **1** chase; go after:
Wareware wa sono otoko o otta
*ga tsukamaeru koto ga dekina-
katta.* (われわれはその男を追ったがつかま
えることができなかった) We *chased* the
man but could not catch him.
2 drive away:
Kare wa sono chii o owareta. (彼
はその地位を追われた) He *was driven*
from his position.

o・「u² おう (負う) *vt.* (o・i-; ow・a-;
ot-te C) **1** carry (a load) on one's
back:
Kare wa sono omoi ni o otte *aruita.* (彼はその重い荷を負って歩いた) He
walked *with* the heavy burden *on
his back.* (⇨ seou)
2 assume (responsibility):
Dare ga sono sekiniñ o ou *no desu
ka?* (だれがその責任を負うのですか)
Who is going to *assume* the re-

sponsibility?
3 get wounded [injured]; suffer
(an injury):
juushoo o ou (重傷を負う) *suffer*
severe injury / *soñgai o* ou (損害を
負う) *suffer* a loss.
4 owe:
Watashi wa kare ni ooku o otte
iru. (私は彼に多くを負っている) I *owe*
him a lot.

o-「wabi おわび (お詫び) *n.* (*polite*)
apology:
*Heñji ga okuremashita koto o ko-
koro kara o-wabi mooshiagemasu.*
(返事が遅れましたことを心からおわび申し
上げます) Please accept my sincere
apologies for the delay in answering your letter. (⇨ wabi)

o-「wañ おわん (お椀) *n.* = wañ¹.

o「wari おわり (終わり) *n.* end;
close:
*Kore de watashi no hanashi wa
owari desu.* (これで私の話は終わりで
す) This is the *end* of my story. /
Futari no naka mo kore de owari
deshoo. (二人の仲もこれで終わりでしょ
う) The relationship between the
couple will come to *end* because
of this. / *Nijus-seeki mo* owari *ni
chikazuite imasu.* (二十世紀も終わ
りに近づいています) The twentieth
century is drawing to a *close.*
(↔ hajime) (⇨ owaru)

o「war・u おわる (終わる) *vi.* (owa-
r・i-; owar・a-; owat-te C)
finish; end; be over:
Sooji wa moo sugu owarimasu.
(掃除はもうすぐ終わります) The clean-
ing will *finish* in a moment. /
Gakkoo ga owatte *kara hoñya ni
yotta.* (学校が終わってから本屋に寄っ
た) I dropped in at a bookstore
after school was over. / *Sono jikkeñ wa shippai ni* owatta. (その実
験は失敗に終わった) The experi-
ment *ended* in failure. / *Shikeñ
wa* owarimashita. (試験は終わりまし
た) The examination *is over.*

《⇨ oeru; owari)》

o⌐**ya**⌐ おや（親）*n.* parent(s):
Kare wa oya *no chuukoku ni shita-gawanakatta.*（彼は親の忠告に従わなかった）He didn't follow his *parents*' advice. / chichi-oya（父親）a *father* / haha-oya（母親）a *mother* / oya-*gaisha*（親会社）a *parent company.*《↔ ko》

o⌐**ya**´⌐ おや *int.* oh; oh dear; dear me; good heavens:
Oya´, are wa nañ no oto da?（おやっ、あれは何の音だ）*Oh!* What's that sound?

o⌐**yako** おやこ（親子）*n.* parent and child:
oyako *no aijoo*（親子の愛情）the affection between *parent and child* / oyako *no kizuna*（親子のきずな）the ties between *parent and child.*

o⌐**yakodoñ** おやこどん（親子どん）*n.* ⇨ doñburi.

o⌐**yaoya** おやおや *int.* well; oh; oh dear; good heavens: ★ Intensive equivalent of '*oya*¹.'
Oyaoya, mata zañgyoo desu ka?（おやおや、また残業ですか）*Well, well,* you are working overtime again? / *Oyaoya, kore wa odoroita.*（おやおや、これは驚いた）*Good heavens!* This is a big surprise.《⇨ oya¹》

o⌐**yasumi nasa**⌐**i** おやすみなさい（お休みなさい）Good night; Sleep well.

o⌐**ya**⌐**tsu** おやつ（お八つ）*n.* **1** coffee [tea] break:
Oyatsu ni shimashoo.（おやつにしましょう）Let's have a *coffee break.*
2 snack; refreshments:
Kodomo-tachi wa sañ-ji ni oyatsu *o tabeta.*（子どもたちは3時におやつを食べた）The children had a *snack* at three in the afternoon.

o⌐**yayubi** おやゆび（親指）*n.* thumb. ★ In Japanese, the thumb is considered one of the fingers.《⇨ yubi (illus.)》

o⌐**yobi** および（及び）*conj.* (formal) and; both...and...:
Shimee oyobi *juusho o kinyuu no koto.*（氏名および住所を記入のこと）Enter *both* name *and* address.《⇨ soshite; to²》

o⌐**yobos**⌐**u** およぼす（及ぼす）*vt.* (oyobosh·i-; oyobos·a-; oyobosh·i-te Ⓒ) exert (influence); cause (harm):
Kono yoo na eega wa seeshooneñ ni warui eekyoo o oyoboshimasu.（このような映画は青少年に悪い影響を及ぼします）This kind of film will *have* a bad influence on youth. / *Kono jikeñ ga ryookoku no kañkee ni* oyobosu *eekyoo wa ookii.*（この事件が両国の関係に及ぼす影響は大きい）This incident will *have* a great influence on relations between the two countries.《⇨ oyobu》

o⌐**yob**⌐**u** およぶ（及ぶ）*vi.* (oyob·i-; oyob·a-; oyoñ-de Ⓒ) **1** extend; spread; reach:
Kare no keñkyuu wa hiroi hañi ni oyoñde imasu.（彼の研究は広い範囲に及んでいます）His researches *extend* over a wide field. / *Kaimeñ no oseñ wa suu-juk-kiro ni mo* oyoñda.（海面の汚染は数10キロにも及んだ）The sea pollution *spread* over tens of kilometers.《⇨ oyobosu》
2 (of time) last:
Kare no shukuji wa sañjup-puñ ni mo oyoñda.（彼の祝辞は30分にも及んだ）His congratulatory address *lasted* all of thirty minutes.
3 match:
Suugaku de wa kare ni oyobu *mono wa imaseñ.*（数学では彼に及ぶ者はいません）There is no one who can *match* him in math.
4 (in the negative) do not need:
Anata wa kuru ni wa oyobimaseñ.（あなたは来るには及びません）You *don't need* to come.

o⌈yo⌉g·u およぐ（泳ぐ）*vi.* (oyog·i-; oyog·a-; oyo·i-de Ⓒ) **1** swim: *Ike ni koi ga* oyoide iru.（池にこいが泳いでいる）Carp *are swimming* in the pond. / *Kare wa kawa o* oyoide watatta.（彼は川を泳いで渡った）He *swam* across the river.

o-⌈**yomesañ**⌉ およめさん（お嫁さん）*n.* bride. 《⇨ yome》

o⌈**yoso**⌉ およそ（凡そ）*adv.* **1** about; nearly: *Kañkyaku wa* oyoso *gomañ-niñ datta.*（観客はおよそ5万人だった）The number of spectators was *about* 50,000.

2 (with a negative) quite; entirely: *Soñna koto o shite mo* oyoso *imi ga arimaseñ.*（そんなことをしてもおよそ意味がありません）Even if you did that kind of thing, it would be *quite* meaningless. / *Kare wa* oyoso *buñgaku to wa eñ ga arimaseñ.*（彼はおよそ文学とは縁がありません）He has *absolutely* no knowledge of literature.

oyoso no (～の) approximate: *Oyoso no shusseki-sha no kazu o oshiete kudasai.*（およその出席者の数を教えてください）Please tell me the *approximate* number of people who will be present. / *Sore ni tsuite wa* oyoso no *keñtoo ga tsuite imasu.*（それについてはおよその見当がついています）I have an *approximate* idea about that.

o-⌈**yu**⌉ おゆ（お湯）*n.* hot water. 《⇨ yu》

o-⌈**zooni**⌉ おぞうに（お雑煮）*n.* = zooni.

P

-pa ぱ (羽) *suf.* counter for birds and rabbits. 《⇨ -wa》

pa⌐ama パーマ *n.* permanent wave; perm:
Kami ni paama *o kakete moratta.* (髪にパーマをかけてもらった) I *had* my hair *permed.*

pa⌐ase⌐nto パーセント *n.* percent; per cent:
*jup-*paasento *no waribiki* (10% の割り引き) a discount of ten *percent.* 《⇨ bu²; wari》

pa⌐atii パーティー *n.* **1** (of an occasion) party:
paatii *o hiraku* [*okonau*] (パーティーを開く[行う]) give a *party* / *Konban watashi-tachi wa* paatii *o shimasu.* (今晩私たちはパーティーをします) We are having a *party* tonight.
2 (of a group) party:
Kita Arupusu e mukatta paatii *wa soonan shita rashii.* (北アルプスへ向かったパーティーは遭難したらしい) The *party* which left for the Northern Japan Alps seems to have met with an accident. 《⇨ ikkoo¹》

pa⌐chinko パチンコ *n.* pinball (game); pachinko:
pachinko *o suru* (パチンコをする) play *pachinko* / pachinko-*ya* (パチンコ屋)

PACHINKO

a *pinball* house [parlor].

pa⌐chipachi ぱちぱち *adv.* (～ to) (the sound or action of crackling, clapping, etc.):
Kareki ga pachipachi (*to*) *moeta.* (枯れ木がぱちぱち(と)燃えた) The dry trees burned *with a crackling sound.* / *Jinja de ogamu toki wa* pachipachi *to ni-kai te o tataki-masu.* (神社で拝むときはぱちぱちと2回手をたたきます) We *clap* our hands together twice when we pray at a shrine.
pachipachi saseru (～させる) *vt.* blink: *Kanojo wa me o* pachi-pachi *saseta.* (彼女は目をぱちぱちさせた) She *blinked* her eyes.

-pai ぱい (杯) *suf.* counter for glassfuls or cupfuls. 《⇨ -hai》

pa⌐ipu パイプ *n.* **1** pipe:
Kono paipu *wa nani-ka ga tsu-matte iru.* (このパイプは何かが詰まっている) Something is stopping up this *pipe.*
2 pipe; cigarette holder:
Kare wa paipu *o fukashite ita.* (彼はパイプをふかしていた) He was smoking a *pipe.*
3 mediator:
Kare ga ryoosha no aida no paipu-*yaku o tsutometa.* (彼が両者の間のパイプ役をつとめた) He acted as the *mediator* between the two parties.

-paku ぱく (泊) *suf.* counter for overnight stays. 《⇨ -haku》

pa⌐n パン *n.* bread; toast; roll; bun:
pan *ik-kin* (パン1斤) a loaf of *bread* / pan *ichi-mai* (パン1枚) a slice of *bread.* / pan *o yaku* (パンを焼く) bake [toast] *bread.*

pa⌐nfure⌐tto パンフレット *n.* pamphlet; brochure; leaflet.

pa⌐ñjii パンジー *n.* pansy.

pa⌐ñku パンク *n.* flat tire; puncture:
Gasoriñ sutañdo de pañku *o naoshite moratta.* (ガソリンスタンドでパンクを直してもらった) I had the *flat tire* fixed at a service station.

pañku suru (~する) *vi.* have a flat tire; be punctured: *Kesa wa jiteñsha ga* pañku shite, *gakkoo ni okurete shimatta.* (今朝は自転車がパンクして、学校に遅れてしまった) This morning I ended up being late for school because my bicycle *had a puncture.*

pa⌐ñtii パンティー *n.* panties.

pa⌐norama パノラマ *n.* panorama.

pa⌐ñtii-suto⌐kkiñgu パンティーストッキング *n.* panty hose.

pa⌐ñtoma⌐imu パントマイム *n.* pantomime.

pa⌐ñtsu パンツ *n.* underpants; briefs; shorts: ★ Not usually used for '*trousers.*'
pañtsu *o haku* [*nugu*] (パンツをはく[脱ぐ]) put on [take off] *shorts.*

pa⌐ñya パンや (パン屋) *n.* bakery; baker.

pa⌐pa パパ *n.* dad; daddy; papa; father. 《⇨ mama²》

pa⌐rapara¹ ぱらぱら *adv.* (~ to)
1 (the sound or action of droplets or small objects falling or pages being turned):
Ame ga parapara (to) *futte kita.* (雨がぱらぱら(と)降って来た) The rain has started to *spatter down.* / *Kare wa sono atarashii zasshi o* parapara (to) *mekutta.* (彼はその新しい雑誌をぱらぱら(と)めくった) He *flipped* through the new magazine. / *Shio o niku ni* parapara to *furikaketa.* (塩を肉にぱらぱらと振りかけた) I *sprinkled* salt over the meat.

pa⌐rapara² ぱらぱら *adv.* (the state of being sparse):
Dono sharyoo mo jookyaku wa parapara *datta.* (どの車両も乗客はば

らぱらだった) There were *just a few* passengers on every train.

pa⌐sapasa¹ ぱさぱさ *adv.* (~ to; ~ suru) (the state of being dry and bland):
Kono pañ wa pasapasa shite iru. (このパンはぱさぱさしている) This bread *is all dried up.*

pa⌐sapasa² ぱさぱさ *adv.* dry and brittle:
Kami ga pasapasa *da.* (髪がぱさぱさだ) My hair is *dry and brittle.*

pa⌐sokoñ パソコン *n.* personal computer. ★ From '*paasonaru-koñpyuutaa.*'

pa⌐su パス *n.* pass:
Watashi wa sono yuueñchi no pasu *o motte imasu.* (私はその遊園地のパスを持っています) I have a *pass* for the amusement park.

pasu suru (~する) *vt., vi.* **1** succeed; pass: *shikeñ ni* pasu suru (試験にパスする) *pass* an exam.
2 make a pass (with a ball, etc.):
booru o pasu suru (ボールをパスする) *pass* a ball.
3 (in playing cards) pass.

pa⌐supo⌐oto パスポート *n.* passport:
pasupooto *o shiñsee suru* (パスポートを申請する) apply for a *passport* / pasupooto *o kooshiñ suru* (パスポートを更新する) renew one's *passport* / pasupooto *o koofu suru* (パスポートを交付する) issue a *passport* / Pasupooto *o haikeñ itashimasu.* (パスポートを拝見いたします) May I see your *passport?* / *Watashi no* pasupooto *wa raigetsu kiremasu.* (私のパスポートは来月切れます) My *passport* will expire next month. 《⇨ ryokeñ》

-patsu ぱつ (発) *suf.* counter used with bullets, shells and large fireworks. 《⇨ -hatsu²》

pa⌐tto ぱっと *adv.* suddenly; all at once; quickly:
Ii kañgae ga patto *ukañda.* (いい考えがぱっと浮かんだ) A great idea *sud-*

denly occurred to me. / *Akari ga* patto *tsuita*. (明かりがぱっとついた) A light *suddenly* came on. / *Hi ga* patto *moe-agatta*. (火がぱっと燃え上がった) The fire *suddenly* flared up. / *Sono uwasa wa* patto *hirogatta*. (そのうわさはぱっと広がった) The rumor spread *quickly*.

patto shinai (〜しない) unattractive; inconspicuous; dull: *Gakusee no toki no kare wa amari* patto shinakatta. (学生のときの彼はあまりぱっとしなかった) He *was* rather *dull* when he was a student.

pe¹chakucha ぺちゃくちゃ *adv.* (〜 to) (used to express the manner of chattering [prattling]): *Oñna-no-ko-tachi wa deñsha no naka de* pechakucha (to) *shabette ita*. (女の子たちは電車の中でぺちゃくちゃ(と)しゃべっていた) The girls *were chattering away* in the train.

pe⌐eji ページ (頁) *n.* page: peeji *o mekuru* (ページをめくる) turn a *page* / *Tekisuto no juuni* peeji *o hiraki nasai*. (テキストの 12 ページを開きなさい) Open your textbooks at *page* 12. / *Sono shashiñ wa sañ* peeji *ni dete imasu*. (その写真は 3 ページに出ています) The picture appears on *page* 3.

pe⌐epaa-te¹suto ペーパーテスト *n.* written test.

pe¹kopeko¹ ぺこぺこ *a.n.* (〜 na, ni) (the state of being hungry): *Onaka ga* pekopeko *da*. (おなかがぺこぺこだ) I am very *hungry*.

pe¹kopeko² ぺこぺこ *adv.* (〜 to; 〜 suru) bow humbly: ★ Used to express the action of bowing. pekopeko (*to*) *atama o sageru* (ぺこぺこ(と)頭を下げる) bow *servilely* / *Kare wa jooshi ni itsu-mo* pekopeko *shite iru*. (彼は上司にいつもぺこぺこしている) He *is* always *bowing and scraping* to his boss.

pe¹ñ ペン *n.* pen: ★ A general word referring to fountain pens, ballpoint pens, etc. peñ *de kaku* (ペンで書く) write with a *pen*. (⇨ mañneñhitsu)

-peñ ぺん (遍) *suf.* counter for the number of times. (⇨ -heñ)

pe¹ñchi ペンチ *n.* cutting pliers.

pe¹ñki ペンキ *n.* paint: *kabe ni* peñki *o nuru* (壁にペンキを塗る) *paint* a wall / *Teñjoo no* peñki *ga hagarete kita*. (天井のペンキがはがれてきた) The *paint* is coming off the ceiling. / *Peñki* nuritate. (*sign*) (ペンキ塗りたて) Wet *Paint*.

Peñki nuritate ni tsuki go-chuui negaimasu. (Wet paint, so take care.)

PEÑKI NURITATE SIGN

pe¹rapera¹ ぺらぺら *a.n.* (〜 na, ni) fluent; glib; voluble: *Kare wa Nihoñgo ga* perapera *desu*. (彼は日本語がぺらぺらです) His Japanese is *fluent*
— *adv.* (〜 to) talkatively; noisily: *Tsumaranai koto o* perapera (to) *shaberu na*. (つまらない事をぺらぺら(と)しゃべるな) Do not *prattle on* about trifling matters. (⇨ berabera)

pe¹rapera² ぺらぺら *a.n.* (〜 na/ no, ni) (of paper, board, etc.) thin; flimsy: *Kono biñseñ wa* perapera *da*. (この便せんはぺらぺらだ) This letter paper is very *thin*.

pe¹resutoro¹ika ペレストロイカ *n.* perestroika.

pi⌐ano ピアノ *n.* piano: piano *o hiku* (ピアノを弾く) play the

piano / piano *ni awasete utau* (ピア
ノに合わせて歌う) sing to the *piano*.

pi˺chipichi ぴちぴち *adv.* (～ to;
～ suru) (the state of being
young, fresh and vigorous):
Sono shoojo wa pichipichi *(to)*
shite ita. (その少女はぴちぴち(と)してい
た) The girl was *young and fresh.*
/ *Ebi ga ami no naka de* pichipichi
(to) hanete ita. (えびが網の中でぴちぴ
ち(と)跳ねていた) The prawns in the
net *were jumping all around.*

pi˺i-kee-o˺o ピーケーオー *n.*
= PKO.

pi˺imañ ピーマン *n.* green pepper; pimento.

pi˺ipii ぴいぴい *adv.* (～ to; ～
suru) **1** (the song of birds):
Hayashi no naka de tori ga piipii
(to) naite iru. (林の中で鳥がぴいぴい
(と)鳴いている) Birds *are chirping* in
the woods.
2 (of a financial condition) badly
off; hard up:
Kare wa ima piipii *shite iru.* (彼は
今ぴいぴいしている) He *is short of*
money right now.

pi˺kapika[1] ぴかぴか *a.n.* (～ na/no,
ni) shining; glittering:
Kuruma o arattara, pikapika *ni*
natta. (車を洗ったら、ぴかぴかになった)
When I washed the car, it became *shiny.* / *Kare wa itsu-mo*
kutsu o pikapika *ni migaku.* (彼は
いつも靴をぴかぴかに磨く) He always
polishes his shoes until they
shine.

pi˺ka˺pika[2] ぴかぴか *adv.* (～ to)
(the state of glittering, twinkling,
etc.):
Kiñ-medaru ga hi o ukete pikapika hikatte ita. (金メダルが日を受けて
ピカピカ光っていた) The gold medal
was glittering in the sun. / *Ina-*
zuma ga tooku de pikapika to hikatta. (稲妻が遠くでピカピカと光った)
There was a flash of lightning in
the distance.

-piki ぴき (匹) *suf.* counter for
small animals, fish and insects.
《⇨ -hiki》

pi˺kunikku ピクニック *n.* picnic:
★ Used for a pleasure trip which
includes a picnic. Not used in
the sense of a meal out of doors.
Kinoo wa kazoku de pikunikku *ni*
ikimashita. (きのうは家族でピクニック
に行きました) Our family went on a
picnic yesterday.

pi˺kupiku ぴくぴく *adv.* (～ to;
～ suru) (the state of twitching):
Inu no hana ga pikupiku *(to) ugo-*
ita. (犬の鼻がぴくぴく(と)動いた) The
dog's nose *twitched.* / *Uki ga*
pikupiku *shite iru.* (浮きがぴくぴくして
いる) The float *is bobbing up and*
down.

pi˺ñ ピン *n.* pin; hairpin.

pi˺ñku ピンク *n.* pink:
piñku *no seetaa* (ピンクのセーター) a
pink sweater. 《⇨ momoiro》

> ┌─ **USAGE** ─┐
> Suggests something risqué,
> like 'blue' in English. *e.g.*
> piñku-*eega* (ピンク映画) a *porno-*
> *graphic* movie.

pi˺ñpoñ ピンポン *n.* ping-pong;
table tennis:
Watashi-tachi wa himatsubushi ni
piñpoñ *o shita.* (私たちはひまつぶしにピ
ンポンをした) We played *table tennis*
to kill time. 《⇨ takkyuu》

pi˺ñto ピント *n.* focus:
piñto *ga amai* [*zurete iru*] (ピントが
あまい[ずれている]) be out of *focus* /
Kono shashiñ wa piñto *ga atte iru*
[*inai*]. (この写真はピントが合っている[い
ない]) This picture is [not] in *fo-*
cus. / *Kono kamera wa* piñto *o*
awaseru no ga muzukashii. (このカ
メラはピントを合わせるのが難しい) This
camera is difficult to *focus.*
piñto-hazure (～外れ) be wide of
the mark: *Kare no iu koto wa*
piñto-hazure *da.* (彼の言うことはピン

ト外れだ) What he says *is off the point.* 《⇨ mato》

pi｢sutoru ピストル *n.* pistol; revolver; gun:
pisutoru *o hassha suru* (ピストルを発射する) fire a *pistol*.

pi｢ta｣ri ぴたり *adv.* (~ to)
1 closely; tightly:
Futari wa pitari *to kata o yoseatte suwatta.* (二人はぴたりと肩を寄せ合って座った) The two of them sat *closely* together, shoulder to shoulder. / *Mado o* pitari (to) *shime nasai.* (窓をぴたり(と)閉めなさい) Shut the window *tightly.*
2 suddenly; right away:
Sono kusuri o noñdara, itami ga pitari (to) *tomatta.* (その薬を飲んだら、痛みがぴたりと止まった) The pain *went right away* after I took the medicine.
3 exactly perfectly:
Yosoo ga pitari (to) *atatta.* (予想がぴたり(と)当たった) My forecast hit the mark *exactly.* / *Keesañ ga* pitari (to) *atta.* (計算がぴたり(と)合った) The calculation was *exactly* right.

pi｢tchaa ピッチャー *n.* pitcher.

pi｢tchi ピッチ *n.* pace; speed:
Shigoto no pitchi *o agenakereba naranai.* (仕事のピッチを上げなければならない) We have to speed up the *pace* of our work. / *Koosoo-biru ga kyuu*-pitchi *de keñsetsu sarete iru.* (高層ビルが急ピッチで建設されている) High-rise buildings are being built at a fast *pace.*

pi｢tta｣ri ぴったり *adv.* (~ no, to; ~ suru) **1** = pitari.
2 right:
Kono fuku wa anata ni pittari *desu.* (この服はあなたにぴったりです) These clothes are *just right* for you.

PKO *n.* abbreviation of 'Peace Keeping Operations' (国連平和維持活動 = *Kokureñ heewa iji*

katsudoo). ★ Usually appears as 'PKO' even within Japanese script.

-po ほ (歩) *suf.* counter for steps. 《⇨ -ho》

po｢kapoka ぽかぽか *adv.* (~ to; ~ suru) **1** (the state of being nice and warm):
Yooki ga pokapoka *shite ite kimochi ga ii.* (陽気がぽかぽかしていて気持ちがいい) The weather is *nice and warm.* / *Oñseñ ni haittara, shibaraku karada ga* pokapoka *shite ita.* (温泉に入ったら、しばらく体がぽかぽかしていた) After I had bathed in the hot spring, I felt *nice and warm* for quite a while.
2 (of beating) repeatedly:
Boku wa ani ni pokapoka (to) *nagurareta.* (ぼくは兄にぽかぽか(と)殴られた) I received a *rain of blows* from my older brother.

po｢ke｣tto ポケット *n.* pocket:
hañkachi o poketto *ni shimau* (ハンカチをポケットにしまう) put a handkerchief into one's *pocket* / poketto *kara techoo o dasu* (ポケットから手帳を出す) take a notebook from one's *pocket.*

po｢kka｣ri ぽっかり *adv.* (~ to)
1 (the state of floating):
Shiroi kumo ga sora ni pokkari (to) *ukañde iru.* (白い雲が空にぽっかり(と)浮かんでいる) There *is* a white cloud *suspended* in the sky.
2 (the state of being wide open):
Michi ni ana ga pokkari *aite ita.* (道に穴がぽっかり開いていた) There *was* a hole *gaping wide open* in the road.

-poñ ほん (本) *suf.* counter for long cylindrical objects. 《⇨ -hoñ》

po｢ñdo ポンド *n.* **1** pound sterling:
Poñdo wa ima ikura desu ka? (ポンドは今いくらですか) What's the exchange rate for the *pound* now? / *Poñdo ga neagari [nesagari] shita.*

（ポンドが値上がり[値下がり]した）The value of *pound* sterling has risen [fallen].

2 pound (unit of weight).

po¹ñpu ポンプ *n.* pump: poñpu de *mizu o* kumi-dasu（ポンプで水をくみ出す）*pump* water out.

-ppo¹i っぽい *suf.* (*a.*) (-ku) [attached to a noun, the continuative base of a verb, or the stem of an adjective] **1** something like; resembling; -ish: shiro-ppoi *fuku*（白っぽい服）*whitish* clothes / *Kare ni wa* kodomo-ppoi *tokoro ga aru.*（彼には子どもっぽいところがある）He has some *childish* points.

2 tending; looking: kiza-ppoi（きざっぽい）*affected* / shime-ppoi（湿っぽい）*dampish* / zoku-ppoi（俗っぽい）*vulgar* / okori-ppoi *seekaku*（怒りっぽい性格）an *irritable* disposition / yasu-ppoi *fuku*（安っぽい服）*cheap-looking* clothes. / *Niwa ga* hokori-ppoku *natta no de mizu o miata.*（庭がほこりっぽくなったので水をまいた）The garden became *dusty*, so I sprinkled it with water.

po¹sutaa ポスター *n.* poster; bill: posutaa *o haru* [*hagasu*]（ポスターをはる[はがす]）put up [take down] a *poster*.

po¹suto ポスト *n.* mailbox:

NEW-AND OLD-STYLE POSUTO

tegami o posuto *ni ireru*（手紙をポストに入れる）put a letter into a *mailbox*.

po¹tsupotsu ぽつぽつ *adv.* (～ to) **1** (the state of small drops falling): *Ame ga* potsupostu futte *kita.*（雨がぽつぽつ降ってきた）The rain started *splattering down in drops*.

2 (the state of things occurring sporadically): *Joohoo ga* potsupostu haitte kita.（情報がぽつぽつ入ってきた）The reports *trickled in*.

po¹tto ポット *n.* thermos [vacuum] bottle; teapot; coffee pot.

-puñ ぶん（分）*suf.* counter for minutes.《⇨ fuñ¹ (table)》

pu¹ñpuñ ぷんぷん *adv.* (～ to; ～ suru) **1** a strong smell: *Kono hana wa* puñpuñ (to) niou.（この花はぷんぷん（と）におう）This flower *gives off a strong scent*. / *Kanojo wa koosui o* puñpuñ (to) sasete ita.（彼女は香水をぷんぷん（と）させていた）She *smelt strongly* of perfume.

2 (the state of being angry): *Kare wa* okotte puñpuñ shite iru.（彼は怒ってぷんぷんしている）He *is absolutely furious*. / *Soñna koto de* puñpuñ suru na.（そんなことでぷんぷんするな）Don't *get angry* about such a thing.

pu¹ragu プラグ *n.* electric plug: *airoñ no* puragu o sashikomu（アイロンのプラグを差し込む）*plug in* the iron.

pu¹rañ プラン *n.* plan: purañ *o tateru*（プランを立てる）make a *plan* / *Natsu-yasumi no* purañ *wa dekimashita ka?*（夏休みのプランはできましたか）Have you worked out the *plans* for your summer vacation?《⇨ keekaku》

pu¹rasu プラス *n.* **1** plus: *Sañ* purasu *ni wa go desu.*（3 プラス 2 は 5 です）Three *plus* two makes

five. / purasu-*kigoo* (プラス記号) a *plus* sign.
2 advantage; gain; asset: *Sono hoohoo no* purasu *to mainasu o kañgaete mi nasai.* (その方法のプラスとマイナスを考えてみなさい) Think over the *advantages* and disadvantages of doing it that way. / *Kono koto wa wareware ni totte* purasu *ni naru deshoo.* (このことはわれわれにとってプラスになるでしょう) This is likely to become an *asset* to us. 《↔ mainasu》
purasu suru (～する) *vt.* add: *Sorezore no gookee ni go o* purasu *shite kudasai.* (それぞれの合計に5をプラスしてください) Please *add* five to each of the totals.
purasu mainasu (～マイナス) plus and minus: *Kore de* purasu *mainasu zero da.* (これでプラスマイナスゼロだ) This makes us *even.*

pu⌈rasuchi⌉kku プラスチック *n.* plastic. ★ Refers only to rigid substances; vinyl is called '*biniiru.*' 《⇨ biniiru (table)》 purasuchikku *no kappu* (プラスチックのカップ) a *plastic* cup.

pu⌈rattoho⌉omu プラットホーム *n.* railroad station platform: Purattohoomu *de deñsha o matta.* (プラットホームで電車を待った) I waited on the *platform* for the train. 《⇨ hoomu》

pu⌈re⌉zeñto プレゼント *n.* present; gift: *Kurisumasu* purezeñto (クリスマスプレゼント) a Christmas *present.*
purezeñto suru (～する) *vt.* give a present: *Watashi wa chichi no tañjoobi ni nekutai o* purezeñto *shita.* (私は父の誕生日にネクタイをプレゼントした) I *gave* my father a necktie *as a present* on his birthday. 《⇨ miyage; okurimono》

-puri ぷり (振り) *suf.* = -buri.

pu⌈riñto プリント *n.* **1** handout; copy; mimeographed copy: *kaigi-yoo no* puriñto *o kubaru* (会議用のプリントを配る) give out *handouts* for a conference.
puriñto suru (～する) *vt.* make a handout [copy]: *Señsee wa shikeñ moñdai o* puriñto *shita.* (先生は試験問題をプリントした) The teacher *made copies* of the exam questions.
2 (of a photograph) print.

pu⌈ripuri ぷりぷり *adv.* (～ to; ～ suru) (the state of being angry): *Otto ga gorufu ni bakari dekakeru to itte, kanojo wa* puripuri *shite ita.* (夫がゴルフにばかり出かけると言って,彼女はぷりぷりしていた) She *was very angry*, complaining that her husband was always going off to play golf.

pu⌉ro[1] プロ *n.* professional; pro: puro *ni naru* (プロになる) turn *professional* / pro-*yakyuu* (プロ野球) *professional* baseball / pro-*gorufaa* (プロゴルファー) a *professional* golfer. 《↔ ama》

pu⌉ro[2] プロ *n.* theatrical agency. ★ Originally from the shortened form of English, 'production.'

pu⌈rogu⌉ramu プログラム *n.* program: *oñgakukai no* puroguramu (音楽会のプログラム) a concert *program* / *Tsugi no* puroguramu *wa nañ desu ka?* (次のプログラムは何ですか) What is next on the *program?*

pu⌉uru プール *n.* swimming pool.

pyu⌉upyuu ぴゅうぴゅう *adv.* (～ to) (used to express a shrill sound): *Soto wa tsumetai kaze ga* pyuupyuu *(to) fuite ita.* (外は冷たい風がぴゅうぴゅう(と)吹いていた) The cold wind *was whistling* outside.

R

-ra ら（等）*suf.* **1** (used to form the plural of a noun referring to a person):

USAGE

Used with reference to equals or subordinates. '*-tachi*' is more common.

---

boku-ra (僕ら) *we*; *us* / kare-ra (彼ら) *they*; *them* / kodomo-ra (子どもら) *children*.
2 (used to form the plural of a pronoun referring to a thing): kore-ra (これら) *these* / sore-ra (それら) *those*.

ra¹ameñ ラーメン *n.* Chinese noodles. ★ One of the most popular foods in Japan. 《⇨ chuuka-soba; iñsutañto-raameñ》

RAAMEÑ

ra¹igetsu らいげつ（来月）*n.* next month:
Nyuugaku shikeñ wa raigetsu *no tsuitachi desu.*（入学試験は来月の一日です）The entrance examination is on the first of *next month.* / *Tanaka-sañ wa* raigetsu *Chuugoku e ikimasu.*（田中さんは来月中国へ行きます）Mrs.Tanaka is going to China *next month.* 《⇨ koñgetsu》

ra¹imu¹gi ライむぎ（ライ麦）*n.* rye. 《⇨ mugi (table)》

ra¹ineñ らいねん（来年）*n.* next year:
Kono hashi wa raineñ *no sañgatsu ni kañsee shimasu.*（この橋は来年の三月に完成します）This bridge will be completed in March *next year.* / *Kanojo wa* raineñ *daigaku o sotsugyoo shimasu.*（彼女は来年大学を卒業します）She is graduating from university *next year.* 《⇨ kotoshi (table)》

ra¹inichi らいにち（来日）*n.* visit to Japan:
Indo gaishoo no rainichi（インド外相の来日）the *visit* of the Indian Foreign Minister *to Japan.*
rainichi suru （〜する）*vi.* visit [come to] Japan: *Sono rokku kashu wa ku-gatsu ni* rainichi shimasu.（そのロック歌手は九月に来日します）That rock singer *is coming to Japan* in September.

ra¹ishuu らいしゅう（来週）*n.* next week:
Kaigi wa raishuu *no getsuyoo desu.*（会議は来週の月曜です）The meeting is on Monday of *next week.* / *Kare wa* raishuu *Okayama kara kaette kimasu.*（彼は来週岡山から帰って来ます）He returns from Okayama *next week.* 《⇨ shuu (table)》

ra¹isu ライス *n.* cooked [boiled] rice. ★ Refers to cooked rice served on Western plates. When referring to rice served in Japanese-style bowls, use the word '*gohañ.*' 《⇨ kome (table)》

ra¹itaa ライター *n.* cigarette lighter:
raitaa *de tabako ni hi o tsukeru* （ライターでたばこに火をつける）light a cigarette with a *lighter.*

ra｢jio ラジオ *n.* radio:
rajio o kakeru (ラジオをかける) play the *radio* / rajio o tsukeru [kesu] (ラジオをつける[消す]) turn on [off] the *radio* / rajio o kiku (ラジオを聞く) listen to the *radio* / Sono nyuusu wa rajio de kikimashita. (そのニュースはラジオで聞きました) I heard that news on the *radio*.

ra｢ke｣tto ラケット *n.* racket:
raketto de booru o utsu (ラケットでボールを打つ) hit a ball with a *racket*.

ra｢kkyoo らっきょう *n.* baker's garlic. ★ A kind of onion similar to a shallot. The pickled bulb is called '*rakkyoo no tsukemono*.'

RAKKYOO

ra｢ku｣ らく (楽) *n.* ease; comfort; relief:
Yoñjuu-neñ hataraita kara moo raku o shitai. (40年働いたからもう楽をしたい) I have been working for forty years, so I *want to take it easy* now.
—*a.n.* (～ na, ni) **1** comfortable; easy:
Doozo o-raku ni shite kudasai. (どうぞお楽にしてください) Please make yourself *comfortable*. / Kusuri o noñdara, raku ni narimashita. (薬を飲んだら、楽になりました) I felt more *comfortable* after taking the medicine. / Kanojo no seekatsu wa raku ja nai. (彼女の生活は楽じゃない) Her life is not *easy*.
2 simple; easy:
Motto raku na shigoto o shitai. (もっと楽な仕事をしたい) I want to get an *easier* job. / Kono nimotsu o

hakobu no wa raku desu. (この荷物を運ぶのは楽です) It is quite *easy* to carry this baggage. / Kare wa sono moñdai o raku ni toita. (彼はその問題を楽に解いた) He solved the problem *easily*.

ra｢kudai らくだい (落第) *n.* failure; flunking:
Kare wa kañtoku to shite wa rakudai da. (彼は監督としては落第だ) As the team's manager, he is a *failure*. / rakudai-see (落第生) a *failed* student / rakudai-teñ (落第点) a *failing* mark.
rakudai suru (～する) *vi.* fail; flunk; repeat the same grade in school: Sono gakusee wa suugaku no teñ ga warukute rakudai shita. (その学生は数学の点が悪くて落第した) The student *failed*, because his score in math was poor.

ra｢kugo らくご (落語) *n.* comic story. ★ Told by a professional raconteur and with a witty ending.

RAKUGO

ra｢kunoo らくのう (酪農) *n.* dairy farming.

ra｢kuseñ らくせん (落選) *n.* defeat in an election:
Kare wa rakuseñ o kakugo shite iru. (彼は落選を覚悟している) He is resigned to *defeat in the election*. 《↔ tooseñ》
rakuseñ suru (～する) *vt.* **1** be defeated: Koñdo no señkyo de

geñshoku no chiji ga rakuseñ shita. (今度の選挙で現職の知事が落選した) The incumbent governor *was not elected* in the recent election.

2 be rejected: *Kanojo no e wa* rakuseñ shita. (彼女の絵は落選した) Her painting *was rejected.*

rañ[1] らん (欄) *n.* column; space: *rañ ni namae o kakikomu* (欄に名前を書き込む) write one's name in the *allotted space* / *kookoku-*rañ (広告欄) the advertising *columns* / *toosho-*rañ (投書欄) the letters-to-the-editor *column.*

rañ[2] らん (蘭) *n.* orchid.

rañboo らんぼう (乱暴) *n.* violence; rudeness: *rañboo o hataraku* (乱暴を働く) use *violence.*

rañboo suru (～する) *vi.* **1** use violence; behave rudely: *Yowai mono ni* rañboo suru *no wa hikyoo desu.* (弱い者に乱暴するのはひきょうです) It is cowardly to *use violence* against weak people.

2 violate; rape: *josee ni* rañboo suru (女性に乱暴する) *rape* a woman.

— *a.n.* (～ na, ni) violent; rude; rough; reckless: rañboo *na kotoba* (乱暴な言葉) *rough* language / rañboo *na uñteñ* (乱暴な運転) *reckless* driving / *Ano ko wa* rañboo *da.* (あの子は乱暴だ) That child is *rude and rough.* / *Kono hako o* rañboo *ni atsukawanai de kudasai.* (この箱を乱暴に扱わないでください) Please *handle* this box *with due care.*

rañchi ランチ *n.* lunch: rañchi *o taberu* (ランチを食べる) eat *lunch.* (⇨ chuushoku)

rañpu[1] ランプ *n.* lamp: rañpu *o tsukeru [kesu]* (ランプをつける[消す]) turn on [off] a *lamp.*

rañpu[2] ランプ *n.* exit [entrance] ramp of an expressway.

rañshi らんし (卵子) *n.* ovum. (⇨ seeshi[1])

-rareru られる *infl. end.* [attached to the negative base of a vowel-stem verb and '*kuru,*' and itself inflected like a vowel-stem verb] (⇨ -reru)

1 (indicates the passive) be...-ed: *Kanojo wa señsee ni* homerareta. (彼女は先生に褒められた) She *was praised* by her teacher. / *Watashi wa isha ni tabako o* kiñjirarete imasu. (私は医者にたばこ禁じられています) I *am forbidden* by my doctor to smoke. / *Kare no añ ga kaigi de* mitomerareta. (彼の案が会議で認められた) His plan *was approved* at the meeting.

2 (indicates a sense of suffering, loss, etc.): ★ Usually used with reference to unfavorable occurrences.
Kitaku no tochuu de ame ni furareta. (帰宅の途中で雨に降られた) I *was caught* in the rain on my way home. / *Okyaku ni nagaku* irarete *meewaku datta.* (お客に長くいられて迷惑だった) I was annoyed because the visitor *stayed* long.

3 (indicates the potential) can: *Kono mi wa* taberaremaseñ. (この実は食べられません) You *cannot eat* this fruit. / *Ashita no kaigi ni wa* deraremasu *ka?* (あしたの会議には出られますか) *Can* you *attend* the meeting tomorrow?

4 (indicates the natural potential): ★ Used when something naturally or involuntarily comes to mind.
Chichi no byooki no koto ga añjirareru. (父の病気のことが案じられる) I *cannot help worrying* about my father's illness. / *Nani-ka kikeñ ga* kañjirareta. (何か危険が感じられた) I *felt* some danger.

5 (indicates the honorific): *Tanaka-sañ no kawari ni Yamada-*

sañ ga korareru (＝ o-ide ni naru) *soo desu.* (田中さんの代わりに山田さんが来られるそうです) I hear that Mr. Yamada will *come* in place of Mr. Yamada. / *Chuugoku ni wa itsu dekakeraremasu* (＝ o-ide ni narimasu) *ka?* (中国にはいつ出かけられますか) When *are* you *going* to China?

ra「shi」・i らしい *a.* (-ku) [follows a noun, adjective, adjectival noun, the dictionary form or the *ta*-form of a verb or the copula]
1 look like; seem: ★ Similar to '*yoo ni mieru.*'
Kono ike wa kanari fukai rashii. (この池はかなり深いらしい) This pond *seems* rather deep. / *Kanojo wa gakusee* rashiku *miemasu ga, moo kekkoñ shite imasu.* (彼女は学生らしく見えますが, もう結婚しています) She *looks like* a student, but in fact she is already married. / *Kono tegami wa Furañsu kara kita* rashii. (この手紙はフランスから来たらしい) This letter is *apparently* from France. / *Kare wa soko e itta koto ga aru* rashikatta. (彼はそこへ行ったことがあるらしかった) It *seemed* that he had been there.
2 they say; I hear: ★ Similar to '*soo da*' for reporting messages.
Kanojo wa byooki rashii. (彼女は病気らしい) *I hear* that she is sick. / *Terebi ni yoru to sakura ga saki-hajimeta* rashii. (テレビによると桜が咲き始めたらしい) According to the television, it *seems* that the cherry trees have started blossoming. / *Kare wa kaisha o yameru* rashii. (彼は会社を辞めるらしい) *They say* that he is leaving the company.

-rashi「i・i -らしい *suf.* (a.) (-ku) typical of; just like; befitting: ★ Added to a noun to make an adjective.
otoko-rashii *taido* (男らしい態度) a *manly* attitude / kodomo-rashii *kao* (子どもらしい顔) a *childish* face

/ *Soñna koto o suru nañte* kimi-rashiku *nai.* (そんなことをするなんて君らしくない) It is not *like you* to do such a thing. / *Kyoo wa hoñtoo ni* haru-rashii *teñki desu ne.* (きょうは本当に春らしい天気ですね) Today it is *real spring* weather, isn't it?

ra「sshu-a」waa ラッシュアワー *n.* rush hour:
Asa no rasshu-awaa *wa saketa hoo ga yoi.* (朝のラッシュアワーは避けたほうがよい) You had better avoid the morning *rush hour.*

re「e[1] れい (例) *n.* **1** example; instance:
Gutai-teki na ree *o ikutsu-ka agete kudasai.* (具体的な例をいくつか上げてください) Please give me some concrete *examples.*
2 case:
Kore wa mare na ree *desu.* (これはまれな例です) This is a rare *case.*
3 custom; habit; practice:
Soo suru no ga Nihoñ no ree *desu.* (そうするのが日本の例です) It is a Japanese *custom* to do so.

re「e[2] れい (礼) *n.* **1** thanks; gratitude:
ree *o noberu* (礼を述べる) express one's *thanks* / *Sassoku go-heñji o itadaki,* o-ree *mooshiagemasu.* (早速ご返事をいただき, お礼申し上げます) *Thank you very much* for your prompt reply. / *Kore wa hoñno* o-ree *no shirushi desu.* (これはほんのお礼のしるしです) This is just a token of my *gratitude.* 《⇨ o-ree》
2 reward; fee:
Watashi wa o-ree *ni ichimañ-eñ kare ni ageta.* (私はお礼に1万円彼にあげた) I gave him 10,000 yen as a *reward.*

re「e[3] れい (礼) *n.* bow; salute:
Seeto-tachi wa señsee ni ree *o shita.* (生徒たちは先生に礼をした) The pupils *bowed* to the teacher.

re「e[4] れい (零) *n.* zero; naught:
Shikeñ wa ree-teñ *datta.* (試験は0

点だった) I got *zero* on the test. / *Oñdo wa choodo* ree-*do desu.*(温度はちょうど零度です) The temperature is exactly *zero* degrees.

re⌐eboo れいぼう(冷房) *n.* air conditioning:
Kono deñsha ni wa reeboo *ga haitte imasu.* (この電車には冷房が入っています) This train has *air conditioning* in it. / *Kono heya wa* reeboo *ga kiki-sugite iru.* (この部屋は冷房がききすぎている) The *air conditioning* in this room is too strong.
reeboo suru (～する) *vt.* air-condition: *Kaigishitsu wa* reeboo shite *arimasu ka?* (会議室は冷房してありますか) *Is* the conference room *air-conditioned?* 《↔ dañboo》

re⌐ebuñ れいぶん(例文) *n.* example; illustrative sentence.

re⌐egai れいがい(例外) *n.* exception:
Kono baai wa reegai *desu.*(この場合は例外です) This case is an *exception.* / *Kaisha wa* reegai *o mitomenakatta.*(会社は例外を認めなかった) The company didn't recognize any *exceptions.*

re⌐egi れいぎ(礼儀) *n.* manners; courtesy; politeness:
Ano hito wa reegi *o shiranai.*(あの人は礼儀を知らない) He does not understand the meaning of *manners.* / *Reejoo wa dasu no ga* reegi *da.*(礼状は出すのが礼儀だ) It is a matter of *courtesy* to write a letter of thanks.

re⌐eka れいか(零下) *n.* below zero:
reeka *ni naru* (零下になる) drop *below zero* / reeka *juugo-do* (零下15度) fifteen degrees *below zero.*

re⌐ekiñ れいきん(礼金) *n.* reward; fee; thank-you money. ★ Money given to the landlord when renting an apartment or house. It is not refundable. 《⇨ shikikiñ;

yachiñ》

re⌐ekoku れいこく(冷酷) *a.n.* (～ na, ni) cruel; heartless; coldhearted:
reekoku *na kee-eesha* (冷酷な経営者) a *heartless* manager.

re⌐ekyaku れいきゃく(冷却) *n.* cooling; refrigeration:
reekyaku-ki (冷却器) a *cooler* / reekyaku *kikañ* (冷却期間) a *cooling-off* period.
reekyaku suru (～する) *vi., vt.* cool; chill; refrigerate: *mizu o* reekyaku suru (水を冷却する) *chill* water. (↔ kanetsu')

re⌐eñ-ko⌐oto レーンコート *n.* raincoat:
Kanojo wa reeñ-kooto *o kite ita.* (彼女はレーンコートを着ていた) She was wearing a *raincoat.* 《⇨ kooto'》

re⌐esee れいせい(冷静) *a.n.* (～ na, ni) calm; cool-headed:
reesee *na hañdañ* (冷静な判断) a *cool* judgment / reesee *ni koodoo suru* (冷静に行動する) act *calmly* / *Haha wa itsu-mo* reesee *desu.*(母はいつも冷静です) My mother is always *calm and composed.*

re⌐esu' レース *n.* race:
reesu *ni katsu* [*makeru*] (レースに勝つ[負ける]) win [lose] a *race.*

re⌐esu² レース *n.* lace:
reesu *o amu* (レースを編む) crochet *lace* / reesu *no kaateñ* (レースのカーテン) a *lace* curtain.

re⌐etañ れいたん(冷淡) *a.n.* (～ na, ni) cold; indifferent; coldhearted:
reetañ *na heñji* (冷淡な返事) a *cold* reply / *Kare wa watashi no shakkiñ no mooshikomi o* reetañ *ni kotowatta.* (彼は私の借金の申し込みを冷淡に断った) He *coldly* turned down my requests for a loan.

re⌐etoo れいとう(冷凍) *n.* freezing; refrigeration:
reetoo-*niku* (冷凍肉) *frozen* meat.

reetoo suru (〜する) *vt.* freeze; refrigerate: *Sakana wa* reetoo shite *hozoñ shimasu.* (魚は冷凍して保存します) They *freeze* the fish to preserve it.

re⌈eto⌉oko れいとうこ (冷凍庫) *n.* freezer. 《⇨ reezooko》

re⌈ezoo れいぞう (冷蔵) *n.* cold storage; refrigeration: reezoo-*soochi* (冷蔵装置) a *refrigeration* plant.

reezoo suru (〜する) *vt.* refrigerate: *Kono shokuhiñ wa* reezoo shite oite *kudasai.* (この食品は冷蔵しておいてください) Please *keep* this food *in cold storage*.

re⌈ezo⌉oko れいぞうこ (冷蔵庫) *n.* refrigerator; icebox: *bataa o* reezooko *ni shimau* (バターを冷蔵庫にしまう) keep the butter in the *refrigerator*. 《⇨ reetooko》

-reki れき (歴) *suf.* career; experience; history: *gaku*-reki (学歴) one's academic *career* / *shoku*-reki (職歴) one's working *experience* / *uñteñ*-reki (運転歴) a driver's *record* / *hikoo*-reki (飛行歴) one's *experience* of flying.

re⌈kishi れきし (歴史) *n.* history: *Daigaku de Nihoñ no* rekishi *o beñkyoo shite imasu.* (大学で日本の歴史を勉強しています) I am studying Japanese *history* at college.
★ '*Nihoñ no rekishi*' is often shortened to '*Nihoñ-shi.*'

re⌈kishi-teki れきしてき (歴史的) *a.n.* (〜 na, ni) historic: rekishi-teki *na jikeñ* (歴史的な事件) a *historic* event / *Kore wa* rekishi-teki *ni yuumee na o-tera desu.* (これは歴史的に有名なお寺です) This is a *historically* famous temple.
★ The Japanese equivalent to '*historical*' is '*rekishi-joo no.*' 《⇨ rekishi》

re⌈ko⌉odo レコード *n.* record; disk:

rekoodo *o kakeru* (レコードをかける) play a *record* / rekoodo *o kiku* (レコードを聞く) listen to a *record*.

re⌈kurie⌉eshoñ レクリエーション *n.* recreation: Rekurieeshoñ *ni haikiñgu ni itta.* (レクリエーションにハイキングに行った) We went hiking for *recreation*.

re⌈moñ レモン *n.* lemon. ★ In Japan the word suggests something fresh and pleasant.

re⌈ñai れんあい (恋愛) *n.* love: *Futari wa* reñai-chuu *desu.* (二人は恋愛中です) Those two *are in love*. / reñai-*shoosetsu* (恋愛小説) a *romantic* novel.

reñai suru (〜する) *vi.* fall in love: *Sono shoojo wa* reñai shita *koto ga nakatta.* (その少女は恋愛したことがなかった) The girl *had never been in love*.

re⌈ñga れんが (煉瓦) *n.* brick: reñga *o tsumu* (れんがを積む) lay *bricks*.

re⌈ñgoo れんごう (連合) *n.* coalition; alliance; union: *yatoo no* reñgoo (野党の連合) a *coalition* of the opposition parties / reñgoo-*koku* (連合国) the *Allied* Powers.

reñgoo suru (〜する) *vi., vt.* combine; ally; unite: *Heewa o mamoru tame ni sekai no kuni ga* reñgoo su beki desu. (平和を守るために世界の国が連合すべきです) The countries of the world *should join together* to preserve peace.

Re⌈ñgoo れんごう (連合) *n.* Japanese Trade Union Confederation; JTUC. ★ Shortened form of '*Nihoñ Roodookumiai Reñgookai*' (日本労働組合連合会).

re⌈ñjitsu れんじつ (連日) *adv.* (〜 no) every day; day after day: Reñjitsu *no ame de kawa no mizu ga fueta.* (連日の雨で川の水が増えた) Because of the *continual days* of rain, the river rose. / *Gekijoo wa*

reñjitsu *mañiñ desu.* (劇場は連日満員です) The theater is full *day after day.*
reñjitsu reñya (～連夜) day and night.

reˈñpoo れんぽう (連邦) *n.* federation; union:
reñpoo-*seefu* (連邦政府) a *federal* government.

reˈñraku れんらく (連絡) *n.* connection; contact:
Kare to no reñraku *wa toremashita ka?* (彼との連絡はとれましたか) *Could* you *get in touch with* him? / *Geñchi kara kuwashii* reñraku *ga arimashita.* (現地から詳しい連絡がありました) We received a detailed *report* from the scene. / *Kono deñsha wa orita ato, basu to no* reñraku *ga warui.* (この電車は降りたあと, バスとの連絡が悪い) After getting off this train, the *connection* with the bus is bad.
reñraku suru (～する) *vi., vt.* connect; contact; get in touch: *Eki ni tsuitara,* reñraku shite *kudasai.* (駅に着いたら, 連絡してください) Please *phone* me when you arrive at the station. / *Kono fune wa ressha to* reñraku shimasu *ka?* (この船は列車と連絡しますか) Does this boat *connect* with the train?

reˈñshuu れんしゅう (練習) *n.* practice; drill; exercise; training; rehearsal:
Kanojo wa piano no reñshuu *ni hageñde imasu.* (彼女はピアノの練習に励んでいます) She is working hard at her piano *practice.* / *Kyoo kateta no wa kibishii* reñshuu *no okage desu.* (きょう勝てたのは厳しい練習のおかげです) The fact that we won today was due to our hard *training.* / reñshuu-*jiai* (練習試合) a *practice* game / reñshuu-*moñdai* (練習問題) a *practice* exercise [drill].
reñshuu suru (～する) *vt.* prac-
tice; drill; train; rehearse: *Shiai ni katsu ni wa motto* reñshuu shinakereba *dame desu.* (試合に勝つにはもっと練習しなければだめです) In order to win the match, we *have to train harder.*

reˈñsoo れんそう (連想) *n.* association of ideas:
Kono kotoba wa reñsoo *ga yoku nai.* (この言葉は連想が良くない) This word does not have a pleasant *connotation.* / reñsoo-*geemu* (連想ゲーム) a *word association* game.
reñsoo suru (～する) *vt.* remind; bring to mind; associate: *Kono e o mite, nani o* reñsoo shimasu *ka?* (この絵を見て, 何を連想しますか) *What comes to mind* when you look at this picture?

reˈñtai-hoshooniñ れんたいほしょうにん (連帯保証人) *n.* surety; person who accepts responsibility for another.

reˈñtogeñ レントゲン *n.* X-rays; Roentgen rays:
reñtogeñ *shashiñ o toru* (レントゲン写真を撮る) take an *X-ray* photograph / *Kinoo* reñtogeñ *keñsa o uketa.* (きのうレントゲン検査を受けた) I had an *X-ray* examination yesterday.

reˈñzoku れんぞく (連続) *n.* continuation; succession; series:
Jikkeñ wa shippai no reñzoku *datta.* (実験は失敗の連続だった) Our experiments were a *succession* of failures. / *Kore de itsuka* reñzoku *no ame desu.* (これで5日連続の雨です) It has now rained for *five consecutive days.*
reñzoku suru (～する) *vi.* continue: *Satsujiñ jikeñ ga* reñzoku shite *okotta.* (殺人事件が連続して起こった) The murders occurred *in succession.*

reˈñzu レンズ *n.* lens:
totsu [*oo*] reñzu (凸[凹]レンズ) a convex [concave] *lens.*

re「po」oto レポート *n.* **1** term
paper; written report: ★ Students commonly call their term
papers '*repooto*.'
Repooto *wa getsuyoo made ni teeshutsu shimasu.*（レポートは月曜まで
に提出します）I will submit my
paper by Monday. 《⇨ roñbuñ》
2 news report:
Geñchi kara no repooto *ni yoreba,
taifuu wa sakumotsu ni ooki-na
higai o ataeta soo desu.*（現地からの
レポートによれば、台風は作物に大きな被
害を与えたそうです）According to
reports from the area, the typhoon did great damage to crops.
repooto suru（～する）*vt.* report;
cover: *Terebi no kisha ga jikeñ
geñba kara* repooto *shite ita.*（テレ
ビの記者が事件現場からレポートしてい
た）The TV correspondent *was
reporting* from the scene of the
occurrence.

-reru れる *infl. end.* [attached to
the negative base of a consonant-
stem verb, and itself inflected
like a vowel-stem verb. '*Suru*'
becomes '*sareru*.'] 《⇨ -rareru》
1 (indicates the passive) be...-ed:
Watashi wa inu ni te o kamareta.
（私は犬に手をかまれた）I *was bitten*
on the hand by a dog. / *Kare wa
kanojo no paatii ni* shootai sareta.
（彼は彼女のパーティーに招待された）He
got invited to her party. / *Watashi wa o-kane o* nusumareta.（私は
お金を盗まれた）I *had* my money
stolen. / *Shisoo wa kotoba ni yotte
hyoogeñ* sareru.（思想は言葉によって
表現される）Thoughts *are expressed*
by means of words. / *Inu no nakigoe de kodomo ga* okosareta.（犬
の鳴き声で子どもが起こされた）The
child *was awakened* by a dog's
barking. 《⇨ sareru》
2 (indicates a sense of suffering,
loss, etc.): ★ Usually used with
reference to unfavorable occur-

rences.
Otto ni shinarete, *kanojo wa mekkiri fuketa.*（夫に死なれて、彼女はめっ
きり老けた）She aged quickly after
her husband *died.* / *Yuube wa
akañboo ni* nakarete, *yoku nemurenakatta.*（夕べは赤ん坊に泣かれて、よ
く眠れなかった）I could not sleep
well last night because the baby
was crying.
3 (indicates the potential) can:
Kono saki wa ikaremaseñ.（この先
は行かれません）You *cannot go* any
further than this.
4 (indicates the natural potential): ★ Used when something
naturally or involuntarily comes
to mind.
*Koñdo no shiai de wa kare no ka-
tsuyaku ga* kitai sareru.（今度の試
合では彼の活躍が期待される）A re-
markable performance *is expected*
of him in the coming match. /
Kono keshiki o miru to kyokyoo ga
omoidasareru.（この景色を見ると故郷
が思い出される）Whenever I look at
this scenery I *am reminded* of my
home town.
5 (indicates the honorific):
Shachoo wa moo kitaku saremashita.（社長はもう帰宅されました）The
president *has* already *left* for
home. / *Sono kabañ wa doko de*
kawareta *no desu ka?*（そのかばんは
どこで買われたのですか）Where *did*
you *buy* that bag?

re「ssee れっせい（劣勢）*n.* inferiority; inferior position:
ressee *o bañkai suru*（劣勢を挽回す
る）rally from an *inferior position.*
— *a.n.* (～ na, ni) inferior:
Chikara de wa kare no hoo ga ressee *datta.*（力では彼のほうが劣勢だっ
た）He was *inferior* in strength.
《↔ yuusee》
re「ssha れっしゃ（列車）*n.* railroad
[railway] train: ★ Usually refers
to a long-distance train.

nobori [*kudari*] *ressha* (上り[下り] 列車) an up [a down] *train* / *Kono ressha wa itsu hassha shimasu ka?* (この列車はいつ発車しますか) When does this *train* leave? / *Saishuu no* ressha *ni maniatta.* (最終の列車に間に合った) I caught the last *train.* 《⇨ deñsha; kisha²》

re｜sutorañ レストラン *n.* restaurant:
resutorañ *de shokuji o suru* (レストランで食事をする) dine at a *restaurant.* 《⇨ shokudoo》

re｜tsu れつ (列) *n.* row; line; queue:
Nyuujookeñ o motomeru hito ga nagai retsu *o tsukutta.* (入場券を求める人が長い列をつくった) Those seeking tickets have formed a long *queue.* / Retsu *ni warikomanai de kudasai.* (列に割り込まないでください) Please don't break into the *line.* 《⇨ gyooretsu》

-retsu れつ (列) *suf.* counter for rows or columns:
*ichi-*retsu (1 列) one *row* / *ni-*retsu (2 列) two *rows* / *zeñ-*retsu (前列) the front *row* / *koo-*retsu (後列) the back *row* / *Yoko ni ichi-*retsu *ni narabi nasai.* (横に1列に並びなさい) Please get into one *line* across. / *Kootsuu juutai de kuruma wa ni-*retsu *ni natte, noronoro to susuñda.* (交通渋滞で車は2列になって, のろのろと進んだ) Because of the traffic jam, the vehicles slowly crawled forward in two *lane.*

re｜tteru レッテル *n.* 1 label:
'*gekiyaku*' *no* retteru *o biñ ni haru* (「劇薬」のレッテルをびんにはる) put a *label* of 'poison' on a bottle:
2 (*fig.*) label:
Kare wa kechi da to iu retteru *o hararete iru.* (彼はけちだというレッテルをはられている) He *is labeled* as a stingy man.

re｜ttoo¹ れっとう (列島) *n.* chain of islands; archipelago:

Nihoñ rettoo (日本列島) the Japanese *Archipelago.* 《⇨ guñtoo》

re｜ttoo² れっとう (劣等) *n.* inferiority; low grade:
rettoo-*hiñ* (劣等品) *inferior* articles / rettoo-*kañ* (劣等感) an *inferiority* complex / rettoo-*see* (劣等生) a *poor* student.

ri｜boñ リボン *n.* ribbon:
Kami no ke o riboñ *de ushiro ni musuñda.* (髪の毛をリボンで後ろに結んだ) I tied my hair back with a *ribbon.*

ri｜eki りえき (利益) *n.* 1 profit; gains:
Kabu o utte, juumañ-eñ no rieki *o eta.* (株を売って, 10万円の利益を得た) I sold the shares and made a *profit* of 100,000 yen. / *Rieki yori soñshitsu no hoo ga haruka ni ookikatta.* (利益より損失のほうがはるかに大きかった) The losses were much greater than the *gains.*
《↔ kessoñ》
2 benefit; good:
Kono torihiki ga otagai no rieki *ni naru koto o nozomimasu.* (この取引がお互いの利益になることを望みます) I hope this business will prove of mutual *benefit.*

ri｜juñ りじゅん (利潤) *n.* profit:
rijuñ *o tsuikyuu suru* (利潤を追求する) pursue *profits.*

ri｜ka りか (理科) *n.* 1 science; natural science:
rika *no jikañ* (理科の時間) a *science* class / rika *no shikeñ* (理科の試験) an examination in *science.*
2 the department of science:
Kare wa rika-kee *ni susuñda.* (彼は理科系に進んだ) He took the *science course.* 《⇨ buñka²》

ri｜kai りかい (理解) *n.* understanding; appreciation:
Sono señsee wa seeto ni rikai *ga arimasu.* (その先生は生徒に理解があります) That teacher has an *understanding* of his pupils. / *Kare no koodoo wa* rikai *ni kurushimu.* (彼

の行動は理解に苦しむ) His behavior *baffles* me. / rikai-*ryoku* (理解力) the ability to *understand*. 《↔ mu-rikai》

rikai suru (〜する) *vt.* understand; appreciate: *Kare wa watashi no iu koto o* rikai shite kureta. (彼は私の言うことを理解してくれた) He *understood* what I said. / *Kono buñshoo wa* rikai shi-nikui. (この文章は理解しにくい) This sentence *is difficult to understand*.

ri「**kishi** りきし (力士) *n.* sumo wrestler. 《⇨ sumoo》

ri「**koñ** りこん (離婚) *n.* divorce: rikoñ *tetsuzuki* (離婚手続き) *divorce* procedures.

　rikoñ suru (〜する) *vi.* get divorced: *Futari wa señgetsu* rikoñ shimashita. (二人は先月離婚しました) They *got divorced* last month. / *Kanojo wa otto to* rikoñ shita. (彼女は夫と離婚した) She *got a divorce* from her husband.

ri「**koo** りこう (利口) *a.n.* (〜 na, ni) clever; wise; smart: rikoo *na ko* (利口な子) a *clever* child / rikoo *na yarikata* (利口なやり方) a *clever* way of doing something / *Kono inu wa totemo* rikoo *desu.* (この犬はとても利口です) This dog is very *intelligent*. / Rikoo *na mono dake ga shusse suru to wa kagiranai.* (利口な者だけが出世するとは限らない) It does not necessarily follow that only *smart* people are promoted.

ri「**ku** りく (陸) *n.* land; shore: riku *ni sumu doobutsu* (陸に住む動物) an animal living on *land* / Riku *ga miete kita.* (陸が見えてきた) *Land* came into sight. 《↔ umi¹》

ri「**ku**「**guñ** りくぐん (陸軍) *n.* army. 《⇨ kaiguñ; kuuguñ》

ri「**kujoo** りくじょう (陸上) *n.* **1** land; shore: Rikujoo *o itta hoo ga añzeñ desu.* (陸上を行ったほうが安全です) It is safer to go by *land*. / rikujoo-*kiñmu* (陸上勤務) *shore* duty. 《↔ kaijoo²》

　2 = rikujoo-kyoogi.

ri「**kujoo-kyo**「**ogi** りくじょうきょうぎ (陸上競技) *n.* track and field; track-and-field events: rikujoo-kyoogi-*joo* (陸上競技場) an *athletic field*.

ri「**kutsu** りくつ (理屈) *n.* **1** reason; logic: *Kare no iu koto wa* rikutsu *ni atte iru.* (彼の言うことは理屈に合っている) What he says is in conformity with *logic*. / *Kono moñdai wa* rikutsu *de wa warikirenai.* (この問題は理屈では割り切れない) This matter cannot be explained by *reason*.

　2 argument: *Kare wa nañ ni de mo* rikutsu *o iu.* (彼は何にでも理屈を言う) He puts forth an *argument* about everything.

ri「**ñgo** りんご (林檎) *n.* apple.

ri「**ñji** りんじ (臨時) *n.* **1** special; extraordinary: *Kyoo wa* riñji *no shuunyuu ga atta.* (きょうは臨時の収入があった) Today I got some *unexpected* money. / riñji-*ressha* (臨時列車) a *special* train / riñji-*kyuugyoo* (臨時休業) an *unscheduled* holiday / riñji-*sookai* (臨時総会) an *extraordinary* general meeting.

　2 temporary; provisional: Riñji *no shigoto ga mitsukatta.* (臨時の仕事が見つかった) I got a *temporary* job. 《⇨ riñji ni》

ri「**ñjiñ** りんじん (隣人) *n.* one's neighbor; people in the neighborhood: Riñjiñ *to wa nakayoku yatte imasu.* (隣人とは仲よくやっています) I am getting along well with my *neighbors*. / *Kare wa* riñjiñ *ga dare da ka mo shiranai.* (彼は隣人がだれだかも知らない) He even does not know *who lives next-door*.

ri「ñji ni りんじに (臨時に) *adv.* temporarily; specially; provisionally: *Kare o* riñji ni *yatotta.* (彼を臨時に雇った) We employed him *temporarily.* 《⇨ riñji)

Ri「ñya¹-choo りんやちょう (林野庁) *n.* Forestry Agency: Riñya-choo *chookañ* (林野庁長官) the Director General of the *Forestry Agency.* 《⇨ choo⁴ (table)》

ri「ppa りっぱ (立派) *a.n.* (~ na, ni) 1 respectable; worthy; praiseworthy; honorable: rippa *na gyooseki* (りっぱな業績) *praiseworthy* achievements / *Sono toki no kare no koodoo wa* rippa *datta.* (そのときの彼の行動はりっぱだった) His behavior on that occasion was *highly commendable.*
2 wonderful; magnificent; splendid; excellent: Rippa *na biru desu ne.* (りっぱなビルですね) This is a *splendid* building, isn't it? / *Tanaka-sañ wa suiee no* rippa *na kiroku o nokoshimashita.* (田中さんは水泳のりっぱな記録を残しました) Mr. Tanaka established some *outstanding* swimming records. / *Kare wa* rippa *ni jibuñ no yakume o hatashita.* (彼はりっぱに自分の役目を果たした) He performed his duties *superbly.*

ri「ppoo¹ りっぽう (立方) *n.* cube: *Kono tañku ni wa mizu ga go-rippoo-meetoru hairimasu.* (このタンクには水が 5 立方メートル入ります) This tank holds five *cubic* meters of water. / rippoo-*koñ* (立方根) a *cube* root / rippoo-tai (立方体) a *cube.* 《↔ heehoo)

ri「ppoo² りっぽう (立法) *n.* law making; legislation: Rippoo-*kikañ wa kokkai desu.* (立法機関は国会です) The *law-making* organ is the Diet. / rippoo-fu (立法府) a *legislature.* 《⇨ sañkeñbuñritsu)

ri「reki りれき (履歴) *n.* one's per-

sonal history; one's career: *Kare wa doñna* rireki *no hito desu ka?* (彼はどんな履歴の人ですか) What kind of *background* does he have? 《⇨ keereki)

ri「re¹kisho りれきしょ (履歴書) *n.* personal history; curriculum vitae.

ri「riku りりく (離陸) *n.* take-off (of an airplane). ririku suru (~する) *vi.* take off: *Hikooki wa sañjip-puñ okurete* ririku shita. (飛行機は 30 分遅れて離陸した) The airplane *took off* thirty minutes behind schedule. 《↔ chakuriku)

ri「roñ りろん (理論) *n.* theory: riroñ *o jissai ni ooyoo suru* (理論を実際に応用する) apply *theory* to practice.

ri「see りせい (理性) *n.* reason: risee *o ushinau* (理性を失う) lose one's *reason.*

ri「shi りし (利子) *n.* interest: rishi *o shiharau* (利子を支払う) pay *interest* / *Tooza-yokiñ ni wa* rishi *ga tsukanai.* (当座預金には利子がつかない) A checking account yields no *interest.* / *Go-paaseñto no* rishi *de kane o karita.* (5% の利子で金を借りた) I borrowed money at five percent *interest.* 《↔ gañkiñ)

ri「soku りそく (利息) *n.* = rishi.

ri「soo りそう (理想) *n.* ideal: takai risoo *o idaku* (高い理想を抱く) have lofty *ideals* / *Kimi no* risoo *o jitsugeñ suru no wa muzukashii.* (君の理想を実現するのは難しい) It is difficult to realize your *ideals* / *Anata no* risoo *no otto to wa doñna hito desu ka?* (あなたの理想の夫とはどんな人ですか) What kind of person is your *ideal* of a husband?

ri「soo-teki りそうてき (理想的) *a.n.* (~ na, ni) ideal: *Shoojo wa* risoo-teki *na oñgaku-kyooiku o uketa.* (少女は理想的な音

楽教育を受けた) The girl received an *ideal* musical education. / *Kono basho wa teñtai-kañsoku ni risoo-teki da.* (この場所は天体観測に理想的だ) This spot is *ideal* for astronomical observations.

ri⌐sshiñ-shusse りっしんしゅっせ (立身出世) *n.* success in life: *Haha-oya wa musuko no* risshiñ-shusse *o yorokoñda.* (母親は息子の立身出世を喜んだ) The mother was delighted at her son's *success in life.* / risshiñ-shusse-shugi (立身出世主義) the *cult of success.*

risshiñ-shusse suru (〜する) *vi.* succeed in life: *Kare wa* risshiñ-shusse suru *koto dake o kañgaete iru.* (彼は立身出世することだけを考えている) He thinks of nothing but *getting ahead in life.* (⇨ shusse)

-ritsu りつ (率) *suf.* rate; percentage; proportion: *shitsugyoo*-ritsu (失業率) the unemployment *rate* / *toohyoo*-ritsu (投票率) the voter *turnout* / *keezai seechoo*-ritsu (経済成長率) the *rate* of economic growth. (⇨ wariai)

ri⌐ttaa リッター *n.* liter. ★ Often used when referring to gasoline. (⇨ rittoru)

ri⌐ttai りったい (立体) *n.* three-dimensional object; solid: rittai-*eega* (立体映画) a *three-dimensional* film / rittai-*oñkyoo* (立体音響) *stereophonic* sound.

ri⌐ttai-ko⌐osa (立体交差) *n.* two-level crossing; overpass system.

ri⌐ttai-teki りったいてき (立体的) *a.n.* (〜 na, ni) solid; three-dimensional.

ri⌐ttoru リットル (立) *n.* liter: *mizu ni*-rittoru (水2リットル) two *liters* of water. (⇨ rittaa)

ri⌐yoo りよう (利用) *n.* use; utilization: *kaku enerugii no heewa* riyoo (核

エネルギーの平和利用) the peaceful *use* of nuclear energy.

riyoo suru (〜する) *vt.* use; utilize; make use of; take advantage of: *Kono toshokañ wa dare de mo* riyoo suru *koto ga dekimasu.* (この図書館はだれでも利用することができます) Anybody can *use* this library. / *Kare wa yoka o yuukoo ni* riyoo shite iru. (彼は余暇を有効に利用している) He *makes full use of* his leisure time. / *Ano hito wa watashi o* riyoo shite iru *no da to kizuita.* (あの人は私を利用しているのだと気づいた) I became aware that he *was taking advantage of* me.

ri⌐yuu りゆう (理由) *n.* reason; cause: riyuu *o ageru* (理由を挙げる) give a *reason* / *Doo iu* riyuu *de tsutome o yameta ñ desu ka?* (どういう理由で勤めを辞めたんですか) What is your *reason* for quitting your job? / *Hañtai suru nani-ka tokubetsu no* riyuu *de mo aru ñ desu ka?* (反対する何か特別の理由でもあるんですか) Do you have any particular *reason* to oppose it? / *Kare ga okoru* riyuu *wa juubuñ ni aru.* (彼が怒る理由は十分にある) He has good *cause* to be angry.

ri⌐zumu リズム *n.* rhythm: *Sono kyoku no* rizumu *ni notte odotta.* (その曲のリズムにのって踊った) We danced to the *rhythm* of the music.

ro⌐bii ロビー *n.* lobby: *Hoteru no* robii *de o-ai shimashoo.* (ホテルのロビーでお会いしましょう) Let's meet in the *lobby* of the hotel.

ro⌐kka⌐kukee ろっかくけい (六角形) *n.* hexagon.

ro⌐kotsu ろこつ (露骨) *a.n.* (〜 na, ni) frank; candid; plain; open: rokotsu *na kotoba* (露骨な言葉) *plain* words / rokotsu *ni hyoogeñ suru* (露骨に表現する) express something *frankly* / *Kare wa* rokotsu *ni fumañ o arawashita.* (彼は露骨に不満を表した) He expressed his dissatisfaction *openly.*

ro⌈ku⌉ ろく (六) *n.* six: roku-*ji* (6 時) *six* o'clock / roku-bañme (六番目) the *sixth.* 《⇨ muttsu; suu² (table)》

ro⌈ku ni⌉ ろくに (碌に) *adv.* (with a negative) (not) well; (not) properly; hardly: *Kare wa* roku ni *kañgaezu ni, iitai koto o iu.* (彼はろくに考えずに, 言いたいことを言う) He says just what he wishes to, without thinking it over *properly.* / *Kyoo wa isogashikute,* roku ni *shokuji o shite imasen.* (きょうは忙しくて, ろくに食事をしていません) I have been so busy today that I haven't eaten *properly.* 《⇨ rokuroku》

ro⌈ku-gatsu⌉ ろくがつ (六月) *n.* June: Roku-gatsu *wa ame ga ooi.* (六月は雨が多い) We have a lot of rain in *June.* 《⇨ tsuki¹ (table)》

ro⌈kumaku⌉ ろくまく (肋膜) *n.* pleura.

ro⌈ku-na⌉ ろくな (碌な) *attrib.* (with a negative) (no) good: *Kono heñ ni wa* roku-na *shokudoo ga nai.* (この辺にはろくな食堂がない) There are no *good* restaurants around here. / *Kotoshi wa* roku-na koto *ga nakatta.* (今年はろくなことがなかった) *Nothing good* has happened to me this year. / *Uso o tsuku to* roku-na *niñgeñ ni narenai yo.* (うそをつくとろくな人間になれないよ) If you tell lies, you will turn out to be a *worthless* person.

ro⌈kuoñ⌉ ろくおん (録音) *n.* recording; transcription: *Kore wa* rokuoñ *ga yoku nai.* (これは録音が良くない) The *recording* on this is no good. / rokuoñ-*ki* (録音機) a *recording* machine.

rokuoñ suru (～する) *vt.* record;

tape: *Kono uta wa rajio kara* rokuoñ *shimashita.* (この歌はラジオから録音しました) I *recorded* this song from the radio.

ro⌈kuroku⌉ ろくろく *adv.* (with a negative) (not) well; hardly; scarcely: *Yuube wa* rokuroku *nenakatta.* (ゆうべはろくろく寝なかった) I slept *badly* last night. / *Kare wa koñgakki wa* rokuroku *beñkyoo shite inai.* (彼は今学期はろくろく勉強していない) He has *hardly* studied this semester.

-roñ ろん (論) *suf.* theory; essay; comment: kyooiku-roñ (教育論) educational *theory* / buñgaku-roñ (文学論) an *essay* on literature.

ro⌈ñbuñ⌉ ろんぶん (論文) *n.* essay; thesis; paper: *jiñshu-sabetsu ni kañsuru* roñbuñ (人種差別に関する論文) an *essay* on racial discrimination / hakase-roñbuñ (博士論文) a doctoral *dissertation.* 《⇨ repooto》

ro⌈ñji·ru⌉ ろんじる (論じる) *vt.* (roñji-te Ⓥ) discuss; argue; treat: *Watashi-tachi wa kore kara no seeji o* roñjita. (私たちはこれからの政治を論じた) We *discussed* future political affairs. / *Kono roñbuñ wa heewa-moñdai o* roñjite imasu. (この論文は平和問題を論じています) This essay *discusses* the problems of peace.

ro⌈ñri⌉ ろんり (論理) *n.* logic: *Kimi no* roñri *ni wa tsuite ikemaseñ.* (君の論理にはついていけません) I cannot follow your *logic.*

ro⌈ñri-teki⌉ ろんりてき (論理的) *a.n.* (～ na, ni) logical: *Kare wa* roñri-teki *na setsumee o shita.* (彼は論理的な説明をした) He gave a *logical* explanation.

ro⌈o⌉ ろう (労) *n.* labor; pains; trouble: *Kanojo wa kesshite* roo *o oshi-*

manai. (彼女は決して労を惜しまない) She never spares *pains.* / *Kaisha wa kare no naganeñ no roo ni mukuita.* (会社は彼の長年の労に報いた) The company rewarded him for his long years of *service.*

ro「odoo ろうどう (労働) *n.* (manual) labor; work: *Watashi-tachi wa ichinichi hachi-jikañ roodoo desu.* (私たちは1日8時間労働です) We *work* eight hours a day. / roodoo-*jikañ* [*jookeñ*] (労働時間[条件]) *working* hours [conditions].
 roodoo suru (～する) *vi.* labor; work: *Wareware wa* roodoo shi-te, *chiñgiñ o ete iru.* (われわれは労働して、賃金を得ている) We *do* our *work* and get wages.

Ro「odoo-da」ijiñ (労働大臣) *n.* Minister of Labor.

ro「odoo-ku」miai ろうどうくみあい (労働組合) *n.* labor union; trade union: roodoo-kumiai *o soshiki suru* (労働組合を組織する) organize a *labor union.* (⇨ kumiai)

ro「odo」osha ろうどうしゃ (労働者) *n.* laborer; worker.

Ro「odo」o-shoo ろうどうしょう (労働省) *n.* Ministry of Labor. (⇨ shoo¹ (table))

ro「ogo ろうご (老後) *n.* one's old age: *Roogo o tanoshiku sugoshitai.* (老後を楽しく過ごしたい) I want to live happily in *my old age.*

ro「ohi ろうひ (浪費) *n.* waste; extravagance: *Soñna hoñ o yomu no wa jikañ no roohi desu.* (そんな本を読むのは時間の浪費です) It is a *waste* of time to read such a book.
 roohi suru (～する) *vt.* waste: *Kare wa tsumaranai koto ni o-kane o roohi shita.* (彼はつまらないことにお金を浪費した) He *wasted* his money on trifles. (↔ setsuyaku)

ro「ojiñ ろうじん (老人) *n.* old people; aged man [woman]; the aged: roojiñ *ni seki o yuzuru* (老人に席を譲る) give one's seat to an *old man* / Roojiñ *wa itawaranakereba naranai.* (老人はいたわらなければならない) We must be kind to *old people.* (↔ wakamono)

ro「ojiñ-ho」omu ろうじんホーム (老人ホーム) *n.* home for old people; nursing home for the aged.

ro「oka ろうか (廊下) *n.* corridor; passage: *Rooka wa shizuka ni aruki nasai.* (廊下は静かに歩きなさい) Walk quietly along the *corridor.*

ro「oma」ji ローマじ (羅馬字) *n.* Roman letters; Roman alphabet: *Namae o roomaji de kaite kudasai.* (名前をローマ字で書いてください) Please write your name in *Roman letters.* (⇨ table (inside front cover))

ro「oryoku ろうりょく (労力) *n.* labor; effort; service: *Koñpyuutaa ga ooi-ni rooryoku o habuite kureru.* (コンピューターが大いに労力を省いてくれる) Computers save us a lot of *labor.* / *Rooryoku wa itsu de mo teekyoo shimasu.* (労力はいつでも提供します) I am ready to offer my *services* any time.

ro「oso」ku ろうそく (蠟燭) *n.* candle; taper: roosoku *o tsukeru* [*kesu*] (ろうそくをつける[消す]) light [put out] a *candle.*

Ro「shia ロシア (露西亜) *n.* Russia; the Russian Republic.

Ro「shiago ロシアご (ロシア語) *n.* Russian language; Russian.

Ro「shia」jiñ ロシアじん (ロシア人) *n.* Russian; the Russians.

Ro「shia-kyoowa」koku ロシアきょうわこく (ロシア共和国) *n.* Russian Federation.

ro⌈shutsu　ろしゅつ（露出）*n.*
1 outcropping:
iwa no roshutsu（岩の露出）an *outcropping* of rock.
2 exposure:
Kono shashiñ wa roshutsu *ga fusoku shite iru.*（この写真は露出が不足している）This picture is *underexposed.*
roshutsu suru（〜する）*vt.* expose; bare: *hada o* roshutsu *suru*（肌を露出する）*bare* one's body.

ru⌉i　るい（類）*n.* kind; sort.
《⇨ shurui》

ru⌈iji　るいじ（類似）*n.* similarity; likeness; resemblance:
ruiji-*hiñ*（類似品）an *imitation* / ruiji-*teñ*（類似点）a point of *similarity.*
ruiji suru（〜する）*vi.* be similar [alike]; resemble: *Kono futatsu no e wa yoku* ruiji *shite iru.*（この二つの絵はよく類似している）These two pictures *look very much alike.*
《⇨ niru²》

ru⌉su　るす（留守）*n.* absence:
Chichi wa rusu *desu.*（父は留守です）My father *is not at home* now. / *Ashita kara mikka-kañ ie o* rusu *ni shimasu.*（あしたから3日間家を留守にします）I *will be away* from home for three days from tomorrow. / Rusu *no aida, neko no sewa o tonari no okusañ ni tanoñda.*（留守の間，猫の世話を隣の奥さんに頼んだ）I asked the lady next door to look after my cat while I *was away.*

ru⌈subañ　（留守番）*n.* looking after the house during a person's absence:
Watashi ga rusubañ *o shimasu.*（私が留守番をします）I *will take care of* the house while you are out. / rusubañ-*deñwa*（留守番電話）a *telephone answering machine.*

ru⌉uru　ルール *n.* rule:
ruuru *o mamoru*（ルールを守る）ob-serve a *rule* / ruuru *ni shitagau*（ルールに従う）follow a *rule* / *Sore wa* ruuru *ihañ desu.*（それはルール違反です）That's against the *rules.*
《⇨ kisoku》

ru⌉uto　ルート *n.* **1** route; channel:
Kare wa betsu no ruuto *de Oosaka e itta.*（彼は別のルートで大阪へ行った）He went to Osaka by another *route.* / *Ima gaikoo* ruuto *o tsuujite kooshoo-chuu desu.*（いま外交ルートを通じて交渉中です）The negotiations are continuing through diplomatic *channels.*
2 (of mathematics) root.

rya⌉ku　りゃく（略）*n.* abbreviation; omission:
"Kokureñ" wa "Kokusai-reñgoo" no ryaku *desu.*（「国連」は「国際連合」の略です）"UN" is an *abbreviation* of "United Nations."
《⇨ shooryaku; tañshuku》

rya⌈kugo　りゃくご（略語）*n.* abbreviated word; abbreviation:
Kono ryakugo *wa doo iu imi desu ka?*（この略語はどういう意味ですか）What does this *abbreviation* stand for?

rya⌈ku·s·u　りゃくす（略す）*vt.* (ryakush·i-; ryakus·a-; ryakush·i-te Ⓒ) abbreviate:
Kokusai Deñshiñ Deñwa Kabushikigaisha wa ryakushite *kee-dii-dii to yobaremasu.*（国際電信電話株式会社は略してKDDと呼ばれます）The Kokusai Denshin Denwa Co., Ltd. is called KDD *for short.* / *Enu-etchi-kee wa Nihoñ Hoosoo Kyookai o* ryakushita *mono desu.*（NHKは日本放送協会を略したものです）NHK is an *abbreviation* of Nihon Hoso Kyokai.

ryo⌈hi　りょひ（旅費）*n.* traveling expenses.

ryo⌈kaku　りょかく（旅客）*n.* passenger; traveler. ★ Also pronounced '*ryokyaku.*'

ryo⌈ka⌉kuki りょかくき（旅客機）*n.*
passenger plane. ★ Also pronounced '*ryokakki.*'

ryo⌈kañ りょかん（旅館）*n.* Japanese inn:

─(CULTURE)─

The rooms have tatami floors, and the rate usually includes breakfast and dinner.

Kyooto de wa ryokañ *ni tomarimashita.*（京都では旅館に泊まりました）I put up at a *Japanese inn* in Kyoto.

RYOKAÑ

ryo⌈keñ りょけん（旅券）*n.* passport:
ryokeñ *o shiñsee suru*（旅券を申請する）apply for a *passport* / *Kono* ryokeñ *wa raigetsu kigeñ ga kiremasu.*（この旅券は来月期限が切れます）This *passport* expires next month. 《⇨ pasupooto》

ryo⌈koo りょこう（旅行）*n.* trip; journey; tour; travel:
Yamada-sañ wa kaigai ryokoo *ni dekakemashita.*（山田さんは海外旅行に出かけました）Mr. Yamada set out on an overseas *trip.* / *Kare wa itsu* ryokoo *kara kaerimasu ka?*（彼はいつ旅行から帰りますか）When will he return from his *journey?*
ryokoo suru（～する）*vi.* travel; make a trip: *Watashi wa kuruma de Nihoñ-juu achi-kochi* ryokoo

shimashita.（私は車で日本中あちこち旅行しました）I *traveled* all over Japan by car. / ryokoo-*añnai(sho)*（旅行案内（書））a guidebook for *travelers* / ryookoo-*añnaijo*（旅行案内所）a *tourist* bureau / ryokoo-*gyoosha*（旅行業者）a *travel* agent.

-ryoku りょく（力）*suf.* power:
sui-ryoku（水力）hydraulic *power* / *seeji*-ryoku（政治力）political *power.*

ryo⌈kucha りょくちゃ（緑茶）*n.* green tea. 《⇨ o-cha (table)》

ryo⌈kyaku りょきゃく（旅客）*n.* = ryokaku.

ryo⌈o⌉¹ りょう（量）*n.* **1** quantity; amount:
ryoo *ga masu [heru]*（量が増す[減る]）the *quantity* increases [decreases] / ryoo *ga ooi [sukunai]*（量が多い[少ない]）be large [small] in *quantity* / *Sekiyu no* ryoo *ni wa kagiri ga aru.*（石油の量には限りがある）There is a limit to the *amount* of oil. 《↔ shitsu》
2 volume:
Kootsuu no ryoo *ga sañ-neñ de ni-bai ni natta.*（交通の量が3年で2倍になった）The *volume* of traffic doubled in three years.

ryo⌈o⌉² りょう（寮）*n.* dormitory:
Musuko wa gakkoo no ryoo *ni imasu.*（息子は学校の寮にいます）My son lives in a school *dormitory.* / *Kono kaisha ni wa dokushiñ*-ryoo *ga arimasu.*（この会社には独身寮があります）This company has a *dormitory* for single people.

ryo⌈o⌉³ りょう（良）*n.* (of a grade rating) being good or satisfactory; B or C in schoolwork:
Suugaku wa ryoo *datta.*（数学は良だった）I got a *B* in mathematics. 《⇨ seeseki (table)》

ryo⌈o⌉⁴ りょう（猟）*n.* shooting; hunting:
ryoo *ni dekakeru*（猟に出かける）go *shooting [hunting]* / *Kono yama*

wa ryoo *ga kiñjirarete imasu.* (この山は猟が禁じられています) *Shooting* is not allowed on this mountain.

ryo⌐o⌐ りょう(漁) *n.* **1** fishing; fishery:
ryoo *ni iku* (漁に行く) go *fishing.*
2 catch:
Kyoo wa ryoo *ga sukunakatta.* (きょうは漁が少なかった) We had a poor *catch* today.

ryo⌐o- りょう(両) *pref.* both:
ryoo-*koku* (両国) *both* countries / ryoo-*niñ* (両人) *both* people.

-ryoo りょう(料) *suf.* charge; fee; rate:
deñwa-ryoo (電話料) a telephone *charge* / *jugyoo*-ryoo (授業料) a tuition *fee* / *chuusha*-ryoo (駐車料) a parking *fee* / *nyuujoo*-ryoo (入場料) an admission *fee* / *tesuu*-ryoo (手数料) a *commission.*
《⇨ -chiñ; -dai²》

ryo⌐oashi りょうあし(両足) *n.* both feet [legs]. 《⇨ ryoote》

ryo⌐odo りょうど(領土) *n.* territory; possession; domain:
hoppoo-ryoodo *o meguru kooshoo* (北方領土をめぐる交渉) negotiations about the Northern *Territories* / *Kono shima wa Nihoñ no* ryoodo *desu.* (この島は日本の領土です) This island is Japanese *territory.* / *Sono kuni wa moto Igirisu no* ryoodo *datta.* (その国はもとイギリスの領土だった) That country was formerly a British *possession.*

ryo⌐ogae りょうがえ(両替) *n.* money exchange:
Ryoogae no tesuuryoo wa ikura desu ka? (両替の手数料はいくらですか) How much is the commission on *exchange transactions*? / ryoo-gae-ki (両替機) a machine for changing bills and large-denomination coins into small change. 《⇨ photo (right)》

ryoogae suru (〜する) *vt.* exchange; change: *ichimañ-eñ*

RYOOGAE-KI

satsu o señ-eñ satsu ni ryoogae *suru* (一万円札を千円札に両替する) *change* a 10,000-yen bill to 1,000-yen bills / *Hoteru de mo doru o eñ ni* ryoogae *shite kuremasu.* (ホテルでもドルを円に両替してくれます) Even at hotels they will *change* dollars into yen for you.

ryo⌐ogawa りょうがわ(両側) *n.* both sides:
Kono michi no ryoogawa *wa chuusha kiñshi desu.* (この道の両側は駐車禁止です) Parking is prohibited on *both sides* of this road.
《⇨ katagawa》

ryo⌐ohashi りょうはし(両端) *n.* both ends:
Tsuna no ryoohashi *ni musubime o tsukutta.* (綱の両端に結び目を作った) I tied knots at *both ends* of the rope. 《↔ katahashi》

ryo⌐oho⌐o りょうほう(両方) *n.* both; both parties [sides]:
Ryoohoo kudasai. (両方下さい) Please give me *both.* / *Suzuki-sañ wa Chuugokugo to Doitsugo no* ryoohoo *ga hanasemasu.* (鈴木さんは中国語とドイツ語の両方が話せます) Miss Suzuki can speak *both* Chinese and German. / *Gichoo wa sañsee to hañtai,* ryoohoo *no ikeñ o kikanakereba naranai.* (議長は賛成と反対、両方の意見を聞かなければならない) The chairman must listen to *both* the opinions of

those in favor and those against. / *Kare wa jookañ gekañ, ryoohoo tomo yoñde shimatta.* (彼は上巻下巻, 両方とも読んでしまった) He read *both* Volume 1 and Volume 2. / *Watashi wa* ryoohoo *tomo hoshiku arimaseñ.* (私は両方とも欲しくありません) I do not want *either* of them. 《↔ katahoo》

ryoˈoji りょうじ (領事) *n.* consul. 《⇨ taishi (table)》

ryoˈojiˈkañ りょうじかん (領事館) *n.* consulate. 《⇨ taishikañ (table)》

ryoˈokai¹ りょうかい (了解) *n.* understanding; agreement; consent: *Ryoosha no aida ni wa añmoku no* ryookai *ga atta.* (両者の間には暗黙の了解があった) There was a tacit *understanding* between the two parties. / *Sono keñ ni tsuite wa ue no hito no* ryookai *o toranakereba narimaseñ.* (その件については上の人の了解をとらなければなりません) With regard to the matter, we have to obtain our superior's *consent.*
  ryookai suru (～する) *vt.* understand; consent: *Anata no ito wa* ryookai shimashita. (あなたの意図は了解しました) I *understood* your intention.

ryoˈokai² りょうかい (領海) *n.* territorial waters.

ryoˈokiñ りょうきん (料金) *n.* rate; charge; fee; fare: *Nimotsu no tsuika* ryookiñ *o harawanakereba naranakatta.* (荷物の追加料金を払わなければならなかった) I had to pay a supplementary baggage *charge.* / Ryookiñ *wa irimaseñ.* (料金はいりません) It is free of *charge.* / *Yuubiñ-*ryookiñ *ga raigetsu kara neagari shimasu.* (郵便料金が来月から値上がりします) Postal *rates* will go up next month. / *Oosaka made no* ryookiñ *wa ikura desu ka?* (大阪までの料金はいくらですか) How much is the *fare* to Osaka? /

ryookiñ-jo (料金所) a *tollgate.*

RYOOKIÑ-JO

ryoˈokoo りょうこう (良好) *a.n.* (～ na, ni) good; excellent; satisfactory: ryookoo *na keeka* (良好な経過) *satisfactory* progress / *Kotoshi no kome no shuukaku wa* ryookoo *deshita.* (今年の米の収穫は良好でした) The rice harvest this year was *excellent.* 《⇨ yoi¹》

ryoˈori りょうり (料理) *n.* cooking; cookery; cuisine; dish; food: ryoori *o dasu* (料理を出す) serve *food* / ryoori *o narau* (料理を習う) learn *cooking* / *Kanojo wa* ryoori *ga joozu desu.* (彼女は料理が上手です) She is good at *cooking.* / *Kono* ryoori *wa umai* [*mazui*]. (この料理はうまい[まずい]) This *food* tastes delicious [does not taste good]. / ryoori-*ya* (料理屋) a *Japanese restaurant.*
  ryoori suru (～する) *vt.* cook; prepare: *Kanojo wa watashi-tachi ni sakana o* ryoori shite kureta. (彼女は私たちに魚を料理してくれた) She *cooked* some fish for us.

ryoˈosañ りょうさん (量産) *n.* mass production: *Kono shoohiñ wa* ryoosañ *ga dekimaseñ.* (この商品は量産ができません) These goods cannot be *mass-produced.*
  ryoosañ suru (～する) *vt.* mass-produce: *Sono koojoo de wa yushutsu-yoo ni ootobai o* ryoosañ

suru *koto ni kimeta.* (その工場では輸出用にオートバイを量産することに決めた) At the factory, they decided to *mass-produce* motorbikes for export.

ryo¬osha りょうしゃ (両者) *n.* both of the two people; each other:
Ryoosha *wa sono moñdai o nesshiñ ni toogi shita.* (両者はその問題を熱心に討議した) *Both of them* discussed the problem in earnest. / Ryoosha *no setsumee ga kuichigatte ita.* (両者の説明が食い違っていた) Their accounts contradicted *each other.*

ryo¬oshi りょうし (漁師) *n.* fisherman.

ryo¬oshiñ[1] りょうしん (両親) *n.* one's parents:
Ryooshiñ *wa mada keñzai desu.* (両親はまだ健在です) My *parents* are still hale and hearty.

ryo¬oshiñ[2] りょうしん (良心) *n.* conscience:
Ryooshiñ *ni yamashii koto wa arimaseñ.* (良心にやましいことはありません) I have a clear *conscience.* / Kare *wa* ryooshiñ *ni itami o kañjite ita.* (彼は良心に痛みを感じていた) He felt a pang of *conscience.*

ryo¬oshu りょうしゅ (領主) *n.* feudal lord.

ryo⌐oshuusho りょうしゅうしょ (領収書) *n.* receipt:
Ryooshuusho *o moraemasu ka?* (領収書をもらえますか) May I have a *receipt,* please?

ryo⌐oshuushoo りょうしゅうしょう (領収証) *n.* voucher; receipt.
《⇨ photo (right)》

ryo⌐ote りょうて (両手) *n.* both hands; both arms:
Kare *wa* ryoote *o hirogete, watashi no iku michi o jama shita.* (彼は両手を広げて, 私の行く道をじゃました) He stood in my way with his *arms* stretched out. / Watashi *wa roopu o* ryoote *de tsukañda.* (私は

ロープを両手でつかんだ) I grasped the rope with *both hands.* 《⇨ katate; ryooashi》

RYOOSHUUSHOO

ryu⌐kkusa¬kku リュックサック *n.* rucksack:
ryukkusakku *o seou* (リュックサックを背負う) carry a *rucksack* on one's back.

ryu¬u りゅう (龍) *n.* dragon.

-ryuu りゅう (流) *suf.* **1** style; type; way:
Nihoñjiñ-ryuu *no kañgaekata* (日本人流の考え方) a Japanese *way* of thinking / jiko-ryuu (自己流) one's own *way* (of doing things).
2 class; rate; grade:
ichi-ryuu (一流) first *class* / ni-ryuu (二流) second *rate* / chuu-ryuu (中流) middle *grade* / joo-ryuu (上流) upper *class.*
3 flow; stream; current:
deñ-ryuu (電流) electric *current* / sui-ryuu (水流) a *stream* of water / hoñ-ryuu (本流) the main *course* of a river / shi-ryuu (支流) a *tributary.*

ryu⌐uchijoo りゅうちじょう (留置場) *n.* detention house; lockup:
ruuchijoo *ni irerareru* (留置場に入れられる) be locked up in a *jail.*

ryu⌐udo¬oshoku りゅうどうしょく (流動食) *n.* liquid food [diet]:
Watashi *wa byooiñ de* ryuudooshoku *o torasareta.* (私は病院で流動食をとらされた) I was put on a *liquid diet* in the hospital.

ryu⌐ugaku りゅうがく (留学) *n.*

studying abroad:
Musuko wa Doitsu ni ryuugaku-
chuu desu. (息子はドイツに留学で
す) My son is *studying* in Ger-
many.

ryuugaku suru (〜する) *vi.* study
abroad; go abroad for study:
*Watashi wa Supeiñgo o beñkyoo
suru tame ni Supeiñ ni* ryuugaku
suru *tsumori desu.* (私はスペイン語を
勉強するためにスペインに留学するつもりで
す) I intend to *go* to Spain *to*
study Spanish.

ryuᵣugaᵏkusee りゅうがくせい (留
学生) *n.* student studying
abroad; foreign student.

ryuᵣuhyoo りゅうひょう (流氷) *n.*
drift ice; ice floe.

ryuᵣukañ りゅうかん (流感) *n.* influenza; flu:
ryuukañ *ni kakaru* (流感にかかる)
catch *influenza.*

ryuᵣukoo りゅうこう (流行) *n.*
fashion; vogue; fad:
Ryuukoo wa sugu ni kawarimasu.
(流行はすぐに変わります) *Fashions*
soon change. / *Watashi-tachi wa*
ryuukoo *o oi-yasui.* (私たちは流行を
追いやすい) We are too apt to take
up *fashions.* / *Kono kata no booshi wa moo* ryuukoo-*okure desu.*
(この型の帽子はもう流行遅れです) This
style of hat is already out of
fashion. / ryuukoo-*ka* (流行歌) a
popular song.

ryuukoo suru (〜する) *vi.* come
into fashion; be in fashion; be
popular: *Mini-sukaato ga mata*
ryuukoo shite imasu. (ミニスカートが
また流行しています) Mini-skirts *have*
once again *come back into fashion.*
/ *Ima iñfurueñza ga* ryuukoo shite
imasu. (今インフルエンザが流行していま
す) The flu *is going around.*

ryuᵣuneñ りゅうねん (留年) *n.* remaining in the same class.

ryuuneñ suru (〜する) *vi.* repeat
the same class for another year:
*Kare wa shuushoku shinai de
ichi-neñ* ryuuneñ shita. (彼は就職し
ないで 1 年留年した) He did not get
a job and *stayed at the university*
for another year.

ryuᵣuniñ りゅうにん (留任) *n.* remaining in office.

ryuuniñ suru (〜する) *vi.* remain
in office: *Juuyaku wa zeñiñ*
ryuuniñ suru *koto ni kimatta.* (重
役は全員留任することに決まった) It
was decided that all the executives would *remain in office.*

S

sa¹ さ（差）*n.* difference; gap; margin:
Takushii de itte mo chikatetsu de itte mo taishite sa wa arimaseñ. (タクシーで行っても地下鉄で行ってもたいして差はありません) It makes little *difference* whether you go by taxi or by subway. / *Neñree no sa wa ki ni shite imaseñ.* (年令の差は気にしていません) I don't mind the age *gap.* / *Sono uma wa hana no sa de katta.* (その馬は鼻の差で勝った) The horse won the race *by a nose.*
《⇨ chigai》

sa² さ *p.* **1** (used when casually emphasizing one's thoughts or opinions):
Kyoo dekinakereba, ashita suru sa. (きょうできなければ, あしたするさ) If I can't do it today, *well* then, I'll do it tomorrow. / *Kitto kare kara reñraku ga aru sa.* (きっと彼から連絡があるさ) He will certainly get in touch with you. / *Akirameru yori shikata ga nai sa.* (あきらめるよりしかたがないさ) There is nothing left to do but give up.
2 (used to indicate a strong reaction):
Nani o baka na koto o itte iru no sa. (何をばかなことを言っているのさ) What nonsense you are talking! / *Nani sa, añna yatsu.* (何さ, あんなやつ) I'll have nothing to do with such a fellow.
3 (used after a phrase to hold the attention of the listener):
Kono aida karita hoñ sa, moo yoñjatta. (この間借りた本さ, もう読んじゃった) The book I borrowed from you the other day... *Well*, I've already read it. / *Tanaka-sañ to sa, Giñza de sa, eega michatta.*

(田中さんとさ, 銀座でさ, 映画見ちゃった) With Mr. Tanaka, in Ginza, I saw a film.
...to [tte] sa (...と[って]～) (used to report what others have said):
★ Sometimes used in a slighting manner.
Tanaka-sañ wa byooki na ñ da to [tte] sa. (田中さんは病気なんだと[って]さ) I've heard that Mr. Tanaka is sick. / *Kare, shikeñ wa zeñzeñ dekinakatta ñ da to [tte] sa.* (彼, 試験は全然できなかったんだと[って]さ) According to him, he just could not do the exam.

-sa さ *suf.* (*n.*) [added to the stem of an adjective or to an adjectival noun to form a noun]
atsu-sa (暑さ) *heat* / samu-sa (寒さ) *cold* / taka-sa (高さ) *height* / fuka-sa (深さ) *depth* / shiñsetsu-sa (親切さ) *kindness* / shoojiki-sa (正直さ) *honesty.*

sa¹ さあ *int.* now; here; well; come on:
Saa, hajimeyoo. (さあ, 始めよう) *Okay*, let's start. / *Saa, deñsha ga kita zo.* (さあ, 電車が来たぞ) *Well*, here comes the train. / *Saa, watashi ni wa yoku wakarimaseñ.* (さあ, 私にはよくわかりません) *Let me see.* I'm afraid I don't know.
《⇨ sate》

sa¹**abisu** サービス *n.* **1** service:
Kono ryokañ wa saabisu *ga yoi [warui].* (この旅館はサービスが良い[悪い]) The *service* at this Japanese inn is good [poor].
2 discount; no charge; extra:
★ Note this usage that differs from the original English meaning of the word.
Kore wa saabisu *nedañ desu.* (これ

はサービス値段です) This is a *special price*. / *Kono eñpitsu o* saabisu *ni agemasu*. (この鉛筆をサービスにあげます) I will throw in this pencil as an *extra*.

saabisu (o) suru (〜(を)する) *vi.*, *vt.* **1** give a service; attend to: *Kinoo wa katee* saabisu *o shimashita*. (きのうは家庭サービスをしました) I *devoted myself to looking after* my family yesterday.

2 make a discount; give away for nothing: *Hyaku-eñ* saabisu *itashimasu*. (100円サービスいたします) I will *give you a discount* of 100 yen. / *Kono shina o* saabisu *shimasu*. (この品をサービスします) I will *let you have this for nothing*.

sa⌈abisu⌉ryoo サービスりょう (サービス料) *n.* service charge: *Kono seekyuusho ni wa* saabisu-ryoo *ga fukumarete imasu ka?* (この請求書にはサービス料が含まれていますか) Is the *service charge* included in this bill?

sa⌈akuru サークル *n.* club: ★ From English, 'circle.' *eñgeki* saakuru *ni hairu* (演劇サークルに入る) join a dramatic *club* / saa-kuru-*katsudoo* (サークル活動) *club* activities (at college).

sa⌈baku さばく (砂漠) *n.* desert.

sa⌈bi⌉ さび (錆び) *n.* rust; tarnish: sabi *ga tsuku* (さびがつく) gather *rust* / sabi *o otosu* (さびを落とす) clean off *rust* / *Mi kara deta* sabi. (*saying*) (身から出たさび) You have to reap what you have sown.

sa⌈bi⌉·ru さびる (錆びる) *vi.* (sabi-te [V]) rust; get rusty: *Naifu ga* sabite shimatta. (ナイフがさびてしまった) My knife *has gotten rusty*.

sa⌈bishi⌉·i さびしい (寂しい・淋しい) *a.* (-ku) lonely; forlorn; deserted: sabishii *mura* (寂しい村) a *deserted*

village / sabishii *seekatsu* (寂しい生活) a *lonely* life / *Koko wa yoru ni naru to* sabishiku *narimasu*. (ここは夜になると寂しくなります) It becomes *deserted* here at night. / *Hanashi aite ga inai no de paatii de wa* sabishii *omoi o shita*. (話相手がいないのでパーティーでは寂しい思いをした) I felt *lonely* at the party, because there was no one to talk to. (↔ nigiyaka)

sa⌈bo⌉r·u サボる *vt.* (sabor·i-; sabor·a-; sabot-te [C]) (*colloq.*) play truant [hooky]; loaf on the job: ★ From French '*sabotage*.' *Kare wa yoku jugyoo o* saboru. (彼はよく授業をサボる) He often *cuts* classes. / *Saboranai de, shigoto o chañto yari nasai*. (サボらないで, 仕事をちゃんとやりなさい) Do the job properly *without slacking*.

sa⌈boteñ サボテン (仙人掌) *n.* cactus. ★ Sometimes pronounced '*shaboteñ*.'

sa⌈dama⌉r·u さだまる (定まる) *vi.* (sadamar·i-; sadamar·a-; sada-mat-te [C]) be decided; be fixed: *Kaigi no nittee ga* sadamattara, *o-shirase shimasu*. (会議の日程が定まったら, お知らせします) I will let you know when the schedule of the meeting *is fixed*. / *Kono natsu wa teñkoo ga* sadamaranai. (この夏は天候が定まらない) This summer the weather *is* quite *changeable*. (⇒ sadameru)

sa⌈dame⌉·ru さだめる (定める) *vt.* (sadame-te [V]) **1** provide; stipulate; lay down: *Nihoñ-koku keñpoo wa señsoo hooki o* sadamete iru. (日本国憲法は戦争放棄を定めている) The Japanese Constitution *stipulates* the renunciation of war.

2 decide (an aim, goal, etc.); fix; set: *nerai o* sadameru (ねらいを定める) *take* aim / *Shoorai no mokuhyoo*

wa hayaku sadameta *hoo ga yoi.*
（将来の目標は早く定めたほうがよい）
You had better *decide* on your
future goals at an early stage.
《⇨ sadamaru》

saˈdoo さどう（茶道）*n.* tea ceremony. 《⇨ cha-no-yu》

SADOO

saˈe さえ *p.* **1** (not) even:
★ Used for extreme examples.
*Ichi-nichi-juu tabemono mo mo-
chiroñ, mizu* sae *kuchi ni shinakatta.* （一日中食べ物はもちろん, 水さえ
口にしなかった）No food of course,
but not *even* water, passed my
lips all day long. / *Ano kodomo
wa otona de* sae *yomenai yoo na
ji ga yomeru.* （あの子どもは大人でさえ
読めないような字が読める）That child
can read the kinds of Chinese
characters that not *even* adults
can. / *Soñna machigai wa kodomo de* sae *shimaseñ.* （そんな間違いは
子どもでさえしません）*Even* a child
would not make that kind of mistake.

  sae ...-ba [**-tara**] （～...ば[たら]）
(just) as long as; if only: ★ Used
to indicate an emphatic condition. *O-kane* sae *areba, nañ de
mo dekiru.* （お金さえあれば, 何でもでき
る）*Just as long as you have* money, you can do anything. / *Ame
ga furi* sae *shinakereba, dekake-
mashoo.* （雨が降りさえしなければ, 出か
けましょう）Let's go out, *provided*

it doesn't rain. / *Mawari ga shizuka de* sae *areba, heya ga tashoo
semakute mo kamaimaseñ.* （周りが
静かでさえあれば, 部屋が多少狭くてもか
まいません）*So long as* the surroundings are quiet, I do not
mind if the room is a bit small. /
Moo sukoshi beñkyoo sae *sureba,
shikeñ ni ukatta ñ da kedo.* （もう少
し勉強さえすれば, 試験に受かったんだけ
ど）*If only* I had studied a little
harder, I would have passed the
examination. / *Sore ga nisemono
to shitte* sae *itara, kaimaseñ deshita.* （それが偽物と知ってさえいたら, 買
いませんでした）*If only* I had known
that it was a forgery, I would not
have bought it.

saˈegiˈr·u さえぎる（遮る）*vt.* (sae-
gir·i-; saegir·a-; saegit-te Ⓒ)
interrupt; obstruct; block:
hanashi o saegiru （話をさえぎる）
interrupt a conversation / *shikai
o* saegiru （視界をさえぎる）*block* a
person's view / *Kaateñ de hikari
o* saegitta. （カーテンで光をさえぎった）I
blocked out the light with a curtain. / *Soto no soo-oñ o* saegiru *tame ni, mado o shimeta.* （外の騒音を
さえぎるために, 窓を閉めた）I closed
the window to *shut out* the outside noise.

saˈezuˈr·u さえずる（囀る）*vi.* (sae-
zur·i-; saezur·a-; saezut-te Ⓒ)
(of a bird) sing; twitter; chirp;
warble:
Kotori ga doko-ka de saezutte *iru.*
（小鳥がどこかでさえずっている）There
are birds *singing* somewhere.

Saˈgaˈ-keñ さがけん（佐賀県）*n.*
Saga Prefecture. Located in the
northwest of Kyushu, facing the
Sea of Japan on the north and
Ariake Bay on the south. Nota-
ble industries include rice farm-
ing and ceramics. Capital city:
Saga. 《⇨ map (A5)》

saˈgaˈr·u さがる（下がる）*vi.* (sa-

gar·i-; sagar·a-; sagat-te C)
1 go down; fall; lower; drop:
Kioñ ga kyuu ni sagatta. (気温が急に下がった) The temperature *has suddenly gone down.* / *Bukka wa sugu ni wa* sagaranai deshoo. (物価はすぐには下がらないでしょう) Prices *are unlikely to come down* soon. / *Eñ ga agattari* sagattari shite iru. (円が上がったり下がったりしている) The yen *is rising and falling,* rising and *falling.* 《↔ agaru》《⇨ sageru》
2 step back; stand back:
Ressha ga tsuuka shimasu kara ushiro ni sagatte *kudasai.* (列車が通過しますから後ろに下がってください) There is a train coming through, so please *step back.* (*station announcement*)

sa「gas·u さがす (捜す・探す) *vt.*
(sagash·i-; sagas·a-; sagash·i-te C)) look for; seek; search:
megane o sagasu (眼鏡をさがす) *look for* one's glasses / *Keesatsu wa yukue-fumee no oñna-no-ko o* sagashite iru. (警察は行方不明の女の子を捜している) The police *are looking for* the missing girl. / *Kurayami no naka de deñki no suitchi o* sagashita. (暗闇の中で電気のスイッチを探した) I *searched* in the darkness for a light switch.

sa「ge」·ru さげる (下げる) *vt.* (sage-te V)) **1** lower; pull down:
buraiñdo o sageru (ブラインドを下げる) *pull down* the blinds / *nedañ o* sageru (値段を下げる) *lower* the price / *Kare ni wa atama o* sagetaku nai. (彼には頭を下げたくない) I *don't want to bow down* to him. 《⇨ sagaru》
2 hang; wear:
Sono ko wa kata kara kabañ o sagete ita. (その子は肩からかばんを下げていた) The boy *had* a bag *hanging* from his shoulder. / *Kazuko-sañ wa itsu-mo peñdañto o* sagete iru. (和子さんはいつもペンダントを下げている)

Kazuko always *wears* a pendant. 《⇨ sagaru》
3 move back; draw back:
Sono teeburu o ushiro e sagete *kudasai.* (そのテーブルを後ろへ下げてください) Please *move* the table *back.*
4 clear away (dishes); take away:
Kono sara wa o-sage shite *yoroshii desu ka?* (この皿はお下げしてよろしいですか) Is it all right if I *clear away* these plates?

sa「gi」¹ さぎ (詐欺) *n.* fraud; swindle:
Kare wa sagi *o hataraite, tsukamatta.* (彼は詐欺を働いて，捕まった) He was arrested on charges of *fraud.* / *Kanojo wa* sagi *ni atte nijuumañ-eñ damashi-torareta.* (彼女は詐欺にあって 20 万円だましとられた) She was cheated out of 200,000 yen in a *swindle.* / sagi-shi (詐欺師) a *swindler.*

sa「gi」² さぎ (鷺) *n.* heron.

sa「gur·u さぐる (探る) *vt.* (sagur·i-; sagur·a-; sagut-te C))
1 grope for; fumble for; feel for:
Kare wa poketto o sagutte, *kippu o sagashita.* (彼はポケットを探って，切符を探した) *Groping* in his pocket, he searched for the ticket.
2 sound out (a person's intention); feel out:
Kanojo wa kare no hoñshiñ o saguroo *to shita.* (彼女は彼の本心を探ろうとした) She tried to *feel out* his real intentions.

sa「gyoo さぎょう (作業) *n.* (factory) work; operation:
Sagyoo wa ku-ji ni hajimarimasu. (作業が 9 時に始まります) *Work* starts at 9:00. / *Sagyoo-chuu wa herumetto o kaburanakereba narimaseñ.* (作業中はヘルメットをかぶらなければなりません) You have to wear a hard hat while you *are at work.* / sagyoo-jikañ (作業時間) *working* hours.

sagyoo suru (〜する) *vi.* work: *Chuui shite,* sagyoo shite *kudasai.* (注意して, 作業してください) Please *carry out your work* with care.

sa⌐i さい (際) *n.* time; occasion: *Resepushoñ no* sai *kare ni aimashita.* (レセプションの際彼に会いました) I met him on the *occasion* of the reception. / *Hijoo no* sai *wa kono botañ o oshite kudasai.* (非常の際はこのボタンを押してください) Press this button in *case* of emergency.

sa⌐i-[1] さい (再) *pref.* re-; again: sai-*nyuukoku* (再入国) *re*-entry into a country / sai-*koñ* (再婚) *re*-marriage / sai-*riyoo* (再利用) *re*-use / sai-*teeañ* (再提案) *re*-submitting a proposal.

sa⌐i-[2] さい (最) *pref.* (often translated into English as most..., -est): sai-*dai* (最大) the larg*est*; sai-*shoo* (最小) the small*est* / sai-*zeñ* (最善) the *best* / sai-*aku* (最悪) the *worst* / sai-*juuyoo* (最重要) the *most* important.

-sai[1] さい (歳) *suf.* age; years old: *Haha wa juuhas*-sai *de kekkoñ shimashita.* (母は 18 歳で結婚しました) My mother married at the *age* of eighteen. / *Kare ni wa go*-sai *no oñna-no-ko ga imasu.* (彼には 5 歳の女の子がいます) He has a five-year-*old* daughter. / *Anata wa nañ*-sai *desu ka?* (あなたは何歳ですか) How *old* are you?

-sai[2] さい (祭) *suf.* festival; anniversary: *gojuu-neñ*-sai (50 年祭) the fiftieth *anniversary* / *buñka*-sai (文化祭) a cultural *festival* / *gakueñ*-sai (学園祭) a school *festival* / *geejutsu*-sai (芸術祭) a *festival* of art. 《⇨ matsuri (photo)》

sa⌐ibai さいばい (栽培) *n.* growing; cultivation: *ichigo no* saibai (いちごの栽培) strawberry *growing*.
  saibai suru (〜する) *vt.* grow;

raise; cultivate: *Kare wa oñshitsu de bara o* saibai *shite imasu.* (彼は温室でばらを栽培しています) He *grows* roses in a greenhouse.

sa⌐ibañ さいばん (裁判) *n.* trial; judgment: saibañ *ni katsu* [*makeru*] (裁判に勝つ[負ける]) win [lose] a *suit* / *Sono jikeñ wa geñzai* saibañ-*chuu desu.* (その事件は現在裁判中です) The case is now on *trial*. / *Sono fuñsoo wa* saibañ *ni mochikomareta.* (その紛争は裁判にもちこまれた) The dispute was brought into *court*.

sa⌐iba⌐ñkañ さいばんかん (裁判官) *n.* judge.

sa⌐ibañsho さいばんしょ (裁判所) *n.* courthouse; a court of justice.

sa⌐iboo さいぼう (細胞) *n.* (of biology) cell.

sa⌐ichuu さいちゅう (最中) *n.* (in) the middle (of): *Eñkai no* saichuu *ni kare wa seki o tatta.* (宴会の最中に彼は席を立った) He left his seat in the *middle* of the party. / *Kaigi o shite iru* saichuu *ni deñwa ga natta.* (会議をしている最中に電話が鳴った) The telephone rang *just as* we *were in conference*.

sa⌐idaa サイダー *n.* soda pop. ★ From English 'cider,' but not made from apples and non-alcoholic.

sa⌐idai さいだい (最大) *n.* the largest [biggest]; the greatest; maximum: *Kore wa sekai de* saidai *no tañkaa desu.* (これは世界で最大のタンカーです) This is the *largest* tanker in the world. / *Higai wa* saidai *ni mitsumotte mo hyakumañ-eñ deshoo.* (被害は最大に見積もっても 100 万円でしょう) The estimate of the damage will be a million yen, *maximum*. 《↔ saishoo⌐》

sa⌐idañ さいだん (裁断) *n.* **1** cutting:

saidañ-*ki* (裁断機) a cutting machine.

2 decision; judgment: *Sono moñdai wa shachoo no saidañ o aogu koto ni shita.* (その問題は社長の裁断を仰ぐことにした) We submitted the problem to the president's *judgment.*

saidañ suru (〜する) *vt.* **1** cut out: *katagami ni awasete nuno o* saidañ suru (型紙に合わせて布を裁断する) *cut out* cloth according to a pattern.

2 decide; judge: *Sono keñ wa shushoo ga* saidañ shimasu. (その件は首相が裁断します) The prime minister will *give a decision* regarding that matter.

sa⌐ifu さいふ (財布) *n.* wallet; (coin) purse: *Saifu o doko-ka de otoshite shimatta.* (財布をどこかで落としてしまった) I've dropped my *wallet* somewhere.

saifu no himo o yurumeru [shimeru] (〜のひもをゆるめる[しめる]) loosen [tighten] one's purse strings.

sa⌐igai さいがい (災害) *n.* disaster; calamity: saigai *o ukeru [koomuru]* (災害を受ける[被る]) suffer from a *disaster* / saigai-*chi* (災害地) a *disaster* area.

sa⌐igo[1] さいご (最後) *n.* **1** the last; the end: *Kono monogatari no* saigo *wa doo naru ñ desu ka?* (この物語の最後はどうなるんですか) What happens at the *end* of this story? / *Kore ga* saigo *no chañsu desu.* (これが最後のチャンスです) This is the *last* chance. / *Saigo ni kono heya o deta no wa dare desu ka?* (最後にこの部屋を出たのはだれですか) Who was it that left this room *last*? / *Saigo made zeñryoku o tsukushimasu.* (最後まで全力を尽くします) I will do my very

best right up to the *end.* (↔ saisho)

2 once: ★ Used like a conjunction. *Kare ni kane o kashitara* saigo, *kaeshite moraemaseñ.* (彼に金を貸したら最後, 返してもらえません) *Once* you lend him money, you can never get it back.

sa⌐igo[2] さいご (最期) *n.* end of one's life: *Kare wa hisañ na* saigo *o togeta.* (彼は悲惨な最期を遂げた) He *died* in misery.

sa⌐ihoo さいほう (裁縫) *n.* sewing; needlework: *Haha wa* saihoo *ga joozu datta.* (母は裁縫が上手だった) My mother was good at *sewing.* / *Saihoo wa doko de naraimashita ka?* (裁縫はどこで習いましたか) Where did you learn *needlework*?

saihoo suru (〜する) *vi.* sew; do needlework: *Saikiñ wa* saihoo suru *koto wa metta ni arimaseñ.* (最近は裁縫することはめったにありません) I seldom *do needlework* these days.

sa⌐ijitsu さいじつ (祭日) *n.* national holiday; festival day. (⇒ shukujitsu (table))

sa⌐ijoo さいじょう (最上) *n.* the best: *Kare no shita koto wa* saijoo *no hoohoo de wa nai.* (彼のしたことは最上の方法ではない) What he has done is not the *best* way. / *Kore wa* saijoo *no shina desu.* (これは最上の品です) This is the *highest* quality article. (↔ saitee)

sa⌐ikai さいかい (再開) *n.* reopening; resumption: kaigi no saikai (会議の再開) the *resumption* of a meeting.

saikai suru (〜する) *vt.* reopen; resume: *Kaigi wa gogo ni-ji ni* saikai saremasu. (会議は午後2時に再開されます) The meeting will *be* *reconvened* at 2:00 P.M.

saˈikeñ さいけん (再建) *n.* reconstruction; rebuilding:
furui jiñja no saikeñ (古い神社の再建) the *rebuilding* of an old shrine.
saikeñ suru (～する) *vt.* reconstruct; rebuild: *Jishiñ de kowasareta machi wa kañzeñ ni* saikeñ *saremashita.* (地震で壊された町は完全に再建されました) The town which had been destroyed by an earthquake *was* completely *reconstructed.*

saˈikiñ¹ さいきん (最近) *n.* recent date:
Saikiñ *no deñki-seehiñ wa tsukaikata ga fukuzatsu de muzukashii.* (最近の電気製品は使いかたが複雑で難しい) *Modern* electric appliances are complex and difficult to use. / *Watashi wa* saikiñ *made sono koto o shirimaseñ deshita.* (私は最近までそのことを知りませんでした) I didn't know about that until *recently.*
— *adv.* recently; lately:
Saikiñ *yatto Nihoñgo no shiñbuñ ga yomeru yoo ni narimashita.* (最近やっと日本語の新聞が読めるようになりました) Just *recently*, I have at last become able to read Japanese newspapers. / Saikiñ *go-neñkañ de bukka wa it-teñ-go-bai ni natta.* (最近5年間で物価は1.5倍になった) In the *last* five years, prices have increased one and a half times.

saˈikiñ² さいきん (細菌) *n.* germ; bacteria:
saikiñ-*señ* (細菌戦) *biological* warfare.

saˈikoo さいこう (最高) *n.* **1** the highest:
Kare wa saikoo *no seeseki de gookaku shita.* (彼は最高の成績で合格した) He passed the examination with the *highest* mark. / *Nihoñ de* saikoo *no yama wa Fuji-sañ desu.* (日本で最高の山は富士山です) The *highest* mountain in Japan is Mt. Fuji. / *Kyoo wa kotoshi* saikoo *no atsusa datta.* (きょうは今年最高の暑さだった) Today it was the *highest* temperature of the year. ((↔ saitee))
2 best; supreme; maximum:
Kare wa hyaku-meetoru kyoosoo de jibuñ no saikoo *kiroku o dashita.* (彼は100メートル競争で自分の最高記録を出した) He set his *best* record in the hundred-meter sprint. / *Kono dooro de no* saikoo *sokudo wa gojuk-kiro desu.* (この道路での最高速度は50キロです) The *maximum* speed on this road is 50 km/h. / *Kyoo no kibuñ wa* saikoo *da.* (きょうの気分は最高だ) I *feel on top of the world* today.

Saˈikoˈosai さいこうさい (最高裁) *n.* Supreme Court. ★ Shortened form of 'Saikoo-saibañsho.'

Saˈikoo-saibañsho さいこうさいばんしょ (最高裁判所) *n.* Supreme Court.

saˈiku さいく (細工) *n.* **1** work; workmanship:
Kono kagu no saiku *wa subarashii.* (この家具の細工はすばらしい) The *workmanship* of this furniture is excellent.
2 artifice; tactics:
Ano hito no saiku *wa te ga koñde iru.* (あの人の細工は手が込んでいる) He uses very skillful *tactics.*

saiˈkuriñgu サイクリング *n.* cycling:
saikuriñgu *ni iku* (サイクリングに行く) go *cycling.*

saˈikuru サイクル *n.* cycle. ((⇨ shuuki¹))

saˈiñ サイン *n.* **1** signature; autograph:

CULTURE

Comes from English, 'sign,' but used as a noun in Japanese. Sometimes refers to a signa-

ture and sometimes to simply writing one's name. A personal seal is put on Japanese documents instead of a signature.

Kore ga ano sutaa no saiñ *desu.* (これがあのスターのサインです) This is the *autograph* of that star. (⇨ *shomee*))
2 sign; signal:
rañnaa ni toorui no saiñ *o dasu* (ランナーに盗塁のサインを出す) *signal* a runner to steal (*in baseball*) / *Watashi wa kanojo ni "damatte iro" to* saiñ *o okutta.* (私は彼女に「だまっていろ」とサインを送った) I *signaled* her to keep quiet.
saiñ suru (〜する) *vi.* sign; autograph: *Watashi wa sono keeyakusho ni* saiñ *shita.* (私はその契約書にサインした) I *signed* the contract. / *Sumimaseñ ga* saiñ *shite kudasai.* (すみませんが, サインしてください) Excuse me, but may I have your *autograph*?

sa⌐inaⁿ さいなん (災難) *n.* misfortune; disaster; accident: saiñañ *ni au* (災難に遭う) meet with a *misfortune* / saiñañ *o manugareru* (災難を免れる) escape a *disaster* / *Kanojo no musume wa omoigakenai* sainañ *de nakunatta.* (彼女の娘は思いがけない災難で亡くなった) Her daughter lost her life in an unforeseen *accident*.

sa⌐inoo さいのう (才能) *n.* ability; talent; gift: sainoo *o hakki suru* (才能を発揮する) give full play to one's *ability* / *Kare wa hijoo ni* sainoo *no aru pianisuto desu.* (彼は非常に才能のあるピアニストです) He is a pianist of great *talent*. / *Kanojo wa e no* sainoo *ga aru.* (彼女は絵の才能がある) She has a *gift* for painting.

sa⌐ireñ サイレン *n.* siren: saireñ *o narasu* (サイレンを鳴らす) sound a *siren* / *Tooku de* saireñ

no oto ga kikoeru. (遠くでサイレンの音が聞こえる) I hear the distant sound of a *siren*.

sa⌐isañ さいさん (採算) *n.* profit; gain:
Kono nedañ de saisañ *o toru no wa muzukashii.* (この値段で採算を取るのは難しい) It is hard to make a *profit* at this price. / *Kare wa* saisañ *o mushi shite, sono hoñ o dashita.* (彼は採算を無視して, その本を出した) He published the book, without thinking of *profit*. / saisañ-*teñ* (採算点) the *break-even* point. (⇨ *rieki*))

sa⌐iseñ さいせん (賽銭) *n.* offertory; money offering:
jiñja ni saiseñ *o ageru* (神社にさい銭をあげる) make a *money offering* at a shrine / saiseñ-*bako* (さい銭箱) an *offertory* box [chest].

SAISEÑ-BAKO

sa⌐ishi さいし (妻子) *n.* one's wife and children; a man's family:
Kare wa saishi *o yashinau no ni juubuñ na shuunyuu ga arimasu.* (彼は妻子を養うのに十分な収入があります) He has quite enough income to support his *family*.

sa⌐ishite さいして (際して) on the occasion of:
Shuppatsu ni saishite *señsee kara chuui ga atta.* (出発に際して先生から注意があった) The teacher gave us advice *when* we were going to depart. / *Kikeñ ni* saishite *mo kare wa ochitsuite ita.* (危険に際しても

彼は落ちついていた) He remained calm even *in the face of* danger.

sa⌐isho さいしょ (最初) *n.* **1** beginning; start:
Sono hoñ wa saisho *kara saigo made yomimashita.* (その本は最初から最後まで読みました) I have read the book from *beginning* to end. / *Nañ de mo* saisho *wa muzukashii.* (何でも最初は難しい) Everything is difficult at the *start.* ((↔ saigo¹))
2 (the) first:
Sono sakka no saisho *no sakuhiñ wa nañ desu ka?* (その作家の最初の作品は何ですか) What is that author's *first* work? / *Saisho ni hatsugeñ shita no wa Yamada-sañ desu.* (最初に発言したのは山田さんです) It was Mr. Yamada who spoke *first.* / *Kare wa* saisho *wa sono añ ni hañtai datta.* (彼は最初はその案に反対だった) *Originally,* he was against the idea.

sa⌐ishoku さいしょく (菜食) *n.* vegetable diet:
saishoku-shugisha (菜食主義者) a *vegetarian.*
saishoku suru (～する) *vi.* live on vegetables: *Watashi wa* saishoku *shite imasu.* (私は菜食しています) I *only eat fruit and vegetables.*

sa⌐ishoo¹ さいしょう (最小) *n.* the smallest; minimum:
Higai wa saishoo *ni kuitometa.* (被害は最小にくい止めた) We kept the damage to a *minimum.* / *Kore wa sekai* saishoo *no rajio desu.* (これは世界最小のラジオです) This is the *smallest* radio in the world. ((↔ saidai))

sa⌐ishoo² さいしょう (最少) *n.* the least; the smallest:
Kare wa guruupu no naka de neñree ga saishoo *desu.* (彼はグループのなかで年令が最少です) He is the *youngest* in the group. / *Kotoshi no rieki wa kono sañ-neñkañ de* saishoo *datta.* (今年の利益はこの3

年間で最少だった) This year's profit was the *smallest* in the past three years.

sa⌐ishuu¹ さいしゅう (最終) *n.* the last; the final:
Kore ga saishuu *no kettee desu.* (これが最終の決定です) This is our *final* decision. / *Kare wa* saishuu-kai ni hoomurañ o utta. (彼は最終回にホームランを打った) He hit a home run in the *last* inning. / *Watashi wa nañ to ka* saishuu *ressha ni maniatta.* (私はなんとか最終列車に間に合った) I was barely in time for the *last* train.

sa⌐ishuu² さいしゅう (採集) *n.* collection:
shokubutsu saishuu *ni dekakeru* (植物採集に出かける) go out plant *collecting.*
saishuu suru (～する) *vt.* collect; gather: *Kare wa koñchuu o* saishuu *shite imasu.* (彼は昆虫を採集しています) He *collects* insects.

sa⌐isoku さいそく (催促) *n.* demand; reminder:
yachiñ no saisoku (家賃の催促) a *request* for payment of the rent.
saisoku suru (～する) *vt.* press; urge; ask: *Watashi wa kare ni kashita kane no heñsai o* saisoku *shita.* (私は彼に貸した金の返済を催促した) I *pressed* him to repay the money I loaned him.

Sa⌐itama¹-keñ さいたまけん (埼玉県) *n.* Saitama Prefecture. Located in the middle west of the Kanto district, bordered on the south by Tokyo. The capital city, Urawa (浦和), has developed into a satellite city of Tokyo. ((⇨ map (F4)))

sa⌐itee さいてい (最低) *n.* **1** the lowest:
Señgetsu wa uriage ga saitee *datta.* (先月は売上が最低だった) Last month sales were the *lowest.*
2 the worst; minimum:

Shikeñ wa saitee *no deki datta.* (試験は最低の出来だった) I got the *worst* mark in the examination. / *Kanojo no manaa wa* saitee *datta.* (彼女のマナーは最低だった) Her manners were *terrible.* / *Shuuri ni wa* saitee *is-shuukañ kakarimasu.* (修理には最低1週間かかります) The repairs will take *at least* a week. / saitee-*chiñgiñ* (最低賃金) the *minimum* wage / saitee-*kioñ* (最低気温) the *minimum* temperature. 《↔ saikoo》

sa⌈iteñ さいてん (採点) *n.* grading; marking; scoring: *Yamada señsee wa* saiteñ *ga amai [karai].* (山田先生は採点が甘い[辛い]) Mr. Yamada is generous [severe] in *grading.*

 saiteñ suru (〜する) *vt.* grade; mark; score: *Señsee wa kyoo no shikeñ o* saiteñ *shite iru tokoro desu.* (先生はきょうの試験を採点しているところです) The teacher *is grading* today's exam.

sa⌈iwai さいわい (幸い) *a.n.* (〜 na, ni) happy; lucky; fortunate: *Sono hoñ o o-kashi itadakereba* saiwai *desu.* (その本をお貸しいただければ幸いです) I would be very *happy* if you lent me the book. / *Kare ga ie ni ita no wa* saiwai *datta.* (彼が家にいたのは幸いだった) It was *lucky* he was at home. / *Saishuu deñsha ni maniatta no wa* saiwai *datta.* (最終電車に間に合ったのは幸いだった) I was *fortunate* to be able to catch the last train.

— *adv.* happily; luckily; fortunately: ★ Often used in the form '〜 *ni mo.*' *Saiwai chichi no shujutsu wa seekoo shimashita.* (幸い父の手術は成功しました) *Fortunately*, our father's operation was successful. / *Saiwai (ni mo) o-teñki ni megumaremashita.* (幸い(にも)お天気に恵まれました) *Fortunately*, we were

blessed with good weather. 《⇨ shiawase》

sa⌈iyoo さいよう (採用) *n.* adoption; acceptance; employment: saiyoo-*shikeñ* (採用試験) an *employment* examination.

 saiyoo suru (〜する) *vt.* adopt; accept; employ: *Sono kaisha wa joshi o juu-mee* saiyoo *shita.* (その会社は女子を10名採用した) The company *took on* ten women. / *Watashi no añ wa kaigi de* saiyoo *saremashita.* (私の案は会議で採用されました) My proposal *was accepted* at the meeting.

sa⌈ji⌉ さじ (匙) *n.* spoon: *shio hito-*saji (塩一さじ) a *spoonful* of salt / saji *de sukuu* (さじですくう) take up in a *spoon.*

 saji-kageñ (さじかげん) consideration: *Kare wa toshiyori desu kara* saji-kageñ *shite yatte kudasai.* (彼は年寄りですからさじかげんしてやってください) Please *make allowances* for him, because he is old.

 saji o nageru (〜を投げる) give up: *Saji o nageru no wa mada hayai.* (さじを投げるのはまだ早い) It is too early to *throw in the sponge.*

sa⌈ka⌉ さか (坂) *n.* slope; hill: saka *o agaru [kudaru]* (坂を上がる[下る]) go up [down] a *slope* / *Jiteñsha o oshite,* saka *o nobotta.* (自転車を押して、坂を上った) I pushed my bicycle up the *hill.*

sa⌈kae⌉・ru さかえる (栄える) *vi.* (sakae-te Ⅴ) prosper; flourish; thrive: *Kare no shoobai wa* sakaete *imasu.* (彼の商売は栄えています) His business *is prospering.* / *Mukashi wa kono machi mo* sakaete *imashita.* (昔はこの町も栄えていました) In the old days this town *used to be flourishing as well.*

sa⌈ka⌉i さかい (境) *n.* border; boundary: *Edogawa wa Tookyoo-to to*

Chiba-keñ no sakai *desu.* (江戸川は東京都と千葉県の境です) The Edo River is the *border* between metropolitan Tokyo and Chiba Prefecture. / Sakai *o sessuru kuni no aida de wa fuñsoo ga okoriyasui.* (境を接する国の間では紛争が起こりやすい) Conflicts are liable to occur between countries having a common *border.*

sakai ni (〜に) since: *Ku-gatsu o* sakai ni *booeki kuroji wa geñshoo shite imasu.* (九月を境に貿易黒字は減少しています) The trade surplus has been decreasing *since* September.

sa⌜kañ さかん (盛ん) *a.n.* (〜 na, ni) **1** prosperous; flourishing; thriving:
Kono chihoo wa seemitsu-kikaikoogyoo ga sakañ *desu.* (この地方は精密機械工業が盛んです) The precision machinery and instruments industry is *flourishing* in this area.
2 energetic; active; vigorous:
Chichi wa oite masumasu sakañ *desu.* (父は老いてますます盛んです) My father is getting more *active* as he grows older. / *Kanojo wa ima* sakañ *ni e o kaite imasu.* (彼女は今盛んに絵をかいています) She now *actively* paints pictures. / *Yuki ga* sakañ *ni futte iru.* (雪が盛んに降っている) It is snowing *heavily.*
3 popular; enthusiastic:
Nihoñ wa yakyuu ga sakañ *desu.* (日本は野球が盛んです) Baseball is *popular* in Japan. / *Sono kashu wa* sakañ *na hakushu o uketa.* (その歌手は盛んな拍手を受けた) The singer won *enthusiastic* applause.

sa⌜kana[1] さかな (魚) *n.* fish:
Sakana *o te de tsukamaeta.* (魚を手で捕まえた) I caught a *fish* with my hands. / *Koko de* sakana o tsuru *no wa kiñshi sarete imasu.* (ここで魚を釣るのは禁止されています)

Fishing is not allowed here. (⇨ sakanaya))

sa⌜kana[2] さかな (肴) *n.* side dish: ★ Relishes eaten as an accompaniment to drinking.
Yakitori o sake no sakana *ni, ippai noñda.* (焼き鳥を酒のさかなに, 一杯飲んだ) I had a drink, with 'yakitori' as a *side dish.*

sa⌜kanaya さかなや (魚屋) *n.*
1 fish dealer; fishmonger.
2 fish shop.

SAKANAYA (shop)

sa⌜kanobo⌝r·u さかのぼる (遡る) *vi.* (-nobor·i-; -nobor·a-; -nobot-te ⓒ) **1** go [sail] upstream:
Wareware wa kawa o ichi-jikan sakanobotta. (われわれは川を1時間さかのぼった) We *went* an hour *upstream.*
2 (of a practice, convention, custom, etc.) go back; date from:
Kono fuushuu wa Edo jidai made sakanoborimasu. (この風習は江戸時代までさかのぼります) This custom *goes back* as far as the Edo period.

sa⌜kari さかり (盛り) *n.* **1** the height:
Ima ga choodo natsu no sakari *desu.* (今がちょうど夏の盛りです) Now is just the *height* of summer. / *Sakura no hana wa* sakari *o sugimashita.* (桜の花は盛りを過ぎました) The cherry blossoms are now past their *best.*
2 prime; bloom; flower:
Kimi-tachi wa ima ga wakai

sakari *da*. (君たちは今が若い盛りだ) Now is the *prime* of your youth for all of you. / *Kare wa* hataraki-zakari *ni nakunatta*. (彼は働き盛りに亡くなった) He died in his *prime*.
★ '*Sakari*' usually changes to '*zakari*' in compounds.
3 (of animals) heat; rut:
sakari *ga tsuku* (盛りがつく) go on *heat*.

sa⌐kariba さかりば (盛り場) *n.* the busiest quarters of a city; amusement quarters.

sa⌐kasa さかさ (逆さ) *n.* inversion; reverse:
Biñ o sakasa ni shite, *naka o kara ni shita*. (びんを逆さにして、中を空にした) I *inverted* the bottle and emptied it. / *Kono hako wa* sakasa *ni shinai de kudasai*. (この箱は逆さにしないでください) Don't turn this box *upside down*.

sa⌐kaya さかや (酒屋) *n.*
1 liquor store; sake shop.
2 sake dealer.

sa⌐kazuki¹ さかずき (杯) *n.* sake cup:
sakazuki *ni sake o tsugu* (杯に酒をつぐ) fill a *sake cup*. 《⇨ tokkuri (photo)》

sa⌐ke¹ さけ (酒) *n.* **1** sake; fermented rice beverage:
Sake *to biiru to dochira ga ii desu ka?* (酒とビールとどちらがいいですか) Which would you like, *sake* or beer?
2 alcoholic drink; liquor:
Kare wa sake *ni tsuyoi* [*yowai*]. (彼は酒に強い[弱い]) He can [can't] hold his *drink*. / *Watashi wa* sake *mo tabako mo yarimaseñ*. (私は酒もたばこもやりません) I neither *drink* nor smoke.

sa⌐ke² さけ (鮭) *n.* salmon:
★ Sometimes pronounced '*shake*.'
sake *no kañzume* (鮭の缶詰) a can of *salmon*.

sa⌐kebi(go⌐e) さけび(ごえ) (叫び (声) *n.* cry; shout; yell; scream; shriek:
señsoo ni hañtai suru sakebi (戦争に反対する叫び) a *cry* against the war / '*Tasukete*' *to iu* sakebigoe *ga kikoeta*. (「助けて」という叫び声が聞こえた) I heard a *shout* of 'help.' 《⇨ sakebu》

sa⌐ke⌐b·u さけぶ (叫ぶ) *vi.* (sakeb·i-; sakeb·a-; sakeñ-de C)
shout; cry out; yell; scream:
Kanojo wa tasuke o motomete sakeñda. (彼女は助けを求めて叫んだ) She *cried out* for help. / *Kare wa ureshikute, omowazu* '*Yatta*' *to* sakeñda. (彼はうれしくて、思わず「やった」と叫んだ) He was overjoyed so could not help *shouting out* " I succeeded! " / *Demotai wa señsoo hañtai o* sakebi-nagara *kooshiñ shita*. (デモ隊は戦争反対を叫びながら行進した) The demonstrators marched along, *shouting out* against the war.

sa⌐ke⌐·ru¹ さける (避ける) *vi.* (sake-te V) avoid; avert; evade; shun:
Sono jiko o sakeru *no wa fukanoo datta*. (その事故を避けるのは不可能だった) It was impossible to *avert* the accident. / *Samui hi no gaishutsu wa* sakete *kudasai*. (寒い日の外出は避けてください) When it is cold, please *avoid* going out.
sakete toorenai michi (避けて通れない道) a problem that cannot be avoided.

sa⌐ke⌐·ru² さける (裂ける) *vi.* (sake-te V) tear; split; rip:
Shatsu ga kugi ni hikkakatte, sakete *shimatta*. (シャツがくぎに引っかかって、裂けてしまった) My shirt got caught on a nail and *ripped*. 《⇨ saku²》

sa⌐ki さき (先) *n.* **1** point; tip; end; head:
eñpitsu no saki (鉛筆の先) the *point* of a pencil / *yubi no* saki

(指の先) the *tip* of a finger / *boo no* saki (棒の先) the *end* of a stick.

2 future:

Saki *no koto wa wakarimaseñ.* (先のことはわかりません) I do not know what will happen in the *future.* / *Kimi-tachi wakai hito ni wa* saki *ga aru.* (君たち若い人には先がある) You young people have your *futures* in front of you.

3 (～ ni) in advance; beforehand:

Saki *ni daikiñ o haratte kudasai.* (先に代金を払ってください) Please pay *in advance.* / Saki *ni shokuji o shimashoo.* (先に食事をしましょう) Let's eat *first.* ((↔ ato¹))

4 ahead;

Chichi wa saki *ni dekakemashita.* (父は先に出かけました) My father left *ahead* of us. / *Kono* saki *no dooro wa kooji-chuu desu.* (この先の道路は工事中です) The road *ahead* is under construction. / *Doozo o-saki ni.* (どうぞお先に) *After you.* / *O-saki ni shitsuree shimasu.* (お先に失礼します) Excuse me, but I *must be going now.*

5 previous; former:

saki *no shushoo* (先の首相) the *former* prime minister / *Watashi ga* saki *ni nobeta-toori yatte gorañ nasai.* (私が先に述べた通りやってごらんなさい) Try to do it just as I told you *previously.*

saki o arasou (～を争う) fight for the lead: *Kare-ra wa nyuujookeñ o te ni ireru tame ni,* saki o arasotta. (彼らは入場券を手に入れるために, 先を争った) They *vied with each other* to get admission tickets.

saki o kosareru (～を越される) be bested: *Aite ni* saki o kosarenai *yoo ni gañbatta.* (相手に先を越されないようにがんばった) We made every effort *not to be bested* by our opponents.

sa⌐kihodo さきほど (先程) *n., adv.*

(*formal*) a little while ago; some time ago: ★ A little more formal than '*sakki*.'

Shujiñ wa sakihodo *dekakemashita.* (主人は先ほど出かけました) My husband left home *a little while ago.* / Sakihodo *kara Tanaka-sañ ga oosetsuma de o-machi desu.* (先ほどから田中さんが応接間でお待ちです) Mr. Tanaka has been waiting *for a while* in the reception room. / Sakihodo *no hanashi ni modoshimashoo.* (先ほどの話にもどしましょう) Let's return to what we were discussing *previously.* ((⇨ sakki))

sa⌐kka さっか (作家) *n.* writer; author; novelist.

sa⌐kkaa サッカー *n.* soccer; association football. ((⇨ futtobooru))

sa⌐kkaku さっかく (錯覚) *n.* illusion; imagination:

Sore wa kimi no me no sakkaku *desu.* (それは君の目の錯覚です) It is an optical *illusion* you are seeing.

sakkaku suru (～する) *vi.* have an illusion: *Kyoo wa yasumi da to* sakkaku shite ita. (きょうは休みだと錯覚していた) I *was under the misapprehension* that today was a holiday.

sa⌐kki さっき *n., adv.* a little while ago; some time ago:

Kanojo wa sakki *kaerimashita.* (彼女はさっき帰りました) She left for home *a little while ago.* / Sakki *kara nañ-do mo deñwa ga arimashita yo.* (さっきから何度も電話がありましたよ) *For some time now* there have been a lot of telephone calls for you. / Sakki *no hanashi wa wasurete kudasai.* (さっきの話は忘れてください) Please forget what we were *previously* talking about. ((⇨ sakihodo))

sa⌐kkyoku さっきょく (作曲) *n.* musical composition:

Kono uta wa dare no sakkyoku *desu ka?* (この歌はだれの作曲ですか)

Whose *composition* is this song? / sakkyoku-ka (作曲家) a *composer*.

sakkyoku suru (〜する) *vi.*, *vt.* compose; write music: *Kono uta wa Kitahara Hakushuu ga saku-shi shi, Yamada Koosaku ga* sak-kyoku shimashita. (この歌は北原白秋が作詞し、山田耕筰が作曲しました) Hakushu Kitahara wrote the lyrics of this song and Kosaku Yamada *put it to music*.

sa⌐k·u[1] さく (咲く) *vi.* (sak·i-; sa-k·a-; sa·i-te [C]) blossom; come out; bloom: *Kono hana wa go-gatsu-goro ni* sakimasu. (この花は五月ごろに咲きます) These flowers *come out* around May.

sa⌐k·u[2] さく (裂く) *vt.* (sak·i-; sa-k·a-; sa·i-te [C]) 1 tear; split; rip; rend: *Kanojo wa okotte, sono hañkachi o* saita. (彼女は怒って、そのハンカチを裂いた) She *tore* the handkerchief in anger. (⇨ *sakeru*[2])
2 separate; break up (relation, friendship, etc.): *Ano futari no naka o* saku koto wa dekimaseñ. (あの二人の仲を裂くことはできません) *Nothing can come between* the two of them.

sa⌐ku[3] さく (柵) *n.* fence; railing: *Ie no mawari ni* saku *o megura-shita.* (家のまわりにさくをめぐらした) I set up a *fence* around the house.

sa⌐ku[4] さく (策) *n.* plan; scheme; measure; policy: saku *o neru* (策を練る) carefully work out a *plan* / *Nani-ka yoi* saku *wa arimasu ka?* (何か良い策はありますか) Do you have any good *plan*? / *Watashi-tachi wa bañzeñ no* saku *o koojita.* (私たちは万全の策を講じた) We adopted a surefire *measure*. / *Sore wa saizeñ no* saku *to wa omoemaseñ.* (それは最善の策とは思えません) I can't believe that is the best *policy*.

saku ga tsukiru (〜がつきる) exhaust one's resources: *Moo* saku ga tsukimashita. (もう策が尽きました) I *am* now *at my wits' end*.

sa⌐ku[5] さく (割く) *vt.* (sak·i-; sa-k·a-; sa·i-te [C]) spare (time); give: *Isogashikute, ima no tokoro zeñ-zeñ jikañ ga* sakemaseñ. (忙しくて、今のところ全然時間が割けません) I am too busy to spare any time at present. / *O-wabi no tame ni zas-shi no ichi-peeji o* saita. (おわびのために雑誌の1ページを割いた) We *used* one page of the magazine for our apology.

sa⌐ku- さく (昨) *pref.* last: saku-jitsu (昨日) *yesterday* / saku-neñ (昨年) *last* year. 《↔ yoku-》

sa⌐kubañ さくばん (昨晩) *n.* (*formal*) last night; yesterday evening. 《⇨ bañ[1] (table)》

sa⌐kubuñ さくぶん (作文) *n.* essay; composition: *'Yuujoo' to iu dai de* sakubuñ *o kaita.* (「友情」という題で作文を書いた) I wrote an *essay* on 'friendship.'

sa⌐kugara さくがら (作柄) *n.* crop; the crops: *Kotoshi no ine no* sakugara *wa ryookoo desu.* (ことしの稲の作柄は良好です) This year's rice *crop* is good.

sa⌐kuhiñ さくひん (作品) *n.* work; production; creation: *Kare no* sakuhiñ *no teñrañ-kai ga aki ni hirakaremasu.* (彼の作品の展覧会が秋に開かれます) An exhibition of his *works* will be held in autumn. / *Kore ga watashi no sai-sho no* sakuhiñ *desu.* (これが私の最初の作品です) This is my first *creation*.

sa⌐kuiñ さくいん (索引) *n.* index: *Sono kotoba o* sakuiñ *de sagashita.* (その言葉を索引で探した) I looked for the word in the *index*.

sa⌐ku⌐jitsu さくじつ (昨日) *n.* (*for-*

mal) yesterday. 《⇨ kyoo (table)》

sa⌐ku⌐motsu さくもつ（作物）*n.*
crops; farm products:
Kotoshi wa sakumotsu *no deki ga
yosa-soo desu.*（今年は作物のできがよ
さそうです）The *crops* seem promising this year.

sa⌐kuneñ さくねん（昨年）*n.* (*formal*) last year. 《⇨ kotoshi (table)》

sa⌐kura さくら（桜）*n.* cherry
tree; cherry blossoms:
Sakura wa mañkai desu.（桜は満開
です）The *cherry blossoms* are fully
open. ★ The cherry blossom is
Japan's national flower. Japanese
much admire its pink blossoms.
《⇨ hanami (photo)》

SAKURA

sa⌐kusee¹ さくせい（作成）*n.*
drawing up; making out.
sakusee suru (〜する) *vt.* draw
up; make out: *keekakusho [keeyakusho] o* sakusee suru（計画書
[契約書]を作成する）*draw up* a plan
[contract] / *risuto [shiñdañsho] o*
sakusee suru（リスト[診断書]を作成す
る）*make out* a list [medical certificate] / *Sono shorui wa ni-tsuu*
sakusee shite *kudasai.*（その書類は
2通作成してください）Please *draw
up* the document in duplicate.

sa⌐kusee² さくせい（作製）*n.*
= seesaku¹.

sa⌐kuseñ さくせん（作戦）*n.* strategy; tactics; operations:
Kochira no sakuseñ *wa aite chiimu ni yomarete iru yoo da.*（こちら
の作戦は相手チームに読まれているようだ）

Our *strategy* seems to have been
read by the opposing team. /
Kare-ra wa señkyo no sakuseñ *o
netta.*（彼らは選挙の作戦を練った）
They carefully worked out their
tactics for the election.

sa⌐kusha さくしゃ（作者）*n.* author; writer; artist:
Kono uta no sakusha *wa fumee
desu.*（この歌の作者は不明です）The
writer of this song is unknown.

sa⌐kushi さくし（作詞）*n.* writing
a lyric [song]:
sakushi-ka [-sha]（作詞家[者]）a
songwriter.

sa⌐ku⌐ya さくや（昨夜）*n.* last
night; yesterday evening:
Sakuya kiñjo ni kaji ga arimashita.
（昨夜近所に火事がありました）There
was a fire in the neighborhood
last night. / *Sakuya wa hachi-ji ni
ie ni kaerimashita.*（昨夜は8時に家
に帰りました）I came home at eight
last night. 《⇨ koñya》

-sama さま（様）*suf.* ★ Polite
equivalent of '-*sañ*¹.'
1 Mr.; Mrs.; Miss: ★ Used
when paging someone but more
of a written than conversational
form.
*Tanaka-*sama（田中様）*Mr. [Mrs.;
Miss] Tanaka / Tanaka Ichiroo-*
sama（田中一郎様）*Mr.* Ichiro
Tanaka.
2 (used to express respect):
★ Added to a kinship word or a
name signifying a post or position.
*oji-*sama（おじ様）*uncle* / *shichoo-*
sama（市長様）*mayor.*
3 (used to express appreciation):

┌─ USAGE ─────────┐
Added to a word meaning
labor or hard work. Not used
when speaking to one's superiors, but '-*sama deshita*' is
often used to superiors.
└──────────────────┘

Otsukare-sama.（お疲れさま）*You must be very tired.* / Go-kuroo-sama.（ご苦労さま）*I appreciate your help.*

sa⌐ma┐s·u¹ さます（冷ます）*vt.* (sa-mash·i-; samas·a-; samash·i-te Ⓒ) **1** cool:
o-yu o samasu（お湯を冷ます）*cool hot water* / *Yooki wa* samashite *kara, moto no basho ni modoshite kudasai.*（容器は冷ましてから、元の場所に戻してください）Please return the pan to the place where it was after *cooling* it. 《⇨ sameru¹》
2 spoil; dampen:
Kodomo-tachi no netsui o samasu *yoo na koto o itte wa ikemaseñ.*（子どもたちの熱意を冷ますようなことを言ってはいけません）You mustn't say anything which will *dampen* the children's enthusiasm.
《⇨ sameru¹》

sa⌐ma┐s·u² さます（覚ます）*vt.* (sa-mash·i-; samas·a-; samash·i-te Ⓒ) **1** wake up; awake:
Heñ na yume o mite, me o sama-shita.（変な夢を見て、目を覚ました）I had a strange dream and *woke up.* 《⇨ sameru²》
2 awaken; sober up:
hito no mayoi o samasu（人の迷いを覚ます）*bring someone to his senses* / *Yoi o* samashite *kara, uñteñ shi nasai.*（酔いを覚ましてから、運転しなさい）Please drive your car after you *have sobered up.* 《⇨ sameru²》

sa⌐matage┐·ru さまたげる（妨げる）*vt.* (samatage-te Ⓥ) disturb; obstruct; prevent:
Soo-oñ ga akachañ no nemuri o samatageta.（騒音が赤ちゃんの眠りを妨げた）The noise *disturbed* the baby's sleep. / *Kare-ra wa giji no shiñkoo o* samatage-*yoo to shite iru.*（彼らは議事の進行を妨げようとしている）They are trying to *obstruct* the proceedings.

sa⌐ma┐zama さまざま（様々）*a.n.*

(~ na, ni) various; different; all kinds of:
samazama *na moñdai*（さまざまな問題）*all kinds of* problems / Sama-zama *na hito ga* samazama *na ikeñ o motte iru.*（さまざまな人がさまざまな意見を持っている）*Different* people hold *various* opinions.
《⇨ iroiro¹》

sa⌐me┐·ru¹ さめる（冷める）*vi.* (sa-me-te Ⓥ) **1** cool; get cold:
Suupu ga samete *shimatta.*（スープが冷めてしまった）The soup *has gotten cold.* / Samenai *uchi ni o-agari kudasai.*（冷めないうちにお上がりください）Help yourself before it *gets cold.* ★ Expression used when inviting people to help themselves to food. 《⇨ samasu¹》
2 (of a feeling, enthusiasm, etc.) cool down:
Futari no ai wa samete *shimatta.*（二人の愛は冷めてしまった）Their love *has cooled.* / *Kare no gorufu netsu wa* sameta *yoo da.*（彼のゴルフ熱は冷めたようだ）He seems to *have lost* his enthusiasm for golf.

sa⌐me┐·ru² さめる（覚める）*vi.* (sa-me-te Ⓥ) **1** wake up; awake:
Kesa wa go-ji ni me ga sameta.（今朝は5時に目が覚めた）I *woke up* at five this morning.
2 come to one's senses; sober up:
Kare no kotoba de mayoi ga sa-meta.（彼の言葉で迷いが覚めた）His words *brought* me *to my senses.* / *Yoi wa* samemashita *ka?*（酔いは覚めましたか）*Have you sobered up?*
《⇨ samasu²》

sa⌐me┐·ru³ さめる（褪める）*vi.* (sa-me-te Ⓥ) (of color) fade; go out:
iro ga sameru（色がさめる）*be discolored.*

sa⌐mu┐·i さむい（寒い）*a.* (-ku) cold; chilly; freezing:
samui *chihoo*（寒い地方）a *cold* region / *Kinoo wa totemo* samu-

katta.(きのうはとても寒かった) It was very *cold* yesterday. / *Samuku natta no de deñki-gotatsu o da-shita.*(寒くなったので電気ごたつを出した) It got *cold* so I took out the electric foot warmer. 《⇨ samusa》

atsui (暑い / 熱い)	hot
atatakai (暖かい / 温かい)	warm
suzushii (涼しい)	cool
samui (寒い) (of atmosphere)	cold
tsumetai (冷たい) (of the touch)	

sa⌈muke⌉ さむけ (寒気) *n.* chill; cold fit:
Samuke ga suru.(寒気がする) I have a *chill*. / *Kyoofu de senaka ni samuke o oboeta [kañjita].*(恐怖で背中に寒気を覚えた[感じた]) I felt a *chill* of fear run down my spine.

sa⌉musa さむさ (寒さ) *n.* cold; cold weather:
Dañdañ samusa ga kibishiku natte kita.(だんだん寒さが厳しくなってきた) The *cold* has gradually gotten more severe. / *Toshi o toru to samusa ga mi ni shimiru.*(年を取ると寒さが身にしみる) As you get older, you feel the *cold* in your bones. / *Boku wa samusa ni yowai.*(僕は寒さに弱い) I really feel the *cold*. 《↔ atsusa¹》《⇨ samui (table)》

sa⌈ñ⌉¹ さん (三・参) *n.* three; third:
eñpitsu sañ-boñ (鉛筆 3 本) *three* pencils / *sañ-neñ* (3 年) *three* years / *sañ-kai* (3 階) the *third* floor. 《⇨ suu² (table)》

sa⌈ñ⌉² さん (酸) *n.* acid. 《↔ aru-kari》

-sañ¹ さん *suf.* **1** (used to express respect and friendliness):
★ Added to a family or given name.
Yamamoto-sañ (山本さん) *Mr.*

(*Mrs.*; *Miss*) Yamamoto / *Yama-moto Kazuko-sañ* (山本和子さん) *Miss* Kazuko Yamamoto / *Kazuko-sañ* (和子さん) *Kazuko.*
2 (used after a kinship word in certain set phrases):
oji-sañ (おじさん) *uncle* / *oba-sañ* (おばさん) *aunt.*
3 (used to express appreciation in certain set phrases): ★ Not used when speaking to one's superiors.
Otsukare-sañ.(お疲れさん) *You must be tired.* / *Go-kuroo-sañ.* (ご苦労さん) *Thank you for your help.* 《⇨ -sama》

-sañ² さん (山) *suf.* Mount; Mt.
★ Attached to the name of a mountain.
Fuji-sañ (富士山) *Mt.* Fuji / *Shirane-sañ* (白根山) *Mt.* Shirane. 《⇨ -yama》

sa⌈ñbutsu さんぶつ (産物) *n.* product; produce:
Riñgo wa kono chihoo no juuyoo na sañbutsu desu.(りんごはこの地方の重要な産物です) Apples are an important *product* of this district.

sa⌈ñchi さんち (産地) *n.* producing district; production center:
Kono atari wa o-cha no sañchi to shite shirarete imasu.(この辺りはお茶の産地として知られています) This area is known as a *tea-producing district.* / *Yasai wa sañchi choku-soo desu.*(野菜は産地直送です) The vegetables are delivered directly from the *producing districts.*

sa⌉ñdaru サンダル *n.* sandals:
sañdaru *o haku [nugu]* (サンダルをはく[脱ぐ]) put on [take off] *sandals.*

sa⌉ñdo サンド *n.* = sañdoitchi.

sa⌈ñdoi⌉tchi サンドイッチ *n.* sandwich: ★ Often contracted to 'sando.'
hamu sañdoitchi (ハムサンドイッチ) a ham *sandwich.*

sa⌈ñfujiñka さんふじんか (産婦人

科) *n.* obstetrics and gynecology: saⁿfujiⁿka¹-i (産婦人科医) an *obstetrician and gynecologist.*
《⇨ fujiⁿka; byooiⁿ (table)》

saⁿ-gatsu さんがつ (三月) *n.* March:
Hina matsuri wa san-gatsu *mikka desu.* (ひな祭りは三月三日です) The Doll Festival is on *March* 3.
《⇨ tsuki¹ (table)》

Saⁿgiⁿiⁿ さんぎいん (参議院) *n.* the House of Councilors:
Sañgiiñ *giiñ* (参議院議員) a member of *the House of Councilors.*
《⇨ Shuugiiñ; kokkai)》

saⁿgo さんご (珊瑚) *n.* coral.

saⁿgyoo さんぎょう (産業) *n.* industry:
Kono kuni wa sangyoo *ga sakañ da.* (この国は産業が盛んだ) *Industry is thriving in this country.* / *jidoosha-*sangyoo (自動車産業) the automobile *industry.*

Saⁿiⁿ さんいん (山陰) *n.* the northern part of the Chugoku district. It comprises Tottori and Shimane prefectures, and the northern part of Yamaguchi Prefecture. 《⇨ Sañyoo; map (C4)》

saⁿka¹ さんか (参加) *n.* participation; joining:
Miñna ni tooroñkai e no sañka *o yobikaketa.* (みんなに討論会への参加を呼びかけた) We encouraged everyone to *take part* in the debate. / *Watashi wa tenisu no shiai ni* sañka *o mooshikoñda.* (私はテニスの試合に参加を申し込んだ) I *sent in my name* for the tennis tournament.
sañka suru (〜する) *vi.* participate; take part in; join: *Kanojo wa beñroñ taikai ni* sañka *shita.* (彼女は弁論大会に参加した) She *joined* in the speech contest.
《⇨ deru》

saⁿka² さんか (酸化) *n.* oxidation:
hyoomeñ no sañka *o fusegu* (表面の酸化を防ぐ) protect a surface from *oxidation* / sañka-*butsu* (酸化物) *oxide* compound / sañka *booshi-zai* (酸化防止剤) an *antioxidant* / sañka-*zai* (酸化剤) an *oxidizing* agent.
sañka suru (〜する) *vi.* oxidize:
Tetsu wa mizu ni irete oku to, sugu sañka suru. (鉄は水に入れておくと，すぐ酸化する) If you leave iron in water, it *oxidizes* rapidly.

saⁿkaku さんかく (三角) *n.* triangle:
sañkaku-*joogi* (三角定規) a *set square* / sañkaku-*kañkee* (三角関係) the eternal love *triangle.*
《⇨ shikaku²》

saⁿkakukee さんかくけい (三角形) *n.* triangle:
*see-*sañkakukee (正三角形) an equilateral *triangle* / *chokkaku-*sañkakukee (直角三角形) a right *triangle.*

saⁿkeⁿ-buⁿritsu さんけんぶんりつ (三権分立) *n.* separation of the three powers of administration, legislation, and judicature.
《⇨ shihoo²; gyoosee; rippoo²》

saⁿketsu さんけつ (酸欠) *n.* oxygen shortage.

saⁿkoo さんこう (参考) *n.* reference; information; consultation:
Kono shiryoo wa totemo sañkoo *ni narimashita.* (この資料はとても参考になりました) This information *was* very *helpful.* / *Kono hoñ o* sañkoo *ni shi nasai.* (この本を参考にしなさい) You *should refer* to this book. / *Go-*sañkoo *made ni kare no juusho o o-oshie itashimasu.* (ご参考までに彼の住所をお教えいたします) For your *information*, I will give you his address. / sañkoo-*buñkeñ* (参考文献) a *bibliography.*

saⁿkoosho さんこうしょ (参考書) *n.* **1** study-aid book; student handbook. ★ Usually called '*gakushuu-sankoosho.*' Books

necessary for preparing for examinations are called '*juken-sankoosho*.'
2 reference book.

sa⌈nmyaku さんみゃく (山脈) *n.* mountain range [chain].

sa⌈npai さんぱい (参拝) *n.* visit to a shrine or temple for worship: *Watashi wa Meeji-jinguu e* sanpai *ni itta*. (私は明治神宮へ参拝に行った) I visited the Meiji Shrine to *offer up prayers*. 《⇨ omairi》
sanpai suru (〜する) *vi.* go and worship: *Ganjitsu ni wa jinja e itte* sanpai shimasu. (元日には神社へ行って参拝します) We *go and worship* at shrines on New Year's Day.

SANPAI

sa⌈npatsu さんぱつ (散髪) *n.* men's haircut; men's hairdressing:
Tokoya e sanpatsu *ni itte kimasu.* (床屋へ散髪に行ってきます) I'm going to the barbershop to *get a hair cut.*
sanpatsu suru (〜する) *vi.* have a haircut: *Watashi wa kinoo* sanpatsu shita. (私はきのう散髪した) I *had a haircut* yesterday.

sa⌈npo さんぽ (散歩) *n.* walk; stroll:
Asa no sanpo *wa kimochi ga yoi.* (朝の散歩は気持ちが良い) A morning *walk* is refreshing.
sanpo suru (〜する) *vi.* take a

walk: *Watashi wa mainichi yuugata inu o tsurete,* sanpo shimasu. (私は毎日夕方犬を連れて, 散歩します) I *go out* with the dog *for a walk* every evening.

sa⌈nryuu さんりゅう (三流) *n.* third-class; third-rate:
sanryuu *ryokan* (三流旅館) a *third-class* Japanese inn. 《⇨ ichiryuu; niryuu》

sa⌈nsee¹ さんせい (賛成) *n.* agreement; approval; support; favor:
Sansee *no baai wa te o agete kudasai.* (賛成の場合は手を上げてください) If you are in *favor*, please raise your hand. / *Anata wa kono an ni* sansee *desu ka, hantai desu ka?* (あなたはこの案に賛成ですか, 反対ですか) Are you *for* or against this proposal? / Sansee *tasuu to mitomemasu.* (賛成多数と認めます) I recognize that the '*ayes*' are in the majority. 《↔ hantai》
sansee suru (〜する) *vt.* agree; approve; be in favor: *Watashi wa kare no iken ni* sansee shimasu. (私は彼の意見に賛成します) I *agree* with his opinion.

sa⌈nsee² さんせい (三世) *n.* Sansei; the third generation of Japanese immigrants; a member of this generation. 《⇨ issee²; nisee》

sa⌈nshoo さんしょう (参照) *n.* reference:
Juugo-peeji sanshoo. (15 ページ参照) *See* page 15.
sanshoo suru (〜する) *vt.* see; refer to: *Kuwashii koto wa tsugi no sankoosho o* sanshoo shite *kudasai.* (詳しいことは次の参考書を参照してください) Please *refer to* the following reference works for details.

sa⌈nso さんそ (酸素) *n.* oxygen:
sanso-*kyuunyuu* (酸素吸入) *oxygen* inhalation.

sa⌈nsu¹u さんすう (算数) *n.* arithmetic:

Sañsuu *wa nigate desu.*(算数は苦手です) I'm not good at *arithmetic.*

sa˻ñtoo さんとう(三等) *n.* third class; third prize; third place: *Kare wa kuji de* sañtoo *ni natta.* (彼はくじで三等になった) He drew the *third* prize in the lottery. 《⇨ ittoo; nitoo》

Sa˻ñyoo さんよう(山陽) *n.* Sanyo, the southern part of the Chugoku district. It comprises Okayama and Hiroshima prefectures, and the southern part of Yamaguchi Prefecture. 《⇨ Sañiñ; map (C4)》

sa˻ñzañ さんざん(散々) *a.n.* (~ na) severe; terrible: *Tozañ wa ame de* sañzañ *datta.* (登山は雨でさんざんだった) Our mountain climbing was *ruined* by the rain.
— *adv.* severely; terribly: *Sono seeto wa señsee ni* sañzañ *shikarareta.*(その生徒は先生にさんざんしかられた) The pupil was *severely* scolded by his teacher.

sa˻o[1] さお(竿) *n.* pole; rod: ★ Pronounced '*zao*' when preceded by another word to make a compound. *tsuri-*zao (釣り竿) a fishing *rod* / *take-*zao (竹竿) a bamboo *pole.*

sa˻ppa˻ri[1] さっぱり *adv.* (~ suru)
1 feel refreshed: *Furo ni haittara,* sappari *shita.*(ふろに入ったら, さっぱりした) I felt *nice and fresh* after taking a bath.
2 (of clothes) neat: *Kanojo wa itsu-mo* sappari *shita fukusoo o shite iru.*(彼女はいつもさっぱりした服装をしている) She is always dressed *neatly.*
3 (of personality) frank; openhearted: *Kare wa* sappari *shita seekaku o shite iru.*(彼はさっぱりした性格をしている) He has a *frank and openhearted* nature.

4 (of a dish, taste, etc.) simple; plain; light: *Kono ryoori wa* sappari *shita aji o shite iru.*(この料理はさっぱりした味をしている) This dish has a *plain, simple* taste.

sa˻ppa˻ri[2] さっぱり *adv.* **1** no good: *Shikeñ no kekka wa* sappari *datta.* (試験の結果はさっぱりだった) The exam result was *no good.*
2 (with a negative) not at all: *Roshiago wa* sappari *wakarimaseñ.*(ロシア語はさっぱりわかりません) I do not understand Russian *at all.* 《⇨ sukoshi mo》

Sa˻pporo さっぽろ(札幌) *n.* capital of Hokkaido, a commercial center. 《⇨ map (B2)》

sa˻ra さら(皿) *n.* plate; dish; platter; saucer: *suupu hito-*sara (スープ一皿) a *plate* of soup. ★ Sets of Japanese dishes are sold in units of five, not six.

sa˻ra ni さらに(更に) *adv.* further; even [still] more: *Sono keñ wa* sara ni *shiraberu hitsuyoo ga arimasu.*(その件はさらに調べる必要があります) We need to examine the matter *further.* / *Yoru ni naru to, ame wa* sara ni *tsuyoku natta.*(夜になると, 雨はさらに強くなった) The rain became *even* heavier as night fell. / *Sono kaisha wa nooyaku no hoka,* sara ni *iyakuhiñ mo atsukau yoo ni natta.*(その会社は農薬のほか, さらに医薬品も扱うようになった) The company has started to deal in pharmaceuticals *in addition to* agricultural chemicals.

sa˻rada サラダ *n.* salad: sarada *o tsukuru* (サラダを作る) make a *salad* / *yasai-*sarada (野菜サラダ) a vegetable *salad.*

sa˻raineñ さらいねん(再来年) *n.* the year after next: *Musuko wa* saraineñ *daigaku o*

sotsugyoo shimasu. (息子は再来年大学を卒業します) My son will graduate from college *the year after next.* / *Oriñpikku wa* saraineñ *ni hirakaremasu.* (オリンピックは再来年に開かれます) The Olympics will be held *the year after next.*
《⇨ kotoshi》

sa⌐raishuu さらいしゅう (再来週) *n.* the week after next:
Shikeñ wa saraishuu *(ni) hajimarimasu.* (試験は再来週(に)始まります) The examinations start *the week after next.* / Saraishuu *no kyoo made ni shiagete kudasai.* (再来週のきょうまでに仕上げてください) Please finish it by *two weeks from today.*
《⇨ shuu¹ (table)》

sarari⌐imañ サラリーマン *n.* office worker; white-collar worker; salaried worker. ★ Refers to male workers. Female workers are often called '*oo-eru*' (OL).
《⇨ oo-eru》

sa⌐rasara さらさら *adv.* (~ to) (the sound or state of moving or proceeding smoothly):
Ogawa no sarasara (to) *nagareru oto ga kikoeru.* (小川のさらさら(と)流れる音が聞こえる) I can hear the *murmur* of the stream as it *flows* along. / *Kaze de ki no ha ga* sarasara to *natte iru.* (風で木の葉がさらさらと鳴っている) The leaves are *rustling* in the wind. / *Kare wa tegami ni* sarasara to *saiñ shita.* (彼は手紙にさらさらとサインした) He signed the letter *with a flourish.*

sa⌐ra·u¹ さらう (攫う) *vt.* (sara·i-; saraw·a-; sarat-te C) 1 sweep away:
Kodomo ga nami ni sarawareta. (子どもが波にさらわれた) A child *was swept away* by the waves.
2 kidnap:
Kare no hitori musume ga sarawareta. (彼の一人娘がさらわれた) His only daughter *was kidnapped.*

3 carry off (a victory); win (popularity, etc.):
Shiñjiñ ga yuushoo o saratta. (新人が優勝をさらった) The newcomer *carried off* the championship. / *Sono sutaa wa wakamono no niñki o* saratta. (そのスターは若者の人気をさらった) The star *won* the popularity of the young.

sa⌐ra·u² さらう (浚う) *vt.* (sara·i-; saraw·a-; sarat-te C) clean; dredge:
Watashi-tachi wa sono ike o saratta. (私たちはその池をさらった) We *dredged* the pond.

sare-ru される *vt.* (sare-te V)
1 (honorific equivalent of '*suru*'):
Señsee mo shusseki sareru *soo desu.* (先生も出席されるそうです) I hear that the teacher will also *be present.*
2 be done: ★ The passive of '*suru.*'
Watashi wa kare ni ijiwaru sareta. (私は彼に意地悪された) I *was treated* meanly by him.

sa⌐r·u¹ さる (去る) *vi.* (sar·i-; sar·a-; sat-te C) leave; pass; resign:
Kanojo wa kinoo Nihoñ o satte *Supeiñ e mukatta.* (彼女はきのう日本を去ってスペインへ向かった) Yesterday she *left* Japan for Spain. / *Kare wa koñgetsu-matsu ni shoku o* sarimasu. (彼は今月末に職を去ります) He will *retire* from his job at the end of this month. / *Taifuu wa* sarimashita. (台風は去りました) The typhoon *has passed.* / *Ha no itami ga* satta. (歯の痛みが去った) The pain in my tooth *has gone.*

sa⌐ru² さる (猿) *n.* monkey; ape.

sa⌐ru- さる (去る) *pref.* last:
saru *go-gatsu* (去る五月) *last* May / *Sono jikeñ wa* saru *itsuka ni okotta.* (その事件は去る五日に起こった) The incident occurred on the

fifth of *this* [*last*] month.

sa⌐sae·ru ささえる（支える）*vt.* (sa-sae-te Ⓥ) **1** prop up:
Kare wa tana o boo de sasaeta. (彼は棚を棒で支えた) He *propped up* the shelf with a stick.
2 support (a family, group, organization, etc.):
Kare wa hitori de roku-niñ kazoku o sasaete iru. (彼は一人で6人家族を支えている) He *supports* a family of six by himself.

sa⌐sa⌐r·u ささる（刺さる）*vi.* (sasar·i-; sasar·a-; sasat-te Ⓒ) stick; prick:
Hari ga yubi ni sasatta. (針が指に刺さった) A needle *pricked* my finger.

sa⌐sa⌐yaka ささやか *a.n.* (~ na, ni) small; humble; modest:
shomiñ no sasayaka *na negai* (庶民のささやかな願い) a *modest* request from common folk / *Watanabe-sañ no tame ni* sasayaka *na kañgee-kai o moyooshitai to omoimasu.* (渡辺さんのためにささやかな歓迎会を催したいと思います) We would like to have a *small* welcome party for Miss Watanabe. / *Kare-ra wa* sasayaka *ni kurashite imasu.* (彼らはささやかに暮らしています) They live in a *humble* way.

saserare·ru させられる *vt.* (-rare-te Ⓥ) be made to do:
Watashi wa toire no sooji o saserareta. (私はトイレの掃除をさせられた) I *was made* to clean the toilet. / *Kanojo wa doñna shigoto o* saserareru *no ka shiñpai datta.* (彼女はどんな仕事をさせられるのか心配だった) She was anxious about what kind of work she was going to *be made to do.* / *Paatii de jiko-shookai* saserarete *hazukashikatta.* (パーティーで自己紹介させられて恥ずかしかった) I felt shy when I *was made* to introduce myself at the party. 《⇨ saseru; -rareru》

sase·ru させる *vt.* (sase-te Ⓥ) **1** make someone do; cause someone to do:
Otooto ni shigoto o saseta. (弟に仕事をさせた) I *made* my younger brother *do* some work. / *Koochi wa señshu ni mainichi* reñshuu saseta. (コーチは選手に毎日練習させた) The coach *made* the players *practice* every day. / *Soñna koto wa kare ni* sase *nasai.* (そんなことは彼にさせなさい) You had better *make* him *do* such a thing.
2 let someone do; allow someone do:
Watashi wa kare-ra ni yaritai-yoo ni saseta. (私は彼らにやりたいようにさせた) I *let* them *do* as they wished. / *Sore wa watashi ni* sasete *kudasai.* (それは私にさせてください) Please *allow* me *to do* it.

-sase·ru させる *infl. end.* (-sase-te Ⓥ) [attached to the negative base of a vowel-stem verb and '*kuru*,' and itself inflected like a vowel-stem verb]
1 make someone do; cause someone to do:
Kare no kañgae o kaesaseru *no wa muzukashii.* (彼の考えを変えさせるのはむずかしい) It is difficult to *make* him *change* his mind. / *Anata ga korarenakereba, dare-ka hoka no hito o* kosasete *kudasai.* (あなたが来られなければだれかほかの人を来させてください) If you can't come, please *have* someone else *come.* 《⇨ -seru》
2 let someone do; allow someone to do:
Sono ko ni suki na dake tabesasete *yari nasai.* (その子に好きなだけ食べさせてやりなさい) *Let* the child *eat* as much as he likes. 《⇨ -seru》

sa⌐shiage·ru さしあげる（差し上げる）*vt.* (-age-te Ⓥ) (*honorific*) give; present:
Seekai no kata ni wa shoohiñ o

sashiagemasu.（正解の方には賞品を差し上げます）We will *present* a prize to the person who answers correctly. / *Nani o* sashiagemashoo *ka?* (*at a store*)（何を差し上げましょうか）*May I help you?*

sa⌈shidas·u さしだす（差し出す）*vt.* (-dash·i-; -das·a-; -dash·i-te Ⓒ) **1** hold up; reach out: *Sono seerusumañ wa meeshi o* sashidashita.（そのセールスマンは名刺を差し出した）The salesman *held out* his business card. / *Kanojo wa te o* sashidashite *akushu o motometa.*（彼女は手を差し出して握手を求めた）She *held out* her hand for a handshake.
2 hand in; present; submit: *Kono shorui o ashita zeemusho ni* sashidasanakereba narimaseñ.（この書類をあした税務署に差し出さなければなりません）I *have to submit* these documents tomorrow to the tax office.

sa⌈shi⌉hiki さしひき（差し引き）*n.* balance; total: Sashihiki *ikura ni narimasu ka?*（差し引きいくらになりますか）How much does it come to *all together?* (⇨ gookee)
sashihiki suru（～する）*vi.* balance: Sashihiki suru *to goseñ-eñ no kuroji ni narimasu.*（差し引きすると5千円の黒字になります）If we *work out the balance*, we end up with 5,000 yen to the good.

sa⌈shimi⌉ さしみ（刺身）*n.* slices of raw fish for eating: *maguro [tai] no* sashimi（まぐろ[鯛]の刺身）*sliced raw* tuna [sea bream]. ((⇨ photo (right)))

sa⌈shitsukae さしつかえ（差し支え）*n.* (with a negative) difficulty; obstruction; harm: Sashitsukae nakereba, *ashita kite kudasai.*（差し支えなければ、あした来てください）*If it is not inconvenient,* I would like you to come tomor-

SASHIMI

row. / *Kono kyuujoo wa yane ga aru kara ame ga futte mo* sashitsukae arimaseñ.（この球場は屋根があるから雨が降っても差し支えありません）Since this ball park has a roof, the rain *does not interfere* with the game. ((⇨ sashitsukaeru))

sa⌈shitsukae·ru さしつかえる（差し支える）*vi.* (-tsukae-te Ⓥ) interfere; affect: *Chooshoku o tabenai to karada ni* sashitsukaemasu *yo.*（朝食を食べないと体に差し支えますよ）If you don't eat breakfast, it will *affect* your health. ((⇨ sashitsukae))

sa⌈shizu さしず（指図）*n.* directions; instructions; orders: *Kare no* sashizu *wa ukemaseñ.*（彼の指図は受けません）I will not take *orders* from him. / *Dare no* sashizu *de soo shita ñ desu ka?*（だれの指図でそうしたんですか）On whose *instructions* did you do that?
sashizu suru（～する）*vt.* direct; instruct; order: *Señsee wa seeto ni sugu heya kara deru yoo ni* sashizu shita.（先生は生徒にすぐ部屋から出るように指図した）The teacher *instructed* the students to go out of the room immediately. / *Watashi wa hito kara are kore* sashizu saretaku nai.（私は人からあれこれ指図されたくない）I *do not want to be told* by anyone to do this and that.

sa⌈so·u さそう（誘う）*vt.* (saso·i-; sasow·a-; sasot-te Ⓒ) **1** invite;

ask; allure; tempt:
shokuji ni sasou(食事に誘う)*invite* (a person) to dinner / *Watashi wa sukii ni ikoo to kanojo o* sasotta.(私はスキーに行こうと彼女を誘った) I *asked* her to come skiing.

2 cause (tears, laughter, etc.):
Sono eega wa kañkyaku no namida o sasotta.(その映画は観客の涙を誘った) The film *moved* the audience to tears.

sa⌐ssa to さっさと *adv.* quickly; promptly:
Sassa to aruki nasai.(さっさと歩きなさい) Walk *quickly.* / *Jikañ ga kuru to kare-ra wa* sassa to *shigoto o yameta.*(時間が来ると彼らはさっさと仕事をやめた) When the time came, they *promptly* stopped working.

sa⌐sshi さっし (察し) *n.* understanding; guess; judgment:
Kare wa sasshi *ga ii* [*warui*].(彼は察しがいい[悪い]) He is quick [slow] to *understand.* / *Kanojo no toshi wa* sasshi *ga tsukimasu.*(彼女の年は察しがつきます) It is not difficult to *guess* her age. 《⇨ sassuru》

sa⌐ssoku さっそく (早速) *adv.* immediately; promptly:
Go-chuumoñ no shina wa sassoku *o-todoke shimasu.*(ご注文の品は早速お届けします) We will *immediately* deliver the goods you have ordered. / *Watashi wa kanojo no tegami ni* sassoku *heñji o kaita.*(私は彼女の手紙に早速返事を書いた) I *promptly* replied to her letter.

sa⌐ssoo to さっそうと *adv.* smartly; dashingly:
Kare wa atarashii fuku de sassoo to *arawareta.*(彼は新しい服でさっそうと現れた) He showed up *smartly* dressed in a new suit. / *Kodomotachi wa* sassoo to *kooshiñ shita.*(子どもたちはさっそうと行進した) The children marched *with light steps.*

sa⌐ss·uru さっする (察する) *vt.* (sassh·i-; sassh·i-; sassh·i-te

Ⅰ) **1** guess; presume; suppose:
Watashi wa kare ga nani-ka kakushite iru to sasshita.(私は彼が何か隠していると察した) I *guessed* that he was hiding something. / *Sassuru tokoro, kare wa kanari soñ o shita rashii.*(察するところ, 彼はかなり損をしたらしい) *According to what I have gathered*, it seems that he has lost a considerable amount. 《⇨ sasshi》

2 appreciate; understand:
*O-kimochi wa o-*sasshi *itashimasu.*(お気持ちはお察しいたします) I *appreciate* how you feel.

sa⌐s·u[1] さす (指す) *vt.* (sash·i-; sas·a-; sash·i-te Ⓒ) **1** point; show; indicate:
Dore ga hoshii ka, yubi de sashi *nasai.*(どれが欲しいか, 指で指しなさい) *Point* to the one you want. / *Tokee no hari ga juuni-ji o* sashite *iru.*(時計の針が12時を指している) The hands of the clock *show* twelve o'clock.

2 mean; refer to:
Anata no koto o sashite, *itta wake de wa arimaseñ.*(あなたのことを指して, 言った訳ではありません) I do not mean to imply that I *was referring to* you.

3 (in a classroom) call on:
Kare wa kurasu de yoku señsee ni sasareru.(彼はクラスでよく先生に指される) In class, he *is often called on* by the teacher.

sa⌐s·u[2] さす (刺す) *vt.* (sash·i-; sas·a-; sash·i-te Ⓒ) **1** stab; pierce; thrust:
Sono otoko wa kanojo o naifu de sashita.(その男は彼女をナイフで刺した) The man *stabbed* her with a knife.

2 (of an insect) sting; bite:
Hachi ni te o sasareta.(蜂に手を刺された) I *was stung* on the hand by a bee.

3 (in baseball) throw out:
Rañnaa wa sañrui de sasareta.(ラ

ンナーは 3 塁で刺された) The runner *was thrown out* at third base.

sa「suga さすが (流石) *adv.*

1 (〜 ni) truly; indeed:
Sasuga ni *Fuji-sañ wa utsukushii*. (さすがに富士山は美しい) Mt. Fuji is *truly* beautiful. / *Nihoñ no natsu wa* sasuga ni *mushiatsui*. (日本の夏はさすがに蒸し暑い) Japanese summers are *indeed* muggy.

2 (〜 no) even:
Sasuga no *kare mo tsui ni maketa*. (さすがの彼もついに負けた) *Even* he finally suffered a defeat.

3 (〜 ni/wa) just as one might expect:
Sasuga wa *taika da. Migoto na e da*. (さすがは大家だ. みごとな絵だ) *That's just what one would expect* of a master. It's a wonderful painting.

sa「tchuuzai さっちゅうざい (殺虫剤) *n.* insecticide.

sa「te さて *int.* now; well:
★ Used at the beginning of a sentence.
Sate, *tsugi no gidai ni utsurimasu*. (さて, 次の議題に移ります) *Now* we are going to move on to the next topic. / Sate, *doo shita mono ka?* (さて, どうしたものか) *And now*, what shall we do?

sa「te-wa さては *adv.* well; then; surely:
Sate-wa, *aitsu ore o damashita na*. (さては, あいつおれをだましたな) *Well*, that guy cheated me.

sa「toimo さといも (里芋) *n.* taro. 《⇨ imo (illus.)》

sa「to「o さとう (砂糖) *n.* sugar:
Koohii ni wa satoo *o iremasu ka?* (コーヒーには砂糖を入れますか) Would you like *sugar* in your coffee? / *Watashi wa* satoo *o hikaete imasu*. (私は砂糖を控えています) I am careful not to take too much *sugar*.

sa「tor・u さとる (悟る) *vt.* (sator・i-; sator・a-; satot-te ⓒ) **1** realize; find:
Koto no juudai-sa o satotta. (事の重大さを悟った) I *realized* the importance of the matter.

2 sense (danger):
Kikeñ o satotte, *kare wa sugu nigeta*. (危険を悟って, 彼はすぐ逃げた) *Sensing* danger, he quickly escaped.

sa「tsu さつ (札) *n.* paper money; bill; note:
señ-eñ satsu (千円札) a 1,000-yen *bill*. ★ '*O-satsu*' is more common when used independently. 《⇨ shihee (photo)》

-satsu さつ (冊) *suf.* volume; copy: ★ Counter for books and magazines.
Kono jisho wa ni-satsu ni wakarete imasu. (この辞書は 2 冊に分かれています) This dictionary is divided into two *volumes*. / Watashi wa zasshi o sañ-satsu totte imasu. (私は雑誌を 3 冊とっています) I subscribe to *three* magazines.

sa「tsutaba さつたば (札束) *n.* roll [wad] of bills:
satsutaba o kazoeru (札束を数える) count a *wad of money*.

sa「tsuee さつえい (撮影) *n.* photographing; shooting:
Koko de wa butsuzoo no satsuee wa kiñshi sarete imasu. (ここでは仏像の撮影は禁止されています) *Taking photographs* of the Buddhist image is prohibited here.

satsuee suru (〜する) *vt.* take a picture; photograph; shoot:
Sono kañtoku wa ima atarashii eega o satsuee shite imasu. (その監督は今新しい映画を撮影しています) The director *is* now *shooting* a new movie.

sa「tsujiñ さつじん (殺人) *n.* homicide; murder:
satsujiñ o okasu (殺人を犯す) commit *murder* / satsujiñ-jikeñ (殺人

事件) a *murder* case / satsujiñ-hañ (殺人犯) a *murderer*.

sa⌈tsumaimo さつまいも *n.*
sweet potato. 《⇨ imo (illus.)》

sa⌉tto さっと *adv.* quickly; suddenly:
hooreñsoo o satto *yuderu* (ほうれん草をさっとゆでる) boil spinach *quickly* / *Doa ga* satto *hiraita*. (ドアがさっと開いた) The door opened *suddenly*. / *Ame ga* satto *futte kita*. (雨がさっと降ってきた) A shower came on *suddenly*.

sa⌈wagashi⌉·i さわがしい (騒がしい) *a.* (-ku) noisy; boisterous:
Kodomo-tachi no koe ga sawagashii. (子どもたちの声が騒がしい) The children's voices are very *noisy*. / *Koko wa* sawagashikute, *hanashi ga dekimaseñ*. (ここは騒がしくて、話ができません) It is too *noisy* here for us to talk. / *Kono mura mo dañdañ* sawagashiku *natte kita*. (この村もだんだん騒がしくなってきた) This village, too, has become *noisier* bit by bit. 《⇨ sawagi; sawagu》

sa⌉wagi さわぎ (騒ぎ) *n.* noise; clamor; uproar:
Tonari no heya kara sugoi sawagi *ga kikoeru*. (隣の部屋からすごい騒ぎが聞える) I can hear a terrible *racket* from the next room. / *Kore wa ittai nañ no* sawagi *desu ka?* (これはいったい何の騒ぎですか) What on earth is this *uproar*? / *Kono* sawagi *o okoshita no wa dare desu ka?* (この騒ぎを起こしたのはだれですか) Who is it that created this *uproar*? 《⇨ sawagu; sawagashii》

...dokoro no sawagi de wa nai (...どころの〜ではない) be out of the question: *Isogashikute, natsuyasumi* dokoro no sawagi de wa nai. (忙しくて、夏休みどころの騒ぎではない) I am so busy that taking a summer holiday *is out of the question*.

sa⌈wa⌉g·u さわぐ (騒ぐ) *vi.* (sawa-g·i-; sawag·a-; sawa·i-de [C])
1 make a noise; clamor:
Soñna ni sawaganai de *kudasai*. (そんなに騒がないでください) *Don't make* such *a noise*. / *Kare-ra wa sono hooañ ni hañtai shite* sawa-ida. (彼らはその法案に反対して騒いだ) They *clamored* in protest against the bill.
2 make merry:
Miñna de uta o utatte sawaida. (みんなで歌を歌って騒いだ) We all sang and *made merry*. 《⇨ sawagi》
3 make a fuss:
Ano kashu wa ima masukomi de sawagarete imasu. (あの歌手は今マスコミで騒がれています) *A great fuss is* now *made of* that singer by the media. 《⇨ sawagi》

sa⌈war·u¹ さわる (触る) *vi.* (sawar·i-; sawar·a-; sawat-te [C])
touch; feel:
Teñjihiñ ni sawaranai de *kudasai*. (展示品に触らないでください) *Don't touch* the articles on display. / *Kono kire wa* sawaru *to kinu no yoo da*. (このきれは触ると絹のようだ) If you *touch* this cloth, it is like silk.

sa⌈war·u² さわる (障る) *vi.* (sawar·i-; sawar·a-; sawat-te [C])
1 hurt (a person's feelings); get on (a person's nerves); offend:
Kanojo no kotoba ga kare no ki ni sawatta. (彼女の言葉が彼の気にさわった) Her words *hurt* his feelings.
2 affect; be harmful (to health):
Nomi-sugi wa karada ni sawaru. (飲み過ぎは体にさわる) Drinking to excess *affects* the health.

sa⌈wa⌉yaka さわやか (爽やか) *a.n.* (〜 na, ni) fresh; refreshing; crisp; pleasant:
sawayaka *na asa no kuuki* (さわやかな朝の空気) the *refreshing* morning air / *Ano hito no hanashikata wa* sawayaka *da*. (あの人の話し方はさわやかだ) His way of speaking is *clear and crisp*.

sa「yona「ra さよなら (*informal*)
Goodbye. 《⇒ sayoonara》

sa「yoo さよう (作用) *n.* action;
operation; function:
sayoo *to* hañ-sayoo (作用と反作用)
action and reaction / *Shio wa iñryoku no* sayoo *de okorimasu.* (潮
は引力の作用で起こります) Tides are
caused by the *action* of gravity. /
*kokyuu-*sayoo (呼吸作用) respiratory *action.*

sa「yoona「ra さようなら (左様なら)
Goodbye; So long:
Sayoonara, *o-geñki de.* (さようなら,
お元気で) *Goodbye*, all that best!

sa「yuu さゆう (左右) *n.* right and
left:
Michi o wataru toki wa sayuu *o
yoku mi nasai.* (道を渡るときは左右を
よく見なさい) Carefully look *right
and left* before crossing the
street. / *Hikooki ga totsuzeñ* sayuu *ni yureta.* (飛行機が突然左右に
揺れた) The plane suddenly rolled
from side to side. 《⇒ jooge; ue-
shita》

sayuu suru (～する) decide; influence; control: *Sono moñdai
ga señkyo o ookiku* sayuu shita.
(その問題が選挙を大きく左右した)
That matter greatly *influenced*
the election. / *Kono kooto wa
yane ga aru no de teñkoo ni* sayuu
saremaseñ. (このコートは屋根があるの
で天候に左右されません) Since this
court has a roof, the weather
makes no difference.

sa「zo さぞ *adv.* surely; I am
sure:
Okaasañ wa sazo *yorokoñda deshoo.* (お母さんはさぞ喜んだでしょう) *I
am sure* your mother was very
pleased. / *Nagai tabi de* sazo *tsukareta deshoo.* (長い旅でさぞ疲れたで
しょう) You *must be* tired from
your long trip.

sa「zuka「r・u さずかる (授かる) *vi.*
(sazukar・i-; sazukar・a-; sazukat-

te C) be given [awarded]; be
blessed with:
*Kare wa naganeñ no kooseki ni ta-
ishite tokubetsu no shoo o* sazukatta. (彼は長年の功績に対して特別の
賞を授かった) He *was conferred* special honors for his years of service. / *Kotoshi Buñka-kuñshoo o*
sazukatta *no wa go-niñ desu.* (こと
し文化勲章を授かったのは 5 人です)
There were five people who *were
awarded* the Order of Culture
this year. / *Kanojo wa oñna-no-ko
o* sazukatta. (彼女は女の子を授かった)
She *was blessed with* the birth of
a girl. 《⇒ sazukeru》

sa「zuke「・ru さずける (授ける) *vt.*
(sazuke-te V) award; confer;
grant:
Sono gaka wa Buñka-kuñshoo o
sazukerareta. (その画家は文化勲章を
授けられた) That painter *was
awarded* the Order of Culture.
《⇒ sazukaru》

se せ (背) *n.* **1** back:
uma no se *ni noru* (馬の背に乗る)
ride on a horse's *back* / se *o nobasu* (背を伸ばす) straighten one's
back / *Kare wa omoi ryukku o* se
ni otte, yama o nobotta. (彼は重いリ
ュックを背に負って, 山を登った) He
climbed the mountain with a
heavy rucksack on his *back.*
《⇒ senaka》
2 = see[1].

se「biro せびろ (背広) *n.* business
suit; lounge suit:
daburu no sebiro (ダブルの背広) a
double-breasted *suit* / sebiro *no
mitsuzoroi* (背広の三つぞろい) a
three-piece *suit.*

se「dai せだい (世代) *n.* generation:
Ano señshu to watashi wa doo
sedai *da.* (あの選手と私は同世代だ)
That player and I are of the
same *generation.* / *Tsugi no* sedai
no hito-tachi ni ooi-ni kitai shite

imasu. (次の世代の人たちにおおいに期待しています) I expect much from the next *generation.*

se｜e[1] せい (背) *n.* height of a person; stature:

see *ga nobiru* (背が伸びる) grow in *stature* / *Kare wa watashi yori* see *ga takai* [*hikui*]. (彼は私より背が高い[低い]) He *is taller* [*shorter*] than me. 《⇨ se》

se｜e[2] せい (性) *n.* sex: ★ The act of sex is called '*sekkusu*.'

see *no sabetsu* (性の差別) *sexual* discrimination / see-*kyooiku* (性教育) *sex* education.

se｜e[3] せい (姓) *n.* family name; surname. 《⇨ myooji (table)》

se｜e[4] せい (精) *n.* energy; vigor.

see o dasu (〜を出す) work hard: see *o dashite beñkyoo suru* (精を出して勉強する) study *harder.*

se｜e[5] せい (所為) *n.* **1** blame; fault:

Sore wa watashi no see *de wa arimaseñ.* (それは私のせいではありません) It's not my *fault.* / *Miñna wa sono jiko o kare no* see *ni shita.* (みんなはその事故を彼のせいにした) They all *blamed* the accident on him.

2 because of; due to: ★ Indicates an unfavorable cause or reason.

Deñsha ga okureta no wa yuki no see *desu.* (電車が遅れたのは雪のせいです) The train was late *because of* the snow. / *Kare ga shippai shita no wa taimañ no* see *da.* (彼が失敗したのは怠慢のせいだ) His failure is *due to* his negligence. 《⇨ okage》

-see せい (製) *suf.* made in [by; of]; -made:

garasu-see *no kabiñ* (ガラス製の花瓶) a vase *made* of glass / *Nihoñ*-see *no kamera* (日本製のカメラ) a Japanese-*made* camera.

se｢ebetsu せいべつ (性別) *n.* distinction of sex:

Seebetsu *ni kañkee naku dare de mo oobo dekimasu.* (性別に関係なくだれでも応募できます) Anyone can apply, regardless of *sex.* / *Pañda no akachañ no* seebetsu *wa mada wakarimaseñ.* (パンダの赤ちゃんの性別はまだわかりません) The *sex* of the baby panda has not been determined yet.

se｢ebi せいび (整備) *n.* maintenance; repair; improvement:

kuruma no seebi (車の整備) motor vehicle *maintenance* / *kañkyoo no* seebi (環境の整備) *improvement* of the environment / seebi-*koojoo* (整備工場) a *repair* shop.

seebi suru (〜する) *vt.* maintain; service; improve: *Watashi wa kuruma o* seebi *shite moratta.* (私は車を整備してもらった) I *had* my car *serviced.* / *Gurañdo o* seebi *suru no wa watashi-tachi no tsutome desu.* (グランドを整備するのは私たちの務めです) It is our duty to *look after* the sports ground.

se｢ebo せいぼ (歳暮) *n.* year-end gift: ★ Usually with '*o-*.' Japanese people customarily send '*o-seebo*' to those to whom they feel indebted. 《⇨ chuugeñ》

se｜ebuñ せいぶん (成分) *n.* ingredient; component:

kusuri no seebuñ (薬の成分) the *ingredients* of a medicine.

se｜ebutsu せいぶつ (生物) *n.* living thing; creature.

se｜ebyoo せいびょう (性病) *n.* venereal disease.

se｢echoo せいちょう (成長) *n.* growth:

Kono ki wa seechoo *ga hayai.* (この木は成長が速い) This tree *grows quickly.* / *Kono kuni no keezai no* seechoo *wa mezamashii.* (この国の経済の成長はめざましい) This country's economic *growth* is striking.

seechoo suru (〜する) *vi.* grow: *Musuko wa* seechoo *shite, ichi-*

niñ-mae ni narimashita. (息子は成長して，一人前になりました) My son *has grown up* to be a fully independent man.

se˺edo せいど（制度）*n.* system; institution:

atarashii seedo o mookeru (新しい制度を設ける) establish a new *system* / *seedo o haishi suru* (制度を廃止する) abolish a *system* / *kyooiku*-seedo (教育制度) an educational *system* / *seeji*-seedo (政治制度) political *institutions.*

se˺e-eki せいえき（精液）*n.* semen; sperm.

se˺efu せいふ（政府）*n.* government; administration:

Ima no seefu *wa zoozee o kañgaete iru.* (今の政府は増税を考えている) The present *government* is considering a tax increase. / seefu *tookyoku* (政府当局) the *government* authorities.

se˺efuku[1] せいふく（制服）*n.* uniform:

Seeto wa miñna seefuku *o kite iru.* (生徒はみんな制服を着ている) The pupils are all in *uniform.*

se˺efuku[2] せいふく（正副）*n.* original and duplicate:

shorui o seefuku *ni-tsuu sakusee suru* (書類を正副2通作成する) make out documents in *duplicate* / seefuku *gichoo* (正副議長) the *chairman and vice-chairman.*

se˺egeñ せいげん（制限）*n.* restriction; limit:

Oobo ni wa neñree no seegeñ *ga arimasu.* (応募には年齢の制限があります) There is an age *limit* for applications. / *Kono shina no kazu ni wa* seegeñ *ga arimasu.* (この品の数には制限があります) These goods *are limited* in number. / seegeñ-*jikañ* [*sokudo*] (制限時間[速度]) a time [speed] *limit.*

seegeñ suru （〜する）*vt.* restrict; limit: *Nihoñ wa yunyuu o* seegeñ

shite iru *to hinañ sarete iru.* (日本は輸入を制限していると非難されている) Japan is criticized for *restricting* imports. / *Watashi wa* shokuji o seegeñ shite imasu. (私は食事を制限してます) I *am on a diet.*

se˺egi せいぎ（正義）*n.* justice; right:

seegi *no mikata* (正義の味方) a champion of *right* / *Seegi no tatakai nado to iu mono wa soñzai shinai.* (正義の戦いなどというものは存在しない) Such a thing as a fight for *justice* does not exist. / seegi-*kañ* (正義感) a sense of *justice.*

se˺ehiñ せいひん（製品）*n.* product; article; goods:

Seehiñ *no hañbuñ wa yushutsu shite imasu.* (製品の半分は輸出しています) We export half of our *products.* / *Nihoñ*-seehiñ (日本製品) *articles* made in Japan / *gaikoku*-seehiñ (外国製品) foreign *products* / *deñki*-seehiñ (電気製品) electric *appliances.*

se˺eho˺okee せいほうけい（正方形）*n.* square.

se˺eiku せいいく（成育・生育）*n.* growth: ★ '成育' is usually used for animals and '生育' for plants.

sakana no seeiku (魚の成育) the *growth* of fish / *Kotoshi wa kyabetsu no* seeiku *ga ryookoo da.* (今年はキャベツの生育が良好だ) The cabbages are showing very satisfactory *growth* this year.

seeiku suru （〜する）*vt., vi.* grow: *Ine wa juñchoo ni* seeiku *shite imasu.* (稲は順調に生育しています) The rice plants *are coming along* nicely.

se˺eji せいじ（政治）*n.* politics; government; administration:

Seeji ni mukañshiñ na hito ga ooi. (政治に無関心な人が多い) Many people are indifferent to *politics.* / seeji-*katsudoo* (政治活動) *political* activity / *miñshu*-seeji (民主政治)

democratic *government*.

se⌐ejika せいじか (政治家) *n.*
statesman; politician.

se⌐ejiñ せいじん (成人) *n.* adult;
grown-up:
seejiñ-*eega* (成人映画) an *adult*
movie / seejiñ-*shiki* (成人式) a
coming-of-age ceremony.
seejiñ suru (〜する) *vi.* become
an adult; come of age: *Kodomo
wa sañ-niñ tomo* seejiñ shimashita.
(子どもは 3 人とも成人しました) All
three of my children *have
reached adulthood.*

se⌐ejiñbyoo せいじんびょう (成人
病) *n.* adult diseases; diseases
which are often connected with
aging.

Se⌐ejiñ-no-hi⌐ (成人の日) *n.*
Coming-of-Age Day (Jan. 15).
《⇨ shukujitsu (table)》

se⌐ejitsu せいじつ (誠実) *a.n.*
(〜 na, ni) sincere; honest; faithful:
seejitsu *na hitogara* (誠実な人柄)
an *honest* personality / *Kare wa
yakusoku o* seejitsu *ni jikkoo
shita.* (彼は約束を誠実に実行した) He
faithfully carried out his promise.

se⌐ejoo せいじょう (正常) *a.n.*
(〜 na, ni) normal; ordinary:
seejoo *na niñgen* (正常な人間) a
psychologically normal individual
/ *Kare no ishiki wa* seejoo *ni modotta.* (彼の意識は正常に戻った) He
returned to his *normal senses.* /
Taioñ wa seejoo *desu.* (体温は正常
です) My temperature is *normal.* /
Kikai wa zeñbu seejoo *ni ugoite
imasu.* (機械は全部正常に動いていま
す) The machinery is all working
normally.

se⌐ejooka せいじょうか (正常化) *n.*
normalization.
seejooka suru (〜する) *vt.* normalize: *Seefu wa sono kuni to no
kokkoo o* seejooka shiyoo *to do-*

ryoku shite iru. (政府はその国との国
交を正常化しようと努力している) The
government is making efforts to
normalize diplomatic relations
with that contry.

se⌐ejuku せいじゅく (成熟) *n.* ripeness; maturity:
kudamono no seejuku (果物の成熟)
the *ripeness* of a fruit.
seejuku suru (〜する) *vt.* ripen;
mature: *Kono riñgo wa mada
juubuñ ni* seejuku shite imaseñ.
(このりんごはまだ十分に成熟していません)
This apple *is not* yet fully *ripe.* /
Saikiñ no kodomo wa seejuku suru
no ga hayai. (最近の子どもは成熟する
のが早い) Children these days
mature rapidly.

se⌐ekai せいかい (正解) *n.* correct
answer.

se⌐ekaku¹ せいかく (性格) *n.* character; disposition; personality:
Ano ko wa sunao na seekaku *o
shite iru.* (あの子は素直な性格をしてい
る) That child has a gentle *character.* / *Kare wa* seekaku *ga akarui
[kurai].* (彼は性格が明るい[暗い]) He
has a cheerful [gloomy] *disposition.* / *Kono buñshoo ni wa kare
no* seekaku *ga dete iru.* (この文章に
は彼の性格が出ている) His *personality* is revealed in these writings.

se⌐ekaku² せいかく (正確) *a.n.*
(〜 na, ni) correct; accurate; precise; exact:
Shiñbuñ no kiji ga itsu-mo seekaku *to wa kagiranai.* (新聞の記事がい
つも正確とは限らない) Newspaper
reports are not always *accurate.* /
Kono shigoto wa seekaku-sa *ga
yookyuu sareru.* (この仕事は正確さが
要求される) This work requires
accuracy. / *Kono tokee wa* seekaku *desu.* (この時計は正確です) This
watch is *accurate.* / Seekaku *na
jikañ o oshiete kudasai.* (正確な時
間を教えてください) Please tell me
the *correct* time. / *Keesañ wa* see-

kaku *ni shite kudasai.* (計算は正確にしてください) Please do the calculations *correctly.* 《↔ fuseekaku》

se⌐ekatsu せいかつ (生活) *n.* life; living; livelihood:
zeetaku na seekatsu (ぜいたくな生活) a *life* of luxury / seekatsu *o kiritsumeru* (生活を切り詰める) cut back on *daily expenses* / Seekatsu *ga kurushii* [*raku da*]. (生活が苦しい [楽だ]) *Life* is hard [easy]. / *Ryooshiñ wa inaka de heewa na* seekatsu *o okutte imasu.* (両親は田舎で平和な生活を送っています) My parents lead a quiet *life* in the country. / *Kare wa* mainichi no seekatsu ni komatte iru *rashii.* (彼は毎日の生活に困っているらしい) He seems to be having a *difficult time getting by.* / seekatsu-*hi* (生活費) *living* expenses / seekatsu-*suijuñ* (生活水準) the standard of *living.* 《⇨ seekee¹》

seekatsu (o) suru (〜 (を) する) *vi.* live; make a living: *Musume wa jibuñ no kyuuryoo de* seekatsu shite imasu. (娘は自分の給料で生活しています) My daughter *gets by* on her salary.

se⌐ekee¹ せいけい (生計) *n.* one's living; one's livelihood:
seekee *o tateru* (生計を立てる) make *one's living* / *Kanojo wa suupaa de hataraite* seekee *o tasukete iru.* (彼女はスーパーで働いて生計を助けている) She helps *support her family* by working at a supermarket.

se⌐ekee² せいけい (整形) *n.* orthopedic surgery; plastic surgery:
hana no seekee-*shujutsu* (鼻の整形手術) *plastic surgery* on the nose.

seekee suru (〜する) *vt.* have plastic surgery: *Kanojo wa* seekee shitara *bijiñ ni natta.* (彼女は整形したら美人になった) She became a beauty *after having cosmetic surgery.*

se⌐ekee-ge⌐ka せいけいげか (整形外科) *n.* orthopedics. 《⇨ byooiñ (table)》

se⌐ekeñ せいけん (政権) *n.* political power:
seekeñ *o nigiru* [*ushinau*] (政権を握る [失う]) come into [lose] *power* / *Hoshutoo ga geñzai* seekeñ *o nigitte iru.* (保守党が現在政権を握っている) The conservative party is now in *power.*

se⌐eketsu せいけつ (清潔) *a.n.*
(〜 na, ni) **1** clean; neat:
seeketsu *na minari* (清潔な身なり) a *clean and neat* appearance / *Toire wa itsu-mo* seeketsu *ni shite oki nasai.* (トイレはいつも清潔にしておきなさい) Please keep the toilet *clean.* 《↔ fuketsu》
2 honest:
seeketsu *na seejika* (清潔な政治家) an *honest* politician.

se⌐eki せいき (世紀) *n.* century:
kigeñ-zeñ yoñ-seeki (紀元前 4 世紀) the fourth *century* B.C. / *ni-jyuu is*-seeki (21 世紀) the twenty-first *century.* 《⇨ hi¹ (table)》

se⌐ekoo¹ せいこう (成功) *n.* success; prosperity; achievement:
seekoo *o osameru* (成功をおさめる) achieve *success* / *Anata no* seekoo *wa machigai arimaseñ.* (あなたの成功は間違いありません) You are certain of *success.* / *Go-*seekoo *o inorimasu.* (ご成功を祈ります) I wish you *success.*

seekoo suru (〜する) *vi.* succeed; be successful: *Kare no jigyoo wa* seekoo shita. (彼の事業は成功した) His business *was a success.* / *Ikeda-shi wa oñgakuka to shite* seekoo shita. (池田氏は音楽家として成功した) Mr. Ikeda *achieved success* as a musician. 《↔ shippai》

se⌐ekoo² せいこう (性交) *n.* sexual intercourse.
seekoo suru (〜する) *vi.* have sexual intercourse.

se⌐eko⌐oi せいこうい（性行為）*n.* sexual act.

se⌐ekyuu せいきゅう（請求）*n.* demand; claim; request: *soñgai-baishoo no* seekyuu (損害賠償の請求) a *claim* for damages / seekyuu *ni oojiru* (請求に応じる) comply with a *request* / seekyuu-sho (請求書) a *bill*; a *request for payment.*

SEEKYUUSHO

seekyuu suru (～する) *vt.* demand; claim; request; charge: *mihoñ o* seekyuu suru (見本を請求する) *request* a sample / *kootsuu-hi o* seekyuu suru (交通費を請求する) *make a claim* for travel expenses / *Terebi no shuuri ni goseñ-eñ* seekyuu sareta. (テレビの修理に5千円請求された) I *was charged* 5,000 yen for the repair of the TV set.

se⌐emee¹ せいめい（生命）*n.* life: *Kanojo no* seemee *wa abunai.* (彼女の生命は危ない) Her *life* is in danger. / *Sono jiko de ooku-no hito ga* seemee *o ushinatta.* (その事故で多くの人が生命を失った) Many people lost their *lives* in the accident. / *Kare no* seemee *ni betsujoo wa nakatta.* (彼の生命に別条はなかった) There was no fear for his *life.*

se⌐emee² せいめい（姓名）*n.* one's full name: seemee *o itsuwaru* (姓名を偽る) give a false *name.* (⇨ namae)

se⌐emee³ せいめい（声明）*n.* statement; declaration; announcement: *Seefu wa oshoku jikeñ ni tsuite* seemee *o dashita.* (政府は汚職事件について声明を出した) The government made a *statement* on the corruption case. / seemee-*sho* (声明書) an official written *statement.*

se⌐emitsu せいみつ（精密）*a.n.* (～ na, ni) precise; detailed; minute: seemitsu *na chizu* (精密な地図) a *detailed* map / seemitsu *ni shiraberu* (精密に調べる) investigate *very closely* / seemitsu-*kikai* (精密機械) a *precision* machine / seemitsu-*keñsa* (精密検査) a *detailed* (health) examination.

se⌐emoñ せいもん（正門）*n.* front gate; main entrance.

se⌐eneñ¹ せいねん（青年）*n.* youth; young man: *Kare wa sono tooji juuhas-sai no* seeneñ *datta.* (彼はその当時18歳の青年だった) He was a *youth* of eighteen at that time. / *Kare no musuko wa shoorai yuuboo na* seeneñ *desu.* (彼の息子は将来有望な青年です) His son is a *young man* with a promising future. / seeneñ *dañjo* (青年男女) *young* men and women. (⇨ shooneñ)

se⌐eneñ² せいねん（成年）*n.* full age; majority: *Uchi no musume wa raineñ* seeneñ *ni tasshimasu.* (うちの娘は来年成年に達します) Our daughter will *come of age* next year. (⇨ seejiñ)

se⌐eneñga⌐ppi せいねんがっぴ（生年月日）*n.* date of one's birth.

se⌐enoo せいのう（性能）*n.* efficiency; performance; power: *Kono kamera no* seenoo *wa yoi.* (このカメラの性能は良い) This camera *works well.* / *Motto* seenoo *no yoi koñpyuutaa ga hoshii.* (もっと性能の

よいコンピューターが欲しい）I want a more *efficient* computer.

se｜eoñ せいおん（清音）*n.* voiceless sound. ★ Japanese syllables with a consonant that is not voiced, *i.e.* か (*ka*), さ (*sa*), ち (*chi*), ほ (*ho*). 《⇨ dakuoñ; hañdakuoñ; inside front cover》

se｜era｜afuku セーラーふく（セーラー服）*n.* sailor suit [blouse]; middy blouse and skirt. ★ A school uniform worn by Japanese junior or senior high school girls.

SEERAAFUKU

se｜ereki せいれき（西暦）*n.* Christian era; A.D: *Seeneñgappi o* seereki *de kaite kudasai.*（生年月日を西暦で書いてください）Please write the date of your birth according to the *Christian era.* / Seereki *señ-kyuuhyaku-gojuu-neñ wa Shoowa nijuu-go-neñ ni atarimasu.*（西暦 1950 年は昭和 25 年にあたります）The *year* 1950 corresponds to the twenty-fifth year of Showa.

se｜eri[1] せいり（整理）*n.* tidying up; putting things in order: seeri *seetoñ*（整理整頓）*tidiness* and good order / seeri-*dañsu*（整理だんす）a *commode*; a *chest of drawers* / seeri-*keñ*（整理券）a *numbered order ticket.* ★ Given out to avoid making people wait in a queue.

seeri suru（～する）*vt.* **1** tidy up; put in order; arrange: *Heya o kiree ni* seeri *shi nasai.*（部屋をきれいに整理しなさい）*Tidy* your room *up* properly. / *Kaado o arufabetto-juñ ni* seeri *shita.*（カードをアルファベット順に整理した）I *arranged* the cards in alphabetical order.
2 cut down; reduce: *Kaisha wa juugyooiñ o* seeri *suru kañgae da.*（会社は従業員を整理する考えだ）The company is considering *reducing* the number of employees.

se｜eri[2] せいり（生理）*n.* **1** physiology.
2 menses: seeri *ni naru*（生理になる）have one's monthly *period.*

se｜eritsu せいりつ（成立）*n.* coming into existence; formation; conclusion: *iiñkai no* seeritsu（委員会の成立）the *setting up* of a committee / *hooañ no* seeritsu *o miokuru*（法案の成立を見送る）delay the *passage* of a bill.

seeritsu suru（～する）*vi.* come into existence; be formed; be concluded: *Atarashii naikaku ga* seeritsu *shita.*（新しい内閣が成立した）A new cabinet *was formed.* / *Kotoshi no yosañ ga* seeritsu *shita.*（今年の予算が成立した）This year's budget *has been approved.* / *Ryookoku-kañ ni jooyaku ga* seeritsu *shita.*（両国間に条約が成立した）A treaty *was concluded* between the two countries. / *Shussekisha ga tarinakute, kaigi wa* seeritsu *shinakatta.*（出席者が足りなくて、会議は成立しなかった）Since there were not enough people present, the meeting *was not held.* / *Futari no koñyaku ga* seeritsu *shimashita.*（二人の婚約が成立しました）The couple's engagement *is now official.*

se⌐eryoku せいりょく (勢力) *n.*
influence; power; strength:
*Kare wa zaikai de seeryoku o fu-
rutte iru.* (彼は財界で勢力をふるってい
る) He has a great deal of *influence* in the business world. / Seeryoku *arasoi ni wa makikomaretaku nai.* (勢力争いには巻き込まれたく
ない) I don't like to be involved in
a *power* struggle. / *Taifuu no* seeryoku *wa shidai ni otoroeta.* (台風
の勢力は次第に衰えた) The strength
of the typhoon *has* gradually *di-
minished.*

se⌐e-sa⌐betsu せいさべつ (性差別)
n. sexism; sex discrimination.

se⌐esaku[1] せいさく (製作) *n.* manufacture; production of machinery:
seesaku-*hi* (製作費) the cost of
manufacture / seesaku-jo (製作所)
a *factory*; a *workshop.*
seesaku suru (～する) *vt.* manufacture; produce: *Kono koojoo
de wa terebi no buhiñ o* seesaku
shite iru. (この工場ではテレビの部品を
製作している) They *produce* television components at this factory.

se⌐esaku[2] せいさく (制作) *n.* production of works of art:
terebi-bañgumi no seesaku (テレビ
番組の制作) the *production* of a
TV program.
seesaku suru (～する) *vt.* produce: *Sono kañtoku wa atarashii
eega o* seesaku shite imasu. (その監
督は新しい映画を制作しています) The
director *is making* a new movie.

se⌐esaku[3] せいさく (政策) *n.*
policy:
Sookyuu ni keezai seesaku *o tateru hitsuyoo ga arimasu.* (早急に
経済政策を立てる必要があります) It is
necessary to establish an economic *policy* without delay. / *gaikoo* seesaku (外交政策) a foreign
policy.

se⌐esañ せいさん (生産) *n.* pro-

duction; output:
Sakumotsu no seesañ *ga zoodai
[teeka] shita.* (作物の生産が増大[低
下]した) The *output* of farm products has increased [declined].

seesañ suru (～する) *vt.* produce;
manufacture: *Kono koojoo de wa
tsuki ni goseñ-dai no terebi ga
seesañ sarete imasu.* (この工場では
月に 5,000 台のテレビが生産されていま
す) Five thousand television sets
are produced per month at this
factory. 《↔ shoohi》

se⌐esañ⌐sha せいさんしゃ (生産者)
n. producer; maker; manufacturer:
seesañsha-*kakaku* (生産者価格) a
producer price. 《⇨ shoohisha》

se⌐eseki せいせき (成績) *n.*
school record; grade; result:
Seeseki *ga agatta [sagatta].* (成績
が上がった[下がった]) My *grades*
improved [got worse]. / *Kanojo
wa gakkoo no* seeseki *ga yoi
[warui].* (彼女は学校の成績が良い[悪
い]) Her school *grades* are good
[poor]. / *Shikeñ no* seeseki *ni gakkari shita.* (試験の成績にがっかりした)
I was disappointed at the *results*
of the examination.

TYPICAL SEESEKI

yuu (優)	A (excellent)
ryoo (良)	B (good)
	C (satisfactory)
ka (可)	D (just passed)
	E (conditionally passed)
fuka (不可)	F (failed)

se⌐eshi[1] せいし (生死) *n.* life and
death:
seeshi *ni kakawaru moñdai* (生死
にかかわる問題) a matter of *life and
death* / *Kare no* seeshi *wa fumee
desu.* (彼の生死は不明です) Nobody

knows whether he is *alive or not*.

se⌈eshi[2] せいし (制止) *n.* holding back; control:
Kare wa kakari no hito no seeshi *o mushi shite, saku no naka e haitta.* (彼は係りの人の制止を無視して、さくの中に入った) He ignored the *orders* of the person in charge and entered inside the fence.
seeshi suru (〜する) *vt.* stop; hold back; restrain: *Keekañ wa guñshuu o* seeshi shita. (警官は群衆を制止した) The policemen *held back* the crowd.

seeshi[3] せいし (精子) *n.* sperm. (⇨ rañshi)

se⌈eshiki せいしき (正式) *a.n.* (〜 na, ni) formal; official; regular:
seeshiki *na happyoo* (正式な発表) an *official* announcement / *Shuushoku wa mada* seeshiki *ni kimatte imaseñ.* (就職はまだ正式に決まっていません) My employment has not been *officially* confirmed yet. / *Ano futari wa mada* seeshiki *ni kekkoñ shite imaseñ.* (あの二人はまだ正式に結婚していません) The two of them are not yet married *legally*.

se⌉eshiñ せいしん (精神) *n.*
1 mind; soul:
Kare no seeshiñ *wa seejoo desu.* (彼の精神は正常です) He is of sound *mind*. / seeshiñ-*byoo* (精神病) a *mental* disease / seeshiñ-*eesee* (精神衛生) *mental* hygiene / seeshiñ-*igaku* (精神医学) *psychiatry* / seeshiñ-*ryoku* (精神力) *mental* power.
2 spirit.
keñpoo no seeshiñ (憲法の精神) the *spirit* of the constitution.

se⌈eshiñ-teki せいしんてき (精神的) *a.n.* (〜 na, ni) mental; spiritual:
Chichi-oya no shi wa kare ni totte ooki-na seeshiñ-teki *dageki datta.*

(父親の死は彼にとって大きな精神的打撃だった) His father's death was a great *mental* blow to him. / *Kanojo wa* seeshiñ-teki *ni tsukarete ita.* (彼女は精神的に疲れていた) She was *mentally* exhausted.

se⌈eshitsu せいしつ (性質) *n.*
1 nature; disposition; character:
Kare wa yooki na seeshitsu *no otoko da.* (彼は陽気な性質の男だ) He is a man of a cheerful *disposition*. / *Inu to neko wa* seeshitsu *ga chigau.* (犬と猫は性質が違う) Dogs and cats have different *natures*.
2 property; quality:
abura ga mizu ni uku to iu seeshitsu *o riyoo suru* (油が水に浮くという性質を利用する) make use of oil's *property* of floating on water.

se⌈esho[1] せいしょ (清書) *n.* fair copy; making a fair copy:
Kanojo ni geñkoo no seesho *o tanoñda.* (彼女に原稿の清書を頼んだ) I asked her to make a *fair copy* of my draft.
seesho suru (〜する) *vt.* make a fair copy: *Waapuro de tegami o* seesho shita. (ワープロで手紙を清書した) I *made a fair copy* of the letter with the word processor.

se⌈esho[2] せいしょ (聖書) *n.* the Bible; Testament:
kyuuyaku seesho (旧約聖書) the Old *Testament* / *shiñyaku* seesho (新約聖書) the New *Testament*.

se⌈eshuñ せいしゅん (青春) *n.* youth; the period of adolescence:
Kare wa mada seeshuñ *no yume o idaite iru.* (彼はまだ青春の夢を抱いている) He still cherishes his dream of *youth*. / *Kanojo wa* seeshuñ *jidai o Oosutoraria de sugoshita.* (彼女は青春時代をオーストラリアで過ごした) She spent her *youth* in Australia.

se⌈esoo せいそう (清掃) *n.* cleaning:

seesoo-sha (清掃車) a *garbage truck*; a *dustcart* / Seesoo-*chuu.* (*sign*) (清掃中) *Cleaning.*

seesoo suru (～する) *vt.* clean: *heya* [*dooro*] *o* seesoo suru (部屋 [道路]を清掃する) *clean* a room [street]. 《⇨ sooji》

TOIRE SEESOO-CHUU SIGN

se⌐etaa セーター *n.* sweater: seetaa *o kiru* [*nugu*] (セーターを着る [脱ぐ]) put on [take off] a *sweater* / *Kanojo wa akai* seetaa *o kite ita.* (彼女は赤いセーターを着ていた) She was wearing a red *sweater.*

se⌐etee せいてい (制定) *n.* enactment; establishment: *atarashii hooritsu no* seetee (新しい法律の制定) the *enactment* of a new law.

seetee suru (～する) *vt.* enact; establish: *Nihoñ no ima no keñpoo wa señ-kyuuhyaku-yoñjuuroku-neñ ni* seetee saremashita. (日本の今の憲法は1946年に制定されました) Japan's present constitution *was established* in 1946.

se⌐e-teki せいてき (性的) *a.n.* (～ na, ni) sex; sexual; sexy: see-teki *ni soojuku na kodomo* (性的に早熟な子ども) a *sexually* precocious child / see-teki *iyagarase* (性的いやがらせ) *sexual* harassment / see-teki *hañzai* (性的犯罪) a *sex* crime / *Kanojo wa* see-teki (*na*)

miryoku ga aru. (彼女は性的(な)魅力がある) She has *sex* appeal.

se⌐eteñ せいてん (晴天) *n.* fair weather: *Saiwai* seeteñ *ni megumaremashita.* (幸い晴天に恵まれました) Fortunately, we were favored with *lovely weather.* 《↔ uteñ》

se⌐etetsu せいてつ (製鉄) *n.* iron manufacture: seetetsu-jo (製鉄所) an *ironworks.*

se⌐eto せいと (生徒) *n.* pupil; student: ★ College students are called '*gakusee.*' *Kono kurasu ni wa* seeto *ga sañjuu-niñ imasu.* (このクラスには生徒が30人います) There are thirty *pupils* in this class. / dañshi-seeto (男子生徒) a *schoolboy* / joshi-seeto (女子生徒) a *schoolgirl.*

se⌐etoñ せいとん (整頓) *n.* order. **seetoñ suru** (～する) *vt.* put in order; tidy up: *Tsukue no ue o* seetoñ *shi nasai.* (机の上を整とんしなさい) *Tidy up* the top of your desk. / *Heya wa itsu-mo* seetoñ *shite imasu.* (部屋はいつも整とんしています) I always *keep* my room *neat and clean.*

se⌐etoo¹ せいとう (正当) *a.n.* (～ na, ni) just; right; good; fair: *Kare ni wa* seetoo *na riyuu ga arimasu.* (彼には正当な理由があります) He has a *good* reason. / *Kono e o* seetoo *ni hyooka shite kudasai.* (この絵を正当に評価してください) Please make a *fair* appraisal of this picture. / *Kare no yookyuu wa* seetoo *da to omoimasu.* (彼の要求は正当だと思います) I think his demands are *reasonable.* 《↔ futoo》

se⌐etoo² せいとう (政党) *n.* political party: seetoo-*seeji* (政党政治) *party* politics. 《⇨ table (next page)》

se⌐eyaku せいやく (制約) *n.*

restriction; restraint; limitation: *hooritsu-joo no* seeyaku o ukeru (法律上の制約を受ける) *be legally restricted* / *Yosañ ni wa* seeyaku *ga arimasu.* (予算には制約があります) There are budgetary *limitations.*

seeyaku suru (〜する) *vt.* limit; restrict; restrain: ★ Often used in the passive. *Anata no koodoo no jiyuu wa sukoshi mo* seeyaku saremaseñ. (あなたの行動の自由は少しも制約されません) Your freedom of action *is not limited* in any way.

Se⌐eyoo せいよう (西洋) *n.* the West:
seeyoo *shokoku* (西洋諸国) the *Western* countries / seeyoo-*ryoori* (西洋料理) *Western* cooking / seeyoo-*buñmee* (西洋文明) *Western* civilization. (↔ Tooyoo)

Se⌐eyo⌐ojiñ せいようじん (西洋人) *n.* Westerner; European. (↔ Tooyoojin)

se⌐eza せいざ (正座) *n.* sitting in a formal posture. ★ To sit upright on the floor with one's shins folded under the haunches and the knees facing out. It is the typical sitting postion for formal situations.

se⌐ezee せいぜい (精々) *adv.*
1 as...as possible:
Koohai ni makenai yoo ni seezee *beñkyoo shi nasai.* (後輩に負けないように せいぜい勉強しなさい) Study *as* hard *as possible* so as not to be beaten by your juniors. / Seezee *o-yasuku shite okimasu.* (せいぜいお 安くしておきます) We will give you *as* big a discount as *possible.*
2 (of cost, time quantity, etc.) at (the) best [most]:
Ryokoo no hiyoo wa seezee *go-mañ-eñ gurai deshoo.* (旅行の費用 はせいぜい5万円ぐらいでしょう) The trip will cost about 50,000 yen *at the most.* / *Soko made iku no ni kakatte mo,* seezee *ichi-jikañ desu.* (そこまで行くのにかかっても, せいぜい 1時間です) You can get there in an hour *at the most.*

se⌐ezoñ せいぞん (生存) *n.* existence; survival:
Kyuu-niñ-chuu go-niñ no seezoñ *ga kakuniñ sareta.* (9人中5人の生 存が確認された) The *survival* of five people out of the nine was confirmed. / seezoñ-*kyoosoo* (生 存競争) the struggle for *existence* / seezoñ-*sha* (生存者) a survivor.

seezoñ suru (〜する) *vi.* exist; survive; live: *Tsuki ni wa seebutsu wa* seezoñ *shinai.* (月には生物は 生存しない) *No* life *exists* on the moon.

se⌐ezoo せいぞう (製造) *n.* manufacture; production:
Seezoo *to hañbai wa wakarete imasu.* (製造と販売は分かれています) *Production* and sales are separate. / seezoo-*gyoo* (製造業) the *manufacturing* industry / seezoo-*moto* (製造元) a *producer*; a *manufacturer* / seezoo-*neñgappi* (製造年月

SEETOO

Jiyuu Miñshutoo	(自由民主党)	Liberal Democratic Party
Nihoñ Shakaitoo	(日本社会党)	Social Democratic Party of Japan
Koomeetoo	(公明党)	Komeito Party
Miñshatoo	(民社党)	Japan Democratic Socialist Party
Nihoñ Kyoosañtoo	(日本共産党)	Japanese Communist Party
Shakai Miñshu Reñgoo (社会民主連合)		United Social Democratic Party

日) the date of *manufacture*.

seezoo suru (〜する) *vt.* manufacture; produce; make: *Kono koojoo de wa yushutsu-yoo no kuruma o* seezoo shite imasu. (この工場では輸出用の車を製造しています) At this factory they *produce* vehicles for export.

se˺kai せかい (世界) *n.* **1** the world:
sekai *o is-shuu suru* (世界を一周する) go around the *world* / *Sono kaisha wa* sekai *kakuchi ni shiteñ ga aru.* (その会社は世界各地に支店がある) The company has its branch offices all over the *world.* / sekai-*ryokoo* (世界旅行) a round-the-*world* trip / sekai-*taiseñ* (世界大戦) a *world* war.
2 circle; sphere; realm:
seeji no sekai (政治の世界) political *circles* / *shi no* sekai (詩の世界) the *world* of poetry.

se˺kaseka せかせか *adv.* (〜 to; 〜 suru) (the state of being restless or busy):
sekaseka (to) aruku (せかせか(と)歩く) *bustle along* / *Kare wa itsu-mo* sekaseka *shite iru.* (彼はいつもせかせかしている) He is always *restless.*

se˹ka˺s·u せかす (急かす) *vt.* (sekash·i-; sekas·a-; sekash·i-te [C]) hurry; rush; press:
Soñna ni sekasanai de *kudasai.* (そんなにせかさないでください) Please *don't rush* me like that. / *Añmari shokuniñ o* sekasu *to shigoto ga zatsu ni naru osore ga arimasu.* (あんまり職人をせかすと仕事が雑になる恐れがあります) If you *press* a craftsman *too hard,* I am afraid his work will become sloppy. (⇨ seku)

se˺keñ せけん (世間) *n.* the world; the public; society:
Kanojo wa amari sekeñ *o shiranai.* (彼女はあまり世間を知らない) She does not know much about the *world.* / *Kare no hatsumee wa* se-keñ *no chuumoku o atsumeta.* (彼の発明は世間の注目を集めた) His invention attracted *public* attention. / *Sono doroboo wa* sekeñ *o sawagaseta.* (その泥棒は世間を騒がせた) The thief *caused a great sensation.*

se˺ki[1] せき (席) *n.* seat; one's place:
seki *ni tsuku* (席に着く) take one's *seat* / seki *o tatsu [hanareru]* (席を立つ[離れる]) stand up from [leave] one's *seat* / seki *e modoru* (席へ戻る) return to one's *seat* / seki *o yoyaku suru* (席を予約する) reserve a *seat* / *Kono* seki *wa aite imasu ka?* (この席は空いていますか) Is this *seat* vacant? / *Kono* seki *o totte oite kudasai.* (この席をとっておいてください) Please keep this *seat* for me. / *Kare wa* seki *o kette, kaijoo kara deta.* (彼は席をけって、会場から出た) Kicking his *seat,* he walked out of the hall.

se˹ki˺[2] せき (咳) *n.* cough; coughing:
seki *ga deru* (せきが出る) suffer from a *cough* / *Seki ga tomaranai.* (せきが止まらない) I am unable to stop *coughing.* / *Kodomo no* seki *ga hidoi.* (子どものせきがひどい) Our child has a bad *cough.* / *Byooniñ wa hageshiku* seki *o shita.* (病人は激しくせきをした) The patient *coughed* badly. / seki-*dome* (せき止め) *cough* medicine.

-seki せき (隻) *suf.* counter for large ships:
guñkañ is-seki (軍艦一隻) *a* warship.

se˹kiba˺rai せきばらい (咳払い) *n.* cough.
sekibarai (o) suru (〜(を)する) *vi.* clear one's throat.

se˺kidoo せきどう (赤道) *n.* equator.

se˺kigaiseñ せきがいせん (赤外線) *n.* infrared rays. (↔ shigaiseñ)

se⌈kijuuji せきじゅうじ (赤十字) *n.*
the Red Cross:
Nihoñ Sekijuujisha (日本赤十字社)
the Japanese *Red Cross Society.*

se⌈kiniñ せきにん (責任) *n.* responsibility; duty; obligation; liabil-
ity:
sekiniñ ga aru (責任がある) *be responsible* for / sekiniñ o toru (責任
をとる) take *responsibility* for / sekiniñ o nogareru (責任を逃れる)
shirk one's *responsibility* / *Sono
koto ni tsuite ooi-ni* sekiniñ *o kañjite imasu.* (そのことについておおいに責
任を感じています) I feel a great deal
of *responsibility* for that. / *Kare
wa jibuñ no* sekiniñ *o rippa ni
hatashita.* (彼は自分の責任を立派に
果たした) He has performed his
duty very well. / *Sono jiko no* sekiniñ *wa uñteñsha ni aru.* (その事故
の責任は運転者にある) The *blame*
for the accident lies with the
driver.

se⌈kita⌉ñ せきたん (石炭) *n.* coal:
sekitañ o horu (石炭を掘る) mine
coal / sekitañ o taku (石炭をたく)
burn *coal.*

se⌈kitate·ru せきたてる (急き立てる)
vt. (-tate-te Ⅴ) urge; hurry; hasten; press:
*Hayaku repooto o kaku yoo ni ka-
re o* sekitateta. (早くレポートを書くよ
うに彼をせきたてた) I *urged* him to
write his school report soon. /
Soñna ni sekitatenai *de kudasai.*
(そんなにせきたてないでください) *Don't
hurry* me like that.

se⌈kiyu せきゆ (石油) *n.* petroleum; kerosene:
sekiyu-*sutoobu* (石油ストーブ) a *kerosene* heater.

se⌈kkaku せっかく (折角) *adv.*

1 in spite of one's efforts:
Sekkaku *kita no ni doobutsu-eñ
wa yasumi datta.* (せっかく来たのに動
物園は休みだった) Although we *took
the trouble* to come, the zoo was

closed. / Sekkaku *no doryoku mo
muda ni natte shimatta.* (せっかくの
努力もむだになってしまった) The
greatest efforts we had made
turned out to be in vain.

2 (~ no) kind:
Sekkaku no *o-maneki desu ga sono hi wa tsugoo ga tsukimaseñ.*
(せっかくのお招きですがその日は都合がつ
きません) Thank you very much
for your *kind* invitation, but I
cannot make it on that day. / Sekkaku *desu ga, o-kotowari itashimasu.* (せっかくですが, お断わりいたしま
す) It is *kind* of you, but I must
decline.

3 (~ no) precious; rare:
Sekkaku no *kikai o nogashita.* (せっ
かくの機会を逃した) I let a *rare* opportunity slip by. / Sekkaku no
shiai ga ame de chuushi to natta.
(せっかくの試合が雨で中止となった)
The game *that we had been looking forward to* was canceled due
to rain.

se⌈kkee せっけい (設計) *n.* plan;
design:
seekatsu no sekkee *o tateru* (生活
の設計を立てる) make a *plan* for
one's life / sekkee-*zu* (設計図) a
plan; a blueprint.

sekkee suru (~する) *vt.* plan;
design: *Kono uchi wa watashi ga*
sekkee shimashita. (この家は私が設
計しました) I *designed* this house. /
Kono kuruma wa muda naku sekkee sarete imasu. (この車は無駄なく
設計されています) This car *is designed* with no frills.

se⌈kkeñ せっけん (石鹸) *n.* soap:
Sekkeñ *de te o arai nasai.* (せっけん
で手を洗いなさい) Wash your hands
with *soap*. / *kona-*sekkeñ (粉せっけ
ん) *soap* powder.

se⌈kkiñ せっきん (接近) *n.* approach; access.

sekkiñ suru (~する) *vi.* approach; come [go] near: *Taifuu*

ga Kañtoo chihoo ni sekkiñ shite imasu.(台風が関東地方に接近しています) The typhoon *is approaching* the Kanto Region. / *Ryoo chiimu no* jitsuryoku wa sekkiñ shite iru.(両チームの実力は接近している) The two teams *are becoming more evenly matched.*

se「kkusu セックス *n.* sexual intercourse; sex: ★ Japanese '*sekkusu*' is used only in this meaning. sekkusu *no hanashi o suru* (セックスの話をする) talk about *sex*.

... to sekkusu (o) suru (…と〜(を)する) *vi.* have sex with ....

se「kkyoku-teki せっきょくてき(積極的) *a.n.* (〜 na, ni) positive; active; aggressive: sekkyoku-teki *na seekaku* (積極的な性格) a *positive* personality / *Kare wa sono keekaku ni* sekkyoku-teki *ni sañsee shita.*(彼はその計画に積極的に賛成した) He was *strongly* in favor of the plan. / *Kanojo wa nañ ni taishite mo* sekkyoku-teki *desu.*(彼女は何に対しても積極的です) She is *positive* in everything. 《↔ shookyoku-teki》

se「k·u せく(急く) *vi.* (sek·i-; sek·a-; se·i-te [C]) hurry; be impatient: *Soñna ni* seku *hitsuyoo wa arimaseñ.*(そんなにせく必要はありません) You don't need to *be in* such *a hurry.* / *Aa, ki ga* seku.(ああ, 気がせく) Oh, I cannot restrain my *impatience.* 《⇒ sekasu》

se「kuhara セクハラ *n.* sexual harassment. ★ Shortened form of '*sekusharu harasumeñto*' (sexual harassment).

se「ma」·i せまい(狭い) *a.* (-ku) small; narrow: semai *apaato* (狭いアパート) a *small* apartment / *Nihoñ wa* semai *shimaguni desu.*(日本は狭い島国です) Japan is a *small* island country. ★ Although Japan is a large country, it is customary for the Japanese to refer to it in these terms. *Dooro ga* semakute, *uñteñ shinikui.*(道路が狭くて, 運転しにくい) The road is so *narrow* that it is difficult to drive along it. / *Kare wa shiya ga* semai.(彼は視野が狭い) He has *narrow* views. 《↔ hiroi》

se「ma」r·u せまる(迫る) *vi.* (semar·i-; semar·a-; semat-te [C]) **1** draw near; approach; be at hand: *Shuppatsu no hi ga* sematte kita.(出発の日が迫ってきた) The day of departure *is drawing near.* / *Shikeñ wa ato mikka ni* sematta.(試験はあと3日に迫った) The examination *is only three days off.* **2** force; press; urge: *Daijiñ wa sono jikeñ no sekiniñ o totte, jiniñ o* semarareta.(大臣はその事件の責任をとって, 辞任を迫られた) The minister *was urged* to take responsibility for the affair and resign.

se「meñto セメント *n.* cement: semeñto *o nuru* (セメントを塗る) cover with *cement.*

se「me」·ru[1] せめる(攻める) *vt.* (seme-te [V]) attack; invade: *Teki wa ushiro kara* semete kita.(敵は後ろから攻めて来た) The enemy *attacked* us from behind. 《↔ mamoru》

se「me」·ru[2] せめる(責める) *vt.* (seme-te [V]) blame; accuse; criticize: *Kare wa watashi no mudañ kesseki o* semeta.(彼は私の無断欠席を責めた) He *criticized* me for being absent without permission. / *Señsee wa kare no fuchuui o* semeta.(先生は彼の不注意を責めた) The teacher *criticized* him for his carelessness.

se「mete せめて *adv.* at least; just; only:

Semete *neñ ni ni-kai wa keñshiñ o uketa hoo ga yoi.*(せめて年に2回は検診を受けたほうがよい)You should undergo a medical examination twice a year *at least.* / *Ato futsuka, ie* semete *ato ichi-nichi matte kudasai.*(あと2日, いえ せめてあと1日待ってください)Please wait two more days—or even *just* one. / Semete *ato ichimañ-eñ areba, ano fuku ga kaeru ñ da ga.*(せめてあと1万円あれば, あの服が買えるんだが)I could buy that suit *if* I had just 10,000 yen more.

se⌐mi せみ(蟬) *n.* cicada.

se⌐ñ¹ せん(線) *n.* line:
señ *o hiku* (線を引く) draw a *line.*

se⌐ñ² せん(千) *n.* one thousand. 《⇨ suu² (table)》

se⌐ñ³ せん(栓) *n.* stopper; cork:
señ o nuku (栓を抜く) *uncork* / ga-su [suidoo] no señ *o hiraku [shimeru]* (ガス[水道]の栓を開く[締める]) turn on [off] the *gas [water]* / *Oyogu mae ni mimi ni* señ o shita. (泳ぐ前に耳に栓をした)I *plugged* my ears before swimming. / *Biñ o tsukattara,* señ *o shite oki nasai.*(びんを使ったら, 栓をしておきなさい)Put the *stopper* in the bottle after using it.

se⌐ñ⁴ せん(選) *n.* selection:
señ ni hairu [moreru] (選に入る[漏れる]) *be [not] selected.*

-señ せん(線) *suf.* transport system; line:
Chuuoo-señ no deñsha (中央線の電車) trains on the Chuo *Line.* 《⇨ -bañseñ》

se⌐naka せなか(背中) *n.* back:
Kanojo wa senaka *ni akañboo o obutte ita.*(彼女は背中に赤ん坊をおぶっていた)She was carrying a baby on her *back.* 《⇨ jiñtai (illus.)》

se⌐ñbazu⌐ru せんばづる(千羽鶴) *n.* a thousand folded paper cranes on a string. ★ Often used in praying for recovery from illness. 《⇨ tsuru³》

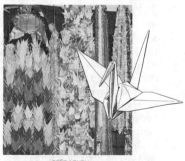

SEÑBAZURU

se⌐ñbee せんべい(煎餅) *n.* Japanese rice cracker.

SEÑBEE

se⌐ñcha せんちゃ(煎茶) *n.* green tea of middle grade. 《⇨ o-cha (table)》

se⌐ñchi センチ *n.* centimeter:
★ Shortened form of '*senchi-meetoru.*'
*Kono himo wa nagasa ga hachi-jus-*señchi *arimasu.*(このひもは長さが80センチあります)This cord is eighty *centimeters* long.

se⌐ñchi-me⌐etoru センチメートル(糎) *n.* centimeter. ★ The shortened form '*señchi*' is more common. 《⇨ señchi》

se⌐ñchoo せんちょう(船長) *n.* captain (of a ship).

Se⌐ñdai せんだい(仙台) *n.* the capital of Miyagi Prefecture. ★ The economic, political and cultural center of the Tohoku district of northeastern Honshu. 《⇨ map (G2)》

se⌐ñdatte せんだって *n.* = señjitsu.

se⌐ñdeñ せんでん(宣伝) *n.* advertisement; publicity; propaganda: Señdeñ *ga yokatta no de nyuujookeñ wa sugu urikireta.*(宣伝が良かったので入場券はすぐ売り切れた)The *publicity* was good, so the tickets quickly sold out. / *Sono shohyoo wa* señdeñ *ni riyoo sareta.*(その書評は宣伝に利用された)The review was used to *advertise* the book. / señdeñ-*kaa*(宣伝カー)an *advertising* van.

　señdeñ (o) suru (〜(を)する) *vt.* advertise; propagandize: *Sono kaisha wa terebi de sakañ ni shiñseehiñ o* señdeñ *shite iru.*(その会社はテレビで盛んに新製品を宣伝している)That company *is* widely *advertising* its new product on television. 《⇨ kookoku》

se⌐ñge⌐ñ せんげん(宣言) *n.* declaration; proclamation; announcement: *dokuritsu-*señgeñ(独立宣言)a *declaration* of independence.

　señgeñ (o) suru (〜(を)する) *vt.* declare; proclaim; announce: *chuuritsu o* señgeñ *suru*(中立を宣言する) *declare* one's neutrality.

se⌐ñgetsu せんげつ(先月) *n.* last month: Señgetsu *wa isogashikatta.*(先月は忙しかった)I was busy *last month.* / Señgetsu *no uriage wa mokuhyoo ni tasshinakatta.*(先月の売り上げは目標に達しなかった)*Last month's* sales did not attain the target. 《↔ koñgetsu; raigetsu》

se⌐ñgo せんご(戦後) *n.* the postwar period; after the war: *Kare wa* señgo-*umare desu.*(彼は戦後生まれです)He was born *after the war.* / Señgo *no Nihoñ no keezai hatteñ wa mezamashikatta.*(戦後の日本の経済発展はめざましかった)The *postwar* economic development of Japan was remarkable. 《↔ señzeñ》

Se⌐ñgoku-ji⌐dai せんごくじだい(戦国時代) *n.* Sengoku Period (ca. 1480 to ca. 1570). 《⇨ jidai (table)》

se⌐ñi せんい(繊維) *n.* fiber: *goosee[kagaku]-*señi(合成[化学]繊維)synthetic [chemical] *fiber.*

se⌐ñjitsu せんじつ(先日) *n.* the other day; a few days ago; some time ago: Señjitsu *wa o-sewa ni narimashita.*(先日はお世話になりました)You were very kind to me *the other day.* / *Kore ga* señjitsu *no o-yakusoku no shina desu.*(これが先日のお約束の品です)These are the items we promised you *a few days ago.* / *Kono hoñ wa* señjitsu *deta bakari desu.*(この本は先日出たばかりです)This book came out just *the other day.*

se⌐ñjitsu wa do⌐omo せんじつはどうも(先日はどうも) ★ Used when thanking someone or apologizing for something which happened a few days previously. Señjitsu wa doomo.(先日はどうも)*Thank you very much for the other day.* ★ The usual response is '*Iie kochira koso.*' (It is I who should thank you.) 《⇨ doomo》

se⌐ñkoo せんこう(専攻) *n.* academic specialty; special field; major: Señkoo *wa nañ desu ka?*(専攻は何ですか)What is your *field of expertise?* / señkoo-*kamoku*(専攻科目)an academic *major*; one's *specialty.*

　señkoo suru (〜する) *vt.* major in; specialize in: *Watashi wa daigaku de hooritsu o* señkoo *shimashita.*(私は大学で法律を専攻しました)I *majored* in law at university.

se⌐ñkyo せんきょ(選挙) *n.* election: señkyo *ni deru*(選挙に出る)run in an *election* / señkyo *ni katsu [makeru]*(選挙に勝つ[負ける])win [lose] in an *election* / *Watashi wa* señ-kyo *de kurasu-iiñ ni* erabareta.(私は選挙でクラス委員に選ばれた) I *was elected* a member of our class committee. / *Koñdo no nichiyoo ni chiji no* señkyo *ga arimasu.*(今度の日曜に知事の選挙があります) A gubernatorial *election* is to be held this Sunday. / señkyo-*keñ* (選挙権) the right *to vote* / señkyo-*uñ-doo* (選挙運動) an *election* campaign.

señkyo suru (～する) *vt.* elect; vote for: *Watashi-tachi wa kai-choo o erabu no ni sañ-kai* señkyo shita.(私たちは会長を選ぶのに3回選挙した) We *voted* three times to elect a chairman.

se⸢ñmeñ せんめん (洗面) *n.* washing one's face: señmeñ *o sumasu* (洗面を済ます) have a *wash* / señmeñ-*doogu* (洗面道具) one's *washing* things.

señmeñ suru (～する) *vi.* wash one's face: *reesui de* señmeñ suru (冷水で洗面する) *wash one's face* with cold water.

se⸢ñmeñjo せんめんじょ (洗面所) *n.*
1 washroom; lavatory.

───── **CULTURE** ─────
In an ordinary Japanese house, the bathtub and the toilet are installed in separate rooms.

2 washstand.

se⸢ñme⸢ñki せんめんき (洗面器) *n.* washbowl; washbasin.

se⸢ñmoñ せんもん (専門) *n.* specialty; special subject: *Kare no* señmoñ *wa keezaigaku desu.*(彼の専門は経済学です) His *specialty* is economics. / *Watashi wa Nihoñ no rekishi o* señmoñ *ni keñkyuu shitai.*(私は日本の歴史を専門に研究したい) I'd like to make a *special study* of Japanese history.

se⸢ñmoñka せんもんか (専門家) *n.* specialist; expert; professional.

se⸢ñmu (**to⸢rishimari⸣yaku**) せんむ(とりしまりやく) (専務(取締役)) *n.* senior [executive] managing director; senior vice president. 《⇨ kaisha (table)》

se⸢ñnuki[1] せんぬき (栓抜き) *n.* corkscrew; bottle opener.

se⸢nobi せのび (背伸び) *n.* standing on tiptoe.

senobi (**o**) **suru** (～(を)する) *vi.*
1 stand on tiptoe; stretch oneself: Senobi sureba, *sono hoñ ga toremasu.*(背伸びすれば、その本が取れます) If you *stretch up*, you can get the book.
2 (*fig.*) aim too high: *Kare wa itsu-mo* senobi shite *shippai suru.* (彼はいつも背伸びして失敗する) He always *aims too high*, and fails.

se⸢ñpai せんぱい (先輩) *n.* one's senior; elder: *Kare wa watashi no sañ-neñ* señ-pai *desu.*(彼は私の3年先輩です) He is my *senior* by three years. 《↔ koohai》

se⸢ñpu⸣uki せんぷうき (扇風機) *n.* electric fan: señpuuki *o kakeru [tsukeru]* (扇風機をかける[つける]) turn on an *electric fan* / señpuuki *o tomeru [ke-su]* (扇風機を止める[消す]) turn off an *electric fan.*

se⸢ñro せんろ (線路) *n.* railroad [railway] track; line: señro *o shiku* (線路を敷く) lay *railroad tracks.*

se⸢ñryoo[1] せんりょう (占領) *n.* occupation; possession; capture: señryoo-*guñ* (占領軍) an army of *occupation.*

señryoo suru (～する) *vt.* occupy; have all to oneself: *Señgo, reñgoo-guñ ga Nihoñ o* señryoo shita.(戦後、連合軍が日本を占領した) After the war, the Allied Forces *occupied* Japan. / *Kare wa sono heya o hitori de* señryoo shite iru.(彼はその部屋を独りで占領し

ている) He *keeps* the room *all to himself.*

se⌐ñryo¬o² せんりょう (染料) *n.* dye; dyestuffs.

se⌐ñse¬e せんせい (先生) *n.*
1 teacher; professor:
Nihoñgo no señsee (日本語の先生) a *teacher* of Japanese / *Tanaka-sañ wa jitaku de ikebana no* señsee *o shite imasu.* (田中さんは自宅で生け花の先生をしています) Mrs. Tanaka *teaches* flower arrangement at her home. / *Señsee, shitsumoñ shite mo ii desu ka?* (先生, 質問してもいいですか) *Sir [Ma'am],* may I ask you a question? ★ '*Señsee*' is also used to address artists writers, politicians, etc.
2 doctor:
Yamada señsee *wa gogo wa kyuu-shiñ desu.* (山田先生は午後は休診です) *Doctor* Yamada will see no patients this afternoon. 《⇨ isha》

se⌐ñshi せんし (戦死) *n.* death in battle:
meeyo no señshi (名誉の戦死) a glorious *death* in battle / señshi-sha (戦死者) the *war dead.*
señshi suru (～する) *vi.* be killed in war: *Sofu wa* señshi shimashi-ta.* (祖父は戦死しました) My grandfather *was killed in action.*

se⌐ñshu せんしゅ (選手) *n.* player; athlete:
yakyuu no señshu (野球の選手) a baseball *player* / *Oriñpikku no* señshu (オリンピックの選手) an Olympic *competitor.*

se⌐ñshuu せんしゅう (先週) *n.* last week:
Señshuu wa wariai hima deshita. (先週はわりあい暇でした) I had quite a bit of free time *last week.* / *Señ-shuu no doyoo wa ie ni imashita.* (先週の土曜は家にいました) I was at home *last* Saturday. 《⇨ shuu¹ (table)》

se⌐ñshu¬uraku せんしゅうらく (千

秋楽) *n.* the last day of a Grand Sumo Tournament; the last day of a public performance. 《⇨ sumoo》

se⌐ñsoo せんそう (戦争) *n.* war; battle; fight:
señsoo *ni iku* (戦争に行く) go off to *war* / señsoo *ni katsu [makeru]* (戦争に勝つ[負ける]) win [lose] a *war* / señsoo *no hooki* (戦争の放棄) renunciation of *war* / Señsoo *ga hajimatta [okotta].* (戦争が始まった[起こった]) The *war* broke out. / Señsoo *ga owatta.* (戦争が終わった) The *war* ended. / señsoo-*jootai* (戦争状態) a state of *war.*
《↔ heewa》
señsoo (o) suru (～(を)する) *vi.* make war; go to war: *Ima de mo otagai ni* señsoo *o shite iru kuni ga ikutsu-ka arimasu.* (今でもお互いに戦争をしている国がいくつかあります) Even now there are some countries which *are* still *at war* with each other.

se⌐ñsu せんす (扇子) *n.* folding fan:
señsu *o tsukau* (扇子を使う) *fan oneself.* 《⇨ uchiwa》

SEÑSU

se⌐ñtaa センター *n.* **1** center:
shoppiñgu señtaa (ショッピング・センター) a shopping *center.*
2 (of baseball) center field; center fielder.

se⌐ñtaku¹ せんたく (洗濯) *n.*

wash; washing; laundry:
Kono zuboñ o señtaku *ni dashite
kudasai.*(このズボンを洗濯に出してくだ
さい) Please send these trousers to
the *laundry.* / *Kono kiji wa* señtaku *ga kiku.*(この生地は洗濯がきく)
This material is *washable.* / señ-
taku-*sekkeñ*(洗濯せっけん) *laundry*
soap.

señtaku suru (～する) *vt.* wash;
do the laundry： *Seetaa o* señtaku
shitara, *chijiñde shimatta.*(セーター
を洗濯したら, 縮んでしまった) The
sweater shrank when I *washed* it.

se⌐ñtaku² せんたく(選択) *n.*
choice; selection; option:
shokugyoo no señtaku(職業の選
択) *choice* of occupation / *Kono
keñ ni tsuite wa* señtaku *no yochi
wa arimaseñ.*(この件については選択の
余地はありません) We have no room
for *choice* in this matter. / señ-
taku-*kamoku*(選択科目) an *elec-
tive* [*optional*] school subject.

señtaku suru (～する) *vt.* choose;
select： *Sañ-kamoku no naka kara
ni-kamoku* señtaku suru *koto ni
natte imasu.*(3科目の中から2科目
選択することになっています) We have
to *choose* two courses from
among these three.

se⌐ñtakuki せんたくき(洗濯機) *n.*
washing machine; washer:
señtakuki *de shitagi o arau*(洗濯
機で下着を洗う) wash underwear in
a *washing machine.*

se⌐ñtakumono せんたくもの(洗濯
物) *n.* laundry; washing:
señtakumono *o hosu*(洗濯物を干す)
hang the *washing* out to dry /
señtaku-*mono o toriireru*(洗濯物を
取り入れる) take in the *washing.*

se⌐ñteñ-teki せんてんてき(先天的)
a.n. (～ na, ni) native; innate;
inborn:
señteñ-teki *na sainoo*(先天的な才
能) *innate* talent / *Kare wa* supootsu *ni* señteñ-teki *ni sugurete iru.*

(彼はスポーツに先天的に優れている) He
naturally excels at sports.
《↔ kooteñ-teki》

se⌐ñtoo¹ せんとう(先頭) *n.* the
head; the lead:
señtoo *o kiru*(先頭をきる) take the
lead / *ikkoo no* señtoo *ni tatte aruku*(一行の先頭に立って歩く) walk at
the *head* of the group.

se⌐ñtoo² せんとう(戦闘) *n.* battle;
combat; fight; action:
señtoo *ni sañka suru*(戦闘に参加す
る) take part in *combat* / señtoo *o
kaishi* [*chuushi*] *suru*(戦闘を開始
[中止]する) commence [cease] *hos-
tilities* / señtoo-ki(戦闘機) a *fight-
er plane.*

se⌐ñtoo³ せんとう(銭湯) *n.* public
bath. ★ A neighborhood institution originally used by those
who have no bathing facilities in
their homes. The men's and
women's bathing areas are

outside

inside

SEÑTOO

separate. 《⇨ furo; furoya》

se￢nzai せんざい (洗剤) *n.* detergent:
chuusee-senzai (中性洗剤) a neutral *detergent.*

se￢nzen せんぜん (戦前) *n.* the prewar period; before the war:
senzen *no kyooiku* (戦前の教育) *prewar* education / *Sore wa* senzen *ni ryuukoo shita uta desu.* (それは戦前に流行した歌です) That is a song that was popular *before the war.* 《↔ sengo》

se￢nzo せんぞ (先祖) *n.* ancestor; forefathers:
senzo daidai *no haka* (先祖代々の墓) the *family* tomb. 《⇨ shison》

se￢o·u せおう (背負う) *vt.* (seo·i-; seow·a-; seot-te Ⓒ) **1** carry (a load) on one's back:
Kare wa ooki-na nimotsu o seotte *ita.* (彼は大きな荷物を背負っていた) He *was carrying* a heavy load *on his back.*
2 shoulder (responsibility):
Kare wa sono shippai no sekinin o hitori de seotta. (彼はその失敗の責任を一人で背負った) He *shouldered* all the responsibility for the failure. / *Nihon no shoorai o* seou *no wa kimi-tachi da.* (日本の将来を背負うのは君たちだ) It is you all who *shoulder* the future of Japan. 《⇨ ou²》

se￢rifu せりふ (台詞) *n.* words; one's lines:
serifu *o iu* (せりふを言う) speak one's *part* / serifu *o wasureru* (せりふを忘れる) forget one's *lines.*

se￢ron せろん (世論) *n.* public opinion. 《⇨ yoron》

-se·ru せる *infl. end.* (-se-te Ⓥ) [attached to the negative base of a consonant-stem verb and itself inflected like a vowel-stem verb]
1 make someone do; cause someone to do:
Watashi no kawari ni kanai o ika-setara *doo narimasu ka?* (私の代わりに家内を行かせたらどうなりますか) What will happen if I *make* my wife *go* instead of me. / *Kare ni sugu henji o* kakasemasu. (彼にすぐ返事を書かせます) I'll *make* him *write* his answer immediately. / *Kanojo wa watashi o nan-jikan mo* mataseta. (彼女は私を何時間も待たせた) She *made* me *wait* for hours. 《⇨ -saseru》
2 let someone do; allow someone to do:
Kodomo-tachi wa soto de asobaseru *ni kagirimasu.* (子どもたちは外で遊ばせるに限ります) Nothing is better than *letting* the children *play* outdoors. / *Watashi ni mo kono hon o* yomasete *kudasai.* (私にもこの本を読ませてください) Please *allow me as well to read* this book.

se￢sse to せっせと *adv.* hard; busily:
Kanojo wa itsu-mo sesse to *hataraite iru.* (彼女はいつもせっせと働いている) She always works *diligently.* / *Kare wa* sesse to *Nihongo no benkyoo ni hagende iru.* (彼はせっせと日本語の勉強に励んでいる) He is working away *very hard* at his Japanese studies.

se￢sshi せっし (摂氏) *n.* Celsius; centigrade: ★ The Fahrenheit scale is not used in Japan. 《⇨ ondo (table)》

$$C = (F - 32) \div 9 \times 5$$
$$F = C \div 5 \times 9 + 32$$

C	F	C	F
100°	212°	30.0°	86°
90°	194°	20.0°	68°
80°	176°	10.0°	50°
70°	158°	0.0°	32°
60°	140°	−10.0°	14°
50°	122°	−17.8°	0°
40°	104°	−20.0°	−4°

sesshi *nijuuhachi-do* (摂氏 28 度)
twenty-eight degrees *centigrade.*

se⌐sshoku せっしょく (接触) *n.*
1 contact; touch; connection:
Kono puragu wa sesshoku ga wa-rui. (このプラグは接触が悪い) This
plug gives a bad *connection.* / ses-shoku-jiko (接触事故) a *slight colli-sion.*
2 contact with a person:
Watashi wa seejika to wa ses-shoku ga arimaseñ. (私は政治家とは
接触がありません) I have no *contact*
with politicians.
sesshoku suru (～する) *vi.*
1 contact; touch: *Kare no jiteñ-sha ga kuruma to sesshoku shite, kare wa taoreta.* (彼の自転車が車と
接触して, 彼は倒れた) His bicycle
bumped into a car and he fell
over.
2 get in touch:
*Kare wa kañkeesha ni sesshoku
shite, joohoo o atsumeta.* (彼は関係
者に接触して, 情報を集めた) He *got
in touch* with the persons con-cerned and collected the infor-mation.

se⌐ssui せっすい (節水) *n.* water
saving:
Mizu-busoku no tame sessui o o-negai shimasu. (水不足のため節水を
お願いします) On account of the
water shortage, we request that
you *save water.*
sessui suru (～する) *vi.* save
water: *Ame ga furanai no de ses-sui suru hitsuyoo ga aru.* (雨が降ら
ないので節水する必要がある) Since we
have had no rain, we have to *use
water sparingly.*

se⌐ss·uru せっする (接する) *vi.*
(sessh·i-; sessh·i-; sessh·i-te
①) **1** touch:
Deñseñ ga noki ni sesshite iru. (電
線が軒に接している) The electric
wire *touches* the eaves.
2 come into contact with (a per-

son); see:
*Kare wa sakka to sessuru kikai ga
ooi.* (彼は作家と接する機会が多い) He
has many chances to *come into
contact with* novelists.
3 attend to (a guest, customer,
etc.); deal with:
*Kanojo wa o-kyaku ni sessuru no
ga joozu da.* (彼女はお客に接するのが
上手だ) She is good at *dealing
with* customers.
4 border; abut:
Nihoñ wa dono gaikoku to mo ses-shite imaseñ. (日本はどの外国とも接
していません) Japan does not *border*
any foreign countries.

se⌐tchi せっち (設置) *n.* forma-tion; establishment; installation:
daigaku no setchi-*kijuñ* (大学の設
置基準) the official requirements
for the *establishment* of a college.
setchi suru (～する) *vt.* form; es-tablish; install: *iiñkai o* setchi su-ru (委員会を設置する) *set up* a com-mittee / *Sono hoteru wa kaku he-ya ni supuriñkuraa o* setchi shita.
(そのホテルは各部屋にスプリンクラーを設
置した) The hotel *has installed*
sprinklers in every room.

se⌐tomono せともの (瀬戸物) *n.*
china; porcelain; earthenware:
setomono *no chawañ* (瀬戸物の茶
碗) a *china* teacup / setomono-*ya*
(瀬戸物屋) a *china* shop.

se⌐tsu¹ せつ (説) *n.* **1** theory:
atarashii setsu *o tateru* (新しい説を
立てる) put forward a new *theory* /
Ooku-no hito ga kare no setsu *o
shiji shite imasu.* (多くの人が彼の説
を支持しています) Many people sup-port his *theory.*
2 opinion; view:
Kare wa jibuñ no setsu *o magena-katta.* (彼は自分の説を曲げなかった)
He didn't change his own *views.*
/ *Sore ni tsuite wa* setsu *ga waka-rete imasu.* (それについては説が分れてい
ます) *Opinion* is divided about it.

se⌐tsu[2] せつ（節）*n.* **1** occasion; time; when:
Kochira e o-ide no setsu wa zehi o-tachiyori kudasai.（こちらへお出での節はぜひお立ち寄りください）By all means, please drop in *when* you happen to be in the neighborhood. / *Sono* setsu *wa go-kyoo-ryoku arigatoo gozaimashita.*（その節はご協力ありがとうございました）Thank you very much for your cooperation on that *occasion*.
2 (of grammar) clause:
*shu-*setsu（主節）the main *clause* / *juuzoku-*setsu（従属節）a dependent *clause*.
3 section; paragraph; phrase:
*Tekisuto no dai sañ-*setsu *o hiraki nasai.*（テキストの第3節を開きなさい）Please open your textbook to *section* three.
4 one's principles:
Kare wa jibuñ no setsu *o mageru yoo na otoko de wa nai.*（彼は自分の節を曲げるような男ではない）He is not the sort of man who compromises on *his principles*.

se⌐tsubi せつび（設備）*n.* equipment; facilities; accommodations:
kiñdai-teki na setsubi *no totonotta koojoo*（近代的な設備の整った工場）a factory equipped with modern *facilities* / *Kono ryokañ wa* setsubi *ga yoi [warui].*（この旅館は設備が良い[悪い]）This Japanese inn has good [poor] *facilities*. / setsubi-*tooshi*（設備投資）*plant* investment.
setsubi suru（～する）*vt.* equip; accommodate: *Subete no heya ni kuuraa o* setsubi shite *hoshii to omou.*（すべての部屋にクーラーを設備してほしいと思う）We want to *have* air conditioners *put* into all the rooms.

se⌐tsubuñ せつぶん（節分）*n.* the day before the start of spring.

Usually falls on February 2 or 3. On the evening of this day, Japanese conduct the 'Bean-Throwing' ceremony and scatter roasted soybeans to drive away evil spirits.

se⌐tsudañ せつだん（切断）*n.* cutting; severance; amputation:
kata-ude no setsudañ（片腕の切断）the *amputation* of one arm.
setsudañ suru（～する）*vt.* cut off; sever; amputate: *deñwaseñ o* setsudañ suru（電話線を切断する）*cut* a telephone wire / *Saiaku no baai, kare no ashi wa* setsudañ *shinakereba naranai ka mo shirenai.*（最悪の場合，彼の足は切断しなければならないかもしれない）In the worst case, we may have to *amputate* his foot.

se⌐tsudeñ せつでん（節電）*n.* power saving:
Setsudeñ *ni go-kyooryoku kudasai.*（節電にご協力ください）Please cooperate by *economizing on electricity*.
setsudeñ suru（～する）*vi.* save electricity: Setsudeñ suru *tame ni kuuraa o tometa.*（節電するためにクーラーを止めた）I turned off the air conditioner to *save electricity*.

se⌐tsujoku せつじょく（雪辱）*n.* vindication of one's honor; revenge:
setsujoku o hatasu（雪辱を果たす）*get even*; *avenge oneself*.
setsujoku (o) suru（～（を）する）*vi.* redeem one's honor; avenge one's loss: *Watashi-tachi wa kono mae no shiai no* setsujoku o shita.（私たちはこの前の試合の雪辱をした）We *got revenge* for our defeat in the previous match.

se⌐tsumee せつめい（説明）*n.* explanation; illustration:
Sono keñ ni tsuite anata no setsu-

mee *ga hoshii.*(その件についてあなたの説明が欲しい) I would like to have your *explanation* about that matter. / *Kare no koodoo wa* setsumee *o yoo suru.*(彼の行動は説明を要する) His behavior needs *explanation.* / *Shujutsu ni tsuite isha kara* setsumee *ga atta.*(手術について医者から説明があった) We received an *explanation* from the doctor about the operation. / setsumee-sho (説明書) an *explanatory* leaflet; written *instructions.*

setsumee (o) suru (〜(を)する) *vt.* explain; illustrate; demonstrate: *Kono tañgo no imi o* setsumee *shite kudasai.*(この単語の意味を説明してください) Please *explain* the meaning of this word. / *Señsee wa furiko no uñdoo o zu de* setsumee *shita.*(先生は振り子の運動を図で説明した) The teacher *illustrated* the movement of a pendulum with a diagram.

se┌tsuritsu せつりつ (設立) *n.* establishment; foundation: *atarashii gakkoo no* setsuritsu (新しい学校の設立) the *foundation* of a new school.

setsuritsu suru (〜する) *vt.* set up; establish; found: *Kono kaisha wa rokujuu-neñ mae ni* setsuritsu *saremashita.*(この会社は60年前に設立されました) This company *was founded* sixty years ago.

se┌tsuyaku せつやく (節約) *n.* economy; saving; thrift: *Kono kikai o tsukaeba, ooi ni jikañ no* setsuyaku *ni narimasu.*(この機械を使えば、おおいに時間の節約になります) If you use this machine, you can make great *savings* in time.

setsuyaku suru (〜する) *vt.* economize; save; cut down: *gasu [deñki] o* setsuyaku *suru* (ガス[電気]を節約する) *economize* on gas [electricity] / *Aruite, takushii-dai o* se-

tsuyaku shita.(歩いて、タクシー代を節約した) I *saved* on the taxi fare by walking. 《↔ roohi》《⇨ keñyaku》

se┌tsuzoku せつぞく (接続) *n.* connection; joining; link: *Kono koodo wa* setsuzoku *ga doko-ka warui.*(このコードは接続がどこか悪い) There is something wrong with the *connection* of this electrical cord. / *Tsugi no eki de kono deñsha ni* setsuzoku *wa arimasu ka?*(次の駅でこの電車に接続はありますか) Is there a *connection* with this train at the next station?

setsuzoku suru (〜する) *vi., vt.* join; connect: *paipu o* setsuzoku *suru* (パイプを接続する) *join* two pipes / *Takasaki-señ wa kono eki de Toohoku-señ to* setsuzoku *shimasu.*(高崎線はこの駅で東北線と接続します) The Takasaki Line *joins* the Tohoku Line at this station. / *Kono basu wa shuuteñ de saishuu deñsha ni* setsuzoku *shimasu.*(このバスは終点で最終電車に接続します) At the last stop, this bus *connects* with the last train.

se┌tsuzoku┐shi せつぞくし (接続詞) *n.* (of grammar) conjunction.

se┌wa┐ せわ (世話) *n.* **1** care: *Rusu no aida kodomo no* sewa *o yoroshiku o-negai shimasu.*(留守の間子どもの世話をよろしくお願いします) I would like to ask you to take *care* of my child while I am out. / *Oosaka ni itta toki, obasañ no* sewa *ni narimashita.*(大阪に行ったときおばさんの世話になりました) When I went to Osaka, I *was looked after* by my aunt.
2 trouble: *Hito ni* sewa *o kakenai yoo ni shinasai.*(人に世話をかけないようにしなさい) Be careful not to cause *trouble* to others. / *Doomo o-sewa o kakemashita.*(どうもお世話をかけました) I'm sorry to *have troubled you.*

3 help; kindness:
Anata no o-toosañ ni wa taiheñ o-sewa ni natte imasu. (あなたのお父さんには大変お世話になっています) I do appreciate the *help* I always receive from your father. / *Kono-tabi wa taiheñ o-sewa ni nari, arigatoo gozaimashita.* (この度は大変お世話になり、ありがとうございました) Thank you very much for *what you* recently *did* for me.
4 recommendation; introduction:
Anata no o-toosañ no o-sewa de, kono kaisha ni hairu koto ga dekimashita. (あなたのお父さんのお世話で、この会社に入ることができました) I was able to join this firm on the *recommendation* of your father.
sewa ga yakeru (〜がやける) be troublesome: *Uchi no ko wa hoñtoo ni sewa ga yakeru.* (うちの子はほんとうに世話がやける) Our child is really *troublesome*.
sewa (o) suru (〜(を)する) *vt.*
1 take care of; look after; attend: *Dare ga sono roojiñ no sewa o shimasu ka?* (だれがその老人の世話をしますか) Who *looks after* the old man? / *Kañgofu-sañ ga sono byooniñ no sewa o shite imasu.* (看護婦さんがその病人の世話をしています) A nurse *is attending* the patient.
2 recommend; introduce: *Ueki-ya-sañ ga ii daiku-sañ o sewa shite kureta.* (植木屋さんがいい大工さんを世話してくれた) Our gardener was kind enough to *recommend* a good carpenter.
Yokee na o-sewa da. (余計なお世話だ) Mind your own business.
-sha しゃ (車) *suf.* car; vehicle: *jidoo*-sha (自動車) a motor *vehicle* / *ka*-sha (貨車) a freight *car* / * res*-sha (列車) a long-distance *train*.
sha⌈beˈr·u しゃべる (喋る) *vi.* (shaber·i-; shaber·a-; shabet-te C)

chat; chatter; talk:
Kanojo wa itsu-mo yoku shaberu. (彼女はいつもよくしゃべる) She *is* always very *talkative*. / *Watashi-tachi wa noñdari tabetari shinagara shabetta.* (私たちは飲んだり食べたりしながらしゃべった) We *chatted* over our food and drink. / *Kono koto wa dare ni mo shaberanai de kudasai.* (このことはだれにもしゃべらないでください) Please *do not tell* anyone about this. 《⇨ hanasu¹》
sha⌈bushabu しゃぶしゃぶ *n.* thin slices of beef and vegetables cooked portion by portion in boiling water on the table.
★ Dipped in special sauce before eating.

SHABUSHABU

sha⌈choo しゃちょう (社長) *n.* president of a company; managing director:
Koko no shachoo wa donata desu ka? (ここの社長はどなたですか) Who is the *president* of this company? / *fuku*-shachoo (副社長) an executive vice-*president*. ★ Subordinates usually call their chief by the official title, not by name. 《⇨ kaisha (table)》
sha⌈dañ しゃだん (遮断) *n.* cutting off; interruption:
shadañ-ki (遮断機) a railroad *crossing gate*.
shadañ suru (〜する) *vt.* cut off; interrupt; hold up: *Sono jiko no tame ni kootsuu ga ichiji shadañ sareta.* (その事故のために交通が一時

遮断された) Owing to the accident, traffic *was* temporarily *interrupted*.

sha⌈doo しゃどう (車道) *n.* roadway; carriageway:
Shadoo *o yokogiru toki wa sayuu o yoku mi nasai*. (車道を横切るときは左右をよく見なさい) Look right and left carefully when you cross the *roadway*. (↔ hodoo)

sha⌈gai しゃがい (車外) *n.* outside a car [train]:
shagai *no fuukee* (車外の風景) the view *from a train*. (⇨ shanai)

sha⌈gam·u しゃがむ *vi.* (shagam·i-; shagam·a-; shagañ-de C) crouch; squat:
Mae ni iru hito wa shagañde *kudasai*. (前にいる人はしゃがんでください) Will the people in front please *crouch down*?

sha⌈iñ しゃいん (社員) *n.* company employee:
Anata wa koko no shaiñ *desu ka?* (あなたはここの社員ですか) Are you an *employee* of this company?
★ '*Kaishaiñ*' is considered an occupational category.

sha⌈kai しゃかい (社会) *n.* society; the world:
shakai *no ruuru ni shitagau* (社会のルールに従う) obey the rules of *society* / shakai *ni deru* (社会に出る) go out into the *world* / shakai-*hoshoo* (社会保障) *social* welfare guarantee / shakai-*ka* (社会科) *social* studies / shakai-*kagaku* (社会科学) *social* science / shakai-*kyooiku* (社会教育) *adult* education / shakai-*shugi* (社会主義) *socialism* / shakai-shugisha (社会主義者) a *socialist*.

Sha⌈kaihoke⌉ñ-choo しゃかいほけんちょう (社会保険庁) *n.* Social Insurance Agency:
Shakaihokeñ-choo *chookañ* (社会保険庁長官) the Director General of the *Social Insurance Agency*.

(⇨ choo⁴ (table))

Sha⌈kai Mi⌈ñshu Re⌉ñgoo しゃかいみんしゅれんごう (社会民主連合) *n.* United Social Democratic Party. (⇨ seetoo² (table))

Sha⌈kaitoo しゃかいとう (社会党) *n.* = Nihoñ Shakaitoo. (⇨ seetoo² (table))

sha⌈kki⌉ñ しゃっきん (借金) *n.* debt; loan:
Watashi wa yaku hyakumañ-eñ shakkiñ *ga aru*. (私は約100万円借金がある) I am in *debt* for about a million yen. / Shakkiñ *o hayaku kaeshi nasai*. (借金を早く返しなさい) Please repay your *loan* soon. / *Kare wa* shakkiñ *de kubi ga mawaranai*. (彼は借金で首が回らない) He is up to his ears in *debt*.
shakkiñ (o) **suru** (〜を する) *vi.* borrow money: *Kare kara ichimañ-eñ* shakkiñ *shita*. (彼から1万円借金した) I *borrowed* 10,000 yen from him. / *Doko-ka kara* shakkiñ *shinakereba, ie wa tachimaseñ*. (どこかから借金しなければ、家は建ちません) One cannot build a house *without borrowing money* from somewhere.

sha⌉kkuri しゃっくり *n.* hiccup:
Shakkuri *ga tomaranai*. (しゃっくりが止まらない) My *hiccups* won't stop. / *Kare wa nañdo-mo* shakkuri *o shita*. (彼は何度もしゃっくりをした) He *has hiccupped* a number of times.

sha⌉ko しゃこ (車庫) *n.* garage; carbarn:
kuruma o shako *ni ireru* (車を車庫に入れる) drive a car into the *garage*. (⇨ gareeji)

sha⌉meñ しゃめん (斜面) *n.* slope; slant:
yama no shameñ *o noboru* (山の斜面を登る) go up the *slope* of a mountain / *sukii de* shameñ *o suberi-oriru* (スキーで斜面を滑り降りる) ski down a *slope*.

Sha⌈mi⌉ñreñ しゃみんれん (社民連)

n. = Shakai Miñshu Reñgoo.

sha｜nai しゃない（車内）*n.* inside a vehicle [train]:
Shanai *wa kiñeñ desu.*（車内は禁煙です）Smoking is prohibited *in the train* [bus]. / shanai-*hañbai*（車内販売）sales of food *aboard a train.*《↔ shagai》

sha⌐re しゃれ *n.* joke; witty remark; pun:
share *o iu* [*tobasu*]（しゃれを言う[とばす]）crack a *joke* / *Dare mo watashi no* share *ga wakaranakatta.*（だれも私のしゃれがわからなかった）Nobody understood my *joke.*

sha⌐riñ しゃりん（車輪）*n.* wheel:
jiteñsha no shariñ（自転車の車輪）the *wheels* of a bicycle.

sha⌐ryoo しゃりょう（車両）*n.* vehicle; railway car:
Kono dooro wa sharyoo *tsuukoo-dome desu.*（この道路は車両通行止めです）This road is closed to *vehicles.* / *Dono* sharyoo *mo mañiñ datta.*（どの車両も満員だった）Every *carriage* was full of passengers.

sha⌐see しゃせい（写生）*n.* sketch; sketching:
shasee-*choo*（写生帳）a *sketch-book*; a *sketchpad.*
 shasee suru（～する）*vt.* sketch:
Watashi wa Fuji-sañ o shasee shita.（私は富士山を写生した）I *made a sketch* of Mt. Fuji.

sha⌐setsu しゃせつ（社説）*n.* editorial; leading article.

sha⌐shiñ しゃしん（写真）*n.* photograph; picture:
yama no shashiñ *o toru*（山の写真を撮る）take a *photograph* of mountains / *Watashi-tachi wa kare ni* shashiñ *o totte moratta.*（私たちは彼に写真を撮ってもらった）We had our *picture* taken by him.

sha⌐shi｜ñki しゃしんき（写真機）*n.* camera.《⇨ kamera》

sha⌐shoo しゃしょう（車掌）*n.* train [bus] conductor; guard.

sha⌐tai しゃたい（車体）*n.* body of a car; frame:
jiteñsha no shatai（自転車の車体）the *frame* of a bicycle.

sha｜tsu シャツ *n.* shirt; undershirt; underwear: ★ The type of shirt with which one wears a necktie is called '*waishatsu.*'
shatsu *o kiru* [*nugu*]（シャツを着る[脱ぐ]）put on [take off] one's *shirt.*

shi[1] し *p.* **1** and (also): ★ Used for emphatic listing.
Ano mise wa ryoori ga oishii shi, *fuñiki mo ii.*（あの店は料理がおいしいし，雰囲気もいい）The food in that restaurant is good, *and also* there is a pleasant atmosphere. / *Yamamoto-sañ wa yasashii* shi, *shiñsetsu da.*（山本さんは優しいし，親切だ）Mr. Yamamoto is gentle, *and* kind, *too.* / *Kyoo wa nichiyoo da* shi, *teñki mo ii* shi, *doko-ka e iki-mashoo.*（きょうは日曜だし，天気もいいし，どこかへ行きましょう）Today is Sunday, *and what's more* the weather is also fine, *so* let's go somewhere. / *Hi wa kureru* shi, *ame wa futte kuru* shi, *takushii wa konai* shi, *doo ni mo naranakatta.*（日は暮れるし，雨は降ってくるし，タクシーは来ないし，どうにもならなかった）The sun had set, *and* it began to rain, *and* there was no taxi, *so* there was nothing I could do.
《⇨ to²; to ka》
2 (used at the end of an incomplete sentence in order to leave the rest to the imagination of the listener):
Asobi ni ikitai shi, *o-kane wa nai* shi...（遊びに行きたいし，お金はないし...）I want to go off and enjoy myself, but I have no money, so... / *Basu mo takushii mo konai* shi... *Doo shiyoo.*（バスもタクシーも来ないし...どうしよう）There are no buses or taxis... What shall I do?

shi[12] し（市）n. city:
Kamakura-shi（鎌倉市）the *City*
of Kamakura.《⇨ machi (table)》

shi[13] し（詩）n. poem; poetry;
verse:
shi *o kaku [tsukuru]*（詩を書く[作
る]）write a *poem*.

shi[14] し（四）n. four. ★'四' is
usually pronounced 'yoñ,' as the
pronunciation 'shi' suggests
'death.'《⇨ suu² (table)》

shi[15] し（氏）n. 1 Mr:
Suzuki-shi ga gichoo ni erabareta.
（鈴木氏が議長に選ばれた）*Mr.* Suzu-
ki was elected chairman. / *Aoki-
shi fusai mo sono kai ni shusseki
shita.*（青木氏夫妻もその会に出席した）
Mr. and Mrs. Aoki were also
present at the party.
2 family:
Tokugawa-shi（徳川氏）the Tokugawa *family*.

shi[16] し（氏）n. he; him:
Shi *no keñkoo o shukushite, kañpai shiyoo.*（氏の健康を祝して, 乾杯し
よう）Let's toast *his* health.

shi[17] し（死）n. death:
Karoo ga kare no shi *o maneita.*
（過労が彼の死を招いた）Overwork
caused his *death*. / *Abunai tokoro
de* shi *o manugareta.*（危ないところで
死を免れた）I narrowly escaped
death.

shiᒐage しあげ（仕上げ）n. finish:
Kono teeburu wa shiage *ga suteki
da.*（このテーブルは仕上げがすてきだ）
This table has a nice *finish*. /
*Sukoshi te o kuwaete, e no saigo
no* shiage o shita.（少し手を加えて,
絵の最後の仕上げをした）I made
some small alterations and *finished off* the painting.《⇨ shia-
geru》

shiᒐageᒐ·ru しあげる（仕上げる）vt.
(shiage-te Ⅴ) finish; complete:
Kono shigoto wa kyoo-juu ni shiagemasu.（この仕事はきょう中に仕上げ
ます）I am going to *finish* this

work today.《⇨ shiage》

shiᒐai しあい（試合）n. match;
game; bout; competition:
shiai *ni katsu [makeru]*（試合に勝つ
[負ける]）win [lose] a *match* / shiai
ni deru（試合に出る）take part in a
game / *Kyoo no gogo wa sofuto-
booru no* shiai *ga arimasu.*（きょうの
午後はソフトボールの試合があります）
We are going to have a softball
game this afternoon.

shiai (o) suru（〜を(を)する）vi. play
a game; have a match; compete:
*Kare no chiimu wa uchi to rai-
shuu* shiai suru *koto ni natte imasu.*（彼のチームはうちと来週試合すること
になっています）His team is scheduled to *have a match* against
ours next week.

shiᒐasaᒐtte しあさって n. three
days from today:
Shiasatte wa shukujitsu desu.（し
あさっては祝日です）*Three days from
now* is a national holiday. / *Shiasatte kare wa Chuugoku e shuppatsu shimasu.*（しあさって彼は中国へ
出発します）He leaves for China in
three days.《⇨ kyoo (table)》

shiᒐawase しあわせ（幸せ）n. happiness; blessing; fortune:
O-futari no shiawase *o negatte orimasu.*（お二人の幸せを願っております）I
wish both of you every *happiness*.
— *a.n.* (〜 na, ni) happy; fortunate; lucky:
Watashi wa ima shiawase *desu.*
（私は今幸せです）I am very *happy*
now. / *Futari wa* shiawase *ni
kurashite imasu.*（二人は幸せに暮ら
しています）The two of them are
living *happily*.《↔ fushiawase》
《⇨ koofuku》

shiᒐba しば（芝）n. turf; grass:
shiba *o karu*（芝を刈る）mow the
grass.

shiᒐbafu しばふ（芝生）n. lawn;
grass:
Shibafu ni hairanai koto. (*sign*)（芝

生に入らないこと) Keep Off the *Grass.*

shi「bai しばい (芝居) *n.* **1** play; drama; performance:
shibai *o mi ni iku* (芝居を見に行く) go to see a *play* / *Sono* shibai *wa atatta* [*ukenakatta*]. (その芝居は当った[受けなかった]) The *play* was a success [flop]. / *Sono yakusha wa ii* shibai *o shita.* (その役者はいい芝居をした) The actor *played* his part very well.
2 put-on; acting:
Ani ga okotta no wa shibai *desu.* (兄が怒ったのは芝居です) My brother's anger is just a *put-on.*

shi「ba「raku しばらく (暫く) *adv.*
1 for a while [minute]:
Shibaraku, *o-machi kudasai.* (しばらく、お待ちください) Please wait *a little while.* / Shibaraku *sureba chichi wa modorimasu.* (しばらくすれば父は戻ります) My father will be back *in a minute.*
2 for the time being:
Shibaraku *kono hoteru ni taizai shimasu.* (しばらくこのホテルに滞在します) I will be staying in this hotel *for the time being.*
Shibaraku (buri) desu ne. (〜(ぶり)ですね) I haven't seen you for a long time. ★ Expression used when meeting someone after a long time.

shi「ba「r・u しばる (縛る) *vt.* (shibar・i-; shibar・a-; shibat-te C̄)
1 tie; bind:
Tsutsumi o himo de shibatta. (包みをひもで縛った) I *tied up* the parcel with string. / *Kare wa teashi o* shibararete ita. (彼は手足を縛られていた) He *was bound* hand and foot. / *Kanojo wa kizuguchi o hootai de* shibatta. (彼女は傷口を包帯でしばった) She *wrapped* a bandage around the wound.
2 (of time) restrict; bind:
jikañ ni shibarareru (時間に縛られ

る) *be restricted* by time.

shi「bashiba しばしば (屡々) *adv.* many times; often; frequently:
Hokkaidoo ni wa shibashiba *ikimashita.* (北海道にはしばしば行きました) I have *often* been to Hokkaido. / *Kanojo wa* shibashiba *chikoku suru.* (彼女はしばしば遅刻する) She is *frequently* late. / *Saikiñ wa roojiñ iryoo no koto ga* shibashiba *wadai ni naru.* (最近は老人医療のことがしばしば話題になる) The medical treatment of old people *often* becomes a topic of discussion these days.

shi「basu しバス (市バス) *n.* city bus. ★ This is a bus operated by a city. (⇨ shideñ)

shi「bire「・ru しびれる (痺れる) *vi.* (shibire-te V̄) be numbed; be paralyzed:
Samukute, te no yubi ga shibirete shimatta. (寒くて、手の指がしびれてしまった) My fingers *are numb* with cold. / *Ashi ga* shibirete *tatenai.* (足がしびれて立てない) I cannot stand up because my feet *are asleep.*

shi「boo¹ しぼう (志望) *n.* wish; desire; plan:
Kare wa beñgoshi shiboo *da.* (彼は弁護士志望だ) He *wishes* to be a lawyer. / *Musuko wa* shiboo-*doori sono daigaku ni hairemashita.* (息子は志望通りその大学に入れました) My son could enter the college that *he had hoped to.* / *Kare wa shoorai no* shiboo *ni tsuite watashi ni katatta.* (彼は将来の志望について私に語った) He spoke to me about his future *plans.* / shiboo-*sha* (志望者) an *applicant.*
shiboo suru (〜する) *vt.* want; desire; plan: *Kono kurasu de seejika o* shiboo suru *hito wa sukunai.* (このクラスで政治家を志望する人は少ない) In this class, there are few people who *want* to be politicians.

shi「boo² しぼう(死亡) *n.* death:
shiboo-*jiko* (死亡事故) a *fatal* accident / shiboo-*ritsu* (死亡率) the
death rate / shiboo-*sha* (死亡者)
the *deceased*.
　shiboo suru (〜する) *vi.* die; be
killed: *Sono jiko de go-niñ* shiboo shita. (その事故で 5 人死亡した)
Five people *died* in the accident.
《⇨ shinu》

shi「boo³ しぼう(脂肪) *n.* fat;
grease:
shiboo *ga tsuku* (脂肪が付く) put
on *fat* / shiboo *o toru* (脂肪を取る)
get rid of *fat* / *Kono niku wa* shiboo ga ooi. (この肉は脂肪が多い)
This meat is *fatty.* 《⇨ abura²》

shi「bo」ru しぼる(絞る) *vt.* (shibor·i-; shibor·a-; shibot-te [C])
1 squeeze; press:
remoñ o shiboru (レモンを絞る)
squeeze a lemon / *gureepufuruu-tsu no juusu o* shiboru (グレープフル
ーツのジュースを絞る) *squeeze* the
juice from a grapefruit.
2 wring:
Nureta taoru o shibotte, *hoshita.*
(濡れたタオルを絞って、干した) I *wrung*
the wet towel and put it out to
dry.

shi「ibu」·i しぶい(渋い) *a.* (-ku)
1 (of taste) bitter; sharp and
astringent:
shibui *o-cha* (渋いお茶) *bitter* tea /
Kono kaki wa shibui. (このかきは渋
い) This persimmon has a *sharp,
astringent* taste. 《⇨ aji¹ (table)》
2 (of color) sober; quiet; refined:
shibui *iro* (渋い色) a *restrained*
color / shibui *iro no chawañ* (渋い
色の茶わん) a teacup of *sober, but
tasteful*, color / *Kare wa itsu-mo*
shibui *fukusoo o shite iru.* (彼はいつ
も渋い服装をしている) He is always
dressed in *quiet good taste.*
3 (of countenance) sullen:
shibui *heñji* (渋い返事) a *sullen* answer / *Kozukai o motto nedattara,
chichi wa* shibui *kao o shita.* (こづ
かいをもっとねだったら、父は渋い顔をした)
My father made a *sour* face when
I asked for more pocket money.
4 tight-fisted:
Ano hito wa kane ni shibui. (あの人
は金に渋い) He is *stingy.*

shi「bu」r·u しぶる(渋る) *vi.* (shibur·i-; shibur·a-; shibut-te [C])
hesitate; be reluctant:
Kare wa kanojo ni au no o shibutta. (彼は彼女に会うのを渋った) He
was reluctant to meet her.

shi「chi」 しち(七) *n.* seven.
《⇨ nana; nanatsu; suu² (table)》

Shi「chi-fuku」jiñ しちふくじん(七
福神) *n.* the Seven Gods of
Good Luck. ★ They always
appear aboard a treasure ship ('*ta-
kara-bune*').

SHICHI-FUKUJIÑ

shi「chi-gatsu」 しちがつ(七月) *n.*
July:
Tanabata matsuri wa shichi-gatsu
ni arimasu. (七夕祭りは七月にありま
す) The Star Festival is celebrated in *July.* 《⇨ tsuki¹ (table)》

shi「cho」o¹ しちょう(市長) *n.*
mayor:
Nagoya shichoo (名古屋市長) the
Mayor of Nagoya.

shi「cho」o² しちょう(支庁) *n.* the
regional branch of a government
agency.

shi「cho」o³ しちょう(市庁) *n.* = shiyakusho.

shiˈdai しだい（次第）*n.* **1** the instant; the moment: ★ Follows the continuative base of a verb. *Kekka ga wakari shidai o-shirase shimasu.* （結果がわかり次第お知らせします） We will inform you *as soon as* we know the results. **2** being dependent: *Seekoo suru ka shinai ka wa anata no doryoku shidai desu.* （成功するかしないかはあなたの努力次第です） Whether you succeed or not *depends* on your own efforts. | *Kettee wa kimi shidai da.* （決定は君次第だ） The decision is *up to* you. **3** circumstances: *Koo-iu shidai de asu no kaigi ni wa shusseki dekimaseñ.* （こういう次第であすの会議には出席できません） Under these *circumstances*, I cannot attend tomorrow's meeting. 《⇨ wake》 **4** order; program: *shiki-shidai* （式次第） the *program* of a ceremony.

shiˈdai ni しだいに（次第に）*adv.* gradually: *Taifuu no sekkiñ de fuu-u ga shidai ni tsuyoku natte kita.* （台風の接近で風雨がしだいに強くなってきた） The wind and rain have *gradually* become stronger with the approach of the typhoon.

shiˈdareyaˈnagi しだれやなぎ（垂れ柳）*n.* weeping willow.

shiˈdeñ してん（市電）*n.* streetcar; tram. ★ This is a streetcar operated by a city. 《⇨ shibasu》

shiˈdoo[1] しどう（指導）*n.* guidance; direction; leadership; instruction: *Joñ wa Tanaka kyooju no shidoo o ukete Nihoñ-shi o keñkyuu shimashita.* （ジョンは田中教授の指導を受けて日本史を研究しました） John studied Japanese history under the *guidance* of Professor Tanaka. | *Atarashii koochi no shidoo no moto de señshu-tachi wa chikara o tsuketa.* （新しいコーチの指導の下で選手たちは力をつけた） Under the *direction* of the new coach, the athletes developed their ability and skill. | *Shi-gatsu kara Toda señsee ga shidoo ni atararemasu.* （四月から戸田先生が指導にあたられます） From April, Mr. Toda is scheduled to be the teacher in *charge* of us. | *shidoo-sha* （指導者） a *leader*; a *guide*.

shidoo suru （〜する）*vt.* guide; direct; coach; instruct; teach: *Kare wa watashi ni tenisu o shidoo shite kureta.* （彼は私にテニスを指導してくれた） He *coached* me in tennis.

shiˈdoo[2] しどう（私道）*n.* private road [path]: *Shidoo ni tsuki kuruma no toorinuke o kiñzu.* （*sign*）（私道につき車の通り抜けを禁ず） This is a *private road*. Vehicles are not allowed to pass through.

shiˈgai[1] しがい（市街）*n.* the streets; city; town: *Shigai wa matsuri de nigiwatte ita.* （市街は祭りでにぎわっていた） The *streets* were crowded with people enjoying the festival. | *kyuu-shigai* （旧市街） the old *section* of a city.

shiˈgai[2] しがい（市外）*n.* suburbs; outskirts: *Ooku no hito ga shigai no ie kara toshiñ no kaisha ni kayotte iru.* （多くの人が市外の家から都心の会社に通っている） Many people commute from their homes in the *suburbs* to their offices in the heart of the city. | *shigai-deñwa* （市外電話） an *out-of-town* telephone call. 《↔ shinai》《⇨ koogai[1]》

shiˈgaiseñ しがいせん（紫外線）*n.* ultraviolet rays. 《↔ sekigaiseñ》

Shiˈgaˈ-keñ しがけん（滋賀県）*n.* Shiga Prefecture. Located in the northeast of the Kinki district. Lake Biwa, the largest lake in Japan, is located in the center of the prefecture. Capital city: Otsu (大津). (⇨ map (E4))

shi「gamitsu」k·u しがみつく *vi.* (-tsuk·i-; -tsuk·a-; -tsu·i-te C) cling to; hang [hold] on to: *Kare wa sono tsuna ni shigami-tsuita.* (彼はその綱にしがみついた) He *held on to* the rope. / *Sono ko wa haha-oya ni shigamitsuite, naita.* (その子は母親にしがみついて, 泣いた) *Clinging to* her mother, the child cried.

shi-「gatsu」 しがつ(四月) *n.* April: *Nihoñ de wa shiñ-gakki wa shi-gatsu ni hajimaru.* (日本では新学期は四月に始る) In Japan, the first school term begins in *April.* (⇨ tsuki¹ (table))

shi「geki しげき(刺激) *n.* stimulation; stimulus; incentive: *Kanojo no seekoo wa watashi ni totte yoi shigeki ni natta.* (彼女の成功は私にとって良い刺激になった) Her success provided a good *stimulus* to me. / *Kono mura no shigeki no nai seekatsu ni akimashita.* (この村の刺激のない生活に飽きました) I am fed up with the *dull* life in this village.

shigeki suru (〜する) *vt.* stimulate; excite; provoke: *Arukooru wa shokuyoku o shigeki suru.* (アルコールは食欲を刺激する) Alcohol *stimulates* the appetite. / *Sono moñ-dai o mochidasu to, aite-gawa o shigeki suru osore ga arimasu.* (その問題を持ち出すと, 相手側を刺激する恐れがあります) If we bring up that problem, it is likely to *provoke* the other party.

shi」geñ しげん(資源) *n.* resources: *shigeñ ni tomu [toboshii]* (資源に富む[乏しい]) be rich [poor] in re-

sources / *teñneñ-shigeñ o kaihatsu suru* (天然資源を開発する) develop natural *resources.*

Shi「geñ-enerugi」i-choo しげんエネルギーちょう(資源エネルギー庁) *n.* Agency of Natural Resources and Energy: *Shigeñ-enerugii-choo chookañ* (資源エネルギー庁長官) the Director General of the *Agency of Natural Resources and Energy.* (⇨ choo⁴ (table))

shi「ge」r·u しげる(茂る) *vi.* (shi-ger·i-; shiger·a-; shiget-te C) (of plants) grow thickly; (of weeds) be overgrown: *Kare no uchi no ura ni wa ki ga shigette imasu.* (彼の家の裏には木が茂っています) The trees *grow thickly* in the back of his house.

shi「goto しごと(仕事) *n.* 1 work; job; business: *Kyoo no shigoto wa owarimashita.* (きょうの仕事は終わりました) Today's *work* is over. / *Chichi wa nichiyoo mo shigoto o shite imasu.* (父は日曜も仕事をしています) My father *works* even on Sundays. / *Saikiñ shigoto wa umaku itte imasu.* (最近仕事はうまくいっています) The *job* has recently been going along smoothly. / *Watashi wa raishuu shigoto de Kumamoto e ikimasu.* (私は来週仕事で熊本へ行きます) I am going to Kumamoto on *business* next week. / *Kare wa shigoto no dekiru hito desu.* (彼は仕事のできる人です) He is an *able worker.* 2 position; work; job; employment: *"O-shigoto wa nañ desu ka?"* *"Kaishaiñ desu."* (「お仕事は何ですか」「会社員です」) "What is *your job*?" "I am a company employee." / *Kare wa ima shigoto o saga-shite iru tokoro desu.* (彼は今仕事を探しているところです) He is now seeking *employment.*

shiˈhai しはい（支配）*n.* rule; government; control:
Too-oo ni okeru sono kuni no shihai wa owatta. (東欧におけるその国の支配は終わった) The *rule* of that country in Eastern Europe has ended. / shihai-sha (支配者) a *ruler*.
shihai suru (〜する) *vt.* rule; govern; control; dominate:
Sono kuni wa dokusai-sha ni yotte shihai sarete ita. (その国は独裁者によって支配されていた) That country *was controlled* by a dictator.

shiˈhaˈinin̄ しはいにん（支配人）*n.* manager:
resutoran̄ [hoteru] no shihainin̄ (レストラン[ホテル]の支配人) a restaurant [hotel] *manager*.

shiˈharai しはらい（支払い）*n.* payment:
shiharai o sumasu (支払いを済ます) complete *payment* / *shiharai o nobasu* (支払いを延ばす) put off *payment* / *Shiharai wa getsumatsu ni narimasu.* (支払いは月末になります) *Payment* will be made at the end of the month. 《⇨ shiharau》

shiˈharaˈ·u しはらう（支払う）*vt.* (-hara·i-; -haraw·a-; -harat-te Ⓒ) pay; defray:
Kon̄getsu wa gasu-dai ni ichiman̄-en̄ shiharatta. (今月はガス代に1万円支払った) This month I *paid* 10,000 yen for gas. 《⇨ harau; shiharai》

shiˈhatsu しはつ（始発）*n.* **1** the first train; the first run:
Shihatsu kara shoogo made sutoraiki desu. (始発から正午までストライキです) They will stage a strike from the *first run* till noon. 《↔ shuuden̄(sha); shuusha》
2 starting:
Sono ressha wa Shin̄juku shihatsu desu. (その列車は新宿始発です) That train *starts* from Shinjuku. / shi-

hatsu-*eki* (始発駅) the *starting* station.

shiˈhee しへい（紙幣）*n.* paper money. 《⇨ satsu; kooka[3]》

SHIHEE IN CURRENT USE

shiˈhon̄ しほん（資本）*n.* capital; fund:
Kare wa jibun̄ no o-kane o shihon̄ ni shite, shoobai o hajimeta. (彼は自分のお金を資本にして、商売を始めた) He used his own money as *capital* and started his business. / *Kono kaisha no shihon̄-kin̄ wa ichioku-en̄ desu.* (この会社の資本金は1億円です) This company *is capitalized* at 100 million yen. / shihon̄-ka (資本家) a *capitalist* / shihon̄-shugi (資本主義) *capitalism*.

shiˈhoˈo[1] しほう（四方）*n.* all sides; all around:
Sono mura wa shihoo o yama ni kakomarete iru. (その村は四方を山に囲まれている) The village is surrounded *on all sides* by mountains. / *Yamakaji de go-kiro shihoo ga yaketa.* (山火事で5キロ四方が焼けた) The area within a *radius* of five kilometers was destroyed by a hill fire.

shihoo-happoo (〜八方) all sides

[directions]: *Kodomo-tachi wa*
shihoo-happoo *e nigeta.* (子どもたち
は四方八方へ逃げた) The children
ran away *in all directions.*

shi꜒hoo² しほう（司法） *n.* juris-
diction:
shihoo-*keñ* （司法権） *judicial*
power / shihoo-*shikeñ* （司法試験）
a *bar* examination. 《⇨ sañkeñ-
buñritsu》

shi꜒i-di꜒i シーディー *n.* =CD.

shi꜒iñ しいん（子音） *n.* consonant.
《⇨ appendixes; boiñ》

shi꜒ire しいれ（仕入れ） *n.* stock-
ing; buying in:
Shiire *no tañtoo wa dare desu ka?*
（仕入れの担当は誰ですか）Who is in
charge of *purchasing*? / *Kono shina no* shiire *kakaku wa ikura
desu ka?* （この品の仕入れ価格はいくら
ですか）What is the *buying* price of
this article? 《⇨ shiireru》

shi꜒ire꜒·ru しいれる（仕入れる）*vt.*
(shiire-te Ⓥ) **1** stock (goods);
lay in stock:
Sorosoro fuyumono o shiireru *jiki
desu.* （そろそろ冬物を仕入れる時期で
す）It's now time to *stock up* with
winter goods. 《⇨ shiire》
2 get (information):
Doko de sono joohoo o shiire-
mashita ka? （どこでその情報を仕入れ
ましたか）Where did you *get* that
information?

shi꜒i꜒·ru しいる（強いる）*vt.* (shii-te
Ⓥ) force; compel; press:
Kare wa jishoku o shiirareta. （彼は
辞職を強いられた）He *was forced* to
resign.

shi꜒ite しいて（強いて）*adv.* against
one's will; forcibly:
Shiite *soñna koto o suru hitsuyoo
wa arimaseñ.* （しいてそんなことをする必
要はありません）You don't have to
do that *against your will.* / *Ryoohoo onaji kurai desu ga* shiite *ieba, kochira no hoo ga suki desu.*
（両方同じくらいですがしいて言えば、こち

らの方が好きです）They are both
pretty much the same, but *if I
must choose*, I like this more.

shi꜒ito-be꜒ruto シートベルト *n.*
seat belt:
shiito-beruto *o shimeru* （シートベル
トを締める）fasten a *seat belt.*

shi꜒itsu シーツ *n.* bed sheet:
beddo ni shiitsu *o shiku* （ベッドにシ
ーツを敷く）put *sheets* on a bed.

shi꜒izuñ シーズン *n.* season:
Yakyuu no shiizuñ *wa owarimashita.* （野球のシーズンは終わりました）
The baseball *season* is over. /
Kaki wa ima ga shiizuñ *desu.* （カキ
は今がシーズンです）Oysters are now
in *season.*

shi꜒izuñ-o꜒fu シーズンオフ *n.* off-
season:
Ima wa shiizun-ofu *da kara, ryokañ ni yasuku tomaremasu.* （今はシ
ーズンオフだから、旅館に安く泊まれます）
Since it is *out of season*, you can
stay at an inn at cheap rates.

shi꜒ji¹ しじ（指示）*n.* directions;
instructions:
shiji *o ataeru* [*ukeru*] （指示を与える
[受ける]）give [receive] *instructions*
/ *Keesatsukañ no* shiji *ni shitagatte kudasai.* （警察官の指示に従っ
てください）Please follow the *instructions* of the police. / *Iiñchoo
wa suto no* shiji *o dashita.* （委員長
はストの指示を出した）The chairman
issued *instructions* for a strike.
shiji suru （〜する）*vt.* direct; instruct; indicate: *Watashi wa kodomo-tachi ni heya no kagi o
kakete oku yoo ni* shiji shita. （私は
子どもたちに部屋の鍵をかけておくように
指示した）I *instructed* the children
to keep the room locked.

shi꜒ji² しじ（支持）*n.* support;
backing:
Shushoo wa kokumiñ no shiji *o
ushinatte* [*ete*] *iru.* （首相は国民の支
持を失って[得て]いる）The prime
minister has lost [has] the *sup-*

port of the people. / *Koohosha wa* shiji *o uttaeta.*(候補者は支持を訴えた) The candidate appealed for *support.*

shiji suru (〜する) *vt.* support; back up: *Watashi wa anata no ikeñ o* shiji *shimasu.*(私はあなたの意見を支持します) I *support* your opinion.

shi⌐jiñ しじん (詩人) *n.* poet: *joryuu*-shijiñ (女流詩人) a female *poet.*

shi⌐jitsu しじつ (手術) *n.* = shujutsu.

shi⌐joo しじょう (市場) *n.* market: *shiñ-seehiñ o* shijoo *ni dasu* (新製品を市場に出す) put a new product on the *market* / *kaigai*-shijoo *o hirogeru* (海外市場を広げる) expand a foreign *market* / shijoo-*choosa* (市場調査) a *market* survey.

shi⌐juu しじゅう (始終) *adv.* always; very often: *Kare wa* shijuu *fuhee bakari itte iru.*(彼はしじゅう不平ばかり言っている) He does nothing but complain *all the time.* / *Chichi wa* shijuu *gorufu ni itte iru.*(父はしじゅうゴルフに行っている) My father is *always* off playing golf.

shi⌐ka[1] しか (鹿) *n.* deer; stag; hind.

shi⌐ka[2] しか (歯科) *n.* dentistry: shika-i (歯科医) a *dentist.* 《⇨ haisha[1]; byooiñ (table)》

shika[3] しか *p.* **1** only; except for: ★ Used after a noun or counter in negative sentences. *Kanojo wa kodomo ga hitori* shika *inakatta.*(彼女は子どもが一人しかいなかった) She had *only* one child. / *Yuube wa sañ-jikañ* shika *nenakatta.*(ゆうべは3時間しか寝なかった) Last night I slept *but* three hours. / *Kore wa kono mise de* shika *utte imaseñ.*(これはこの店でしか売っていません) This is sold *nowhere but* at this shop. 《⇨ dake;

nomi[2]; bakari》

2 no other way: ★ Used after a verb in the dictionary form. *Koo nattara moo yaru* shika *arimaseñ.*(こうなったらもうやるしかありません) If such is the case, there is *nothing* for us *but* to go ahead and do it. / *Dare ni mo tayorazu, jibuñ de yaru* shika *arimaseñ.*(だれにも頼らず、自分でやるしかありません) I have *no* choice *but* to do it alone, relying on no one.

shi⌐kaeshi しかえし (仕返し) *n.* revenge; retaliation: *Kare wa* shikaeshi *ni atama o nagurareta.*(彼はしかえしに頭を殴られた) He was hit on the head in *revenge.*

shikaeshi (o) suru (〜を)する) *vi.* revenge; get back at: *Kare ni kono* shikaeshi o shite *yaru zo.*(彼にこのしかえしをしてやるぞ) I'll *get back* at him for this.

shi⌐kai しかい (司会) *n.* master of ceremonies; chairperson: *Kyoo no kaigi no* shikai *wa dare desu ka?* (きょうの会議の司会はだれですか) Who will be the *chairperson* at today's conference? / *Kyoo wa watashi ga* shikai *o shimasu.* (きょうは私が司会をします) Today I will *take the chair* at the meeting. / *Kare wa sono bañgumi no* shikai *o tsutometa.*(彼はその番組の司会をつとめた) He acted as the *emcee* of the program. / shikai-sha (司会者) a *master of ceremonies*; an *M.C.*

shi⌐kake しかけ (仕掛け) *n.* device; mechanism; gadget: *Kono niñgyoo wa doñna* shikake *de ugoku no desu ka?* (この人形はどんなしかけで動くのですか) What *device* makes this doll move? / *Kono poñpu no* shikake *wa kañtañ desu.* (このポンプのしかけは簡単です) The *mechanism* of this pump is simple. / *Kono* shikake *wa umaku dekite iru.*(このしかけはうまくできてい

る) This *gadget* works very well.

shiｒkakeｌ·ru しかける (仕掛ける) *n.*
(-kake-te Ⓥ) **1** start (a quarrel):
*Kare wa watashi ni keñka o shika-
kete kita.* (彼は私にけんかをしかけてき
た) He *picked* a quarrel with me.
2 set (a trap); plant (a bomb):
*Watashi wa kare-ra ga shikaketa
wana ni hamatta.* (私は彼らがしかけた
わなにはまった) I fell into the trap
they *set*.

shiｒkaku[1] しかく (資格) *n.* **1** qualification; capacity:
*Yamada-sañ wa Nihoñgo-kyooshi
no shikaku ga arimasu.* (山田さんは
日本語教師の資格があります) Mr. Ya-
mada has *qualifications* as a teacher of Japanese. / *Kare wa sono
kai ni kojiñ no shikaku de shusseki shita.* (彼はその会に個人の資格で
出席した) He attended the meeting in his private *capacity*.
2 license; certificate:
*Isha no shikaku o toru no wa mu-
zukashii.* (医者の資格を取るのは難し
い) It is difficult to get a doctor's
license.

shiｒkaku[2] しかく (四角) *a.n.*
(~ **na, ni**) square:
shikaku na teeburu (四角なテーブル)
a *square* table / *kami o shikaku ni
kiru* (紙を四角に切る) cut a piece of
paper into a *square*. 《⇨ shikakui》

shiｒkaku[3] しかく (死角) *n.* dead
angle; blind spot:
*Sono jiteñsha wa torakku no uñ-
teñshu no shikaku ni haitte, hikareta.* (その自転車はトラックの運転手の
死角に入って, ひかれた) The bicycle
was hit by the truck because it
entered the driver's *blind spot*.

shiｒkakuｌ·i しかくい (四角い) *a.*
(-ku) square:
shikakui teeburu (四角いテーブル) a
square table / *Kono kami o shika-
kuku kiri nasai.* (この紙を四角く切り
なさい) Cut this piece of paper into
squares. 《⇨ shikaku[2]; marui》

shikaｌkukee しかくけい (四角形)
n. quadrangle; tetragon.

shiｒkame·ru しかめる *vt.* (shi-
kame-te Ⓥ) frown; grimace:
*Kanojo wa sono shirase o kiite,
kao o shikameta.* (彼女はその知らせを
聞いて, 顔をしかめた) She *frowned*
on hearing the news.

shiｒkaｌmo しかも (然も) *conj.*
1 moreover; besides:
Kanojo wa shigoto ga hayai. Shikamo *shiñchoo da.* (彼女は仕事が速
い. しかも慎重だ) She does her
work very quickly; *moreover*, she
is careful. / *Kuraku nari,* shikamo *ame ga futte kita.* (暗くなり, しか
も雨が降ってきた) It has become
dark, *and what's more*, it has
started to rain.
2 yet; still; nevertheless:
*Kare wa kikeñ ni chokumeñ shi,
shikamo heezeñ to shite ita.* (彼は
危険に直面し, しかも平然としていた)
He faced dangers, *and yet* he still
remained calm.

shiｒkar·u しかる (叱る) *vt.* (shikar-
r·i-; shikar·a-; shikat-te Ⓒ)
scold; reprove:
*Chikoku shite señsee ni shikara-
reta.* (遅刻して先生にしかられた) I arrived late and *was scolded* by my
teacher. / *Haha-oya wa gyoogi no
warui kodomo o shikatta.* (母親は
行儀の悪い子どもをしかった) The
mother *scolded* her bad-man-
nered child.

shiｒkaｌshi しかし (然し) *conj.* but;
however:
*Wareware wa ichi-jikañ hodo
matta.* Shikashi *ame wa yamana-
katta.* (われわれは1時間ほど待った. し
かし雨はやまなかった) We waited for
about an hour, *but* the rain did
not let up. / *Tashika ni kare wa
shigoto ga hayai.* Shikashi *shoo-
shoo zatsu da.* (確かに彼は仕事が速い.
しかし少々雑だ) He is a quick worker, to be sure. *But* his work is a

little sloppy.

shi⌐kashi-na⌐gara しかしながら
(然し乍ら) *conj.* however; but.
★ More formal than '*shikashi.*'

shi⌐kata しかた (仕方) *n.* way;
method:
Señsee ga tadashii beñkyoo no shikata *o oshiete kureta.* (先生が正しい
勉強のしかたを教えてくれた) The
teacher told us the right *way of
studying.* / *Kono jidoosha no
uñteñ no* shikata *o shitte imasu
ka?* (この自動車の運転のしかたを知って
いますか) Do you know *how to*
drive this car?

shi⌐kata-na⌐·i しかたない (仕方ない)
a. (-ku)

> **USAGE**
>
> Polite forms are '*shikatanai
> desu*' and '*shikata arimaseñ.*'
> '*Shikata ga nai*' is also used in
> the same meaning.

1 (*pred.*) cannot help doing; be
no use doing:
Shikata-nai. Akirameyoo. (仕方ない.
あきらめよう) It *cannot be helped.*
Let's give it up. / *Suñda koto wa*
shikata-nai. (済んだことは仕方ない)
What is done, *is done.* / *Ima soko
e itte mo,* shikata-nai. (今そこへ行っ
ても，仕方ない) It's *no use* going
there now.
2 (-ku) unwillingly; against
one's will:
Watashi wa shikata-naku *sañsee
shita.* (私は仕方なく賛成した) I approved it *reluctantly.*
-te shikata-nai (て〜) be dying
to do: *Ikitakute shikata-nai.* (行き
たくて仕方ない) I'm *dying to go*
there.

shi⌐ke⌐e けい (死刑) *n.* death
penalty:
shikee o señkoku sareru (死刑を宣
告される) be sentenced to *death* /
shikee-shuu (死刑囚) a prisoner
condemned to death.

shi⌐ke⌐ñ しけん (試験) *n.* examination; test:
shikeñ o ukeru (試験を受ける) take
an *examination* / shikeñ *ni ukaru*
[*gookaku suru*] (試験に受かる[合格す
る]) pass an *examination* / shikeñ
ni ochiru (試験に落ちる) fail an *examination* / *Kyoo wa suugaku no*
shikeñ *ga arimasu.* (きょうは数学の
試験があります) We have a math
test today. / *Kono moñdai wa* shikeñ *ni desoo da.* (この問題は試験に
出そうだ) This question is likely to
appear in the *examination.*

shikeñ (o) suru (〜(を)する) *vt.*
test; experiment: *Natsu-yasumi
no mae ni* shikeñ o suru *señsee
mo imasu.* (夏休み前に試験をする先
生もいます) There are some teachers who *give tests* before the summer vacation. / *Seenoo ni tsuite
wa* shikeñ o shite *minai to wakarimaseñ.* (性能については試験をしてみな
いとわかりません) We cannot gauge
the performance until we *test* it.

shi⌐keñkañ しけんかん (試験管) *n.*
test tube.

shi⌐ki⌐[1] しき (四季) *n.* the four seasons:
Kono kooeñ wa shiki *o tsuujite
utsukushii.* (この公園は四季を通じて
美しい) This park is beautiful in
all seasons. 《⇨ kisetsu (table)》

shiki	haru （春）	spring
	natsu （夏）	summer
	aki （秋）	autumn
	fuyu （冬）	winter

shi⌐ki⌐[2] しき (指揮) *n.* **1** command; direction:
shiki o toru (指揮をとる) assume
command / *Kare-ra wa shachoo no
shiki de kooshoo o hajimeta.* (彼ら
は社長の指揮で交渉を始めた) They
started negotiations under the
leadership of the president.

2 conducting musicians: *Sono kookyoo-gakudañ wa Ozawa Seeji no shiki de Beetoobeñ no 'Dai-ku' o eñsoo shita.*(その交響楽団は小沢征爾の指揮でベートベンの「第九」を演奏した) The symphony orchestra played Beethoven's Symphony No. 9 under the *baton* of Seiji Ozawa. / shiki-sha (指揮者) a *conductor.*

shiki suru (～する) *vt.* **1** command; direct: *Taichoo wa kuruma no ue kara kidootai o shiki shita.*(隊長は車の上から機動隊を指揮した) The commander *directed* the riot squad from the top of the vehicle.
2 conduct: *Ani wa chiisa-na koorasu o shiki shite iru.*(兄は小さなコーラスを指揮している) My elder brother *conducts* a small chorus group.

shi「ki」[3] しき(式) *n.* **1** ceremony: shiki o okonau (式を行う) hold a *ceremony* / shiki ni deru (式に出る) attend a *ceremony.* 《⇨ -shiki》
2 expression; formula: shiki de arawasu (式で表す) express something in a *formula.*

-shiki しき(式) *suf.* **1** ceremony: *nyuugaku-*shiki (入学式) a school entrance *ceremony* / *sotsugyoo-*shiki (卒業式) a graduation *ceremony* / *kekkoñ-*shiki (結婚式) a wedding *ceremony.*
2 way; style; fashion: *Nihoñ-*shiki *no toire* (日本式のトイレ) a Japanese-*style* toilet / *Chuugoku-*shiki *no ryoori* (中国式の料理) Chinese-*style* cooking.

shi「kibu」toñ しきぶとん(敷き布団) *n.* mattress; sleeping pad. 《⇨ futoñ (illus.)》

shi「kichi しきち(敷地) *n.* site; lot; ground: *Semai* shikichi *ni ie ga ni-keñ tatte iru.*(狭い敷地に家が2軒建っている) There are two houses standing on a small *lot.*

shi「ki」kiñ しききん(敷金) *n.* deposit: ★ Money paid to a landlord as a pledge for the rental contract. It is returnable. shikikiñ o ireru (敷金を入れる) make a *deposit.* 《⇨ reekiñ》

shi「ki」ñ しきん(資金) *n.* fund; capital: shikiñ o chootatsu suru (資金を調達する) raise *funds* / shikiñ ga tarinai (資金が足りない) be short of *funds* / *Kare wa* shikiñ *atsume ni isogashii.*(彼は資金集めに忙しい) He is busy collecting *funds.*

shi「kiri しきり(仕切り) *n.* **1** partition; compartment: *heya no* shikiri *o toru* (部屋の仕切りを取る) remove the *partitions* of a room / *Heya ni* shikiri o shite mittsu ni waketa.*(部屋に仕切りをして3つに分けた) We divided the room into three by *partitioning* it. 《⇨ shikiru》
2 (of sumo wrestling) the warm-up process before a bout: shikiri-*naoshi o suru* (仕切り直しをする) *toe the mark* again.

shi「kiri ni しきりに(頻りに) *adv.* very often; continually; eagerly: *Kare wa* shikiri ni *watashi o tazunete kuru.*(彼はしきりに私を訪ねて来る) He comes to see me *very often.* / *Señsee wa* shikiri ni *sono hoñ o susumeta.*(先生はしきりにその本を勧めた) The teacher *strongly* recommended that book.

shi「ki」r·u しきる(仕切る) *vt.* (shikir·i-; shikir·a-; shikit-te [C]) divide; parition: *Kaateñ de heya o futatsu ni* shikitta.*(カーテンで部屋を2つに仕切った) I *divided* the room into two with curtains. 《⇨ shikiri》

shi「kisai しきさい(色彩) *n.* color; coloration; coloring: shikisai ni tomu [toboshii] (色彩に富む[乏しい]) be *colorful [colorless]*

/ *Kanojo wa ii* shikisai-*kañkaku o shite iru.*(彼女はいい色彩感覚をしている) She has a good sense of *color.*

shi「kka」ri しっかり *adv.* (~ to; ~ suru) **1** firmly; tightly:
Kono tsuna ni shikkari *(to) tsukamari nasai.* (この綱にしっかり(と)つかまりなさい) Please take hold of this rope *firmly.*
2 hard; steadily; bravely:
Shikkari *(to) beñkyoo shi nasai.* (しっかり(と)勉強しなさい) Study *hard.* / Shikkari shi nasai. (しっかりしなさい) *Pull yourself together.*
shikkari shite iru [shita] (~している[した]) firm; reliable:
Kono tatemono wa kiso ga shikkari shite iru. (この建物は基礎がしっかりしている) The foundations of this building *are firm.* / *Kare wa* shikkari shita *jiñbutsu desu.* (彼はしっかりした人物です) He is a *reliable* person.

shi「kke」 しっけ (湿気) *n.* moisture; humidity; damp:
shikke no aru *heya* (湿気のある部屋) a *damp* room / shikke no nai *tokoro* (湿気のない所) a *dry* place / *Kyoo wa* shikke ga ooi. (きょうは湿気が多い) It is very *humid* today.

shi「kki」¹ しっき (漆器) *n.* lacquerware. 《⇨ urushi》

shi「kki」² しっき (湿気) *n.* = shikke.

Shi「ko」ku しこく (四国) *n.* the smallest of the four principal islands of Japan, south of Honshu and east of Kyushu. It comprises Kagawa, Tokushima, Kochi and Ehime prefectures. 《⇨ map (C5)》

shi「k·u しく (敷く) *vt.* (shik·i-; shik·a-; shi·i-te Ⓒ) lay; spread; cover; stretch:
yuka ni juutañ o shiku (床にじゅうたんを敷く) *lay* a carpet on the floor / *michi ni jari o* shiku (道に砂利を敷く) *spread* gravel on a road / *futoñ o* shiku (ふとんを敷く) *lay down* a

futon / *Doozo zabutoñ o* shiite *kudasai.* (どうぞ座布団を敷いてください) Please *take* a cushion and sit down.

shi「kuji」r·u しくじる *vt.* (-jir·i-; -jir·a-; -jit-te Ⓒ) fail; blunder; make a mistake:
Kare wa shikeñ ni shikujitta. (彼は試験にしくじった) He *failed* in the examination.

shi「kumi しくみ (仕組み) *n.* structure; mechanism; setup:
niñgeñ no karada no shikumi (人間の体のしくみ) the *structure* of a human body / *koñpyuutaa no* shikumi (コンピューターのしくみ) the *working* of a computer / *kaisha no* shikumi (会社のしくみ) the *setup* of a company.

shi「ku」shiku しくしく *adv.*
shikushiku (to) itamu (~(と)痛む) have a dull pain: *I ga* shikushiku (to) itamu. (胃がしくしく(と)痛む) I *have a dull pain* in the stomach.
shikushiku (to) naku (~(と)泣く) sob; weep: *Sono ko wa maigo ni natte,* shikushiku (to) naite ita. (その子は迷子になって、しくしく(と)泣いていた) The child got lost and *was sobbing.*

shi「kyuu」¹ しきゅう (至急) *n., adv.* urgently; immediately:
shikyuu *no yooji* (至急の用事) *urgent* business / Shikyuu go-heñji o *kudasai.* (至急ご返事を下さい) Please let us have your reply *promptly.* / Shikyuu (至急) *Urgent.* ★ Usually written on a document, envelope, etc.

shi「kyuu」² しきゅう (子宮) *n.* womb; uterus:
shikyuu-*gañ* (子宮がん) *uterine* cancer. 《⇨ gañ》

shi「kyuu」³ しきゅう (四球) n. (of baseball) base on balls; walk.

shi「ma」¹ しま (島) *n.* island:
shima *ni sumu juumiñ* (島に住む住

民) the inhabitants of an *island* / shima-*guni* (島国) an *island* country.

shi「ma」² しま (縞) *n.* stripe: *aoi* shima *no nekutai* (青い縞のネクタイ) a tie with blue *stripes* / shima *no aru shatsu* (縞のあるシャツ) a *striped* shirt.

shimai¹ しまい (姉妹) *n.* sisters: *sañ-niñ* shimai (三人姉妹) three *sisters* / shimai-*toshi* (姉妹都市) a *sister* city. 《⇨ kyoodai》

shi「mai² しまい (仕舞い) *n.* end: *Hanashi o* shimai *made kike.* (*rude*) (話をしまいまで聞け) Listen until I *finish* what I'm saying. / *Hajime kara* shimai *made kare wa damatte ita.* (始めからしまいまで彼は黙っていた) He kept silent from beginning to *end.* 《⇨ oshimai》

shi「mai ni」 wa (しまいには) *adv.* finally: *Kare-ra no giroñ wa* shimai ni wa *naguriai ni natta.* (彼らの議論はしまいには殴り合いになった) Their argument *ended in a fight.*

Shi「mane」-keñ しまねけん (島根県) *n.* Shimane Prefecture. Located in the northwest of the Chubu district, facing the Sea of Japan on the north. The capital city, Matsue (松江), is an important trading center. 《⇨ map (C4)》

shi「ma」r·u¹ しまる (閉まる) *vi.* (shimar·i-; shimar·a-; shimat-te Ⓒ) **1** close; be closed: *Kono doa wa jidoo-teki ni* shimarimasu. (このドアは自動的に閉まります) This door *closes* automatically. / *Mado wa zeñbu* shimatte imasu. (窓はぜんぶ閉まっています) All the windows *are closed.* 《⇨ shimeru¹》 **2** (of a shop) shut: *Sono mise wa hachi-ji ni* shimarimasu. (その店は8時に閉まります) That shop *shuts* at eight. / *Depaato wa mada* shimatte ita. (デパート

はまだ閉まっていた) The department store *was not open* yet. 《⇨ shimeru¹》

shi「ma」r·u² しまる (締まる) *vi.* (shimar·i-; shimar·a-; shimat-te Ⓒ) **1** be tightened; become firm: *Neji wa shikkari* shimatte imasu. (ねじはしっかり締まっています) The screws *are* good and *tight.* 《⇨ shimeru²》 / *Kare wa* shimatta *karada o shite iru.* (彼は締まった体をしている) He has a *firm* body. **2** become tense: *Kyoo no kare wa* shimatte iru. (きょうの彼は締まっている) He *is tense* today. / *Saa,* shimatte ikoo. (さあ、締まっていこう) Now, *let's pull ourselves together.* **3** be frugal: *Kanojo wa nakanaka* shimatte iru. (彼女はなかなか締まっている) She *is* very *frugal* with money.

shi「ma」su します do: ★ Polite form of 'suru.' *Daigaku o detara nani o* shimasu *ka?* (大学を出たら何をしますか) What will you *do* after college? / *Watashi wa sono kai ni shusseki* shimaseñ deshita. (私はその会に出席しませんでした) I *did not* attend that party. 《⇨ suru¹》

shi「matsu しまつ (始末) *n.* disposal; management; settlement: shimatsu o tsukeru (始末をつける) *settle* (one's accounts); *wind up* (a business) / *Kono ko wa* shimatsu ni oenai. (この子は始末に負えない) This child is *unmanageable.*

shimatsu ga warui (〜が悪い) be impossible to handle: *Yopparai wa* shimatsu ga warui. (酔っぱらいは始末が悪い) Drunkards are *difficult to deal with.*

shimatsu (o) suru (〜(を)する) *vt.* dispose of; tidy up; put in order: *gomi no* shimatsu o suru (ごみの始末をする) *dispose of* the garbage / *Soto e iku mae ni kono omocha o* shimatsu shi nasai. (外へ行く前にこのおもちゃを始末しなさい) *Tidy up* these toys before going out.

shi⌈matsusho しまつしょ (始末書) *n.* written apology: ★ Submitted to superiors by those who have caused an accident or made a blunder.
Kare wa kaisha ni soōgai o ataete, shimatsusho *o kakasareta.* (彼は会社に損害を与えて, 始末書を書かされた) He caused a loss to his company and was made to write an *apology.*

shi⌈ma⌉tta しまった *int.* gosh!; oh no!:
Shimatta! *Teeki o wasureta.* (しまった. 定期を忘れた) *Gosh!* I have forgotten my commuter pass.

shi⌈ma·u[1] しまう (仕舞う) *vi.* (shima·i-; shimaw·a-; shimat-te ⓒ) stop (work); leave off:
Kyoo wa itsu-mo yori hayaku shigoto o shimatta. (きょうはいつもより早く仕事をしまった) Today I *left off* working earlier than usual.

shima·u[2] しまう (仕舞う) (shima·i-; shimaw·a-; shimat-te ⓒ) ★ Follows the *te*-form of a verb. In conversation '*-te+shimau*' becomes '*-chau,*' and '*-de+shimau*' becomes '*-jau.*'
1 have done; (have) finished doing: ★ Used to emphasize the recent completion or occurrence of an action.
Shukudai wa moo yatte shimaimashita (yat-chaimashita). (宿題はもうやってしまいました(やっちゃいました)) I *have* already *finished* my homework. / *Moratta tokee o nakushite* shimatta (nakushi-chatta). (もらった時計をなくしてしまった(なくしちゃった)) I *have lost* the watch presented to me.
2 end up doing; go and do: ★ Used in reference to unfavorable consequences.

Kotori ga shiōde shimatta (shiō-jatta). (小鳥が死んでしまった(死んじゃった)) The bird *finally died.* / *Ukkari garasu o* watte shimatta (wat-chatta). (うっかりガラスを割ってしまった(割っちゃった)) I carelessly *went and broke* the glass.

shi⌈ma·u[3] しまう (仕舞う) *vi.* (shima·i-; shimaw·a-; shimat-te ⓒ) put away; put back; keep:
Tsukatta mono wa moto no basho ni shimai nasai. (使った物は元の場所にしまいなさい) *Put* the things you have used *back* in their original place. / *Seōpuuki wa monooki ni* shimaimashita. (扇風機は物置にしまいました) I *put* the electric fan *away* in the storeroom.

shi⌈mauma しまうま (縞馬) *n.* zebra.

shi⌉mee[1] しめい (氏名) *n.* full name: ★ Literally 'family name' (氏) and 'personal name' (名).
Koko ni juusho shimee *o kaite kudasai.* (ここに住所氏名を書いてください) Please write your *name* and address here. 《⇨ namae》

shi⌉mee[2] しめい (使命) *n.* mission:
shimee *o hatasu* (使命を果たす) carry out one's *mission* / *Kare wa tokubetsu no* shimee *o obite, Ejiputo e hakeō sareta.* (彼は特別の使命を帯びて, エジプトへ派遣された) He was sent to Egypt on a special *mission.*

shi⌈mee[3] しめい (指名) *n.* nomination; designation; appointment:
shimee *o ukeru* (指名を受ける) receive a *nomination* / shimee-*tehai* (指名手配) instituting a search for an *identified criminal.*
shimee suru (～する) *vt.* nominate; designate; name: *Iiōkai wa Yamada-saō o gichoo ni* shimee shita. (委員会は山田さんを議長に指名した) The committee *desig-*

nated Mr. Yamada as chairman.

shi⌈mekiri しめきり（締め切り）n.
1 deadline:
Oobo no shimekiri wa sañ-gatsu tooka desu.（応募の締め切りは 3 月 10 日です）The *deadline* for applications is March 10. / *Nañ to ka geñkoo no shimekiri ni maniatta.* （何とか原稿の締め切りに間に合った）I managed to make the *deadline* for the manuscript. 《⇨ shime-kiru²》
2 (*sign*) Closed; No Entrance.

shi⌈mekir·u¹ しめきる（閉め切る）vt.
(-kir·i-; -kir·a-; -kit-te Ⓒ) close [shut] up:
Ame ga hidoi no de amado o shi-mekitte oita.（雨がひどいので雨戸をしめきっておいた）The rain was so heavy that I *kept* the shutters *closed*.

shi⌈mekir·u² しめきる（締め切る）vt.
(-kir·i-; -kir·a-; -kit-te Ⓒ) close:
Boshuu wa koñgetsu ippai de shi-mekirimasu.（募集は今月いっぱいで締め切ります）Applications will *be closed* at the end of this month. 《⇨ shimekiri》

shi⌈menawa しめなわ（注連縄）n.
sacred straw festoon.

─CULTURE─

A twisted rice-straw rope hung with strips of white paper. It is usually strung up in front of a Shinto shrine or a family Shinto altar to ward off evil spirits.

SHIMENAWA

---

shi⌈meppo¹·i しめっぽい（湿っぽい）
a. (-ku) 1 wet; damp; humid; moist:
Kono taoru wa shimeppoi.（このタオルはしめっぽい）This towel is *damp*. / *Mado o akete oitara, heya ga shi-meppoku natte shimatta.*（窓を開けておいたら、部屋がしめっぽくなってしまった）The room got rather *damp* because I left the windows open.
2 gloomy:
Kyoo wa shimeppoi hanashi wa yameyoo.（きょうはしめっぽい話はやめよう）Let's put *gloomy* topics aside today.

shi⌈me¹·ru¹ しめる（閉める）vt.
(shime-te Ⓥ) close; shut:
Mado o shimete kudasai.（窓を閉めてください）Please *shut* the window. / *Doa wa shimete arimasu ka?*（ドアは閉めてありますか）*Is* the door *closed?* 《⇨ shimaru¹》

shi⌈me¹·ru² しめる（締める）vt.
(shime-te Ⓥ) 1 fasten:
Kuruma o uñteñ suru toki wa shiito-beruto o shimenakereba narimaseñ.（車を運転するときはシートベルトを締めなければなりません）You *have to fasten* your seatbelt when driving.
2 put on (neckties, belts, etc.):
★ '*shimete iru*' = wear.
nekutai o shimeru（ネクタイを締める）*put on* a tie / *Kare wa akai neku-tai o shimete ita.*（彼は赤いネクタイを締めていた）He *was wearing* a red tie. 《⇨ kiru² (table)》
3 lock:
doa no kagi o shimeru（ドアの鍵を締める）*lock* a door. 《⇨ shimaru²》
4 add up; total:
Shimete ichimañ goseñ-eñ ni nari-masu.（締めて 1 万 5 千円になります）*Adding it up*, it comes to 15,000 yen.

shi⌈mer·u³ しめる（湿る）vi. (shi-mer·i-; shimer·a-; shimet-te Ⓒ) get damp; get moist:

Kono taoru wa mada shimette imasu. (このタオルはまだ湿っています) This towel *is* still *damp.*

shi⌐me¬・ru⁴ しめる (占める) *vt.* (shime-te Ⓥ) occupy; hold: *Kare wa kaisha de juuyoo na chii o* shimete imasu. (彼は会社で重要な地位を占めています) He *occupies* an important position in the company. / *Kono seetoo wa kokkai de kahañsuu o* shimete iru. (この政党は国会で過半数を占めている) This party *holds* the majority in the Diet.

shi⌐me¬s・u しめす (示す) *vt.* (shimesh・i-; shimes・a-; shimesh・i-te Ⓒ) show; point out; indicate: *seei o* shimesu (誠意を示す) *show* one's sincerity / *jitsuree o* shimesu (実例を示す) *give* an actual example / *Kare wa sono basho o chizu de* shimeshita. (彼はその場所を地図で示した) He *indicated* the place on the map. / *Kanojo wa jibuñ de kaita e o yubi de* shimeshita. (彼女は自分でかいた絵を指で示した) She *pointed* to the picture she painted. / *Taioñkee wa sañjuukyuu-do o* shimeshite ita. (体温計は 39 度を示していた) The clinical thermometer *showed* 39 degrees.

shi⌐mi しみ (染み) *n.* stain; spot; blot: *Shatsu ni iñku no* shimi *ga tsuite imasu yo.* (シャツにインクの染みがついていますよ) You have ink *stains* on your shirt. / *Kono* shimi *o nuku no wa muzukashii.* (この染みを抜くのは難しい) It is difficult to take out this *stain.*

shi⌐miji¬mi しみじみ *adv.* (~ to) deeply; really; keenly; quietly: *Byooki o shite,* shimijimi (to) *keñkoo no taisetsu na koto ga wakatta.* (病気をして、しみじみ(と)健康の大切なことがわかった) I *keenly* realized the importance of good health

when I became ill. / *Kare to shoorai ni tsuite* shimijimi (to) *hanashiatta.* (彼と将来についてしみじみ(と)話し合った) I had a *heart-to-heart* talk with him about our future.

shi¬miñ しみん (市民) *n.* citizen: shimiñ-keñ (市民権) *citizenship.*

shi⌐mi・ru しみる (染みる) *vi.* (shimi-te Ⓥ) **1** smart; sting; (of medicine) irritate: *Kono kusuri wa sukoshi* shimimasu. (この薬は少ししみます) This medicine *stings* a little. / *Kemuri ga me ni* shimiru. (煙が目にしみる) The smoke *irritates* my eyes. **2** (of kindness, gentleness) touch: *Kare no shiñsetsu ga mi ni* shimita. (彼の親切が身にしみた) His kindness *deeply touched* me. **3** (of cold) pierce: *Samusa ga mi ni* shimita. (寒さが身にしみた) The cold *chilled* me to the bone.

shi⌐mo¬¹ しも (霜) *n.* frost: *Kesa wa* shimo *ga orita.* (今朝は霜がおりた) We had *frost* this morning.

shimo² しも *p.* (used with a negative) (not) always; (not) necessarily: ★ Used mainly with '*kanarazu*' or '*dare.*' *Jii-enu-pii ga sekai dai-ni-i da kara to itte, Nihoñjiñ ga* dare shimo *kanemochi da to iu wake de wa nai.* (GNP が世界第 2 位だからといって、日本人がだれしも金持ちだというわけではない) Even if Japan's GNP is the second highest in the world, it doesn't mean that *every* Japanese is rich. / *Doryoku shite mo,* kanarazu shimo *seekoo suru to wa kagiranai.* (努力しても、必ずしも成功するとは限らない) Even if you make every effort, it *doesn't always follow* that you will succeed.

shi⌐mo- しも (下) *pref.* **1** lower:

shimo-*te* (下手) the *lower* part; the left of the stage / shimo-*za* (下座) a *lower* seat. 《↔ kami-》
2 the second:
shimo-*hañki* (下半期) the *second* half of the year. 《↔ kami-》
3 last:
shimo-*futa-keta* (下2桁) the *last* two figures.

shi⸢moñ しもん (指紋) *n.* fingerprints.

shi⸢ñ¹ しん (芯) *n.* core; lead; wick:
riñgo no shiñ (りんごのしん) an apple *core* / *eñpitsu no* shiñ (鉛筆のしん) the *lead* of a pencil / *roosoku no* shiñ (ろうそくのしん) the *wick* in a candle.

shi⸢ñ² しん (心) *n.* heart; spirit:
Kare wa shiñ *wa yasashii hito da.* (彼は心はやさしい人だ) He is kind at *heart.* / *Kore wa* shiñ *no tsukareru shigoto da.* (これは心の疲れる仕事だ) This is *mentally* exhausting work. / *Kanojo wa nakanaka* shiñ *ga tsuyoi.* (彼女はなかなか心が強い) She *has* a pretty *strong character.* 《⇨ kokoro》

shi⸢ñ- しん (新) *pref.* new:
shiñ-*gakki* (新学期) a *new* school term / shiñ-*kiroku* (新記録) a *new* record / shiñ-*seehiñ* (新製品) a *new* product / shiñ-*sha* (新車) a *new* car.

shi⸢na しな (品) *n.* **1** article; goods:
Kono shina *wa yoku ureru to omoimasu.* (この品はよく売れると思います) I think this *article* will sell well. / *Chuumoñ-shita* shina *ga mada todokanai.* (注文した品がまだ届かない) The *goods* I ordered have not been delivered yet.
2 quality; brand:
Kono kabañ wa shina *ga yoi [warui].* (このカバンは品が良い[悪い]) This bag is of good [bad] *quality.*

shi⸢nabi·ru しなびる (萎びる) *vi.*

(shinabi-te Ⅴ) wither; shrivel:
Kabiñ no hana ga shinabite shimatta. (花瓶の花がしなびてしまった) The flowers in the vase *have withered.*

shi⸢nai しない (市内) *n.* city; within the city: ★ This only applies to a city which is designated as '*shi*.' 《⇨ tonai》
Musuko wa shinai *no kookoo ni kayotte imasu.* (息子は市内の高校に通っています) My son goes to a high school *in the city.* / shinai-*deñwa* (市内電話) a *local* phone call. 《↔ shigai²》

shi⸢namono しなもの (品物) *n.* article; goods. 《⇨ shina》

Shi⸢nano⸣gawa しなのがわ (信濃川) *n.* the Shinano River.
★ The longest river in Japan; it flows into the Sea of Japan at Niigata.

shi⸢na⸣yaka しなやか *a.n.* (~ na, ni) soft and tender; flexible; supple:
shinayaka *na eda* (しなやかな枝) a *supple* branch / shinayaka *ni odoru* (しなやかに踊る) dance *gracefully* / *Kanojo wa doosa ga* shinayaka *da.* (彼女は動作がしなやかだ) Her movements are *lithe and lissom.*

shi⸢ñ-Bee しんべい (親米) *n.* pro-American:
shiñ-Bee *gaikoo* (親米外交) *pro-American* diplomacy. 《↔ hañ-Bee》

shi⸢ñboo しんぼう (辛抱) *n.* patience; endurance; perseverance:
Kimi wa shiñboo *ga tarinai.* (君は辛抱が足りない) You lack *patience.* 《⇨ gamañ》

shiñboo suru (~する) *vi., vt.* be patient; endure; persevere: *Ato go-fuñ* shiñboo shi nasai. (あと5分辛抱しなさい) Just *be patient* for another five minutes. / *Watashi wa moo* shiñboo dekimaseñ. (私は

もう辛抱できません）I *can endure it no longer.*

shi⌐ñboozuyo⌐·i しんぼうづよい（辛抱強い）*a.* (-ku) patient; persevering; tenacious: *Ano hito wa* shiñboozuyoi. (あの人は辛抱強い) He is *patient.* / *Watashi wa* shiñboozuyoku *kanojo no heñji o matta.* (私は辛抱強く彼女の返事を待った）I *patiently* waited for her answer.

shi⌐ñbuñ しんぶん（新聞）*n.* newspaper; paper: shiñbuñ *o yomu* (新聞を読む) read a *newspaper* / shiñbuñ *o toru* (新聞を取る) take a *newspaper* / shiñbuñ *o haitatsu suru* (新聞を配達する) deliver *newspapers* / shiñbuñ-*sha* (新聞社) a *newspaper* company. (⇨ furushiñbuñ)

shi⌐ñchiku しんちく（新築）*n.* new building; new construction: shiñchiku *no ie* (新築の家) a *newly built* house / shiñchiku-chuu *no ie* (新築中の家) a house *under construction* / shiñchiku-*iwai* (新築祝い) a present to commemorate a *new house*; a *housewarming party.*
shiñchiku suru (～する) *vt.* build; construct: *Raineñ wa ie o* shiñchiku suru *yotee desu.* (来年は家を新築する予定です) We plan to *build* a house next year.

shi⌐ñchoo[1] しんちょう（身長）*n.* stature; height: shiñchoo *o hakaru* (身長を測る) measure one's *height* / Shiñchoo *wa dono kurai desu ka?* (身長はどのくらいですか) How *tall* are you? / *Kare wa* shiñchoo *ga hyaku-hachijus-señchi aru.* (彼は身長が180センチある) He is 180 centimeters *tall.*
shi⌐ñchoo[2] しんちょう（慎重）*a.n.* (～ na, ni) careful; cautious; prudent: *Tanaka-sañ wa* shiñchoo *na hito*

da ga ketsudañ wa hayai. (田中さんは慎重な人だが決断は速い) Mr. Tanaka is *cautious*, but quick at making decisions. / *Iiñkai wa kisoku no kaisee ni tsuite* shiñchoo *ni keñtoo shita.* (委員会は規則の改正について慎重に検討した) The committee *carefully* considered the amendment to the regulations. / *Shiñchoo ni koodoo shite kudasai.* (慎重に行動してください) Please act *discreetly.* (↔ keesotsu)

> **⸨USAGE⸩**
> '*Shiñchoo ni keñtoo shimasu.*' is a set phrase often used when implying a negative reply. The noun form '*shiñchoosa*' is also used. *e.g. Kare no hatsugeñ wa seejika to shite no* shiñchoosa *o kaite iru.* (彼の発言は政治家としての慎重さを欠いている) His remark is lacking in the *prudence* of a statesman.

shi⌐ñchuu しんちゅう（真鍮）*n.* brass: *Kono totte wa* shiñchuu *de dekite imasu.* (この取っ手は真ちゅうでできています) This doorknob is made of *brass.*

shi⌐ñdai しんだい（寝台）*n.* bed; berth: *Watashi wa ue* [*shita*] *no* shiñdai *de nemashita.* (私は上[下]の寝台で寝ました) I slept in the upper [lower] *berth.* / shiñdai-*sha* (寝台車) a *sleeping* car.

shi⌐ñdañ しんだん（診断）*n.* diagnosis: *isha no* shiñdañ *o ukeru* (医者の診断を受ける) *have* (one's case) *diagnosed* by a doctor / shiñdañ-*sho* (診断書) a *medical* certificate.
shiñdañ suru (～する) *vt.* diagnose: *Isha wa kañja o haigañ to* shiñdañ *shita.* (医者は患者を肺がんと診断した) The doctor *diagnosed* the patient as having lung cancer.

shi⌐ñdo¹ しんど (震度) *n.* seismic
intensity; intensity of a quake on
the Japanese scale of eight:
Kesa shiñdo sañ *no jishiñ ga atta.*
(けさ震度 3 の地震があった) This
morning we had an earthquake
with an *intensity of three on the
Japanese scale.*

shi⌐ñdo² しんど (進度) *n.* progress:
shiñdo *ga hayai* [*osoi*] (進度が速い
[遅い]) make fast [slow] *progress* /
Shiñdo *wa kamoku ni yotte machimachi desu.* (進度は科目によってまち
まちです) *Progress* differs according
to the subject.

shi⌐ñdoo¹ しんどう (振動) *n.* vibration; swing; oscillation:
shiñdoo-*suu* (振動数) the number
of *vibrations.*
shiñdoo suru (～する) *vt.* vibrate;
swing; oscillate: *Basu wa dekoboko michi de sayuu ni hageshiku*
shiñdoo shita. (バスはでこぼこ道で左
右に激しく振動した) The bus vio-
lently *swayed* from side to side
on the bumpy road.

shi⌐ñdoo² しんどう (震動) *n.*
quake; tremor:
jishiñ ni yoru shiñdoo (地震による
震動) *tremors* from an earthquake.
shiñdoo suru (～する) *vi.* shake;
quake; tremble: *Kono hashi wa
kuruma ga tooru toki* shiñdoo shimasu. (この橋は車が通るとき震動しま
す) This bridge *shakes* when cars
cross it.

shi⌐ñfu⌐zeñ しんふぜん (心不全) *n.*
heart failure.

shi⌐ñga⌐kki しんがっき (新学期) *n.*
new school term. 《⇨ gakki¹》

shi⌐ñgaku しんがく (進学) *n.* going on to a school of the next
higher level.
shiñgaku suru (～する) *vi.* enter a
school of a higher grade: *Koko
no kookoo no seeto no hotoñdo wa
daigaku e* shiñgaku shimasu. (ここ

の高校の生徒のほとんどは大学へ進学し
ます) Almost all the students at
this high school *continue on to
college.*

shi⌐ñgoo しんごう (信号) *n.* signal; traffic light:
shiñgoo *o mamoru* [*mushi suru*]
(信号を守る[無視する]) observe
[ignore] a *traffic signal* / Shiñgoo
ga aka kara ao ni kawatta. (信号が
赤から青に変わった) The *traffic light*
changed from red to green.

shi⌐ñnimonogu⌐rui しにものぐるい
(死に物狂い) *n.* desperation:
shinimonogurui *no doryoku* (死に
物狂いの努力) *desperate* efforts /
shinimonogurui *ni* [*de*] *nigeru* (死
に物狂いに[で]逃げる) run away *for
dear life* / *Tooji wa ikiru tame ni*
shinimonogurui datta. (当時は生きる
ために死に物狂いだった) In those
days, we *struggled frantically*
just to stay alive.

shi⌐ñjiñ しんじん (新人) *n.* new
star; new employee; rookie:
Kanojo wa koñgetsu debyuu-shita
shiñjiñ *desu.* (彼女は今月デビューした
新人です) She is a *new star* who
made her debut this month. /
Kotoshi no shiñjiñ *wa otonashii.*
(今年の新人はおとなしい) This year's
new employees are meek and obedient. / shiñjiñ-*kashu* (新人歌手) a
new singer.

shi⌐ñji⌐·ru しんじる (信じる) *vt.*
(shiñji-te Ⅴ) **1** believe:
Anata no iu koto o shiñjimasu. (あ
なたの言うことを信じます) I *believe*
what you say. / *Anata wa yuuree
o* shiñjimasu *ka?* (あなたは幽霊を信じ
ますか) Do you *believe* in ghosts? /
Soñna koto wa shiñjiraremaseñ.
(そんなことは信じられません) I just *can
not believe* that kind of thing.
2 trust:
Watashi wa kare o shiñjite imasu.
(私は彼を信じています) I *trust* him.
3 be sure; be confident:

Kanojo wa kitto seekoo suru to shiñjimasu. (彼女はきっと成功すると信じます) I *am confident* that she will succeed.
4 believe in (religions): *Watashi wa bukkyoo o* shiñjite imasu. (私は仏教を信じています) I *believe in* Buddhism.

shiˈñjitsu しんじつ (真実) *n.* truth; reality; fact: *Kare wa yuuki o dashite,* shiñjitsu *o katatta.* (彼は勇気を出して, 真実を語った) He plucked up his courage and spoke the *truth.*
⟪⇨ shiñsoo⟫

shiˈñju しんじゅ (真珠) *n.* pearl: shiñju *no kubikazari* (真珠の首飾り) a *pearl* necklace.

Shiˈñjuku しんじゅく (新宿) *n.* a major business, hotel, and entertainment center in Tokyo.
★ Well known for its high-rise buildings. The Tokyo Metropolitan Government buildings (including the highest building in Japan) are located here.

shiˈñjuu しんじゅう (心中) *n.* double suicide; taking someone into death with one:

(CULTURE)
The most usual case is that of a man and a woman whose love has not been fulfilled; often taken up as the theme of traditional Japanese dramas.

Kanojo wa kodomo no byooki o ku ni shite, shiñjuu *o hakatta.* (彼女は子どもの病気を苦にして, 心中を図った) Worrying too much about her child's illness, she attempted to *kill herself and her child.*
shiñjuu suru (〜する) *vi.* commit a double suicide. ⟪⇨ muri-shiñjuu⟫

Shiˈñkaˈñseñ しんかんせん (新幹線) *n.* the Shinkansen; bullet train:

Señdai made Shiñkañseñ *de ikimashita.* (仙台まで新幹線で行きました) I went to Sendai on the *Shinkansen.* / *Tookaidoo* Shiñkañseñ (東海道新幹線) the *New* Tokaido *Line.*

SHIÑKAÑSEÑ

shiˈñkee しんけい (神経) *n.*
1 nerve: *Kare wa me no* shiñkee *o yararete imasu.* (彼は目の神経をやられています) His visual *nerves* are damaged.
2 sensitivity: shiñkee ga surudoi [nibui] (神経が鋭い[鈍い]) *be sensitive [insensitive].*
shiñkee ga futoi (〜が太い) be bold: *Kare wa* shiñkee ga futoi. (彼は神経が太い) He *has a lot of nerve.*
shiñkee ga hosoi (〜細い) be oversensitive: *Kanojo wa* shiñkee ga hoso-suguru. (彼女は神経が細すぎる) She is *too sensitive.*
shiñkee ni sawaru (〜にさわる) get on one's nerves: *Ano soo-oñ wa* shiñkee ni sawaru. (あの騒音は神経にさわる) That noise *gets on my nerves.*

shiˈñkeeka しんけいか (神経科) *n.* neurology: shinkeeka-i (神経科医) a *neurologist.* ⟪⇨ byooiñ (table)⟫

shiˈñkeˈeshitsu しんけいしつ (神経質) *a.n.* (〜 na, ni) nervous: shiñkeeshitsu *na hito* (神経質な人) a *nervous* person / *Hito no iu koto ni amari* shiñkeeshitsu *ni naru na.* (人の言うことにあまり神経質になるな)

Don't *bother too much* about what others say.

shi「ñkeñ しんけん (真剣) *a.n.*
(～ na, ni) serious; earnest: shiñkeñ *na kao* (真剣な顔) a *serious* expression / *Watashi wa* shiñkeñ *desu.* (私は真剣です) I am *serious.* / *Kono koto wa motto* shiñkeñ *ni kañgaete kudasai.* (このことはもっと真剣に考えてください) Please take this matter more *seriously.* 《⇨ shiñkoku》

shi「ñkiñ-ko」osoku しんきんこうそく (心筋梗塞) *n.* myocardial infarction.

shi「ñkoku しんこく (深刻) *a.n.*
(～ na, ni) serious; grave: shiñkoku *na moñdai* (深刻な問題) a *serious* problem / shiñkoku *na kao-tsuki* (深刻な顔つき) a *grave* countenance / *Jitai wa* shiñkoku *desu.* (事態は深刻です) The situation is *grave.* / *Amari* shiñkoku *ni naranai de kudasai.* (あまり深刻にならないでください) Please do not get too *serious* about it. 《⇨ shiñkeñ》

shi「ñkoñ しんこん (新婚) *n.*
newly-married: *Ano futari wa* shiñkoñ *hoyahoya desu.* (あの二人は新婚ほやほやです) They are *recently married.* / shiñkoñ-*ryokoo* (新婚旅行) a *honeymoon* / shiñkoñ-*fuufu* (新婚夫婦) the *newlyweds.*

shi「ñkoo[1] しんこう (進行) *n.*
progress; advance: *kooji no* shiñkoo *ga hayai* [*osoi*] (工事の進行が早い[遅い]) the *progress* of construction is fast [slow] / *kuruma no* shiñkoo *o samatageru* (車の進行を妨げる) block the *progress* of a car / *byooki no* shiñkoo *o kuitomeru* (病気の進行を食い止める) halt the *advance* of an illness / Shiñkoo *hookoo ni mukatte* migi [*hidari*] *ni Fuji-sañ ga miemasu.* (進行方向に向かって右[左]に富士山が見えます) You can see Mt.

Fuji on the right [left] *up ahead.* / shiñkoo-gakari (進行係) a *program director*; a *master of ceremonies.*

shiñkoo suru (～する) *vi.* move; progress; advance: *Shigoto wa juñchoo ni* shiñkoo *shite imasu.* (仕事は順調に進行しています) The job *is going ahead* smoothly. / *Byooki wa shujutsu ga fukanoo na tokoro made* shiñkoo *shite shimatte ita.* (病気は手術が不可能なところまで進行してしまっていた) The disease *had progressed* to a stage at which it was impossible to operate.

shiñkoo[2] しんこう (信仰) *n.* faith; belief: shiñkoo *o motsu* (信仰を持つ) have a *faith* / shiñkoo *o suteru* (信仰を捨てる) renounce one's *faith* / shiñkoo *no jiyuu* (信仰の自由) freedom of *belief* / *Ano hito wa* shiñkoo *ga atsui.* (あの人は信仰が厚い) He is a man of deep *faith.*

shiñkoo suru (～する) *vt.* believe in: *Watashi wa bukkyoo o* shiñkoo *shite imasu.* (私は仏教を信仰しています) I *believe in* Buddhism. 《⇨ shiñjiru》

shi「ñkuu しんくう (真空) *n.* vacuum.

shi「ñkuukañ しんくうかん (真空管) *n.* vacuum tube; valve.

shi」ñneñ[1] しんねん (新年) *n.* new year; the New Year: shiñneñ *o iwau* (新年を祝う) celebrate the *New Year* / Shiñneñ *omedetoo gozaimasu.* (新年おめでとうございます) I wish you a happy *New Year.* 《⇨ shoogatsu》

shi」ñneñ[2] しんねん (信念) *n.* belief; faith; conviction: shiñneñ *o tsuranuku* [*magenai*] (信念を貫く[曲げない]) stick to [do not deviate from] one's *faith* / *Doryoku wa mukuirareru to iu no ga watashi no* shiñneñ *desu.* (努力は

報いられるというのが私の信念です) It is my *belief* that effort is rewarded.

shiˈñnyuu しんにゅう (侵入) *n.* invasion; intrusion; raid: *teki no* shiñnyuu *o fusegu* (敵の侵入を防ぐ) prevent the *invasion* of the enemy.

　shiñnyuu suru (〜する) *vi.* invade; intrude; raid: *Doroboo wa mado kara heya ni* shiñnyuu *shita.* (泥棒は窓から部屋に侵入した) The burglar *broke into* the room through a window.

shiˈ-noo-koo-shoo しのうこうしょう (士農工商) *n.* the four classes in Japanese feudal society, from the highest to the lowest; warriors, farmers, artisans, and merchants.

shi	bushi	warriors
noo	noomiñ	farmers
koo	shokuniñ	artisans
shoo	shooniñ	merchants

shiˈñpai しんぱい (心配) *n.* **1** anxiety; worry; concern; uneasiness: *Taifuu ga Nihoñ o osou* shiñpai *wa nai.* (台風が日本を襲う心配はない) There is no *fear* of the typhoon coming to Japan. / *Otooto wa oya ni* shiñpai *bakari kakete iru.* (弟は親に心配ばかりかけている) My younger brother is always causing my parents *anxiety*.
2 care; help: *Ojisañ ga shuushoku no* shiñpai *o shite kureta.* (おじさんが就職の心配をしてくれた) My uncle *helped* me find employment.

　shiñpai suru (〜する) *vt.* worry; fear; care; be troubled: *Jiko o okoshita no de wa nai ka to zuibuñ* shiñpai *shimashita.* (事故を起こしたのではないかとずいぶん心配しました)

I *was* very *worried* that you may have caused an accident. / *Tomaru tokoro wa* shiñpai *shinai de kudasai.* (泊まるところは心配しないでください) Please *don't worry* about somewhere to stay for the night.
— *a.n.* (〜 na) worried; anxious; uneasy: *Kodomo ga kega o shinai ka to* shiñpai *da.* (子どもがけがをしないかと心配だ) I'*m worried* that the children might get injured. / *Shikeñ no kekka ga* shiñpai *de yoku nemurenakatta.* (試験の結果が心配でよく眠れなかった) I *felt anxious* about the results of the exam, and couldn't sleep well. (⇨ fuañ)

shiˈñpañ しんぱん (審判) *n.*
1 (of sports) umpire; referee: *Kare ga sono shiai no* shiñpañ *o tsutometa.* (彼がその試合の審判をつとめた) He acted as *umpire* for the game.
2 judgment: *kainañ ni tsuite* shiñpañ *o kudasu* (海難について審判を下す) pass *judgment* on a marine accident.

shiˈñpi しんぴ (神秘) *n.* mystery.

shiˈñpi-teki しんぴてき (神秘的) *a.n.* (〜 na, ni) mysterious: *Sono gishiki wa doko to naku* shiñpi-teki *na tokoro ga aru.* (その儀式はどことなく神秘的なところがある) There is something *mysterious* about that ritual.

shiˈñpo しんぽ (進歩) *n.* progress; advance; improvement: *kagaku no* shiñpo (科学の進歩) the *advance* of science / shiñpo *o togeru* (進歩を遂げる) make *progress*.
　shiñpo suru (〜する) *vi.* progress; advance; improve: *Igaku wa ichijirushiku* shiñpo *shite iru.* (医学は著しく進歩している) Medicine *is making* remarkable *progress*.

shiˈñpo-teki しんぽてき (進歩的) *a.n.* (〜 na, ni) progressive; advanced:

shiñpo-teki *na hito* (進歩的な人) a person of *progressive* ideas / *Kare no kañgae wa* shiñpo-teki *da.* (彼の考えは進歩的だ) His thinking is *forward-looking.* ((↔ hoshu-teki))

shi⌐ñpu¹ しんぷ (神父) *n.* father. ★ A priest or clergyman in the Roman Catholic church. ((⇨ bokushi))

shi⌐ñpu² しんぷ (新婦) *n.* bride. ★ Used only at a wedding ceremony or reception. ((⇨ shiñroo))

shi⌐ñrai しんらい (信頼) *n.* trust; confidence:
shiñrai *o uragiru* (信頼を裏切る) betray a *trust* / shiñrai *ni kotaeru* (信頼にこたえる) live up to (a person's) *expectations* / shiñrai-*kañkee* (信頼関係) a relationship based on *trust.*
　shiñrai suru (～する) *vt.* trust; rely on: *Kare o* shiñrai *shite, zeñbu makase nasai.* (彼を信頼して、全部まかせなさい) *Put your faith* in him and leave everything to him. / *Sono joohoo wa* shiñrai *dekimasu.* (その情報は信頼できます) The information *is reliable.*

shi⌐ñri¹ しんり (心理) *n.* state of mind; psychology:
Kodomo no shiñri *wa wakaranai.* (子どもの心理はわからない) I cannot understand the *state of mind* of a child. / shiñri-*gaku* (心理学) *psychology.*

shi⌐ñri² しんり (真理) *n.* truth:
shiñri *o tañkyuu suru* (真理を探求する) seek the *truth* / *Kimi no iu koto ni wa ichimeñ no* shiñri *ga aru.* (君の言うことには一面の真理がある) There is some *truth* in what you say.

shi⌐ñriñ しんりん (森林) *n.* forest; woods. ((⇨ mori; hayashi))

shi⌐ñroo しんろう (新郎) *n.* bridegroom; groom: ★ Used only at a wedding ceremony or reception.

shiñroo *shiñpu* (新郎新婦) the bride and *groom.* ((⇨ shiñpu))

shi⌐ñrui しんるい (親類) *n.* relative; relation:
chikai [tooi] shiñrui (近い[遠い]親類) a near [distant] *relative* / *Kanojo wa watashi no haha-kata no* shiñrui *desu.* (彼女は私の母方の親類です) She is a *relative* on my mother's side. ((⇨ kazoku (table)))

shi⌐ñryaku しんりゃく (侵略) *n.* invasion; aggression:
shiñryaku *kara kuni o mamoru* (侵略から国を守る) defend a country against *invasion* / *keezai*-shiñryaku (経済侵略) an act of economic *aggression* / shiñryaku-*señsoo* (侵略戦争) a war of *aggression.*
　shiñryaku suru (～する) *vt.* invade: *Kare-ra wa sono kuni o* shiñryaku *suru no ga mokuteki de guñtai o okurikoñda.* (彼らはその国を侵略するのが目的で軍隊を送り込んだ) They sent in an army with the intention of *invading* the country.

shi⌐ñryoo しんりょう (診療) *n.* medical treatment:
shiñryoo o ukeru (診療を受ける) *be treated* / shiñryoo-*jikañ* (診療時間) *consultation* hours / shiñryoo-jo (診療所) a *clinic*; a *dispensary.* ((⇨ chiryoo))
　shiñryoo suru (～する) *vt.* treat: *Kono byooiñ wa heejitsu wa gozeñ ku-ji kara gogo go-ji made* shiñryoo *shite imasu.* (この病院は平日は午前9時から午後5時まで診療しています) This hospital on weekdays *treats* patients from 9:00 A.M. to 5:00 P.M.

shi⌐ñsatsu しんさつ (診察) *n.* medical examination:
shiñsatsu o ukeru (診察を受ける) *be examined* by a doctor / shiñsatsu-*keñ* (診察券) a *consultation* ticket / shiñsatsu-*shitsu* (診察室) a *consulting* room.

shiñsatsu suru (～する) vt. examine; see: *Isha wa kañja o hitori hitori teenee ni* shiñsatsu shita. (医者は患者をひとりひとり丁寧に診察した) The doctor carefully *examined* each patient.

shi「ñsee[1] しんせい (申請) n. application; request: *pasupooto no* shiñsee (パスポートの申請) an *application* for a passport / shiñsee-*sho* (申請書) an *application* form; a written *application*.

shiñsee (o) suru (～(を)する) vt. apply for: *Shiyakusho ni juumiñ-hyoo no koofu o* shiñsee shita. (市役所に住民票の交付を申請した) I *applied* for a copy of my residence certificate at the municipal office.

shi「ñsee[2] しんせい (神聖) a.n. (～ na) sacred; holy; divine: shiñsee *na basho* (神聖な場所) a *holy* place.

shi「ñseki しんせき (親戚) n. relative; relation. 《⇨ shiñrui》

shi「ñseñ しんせん (新鮮) a.n. (～ na, ni) fresh; new; green: shiñseñ *na yasai* (新鮮な野菜) *fresh* vegetables / *Inaka no kuuki wa* shiñseñ *desu.* (田舎の空気は新鮮です) Country air is *clean and fresh.*

shi「ñsetsu しんせつ (親切) n. kindness; kindliness; tenderness: *Go-*shiñsetsu *wa wasuremaseñ.* (ご親切は忘れません) I will never forget your *kindness.* / *Kanojo no* shiñsetsu *ga mi ni shimita.* (彼女の親切が身にしみた) Her *kindness* touched my heart.
— a.n. (～ na, ni) kind; kindly; friendly; hospitable: *Nihoñ de wa miñna ga* shiñsetsu *ni shite kuremashita.* (日本ではみんなが親切にしてくれました) Everyone was *kind* to me in Japan. / Shiñse-

tsu *na hito ga michi o oshiete kureta.* (親切な人が道を教えてくれた) A *kind* person showed me the way. 《↔ fushiñsetsu》

shi「ñshi しんし (紳士) n. gentleman: *Kare wa totemo* shiñshi *to wa ienai.* (彼はとても紳士とはいえない) You can certainly not call him a *gentleman.*

shi「ñshiki しんしき (神式) n. Shinto rites: *Kanojo no kekkoñshiki wa* shiñshiki *de okonawareta.* (彼女の結婚式は神式で行われた) Her wedding was held according to *Shinto rites.* 《⇨ busshiki》

shi「ñshiñ しんしん (深々) adv. (～ to) (the state of increasing darkness or cold, or snow falling): *Yoru ga* shiñshiñ *to fukete iku.* (夜がしんしんと更けていく) The night *is getting far advanced.* / *Yuki ga* shiñshiñ *to futte iru.* (雪がしんしんと降っている) The snow is falling *thick and fast.*

shi「ñshitsu しんしつ (寝室) n. bedroom.

shi「ñshoku しんしょく (浸食) n. erosion.
shiñshoku suru (～する) vt. erode: *Kono hora-ana wa kaisui de* shiñshoku sarete *dekita mono desu.* (この洞穴は海水で浸食されてできたものです) This is a cave that was formed by *being eroded* by seawater.

shi「ñsho「osha しんしょうしゃ (身障者) n. abbreviation for '*shiñtai-shoogaisha.*' 《⇨ shiñtai-shoogaisha》

shi「ñshutsu しんしゅつ (進出) n. advance: *Sono kaisha wa kaigai* shiñshutsu *o keekaku shite iru.* (その会社は海外進出を計画している) The firm is planning to *expand* its business overseas.

shiñshutsu suru (～する) *vt.* advance; make one's way: *kesshoo-señ ni* shiñshutsu suru (決勝戦に進出する) *advance* to the finals / *Saikiñ Kañkoku no seehiñ ga Nihoñ ni* shiñshutsu shite kite iru. (最近韓国の製品が日本に進出してきている) Goods produced in South Korea *have* recently *been flowing* into Japan.

shiⁿsoo しんそう (真相) *n.* the truth; fact: Shiñsoo *wa itsu-ka akiraka ni naru deshoo*. (真相はいつか明らかになるでしょう) The *truth* will come out some day. / *Sono* shiñsoo *wa dare mo shirimaseñ*. (その真相はだれも知りません) Nobody knows the *true facts.*

shiⁿtai しんたい (身体) *n.* body; constitution: *Kare wa* shiñtai *kyookeñ da*. (彼は身体強健だ) He has a strong *body.* / shiñtai-*keñsa* (身体検査) a *physical* examination.

shiⁿtai-shoogaⁿisha (身体障害者) *n.* physically handicapped person; disabled person.

Shiⁿtoo しんとう (神道) *n.* Shintoism; Shinto. ★ The indigenous religion of Japan, featuring the worship of nature and ancestors.

shiⁿ·u しぬ (死ぬ) *vi.* (shin·i-; shin·a-; shiñ-de Ⓒ) die; be killed: ★ A rather blunt expression. 'Nakunaru' is more polite. *Chichi wa gañ de shinimashita*. (父はがんで死にました) My father *died of* cancer. / *Kare wa kootsuu jiko de* shiñda. (彼は交通事故で死んだ) He *was killed* in a traffic accident. / *Anata no go-oñ wa* shinu made *wasuremaseñ*. (あなたのご恩は死ぬまで忘れません) I will never forget your kindness *as long as I live.* (↔ ikiru) (⇒ shiboo²)

shiⁿya-hoⁿosoo しんやほうそう (深夜放送) *n.* late-night broadcasting.

shiⁿyoo しんよう (信用) *n.* confidence; trust; faith; reliance: shiñyoo *o eru* (信用を得る) gain (a person's) *confidence* / shiñyoo *o nakusu* [*ushinau*] (信用をなくす[失う]) lose one's *good name* / *Sore wa kaisha no* shiñyoo *ni kakawaru moñdai desu*. (それは会社の信用にかかわる問題です) That is a problem which affects the *reputation* of our company. / *Kare wa miñna ni* shiñyoo *ga aru*. (彼はみんなに信用がある) He *is trusted* by everyone.

shiñyoo suru (～する) *vt.* trust; put confidence in; rely on: *Kare no kotoba o* shiñyoo *shite, hidoi me ni atta*. (彼の言葉を信用して, ひどい目にあった) I had a terrible experience through *relying* on what he had said. / *Tetsuzuki wa* shiñyoo *dekiru hito ni tanomi nasai*. (手続きは信用できる人に頼みなさい) For the paperwork, ask someone you *can trust.*

shiⁿyoo-kuⁿmiai しんようくみあい (信用組合) *n.* credit union (association). ★ Operates as a bank for medium and small-sized enterprises.

shiⁿyuu しんゆう (親友) *n.* close friend; one's best friend: *Kare wa watashi no naganeñ no* shiñyuu *desu*. (彼は私の長年の親友です) He is a *close friend* of many years.

shiⁿzeñ しんぜん (親善) *n.* friendship; goodwill: *Kare wa kokusai-*shiñzeñ *no tame ni tsukushita*. (彼は国際親善のために尽くした) He devoted himself to the promotion of international *friendship.* / shiñzeñ-*jiai* (親善試合) a game to promote *goodwill.*

shiⁿzeñ-keⁿkkoñ しんぜんけっこん (神前結婚) *n.* wedding according to Shinto rites.

shi「ñzoo しんぞう（心臓）*n.* heart:
Chichi wa shiñzoo *ga warui.*（父は
心臓が悪い）My father has *heart*
trouble. / *Sore o mite,* shiñzoo *ga
dokidoki shita.*（それを見て、心臓がど
きどきした）My *heart* thumped at
the sight. / shiñzoo-*byoo*（心臓病）
heart disease / shiñzoo-*hossa*（心
臓発作）a *heart* attack / shiñzoo-
mahi（心臓麻痺）*heart* failure.
　shiñzoo ga tsuyoi [yowai]（～が
強い[弱い]）be bold [timid]: *Kare
wa* shiñzoo ga tsuyoi.（彼は心臓が
強い）He is *stout-hearted.* / *Watashi wa* shiñzoo ga yowai *kara totemo soñna koto wa dekimaseñ.*
（私は心臓が弱いからとてもそんなことはで
きません）I am too *shy* to do a thing
like that.

shi「ñz·u¹ru しんずる（信ずる）*vt.*
(shiñj·i-; shiñj·i-; shiñj·i-te ①)
= shiñjiru.

shi「o¹¹ しお（塩）*n.* salt:
Sono shio *o mawashite kudasai.*
（その塩を回してください）Please pass
me the *salt.* / *Kore wa* shio *ga
kiki-sugite iru.*（これは塩が効きすぎて
いる）There is too much *salt* in
this.

shi「o¹² しお（潮）*n.* tide:
shio *no michi-hi*（潮の満ち干）the
ebb and flow of the *tide* / Shio *ga
michite kuru [hiite iku].*（潮が満ちて
来る[引いて行く]）The *tide* is coming in [going out].

shi「okara¹·i しおからい（塩辛い）*a.*
(-ku) salty. 《⇒ karai; aji¹ (table)》

shi「oñ しおん（子音）*n.* = shiiñ.

shi「ore·ru しおれる（萎れる）*vi.*
(shiore-te ⓥ) **1** (of a plant)
wither; wilt; fade:
Mizu ga nakute, hana ga shiorete
shimatta.（水がなくて、花がしおれてしま
った）The flowers *have withered*
for lack of water. 《⇒ kareru》
　2 (of a person) be dejected:
Hideo wa señsee ni shikararete,

shiorete iru.（秀雄は先生にしかられて、
しおれている）Hideo *is dejected*, because he was scolded by his
teacher.

shi「ppai しっぱい（失敗）*n.* failure; mistake:
Sono keekaku wa shippai *ni
owatta.*（その計画は失敗に終わった）
The plan ended in *failure.* /
Kare o gichoo ni erañda no wa
shippai *datta.*（彼を議長に選んだのは
失敗だった）Electing him chairman
was a *mistake.*
　shippai suru（～する）*vi.* fail:
*Kanojo wa uñteñ meñkyo no shi-
keñ ni ni-do* shippai shita.（彼女は
運転免許の試験に2度失敗した）She
failed her driving-test twice.
《↔ seekoo¹》

shi「ppitsu しっぴつ（執筆）*n.*
writing:
Kare wa shippitsu *ga hayai [osoi].*
（彼は執筆が速い[遅い]）He is fast
[slow] in *writing.* / *Watashi wa
sono zasshi ni* shippitsu *o tanomareta.*（私はその雑誌に執筆を頼まれ
た）I was asked to *write* for that
magazine. / *Sono sakka wa atarashii sakuhiñ o* shippitsu-chuu *desu.*
（その作家は新しい作品を執筆中です）
The author *is writing* a new
work. / shippitsu-*sha*（執筆者）a
writer; an *author.*
　shippitsu suru（～する）*vt.* write:
hoñ [roñbuñ] o shippitsu suru（本
[論文]を執筆する）*write* a book [an
essay].

shi「ppo¹ しっぽ（尻尾）*n.* tail:
Sono inu wa watashi o mite,
shippo *o futta.*（その犬は私を見て、し
っぽを振った）The dog wagged its
tail when it saw me.
　shippo o dasu（～を出す）show
one's true self: *Tootoo kare wa*
shippo *o dashita.*（とうとう彼はしっぽ
を出した）At last he *showed his
true character.*
　shippo o tsukamu（～をつかむ）

find a person's fault: *Kare wa
shippo o tsukamarete iru no de
kanojo ni noo to ienai.* (彼はしっぽを
つかまれているので彼女にノーと言えない)
Since *she has something on him,*
he cannot say 'no' to her.

shi⌐rabe[1] しらべ (調べ) *n.* examination; investigation; questioning.
*Sono otoko wa keesatsu no shi-
rabe ni taishite mokuhikeñ o tsukatta.* (その男は警察の調べに対して黙
秘権を使った) In response to police
questioning, the man exercised
his right to silence. 《⇒ shiraberu》

shi⌐rabe[2] しらべ (調べ) *n.* melody; tune:
natsukashii Nihoñ no shirabe (懐か
しい日本の調べ) an old-time Japanese *melody.*

shi⌐rabemono しらべもの (調べ物)
n. something to check up on:
*Kanojo wa toshokañ de shirabe-
mono o shite imasu.* (彼女は図書館
で調べ物をしています) She *is checking
up on something* in the library.

shi⌐rabe[1]**·ru** しらべる (調べる) *vt.*
(shirabe-te [V]) 1 examine; inspect; investigate:
*Keesatsu wa kaji no geñiñ o shira-
bete imasu.* (警察は火事の原因を調べ
ています) The police *are investigating* the cause of the fire. /
*Zee-
kañ de mochimono o shiraberareta.* (税関で持ち物を調べられた) My
belongings *were examined* at customs. 《⇒ shirabe[1]》
2 consult (a reference book);
look up:
*Kare wa sono go no imi o jisho de
shirabeta.* (彼はその語の意味を辞書で
調べた) He *consulted* the dictionary for the meaning of the
word.

shi⌐rase しらせ (知らせ) *n.* news;
information; report:
yoi [warui] shirase (良い[悪い]知ら
せ) good [bad] *news* / *Kare kara*

nani-ka shirase ga arimashita ka?
(彼から何か知らせがありましたか) Has
there been any *news* from him? /
*Kichoo na o-shirase arigatoo go-
zaimashita.* (貴重なお知らせありがとう
ございました) Thank you for the
valuable *information.* 《⇒ shira-
seru》

shi⌐rase·ru しらせる (知らせる) *vt.*
(shirase-te [V]) let know; inform; tell; report:
Eki ni tsuitara, shirasemasu. (駅に
着いたら、知らせます) I will *let you
know* when I have arrived at the
station. / *Dare mo sono koto o
shirasete kurenakatta.* (だれもそのこ
とを知らせてくれなかった) Nobody *has
told* me about that. / *Sono jiko
wa keesatsu ni shiraseta hoo ga
yoi.* (その事故は警察に知らせたほうがよ
い) You had better *report* the accident to the police. 《⇒ shirase》

shi⌐razu-shi⌐razu しらずしらず
(知らず知らず) *adv.* (~ ni) without
knowing it; unconsciously:
*Kodomo wa shirazu-shirazu (ni)
kotoba o oboeru.* (子どもは知らず知ら
ず(に)言葉を覚える) Children learn
language *unconsciously.* / *Kare
wa shirazu-shirazu no uchi ni aku
no michi ni haitte shimatta.* (彼は
知らず知らずのうちに悪の道に入ってしま
った) *Before he realized it,* he had
ended up on the path of wicked-
ness.

shi⌐ri[1] しり (尻) *n.* buttocks; bottom: ★ Often with 'o-'.
kodomo no shiri o butsu (子どものし
りをぶつ) beat a child on the *buttocks* / shiri-*mawari* (しりまわり)
one's *hip* measurement.
《⇒ jiñtai (illus.); koshi (illus.)》

shi⌐riai しりあい (知り合い) *n.*
acquaintance:
Ano hito wa tañ-naru shiriai desu.
(あの人は単なる知り合いです) He is
just an *acquaintance.* / *Kare to
wa guuzeñ shiriai ni narimashita.*

(彼とは偶然知り合いになりました) I *got acquainted* with him by chance.

shi¬riizu シリーズ *n.* series; serial.

shi¬ritsu¹ しりつ（私立）*n.* private: ★Sometimes '*watakushi-ritsu*' to distinguish it from '*shiritsu²*'（市立）.
shiritsu *no gakkoo*（私立の学校）a *private* school / shiritsu-*daigaku*（私立大学）a *private* university [college]. 《↔ kooritsu¹》

shi¬ritsu² しりつ（市立）*n.* municipal: ★Sometimes '*ichiritsu*' to distinguish it from '*shiritsu¹*'（私立）.
shiritsu *no gakkoo*（市立の学校）a *municipal* school / shiritsu *no toshokañ*（市立の図書館）a *municipal* library.

shi¬ro¹ しろ（白）*n.* **1** white:
shiro *no seetaa*（白のセーター）a *white* sweater. 《↔ kuro》
2 innocence:
Kare wa zettai ni shiro *da to omou.*（彼は絶対に白だと思う）I am quite sure that he is *innocent*. 《↔ kuro》

shi¬ro² しろ（城）*n.* castle.

SHIRO

shi¬ro¹·i しろい（白い）*a.* (-ku) white; (of skin) fair; (of hair) gray:
shiroi *kiku*（白い菊）a *white* chrysanthemum / *Suzuki-sañ wa iro ga* shiroi.（鈴木さんは色が白い）Miss Suzuki has *fair* skin. / *Saikiñ kami ga* shiroku *nari-hajimeta.*（最近髪が白くなり始めた）My hair has recently started to turn *gray*.

shi¬ro-kuro しろくろ（白黒）*n.* black and white: ★Note that the Japanese word order is opposite from the English.
shiro-kuro *no fuirumu*（白黒のフイルム）*black-and-white* film / shiro-kuro *no terebi*（白黒のテレビ）a *black-and-white* television.
shiro-kuro o tsukeru（～をつける）make clear which is right: *Sono keñ wa hakkiri* shiro-kuro o tsuketa *hoo ga ii.*（その件ははっきり白黒をつけたほうがいい）You had better clearly *decide on the merits* of that case.

shi¬rooto しろうと（素人）*n.* amateur; layman:
Watashi wa shashiñ wa shirooto *desu.*（私は写真は素人です）I am an *amateur* in photography. / *Reñga o tsumu no wa* shirooto *ni wa muzukashii.*（れんがを積むのは素人には難しい）It is difficult for a *non-professional* to lay bricks. / *Kanojo no eñgi wa* shirooto-*banare shite iru.*（彼女の演技は素人ばなれしている）Her performance is very far from being *amateurish*. 《↔ kurooto》

shi¬r·u¹ しる（知る）*vt.* (shir·i-; shir·a-; shit-te Ⓒ) **1** know; have knowledge of; be acquainted with: ★The form '*shitte iru*' is used rather than '*shiru*.'
Kanojo no deñwa bañgoo o shitte imasu *ka?*（彼女の電話番号を知っていますか）Do you *know* her phone number? / *Kare wa Nihoñgo o sukoshi* shitte imasu.（彼は日本語を少し知っています）He *knows* a bit of Japanese. / *Watashi wa kare no koto o yoku* shitte imasu.（私は彼のことをよく知っています）I *am* well

acquainted with him. / *Kono heñ no koto wa yoku* shirimaseñ. (この辺のことはよく知りません) I *do not know* this area very well. / *Kare ga nyuuiñ shite iru to wa* shiranakatta. (彼が入院しているとは知らなかった) I *did not know* that he was in the hospital. / *Sono kashu no na wa miñna ni* shirarete imasu. (その歌手の名はみんなに知られています) The name of the singer *is known* to everybody.
2 realize; notice; be aware: *Koñna ni osoi to wa* shiranakatta. (こんなに遅いとは知らなかった) I *did not realize* it was this late. / *Watashi wa jibuñ no ketteñ o* shitte imasu. (私は自分の欠点を知っています) I *am aware of* my shortcomings.
3 discover; find: *Kare wa jibuñ ga machigatte iru koto o* shitta. (彼は自分が間違っていることを知った) He *found* that he was wrong.

shi⌐ru² しる(汁) *n.* juice; soup: *remoñ no shiru o shiboru* (レモンの汁を絞る) squeeze the *juice* from a lemon. (⇨ misoshiru (photo))

shi⌐rubaa-shi⌐ito シルバーシート *n.* seat reserved for the elderly or handicapped on trains or buses. ★ Literally 'silver seat.'

SHIRUBAA-SHIITO

shi⌐ruko¹ しるこ(汁粉) *n.* sweet thick soup made from red beans with pieces of rice cake. ★ Often with 'o-.'

SHIRUKO

shi⌐rushi しるし(印) *n.* **1** mark; check; sign: *Watashi wa muzukashii tañgo ni eñpitsu de* shirushi *o tsuketa.* (私は難しい単語に鉛筆で印をつけた) I *marked* the difficult words with a pencil. / *Aka wa kikeñ no* shirushi *desu.* (赤は危険の印です) Red is a *sign* of danger.
2 token: *Tsumaranai mono desu ga, kañsha no* shirushi *ni o-okuri shimashita.* (つまらない物ですが, 感謝の印にお送りしました) I have sent you a small present as a *token* of my gratitude.

shi⌐rus·u しるす(記す) *vt.* (shirush·i-; shirus·a-; shirush·i-te ⒞) *(formal)* write down: *Kare wa shusseki-sha no namae o nooto ni* shirushita. (彼は出席者の名前をノートに記した) He *wrote down* the names of those present in his notebook. (⇨ kaku¹)

shi⌐ryoo しりょう(資料) *n.* material; data: *roñbuñ no tame no* shiryoo *o atsumeru* (論文のための資料を集める) collect *material* for an essay / shiryoo *o buñseki suru* (資料を分析する) analyze *data.*

shi⌐satsu しさつ(視察) *n.* inspection; observation: *Daijiñ ga geñchi made* shisatsu *ni dekaketa.* (大臣が現地まで視察に出かけた) The minister departed for an on-the-spot *inspection.*
shisatsu suru (〜する) *vt.* inspect; observe: *Choosadañ wa*

jiko geñba o shisatsu shita. (調査団は事故現場を視察した) The commission of enquiry *inspected* the scene of the accident.

shi「see しせい (姿勢) *n.* posture; carriage; position:
Kare wa shisee *ga ii* [*warui*]. (彼は姿勢がいい[悪い]) He has fine [poor] *posture.* / Shisee o tadashi nasai. (姿勢を正しなさい) *Straighten up!*

shi「señ しせん (支線) *n.* branch line (of a railroad).

shi」setsu しせつ (施設) *n.* **1** facilities:
Kono machi ni wa subarashii goraku shisetsu *ga aru.* (この町にはすばらしい娯楽施設がある) There are excellent recreational *facilities* in this town.
2 (*euphemistically*) institution; home; mental hospital:
Kare wa haha-oya o shisetsu *ni ireta.* (彼は母親を施設に入れた) He put his mother into an *institution.*

shi」sha[1] ししゃ (死者) *n.* dead person; the dead:
Sono jiko de shisha *ga go-mee deta.* (その事故で死者が5名出た) The accident caused five *deaths.* / *Kono jiko ni yoru* shisha *wa hyakunijuu-niñ desu.* (この事故による死者は120人です) The *death* toll in this accident is 120.

shi」sha[2] ししゃ (支社) *n.* branch office. (⇨ shiteñ)

shi」sha-gonyuu ししゃごにゅう (四捨五入) *n.* rounding off.
★ To round up to the nearest whole number when the figure is 5 and above, and round down when the figure is 4 and below.
shisha-gonyuu suru (〜する) *vt.* round off: *Roku teñ sañ-goo o shoosuu dai ni-i de* shisha-gonyuu suru *to roku teñ yoñ ni narimasu.* (6.35 を小数第2位で四捨五入すると6.4になります) When 6.35 is *round-*

ed off to one decimal place, it becomes 6.4. (⇨ kiriageru; kirisuteru; shoosuu[2])

shi「sho」osha ししょうしゃ (死傷者) *n.* casualties:
Sono jiko de tasuu no shishoosha *ga deta.* (その事故で多数の死傷者が出た) There were many *dead and injured* in the accident.

shi「shutsu ししゅつ (支出) *n.* expenditure; outgoings; expense:
shishutsu *o kiritsumeru* (支出を切り詰める) cut down on *expenses* / *shuunyuu to* shishutsu *no barañsu o toru* (収入と支出のバランスをとる) achieve a balance between income and *expenditure.* (↔ shuunyuu)
shishutsu suru (〜する) *vt.* pay; expend: *Yosañ kara tsuushiñ-hi o* shishutsu shita. (予算から通信費を支出した) We *paid out* expenses for postage and communications from the budget.

shi「shuu ししゅう (刺繍) *n.* embroidery:
shishuu-iri *no hañkachi* (ししゅう入りのハンカチ) an *embroidered* handkerchief / shishuu-ito (ししゅう糸) *embroidery* thread.
shishuu (o) suru (〜(を)する) *vt.* embroider: *Sukaafu ni namae o* shishuu shita. (スカーフに名前をししゅうした) I *embroidered* my name on my scarf.

shi」soku しそく (四則) *n.* the four basic operations of arithmetic. (⇨ keesañ)

shi」soñ しそん (子孫) *n.* descendant; offspring. (↔ señzo)

shi「soo しそう (思想) *n.* thought; idea:
Kare wa kageki na shisoo *o idaite iru.* (彼は過激な思想を抱いている) He has radical *ideas.* / shisoo *no jiyuu* (思想の自由) freedom of *thought* / shisoo-ka (思想家) a

thinker.

shi「sso] しっそ(質素) *a.n.* (~ na, ni) simple; plain; homely: *Kare no seekatsu wa shisso desu.* (彼の生活は質素です) His way of living is *plain and simple.* / *Kanojo wa itsu-mo shisso na minari o shite iru.* (彼女はいつも質素な身なりをしている) She is always *plainly* dressed. / *Ryooshiñ wa inaka de shisso ni kurashite imasu.* (両親は田舎で質素に暮らしています) My parents live a *simple* life in the country.

shi「su]u しすう(指数) *n.* index number: *bukka-shisuu* (物価指数) a price *index.*

shi「ta] した(下) *n.* **1** under; below: *Ki no shita de inu ga nete iru.* (木の下で犬が寝ている) There is a dog asleep *under* the tree. / *Kare wa uwagi no shita ni chokki o kite ita.* (彼は上着の下にチョッキを着ていた) He was wearing a vest *under* his jacket. / *Taiyoo ga chiheeseñ no shita ni shizuñda.* (太陽が地平線の下に沈んだ) The sun went down *below* the horizon. / *Suugaku no shikeñ no teñ wa heekiñ yori shita datta.* (数学の試験の点は平均より下だった) My score in the mathematics test was *below* the average. 《↔ ue¹》
2 down; downward: *Kono erebeetaa wa shita e ikimasu.* (このエレベーターは下へ行きます) This elevator is going *down.* / *Raito o shita ni mukete kudasai.* (ライトを下に向けてください) Please turn the light so it faces *down.* 《↔ ue¹》
3 junior; younger: *Kanai wa mittsu shita desu.* (家内は3つ下です) My wife is three years *younger* than me. / *Ichibañ shita no musume wa mada shooga-*

kusee desu. (いちばん下の娘はまだ小学生です) Our *youngest* daughter is still an elementary school pupil. / *Kare wa shita no mono o mikudasu keekoo ga aru.* (彼は下の者を見下す傾向がある) He is inclined to look down on those who are *junior* to him. 《↔ ue¹》

shi「ta]² した(舌) *n.* tongue: *shita o dasu* (舌を出す) put out one's *tongue.*
shita ga mawaru (~が回る) talk a lot: *Kanojo wa yoku shita ga mawaru.* (彼女はよく舌が回る) She *has a glib tongue.*
shita o maku (~を巻く) be filled with admiration: *Kare no kiokuryoku ni wa shita o maita.* (彼の記憶力には舌を巻いた) I *was amazed* by his good memory.
shita tarazu (~足らず) sketchy: *Kono setsumee wa shita tarazu da.* (この説明は舌足らずだ) This explanation *is inadequate.*

shi「tagae]・ru したがえる(従える) *vt.* (shitagae-te Ⅴ) make (a person) follow; be accompanied by: *Shachoo wa buka o suu-niñ shitagaete, koojoo o shisatsu shita.* (社長は部下を数人従えて, 工場を視察した) The president conducted an inspection of the factory *attended by* a number of his subordinates. 《⇒ shitagau》

shi「tagaki したがき(下書き) *n.* draft: *shitagaki o seesho suru* (下書きを清書する) make a fair copy of a *draft.*
shitagaki (o) suru (~(を)する) *vt.* make a rough copy; draft: *Supiichi no shitagaki o shita.* (スピーチの下書きをした) I *made a draft* of my speech.

shi「tagatte]¹ したがって(従って)
★ Used in the pattern '*...ni shitagatte.*' **1** in accordance with: *Subete, kare no sashizu ni shitagatte okonatta.* (すべて, 彼の指図に従

って行った) We have done everything *in accordance with* his instructions. 《⇨ shitagau》

2 as:

Taifuu no sekkiñ ni shitagatte, *fuu-u ga tsuyoku natta.* (台風の接近に従って、風雨が強くなった) *As the* typhoon drew nearer, the wind got stronger and the rain heavier. 《⇨ tsurete》

shiˈtagatte² したがって (従って) *conj.* (*formal*) therefore; consequently; accordingly: ★ Used at the beginning of a sentence. *Sañ-gatsu juugo-nichi wa wagasha no sooritsu kineñbi ni ataru. Shitagatte kyuugyoo to suru.* (三月十五日はわが社の創立記念日に当たる。従って休業とする) March 15 is the anniversary of the founding of our company. *Accordingly*, we will be closed for business.

shiˈtaga·u したがう (従う) *vi.* (shitaga·i-; shitagaw·a-; shitagat-te Ⓒ) obey; follow; observe: *meeree ni* shitagau (命令に従う) *obey* an order / *chuukoku ni* shitagau (忠告に従う) *follow* advice / *kisoku ni* shitagau (規則に従う) *observe* a regulation / *liñkai no kettee ni* shitagaimasu. (委員会の決定に従います) We will *abide by* the decision of the committee. 《⇨ shitagaeru》

shiˈtagi したぎ (下着) *n.* underwear; underclothes: shitagi *o kiru* [*nugu*] (下着を着る[脱ぐ]) put on [take off] one's *underclothes* / shitagi *o torikaeru* (下着を取り替える) change one's *underwear*.

shiˈtai したい (死体) *n.* dead body; corpse: *Kare wa* shitai *to natte hakkeñ sareta.* (彼は死体となって発見された) He was found *dead*.

shiˈtaku したく (支度) *n.* preparation; arrangements:

Shitaku wa dekimashita ka? (したくはできましたか) *Are you ready?* / *Yuuhañ no* shitaku ga dekimashita. (夕飯のしたくができました) Dinner *is ready*. / shitaku-kiñ (支度金) an *outfit* allowance.

shitaku (**o**) **suru** (〜を)する) *vi.* prepare; get ready: *Hayaku gakkoo e iku* shitaku o shi nasai. (早く学校へ行くしたくをしなさい) Hurry up and *get ready* to go to school.

shiˈtamachi したまち (下町) *n.*

1 the lower section of a city.

2 the old part of Tokyo.

★ Such as Asakusa and Kanda where family industries and commerce used to thrive. 《↔ yamanote》

shiˈtashi¹**·i** したしい (親しい) *a.* (-ku) friendly; familiar; intimate; close: shitashii *tomodachi* (親しい友だち) a *good* friend / shitashii *kañkee* (親しい関係) *close* relations / shitashiku *tsukiau* (親しくつき合う) be on *good* terms / *Anata wa Yamadasañ to* shitashii *desu ka?* (あなたは山田さんと親しいですか) Are you on *close* terms with Mr. Yamada? / *Ano hito to wa itsu* shitashiku *natta ñ desu ka?* (あの人とはいつ親しくなったんですか) When did you *become friends* with her?

shitashiku suru (親しくする) *vi.* be on good terms: *Kare wa watashi-tachi ni toku ni* shitashiku shite *kureta.* (彼は私たちに特に親しくしてくれた) He *treated* us in an exceptionally *friendly way*.

shiˈtashimi したしみ (親しみ) *n.* friendly feeling; affection: *Watashi wa kanojo no hitogara ni* shitashimi o kañjita. (私は彼女の人柄に親しみを感じた) I *felt myself drawn* to her because of her personality. 《⇨ shitashimu》

shiˈtashi¹**m·u** したしむ (親しむ) *vi.* (-shim·i-; -shim·a-; -shiñ-de Ⓒ)

1 be familiar [intimate]:
Sono otogibanashi wa kodomo-tachi ni shitashimarete imasu. (そのおとぎ話は子どもたちに親しまれています) That fairy tale *is familiar* to children.
2 enjoy; take an interest:
Kanojo wa suisaiga ni shitashiñde imasu. (彼女は水彩画に親しんでいます) She *enjoys* painting with watercolors. / *Aki wa dokusho ni* shitashimu *no ni, yoi kisetsu desu.* (秋は読書に親しむのに, 良い季節です) Autumn is a good season to *enjoy* reading. 《⇨ shitashimi》

shiˈtateˈ‧ru したてる (仕立てる) *vt.* (shitate-te [V]) **1** tailor; make:
Kare wa atarashii suutsu o it-chaku shitateta. (彼は新しいスーツを一着仕立てた) He *had* a suit *made*.
2 raise; educate; train (a person):
Kanojo wa oñnade hitotsu de musuko o ichiniñ-mae ni shitateta. (彼女は女手一つで息子を一人前に仕立てた) She *raised* her son to manhood all by herself.

shiˈtauke したうけ (下請け) *n.* subcontract; subcontractor:
Kare wa sono shigoto o shitauke *ni dashita.* (彼はその仕事を下請けに出した) He gave the work to a *subcontractor*. / *Uchi wa sono kaisha no* shitauke *o shite imasu.* (うちはその会社の下請けをしています) We *subcontract* for that firm. / shitauke-koojoo (下請け工場) a *subcontracting* factory.

shiˈtee してい (指定) *n.* appointment; designation:
shitee *o ukeru* (指定を受ける) receive a *designation* / shitee *o hazusu* (指定をはずす) have a *designation* removed / *Shitee no basho ni* shitee *no jikañ ni kite kudasai.* (指定の場所に指定の時間に来てください) Please come to the *designated* place at the *appointed* time. / *Ko-*

chira no shitee-*doori ni shite kudasai.* (こちらの指定通りにしてください) Please do it according to our *directions*. / *Toku ni seki no* shitee *wa arimaseñ.* (特に席の指定はありません) There are no seats specially *reserved*. / shitee-*seki* (指定席) a *reserved* seat.

shitee suru (〜する) *vt.* appoint; designate; specify: *Sono tatemono wa kokuhoo ni* shitee *sareta.* (その建物は国宝に指定された) The building *was designated* a National Treasure.

shiˈteki してき (指摘) *n.* indication:
ayamari no shiteki *o ukeru* (誤りの指摘を受ける) *have* one's mistakes *pointed out*.

shiteki suru (〜する) *vt.* point out; indicate: *Watashi wa sono shoohiñ no ketteñ o* shiteki *shita.* (私はその商品の欠点を指摘した) I *pointed out* the defects in the merchandise.

shiˈteñ してん (支店) *n.* branch office [store; shop].

shiˈtetsu してつ (私鉄) *n.* private railroad [railway].

shiˈtoˈshito しとしと *adv.* (〜 to) (the state of fine rain falling):
Ame ga shitoshito (*to*) *futte iru.* (雨がしとしと(と)降っている) The rain is falling *softly*.

shiˈtoˈyaka しとやか (淑やか) *a.n.* (〜 na, ni) graceful; gentle:
Suzuki-sañ wa shitoyaka *na josee desu.* (鈴木さんはしとやかな女性です) Miss Suzuki is a *graceful and modest* woman. / *Kanojo wa* shitoyaka *ni furumatta.* (彼女はしとやかにふるまった) She bore herself *in a ladylike manner*.

shiˈtsu しつ (質) *n.* quality:
Ryoo yori mo shitsu *ga taisetsu desu.* (量よりも質が大切です) *Quality* matters more than quantity. / *Kono sekitañ wa* shitsu *ga ii* [wa-

rui].(この石炭は質がいい[悪い]) This coal is of good [poor] *quality*. 《↔ ryoo¹》

-shitsu しつ（室）*suf.* room: *kyoo*-shitsu（教室）a class*room* / *yoku*-shitsu（浴室）a bath*room* / *machiai*-shitsu（待合室）a waiting *room* / *oosetsu*-shitsu（応接室）a drawing *room*.

shi⌈tsuboo しつぼう（失望）*n.* disappointment; discouragement: shitsuboo no amari *jisatsu suru*（失望のあまり自殺する）commit suicide *out of despair*.

shitsuboo suru（～する）*vi.* be disappointed: *Kare wa sono shirase o kiite,* shitsuboo shita.（彼はその知らせを聞いて、失望した）He *was disappointed* at hearing the news.

shi⌈tsu⌉do しつど（湿度）*n.* humidity: Shitsudo *ga agatta [sagatta].*（湿度が上がった[下がった]）The *humidity* rose [declined]. / *Kyoo wa* shitsudo *ga takai [hikui].*（きょうは湿度が高い[低い]）The *humidity* is high [low] today.

shi⌈tsu⌉gai しつがい（室外）*n.* outside a room; outdoors. 《↔ shitsunai》

shi⌈tsugyoo しつぎょう（失業）*n.* unemployment: Shitsugyoo *ga fuete [hette] iru.*（失業が増えて[減って]いる）*Unemployment* is increasing [decreasing]. / shitsugyoo-sha（失業者）the *unemployed* / shitsugyoo-*taisaku*（失業対策）a measure against *unemployment* / shitsugyoo-*hokeñ*（失業保険）*unemployment* insurance.

shitsugyoo suru（～する）*vt.* lose one's job; be out of work: *Kaisha ga tsuburetara, watashi wa* shitsugyoo shite *shimaimasu.*（会社がつぶれたら、私は失業してしまいます）If the company goes under, I will end up *being out of work*.

shi⌈tsuke しつけ（躾）*n.* training;

discipline; manners: *katee no* shitsuke（家庭のしつけ）home *discipline* / *Kono ko wa* shitsuke ga yoi [warui].（この子はしつけが良い[悪い]）This child is *well-[ill-]mannered*. / *Chichi wa* shitsuke *ga kibishikatta.*（父はしつけが厳しかった）My father was very particular about our *upbringing*. / *Kodomo ni wa shikkari* shitsuke *o suru koto ga taisetsu desu.*（子どもにはしっかりしつけをすることが大切です）It is important to teach children *proper behavior*.

shi⌈tsukko⌉·i しつっこい *a.* (-ku) = shitsukoi.

shi⌈tsuko⌉·i しつこい *a.* (-ku)
1 persistent; stubborn; importunate: shitsukoi *hito*（しつこい人）an *obstinate* person / *Onaji koto o* shitsukoku *iwanai de kudasai.*（同じことをしつこく言わないでください）Please stop going *on and on* about the same thing.
2 (of food) heavy; cloying; greasy: *Saikiñ* shitsukoi *mono wa iya ni natte kimashita.*（最近しつこい物はいやになってきました）I have recently come to dislike *greasy* foods.

shi⌈tsumoñ しつもん（質問）*n.* question; inquiry: *Nani-ka* shitsumoñ *wa arimaseñ ka?*（何か質問はありませんか）Aren't there any *questions*? / *Shitsumoñ ni kotaete kudasai.*（質問に答えてください）Please answer the *question*.

shitsumoñ suru（～する）*vt., vi.* ask a question: "*Shitsumoñ shite mo yoroshii desu ka?*" "*Doozo.*"（「質問してもよろしいですか」「どうぞ」）"May I *ask a question*?" "Yes, of course." / *Wakaranai tokoro o señsee ni* shitsumoñ shita.（わからないところを先生に質問した）I *asked* the teacher about the points I did not understand.

shi「tsu¹nai しつない (室内) *n.* inside a room:
Shitsunai *no oñdo wa sañjuu-sañdo made agatta.* (室内の温度は 33 度まで上がった) The temperature in the room rose to thirty-three degrees. / shitsunai-*puuru* (室内プール) an indoor swimming pool / shitsunai-*sooshoku* (室内装飾) interior decoration. 《⇨ shitsugai》

shi「tsuoñ しつおん (室温) *n.* room temperature. 《⇨ oñdo (table)》

shi「tsu¹ree しつれい (失礼) *n.* impoliteness:
Soñna koto o sureba, shitsuree *ni narimasu.* (そんな事をすれば、失礼になります) It would be *impolite* of you to do such a thing. / Shitsuree *o shoochi de, o-kiki shimasu.* (失礼を承知で、お聞きします) I know it is *impolite,* but, nevertheless, I would like to ask you something.
shitsuree suru (〜する) *vi.* **1** I'm sorry; Excuse me:
Kinoo wa rusu o shite, shitsuree shimashita. (きのうは留守をして、失礼しました) I *am sorry* that I was not at home yesterday. / *Chotto* shitsuree shimasu. (ちょっと失礼します) *Excuse me,* please. / *Kooto o kita mama de* shitsuree shimasu. (コートを着たままで失礼します) *Please forgive me* for not taking off my overcoat.
2 I must be going:
O-saki ni shitsuree shimasu. (お先に失礼します) Now *I must be going.*
— *a.n.* (〜 na) impolite; discourteous; rude:
shitsuree *na hito* (失礼な人) a *discourteous* person / shitsuree *na taido* (失礼な態度) an *impolite* attitude / *Hito no mae o damatte tooru no wa* shitsuree *desu.* (人の前を黙って通るのは失礼です) It is *rude* to pass in front of others without saying anything. / Shitsuree *desu ga o-namae o oshiete kudasai.* (失

礼ですがお名前を教えてください) *Excuse me,* but could you please tell me your name? / *O-kyaku-sama ni* shitsuree *na koto o itte wa ikemaseñ.* (お客様に失礼なことを言ってはいけません) You must not make *rude* remarks to our customers.

shi「tto しっと (嫉妬) *n.* jealousy; envy:
shitto *ni moeru* (しっとに燃える) burn with *jealousy* / shitto-bukai *hito* (しっと深い人) a *jealous* person.
shitto suru (〜する) *vt.* be jealous of; envy: *Kare wa kimi no seekoo o* shitto *shite iru.* (彼はきみの成功をしっとしている) He *is jealous* of your success.

shi「wa しわ (皺) *n.* **1** wrinkle:
Roojiñ no kao wa shiwa-*darake datta.* (老人の顔はしわだらけだった) The old man's face was covered with *wrinkles.* / *Kare wa hitai ni* shiwa *o yoseta.* (彼は額にしわを寄せた) He *wrinkled* his forehead.
2 crease:
Kanojo wa airoñ de zuboñ no shiwa *o nobashita.* (彼女はアイロンでズボンのしわを伸ばした) She ironed out the *creases* in the trousers / Shiwa *ni natta kami o nobashita.* (しわになった紙を伸ばした) I smoothed out the *crumpled* paper.

shi「waza しわざ (仕業) *n.* one's doing; work:
Kore wa dare no shiwaza *desu ka?* (これは誰のしわざですか) Whose *doing* is this? / *Kore wa kare no* shiwaza *ni chigainai.* (これは彼のしわざにちがいない) This must be his *doing.*

shi「ya¹kusho しやくしょ (市役所) *n.* municipal [city] office; city hall. 《⇨ kuyakusho》

shi「yoo¹ しよう (使用) *n.* use; employment:
Kono heya wa shiyoo-chuu *desu.* (この部屋は使用中です) This room *is occupied.* / *Kono rajio no* shiyoo-

hoo *ga wakarimaseñ.* (このラジオの使用法がわかりません) I don't know *how to use* this radio. / shiyoo-niñ (使用人) an *employee* / shiyoo-ryoo (使用料) the *rent* / shiyoo-sha (使用者) a *user*; a *consumer*; an *employer*.

shiyoo suru (～する) *vt.* use; employ: *Kono deñwa o shiyoo shite mo yoroshii desu ka?* (この電話を使用してもよろしいですか) May I *use* this telephone? / *Kono toire wa shiyoo suru koto ga dekimaseñ.* (このトイレは使用することができません) This toilet *is not in use*. 《⇨ tsukau》

shi「yoo[2] しよう (私用) *n.* private use; private business: shiyoo *no deñwa* (私用の電話) a *private* telephone call / *Kiñmujikañ-chuu ni kare wa* shiyoo *de gaishutsu shita.* (勤務時間中に彼は私用で外出した) He went out on *personal errands* during working hours.

shi「yoo ga na」・i しようがない (仕様がない) *a.* (-ku) ★ Also pronounced 'shoo ga nai.' Polite forms are '*shiyoo ga nai desu*' and '*shiyoo ga arimaseñ.*'
1 (*pred.*) be helpless; have no choice: *Dame nara*, shiyoo ga nai. *Hoka no hito ni tanomimasu.* (だめなら, しようがない. 他の人に頼みます) If your answer is 'No,' *there is no more to be said*. I will ask someone else. / *Shiyoo ga nakute, soo shimashita.* (しようがなくて, そうしました) I *had no choice* but to do it like that. 《⇨ shikata-nai》
2 (*attrib.*) good-for-nothing: *Aitsu wa* shiyoo ga nai *yatsu da.* (あいつはしようがないやつだ) He is a *good-for-nothing*.

shi「yuu しゆう (私有) *n.* private possession: shiyuu-*zaisañ* (私有財産) *private*

property / shiyuu-*chi* (私有地) *private* land.

shi「zai しざい (資材) *n.* material; raw material: *keñchiku*-shizai (建築資材) building *materials*.

shi「zeñ しぜん (自然) *n.* nature: shizeñ *o mamoru* (自然を守る) protect *nature* / *Hokkaidoo ni wa mada* shizeñ *ga nokotte iru.* (北海道にはまだ自然が残っている) The *natural* environment still survives in Hokkaido. / shizeñ-*hakai* (自然破壊) the destruction of *nature* / shizeñ-*hogo* (自然保護) the conservation of *nature* / shizeñ-*kagaku* (自然科学) *natural* science / shizeñ-*shokuhiñ* (自然食品) *natural* foods.
— *a.n.* (～ na, ni) natural; naturally: shizeñ *na eñgi* (自然な演技) *natural* acting / shizeñ *ni furumau* (自然に振る舞う) behave *naturally* / *Kono ii-kata no hoo ga Nihoñgo to shite* shizeñ *desu.* (この言い方のほうが日本語として自然です) This is a more *natural* way of saying it in Japanese. 《↔ fushizeñ》
— *adv.* naturally; automatically: *Shussekisha ga sukunakatta no de kai wa* shizeñ *chuushi ni natta.* (出席者が少なかったので会は自然中止になった) There were few people present, so the meeting was *automatically* canceled.

shi「zeñ ni しぜんに (自然に) *adv.* of oneself; automatically; spontaneously: *Kaze wa* shizeñ ni *naotta.* (かぜは自然に治った) My cold cured *itself*. / *Kono gaitoo wa kuraku naru to*, shizeñ ni *teñtoo shimasu.* (この街灯は暗くなると, 自然に点灯します) These street lights go on *automatically* when it gets dark.

shi「zeñ to しぜんと (自然と) *adv.*

naturally; automatically: *Kodomo-tachi wa* shizeñ *to naka-yoshi ni natta.* (子どもたちは自然と仲良しになった) The children *naturally* became friendly. ((⇨ shizeñ ni))

shiˈzuka しずか (静か) *a.n.* (~ na, ni) **1** quiet; still: shizuka *na heya* (静かな部屋) a *quiet* room / *Chooshuu wa* shizuka *datta.* (聴衆は静かだった) The audience was *still*. / *Shizuka ni* shi *nasai.* (静かにしなさい) Please be *quiet*. ((↔ yakamashii))
2 calm; soft: shizuka *na koe* (静かな声) a *soft* voice / *Akañboo ga* shizuka *ni nemutte iru.* (赤ん坊が静かに眠っている) The baby is sleeping *peacefully*. / *Kyoo no umi wa* shizuka *da.* (きょうの海は静かだ) The sea is *calm* today.

shiˈzuku[1] しずく (滴) *n.* drop: *Ame no* shizuku *ga hoo ni atatta.* (雨のしずくがほおにあたった) A *drop* of rain struck my cheek. / *Jaguchi kara* mizu no shizuku *ga ochite iru.* (蛇口から水のしずくが落ちている) *Water is dripping* from the tap.

shiˈzumaˈr·u しずまる (静まる) *vi.* (shizumar·i-; shizumar·a-; shizumat-te [C]) calm [quiet] down; subside: *Kaze ga* shizumatta. (風が静まった) The wind *has died down*. / *Soodoo ga* shizumatta. (騒動が静まった) The disturbance *subsided*. ((⇨ shizumeru²))

shiˈzume·ru[1] しずめる (沈める) *vt.* (shizume-te [V]) sink; submerge: *fune o* shizumeru (船を沈める) *sink* a ship / *Kare wa suichuu ni karada o* shizumeta. (彼は水中に体を沈めた) He *submerged* himself in the water. ((⇨ shizumu))

shiˈzume·ru[2] しずめる (静める) *vt.* (shizume-te [V]) calm; quiet; soothe; appease:

ikari o shizumeru (怒りを静める) *soothe* someone's anger / *Kare wa koofuñ shita kañkyaku o* shizumeta. (彼は興奮した観客を静めた) He *calmed* the excited spectators. ((⇨ shizumaru))

shiˈzum·u しずむ (沈む) *vi.* (shizum·i-; shizum·a-; shizuñ-de [C]) **1** sink; go down: *Sono fune wa akkenaku* shizuñde *shimatta.* (その船はあっけなく沈んでしまった) The ship *sank* quickly. / *Taiyoo ga* shizumanai *uchi ni kaeroo.* (太陽が沈まないうちに帰ろう) Let's go home *before* the sun *goes down*. ((⇨ shizumeru¹))
2 be depressed: *Kare wa naze-ka* shizuñde *ita.* (彼はなぜか沈んでいた) He *was depressed* for some reason or other.

Shiˈzuoka[1]**-keñ** しずおかけん (静岡県) *n.* Shizuoka Prefecture. Located in the Chubu district between Tokyo and Osaka, facing the Pacific on the south. Izu Peninsula, with its many hot spas, is located in the eastern part of the prefecture. Capital city: Shizuoka. ((⇨ map (F4)))

sho- しょ (諸) *pref.* various: sho-*koku* (諸国) *various* countries / sho-*señsee* (諸先生) *teachers*. ((⇨ kaku-))

-sho[1] しょ (所) *suf.* place; office; institute: juu-sho (住所) an *address* / jimu-sho (事務所) an *office* / saibañ-sho (裁判所) a law *court*. ((⇨ -jo))

-sho[2] しょ (書) *suf.* writing; letter; book: buñ-sho (文書) a *document* / doku-sho (読書) *reading* / see-sho (聖書) the *Holy Bible*.

shoˈbatsu しょばつ (処罰) *n.* punishment: shobatsu *o ukeru* (処罰を受ける) receive *punishment* / shobatsu *ni atai suru* (処罰に値する) deserve

punishment.
shobatsu suru (～する) *vt.* punish: ★ Often used in the passive. *Sake o noñde, kuruma o uñteñ suru to,* shobatsu saremasu. (酒を飲んで、車を運転すると、処罰されます) If you drink and drive, you will *be punished.*

sho⌐buñ しょぶん (処分) *n.* **1** disposal:
Gomi no shobuñ *ni komatte imasu.* (ごみの処分に困っています) I do not know what to do about *getting rid of* the rubbish.
2 punishment:
Kare wa uñteñ meñkyo-teeshi no shobuñ o uketa. (彼は運転免許停止の処分を受けた) He *was punished* by having his driving license suspended. / *Sono gakusee wa* taigaku shobuñ *ni* natta. (その学生は退学処分になった) The student *was expelled from school.*
shobuñ suru (～する) *vt.* **1** dispose of; do away with; get rid of: *ie o* shobuñ suru (家を処分する) *sell off* one's house / *zaisañ o* shobuñ suru (財産を処分する) *dispose of* one's assets / *Furui zasshi o* shobuñ shita. (古い雑誌を処分した) I *threw away* some old magazines.
2 punish; discipline: *Kaisha wa kañkeesha o* shobuñ shita. (会社は関係者を処分した) The company *disciplined* the persons concerned.

sho⌐chi しょち (処置) *n.* measure; treatment; disposal:
ookyuu shochi *o toru* (応急処置をとる) take emergency *measures* / *Moo* shochi nashi *desu.* (もう処置なしです) I *don't know what to do* about this situation.
shochi suru (～する) *vt.* deal with; treat; dispose of: *moñdai o umaku* shochi suru (問題をうまく処置する) *deal with* a problem skillfully / *mushiba o* shochi suru (虫

歯を処置する) *treat* a decayed tooth.

sho⌐chuu-mi⌐mai しょちゅうみまい (暑中見舞い) *n.* summer greeting card. ★ A postcard sent to inquire after a person's health in the hot season.

sho⌐ho しょほ (初歩) *n.* the first step; rudiments:
Nihoñgo kaiwa no shoho (日本語会話の初歩) *first steps* to spoken Japanese / *Nihoñgo o* shoho *kara hajimeta tokoro desu.* (日本語を初歩から始めたところです) I have just started to learn Japanese from the *very beginning.*

sho⌐kki しょっき (食器) *n.* tableware; the dishes:
shokki *o arau* (食器を洗う) wash the *dishes.*

sho⌐kku ショック *n.* shock:
shokku *o ukeru [ataeru]* (ショックを受ける[与える]) get [give] a *shock* / *Sono shirase wa ooki-na* shokku datta. (その知らせは大きなショックだった) The news was a great *shock* to me.

sho⌐koku しょこく (諸国) *n.* various countries:
Kare wa Yooroppa shokoku *o ryokoo shita.* (彼はヨーロッパ諸国を旅行した) He made a tour of European *countries.*

sho⌐kuba⌐ しょくば (職場) *n.* one's place of work; office; one's job:
shokuba *o hooki suru* (職場を放棄する) walk out on one's *job* / *Watashi no* shokuba *de wa taipisuto o motomete imasu.* (私の職場ではタイピストを求めています) In my *office,* we're looking for a typist.

sho⌐ku⌐butsu しょくぶつ (植物) *n.* plant; vegetation:
shokubutsu *o sodateru* (植物を育てる) grow *plants.*

sho⌐kubutsu⌐eñ しょくぶつえん (植物園) *n.* botanical garden. 《⇨ doobutsueñ》

sho￢kudoo しょくどう（食堂） *n.*
dining room; cafeteria; eating
place:
*Chuushoku wa chikaku no shoku-
doo de tabemashita.* (昼食は近くの
食堂で食べました) I ate my lunch at
a nearby *eating place.*

SAMPLE DISPLAY AT SHOKUDOO ENTRANCE

sho￢kudo￢osha しょくどうしゃ（食
堂車） *n.* dining car.

sho￢ku￢gyoo しょくぎょう（職業） *n.*
occupation; profession; job;
business:
*Ano hito no shokugyoo wa nañ
desu ka?* (あの人の職業は何ですか)
What is his *occupation*? / *Kare no
shokugyoo wa beñgoshi desu.* (彼
の職業は弁護士です) He is a lawyer
by *profession.*

sho￢kuhi しょくひ（食費） *n.* food
expenses; board:
*Tsuki ni shokuhi wa dono kurai
kakarimasu ka?* (月に食費はどのくら
いかかりますか) How much do your
food expenses come to every
month?

sho￢kuhiñ しょくひん（食品） *n.*
food; foodstuffs:
shokuhiñ-teñkabutsu (食品添加物)
a *food* additive.

sho￢ku￢iñ しょくいん（職員） *n.*
staff; staff member; personnel:
*Kono shokuba ni wa shokuiñ ga
juu-niñ imasu.* (この職場には職員が
10人います) There are ten *staff
members* in this office. / *shokuiñ-
kaigi* (職員会議) a *staff* meeting /
shokuiñ-shitsu (職員室) a *staff*
room. 《⇨ shaiñ》

sho￢kuji しょくじ（食事） *n.* meal;
diet:
Shokuji wa sumimashita ka? (食事
は済みましたか) Have you finished
your *meal*? / *Shokuji no yooi ga
dekimashita.* (食事の用意ができまし
た) *Dinner* is ready.
shokuji (o) suru (～（を）する) *vi.*
have a meal: *Isogashii no de kañtañ na shokuji o shita.* (忙しいので簡
単な食事をした) I was busy so I *had*
a simple *meal*. / *Kyoo wa soto de
shokuji o shimashoo.* (きょうは外で
食事をしましょう) *Let's eat out* today.

sho￢ku￢motsu しょくもつ（食物） *n.*
food:
shooka no yoi [warui] shokumotsu
(消化の良い[悪い]食物) easily diges-
tible [indigestible] *food* / *Eeyoo
no aru shokumotsu o tori nasai.*
(栄養のある食物をとりなさい) Please
eat nourishing *food.*

sho￢kuniñ しょくにん（職人） *n.*
artisan; craftsman:
shokuniñ-katagi (職人かたぎ) the
artisan spirit. 《⇨ shi-noo-koo-
shoo (table)》

sho￢ku￢ryoo[1] しょくりょう（食料） *n.*
foodstuffs: ★ Often refers to
food other than staples.
shokuryoohiñ-teñ (食料品店) a *gro-
cery* store. 《⇨ shokuryoo[2]》

sho￢ku￢ryoo[2] しょくりょう（食糧） *n.*
food; provisions: ★ Often refers
to staple food.
shokuryoo o takuwaeru (食糧を蓄え
る) lay in *provisions* / *shokuryoo
ga nakunaru* (食糧がなくなる) run
out of *provisions* / *Sono kuni no
shokuryo-moñdai wa shiñkoku
desu.* (その国の食糧問題は深刻です)
The *food* problem in that country is serious. 《⇨ shokuryoo[1]》

Sho￢kuryo￢o-choo しょくりょうち
ょう（食糧庁） *n.* Food Agency:
Shokuryoo-choo chookañ (食糧庁
長官) the Director General of the
Food Agency. 《⇨ choo[4] (table)》

sho「kutaku[1] しょくたく (食卓) *n.*
dining table:
shokutaku *ni tsuku* (食卓につく) sit
at *table* / shokutaku *o katazukeru*
(食卓を片づける) clear the *table*.

sho「kutaku[2] しょくたく (嘱託) *n.*
part-time employee; nonregular
employee: ★ Refers to a person
employed temporarily for spe-
cialized duties.
Kare wa teeneñ-go mo shokutaku
to shite sono kaisha de hataraita.
(彼は定年後も嘱託としてその会社で働
いた) After retirement, he continued to work for that company
as a *nonregular employee*.

sho「kuyoku しょくよく (食欲) *n.*
appetite:
shokuyoku *ga aru* [*nai*] (食欲がある
[ない]) have a good [poor] *appetite*
/ shokuyoku *o ushinau* (食欲を失う)
lose one's *appetite* / shokuyoku *o
sosoru* (食欲をそそる) stimulate the
appetite.

sho「kyuu しょきゅう (初級) *n.* be-
ginner's class:
Nihoñgo no shokyuu *kurasu
[koosu]* (日本語の初級クラス[コース])
the *beginners*' Japanese class
[course] / shokyuu *Nihoñgo* (初級
日本語) Japanese for *beginners*.

《⇨ chuukyuu; jookyuu》

sho「mee しょめい (署名) *n.* signature; autograph:
Koko ni shomee *o onegai itashimasu.* (ここに署名をお願いいたします)
Please *sign your name* here. /
shomee *uñdoo* (署名運動) a *signa-
ture-collecting* campaign.
  shomee suru (〜する) *vi.* sign;
autograph: *keeyakusho ni*
shomee suru (契約書に署名する)
sign a contract. 《⇨ saiñ》

sho」miñ しょみん (庶民) *n.* ordinary citizen; common people;
average person:
Bukka ga sagareba, shomiñ *wa
yorokobu.* (物価が下がれば、庶民は喜
ぶ) If prices go down, the *average
person* will be glad.

sho」motsu しょもつ (書物) *n.*
(*formal*) book. 《⇨ hoñ》

sho」mu しょむ (庶務) *n.* general
affairs:
shomu-*ka* (庶務課) the *general
affairs* section (of a company).

sho」o[1] しょう (省) *n.* ministry:
Gaimu-shoo (外務省) the *Ministry*
of Foreign Affairs. 《⇨ choo[4]
(table)》

sho」o[2] しょう (性) *n.* nature; disposition; temperament.

SHOO

Gaimu-shoo	(外務省)	Ministry of Foreign Affairs
Hoomu-shoo	(法務省)	Ministry of Justice
Jichi-shoo	(自治省)	Ministry of Home Affairs
Keñsetsu-shoo	(建設省)	Ministry of Construction
Koosee-shoo	(厚生省)	Ministry of Health and Welfare
Moñbu-shoo	(文部省)	Ministry of Education
Nooriñ-suisañ-shoo (農林水産省)		Ministry of Agriculture, Forestry and Fisheries
Ookura-shoo	(大蔵省)	Ministry of Finance
Roodoo-shoo	(労働省)	Ministry of Labor
Tsuusañ-shoo	(通産省)	Ministry of International Trade and Industry
Uñyu-shoo	(運輸省)	Ministry of Transport
Yuusee-shoo	(郵政省)	Ministry of Posts and Telecommunications

shoo ni au (〜に合う) be conge-
nial to one: *Nattoo wa watashi no
shoo ni awanai.* (納豆は私の性に合
わない) *Nattoo does not agree with
me.* / *Ima no shigoto wa kare no
shoo ni atte iru yoo da.* (今の仕事は
彼の性に合っているようだ) The pres-
ent work seems to *be suited* to
him.

sho˥o³ しょう (賞) *n.* prize; reward; award:
shoo *o toru* (賞を取る) win a *prize* /
Kare wa sono sakuhiñ de shoo *o
moratta.* (彼はその作品で賞をもらった)
He received a *prize* for his work.

sho˥o⁴ しょう (章) *n.* **1** chapter:
*dai is-*shoo (第1章) *Chapter* 1.
2 badge; emblem:
*kaiiñ-*shoo (会員章) a membership
badge.

sho˥o⁵ しょう (小) *n.* smallness:
Saizu wa dai to shoo *ga arimasu.*
(サイズは大と小があります) There are
two sizes: large and *small.*
《⇨ dai¹; chuu¹ (table)》

sho⌐o- しょう (小) *pref.* small;
minor:
shoo-*gekijoo* (小劇場) a *small* theater / shoo-*kibo* (小規模) *small*
scale / Shoo-*Ajia* (小アジア) Asia
Minor. 《↔ dai¹-》

sho˥obai しょうばい (商売) *n.*
business; trade; occupation:
shoobai *o hajimeru* [*yameru*] (商
売を始める[やめる]) open [close] a
business / *"Go-shoobai wa nañ
desu ka?" "Yaoya desu."* (「ご商売
は何ですか」「やお屋です」) "What is
your *business*?" "I'm a greengrocer." / *Kare no* shoobai *wa hañjoo
shite iru.* (彼の商売は繁盛している)
His *business* is thriving.
　shoobai (**o**) **suru** (〜(を)する) *vi.*
do business; engage in trade;
deal in: *Oji wa Oosaka de* shoobai o shite imasu. (おじは大阪で商売
をしています) My uncle *is doing
business* in Osaka.

sho⌐obeñ しょうべん (小便) *n.*
piss; urine: ★ Often pro-
nounced '*shoñbeñ.*'

> ━━(**USAGE**)━━
> Considered vulgar and advis-
> able not to use in public. '*O-
> shikko*' (rather childish) and
> '*o-shoosui*' (used in the hospi-
> tal) can be used instead.

shoobeñ *ga chikai* (小便が近い)
have frequent *calls of nature* /
Shoobeñ *muyoo* (*sign*) (小便無用)
No *Urinating.*
　shoobeñ (**o**) **suru** (〜(を)する) *vi.*
urinate: *tachi-*shoobeñ o suru (立
ち小便をする) *urinate* in the street.
《↔ daibeñ》

sho⌐oboo しょうぼう (消防) *n.* fire
fighting:
Watashi-tachi wa shoo boo *no kuñreñ o shita.* (私たちは消防の訓練をし
た) We had a *fire* drill. / shooboo-
dañ (消防団) a *fire-fighting* team /
shooboo-*sho* (消防署) a *fire* station / shooboo-*sha* (消防車) a *fire*
engine.

Sho⌐obo˥o-choo しょうぼうちょう
(消防庁) *n.* Fire Defense
Agency:
Shooboo-choo *chookañ* (消防庁長
官) the Director General for the
Fire Defense Agency. 《⇨ choo⁴
(table)》

EMBLEM OF THE SHOOBOO-CHOO

sho˥obu しょうぶ (勝負) *n.* game:
shoobu *ni katsu* [*makeru*] (勝負に
勝つ[負ける]) win [lose] a *game* /
Shoobu *wa tsukimashita.* (勝負はつ
きました) The victor of the *game* is

already decided. / *Futari wa* ii shoobu da.(二人はいい勝負だ) They *are evenly matched.*

shoobu suru (〜する) *vi.* have a game; fight: *Kare to* shoobu shite mo kanaimaseñ.(彼と勝負してもかないません) I *have no chance* against him.

sho⌐ochi しょうち (承知) *n.* knowing; being aware (of); consent: *Kaki ni iteñ shimashita no de,* go-shoochi *kudasai.*(下記に移転しましたので、ご承知ください) Please *note* that we have moved to the address given below. / Go-shoochi no yoo ni, *kare wa señgetsu taishoku shimashita.*(ご承知のように、彼は先月退職しました) *As you know,* he retired last month.

shoochi suru (〜する) *vi.*
1 know; be aware (of); understand: *Sono koto wa* yoku shoochi shite imasu.(そのことはよく承知しています) I *am well aware* of that.
2 consent; agree; permit: *Chichi wa yatto watashi-no keekaku o* shoochi shite kureta.(父はやっと私の計画を承知してくれた) My father finally *agreed* to my plan. / *"Ima sugu ni kite kudasai." "*Shoochi shimashita.*"*(「今すぐに来てください」「承知しました」) *"Please come right away." "All right."* / *Iu koto o kikanai to* shoochi shimaseñ yo.(言うことをきかないと承知しませんよ) If you do not do as you are told, *you'll be sorry for it.*

sho⌐o-chiku¹-bai しょうちくばい (松竹梅) *n.* pine, bamboo and Japanese apricot.

CULTURE
These three plants are used together in making symbolic decorations on happy occasions such as New Year's and at weddings. At a restaurant, they are often used to classify the grade of the dishes: *matsu* (松)＝the most expensive / *take* (竹)＝medium / *ume* (梅)＝ cheap.

sho⌐ochoo しょうちょう (象徴) *n.* symbol: *Teñnoo wa Nihoñkoku no* shoochoo *desu.*(天皇は日本国の象徴です) The Emperor is the *symbol* of Japan.

shoochoo suru (〜する) *vt.* symbolize: *Hato wa heewa o* shoochoo shimasu.(鳩は平和を象徴します) The dove *symbolizes* peace.

sho⌐odaku しょうだく (承諾) *n.* consent; agreement; permission; acceptance: *Sono seeto wa señsee no* shoodaku *o ete, hayaku kaetta.*(その生徒は先生の承諾を得て、早く帰った) The pupil went home early after receiving her teacher's *permission.* / shoodaku-sho (承諾書) a written *consent.*

shoodaku suru (〜する) *vt.* consent; agree; permit; accept: *Señpoo wa kochira no yookyuu o kañtañ ni* shoodaku shita.(先方はこちらの要求を簡単に承諾した) The other party readily *agreed* to our demands.

sho⌐odoku しょうどく (消毒) *n.* disinfection; sterilization: shoodoku-yaku (消毒薬) *disinfectant* / *nikkoo*-shoodoku (日光消毒) *disinfection* by sunlight.

shoodoku suru (〜する) *vt.* disinfect; sterilize: *kizuguchi o* shoodoku suru (傷口を消毒する) *disinfect* a wound / *iryoo-kigu o* shoodoku suru (医療器具を消毒する) *sterilize* medical instruments.

sho⌐o-ene しょうエネ (省エネ) *n.* energy-saving: ★ Shortened form of 'shoo-enerugii.' Shoo-ene *no tame kuuraa o kitta.*(省エネのためクーラーをきった) In order to *save energy,* I turned off the air conditioner.

sho⌐ogai¹ しょうがい（障害）*n.*
1 obstacle; obstruction; barrier:
shoogai *ni butsukaru* (障害にぶつか
る) encounter an *obstacle* / kotoba
no shoogai *o torinozoku* (言葉の障
害を取り除く) remove a language
barrier / *Futari wa ooku no* shoogai *o norikoete, kekkoñ shita.* (二
人は多くの障害を乗り越えて、結婚した)
The two of them overcame
many *obstacles* and got married.
2 defect; impediment:
Kare wa geñgo-shoogai *ga aru.*
(彼は言語障害がある) He has a
speech *defect*.

sho⌐ogai² しょうがい（生涯）*n.*
one's whole life:
Kanojo wa shiawase na shoogai *o
okutta.* (彼女は幸せな生涯を送った)
She led a happy *life*. / *Sono gaka
wa gaikoku de* shoogai *o oeta.* (そ
の画家は外国で生涯を終えた) The
painter ended his *days* in a foreign country. / *Kare wa* shoogai
dokushiñ datta. (彼は生涯独身だっ
た) He remained single *throughout his life*.

sho⌐oga⌐kkoo しょうがっこう（小学
校）*n.* elementary school.
(⇨ gakkoo)

sho⌐ogakukiñ しょうがくきん（奨学
金）*n.* scholarship: ★ The usual
'*shoogakukiñ*' is simply a loan
without interest for school expenses that has to be paid back
after the borrower gets a job.
shoogakukiñ *o mooshikomu* [*ukeru*] (奨学金を申し込む[受ける]) apply
for [receive] a *scholarship* / *Watashi wa* shoogakukiñ *o moratte
imasu.* (私は奨学金をもらっています) I
am on a *scholarship*.

sho⌐oga⌐kusee しょうがくせい（小
学生）*n.* elementary school pupil; schoolchild. (⇨ seeto)

sho⌐o ga na⌐·i しょうがない *a.*
(-ku) = shiyoo ga nai.

sho⌐ogatsu しょうがつ（正月）*n.*
the New Year; January:

> ── CULTURE ──
> In traditional times, it was the
> only vacation, along with '*boñ*,'
> that most Japanese received.
> Even now it has great social
> and religious significance.

Shoogatsu-*yasumi ni wa kuni e
kaerimasu.* (正月休みには国へ帰りま
す) I'll go home during the *New
Year* vacation.

sho⌐ogi しょうぎ（将棋）*n.* Japanese chess:
shoogi *o sasu* (将棋を指す) play
shogi.

shoogi-daoshi ni naru (将棋倒し
になる) fall over like dominoes:
Kodomo-tachi wa shoogi-daoshi
ni natta. (子どもたちは将棋倒しになっ
た) The children *fell over like a
row of dominoes*.

SHOOGI

sho⌐ogo しょうご（正午）*n.* noon;
midday:
Shoogo *ni beru ga narimasu.* (正午
にベルが鳴ります) The bell rings at
noon. / shoogo *no nyuusu* (正午の
ニュース) the *twelve o'clock* news.
(⇨ o-hiru)

sho⌐oguñ しょうぐん（将軍）*n.*
1 general.
2 Shogun. ★ The title of the
chief hereditary military commander in Japan. He was the
real ruler of Japan 1603–1867.

sho⌐ogyoo しょうぎょう（商業）*n.*

commerce; business:
shoogyoo-*kookoo* (商業高校) a
commercial high school / shoo-
gyoo-*toshi* (商業都市) a *commercial* city / shoogyoo-shugi (商業主
義) *commercialism*.

sho⌈ohai しょうはい (勝敗) *n.* result of a game [battle]; victory or
defeat:
Kare no tokuteñ ga shiai no shoo-
hai *o kimeta*. (彼の得点が試合の勝敗
を決めた) His scoring decided the
game.

sho⌈ohi しょうひ (消費) *n.* consumption; expenditure:
Saikiñ kokunai no shoohi *ga nobite iru*. (最近国内の消費が伸びている)
Domestic *consumption* has been
on the rise recently. / shoohi-*zee*
(消費税) a *consumption* tax.
　shoohi suru (〜する) *vt.* consume: *Watashi-tachi wa hitori
atari neñ ni juk-kiro no kome o*
shoohi shite imasu. (私たちは一人あ
たり年に 10 キロの米を消費しています)
We *consume* ten kilograms of rice
per head every year. 《↔ seesañ》

sho⌈ohiñ[1] しょうひん (商品) *n.*
commodity; goods; merchandise:
Kare no mise wa iroiro na shoohiñ *o atsukatte iru*. (彼の店はいろいろ
な商品を扱っている) His store deals
in a variety of *goods*. / shoohiñ
mihoñ (商品見本) a *trade* sample /
shoohiñ-keñ (商品券) a *gift certificate*.

sho⌈ohiñ[2] しょうひん (賞品) *n.*
prize; trophy:
shoohiñ *o morau* [*kakutoku suru*]
(賞品をもらう[獲得する]) get [win] a
prize.

sho⌈ohi⌉sha しょうひしゃ (消費者)
n. consumer:
Kanojo wa shoohisha *o daihyoo
shite, señkyo ni rikkooho shita*.
(彼女は消費者を代表して、選挙に立候
補した) Representing *consumers*,

she ran in the election. / shoohi-
sha-*dantai* (消費者団体) a *consumer* organization / shoohisha-
uñdoo (消費者運動) a *consumer*
movement. 《↔ seesañsha》

sho⌈oji しょうじ (障子) *n.* paper
sliding door; shoji screen. ★ A
sliding screen covered with trans-
lucent paper, used to make up
the partitions or dividing walls
of a Japanese house.

SHOOJI

sho⌈oji⌉ki しょうじき (正直) *n.*
honesty; uprightness:
Shoojiki *ga ichibañ desu*. (正直が
一番です) *Honesty* is the best
policy.
　— *a.n.* (〜 na, ni) honest; frank;
straightforward:
Ano hito wa itsu-mo shoojiki *da*.
(あの人はいつも正直だ) He is always
honest and straightforward. / *Hoñtoo no koto o* shoojiki *ni hanashite
kudasai*. (本当のことを正直に話してく
ださい) Please speak the truth
frankly. / Shoojiki na tokoro, *doo
shite yoi ka wakarimaseñ*. (正直な
ところ、どうしてよいかわかりません) *To
tell you the truth*, I do not know
what to do.

sho⌈oji·ru しょうじる (生じる) *vi.*
(shooji-te Ⅴ) arise; happen;
come about; result:
Gakusee no aida de fumañ ga
shoojita. (学生の間で不満が生じた)
Discontent *arose* among the stu-

dents. / *Doo shite booeki masatsu ga* shoojita *no desu ka?* (どうして貿易摩擦が生じたのですか) Why is it that trade friction *has arisen*? / *Yoi kekka ga* shoojiru *koto o inorimasu.* (よい結果が生じることを祈ります) I pray that a favorable outcome will *occur*.

sho⌈o⌉jo しょうじょ (少女) *n.* young [little] girl:
Kanojo wa shoojo-jidai *o Hokkaidoo de sugoshita.* (彼女は少女時代を北海道で過ごした) She passed her *childhood* in Hokkaido. / shoojo-*shumi* (少女趣味) a *girlish* interest [taste]. 《↔ shoonen》

sho⌈ojoo⌉¹ しょうじょう (賞状) *n.* certificate of merit [commendation]:
Sakuhiñ ga nyuuseñ shite, kare wa shoojoo *o moratta.* (作品が入選して, 彼は賞状をもらった) His work won a prize and he was awarded a *certificate of merit*.

sho⌈ojo⌉o² しょうじょう (症状) *n.* symptom; condition:
Nodo ga itamu no wa kaze no shoojoo *desu.* (のどが痛むのは風邪の症状です) A sore throat is a *symptom* of a cold. / *Kodomo no* shoojoo *wa omotta yori mo yokatta.* (子どもの症状は思ったよりも良かった) The *condition* of the child was better than I had expected.

sho⌈oka⌉¹ しょうか (消化) *n.* digestion:
Kono tabemono wa shooka *ga yoi* [*warui*]. (この食べ物は消化が良い[悪い]) This food is easy [difficult] to *digest*. / shooka-*furyoo* (消化不良) *indigestion* / shooka-*kikañ* (消化器官) the *digestive* organs.
shooka suru (～する) *vi., vt.* digest; assimilate: *Niku wa* shooka suru *no ni jikañ ga kakaru.* (肉は消化するのに時間がかかる) It takes a while for meat to *be digested*. / *Seeto-tachi wa sono hoñ no naiyoo*

o juubuñ ni shooka dekinakatta. (生徒たちはその本の内容を十分に消化できなかった) The pupils *were unable to digest* the contents of the book properly.

sho⌈oka⌉² しょうか (消火) *n.* fire extinguishing [fighting]:
Watashi-tachi wa miñna de shooka ni atatta. (私たちはみんなで消火にあたった) We all *fought the fire*. / shooka-*ki* (消火器) a *fire extinguisher* / shooka-*señ* (消火栓) a *fire hydrant*.
shooka suru (～する) *vt.* extinguish a fire; fight a fire: *Kaji o* shooka suru *no ni sañ-jikañ kakatta.* (火事を消火するのに 3 時間かかった) It took three hours to *put out the fire*.

SHOOKAKI

sho⌈okai⌉¹ しょうかい (紹介) *n.* introduction; presentation:
shookai-*joo* (紹介状) a letter of *introduction* / jiko-shookai (自己紹介) a self-*introduction*.
shookai suru (～する) *vt.* introduce; present: *Yamada-sañ o go-*shookai shimasu. (山田さんをご紹介します) I wish to *introduce* Ms. Yamada. / *Kore wa Nihoñ no buñka o sekai ni* shookai suru *hoñ desu.* (これは日本の文化を世界に紹介する本です) This is a book which *introduces* Japanese culture to the world.

sho⌐okai² しょうかい（商会）*n.*
firm; company:
Sakamoto shookai（坂本商会）Sakamoto & *Co.*

sho⌐oko しょうこ（証拠）*n.* proof;
evidence:
shooko *o dasu [iñmetsu suru]*（証拠を出す[隠滅する]）produce [destroy] *evidence* / *Kare ga sore o yatta to iu* shooko *wa nai.*（彼がそれをやったという証拠はない）There is no *proof* that he did it.

sho⌐okyoku-teki しょうきょくてき（消極的）*a.n.*（〜 na, ni）negative; passive:
shookyoku-teki *na taido*（消極的な態度）a *passive* attitude / shookyoku-teki *ni furumau*（消極的にふるまう）behave in a *negative* way / *Kare wa nanigoto mo* shookyoku-teki *da.*（彼は何事も消極的だ）He is *passive* in everything. / *Kachoo wa watashi no teeañ ni* shookyoku-teki *datta.*（課長は私の提案に消極的だった）The manager was *lukewarm* to my proposal.《↔ sekkyoku-teki》

sho⌐omee¹ しょうめい（証明）*n.*
proof; evidence; testimony:
shoomee-sho（証明書）a *certificate.*
shoomee suru（〜する）*vt.* prove;
testify; certify: *Kare wa jibuñ no mujitsu o* shoomee shita.（彼は自分の無実を証明した）He *proved* his innocence. / *Mibuñ o* shoomee suru *mono o nani-ka o-mochi desu ka?*（身分を証明するものを何かお持ちですか）Do you have anything with you to *prove* your identity?

sho⌐omee² しょうめい（照明）*n.*
lighting; illumination:
teñjihiñ ni shoomee *o ateru*（展示品に照明を当てる）direct a *light* onto an exhibit / *Kono heya wa* shoomee *ga yoi [warui].*（この部屋は照明が良い[悪い]）This room is well [badly] *lighted.* / shoomee-kigu（照明器具）*lights; lighting*

fixtures.
shoomee suru（〜する）*vt.* light;
illuminate: *Kono heya wa motto akaruku* shoomee shita *hoo ga yoi.*（この部屋はもっと明るく照明したほうが良い）It would be better if this room *were* more brightly *lighted.*

sho⌐omeñ しょうめん（正面）*n.*
the front; facade; the area in front:
Sono uchi no shoomeñ *wa dooro ni meñshite iru.*（その家の正面は道路に面している）The *front* of the house faces the road. / *Eki no* shoomeñ *ni fuñsui ga arimasu.*（駅の正面に噴水があります）There is a fountain in *front* of the station. / shoomeñ-*iriguchi*（正面入口）the *front* entrance / shoomeñ-*shoototsu*（正面衝突）a *head-on* collision.《⇨ mae¹》

sho⌐omoo しょうもう（消耗）*n.* exhaustion; consumption:
Juuroodoo de tairyoku no shoomoo *ga hageshikatta.*（重労働で体力の消耗が激しかった）It was hard labor so I *used up* my physical strength very rapidly. / shoomoo-hiñ（消耗品）*expendables.*
shoomoo suru（〜する）*vi., vt.*
exhaust; consume: *Marasoñ de tairyoku ga* shoomoo shite shimatta.（マラソンで体力が消耗してしまった）I *was exhausted* by the marathon race.

sho⌐oneñ しょうねん（少年）*n.*
(little) boy; lad:
Watashi wa shooneñ-*jidai ni kono kawa de yoku oyogimashita.*（私は少年時代にこの川でよく泳ぎました）I often swam in this river in my *childhood.*《↔ shoojo》

sho⌐onika しょうにか（小児科）*n.*
pediatrics:
shoonika-i（小児科医）a *pediatrician.*《⇨ byooiñ (table)》

sho⌐oniñ¹ しょうにん（承認）*n.* approval; recognition; permission:

shooniñ *o eru* [*morau*] (承認を得る
[もらう]) get *permission* / *Kore ni
wa shichoo no* shooniñ *ga hitsuyoo desu*. (これには市長の承認が必要
です) The mayor's *approval* is
necessary for this.

shooniñ suru (～する) *vt.* approve; recognize; permit: *Sono
teeañ o* shooniñ *shita no wa dare
desu ka?* (その提案を承認したのはだれ
ですか) Who is it that *approved* the
proposal? / *Sono kuni wa dokuri-
tsu-koku to shite* shooniñ *sareta.*
(その国は独立国として承認された)
That country *was recognized* as
an independent state.

sho⌐oniñ² しょうにん (商人) *n.*
merchant; tradesman; dealer;
storekeeper; shopkeeper.
《⇒ shi-noo-koo-shoo (table)》

sho⌐oniñ³ しょうにん (証人) *n.* witness:
shooniñ *ni tatsu* (証人に立つ) bear
witness / *Kare wa* shooniñ *to shite
saibañsho ni yobareta.* (彼は証人と
して裁判所に呼ばれた) He was sum-
moned to court as a *witness.*

sho⌐oniñ⁴ しょうにん (昇任) *n.*
promotion:
Shooniñ *omedetoo.* (昇任おめでとう)
Congratulations on your *promotion!*

shooniñ suru (～する) *vi.* be promoted: *Kare ga* shooniñ *suru
chañsu wa arimasu.* (彼が昇任するチ
ャンスはあります) There is a chance
for him to *be promoted.*

sho⌐orai しょうらい (将来) *n.* future; the time [days] to come:
Anata ni wa akarui shoorai *ga aru.*
(あなたには明るい将来がある) You
have a bright *future* in front of
you. / *Shoorai ni sonaete chokiñ o
shi nasai.* (将来に備えて貯金をしなさ
い) Please save money to provide
for the *future.* / *Shoorai nani ga
okoru ka, dare ni mo wakarimaseñ.* (将来何が起こるか, だれにもわかりま

señ) Nobody knows what will
happen in the *future.* 《⇒ mirai》

sho⌐oree しょうれい (奨励) *n.* encouragement:
shooree *o ukeru* (奨励を受ける) receive *encouragement* / shooree-*kiñ*
(奨励金) a subsidy.

shooree suru (～する) *vt.* encourage; recommend: *Uchi no gakkoo de wa supootsu o* shooree
shite imasu. (うちの学校ではスポーツを
奨励しています) Our school *encourages* sports.

sho⌐ori しょうり (勝利) *n.* victory:
attoo-teki na shoori *o osameru* (圧
倒的な勝利をおさめる) gain an over-
whelming *victory* / *Sore wa wareware no dañketsu no* shoori *datta.*
(それはわれわれの団結の勝利だった) It
was a *victory* due to our solidarity. 《↔ haiboku》

sho⌐oryaku しょうりゃく (省略) *n.*
omission; abridgment; abbreviation:
Kono eega ni wa kanari shooryaku *ga aru.* (この映画にはかなり省略があ
る) There are quite a few *cuts* in
this movie. / *'Pasokoñ' wa 'paasonaru-koñpyuutaa' no* shooryaku
desu. (「パソコン」は「パーソナル・コンピ
ューター」の省略です) 'Pasokoñ' is an
abbreviation of '*paasonaru-koñpyuutaa.*' (personal computer) /
Ika shooryaku. (以下省略) The
rest *is omitted.* ★ Formula used
in documents, written materials,
etc.

shooryaku suru (～する) *vt.*
omit; abridge; abbreviate: *Kono
joshi wa* shooryaku *dekimañ.*
(この助詞は省略できません) We *can-
not omit* this particle. / *Komakai
suuji wa* shooryaku *shite, yooteñ
dake o hanashimasu.* (細かい数字は
省略して, 要点だけを話します) I will
ignore the detailed figures and
just talk about the main points.

sho⌐oryo⌐o しょうりょう (少量) *n.*

a small quantity [amount]:
Shooryoo *no shio ga aji o hikitate-masu.* (少量の塩が味を引き立てます)
A little salt brings out the taste.
/ *Biñ ni uisukii ga* shooryoo *no-kotte ita.* (びんにウイスキーが少量残っていた) There was *a bit* of whisky left in the bottle. 《↔ taryoo》

sho⌐osai しょうさい (詳細) *n.* details; particulars:
Shoosai *wa kono pañfuretto o yoñde kudasai.* (詳細はこのパンフレットを読んでください) Please read this brochure for further *details.* / Shoosai *wa ato de o-shirase shimasu.* (詳細は後でお知らせします) We will inform you of the *particulars* later on. 《↔ gaiyoo》
— *a.n.* (~ na, ni) detailed; particular; minute; full.
Kare wa sono añ o shoosai *ni setsumee shita.* (彼はその案を詳細に説明した) He explained the plan *in detail.*

sho⌐osetsu しょうせつ (小説) *n.* novel; story; fiction:
shoosetsu *o yomu* [*kaku*] (小説を読む[書く]) read [write] a *novel* / shoosetsu-ka (小説家) a novelist.

sho⌐osha[1] しょうしゃ (商社) *n.* trading company; business firm:
Kare wa shoosha *ni tsutomete imasu.* (彼は商社に勤めています) He works for a *trading company.*

sho⌐osha[2] しょうしゃ (勝者) *n.* winner; victor:
Kaku-señsoo de wa shoosha *mo haisha mo nai.* (核戦争では勝者も敗者もない) In a nuclear war there are no *winners* nor losers. 《↔ haisha[2]》

sho⌐oshiñ しょうしん (昇進) *n.* promotion:
Shooshiñ *omedetoo.* (昇進おめでとう) Congratulations on your *promotion.*
shooshiñ suru (~する) *vi.* be promoted: *Kare wa kachoo ni* shooshiñ shita. (彼は課長に昇進した)

He *was promoted* to section chief.

sho⌐oshoo しょうしょう (少々) *adv.* a little [few]; a moment [minute]:
Satoo o shooshoo *kuwaete kudasai.* (砂糖を少々加えてください) Please add a *bit* of sugar. / Shoo-shoo *o-machi kudasai.* (少々お待ちください) Please wait *a moment.* 《⇒ shooryoo》

sho⌐osu⌐u[1] しょうすう (少数) *n.* a small number; minority:
Hoñ-no shoosuu *no hito shika hañtai shinakatta.* (ほんの少数の人しか反対しなかった) Only a very *small number* of people were against it. / *Kooeñ o kiki ni kita hito wa* shoosuu *datta.* (講演を聴きに来た人は少数だった) The people who came to listen to the lecture were *few in number.* / shoosuu-ha (少数派) the *minority* / shoosuu-*miñzoku* (少数民族) a *minority* race. 《↔ tasuu》

sho⌐osu⌐u[2] しょうすう (小数) *n.* decimal:
shoosuu-*teñ* (小数点) a *decimal* point / Shoosuu-teñ ika o kiriage nasai. (小数点以下を切り上げなさい) Round up the *fractions* to a whole number.

sho⌐otai[1] しょうたい (招待) *n.* invitation:
Watashi wa gorufu no shootai *o uketa.* (私はゴルフの招待を受けた) I received an *invitation* to golf. / *Hoñjitsu wa kono yoo na seki ni* go-shootai *itadaki, arigatoo gozaimashita.* (本日はこのような席にご招待いただき、ありがとうございました) Thank you very much for *having invited* me here today. / shootai-*joo* (招待状) an *invitation* card; a letter of *invitation* / shootai-keñ (招待券) a *complimentary* ticket.
shootai suru (~する) *vt.* invite:
Watashi wa kanojo no paatii ni shootai sareta. (私は彼女のパーティー

に招待された) I *was invited* to her party.

sho˺otai[2] しょうたい (正体) *n.* a person's true colors [character]; true nature:
Tootoo kare wa shootai *o arawa-shita.* (とうとう彼は正体を現した) At last he has shown *his true colors.* / *Sono buttai no* shootai *wa mada wakatte inai.* (その物体はまだわかっていない) The *true nature* of the object is still unknown.
shootai mo naku nemuru [you] (～もなく眠る[酔う]) be fast asleep [dead drunk]: *Kare wa* shootai mo naku nemutte ita. (彼は正体もなく眠っていた) He *was sleeping like a log.*

sho˺oteñ[1] しょうてん (商店) *n.* store; shop:
shooteñ-*gai* (商店街) a *shopping* center; a *shopping* street / *Yamazaki* shooteñ (山崎商店) Yamazaki's *shop.*

sho˺oteñ[2] しょうてん (焦点) *n.* focus:
shooteñ *ga atte iru* [*inai*] (焦点が合っている[いない]) be in [out of] *focus* / *Chuuoo no hito ni kamera no* shooteñ o awaseta. (中央の人にカメラの焦点を合わせた) I *focused* the camera on the person in the center.

sho˹otoo しょうとう (消灯) *n.* turning off the lights:
shootoo-*jikañ* (消灯時間) *lights-out.*
shootoo suru (～する) *vi.* turn off [put out] the lights: *Kono byooiñ wa ku-ji ni* shootoo suru. (この病院は9時に消灯する) They *turn off the lights* at nine at this hospital.

sho˹ototsu しょうとつ (衝突) *n.*
1 collision; crash:
deñsha no shoototsu-*jiko* (電車の衝突事故) a *collision* between trains.
2 clash; conflict:
rigai no shoototsu (利害の衝突) a *clash* of interests.

shoototsu suru (～する) *vi.*
1 collide; run into; crash:
Torakku to jooyoosha ga shoomeñ-shoototsu shita. (トラックと乗用車が正面衝突した) A truck and a car *collided* head on.
2 clash; conflict: *Watashi wa itsu-mo gañko na chichi to ikeñ ga* shoototsu suru. (私はいつもがんこな父と意見が衝突する) My opinions *are* always *in conflict* with those of my stubborn father. / *Guñ-shuu wa keekañ-tai to* shoototsu shita. (群衆は警官隊と衝突した) The crowd *clashed* with the police.
《⇨ butsukaru》

Sho˹owa しょうわ (昭和) *n.* Showa: ★ The name of a Japanese emperor and of his reign.
Shoowa-*jidai* (昭和時代) the *Showa* era (Dec. 25, 1926—Jan. 7, 1989) / *Watashi wa* Shoowa *juuneñ umare desu.* (私は昭和10年生れです) I was born in the tenth year of *Showa* (=1935).
《⇨ geñgoo (table); jidai (table)》

sho˹oyu しょうゆ (醤油) *n.* soy sauce:
toofu ni shooyu *o kakeru* (とうふにしょうゆをかける) put *soy sauce* on tofu.

sho˺ri しょり (処理) *n.* management; disposal; treatment:
Gomi no shori *wa ooki-na moñdai desu.* (ごみの処理は大きな問題です) Garbage *disposal* is a big problem. / *Sono keñ no* shori *ni wa mada tashoo jikañ ga kakarimasu.* (その件の処理にはまだ多少時間がかかります) It will take a little more time to *deal with* that matter.
shori suru (～する) *vt.* handle; deal with; manage: *Kare-ra wa sono moñdai o jimu-teki ni* shori shita. (彼らはその問題を事務的に処理した) They *handled* the matter in a businesslike manner.

sho˹rui しょるい (書類) *n.* document; papers:

Kaigi no shorui *o totonoenakereba naranai.*(会議の書類を整えなければならない) I have to prepare the *papers* for the meeting. / *Yushutsu no* shorui *wa betsubiñ de yuusoo shimashita.*(輸出の書類は別便で郵送しました) We have sent you the shipping *documents* under separate cover.

sho⌐sai しょさい（書斎）*n.* study: *Kare wa jibuñ no* shosai *o motte imasu.*（彼は自分の書斎を持っています） He has his own *study*.

sho⌐tchuu しょっちゅう *adv.* (*informal*) always; very often: *Kare wa* shotchuu *guchi o koboshite iru.*（彼はしょっちゅうぐちをこぼしている） He is *always* complaining. 《⇨ itsu-mo》

sho⌐toku しょとく（所得）*n.* income; earnings: *Sarariimañ no heekiñ neñkañ* shotoku *wa yaku roppyakumañ-eñ desu.*（サラリーマンの平均年間所得は約600万円です） The average annual *income* of male office workers is about six million yen. / shotoku-*zee*（所得税）an *income* tax.

sho⌐oyo しょうよ（賞与）*n.* = boonasu.

sho⌐yuu しょゆう（所有）*n.* possession; ownership: *Kono tochi wa dare no* shoyuu *desu ka?*（この土地はだれの所有ですか） Who does this land *belong* to? / *Chichi-oya no shigo, sono ie wa kare no* shoyuu *to natta.*（父親の死後，その家は彼の所有となった） On his father's death, he came into *possession* of the house. / shoyuu-*butsu*（所有物）one's *possessions* / shoyuu-*keñ*（所有権）the right of *ownership* / shoyuu-*sha*（所有者） an *owner*.

shoyuu suru （〜する）*vt.* possess; own: *Tanaka-sañ wa koodai na sañriñ o* shoyuu *shite imasu.*（田中さんは広大な山林を所有しています） Mr.

Tanaka *owns* a vast forested mountain area.

sho⌐zoku しょぞく（所属）*n.* one's position [post; place]: *Yatto atarashii* shozoku *ga kimarimashita.*（やっと新しい所属が決まりました） At last I *was assigned* to a new post. / *Enu-etchi-kee* shozoku *no anauñsaa*（NHK所属のアナウンサー） an announcer *with* NHK.

shozoku suru （〜する）*vi.* belong to; be attached to: *Kanojo wa sañgakubu ni* shozoku *shite imasu.*（彼女は山岳部に所属しています） She *belongs* to the mountaineering club. / *Kare wa uchi no prodakushoñ ni* shozoku *shite iru terebi tareñto no hitori desu.*（彼はうちのプロダクションに所属しているテレビタレントの一人です） He is one *of* our agency's TV personalities.

shu⌐¹ しゅ（種）*n.* kind; sort; class; type: *Kono* shu *no hoñ ga yoku urete imasu.*（この種の本がよく売れています） Books of this *kind* are selling well. 《⇨ shurui》

shu⌐² しゅ（主）*n.* the chief [principal] thing: *Kono jigyoo wa kanemooke ga* shu *de wa nai.*（この事業は金もうけが主ではない） It is not the *main purpose* of this enterprise to make money. 《⇨ shu to shite》

shu⌐³ しゅ（主）*n.* the Lord: shu *Iesu Kirisuto*（主イエスキリスト） Jesus Christ, *Our Lord*.

-shu しゅ（酒）*suf.* alcoholic drink: *Nihoñ-*shu（日本酒）Japanese *sake* / budoo-shu（ぶどう酒）*wine* / riñgo-shu（りんご酒）*cider*.

shu⌐bi しゅび（守備）*n.* defense; guard; fielding: shubi *ni tsuku*（守備につく）*take the field* / *Uchi no chiimu wa* shubi *ga yowai* [*katai*].（うちのチームは守備が弱い[堅い]）Our team is weak [strong] in *defense*. / *Ano señshu wa* shubi *ga umai.*（あの選手は守備がうまい）That player is good at *fielding*.

shubi suru（〜する）*vi.* defend; guard: *Koñdo wa wareware ga* shubi suru *bañ da.*（今度はわれわれが守備する番だ）Now it's our turn to *defend*. 《↔ koogeki》

shuˈchoo しゅちょう（主張）*n.* insistence; claim; assertion; opinion:
Kare-ra no shuchoo *wa mottomo da.*（彼らの主張はもっともだ）Their *claim* sounds reasonable. / *Kare wa saigo made* shuchoo *o tooshita.*（彼は最後まで主張を通した）He stuck to his *opinion* to the last.

shuchoo suru（〜する）*vt.* insist; maintain; claim: *Ani wa jibuñ ga tadashii to* shuchoo *shita.*（兄は自分が正しいと主張した）My elder brother *insisted* that he was right. / *Kumiai wa sutoraiki no keñri o* shuchoo *shite iru.*（組合はストライキの権利を主張している）The union *claims* the right to strike.

shuˈdai しゅだい（主題）*n.* subject; theme:
shudai-*ka*（主題歌）a *theme* song.

shuˈdañ しゅだん（手段）*n.* means; measures; step:
Kare-ra wa mokuteki no tame ni wa shudañ *o erabanai.*（彼らは目的のためには手段を選ばない）They are not choosy about what *means* they use to achieve their goals. / *Sono moñdai o kaiketsu suru ni wa omoikitta* shudañ *o toranakereba naranai.*（その問題を解決するには思い切った手段を取らなければならない）We have to take some drastic *measures* to solve that problem.

shuˈee しゅえい（守衛）*n.* guard; doorkeeper.

shuˈeñ しゅえん（主演）*n.* having a leading role; the leading actor [actress]:

Mifune Toshiroo shueñ *no eega*（三船敏郎主演の映画）a movie *starring* Toshiro Mifune / *Shueñ wa dare desu ka?*（主演はだれですか）Who is the *star*?

shueñ suru（〜する）*vi.* play the leading role; star: *Sono eega de wa kañtoku mizukara ga* shueñ *shite iru.*（その映画では監督みずからが主演している）The director himself *plays the leading role* in the movie.

shuˈfu[1] しゅふ（主婦）*n.* housewife.

shuˈfu[2] しゅふ（首府）*n.* capital; metropolis. 《⇨ shuto》

shuˈgi しゅぎ（主義）*n.* principle; doctrine:
Kare wa jibuñ no shugi *o magenakatta.*（彼は自分の主義を曲げなかった）He did not deviate from his *principles*.

shuˈgo しゅご（主語）*n.* (of grammar) subject of a sentence.

shuˈjiñ しゅじん（主人）*n.* **1** storekeeper; employer; owner:
Mise no shujiñ *ni sono nedañ o kiite mita.*（店の主人にその値段を聞いてみた）I asked the *storekeeper* about the price.
2 husband: ★ *shujiñ*＝one's own husband; *go-shujiñ*＝someone else's husband.
Kyoo wa shujiñ *wa gorufu desu.*（きょうは主人はゴルフです）My *husband* went golfing today. / *Yamada-sañ no* go-shujiñ *ga nyuuiñ sareta soo desu.*（山田さんのご主人が入院されたそうです）I hear that Mrs. Yamada's *husband* has been hospitalized. 《⇨ otto; tsuma》

shuˈju しゅじゅ（種々）*n.* many kinds; various:
Sono keekaku wa shuju *no riyuu de chuushi to natta.*（その計画は種々の理由で中止となった）The project was suspended for *a number of* reasons.

shuju zatta na（〜雑多な）all

kinds of: *Depaato wa* shuju zatta
na *shoohiñ o atsukatte imasu.* (デパ
ートは種々雑多な商品を扱っています)
Department stores handle *all
kinds of* goods.

shuᒦjutsu しゅじゅつ (手術) *n.* operation: ★ Often pronounced
'*shijitsu.*'
shujutsu *o ukeru* (手術を受ける) undergo an *operation* / *Kare wa* shu-
jutsu-*go sukkari geñki ni narimashita.* (彼は手術後すっかり元気になりま
した) He completely recovered
after the *operation.* / shujutsu-*shitsu* (手術室) an *operating* theater.
shujutsu (o) suru (～(を)する) *vt.*
operate; be operated on: *Watashi wa kyoneñ i o* shujutsu shimashita. (私は去年胃を手術しました) I
had an operation on my stomach
last year. / *Inoue señsee ga chichi
no* shujutsu *o shimashita.* (井上先
生が父の手術をしました) Dr. Inoue
operated on my father.

shuᒦkañ しゅかん (主観) *n.* sub-
jectivity.

shuᒦkañ-teki しゅかんてき (主観的)
a.n. (～ na, ni) subjective:
Kare wa shukañ-teki *na ikeñ o
nobeta.* (彼は主観的な意見を述べた)
He gave his *subjective* opinion.
《↔ kyakkañ-teki》

shuᒦkketsu しゅっけつ (出血) *n.*
bleeding; hemorrhage:
shukketsu *ga tomaru* (出血が止まる)
bleeding stops / shukketsu *o tomeru* (出血を止める) stop a *hemorrhage* / shukketsu *taryoo de shinu*
(出血多量で死ぬ) die from exces-
sive *bleeding.*
shukketsu dai-saabisu (～大サー
ビス) a 'giving-away' sale.
shukketsu suru (～する) *vt.*
bleed: *Hana kara* shukketsu shite,
nakanaka tomaranai. (鼻から出血し
て、なかなか止まらない) I keep on
bleeding from the nose and it just
won't stop.

shuᒦkkiñ しゅっきん (出勤) *n.* going to work; attendance:
Maiasa shukkiñ *mae ni shiñbuñ o
yomimasu.* (毎朝出勤前に新聞を読み
ます) I read the paper every morning before *leaving for work.* /
shukkiñ-*bo* (出勤簿) an *attendance*
book / shukkiñ-*jikañ* (出勤時間)
the starting time *for work.*
shukkiñ suru (～する) *vt.* go to
work; go [come] to the office:
Kyoo wa hayaku shukkiñ shinakereba naranai. (きょうは早く出勤し
なければならない) I *have to go to work*
earlier than usual today. / *Tanaka-sañ wa mada* shukkiñ shite imaseñ. (田中さんはまだ出勤していません)
Mrs. Tanaka *has not come into
the office* yet.

shuᒦkkoku しゅっこく (出国) *n.*
departure from a country:
Kare wa fuhoo shukkoku *de tsukamatta.* (彼は不法出国で捕まった) He
was arrested for *leaving the country* illegally. / shukkoku-*tetsuzuki*
(出国手続き) *departure* formalities.
shukkoku suru (～する) *vt.* leave
a country; get out of a country:
Ooku no nañmiñ ga fune de shukkoku shita. (多くの難民が船で出国し
た) A lot of refugees *left their
country* by boat. 《↔ nyuukoku》

shuᒦkudai しゅくだい (宿題) *n.*
1 homework; assignment:
natsu-yasumi no shukudai (夏休み
の宿題) *assignments* for the summer vacation / *Kyoo wa takusañ*
shukudai *ga deta.* (きょうはたくさん宿
題が出た) Today we were given a
lot of *homework.* / Shukudai *wa
moo sumasemashita.* (宿題はもう済
ませました) I have already finished
my *homework.* / *Yuushoku-go* shukudai *o shita.* (夕食後宿題をした) I
did my *homework* after dinner.
2 open [pending] question:
*Kono moñdai wa tsugi no kai
made* shukudai ni shite okima-

shoo.（この問題は次の会まで宿題にして
おきましょう）*Let's leave* this matter
as it is until the next meeting.

shuｒkujitsu しゅくじつ（祝日）*n.*
national [legal; public] holiday.
（⇨ table (below); saijitsu）

shuｒkusaiｌjitsu しゅくさいじつ（祝
祭日）*n.* national [public] holiday; red-letter day; festival.
★ Combination of '*shukujitsu*'
（祝日）and '*saijitsu*'（祭日）.

shuｒkushoo しゅくしょう（縮小）*n.*
reduction; curtailment:
guñbi no shukushoo（軍備の縮小）
reduction of armaments / *Kono
kopiiki wa* shukushoo *ga dekimasu.*（このコピー機は縮小ができます）
This copying machine can make
reduced-size copies.

　shukushoo suru（～する）*vt.* re-
　duce; curtail: *Kare-ra wa yosañ
　o* shukushoo *shita.*（彼らは予算を縮
　小した）They *curtailed* their bud-
　get. / *Kaisha wa jiñiñ o* shukushoo
　suru koto o kañgaete iru.（会社は人
　員を縮小することを考えている）The
　company is considering *cutting
　back* on personnel.（↔ kakudai）

shuｒkuｌs･u しゅくす（祝す）*n.* (shu-
kush･i-; shukus･a-; shukush･i-te
Ⓒ) (*formal*) congratulate; celebrate:
Kare no shooshiñ o shukushite *kai*

o hiraita.（彼の昇進を祝して会を開い
た）We gave a party to *celebrate*
his promotion.（⇨ iwau）

shuｒmi しゅみ（趣味）*n.* **1** hobby;
pastime; interest:
Anata no shumi *wa nañ desu ka?*
（あなたの趣味は何ですか）What are
your *hobbies?* / *Watashi no* shumi
wa dokusho desu.（私の趣味は読書
です）My favorite *pastime* is reading.
2 taste:
Kanojo wa kiru mono no shumi *ga
ii* [*warui*].（彼女は着る物の趣味がいい
[悪い]）She has fine [poor] *taste* in
clothes. / *Kono nekutai wa watashi no* shumi *de wa nai.*（このネクタイ
は私の趣味ではない）This tie is not
to my *taste*.

Shuｒñbuñ-no-hiｌ（春分の日）*n.*
Vernal Equinox Day (about
March 21).（⇨ shukujitsu (table)）

shuｒniñ しゅにん（主任）*n.* head;
chief; boss:
*Shuniñ wa ima gaishutsu-chuu
desu.*（主任はいま外出中です）The
chief is out on business. / *Kare
wa koko no kaikee-shuniñ desu.*
（彼はここの会計主任です）He is the
chief accountant of this section.

shuｒñkañ しゅんかん（瞬間）*n.* moment; instant:
Kettee-teki na shuñkañ *ga yatte*

SHUKUJITSU

January	1	Gañjitsu	New Year's Day
January	15	Seejiñ-no-hi	Coming-of-Age Day
February	11	Keñkoku-kineñ-no-hi	National Foundation Day
ca. March	21	Shuñbuñ-no-hi	Vernal Equinox Day
April	29	Midori-no-hi	Greenery Day
May	3	Keñpoo-kineñbi	Constitution Day
May	5	Kodomo-no-hi	Children's Day
September	15	Keeroo-no-hi	Respect-for-the-Aged Day
ca. Sept.	23	Shuubuñ-no-hi	Autumnal Equinox Day
October	10	Taiiku-no-hi	Health-Sports Day
November	3	Buñka-no-hi	Culture Day
November	23	Kiñroo-kañsha-no-hi	Labor Thanksgiving Day
December	23	Teñnoo-tañjoobi	The Emperor's Birthday

kita.(決定的な瞬間がやってきた) The critical *moment* has come. / *Sore wa shuñkañ no dekigoto datta*.(それは瞬間の出来事だった) It was something that happened in an *instant*. / shuñkañ-yuwakashiki (瞬間湯沸かし器) a *gas water-heater*.

...shita shuñkañ (…した〜) the moment: *Hako no futa o aketa* shuñkañ *bakuhatsu shita*.(箱のふたを開けた瞬間爆発した) *The moment* I took off the lid, the box exploded.

shu⌐ñki しゅんき (春季) *n.* spring; springtime: shuñki-*uñdookai* (春季運動会) a *spring* athletic meet. 《⇨ kaki³; shuuki²; tooki⁴》

shu⌐ppañ¹ しゅっぱん (出版) *n.* publication; publishing: shuppañ *no jiyuu* (出版の自由) freedom of the *press* / shuppañ-butsu (出版物) a *publication* / shuppañ-*gyoo* (出版業) the *publishing* business / shuppañ-*sha* (出版社) a *publishing* company; a *publisher*.

shuppañ suru (〜する) *vt.* publish; issue: *Sono hoñ wa raigetsu* shuppañ *saremasu*.(その本は来月出版されます) The book will *come out* next month. 《⇨ dasu (**3**); deru (**1**)》

shu⌐ppañ² しゅっぱん (出帆) *n.* sailing; departure.

shuppañ suru (〜する) *vi.* set sail; leave; depart: *Kono fune wa Amerika e mukete asu* shuppañ *shimasu*.(この船はアメリカへ向けてあす出帆します) This ship *sails* for America tomorrow.

shu⌐ppatsu しゅっぱつ (出発) *n.* departure; start: *Jiko de deñsha no* shuppatsu *ga okureta*.(事故で電車の出発が遅れた) The *departure* of the train was delayed due to an accident. / *Tsugoo de* shuppatsu *o ichi-jikañ hayamemasu*.(都合で出発を一時間早

めます) Owing to circumstances, we will bring forward our *departure* by an hour.

shuppatsu suru (〜する) *vi.* leave; start; depart; set out: *Señdai-yuki no basu wa moo* shuppatsu *shimashita*.(仙台行きのバスはもう出発しました) The bus for Sendai *has* already *left*. 《↔ toochaku》 《⇨ deru (**1**)》

shu⌐ppiñ しゅっぴん (出品) *n.* exhibition; display: shuppiñ-*butsu* (出品物) an item on *display* / shuppiñ-*mokuroku* (出品目録) a list of the *exhibits*.

shuppiñ suru (〜する) *vt.* exhibit; display: *Koñdo no teñrañkai ni wa atarashii sakuhiñ o* shuppiñ *shimasu*.(今度の展覧会には新しい作品を出品します) I will *exhibit* my new work at the coming show.

shu⌐rui しゅるい (種類) *n.* kind; sort; variety: *Watashi wa iroiro na* shurui *no supootsu ni kyoomi o motte imasu*.(私はいろいろな種類のスポーツに興味を持っています) I am interested in *various* kinds of sports. / *Kore wa nañ to iu* shurui *no inu desu ka?* (これは何という種類の犬ですか) What *kind* of dog is this? / *Kono doobutsueñ ni wa arayuru* shurui *no doobutsu ga imasu*.(この動物園にはあらゆる種類の動物がいます) There are all *sorts* of animals in this zoo.

shu⌐sai しゅさい (主催) *n.* sponsorship; promotion: *shi* shusai *no koñsaato* (市主催のコンサート) a concert *sponsored* by the municipal government / *Kono teñrañkai wa doko ga* shusai *desu ka?* (この展覧会はどこが主催ですか) What organization *is sponsoring* this exhibition? / shusai-*sha* (主催者) a *sponsor*; a *promoter*.

shusai suru (〜する) *vt.* organize; sponsor; host: *Kono gyooji wa aru shiñbuñsha ga* shusai *shite* imasu. (この行事はある新聞社が主催しています) A certain newspaper company *is sponsoring* this event.

shuᒐshi しゅし (趣旨) *n.* aim; object; point:
O-hanashi no shushi *wa yoku wakarimashita.* (お話しの趣旨はよくわかりました) I've understood the *point* of what you are saying.

shuᒐshoku しゅしょく (主食) *n.* staple food:
Kome o shushoku ni shite iru kuni wa ooi. (米を主食にしている国は多い) There are many countries where the people live on a *staple diet* of rice.

shuᒐshoo しゅしょう (首相) *n.* prime minister; premier:
shushoo *ni niñmee sareru* (首相に任命される) be appointed *prime minister*. 《⇨ Soori-daijiñ》

shuᒐssañ しゅっさん (出産) *n.* birth; childbirth; delivery:
shussañ *o iwau* (出産を祝う) celebrate the *birth* of a child / Go-shussañ no yotee *wa itsu goro desu ka?* (ご出産の予定はいつごろですか) When *is your baby due?* / shussañ-*kyuuka* (出産休暇) *maternity* leave.
shussañ suru (～する) *vi., vt.* give birth: *Imooto wa señgetsu dañshi o buji* shussañ shimashita. (妹は先月男子を無事出産しました) My younger sister safely *gave birth* to a boy last month.

shuᒐsse しゅっせ (出世) *n.* success in life; promotion:
Kare wa shusse *ga hayakatta.* (彼は出世が早かった) His *promotions* were speedy. / shusse-*saku* (出世作) a work *which brings the writer fame*.
shusse suru (～する) *vi.* succeed in life; be promoted: *Kinodoku da kedo kare no* shusse *suru mikomi wa arimaseñ.* (気の毒だけど彼の出世する見込みはありません) I feel

sorry about it, but there is no chance of his *being promoted*. 《⇨ risshiñ-shusse》

shuᒐssee しゅっせい (出生) *n.* birth: ★ Also pronounced '*shusshoo.*'
shussee-*chi* (出生地) a *birthplace* / shussee-*ritsu* (出生率) a *birthrate* / shussee-*todoke* (出生届) the notification of a *birth* (to the authorities).

shuᒐsseki しゅっせき (出席) *n.* presence; attendance:
shusseki o toru (出席をとる) *call the roll* / *Kyoo no atsumari wa* shusseki *ga sukunakatta.* (きょうの集まりは出席が少なかった) *Attendance* was poor at today's gathering. / shusseki-*sha* (出席者) the people *present*.
shusseki suru (～する) *vt.* attend; be present: *Kinoo no paatii wa* shusseki shimashita *ka?* (きのうのパーティーは出席しましたか) Did you *go to* the party yesterday? / *Doozo o-kigaru ni* shusseki shite *kudasai.* (どうぞお気軽に出席してください) Please feel free to *come along*. 《↔ kesseki》《⇨ deru (3)》

shuᒐsshiñ しゅっしん (出身) *n.*
1 the place where one was born: Go-shusshiñ *wa dochira desu ka?* (ご出身はどちらですか) Where do you *come from?* / *Kare wa Kyooto no* shusshiñ *desu.* (彼は京都の出身です) He *comes from* Kyoto.
2 graduate:
Watashi wa kono daigaku no shusshiñ *desu.* (私はこの大学の出身です) I am a *graduate* of this university.

shuᒐsshoo しゅっしょう (出生) *n.* birth. 《⇨ shussee》

shuᒐtai しゅたい (主体) *n.* main constituent; core:
Sono chiimu wa wakai hito ga shutai ni natte imasu. (そのチームは若い人が主体になっています) The team *is made up mainly* of young players.

shu⌐tchoo しゅっちょう（出張）*n.*
business [official] trip:
*Watashi wa kaigai-shutchoo o
meejirareta.*（私は海外出張を命じられ
た）I was ordered to go on an
overseas *business trip.* / shutchoo-
jo（出張所）a *branch office* (of a
company); a *subsidiary office* (of
a public organization) / shutchoo-
ryohi（出張旅費）expenses for a
business trip / shutchoo-*saki*（出張
先）the destination of a *business
trip.*
   shutchoo suru（〜する）*vi.* make
a business [an official] trip: *Koñshuu wa Okinawa e shutchoo shimasu.*（今週は沖縄へ出張します）This
week I *am making a business trip*
to Okinawa.

shu⌐to しゅと（首都）*n.* capital;
metropolis:
   shuto-*keñ*（首都圏）*Tokyo* and the
surrounding region / shuto-*koosoku-dooro*（首都高速道路）the
Metropolitan Expressway.

shu⌐toku しゅとく（取得）*n.* (*formal*) acquisition:
fudoosañ no shutoku（不動産の取
得）the *acquisition* of real estate.
   shutoku suru（〜する）*vt.* acquire; obtain; get possession of:
*Kare wa ik-kagetsu de uñteñ-
meñkyo o* shutoku shita.（彼は1か
月で運転免許を取得した）He *ob-
tained* a driver's license in a
month.《⇨ toru¹》

shu⌐ to shite しゅとして（主として）
adv. mainly; chiefly; mostly:
Kaiiñ wa shu to shite *shufu desu.*
（会員は主として主婦です）The mem-
bers are *mostly* housewives.

shu⌐tsueñ しゅつえん（出演）*n.*
appearance:
   shutsueñ-*ryoo*（出演料）a *performance* fee / shutsueñ-sha（出演者）
a *performer*; an *actor.*
   shutsueñ suru（〜する）*vi.* appear; perform: *Kono eega ni wa*

uchi no musume ga shutsueñ shite
imasu.（この映画にはうちの娘が出演し
ています）Our daughter *appears* in
this film.

shu⌐tsujoo しゅつじょう（出場）*n.*
participation; entry:
   shutsujoo-sha（出場者）a *participant*; a *contestant* / shutsujoo-
teeshi（出場停止）*suspension* (of an
athlete).
   shutsujoo suru（〜する）*vi.* take
part in; participate in: *Ano hito
wa Oriñpikku ni* shutsujoo shita
señshu desu.（あの人はオリンピックに
出場した選手です）He is an athlete
who *took part* in the Olympics.

shu⌐u¹ しゅう（週）*n.* week:
*Shuu ni nañ-do Nihoñgo no ressuñ
o ukemasu ka?*（週に何度日本語のレ
ッスンを受けますか）How many Jap-
anese lessons do you take a *week?*
《⇨ hi¹ (table)》

señshuu	last week
koñshuu	this week
raishuu	next week
saraishuu	the week after next

shu⌐u² しゅう（州）*n.* state (of the
U.S., Australia, etc.); country.

Shu⌐ubuñ-no-hi⌐ （秋分の日）*n.*
Autumnal Equinox Day (about
Sept. 23).《⇨ shukujitsu (table)》

shu⌐uchaku しゅうちゃく（執着）*n.*
attachment; adherance:
Kare wa kiñseñ ni taisuru shuuchaku *ga tsuyoi.*（彼は金銭に対する
執着が強い）He has a great *attachment* to money.
   shuuchaku suru（〜する）*vi.* adhere to; be attached to: *Kare wa
jibuñ no añ ni saigo made* shuuchaku shite ita.（彼は自分の案に最後
まで執着していた）He *adhered* to his
own plan till the last.

shu⌐uchaku⌐-eki しゅうちゃくえき

(終着駅) *n.* terminal station: *Koko wa basu no* shuuchaku-eki *desu.* (ここはバスの終着駅です) This is the bus *terminal.*

shuˈuchuu しゅうちゅう (集中) *n.* concentration: *Jiñkoo no dai-toshi e no* shuuchuu *o osaeru hitsuyoo ga aru.* (人口の大都市への集中を抑える必要がある) It is necessary to control the *concentration* of population into large cities. / shuuchuu-*goou* (集中豪雨) a *localized* torrential downpour / shuuchuu-*ryoku* (集中力) the power of *concentration.*

shuuchuu suru (〜する) *vi., vt.* concentrate; focus; center: *chuui o* shuuchuu suru (注意を集中する) *focus* one's attention / *Dai-kigyoo wa toshi ni* shuuchuu shite iru. (大企業は都市に集中している) Big business *is concentrated* in the cities. / *Hihañ ga sono seejika ni* shuuchuu shita. (批判がその政治家に集中した) Criticism *centered* on that politician. 《↔ buñsañ》

shuˈudañ しゅうだん (集団) *n.* group; mass: *Kare-ra wa* shuudañ *de achikochi arukimawatta.* (彼らは集団であちこち歩き回った) They wandered in a *group* from place to place. / *Sono hoteru de* shuudañ *shoku-chuudoku ga hassee shita.* (そのホテルで集団食中毒が発生した) *Mass* food poisoning broke out in the hotel. / shuudañ-*keñshiñ* (集団検診) a *group* health check.

shuˈudeˈñ(sha) しゅうでん(しゃ) (終電(車)) *n.* the last train of the day: shuudeñ *ni maniau* (終電に間に合う) be in time for *the last train* / shuudeñ *ni noriokureru* (終電に乗り遅れる) miss *the last train.* 《↔ shi-hatsu》

shuˈugeki しゅうげき (襲撃) *n.* attack; assault; raid: shuugeki o ukeru (襲撃を受ける) *be attacked.*

shuugeki suru (〜する) *vt.* raid; attack: *Kagekiha ga kuukoo no jimusho o* shuugeki shita. (過激派が空港の事務所を襲撃した) The radicals *attacked* the airport office.

Shuˈugiˈiñ しゅうぎいん (衆議院) *n.* the House of Representatives: Shuugiiñ *giiñ* (衆議院議員) a member of the *House of Representatives.* 《⇨ Sañgiiñ; kokkai》

shuˈugoo しゅうごう (集合) *n.*
1 gathering; meeting; assembly: Shuugoo *to kaisañ wa onaji basho desu.* (集合と解散は同じ場所です) The point of *assembly* and dispersal is the same. / shuugoo-*ji-kañ* [*basho*] (集合時間[場所]) the *meeting* time [place].
2 (of mathematics) set: shuugoo-*roñ* (集合論) *set* theory.

shuugoo suru (〜する) *vi.* gather; meet; assemble: *Hachi-ji ni eki-mae-hiroba ni* shuugoo suru *koto ni natte imasu.* (8時に駅前広場に集合することになっています) We are to *rendezvous* in the square in front of the station at eight o'clock. 《↔ kaisañ》

shuˈuheñ しゅうへん (周辺) *n.* vicinity; neighborhood; outskirts: *Watashi-tachi no taihañ wa Too-kyoo* shuuheñ *ni suñde imasu.* (私たちの大半は東京周辺に住んでいます) Most of us live on the *outskirts* of Tokyo.

shuˈui しゅうい (周囲) *n.* **1** circumference: *Kono mizuumi wa* shuui *ga go-kiro arimasu.* (この湖は周囲が5キロあります) This lake is five kilometers in *circumference.*
2 surroundings; circumstances: Shuui *ga urusakute, beñkyoo ga dekinakatta.* (周囲がうるさくて、勉強ができなかった) I couldn't devote

myself to my study because of the noisy *surroundings*. / Shuui *no jijoo de yamunaku, sono keekaku wa chuushi shimashita.* (周囲の事情でやむなく、その計画は中止しました) We were obliged to abandon the plan through force of *circumstance.*

shu⌐ukai しゅうかい（集会）*n.* meeting; assembly; gathering: *Gakusee wa jugyooryoo no neage ni hañtai shite* shuukai *o hiraita.* (学生は授業料の値上げに反対して集会を開いた) The students held a *meeting* of protest against the increase in tuition fees.

shu⌐ukaku しゅうかく（収穫）*n.* crop; harvest: *Kotoshi wa kome no* shuukaku *ga yokatta.* (今年は米の収穫が良かった) This year the rice *harvest* has been good. / *Koñdo no choosa wa ooki-na* shuukaku *ga arimashita.* (今度の調査は大きな収穫がありました) This research *was* very *fruitful.*
shuukaku suru (〜する) *vt.* harvest; crop: *Nashi wa aki ni* shuukaku *saremasu.* (なしは秋に収穫されます) Pears *are harvested* in autumn.

shu⌐ukañ[1] しゅうかん（習慣）*n.* habit; custom; practice: *yoi* shuukañ *o mi ni tsukeru* (良い習慣を身につける) form a good *habit* / *warui* shuukañ *kara nukedasu* (悪い習慣から抜け出す) get out of a bad *habit* / *Hayaku okiru no wa yoi* shuukañ *desu.* (早く起きるのは良い習慣です) It is a good *habit* to get up early. / Shuukañ *wa kuni ni yotte chigaimasu.* (習慣は国によって違います) *Customs* differ from country to country.

shu⌐ukañ[2] しゅうかん（週間）*n.* week: *teñki no* shuukañ-*yohoo* (天気の週間予報) a weather forecast for the *next week* / *Booka* Shuukañ (防火

週間) Fire Prevention *Week* / *Kootsuu Añzeñ* Shuukañ (交通安全週間) Traffic Safety *Week.*

shu⌐ukañshi しゅうかんし（週刊誌）*n.* weekly magazine.

shu⌐uki[1] しゅうき（周期）*n.* cycle; period: *keeki no* shuuki (景気の周期) a business [trade] *cycle* / *shio no* shuuki (潮の周期) tidal *periods.*

shu⌐uki[2] しゅうき（秋季）*n.* fall; autumn: shuuki-*uñdookai* (秋季運動会) an *autumn* athletic meet. 《⇒ tooki[4]; shuñki; kaki[3]》

-shu⌐uki しゅうき（周忌）*suf.* anniversary of a person's death: *Kyoo wa haha no sañ-*shuuki *desu.* (きょうは母の 3 周忌です) Today is the third *anniversary* of our mother's death.

shu⌐ukiñ しゅうきん（集金）*n.* collection of money: *shiñbuñ-dai no* shuukiñ (新聞代の集金) the *collection* of newspaper subscription fees / shuukiñ-*niñ* (集金人) a *money* [*bill*] *collector.*
shuukiñ suru (〜する) *vt.* collect money: *Watashi no shigoto wa jushiñ-ryoo o* shuukiñ *shite, aruku koto desu.* (私の仕事は受信料を集金して、歩くことです) My job is to go around *collecting* television viewing *fees.*

shu⌐uki-teki しゅうきてき（周期的）*a.n.* (〜 na, ni) periodical: *Kono kazañ wa* shuuki-teki *ni bakuhatsu shimasu.* (この火山は周期的に爆発します) This volcano erupts *periodically.*

shu⌐ukyoo しゅうきょう（宗教）*n.* religion: shuukyoo *o shiñjiru* (宗教を信じる) believe in *religion.*

shu⌐umatsu しゅうまつ（週末）*n.* weekend: Shuumatsu *wa Hakone e iku yotee desu.* (週末は箱根へ行く予定です) I plan to go to Hakone on the *weekend*. / *Kare wa* shuumatsu *o ie de sugoshita.*（彼は週末を家で過ごした）He spent the *weekend* at home.（⇨ heejitsu）

-shuˈuneñ しゅうねん（周年）*suf.* anniversary: ★ Used for a happy event.
is-shuuneñ *kineñbi*（一周年記念日）the first *anniversary* / *sooritsu sañjuu-*shuuneñ（創立30周年）the thirtieth *anniversary* of the foundation.

shuˈuniñ しゅうにん（就任）*n.* assumption of office; inauguration: shuuniñ-*eñzetsu*（就任演説）an *inaugural* address.
 shuuniñ suru（～する）*vi.* take office; assume: *Suzuki-shi ga shachoo ni* shuuniñ *shita.*（鈴木氏が社長に就任した）Mr. Suzuki *assumed the post* of company president.

shuˈunyuu しゅうにゅう（収入）*n.* income; earnings; revenue: *Kare wa* shuunyuu *ga ooi [sukunai].*（彼は収入が多い[少ない]）He has a large [small] *income.* / *Nañ to ka* shuunyuu *no hañi-nai de kurashite imasu.*（なんとか収入の範囲内で暮らしています）I manage to get along within my *income.*（↔ shishutsu）

shuunyuu-iñshi しゅうにゅういんし（収入印紙）*n.* revenue stamp. ★ Often called '*iñshi,*' and put on a bond, deed, etc.

SHUUNYUU-IÑSHI

shuˈuri しゅうり（修理）*n.* repair; mending:
Kono kuruma no shuuri *ni wa nijuumañ-eñ kakarimasu.*（この車の修理には20万円かかります）It will cost 200,000 yen for the *repairs* to this car. / *Ano baiku wa* shuuri *ni dashimashita.*（あのバイクは修理に出しました）I put that motorbike in for *repairs.* / shuuri-*koojoo*（修理工場）a *repair* shop.
 shuuri suru（～する）*vt.* repair; mend; fix: *Sorosoro yane o* shuuri *shite morawanakereba naranai.*（そろそろ屋根を修理してもらわなければならない）We have to *get* the roof *repaired* soon.

shuˈuryoo しゅうりょう（終了）*n.* end; close:
Kyoo no eñsoo wa kore de shuuryoo *desu.*（きょうの演奏はこれで終了です）This is the *last* performance of today's concert.
 shuuryoo suru（～する）*vi., vt.* end; close: *Hoñjitsu no eegyoo wa* shuuryoo *shimashita.*（本日の営業は終了しました）We *are closed* for today.（↔ kaishi）

shuˈusee[1] しゅうせい（修正）*n.* amendment; revision; modification:
Yosañ-añ ni oohaba na shuusee *o kuwaete teeshutsu shita.*（予算案に大幅な修正を加えて提出した）We submitted the budget with extensive *revisions.* / shuusee-*añ*（修正案）a proposed *amendment.*
 shuusee suru（～する）*vt.* amend; revise; modify; correct: *eesee no kidoo o* shuusee *suru*（衛星の軌道を修正する）*adjust* the orbit of a satellite / *Liñkai wa sono hoo-añ o* shuusee *shita.*（委員会はその法案を修正した）The committee *revised* the bill.

shuˈusee[2] しゅうせい（習性）*n.* habit; behavior:
saru no shuusee *o keñkyuu suru*

（猿の習性を研究する）study the *behavior* of monkeys / *Kare wa yofukashi ga* shuusee *to natte shimatta.*（彼は夜更かしが習性となってしまった）He got into the *habit* of staying up late at night.

shu⌐usha しゅうしゃ（終車）*n.* the last train [bus]. 《↔ shihatsu》

shu⌐ushi[1] しゅうし（収支）*n.* incomings and outgoings; revenue and expenditure:
Nihoñ no booeki-shuushi wa kuroji desu.（日本の貿易収支は黒字です）Japan's *balance* of trade is in the black. / *Kanojo wa shuushi o awaseru no ni kuroo shita.*（彼女は収支を合わせるのに苦労した）She had difficulty in *making ends meet.*

shu⌐ushi[2] しゅうし（終始）*adv.* from beginning to end; throughout:
Sono chiimu wa shuushi yuusee datta.（そのチームは終始優勢だった）That team had an edge *from beginning to end.*

shuushi suru（〜する）*vi.* remain the same from beginning to end:
Shushoo no eñzetsu wa rakkañroñ ni shuushi shita.（首相の演説は楽観論に終始した）*From start to finish*, the prime minister's speech was optimistic.

shu⌐ushoku しゅうしょく（就職）*n.* finding employment:
Kare no shuushoku *no sewa o shite yatta.*（彼の就職の世話をしてやった）I helped him in *finding employment.* / shuushoku-*shikeñ*（就職試験）an *employment* examination.

shuushoku suru（〜する）*vi.* find work; get a position: *Musuko wa kotoshi giñkoo ni* shuushoku *shimashita.*（息子は今年銀行に就職しました）Our son *obtained a position* at a bank this year.

shu⌐ushokugo しゅうしょくご（修飾語）*n.* (of grammar) modifier; qualifier.

shu⌐ushuu しゅうしゅう（収集）*n.* collection:
shiryoo no shuushuu（資料の収集）the *collection* of data / *gomi no* shuushuu-*bi*（ごみの収集日）a garbage *collection* day.

shuushuu suru（〜する）*vt.* collect: *Doñna shurui no kitte o* shuushuu *shite iru ñ desu ka?*（どんな種類の切手を収集しているんですか）What type of stamps *are* you *collecting*?

shu⌐uteñ しゅうてん（終点）*n.* terminal station; terminus:
Kono chikatetsu no shuuteñ *wa Shibuya desu.*（この地下鉄の終点は渋谷です）The *terminal station* of this subway line is Shibuya.
《↔ kiteñ》

shu⌐utoku⌐butsu しゅうとくぶつ（拾得物）*n.* article found; find:
shuutokubutsu *o keesatsu ni todokeru*（拾得物を警察に届ける）hand in *lost property* to the police.
《⇨ hirou》

shu⌐uyoo しゅうよう（収容）*n.* accommodation; seating:
shuuyoo-*jiñiñ*（収容人員）the number of persons *to be admitted* / shuuyoo-*jo*（収容所）a *concentration* camp.

shuuyoo suru（〜する）*vt.* accommodate; admit: *Kono hoteru wa gohyaku-niñ* shuuyoo *dekimasu.*（このホテルは 500 人収容できます）This hotel *can accommodate* five hundred guests. / *Keganiñ wa chikaku no byooiñ ni* shuuyoo *sareta.*（けが人は近くの病院に収容された）The injured *were admitted* to a nearby hospital.

shu⌐uzeñ しゅうぜん（修繕）*n.* = shuuri.

shu⌐yaku しゅやく（主役）*n.* the leading part [role]; lead:
shuyaku *o tsutomeru* [*eñjiru*]（主役を務める[演じる]）play the *leading role* / *Kanojo wa sono geki de* shu-

yaku o moratta. (彼女はその劇で主役をもらった) She was given the *lead* in the play.

shu「yoo　しゅよう (主要) *a.n.*
(〜 na) important; chief; principal; main:
Kaigi no shuyoo *na gidai wa nañ desu ka?* (会議の主要な議題は何ですか) What are the *main* items on the agenda of the meeting? / shuyoo-*sañgyoo* (主要産業) *major* industries / shuyoo-*toshi* (主要都市) *chief* cities.

so「ba¹　そば (側) *n.* 1 side:
Sono ko wa haha-oya no soba *kara hanareyoo to shinakatta.* (その子は母親のそばから離れようとしなかった) The child wouldn't leave his mother's *side*.
2 (〜 ni) next to; near; beside:
Chuushajoo wa eki no soba *ni arimasu.* (駐車場は駅のそばにあります) The parking lot is *next to* the station. / *Watashi no ie no* soba *ni kooeñ ga arimasu.* (私の家のそばに公園があります) There is a park *near* my house. / *Motto* soba *ni yori nasai.* (もっとそばに寄りなさい) Come *closer* to me.

so「ba²　そば (蕎麦) *n.* buckwheat (noodles):
zaru-soba (ざるそば) *buckwheat noodles,* boiled and served, with pieces of 'nori' (laver) on top.

ZARU-SOBA

so「bie¹·ru　そびえる (聳える) *vi.* (sobie-te Ⅴ) rise; tower:
Me no mae ni sobiete iru *no ga Komagatake desu.* (目の前にそびえているのが駒ケ岳です) That mountain *rising high* before us is Mt. Komagatake.

so「bo　そぼ (祖母) *n.* one's grandmother:
Sobo *wa mimi ga tooi.* (祖母は耳が遠い) My *grandmother* is hard of hearing. 《↔ sofu》
《⇒ kazoku (table)》

so「boku　そぼく (素朴) *a.n.* (〜 na, ni) simple; unsophisticated:
soboku *na hitogara* (素朴な人柄) an *unsophisticated* personality / *Inaka no kurashi wa* soboku *desu.* (いなかの暮らしは素朴です) Country life is *simple and unsophisticated.*

so「chira　そちら *n.* ★ More polite than 'sotchi.'
1 there; over there: ★ Refers to a direction or a place close to the listener.
Sugu sochira *e ukagaimasu.* (すぐそちらへうかがいます) I'll come *over there* right away. / *Sochira ga deguchi desu.* (そちらが出口です) *That way* is the exit. / *Kozutsumi wa* sochira *ni tsukimashita ka?* (小包はそちらに着きましたか) Has the parcel arrived *there*?
2 that one; the other one: ★ Refers to something closer to the listener than the speaker.
Sochira *no o misete itadakemasu ka?* (そちらのを見せていただけますか) May I take a look at *that* one? / *Anata ga susumete kureta* sochira *o moraimasu.* (あなたが勧めてくれたそちらをもらいます) I'll take *that* one you suggested to me.
3 you; your side:
Sochira *no tsugoo no yoi toki ni itsu de mo oide kudasai.* (そちらの都合の良いときにいつでもおいでください) Please come any time when it is

convenient to *you.* / Sochira *wa minasañ o-geñki desu ka?* (そちらはみなさんお元気ですか) Are *your* family all well? 《⇨ achira; kochira》

so「dachi¹ そだち (育ち) *n.*

1 growth:
Kotoshi wa ine no sodachi *ga yoku nai.* (ことしは稲の育ちが良くない) This year the *growth* of rice is not good. 《⇨ sodatsu》

2 upbringing; breeding:
sodachi *no yoi hito* (育ちの良い人) a person of fine *breeding.* / *Watashi wa Tookyoo* sodachi *desu.* (私は東京育ちです) I *grew up* in Tokyo. 《⇨ sodatsu》

so「date]・ru そだてる (育てる) *vt.* (sodate-te Ⓥ) bring up; raise; cultivate; train:
kodomo o sodateru (子どもを育てる) *bring up* a child / *sakumotsu o* sodateru (作物を育てる) *cultivate* a crop / *Kare wa ooku no yuushuu na señshu o* sodateta. (彼は多くの優秀な選手を育てた) He *has trained* many excellent players. 《⇨ sodatsu》

so「da]ts・u そだつ (育つ) *vi.* (sodach・i-; sodat・a-; sodat-te Ⓒ) grow (up):
Riñgo wa koko de wa sodachimaseñ. (りんごはここでは育ちません) Apples *do not grow* here. / *Kare wa Kañda de umare Kañda de* sodatta. (彼は神田で生まれ神田で育った) He was born in Kanda and *grew up* there. 《⇨ sodateru; sodachi》

so「de そで (袖) *n.* sleeve:
Sode *o makuri nasai.* (そでをまくりなさい) Roll your *sleeves* up.

so「e・ru そえる (添える) *vt.* (soe-te Ⓥ) attach; add; garnish:
Okurimono ni tegami o soeta. (贈り物に手紙を添えた) I *attached* a letter to the gift. / *Suteeki ni wa yasai ga* soete atta. (ステーキには野菜が添えてあった) The steak *was garnished* with vegetables.

so「fu そふ (祖父) *n.* one's grandfather:
Sofu *wa hitori de apaato ni suñde imasu.* (祖父は一人でアパートに住んでいます) My *grandfather* lives alone in an apartment. / *Kare wa* sofu *kara Eego o manañda.* (彼は祖父から英語を学んだ) He learned English from his *grandfather.* 《↔ sobo》 《⇨ kazoku (table)》

so「futo-bo]oru ソフトボール *n.* softball:
sofuto-booru *o suru* (ソフトボールをする) play *softball.*

so「futo-kuri]imu ソフトクリーム *n.* soft ice-cream (in a cone).

so「kku]ri そっくり *a.n.* (~ na/no, ni) similar; like:
Kanojo wa haha-oya ni sokkuri *desu.* (彼女は母親にそっくりです) She is *exactly like* her mother. / *Kono zooka wa hoñmono* sokkuri *da.* (この造花は本物そっくりだ) The artificial flowers look *just like* real ones. / *Kono zoo o jitsubutsu* sokkuri *ni tsukutte kudasai.* (この像を実物そっくりに作ってください) Please make this statue *true to life.*
— *adv.* all; wholly; entirely:
Mochimono o sokkuri *nusumareta.* (持ち物をそっくり盗まれた) I had *all* my things stolen. / *Kare wa chichi-oya no zaisañ o* sokkuri *uketsuida.* (彼は父親の財産をそっくり受け継いだ) He inherited his father's *entire* estate.

so「ko¹ そこ *n.* **1** that place; there: ★ Refers to a place near the listener and slightly distant from the speaker.
Suutsukeesu wa soko *ni oite kudasai.* (スーツケースはそこに置いてください) Leave the suitcase *there*, please. / "Soko *wa nañ no heya desu ka?*" "*Ima desu.*" (「そこは何の部屋ですか」「居間です」) "What is *that* room?" "It is the living room." 《⇨ asoko; doko; koko¹》

2 there: ★ Refers to a place previously mentioned.
Saisho wa Oosaka e iki, soko *kara Okayama e ikimasu.* (最初は大阪へ行き, そこから岡山へ行きます) First I go to Osaka, and from *there* to Okayama. / *Kooen e iki,* soko *de minna de bentoo o tabemashita.* (公園へ行き, そこでみんなで弁当を食べました) We went to the park and ate lunch *there.*
3 that: ★ Refers to a subject mentioned by the listener.
Soko *no tokoro o moo ichido itte kudasai.* (そこの所をもう一度言ってください) Will you please repeat *what* you have just said?
4 then; when: ★ Refers to a particular time.
Soko *de kai o owari ni shita.* (そこで会を終わりにした) We broke up the party *then.* / *Dekakeyoo to shitara,* soko *e denwa ga kakatte kita.* (出かけようとしたら, そこへ電話がかかってきた) I was just going out, *when* the telephone rang.

so⌐ko² そこ (底) *n.* **1** bottom:
Kono baketsu wa soko *ni ana ga aite iru.* (このバケツは底に穴があいている) There is a hole in the *bottom* of this bucket. / *Kokoro no* soko *kara o-ree mooshiagemasu.* (心の底からお礼申し上げます) I thank you from the *bottom* of my heart.
2 sole:
Kutsu ni atarashii soko *o tsukete moratta.* (靴に新しい底をつけてもらった) I had new *soles* put on my shoes.
soko o tsuku (〜をつく) reach bottom; run out: *Shikin ga* soko *o tsuita.* (資金が底をついた) Our funds *have run out.*

so⌐ko de そこで *conj.* so; therefore: ★ Used at the beginning of a sentence.
Kare wa kuru koto ga dekimasen. Soko de *watashi ga dairi de mairimashita.* (彼は来ることができません. そ

こで私が代理で参りました) He is unable to come. I have *therefore* come in his place.

so⌐kona⌐·u そこなう (損なう) *vt.*
(sokona·i-; sokonaw·a-; sokonat-te Ⓒ) spoil; ruin; injure:
Kare wa hataraki-sugite kenkoo o sokonatta. (彼は働きすぎて健康を損なった) He *ruined* his health by overworking. / *Watashi wa kanojo no kigen o* sokonawanai *yoo ni ki o tsuketa.* (私は彼女のきげんを損なわないように気をつけた) I took care so that I should *not hurt* her feelings.

-so⌐kona⌐·u そこなう (損なう) (-sokona·i-; -sokonaw·a-; -sokonat-te Ⓒ) miss; fail to (do): ★ Occurs as the second element of compound verbs. Added to the continuative base of a verb.
densha ni nori-sokonau (電車に乗りそこなう) *miss* a train. / *Isogashiku-te sono eega o* mi-sokonatta. (忙しくてその映画を見そこなった) I was so busy that I *missed* the chance to see the movie.

so⌐ko⌐ra そこら *n.* **1** around there:
Megane nara, sokora *ni aru hazu desu.* (眼鏡なら, そこらにあるはずです) As for your glasses, they should be somewhere *around there.*
2 all over the place:
Karada ga sokora-*juu itai.* (体がそこらじゅう痛い) I have aches and pains *all over* my body.
3 approximately; or so:
Sono kamera nara, sanman-en ka sokora *de te ni hairimasu.* (そのカメラなら, 3万円かそこらで手に入ります) That camera is available at 30,000 yen *or so.*

-soku/zoku そく/ぞく (足) *suf.* counter for footgear:
kutsu is-soku (靴1足) *a pair* of shoes / *Kutsushita o* san-zoku *sen-en de katta.* (靴下を3足千円で買った) I bought *three pairs* of

socks for 1,000 yen.

1 i⌐s-soku˥	7 na⌐na˥-soku
2 ni˥-soku	8 ha⌐s-soku˥
3 sa˥ñ-zoku	9 kyu˥u-soku
4 yo˥ñ-soku	10 ji⌐s-soku˥
5 go˥-soku	(ju⌐s-soku˥)
6 ro⌐ku-soku˥	? na˥ñ-zoku

so⌐kubaku そくばく (束縛) *n.* restraint; restriction:
sokubaku *o ukeru* (束縛を受ける) be placed under *restraint* / sokubaku *kara nogareru* (束縛から逃れる) escape from *restrictions.*
sokubaku suru (～する) *vt.* restrain; restrict: *Kono hooañ wa geñroñ no jiyuu o sokubaku suru osore ga aru.* (この法案は言論の自由を束縛する恐れがある) There is a fear that this bill will *restrict* freedom of speech.
so˥kudo そくど (速度) *n.* speed; velocity:
sokudo *o masu* (速度を増す) pick up *speed* / *Taifuu wa sokudo o hayamete, Nihoñ ni chikazuite imasu.* (台風は速度を速めて、日本に近づいています) The typhoon is approaching Japan with increasing *speed.* / *seegeñ*-sokudo (制限速度) *speed* limit. (⇨ sokuryoku; supiido)
so⌐kumeñ そくめん (側面) *n.* side; flank:
teki no sokumeñ *o tsuku* (敵の側面をつく) attack the enemy on the *flank* / *Watashi-tachi wa sokumeñ kara kare o eñjo shita.* (私たちは側面から彼を援助した) We helped him *indirectly.* / *Kare ni soñna* sokumeñ *ga aru to wa shiranakatta.* (彼にそんな側面があるとは知らなかった) I didn't know that there was such a *side* to him.
so⌐kuoñ そくおん (促音) *n.* doubled consonant. ★ Represented in writing by a small '*tsu*' (っ).

e.g. itta (行った). (⇨ appendixes)
so⌐ku˥ryoku そくりょく (速力) *n.* speed:
Kuruma wa shidai ni sokuryoku *o mashita.* (車は次第に速力を増した) The car gradually gathered *speed.* / *Kare wa zeñ*-sokuryoku *de hashitta.* (彼は全速力で走った) He ran at full *speed.* (⇨ sokudo; supiido)
so⌐kuryoo そくりょう (測量) *n.* survey:
Kare no kaisha ni sono tochi no sokuryoo *o tanoñda.* (彼の会社にその土地の測量を頼んだ) We asked his company to make a *survey* of the land. / sokuryoo-gishi (測量技師) a *surveyor* / sokuryoo-zu (測量図) a *survey* map.
sokuryoo suru (～する) *vt.* survey: *Biru o tateru tame ni tochi o* sokuryoo shita. (ビルを建てるために土地を測量した) We *surveyed* the land to put up a building.
so⌐kushiñ そくしん (促進) *n.* promotion; furtherance:
hañbai no sokushiñ *o hakaru* (販売の促進を図る) work out a sales *promotion* / *Kokureñ no shisetsudañ wa sekai heewa no* sokushiñ *ni kookeñ shita.* (国連の使節団は世界平和の促進に貢献した) The UN mission contributed to the *furtherance* of world peace.
sokushiñ suru (～する) *vt.* promote; futher; hasten: *Seefu wa booeki o* sokushiñ suru *seesaku o totte iru.* (政府は貿易を促進する政策をとっている) The government has adopted a policy which *encourages* foreign trade.
so⌐kutatsu そくたつ (速達) *n.* special [express] delivery:
Kono tegami o sokutatsu *ni shite kudasai.* (この手紙を速達にしてください) Please send this letter by *special delivery.* / sokutatsu-*yuubiñ* (速達郵便) *special delivery* mail.
so⌐kutee そくてい (測定) *n.* mea-

surement:

sokutee-*ki* (測定器) a *measuring* instrument.

sokutee suru (〜する) *vt.* measure; check: *kuruma no hayasa o* sokutee suru (車の速さを測定する) *measure* the speed of a car / *chijoo no ichi o* sokutee suru (地上の位置を測定する) *determine* the location of points on the surface of the earth.

so⌐mar·u そまる (染まる) *vi.* (somar·i-; somar·a-; somat-te ⓒ)
1 dye; be tinged:
Kono kiji wa yoku somaru. (この生地はよく染まる) This cloth *takes dye* well. / *Jikeñ no geñba wa chi ni* somatte ita. (事件の現場は血に染まっていた) The scene of the crime *was covered* in blood. 《⇨ someru》
2 be adversely influenced (by one's surroundings):
Sono shooneñ wa shidai ni aku ni somatte itta. (その少年は次第に悪に染まっていった) The boy gradually *became steeped* in vice.

so⌐matsu そまつ (粗末) *a.n.*
(〜 na, ni) **1** poor; plain; humble:
somatsu *na ie* (粗末な家) a *plain*, *simple* house / somatsu *na fuku* (粗末な服) *shabby* clothes / *Kare-ra wa* somatsu *na shokuji o shita.* (彼らは粗末な食事をした) They had a *frugal* meal.
2 careless; rough; rude:
Hoñ o somatsu *ni atsukatte wa ikemaseñ.* (本を粗末に扱ってはいけません) Don't handle books *roughly*. / *Saikiñ wa mono o* somatsu *ni suru hito ga ooi.* (最近は物を粗末にする人が多い) These days there are many people who treat objects *without due respect*.

so⌐me·ru そめる (染める) *vt.* (some-te Ⓥ) dye; tinge:
Kanojo wa kami o chairo ni someta. (彼女は髪を茶色に染めた) She

dyed her hair brown. 《⇨ somaru》

so⌐mosomo そもそも *adv.* in the first place; (what) on earth:
Somosomo *koñna tokoro ni kita no ga machigai da.* (そもそもこんな所に来たのがまちがいだ) *In the first place*, it was wrong of us to come to a place like this. / Somosomo *dare ga koñna koto o iidashita ñ desu ka?* (そもそもだれがこんなことを言い出したんですか) Who *on earth* proposed such a thing? / *Geñiñ wa* somosomo *nañ datta ñ desu ka?* (原因はそもそも何だったんですか) What *on earth* was the cause?

so⌐mu·k·u そむく (背く) *vi.* (somuk·i-; somuk·a-; somu·i-te ⓒ) disobey; disregard; violate:
meeree ni somuku (命令に背く) *disobey* an order / *hooritsu ni* somuku (法律に背く) *disregard* the law / *chuukoku ni* somuku (忠告に背く) *ignore* a warning / *Kare wa ryooshiñ no kitai ni* somuite, *shikeñ ni shippai shita.* (彼は両親の期待に背いて、試験に失敗した) *Contrary to* his parents' hopes, he failed the exam.

so⌐ñ そん (損) *n.* loss:
Kabu o ima uru to gomañ-eñ no soñ *ni naru.* (株を今売ると 5 万円の損になる) If I sell the stock now, I will suffer a *loss* of 50,000 yen.
soñ (o) suru (〜(を)する) *vt.* lose; suffer a loss: *Keeba de nimañ-eñ* soñ (o) shita. (競馬で 2 万円損(を)した) I *lost* 20,000 yen at the races.
— *a.n.* (〜 na, ni) disadvantageous:
soñ *na tachiba* (損な立場) a *disadvantageous* position / soñ *na seekaku* (損な性格) a personality that *handicaps* one / *Soñna koto o suru to* soñ *ni narimasu yo.* (そんなことをすると損になりますよ) If you do something like that it will be to your *disadvantage*. 《↔ toku²》

so⌐nae そなえ (備え) *n.* prepara-

tions; provision; defense:
Jishiñ ni taisuru sonae *wa dai-joobu desu ka?* (地震に対する備えはだいじょうぶですか) *Are* you *well prepared* against earthquakes? / *Roogo no* sonae *ga shiñpai desu.* (老後の備えが心配です) I am worried about *provisons* for my old age. / Sonae areba *urei nashi.* (*saying*) (備えあれば憂いなし) *Lay up* for a rainy day. 《⇨ sonaeru¹》

so「nae」·ru¹ そなえる(備える) *vt.* (sonae-te Ⅴ) **1** prepare; provide:
saigai ni sonaeru (災害に備える) *prepare* against disaster / *Kanojo wa shikeñ ni* sonaete *beñkyoo shite imasu.* (彼女は試験に備えて勉強しています) She is studying *in preparation for* the exam. / *Roogo ni* sonaete *chokiñ shite imasu.* (老後に備えて貯金しています) I am saving up *for* my old age. 《⇨ sonae》
2 equip; furnish:
Kono kyooshitsu ni wa koñpyuutaa ga sonaete *arimasu.* (この教室にはコンピューターが備えてあります) Computers *are installed* in this classroom.

so「nae」·ru² そなえる(供える) *vt.* (sonae-te Ⅴ) offer:
Watashi wa kare no haka ni hana o sonaeta. (私は彼の墓に花を供えた) I *offered* flowers at his grave.

so「naetsuke」 そなえつけ(備え付け) *n.* equipment; fittings:
sonaetsuke *no beddo* (備え付けのベッド) a *fixed* bed / sonaetsuke *no hoñdana* (備え付けの本棚) *built-in* bookshelves / *Doozo* sonaetsuke *no shokki o o-tsukai kudasai.* (どうぞ備え付けの食器をお使いください) Please feel free to use the tableware *kept here.* 《⇨ sonaetsukeru》

so「naetsuke」·ru そなえつける(備え付ける) *vt.* (-tsuke-te Ⅴ) provide; furnish; equip; install:
Kono heya ni wa hitsuyoo na ka-gu ga subete sonaetsukete *arimasu.* (この部屋には必要な家具がすべて備え付けてあります) This room *is* fully *equipped* with all the necessary furniture. 《⇨ sonaetsuke》

so「ñchoo」¹ そんちょう(尊重) *n.* respect; high regard; esteem:
★ The grammatical object is usually inanimate.
jiñkeñ no soñchoo (人権の尊重) *respect* for human rights.
soñchoo suru (〜する) *vt.* respect; make much of: *Hoka no hito no ikeñ mo* soñchoo *shinakereba naranai.* (ほかの人の意見も尊重しなければならない) We *must* also *respect* other people's opinions. 《⇨ soñkee》

so「ñchoo² そんちょう(村長) *n.* village chief; the head of a village.

so「ñdai そんだい(尊大) *a.n.* (〜 na, ni) arrogant; haughty; self-important:
Kare no soñdai *na taido ni hara ga tatta.* (彼の尊大な態度に腹がたった) I got angry at his *arrogant* attitude.

so「ñgai そんがい(損害) *n.* damage; loss:
Taifuu wa sono machi ni ooki-na soñgai *o ataeta.* (台風はその町に大きな損害を与えた) The typhoon caused great *damage* to the town. / *Sono kuni wa señsoo de ooki-na* soñgai *o koomutta.* (その国は戦争で大きな損害をこうむった) The country suffered heavy *losses* in the war.

so「ñkee そんけい(尊敬) *n.* respect; esteem; reverence:
★ The grammatical object is usually a person or the actions of a person.
hitobito no soñkee *o atsumeru* (人人の尊敬を集める) gain the *respect* of others / *Anata no shita koto wa* soñkee *ni atai shimasu.* (あなたのしたことは尊敬に値します) What you have done is worthy of *respect.*

soñkee suru (～する) *vt.* respect; esteem: *Watashi wa Yamada señsee o* soñkee *shite imasu.* (私は山田先生を尊敬しています) I *hold* my teacher, Mr. Yamada, *in high esteem.* (⇨ soñchoo')

soñna そんな *attrib.* **1** such; like that: ★ Refers to something mentioned or done by the listener.
Soñna *kanashi-soo na kao o shinai de kudasai.* (そんな悲しそうな顔をしないでください) Please don't put on *such* a sad look. / Soñna *iikata wa nai deshoo.* (そんな言い方はないでしょう) You should not speak *like that.*
2 that; such: ★ Refers to something mentioned by the listener.
"Kare wa shutchoo-chuu desu." *"*Soñna *hazu wa arimaseñ."* (「彼は出張中です」「そんなはずはありません」) "He is on a business trip." "*That* cannot be true." / *"Murata-sañ ni wa o-ai ni narimashita ka?"* *"*Soñna *kata wa shirimaseñ."* (「村田さんにはお会いになりましたか」「そんな方は知りません」) "Have you met Mr. Murata?" "I don't know a person by *that* name." (⇨ añna; doñna; koñna)

soñna ni そんなに *adv.* that; like that; such; so:
Kono hoñ wa soñna ni *omoshiroku nai.* (この本はそんなにおもしろくない) This book is not *all that* interesting. / *Anata ga* soñna ni *iu no nara, kai ni shusseki shimashoo.* (あなたがそんなに言うのなら、会に出席しましょう) If you insist *so much,* I'll attend the party. / Soñna ni *isogu hitsuyoo wa arimaseñ.* (そんなに急ぐ必要はありません) You needn't be in *such* a hurry. / *Inu wa* soñna ni *tooku made ikimaseñ.* (犬はそんなに遠くまで行きません) The dog doesn't go *so* far. (⇨ añna ni; doñna ni; koñna ni)

sono その *attrib.* **1** the; that: ★ Refers to something which is located away from the speaker and close to the listener.
Sono *shio o totte kudasai.* (その塩をとってください) Could you pass me *the* salt, please. / *Kimi ga motte iru* sono *kasa wa watashi no desu.* (君が持っているその傘は私のです) *That* umbrella you have in your hand is mine.
2 the; that; it: ★ Refers to a person or thing just mentioned.
"Kore wa himitsu desu." "Hoka ni dare ka sono *koto o shitte imasu ka?"* (「これは秘密です」「ほかにだれかそのことを知っていますか」) "This is a secret." "Is there anyone else who knows about *it?*" / *"Uchi wa eki no sugu soba desu." "*Sono *eki wa kyuukoo mo tomarimasu ka?"* (「家は駅のすぐそばです」「その駅は急行も止まりますか」) "My house is near the station." "Do the expresses also stop at *that* station?" (⇨ ano; dono; kono)

sono-aida そのあいだ (その間) *adv.* during the time; in the meantime; all the while:
Sono-aida *nani o shite imashita ka?* (その間何をしていましたか) What were you doing *during that time?* / *Miñna wa utatta ga kare wa* sono-aida *damatte ita.* (みんなは歌ったが彼はその間黙っていた) Everybody sang, but he was *meanwhile* silent. / Sono-aida *zutto ame datta.* (その間ずっと雨だった) It was rainy *all the while.*

sono-hoka そのほか (その他) *n.* the rest; the others:
Sono-hoka *no koto wa watashi ga yarimasu.* (そのほかのことは私がやります) I will do *the rest.* / Sono-hoka *no hito wa koko ni ite kudasai.* (そのほかの人はここにいてください) Will *the others* please remain here? / Sono-hoka *wa irimaseñ.* (そのほかは

要りません〕I do not need any *more*.
—— *adv.* (~ ni) else; besides.
Sono-hoka (*ni*) *nani-ka suru koto ga arimasu ka?*（そのほか(に)何かすることがありますか）Is there anything to do *apart from that*? / *Sono-hoka (ni) nani-ka shitsumoñ wa arimasu ka?*（そのほか(に)何か質問はありますか）Are there *any other* questions?

so⌈no-ma⌉e そのまえ（その前）*n.*, *adv.* before that; in front of a person:
Sono-mae ni mada yaru koto ga aru.（その前にまだやることがある）There is something I have to do *before that*. / *Sono-mae ni aru no wa nañ desu ka?*（その前にあるのは何ですか）What is it that *in front of* you?

so⌈no-mama そのまま（その儘）*n.*
1 the present state [situation]; as it is:
Sono-mama no jootai ga shibaraku tsuzuita.（そのままの状態がしばらく続いた）The *existing* conditions continued for a while. / *Kañja wa sono-mama nekasete oite kudasai.*（患者はそのまま寝かせておいてください）Please leave the patient sleeping *as he is*. / *Hañzai no geñba wa shibaraku sono-mama ni shite okareta.*（犯罪の現場はしばらくそのままにしておかれた）The scene of the crime was left *undisturbed* for a while. / *Sono-mama no kakkoo de paatii e iku tsumori desu ka?*（そのままのかっこうでパーティーへ行くつもりですか）Do you intend to go to the party dressed *like that*? (⇨ mama¹)
2 immediately:
Kodomo wa gakkoo kara kaeru to sono-mama asobi ni dekaketa.（子どもは学校から帰るとそのまま遊びに出かけた）The child came home from school and *immediately* went out to play. (⇨ mama¹)

so⌈no-uchi そのうち（その内）*adv.*

(~ ni) soon; before long; someday; sometime:
Kare wa sono-uchi (ni) yatte kuru deshoo.（彼はそのうち(に)やって来るでしょう）I expect that he will turn up *soon*. / *Sono-uchi mata nomimashoo.*（そのうちまた飲みましょう）Let's get together for a drink *before too long*. / *Sono-uchi ame mo agaru deshoo.*（そのうち雨も上がるでしょう）The rain should let up *soon*.

so⌈no ue そのうえ（その上）*conj.* besides; moreover:
Kare wa yokubari de, sono ue kechi datta.（彼は欲張りで、その上けちだった）He was greedy, and *besides* he was stingy. / *Kanojo wa bijiñ de, sono ue atama ga yoi.*（彼女は美人で、その上頭が良い）She is a beauty, and *moreover* she has brains. / *Sono ue warui koto ni, pasupooto o nakushite shimatta.*（その上悪いことに、パスポートをなくしてしまった）*And what was worse*, I lost my passport.

so⌈ñshitsu そんしつ（損失）*n.* loss:
Soñshitsu no hoo ga rieki yori mo ookikatta.（損失のほうが利益よりも大きかった）The *losses* were greater than the gains. / *Kare no shi wa kokka ni totte ooki-na soñshitsu desu.*（彼の死は国家にとって大きな損失です）His death is a great *loss* to the nation. (⇨ soñ)

so⌈ñzai そんざい（存在）*n.* existence; presence; being:
Anata wa kami no soñzai o shiñjimasu ka?（あなたは神の存在を信じますか）Do you believe in the *existence* of God? / *Kare no soñzai o mushi suru wake ni wa ikimaseñ.*（彼の存在を無視する訳にはいきません）We cannot afford to ignore his *presence*. / *soñzai-riyuu*（存在理由）*raison d'être*.

soñzai suru (~する) *vi.* exist:
Kasee ni wa seebutsu wa soñzai

shimaseñ. (火星には生物は存在しませ
ん) *No* life *exists* on Mars.

so˥o[1] そう *adv.* **1** yes; no:
★ Used to express agreement
with a question, regardless of
whether it is affirmative or negative:
*"Anata wa Doitsu no kata desu
ka?" "Soo desu."* (「あなたはドイツの
方ですか」「そうです」) "Are you German?" *"That's right."* / *"Anata
wa o-sake o nomimaseñ ne?"*
"Soo desu. Zeñzeñ nomimaseñ."
(「あなたはお酒を飲みませんね」「そうです。
全然飲みません」) " You don't drink,
do you?" *"That's right.* I don't
drink at all.*"*
2 so; like that; in that way:
Soo shite kudasai. (そうしてください)
Please do it *like that.* / *Watashi
wa* soo *omoimasu.* (私はそう思いま
す) I think *so.* / *Soo okoranai de
kudasai.* (そう怒らないでください)
Please do not get *so* angry. /
Kono hoñ wa soo *omoshiroku wa
arimaseñ.* (この本はそうおもしろくはあり
ません) This book is not *so* interesting.
soo desu ne (〜ですね) well; let
me see: Soo desu ne, *ato de moo
ichido soodañ shimashoo.* (そうです
ね, あとでもう一度相談しましょう) *Well,*
let us talk about it again once
more.
soo ieba (〜言えば) by the way:
Soo ieba, *anata no o-ko-sañ wa
kotoshi sotsugyoo desu ne?* (そう言
えば, あなたのお子さんは今年卒業ですね)
By the way, your child graduates
this year, doesn't he?
soo[2] そう *n.* they say; I hear; I
understand: ★ Preceded by a
non-polite style predicate in either the present or past tense.
Yamada-sañ wa teñkiñ ni naru
soo *desu.* (山田さんは転勤になるそうで
す) *I hear* that Mr. Yamada is to
be transferred. / *Kamera no shu-*

uri ni wa is-shuukañ kakaru soo
desu. (カメラの修理には一週間かかるそ
うです) *They say* that it will take a
week to repair the camera. /
Kono suupaa wa yasui soo *desu.*
(このスーパーは安いそうです) *I hear*
that this supermarket is cheap. /
Anata wa kono añ ni sañsee da
soo *desu ne.* (あなたはこの案に賛成だ
そうですね) *I understand* that you
are in favor of this proposal.

so˥o[3] そう *int.* really; good:
*"Kuji ni atatta yo." "Soo, yokatta
ne."* (「くじに当たったよ」「そう, よかった
ね」) "I won in the lottery.*"*
"*Really?* That's great! " / *"Sakki
jishiñ ga arimashita." "Soo (desu
ka). Ki ga tsukimaseñ deshita."*
(「さっき地震がありました」「そう(ですか).
気がつきませんでした」) "There was
an earthquake a little while ago. "
"*Really?* I didn't feel it. "

so˥o[4] そう (層) *n.* **1** layer; stratum:
gañseki no soo (岩石の層) a rock
stratum.
2 class; bracket:
chishiki-soo (知識層) the *intelligentsia* / kooshotokusha-soo (高所
得者層) the high income *bracket.*

so˥o- そう (総) *pref.* all; general;
total:
soo-señkyo (総選挙) a *general* election / soo-shotoku (総所得) one's
gross income / soo-jiñkoo (総人口)
the *total* population.

-soo そう *suf.* (*a.n.*) (〜 na, ni)
look; seem; appear: ★ Attached
to the continuative base of a
verb, or the stem of an adjective,
or to an adjectival noun. The
adjectives '*yoi*' and '*nai*' take the
form '*yosa-soo*' and '*nasa-soo.*'
Ame ga furi-soo da. (雨が降りそうだ)
It looks like rain. / *Kono yubiwa
wa* taka-soo da. (この指輪は高そうだ)
This ring *looks expensive.* / *Kare
wa totemo* geñki-soo datta. (彼はと

ても元気そうだった) He *looked very healthy*. / *Kono kawa wa shitsu ga* yosa-soo da. (この革は質が良さそうだ) This leather *seems to be of good quality*. / *Kanojo wa* ureshi-kunasa-soo datta. (彼女はうれしくなさそうだった) She *didn't look too happy*.

so⌐oba そうば (相場) *n.* **1** market price; rate:
Daizu no sooba *ga agatte imasu*. (大豆の相場が上がっています) The *market price* for soybeans is rising. / *Eñ no doru ni taisuru* sooba *wa ikura desu ka?* (円のドルに対する相場はいくらですか) What is the *exchange rate* of the yen against the dollar?
2 speculation:
sooba *ni te o dasu* (相場に手を出す) dabble in *speculation*; be involved in *stocks* / Sooba *de soñ o shita*. (相場で損をした) I have lost money in *speculation*.

so⌐ochi そうち (装置) *n.* device; equipment; apparatus:
Kono fune ni wa reedaa-soochi *ga arimasu*. (この船にはレーダー装置があります) This ship has radar *equipment*. / *Sono heya ni wa* dañboo-soochi *ga nakatta*. (その部屋には暖房装置がなかった) There was no *kind of heating* in the room. / *añzeñ*-soochi (安全装置) a safety *device*.

so⌐odañ そうだん (相談) *n.* talks; consultation; conference:
Sono koto de kanojo kara soodañ *o uketa*. (そのことで彼女から相談を受けた) I *was consulted* by her about the matter. / *Chotto* soodañ *ni notte itadakemasu ka?* (ちょっと相談に乗っていただけますか) May I ask you for some *advice*? / *Soñna koto wa totemo dekinai* soodañ *desu*. (そんなことはとてもできない相談です) That sort of thing is an absolutely impossible *proposal*.

soodañ suru (～する) *vi., vt.* talk; consult; confer: Soodañ shitai *koto ga atte, kimashita*. (相談したいことがあって、来ました) I came here because I have something to *talk over* with you. / *Shiñro ni tsuite wa señsee to* soodañ shi nasai. (進路については先生と相談しなさい) You should *talk* to your teacher about your future.

so⌐odeñ そうでん (送電) *n.* transmission of electricity; power supply:
Jiko no tame, soodeñ *ga tomatta*. (事故のため、送電が止まった) Owing to an accident, the *power supply* was cut off.
soodeñ suru (～する) *vt.* transmit [supply] electricity: *Kono hatsu-deñsho kara wa Tookyoo hoomeñ e* soodeñ sarete imasu. (この発電所からは東京方面へ送電されています) *Electricity is supplied* to the Tokyo area from this power station.

so⌐odoo そうどう (騒動) *n.* disturbance; trouble; riot:
Sono soodoo *o okoshita no wa dare desu ka?* (その騒動を起こしたのはだれですか) Who is it that caused the *disturbance*? / *Keesatsu ga sono* soodoo *o shizumeta*. (警察がその騒動を鎮めた) The police suppressed the *riot*.

so⌐ogeñ そうげん (草原) *n.* grasslands; plain.

so⌐ogo そうご (相互) *n.* mutual; reciprocal:
Sono kai wa soogo *no rikai o fukameru no ni yakudatta*. (その会は相互の理解を深めるのに役立った) The meeting went a long way toward promoting *mutual* understanding. / *Kare-ra wa* soogo *ni tayotte iru*. (彼らは相互に頼っている) They depend on *each other*. (⇨ tagai)

so⌐ogo-no⌐riire そうごのりいれ (相互乗り入れ) *n.* mutual use of each

other's tracks; mutual trackage agreement:
Koko de wa chikatetsu to Jee-aaru-señ ga soogo-noriire *shite imasu.* (ここでは地下鉄と JR 線が相互乗り入れしています) The subway and JR trains *run on each other's tracks* here.

so⌐ogoo そうごう (総合) *n.* synthesis; generalization: soogoo-byooiñ (総合病院) a *general* hospital / soogoo-daigaku (総合大学) a *university* (as opposed to a college) / soogoo-zasshi (総合雑誌) a *general* magazine.

soogoo suru (〜する) *vt.* put together; synthesize: *Shussekisha no ikeñ o* soogoo suru *to kono ketsuroñ ni narimasu.* (出席者の意見を総合するとこの結論になります) If we *consider* what is common to the participants' views, we come to this conclusion.

so⌐oi¹ そうい (相違) *n.* difference; divergence:
Ryoosha no ikeñ ni wa ooki-na sooi *ga arimasu.* (両者の意見には大きな相違があります) There are great *differences* in the views of the two parties. / *Ijoo* sooi arimaseñ. (以上相違ありません) I affirm the above to *be true and correct.*
★ Used when attesting to the veracity of a document.

sooi suru (〜する) *vi.* differ; diverge: *Kare ga itte iru koto wa jijitsu to* sooi shite iru. (彼が言っていることは事実と相違している) What he says *diverges* from the actual facts.

so⌐oi² そうい (総意) *n.* the general opinion [will]; the consensus:
Kore wa wareware shaiñ no sooi *ni yoru mono desu.* (これはわれわれ社員の総意によるものです) This is supported by the *general will* of our company's employees.

so⌐o-iu そういう *attrib.* **1** such; like that; that kind of: ★ Refers to something mentioned by the listener.
"Kinoo Maruyama-sañ to iu kata ga tazunete kimashita." "Soo-iu hito wa shirimaseñ." (「きのう丸山さんという方が訪ねて来ました」「そういう人は知りません」) "A Mrs. Maruyama came to see you yesterday." "I don't know *such* a person."
/ *"Kare wa tokidoki uso o iimasu." "Soo-iu otoko wa shiñyoo dekinai."* (「彼はときどきうそを言います」「そういう男は信用できない」) "He sometimes tells lies." "You can't trust *that sort of* man." / *"Tsugi no ressha ni noritai ñ desu ga." "Soo-iu koto deshitara, eki made kuruma de okurimashoo."* (「次の列車に乗りたいんですが」「そういうことでしたら、駅まで車で送りましょう」) "I want to catch the next train." "If *that* is the case, I'll give you a lift to the station."

2 that: ★ Refers to what the speaker previously mentioned.
Soo-iu *wake de kyoo no kaigi ni wa shusseki dekimaseñ.* (そういう訳できょうの会議には出席できません) *That*'s why I am unable to attend today's meeting.
(⇨ aa-iu; doo-iu; koo-iu)

so⌐oji そうじ (掃除) *n.* cleaning:
Kanojo no heya wa sooji *ga yoku yukitodoite iru.* (彼女の部屋は掃除がよく行き届いている) Her room *is kept very clean.* / sooji-toobañ (掃除当番) the person on *cleaning* duty for the day.

sooji (o) suru (〜(を)する) *vt.* clean; sweep: *Watashi wa mai-asa heya o* sooji shimasu. (私は毎朝部屋を掃除します) I *clean* my room every morning.

so⌐oji⌐ki そうじき (掃除機) *n.* (vacuum) cleaner:
Heya ni soojiki *o kakemashita ka?* (部屋に掃除機をかけましたか)

Have you *vacuumed* your room?

so⌐ojuu そうじゅう (操縦) *n.* operation; maneuvering:
Kare wa hikooki no soojuu *o naratte imasu.* (彼は飛行機の操縦を習っています) He is learning how to *fly* an airplane. / soojuu-seki (操縦席) a *cockpit* / soojuu-shi (操縦士) a *pilot*.
  soojuu suru (～する) *vt.* **1** operate; pilot; fly; steer: *kikai o* soojuu suru (機械を操縦する) *operate* a machine / *hikooki* [*fune*] *o* soojuu suru (飛行機 [船] を操縦する) *pilot* a plane [ship].
  2 control; manage: *Dare-ka ga kage de kare o* soojuu shite iru. (だれかが陰で彼を操縦している) There is someone *controlling* him from behind the scenes.

so⌐okai そうかい (総会) *n.* general meeting:
*kabunushi-*sookai *o hiraku* (株主総会を開く) hold a *general meeting* of stockholders.

so⌐o ka to itte そうかといって *conj.* but; nevertheless; for all that:
Kinoo kara kazegimi desu. Shikashi soo ka to itte, *yasuñde mo iraremaseñ.* (きのうからかぜぎみです。 しかしそうかといって、休んでもいられません) I have had a bit of a cold since yesterday; but I cannot stay away from work *for that reason*.

so⌐okiñ そうきん (送金) *n.* remittance of money:
Oya kara no sookiñ *ga tomatte, komatte imasu.* (親からの送金が止まって、困っています) *The money my parents send me* has stopped, so I am in a fix.
  sookiñ suru (～する) *vi.* send money; remit: *Watashi wa Tookyoo ni iru musuko ni maitsuki* sookiñ shite imasu. (私は東京にいる息子に毎月送金しています) I *send money* to my son in Tokyo every

month.

so⌐oko そうこ (倉庫) *n.* warehouse; storehouse:
Sono shinamono wa sooko *ni azukete arimasu.* (その品物は倉庫に預けてあります) The goods are kept in the *warehouse*.

So⌐omu⌐-choo そうむちょう (総務庁) *n.* Management and Coordination Agency:
Soomu-choo *chookañ* (総務庁長官) the Director General of the *Management and Coordination Agency*. 《⇨ choo⁴ (table)》

so⌐o-oñ そうおん (騒音) *n.* noise; din:
soo-oñ *o tateru* (騒音をたてる) make a *noise* / *Toori no* soo-oñ *ga urusai.* (通りの騒音がうるさい) The *noise* from the street is annoying. / soo-oñ-*koogai* (騒音公害) *noise* pollution.

so⌐ori そうり (総理) *n.* abbreviation for 'Soori-daijiñ.'
Soori-*fu* (総理府) the *Prime Minister*'s Office.

So⌐ori-dai⌐jiñ そうりだいじん (総理大臣) *n.* Prime Minister; Premier.

so⌐oritsu そうりつ (創立) *n.* establishment; foundation:
Watashi wa kono kaisha ni sooritsu *irai tsutomete imasu.* (私はこの会社に創立以来勤めています) I have been working for this company since its *foundation*. / sooritsu *kineñbi* (創立記念日) the anniversary of the *founding*.
  sooritsu suru (～する) *vt.* establish; found: *Kono kaisha wa juu-neñ mae ni* sooritsu saremashita. (この会社は10年前に創立されました) This company *was established* ten years ago.

so⌐oryo⌐oji そうりょうじ (総領事) *n.* consul general. 《⇨ taishi (table)》

so⌐oryooji⌐kañ そうりょうじかん (総領事館) *n.* consulate general:

Nihoñ sooryoojikañ (日本総領事館) the Japanese *Consulate General*. 《⇨ taishikañ (table)》

so⌐osa[1] そうさ (捜査) *n.* criminal investigation; search; manhunt: soosa o susumeru (捜査を進める) proceed with an *investigation* / *Sono hañniñ wa* soosa-chuu *desu.* (その犯人は捜査中です) They *are searching* for the criminal. / soosa-*hoñbu* (捜査本部) the *investigation* headquarters / soosa-reejoo (捜査令状) a *search* warrant.
　soosa suru (～する) *vt.* investigate: *Keesatsu wa sono jikeñ o* soosa shi-hajimeta. (警察はその事件を捜査し始めた) The police *have started investigating* the case.

so⌐osa[2] そうさ (操作) *n.* operation; handling; manipulation: *Kono kikai wa* soosa *ga muzukashii.* (この機械は操作が難しい) The *operation* of this machine is difficult.
　soosa suru (～する) *vt.* operate; handle; manipulate: *kikai o* soosa suru (機械を操作する) *operate* a machine / *kabu o* soosa suru (株を操作する) *manipulate* stocks / *Dare-ka ga choobo o* soosa shita *yoo da.* (だれかが帳簿を操作したようだ) It seems that someone *juggled* the account books.

so⌐o sa そうさ yes; you are correct: ★ Expresses a feeling of pride. *"It-too-shoo o totta soo ne"* *"Soo sa."* (「一等賞を取ったそうね」「そうさ」) " I hear you have gotten first prize." *"Yes, that's right."* 《⇨ soo[3]》

so⌐osaku[1] そうさく (創作) *n.* creation; original work; novel: *Kare wa atarashii sakuhiñ no* soosaku *ni torikakatta.* (彼は新しい作品の創作に取りかかった) He got to work on his new *novel*. / *Sono hanashi wa dare-ka no* soosaku *da.* (その話はだれかの創作だ) That story

is someone's *fabrication*. / soosaku-*katsudoo* (創作活動) *creative* activity.
　soosaku suru (～する) *vt.* create; originate; write: *Kono kabiñ wa kanojo ga* soosaku shita *mono desu.* (この花瓶は彼女が創作したものです) This vase is an *original one made* by her.

so⌐osaku[2] そうさく (捜索) *n.* search; manhunt: *Yukue-fumee no ko no* soosaku *ga asa kara hajimatta.* (行方不明の子の捜索が朝から始まった) The *search* for the missing child began in the morning.
　soosaku suru (～する) *vt.* make a search: *Keesatsu wa sono uchi o* soosaku shita *ga, shooko wa mitsukaranakatta.* (警察はその家を捜索したが, 証拠は見つからなかった) The police *searched* the house, but could not find the evidence.

so⌐oshiki そうしき (葬式) *n.* funeral (service): ★ Often 'o-*sooshiki*.'
　sooshiki o suru [*itonamu*] (葬式をする[営む]) perform a *funeral service* / *kojiñ no* sooshiki o dasu (故人の葬式を出す) give the deceased a *funeral* / *Ooku no hito ga sono* sooshiki *ni sañretsu shita.* (多くの人がその葬式に参列した) A lot of people attended the *funeral*. / *Sooshiki wa chikaku no tera de okonawareta.* (葬式は近くの寺で行われた) The *funeral* was held at a nearby temple.

so⌐o shitara そうしたら *conj.*
1 after that; after all: ★ Used at the beginning of a sentence. *Ichi-jikañ mo matta.* Soo shitara *yatto kare ga arawareta.* (1 時間も待った. そうしたらやっと彼が現れた) I waited a full hour. *After that* he at last showed up.
2 then; if so; in that case: *Motto majime ni beñkyoo shi*

nasai. Soo shitara *baiku o katte agemasu*. (もっともまじめに勉強しなさい. そうしたらバイクを買ってあげます) Try to study more seriously. *If you do*, I will buy you a motorcycle. (⇨ soo sureba)

so⌐o shite そうして *conj.* and then:
Soo shite *kare wa shushoo ni niñ-mee sareta*. (そうして彼は首相に任命された) *And then* he was appointed prime minister. (⇨ soshite)
— *adv.* that way; like that:
Soo shite *yaru no ga ichibañ da*. (そうしてやるのが一番だ) The best way to do it is *like that*.

so⌐oshoku そうしょく（装飾）*n.* decoration; ornament:
Kono tatemono wa sooshoku *ga sukunai*. (この建物は装飾が少ない) This building has few *decorative features*. / sooshoku-hiñ（装飾品）an *ornament*.
sooshoku suru（～する）*vt.* decorate; ornament: *shitsunai o* sooshoku suru（室内を装飾する）*decorate* an interior.

so⌐osoo[1] そうそう *int.* yes; oh; come to think of it; I remember:
Soosoo, *ano hito wa Yamada-sañ desu*. (そうそう, あの人は山田さんです) *Come to think of it*, he is Mr. Yamada.

so⌐osoo[2] そうそう（草々）*n.* Sincerely yours. ★ Polite way of ending a formal letter which begins with '*zeñryaku*.' (⇨ zeñryaku; tegami)

so⌐osu ソース *n.* sauce: ★ In Japan it often refers to a thick brown sauce.
toñkatsu ni soosu *o kakeru*（トンカツにソースをかける）pour *sauce* on a pork cutlet.

so⌐o sure⌐ba そうすれば *conj.* then; if so; in that case: ★ Used at the beginning of a sentence.
Kono kusuri o nomi nasai. Soo

sureba, *sugu yoku narimasu*. (この薬を飲みなさい. そうすれば, すぐよくなります) Take this medicine. *If you do so*, you will soon get better. / *Kono michi o massugu iki nasai*. Soo sureba, *migi ni yuubiñkyoku ga arimasu*. (この道をまっすぐ行きなさい. そうすれば, 右に郵便局があります) Go straight along this road. The post office will *then* be on your right.

so⌐o suru to そうすると *conj.* then; if so; in that case: ★ Used at the beginning of a sentence.
Kare no uchi ni deñwa o shite mita. Soo suru to, *okusañ ga deta*. (彼の家に電話をしてみた. そうすると, 奥さんが出た) I called his home. *Whereupon* his wife answered. / Soo suru to, *kono jikeñ wa naga-biku ka mo shiremaseñ ne*. (そうすると, この事件は長引くかもしれませんね) *If that is so*, it will probably take a long time before this case is solved.

so⌐otoo[1] そうとう（相当）*n.* worth:
Kare ni goseñ-eñ sootoo *no shina o okutta*. (彼に5,000円相当の品を贈った) I presented him with an article *worth* five thousand yen.
...ni sootoo suru（...に～する）*vi.* be equivalent to; correspond to:
Ichi-maruku wa Nihoñ no nañ-eñ ni sootoo *shimasu ka?*（1マルクは日本の何円に相当しますか）What *is* one mark *equivalent* to in Japanese yen? / *Sakana no era wa hito no hai* ni sootoo *shimasu*. (魚のえらは人の肺に相当します) The gills of a fish *correspond* to the lungs of a person. / '*Uma*' ni sootoo suru *Chuugokugo wa nañ desu ka?* (「馬」に相当する中国語は何ですか) What is the *equivalent* Chinese word for 'horse'?

so⌐otoo[2] そうとう（相当）*a.n.* (～ na/no, ni) considerable; quite; decent:

sootoo *na* [*no*] *kiñgaku* (相当な[の] 金額) a *considerable* sum of money / *Kare wa* sootoo *na zaisañ o soozoku shita.* (彼は相当な財産を相続した) He inherited *quite* a fortune. / *Kare no sukii no udemae wa* sootoo *na mono desu.* (彼のスキーの腕前は相当なものです) His skill at skiing is *quite* something.
— *adv.* pretty; a lot: *Kyoo wa* sootoo *atsuku nari-soo da.* (きょうは相当暑くなりそうだ) I think it is going to be *quite* hot today. / *Kare wa* sootoo *soñ o shita yoo da.* (彼は相当損をしたようだ) He seems to have lost *a lot.*

so⌐ozoo¹ そうぞう (想像) *n.* imagination; fancy; supposition; guess: *Watashi no* soozoo *wa atatta* [*hazureta*]. (私の想像は当たった[はずれた]) My *guess* was correct [wrong].

soozoo suru (〜する) *vt.* imagine; fancy; guess: *Soko no keshiki wa* soozoo *shite ita mono to chigatte ita.* (そこの景色は想像していたものと違っていた) The scenery there was different from what I *had imagined.* / *Mizu no nai seekatsu nado* soozoo *dekimaseñ.* (水のない生活など想像できません) I *can't imagine* life without water.

so⌐ozoo² そうぞう (創造) *n.* creation: soozoo-*ryoku* (創造力) *creative* power / soozoo-*sha* (創造者) a *creator.*

soozoo suru (〜する) *vt.* create: *atarashii shakai o* soozoo *suru* (新しい社会を創造する) *create* a new society.

so⌐ozooshi¹∙i そうぞうしい (騒々しい) *a.* (-ku) noisy; boisterous: soozooshii *hito* (騒々しい人) a *noisy* person / *Soto ga* soozooshii. (外が騒々しい) It is *noisy* outside. / *Soozooshikute, yoku kikoemaseñ.* (騒々しくて, よく聞こえません) I can

not hear you well because of the *noise.* / *Kono-goro sono jikeñ de yo-no-naka ga* soozooshii. (このごろ その事件で世の中が騒々しい) Society is in an *uproar* these days because of that scandal. ((⇨ sawagashii))

so⌐ra¹ そら (空) *n.* the sky; the air: *Sora ni wa kumo hitotsu nakatta.* (空には雲一つなかった) There was not a cloud in the *sky.* / *Herikoputaa wa* sora *takaku maiagatta.* (ヘリコプターは空高く舞い上がった) The helicopter soared up into the *sky.* / sora *no tabi* (空の旅) a journey by *air.*

so⌐ra² そら *int.* look; there: ★ Not used to superiors. *Sora, kore o yaru yo.* (そら, これをやるよ) *Look,* I'll give this to you. / *Sora, watashi no itta toori da.* (そら, 私の言ったとおりだ) *There,* I told you so. / *Sora, deñsha ga kuru zo.* (そら, 電車が来るぞ) *Look!* Here comes the train.

so⌐re¹ それ *n.* **1** that; it: ★ Refers to something which is located away from the speaker and close to the listener. *Sore wa dare no hoñ desu ka?* (それはだれの本ですか) Whose book is *that?* / *Anata ga te ni motte iru* sore *wa nañ desu ka?* (あなたが手に持っているそれは何ですか) What is *it* that you have in your hand?
2 that; it: ★ Refers to something mentioned by the listener. *"Jiko no koto shitte imasu ka?"* *"Sore wa itsu no koto desu ka?"* (「事故のこと知っていますか」「それはいつのことですか」) "Do you know about the accident?" "When did *it* take place?" / *"Kare wa soo itte imasu." "Sore wa jijitsu to chigaimasu."* (「彼はそう言っています」「それは事実と違います」) "He says so." "*It* contradicts the facts."

3 it: ★ Refers to something previously mentioned.
Kinoo kasa o kaimashita ga, sore *o doko-ka e okiwasurete shimaimashita.* (きのう傘を買いましたが, それをどこかへ置き忘れてしまいました) I bought an umbrella yesterday, but I have left *it* somewhere. 《⇨ are¹; dore¹; kore》

so⌐re² それ *int.* there; now; look: Sore, *isoge.* (それ, 急げ) *Look,* hurry up! / Sore, *nigero.* (それ, 逃げろ) *Now,* run away!

so⌐re da⌐ kara それだから *conj.* so; that is why: ★ Used at the beginning of a sentence.
Kanojo wa seekaku ga yoi. Sore da kara *tomodachi ga takusañ iru.* (彼女は性格が良い. それだから友だちがたくさんいる) She has a nice personality. *That is why* she has got a lot of friends.

so⌐re de それで *conj.* **1** and; then:
Sore de *anata wa doo omoimasu ka?* (それであなたはどう思いますか) *And* what is your opinion?
2 therefore:
Netsu ga ari, sore de *gakkoo o yasumimashita.* (熱があり, それで学校を休みました) I had a fever, *therefore* I was absent from school.
— *adv.* now:
Sore de *jijoo ga wakarimashita.* (それで事情がわかりました) *Now* I have understood the circumstances.

s⌐ore de⌐ mo それでも *conj.* but; still; nevertheless; however: ★ Used at the beginning of a sentence.
Muzukashii ka mo shirenai. Sore de mo *yaru shika nai.* (難しいかもしれない. それでもやるしかない) It may be difficult. *Nevertheless,* there is nothing for it but to have a go. / Sore de mo *anata wa kare no yuujiñ na no desu ka?* (それでもあなたは彼の友人なのですか) *And yet* you say

that you are his true friend?

so⌐re de⌐ wa それでは *conj.* **1** if that is the case; if so; in that case: ★ Used at the beginning of a sentence.
"Watashi mo sono eega o mitai to omotte imasu." "Sore de wa, issho ni ikimaseñ ka?" (「私もその映画を見たいと思っています」「それでは, 一緒に行きませんか」) "I want to see that movie as well." "*In that case,* shall we go together?"
2 well; then: ★ Used at the beginning of a sentence.
Sore de wa, *kyoo wa kore de owarimasu.* (それでは, きょうはこれで終わります) *Well then,* we will finish here for today.

so⌐re do⌐koro ka それどころか on the contrary: ★ Used at the beginning of a sentence.
"Ima hima desu ka?" "Sore dokoro ka, isogashii saichuu desu." (「今暇ですか」「それどころか, 忙しい最中です」) "Are you free now?" "*Quite the opposite.* I am very busy right now."

so⌐re ja⌐(a) それじゃ(あ) *int.* well (then): 《⇨ de wa²》
Sore jaa, *mata ashita.* (それじゃあ, またあした) *Well,* see you tomorrow.

so⌐re kara それから *conj.* and then; after that; afterward:
Terebi de nyuusu o mite, sore kara *furo ni haitta.* (テレビでニュースを見て, それから風呂に入った) I watched the news on TV, *and then* took a bath. / Sore kara *kare wa doo shimashita ka?* (それから彼はどうしましたか) What did he do *after that?* / *Kare wa* sore kara *ma-mo-naku nakunarimashita.* (彼はそれから間もなく亡くなりました) He died soon *afterward.*

so⌐re-(k)kiri それ(っ)きり *adv.*
1 (with a negative) since:
Sore-(k)kiri *kanojo kara tayori wa arimaseñ.* (それ(っ)きり彼女から便りは

ありません) I haven't heard from her *since then*. 《⇨ are-(k)kiri》

2 all; no more than that: *Shiryoo wa sore-(k)kiri desu ka?* (資料はそれ(っ)きりですか) Is that *all* the material you have? / *Anata no chokiñ wa sore-kkiri shika nai no desu ka?* (あなたの貯金はそれっきりしかないのですか) Are your savings *no more than* that? 《⇨ kore-(k)kiri》

soˈre maˈde それまで (それ迄) up to that time; till then: *Kare no shoobai wa sore made umaku itte ita.* (彼の商売はそれまでうまくいっていた) His business was successful *up to that time*. / *Kanojo wa sore made gaikoku e itta koto ga nakatta.* (彼女はそれまで外国へ行ったことがなかった) She had never been abroad *until then*. / *Sore made ni wa kono shigoto o kañsee sasemasu.* (それまでにはこの仕事を完成させます) I will finish this work *by then*.

sore made suru [yaru] (〜する[やる]) do that much: *Sore made suru [yaru] koto wa nai yo.* (それまでする[やる]ことはないよ) You don't have to *do that much*.

Soˈreñ ソれん (ソ連) *n.* the Soviet Union; the Union of Soviet Socialist Republics. ★ The union before the Commonwealth of Independent States was established. 《⇨ Dokuritsu Kokka Kyoodootai》

soˈre naˈra それなら *conj.* if so; in that case: ★ Used at the beginning of a sentence. *"Ogotte ageru yo." "Sore nara issho ni itte mo ii."* (「おごってあげるよ」「それならいっしょに行ってもいい」) "I'll be glad to treat you." "*If so*, I'll come along with you?"

soˈre ni それに *conj.* and; besides; moreover: ★ Often used at the beginning of a sentence. *Kanojo wa uta ga umai. Sore ni baioriñ mo hiku.* (彼女は歌がうまい. それにバイオリンも引く) She is good at singing, *and* also plays the violin. / *Koko wa yachiñ ga yasui shi, sore ni eki ni mo chikai.* (ここは家賃が安いし, それに駅にも近い) The rent for this house is low, *and moreover* it is near the station. / *Sore ni watashi ni wa mada shakkiñ ga arimasu.* (それに私にはまだ借金があります) *What is more*, I am still in debt.

soˈre toˈmo それとも *conj.* or: *Ocha ni shimasu ka, sore tomo koohii ni shimasu ka?* (お茶にしますか, それともコーヒーにしますか) Do you wish green tea, *or* would you like coffee?

soˈre wa soˈo to それはそうと incidentally; by the way: ★ Used at the beginning of a sentence when changing the subject. *Sore wa soo to, otoosañ no guai wa doo desu ka?* (それはそうと, お父さんの具合はどうですか) *By the way*, how is your father's health? 《⇨ tokoro de》

soˈreˈzore それぞれ *n., adv.* each; respectively: *Sorezore jibuñ no konomi ga arimasu.* (それぞれ自分の好みがあります) *Each* has his own taste. / *Shussekisha wa sorezore ikeñ o nobemashita.* (出席者はそれぞれ意見を述べました) The participants expressed their *respective* views.

soˈrobañ そろばん (算盤) *n.* abacus: *sorobañ de keesañ suru* (そろばんで計算する) calculate on the *abacus*.

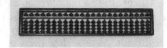

SOROBAN

soˈroeˈ·ru そろえる (揃える) *vt.* (soroe-te Ⅴ) **1** arrange properly;

put in order:

kaado o arufabetto juñ ni soroeru
(カードをアルファベット順にそろえる) *ar-
range* cards *in* alphabetical *order*.
《⇨ sorou》

2 get ready; collect:
Hitsuyoo na shorui wa zeñbu so-
roemashita. (必要な書類は全部そろえ
ました) I *got* all the necessary documents *ready*. 《⇨ sorou》

3 make even:
ki o onaji takasa ni soroeru (木を同
じ高さにそろえる) *make* the trees the
same height / *koe o soroete utau*
(声をそろえて歌う) sing *in chorus*.
《⇨ sorou》

so¹rosoro そろそろ *adv.* **1** (of
time) soon; before long; almost:
Sorosoro *hi ga kuremasu*. (そろそろ
日が暮れます) It will *soon* grow
dark. / Sorosoro *shitsuree shimasu*. (そろそろ失礼します) *Now* I
must be getting along.
《⇨ ma-mo-naku》

2 (~ to) (of movement) slowly;
little by little:
Sono kañja wa sorosoro (to) *aruite itta*. (その患者はそろそろ(と)歩いて
行った) The patient walked away
slowly.

so¹ro¹·u そろう (揃う) *vi.* (soro·i-;
sorow·a-; sorot-te C)
1 gather; meet; assemble:
Zeñiñ jikañ-doori ni sorotta. (全員
時間通りにそろった) Everyone *assembled* at the appointed time.

2 be equal; be even; be uniform:
Kono jagaimo wa ookisa ga sorotte inai. (このじゃがいもは大きさがそろ
っていない) These potatoes *are not
equal* in size. / *Kare-ra wa miñna
fukusoo ga* sorotte ita. (彼らはみんな
服装がそろっていた) Their clothes
were all *the same*. 《⇨ soroeru》

3 be [become] complete:
*Koko ni wa Sheekusupia zeñshuu
ga* sorotte imasu. (ここにはシエークス

ピア全集がそろっています) We *have* a
complete set of Shakespeare's
works here. / *Kare no daigaku ni
wa yuumee na kyooju ga* sorotte
iru. (彼の大学には有名な教授がそろって
いる) His university *has a team* of
famous professors. 《⇨ soroeru》

so¹r·u¹ そる (剃る) *vi.* (sor·i-; so-
r·a-; sot-te C) shave:
Maiasa deñki-kamisori de hige o
sorimasu. (毎朝電気かみそりでひげをそ
ります) Every morning I *shave*
with an electric razor.

so¹r·u² そる (反る) *vi.* (sor·i-; so-
r·a-; sot-te C) warp; curve;
bend:
Kono hoñ wa hyooshi ga sotte iru.
(この本は表紙が反っている) The cover
of this book *is warped*.

so¹señ そせん (祖先) *n.* ancestor;
forefathers:
soseñ o matsuru (祖先を祭る) worship one's *ancestors*. 《↔ shisoñ》
《⇨ señzo》

so¹shiki そしき (組織) *n.* **1** organization; formation; system:
kaisha no soshiki (会社の組織) the
organization of a company.

2 tissue:
soshiki *o ishoku suru* (組織を移植
する) transplant *tissue*.

soshiki suru (~する) *vt.* organize; form; compose: *roodoo-
kumiai o* soshiki suru (労働組合を
組織する) *organize* a labor union /
naikaku o soshiki suru (内閣を組織
する) *form* a cabinet.

so¹shite そして *conj.* and; and
then: ★ A very common word
for connecting words and clauses.
Yamada-sañ, Suzuki-sañ, soshite
*watashi no sañ-niñ de sore o yari-
mashita*. (山田さん, 鈴木さん, そして私
の 3 人でそれをやりました) The three
of us, Yamada, Suzuki *and* I,
did it together. / *Furo ni hairi,*
soshite *sugu ni nemashita*. (風呂に
入り, そしてすぐに寝ました) I took a

bath, *and then* went to bed right away.

so⌈shitsu そしつ (素質) *n.* the makings; quality; aptitude:
Kanojo wa sugureta pianisuto ni naru soshitsu *ga aru.* (彼女は優れたピアニストになる素質がある) She has the *aptitude* to become an excellent pianist. / *Kare ni wa seerusumañ no* soshitsu *wa nai.* (彼にはセールスマンの素質はない) He does not have the *makings* of a salesman.

so⌈shoo そしょう (訴訟) *n.* suit; lawsuit:
soshoo *o okosu* (訴訟を起こす) file a *suit* / soshoo *ni katsu* [*makeru*] (訴訟に勝つ[負ける]) win [lose] a *court case.*

so⌈sog·u そそぐ (注ぐ) *vt., vi.* (sosog·i-; sosog·a-; soso·i-de Ⓒ)
1 pour; water:
potto ni o-yu o sosogu (ポットにお湯を注ぐ) *pour* hot water into a thermos flask.
2 concentrate; devote oneself to; focus:
Kare wa jibuñ no keñkyuu ni zeñ-ryoku o sosoida. (彼は自分の研究に全力を注いだ) He *put* everything into his studies. / *Miñna no shi-señ ga kare ni* sosogareta. (みんなの視線が彼に注がれた) Everyone's gaze *was focused* on him.
3 flow:
Kono kawa wa Taiheeyoo ni so-sogimasu. (この川は太平洋に注ぎます) This river *flows* into the Pacific Ocean.

so⌈sokkashi¹·i そそっかしい *a.* (-ku) hasty; careless; thoughtless:
Kare wa sosokkashikute, *yoku shippai suru.* (彼はそそっかしくて、よく失敗する) He is *careless,* so he often makes blunders. / *Shikeñ de* sosokkashii *machigai o shite shimatta.* (試験でそそっかしい間違いをしてしまった) I made a *careless* mis-

take on the test.

so⌈tchi¹ そっち *n.* ★ Informal equivalent of '*sochira.*'
1 that; over there:
Sotchi *no o misete kudasai.* (そっちのを見せてください) Please show me *that* one. / *Hoñ wa* sotchi *no tana ni nosete kudasai.* (本はそっちの棚に載せてください) Please put the book on the shelf *over there.*
2 you:
Kono moñdai ni tsuite sotchi *no kañgae wa doo desu ka?* (この問題についてそっちの考えはどうですか) What are *your* thoughts on this matter? 《⇨ atchi; dotchi; kotchi》

so⌈tchoku そっちょく (率直) *a.n.* (~ na, ni) frank; straightforward; candid:
Anata no sotchoku *na ikeñ o kikasete kudasai.* (あなたの率直な意見を聞かせてください) Please give me your *frank* opinion. / *Kare wa omotte iru koto o* sotchoku *ni nobeta.* (彼は思っていることを率直に述べた) He *candidly* stated what he thought. / *Sotchoku ni itte, kare no gookaku wa muzukashii to omoimasu.* (率直に言って、彼の合格はむずかしいと思います) To tell you the *truth,* it will be difficult for him to pass the exam.

so⌈to そと (外) *n.* outside; outdoors:
Soto *wa ame desu.* (外は雨です) It is raining *outside.* / *Kodomo-tachi wa* soto *de asoñde imasu.* (子どもたちは外で遊んでいます) The children are playing *outdoors.* / *Kanojo wa boñyari mado no* soto *o mite ita.* (彼女はぼんやり窓の外を見ていた) She was looking *out of the window* vacantly. 《↔ uchi²; naka¹》

so⌈togawa そとがわ (外側) *n.* the outside; exterior:
hako no sotogawa (箱の外側) the *outside* of a box / *Kono doa wa* sotogawa *ni hirakimasu.* (このドアは

外側に開きます）This door opens *outward.* / *Kare no uchi no soto-gawa wa tsuta de oowarete imasu.* （彼の家の外側はつたでおおわれています）The *exterior* of his house is covered with ivy. 《↔ uchigawa》

so⌈tsugyoo そつぎょう（卒業）*n.* graduation: *Sotsugyoo-go wa nani o shimasu ka?* （卒業後は何をしますか）What are you going to do after *graduation?* / sotsugyoo-see （卒業生）a *graduate* / sotsugyoo-*shiki* （卒業式）*graduation* ceremony; *commencement* / sotsugyoo-*shoosho* （卒業証書）a diploma of *graduation.*
　sotsugyoo suru （〜する）*vt.* graduate; finish: *Musuko wa kono sañ-gatsu ni daigaku o sotsugyoo shimasu.* （息子はこの三月に大学を卒業します）Our son *graduates* from university this March. 《↔ nyuu-gaku》

so⌈tto そっと *adv.* quietly; softly; lightly; gently: *Kare wa heya kara sotto dete itta.* （彼は部屋からそっと出て行った）He went out of the room *quietly.* / *Watashi wa kodomo-tachi ni sotto hanashi-kaketa.* （私は子どもたちにそっと話しかけた）I spoke *gently* to the children. / *Kono kabiñ wa koware-yasui kara,* sotto *atsu-katte kudasai.* （この花瓶は壊れやすいから、そっと扱ってください）This vase is fragile, so please handle it *carefully.*
　sotto shite oku （〜しておく）let a person alone; leave a thing as it is: *Kare no koto wa shibaraku* sotto shite okoo. （彼のことはしばらくそっとしておこう）Let's *leave* him *alone* for the time being. / *Sono moñdai wa* sotto shite oita *hoo ga yoi.* （その問題はそっとしておいたほうがよい）We had better *leave* that problem *just as it is.*

so⌈u¹ そう（沿う）*vi.* (so·i-; so-w·a-; sot-te Ⓒ) **1** go [run] along: *Watashi-tachi wa kawa ni* sotte *aruita.* （私たちは川に沿って歩いた）We walked *along* the riverbank. / *Michi wa mizuumi ni* sotte ita. （道は湖に沿っていた）The road *ran along* the lakeside.
　2 be done according to: *Shigoto wa saisho no keekaku ni* sotte *susumerareta.* （仕事は最初の計画に沿って進められた）The work was continued *according to* the original plan.

so⌈u² そう（添う）*vt.* (so·i-; so-w·a-; sot-te Ⓒ) meet (expectations); answer; come up to: *Go-kitai ni* sou *yoo, doryoku ita-shimasu.* （ご期待に添うよう、努力いたします）I will make every effort to *meet* your expectations. / *Watashi wa oya no kiboo ni* sotte, *isha ni natta.* （私は親の希望に添って、医者になった）I became a doctor *in accordance with* my parents' wishes.

su¹ す（巣）*n.* nest; web; comb: *tori no* su （鳥の巣）a bird's *nest* / *kumo no* su （くもの巣）a spider's *web* / mitsubachi no su （蜜蜂の巣）a *honeycomb* / *Tsubame ga noki shita ni* su *o tsukutta.* （つばめが軒下に巣をつくった）Swallows built their *nests* in the eaves. / *Kumo wa mu-shi o tsukamaeru tame ni* su *o ha-ru* [kakeru]. （くもは虫を捕まえるために巣を張る[かける]）Spiders spin *webs* in order to catch insects.

su¹² す（酢）*n.* vinegar: *Kyuuri o* su *ni tsuketa.* （きゅうりを酢に漬けた）I pickled cucumbers in *vinegar.* / su-no-mono （酢の物）a *vinegared* dish.

su⌈barashi⌉·i すばらしい（素晴らしい）*a.* (-ku) wonderful; splendid; excellent: subarashii *keshiki* （すばらしい景色）

a *splendid* view / subarashii *see-seki* (すばらしい成績) *excellent* school grades / *Gochisoo wa* subarashikatta. (ごちそうはすばらしかった) The meal was *wonderful*. / *Kanojo wa* subarashiku *joozu ni Nihoñgo o hanashimasu.* (彼女はすばらしくじょうずに日本語を話します) She can speak Japanese *exceptionally* well.

su「bashiko¹·i すばしこい *a.* (-ku) nimble; quick:
subashikoi *kodomo* (すばしこい子ども) a *nimble* child / *Itazura ga mitsukaru to sono ko wa* subashikoku *nigeta.* (いたずらが見つかるとその子はすばしこく逃げた) The boy *quickly* ran off when his prank was discovered. (⇨ subayai)

su「baya¹·i すばやい (素早い) *a.* (-ku) quick; nimble:
Kare wa doosa ga subayai. (彼は動作がすばやい) He is *quick* in his movements. / *Seefu wa sono jitai ni* subayaku *taioo shita.* (政府はその事態にすばやく対応した) The government *promptly* dealt with the situation. (⇨ subashikoi)

su「be¹r·u すべる (滑る) *vi.* (suber·i-; suber·a-; subet-te C)
1 slip; slide; glide:
Watashi wa subette, *koroñde shimatta.* (私は滑って、転んでしまった) I *slipped* and fell down. / *Booto wa kawa o suberu yoo ni kudatta.* (ボートは川を滑るように下った) The boat came down the river as if *gliding*.
2 fail (an examination):
Kare wa nyuugaku-shikeñ ni subetta. (彼は入学試験に滑った) He *failed* the entrance examination.

su¹bete すべて (全て) *n., adv.* all; everything:
Subete *watashi no sekiniñ desu.* (すべて私の責任です) I am responsible for *everything*. / Subete *no hito ga sono añ ni sañsee shita.* (すべての人がその案に賛成した) *Everyone* agreed to the proposal. / *Kare wa sono jikeñ no* subete *o shitte iru.* (彼はその事件のすべてを知っている) He knows *everything* about the incident. / *Kare no iu koto* subete *ga tadashii wake de wa nai.* (彼の言うことすべてが正しいわけではない) It does not follow that *all* he says is right.

su「dare すだれ (簾) *n.* bamboo blind; reed screen. ★ Traditionally used to screen out the sun and maintain privacy during the summer.

SUDARE

su「de¹ すで (素手) *n.* empty hand; bare hand:
sude *de tatakau* (素手で戦う) fight *unarmed* / *Watashi wa sono sakana o* sude *de tsukamaeta.* (私はその魚を素手で捕まえた) I caught that fish with my *bare hands*.

su¹de ni すでに (既に) *adv.* already; previously; before; long ago:
Deñwa o shitara, kare wa sude ni *dekakete ita.* (電話をしたら、彼はすでに出かけていた) When I telephoned, he had *already* left. / *Zañneñ desu ga sono hi wa* sude ni *yotee ga arimasu.* (残念ですがその日はすでに予定があります) Unfortunately I *already* have a previous arrangement on that day. / *Sono hito ni wa* sude ni *atta koto ga arimasu.* (その人にはすでに会ったことがあります) I have met her *previously*.

su⌐e すえ（末）*n*. 1 end:
Koñgetsu sue *ni kare wa Burajiru
e ikimasu.*（今月末に彼はブラジルへ行
きます）He is leaving for Brazil at
the *end* of this month.
2 after: ★ Follows the past of a
verb.
Yoku kañgaeta sue *o-kotae itashimasu.*（よく考えた末お答えいたします）I
will give a reply *after* thinking it
over carefully.
3 youngest child:
sue *no musuko*（末の息子）the
youngest son.

su⌐ekko すえっこ（末っ子）*n*. the
youngest child.

su⌐e·ru すえる（据える）*vt*. (sue-te
Ⓥ) 1 set; place; fix:
Tokonoma ni boñsai o sueta.（床の
間に盆栽を据えた）I *placed* a bonsai
in the *alcove*. / *Hoñbako o heya
no sumi ni* sueta.（本箱を部屋の隅に
据えた）I *placed* a bookcase in a
corner of the room.
2 appoint:
*Shachoo wa jibuñ no musuko o
kookeesha ni* sueta.（社長は自分の
息子を後継者に据えた）The presi-
dent *appointed* his son as his successor.

su⌐gasugashi¹·i すがすがしい（清
清しい）*a*. (-ku) fresh; refreshing;
bracing:
sugasugashii *kaze*（すがすがしい風）a
refreshing breeze / *Yoku nemureta no de kesa wa* sugasugashii.
（よく眠れたのでけさはすがすがしい）I
slept well, so I feel *refreshed* this
morning.

su⌐gata すがた（姿）*n*. figure;
shape:
Watashi wa mae o iku otoko no
sugata *ni mioboe ga atta.*（私は前を
行く男の姿に見覚えがあった）I recog-
nized the *figure* of the man walking ahead of me. / *Kare wa* misuborashii sugata *o shite ita.*（彼はみ
すぼらしい姿をしていた）He *looked*

shabby. / *Fuji-sañ wa* sugata *ga
utsukushii.*（富士山は姿が美しい）Mt.
Fuji is beautiful in *shape.*

sugata o arawasu（〜を現す）
appear; come into view: *Kare
wa sono kai ni* sugata o arawashita.（彼はその会に姿を現した）He
appeared at the party.

sugata o kesu（〜を消す）disap-
pear: *Kanojo wa totsuzeñ* sugata
o keshita.（彼女は突然姿を消した）
She suddenly *disappeared.*

su⌐gi すぎ（杉）*n*. Japanese cedar.

-sugi すぎ（過ぎ）*suf*. 1 (of times
and dates) past; after:
Ima hachi-ji go-fuñ-sugi *desu.*（今
8時5分過ぎです）It is now five
past eight. / *Go-ji*-sugi *ni moo
ichi-do deñwa shimasu.*（5時過ぎに
もう一度電話します）*After* five
o'clock I will phone once more. /
Tooka-sugi *ni reñraku itashimasu.*
（10日過ぎに連絡いたします）I will get
in touch with you *after* the tenth.
《↔ -mae¹》
2 (of age) over; past:
Chichi wa nanajuu-sugi *desu.*（父は
70過ぎです）My father *is over* seventy. 《↔ -mae》
3 too much: ★ Added to the
continuative base of a verb.
Tabe-sugi *wa keñkoo ni yoku arimaseñ.*（食べ過ぎは健康に良くありませ
ん）Eating *too much* is not good
for the health. 《⇒ -sugiru》

su⌐gi¹·ru すぎる（過ぎる）*vi*. (sugite Ⓥ) 1 (of time) pass; be over:
Are kara ni-neñ (ga) sugimashita.
（あれから2年(が)過ぎました）Since
then two years *have passed.* /
Natsu ga sugi, *aki ni natta.*（夏が過
ぎ、秋になった）Summer *is over* and
autumn has come. / *Toki ga doñdoñ* sugite iku.（時がどんどん過ぎて行
く）Time *flies.*
2 pass through:
Ressha wa moo Hiroshima o sugimashita.（列車はもう広島を過ぎました）

The train *has* already *passed through* Hiroshima.
3 be past:
Kare wa go-juu o sugite iru *to omoimasu.*(彼は50を過ぎていると思います) I think he *is past* fifty.

-sugi·ru -すぎ(過ぎる)(-sugi-te V) over-; too much: ★ Occurs as the second element of compound verbs. Added to the continutive base of a verb or the stem of an adjective.
hataraki-sugiru (働きすぎる) *over*work / *tabe*-sugiru (食べすぎる) *over*-eat / *Kono hako wa* omosugite, *hakobenai.*(この箱は重すぎて，運べない) This box is *too heavy* to carry.

su⌈go⌉·i すごい(凄い) *a.* (-ku)
1 (*informal*) great; superb; fantastic:
sugoi *bijin* (すごい美人) a *great* beauty / *Shinjuku wa* sugoi *hito datta.*(新宿はすごい人だった) There was a *large* crowd in Shinjuku. / Sugoi *tatemono desu ne.*(すごい建物ですね) This is a *fantastic* building, isn't it?
2 drastic; dreadful; horrible:
kabu no sugoi *booraku* (株のすごい暴落) a *drastic* slump in stocks / sugoi *jishin* (すごい地震) a *frightful* earthquake.
3 (-ku) awfully; terribly; extremely:
Kyoo wa sugoku *samui.*(きょうはすごく寒い) It is *awfully* cold today. / *Kono hon wa* sugoku *omoshiroi.*(この本はすごくおもしろい) This book is *terribly* interesting.

su⌈goroku⌉ すごろく(双六) *n.* a type of a board game.

> **CULTURE**
> Players move their marker the number of places indicated by dice, following travelogue pictures printed on a board or on paper. The person who first reaches the end of the journey wins. Usually played during the New Year holiday.

SUGOROKU

su⌈go⌉s·u すごす(過ごす) *vt.* (sugosh·i-; sugos·a-; sugosh·i-te C) pass; spend; idle away:
Watashi-tachi wa tento de ichi-ya o sugoshita.(私たちはテントで一夜を過ごした) We *spent* the night in a tent. / *Natsu-yasumi wa dono yoo ni* sugoshimasu *ka?* (夏休みはどのように過ごしますか) How are you going to *spend* your summer vacation? / *Ikaga* o-sugoshi *desu ka?* (いかがお過ごしですか) How *are* you *getting along?*

su⌈gosugo すごすご *adv.* (～ to) dejectedly; with a heavy heart:
Shakkin o kotowararete kare wa sugosugo *(to) hikisagatta.*(借金を断られて彼はすごすご(と)引き下がった) Having been refused a loan, he *dejectedly* withdrew.

su⌈gu すぐ(直ぐ) *adv.* **1** (of time) at once; right away; soon:
Sugu *hajimeyoo.*(すぐ始めよう) Let's start *at once.* / Sugu *ikimasu.*(すぐ行きます) I am coming *in a minute.* / *Kodomo wa gakkoo kara kaeru to* sugu *asobi ni itta.*(子どもは学校から帰るとすぐ遊びに行った) The child went out to play *as soon as* he returned from school. / *Moo* sugu *shoogatsu desu.*(もうすぐ正月です) The New Year will *soon* be here.
2 (of distance) just; right:
Eki wa sugu *soko desu.*(駅はすぐそ

こです) The station is *just* over there. / *Kagi wa* sugu *me no mae ni atta.* (鍵はすぐ目の前にあった) The key was *right* in front of me.
3 easily; readily:
Kare wa sugu *okoru.* (彼はすぐ怒る) He gets angry *easily.* / Sugu *añji ni kakaru hito ga iru.* (すぐ暗示にかかる人がいる) There are some people who are *readily* influenced by suggestions.

su「gure」・ru すぐれる (優れる) *vi.*
(sugure-te Ⅴ) excel; surpass:
Kanojo wa piano no eñsoo ni sugurete iru. (彼女はピアノの演奏に優れている) She *excels* in playing the piano. / *Hiñshitsu de wa kono hoo ga sore yori* sugurete imasu. (品質ではこのほうがそれより優れています) This *is much better* than that in quality.

su「ibokuga すいぼくが (水墨画) *n.*
a drawing in Indian ink.
《⇨ sumie (photo)》

su「ibuñ すいぶん (水分) *n.* water; moisture; juice:
Atsui toki wa suibuñ *o toranakereba ikemaseñ.* (暑いときは水分をとらなければいけません) You have to drink *liquids* when it is hot. / *Momo yori nashi no hoo ga* suibuñ *ga ooi.* (桃よりなしの方が水分が多い) Pears have more *juice* than peaches. / suibuñ *no ooi kudamono* (水分の多い果物) *juicy* fruit.

su「ichoku すいちょく (垂直) *a.n.*
(〜 na, ni) perpendicular; vertical:
suichoku *no zeppeki* (垂直の絶壁) a *perpendicular* cliff / suichoku *na señ o hiku* (垂直な線を引く) draw a *vertical* line / *hashira o* suichoku *ni tateru* (柱を垂直に立てる) fix a pole *vertically*. 《⇨ suihee》

su「ichuu すいちゅう (水中) *n.* underwater; in the water:
suichuu *ni tobikomu* (水中に飛び込む) jump *into the water* / *Kare wa*

suichuu *o mogutte oyoida.* (彼は水中をもぐって泳いだ) He swam *underwater.* / suichuu-*megane* (水中眼鏡) *swimming* goggles / suichuu-*kamera* (水中カメラ) an *underwater* camera.

su「ideñ すいでん (水田) *n.* paddy; paddy field:
suideñ *o tagayasu* (水田を耕す) plow a *paddy field.* 《⇨ ta¹; tañbo》

SUIDEÑ

su「idoo すいどう (水道) *n.* **1** water supply [service]:
suidoo o dasu [tomeru] (水道を出す [止める]) *turn on* [*off*] *the faucet* / *Kono* suidoo no mizu *wa nomemasu ka?* (この水道の水は飲めますか) Is this *tap water* good to drink? / *Suidoo ga nai kara, ido kara mizu o kuñde imasu.* (水道がないから, 井戸から水をくんでいます) Since we have no *piped water*, we draw water from the well.
2 channel:
Buñgo-suidoo (豊後水道) the Bungo *Channel*.

su「idookañ すいどうかん (水道管) *n.* water pipe; water main.

su「iee すいえい (水泳) *n.* swimming; bathing:
Kare wa suiee *ga tokui desu.* (彼は水泳が得意です) He is good at *swimming.* / *Watashi wa mainichi puuru e* suiee *ni ikimasu.* (私は毎日プールへ水泳に行きます) I go *swimming* in the pool every day. / suiee-señshu (水泳選手) a *swimmer in a race*.

suiee (o) **suru** (～(を)する) *vi.*
swim: *Kodomo no koro kono kawa de yoku* suiee *o shimashita.*
(子どものころこの川でよく水泳をしました)
I used to *swim* in this river when
I was a child.

su⌐igara すいがら(吸い殻) *n.* cigarette butt [end]:
Haizara wa suigara *de ippai datta.*
(灰皿は吸い殻でいっぱいだった) The
ashtray was full of *butts*.

su⌐igiñ すいぎん(水銀) *n.* mercury:
suigiñ-*oñdokee* (水銀温度計) a *mercury* thermometer.

su⌐ihee すいへい(水平) *a.n.*
(～ na, ni) horizontal; level:
gakubuchi o suihee ni suru (額縁を
水平にする) *straighten* a picture
frame / *Kono yuka wa* suihee *de
nai.* (この床は水平でない) This floor
is not *level.* ((⇨ suichoku))

su⌐iheeseñ すいへいせん(水平線)
n. horizon: ★ The line where
the sky and the sea meet.
Fune ga suiheeseñ *no ue ni arawareta.* (船が水平線の上に現れた) A
ship appeared on the *horizon.*
((⇨ chiheeseñ (table)))

su⌐iji すいじ(炊事) *n.* cooking;
kitchen work:
Watashi wa kanojo no suiji *o tetsudatta.* (私は彼女の炊事を手伝った) I
helped her with the *cooking.* /
suiji-*ba* (炊事場) a *kitchen* / suiji-
doogu (炊事道具) *kitchen* utensils.
suiji (o) **suru** (～する) *vi.* cook:
Watashi wa ima jibuñ de suiji (o)
shite imasu. (私は今自分で炊事(を)し
ています) I *cook* for myself these
days. ((⇨ ryoori))

su⌐ijuñ すいじゅん(水準) *n.* level;
standard:
*Sono kuni no seekatsu-*suijuñ *wa
takai.* (その国の生活水準は高い) The
standard of living in that country is high. / *Hiñshitsu wa mada*
suijuñ *ni tasshite inai.* (品質はまだ水
準に達していない) The quality is not

yet up to *standard.* / *Sono otoko-
no-ko no chinoo wa nami no* suijuñ
ijoo [ika] datta. (その男の子の知能は
並の水準以上[以下]だった) The
boy's intelligence was above [below] the *average.*

su⌐ika すいか(西瓜) *n.* watermelon. ★ Japanese watermelons are
rounder than Western ones.

SUIKA

su⌐imeñ すいめん(水面) *n.* the
water surface:
Suimeñ *ni nani-ka ga uite iru.* (水
面に何かが浮いている) Something is
floating *on the water.* / *Ooki-na
koi ga* suimeñ *ni ukabi-agatta.* (大
きなこいが水面に浮かび上がった) A
large carp came up to the *surface
of the water.*

su⌐imiñ すいみん(睡眠) *n.* sleep:
suimiñ *o toru* (睡眠をとる) have a
sleep / suimiñ *o samatageru* (睡眠
を妨げる) disturb someone's *sleep* /
Kare wa suimiñ-*busoku de nemu-
soo na kao o shite iru.* (彼は睡眠不
足で眠そうな顔をしている) He looks
drowsy from lack of *sleep.* / sui-
miñ-*jikañ* (睡眠時間) hours of
sleep / suimiñ-*yaku* (睡眠薬) a
sleeping drug [pill].
suimiñ suru (～する) *vi.* sleep:
Suimiñ *shite iru toki mo noo wa*

hataraite imasu.（睡眠しているときも脳は働いています）The brain is active even when you *are asleep.*

su⌐ioñ すいおん（水温）*n.* water temperature. 《⇨ oñdo (table)》

su⌐iri すいり（推理）*n.* reasoning; inference; guess: *Anata no* suiri *wa tadashii [machigatte iru].*（あなたの推理は正しい[間違っている]）Your *reasoning* is correct [wrong]. / suiri-shoosetsu（推理小説）a *mystery*; a *detective story.*
suiri suru (〜する) *vt.* reason; infer; deduce: *Kono jijitsu kara anata wa doo* suiri shimasu *ka?*（この事実からあなたはどう推理しますか）What do you *deduce* from this fact? / *Yoku soko made* suiri shimashita *ne.*（よくそこまで推理しましたね）You did well to *reason* things *out* to that extent.

su⌐iryoku すいりょく（水力）*n.* waterpower: suiryoku *hatsudeñsho*（水力発電所）a *hydroelectric power* plant. 《↔ karyoku》

su⌐iryoo すいりょう（推量）*n.* guess; surmise; inference: Suiryoo *ga atatta [hazureta].*（推量が当たった[外れた]）My *guess* was right [wrong].
suiryoo suru (〜する) *vt.* guess; surmise; conjecture: *Koe no chooshi kara sono hito no kimochi o* suiryoo suru *koto ga kanoo desu.*（声の調子からその人の気持ちを推量することが可能です）It is possible to *guess* a person's feelings from their tone of voice. 《⇨ suisoku》

suisa⌐ñbutsu すいさんぶつ（水産物）*n.* marine products.

Su⌐isa⌐ñ-choo すいさんちょう（水産庁）*n.* Fisheries Agency: Suisañ-choo *chookañ*（水産庁長官）the Director General of the *Fisheries Agency.* 《⇨ choo⁴ (table)》

su⌐iseñ¹ すいせん（推薦）*n.* recom-

mendation: *Kare wa kyooju no* suiseñ *de kono kaisha ni haitta.*（彼は教授の推薦でこの会社に入った）He entered this company on the professor's *recommendation.* / suiseñ-joo（推薦状）a letter of *recommendation* / suiseñ-*nyuugaku*（推薦入学）entering college by *recommendation.*
suiseñ suru (〜する) *vt.* recommend: *Señsee ga kono jisho o* suiseñ shite kuremashita.（先生がこの辞書を推薦してくれました）Our teacher *recommended* this dictionary to us.

su⌐iseñ² すいせん（水仙）*n.* narcissus; daffodil.

su⌐iseñ-be⌐ñjo すいせんべんじょ（水洗便所）*n.* flush toilet. 《⇨ beñjo》

su⌐ishiñ すいしん（推進）*n.* propulsion; drive: suishiñ-*ryoku*（推進力）*driving force.*
suishiñ suru (〜する) *vt.* propel; push on with: *Kono keekaku wa nañ to shite mo* suishiñ shinakereba naranai.（この計画はなんとしても推進しなければならない）We *have to push ahead* with this plan at any cost.

su⌐ishitsu すいしつ（水質）*n.* quality of water: suishitsu-*keñsa*（水質検査）examination of *water*; *water* analysis.

su⌐ishoo すいしょう（水晶）*n.* crystal.

su⌐iso すいそ（水素）*n.* hydrogen.

su⌐isoku すいそく（推測）*n.* guess; conjecture: *Anata no* suisoku *wa atarimashita [hazuremashita].*（あなたの推測は当たりました[外れました]）Your *guess* was right [wrong]. / *Sono geñiñ wa daitai* suisoku ga tsukimasu.（その原因はだいたい推測がつきます）I *can* pretty much *guess* what the cause was. / *Sore wa tañ-naru* suisoku ni suginai.（それは単なる推測に過ぎない）

That is nothing more than mere *supposition*.

suisoku suru (～する) *vt.* guess; conjecture: *Tatta kore dake no shiryoo kara* suisoku suru *koto wa kikeñ desu.* (たったこれだけの資料から推測することは危険です) It is risky to *make inferences* from only these data.

su⌐isui すいすい *adv.* (～ to) lightly; easily: *Ike de koi ga* suisui (to) *oyoide iru.* (池でこいがすいすい(と)泳いでいる) The carp *are gliding* through the pond. / *Kare wa* suisui (to) *shusse shita.* (彼はすいすい(と)出世した) He *smoothly* rose through the ranks.

su⌐itchi スイッチ *n.* switch: *hiitaa no* suitch *o ireru [kiru]* (ヒーターのスイッチを入れる[切る]) *switch on [off]* a heater.

su⌐ito⌐r·u すいとる (吸い取る) *vt.* (-tor·i-; -tor·a-; -tot-te Ⓒ) suck up; soak up; absorb: *Shiñbuñshi wa mizu o yoku* suitorimasu. (新聞紙は水をよく吸い取ります) Newspaper *absorbs* water well.

su⌐iyo⌐o(bi) すいよう(び)(水曜(日)) *n.* Wednesday: *Kare wa* suiyoobi *no gogo ni kimasu.* (彼は水曜日の午後に来ます) He comes on *Wednesday* afternoons. 《⇨ yoobi (table)》

su⌐ji すじ (筋) *n.* **1** line; stripe: suji *o hiku* (筋を引く) draw a *line* / *Kare wa akai* suji *no haitta tii-shatsu o kite ita.* (彼は赤い筋の入ったTシャツを着ていた) He wore a T-shirt with red *stripes*.
2 muscle; tendon; sinew: *Ashi no* suji *o itamete shimatta.* (足の筋を痛めてしまった) I have hurt a *tendon* in my leg. / *Kubi no* suji *ga itai.* (首の筋が痛い) I *have a crick* in my neck.
3 string: *mame no* suji *o toru* (豆の筋を取る) remove the *strings* from beans.
4 story; plot: *Hanashi no* suji *wa heeboñ datta.* (話の筋は平凡だった) The *story* was commonplace.
5 sense; logic: *Kimi no iu koto wa* suji *ga tooranai.* (君の言うことは筋が通らない) There is no *sense* in what you say.

su⌐ka⌐afu スカーフ *n.* head scarf: *Akai* sukaafu *o shite iru no ga Suzuki-sañ desu.* (赤いスカーフをしているのが鈴木さんです) The person wearing the red *scarf* is Mrs. Suzuki.

su⌐ka⌐ato スカート *n.* skirt: sukaato *o haku* [nugu] (スカートをはく[脱ぐ]) put on [take off] one's *skirt*.

su⌐ke⌐eru スケール *n.* scale; caliber: sukeeru *no ooki-na jigyoo* (スケールの大きな事業) a large-*scale* enterprise / sukeeru *no ookii* [chiisai] *hito* (スケールの大きい[小さい]人) a man of high [low] *caliber*.

su⌐keeto スケート *n.* ice skating: ★ From English skate, but it refers to the action of skating, not the boots. *Watashi wa* sukeeto *ga suki desu.* (私はスケートが好きです) I like *ice skating*. / *Kinoo wa mizuumi e* sukeeto *ni ikimashita.* (きのうは湖へスケートに行きました) I went *skating* on the lake yesterday. / *Hisashiburi ni* sukeeto *o shimashita.* (久しぶりにスケートをしました) I enjoyed *skating* for the first time in quite a while. / sukeeto-*gutsu* (スケート靴) a pair of *skates* / sukeeto-*riñku* (スケートリンク) a *skating* rink.

su⌐ke⌐juuru スケジュール *n.* schedule; program: *Shigoto no* sukejuuru *wa tatemashita ka?* (仕事のスケジュールは立てましたか) Have you worked out your work *schedule*? / *Raishuu wa* sukejuuru *ga tsumatte imasu.* (来週はスケジュールが詰まっています) I have a tight *schedule* next week. / *Subete* sukejuuru-doori *umaku ikimashita.* (すべてスケジュールどおりうまくいきました) Everything went smoothly *as scheduled.* / sukejuuru-*hyoo* (スケジュール表) a table of one's *schedule.*

su⌐ki⌐¹ すき(好き) *a.n.* (~ na, ni) like; be fond of; love: suki *na supootsu* (好きなスポーツ) one's *favorite* sport / suki *na haiyuu* (好きな俳優) an actor one *likes* / *Tanaka-sañ wa e o kaku no ga* suki desu. (田中さんは絵をかくのが好きです) Ms. Tanaka *likes* to paint. / *Watashi wa atarashii señsee ga dañdañ* suki ni natta. (私は新しい先生がだんだん好きになった) I gradually *took to* the new teacher. / *Watashi ni wa* suki *na hito ga imasu.* (私には好きな人がいます) I have someone I *love.* / *Itsu de mo* suki *na toki ni kite kudasai.* (いつでも好きなときに来てください) Please come whenever you *like.* 《⇨ daisuki》

suki na yoo ni (~ように) as one likes: *Oya no iu koto o kikanai no nara* suki na yoo ni *shi nasai.* (親の言うことを聞かないのなら好きなようにしなさい) If you are not going to listen to your parents, do *as you like.* / *Anata no* suki na yoo ni *sekkee shite kudasai.* (あなたの好きなように設計してください) Please design it *as you wish.* 《↔ kirai》

su⌐ki⌐² すき(隙) *n.* **1** unguarded moment; chance: suki o miseru (すきを見せる) *be off one's guard* / suki *o ukagau* (すきをうかがう) watch for a *chance* / *Dare mo inai* suki ni *tsumamigui o shita.* (だれもいないすきにつまみ食いをした) I took some snacks *while no one was around.*

2 fault; flaw: *Kare no toobeñ ni wa* suki *ga nakatta.* (彼の答弁にはすきがなかった)

There were no *flaws* in his answer.

3 space; room: *Suutsukeesu wa ippai de sono hoñ o ireru* suki *wa arimaseñ.* (スーツケースはいっぱいでその本を入れるすきはありません) The suitcase is full and there is no *room* for the book.

su⌐ki⌐³ すき(鋤) *n.* plow; spade.

su⌐ki⌐i スキー *n.* **1** ski: sukii *o haku* [*nugu*] (スキーをはく[脱ぐ]) put on [take off] *skis.*

2 skiing: sukii *ni iku* (スキーに行く) go *skiing* / *Fuyu-yasumi wa mainichi* sukii *o shimashita.* (冬休みは毎日スキーをしました) During the winter vacation I *skied* every day. / sukii-*joo* (スキー場) a *skiing* ground.

su⌐kima すきま(隙間) *n.* **1** opening; gap; space: *Kabe no* sukima *kara naka o nozoita.* (壁のすき間から中をのぞいた) I peeped inside through an *opening* in the wall / sukima-kaze (すき間風) a *draft.*

2 chink; crack: *mado-garasu no* sukima (窓ガラスのすき間) a *crack* between windowpanes.

su⌐kito⌐or·u すきとおる(透き通る) *vi.* (-toor·i-; -toor·a-; -toot-te Ⓒ) be transparent; be seen through: sukitootta *garasu* (透き通ったガラス) *transparent* glass / *Ogawa no mizu ga* sukitoote iru. (小川の水が透き通っている) The water in the stream *is clear.*

su⌐kiyaki すきやき(すき焼き) *n.* sukiyaki. ★ A dish of sliced meat and vegetables cooked in a shallow iron pan. 《⇨ photo (next page)》

su⌐ki⌐zuki すきずき(好き好き) *n.* a matter of taste: *Hito ni wa sorezore* sukizuki *ga arimasu.* (人にはそれぞれ好き好きがあり

SUKIYAKI

ます) People have their *different tastes*.

su⌐kka⌐ri すっかり *adv.* completely; perfectly:
Sono koto o sukkari *wasurete ita.* (そのことをすっかり忘れていた) I had *completely* forgotten about it. / *Kare wa moo* sukkari *yoku narimashita.* (彼はもうすっかりよくなりました) He has already recovered *completely*.

su⌐kki⌐ri すっきり *adv.* (~ to; ~ suru) (the state of being refreshed, neat, clear-cut or simple):
Furo ni haittara, kibuñ ga sukkiri *shita.* (ふろに入ったら、気分がすっきりした) I felt *refreshed* after taking a bath. / *Doomo kare no setsumee wa* sukkiri *shinai teñ ga aru.* (どうも彼の説明はすっきりしない点がある) There is something *unclear* about his explanation.

su⌐ko⌐shi すこし (少し) *n., adv.*
1 a few [little]; some:
Kaijoo ni wa hito ga sukoshi *shika inakatta.* (会場には人が少ししかなかった) There were only *a few* people in the hall. / *O-cha o moo* sukoshi *kudasai.* (お茶をもう少し下さい) Please give me a *little* more tea. / *Sukoshi de mo o-yaku ni tateba saiwai desu.* (少しでもお役に立てば幸いです) I'll be delighted if I can help you even *a little*.
《↔ takusañ》
2 a bit; somewhat:

Watashi wa Nihoñgo ga sukoshi *wakarimasu.* (私は日本語が少しわかります) I understand Japanese *a bit*. / *Kono michi o* sukoshi *iku to hashi ni demasu.* (この道を少し行くと橋に出ます) Go along this road *a bit* and you will come to a bridge. / *Kare wa* sukoshi *wa yoku narimashita ka?* (彼は少しは良くなりましたか) Has he got *somewhat* better?
3 a short time:
Kono heñ de sukoshi *yasumimashoo.* (この辺で少し休みましょう) Let's take *a short* rest somewhere around here. / *Sukoshi shitara, ikimasu.* (少ししたら、行きます) I'll come in *a little while*.

su⌐ko⌐shi mo すこしも (少しも) *adv.* (with a negative) (not) at all; (not) in the least:
Kare ni wa sukoshi mo *doojoo no yochi wa nai.* (彼には少しも同情の余地はない) He deserves no sympathy *at all*. / *Sono eega wa* sukoshi mo *omoshiroku nakatta.* (その映画は少しもおもしろくなかった) The film was *not in the least* interesting.

su⌐koshi-zu⌐tsu すこしずつ (少しずつ) *adv.* little by little; gradually:
Kanojo no byooki wa sukoshi-zutsu *yoku natte imasu.* (彼女の病気は少しずつ良くなっています) She is *gradually* getting over her illness. / *Sukoshi-zutsu tabe nasai yo.* (少しずつ食べなさいよ) Eat it *little by little*.

su⌐k·u¹ すく (空く) *vi.* (suk·i-; suk·a-; su·i-te Ⓒ) **1** become less crowded:
Deñsha wa suite ita. (電車はすいていた) The train *was* rather *empty*.
2 (of a stomach) become empty:
Onaka ga sukimashita. (おなかがすきました) I feel *hungry*.

su⌐k·u² すく (好く) *vt.* (suk·i-; suk·a-; su·i-te Ⓒ) like; love:
Kanojo no hanashikata wa doomo

sukanai. (彼女の話し方はどうも好かな
い) I just *don't like* the way she
talks. / *Kare wa miñna ni* suka-
rete iru. (彼はみんなに好かれている) He
is liked by everybody.

su̱「kui すくい (救い) *n.* **1** help; rescue:
Kanojo wa sukui *o motomete sakeñda*. (彼女は救いを求めて叫んだ)
She cried out for *help*. / *Dare mo
oborete iru hito ni* sukui *no te o
nobeyoo to shinakatta*. (だれも溺れて
いる人に救いの手を伸べようとしなかった)
No one made any attempt to *save*
the drowning man. 《⇨ sukuu¹》
2 relief; saving grace:
*Sono jiko de shisha ga denakatta
no ga* sukui *datta*. (その事故で死者が
でなかったのが救いだった) It was a
great *relief* that there were no
fatalities in the accident. / *Kare
ga hañsee shita no ga* sukui *datta*.
(彼が反省したのが救いだった) The fact
that he expressed his regret was
a *saving grace*.

su̱「kuna¹·i すくない (少ない) *a.*
(-ku) few; little; small; scarce;
short:
wakamono no sukunai *mura* (若者
の少ない村) a village with *few*
young people / *Koñgetsu wa
ame ga* sukunakatta. (今月は雨が少
なかった) We have had *little* rain
this month. / *Kono machi wa jiñkoo ga* sukunai. (この町は人口が少な
い) This town has a *small* population. / *Sono jikeñ ni kañshiñ o
motte iru hito wa* sukunaku nai. (そ
の事件に関心を持っている人は少なくな
い) Not a *few* people are interested in that case. 《↔ ooi》

su̱「ku¹naku-tomo すくなくとも
(少なくとも) *adv.* at least; not less
than:
Kono kimono wa sukunaku-tomo
sañjuumañ-eñ wa shimasu. (この着
物は少なくとも 30 万円はします) This
kimono costs *at least* 300,000 yen.

/ Sukunaku-tomo *oree no tegami
gurai wa kaki nasai*. (少なくともお礼
の手紙ぐらいは書きなさい) *At least*
you should write a letter of
thanks.

su̱「kuri¹iñ スクリーン *n.* screen:
Watashi wa sukuriiñ *ni suraido o
utsushita*. (私はスクリーンにスライドを
映した) I projected slides onto the
screen.

su̱「ku·u¹ すくう (救う) *vt.* (suku·i-;
sukuw·a-; sukut-te Ⓒ) save; rescue; help:
Isha wa watashi no inochi o sukutte kureta. (医者は私の命を救ってく
れた) The doctor *saved* my life. /
Kare wa watashi o kukyoo kara
sukutte kureta. (彼は私を苦境から救
ってくれた) He *helped* me out of
difficulty. 《⇨ sukui》

su̱「ku·u² すくう (掬う) *vt.* (suku·i-;
sukuw·a-; sukut-te Ⓒ) scoop
(up); dip (up); ladle:
sakana o ami de sukuu (魚を網です
くう) *catch* fish in a net / *Mizu o te
de* sukutte noñda. (水を手ですくって
飲んだ) I *scooped up* some water in
my hands and drank it.

su̱「ma¹ato スマート *a.n.* (~ na,
ni) nice-looking; stylish; slender: ★ From English 'smart.'
sumaato *na karada(-tsuki)* (スマート
な体(つき)) a *slim* figure / sumaato
na yarikata (スマートなやり方) a *clever* way of doing something / *Koi
iro no fuku o kiru to* sumaato *ni
miemasu yo*. (濃い色の服を着るとスマ
ートに見えますよ) You would look
stylish in dark colored clothes. /
Kanojo wa itsu-mo fukusoo ga
sumaato *da*. (彼女はいつも服装がスマ
ートだ) Her clothes are always *chic*.
《⇨ iki²》

su̱¹mai すまい (住まい) *n.* **1** address:
O-sumai wa dochira desu ka? (お
住まいはどちらですか) May I ask
where you live?

2 home; house; residence:
Koko wa kari no sumai *desu.* (ここは仮の住まいです) This is my temporary *residence*.

su「ma」na·i すまない (済まない) *a.* (-ku) sorry; inexcusable:
Kimi ni wa hoñtoo ni sumanai *koto o shimashita.* (君には本当にすまないことをしました) I really did something *unpardonable* to you. / *Go-meewaku o kakete,* sumanaku *omotte imasu.* (ご迷惑をかけて、すまなく思っています) I feel *sorry* for causing you so much trouble.
《⇨ sumimaseñ》

su「mase」·ru すませる (済ませる) *vt.* (sumase-te ▽) **1** finish; get through:
Moo chuushoku wa sumasemashita ka? (もう昼食は済ませましたか) *Have* you *finished* lunch yet? / *Kono shigoto wa asu made ni* sumasemasu. (この仕事はあすまでに済ませます) I will *get through with* this work by tomorrow.
《⇨ sumasu¹》

2 get along; manage:
Koñgetsu wa kore dake no kozukai de sumase *nasai.* (今月はこれだけのこづかいで済ませなさい) This month please *manage* on just this amount of spending money.

su「ma」s·u¹ すます (済ます) *vt.* (sumash·i-; sumas·a-; sumash·i-te ©) **1** finish; settle:
Kare wa shiharai o sumasanai *de dete ikoo to shita.* (彼は支払いを済まさないで出て行こうとした) He tried to leave *without paying* the bill.
《⇨ sumaseru》

2 manage (with); make do:
Nihoñgo no beñkyoo ni jisho nashi de sumasu *koto wa dekimaseñ.* (日本語の勉強に辞書なしで済ますことはできません) In studying Japanese, one cannot *do* without a dictionary.

su「ma」s·u² すます (澄ます) *vi.* (su-mash·i-; sumas·a-; sumash·i-te ©) put on airs:
Kanojo wa sumashite ita. (彼女は澄ましていた) She *was prim and proper.* / *Kare wa* sumashita kao o shite, *hiniku o itta.* (彼は澄ました顔をして、皮肉を言った) He made an ironic remark *with a straight face.*

su「mi」¹ すみ (隅) *n.* corner:
Terebi o heya no sumi *ni oita.* (テレビを部屋の隅に置いた) I placed the TV set in a *corner* of the room.

sumi kara sumi made (〜から〜まで) everywhere: Sumi kara sumi made *sagashi nasai.* (隅から隅まで捜しなさい) Search *every nook and cranny.*

su「mi」² すみ (炭) *n.* charcoal:
sumi *o yaku* (炭を焼く) make *charcoal.*

su「mi」³ すみ (墨) *n.* India [Chinese] ink; ink stick:
suzuri de sumi *o suru* (すずりで墨をする) rub an *ink stick* on an inkstone / sumi *de kaku* (墨で書く) write in *India ink.* 《⇨ suzuri》

su「mi」e すみえ (墨絵) *n.* India-ink painting. 《⇨ suibokuga》

SUMIE

su「mimase」ñ すみません **1** excuse [pardon] me; I'm sorry: Sumimaseñ *ga, moo ichi-do itte kudasai.* (すみませんが、もう一度言ってください) *Excuse me,* but will you please repeat that? / *Go-meewaku*

o o-kakeshite, sumimaseñ. (ご迷惑
をおかけして, すみません) *I am sorry*
for causing you a lot of trouble.
2 thank you:
Tetsudatte itadaite, sumimaseñ.
(手伝っていただいて, すみません) *Thank
you* very much for helping me.
《⇨ arigatoo》

su⌐mire すみれ (菫) *n.* violet
(flower).

su⌐moo すもう (相撲) *n.* sumo
wrestling:

CULTURE

Traditional Japanese wrestling.
The wrestler loses when he is
forced out of the ring or when
he touches the ground with
any part of his body except the
soles of his feet.

Kare to sumoo o totta. (彼と相撲を
とった) I *wrestled* with him.

SUMOO BOUT

su⌐m·u¹ すむ (住む) *vi.* (sum·i-;
sum·a-; suñ-de ⒸⒷ) live; reside:
★ Used in the '*-te iru*' form
when referring to where a person
currently lives.
Kare wa doko ni suñde iru *ñ desu
ka?* (彼はどこに住んでいるんですか)
Where *does* he *live?* / *Watashi wa
haha to apaato ni* suñde imasu. (私
は母とアパートに住んでいます) I *am living* with my mother in an apartment. / *Sumeba miyako da.*
(*saying*) (住めば都だ) There is no
place like home.

su⌐m·u² すむ (済む) *vi.* (sum·i-;
sum·a-; suñ-de ⒸⒷ) be finished;
come to an end; get through:
Yatto shigoto ga suñda. (やっと仕事
が済んだ) At last work *is finished.* /
Kaigi wa moo sumimashita *ka?*
(会議はもう済みましたか) *Has* the
meeting *finished* yet? / *Koñgetsu
wa akaji nashi de* suñda. (今月は赤
字なしで済んだ) We *have gotten
through* this month without going into the red.

su⌐m·u³ すむ (澄む) *vi.* (sum·i-;
sum·a-; suñ-de ⒸⒷ) become
clear:
Koñya wa sora ga suñde ite, *hoshi
ga yoku mieru.* (今夜は空が澄んでい
て, 星がよく見える) Tonight the sky
is clear and the stars are clearly
visible.

su⌐na すな (砂) *n.* sand; grain of
sand:
suna *de asobu* (砂で遊ぶ) play in
the *sand.*

su⌐nao すなお (素直) *a.n.* (~ na,
ni) gentle; mild; obedient:
Kare no musuko wa seeshitsu ga
sunao *da.* (彼の息子は性質が素直だ)
His son has a *gentle* nature. /
Sono ko wa watashi no iu koto o
sunao *ni kiita.* (その子は私の言うこと
を素直に聞いた) The child listened
obediently to what I said.

su⌐na⌐wachi すなわち (即ち) *conj.*
(*formal*) that is (to say); namely:
Nihoñ no shuto, sunawachi *Tookyoo* (日本の首都, すなわち東京) the
capital of Japan, *that is to say,*
Tokyo / *Sono jiko wa mikka mae,*
sunawachi *kiñyoobi ni okotta.* (そ
の事故は3日前, すなわち金曜日に起こ
った) The accident happened
three days ago, *that is,* on Friday.

su⌐ne¹ すね (脛) *n.* shank; shin.
sune o kajiru (~ をかじる) be dependent on: *oya no* sune o kajiru
(親のすねをかじる) *sponge off* one's
parents. 《⇨ jiñtai (illus.)》

su「ñpoo すんぽう（寸法）*n.* measure; measurements; size:
Kono kutsu wa suñpoo *ga pittari da.* (この靴は寸法がぴったりだ) The *size* of these shoes is just right. / *Kono shatsu wa* suñpoo *ga awanai.* (このシャツは寸法が合わない) This shirt *does not fit me.* / *Yoofuku o tsukuru no ni* suñpoo *o totte moratta.* (洋服を作るのに寸法をとってもらった) I had my *measurements* taken for a suit to be made. / *Kono suutsukeesu no* suñpoo *wa dono kurai desu ka?* (このスーツケースの寸法はどのくらいですか) What are the *measurements* of this suitcase? 《⇨ ookisa》

su「ñzeñ すんぜん（寸前）*n.* just [right] before:
Kare-ra wa fune ga shizumu sunzeñ *ni booto ni notta.* (彼らは船が沈む寸前にボートに乗った) They got into the boat *just before* the ship sank. / *Sono kaisha wa toosañ* sunzeñ *datta.* (その会社は倒産寸前だった) The company was *on the verge* of bankruptcy.

su「pa「supa すぱすぱ *adv.* (~ to) (with) quick puffs: ★ Used to express the action of smoking heavily.
tabako o supasupa *(to) suu* (たばこをすぱすぱ(と)吸う) *puff away* at a cigarette.

Su「pe「iñ スペイン *n.* Spain.

Su「peiñgo スペインご（スペイン語）*n.* Spanish.

Su「pei「ñjiñ スペインじん（スペイン人）*n.* Spaniard; the Spanish.

su「piido スピード *n.* speed:
supiido o ageru [otosu] (スピードを上げる[落とす]) *accelerate* [*decelerate*] / *Ano pitchaa no tama wa* supiido *ga aru.* (あのピッチャーの球はスピードがある) That pitcher *pitches very fast* balls. / *Soñna ni* supiido *o dasu to abunai.* (そんなにスピードを出すと危ない) It is dangerous to drive at such a *speed.* / *furu-*supiido (フルスピード) full *speed* / supiido-*ihañ* (スピード違反) a *speeding* violation. 《⇨ hayasa; sokudo》

su「pi「ikaa スピーカー *n.* speaker; loudspeaker:
Sono anauñsu wa supiikaa *de kikimashita.* (そのアナウンスはスピーカーで聞きました) We heard the announcement over the *loudspeaker.*

su「po「otsu スポーツ *n.* sport(s):
Daigaku de wa doñna supootsu *o shimashita ka?* (大学ではどんなスポーツをしましたか) What *sports* did you do in college? / supootsu-*kaa* (スポーツカー) a *sports* car / supootsu-*shiñbuñ* (スポーツ新聞) a *sports* paper.

su「ppa「-i すっぱい（酸っぱい）*a.* (-ku) acid; sour; vinegary:
suppai *kudamono* (すっぱい果物) *acid* fruit / *Kono budoo wa* suppai. (このぶどうはすっぱい) These grapes taste *sour.* / *Gyuunyuu wa kusaru to* suppaku *naru.* (牛乳は腐るとすっぱくなる) Milk becomes *sour* when it goes off. 《⇨ aji¹ (table)》

su「puri「ñkuraa スプリンクラー *n.* sprinkler:
spuriñkuraa *o setchi suru* (スプリンクラーを設置する) install *sprinklers.*

su「pu「uñ スプーン *n.* spoon:
supuuñ *ni-hai no satoo* (スプーン2杯の砂糖) two *spoonfuls* of sugar.

su「ra すら *p.* even; if only: ★ Used for extreme examples.
Ano hito wa kañji wa mochiroñ, hiragana sura *yomenai.* (あの人は漢字はもちろん、平仮名すら読めない) He can not *even* read 'hiragana,' not to mention 'kanji.' / *Kodomo ni* sura *dekiru no da kara anata ni dekinai wake ga nai.* (子どもにすらできるのだからあなたにできない訳がない) *Even* a child can do it, so there is no reason you can't. 《⇨ sae》

su「raido スライド *n.* slide; transparency:

suraido-*eeshaki* (スライド映写機) a *slide* projector.

su￢rasura すらすら *adv.* (～ to) smoothly; easily; fluently; readily:
Shigoto wa omotta yori surasura (*to*) *susuñda.* (仕事は思ったよりすらすら(と)進んだ) The job progressed more *smoothly* than we had imagined. / *Kare wa sono suugaku no moñdai o* surasura (*to*) *toita.* (彼はその数学の問題をすらすら(と)解いた) He *easily* solved the mathematics problems. / *Sono ko wa jibuñ no ayamachi o* surasura (*to*) *mitometa.* (その子は自分の過ちをすらすら(と)認めた) The boy *readily* acknowledged his mistake.

su￢rechiga·u すれちがう (すれ違う) *vi.* (-chiga·i-; -chigaw·a-; -chigat-te C) pass by:
Michi de señsee to surechigatta. (道で先生とすれ違った) I *passed* my teacher on the road. / *Nobori deñsha to kudari deñsha ga* surechigatta. (上り電車と下り電車がすれ違った) The up train and the down train *passed each other*.

su￢ri すり (掏摸) *n.* pickpocket:
Deñsha de suri *ni yarareta.* (電車ですりにやられた) I *got my pocket picked* in the train. 《⇨ suru⁴》

su￢ri￢ppa スリッパ *n.* scuffs; mules. ★ From English 'slippers.'

SURIPPA

su￢ro￢gañ スローガン *n.* slogan:

Demotai wa 'señsoo hañtai' no suroogañ *o kakagete, kooshiñ shita.* (デモ隊は「戦争反対」のスローガンを掲げて, 行進した) The demonstrators marched holding aloft the *slogan* of 'Down with war.'

s·u￢ru¹ する *vt.* (sh·i-; sh·i-; sh·i-te I) **1** do (something):
kaimono o suru (買い物をする) *do* the shopping / *señtaku o* suru (洗濯をする) *do* the washing / *shukudai o* suru (宿題をする) *do* one's homework.
2 have (a wash, walk, etc.):
shokuji o suru (食事をする) *have* a meal / *oshaberi o* suru (おしゃべりをする) *have* a chat / *keñka o* suru (けんかをする) *have* a fight / *Watashi wa sono keñ ni tsuite kare to hanashi o shita.* (私はその件について彼と話をした) I *had* a talk with him about that matter.
3 take (a bath, break, etc.):
nyuuyoku suru (入浴する) *take* a bath / *hirune o* suru (昼寝をする) *take* a nap / *Watashi wa dare ga kuru ka chuumoku* shita. (私はだれが来るか注目した) I *took* note of who came.
4 make (a decision, discovery, etc.):
yakusoku o suru (約束をする) *make* a promise / *iiwake o* suru (言い訳をする) *make* excuses / *juñbi o* suru (準備をする) *make* preparations.
5 play (baseball, chess, etc.):
yakyuu o suru (野球をする) *play* baseball / *torañpu o* suru (トランプをする) *play* cards.
6 (of an article, goods, etc.) cost:
Kono tokee wa ikura shimashita *ka?* (この時計はいくらしましたか) How much *did* this watch *cost*? / *Kono yubiwa wa sañmañ-eñ* shimashita. (この指輪は3万円しました) This ring *cost* me 30,000 yen.
7 put on (a scarf, gloves, etc.):
tebukuro o suru (手袋をする) *put on*

gloves / *Kanojo wa kiiroi mafuraa o* shite *ita.*(彼女は黄色いマフラーをしていた) She *was wearing* a yellow muffler. 《⇨ kiru² (table)》

...ga suru (...が〜) there is...: *Yoi kaori ga suru.*(良い香りがする) *There is* a nice smell. / *Henna oto ga suru.*(変な音がする) *There is* a strange sound.

...koto ni suru (...ことに〜) decide: *Atarashii terebi o kau* koto ni shi-mashita.(新しいテレビを買うことにしました) I *have decided* to buy a new television.

...ni shite mo (...にしても) even if: *Isogashii* ni shite mo, *heñji wa sugu ni dashi nasai.*(忙しいにしても, 返事はすぐに出しなさい) *Even if* you are busy, you should write your reply right away.

...ni shite wa (...にしては) consid-ering: *Kare wa go-juu* ni shite wa, *wakaku mieru.*(彼は50にしては, 若く見える) He looks young *con-sidering* he is fifty years old.

...ni suru (...に〜) **1** make into: *Tanaka-sañ o gichoo* ni shima-shoo.(田中さんを議長にしましょう) *Let's make* Mr. Tanaka the chair-man.

2 choose; decide: *"Kimi wa nani* ni suru." *"Boku wa toñkatsu* ni suru."(「君は何にする」「ぼくはとんかつにする」) "What *would* you *like to* eat?" "I'll *have* a pork cutlet."

...o shite iru (...をしている) **1** be doing: *Haha wa señtaku o* shite imasu.(母は洗濯をしています) My mother *is doing* the washing. / *Asoko de oshaberi o* shite iru *no wa dare desu ka?*(あそこでおしゃべりをしているのはだれですか) Who is it *talking* over there?

2 work as; be engaged: *Ani wa isha o* shite imasu.(兄は医者をしています) My older brother *is* a doc-tor.

3 have (a shape, color, etc.):

Kanojo wa ooki-na me o shite iru.(彼女は大きな目をしている) She *has* large eyes. / *Sono hana wa doñna iro o* shite imasu *ka?*(その花はどんな色をしていますか) What *is* the color of that flower?

...shite iru (...している) be doing: *Hanako wa ima heya o* sooji shite imasu.(花子は今部屋を掃除しています) Hanako *is* now *cleaning* her room.

...to shitara (...としたら) as; when: *Dekakeyoo* to shitara, *deñwa ga kakatte kita.*(出かけようとしたら, 電話がかかってきた) *As* I was about to go out, there was a phone call.

...to sureba (...とすれば) if: *Ryo-koo suru* to sureba, *doko e ikima-su ka?*(旅行するとすれば, どこへ行きますか) *If* you were to take a trip, where would you like to go?

USAGE

Note the following types of usage.
1 noun+*suru*
beñkyoo suru (study)
2 adverb+*suru*
hakkiri suru (become clear)
---

su˥r·u² する(刷る) *vt.* (sur·i-; su-r·a-; sut-te Ⓒ) print: *Kono meeshi wa doko de* surima-shita *ka?* (この名刺はどこで刷りましたか) Where *did* you *get* this name card *printed*? / *Kono hoñ wa sho-hañ o sañzeñ-bu* surimashita. (この本は初版を3,000部刷りました) We *printed* 3,000 copies of the first edition of this book.

su˥r·u³ する(擦る) *vt.* (sur·i-; su-r·a-; sut-te Ⓒ) **1** strike (a match); rub: *matchi o* suru (マッチをする) *strike* a match / *sumi o* suru (墨をする) *rub* down an inkstick.

2 lose (at gambling): *Kare wa keeba de taikiñ o* sutta. (彼は競馬で大金をすった) He *lost* a lot of money at the races.

su⌐r·u⁴ する (掏る) *vt.* (sur·i-; su-r·a-; sut-te Ⓒ) pick; lift: *Watashi wa deñsha no naka de saifu o surareta.* (私は電車の中で財布をすられた) I *had* my wallet *lifted* in the train. ((⇨ suri))

su⌐rudo⌐·i するどい (鋭い) *a.* (-ku)
1 (of a blade, a claw, etc.) sharp; keen: surudoi *ha* (鋭い刃) a *sharp* blade / *neko no* surudoi *tsume* (ねこの鋭いつめ) the *sharp* claws of a cat.
2 (of a look, pain, etc.) sharp; acute: surudoi *metsuki* (鋭い目つき) a *sharp* look / surudoi *itami* (鋭い痛み) an *acute* pain / *Ikeñ ga* suru-doku *tairitsu shita.* (意見が鋭く対立した) Opinion was very *sharply* divided.
3 (of a person etc.) sharp; alert: surudoi *hihañ* (鋭い批判) *sharp* criticism / *Sore ni ki ga tsuku to wa nakanaka* surudoi *desu ne.* (それに気がつくとはなかなか鋭いですね) It is pretty *sharp* of you to notice that. ((↔ nibui))

su⌐rume するめ (鯣) *n.* dried squid. ((⇨ ika²))

SURUME

su⌐rusuru するする *adv.* (～ to) easily; smoothly: *Obi ga* surusuru (*to*) *toketa.* (帯がするする(と)解けた) The obi *easily* came undone. / *Saru wa* suru-suru (*to*) *ki ni nobotta.* (猿はするする(と)木に登った) The monkey climbed up the tree *with perfect ease.*

su⌐ru to すると *conj.* **1** and;

then: ★ Used at the beginning of a sentence.
Kare wa neyoo to shite ita. Suru to *deñwa ga natta.* (彼は寝ようとしていた. すると電話が鳴った) He was going to sleep. *Just then* the telephone rang.
2 in that case: ★ Used at the beginning of a sentence.
"*Ashita no yohoo wa ame desu.*" "Suru to *uñdookai wa chuushi desu ne.*" (「あしたの予報は雨です」「すると運動会は中止ですね」) "Tomorrow the forecast is for rain." "*In that case*, we will have to cancel the athletic meet, won't we?"

su⌐shi¹ すし (寿司・鮨) *n.* sushi: ★ Vinegared rice balls topped with slices of raw fish and vegetables.
sushi *o nigiru* (すしを握る) make *sushi* / sushi-*ya* (すし屋) a *sushi* bar [shop].

INSIDE A SUSHIYA

SUSHI

su⌐so すそ (裾) *n.* **1** hem; bottom:
sukaato no suso (スカートのすそ) the

hem of a skirt / *kimono no* suso
(着物のすそ) the *hem* of a kimono.
2 foot:
yama no suso (山のすそ) the *foot* of
a mountain.

su⌈su すす (煤) *n.* soot:
Eñtotsu no susu *o haratta.* (煙突の
すすを払った) I cleared the *soot*
from the chimney. / susu-darake
no teñjoo (すすだらけの天井) a *sooty*
ceiling.

su⌈sume·ru¹ すすめる (進める) *vt.*
(susume-te ⟨V⟩) **1** proceed with
(a procedure, project, etc.); carry
forward:
Kare-ra wa kooshoo o susumeru
koto ni kimeta. (彼らは交渉を進める
ことに決めた) They decided to *proceed with* the negotiations. /
Kono keekaku wa isoide susumeru *hitsuyoo ga arimasu.* (この計
画は急いで進める必要があります) It is
necessary to *carry forward* this
plan hurriedly. 《⇨ susumu》
2 promote; further:
Wareware wa sekai heewa o susu-
menakereba *naranai.* (われわれは世
界平和を進めなければならない) We
have to promote world peace.
3 put forward (the hand of a
clock [watch]):
Tokee no hari o go-fuñ susumeta.
(時計の針を5分進めた) I *put the*
hands of my watch five minutes
forward. 《↔ okuraseru》《⇨ su-
sumu》

su⌈sume·ru² すすめる (勧める) *vt.*
(susume-te ⟨V⟩) **1** advise; suggest; persuade:
*Watashi wa kare ni tabako o ya-
meru yoo* susumeta. (私は彼にたばこ
をやめるよう勧めた) I *advised* him to
give up smoking.
2 recommend:
Señsee wa sono jisho o seeto ni
susumeta. (先生はその辞書を生徒に勧
めた) The teacher *recommended*
that dictionary to the pupils.

3 offer (a dish, drink, etc.):
Kare wa kanojo ni sake o susumeta. (彼は彼女に酒を勧めた) He
offered her some sake.
4 tell; ask; invite:
*Kare wa watashi ni kutsurogu
yoo* susumeta. (彼は私にくつろぐよう
勧めた) He *told* me to make
myself comfortable.

su⌈sum·u すすむ (進む) *vi.* (su-
sum·i-; susum·a-; susuñ-de ⟨C⟩)
1 proceed; travel:
Watashi-tachi wa kita ni mukatte
susuñda. (私たちは北に向かって進んだ)
We *proceeded* northward. / *Hikari wa oto yori hayaku* susumu.
(光は音より速く進む) Light *travels*
faster than sound.
2 (of a clock [watch]) gain; be
fast:
*Kono tokee wa ik-kagetsu ni go-
fuñ* susumimasu. (この時計は一か月
に5分進みます) This clock *gains*
five minutes a month. / *Kimi no
tokee wa ni-fuñ* susuñde iru *yo.* (君
の時計は2分進んでいるよ) Your
watch *is* two minutes *fast.*
《↔ okureru》《⇨ susumeru》
3 (of a procedure, project, etc.)
make progress; advance:
Keekaku wa juñchoo ni susuñde
imasu *ka?* (計画は順調に進んでいます
か) *Are* your plans *advancing*
smoothly? / *Kagaku-gijutsu wa
higoto ni* susuñde iru. (科学技術は
日ごとに進んでいる) Scientific technology *advances* day by day.
4 (of diseases) get worse:
Kare no byooki wa daibu susuñde
iru. (彼の病気はだいぶ進んでいる) His
illness *has gotten* considerably
worse.
5 (of appetite) be good:
Kyoo wa shoku ga susumanai. (き
ょうは食が進まない) I *do not have a
good appetite* today.

su⌈sur·u すする (啜る) *vt.* (susur-
r·i-; susur·a-; susut-te ⟨C⟩) sip;

slurp; suck:

o-cha o susuru (お茶をすする) *sip* tea / hana o susuru (鼻をすする) *sniffle* / Nihoñ de wa soba o susuru toki oto o tateru no wa warui koto de wa arimaseñ. (日本ではそばをすすると き音を立てるのは悪いことではありません) In Japan, it is not bad manners to make a noise while *sucking in* noodles.

su⌐ta⌐a　スター　n. actor [actress, singer, player, etc.]; star:

> ┌─ USAGE ─┐
> 'Sutaa' comes from English 'star,' but it does not necessarily refer to a person who plays a leading and brilliant part.

Kanojo wa eega sutaa *ni naritai to* omotte iru. (彼女は映画スターになりた いと思っている) She longs to be a movie *actress*.

su⌐ta⌐ato　スタート　n. start; getaway:

Sono uma wa yoi sutaato *o kitta.* (その馬はよいスタートを切った) The horse got off to a good *start.* / sutaato-*raiñ* (スタートライン) the *starting* line.

sutaato suru (～する) *vi.* start; begin: *Shi-gatsu kara atarashii gakuneñ ga* sutaato shimasu. (四 月から新しい学年がスタートします) A new academic year *starts* in April.

su⌐tairi⌐suto　スタイリスト　n.
1 fashion-conscious person.
2 adviser on the hairstyle and clothes of models and actors.

su⌐ta⌐iru　スタイル　n. **1** figure: Kanojo wa sutairu *ga ii.* (彼女はスタ イルがいい) She has a good *figure.*
2 style: Seekatsu no sutairu *ga kawatta.* (生活のスタイルが変わった) Life-*styles* have changed.

su⌐ta⌐jiamu　スタジアム　n. stadium.

su⌐ta⌐suta　すたすた　*adv.* (～ to) briskly; hurriedly: ★ Used to express a way of walking.
Kare wa sutasuta *to toori no hoo e* aruite itta. (彼はすたすたと通りの方へ 歩いて行った) He walked *briskly* toward the street.

su⌐te⌐eji　ステージ　n. stage: suteeji *ni tatsu* (ステージに立つ) appear on the *stage.*

su⌐te⌐eki　ステーキ　n. steak; beefsteak:
Suteeki *wa yoku yaite kudasai.* (ス テーキはよく焼いてください) I'd like to have my *steak* well-done. ((⇨ bifuteki))

su⌐teki　すてき (素敵) *a.n.* (～ na) nice; splendid; marvelous; great:
suteki *na keshiki* (すてきな景色) *beautiful* scenery / suteki *na* josee (すてきな女性) a *wonderful* woman / Kimi no aidea wa suteki *da.* (君のアイデアはすてきだ) That idea of yours is *brilliant.*

su⌐tereo　ステレオ　n. stereo: stereo *o kakeru* (ステレオをかける) play a *stereo* / sutereo *de rokuoñ* suru (ステレオで録音する) record in *stereo.*

su⌐te-ru　すてる (捨てる) *vt.* (sutete Ⓥ) **1** throw away; cast off; dump:
Kono reezooko o suteru *no wa mottainai.* (この冷蔵庫を捨てるのはもったい ない) It is a waste to *throw away* this refrigerator. / Gomi wa gomibako ni sutete kudasai. (ごみはごみ 箱に捨ててください) *Put* the rubbish in the dustbin. / Gomi o suteru *na.* (sign) (ごみを捨てるな) No *Dumping* Here.

2 abandon; give up; forsake:
inochi o suteru (命を捨てる) *throw away* one's life / meeyo o suteru (名誉を捨てる) *forsake* one's honor / kazoku o suteru (家族を捨てる) *abandon* one's family.

su⌈to⌉ スト *n.* strike:
Kumiai wa chiñage o yookyuu shite, suto *ni haitta.* (組合は賃上げを要求して, ストに入った) Demanding a wage hike, the union went on *strike.* (⇨ sutoraiki)

su⌈to⌉obu ストーブ *n.* heater:
★ Comes from English 'stove' but never refers to an apparatus for cooking food.
sutoobu *o tsukeru* [*kesu*] (ストーブをつける[消す]) turn on [off] a *heater* / *sekiyu*-sutoobu (石油ストーブ) a kerosene *heater.*

su⌈to⌉ppu ストップ *n.* stop; halt:
Sono keekaku wa shiñkoo ni su-toppu ga kakatta. (その計画は進行にストップがかかった) The development of the project was brought to a *halt.*
sutoppu suru (〜する) *vi.* stop:
Suto no tame, kootsuu wa sutoppu *shite imasu.* (ストのため, 交通はストップしています) Because of the strike, transport *is at a standstill.*

su⌈toppu-uo⌉tchi ストップウォッチ *n.* stopwatch.

su⌈tora⌉iki ストライキ *n.* strike:
Kare-ra wa roodoo-jookeñ no kai-zeñ o motomete, sutoraiki *o oko-natta.* (彼らは労働条件の改善を求めて, ストライキを行った) They went on *strike,* calling for better working conditions. / *Sutoraiki wa ma-mo-naku chuushi sareta.* (ストライキは間もなく中止された) The *strike* was soon called off. (⇨ suto)

su⌈tora⌉iku ストライク *n.* (of base-ball) strike:
Kare wa sutoraiku *o minogashite sañshiñ shita.* (彼はストライクを見逃して三振した) He was called out on *strikes.* (↔ booru²)

su⌈to⌉resu ストレス *n.* stress:
Kare wa sutoresu *ga tamatte iru yoo da.* (彼はストレスがたまっているようだ) He seems to be under much *stress.*

su⌈tto すっと *adv.* (〜 suru) feel refreshed [relieved]:
Setsujoku o hatashite, mune ga sutto *shita.* (雪辱を果たして, 胸がすっとした) Since we got even with them, our feelings *were placated.* / *Nayami o uchiakete* kimochi ga sutto shita. (悩みを打ち明けて気持ちがすっとした) *A burden was removed from my mind* after I disclosed my worries. / *Shiñseñ na kuuki o suttara, atama ga* sutto *shita.* (新鮮な空気を吸ったら, 頭がすっとした) My head *cleared* after I took a breath of fresh air.

su·⌈u⌉¹ すう (吸う) *vt.* (su·i-; su-w·a-; sut-te C) **1** breathe (in):
asa no shiñseñ na kuuki o suu (朝の新鮮な空気を吸う) *breathe* the fresh morning air / *iki o sutte haku* (息を吸って吐く) *breathe in* and breathe out.
2 sip; sup; suck; absorb:
Akañboo ga haha-oya no chichi o sutte iru. (赤ん坊が母親の乳を吸っている) A baby *is sucking* at her mother's breast. / *Spoñji wa mizu o yoku* suu. (スポンジは水をよく吸う) Sponges *absorb* water well.
3 smoke:
Tabako o sutte mo ii desu ka? (たばこを吸ってもいいですか) May I *smoke?*

su⌈u⌉² すう (数) *n.* number:
seeto[*shussekisha*]-suu (生徒[出席者]数) the *number* of pupils [attendants]. (⇨ table (next page); kazu)

su⌈ugaku すうがく (数学) *n.* mathematics.

su⌈uhai すうはい (崇拝) *n.* worship; admiration; cult:
kojiñ-suuhai (個人崇拝) a personality *cult* / suuhai-sha (崇拝者) a *worshipper*; an *avid admirer.*
suuhai suru (〜する) *vt.* worship; admire; adore: *guuzoo o* suuhai suru (偶像を崇拝する) *worship* an idol / *Ano hito wa watashi ga* suu-

hai shite iru *kagakusha no hitori desu.*(あの人は私が崇拝している科学者の一人です) He is one of the scientists I *admire.*

su⌐uji すうじ (数字) *n.* numeral; figure:

Kono risuto ni wa suuji *no machigai ga aru.*(このリストには数字の間違いがある) There are some *numerical* errors in this list. / *arabia* [*rooma*]-*suuji* (アラビア[ローマ]数字) Arabic [Roman] *numerals.*

suuji ni tsuyoi [yowai] (〜に強い[弱い]) be good [poor] at figures.

su⌐upaa(-ma⌐aketto) スーパー (マーケット) *n.* supermarket:

Kaimono wa kono suupaa *de shite imasu.*(買い物はこのスーパーでしています) I do my shopping at this supermarket.

su⌐upu スープ *n.* soup; broth: suupu *o nomu* (スープを飲む) have [eat] *soup.*

su⌐ushi すうし (数詞) *n.* (of grammar) numeral.

su⌐utsu スーツ *n.* suit:

Natsu no suutsu *o it-chaku shiñchoo shimashita.*(夏のスーツを1着新調しました) I had a new summer *suit* made.

su⌐war·u すわる (座る) *vi.* (suwar·i-; suwar·a-; suwat-te [C]) sit (down); take a seat:

isu ni suwaru (いすに座る) *sit* in a chair / *tatami ni* suwaru (畳に座る) *sit* on the tatami / *Doozo o-suwari kudasai.*(どうぞお座りください) Please *take a seat.* / *Deñsha ni*

suu

1	i⌐chi⌐ (一)		100	hya⌐ku⌐ (百)
2	ni⌐ (二)		200	ni-⌐hyaku
3	s⌐añ (三)		300	sañ⌐-byaku
4	shi⌐, yo⌐ñ (四)		400	yoñ⌐-hyaku
5	go⌐ (五)		500	go-⌐hyaku
6	ro⌐ku⌐ (六)		600	rop-⌐pyaku
7	na⌐na, shi⌐chi⌐ (七)		700	na⌐na⌐-hyaku
8	ha⌐chi⌐ (八)		800	hap-⌐pyaku
9	ku⌐, kyu⌐u (九)		900	kyu⌐u-hyaku
10	ju⌐u (十)		1,000	se⌐ñ (千)
11	ju⌐u-ichi⌐		2,000	ni-⌐se⌐ñ
12	ju⌐u-ni⌐		3,000	sa⌐ñ-ze⌐ñ
13	ju⌐u-sañ		4,000	yo⌐ñ-se⌐ñ
14	ju⌐u-shi⌐, ju⌐u-yoñ⌐		5,000	go-⌐se⌐ñ
15	ju⌐u-go		6,000	ro⌐ku-se⌐ñ
16	ju⌐u-roku⌐		7,000	na⌐na-se⌐ñ
17	ju⌐u-shichi⌐, ju⌐u-na⌐na		8,000	ha⌐s-se⌐ñ
18	ju⌐u-hachi⌐		9,000	kyu⌐u-se⌐ñ
19	ju⌐u-ku, ju⌐u-kyu⌐u		10,000	i⌐chi-ma⌐ñ (1万)
20	ni⌐-juu		100,000	ju⌐u-ma⌐ñ
30	sa⌐ñ-juu		1,000,000	hya⌐ku-ma⌐ñ
40	yo⌐ñ-juu		10,000,000	se⌐ñ-ma⌐ñ
50	go-⌐ju⌐u		100,000,000	i⌐chi⌐-oku (1億)
60	ro⌐ku-ju⌐u		1,000,000,000	ju⌐u-oku
70	shi⌐chi-ju⌐u, na⌐na⌐-juu		10,000,000,000	hya⌐ku⌐-oku
80	ha⌐chi-ju⌐u		100,000,000,000	se⌐ñ-oku
90	kyu⌐u-juu		1000,000,000,000	i⌐t-choo (1兆)

notta ga zutto suwarenakatta. (電
車に乗ったがずっと座れなかった) I got
on the train but *could not get a
seat* the whole way. (⇨ kakeru¹)

su⌐yasuya すやすや *adv.* (~ to)
calmly; quietly; peacefully:
★ Used to express the state of
sleeping:
Akañboo wa suyasuya (*to*) *nemutte imasu.* (赤ん坊はすやすや(と)眠
っています) The baby is sleeping
peacefully.

su⌐zu¹ すず(鈴) *n.* bell:
suzu *o narasu* (鈴を鳴らす) ring a
bell.

su⌐zu² すず(錫) *n.* tin.

su⌐zume すずめ(雀) *n.* sparrow.

su⌐zuri¹ すずり(硯) *n.* inkstone:
suzuri *de sumi o suru* (すずりで墨を
する) rub an Indian ink stick on
an *inkstone* / suzuri-bako (すずり箱)

an *inkstone box.*

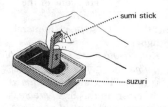

sumi stick

suzuri

SUZURI

su⌐zushi¹·i すずしい(涼しい) *a.*
(-ku) cool; refreshing:
Kono heya wa suzushii. (この部屋は
涼しい) This room is *cool.* / *Asa-
bañ* suzushiku *natte kita.* (朝晩涼し
くなってきた) The mornings and
evenings have become *cool.*
((↔ atatakai))((⇨ samui (table)))

T

ta¹ た（田）*n*. (rice) paddy:
ta *o tagayasu*（田を耕す）plow a
rice field.《⇨ suideñ (photo)》

ta² た（他）*n*. the rest; the other;
the others:
Hitotsu dake nokoshi, ta *wa suteta.*（一つだけ残し他は捨てた）I kept
one and discarded *the others.* /
Ta *no mono wa doko e ikimashita
ka?*（他の者はどこへ行きましたか）
Where did the *other* people go?
《⇨ hoka》

-ta た *infl. end.* [attached to verbs,
adjectives, and the copula]

> ─（**USAGE**）─
>
> The *ta*-form of a verb is made
> by dropping the final '*-te*' of
> the *te*-form of a verb and add-
> ing '*-ta.*' When the *te*-form is
> '*-de,*' add '*-da.*' The *ta*-form of
> an adjective is made by drop-
> ping the final '*-i,*' and adding
> '*-katta.*' The *ta*-form of the cop-
> ula is '*datta.*' 《⇨ appendixes》

1 (indicates an action or a situation in the past):
Kesa wa go-ji ni okita.（今朝は5時
に起きた）I *got up* at five this morning. / *Kare no eñzetsu wa* subarashikatta.（彼の演説はすばらしかった）
His speech *was excellent.* / *Sono
hoñ wa moo* yomimashita.（その本
はもう読みました）I *have* already
read that book. / *Umi wa shizuka*
datta.（海は静かだった）The sea *was*
calm.

2 (indicates an action or a situation which is just finished or
completed):
Kare wa ima dekaketa tokoro
desu.（彼は今出かけたところです）He
has just *gone out.* / *Eki ni* tsuita

toki deñwa o kudasai.（駅に着いたと
き電話を下さい）Please call me
when you *have arrived* at the station. 《⇨ -tara》

3 (used to ask for confirmation
or agreement):
Kore wa kimi no datta ne.（これは君
のだったね）This *is* yours, isn't it? /
Go-chuumoñ no shina wa kore
deshita ne.（ご注文の品はこれでしたね）
This *is* the article you ordered,
isn't it?

4 (used to make a clause which
modifies a noun):
Ano shiroi fuku o kita *hito wa
dare desu ka?*（あの白い服を着た人は
だれですか）Who is that person *in
white?* / *Kore ga kanojo no* kaita e
desu.（これが彼女のかいた絵です）This
is the picture she *drew.*

ta⌐**ba** たば（束）*n*. bundle; bunch:
tegami no taba（手紙の束）a *bundle*
of letters / *kagi no* taba（鍵の束）a
bunch of keys.

ta⌐**bako** たばこ（煙草）*n*. cigarette; cigar; tobacco:
tabako *ni hi o tsukeru*（たばこに火を
つける）light a *cigarette* / *Tabako o*
sutte *mo ii desu ka?*（たばこを吸って
もいいですか）Do you mind if I
smoke? / *Tabako wa yamemashita.*
（たばこはやめました）I gave up *smoking.* / *Tabako wa hai to shiñzoo ni
gai ga arimasu.*（たばこは肺と心臓に
害があります）*Smoking* is harmful to
your lungs and heart.

ta⌐**bane**⌐·**ru** たばねる（束ねる）*vt*.
(tabane-te Ⅴ) bundle; tie up in
a bundle:
ki no eda o tabaneru（木の枝を束ね
る）*bundle up* branches / *Kono
shiñbuñ o* tabanete *kudasai.*（この
新聞を束ねてください）Please *bundle*

up these newspapers.

ta¦bemo¬no たべもの (食べ物) *n.* food:

Kare-ra wa somatsu na tabemono de mañzoku shite ita. (彼らは粗末な食べ物で満足していた) They were content with poor *food.* / *Nani-ka tabemono o kudasai.* (何か食べ物を下さい) Please give me *something to eat.*

ta¦be¬·ru たべる (食べる) *vt.* (tabe-te Ⅴ) **1** eat; have:

sashimi o taberu (さしみを食べる) *eat* slices of raw fish / *o-hiru o taberu* (お昼を食べる) *have* lunch / *Tanaka-sañ wa yoku taberu.* (田中さんはよく食べる) Mr. Tanaka *eats* a lot. / *Ano mise de sañdoitchi de mo tabemashoo.* (あの店でサンドイッチでも食べましょう) *Let's have* some sandwiches or something at that shop. 《⇨ kuu; meshiagaru》

2 live on:

Hito-tsuki gomañ-eñ de wa tabete ikemaseñ. (ひと月5万円では食べていけません) One *cannot live* on fifty thousand yen a month.

ta¦bi¬¹ たび (旅) *n.* trip; journey; tour; travel:

fune no tabi (船の旅) a sea *voyage* / *basu no tabi* (バスの旅) a bus *tour* / *tabi ni deru* (旅に出る) set out on a *journey* / *Sora no tabi wa hajime-te desu.* (空の旅は初めてです) This is my first airplane *trip.* / *Watashi wa Nihoñ-juu iroiro na tokoro ni tabi o shimashita.* (私は日本中いろいろな所に旅をしました) I *have traveled* widely throughout Japan. 《⇨ ryokoo》

ta¦bi¬² たび (足袋) *n.* Japanese socks. ★ The front part is separated into two, the big toe and the other four toes. Usually worn with kimono. 《⇨ photo (right)》

ta¦bi¬³ たび (度) *n.* **1** every time:

Kono shashiñ o miru tabi ni na-kunatta chichi o omoidasu. (この写

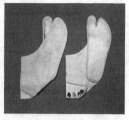

TABI

真を見るたびに亡くなった父を思い出す) *Every time* I look at this photo I recall my dead father. / *Jikkeñ wa nañ-do mo yatta ga sono tabi ni shippai shita.* (実験は何度もやったがその度に失敗した) I repeatedly carried out the experiment, but *every time* I failed.

2 occasion:

Kono tabi wa go-kekkoñ omede-too gozaimasu. (この度はご結婚おめでとうございます) Congratulations on this, the *occasion* of your wedding.

-¬tabi たび (度) *suf.* counter for the number of times.

Hito-tabi tsuita shuukañ wa ya-me-nikui. (一たびついた習慣はやめにくい) *Once* you pick up a habit, it is difficult to get rid of it. / *Jikkeñ wa mi-tabi yarimashita ga dame deshita.* (実験は三たびやりましたがだめでした) We carried out the experiment three *times,* but it was in vain. 《⇨ -do》

ta¦bitabi たびたび (度々) *adv.* often; many times; repeatedly:

Kare to wa saikiñ tabitabi atte imasu. (彼とは最近たびたび会っています) Lately I have met with him *often.* 《⇨ shibashiba》

ta¦boo たぼう (多忙) *a.n.* (~ na/no) busy:

taboo na mainichi (多忙な毎日) a *busy* daily life / *Taboo de sono kaigi ni wa deraremaseñ.* (多忙でその会議には出られません) I cannot attend the meeting because I am very *busy*. / Go-taboo *no tokoro o-atsumari itadaki, arigatoo gozaimasu.*(ご多忙のところお集まりいただき，ありがとうございます) Thank you very much for coming here when you are all so *busy*. 《⇨ isogashii》

ta⌈buñ たぶん（多分）*adv.* probably; perhaps; maybe:
Gogo wa tabuñ ame ni naru deshoo.(午後はたぶん雨になるでしょう) It will *probably* rain in the afternoon. / Tabuñ *kanojo wa konai deshoo.*(たぶん彼女は来ないでしょう)*Maybe* she won't come. 《⇨ osoraku; tashika》

-⌉tachi たち（達）*suf.* [attached to nouns indicating people and animals] (indicates the plural):
★ Note there are two uses; *señsee-tachi* ＝the teachers / the teacher(s) and others. When attached to people's names; *Kaneko-sañ-tachi*＝Mr. Kaneko and those with him.
kodomo-tachi（子どもたち）*children*/ doobutsu-tachi（動物たち）*animals.*

ta⌈chiagar·u たちあがる（立ち上がる）*vi.* (-agar·i-; -agar·a-; -agatte ⓒ) **1** stand up:
Kare wa isu kara tachiagatta.（彼はいすから立ち上がった）He *stood up* from the chair.
2 rise up:
Kokumiñ wa dokusai-seeji ni taishite tachiagatta.（国民は独裁政治に対して立ち上がった）The people *rose up* against the dictatorship.

ta⌈chiba⌉ たちば（立場）*n.* **1** position; situation:
Kochira no tachiba *mo rikai shite kudasai.*（こちらの立場も理解してくださ い）I hope you will understand our *position*. / *Watashi-tachi wa ima muzukashii* tachiba *ni arimasu.*（私たちは今むずかしい立場にあります）We are now in a difficult *situation*. / *Watashi no* tachiba *de wa kore ijoo wa iemaseñ.*（私の立場では

これ以上は言えません）I am not in a *position* to make further comments.
2 standpoint:
Chigatta tachiba *kara arayuru kanoosee o kañgaemashita.*（違った立場からあらゆる可能性を考えました）We considered all possibilities from a different *standpoint*.

ta⌈chidomar·u たちどまる（立ち止まる）*vi.* (-domar·i-; -domar·a-; -domat-te ⓒ) stop; pause; stand still:
Kare wa tachidomatte, *sono e o mitsumeta.*（彼は立ち止まって，その絵を見つめた）He *stopped* and gazed at the picture.

ta⌈chiiri たちいり（立ち入り）*n.* entrance; entry:
tachiiri *keñsa o suru*（立ち入り検査をする）make an *on-the-spot* inspection / *Koko wa* tachiiri *kiñshi desu.*（ここは立ち入り禁止です）This area is *off-limits*. / *Shibafu-nai* tachiiri *kiñshi.*（*sign*）（芝生内立ち入り禁止）*Keep Off* the Grass. 《⇨ tachiiru》

TACHIIRI KIÑSHI SIGN

ta⌈chii⌉r·u たちいる（立ち入る）*vi.* (-ir·i-; -ir·a-; -it-te ⓒ) **1** trespass; enter:
Taniñ no tochi ni mudañ de tachiitte *wa ikemaseñ.*（他人の土地に無断で立ち入ってはいけません）You must not *trespass* on other

people's land. (⇨ tachiiri)
2 meddle; pry into:
Kono moñdai ni wa tachiiritaku *arimaseñ.* (この問題には立ち入りたくありません) I don't wish to *meddle* in this problem. / Tachiitta *koto o kiku yoo desu ga, kuruma wa o-mochi desu ka?* (立ち入ったことを聞くようですが、車はお持ちですか) Excuse me if I'm too *inquisitive*, but do you have a car?

ta⌐chimachi たちまち (忽ち) *adv.*
in a moment; in no time:
Kineñ-kitte wa tachimachi *uri-kireta.* (記念切手はたちまち売り切れた) The commemorative stamps were sold out *in no time.*

ta⌐chisar·u たちさる (立ち去る) *vi.*
(-sar·i-; -sar·a-; -sat·te C)
leave; go away:
Kanojo wa sayonara mo iwanai de, tachisatta. (彼女はさよならも言わないで、立ち去った) She *left* without even saying good-bye.

ta⌐chisuku⌐m·u たちすくむ (立ち竦む) *vi.* (-sukum·i-; -sukum·a-; -sukuñ-de C) be [stand] petrified:
Osoroshii kookee o mite, watashi wa sono ba ni tachisukuñde shimatta. (恐ろしい光景を見て、私はその場に立ちすくんでしまった) I *stood rooted* to the spot at the horrible sight.

ta⌐chiyor·u たちよる (立ち寄る) *vi.*
(-yor·i-; -yor·a-; -yot·te C)
drop in; stop by:
Kiñjo ni korareta toki wa tachi-yotte *kudasai.* (近所に来られたときは立ち寄ってください) When you are in the neighborhood, please *drop in.*

ta⌐da¹ ただ (唯) *adv.* only; simply; just:
Ima wa tada *kekka o matsu bakari desu.* (今はただ結果を待つばかりです) There is nothing to be done now but *simply* wait for the results. / *Kare no Nihongo no tassha na no ni wa* tada *odoroku bakari*

desu. (彼の日本語の達者なのにはただ驚くばかりです) I am *just* amazed at his fluency in Japanese.

ta⌐da² ただ (只) *n.* no charge; free:
Kono katarogu wa tada *desu.* (このカタログはただです) There is *no charge* for this catalog. / *Kippu o* tada *de moratta.* (切符をただでもらった) I got the ticket *for nothing.*

ta⌐dachi ni ただちに (直ちに) *adv.*
at once; immediately; directly:
Ikkoo wa tadachi ni *shuppatsu shita.* (一行はただちに出発した) The party *immediately* set out. / *Kore o motte* tadachi ni *kare no shippai to wa dañgeñ dekinai.* (これをもってただちに彼の失敗とは断言できない) For this reason we cannot *directly* conclude that it's his mistake. (⇨ sugu)

ta⌐da⌐ima¹ ただいま (唯今) *n., adv.*
now; (at) present; soon:
Tadaima no jikoku wa ku-ji juu-go-fuñ desu. (ただいまの時刻は9時15分です) The time *now* is fifteen minutes past nine. / *Tadaima no tokoro ijoo wa arimaseñ.* (ただいまのところ異常はありません) *So far* everything is all right. / *Tadaima mairimasu.* (ただいま参ります) I am coming *soon.*

ta⌐daima² ただいま I'm home.; I've just gotten back. ★ A greeting used by a person who has just come home. (⇨ okaeri nasai)

ta⌐dashi ただし (但し) *conj.* but; however; provided:
Sono reñraku wa kikimashita. Tadashi kanojo ni wa mada tsutaete imaseñ. (その連絡は聞きました。ただし彼女にはまだ伝えていません) I have received the message. *However,* I have not told her yet. / *Sono shigoto wa hikiukete mo ii desu yo. Tadashi kimi mo tetsudatte kurereba ne.* (その仕事は引き受けてもいいですよ。ただし君も手伝ってくれ

れ ば ね) I'm willing to accept the job, *provided* you help me.

ta⌐dashi⌐·i ただしい (正しい) *a.* (-ku) correct; right; proper: tadashii *kotae* (正しい答え) the *right* answer / tadashiku *rikai suru* (正しく理解する) understand *correctly* / *Kimi no handan wa* tadashikatta. (きみの判断は正しかった) Your decision was *correct*.

ta⌐da⌐s·u ただす (正す) *vt.* (tadash·i-; tadas·a-; tadash·i-te ⓒ) 1 correct; rectify: *Tsugi no bun no ayamari o* tadashi nasai. (次の文の誤りを正しなさい) *Correct* the errors in the following sentences.
2 reform; straighten: *okonai o* tadasu (行いを正す) *reform* one's conduct / *Shisee o* tadashi nasai. (姿勢を正しなさい) *Straighten* your posture.

ta⌐dayo⌐·u ただよう (漂う) *vi.* (tadayo·i-; tadayow·a-; tadayot-te ⓒ) 1 drift; float: *Shiroi booto ga kaijoo o* tadayotte ita. (白いボートが海上を漂っていた) There *was* a white boat *afloat* on the sea.
2 be filled with: *Kaijoo ni wa nekki ga* tadayotte ita. (会場には熱気が漂っていた) The hall *was alive* with excitement.

ta⌐doo⌐shi たどうし (他動詞) *n.* transitive verb. 《⇨ appendixes》

ta⌐doritsu⌐k·u たどりつく (辿り着く) *vi.* (-tsuk·i-; -tsuk·a-; -tsu·i-te ⓒ) manage to arrive; work one's way: *Watashi-tachi wa yatto mokuteki-chi ni* tadoritsuita. (私たちはやっと目的地にたどり着いた) At last we *made our way to* our destination. / *Ko-ya ni* tadoritsuita *toki, kare wa furafura datta*. (小屋にたどり着いたとき, 彼はふらふらだった) When he *managed to arrive* at the hut, he was groggy.

ta⌐e⌐·ru¹ たえる (耐える) *vi.* (tae-te ⓥ) bear; stand; endure: *Kono samusa ni wa* taerarenai. (この寒さには耐えられない) I *cannot bear* this cold. / *Kanojo wa mamahaha no ijime ni* taeta. (彼女は継母のいじめに耐えた) She *endured* her stepmother's ill-treatment. / *Yuka wa hon no omomi ni* taerarenakatta. (床は本の重みに耐えられなかった) The floor *was not strong enough to bear* the weight of the books.

ta⌐e⌐·ru² たえる (絶える) *vi.* (tae-te ⓥ) 1 become extinct; die out: *Kono shu no doobutsu wa* taete, *ima wa imasen*. (この種の動物は絶えて, 今はいません) This species of animal, *being extinct*, no longer exists.
2 (of contact, relations, etc.) be cut off; come to an end: *Denwa no koshoo de kare to no renraku ga* taeta. (電話の故障で彼との連絡が絶えた) With the phone out of order, communication with him *was broken*.

ta⌐ezu たえず (絶えず) *adv.* always; continually; constantly: *Kono dooro wa kuruma ga* taezu *tootte iru*. (この道路は車が絶えず通っている) Cars pass along this road *incessantly*.

ta⌐gai たがい (互い) *n.* each other; one another: ★ Often with '*o-*.' *Wareware wa* o-tagai *no tansho o shitte iru*. (われわれはお互いの短所を知っている) We know *each other*'s weaknesses. / *Kare-ra wa* o-tagai *ni* tasukeatta. (彼らはお互いに助け合った) They helped *each other*.

-taga⌐r·u たがる *suf.* (*vi.*) (-tagar·i-; -tagar·a-; -tagat-te ⓒ) [attached to the continuative base of a verb] want (to do); be eager (to do): ★ Indicates the wishes and hopes of a person other than the speaker. *Kare wa nan de mo* shiritagaru.

（彼は何でも知りたがる）He *is eager to know* everything. / *Kodomo-tachi wa haha-oya ni aitagatte iru.*（子どもたちは母親に会いたがっている）The children *want to meet* their mother.

ta⌐gaya⌐s·u たがやす（耕す）*vt.* (tagayash·i-; tagayas·a-; tagayash·i-te Ⓒ) cultivate; till; plow:
tochi o tagayasu（土地を耕す）*cultivate* land / *hatake o tagayasu*（畑を耕す）*plow* a field.

ta⌐gu⌐r·u たぐる（手繰る）*vt.* (tagur·i-; tagur·a-; tagut-te Ⓒ) haul in [up]; draw in:
tsuna o taguru（綱をたぐる）*haul up* a rope.

ta⌐i¹ たい（対）*n.* versus; between:
Jaiañtsu tai Taigaasu no shiai（ジャイアンツ対タイガースの試合）a game *between* the Giants and the Tigers / *Uchi no chiimu wa sañ tai ni de katta.*（うちのチームは3対2で勝った）Our team won by a score of three *to* one.

ta⌐i² たい（鯛）*n.* sea bream.
★ Since the name of the fish is associated with the word '*medetai*' (happy), it is customarily served on happy occasions.

ta⌐i³ たい（隊）*n.* party; company; band:
tai o kumu（隊を組む）form a *party* (of men) / *soosaku-tai*（捜索隊）a search *party*.

Ta⌐i タイ（泰）*n.* Thailand.

-ta·i たい *infl. end.* (-ku) [attached to the continuative base of a verb] want (to do); would like (to do): ★ Indicates the speaker's wishes or a desire to do something.
Watashi wa nani-ka uñdoo ga [o] *shitai.*（私は何か運動が[を]したい）I *want to do* some exercise. 《⇨ ga¹》 / *Kono mizu o nomitai no desu ga, nomemasu ka?*（この水を飲みたいので

すが, 飲めますか）I'*d like to drink* this water, but is it good for drinking? / *Kyoo wa ikitaku arimaseñ.*（きょうは行きたくありません）I *don't wish to* go today. / *Sono hoñ o itsu-ka yomitai to omotte imasu.*（その本をいつか読みたいと思っています）I *want to read* that book some day. / *Ano hito to ryokoo ni ikitai.*（あの人と旅行に行きたい）I *want to go* on a trip with her. / *Nakitai kimochi da.*（泣きたい気持ちだ）I *feel like* crying. / *Hayaku kekka o shiritakatta.*（早く結果を知りたかった）I *was anxious to know* the result soon.

ta⌐idañ たいだん（対談）*n.* talk between two people; interview:
taidañ-bañgumi（対談番組）a (television) *talk* show.
taidañ suru (〜する) *vi.* have a talk: *Sono futari no sakka ga terebi de taidañ suru no o mimashita.*（その二人の作家がテレビで対談するのを見ました）I saw the two authors *having a talk* on television.

ta⌐ido たいど（態度）*n.* attitude; manner; behavior:
taido o kaeru（態度を変える）change one's *attitude* / *taido o kimeru*（態度を決める）determine one's *attitude* / *tsuyoi taido o toru*（強い態度をとる）adopt a firm *attitude* / *Sono ko wa jugyoo-chuu taido ga warukatta.*（その子は授業中態度が悪かった）The child *behaved badly* in class. / *Ano hito wa itsu-mo taido ga ookii.*（あの人はいつも態度が大きい）His *attitude* is always arrogant.

ta⌐ifu⌐u たいふう（台風）*n.* typhoon:
Taifuu ga Kañtoo chihoo o osotta.（台風が関東地方を襲った）The *typhoon* hit the Kanto district.

ta⌐igai たいがい（大概）*n.* (〜 no) most; nearly all:
Eki made taigai wa jitensha de

ikimasu. (駅までたいがいは自転車で行きます) *In most cases*, I go to the station by bicycle. / *Taigai no otoko-no-ko wa ootobai ni kañshiñ ga aru.* (たいがいの男の子はオートバイに関心がある) *Most* boys are interested in motorbikes.
— *adv.* usually; generally: *Nichiyoobi wa* taigai *ie ni imasu.* (日曜日はたいがい家にいます) On Sundays I am *generally* at home. (⇨ taitee)

ta⌐igaku たいがく (退学) *n.* withdrawal from school; expulsion from school: taigaku-*shobuñ* (退学処分) *expulsion* from school / taigaku-*todoke* (退学届) a notice of *withdrawal from school*. (⇨ teegaku¹)
taigaku suru (～する) *vi.* leave school: *Kare wa katee no jijoo de* taigaku *shimashita.* (彼は家庭の事情で退学しました) He *left school* for family reasons. / *Go-niñ no gakusee ga kisoku ihañ de* taigaku saserareta. (五人の学生が規則違反で退学させられた) Five students *were expelled* from school because of their violation of the rules.

ta⌐iguu たいぐう (待遇) *n.* **1** treatment; terms; pay: taiguu *o kaizeñ suru* (待遇を改善する) give (a person) better *treatment* / *Soko de no* taiguu *wa hidokatta.* (そこでの待遇はひどかった) The *treatment* I got there was terrible. / *Ano kaisha wa* taiguu *ga yoi* [*warui*]. (あの会社は待遇が良い[悪い]) That company *pays* its employees *well* [*badly*]. / *Sono kaisha wa kare o buchoo-*taiguu *de mukaeta.* (その会社は彼を部長待遇で迎えた) The company employed him on the same *terms* as those of a general manager.
2 service: *Kono ryokañ wa* taiguu *ga yoi.* (こ

の旅館は待遇が良い) The *service* at this inn is good.
taiguu suru (～する) *vt.* treat; pay: *Watashi-domo de wa kakuji no jitsuryoku ni oojite* taiguu shimasu. (私どもでは各自の実力に応じて待遇します) We *pay* each person according to his or her ability.

Ta⌐ihe⌐eyoo たいへいよう (太平洋) *n.* Pacific Ocean. (⇨ Taiseeyoo)

Ta⌐iheeyoo-se⌐ñsoo たいへいようせんそう (太平洋戦争) *n.* World War II (especially the Pacific Theater).

ta⌐iheñ たいへん (大変) *a.n.* (～ na) **1** very; awful; terrible: *Ryokoo de wa* taiheñ *na keekeñ o shimashita.* (旅行ではたいへんな経験をしました) I had an *awful* experience during the trip. / *Kinoo no atsusa wa* taiheñ *na mono deshita.* (きのうの暑さはたいへんなものでした) Yesterday's heat was something *terrible*.
2 (of quantity) a lot of: *Sono shoobai ni wa* taiheñ *na shikiñ ga iru.* (その商売にはたいへんな資金がいる) You need *a lot of* funds for that business.
3 hard; difficult: *Kare o settoku suru no wa* taiheñ *desu.* (彼を説得するのはたいへんです) It is *hard* to persuade him.
4 serious; grave: Taiheñ *na machigai o shite shimatta.* (たいへんな間違いをしてしまった) I have made a *serious* mistake.
Taiheñ da (～だ) Good heavens!: Taiheñ da. *Tonari ga kaji da.* (大変だ。隣が火事だ) *Good heavens!* There is a fire next door.
— *adv.* (～ ni) very much; greatly; extremely: Taiheñ (*ni*) *yoku dekimashita.* (たいへん(に)よくできました) You did *very well.* / Taiheñ *o-sewa ni narimashita.* (たいへんお世話になりました) I

am *very much* obliged to you for your kindness. / *Watashi wa Nihoñ-buñgaku ni* taiheñ *kañshiñ ga arimasu.* (私は日本文学にたいへん関心があります) I have a *very deep* interest in Japanese literature.

ta⌐iho たいほ (逮捕) *n.* arrest: taiho-*joo* (逮捕状) an *arrest* warrant.

taiho suru (～する) *vt.* arrest: *Sono otoko wa nusumi no geñkoo-hañ de* taiho *sareta.* (その男は盗みの現行犯で逮捕された) That man *was arrested* in the act of stealing.

ta⌐ihoo たいほう (大砲) *n.* heavy gun; cannon: taihoo *o utsu* (大砲を撃つ) fire a *gun.*

ta⌐iiku たいいく (体育) *n.* physical education: taiiku *no jugyoo* (体育の授業) a *physical education* class / taiiku-*kañ* (体育館) a *gymnasium.*

Ta⌐iiku-no-hi (体育の日) *n.* Health-Sports Day (Oct. 10). 《⇨ shukujitsu (table)》

ta⌐iiñ たいいん (退院) *n.* leaving the hospital: *Kanojo no* taiiñ *wa itsu desu ka?* (彼女の退院はいつですか) When *is* she *leaving* the hospital? / *Taiiñ omedetoo gozaimasu.* (退院おめでとうございます) Congratulations on your *discharge from the hospital.*

taiiñ suru (～する) *vi.* leave the hospital; be discharged from the hospital: *Okagesama de chichi wa kinoo* taiiñ *shimashita.* (おかげさまで父はきのう退院しました) I am glad to say that my father *left the hospital* yesterday. 《↔ nyuuiñ》

ta⌐iji たいじ (退治) *n.* getting rid of; extermination:

taiji suru (～する) *vt.* get rid of; exterminate: *gokiburi o* taiji *suru* (ごきぶりを退治する) *get rid of* cockroaches.

Ta⌐i⌐jiñ タイじん (タイ人) *n.* a Thai.

ta⌐ijoo たいじょう (退場) *n.* leaving; exit: *Kare wa shiñpañ ni* taijoo *o mee-jirareta.* (彼は審判に退場を命じられた) He *was thrown out* of the game by the umpire.

taijoo suru (～する) *vi.* leave; exit: *butai kara* taijoo suru (舞台から退場する) *leave* the stage / *Kare wa seki o kette* taijoo *shita.* (彼は席をけって退場した) Kicking the chair, he *walked out* of the room. 《⇨ nyuujoo》

ta⌐ijuu たいじゅう (体重) *n.* one's body weight: taijuu *ga fueru [heru]* (体重が増える[減る]) gain [lose] *weight* / taijuu *o hakaru* (体重を測る) *weigh oneself* / *Taijuu wa rokujuu-go kiro arimasu.* (体重は65キロあります) I *weigh* sixty-five kilograms.

ta⌐ika たいか (大家) *n.* authority; expert; great master.

ta⌐ikai たいかい (大会) *n.* **1** convention; mass [general] meeting: *Too no* taikai *ga chikai uchi ni hirakaremasu.* (党の大会が近いうちに開かれます) The party *convention* will be held in the near future. **2** tournament; contest: *tenisu-*taikai (テニス大会) a tennis *tournament* / *beñroñ-*taikai (弁論大会) a speech *contest.*

ta⌐ikaku たいかく (体格) *n.* physique; constitution; build: *gasshiri shita* taikaku *no hito* (がっしりした体格の人) a man of strong *build.*

ta⌐ikee たいけい (体系) *n.* system; organization: taikee no totonotta *riroñ* (体系の整った理論) a *well-constructed* theory.

ta⌐ikee-teki たいけいてき (体系的) *a.n.* (～ na, ni) systematic: *Kare no roñbuñ wa* taikee-teki *de nai.* (彼の論文は体系的でない) His thesis is not *systematic.* / *Watashi wa Nihoñgo no buñpoo o* taikee-teki *ni manañda.*（私は日本語の文法を体系的に学んだ）I studied Japanese grammar *systematically.*

ta⌐ikeñ　たいけん（体験）*n.* personal experience:
taikeñ *o ikasu*（体験を生かす）make use of one's *experience* / taikeñ-*gakushuu*（体験学習）learning by *experience.*

taikeñ suru（〜する）*vt.* experience; undergo: *Watashi wa kore made ooku no koññañ o* taikeñ shite kimashita.（私はこれまで多くの困難を体験してきました）Up to now, I *have come through* a lot of difficulties.

ta⌐ikiñ　たいきん（大金）*n.* large sum of money:
Kare wa sono señkyo de taikiñ *o baramaita.*（彼はその選挙で大金をばらまいた）He spread around *a great deal of money* at the election. / *Juumañ-eñ wa watashi ni totte* taikiñ *desu.*（10万円は私にとって大金です）One hundred thousand yen is *a large sum of money* to me.

ta⌐iko　たいこ（太鼓）*n.* drum:
taiko *o tataku*（太鼓をたたく）beat a *drum.*

BEATING A TAIKO

ta⌐ikoo　たいこう（対抗）*n.* competition; rivalry:
taikoo-*ba*（対抗馬）a *rival* horse; a *rival* candidate in an election / taikoo-*ishiki*（対抗意識）*competitive* spirit.

taikoo suru（〜する）*vi.* match; equal; compete: *Suupaa ni* taikoo shite, *kaku shooteñ wa baageñ o hajimeta.*（スーパーに対抗して、各商店はバーゲンを始めた）*To compete* with the supermarket, each shop started giving reductions.

ta⌐ikutsu　たいくつ（退屈）*a.n.* (〜 na) tedious; boring; dull: taikutsu *na hanashi*（退屈な話）a *tedious* story / *Sono eega wa* taikutsu *datta.*（その映画は退屈だった）The movie was *boring.* / *Nani mo suru koto ga nakute,* taikutsu *da.*（何もすることがなくて、退屈だ）With nothing to do, I am *bored.*

taikutsu suru（〜する）*vi.* be bored; be weary: *Kare no nagai hanashi ni wa* taikutsu shita.（彼の長い話には退屈した）I *got bored* with his long drawn-out story. 《⇨ akiru》

ta⌐ioñ　たいおん（体温）*n.* body temperature:
taioñ *o hakaru*（体温を測る）take a person's *temperature.* 《⇨ oñdo (table)》

ta⌐ioñkee　たいおんけい（体温計）*n.* clinical thermometer.

ta⌐ipu¹　タイプ *n.* type; kind: *gakusha* taipu *no hito*（学者タイプの人）a scholarly *kind* of person / *Watashi wa ano* taipu *no hito wa nigate desu.*（私はあのタイプの人は苦手です）I just cannot get along with that *type* of person.

ta⌐ipu²　タイプ *n.* typewriter; typing:
tegami o taipu *de utsu*（手紙をタイプで打つ）*type* a letter / *Anata wa* taipu *ga dekimasu ka?*（あなたはタイプができますか）Can you *type?*

taipu suru（〜する）*vt.* type: *Kono geñkoo o* taipu shite *kudasai.*（この原稿をタイプしてください）Please *type up* this manuscript.

ta⌐ipura⌐itaa　タイプライター *n.* typewriter:

tegami o taipuraitaa *de utsu* (手紙をタイプライターで打つ) write a letter on a *typewriter*.

ta⌐ira たいら（平ら）*a.n.* (~ na, ni) flat; even; level:
taira *na ita* (平らな板) a *flat* board / *Kono heñ wa* taira *na tochi ga sukunai.* (この辺は平らな土地が少ない) There is little *flat* land around here. / *Hyoomeñ o* taira *ni shite kudasai.* (表面を平らにしてください) Please make the surface *level*.

ta⌐iriku たいりく（大陸）*n.* continent.

ta⌐iritsu たいりつ（対立）*n.* opposition; antagonism; confrontation:
Ryoosha wa ima tairitsu *jootai ni aru.* (両者は今対立状態にある) The two of them are in a state of *confrontation*. / *Roo-shi no* tairitsu *ga fukamatte iru.* (労使の対立が深まっている) The *antagonism* between labor and management has become pronounced.
tairitsu suru (~する) *vi.* be opposed; confront: *rigai ga* tairitsu suru (利害が対立する) interests *are in conflict* / *Kare to chichi-oya no ikeñ wa makkoo kara* tairitsu shite ita. (彼と父親の意見は真っ向から対立していた) His and his father's opinions *were in* direct *confrontation*.

ta⌐iryoku たいりょく（体力）*n.* physical strength; powers:
tairyoku *o tsukeru* (体力をつける) build up one's *strength* / *Watashi wa amari* tairyoku *ga nai.* (私はあまり体力がない) I do not have much *physical strength*. / *Kare wa saikiñ* tairyoku *ga otoroete kite iru.* (彼は最近体力が衰えてきている) His *physical powers* are failing these days.

ta⌐iryoo たいりょう（大量）*n.* a large quantity:
Koñpyuutaa wa tairyoo *no kami o shoohi suru.* (コンピューターは大量の紙を消費する) Computers use *a large quantity* of paper. / *Kare wa sono shina o* tairyoo *ni kaikoñda.* (彼はその品を大量に買い込んだ) He bought up those goods in *bulk*.
(↔ shooryoo)

ta⌐isaku たいさく（対策）*n.* measure; countermeasure:
Kootsuu-jiko ni taishite, nañra ka no taisaku *o kañgaenakereba naranai.* (交通事故に対して, なんらかの対策を考えなければならない) We have to work out some *measures* against traffic accidents. / *Soo-oñ koogai ni taishite, nani mo* taisaku *ga koojirarete inai.* (騒音公害に対して, 何も対策が講じられていない) No *measures* have been taken to deal with the noise pollution.

ta⌐isee たいせい（体制）*n.* system; structure; establishment:
atarashii seeji-taisee *o kakuritsu suru* (新しい政治体制を確立する) establish a new political *system* / *Kare wa* taisee *ni hañtai shite iru hitori da.* (彼は体制に反対している一人だ) He is one of those who are against the *establishment*.
(↔ hañ-taisee)

Ta⌐ise⌐eyoo たいせいよう（大西洋）*n.* Atlantic Ocean.
(⇨ Taiheeyoo)

ta⌐iseki たいせき（体積）*n.* volume; capacity:
Kono tsutsumi no taiseki *wa yaku hyakunijuu-rippoo-señchi arimasu.* (この包みの体積は約 120 立方センチあります) The *volume* of this package is about 120 cubic centimeters.
(⇨ meñseki)

ta⌐iseñ たいせん（大戦）*n.* great war:
dai ni-ji sekai taiseñ (第二次世界大戦) the Second World *War*.

ta⌐isetsu たいせつ（大切）*a.n.* (~ na, ni) important; valuable; precious:
Taisetsu *na koto o wasurete ima-*

shita. (大切なことを忘れていました) I've forgotten something *important.* / *Kore wa watashi ga* taisetsu ni shite iru *e desu.* (これは私が大切にしている絵です) This is the picture that I *treasure.* / *Mizu o* taisetsu ni shiyoo. (水を大切にしよう) *Let's not waste* water. (⇨ daiji¹)

ta˥isha たいしゃ (退社) *n.* leaving one's office; resignation; retirement.

taisha suru (〜する) *vi.* leave one's office; resign; retire: *Watashi wa mainichi go-ji-haṅ ni* taisha shimasu. (私は毎日5時半に退社します) I *leave* my office at half past five every day. / *Kare wa teeneṅ de* taisha shimashita. (彼は定年で退社しました) He reached the age limit and *retired.* 《↔ nyuusha》《⇨ taishoku》

ta˥ishi たいし (大使) *n.* ambassador:
chuunichi Amerika taishi (駐日アメリカ大使) the American *ambassador* to Japan.

taishi	(大使)	ambassador
kooshi	(公使)	minister
ryooji	(領事)	consul

ta˥ishikaṅ たいしかん (大使館) *n.* embassy:
Tookyoo no Igirisu taishikaṅ (東京のイギリス大使館) the British *embassy* in Tokyo.

taishikaṅ	(大使館)	embassy
kooshikaṅ	(公使館)	legation
ryoojikaṅ	(領事館)	consulate

ta˥ishita たいした (大した) *attrib.*
1 a lot of; great:
Hyakumaṅ-eṅ to ieba, taishita *kiṅgaku desu.* (100万円といえば、たいした金額です) A million yen is a *considerable* sum of money. / *Kare no shageki no udemae wa* taishita

mono da. (彼の射撃の腕前はたいしたものだ) His skill in shooting is *quite* something.
2 (with a negative) not very; not much of:
Kare no kega wa taishita *koto wa nakatta.* (彼のけがはたいしたことはなかった) His injury was *nothing* serious. / *Kare wa* taishita *shoosetsuka de wa arimaseṅ.* (彼はたいした小説家ではありません) He is not *much of* a novelist.

ta˥ishite¹ たいして (大して) *adv.* (with a negative) (not) very (much):
Taishite *o-yaku ni tatezu, mooshiwake arimaseṅ.* (たいしてお役に立てず、申し訳ありません) I am sorry that I could not be of *much* assistance. / *Sono shirase o kiite mo, kare wa* taishite *yorokobanakatta.* (その知らせを聞いても、彼はたいして喜ばなかった) Even when he heard the news, he was not *particularly* happy. / Taishite *eraku mo nai no ni kare wa soṅdai da.* (たいして偉くもないのに彼は尊大だ) Although he is not *such* a great person, he is arrogant.

ta˥ishite² たいして (対して)
★ Used in the pattern '*...ni taishite.*' **1** to; against; regarding: ★ Used in expressions of reference.
Go-shitsumoṅ ni taishite *o-kotae shimasu.* (ご質問に対してお答えします) I will reply *to* your question. / *Wareware wa kaisha no hooshiṅ ni* taishite *tsuyoku haṅtai shita.* (われわれは会社の方針に対して強く反対した) We firmly opposed the company's policy. / *Soo iu iikata wa aite ni* taishite *shitsuree desu.* (そういう言い方は相手に対して失礼です) Such a way of speaking is rude *to* the other person. / *Sono rikishi wa yokozuna ni* taishite *zeṅseṅ shita.* (その力士は横綱に対して善戦し

た) The sumo wrestler put up a good fight *against* the grand champion. 《⇨ taisuru》

2 in contrast to:

Sono keekaku ni neñchoosha ga sañsee shita no ni taishite, *wakai hito-tachi wa hañtai shita.* (その計画に年長者が賛成したのに対して、若い人たちは反対した) *In contrast to* the elderly people's support of the plan, the young were against it.

ta⸢ishoku たいしょく (退職) *n.* retirement; resignation:

Taishoku-go wa doo sareru ñ desu ka? (退職後はどうされるんですか) What are you going to do after *retirement*? / taishoku-*kiñ* (退職金) *severance* pay; a *retirement* allowance.

taishoku suru (〜する) *vi.* retire; resign: *Chichi wa kyoneñ teeneñ de* taishoku shimashita. (父は去年定年で退職しました) Last year my father *left his company* at the retirement age. 《⇨ taisha》

ta⸢ishoo¹ たいしょう (対象) *n.* object; subject:

Kare no keñkyuu no taishoo *wa Nihoñ-tee-eñ desu.* (彼の研究の対象は日本庭園です) The *object* of his study is the Japanese garden. / *Kono shina wa kazee no* taishoo ni narimasu. (この品は課税の対象になります) These goods *are subject to* taxation. / *Kono zasshi wa wakai josee o* taishoo ni shite imasu. (この雑誌は若い女性を対象にしています) This magazine *is intended* for young women.

ta⸢ishoo² たいしょう (対照) *n.* contrast; comparison:

Kono e wa mee-añ no taishoo *ga hakkiri shite iru.* (この絵は明暗の対照がはっきりしている) There is a sharp *contrast* between light and shade in this picture. / *Shiroi kabe ga kuroi kagu to utsukushii* taishoo *o nashite iru.* (白い壁が黒い家具と美しい対照をなしている) The white walls make a lovely *contrast* with the black furniture.

taishoo suru (〜する) *vt.* contrast; compare: *hoñyaku o geñbuñ to* taishoo suru (翻訳を原文と対照する) *compare* a translation with the original text / *choobo o geñbo to* taishoo suru (帳簿を原簿と対照する) *compare* the account books with the original ledger.

ta⸢ishoo³ たいしょう (対称) *n.* symmetry.

ta⸢ishoo⁴ たいしょう (大将) *n.* general; admiral: ★ For specificity, add the name of the service before the rank.

kaiguñ-taishoo (海軍大将) *admiral.*

Ta⸢ishoo たいしょう (大正) *n.* Taisho:

Taishoo-*jidai* (大正時代) the *Taisho* era (1912–1926) / Taishoo-teñoo (大正天皇) the *Taisho* Emperor. 《⇨ geñgoo (table); jidai (table)》

ta⸢ishuu たいしゅう (大衆) *n.* the general public; the people; the masses:

Sono seesaku wa taishuu *no shiji o erarenakatta.* (その政策は大衆の支持を得られなかった) The policy failed to get the support of *the people.* / taishuu-*sha* (大衆車) a *popular* car / taishuu-*shokudoo* (大衆食堂) a *cheap* restaurant / taishuu-*uñdoo* (大衆運動) a *mass* movement.

ta⸢isoo¹ たいそう (体操) *n.* gymnastics; physical exercise; calisthenics:

Kanojo wa biyoo to keñkoo no tame ni taisoo *o shite imasu.* (彼女は美容と健康のために体操をしています) She does *exercise* for beauty and health. / taisoo-*kyoogi* (体操競技) a *gymnastic* competition / taisoo-señshu (体操選手) a *gymnast.* 《⇨ uñdoo》

ta⌐isoo² たいそう（大層）*adv.* very (much); greatly:

Kanojo wa sono e ga taisoo ki ni itte iru yoo datta.（彼女はその絵がたいそう気に入っているようだった）She seemed to like the picture *very much*. 《⇨ hijoo》

ta⌐is·u⌐ru たいする（対する）*vi.* (ta-ish·i-; tais·a-; taish·i-te ⓒ)

...ni taisuru (...に〜) to; against: *Sono mondai ni taisuru taisaku o tatenakereba naranai.*（その問題に対する対策を立てなければならない）We have to work out countermeasures *against* the problem. 《⇨ taishite²》

ta⌐itee たいてい（大抵）*n.* (〜 no) most; just about:

Taitee no kodomo wa chokoreeto ga suki desu.（たいていの子どもはチョコレートが好きです）*Most* children like chocolate. / *Kanojo wa taitee no shigoto wa konashimasu.*（彼女はたいていの仕事はこなします）She can handle *just about* any kind of work.

— *adv.* usually; generally: *Chichi wa nichiyoobi wa taitee gorufu ni ikimasu.*（父は日曜日はたいていゴルフに行きます）My father *usually* goes off to play golf on Sundays. 《⇨ taigai》

ta⌐itoo たいとう（対等）*a.n.* (〜 na/no, ni) equal; even:

otagai ni taitoo no tachiba de hanashiau（お互いに対等の立場で話し合う）talk with each other on an *equal* footing / *Kono shokuba de wa minna ga taitoo desu.*（この職場ではみんなが対等です）Everyone is *equal* in this workplace. / *Ware-ware wa aite chiimu to taitoo ni tatakatta.*（われわれは相手チームと対等に戦った）We competed on *equal terms* against the other team. 《⇨ byoodoo》

Ta⌐iwa⌐n たいわん（台湾）*n.* Taiwan.

Ta⌐iwan⌐jin たいわんじん（台湾人）*n.* Taiwanese.

ta⌐iya タイヤ *n.* tire:

taiya ni kuuki o ireru（タイヤに空気を入れる）pump up a *tire* / *taiya o torikaeru*（タイヤを取り替える）change *tires* / *Taiya ga panku shita.*（タイヤがパンクした）I got a flat *tire*.

ta⌐iyaku たいやく（大役）*n.* important task [duty]:

taiyaku o hatasu（大役を果たす）carry out an *important duty*.

ta⌐iyoo¹ たいよう（太陽）*n.* the sun:

Taiyoo wa higashi kara nobori, nishi ni shizumu.（太陽は東から昇り，西に沈む）*The sun* rises in the east and sets in the west. / *taiyoo-denchi*（太陽電池）a *solar* battery / *taiyoo-netsu*（太陽熱）*solar* heat.

ta⌐iyoo² たいよう（大洋）*n.* ocean: *taiyoo-koorosen*（大洋航路船）an *ocean* liner.

ta⌐iyoo-ne⌐nsuu たいようねんすう（耐用年数）*n.* period of durability; life:

Kono terebi no taiyoo-nensuu wa juu-nen desu.（このテレビの耐用年数は10年です）The *life* of this television is ten years.

ta⌐izai たいざい（滞在）*n.* stay; visit:

Kanazawa ni wa is-shuukan taizai no yotee desu.（金沢には一週間滞在の予定です）We plan to *stay* in Kanazawa for a week. / *Sono jiken wa watashi ga Pekin taizai-chuu ni okimashita.*（その事件は私が北京滞在中に起きました）That incident took place *while I was staying* in Beijing.

taizai suru (〜する) *vi.* stay: *Watashi mo sono hoteru ni is-shuukan taizai shita koto ga arimasu.*（私もそのホテルに一週間滞在したことがあります）I also *stayed* at the hotel for a week.

ta⌈ka たか (鷹) *n.* hawk; falcon.

ta⌈ka⌉·i たかい (高い) *a.* (-ku)
1 high; tall; lofty:
takai *tatemono* (高い建物) a *tall* building / *Tanaka-sañ wa se ga* takai. (田中さんは背が高い) Mr. Tanaka is *tall.* / *Fuji-sañ wa Nihoñ de ichibañ* takai *yama desu.* (富士山は日本で一番高い山です) Mt. Fuji is the *highest* mountain in Japan. / *Hikooki ga sora* takaku *toñde iru.* (飛行機が空高く飛んでいる) The plane is flying *high* in the sky. (（↔ hikui)) (（⇨ takasa)）
2 expensive; high; dear:
teedo no takai *gakkoo* (程度の高い学校) a school of *high* academic standing / *Tookyoo wa bukka ga* takai. (東京は物価が高い) The price of goods in Tokyo is *high.* / *Kono yubiwa wa* takakute, *watashi ni wa kaemaseñ.* (この指輪は高くて、私には買えません) This ring is too *expensive* for me to buy. / *Kare no kaisha wa kyuuryoo ga* takai *rashii.* (彼の会社は給料が高いらしい) The salary in his company is apparently *good.* (（↔ yasui)）
3 (of status, position, degree, etc.) high:
takai *risoo* (高い理想) *high* ideals / takai *seekatsu suijuñ* (高い生活水準) a *high* standard of living / *Kachoo wa Suzuki-sañ o* takaku *hyooka shite iru.* (課長は鈴木さんを高く評価している) The manager thinks *highly* of Mr. Suzuki. (（↔ hikui)）
4 (of sound, voice) loud; high-pitched:
Koe ga takai. *Hito ni kikareru zo.* (声が高い。人に聞かれるぞ) Your voice is too *loud.* You will be overheard.

ta⌈ka⌉kukee たかくけい (多角形) *n.* polygon.

ta⌈kama⌉r·u たかまる (高まる) *vi.* (takamar·i-; takamar·a-; taka-mat-te Ⓒ) rise; increase:
Sono hoñ de kanojo no meesee ga takamatta. (その本で彼女の名声が高まった) Her fame *grew* because of the book. / *Ryookoku no aida no seeji-teki kiñchoo ga* takamatte iru. (両国の間の政治的緊張が高まっている) Political tensions between the two countries *are increasing.* (（⇨ takameru)）

ta⌈kame⌉·ru たかめる (高める) *vt.* (takame-te Ⓥ) raise; increase; improve:
koe o takameru (声を高める) *raise* one's voice / *kokumiñ no seekatsu-suijuñ o* takameru (国民の生活水準を高める) *increase* the people's standard of living / *kyooyoo o* takameru (教養を高める) *improve* one's cultural level / *shaiñ no shiki o* takameru (社員の士気を高める) *raise* the morale of the employees. (（⇨ takamaru)）

ta⌈kara⌉ たから (宝) *n.* treasure:
Kanojo ni totte, kodomo wa takara *desu.* (彼女にとって、子どもは宝です) To her, her child is her *treasure.* / *Kaizoku ga kono shima ni* takara *o kakushita to iwarete imasu.* (海賊がこの島に宝を隠したと言われています) It is said that pirates hid *treasure* on this island. (（⇨ takaramono)）

ta⌈kara⌉kuji たからくじ (宝くじ) *n.* public lottery (ticket):
takarakuji *ni hazureru* (宝くじに外れる) win nothing in a *lottery* / *Watashi wa* takarakuji *de juumañ-eñ ateta.* (私は宝くじで10万円当てた) I won a hundred thousand yen in a *public lottery.* (（⇨ kuji)）

TAKARAKUJI

ta⌐karamono¹ たからもの (宝物) *n.*
treasure; heirloom:
Kono e wa uchi ni tsutawaru takaramono *desu.* (この絵はうちに伝わる
宝物です) This picture is an *heirloom* which has been handed
down in our family. 《⇨ takara》

ta⌐kasa たかさ (高さ) *n.* **1** height;
altitude:
Ano biru no takasa *wa dono kurai
arimasu ka?* (あのビルの高さはどのくら
いありますか) What is the *height* of
that building? / *Kono tsukue no*
takasa *o hakatte kudasai.* (この机の
高さを測ってください) Will you please
measure the *height* of this desk?
《↔ haba》《⇨ takai》
2 high cost [price]:
Nihon ni kite seekatsu-hi no takasa *ni odorokimashita.* (日本に来
て生活費の高さに驚きました) When I
arrived in Japan, I was amazed at
the *high cost* of living. 《⇨ takai》
3 pitch; loudness:
oto no takasa *o choosetsu suru* (音
の高さを調節する) control the *pitch*
[*loudness*] of the sound.

ta⌐ke¹ たけ (竹) *n.* bamboo:
take-*yabu* (竹やぶ) a *bamboo* thick-
et / take-*zaiku* (竹細工) *bamboo*
work / take-*zao* (竹ざお) a *bamboo*
pole.

TAKE-YABU

ta⌐ke¹² たけ (丈) *n.* **1** length:
kimono no take (着物の丈) the
length of a kimono / *sukaato no*
take o mijikaku suru (スカートの丈を
短くする) *shorten* a skirt.
2 height:
take ga nobiru (丈がのびる) *grow
tall*.

ta⌐ki たき (滝) *n.* waterfall:
Nikkoo no Kegon no taki (日光の
華厳の滝) the Kegon *Falls* in
Nikko.

ta⌐kibi たきび (焚火) *n.* open-air
fire; bonfire:
takibi *ni ataru* (たき火にあたる)
warm oneself at a *fire* / *Ochiba o
atsumete,* takibi *o shita.* (落葉を集
めて、たき火をした) I gathered up the
fallen leaves and made a *fire*.

ta⌐kkyuu たっきゅう (卓球) *n.*
table tennis; ping-pong:
takkyuu *no shiai* (卓球の試合) a
table tennis match / *Kyoo wa hisashiburi ni* takkyuu *o shimashita.*
(きょうは久しぶりに卓球をしました)
Today, for the first time in a
long while, I played *table tennis*.
/ takkyuu-*dai* (卓球台) a *ping-pong*
table. 《⇨ pinpon》

ta⌐kkyuubin たっきゅうびん (宅急
便) *n.* (*trade name*) express
home delivery:
Gorufu doogu o takkyuubin *de
uchi e okutta.* (ゴルフ道具を宅急便で
家へ送った) I *had* my golf clubs
home-delivered.

ta⌐ko¹ たこ (蛸) *n.* octopus.
★ A favorite food in Japan. It is
boiled, vinegared or cooked with
vegetables.

ta⌐ko² たこ (凧)
n. kite:

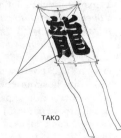

TAKO

tako *o ageru* [*orosu*] (たこを揚げる
[下ろす]) fly [draw in] a *kite*.

ta⌐ko³ たこ (胼胝) *n*. callus.

ta⌐k·u¹ たく (炊く) *vt*. (tak·i-; ta-
k·a-; ta·i-te Ⓒ) cook (rice); boil:
Kesa wa hayaku okite gohañ o
taita. (今朝は早く起きてご飯を炊いた)
I got up early this morning and
cooked the rice.

ta⌐k·u² たく (焚く) *vt*. (tak·i-; ta-
k·a-; ta·i-te Ⓒ) burn (fuel):
sekitañ [*maki*] *o* taku (石炭[まき]を
たく) *burn* coal [firewood].

ta⌐ku³ たく (宅) *n*. ⇨ otaku.

ta⌐kumashi⌐·i たくましい (逞しい) *a*.
(-ku) 1 strong; robust:
takumashii *wakamono* (たくましい若
者) a *strong* youngster / *Kare wa*
takumashii *karada o shite iru*. (彼
はたくましい体をしている) He has a *robust* physique. / *Kare no musuko
wa* takumashiku *seechoo shita*. (彼
の息子はたくましく成長した) His son
grew up into a *robust* young man.
2 powerful:
takumashii *soozooryoku* (たくましい
想像力) a *powerful* imagination.

ta⌐kumi たくみ (巧み) *a.n*. (~ na,
ni) skillful; clever:
takumi *na soosa* (巧みな操作) a *skillful* handling / *hoochoo o* takumi
ni tsukau (包丁を巧みに使う) wield a
kitchen knife with *skill* / *moñdai
o* takumi *ni shori suru* (問題を巧み
に処理する) *skillfully* deal with a
problem.

ta⌐kusa⌐ñ たくさん (沢山) *n., adv*.
1 many; much; a lot of:
Yuueñchi ni wa hito ga takusañ
imashita. (遊園地には人がたくさんいま
した)=*Yuueñchi ni wa* takusañ *no
hito ga imashita*. (遊園地にはたくさん
の人がいました) There were *a lot of*
people in the amusement park.
★ The first of these patterns is
usually more natural Japanese. /
Kare wa hoñ o takusañ *motte
imasu*. (彼は本をたくさん持っています)

He has *a lot of* books. 《↔ sukoshi; shooshoo》
2 enough; sufficiently:
Biiru wa kekkoo desu. Moo takusañ *itadakimashita*. (ビールは結構で
す. もうたくさんいただきました) No
more beer, thanks. I've already
had *quite enough*. / *Kare no jimañ-banashi wa moo* takusañ *da*.
(彼の自慢話はもうたくさんだ) I have
had *enough* of his boasting. /
Moo takusañ! (もうたくさん!) I *can't
stand it* any longer.

ta⌐kushii タクシー *n*. taxi:
Takushii *o yoñde kudasai*. (タクシー
を呼んでください) Please call me a
taxi. / Takushii *de Shiñjuku made
ikimashoo*. (タクシーで新宿まで行きま
しょう) Let's go to Shinjuku by
taxi. / *Koko de* takushii *o hiroe-
masu ka?* (ここでタクシーを拾えますか)
Can we get a *taxi* here? / taku-
shii-*noriba* (タクシー乗り場) a *taxi*
stand. 《⇨ haiyaa》

TAKUSHII NORIBA

ta⌐kuwae⌐·ru たくわえる (蓄える)
vt. (takuwae-te Ⓥ) save; put
away; store:
roogo no seekatsu-shikiñ o takuwaeru (老後の生活資金を蓄える)
save money to provide for one's
old age / *Fuyu ni sonaete, neñryoo o* takuwaete *okanakereba
naranai*. (冬に備えて, 燃料を蓄えておか
なければならない) We have to *store*

up fuel for the winter.

ta⌐ma⌐¹ たま（球）*n.* **1** (of base-ball, billiards, etc.) ball: *Kare wa hayai* tama *o nageru.*（彼は速い球を投げる）He throws a fast *ball.* / *Dare mo kare no* tama *o utenakatta.*（だれも彼の球を打てなかった）Nobody could hit his *ball.*
2 light bulb: tama *o torikaeru*（球を取り替える）change a *bulb* / *Tama ga kireta.*（球が切れた）The *bulb* has burned out.（⇨ deñkyuu）

ta⌐ma⌐² たま（玉）*n.* ball; bead: *keito no* tama（毛糸の玉）a *ball* of wool / tama *no ase*（玉の汗）*beads* of sweat.
tama ni kizu（～にきず）only fault [defect]: *Kare wa seekaku no yowai no ga* tama ni kizu *da.*（彼は性格の弱いのが玉にきずだ）A weakness in character is his *only defect.*

ta⌐ma⌐³ たま（弾）*n.* bullet: tama *ni ataru*（弾に当たる）be hit by a *bullet.*

ta⌐ma⌐go たまご（卵）*n.* egg: tamago *o umu*（卵を産む）lay an *egg* / tamago *o kaesu*（卵をかえす）hatch an *egg* / tamago *o waru*（卵を割る）break an *egg* / tamago *o yaku* [*yuderu*]（卵を焼く[ゆでる]）fry [boil] an *egg* / tamago-yaki（卵焼き）an *omelet.*（⇨ yude-tamago）

ta⌐mago-doñ たまごどん（卵どん）*n.* ⇨ doñburi

ta⌐mane⌐gi たまねぎ（玉葱）*n.* onion.（⇨ negi）

ta⌐ma ni たまに *adv.*（～ wa）once in a while; occasionally; rarely: *Kare to wa* tama ni *shika aimaseñ.*（彼とはたまにしか会いません）I meet him only *rarely.* / Tama ni *wa asobi ni kite kudasai.*（たまには遊びに来てください）Please come over to our house *from time to time.*

ta⌐marana·i たまらない（堪らない）*a.*

(-ku) ★ Polite forms are '*tamaranai desu*' and '*tamarimaseñ.*' unbearable; intolerable: *Kono atsusa wa* tamaranai.（この暑さはたまらない）This heat is *unbearable.* / *Bukka ga koo takakute wa* tamaranai.（物価がこう高くてはたまらない）It is *intolerable* that prices are this high.

-te tamaranai（て～）**1** so...that one cannot stand...: *Sabishikute* tamaranai.（寂しくてたまらない）I *am so lonely that* I *cannot stand* it. / *Musuko ga daigaku ni gookaku shita no de kanojo wa* ureshikute tamaranakatta.（息子が大学に合格したので彼女はうれしくてたまらなかった）She *was beside herself with joy* because her son passed his university entrance exam.
2 be eager; be dying: *Kanojo ni* aitakute tamaranai.（彼女に会いたくてたまらない）I *am dying to see* her. / *Jibuñ no kuruma ga* hoshikute tamaranai.（自分の車が欲しくてたまらない）I *cannot wait to have* my own car.

ta⌐mar·u⌐¹ たまる（溜まる）*vi.* (tamar·i-; tamar·a-; tamat-te Ⓒ) collect; pile up; accumulate; gather: *Tana no ue ni hokori ga* tamatta.（棚の上にほこりがたまった）Dust *has collected* on the shelf. / *Shigoto* [*Shakkiñ*] *wa sugu ni* tamaru.（仕事[借金]はすぐにたまる）The work [debt] soon *piles up.*（⇨ tameru¹）

ta⌐mar·u⌐² たまる（貯まる）*vi.* (tamar·i-; tamar·a-; tamat-te Ⓒ) be saved: *Kare wa daibu o-kane ga* tamatta *yoo da.*（彼はだいぶお金がたまったようだ）He seems to *have saved up* quite a bit of money.（⇨ tameru²）

ta⌐mashii たましい（魂）*n.* soul; spirit: *Kanojo wa shiñdara,* tamashii *wa teñgoku e iku to shiñjite iru.*（彼女

は死んだら、魂は天国へ行くと信じている）She believes that the *soul* goes to heaven when you die.

ta⌈**matama** たまたま(偶々) *adv.* by chance:

Depaato de tamatama *mukashi no tomodachi ni atta.* (デパートでたまたま昔の友だちに会った) I met *by chance* an old friend at the department store. / *Koñkai wa* tamatama *umaku ikimashita ga, itsu-mo koo to wa kagirimaseñ yo.* (今回はたまたまうまくいきましたが、いつもこうとは限りませんよ) Things *happened* to go well this time, but it does not necessarily follow that it will always be like this.

ta⌈**me**⌉ ため (為) *n.* **1** for the sake of; for the benefit of:

Soñna koto o shite mo tame *ni naranai.* (そんなことをしてもためにならない) Even if you do something like that, it will not be *beneficial*. / *Watashi wa kimi no* tame *ni, soo shita no desu.* (私は君のために、そうしたのです) I did so *for* your own *sake*. / *Kono hoñ wa kimi no* tame *ni naru yo.* (この本はきみのためになるよ) This book will *be good* for you. / *Keñkoo no* tame ni naru *koto o nani-ka shite imasu ka?* (健康のためになることを何かしていますか) Is there anything you are doing *for* your health?

2 for the purpose of; in order to:

Kanojo wa ryokoo e iku tame *ni, o-kane o tamete iru.* (彼女は旅行へ行くために、お金をためている) She is saving money *for the purpose of* going on a trip. / *Kare ga Chuugoku e iku no wa Chuugokugo o beñkyoo suru* tame *da.* (彼が中国へ行くのは中国語を勉強するためだ) The purpose of his going to China is *to* study Chinese.

3 because of; owing to; as a result of:

Byooki no tame *ni, paatii ni derarenakatta.* (病気のために、パーティーに出られなかった) I could not attend the party *because of* my illness. / *Jiko no* tame *ni, ressha ga okureta.* (事故のために、列車が遅れた) *Owing to* an accident, the train was delayed. / *Bukka ga agatta no wa iñfure no* tame *da.* (物価が上がったのはインフレのためだ) The increase in prices is *due to* inflation.

⌈ **USAGE** ⌉

When a noun comes before '*tame,*' the interpretation depends on the context. *e.g. Gorufujoo keñsetsu no* tame, *yama o kuzushita.* (ゴルフ場建設のため、山をくずした) They destroyed hills *in order to* build a golf course. / *Gorufujoo keñsetsu no* tame, *kañkyoo ga hakai sareta.* (ゴルフ場建設の為、環境が破壊された) The environment was destroyed *as a result of* the building of a golf course.

ta⌈**mei**⌉**ki** ためいき (ため息) *n.* sigh:

ooki-na tameiki *o tsuku* (大きなため息をつく) give a deep *sigh* / *Kanojo wa gakkari shite,* tameiki *o morashita.* (彼女はがっかりして、ため息をもらした) She let out a *sigh* because she was disappointed.

ta⌈**mera**⌉**·u** ためらう (躊躇う) *vi.* (tamera·i-; tameraw·a-; tamerat-te Ⓒ) hesitate; waver; hang back:

Kanojo wa soko e iku no o tameratta. (彼女はそこへ行くのをためらった) She *hesitated* about going there. / *Kare wa tsugi ni nani o iu beki ka* tameratta. (彼は次に何を言うべきかためらった) He *hesitated* over what he should say next.

《⇨ chuucho》

ta⌈**me·ru**⌉**¹** ためる (溜める) *vt.* (tame-te Ⓥ) store; cumulate:

Sono shima no hito-tachi wa ama-mizu o tamete *iñryoosui ni shite imasu.* (その島の人たちは雨水をためて飲料水にしています) The people on the island *collect and store* rainwater and use it for drinking water. / *Kanojo wa me ni namida o* tamete ita. (彼女は目に涙をためていた) Her eyes *were filled* with tears. 《⇨ tamaru¹》

ta⌐me·ru² ためる（貯める）*vt.* (tame-te Ⅴ) save; amass: *ryokoo no tame ni kane o* tameru (旅行のために金をためる) *save* money for a trip / *Sono roojiñ wa taikiñ o* tameta. (その老人は大金をためた) The old man *amassed* a fortune. 《⇨ tamaru²》

ta⌐meshi¹ **ni** ためしに（試しに）*adv.* tentatively; on trial: *Kau mae ni* tameshi ni *sono kutsu o haite mita.* (買う前に試しにその靴を履いてみた) I *tried on* the shoes before I bought them. / *Atarashii koñpyuutaa o* tameshi ni *is-shuu-kañ tsukatte mita.* (新しいコンピュータを試しに一週間使ってみた) I used the new computer *on trial* for a week.

ta⌐me⌐s·u ためす（試す）*vt.* (tamesh·i-; tames·a-; tamesh·i-te C) try; test: *Kore wa kare no nooryoku o* tamesu ii chañsu da. (これは彼の能力を試すいいチャンスだ) This is a good chance to *test* his ability. / *Doozo kono fuku o* o-tameshi *kudasai.* (どうぞこの服をお試しください) Please *try* these clothes on. / *Kare no yuuki o* tameshite miyoo. (彼の勇気を試してみよう) *Let's put* his courage *to the test.*

ta⌐mo⌐ts·u たもつ（保つ）*vi.* (tamoch·i-; tamot·a-; tamot-te C) keep; hold; maintain; preserve; retain: *heya no oñdo o ittee ni* tamotsu (部屋の温度を一定に保つ) *maintain*

a room at a constant temperature / *sekai heewa o* tamotsu (世界平和を保つ) *keep* world peace / *igeñ o* tamotsu (威厳を保つ) *maintain* one's dignity / *Keñkoo [Wakasa] o* tamotsu *ni wa kisoku tadashii seekatsu ga taisetsu desu.* (健康[若さ]を保つには規則正しい生活が大切です) A well regulated life is important in *staying* healthy [young].

ta⌐na たな（棚）*n.* shelf; rack: *Kore o soko no* tana *ni agete [nosete] kudasai.* (これをそこの棚に上げて[載せて]ください) Please put this on that *shelf.* / *Kabe ni* tana *o toritsu-keta.* (壁に棚を取り付けた) I fixed a *shelf* to the wall.

tana-age (ni) suru (棚上げ(に)する) set aside; shelve: *Sono keekaku wa* tana-age *sarete shimatta.* (その計画は棚上げされてしまった) The plan *has been shelved.*

ta⌐nabata たなばた（七夕）*n.* the Star Festival celebrated on July 7. ★ Also called '*tanabata-matsuri.*' 《⇨ ama-no-gawa》

(CULTURE)

In the legend, the two stars, who are lovers, Vega and Altair, cross the Milky Way once a year on the seventh night of July in order to meet.

---

ta⌐ñbo たんぼ（田圃）*n.* rice paddy. 《⇨ ta¹; suideñ (photo)》

ta⌐ñchoo たんちょう（単調）*a.n.* (~ na, ni) monotonous; dull: *Kono heñ no fuukee wa* tañchoo *desu.* (この辺の風景は単調です) The scenery around here is *monotonous.* / *Tañchoo na seekatsu ni wa akimashita.* (単調な生活には飽きました) I am tired of my *dull* life.

ta⌐ne たね（種）*n.* **1** seed: tane *o maku* (種をまく) sow [plant] *seeds.*

2 cause; source:

Musume no koto ga itsu-mo shiñpai no tane desu.(娘のことがいつも心配の種です) Our daughter is always a *cause* of anxiety.

ta⌐ñgo たんご (単語) *n.* word; vocabulary:
tañgo no imi o jisho de shiraberu (単語の意味を辞書で調べる) look up the meaning of a *word* in the dictionary.

ta⌐ni¹ たに (谷) *n.* valley; gorge.

ta⌐ñi たんい (単位) *n.* **1** unit:
Eñ ga Nihoñ no tsuuka no tañi *desu.*(円が日本の通貨の単位です) The yen is the *unit* of Japanese currency. / *Kono hyoo no kiñgaku wa señ-eñ* tañi *desu.*(この表の金額は千円単位です) The money in this table is shown in *units* of one thousand yen.
2 (of a school) credit:
*Sotsugyoo made ni ato ni-*tañi *toranakereba naranai.*(卒業までにあと2単位とらなければならない) I have to earn two more *credits* by graduation.

ta⌐niñ たにん (他人) *n.* others; unrelated person:
Taniñ ni meewaku o kakenai yoo ni ki o tsuke nasai.(他人に迷惑をかけないように気をつけなさい) Be careful not to cause trouble to *others.*

ta⌐ñjoo たんじょう (誕生) *n.* birth:
shiñ-seekeñ no tañjoo (新政権の誕生) the *birth* of a new government / *tañjoo-iwai* (誕生祝い) a *birthday* present.
tañjoo suru (〜する) *vi.* be born:
Sono fuufu ni chuunañ ga tañjoo *shita.*(その夫婦に長男が誕生した) Their first son *was born* to them.

ta⌐ñjo⌐obi たんじょうび (誕生日) *n.* birthday:
Tañjoobi omedetoo.(誕生日おめでとう) Happy *birthday* to you!

ta⌐ñjuñ たんじゅん (単純) *a.n.* (〜 na, ni) **1** simple:
tañjuñ na keesañ (単純な計算) a

simple calculation / *Kore wa tañjuñ ni kaiketsu dekiru moñdai de wa nai.*(これは単純に解決できる問題ではない) This is not a problem that can be *easily* solved. / *Tañjuñ ni kañgaereba, kare no itte iru koto wa tadashii.*(単純に考えれば, 彼の言っていることは正しい) In *simple* terms, what he says is right.
2 (of people, ways of thinking, etc.) simple-minded:
tañjuñ na hito (単純な人) a *simple-minded* person.

ta⌐ñka¹ たんか (単価) *n.* unit price:
tañka o sageru (単価を下げる) lower the *unit price.*

ta⌐ñka² たんか (担架) *n.* stretcher:
Kare wa tañka *de hakobareta.*(彼は担架で運ばれた) He was carried on a *stretcher.*

ta⌐ñka³ たんか (短歌) *n.* Japanese poem consisting of 31 syllables.
★ The syllables are arranged in five lines of 5, 7, 5, 7 and 7.
《⇨ next page》

ta⌐ñkeñ たんけん (探検) *n.* exploration; expedition:
Nañkyoku tañkeñ (南極探検) an Antarctic *exploration* / tañkeñ-ka (探検家) an *explorer.*
tañkeñ suru (〜する) *vt.* explore:
Shooneñ-tachi wa sono chiisa-na shima o tañkeñ *shita.*(少年たちはその小さな島を探検した) The boys *explored* the small island.

ta⌐ñki¹ たんき (短期) *n.* a short (period) of time:
Tañki no kashitsuke o mooshikoñda.(短期の貸し付けを申し込んだ) I asked for a *short-term* loan. / *Kare wa* tañki-*kañ de Nihoñgo o shuutoku shita.*(彼は短期間で日本語を習得した) He mastered Japanese in a *short time.* 《↔ chooki》

ta⌐ñki² たんき (短気) *n., a.n.* (〜 na) short temper; short-tempered:

tañki o okosu (短気を起こす) *lose one's temper* / *Chichi wa* tañki *de, sugu okoru.* (父は短気で、すぐ怒る) My father is *short-tempered*, so he gets angry easily.

ta⌐ñkoo たんこう (炭鉱) *n.* coal mine.

ta⌐ñ-naru たんなる (単なる) *attrib.* mere; simple; only:
Sore wa tañ-naru *uwasa desu.* (それは単なるうわさです) That is a *mere* rumor. / *Kare ga itte iru no wa* tañ-naru *iiwake ni suginai.* (彼が言っているのは単なる言い訳に過ぎない) What he says is *nothing more* than an excuse.

ta⌐ñ ni たんに (単に) *adv.* only; merely; simply:
Watashi wa tañ ni *shitte iru koto o hanashita dake desu.* (私は単に知っていることを話しただけです) I have just told them *only* what I know. 《⇨ tada¹》

ta⌐ no たの (他の) *attrib.* other; another:
ta no *hito* [*moñdai*] (他の人 [問題]) *another* person [problem] / ta no *gidai* (他の議題) *another* topic for discussion. 《⇨ hoka》

ta⌐nomi たのみ (頼み) *n.* request; favor:
Anata ni tanomi *ga aru no desu ga.* (あなたに頼みがあるのですが) I have a *favor* to ask of you. / *Watashi wa kare no* tanomi *o kotowatta.* (私は彼の頼みを断った) I declined his *request.* 《⇨ tanomu》

tanomi no tsuna (〜の綱) one's only [last] hope: *Watashi no* tanomi no tsuna *wa kireta.* (私の頼みの綱は切れた) My *one and only hope* is gone.

ta⌐nomoshi⌐·i たのもしい (頼もしい) *a.* (-ku) reliable; promising; trustworthy:
Musuko-sañ mo tanomoshiku *narimashita ne.* (息子さんも頼もしくなりましたね) Your son has grown into a *reliable* youth, hasn't he? / *Kotoshi wa* tanomoshii *shiñnyuu-shaiñ ga ooi.* (ことしは頼もしい新入社員が多い) Many of the new employees this year look *promising.*

ta⌐no⌐m·u たのむ (頼む) *vt.* (ta-nom·i-; tanom·a-; tanoñ-de Ⓒ)
1 ask (a favor); beg:
Anata ni tanomitai *koto ga aru no desu ga.* (あなたに頼みたいことがあるのですが) There is something I *want to ask* of you. / *Watashi wa kare ni tasuke o* tanoñda. (私は彼に助けを頼んだ) I *asked* him for assistance. 《⇨ tanomi》
2 order (goods); call (in); hire:
Hoñya ni hoñ o tanoñda *ga shinagire datta.* (本屋に本を頼んだが品切れだった) I *ordered* a book at the bookshop, but it was out of stock.

TAÑKA

Hisakata no	ひさかたの
hikari nodokeki	ひかりのどけき
haru no hi ni	はるのひに
shizu kokoronaku	しづこころなく
hana no chirurañ	はなのちるらむ

久方の光のどけき春の日にしづ心なく花の散るらむ

(紀　友則)

On such a calm and quiet day in the spring, why do the cherry blossoms fall in a hurry.

(Ki no Tomonori)

/ *Takushii o* tanoñde *kudasai.*(タクシーを頼んでください) Please *call a* taxi. / *Isha o* tanomimasu.(医者を頼みます) I will *call* a doctor.

ta⌐noshi⌐·i たのしい（楽しい）*a.* (-ku) enjoyable; cheerful; happy:
Oñgaku o kiku no wa tanoshii.(音楽を聞くのは楽しい) Listening to music is *enjoyable.* / *Moo sugu* tanoshii *shoogatsu ga yatte kuru.* (もうすぐ楽しい正月がやって来る) Soon the New Year, which is so *enjoyable*, will be upon us. / *Kinoo no eñsoku wa totemo* tanoshikatta. (きのうの遠足はとても楽しかった) Yesterday's outing was great *fun.* / *Kyoo wa ichi-nichi* tanoshiku *sugoshita.*(きょうは一日楽しく過ごした) I had a *great* time today. （⇨ tanoshimi; tanoshimu）

ta⌐noshi⌐mi たのしみ（楽しみ）*n.*
1 pleasure; enjoyment; amusement; diversion:
Dokusho wa jiñsee no tanoshimi *no hitotsu desu.*(読書は人生の楽しみの一つです) Reading is one of the *pleasures* of life. / *Nichiyoobi ni doraibu suru no ga kare no* tanoshimi *desu.*(日曜日にドライブするのが彼の楽しみです) Going for a drive on Sundays is his *diversion.*
（⇨ tanoshii; tanoshimu）
2 hope; expectation:
Kodomo no shoorai ga tanoshimi desu.(子どもの将来が楽しみです) I *look forward to* my children's future. / *O-ai dekiru no o* tanoshimi *ni shite imasu.*(お会いできるのを楽しみにしています) I *am looking forward to* seeing you.

ta⌐noshi⌐m·u たのしむ（楽しむ）*vt., vi.* (-shim·i-; -shim·a-; -shiñ-de Ⓒ) enjoy; have a good time:
Doosookai de ooi-ni tanoshiñda. (同窓会で大いに楽しんだ) At the school reunion, we really *enjoyed ourselves.* / *Kanojo wa ima no shi-*

goto o tanoshiñde imasu.(彼女は今の仕事を楽しんでいます) She *takes great pleasure* in doing her present job. （⇨ tanoshii; tanoshimi）

ta⌐ñpaku⌐shitsu たんぱくしつ（蛋白質）*n.* protein.

ta⌐ñseñ たんせん（単線）*n.* single track:
tañseñ *no tetsudoo*(単線の鉄道) a *single-track* railroad. （↔ fukuseñ）

ta⌐ñshiñ-fu⌐niñ たんしんふにん（単身赴任）*n.* taking up a new post and leaving one's family behind:
tañshin-funiñsha(単身赴任者) a *business bachelor.*

tañshiñ-funiñ suru （～する）*vi.* leave for a new post by oneself:
Kare wa shi-gatsu kara Hokkaidoo e tañshiñ-funiñ suru *koto ni natte iru.*(彼は四月から北海道へ単身赴任することになっている) In April he is going to be transferred to Hokkaido and will have to *take up a bachelor life.*

ta⌐ñsho たんしょ（短所）*n.* shortcomings; weak point; fault:
Dare de mo nañra ka no tañsho *wa aru.*(だれでもなんらかの短所はある) Everybody has some *shortcomings.* / *Ki no mijikai no ga kare no* tañsho *desu.*(気の短いのが彼の短所です) A quick temper is his *weak point.* （↔ choosho）

ta⌐ñshuku たんしゅく（短縮）*n.* shortening; curtailment; reduction:
Kono kikai o irereba, roodoo jikañ no tañshuku *ni narimasu.*(この機械を入れれば，労働時間の短縮になります) If we can install this machine, it will lead to a *reduction* in working hours. / tañshuku-*jugyoo*(短縮授業) *shortened* school classes. （↔ eñchoo）

tañshuku suru （～する）*vt.* shorten; reduce: *Tooteñ de wa eegyoo-jikañ o* tañshuku *shite, go-ji ni heeteñ shimasu.*(当店では営業時

間を短縮して, 5 時に閉店します) At our shop we *have shortened* business hours, and therefore close at five o'clock. / *Kare wa sekai-kiroku o go-byoo* tañshuku *shita.* (彼は世界記録を 5 秒短縮した) He *broke* the world record by five seconds.

ta¹ñso たんそ (炭素) *n.* carbon.

ta⌐ñsu たんす (箪笥) *n.* chest of drawers; wardrobe:
Waishatsu wa tañsu *ni shimaimashita.* (ワイシャツはたんすにしまいました) I put away my shirts in the *chest of drawers.*

TAÑSU

ta⌐ñto たんと *adv.* many; much:
★ Used mainly by older people.
Kozukai wa mada tañto *arimasu.* (こづかいはまだたんとあります) I still have *a lot of* pocket money. / *Sono ko o* tañto *shikatte kudasai.* (その子をたんとしかってください) I would like you to give the child a *good* scolding.

ta⌐ñtoo たんとう (担当) *n.* charge:
Kono shigoto wa dare no tañtoo *desu ka?* (この仕事は誰の担当ですか) *Who is responsible* for this job? / tañtoo-*sha* (担当者) the person *in charge.*

tañtoo suru (〜する) *vt.* be in charge (of); take charge (of):
Kanojo wa kaikee o tañtoo *shite imasu.* (彼女は会計を担当しています) She *is in charge of* accounting. /

Watashi wa suugaku o tañtoo *shite imasu.* (私は数学を担当しています) I *teach* mathematics.

ta¹nuki たぬき (狸) *n.* raccoon dog. ★ In Japan, tradition says that raccoon dogs and foxes bewitch people. (⇨ kitsune)

DECORATIVE TANUKI STATUE

ta⌐ore¹·ru たおれる (倒れる) *vi.* (ta-ore-te Ⓥ) **1** fall; topple:
Taifuu de taiboku ga taoreta. (台風で大木が倒れた) A big tree *fell down* in the typhoon. / *Kanojo wa subette,* taoreta. (彼女は滑って, 倒れた) She slipped and *fell.* / *Oshoku jikeñ de naikaku ga* taoreta. (汚職事件で内閣が倒れた) The cabinet *fell* because of the corruption case. (⇨ taosu)
2 become sick; (of a person) die; be killed:
Ooku no seeto ga atsusa de taoreta. (多くの生徒が暑さで倒れた) A lot of students *fainted* because of the heat. / *Karoo de taoreru sarariimañ ga ooi.* (過労で倒れるサラリーマンが多い) There are many office workers who *collapse* from overwork.

ta¹oru タオル *n.* towel:
Kono taoru *de te o fuki nasai.* (このタオルで手をふきなさい) Please dry your hands with this *towel.*

ta⌐o¹s·u たおす (倒す) *vt.* (taosh·i-; taos·a-; taosh·ite Ⓒ) **1** throw [push] down; knock down; tip:
Kare wa chooseñsha o appaa de

taoshita. (彼は挑戦者をアッパーで倒した) He *knocked* the challenger down with an uppercut. / *Kabiñ o taosanai yoo ni ki o tsuke nasai.* (花瓶を倒さないように気をつけなさい) Be careful not to *tip* the vase *over.* ((⇨ taoreru))

2 beat; defeat; overthrow: *Kare wa yokozuna o* taoshita. (彼は横綱を倒した) He *beat* the sumo grand champion. / *Kokumiñ wa dokusai-seekeñ o* taoshita. (国民は独裁政権を倒した) The people *overthrew* the dictatorship. ((⇨ taoreru))

ta⌈ppu⌉ri たっぷり *adv.* (～ to) fully; enough; in plenty: *Sono kooji wa* tappuri *ni-ka-getsu kakarimasu.* (その工事はたっぷり2か月かかります) The construction work will take two *full* months. / *Kare wa jishiñ* tappuri *da.* (彼は自信たっぷりだ) He is *full* of confidence. / *Doozo* tappuri (*to*) *meshiagatte kudasai.* (どうぞたっぷり(と)召し上がってください) Please eat your *fill.* / *Yosañ wa* tappuri (*to*) *arimasu.* (予算はたっぷり(と)あります) We have *ample* funds.

-tara たら *infl. end.* [attached to verbs, adjectives, and the copula]

───── **USAGE** ─────
The *tara*-form of a verb is made by dropping the final '*-te*' of the *te*-form of a verb and adding '*-tara.*' When the *te*-form is '*-de,*' add '*-dara.*' The *tara*-form of an adjective is made by dropping the final '*-i,*' and adding '*-kattara.*' The *tara*-form of the copula is '*dattara.*'

1 if:
───── **USAGE** ─────
Note that the action or situation indicated by the verb in the first clause must precede

that indicated in the second clause. '*Tara*' has fewer restrictions than '*-ba*' and '*to*' regarding the type of clause that may follow it. ((⇨ -ba¹; to¹))

a (used in a conditional sentence): *Osoku* nattara, *deñwa shi nasai.* (遅くなったら、電話しなさい) Please phone *if* you are going to be late. / *Kirai* dattara, *tabenakute mo ii desu yo.* (嫌いだったら、食べなくてもいいですよ) *If* you do not like it, you don't have to eat it. / *Amari* takaku nakattara, *kono nekutai o kaitai to omoimasu.* (あまり高くなかったら、このネクタイを買いたいと思います) *If it is not too expensive*, I would like to buy this necktie.

b (used in unreal or imaginary conditionals): ★ The second clause is often in the past. *Kodomo ga ikite* itara, *moo shoo-gakkoo e itte ita daroo.* (子どもが生きていたら、もう小学校へ行っていただろう) *If* my child were alive, he would already be attending elementary school. / *Ano toki moo sukoshi chuui shite* itara, *jiko wa fusegeta daroo.* (あのときもう少し注意していたら、事故は防げただろう) *If* you had been a bit more careful, you would most likely have been able to avoid the accident. / *Takara-kuji ni* atattara, *ii no ni.* (宝くじにあたったら、いいのに) *If only* I had won the lottery! / *Byooki de* nakattara, *ryokoo e ikeru ñ da ga.* (病気でなかったら、旅行へ行けるんだが) If I *were not ill*, I would be able to go on a trip. ((⇨ -ba¹; to¹))

c (used in fixed, introductory expressions): Yoroshikattara, *kono heya o o-tsukai kudasai.* (よろしかったら、この部屋をお使いください) *If it is convenient for you*, please use this room. / Moshi ka shitara, *anata wa Maeda-sañ de wa arimaseñ ka?* (もしかしたら, あなたは前田さんではありませんか) *If my memory is correct*, you are Mr. Maeda, aren't you?

2 when:

a (used to indicate a cause or reason): ★The second clause is often in the past.

Kanojo ni okurimono o shitara, *totemo yorokoñde kureta.* (彼女に贈物をしたら, とても喜んでくれた) *When* I gave her a present, she was very pleased. / *Señzai o* tsukawanakattara, *kiree ni naranakatta.* (洗剤を使わなかったら, きれいにならなかった) *Since* I used no detergent, it did not come out clean.

b (used when an action occurs immediately after the *tara*-clause):

Shujiñ ga kaettara, *soodañ shite mimasu.* (主人が帰ったら, 相談してみます) *When* my husband comes home, I will discuss it with him. / *Kuukoo ni* tsuitara, *o-deñwa shimasu.* (空港に着いたら, お電話します) I will phone you *on arriving* at the airport. / *Daigaku o* detara, *deñkigaisha ni shuushoku shimasu.* (大学を出たら, 電気会社に就職します) *Once* I leave university, I am going to enter an electrical manufacturing company.

c (used when the action in the *tara*-clause leads to an unexpected occurrence): ★ The second clause is in the past.

Yamada no uchi e ittara, *rusu datta.* (山田の家へ行ったら, 留守だった) I went to Yamada's, but he was not at home. / *Sono hoñ o* yoñde mitara, *omotta yori omoshirokatta.* (その本を読んでみたら, 思ったよりおもしろかった) *When* I started reading the book, it was more interesting than I had expected. /

Kinoo Giñza e ittara, *battari Tanaka-sañ ni atta.* (きのう銀座へ行ったら, ばったり田中さんに会った) I went to Ginza yesterday *and* bumped into Miss Tanaka.

-tara (doo desu ka) (～(どうですか)) what about; why don't you: *Koko de* mattara, doo deshoo. (ここで待ったら, どうでしょう) *What about if* we wait here? / *Asoko no koobañ de* kiite mitara, doo deshoo. (あそこの交番で聞いてみたら, どうでしょう) *Why don't you try asking* at the police box over there? / *Atama ga itakattara, gakkoo o* yasuñdara (doo desu ka)?. (頭が痛かったら, 学校を休んだら(どうですか)) If you have a headache, *why don't you take the day off* school?

-taraba たらば *infl. end.* =-tara.

ta⌐ra⌐s·u たらす (垂らす) *vt.* (tarash·i-; taras·a-; tarash·i-te Ⓒ)

1 (of liquid) drop; drip: *Kare wa hitai kara ase o* tarashite ita. (彼は額から汗を垂らしていた) He had sweat *dripping* from his brow. 《⇨ tareru》

2 hang down: *Okujoo kara oo-uridashi no maku o* tarashita. (屋上から大売り出しの幕を垂らした) We *hung down* a banner advertising a bargain sale from the roof. 《⇨ tareru》

-ta⌐razu たらず (足らず) *suf.* less than; not more than: *hyaku-peeji-tarazu no hoñ* (100 ページ足らずの本) a book of *less than* 100 pages / *ichi-kiro-tarazu no kyori* (1キロ足らずの距離) a distance of *less than* a kilometer / *Sañjuppuñ-tarazu de modorimasu.* (30 分足らずで戻ります) I will be back in *less than* thirty minutes.

ta⌐remaku たれまく (垂れ幕) *n.* banner hanging vertically; drop curtain. 《⇨ photo (next page)》

ta⌐re⌐·ru たれる (垂れる) *vi.* (tarete Ⓥ) **1** drip; drop:

TAREMAKU

Jaguchi kara mizu ga tarete *ima-su.* (蛇口から水が垂れています) Water *is dripping* from the faucet. 《⇨ tarasu》

2 hang; dangle:
Kanojo no kami wa kata made tarete ita. (彼女の髪は肩まで垂れていた) Her hair *hung down* to her shoulders. / *Depaato no kabe ni baageñ no taremaku ga* tarete ita. (デパートの壁にバーゲンの垂れ幕が垂れていた) A banner with bargain sale on it *hung* on the wall of the department store. 《⇨ tarasu》

-tari たり *infl. end.* [attached to verbs, adjectives, and the copula] ★ The *tari*-form is made by adding '*ri*' to the *ta*-form, and is normally followed by '*suru*.'
1 (indicates state(s) or action(s) occurring simultaneously or in succession): ★ Used usually in pairs, '*...-tari ...-tari*.'
Sono heya ni wa hito ga detari haittari shite ita. (その部屋には人が出たり入ったりしていた) Some people *were going into* the room, and others *were coming out*. / *Terebi o* mitari *rajio o* kiitari *suru hima mo nai.* (テレビを見たりラジオを聞いたりする暇もない) I have no time to even *watch* TV or *listen* to the radio. / *Yyuube wa* noñdari tabetari *tano-shikatta.* (ゆうべは飲んだり食べたり楽しかった) I had a very good time last

evening, *drinking* and *eating*. / *Koñshuu wa* ame dattari, yuki dat-tari, *ii teñki ga nakatta.* (今週は雨だったり、雪だったり、いい天気がなかった) This week it *has been raining* and *snowing*, and we have had no fine weather. / *Kutsu wa* ookikat-tari chiisakattari, *tekitoo na no ga nakatta.* (靴は、大きかったり、小さかったり、適当なのがなかった) Some shoes were *too big*, and others were *too small*, and I was not able to find any suitable ones.
2 (indicates an example): ★ Often followed by '*nado*.'
Watashi wa donattari *nado shima-señ.* (私はどなったりなどしません) I will not do such a thing as *shouting*. / *Dare-ka ni* miraretari (*nado*) *suru to hazukashii.* (だれかに見られたり(など)すると恥ずかしい) I will feel em-barrassed if I *am seen* by some-one.

taˈriˈru たりる (足りる) *vi.* (tari-te Ⓥ) be enough; be sufficient:
Ichimañ-eñ areba, kootsuu-hi wa tarimasu. (1万円あれば、交通費は足ります) If you have 10,000 yen, it will *be enough* to cover the travel expenses. / *Sono hoñ o kau no ni o-kane ga* tarinakatta. (その本を買うのにお金が足りなかった) I *did not have enough money* to buy the book. / *Hitode ga* tarinai. (人手が足りない) *We are short-handed.*

taˈryoo たりょう (多量) *a.n.* (~ na/no, ni) a large quantity [amount] (of):
taryoo *no shukketsu* (多量の出血) a *great* loss of blood / *Remoñ wa bitamiñ o* taryoo ni fukuñde iru. (レモンはビタミンを多量に含んでいる) Lemons *are rich* in vitamins. 《⇨ tairyoo》《↔ shooryoo》

taˈshika たしか (確か) *a.n.* (~ na, ni) sure; certain; positive:
Kare ga kuru no wa tashika desu. (彼が来るのは確かです) It is *certain*

that he will come. / *Sore wa ta-shika da to omoimasu ka?* (それは確かだと思いますか) Do you feel *sure* about that? / *Sore wa* tashika *na joohoo desu.* (それは確かな情報です) That is a *reliable* piece of information. / *Kare wa* tashika *ni soo iimashita.* (彼は確かにそう言いました) He *certainly* said so. / *Kare wa* tashika *ni jitsuryoku wa aru ga ketsudañryoku ni toboshii.* (彼は確かに実力はあるが決断力に乏しい) He *undoubtedly* has ability, but he is indecisive. 《↔ futashika》

— *adv.* probably; perhaps; possibly:
Ano hito wa tashika *watashi yori wakai hazu desu.* (あの人は確か私より若いはずです) He is younger than me, *if I'm not mistaken.* / *Sono tegami ga kita no wa* tashika *getsuyoobi deshita.* (その手紙が来たのは確か月曜日でした) *If I remember correctly,* the letter arrived on Monday 《⇨ osoraku; tabuñ》.

ta⌐shikame⌐·ru たしかめる (確かめる) *vt.* (tashikame-te Ⓥ) make sure; confirm; check:
*Wasuremono ga nai ka doo ka, moo ichi-do o-*tashikame *kudasai.* (忘れ物がないかどうか, もう一度お確かめください) Please *make sure* once again that you haven't left anything. / *Jisho o hiite, sono imi o* tashikame *nasai.* (辞書を引いて, その意味を確かめなさい) Use your dictionary and *check* the meaning.

ta⌐shi⌐zañ たしざん (足し算) *n.* (of mathematics) addition:
tashizañ *o suru* (足し算をする) *add.* 《↔ hikizañ》《⇨ keesañ (table)》

ta⌐shoo たしょう (多少) *n.* a large or small number; a large or small quantity:
Sañkasha no tashoo *de ryookiñ ga kawarimasu.* (参加者の多少で料金が変わります) The fee varies according to the *number* of participants.

/ *Kiñgaku no* tashoo *wa kamaimaseñ ga, go-kifu o o-negai itashimasu.* (金額の多少はかまいませんが, ご寄付をお願いいたします) We ask for your donations, no matter *what the sum is.* / *Tashoo no fubeñ wa gamañ shite kudasai.* (多少の不便はがまんしてください) Please put up with *a degree* of inconvenience.

— *adv.* some; a little; a few:
Nihoñ ni wa tashoo *shiriai ga imasu.* (日本には多少知り合いがいます) I have *a few* acquaintances in Japan. / *Sake wa mada* tashoo *nokotte imasu.* (酒はまだ多少残っています) There is still *a bit* of sake left.

ta⌐ssha たっしゃ (達者) *a.n.* (〜 na, ni) **1** healthy; in good health:
Sobo wa hachijus-sai desu ga tassha *desu.* (祖母は80歳ですが達者です) Although my grandmother is eighty, she is very *healthy.* / *Ryooshiñ wa inaka de* tassha *ni kurashite imasu.* (両親はいなかで達者に暮らしています) My parents are living in the country in *excellent health.*

2 proficient; expert; well:
gee no tassha *na yakusha* (芸の達者な役者) an *accomplished* actor / *Kanojo wa suiee ga* tassha *desu.* (彼女は水泳が達者です) She is an *expert* swimmer. / *Kare wa Nihoñgo o* tassha *ni hanashimasu.* (彼は日本語を達者に話します) He speaks Japanese *proficiently.*

tas⌐s·uru たっする (達する) *vi., vt.* (tassh·i-; tassh·i-; tassh·i-te Ⓘ) **1** reach; arrive:
Ikkoo wa choojoo ni tasshita. (一行は頂上に達した) The party *reached* the summit.

2 amount; reach:
Higai wa hyakumañ-eñ ni tasshi-ta. (被害は100万円に達した) The damage *amounted* to one million

yen. / *Shikiñ-kañpa wa moku-hyoo-gaku ni* tasshita. (資金カンパは目標額に達した) The fund-raising drive *reached* the target figure.
3 attain; achieve:
Wareware wa mokuteki o tasshita. (われわれは目的を達した) We *attained* our purpose.

ta⌐s·u たす (足す) *vt.* (tash·i-; tas·a-; tash·i-te Ⓒ) add; plus:
Suupu ni sukoshi shio o tashita. (スープに少し塩を足した) I *added* a little salt to the soup. / *Ni tasu sañ wa go.* (2 足す 3 は 5) *Adding* three to two makes five. 《↔ hiku¹》《⇨ keesañ (table)》

ta⌐suka⌐r·u たすかる (助かる) *vi.* (tasukar·i-; tasukar·a-; tasukatte Ⓒ) **1** be saved; be rescued; survive:
Hikooki-jiko de futari no inochi ga kiseki-teki ni tasukatta. (飛行機事故で二人の命が奇跡的に助かった) Two people miraculously *survived* the plane crash. 《⇨ tasukeru》
2 (of aid, help, cooperation, etc.) be helpful:
Anata no go-kyooryoku ga areba, hijoo ni tasukarimasu. (あなたのご協力があれば，非常に助かります) If we have your cooperation it will *be a great help.* / *"De wa nijuumañ-eñ go-yoodate itashimashoo." "Tasu-karimasu. Doomo arigatoo gozaimasu."* (「では 20 万円ご用立ていたしましょう」「助かります。どうもありがとうございます」) "Then, I will lend you 200,000 yen." "It *helps* me out of my difficulties. Thank you very much." 《⇨ tasukeru》

ta⌐suke⌐·ru たすける (助ける) *vt.* (tasuke-te Ⓥ) **1** help; assist; support:
Kanojo ga nimotsu o hakobu no o tasukete yatta. (彼女が荷物を運ぶのを助けてやった) I *helped* her carry the baggage. 《⇨ tasukaru》

2 save; rescue:
Kare wa oboreyoo to shite iru ko-domo o tasuketa. (彼はおぼれようとしている子どもを助けた) He *saved* the child who was about to drown. 《⇨ tasukaru》
3 promote; encourage:
Kono hiryoo wa ha no seechoo o tasukemasu. (この肥料は葉の生長を助けます) This fertilizer *promotes* leaf growth.

ta⌐su⌐u たすう (多数) *n.* a large [great] number; majority:
Sono shuukai ni wa tasuu *no hito ga shusseki shimashita.* (その集会には多数の人が出席しました) A *large number* of people attended the meeting. / *Sañsee* tasuu *de sono giañ wa kaketsu sareta.* (賛成多数でその議案は可決された) The bill was passed by a *majority.* / *Sono kañshuu wa wakamono ga* tasuu *o shimeta.* (その観衆は若者が多数を占めた) Young people made up *most* of the audience. / tasuu-ha (多数派) the *majority* / tasuu-ketsu (多数決) a decision by *majority vote.* 《↔ shoosuu¹》

ta⌐takai たたかい (戦い) *n.* **1** war; battle:
tatakai *ni katsu [makeru]* (戦いに勝つ[負ける]) win [lose] a *battle.* 《⇨ tatakau》
2 struggle:
hiñkoñ to no tatakai (貧困との戦い) the *struggle* against poverty. 《⇨ tatakau》

ta⌐taka·u たたかう (戦う) *vi.* (tataka·i-; tatakaw·a-; tatakat-te Ⓒ) **1** fight; struggle:
Shokumiñchi no hito-tachi wa dokuritsu no tame ni tatakatta. (植民地の人たちは独立のために戦った) The people of the colony *fought* for independence. / *Kare-ra wa koñnañ to* tatakatta. (彼らは困難と戦った) They *struggled* against difficulties. 《⇨ tatakai》

2 (of a game, match) play:
Jaiañtsu wa Taigaasu to tatakatte *hikiwaketa.*(ジャイアンツはタイガースと戦って引き分けた) The Giants *played* against the Tigers and the game ended in a draw.

ta⌐ta⌐k·u たたく(叩く) *vt.* (tatak·i-; tatak·a-; tata·i-te C)
1 beat; hit; knock; slap:
taiko o tataku(太鼓をたたく) *beat* a drum / *Dare-ka ga doa o* tataite *iru.*(誰かがドアをたたいている) Someone *is knocking* on the door. / *Kare wa musuko no atama o* tataita.(彼は息子の頭をたたいた) He *hit* his son on the head.
2 attack; criticize:
Yatoo wa seefu no seesaku o tataita.(野党は政府の政策をたたいた) The opposition *attacked* the government's policy.

ta⌐tami たたみ(畳) *n.* tatami (mat):

> **(─ CULTURE ─)**
>
> A thick rectangular floor mat made of rice straw covered with woven rush grass. Though the size differs by region and by the type of building it is used in, the typical '*tatami*'. mat in a Tokyo-area house measures approximately 5 cm thick, 90 cm in width, and 180 cm in length. When counting tatami mats, '*mai*' is used (*ichi-mai, ni-mai,* etc.), but '*joo*' is used for the standard unit of size in speaking of Japanese rooms (*roku-joo, hachi-joo,* etc.) ((⇨ -joo⁵ (photo)))

Sono heya ni wa tatami *ga shiite atta.*(その部屋にはたたみが敷いてあった) There was *tatami* laid in that room.
((⇨ washitsu (photo)))

ta⌐tam·u たたむ(畳む) *vt.* (tatam·i-; tatam·a-; tatañ-de C)

1 fold; double:
kooto o tatamu(コートをたたむ) *fold* a coat / *hañkachi o yottsu ni* tatamu(ハンカチを四つにたたむ) *fold* a handkerchief in four / *futoñ o* tatamu(ふとんをたたむ) *fold up* a futon.
2 collapse (a desk, umbrella, etc.):
kasa o tatamu(傘をたたむ) *collapse* an umbrella.
3 close down (a shop):
Kare wa mise o tatañda.(彼は店をたたんだ) He *closed down* his shop.

ta⌐te たて(縦) *n.* length: ★ The vertical distance from end to end.
tate *no señ o hiku*(縦の線を引く) draw a *vertical* line / *Kono tsukue wa yoko ga kyuujus-señchi* tate *ga rokujus-señchi arimasu.*(この机は横が90センチ縦が60センチあります) This desk measures 90 centimeters in width and 60 in *length.* / *Tate ichi-retsu ni narabi nasai.*(縦一列に並びなさい) Line up *behind each other.* ((↔ yoko))

ta⌐tegaki たてがき(縦書き) *n.* vertical writing:
tategaki *no kañbañ*(縦書きの看板) a sign written *vertically.*
((↔ yokogaki))

TATEGAKI KAÑBAÑ

ta⌐tekae·ru たてかえる(立て替える) *vt.* (-kae-te V) pay (for someone else); lend:
Tonari no hito ga shiñbuñ-dai o

tatekaete kureta. (隣の人が新聞代を立て替えてくれた) My neighbor *paid* the newspaper bill *for* me. / *Sono kaihi o* tatekaete oite *kuremaseñ ka?* (その会費を立て替えておいてくれませんか) Will you please *lend* me the money to pay the membership fee?

ta⌐temae たてまえ (建て前) *n.* principle; theory; opinion; official stance:
tatemae *to hoññe* (建て前と本音) the *principle* and the practice / Tatemae *wa soo desu ga geñjitsu wa chigaimasu.* (建て前はそうですが現実は違います) The *principle* is thus, but the reality is different. / *Kare wa* tatemae *ni kodawatte iru.* (彼は建て前にこだわっている) He is sticking to his *official stance*.
((↔ hoññe))

ta⌐te⌐mono たてもの (建物) *n.* building.

ta⌐te⌐ru¹ たてる (立てる) *vt.* (tate-te Ⓥ) **1** set up; put up; stand:
tatefuda o tateru (立て札を立てる) *put up* a notice board / *keeki ni roosoku o* tateru (ケーキにろうそくを立てる) *stand* candles on a cake / *hata o* tateru (旗を立てる) *hoist* a flag.
((⇨ tatsu¹))
2 raise (dust); make (a noise):
oto o tateru (音を立てる) *make* a noise / *koe o* tateru (声を立てる) *raise* one's voice / *hokori o* tateru (ほこりを立てる) *raise* dust.
((⇨ tatsu¹))
3 make (a plan):
Natsu-yasumi no keekaku wa tatemashita *ka?* (夏休みの計画は立てましたか) *Have* you *made* plans for your summer vacation?
((⇨ tatsu¹))

ta⌐te⌐ru² たてる (建てる) *vt.* (tate-te Ⓥ) build; erect:
ie o tateru (家を建てる) *build* a house / *Kono tera wa juugo-seeki ni* taterareta *mono desu.* (この寺は

15世紀に建てられたものです) This temple is one which *was built* in the fifteenth century. (⇨ keñchiku; tatsu²)

ta⌐teuri-ju⌐utaku たてうりじゅうたく (建て売り住宅) *n.* ready-built house: ★ Often called '*tateuri*.'
tateuri-juutaku *o kau* (建て売り住宅を買う) buy a *ready-built house*.

ta⌐to⌐e¹ たとえ (譬え・例え) *n.* simile; metaphor; example:
Kare wa tatoe *o hiite, setsumee shita.* (彼はたとえを引いて, 説明した) He explained using *examples*.

ta⌐toe² たとえ (仮令) *adv.* even if; no matter what...:
Tatoe *anata ga hañtai shite mo watashi wa ikimasu.* (たとえあなたが反対しても私は行きます) *Even if* you are against it, I'm going. / Tatoe *nani ga okoroo to, watashi no kesshiñ wa kawarimaseñ.* (たとえ何が起ころうと, 私の決心は変わりません) *No matter what happens*, my determination will not alter. / Tatoe *doko ni sumoo to anata no go-shiñsetsu wa wasuremaseñ.* (たとえどこに住もうとあなたのご親切は忘れません) *Wherever I may live*, I will never forget your kindness.

ta⌐to⌐eba たとえば (例えば) *adv.* for example [instance]; such as:
Watashi wa uñdoo ga suki desu. Tatoeba *suiee to ka tenisu to ka.* (私は運動が好きです. 例えば水泳とかテニスとか) I like sports, *for example*, swimming and tennis, and so on. / Tatoeba *ima kyuu ni ooki-na jishiñ ga kitara, anata wa doo shimasu ka?* (例えば今急に大きな地震が来たら, あなたはどうしますか) *Suppose* there was suddenly a strong earthquake, what would you do?

ta⌐toe⌐ru たとえる (譬える・例える) *vt.* (tatoe-te Ⓥ) compare to; use a simile [metaphor]:
Hana ni tatoereba *kanojo wa yuri no hana da.* (花にたとえれば彼女は百

合の花だ) If you *were to compare* her to a flower, she would be a lily.

-ta[1] **tote** たとて = -tatte.

ta[1]**ts·u**[1] たつ (立つ) *vi.*, *vt.* (ta-ch·i-; tat·a-; tat-te Ⓒ) **1** (of a person or an animal) stand; stand up:

Kare wa madobe ni tatte *ita.* (彼は窓辺に立っていた) He *was standing* by the window. / *Kanojo wa seki o* tatte, *watashi no hoo e yatte ki-ta.* (彼女は席を立って、私の方へやって来た) She *got up* from her seat and came over toward me.

2 (of a thing) stand:

Sono kooen ni wa doozoo ga tatte *imasu.* (その公園には銅像が立っています) A bronze statue *stands* in the park. 《⇨ tateru[1]》

3 (in an election) run; stand:

Kondo no senkyo ni wa dare ga tachimasu *ka?* (今度の選挙には誰が立ちますか) Who *is running* in the coming election? 《⇨ tateru[1]》

4 (of steam, smoke, dust, etc.) rise:

Entotsu kara kemuri ga tatte *iru.* (煙突から煙が立っている) Smoke *is rising* from the chimney. / *Hoko-ri ga* tatanai *yoo ni niwa ni mizu o maita.* (ほこりが立たないように庭に水をまいた) I sprinkled water in the garden so that dust would not *rise up.* 《⇨ tateru[1]》

ta[1]**ts·u**[2] たつ (建つ) *vi.* (tach·i-; tat·a-; tat-te Ⓒ) be built; be erected; be set up:

Kinjo ni manshon ga tatta. (近所にマンションが建った) A condominium *was built* in my neighborhood. / *Kono uchi wa* tatte *kara nijuu-nen ni narimasu.* (この家は建ってから20年になります) Twenty years have passed since this house *was built.* 《⇨ tateru[2]》

ta[1]**ts·u**[3] たつ (絶つ) *vt.* (tach·i-; tat·a-; tat-te Ⓒ) break off;

sever; cut off:

Ryookoku wa gaikoo kankee o tatta. (両国は外交関係を絶った) The two countries *broke off* diplomatic relations. / *Sore irai kare wa shoosoku o* tatte *iru.* (それ以来彼は消息を絶っている) He *has not been heard of* since then.

ta[1]**ts·u**[4] たつ (経つ) *vi.* (tach·i-; tat·a-; tat-te Ⓒ) (of time) pass by; go by:

Toki ga tatsu *no wa hayai.* (時がたつのは速い) Time *passes* quickly. / *Chichi-oya ga nakunatte kara san-nen* tatta. (父親が亡くなってから3年たった) Three years *have passed* since my father died. / *Kare wa is-shuukan* tatanai *uchi ni genki ni natta.* (彼は1週間たたないうちに元気になった) He got well *before* a week *had passed.* 《⇨ keeka》

ta[1]**ts·u**[5] たつ (発つ) *vt.* (tach·i-; tat·a-; tat-te Ⓒ) start; leave:

Kare wa Nyuu Yooku o tatte, *Too-kyoo e mukatta.* (彼はニューヨークを発って、東京へ向かった) He *left* New York and headed for Tokyo. / *Watashi wa asu san-ji ni* tachi-masu. (私はあす3時に発ちます) I *depart* at three tomorrow.

ta[1]**ts·u**[6] たつ (断つ) *vt.* (tach·i-; tat·a-; tat-te Ⓒ) quit; give up (smoking, alcohol, etc.):

Kare wa sake mo tabako mo tatta. (彼は酒もたばこも断った) He *has given up* both drinking and smoking.

ta[1]**tta** たった *adv.* only; just; no more than:

Kono tokee wa tatta *sanzen-en de kaimashita.* (この時計はたった3千円で買いました) I bought this watch for *just* 3,000 yen. / *Hokkaidoo e wa* tatta *ichi-do itta-kiri desu.* (北海道へはたった1度行ったきりです) I have been to Hokkaido *only* once —and that's all. / *Eki made koko kara* tatta *go-fun desu.* (駅までここからたった5分です) It takes *no more than* five minutes from here to the station.

-tatte たって (colloquial variant of '*-te mo*') even if:

> ──(**USAGE**)──
> Usually used to suggest that however favorable the condition is, it is nevertheless insufficient. '*-ta tote*' is a written variant.

Ikura kañkyoo ga yokutatte, *eki kara tooi no ga moñdai da.*（いくら環境が良くたって，駅から遠いのが問題だ）*No matter how nice* the surroundings may be, being far from the station is the problem. / Isogashikutatte, *shokuji no jikañ gurai wa aru yo.*（忙しくたって，食事の時間ぐらいはあるよ）*Even if* I am busy, I have enough time to eat. / *Ima kara* dekaketatte, *moo deñsha wa nai yo.*（今から出かけたって，もう電車はないよ）*Even if* you left now, there would no longer be a train. 《⇨ -te mo》

ta⌐ue⌐ たうえ（田植え）*n.* rice-planting; transplantation of rice seedlings:
taue o suru（田植えをする）*transplant rice.*

TAUE

ta⌐wamure⌐·ru たわむれる（戯れる）*vi.* (tawamure-te Ⓥ) (*literary*) play; sport; joke:
Koinu ga sañ-biki niwa de tawamurete iru.（子犬が3匹庭でたわむれている）There are three puppies

playing in the garden.

ta⌐wara⌐ たわら（俵）*n.* straw bag.

ta⌐yasu⌐·i たやすい *a.* (-ku) easy; simple:
tayasui *shigoto*（たやすい仕事）an *easy* task / *Koñna moñdai wa* tayasuku *tokemasu.*（こんな問題はたやすく解けます）I can *easily* solve a problem like this. 《⇨ yasahii⌐》

ta⌐yori[1] たより（便り）*n.* letter; news:
O-tayori *arigatoo gozaimashita.*（お便りありがとうございました）Thank you very much for your *letter.* / *Musuko kara nagai koto* tayori ga nai.（息子から長いこと便りがない）I *haven't heard* from my son for a long time. / *Haha ni wa tsuki ni ichi-do* tayori o shite imasu.（母には月に一度便りをしています）I *write* to my mother once a month.

ta⌐yori[2] たより（頼り）*n.* reliance; dependence; trust:
Kane dake ga tayori da.（金だけが頼りだ）Money is the only *sure thing.* / *Kimi o* tayori ni shite iru yo.（君を頼りにしているよ）I *am relying* on you. 《⇨ tayoru》

tayori ni naru [naranai] (～になる［ならない］) reliable [unreliable]:
Ano hito wa iza to iu toki, tayori ni naru.（あの人はいざというとき，頼りになる）He is *reliable* when you are in a pinch. / *Aitsu wa itsu-mo* tayori ni naranai.（あいつはいつも頼りにならない）That fellow *can never be counted on.*

ta⌐yo⌐r·u たよる（頼る）*vt.* (tayor·i-; tayor·a-; tayot-te Ⓒ) rely [count] on; depend on:
Kare wa mada oya ni tayotte iru.（彼はまだ親に頼っている）He still *depends* on his parents. / *Kanojo wa tomo-dachi o* tayotte, *Nihoñ e kita.*（彼女は友達を頼って，日本へ来た）She came to Japan, *counting on* her friend. 《⇨ tayori[2]》

ta⌐zune⌐·ru[1] たずねる（尋ねる）*vt.*

(tazune-te Ⅴ) **1** ask; inquire; question:

Otoko-no-ko ni yuubiñkyoku e iku michi o tazuneta. (男の子に郵便局へ行く道を尋ねた) I *asked* the boy the way to the post office. / *Kare wa watashi no haha no koto o tazuneta.* (彼は私の母のことを尋ねた) He *asked* after my mother. / *Isha wa watashi no shoojoo ni tsuite tazuneta.* (医者は私の症状について尋ねた) The doctor *asked* me about my symptoms.

2 look for; search for (a person): *Sono hito-tachi wa nikushiñ o tazunete, Chuugoku kara yatte kimashita.* (その人たちは肉親を尋ねて、中国からやって来ました) Those people came from China, *looking for* their relatives.

ta「zune」・ru² たずねる（訪ねる）*vt.* (tazune-te Ⅴ) visit; call on [at]; come [go round] to see:

Kinoo Suzuki-sañ o tazunemashita. (きのう鈴木さんを訪ねました) I *visited* Mr. Suzuki yesterday. / *Kare wa kaisha ni watashi o tazunete kita.* (彼は会社に私を訪ねて来た) He *came* to the company *to see* me.

te¹ て（手）*n.* **1** hand: te *o ageru [furu]* (手を上げる[振る]) raise [wave] one's *hand* / te *o nobasu [sashidasu]* (手を伸ばす[差し出す]) stretch [hold out] one's *hand* / *Kare wa* te *ni hanataba o motte ita.* (彼は手に花束を持っていた) He had a bouquet in his *hand*. / *Teñjihiñ ni wa* te *o furenai de kudasai.* (展示品には手を触れないでください) Please *do not touch* the articles exhibited. / *Nani-ka ga* te *ni fureta.* (何かが手に触れた) I felt something touch my *hand*. 《⇨ jiñtai (illus.)》

2 means; way:

Keesatsu wa arayuru te *o tsukushite, sono ko o sagashita.* (警察は

O-TE O FURENAI DE KUDASAI.
(Please don't touch.)

あらゆる手を尽くして、その子を探した) The police tried every possible *means* to find the child. / *Sore yori hoka ni* te *wa arimaseñ.* (それよりほかに手はありません) There is no other *way* than that.

3 kind; brand:

Kono te *no mono ga yoku uremasu.* (この手のものがよく売れます) Articles of this *kind* sell very well.

te ga denai (〜が出ない) cannot possibly buy: *Kono yubiwa wa takakute* te ga denai. (この指輪は高くて手が出ない) This ring is very expensive, and I *can not afford to buy it*.

te ga mawaru (〜が回る) be on a person's track: *Moo keesatsu no* te ga mawatte imasu. (もう警察の手が回っています) The police *have* already *taken up the case*.

te ni ase nigiru (〜に汗握る) breathtaking: te ni ase nigiru *kyoosoo* (手に汗握る競争) a *breathtaking* race.

te ni ireru (〜に入れる) get; obtain: *Kono kabiñ wa doko de* te ni iremashita *ka?* (この花瓶はどこで手に入れましたか) Where did you *obtain* this vase?

te no koñda (〜の込んだ) carefully worked-out: *Kore wa* te no koñda *dezaiñ da.* (これは手の込んだデザインだ) This is an *elaborate* design.

te o dasu (〜を出す) start; dabble: *Kare wa kabu ni* te o dashite, *soñ o shita.* (彼は株に手を出して、損をした) He *dabbled* in stocks and lost money.

te o kiru (〜を切る) wash one's hands (of): *Ano hito to wa* te o kirimashita. (あの人とは手を切りました) I *broke off* with him.

te o nuku (〜を抜く) cut corners: *Shigoto no* te o nukanai *yoo ni.* (仕事の手を抜かないように) Make sure you *don't cut corners* in your work.

te o tsukeru (〜をつける) start; set about: *Sono shigoto ni wa mada* te o tsukete imaseñ. (その仕事にはまだ手をつけていません) I *have not started* on the work.

te o yaku (〜を焼く) have difficulty in handling: *Sono moñdai ni wa* te o yaite imasu. (その問題には手を焼いています) I *have difficulty in dealing with* that problem.

-te て *infl. end.* [attached to the *ku*-form of an adjective. For the *te*-form of verbs, see appendixes.] ★ The *te*-form of the copula is '*de*.'

1 and: ★ Used to link similar items in a parallel relationship. *Terebi no nyuusu wa* hayakute *seekaku da.* (テレビのニュースは速くて正確だ) The news on TV is *quick and* correct. / *Teñpura wa* oishikute *eeyoo ga aru.* (てんぷらはおいしくて栄養がある) Tempura is *delicious and* nutritious. / *Kono heya wa* hirokute *rippa da.* (この部屋は広くてりっぱだ) This room is *large and* splendid. 《⇨ sore kara; soshite》

2 since; after: ★ Used to indicate a temporal sequence. Similar to '*-te kara*,' but '*-te*' suggests that the action in the second clause immediately follows that in the first clause. *Kanojo wa daigaku o* dete, *sugu kekkoñ shita.* (彼女は大学を出て、す

ぐ結婚した) She got married soon *after* graduating from college. / *Nihoñ ni* kite, *moo sañ-neñ ni narimasu.* (日本に来て、もう3年になります) It is already three years *since* I came to Japan.

3 with: ★ Used when two actions occur almost simultaneously. The verb in the *te*-form describes the means or appearance of the action indicated by the verb following it. 《⇨ -nagara》 *Kare wa udegumi o* shite, *nani-ka kañgaete ita.* (彼は腕組みをして、何か考えていた) He was thinking about something *with* his arms folded.

4 because; since: ★ Used to indicate a cause or reason. The causal relationship is weaker than with '*kara*' and '*no de*.' Note that the second clause cannot express a wish, request, order, etc. 《⇨ kara⁴; no de》 *Kinoo no bañ wa* atsukute, *nemurenakatta.* (きのうの晩は暑くて、眠れなかった) I could not sleep last night *for* the heat. / *Koko wa eki ni* chikakute, *beñri da.* (ここは駅に近くて、便利だ) This place is convenient, *being* near the station. / *Kono karee wa* karakute *taberarenai.* (このカレーは辛くて食べられない) This curry is *too hot* for me *to* eat. / *Kyoo wa* shokuyoku ga nakute, *nani mo tabetaku nai.* (きょうは食欲がなくて、何も食べたくない) Today I *have a poor appetite, and* don't want to eat anything. / *Sumimaseñ,* okuremashite. (すみません、遅れまして) I am sorry *for being late.*

5 by; on: ★ Used to indicate a means or method. *Kanojo wa jiteñsha ni* notte, *kaimono ni ikimashita.* (彼女は自転車に乗って、買い物に行きました) She went shopping *by* bicycle. / *Eki made* aruite, *juugo-fuñ desu.* (駅まで歩いて、15分です) It takes fifteen minutes to go to the station *on foot*.

6 but: ★ Used to indicate a contrast or opposition. The contrastive relationship is weaker than with '*no ni*' or '*ga*.'
Koñna ni doryoku shite, *mada dekinai*. (こんなに努力して、まだできない) I have tried so hard, *but* I still cannot do it. / *Jus-satsu mo hoñ o* katte, *mada is-satsu mo yoñde imaseñ*. (10冊も本を買って、まだ1冊も読んでいません) I bought as many as ten books, *but* have not yet read even one.

7 (used with other verbs such as '*iru*,' '*miru*,' '*oku*,' '*morau*,' '*ageru*,' '*kureru*,' etc.): ★ The *te-*form plus verb form one unit, and there is no pause between the two elements.
Ima Nihoñgo o naratte imasu. (今日本語を習っています) I am now *studying* Japanese. / *Nihoñ-shoku o tabete mimashita ka?* (日本食を食べてみましたか) Have you *tried eating* Japanese food? / *Raishuu made ni kono jiteñsha o* naoshite oite *kudasai*. (来週までにこの自転車を直しておいてください) Please *have* this bicycle *repaired* by next week. / *Kono kamera wa chichi ni* katte moraimashita. (このカメラは父に買ってもらいました) My father *bought* this camera *for me*. / *Sono nimotsu o* motte agemashoo *ka?* (その荷物を持ってあげましょうか) Shall I *carry* those bags *for you?* / *Dare mo* tetsudatte kurenakatta. (だれも手伝ってくれなかった) No one would *help me*.

te⌐a⌐rai てあらい (手洗い) *n.* toilet; restroom; lavatory:
Tearai *wa doko desu ka?* (手洗いはどこですか) Where is the *restroom?*
《⇨ o-tearai (photo)》

te⌐-ashi てあし (手足) *n.* hand and foot; arms and legs; limbs:

Kare wa te-ashi *o shibararete, ugokenakatta*. (彼は手足を縛られて、動けなかった) Having been bound *hand and foot*, he could not move. / *Watashi no chichi wa* te-ashi *ga kikanai*. (私の父は手足が利かない) My father has lost the use of his *limbs*. / *Kanojo wa kare no* te-ashi to natte *tsukaeta*. (彼女は彼の手足となって仕えた) She waited on him *hand and foot*.

te⌐ate てあて (手当て) *n.* **1** medical treatment [care]:
ookyuu-teate *o ukeru* (応急手当てを受ける) receive first *aid*.
2 allowance; bonus:
juutaku[*tsuukiñ*]-teate (住宅[通勤]手当て) a housing [commuting] *allowance* / *chooka-kiñmu*-teate (超過勤務手当て) *extra pay* for overtime / *neñmatsu*-teate (年末手当て) a year-end *bonus*.
《⇨ boonasu; shooyo》
teate (o) suru (〜(を)する) *vt.* treat (an illness): *Kanojo wa kodomo no kega no* teate o shita. (彼女は子どものけがの手当てをした) She *treated* her child's injury.

te⌐bana⌐s·u てばなす (手放す) *vt.* (-banash·i-; -banas·a-; -banash·i-te Ⓒ) part with; sell; give up:
Kare wa tsui ni sono tochi o tebanashita. (彼はついにその土地を手放した) In the end, he *parted with* the land. / *Sono e o* tebanasu *tsumori wa arimaseñ*. (その絵を手放すつもりはありません) I have no intention of *selling* that picture.

te⌐baya⌐·i てばやい (手早い) *a.* (-ku) quick:
Kanojo wa shigoto ga tebayai. (彼女は仕事が手早い) She is *quick* at her work. / *Kare wa* tebayaku *heya o katazuketa*. (彼は手早く部屋を片づけた) He *quickly* straightened up his room.

te⌐biki てびき (手引き) *n.* guide;

guidebook; handbook:
gakushuu no tebiki (学習の手引き)
a study *guide* / tebiki-sho (手引き
書) a *manual* / *Watashi wa Nihongo no buñpoo no yoi* tebiki *o sagashite imasu.* (私は日本語の文法の
よい手引きを探しています) I am look-
ing for a good *guide* to Japanese
grammar.
tebiki (o) suru (〜(を)する) *vt.*
help: *Naibu no mono ga gootoo
no* tebiki *o shita rashii.* (内部の者が
強盗の手引きをしたらしい) Apparent-
ly someone on the inside *helped*
in the robbery.

te⌐bu⌐kuro てぶくろ (手袋) *n.*
glove:
tebukuro *o hameru [hazusu]* (手袋
をはめる[はずす]) put on [take off]
one's *gloves* / *Keekañ wa shiroi*
tebukuro *o shite ita.* (警官は白い手
袋をしていた) The policeman had
white *gloves* on. 《↔ kutsushita》

te⌐buri てぶり (手振り) *n.* gesture;
signs:
Watashi-tachi wa teburi *de hanashita.* (私たちは手振りで話した) We
talked by *gestures.* 《⇨ miburi》

te⌐chi⌐gai てちがい (手違い) *n.*
mistake; fault; accident:
Techigai no nai yoo ni shi nasai.
(手違いのないようにしなさい) Be care-
ful not to make a *mistake.* / *Sore
wa watashi-domo no* techigai *deshita.* (それは私どもの手違いでした) It
was our *fault.* / *Nani-ka no* techigai *de sono tegami wa todokana-
katta.* (何かの手違いでその手紙は届かな
かった) The letter was not delivered owing to some *accident.*

te⌐choo てちょう (手帳) *n.* small
notebook; pocket diary:
Kanojo no deñwa bañgoo o techoo
ni kakitometa. (彼女の電話番号を手
帳に書き留めた) I put her phone
number down in my *notebook.*

te⌐da⌐suke てだすけ (手助け) *n.*
help; assistance:

Sono ko wa tachiagaru toki, mada
tedasuke *ga hitsuyoo desu.* (その子
は立ち上がるとき、まだ手助けが必要です)
The child still needs *assistance*
when he stands up.
tedasuke (o) suru (〜(を)する) *vt.*
help; assist: *Shorui no Nihoñgo
ga wakaranai no o mite, sono hito
ga* tedasuke *shite kureta.* (書類の日
本語がわからないのを見て、その人が手助
けしてくれた) That person *assisted*
me when she saw that I had not
understood the Japanese in the
documents.

te⌐eañ ていあん (提案) *n.* proposal; suggestion; motion:
teeañ *o shiji suru* (提案を支持する)
second a *proposal.*
teeañ (o) suru (〜(を)する) *vt.* propose; suggest; move: *Kare wa
betsu no kikaku o* teeañ *shita.* (彼
は別の企画を提案した) He *proposed*
an alternative plan.

te⌐eboo ていぼう (堤防) *n.* riverbank; embankment; levee:
teeboo *o kizuku* (堤防を築く) build
a *bank.* 《⇨ dote》

te⌐eburu テーブル *n.* table:
teeburu *ni tsuku* (テーブルにつく) sit
at *table.*

te⌐eburu-ku⌐rosu テーブルクロス
n. tablecloth.

te⌐echi ていち (低地) *n.* lowlands;
low ground. 《↔ koochi³》

te⌐edeñ ていでん (停電) *n.* blackout; power failure; power cut:
Sakuya wa teedeñ *ga atta.* (昨夜は
停電があった) We had a *blackout*
last night. / *Teedeñ de koñpyuutaa ga tsukaenakatta.* (停電でコンピ
ューターが使えなかった) I was not able
to use the computer because of a
power failure.
teedeñ suru (〜する) *vi.* fail; be
cut off: *Kaminari de ichiji* teedeñ *shimashita.* (雷で一時停電しまし
た) The *power failed* for a while
because of the lightning. / *Kono*

chiku wa asu no gogo teedeñ shimasu.(この地区はあすの午後停電します) The *electricity supply* in this area *will be suspended* tomorrow afternoon.

te⌈edo ていど (程度) *n.* degree; extent; standard; level:
Teedo *ga takai* [*hikui*].(程度が高い [低い]) The *level* is high [low]. / *Sore ga yoi ka warui ka wa* teedo *no moñdai desu.*(それが良いか悪いかは程度の問題です) It is a question of *degree* whether it is good or bad. / *Sono uwasa wa aru* teedo *made hoñtoo desu.*(そのうわさはある程度まで本当です) The rumor is true to some *extent*. / *Kono suugaku no moñdai wa daigaku* teedo *desu.*(この数学の問題は大学程度です) This math problem is of college *level*. / *seekatsu*-teedo (生活程度) the *standard* of living.

te⌈egaku[1] ていがく (停学) *n.* suspension from school (as punishment):
Kare wa ichi-neñkañ teegaku *ni natta.*(彼は1年間停学になった) He *was suspended from school* for a year. 《⇒ taigaku》

te⌈egaku[2] ていがく (低額) *n.* small sum of money:
teegaku *no chiñgiñ de gamañ suru* (低額の賃金でがまんする) make do with *low* wages / teegaku-*shotokusha* (低額所得者) a person with a *low income*. 《⇒ koogaku》

te⌈eiñ ていいん (定員) *n.* capacity; the fixed number:
Kono basu no teeiñ *wa sañjuu-niñ desu.*(このバスの定員は30人です) The seating *capacity* of this bus is thirty. / *Oobosha wa moo sugu* teeiñ *ni tasshimasu.*(応募者はもうすぐ定員に達します) The number of applicants will soon reach the limit. / *Sono fune wa* teeiñ *o koete ita.*(その船は定員を超えていた) The ship *was overloaded*.

te⌈eka[1] ていか (低下) *n.* fall off; decline; deterioration:
Chiñgiñ no hikisage wa saabisu no teeka *o maneku.*(賃金の引き下げはサービスの低下を招く) The wage cut will bring about a *deterioration* in service.

teeka suru (〜する) *vi.* fall; drop; lower: *Kioñ ga kyuu ni go-do gurai* teeka shita.(気温が急に5度ぐらい低下した) The temperature suddenly *dropped* about five degrees. / *Saikiñ no daigakusee no gakuryoku wa* teeka *shite kite imasu.*(最近の大学生の学力は低下してきています) The academic ability of modern college students *has been declining*. 《↔ jooshoo》

te⌈eka[2] ていか (定価) *n.* fixed [list] price:
teeka *de uru* (定価で売る) sell at the *fixed price* / teeka *no ni-waribiki* (定価の2割引き) a discount of twenty percent off the *list price*.

te⌈eki ていき (定期) *n.* **1** fixed period:
Watashi-tachi wa kaigoo o teeki *ni hiraite imasu.*(私たちは会合を定期に開いています) We hold meetings at *regular intervals*. / teeki-*biñ* (定期便) a *regular* (bus) service / teeki-*shikeñ* (定期試験) an examination held at *regular intervals*. **2** commutation [season] ticket: *sañ-ka-getsu* teeki (3か月定期) a *commutation ticket* good for three months. 《⇒ teekikeñ》

te⌈eki⌉keñ ていきけん (定期券) *n.* commutation [season] ticket. 《⇒ kaisuukeñ》

te⌈ekoku ていこく (定刻) *n.* the scheduled [appointed] time:
Kaigi wa teekoku *ni hajimatta.*(会議は定刻に始まった) The meeting was held at the *scheduled time*. / *Ressha wa* teekoku *ni go-fuñ okurete toochaku shita.*(列車は定刻に5分遅れて到着した) The train arrived

five minutes behind *time*.

te⌈ekoo ていこう (抵抗) *n.* **1** resistance; opposition:
Sono keekaku wa omowanu teekoo *ni atta.* (その計画は思わぬ抵抗にあった) The plan met with unexpected *resistance*.
2 reluctance:
Kare ni au no wa nañto-naku teekoo *o kañjimasu.* (彼に会うのは何となく抵抗を感じます) I *am* rather *reluctant* to meet him.
teekoo suru (～する) *vi.* resist; oppose: *Yatoo wa seefu ni* teekoo shite *kaigi ni denakatta.* (野党は政府に抵抗して会議に出なかった) To *oppose* the government, the opposition did not attend the meeting.

te⌈ekyoo ていきょう (提供) *n.* offer; sponsorship:
teekyoo *o ukeru* (提供を受ける) accept an *offer* / *Kono bañgumi wa gorañ no kaku-sha no* teekyoo *de o-okuri shimashita.* (この番組はご覧の各社の提供でお送りしました) This program was broadcast with the *sponsorship* of the following companies. / *Yamanaka Shookai no* teekyoo (山中商会の提供) *Courtesy* of Yamanaka & Co.
teekyoo suru (～する) *vt.* offer; provide; donate: *Kare wa kichoo na joohoo o* teekyoo shite kureta. (彼は貴重な情報を提供してくれた) He *provided* us with invaluable information.

te⌈ekyu⌉ubi ていきゅうび (定休日) *n.* regular holiday:
Kono depaato wa getsuyoo ga teekyuubi desu. (このデパートは月曜が定休日です) This department store *is closed* on Mondays.

te⌈ema テーマ *n.* theme; subject; topic:
roñbuñ no teema (論文のテーマ) the *theme* of a thesis / *Kyoo no tooroñ no* teema *wa nañ desu ka?* (きょうの討論のテーマは何ですか) What is the

subject of today's discussion? / *Tsugi no* teema *ni utsurimasu.* (次のテーマに移ります) Let's now turn to the next *topic*.

te⌈enee ていねい (丁寧) *a.n.* (～ na, ni) **1** polite; courteous; kind:
teenee *na kotobazukai* (丁寧な言葉づかい) *polite* language / teenee *ni ojigi suru* (丁寧におじぎする) bow *politely* / *Sono hito wa* teenee *ni michi o oshiete kureta.* (その人は丁寧に道を教えてくれた) He explained the way to me *courteously*.
2 careful; close; thorough:
teenee *na choosa* (丁寧な調査) a *thorough* investigation / *kañji o* teenee *ni kaku* (漢字を丁寧に書く) write Chinese characters *carefully*

te⌈eneego ていねいご (丁寧語) *n.* polite word [expression].
★ This comprises honorific and humble polite expressions. *e.g.* (*honorific polite*) gorañ ni narimasu (see), etc. / (*humble polite*) mairimasu (come), etc.

te⌈eneñ ていねん (定年) *n.* retirement age; age limit:
Uchi no kaisha wa rokujus-sai ga teeneñ *desu.* (うちの会社は60歳が定年です) The *retirement age* at our company is sixty. / *Kare wa raineñ* teeneñ *ni naru.* (彼は来年定年になる) He reaches *retirement age* next year. / *Chichi wa* teeneñ *de taishoku shimashita.* (父は定年で退職しました) My father retired because he reached the *age limit*.

te⌈eoñ ていおん (低温) *n.* low temperature:
Kono kusuri wa teeoñ *de hozoñ no koto.* (この薬は低温で保存のこと) Store this medicine at *low temperature*. (↔ koo-oñ)

te⌈epu テープ *n.* **1** (of a cassette, video, etc.) tape:
teepu *o kakeru* (テープをかける) play

a *tape* / *bideo ni* teepu *o ireru* (ビデオにテープを入れる) insert a *tape* into a videocassette recorder.

2 ticker tape; ribbon:
teepu *o nageru* (テープを投げる) fling *ticker tape* / *kaitsuushiki de* teepu *o kiru* (開通式でテープを切る) cut the *ribbon* at the opening ceremony (of a railroad).

3 adhesive tape:
posutaa o kabe ni teepu *de haru* (ポスターを壁にテープではる) stick a poster on the wall with *tape*.

teepu ni toru (〜にとる) record on tape [videotape]: *Kare no kooen wa* teepu *ni torimashita ka?* (彼の講演はテープにとりましたか) *Have* you *recorded* his lecture on tape?

te⌐epu-reko⌐odaa テープレコーダー *n.* tape recorder:
teepu-rekoodaa *o kakeru* (テープレコーダーをかける) play a *tape recorder*.

te⌐eryuujo ていりゅうじょ (停留所) *n.* bus [streetcar] stop: ★ A train station is '*eki*.'
Tsugi no teeryuujo *de oroshite kudasai.* (次の停留所で降ろしてください) Please let me off at the next *stop*. 《⇨ basutee (photo); eki》

TEERYUUJO FOR STREETCARS

te⌐esai ていさい (体裁) *n.* appearance; show; style:
Kanojo wa teesai *o ki ni shite ita.* (彼女は体裁を気にしていた) She was worrying about *appearances*. / *Kare wa* teesai *no ii fuku o kite ita.* (彼は体裁のいい服を着ていた) He

was wearing a suit which looked *nice*. / teesai-*ya* (体裁家) a *poseur*. 《⇨ kakkoo¹》

teesai ga warui (〜が悪い) feel awkward: *Kare to kutsu o machigaete* teesai *ga warukatta.* (彼と靴を間違えて体裁が悪かった) I mistook his shoes for mine and *felt awkward*.

te⌐esee ていせい (訂正) *n.* correction; revision:
shinbun no teesee-*kiji* (新聞の訂正記事) a *correction* to a previous newspaper article.

teesee suru (〜する) *vt.* correct: *Tsugi no bun no ayamari o* teesee *shi nasai.* (次の文の誤りを訂正しなさい) *Correct* the errors in the following sentences. / *Sakihodo no 'Tookyuu' wa 'Tookyoo' no ayamari deshita. Owabi shite* teesee *shimasu.* (先ほどの「東急」は「東京」の誤りでした。お詫びして訂正します) The previous "Tokyu" was a mistake for "Tokyo." *Please note the correction* and accept our apologies. (*television announcement*) 《⇨ naosu¹》

te⌐esha ていしゃ (停車) *n.* (train, bus) stop:
Tsugi no teesha-*eki wa Utsunomiya desu.* (次の停車駅は宇都宮です) The next station *this train stops at* is Utsunomiya. / teesha-*jikan* (停車時間) the duration of a *stop* / *kakueki-*teesha (各駅停車) a *local train*. 《↔ hassha》

teesha suru (〜する) *vi.* stop: *Kono ressha wa Nagoya de ippun-kan* teesha *shimasu.* (この列車は名古屋で1分間停車します) This train *will stop* at Nagoya for one minute. / *Kyuu-*teesha *suru koto ga arimasu kara tesuri ni o-tsukamari kudasai.* (急停車する事がありますから手すりにおつかまりください) Please hold onto the handrail in case we *have to stop* suddenly.

teˈeshi ていし（停止）*n.* **1** stop; halt:
kuruma ni teeshi *o meejiru* (車に停止を命じる) order a car to *halt* / teeshi-shiñgoo (停止信号) a *stoplight* / teeshi-señ (停止線) a stop line. 《↔ zeñshiñ¹》
2 suspension; cessation:
kaku-jikkeñ no teeshi (核実験の停止) the *suspension* of nuclear tests / *yushutsu no* teeshi (輸出の停止) the *suspension* of exports.

teeshi suru (～する) *vi., vt.*
1 stop; halt: *Mae no kuruma ga totsuzeñ* teeshi shita. (前の車が突然停止した) The car in front suddenly *stopped*.
2 suspend:
Watashi wa unteñ-meñkyo o ikka-getsu teeshi sareta. (私は運転免許を1か月停止された) I *had* my driving license *suspended* for one month. / *Kare wa señkyo-ihañ de koomiñkeñ o ichi-neñkañ* teeshi sareta. (彼は選挙違反で公民権を1年間停止された) He *was deprived of* his civil rights for a year because of a violation of the election law.

teˈeshiˈsee ていせい（低姿勢）*n.* modest attitude; low profile:
Kare wa watashi-tachi ni taishite teeshisee *datta*. (彼は私たちに対して低姿勢だった) He assumed a *modest attitude* to us. / *Utagai o kakerareta giiñ wa* teeshisee *datta*. (疑いをかけられた議員は低姿勢だった) The Diet member under suspicion kept a *low profile*. 《↔ kooshisee》

teˈeshoku ていしょく（定食）*n.* fixed meal; table d'hôte:
O-hiru wa teeshoku *o tabemashita*. (お昼は定食を食べました) I ate a *table d'hôte* for lunch.
《⇨ photo (right)》

teˈeshutsu ていしゅつ（提出）*n.* submission; presentation:
Gañsho no teeshutsu *wa kigeñ*

TYPICAL TEESHOKU

geñshu desu. (願書の提出は期限厳守です) Please strictly observe the deadline for *turning in* your application forms. / *shorui no* teeshutsu-*saki* (書類の提出先) the place to which documents must *be submitted*.

teeshutsu suru (～する) *vt.* submit; turn [send] in; present: *gañsho o* teeshutsu suru (願書を提出する) *submit* an application / *jihyoo o* teeshutsu suru (辞表を提出する) *hand in* one's resignation / *shooko o* teeshutsu suru (証拠を提出する) *supply* proof / *Watashi wa ashita repooto o* teeshutsu shinakereba narimaseñ. (私はあしたレポートを提出しなければなりません) I *must hand in* my school report tomorrow.

teˈgaˈkari てがかり（手掛かり）*n.* clue; key; track:
tegakari *o tsukamu* (手掛かりをつかむ) find a *clue* / *Kore ga sono moñdai o toku* tegakari *desu*. (これがその問題を解く手がかりです) This is the *key* to solving the problem. / *Hañniñ wa nani mo* tegakari *o nokosanakatta*. (犯人は何も手がかりを残さなかった) The culprit left no *traces* behind.

teˈgami てがみ（手紙）*n.* letter:
Kare wa sugu ni sono tegami *no heñji o dashita*. (彼はすぐにその手紙の返事を出した) He answered the *letter* promptly. / *Anata no* tegami

wa mada uketotte imaseñ. (あなたの手紙はまだ受け取っていません) I have not received your *letter* yet. / *Kuwashii koto wa* tegami *de o-shirase shimasu.* (詳しいことは手紙でお知らせします) I will let you know the details by *letter.*

FORM OF A JAPANESE LETTER

① Opening phrase　② Text
③ Closing phrase　④ Date
⑤ Name of sender　⑥ Addressee
Examples of opening and closing phrases:
　haikee (拝啓)—keegu (敬具)
　zeñryaku (前略)—soosoo (草々)

te「gara¹ てがら (手柄) *n.* credit; meritorious deed:
Kono seekoo wa kimi no tegara *da.* (この成功は君の手柄だ) *Credit* for this success goes to you. / *Kare wa kisha to shite* tegara *o tateta.* (彼は記者として手柄をたてた) He *distinguished himself* as a reporter.

te「garu てがる (手軽) *a.n.* (~ na, ni) handy; easy; light:
tegaru *na jisho* (手軽な辞書) a *handy* dictionary / tegaru *na shokuji* (手軽な食事) a *light* meal / tegaru *ni ikeru haikiñgu koosu* (手軽に行けるハイキングコース) a hiking trail one can follow *without much difficulty.*

te「giwa¹ てぎわ (手際) *n.* skill; craftsmanship; efficiency:
Kare wa tegiwa yoku *sono kooshoo o matometa.* (彼は手ぎわよくその交渉をまとめた) He concluded the negotiations *with skill.* / *Nani o suru ni mo* tegiwa *no warui hito ga iru mono da.* (何をするにも手ぎわの悪い人がいるものだ) There are those who are *poor* at everything.

te「hai てはい (手配) *n.* arrangements; preparations:
Kaijoo no yoyaku no tehai *wa sumimashita ka?* (会場の予約の手配は済みましたか) Have you made the *arrangements* for reserving the hall?
tehai (o) suru (~(を)する) *vt.*
1 arrange; prepare:
yado o tehai suru (宿を手配する) *make arrangements* for accommodations / *Kuruma no* tehai o shite *kudasai.* (車の手配をしてください) Please *get* the car *ready.*
2 search: *Sono jikeñ no yoogisha wa zeñkoku ni* tehai sarete *imasu.* (その事件の容疑者は全国に手配されています) The suspect in that case *is being searched for* nationwide.

te「hazu てはず (手筈) *n.* arrangements; plan; program:
Kaigi no tehazu *wa totonoimashita ka?* (会議の手はずは整いましたか) Have you made *arrangements* for the meeting? / *Ryokoo no* tehazu *ga kurutte shimatta.* (旅行の手はずが狂ってしまった) The *plans* for the trip went wrong.

te「ho「ñ てほん (手本) *n.* model; example; pattern:

Tehoñ *o hitotsu shimeshite kuda-sai.*(手本を一つ示してください) Please give us an *example.* / *Watashi-tachi wa kare o* tehoñ *ni shita.*(私たちは彼を手本にした) We took him as our *model.*

te⌐ire⌐ ていれ(手入れ) *n.* **1** care: *hada no* teire (肌の手入れ) skin *care* / *Kono niwa wa* teire *ga yuki-todoite iru.*(この庭は手入れが行き届いている) This garden *is well cared for.*

2 raid; crackdown: *Keesatsu no* teire *ga atte, futari taiho sareta.*(警察の手入れがあって，二人逮捕された) There was a police *raid* and two people were arrested.

teire (o) suru (～(を)する) *vt.* **1** take care of; care for; repair: *kami no* teire o suru (髪の手入れをする) *groom* one's hair / *Kono jiteñ-sha wa dare ga* teire o shite imasu *ka?*(この自転車はだれが手入れをしていますか) Who *cares for* this bicycle? / *Amamori ga suru no de yane o* teire shinakereba naranai.(雨もりがするので屋根を手入れしなければならない) The rain is leaking through, so I *have to repair* the roof.

2 raid; crack down on: *Keesatsu wa sakuya booryoku-dañ no honbu o* teire shita.(警察は昨夜暴力団の本部を手入れした) The police *raided* the gangster head-quarters last night.

-te i⌐tadaku [i⌐tadakeru] ていただく[いただける](て頂く・て戴く[頂ける・戴ける]) *(humble)* have something done for one; be allowed to do something: 《⇨ itadaku》

(USAGE)
Used when asking a favor of a person, who is higher in status. When the person is equal or lower in status, '-te morau' is used.

O-kane o sukoshi kashite itadaki-tai *ñ desu ga.*(お金を少し貸していただきたいんですが) I would appreciate it if you lent me some money. / *Eki e iku michi o* oshiete itadakemasu *ka?*(駅へ行く道を教えていただけますか) Would you be kind enough to tell me the way to the station? / *Kono denwa o tsukawasete* itadake-masu *ka?*(この電話を使わせていただけますか) May I be allowed to use this telephone?

te⌐jina てじな(手品) *n.* magic; conjuring trick: *Kare wa* tejina *ga umai.*(彼は手品がうまい) He is good at *conjuring tricks.* / *Kare wa* tejina *de booshi kara usagi o toridashita.*(彼は手品で帽子からうさぎを取り出した) He *conjured* a rabbit out of his hat. / *Señsee wa seeto ni ikutsu-ka* tejina *o shite miseta.*(先生は生徒にいくつか手品をして見せた) The teacher showed his pupils some *magic tricks.* / tejina-shi (手品師) a *conjurer.*

te⌐juñ てじゅん(手順) *n.* plan; order; process; arrangement: tejuñ *o kimeru* (手順を決める) work out a *plan* / *Subete wa* tejuñ-*doori umaku itta.*(すべては手順どおりうまくいった) Everything went well according to *plan.* / *Kare wa* tejuñ *o machigaeta.*(彼は手順を間違えた) He did it in the wrong *order.* / *Kore wa hañga o tsukuru* tejuñ *o kaisetsu shita hoñ desu.*(これは版画を作る手順を解説した本です) This is a book which explains the *process* of woodblock printmaking.

te⌐ka⌐geñ てかげん(手加減) *n.* allowance; discretion; consideration.

tekageñ (o) suru (～(を)する) *vt.* make allowances; use discretion; take into consideration: *Kare no toshi no koto o kañgaete,* tekageñ (o) shite yari nasai.(彼の年のことを

考えて, 手加減(を)してやりなさい) You *should make allowances* for his age. / *Señsee wa sono keñ no atsukai de* tekageñ *shite kureta.* (先生はその件の扱いで手加減してくれた) The teacher *showed discretion* in handling the matter.

-te kara てから [*te*-form of a verb plus the particle '*kara*'] and then; since: ★ Indicates a temporal sequence with the action in the first clause occurring first. *Kono kaisha ni* haitte kara, *koñpyuutaa o naraimashita.* (この会社に入ってから, コンピューターを習いました) I joined this company *and then* learned how to use a computer. / *Daigaku o sotsugyoo* shite kara, *moo juu-neñ ni narimasu.* (大学を卒業してから, もう10年になります) It is already ten years *since* I graduated from college.

> **USAGE**
>
> Note the difference between '*-te kara*' and '*-ta kara*.' The former is concerned with temporal relationships, and the latter with causal ones. *e.g. Nihoñ e itte kara, Nihoñgo o beñkyoo shita.* (日本へ行ってから, 日本語を勉強した) I went to Japan *and then* studied Japanese. / *Nihoñ e itta kara, Nihoñgo no beñkyoo ga dekita.* (日本へ行ったから, 日本語の勉強ができた) I went to Japan, *therefore* I could study Japanese. 《⇨ kara³》

te⌐kateka てかてか *a.n.* (~ na, ni) (of surfaces, etc.) shiny: *Kare no zuboñ no shiri wa* tekateka *ni hikatte ita.* (彼のズボンのしりはてかてかに光っていた) The seat of his trousers was *shiny*.

te⌐kazu てかず (手数) *n.* trouble. 《⇨ tesuu》

te⌐ki てき (敵) *n.* enemy; opponent; rival:

Teki *wa ushiro kara semete kita.* (敵は後ろから攻めてきた) The *enemy* attacked us from behind. / *Ano hito o* teki *ni mawasu no wa furi desu.* (あの人を敵に回すのは不利です) It will be to your disadvantage to make an *enemy* of him. 《↔ mikata²》

...no teki de wa nai (...の~ではない) be no match for: *Kare wa kimi* no teki de wa nai. (彼は君の敵ではない) He *is no match for* you.

-teki てき (的) *suf.* (a.n.) (~ na, ni) concerning; having a certain character; resembling: ★ Added to a noun, usually of Chinese origin. '*-teki na* [*ni*]' is often equivalent to English '*-al* [*-ally*].' kyooiku-teki (*na*) *keñchi* (教育的(な)見地) an *educational* point of view / roñri-teki *ni setsumee suru* (論理的に説明する) explain *logically* / hi-niñgeñ-teki *na taido* (非人間的な態度) an *inhuman* attitude / ippañ-teki *na kañgae* (一般的な考え) a *common* notion.

te⌐kigi てきぎ (適宜) *a.n.* (~ na, ni), *adv.* appropriate; proper; suitable:
tekigi *na shochi o toru* (適宜な処置をとる) adopt *appropriate* measures / *Garakuta wa* tekigi (*ni*) *shobuñ shite kudasai.* (がらくたは適宜(に)処分してください) Please dispose of the junk *at your discretion*.

te⌐kii てきい (敵意) *n.* hostility; enmity:
tekii *o idaku* (敵意を抱く) have a *hostile feeling* / *Watashi wa kare ni taishite nañ no* tekii *mo motte imaseñ.* (わたしは彼にたいして何の敵意も持っていません) I have no *hostility* toward him. 《↔ kooi²》

te⌐kikaku てきかく (的確) *a.n.* (~ na, ni) accurate; exact; precise:
Kare no setsumee wa tekikaku

datta. (彼の説明は的確だった) His explanation was *accurate.* / *Isha wa* tekikaku *na shiji o ataeta.* (医者は的確な指示を与えた) The doctor gave *precise* directions.

te「kisee てきせい (適性) *n.* aptitude:
Watashi ni wa beñgoshi ni naru tekisee *wa arimaseñ.* (私には弁護士になる適性はありせん) I don't have the *aptitude* to become a lawyer. / tekisee-keñsa (適性検査) an *aptitude* test.

te「kisetsu てきせつ (適切) *a.n.* (～ na, ni) suitable; appropriate; proper:
tekisetsu *na hañdañ* (適切な判断) an *appropriate* judgment / *Kare wa sono moñdai o* tekisetsu *ni shochi shita.* (彼はその問題を適切に処置した) He dealt with the problem in a *proper manner.* / *Kono baai sono kotoba wa* tekisetsu *de* (*wa*) *arimaseñ.* (この場合その言葉は適切で(は)ありません) That expression is not *suitable* in this case.

te「kis·u「ru てきする (適する) *vi.* (tekish·i-; tekis·a-; tekish·i-te ⓒ) be suitable; be good:
★ Used in the pattern '... *ni tekisuru.*'
Kono shokubutsu wa shokuyoo ni tekishite imasu. (この植物は食用に適しています) This plant *is good* for food. / *Kono kawa wa oyogi ni wa* tekisanai. (この川は泳ぎには適さない) This river *is unsuitable* for swimming in.

te「kisuto テキスト *n.* textbook:
★ Shortened form of '*tekisuto bukku*' (textbook).
Tekisuto *no juugo peeji o hiraki nasai.* (テキストの 15 ページを開きなさい) Open your *textbooks* to page 15. (⇨ kyookasho)

te「kitoo てきとう (適当) *a.n.* (～ na, ni) **1** suitable; good:
Tsuuyaku o sagashite iru ñ desu

ga, tekitoo *na hito o shirimaseñ ka?* (通訳を探しているんですが, 適当な人を知りませんか) I am looking for an interpreter. Do you know any *suitable* person? / *Gaikokujiñ no tame no jisho de nani-ka* tekitoo *na no wa arimaseñ ka?* (外国人のための辞書で何か適当なのはありませんか) Aren't there any *good* dictionaries for foreigners? (↔ futekitoo) (⇨ fusawashii)

2 (of work, method, etc.) irresponsible; taking things easy:
Muri shinai de, tekitoo *ni yaroo.* (無理しないで, 適当にやろう) *Let's take it easy* and not push ourselves too hard. / *Anata tte* tekitoo *na hito ne.* (あなたって適当な人ね) You're *not a serious* person, are you? / *Añkeeto ni* tekitoo *ni kinyuu shita.* (アンケートに適当に記入した) I filled out the questionnaire *half-heartedly.*

te「kiyoo てきよう (適用) *n.* application:
hoo no tekiyoo *o nogareru* (法の適用を逃れる) avoid the law *being applied* to oneself.

tekiyoo suru (～する) *vt.* apply:
Kono baai sono kisoku o tekiyoo *suru no wa muri desu.* (この場合その規則を適用するのは無理です) It is very difficult to *apply* that provision in this case.

te「kkiñ てっきん (鉄筋) *n.* steel rod [bar]:
tekkiñ-koñkuriito (鉄筋コンクリート) *ferroconcrete.*

te「kkyoo てっきょう (鉄橋) *n.* iron bridge; railroad bridge:
tekkyoo *o kakeru* [*wataru*] (鉄橋をかける[渡る]) build [cross] a *railroad bridge.*

te「ko てこ (梃子) *n.* lever:
Kare-ra wa teko *de sono ishi o mochiageta.* (彼らはてこでその石を持ち上げた) They raised the stone with a *lever.* / *Watashi wa dorai-*

baa o teko *ni shite, hako no futa o aketa.* (私はドライバーをてこにして，箱のふたをあけた) I used a screwdriver as a *lever* to lift the lid of the box. **teko de mo ugokanai** (〜でも動かない) persist in one's opinion： *Kare wa iya da to ittara,* teko de mo ugokanai. (彼はいやだと言ったら，てこでも動かない) Once he has said no, he *won't budge an inch.*

te⌐kubi てくび（手首）*n.* wrist： *Kanojo wa sono ko no* tekubi *o tsukañda.* (彼女はその子の手首をつかんだ) She took the boy by the *wrist.* 《⇨ jiñtai (illus.)》

te⌐ma⌐ てま（手間）*n.* time; labor; trouble： *Sono mokee o kumitateru no ni, zuibuñ* tema *ga kakatta.* (その模型を組み立てるのに，ずいぶん手間がかかった) It took a lot of *time and labor* to assemble the model. / *Kono yoo ni sureba, daibu* tema *ga habukemasu.* (このようにすれば，だいぶ手間が省けます) If you do it like this, you will be able to save a lot of *trouble.*

tema hima kakeru (〜暇かける) spend time and energy： *Kono sakuhiñ wa* tema hima kakete *tsukutta mono desu.* (この作品は手間暇かけて作ったものです) This is a work I *spent much time and effort* on making.

te⌐mae てまえ（手前）*n.* **1** (〜 ni, de) this side; before： *Hijoo no baai wa kono hañdoru o* temae ni *hiki nasai.* (非常の場合はこのハンドルを手前に引きなさい) Pull this handle *toward you* in an emergency. / *Koosateñ no* temae *de tomatte kudasai.* (交差点の手前で止まってください) Please stop the car *before* you come to the intersection. / *Shuuteñ no hitotsu* temae *de ori nasai.* (終点の一つ手前で降りなさい) Please get off at the stop *before* the last.

2 presence： *Ryooshiñ no* temae *sono ko wa otonashiku shite ita.* (両親の手前その子はおとなしくしていた) The child remained quiet in the *presence* of her parents.

3 (*humble*) I; we： ★ Sometimes refers to 'you,' but this usage is very rude. *Sono shina wa* temae-domo *de wa atsukatte imaseñ.* (その品は手前どもでは扱っていません) *We* don't handle those articles at this shop.

te⌐mane⌐ki てまねき（手招き）*n.* beckoning： *Watashi wa* temaneki *de kare o heya no naka ni* yoñda. (私は手招きで彼を部屋の中に呼んだ) I *beckoned* him into the room. **temaneki suru** (〜する) *vt.* beckon： *Dare-ka ga tooku de* temaneki shite iru. (だれかが遠くで手招きしている) There is someone in the distance *beckoning* to us. ★ The beckoning gesture is made with the palm down, repeatedly bringing the fingers downward.

TEMANEKI

-te mo ても [*te*-form of a verb or adjective plus the particle '*mo*'] **1** (even) if; though： *Ame ga* futte mo *shiai wa arimasu.* (雨が降っても試合はあります) *Even if* it rains, we will have the game. / *Ashita wa* yasuñde mo *ii desu ka?* (あしたは休んでもいいですか) Is it all right *if* I take the day off tomorrow? / *Ikitaku* nakute mo, *ikanakereba narimaseñ.* (行きたくなくて

も, 行かなければなりません) You must
go, *even though* you don't want
to. (⇨ tatoe²))

2 however; whatever:
Doñna ni *sono shigoto ga* tsura-
kute mo *watashi wa yarimasu.* (ど
んなにその仕事がつらくても私はやります)
I will carry out the task *however
painful it is.* / *Itsu deñwa shite
mo kare wa rusu desu.* (いつ電話し
ても彼は留守です) *No matter* when I
phone him, he is not home. / *Kore wa shite mo, shinakute mo ii
desu yo.* (これはしても, しなくてもいいで
すよ) It does not matter *whether*
you *do* this *or not.*

-te morau てもらう ⇨ morau.

te⌐moto¹ てもと(手元) *n.* hand:
Kare wa itsu-mo jisho o temoto *ni
oite iru.* (彼はいつも辞書を手元に置い
ている) He always keeps a dictionary at *hand.* / *Temoto ni soñna
taikiñ wa arimaseñ.* (手元にそんな大
金はありません) I don't have such a
large sum of money on *hand.*

temoto ga kuruu (〜が狂う) miss
one's aim.

teñ¹ てん(点) *n.* **1** dot; spot:
Chizu no kono akai teñ *wa nañ
desu ka?* (地図のこの赤い点は何です
か) What is this red *dot* on the
map?

2 score; grade; mark:
Kare wa shikeñ de hachijuu-go-
teñ *o totta.* (彼は試験で85点を取っ
た) He got a *score* of eighty-five
on the examination. / *Ano señsee
wa* teñ *ga amai* [*karai*]. (あの先生は
点が甘い[辛い]) That teacher is generous [severe] in *scoring.*

3 score; run:
*Sono chiimu wa saishuu kai ni
sañ* teñ *totta.* (そのチームは最終回に3
点取った) The team scored three
runs in the last inning.

4 point; respect:
Sono teñ *ni moñdai ga aru.* (その点
に問題がある) There is a problem

on that *point.* / *Kono futatsu no e
wa aru* teñ *de nite iru.* (この二つの絵
はある点で似ている) These two pic-
tures are similar in some *respects.*

teñ² てん(天) *n.* **1** the sky:
teñ *o aogu* (天を仰ぐ) look up at
the *sky.*

2 Heaven; Providence:
Watashi wa uñ o teñ *ni makaseta.*
(私は運を天にまかせた) I left my fate
in the hands of *Providence.*

-teñ¹ てん(店) *suf.* store; shop;
office:
sho-teñ (書店) a bookstore / kissa-
teñ (喫茶店) a coffee *shop* / shi-teñ
(支店) a branch *office* / bai-teñ (売
店) a (newspaper) *stand*; a *kiosk* /
iñshoku-teñ (飲食店) a *restaurant*
/ dairi-teñ (代理店) an *agency*; a
representative office.

-teñ² てん(展) *suf.* exhibition:
ko-teñ (個展) a one-man *show* /
Yokoyama Taikañ-teñ (横山大観
展) an *exhibition* of Taikan Yokoyama's works / kokuhoo-teñ (国宝
展) an *exhibition* of National
Treasures.

te⌐na⌐oshi てなおし(手直し) *n.* re-
adjustment; rectification; alteration; improvement:
Kono keekaku wa tenaoshi *ga hitsuyoo desu.* (この計画は手直しが必
要です) This plan needs some *im-
provements.* (⇨ teesee)

tenaoshi suru (〜する) *vt.* read-
just; rectify; alter; improve:
Watashi wa zuboñ no nagasa o
tenaoshi *shite moratta.* (私はズボン
の長さを手直ししてもらった) I *had* the
length of my trousers *altered.* /
Kaisha wa soshiki o tenaoshi *suru
koto ni kimeta.* (会社は組織を手直し
することに決めた) The company de-
cided to *reorganize* the system.

te⌐ñchi てんち(天地) *n.* **1** heaven
and earth; universe:
teñchi-soozoo (天地創造) the creation of the *universe.*

2 land; world:
jiyuu no teñchi (自由の天地) a free *land* / *atarashii* teñchi *o moto-mete umi o wataru* (新しい天地を求めて海を渡る) sail across the ocean in search of a new *world*.
3 top and bottom:
Kono shashiñ wa teñchi *ga gyaku da.* (この写真は天地が逆だ) This photo is *upside down.* / Teñchi-muyoo (*sign*) (天地無用) *This Side Up/Do Not Turn Over.*

TEÑCHI-MUYOO SIGN

te⌐ñdoñ てんどん (天どん) *n.* ⇨ doñburi.

te⌐ñgoku てんごく (天国) *n.* heaven; Heaven; paradise. ((↔ jigoku))

te⌐ni⌐motsu てにもつ (手荷物) *n.* carry-on baggage; hand luggage: tenimotsu-azukarijo (手荷物預かり所) a *checkroom*; a *left-luggage office.*

te⌐ñiñ てんいん (店員) *n.* sales-clerk; salesman; saleswoman.

te⌐nisu テニス *n.* tennis: *Suzuki-sañ wa* tenisu *ga joozu da.* (鈴木さんはテニスが上手だ) Miss Suzuki is good at *tennis.* / *Kinoo wa Yamada-sañ to* tenisu *o shita.* (きのうは山田さんとテニスをした) I played *tennis* with Mr. Yamada yesterday.

Te⌐ñjiñsama⌐ てんじんさま (天神様) *n.* the deified spirit of Sugawara Michizane (菅原道真).

──(CULTURE)──
A scholar in the ninth century, he is prayed to as the deity of learning by students who wish to pass entrance exams. The shrine, '*Teñmañguu* (天満宮),' is also called '*Teñjiñsama*' (Tenjin Shrine). ((⇨ ema))

te⌐ñjoo てんじょう (天井) *n.* ceiling; roof:
Kono uchi wa teñjoo *ga takai [hikui].* (この家は天井が高い[低い]) This house has high [low] *ceilings.*

te⌐ñkai てんかい (展開) *n.* development.
teñkai suru (〜する) *vi., vt.* develop; unfold; spread out: *Hirobiro to shita heegeñ ga me no mae ni* teñkai shita. (広々とした平原が目の前に展開した) A broad plain *spread out* before our eyes. / *Giroñ wa igai na hookoo ni* teñkai shita. (議論は意外な方向に展開した) The argument *developed* in an unexpected direction.

te⌐ñkee てんけい (典型) *n.* type; model; specimen:
Ano hito wa shiñshi no teñkee *desu.* (あの人は紳士の典型です) He is the very *model* of a gentleman.

te⌐ñkee-teki てんけいてき (典型的) *a.n.* (〜 na, ni) typical; model: *Sushi wa* teñkee-teki *na Nihoñ ryoori no hitotsu desu.* (すしは典型的な日本料理の一つです) Sushi is one of the *typical* Japanese dishes.

te⌐ñkeñ てんけん (点検) *n.* examination; check; inspection:
*kuruma no teeki-*teñkeñ (車の定期点検) the periodic *inspection* of a car.
teñkeñ suru (〜する) *vt.* examine; check; inspect: *Kono koojoo de wa subete no kikai o maitsuki ik-kai* teñkeñ *shite imasu.* (この工場ではすべての機械を毎月1回点検しています) At this factory, we *check* all the machinery once a month.

/ *Gasoriñ-sutañdo de kuruma o* teñkeñ shite moratta. (ガソリンスタンドで車を点検してもらった) I *had* my car *checked* at a gas station. (⇨ shiraberu)

te⌐ñki てんき (天気) *n.* **1** weather: *Yama no* teñki *wa kawari-yasui.* (山の天気は変わりやすい) The *weather* in the mountains is changeable. / Teñki *wa kudarizaka desu.* (天気は下り坂です) The *weather* has changed for the worse. / *Koko ni, sañ-nichi wa* teñki *no ooki-na kuzure wa nai moyoo desu.* (ここ 2, 3 日は天気の大きな崩れはないもようです) The *weather* is unlikely to get worse over the next two or three days. / teñki-*gaikyoo* (天気概況) general *weather* conditions / teñki-*zu* (天気図) a *weather* map. **2** fine weather: *Kyoo wa* teñki *da.* (きょうは天気だ) It's *fine* today. (⇨ kaisee[2])

te⌐ñkiñ てんきん (転勤) *n.* transfer: *Kare wa hoñsha e* teñkiñ *ni narimashita.* (彼は本社へ転勤になりました) He *was moved* to the head office. **teñkiñ suru** (～する) *vi.* be transferred: *Shi-gatsu kara Hokkaidoo e* teñkiñ *shimasu.* (四月から北海道へ転勤します) I *am being posted* to Hokkaido in April.

te⌐ñki-yo⌐hoo てんきよほう (天気予報) *n.* weather forecast [report].

te⌐ñkoo てんこう (天候) *n.* weather conditions. (⇨ teñki)

te⌐ñmo⌐ñgaku てんもんがく (天文学) *n.* astronomy.

te⌐ñneñ てんねん (天然) *n.* nature: teñneñ-*gasu* (天然ガス) *natural* gas / teñneñ-*kineñbutsu* (天然記念物) a *Natural* Monument / teñneñ-*sañ no unagi* (天然産のうなぎ) *natural, not cultured,* eels / teñneñ-*shigeñ* (天然資源) *natural* resources.

te⌐ñno⌐o てんのう (天皇) *n.* emperor: ★ This only refers to the Emperor of Japan. The emperor of other countries is called, '*kootee.*' Teñnoo-heeka (天皇陛下) *His Majesty the Emperor.* (⇨ kookyo)

Te⌐ñnoo-tañjo⌐obi (天皇誕生日) *n.* the Emperor's Birthday (Dec. 23). (⇨ shukujitsu (table))

te-⌐no⌐-hira てのひら (手の平) *n.* the flat of the hand; palm. **te-no-hira o kaesu** (～を返す) suddenly change one's tune: *Kare wa* te-no-hira o kaesu *yoo ni taido o kaeta.* (彼は手の平を返すように態度を変えた) He changed his attitude *quite abruptly.*

te⌐ñpo テンポ *n.* tempo; pace; speed: teñpo *no osoi kyoku* (テンポの遅い曲) a tune in slow *tempo* / *Kare wa nani o suru ni mo* teñpo *ga noroi.* (彼は何をするにもテンポがのろい) He is *slow-paced* in everything he does.

te⌐ñpura てんぷら (天ぷら) *n.* tempura. ★ A dish of seafood and vegetables, which are dipped in batter and deep-fried.

TEÑPURA

te⌐ñra⌐ñkai てんらんかい (展覧会) *n.* exhibition; show: teñrañkai *o hiraku* (展覧会を開く) hold an *exhibition* / *sakuhiñ o* teñrañkai *ni shuppiñ suru* (作品を展覧会に出品する) submit one's work for an *exhibition* / teñrañkai-*joo* (展覧会場) an *exhibition* hall.

te⌈ńsai[1] てんさい (天災) *n.* natural disaster [calamity]:
Końdo no jiko wa teńsai *desu.* (今度の事故は天災です) This accident was an *act of God*.

te⌈ńsai[2] てんさい (天才) *n.* genius.

te⌈ńshi てんし (天使) *n.* angel.

te⌈ńshoku てんしょく (転職) *n.* change of one's job:
Watashi wa teńshoku *o kańgaete imasu.* (私は転職を考えています) I am thinking of *taking up another job*.
teńshoku suru (～する) *vi.* change one's occupation: *Kare wa kaisha o yamete seńsee ni* teńshoku shita. (彼は会社をやめて先生に転職した) He quit his company and *became* a teacher.

te⌈ńsu⌉u てんすう (点数) *n.* mark; point; score:
Kare wa shikeń de ii teńsuu *o totta.* (彼は試験でいい点数を取った) He got a good *mark* on the test. / *Kyoo no shiai wa* teńsuu *ga hirakisugite omoshiroku nakatta.* (きょうの試合は点数が開き過ぎて面白くなかった) Today's game was not interesting since the *score* was lopsided. 《⇨ teń[1]》

te⌈ńteki てんてき (点滴) *n.* intravenous drip infusion:
Kare wa ima teńteki *o ukete imasu.* (彼は今点滴を受けています) He is now on an *intravenous drip*.

te⌈ńto テント *n.* tent:
teńto *o haru* [*tatamu*] (テントを張る[畳む]) pitch [take down] a *tent*.

te⌈ńtoo てんとう (点灯) *n.* lighting.
teńtoo suru (～する) *vt., vi.* turn [switch] on a light; be turned on: *Kinoo wa* teńtoo shita mama *nete shimatta.* (きのうは点灯したまま寝てしまった) Last night I went to sleep *with the lights on*.

te⌈nugui てぬぐい (手拭) *n.* hand towel. ★ It is made of rough cotton cloth.

te⌈o⌉kure ておくれ (手遅れ) *n.* being too late; being beyond cure: *Ima to natte wa* teokure *desu.* (今となっては手遅れです) It is *too late* now. / *Zańneń nagara kanojo wa* teokure *desu.* (残念ながら彼女は手遅れです) I regret it, but she is *beyond help*.

te⌈ppań てっぱん (鉄板) *n.* iron [steel] plate:
niku o teppań *de yaku* (肉を鉄板で焼く) grill meat on an *iron plate* / teppań-*yaki* (鉄板焼き) meat and vegetables cooked on an *iron plate*.

te⌈ppoo てっぽう (鉄砲) *n.* gun:
teppoo *o utsu* (鉄砲を撃つ) fire a *gun*.

te⌈ra] てら (寺) *n.* (Buddhist) temple. ★ Also 'o-tera.' 《⇨ jińja》

TERA

te⌈rashiawase]**·ru** てらしあわせる (照らし合わせる) *vt.* (-awase-te [V]) compare with; check; test by comparison:
Kanojo wa hońyaku to geńbuń o terashiawasete mita. (彼女は翻訳と原文を照らし合わせてみた) She *compared* the translation with the original. / *Watashi wa kare to kotae o* terashiawaseta. (私は彼と答えを照らし合わせた) I *checked* my answers with his.

te⌈ra]**s·u** てらす (照らす) *vt.* (terash·i-; teras·a-; terash·i-te [C]) light; shine; illuminate:
Michi o kaichuu-deńtoo de terashita. (道を懐中電灯で照らした) I *lighted* the path with a flashlight. 《⇨ teru》

te⌐rebi テレビ *n.* **1** television
(set); TV:
terebi *o tsukeru* [*kesu*] (テレビをつけ
る[消す]) turn on [off] a *TV*.
2 television (program); TV:
Sono tenisu no shiai wa terebi *de
mimashita.* (そのテニスの試合はテレビで
見ました) I watched the tennis
match on *television*. / terebi-*bañgumi* (テレビ番組) a *television* program / terebi-*geemu* (テレビゲーム)
a *video game*.

te⌐rehoñ-ka⌐ado テレホンカード *n.*
telephone card. ★ A prepaid
plastic card against which charges
are debited when using a public
phone. These public phones are
always colored green.

TEREHOÑ-KAADO

te⌐r·u てる(照る) *vi.* (ter·i-; te-
r·a-; tet-te Ⓒ) shine; blaze:
Taiyoo ga kañkañ to tette iru. (太
陽がかんかんと照っている) The sun *is
shining* brightly. (⇨ terasu)

te⌐ruteru-bo⌐ozu てるてるぼうず
(照る照る坊主) *n.* a simple, small
doll, which children hang outside in the hope of it bringing
good weather. (⇨ photo (right))

te⌐saki てさき(手先) *n.* **1** finger;
hand:
Kare wa tesaki *ga kiyoo* [*bukiyoo*] *da.* (彼は手先が器用[不器用]だ)
He is good [clumsy] with his
hands.
2 tool; agent:
booryokudañ no tesaki (暴力団の手

TERUTERU-BOOZU

先) the *tool* of a criminal gang /
*Kare no tesaki to shite hataraku
no wa gomeñ desu.* (彼の手先として
働くのはごめんです) I refuse to act *on
his behalf*.

te⌐suri てすり(手摺り) *n.* rail;
handrail:
tesuri *ni tsukamaru* (手すりにつかま
る) hold on to a *rail*.

te⌐suto テスト *n.* test; quiz:
tesuto *o ukeru* (テストを受ける) take
a *test* / tesuto *ni gookaku suru* (テ
ストに合格する) pass a *test* / *Kyoo
wa kañji no* tesuto *ga atta.* (きょうは
漢字のテストがあった) We had a *test*
on Chinese characters today.
(⇨ shikeñ)
tesuto (o) suru (～(を)する) *vt.*
give a test: *kikai no seenoo o*
tesuto suru (機械の性能をテストする)
test the performance of a machine / *Señsee ga kakitori no* tesuto o shita. (先生が書き取りのテスト
をした) Our teacher *gave* us a dictation *test*.

te⌐suu てすう(手数) *n.* trouble:
Kare no okage de daibu tesuu *ga
habuketa.* (彼のおかげでだいぶ手数が省
けた) Thanks to him, we were
able to save much *trouble*.
o-tesuu desu ga (お～ですが) I am
sorry to trouble you: O-tesuu
desu ga *kono tegami o dashite
kudasai.* (お手数ですがこの手紙を出し
てください) *I am sorry to trouble*

you, but would you mail this letter for me?

te⌈su⌉uryoo てすうりょう（手数料）
n. **1** commission:
Kare ni go-paaseñto no tesuuryoo *o haratta.*（彼に5％の手数料を払った）I paid him a five percent *commission*.
2 service charge.

te⌈tsu てつ（鉄）*n.* iron:
tetsu *no moñ*（鉄の門）an *iron* gate.

te⌈tsubiñ てつびん（鉄瓶）*n.* iron kettle.《⇨ hibachi (illus.)》

te⌈tsuboo てつぼう（鉄棒）*n.*
1 horizontal bar.
2 iron bar.

te⌈tsuda⌉i てつだい（手伝い）*n.*
1 help; assistance:
*Nani-ka o-*tetsudai *suru koto wa arimasu ka?*（何かお手伝いすることはありますか）Is there anything I can *help* you do?《⇨ tetsudau》
2 help(er); assistant:
Dare-ka tetsudai *o yokoshite kudasai.*（だれか手伝いをよこしてください）Please send *someone to help*.

te⌈tsuda⌉·u てつだう（手伝う）*vt.*
(tetsuda·i-; tetsudaw·a·-; tetsudat-te Ⓒ) help; assist:
Watashi wa kanojo no shigoto o tetsudatta.（私は彼女の仕事を手伝った）I *helped* her with her work. / *Kono nimotsu o hakobu no o* tetsudatte *kudasai.*（この荷物を運ぶのを手伝ってください）Please *help* me carry this baggage.《⇨ tetsudai》

te⌈tsudoo てつどう（鉄道）*n.* railroad; railway:
tetsudoo *o shiku*（鉄道を敷く）build a *railroad* / *Sono machi made* tetsudoo *ga kaitsuu shita.*（その町まで鉄道が開通した）A *railroad* was extended to that town.《⇨ Shiñkañseñ》

te⌈tsu⌉gaku てつがく（哲学）*n.*
philosophy:
Kare wa jibuñ no tetsugaku *o motte iru.*（彼は自分の哲学を持ってい

る）He has his own *philosophy*. / tetsugaku-sha（哲学者）a *philosopher*.

te⌈tsuya てつや（徹夜）*n.* staying up all night:
tetsuya *no beñkyoo*（徹夜の勉強）*all night* study / tetsuya *de kañbyoo suru*（徹夜で看病する）sit up looking after a sick person *all night*.

tetsuya suru（～する）*vi.* stay up all night: *Yuube wa* tetsuya *shite, repooto o kaita.*（ゆうべは徹夜して, レポートを書いた）I *stayed up all last night* finishing off my paper.

te⌈tsu⌉zuki てつづき（手続き）*n.*
procedure; formalities:
rikoñ no tetsuzuki *o toru*（離婚の手続きをとる）take the necessary *steps* to obtain a divorce / *Moo nyuugaku no* tetsuzuki *wa sumimashita ka?*（もう入学の手続きは済みましたか）Have you already completed your school entrance *procedures*? / *Kuukoo de nyuukoku no* tetsuzuki *o shita.*（空港で入国の手続きをした）I *went through* immigration *formalities* at the airport.

te⌈ttee てってい（徹底）*n.* thoroughness; completeness:
Shushi no tettee *o hakaru tame ni miñna ni chirashi o kubatta.*（趣旨の徹底を図るためにみんなにちらしを配った）We distributed handbills to ensure that *everyone would understand* our intentions.

tettee suru（～する）*vi.* be thorough; be complete: *Ano hito no kañgae wa* tettee *shite iru.*（あの人の考えは徹底している）His way of thinking is *consistent*. / *Kare wa* tettee *shita goorishugisha da.*（彼は徹底した合理主義者だ）He is an *out-and-out* rationalist. / *Kooshuu-dootoku wa kodomo no uchi ni* tettee *saseru hitsuyoo ga arimasu.*（公衆道徳は子どものうちに徹底させる必要があります）It is necessary to *inculcate* public morality in childhood.

te⌐ttee-teki てっていてき (徹底的) *a.n.* (～ na, ni) thorough; exhaustive:

tettee-teki *na kaikaku* (徹底的な改革) a *thoroughgoing* reform / *Keesatsu wa sono jiko no geñiñ o* tettee-teki *ni choosa shita.* (警察はその事故の原因を徹底的に調査した) The police *exhaustively* investigated the cause of the accident.

-te wa ては [*te*-form of a verb or adjective plus the particle '*wa*']
1 (the '*-te wa*' clause indicates a condition and the following clause the natural or obvious result or conclusion):
Soñna ni tsukarete ite wa, *shigoto ni naranai.* (そんなに疲れていては、仕事にならない) *If* you are so tired, you will not be able to do your job properly. / *Koo* atsukute wa *nooritsu ga sagaru.* (こう暑くては能率が下がる) *With it hot like this,* efficiency decreases. / *Shiñde* shimatte wa *nañ ni mo naranai.* (死んでしまっては何にもならない) There is no point *in* dying.
2 (used to indicate an objection or prohibition):
Abunai tokoro e itte wa ikemaseñ. (危ない所へ行ってはいけません) You *must not go* to dangerous places. / *Soñna koto o* sarete wa *komarimasu.* (そんなことをされては困ります) *Your doing* something like that puts me in an awkward position.
-nakute wa naranai [dame da] (なくてはならない[だめだ]) must; should: ★ The form '*-nakereba*' is used similarly. (⇨ -ba¹)
Ashita made ni kono repooto o kañsee shinakute wa naranai. (あしたまでにこのレポートを完成しなくてはならない) I *have to* complete this report by tomorrow. / *Kodomo wa hayaku* nenakute wa dame desu.

(子どもは早く寝なくてはだめです) Children *should go to bed* early. / *Tegami wa morattara sugu heñji o* dasanakute wa dame da. (手紙はもらったらすぐ返事を出さなくてはだめ) You *must* give an answer to a letter as soon as you have received it.

-te wa...shita mono da (～...したものだ) when...used to do:
Itazura o shite wa, *chichi ni* shikarareta mono desu. (いたずらをしては、父に叱られたものです) *Whenever* I did something naughty, I *used to be scolded* by my father. / *Gakkoo o* sabotte wa, *eega o mi ni* itta mono da. (学校をさぼっては、映画を見に行ったものだ) *Cutting* classes, we *used to go off* to the movies. ★ Note: '*-te wa*' becomes '*-cha*' in informal speech, and '*de wa*' becomes '*ja.*' *e.g. Soko e* itcha ikenai yo. (そこへ行っちゃいけないよ) Don't *go* there. (⇨ de wa¹)

te⌐wake¹ てわけ (手分け) *n.* division of labor.

tewake suru (～する) *vi.* divide; separate; share: *Kono shigoto wa* tewake shite *yaroo.* (この仕事は手分けしてやろう) Let's *divide* this work among us. / *Watashi-tachi wa* tewake shite, *sono maigo no ko o sagashita.* (私たちは手分けして、その迷子の子を探した) We *split up into groups* and looked for the lost child.

te⌐za¹wari てざわり (手触り) *n.* feel; touch:
Kono kawa wa tezawari *ga yawarakai.* (この皮は手触りが柔らかい) This leather is soft to the *touch.* / *Kono juutañ wa biroodo no yoo na* tezawari *da.* (このじゅうたんはビロードのような手触りだ) This carpet *feels* like velvet.

ti⌐sshu-pe¹epaa ティッシュペーパー *n.* tissue; Kleenex (*trademark*). ★ Also called simply '*tis-*

shu.' 《⇨ chirigami》

to¹ と *p*. **1** with; from: ★ Used after a noun.

Watashi wa kare to *yoku tenisu o shimasu.*（私は彼とよくテニスをします）I often play tennis *with* him. / *Tanaka-sañ wa okusañ* to *wakareta soo desu.*（田中さんは奥さんと別れたそうです）I hear that Mr. Tanaka has separated *from* his wife. / *Yamada wa yuujiñ no imooto* to *kekkoñ shita.*（山田は友人の妹と結婚した）Yamada married the younger sister of a friend of mine. / *Watashi wa tomodachi* to *beñkyoo shita.*（私は友だちと勉強した）I studied *together with* my friend. / *Kanojo to eega o mi ni itta.*（彼女と映画を見に行った）I went to a movie *with* her.

USAGE

Note the difference between: *Suzuki wa Yamada* to *keñka shita.* (Suzuki quarreled *with* Yamada.) and *Suzuki* to *Yamada wa keñka shita.* (Suzuki *and* Yamada quarreled.) With verbs which necessarily imply a mutual action (*e.g. kekkoñ suru*, *rikoñ suru*, *wakareru*, *keñka suru*), only '*to*' is used. With other verbs (*e.g. hanasu*, *au*, *soodañ suru*), '*to*' and '*ni*' are both used, but with a difference of meaning: *Kare to hanasu.* (He and I speak *with* each other.) / *Kare ni hanasu.* (I speak *to* him.)

---

2 to; into: ★ Used to indicate a resulting change.

Kaji de subete ga hai to *natta.*（火事ですべてが灰となった）Everything was reduced *to* ashes in the fire. / *Osorete ita koto ga jijitsu* to *natta.*（恐れていたことが事実となった）What I had been afraid of became a reality. / *Miñna ichidañ* to *natte*

tatakatta.（みんな一団となって戦った）We all fought together *as* a group. ★ In the above examples, '*ni*' can also be used.

3 from; as; to: ★ Used in expressing difference, similarity, or comparison.

Kore to *onaji mono o kudasai.*（これと同じ物を下さい）Please give me the same one *as* this. / *Kare wa niisañ* to *seekaku ga chigau.*（彼は兄さんと性格が違う）He differs *from* his older brother in character. / *Ima no shigoto wa mae no* to *kurabete, yarigai ga arimasu.*（今の仕事は前のと比べて、やりがいがあります）Compared *to* my previous job, the present one is more rewarding. ★ In the case of '*kuraberu*,' '*ni*' can also be used.

4 that: ★ Used as a quotative particle.

Kare ni ashita yasumu to *tsutaete kudasai.*（彼にあした休むと伝えてください）Please tell him *that* I am taking tomorrow off. / *Ashita wa hareru* to *omoimasu.*（あしたは晴れると思います）I think it will be fine tomorrow. / *Kare wa kono keñ ni tsuite nañ* to *itte imashita ka?*（彼はこの件について何と言っていましたか）What has he said about this matter?

USAGE

Japanese does not distinguish as clearly as English between direct and reported speech. *Kare wa kuru to itta.* ＝ He said, "I'll come." / He said that he would come.

---

5 (used after adverbs, especially those signifying state, condition or manner and after onomatopoeias):

Motto yukkuri to *hanashite kudasai.*（もっとゆっくりと話してください）Please speak more *slowly*. / *Ame*

to

ga shitoshito to futte imasu. (雨が しとしとと降っています) It *is drizzling.* / *Dokañ to ooki-na oto ga shita.* (ド カンと大きな音がした) There was a loud *bang.* ★ In the case of ono-matopoeias, '*to*' can sometimes be followed by '*iu*.' e.g. *dokañ* to *iu oto.*

to² と *p.* and: ★ Used to enu-merate or list two or more nouns. *naifu* to *fooku* (ナイフとフォーク) a knife *and* fork / *chichi* to *haha* (父 と母) my father *and* mother / *Koñ-shuu wa getsuyoo* to *kiñyoo ni kaigi ga arimasu.* (今週は月曜と金 曜に会議があります) We have meet-ings on Monday *and* Friday of this week. 《⇨ dano; to ka; ya¹》

> **USAGE**
>
> Note the difference between '*to*' and '*ya*.' *Kinoo wa sake* to *biiru o noñda.* (We drank sake *and* beer yesterday.) / *Kinoo wa sake* ya *biiru o noñda.* (We drank sake, beer, *and so on* yes-terday.)

to³ と (戸) *n.* door: to *o akeru* [*shimeru*] (戸を開ける[閉 める]) open [close] a *door* / to *o ta-taku* (戸をたたく) knock at a *door.*

to⁴ と (都) *n.* metropolis. ★ An administrative division of Japan, but only used with reference to Tokyo. 《⇨ Tookyoo-to》

to⌐bas·u¹ とばす (飛ばす) *vt.* (tobash·i-; tobas·a-; tobash·i-te Ⓒ) **1** fly; let [make] fly: *Shooneñ wa mokee hikooki o* to-bashite ita. (少年は模型飛行機を飛 ばしていた) The boy *was flying* a model airplane. **2** blow off: *Kaze de señtakumono ga* toba-sareta. (風で洗濯物が飛ばされた) The washing *was blown down* by the wind. **3** drive fast:

Kare wa moo-supiido de baiku o tobashita. (彼は猛スピードでバイクを飛 ばした) He *drove* his motorbike at a furious speed. **4** skip; omit: *Watashi wa sono shoosetsu o* to-basanai *de yoñda.* (私はその小説を 飛ばさないで読んだ) I read the novel *without skipping.* **5** make (a joke); spread: *joodañ o* tobasu (冗談を飛ばす) *crack* a joke / *dema o* tobasu (デマ を飛ばす) *spread* a false rumor. **6** sputter; splash: *doromizu o* tobasu (泥水を飛ばす) *splash* muddy water / *Kare wa tsuba o* tobashi-nagara *shabetta.* (彼はつばを飛ばしながらしゃべった) He talked on, *sputtering.*

to⌐basu² とバス (都バス) *n.* a bus or the bus transportation system operated by the Tokyo Metropo-litan Government.

to⌐biaga⌐r·u とびあがる (飛び上がる) *vi.* (-agar·i-; -agar·a-; -agat-te Ⓒ) **1** jump; leap; spring to one's feet: *Kanojo wa* tobiagatte *yorokoñda.* (彼女は飛び上がって喜んだ) She *jumped* for joy. / *Kare wa odo-roite* tobiagatta. (彼は驚いて飛び上が った) He *sprang to his feet* in sur-prise. **2** fly up: *Hibari ga mugibatake kara* tobia-gatta. (ひばりが麦畑から飛び上がった) A skylark *flew up* from the wheat field.

to⌐bida⌐s·u とびだす (飛び出す) *vi.* (-dash·i-; -das·a-; -dash·i-te Ⓒ) jump out; run out; rush out: *Seeto-tachi wa kyooshitsu kara kootee e* tobidashita. (生徒たちは教 室から校庭へ飛び出した) The pupils *rushed out* of the classroom onto the playground. / *Dooro ni* tobi-dasu *no wa kikeñ desu.* (道路に飛び 出すのは危険です) It is dangerous to *run out* into the street.

to「biko」m·u とびこむ（飛び込む）*vi.*
(-kom·i-; -kom·a-; -koñ-de Ⓒ)
jump [plunge] into; dive into:
Kare wa puuru ni tobikoñda.（彼は
プールに飛び込んだ）He *jumped into*
the pool. / *Tsubame ga ie ni* tobi-
koñde *kita*.（つばめが家に飛び込んで来
た）A swallow came *flying into*
the house.

to「bimawa」r·u とびまわる（飛び回
る）*vt.* (-mawar·i-; -mawar·a-;
-mawat-te Ⓒ) fly about; bustle
about; romp about:
Toñbo ga takusañ sora o tobima-
watte ita.（とんぼがたくさん空を飛び回
っていた）A lot of dragonflies *were
flying about* in the air. / *Kare wa
shigoto de ichinichi-juu* tobima-
watte imasu.（彼は仕事で一日中飛び
回っています）He *bustles about* all
day long with his work.

to「bino」k·u とびのく（飛び退く）*vi.*
(-nok·i-; -nok·a-; -no·i-te Ⓒ)
jump back [aside]:
Kare wa tobinoite *jidoosha o yoketa*.（彼は飛びのいて自動車をよけた）
He *jumped aside* and avoided a
car.

to「bino」r·u とびのる（飛び乗る）*vi.*
(-nor·i-; -nor·a-; -not-te Ⓒ)
jump on [into] (a vehicle):
Kare wa awatete basu ni tobi-
notta.（彼はあわててバスに飛び乗った）
He hurriedly *jumped onto* the
bus.《↔ tobioriru》

to「biori」·ru とびおりる（飛び下りる）
vi. (-ori-te Ⓥ) jump down; leap
down:
Kare wa mado kara tobiorita.（彼
は窓から飛び下りた）He *jumped
down* from the window.《↔ to-
binoru》

to「bira とびら（扉）*n.* **1** door:
tobira *o hiraku* [*shimeru*]（扉を開く
[閉める]）open [close] a *door*.
2 (of a book) title page.

to「bita」ts·u とびたつ（飛び立つ）*vi.*
(-tach·i-; -tat·a-; -tat-te Ⓒ) fly
away; (of an airplane) take off:
Suzume ga issee ni tobitatta.（すず
めがいっせいに飛び立った）Sparrows
flew away all together. / *Hikooki
wa teekoku ni* tobitachimashita.
（飛行機は定刻に飛び立ちました）The
airplane *took off* on time.

to「bitsu」k·u とびつく（飛び付く）*vi.*
(-tsuk·i-; -tsuk·a-; -tsu·i-te Ⓒ)
jump at; leap at:
Neko ga kotori ni tobitsuita.（猫が
小鳥に飛びついた）The cat *jumped
at* the bird. / *Kare wa wareware
no teeañ ni* tobitsuita.（彼はわれわれ
の提案に飛びついた）He *jumped at*
our proposal.

to「boshi」·i とぼしい（乏しい）*a.*
(-ku) scanty; scarce; poor:
Sono kuni wa teñneñ shigeñ ga
toshii.（その国は天然資源が乏しい）
The natural resources in that
country are *scarce*. / *Kimi wa mada keekeñ ga* toboshii.（きみはまだ経
験が乏しい）You are still *lacking* in
experience. / *Getsumatsu ni naru
to kozukai ga* toboshiku naru.（月
末になるとこづかいが乏しくなる）My
spending money runs *short* as
the end of the month approaches.

to「botobo とぼとぼ *adv.* (〜 to)
(a weary or weak way of walking):
tobotobo (to) aruku（とぼとぼ（と）歩
く）*plod along*.

to「b·u[1] とぶ（飛ぶ）*vi.* (tob·i-; to-
b·a-; toñ-de Ⓒ) **1** (of a bird, aircraft) fly:
Tori ga sora o toñde iru.（鳥が空を
飛んでいる）Birds *are flying* in the
sky. / *Kono ryokakki wa Tookyoo
to Nyuu Yooku no aida o* tobimasu.（この旅客機は東京とニューヨークの
間を飛びます）This passenger plane
flies between Tokyo and New
York.
2 (of a person) fly; travel by
plane:

Kare wa Sapporo made hikooki de toñda. (彼は札幌まで飛行機で飛んだ) He *flew* to Sapporo by plane.
3 rush; fly:
Kare wa jiko no geñba e toñda. (彼は事故の現場へ飛んだ) He *rushed* to the scene of the accident.

to⌈b·u[2] とぶ (跳ぶ) *vi.* (tob·i-; to-b·a-; toñ-de C) jump; leap; hop:
Kodomo-tachi ga toñdari *hanetari* shite iru. (子どもたちが跳んだりはねたりしている) The children *are jumping* and leaping around.

to⌈chi とち (土地) *n.* **1** land; lot:
Tookyoo no tochi *wa taka-sugiru.* (東京の土地は高すぎる) The price of *land* in Tokyo is too high. / *Kare wa* tochi-*tsuki no uchi o katta.* (彼は土地つきの家を買った) He bought a house with the *land*.
2 soil:
tochi *o tagayasu* (土地を耕す) culti-vate the *soil*.
3 place:
Kono tochi *ni kita no wa hajimete desu.* (この土地に来たのは初めてです) This is the first time that I've visited this *place*.

To⌈chigi⌉-keñ とちぎけん (栃木県) *n.* Tochigi Prefecture. Located in the north of Kanto district. Nikko, famous for Toshogu Shrine, lies in the northwestern part. Capital city: Utsunomiya (宇都宮). 《⇨ map (F3)》

To⌉choo とちょう (都庁) *n.* the Tokyo Metropolitan Government (Office). 《⇨ photo (right)》

to⌈chuu とちゅう (途中) *n.* on the way; halfway:
Gakkoo kara kaeru tochuu *hoñya ni yotta.* (学校から帰る途中本屋に寄った) I dropped into a bookstore *on my way* back from school. / *Sono keekaku wa* tochuu *de chuu-shi ni natta.* (その計画は途中で中止になった) The project was halted

TOCHOO

halfway through. / *Yuubiñkyoku wa eki e iku* tochuu *ni arimasu.* (郵便局は駅へ行く途中にあります) The post office is *on the way* to the station. / *Tochuu made go-issho shimashoo.* (途中までごいっしょしましょう) I'll go *part of the way* with you.

to⌈chuu-ge⌉sha とちゅうげしゃ (途中下車) *n.* (train) stopover:
Kono kippu de wa tochuu-gesha *dekimaseñ.* (この切符では途中下車できません) You are not allowed to make a *stopover* with this ticket.
tochuu-gesha suru (〜する) *vi.* stop over.

to⌈dana とだな (戸棚) *n.* cup-board; closet:
Shokki wa todana *ni shimaima-shita.* (食器は戸棚にしまいました) I put the dishes in the *cupboard*. / *Irui wa kono* todana *ni shimatte arimasu.* (衣類はこの戸棚にしまってあります) The clothes are kept in this *closet*.

to⌈den とでん (都電) *n.* a streetcar or the streetcar system operated by the Tokyo Metropolitan Government. 《⇨ tobasu[2]》

to⌈doke⌉·ru とどける (届ける) *vt.* (todoke-te V) **1** send; deliver; take; bring:
Kono kagu o jitaku made todo-

kete *kudasai*. (この家具を自宅まで届けてください) Please *deliver* this furniture to my house. / *Watashi wa sono tegami o señsee ni todoketa.* (私はその手紙を先生に届けた) I *took* the letter to my teacher. 《⇨ todoku》

2 report; notify.
Toonañ o keesatsu ni todoketa. (盗難を警察に届けた) I *reported* the theft to the police.

to「do¬k·u とどく (届く) *vi.* (todok·i·; todok·a·; todo·i·te [C])
1 arrive; get to:
Sokutatsu [Takkyuubiñ] ga todokimashita. (速達[宅急便]が届きました) A special delivery [An express home delivery] *has arrived.* 《⇨ todokeru》

2 reach:
Tana no ano hoñ ni te ga todokimasu ka? (棚のあの本に手が届きますか) *Can* you *reach* that book on the shelf?

to-「doo-fu-ke¬ñ とどうふけん (都道府県) *n.* all the major administrative divisions within Japan. 《⇨ map (inside back cover)》

to「ga¬r·u とがる (尖る) *vi.* (togar·i·; togar·a·; togat·te [C]) taper off to a point; be sharp:
★ Often pronounced '*toñgaru.*'
Take no ha no saki wa togatte iru. (竹の葉の先は尖っている) The tip of a bamboo leaf *is pointed.*

to「ge¬ とげ (刺) *n.* prick; splinter:
bara no toge (バラのとげ) a *thorn* from a rosebush / *saboteñ no* toge (サボテンのとげ) a cactus *spine* / Toge *ga yubi ni sasatta.* (とげが指に刺さった) I got a *splinter* in my finger. / *Yubi no toge o nuita.* (指のとげを抜いた) I pulled out the *splinter* in my finger.

to「ge¬·ru とげる (遂げる) *vt.* (toge·te [V]) accomplish; achieve; attain; realize:
nozomi o togeru (望みを遂げる) *at-*tain one's wish / *Kare-ra wa mokuteki o togeta.* (彼らは目的を遂げた) They *accomplished* their purpose.

to「gire¬·ru とぎれる (途切れる) *vi.* (togire·te [V]) break; be interrupted:
Deñwa ga natte, kaiwa ga togireta. (電話が鳴って、会話が途切れた) The phone rang and our conversation *was interrupted.*

to「g·u とぐ (研ぐ) *vt.* (tog·i·; tog·a·; to·i·de [C]) **1** sharpen; whet; grind:
Toishi de naifu o toida. (といしでナイフを研いだ) I *sharpened* the knife on a whetstone.

2 wash (rice):
kome o togu (米を研ぐ) *wash* rice.

to「ho とほ (徒歩) *n.* walking:
Eki made toho *de jup-puñ desu.* (駅まで徒歩で10分です) It takes ten minutes to *walk* to the station. / *Watashi-tachi wa soko made* toho *de ikimashita.* (私たちはそこまで徒歩で行きました) We went there on *foot.*

to「i とい (問い) *n.* question:
Tsugi no toi *ni kotae nasai.* (次の問いに答えなさい) Answer the following *questions.* 《↔ kotae》

to「iawase といあわせ (問い合わせ) *n.* inquiry:
Sono moñdai ni tsuite takusañ no toiawase *ga kita.* (その問題についてたくさんの問い合わせがきた) We received many *inquiries* about the problem. / *Watashi wa ressha no jikoku ni tsuite* toiawase *o shita.* (私は列車の時刻について問い合わせをした) I made an *inquiry* about train times. 《⇨ toiawaseru》

to「iawase¬·ru といあわせる (問い合わせる) *vt.* (-awase·te [V]) inquire; make inquiries:
Sono hoñ ga aru ka shoteñ ni toiawaseta. (その本があるか書店に問い合わせた) I *inquired* at a bookstore

whether the book was there. /
Biza ni tsuite taishikañ ni toiawaseta.（ビザについて大使館に問い合わせ
た）I *made inquiries* to the embassy about a visa. 《⇨ toiawase》

to「ika」es·u といかえす（問い返す）*vi.*
(-kaesh·i-; -kaes·a-; -kaesh·i-te
[C]) ask again; ask back; repeat
one's question:
Kikitorenakatta no de, kare ni toi-
kaeshita.（聞き取れなかったので，彼に
問い返した）I couldn't catch what
he said, so I *asked* him *again*.

to「ire トイレ *n.* toilet; lavatory:
Toire wa doko desu ka?（トイレはど
こてすか）Where is the *toilet?*

to「iretto-pe」epaa トイレットペー
パー *n.* toilet paper [roll].

to「ishi といし（砥石）*n.* whetstone:
toishi *de hoochoo o togu*（といして
包丁を研ぐ）sharpen a kitchen
knife on a *whetstone*.

to「itada」s·u といただす（問い質す）
vt. (-tadash·i-; -tadas·a-; -ta-
dash·i-te [C]) question closely;
inquire:
*Sono joohoo o doko de eta ka ka-
re ni* toitadashita.（その情報をどこで
得たか彼に問いただした）I *questioned*
him *closely* about where he got
the information.

to itte といって *conj.* but; however:
*Sono shigoto wa soñna ni muzuka-
shiku arimaseñ. To itte is-shuukañ de wa dekimaseñ.*（その仕事はそ
んなに難しくありません．といって1週間で
はできません）That work is not so
difficult. *However*, it is impossible to do it in a week.

to i「u」ko「to」da ということだ
(*polite*＝'to iu koto desu')
people say that...; it is said that...;
I hear that..:
*Yamada-sañ wa hitori de Fuji-sañ
ni nobotta* to iu koto desu.（山田さ
んは一人で富士山に登ったということで

す）*I hear that* Mr. Yamada
climbed Mt. Fuji by himself. /
*Saikiñ no seekatsu-suijuñ wa mae
yori yoi* to iu koto da.（最近の生活
水準は前より良いということだ）*It is
said that* the standard of living
these days is higher than previously. 《⇨ koto¹》

to「jikome」·ru とじこめる（閉じ込め
る）*vt.* (-kome-te [V]) shut up;
lock up; confine:
*Kootsuu juutai de kuruma ni ni-
jikañ mo* tojikomerareta.（交通渋
滞で車に2時間も閉じ込められた）We
were stuck in the car for two
whole hours because of the traffic jam.

to「jikomi とじこみ（綴じ込み）*n.*
file:
shiñbuñ no tojikomi（新聞のとじ込
み）a newspaper *file* / *zasshi no*
tojikomi-kookoku（雑誌のとじ込み広
告）an advertisement *bound into* a
magazine. 《⇨ tojikomu》

to「jiko」m·u とじこむ（綴じ込む）*vt.*
(-kom·i-; -kom·a-; -koñ-de [C])
file; keep on file:
Kono shorui o tojikoñde *kudasai.*
（この書類を綴じ込んでください）Please
file these papers. 《⇨ tojikomi》

to「ji」mari とじまり（戸締まり）*n.*
locking of doors:
Tojimari o tashikamemashita ka?
（戸締まりを確かめましたか）Have you
checked *all the doors are locked?*
tojimari (o) suru (～(を)する) *vi.*
lock up: *Dekakeru toki wa geñjuu ni* tojimari suru *yoo ni.*（出かけ
るときは厳重に戸締まりするように）Be
very careful about *locking up*
when leaving home.

to「ji」·ru¹ とじる（閉じる）*vt.* (toji-te
[V]) close; shut:
me o tojiru（目を閉じる）*close* one's
eyes / *hoñ o* tojiru（本を閉じる）*shut*
a book / *mise o* tojiru（店を閉じる）
close a store / *maku o* tojiru（幕を閉
じる）*draw* the curtains / *futa o*

tojiru（ふたを閉じる）*put on* a lid / *kuchi o* tojiru（口を閉じる）*shut* one's mouth.

to「ji˥·ru² とじる（綴じる）*vt.* (toji-te V̄) bind; keep on file:
Kono pañfuretto o hotchikisu de tojite *kudasai.*（このパンフレットをホッチキスで綴じてください）Please *staple* this pamphlet together.

to「ka とか（都下）*n.* **1** Tokyo Metropolitan area.
2 the cities, towns and villages other than those in the 23 wards of Tokyo.（⇨ ku²）

to ka とか *p.* **1** and; or: ★ Used to link representative examples of a class.
Yasumi ni wa tenisu to ka *gorufu o shimasu.*（休みにはテニスとかゴルフをします）I go in for sports *like* tennis *and* golf on holidays. / *Asoñ-de bakari inai de tama ni wa sooji* to ka *señtaku* to ka *shitara doo desu ka?*（遊んでばかりいないでたまには掃除とか洗濯とかしたらどうですか）Instead of just enjoying yourself, what about doing *something like* the cleaning *or* washing once in a while? ★ Note that the second '*to ka*' is optional.（⇨ ya¹）
2 or someone [something]: ★ Used when unable to recall something accurately.
Tanaka-sañ to ka *iu hito kara deñ-wa ga arimashita.*（田中さんとかいう人から電話がありました）There was a phone call from a Mr. Tanaka *or* someone. / *Yamada-sañ wa ashita kuru* to ka *itte imashita.*（山田さんはあした来るとか言っていました）Miss Yamada said *something to the effect* that she would come tomorrow.

to「kai とかい（都会）*n.* city; town:
*Tookyoo wa dai-*tokai *desu.*（東京は大都会です）Tokyo is a big *city*. / *Watashi wa* tokai *no seekatsu yori inaka no seekatsu no hoo ga*

suki desu.（私は都会の生活よりいなかの生活のほうが好きです）I like rural life better than *urban* life.

to「kaku とかく（兎角）*adv.* having a tendency; being likely:
Wareware wa tokaku *jikañ o muda ni shi-gachi desu.*（われわれはとかく時間をむだにしがちです）We *are apt* to waste time. ★ '*Tokaku ... (shi) gachi*' is a very common pattern.

to「ka˥s·u とかす（溶かす）*vt.* (toka-sh·i-; tokas·a-; tokash·i-te Ⓒ) melt; dissolve; liquefy; fuse; thaw:
namari o tokasu（鉛を溶かす）*melt* lead / *satoo o mizu ni* tokasu（砂糖を水に溶かす）*dissolve* sugar in water / *Furaipañ de bataa o* toka-shita.（フライパンでバターを溶かした）I *melted* the butter in a frying pan.（⇨ tokeru¹）

to「kee とけい（時計）*n.* clock; watch: ★ '*Tokee*' is a general word for watches and clocks.
Kono tokee *wa ni-fuñ susuñde [okurete] iru.*（この時計は2分進んで[遅れて]いる）This *clock* is two minutes fast [slow]. / *Kono* tokee *wa ik-ka-getsu ni ni-fuñ susumu [oku-reru].*（この時計は1カ月に2分進む[遅れる]）This *watch* gains [loses] two minutes a month. / *Tokee o rajio no jihoo ni awaseta.*（時計をラジオの時報に合わせた）I set my *watch* by the radio time signal. / *Tokee ga tomatte shimatta.*（時計が止まってしまった）My *watch* has stopped.

tokee	watch	udedokee (wristwatch) kaichuudokee (pocket watch)
	clock	kakedokee (wall clock) okidokee (table clock)

to«kekom·u とけこむ（溶け込む）*vi.*
(-kom·i-; -kom·a-; -koñ·de [C])
1 melt; dissolve:
shio ga tokekoñda *mizu*（塩が溶け
込んだ水）water in which salt *is dissolved.*
2 adapt oneself (to the environment):
*Kanojo wa kurasu ni tokekomu
koto ga nakanaka dekinakatta.*（彼
女はクラスに溶け込むことがなかなかできな
かった）She just *could not fit in*
with the rest of the class.

to«ke»·ru[1] とける（溶ける）*vi.* (toke-
te [V]) melt; dissolve:
Hi ga deta no de yuki wa sugu ni
toketa.（日が出たので雪はすぐに溶けた）
The sun came out, so the snow
soon *melted.* / *Satoo wa mizu ni*
tokemasu.（砂糖は水に溶けます）
Sugar *dissolves* in water. 《⇨ to-
kasu》

to«ke»r·u[2] とける（解ける）*vi.* (toke-
te [V]) **1** (of a problem) be
solved:
Kono moñdai wa nakanaka toke-
nai.（この問題はなかなか解けない）This
problem *is not* easily *solved.*
《⇨ toku[1]》
2 (of a knot) come loose; come
untied:
Kutsu no himo ga toketa.（靴のひも
が解けた）My shoelaces *came undone.* 《⇨ toku[1]》
3 (of suspicion) be cleared; disappear:
Kare e no utagai wa toketa.（彼へ
の疑いは解けた）The suspicions
about him *disappeared.* 《⇨ toku[1]》

to«ki»[1] とき（時）*n.* **1** time; hour:
Sono moñdai wa toki *ga kaiketsu
shite kureru deshoo.*（その問題は時
が解決してくれるでしょう）*Time* will
take care of the problem. / *Watashi-tachi wa kanojo no uchi de
tanoshii* toki *o sugosu koto ga
dekita.*（私たちは彼女の家で楽しい時を
過ごすことができた）We could have a

good *time* at her house.
2 when; while:
Shitsumoñ ga aru toki *wa te o age
nasai.*（質問があるときは手を上げなさい）
When you have a question,
please raise your hand. / *Watashi
ga rusu no* toki *nani-ka arimashita ka?*（私が留守のとき何かありました
か）Did anything happen *while* I
was out? / *O-hima na* toki *itsu de
mo o-tachiyori kudasai.*（お暇なとき
いつでもお立ち寄りください）Please
drop in at our house *whenever*
you are free.
3 occasion; case:
Kono omedetai toki *ni atari, o-
iwai no kotoba o mooshiagemasu.*
（このおめでたいときにあたり、お祝いの言葉
を申し上げます）On this happy *occasion, I* wish to express my congratulations. / *Hijoo no* toki *wa
kono doa o akete kudasai.*（非常の
ときはこのドアを開けてください）Please
open this door *in the event of* an
emergency.

to«kidoki ときどき（時々）*adv.*
from time to time; once in a
while:
Kare wa tokidoki *watashi no ie e
kimasu.*（彼はときどき私の家へ来ます）
He comes to my house *from time
to time.* / *Tokidoki soo-iu koto ga
arimasu.*（ときどきそういうことがありま
す）That kind of thing happens
once in a while.

to«ki» ni wa ときには（時には）*adv.*
sometimes; at times; once in a
while:
*Toki ni wa dare datte machigai o
shimasu.*（時には誰だって間違いをしま
す）Everyone makes mistakes *at
times.*

to ki»tara ときたら as for: ★ Follows a noun and used to mark
the topic of a sentence. Implies a
degree of criticism.
Uchi no ko to kitara, *mainichi terebi bakari mite imasu.*（うちの子と

きたら, 毎日テレビばかり見ています)
When it comes to our child, he does nothing but watch television all day. / *Kimura-sañ to kitara, yakusoku o yabutte mo, ayamaroo to shinakatta.* (木村さんときたら, 約束を破っても, 謝ろうとしなかった) *As for* Mr. Kimura, he wouldn't think of apologizing, even if he broke a promise.

to「kkeñ とっけん (特権) *n*. privilege:
tokkeñ-*kaikyuu* (特権階級) the *privileged* classes.

to「kku ni とっくに (疾っくに) *adv.* long ago; a long time ago:
Kare wa tokku ni *dekakemashita.* (彼はとっくに出かけました) He left *long ago.* / *Sono zasshi wa* tokku ni *urikiremashita.* (その雑誌はとっくに売り切れました) That magazine sold out a *long time ago.*

to「kkuri とっくり (徳利) *n*. sake flask. 《⇨ sakazuki》

TOKKURI AND SAKAZUKI

to¹kkyo とっきょ (特許) *n*. patent:
tokkyo *o shiñsee suru* (特許を申請する) apply for a *patent* / tokkyo *o toru* (特許を取る) take out a *patent* / *Tookyoo* Tokkyo-*kyoku* (東京特許局) Tokyo *Patent* Office. ★ This is a well-known tongue twister.

To「kkyo¹-choo とっきょちょう (特許庁) *n*. Patent Office:
Tokkyo-choo *chookañ* (特許庁長官) the Director General of the *Patent Office.* 《⇨ choo⁴ (table)》

to「kkyuu とっきゅう (特急) *n*. lim-

ited [special] express. 《⇨ kyuukoo¹ (table)》

to「ko とこ (床) *n*. bed:
toko *o shiku* (床を敷く) prepare a *bed* / toko *o ageru* (床をあげる) put away the *bedding.* 《⇨ futoñ》
toko ni tsuku (〜につく) **1** go to bed.
2 be sick in bed: *Kare wa byooki de* toko ni tsuite imasu. (彼は病気で床についています) He *is sick in bed.*

to「konoma とこのま (床の間) *n*. tokonoma; alcove in a Japanese house. ★ Scrolls, artistic ornaments, flower arrangements, etc. are placed in the tokonoma, which is a small alcove with a slightly raised floor. 《⇨ washitsu (photo)》

TOKONOMA

to「koro¹ de ところで *p*. [follows the past tense of a verb, adjective, or the copula]
even if: ★ The first clause introduces a condition and the second clause specifies a disagreeable or unfavorable consequence.
Imasara hañsee shita tokoro de, *okite shimatta koto wa moo shikata ga nai.* (いまさら反省したところで, 起きてしまったことはもう仕方がない) *Even if* you look back on it at this stage, what has happened cannot now be undone. / *Kore kara isshoo-keñmee yatta* tokoro

de, *moo maniawanai daroo*. (これか
ら一生懸命やったところで、もう間に合わ
ないだろう) *Even if* you were to do
your best from now on, it would
be too late. / *Ikura tanoñda* tokoro de, *ano hito wa tasukete kurenai daroo*. (いくら頼んだところで、あの
人は助けてくれないだろう) *No matter*
how much we ask him, I am
afraid he will not help us. / *Dame
datta* tokoro de, *motomoto desu*.
(だめだったところで、もともとです) *Even
if* we fail, we will lose nothing.
-**ta** [-**da**] **tokoro de wa** (た[だ]〜
は) as far as; according to:
★ The first clause puts a limit on
the personal opinion or prediction in the second clause.
Watashi no kiita tokoro de wa,
mata kabu ga sagaru rashii. (私の
聞いたところでは、また株が下がるらしい)
As far as I have heard, stocks
will apparently continue to fall in
value. / *Shiñbuñ de* yoñda tokoro
de wa, *kono natsu wa mizu-busoku da soo desu*. (新聞で読んだとこ
ろでは、この夏は水不足だそうです) *Ac-
cording to what I have read* in
the newspapers, there will be a
water shortage this summer.
— *conj.* **1** well; now: ★ Used
at the beginning of a sentence.
Tokoro de *koñdo wa nani o shimasu ka?* (ところで今度は何をしますか)
Well, what shall we do this time?
2 by the way: ★ Used at the
beginning of a stentence.
Tokoro de *okaasañ wa o-geñki
desu ka?* (ところでお母さんはお元気で
すか) *By the way*, is your mother
in good health?

to「korodo¹koro ところどころ (所
所) *n., adv.* here and there;
several places:
Kono kooeñ ni wa tokorodokoro
ni kadañ ga arimasu. (この公園には
ところどころに花壇があります) There
are flowerbeds *here and there* in

this park. / *Kimi no sakubuñ wa*
tokorodokoro (*ni*) *machigai ga
aru*. (君の作文はところどころ(に)間違い
がある) Your composition has mistakes in *several places*.

to「koro¹ ga ところが *p.* when:
★ Follows the past tense of a
verb, adjective or the copula.

⸺(USAGE)⸺
The first and second clauses
are related in terms of time,
cause or opportunity. The
second clause strongly suggests a realization or discovery
occasioned by the action or
state in the first clause. Similar
to '-*tara*.' 《⇨ -tara》

*Kinoo Yamada no uchi ni deñwa
shita* tokoro ga, *okusan ga dete,
kare wa shutchoo-chuu to no koto
datta*. (きのう山田の家に電話したところ
が、奥さんがでて、彼は出張中とのことだっ
た) *When* I phoned Mr. Yamada's house yesterday, his wife answered and said that he was
away on a business trip. / *Kare
no uchi ni itta* tokoro ga, *kare wa
dekaketa ato datta*. (彼の家に行った
ところが、彼は出かけたあとだった) *When*
I got to his house, he had already left.

— *conj.* but; while: ★ Used at
the beginning of a sentence.
Chichi wa otooto ni wa yasashii.
Tokoro ga *boku ni wa kibishii*. (父
は弟には優しい。ところが僕には厳しい)
My father is very gentle with my
younger brother, *but* he is really
strict with me. / *Miñna ga Kazuko o kurasu iiñ ni erañda*. Tokoro
ga *kanojo wa iya da to itta*. (みんな
が和子をクラス委員に選んだ。ところが彼
女はいやだと言った) They elected
Kazuko one of the class monitors.
But she refused.

to「koya とこや (床屋) *n.* barbershop; barber:

tokoya *ni iku* (床屋に行く) go to the *barbershop*.

to「k·u¹　とく (解く) *vt.* (tok·i-; to-k·a-; to·i-te Ⓒ) **1** untie; undo; unpack; loosen:
himo no musubime o toku (ひもの結び目を解く) *untie* the knot in a piece of string / *nimotsu o toku* (荷物を解く) *unpack* one's baggage. 《⇨ tokeru²》

2 solve (a problem):
Kono moñdai o toku koto ga dekimasu ka? (この問題を解くことができますか) *Can* you *solve* this problem? 《⇨ tokeru²; kaitoo²》

3 dismiss; discharge; relieve:
Kare wa ma-mo-naku geñzai no niñmu o tokareru deshoo. (彼は間もなく現在の任務を解かれるでしょう) He will *be relieved* of his current duties very soon.

to「ku²　とく (得) *n.* profit; benefit:
Koñgetsu wa kabu de daibu toku o shita. (今月は株でだいぶ得をした) I *made a lot of money* from stocks this month.
— *a.n.* (～ na, ni) profitable; advantageous; economical:
toku na tachiba (得な立場) an *advantageous* position / *toku na kaimono* (得な買物) a *good* buy / *Kono sai wa kachoo no iu toori ni shita hoo ga toku da yo.* (この際は課長のいうとおりにしたほうが得だよ) In this case, it will be *to your interest* to follow the advice of your section chief. 《↔ soñ》

to「k·u³　とく (説く) *vt.* (tok·i-; to-k·a-; to·i-te Ⓒ) persuade; talk into; preach:
Kyooshi wa sono ko ni yowaimono ijime o shinai yoo ni toite kikaseta. (教師はその子に弱い者いじめをしないように説いて聞かせた) The teacher *lectured* the boy about not bullying weak people. / *Boo-sañ wa watashi-tachi ni hotoke no michi o toita.* (坊さんは私たちに仏の

道を説いた) The priest *preached* the way of Buddha to us.

to「kubai　とくばい (特売) *n.* sale; bargain sale:
Tokubai de nekutai o katta. (特売でネクタイを買った) I bought a tie at a *sale*. / *Kyoo wa gyuuniku no tokubai ga arimasu.* (きょうは牛肉の特売があります) They have *special prices* on beef today. / tokubai-*bi* (特売日) a *special bargain* day / tokubai-*hiñ* (特売品) *sale* items / tokubai-*joo* (特売場) a *bargain* counter.

tokubai (o) suru (～(を)する) *vt.* sell at a special price: *Sono depaato de wa ima fuyumono no tokubai o shite imasu.* (そのデパートでは今冬物の特売をしています) At that department store they *are* now *selling* winter clothing *at reduced prices*.

to「kubetsu　とくべつ (特別) *a.n.* (～ na/no, ni), *adv.* special; extra; particular; exceptional:
tokubetsu *na riyuu* (特別な理由) a *special* reason / tokubetsu *na chuui* (特別な注意) *particular* care / *Kanojo wa* tokubetsu *da.* (彼女は特別だ) She is an *exception*. / *Kono seetaa wa* tokubetsu *(ni) yasui.* (このセーターは特別(に)安い) This sweater is *exceptionally* cheap. / *Tokubetsu (ni) kirai na tabemono wa arimaseñ.* (特別(に)きらいな食べ物はありません) There is no food that I *particularly* dislike.

to「kuchoo　とくちょう (特徴) *n.* characteristic; feature:
Kono riñgo wa katachi no chiisai no ga tokuchoo desu. (このりんごは形の小さいのが特徴です) This type of apple is *characteristic* for being small in size. / *Kanojo wa* tokuchoo *no aru koe o shite iru.* (彼女は特徴のある声をしている) She has a *characteristic* voice. / *Sono hañniñ no* tokuchoo *o oboete imasu*

ka? (その犯人の特徴を覚えていますか) Do you remember any *distinguishing features* of the criminal? ((⇨ tokushoku))

to「ku」i とくい（得意）*a.n.* (～ na/ no, ni) **1** good; favorite: *Kanojo wa ryoori ga tokui desu.* (彼女は料理が得意です) She is *good* at cooking. / *Kare wa jibuñ no tokui na uta o utatta.* (彼は自分の得意な歌を歌った) He sang his *best* song.
2 proud; triumphant: *Kare wa jibuñ no keekeñ o tokui ni natte hanashita.* (彼は自分の経験を得意になって話した) He talked about his experiences in a *proud manner.* / *Kare wa gorufu de yuushoo shite,* tokui ni natte iru. (彼はゴルフで優勝して、得意になっている) He *is elated* at winning the golf tournament.

to「kuisaki とくいさき（得意先）*n.* custom; customer: *Kare wa* tokuisaki *o mawatte imasu.* (彼は得意先を回っています) He is making the rounds of the *customers.*

to「ku ni とくに（特に）*adv.* specially; especially; particularly: *Kotoshi no natsu wa* toku ni *atsukatta.* (今年の夏は特に暑かった) This summer was *especially* hot. / *Kono keeki wa* toku ni *anata no tame ni tsukutta mono desu.* (このケーキは特にあなたのために作ったものです) This is a cake that I made *especially* for you. / Toku ni *mooshiageru koto wa arimaseñ.* (特に申し上げることはありません) I have nothing *in particular* to say. ((⇨ tokubetsu))

To「kushima」-keñ とくしまけん（徳島県）*n.* Tokushima Prefecture. Located in the east of Shikoku. The capital city, Tokushima, is noted for the famous '*Awa-odori*' (Awa-dance).
((⇨ map (D5)))

to「kushoku とくしょく（特色）*n.* characteristic; feature: *Kono jisho wa ikutsu ka* tokushoku *ga arimasu.* (この辞書はいくつか特色があります) This dictionary contains several *special features.* / *Ano tatemono wa* tokushoku no aru *katachi o shite iru.* (あの建物は特色のある形をしている) That building has a *characteristic* shape. ((⇨ tokuchoo))

to「kushu とくしゅ（特殊）*a.n.* (～ na, ni) special; particular; unique; unusual: tokushu *na jijooo* (特殊な事情) *special* circumstances / *Kono seehiñ wa* tokushu *na zairyoo o tsukatte imasu.* (この製品は特殊な材料を使っています) This product uses *special* materials.

to「kutee とくてい（特定）*n.* specification: *Kono shina wa* tokutee *no mise de shika utte imaseñ.* (この品は特定の店でしか売っていません) This article is sold only at *specific* stores. / *Tokutee no gaaru-fureñdo wa imaseñ.* (特定のガールフレンドはいません) I have no *steady* girlfriend.

tokutee suru (～する) *vt.* specify: *Sono kaisha wa meekaa o* tokutee *shite kita.* (その会社はメーカーを特定してきた) The company *specified* the manufacturer. / *Ima no tokoro hañniñ o* tokutee suru *koto wa dekimaseñ.* (いまのところ犯人を特定することはできません) We are at present unable to *determine the identity* of the criminal.

to「kuyuu とくゆう（特有）*a.n.* (～ na/no, ni) peculiar; characteristic; proper: *kono chihoo* tokuyuu *no sake* (この地方特有の酒) the sake *peculiar* to this district / *Kono o-matsuri wa Nihoñ* tokuyuu *no mono desu.* (このお祭りは日本特有のものです) This festival is *peculiar* to Japan. 《⇨ dokutoku》

to「mar·u[1] とまる (止まる) *vi.* (tomar·i-; tomar·a-; tomat-te ⓒ)
1 (of a moving thing) stop; pull up:
Takushii ga ie no mae ni tomatta. (タクシーが家の前に止まった) The taxi *stopped* in front of my house. / *Kono deñsha wa kaku eki ni* tomarimasu. (この電車は各駅に止まります) This train *stops* at every station. / *Tokee ga* tomatte iru. (時計が止まっている) The clock *has stopped.* 《⇨ tomeru[1]》
2 cease; stop:
Suidoo no mizumore ga tomatta. (水道の水漏れが止まった) The leak in the water pipe *has stopped.* / *Kata no itami ga* tomatta. (肩の痛みが止まった) The pain in my shoulder *has gone.* 《⇨ tomeru[1]》
3 (of electricity or water supply) fail; be cut off:
Jiko de deñki ga tomatta. (事故で電気が止まった) The electricity *failed* because of an accident. 《⇨ tomeru[1]》
4 (of a bird) perch; alight; settle:
Suzume ga ichi-wa ki no eda ni tomatte iru. (すずめが一羽木の枝に止まっている) A sparrow *is perching* on the branch.

to「mar·u[2] とまる (泊まる) *vi.* (tomar·i-; tomar·a-; tomat-te ⓒ)
1 (of a person) stay; lodge:
Yuube wa inaka no ryokañ ni tomatta. (ゆうべは田舎の旅館に泊まった) Last night I *stayed* at a country inn. 《⇨ tomeru[2]》
2 (of a ship) lie at anchor:
Gaikoku no kyakuseñ ga minato ni tomatte iru. (外国の客船が港に泊まっている) There is a foreign passenger ship *anchored* in the harbor.

to「mato トマト *n.* tomato.

to「me·ru[1] とめる (止める) *vt.* (tome-te Ⓥ) **1** stop; bring to a halt; park:
Hoteru no mae de kuruma o tometa. (ホテルの前で車を止めた) I *stopped* the car in front of the hotel. / *Koko ni kuruma o* tomete *wa ikemaseñ.* (ここに車を止めてはいけません) You cannot *park* your car here. / *Te o agete, takushii o* tometa. (手を上げて、タクシーを止めた) I *flagged down* a taxi. 《⇨ tomaru[1]》
2 stop; forbid; prohibit:
Futari no keñka wa tomeru *koto ga dekinakatta.* (二人のけんかは止めることができなかった) I could not *stop* their quarrel. / *Koko de no satsuee wa* tomerarete imasu. (ここでの撮影は止められています) It *is forbidden* to take photographs here.

to「me·ru[2] とめる (泊める) *vt.* (tome-te Ⓥ) lodge; put up; accommodate:
Kare o sono bañ uchi ni tomete yatta. (彼をその晩家に泊めてやった) I *put* him *up* for the night. / *Kono hoteru wa gohyaku-niñ* tomeru *koto ga dekimasu.* (このホテルは5百人泊めることができます) This hotel can *accommodate* 500 people. 《⇨ tomaru[2]》

to「me·ru[3] とめる (留める) *vt.* (tome-te Ⓥ) pin; tape; fasten:
Posutaa o kabe ni byoo de tometa. (ポスターを壁にびょうで留めた) I *fixed* the poster to the wall with tacks.

to「mi とみ (富) *n.* wealth; riches; fortune:
Kare wa tochi no baibai de tomi *o kizuita.* (彼は土地の売買で富を築いた) He heaped up *riches* by buying and selling land.

tomo[1] とも *p.* **1** all; both:
Watashi no kyoodai wa sañ-niñ tomo *isha desu.* (私の兄弟は3人とも医者です) *All* three of my brothers are doctors. / *Machida-sañ go-fuufu wa futari* tomo *gorufu ga*

joozu desu. (町田さんご夫婦は二人とも ゴルフが上手です) *Both* Mr. and Mrs. Machida are good at golf.

2 at the ...-est: ★ Indicates an approximate limit.

Sukunaku tomo *ichi-nichi ichi-jikañ wa uñdoo o shita hoo ga yoi.* (少なくとも 1 日 1 時間は運動をしたほうが良い) You should do *at least* one hour's exercise every day. / Osoku tomo *juu-ji made ni kitaku shi nasai.* (遅くとも 10 時までに帰宅しなさい) Be sure to get back home by ten *at the latest.*

3 no matter where [what; how]: ★ A slightly old form of 'te mo.'

Doñna ni taiheñ de aroo tomo, *akiramete wa ikemaseñ.* (どんなに大変であろうとも，あきらめてはいけません) *However* hard things may be, you must not give up. / *Dare ga koyoo* tomo, *doa o akete wa ikemaseñ.* (だれが来ようとも，ドアを開けてはいけません) *No matter* who comes, you must not open the door.

...tomo aroo hito ga (...～あろう人が) someone like: ★ Used when criticizing the person in question for uncharacteristic behavior.

Anata tomo aroo hito ga *naze soñna koto o shita ñ desu ka?* (あなたともあろう人がなぜそんなことをしたんですか) How could *someone like* you have done such a thing? / *Keesatsukañ* tomo aroo hito ga, *soñna hidoi koto o suru hazu ga arimaseñ.* (警察官ともあろう人が，そんなひどいことをするはずがありません) It is hard to imagine that a policeman, *of all people,* would do such a terrible thing.

tomo² とも *p.* certainly; sure; of course: ★ Used when confidently expressing one's opinions or thoughts. Used mainly by men.

"Tetsudatte kurenai ka?" "Ii tomo." (「手伝ってくれないか」「いいと

も」) "Won't you give me a hand?" "*Only too* pleased to." / *"Ikimasu ka?" "Ee, ikimasu* tomo." (「行きますか」「ええ，行きますとも」) "Are you going?" "Yes, I *certainly* am." / *"Haitte mo yoroshii desu ka?" "Ii desu* tomo." (「入ってもよろしいですか」「いいですとも」) "Is it all right if I come in." "It's *perfectly* all right."

★ Sometimes used with the particle 'sa.' *"Kono shigoto kimi ga shite kureru?" "Ii* tomo sa." (「この仕事君がしてくれる」「いいともさ」) "Will you do this job for me?" "Yes, *of course* I will."

to⌐mo³ とも (友) *n.* friend: *Kare wa shoogai no* tomo *o ushinatta.* (彼は生涯の友を失った) He lost his lifelong *friend.*

to⌐mo- とも (共) *pref.* along [together] with: tomo-bataraki-*katee* (共働き家庭) a *two-paycheck* family / tomo-*gui* (共食い) feeding *on each other; cannibalism.*

-tomo とも (共) *suf.* **1** both; all; neither; none: *Watashi-tachi wa futari-*tomo *geñki desu.* (私たちは二人とも元気です) *Both* of us are well. / *Ano hito-tachi wa futari-*tomo *kimaseñ.* (あの人たちは二人とも来ません) *Neither* of them is coming. / *Watashi no kodomo wa sañ-niñ-*tomo *shoogakusee desu.* (私の子どもは三人とも小学生です) *All* three of my children are elementary school pupils.

2 including: *Kono yadoya no ryookiñ wa shokuhi-*tomo *ip-paku ichimañ-eñ desu.* (この宿屋の料金は食費とも一泊 1 万円です) The charge for one night at this inn is 10,000 yen, *including* the cost of meals.

to⌐mo⌐ba⌐taraki ともばたらき (共働き) *n.* husband and wife both working:

tomobataraki *no katee* (共働きの家庭) a *two-paycheck* family / *Futari tomo kodomo ga umarete mo,* tomobataraki *o tsuzukete imasu.* (二人とも子どもが生まれても, 共働きを続けています) Both of them have continued *working* even after their child was born.

to｢**modachi** ともだち (友達) *n.* friend; companion: *Kare wa mukashi kara no* tomodachi *no hitori desu.* (彼は昔からの友達の一人です) He is one of my *friends* of long standing. / *Kare wa kimi to* tomodachi *ni naritagatte imasu.* (彼は君と友達になりたがっています) He wants to make *friends* with you. / *Yoi* tomodachi *o mochi nasai.* (良い友達を持ちなさい) Keep good *company*.

to｢**mokaku** ともかく *adv.*
1 = tonikaku.
2 regardless of; apart from: *Hoka no hito wa* tomokaku, *watashi wa hañtai desu.* (他の人はともかく, 私は反対です) *Regardless of* the others, I am against it. / *Nedañ wa* tomokaku, *sutairu ga ki ni irimaseñ.* (値段はともかく, スタイルが気に入りません) *Never mind* the price—I don't like the style.

to｢**moka**｢**segi** ともかせぎ (共稼ぎ) *n.* = tomobataraki.

to｢**mona**｢**u** ともなう (伴う) *vi.* (-na·i-; -naw·a-; -nat-te Ⓒ)
1 take; bring; be accompanied: *Kare wa kazoku o* tomonatte *doraibu ni dekaketa.* (彼は家族を伴ってドライブに出かけた) He went for a drive *with* his family.
2 bring about (danger); go together; involve: *Kono shigoto wa kikeñ o* tomonaimasu. (この仕事は危険を伴います) This work *involves* danger.

to｢**mo ni** ともに (共に) *adv.* **1** together; with: *Señsee wa seeto to* tomo ni *kyoo-* shitsu no sooji o shita.* (先生は生徒とともに教室の掃除をした) The teacher cleaned the classroom *together* with the students. / *Shushoo wa fujiñ to* tomo ni *resepushoñ ni shusseki shita.* (首相は夫人とともにレセプションに出席した) The prime minister attended the reception *with* his wife. / *Watashi wa kare to kuroo o* tomo ni *shita.* (私は彼と苦労を共にした) I *shared* troubles with him.
2 both; as well as: *Watashi-tachi futari wa* tomo ni *shikeñ ni ukarimashita.* (私たち二人はともに試験に受かりました) We *both* passed the examination. / *Kare wa daigaku kyooju de aru to* tomo ni *sakka de mo aru.* (彼は大学教授であるとともに作家でもある) He is a writer *as well as* being a university professor.
3 as: *Toshi o toru to* tomo ni *kiokuryoku wa otoroemasu.* (年をとるとともに記憶力は衰えます) *As* one grows older, one's memory becomes poor.

to｢**mor·u** ともる (点る) *vt.* (tomor·i-; tomor·a-; tomot-te Ⓒ) be lit; burn: *Sono koya ni wa rañpu ga* tomotte ita.* (その小屋にはランプがともっていた) A lamp *was burning* in the cabin. (⇨ tsuku｢)

to｢**m·u** とむ (富む) *vi.* (tom·i-; tom·a-; toñ-de Ⓒ) abound (in); be rich (in): ★ Used in the pattern '... *ni tomu.*' *Sono kuni wa koobutsu-shigeñ ni* toñde iru. (その国は鉱物資源に富んでいる) The country *is rich* in mineral resources. / *Kare no supiichi wa yuumoa ni* toñde ita. (彼のスピーチはユーモアに富んでいた) His speech *was full* of humor.

to｢**ñ** トン *n.* ton; tonne: *yoñ-*toñ-*zumi no torakku* (4トン積

みのトラック) a four-*ton* truck / *juu-mañ*-toñ *no tañkaa* (10万トンのタンカー) a tanker of 100,000 *tons*.

to「nae˥・ru となえる(唱える) *vt.* (tonae-te Ⓥ) **1** recite; chant; utter:

neñbutsu o tonaeru (念仏を唱える) *chant* (Buddhist) prayers / *bañzai o* tonaeru (万歳を唱える) *cry* 'banzai.'

2 advocate; advance:

Kare wa atarashii riroñ o tonaete *iru.* (彼は新しい理論を唱えている) He *advocates* a new theory. / *Watashi no ikeñ ni igi o* tonaeru *hito wa inakatta.* (私の意見に異議を唱える人はいなかった) There was nobody who *raised* objections to my opinion.

to「nai とない(都内) *n.* (within) the Tokyo Metropolitan area:

Kare wa tonai *no hoteru ni tomatte imasu.* (彼は都内のホテルに泊まっています) He is staying at a hotel *in Tokyo.* 《⇨ shinai》

to na˥reba となれば ⇨ to sureba.

to「nari となり(隣) *n.* **1** next-door neighbor; the house next door:

Tonari *ni wa dare ga suñde iru ñ desu ka?* (隣にはだれが住んでいるんですか) Who is it living *next door* to you? / *Yamada-sañ to watashi-domo wa* tonari *dooshi desu.* (山田さんと私どもは隣どうしです) The Yamadas and we are *next-door* neighbors.

2 next:

Tonari *no seki wa aite imasu ka?* (隣の席は空いていますか) Is that seat *next* to you free?

to「naria˥wase となりあわせ(隣り合わせ) *n.* being side by side:

Watashi wa kanojo to tonariawase *ni suwatta.* (私は彼女と隣り合わせに座った) I sat *side by side* with her. / *Sore wa shi to* tonariawase *no bookeñ datta.* (それは死と隣り合わせの冒険だった) It was an adventure in

which we *faced* death.

to na˥ru to となると ⇨ to sureba.

to「ñbo とんぼ *n.* dragonfly.

toñbo-gaeri (〜返り) **1** somersault: toñbo-gaeri *o suru.* (とんぼ返りをする) turn a *somersault*.

2 quick round trip: Toñbo-gaeri *de Nagano e itte kimashita.* (とんぼ返りで長野へ行ってきました) I made a *quick visit* to Nagano.

to「ñda とんだ *attrib.* terrible; unexpected; serious:

Watashi wa toñda *jikeñ ni maki-komarete shimatta.* (私はとんだ事件に巻き込まれてしまった) I was involved in a *serious* affair. / *Sore wa* toñda *sainañ deshita ne.* (それはとんだ災難でしたね) It was *quite* an unfortunate occurrence, wasn't it? / Toñda *koto ni natte kita.* (とんだことになってきた) Things have turned out *badly*. 《⇨ toñde mo nai》

to「ñde mo na˥・i とんでもない **1** absurd; outrageous; terrible; unexpected:

Toñde mo nai *koto ga okita.* (とんでもないことが起きた) Something completely *unexpected* occurred. / *Soñna koto o iu nañte* toñde mo nai *yatsu da.* (そんな事を言うなんてとんでもないやつだ) What an *outrageous* person he is to say something like that.

2 (used to express strong negation):

"Watanabe-sañ wa rikoñ shita soo desu ne." "Toñde mo nai." (「渡辺さんは離婚したそうですね」「とんでもない」) "I hear Mrs. Watanabe got divorced." "*Goodness, no!*" / *"Mookatte iru yoo desu ne." "Toñde mo nai. Shakkiñ darake desu.* (「もうかっているようですね」「とんでもない。借金だらけです」) "It seems that you are making a lot of money." "*You are joking.* I am deeply in debt." / *"Taiheñ o-*

sewa ni narimashita." "Toñde mo arimaseñ" (「大変お世話になりました」「とんでもありません」) "Thank you for all your assistance." "*Not at all.*"

To⌐negawa とねがわ (利根川) *n.* the Tone River, one of the largest rivers in Japan; flows into the Pacific Ocean.

to⌐nga⌐r·u とんがる = togaru.

to⌐nikaku とにかく (兎に角) *adv.* anyway; in any case; at any rate: Tonikaku *kono shigoto o katazuke-mashoo.* (とにかくこの仕事を片づけましょう) *Anyway*, let's finish up this work. / Tonikaku *zeñryoku o tsu-kushimasu.* (とにかく全力を尽くします) *At any rate*, I will do my best. / Tonikaku *anata wa sono kaigi ni shusseki shinakereba narimaseñ.* (とにかくあなたはその会議に出席しなければなりません) *In any case*, you have to attend the meeting.

to⌐ñkatsu とんカツ (豚カツ) *n.* deep-fried breaded pork cutlet.

to⌐ñneru トンネル *n.* tunnel: toñneru *o toorinukeru* (トンネルを通り抜ける) pass through a *tunnel*.

tono ko⌐to⌐ da とのことだ I hear that...; they say that...: *Jee-aaru no uñchiñ heñkoo wa sugu ni jisshi sareru to no koto desu.* (JRの運賃変更はすぐに実施されるとのことです) *They say that* the changes in JR fares will soon be put into effect. / *Sono jikkeñ wa seekoo shita to no koto da.* (その実験は成功したとのことだ) *I hear that* the experiment succeeded.

┌─── **USAGE** ───┐
A formal alternative for '*soo da.*' But note that with '*to no koto da*' the source of the report is not usually given. The polite equivalent is '*to no koto desu.*' (⇨ koto¹)
└────────────────┘

to⌐ñtoñ¹ とんとん *adv.* (~ to)

(the sound of a quick light strike): Toñtoñ *to doa o nokku suru oto ga kikoeta.* (とんとんとドアをノックする音が聞こえた) I heard a *knocking* at the door.

to⌐ñtoñ² とんとん *a.n.* (~ na, ni) (*informal*) even; equal; the same: *Keehi o sashihiku to soñ-eki wa* toñtoñ *desu.* (経費を差し引くと損益はとんとんです) If we deduct the expenses, gains and losses are *equal*.

to⌐ñya とんや (問屋) *n.* wholesale store; wholesaler. (⇨ oroshi)

to⌐o¹ とう (十) *n.* ten: ★ Used when counting. too-ka (十日) *ten* days. (⇨ juu¹; kazu (table))

to⌐o² とう (党) *n.* (political) party: too *o kessee suru* (党を結成する) form a political *party* / too *ni hairu* (党に入る) join a *party* / too *o dattai suru* (党を脱退する) leave a *party*. (⇨ seetoo² (table))

to⌐o³ とう (塔) *n.* tower; pagoda; steeple. (⇨ gojuu-no-too (photo))

too- とう (当) *suf.* this; current: too-chi (当地) *this* city [town; country] / too-neñ (当年) *this* [the *current*] year / too-gekijoo (当劇場) *this* theater / too-teñ (当店) *this* store.

-too¹ とう (等) *suf.* **1** class; grade: it-too (1等) first *class* / ni-too (2等) second *class*.
2 prize: *Kyoosoo de* it-too *ni natta.* (競争で1等になった) I won first *prize* in the race.

-too² とう (頭) *suf.* counter for large animals: uma it-too (馬1頭) one horse / ushi go-too (牛5頭) five *head* of cattle / suu-too *no zoo* (数頭の象) *several* elephants. (⇨ -hiki)

to⌐oañ とうあん (答案) *n.* examination answer sheet:
tooañ *o teeshutsu suru* (答案を提出する) hand in one's *paper* / tooañ *o saiteñ suru* (答案を採点する) mark the *papers* / tooañ-*yooshi* (答案用紙) an *answer* sheet. 《↔ moñdai》 《⇨ kotae》

to⌐obañ とうばん (当番) *n.* turn; duty:
Kyoo no toobañ *wa dare desu ka?* (きょうの当番はだれですか) Who is on *duty* today? / *Is-shuukañ ni ichi-do sooji* toobañ *ni atarimasu.* (一週間に一度掃除当番にあたります) I take my *turn* to clean the room once a week.

to⌐obuñ とうぶん (当分) *adv.* for the time being; for some time:
Kyooto ga ki ni irimashita kara, toobuñ *taizai suru tsumori desu.* (京都が気に入りましたから, 当分滞在するつもりです) I have taken a liking to Kyoto, so I intend to stay here *for the time being.* / *Tsugoo ni yori,* toobuñ *kyuugyoo itashimasu.* (都合により, 当分休業いたします) Owing to circumstances, we have *temporarily* stopped doing business.

to⌐ochaku とうちゃく (到着) *n.* arrival:
Jiko no tame, ressha no toochaku *ga okureta.* (事故のため, 列車の到着が遅れた) Because of the accident, the *arrival* of the train was delayed. / toochaku-*jikoku* (到着時刻) the *arrival* time / toochaku-*hoomu* (到着ホーム) the *arrival* platform.
toochaku suru (〜する) *vi.* arrive: *Choosadañ wa yokujitsu mokutekichi ni* toochaku shimashita. (調査団は翌日目的地に到着しました) The team of investigators *arrived* at their destination the next day. / *Ichi-bañ-señ ni Too-kyoo-yuki ga* toochaku shimasu.

(1 番線に東京行きが到着します) The train for Tokyo *is arriving* at track no. 1. 《↔ shuppatsu》 《⇨ tsuku¹》

to⌐odai とうだい (灯台) *n.* lighthouse.

to⌐ofu とうふ (豆腐) *n.* soybean curd; tofu.

TOOFU

to⌐oga⌐rashi とうがらし (唐辛子) *n.* red pepper.

to⌐oge⌐ とうげ (峠) *n.* **1** the top of a mountain pass:
Tooge *kara no nagame wa subarashii.* (峠からの眺めは素晴らしい) The view from the *top of the pass* is wonderful.
2 peak; height:
Atsusa wa ima ga tooge *da.* (暑さは今が峠だ) Now is *the hottest time* of the year.
tooge o kosu [koeru] (〜を越す [越える]) **1** cross over a peak.
2 get over the hump; overcome a difficulty: *Kañja no yoodai wa* tooge *o koshimashita.* (患者の容体は峠を越しました) The condition of the patient *has passed the crisis.*

To⌐ohoku とうほく (東北) *n.*
1 the northeast.
2 the northeastern district of Japan. It comprises Aomori, Akita, Iwate, Yamagata, Miyagi and Fukushima prefectures.
《⇨ map (G2)》

to⌐ohyoo とうひょう (投票) *n.* vote; poll; ballot:
toohyoo *de kimeru* (投票で決める) decide by *vote* / toohyoo-*bi* (投票日) a *voting* day / toohyoo-*jo* (投票

所) a *polling* station / toohyoo-ritsu (投票率) *voter* turnout / too-hyoo-yooshi (投票用紙) a *ballot*.

toohyoo (o) suru (〜(を)する) *vi.* vote; cast a vote: *Mada dare ni toohyoo suru ka kimete imaseñ.* (まだだれに投票するか決めていません) I have not yet decided who I will *vote* for. / *Sono añ ni sañsee [hañtai] no toohyoo o shita.* (その案に賛成[反対]の投票をした) I *voted* for [against] the proposal.

to⌐o·i とおい (遠い) *a.* (-ku) **1** far; distant; a long way:
tooi *kuni* (遠い国) a *distant* country / *Sono daigaku wa eki kara tooi.* (その大学は駅から遠い) The university is a *long way* from the station. (↔ chikai¹)
2 (of time, relation, etc.) remote; distant:
tooi *mukashi* (遠い昔) the *remote* past / *Damu no kañsee wa mada tooi hanashi da.* (ダムの完成はまだ遠い話だ) The completion of the dam is *a long way off.* / *Kono machi ni tetsudoo ga kaitsuu suru no mo tooku nai deshoo.* (この町に鉄道が開通するのも遠くないでしょう) It will not be *long* before the railway is extended to this town. / tooi *shiñseki* (遠い親戚) a *distant* relative.

to⌐oitsu とういつ (統一) *n.* unity; unification; standardization:
Kumiai no iiñchoo wa tooitsu *to dañketsu o uttaeta.* (組合の委員長は統一と団結を訴えた) The chairman of the union appealed for *unity* and solidarity. / tooitsu-chihoo-señkyo (統一地方選挙) *unified* local elections.
tooitsu suru (〜する) *vt.* unify; standardize: *kokka o* tooitsu *suru* (国家を統一する) *unify* a nation / *kakaku o* tooitsu *suru* (価格を統一する) *standardize* prices / *ikeñ o* tooitsu *suru* (意見を統一する) *coordinate* opinions / *Too-zai Doitsu*

wa señ kyuuhyaku kyuujuu-neñ ni tooitsu shita. (東西ドイツは1990年に統一した) East and West Germany *were unified* in 1990.

to⌐oji¹ とうじ (当時) *n.* at that time; then:
Tooji *wa shokuryoo ga fusoku shite ita.* (当時は食料が不足していた) *At that time* there was a shortage of food. / *Kuroo no ookatta* tooji *ni kurabereba, ima no wakai hito wa shiawase da.* (苦労の多かった当時に比べれば, 今の若い人は幸せだ) Compared with the many hardships of *those days*, young people today are very fortunate. / Tooji, *watashi wa shoogakusee deshita.* (当時, 私は小学生でした) I was *then* a pupil at elementary school.

to⌐oji² とうじ (冬至) *n.* the winter solstice (about December 22). (⇨ geshi)

to⌐ojitsu とうじつ (当日) *n.* that day; the very day:
Saiwai shiai no toojitsu *wa yoi teñki datta.* (幸い試合の当日は良い天気だった) Fortunately the weather was very good on *the day* of the match. / *Kare wa* toojitsu *ni natte, kesseki no reñraku o shite kita.* (彼は当日になって, 欠席の連絡をしてきた) When *the day* came he reported that he would be absent.

to⌐ojoo とうじょう (登場) *n.* appearance; entrance:
Kañkyaku wa kare no totsuzeñ no toojoo *ni odoroita.* (観客は彼の突然の登場に驚いた) The audience was surprised by his sudden *appearance.* / toojoo-jiñbutsu (登場人物) *the cast* (of a play). (↔ taijoo)
toojoo suru (〜する) *vi.* appear; enter: *Shuyaku ga butai no kamite kara* toojoo shita. (主役が舞台の上手から登場した) The leading player *came on* from the right of the stage. / *Kono kamera no shiñgata ga chikaku* toojoo suru *yotee*

desu. (このカメラの新型が近く登場する予定です) A new model of this camera is expected to *appear* in the near future.

to⌐oka とおか（十日）*n.* ten days; the tenth day of the month: *Kare wa ato* tooka *no yuuyo o motometa.* (彼はあと10日の猶予を求めた) He asked for another *ten days'* grace. / *Juu-gatsu* tooka (10月10日) October *10.* 《⇨ tsuitachi (table)》

To⌐okai とうかい（東海）*n.* Tokai, the district which comprises the three prefectures of Aichi, Gifu and Shizuoka. 《⇨ map (E4)》

To⌐oka⌐idoo とうかいどう（東海道）*n.* the road from Nihonbashi bridge in the center of Tokyo to Sanjo-ohashi bridge in Kyoto. In former times the road had fifty-three stages. ★ The Tokaido Line of the Japan Railway runs from Tokyo to Kobe.

to⌐okee とうけい（統計）*n.* statistics: tookee *o toru* (統計をとる) collect *statistics* / Tookee *ni yoreba sekai no jinkoo wa zooka shite iru.* (統計によれば世界の人口は増加している) According to the *statistics,* the population of the world is increasing.

to⌐oki¹ とうき（陶器）*n.* earthenware; pottery; ceramics: tooki *no chawan* (陶器の茶碗) a *ceramic* bowl. 《⇨ jiki³》

to⌐oki² とうき（登記）*n.* registration (of a house or land): tooki-*bo* (登記簿) a *register* book / tooki-*jo* (登記所) a *registry* office.
tooki suru (～する) *vt.* register: *atarashiku katta ie* [*tochi*] *o* tooki suru (新しく買った家[土地]を登記する) *register* a newly-bought house [land].

to⌐oki³ とうき（投機）*n.* speculation (in stocks); venture: *E wa* tooki *no taishoo ni naru.* (絵は投機の対象になる) Paintings become the object of *speculation.* / Tooki-teki *na jigyoo ni wa te o dasanai hoo ga yoi.* (投機的な事業には手を出さないほうがよい) You had better not concern yourself with *speculative* enterprises.

to⌐oki⁴ とうき（冬季）*n.* winter; wintertime: tooki *Orinpikku* (冬季オリンピック) the *Winter* Olympics. 《⇨ kaki³; shunki; shuuki²》

to⌐okoo とうこう（登校）*n.* school attendance: Tookoo no tochuu *de ame ga futte kita.* (登校の途中で雨が降ってきた) It began to rain *on my way to school.* / tookoo-*kyohi* (登校拒否) refusal to *attend school.*
tookoo suru (～する) *vi.* go to school: *Ashita wa hachi-ji made ni* tookoo shinakereba naranai. (あしたは8時までに登校しなければならない) We *have to be at school* before eight o'clock tomorrow morning. 《↔ gekoo》

to⌐oku とおく（遠く）*n.* a long way (off): *Amari* tooku *made asobi ni itte wa ikemasen.* (あまり遠くまで遊びに行ってはいけません) You must not go and play too *far off.* / Tooku *ni hanabi ga mieta.* (遠くに花火が見えた) I could see fireworks in *the distance.* 《↔ chikaku》

to⌐okyoku とうきょく（当局）*n.* the authorities: *shi-*tookyoku *kara kyoka o morau* (市当局から許可をもらう) get permission from the ciy *authorities.*

To⌐okyo⌐o-to とうきょうと（東京都）*n.* Tokyo Metropolis, the capital of Japan. Located almost in the center of Japan, it comprises 26 cities (*shi*), 23 wards (*ku*), which are under own autonomous political administration, 7 towns (*machi*) and 8 villages (*mura*). Sometimes 'Tokyo' is used to refer only to the above 23 wards. 《⇨ map (F4)》

to˺oma˺wari とおまわり (遠回り) *n.* roundabout way; detour: *Kono michi o iku to* toomawari *ni narimasu.* (この道を行くと遠回りになります) If we go this way it will be *farther.*
  toomawari (o) suru (〜(を)する) *vi.* make a detour: *Dooro ga kooji-chuu na no de* toomawari (o) *shita.* (道路が工事中なので遠回り(を)した) The road was being repaired, so I *came the long way round.* (↔ chikamichi》

to˺omee とうめい (透明) *a.n.* (〜 na, ni) transparent; clear: toomee *na garasu* (透明なガラス) *transparent* glass. 《⇨ sukitooru》

to˺oniñ とうにん (当人) *n.* **1** the person concerned: *Sono keñ ni tsuite wa* tooniñ *ni kiita hoo ga yoi.* (その件については当人に聞いたほうがよい) We had better ask *the person concerned* about the matter. / *Yagate moñdai no* tooniñ *ga arawareta.* (やがて問題の当人が現れた) After a while, *the person in question* appeared.
2 oneself: *Sono uwasa ni* tooniñ *wa heeki datta.* (そのうわさに当人は平気だった) He *himself* was indifferent to the rumor. 《⇨ hoñniñ》

to˺ori[1] とおり (通り) *n.* street; road: *Kono* toori *o iku to eki ni demasu.* (この通りを行くと駅に出ます) If you follow this *road*, you'll arrive at the station. / *Yuubiñkyoku wa kono* toori *no mukoo gawa desu.* (郵便局はこの通りの向こう側です) The post office is on the other side of this *street.* / *Kono* toori *wa itsu-mo hito de koñzatsu shite iru.* (この通りはいつも人で混雑している) This

street is always crowded.

to˺ori[2] とおり (通り) *n.* as; like: *Kare wa itsu-mo no* toori *ku-ji ni shussha shita.* (彼はいつものとおり9時に出社した) He came to the office at nine *as* usual. / *Watashi wa tada iwareta* toori *ni shita dake desu.* (私はただ言われたとおりにしただけです) I've only done *as* I was told.

-toori/doori とおり/どおり *suf.*
1 kind; sort: *sañ*-toori *no chigatta hoohoo* (三とおりの違った方法) three different *kinds* of methods / *Jikkeñ wa iku*-toori *mo yatte mimashita.* (実験はいくとおりもやってみました) We carried out the experiment in many different *ways.*
2 about; approximately: *Shigoto wa hachi-bu*-doori *owari-mashita.* (仕事は8分どおり終わりました) *About* eighty percent of the work has been finished.

to˺orikakar·u とおりかかる (通り掛かる) *vi.* (-kakar·i-; -kakar·a-; -kakat-te Ⓒ) pass by casually; come along: *Tachibanashi o shite iru tokoro e tamatama kanojo ga* toorikakatta. (立ち話をしているところへたまたま彼女が通りかかった) She happened to *pass by* us while we stood talking.

to˺orinuke とおりぬけ (通り抜け) *n.* passing through; through passage: Toorinuke *kiñshi.* (sign) (通り抜け禁止) No *Thoroughfare.* 《⇨ toorinukeru; photo (next page)》

to˺orinuke˺·ru とおりぬける (通り抜ける) *vi.* (-nuke-te Ⓥ) go [pass] through: *Toñneru o* toorinuketara *Fuji-sañ ga mieta.* (トンネルを通り抜けたら富士山が見えた) When we *passed through* the tunnel, we could see Mt. Fuji.

to˺orisugi·ru とおりすぎる (通り過

TOORINUKE KINSHI SIGN

ぎる）*vi.* (-sugi-te V) pass; go by; go past:
Kare wa wakime mo furazu ni, watashi no mae o toorisugita. (彼はわき目もふらずに, 私の前を通り過ぎた) He *passed* in front of me without even looking aside.
《⇨ tooru》

to¬oroku とうろく（登録）*n.* registration; entry:
Sono meebo ni o-namae no tooroku wa sumimashita ka? (その名簿にお名前の登録はすみましたか) *Have* you *entered* your name in the roll? / tooroku-*bangoo* (登録番号) a *registration* number / tooroku-*shoohyoo* (登録商標) a *registered* trademark.
tooroku suru (～する) *vt.* register; enter: *shoohyoo o* tooroku suru (商標を登録する) *register* a trademark / *Watashi wa sono kontesuto ni* tooroku shita. (私はそのコンテストに登録した) I *entered my name* for the contest.

to¬oron とうろん（討論）*n.* discussion; debate; argument:
tooron *o hajimeru* [*uchikiru*] (討論を始める[打ち切る]) open [close] the *discussion* / tooron *o kasaneru* (討論を重ねる) hold prolonged *discussion* / tooron-kai (討論会) a *debate*; a *panel discussion.*
tooron suru (～する) *vi.* discuss;

debate; argue: *Iinkai wa sono mondai ni tsuite ichinichi-juu* tooron shita. (委員会はその問題について一日中討論した) The committee *argued* about the matter for a whole day.

to¬or·u とおる（通る）*vi.* (toor·i-; toor·a-; toot-te C) **1** (of a vehicle) go; pass:
Kono dooro wa jidoosha ga yoku toorimasu. (この道路は自動車がよく通ります) Many cars *pass* along this road. / *Kono basu wa Ueno o* toorimasu *ka?* (このバスは上野を通りますか) *Does* this bus *go* to Ueno?
2 (of a bill, proposal, etc.) pass; be approved:
shiken ni tooru (試験に通る) *pass* an examination / *Kaisee-an wa kinoo iinkai o* tootta. (改正案はきのう委員会を通った) The amended bill *passed* the committee yesterday. 《⇨ toosu》
3 (of a public vehicle) run:
Densha wa nijup-pun goto ni tootte imasu. (電車は20分毎に通っています) The trains *come by* every twenty minutes.
4 (of a word, sentence, passage, etc.) make sense:
Kono bunshoo wa imi ga tooranai. (この文章は意味が通らない) This sentence *does not convey* any meaning.
5 (of a voice) carry:
Kare no koe wa yoku tooru. (彼の声はよく通る) His voice *carries* well.

to¬osan とうさん（父さん）*n.* (*informal*) father; dad; daddy. ★ A family term. 《↔ kaasan》《⇨ chichi¹; o-toosan》

to¬osee とうせい（統制）*n.* control; regulation:
toosee *o tsuyomeru* [*yurumeru*] (統制を強める[ゆるめる]) tighten [loosen] *controls* / toosee *o kaijo suru* (統制を解除する) lift *controls* / *Undookai wa* yoku toosee ga to-

rete ita. (運動会はよく統制がとれていた) The sports meeting *was well organized.* / toosee-*keezai* (統制経済) a *controlled* economy.

toosee suru (～する) *vt.* control; regulate: *Tochi no nedañ wa* toosee suru *hitsuyoo ga aru.* (土地の値段は統制する必要がある) It is necessary to *control* land prices.
《⇨ seegeñ》

to「oseñ とうせん (当選) *n.* **1** election; win in an election: *Suzuki-shi no* tooseñ *ga kakujitsu ni natta.* (鈴木氏の当選が確実になった) Mr. Suzuki's *election* has become a sure thing. 《↔ rakuseñ》

2 winning a prize: tooseñ-*sha* (当選者) the *winner of a prize.*

tooseñ suru (～する) *vi.* **1** be elected: *Yamada-shi ga shichoo ni* tooseñ shita. (山田氏が市長に当選した) Mr. Yamada *was elected* mayor. 《↔ rakuseñ》

2 win a prize: *Kono keñshoo ni* tooseñ suru *to juumañ-eñ moraemasu.* (この懸賞に当選すると10万円もらえます) If you *win this prize*, you will be able to get 100,000 yen. 《⇨ ataru》

to「oshi とうし (投資) *n.* investment: tooshi-*ka* (投資家) an *investor* / tooshi-*shiñtaku* (投資信託) an *investment* trust.

tooshi suru (～する) *vi.* invest; put money in: *Kare wa sono jigyoo ni gohyakumañ-eñ* tooshi shita. (彼はその事業に500万円投資した) He *invested* five million yen in the business.

to「osho とうしょ (投書) *n.* letter; complaint [suggestion] by letter: *Sono shiñbuñ ni takusañ no* toosho *ga yoserareta.* (その新聞にたくさんの投書が寄せられた) A lot of *letters* were sent in to the newspaper. /

toosho-*rañ* (投書欄) the *letters* column.

toosho suru (～する) *vi., vt.* write in (to a newspaper): *Sono zasshi ni* toosho shita *ga, saiyoo sarenakatta.* (その雑誌に投書したが, 採用されなかった) I *wrote in* to the magazine, but my letter was not accepted.

to「os·u とおす (通す) *vt.* (toosh·i-; toos·a-; toosh·i-te ⓒ) **1** let (a person) pass: *Sumimaseñ ga chotto* tooshite *kudasai.* (すみませんがちょっと通してください) Excuse me, but would you *let* me *pass*, please? / *Shuee ga watashi-tachi o* toosanakatta. (守衛が私たちを通さなかった) The guard *did not let* us *in.* 《⇨ tooru》

2 let in; admit: *Biniiru wa hikari wa* toosu *ga mizu mo kuuki mo* toosanai. (ビニールは光は通すが水も空気も通さない) Plastic sheets *let in* light, but *let through* neither water nor air. 《⇨ tooru》

3 show in (a guest, etc.); usher in: *O-kyaku-sañ o heya ni* tooshi nasai. (お客さんを部屋に通しなさい) Please *show* the guest into the room.

4 thread; pierce: *Watashi wa megane o kakenai to hari ni ito o* toosu *koto ga dekimaseñ.* (私は眼鏡をかけないと針に糸を通すことができません) I can not *thread* a needle unless I put on my glasses. 《⇨ tooru》

5 approve; pass (a bill): *Seefu wa ima no kokkai de sono giañ o* toosu *tsumori de iru.* (政府は今の国会でその議案を通すつもりでいる) The government intends to *pass* the bill in the current session of the Diet. 《⇨ tooru》

6 stick to (one's opinion); persist:

Kare wa akumade jibuñ no shu-choo o toosoo *to shita.*（彼はあくまで自分の主張を通そうとした）He persistently *stuck* to his assertion. 《⇨ tooru》

7 continue; remain (in a certain state):
Kare wa isshoo dokushiñ de too-shita.（彼は一生独身で通した）He *remained* single all his life. 《⇨ tooru》

to¹osuto トースト *n.* toast:
toosuto *ni bataa o nuru*（トーストにバターを塗る）spread butter on *toast*.

to¹otatsu とうたつ（到達）*n.* arrival; attainment:
Mokuhyoo tootatsu *made ni wa mada jikañ ga kakarimasu.*（目標到達までにはまだ時間がかかります）It will take some time before we *reach* our goal.

tootatsu suru (〜する) *vi.* reach; attain: *Kare to watashi wa onaji ketsuroñ ni* tootatsu shita.（彼と私は同じ結論に到達した）He and I *arrived* at the same conclusion.

to¹otee とうてい（到底）*adv.* (with a negative) not possibly; by any means:
Soñna koto wa tootee *fukanoo desu.*（そんなことはとうてい不可能です）That kind of thing is *quite* impossible. 《⇨ totemo》

to¹oteñ とうてん（読点）*n.* Japanese-language comma (、). ★ An English-language comma (,) is called '*koñma.*' 《⇨ kutooteñ》

to¹oto¹bu とうとぶ（尊ぶ）*vt.* (-to-b·i-; -tob·a-; -toñ-de C) value; respect:
oya o tootobu（親を尊ぶ）*respect* one's parents / *inochi o* tootobu（命を尊ぶ）*value* life.

to¹oto¹·i とうとい（尊い・貴い）*a.* (-ku) precious; valuable; noble:
tootoi *kyookuñ*（貴い教訓）an *invaluable* lesson / tootoi *gisee*（尊い犠牲）a *high* sacrifice.

to¹otoo とうとう（到頭）*adv.*
★ More informal than '*tsui ni*'
1 at last; finally:
Kare wa tootoo *sono añ o akirameta.*（彼はとうとうその案をあきらめた）*At last* he gave up the plan. / *Miñna ga nozoñde ita hashi ga* tootoo *kañsee shita.*（みんなが望んでいた橋がとうとう完成した）The bridge that everyone had longed for was *finally* completed.
2 after all:
Kanojo wa tootoo *sugata o misenakatta.*（彼女はとうとう姿を見せなかった）She did not show up *after all*.

To¹oyoo とうよう（東洋）*n.* the Orient; the East:
Tooyoo *shokoku*（東洋諸国）*Oriental* [*Eastern*] countries. 《↔ Seeyoo》

To¹oyo¹ojiñ とうようじん（東洋人）*n.* an Oriental. 《↔ Seeyoojiñ》

to¹ozai とうざい（東西）*n.* east and west:
Kooeñ no toozai *ni fuñsui ga arimasu.*（公園の東西に噴水があります）There are fountains on the *east and west* sides of the park. / too-zai-*nañ-boku*（東西南北）north, south, *east and west*. ★ Note that the Japanese word order is different from the English. 《↔ nañboku》

to¹ozaka¹r·u とおざかる（遠ざかる）*vi.* (-zakar·i-; -zakar·a-; -zakat-te C) **1** go away; fade away:
Basu wa dañdañ toozakate itta.（バスはだんだん遠ざかっていった）The bus gradually *disappeared*. / *Kyuukyuusha no saireñ ga* toozakatta.（救急車のサイレンが遠ざかった）The sound of the ambulance siren *faded away*.
2 keep away:
Saikiñ gorufu kara toozakatte imasu.（最近ゴルフから遠ざかっています）I *haven't played* golf recently. 《⇨ toozakeru》

to⌈ozake⌉·ru とおざける (遠ざける) *vt.* (-zake-te Ⓥ) keep away; avoid; ward off: *Kare wa yuujiñ o* toozakete iru. (彼は友人を遠ざけている) He *keeps* his friends *at a distance.* / *Chichi-oya wa musuko o warui nakama kara* toozakeyoo to shita. (父親は息子を悪い仲間から遠ざけようとした) The father *tried to keep* his son *away* from bad company. (⇨ too-zakaru)

to⌈ozeñ⌉ とうぜん (当然) *a.n.* (～ na/no, ni) reasonable; natural; expected: toozeñ *no kekka* (当然の結果) an *expected* result / toozeñ *no keñri* (当然の権利) a *natural* right / *Watashi-tachi ga saibañ ni katsu no wa* toozeñ *desu.* (私たちが裁判に勝つのは当然です) It is only *natural* that we should win the lawsuit. / *Kare ga erabareru no wa* toozeñ *no koto to omowarete ita.* (彼が選ばれるのは当然のことと思われていた) It was considered *natural* that he was chosen.
— *adv.* naturally; of course: Toozeñ, *kimi mo iku beki da.* (当然、きみも行くべきだ) *Of course,* you should go, too.

to⌈ppa⌉ とっぱ (突破) *n.* break-through; overcoming.
toppa suru (～する) *vt.* break through; overcome: *nañkañ o* toppa suru (難関を突破する) *over-come* a difficulty / *Sono kuruma wa hijooseñ o* toppa shite, *nigeta.* (その車は非常線を突破して、逃げた) The car *broke through* the police cordon and disappeared. / *Kañ-shuu wa gomañ-niñ o* toppa shita. (観衆は 5 万人を突破した) The spec-tators *were more than* fifty thou-sand.

to⌈ppu⌉ トップ *n.* top; first: *Kurasu no* toppu *wa dare desu ka?* (クラスのトップはだれですか) Who

is at the *top* of your class? / *Kare wa* toppu *de gooru-iñ shita.* (彼はトップでゴールインした) He reached the finish line *first.*

to⌈ra⌉ とら (虎) *n.* tiger.

to⌈rae⌉·ru とらえる (捕らえる) *vt.* (torae-te Ⓥ) **1** catch; arrest: *Keesatsu wa sono doroboo o* toraeta. (警察はその泥棒を捕らえた) The police *caught* the thief. ((⇨ tsukamaeru))
2 capture: *Kanojo no eñgi wa kañshuu no kokoro o* toraeta. (彼女の演技は観衆の心を捕らえた) Her performance *captured* the hearts of the audi-ence.

to⌈ra⌉kku トラック *n.* truck; lorry.

to⌈ra⌉ñpu トランプ *n.* playing cards: ★ Not used in the sense of 'trump(s),' as in bridge or whist.
torañpu *o kiru* [*kubaru*] (トランプを切る[配る]) shuffle [deal] the *cards* / torañpu *de uranau* (トランプで占う) tell a fortune with *cards* / *Hima tsubushi ni* torañpu *o shiyoo.* (暇つぶしにトランプをしよう) Let's play *cards* to help kill time.

to⌈re⌉·ru¹ とれる (取れる) *vi.* (tore-te Ⓥ) **1** come off; be removed: *Shatsu no botañ ga* toreta. (シャツのボタンがとれた) A button *has come off* my shirt. / *Kono shimi wa nakanaka* torenai. (このしみはなかなかとれない) This stain just *will not come out.*
2 (of pains) go away: *Kizu no itami ga* toreta. (傷の痛みがとれた) The pain from the cut *has gone away.*
3 (of a word, sentence, passage, etc.) can be interpreted: *Kono buñ wa futatsu no imi ni* to-reru. (この文は二つの意味にとれる) This sentence *can be interpreted* in two ways.

to⌈re⌉·ru² とれる (捕れる) *vi.* (tore-

te ⟨V⟩ (of an animal) be caught:
Kono kawa de wa unagi ga toremasu. (この川ではうなぎがとれます) Eels
are caught in this river.

to⌐re⌐·ru³ とれる (採れる) *vi.* (tore-
te ⟨V⟩) (of a plant) be produced;
be grown:
Kotoshi wa mikañ ga takusañ toremashita. (今年はみかんがたくさんとれ
ました) Mandarin oranges *have
been produced* in large quantities
this year.

to⌐ri とり (鳥) *n.* **1** bird; fowl;
poultry.
2 chicken. (⟹ toriniku)

to⌐ria⌐ezu とりあえず (取り敢えず)
adv. first of all; for the present:
Toriaezu *biiru o sañ-boñ kudasai.*
(とりあえずビールを3本下さい) *To start
with,* please give us three bottles
of beer. / *Shuuri ga owaru made,*
toriaezu *kono soojiki o tsukatte
kudasai.* (修理が終わるまで、とりあえず
この掃除機を使ってください) Please
use this vacuum cleaner *for now,*
until yours has been repaired.

to⌐riage·ru とりあげる (取り上げる)
vt. (-age-te ⟨V⟩) **1** pick up:
juwaki o toriageru (受話器を取り上
げる) *pick up* the telephone receiver.
2 adopt (a proposal); accept (an
opinion):
Iiñkai wa kare no teeañ o toria-
geta. (委員会は彼の提案を取り上げた)
The committee *adopted* his proposal.
3 take up for discussion:
Sono moñdai wa tsugi ni toriage-
masu. (その問題は次に取り上げます)
We will *take up* that problem
next.
4 deprive (someone of a qualification, license, etc.); cancel:
shikaku o toriageru (資格を取り上げ
る) *cancel* someone's license /
Kare wa uñteñ-meñkyoshoo o
toriagerareta. (彼は運転免許証を取

り上げられた) He *was deprived* of
his driver's license.

to⌐riatsukai とりあつかい (取り扱い)
n. treatment; handling:
Kare wa hidoi toriatsukai *o uketa.*
(彼はひどい取り扱いを受けた) He re-
ceived very nasty *treatment.* /
Toriatsukai *chuui (sign)* (取り扱い
注意) *Handle* With Care. (⟹ to-
riatsukau)

TORIATSUKAI CHUUI SIGN

to⌐riatsuka·u とりあつかう (取り扱
う) *vt.* (-atsuka·i-; -atsukaw·a-;
-atsukat-te ⟨C⟩) treat; handle;
deal in [with]:
Kono shinamono wa chuui shite
toriatsukatte *kudasai.* (この品物は
注意して取り扱ってください) Please
handle these goods with care. /
*Kono mise de wa arukooru-iñryoo
wa* toriatsukatte *imaseñ.* (この店で
はアルコール飲料は取り扱っていません)
At this shop we do not *deal in*
alcoholic drinks. / *Gaikoku-
yuubiñ wa dono madoguchi de*
toriatsukatte *imasu ka?* (外国郵便
はどの窓口で取り扱っていますか) At
what window do they *handle*
foreign mail? (⟹ toriatsukai)

to⌐ridas·u とりだす (取り出す) *vt.*
(-dash·i-; -das·a-; -dash·i-te ⟨C⟩)
take out; pick out; produce:
Kanojo wa baggu kara techoo o
toridashita. (彼女はバッグから手帳を
取り出した) She *took out* a small
notebook from her bag.

to⌐rihazus·u とりはずす (取り外す)
vt. (-hazush·i-; -hazus·a-; -hazu-
sh·i-te ⟨C⟩) take away; remove:

Matsuri ga owari, kazari o toriha-zushita. (祭りが終わり、飾りを取り外した) The festival finished and we *removed* the decorations.

to「ri¬hiki とりひき（取り引き）*n.* business; dealings; transaction: *Uchi no kaisha wa sono kaisha to* torihiki *ga arimasu.* (うちの会社はその会社と取り引きがあります) Our company has *business dealings* with that company. / torihiki-*giñkoo* (取引銀行) the bank *one deals with* / torihiki-*saki* (取引先) a *business* connection; a *customer*.
torihiki (o) suru (〜(を)する) *vi.*, *vt.* do business; make a deal: *Sono kaisha to* torihiki shite imasu ga, gaku wa wazuka desu. (その会社と取り引きしていますが、額はわずかです) We *do business* with that firm, but the amount is small. / *Kare-ra wa ura de nani-ka* torihiki *o shite iru rashii.* (彼らは裏で何か取り引きをしているらしい) They seem to *have* some kind of *dealings* behind the scenes.

to「rii とりい（鳥居）*n.* torii.
★ The gateway at the entrance of a Shinto shrine.

TORII

to「riire¬・ru とりいれる（取り入れる）*vt.* (-ire-te Ⓥ) **1** take in: *Ame ga futte kita no de señtaku-mono o* toriireta. (雨が降ってきたので洗濯物を取り入れた) It started to rain, so I *took in* the washing.
2 gather in (a crop); harvest: *Kome wa aki ni* toriiremasu. (米は秋に取り入れます) We *harvest* rice in autumn.
3 adopt (an idea, opinion, etc.); introduce: *Nihoñ wa Oobee kara ooku no shisoo o* toriireta. (日本は欧米から多くの思想を取り入れた) Japan has *borrowed* many ideas from Western countries. / *Shitsunai-sooshoku ni tsuite wa kanojo no ikeñ o oohaba ni* toriiremashita. (室内装飾については彼女の意見を大幅に取り入れました) As for the interior decoration, we *adopted* a lot of her ideas.

to「rikae とりかえ（取り替え）*n.* exchange; replacement: *Shinamono no* torikae *ni wa ryoo-shuusho ga hitsuyoo desu.* (品物の取り替えには領収書が必要です) A receipt is necessary for the *exchange* of articles. / *Surihetta buhiñ wa* torikae *ga dekimasu.* (すり減った部品は取り替えができます) The worn-out part *is replaceable.* (⇨ torikaeru)

to「rikae・ru とりかえる（取り替える）*vt.* (-kae-te Ⓥ) change; exchange; replace; renew: *Shitagi wa mainichi* torikaemasu. (下着は毎日取り替えます) I *change* my underwear every day. / *Watashi wa kare to seki o* torikaeta. (私は彼と席を取り替えた) I *swapped* seats with him. / *Kanojo wa tee-buru-kurosu o atarashii no to* torikaeta. (彼女はテーブルクロスを新しいのと取り替えた) She *changed* the tablecloth for a new one. (⇨ torikae)

to「rikaes・u とりかえす（取り返す）*vt.* (-kaesh・i-; -kaes・a-; -kaesh・i-te Ⓒ) get back; recover; regain: *Watashi wa kare kara sono jisho o* torikaeshita. (私は彼からその辞書を取り返した) I *got* the dictionary *back* from him.
torikaeshi no tsukanai (取り返しのつかない) irrecoverable; fatal:

Watashi wa torikaeshi no tsukanai *shippai o shite shimatta.*（私は取り返しのつかない失敗をしてしまった）I have made an error *that I cannot put right.*

to┌**rikakar·u** とりかかる（取り掛かる）*vi.* (-kakar·i-; -kakar·a-; -kakatte Ⓒ) begin; start; set about: *Watashi-tachi wa chuushoku-go sugu ni shigoto ni* torikakatta.（私たちは昼食後すぐに仕事に取りかかった）We *set about* doing the job right after lunch. / *Saa shigoto ni* torikakaroo.（さあ仕事に取りかかろう）Now *let's get down* to work.

to┌**rikakom·u** とりかこむ（取り囲む）*vt.* (-kakom·i-; -kakom·a-; -kakoñ-de Ⓒ) surround; gather around: *Kare wa oozee no fuañ ni* torikakomareta.（彼は大勢のファンに取り囲まれた）He *was surrounded* by a great number of his fans.

to┌**rikeshi** とりけし（取り消し）*n.* cancellation; withdrawal: *chuumoñ no* torikeshi（注文の取り消し）*cancellation* of an order / *hatsugeñ no* torikeshi（発言の取り消し）*withdrawal* of a remark.（⇨ torikesu）

to┌**rikes·u** とりけす（取り消す）*vt.* (-kesh·i-; -kes·a-; -kesh·i-te Ⓒ) cancel; take back; withdraw: *Mikka no yoyaku o* torikeshitai *no desu ga.*（三日の予約を取り消したいのですが）I *would like to cancel* the reservation for the third. / *Daijiñ wa moñdai no hatsugeñ o* torikeshita.（大臣は問題の発言を取り消した）The minister *withdrew* his controversial remark.（⇨ torikeshi）

to┌**rikumi** とりくみ（取り組み）*n.*
1 measures: *Seefu no fukushi moñdai ni taisuru* torikumi *wa namanurui.*（政府の福祉問題に対する取り組みは生ぬるい）The *measures* the government

are taking regarding welfare problems are half-hearted.（⇨ torikumu）
2 (of sumo wrestling) match; bout: *yokozuna dooshi no* torikumi（横綱同士の取り組み）a *match* between grand champion sumo wrestlers.（⇨ torikumu）

to┌**rikum·u** とりくむ（取り組む）*vi.* (-kum·i-; -kum·a-; -kuñ-de Ⓒ) wrestle with; tackle; be engaged in: *Kare wa ima sono moñdai ni* torikuñde imasu.（彼は今その問題に取り組んでいます）He *is* now *tackling* the problem.（⇨ torikumi）

to┌**rimak·u** とりまく（取り巻く）*vt.* (-mak·i-; -mak·a-; -ma·i-te Ⓒ) surround: *Watashi-tachi o* torimaku *joosee wa kibishii.*（私たちを取り巻く情勢は厳しい）The circumstances *surrounding* us are harsh. / *Señsee wa seeto-tachi ni* torimakareta.（先生は生徒たちに取り巻かれた）The teacher *was surrounded* by her pupils.

to┌**rimodo┐s·u** とりもどす（取り戻す）*vt.* (-modosh·i-; -modos·a-; -modosh·i-te Ⓒ) get back; recover; regain: *ishiki o* torimodosu（意識を取り戻す）*recover* consciousness / *Kare wa shidai ni keñkoo o* torimodoshita.（彼は次第に健康を取り戻した）He gradually *regained* his health.

to┌**rinigas·u** とりにがす（取り逃がす）*vt.* (-nigash·i-; -nigas·a-; -nigash·i-te Ⓒ) fail to catch; miss: *Keesatsu wa yoogisha o* toriniga-shita.（警察は容疑者を取り逃がした）The police *failed to arrest* the suspect. / *Sekkaku no kikai o* torinigashite shimatta.（せっかくの機会を取り逃がしてしまった）I *have let* a rare opportunity *slip by.*（⇨ nigasu）

to「riniku とりにく(鶏肉) *n.* chicken meat; poultry.

to「rinozo」k·u とりのぞく(取り除く) *vt.* (-nozok·i-; -nozok·a-; -nozo-i-te C) take away; remove: *dooro kara shoogaibutsu o torino-zoku* (道路から障害物を取り除く) *get rid of* an obstacle from a road / *Watashi wa kanojo no fuañ o tori-nozoku koto ga dekinakatta.* (私は彼女の不安を取り除くことができなかった) I was unable to *dispel* her anxiety.

to「rishimari とりしまり(取り締まり) *n.* control; regulation; crackdown: *kootsuu-ihañ no* torishimari (交通違反の取り締まり) a *crackdown* on traffic offenders / *Nihoñ de wa mayaku no* torishimari *ga kibishii.* (日本では麻薬の取り締まりが厳しい) In Japan, narcotics *control* is strict. 《⇨ torishimaru》

to「rishimari」yaku とりしまりやく (取締役) *n.* director (of a company). 《⇨ kaisha (table)》

to「rishima」r·u とりしまる(取り締まる) *vt.* (-shimar·i-; -shimar·a-; -shimat-te C) control; crack down: *booryoku o* torishimaru (暴力を取り締まる) *control* violent actions / *Ima yopparai-uñteñ o* torishimatte imasu. (今酔っ払い運転を取り締まっています) They *are* now *cracking down* on drunken driving. 《⇨ torishimari》

to「rishirabe とりしらべ(取り調べ) *n.* questioning; investigation; examination: *Kare wa keesatsu de* torishirabe *o uketa.* (彼は警察で取り調べを受けた) He *was questioned* at the police station. / *Keesatsu no* torishirabe *wa kibishikatta.* (警察の取り調べは厳しかった) The *investigation* by the police was very thorough. 《⇨ torishiraberu》

to「rishirabe」·ru とりしらべる(取り調べる) *vt.* (-shirabe-te V) examine (a suspect, etc.); investigate; inquire into: *Keesatsu wa yoogisha o* torishirabete iru. (警察は容疑者を取り調べている) The police *are examining* the suspect. 《⇨ torishirabe》

to「ritsugi とりつぎ(取り次ぎ) *n.* agency; agent: *Too-teñ wa takuhaibiñ no* toritsu-gi *o shite imasu.* (当店は宅配便の取り次ぎをしています) Our shop is an *agency* for handling express delivery parcels. 《⇨ toritsugu》
toritsugi ni deru (〜に出る) answer: *Beru o narashita ga dare mo* toritsugi ni dete konakatta. (ベルを鳴らしたがだれも取り次ぎに出て来なかった) I rang the bell, but nobody *answered.*

to「ritsu」g·u とりつぐ(取り次ぐ) *vt.* (-tsug·i-; -tsug·a-; -tsu·i-de C) **1** act as an agent: *Go-chuumoñ wa watashi-domo ga* toritsuide orimasu. (ご注文は私どもが取り次いでおります) We will *act as agent* for what you order. 《⇨ to-ritsugi》
2 convey (a message, telephone, etc.); answer: *Anata no kañgae wa shachoo ni* toritsuide okimasu. (あなたの考えは社長に取り次いでおきます) I will *convey* your ideas to the president. / *Deñwa wa dare ga* toritsugima-shita *ka?* (電話はだれが取り次ぎましたか) Who *answered* the phone? 《⇨ toritsugi》

to「ritsuke·ru とりつける(取り付ける) *vt.* (-tsuke-te V) **1** install; furnish; equip; fit: *Eakoñ o heya ni* toritsukete mo-ratta. (エアコンを部屋に取り付けてもらった) I *had* an air conditioner *installed* in my room.
2 obtain (consent, permission, etc.):

Sono koto ni kañshite chichi no dooi o toritsuketa.(そのことに関して父の同意を取り付けた) I *obtained* my father's consent regarding that matter.

to⌐robi とろび (とろ火) *n.* very slow heat; low fire:
mame o torobi *de niru* (豆をとろ火で煮る) simmer beans over *low heat.*

to⌐r·u¹ とる (取る・執る) *vt.* (tor·i-; tor·a-; tot-te ⓒ) **1** take; take hold of; seize:
Kare wa hoñdana kara jisho o totta.(彼は本棚から辞書を取った) He *took* a dictionary from the bookshelf. / *Haha-oya wa kodomo no ude o* totta.(母親は子どもの腕を取った) The mother *took* her child by the arm. / *Shio o* totte *kudasai.* (塩を取ってください) Please *pass* me the salt.
2 get; take; receive; obtain; win:
Kyoo wa yasumi o torimashita.(きょうは休みをとりました) I *took* a day off today. / *Kanojo wa supiichi koñtesuto de ittoo o* totta.(彼女はスピーチコンテストで一等をとった) She *won* first prize in the speech contest.
3 take off; remove:
Kare wa booshi o totte, *aisatsu shita.*(彼は帽子をとって, 挨拶した) He *took off* his hat and greeted me. / *Mado no yogore o* tori nasai. (窓の汚れをとりなさい) *Please get* the dirt *off* the window.
4 steal; rob:
Watashi wa jiteñsha o dare-ka ni torareta.(私は自転車をだれかにとられた) I *had* my bicycle *stolen* by someone. 《⇨ nusumu》
5 subscribe to (a newspaper, magazine); buy:
Watashi mo onaji shiñbuñ o totte *imasu.*(私も同じ新聞をとっています) I also *take* the same newspaper.

6 eat; have:
Bitamiñ no aru mono o tori nasai. (ビタミンのあるものをとりなさい) *Eat* things containing vitamins. / *Moo chuushoku wa* torimashita *ka?*(もう昼食はとりましたか) *Have* you already *had* lunch?
7 take; make out; interpret; understand:
Watashi ga itta koto o waruku toranai de *kudasai.*(私が言ったことを悪くとらないでください) *Do not take* my words amiss.
8 take up; occupy (a place):
Kono tsukue wa basho o tori-*sugiru.*(この机は場所をとり過ぎる) This desk *takes up* too much space. 《⇨ shimeru⁴》
9 record; write down:
bañgumi o bideo ni toru (番組をビデオにとる) *record* a program on video / *kiroku o* toru (記録をとる) *keep records* / *nooto o* toru (ノートをとる) *take* notes.
10 charge (a fare, fee, etc.); demand:
Ano ryokañ wa ip-paku nimañ-eñ mo torimasu.(あの旅館は一泊2万円もとります) That inn *charges* all of 20,000 yen for one night. / *Chuu-sha-ihañ de bakkiñ o* torareta.(駐車違反で罰金をとられた) I *was fined* for a parking violation.

to⌐r·u² とる (捕る) *vt.* (tor·i-; to-r·a-; tot-te ⓒ) catch (an animal, fish, etc.); get:
Kawa e sakana o tori ni ikimaseñ ka?(川へ魚をとりに行きませんか) Won't you come to the river for *fishing*?

to⌐r·u³ とる (採る) *vt.* (tor·i-; to-r·a-; tot-te ⓒ) **1** gather; pick (a plant):
Budoo-eñ de budoo o takusañ tori-mashita.(ぶどう園でぶどうをたくさんとりました) We *picked* a lot of grapes in the vineyard.
2 adopt (a proposal, suggestion,

etc.); choose; employ; engage: *Kimi no añ o* toroo. (君の案をとろう) *Let's adopt* your proposal. / *Eego no dekiru hito o* toritai. (英語のできる人をとりたい) We *want to employ* someone who can speak English.

to˺r·u⁴　とる (撮る) *vt.* (tor·i-; to-r·a-; tot-te Ⓒ) take (a picture): *eega o* toru (映画をとる) *shoot* a film / *Anata no shashiñ o* torasete *kudasai*. (あなたの写真を撮らせてください) Please *let* me *take* your picture. / *Kono butsuzoo no shashiñ o* totte *mo ii desu ka?* (この仏像の写真を撮ってもいいですか) May I *take* a picture of this Buddhist image? 《⇨ satsuee》

to˺ryoo　とりょう (塗料) *n.* paint. 《⇨ peñki》

to˺shi¹¹　とし (年) *n.* **1** year: toshi *no hajime* [*kure*] (年の初め[暮れ]) the beginning [end] of the *year* / *Toshi ga tatsu ni tsure, so-no jikeñ wa wasurerareta*. (年がたつにつれ、その事件は忘れられた) As the *years* went by, the incident was forgotten. / *Chichi wa watashi ga kekkoñ shita* toshi *ni taishoku shimashita*. (父は私が結婚した年に退職しました) My father retired in the *year* I got married.
2 age: toshi *o toru* (年を取る) *grow old* / *Ano hito no* toshi *wa ikutsu daroo?* (あの人の年はいくつだろう) What would his *age* be?

to˺shi²　とし (都市) *n.* city; towns and cities: *Wakai hito-tachi wa* toshi *no seekatsu ni akogareru*. (若い人たちは都市の生活にあこがれる) Young people yearn for *city* life. / toshi-*gasu* (都市ガス) *city* gas / toshi-*keekaku* (都市計画) *city* planning.

to˺shigoro　としごろ (年頃) *n.*
1 marriageable age: *Kare ni wa* toshigoro *no musume-sañ ga iru*. (彼には年ごろの娘さんがい

る) He has a daughter of *marriageable age*.
2 about the same age: *Watashi ni mo añta to onaji* toshigoro *no musuko ga imasu*. (私にもあんたと同じ年ごろの息子がいます) I also have a son *of your age*.

to˺shiñ　としん (都心) *n.* the heart [center] of Tokyo: *Kaisha wa* toshiñ *ni arimasu*. (会社は都心にあります) My office is in *the center of Tokyo*. 《↔ toka》

to˺shi-shita　としした (年下) *n.* junior in age: *Kare wa watashi yori sañ-sai* toshi-shita *desu*. (彼は私より3歳年下です) He is three years my *junior*. / *Watashi wa anata yori* toshi-shita *desu*. (私はあなたより年下です) I am *younger* than you. 《↔ toshi-ue》

to shi˺ta˺ra　としたら = to sureba.

to shite　として **1** as; for: ★ Indicates a role, position or qualification. *Yamamoto-shi wa taishi* to shite *Chuugoku ni hakeñ sareta*. (山本氏は大使として中国に派遣された) Mr. Yamamoto was sent to China *as* ambassador. / *Kare wa sono hako o isu* to shite *tsukatta*. (彼はその箱を椅子として使った) He used the box *for* a chair. / *Watashi* to shite *wa koñdo no kettee ni sañsee dekimaseñ*. (私としては今度の決定に賛成出来ません) *As for* me, I cannot agree to the present decision.
2 not even a ... ★ Used after words such as 'hitori', 'ichi-nichi,' 'ichi-do,' etc. with a negative. *Dare hitori* to shite *kare o tasuke-yoo to shinakatta*. (だれ一人として彼を助けようとしなかった) *Not a single* person tried to help him. / *Kano-jo ga otto no buji o inoranai hi wa ichi-nichi* to shite *nakatta*. (彼女が夫の無事を祈らない日は一日としてなかった) There was *not even a* single

day on which she did not pray
for her husband's safety.

to⌐shito⌐tta としとった (年とった)
old; aged:
toshitotta *ryooshiñ* (年とった両親)
one's *aged* parents.

to⌐shi⌐tsuki としつき (年月) *n.*
years:
*Sono toñneru o tsukuru no ni na-
gai* toshitsuki *ga kakatta.* (そのトン
ネルを作るのに長い年月がかかった) It
took many *years* to build the tunnel. ((⇨ neñgetsu))

to⌐shi-ue としうえ (年上) *n.* senior in age:
Kare wa kanojo yori go-sai toshi-
ue *desu.* (彼は彼女より5歳年上です)
He is five years her *senior.* / *Sañ-
niñ no naka de Tanaka-sañ ga ichibañ* toshi-ue *desu.* (三人の中で田中
さんがいちばん年上です) Miss Tanaka
is *the oldest* of the three.
((↔ toshi-shita))

to⌐shiyori⌐ としより (年寄り) *n.*
old person [people]:
Kanojo wa toshiyori *ni seki o yuzutta.* (彼女は年寄りに席を譲った)
She gave up her seat to an *old
man.* ((↔ wakamono))

to⌐sho としょ (図書) *n.* books:
tosho-*mokuroku* (図書目録) a catalog of *books.* ((⇨ hoñ))

to⌐shokañ としょかん (図書館) *n.*
(public) library:
toshokañ *de hoñ o kariru* (図書館
で本を借りる) borrow a book from
the *library* / toshokañ-choo (図書
館長) a chief librarian; the director of a library. ((⇨ toshoshitsu))

to⌐sho⌐keñ としょけん (図書券) *n.*
book token. ★ Often given as a
gift. ((⇨ photo (right)))

to⌐sho⌐shitsu としょしつ (図書室)
n. library; reading room.
★ Usually refers to a library in a
school or an office. ((⇨ toshokañ))

to⌐ssa とっさ (咄嗟) *n.* (~ no)
sudden; instant:

TOSHOKEÑ

Hijoo no toki wa tossa *no hañdañ
ga hitsuyoo desu.* (非常のときはとっさ
の判断が必要です) In emergency
cases, *instant* decisions are necessary. / *Sore wa* tossa *no dekigoto
de, fusegu koto wa dekimaseñ deshita.* (それはとっさの出来事で、防ぐこと
はできませんでした) That was an *unexpected* occurrence, so we could
not guard against it.

to⌐ssa ni とっさに (咄嗟に) *adv.*
immediately; instinctively:
Kare wa sono shitsumoñ ni tossa
ni *kotaerarenakatta.* (彼はその質問に
とっさに答えられなかった) He could
not answer the question *immediately.* / *Watashi wa sono kuruma
o* tossa ni *yoketa.* (私はその車をとっ
さによけた) I *instinctively* dodged
the car.

to su⌐reba とすれば if; supposing; on the assumption that...:

─(**USAGE**)─
The particle '*to*' plus the provisional of '*suru*.' The second
clause indicates a judgment or
inference based on the supposition in the first clause.

Tanaka ga dame to sureba, *dare
ni kono shigoto o tanomoo ka?* (田
中がだめとすれば、だれにこの仕事を頼もう
か) *Supposing* Tanaka were not
available, who would we ask to

do this job? / *Kimi ga dekinai to sureba, tabuñ dare ni mo dekinai deshoo.* (君ができないとすれば、たぶんだれにもできないでしょう) *If* you are unable to do this, I doubt that anyone can.

★ '*To suru to*,' '*to shitara*,' '*to nareba*,' and '*to naru to*' are also used similarly. 《⇒ -tara; to¹》

to su⌐ru to とすると = to sureba.

to⌐tañ¹ とたん（途端）*n.* the moment; just as...:

Furo ni hairoo to shita totañ (*ni*) *deñwa ga naridashita.* (ふろに入ろうとしたとたん(に)電話が鳴りだした) *Just as* I was about to get into the bath, the phone started ringing.

to⌐tañ² トタン *n.* galvanized iron.

tote とて *p.* even if:

┌─ **USAGE** ─────────────┐
Used when a fact is presented or an assumption made but the subsequent result or inference is contrary to expectation.
└──────────────────────────┘

Shigoto ga iya da tote *yameru wake ni wa ikanai.* (仕事がいやだとてやめる訳にはいかない) *Even if* you don't like the job, it won't do for you to quit. / *Shippai shita* tote *gakkari suru na.* (失敗したとてがっかりするな) *Even if* you've failed, do not be discouraged.

...koto tote (...こと〜) for; since: ★ Indicates that the first clause is the cause or reason for the second one. Slightly formal. *Shiranai* koto tote *shitsuree shimashita.* (知らないこととて失礼しました) Please forgive me *for* not knowing. / *Nani-shiro hajimete no* koto tote *iroiro taiheñ deshita.* (何しろ初めてのこととていろいろ大変でした) Anyway, things were very difficult, *since* it was the first time.

to⌐temo とても *adv.* ★ Also '*tottemo*.' **1** very; really; awfully; extremely:

Kono hoñ wa totemo *omoshiroi.* (この本はとてもおもしろい) This book is *very* interesting. / *Kesa wa* totemo *samukatta.* (今朝はとても寒かった) It was *awfully* cold this morning.

2 (with a negative) not possibly; by any means:

Koñna muzukashii moñdai wa totemo *tokemaseñ.* (こんな難しい問題はとても解けません) I cannot *possibly* solve this sort of difficult problem.

to⌐tonoe⌐·ru ととのえる（整える・調える）*vt.* (-noe-te Ⓥ) **1** prepare; get ready:

chooshoku o totonoeru (朝食を整える) *prepare* breakfast / *Kanojo wa beddo o* totonoeta. (彼女はベッドを整えた) She *made* the bed. 《⇒ totonou》

2 make tidy; dress:

Kanojo wa gaishutsu suru mae ni kami o totonoeta. (彼女は外出する前に髪を整えた) She *arranged* her hair before going out.

3 settle; arrange:

Kare wa futari no eñdañ o umaku totonoeta. (彼は二人の縁談をうまく整えた) He skillfully *arranged* their marriage. 《⇒ totonou》

to⌐tono⌐·u ととのう（整う・調う）*vi.* (-no·i-; -now·a-; -not-te Ⓒ) **1** be ready; be prepared; be completed:

Yuushoku no shitaku ga totonoimashita. (夕食の支度が整いました) Dinner *is ready.* / *Juñbi ga sukkari* totonotta. (準備がすっかり整った) The arrangements *are* fully *completed.* 《⇒ totonoeru》

2 be settled; be arranged:

Yamada-sañ to Tanaka-sañ no aida de eñdañ ga totonotta. (山田さんと田中さんの間で縁談が整った) A marriage *has been arranged* between Mr. Yamada and Miss Tanaka. / *Sono keeyaku wa* to-

tonowanakatta.（その契約は整わなかった）The contract *was not concluded*. 《⇨ totonoeru》

to⌐tsuzeñ とつぜん（突然）*a.n.* (~ na/no, ni) sudden; abrupt; unexpected:
Chichi no shi wa amari ni mo totsuzeñ *datta*.（父の死はあまりにも突然だった）My father's death was all too *sudden*. / Totsuzeñ *no yotee no heñkoo de mina-sama ni go-meewaku o o-kake shimashita*.（突然の予定の変更で皆様にご迷惑をおかけしました）We are sorry to have put you to inconvenience by the *sudden* change in the schedule.
— *adv.* suddenly; abruptly; unexpectedly: Totsuzeñ *deñwa ga natta*.（突然電話が鳴った）*Suddenly* the phone rang. / *Ressha ga* totsuzeñ *tomatta*.（列車が突然止まった）The train stopped *abruptly*.

to⌐tte[1] とって to; for: ★ Used in making judgments or evaluations. Used in the pattern '*...ni totte*.' Before a noun '*...ni totte no*.'
Kagaku-gijutsu no shiñpo wa waga kuni ni totte *kakasenai mono desu*.（科学技術の進歩はわが国にとって欠かせないものです）The progress of technology is something that is indispensable *for* our country. / *Kaigai-ryokoo wa watashi ni* totte *wasurerarenai omoide desu*.（海外旅行は私にとって忘れられない思い出です）The overseas trip is an unforgettable memory *to* me. / *Seeto no shiñpo wa kyooshi ni* totte *no yorokobi desu*.（生徒の進歩は教師にとっての喜びです）The progress of a pupil is a joy *to* his teachers.

to⌐tte[2] とって（取っ手）*n.* handle; knob; pull; grip:
nabe no totte（なべの取っ手）the *handle* of a pan / doa no totte（ドアの取っ手）a *doorknob* / hikidashi no totte（引き出しの取っ手）the *pull*

of a drawer.

tottemo とっても ＝ totemo.

To⌐ttori⌐-keñ とっとりけん（鳥取県）*n.* Tottori Prefecture. Located in the northeast of the Chugoku district, facing the Sea of Japan on the north. The ranges of dunes on the sea coast are well-known. Capital city: Tottori. 《⇨ map (C4)》

to⌐u とう（問う）*vt.* (to·i-; tow·a-; to·u-te Ⓒ) **1** ask; inquire:
hito no añpi o tou（人の安否を問う）*ask* about a person's safety. 《⇨ tazuneru[1]》
2 (in the negative) care; mind:
Nedañ wa toimaseñ.（値段は問いません）I *don't care* about the price.

to wa ka⌐gira⌐nai とはかぎらない（とは限らない）not necessarily; not always: ★ This phrase is often preceded by '*kanarazu shimo*.' The polite equivalent is '*to wa kagirimaseñ*.'
Takai mono ga ii to wa kagiranai.（高いものがいいとは限らない）Expensive things are *not necessarily* good. / *Kanemochi ga kanarazu shimo koofuku* to wa kagiranai.（金持ちが必ずしも幸福とは限らない）The rich are *not always* happy. 《⇨ kagiru》

To⌐yama⌐-keñ とやまけん（富山県）*n.* Toyama Prefecture. Located almost in the center of the Chubu district, facing the Sea of Japan on the north. The capital city, Toyama, is famous for pharmaceuticals. 《⇨ map (E3)》

to⌐zañ とざん（登山）*n.* mountain climbing; going up a mountain:
Fuyu no tozañ *wa nadare ga ki-keñ desu*.（冬の登山はなだれが危険です）When *climbing* in winter, avalanches can be dangerous. / to-zañ-*doo*（登山道）a path *up a mountain* / tozañ-*guchi*（登山口）the spot from which a *mountain*

ascent starts / tozañ-*ka* (登山家) a *mountain* climber.

toza͡ñ (o) suru (～(を)する) *vi.* climb a mountain: *Kono toshi de* tozañ suru *no wa muri desu.* (この年で登山するのは無理です) It is very hard to *climb a mountain* at this age.

tsu͡ba つば (唾) *n.* spit; saliva: *Michi ni* tsuba *o haite wa ikemase͡ñ.* (道につばを吐いてはいけません) You mustn't *spit* on the street. / *Kare wa* tsuba *o tobashi-nagara hayakuchi de shabetta.* (彼はつばを飛ばしながら早口でしゃべった) He talked fast, *sputtering away.*

tsu͡baki[1] つばき (唾) = tsuba.

tsu͡baki[2] つばき (椿) *n.* camellia.

TSUBAKI

tsu͡bame つばめ (燕) *n.* swallow (bird).

tsu͡basa つばさ (翼) *n.* wing: tsubasa *o hirogeru [tatamu]* (翼を広げる[たたむ]) spread [fold] the *wings* / *hikooki no* tsubasa (飛行機の翼) the *wings* of an airplane.

tsu͡bo[1] つぼ (壺) *n.* pot; jar; vase: *satoo-*tsubo (砂糖つぼ) a sugar *pot.*

tsu͡bo[2] つぼ (坪) *n.* tsubo. ★ Unit of area. 1 tsubo = 3.3 square meters.

tsu͡bomi[1] つぼみ (蕾) *n.* flower bud: tsubomi *o dasu* (つぼみを出す) put forth *buds* / *Sakura no ki ga* tsu-

bomi *o motte iru.* (桜の木がつぼみを持っている) The cherry trees are in *bud.*

tsu͡bu つぶ (粒) *n.* grain; drop: *kome[mugi]-*tsubu (米[麦]粒) *grains* of rice [wheat] / *oo-*tsubu *no ame* (大粒の雨) large *drops* of rain.

tsubu ga sorou (～がそろう) **1** be all the same size: tsubu ga sorotta *ri͡ñgo* (粒がそろったりんご) apples of *uniform size.*

2 be all excellent: *Kotoshi no shi͡ñji͡ñ-se͡ñshu wa* tsubu ga sorotte iru. (今年の新人選手は粒がそろっている) The rookies this year *are all good players.*

-tsubu -つぶ (粒) *suf.* counter for grain and small round objects: *kome hito-*tsubu (米1粒) *a grain* of rice / *mame go-*tsubu (豆5粒) *five* beans.

tsu͡bure·ru つぶれる (潰れる) *vi.* (tsubure-te ⊽) **1** be crushed; be smashed; collapse: *Jisuberi de sañ-ge͡ñ ga* tsubureta. (地すべりで3軒がつぶれた) Three houses *were crushed* in the landslide. (⇨ tsubusu)

2 go bankrupt: *Kare no kaisha wa* tsuburemashita. (彼の会社はつぶれました) His company *went bankrupt.* (⇨ tsubusu)

tsu͡bur·u つぶる (瞑る) *vt.* (tsubur·i-; tsubur·a-; tsubut-te ⊆) close [shut] (one's eyes): *Me o* tsubutta *ga nemurenakatta.* (目をつぶったが眠れなかった) I *closed* my eyes, but could not sleep.

tsu͡bus·u つぶす (潰す) *vt.* (tsubush·i-; tsubus·a-; tsubush·i-te ⊆) **1** crush; smash: *Kare wa hako o fu͡ñzukete* tsubushita. (彼は箱を踏んづけてつぶした) He stepped on the box and *crushed* it. / *Kono ryoori ni wa* tsubushita

jagaimo o tsukaimasu. (この料理に
はつぶしたじゃがいもを使います) We use
mashed potatoes for this dish.
《⇨ tsubureru》

2 thwart (a plan, project, etc.);
ruin:
*Kare-ra wa wareware no keekaku
o tsubusoo to shite iru.* (彼らはわれわ
れの計画をつぶそうとしている) They are
trying to *thwart* our plan. 《⇨ tsu-
bureru》

3 kill [pass] (time):
*Watashi-tachi wa toranpu o shite
hima o tsubushita.* (私たちはトランプ
をして暇をつぶした) We *killed* time
playing cards. / *Hima tsubushi ni
sanpo ni deta.* (暇つぶしに散歩に出た)
I went for a walk to *pass* the
time.

tsu⌈buyaki つぶやき(呟き) *n.*
mutter; murmur; grumble.
《⇨ tsubuyaku》

tsu⌈buyak·u つぶやく(呟く) *vi.*
(tsubuyak·i-; tsubuyak·a-; tsu-
buya·i-te C) murmur; mutter;
grumble:
*Kare wa nani-ka hitori de tsubu-
yaita.* (彼は何か一人でつぶやいた) He
muttered something to himself. /
*Nani o butsubutsu tsubuyaite iru
no?* (何をぶつぶつつぶやいているの)
What *are* you *grumbling* about?
《⇨ tsubuyaki》

tsu⌈chi⌉ つち(土) *n.* **1** earth;
soil; mud:
uekibachi ni tsuchi o ireru (植木鉢
に土を入れる) put *soil* in a flower-
pot / *Zubon ni tsuchi ga tsuite
iru yo.* (ズボンに土がついているよ)
There's *dirt* on your trousers.

2 the ground:
bokoku no tsuchi o fumu (母国の土
を踏む) stand on the *ground* of
one's homeland.

tsuchi ga tsuku (～がつく) be
beaten in sumo wrestling: *Yokozuna wa mikka-me ni tsuchi ga
tsuita.* (横綱は三日目に土がついた)

The grand champion wrestler
was beaten on the third day.

tsu⌉e つえ(杖) *n.* stick; cane:
tsue o tsuite aruku (杖をついて歩く)
walk with a *stick*.

tsu⌈geguchi つげぐち(告げ口) *n.*
tattle; talebearing.
tsugeguchi (o) suru (～を)する)
vt. tell on; let on: *Dare-ka ga
watashi no koto o tsugeguchi shita
rashii.* (だれかが私のことを告げ口したら
しい) Apparently someone has
told on me.

tsu⌈ge·ru つげる(告げる) *vt.* (tsu-
ge-te V) tell; inform:
*Kare wa mita toori no koto o kee-
satsu ni tsugeta.* (彼は見たとおりのこ
とを警察に告げた) He *reported* it to
the police just as he had seen it. /
*Watashi wa kanojo ni wakare o
tsugeta.* (私は彼女に別れを告げた) I
said goodbye to her.

tsu⌈gi⌉ つぎ(次) *n.* next:
Tsugi no kata doozo. (次の方どうぞ)
Next person, please. / *Tsugi (no
eki) wa Ueno desu.* (次(の駅)は上野
です) The *next* station is Ueno. /
*Watashi wa kare no tsugi ni wa-
kai.* (私は彼の次に若い) *Next to* him,
I'm the youngest.

tsugi kara tsugi e (to) (～から～
へ(と)) one after another: *Tsugi
kara tsugi e (to) tabemono ga dete
kita.* (次から次へ(と)食べ物が出て来た)
The dishes of food appeared *one
after another*.

tsu⌈giko⌉m·u つぎこむ(注ぎ込む)
vt. (-kom·i-; -kom·a-; -kon-de
C) put into; invest:
*Kare wa zenryoku o sono shiai ni
tsugikonda.* (彼は全力をその試合につ
ぎ込んだ) He *put* all his energy
into the match. / *Kanojo wa chokin o kabu ni tsugikonda.* (彼女は
貯金を株につぎ込んだ) She *invested*
her savings in stocks.

tsu⌈gime つぎめ(継ぎ目) *n.* joint;
seam:

reeru no tsugime (レールの継ぎ目) rail *joints* / tsugime no nai *paipu* (継ぎ目のないパイプ) a *jointless* pipe / *Isu no* tsugime *ga yuruñde iru.* (いすの継ぎ目がゆるんでいる) The *joints* of the chair are loose.

tsu「gi¹tsugi つぎつぎ (次々) *adv.* (~ ni, to) one after another; in succession:
Tsugitsugi *ni señshu-tachi ga nyuujoo shita.* (次々に選手たちが入場した) The competitors entered *one after another.* / *Hikooki wa* tsugitsugi *ni chakuriku shita.* (飛行機は次々に着陸した) The planes landed *one after the other.* / *Kare wa* tsugitsugi *ni* [*to*] *shiñ-kiroku o tsukutta.* (彼は次々に[と]新記録を作った) He established *one* new record *after another.*

tsu「goo つごう (都合) *n.* convenience; opportunity; circumstances:
Sochira no go-tsugoo *wa ikaga desu ka?* (そちらのご都合はいかがですか) When will it *be convenient* for you? / *Anata no* tsugoo *no yoi* [*warui*] *hi o oshiete kudasai.* (あなたの都合の良い[悪い]日を教えてください) Please tell me which day is *convenient* [*inconvenient*] for you. / *Kanojo wa katee no* tsugoo *de sono shigoto o yameta.* (彼女は家庭の都合でその仕事を辞めた) She quit her job due to family *reasons.*

tsugoo ga tsuku (~ がつく) suit one's convenience: Tsugoo ga tsuki shidai, *o-ukagai shimasu.* (都合がつきしだい、おうかがいします) I'll come to see you *as soon as it is convenient.* / *Zañneñ desu ga* tsugoo ga tsukimaseñ. (残念ですが都合がつきません) I am sorry, but I *can not find time.*

tsugoo o tsukeru (~ をつける) manage to do: *Watashi wa nañ to ka* tsugoo *o tsukete sono paatii ni deru tsumori desu.* (私は何とか都合をつけてそのパーティーに出るつもりです) I will somehow *manage* to come to the party.

tsugoo suru (~ する) *vt.* accommodate: *Ikura-ka o-kane o* tsugoo shite *itadakemaseñ ka?* (いくらかお金を都合していただけませんか) Would you be kind enough to *lend* me some money?

tsu「g・u¹ つぐ (注ぐ) *vt.* (tsug・i-; tsug・a-; tsu・i-de ⒸＩ) pour; fill: *gurasu ni waiñ o* tsugu (グラスにワインをつぐ) *pour* wine into a glass / *Kanojo wa o-cha o* tsuide kureta. (彼女はお茶をついでくれた) She *poured* me some tea.

tsu「g・u² つぐ (次ぐ) *vi.* (tsug・i-; tsug・a-; tsu・i-de ⒸＩ) be [come] next to: ★ Used in the patterns '... *ni tsugu*' and '... *ni tsuide.*' *Koko wa Tookyoo ni* tsugu *daitokai desu.* (ここは東京に次ぐ大都会です) *Next* to Tokyo, this is the biggest city. / *Kare ni* tsuide, *Yamada-sañ ga gooru-iñ shita.* (彼に次いで、山田さんがゴールインした) Mr. Yamada crossed the finishing line *after* him. / *Tone-gawa wa Shinano-gawa ni* tsuide *nagai kawa desu.* (利根川は信濃川に次いで長い川です) The Tone River is the *next* longest river after the Shinano River.

tsu「g・u³ つぐ (継ぐ) *vt.* (tsug・i-; tsug・a-; tsu・i-de ⒸＩ) succeed; inherit; take over: *Kare wa kagyoo o* tsuida. (彼は家業を継いだ) He *succeeded* to the family business. / *Watashi no shoobai o* tsugu *hito wa moo imaseñ.* (私の商売を継ぐ人はもういません) There is no longer anyone to *take over* my business.

tsu「i¹ つい (対) *n.* pair: *Kono yunomi-jawañ wa* tsui *ni natte imasu.* (この湯飲み茶わんは対になっています) These teacups make a *pair.*

tsu⌐i[2] つい *adv.* **1** (of time and distance) just; only: Tsui *sakihodo koko ni tsuita toko-ro desu.* (つい先ほどここに着いたところです) I got here *just* a little while ago. / Tsui *kono saki de Tanaka-sañ ni aimashita.* (ついこの先で田中さんに会いました) I came across Mr. Tanaka *just* a little way ahead of you.
2 carelessly; by mistake: *Sono tegami o dasu no o* tsui *wa-surete shimatta.* (その手紙を出すのをつい忘れてしまった) I *carelessly* forgot to mail the letter. / Tsui *hoñtoo no koto o itte shimatta.* (ついほんとうのことを言ってしまった) I *unintentionally* revealed the truth.

-tsui つい (対) *suf.* counter for a pair: *it-*tsui *no yunomi-jawañ* (一対の湯飲み茶碗) a *pair* of teacups.

tsu⌐ide[1] ついで (序で) *n.* chance; opportunity; convenience: *Sono hoñ o o-kaeshi itadaku no wa* tsuide *no toki de kekkoo desu.* (その本をお返しいただくのはついでのときで結構です) It will be perfectly all right if you return the book at your *convenience*.

tsu⌐ide[2] ついで (次いで) *adv.* next to; after: *Nihoñ de Fuji-sañ ni* tsuide *takai yama wa doko desu ka?* (日本で富士山に次いで高い山はどこですか) What is the next highest mountain in Japan *after* Mt. Fuji? / *Daitoo-ryoo ni* tsuide *shushoo ga eñzetsu shita.* (大統領に次いで首相が演説した) The prime minister gave his speech *after* that of the president.

tsu⌐ide ni ついでに (序でに) *adv.* while; on the way: *Hoñya e iku* tsuide ni *kitte mo katte kimasu.* (本屋へ行くついでに切手も買って来ます) I will buy some stamps *on my way* to the book-store. / *Kiñjo ni kita* tsuide ni

tachiyorimashita. (近所に来たついでに立ち寄りました) I dropped in *while* I was in the neighborhood. / Tsuide ni *to itte wa shitsuree de-su ga, kono hoñ mo kashite kuda-sai.* (ついでにと言っては失礼ですが、この本も貸してください) It may be rude to ask *now*, but will you lend me this book, too?

tsu⌐ihoo ついほう (追放) *n.* exile; expulsion; purge: *Sono shoosetsuka wa kokugai* tsui-hoo ni natta. (その小説家は国外追放になった) That novelist *was exiled* from her country.

tsuihoo suru (～する) *vt.* exile; banish; deport; oust: *Kare wa kokoku kara* tsuihoo sareta. (彼は故国から追放された) He *was exiled* from his native country. / *Kare o shokuba kara* tsuihoo suru *koto wa dekimaseñ.* (彼を職場から追放することはできません) We cannot *make* him *leave* his place of work.

tsu⌐ika ついか (追加) *n.* addition; supplement: Tsuika *no chuumoñ wa haitatsu ga okuremasu.* (追加の注文は配達が遅れます) The delivery of *additional* orders will be delayed. / tsui-ka-*ryookiñ* (追加料金) an *additional* charge / tsuika-*yosañ* (追加予算) a *supplementary* budget.

tsuika suru (～する) *vt.* add; sup-plement: *Biiru o ato ni-hoñ* tsui-ka shite *kudasai.* (ビールをあと2本追加してください) Please *bring us two more bottles* of beer. / *Meebo ni kare no namae ga* tsuika sareta. (名簿に彼の名前が追加された) His name *was added* to the list.

tsu⌐i ni ついに (遂に) *adv.* **1** at last; finally: *Wareware wa* tsui ni *mokuhyoo o tassee shita.* (われわれはついに目標を達成した) We *at last* achieved our goal. / *Sono otoko wa* tsui ni *tsu-mi o mitometa.* (その男はついに罪を認

めた) He *finally* admitted to his crime.

2 (with a negative) after all: *Kanojo ni nañ-do mo tegami o dashita ga,* tsui ni *heñji ga konakatta.* (彼女に何度も手紙を出したが,ついに返事がこなかった) I wrote her many times, but *ended up* getting no answer.

tsuˈiraku ついらく (墜落) *n.* (of airplanes) fall; crash: tsuiraku-*geñba* (墜落現場) a *crash* site / tsuiraku-jiko (墜落事故) a *plane crash.*

tsuiraku suru (～する) *vi.* fall; crash: *Sono hikooki wa yama ni* tsuiraku shita. (その飛行機は山に墜落した) The plane *crashed* into the mountain.

tsuˈitachi¹ ついたち (一日) *n.* the first day of the month: *Go-gatsu* tsuitachi *wa Mee-dee desu* (五月一日はメーデーです) May 1 is May Day. (⇨ table (below)》

tsuˈite ついて (就いて) ★ Used in the pattern '*…ni tsuite.*' Before a noun '*…ni tsuite no.*'

1 about; on; concerning: ★ Indicates the topic under discussion.
Atarashii seefu ni tsuite *doo omoimasu ka?* (新しい政府についてどう思いますか) What do you think *about* the new government? / *Watashi wa Nihoñ no kiñdai-buñgaku ni* tsuite *roñbuñ o kakimashita.* (私は日本の近代文学について論文を書きました) I wrote a thesis *on* modern Japanese literature. / *Sono keñ ni* tsuite *no kiji o shiñbuñ de yomimashita.* (その件についての記事を新聞で読みました) I read an article in the newspaper *concerning* that matter.

2 per; for: ★ Indicates proportions or ratios. Also in the pattern '*…ni tsuki.*'
Sañka hiyoo wa hitori ni tsuite *rokuseñ-eñ desu.* (参加費用は一人について6千円です) The participation fee is 6,000 yen *for* each person. / *Chuusha-ryookiñ wa ichi-jikañ ni* tsuki *sañbyaku-eñ desu.* (駐車料金は1時間につき300円です) The parking fee is 300 yen *per* hour.

tsuˈiyaˈsˑu ついやす (費やす) *vt.* (tsuiyashˑiˑ; tsuiyasˑaˑ; tsuiyashˑiˑte [C]) spend (time, money); waste; consume:
Kare wa sono jigyoo ni ooku no jikañ to kane o tsuiyashita. (彼はその事業に多くの時間と金を費やした) He *spent* a lot of time and money on the business. / *Muda na jikañ o* tsuiyasanai *yoo ni shi nasai.* (むだな時間を費やさないようにしなさい) Make sure you *don't waste* time.

tsuˈkaeˈˑru¹ つかえる (支える) *vi.* (tsukaeˑte [V]) **1** be choked; be stopped; be blocked:

DAYS OF THE MONTH

1st	tsuˈitachi¹	11th	juˈu-ichi-nichi¹	21st	niˈjuu-ichi-nichi
2nd	fuˈtsuka	12th	juˈu-ni-nichi¹	22nd	niˈjuu-ni-nichi
3rd	miˈkka	13th	juˈu-saˈñ-nichi	23rd	niˈjuu-sañ-nichi
4th	yoˈkka	14th	juˈu-yokka	24th	niˈjuu-yokka
5th	iˈtsuka	15th	juˈu-go-nichi	25th	niˈjuu-go-nichi
6th	muˈika	16th	juˈu-roku-nichi¹	26th	niˈjuu-roku-nichi
7th	naˈnu[o]ka	17th	juˈu-shichi-nichi¹	27th	niˈjuu-shichi-nichi
8th	yoˈoka	18th	juˈu-hachi-nichi¹	28th	niˈjuu-hachi-nichi
9th	koˈkonoka¹	19th	juˈu-ku-nichi	29th	niˈjuu-ku-nichi
10th	toˈoka	20th	haˈtsuka	30th	saˈñjuˈu-nichi
				31st	saˈñjuu-ichi-nichi

Gesuikañ ni nani-ka ga tsukaete iru. (下水管に何かがつかえている) There is something *blocking* the drain. / *Kono saki, kuruma ga* tsukaete imasu. (この先、車がつかえています) The traffic *is blocked* ahead. / *Kotoba ga* tsukaete *dete konakatta.* (言葉がつかえて出てこなかった) I *faltered* and the words did not come out.

2 be too big to go into: *Piano wa doa ni* tsukaete *naka ni hairanakatta.* (ピアノはドアにつかえて中に入らなかった) The piano *was too big* for the door and could not go into the room.

tsu⌈kae·ru[2] つかえる (仕える) *vi.* (tsukae-te ⟨V⟩) serve; wait on: *Kanojo wa juugo-neñ-kañ sono ie ni* tsukaeta. (彼女は15年間その家に仕えた) She *served* in that house for fifteen years.

tsu⌈kai つかい (使い) *n.* **1** errand: *Kodomo o* tsukai *ni yatta.* (子どもを使いにやった) I sent the child on an *errand*. / *O-*tsukai *ni itte kuremasu ka?* (お使いに行ってくれますか) Will you go on an *errand* for me?

2 messenger; bearer: *Sono shorui wa* tsukai *no mono ni watashite kudasai.* (その書類は使いの者に渡してください) Please hand the papers to the *messenger*.

tsu⌈kaihata]s·u つかいはたす (使い果たす) *vt.* (-hatash·i-; -hatas·a-; -hatash·i-te ⟨C⟩) use up; exhaust: *Kozukai o* tsukaihatashite shimatta. (小遣いを使い果たしてしまった) I *have used up* all my pocket money.

tsu⌈kaikomi つかいこみ (使い込み) *n.* embezzlement; misappropriation: *Kare wa kaisha no kane no* tsukaikomi *ga mitsukatte kubi ni natta.* (彼は会社の金の使い込みが見つかって首になった) His *embezzlement* of the company funds was found out,

and he was fired. ((⇒ tsukaikomu))

tsu⌈kaiko]m·u つかいこむ (使い込む) *vt.* (-kom·i-; -kom·a-; -koñ-de ⟨C⟩) embezzle: *Kanojo wa kaisha no kane o* tsukaikoñda. (彼女は会社の金を使い込んだ) She *embezzled* company money. ((⇒ tsukaikomi))

tsu⌈kaikona]s·u つかいこなす (使いこなす) *vt.* (-konash·i-; -konas·a-; -konash·i-te ⟨C⟩) make good use of; have a good command of: *Kanojo wa Nihoñgo o umaku* tsukaikonashite iru. (彼女は日本語をうまく使いこなしている) She *has a* very *good command* of Japanese.

tsu⌈kainare]·ru つかいなれる (使い慣れる) *vi.* (-nare-te ⟨V⟩) be accustomed to using: *Kono waapuro wa* tsukainarete imasu. (このワープロは使い慣れています) I *am accustomed to using* this word processor.

tsu⌈kaisute つかいすて (使い捨て) *n.* throwaway; disposable: tsukaisute *kamera* (使い捨てカメラ) a *throwaway* camera / tsukaisute *raitaa* (使い捨てライター) a *disposable* lighter.

tsu⌈kamae·ru つかまえる (捕まえる) *vt.* (tsukamae-te ⟨V⟩) catch; arrest: *Kare wa sono sakana o sude de* tsukamaeta. (彼はその魚を素手で捕まえた) He *caught* the fish with his bare hands. / *Keesatsu-kañ ga suri o geñkoohañ de* tsukamaeta. (警察官がすりを現行犯で捕まえた) The policeman *arrested* the pickpocket in the act. / *Koko de takushii o* tsukamaemashoo. (ここでタクシーを捕まえましょう) *Let's catch* a taxi here. ((⇒ tsukamaru))

tsu⌈kamar·u つかまる (捕まる) *vi.* (tsukamar·i-; tsukamar·a-; tsukamat-te ⟨C⟩) be caught; be arrested: *Sono seeto wa kañniñgu o shite* *iru tokoro o* tsukamatta.（その生徒はカンニングをしているところを捕まった）The pupil *was caught* in the act of cheating.《⇨ tsukamaeru》

tsu⌐ka⌐m·u つかむ（攫む）*vt.* (tsukam·i-; tsukam·a-; tsukañ-de C)
1 catch; hold:
Kare wa ikinari watashi no ude o tsukañda.（彼はいきなり私の腕をつかんだ）He suddenly *caught* me by the arm.
2 get (money); grasp (a meaning, intention, etc.); seize (an opportunity):
taikiñ o tsukamu（大金をつかむ）*get* a large sum of money / *chañsu o* tsukamu（チャンスをつかむ）*seize* a chance / *imi o* tsukamu（意味をつかむ）*grasp* the meaning / *Sono shiñsoo wa mada* tsukañde imaseñ.（その真相はまだつかんでいません）We *have not found* the truth yet.
3 hold onto; take hold of:
Hitogomi de sono ko wa chichioya no te ni tsukamatte ita.（人混みでその子は父親の手につかまっていた）The child *was holding* onto his father's hand in the crowd.

tsu⌐kare つかれ（疲れ）*n.* fatigue; tiredness; exhaustion:
Hataraki-sugite, tsukare ga deta.（働きすぎて、疲れが出た）I *feel tired* because I have worked too hard. / *Ni, sañ-nichi yasuñdara,* tsukare ga toreru deshoo.（2, 3 日休んだら、疲れがとれるでしょう）If you rest for a couple of days, you will recover from your *fatigue*.《⇨ tsukareru》

tsu⌐kare⌐·ru つかれる（疲れる）*vi.* (tsukare-te V) get tired; be tired out; be exhausted:
Kyoo wa zañgyoo de tsukaremashita.（きょうは残業で疲れました）Today I *am tired* from overtime work. / *Tsukareta yoo desu ne. Yasuñde kudasai.*（疲れたようですね。休んでください）You look *tired*. Take a rest.《⇨ tsukare》

tsu⌐ka·u つかう（使う）*vt.* (tsukai-; tsukaw·a-; tsukat-te C)
1 use:
Kono-goro no kodomo wa hashi o tsukau *no ga heta da.*（このごろの子どもは箸を使うのがへただ）Children these days are bad at *using* chopsticks. / *Kanojo wa waapuro o* tsukatte *tegami o kaita.*（彼女はワープロを使って手紙を書いた）She *used* a wordprocessor to write the letter.
2 spend (money, time); use:
Sono o-kane wa zeñbu tsukatte shimaimashita.（そのお金は全部使ってしまいました）I *have spent* all the money. / *Jikañ o yuukoo ni* tsukai nasai.（時間を有効に使いなさい）*Use* your time efficiently.
3 employ; handle:
Sono mise wa isogashii toki ni wa arubaito o tsukau.（その店は忙しいときにはアルバイトを使う）At busy periods they *employ* part-timers at that shop. / *Kanojo wa hito o* tsukau *no ga umai.*（彼女は人を使うのがうまい）She is good at *dealing with* people.
4 speak (a language); write:
Eego o tsukatte *mo ii desu ka?*（英語を使ってもいいですか）Is it all right if I *speak* English?
5 use (a nonmaterial thing):
atama o tsukau（頭を使う）*use* one's head / *ki o* tsukau（気を使う）*worry* about / *shiñkee o* tsukau（神経を使う）*pay* careful attention to.

tsu⌐kekuwae⌐·ru つけくわえる（付け加える）*vt.* (-kuwae-te V) add; append:
Hoka ni nani-ka tsukekuwaeru *koto wa arimasu ka?*（ほかに何かつけ加えることはありますか）Is there anything else to *add*?

tsu⌐kemono つけもの（漬け物）*n.* pickles: ★ Vegetables pickled in salt and rice bran.
kyuuri no tsukemono（きゅうりの漬け

物) *pickled* cucumbers.

tsu「ke⌐**·ru**¹ つける（付ける）*vt.*
(tsuke-te Ⓥ) **1** attach (medicine); apply; spread (butter,
jam):
Kare wa suutsukeesu ni nafuda o
tsuketa.（彼はスーツケースに名札をつけ
た）He *attached* a name tag to his
suitcase. / *Ashi ni mizumushi no
kusuri o* tsuketa.（足に水虫の薬をつ
けた）I *applied* the medicine for
athlete's foot to my feet. / *Pañ ni
bataa o* tsukete *kudasai.*（パンにバタ
ーをつけてください）Please *spread* butter on the bread.
2 fix (equipment); install:
Kuruma ni eakoñ o tsukete moratta.（車にエアコンをつけてもらった）I
had an air conditioner *installed*
in my car.
3 write (a memo, diary, etc.):
memo o tsukeru（メモをつける）*take* a
note / *Kanai wa mainichi nikki o*
tsukete imasu.（家内は毎日日記をつ
けています）My wife *writes* a diary
every day.
4 give (a mark); grade:
*Señsee wa kare no tooañ ni ii teñ
o* tsuketa.（先生は彼の答案にいい点を
つけた）The teacher *gave* his answer a high mark.
5 tail; follow:
Kanojo wa dare-ka ni tsukerarete
ita.（彼女はだれかにつけられていた）She
was being followed by someone.

tsu「ke⌐**·ru**² つける（着ける）*vt.*
(tsuke-te Ⓥ) **1** put on (a dress,
ring, etc.): ★ '*tsukete iru*'＝wear.
*Kanojo wa atarashii doresu o mi
ni* tsuketa.（彼女は新しいドレスを身に
着けた）She *put on* a new dress. /
Kanojo wa iyariñgu o tsukete ita.
（彼女はイヤリングを着けていた）She
was wearing earrings. 《⇨ kiru²
(table)》
2 drive (a car) up to; draw (a
ship) alongside:
Geñkañ ni kuruma o tsuketa.（玄関

に車を着けた）I *drove* my car up to
the entrance. / *Fune o gañpeki ni*
tsuketa.（船を岸壁に着けた）We
brought the ship *alongside* the
quay.

tsu「ke⌐**·ru**³ つける（点ける）*vt.*
(tsuke-te Ⓥ) switch on: light;
set fire:
deñki o tsukeru（電気をつける）
switch on the electricity / *tabako
ni hi o* tsukeru（たばこに火をつける）
light a cigarette / *Dare-ka ga sono
furui koya ni hi o* tsuketa.（だれかが
その古い小屋に火をつけた）Someone
set fire to the old hut. 《⇨ tsuku⁴》

tsu「ke⌐**·ru**⁴ つける（漬ける）*vt.* (tsuke-te Ⓥ) pickle; preserve:
Niku o shio ni tsukete *hozoñ shita.*
（肉を塩に漬けて保存した）I *salted* the
meat to preserve it.

tsu「ki¹ つき（月）*n.* month:
Yachiñ wa tsuki *juumañ-eñ desu.*
（家賃は月 10 万円です）The rent is
100,000 yen a *month*. / *Kare wa*
tsuki *ni ik-kai Oosaka e ikimasu.*
（彼は月に一回大阪へ行きます）He
goes to Osaka once a *month.*
《⇨ hi¹ (table)》

January	i「chi-gatsu⌐
February	ni-「gatsu⌐
March	sa⌐ñ-gatsu
April	shi-「gatsu⌐
May	go⌐-gatsu
June	ro「ku-gatsu⌐
July	shi「chi-gatsu⌐
August	ha「chi-gatsu⌐
September	ku⌐-gatsu
October	ju「u-gatsu⌐
November	ju「u-ichi-gatsu⌐
December	ju「u-ni-gatsu⌐

tsu「ki¹² つき（月）*n.* the moon:
Tsuki ga deta.（月が出た）*The moon*
has come out. / *Tsuki ga nishi ni
shizuñda.*（月が西に沈んだ）*The
moon* has set in the west. / *Tsuki
ga akaruku kagayaite iru.*（月が明

るく輝いている) *The moon* is shining brightly.

tsu⌐ki¹³ つき(付き) *n.* **1** adherence; stickiness:
Kono nori wa tsuki *ga yoi* [*warui*]. (この糊は付きが良い[悪い]) This glue *sticks well* [*badly*].
2 combustion:
Kono raitaa wa tsuki *ga warui*. (このライターは付きが悪い) This lighter *does not light easily.*

-tsuki つき(付き) *suf.* with:
*tochi-*tsuki *no ie* (土地付きの家) a house *with* the land / *Kono rajio wa ichi-neñ-kañ no hoshoo-*tsuki *desu.* (このラジオは1年間の保証付きです) This radio comes *with* a one-year guarantee.

tsu⌐kiai つきあい(付き合い) *n.* association; friendship; acquaintance:
tsukiai *ga hiroi* [*semai*] (つきあいが広い[狭い]) have many [few] *acqaintances* / *Kare to wa* nagai tsukiai desu. (彼とは長いつきあいです) I *have known him* for a long time. / *Kare wa* tsukiai *de yoku sake o nomu.* (彼はつきあいでよく酒を飲む) He often drinks *socially.*
《⇨ tsukiau》

tsu⌐kiatari つきあたり(突き当たり) *n.* the end:
Sono mise wa kono michi no tsukiatari *ni arimasu.* (その店はこの道の突き当たりにあります) That store is at the *end* of this street.

tsu⌐kiata⌐r·u つきあたる(突き当たる) *vi.* (-atar·i-; -atar·a-; -atat-te Ⓒ) **1** run into; collide; run against:
Torakku ga deñchuu ni tsukiatatta. (トラックが電柱に突き当たった) The truck *ran into* a utility pole.
2 face (a problem, difficulties, etc.):
Kare wa muzukashii moñdai ni tsukiatatta. (彼はむずかしい問題に突き当たった) He *came up* against a tough problem.

tsu⌐kia⌐·u つきあう(付き合う) *vi.* (-a·i-; -aw·a-; -at-te Ⓒ) associate with; keep company with:
warui nakama to tsukiau (悪い仲間とつきあう) *keep company* with a bad lot / *Ano hito to wa* tsukiawanai hoo ga yoi. (あの人とはつきあわない方がよい) You had better *not associate* with him. / *Saikiñ kanojo wa otoko-no-ko to* tsukiau *yoo ni natta.* (最近彼女は男の子とつきあうようになった) She has recently started to *go out* with boys.
《⇨ tsukiai》

tsu⌐kiawase⌐·ru つきあわせる(突き合わせる) *vt.* (-awase-te Ⓥ) compare; check:
Futatsu no jisho o tsukiawasete *mita.* (二つの辞書を突き合わせてみた) I *compared* the two dictionaries. / *Kono koosee-zuri o geñkoo to* tsukiawasete *kudasai.* (この校正刷りを原稿と突き合わせてください) Please *check* this galley proof against the manuscript.

tsu⌐kigime つきぎめ(月極め) *n.* (of payment) monthly:
Watashi wa chuushajoo o tsukigime *de karite iru.* (私は駐車場を月ぎめでかりている) I rent a parking space *by the month.*

(Monthly Parking)
TSUKIGIME YUURYOO CHUUSHAJOO

tsu⌐ki⌐hi つきひ(月日) *n.* time; years:
Tsukihi *wa tatsu no ga hayai.* (月日はたつのが早い) *Time* flies. / *Are kara* sañ-neñ *no* tsukihi *ga nagareta.* (あれから3年の月日が流れた) *Three years* have passed since then. 《⇨ neñgetsu》

tsu「kioto¹s·u つきおとす (突き落とす) *vt.* (-otosh·i-; -otos·a-; -oto-sh·i-te Ⓒ) push over; thrust down:
gake kara hito o tsukiotosu (がけから人を突き落とす) *push* a person *off* a cliff.

tsu「ki¹·ru つきる (尽きる) *vi.* (tsu-ki-te Ⓥ) run out; be exhausted:
Shikiñ ga tsukite shimatta. (資金が尽きてしまった) The funds *have run out.*

tsu「kisa¹s·u つきさす (突き刺す) *vt.* (-sash·i-; -sas·a-; -sash·i-te Ⓒ) stick; pierce; stab:
fooku de niku o tsukisasu (フォークで肉を突き刺す) *stick* a fork into a piece of meat / *Kare wa sono otoko no mune ni naifu o tsukisashita.* (彼はその男の胸にナイフを突き刺した) He *stuck* a knife into the man's chest.

tsu「kisoi つきそい (付き添い) *n.* attendance; attendant; escort:
Tsukisoi no josee wa donata desu ka? (付き添いの女性はどなたですか) Who is the woman *with* him? / *Roku-sai ika no kodomo wa ryooshiñ no tsukisoi ga hitsuyoo desu.* (6才以下の子どもは両親の付き添いが必要です) Children six and under must *be accompanied* by their parents. (⇨ tsukisou)

tsu「kiso·u つきそう (付き添う) *vt.* (-so·i-; -sow·a-; -sot-te Ⓒ) accompany; attend; escort:
Haha-oya wa byooki no kodomo ni tsukisotta. (母親は病気の子どもに付き添った) The mother *attended* her sick child. / *Kare wa ryooshiñ ni tsukisowarete, heya ni haitte kita.* (彼は両親に付き添われて、部屋に入って来た) He came into the room *accompanied* by his parents. (⇨ tsukisoi)

tsu「kitoba¹s·u つきとばす (突き飛ばす) *vt.* (-tobash·i-; -tobas·a-; -tobash·i-te Ⓒ) thrust away; send flying:
Kare wa watashi o tsukitobashita. (彼は私を突き飛ばした) He *pushed* me *away*.

tsu「kitome¹·ru つきとめる (突き止める) *vt.* (-tome-te Ⓥ) trace; locate; ascertain:
Uwasa no dedokoro o tsukitometa. (うわさの出所を突き止めた) I *traced* the source of the rumor. / *Keesatsu wa hañniñ no ibasho o tsukitometa.* (警察は犯人の居場所を突き止めた) The police *located* the criminal's whereabouts. / *Sono koshoo no geñiñ o tsukitomeru koto wa dekinakatta.* (その故障の原因を突き止めることはできなかった) We could not *ascertain* the cause of the breakdown.

tsu「kitsuke¹·ru つきつける (突き付ける) *vt.* (-tsuke-te Ⓥ) point (a weapon); confront with (evidence):
Watashi wa kare ni shooko o tsukitsuketa. (私は彼に証拠を突きつけた) I *confronted* him with the proof. / *Sono otoko wa watashi ni pisutoru o tsukitsuketa.* (その男は私にピストルを突きつけた) The man *pointed* a pistol at me.

tsu「kko¹m·u つっこむ (突っ込む) *vi.* (-kom·i-; -kom·a-; -koñ-de Ⓒ) thrust into; dip into; run into:
Kare wa poketto ni te o tsukkoñda. (彼はポケットに手を突っ込んだ) He *dipped* his hand into his pocket.
tsukkoñda (突っ込んだ) penetrating: *Kare wa tsukkoñda shitsumoñ o shita.* (彼は突っ込んだ質問をした) He asked a *penetrating* question.

tsu「k·u¹ つく (着く) *vi.* (tsuk·i-; tsuk·a-; tsu·i-te Ⓒ) **1** arrive (at); get (to); reach:
Ikkoo wa buji, sañchoo ni tsuita. (一行は無事、山頂に着いた) The party safely *arrived* at the summit. / *Watashi no tegami wa moo*

tsukimashita *ka?* (私の手紙はもう着きましたか) *Has* my letter *reached* you yet?
2 touch; reach:
Teñjoo ga hikui no de atama ga tsuki-soo *da.* (天井が低いので頭がつきそうだ) The ceiling is so low that my head almost *touches* it.
3 sit down; take a seat:
seki ni tsuku (席に着く) *take* a seat / *shokutaku ni* tsuku (食卓に着く) *sit down* to a meal.

tsuˈkˑu² つく (付く) *vi.* (tsukˑiˑ; tsukˑaˑ; tsuˑiˑte [C]) **1** stick; adhere:
Kore wa nori de wa tsukimaseñ. (これは糊では付きません) We *cannot stick* these with paste.
2 be stained:
Te ni iñku ga tsuite imasu *yo.* (手にインクが付いていますよ) Your hands *are stained* with ink. / *Kare no waishatsu ni kuchibeni ga* tsuite ita. (彼のワイシャツに口紅が付いていた) *There was* lipstick on his shirt.
3 have; carry; include:
Kaku heya ni basu, toire ga tsuite imasu. (各部屋にバス, トイレが付いています) Each room *has* a bath and toilet. / *Kono zasshi ni wa furoku ga* tsuite imasu. (この雑誌には付録が付いています) This magazine *has* a supplement.
4 take the side of; side with:
Watashi ga tsuite iru *kara añshiñ shi nasai.* (私が付いているから安心しなさい) Since I *am at your side*, set your mind at ease.
5 (of seed, fruit, etc.) bear; yield; take root; bear (interest):
Niwa no kuri no ki ni mi ga takusañ tsuita. (庭の栗の木に実がたくさん付いた) The chestnut tree in the garden *bore* a lot of chestnuts. / *Giñkoo no yokiñ ni rishi ga* tsuita. (銀行の預金に利子が付いた) My bank account *bore* interest.

tsuˈkˑu³ つく (就く) *vi.* (tsukˑiˑ; tsukˑaˑ; tsuˑiˑte [C]) **1** take; hold; be engaged:
Kanojo wa too no iiñchoo no chii ni tsuita. (彼女は党の委員長の地位に就いた) She *took* the post of party chairperson. / *Yamada-sañ wa kyooshoku ni* tsuite iru. (山田さんは教職に就いている) Miss Yamada *is* in the teaching profession.
2 take lessons from; study under (a person):
Kanojo wa iemoto ni tsuite *ikebana o naratte imasu.* (彼女は家元に就いて生け花を習っています) She *is taking* lessons in flower arrangement *from* the master.

tsuˈkˑu⁴ つく (点く) *vi.* (tsukˑiˑ; tsukˑaˑ; tsuˑiˑte [C]) **1** catch fire; be lighted:
Mokuzoo no ie wa hi ga tsuki-yasui. (木造の家は火がつきやすい) Wooden houses easily *catch* fire. / *Jishiñ no ato too-ka shite, deñki ga* tsuita. (地震の後10日して, 電気がついた) Ten days after the earthquake, the electricity *came on.* (⇨ tsukeru³)

tsuˈkˑu⁵ つく (突く) *vt.* (tsukˑiˑ; tsukˑaˑ; tsuˑiˑte [C]) **1** poke; stab; prick; spear:
Kare wa watashi no wakibara o hiji de tsuita. (彼は私の脇腹をひじで突いた) He *poked* me in the ribs with his elbow.
2 toll (a bell); strike; bounce (a ball):
mari o tsuku (まりをつく) *bounce* a ball / *Kodomo-tachi wa kawaru-gawaru kane o* tsuita. (子どもたちは代わる代わる鐘をついた) The children *struck* the bell by turns.

tsuˈkˑu⁶ つく (吐く) *vt.* (tsukˑiˑ; tsukˑaˑ; tsuˑiˑte [C]) tell; sigh:
uso o tsuku (うそをつく) *tell* a lie / *tameiki o* tsuku (ため息をつく) *give* a sigh.

tsuˈkue つくえ (机) *n.* desk:
tsukue *ni mukatte beñkyoo suru*

(机に向かって勉強する) study at one's *desk*.

tsu「kuri¹ つくり (旁) *n.* the right-hand element of a Chinese character. ★ Often the phonetic element of the character. 《⇨ bushu (table)》

tsu「kuriage」・ru つくりあげる (作り上げる) *vt.* (-age-te V̄) complete; finish; build [make] up:
Sono mokee-hikooki o tsukuri-ageru no ni sañ-shuukañ kakatta. (その模型飛行機を作り上げるのに3週間かかった) It took three weeks to *complete* that model airplane. / *Kanojo wa sono hanashi o umaku* tsukuriageta. (彼女はその話をうまく作り上げた) She skillfully *made up* that story.

tsu「ku」r・u¹ つくる (作る) *vt.* (tsu-kur・i-; tsukur・a-; tsukut-te C̄)
1 make; form; shape; manufacture: 《⇨ tsukuru²》
Ki de inugoya o tsukutta. (木で犬小屋を作った) I *made* a kennel of wood. / *Sono koojoo wa ootobai o* tsukutte imasu. (その工場はオートバイを作っています) That factory *manufactures* motorbikes.
2 write; compose; make:
shi o tsukuru (詩を作る) *write* a poem / *añ o* tsukuru (案を作る) *make* a plan / *keeyakusho o* tsu-kuru (契約書を作る) *draw up* a contract.
3 grow; raise:
kome [yasai] o tsukuru (米[野菜]を作る) *grow* rice [vegetables].
4 form; organize:
retsu o tsukuru (列を作る) *form* a line / *roodoo-kumiai o* tsukuru (労働組合を作る) *organize* a labor union.
5 cook; make:
Kono keeki wa dare ga tsukurima-shita ka? (このケーキはだれが作りましたか) Who *made* this cake? / *Kyoo wa watashi ga yuushoku o* tsukuri-

masu. (きょうは私が夕食を作ります) I will *cook* dinner today.

tsu「ku」r・u² つくる (造る) *vt.* (tsu-kur・i-; tsukur・a-; tsukut-te C̄)
★ The Chinese character '造' is chiefly used with reference to construction work and manufactured products.
1 build; construct:
ie o tsukuru (家を造る) *build* a house / *hashi o* tsukuru (橋を造る) *construct* a bridge.
2 mint; coin:
kooka o tsukuru (硬貨を造る) *mint* coins / *shihee o* tsukuru (紙幣を造る) *print* paper money / *shiñgo o* tsukuru (新語を造る) *coin* a new word.
3 create:
atarashii toshi o tsukuru (新しい都市を造る) *create* a new city / *tee-eñ o* tsukuru (庭園を造る) *create* a garden.
4 brew:
biiru o tsukuru (ビールを造る) *brew* beer.

tsu「ku」s・u つくす (尽くす) *vt.* (tsu-kush・i-; tsukus・a-; tsukush・i-te C̄) **1** exhaust (energy); use up; consume:
Kare wa zeñryoku o tsukushita. (彼は全力を尽くした) He *has done* his best.
2 devote oneself; serve:
Kanojo wa byooki no otto no tame ni tsukushita. (彼女は病気の夫のために尽くした) She *did all she could* for her sick husband.

tsu「kuzu」ku つくづく *adv.* (~ to)
1 (of dislike) utterly; really:
Wabishii tañshiñ-funiñ ga tsuku-zuku iya ni natta. (わびしい単身赴任がつくづくいやになった) I was transferred to this present post, leaving my family behind, and I am *utterly* disgusted at this lonely life.
2 carefully; intently:

Watashi wa kore made no jiñsee o tsukuzuku (to) furikaette mita. (私はこれまでの人生をつくづく(と)振り返ってみた) I *carefully* looked back on my life so far. / *Kanojo wa sono e o tsukuzuku (to) nagameta.* (彼女はその絵をつくづく(と)眺めた) She looked at the picture *intently*.

tsu⌐ma つま (妻) *n.* wife:
★ '*Tsuma*' refers to one's own wife, or is used as a generic term for wife. '*Kanai*' is used only in the first sense. 《⇨ kazoku (table)》 *Tsuma wa paato de hataraite imasu.* (妻はパートで働いています) My *wife* works part-time. / *Otto ga shiboo shita baai, tsuma ga sono isañ no hañbuñ o soozoku shimasu.* (夫が死亡した場合，妻がその遺産の半分を相続します) When the husband dies, the *wife* inherits half of his estate. 《↔ otto》

tsu⌐mami¹ つまみ (摘まみ) *n.*
1 knob:
tsumami o mawasu (つまみを回す) turn a *knob*.
2 pinch:
hito-tsumami *no shio* (一つまみの塩) a *pinch* of salt. 《⇨ tsumamu》

tsu⌐mami² つまみ *n.* light snacks; hors d'oeuvre: ★ Something that goes well with alcoholic beverages, such as nuts, small crackers, etc.
Kanappe ga sake no tsumami ni deta. (カナッペが酒のつまみに出た) Canapés *were served with drinks.*

tsu⌐mamigui つまみぐい (つまみ食い) *n.* eating with the fingers; sneaking a bite of food.
tsumamigui suru (〜する) *vt.* eat secretly: *Kono keeki o tsumamigui shita no wa dare desu ka?* (このケーキをつまみ食いしたのはだれですか) Who is it that *ate* this cake *on the sly?*

tsu⌐mam·u つまむ (摘まむ) *vt.* (tsu-mam·i-; tsumam·a-; tsumañ-de

⌐C) pick up; pinch:
Kamikuzu o tsumañde *kuzukago ni ireta.* (紙くずをつまんでくずかごに入れた) I *picked up* the scraps of paper and put them into the litter bin. / *Kanojo wa piinattsu o* tsumañde *tabeta.* (彼女はピーナッツをつまんで食べた) She ate the peanuts, *picking them up with her fingers.* / *Doozo,* tsumañde *kudasai.* (どうぞ，つまんでください) Please *help yourself* to the snacks. 《⇨ tsumami¹》

tsu⌐mara·na·i つまらない (詰まらない) *a.* (-ku) **1** uninteresting; boring:
tsumaranai *hoñ* (つまらない本) a *boring* book / *Sono shiai wa* tsumaranakatta. (その試合はつまらなかった) The match was *not exciting.* / *Suru koto mo naku, hitori de ie ni iru no wa* tsumaranai. (することもなく，ひとりで家にいるのはつまらない) It is *boring* staying at home with nothing to do. 《↔ omoshiroi》
2 trifling; foolish; worthless:
Tsumaranai koto de nayamu no wa yame nasai. (つまらないことで悩むのはやめなさい) Stop worrying about *trifles.* / *Tsumaranai machigai o shite shimatta.* (つまらない間違いをしてしまった) I have made a *silly* mistake. / *Tsumaranai mono desu ga doozo.* (つまらないものですがどうぞ) This is *nothing special*, but I hope you will accept it. ★ '*Tsumaranai mono*' literally means, 'a trifling thing.' This is a set phrase used when giving a present.

tsu⌐mari¹ つまり (詰まり) *conj.* that is; in short; in a word; after all:
Tsumari sore ga kimi no iitai koto desu ne. (つまりそれが君の言いたいことですね) *In short*, that is what you want to say, isn't it? / *Kare wa sono kaigi ni shusseki shinakatta. Tsumari sono keekaku ni wa sañ-*

see de nai to iu koto da. (彼はその会議に出席しなかった。つまりその計画には賛成でないということだ) He did not attend the meeting. *That means* that he does not agree with the plan.

tsu⌈maˉr·u つまる (詰まる) *vi.* (tsumar·i-; tsumar·a-; tsumat-te C)
1 be stopped; be choked up; clog:
Gesui ga tsumatte iru. (下水が詰まっている) The drains *are blocked.* / *Kaze o hiite, hana ga tsumatta.* (かぜをひいて，鼻が詰まった) I have a cold so my nose *is stuffed up.*
2 be full; be filled up; be packed:
Kabañ no naka wa shorui ga ippai tsumatte ita. (かばんの中は書類がいっぱい詰まっていた) The briefcase *was packed* full of papers. 《⇨ tsumeru》

tsu⌈masaki つまさき (爪先) *n.* tiptoe; tip:
tsumasaki de aruku (つま先で歩く) walk on *tiptoe.* 《⇨ jiñtai (illus.)》

tsu⌈mazuk·u つまずく (躓く) *vi.* (-zuk·i-; -zuk·a-; -zu·i-te C)
1 stumble; trip:
Ishi ni tsumazuite koroñde shimatta. (石につまずいて転んでしまった) I *stumbled* on a stone and fell.
2 (of a project, plan, etc.) fail; go wrong:
Watashi-tachi no keekaku wa saisho kara tsumazuita. (私たちの計画は最初からつまずいた) Our plan *went wrong* from the beginning.

tsu⌈me つめ (爪) *n.* nail; claw:
tsume o kamu (爪をかむ) bite one's *nails* / *te no tsume o kiru* (手の爪を切る) cut one's *fingernails.*

tsu⌈mekake·ru つめかける (詰めかける) *vt.* (-kake-te V) besiege; throng; crowd:
Kisha-tachi ga shuzai no tame ni keesatsu ni tsumekaketa. (記者たちが取材のために警察に詰めかけた) Re-

porters *besieged* the police station to cover the news. / *Oozee no hito ga sono kaijoo ni* tsumeka-keta. (おおぜいの人がその会場に詰めかけた) A throng *gathered* in the hall.

tsu⌈me⌉·ru つめる (詰める) *vt.* (tsume-te V) **1** pack; stuff; fill; plug; stop:
Dañbooru-bako ni hoñ o tsumeta. (段ボール箱に本を詰めた) I *packed* the books in the cardboard boxes. / *Biñ ni mizu o tsumeta.* (瓶に水を詰めた) I *filled* the bottle with water. 《⇨ tsumaru》
2 move over; stand [sit] closer:
Moo sukoshi oku e tsumete kudasai. (もう少し奥へ詰めてください) Will you *move back* a little more, please?
3 shorten (time); cut (hair):
Yasumi-jikañ o go-fuñ-kañ tsumeta. (休み時間を5分間詰めた) They *shortened* the rest period by five minutes. / *Kanojo wa kami o sukoshi tsumeta.* (彼女は髪を少し詰めた) She slightly *shortened* her hair.

tsu⌈meta·i つめたい (冷たい) *a.* (-ku) **1** (of temperature) cold; cool; chilly:
tsumetai nomimono (冷たい飲み物) a *cold* drink / *tsumetai kaze* (冷たい風) a *chill* wind / *Samusa de te ga tsumetaku natta.* (寒さで手が冷たくなった) My hands were *freezing* from the cold. 《↔ atsui¹》 《⇨ samui (table)》
2 (of a person's attitude) cold; cool:
tsumetai kotoba (冷たい言葉) *cold* words / *tsumetai hito* (冷たい人) a *coldhearted* person / *Watashi wa tsumetaku atsukawareta.* (私は冷たく扱われた) I got the *cold* shoulder. 《↔ atatakai》

tsu⌈mi つみ (罪) *n.* sin; crime; offense:
tsumi o okasu (罪を犯す) commit a

sin [*crime*] / *Kanojo ni* tsumi *wa nai.* (彼女に罪はない) She *is innocent.*

...ni tsumi o kiseru (...に～を着せる) put the blame on: *Kare wa kanojo* ni tsumi o kiseta. (彼は彼女に罪を着せた) He *put the blame on* her.

tsu⌈mori つもり (積もり) *n.* **1** intention; purpose; idea: *Doo-iu* tsumori *desu ka?* (どういうつもりですか) What do you *mean* by that? / *Joodañ no* tsumori *de itta dake desu.* (冗談のつもりで言っただけです) I only said it *as a joke.* / *Jikañ-doori ni tsuku* tsumori *datta ñ desu ga.* (時間どおりに着くつもりだったんですが) I *intended* to arrive on time, but... / *Sono koto wa kare ni iwanai* tsumori *desu.* (そのことは彼に言わないつもりです) I do not *plan* to tell him about that. / *Sono kai ni shusseki suru* tsumori *wa arimaseñ.* (その会に出席するつもりはありません) I have no *intention* of attending the party.

2 thought; expectation; conviction: *Kare ni kite moraeru* tsumori *de ita.* (彼に来てもらえるつもりでいた) I *expected* that he would come. / *Watashi wa shikeñ ni ukaru* tsumori *desu.* (私は試験に受かるつもりです) I *expect* to pass the exam. / *Kanojo wa jibuñ de bijiñ no* tsumori *de iru.* (彼女は自分で美人のつもりでいる) She *is convinced* she is a beauty.

3 attitude; frame of mind: *Koñdo shippai shitara, kubi da kara sono* tsumori *de.* (今度失敗したら, 首だからそのつもりで) If you fail again, you will be fired, so *be prepared* for that. / *Abunai kara sono* tsumori *de ki o tsuke nasai.* (危ないからそのつもりで気をつけなさい) It's dangerous, so *bear that in mind* and be careful.

tsu⌈mor·u つもる (積もる) *vi.* (tsumor·i-; tsumor·a-; tsumot-te Ⓒ) accumulate; be piled up: *Yuki ga takusañ* tsumotta. (雪がたくさん積もった) The snow *lies* very deep. / *Sono kaisha no akaji wa* tsumori tsumotte, *ichioku-eñ ni natta.* (その会社の赤字は積もり積もって, 1億円になった) The deficit of the company *piled up and up* to 100 million yen.

tsu⌈m·u¹ つむ (積む) *vt.* (tsum·i-; tsum·a-; tsuñ-de Ⓒ) **1** pile; heap; stack: *Tsukue no ue ni shorui ga yama to* tsuñde aru. (机の上に書類が山と積んである) The documents *are piled up* on the desk in a heap.

2 load: *Torakku ni hikkoshi no nimotsu o* tsuñda. (トラックに引っ越しの荷物を積んだ) We *loaded* the truck with the things we were moving to our new house.

3 accumulate (experience, exercise, etc.): *keekeñ o* tsumu (経験を積む) *accumulate* experience / *Kare no shiñ-kiroku wa kibishii reñshuu o* tsuñda *seeka desu.* (彼の新記録は厳しい練習を積んだ成果です) His new record is the result of his *repeated* hard training.

tsu⌈m·u² つむ (摘む) *vt.* (tsum·i-; tsum·a-; tsuñ-de Ⓒ) pick; gather; pluck; nip: *Kodomo-tachi wa nohara de hana o* tsuñda. (子どもたちは野原で花をつんだ) The children *gathered* flowers in the field.

tsu⌈na¹ つな (綱) *n.* rope; cord: tsuna *o haru* [*taguru*] (綱を張る[たぐる]) stretch [haul in] a *rope* / *Tsutsumi o* tsuna *de shibatta.* (包みを綱でしばった) I tied the parcel with a *cord.*

tsu⌈nagari つながり (繋り) *n.* connection; relation:

Sono futatsu no jikeñ ni wa tsunagari *ga aru.*(その2つの事件にはつながりがある) There is some *connection* between the two cases. / *Kanojo to wa nañ no* tsunagari *mo arimaseñ.*(彼女とは何のつながりもありません) I don't have any *dealings* with her. 《⇨ tsunagaru》

tsu⌐nagar·u つながる (繋がる) *vi.* (tsunagar·i-; tsunagar·a-; tsunagat-te C) **1** connect; link: *Atarashii hashi de Hoñshuu to Shikoku ga* tsunagatta.(新しい橋で本州と四国がつながった) Honshu and Shikoku *were linked* by new bridges. / *Deñwa ga* tsunagarimashita.(電話がつながりました) Your party *is on the line.* 《⇨ tsunagu》 **2** be related; be linked: *Watashi wa kare to chi ga* tsunagatte imasu.(私は彼と血がつながっています) I *am related* to him by blood. 《⇨ tsunagari》

tsu⌐nage·ru つなげる (繋げる) *vt.* (tsunage-te V) = tsunagu.

tsu⌐nag·u つなぐ (繋ぐ) *vt.* (tsunag·i-; tsunag·a-; tsuna·i-de C) **1** tie; fasten; chain: *Inu o ki ni* tsunaida.(犬を木につないだ) I *tied* the dog to a tree. 《⇨ tsunagaru》 **2** connect; join: *Kono hoosu o shookaseñ ni* tsunagi nasai.(このホースを消火栓につなぎなさい) *Connect* this hose to the fire hydrant. / *Futari wa te o* tsunaide *aruite ita.*(二人は手をつないで歩いていた) The two were walking *hand in hand.* / *Deñwa o* tsunagimashita.(電話をつなぎました) I've *put* the call *through.*

tsu⌐nami つなみ (津波) *n.* tidal wave; tsunami: tsunami *ni osowareru* (津波に襲われる) be struck by a *tidal wave.*

tsu⌐ne ni つねに (常に) *adv.* (*slightly formal*) always; habitually:

Kare wa tsune ni *keñkoo-iji ni tsutomete iru.*(彼は常に健康維持に努めている) He is *always* careful about keeping himself in good health. / *Yuutoosee ga* tsune ni *seekoo suru to wa kagiranai.*(優等生が常に成功するとは限らない) It does not necessarily follow that honor students *always* succeed. 《⇨ itsu-mo》

tsu⌐ne⌐r·u つねる (抓る) *vt.* (tsuner·i-; tsuner·a-; tsunet-te C) pinch; nip: *Kanojo wa watashi no ude o* tsunetta.(彼女は私の腕をつねった) She *pinched* me on the arm.

tsu⌐no⌐ つの (角) *n.* horn; antler.

tsu⌐ra·i つらい (辛い) *a.* (-ku) hard; tough; painful; bitter: tsurai *shigoto* (つらい仕事) *hard* work / tsurai *omoi o suru* (つらい思いをする) have a *bitter* experience / *Kono kanashii shirase o kanojo ni tsutaeru no wa* tsurai.(この悲しい知らせを彼女に伝えるのはつらい) It is *heartbreaking* to tell her this sad news. / *Kare wa buka ni* tsuraku *atatta.*(彼は部下につらく当たった) He treated his subordinates *harshly.*

tsu⌐rane⌐·ru つらねる (連ねる) *vt.* (-ne-te V) line; range: *Tateuri-juutaku ga noki o* tsuranete iru.(建売り住宅が軒を連ねている) The ready-made houses *stand in line.* / *Kare mo sono uñdoo no hokkiniñ to shite na o* tsuraneta.(彼もその運動の発起人として名を連ねた) He also *put down* his name as one of the originators of the campaign.

tsu⌐ranu⌐k·u つらぬく (貫く) *vt.* (-nuk·i-; -nuk·a-; -nu·i-te C) **1** pierce; run through; penetrate: *Tama wa kabe o* tsuranuita.(弾は壁を貫いた) The bullet *went through* the wall. / *Kawa wa machi no chuushiñ o* tsuranuite imasu.(川は町の中心を貫いています) The river *runs through* the center of the town.

2 carry through; accomplish: *Kare wa jibuñ no shiññeñ o tsuranuita.* (彼は自分の信念を貫いた) He *maintained* his convictions *to the end.*

tsuˈre つれ (連れ) *n.* companion: *Tsure ga matte imasu no de shitsuree shimasu.* (連れが待っていますので失礼します) My *companion* is waiting so I'm afraid I have to leave now. / *Kare no tsure no josee o shitte imasu ka?* (彼の連れの女性を知っていますか) Do you know the woman *who is with* him?

tsuˈre·ru つれる (連れる) *vt.* (tsure-te [V]) take (a person); bring (a person); be accompanied: *Watashi wa kodomo o doobutsueñ e tsurete itta.* (私は子どもを動物園へ連れて行った) I *took* the children to the zoo.

tsuˈrete つれて *conj.* accordingly; consequently.

...ni tsurete (...に〜) as...: *Toshi o toru ni tsurete tairyoku ga yowaru.* (年を取るにつれて体力が弱る) *As* one grows older, one's strength decreases.

tsuˈri[1] つり (釣り) *n.* fishing; angling: *Kawa e tsuri ni ikimashoo.* (川へ釣りに行きましょう) Let's go to the river to *fish.* / *Kinoo wa ichinichi-juu tsuri o shite sugoshimashita.* (きのうは一日中釣りをして過ごしました) I spent the whole of yesterday *fishing.* / tsuri-bari (釣り針) a *fishhook* / tsuri-ito (釣り糸) a *fishline* / tsuri-zao (釣ざお) a *fishing* rod.

tsuˈri[2] つり (釣り) *n.* change: ★ Often with '*o-*.' *Tsuri o morau no o wasureta.* (つりをもらうのを忘れた) I forgot to get the *change.* 《⇨ o-tsuri》

tsuˈriai つりあい (釣り合い) *n.* bal-

ance; proportion; harmony: *tsuriai ga toreru* (つり合いがとれる) come to a *balance* / tsuriai ga ii [warui] (つり合いがいい[悪い]) *well* [*ill*]-*balanced* / *Shuushi no tsuriai no toreta yosañ o kumu koto ga dekita.* (収支のつり合いのとれた予算を組むことができた) We were able to put together a budget which *balances* revenue and expenditure. 《⇨ tsuriau》

tsuˈriaˈ·u つりあう (釣り合う) *vi.* (-a·i-; -aw·a·; -at-te [C]) balance; be in proportion; be in harmony; match: *Nihoñ no yushutsu-gaku to yunyuu-gaku ga tsuriatte inai to iwareru.* (日本の輸出額と輸入額が釣り合っていないと言われる) It is said that Japan's exports and imports do not *balance.* 《⇨ tsuriai》

tsuˈribashi つりばし (吊り橋) *n.* rope bridge; suspension bridge.

tsuˈriseñ つりせん (釣り銭) *n.* small change: *Tsuriseñ no nai yoo ni o-negai shimasu.* (つり銭のないようにお願いします) Please have the *exact amount* ready. 《⇨ o-tsuri》

tsuˈr·u[1] つる (釣る) *vt.* (tsur·i-; tsur·a-; tsut-te [C]) fish; angle; catch: *Kinoo wa kawa e sakana o tsuri ni ikimashita.* (きのうは川へ魚を釣りに行きました) Yesterday I went to the river to *fish.* / *Kore ga kinoo tsutta sakana desu.* (これがきのう釣った魚です) This is the fish I *caught* yesterday.

tsuˈr·u[2] つる (吊る) *vt.* (tsur·i-; tsur·a-; tsut-te [C]) hang; suspend: *kaateñ o tsuru* (カーテンをつる) *hang* curtains / *kubi o tsuru* (首をつる) *hang* oneself. 《⇨ tsurusu》

tsuˈru[3] つる (鶴) *n.* crane. ★ Cranes and turtles are symbols of longevity in Japan. A popular saying goes, '*Tsuru wa señ-neñ, kame wa mañ-neñ.*' (鶴は千年、亀は万年) Cranes live one thousand years, and turtles ten thousand years.

tsu⌈rus·u つるす (吊す) *vt.* (tsu-rush·i-; tsurus·a-; tsurush·i-te Ⓒ) hang; suspend:
Kanojo wa señtakumono o heya no naka ni tsurushita. (彼女は洗濯物を部屋の中につるした) She *hung* the washing in the room. 《⇨ tsuru²》

tsu⌈tae·ru つたえる (伝える) *vt.* (tsutae-te Ⓥ) **1** tell; inform; notify; communicate:
Señsee wa seeto ni raishuu tesuto o suru to tsutaeta. (先生は生徒に来週テストをすると伝えた) The teacher *informed* the pupils that they would have a test next week. / *Minasañ ni yoroshiku o-tsutae kudasai.* (みなさんによろしくお伝えください) Please *give* everyone my regards.
2 hand down (a tale, custom, religion, etc.); introduce:
Kore wa kono chihoo ni mukashi kara tsutaerarete iru hanashi desu. (これはこの地方に昔から伝えられている話です) This is a tale that *has been handed down* in this area from the old days. 《⇨ tsutawaru》
3 transmit; introduce:
Bukkyoo wa Chooseñ-hañtoo kara Nihoñ ni tsutaerareta. (仏教は朝鮮半島から日本に伝えられた) Buddhism *was introduced* into Japan from the Korean Peninsula. 《⇨ tsutawaru》
4 conduct; transmit:
Doo wa deñki o tsutaeru. (銅は電気を伝える) Copper *conducts* electricity.

tsu⌈ta·u つたう (伝う) *vt.* (tsuta·i-; tsutaw·a-; tsutat-te Ⓒ) go along:
yane o tsutatte nigeru (屋根を伝っ て逃げる) flee from roof *to* roof.

tsu⌈tawar·u つたわる (伝わる) *vi.* (tsutawar·i-; tsutawar·a-; tsutawat-te Ⓒ) **1** (of information, rumor, etc.) spread; travel; circulate: 《⇨ tsutaeru》
Sono uwasa wa machi-juu ni tsutawatta. (そのうわさは町中に伝わった) The rumor *has spread* all over town. / *Geñchi kara wa nañ no joo-hoo mo tsutawatte kimaseñ.* (現地からは何の情報も伝わってきません) So far *no* information *has been received* from the scene.
2 (of a tale, tradition, etc.) come down; be handed down:
Kore wa mukashi kara tsutawatte iru hanashi desu. (これは昔から伝わっている話です) This is a tale *handed down* from the old days. 《⇨ tsutaeru》
3 be transmitted; be introduced:
Bukkyoo ga Nihoñ ni tsutawatta no wa roku-seeki nakaba desu. (仏教が日本に伝わったのは6世紀半ばです) It is in the mid-sixth century that Buddhism *was introduced* into Japan. 《⇨ tsutaeru》

tsu⌈toma⌉r·u つとまる (勤まる) *vi.* (-mar·i-; -mar·a-; -mat-te Ⓒ) be fit; be equal:
Sono shigoto ga watashi ni tsutomaru ka doo ka shiñpai desu. (その仕事が私に勤まるかどうか心配です) I am worried whether I *am equal* to the job.

tsu⌈tome⌉¹ つとめ (勤め) *n.* work; job:
O-tsutome wa dochira desu ka? (お勤めはどちらですか) Where do you *work*? / *Kyoo wa tsutome o yasuñda.* (きょうは勤めを休んだ) I took today off *work*. 《⇨ tsutomeru¹》

tsu⌈tome⌉² つとめ (務め) *n.* duty; task:
Kare wa tsutome o rippa ni hatashita. (彼は務めを立派に果たした) He

discharged his *duties* splendidly. (⇨ tsutomeru²)

tsu⌈tome⌉·ru¹ つとめる (勤める) *vt.* (-me-te Ⓥ) work for; serve:
Kanojo wa shoojigaisha ni tsutomete imasu. (彼女は商事会社に勤めています) She *works for* a trading company. (⇨ tsutome¹)

tsu⌈tome⌉·ru² つとめる (務める) *vt.* (-me-te Ⓥ) act as:
Kare wa kaigi de gichoo o tsutometa. (彼は会議で議長を務めた) He *acted* as chairman at the conference. (⇨ tsutome²)

tsu⌈tome⌉·ru³ つとめる (努める) *vt.* (-me-te Ⓥ) try; make efforts; endeavor:
Watashi wa keñkoo-iji ni tsutomete imasu. (私は健康維持に努めています) I *try* to keep in good health. / *Kaisha wa akaji no kaishoo ni tsutomete iru.* (会社は赤字の解消に努めている) Our company *is making efforts* to get out of the red.

tsu⌈tomesaki つとめさき (勤め先) *n.* one's place of employment:
Kare wa señgetsu tsutomesaki o kaemashita. (彼は先月勤め先を替えました) He changed his *job* last month. / *Anata no o-tsutomesaki wa dochira desu ka?* (あなたのお勤め先はどちらですか) Where do you *work*? (⇨ kaisha)

tsu⌈tsu つつ (筒) *n.* pipe; tube; cylinder:
take no tsutsu (竹の筒) a bamboo *tube.*

tsu⌈tsu⌉k·u つつく (突つく) *vt.* (tsu-tsuk·i-; tsutsuk·a-; tsutsu·i-te Ⓒ) poke; peck; nudge:
Niwatori ga esa o tsutsuite iru. (にわとりがえさをつついている) The hen *is pecking* at the feed. / *Dare-ka ga watashi no senaka o tsutsuita.* (誰かが私の背中をつついた) Someone *poked* me in the back.

tsu⌈tsu⌉m·u つつむ (包む) *vt.* (tsu-tsum·i-; tsutsum·a-; tsutsuñ-de Ⓒ) 1 wrap; pack:
Kanojo wa sono hako o shiñbuñshi ni tsutsuñda. (彼女はその箱を新聞紙に包んだ) She *wrapped up* the box in newspaper. / *Kore o* okuri-mono-yoo ni tsutsuñde *kudasai.* (これを贈り物用に包んでください) Please *gift-wrap* this.

2 cover; veil:
Yama zeñtai ga moya ni tsutsumarete ita. (山全体がもやに包まれていた) The whole mountain *was covered* in mist. / *Sono jikeñ wa izeñ nazo ni tsutsumarete imasu.* (その事件は依然なぞに包まれています) The affair *is* still *shrouded* in mystery.

tsu⌈tsushimi⌉ つつしみ (慎み) *n.* modesty; prudence; discretion; self-control:
Kanojo wa tsutsushimi *ni kakeru tokoro ga aru.* (彼女は慎みに欠けるところがある) She lacks *modesty.* / *Kare wa yotte,* tsutsushimi *o wasureta.* (彼は酔って, 慎みを忘れた) He got drunk and lost his *self-control.* (⇨ tsutsushimu)

tsu⌈tsushi⌉m·u つつしむ (慎む) *vt.* (-shim·i-; -shim·a-; -shiñ-de Ⓒ) 1 be careful; be discreet; be prudent; be cautious:
Koodoo o tsutsushimi *nasai.* (行動を慎みなさい) *Be prudent* in your conduct.

2 refrain from; be moderate:
Sake wa tsutsushiñda *hoo ga ii desu yo.* (酒は慎んだほうがいいですよ) You had better *cut down on* your drinking. (⇨ tsutsushimi)

tsu⌈u つう (通) *n.* authority; expert:
Ano hito wa kabuki no tsuu *desu.* (あの人は歌舞伎の通です) He is an *authority* on kabuki. / *Kare wa Nihoñ* tsuu *desu.* (彼は日本通です) He is *very well-informed* about Japan.

tsu⌈uchi つうち (通知) *n.* notice;

notification; information:
Gookaku no tsuuchi *wa mada uke-totte imaseñ.*(合格の通知はまだ受け取っていません) I have not yet received the *notification* that I passed the examination. / *Kare kara nani-ka* tsuuchi *ga arimashita ka?*(彼から何か通知がありましたか) *Have you heard* anything from him? / tsuuchi*-hyoo* (通知表) a *report* card.

tsuuchi suru (〜する) *vt.* notify; inform: *Kuwashii koto wa ato de* tsuuchi *shimasu.*(詳しいことは後で通知します) We will *inform* you of the details later. / *Kare wa sono kai ni derarenai to* tsuuchi *shite kita.*(彼はその会に出られないと通知してきた) He *notified* me that he would be unable to attend the party.

tsu⌈ugaku つうがく (通学) *n.* traveling to school; attending school:
Tsuugaku ni dono kurai kakarimasu ka?(通学にどのくらいかかりますか) How long does it take to *get to school?*

tsuugaku suru (〜する) *vi.* go to school: *Watashi wa jiteñsha de* tsuugaku *shite imasu.*(私は自転車で通学しています) I *go to school* by bicycle. (⇨ tsuukiñ)

tsu⌈uji つうじ (通じ) *n.* bowel movement; evacuation; stool:
★ Often used with '*o-*' in a hospital.
*O-*tsuuji *wa arimashita ka?*(お通じはありましたか) Did you have a *bowel movement?* / *Watashi wa koko mikka-kañ* tsuuji *ga nai.*(私はここ3日間通じがない) I *have been constipated* these three days.

tsu⌈uji・ru つうじる (通じる) *vi.* (tsuuji-te Ⅴ) **1** lead; run:
Kono michi wa eki e tsuujite *imasu.*(この道は駅へ通じています) This road *leads* to the station. /

Soko kara saki wa tetsudoo ga tsuujite *imaseñ.*(そこから先は鉄道が通じていません) The railroad *does not run* beyond there. / *Aomori to Hakodate no aida ni wa toñneru ga* tsuujite *imasu.*(青森と函館の間にはトンネルが通じています) A tunnel *connects* Aomori and Hakodate.
2 (of a telephone) get through:
Kanojo no uchi ni deñwa o shita ga tsuujinakatta.(彼女の家に電話をしたが通じなかった) I telephoned her house but I *could not get through.*
3 be understood; make oneself understood:
Kanojo no Nihoñgo wa yoku tsuujita.(彼女の日本語はよく通じた) Her Japanese *was* easily *understood.* / *Watashi no iu koto ga aite ni* tsuujinakatta.(私の言うことが相手に通じなかった) I *could not make myself understood* to the other party.
4 be well-informed; be familiar:
Kare wa sono kaisha no naibu-jijoo ni tsuujite *iru.*(彼はその会社の内部事情に通じている) He *is well-informed* on the internal affairs of the company.

...o tsuujite (...を通じて) through:
Kyoo wa ichi-neñ o tsuujite *ichi-bañ hi no nagai hi desu.*(きょうは一年を通じていちばん日の長い日です) Today is the day which is the longest *of* the year. / *Sono jikeñ wa masukomi o* tsuujite, *ichihayaku hoodoo sareta.*(その事件はマスコミを通じて、いち早く報道された) The affair was promptly reported *through* the news media.

tsu⌈ujoo つうじょう (通常) *n., adv.* usually; generally:
Shiyakusho wa tsuujoo *ku-ji kara hajimarimasu.*(市役所は通常9時から始まります) The city office *usually* opens at nine. / *Neñmatsu mo* tsuujoo*-doori eegyoo itashimasu.*(年末も通常どおり営業いたします) We

will be conducting business *as usual* at the end of the year. / tsuujoo-*kokkai* (通常国会) an *ordinary* Diet session. (⇨ futsuu¹)

tsuˈuka つうか (通過) *n.* passage: *hooañ no* tsuuka (法案の通過) the *passage* of a bill / tsuuka-*eki* (通過駅) a station *at which the train does not stop* / tsuuka-*ressha* (通過列車) a *through* train.

 tsuuka suru (〜する) *vi.* pass: *Watashi-tachi wa kuruma de toñneru o* tsuuka shita. (私たちは車でトンネルを通過した) We *passed* through the tunnel in a car. / *Kyuukoo wa kono eki o* tsuuka shimasu. (急行はこの駅を通過します) The express *does not stop* at this station. / *Sono hooañ wa Shuugiiñ o* tsuuka shita. (その法案は衆議院を通過した) The bill *passed* the House of Representatives.

tsuˈuki つうき (通気) *n.* ventilation; air permeability: tsuuki *no yoi kutsu* (通気の良い靴) shoes that *breathe well* / *Kono heya wa* tsuuki *ga yoi [warui].* (この部屋は通気が良い[悪い]) This room *is* well[poorly]-*ventilated.* / tsuuki-koo (通気孔) a *vent*.

tsuˈukiñ つうきん (通勤) *n.* commutation; going to work: *Mañiñ deñsha de no* tsuukiñ *wa tsurai.* (満員電車での通勤はつらい) *Commuting* in a crowded train is unbearable. / tsuukiñ-*deñsha* (通勤電車) a *commuter* train / tsuukiñ-*jikañ* (通勤時間) the time *it takes to get to work* / tsuukiñ-*teeki* (通勤定期) a *commuter* pass.

 tsuukiñ suru (〜する) *vi.* commute; go to work: *Kare wa kuruma de* tsuukiñ shite imasu. (彼は車で通勤しています) He *goes to work* by car.

tsuˈukoo つうこう (通行) *n.* passing; passage; traffic: *Kono dooro wa kuruma no* tsuu-

koo *ga hageshii.* (この道路は車の通行が激しい) The *traffic* on this road is very heavy. / Tsuukoo no jama *o shinai de kudasai.* (通行のじゃまをしないでください) Please don't stand *in my way.* / *Kono michi wa ippoo-*tsuukoo *desu.* (この道は一方通行です) This is a *one-way* street. / *Migigawa* tsuukoo *o mamorimashoo.* (右側通行を守りましょう) Keep *to the right.* / *Kono saki wa* tsuukoo-dome *desu.* (この先は通行止めです) The road *is closed* ahead. / tsuukoo-*niñ* (通行人) a *passerby*; a *pedestrian* / tsuukoo-*ryookiñ* (通行料金) a *toll*.

 tsuukoo suru (〜する) *vi.* pass; go along: *Sharyoo wa koko o* tsuukoo suru *koto ga dekimaseñ.* (車両はここを通行することができません) Vehicles *cannot pass through* here.

(No thoroughfare for vehicles)
SHARYOO TSUUKOODOME SIGN

tsuˈu-piˈisu ツーピース *n.* two-piece woman's suit: tsuu-piisu *no mizugi* (ツーピースの水着) a *two-piece* bathing suit.

tsuˈuro つうろ (通路) *n.* passage; way; aisle: Tsuuro *ni mono o oite wa ikemaseñ.* (通路に物を置いてはいけません) You mustn't leave things in the *aisle.* / Tsuuro *o akete kudasai.* (通路を空けてください) Please clear the *way.*

Tsu⌈usañ-da⌉ijiñ (通産大臣) *n.* Minister of International Trade and Industry.

Tsu⌈usañ⌉-shoo (通産省) *n.* Ministry of International Trade and Industry. ★ Abbreviation: MITI. 《⇒ shoo¹ (table)》

tsu⌈ushiñ つうしん (通信) *n.* correspondence; communication: *Gaikoku to no tsuushiñ ni fakkusu wa beñri desu.* (外国との通信にファックスは便利です) Fax is very useful in *communicating* with foreign countries. / tsuushiñ-*eesee* (通信衛星) a *communications* satellite / tsuushiñ-*hañbai* (通信販売) *mail order* sales / tsuushiñ-*kyooiku* (通信教育) education by *correspondence*; *distance learning.*

tsuushiñ suru (〜する) *vi.* correspond; communicate: *Sono shima to wa museñ de tsuushiñ shite imasu.* (その島とは無線で通信しています) We *communicate* with the island by radio.

tsu⌈uyaku つうやく (通訳) *n.* interpretation; interpreter: *Watashi wa Suzuki-sañ ni tsuuyaku o tanoñda.* (私は鈴木さんに通訳を頼んだ) I asked Mr. Suzuki to *interpret* for me. / *Shoodañ wa tsuuyaku o tooshite okonawareta.* (商談は通訳を通して行なわれた) The business negotiations were conducted through an *interpreter.*

tsuuyaku suru (〜する) *vt.* interpret: *Kanojo wa watashi no iu koto o Chuugokugo ni tsuuyaku shita.* (彼女は私の言うことを中国語に通訳した) She *interpreted* what I said into Chinese. 《⇒ doojitsuuyaku》

tsu⌈uyoo つうよう (通用) *n.* popular use; circulation; currency: *Kono kaisuukeñ no tsuuyoo kikañ wa ik-ka-getsu desu.* (この回数券の通用期間は1か月です) The term of *validity* of these coupon tickets

is one month. / tsuuyoo-moñ (通用門) a *side entrance.*

tsuuyoo suru (〜する) *vi.* be used; be accepted; be valid: *Kono kurejitto kaado wa sekaijuu de tsuuyoo shimasu.* (このクレジットカードは世界中で通用します) This credit card *is valid* worldwide. / *Sono kañgae wa sekeñ de wa tsuuyoo shimaseñ.* (その考えは世間では通用しません) That way of thinking *is not accepted* in society. / *Kono kippu wa mikka-kañ tsuuyoo shimasu.* (この切符は3日間通用します) This ticket *is valid* for three days.

tsu⌈ya つや (艶) *n.* gloss; luster; polish: *Kanojo wa tsuya no aru kami o shite iru.* (彼女はつやのある髪をしている) She has *glossy* hair. / *Shiñju o migaite, tsuya o dashita.* (真珠を磨いて, つやを出した) I polished the pearl to bring out its *luster.*

tsu⌈yo⌉·i つよい (強い) *a.* (-ku) **1** strong; powerful; intense: tsuyoi *kaze* [*nioi*] (強い風[におい]) a *strong* wind [smell] / tsuyoi *hizashi* (強い日ざし) *intense* sunlight / *Kono chiimu wa riigu de ichibañ tsuyoi.* (このチームはリーグでいちばん強い) This team is the *strongest* in the league. / *Kanojo wa ishi ga tsuyoi.* (彼女は意志が強い) She has a *strong* will. / *Tookyoku wa sono kaisha ni tsuyoi atsuryoku o kaketa.* (当局はその会社に強い圧力をかけた) The authorities put *great* pressure on the company. / *Watashi wa i ga amari tsuyoku nai.* (私は胃があまり強くない) I have a *delicate* stomach. (↔ yowai) 《⇒ tsuyosa》 **2** (...ni) be good at: *Kanojo wa Chuugokugo ni tsuyoi.* (彼女は中国語に強い) She is *good* at Chinese. / *Kare wa suuji ni tsuyoi.* (彼は数字に強い) He is *good* at figures. 《↔ yowai》

3 (...ni) be able to resist; withstand:

Kono biniiru-bukuro wa mizu ni tsuyoi. (このビニール袋は水に強い) This plastic bag is *waterproof*. / *Watashi wa kitaguni umare na no de samusa ni* tsuyoi. (私は北国生まれなので寒さに強い) I can *easily stand* the cold since I was born in a northern land. (↔ yowai) (⇨ tsuyosa)

tsu⌐yoki つよき (強気) *a.n.* (~ na, ni) bold; aggressive; optimistic:

tsuyoki *ni deru* (強気に出る) take an *aggressive* attitude / tsuyoki *na koodoo* (強気な行動) a *bold* action / *Kare wa itsu-mo* tsuyoki *da.* (彼はいつも強気だ) He is always *firm and resolute*. (↔ yowaki)

tsu⌐yoma⌐r·u つよまる (強まる) *vi.* (-mar·i-; -mar·a-; -mat-te Ⓒ) become strong; increase in power [strength]:

Taifuu no sekkiñ ni yori fuu-u ga tsuyomatta. (台風の接近により風雨が強まった) As the typhoon approached, the wind *grew stronger* and the rain *became heavier*. / *Seefu ni taisuru fumañ no koe ga* tsuyomatte iru. (政府に対する不満の声が強まっている) The voices of dissatisfaction against the government *have been growing louder*. (⇨ tsuyomeru)

tsu⌐yome⌐·ru つよめる (強める) *vt.* (-me-te Ⓥ) strengthen; intensify; emphasize:

ryookoku no musubitsuki o tsuyomeru (両国の結びつきを強める) *strengthen* the ties between two countries / *hañtai-uñdoo o* tsuyomeru (反対運動を強める) *intensify* an opposition campaign / *gasu no hi o* tsuyomeru (ガスの火を強める) *turn up* the gas. (↔ yowameru) (⇨ tsuyomaru)

tsu⌐yosa つよさ (強さ) *n.*

strength; power:

tsuna no tsuyosa (綱の強さ) the *strength* of a rope / *kaze no* tsuyosa *o hakaru* (風の強さを測る) measure the *force* of the wind / *Aite chiimu no* tsuyosa *wa wakaranai.* (相手チームの強さはわからない) We don't know *how strong* the opposing team is. (⇨ tsuyoi)

tsu⌐yu¹ つゆ (露) *n.* dew; dewdrop:

tsuyu *ni nureru* (露にぬれる) be wet with *dew* / *Tsuyu ga orita.* (露が降りた) The *dew* has fallen.

tsu⌐yu² つゆ (梅雨) *n.* the rainy season: ★ The period from June to July, when there are many rainy days.

Moo tsuyu *ni haitta rashii.* (もう梅雨に入ったらしい) It seems that the *rainy season* has set in. / *Tsuyu wa moo sugu akeru deshoo.* (梅雨はもうすぐ明けるでしょう) The *rainy season* should soon be over. (⇨ uki¹)

tsu⌐yu³ つゆ (汁) *n.* soup; sauce; juice. ★ Often called '*o-tsuyu*.' (⇨ shiru²)

tsu⌐zuke·ru つづける (続ける) *vt.* (tsuzuke-te Ⓥ) continue; go on; keep up:

Doozo hanashi o tsuzukete *kudasai.* (どうぞ話を続けてください) *Go on* with your story, please. / *Kare wa ichinichi-juu shigoto o* tsuzuketa. (彼は一日中仕事を続けた) He *continued* working all day long. / *Kyuukee no ato, mata hanashiai o* tsuzuketa. (休憩のあと、また話し合いを続けた) We *resumed* our discussion after a break. (⇨ tsuzuku)

tsu⌐zuki つづき (続き) *n.* continuance; continuation; sequel:

Sono hanashi no tsuzuki *ga kikitai.* (その話の続きが聞きたい) I want to hear the *rest* of the story. / *Tsuzuki wa ji-goo.* (続きは次号) *To be continued* in the next issue (of

this magazine). ((⇨ tsuzuku))

tsu⌐zuk·u つづく (続く) *vi.* (tsu-
zuk·i-; tsuzuk·a-; tsuzu·i-te [C])
1 continue; go on; last:
Seeteñ ga is-shuukañ tsuzuita. (晴
天が一週間続いた) The fine weath-
er *continued* for a week. ((⇨ tsuzukeru; tsuzuki))
2 follow:
Watashi-tachi wa kare ni tsuzuite
sono heya ni haitta. (私たちは彼に続
いてその部屋に入った) We went into
the room, *following* him.
3 lead; extend:
*Kono namikimichi wa ichi-kiro
hodo* tsuzukimasu. (この並木道は1
キロほど続きます) This avenue of
trees *extends* for about one kilometer.

tsu⌐zumi¹ つづみ (鼓) *n.* Japanese
hand drum. ★ Beaten with the
fingertips.

TSUZUMI

tta⌐ra¹ ったら *p.* (used to mark
the topic of a sentence): ★ Follows a noun or the dictionary
form of a verb. An informal
form mainly used by women.
Uchi no ko ttara, *asoñde bakari*

ite, sukoshi mo beñkyoo shinai. (う
ちの子ったら, 遊んでばかりいて, 少しも勉
強しない) *That child of ours!* He
plays around all the time, and
does not study one bit. / *Kimura-
sañ ttara, kazoku de sekai ryokoo
suru ñ desu tte.* (木村さんったら, 家
族で世界旅行するんですって) Is it true
that *Mr. Kimura* is going on a
round-the-world trip with his
family?

...ttara nai (...～ない) (used for
emphasis or exaggeration):
Nichiyoo no depaato wa koñde iru
ttara nai *wa.* (日曜のデパートは込んで
いるったらないわ) The department
stores on Sundays *are absolutely
jam-packed* with people! / *Kono
tokoro mainichi* isogashii ttara
nai. (このところ毎日忙しいったらない)
These days I *am rushed off my
feet* every day!

(t)tara² (っ)たら *p.* = (t)teba.

(t)teba (っ)てば *p.* (used when
emphasizing one's thoughts or
opinions to someone who appears not to understand):
★ Sometimes used as a retort or
contradiction. Use '*teba*' after '*ñ,*'
otherwise '*tteba.*'
"Hayaku ikoo yo." "Wakatte iru
tteba." (「早く行こうよ」「わかっているっ
てば」) "Let's hurry up and get
along." "Okay, okay, *I understand.*" / *"Kore tabecha ikenai yo."
"Tabemaseñ teba."* (「これ食べちゃい
けないよ」「食べませんてば」) "You
must not eat this." "I am not
going to eat it, *I tell you.*" / *Shizuka ni shinasai* tteba. (静かにしなさ
いってば) Be quiet, *I say!*

U

-u う *infl. end.* = -oo.

u˹ba˺·u うばう (奪う) *vt.* (uba·i-; ubaw·a-; ubat-te Ⓒ) take by force; snatch; rob; deprive: *Sono otoko wa kanojo no handobaggu o ubatte, nigeta.* (その男は彼女のハンドバッグを奪って、逃げた) The man *snatched* her handbag and made off. / *Kare-ra wa jiyuu o ubawareta.* (彼らは自由を奪われた) They *were deprived* of freedom. / *Sono hikooki jiko de ooku no jinmee ga ubawareta.* (その飛行機事故で多くの人命が奪われた) Many lives *were lost* in the airplane accident.

u˹chi[1] うち (家) *n.* **1** house: *Kono uchi wa tatete kara sanjuunen ni narimasu.* (この家は建ててから30年になります) It is thirty years since this *house* was built. / *Atarashii uchi ni wa itsu hikkoshi desu ka?* (新しい家にはいつ引っ越しですか) When are you moving to your new *house*? 《⇨ ie[1]》

2 home: *Kinoo wa ichinichi-juu uchi ni imashita.* (きのうは一日中家にいました) I stayed at *home* all day yesterday. / *Kodomo-tachi wa moo uchi ni kaerimashita.* (子どもたちはもう家に帰りました) The children have already gone *home*.

3 family: *Kare no uchi wa minna genki desu.* (彼の家はみんな元気です) His *family* are all fine.

4 (～ no) my; our: uchi no *chichi* (うちの父) *my* father / uchi no *gakkoo* [*kaisha*] (うちの学校[会社]) *our* school [company].

u˹chi[2] うち (内) *n.* **1** inside: *Kanojo wa heya no uchi kara kagi o kaketa.* (彼女は部屋のうちから鍵をか

けた) She locked the door from *inside* the room. 《↔ soto》 《⇨ naka[1]》

2 (～ ni) in; within; before: *Ni, san-nichi no uchi ni kono shigoto wa owarimasu.* (二、三日のうちにこの仕事は終わります) I will finish this job *within* two or three days. / *Kuraku naranai uchi ni kaerimashoo.* (暗くならないうちに帰りましょう) Let's go back *before* it gets dark.

3 (～ kara) of; out of: *Kono itsutsu no uchi kara hitotsu tori nasai.* (この五つのうちから一つ取りなさい) Take one *out of* these five.

u˹chiake·ru うちあける (打ち明ける) *vt.* (-ake-te Ⓥ) confide; confess; unburden: *Kare wa watashi ni tagaku no shakkin ga aru koto o uchiaketa.* (彼は私に多額の借金があることを打ち明けた) He *confessed* to me that he had heavy debts.

u˹chiawase うちあわせ (打ち合わせ) *n.* arrangement: *Kaigi no uchiawase wa moo sumimashita ka?* (会議の打ち合わせはもう済みましたか) Have the *arrangements* for the meeting been completed yet? 《⇨ uchiawaseru》

u˹chiawase·ru うちあわせる (打ち合わせる) *vt.* (-awase-te Ⓥ) arrange; make arrangements: *shiki no shidai o uchiawaseru* (式の次第を打ち合わせる) *make arrangements* for the order of speeches and events during a ceremony. 《⇨ uchiawase》

u˹chigawa うちがわ (内側) *n.* the inside; interior: *hako no uchigawa* (箱の内側) the *inside* of a box / *Kono kooto wa uchigawa ga ke desu.* (このコートは

内側が毛です) This coat is fur on the *inside*. / *Kono doa wa* uchigawa *ni hirakimasu*. (このドアは内側に開きます) This door opens *inward*. ((↔ sotogawa))

u⌐**chikeshi** うちけし (打ち消し) *n.* denial; negation:
Kanojo wa sono uwasa no uchikeshi *ni kushiñ shite iru*. (彼女はそのうわさの打ち消しに苦心している) She is taking great pains to *deny* the rumor. ((⇨ uchikesu))

u⌐**chikes·u** うちけす (打ち消す) *vt.*
(-kesh·i-; -kes·a-; -kesh·i-te C)
deny; negate:
Kare wa sono jikeñ to no tsunagari o uchikeshita. (彼はその事件とのつながりを打ち消した) He *denied* that he had anything to do with the affair. ((⇨ uchikeshi))

u⌐**chikir·u** うちきる (打ち切る) *vt.*
(-kir·i-; -kir·a-; -kit-te C) discontinue; break off:
Roodoosha-gawa wa kooshoo o uchikitte, *suto ni haitta*. (労働者側は交渉を打ち切って, ストに入った) The workers *broke off* negotiations and went on strike.

u⌐**chikom·u** うちこむ (打ち込む) *vt.*
(-kom·i-; -kom·a-; -koñ-de C)
1 drive; shoot; smash:
jimeñ ni kui o uchikomu (地面にくいを打ち込む) *drive* a stake into the ground.
2 devote oneself to:
Kare wa eega no seesaku ni uchikoñde *iru*. (彼は映画の製作に打ち込んでいる) He *devotes himself to* making films.

u⌐**chiwa**¹ うちわ (内輪) *n.* **1** private; family:
uchiwa *dake no atsumari* (内輪だけの集まり) a *private* meeting / uchiwa *dake no kekkoñ-shiki* (内輪だけの結婚式) a *family* wedding / *Sono keñ wa* uchiwa *de kaiketsu shimashita*. (その件は内輪で解決しました) We settled the matter *among our-*

selves. ((⇨ naibu))
2 conservative; moderate:
Hiyoo wa uchiwa *ni mitsumotte, gojuumañ-eñ kakarimasu*. (費用は内輪に見積もって, 50万円かかります) *Conservatively* estimated, the cost is half a million yen.

uchiwa-mome (～もめ) internal trouble; a family quarrel.

u⌐**chi**¹**wa**² うちわ (団扇) *n.* round paper and bamboo fan:
uchiwa *de aogu* (うちわであおぐ) use a *fan*. ((⇨ señsu))

UCHIWA

u⌐**chiwake** うちわけ (内訳) *n.* breakdown; item; detail:
Kare wa shishutsu no uchiwake *o watashi ni shimeshita*. (彼は支出の内訳を私に示した) He showed me the *breakdown* of expenditures. / *Seekyuusho ni wa* uchiwake *o kaite kudasai*. (請求書には内訳を書いてください) Please *itemize* all the charges on the bill.

u⌐**chuu** うちゅう (宇宙) *n.* the universe; the cosmos; space:
uchuu-*hikoo* (宇宙飛行) *space* flight.

u⌐**de**¹ うで (腕) *n.* **1** arm; forearm:
Kare wa futoi ude *o shite iru*. (彼は太い腕をしている) He has thick *arms*. / *Kanojo wa* ude *ni neko o daite ita*. (彼女は腕に猫を抱いていた) She was carrying a cat in her *arms*. / *Watashi wa* ude *o nobashite, sono biñ o totta*. (私は腕を伸ばして, その瓶

をとった) I *reached out* and took the bottle. 《⇨ jiñtai (illus.)》

2 ability; skill:
Subete wa kimi no ude *shidai desu.*(すべては君の腕しだいです) Everything depends on your *ability.* / *Kare wa saikiñ gorufu no* ude *ga agatta.*(彼は最近ゴルフの腕が上がった) He has recently improved his *skill* in golf. / *Yamada-shi wa* ude *no ii beñgoshi desu.*(山田氏は腕のいい弁護士です) Mr. Yamada is a *very competent* lawyer. 《⇨ udemae》

u⌈dedo⌉kee うでどけい (腕時計) *n.* wristwatch:
Shachoo wa kiñ no udedokee *o shite iru.*(社長は金の腕時計をしてる) The president of our company wears a gold *watch.* 《⇨ tokee (table)》

u⌈degumi⌉ うでぐみ (腕組み) *n.* folding one's arms:
Señsee wa udegumi *o shite kañgaete ita.*(先生は腕組みをして考えていた) Our teacher was thinking with his *arms folded.*

u⌈demae うでまえ (腕前) *n.* skill; ability:
Kare wa migoto na uñteñ no udemae *o hiroo shita.*(彼は見事な運転の腕前を披露した) He showed great *skill* at driving. / *Ano hito no tenisu no* udemae *wa doo desu ka?* (あの人のテニスの腕前はどうですか) *How good* is he at playing tennis? 《⇨ ude》

u⌈doñ うどん *n.* noodles:
udoñ *o yuderu* (うどんをゆでる) boil *noodles.* 《⇨ photo (right)》

u⌈e[1] うえ (上) *n.* **1** on:
Kanojo wa yuka no ue *ni juutañ o shiita.*(彼女は床の上にじゅうたんを敷いた) She laid a carpet *on* the floor. 《↔ shita[1]》

2 over; above:
Hikooki wa yama no ue *o toñde ita.*(飛行機は山の上を飛んでいた) The

UDOÑ

plane was flying *over* the mountain. / *Tsuki ga oka no* ue *ni nobotta.*(月が丘の上に昇った) The moon rose *above* the hill. 《↔ shita[1]》

3 up; upstairs:
Kanojo wa esukareetaa de ue *ni ikimashita.*(彼女はエスカレーターで上に行きました) She went *up* in the escalator. / Ue *de dare-ka ga sawaide iru.*(上でだれかが騒いでいる) There's someone making a noise *upstairs.* 《↔ shita[1]》

4 top:
yama no ue (山の上) the *top* of a mountain / *Sono hoñ wa ichibañ* ue *no tana ni arimasu.*(その本はいちばん上の棚にあります) The book is on the *top* shelf. 《↔ shita[1]》

5 senior; older:
Shujiñ wa watashi yori go-sai ue *desu.*(主人は私より5歳上です) My husband is five years *older* than me. / *Ichibañ* ue *no musuko wa daigakusee desu.*(いちばん上の息子は大学生です) Our *eldest* son is a university student. 《↔ shita[1]》

6 superior:
Kono koocha no hoo ga sore yori shitsu ga ue *desu.*(この紅茶の方がそれより質が上です) This tea is *superior* in quality to that one. 《⇨ otoru》

7 after:
Sono koto wa ryooshiñ to soodañ

no ue *kimemasu.*(そのことは両親と相談の上決めます) I will decide that matter *after* discussing it with my parents.

u￢e￣¹² うえ(飢え) *n.* hunger; starvation:

Sekai ni wa ue *de kurushiñde iru hito ga oozee iru.*(世界には飢えて苦しんでいる人がおおぜいいる) In the world there are many people who are suffering from *starvation.* (⇨ ueru²)

u￢e￣etoresu ウエートレス *n.* waitress. ★ When calling a waitress in a restaurant, say '*Chotto, suimaseñ.*'

u￢eki うえき(植木) *n.* garden tree [plant]; potted plant:
ueki *no teire o suru*(植木の手入れをする) trim and train *plants* / ueki-ya(植木屋) *a gardener.*

u￢e·ru¹ うえる(植える) *vt.* (ue-te Ⅴ) plant; sow; grow:
Kootee ni sakura no ki o ueta.(校庭に桜の木を植えた) We *planted* cherry trees in the school grounds.

u￢e￣·ru² うえる(飢える) *vi.* (ue-te Ⅴ) be [go] hungry; starve:
Uete iru hito no koto o omoeba, tabemono o muda ni dekinai.(飢えている人のことを思えば、食べ物をむだにできない) When we think of those who *are starving*, we cannot waste food. / *Sono ko wa aijoo ni* uete ita.(その子は愛情に飢えていた) That child *craved* affection. (⇨ ue²)

u￢e￣-shita うえした(上下) *n.* up and down:
Kono e wa ue-shita *ga gyaku desu.*(この絵は上下が逆です) This picture is *upside-down.* (↔ sayuu) (⇨ jooge)

u￢gai うがい(含嗽) *n.* gargling:
Ugai *wa kaze no yoboo ni narimasu.*(うがいはかぜの予防になります) *Gargling* prevents colds. / *Watashi wa soto kara kaette kuru to*

itsu-mo ugai o shimasu.(私は外から帰って来るといつもうがいをします) When I come back home, I always *gargle.*

u￢goka￣s·u うごかす(動かす) *vt.* (ugokash·i-; ugokas·a-; ugokash·i-te Ⓒ) **1** move:
Kono tsukue o mado no hoo e ugokashimashoo.(この机を窓の方へ動かしましょう) *Let's move* this desk toward the window.
2 operate (a machine, vehicle, etc.); run; start:
Kono kikai wa doo yatte ugokasu *ñ desu ka?*(この機械はどうやって動かすんですか) What is it that I do to *start* this machine? (⇨ ugoku)
3 (of feelings, emotions) touch; move; influence:
Sono tegami wa kanojo no kokoro o ugokashita.(その手紙は彼女の心を動かした) That letter *touched* her heart. (⇨ ugoku)

u￢goki￣¹ うごき(動き) *n.* **1** movement; motion:
Shiai no toki no señshu-tachi no ugoki *wa yokatta.*(試合のときの選手たちの動きは良かった) The *movements* of the players in the match were quite good. (⇨ ugoku)
2 activity; action:
Keesatsu wa booryokudañ no ugoki *o shirabete iru.*(警察は暴力団の動きを調べている) The police are investigating the *activities* of criminal gangs. / *Kazañ no ik-ka-getsu no* ugoki *o kiroku shita.*(火山の1か月の動きを記録した) We recorded a month's *activity* of the volcano.
3 trend; development:
Seejika wa yo no naka no ugoki *ni biñkañ desu.*(政治家は世の中の動きに敏感です) Politicians are sensitive to social *trends.* (⇨ ugoku)

u￢go￣k·u うごく(動く) *vi.* (ugok·i-; ugok·a-; ugo·i-te Ⓒ) **1** move; budge; stir:

Kare wa kega o shite, ugokemaseñ. (彼はけがをして, 動けません) He has hurt himself and *cannot move.* (⇨ ugokasu; ugoki)

2 (of a machine, vehicle, etc.) work; run:
Kono kuruma wa deñki de ugokimasu. (この車は電気で動きます) This car *runs* on electricity. / *Kono erebeetaa wa* ugoite imasu *ka?* (このエレベーターは動いていますか) *Is* this elevator *working?* (⇨ ugokasu)

3 act; get about:
Ima ugoku *no wa keñmee de wa arimaseñ.* (今動くのは賢明ではありません) It is not wise to *act* now.

4 (of feelings, emotions) be influenced; be moved; be touched:
Kare no kotoba ni watashi no kokoro wa ugoita. (彼の言葉に私の心は動いた) His words *swayed* my feelings. (⇨ ugoki; ugokasu)

uˈiˈsukiˈi ウイスキー *n.* whisk(e)y:
uisukii *no mizuwari* (ウイスキーの水割り) *whisky* and water.

uˈkabe·ru うかべる (浮かべる) *vt.* (ukabe-te [V]) **1** float; set afloat:
Kodomo-tachi wa ikada o kawa ni ukabeta. (子どもたちはいかだを川に浮かべた) The children *floated* a raft on the river. (⇨ ukabu)

2 show (one's feeling); express:
Sore o kiite, kare wa fumañ no iro o kao ni ukabeta. (それを聞いて, 彼は不満の色を顔に浮かべた) When he heard that, dissatisfaction *showed* on his face. / *Oñna-no-ko wa emi o* ukabete, *sono okurimono o uketotta.* (女の子は笑みを浮かべて, その贈り物を受け取った) The girl received the present *with* a smile. (⇨ ukabu)

3 recall (memory); recollect:
Watashi wa kookoo jidai no tanoshikatta omoide o atama ni ukabeta. (私は高校時代の楽しかった思い出を頭に浮かべた) I *recalled* the happy memories of my high school days. (⇨ ukabu)

uˈkab·u うかぶ (浮かぶ) *vt.* (ukab·i-; ukab·a-; ukañ-de [C])
1 float:
Mizuumi ni wa booto ga nañ-soo ka ukañde *ita.* (湖にはボートが何そうか浮かんでいた) There were several boats *floating* on the lake. (⇨ ukaberu)

2 (of an idea) come into; occur:
Meeañ ga atama ni ukañda. (名案が頭に浮かんだ) A good idea *came into* my head. (⇨ ukaberu)

3 (of tears, countenance) appear:
Kanojo no me ni namida ga ukañda. (彼女の目に涙が浮かんだ) Tears *appeared* in her eyes. / *Sore o kiite, kare no kao ni hotto shita hyoojoo ga* ukañda. (それを聞いて, 彼の顔にほっとした表情が浮かんだ) An expression of relief *appeared* on his face on hearing that. (⇨ ukaberu)

uˈkaga·u うかがう (伺う) *vt.* (ukaga·i-; ukagaw·a-; ukagat-te [C])
1 (*humble*) visit; call on [at]:
Asu o-taku ni ukagatte *mo yoroshii desu ka?* (あすお宅にうかがってもよろしいですか) Is it all right if I *call on* you at home tomorrow?

2 (*humble*) ask:
Ukagaitai *koto ga aru ñ desu ga.* (うかがいたいことがあるんですが) There are some questions I'*d like to ask* you. / *Chotto* ukagaimasu *ga, yuubiñkyoku wa doko desu ka?* (ちょっとうかがいますが, 郵便局はどこですか) *Excuse me*, but where is the post office?

3 (*humble*) hear; be told:
Anata wa teñkiñ sareta to ukagatte *orimasu ga.* (あなたは転勤されたとうかがっておりますが) I *hear* that you have been transferred.

uˈkeire·ru うけいれる (受け入れる) *vt.* (-ire-te [V]) accept (a demand, request, proposal, etc.); grant:
Kare-ra wa wareware no yookyuu o ukeireta. (彼らはわれわれの要求を受

け入れた) They *accepted* our demands. / *Watashi no teean wa* ukeirerarenakatta. (私の提案は受け入れられなかった) My proposal *was not accepted*.

u「kemi」 うけみ (受け身) *n.* **1** passive:
Kanojo wa nani o suru ni mo ukemi *da.* (彼女は何をするにも受け身だ) She is *passive* in everything she does.
2 passive sentence.
《⇨ -rareru; -reru》

u「kemochi うけもち (受け持ち) *n.* charge; responsibility:
Kono kurasu wa Tanaka sensee no ukemochi *desu.* (このクラスは田中先生の受け持ちです) This class is in the *charge* of Mr. Tanaka. / *Kondo watashi no* ukemochi *no basho ga kawarimashita.* (今度私の受け持ちの場所が変わりました) My area of *responsibility* has recently changed.
《⇨ ukemotsu》

u「kemots・u うけもつ (受け持つ) *vt.* (-moch・i-; -mot・a-; -mot-te Ⓒ) take charge of; be in charge of:
Dare ga kono kurasu o ukemotte *imasu ka?* (だれがこのクラスを受け持っていますか) Who *is in charge of* this class? 《⇨ ukemochi》

u「ke」・ru うける (受ける) *vt.* (uke-te Ⓥ) **1** catch:
Kare wa booru o katate de uketa. (彼はボールを片手で受けた) He *caught* the ball in one hand.
2 receive (an invitation); get; obtain (permission):
Watashi wa sono kai no shootai o ukete imasen. (私はその会の招待を受けていません) I *have* not *received* an invitation to that party. / *Watashi-tachi wa sono e o fukusee suru kyoka o* ukete imasu. (私たちはその絵を複製する許可を受けています) We *have* permission to reproduce that picture.
3 suffer:

Sono mura wa taifuu de ooki-na higai o uketa. (その村は台風で大きな被害を受けた) The village *suffered* heavy damage from the typhoon.
4 take (an examination); sit for:
Kanojo wa sono daigaku no nyuugaku shiken o uketa. (彼女はその大学の入学試験を受けた) She *took* the entrance exam to the university.
5 *vi.* be popular:
Sono sakka no shoosetsu wa josee no aida de ukete iru. (その作家の小説は女性の間で受けている) That author's novels *are popular* among women.

...o o-uke suru (...をお受けする) (*humble*) accept: *Anata no go-shootai o yorokonde* o-uke shimasu. (あなたのご招待を喜んでお受けします) I am very happy to *accept* your invitation. / *Tsutsushinde, kono taiyaku o* o-uke itashimasu. (謹んで、この大役をお受けいたします) I humbly *accept* this important task.

u「ketome・ru うけとめる (受け止める) *vt.* (-tome-te Ⓥ) **1** catch; stop; take:
booru o uketomeru (ボールを受け止める) *catch* a ball.
2 take (a situation); deal with:
Seefu wa jitai o reesee ni uketomete iru. (政府は事態を冷静に受け止めている) The government *takes* the situation calmly.

u「ketori うけとり (受取) *n.* **1** accepting:
Kare wa sono okurimono no uketori *o kobanda.* (彼はその贈り物の受け取りを拒んだ) He refused to *accept* the gift. 《⇨ uketoru》
2 receipt:
Kaimono no uketori *o morau no o wasureta.* (買物の受取をもらうのを忘れた) I forgot to get a *receipt* for what I had bought.
《⇨ ryooshuushoo (photo)》

u「ketor・u うけとる (受け取る) *vt.* (-tor・i-; -tor・a-; -tot-te Ⓒ) **1** re-

ceive; get; take; accept:
Sono tegami wa mada uketotte *imaseñ.* (その手紙はまだ受け取っていません) I *have not received* the letter yet. / *Riyuu no nai okurimono wa uketoru koto ga dekimaseñ.* (理由のない贈り物は受け取ることができません) I *cannot accept* a present given without reason. (⇨ uketori)

2 interpret; take:
Ima no wa joodañ to shite uketotte kudasai. (今のは冗談として受け取ってください) Please *take* what I have just said as a joke.

u「ketsugi うけつぎ (受け継ぎ) *n.* succession; inheritance. (⇨ uketsugu)

u「ketsug·u うけつぐ (受け継ぐ) *vt.* (-tsug·i-; -tsug·a-; -tsu·i-de C) succeed to; inherit:
Otto ga shiñda ato, tsuma ga jigyoo o uketsuida. (夫が死んだ後, 妻が事業を受け継いだ) The wife *succeeded to* the business after her husband's death. / *Kare no hitorimusume ga sono zaisañ o uketsuida.* (彼のひとり娘がその財産を受け継いだ) His only daughter *inherited* the estate. (⇨ uketsugi)

u「ketsuke うけつけ (受付) *n.*
1 receptionist; reception desk:
Kanojo wa byooiñ no uketsuke o shite imasu. (彼女は病院の受付をしています) She works as a *receptionist* in a hospital. / *Kono shorui wa uketsuke ni dashite kudasai.* (この書類は受付に出してください) Please hand in these papers at the *reception desk*. / *Hoñjitsu no uketsuke wa owarimashita.* (本日の受付は終わりました) *The office* has closed for the day.

2 acceptance:
Ashita kara mooshikomi no uketsuke o shimasu. (あしたから申し込みの受付をします) We will *accept* applications from tomorrow. (⇨ uketsukeru; ukeireru)

u「ketsuke·ru うけつける (受け付ける) *vt.* (-tsuke-te V) accept; receive:
Gañsho wa koñgetsu-matsu made uketsukemasu. (願書は今月末まで受け付けます) We *accept* applications until the end of this month. / *Kanojo wa hito no chuukoku o uketsukenai.* (彼女は人の忠告を受けつけない) She *will not heed* other people's warnings. (⇨ uketsuke)

u「ki[1] うき (雨季) *n.* the rainy season:
Uki ni haitta yoo da. (雨季に入ったようだ) It seems that we have entered *the rainy season*. / *Yatto uki ga aketa.* (やっと雨季が明けた) At last *the rainy season* is over. (↔ kañki[2]) (⇨ tsuyu[2])

u「ki[2] うき (浮き) *n.* float (on a fishing line).

u「kka]ri うっかり *adv.* (~ to; ~ suru) carelessly; inadvertently:
Ukkari (to) kare no yakusoku o wasurete shimatta. (うっかり(と)彼の約束を忘れてしまった) I *carelessly* forgot my appointment with him. / *Ukkari shite, himitsu o shabette shimatta.* (うっかりして, 秘密をしゃべってしまった) I *inadvertently* revealed the secret.

u「k·u うく (浮く) *vi.* (uk·i-; uk·a-; u·i-te C) **1** float; rise to the surface:
Koruku wa mizu ni ukimasu. (コルクは水に浮きます) Cork *floats* on water. / *Fuuseñ ga kuuchuu ni uite iru.* (風船が空中に浮いている) A balloon *is floating* in the air.

2 (of cost, expense) be saved:
Kare no kuruma ni nosete moratta no de takushii-dai ga uita. (彼の車に乗せてもらったのでタクシー代が浮いた) I got a lift in his car, so the taxi fare *was saved*.

u「ma[1] うま (馬) *n.* horse:
uma ni noru (馬に乗る) ride a *horse*

/ uma *ni matagaru* (馬にまたがる) sit astride a *horse* / uma *kara oriru* (馬から降りる) dismount from a *horse* / *Kare wa* uma ni notte *machi made itta.* (彼は馬に乗って町まで行った) He went to town *on horseback.*

uma ga au (〜が合う) get along well: *Yamada to wa doo-iu wake ka* uma ga au. (山田とはどういう訳か馬が合う) I don't know why, but I *get along well* with Yamada.

uma no mimi ni neñbutsu (〜の耳に念仏) don't listen to: *Kare ni chuui shite mo,* uma no mimi ni neñbutsu *datta.* (彼は注意しても，馬の耳に念仏だった) He *was deaf* to my warning.

u˺ma˼·i うまい *a.* (-ku) **1** skillful; good:
Suzuki-sañ wa sukii ga umai. (鈴木さんはスキーがうまい) Mr. Suzuki is *good* at skiing. / *Kare wa uñteñ ga* umaku *natta.* (彼は運転がうまくなった) He has become *skillful* at driving. ((⇨ joozu))
2 (of an idea, a project, etc.) great; good:
Sore wa umai *kañgae da.* (それはうまい考えだ) That is a *great* idea.
3 (of food) delicious; good:
★ Used mainly by men.
Kono meroñ wa umai. (このメロンはうまい) This melon is *delicious.*
4 successful; profitable; lucky:
Subete umaku *ikimashita.* (すべてうまくいきました) Everything worked out *well.* / *Nani-ka* umai *hanashi wa arimaseñ ka?* (何かうまい話はありませんか) Haven't you heard anything *favorable?*

u˺mare うまれ (生まれ) *n.* birth; descent:
Kanojo wa umare *ga yoi.* (彼女は生まれが良い) She is of good *birth.* / *O-umare wa dochira desu ka?* (お生まれはどちらですか) Where do you *come from?* / *Watashi wa* umare *mo sodachi mo Tookyoo desu.* (私は生まれも育ちも東京です) I *was born* and brought up in Tokyo.
((⇨ umareru))

u˺mare·ru うまれる (生まれる) *vi.*
(umare-te V) **1** be born:
Watashi ga umareta *no wa señkyuuhyaku rokujuu-neñ desu.* (私が生まれたのは 1960 年です) The year I *was born* was 1960. / *Kanojo wa moo sugu kodomo ga* umaremasu. (彼女はもうすぐ子どもが生まれます) A child *will* soon *be born* to her.
((↔ shinu)) ((⇨ umu¹; umare))
2 come into existence:
Kuudetaa de guñji-seekeñ ga umareta. (クーデターで軍事政権が生まれた) A military government *came into existence* through a coup d'état.
((⇨ umare; umu¹))

u˺maretsuki うまれつき (生まれ付き) *n., adv.* by nature:
umaretsuki *no sainoo* (生まれつきの才能) a *natural* talent / *Kanojo no koe ga ii no wa* umaretsuki *desu.* (彼女の声がいいのは生まれつきです) Her fine voice is something she *was born with.*

u˺mar·u うまる (埋まる) *vt.* (umar·i·; umar·a-; umat-te C) be buried; be filled up:
Yamakuzure de go-niñ ga umatta. (山崩れで 5 人が埋まった) Five people *were buried* by the landslide. / *Kaijoo wa hito de* umatta. (会場は人で埋まった) The hall *was filled* with people. ((⇨ umeru))

u˺me うめ (梅) *n.* ume; Japanese apricot; *Prunus mume.* ★ Often mistakenly called 'plum.'
ume *no ki* (梅の木) an *ume* tree.
((⇨ illus. (next page)))

u˺meboshi うめぼし (梅干し) *n.* pickled Japanese apricot.
((⇨ photo (next page)))

u˺mekigo˺e うめきごえ (呻き声) *n.* groan; moan:
Dare-ka no umekigoe *ga suru.* (だれ

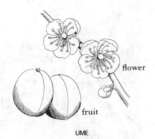

flower

fruit

UME

UMEBOSHI

かのうめき声がする) I hear someone's *groans*.

u˺me˺k·u うめく（呻く）*vi.* (ume-k·i-; umek·a-; ume·i-te C̲) groan:
Kare wa ashikubi o kujiki, itakute umeita.（彼は足首をくじき、痛くてうめいた）He sprained his ankle and *groaned* in pain.

u˺me·ru うめる（埋める）*vt.* (ume-te V̲) **1** bury; fill in:
Kanojo wa gomi o atsumete, niwa ni umeta.（彼女はごみを集めて、庭に埋めた）She gathered up the trash and *buried* it in the garden. / *Kuuran o tekitoo na go de* ume nasai.（空欄を適当な語で埋めなさい）*Fill in* the blanks with a suitable word. 《⇨ uzumeru》
2 make up for (a loss, deficit):
Akaji o umenakereba naranai.（赤字を埋めなければならない）We *have to make up* the deficit. 《⇨ umaru》

u˺metate うめたて（埋め立て）*n.* land reclamation:
umetate-*kooji*（埋め立て工事）*reclamation* work / umetate-*chi*（埋め立て地）*reclaimed* land.
《⇨ umetateru》

u˺metate˺·ru うめたてる（埋め立てる）*vt.* (-tate-te V̲) reclaim; fill up; recover:
Umi o umetatete, *koojoo o tsukuru keekaku desu.*（海を埋め立てて、工場を作る計画です）It is a plan to *reclaim* land from the sea and build a factory. 《⇨ umetate》

u˺mi[1] うみ（海）*n.* sea; ocean:
umi *de oyogu*（海で泳ぐ）swim in *the sea* / *Kyoo no* umi *wa odayaka da* [*arete iru*].（きょうの海は穏やかだ［荒れている］）*The sea* today is calm [rough]. 《↔ riku》

u˺mi[2] うみ（膿）*n.* pus; discharge:
Kizu ga umi *o motte iru.*（傷がうみをもっている）The wound has formed *pus.* / *Kono odeki wa hayaku* umi *o dashita hoo ga ii.*（このおできは早くうみを出したほうがいい）You had better press out the *pus* from this boil soon. 《⇨ umu[2]》

u˺m·u[1] うむ（生む）*vt.* (um·i-; um·a-; uñ-de C̲) **1** give birth to; breed; lay:
Kanojo wa oñna-no-ko o uñda.（彼女は女の子を生んだ）She *gave birth to* a girl. / *Kono niwatori wa mainichi tamago o* umimasu.（このにわとりは毎日卵を生みます）This chicken *lays* an egg every day. 《⇨ umareru》
2 produce; give rise to; yield:
Kare wa Nihoñ ga uñda *saidai no sakka no hitori desu.*（彼は日本が生んだ最大の作家の一人です）He is one of the greatest authors Japan *has produced.* / *Mazushisa ga hañzai o* umu *koto ga ooi.*（貧しさが犯罪を生むことが多い）Poverty often *gives rise to* crime. / *Kono tooshi wa rieki o* umi-soo *mo nai.*（この投資は利益を生みそうもない）This investment does not seem likely to *yield* a profit. 《⇨ umareru》

u˺m·u[2] うむ（膿む）*vi.* (um·i-; um·a-; uñ-de C̲) suppurate; fester; form pus:

Kizu ga uñde kita. (傷がうんできた) The wound *has suppurated.* ((⇨ umi²))

u⌐mu³ うむ (有無) *n.* existence; presence:
Anata no keekeñ no umu wa toimaseñ. (あなたの経験の有無は問いません) We do not mind *whether you have experience or not.*

umu o iwasezu (～を言わせず) willy-nilly; forcibly: Umu o iwasezu, *kare ni sono shigoto o yaraseta.* (有無を言わせず, 彼にその仕事をやらせた) I forced him to do the job, *irrespective of whether or not he wanted to.*

u⌐ñ¹ うん (運) *n.* luck; fortune; chance:
Kare wa uñ ga ii [warui]. (彼は運がいい[悪い]) He is *lucky [unlucky]*. / Uñ *ga muite kita zo.* (運が向いてきたぞ) *Luck* has turned in my favor. / *Kare mo* uñ *no tsuki da.* (彼も運のつきだ) His *luck* has run out. / Uñ-yoku *shuu-deñsha ni maniatta.* (運よく終電車に間に合った) *Luckily,* I caught the last train. / Uñ-waruku *sono hoñ wa shinagire datta.* (運悪くその本は品切れだった) *Unfortunately,* the book was out of stock.

u⌐ñ² うん *int.* (*informal*) all right:
*"Kore tetsudatte kureru kai." "*Uñ, *ii yo."* (「これ手伝ってくれるかい」「うん, いいよ」) *"Can you help me with this?" "Okay, fine."*

uñ to iu (～と言う) say yes; *Kare wa nakanaka* uñ to iwanakatta. (彼はなかなかうんと言わなかった) He *just would not say yes.*

u⌐nagi うなぎ (鰻) *n.* eel:
unagi *no kabayaki* (うなぎのかば焼き) broiled *eel* / unagi-*doñburi* (うなぎどんぶり) a bowl of rice topped with broiled *eel* / unajuu (うな重) broiled eel on rice in a lacquered box. ((⇨ photo (right)))

u⌐na⌐r·u うなる (唸る) *vi.* (unar·i-; unar·a-; unat-te [C]) **1** groan;

UNAJUU

UNAGI KABAYAKI SIGN

moan; growl:
Kare wa kurushiñde unatte ita. (彼は苦しんでうなっていた) He *was groaning* with pain.
2 (of a motor, engine, etc.) howl; roar:
Torakku ga unari-nagara *saka o nobotte itta.* (トラックがうなりながら坂を上って行った) The truck climbed the slope *with a loud noise.*

u⌐nazuk·u うなずく (頷く) *vi.* (unazuk·i-; unazuk·a-; unazu·i-te [C]) nod; approve:
Kare wa shoodaku shite, unazuita. (彼は承諾して, うなずいた) He *nodded* in agreement.

u⌐ñchiñ うんちん (運賃) *n.* fare; charge; freight:
Tookyoo kara Oosaka made no uñchiñ *wa ikura desu ka?* (東京から大阪までの運賃はいくらですか) How much is the *fare* from Tokyo to Osaka? ((⇨ ryookiñ))

u⌐ñdoo うんどう (運動) *n.* **1** exercise; sport:
Aruku no wa ii uñdoo *desu.* (歩くのはいい運動です) Walking is good *exercise.* / uñdoo-*busoku* (運動不足) lack of *exercise* / uñdoo-gutsu (運動靴) *sneakers.*
2 movement; campaign:
Kaku-chi de koogai hañtai no uñdoo *ga okite imasu.* (各地で公害反対の運動が起きています) Anti-pol-

lution *campaigns* have started in various districts. / seeji-uṅdoo (政治運動) a political *movement* / seṅkyo-uṅdoo (選挙運動) an election campaign.

uṅdoo (o) suru (～(を)する) *vi.*
1 take exercise: *Isha kara* motto uṅdoo (o) suru *yoo ni iwareta.* (医者からもっと運動(を)するように言われた) I was told by my doctor to *do more exercise.*
2 campaign:
Kaṅkeesha wa hooaṅ seeritsu no tame ni, sakaṅ ni uṅdoo shite iru. (関係者は法案成立のために，盛んに運動している) The interested parties *are campaigning* vigorously for the passage of the bill.

u⌐ṅdoojoo うんどうじょう (運動場) *n.* playground; playing field: uṅdoojoo *ni atsumaru* (運動場に集まる) assemble in the *playground.*

u⌐ṅdo⌐okai うんどうかい (運動会) *n.*
1 sports day:
Uṅdookai *wa maitoshi juu-gatsu ni okonawaremasu.* (運動会は毎年10月に行われます) Our *sports day* is held every year in October.
2 athletic meet.

UṄDOOKAI SCENE

u⌐ṅee うんえい (運営) *n.* management; operation; administration: *Kare wa kaisha no* uṅee *ni shippai shita.* (彼は会社の運営に失敗した) He failed in the *management* of the company. / uṅee-*hi* (運営費) *operating* expenses / uṅee-*iiṅkai*

(運営委員会) a *steering* committee.

uṅee (o) suru (～(を)する) *vt.* manage; operate; administer: *jigyoo o* uṅee suru (事業を運営する) *manage* a business.

u⌐ṅga うんが (運河) *n.* canal.

u⌐ṅmee うんめい (運命) *n.* fate; destiny:
Uṅmee *ni mi o makaseru shika nai.* (運命に身をまかせるしかない) There is nothing for it but to resign ourselves to *fate.* ((⇨ uṅ))

u⌐ṅpaṅ うんぱん (運搬) *n.* carriage; conveyance; transport: *kamotsu no* uṅpaṅ (貨物の運搬) the *carriage* of goods.

uṅpaṅ suru (～する) *vt.* carry; convey; transport: *Kazai-doogu wa subete torakku de* uṅpaṅ shite moratta. (家財道具はすべてトラックで運搬してもらった) I *had* all the household goods *moved* by truck.

u⌐ṅteṅ うんてん (運転) *n.* driving; operation:
*Watashi wa itsu-mo aṅzeṅ-*uṅteṅ *o kokorogakete imasu.* (私はいつも安全運転を心がけています) I always take care to *drive* safely. / *Kono erebeetaa wa ima* uṅteṅ *ga tomatte imasu.* (このエレベーターは今運転が止まっています) This elevator *is not running* now. / *Kono kikai wa shirooto ni wa* uṅteṅ *dekimaseṅ.* (この機械は素人には運転できません) An inexperienced person cannot *operate* this machine.

uṅteṅ (o) suru (～(を)する) *vi., vt.* drive; run; operate: *Ki o tsukete* uṅteṅ shi nasai. (気をつけて運転しなさい) *Please drive* carefully. / *Neṅmatsu ni wa riṅji deṅsha ga* uṅteṅ saremasu. (年末には臨時電車が運転されます) Special trains *are run* at the year-end.

u⌐ṅte⌐ṅshu うんてんしゅ (運転手) *n.* driver; chauffeur; motorman: *takushii [torakku] no* uṅteṅshu (タクシー[トラック]の運転手) a taxi

[truck] *driver* / *basu no* uñteñshu
(バスの運転手) a bus *driver* / *kikañ-
sha no* uñteñshu (機関車の運転手)
an *engineer*; a *engine driver*.

u⌐ñto うんと *adv.* (*informal*)
hard; severely; much:
Ii ko da kara uñto *beñkyoo shi nasai yo.* (いい子だからうんと勉強しなさい
よ) You are a good boy, so make
sure you study *hard*. / *Kare wa
zaisañ o* uñto *motte iru.* (彼は財産
をうんと持っている) He has a *large*
fortune.

u⌐nubore うぬぼれ（自惚れ）*n.*
conceit; self-conceit; vanity:
Kanojo wa unubore *ga tsuyoi.* (彼
女はうぬぼれが強い) She is full of *conceit*. (⇨ unuboreru)

u⌐nubore·ru うぬぼれる（自惚れる）
vi. (unubore-te Ⓥ) flatter oneself; be conceited:
Kare wa jibuñ ni sainoo ga aru to
unuborete ita. (彼は自分に才能がある
とうぬぼれていた) He *fancied himself*
to have talent. (⇨ unubore)

u⌐ñyu うんゆ（運輸）*n.* transport:
uñyu-*gaisha* (運輸会社) a *transport*
company.

U⌐ñyu-da⌐ijiñ うんゆだいじん（運輸
大臣）*n.* Minister of Transport.

U⌐ñyu⌐-shoo うんゆしょう（運輸省）
n. Ministry of Transport.
(⇨ shoo¹ (table))

u⌐o うお（魚）*n.* fish. (⇨ sakana)

u⌐oi⌐chiba うおいちば（魚市場）*n.*
fish market. (⇨ ichiba (photo))

u⌐ra うら（裏）*n.* **1** back; the
wrong side; the reverse:
fuutoo no ura (封筒の裏) the *back*
of an envelope / *Kochira wa kami
no* ura *desu.* (こちらは紙の裏です)
This is the *wrong side* of the
paper. / *Ura ni tsuzuku.* (裏に続く)
Please turn over. (↔ omote)
2 back door:
Kare wa ura *kara dete itta.* (彼は裏
から出て行った) He left through the
back door. (↔ omote)

3 back; rear:
Uchi no ura *ni wa kawa ga nagarete imasu.* (家の裏には川が流れていま
す) There is a stream running
past the *back* of our house.
(↔ mae)
4 (of baseball) the second half:
Kyuu-kai no ura *o nokosu nomi to
narimashita.* (9回の裏を残すのみとな
りました) There is now only *the
second half* of the ninth inning
left. (↔ omote)
5 hidden part; shady side:
ura *no imi* (裏の意味) a *hidden*
meaning / *Kare wa sono keekaku
no* ura *o minuita.* (彼はその計画の裏
を見抜いた) He figured out the *secret* part of the plan.

ura o kaku (～をかく) outsmart:
Kare wa watashi no ura *o kakoo
to shita.* (彼は私の裏をかこうとした)
He tried to *outwit* me.

u⌐raga⌐eshi うらがえし（裏返し）*n.*
inside out:
Kimi no seetaa wa uragaeshi *desu
yo.* (君のセーターは裏返しですよ) Your
sweater is *inside out*. / *Shatsu o*
uragaeshi *ni kite shimatta.* (シャツを
裏返しに着てしまった) I put my undershirt on *inside out*.
(⇨ uragaesu)

u⌐raga⌐es·u うらがえす（裏返す）*vt.*
(-gaesh·i-; -gaes·a-; -gaesh·i-te
Ⓒ) turn over; turn inside out:
kami o uragaesu (紙を裏返す) *turn
over* a sheet of paper / *Anata wa
kutsushita o* uragaeshite *haite
imasu yo.* (あなたは靴下を裏返してはい
ていますよ) You are wearing your
socks *inside out*. (⇨ uragaeshi)

u⌐ragi⌐r·u うらぎる（裏切る）*vt.*
(-gir·i-; -gir·a-; -git-te Ⓒ)
betray; disappoint (someone's
hopes):
Kare wa watashi o uragitta. (彼は
私を裏切った) He *betrayed* me. /
Kekka wa wareware no kitai o
uragitta. (結果はわれわれの期待を裏切

った）The result *fell short of* our expectations.

uˈraguchi うらぐち（裏口）*n.* back door [entrance]:
Kare wa uraguchi kara dete ikimashita.（彼は裏口から出て行きました）He went out by the *back door.*

urˈaguchi-nyuˈugaku うらぐちにゅうがく（裏口入学）*n.* backdoor admission to a university:
Kono daigaku wa uraguchi-nyuugaku o shiyoo to shite mo dame desu.（この大学は裏口入学をしようとしてもだめです）It is no use trying to *buy your way into this university.*

uˈramiˈ うらみ（恨み）*n.* grudge; spite; ill-feeling:
Watashi wa anata ni nañ no urami *mo motte imaseñ.*（私はあなたに何の恨みも持っていません）I hold absolutely no *grudges* against you. 《⇨ uramu》

uˈramoñ うらもん（裏門）*n.* back [rear] gate. 《↔ omotemoñ》

uˈraˈm·u うらむ（恨む）*vt.* (ura-m·i-; uram·a-; urañ-de Ⓒ) bear a grudge; think ill of:
Kanojo wa kimi o sugoku urañde *iru yo.*（彼女は君をすごく恨んでいるよ）She *bears* deep *resentment* toward you. / *Warugi wa nakatta ñ da. Watashi o* uramanai de *kure.*（悪気はなかったんだ. 私を恨まないでくれ）I meant no harm. Please *do not hold a grudge* against me. 《⇨ urami》

uˈra-omote うらおもて（裏表）*n.* the top side and the bottom side; both sides:
kami no ura-omote *ni iñsatsu suru*（紙の裏表に印刷する）print on *both sides* of the paper.
ura-omote ga aru（〜がある）two-faced: *Ano hito wa* ura-omote *ga aru.*（あの人は裏表がある）He is a *double-dealer.*

uˈrayamashiˈ·i うらやましい（羨ましい）*a.* (-ku) envious; jealous:

urayamashii *seekatsu*（うらやましい生活）a life *to be envied* / *Anata no nagai kyuuka ga* urayamashii.（あなたの長い休暇がうらやましい）I am *jealous* of your long holidays. / *Kanojo wa sono hanashi o kiite,* urayamashiku *omotta.*（彼女はその話を聞いて, うらやましく思った）She felt *jealous* when she heard the story. / *Ano futari wa* urayamashii *hodo naka ga ii.*（あの二人はうらやましいほど仲がいい）The two of them get on so well together that I feel *envious.* 《⇨ urayamu》

uˈrayaˈm·u うらやむ（羨む）*vt.* (ura-yam·i-; urayam·a-; urayañ-de Ⓒ) envy; be envious:
Miñna kare no zaisañ o urayañda.（みんな彼の財産をうらやんだ）Everyone *envied* him his fortune. 《⇨ urayamashii》

uˈre·ru¹ うれる（売れる）*vi.* (ure-te Ⓥ) **1** sell; be sold:
Sono hoñ wa yoku urete imasu.（その本はよく売れています）That book *is selling* well.
2 (of an entertainer, etc.) be popular; be famous:
Sono kashu no na wa sekeñ ni yoku urete imasu.（その歌手の名は世間によく売れています）The name of the singer *is well known* to everybody.

uˈreˈ·ru² うれる（熟れる）*vi.* (ure-te Ⓥ) ripen:
Kono suika wa mada urete inai.（このすいかはまだ熟れていない）This watermelon *is not ripe* yet.

uˈreshiˈ·i うれしい（嬉しい）*a.* (-ku) glad; happy; pleased:
Anata ni o-ai dekite, ureshii *desu.*（あなたにお会いできて, うれしいです）I am very *glad* to meet you. / *Oide itadakereba,* ureshiku *omoimasu.*（お出でいただければ, うれしく思います）I would be *delighted* if you could come. / *Kare ga umaku itta to kiite,* ureshikatta.（彼がうまくいったと

聞いて, うれしかった) I was *happy* to hear that he had succeeded.

uˈri うり (瓜) *n.* type of melon; vegetable such as a gourd, squash, cucumber, etc.

uri-futatsu (うり二つ) double(s); look-alike(s): *Kare to kare no nii-sañ wa* uri-futatsu *da.*(彼と彼の兄さんはうり二つだ) He and his older brother *are as alike as two peas in the pod.*

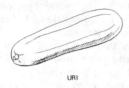

URI

uˈriage うりあげ (売り上げ) *n.* sales; proceeds; turnover: uriage *o nobasu* (売り上げを伸ばす) increase the *sales* / *Koñgetsu no* uriage *wa sañbyakumañ-eñ datta.* (今月の売り上げは 300 万円だった) *Proceeds* for this month were three million yen. / *Otaku no kaisha no neñkañ* uriage *wa dono kurai desu ka?* (お宅の会社の年間売り上げはどのくらいですか) How much is the annual *turnover* of your company?

uˈriba うりば (売り場) *n.* counter; department; office: *omocha [buñboogu]* uriba (おもちゃ[文房具]売り場) the toy [stationery] *department* / *Kippu* uriba *wa doko desu ka?* (切符売り場はどこですか) Where is the ticket *office?*

uˈridashi うりだし (売り出し) *n.* opening sale; bargain [special] sale: *Natsu-mono no* uridashi *ga hajimatta.*(夏物の売り出しが始まった) The *sale* of summer goods has started. / *neñmatsu* oo-uridashi (年末大売り出し) a year-end *bargain sale.* (⇨ uridasu)

uridashi-chuu no (～中の) up-and-coming: *Kanojo wa ima* uri-dashi-chuu no *kashu desu.* (彼女は今売り出し中の歌手です) She is a singer *coming into popularity.* 《⇨ niñki》

uˈridaˈs·u うりだす (売り出す) *vt.* (-dash·i-; -das·a-; -dash·i-te C)
1 put on sale; offer for sale: *Kono kuruma wa* uridashita *bakari desu.* (この車は売り出したばかりです) This car *has* just *been put on sale.* 《⇨ uridashi》
2 win a reputation; become popular: *Sono kashu wa atarashii kyoku de* uridashita.(その歌手は新しい曲で売り出した) The singer *made her reputation* with a new song. 《⇨ uridashi》

uˈrikire うりきれ (売り切れ) *n.* sell-out; being out of stock: *Sono shiai no nyuujookeñ wa* urikire desu.(その試合の入場券は売り切れです) The tickets for the match *have sold out.* 《⇨ urikireru》

uˈrikireˈ·ru うりきれる (売り切れる) *vi.* (-kire-te V) be sold out; be out of stock: *Sono zasshi no shiñneñ-goo wa* urikiremashita.(その雑誌の新年号は売り切れました) The New Year issue of that magazine *has been sold out.* 《⇨ urikire》

uˈrimono うりもの (売り物) *n.*
1 article for sale: *Kono shina wa* urimono *de wa ari-maseñ.* (この品は売り物ではありません) This *article* is not *for sale.*
2 selling point: *Kono mise wa saabisu ga* urimono *desu.* (この店はサービスが売り物です) Good service is the *selling point* of this store.

uˈroko うろこ (鱗) *n.* (of fish) scale.

uˈrouro うろうろ *adv.* (～ to; ～ suru) (an aimless or uneasy way of walking):

Heñ na otoko ga urouro (*to*) aruki-
mawatte iru *kara, ki o tsuketa hoo
ga yoi.* (変な男がうろうろ(と)歩き回って
いるから, 気をつけたほうがよい) There is
a strange fellow *hanging around,*
so you had better be careful.

u｢r･u¹ うる (売る) *vt.* (ur･i-; ur･a-;
ut-te Ⓒ) **1** sell:
Kare no mise wa buñboogu o utte
iru. (彼の店は文房具を売っている) His
store *sells* stationery. / *Watashi
wa ano rajio o ichimañ-eñ de kare
ni* utta. (私はあのラジオを1万円で彼に
売った) I *sold* him that radio for
10,000 yen. 《↔ kau¹》
2 betray (one's country, organization, friend, etc.); sell out:
Kare wa supai to natte, kuni o
utta. (彼はスパイとなって, 国を売った)
He became a spy and *betrayed*
his country.

u｢ru² うる (得る) *vt.* (e-te Ⓥ) (*literary*) gain:
Kare no hanashi wa uru *tokoro ga
ookatta.* (彼の話は得る所が多かった)
There was much to *gain* from
his talk. 《⇨ eru》

u｢rusa｣･i うるさい (煩い) *a.* (-ku)
1 noisy:
urusai *kodomo-tachi* (うるさい子ども
たち) *noisy* children / *Yuube wa
inu ga* urusaku *hoete ita.* (ゆうべ犬
がうるさくほえていた) There was a
dog barking *noisily* last night. /
Urusai zo. (うるさいぞ) Stop that
noise! 《⇨ yakamashii》
2 (of a demand, a request, etc.)
annoying; nagging:
*Kodomo ga omocha o katte kure
to* urusai. (子どもがおもちゃを買ってくれ
とうるさい) My child is *pestering*
me to buy him a toy. / *Haha wa
itsu-mo beñkyoo shiro to* urusaku
iu. (母はいつも勉強しろとうるさく言う)
My mother is always *on at* me
with her "Study, study." 《⇨ ya-
kamashii》
3 strict:

Watashi-tachi no señsee wa urusai.
(私たちの先生はうるさい) Our teacher
is *strict.*
4 particular:
Chichi wa koohii no aji ni urusai.
(父はコーヒーの味にうるさい) My fa-
ther is *particular* about the taste
of his coffee.

u｢rushi うるし (漆) *n.* Japanese
lacquer; japan. 《⇨ shikki¹》

u｢ryoo うりょう (雨量) *n.* rainfall;
precipitation.

u｢sagi うさぎ (兎) *n.* rabbit; hare.

u｢shi うし (牛) *n.* cattle; bull;
cow; ox:
ushi *no chichi o shiboru* (牛の乳を
絞る) milk a *cow.*

u｢shina･u うしなう (失う) *vt.* (ushi-
na･i-; ushinaw･a-; ushinat-te
Ⓒ) **1** lose; be deprived of:
*Kanojo wa kodomo no toki, chi-
chi-oya o* ushinatta. (彼女は子どもの
とき, 父親を失った) She *lost* her
father when she was a child. /
Fukeeki ni wa shoku o ushinau
hito ga ooi. (不景気には職を失う人が
多い) In hard times, there are
many people who *lose* their jobs.
2 miss (an opportunity):
Watashi wa zekkoo no kikai o
ushinatte shimatta. (私は絶好の機
会を失ってしまった) I *have missed* a
golden opportunity.

u｢shiro うしろ (後ろ) *n.* **1** back;
rear:
ushiro *kara go-bañme no retsu* (後
ろから5番目の列) the fifth row
from the *back* / *Watashi wa kuruma no* ushiro *no seki ni suwatta.*
(私は車の後ろの席に座った) I sat in
the *back* seat of the car. / *Moo
sukoshi* ushiro *ni sagatte kudasai.*
(もう少し後ろに下がってください) Please
move *back* a bit more. 《↔ mae》
2 behind:
Ushiro kara osanai de kudasai. (後
ろから押さないでください) Stop push-
ing from *behind.* / *Kodomo wa*

chichi-oya no ushiro *ni tsuite aruite ita.* (子どもは父親の後ろについて歩いていた) The child was walking along *behind* her father. ⟪↔ mae⟫

uˈshiroˈashi うしろあし (後ろ足) *n.* hind leg. ⟪↔ maeashi⟫

uˈso うそ (嘘) *n.* **1** lie; fib:

> **USAGE**
> In some situations, '*uso*' has lost the original sense of 'lie,' and is often used, especially by young people, as a response meaning 'Is that really true?'

Kare wa heeki de uso *o tsuku.* (彼は平気でうそをつく) He makes no bones about telling *lies.* / *"Kare wa chikaku kekkoñ suru soo da yo." "*Uso *deshoo."* (「彼は近く結婚するそうだよ」「うそでしょう」) "I hear that he is getting married quite soon." "*No kidding.*"

2 falseness:
Sono uwasa wa uso *da to wakatta.* (そのうわさはうそだとわかった) I found out that the rumor was *false.*

uˈsugi うすぎ (薄着) *n.* being lightly dressed:
Watashi wa dochira ka to ieba, neñjuu usugi *desu.* (私はどちらかと言えば, 年中薄着です) I would say that I am rather *lightly clothed* all the year round. ⟪↔ atsugi⟫
usugi (o) suru (～(を)する) *vi.* be lightly dressed; wear light clothes: *Kono samui no ni* usugi o suru *no wa karada ni yoku arimaseñ.* (この寒いのに薄着をするのは体によくありません) It is not good for your health to *wear light clothes* when it is this cold.

uˈsugura·i うすぐらい (薄暗い) *a.* (-ku) dim; dusky:
usugurai *heya* (薄暗い部屋) a *dimly-lit* room / *Dañdañ* usuguraku *natte kita.* (だんだん薄暗くなってきた) It gradually got *dark.* ⟪⇨ kurai[1]⟫

uˈsu·i うすい (薄い) *a.* (-ku)
1 thin:
usui *kami* [*hoñ*] (薄い紙[本]) a *thin* sheet of paper [book]. ⟪↔ atsui[3]⟫
2 (of taste) weak; thin; lightly-seasoned:
Kono koohii wa usui. (このコーヒーは薄い) This coffee is *weak.* / *Suupu ga* usui. (スープが薄い) The soup is *watery.* / *Dasareta ryoori wa aji ga* usukatta. (出された料理は味が薄かった) The dishes served *lacked flavor.* ⟪↔ koi[1]⟫
3 (of color) light:
usui *midori iro* (薄い緑色) *light* green. ⟪↔ koi[1]⟫
4 thin; sparse:
Chichi no kami ga usuku *natte kita.* (父の髪が薄くなってきた) My father's hair has gotten *thin.*
5 (of possibility) few; little:
Kare no tooseñ no nozomi wa usui. (彼の当選の望みは薄い) There is *little* hope of his being elected.

uˈsume·ru うすめる (薄める) *vt.* (usume-te [V]) dilute; water down:
Kanojo wa koohii o oyu de usumeta. (彼女はコーヒーをお湯で薄めた) She *made* the coffee *weaker* by adding hot water.

uˈtaˈ うた (歌) *n.* **1** song:
Kanojo wa watashi no suki na uta *o utatta.* (彼女は私の好きな歌を歌った) She sang my favorite *song.* / *Watashi wa Misora Hibari no* uta *ga suki desu.* (私は美空ひばりの歌が好きです) I love the *songs* of Hibari Misora. ⟪⇨ utau⟫
2 'tanka' poem:
uta *o yomu* (歌を詠む) compose a '*tanka*' *poem.* ⟪⇨ tañka[3]⟫

uˈtagai うたがい (疑い) *n.*
1 doubt:
Kimi no seekoo wa utagai *arimaseñ.* (きみの成功は疑いありません) I have no *doubt* about your success. ⟪⇨ utagau⟫
2 suspicion:

utagai o idaku (疑いを抱く) have a *suspicion* / utagai o harasu (疑いを晴らす) clear a *suspicion* / Watashi ni utagai o kakenai de kudasai. Watashi wa nani mo shite imaseñ. (私に疑いをかけないでください. 私は何もしていません) Please don't throw *suspicion* on me. I have not done anything at all. (⇨ utagau)

u｢**taga·u** うたがう (疑う) *vt.* (uta-ga·i-; utagaw·a·-; utagat-te Ⓒ) doubt; suspect: Kare wa watashi no iu koto o utagatte iru yoo da. (彼は私の言うことを疑っているようだ) It seems that he *doubts* what I say. / Miñna kare ga sono jikeñ ni kañkee ga aru mono to utagatte iru. (みんな彼がその事件に関係があるものと疑っている) Everybody *suspects* that he has some connection with the affair. ((⇨ utagai))

u｢**tago｣e** うたごえ (歌声) *n.* singing voice.

u｢**ta·u** うたう (歌う) *vt.* (uta·i-; utaw·a·-; utat-te Ⓒ) sing: Haha-oya wa komori-uta o utatte ita. (母親は子守歌を歌っていた) The mother *was singing* a lullaby. / Saa ooki-na koe de utaimashoo. (さあ, 大きな声で歌いましょう) Now, *let's sing* in a loud voice. ((⇨ uta))

u｢**teñ** うてん (雨天) *n.* rainy weather; rain: Uteñ *no baai wa eñsoku wa chuushi desu.* (雨天の場合は遠足は中止です) In the event of *rain*, the excursion will be canceled. / Shiai wa uteñ juñeñ *desu.* (試合は雨天順延です) The game *will be put off until the first fine day.* (↔ seeteñ; doñteñ))

u｢**ts·u**[1] うつ (打つ) *vt.* (uch·i-; ut·a·-; ut-te Ⓒ) **1** hit; strike; knock: batto de booru o utsu (バットでボールを打つ) *hit* a ball with a bat / kana-zuchi de kugi o utsu (金づちでくぎを

打つ) *strike* a nail with a hammer / Sono ko wa koroñde kabe de atama o utta. (その子はころんで壁で頭を打った) The child fell and *knocked* his head against the wall. **2** (of a clock) strike: Tokee ga choodo hachi-ji o utta. (時計がちょうど8時を打った) The clock *has* just *struck* eight.

u｢**ts·u**[2] うつ (撃つ) *vt.* (uch·i-; ut·a·-; ut-te Ⓒ) shoot; fire: Keekañ wa nigete iku hañniñ o pisutoru de utta. (警官は逃げていく犯人をピストルで撃った) The policeman *shot* the escaping criminal with his pistol. / Ryooshi wa kuma o neratte, raifuru o utta. (猟師は熊をねらって, ライフルを撃った) The hunter aimed at the bear and *fired* his rifle.

u｢**tsukushi｣·i** うつくしい (美しい) *a.* (-ku) (*slightly literary*) beautiful; pretty; handsome: utsukushii josee (美しい女性) a *beautiful* woman / utsukushii keshiki (美しい景色) *lovely* scenery / utsukushii koe (美しい声) a *sweet* voice / utsukushii yuujoo (美しい友情) a *beautiful* friendship / Hanayome wa itsu-mo yori issoo utsukushiku mieta. (花嫁はいつもよりいっそう美しく見えた) The bride looked even more *beautiful* than usual. ((⇨ kiree))

u｢**tsumuk·u** うつむく (俯く) *vi.* (-muk·i-; -muk·a·-; -mu·i-te Ⓒ) look down; hang one's head: Sono oñna-no-ko wa hazukashi-gatte utsumuita. (その女の子は恥ずかしがってうつむいた) The girl shyly *lowered her head.*

u｢**tsurikawari** うつりかわり (移り変わり) *n.* change; transition: kisetsu no utsurikawari (季節の移り変わり) the *changes* of the seasons / ryuukoo no utsurikawari (流行の移り変わり) *changes* in fashion.

u｢**tsu｣r·u**[1] うつる (移る) *vi.* (utsu-

r·i-; utsur·a-; utsut·te Ⓒ)
1 move; shift:
Watashi-tachi wa seṅgetsu shiṅ-kyo ni utsurimashita.(私たちは先月新居に移りました) Last month we *moved* into our new house. / *Achira no seki ni* utsurimashoo.(あちらの席に移りましょう) *Let's move* to the seats over there. 《⇨ utsusu¹》
2 move on to (a new topic, subject, etc.):
Sore kara wadai wa kanojo no koṅyaku no hanashi ni utsutta.(それから話題は彼女の婚約の話に移った) Then our talk *turned* to her engagement. 《⇨ utsusu¹》
3 be infected; catch:
Kaze wa utsuriyasui.(かぜはうつりやすい) Colds *are catching*. 《⇨ utsusu¹》

u⌐tsu⌐r·u² うつる (写る) vi. (utsu-r·i-; utsur·a-; utsut·te Ⓒ) (of a photograph) be taken; come out:
Kono shashiṅ wa yoku utsutte *imasu ne.*(この写真はよく写っていますね) This photo *has come out* well, hasn't it? / *Sono shashiṅ ni wa kare no uchi ga* utsutte ita.(その写真には彼の家が写っていた) His house *was in the photograph.* 《⇨ utsu-su²》

u⌐tsu⌐r·u³ うつる (映る) vi. (utsu-r·i-; utsur·a-; utsut·te Ⓒ) be reflected; be mirrored:
Fuji-saṅ ga mizuumi ni utsutte ita.(富士山が湖に映っていた) Mt. Fuji *was reflected* in the lake. 《⇨ utsusu³》

u⌐tsu⌐s·u¹ うつす (移す) vt. (utsu-sh·i-; utsus·a-; utsush·i-te Ⓒ)
1 move; transfer:
Kare wa terebi o heya no sumi ni utsushita.(彼はテレビを部屋の隅に移した) He *moved* the television into a corner of the room. / *Mizusashi no mizu o koppu ni* utsushita.(水差しの水をコップに移した) I *poured*

the water from the pitcher into the glass. / *Kare wa Sapporo no shisha ni* utsusareta.(彼は札幌の支社に移された) He *was transferred* to the Sapporo branch. 《⇨ utsuru¹》
2 give; infect:
Watashi wa anata ni kaze o utsu-sareta.(私はあなたにかぜをうつされた) I *got* a cold from you. 《⇨ utsuru¹》

u⌐tsu⌐s·u² うつす (写す) vt. (utsu-sh·i-; utsus·a-; utsush·i-te Ⓒ)
1 photograph:
Watashi-tachi no shashiṅ o utsu-shite *kudasai.*(私たちの写真を写してください) Please *take* a photo of us. 《⇨ utsuru²》
2 copy; trace:
Kokubaṅ ni kaite aru koto o nooto ni utsushi nasai.(黒板に書いてあることをノートに写しなさい) *Copy* what is written on the blackboard into your notebooks. / *Kanojo wa usui kami o e no ue ni nosete, sore o* utsushita.(彼女は薄い紙を絵の上にのせて、それを写した) She put a thin sheet of paper over the picture and *traced* it.

u⌐tsu⌐s·u³ うつす (映す) vt. (utsu-sh·i-; utsus·a-; utsush·i-te Ⓒ) reflect; mirror; project:
Kare wa suraido o sukuriiṅ ni utsushita.(彼はスライドをスクリーンに映した) He *projected* the slides onto the screen. 《⇨ utsuru³》

u⌐tsuwa うつわ (器) n. **1** container; vessel:
utsuwa *ni kudamono o moru* (器に果物を盛る) heap fruit into a *bowl*.
2 ability; caliber:
Kare wa kaṅtoku no utsuwa *de wa nai.*(彼は監督の器ではない) He does not have *what it takes* to be team manager.

u⌐ttae うったえ (訴え) n. **1** lawsuit; legal action:
Kare wa wareware no kaisha ni taishite soṅgai-baishoo no uttae *o okoshita.*(彼はわれわれの会社に対して

損害賠償の訴えを起こした) He brought an *action* for damages against our company. (⇨ uttaeru)

2 appeal; complaint:
Dare mo kanojo no uttae *o kiite yaroo to shinakatta.* (だれも彼女の訴えを聞いてやろうとしなかった) No one would listen to her *complaint*. (⇨ uttaeru)

u「ttae·ru うったえる (訴える) *vt.* (uttae-te Ⓥ) **1** bring an action; file a suit:
Kare wa meeyo-kisoñ de sono zasshi o uttaeta. (彼は名誉棄損でその雑誌を訴えた) He *sued* the magazine for libel. (⇨ uttae)

2 complain (illness, etc.):
Kanojo wa neñjuu zutsuu o uttaete iru. (彼女は年中頭痛を訴えている) She *is* always *complaining* of headaches.

3 appeal; protest (one's innocence):
Hikoku wa muzai o uttaeta. (被告は無罪を訴えた) The defendant *protested* his innocence. / *Kare no kooeñ wa chooshuu no kokoro ni tsuyoku* uttaeta. (彼の講演は聴衆の心に強く訴えた) His address *appealed* strongly to the feelings of the audience. / *Seefu wa kokumiñ ni shoo-ene o* uttaeta. (政府は国民に省エネを訴えた) The government *made an appeal* to the nation to save energy.

4 resort (to violence):
Doñna baai de mo booryoku ni uttaete *wa ikemaseñ.* (どんな場合でも暴力に訴えてはいけません) Whatever the situation, you must not *resort* to violence. (⇨ uttae)

u「ttooshi¹·i うっとうしい (鬱陶しい) *a.* (-ku) gloomy; depressing; annoying:
ame de uttooshii *teñki* (雨でうっとうしい天気) rainy and *depressing* weather / *Nagai kami wa* uttooshii. (長い髪はうっとうしい) Long

hair is a *nuisance*. / *Ano hito to tsukiau no ga* uttooshiku natte kita. (あの人とつき合うのがうっとうしくなってきた) I *have had quite enough* of associating with him.

u「uru ウール *n.* wool:
uuru *no kutsushita* (ウールの靴下) *woolen* socks.

u「wagi うわぎ (上着) *n.* coat; jacket:
uwagi *o kiru* [*nugu*] (上着を着る[脱ぐ]) put on [take off] one's *coat*.

u「waki うわき (浮気) *n.* being fickle; being unfaithful.
uwaki (o) suru (~(を)する) *vi.* have an affair; be unfaithful:
Kare wa tsuma ni kakurete, uwaki (o) shita. (彼は妻に隠れて, 浮気(を)した) He *had an affair*, unknown to his wife. / *Kanojo wa shokuba no dañsee to* uwaki (o) shite iru. (彼女は職場の男性と浮気(を)している) She *fools around* with a man at work.
— *a.n.* (~ na) fickle; unfaithful:
uwaki *na hito* (浮気な人) a person of *easy virtue*.

u「wasa うわさ (噂) *n.* rumor; gossip; hearsay:
Sono uwasa *wa kiñjo-juu ni sugu hiromatta.* (そのうわさは近所中にすぐ広まった) The *rumor* soon spread right through the neighborhood. / *Dare ga soñna* uwasa *o tateta no daroo ka?* (だれがそんなうわさをたてたのだろうか) I wonder who it is that started a *rumor* like that. / *Kare wa taishoku suru to iu* uwasa *desu.* (彼は退職するといううわさです) There is a *story going around* that he will resign.
uwasa (o) suru (~(を)する) *vi.* talk about; gossip about: *Karera ga kimi no* uwasa *o shite iru no o kikimashita.* (彼らが君のうわさをしているのを聞きました) I heard them *talking about* you.

u⌈yama⌉·u うやまう (敬う) *vt.*
(-ma·i-; -maw·a-; -mat·te Ⓒ)
respect; worship:
ryooshiñ o uyamau (両親を敬う) *re-spect* one's parents.

u⌈zu⌉maki うずまき (渦巻) *n.*
whirlpool; eddy.

u⌈zumar·u うずまる (埋まる) *vi.*
(-mar·i-; -mar·a-; -mat·te Ⓒ)
1 be buried:
Dooro ga yuki ni uzumatte, *waka-ranakatta.* (道路が雪にうずまって, わからなかった) I could not find the road as it *was buried* under the snow. (⇨ uzumeru)
2 be filled; overflow:
Hiroba wa oozee no guñshuu de uzumatta. (広場は大勢の群衆でうずまった) The plaza *was overflowing* with people. (⇨ umeru; uzumeru)

u⌈zume·ru うずめる (埋める) *vt.*
(-me·te Ⓥ) bury. (⇨ umeru)

u⌈zumore·ru うずもれる (埋もれる)
vi. (-more·te Ⓥ) be buried:
Dooro wa yuki ni uzomorete ita.
(道路は雪にうずもれていた) The road *was covered* with snow.

W

wa¹¹ わ（輪）*n.* circle; ring; loop: *himo de* wa *o tsukuru* (ひもで輪をつくる) make a *loop* in a string / *Miñna de* wa *ni natte odotta.* (みんなで輪になって踊った) We danced in a *ring*.

wa¹² わ（和）*n.* **1** unity; harmony: *Kono keekaku o seekoo saseru ni wa* hito no wa *ga taisetsu desu.* (この計画を成功させるには人の和が大切です) In order to make a success of this project, *good teamwork* is important.
2 sum; total: wa *o motomeru* (和を求める) work out the *sum*.

wa³ わ *p.* **1** (used to mark the topic of a sentence):

> **USAGE**
> Used when the speaker wants to add something new about the topic. 《⇨ ga¹》

Kore wa *watashi no jisho desu.* (これは私の辞書です) *This* is my dictionary. / Watashi wa *daigaku-see desu.* Señkoo wa *Nihoñ-buñ-gaku desu.* (私は大学生です。専攻は日本文学です) *I* am a college student. *My major* is Japanese literature. / Tanaka-sañ wa *doko ni imasu ka?* (田中さんはどこにいますか) Where is *Miss Tanaka*?

> **USAGE**
> '*Wa*' is not used in a clause that modifies a noun. *e.g.* *Anata* ga [not wa] *suki na tabemono wa nañ desu ka?* (あなたが好きな食べ物は何ですか) What kind of food do you like?

2 (used in making contrasts and comparisons):
Ame wa *futte imasu ga* kaze wa *arimaseñ.* (雨は降っていますが風はありません) *Raining it is*, but there is no *wind*. / Tanaka-sañ to wa *yo-ku hanashimasu ga* Yamada-sañ to wa *amari hanashimaseñ.* (田中さんとはよく話しますが山田さんとはあまり話しません) *With Tanaka*, I often speak but not so often *with Yamada*.

3 (used with a negative in a contrastive sense):
Watasha wa *tabako wa suimaseñ.* (私はたばこは吸いません) I *don't smoke* (but I do drink). / Kanojo ga *kek-koñ shita to wa* shiranakatta. (彼女が結婚したとは知らなかった) I did not know *that she had got married*.

4 (used to indicate a limit):
★ With a counter.
Kono nekutai wa goseñ-eñ wa *su-ru daroo.* (このネクタイは5千円はするだろう) I suppose this tie will cost *at least* 5,000 yen. / *Koko kara eki made jup-puñ* wa *kakarima-señ.* (ここから駅まで10分はかかりません) It does not take *as much as* ten minutes from here to the station.

wa⁴ わ *p.* **1** (used to indicate emotions, such as admiration):
★ Used mainly by women. The form '*waa*' is more emphatic. *Watashi mo gaikoku e* ikitai wa. (私も外国へ行きたいわ) I too *want to* go abroad. / *Hana ga* kiree da wa. (花がきれいだわ) The flowers *are beautiful.* / Aitai waa. (会いたいわあ) *I do want to meet you!*

2 (used for slight emphasis):
★ Used mainly by women.
Watashi ga iku wa. (私が行くわ) I

am going. | *Kinoo Yamada-sañ ni* aimashita wa. (きのう山田さんに会いましたわ) I *met* Mr. Yamada yesterday. | *Moo ni-do to añna koto* shimaseñ wa. (もう二度とあんなことしませんわ) I *will never do* that kind of thing again.

> **USAGE**
>
> Sometimes used with other particles. *Watashi ga* suru wa yo. (私がするわよ) I *will do it, I tell you.* | *Ashita* kuru wa ne? (あした来るわね) You *will come* tomorrow, *won't you?* 《⇨ ne³; yo³》

3 (used to emphasize emotions or feelings of surprise): *Deñsha de ashi o* fumareru wa, *saifu o* nusumareru wa, *kyoo wa hidoi hi datta.* (電車で足を踏まれるわ, 財布を盗まれるわ, きょうはひどい日だった) My foot *got stepped on* in the train and my purse *was stolen.* What an awful day it has been today! | *Hito ga* iru wa, iru wa, *ashi no fumiba mo nai kurai datta.* (人がいるわ, いるわ, 足の踏み場もないくらいだった) There were *people, people* everywhere—there was hardly space to even stand.

-wa/ba/pa わ(羽)/ば/ぱ *suf.* counter for birds and rabbits.

1	ichi⌐-wa	7	na⌐na⌐-wa
2	ni⌐-wa	8	ha⌐chi⌐-wa
3	sa⌐ñ-ba	9	kyu⌐u-wa
4	yo⌐ñ-wa	10	ji⌐p-pa
5	go⌐-wa		(ju⌐p-pa)
6	ro⌐ku⌐-wa	?	na⌐ñ-ba

wa⌐a わあ *int.* hurray; hurrah; gee; wow: *Waa, sugoi.* (わあ, すごい) *Wow,* that is great. | *Kodomo-tachi wa yorokoñde "waa" to sakeñda.* (子どもたちは喜んで「わあ」と叫んだ) The children joyfully shouted out,

"*Hurrah.*"

wa⌐apuro ワープロ *n.* word processor: *waapuro o utsu [tsukau]* (ワープロを打つ[使う]) use [operate] a *word processor* | *Kono shorui wa* waapuro *de sakusee shimashita.* (この書類はワープロで作成しました) I prepared these documents on a *word processor.*

wa⌐bi わび(詫び) *n.* apology: ★ Often 'o-wabi.' *Watashi wa kare ni* wabi *o ireta.* (私は彼にわびを入れた) I made my *apologies* to him. | *Kokoro kara* o-wabi itashimasu. (心からおわびいたします) I *apologize* to you from the bottom of my heart. | wabi-*joo* (わび状) a letter of *apology.* 《⇨ wabiru》

wa⌐bi·ru わびる(詫びる) *vt.* (wabite Ⓥ) apologize; make an apology: *Watashi wa kare ni nani mo* wabiru *koto wa arimaseñ.* (私は彼に何もわびることはありません) I have nothing to *apologize* to him about. 《⇨ wabi》

wa⌐bishi⌐i わびしい(侘びしい) *a.* (-ku) lonely; miserable; dreary: *Sono roojiñ wa hitori de* wabishi-ku *kurashite ita.* (その老人はひとりでわびしく暮らしていた) That old man was leading a *lonely* life by himself. | *Kanojo ni* wabishii *omoi o sasetaku nai.* (彼女にわびしい思いをさせたくない) I don't wish to make her feel *miserable.* | *Oka no fumoto ni* wabishii *ie ga ik-keñ tatte ita.* (丘のふもとにわびしい家が一軒建っていた) There was a *shabby* house standing at the foot of the hill. 《⇨ mijime; sabishii》

wa⌐buñ わぶん(和文) *n.* Japanese; Japanese writing: *wabuñ-eeyaku* (和文英訳) translation from Japanese into English.

wa⌐dai わだい(話題) *n.* topic; sub-

ject of conversation:
Wadai o kaemashoo. (話題を変えま
しょう) Let's change the *topic*. /
*Watashi-tachi no aida de kanojo
no koto ga* wadai *ni natta.* (私たちの
間で彼女のことが話題になった) She
became the *subject* of our conversation. / *Kore ga* wadai *no shiñ-
seehiñ desu.* (これが話題の新製品で
す) This is the new product that
everyone is talking about.

wa⌈dakamari わだかまり (蟠り) *n.*
bad feeling; grudge:
*Watashi wa kare ni taishite nañ
no* wadakamari *mo arimaseñ.* (私
は彼に対して何のわだかまりもありません)
I have no *bad feelings* against
him. / *Watashi-tachi wa o-tagai
ni* wadakamari naku *hanashiatta.*
(私たちはお互いにわだかまりなく話し合っ
た) We talked with each other
frankly.

wa⌈ee-ji˥teñ わえいじてん (和英辞
典) *n.* Japanese-English dictionary for Japanese people:
waee-jiteñ *o hiku* (和英辞典を引く)
consult a Japanese-English dictionary. 《⇨ eenichi-jiteñ; eewa-
jiteñ; nichiee-jiteñ》

wafuku わふく (和服) *n.* kimono;
traditional Japanese costume.
★ More formal than 'kimono.'
《⇨ kimono》

WAFUKU

wa⌈fuu わふう (和風) *n.* Japanese
style:
wafuu *no ie* (和風の家) a *Japanese-
style* house / wafuu-*ryoori* (和風料
理) *Japanese-style* cooking.
《⇨ yoofuu》

wa⌈ga わが (我が) *attrib.* my;
our:
waga-*sha* (わが社) *our* company /
waga-*ya* (わが家) *our* house / wa-
ga-*ko* (わが子) *our* child / waga-
kuni (わが国) *our* country.

wa⌈gamama˥ わがまま (我儘) *n.*
selfishness; willfulness:
wagamama *o toosu* (わがままを通す)
get one's way / Wagamama *o itte
wa ikemaseñ.* (わがままを言ってはいけ
ません) Don't *insist on your own
way.* 《⇨ katte²》
— *a.n.* (~ na, ni) selfish; willful; egoistic: wagamama *na kañgae* (わがままな考え) a *selfish* way of
thinking / wagamama *ni furumau*
(わがままにふるまう) behave *just as
one pleases* / *Uchi no ko wa* wagamama *de komaru.* (うちの子はわがまま
で困る) Our child is *willful*, so we
have a hard time with him.

wa⌈ga˥shi わがし (和菓子) *n.* Japanese confectionery. 《↔ yoo-
gashi》

WAGASHI

wa⌈gomu わゴム (輪ゴム) *n.* rubber band:
shorui ni wagomu *o kakeru* (書類

に輪ゴムをかける) put a *rubber band* around papers.

waˈiñ ワイン *n.* wine: *aka* [*shiro*] waiñ (赤[白]ワイン) red [white] *wine*.

waˈishatsu ワイシャツ *n.* shirt; dress shirt: ★ Refers to a shirt with which a tie can be worn. waishatsu *o kiru* [*nugu*] (ワイシャツを着る[脱ぐ]) put on [take off] a *shirt* / *hañsode no* waishatsu (半袖のワイシャツ) a short-sleeved *shirt* / *Kare wa* waishatsu-sugata *de hataraita.* (彼はワイシャツ姿で働いた) He worked in his *shirtsleeves.*

waˈiwai わいわい *adv.* (~ to) noisily; boisterously: *Kodomo-tachi wa* waiwai (*to*) *sawaide ita.* (子どもたちはわいわい(と)騒いでいた) The children were making *a lot of noise.* / *Kare-ra wa nani o* waiwai *itte iru ñ da?* (彼らは何をわいわい言っているんだ) What are they making such a *fuss* about?

waˈka わか (和歌) *n.* = *tañka*[3].

waˈkaˈ·i わかい (若い) *a.* (-ku)
1 young; youthful: wakai *hito* (若い人) a *young* person / *Haha wa chichi yori go-sai* wakai. (母は父より5歳若い) My mother is five years *younger* than my father. / Wakai *toki ni karada o kitae nasai.* (若いときに体を鍛えなさい) Build up your body while you are *young.* / *Sofu wa mada ki ga* wakai. (祖父はまだ気が若い) My grandfather still has a *youthful* spirit.
2 immature; inexperienced; green: *Soñna koto o iu nañte kimi mo mada* wakai. (そんなことを言うなんてきみもまだ若い) You are still *green* to say that sort of thing.
3 (of numbers) low: *Bañgoo no* wakai *juñ ni narañde kudasai.* (番号の若い順に並んでくださ

い) Please line up starting with those holding the *lower* numbers.

waˈkaˈme わかめ (若布) *n.* wakame (*Undaria pinnatifida*) seaweed. ★ Often served in miso soup.

waˈkamono わかもの (若者) *n.* young people; youth. ((↔ roojiñ; toshiyori))

waˈkareˈ わかれ (別れ) *n.* parting; separation; farewell: Wakare *ni saishite, watashi-tachi wa kare ni tokee o okutta.* (別れに際して, 私たちは彼に時計を贈った) We presented him with a watch on *parting.* / *Moo* o-wakare *shina-kereba narimaseñ.* (もうお別れしなければなりません) Now, I *have to say good-bye.* ((⇨ wakareru))

waˈkareˈ·ru[1] わかれる (分かれる) *vi.* (wakare-te Ⅴ) branch off; divide; fork; split: *Kono kawa wa yaku ni-kiro saki de futatsu ni* wakaremasu. (この川は約2キロ先で二つに分かれます) This river *divides* about two kilometers ahead. / *Michi ga* wakaretara, *migi no michi o iki nasai.* (道が分かれたら, 右の道を行きなさい) When the road *forks*, follow the right-hand branch. / *Chiimu wa futatsu ni* wakarete, *koohaku-jiai o okonatta.* (チームは2つに分かれて, 紅白試合を行なった) The members of the team *split* into red and white groups and played the game. ((⇨ wakeru))

waˈkareˈ·ru[2] わかれる (別れる) *vi.* (wakare-te Ⅴ) part; say goodbye; separate; divorce: *Watashi wa eki de kanojo to* wakareta. (私は駅で彼女と別れた) I *parted* from her at the station. / *Futari wa kekkoñ shite, ni-neñ de* wakareta. (二人は結婚して, 2年で別れた) They *separated* two years after getting married. ((⇨ wakare))

waˈkaˈr·u わかる（分かる・判る・解る）*vi.* (wakar·i-; wakar·a-; wakatte Ⓒ) **1** understand:
Watashi no itte iru koto ga wakarimasu *ka?* (私の言っていることがわかりますか) *Do* you *understand* what I am saying? / *Watashi wa Nihoñgo ga* wakarimaseñ. (私は日本語がわかりません) I *don't understand* Japanese.
2 know:
Ano hito wa dare ka wakarimasu *ka?* (あの人はだれかわかりますか) *Do* you *know* who he is? / *Ashita no koto wa* wakarimaseñ. (あしたのことはわかりません) *Nobody knows* what will happen tomorrow.
3 turn out; prove:
Kekkyoku kare wa mujitsu to wakatta. (結局彼は無実とわかった) He *turned out* to be innocent after all.

waˈkasˈu わかす（沸かす）*vt.* (wakash·i-; wakas·a-; wakash·i-te Ⓒ) **1** boil; heat:
yu o wakasu (湯を沸かす) *boil* water / *furo o* wakasu (ふろを沸かす) *get* a bath *ready*. 《⇨ waku²》
2 excite:
Kare no subarashii puree wa kañshuu o wakashita. (彼のすばらしいプレーは観衆を沸かした) His fine play *excited* the spectators. 《⇨ waku²》

waˈkawakashiˈ·i わかわかしい（若若しい）*a.* (-ku) youthful; fresh:
Ano hito wa toshi no wari ni wakawakashii. (あの人は年の割に若々しい) He is *young* for his age. 《⇨ wakai》

Waˈkayamaˈ-keñ わかやまけん（和歌山県）*n.* Wakayama Prefecture. Located in the Kinki district, on the southwest end of the Kii Peninsula. The chief industry is timber but citrus production is also important. Capital city: Wakayama. 《⇨ map (D5)》

waˈke わけ（訳）*n.* **1** reason; cause; grounds:
Futari no rikoñ no wake *o shiritai.* (二人の離婚の訳を知りたい) I'd like to know the *reason* for their divorce. / Doo-iu wake *de shigoto o kotowatta ñ desu ka?* (どういう訳で仕事を断ったんですか) *Why* did you turn down the job?
2 case; circumstances:
Soo-iu wake *nara, dekiru dake no koto wa shimasu.* (そういう訳なら、できるだけのことはします) If that is the *case*, I will do what I can. / *Koo-iu* wake *desu kara go-yooboo ni wa oojiraremaseñ.* (こういう訳ですからご要望には応じられません) Under these *circumstances*, we are unable to meet your request. 《⇨ jijoo》
3 meaning:
Kono buñ wa nani o itte iru no ka wake *ga wakaranai.* (この文は何を言っているのか訳がわからない) I cannot make out the *meaning* of this sentence.
4 sense:
Shachoo wa wake *no wakaru hito desu.* (社長は訳のわかる人です) Our president is a *sensible* man.

waˈke de wa nai わけではない（訳ではない）(*polite*＝wake de wa arimaseñ) do not mean that...; it is not (exactly) that...:
Sono shigoto ga iya to iu wake de wa nai. (その仕事がいやという訳ではない) I *do not mean that* I dislike the job. / *Sono kisoku wa shiranai* wake de wa arimaseñ. (その規則は知らない訳ではありません) *It is not that* I don't know the rules. 《⇨ wake》

waˈke ni wa iˈkanai わけにはいかない（訳にはいかない）(*polite*＝wake ni wa ikimaseñ) **1** cannot; must not: ★ Indicates a moral, not physical, inability or prohibition.
Kare no teeañ wa kotowaru wake ni wa ikanai. (彼の提案は断るわけに

はいかない) We *cannot really* decline his proposal. / *Damatte dekakeru* wake ni wa ikimaseñ. (黙って出かけるわけにはいきません) We *can not* just walk out without saying anything.

2 must; cannot help but...: ★ The verb preceding '*wake*' is in the negative.

Kyoo wa ikanai wake ni wa ikanai. (きょうは行かないわけにはいかない) Today *it just won't do* if I don't go. / *Kanojo kara reñraku ga nai no de shiñpai shinai* wake ni wa ikimaseñ. (彼女から連絡がないので心配しないわけにはいきません) So far I have heard nothing from her, so I *cannot help* worrying.

wa⌐ke⌐·ru わける (分ける) *vt.* (wake-te Ⅴ) **1** divide; distribute; share:

Seeto-tachi o yottsu no guruupu ni waketa. (生徒たちを4つのグループに分けた) We *divided* the pupils into four groups. / *Watashi-tachi wa rieki o miñna de* wakeru *koto ni shita.* (私たちは利益をみんなで分けることにした) We decided to *divide* the profits among everyone. / *Kare wa tochi o musuko-tachi ni* waketa. (彼は土地を息子たちに分けた) He *distributed* his land among his sons. / *Sono chokoreeto o tomodachi ni mo* wakete *age nasai.* (そのチョコレートを友だちにも分けてあげなさい) *Share* the chocolate with your friends as well. ((⇨ wakeru¹))

2 classify: *Zoosho o bumoñ-betsu ni* waketa. (蔵書を部門別に分けた) I *classified* the book collection according to the different categories.

wa⌐ke wa nai わけはない (訳はない) (*polite*＝wake wa arimaseñ) **1** there is no reason for...; it cannot be ...:

Kare ga soñna ni isogashii wake

wa nai. (彼がそんなに忙しいわけはない) It *cannot be* that he is so busy. / *Miki-sañ ga byooki no* wake wa arimaseñ. (三木さんが病気のわけはありません) I *can't believe* that Mr. Miki is sick. / *Chañto setsumee shita kara,* wakaranai wake wa nai. (ちゃんと説明したから、わからないわけはない) I explained it properly, so *there is no reason* for you not to understand it.

2 easy; simple: *Jiteñsha ni noru no nañ ka* wake wa nai. (自転車に乗るのなんかわけはない) It is *quite easy* to ride a bicycle. / *Koñna moñdai o toku no wa* wake wa nai. (こんな問題を解くのはわけはない) This problem *is simple* to solve.

wa⌐ki⌐ わき (脇) *n.* **1** under one's arm:

Kanojo wa waki *ni hoñ o kakaete ita.* (彼女はわきに本を抱えていた) She was carrying some books *under her arm.*

2 side: Waki *e doite kudasai.* (わきへどいてください) Please step *aside.* / *Chuushajoo wa sono mise no* waki *ni arimasu.* (駐車場はその店のわきにあります) The parking lot is at the *side* of the shop. / *Kare wa* waki *kara sugu ni kuchi o dasu.* (彼はわきからすぐに口を出す) He soon *meddles* in our affairs.

wa⌐kibara わきばら (わき腹) *n.* one's side:

Wakibara *ga itai.* (わき腹が痛い) I feel a pain in *my side.* / *Kare wa watashi no* wakibara *o tsutsuite chuui shita.* (彼は私のわき腹をつついて注意した) He cautioned me by poking me in *the ribs.*

wa⌐kimi⌐ わきみ (脇見) *n.* looking away; glancing aside: wakimi-*uñteñ* (わき見運転) driving a car *without keeping one's eyes on the road.*

wakimi (o) suru (〜(を)する) *vi.*
look away: *Shikeñ-chuu wa* wakimi shite *wa ikemaseñ.* (試験中は
わき見してはいけません) Don't *look
around* during the examination.

waˈki-noˈ-shita わきのした (脇の
下) *n.* armpit:
waki-no-shita *ni ase o kaku* (わきの
下に汗をかく) sweat *under one's
arms.* 《⇨ jiñtai (illus.)》

waˈku¹ わく (枠) *n.* **1** frame:
Mado no waku *ga hokori-darake
da.* (窓の枠がほこりだらけだ) The window *frames* are covered with
dust.
2 limit:
Yosañ ni wa waku *ga arimasu.* (予
算には枠があります) There are *limits*
to the budget.
waku ni hamatta (〜にはまった)
stereotyped; conventional: *Dore
mo* waku ni hamatta *añ de, shiñ-
señmi ga nai.* (どれも枠にはまった案で、
新鮮味がない) They are all *stereotyped* plans and there is nothing
novel.

waˈkˈuˈ² わく (沸く) *vi.* (wak·i-;
wak·a-; wa·i-te 〇) **1** boil; be
heated:
O-yu ga waite imasu. (お湯が沸いて
います) The water *is boiling.* / *Furo
wa* waite imasu *ka?* (ふろは沸いてい
ますか) *Is* the bath *ready?* 《⇨ wa-
kasu》
2 be excited:
Kuni-juu ga Oriñpikku de waita.
(国中がオリンピックで沸いた) The
whole country *was excited* over
the Olympic Games. 《⇨ wakasu》

waˈkuwaku わくわく *adv.*
(〜 suru [saseru]) (used to express excitement, joy, expectation or happiness):
*Hisashiburi ni kikoku suru koto o
kañgaeru to* wakuwaku suru. (久し
ぶりに帰国することを考えるとわくわくす
る) I *get excited* when I think of
returning to my country after

being away a long time. / *Watashi wa mune o* wakuwaku sase-
nagara *kanojo no tegami o yoñda.*
(私は胸をわくわくさせながら彼女の手紙
を読んだ) I read her letter *with my
heart beating.*

waˈñ¹ わん (椀) *n.* bowl: ★ Often
'*o-wañ.*'
*Misoshiru wa ki no o-*wañ *de
dashimasu.* (みそ汁は木のおわんで出し
ます) You serve miso soup in a
wooden *bowl.*

with a lid　　without a lid
O-WAÑ

waˈñ² わん (湾) *n.* bay; gulf:
Tookyoo wañ (東京湾) Tokyo
Bay.

waˈna わな (罠) *n.* trap; snare:
wana *o shikakeru* (わなを仕掛ける)
set a *trap* / wana *ni kakaru* (わなに
かかる) be caught in a *trap* / *Watashi wa kare no* wana *ni hamatta.*
(私は彼のわなにはまった) I fell into his
trap.

Waˈñgañ-seˈñsoo わんがんせんそ
う (湾岸戦争) *n.* the Gulf War.

waˈni わに (鰐) *n.* crocodile; alligator:
wani-*gawa no beruto* (ワニ皮のベル
ト) a *crocodile* [an *alligator*]
leather belt.

waˈñpiˈisu ワンピース *n.* dress;
female one-piece garment:
Kanojo wa guriiñ no wañpiisu *o
kite ita.* (彼女はグリーンのワンピースを
着ていた) She wore a green *dress.*

waˈñwañ わんわん **1** bow-wow:
★ An imitation of the barking of
a dog.
Inu ga wañwañ (to) *hoete iru.* (犬
がわんわん(と)ほえている) A dog *is*

barking. (⇨ hoeru)

2 (young children's word) doggie.

wa┌ra わら (藁) *n.* straw:
wara-*zaiku* (わら細工) *straw* work / wara-*buki no ie* (わらぶきの家) a house with a *straw*-thatched roof.

wa┌rai わらい (笑い) *n.* laugh; laughter:
warai *o koraeru* (笑いをこらえる) suppress one's *laughter* / *Amari okashii no de* warai *ga tomaranakatta.* (あまりおかしいので笑いが止まらなかった) It was so funny that my *laughter* wouldn't stop. (⇨ warau)

wa┌raigo┐e わらいごえ (笑い声) *n.* laughing voice; laughter:
dotto iu waraigoe (どっという笑い声) peals of *laughter* / *Ni-kai de* waraigoe *ga shita.* (二階で笑い声がした) *Laughter* was heard upstairs. (↔ nakigoe)

wa┌ra·u わらう (笑う) *vi.* (wara·i-; waraw·a-; warat-te C)
1 laugh; grin; smile:
Kare no joodañ de miñna ga waratta. (彼の冗談でみんなが笑った) We all *laughed* at his joke. / *Sono ko wa purezeñto o moratte, nikkori* waratta. (その子はプレゼントをもらって, にっこり笑った) The child *grinned* on getting his present. (⇨ warai)
2 laugh at; ridicule; make fun of:
Kare wa majime na ñ da kara waratte *wa ikenai.* (彼はまじめなんだから笑ってはいけない) Since he is serious, we should not *laugh.* / *Miñna kanojo no okashi-na booshi no koto o* waratta. (みんな彼女のおかしな帽子のことを笑った) Everyone *ridiculed* her strange hat.

wa┌re-na┌gara われながら (我ながら) *adv.* if I do say so myself:
Ware-nagara yoku yatta to omoimasu. (われながらよくやったと思います) I think I did rather well, *if I may so.* / *Soñna machigai o shite,* wa-re-nagara *hazukashii.* (そんな間違いをして, われながら恥ずかしい) I am ashamed *of myself* for having made such a mistake.

wa┌re·ru われる (割れる) *vi.* (wa-re-te V) **1** break; smash:
Sara o otoshita ga warenakatta. (皿を落としたが割れなかった) I dropped the plate, but it *didn't break.* (⇨ kowareru; waru)
2 (of opinions, organization, group, etc.) be divided; split:
Ikeñ ga futatsu ni wareta. (意見が二つに割れた) Opinion *was divided* into two camps. (⇨ wakareru)

wa┌reware われわれ (我々) *n.* (*formal*) = watashi-tachi.
we: ★ 'wareware no'=our; 'wareware o'=us. Used mainly by men.
Wareware wa geñroñ no jiyuu no tame ni tatakau. (われわれは言論の自由のために闘う) *We* will fight for freedom of speech. / *Wareware no yookyuu wa seetoo na mono desu.* (われわれの要求は正当なものです) *Our* demands are just ones.

wa┌ri わり (割) *n.* **1** rate; ratio:
Sañsee to hañtai no wari *wa sañ tai ni datta.* (賛成と反対の割は3対2だった) The *ratio* of supporters and opponents was three to two. / *Basu wa ichi-jikañ ni san-boñ no* wari *de hashitte imasu.* (バスは1時間に3本の割で走っています) The buses run at the *rate* of three an hour. (⇨ wariai)
2 (unit of ratio) ten percent:
Genkiñ nara, ni-wari *hikimasu.* (現金なら, 2割引きます) If you pay in cash, we will give you a discount of *twenty percent.* / *Unchiñ ga* ichi-wari *neage ni natta.* (運賃が1割値上げになった) Fares were raised by *ten percent.* (⇨ bu)
wari ni awanai (〜に合わない) do not pay; be unprofitable: *Sono shigoto wa* wari ni awanakatta.

(その仕事は割に合わなかった) The job *didn't pay.* 《⇨ wari ni》

wa⌐riai わりあい (割合) *n.* rate; ratio; percentage:
Kono gakkoo no dañshi to joshi no wariai *wa go tai yoñ desu.* (この学校の男子と女子の割合は5対4です) The *ratio* of boys to girls at this school is five to four. / *Shio to satoo no* wariai *wa dono kurai desu ka?* (塩と砂糖の割合はどのくらいですか) What is the *ratio* of salt to sugar? 《⇨ wari》
— *adv.* comparatively; relatively:
Suugaku no moñdai wa wariai *yasashikatta.* (数学の問題は割合やさしかった) The math problem was *comparatively* easy. / *Kyoo wa* wariai (ni) *suzushii.* (きょうは割合(に)涼しい) It is *fairly* cool today.

wa⌐riate わりあて (割り当て) *n.* assignment; allotment: quota:
Kifu no wariate *wa dono kurai desu ka?* (寄付の割り当てはどのくらいですか) How much is the *amount alloted* toward contributions? / *Yunyuu no* wariate *wa fuete imasu.* (輸入の割り当ては増えています) The import *quotas* are increasing. 《⇨ wariateru》

wa⌐riate¹·ru わりあてる (割り当てる) *vt.* (-ate-te Ⓥ) assign; allot; allocate:
Watashi wa yakkai na shigoto o wariaterareta. (私はやっかいな仕事を割り当てられた) I *was assigned* a troublesome task. / *Yosañ no roku-teñ-go paaseñto ga booee-hi ni* wariaterareta. (予算の 6.5% が防衛費に割り当てられた) Six point five percent of the budget *was allocated* to national defense expenditure. 《⇨ wariate》

wa⌐riba¹shi わりばし (割り箸) *n.* disposable wooden chopsticks. 《⇨ photo (right)》

wa⌐ribiki わりびき (割引) *n.* dis-

WARIBASHI
Wrapped in paper, and split when using.

count; reduction:
*Watashi wa kono kamera o ni-*waribiki *de kaimashita.* (私はこのカメラを2割引で買いました) I bought this camera at a twenty *percent discount.* / *Kono shoohiñ wa* waribiki *ni natte imasu.* (この商品は割引になっています) There is a *discount* on these articles. / waribiki-*keñ* (割引券) a *discount* ticket / waribiki-*ritsu* (割引率) the size of a *discount* / waribiki-*ryookiñ* (割引料金) a *discount* rate.

waribiki (o) suru (～(を)する) *vt.* reduce; discount: *Kono keñ o miseru to* waribiki *shite kureru soo desu.* (この券を見せると割引してくれるそうです) I hear that if you show this coupon, they will *give you a reduced rate.* 《⇨ waribiku》

wa⌐ribi¹k·u わりびく (割り引く) *vt.* (-bik·i-; bik·a-; -bi·i·te Ⓒ) discount; reduce:
Geñkiñ nara waribikimasu. (現金なら割り引きます) We will *make a discount* if you pay in cash. / *Sono mise wa nijup-paaseñto* waribiite *kureta.* (その店は20% 割り引いてくれた) That store *gave me* a twenty percent *discount.* 《⇨ waribiki》

waribiite kiku (割り引いて聞く) don't take a person's story at face value: *Kare no hanashi wa* waribiite kiita *hoo ga yoi.* (彼の話は割り引いて聞いたほうがよい) You had better take what he says *with a grain of salt.*

wa⌐rikañ わりかん (割り勘) *n.*

each paying his [her] own way:
Kañjoo wa warikañ *ni shimashoo.*
(勘定は割り勘にしましょう) *Let's split*
the bill.

waˈrikoˈmˈu わりこむ (割り込む) *vi.*
(-kom·i-; -kom·a-; -koñ-de [C])
1 squeeze oneself:
mañiñ deñsha ni warikomu (満員
電車に割り込む) *squeeze oneself* into
a crowded train.
2 jump a line; cut in:
Retsu ni warikomanai *de kudasai.*
(列に割り込まないでください) Please
don't jump the line. / *Ootobai ga
kuruma no mae ni* warikoñde kita.
(オートバイが車の前に割り込んできた) A
motorcycle *cut in* in front of my
car.
3 break into (a conversation):
*Kanojo wa wareware no hanashi
ni* warikoñde kita. (彼女はわれわれの
話に割り込んできた) She *broke into*
our conversation.

waˈri ni わりに (割に) *adv.*
1 comparatively; rather; fairly:
Kono nekutai wa wari ni *yasu-
katta.* (このネクタイは割に安かった)
This necktie was *comparatively*
cheap. / *Kare wa* wari ni *kimuzukashii.* (彼は割に気むずかしい) He is
rather hard to please.
2 in proportion to; for:
Kare wa toshi no wari ni *fukete
mieru.* (彼は年の割に老けて見える) He
looks old *for* his age. / *Kore wa
nedañ no* wari ni *shitsu ga yoi.* (こ
れは値段の割に質がよい) *Considering*
the price, the quality of this is
good. / *Kare wa katte na koto o iu*
wari ni *shigoto o shinai.* (彼は勝手
なことを言う割に仕事をしない) He
does not do much work, *compared to* all the talking he does.

waˈriˈzañ わりざん (割り算) *n.* (of
arithmetic) division:
warizañ *o suru* (割り算をする) *divide.*
《⇨ keesañ (table); waru》

waˈr·u わる (割る) *vt.* (war·i-; wa-

r·a-; wat-te [C]) **1** break; smash:
Sumimaseñ, madogarasu o watte
shimaimashita. (すみません、窓ガラス
を割ってしまいました) I am sorry, but
I *have broken* the window.
《⇨ wareru》
2 split; chop:
Mukashi wa maki o watte, *neñryoo ni shita.* (昔はまきを割って、燃
料にした) In the old days people
used to *chop* logs to use as fuel.
3 divide:
Juu-ni waru *yoñ wa sañ desu.* (12
割る4は3です) Twelve *divided* by
four is three. 《⇨ keesañ (table)》
4 dilute:
Uisukii o mizu de watte *noñda.*
(ウイスキーを水で割って飲んだ) I *di-
luted* the whisky with water and
drank it. 《⇨ mizuwari》

waˈrugiˈ わるぎ (悪気) *n.* evil
intention; ill will; malice:
Kare ni wa nañ no warugi *mo
nakatta to wakatta.* (彼には何の悪気
もなかったとわかった) It turned out
that he did it without any *evil
intention.* / *Watashi wa* warugi
*ga atte soñna koto o itta no de wa
arimaseñ.* (私は悪気があってそんなこと
を言ったのではありません) I didn't say
that kind of thing out of *malice.*

waˈruˈ·i わるい (悪い) *a.* (-ku)
1 bad; evil; wrong:
warui *shuukañ* (悪い習慣) a *bad*
habit / *Uso o tsuku no wa* warui
koto desu. (うそをつくのは悪いことです)
It is *wrong* to tell a lie. / *Kare wa*
warui *koto o shite, keesatsu ni tsukamatta.* (彼は悪いことをして、警察につ
かまった) He committed a *crime*
and was caught by the police.
《↔ yoi¹》
2 (of quality, weather, harvest)
bad; poor; inferior:
Kono tamago wa waruku *natte iru.*
(この卵は悪くなっている) This egg is
bad. / *Kotoshi wa kome no shuukaku ga* warukatta. (今年は米の収

穫が悪かった）This year's rice harvest was *poor*. / *Hatsuoñ ga* warui *to tsuujinai koto ga arimasu.*（発音が悪いと通じないことがあります）You sometimes cannot make yourself understood if your pronunciation is *poor*. 《⇨ yoi¹》

3 (of situation, state, etc.) bad; sick; ill-timed:
Kyoo wa buchoo no kigeñ ga warui.（きょうは部長の機嫌が悪い）The general manager is in a *bad* mood today. / *Kono kuruma wa eñjiñ no guai ga* warui.（この車はエンジンのぐあいが悪い）There is something *wrong* with the engine of this car. / *Kyoo wa i no chooshi ga* warui.（きょうは胃の調子が悪い）I have an *upset* stomach today. / *Jitai wa masumasu* waruku *natta.*（事態はますます悪くなった）The situation went from bad to *worse*. 《↔ yoi¹》

4 (of luck) bad; unlucky:
Kare wa uñ *ga* warukatta *dake da.*（彼は運が悪かっただけだ）He was just *unlucky*. / *Waruku suru to deñsha ni maniawanai ka mo shirenai.*（悪くすると電車に間に合わないかも知れない）If we are *unlucky*, we may not be in time for the train. 《↔ yoi¹》

5 troublesome; harmful:
Warui kedo tetsudatte moraemasu ka?（悪いけど手伝ってもらえますか）I am *sorry* to bother you, but could you give me a hand? / *Soñna koto o suru to Suzuki-sañ ni* warui *desu yo.*（そんなことをすると鈴木さんに悪いですよ）If you do something like that, it will cause Mr. Suzuki a lot of *trouble*. / *Tabako wa keñkoo ni* warui.（たばこは健康に悪い）Cigarettes are bad for the health.

waruku iu（悪く言う）speak ill of: *Hoka no hito no koto o* waruku iu *no wa yoshi nasai.*（ほかの人のことを悪く言うのはよしなさい）Don't *speak*
ill of other people.

waruku omou（悪く思う）think ill of: *Waza-to yatta no de wa nai no de,* waruku omowanai *de kudasai.*（わざとやったのではないので、悪く思わないでください）I didn't do it on purpose, so please *do not blame* me.

waˈruˈkuchi わるくち（悪口）*n.* slander:
Kage de hito no warukuchi *o iu no wa yoshi nasai.*（かげで人の悪口を言うのはよしなさい）Stop *speaking ill of* others behind their backs.

waˈsai わさい（和裁）*n.* Japanese dressmaking; kimono making. 《↔ yoosai》

waˈshitsu わしつ（和室）*n.* Japanese-style room. 《↔ yooshitsu》《⇨ photo (next page)》

waˈsho わしょ（和書）*n.* book published in the Japanese language; Japanese book. 《⇨ yoosho》

waˈshoku わしょく（和食）*n.* Japanese food:
Watashi wa yooshoku yori, washoku *no hoo ga suki desu.*（私は洋食より、和食のほうが好きです）I like *Japanese food* better than Western food. 《↔ yooshoku²》

waˈsuremono わすれもの（忘れ物）*n.* something left behind:
Watashi wa yoku deñsha ni wasuremono *o suru.*（私はよく電車に忘れ物をする）I often *forget things* on the train. / *Wasuremono no nai yoo ni chuui shi nasai.*（忘れ物のないように注意しなさい）Make sure that you *take all your belongings with you.* / wasuremono-*toriatsukaijo*（忘れ物取り扱い所）a *lost-and-found*

WASUREMONO-TORIATSUKAIJO SIGN

office. 《⇨ okiwasureru; wasureru》

waˈsure·ru わすれる (忘れる) *vt.*
(wasure-te [V]) **1** forget:
Yuube wa akari o kesu no o wa-surete shimatta. (ゆうべは明りを消すのを忘れてしまった) I *forgot* to turn out the lights last night. / *Jisho o gakkoo ni wasurete kita.* (辞書を学校に忘れてきた) I *forgot* my dictionary at school. / *Kono tegami o wasurezu ni, posuto ni irete kudasai.* (この手紙を忘れずに, ポストに入れてください) Please *do not forget* to post this letter.
2 leave behind:
Deñsha no naka ni kasa o wasu-rete shimatta. (電車の中に傘を忘れてしまった) I *have left* my umbrella on the train.

waˈta¹ わた (綿) *n.* cotton:
futoñ ni wata o tsumeru (ふとんに綿を詰める) stuff *cotton* into a futon.

waˈtakushi わたくし (私) *n.*
= watashi.

waˈtakushi-doˈmo わたくしども (私共) *n.* (*humble*) we; our company [office; store]: ★ Used by service personnel.
Watakushi-domo wa yoosho o atsukatte orimaseñ. (私どもは洋書を

扱っておりません) *We* do not handle foreign books.

waˈtakushiˈritsu わたくしりつ (私立) *n.* = shiritsu¹.

waˈtar·u わたる (渡る) *vi.* (watar·i-; watar·a-; watat-te [C])
1 cross; go across; go over:
Kare wa dooro o hashitte watatta. (彼は道路を走って渡った) He ran *across* the street. / *Kono kawa wa nagare ga kyuu de, oyoide watare-maseñ.* (この川は流れが急で, 泳いで渡れません) This river is too rapid to *swim across*.
2 (of a bird) migrate; (of religion, custom, etc.) be introduced:
Fuyu ni naru to tsubame wa minami e watatte ikimasu. (冬になるとつばめは南へ渡って行きます) When winter comes, swallows *migrate* southward. / *Kirisuto-kyoo wa itsu Nihoñ ni watatte kimashita ka?* (キリスト教はいつ日本に渡って来ましたか) When *did* Christianity *come* to Japan?

waˈtashi わたし (私) *n.* (*polite*= watakushi) I: ★ 'watashi no' = my; 'watashi o' = me. Words indicating personal reference are

kakejiku

shooji

zataku

zabutoñ

tokonoma

tatami

WASHITSU

less commonly used in Japanese than in English.
(Watashi *wa*) *kinoo Yamada-sañ ni aimashita.*（（私は）きのう山田さんに会いました）*I* met Mr. Yamada yesterday.
The following are situations in which the use of '*watashi*' is natural:
1 (when contrasting oneself with someone else):
"*Watashi wa biiru ni shimasu."* "*Jaa,* watashi *mo." "Watashi wa uisukii ni shimasu."* (at a restaurant) (「私はビールにします」「じゃ, 私も」「私はウイスキーにします」) *"I'll* have beer." "*Me,* too." "*I'll* have whisky." / Watashi ni *mo misete kudasai.* (私にも見せてください) Please let *me* have a look at it, too. / *"Dare-ka tabako o kai ni itte kuremaseñ ka?"* "Watashi *ga ikimashoo."* (「だれかたばこを買いに行ってくれませんか」「私が行きましょう」) "Won't someone go and buy a pack of cigarettes for me?" "*I'll* go." / *"Nañ de koñna tokoro ni iru ñ desu ka?"* "*Anata o matte ita ñ desu yo."* "Watashi *o desu ka?"* "*Soo desu yo."* (「何でこんな所にいるんですか」「あなたを待っていたんですよ」「私をですか」「そうですよ」) "Why are you here?" "I was waiting for you." "For *me*?" "Yes." / *"Kono kasa wa dare no desu ka?"* "*Sore wa* watashi no *desu."* (「この傘はだれのですか」「それは私のです」) "Whose umbrella is this?" "It's *mine.*"
2 (when mentioning oneself for the first time): ★ When the topic is already about oneself, '*watashi*' is normally not used. Watashi *wa Suzuki to iimasu. Señdai kara kimashita.* (私は鈴木と言います. 仙台から来ました) *My name* is Suzuki. I come from Sendai. / *Hajimemashite.* (Watashi *wa*)

Yamada to mooshimasu. (初めまして. (私は)山田と申します) How do you do? *My name* is Yamada.

wa⌈tashibu⌉ne わたしぶね（渡し船）*n.* ferry. ★ A small boat used to carry passengers across a river. (⇨ *fune*))

WATASHIBUNE

wa⌈tashi⌉-tachi わたしたち（私達）*n.* we: ★ 'watashi-tachi no' = our; 'watashi-tachi o' = us. Watashi-tachi *wa yoku issho ni asoñda mono desu.* (私たちはよくいっしょに遊んだものです) *We* often used to play together. / *Kore ga* watashi-tachi no *atarashii ie desu.* (これが私たちの新しい家です) This is *our* new house.

wa⌈tas·u わたす（渡す）*vt.* (watash·i-; watas·a-; watash·i-te C)
1 give; hand over:
Kono tegami o kanojo ni watashite *kudasai.* (この手紙を彼女に渡してください) Please *give* her this let-

ter.

2 lay (a board); stretch (a rope, bridge, etc., between): *ana ni ita o* watasu (穴に板を渡す) *lay* a plank across a hole / *ogawa ni hashi o* watasu (小川に橋を渡す) *build* a bridge over a brook / *eda kara eda e tsuna o* watasu (枝から枝へ綱を渡す) *stretch* a rope from branch to branch.

wa˥za-to わざと (態と) *adv.* on purpose; intentionally; deliberately: Waza-to *soo shita no de wa arimaseñ.* (わざとそうしたのではありません) I did not do it *on purpose.* / *Kanojo wa* waza-to *shiranai furi o shita.* (彼女はわざと知らないふりをした) She *deliberately* pretended not to notice.

waza-to-rashii (〜らしい) put-on; unnatural: *Kare no taido wa* waza-to-rashikatta. (彼の態度はわざとらしかった) His manner seemed *put-on.*

wa˥zawaza わざわざ (態々) *adv.* specially; expressly: *O-isogashii tokoro o* wazawaza *oide itadaki, arigatoo gozaimasu.* (お忙しいところをわざわざお出でいただき, ありがとうございます) Thank you very much for *taking the trouble* to come here when you are so busy. / *Kare wa sono shiai o miru tame ni,* wazawaza *Tookyoo kara Oosaka made itta.* (彼はその試合を見るために, わざわざ東京から大阪まで行った) He went *all the way* to Osaka from Tokyo to see the game.

wa˥zuka わずか (僅か) *a.n.* (〜 na, ni) few; little; slight: *Hoñno* wazuka *na hito ga sono kai ni shusseki shita.* (ほんのわずかな人がその会に出席した) Only *a few* people attended the party. / *Kare ga seekoo suru chañsu wa* wazuka *da.* (彼が成功するチャンスはわずかだ) There is a *slim* chance that he will succeed. / *Watashi no suutsukeesu wa kimi no yori* wazuka *ni ookii.* (私のスーツケースはきみのよりわずかに大きい) My suitcase is *slightly* bigger than yours.

— *adv.* only: *Kyooto ni wa* wazuka *mikka ita dake deshita.* (京都にはわずか三日いただけでした) I was in Kyoto for *only* three days. / *Ima wa* wazuka *señ-eñ shika motte imaseñ.* (今はわずか千円しか持っていません) Now I have *only* one thousand yen.

Y

ya¹ や *p.* and: ★ Used to link nouns which are representative of their class.
Sono o-kane de hoñ ya jisho o kaimashita. (そのお金で本や辞書を買いました) I bought books, dictionaries, *and the like*, with that money. / *Nihoñ de wa Kyooto ya Nara e ikitai desu.* (日本では京都や奈良へ行きたいです) In Japan, I want to go to *places like* Kyoto *and* Nara.
《⇨ dano; to²; to ka》

ya² や *p.* as soon as: ★ Follows the dictionary form of a verb. Also 'ya ina ya.' 《⇨ ina》
Kare wa uchi ni kaeru ya (ina ya) kabañ o oite, mata tobidashite itta. (彼は家に帰るや(いなや)かばんを置いて、また飛び出して行った) *No sooner* had he come home *than* he put down his bag and rushed out again. / *Musume wa watashi no kao o miru ya (ina ya) nakidashita.* (娘は私の顔を見るや(いなや)泣き出した) My daughter started crying *as soon as* she saw my face.

ya³ や *p.* **1** (used in orders, requests or invitations): ★ Used by men.
Chotto tetsudatte kure ya. (ちょっと手伝ってくれや) *Here!* Give us a hand. / *Sorosoro dekakeyoo ya.* (そろそろ出かけようや) Now let's get going.
2 (used at the end of a sentence to add a note of informality to judgments, or statements of emotion or feeling): ★ Used by men.
Aa tsumañnai ya. (ああ、つまんないや) Oh, how boring! / *Sappari wakaranai ya.* (さっぱりわからないや) I just don't understand! / *Boku wa ikitaku nai ya.* (ぼくは行きたくないや) I

tell you, I don't want to go.
3 (used by older people in addressing family members and those junior to them):
Hanako ya, chotto kite okure. (花子や、ちょっと来ておくれ) Hanako! Come over here. / *Taroo ya, chotto tetsudatte.* (太郎や、ちょっと手伝って) Come on Taro! Lend a hand.

ya¹⁴ や (矢) *n.* arrow:
ya o iru (矢を射る) shoot an *arrow* / *Ya ga mato ni atatta.* (矢が的に当たった) The *arrow* hit the target.
《↔ yumi》

ya' やっ *int.* **1** aha: ★ An exclamation of satisfaction or surprise.
Ya', mitsuketa. (やっ、見つけた) *Aha!* I have found it.
2 hi; ya:
Ya', hisashiburi da ne. (やっ、久しぶりだね) *Hi!* It has been a long time, hasn't it?

-ya -や (屋) *suf.* store; shop; person:
yao-ya (八百屋) a *greengrocery* / *sakana-ya* (魚屋) a fish *shop* / *seeji-ya* (政治屋) a *professional politician.*

ya¹a やあ *int.* (*informal*) hi; hello:
Yaa, o-geñki desu ka? (やあ、お元気ですか) *Hi,* how are you?

ya「bañ やばん (野蛮) *a.n.* (~ na, ni) savage; barbarous:
yabañ na kooi (野蛮な行為) a *barbarous* act / *yabañ ni furumau* (野蛮に振る舞う) behave like a *savage* / *yabañ-jiñ* (野蛮人) a *barbarian.*

ya「bure「・ru¹ やぶれる (破れる) *vi.* (yabure-te Ⓥ) **1** tear; be torn; rip; be ripped:
Kono peeji wa yaburete iru. (このペ

－ジは破れている) This page *is torn*. / *Uwagi no sode ga kugi ni hikkakatte* yaburete shimatta. (上着のそでがくぎに引っ掛かって破れてしまった) The sleeve of my jacket caught on a nail and *was ripped*. / *Kono kiji wa* yabure-yasui. (この生地は破れやすい) This material *is* easily *torn*. (⇨ yaburu¹)

2 (of relationship, balance, etc.) break down; come to nothing: *Nichi-Bee-kañ no booeki no kiñkoo ga* yabureta. (日米間の貿易の均衡が破れた) The Japanese-American trade balance *became lopsided*. / *Kanojo no kekkoñ seekatsu wa sañ-neñ de* yabureta. (彼女の結婚生活は 3 年で破れた) Her married life *came to an end* after three years. (⇨ yaburu¹)

ya⌈bure⌉·ru² やぶれる (敗れる・破れる) *vi.* (yabure-te Ⓥ) (of a competitor) lose; be beaten: *Kinoo no shiai de uchi no chiimu wa kare no chiimu ni* yabureta. (きのうの試合でうちのチームは彼のチームに敗れた) Our team *was beaten* by his team in yesterday's game. / *Sono seejika wa koñdo no señkyo de* yabureta. (その政治家は今度の選挙で敗れた) The politician *was defeated* in this election. (⇨ yaburu²)

ya⌈bu⌉r·u¹ やぶる (破る) *vt.* (yabur·i-; yabur·a-; yabut-te Ⓒ) **1** tear; rip; break: *Akañboo ga shooji o* yabutta. (赤ん坊が障子を破った) The baby *ripped* the paper sliding door. / *Kare wa sono tegami o* yabutte *suteta*. (彼はその手紙を破って捨てた) He *ripped up* the letter and threw it away. (⇨ yaburu¹)

2 break (a promise, agreement, record, etc.): *Gootoo wa mado o* yabutte *haitta*. (強盗は窓を破って入った) The burglar *broke* the window and entered. / *Kanojo wa kesshite yaku-soku o* yaburanai. (彼女は決して約束を破らない) She *never breaks* promises. / *Sono kiroku wa too-buñ* yaburarenai *deshoo*. (その記録は当分破られないでしょう) That record will probably *not be broken* for some time.

ya⌈bu⌉r·u² やぶる (敗る・破る) *vt.* (yabur·i-; yabur·a-; yabut-te Ⓒ) beat; defeat: *Taigaasu wa Jaiañtsu o yoñ tai ichi de* yabutta. (タイガースはジャイアンツを 4 対 1 で破った) The Tigers *beat* the Giants 4 to 1. (⇨ yabureru²)

ya⌈chiñ やちん (家賃) *n.* (of an apartment, house, etc.) rent: *Kono heya no* yachiñ *wa ikura desu ka?* (この部屋の家賃はいくらですか) What is the *rent* on this room? / *Koñgetsu no* yachiñ *wa mada haratte imaseñ*. (今月の家賃はまだ払っていません) I haven't paid my *rent* for this month. / *Yachiñ ga tsuki juumañ-eñ ni agatta*. (家賃が月 10 万円に上がった) My *rent* has gone up to 100,000 yen a month.

ya⌈do やど (宿) *n.* **1** inn; hotel: *Watashi wa eki no chikaku ni* yado *o totta*. (私は駅の近くに宿をとった) I stayed at a *hotel* near the station. / *Kono atari de* yado *o sagasu no wa taiheñ desu*. (この辺りで宿を探すのは大変です) It is difficult to find a *place to stay* around here. **2** lodging: *Watashi wa kare ni hito-bañ* yado *o kashite yatta*. (私は彼に一晩宿を貸してやった) I gave him a night's *lodging*.

ya⌈doya やどや (宿屋) *n.* Japanese-style hotel; Japanese inn: yadoya *ni tomaru* (宿屋に泊まる) stay at a *Japanese inn*. (⇨ yado)

ya⌈gate やがて *adv.* by and by; before long; in the course of time:

Yagate *kare mo kuru daroo.*（やがて
彼も来るだろう）He also will be arriving *by and by.* / *Kaze wa* yagate *naorimashita.*（かぜはやがて治りまし
た）My cold got better *after a
while.* / *Nihoñ ni kite* yagate *sañ-
neñ ni narimasu.*（日本に来てやがて
3年になります）It will *soon* be three
years since I came to Japan.

ya⌐gu　やく（夜具）*n.* bedding;
bedclothes.《⇨ futoñ (illus.)》

ya⌐ha⌐ri　やはり *adv.* (*intensive =
yappari*) **1** as expected:
*Yahari anata ga yosoo shita toori
ni narimashita.*（やはりあなたが予想し
た通りになりました）Things turned
out *just as you had expected.*
2 still; nonetheless; after all:
Kare wa ima mo yahari *Kamakura ni suñde imasu.*（彼は今もやは
り鎌倉に住んでいます）He *still* lives
in Kamakura. / *Watashi wa* yahari *sore ni hañtai desu.*（私はやはり
それに反対です）I am against it *nonetheless.* / *Sake wa* yahari *Nada da.*
（酒はやはり灘だ）*Whatever you may
say,* the best sake comes from
Nada.
3 too; also: ★ In the pattern
'*...mo yahari.*'
Anata mo yahari *kaze o hiita ñ
desu ka?*（あなたもやはりかぜをひいたん
ですか）Have you caught a cold *as
well*? / *Kare no musuko mo* yahari
señsee desu.（彼の息子もやはり先生で
す）His son is *also* a teacher.

ya⌐i　やい *int.* (*rude*) hey:
Yai, kono itazurakko. Dete koi.（や
い、このいたずらっ子。出て来い）*Hey,
you rascal. Come on out!*

ya⌐ji　やじ（野次）*n.* jeering; hoot.
《⇨ yajiru》

ya⌐ji⌐r·u（野次る）*vt.* (yajir·i-;
yajir·a-; yajit-te Ⓒ) jeer; hoot;
boo:
Enzetsusha wa chooshuu ni yaji-
rareta.（演説者は聴衆にやじられた）
The speaker *was booed* by the

audience.《⇨ yaji》

ya⌐ji⌐rushi　やじるし（矢印）*n.* arrow sign:
yajirushi ni shitagatte susumu（矢
印に従って進む）follow the *arrows.*

ya⌐jiuma　やじうま（野次馬）*n.* curious onlooker; rubberneck:
yajiuma-koñjoo（やじ馬根性）*curiosity.*《⇨ kookishiñ》

ya⌐kamashi⌐·i　やかましい（喧しい）
a. (-ku) **1** noisy; loud:
Rajio no oto ga yakamashii.（ラジオ
の音がやかましい）The sound of the
radio is *noisy.* / *Soto ga* yakamashii *kedo nani-ka atta ñ desu ka?*
（外がやかましいけど何かあったんですか）
There is a lot of *noise* outside.
Has something happened?
《↔ shizuka》《⇨ urusai》
2 (of a rule, a regulation, etc.)
strict:
Kono gakkoo wa kisoku ga yakamashii.（この学校は規則がやかましい）
The rules at this school are very
strict. / *Kachoo wa jikañ ni* yakamashii.（課長は時間にやかましい）Our
section chief is very *strict* about
punctuality.
3 (of a person) particular:
Shujiñ wa tabemono ni yakamashii.（主人は食べ物にやかましい）My
husband is very *particular* about
food.《⇨ urusai》

ya⌐kañ¹　やかん（夜間）*n.* night;
nighttime:
*Yakañ no gaishutsu wa kiñjirare-
te imasu.*（夜間の外出は禁じられていま
す）Going out at *night* is forbidden. / *yakañ-bu*（夜間部）*night*
school.《↔ hiruma》

ya⌐kañ²　やかん（薬缶）*n.* teakettle;
kettle:
yakañ o hi ni kakeru（やかんを火にか
ける）put a *kettle* over the fire /
yakañ de yu o wakasu（やかんで湯を
わかす）boil water in a *kettle.*

ya⌐kedo　やけど（火傷）*n.* burn;
scald:

Kare no yakedo *wa naoru made jikañ ga kakatta.* (彼のやけどは治るまで時間がかかった) His *burns* took a long time to heal. / yakedo *no ookyuu-teate* (やけどの応急手当) first-aid treatment for a *burn*.
yakedo suru (〜する) *vi.* get burned; get scalded: *Sono ko wa nettoo de te o* yakedo *shita.* (その子は熱湯で手をやけどした) The child *scalded* his hand with boiling water.

ya⌐ke·ru やける (焼ける) *vi.* (yakete V) **1** burn; be burned: *Sono mise wa sakuya no kaji de* yaketa. (その店は昨夜の火事で焼けた) That shop *burned down* in last night's fire. (⇨ yaku¹)
2 be broiled; be grilled; be roasted; be baked; be toasted: *Keeki ga* yaketa. (ケーキが焼けた) The cake *was done.* / *Pañ no* yakeru *nioi ga suru.* (パンの焼けるにおいがする) I can smell bread *baking.* (⇨ yaku¹)
3 be tanned; get sunburned: *Irojiro no hito wa sugu* hi ni yakeru. (色白の人はすぐ日に焼ける) Fair-skinned people *get tanned* easily. / *Umi ni oyogi ni itte,* hi ni yaketa. (海に泳ぎに行って、日に焼けた) I *got sunburned* when I went swimming in the sea. (⇨ yaku¹)
4 be discolored: *Kono kiji wa iro ga* yake-yasui. (この生地は色が焼けやすい) This cloth *quickly becomes discolored.*

ya⌐kimashi やきまし (焼き増し) *n.* additional print of a photo: *Kono shashiñ wa itsu de mo* yakimashi *dekimasu.* (この写真はいつでも焼き増しできます) We can *make more copies* of this photo any time.
yakimashi suru (〜する) *vt.* make an additional print [copy]: *Kono shashiñ o go-mai* yakimashi shite kudasai. (この写真を5枚焼き増しして

ください) Please *make* five *prints* of this photo.

ya⌐kimochi⌐ やきもち (焼き餅) *n.* toasted rice cake. (⇨ mochi)
yakimochi o yaku (〜を焼く) get jealous: *Kanojo wa watashi ga hoka no oñna no hito to hanasu to* yakimochi o yaku. (彼女は私がほかの女の人と話すと焼き餅を焼く) She *gets jealous* when I talk to other women.

ya⌐kitori やきとり (焼き鳥) *n.* chunks of chicken barbecued on a bamboo skewer: ★ Various entrails and parts of pork are also served in the same way.
yakitori-ya (焼き鳥屋) a *yakitori restaurant.* (⇨ choochiñ)

YAKITORI

ya⌐kkai やっかい (厄介) *n.* burden; trouble: *hoka no hito ni* yakkai *o kakeru* (ほかの人にやっかいをかける) cause other people a lot of *trouble* / yakkai-mono (やっかい者) an *unmanageable person*; a *burden.*
— *a.n.* (〜 na, ni) troublesome; burdensome: yakkai *na shigoto* (やっかいな仕事) a *troublesome* job / *Moñdai ga* yakkai *ni natte kita.* (問題がやっかいになってきた) The problem has become rather *complicated.*
yakkai ni naru (やっかいになる) depend on; stay: *Kare wa mada oya no* yakkai ni natte iru. (彼はまだ親のやっかいになっている) He *is* still *dependent* on his parents. / *Kotoshi no natsu wa is-shuukañ oji no tokoro ni* yakkai ni natta. (ことしの

夏は一週間おじの所にやっかいになった）
This summer I *stayed* at my uncle's place for a week.

ya⌈kki やっき（躍起）*a.n.* （〜 ni） eager; excited; heated; vehement:
Kare-ra wa hito-mooke shiyoo to yakki ni [to] natte iru. （彼らは一もうけしようと躍起に[と]なっている）They *are eager* to make a big profit. / *Kare wa yakki ni natte, sono uwasa o hitee shita.* （彼は躍起になって、そのうわさを否定した）He *vehemently* denied the rumor.

ya⌈kkyoku やっきょく（薬局）*n.* pharmacy; drugstore.

ya⌈k·u˥ やく（焼く）*vt.* （yak·i-; ya-k·a-; ya·i-te Ⓒ） **1** burn:
Kimitsu-shorui o yaita. （機密書類を焼いた）I *burned* the classified documents. （⇨ yakeru）
2 tan; get a tan:
Kanojo wa umi e itte, hada o yaita. （彼女は海へ行って、肌を焼いた）She went to the seaside and *got a tan.* （⇨ yakeru）
3 broil; grill; roast; bake; toast; barbecue:
suteeki o yaku （ステーキを焼く）*grill* a steak / *Oobuñ de pañ o yaita.* （オーブンでパンを焼いた）I *baked* bread in the oven. （⇨ yakeru）

ya⌈ku˥¹² やく（役）*n.* **1** role; part:
Kanojo no musuko wa ooji no yaku o eñjita. （彼女の息子は王子の役を演じた）Her son played the *part* of a prince.
2 position; post:
Kare wa buchoo no yaku o ataera-reta. （彼は部長の役を与えられた）He was given the *post* of general manager.

yaku ni tatsu （〜に立つ）be use-ful: *Anata no hiñto wa yaku ni tachimashita.* （あなたのヒントは役に立ちました）Your hint *was very help-ful.* / *Kono hoñ wa amari* yaku ni tatanakatta. （この本はあまり役に立た

なかった）This book *was not much help.*

ya⌈ku˥³ やく（約）*adv.* about; some; nearly:
Koko kara eki made yaku *ni-kiro arimasu.* （ここから駅まで約２キロあります）It is *about* two kilometers from here to the station. / *Hooru ni wa* yaku *nijuu-niñ no hito ga imashita.* （ホールには約20人の人がいました）There were *some* twenty peo-ple in the hall.

ya⌈ku˥⁴ やく（訳）*n.* translation:
Kanojo wa yaku *ga umai [heta da].* （彼女は訳がうまい[へただ]）She is good [poor] at *translation.* / *Kono hoñ no Nihoñgo* yaku *wa mada dete imaseñ.* （この本の日本語訳はまだ出ていません）The Japanese *translation* of this book has not been pub-lished yet. （⇨ hoñyaku; yakusu）

-yaku やく（薬）*suf.* medicine; drug; pill:
shiñ-yaku （新薬）a new *drug* / *sui-miñ-yaku* （睡眠薬）a sleeping *pill* / *doku-yaku* （毒薬）*poison.*

ya⌈kuda⌈ts·u やくだつ（役立つ）*vi.* （-dach·i-; -dat·a-; -dat·te Ⓒ） be of use; be useful; be helpful:
Kono hoñ wa Nihoñgo no beñkyoo ni taiheñ yakudachimasu. （この本は日本語の勉強に大変役だちます）This book *is* very *useful* in the study of Japanese.

ya⌈kugo やくご（訳語）*n.* word; term; equivalent translation:
Kono Nihoñgo ni pittari no Eego no yakugo *wa arimaseñ.* （この日本語にぴったりの英語の訳語はありません）There is no really suitable En-glish *word* for this Japanese term.

ya⌈kuhiñ やくひん（薬品）*n.* med-icine; drug; chemical. （⇨ kusuri）

ya⌈kume やくめ（役目）*n.* duty; role:
Jibuñ no yakume *wa chañto yari nasai.* （自分の役目はちゃんとやりなさい）Carry out your *duties* properly. /

Kare wa sono fuñsoo de chootee-sha no yakume *o hatashita.* (彼はその紛争で調停者の役目を果たした) He played the *role* of arbitrator in the dispute. / *Choonañ wa otooto-tachi ni taishite chichi-oya no* yakume o hatashita. (長男は弟たちに対して父親の役目を果たした) The oldest son *acted* as father to his younger brothers.

ya⌐kuniñ やくにん (役人) *n.* government official; public servant: *Gaimu-shoo no* yakuniñ (外務省の役人) an *official* in the Ministry of Foreign Affairs.

ya⌐kusha やくしゃ (役者) *n.* actor; actress: ★ Less formal than '*haiyuu*.'
Kare wa yakusha *ni naritagatte iru.* (彼は役者になりたがっている) He wants to become an *actor.*
《⇨ haiyuu》
yakusha ga ichimai ue (～が一枚上) be better than: *Ano hito wa watashi yori* yakusha ga ichi-mai ue da. (あの人は私より役者が一枚上だ) He is a *cut above* me.

ya⌐kusho やくしょ (役所) *n.* government office:
Chichi wa yakusho *ni tsutomete imasu.* (父は役所に勤めています) My father works at a *government office.* / *shi*-yakusho (市役所) a city *hall* / *ku*-yakusho (区役所) a ward *office.*

ya⌐kusoku やくそく (約束) *n.* promise; engagement; appointment:
yakusoku *o mamoru* [*yaburu*] (約束を守る[破る]) keep [break] a *promise* / *Koñbañ wa kare to au* yakusoku *ga arimasu.* (今晩は彼と会う約束があります) I have an *appointment* to see him this evening. / *Kanojo wa* yakusoku *no jikañ ni arawarenakatta.* (彼女は約束の時間に現れなかった) She did not turn up at the *appointed* time.

yakusoku ga chigau (～が違う) different from what was promised: *Sore de wa* yakusoku ga chi-gaimasu. (それでは約束が違います) That being so, *it's contrary to your promise.*
yakusoku suru (～する) *vt.* promise; make an appointment: *Watashi wa kare ni kyooryoku o* yaku-soku shita. (私は彼に協力を約束した) I *promised* him my cooperation. / *Chichi wa watashi ni kuruma o katte kureru to* yakusoku shite kureta. (父は私に車を買ってくれると約束してくれた) My father *promised* me that he would buy me a car.

ya⌐ku·s·u やくす (訳す) *vt.* (yaku-sh·i-; yakus·a-; yakush·i-te C) translate; put...into...:
Tsugi no Eego o Nihoñgo ni yaku-shi nasai. (つぎの英語を日本語に訳しなさい) *Put* the following English *into* Japanese. / *Kono hoñ wa sañ-ka-kokugo ni* yakusarete imasu. (この本は三か国語に訳されています) This book *has been translated* into three languages. 《⇨ yaku》

ya⌐kuwari やくわり (役割) *n.* part; role:
Kare wa sono señkyo-uñdoo de juuyoo na yakuwari *o hatashita.* (彼はその選挙運動で重要な役割を果たした) He played an important *role* in the election campaign.

ya⌐kyuu やきゅう (野球) *n.* baseball:
Yakyuu *wa shita koto wa arima-señ ga, miru no wa suki desu.* (野球はしたことはありませんが、見るのは好きです) I have never played *baseball*, but I like to watch it. / yakyuu *no señshu* (野球の選手) a *baseball* player / yakyuu-joo (野球場) a *ballpark.*

ya⌐ma やま (山) *n.* **1** mountain; hill: ★ A hill with a gentle slope and lower than '*yama*' is called '*oka*.'

yama *ni noboru* (山に登る) climb a *mountain* / yama *o kudaru* (山を下る) descend a *mountain* / *natsu-yasumi o* yama *de sugosu* (夏休みを山で過ごす) spend one's summer vacation in the *mountains*. 《⇨ oka》

2 heap; pile:
gomi no yama (ごみの山) a trash *heap* / *hoñ no* yama (本の山) a *pile* of books.

3 climax; juncture:
Sono jikeñ wa yama *o mukaeta.* (その事件は山を迎えた) The affair has reached a critical *juncture*.

4 guess:
Yama *ga atatta [hazureta].* (やまが当たった[はずれた]) My *guess* hit [missed] the mark.

-yama やま (山) *suf.* Mount; Mt.
★ Added to the name of a mountain.
Mihara-yama (三原山) *Mount* Mihara / *Asama*-yama (浅間山) *Mount* Asama. 《⇨ -sañ²》

Ya「magata」-keñ やまがたけん (山形県) *n.* Yamagata Prerecture. Located in the southwest section of the Tohoku district, facing the Sea of Japan. The production of cherries, grapes and pears is the highest in Japan. Capital city: Yamagata. 《⇨ map (G2)》

Ya「maguchi」-keñ やまぐちけん (山口県) *n.* Yamaguchi Prefecture. Located at the west end of Honshu. In the central region, there is the largest limestone plateau in Japan with many stalactite caves. Capital city: Yamaguchi. 《⇨ map (B4)》

ya「maimo やまいも (山芋) *n.* yam. 《⇨ imo (illus.)》

ya「maku」zure やまくずれ (山崩れ) *n.* landslide.
Totsuzeñ yamakuzure *ga okita.* (突然山崩れが起きた) Suddenly a *landslide* occurred.

Ya「manashi」-keñ やまなしけん (山梨県) *n.* Yamanashi Prefecture. Located in the southeast section of the Chubu district, surrounded by mountain ranges. The Fuji Five Lakes lie here at the foot of Mt. Fuji. Capital city: Kofu (甲府). 《⇨ map (F4)》

ya「manote やまのて (山の手) *n.*
1 the hilly section of a city.
2 the residential section of a city; uptown. 《↔ shitamachi》

ya「mawake」 やまわけ (山分け) *n.* equal division; going halves. 《⇨ buñpai》

yamawake (ni) suru (〜(に)する) *vt.* divide equally; go shares:
Mooke wa futari de yamawake ni shiyoo. (もうけは二人で山分けにしよう) Let's *split* the profit *fifty-fifty*. / *Moratta o-kane wa miñna de* yamawake shita. (もらったお金はみんなで山分けした) We *divided* the money received *equally* among ourselves.

ya「me・ru」¹ やめる (止める) *vt.* (ya-me-te Ⓥ) **1** stop; discontinue:
Oshaberi o yame nasai. (おしゃべりをやめなさい) *Stop* your chattering! / *Sono shiñbuñ wa toru no o* yame-mashita. (その新聞は取るのをやめました) I *stopped* taking that newspaper. 《⇨ yamu¹》

2 give up; abandon:
Kare wa keñkoo no tame ni taba-ko o yameta. (彼は健康のためにたばこをやめた) He *gave up* smoking for his health. / *Sono keekaku wa* yameru *koto ni narimashita.* (その計画はやめることになりました) It has been decided to *give up* the plan. 《⇨ akirameru》

ya「me・ru」² やめる (辞める) *vt.* (ya-me-te Ⓥ) resign; quit:
Yamada-sañ wa shachoo o ya-meta. (山田さんは社長を辞めた) Mr. Yamada *resigned* his position as president. / *Kare wa chuuto de*

gakkoo o yameta. (彼は中途で学校
を辞めた) He *dropped out* of school.
/ *Kare wa kaisha o* yamesasera-
reta. (彼は会社を辞めさせられた) He
was forced to quit the company.

ya⸢mi⸣[1] やみ (闇) *n.* **1** darkness:
Kare-ra wa yami *ni magirete, ni-
gesatta.* (彼らはやみにまぎれて、逃げ去
った) They ran away under cover
of *darkness.*
2 black-marketing; illegal trade:
shinamono o yami *de uru* [*kau*]
(品物をやみで買う[売る]) sell [buy]
goods on the *black market.*

ya⸢m·u⸣[1] やむ (止む) *vi.* (yam·i-;
yam·a-; yañ-de Ⓒ) stop; die
down:
Ame ga yandara *dekakeyoo.* (雨が
やんだら出かけよう) Let's go out
when the rain *has stopped.* / *Kaze
ga* yañda. (風がやんだ) The wind
has died down. / *Mono-oto ga*
yañda. (物音がやんだ) The sound
ceased. / *Sawagi ga* yañda. (騒ぎが
やんだ) The noise *died down.* /
Nakigoe ga yañda. (泣き声がやんだ)
The crying *stopped.* / *Hanashigoe ga* yañda. (話し声がやんだ) The
voices *stopped.* (⇨ yameru[1])

ya⸢m·u⸣[2] やむ (病む) *vt., vi.* (ya-
m·i-; yam·a-; yañ-de Ⓒ) be
taken sick; suffer from:
Kanojo wa zeñsoku o yañde imasu.
(彼女はぜんそくを病んでいます) She *is
suffering from* asthma.

ya⸢mu⸣naku やむなく *adv.* =
yamu o ezu.

ya⸢mu o e⸣nai やむをえない (やむを
得ない) unavoidable; inevitable:
*Yamu o enai jijoo de, kai ni wa
kesseki sasete itadakimasu.* (やむを
えない事情で、会には欠席させていただき
ます) Because of *unavoidable* circumstances, please excuse me
from attending the party. / *Kare
ga shippai shita no wa* yamu o
emaseñ. (彼が失敗したのはやむをえませ
ん) It is *inevitable* that he failed.

ya⸢mu o e⸣zu やむをえず (やむを得
ず) *adv.* reluctantly; unwillingly:
Kare ga yasuñda no de, yamu o
ezu *watashi ga gichoo no yaku o
hikiuketa.* (彼がやすんだので、やむをえず
私が議長の役を引き受けた) Since
he was absent, I *reluctantly* took on
the post of chairman. / *Jijoo ga
atte, kanojo wa* yamu o ezu *taishoku shita.* (事情があって、彼女はや
むをえず退職した) Owing to circumstances, she *unwillingly* quit her
job.

ya⸣ne やね (屋根) *n.* roof:
yane *ni noboru* (屋根に上る) climb
onto a *roof* / *kawara de* yane *o
fuku* (かわらで屋根をふく) cover a
roof with tiles.

ya⸣nushi やぬし (家主) *n.* landlord; landlady:
Kono uchi no yanushi *wa dare
desu ka?* (この家の家主はだれですか)
Who is the *owner* of this house?

ya⸢oya やおや (八百屋) *n.*
1 vegetable store; greengrocery:
2 greengrocer.

YAOYA

ya⸢ppa⸣ri やっぱり *adv.* (*intensive*) = yahari.

yara やら *p.* what with...:
★ Used in the pattern '...*yara*...
yara' to link nouns or verbs
which are representative of their
class.
Beñkyoo yara*, arubaito* yara *de,
kono-goro isogashii.* (勉強やら、アル
バイトやらで、このごろ忙しい) *What
with* my studies *and* my part-
time job, I am busy these days. /

Deñwa ga naru yara, *tomodachi ga kuru* yara de, *ichi-nichi-juu isogashikatta.* (電話がなるやら，友だちが来るやらで，一日中忙しかった) *With the* phone ringing *and* my friends coming around, I was busy all day. 《⇨ ya¹》

ya⌐reyare やれやれ *int.* well: ★ Used to express a sigh of relief. *Yareyare, yatto shigoto ga owatta.* (やれやれ，やっと仕事が終わった) *Well, well,* the job is at last finished.

ya⌐rikata やりかた (やり方) *n.* way; method: *Sono yarikata o oshiete kudasai.* (そのやり方を教えてください) Please show me *how to do* it. / *Seekoo mo shippai mo yarikata shidai desu.* (成功も失敗もやり方しだいです) Success or failure depends on *how you do* it. / *Kare wa kare dokutoku no yarikata o shite, seekoo shimashita.* (彼は彼独特のやり方をして，成功しました) He succeeded by doing it in his own special *way.*

ya⌐rikome·ru やりこめる (遣り込める) *vt.* (-kome-te Ⓒ) argue a person down: *Kare ga jimañ suru no de yarikomete yatta.* (彼が自慢するのでやり込めてやった) As he boasted too much, I *talked him down.*

ya⌐rinaoshi やりなおし (やり直し) *n.* redoing; doing over again: *Suñda koto wa yarinaoshi ga kikimaseñ.* (済んだことはやり直しがききません) What is done *cannot be undone.* / *Kachoo wa kare ni sono shigoto no yarinaoshi o meejita.* (課長は彼にその仕事のやり直しを命じた) The manager told him to *do* the job *once more.* 《⇨ yarinaosu》

ya⌐rinao⌐s·u やりなおす (やり直す) *vt.* (-naosh·i-; -naos·a-; -naosh·i-te ⒸⒸ) do over again; make a fresh start: *Sono shigoto o saisho kara yarinaoshimashita.* (その仕事を最初から

やり直しました) I *did* the work *over* from the beginning. / *Sono ki ni nareba, jiñsee wa yarinaosu koto ga dekimasu.* (その気になれば人生はやり直すことができます) If you have the inclination to do so, you can *make a fresh start* in life. 《⇨ yarinaoshi》

ya⌐ri⌐tori やりとり (やり取り) *n.* exchange: *okurimono no yaritori* (贈り物のやり取り) an *exchange* of presents / *hageshii kotoba no yaritori* (激しい言葉のやり取り) a violent *exchange* of words / *Kanojo to wa mada tegami no yaritori o shite imasu.* (彼女とはまだ手紙のやり取りをしています) I *am* still *exchanging* letters with her.

ya⌐r·u¹ やる (遣る) *vt.* (yar·i-; yar·a-; yat-te ⒸⒸ) 1 do; play: ★ More informal than 'suru.' *Shukudai o yarimashita ka?* (宿題をやりましたか) Have you *done* your homework? / *Tenisu o yarimashoo.* (テニスをやりましょう) *Let's play* tennis.
2 keep; run: *Chichi wa hoñya o yatte imasu.* (父は本屋をやっています) My father *runs* a bookstore.
3 eat; drink; have; smoke: *Kare wa tabako wa yaranai ga, sake wa yaru.* (彼はたばこはやらないが，酒はやる) He *does not* smoke, but *drinks.*

ya⌐r·u² やる (遣る) *vt.* (yar·i-; yar·a-; yat-te ⒸⒸ) 1 give: ★ Never used toward one's superiors. *kodomo ni o-kashi o yaru* (子どもにお菓子をやる) *give* candy to a child / *inu ni esa o yaru* (犬にえさをやる) *feed* the dog / *hana ni mizu o yaru* (花に水をやる) *water* the flowers. 《⇨ ageru¹》
2 send: *Watashi wa musume ni tegami o yatta.* (私は娘に手紙をやった) I *sent* a

letter to my daughter. / *Kare wa musuko o ika-daigaku ni* yatta. (彼は息子を医科大学にやった) He *sent* his son to a medical college.

ya⌈sai やさい（野菜）*n.* vegetable; greens:
yasai *o tsukuru* (野菜を作る) grow *vegetables* / yasai-*sarada[suupu]* (野菜サラダ[スープ]) *vegetable* salad [soup].

YASAI

ya⌈sashi·i[1] やさしい（易しい）*a.* (-ku) easy; simple; plain:
Kono hoñ wa yasashii *Nihoñgo de kaite arimasu.* (この本はやさしい日本語で書いてあります) This book is written in *easy* Japanese. / *Kyoo no tesuto wa* yasashikatta. (きょうのテストはやさしかった) Today's test was *easy*.

ya⌈sashi·i[2] やさしい（優しい）*a.* (-ku) gentle; tender; kind:
kimochi no yasashii *hito* (気持ちの優しい人) a *kindhearted* person / yasashii *koe* (優しい声) a *sweet* voice / *Kare wa* yasashii *me o shite iru.* (彼は優しい目をしている) He has *gentle* eyes. / *Kanojo wa watashi ga komatte iru toki* yasashiku *shite kureta.* (彼女は私が困っているとき優しくしてくれた) She was *kind* to me when I was in a difficult situation.

ya⌈se·ru やせる（痩せる）*vi.* (yase-

te Ⓥ) lose weight; become thin:
Kanojo wa totemo yasete iru. (彼女はとてもやせている) She *is* very *thin*. / *Watashi wa saikiñ go-kiro* yase-mashita. (私は最近5キロやせました) I *have* recently *lost* five kilograms. / yaseta *hito [uma]* (やせた人[馬]) a *lean* person [horse].

ya⌈shiki[1] やしき（屋敷）*n.* mansion; residence; premises:
Kare wa ooki-na yashiki *ni suñde iru.* (彼は大きな屋敷に住んでいる) He lives in a large *mansion*.

ya⌈shiñ やしん（野心）*n.* ambition:
Kare wa chiji ni naritai to iu yashiñ *o motte iru.* (彼は知事になりたいという野心を持っている) He has *ambitions* of becoming prefectural governor. / yashiñ-*ka* (野心家) an *ambitious* person.

ya⌈shina·u やしなう（養う）*vt.* (yashina·i-; yashinaw·a-; yashinat-te Ⓒ) 1 support; sustain; feed:
Watashi wa kazoku go-niñ o ya-shinawanakereba naranai. (私は家族5人を養わなければならない) I *must support* a family of five.
2 bring up:
Sono kodomo wa shiñseki no uchi de yashinawareta. (その子どもは親戚の家で養われた) The child *was brought up* in the home of his relatives.
3 cultivate; develop; build up:
jitsuryoku o yashinau (実力を養う) *cultivate* one's proficiency / *Kare wa mainichi suiee o shite tairyo-ku o* yashinatta. (彼は毎日水泳をして体力を養った) He *built up* his physical strength by swimming every day.

ya⌈su⌉·i やすい（安い）*a.* (-ku) cheap; low; inexpensive; reasonable:
Watashi wa yasui *kuruma o katta.* (私は安い車を買った) I bought a

cheap car. / *Moo sukoshi* yasuku *narimaseñ ka?* (もう少し安くなりませんか) Can't you make it a little *cheaper?* / *Sono nedañ nara* yasui. (その値段なら安い) If that is the price, it's *cheap.* / *Kyuuryoo ga* yasukute *taiheñ da.* (給料が安くてたいへんだ) Since my salary is *low*, I am having a hard time. 《↔ takai》

-yasu¹·i やすい（易い）*suf.* (*a.*) (-ku) easy; apt: ★ Added to the continuative base of a verb.
Kare no buñshoo wa yomi-yasui. (彼の文章は読みやすい) His prose is *easy* to read. / *Kono soojiki wa koware*-yasui. (この掃除機は壊れやすい) This vacuum cleaner is *apt* to break down. 《↔ -nikui》

ya「sume¹·ru やすめる（休める）*vt.* (yasume-te V̄) rest; relax:
karada o yasumeru (体を休める) *rest* one's body / *Dokusho no ato wa me o* yasumeru *to yoi.* (読書のあとは目を休めるとよい) It is good to *rest* your eyes after reading. / *Watashi wa shibaraku* shigoto no te o yasumeta. (私はしばらく仕事の手を休めた) I *took a rest* from my work for a while. 《⇨ yasumu》

ya「sumi¹ やすみ（休み）*n.* **1** rest; break; respite:
Kono heñ de ichi-jikañ no yasumi *o torimashoo.* (この辺で1時間の休みをとりましょう) Let's take an hour's *break* at this stage. / *Watashi-tachi wa* yasumi *nashi de sañ-jikañ aruita.* (私たちは休みなしで3時間歩いた) We walked three hours without a *rest.* 《⇨ yasumu》
2 absence:
Kare wa kyoo wa yasumi desu. (彼はきょうは休みです) He *is absent* today. 《⇨ yasumu》
3 being closed:
Kono depaato wa suiyoobi ga yasumi desu. (このデパートは水曜日が休みです) This department store *is closed* on Wednesdays. / *Asu wa*

gakkoo ga yasumi desu. (あすは学校が休みです) We *have no school* tomorrow. 《⇨ yasumu》
4 holiday; vacation:
Kanojo wa yasumi *o totte, kaigai ryokoo e ikimashita.* (彼女は休みをとって、海外旅行へ行きました) She took a *holiday* and went on an overseas trip. 《⇨ kyuuka》

ya「sumono やすもの（安物）*n.* cheap article:
yasumono *no tokee* (安物の時計) a *cheap* watch / *Yasumono o kau to kekkyoku takaku tsuku.* (安物を買うと結局高くつく) *Cheaper things* cost you more in the long run.

ya「su¹m·u やすむ（休む）*vi.* (yasum·i-; yasum·a-; yasuñ-de ⓒ)
1 take a rest; relax:
Tsukareta no de sukoshi yasumoo. (疲れたので少し休もう) I'm tired; *let's rest* a bit. 《⇨ yasumeru; yasumi》
2 be absent; stay away; take a holiday:
Kyoo kanojo wa kaze de kaisha o yasuñda. (きょう彼女はかぜで会社を休んだ) Today she *stayed away* from the office with a cold. 《⇨ yasumi》
3 go to bed; sleep:
Yuube wa yoku o-yasumi *ni naremashita ka?* (ゆうべはよくお休みになれましたか) *Did* you *sleep* well last night? / *Ashita wa hayai kara koñya wa hayaku* yasumoo. (あしたは早いから今夜は早く休もう) We must get up early tomorrow, so *let's go to bed* early tonight. 《⇨ neru¹》
O-yasumi nasai. (お休みなさい) Good night.

ya「suppo¹·i やすっぽい（安っぽい）*a.* (-ku) cheap; shoddy; tawdry:
yasuppoi *kabañ* (安っぽいかばん) a *cheap-looking* bag / *Kono nekutai wa nedañ no wari ni* yasuppoku *mieru.* (このネクタイは値段の割に安っぽく見える) Considering the price,

this tie looks rather *shoddy*.

ya⌐tara ni やたらに (矢鱈に) *adv.*
freely; haphazardly; thought-
lessly; at random:
Hoshii kara to itte, yatara ni *mono o kau mono de wa arimaseñ.*
(欲しいからといって、やたらに物を買うもの
ではありません) However much you
may want it, one does not buy
things *indiscriminately*.

ya⌐too やとう (野党) *n.* the opposition party; the opposition:
yatoo *giiñ* (野党議員) a member
of *the opposition* (in the Diet).
《↔ yotoo》

ya⌐to⌐·u やとう (雇う) *vt.* (yato·i-;
yatow·a-; yatot-te C) employ;
hire:
*Sono kaisha wa uñteñshu o sañ-
niñ* yatotte iru. (その会社は運転手を
3人雇っている) That company *em-
ploys* three drivers. / *Kare wa
hisho o* yatotta. (彼は秘書を雇った)
He *hired* a secretary.

ya⌐tsu やつ (奴) *n.* (sometimes
derog.) fellow; guy; chap:
Aitsu wa jitsu ni ii [iya na] yatsu
da. (あいつは実にいい[いやな]やつだ) He
is really a nice [disgusting] *guy.* /
Soñna koto o suru baka na yatsu
ga aru ka. (そんなことをするばかなやつが
あるか) How could *you* have done
such a silly thing!

ya⌐tte ku⌐ru やってくる (やって来る)
vi. (ki-; ko-; ki-te 1) **1** come
along; appear; turn up:
Inaka kara haha ga yatte kita. (い
なかから母がやって来た) My mother
has come up from the country. /
Kare wa ichi-jikañ go ni yatte
kita. (彼は1時間後にやって来た) He
turned up an hour later. 《⇨ kuru》
2 continue to do:
Ima made doo ni ka yatte korareta *no mo mina-sama no okage
desu.* (今までどうにかやって来られたのも
皆様のおかげです) It is thanks to you
all that I have managed to *get*

where I am now. / *Moo juu-neñ
kono shigoto o* yatte kimashita. (も
う10年この仕事をやって来ました) I
have already *been doing* this job
for ten years.

ya⌐tto やっと *adv.* **1** at last;
finally:
Yatto *mokuhyoo ga tassee dekita.*
(やっと目標が達成できた) *At last*, we
were able to attain our objective.
/ *Kare wa* yatto *nyuugaku-shikeñ
ni gookaku shita.* (彼はやっと入学試
験に合格した) He *finally* passed
the school entrance exam. / *Juu-
neñ kakatte,* yatto *shakkiñ o
harai-oeta.* (10年かかって、やっと借金
を払い終えた) It took ten years to *fi
nally* finish repaying the loan.
2 just; barely:
Watashi-tachi wa yatto *no koto
de yamagoya ni tadoritsuita.* (私た
ちはやっとのことで山小屋にたどりついた)
We *barely* managed to get to the
mountain hut. / *Kyoo wa tsukarete aruku no mo* yatto *datta.*
(きょうは疲れて歩くのもやっとだった)
Today I was so tired that even
walking was an *effort.* 《⇨ yoo-
yaku》

yat⌐tsu やっつ (八つ) *n.* eight:
★ Used when counting.
Kono riñgo o yattsu *kudasai.* (この
りんごを8つ下さい) Can I have *eight*
of these apples? / yattsu-me (八つ
目) *the eighth.* 《⇨ kazu (table)》

ya⌐ttsuke⌐·ru やっつける *vt.* (yat-
tsuke-te V) beat; criticize:
Aitsu o yattsukete *yaru zo.* (あいつ
をやっつけてやるぞ) I will *let that fellow have it*!

ya⌐wara⌐ka やわらか (柔らか) *a.n.*
(~ na, ni) **1** soft; tender:
yawaraka *na kusshoñ* (柔らかなクッ
ション) a *soft* cushion. 《↔ katai》
2 gentle; mild:
yawaraka *na hizashi* (柔らかな日ざ
し) *mild* sunshine / *Kare no hyoojoo wa* yawaraka *datta.* (彼の表情

は柔らかだった) He had a *gentle* expression.

3 flexible; supple: yawaraka *na karada* (柔らかな体) a *supple* body. 《⇨ yawarakai》

ya「waraka」・i やわらかい (柔かい・軟かい) *a.* (-ku) **1** soft; tender: yawarakai *beddo* (柔らかいベッド) a *soft* bed / yawarakai *niku* (柔らかい肉) *tender* meat. 《↔ katai》

2 gentle; mild: Yawarakai *asa no hizashi ga heya ni sashikoñde kita.* (柔らかい朝の日ざしが部屋に差し込んできた) The *gentle* morning sunlight came into the room.

3 (of a way of thinking, etc.) flexible; supple: *Kare no kañgaekata wa mada* yawarakai. (彼の考え方はまだ柔らかい) He is still *flexible* in his thinking. / *Kodomo wa karada ga* yawarakai. (子供は体が柔らかい) Children have *supple* bodies. 《↔ katai》《⇨ yawaraka》

ya「ya やや (稍) *adv.* a little; somewhat: *Kinoo ni kurabete kesa wa* yaya *atatakai.* (きのうに比べて今朝はやや暖かい) Compared to yesterday, it is *a little* warmer this morning. / *Keeki wa* yaya *yoku natte imasu.* (景気はややよくなっています) Business conditions are improving *slightly.* 《⇨ sukoshi》

ya「yakoshi」・i ややこしい *a.* (-ku) (*colloq.*) complicated; intricate; complex: yayakoshii *moñdai* (ややこしい問題) a *complicated* problem / *Kare wa* yayakoshii *jikeñ ni makikomareta.* (彼はややこしい事件に巻き込まれた) He got involved in a *troublesome* affair. / *Kore wa* yayakoshii *koto ni natta.* (これはややこしいことになった) Now things are in a *mess.*

Ya「yoi-ji」dai やよいじだい (弥生時代) *n.* Yayoi Period (ca. 300 B.C.

to A.D. 300)： Yayoi-shiki *doki* (弥生式土器) *Yayoi* ware. 《⇨ jidai (table)》

yo[1] よ (世) *n.* **1** world: *kono [ano]* yo (この[あの]世) this [the other] *world.*

2 times; age: *Yo wa koñpyuutaa no jidai desu.* (世はコンピューターの時代です) This is the *age* of computers. 《⇨ yo-no-naka》

yo mo sue (〜も末) a degenerate age: Yo mo sue *da.* (世も末だ) What a *degenerate age* this is!

yo ni deru (〜に出る) make one's debut: *Kare wa hatachi no toki, shoosetsuka to shite* yo ni deta. (彼は二十歳のとき, 小説家として世に出た) When he was twenty, he *made his debut* as a novelist.

yo o saru (〜を去る) pass away: *Sono haiyuu wa wakaku-shite* yo o satta. (その俳優は若くして世を去った) The actor *died* young.

yo[2] よ (夜) *n.* night: *Sono yo wa yuki ga futte ita.* (その夜は雪が降っていた) It was snowing that *night.* / *Yo mo fukete kita no ni kare wa mada kaeranai.* (夜もふけてきたのに彼はまだ帰らない) *It's getting late,* but he has not come home yet. / *Moo sugu* yo *ga akemasu.* (もうすぐ夜が明けます) *The day will soon break.* 《↔ hiru (table)》《⇨ yoru[1]》

yo[3] よ *p.* **1** (used when emphasizing one's thoughts, feeling or opinions, or when reminding someone of something): *Hayaku shinai to okuremasu* yo. (早くしないと遅れますよ) *Look,* you will be late unless you hurry up. / *Ano eega wa omoshiroi desu* yo. (あの映画は面白いですよ) *I can guarantee* the movie is exciting. / *Soñna shigoto wa iya desu* yo. (そんな仕事はいやですよ) I hate that kind of job.

2 (used to indicate an invitation or order):
Issho ni ikimashoo yo. (いっしょに行きましょうよ) *Come on,* let us go together. / *Soko e itte wa ikemaseñ* yo. (そこへ行ってはいけませんよ) You *really* must not go there. / *Kotchi ni koi* yo. (by men) (こっちに来いよ) Come here. / *Soñna koto iu na* yo. (by men) (そんなこと言うなよ) Don't say that sort of thing.
3 (used to indicate disapproval of someone's thoughts or actions):
Soko de nani o shite iru ñ da yo. (by men) (そこで何をしているんだよ) What are you up to there? / *Nani shite iru no* yo. (by women) (何しているのよ) What is it that you are doing? / *Nañ da* yo. (by men) (何だよ) What is it? / *Nani* yo. (by women) (何よ) What is it?
4 (formal) (used as a form of address):
Waga ko yo. (我が子よ) Oh, my child! / *Kami* yo. (神よ) Oh, God!

> **USAGE**
> Sometimes used with other particles. *Wakarimasu* yo ne. (わかりますよね) You *do* understand, don't you? / *Soñna koto kare ni dekiru ka* yo. (そんなこと彼にできるかよ) You *really* think he can do something like that?
> ((⇨ ka³; ne³))

-yo よ (余) suf. over; more than: *juu-niñ-yo* (10人余) *more than* ten people / *nijuu-yo-neñ* (20余年) *more than* twenty years.

yoˈakeˈ よあけ (夜明け) n. dawn; daybreak:
Kare wa yoake mae ni ie o demashita. (彼は夜明け前に家を出ました) He left home before *dawn.*

yoˈbi よび (予備) n. spare; extra:
yobi *no taiya [kagi]* (予備のタイヤ[鍵]) a *spare* tire [key] / *Neñ no ta-* me yobi *no okane o motte iki nasai.* (念のため予備のお金を持って行きなさい) Take some *extra* money with you just in case. / yobi-*chishiki* (予備知識) *elementary* knowledge / yobi-*hi* (予備費) a *reserve* fund / yobi-*kooshoo* (予備交渉) *preliminary* negotiations. ((⇨ yooi¹))

yoˈbidashi よびだし (呼び出し) n.
1 summons:
Kare wa keesatsu kara yobidashi *o uketa.* (彼は警察から呼び出しを受けた) He got a *summons* from the police to appear. ((⇨ yobidasu))
2 paging: ★ Usually 'o-yobidashi.'
Suzuki-sama o o-yobidashi *itashimasu. Furoñto made oide kudasai.* (鈴木さまをお呼び出しいたします. フロントまでおいでください) *Paging* Mr. Suzuki. Please come to the front desk. ((⇨ yobidasu))
3 (of sumo wrestling) match announcer.

yoˈbidaˈsˈu よびだす (呼び出す) vt. (-dash·i-; -das·a-; -dash·i-te C)
1 call; page:
Robii de kare o yobidashite *moratta.* (ロビーで彼を呼び出してもらった) I *had* him *paged* in the lobby. / *Sono seeto wa tabako o sutte, señsee ni* yobidasareta. (その生徒はたばこを吸って, 先生に呼び出された) The pupil *was called* before the teacher for smoking. ((⇨ yobidashi))
2 call [ring] up:
Taroo o deñwa-guchi ni yobidashite *kudasai.* (太郎を電話口に呼び出してください) Please *call* Taro to the phone. ((⇨ yobidashi))
3 summon:
Kare wa saibañsho ni yobidasareta. (彼は裁判所に呼び出された) He *was summoned* to court. ((⇨ yobidashi))

yoˈbikake よびかけ (呼び掛け) n. appeal; plea:

Watashi-tachi wa kaku-jikkeñ hañtai no yobikake *o okonatta.* (私たちは核実験反対の呼びかけを行った) We made an *appeal* against a nuclear test. / *Shusaisha no* yobikake *ni oojite ooku no hito ga sono taikai ni sañka shita.* (主催者の呼びかけに応じて多くの人がその大会に参加した) In response to *appeals* by the promoter, a lot of people attended the convention. ((⇨ yobikakeru))

yo⌐bikake⌐·ru よびかける (呼び掛ける) *vt.* (-kake-te V) **1** call (out); address:
Toori de shiranai hito ni yobikakerarete, *gyotto shita.* (通りで知らない人に呼びかけられて, ぎょっとした) I was startled when a stranger on the street *called out* to me. ((⇨ yobikake)) **2** appeal to (the public):
Shichoo wa shimiñ ni kootsuu jiko booshi o yobikaketa. (市長は市民に交通事故防止を呼びかけた) The mayor *appealed* to the residents to prevent traffic accidents. ((⇨ yobikake))

yo⌐bikoo よびこう (予備校) *n.* cramming school. ★ A school for students who wish to pass the university entrance exam.

yo⌐bisute よびすて (呼び捨て) *n.* (calling a person's name without any title of courtesy): ★ Shows either friendliness or disrespect.
Kare wa buka o yobisute *ni shite iru.* (彼は部下を呼び捨てにしている) He *drops the 'Mister' or 'Miss' when addressing* those working under him.

yo⌐boo よぼう (予防) *n.* prevention; precaution; protection:
Yoboo wa chiryoo ni masarimasu. (予防は治療に勝ります) *Prevention* is better than cure. / yoboo-*igaku* (予防医学) *preventive* medicine.
yoboo suru (〜する) *vt.* prevent;

protect: *Ha o migaite mushiba o* yoboo *shi nasai.* (歯をみがいて虫歯を予防しなさい) Brush your teeth to *prevent* tooth decay.

yo⌐boo-chu⌐usha よぼうちゅうしゃ (予防注射) *n.* preventive shot [injection].

yo⌐b·u よぶ (呼ぶ) *vt.* (yob·i-; yob·a-; yoñ-de C) **1** call; call [cry] out:
Dare-ka ga watashi no na o yoñda. (だれかが私の名を呼んだ) Someone *called* my name. / *Nani-ka moñdai ga attara, watashi o* yoñde *kudasai.* (何か問題があったら, 私を呼んでください) If you have any problems, please *call* me. / *Takushii o* yobimashoo ka? (タクシーを呼びましょうか) *Shall* I *call* a taxi?
2 invite:
Paatii ni wa kare o yobitai. (パーティーには彼を呼びたい) I *would like to invite* him to the party.
3 give a name; call:
Chikamatsu wa Nihoñ no Sheekusupia to yobareru *koto ga arimasu.* (近松は日本のシェークスピアと呼ばれることがあります) Chikamatsu *is* often *called* the Shakespeare of Japan.

yo⌐buñ よぶん (余分) *a.n.* (〜 na, ni) extra; spare; additional:
Ima wa yobuñ *na jikañ wa arimaseñ.* (今は余分な時間はありません) There is no time *to spare* now. / *Yaoya wa watashi ni riñgo o ikko* yobuñ *ni kureta.* (やおやは私にりんごを1個余分にくれた) The greengrocer gave me an *extra* apple. ((⇨ yokee))

yo⌐chi よち (余地) *n.* room; space:
Kare no yuuzai wa utagai no yochi *ga arimaseñ.* (彼の有罪は疑いの余地がありません) There's no *room* to doubt his guilt. / *Mada ikuraka kaizeñ no* yochi *ga arimasu.* (まだいくらか改善の余地があります) There is some *room* for improvement. /

Kono heya ni wa hoñbako o oku yochi *wa arimaseñ.*(この部屋には本箱を置く余地はありません) There's no *space* for a bookcase in this room.

yoˈchiyochi よちよち *adv.* (~ to) (the unsteady gait of a young child):
Akañboo ga yochiyochi aruki-hajimeta.(赤ん坊がよちよち歩き始めた) The baby *began to toddle.*

yoˈfuˈkashi よふかし(夜更かし) *n.* staying up late at night:
Yofukashi *wa karada ni yoku arimaseñ.*(夜更かしは体によくありません) *Keeping late hours* is not good for you.

yofukashi suru (~する) *vi.* stay up late at night; keep late hours:
Yuube wa hoñ o yoñde, yofukashi shita *no de kyoo wa nemui.*(ゆうべは本を読んで、夜更かししたのできょうは眠い) I am sleepy today because I *stayed up late* reading last night.
(↔ asaneboo)

yoˈfuke よふけ(夜更け) *n.* late hours of the night; midnight:
Yofuke *ni kare ga tazunete kita.*(夜更けに彼が訪ねて来た) He came to see me *late at night.*

yoˈgore よごれ(汚れ) *n.* dirt; stain; soil:
Zuboñ no yogore *o aratte otoshita.*(ズボンの汚れを洗って落とした) I washed off the *dirt* on the trousers. / *Kono iro wa* yogore *ga medatanai.*(この色は汚れが目立たない) *Dirty marks* don't stand out on this color. (⇨ yogoreru)

yoˈgore·ru よごれる(汚れる) *vi.* (yogore-te V) **1** become dirty; be soiled; be stained:
Nukarumi o aruite, kutsu ga yogoreta.(ぬかるみを歩いて、靴が汚れた) My shoes *became dirty* from walking on the muddy road. / *Sono* yogoreta *te o arai nasai.*(その汚れた手を洗いなさい) Wash those *dirty* hands!
(⇨ yogosu; yogore)

2 be polluted:
Kono kawa wa koojoo no haisui de yogorete iru.(この川は工場の排水で汚れている) This river *is polluted* by waste from the factory.
(⇨ yogosu; yogore)

yoˈgos·u よごす(汚す) *vt.* (yogosh-i-; yogos-a-; yogosh-i-te C) **1** make dirty; soil; stain:
Kono hoñ o yomu toki ni yogosanai *yoo ni ki o tsukete kudasai.*(この本を読むときに汚さないように気をつけてください) Please be careful *not to dirty* this book when you read it. / *Sono ko wa aisukuriimu de fuku o* yogoshite shimatta.(その子はアイスクリームで服を汚してしまった) The girl *soiled* her dress with ice cream. (⇨ yogoreru)

2 pollute:
Baieñ ga kuuki o yogoshite iru.(煤煙が空気を汚している) Soot and smoke *are polluting* the air.
(⇨ yogoreru)

yoˈhodo よほど(余程) *adv.* **1** very; much; greatly:
Kare wa yohodo *noñda to miete, furafura shite ita.*(彼はよほど飲んだとみえて、ふらふらしていた) He seemed to have drunk *a lot* and was unsteady on his feet. / *Kanojo wa ima no shigoto ga* yohodo *ki ni itte iru yoo da.*(彼女は今の仕事がよほど気に入っているようだ) She seems *very* pleased with her present job.

2 nearly; almost:
Yohodo *tsutome o yameyoo ka to omoimashita ga omoitodomari-mashita.*(よほど勤めをやめようかと思いましたが思いとどまりました) I *almost* decided to quit my job, but I changed my mind.

yohodo no koto (~のこと) exceptional reason: *Kare wa* yohodo no koto *ga nai kagiri okorimaseñ.*(彼はよほどのことがない限り怒りません) He never gets angry unless *there is some good reason.*

yo⌐hoo よほう（予報）*n.* forecast:
Teñki-yohoo ga atatta [hazureta].
（天気予報が当たった[外れた]）The
weather *forecast* was right
[wrong]. / *Teñki no chooki-yohoo
wa ate ni naranai.*（天気の長期予報
は当てにならない）The long-range
weather *forecast* is not reliable.
yohoo suru（～する）*vt.* forecast:
*Terebi de wa gogo kara ame ni
naru to yohoo shite ita.*（テレビでは
午後から雨になると予報していた）On
television they *forecasted* that the
rain would begin in the afternoon.

yo⌐i·i¹ よい（良い・善い）*a.* (-ku)
★ More formal than '*ii.*'
1 good; excellent:
Sore wa yoi kañgae desu.（それは良
い考えです）That's a *good* idea. /
*Kare no eñzetsu wa totemo yo-
katta.*（彼の演説はとても良かった）His
speech was *excellent*.
2 good; well:
Anata ni yoi shirase ga arimasu.
（あなたに良い知らせがあります）There is
some *good* news for you. / *Kanojo
wa sodachi ga yoi.*（彼女は育ちが良
い）She is *well* bred. 《↔ warui》
3 (of quality, weather, harvest)
good; fine:
*Watashi wa shitsu no yoi mono
dake o erañda.*（私は質の良いものだけ
をえらんだ）I selected only those
items of *good* quality. / *Kinoo wa
teñki ga yokatta ga, kyoo wa ame
da.*（きのうは天気が良かったが、きょうは
雨だ）Yesterday it was *fine*, but
today it is rainy. 《↔ warui》
4 (of a situation or condition)
good; fine:
*Kyoo wa karada no chooshi ga
amari yoku nai.*（きょうは体の調子が
あまり良くない）Today my physical
condition is not so *good*. / *Chichi
no guai wa yoku natte kimashita.*
（父のぐあいはよくなってきました）My
father's condition *has improved*. /

Keeki wa yoku natte imasu.（景気
はよくなっています）Business condi-
tions are getting *better*. 《↔ wa-
rui》
5 (of a choice, method, etc.)
right; suitable:
*Ueno e iku ni wa kono basu de
yoi no desu ka?*（上野へ行くにはこの
バスでよいのですか）Is this bus *okay* if
I want to go to Ueno? / *Koko wa
sakana-tsuri ni yoi basho desu.*（こ
こは魚釣りに良い場所です）This is a
good place for fishing.
6 (of luck) good; lucky:
*Uñ-yoku kanojo ni au koto ga de-
kita.*（運良く彼女に会うことができた）
Luckily I was able to meet her.
《↔ warui》

... hoo ga yoi（...ほうが～）had better: *Ima wa kanojo ni awanai hoo
ga yoi.*（今は彼女に会わないほうがよい）
You *had better* not see her now.
/ *Kimi wa sugu ni isha ni itta hoo
ga yoi.*（きみはすぐに医者に行ったほうが
よい）You *should* go and see a doctor without delay. 《⇒ hoo ga ii》
-te mo yoi（ても～）can; may:
*Kono arubamu o mite mo yoi de-
su ka?*（このアルバムを見てもよいですか）
Can I *have a look* at this photo
album?

yo⌐i² よい（酔い）*n.* drunkenness;
intoxication:
Dañdañ yoi ga mawatte kita.（だん
だん酔いが回ってきた）Gradually the
alcohol began to have an effect on
me. 《⇒ you》

yo⌐isho よいしょ *int.* heave ho;
here we go. ★ Used when moving something heavy, often by
two or more people together.

yo⌐jinobor·u よじのぼる（よじ登る）
vi. (-nobor·i-; -nobor·a-; -nobot-
te Ⓒ) climb (up); clamber (up):
ki ni [o] yojinoboru（木に[を]よじ登
る）*climb up* a tree / *Watashi-tachi
wa sono gake o yojinobotta.*（私た
ちはそのがけをよじ登った）We *climbed*

up that cliff. 《⇨ noboru³》

yo「jire」·ru よじれる（捩れる）*vi.* (yo-jire-te ⊻) be twisted:
Nekutai ga yojirete *imasu yo.* (ネクタイがよじれていますよ) Your necktie *is twisted.*

yo「ka よか（余暇）*n.* leisure; free [spare] time:
Yoka wa moppara dokusho ni atete imasu. (余暇はもっぱら読書にあてています) I devote nearly all my *leisure time* to reading. / *Kare wa* yoka *ni tenisu o tanoshiñde imasu.* (彼は余暇にテニスを楽しんでいます) He enjoys playing tennis in his *free time.*

yo「kee よけい（余計）*a.n.* (~ na) unnecessary; needless:
Yokee na koto wa shaberanai yoo ni shi nasai. (よけいなことはしゃべらないようにしなさい) Be careful not to make *uncalled-for* remarks. / *Yokee na o-sewa desu.* (よけいなお世話です) It's *none* of your business.
—*adv.* (~ ni) (the) more; extra; too many [much]:
Ukkari shite o-tsuri o yokee *ni yatte shimatta.* (うっかりしておつりをよけいにやってしまった) I inadvertently gave *too much* change. / *Suru na to iwareru to* yokee (*ni*) *shitaku naru mono desu.* (するなと言われるとよけい(に)したくなるものです) When we are told not to do something, we are inclined to want to do it *all the more.* 《⇨ yobuñ》

yo「ke」·ru よける（避ける）*vt.* (yo-ke-te ⊻) avoid; dodge:
kaze o yokeru (風をよける) *avoid* the wind / *ame o* yokeru (雨をよける) *seek shelter* from the rain / *Mizutamari o* yoke-nagara *aruita.* (水たまりをよけながら歩いた) I walked along, *avoiding* the puddles. / *Kare wa kuruma o* yokeru *tame ni waki e tobinoita.* (彼は車をよけるためにわきへ飛びのいた) He jumped aside to *dodge* the car.

yo「ki よき（予期）*n.* anticipation; expectation:
Yoki ni hañshite, shussekisha wa sukunakatta. (予期に反して、出席者は少なかった) Contrary to *expectations,* few people attended.
《⇨ yosoo》
yoki suru (~する) *vt.* expect; anticipate: *Sono shigoto wa* yoki *shite ita yori hayaku owarimashita.* (その仕事は予期していたより早く終わりました) The job was finished more quickly than we *had anticipated.* / *Soñna koto wa* zeñzeñ yoki *shite imaseñ deshita.* (そんなことは全然予期していませんでした) We *had never expected* anything like that.

yo「kiñ よきん（預金）*n.* deposit; money on deposit; savings:

(USAGE)
A deposit in a bank is generally called '*yokiñ,*' and savings put in the post office are called '*chokiñ.*'

---

yokiñ *o hikidasu* [orosu] (預金を引き出す[おろす]) withdraw one's *savings* / *Watashi wa kono giñkoo ni sukoshi* yokiñ *ga arimasu.* (私はこの銀行に少し預金があります) I have a small *deposit* in this bank. / yokiñ-tsuuchoo (預金通帳) a *bankbook.*
yokiñ suru (~する) *vi., vt.* deposit: *Kinoo juumañ-eñ* yokiñ *shimashita.* (きのう10万円預金しました) I *made a deposit* of 100,000 yen yesterday. 《⇨ chokiñ》

yo「kka よっか（四日）*n.* four days; the fourth day of the month:
Kare wa yokka *mae ni ryokoo ni dekakemashita.* (彼は4日前に旅行に出かけました) He went on a trip *four days* ago. / *Hachigatsu* yokka (八月四日) August 4. 《⇨ tsuitachi (table)》

yo「ko よこ（横）*n.* 1 width:
★ The horizontal distance from

side to side.

*Kono kami wa yoko ga juuhachi-
señchi, tate ga nijuusañ-señchi
arimasu.* (この紙は横が 18 センチ, 縦が
23 センチ, あります) This sheet of paper is eighteen centimeters in
width and twenty-three in length.
《↔ tate》

2 side:

*Kanojo wa watashi no yoko ni su-
watta.* (彼女は私の横に座った) She
sat at my *side.* / *Kuruma o uñteñ
suru toki wa yoko o minai de mae
o mi nasai.* (車を運転するときは横を見
ないで前を見なさい) When you're
driving a car, look straight ahead,
without turning aside.

3 (~ ni) sideways; crossways:
Kani wa yoko ni aruku. (かには横に
歩く) Crabs walk *sideways.* / *Yoko
ni señ o ip-poñ hiki nasai.* (横に線
を一本引きなさい) Draw a line *hori-
zontally.*

yoˈkogaki よこがき (横書き) *n.*
horizontal writing. 《↔ tategaki》

yoˈkogao よこがお (横顔) *n.* (of a
face) profile.

yoˈkogiˈr·u よこぎる (横切る) *vt.*
(-gir·i-; -gir·a-; -git-te Ⓒ) cross;
go across:
dooro o yokogiru (道路を横切る)
cross a road / *Me no mae o ootobai ga yokogitte itta.* (目の前をオー
トバイが横切って行った) Motorcycles
passed by in front of me.

Yoˈkohama よこはま (横浜) *n.*
capital of Kanagawa Prefecture.
A major Japanese seaport.
《⇨ map (F4)》

yoˈkoˈs·u よこす (寄越す) *vt.* (yo-
kosh·i-; yokos·a-; yokosh·i-te
Ⓒ) **1** send; hand over: ★ The
recipient is the speaker.
*Musuko wa metta ni tegami o yo-
kosanai.* (息子はめったに手紙をよこさ
ない) My son *rarely sends* me letters. / *Sono naifu o kochira ni yo-
koshi nasai.* (そのナイフをこちらによこし

なさい) Please *hand* that knife *over*
to me.

2 make a person come to the
speaker or writer:
*O-ko-sañ o itsu de mo uchi e asobi
ni yokoshite kudasai.* (お子さんをい
つでもうちへ遊びによこしてください)
Please *send* your child to play at
our house anytime.

yoˈkuˈ[1] よく (欲) *n.* greed; ava-
rice; desire:
Kare wa yoku ga fukai. (彼は欲が深
い) He *is greedy.* / *Yoku o dasu to
shippai shimasu yo.* (欲を出すと失
敗しますよ) If you *are too greedy,*
you will fail.

yoku o ieba (~を言えば) I wish:
*Yoku o ieba, kare ni wa moo suko-
shi gañbatte moraitai.* (欲を言えば,
彼にはもう少しがんばってもらいたい) *If I
am not asking too much,* I would
like him to try a bit harder.

yoˈkuˈ[2] よく (良く) *adv.* **1** well;
fully; thoroughly:
Yoku dekimashita. (よくできました)
Well done! / *Yamada-sañ wa
yoku shitte imasu.* (山田さんはよく知
っています) I know Miss Yamada
very well. / *Ossharu koto wa yoku
wakarimashita.* (おっしゃることはよくわ
かりました) I understand *perfectly*
what you say.

2 kindly; favorably:
*Kare wa itsu-mo watashi ni yoku
shite kuremasu.* (彼はいつも私によくし
てくれます) He always treats me
kindly. / *Kanojo wa anata no koto
o yoku itte mashita yo.* (彼女はあな
たのことをよく言ってましたよ) She
spoke *highly* of you. 《⇨ warui》

3 (used to express wonder, or
disapproval):
Yoku kega o shimaseñ deshita ne.
(よくけがをしませんでしたね) It's *a miracle* that you were not injured, isn't
it? / *Kimi wa yoku soñna koto ga
ieru ne.* (君はよくそんなことが言えるね)
I am amazed you can say some-

thing like that.

yo˥ku³ よく *adv.* frequently; often:
Kare wa yoku *kaze o hiku.* (彼はよくかぜを引く) He *often* catches colds. / *Kodomo no koro kono heñ de* yoku *asobimashita.* (子どものころこの辺でよく遊びました) I *often* played around here when I was a child. / *Watashi wa shigoto de* yoku *Koobe e ikimasu.* (私は仕事でよく神戸へ行きます) I *frequently* go to Kobe on business.

yo˥ku- よく (翌) *pref.* next; following:
yoku-*go-gatsu tooka* (翌 5 月 10 日) the *following* day, that is, May 10.

-yoku よく (欲) *suf.* desire; lust:
chishiki-yoku (知識欲) *thirst* for knowledge / *kiñseñ*-yoku (金銭欲) *desire* for money / *keñryoku*-yoku (権力欲) a *lust* for power.

yo˥kuasa よくあさ (翌朝) *n.* the next [following] morning:
Yokuasa *kare wa hayaku okite shuppatsu shita.* (翌朝彼は早く起きて出発した) *The following morning* he got up early and set off. 《↔ kesa》

yo˥kubari¹ よくばり (欲張り) *a.n.* (~ *na, ni*) greedy; avaricious:
yokubari *na hito* (欲張りな人) an *avaricious* person / *Kimi mo* yokubari *da ne.* (君も欲張りだね) You *are grasping*, aren't you? 《↔ muyoku》《⇨ yokubaru》

yo˥kuba˥r·u よくばる (欲張る) *vi.* (-bar·i-; -bar·a-; -bat-te [C]) be greedy; be avaricious:
Sono ko wa yokubatte *motto hoshii to itta.* (その子は欲ばってもっと欲しいと言った) That child *was greedy* and asked for more. / *Soñna ni* yokubaru *mono de wa arimaseñ.* (そんなに欲ばるものではありません) You should not *try to get so much*. 《⇨ yokubari》

yo˥kuboo よくぼう (欲望) *n.* de-sire; appetite; craving:
yokuboo *o mitasu [osaeru]* (欲望を満たす[抑える]) satisfy [overcome] one's *cravings* / *Niñgeñ no* yokuboo *ni wa kagiri ga nai.* (人間の欲望には限りがない) There's no limit to human *desires*.

yo˥kuchoo よくちょう (翌朝) *n.* (*formal*) the next [following] morning. 《⇨ yokuasa》

yo˥kugetsu よくげつ (翌月) *n.* the next [following] month:
Shiharai wa yokugetsu *matsu desu.* (支払いは翌月末です) Payment should be made at the end of *the next month*. 《↔ señgetsu》

yo˥kujitsu よくじつ (翌日) *n.* the next [following] day:
Shiai wa ame no tame yokujitsu *ni eñki sareta.* (試合は雨のため翌日に延期された) The game was put off until *the following day* because of rain. / *Yokujitsu* (*wa*) *doko e ikimashita ka?* (翌日(は)どこへ行きましたか) Where did you go *the next day?* 《↔ zeñjitsu》《⇨ akuruhi》

yo˥kuneñ よくねん (翌年) *n.* the next [following] year:
Kare wa sono yokuneñ *taisha shita.* (彼はその翌年退社した) He left the company *the following year*. 《↔ kyoneñ》《⇨ akurutoshi》

yo˥kushitsu よくしつ (浴室) *n.* bathroom; bath: ★ In Japanese houses, the bath and toilet are in separate rooms.
Yokushitsu *de shawaa o abita.* (浴室でシャワーを浴びた) I took a shower in the *bathroom*. 《⇨ furoba (photo)》

yo˥kushuu よくしゅう (翌週) *n.* the next [following] week.

yo˥me よめ (嫁) *n.* **1** bride:
musume o yome *ni yaru* (娘を嫁にやる) *give* one's daughter *in marriage* / *Musume wa roku-gatsu ni* yome *ni ikimashita.* (娘は 6 月に嫁に行きました) My daughter *got*

married in June. 《↔ muko》

2 daughter-in-law:
Uchi no yome *wa ryoori ga joozu da.* (うちの嫁は料理がじょうずだ) My *daughter-in-law* is a good cook. 《↔ muko》

yo⌐mi⌐ よみ (読み) *n.* **1** reading:
Kare wa hoñ no yomi *ga osoi.* (彼は本の読みが遅い) He is a *slow reader.* 《⇨ yomu》

2 judgment; calculation; insight:
Kare wa yomi *ga fukai [asai].* (彼は読みが深い[浅い]) He is a man of deep [shallow] *insight.* / Yomi *ga atatta.* (読みが当たった) I *have guessed right.* / *Kare no* yomi *wa hazureta.* (彼の読みは外れた) His *judgment* has proved to be wrong. 《⇨ yomu》

yo⌐miga⌐er·u よみがえる (蘇る) *vi.* (-gaer·i-; -gaer·a-; -gaet-te C)
1 come back to life; come to oneself:
Sono shoojo wa kiseki-teki ni yomigaetta. (その少女は奇跡的によみがえった) The young girl miraculously *came back to life.*

2 (of memory, impression, etc.) revive; be refreshed:
Kono shashiñ o miru to, tooji no omoide ga yomigaette kuru. (この写真を見ると当時の思い出がよみがえってくる) When I look at this picture, the memories of that time *come back* to me.

yo⌐mi-kaki よみかき (読み書き) *n.* reading and writing:
gakkoo de yomi-kaki *o narau* (学校で読み書きを習う) learn *how to read and write* at school / yomi-kaki *sorobañ* (読み書きそろばん) the three R's [*reading, writing,* and arithmetic].

yo⌐mikata よみかた (読み方) *n.* reading; pronunciation; interpretation:
Kono kañji no yomikata *o oshiete*

kudasai. (この漢字の読み方を教えてください) Can you tell me *how to read* this Chinese character? / *Kono ji no* yomikata *ga wakarimaseñ.* (この字の読み方がわかりません) I don't know *how to pronounce* this letter.

yo⌐m·u よむ (読む) *vt.* (yom·i-; yom·a-; yoñ-de C) **1** read:
hoñ o yomu (本を読む) *read a book* / *gurafu o* yomu (グラフを読む) *read a graph* / *memori o* yomu (目盛りを読む) *read gradations on a scale* / *koe o dashite* yomu (声を出して読む) *read aloud* / *Kono hoñ wa wakai hito no aida de yoku* yomarete imasu. (この本は若い人の間でよく読まれています) This book *is* widely *read* among young people. / *Haha wa yoku doowa o* yoñde *kuremashita.* (母はよく童話を読んでくれました) My mother frequently used to *read* me children's stories. / *Kono kañji wa nañ to* yomimasu *ka?* (この漢字は何と読みますか) How *do* you *read* this Chinese character? 《⇨ yomi》

2 read (a person's intention, mind, etc.); fathom:
hito no kaoiro o yomu (人の顔色を読む) *read a person's face* / *Kare no kañgae ga* yomenai. (彼の考えが読めない) I *cannot fathom* his thoughts.

yo⌐ñ よん (四) *n.* four:
Uchi ni wa neko ga yoñ-hiki iru. (うちには猫が四匹いる) We have *four* cats. 《⇨ shi⁴; suu² (table)》

yo⌐naka⌐ よなか (夜中) *n.* midnight; the middle of the night:
Yonaka *ni kaji ga atta.* (夜中に火事があった) A fire broke out in *the middle of the night.* 《↔ yoake》

yo⌐ñkyuu よんきゅう (四球) *n.* = shikyuu³.

yo-⌐no⌐-naka よのなか (世の中) *n.* the world; times; society:
Kare wa yo-no-naka *no koto o* yo-

ku shitte iru. (彼は世の中のことをよく知っている) He has seen much of *the world.* / *Yo-no-naka wa kawaru no ga hayai.* (世の中は変わるのが早い) *Times* change quickly. / *Nani-ka* yo-no-naka *no tame ni naru koto o shitai.* (何か世の中のためになることをしたい) I want to do something to improve our *society.* 《⇒ yo¹》

yo¹o¹ よう(用) *n.* something to do; business:
Koñbañ wa yoo *ga arimasu.* (今晩は用があります) I have *something to do* this evening. / *Chotto* yoo *ga atte Tookyoo made kimashita.* (ちょっと用があって東京まで来ました) I came up to Tokyo on *some business.* / *Ashita wa* yoo *ga arimaseñ.* (あしたは用がありません) I *am free* tomorrow. / *Nani-ka go-*yoo *desu ka?* (何かご用ですか) Is there *anything I can do for you?* / *Gogo wa chichi ni tanomareta* yoo *o shinakereba narimaseñ.* (午後は父に頼まれた用をしなければなりません) This afternoon I have to do *something* that my father asked me to.
yoo ga nai (〜がない) be no longer useful: *Kono taipuraitaa wa moo* yoo *ga arimaseñ.* (このタイプライターはもう用がありません) I *do not need* this typewriter anymore.
yoo o nasanai (〜をなさない) be of no use: *Kono kasa wa* yoo *o nasanai.* (この傘は用をなさない) This umbrella *is useless.*
yoo o tasu (〜を足す) go to the toilet: *Chotto* yoo *o tashite kimasu.* (ちょっと用を足してきます) Excuse me, *I'm going to the toilet.* ★ Slightly vulgar.

yoo² よう(様) *a.n.* (〜 na, ni)
1 seem; look: ★ Used to indicate a judgment based on sight, sound, or smell.
Kare wa sono koto o zeñzeñ oboete inai yoo da. (彼はそのことを全然

覚えていないようだ) He *does not seem* to remember that at all. / *Yamada-sañ wa tsukarete iru* yoo desu. (山田さんは疲れているようです) Mr. Yamada *looks* tired.
2 like; similar to; of the kind:
Watashi mo kare no yoo na *kashu ni naritai.* (私も彼のような歌手になりたい) I wish to be a singer *like* him. / *Yama no* yoo na *nami ga oshiyosete kita.* (山のような波が押し寄せて来た) *Mountainous* waves came surging in.
3 to the effect that:
Kanojo wa soñna yoo na *koto o itta.* (彼女はそんなようなことを言った) She said something *to that effect.* / *Yamada-sañ ga kaisha o yameru* yoo na *hanashi o kikimashita.* (山田さんが会社を辞めるような話を聞きました) I heard something *to the effect* that Miss Yamada was leaving the company.
4 such; sort: ★ Usually in a negative expression, often with 'kesshite.'
Kare wa sono yoo na *koto wa iimaseñ deshita.* (彼はそのようなことは言いませんでした) He said no *such* thing. / *Watashi wa kesshite uso o tsuku* yoo na *niñgeñ de wa arimaseñ.* (私は決してうそをつくような人間ではありません) I am certainly not the *sort of* person who tells lies.
yoo ni (〜に) **1** as; like: *Watashi wa itsu-mo no* yoo ni *roku-ji ni okimashita.* (私はいつものように6時に起きました) I got up at six *as* usual. / *Kare wa komanezumi no* yoo ni *yoku hataraku.* (彼はこまねずみのようによく働く) He works *like* a beaver. / *Go-shoochi no* yoo ni, *koñkai no jiko wa fuchuui ni yoru mono desu.* (ご承知のように、今回の事故は不注意によるものです) *As* you are well aware, this was an accident caused by negligence.
2 so that; so as to: *Miñna ni ki-*

koeru yoo ni *ooki-na koe de hana-shite kudasai.*(みんなに聞こえるように大きな声で話してください) Please speak in a loud voice *so that* everyone can hear you. / *Wasure-mono no nai* yoo ni *go-chuui kudasai.*(忘れ物のないようにご注意ください) Please make sure *that* you do not forget your belongings.

yoo ni iu [tanomu] (～に言う[頼む]) tell [ask]: *Kodomo ni rusuban suru* yoo ni *itta.*(子どもに留守番するように言った) I *told* the child to look after the house during my absence.

yoo ni naru (～になる) reach the point where: *Nihongo ga hana-seru* yoo ni *narimashita.*(日本語が話せるようになりました) I *have reached the stage* at which I can speak Japanese. / *Akachan wa arukeru* yoo ni *narimashita ka?*(赤ちゃんは歩けるようになりましたか) *Has* your baby *started walking?*

yoo ni shite iru (～にしている) make it a rule: *Watashi wa maiasa bitamin-zai o nomu* yoo ni *shite imasu.*(私は毎朝ビタミン剤を飲むようにしています) I *make it my practice* to take vitamin pills every morning. / *Shokuji no ato wa ha o migaku* yoo ni *shite imasu.*(食事の後は歯を磨くようにしています) I *make it a rule* to brush my teeth after meals.

-yoo よう *infl. end.* [attached to the continuative base of a vowel-stem verb. Irregular verbs are '*shiyoo*' and '*koyoo*'] (⇨ -oo)
1 intend; want:
Ashita wa hayaku okiyoo.(あしたは早く起きよう) I *will get up* early tomorrow. / *Kinoo koyoo to omoi-mashita ga, yooji ga atte dame de-shita.*(きのう来ようと思いましたが, 用事があってだめでした) Yesterday I *intended to come*, but I couldn't because of business. / *Kare o ta-*

zuneru no wa yameyoo *to omoi-masu.*(彼を訪ねるのはやめようと思います) I *have given up the idea* of going to visit him.
2 let's:
Moo ichi-do yatte miyoo.(もう一度やってみよう) *Let's try* it once more. / *Issho-ni terebi o* miyoo.(一緒にテレビを見よう) *Let's watch* TV together.

-(y)oo to suru ((よう)～とする) be about to; try: *Uchi o* deyoo to shita *toki, denwa ga natta.*(家を出ようとしたとき, 電話が鳴った) When I *was about to* leave home, the telephone rang. / *Sono doa o* akeyoo to shita *ga, kagi ga kakatte ita.*(そのドアを開けようとしたが, 鍵がかかっていた) I *tried* to open the door, but it was locked.

yo゠obi ようび(曜日) *n.* day of the week:
"*Kyoo wa nan* yoobi *desu ka?*" "*Suiyoobi desu.*"(「きょうは何曜日ですか」「水曜日です」) "What *day of the week* is it today?" "It's *Wednesday.*"

ni゠chiyo゠o(bi)	日曜(日)	Sunday
ge゠tsuyo゠o(bi)	月曜(日)	Monday
ka゠yo゠o(bi)	火曜(日)	Tuesday
su゠iyo゠o(bi)	水曜(日)	Wednesday
mo゠kuyo゠o(bi)	木曜(日)	Thursday
ki゠nyo゠o(bi)	金曜(日)	Friday
do゠yo゠o(bi)	土曜(日)	Saturday

yo゠oboo ようぼう(要望) *n.* request; requirement:
yooboo *ni oojiru [kotaeru]* (要望に応じる[応える]) meet a person's *requirements* / *Kumiai wa roodoo-jikan tanshuku no* yooboo *o da-shita.*(組合は労働時間短縮の要望を出した) The labor union made a *request* for the shortening of working hours.

yooboo suru (～する) *vt.* ask for;

request: *Watashi-tachi wa tsugi no sañ-teñ o yooboo shimasu.*(私たちは次の3点を要望します) We *make* the following three *requests*.

yo⌐obuñ ようぶん (養分) *n.* nourishment; nutriment: *Shokubutsu wa ne kara yoobuñ o toru.*(植物は根から養分をとる) Plants draw *nourishment* through their roots.

yo⌐ochi ようち (幼稚) *a.n.* (~ na, ni) childish; immature: yoochi *na kañgae*(幼稚な考え) a *childish* way of thinking / *Kare wa toshi no wari ni* yoochi *da.*(彼は年の割に幼稚だ) He is rather *childish* for his age.

yo⌐ochi⌐eñ ようちえん (幼稚園) *n.* kindergarten: *Musuko wa kiñjo no* yoochieñ *e itte imasu.*(息子は近所の幼稚園へ行っています) My son goes to a *kindergarten* in the neighborhood. 《⇨ gakkoo》

yo⌐oda⌐i ようだい (容体) *n.* condition of a patient: *Kañja no* yoodai *wa yoku natte imasu.*(患者の容体はよくなっています) The *condition* of the patient is improving. / *Kare no* yoodai *ga kyuu ni waruku natta.*(彼の容体が急に悪くなった) His *condition* has taken a sudden change for the worse.

yo⌐odate⌐·ru ようだてる (用立てる) *n.* (-date-te [C]) lend (money): *Ichimañ-eñ bakari* yoodatete *itadakereba, arigataku omoimasu.*(一万円ばかり用立てていただければ, ありがたくおもいます) I would appreciate it if you *could lend* me about 10,000 yen.

yo⌐ofuku ようふく (洋服) *n.* Western clothes; suit; dress: *Kanojo wa shiñchoo no* yoofuku *o kite ita.*(彼女は新調の洋服を着ていた) She wore a new *dress*. 《↔ wafuku; kimono》

yo⌐ofuu ようふう (洋風) *n.* Western style: yoofuu *no ie*(洋風の家) a *Western-style* house. 《↔ wafuu》

yo⌐oga ようが (洋画) *n.* **1** Western [European] painting; oil painting. 《↔ Nihoñga》 **2** foreign film. 《↔ Nihoñ eega》

yo⌐oga⌐shi ようがし (洋菓子) *n.* cake; Western-style confectionery. 《↔ wagashi》

yo⌐ogi ようぎ (容疑) *n.* suspicion: yoogi *o ukeru*(容疑を受ける) *be suspected* / yoogi *o harasu*(容疑を晴らす) dispel *suspicion* / *Sono otoko wa satsujiñ no* yoogi *de taiho sareta.*(その男は殺人の容疑で逮捕された) That man was arrested on *suspicion* of murder. / yoogi-sha (容疑者) a *suspect*.

yo⌐ogo[1] ようご (用語) *n.* term; word; terminology: *Kare wa hooritsu-*yoogo *ni kuwashii.*(彼は法律用語に詳しい) He is familiar with legal *terms*. / *Koñpyuutaa de tsukawareru* yoogo *wa wakari-nikui.*(コンピューターで使われる用語はわかりにくい) The *jargon* used with computers is hard to understand.

yo⌐ogo[2] ようご (擁護) *n.* support; protection.
yoogo suru (~する) *vt.* support; protect: *keñpoo* [*miñshu-shugi*] *o* yoogo suru (憲法[民主主義]を擁護する) *support* the constitution [democracy].

yo⌐ogu ようぐ (用具) *n.* tool; instrument: *Yoogu wa tsukattara, moto no basho ni oki nasai.*(用具は使ったら, 元の場所に置きなさい) Put the *tools* back when you are done with them. / *Kare no mise wa supootsu-*yoogu *o atsukatte imasu.*(彼の店はスポーツ用具を扱っています) His shop deals in sporting *goods*.

yo⌐ogu⌐ruto ヨーグルト *n.* yogurt.

yo⌐oi[1] ようい（用意）*n.* preparation; arrangement; readiness: *Shuppatsu no* yooi *wa dekimashita ka?*（出発の用意はできましたか）*Are you ready* to leave? / *Shokuji no* yooi *ga dekimashita.*（食事の用意ができました）The meal *is on the table.*

yooi (o) suru（～（を）する）*vt.* prepare; arrange; get ready: *paatii no* yooi *o suru*（パーティーの用意をする）*arrange* everything for a party / *ryokoo no* yooi *o suru*（旅行の用意をする）*prepare* for a journey / *o-kane o* yooi *suru*（お金を用意する）*get* money *ready.*

yo⌐oi[2] ようい（容易）*a.n.* (～ na, ni) easy; simple: yooi *na shigoto*（容易な仕事）an *easy* task / *Kono kawa o oyoide wataru no wa* yooi *de nai.*（この川を泳いで渡るのは容易でない）It is not *easy* to swim across this river. / *Kore wa* yooi *ni kaiketsu dekiru moñdai de wa arimaseñ.*（これは容易に解決できる問題ではありません）This is not a problem that can be solved *easily.* 《⇨ kañtañ》

yo⌐oji[1] ようじ（用事）*n.* business; things to do; engagement: *Chichi wa* yooji *de gaishutsu shite imasu.*（父は用事で外出しています）Our father is out on *business.* / *Kyoo wa toku ni* yooji *wa arimaseñ.*（きょうは特に用事はありません）Today I *have nothing particular to do.* / *Hoka ni* yooji *ga arimasu no de kore de shitsuree shimasu.*（ほかに用事がありますのでこれで失礼します）I have another *engagement,* so please excuse me now. / *Jibuñ no* yooji *o sumashite kara ukagaimasu.*（自分の用事をすましてから伺います）I'll come and see you after finishing *what I have to do.* 《⇨ yoo¹》

yo⌐oji[2] ようじ（幼児）*n.* infant; very young child: *Roku-sai no* yooji *ga yuukai sareta.*（6歳の幼児が誘拐された）A six-year-old *child* was kidnapped. / yooji-*kyooiku*（幼児教育）*preschool* education.

yo⌐ojiñ ようじん（用心）*n.* care; caution; precaution: *Hi no moto ni* go-yoojiñ.（火の元にご用心）*Be careful* with fire. / yoojiñ-*boo*（用心棒）a *bodyguard*; a *bouncer.*

yoojiñ suru（～する）*vi.* take care; be careful: *Kaze o hikanai yoo ni* yoojiñ *shi nasai.*（風邪を引かないように用心しなさい）*Take care* not to catch a cold. / *Ashimoto ni* yoojiñ *shite kudasai.*（足元に用心してください）Please *mind* your step.

yo⌐ojiñbuka⌐i ようじんぶかい（用心深い）*a.* (-ku) cautious; watchful; careful: *Kagi o yottsu mo tsukeru nañte zuibuñ* yoojiñbukai *hito da.*（かぎを四つもつけるなんてずいぶん用心深い人だ）What a *cautious* person you are to put four locks on the door. 《⇨ chuuibukai; shiñchoo²》

yo⌐oka ようか（八日）*n.* eight days; the eighth day of the month: *Soko made fune de* yooka *kakarimasu.*（そこまで船で8日かかります）It takes *eight days* to go there by ship. / *O-tegami wa roku-gatsu* yooka *ni uketorimashita.*（お手紙は6月8日に受け取りました）I received your letter on June *8.* 《⇨ tsuitachi (table)》

yo⌐okee ようけい（養鶏）*n.* poultry farming; chicken raising: yookee-*joo*（養鶏場）a *poultry* farm.

yo⌐oke⌐ñ ようけん（用件）*n.* business: *Toriaezu* yookeñ *nomi de shitsuree shimasu.* (formal)（とりあえず用件のみで失礼します）Anyway, please excuse my leaving immediately after completing the *business at hand*. / *De wa* yookeñ *ni hairimashoo*. (では用件に入りましょう) Now, let's get down to *business*. / *Go-yookeñ wa nañ deshoo ka?* (ご用件は何でしょうか) *What can I do for you?*

yo˺oki[1] ようき (容器) *n.* container: yooki *ni ireru* (容器に入れる) put into a *container* / yooki *kara dasu* (容器から出す) take out of a *container*.

yo˺oki[2] ようき (陽気) *a.n.* (~ na, ni) cheerful; lively; merry: yooki *na kazoku* (陽気な家族) a *cheerful* family / *Ano hito wa itsu-mo* yooki *da*. (あの人はいつも陽気だ) He is always *cheerful*. / *Suzuki-sañ wa sake o nomu to* yooki *ni naru*. (鈴木さんは酒を飲むと陽気になる) Mr. Suzuki becomes *merry* when he drinks.

yo˺oki[3] ようき (陽気) *n.* weather: *Ii* yooki *desu ne*. (いい陽気ですね) Pleasant *weather*, isn't it? / *Hokkaidoo no hoo no* yooki *wa ikaga desu ka?* (北海道の方の陽気はいかがですか) How is the *weather* in Hokkaido?

yo˺okyuu ようきゅう (要求) *n.* demand; requirement; claim: yookyuu *o mitasu* (要求を満たす) meet a person's *requirements* / *Kare wa wareware no* yookyuu *ni oojita*. (彼はわれわれの要求に応じた) He acceded to our *demands*.
yookyuu suru (~する) *vt.* demand; require; claim: *Kumiai wa chiñgiñ no neage o* yookyuu *shite iru*. (組合は賃金の値上げを要求している) The union *is demanding* a wage hike. / *Watashi-tachi wa sono shitsumoñ ni taisuru kaitoo o* yookyuu *shita*. (私たちはその質問に対する回答を要求した) We *requested* an answer to the question. 《⇨ motomeru》

yo˺omoo ようもう (羊毛) *n.* wool:

yoomoo no *moofu* (羊毛の毛布) a *wool* blanket.

yo˺o-oñ ようおん (拗音) *n.* palatalized consonant. ★ The palatalized sound is represented by a smaller や, ゆ and よ (ャ, ュ, ョ) after the *i*-row *kana* letter of the appropriate consonant: *kya* (きゃ), *kyu* (きゅ), *kyo* (きょ). 《⇨ inside front cover; appendixes》

Yo˺oro˺ppa ヨーロッパ *n.* Europe: Yooroppa-*jiñ* (ヨーロッパ人) a *European* / Yooroppa-*tairiku* (ヨーロッパ大陸) the *European* Continent.

yo˺oryo˺o[1] ようりょう (要領) *n.*
1 point; essentials: *Kare no setsumee wa* yooryoo *o ete iru*. (彼の説明は要領を得ている) His explanation is to the *point*.
2 knack: *Yatto kuruma no uñteñ no* yooryoo *ga wakatta*. (やっと車の運転の要領がわかった) At last I got the *knack* of driving a car.
yooryoo ga ii [warui] (~がいい [悪い]) clever [clumsy]: *Kare wa* yooryoo ga ii [warui]. (彼は要領がいい [悪い]) He is *quick and smart* [*slow and dull*].

yo˺oryo˺o[2] ようりょう (容量) *n.* capacity; volume; bulk: *tañku no* yooryoo (タンクの容量) the *capacity* of a tank. 《⇨ taiseki》

yo˺osai ようさい (洋裁) *n.* dressmaking: yoosai-*gakkoo* (洋裁学校) a *dressmaking* school. 《↔ wasai》

yo˺osee ようせい (養成) *n.* training; education: *kyooiñ* yoosee *daigaku* (教員養成大学) a teacher *training* college.
yoosee suru (~する) *vt.* train; educate; foster: *Kono gakkoo de wa kañgofu o* yoosee *shite imasu*. (この学校では看護婦を養成しています) They *train* nurses at this school.

yo˺oshi[1] ようし (要旨) *n.* outline;

summary; the gist:

Kare no eñzetsu no yooshi *o oshiete kudasai.*（彼の演説の要旨を教えてください）Please give me the *gist* of his speech.

yo⌐oshi[2]　ようし（養子）*n.* adopted [foster] child:

Kare wa sono uchi no yooshi *ni natta.*（彼はその家の養子になった）He *was adopted* into that family.

yo⌐oshitsu　ようしつ（洋室）*n.* Western-style room.《↔ washitsu》

yo⌐osho　ようしょ（洋書）*n.* book published in a Western language.《↔ washo》

yo⌐oshoku[1]　ようしょく（養殖）*n.* culture; farming:

Kono mizuumi wa unagi no yooshoku *de yuumee desu.*（この湖はうなぎの養殖で有名です）This lake is famous for its eel *culture.* / yooshoku-*shiñju*（養殖真珠）a *cultured* pearl.

yooshoku suru（～する）*vt.* raise; farm: *masu o* yooshoku suru（ますを養殖する）*raise* trout.

yo⌐oshoku[2]　ようしょく（洋食）*n.* Western food; Western dishes.《↔ washoku》

yo⌐oso　ようそ（要素）*n.* element; factor; constituent:

Geñka wa kakaku kettee no juuyoo na yooso *desu.*（原価は価格決定の重要な要素です）The cost is an important *factor* in setting the price. / *Kono hiryoo wa shokubutsu no seechoo ni hitsuyoo na* yooso *o subete fukuñde imasu.*（この肥料は植物の成長に必要な要素をすべて含んでいます）This fertilizer has all the *elements* that are necessary for plant growth.

yo⌐osu　ようす（様子）*n.* **1** condition; state:

Byooniñ no yoosu *ga shiñpai desu.*（病人の様子が心配です）I am worried about the *condition* of the patient. / *Kare no ie wa hidoi* yoosu *datta.*（彼の家はひどい様子だった）His house was in a bad *state*.

2 appearance; looks:

Sono biru de, machi no yoosu *ga kawatta.*（そのビルで、町の様子が変わった）With that building, the *look* of the town has changed. / *Kanojo wa shiawase-soo na* yoosu *o shite ita.*（彼女は幸せそうな様子をしていた）She *looked* very happy.

yo⌐o-su⌐ru ni　ようするに（要するに）*adv.* in short; in a word; after all:

Kono jigyoo wa yoo-suru ni *shikiñ ga tarinai tame ni shippai shita ñ da.*（この事業は要するに資金が足りないために失敗したんだ）This business failed, *to put it simply*, because of a lack of funds. / *Yoo-suru ni kimi wa nani ga shitai ñ da?*（要するにきみは何がしたいんだ）What do you want to do, *actually*?

yo⌐ote⌐ñ　ようてん（要点）*n.* point; essence; the gist:

O-hanashi no yooteñ *wa tsukamemashita.*（お話の要点はつかめました）I got the *point* of your talk. / *Kare no supiichi wa mijikakute, shikamo* yooteñ *ga shiborarete ita.*（彼のスピーチは短くて、しかも要点がしぼられていた）His speech was short, and what's more, he kept to the *point*.

yo⌐oto　ようと（用途）*n.* use:

Purasuchikku wa yooto *ga hiroi.*（プラスチックは用途が広い）Plastics have many *uses*.

yo⌐oyaku　ようやく（漸く）*adv.*

1 at last; finally:

Watashi-tachi wa yooyaku *mokutekichi ni tsuita.*（私たちはようやく目的地に着いた）We *finally* reached our destination. / *Yooyaku harurashiku natte kita.*（ようやく春らしくなってきた）It has *at last* become just like spring.

2 barely; with difficulty:

Saishuu-deñsha ni yooyaku *ma-niaimashita.* (最終電車にようやく間に合いました) I was *barely* in time for the last train. 《⇨ yatto》

yoꜝpparai よっぱらい (酔っぱらい) *n.* drunken person; drunk: yopparai-*uñteñ* (酔っぱらい運転) *drunken* driving.

yoꜝreꜜba よれば (依れば) according to: ★ Indicates the source or authority of information received. Used in the pattern '*...ni yoreba.*' Also '*...ni yoru to.*'
Teñki-yohoo ni yoreba, *ashita wa ame ni naru rashii.* (天気予報によれば, あしたは雨になるらしい) *According to* the weather forecast, tomorrow it will apparently rain. / *Shiñ-buñ ni* yoreba, *keeki wa yoku na-ru soo desu.* (新聞によれば, 景気はよくなるそうです) The papers *say* the business climate will improve.

yoꜝri より *p.* **1** ...than: ★ Used to make comparisons.
Watashi wa koohii yori *koocha no hoo ga suki desu.* (私はコーヒーよりも紅茶のほうが好きです) I like coffee rather *than* tea. / *Tanaka-sañ* yori *Yamada-sañ no hoo ga nesshiñ desu.* (田中さんより山田さんのほうが熱心です) Mr. Yamada is more earnest *than* Mr.Tanaka. / *Kore* yori *ookii no wa arimasu ka?* (これより大きいのはありますか) Is there a bigger one *than* this?
2 (*formal*) at; from; than: ★ Indicates a point of origin in time or space. 《⇨ kara³》
Kyoo no kaigi wa sañ-ji yori *haji-memasu.* (きょうの会議は3時より始めます) We will start today's meeting *at* three. / *Koko* yori *saki ni haitte wa ikemaseñ.* (ここより先に入ってはいけません) You must not go in any further *than* this.

...yori (**hoka ni**) **...ga nai** (...～(ほかに)...がない) have no alternative but to (do):

Hitori de wa dekinai kara, dare ka ni tanomu yori (hoka ni) *te ga nai.* (一人ではできないから, だれかに頼むより(ほかに)手がない) I cannot do it by myself, so I *cannot avoid ask-ing for someone's help.* / *Kono byooki wa* shujutsu suru yori (hoka ni) *hoohoo ga arimaseñ.* (この病気は手術するより(ほかに)方法がありません) With this illness *there is nothing for it but to have an operation.*

yoꜝrikakaꜜrꜟu よりかかる (寄り掛かる) *vi.* (-kakar·i-; -kakar·a-; -ka-kat-te Ⓒ) **1** lean on; recline against:
Kare wa kabe ni yorikakatte ita. (彼は壁に寄り掛かっていた) He *was leaning against* the wall.
2 rely on:
Kare wa mada oya ni yorikakatte iru. (彼はまだ親に寄り掛かっている) He still *relies on* his parents.

yoꜝrimichi よりみち (寄り道) *n.* dropping in; stopover.
yorimichi (**o**) **suru** (～(を)する) *vi.* drop in; make a stopover: *Gak-koo no kaeri ni, tomodachi no to-koro e* yorimichi o shita. (学校の帰りに, 友だちの所へ寄り道をした) I *dropped in* on a friend on the way back from school.

yoꜝriwakeꜜrꜟu よりわける (選り分ける) *vt.* (-wake-te Ⓥ) sort out; classify:
Tamago o ookisa de yoriwaketa. (卵を大きさより分けた) I *sorted* the eggs according to size.

yoꜝroi よろい (鎧) *n.* armor. 《⇨ photo (next page)》

yoꜝrokeꜜrꜟu よろける *vi.* (-ke-te Ⓥ) stagger; totter; stumble:
Sono roojiñ wa yorokete *koroñda.* (その老人はよろけてころんだ) The old man *staggered* and fell over.

yoꜝrokobi よろこび (喜び) *n.* joy; pleasure; delight; rapture:
Kanojo wa yorokobi *ni afureta kao o shite ita.* (彼女は喜びにあふれた

YOROI

顔をしていた) She wore an expression overflowing with *joy*. / *Watashi no kokoro wa* yorokobi *ni hazuñda*. (私の心は喜びに弾んだ) My heart jumped with *joy*. 《↔ kanashimi》《⇨ yorokobu》

yo⌐roko⌐b·u よろこぶ (喜ぶ) *vi.* (-kob·i-; -kob·a-; -koñ-de C) be glad; be pleased; be delighted: *Ryooshiñ wa sono shirase o kiite,* yorokoñda. (両親はその知らせを聞いて, 喜んだ) My parents *were delighted* at hearing the news. 《⇨ yorokobi》

yorokoñde ... suru (喜んで...する) be glad to do: Yorokoñde *o-tetsudai shimasu*. (喜んでお手伝いします) I will *be glad to* help you.

yo⌐roñ よろん (世論) *n.* public opinion: yoroñ *o kañki suru* (世論を喚起する) arouse *public opinion* / Yoroñ *wa seefu no seesaku ni hañtai desu*. (世論は政府の政策に反対です) *Public opinion* is against the government's policy. / yoroñ-*choosa* (世論調査) a *public opinion* poll.

yo⌐roshi·i よろしい (宜しい) *a.* (-ku) ★ Formal alternative of '*ii*.'
1 all right; fine; good: *Juñbi wa* yoroshii *deshoo ka?* (準備はよろしいでしょうか) You are *ready*, I assume? / Yoroshii. *Watashi ga sekiniñ o mochimasu*. (よろしい. 私が責任を持ちます) *All right*. I will take the responsibility. / "*Nani-ka kaku mono o kashite kudasai.*" "*Eñpitsu de* yoroshii *desu ka?*" (「何か書くものを貸してください」「鉛筆でよろしいですか」) "Can you lend me something to write with?" "Will a pencil *do*?" / Yoroshikattara, *koohii de mo nomimaseñ ka?* (よろしかったら, コーヒーでも飲みませんか) *If it is all right with you*, why don't we have a cup of coffee, or something?
2 had better; should: *Kare no iu toori ni shita hoo ga* yoroshii *desu yo*. (彼の言うとおりにしたほうがよろしいですよ) You *had better* do as he tells you.
3 can; may: *Kono deñwa o tsukatte mo* yoroshii *desu ka?* (この電話を使ってもよろしいですか) *May* I use this telephone? 《⇨ yoi¹》

yo⌐roshiku よろしく (宜しく) *adv.*
1 (used to express one's hopes for friendship or favor):

(USAGE)

A common expression used when requesting another person's favorable consideration in the future.

Hajimemashite. Doozo yoroshiku *o-negai shimasu*. (始めまして. どうぞよろしくお願いします) How do you do? *Nice to meet you.* ★ Greeting used when first meeting someone. / *Kono shigoto o* yoroshiku *tanomimasu*. (この仕事をよろしく頼みます) *I would be grateful for your help* with this job. / *Musuko o doo-ka* yoroshiku *o-negai shimasu*. (息子をどうかよろしくお願いします) *I should be obliged if you would do what you can* for my son. / *Kotoshi mo* yoroshiku *o-*

negai itashimasu. (今年もよろしくお願いいたします) *I hope I can rely on your cooperation* this year, as well.
2 (used to express one's regards or best wishes):
O-toosañ ni mo yoroshiku *o-tsutae kudasai.* (お父さんにもよろしくお伝えください) Please give my *regards* to your father. / *Haha kara mo* yoroshiku *to no koto desu.* (母からもよろしくとのことです) My mother asked me to send you her *best wishes.*

yoˈroyoro よろよろ *adv.* (~ to; ~ suru) staggeringly; totteringly; falteringly:
Sono byooniñ wa yoroyoro *(to) tachiagatta.* (その病人はよろよろ(と)立ち上がった) The patient *unsteadily* rose to his feet.

yoˈru[1] よる (夜) *n.* night:
Kare wa yoru *osoku made hataraita.* (彼は夜遅くまで働いた) He worked till late at *night.*
《↔ asa[1]》《⇨ bañ[1] (table)》

yoˈrˈu[2] よる (寄る) *vi.* (yor·i-; yor·a-; yot-te [C]) **1** draw near; come [go] close:
Samui kara motto sutoobu no soba ni yori nasai. (寒いからもっとストーブのそばに寄りなさい) As it is cold, please *come closer* to the heater.
2 drop in:
Zehi ichido watashi no uchi ni o-yori kudasai. (ぜひ一度私の家にお寄りください) By all means, please *drop in* to our house some time. / *Tochuu Oosaka ni* yotte *kara, Koobe ni ikimashita.* (途中大阪に寄ってから, 神戸に行きました) After *stopping off* at Osaka, I went on to Kobe.

yoˈrˈu[3] よる (因る) *vi.* (yor·i-; yor·a-; yot-te [C]) **1** depend:
Hoosaku ka fusaku ka wa teñkoo ni yorimasu. (豊作か不作かは天候によります) Whether the crop is abundant or poor *depends* on the weather. 《⇨ shidai》
2 be based; according to:
Kono monogatari wa jijitsu ni yotte *kakaremashita.* (この物語は事実によって書かれました) This story was written, *based* on fact. / *Teñki-yohoo ni* yoreba *ashita wa ame desu.* (天気予報によればあしたは雨です) *According to* the weather report, it will rain tomorrow.
3 be caused; owing to:
Kaji wa tabako no fushimatsu ni yoru *mono datta.* (火事はたばこの不始末によるものだった) The fire was one *caused by* not extinguishing a cigarette. / *Oo-yuki ni* yori *ressha wa futsuu ni natta.* (大雪により列車は不通になった) *Owing to* the heavy snowfall, train service was suspended. / *Taifuu ni* yoru *higai wa ookikatta.* (台風による被害は大きかった) The damage *from* the typhoon was heavy.
... ni yotte (...によって) by: '*Geñji monogatari*' *wa Murasaki Shikibu ni* yotte *kakareta.* (「源氏物語」は紫式部によって書かれた) 'The Tale of Genji' was written *by* Murasaki Shikibu. 《⇨ yotte》

yoˈsañ よさん (予算) *n.* budget:
raineñ-do no yosañ (来年度の予算) the *budget* for the next year / yosañ *o tateru* (予算を立てる) make a *budget* / *Paatii wa* yosañ-nai de *dekimashita.* (パーティーは予算内でできました) We were able to give the party within the limits of the *budget.*

yoˈseatsume よせあつめ (寄せ集め) *n.* medley; odds and ends:
yoseatsume *no chiimu* (寄せ集めのチーム) a *scratch* team. 《⇨ yoseatsumeru》

yoˈseatsumeˈ·ru よせあつめる (寄せ集める) *vt.* (-atsume-te [V]) collect; gather up; bring together.
Ochiba o yoseatsumete *moyashita.* (落ち葉を寄せ集めて燃やした) I *gath-*

ered up the fallen leaves and burned them. / *Kono hoñ wa iro-iro na zasshi no kiji o yoseatsume-ta mono desu.* (この本はいろいろな雑誌の記事を寄せ集めたものです) This book is one consisting of articles *collected* from various magazines. (⇨ yoseatsume)

yoˈseˑru よせる(寄せる) *vt.* (yose-te Ⓥ) **1** bring [draw] up: *Akari o motto hoñ no soba e yose nasai.* (あかりをもっと本のそばへ寄せなさい) *Bring* the light *closer* to the book.
2 put [push] aside: *Tsukue o mado no waki ni yoseta.* (机を窓のわきに寄せた) I *put* the desk *next to* the window.

yoˈshi よし(良し・好し) *int.* well; good; all right; OK: ★ Used to express one's determination when starting something. *Yoshi, soo shiyoo.* (よし、そうしよう) *Well*, let's do so.

yoˈshiˈashi よしあし(善し悪し) *n.* good or bad; right or wrong: *koto no* yoshiashi *o kubetsu suru* (事のよしあしを区別する) *tell the good from the bad* / *Yoshiashi wa betsu to shite, tonikaku soko e itte miyoo.* (よしあしは別として、とにかくそこへ行ってみよう) *Whether it is good or bad*, let's go there anyway.
yoshiashi da (〜だ) have good and bad points: *Hima ga aru no mo* yoshiashi da. (暇があるのもよしあしだ) *It is not always good* to have ample leisure time.

yoˈshiyoshi よしよし *int.* (used when consoling someone): *Yoshiyoshi. Moo nakanai de.* (よしよし。もう泣かないで) *Come come.* You must stop crying now.

yoˈshuu よしゅう(予習) *n.* preparation (of one's lessons): *Yoshuu to fukushuu wa dochira mo taisetsu desu.* (予習と復習はどちらも大切です) Both *preparation* and

review are important.
yoshuu (o) suru (〜(を)する) *vt.* prepare one's lessons: *Ashita no jugyoo no yoshuu o shinakereba naranai.* (あしたの授業の予習をしなければならない) I *have to prepare* for tomorrow's class. (↔ fukushuu)

yoˈso よそ(他所) *n.* **1** another place; some other place: *Doko-ka yoso no mise o sagashimashoo.* (どこかよその店を探しましょう) Let's look for *some other* shop. / *Yoso ni itte asobi nasai.* (よそに行って遊びなさい) Go off and play *somewhere else.*
2 another person: yoso no hito (よその人) a *stranger* / *kodomo o* yoso *ni azukeru* (子どもをよそに預ける) leave one's child in the care of *another.*
... o yoso ni (...を〜に) ignoring; neglecting: *Ryooshiñ no shiñpai o* yoso ni *kare wa yoru osoku dekaketa.* (両親の心配をよそに彼は夜遅く出かけた) *Ignoring* his parents' concern, he went out late at night.

yoˈsoo (予想) *n.* expectation; anticipation; guess: *Yosoo ga atarimashita [hazurema-shita].* (予想が当りました[外れました]) My *guess* proved right [wrong]. / *Kekka wa* yosoo-doori *deshita.* (結果は予想どおりでした) The result was *as we had expected.* / *Koñ-getsu no rieki wa* yosoo *ijoo [ika] deshita.* (今月の利益は予想以上[以下]でした) This month's profit was greater [less] than *we had anticipated.* / *Sono chiimu wa* yosoo *ni hañshite, makete shimatta.* (そのチームは予想に反して、負けてしまった) That team lost the game, contrary to our *expectations.*
yosoo suru (〜する) *vt.* expect; anticipate; guess: *Shoorai nani ga okoru ka dare mo* yosoo suru *koto wa dekimaseñ.* (将来何が起こ

るかだれも予想することはできません）
Nobody can *predict* what will
happen in the future.

yo⌐s·u よす (止す) *vt.* (yosh·i-;
yos·a-; yosh·i-te C) stop; give
up; quit:
tabako o yosu (たばこをよす) *give up*
smoking / *gakkoo o yosu* (学校をよ
す) *quit* school / *Soñna baka na
mane wa* yoshi nasai. (そんなばかなま
ねはよしなさい) *Stop* behaving in
such a ridiculous manner.
《⇨ yameru¹》

yo⌐tee よてい (予定) *n.* plan;
schedule; program:
yotee *o tateru* (予定を立てる) make
a *plan* / yotee *o heñkoo suru* (予定
を変更する) change a *schedule* /
Kyoo no yotee *wa doo natte imasu ka?* (きょうの予定はどうなっています
か) What are the *plans* for today?
/ *Kaigi wa juu-ji kara no* yotee
desu. (会議は 10 時からの予定です)
The meeting *is scheduled* to start
at ten. / *Ressha wa* yotee *yori
ichi-jikañ okurete toochaku shimashita.* (列車は予定より 1 時間遅れて到
着しました) The train arrived one
hour behind *schedule*. / *Subete
wa* yotee-doori *umaku ikimashita.*
(すべては予定どおりうまくいきました)
Everything went smoothly *as
planned*.
　yotee suru (〜する) *vt.* plan;
schedule; expect: *Riñji no kaigi
wa mokuyoobi no gogo ni* yotee
shite imasu. (臨時の会議は木曜日の
午後に予定しています) We *have
scheduled* an extraordinary meeting for Thursday afternoon.

yo⌐too よとう (与党) *n.* the ruling
[government] party:
yotoo *giiñ* (与党議員) a member
of the *ruling* party. 《↔ yatoo》

yo⌐tsukado よつかど (四つ角) *n.*
crossroads; intersection:
yotsukado *o hidari ni magaru* (四
つ角を左に曲がる) turn to the left at
an *intersection*.

yo⌐tte よって (依って) ★ Used in
the pattern '...*ni yotte*.'
1 by: ★ Used with a passive
verb and indicates the agent of a
passive sentence.
*Kono zoo wa yuumee na chooko-
kuka ni* yotte *tsukurareta mono
desu.* (この像は有名な彫刻家によって
作られたものです) This statue is one
that was made *by* a famous sculp-
tor. 《⇨ yoru³》
2 because of; due to: ★ Indicates cause or reason.
Señsoo ni yotte *ooku no hito ga
nikushiñ o ushinaimashita.* (戦争に
よって多くの人が肉親を失いました)
Many people lost their families
because of the war. / *Koñpyuutaa
no doonyuu ni* yotte *shigoto no
nooritsu ga agatta.* (コンピューターの
導入によって仕事の能率があがった)
Work efficiency has increased
due to the introduction of computers. 《⇨ de¹》
3 with; by; through; of: ★ Indicates means, method or material.
Miñna no kyooryoku ni yotte *sono
shigoto wa hayaku owatta.* (みんな
の協力によってその仕事は早く終わった)
The work was finished early
with the cooperation of everyone.
/ *Kono niñgyoo wa kami ni* yotte
dekite imasu. (この人形は紙によってで
きています) This doll is made *of*
paper.
4 (differ) from...to...: ★ Used in
expressions indicating variety or
disparity.
Fuuzoku shuukañ wa kuni ni yotte *chigaimasu.* (風俗習慣は国によっ
て違います) Manners and customs
vary *from* country *to* country. /
Hito ni yotte *kañgae-kata ni chigai ga arimasu.* (人によって考え方に
違いがあります) There are differences in thinking *between* people.

USAGE

In **1, 2** and **3** '*ni yori*' can also be used. Before a noun '*...ni yoru.*' *e.g. kasai ni* yoru *higai* (火災による被害) damage *caused by* fire / *piano ni* yoru *eñsoo* (ピアノによる演奏) a piano recital.

yo⌈ttsu⌉ よっつ（四つ）*n.* four: ★ Used when counting. *Keeki o* yottsu *ni kitta.* (ケーキを四つに切った) I cut the cake into *four*. / yottsu-me （四つ目）*the fourth.* 《⇨ kazu (table)》

yo⌉·u よう（酔う）*vi.* (yo·i-; yo-w·a-; yot-te Ⓒ) **1** get tipsy; become drunk: *Kanojo wa sugu ni sake ni* yotte shimau. (彼女はすぐに酒に酔ってしまう) She *gets tipsy* very quickly. 《⇨ yoi²; yowaseru》 **2** get sick: *fune* [*kuruma*] *ni* you (船[車]に酔う) *get seasick* [*carsick*] / *Anata wa norimono ni* yoimasu *ka?* (あなたは乗り物に酔いますか) *Are* you *subject to* motion *sickness*? **3** be intoxicated; be elated: *Señshu-tachi wa shoori ni* yotte ita. (選手たちは勝利に酔っていた) The players *were elated* at the victory.

yo⌈wa⌉·i よわい（弱い）*a.* (-ku) **1** weak: *Haha wa karada ga* yowai. (母は体が弱い) My mother is physically *weak*. / *Kare wa ishi ga* yowai *no de sugu akirameru.* (彼は意志が弱いのですぐあきらめる) He is *weak*-willed so he gives up easily. 《↔ tsuyoi》 **2** dim; low: yowai *hikari* (弱い光) a *dim* light / *Gasu no hi o* yowaku shi nasai. (ガスの火を弱くしなさい) *Turn down* the gas. 《↔ tsuyoi》 **3** (...ni) (of knowledge, etc.) be poor at; weak: *Watashi wa kañji ni* yowai. (私は漢字に弱い) I *am poor* at Chinese

characters. **4** (...ni) be affected easily: *Chichi wa sake ni* yowai. (父は酒に弱い) My father *cannot hold* his liquor very well. / *Kanojo wa norimono ni* yowai. (彼女は乗り物に弱い) She gets carsick *easily*. / *Nairoñ wa netsu ni* yowai. (ナイロンは熱に弱い) Nylon is *not resistant to* heat. 《↔ tsuyoi》

yo⌈waki よわき（弱気）*a.n.* (~ na, ni) weak-minded; timid; pessimistic: *Kare wa doomo* yowaki *da.* (彼はどうも弱気だ) He is somewhat *weak-minded*. / *Daiji na shiai o mae ni shite,* yowaki *ja dame da.* (大事な試合を前にして、弱気じゃだめだ) With an important match coming up, it won't do to *lose confidence*. 《↔ tsuyoki》

yo⌈wame⌉·ru よわめる（弱める）*vt.* (yowame-te Ⓥ) weaken; turn down: *Reeboo o* yowamete *mo ii desu ka?* (冷房を弱めてもいいですか) Do you mind if I *turn down* the air conditioner? / *Tabako to arukooru wa shiñzoo o* yowamemasu. (たばことアルコールは心臓を弱めます) Cigarettes and alcohol *weaken* the heart. 《↔ tsuyomeru》 《⇨ yowaru》

yo⌈wa⌉r·u よわる（弱る）*vi.* (yo-war·i-; yowar·a-; yowat-te Ⓒ) **1** become weak; weaken: *Toshi o toru to karada ga* yowatte kimasu. (年をとると体が弱ってきます) One's body *becomes weaker* with age. 《⇨ yowameru》 **2** be perplexed; be in a fix: *Kodomo ni nakarete,* yowatta. (子どもに泣かれて、弱った) I *was at a loss* when the child was crying. / *Tookyoo no atsusa ni wa* yowarimashita. (東京の暑さには弱りました) I *did not know what to do* about Tokyo's heat.

yoˈwaseˈ·ru よわせる (酔わせる) *vt.*
(yowase-te ▽) **1** make a person
drunk:
*Kare wa kanojo ni muri ni sake o
nomasete yowaseta.* (彼は彼女にむ
りに酒を飲ませて酔わせた) He forced
alcohol on her and *got her drunk.*
《⇨ you'》
2 charm; enchant:
*Kare no eñsoo wa choochuu o yo-
waseta.* (彼の演奏は聴衆を酔わせた)
His performance *enchanted* the
audience. 《⇨ you'》

yoˈyaku よやく (予約) *n.* **1** reservation; booking:
yoyaku *o toru* [*torikesu*] (予約をとる
[取り消す]) make [cancel] a *reservation* / *Koñshuu wa kono hoteru
wa* yoyaku de ippai desu. (今週はこ
のホテルは予約でいっぱいです) This
hotel *is fully booked* this week. /
Kono kagu wa yoyaku-zumi desu.
(この家具は予約済みです) This item
of furniture *has already been sold.*
/ yoyaku-kiñ (予約金) a *deposit*; a
down payment / yoyaku-seki (予約
席) a *reserved* seat.
2 subscription:
Kono zasshi wa yoyaku *ga hitsuyoo desu.* (この雑誌は予約が必要です)
You need a *subscription* to get
this magazine.
3 appointment.
yoyaku suru (～する) *vt.* **1** reserve; book: *Sono hoteru ni heya
o* yoyaku shimashita *ka?* (そのホテル
に部屋を予約しましたか) *Have* you
reserved a room at the hotel?
2 subscribe: *Sono zasshi wa nineñ-kañ* yoyaku suru *to sañjup-
paaseñto no waribiki ga arimasu.*
(その雑誌は2年間予約すると30%の
割引があります) You can get a thirty percent discount if you *subscribe* to that magazine for two
years.
3 make an appointment: *Haisha
ni wa ni-ji ni* yoyaku shimashita.

(歯医者には2時に予約しました) I
made an appointment with the
dentist for two o'clock.

yoˈyuu よゆう (余裕) *n.* margin;
room; leeway:
Ressha no norikae ni jup-puñ yoyuu *o mite oita.* (列車の乗り換えに10
分余裕を見ておいた) I allowed a *margin* of ten minutes for changing
trains. / *Koko ni wa soñna ni
ooki-na teeburu o oku* yoyuu *wa
arimaseñ.* (ここにはそんなに大きなテーブ
ルを置く余裕はありません) There is no
room here to place such a large
table. / *Atarashii kamera o kau*
yoyuu wa arimaseñ. (新しいカメラを
買う余裕はありません) I *cannot afford*
to buy a new camera.

yu' ゆ (湯) *n.* **1** hot water: ★ Often '*o-yu.*'

(o-)yu (hot water)	water
mizu (cold water)	

yu *o wakasu* (湯を沸かす) boil *water*
/ *Mizu de naku,* o-yu *o kudasai.*
(水でなく, お湯を下さい) Give me *hot
water*, not cold water, please.
2 (hot) bath. 《⇨ furoba (photo)》

-yu ゆ (油) *suf.* oil:
seki-yu (石油) *petroleum* / too-yu
(灯油) *kerosene.*

yuˈbiˈ ゆび (指) *n.* finger; thumb;
toe:
yubi *ni yubiwa o hameru* (指に指輪

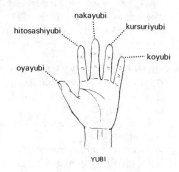

YUBI

をはめる) put a ring on one's *finger* / yubi *de kazoeru* (指で数える) count on one's *fingers*.

yu⌐bisa⌐s·u ゆびさす (指さす) *vt.* (-sash·i-; -sas·a·-; -sash·i-te Ⓒ) point to [at]: *kabe no e o* yubisasu (壁の絵を指さす) *point to* a picture on the wall / *Hito o* yubisasu *no wa shitsuree desu.* (人を指さすのは失礼です) It is rude to *point at* people. / *Omawari-san wa eki made no michi o* yubisashite oshiete kureta. (お巡さんは駅までの道を指さして教えてくれた) The policeman *indicated* the way to the station for me.

yu⌐biwa ゆびわ (指輪) *n.* ring: yubiwa *o hameru* [*nuku*] (指輪をはめる[抜く]) put on [take off] a *ring* / *Kanojo wa konyaku-yubiwa o shite ita.* (彼女は婚約指輪をしていた) She was wearing an engagement *ring*.

yu⌐dan ゆだん (油断) *n.* carelessness; inattention; negligence: *Chotto shita* yudan *ga moto de ooki-na jiko ni natta.* (ちょっとした油断がもとで大きな事故になった) A little *carelessness* led to a serious accident.

yudan suru (〜する) *vi.* be careless; be inattentive; be negligent: *Kuruma o unten suru toki wa* yudan shite *wa ikemasen.* (車を運転するときは油断してはいけません) When you are driving, you must not *let your attention wander*.

yu⌐de⌐·ru ゆでる (茹でる) *vt.* (yu-de-te Ⓥ) boil: *tamago o* yuderu (卵をゆでる) *boil* an egg / yudeta *hoorenso* (ゆでたほうれん草) *boiled* spinach.

yu⌐de-ta⌐mago ゆでたまご (茹卵) *n.* boiled egg. (⇨ hanjuku)

yu⌐e ni ゆえに (故に) *conj.* (*formal*) therefore; consequently; hence: Yue ni *kare no setsu wa machigatte iru.* (ゆえに彼の説は間違っている)

Consequently, his theory is wrong.

yu⌐game·ru ゆがめる (歪める) *vt.* (yugame-te Ⓥ) distort; twist: *kao o* yugameru (顔をゆがめる) *screw up* one's face / *Juken kyoosoo ga honrai no kyooiku o* yugamete iru. (受験競争が本来の教育をゆがめている) Competition in the entrance exams *is distorting* the fundamentals of education. (⇨ yugamu)

yu⌐gam·u ゆがむ (歪む) *vi.* (yugam·i-; yugam·a·-; yugan-de Ⓒ) be twisted; be distorted; be warped; lean: *Kono kagami wa zoo ga* yugande *utsuru.* (この鏡は像がゆがんで映る) This mirror reflects a *distorted* image. / *Kanja no kao wa kutsuu de* yugande ita. (患者の顔は苦痛でゆがんでいた) The patient's face *was contorted* with pain. / *Kare wa seekaku ga* yugande iru. (彼は性格がゆがんでいる) He has a *warped* personality. (⇨ yugameru)

yu⌐ge ゆげ (湯気) *n.* steam: *Yakan kara* yuge *ga dete iru.* (やかんから湯気が出ている) *Steam* is rising from the kettle.

yu⌐i-itsu ゆいいつ (唯一) *n.* one and only: *Kare ga sono jiko no* yui-itsu *no seezonsha desu.* (彼がその事故の唯一の生存者です) He is the *sole* survivor of that accident. / *Kare no* yui-itsu *no tanoshimi wa tsuri desu.* (彼の唯一の楽しみは釣りです) His *only* pastime is fishing.

yu⌐ka ゆか (床) *n.* floor: *itabari no* yuka (板張りの床) a boarded *floor* / *Yuka ni wa atsui juutan ga shiite atta.* (床には厚いじゅうたんが敷いてあった) The *floor* was covered with a thick carpet.

yu⌐kai ゆかい (愉快) *a.n.* (〜 na, ni) pleasant; enjoyable; jolly; amusing:

yukai *na nakama* (愉快な仲間) *pleasant* company / *Kyoo no paatii wa yukai datta.* (きょうのパーティーは愉快だった) The party today was *enjoyable.* / *Tanaka-saṅ wa hoṅtoo ni yukai na hito da.* (田中さんはほんとうに愉快な人だ) Mr. Tanaka is really a *jolly* person. 《↔ fuyukai》

yu⌐kata ゆかた (浴衣) *n.* informal summer kimono. ★ An unlined cotton kimono with simple patterns of deep blue.

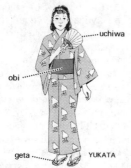

uchiwa

obi

geta   YUKATA

yu⌐ketsu ゆけつ (輸血) *n.* blood transfusion:
yuketsu *o ukeru* (輸血を受ける) receive a *blood transfusion.*
yuketsu suru (〜する) *vi.* transfuse: *Isha wa sono kaṅja ni yuketsu shita.* (医者はその患者に輸血した) The doctor *gave* the patient a *blood transfusion.*

yu⌐ki¹ ゆき (雪) *n.* snow:
Yuki *ga futte kita.* (雪が降ってきた) It *has begun to snow.* / Yuki *ga yaku go-seṅchi tsumotta.* (雪が約5センチ積もった) The *snow* was about five centimeters deep. / *Kotoshi wa* yuki *ga ookatta.* (今年は雪が多かった) We have had a lot of *snow* this year.

yu⌐ki² ゆき (行き) *n.* (=iki²) going (to a destination):
Deṅsha wa yuki *wa koṅde ita ga, kaeri wa suite ita.* (電車は行きはこんでいたが, 帰りはすいていた) The train was crowded *on the way there,* but not crowded on the way back. / *Koṅdo no ryokoo wa* yuki *mo* kaeri *mo hikooki deshita.* (今度の旅行は行きも帰りも飛行機でした) On my recent trip, I took an airplane *both ways.* 《↔ kaeri》《⇨ yuku》

-yuki ゆき (行き) *suf.* bound for:
*Oosaka-*yuki *no ressha* (大阪行きの列車) a train *bound for* Osaka / *Kono basu wa* doko-yuki *desu ka?* (このバスはどこ行きですか) *Where* does this bus *go?*

yu⌐kichigai ゆきちがい (行き違い) *n.*
1 crossing each other:
Tegami ga yukichigai *ni natte shimatta.* (手紙が行き違いになってしまった) Our letters *have crossed each other.* / *Tochuu de otagai ni* yukichigai *ni natta yoo da.* (途中でお互いに行き違いになったようだ) We seem to *have missed each other* on the way.
2 misunderstanding:
Futari no aida ni wa yukichigai *ga atta.* (二人の間には行き違いがあった) There was some *misunderstanding* between the two of them.

yu⌐kidomari ゆきどまり (行き止まり) *n.* dead end:
Kono michi wa yukidomari *desu.* (この道は行き止まりです) This road comes to a *dead end.*

yu⌐kisaki ゆきさき (行き先) *n.* = yukusaki.

yu⌐kku⌐ri ゆっくり *adv.* (〜 to)
1 slowly; without hurry; leisurely:
Roojiṅ wa yukkuri *(to) aruite ita.* (老人はゆっくり(と)歩いていた) The old man was walking *slowly.* / *Kore kara* yukkuri *(to) iimasu kara watashi no iu koto o kakitotte kudasai.* (これからゆっくり(と)言いますから私の言う事を書き取ってください) Now I will speak *slowly,* so take down what I say. / *Watashi-tachi wa kaigaṅ*

de ichi-nichi o yukkuri (*to*) *sugoshita*. (私たちは海岸で一日をゆっくり(と)過ごした) We passed the day at the seaside in a *leisurely fashion*.
2 good; plenty of:
Yuube wa yukkuri *nemuremashita*. (夕べはゆっくり眠れました) Last night I was able to have a *good* sleep. / *Futari wa sake o nomi-nagara* yukkuri *hanashita*. (二人は酒を飲みながらゆっくり話した) The two of them had a *long* talk over drinks. / *Deñsha ni wa* yukkuri *maniaimasu*. (電車にはゆっくり間に合います) We are in *plenty* of time for the train.

yukkuri suru (〜する) *vi.* take one's time; stay long: *Doozo* yukkuri *shite itte kudasai*. (どうぞゆっくりしていってください) Please *take your time.* / *Zañneñ-nagara ima wa* yukkuri *shite iraremaseñ*. (残念ながら今はゆっくりしていられません) Unfortunately, there is *no time to spare* now.

yu⌈k·u ゆく (行く) *vi.* (yuk·i-; yuk·a-; it-te Ⓒ) = iku.

yu⌈kue ゆくえ (行方) *n.* whereabouts:
Kanojo no yukue *o go-zoñji desu ka?* (彼女の行方をご存じですか) Do you know her *whereabouts*? / *Keesatsu de wa kare no* yukue *o sagashite iru*. (警察では彼の行方を探している) The police are searching for *him*.

yu⌈kue-fu⌉mee ゆくえふめい (行方不明) *n.* missing:
Yama de go-niñ ga yukue-fumee *ni natta*. (山で5人が行方不明になった) Five people *have gone missing* in the mountains.

yu⌈kusaki ゆくさき (行く先) *n.* destination; whereabouts:
Kono basu no yukusaki *wa doko desu ka?* (このバスの行く先はどこですか) What is the *destination* of this bus? / *Kare wa* yukusaki *fumee desu*. (彼は行く先不明です) His

whereabouts are unknown. / *Kare wa* yukusaki *o tsugezu ni, ie o dete itta*. (彼は行く先を告げずに, 家を出て行った) He left home without telling us *where he was going*.

yu⌈kusue ゆくすえ (行く末) *n.* future:
Kare wa musuko no yukusue *o shiñpai shite iru*. (彼は息子の行く末を心配している) He is anxious about his son's *future*.

yu⌈me⌉ ゆめ (夢) *n.* **1** dream:
Watashi wa tokidoki shikeñ no yume *o miru*. (私はときどき試験の夢を見る) I sometimes have a *dream* about the examination. / *Osoroshii* yume *kara sameta*. (恐ろしい夢から覚めた) I awoke from a frightening *dream*.
2 ambition; dream:
Isha ni naru no ga kare no yume *desu*. (医者になるのが彼の夢です) It is his *dream* to become a doctor.

yu⌈mi⌉ ゆみ (弓) *n.* bow:
yumi *o hiku* (弓を引く) draw a *bow* / yumi *o iru* (弓を射る) *shoot an arrow.* 《↔ ya⁴》

Yu⌈ne⌉suko ユネスコ *n.* UNESCO; the United Nations Educational, Scientific, and Cultural Organization.

yu⌈nomi⌉ ゆのみ (湯呑) *n.* cup; teacup. 《⇨ chawañ》

YUNOMI

yu⌈nyuu ゆにゅう (輸入) *n.* import; importation:
kome no yunyuu *moñdai* (米の輸入問題) the issue of rice *imports* / *noosañbutsu no* yunyuu *o fuyasu* [*herasu*] (農産物の輸入を増やす[減らす]) increase [decrease] the *impor-*

tation of farm products / yunyuu-
chooka (輸入超過) an unfavorable
balance of *trade* / yunyuu-*hiñ* (輸
入品) *imported* goods.

yunyuu suru (〜する) *vt.* import:
*Nihoñ wa ooku no kuni kara sho-
kuryoo-hiñ o* yunyuu *shite imasu.*
(日本は多くの国から食料品を輸入して
います) Japan *imports* food from a
large number of countries.
《↔ yushutsu》

yuˈre·ru ゆれる (揺れる) *vi.* (yurete V) **1** shake; tremble; sway:
Jishiñ de ie ga hidoku yureta. (地
震で家がひどく揺れた) The house
shook violently because of the
earthquake. / *Ki no eda ga kaze
ni* yurete iru. (木の枝が風に揺れてい
る) The branches of the tree *are
swaying* in the wind. / *Basu ga
hidoku* yurete, *kimochi ga waruku natta.* (バスがひどく揺れて、気持ち
が悪くなった) The bus *swayed* so
violently that I began to feel sick.
2 waver:
*Sono moñdai de kanojo no kokoro
wa* yurete iru. (その問題で彼女の心は
揺れている) Her heart *is wavering*
over that problem.

yuˈru·i ゆるい (緩い) *a.* (-ku)
1 loose; lax:
Kono neji wa yurui. (このねじはゆるい)
This screw is *loose.* / *Kono kutsu
wa boku ni wa sukoshi* yurui. (この
靴はぼくには少しゆるい) These shoes
are a little *too big* for me. 《↔ ki-
tsui》《⇨ yurumu》
2 gentle:
Sono shikichi wa yurui *shameñ ni
natte iru.* (その敷地はゆるい斜面になっ
ている) The site forms a *gentle*
slope. 《↔ kyuu》
3 slow:
Kare wa yurui *tama o nageta.* (彼は
ゆるい球を投げた) He pitched a *slow*
ball. 《↔ hayai》

yuˈrume·ru ゆるめる (緩める) *vt.*
(yurume-te V) **1** loosen; unfas-

ten; relax:
beruto o yurumeru (ベルトをゆるめる)
loosen one's belt / *Kata no chikara
o* yurume nasai. (肩の力をゆるめなさ
い) *Relax* your shoulders. 《⇨ yu-
rumu; yurui》
2 make less strict; relax:
Tookyoku wa keekai o yurumeta.
(当局は警戒をゆるめた) The authori-
ties *relaxed* their vigilance.
《⇨ yurumu》
3 slow down:
*Kuruma wa sakamichi de supiido
o* yurumeta. (車は坂道でスピードをゆる
めた) The car *slowed down* on the
slope.

yuˈruˈm·u ゆるむ (緩む) *vi.* (yu-
rum·i-; yurum·a-; yuruñ-de V)
1 become loose; loosen:
Nekutai ga yuruñde imasu yo. (ネク
タイがゆるんでいますよ) Your necktie
is loose. 《⇨ yurumeru》
2 soften; abate:
Bee-Chuu no kiñchoo ga yuruñda.
(米中の緊張がゆるんだ) American-
Chinese tensions *abated.* / *Samusa ga* yuruñde kita. (寒さがゆる
んできた) It *has become less* cold.

yuˈrushi ゆるし (許し) *n.* permission; pardon:
Kanojo wa oya no yurushi *o ete
gaikoku e itta.* (彼女は親の許しを得
て外国へ行った) She got *permission*
from her parents and went
abroad. / *Doo-ka o-*yurushi *kudasai.* (どうかお許しください) I beg your
pardon. 《⇨ kyoka; yurusu》

yuˈruˈs·u ゆるす (許す) *vt.* (yurus-
sh·i-; yurus·a-; yurush·i-te C)
1 permit; allow:
*Kanojo wa byooiñ kara gaishutsu
o* yurusareta. (彼女は病院から外出を
許された) She *was allowed* to leave
the hospital for a short period of
time. 《⇨ yurushi》/ *Jikañ ga* yurusu *kagiri sono keñkyuu o tsuzu-
ketai.* (時間が許す限りその研究を続け
たい) I want to continue that

research as long as time *permits*.
2 forgive:
Watashi wa kare no kooi o yurusu
koto ga dekinai. (私は彼の行為を許
すことができない) I *cannot forgive*
what he did. / *Go-busata o* o-yurushi *kudasai.* (ごぶさたをお許しくださ
い) *Forgive* me for not contacting
you for so long.

yu⌐ru⌐yaka ゆるやか (緩やか) *a.n.*
(～ na, ni) gentle; slow:
yuruyaka *na saka* (ゆるやかな坂) a
gentle slope / *Ooki-na kawa wa
nagare ga* yuruyaka *desu.* (大きな川
は流れがゆるやかです) Large rivers
flow *slowly.* / *Kisoku ga* yuruyaka
ni natta. (規則がゆるやかになった) The
regulations became *less strict.*
((↔ kitsui))

yu⌐sabur⌐u ゆさぶる (揺さぶる) *vt.*
(-bur·i-; -bur·a-; -but-te Ⓒ)
shake; move:
*Kodomo-tachi wa omoshirogatte
tsuribashi o* yusabutta. (子どもたちは
おもしろがってつり橋をゆさぶった) The
children *shook* the rope bridge
for fun. / *Sono jiken wa naikaku
o* yusabutta. (その事件は内閣を揺さぶ
った) The incident *rocked* the
cabinet. ((⇨ yusuru¹))

yu⌐shutsu ゆしゅつ (輸出) *n.* export; exportation:
Kuruma no yushutsu *wa nobite
imasu.* (車の輸出は伸びています) The
export of cars is increasing. / yu-
shutsu-*chooka* (輸出超過) an excess of *imports* / yushutsu-hiñ (輸
出品) goods for *export.*
  yushutsu suru (～する) *vt.* export: *Nihoñ wa iroiro na kuni e
jidoosha o* yushutsu *shite imasu.*
(日本はいろいろな国へ自動車を輸出して
います) Japan *exports* automobiles
to many countries. ((↔ yunyuu))

yu⌐soo ゆそう (輸送) *n.* transport;
transportation:
yusoo-*ki* (輸送機) a *transport*
plane / yusoo-*señ* (輸送船) a *trans-*

port ship.
  yusoo suru (～する) *vt.* transport;
carry: *Ressha-jiko no tame, jookyaku wa basu de* yusoo *sareta.*
(列車事故のため, 乗客はバスで輸送され
た) On account of the train accident, the passengers *were carried*
by bus.

yu⌐sug⌐u ゆすぐ (濯ぐ) *vt.* (yusu-
g·i-; yusug·a-; yusu·i-de Ⓒ)
rinse out; wash out:
señtakumono o yusugu (洗濯物をゆ
すぐ) *rinse* one's laundry / *Gaishutsu kara kaettara, kuchi o* yusugi
nasai. (外出から帰ったら, 口をゆすぎな
さい) When you come home after
being out, *rinse out* your mouth.
★ Japanese children are taught
this as an item of personal hygiene.

yu⌐sur⌐u¹ ゆする (揺する) *vt.* (yu-
sur·i-; yusur·a-; yusut-te Ⓒ)
shake; rock:
Ki o yusutte, *mi o otoshita.* (木を揺
すって, 実を落とした) I *shook* the tree
causing the fruit to fall. / *Haha-
oya wa kodomo o* yusutte *okoshita.* (母親は子どもを揺すって起こした)
The mother *shook* her child
awake. ((⇨ yusaburu))

yu⌐sur⌐u² ゆする (強請る) *vt.* (yu-
sur·i-; yusur·a-; yusut-te Ⓒ)
extort; blackmail:
Kare wa kanojo kara taikiñ o
yusutta. (彼は彼女から大金をゆすった)
He *blackmailed* her out of a large
sum of money.

yu⌐taka ゆたか (豊か) *a.n.* (～ na,
ni) abundant; ample; rich; affluent:
yutaka *na shigeñ* (豊かな資源) *abundant* resources / yutaka *na sainoo*
(豊かな才能) *a wealth of* talent /
Yamada-sañ wa yutaka *na katee
ni sodatta.* (山田さんは豊かな家庭に育
った) Miss Yamada grew up in an
affluent family. / *Ano o-isha-sañ
wa keekeñ ga* yutaka *desu.* (あのお

医者さんは経験が豊かです) That doctor is *rich* in experience. / *Geejutsu wa hito no kokoro o* yutaka ni suru.(芸術は人の心を豊かにする) The arts *enrich* our spirits.《↔ mazushii; toboshii》

yuˈttaˈri ゆったり *adv.* (~ to; ~ suru) at ease; comfortably; loosely:
Guriiñsha no zaseki ni yuttari *to suwatta.*(グリーン車の座席にゆったりと座った) I sat *comfortably* in a first class train seat. / *Tama ni wa* yuttari (*to*) *shita kibuñ o ajiwaitai.*(たまにはゆったり(と)した気分を味わいたい) Once in a while I would like to savor the pleasure of being *completely at ease.* / *Kare wa* yuttari (*to*) *shita yukata o kite ita.*(彼はゆったり(と)したゆかたを着ていた) He was wearing a *loose*-fitting 'yukata.'

yu·ˈu[1] いう (言う) *vi.* (i·i-; yuw·a-; yut-te C) = iu.

yuˈu[2] ゆう (優) *n.* (of a grade, rating) being excellent; A (in schoolwork):
Suugaku de yuu *o totta.*(数学で優をとった) I got an *A* in mathematics.《⇨ seeseki (table)》

yuˈube[1] ゆうべ (夕べ) *n.* yesterday evening; last night:
Yuube wa atsukute nemurenakatta.(ゆうべは暑くて眠れなかった) *Last night* I couldn't sleep because it was so hot. / *Yuube eki de Itoosañ ni aimashita.*(ゆうべ駅で伊藤さんに会いました) *Yesterday evening*, I met Mr. Ito at the station.

yuˈube[2] ゆうべ (夕べ) *n.* (*literary*) evening:
oñgaku no yuube (音楽の夕べ) a musical *evening.*

yuˈubiñ ゆうびん (郵便) *n.* **1** mail [postal] service; mail:
kokunai[*gaikoku*]-yuubiñ (国内[外国]郵便) domestic [overseas] *mail* / yuubiñ-*bañgoo* (郵便番号) *zip* [*postal*] code / yuubiñ-*chokiñ* (郵

便貯金) *postal* savings / yuubiñ-*kawase* (郵便為替) a *postal* money order / yuubiñ-*uke* (郵便受け) a *mail*box.
2 postal matter; mail:
Watashi-ate no yuubiñ *wa kite imasu ka?*(私宛の郵便は来ていますか) Is there any *mail* for me? / *Getsuyoo ni wa* yuubiñ *ga takusañ kimasu.*(月曜には郵便がたくさんきます) We receive a lot of *mail* on Mondays. / *Yuubiñ wa moo dashimashita.*(郵便はもう出しました) I *have* already *mailed* the letters.

yuˈubiˈñbutsu ゆうびんぶつ (郵便物) *n.* = yuubiñ (**2**).

yuˈubiˈñkyoku ゆうびんきょく (郵便局) *n.* post office. ★ 〒 is the emblem of '*yuubiñkyoku*' and '*Yuusee-shoo.*'《⇨ Yuusee-shoo》

YUUBIÑ KYOKU

yuˈuboku ゆうぼく (遊牧) *n.* nomadism:
yuuboku-*miñzoku* (遊牧民族) a *nomadic* tribe / yuuboku-*seekatsu* (遊牧生活) a *nomadic* life.

yuˈuboo ゆうぼう (有望) *a.n.* (~ na, ni) promising; hopeful:
yuuboo *na wakamono* (有望な若者) a *promising* young person / *Kono kabu wa* yuuboo *desu.*(この株は有望です) These stocks are *promising.*

yuˈudachi ゆうだち (夕立) *n.* sudden, heavy shower on a summer afternoon:
Uchi ni kaeru tochuu de yuudachi *ni atta.*(家に帰る途中で夕立にあった) I was caught in a *shower* on my way home. / yuudachi-*gumo* (夕立

雲) a *shower* cloud.

yu「udoku ゆうどく (有毒) *a.n.*
(~ na, ni) poisonous:
yuudoku (*na*) *gasu* (有毒(な)ガス) *poisonous* gas / *Kono kinoko wa* yuudoku *desu.* (このきのこは有毒です)
These mushrooms are *poisonous*.

yu「ueki ゆうえき (有益) *a.n.* (~ na,
ni) useful; helpful; instructive:
yuueki *na hanashi* (有益な話) an
instructive talk / *Anata no chuukoku wa totemo* yuueki *deshita.*
(あなたの忠告はとても有益でした) Your
advice was very *helpful.* / *O-kane
wa* yuueki *ni tsukai nasai.* (お金は
有益に使いなさい) Make *good use* of
your money. (↔ mueki)

yu「ugai ゆうがい (有害) *a.n.*
(~ na, ni) harmful; injurious;
bad:
seeshoonen ni yuugai *na zasshi*
(青少年に有害な雑誌) a magazine
harmful to young people / *Tabako wa kenkoo ni* yuugai *desu.* (たば
こは健康に有害です) Smoking is *injurious* to the health. (↔ mugai)

yu「ugata ゆうがた (夕方) *n.* evening:
Yuugata (*ni*) *ame ga furidashita.*
(夕方(に)雨が降りだした) It began to
rain in the *evening.* (⇨ ban[1];
yuube[1])

yu「ugure ゆうぐれ (夕暮れ) *n.*
evening. (⇨ yuugata)

yu「uhan ゆうはん (夕飯) *n.* supper; dinner. (⇨ yuushoku)

yu「uhi ゆうひ (夕日) *n.* the
evening [setting] sun. (⇨ asahi)

yu「ujin ゆうじん (友人) *n.* friend:
Shichoo wa chichi no yuujin *desu.*
(市長は父の友人です) The mayor is
a *friend* of my father.

yu「ujoo ゆうじょう (友情) *n.*
friendship:
Kare to no yuujoo *wa eekyuu ni
kawarimasen.* (彼との友情は永久に
変わりません) My *friendship* with
him will never change.

yu「ukai ゆうかい (誘拐) *n.* kidnapping; abduction:
yuukai-han (誘拐犯) a *kidnapper* /
yuukai-jiken (誘拐事件) a *kidnapping*.
yuukai suru (~する) *vt.* kidnap;
abduct: *Nana-sai no kodomo ga
minoshirokin meate ni* yuukai *sareta.* (七歳の子どもが身代金目当てに
誘拐された) A seven-year-old child
was kidnapped and held for ransom.

yu「ukan[1] ゆうかん (勇敢) *a.n.*
(~ na, ni) brave; courageous:
yuukan *na otoko-no-ko* (勇敢な男の
子) a *brave* boy / yuukan *ni tatakau* (勇敢に闘う) fight *courageously*
/ *Oboreru ko o tasuketa kare wa*
yuukan *datta.* (溺れる子を助けた彼は
勇敢だった) The man who saved
the drowning child was *brave*.

yu「ukan[2] ゆうかん (夕刊) *n.* evening paper; the evening edition
of a newspaper. (↔ chookan[1])

yu「uki ゆうき (勇気) *n.* courage;
bravery:
Yuuki *o dashi nasai.* (勇気を出しな
さい) *Be brave!* / *Kare no kotoba
de* yuuki *ga deta.* (彼の言葉で勇気が
出た) His words gave me a lot of
courage. / *Sore o suru ni wa* yuuki
ga iru. (それをするには勇気がいる) You
need *courage* to do that.

yu「ukoo[1] (友好) *n.* friendly relationship; friendship:
Nichi-Bee no yuukoo-kankee (日米
の友好関係) *friendly relations* between Japan and the United
States / *Sono taikai wa sankasha
no* yuukoo *o fukameru no ni ooi-ni
yakudatta.* (その大会は参加者の友好
を深めるのに大いに役立った) The convention went a long way toward
promoting *friendship* among the
participants.

yu「ukoo[2] ゆうこう (有効) *a.n.*
(~ na, ni) effective; valid:
Kono pasupooto wa hachi-gatsu

made yuukoo *desu.*(このパスポートは8月まで有効です) This passport is *valid* until August. / *Jikañ wa* yuukoo *ni tsukai nasai.*(時間は有効に使いなさい) Make sure you use your time *efficiently.* 《↔ mukoo》

yu⌐umee ゆうめい (有名) *a.n.* (~ na, ni) famous; well-known; notorious:
Kono tatemono wa sekai-teki ni yuumee *desu.*(この建物は世界的に有名です) This building is *famous* worldwide. / *Ano hito ga* yuumee *na bijutsu hyooroñka desu.*(あの人が有名な美術評論家です) He is a *famous* art critic. / *Kare wa wakai toki sakka to shite* yuumee *ni natta.*(彼は若いとき作家として有名になった) He became *famous* as a novelist when he was young. / *Sono toshi wa hañzai ga ooi koto de* yuumee *desu.*(その都市は犯罪の多いことで有名です) That city is *notorious* for its many crimes. 《↔ mumee》

yu⌐umeshi ゆうめし (夕飯) *n.* (*informal*) supper; dinner. 《⇒ yuushoku》

yu⌐umoa ユーモア *n.* humor; joke:
Kare wa yuumoa *no señsu ga nai.*(彼はユーモアのセンスがない) He has no sense of *humor.* / *Yamada-shi no eñzetsu wa* yuumoa *ni toñde ita.*(山田氏の演説はユーモアに富んでいた) Mr. Yamada's speech was full of *humor.*

yu⌐unoo ゆうのう (有能) *a.n.* (~ na) able; capable; competent:
yuunoo *na jiñbutsu* (有能な人物) an *able* person / *Kare no hisho wa taiheñ* yuunoo *desu.*(彼の秘書はたいへん有能です) His secretary is exceedingly *competent.* 《↔ munoo》

yu⌐uri ゆうり (有利) *a.n.* (~ na, ni) advantageous; favorable:
Kare wa watashi ni yuuri *na shoo-*

geñ *o shita.* (彼は私に有利な証言をした) He testified *in my favor.* / *O-kane wa giñkoo ni nagaku azuketa hoo ga* yuuri *desu.*(お金は銀行に長く預けた方が有利です) It is *more profitable* to deposit your money in the bank for a long period of time. / *Kooshoo wa* yuuri *ni susumeru koto ga dekita.*(交渉は有利に進めることができた) We were able to conduct the negotiations *favorably.* 《↔ furi¹》

yu⌐uryoku ゆうりょく (有力) *a.n.* (~ na, ni) influential; strong; leading:
yuuryoku *na seejika* (有力な政治家) an *influential* politician / yuuryoku *na shooko* (有力な証拠) *strong* evidence / *Koñdo no señkyo de wa kare ga* yuuryoku *desu.*(今度の選挙では彼が有力です) He is *likely* to be elected in this election. 《↔ muryoku》

yuuryoo (有料) *n.* charge:
Kono teñrañkai wa yuuryoo *desu.*(この展覧会は有料です) There is a *charge* for this exhibition. / yuuryoo-*toire* (有料トイレ) a *pay* toilet / yuuryoo-*dooro* (有料道路) a *toll* road. 《↔ muryoo》

yu⌐usee ゆうせい (優勢) *n.* superiority; lead:
yuusee *o tamotsu* (優勢を保つ) retain one's *superiority.*
— *a.n.* (~ na, ni) superior; leading:
Dochira ga yuusee *desu ka?* (どちらが優勢ですか) Which one is *superior?* / *Wareware no chiimu wa saisho kara* yuusee *datta.*(われわれのチームは最初から優勢だった) Our team *led* from the beginning. 《↔ ressee》

Yu⌐usee-da⌐ijiñ (郵政大臣) *n.* Minister of Posts and Telecommunications.

Yu⌐use⌐e-shoo ゆうせいしょう (郵政省) *n.* Ministry of Posts and

Telecommunications.
《⇨ shoo[1] (table)》

yu⌐useñ ゆうせん (優先) *n.* priority; precedence; preference: yuuseñ-keñ (優先権) the *priority* / yuuseñ-*juñi* (優先順位) the order of *priority*.
  yuuseñ suru (〜する) *vi.* have priority; take precedence: *liñkai wa sono moñdai o* yuuseñ shite *toriageru koto ni shita.* (委員会はその問題を優先して取り上げることにした) The committee decided to deal with that problem *on a priority basis.*

yu⌐useñ-ho⌐osoo ゆうせんほうそう (有線放送) *n.* closed-circuit [cable] broadcasting.

yu⌐ushoku ゆうしょく (夕食) *n.* supper; dinner: yuushoku *o taberu* [*toru*] (夕食を食べる[とる]) have *supper* / Yuushoku *ni sakana o tabeta.* (夕食に魚を食べた) I had fish for *dinner.*
《⇨ yuumeshi; bañsañ》

yu⌐ushoo ゆうしょう (優勝) *n.* victory; championship: yuushoo *o kazaru* [*nogasu*] (優勝を飾る[逃す]) win [fail to win] the *championship* / *Sono chiimu wa* yuushoo *o neratte iru.* (そのチームは優勝をねらっている) The team is aiming for the *championship.* / yuushoo-sha (優勝者) the *winner.*
  yuushoo suru (〜する) *vi.* win the victory [championship]: *Kanojo wa tenisu de ni-neñ reñzoku* yuushoo shita. (彼女はテニスで2年連続優勝した) She *won* the tennis *championship* two years running. / *Beñroñ-taikai de wa dare ga* yuushoo shimashita *ka?* (弁論大会ではだれが優勝しましたか) Who *won first prize* in the speech contest?

yu⌐ushuu ゆうしゅう (優秀) *a.n.* (〜 na) excellent; superior; outstanding: yuushuu *na seeseki de sotsugyoo*

suru (優秀な成績で卒業する) graduate with an *excellent* academic record / *Kare no musuko wa* yuushuu *da.* (彼の息子は優秀だ) His son is *outstanding.*

yu⌐usoo ゆうそう (郵送) *n.* sending by mail [post]: yuusoo-ryoo (郵送料) *postage.*
  yuusoo suru (〜する) *vt.* mail [post]; send by mail [post]: *Shashiñ wa ato de* yuusoo shimasu. (写真は後で郵送します) I will *mail* you the photos afterward.

yu⌐utoo ゆうとう (優等) *n.* academic honors: yuutoo *de daigaku o sotsugyoo suru* (優等で大学を卒業する) graduate from college with *honors* / yuutoo-*see* (優等生) an *honor* student.

yu⌐u-utsu ゆううつ (憂鬱) *a.n.* (〜 na, ni) depressing; gloomy; melancholy: *Mainichi teñki ga warukute* yuuutsu *da.* (毎日天気が悪くてゆううつだ) I feel *gloomy* because of the long spell of bad weather. / *Kare wa* yuu-utsu-*soo na kao o shite ita.* (彼はゆううつそうな顔をしていた) He looked *depressed.* / *Sono hanashi o kiite,* yuu-utsu *ni natta.* (その話を聞いて, ゆううつになった) I sank into a state of *melancholy* on hearing the news.

yu⌐uwaku ゆうわく (誘惑) *n.* temptation; lure; seduction: yuuwaku *ni katsu* [*makeru*] (誘惑に勝つ[負ける]) overcome [give in to] *temptation* / yuuwaku *to tatakau* (誘惑と闘う) resist the *temptation.*
  yuuwaku suru (〜する) *vt.* tempt; lure; seduce (a woman): *Kare-ra wa kiñseñ de watashi o* yuuwaku shiyoo to shita. (彼らは金銭で私を誘惑しようとした) They *attempted to win me over* with money.

yu⌐uyake ゆうやけ (夕焼け) *n.*

glow of the sunset:
Sora wa yuuyake *de makka datta.*
(空は夕焼けで真っ赤だった) The sky
was deep-red with the *glow of the
sunset.* 《↔ asayake》

yu⌐uyu⌐u ゆうゆう（悠々）*adv.*
(〜 to) **1** easily; without difficulty:
Ima ikeba, saishuu-deñsha ni yuuyuu *(to) noremasu.* (今行けば、最終
電車にゆうゆう（と）乗れます) If you go
now, you can *easily* catch the last
train. / *Kare nara sono gakkoo ni*
yuuyuu *(to) hairemasu.* (彼ならその学
校にゆうゆう（と）入れます) If it's him,
he can get into that school *without any difficulty* at all. / *Kono
basu wa* yuuyuu *gojuu-niñ noremasu.* (このバスはゆうゆう 50 人乗れま
す) Fifty people can *quite easily*
get on this bus.
2 calmly; sedately; leisurely.
Kare wa sono ba kara yuuyuu *to
tachisatta.* (彼はその場からゆうゆうと立
ち去った) He *calmly* went away
from the spot. / *Ima wa* yuuyuu *to
suwatte iru baai de wa arimaseñ.*
（今はゆうゆうと座っている場合ではありま
せん) Now is not the time for us
to *leisurely* sit back.

yu⌐uzuu ゆうずう（融通）*n.*
1 adaptability; flexibility:
Ano hito wa yuuzuu *ga kiku [kika-
nai].* (あの人は融通がきく[きかない]) He
is flexible and versatile [*rigid and
literal-minded*].

2 accommodation; financing:
Kare ni hyakumañ-eñ no yuuzuu *o
tanoñda ga kotowarareta.* (彼に 100
万円の融通を頼んだが断わられた) I
asked him for a million yen of
financing but was turned down.
yuuzuu suru (〜する) *vt.* accommodate; lend: *Suzuki-sañ ga
nijuumañ-eñ* yuuzuu *shite kuremashita.* (鈴木さんが 20 万円融通してくれ
ました) Miss Suzuki *lent* me
200,000 yen.

yu⌐zur·u ゆずる（譲る）*vt.* (yuzur-
r·i-; yuzur·a-; yuzut-te ⊂)
1 hand over; transfer:
Kare wa musuko ni tochi o yuzutta. (彼は息子に土地を譲った) He
transferred the property to his
son. / *Sono seejika wa kooshiñ ni
michi o* yuzutta. (その政治家は後進
に道を譲った) The politician *made
way* for the younger generation.
2 give; offer; sell:
*Shooneñ wa basu de roojiñ ni seki
o* yuzutta. (少年はバスで老人に席を譲
った) The boy *gave up* his seat to
an elderly person on the bus. /
*Kare wa watashi ni waapuro o
yasuku* yuzutte kureta. (彼は私にワ
ープロを安く譲ってくれた) He *sold* his
word processor to me cheaply.
3 concede; make a concession:
Sono teñ wa yuzuremaseñ. (その点
は譲れません) I *cannot concede* that
point.

Z

za⌐azaa ざあざあ *adv.* (~ to)
hard: ★ The sound of heavy
rainfall.
Ame ga zaazaa (to) *futte kita.* (雨
がざあざあ(と)降ってきた) The rain
began to pour down.

za⌐buñ ざぶん *adv.* (~ to) with a
splash: ★ The sound of a heavy
object falling into water.
Kare wa zabuñ *to kawa ni ochita.*
(彼はざぶんと川に落ちた) He fell into
the river *with a splash.*

za⌐bu⌐toñ ざぶとん (座布団) *n.*
cushion for sitting on.

ZABUTOÑ

za⌐da⌐ñkai (座談会) *n.* discussion meeting; round-table talk:
zadañkai *o hiraku* (座談会を開く)
hold a *round-table talk.*

-zai ざい (剤) *suf.* medicine; drug;
dose:
yaku-zai (薬剤) a *medicine* / ge-zai
(下剤) a *laxative* / joo-zai (錠剤) a
tablet.

za⌐igaku ざいがく (在学) *n.* being
in school [college]:
Kare wa zaigaku-chuu *ni Nihoñ-
juu o ryokoo shita.* (彼は在学中に日
本中を旅行した) He traveled all
over Japan *during his school days.*
/ zaigaku-shoomeesho (在学証明
書) a certificate of *attendance at a
school.*
　zaigaku suru (~する) *vi.* attend a
school; be in school: *Musuko*

wa Tookyoo no daigaku ni zaigaku shite imasu. (息子は東京の大
学に在学しています) My son *is at-
tending* a college in Tokyo.

za⌐iko ざいこ (在庫) *n.* stock:
zaiko *o shiraberu* (在庫を調べる)
take *stock* / *Kono shina wa* zaiko
ga juubuñ arimasu. (この品は在庫が
十分あります) We have a good *stock*
of this article. / *Sono hoñ wa* zaiko *ga kirete imasu.* (その本は在庫が
切れています) The book is out of
stock.

za⌐imoku ざいもく (材木) *n.* wood;
lumber; timber:
zaimoku-okiba (材木置き場) a *lum-
beryard.*

za⌐iryo⌐o ざいりょう (材料) *n.* material; stuff; ingredient:
Kono kagu wa yoi zairyoo *de dekite iru.* (この家具は良い材料ででき
ている) This furniture is made of
good *materials.* / *Washi no* zairyoo *wa nañ desu ka?* (和紙の材料
は何ですか) What *materials* are
used to make Japanese paper? /
Kanojo wa keeki no zairyoo *o kai
ni dekakemashita.* (彼女はケーキの材
料を買いに出かけました) She went
out to buy the *ingredients* for a
cake.

za⌐isañ ざいさん (財産) *n.* property; fortune:
Kare no zaisañ *wa dare ga soozoku suru no desu ka?* (彼の財産は
だれが相続するのですか) Who is it that
inherits his *property?* / *Kare wa
tochi o utte, hito-*zaisañ *tsukutta.*
(彼は土地を売って、ひと財産作った) He
made a *tidy sum* selling his land.
/ *Watashi wa kanojo no* zaisañ *meate ni kekkoñ shita no de wa arimaseñ.* (私は彼女の財産目当てに結婚

したのではありません) It is not that I married her for her *money*.

za⌐isee ざいせい (財政) *n.* finance: *Kono kaisha no* zaisee *wa keñzeñ desu.* (この会社の財政は健全です) This firms's *finances* are sound. / *Wareware no kurabu wa ima* zaisee *ga kurushii.* (われわれのクラブはいま財政が苦しい) Our club is now in *financial* difficulties.

za⌐iseki¹ ざいせき (在籍) *n.* registration; enrollment: zaiseki-*sha* (在籍者) a *registered* person / zaiseki-*shoomeesho* (在籍証明書) a certificate of (student) *registration*.

zaiseki suru (〜する) *vi.* be registered; be enrolled: *Kare wa mada kono daigaku ni* zaiseki *shite imasu ka?* (彼はまだこの大学に在籍していますか) *Is* he still *registered* in this university?

za⌐iseki² ざいせき (在席) *n.* being at one's own seat [desk].

zaiseki suru (〜する) *vi.* be at one's desk: *Kachoo wa tadaima* zaiseki *shite orimaseñ.* (課長はただいま在席しておりません) The section chief *is not at his desk* now.

za⌐itaku ざいたく (在宅) *n.* being at home: ★ Often with 'go-.' *Yukari-sañ wa* go-zaitaku *desu ka?* (ゆかりさんはご在宅ですか) Is Yukari *at home?*

zaitaku suru (〜する) *vi.* be at home: *Chichi wa* zaitaku *shite imasu.* (父は在宅しています) My father *is at home.*

za⌐kka ざっか (雑貨) *n.* sundries; miscellaneous goods: zakka-*teñ* (雑貨店) a *general* store.

za⌐kkubarañ ざっくばらん *a.n.* (〜 na, ni) (*informal*) frank; candid; outspoken: zakkubarañ *na hito* (ざっくばらんな人) an *outspoken* person / *Zakkubarañ ni hanashite kudasai.* (ざっくばらんに話してください) Speak *frankly,*

please. ((⇨ sotchoku))

za⌐ndaka ざんだか (残高) *n.* balance; the remainder: *Geñzai no yokiñ* zañdaka *wa juumañ-eñ desu.* (現在の預金残高は10万円です) My current bank *balance* is 100,000 yen.

za⌐ñgyoo ざんぎょう (残業) *n.* overtime (work): *Kare wa* zañgyoo *ga tsuzuki, tsukarete iru.* (彼は残業が続き, 疲れている) His *overtime work* has been continuing and he is exhausted. / zañgyoo-*teate* (残業手当) *overtime* pay.

zañgyoo (o) suru (〜(を)する) *vi.* work overtime: *Kare wa maibañ osoku made* zañgyoo *shite iru.* (彼は毎晩遅くまで残業している) He *does overtime* late every evening.

za⌐ñkoku ざんこく (残酷) *a.n.* (〜 na, ni) cruel; atrocious; brutal: zañkoku *na kooi* (残酷な行為) a *brutal* act / zañkoku *na koto o iu* (残酷なことを言う) say something *heartless* / *Doobutsu o* zañkoku *ni atsukatte wa ikemaseñ.* (動物を残酷に扱ってはいけません) You mustn't treat animals *cruelly.*

za⌐ñne⌐ñ ざんねん (残念) *a.n.* (〜 na, ni) sorry; regrettable; repentant: *Anata ga paatii ni derarenai no wa* zañneñ *desu.* (あなたがパーティーに出られないのは残念です) I am *sorry* that you cannot come to the party. / *Sekkaku no chañsu o nogashite,* zañneñ *na koto o shita.* (せっかくのチャンスを逃して, 残念なことをした) I *regret* that I missed a great chance.

zañneñ-nagara (残念ながら) regrettably; unfortunately: *Zanneñ-nagara go-yooboo ni wa oojiraremaseñ.* (残念ながらご要望には応じられません) *We regret to say* that we cannot meet your requirements.

za⌈ppi ざっぴ（雑費）*n.* miscellaneous [sundry] expenses; incidental expenses:
Soo hiyoo wa zappi *mo fukumete, gomañ-eñ desu.*（総費用は雑費も含めて、5万円です）The total comes to 50,000 yen, including *sundry expenses.*

-za⌈ru o ⌈e⌉nai ざるをえない（ざるを得ない）(*polite=*'*-zaru o emaseñ*') cannot help; have no choice but:
★ Attached to the negative base of a verb. Note the irregular form of '*suru,*' '*sezaru o enai.*'
Koñdo no baai wa kare ni ayamarazaru o enakatta.（今度の場合は彼に謝らざるをえなかった）In this case, we *had no choice but to apologize* to him. / *Yukidomari datta no de* modorazaru o enakatta.（行き止まりだったので戻らざるをえなかった）It was a dead end, so *there was nothing for it but to go back.*

za⌈seki ざせき（座席）*n.* seat:
zaseki *o yoyaku suru*（座席を予約する）reserve a *seat* / *Tsuuro-gawa no* zaseki *ni shite kudasai.*（通路側の座席にしてください）I'd like to have an aisle *seat.* / zaseki-*shiteekeñ*（座席指定券）a reserved-*seat* ticket. 《⇨ seki¹》

za⌈setsu ざせつ（挫折）*n.* setback; collapse:
Watashi wa umarete hajimete zasetsu-kañ *o ajiwatta.*（私は生まれて初めて挫折感を味わった）I experienced a serious *setback* for the first time in my life.
zasetsu suru（～する）*vi.* miscarry; collapse: *Kanojo wa gaka o kokorozashita ga tochuu de* zasetsu shita.（彼女は画家を志したが途中で挫折した）She aspired to become an artist, but *became discouraged* along the way.

za⌈shiki⌉ ざしき（座敷）*n.* tatami-matted reception room with a 'tokonoma.'《⇨ washitsu (photo)》

za⌈shoo ざしょう（座礁）*n.* stranding; going aground.
zashoo suru（～する）*vi.* go [run] aground: *Tañkaa ga* zashoo shita.（タンカーが座礁した）A tanker *has run aground.*

za⌈sshi ざっし（雑誌）*n.* magazine; periodical:
zasshi *o yoyaku koodoku suru*（雑誌を予約購読する）subscribe to a *magazine* / *Doñna* zasshi *o totte imasu ka?*（どんな雑誌をとっていますか）What kind of *magazine* do you take?

za⌈ssoo ざっそう（雑草）*n.* weed:
niwa no zassoo o toru（庭の雑草をとる）*weed* the garden.《⇨ kusa》

za⌈taku ざたく（座卓）*n.* a low table placed in a Japanese-style room.《⇨ washitsu (photo)》

za⌈tsu ざつ（雑）*a.n.*（～ na, ni）careless; sloppy; slipshod; rough:
Kare wa shigoto ga zatsu da.（彼は仕事が雑だ）He is *careless* in his work. / *Kono ie no tsukuri wa* zatsu da.（この家の作りは雑だ）The construction of this house is *crude.*

za⌈tsudañ ざつだん（雑談）*n.* chat; light conversation:
Kanojo-tachi wa sugu ni zatsudañ *o hajimeta.*（彼女たちはすぐに雑談を始めた）The women soon started *chatting.*
zatsudañ (o) suru（～を)する）*vi.* have a chat: *Watashi-tachi wa o-cha o nomi-nagara* zatsudañ o shita.（私たちはお茶を飲みながら雑談をした）We *talked about this and that* over a cup of tea.

za⌈tsuoñ ざつおん（雑音）*n.* noise; static:
Kono rajio wa zatsuoñ *ga hairu.*（このラジオは雑音が入る）This radio picks up a lot of *static.*

za⌈tto ざっと *adv.* **1** briefly; roughly:

Sono shorui ni wa zatto *me o too-shimashita.* (その書類にはざっと目を通しました) I *briefly* looked through the papers.
2 about; approximately:
Kare no soobetsu-kai ni wa zatto *nihyaku-niñ atsumatta.* (彼の送別会にはざっと 200 人集まった) There were *about* 200 people at his farewell party.

za⌐ttoo ざっとう (雑踏) *n.* crowd; throng; congestion.
zattoo suru (〜する) *vi.* be crowded; be thronged: *Toori wa kaimono-kyaku de* zattoo *shite ita.* (通りは買物客で雑踏していた) The street *was crowded* with shoppers.

za⌐wazawa ざわざわ *adv.*
(〜 to) **1** (the murmur heard when many people are together): *Kaijoo-nai wa* zawazawa (*to*) *shite ita.* (会場内はざわざわ(と)していた) There was a *stirring* in the hall. 《⇨ gayagaya》
2 (the sound of leaves rustling in the wind):
Tsuyoi kaze ni ki no ha ga zawazawa (*to*) *yurete iru.* (強い風に木の葉がざわざわ(と)揺れている) The leaves *are rustling* in the strong wind.

za⌐yaku ざやく (座薬) *n.* suppository.

ze ぜ *p.* (*colloq.*) (used to emphasize one's opinions or wishes):
★ Used only by men.

─── USAGE ───
Both '*ze*' and '*zo*' are assertive particles which imply camaraderie and should be used only to close friends and those of lower status. '*Ze*' is softer than '*zo.*'

Sorosoro dekakeyoo ze. (そろそろ出かけようぜ) *Well*, let's be going now. / *Ashita mata kuru* ze. (あしたまた来るぜ) *You can be sure* I will be back tomorrow.

ze⌐e ぜい (税) *n.* tax; taxation:
Kono kakaku ni wa zee *ga fukumarete imasu ka?* (この価格には税が含まれていますか) Is the *tax* included in this price? / *Kanojo no gesshuu wa* zee-komi *de nijuumañ-eñ desu.* (彼女の月収は税込みで 20 万円です) Her monthly income is 200,000 yen before *taxes.* / zee-*ritsu* (税率) a *tax* rate. 《⇨ zeekiñ》

ze⌐ekañ ぜいかん (税関) *n.* customs; customhouse:
Zeekañ no tetsuzuki wa sumimashita ka? (税関の手続きは済みましたか) Are you through with the *customs* formalities? / *Kare wa* zeekañ *de nimotsu o shiraberareta.* (彼は税関で荷物を調べられた) His baggage was inspected at *customs.* / zeekañ-*shiñkokusho* (税関申告書) a *customs* declaration.

ze⌐ekiñ ぜいきん (税金) *n.* tax; duty:
zeekiñ *o osameru* [*shiharau*] (税金を納める[支払う]) pay a *tax* / *Kore ni wa* zeekiñ *ga kakarimaseñ.* (これには税金がかかりません) There is no *tax* on this.

ze⌐emu⌐sho ぜいむしょ (税務署) *n.* tax office.

ze⌐etaku ¹ ぜいたく (贅沢) *n.* luxury; extravagance:
Watashi ni soñna zeetaku *wa dekimaseñ.* (私にそんなぜいたくはできません) I cannot afford such *luxury.* / *Amari* zeetaku *o iu na.* (あまりぜいたくを言うな) You *are asking too much.*
── *a.n.* (〜 na, ni) luxurious; extravagant; lavish: zeetaku *na shokuji* (ぜいたくな食事) an *extravagant* meal / zeetaku *na kurashi o suru* (ぜいたくな暮らしをする) live a *luxurious* life / *Kanojo ga kiru mono ga* zeetaku *da.* (彼女は着るものがぜいたくだ) The clothes she wears are *extravagant.*

ze⌐hi ¹ ぜひ (是非) *adv.* surely; by

all means; at any cost:
Kai ni wa zehi *shusseki shite ku-dasai.* (会にはぜひ出席してください) *Be sure* to attend the party. / *Chika-ku ni kita toki wa* zehi *yotte kuda-sai.* (近くに来たときはぜひ寄ってください) Please *make sure* that you drop in when you are in the neighbor-hood. / *Kono shigoto wa getsuma-tsu made ni* zehi *shiagete kudasai.* (この仕事は月末までにぜひ仕上げてください) Please finish this job *with-out fail* by the end of this month. / *Ano atarashii koñpyuutaa ga* zehi *hoshii.* (あの新しいコンピューターがぜひ欲しい) I want to buy that new computer *at any cost.*

ze⌐hi² ぜひ (是非) *n.* right and/or wrong:
Watashi-tachi wa sono seedo no zehi *ni tsuite roñjita.* (私たちはその制度の是非について論じた) We argued about the *rights and wrongs* of the system.

ze⌐hi-tomo ぜひとも (是非共) *adv.* an emphatic form of '*zehi.*'
《⇨ zehi¹》

ze⌐kkoo¹ ぜっこう (絶好) *n.* (~ no) ideal; perfect:
Kyoo wa haikiñgu ni zekkoo *no teñki desu.* (きょうはハイキングに絶好の天気です) Today it's *perfect* weath-er for going on a hike. / *Watashi wa* zekkoo *no chañsu o nogashite shimatta.* (私は絶好のチャンスを逃してしまった) I have let a *golden* oppor-tunity slip by.

ze⌐kkoo² ぜっこう (絶交) *n.* breach; breaking off relations:
Ano jikeñ irai kanojo to wa zek-koo *jootai desu.* (あの事件以来彼女とは絶交状態です) Since that inci-dent my *relationship* with her *is off.* / *Moo kimi to wa* zekkoo *da.* (もう君とは絶交だ) I *am through* with you.
zekkoo suru (~する) *vi.* break up with: *Sono keñka ga moto de*

futari wa zekkoo *shite shimatta.* (そのけんかがもとで二人は絶交してしまった) They *broke with each other* because of that argument.

ze⌐kkyoo ぜっきょう (絶叫) *n.* shout; scream; exclamation.

ze⌐ñ¹ ぜん (善) *n.* good; right:
zeñ *to aku* (善と悪) *right* and wrong / *Zeñ wa isoge.* (善は急げ) (*saying*) (善は急げ) The sooner, *the better.*
《↔ aku³》《⇨ zeñaku》

ze⌐ñ² ぜん (禅) *n.* Zen:
zeñ-*dera* (禅寺) a temple of *Zen Buddhism* / zeñ-*shuu* (禅宗) the *Zen* school of Buddhism / zeñ-*soo* (禅僧) a *Zen* priest.

ze⌐ñ-¹ ぜん (全) *pref.* all; whole:
zeñ-*do* (全土) the *whole* land / zeñ-*sekai* (全世界) the *whole* world / zeñ-*zaisañ* (全財産) one's *whole* fortune.

ze⌐ñ-² ぜん (前) *pref.* the former; ex-:
zeñ-*Soori-daijiñ* (前総理大臣) the *former* prime minister. ★ 'Moto *(no) Soori-daijiñ*' is *a previous* prime minister. 《⇨ moto²》

-zeñ ぜん (前) *suf.* before:
señ-zeñ (戦前) *before* the war / shoku-zeñ (食前) *before* a meal.

ze⌐ñaku ぜんあく (善悪) *n.* right and wrong; good and evil:
zeñaku *o wakimaeru* [*kubetsu su-ru*] (善悪をわきまえる[区別する]) tell *right* from *wrong.* 《⇨ zeñ》

ze⌐ñbu ぜんぶ (全部) *n.* all; every-thing; total:
Sore de zeñbu *desu.* (それで全部です) That's *all.* / *Sono sakka no saku-hiñ wa* zeñbu *yomimashita.* (その作家の作品は全部読みました) I have read *all* that author's works. / *Zeñbu de ikura desu ka?* (全部でいくらですか) How much is it *all to-gether?*

ze⌐ñgo ぜんご (前後) *n.* before and after; in front and in the rear; back and forth:

zeñgo *o yoku chuui shite miru* (前
後をよく注意して見る) look carefully
in front and behind / *ude o* zeñgo
ni furu (腕を前後に振る) wave one's
arms *back and forth* / *teki o* zeñgo *kara semeru* (敵を前後から攻める)
attack the enemy from *the front
and the rear*.

zeñgo o wasureru (～を忘れる)
forget oneself: *Kare wa ikari de*
zeñgo *o wasureta.* (彼は怒りで前後
を忘れた) He *was beside himself*
with rage.

zeñgo suru (～する) *vi*. be reversed: *Kare no hanashi wa yoku*
zeñgo *suru.* (彼の話はよく前後する)
His stories often *get confused*.

-zeⁿgo ぜんご (前後) *suf*. about;
around:
*yoñjus-sai-*zeñgo (40 歳前後) *about*
forty years old / *Kare wa moku-
yoobi-*zeñgo *ni kaette kimasu.* (彼
は木曜日前後に帰って来ます) He is
coming back *around* Thursday.

zeⁿhañ ぜんはん (前半) *n*. the
first half:
nijus-seeki zeñhañ (20 世紀前半)
the first half of the twentieth
century / *Sono hoñ wa* zeñhañ
shika yoñde imaseñ. (その本は前半
しか読んでいません) I have read only
the first part of the book. / *Reesu
wa* zeñhañ *ga owatta tokoro desu.*
(レースは前半が終わったところです) *The
first half* of the race has just
been completed. 《↔ koohañ》

zeⁿiñ ぜんいん (全員) *n*. all the
members:
Zeñiñ ga sono añ ni sañsee shita.
(全員がその案に賛成した) *All the
members* agreed to the proposal. /
Zeñiñ buji ni kitaku shimashita.
(全員無事に帰宅しました) *Everyone*
safely returned home.

zeⁿjitsu ぜんじつ (前日) *n*. the
day before; the previous day:
Shuppatsu no zeñjitsu *ni yotee ga
heñkoo ni natta.* (出発の前日に予定

が変更になった) The schedule was
changed *the day before* departure.
/ *Shiai no* zeñjitsu *made ame ga
futta.* (試合の前日まで雨が降った) It
rained up to *the day before* the
game. 《↔ yokujitsu》

zeⁿkai ぜんかい (全快) *n*. complete recovery:
Kanojo no zeñkai *made, ni-shuukañ kakaru deshoo.* (彼女の全快まで,
2 週間かかるでしょう) Two weeks of
hospital treatment will be necessary for her *complete recovery*.

zeñkai suru (～する) *vi*. recover
completely: *Okagesama de byooki wa* zeñkai *itashimashita.* (おかげ
さまで病気は全快いたしました) I *have
completely gotten over* my illness,
thank you.

zeⁿki ぜんき (前期) *n*. the first
half year; the first term [semes-
ter]:
Kyoo zeñki *no shikeñ ga atta.* (きょ
う前期の試験があった) We had the
first-term exams today.
《↔ kooki》

zeⁿkoku ぜんこく (全国) *n*. the
whole country; all parts of the
country:
Sono koñkuuru ni zeñkoku *kara
daihyoo ga atsumatta.* (そのコンクー
ルに全国から代表が集まった) Repre-
sentatives from *the whole country*
came together for the contest. /
Kare no na wa zeñkoku *ni shirarete imasu.* (彼の名は全国に知られてい
ます) His name is known *all over
the country.* / *Zeñkoku Kookoo
Yakyuu Taikai* (全国高校野球大会)
the *National* Senior High
School Baseball Tournament.

zeⁿkoku-teki ぜんこくてき (全国
的) *a.n.* (～ na, ni) nationwide;
all over the country:
zeñkoku-teki *na choosa o okonau*
(全国的な調査を行なう) make a *na-
tionwide* survey / *Teñki wa* zeñkoku-teki *ni kudarizaka desu.* (天

気は全国的に下り坂です）The weather is changing for the worse *all over the country.*

ze⌈ñmetsu ぜんめつ（全滅）*n.* annihilation; total destruction: *Taifuu de sakumotsu ga* zeñmetsu suñzeñ *desu.*（台風で作物が全滅寸前です）The crops were *almost completely destroyed* by the typhoon.
zeñmetsu suru（〜する）*vi.* be annihilated; be totally destroyed: *Gorufujoo no keñsetsu de kichoo na shokubutsu ga* zeñmetsu shita.（ゴルフ場の建設で貴重な植物が全滅した）Valuable flora *was totally destroyed* due to the construction of the golf course. / *Bakugeki de sono mura wa* zeñmetsu shita.（爆撃でその村は全滅した）The village *was wiped out* by bombing.

ze⌈ñpañ ぜんぱん（全般）*n.* the whole: *Nihongo no beñkyoo ni wa Nihoñ buñka* zeñpañ *no chishiki ga hitsuyoo desu.*（日本語の勉強には日本文化全般の知識が必要です）A *general* knowledge of Japanese culture is necessary for study of the language.

ze⌈ñpañ-teki ぜんぱんてき（全般的）*a.n.*（〜 na, ni) on the whole; all in all: *Kotoshi no fuyu wa* zeñpañ-teki *ni atatakai.*（今年の冬は全般的に暖かい）This winter is, *on the whole,* warm.

ze⌈ñryaku ぜんりゃく（前略）*n.* Dear Mr. [Mrs., Miss, Ms.]...; Dear Sir [Sirs, Madam].
★ Used in the salutation of an informal letter. The corresponding complimentary close is '*soo-soo.*'《⇒ tegami; haikee[1]》

ze⌈ñryoku ぜんりょく（全力）*n.* all one's strength: *Kare wa sono sakuhiñ ni* zeñryoku *o katamuketa.*（彼はその作品に全力を傾けた）He devoted *all his energies* to the work. / *Watashi wa* zeñryoku *o komete, sono kui o uchikoñda.*（私は全力をこめて，その杭を打ち込んだ）I drove the stake in with *all my might.* / *Tonikaku* zeñryoku *o tsukushimasu.*（とにかく全力を尽くします）Anyway, I will *do my best.*

ze⌈ñsha ぜんしゃ（前者）*n.* the former: 《↔ koosha[2]》 *Kyuushuu to Shikoku de wa* zeñsha *no hoo ga meñseki ga hiroi.*（九州と四国では前者のほうが面積が広い）Of Kyushu and Shikoku, *the former* is larger in area.

ze⌈ñshiñ[1] ぜんしん（前進）*n.* advance; progress: *Fune wa ryuuhyoo ni habamarete,* zeñshiñ *to kootai o kurikaeshita.*（船は流氷に阻まれて，前進と後退を繰り返した）Obstructed by the ice floes, the ship repeatedly *moved forward* and backward. / *Kiri no tame* zeñshiñ *dekinakatta.*（霧のため前進できなかった）The fog prevented us from *going ahead.*
zeñshiñ suru（〜する）*vi.* go ahead; advance; progress: *Keñkyuu wa sukoshi-zutsu* zeñshiñ *shite imasu.*（研究は少しずつ前進しています）The research *is making progress* little by little.

ze⌈ñshiñ[2] ぜんしん（全身）*n.* the whole body: *Ame de* zeñshiñ *zubunure ni natte shimatta.*（雨で全身ずぶぬれになってしまった）I got soaked *from head to toe* in the rain. / *Sono ko wa* zeñshiñ *doro-darake datta.*（その子は全身泥だらけだった）The child was covered with mud *all over.* / zeñshiñ *ga utsuru kagami*（全身が映る鏡）a *full-length* mirror.

ze⌈ñsoku ぜんそく（喘息）*n.* asthma.

ze⌈ñsoku⌉ryoku ぜんそくりょく（全速力）*n.* full speed: zeñsokuryoku *de hashiru*（全速力で

走る) run at *full speed*.

ze￢ñtai ぜんたい (全体) *n.* the whole; all:

Sono jikeñ de machi zeñtai *ga oosawagi ni natta.* (その事件で町全体が大騒ぎになった) *The whole town* was thrown into confusion by that affair. / *Kono kettee wa* kaiiñ zeñtai *ni shirasenakereba naranai.* (この決定は会員全体に知らせなければならない) We have to inform *all the members* of this decision. / *Kono sakubuñ wa* zeñtai to shite *yoku dekite imasu.* (この作文は全体として良くできています) This essay is *on the whole* well written.

ze￢ñtee ぜんてい (前提) *n.* premise; assumption:

Anata no zeñtee *wa machigatte iru.* (あなたの前提はまちがっている) Your *premise* is wrong. / *Kare wa kookyoo ga tsuzuku to iu* zeñtee *ni tatte, jigyoo o hajimeta.* (彼は好況が続くという前提に立って，事業を始めた) He started his business on the *assumption* that the favorable market conditions would continue.

ze￢ñto ぜんと (前途) *n.* future; one's way:

zeñto yuuboo *na wakamono* (前途有望な若者) a *promising* young man / *Kare-ra no* zeñto *ni wa iroiro na shoogai ga atta.* (彼らの前途にはいろいろな障害があった) There were various obstacles *in their way*.

ze￢ñwañ ぜんわん (前腕) *n.* forearm. 《⇨ ude; jiñtai (illus.)》

ze￢ñzeñ ぜんぜん (全然) *adv.*

1 (with a negative) not at all; never:

Kare ni tsuite wa zeñzeñ *shirimaseñ.* (彼については全然知りません) I know nothing *at all* about him. / *Anata no itte iru koto wa* zeñzeñ *wakarimaseñ.* (あなたの言っていることは全然わかりません) I have *not the*

slightest idea what you are talking about.

2 completely; entirely; altogether:

Watashi no kañgae wa kare no to zeñzeñ *chigaimasu.* (私の考えは彼のと全然違います) My ideas are *completely* different from his.

ze￢ro ゼロ *n.* **1** zero:

Naiseñ-bañgoo wa ichi zero *roku desu.* (内線番号は 106 です) My extension number is 106. 《⇨ ree⁴》

2 nothing:

Kare wa yuumoa no kañkaku ga zero *da.* (彼はユーモアの感覚がゼロだ) He *has no* sense of humor.

zero kara yarinaosu (〜からやり直す) start from scratch: *Watashi wa* zero kara yarinaosu *koto ni kimeta.* (私はゼロからやり直すことに決めた) I have decided to *start from the very beginning*.

ze￢tsuboo ぜつぼう (絶望) *n.* despair; hopelessness:

Kanojo wa zetsuboo *no amari shiñde shimaitai to omotta.* (彼女は絶望のあまり死んでしまいたいと思った) She wanted to die out of *despair*. / *Kare no seezoñ wa* zetsuboo *to omowarete imasu.* (彼の生存は絶望と思われています) His survival is regarded as *hopeless*.

zetsuboo suru (〜する) *vi.* despair; give up hope: *Kare wa jiñsee ni* zetsuboo *shite ita.* (彼は人生に絶望していた) He *gave up* on life.

ze￢tsuboo-teki ぜつぼうてき (絶望的) *a.n.* (〜 na, ni) desperate; hopeless:

Kono shoobai no mitooshi wa zetsuboo-teki *desu.* (この商売の見通しは絶望的です) The outlook for this kind of business is *hopeless*.

ze￢tsueñ ぜつえん (絶縁) *n.*

1 breaking off relations:

zetsueñ-joo (絶縁状) a letter *terminating a relationship*.

2 insulation:

zetsueñ-*teepu* (絶縁テープ) *insulating* tape.

zetsueñ suru (〜する) *vi.* break off relations: *Kare wa furyoo nakama to* zetsueñ *shita.* (彼は不良仲間と絶縁した) He *has broken off relations* with his delinquent friends.

ze⌐ttai ぜったい (絶対) *n.* absoluteness:
Koko de wa kañtoku no meeree wa zettai *desu.* (ここでは監督の命令は絶対です) Around here the team manager's orders are *final.* / *Kono moñdai ni kañshite wa shachoo ga* zettai *no keñgeñ o motte imasu.* (この問題に関しては社長が絶対の権限を持っています) Regarding this matter, the president has *absolute* authority.

ze⌐ttai ni ぜったいに (絶対に) *adv.*
1 absolutely; surely:
Koko nara zettai ni *añzeñ desu.* (ここなら絶対に安全です) Provided you are here, you are *absolutely* safe. / *Kimi no kañgae wa* zettai ni *machigatte iru.* (きみの考えは絶対に間違っている) Your opinion is *absolutely* wrong.
2 (with a negative) never; by no means:
Kono himitsu wa zettai ni *hito ni iimaseñ.* (この秘密は絶対に人に言いません) *Under no circumstances*, will I tell this secret to anybody. / *Subete no hito o mañzoku saseru koto wa* zettai ni *dekinai.* (すべての人を満足させることは絶対にできない) It is *completely* impossible to satisfy everyone.

zo ぞ *p.* **1** (used rhetorically to oneself in confirming an opinion): ★ Used only by men.
Nañ da ka heñ da zo. (何だか変だぞ) *I am sure* something or other is wrong. / *Saa, kyoo wa shigoto o suru* zo. (さあ、きょうは仕事をするぞ) Well, I will do the work today.

2 (used to emphasize one's opinions or wishes): ★ A potentially rude form used to close friends and those of lower status. (⇨ **ze**)
Sorosoro dekakeru zo. (そろそろ出かけるぞ) Well, let's be off now. / *Soñna koto o suru to shippai suru* zo. (そんなことをすると失敗するぞ) If you do that kind of thing, you will fail. ★ Not used for invitations or requests.

-zoi ぞい (沿い) *suf.* along:
*yama-*zoi *no michi* (山沿いの道) a road *along* the foot of a mountain / *kawa-*zoi *o aruku* (川沿いを歩く) walk *along* the bank of a river. (⇨ **sou'**)

zo⌐kugo ぞくご (俗語) *n.* slang; slang word:
'Deka' wa keeji no zokugo *desu.* (「デカ」は刑事の俗語です) '*Deka*' is a *slang word* meaning 'detective.'

zo⌐kus·u⌐ru ぞくする (属する) *vi.* (-sh·i-; -sh·i-; -sh·i-te ①) belong to:
Sakura wa bara-ka ni zokushimasu. (桜はバラ科に属します) Cherries *belong to* the rose family. / *Tanaka daigishi wa Jimiñ-too no Yamada-ha ni* zokusuru. (田中代議士は自民党の山田派に属する) Representative Tanaka *belongs to* the Yamada faction of the Liberal Democratic Party.

zo⌐kuzoku' ぞくぞく (続々) *adv.* (〜 **to**) in succession; one after another:
Kichi kara hikooki ga zokuzoku *(to) tobitatta.* (基地から飛行機が続々と飛び立った) The planes flew away from the base *one after another.* / *Kaijoo e chooshuu ga* zokuzoku *to tsumekaketa.* (会場へ聴衆がぞくぞくと詰めかけた) The audience thronged into the hall *in an endless stream.* / *Natsu ni naru to wakai hito-tachi ga* zoku-zoku *(to) sono shima e ikimasu.* (夏になると若

い人たちが続々(と)その島へ行きます)
When summer comes, young
people set out for that island *in
great numbers.*

zo¹kuzoku² ぞくぞく *adv.*
(～ suru) (the state of feeling
chilliness or being excited):
Netsu ga aru no ka, karada ga
zokuzoku suru. (熱があるのか, 体がぞく
ぞくする) I must have a fever because I *have the shivers.* / *Kesa
wa* zokuzoku suru *hodo samui.* (け
さはぞくぞくするほど寒い) This morn-
ing it is cold enough to *make one
shiver.* / *Sono shiai o mite* zokuzoku shita. (その試合を見てぞくぞく
した) I *was thrilled* with the
match.

zo「ñji¹・ru そんじる (存じる) *vi.* (zo-
ñji-te Ⅴ)

USAGE

Used in the forms 'zoñjimasu'
and 'zonjite.' The plain form
'zonjiru' is never used. The
honorific equivalent is 'gozoñji
desu.' (⇨ gozoñji)

---

1 (*humble*) know:
Yamada-sañ no koto wa yoku zoñ-
jite orimasu. (山田さんのことはよく存
じております) I *know* Mr. Yamada
very well. / *Watashi wa ano kata
wa* zoñjimaseñ. (私はあの方は存じま
せん) I *do not know* that person.
(⇨ shiru¹)
2 (*humble*) hope; feel; think:
Soo shitai to zoñjimasu. (そうしたい
と存じます) I *hope* to do so. / *Kooee
ni* zoñjimasu. (光栄に存じます) I *feel*
honored.

zo「ñza¹i そんざい *a.n.* (～ na, ni)
rude; rough; careless; impolite:
Kare wa kuchi no kikikata ga zoñzai da. (彼は口のききかたがぞんざいだ)
He is *rude* in speech. / *Mono o*
zoñzai *ni atsukatte wa ikemaseñ.*
(物をぞんざいに扱ってはいけません) Do
not handle things *roughly.*

zo¹o ぞう (象) *n.* elephant.

zo「odai ぞうだい (増大) *n.* increase; enlargement:
juyoo no zoodai (需要の増大) an
increase in demand.
zoodai suru (～する) *vi., vt.* increase: *Dai-toshi de hañzai ga*
zoodai shite iru. (大都市で犯罪が増
大している) Crimes *are increasing*
in the big cities. (↔ geñshoo)
(⇨ zooka)

zo「ogeñ ぞうげん (増減) *n.* increase and [or] decrease; fluc-
tuation; variation:
jiñkoo no zoogeñ (人口の増減)
fluctuations in population.
zoogeñ suru (～する) *vi., vt.* increase and [or] decrease; fluctuate; vary: *Uriage wa tsuki-goto
ni* zoogeñ shimasu. (売上は月ごとに
増減します) The sales *vary* from
month to month.

zo「oka ぞうか (増加) *n.* increase:
jiñkoo no zooka (人口の増加) an
increase in population.
zooka suru (～する) *vi., vt.* increase: *Kootsuu-jiko ni yoru shi-
boosha ga* zooka shite imasu. (交
通事故による死亡者が増加しています)
The number of those killed due
to traffic accidents *has been increasing.* (↔ geñshoo¹) (⇨ zoodai)

zo「okiñ ぞうきん (雑巾) *n.* duster;
dust cloth; floor cloth:
yuka ni zookiñ *o kakeru* (床にぞうき
んをかける) clean the floor with a
rag / *Nureta* zookiñ *de tana o
fuita.* (ぬれたぞうきんで棚をふいた) I
wiped the shelves with a damp

ZOOKIÑ-GAKE

cloth. / zookiñ-gake (ぞうきんがけ) *wiping* (the floor).

zo「okyoo （増強） *n.* reinforcement; increase; buildup: *guñjiryoku no* zookyoo (軍事力の増強) an arms *buildup*.

  zookyoo suru (～する) *vt.* reinforce; strengthen: *yusooryoku o* zookyoo suru (輸送力を増強する) *augment* the transport capacity.

zo「oni ぞうに (雑煮) *n.* soup with rice cakes, chicken and vegetables. ★ A traditional New Year dish. (⇨ shoogatsu)

ZOONI

zo「ori ぞうり (草履) *n.* Japanese flat sandals. 《⇨ wafuku (illus.)》

ZOORI

zo「oseñ ぞうせん (造船) *n.* shipbuilding: zooseñ-jo (造船所) a *shipyard*.

zo「osho ぞうしょ (蔵書) *n.* a collection of books; one's personal library.

Zo「ooshoo ぞうしょう (蔵相) *n.* Finance Minister. 《⇨ Ookuradaijiñ; shoo¹ (table)》

zo「oshuu ぞうしゅう (増収) *n.* increase of income [revenue]: *Kaisha wa kotoshi no* zooshuu *o sañ-paaseñto to mite iru.* (会社はことしの増収を3% と見ている) The company expects an *increased profit* of three percent this year. 《⇨ geñshuu》

zo「rozoro ぞろぞろ *adv.* (～ to) in a stream; one after another: *Sono toori wa itsu-mo hito ga* zorozoro (*to*) *aruite iru.* (その通りはいつも人がぞろぞろ(と)歩いている) There is always a *stream* of people passing along this street. / *Kañkoo-kyaku wa* zorozoro (*to*) *basu ni norikoñda.* (観光客はぞろぞろ(と)バスに乗り込んだ) The sightseers got on the bus *one after another*.

zu ず (図) *n.* drawing; figure; diagram; illustration: zu *o kaku* (図をかく) make a *drawing* / zu *de setsumee suru* (図で説明する) explain with an *illustration* / *Yoñ-peeji no*, zu *sañ o sañ-shoo shi nasai.* (4 ページの、図 3 を参照しなさい) Refer to *figure* 3 on page 4.

zu「boñ ズボン *n.* trousers; slacks; pants: zuboñ *o haku* [*nugu*] (ズボンをはく[脱ぐ]) put on [take off] one's *trousers* / zuboñ-*tsuri* (ズボンつり) suspenders; braces.

zu「ibuñ ずいぶん (随分) *adv.* very (much); really; a lot; quite: *Anata no musuko-sañ wa* zuibuñ *se ga takai desu ne.* (あなたの息子さんはずいぶん背が高いですね) Your son is *very* tall, isn't he? / *Kono heñ wa mukashi to* zuibuñ *kawarimashita.* (この辺は昔とずいぶん変わりました) This area has changed *a lot* from the old days. / *Kanojo wa Nihoñgo o hanasu no ga* zuibuñ *umaku natta.* (彼女は日本語を話すのがずいぶんうまくなった) She has *really* become good at speaking Japanese.

zu「ihitsu ずいひつ (随筆) *n.* essay: zuihitsu *o kaku* (随筆を書く) write an *essay*.

-zu ni ずに ⇨ -nai¹.

zuˈñzuñ ずんずん *adv.* (~ to)
quickly; rapidly; on and on:
*Kanojo no byooki wa zuñzuñ (to)
yoku natte imasu.* (彼女の病気はずん
ずん(と)良くなっています) She is get-
ting better *quickly.* / *Kare wa* zuñzuñ *(to) ishidañ o nobotte itta.* (彼
はずんずん(と)石段を上って行った) He
briskly went up the stone steps.

-zurai づらい *suf.* (*a.*) (-ku) hard;
difficult: ★ Added to the continuative base of a verb.
ii-zurai (言いづらい) be *painful* to
say / *Kare wa koe ga chiisai no de
kiki*-zurai. (彼は声が小さいので聞きづ
らい) He speaks in a low voice, so
it is *hard* to catch what he says. /
*Kono hoñ wa ji ga chiisakute yo-
mi*-zurai. (この本は字が小さくて読みづ
らい) This book has small print
and is thus *difficult* to read.
《⇨ -gatai; -nikui》

zuˈrari ずらり *adv.* (~ to) in a
line [row]:
Butai ni odoriko ga zurari *to na-
rañda.* (舞台に踊り子がずらりと並んだ)
The dancers formed a *straight
line* on the stage.

zuˈraˈs·u ずらす *vt.* (zurash·i-;
zuras·a-; zurash·i-te Ⓒ) **1** shift;
move a little:
*Isu o sukoshi migi ni zurashite ku-
dasai.* (いすを少し右にずらしてください)
Please move the chair a bit to
the right. 《⇨ zureru》
2 put off; postpone:
*Nittee o ni, sañ-nichi zurashite ita-
dakemasu ka?* (日程を2, 3日ずらし
ていただけますか) Could you *move
back* the schedule by two or
three days? 《⇨ zureru》

zuˈreˈ·ru ずれる *vi.* (zure-te Ⓥ)
1 be shifted; be not in the right
place:
Kabe no e ga migi ni zurete iru.
(壁の絵が右にずれている) The picture
on the wall *is tilted* to the right.
《⇨ zurasu》

2 be put off:
*Shigoto ga haitte, yotee ga is-
shuukañ* zuremashita. (仕事が入って,
予定が1週間ずれました) Because
some work has come in, my
schedule *is* a week *off.* 《⇨ zurasu》
3 deviate:
Kare no ikeñ wa teema to sukoshi
zurete iru. (彼の意見はテーマと少しずれ
ている) His opinion *is* a bit *off* the
topic. 《⇨ zure》

zuˈreˈ ずれ *n.* difference; gap:
sedai-kañ no zure (世代間のずれ) a
generation *gap* / *jikañ no* zure (時
間のずれ) a time *lag* / *Kare to ryooshiñ no aida ni wa kangaekata no
zure ga atta.* (彼と両親の間には考え方
のずれがあった) There was a *difference* of views between him and
his parents. 《⇨ zureru》

zuˈruˈ·i ずるい *a.* (-ku) cunning;
tricky; unfair:
*Shukudai o niisañ ni yatte morau
nañte* zurui yo. (宿題を兄さんにやって
もらうなんてずるいよ) It's *unfair* of
you to get your brother to do
your homework. / *Nañte zurui
hito da.* (何てずるい人だ) What a
tricky person!

zuˈruzuru ずるずる *adv.* (~ to)
trailingly; draggingly:
*Kanojo wa kimono no suso o zuru-
zuru (to) hikizutte ita.* (彼女は着物の
すそをずるずる(と)引きずっていた) She
walked along with the hem of
her kimono *trailing.* / *Kare wa
zuruzuru (to) heñji o nobashita.* (彼
はずるずる(と)返事を延ばした) He *kept
on* putting off his reply. / *Kare wa
sono iñboo ni zuruzuru to hiki-
komareta.* (彼はその陰謀にずるずると
引き込まれた) He *was dragged* into
the intrigue.

zuˈsañ ずさん (杜撰) *a.n.* (~ na)
careless; slipshod; faulty:
zusañ *na keekaku* (ずさんな計画) a
faulty plan / *Kare wa suru koto
ga* zusañ *da.* (彼はすることがずさんだ)

He does things in a *slipshod manner*.

-zuˈtai づたい (伝い) *suf*. along: *señro*-zutai *no michi* (線路づたいの道) a road *running beside* the railway lines / *kaigañ*-zutai *ni aruku* (海岸づたいに歩く) walk *along* the seashore / *Neko ga yane*-zutai *ni nigeta.* (猫が屋根づたいに逃げた) The cat ran away *from* roof *to* roof.

zuˈtazuta ni ずたずたに *adv*. to pieces; to shreds: *Kare wa sono shorui o* zutazuta ni *yabuita.* (彼はその書類をずたずたに破いた) He tore the papers *to pieces*. / *Jishiñ de dooro wa* zutazuta ni *natta.* (地震で道路はずたずたになった) The road *was completely destroyed* by the earthquake.

-zuˈtsu ずつ (宛) *suf*. **1** of each; for each; to each: ★ Indicates distribution. *Kono kami o hitori*-zutsu *ichi-mai tori nasai.* (この紙を一人ずつ1枚取りなさい) *Each of you* take a sheet of this paper. / *Kodomo-tachi ni sono o-kashi o mittsu*-zutsu *wa oo-sugiru.* (子どもたちにそのお菓子を3つずつは多すぎる) Three *apiece* of those candies for the children is too much.
2 at a time: ★ Indicates repetition: *Hitori*-zutsu *heya o dete itta.* (一人ずつ部屋を出て行った) They left the room, *one by one*. / *Sukoshi*-zutsu *arukeru yoo ni narimashita.* (少しずつ歩けるようになりました) *Little by little* I have reached the stage where I am able to walk. / *Kañji o ichi-nichi* juu-go-zutsu *añki shita.* (漢字を1日10語ずつ暗記した) I memorized *ten* Chinese characters a day.

zuˈtsuu ずつう (頭痛) *n*. headache: *Asa kara* zutsuu *ga suru.* (朝から頭痛がする) I've had a *headache* since this morning.

zutsuu no tane (〜の種) a source of worry: *Shikiñ atsume ga* zutsuu no tane *desu.* (資金集めが頭痛の種です) Fund raising is a *headache* to us.

zuˈtto ずっと *adv*. **1** (with a comparative) much; far: *Kyoo wa kinoo yori* zutto *samui.* (きょうはきのうよりずっと寒い) Today is *much* colder than yesterday. / *Kare wa watashi yori* zutto *wakai.* (彼は私よりずっと若い) He is *much* younger than I. 《⇨ haruka ni》
2 (of time) long: *Kanojo wa* zutto *yasuñde imashita.* (彼女はずっと休んでいました) She was absent *for a long time*. / *Sono hito ni wa* zutto *mae ni atta koto ga arimasu.* (その人にはずっと前に会ったことがあります) I met him a *long* time ago. / *Zutto ato ni natte, sono koto ni ki ga tsukimashita.* (ずっと後になって、そのことに気がつきました) I noticed that a *long* time afterward.
3 all the time; all the way: *Natsu-yasumi wa* zutto *Hokkaidoo ni imashita.* (夏休みはずっと北海道にいました) During the summer vacation, I was in Hokkaido *the whole time*. / *Basu ni noranai de, eki made* zutto *arukimashita.* (バスに乗らないで、駅までずっと歩きました) I walked *all the way* to the station without taking the bus. / *Kare wa kaigi-chuu* zutto *damatte ita.* (彼は会議中ずっと黙っていた) He said nothing *throughout* the meeting.

zuˈuzuushiˈ‧i ずうずうしい (図々しい) *a*. (-ku) impudent; pushy; shameless: *Nañte* zuuzuushii *hito daroo.* (なんてずうずうしい人だろう) What an *impudent* fellow. / *Sono otoko wa* zuu-zuushiku, *uchi ni hairikoñda.* (その男はずうずうしく、家に入り込んだ) That man *had the nerve* to come into our house. 《⇨ atsukamashii》

Guide to Japanese Pronunciation

1. Standard pronunciation of the Japanese language

The variety of Japanese of greatest practical importance for foreign learners is that called **Standard Japanese**. This is understood throughout Japan. The pronunciation of Standard Japanese is based on that of educated people who were born and brought up in Tokyo, or its vicinity.

2. Vowels

2. 1 Short and Long Vowels

The vowel system of Japanese (hereafter abbreviated to J) is much simpler than that of English (abbreviated to E). It consists of five short vowels **i, e, a, o, u**, and the corresponding long vowels. Long vowels may also be interpreted as double vowels, and in this dictionary they are written **ii, ee, aa, oo, uu**. It should be noted that the distinction between short and long vowels is significant in Japanese in that it affects the meanings of words. For example, *i* (stomach) vs. *ii* (good), *tesee* (handmade) vs. *teesee* (correction), *kado* (corner) vs. *kaado* (card), *toru* (take) vs. *tooru* (pass), *kuki* (stem) vs. *kuuki* (air).

In pronouncing a long vowel, foreign learners should nearly double the length of the corresponding short vowel. E speakers are especially advised not to lengthen J short vowels, but to cut them short.

2. 2 i and ii (い, イ and いー, イー)

J **i** is phonetically [i] and [i:]. It is close to the French vowel in *qui, ici*, etc. E short *i*-vowel in words like *sit, miss* is halfway between J **i** and **e**, and, if used, sometimes sounds like **e** to Japanese listeners. It would be better for E-speaking learners to make their *i*-vowel more like long *e*, though they must cut it short. On the other hand, E long *e*-vowel in *be, seat*, etc. can safely be used for J **ii**.

2. 3 e and ee (え, エ and えー, エー)

J **e** is phonetically halfway between [e] and [ɛ], and is close to the short *e*-vowel in *get, less*, etc. The *a*-vowel in *day, late*, etc. can safely be used for J **ee**, though the latter is less diphthongal than the former.

2. 4 a and aa (あ, ア and あー, アー)

Phonetically between [a] and [ɑ], J **a** has rather a wide range. The nearest vowel to this is British (abbreviated to B hereafter) E short *u*-vowel in *cut, fun*, etc. J **a** is halfway between American (abbreviated to A) E short *u*-vowel (*hut, luck*, etc.) and short *o*-vowel (*not, lock*, etc.) The initial part of the long *i*-vowel in *ice, fine*, etc. will also do for J **a**.

Learners are warned against using E short *a*-vowel in *back, man*, etc., since this sometimes sounds a little like **e** to Japanese listeners. E *a*-vowel in words like *father, Chicago* can be used for J **aa**.

2. 5 o and oo (お, オ and おー, オー)

J **o** is phonetically halfway between [o] and [ɔ]. The nearest approach to this vowel is the initial part of A E long *o*-vowel in *go, most*, etc., or the B E *au*-vowel in *cause, law*, etc., but these should be cut short. B E short *o*-vowel in *hot, lock*, etc. is too open for J **o**, and A E short *o*-vowel in *hot, lock*, etc. is more like J **a** than J **o**. The nearest vowel to J **oo** is B E *au*-vowel, A E *au*-vowel being too open. It is also like A E long *o*-vowel in *go, road*, etc., though less diphthongal. British learners (especially those from southern England) should never use their long *o*-vowel in *go, road*, etc., because it sometimes sounds like **au** to Japanese listeners.

2. 6 u and uu (う, ウ and うー, ウー)

J **u** is phonetically [ɯ], that is, it lacks the lip-rounding which accompanies the *u*-vowel of most European languages. Therefore learners are advised not to round the corners of their mouths, but to draw them back when making this vowel. This also holds true in the pronunciation of long **uu**.

2. 7 Devoicing of vowels

J vowels, especially **i** and **u** are often devoiced (i.e. become voiceless) when they do not carry the accent nucleus (see 5.) and occur between voiceless consonants, or occur at the end of a word or an utterance, preceded by a voiceless consonant. The devoicing is represented by a small circle under the phonetic symbols thus [i̥] and [ɯ̥]. For example, *chikara* [tʃi̥kara] (strength), *pittari* [pi̥ttari] (closely), *ashi* [aʃi̥] (reed); *suppai* [sɯ̥ppai] (sour), *futoi* [ɸɯ̥toi] (thick), *karasu* [karasɯ̥], etc. In the final **su** in ...*masu.* or ...*desu.*, **u** is very often devoiced or dropped completely, and the preceding **s** is compensatorily lengthened. However, failure to devoice these **i**'s and **u**'s does not impair any intelligibility.

3. Consonants

3.1 k (**ka** か, カ, **ki** き, キ, **ku** く, ク, **ke** け, ケ, **ko** こ, コ; **kya** きゃ, キャ, **kyu** きゅ, キュ, **kyo** きょ, キョ)

Phoetically [k]. It is like E *k* in *keep*, *cold*, etc., but the aspiration, or *h*-like sound, after J **k** is weaker than in E.

3.2 g (**ga** が, ガ, **gi** ぎ, ギ, **gu** ぐ, グ, **ge** げ, ゲ, **go** ご, ゴ; **gya** ぎゃ, ギャ, **gyu** ぎゅ, ギュ, **gyo** ぎょ, ギョ)

Phonetically [g]. It is like E *g* in *get*, *good*, etc. In the middle of words like *kago* (basket), *agaru* (rise) and in the particle *ga* (が), **g** is often pronounced [ŋ] (as in E *sing*) in traditional standard J, but [ŋ] is currently being replaced by [g]. Foreign learners can safely use [g] in these positions.

3.3 s (**sa** さ, サ, **su** す, ス, **se** せ, セ, **so** そ, ソ)

Phonetically [s], the sound in E *set*, *soon*, etc.

3.4 sh (**shi** し, シ, **sha** しゃ, シャ, **shu** しゅ, シュ, **sho** しょ, ショ)

Phonetically [ʃ]. It is like E *sh* in *shine*, *short*, etc., but lacks the lip-protrusion which often accompanies E *sh*.

3.5 z (**za** ざ, ザ, **zu** ず, ズ, **ze** ぜ, ゼ, **zo** ぞ, ゾ)

At the beginning of words, J **z** is phonetically [dz], like E *ds* in *cards*, *leads*, etc. In the middle of words it is usually [z], like E *z* in *zone*, *lazy*, etc. However, *z* is always intelligible in all positions.

3.6 j (**ji** じ, ジ; **ja** じゃ, ジャ, **ju** じゅ, ジュ, **jo** じょ, ジョ)

Phonetically [dʒ], the sound in E *judge*, *George*, etc.

3.7 t (**ta** た, タ, **te** て, テ, **to** と, ト)

Phonetically dental [t] with the tip of the tongue against the front upper teeth, rather than against the teethridge as in the E *t* in *time*, *talk*, etc., which, however, can safely be used. The aspiration after J **t** is weaker than in E. American learners are warned against using their *t* before a weak vowel as in words like *city*, *matter*, because it sometimes sounds like **r** to Japanese listeners.

3.8 d (**da** だ, ダ, **de** で, デ, **do** ど, ド)

Phonetically [d] pronounced in the same way as J **t** but with voice. However, the E *d* as in in *dark*, *date*, etc., can safely be used for J **d**. Again, Americans should avoid using their *d* before a weak vowel as in *ladder*, *pudding*, etc., since it sometimes sounds like **r** to Japanese listeners.

3.9 ch (**chi** ち, チ; **cha** ちゃ, チャ, **chu** ちゅ, チュ, **cho** ちょ, チョ)

Phonetically [tʃ], the sound in E *church*, *nature*, etc.

3.10 ts (**tsu** つ, ツ)

Phonetically [ts], the sound in E *cats*, *roots*, etc. English speakers often find it difficult to say [ts] initially as in *tsuzuku* (continue), *tsuru* (crane). You can practice this sound by saying it in words like *cat's-eye* and then omitting the first part of that word (*ca*).

3.11 n (**na** な, ナ, **ni** に, ニ, **nu** ぬ, ヌ, **ne** ね, ネ, **no** の, ノ; **nya** にゃ, ニャ, **nyu** にゅ, ニュ, **nyo** にょ, ニョ)

Phonetically dental [n], not alveolar as the E *n* in *night*, *none*, etc., but this causes no practical problems. It is more important that foreign learners should distinguish this sound from **ñ** treated in 3.20.

3.12 h (**ha** は, ハ, **hi** ひ, ヒ, **he** へ, ヘ, **ho** ほ, ホ; **hya** ひゃ, ヒャ, **hyu** ひゅ, ヒュ, **hyo** ひょ, ヒョ)

Phonetically [h], the sound in E *house*, *hold*, etc. To be more exact, the **h** before **i** and **y** is phonetically [ç], the sound heard in German *ich*. [ç] is accompanied by more friction in the mouth than E *h*.

3.13 f (**fu** ふ, フ)

Phonetically [ɸ]. Though spelled with **f**, it is slightly different from the *f* in European languages. While European *f* is formed with the lower lip against the upper teeth, the J **f** is produced with the upper and the lower lips close together. The friction sound of J **f** is weaker than European *f*.

3.14 b (**ba** ば, バ, **bi** び, ビ, **bu** ぶ, ブ, **be** べ, ベ, **bo** ぼ, ボ; **bya** びゃ, ビャ, **byu** びゅ, ビュ, **byo** びょ, ビョ)

Phonetically [b]. Like E *b* in *be*, *ball*, etc.

3.15 p (**pa** ぱ, パ, **pi** ぴ, ピ, **pu** ぷ, プ, **pe** ぺ, ペ, **po** ぽ, ポ; **pya** ぴゃ, ピャ, **pyu** ぴゅ, ピュ, **pyo** ぴょ, ピョ)

Phonetically [p]. It is like E *p* in *pay*, *post*, etc., but the aspiration after J **p** is weaker than in E.

3.16 m (**ma** ま, マ, **mi** み, ミ, **mu** む, ム, **me** め, メ, **mo** も, モ; **mya** みゃ, ミャ, **myu** みゅ, ミュ, **myo** みょ, ミョ)

Phonetically [m], the sound in E *meet*, *most*, etc.

3.17 y (**ya** や, ヤ, **yu** ゆ, ユ, **yo** よ, ヨ)

Phonetically [j], the semivowel corresponding to the vowel **i** [i].

It is like the sound in E *yes*, *you*, etc. **ya**, **yu**, **yo** can follow consonants such as **p**, **b**, **k**, **g**, **h**, **m**, **n** and form one syllable. In that case the resulting combinations are called **yoo-oñ**.

3. 18   r (**ra** ら, ラ, **ri** り, リ, **ru** る, ル, **re** れ, レ, **ro** ろ, ロ; **rya** り や, リャ, **ryu** りゅ, リュ, **ryo** りょ, リョ)

Phonetically, J **r** is often a retroflex stop [ɖ] initially and flap [ɾ] between vowels. Unlike E and other European *r*, it is made with a single tap of the tip of the tongue against the front upper teeth. It sometimes sounds like *d* to a European ear.

3. 19   w (**wa** わ, ワ)

Phonetically [ɰ], the semivowel corresponding to the vowel **u** [ɯ]. Like J **u**, it lacks lip-rounding which usually accompanies European *w*-sound.

3. 20   ñ (ん, ン)

ñ is peculiar to J. Learners should never confuse this sound with **n** treated in 3.11. Though usually spelled with the same letter **n** in the Roman alphabet, **n** and **ñ** are quite different in J. While **n** is a pure consonant and is always followed by a vowel or **y**, **ñ** appears word-finally, before a consonant, a vowel, and **y**, but never at the beginning of a word. **ñ** is called **hatsuoñ**. It is always long enough to make a syllable by itself (see 4). Besides, **ñ** has the following varieties according to the position in which it appears. The phonetic property common to all the following variants is that they are syllabic nasals. Thus,

(1) in word-final position: Phonetically syllabic [ɴ], a rather difficult sound for foreign learners. It is made further back than E *ng* [ŋ] (between the backmost part of the tongue and uvula). Examples *eñ* (yen), *hoñ* (book).

(2) before **z**, **j**, **t**, **d**, **ch**, **ts**, **n**, and **r**: Phonetically syllabic [n], nearly the same as E *n*, but longer. Examples *bañzai* (hurrah), *heñji* (answer), *kañtoku* (manager), *koñdo* (this time), *deñchi* (cell), *kañtsuu* (penetration), *oñna* (woman), *señro* (rail).

(3) before **f**, **b**, **p**, and **m**: Phonetically syllabic [m], the same as E *m*, but longer. Examples *iñfure* (inflation), *biñboo* (poverty), *kiñpatsu* (blonde), *koñmori* (thickly).

(4) before **k** and **g**: Phonetically syllabic [ŋ], the same as E *ng*, but longer. Examples *keñka* (quarrel), *sañgo* (coral).

(5) before **s** and **sh**: To be phonetically exact, a nasalized vowel [ĩ], but learners may use [ɴ] in this position. Examples *keñsa* (inspection), *deñsha* (electric train). English-speaking peo-

ple are advised not to use their *n* here, because they often insert a *t*-sound between *n* and the following *s* or *sh*. The result is *nts* or *nch*, which may sometimes be unintelligible to a Japanese listener.

(6) before **h**, **y**, **w**, and a vowel: Phonetically nasalized vowels like [ĩ], [ẽ], [ũ], etc. Learners, however, may use [N] in these positions. Examples *hañhañ* (fifty-fifty), *pañya* (bakery), *deñwa* (telephone), *heñi* (variation), *dañatsu* (oppression). They should never use *n* in these positions, since the resulting pronunciation would often be unintelligible. Note the following distinctions: *hiñi* (dignity) vs. *hi ni* (by a day), *kiñeñ* (no smoking) vs. *kineñ* (commemoration), *fuñeñ* (smoke of a volcano) vs. *funeñ* (non-flammable).

3.21 Double consonants (っ, ッ)

In J, double consonants appear in the combination of **kk**, **ss**, **ssh** (sh+sh), **tt**, **tch** (t+ch), **tts** (t+ts), and **pp** as in *sekkeñ* (soap), *bessoo* (villa), *issho* (together), *kitto* (certainly), *itchi* (agreement), *mittsu* (three), *suppai* (sour). English-speaking learners are warned against regarding them as single consonants as in *lesson*, *butter*, *catcher*, etc. They should pronounce them twice as the *c*'s in *thick cloud*, *sh*'s in *reddish shoes*, *t*'s in *hot tea*, *tch* in *hit children*, *p*'s in *hope peace*, etc. To Japanese ears, the first part of a double consonant is considered an independent sound and is counted as consituting another syllable (see 4.). For example, while the second **t** in *kitto* (certainly) is the "normal" **t**, the first **t** is regarded as an independent sound referred to as **sokuoñ** and is written with a smaller *kana* letter っ, ッ (the Roman letter **q** is used by some linguists to represent it, as in *kiqto*), and the word is counted as making three syllables (not two). Likewise, *sekkeñ* (i.e. *seqkeñ*) constitutes three syllables. Note the following distinctions between single and double consonants: *sekeñ* (world) vs. *sekkeñ* (soap), *sasoo to* (in order to stab) vs. *sassoo to* (smartly), *hato* (pigeon) vs. *hatto* (surprisedly), *ichi* (location) vs. *itchi* (agreement), *mitsu* (honey) vs. *mittsu* (three), *supai* (spy) vs. *suppai* (sour).

4. Syllables

J syllables (to be more exact, beats, or technically, morae) are normally composed of a consonant and a vowel in that order, the exceptions being **ñ** ん, ン (see 3.20) and **q** っ, ッ (see 3.21).

See the table of the J syllabary on the front endpaper. J syllables tend to be of nearly equal length, though **ñ** and **q** are usually pronounced slightly shorter. Thus, *teashi* (limbs) (three syllables) is said nearly three times longer than *te* (hand) (one syllable).

5. Accent

J does not have an accent system of strong and weak stress like E, and each syllable is said with nearly equal strength. Instead, J has a pitch accent system. The degrees of the pitch of voice depend on the rate of vibration of the vocal cords. When the vibration is fast the pitch is high, and when the rate is slow the pitch is low. The accent patterns of standard J are most clearly explained in terms of two significant levels of pitch: **high** and **low**, and the **accent nucleus**. Words are divided into two classes: words with and without an accent nucleus. In all words which have an accent nucleus, the syllable where the nucleus falls and the preceding syllables (except the first one which is automatically low) are pronounced high, and every syllable that follows the nucleus is said low. In this dictionary accent nucleus is marked with ˥, and the automatic rise on the second syllable is marked with ˹. Thus,

(1) Words with an accent nucleus on the first syllable are: *hi*˥ (fire), *ne*˥*ko* (cat), *i*˥*nochi* (life), *so*˥*rososo* (slowly).

(2) Words with a nucleus on the second syllable are: *i*˹*nu*˥ (dog), *ko*˹*ko*˥*ro* (mind), *i*˹*ke*˥*bana* (flower arrangement).

(3) Words with a nucleus on the third syllable are: *o*˹*toko*˥ (man), *a*˹*maga*˥*sa* (umbrella), *ka*˹*rai*˥*bari* (bravado).

(4) Words with a nucleus on the fourth syllable are: *o*˹*tooto*˥ (younger brother), *wa*˹*tashibu*˥*ne* (ferry boat), *shi*˹*dareya*˥*nagi* (weeping willow).

(5) Words without an accent nucleus are automatically pronounced with the first syllable low and all the succeeding syllables are kept high (though actually with a slight gradual descent). They are: *hi* (day), *u*˹*shi* (cattle), *ka*˹*tachi* (shape), *to*˹*modachi* (friend). Compare the following pair of phrases: *hi*˥ *ga* (the fire is...) and *hi* ˹*ga* (the day is...), the former *hi* having a nucleus on it, the latter *hi* without a nucleus.

A word may lose its original accent pattern when it becomes a part of a compound word which then has its own accent pattern as a single word. Thus, *ga*˹*ikoku* (foreign country) and *yu*˹*ubiñ* (mail) but *ga⌈ikoku-yu⌉ubiñ* (foreign mail), *o⌉ñgaku* (music) and *ga⌈kkoo* (school), but *o⌈ñgaku-ga⌉kkoo* (music school), and so on. In this dictionary, only those compounds given as main entries are marked with accent.

Outline of Japanese Grammar

1 Noun

Japanese nouns have no gender or case. There is no distinction between singular and plural: *hoñ* (本) means 'a book' or 'books.' But some suffixes are used to indicate the plural: *kare-ra* (they), *kodomo-tachi* (children). Some nouns are capable of forming plurals by reduplication, sometimes with sound changes: *yama-yama* (mountains), and *hito-bito* (people).

1. 1 There is a large class of nouns whose function is chiefly grammatical. They are used in making phrases in which these nouns are preceded by a modifier. For example, *kita toki* (when I came), *mita koto* (what I saw), *nani-ka taberu mono* (something to eat), etc. Other examples of such nouns are *aida, tame, tokoro, wake,* etc.

2 Verb

Verbs are classified into the following three groups: consonant-stem verbs, vowel-stem verbs and irregular verbs.

2. 1 Consonant-stem verb (*u*-verbs)

The verbs in this group have a consonant preceding final '*u*' in the dictionary form. Note that all verbs ending in vowel plus '*u*' in their dictionary form are also consonant stem verbs; the original '*w*' in these verbs has simply been lost in the modern language: *kawu* > *kau, hirowu* > *hirou*, etc.

Consonant-stem verbs are marked C̄ in this dictionary.

2. 2 Vowel-stem verb (*ru*-verbs)

The verbs in this group end with a final '-*ru*' preceded by '*i*' or '*e*' in the dictionary form. However, not all verbs that end thus are vowel-stem verbs, since there are some consonant-stem verbs which end with '-*iru*' or '-*eru.*'

> *hairu* (enter), *hashiru* (run), *iru* (need), *kiru* (cut), *shiru* (know), *kaeru* (return).

Vowel-stem verbs are marked V̄ in this dictionary.

2. 3 Irregular verb

There are only two irregular verbs, *suru* (do) (and those verbs formed with *suru*: *meñsuru*, *tassuru*, etc.) and *kuru* (come), which are irregular only in their stems.

Irregular verbs are marked ⊡ in this dictionary.

3 Conjugations of Verbs
Basic Verb Forms

	Ending	Consonant-stem verbs		Vowel-stem verb	Irregular verb	Irregular verb
Dictionary form	-u	kak·u (write)	yob·u (call)	tabe·ru (eat)	s·uru (do)	k·uru (come)
masu-form	-masu	kaki-masu	yobi-masu	tabe-masu	shi-masu	ki-masu
Negative	-nai	kaka-nai	yoba-nai	tabe-nai	shi-nai	ko-nai
te-form	-t[d]e	kai-te	yoñ-de	tabe-te	shi-te	ki-te
ta-form	-t[d]a	kai-ta	yoñ-da	tabe-ta	shi-ta	ki-ta
tara-form	-t[d]ara	kai-tara	yoñ-dara	tabe-tara	shi-tara	ki-tara
tari-form	-t[d]ari	kai-tari	yoñ-dari	tabe-tari	shi-tari	ki-tari
Desiderative	-tai	kaki-tai	yobi-tai	tabe-tai	shi-tai	ki-tai
Provisional	-ba	kake-ba	yobe-ba	tabere-ba	sure-ba	kure-ba
Tentative	-oo -yoo	kak-oo	yob-oo	tabe-yoo	shi-yoo	ko-yoo
Imperative	-e -ro	kak-e	yob-e	tabe-ro	shi-ro	ko-i
Potential	-eru -rareru	kak-eru	yob-eru	tabe-rareru	(dekiru)	ko-rareru
Passive	-reru -rareru	kaka-reru	yoba-reru	tabe-rareru	sa-reru	ko-rareru
Causative	-seru -saseru	kaka-seru	yoba-seru	tabe-saseru	sa-seru	ko-saseru
Causative-passive	-serareru -saserareru	kaka-sera-reru	yoba-sera-reru	tabe-saserareru	saserareru	ko-saserareru

3.1 Dictionary form
This is the form by which verbs are listed in the dictionary. The dictionary form of all Japanese verbs ends in '*u*.' This form is in fact the non-past tense of a verb.

Watashi wa iku. (I go/will go.)

3.2 Continuative form (*masu*-form)

The continuative base of a consonant-stem verb is made by replacing the final '*u*' with '*i*': *kaku* (write) > *kaki-masu*. In the case of a vowel-stem verb, it is made by dropping the final '*ru*': *taberu* (eat) > *tabe-masu*. Irregular verbs are: *suru* (do) > *shi-masu*, *kuru* (come) > *ki-masu*. The following five formal, polite verbs are slightly irregular in dropping '*r*' in their continuative forms.

gozaru (be)	*gozari-masu* > *gozai-masu*
irassharu (go, come)	*irasshari-masu* > *irasshai-masu*
kudasaru (give)	*kudasari-masu* > *kudasai-masu*
nasaru (do)	*nasari-masu* > *nasai-masu*
ossharu (say)	*osshari-masu* > *osshai-masu*

'-*masu*' is used to make the tone of speech polite, and has no concrete meaning in itself.

The conjugation of '-*masu*'

Negative	-maseñ
te-form	-mashi-te
ta-form	-mashi-ta
ba-form	-masure-ba
Tentative	-mashoo

3.3 Negative form (*nai*-form)

The negative base of a consonant-stem verb is made by replacing the final '*u*' with '*a*': *kaku* (write) > *kaka-nai*. In modern Japanese '*w*' is retained only before '*a*,' so those verbs which end in vowel plus '*u*' in the dictionary form in the modern language, but which had an original '*w*' (see 2.1), retain this in the negative form: *ka(w)u* > *kawa-nai*, *hiro(w)u* > *hirowa-nai*. In the case of a vowel-stem verb, the negative base is made by dropping the final '*ru*': *taberu* (eat) > *tabe-nai*. Irregular verbs are: *suru* (do) > *shi-nai*, *kuru* (come) > *ko-nai*.

The conjugation of '*nai*'

te-form	-naku-te
ta-form	-nakat-ta
ba-form	-nakere-ba

3.4 Gerund (*te*-form)

In the case of a vowel-stem verb, the gerund is made by adding '*te*' to the stem.

In the consonant-stem conjugation, however, the verbs undergo sound changes according to the final consonant of the stem.

ka-	ku	ka-	i	-te	write
oyo-	gu	oyo-	i	-de	swim
to-	bu	to-	ñ	-de	jump
no-	mu	no-	ñ	-de	drink
shi-	nu	shi-	ñ	-de	die
hana-	su	hana-	shi	-te	speak
ka-	u	ka-	t	-te	buy
no-	ru	no-	t	-te	ride
ma-	tsu	ma-	t	-te	wait

For the uses of the *te*-form, see under the main entry for '-*te*.' The past tense (*ta*-form) is simply made be replacing the '-*te*' with '-*ta*.'

3.5 Provisional form (*ba*-form)

The provisional form of a verb is made by replacing the final '-*u*' with '*e*' and adding '-*ba*.' This is equivalent to stating that the *ba*-form of a verb is made by dropping the final '-*u*' and adding '-*eba*': *kaku* (write) > *kake-ba*, *taberu* (eat) > *tabere-ba*. Irregular verbs are *suru* (do) > *sure-ba* and *kuru* (come) > *kure-ba*.

This form is also called the conditional form. It indicates the circumstances under which the situation or action in the main clause will be possible.

3.6 Tentative form

The tentative form of a consonant-stem verb is made by changing the final '*u*' to '*oo*': *kaku* (write) > *kak-oo*. In the case of a vowel-stem verb, it is made by changing the final '-*ru*' to '-*yoo*': *taberu* (eat) > *tabe-yoo*. Irregular verbs are *suru* (do) > *shi-yoo*, *kuru* (come) > *ko-yoo*. This form conveys the probable mood and indicates possibility, probability, belief, doubt, etc.

3.7 Imperative form

The imperative form of a consonant-stem verb is made by replacing the final '*u*' with '*e*': *kaku* (write) > *kak-e*. In the case of a vowel-stem verb, it is made by replacing the final '*ru*' with '*ro*': *taberu* (eat) > *tabe-ro*. The irregular verbs are *suru* (do) > *shi-ro* and *kuru* (come) > *ko-i*. This form constitutes a brusque imperative.

The imperative forms of the formal, polite verbs are as follows:

>
> *gozaru* (be)   no form
>
> *irassharu* (go, come) > *irasshai*
>
> *kudasaru* (give)   > *kudasai*
>
> *nasaru* (do)   > *nasai*
>
> *ossharu* (say)   > *osshai*

3.8 Other verb forms

Forms not dealt with in this 'Outline' can be referred to under the relevant 'ending' in the body of the dictionary.

4 Intransitive and transitive verbs

4.1 Intransitive verb (*vi.*)

An intransitive verb is a verb which is used without a direct object: *aku* (open), *tomaru* (stop), *iku* (go), *kuru* (come), etc.

4.2 Transitive verb (*vt.*)

A transitive verb is a verb which is used with a direct object. The object is usually followed by the particle '*o*.' However, it does not necessarily follow that every noun followed by '*o*' is a direct object, since '*o*' can also denote a location: *kado o magaru* (turn a corner).

Many transitive verbs have intransitive verb partners: *okosu* (wake) / *okiru* (get up), *miru* (look at) / *mieru* (be visible).

Pairs of transitive and intransitive verbs

vt.	*vi.*	Examples
-eru	-aru	ageru (raise) / agaru (rise)
-eru	-u	tsukeru (attach) / tsuku (stick)
-u	-eru	toru (take) / toreru (be taken)
-asu	-u	chirasu (scatter) / chiru (be scattered)
-su	-ru	kaesu (return) / kaeru (come back)

In the case of a small number of verbs, the transitive and intransitive forms are the same: *owaru* (end), *hiraku* (open), etc.

Among the large class of verbs formed by noun plus *suru*, some are transitive, some are intransitive, and some are both transitive and intransitive.

sakusee suru (*vt.*) (I) make (something).

shippai suru (*vi.*) (I) fail.

teñkai suru (*vt.*) (I) develop (something).

(*vi.*) (Something) develops.

5 Copula

The informal form is *da* and the polite form is *desu*.

The conjugation of the copula

	informal	polite
Sentence final form	da	desu
Negative	de nai (ja nai)	de wa arimaseñ (ja arimaseñ)
te-form	de	deshite
ta-form	datta	deshita
ba-form	nara (ba)	deshitara (ba)

6 Adjective

The dictionary form of adjectives ends with '*i*.' Adjectives occur in attributive position: *Kore wa furui kuruma desu.* (This is an old car.), or in predicative position: *Kono kuruma wa furui.* (This car is old.) An adjective can stand by itself as a complete sentence. For example, *Furui* means '(Something) is old.'

Basic adjective forms

Dict. form	samu·i (cold)
ku-form	samu-ku
Negative	samu-kunai
te-form	samu-kute
ta-form	samu-katta
ba-form	samu-kereba

7 Adjectival noun

Adjectival nouns have some functions that ordinary nouns have, and other functions which are similar to adjectives. This class of words is sometimes simply called 'na word,' since the word 'na' is used to link an adjectival noun to the following noun or adjectival noun which it modifies. An adjectival noun followed by 'ni' is an adverb. In this dictionary, 'na' is treated as a variant of the copula and 'ni' is a particle indicating manner, and they are written separately: *shizuka na umi* (calm sea), *shizuka ni aruku* (walk quietly).

8 Adverb

Adverbs modify verbs, adjectives and other adverbs. There are true adverbs and derived adverbs. True adverbs include *sugu* (immediately), *mattaku* (very much), *hakkiri* (clearly), etc.
Derived adverbs:
1 Adjectival nouns with the particle '*ni*.'
   shizuka ni (quietly)
2 The *ku*-form of adjectives.
   hayaku (early), *osoku* (slowly), etc.
3 The *te*-form of verbs.
   aratamete (again), *kononde* (willingly), etc.

9 Interrogative words

When interrogative words are followed by the particles '*ka*' or '*mo*,' or the gerund of the copula plus '*mo*' (i.e. *de mo*), the resulting combinations take on a variety of meanings.

	with 'ka'	with 'mo'		with 'de mo'
		(affirm. verb)	(neg. verb)	
dare (who)	someone	everyone	no one	anyone
dore (which of three or more)	some (one)	every one	none	any one
dochira (which of two)	either	both	neither	either
doo (how)	somehow	every way	no way	any way
doko (where)	somewhere	everywhere	nowhere	anywhere
itsu (when)	sometime	always	never	any time
nani (what)	something	(not used)	nothing	anything

10 Attributive

Attributive refers to a class of words which do not change their form. Some of these correspond to English pronominal adjectives: *kono* (this), *sono* (that), *ano* (that over there), *dono* (which), *koñna* (this kind of), *soñna* (that kind of), *añna* (that kind of), *doñna* (what kind of). *Ooki-na* (large), *chiisa-na* (small), *okashi-na* (funny), etc. are also considered attributives. They cannot be classified as adjectival nouns, even though they are followed by '*na*,' because *ooki*, *chiisa* and *okashi* without '*na*' can neither be used as nouns nor be followed by the copula *da* (*desu*).

ko- here (near the speaker)	so- there (far from the speaker and near the listener)	a- over there (far from both speaker and listener)	do- question
kore this (one)	sore that (one)	are that (one)	dore? which (one)?
kono this	sono that	ano that (over there)	dono? which?
koko here	soko there	asoko over there	doko? where?
kochira this side	sochira that side	achira that side	dochira? which side?
koñna this kind of	soñna that kind of	añna that kind of	doñna? what kind of?
koo like this	soo like that	aa like that	doo? how?

11 Conjunction

A conjunction is a word or phrase which is used to link words, phrases, clauses, or sentences. Many Japanese conjunctions are a combination of two or more words: *sore de* (therefore), *soo suru to* (then).

12 Inflected ending

Inflected endings are attached to a base of a verb, the stem of a verb or adjective, or the copula in order to give a wide range of additional meanings to that verb, adjective or copula: '*-ba*' in *ikeba*, '*-nai*' in *oishikunai*, '*-ta*' in *deshita*, etc.

13 Particle

Particles (*wa, ga, mo, o*, etc.) are unchanging in form and used to indicate the topic, subject, object, etc. of a Japanese sentence as well as functioning in a way similar to prepositions in English: *kara* (away from), *ni* (toward), etc. They are placed after a noun, clause, or sentence, and are sometimes called 'postpositions.'

14 Interjection

An interjection is a word which expresses a strong feeling such as surprise, pain, horror and so on.

   aa (oh), *iya* (no), *hora* (look), etc.

15 Prefix

A prefix is a meaning element or a group of meaning elements added to the beginning of a word to form a new word. The new word is written as one word, or sometimes a hyphen is used.

   dai- (big), *doo-* (the same), *sai-* (again), etc.

16 Suffix

A suffix is a meaning element or a group of meaning elements added to the end of another word to form a new word. suf. (*a.*) and suf (*a.n.*) indicate that the derived forms are an adjective or adjectival noun respectively.

   -dañ (group), *-juu* (through), *-ryuu* (style), etc.

Essential English-Japanese Vocabulary List

Use this list to determine the basic translation of English words that you do not know in Japanese. Additional information, usage notes, and references to synonyms may be found under the entry in the main dictionary.

A
able dekiru
about yaku; oyoso
above ue
abroad gaikoku
absent kesseki; yasumu
accident jiko
account kañjoo
add kuwaeru; tasu
address juusho
advertisement kookoku
advice jogeñ
afraid omou; osoreru
after ato; nochi
afternoon gogo
again futatabi
against hañtai
age neñree; toshi
ago mae
agree dooi
air kuuki
airplane hikooki
airport kuukoo
all subete; zeñbu
allow yurusu
all right yoi
almost hotoñdo
alone hitori
already sude ni
also mata
although keredo
always itsu-mo
among aida
amount gaku
and soshite; to
angry okoru
another hoka
answer heñji; kotae
any dore
anybody dare mo

anyone dare-ka
anything nani-ka
apartment apaato
apply mooshikomu
appointment yakusoku
April shi-gatsu
area chiiki; meñseki
arm ude
around mawari
arrive tsuku
art bijutsu
as to shite
ask kiku; tazuneru
at de; ni
attend shusseki
attention chuui
audience chooshuu
August hachi-gatsu
automobile jidoosha
automatic jidoo
autumun aki
average heekiñ
avoid sakeru
aware kizuku

B
baby akañboo
back ushiro
bad warui
bag fukuro; kabañ
baggage nimotsu
bank giñkoo
basis kiso
bath furo
bathroom yokushitsu
battery deñchi
beach kaigañ
be aru; iru
beard hige

beautiful utsukushii
because da kara
become naru
bed beddo
before mae
begin hajimeru
bedroom shiñshitsu
behind ushiro
believe shiñjiru
below shita
beside soba
best saikoo
better yoi
between aida
beyond koeru
bicycle jiteñsha
big ookii
bill kañjoo
bird tori
birthday tañjoobi
bit sukoshi
bite kamu
black kuro
blanket moofu
blood chi
blue aoi
boat booto
body jiñtai; karada
book hoñ
born umareru
borrow kariru
both ryoohoo
bottle biñ
bow ojigi
box hako
boy otoko-no-ko
brake bureeki
bread pañ
break kowasu
breakfast chooshoku
breath iki
bride hanayome

bridge hashi
biright akarui
bring motte kuru
brother kyoodai
brown chairo
build tateru
burn moyasu
bus basu
busy isogashii
but shikashi
butter bataa
buy kau
by de; ni; yoru

C

call yobu
camera kamera
can dekiru; kañ
cancel torikesu
car kuruma
care shiñpai
careful chuui
carry hakobu
case baai
cash geñkiñ
catch tsukamu
cause geñiñ
center chuushiñ
certificate shoomee-
    sho
chair isu
change kaeru
character kañji
charge ryookiñ
cheap yasui
child kodomo
choose erabu
chopsticks hashi
church kyookai
cigarette tabako
city shi
climb noboru
climate kikoo
clock tokee
close chikai; shimeru
clothing kimono
coin kooka
cold kaze; samui
collect atsumeru
college daigaku
color iro
come kuru

comfortable kaiteki
company kaisha
condition jookeñ;
    jootai
consider kañgaeru
consulate ryoojikañ
contain fukumu
continue tsuzukeru
conversation kaiwa
cook ryoori
cool suzushii
corner kado; sumi
correct tadashii
cost hiyoo
count kazoeru
country inaka; kuni
cover kakeru
cream kuriimu
cross yokogiru
crowd komu
cry naku
custom shuukañ
customer kyaku
cut kiru

D

damage soñgai
dangerous abunai
dark kurari
date hinichi
daughter musume
day hi; hiruma
December juuni-
    gatsu
decision kettee
deep fukai
delay okureru
delicious oishii
deliver watasu
demand yookyuu
dentist haisha
deny hitee
dapartment store
    depaato
depend tayoru
depth fukasa
desk tsukue
detail shoosai
dictionary jisho
die shinu
difference chigai
different chigau

difficult muzukashii
dining room shoku-
    doo
dinner yuushoku
direction hookoo
dirty kitanai
discount waribiki
discover mitsukeru
discuss hanashiau
disease byooki
dish ryoori
distance kyori
divide wakeru
do suru
doctor isha
dollar doru
door doa
double bai
doubt utagau
down shita
dozen daasu
draw hiku
drink nomu
drive uñteñ
drugstore yakkyoku
dry kawaku
during aida

E

each kaku
ear mimi
early hayai
earthquake jishiñ
east higashi
easy yasashii
eat taberu
education kyooiku
effort doryoku
egg tamago
eight hachi; yattsu
either dochira-ka
electric deñki
elevator erebeetaa
embassy taishikañ
emergency kiñkyuu
else hoka
employ yatou
empty kara
end owari
enjoy tanoshimu
enough juubuñ
enter hairu